THE WAY

Complete
Catholic
Edition
including the
Deuterocanonical
Books

An illustrated edition of
The Living Bible
as developed by the editors of
Campus Life Magazine,
Youth for Christ International

Foreword to the Catholic Edition
by Keith Clark, O.F.M.Cap.

TYNDALE HOUSE PUBLISHERS
Wheaton, Illinois

OUR SUNDAY VISITOR
Huntington, Indiana

Nihil Obstat: REV. LAWRENCE A. GOLLNER
Censor Librorum
Imprimatur: LEO A. PURSLEY
Bishop of Fort Wayne-South Bend
January 9, 1976

*The Way, Complete Catholic Edition
including the Deuterocanonical Books*

Fourth printing, June 1979

230,000 copies in print

Library of Congress Catalog Card Number 76-3289
ISBN 0-87973-831-6

Printed in the United States of America

Introduction

Every vernacular version of the Bible is a translation from the original Greek or Hebrew which in some cases may be a translation from an even earlier Aramaic version of the Scriptures. If these vernacular translations are judged good or bad on the basis of their literal translation from the original languages, the question of good or bad translations should be left entirely to linguists. In such a case, no translation would be accepted as perfect, because the idioms of one language remain unintelligible in a translation to another language.

Vernacular versions of the Bible have been accepted by the various Churches or rejected by them on the basis of Doctrinal implications of the translations. The acceptance of a vernacular translation by a Church means that the wording is not inimical to the Doctrinal traditions of that Church. Thus the question of good or bad translation is no longer a linguistic question, but a Doctrinal one.

Genuine care and concern for the purity of a Doctrinal tradition has in the history of Christianity been the cause of serious dispute among the Churches. Translations of the Scripture have been undertaken from a Doctrinal bias born out of this genuine concern.

This present volume departs radically from this history of Scriptural translations. It is born out of a sincere desire to have the Word of God reach as many people as possible, and in a language that is our own. Perhaps more than other translations, this translation cannot be used as a basis for Doctrinal or traditional disputes. More than other English versions of the Bible, this one freely departs from a literal translation from the original languages. People from various Doctrinal traditions may rejoice or be chagrined at the particular translations found within this volume, depending on whether or not the translation supports their particular Doctrinal bias. Most readers of the Bible who choose this translation will not be interested in such technical, theological considerations. They will be looking for spirit and life from the Word of God. We rejoice in our chance to encourage and help those who approach the Scriptures for this reason. We caution those who wish to engage in theological disputes not to use this volume. But we gladly join in cooperation with all those whose sincere interest is to make the Word of God available in a truly American style.

Father Keith Clark, O.F.M.Cap.

THE WAY

Terry White

"The cosmos is a gigantic flywheel making 10,000 revolutions per minute. Man is a sick fly taking a dizzy ride on it."
—*H. L. Mencken*

"The world will not end with a bang,

but with a whimper." –*T.S. Eliot*

I heard one-third of the world is gradually starving. There's no way life can make sense when things like that exist. And think of all the wars each year. I'd like to change things, but every action is ultimately futile!"

–*a young American*

"The world is a bad place, a very bad place to live. Oh, but I don't want to die." –*the BeeGees*

Today we watch war's shattered children groaning on the six o'clock news, their cries mingling with our dinner conversation. We hear people rail at one another and plot the bombing of each other's families. We suddenly realize that we Americans are ripping up our environment, leaving only a memory.

And we listen to commentators and professors explain the world's problems—and blatantly contradict each other. We watch friends in despair, finding no wholeness, no meaning.

So much of our modern experience echoes the Scripture: "Before every man there lies a wide and pleasant road he thinks is right, but it ends in death" (Proverbs 16:25).

Is there a way to *life*?

Is there a way to joy, peace, whole-

Two brothers running across America as well as a young couple sitting on the railroad tracks– all must face the question: Where are we headed? (See pages 241 and 733.)

ness, health, direction, purpose?

This book says:

"As for God, his way is perfect; the word of the Lord is true" (2 Samuel 22:31).

"This is the fresh, new, life-giving way which Christ has opened up for us ... to let us into the holy presence of God" (Hebrews 10:20).

"Jesus told him (Thomas), 'I am the Way—yes, and the Truth and the Life. No one can get to the Father except by means of me'" (John 14:6).

How can this be? Don't the circumstances of Planet Earth eliminate any idea of "the goodness of God"? Hasn't science pretty well disproved all these "ancient myths"? Is this book even relevant anymore?

Read it and see for yourself. Here are some of its crucial truths which, despite what you may have been told, have a great deal to do with the 20th century:

▶ The world was not always like this. God made it beautiful. He even made men beautiful, without any hatreds, lusts, or hangups. Men are the ones who rebelled and messed everything up.

▶ God, as seen through the Old Testament (the first three-fourths of the Bible), kept speaking to men. Some listened. Some obeyed. But most went on ignoring him, shuffling for their own answers. No wonder we now have so many conflicting ideologies, religions, and questions of right and wrong.

▶ The Creator God himself invaded our planet. Men weren't getting any closer to the way of life, so God came here in physical form. He was called Jesus, the Christ, the Son of God, Son of man, the Messiah. He made God's way clear. He spent 33 years here; four different biographies are included in the New Testament.

▶ This God-man, Jesus—"it is his power that holds everything together" (Colossians 1:17)—works today, dynamically changing lives, showing the way to real life, revolutionizing people wherever he is welcomed.

He brings a dramatic change in human existence! "Your cup of joy will overflow," he told his followers (John 15:11).

However, this is not an unrealistic, oversimplified book. Not at all. It deals with life, which is complex and mysterious. It's not arranged interview style—one-line questions followed by two-paragraph answers from the Almighty. The deep paradoxes of life and existence can't be neatly wrapped up like that.

Instead, God tells us what we need to know for successful living through a variety of formats: people-stories, poetry, direct messages or prophecies, and most clearly of all, the Earth-visit of Jesus. All have an undeniable ring of truth.

But it's up to us to absorb great truths, far-reaching concepts, overall

perspectives—and allow God to work out their meanings in our lives.

This particular edition of the Bible is among the easiest to understand, since it is a paraphrase. Instead of translating the original Hebrew and Greek texts word for word, the ideas are expressed here as ordinary Americans in the late 20th century would say them—with our idioms, word-pictures, and expressions.

If this is your first experience at getting into the Bible, you may want to read the following pages for some suggestions on what to read first.

The longer you read, the more you will find yourself confronting the way—God's way. He won't necessarily make life problem-free or rosy, but you will understand the meaning and purpose of your existence. And he is ready to create new life in you and empower you to live it.

Life demands leadership, not only on the football field but in everything we do—and how do we know enough to take charge, to keep life from becoming one long rollercoaster ride?
(See pages 296 and 212.)

IF YOU'RE NEW TO THIS BOOK

There's no rule that says you have to read the Bible straight through starting at page one. In fact, if this is one of the first times you've cracked the cover, we'd suggest this sequence:

1. "Mark" (see the table of contents for page numbers). It's the shortest, most fast-moving of the four biographies of Christ which begin the New Testament. It was written by a young man who was probably at times an eyewitness of what Jesus did, and had access to the vast memories of Christ's disciples. This book will give you dramatic introduction to the events that changed the world.

2. A couple of the short letters written by two leaders in the early church: "1 John" talks about how Christians show the love that our world needs so badly, and "James" hits hard on putting our faith in Christ into action.

3. "Romans" is one of the many letters written by Paul, and is the greatest statement on how selfish, arrogant, sinful humans can find acceptance with God.

4. Pick up the first-century story where you left it at the end of "Mark" by reading "Acts"—the dynamic story of the first Christians and how they spread the Good News all over the Roman Empire.

5. "Philippians" is another short note Paul wrote from prison—yet his joyful perspective tells us something about the durability of faith in Christ.

6. "John," the fourth of Jesus' biographies, is more conceptual than the other three. It spends less time on miracles and more time recording Christ's dialogues and statements. His relation with his Father, God, comes through strongly.

7. "Psalms"—maybe not all of them, at first, but read enough to give you a sense of what it means to worship God and pour out your inner feelings to him.

From there on, drop in on Daniel, Genesis, Ephesians, 1 and 2 Timothy, Amos, Proverbs ... To get some ideas on reading the entire volume, see the next page.

Wilmer Zehr

People have often made the Bible out to be some gigantic encyclopedia that nobody ever wades all the way through. Not so. It's a big book, but no bigger than other best sellers of our time.

Actually, you can read the entire Bible in less than 80 hours. Most new readers feel like sitting down and cruising through great sections of it at a time. The whole New Testament is only 275 pages of actual print.

If you want to spread it out, there's an easy plan that will get you through the Bible in a year. You roll along at only 20 pages a week—specifically, 23 chapters a week, which most people arrange as three each day and five on Sunday, when they have a little more reading time. For the sake of balance, you can split each day's reading between Old and New Testaments; in other words, read two books simultaneously (two chapters from Genesis and one from Matthew, etc.).

However you decide to read it, use the check-chart which starts on the next page for x-ing out the chapters as you go. That way, you'll always know where you last read, and when you finally finish the Bible.

You'll soon notice that the Bible is arranged with all the narrative books together, then the poetry, then the prophecy. Here is Dr. Stanley M. Horton's rearrangement of the books in an attempt to put them in chronological order—in other words, in sequence as the events actually happened.

Ways to Read THE WAY

Genesis 1—22
Job
Genesis 23—50
Exodus
Psalm 90
Leviticus
Numbers
Deuteronomy
Psalm 91
Joshua
Judges
Ruth
1 Samuel 1—16:13
Psalm 23
1 Samuel 16:14—19:11
Psalm 59
1 Samuel 19:12—21:15
Psalms 34, 56
1 Samuel 22:1, 2
Psalms 57, 142
1 Samuel 22:3-23
Psalm 52
1 Samuel 23
Psalms 54, 63
1 Samuel 24—31
2 Samuel 1—7
Psalm 30
2 Samuel 8:1-14
Psalm 60
2 Samuel 8:15—12:14
Psalms 51, 32
2 Samuel 12:15—15:37
Psalms 3, 69
2 Samuel 16—20
Psalms 64, 70
2 Samuel 21, 22
Psalm 18
2 Samuel 23, 24
Psalms 4—9, 11—17, 19
—22, 24—29, 31, 35—41,
53, 55, 58, 61, 62, 65, 68,
72, 86, 101, 103, 108—
110, 138—141, 143—145
1 Kings 1—4
Proverbs

Song of Solomon
1 Kings 5—11
Ecclesiastes
1 Kings 12—22
2 Kings 1—14:25
Jonah
2 Kings 14:26-29
Amos
2 Kings 15—25
Psalms 1, 2, 10, 33, 43,
66, 67, 71, 89, 92-100,
102, 104—106, 111—
125, 127—136, 146—150
1 Chronicles 1—16
Psalms 42, 44—50, 73—
85, 87, 88
1 Chronicles 17—29
2 Chronicles 1—21
Obadiah
2 Chronicles 22
Joel
2 Chronicles 23—26:8
Isaiah 1—5
2 Chronicles 26:9-23
Isaiah 6
2 Chronicles 27—32
Isaiah 7—66
Hosea
Micah
Nahum
2 Chronicles 33, 34
Zephaniah
2 Chronicles 35
Habakkuk
Jeremiah 1—6, 11, 12,
26, 7—10, 14—20, 35, 36,
45, 25, 46—49, 13, 22—
24, 27—29, 50, 51, 30—
33, 21, 34, 37—39, 52,
40—44
Lamentations
2 Chronicles 36:1-8
Daniel
2 Chronicles 36:9-21
Psalm 137

Ezekiel
2 Chronicles 36:22, 23
Ezra 1—5:1
Haggai
Zechariah
Psalms 107, 126
Ezra 5:2—6:22
Esther
Ezra 7—10
Nehemiah
Malachi

Matthew
Mark
Luke
John
Acts 1—14
James
Acts 15
Galatians
Acts 16
Philippians
Acts 17:1-10
1 Thessalonians
2 Thessalonians
Acts 17:11—18:11
1 Corinthians
2 Corinthians
Acts 18:12—20:1
Ephesians
Romans
Acts 20:2—28:30
Colossians
Hebrews
Titus
Philemon
1 Timothy
2 Timothy
1 Peter
2 Peter
1 John
2 John
3 John
Jude
Revelation

Used by permission of Gospel Publishing House, Springfield, Mo.

THE OLD TESTAMENT

Genesis	1	2	3	4	5	6	7	8	9	10	11	12	13	14	15	16
	17	18	19	20	21	22	23	24	25	26	27	28	29	30	31	32
	33	34	35	36	37	38	39	40	41	42	43	44	45	46	47	48
	49	50														
Exodus	1	2	3	4	5	6	7	8	9	10	11	12	13	14	15	16
	17	18	19	20	21	22	23	24	25	26	27	28	29	30	31	32
	33	34	35	36	37	38	39	40								
Leviticus	1	2	3	4	5	6	7	8	9	10	11	12	13	14	15	16
	17	18	19	20	21	22	23	24	25	26	27					
Numbers	1	2	3	4	5	6	7	8	9	10	11	12	13	14	15	16
	17	18	19	20	21	22	23	24	25	26	27	28	29	30	31	32
	33	34	35	36												
Deuteronomy	1	2	3	4	5	6	7	8	9	10	11	12	13	14	15	16
	17	18	19	20	21	22	23	24	25	26	27	28	29	30	31	32
	33	34														
Joshua	1	2	3	4	5	6	7	8	9	10	11	12	13	14	15	16
	17	18	19	20	21	22	23	24								
Judges	1	2	3	4	5	6	7	8	9	10	11	12	13	14	15	16
	17	18	19	20	21											
Ruth	1	2	3	4												
1 Samuel	1	2	3	4	5	6	7	8	9	10	11	12	13	14	15	16
	17	18	19	20	21	22	23	24	25	26	27	28	29	30	31	
2 Samuel	1	2	3	4	5	6	7	8	9	10	11	12	13	14	15	16
	17	18	19	20	21	22	23	24								
1 Kings	1	2	3	4	5	6	7	8	9	10	11	12	13	14	15	16
	17	18	19	20	21	22										
2 Kings	1	2	3	4	5	6	7	8	9	10	11	12	13	14	15	16
	17	18	19	20	21	22	23	24	25							
1 Chronicles	1	2	3	4	5	6	7	8	9	10	11	12	13	14	15	16
	17	18	19	20	21	22	23	24	25	26	27	28	29			
2 Chronicles	1	2	3	4	5	6	7	8	9	10	11	12	13	14	15	16
	17	18	19	20	21	22	23	24	25	26	27	28	29	30	31	32
	33	34	35	36												
Ezra	1	2	3	4	5	6	7	8	9	10						
Nehemiah	1	2	3	4	5	6	7	8	9	10	11	12	13			
Esther	1	2	3	4	5	6	7	8	9	10						
Job	1	2	3	4	5	6	7	8	9	10	11	12	13	14	15	16
	17	18	19	20	21	22	23	24	25	26	27	28	29	30	31	32
	33	34	35	36	37	38	39	40	41	42						

Psalms	1	2	3	4	5	6	7	8	9	10	11	12	13	14	15	16
	17	18	19	20	21	22	23	24	25	26	27	28	29	30	31	32
	33	34	35	36	37	38	39	40	41	42	43	44	45	46	47	48
	49	50	51	52	53	54	55	56	57	58	59	60	61	62	63	64
	65	66	67	68	69	70	71	72	73	74	75	76	77	78	79	80
	81	82	83	84	85	86	87	88	89	90	91	92	93	94	95	96
	97	98	99	100	101	102	103	104	105	106	107	108	109	110	111	112
	113	114	115	116	117	118	119	120	121	122	123	124	125	126	127	128
	129	130	131	132	133	134	135	136	137	138	139	140	141	142	143	144
	145	146	147	148	149	150										
Proverbs	1	2	3	4	5	6	7	8	9	10	11	12	13	14	15	16
	17	18	19	20	21	22	23	24	25	26	27	28	29	30	31	
Ecclesiastes	1	2	3	4	5	6	7	8	9	10	11	12				
Song/Solomon	1	2	3	4	5	6	7	8								
Isaiah	1	2	3	4	5	6	7	8	9	10	11	12	13	14	15	16
	17	18	19	20	21	22	23	24	25	26	27	28	29	30	31	32
	33	34	35	36	37	38	39	40	41	42	43	44	45	46	47	48
	49	50	51	52	53	54	55	56	57	58	59	60	61	62	63	64
	65	66														
Jeremiah	1	2	3	4	5	6	7	8	9	10	11	12	13	14	15	16
	17	18	19	20	21	22	23	24	25	26	27	28	29	30	31	32
	33	34	35	36	37	38	39	40	41	42	43	44	45	46	47	48
	49	50	51	52												
Lamentations	1	2	3	4	5											
Ezekiel	1	2	3	4	5	6	7	8	9	10	11	12	13	14	15	16
	17	18	19	20	21	22	23	24	25	26	27	28	29	30	31	32
	33	34	35	36	37	38	39	40	41	42	43	44	45	46	47	48
Daniel	1	2	3	4	5	6	7	8	9	10	11	12				
Hosea	1	2	3	4	5	6	7	8	9	10	11	12	13	14		
Joel	1	2	3													
Amos	1	2	3	4	5	6	7	8	9							
Obadiah	1															
Jonah	1	2	3	4												
Micah	1	2	3	4	5	6	7									
Nahum	1	2	3													
Habakkuk	1	2	3													
Zephaniah	1	2	3													
Haggai	1	2														
Zechariah	1	2	3	4	5	6	7	8	9	10	11	12	13	14		
Malachi	1	2	3	4												

THE NEW TESTAMENT

Matthew	1	2	3	4	5	6	7	8	9	10	11	12	13	14	15	16
	17	18	19	20	21	22	23	24	25	26	27	28				
Mark	1	2	3	4	5	6	7	8	9	10	11	12	13	14	15	16
Luke	1	2	3	4	5	6	7	8	9	10	11	12	13	14	15	16
	17	18	19	20	21	22	23	24								
John	1	2	3	4	5	6	7	8	9	10	11	12	13	14	15	16
	17	18	19	20	21											
Acts	1	2	3	4	5	6	7	8	9	10	11	12	13	14	15	16
	17	18	19	20	21	22	23	24	25	26	27	28				
Romans	1	2	3	4	5	6	7	8	9	10	11	12	13	14	15	16
1 Corinthians	1	2	3	4	5	6	7	8	9	10	11	12	13	14	15	16
2 Corinthians	1	2	3	4	5	6	7	8	9	10	11	12	13			
Galatians	1	2	3	4	5	6										
Ephesians	1	2	3	4	5	6										
Philippians	1	2	3	4												
Colossians	1	2	3	4												
1 Thess.	1	2	3	4	5											
2 Thess.	1	2	3													
1 Timothy	1	2	3	4	5	6										
2 Timothy	1	2	3	4												
Titus	1	2	3													
Philemon	1															
Hebrews	1	2	3	4	5	6	7	8	9	10	11	12	13			
James	1	2	3	4	5											
1 Peter	1	2	3	4	5											
2 Peter	1	2	3													
1 John	1	2	3	4	5											
2 John	1															
3 John	1															
Jude	1															
Revelation	1	2	3	4	5	6	7	8	9	10	11	12	13	14	15	16
	17	18	19	20	21	22										

HOW THE BIBLE

You don't have to read far into the Bible before you recognize it's not like other books. It's not a tightly-woven story like a novel, or a systematic list like a textbook. It includes a diverse batch of styles: poetry, history, sermons, dramatic stories, letters.

Some people dip into a book such as Leviticus or 1 Chronicles and soon give up in confusion. They don't understand why such material is important to them. To appreciate what God is saying to us, it's important to know the whole sweep of the Bible.

In the first place, the Bible isn't one book—it's an entire library, a collection of separate books written on rolled-up scrolls by many authors. Until 100 years after Jesus came, no one had a complete set of all the books in the Bible.

The remarkable thing is that a collection of books written over 1500 years by dozens of different authors would have as much unity as the Bible has. The parts fit together, and God's plan of saving man makes sense as you read through it. (Imagine a book begun back in the 10th century—500 years before Columbus—which was just finished in the 1970s. How do you think a book like that would read?) The Bible's unity is one of the most obvious signs that God was behind the planning and writing of the whole book. By using a variety of men and situations over the years, God developed a complete record of what he wants us to know.

It sometimes helps to subdivide the Bible into groupings of similar books. These groups are the Pentateuch, the history books, the poetic books, the prophets, the Gospels, and Acts, the epistles, and the Revelation. Keeping these groups in mind, whenever you turn to a book like Malachi or 2 Kings, you'll have a general idea of where it fits in the Bible.

THE FIRST FIVE BOOKS: GENESIS—DEUTERONOMY

In the Old Testament God begins with a single couple, Adam and Eve. He puts them in a perfect world with certain rules to obey. They flunk. The first eleven chapters of Genesis mostly record one failure after another. God punishes Adam and Eve, destroys the world with a massive flood, and smashes a misguided rebellion at the tower of Babel.

God reaches down and selects a man named Abraham, to whom he gives some extraordinary promises. He promises that Abraham's descendants will some day become as numerous as sand on a beach, and that they will grow to become a mighty nation with their own land. Thus, God focuses in on one particular set of people, the Jews.

From Genesis on, most of the Old Testament concerns the Jews. Have you ever wondered why our Bible contains so much meticulous detail on the history and culture of the Jews? They have always been a key part of God's plan to prepare the world for the coming of Christ.

FITS TOGETHER

God has a special role for the Jewish race to play in history, and so he carefully works with them.

Within several generations Abraham's descendants begin to proliferate. Soon there are twelve tribes of Israel, and God leads them out of slavery in the remarkable drama of the Exodus. Forty years of wandering in the desert occur before the disgruntled tribes can be molded into a group with the unity and spirit God needs.

In these first five books, God gathers hundreds of thousands of freed Israelis and gives them a culture. He intends far more than simply creating a nation as a world curiosity. He wants to set apart a nation he can call his people—so that all over the world when the word Israelite is mentioned, everyone would know "they belong to Jehovah, the Lord God." In creating that culture, God outlines rules concerning health, food, dress and behavior. These rules and the early Jewish history occupy the first five books of the Bible.

How should we study the first five books of the Bible? Are they merely an interesting history lesson? They must be more because Jesus and Paul and the disciples constantly refer back to God's Word in these books. There are several effective ways of studying this material.

Spiritual Examples. Genesis contains accounts of many characters who tried to follow God. The Bible never glosses over human mistakes nor pretends the godly way is easy. It exposes the wrinkles and flaws of God's people. Of the chief characters in Genesis, Adam is the first sinner, Abraham lies to protect himself, and Jacob is a conniver. Yet God works through their frailty to teach them, and us, about himself. People like Joseph give us sterling examples of how to avoid temptations and concentrate on what really counts in life.

How God Works. God can seem unpredictable from our limited human perspective. For example, consider his promise to Abraham to create a great nation from his descendants. A very excited Abraham waits year after year until finally he concludes his wife is sterile. After twenty-five years of discouragement, he bypasses God's plan and fathers an illegitimate child. Abraham missed God's lessons of trust: that when he makes a promise he will fulfill it, even when all the odds are against it. Even so, through a miracle, God does finally allow Abraham's wife to give birth to the promised son.

What God Is Like. Behind the minute laws and rules of a book like Leviticus, are principles which hint at what God is like. He is a Holy God who must be taken seriously. People of that time had the habit of inventing and discarding gods as they felt like it. God declares that he alone is the true God, worthy of all worship.

In one sense what God ultimately demands—obedience—has not

changed since Old Testament days. But God teaches the Israelites much as a parent must teach a young child—with dozens of clearly-spelled-out rules.

HISTORY BOOKS: JOSHUA—ESTHER

Next come twelve of the most exciting books in the Bible. They're full of conflict, competition, romance, and human drama. Joshua opens a new chapter in Israel's history when he leads them into a productive new land. They don't stroll in and claim the land, however; they have to fight for every inch. Along the way, they learn how dearly it costs to disobey God or rebel against him.

Once Israel has settled comfortably in their lush new land, they splinter off into tribes and begin grumbling. Judges records one of the low points of all Jewish history, when "every man did whatever he thought was right."

Later Israel undergoes a revival under the leadership of Samuel. Under pressure from the people, Samuel anoints Israel's first king, a man named Saul.

Saul is followed by David, one of the most important men in the Old Testament, who is called a man "after God's own heart." David and his son King Solomon lead Israel to its historical zenith. Other kings follow them, showing some flashes of brilliance, but most slide into spiritual decline.

The Walls Come Crashing Down. God has meticulously worked through inconsistent humans to build a kingdom where he is the true God. He blesses Israel through David and Solomon, and a magnificent temple, one of the great wonders of the world, is built as a center of worship.

But in spite of these blessings, decade after decade of civil war, immorality, and disobedience pass. The Jewish ideal of a lasting kingdom begins to fade away as enemies march closer to Israel's borders. God sends prophets—some of the most daring, courageous men in the Bible—to warn his people, but their advice is scorned. Finally, after repeated warnings about what would happen, God allows first the Assyrians and then the Babylonians to devastate Israel.

It surely looks as though all God's promises to the Jews are wiped out. No kingdom, no temple, no nation. A Persian king does allow a partial rebuilding program under Ezra and Nehemiah's direction, but it suffers by comparison with the splendor of the past.

The twelve history books which record Israel's spectacular rise and fall read on several levels. As history, they're as exciting and dramatic as a TV series. The personalities they describe are varied and colorful. But the history books also teach about the character of God. He showers David with forgiveness even after David betrays God by murdering and by stealing a man's wife. Time and again God is seen as a Lover calling his people to return to him. But inevitably Israel gets sidetracked by materialism, selfishness and success. (Sound familiar?)

POETRY BOOKS: JOB—SONG OF SOLOMON

If you did read the Bible straight through, you'd probably breathe a great sigh of relief when you hit the next five books. They provide a beautiful interlude between the violent record of Israel's history and the smoke and thunder of the prophets. God's Word includes a variety of rich art forms in these books. Every English Lit class worth its salt uses selections from them as choice expressions of the human soul in print.

Unlike previous books, the poetry books are not so much concerned with facts of history. Rather, they cut through behavior and speak directly to the inner attitude of the reader.

Job, for example, explores in drama form the inner turmoil of a man who faces suffering. By reading Job's story and identifying with him, we can learn God's viewpoint of suffering, and how he wants us to respond. The Bible does not gloss over Job's agony and the phoniness of his friends' excuses. It shows a real man, writhing in pain, trying his best to cling to a hidden God.

The next book, the Psalms, is the favorite book of many Christians. You can find a psalm to fit any mood—despair, anger, praise, depression, loneliness, sorrow, exuberance. The psalms are songs from the heart to God.

Proverbs is more practical and pungent than the other poetry. It shows what our behavior should be in everyday life. There's hardly a situation you'll run up against in the 20th century which Solomon doesn't refer to in some way. He also contributed the brief books Ecclesiastes and Song of Solomon. Ecclesiastes summarizes the despair of life without God, and Song of Solomon is a beautiful love poem which demonstrates the right attitude about love.

Reading poetry books is not so much an educational experience as an emotional one. For instance, if you're plagued by guilt about something and don't know how to deal with it, you could start by repeating to God Psalm 51. It was composed by David after he confessed his sin of murder and adultery. Nothing expresses the clean sweep of forgiveness more eloquently. Psalms is loaded with such mood poems that seem to cut to the core of where a person is feeling.

THE PROPHETS: ISAIAH—MALACHI

If the history books record Israel's history and the poetry books express individuals' response to God during that history, the prophets give us direct insight into God's viewpoint of what takes place. God calls men of all backgrounds and styles to explain to Israel how he views what is going on. Some, like Amos, are rural farmers; others, like Isaiah, are statesmen. Some speak eloquently, poetically; others are more folksy and down-to-earth. Joel paints vivid images of locusts attacking the nation; Ezekiel whirls off fantastic scenes of wheels and lights.

Despite differences in style, all the prophets hammer home the same theme: Israel as a nation has blown it and their sin cannot go ignored by God. Yet, it isn't too late to repent, and one day everything will change: God will send a Messiah, a Deliverer who will establish a time of peace and prosperity, without the sin and failures that history has shown so far.

You can consider the prophets as sermons from God. To make his message absolutely clear, God uses all sorts of visual symbols to drive it home. Each prophet also has his own special emphasis.

There's much more to the prophets than sermons, however. Wedged in are hundreds of predictions about the future which will keep you scratching your head. Some specific prophecies written back then are just now coming true.

Also, there are some astounding previews of Jesus Christ. Hundreds of years before his birth, prophets predict titles he would be called one day, his birthplace, and the words he would say before his death.

SOMETHING NEW

For a 400-year period, no new writings appear which are added to Scripture. But then, in a brief span, the entire New Testament, twenty-seven books, explodes. The reason? The greatest event in history—when God becomes a man.

Jesus is not just one more attempt by God to get man's attention. He is more than the most wonderful thing God did in history. Unlike the prophets, he is not a good man selected by God to be his spokesman. He is all of God living in flesh and muscle on earth. Jesus makes clear that his coming is the fulfillment of all the books that have gone before. Those intricate instructions on feasts and sacrifices way back in the first five books all point to him. The roller-coaster history of Israel had all occurred to prepare a culture to allow the God-man to enter history.

THE GOSPELS: MATTHEW—JOHN

As if to underscore the significance of Jesus' life, the Bible devotes four books to his activity on earth. They are not biographies in the classical sense. For example, none of them gives a sentence about what Jesus looked like! Yet, in a way they do paint a word portrait. Each man—Matthew, Mark, Luke, and John—brings out new colors and highlights different details.

Each author seems to focus on a different audience also. Mark writes a fast-paced, newspaper-like account of the main events of Jesus' life to suit the busy, consumer-oriented readers of the Roman Empire. Matthew, on the other hand, takes special pains to explain to a Jewish audience just how Jesus' life affects their traditions. He often refers to the Old Testament.

Of the four Gospels, John is the most unique in style. He seems less interested in recording history than in expressing the deep truths which Jesus taught. In fact, he states his purpose in writing: "These are recorded so that you will believe that he is the Messiah, the Son of God, and that believing in him you will have life" (John 20:31).

God has said to Abraham, "I will build a great nation." Jesus introduces a new chapter in history with the statement, "I will build my church." The focus on the Jews expands outward to include the whole world. There is no need to look back for a holy nation. Jesus' kingdom is an internal one, in which race and sex make no difference. He gave his life so that all—Jew and Gentile—might live.

ACTS OF THE APOSTLES

Volume two of Luke's detailed history takes off with Jesus' departure from earth and zeroes in on two apostles, Paul and Peter. The years following the ascension of Jesus are some of the most exciting of history, and the tone of Acts captures the breathless enthusiasm of Jesus' early followers. Seeing Jesus alive again after his execution causes a remarkable turnaround in the downcast disciples.

The church evolves quickly out of the Jewish structure. Soon believers are meeting in homes and electing officers. Peter's experience in chapter 10 establishes once and for all that the Gospel is for the non-Jew as well.

While on earth Jesus had preached mainly a message about the coming Kingdom, a message which was never quite understood. In Acts the disciples begin preaching Jesus. With the Holy Spirit's guidance the apostles begin to see what God had done in history. Previously the apostles had listened to Jesus' teaching and observed the facts of his life and death. Now they take those facts and interpret them, with incredible courage. People's responses to their Good News is what makes Acts such exciting reading. Lives are changed, cities are rocked.

Acts also establishes the authority of one of the most unexpected heroes of the Gospel—the apostle Paul. A radical convert, his experiences could fill an encyclopedia.

Jesus is absent from us physically. But he sent, as he had promised, the Holy Spirit, whose incredible works are recorded in the pages of Acts.

THE EPISTLES: ROMANS—JUDE

Up to now, the New Testament has been mostly action, with a few speeches sandwiched in. The Gospels and Acts lay out plenty of facts. It's up to the Epistles to interpret those facts.

The Epistles aren't complex sermons. They are written as letters, as one disciple of Christ shares insights. Some, such as Romans, the theology book of the Bible, are systematic. Others, like Thessalonians and Galatians and Corinthians, are designed to correct problems in various churches. They breathe with humanity—personality clashes, marital squabbles, jealousies.

Compare Luke's account of Jesus' death with the discussion in Romans 3—6. Luke reports perhaps the most significant moment of history with these nine words, "Jesus shouted out again, dismissed his spirit, and died" (Matthew 27:50). In contrast, Paul explains the fact of Jesus' death at great length, relating its cosmic and personal significance. He personalizes history, showing how Christ died and rose again so that we could be accepted as God's sons. That wooden cross and dark, empty tomb mean something to me—they are God's gift leading to salvation.

The Epistles develop the seed truths which Jesus shared on different occasions in picture form. They show what it means to call God Father. They describe everything involved in becoming a Christian, what it means to be "in Christ." And they give much practical advice on how to handle personal decisions. What is right and wrong? How much of being "spiritual" is personality or attitude? What did Jesus mean when he said he would be coming back?

While reading the Epistles, it helps to also read a Bible study book to find out what spurred the Bible authors to write. For example, Paul in Galatians was responding to people who were trying to make Christianity more legalistic. On the other hand, James wrote to people who claimed you only needed faith; it wasn't necessary to put that faith in action.

THE REVELATION

The last book in the Bible is in a class all by itself. Of all books in the Bible, it may seem strangest to a modern reader. But at the time it was written, this style was a popular one. Jewish authors wrote fantasies about what the "Day of the Lord" would be like, with complex symbols and codes the ancient reader would understand. Revelation, of course, is not a fantasy, but it parallels in style many of these

Jewish books. And to a second-century reader it may not have seemed strange at all.

The Revelation was meant for more than an exercise for prophecy scholars. It consummates the entire New Testament. It pulls away the veil and lets us see the battle raging between God and Satan. Sin and death and corruption still rule the world now—any daily newspaper will prove that. But one day it will change. God will pull out all the stops and decisively defeat evil. The language is symbolic and difficult, but the message is clear. We who are aligned with Christ will be victorious. Jesus will reign forever and ever.

HOW TO STUDY THE BOOKS

If you were stranded on a desert island with nothing but a toothbrush and a Bible, you *might* sit down and read it straight through in a couple of weeks. If so, you would see the grand sweep of the Bible. The symbols of the Old Testament would make sense as you quickly saw them fulfilled and given flesh in the New Testament.

But not very many of us will have such opportunity. Let's face it: usually we dip and choose, sampling the riches of the Bible like a smörgasbord.

As you sample, here are some hints that may help your study.

1. Note the difference between direct and indirect teaching. Direct teaching is like this article—a straight presentation of facts or thoughts. Books like Deuteronomy, Proverbs, and the Epistles, as well as many of the prophets' messages, are direct teaching. They need careful study. Who are they speaking to? Why? What's their message? How does it apply to me?

Indirect teaching can take a variety of forms. It gets a message across, but by telling a story or parable, recording a person's history, or repeating a song. Job, Psalms, Jesus' parables, and the history books belong in this category. They seem lighter reading, and you'll probably find yourself reading faster, with your emotions caught up.

2. Work at fitting the Old Testament and the New Testament together. All through the New Testament are sprinkled references to Old Testament events and quotes from the Old Testament. When you run across them, look them up with the help of a Bible reference book (your pastor could recommend one). They'll help you develop the habit of drawing out the Old Testament's message.

3. Try reading some of the shorter books straight through at one sitting. When Paul wrote Philippians, he wrote one continuous letter to a church. There were no chapter and verse divisions (these were added later for ease in locating passages). Imagine you are a member of the church at Philippi reading this letter for the first time.

4. Hunt up a small group for in-depth Bible study. Your pastor or youth worker or Christian campus leader should know of small group Bible studies. It helps to hear other people telling how the Bible spoke to them. And bouncing ideas around should stimulate you to study the Bible deeper, to discover its true meaning.

When you're
feeling lonely,
left out:
Luke 6.

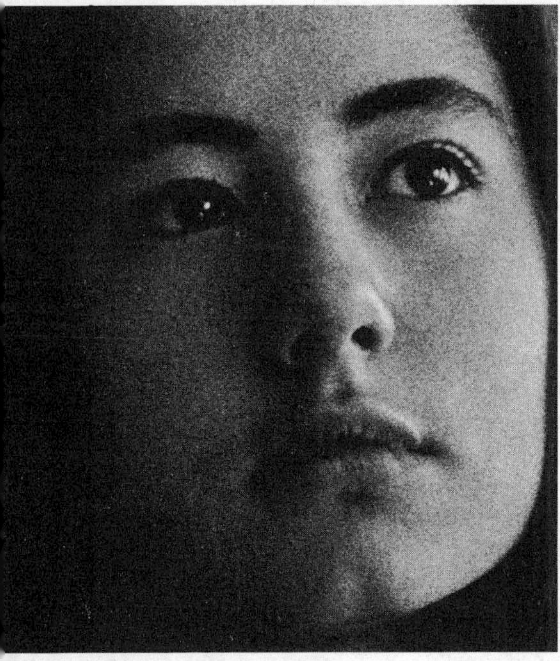

HOW THIS BOOK SPEAKS DIRECTLY TO YOU

Rohn Engh

It's no coincidence that the Bible is the all-time best seller with close to two *billion* copies sold or given away. Parts of it have been translated into 1,280 languages. It's in a class all by itself.

That's because it touches people right where they live, where they hurt. The passages listed here are a few examples of the Bible's facility for getting right to the point.

Philip Yancey

When
you're
not sure
what your
value is,
where
you stand:
*read
Genesis 1,
Romans 4, 5.*

When you wonder what God thinks of you: *Romans 1-3.*

When you want to get right with God: *John 3.*

When you feel guilty: *1 John 1, 2; Psalm 51.*

When you're tired: *Psalm 23.*

When you're hurting: *Hebrews 12.*

When you're tempted: *Daniel 1, James 1, 1 Corinthians 10.*

When you need courage: *Joshua 1, Ephesians 6, Hebrews 13.*

When you're hassled: *Isaiah 26, Philippians 4.*

When you need a little common sense: *Proverbs.*

When you think about injustice: *Hosea, Amos, Micah.*

When you feel a little defeated: *Acts 1-8.*

When you're feeling happy: *Psalms 95–101.*

When
you're
afraid:
*Psalms 27,
91, 121, 139.*

Rohn Engh

When you wonder who Jesus really was: *John 6-10.*

When you're trying to figure out the church: *1 Corinthians 12, Ephesians.*

When you think about death: *1 Corinthians 15, 2 Corinthians 5.*

When you wonder about the world's future: *Matthew 24, 1 Timothy 4, Revelation.*

When you've been offended: *1 Corinthians 6.*

When you wonder about the government: *Romans 13.*

When you're finding it hard to believe: *Hebrews 11, Genesis 12–24.*

When you need to forgive someone: *Philemon.*

When you're trying to figure out what's right and wrong: *Matthew 5–7, Colossians 2*.

When you've said something you shouldn't: *James 3*.

When you're sick: *Mark 1-3, James 5*.

When you feel like copping out: *Jonah*.

When you wonder about God's power: *Exodus 1–15, Isaiah 40*.

When you can't figure out the reasons for suffering: *Job*.

When you wonder what following Jesus is all about: *John 13-16*.

When you're struggling to do right, and can't quite make it: *Romans 7-8*.

When you want to find out what true love is: *1 Corinthians 13*.

When you need to make a decision: *Proverbs 3, James 1*.

CONTENTS

The Old Testament

The New Testament

CONTENTS

Alphabetical List of Books

A Good Place to Be

Philip Yancey

Soil, rocks, plants, animals, people—it's not a bad planet. How did we come to be so lucky? The more we learn of Venus, Mars, and the other way stations in our universe, the more we appreciate Earth.

The Bible's first book, Genesis, tells how it all came about. It doesn't give any dates—it says only that "in the beginning" God was pleased with how it turned out. For awhile, that is. Soon man ruined it, and ever since, Earth has had to endure the greed, hatred, and lust of selfish humanity.

Genesis goes streaking through its first 11 chapters, covering thousands of years—then suddenly settles down to the life of one man, Abraham, and his family. The rest of the book covers no more than 200 years, starting somewhere in the 1900s (*before* Christ, that is!)

As you read about the murder of Abel, the voyage of Noah, the trickiness of Jacob and the skyrocketing career of his son Joseph, you'll get a sense of our beginnings . . . and the God who has put up with us humans for all these centuries . . . .

GENESIS

1 WHEN GOD BEGAN creating[a] the heavens and the earth, [2] the earth was at first[b] a shapeless, chaotic mass,[c] with the Spirit of God brooding over the dark vapors.[d] [3] Then[b] God said, "Let there be light." And light appeared. [4,5] And God was pleased with it, and divided the light from the darkness. So he let it shine for awhile, and then there was darkness again. He called the light "daytime," and the darkness "nighttime." Together they formed the first day.[e]

[6] And God said, "Let the vapors separate[f] to form the sky above and the oceans below." [7,8] So God made the sky, dividing the vapor above from the water below. This all happened on the second day.[g]

[9,10] Then God said, "Let the water beneath the sky be gathered into oceans so that the dry land will emerge." And so it was. Then God named the dry land "earth," and the water "seas." And God was pleased. [11,12] And he said, "Let the earth burst forth with every sort of grass and seed-bearing plant, and fruit trees with seeds inside the fruit, so that these seeds will produce the kinds of plants and fruits they came from." And so it was, and God was pleased. [13] This all occurred on the third day.[h]

[14,15] Then God said, "Let there be bright lights in the sky to give light to the earth and to identify the day and the night; they shall bring about the seasons on the earth, and mark the days and years." And so it was. [16] For God made two huge lights, the sun and moon, to shine down upon the earth—the larger one, the sun, to preside over the day and the smaller one, the moon, to preside through the night; he also made the stars. [17] And God set them in the sky to light the earth, [18] and to preside over the day and night, and to divide the light from the darkness. And God was pleased. [19] This all happened on the fourth day.[i]

[20] Then God said, "Let the waters teem with fish and other life, and let the skies be filled with birds of every kind." [21,22] So God created great sea creatures, and every sort of fish and every kind of bird. And God looked at them with pleasure, and blessed them all. "Multiply and stock the oceans," he told them, and to the birds he said, "Let your numbers increase. Fill the earth!" [23] That ended the fifth day.[j]

[24] And God said, "Let the earth bring forth every kind of animal—cattle and reptiles and wildlife of every kind." And so it was. [25] God made all sorts of wild animals and cattle and reptiles. And God was pleased with what he had done.

[26] Then God said, "Let us make a man[k] —someone like ourselves,[l] to be the master of all life upon the earth and in the skies and in the seas."

[27] So God made man like his Maker.

Like God did God make man;

Man and maid did he make them.

[28] And God blessed them and told them, "Multiply and fill the earth and subdue it; you are masters of the fish and birds and all the animals. [29] And look! I have given you the seed-bearing plants throughout the earth, and all the fruit trees for your food. [30] And I've given all the grass and plants to the animals and birds for their food." [31] Then God looked over all that he had made, and it was excellent in every way. This ended the sixth day.[m]

---

a Or, "In the beginning God created . . ."   b Implied.   c Or, "shapeless and void."
d Or, "over the cloud of darkness," or, "over the darkness and waters," or even, "over the dark, gaseous mass." There is no "right" way to translate these words.   e Literally, "And there was evening and there was morning, one day (or, 'period of time')."   f Literally, "Let there be a dome to divide the waters."
g Literally, "There was evening and there was morning, a second day (or, 'period of time')."
h Literally, "And there was evening and there was morning, a third day (or, 'period of time')."
i Literally, "And there was evening and there was morning, a fourth day (or, 'period of time')."
j Literally, "And there was evening and there was morning, a fifth day (or, 'period of time')."
k Literally, "men."   l Literally, "Let us make man in our image, in our likeness."   m Literally, "And there was evening and there was morning, a sixth day (or, 'period of time')."

2 NOW AT LAST the heavens and earth were successfully completed, with all that they contained. [2] So on the seventh day, having finished his task, God ceased from this work he had been doing, [3] and God blessed the seventh day and declared it holy, because it was the day when he ceased this work of creation.

[4] Here is a summary of the events in the creation of the heavens and earth which the Lord God made.

[5] There were no plants or grain sprouting up across the earth at first, for the Lord God hadn't sent any rain; nor was there anyone to farm the soil. [6] (However, water welled up from the ground at certain places and flowed across the land.)

[7] The time came when the Lord God formed a man's body from the dust of the ground[a] and breathed into it the breath of life. And man became a living person.

[8] Then the Lord God planted a garden in Eden, to the east, and placed in the garden the man he had formed. [9] The Lord God planted all sorts of beautiful trees there in the garden, trees producing the choicest of fruit. At the center of the garden he placed the Tree of Life, and also the Tree of Conscience, giving knowledge of Good and Bad. [10] A river from the land of Eden flowed through the garden to water it; afterwards the river divided into four branches. [11,12] One of these was named the Pishon; it winds across the entire length of the land of Havilah,[b] where nuggets of pure gold are found, also beautiful bdellium and even lapis lazuli. [13] The second branch is called the Gihon, crossing the entire length of the land of Cush. [14] The third branch is the Tigris, which flows to the east of the city of Asher. And the fourth is the Euphrates.

[15] The Lord God placed the man in the Garden of Eden as its gardener, to tend and care for it. [16,17] But the Lord God gave the man this warning: "You may eat any fruit in the garden except fruit from the Tree of Conscience—for its fruit will open your eyes to make you aware of right and wrong, good and bad. If you eat its fruit, you will be doomed to die."

[18] And the Lord God said, "It isn't good for man to be alone; I will make a companion for him, a helper suited to his needs." [19,20] So the Lord God formed from the soil every kind of animal and bird, and brought them to the man to see what he would call them; and whatever he called them, that was their name. But still there was no proper helper for the man. [21] Then the Lord God caused the man to fall into a deep sleep, and took one of his ribs and closed up the place from which he had removed it, [22] and made the rib into a woman, and brought her to the man.

[23] "This is it!" Adam exclaimed. "She is part of my own bone and flesh! Her name is 'woman' because she was taken out of a man." [24] This explains why a man leaves his father and mother and is joined to his wife in such a way that the two become one person.[c] [25] Now although the man and his wife were both naked, neither of them was embarrassed or ashamed.

3 THE SERPENT WAS the craftiest of all the creatures the Lord God had made. So the serpent came to the woman. "Really?" he asked. *"None* of the fruit in the garden? God says you mustn't eat *any* of it?"

[2,3] "Of course we may eat it," the woman told him. "It's only the fruit from the tree at the *center* of the garden that we are not to eat. God says we mustn't eat it or even touch it, or we will die."

[4] "That's a lie!" the serpent hissed. "You'll not die! [5] God knows very well that the instant you eat it you will become like him, for your eyes will be opened—you will be able to distinguish good from evil!"

[6] The woman was convinced. How lovely and fresh looking it was! And it would make her so wise! So she ate some of the fruit and gave some to her husband, and he ate it too. [7] And as they ate it, suddenly they became aware of their nakedness, and were embarrassed. So they strung fig leaves together to cover themselves around the hips.

[8] That evening they heard the sound of

---

a Or, "from a lump of soil," or, "from clods in the soil," or, "from a clod of clay."   b Located along the border of Babylonia.   c Literally, "one flesh."

the Lord God walking in the garden; and they hid themselves among the trees. [9] The Lord God called to Adam, "Why are you hiding?"[a]

[10] And Adam replied, "I heard you coming and didn't want you to see me naked. So I hid."

[11] "Who told you you were naked?" the Lord God asked. "Have you eaten fruit from the tree I warned you about?"

[12] "Yes," Adam admitted, "but it was the woman you gave me who brought me some, and I ate it."

[13] Then the Lord God asked the woman, "How could you do such a thing?"

"The serpent tricked me," she replied.

[14] So the Lord God said to the serpent, "This is your punishment: You are singled out from among all the domestic and wild animals of the whole earth—to be cursed. You shall grovel in the dust as long as you live, crawling along on your belly. [15] From now on you and the woman will be enemies, as will all of your offspring and hers. And I will put the fear of you into the woman, and between your offspring and hers. He shall strike you on your head, while you will strike at his heel."

[16] Then God said to the woman, "You shall bear children in intense pain and suffering; yet even so, you shall welcome your husband's affections, and he shall be your master."

[17] And to Adam, God said, "Because you listened to your wife and ate the fruit when I told you not to, I have placed a curse upon the soil. All your life you will struggle to extract a living from it. [18] It will grow thorns and thistles for you, and you shall eat its grasses. [19] All your life you will sweat to master it, until your dying day. Then you will return to the ground from which you came. For you were made from the ground, and to the ground you will return."

[20] The man named his wife Eve (meaning[b] "The life-giving one"), for he said, "She shall become the mother of all mankind"; [21] and the Lord God clothed Adam and his wife with garments made from skins of animals.

[22] Then the Lord said, "Now that the man has become as we are, knowing good from bad, what if he eats the fruit of the Tree of Life and lives forever?" [23] So the Lord God banished him forever from the Garden of Eden, and sent him out to farm the ground from which he had been taken. [24] Thus God expelled him, and placed mighty angels at the east of the garden of Eden, with a flaming sword to guard the entrance to the Tree of Life.

4 THEN ADAM HAD sexual intercourse with Eve his wife, and she conceived and gave birth to a son, Cain (meaning "I have created"). For, as she said, "With God's help, I have created a man!" [2] Her next child was his brother, Abel.

Abel became a shepherd, while Cain was a farmer. [3] At harvest time Cain brought the Lord a gift of his farm produce, [4] and Abel brought the fatty cuts of meat from his best lambs, and presented them to the Lord. And the Lord accepted Abel's offering, [5] but not Cain's. This made Cain both dejected and very angry, and his face grew dark with fury.

[6] "Why are you angry?" the Lord asked him. "Why is your face so dark with rage? [7] It can be bright with joy if you will do what you should! But if you refuse to obey, watch out. Sin is waiting to attack you, longing to destroy you. But you can conquer it!"

[8] One day Cain suggested to his brother, "Let's go out into the fields." And while they were together there, Cain attacked and killed his brother.

[9] But afterwards the Lord asked Cain, "Where is your brother? Where is Abel?"

"How should I know?" Cain retorted. "Am I supposed to keep track of him wherever he goes?"

[10] But the Lord said, "Your brother's blood calls to me from the ground. What have you done? [11] You are hereby banished from this ground which you have defiled with your brother's blood. [12] No longer will it yield crops for you, even if you toil on it forever! From now on you will be a fugitive

---

a Or, "Where are you?"   b Many Hebrew names are based on puns. In this case for instance, the Hebrew word for *Eve* sounds similar to a Hebrew word that means "life-giving."

and a tramp upon the earth, wandering from place to place."

[13] Cain replied to the Lord, "My punishment is greater than I can bear. [14] For you have banished me from my farm and from you, and made me a fugitive and a tramp; and everyone who sees me will try to kill me."

[15] The Lord replied, "They won't kill you, for I will give seven times your punishment to anyone who does." Then the Lord put an identifying mark on Cain as a warning not to kill him. [16] So Cain went out from the presence of the Lord and settled in the land of Nod, east of Eden.

[17] Then Cain's wife conceived and presented him with a baby son named Enoch; so when Cain founded a city, he named it Enoch, after his son.

[18] Enoch was the father[a] of Irad;
Irad was the father[a] of Mehujael;
Mehujael was the father[a] of Methusael;
Methusael was the father[a] of Lamech;

[19] Lamech married two wives—Adah and Zillah. [20] To Adah was born a baby named Jabal. He became the first of the cattlemen and those living in tents. [21] His brother's name was Jubal, the first musician—the inventor[b] of the harp and flute. [22] To Lamech's other wife, Zillah, was born Tubal-cain. He opened the first foundry[c] forging instruments of bronze and iron.

[23] One day Lamech said to Adah and Zillah, "Listen to me, my wives. I have killed a youth who attacked and wounded me. [24] If anyone who kills Cain will be punished seven times, anyone taking revenge against me for killing that youth should be punished seventy-seven times!"

[25] Later on Eve gave birth to another son and named him Seth (meaning "Granted"); for, as Eve put it, "God has granted me another son for the one Cain killed." [26] When Seth grew up, he had a son and named him Enosh. It was during his life-time that men first began to call themselves "the Lord's people."[d]

5 HERE IS A list of some[a] of the descendants of Adam—the man who was like[b] God from the day of his creation. [2] God created man and woman and blessed them, and called them Man from the start.

[3,4,5] *Adam:* Adam was 130 years old when his son[c] Seth was born, the very image of his father in every way.[d] After Seth was born,[e] Adam lived another 800 years, producing sons and daughters, and died at the age of 930.

[6,7,8] *Seth:* Seth was 105 years old when his son Enosh was born. Afterwards he lived another 807 years, producing sons and daughters, and died at the age of 912.

[9,10,11] *Enosh:* Enosh was ninety years old when his son Kenan was born. Afterwards he lived another 815 years, producing sons and daughters, and died at the age of 905.

[12,13,14] *Kenan:* Kenan was seventy years old when his son Mahalalel was born. Afterwards he lived another 840 years, producing sons and daughters, and died at the age of 910.

[15,16,17] *Mahalalel:* Mahalalel was sixty-five years old when his son Jared was born. Afterwards he lived 830 years, producing sons and daughters, and died at the age of 895.

[18,19,20] *Jared:* Jared was 162 years old when his son Enoch was born. Afterwards he lived another 800 years, producing sons and daughters, and died at the age of 962.

[21-24] *Enoch:* Enoch was sixty-five years old when his son Methuselah was born. Afterwards he lived another 300 years in fellowship with God, and produced sons and daughters; then, when he was

---

a Or, "the ancestor of."　　　b Literally, "He was the father of all such as handle the harp and pipe."
c Literally, "He was the father of all metal workers in bronze and iron."　　　d Or, "This man was the first to invoke the name of Jehovah."　　　5a Literally, "This is the roll of Adam's descendants."
b Literally, "In the likeness of God."　　　c Or, by Hebrew usage, "When his son, the *ancestor* (of Seth) was born." So also in verses 6, 9, 12, 15, 18, 21, 25, 28, 32.　　　d Literally, "In his own likeness, after his image."
e Or, by Hebrew usage, "After this ancestor of Seth was born."

365, and in constant touch with God, he disappeared, for God took him!

²⁵,²⁶,²⁷ *Methuselah:* Methuselah was 187 years old when his son Lamech was born; afterwards he lived another 782 years, producing sons and daughters, and died at the age of 969.

²⁸⁻³¹ *Lamech:* Lamech was 182 years old when his son Noah was born. Lamech named him Noah (meaning "Relief") because he said, "He will bring us relief from the hard work of farming this ground which God has cursed." Afterwards Lamech lived 595 years, producing sons and daughters, and died at the age of 777.

³² *Noah:* Noah was 500 years old and had three sons, Shem, Ham, and Japheth.

6 NOW A POPULATION explosion took place upon the earth. It was at this time that beings from the spirit worldᵃ looked upon the beautiful earth women and took any they desired to be their wives. ³ Then Jehovah said, "My Spirit must not forever be disgraced in man, wholly evil as he is. I will give him 120 years to mend his ways."

⁴ In those days, and even afterwards, when the evil beings from the spirit world were sexually involved with human women, their children became giants, of whom so many legends are told. ⁵ When the Lord God saw the extent of human wickedness, and that the trend and direction of men's lives were only towards evil, ⁶ he was sorry he had made them. It broke his heart.

⁷ And he said, "I will blot out from the face of the earth all mankind that I created. Yes, and the animals too, and the reptiles and the birds. For I am sorry I made them."

⁸ But Noah was a pleasure to the Lord. Here is the story of Noah: ⁹,¹⁰ He was the only truly righteous man living on the earth at that time. He tried always to conduct his affairs according to God's will. And he had three sons—Shem, Ham, and Japheth.

¹¹ Meanwhile, the crime rate was rising rapidly across the earth, and, as seen by God, the world was rotten to the core.

¹²,¹³ As God observed how bad it was, and saw that all mankind was vicious and depraved, he said to Noah, "I have decided to destroy all mankind; for the earth is filled with crime because of man. Yes, I will destroy mankind from the earth. ¹⁴ Make a boat from resinous wood, sealing it with tar; and construct decks and stalls throughout the ship. ¹⁵ Make it 450 feet long, 75 feet wide, and 45 feet high. ¹⁶ Construct a skylight all the way around the ship, eighteen inches below the roof; and make three decks inside the boat—a bottom, middle, and upper deck—and put a door in the side.

¹⁷ "Look! I am going to cover the earth with a flood and destroy every living being —everything in which there is the breath of life. All will die. ¹⁸ But I promise to keep you safe in the ship, with your wife and your sons and their wives. ¹⁹,²⁰ Bring a pair of every animal—a male and a female—into the boat with you, to keep them alive through the flood. Bring in a pair of each kind of bird and animal and reptile. ²¹ Store away in the boat all the food that they and you will need." ²² And Noah did everything as God commanded him.

7 FINALLY THE DAY came when the Lord said to Noah, "Go into the boat with all your family, for among all the people of the earth, I consider you alone to be righteous. ² Bring in the animals, too—a pair of each, except those kinds I have chosen for eating and for sacrifice: take seven pairs of each of them, ³ and seven pairsᵃ of every kind of bird. Thus there will be every kind of life reproducing again after the flood has ended. ⁴ One week from today I will begin forty days and nights of rain; and all the animals and birds and reptiles I have made will die."

⁵ So Noah did everything the Lord commanded him. ⁶ He was 600 years old when the flood came. ⁷ He boarded the boat with his wife and sons and their wives, to escape the flood. ⁸,⁹ With him were all the various kinds of animals—those for eating and sac-

rifice, and those that were not, and the birds and reptiles. They came into the boat in pairs, male and female, just as God commanded Noah.

[10,11,12] One week later, when Noah was 600 years, two months, and seventeen days old, the rain came down in mighty torrents from the sky, and the subterranean waters burst forth upon the earth for forty days and nights. [13] But Noah had gone into the boat that very day with his wife and his sons, Shem, Ham, and Japheth, and their wives. [14,15] With them in the boat were pairs of every kind of animal—domestic and wild —and reptiles and birds of every sort. [16] Two by two they came, male and female, just as God had commanded. Then the Lord God[b] closed the door and shut them in.

[17] For forty days the roaring floods prevailed, covering the ground and lifting the boat high above the earth. [18] As the water rose higher and higher above the ground, the boat floated safely upon it; [19] until finally the water covered all the high mountains under the whole heaven, [20] standing twenty-two feet and more above the highest peaks. [21] And all living things upon the earth perished—birds, domestic and wild animals, and reptiles and all mankind— [22] everything that breathed and lived upon dry land. [23] All existence on the earth was blotted out—man and animals alike, and reptiles and birds. God destroyed them all, leaving only Noah alive, and those with him in the boat. [24] And the water covered the earth 150 days.

8 GOD DIDN'T FORGET about Noah and all the animals in the boat! He sent a wind to blow across the waters, and the floods began to disappear, [2] for the subterranean water sources ceased their gushing, and the torrential rains subsided. [3,4] So the flood gradually receded until, 150 days after it began, the boat came to rest upon the mountains of Ararat. [5] Three months later,[a] as the waters continued to go down,

other mountain peaks appeared.

[6] After another forty days, Noah opened a porthole [7] and released a raven that flew back and forth[b] until the earth was dry. [8] Meanwhile he sent out a dove to see if it could find dry ground, [9] but the dove found no place to light, and returned to Noah, for the water was still too high. So Noah held out his hand and drew the dove back into the boat.

[10] Seven days later Noah released the dove again, [11] and this time, towards evening, the bird returned to him with an olive leaf in her beak. So Noah knew that the water was almost gone. [12] A week later he released the dove again, and this time she didn't come back.

[13] Twenty-nine days after that,[c] Noah opened the door to look, and the water was gone. [14] Eight more weeks went by. Then at last the earth was dry. [15,16] Then God told Noah, "You may all go out. [17] Release all the animals, birds, and reptiles, so that they will breed abundantly and reproduce in great numbers." [18,19] So the boat was soon empty. Noah, his wife, and his sons and their wives all disembarked, along with all the animals, reptiles, and birds—all left the ark in pairs and groups.

[20] Then Noah built an altar and sacrificed on it some of the animals and birds God had designated[d] for that purpose. [21] And Jehovah was pleased with[e] the sacrifice and said to himself, "I will never do it again—I will never again curse the earth, destroying all living things, even though man's bent is always toward evil from his earliest youth, and even though he does such wicked things. [22] As long as the earth remains, there will be springtime and harvest, cold and heat, winter and summer, day and night."

9 GOD BLESSED NOAH and his sons and told them to have many children and to repopulate the earth.

[2,3] "All wild animals and birds and fish will be afraid of you," God told him; "for

---

b Literally, "Jehovah."   8a Literally, "on the first day of the tenth month."   b Apparently lighting from time to time upon carcasses of dead animals floating on the water. The dove which Noah next dispatched would not alight on such floating carrion, and was thus a good indication of the water level.
c Literally, "in the 601st year, in the first month, the first day of the month."   d Literally, "clean," i.e., ritually approved by God.   e Literally, "and Jehovah smelled the delicious odor and said . . ."

I have placed them in your power, and they are yours to use for food, in addition to grain and vegetables. ⁴ But never eat animals unless their life-blood has been drained off. ⁵,⁶ And murder is forbidden. Man-killing animals must die, and any man who murders shall be killed; for to kill a man is to kill one made like God. ⁷ Yes, have many children and repopulate the earth and subdue it."

⁸ Then God told Noah and his sons, ⁹,¹⁰,¹¹ "I solemnly promise you and your children[a] and the animals you brought with you —all these birds and cattle and wild animals—that I will never again send another flood to destroy the earth. ¹² And I seal this promise with this sign: ¹³ I have placed my rainbow in the clouds as a sign of my promise until the end of time, to you and to all the earth. ¹⁴ When I send clouds over the earth, the rainbow will be seen in the clouds, ¹⁵ and I will remember my promise to you and to every being, that never again will the floods come and destroy all life. ¹⁶,¹⁷ For I will see the rainbow in the cloud and remember my eternal promise to every living being on the earth."

¹⁸ The names of Noah's three sons were Shem, Ham, and Japheth. (Ham is the ancestor of the Canaanites.)[b] ¹⁹ From these three sons of Noah came all the nations of the earth.

²⁰,²¹ Noah became a farmer and planted a vineyard, and he made wine. One day as he was drunk and lay naked in his tent, ²² Ham, the father of Canaan, saw his father's nakedness and went outside and told his two brothers. ²³ Then Shem and Japheth took a robe and held it over their shoulders and, walking backwards into the tent, let it fall across their father to cover his nakedness as they looked the other way. ²⁴,²⁵ When Noah awoke from his drunken stupor, and learned what had happened and what Ham, his younger son, had done, he cursed Ham's descendants:[c]

"A curse upon the Canaanites," he
　　swore.
"May they be the lowest of slaves

To the descendants of Shem and
　　Japheth."
²⁶,²⁷ Then he said,
"God bless Shem,
And may Canaan be his slave.[d]
God bless Japheth,
And let him share the prosperity of
　　Shem,
And let Canaan be his slave."
²⁸ Noah lived another 350 years after the flood, ²⁹ and was 950 years old at his death.

10 THESE ARE THE families of Shem, Ham, and Japheth, who were the three sons of Noah; for sons were born to them after the flood.

² The sons[a] of Japheth were:
　　Gomer, Magog, Madai,
　　Javan, Tubal,
　　Meshech, Tiras.
³ The sons of Gomer:
　　Ashkenaz, Riphath, Togarmah.
⁴ The sons of Javan:
　　Elishah, Tarshish,
　　Kittim, Dodanim.
⁵ Their descendants became the maritime nations in various lands, each with a separate language.
⁶ The sons of Ham were:
　　Cush, Mizraim,
　　Put, Canaan.
⁷ The sons of Cush were:
　　Seba, Havilah, Sabtah,
　　Raamah, Sabteca.
　　The sons of Raamah were:
　　Sheba, Dedan.
⁸ One of the descendants[b] of Cush was Nimrod, who became the first of the kings. ⁹ He was a mighty hunter, blessed of God,[c] and his name became proverbial. People would speak of someone as being "like Nimrod—a mighty hunter, blessed of God."[c] ¹⁰ The heart of his empire included Babel, Erech, Accad, and Calneh in the land of Shinar. ¹¹,¹² From there he extended his reign to Assyria. He built Nineveh, Rehoboth-Ir, Calah, and Resen (which is located between Nineveh and Calah), the main city of the empire.

---

a Literally, "your seed."　　　b Ham was not the ancestor of the Negro, as was once erroneously supposed. c Literally, "cursed be Canaan." The Canaanites were Ham's descendants.　　　d Or, "Blessed be Jehovah, the God of Shem . . . and may the Canaanites be Shem's slaves."　　　10a "descendants." b Or, "the son of Cush."　　　c Or, "a mighty hunter against the Lord."

[13,14] Mizraim was the ancestor[d] of the people inhabiting these areas: Ludim, Anamim, Lehabim, Naphtuhim, Pathrusim, Casluhim (from whom came the Philistines), and Caphtorim.

[15-19] Canaan's oldest son was Sidon, and he was also the father of Heth; from Canaan descended these nations: Jebusites, Amorites, Girgashites, Hivites, Arkites, Sinites, Arvadites, Zemarites, Hamathites. Eventually the descendants of Canaan spread from Sidon all the way to Gerar, in the Gaza strip; and to Sodom, Gomorrah, Admah, and Zeboiim, near Lasha.

[20] These, then, were the descendants of Ham, spread abroad in many lands and nations, with many languages.

[21] Eber descended from Shem, the oldest brother of Japheth. [22] Here is a list of Shem's other descendants: Elam, Asshur, Arpachshad, Lud, Aram.

[23] Aram's sons[e] were: Uz, Hul, Gether, Mash.

[24] Arpachshad's son was Shelah, and Shelah's son was Eber.

[25] Two sons were born to Eber: Peleg (meaning "Division," for during his lifetime the people of the world were separated and dispersed), and Joktan (Peleg's brother).

[26-30] Joktan was the father[f] of Almodad, Sheleph, Hazarmaveth, Jerah, Hadoram, Uzal, Diklah, Obal, Abima-el, Sheba, Ophir, Havi-lah, Jobab. These descendants of Joktan lived all the way from Mesha to the eastern hills of Sephar.

[31] These, then, were the descendants of Shem, classified according to their political groupings, languages, and geographical locations. [32] All of the men listed above descended from Noah, through many generations, living in the various nations that developed after the flood.

11 AT THAT TIME all mankind spoke a single language. [2] As the population grew and spread eastward, a plain was discovered in the land of Babylon,[a] and was soon thickly populated.[b] [3,4] The people who lived there began to talk about building a great city, with a temple-tower reaching to the skies—a proud, eternal monument to themselves.

"This will weld us together," they said, "and keep us from scattering all over the world." So they made great piles of hard-burned brick, and collected bitumen to use as mortar.

[5] But when God came down to see the city and the tower mankind was making, [6] he said, "Look! If they are able to accomplish all this when they have just *begun* to exploit their linguistic and political unity, just think of what they will do later! Nothing will be unattainable for them![c] [7] Come, let us go down and give them different languages, so that they won't understand each other's words!"

[8] So, in that way, God scattered them all over the earth; and that ended the building of the city. [9] That is why the city was called Babel (meaning "confusion"), because it was there that Jehovah confused them by giving them many languages, thus widely scattering them across the face of the earth.

[10,11] Shem's line of descendants included Arpachshad, born two years after the flood when Shem was 100 years old; after that he lived another 500 years, and had many sons and daughters.

[12,13] When Arpachshad was thirty-five years old, his son[d] Shelah was born, and after that he lived another 403 years, and had many sons and daughters.

[14,15] Shelah was thirty years old when his son Eber was born, living 403 years after that, and had many sons and daughters.

---

d Or, "father."   e Or, "descendants."   f Or, "ancestor."   11a Literally, "the land of Shinar," located at the mouth of the Persian Gulf.   b Literally, "and they settled there."   c Language is the basis on which science feeds upon itself and grows. This was the beginning of an explosion of knowledge, nipped in the bud because of wrong motives and wrong use of the knowledge gained. Similarity with today's world is significant.   d Or, by Hebrew usage, "there was born to him the ancestor of Shelah, and after that . . ." So also throughout the remainder of the chapter.

16,17 Eber was thirty-four years old when his son Peleg was born. He lived another 430 years afterwards, and had many sons and daughters.

18,19 Peleg was thirty years old when his son Reu was born. He lived another 209 years afterwards, and had many sons and daughters.

20,21 Reu was thirty-two years old when Serug was born. He lived 207 years after that, with many sons and daughters.

22,23 Serug was thirty years old when his son Nahor was born. He lived 200 years afterwards, with many sons and daughters.

24,25 Nahor was twenty-nine years old at the birth of his son Terah. He lived 119 years afterwards, and had sons and daughters.

26 By the time Terah was seventy years old, he had three sons, Abram, Nahor, and Haran. 27 And Haran had a son named Lot. 28 But Haran died young, in the land where he was born (in Ur of the Chaldeans), and was survived by his father.

29 Meanwhile, Abram married his half-sister[e] Sarai, while his brother Nahor married their orphaned niece Milcah,[f] who was the daughter of their brother Haran; and she had a brother named Iscah. 30 But Sarai was barren; she had no children. 31 Then Terah took his son Abram, his grandson Lot (his son Haran's child), and his daughter-in-law Sarai, and left Ur of the Chaldeans to go to the land of Canaan; but they stopped instead at the city of Haran and settled there. 32 And there Terah died at the age of 205.[g]

12 AFTER THE DEATH of Abram's father, God told him, "Leave your own country behind you, and your own people, and go to the land I will guide you to. 2 If you do, I will cause you to become the father of a great nation; I will bless you and make your name famous, and you will be a blessing to many others.[a] 3 I will bless those who bless you and curse those who curse you; and the entire world will be blessed because of you."[b]

4 So Abram departed as the Lord had instructed him, and Lot went too; Abram was seventy-five years old at that time. 5 He took his wife Sarai, his nephew Lot, and all his wealth—the cattle and slaves he had gotten in Haran—and finally arrived in Canaan. 6 Traveling through Canaan, they came to a place near Shechem, and set up camp beside the oak at Moreh. (This area was inhabited by Canaanites at that time.) 7 Then Jehovah appeared to Abram and said, "I am going to give this land to your descendants." And Abram built an altar there to commemorate Jehovah's visit. 8 Afterwards Abram left that place and traveled southward[c] to the hilly country between Bethel on the west and Ai on the east. There he made camp, and made an altar to the Lord and prayed to him. 9 Thus he continued slowly southward to the Negeb, pausing frequently.

10 There was at that time a terrible famine in the land: and so Abram went on down to Egypt to live. 11,12,13 But as he was approaching the borders of Egypt, he asked Sarai his wife to tell everyone that she was his sister! "You are very beautiful," he told her, "and when the Egyptians see you they will say, 'This is his wife. Let's kill him and then we can have her!' But if you say you are my sister, then the Egyptians will treat me well because of you, and spare my life!" 14 And sure enough, when they arrived in Egypt everyone spoke of her beauty. 15 When the palace aides saw her, they praised her to their king, the Pharaoh, and she was taken into his harem.[d] 16 Then Pharaoh gave Abram many gifts because of her—sheep, oxen, donkeys, men and women slaves, and camels.

17 But the Lord sent a terrible plague upon Pharaoh's household on account of her being there. 18 Then Pharaoh called Abram before him and accused him sharply. "What is this you have done to me?" he demanded. "Why didn't you tell me she was your wife? 19 Why were you

---

e Implied. See Genesis 20:12.   f Implied.   g Implied. The Samaritan Pentateuch says that Terah died when he was 145 years old, so that his death occurred in the year of Abraham's departure from Haran. This is more consistent with Genesis 11:26 and 12:4. See also Acts 7:4.   12a Or, "I will make your name so famous that it will be used to pronounce blessings on others."   b Or, "The nations will bless themselves because of you."   c Implied.   d Literally, "into the household of Pharaoh."

willing to let me marry her, saying she was your sister? Here, take her and be gone!" [20] And Pharaoh sent them out of the country under armed escort—Abram, his wife, and all his household and possessions.

13 SO THEY LEFT Egypt and traveled north into the Negeb—Abram with his wife, and Lot, and all that they owned, for Abram was very rich in livestock, silver, and gold. [3,4] Then they continued northward toward Bethel where he had camped before, between Bethel and Ai—to the place where he had built the altar. And there he again worshiped the Lord.

[5] Lot too was very wealthy, with sheep and cattle and many servants.[a] [6] But the land could not support both Abram and Lot with all their flocks and herds. There were too many animals for the available pasture. [7] So fights broke out between the herdsmen of Abram and Lot, despite the danger they all faced[b] from the tribes of Canaanites and Perizzites present in the land. [8] Then Abram talked it over with Lot. "This fighting between our men has got to stop," he said. "We can't afford to let a rift develop between our clans. Close relatives such as we are must present a united front! [9] I'll tell you what we'll do. Take your choice of any section of the land you want, and we will separate. If you want that part over there to the east, then I'll stay here in the western section. Or, if you want the west, then I'll go over there to the east."

[10] Lot took a long look at the fertile plains of the Jordan River, well watered everywhere (this was before Jehovah destroyed Sodom and Gomorrah); the whole section was like the Garden of Eden,[c] or like the beautiful countryside around Zoar in Egypt. [11] So that is what Lot chose—the Jordan valley to the east of them. He went there with his flocks and servants, and thus he and Abram parted company. [12] For Abram stayed in the land of Canaan, while Lot lived among the cities of the plain, settling at a place near the city of Sodom. [13] The men of this area were unusually wicked, and sinned greatly against Jehovah.

[14] After Lot was gone, the Lord said to Abram, "Look as far as you can see in every direction, [15] for I am going to give it all to you and your descendants. [16] And I am going to give you so many descendants that, like dust, they can't be counted! [17] Hike in all directions and explore the new possessions I am giving you." [18] Then Abram moved his tent to the oaks of Mamre, near Hebron, and built an altar to Jehovah there.

14 NOW WAR FILLED the land—
Amraphel, king of Shinar,
Arioch, king of Ellasar,
Ched-or-laomer, king of Elam, and
Tidal, king of Goiim
[2] Fought against:
Bera, king of Sodom,
Birsha, king of Gomorrah,
Shinab, king of Admah,
Shemeber, king of Zeboiim, and
The king of Bela (later called Zoar).
[3] These kings (of Sodom, Gomorrah, Admah, Zeboiim, and Bela) mobilized their armies in Siddim Valley (that is, the valley of the Salt Sea). [4] For twelve years they had all been subject to King Ched-or-laomer, but now in the thirteenth year, they rebelled.

[5,6] One year later, Ched-or-laomer and his allies arrived and the slaughter began. For they were victorious over the following tribes at the places indicated:
The Rephaim in Ashteroth-karnaim;
The Zuzim in Ham;
The Emim in the plain of Kiriathaim;
The Horites in Mount Seir, as far as
    El-paran at the edge of the desert.
[7] Then they swung around to Enmishpat (later called Kadesh) and destroyed the Amalekites, and also the Amorites living in Hazazan-tamar.

[8,9] But now the other army, that of the kings of Sodom, Gomorrah, Admah, Zeboiim, and Bela (Zoar), unsuccessfully[a] attacked Ched-or-laomer and his allies as they were in the Salt Sea Valley (four kings against five). [10] As it happened, the valley was full of asphalt pits. And as the army of the kings of Sodom and Gomorrah fled,

---

a Implied. Literally, "many tents."   b Implied.   c Literally, "the Garden of Jehovah."
14a Implied.

some slipped into the pits, and the remainder fled to the mountains. [11] Then the victors plundered[b] Sodom and Gomorrah and carried off all their wealth and food, and went on their homeward way, [12] taking with them Lot—Abram's nephew[c] who lived in Sodom—and all he owned. [13] One of the men who escaped came and told Abram the Hebrew, who was camping among the oaks belonging to Mamre the Amorite (brother of Eshcol and Aner, Abram's allies).

[14] When Abram learned that Lot had been captured, he called together the men born into his household, 318 of them in all, and chased after the retiring army as far as Dan. [15] That night he successfully attacked them and pursued the fleeing army to Hobah, north of Damascus, [16] and recovered everything—the loot that had been taken, his relative Lot, and all of Lot's possessions, including the women and other captives.

[17] As Abram returned from his strike against Ched-or-laomer and the other kings at the Valley of Shaveh (later called King's Valley), the king of Sodom came out to meet him, [18] and Melchizedek, the king of Salem (Jerusalem), who was a priest of the God of Highest Heaven, brought him bread and wine. [19,20] Then Melchizedek blessed Abram with this blessing:

"The blessing of the supreme God, Creator of heaven and earth, be upon you, Abram; and blessed be God, who has delivered your enemies over to you."

Then Abram gave Melchizedek a tenth of all the spoils.

[21] The king of Sodom told him, "Just give me back my people who were captured; keep for yourself the booty stolen from my city."

[22] But Abram replied, "I have solemnly promised Jehovah, the supreme God, Creator of heaven and earth, [23] that I will not take so much as a single thread from you, lest you say, 'Abram is rich because of what I gave him!' [24] All I'll accept is what these young men of mine have eaten; but give a share of the booty to Aner, Eshcol, and Mamre, my allies."

15 AFTERWARDS JEHOVAH SPOKE to Abram in a vision, and this is what he told him: "Don't be fearful, Abram, for I will defend you. And I will give you great blessings."

[2,3] But Abram replied, "O Lord Jehovah, what good are all your blessings when I have no son? For without a son, some other member of my household[a] will inherit all my wealth."

[4] Then Jehovah told him, "No, no one else will be your heir, for you will have a son to inherit everything you own."

[5] Then God brought Abram outside beneath the nighttime sky and told him, "Look up into the heavens and count the stars if you can. Your descendants will be like that—too many to count!" [6] And Abram believed God; then God considered him righteous on account of his faith.

[7] And he told him, "I am Jehovah who brought you out of the city of Ur of the Chaldeans, to give you this land forever."

[8] But Abram replied, "O Lord Jehovah, how can I be sure that you will give it to me?" [9] Then Jehovah told him to take a three-year-old heifer, a three-year-old female goat, a three-year-old ram, a turtledove and a young pigeon, [10] and to slay them and to cut them apart down the middle, and to separate the halves, but not to divide the birds. [11] And when the vultures came down upon the carcasses, Abram shooed them away.

[12] That evening as the sun was going down, a deep sleep fell upon Abram, and a vision of terrible foreboding, darkness, and horror.

[13] Then Jehovah told Abram, "Your descendants will be oppressed as slaves in a foreign land for 400 years. [14] But I will punish the nation that enslaves them, and at the end they will come away with great wealth. [15] (But you will die in peace, at a ripe old age.) [16] After four generations they will return here to this land; for the wickedness of the Amorite nations living here now[b] will not be ready for punishment until then."

---

b Implied in context.   c Literally, "Abram's brother's son."   15a Or, "Eliezer of Damascus."
b Implied.

¹⁷ As the sun went down and it was dark, Abram saw a smoking fire-pot and a flaming torch that passed between the halves of the carcasses. ¹⁸ So that day Jehovah made this covenant with Abram: "I have given this land to your descendants from the Wadi-el-Arish^c to the Euphrates River. ¹⁹,²⁰,²¹ And I give to them these nations: Kenites, Kenizzites, Kadmonites, Hittites, Perizzites, Rephaim, Amorites, Canaanites, Girgashites, Jebusites."

16 BUT SARAI AND Abram had no children. So Sarai took her maid, an Egyptian girl named Hagar, ²,³ and gave her to Abram to be his second wife.

"Since the Lord has given me no children," Sarai said, "you may sleep with my servant girl, and her children shall be mine."

And Abram agreed. (This took place ten years after Abram had first arrived in the land of Canaan.) ⁴ So he slept with Hagar, and she conceived; and when she realized she was pregnant, she became very proud and arrogant toward her mistress Sarai. ⁵ Then Sarai said to Abram, "It's all your fault. For now this servant girl of mine despises me, though I myself gave her the privilege of being your wife. May the Lord judge you for doing this to me!"^{a}

⁶ "You have my permission to punish the girl as you see fit," Abram replied. So Sarai beat her and she ran away. ⁷ The Angel of the Lord found her beside a desert spring along the road to Shur.

⁸ *The Angel:* "Hagar, Sarai's maid, where have you come from, and where are you going?"

Hagar: "I am running away from my mistress."

⁹⁻¹² *The Angel:* "Return to your mistress and act as you should, for I will make you into a great nation. Yes, you are pregnant and your baby will be a son, and you are to name him Ishmael ('God hears'), because God has heard your woes. This son of yours will be a wild one—free and untamed as a wild ass!

He will be against everyone, and everyone will feel the same towards him. But he will live near the rest of his kin."

¹³ Thereafter^b Hagar spoke of Jehovah—for it was he who appeared to her—as "the God who looked upon me," for she thought, "I saw God and lived to tell it." ¹⁴ Later that well was named "The Well of the Living One Who Sees Me." It lies between Kadesh and Bered.

¹⁵ So Hagar gave Abram a son, and Abram named him Ishmael. ¹⁶ (Abram was eighty-six years old at this time.)

17 WHEN ABRAM WAS ninety-nine years old, God appeared to him and told him, "I am the Almighty; obey me and live as you should. ²,³,⁴ I will prepare a contract between us, guaranteeing to make you into a mighty nation. In fact you shall be the father of not only one nation, but a multitude of nations!" Abram fell face downward in the dust as God talked with him.

⁵ "What's more," God told him, "I am changing your name. It is no longer 'Abram' ('Exalted Father'), but 'Abraham' ('Father of Nations')—for that is what you will be. I have declared it. ⁶ I will give you millions of descendants who will form many nations! Kings shall be among your descendants! ⁷,⁸ And I will continue this agreement between us generation after generation, forever, for it shall be between me and your children as well. It is a contract that I shall be your God and the God of your posterity. And I will give all this land of Canaan to you and them, forever. And I will be your God.

⁹,¹⁰ "Your part of the contract," God told him, "is to obey its terms. You personally and all your posterity have this continual responsibility: that every male among you shall be circumcised; ¹¹ the foreskin of his penis shall be cut off. This will be the proof that you and they accept this covenant. ¹² Every male shall be circumcised on the eighth day after birth. This applies to every foreign-born slave as well as to everyone born in your household. This is a permanent

---

c Literally, "River of Egypt," at the southern border of Judah.   16a Literally, "Let the Lord judge between me and you."   b Implied.

part of this contract, and it applies to all your posterity. [13] All must be circumcised. Your bodies will thus be marked as participants in my everlasting covenant. [14] Anyone who refuses these terms shall be cut off from his people; for he has violated my contract."

[15] Then God added, "Regarding Sarai your wife—her name is no longer 'Sarai' but 'Sarah' ('Princess'). [16] And I will bless her and give you a son from her! Yes, I will bless her richly, and make her the mother of nations! Many kings shall be among your posterity."

[17] Then Abraham threw himself down in worship before the Lord, but inside he was laughing in disbelief![a] "Me, be a father?" he said in amusement. "Me—100 years old? And Sarah, to have a baby at 90?"

[18] And Abraham said to God, "Yes, do bless Ishmael!"

[19] "No," God replied, "that isn't what I said. *Sarah* shall bear you a son; and you are to name him Isaac ('Laughter'), and I will sign my covenant with him forever, and with his descendants. [20] As for Ishmael, all right, I will bless him also, just as you have asked me to. I will cause him to multiply and become a great nation. Twelve princes shall be among his posterity. [21] But my contract is with Isaac, who will be born to you and Sarah next year at about this time."

[22] That ended the conversation and God left. [23] Then, that very day, Abraham took Ishmael his son and every other male—born in his household or bought from outside —and cut off their foreskins, just as God had told him to. [24-27] Abraham was ninety-nine years old at that time, and Ishmael was thirteen. Both were circumcised the same day, along with all the other men and boys of the household, whether born there or bought as slaves.

18 THE LORD APPEARED again to Abraham while he was living in the oak grove at Mamre. This is the way it happened: One hot summer afternoon as he was sitting in the opening of his tent, [2] he suddenly noticed three men coming toward him. He sprang up and ran to meet them and welcomed them.

[3,4] "Sirs," he said, "please don't go any further. Stop awhile and rest here in the shade of this tree while I get water to refresh your feet, [5] and a bite to eat to strengthen you. Do stay awhile before continuing your journey."

"All right," they said, "do as you have said."

[6] Then Abraham ran back to the tent and said to Sarah, "Quick! Mix up some pancakes![a] Use your best flour, and make enough for the three of them!" [7] Then he ran out to the herd and selected a fat calf and told a servant to hurry and butcher it. [8] Soon, taking them cheese and milk and the roast veal, he set it before the men and stood beneath the trees beside them as they ate.

[9] "Where is Sarah, your wife?" they asked him.

"In the tent," Abraham replied.

[10] Then the Lord said, "Next year[b] I will give you and Sarah a son!" (Sarah was listening from the tent door behind him.) [11] Now Abraham and Sarah were both very old, and Sarah was long since past the time when she could have a baby.

[12] So Sarah laughed silently. "A woman my age have a baby?" she scoffed to herself. "And with a husband as old as mine?"

[13] Then God said to Abraham, "Why did Sarah laugh? Why did she say 'Can an old woman like me have a baby?' [14] Is anything too hard for God? Next year, just as I told you, I will certainly see to it that Sarah has a son."

[15] But Sarah denied it. "I didn't laugh," she lied, for she was afraid.

[16] Then the men stood up from their meal and started on toward Sodom; and Abraham went with them part of the way. [17] "Should I hide my plan from Abraham?" God asked. [18] "For Abraham shall become a mighty nation, and he will be a source of blessing for all the nations of the earth. [19] And I have picked him out to have godly descendants and a godly household—men who are just and good—so that I can do for him all I have promised."

[20] So the Lord told Abraham, "I have heard that the people of Sodom and Gomor-

---

a Implied. **18a** Probably some sort of *tortilla*. b Literally, "when life would be due."

rah are utterly evil, and that everything they do is wicked. ²¹ I am going down to see whether these reports are true or not. Then I will know." ²²,²³ So the other two went on toward Sodom, but the Lord remained with Abraham a while. Then Abraham approached him and said, "Will you kill good and bad alike? ²⁴ Suppose you find fifty godly people there within the city—will you destroy it, and not spare it for their sakes? ²⁵ That wouldn't be right! Surely you wouldn't do such a thing, to kill the godly with the wicked! Why, you would be treating godly and wicked exactly the same! Surely you wouldn't do that! Should not the Judge of all the earth be fair?"

²⁶ And God replied, "If I find fifty godly people there, I will spare the entire city for their sake."

²⁷ Then Abraham spoke again. "Since I have begun, let me go on and speak further to the Lord, though I am but dust and ashes. ²⁸ *Suppose there are only forty-five? Will you destroy the city for lack of five?"*

And God said, "I will not destroy it if I find forty-five."

²⁹ Then Abraham went further with his request. *"Suppose there are only forty?"*

And God replied, "I won't destroy it if there are forty."

³⁰ "Please don't be angry," Abraham pleaded. "Let me speak: *suppose only thirty are found there?"*

And God replied, "I won't do it if there are thirty there."

³¹ Then Abraham said, "Since I have dared to speak to God, let me continue— *Suppose there are only twenty?"*

And God said, "Then I won't destroy it for the sake of the twenty."

³² Finally, Abraham said, "Oh, let not the Lord be angry; I will speak but this once more! *Suppose only ten are found?"*

And God said, "Then, for the sake of the ten, I won't destroy it."

³³ And the Lord went on his way when he had finished his conversation with Abraham. And Abraham returned to his tent.

19 THAT EVENING THE two angels came to the entrance of the city of Sodom, and Lot was sitting there as they arrived.

When he saw them he stood up to meet them, and welcomed them.

² "Sirs," he said, "come to my home as my guests for the night; you can get up as early as you like and be on your way again."

"Oh, no thanks," they said, "we'll just stretch out here along the street."

³ But he was very urgent, until at last they went home with him, and he set a great feast before them, complete with freshly baked unleavened bread. After the meal, ⁴ as they were preparing to retire for the night, the men of the city—yes, Sodomites, young and old from all over the city—surrounded the house ⁵ and shouted to Lot, "Bring out those men to us so we can rape them."

⁶ Lot stepped outside to talk to them, shutting the door behind him. ⁷ "Please, fellows," he begged, "don't do such a wicked thing. ⁸ Look—I have two virgin daughters, and I'll surrender them to you to do with as you wish. But leave these men alone, for they are under my protection."

⁹ "Stand back," they yelled. "Who do you think you are? We let this fellow settle among us and now he tries to tell us what to do! We'll deal with you far worse than with those other men." And they lunged at Lot and began breaking down the door.

¹⁰ But the two men reached out and pulled Lot in and bolted the door, ¹¹ and temporarily blinded the men of Sodom so that they couldn't find the door.

¹² "What relatives do you have here in the city?" the men asked. "Get them out of this place—sons-in-law, sons, daughters, or anyone else. ¹³ For we will destroy the city completely. The stench of the place has reached to heaven and God has sent us to destroy it."

¹⁴ So Lot rushed out to tell his daughters' fiancés, "Quick, get out of the city, for the Lord is going to destroy it." But the young men looked at him as though he had lost his senses.

¹⁵ At dawn the next morning the angels became urgent. "Hurry," they said to Lot, "take your wife and your two daughters who are here and get out while you can, or you will be caught in the destruction of the city."

¹⁶ When Lot still hesitated, the angels

seized his hand and the hands of his wife and two daughters and rushed them to safety, outside the city, for the Lord was merciful.

[17] "Flee for your lives," the angels told him. "And don't look back. Escape to the mountains. Don't stay down here on the plain or you will die."

[18,19,20] "Oh no, sirs, please," Lot begged, "since you've been so kind to me and saved my life, and you've granted me such mercy, let me flee to that little village over there instead of into the mountains, for I fear disaster in the mountain. See, the village is close by and it is just a small one. Please, please, let me go there instead. Don't you see how small it is? And my life will be saved."

[21] "All right," the angel said, "I accept your proposition and won't destroy that little city. [22] But hurry! For I can do nothing until you are there." (From that time on that village was named Zoar, meaning "Little City.")

[23] The sun was rising as Lot reached the village. [24] Then the Lord rained down fire and flaming tar from heaven upon Sodom and Gomorrah, [25] and utterly destroyed them, along with the other cities and villages of the plain, eliminating all life—people, plants, and animals alike. [26] But Lot's wife looked back as she was following along behind him, and became a pillar of salt.

[27] That morning Abraham was up early and hurried out to the place where he had stood before the Lord. [28] He looked out across the plain to Sodom and Gomorrah and saw columns of smoke and fumes, as from a furnace, rising from the cities there. [29] So God heeded Abraham's plea and kept Lot safe, removing him from the maelstrom of death that engulfed the cities.

[30] Afterwards Lot left Zoar, fearful of the people there, and went to live in a cave in the mountains with his two daughters. [31] One day the older girl said to her sister, "There isn't a man anywhere in this entire area that our father would let us marry. And our father will soon be too old for having children. [32] Come, let's fill him with wine and then we will sleep with him, so that our clan will not come to an end." [33] So they got him drunk that night, and the older

girl went in and had sexual intercourse with her father; but he was unaware of her lying down or getting up again.

[34] The next morning she said to her younger sister, "I slept with my father last night. Let's fill him with wine again tonight, and you go in and lie with him, so that our family line will continue." [35] So they got him drunk again that night, and the younger girl went in and lay with him, and, as before, he didn't know that anyone was there. [36] And so it was that both girls became pregnant from their father. [37] The older girl's baby was named Moab; he became the ancestor of the nation of the Moabites. [38] The name of the younger girl's baby was Benammi; he became the ancestor of the nation of the Ammonites.

20 NOW ABRAHAM MOVED south to the Negeb, and settled between Kadesh and Shur. One day, when visiting the city of Gerar, [2] he remarked that Sarah was his sister! Then King Abimelech sent for her, and had her brought to him at his palace.

[3] But that night God came to him in a dream and told him, "You are a dead man, for that woman you took is married."

[4] But Abimelech hadn't slept with her yet, so he said, "Lord, will you slay an innocent man? [5] He told me, 'She is my sister,' and she herself said, 'Yes, he is my brother.' I hadn't the slightest intention of doing anything wrong."

[6] "Yes, I know," the Lord replied. "That is why I held you back from sinning against me; that is why I didn't let you touch her. [7] Now restore her to her husband, and he will pray for you (for he is a prophet) and you shall live. But if you don't return her to him, you are doomed to death along with all your household."

[8] The king was up early the next morning, and hastily called a meeting of all the palace personnel and told them what had happened. And great fear swept through the crowd.

[9,10] Then the king called for Abraham. "What is this you've done to us?" he demanded. "What have I done that deserves treatment like this, to make me and my kingdom guilty of this great sin? Who would suspect that you would do a thing

like this to me? Whatever made you think of this vile deed?"

[11,12] "Well," Abraham said, "I figured this to be a godless place. 'They will want my wife and will kill me to get her,' I thought. And besides, she *is* my sister—or at least a half-sister (we both have the same father)—and I married her. [13] And when God sent me traveling far from my childhood home, I told her, 'Have the kindness to mention, wherever we come, that you are my sister.'"

[14] Then King Abimelech took sheep and oxen and servants—both men and women—and gave them to Abraham, and returned Sarah his wife to him.

[15] "Look my kingdom over, and choose the place where you want to live," the king told him. [16] Then he turned to Sarah. "Look," he said, "I am giving your 'brother' a thousand silver pieces as damages for what I did, to compensate for any embarrassment and to settle any claim against me regarding this matter. Now justice has been done."

[17] Then Abraham prayed, asking God to cure the king and queen and the other women of the household, so that they could have children; [18] for God had stricken all the women with barrenness to punish Abimelech for taking Abraham's wife.

21 THEN GOD DID as he had promised, and Sarah became pregnant and gave Abraham a baby son in his old age, at the time God had said; [3] and Abraham named him Isaac (meaning "Laughter!"). [4,5] Eight days after he was born, Abraham circumcised him, as God required. (Abraham was 100 years old at that time.)

[6] And Sarah declared, "God has brought me laughter! All who hear about this shall rejoice with me. [7] For who would have dreamed that I would ever have a baby? Yet I have given Abraham a child in his old age!"

[8] Time went by and the child grew and was weaned; and Abraham gave a party to celebrate the happy occasion. [9] But when Sarah noticed Ishmael—the son of Abraham and the Egyptian girl Hagar—

teasing[a] Isaac, [10] she turned upon Abraham and demanded, "Get rid of that slave girl and her son. He is not going to share your property with my son. I won't have it."

[11] This upset Abraham very much, for after all, Ishmael too was his son.

[12] But God told Abraham, "Don't be upset over the boy or your slave-girl wife; do as Sarah says, for Isaac is the son through whom my promise will be fulfilled. [13] And I will make a nation of the descendants of the slave-girl's son, too, because he also is yours."

[14] So Abraham got up early the next morning, prepared food for the journey, and strapped a canteen of water to Hagar's shoulders and sent her away with their son. She hiked out into the wilderness of Beersheba, wandering aimlessly. [15] When the water was gone she left the child beneath a bush [16] and went off and sat down a hundred yards or so away. "I don't want to watch him die," she said, and burst into tears, sobbing wildly.

[17] Then God answered the lad's cries, and the Angel of God called to Hagar from the sky, "Hagar, what's wrong? Don't be afraid! For God has heard the lad's cries as he is lying there. [18] Go and get the boy and comfort him, for I will make a great nation from his descendants."

[19] Then God opened her eyes and she saw a well; so she refilled the canteen and gave the lad a drink. [20,21] And God blessed the boy and he grew up in the wilderness of Paran, and became an expert archer. And his mother arranged a marriage for him with a girl from Egypt.

[22] About this time King Abimelech, and Phicol, commander of his troops, came to Abraham and said to him, "It is evident that God helps you in everything you do; [23] swear to me by God's name that you won't defraud me or my son or my grandson, but that you will be on friendly terms with my country, as I have been toward you."

[24] Abraham replied, "All right, I swear to it!" [25] Then Abraham complained to the king about a well the king's servants had taken violently away from Abraham's serv-

---

a Or, "mocking"; whether in innocent fun or otherwise is not clear in the text.

ants.

²⁶ "This is the first I've heard of it," the king exclaimed, "and I have no idea who is responsible. Why didn't you tell me before?"

²⁷ Then Abraham gave sheep and oxen to the king, as sacrifices to seal their pact. ²⁸,²⁹ But when he took seven ewe lambs and set them off by themselves, the king inquired, "Why are you doing that?"

³⁰ And Abraham replied, "They are my gift to you as a public confirmation that this well is mine."

³¹ So from that time on the well was called Beer-sheba ("Well of the Oath"), because that was the place where they made their covenant. ³² Then King Abimelech, and Phicol, commander of his army, returned home again. ³³ And Abraham planted a tamarisk tree beside the well, and prayed there to the Lord, calling upon the Eternal God [to witness the covenant[b]]. ³⁴ And Abraham lived in the Philistine country for a long time.

22 LATER ON, GOD tested Abraham's [faith and obedience[a]].

"Abraham!" God called.

"Yes, Lord?" he replied.

² "Take with you your only son—yes, Isaac whom you love so much—and go to the land of Moriah and sacrifice him there as a burnt offering upon one of the mountains which I'll point out to you!"

³ The next morning Abraham got up early, chopped wood for a fire upon the altar, saddled his donkey, and took with him his son Isaac and two young men who were his servants, and started off to the place where God had told him to go. ⁴ On the third day of the journey Abraham saw the place in the distance.

⁵ "Stay here with the donkey," Abraham told the young men, "and the lad and I will travel yonder and worship, and then come right back."

⁶ Abraham placed the wood for the burnt offering upon Isaac's shoulders, while he himself carried the knife and the flint for striking a fire. So the two of them went on together.

⁷ "Father," Isaac asked, "we have the wood and the flint to make the fire, but where is the lamb for the sacrifice?"

⁸ "God will see to it, my son," Abraham replied. And they went on.

⁹ When they arrived at the place where God had told Abraham to go, he built an altar and placed the wood in order, ready for the fire, and then tied Isaac and laid him on the altar over the wood. ¹⁰ And Abraham took the knife and lifted it up to plunge it into his son, to slay him.

¹¹ At that moment the Angel of God shouted to him from heaven, "Abraham! Abraham!"

"Yes, Lord!" he answered.

¹² "Lay down the knife; don't hurt the lad in any way," the Angel said, "for I know that God is first in your life—you have not withheld even your beloved son from me."

¹³ Then Abraham noticed a ram caught by its horns in a bush. So he took the ram and sacrificed it, instead of his son, as a burnt offering on the altar. ¹⁴ Abraham named the place "Jehovah provides"—and it still goes by that name to this day.

¹⁵ Then the Angel of God called again to Abraham from heaven. ¹⁶ "I, the Lord, have sworn by myself that because you have obeyed me and have not withheld even your beloved son from me, ¹⁷ I will bless you with incredible blessings and multiply your descendants into countless thousands and millions, like the stars above you in the sky, and like the sands along the seashore. These descendants of yours will conquer their enemies, ¹⁸ and be a blessing to all the nations of the earth—all because you have obeyed me."

¹⁹ So they returned to his young men, and traveled home again to Beer-sheba.

²⁰⁻²³ After this, a message arrived that Milcah, the wife of Abraham's brother Nahor, had borne him eight sons. Their names were:

Uz, the oldest,
Buz, the next oldest,
Kemuel (father of Aram),
Chesed, Hazo, Pildash, Jidlaph,
Bethuel (father of Rebekah).

²⁴ He also had four other children from

---

b Implied.   22a Implied.

his concubine, Reumah:
> Tebah, Gaham,
> Tahash, Maacah.

23 WHEN SARAH WAS 127 years old, she died in Hebron in the land of Canaan; there Abraham mourned and wept for her. ³ Then, standing beside her body, he said to the men of Heth:

⁴ "Here I am, a visitor in a foreign land, with no place to bury my wife. Please sell me a piece of ground for this purpose."

⁵,⁶ "Certainly," the men replied, "for you are an honored prince of God among us; it will be a privilege to have you choose the finest of our sepulchres, so that you can bury her there."

⁷ Then Abraham bowed low before them and said, ⁸ "Since this is your feeling in the matter, be so kind as to ask Ephron, Zohar's son, ⁹ to sell me the cave of Mach-pelah, down at the end of his field. I will of course pay the full price for it, whatever is publicly agreed upon, and it will become a permanent cemetery for my family."

¹⁰ Ephron was sitting there among the others, and now he spoke up, answering Abraham as the others listened, speaking publicly before all the citizens of the town: ¹¹ "Sir," he said to Abraham, "please listen to me. I will give you the cave and the field without any charge. Here in the presence of my people, I give it to you free. Go and bury your dead."

¹² Abraham bowed again to the men of Heth, ¹³ and replied to Ephron, as all listened: "No, let me buy it from you. Let me pay the full price of the field, and then I will bury my dead."

¹⁴,¹⁵ "Well, the land is worth 400 pieces of silver," Ephron said, "but what is that between friends? Go ahead and bury your dead."

¹⁶ So Abraham paid Ephron the price he had suggested—400 pieces of silver, as publicly agreed. ¹⁷,¹⁸ This is the land he bought: Ephron's field at Mach-pelah, near Mamre, and the cave at the end of the field, and all the trees in the field. They became his permanent possession, by agreement in the presence of the men of Heth at the city gate. ¹⁹,²⁰ So Abraham buried Sarah there, in the field and cave deeded to him by the men of Heth as a burial plot.

24 ABRAHAM WAS NOW a very old man, and God blessed him in every way. ² One day Abraham said to his household administrator, who was his oldest servant, ³ "Swear by Jehovah, the God of heaven and earth, that you will not let my son marry one of these local girls, these Canaanites. ⁴ Go instead to my homeland, to my relatives, and find a wife for him there."

⁵ "But suppose I can't find a girl who will come so far from home?" the servant asked. "Then shall I take Isaac there, to live among your relatives?"

⁶ "No!" Abraham warned. "Be careful that you don't do that under any circumstance. ⁷ For the Lord God of heaven told me to leave that land and my people, and promised to give me and my children this land. He will send his angel on ahead of you, and he will see to it that you find a girl from there to be my son's wife. ⁸ But if you don't succeed, then you are free from this oath; but under no circumstances are you to take my son there."

⁹ So the servant vowedᵃ to follow Abraham's instructions. ¹⁰ He took with him ten of Abraham's camels loaded with samples of the best of everything his master owned, and journeyed to Iraq, to Nahor's village. ¹¹ There he made the camels kneel down outside the town, beside a spring. It was evening, and the women of the village were coming to draw water.

¹² "O Jehovah, the God of my master," he prayed, "show kindness to my master Abraham and help me to accomplish the purpose of my journey. ¹³ See, here I am, standing beside this spring, and the girls of the village are coming out to draw water. ¹⁴ This is my request: When I ask one of them for a drink and she says, 'Yes, certainly, and I will water your camels too!'— let her be the one you have appointed as Isaac's wife. That is how I will know."

¹⁵,¹⁶ As he was still speaking to the Lord

---

a Literally, "put his hand under the thigh of Abraham his master and swore to him that . . ."

about this, a beautiful young girl[b] named Rebekah arrived with a water jug on her shoulder and filled it at the spring. (Her father was Bethuel the son of Nahor[c] and his wife Milcah.) ¹⁷ Running over to her, the servant asked her for a drink.

¹⁸ "Certainly, sir," she said, and quickly lowered the jug for him to drink. ¹⁹ Then she said, "I'll draw water for your camels, too, until they have enough!"

²⁰ So she emptied the jug into the watering trough and ran down to the spring again and kept carrying water to the camels until they had enough. ²¹ The servant said no more, but watched her carefully to see if she would finish the job,[d] so that he would know whether she was the one. ²² Then at last, when the camels had finished drinking, he produced a quarter-ounce gold earring[e] and two five-ounce golden bracelets for her wrists.

²³ "Whose daughter are you, miss?" he asked. "Would your father have any room to put us up for the night?"

²⁴ "My father is Bethuel, the son of Milcah, the wife of Nahor," she replied. ²⁵ "Yes, we have plenty of straw and food for the camels, and a guest room."

²⁶ The man stood there a moment with head bowed, worshiping Jehovah. ²⁷ "Thank you, Lord God of my master Abraham," he prayed; "thank you for being so kind and true to him, and for leading me straight to the family of my master's relatives."

²⁸ The girl ran home to tell her folks,[f] ²⁹,³⁰ and when her brother Laban saw the ring, and the bracelets on his sister's wrists, and heard her story, he rushed out to the spring where the man was still standing beside his camels, and said to him, ³¹ "Come and stay with us, friend;[g] why stand here outside the city when we have a room all ready for you, and a place prepared for the camels!"

³² So the man went home with Laban, and Laban gave him straw to bed down the camels, and feed for them, and water for the camel drivers to wash their feet. ³³ Then supper was served. But the old man said, "I don't want to eat until I have told you why I am here."

"All right," Laban said, "tell us your errand."

³⁴ "I am Abraham's servant," he explained. ³⁵ "And Jehovah has overwhelmed my master with blessings so that he is a great man among the people of his land. God has given him flocks of sheep and herds of cattle, and a fortune in silver and gold, and many slaves and camels and donkeys.

³⁶ "Now when Sarah, my master's wife, was very old, she gave birth to my master's son, and my master has given him everything he owns. ³⁷ And my master made me promise not to let Isaac marry one of the local girls,[h] ³⁸ but to come to his relatives here in this far-off land, to his brother's[i] family, and to bring back a girl from here to marry his son. ³⁹ 'But suppose I can't find a girl who will come?' I asked him. ⁴⁰ 'She will,' he told me—'for my Lord, in whose presence I have walked, will send his angel with you and make your mission successful. Yes, find a girl from among my relatives, from my brother's family. ⁴¹ You are under oath to go and ask. If they won't send anyone, then you are freed from your promise.'

⁴² "Well, this afternoon when I came to the spring I prayed this prayer: 'O Jehovah, the God of my master Abraham, if you are planning to make my mission a success, please guide me in this way: ⁴³ Here I am, standing beside this spring. I will say to some girl who comes out to draw water, "Please give me a drink of water!" ⁴⁴ And she will reply, "Certainly! And I'll water your camels too!" Let that girl be the one you have selected to be the wife of my master's son.'

⁴⁵ "Well, while I was still speaking these words, Rebekah was coming along with her water jug upon her shoulder; and she went down to the spring and drew water and filled the jug. I said to her, 'Please give me a drink.' ⁴⁶ She quickly lifted the jug down from her shoulder so that I could drink, and told me, 'Certainly, sir, and I will water your camels too!' So she did! ⁴⁷ Then I asked her, 'Whose family are you from?' And she

---

b Literally, "a virgin."   c Abraham's brother.   d Implied.   e Literally, "nose-ring."
f Doubtless to tell them that a messenger had arrived from her great-uncle.   g Literally, "blessed of Jehovah."   h Literally, "daughters of the Canaanites."   i Literally, "go into my father's house."

told me, 'Nahor's. My father is Bethuel, the son of Nahor and his wife Milcah.' So I gave her the ring and the bracelets. ⁴⁸ Then I bowed my head and worshiped and blessed Jehovah, the God of my master Abraham, because he had led me along just the right path to find a girl from the family^j of my master's brother. ⁴⁹ So tell me, yes or no. Will you or won't you be kind to my master and do what is right? When you tell me, then I'll know what my next step should be, whether to move this way or that."

⁵⁰ Then Laban and Bethuel replied, "The Lord has obviously brought you here, so what can we say? ⁵¹ Take her and go! Yes, let her be the wife of your master's son, as Jehovah has directed."

⁵² At this reply, Abraham's servant fell to his knees before Jehovah. ⁵³ Then he brought out jewels set in solid gold and silver for Rebekah, and lovely clothing; and he gave many valuable presents to her mother and brother. ⁵⁴ Then they had supper, and the servant and the men with him stayed there overnight. But early the next morning he said, "Send me back to my master!"

⁵⁵ "But we want Rebekah here at least another ten days or so!" her mother and brother exclaimed. "Then she can go."

⁵⁶ But he pleaded, "Don't hinder my return; the Lord has made my mission successful, and I want to report back to my master."

⁵⁷ "Well," they said, "we'll call the girl and ask her what she thinks."

⁵⁸ So they called Rebekah. "Are you willing to go with this man?" they asked her.

And she replied, "Yes, I will go."

⁵⁹ So they told her good-bye, sending along the woman who had been her childhood nurse, ⁶⁰ and blessed her with this blessing as they parted:

"Our sister,
May you become
The mother of many millions!
May your descendants
Overcome all your enemies."

⁶¹ So Rebekah and her servant girls mounted the camels and went with him.

⁶² Meanwhile, Isaac, whose home was in the Negeb, had returned to Beer-lahai-roi. ⁶³ One evening as he was taking a walk out in the fields, meditating, he looked up and saw the camels coming. ⁶⁴ Rebekah noticed him and quickly dismounted.

⁶⁵ "Who is that man walking through the fields to meet us?" she asked the servant.

And he replied, "It is my master's son!"^{k} So she covered her face with her veil. ⁶⁶ Then the servant told Isaac the whole story.

⁶⁷ And Isaac brought Rebekah into his mother's tent, and she became his wife. He loved her very much, and she was a special comfort to him after the loss of his mother.

25 NOW ABRAHAM MARRIED again. Keturah was his new wife, and she bore him several children:

Zimran, Jokshan, Medan,
Midian, Ishbak, Shuah.

³ Jokshan's two sons were Sheba and Dedan. Dedan's sons were Asshurim, Letushim, and Leummim. ⁴ Midian's sons were Ephah, Epher, Hanoch, Abida, and Eldaah.^{a}

⁵ Abraham deeded everything he owned to Isaac; ⁶ however, he gave gifts to the sons of his concubines and sent them off into the east, away from Isaac. ⁷,⁸ Then Abraham died, at the ripe old age of 175, ⁹,¹⁰ and his sons Isaac and Ishmael buried him in the cave of Mach-pelah near Mamre, in the field Abraham had purchased from Ephron the son of Zohar, the Hethite, where Sarah, Abraham's wife was buried.

¹¹ After Abraham's death, God poured out rich blessings upon Isaac. (Isaac had now moved south to Beer-lahai-roi in the Negeb.)

¹²⁻¹⁵ Here is a list, in the order of their births, of the descendants of Ishmael, who was the son of Abraham and Hagar the Egyptian, Sarah's slave girl:

Nebaioth, Kedar, Abdeel,
Mibsam, Mishma, Dumah,
Massa, Hadad, Tema,
Jetur, Naphish, Kedemah.

¹⁶ These twelve sons of his became the

---

j Literally, "my master's brother's daughter."   k Literally, "It is my master."   25a The text adds, "all these were the children of Keturah."

founders of twelve tribes that bore their names. [17] Ishmael finally died at the age of 137, and joined his ancestors.[b] [18] These descendants of Ishmael were scattered across the country from Havilah to Shur (which is a little way to the northeast of the Egyptian border in the direction of Assyria). And they were constantly at war with one another.

[19] This is the story of Isaac's children: [20] Isaac was forty years old when he married Rebekah, the daughter of Bethuel the Aramean from Paddam-aram, sister of Laban. [21] Isaac pleaded with Jehovah to give Rebekah a child, for even after many years of marriage[c] she had no children. Then at last she became pregnant. [22] And it seemed as though children were fighting each other inside her!

"I can't endure this," she exclaimed. So she asked the Lord about it.

[23] And he told her, "The sons in your womb shall become two rival nations. One will be stronger than the other; and the older shall be a servant of the younger!"

[24] And sure enough, she had twins. [25] The first was born so covered with reddish hair that one would think he was wearing a fur coat! So they called him "Esau."[d] [26] Then the other twin was born with his hand on Esau's heel! So they called him Jacob (meaning "Grabber"). Isaac was sixty years old when the twins were born.

[27] As the boys grew, Esau became a skillful hunter, while Jacob was a quiet sort who liked to stay at home. [28] Isaac's favorite was Esau, because of the venison he brought home, and Rebekah's favorite was Jacob.

[29] One day Jacob was cooking stew when Esau arrived home exhausted from the hunt.

[30] *Esau:* "Boy, am I starved! Give me a bite of that red stuff there!" (From this came his nickname "Edom," which means "Red Stuff.")

[31] *Jacob:* "All right, trade me your birthright for it!"

[32] *Esau:* "When a man is dying of starvation, what good is his birthright?"

[33] *Jacob:* "Well then, vow to God that it is mine!"

And Esau vowed, thereby selling all his eldest-son rights to his younger brother. [34] Then Jacob gave Esau bread, peas, and stew; so he ate and drank and went on about his business, indifferent to the loss of the rights he had thrown away.[e]

26 NOW A SEVERE famine overshadowed the land, as had happened before, in Abraham's time, and so Isaac moved to the city of Gerar where Abimelech, king of the Philistines, lived.

[2] Jehovah appeared to him there and told him, "Don't go to Egypt. [3] Do as I say and stay here in this land. If you do, I will be with you and bless you, and I will give all this land to you and to your descendants, just as I promised Abraham your father. [4] And I will cause your descendants to become as numerous as the stars! And I will give them all of these lands; and they shall be a blessing to all the nations of the earth. [5] I will do this because Abraham obeyed my commandments and laws."

[6] So Isaac stayed in Gerar. [7] And when the men there asked him about Rebekah, he said, "She is my sister!" For he feared for his life if he told them she was his wife; he was afraid they would kill him to get her, for she was very attractive. [8] But sometime later, King Abimelech, king of the Philistines, looked out of a window and saw Isaac petting with Rebekah.

[9] Abimelech called for Isaac and exclaimed, "She is your wife! Why did you say she is your sister?"

"Because I was afraid I would be murdered," Isaac replied. "I thought someone would kill me to get her from me."

[10] "How could you treat us this way?" Abimelech exclaimed. "Someone might carelessly have raped her, and we would be doomed." [11] Then Abimelech made a public proclamation: "Anyone harming this man or his wife shall die."

[12] That year Isaac's crops were tremendous—100 times the grain he sowed. For Jehovah blessed him. [13] He was soon a man of great wealth, and became richer and

---

b Literally, "and was gathered to his people."   c Implied in verses 20 and 26.   d Which sounds a little like the Hebrew word for "hair."   e Literally, "thus did Esau consider his birthright to be of no value."

richer. [14] He had large flocks of sheep and goats, great herds of cattle, and many servants. And the Philistines became jealous of him. [15] So they filled up his wells with earth—all those dug by the servants of his father Abraham.

[16] And King Abimelech asked Isaac to leave the country. "Go somewhere else," he said, "for you have become too rich and powerful for us."

[17] So Isaac moved to Gerar Valley and lived there instead. [18] And Isaac redug the wells of his father Abraham, the ones the Philistines had filled after his father's death, and gave them the same names they had had before, when his father had named them. [19] His shepherds also dug a new well in Gerar Valley, and found a gushing underground spring.

[20] Then the local shepherds came and claimed it. "This is our land and our well," they said, and argued over it with Isaac's herdsmen. So he named the well, "The Well of Argument!"[a] [21] Isaac's men then dug another well, but again there was a fight over it. So he called it, "The Well of Anger."[b] [22] Abandoning that one, he dug again, and the local residents finally left him alone. So he called it, "The Well of Room Enough for Us at Last!"[c] "For now at last," he said, "the Lord has made room for us and we shall thrive."

[23] When he went to Beer-sheba, [24] Jehovah appeared to him on the night of his arrival. "I am the God of Abraham your father," he said. "Fear not, for I am with you and will bless you, and will give you so many descendants that they will become a great nation—because of my promise to Abraham, who obeyed me." [25] Then Isaac built an altar and worshiped Jehovah; and he settled there, and his servants dug a well.

[26] One day Isaac had visitors from Gerar. King Abimelech arrived with his advisor, Ahuzzath, and also Phicol, his army commander.

[27] "Why have you come?" Isaac asked them. "This is obviously no friendly visit, since you kicked me out in a most uncivil way."

[28] "Well," they said, "we can plainly see that Jehovah is blessing you. We've decided to ask for a treaty between us. [29] Promise that you will not harm us, just as we have not harmed you, and in fact, have done only good to you and have sent you away in peace; we bless you in the name of the Lord."

[30] So Isaac prepared a great feast for them, and they ate and drank in preparation for the treaty ceremonies. [31] In the morning, as soon as they were up, they each took solemn oaths to seal a non-aggression pact. Then Isaac sent them happily home again.

[32] That very same day Isaac's servants came to tell him, "We have found water" —in the well they had been digging. [33] So he named the well, "The Well of the Oath,"[d] and the city that grew up there was named "Oath,"[e] and is called that to this day.

[34] Esau, at the age of forty, married a girl named Judith, daughter of Be-eri the Hethite; and he also married Basemath, daughter of Elon the Hethite. [35] But Isaac and Rebekah were bitter about his marrying them.

27 ONE DAY, IN Isaac's old age when he was half-blind, he called for Esau his oldest son.

Isaac: "My son?"

Esau: "Yes, father?"

[2,3,4] *Isaac:* "I am an old man now, and expect to die 'most any day. Take your bow and arrows out into the fields and get me some venison, and prepare it just the way I like it—savory and good —and bring it here for me to eat, and I will give you the blessings that belong[a] to you, my first-born son,[a] before I die."

[5] But Rebekah overheard the conversation. So when Esau left for the field to hunt for the venison, [6,7] she called her son Jacob and told him what his father had said to his brother.

[8,9,10] *Rebekah:* "Now do exactly as I tell you. Go out to the flocks and bring me two young goats, and I'll prepare your father's favorite dish from them. Then take it to your father, and after he has enjoyed it he will bless *you* before his

---

a Eseb.   b Sitnah.   c Rehoboth.   d Shibah.   e Beer-sheba.   27a Implied.

death, instead of Esau!"[b]

11,12 *Jacob:* "But mother! He won't be fooled that easily.[b] Think how hairy Esau is, and how smooth my skin is! What if my father feels me? He'll think I'm making a fool of him, and curse me instead of blessing me!"

13 *Rebekah:* "Let his curses be on me, dear son. Just do what I tell you. Go out and get the goats."

14 So Jacob followed his mother's instructions, bringing the dressed kids, which she prepared in his father's favorite way. 15 Then she took Esau's best clothes—they were there in the house—and instructed Jacob to put them on. 16 And she made him a pair of gloves from the hairy skin of the young goats, and fastened a strip of the hide around his neck; 17 then she gave him the meat, with its rich aroma, and some fresh-baked bread. 18 Jacob carried the platter of food into the room where his father was lying.

Jacob: "Father?"

Isaac: "Yes? Who is it, my son—Esau or Jacob?"

19 *Jacob:* "It's Esau, your oldest son. I've done as you told me to. Here is the delicious venison you wanted. Sit up and eat it, so that you will bless me with all your heart!"

20 *Isaac:* "How were you able to find it so quickly, my son?"

Jacob: "Because Jehovah your God put it in my path!"

21 *Isaac:* "Come over here. I want to feel you, and be sure it really is Esau!"

22 (Jacob goes over to his father. He feels him!)

Isaac: (to himself) "The voice is Jacob's, but the hands are Esau's!"

23 (The ruse convinces Isaac and he gives Jacob his blessings):

24 *Isaac:* "Are you really Esau?"

Jacob: "Yes, of course."

25 *Isaac:* "Then bring me the venison, and I will eat it and bless you with all my heart."

(Jacob takes it over to him and Isaac eats; he also drinks the wine Jacob brings him.)

26 *Isaac:* "Come here and kiss me, my son!"

(Jacob goes over and kisses him on the cheek. Isaac sniffs his clothes, and finally seems convinced.)

27,28,29 *Iscac:* "The smell of my son is the good smell of the earth and fields that Jehovah has blessed. May God always give you plenty of rain for your crops, and good harvest of grain, and new wine. May many nations be your slaves. Be the master of your brothers. May all your relatives bow low before you. Cursed are all who curse you, and blessed are all who bless you."

30 (As soon as Isaac has blessed Jacob, and almost before Jacob leaves the room, Esau arrives, coming in from his hunting. 31 He also has prepared his father's favorite dish and brings it to him.)

Esau: "Here I am, father, with the venison. Sit up and eat it so that you can give me your finest blessings!"

32 *Isaac:* "Who is it?"

Esau: "Why, it's me, of course! Esau, your oldest son!"

33 (Isaac begins to tremble noticeably.)

Isaac: "Then who is it who was just here with venison, and I have already eaten it and blessed him with irrevocable blessing?"

34 (Esau begins to sob with deep and bitter sobs.)

Esau: "O my father, bless me, bless me too!"

35 *Isaac:* "Your brother was here and tricked me and has carried away your blessing."

36 *Esau:* (bitterly) "No wonder they call him 'The Cheater.'[c] For he took my birthright, and now he has stolen my blessing. Oh, haven't you saved even one blessing for me?"

37 *Isaac:* "I have made him your master, and have given him yourself and all of his relatives as his servants. I have guaranteed him abundance of grain and wine—what is there left to give?"

38 *Esau:* "Not one blessing left for me? O my father, bless me too."

(Isaac says nothing[d] as Esau weeps.)

39,40 *Isaac:* "Yours will be no life of ease and

---

b Implied.   c "Jacob" means "Cheater."   d This clause appears in some versions, not in others.

luxury, but you shall hew your way with your sword. For a time you will serve your brother, but you will finally shake loose from him and be free."

⁴¹ So Esau hated Jacob because of what he had done to him. He said to himself, "My father will soon be gone, and then I will kill Jacob." ⁴² But someone got wind of what he was planning, and reported it to Rebekah. She sent for Jacob and told him that his life was being threatened by Esau.

⁴³ "This is what to do," she said. "Flee to your Uncle Laban in Haran. ⁴⁴ Stay there with him awhile until your brother's fury is spent, ⁴⁵ and he forgets what you have done. Then I will send for you. For why should I be bereaved of both of you in one day?"

⁴⁶ Then Rebekah said to Isaac, "I'm sick and tired of these local girls. I'd rather die than see Jacob marry one of them."

28 SO ISAAC CALLED for Jacob and blessed him and said to him, "Don't marry one of these Canaanite girls. ² Instead, go at once to Paddan-aram, to the house of your grandfatherᵃ Bethuel, and marry one of your cousins—your Uncleᵇ Laban's daughters. God Almighty bless you and give you many children; may you become a great nation of many tribes! ⁴ May God pass on to you and to your descendants the mighty blessings promised to Abraham. May you own this land where we now are foreigners, for God has given it to Abraham."

⁵ So Isaac sent Jacob away, and he went to Paddan-aram to visit his Uncle Laban, his mother's brother—the son of Bethuel the Aramean.

⁶,⁷,⁸ Esau realized that his father despised the local girls, and that his father and mother had sent Jacob to Paddan-aram, with his father's blessing, to get a wife from there, and that they had strictly warned him against marrying a Canaanite girl, and that Jacob had agreed and had left for Paddan-aram. ⁹ So Esau went to his Uncle Ishmael's family and married two additional wives

from there, besides the wives he already had. One of these new wives was Mahalath, the sister of Nebaioth, and daughter of Ishmael, Abraham's son.

¹⁰ So Jacob left Beer-sheba and journeyed toward Haran. ¹¹ That night, when he stopped to camp at sundown, he found a rock for a headrest and lay down to sleep, ¹² and dreamed that a staircaseᶜ reached from earth to heaven, and he saw the angels of God going up and down upon it.

¹³ At the top of the stairs stood the Lord. "I am Jehovah," he said, "the God of Abraham, and of your father Isaac. The ground you are lying on is yours! I will give it to you and to your descendants. ¹⁴ For you will have descendants as many as dust! They will cover the land from east to west and from north to south; and all the nations of the earth will be blessed through you and your descendants. ¹⁵ What's more, I am with you, and will protect you wherever you go, and will bring you back safely to this land; I will be with you constantly until I have finished giving you all I am promising."

¹⁶,¹⁷ Then Jacob woke up. "God lives here!" he exclaimed in terror. "I've stumbled into his home! This is the awesome entrance to heaven!" ¹⁸ The next morning he got up very early and set his stone headrest upright as a memorial pillar, and poured olive oil over it. ¹⁹ He named the place Bethel ("House of God"), though the previous name of the nearest villageᵈ was Luz.

²⁰ And Jacob vowed this vow to God: "If God will help and protect me on this journey and give me food and clothes, ²¹ and will bring me back safely to my father, then I will choose Jehovah as my God! ²² And this memorial pillar shall become a place for worship; and I will give you back a tenth of everything you give me!"

29 JACOB TRAVELED ON, finally arriving in the land of the East. ² He saw in the distance three flocks of sheep lying beside a well in an open field, waiting to be watered. But a heavy stone covered the mouth of the well. ³ (The custom was that the stone

---

a Literally, "your mother's father."   b Literally, "your mother's brother."   c Literally, "ladder."
d Literally, "of the city."

was not removed until all the flocks were there. After watering them, the stone was rolled back over the mouth of the well again.) [4] Jacob went over to the shepherds and asked them where they lived.

"At Haran," they said.

[5] "Do you know a fellow there named Laban, the son of Nahor?"

"We sure do."

[6] "How is he?"

"He's well and prosperous. Look, there comes his daughter Rachel with the sheep."

[7] "Why don't you water the flocks so they can get back to grazing?" Jacob asked. "They'll be hungry if you stop so early in the day!"

[8] "We don't roll away the stone and begin the watering until all the flocks and shepherds are here," they replied.

[9] As this conversation was going on, Rachel arrived with her father's sheep, for she was a shepherdess. [10] And because she was his cousin—the daughter of his mother's brother—and because the sheep were his uncle's, Jacob went over to the well and rolled away the stone and watered his uncle's flock. [11] Then Jacob kissed Rachel and started crying! [12,13] He explained about being her cousin on her father's side, and that he was her Aunt Rebekah's son. She quickly ran and told her father, Laban, and as soon as he heard of Jacob's arrival, he rushed out to meet him and greeted him warmly and brought him home. Then Jacob told him his story.

[14] "Just think, my very own flesh and blood," Laban exclaimed.

After Jacob had been there about a month, [15] Laban said to him one day, "Just because we are relatives is no reason for you to work for me without pay. How much do you want?" [16] Now Laban had two daughters, Leah, the older, and her younger sister, Rachel. [17] Leah had lovely eyes, but Rachel was shapely, and in every way a beauty. [18] Well, Jacob was in love with Rachel. So he told her father, "I'll work for you seven years if you'll give me Rachel as my wife."

[19] "Agreed!" Laban replied. "I'd rather give her to you than to someone outside the family."

[20] So Jacob spent the next seven years working to pay for Rachel. But they seemed to him but a few days, he was so much in love. [21] Finally the time came for him to marry her.

"I have fulfilled my contract," Jacob said to Laban. "Now give me my wife, so that I can sleep with her."

[22] So Laban invited all the men of the settlement to celebrate with Jacob at a big party. [23] Afterwards, that night, when it was dark, Laban took Leah to Jacob, and he slept with her. [24] (And Laban gave to Leah a servant girl, Zilpah, to be her maid.) [25] But in the morning—it was Leah!

"What sort of trick is this?" Jacob raged at Laban. "I worked for seven years for Rachel. What do you mean by this trickery?"

[26] "It's not our custom to marry off a younger daughter ahead of her sister," Laban replied smoothly.[a] [27] "Wait until the bridal week is over and you can have Rachel too—if you promise to work for me another seven years!"

[28] So Jacob agreed to work seven more years. Then Laban gave him Rachel, too. [29] And Laban gave to Rachel a servant girl, Bilhah, to be her maid. [30] So Jacob slept with Rachel, too, and he loved her more than Leah, and stayed and worked the additional seven years.

[31] But because Jacob was slighting Leah, Jehovah let her have a child, while Rachel was barren. [32] So Leah became pregnant and had a son, Reuben (meaning "God has noticed my trouble"), for she said, "Jehovah has noticed my trouble—now my husband will love me." [33] She soon became pregnant again and had another son and named him Simeon (meaning "Jehovah heard"), for she said, "Jehovah heard that I was unloved, and so he has given me another son." [34] Again she became pregnant and had a son, and named him Levi (meaning "Attachment") for she said, "Surely now my husband will feel affection for me, since I have given him three sons!" [35] Once again she was pregnant and had a son and named him Judah (meaning "Praise"), for she said, "Now I will praise Jehovah!" And then she

---

a Implied from context.

stopped having children.

30 RACHEL, REALIZING SHE was barren, became envious of her sister. "Give me children or I'll die," she exclaimed to Jacob. ² Jacob flew into a rage. "Am I God?" he flared. "He is the one who is responsible for your barrenness."

³ Then Rachel told him, "Sleep with my servant-girl Bilhah, and her children will be mine." ⁴ So she gave him Bilhah to be his wife, and he slept with her, ⁵ and she became pregnant and presented him with a son. ⁶ Rachel named him Dan (meaningᵃ "Justice"), for she said, "God has given me justice, and heard my plea and given me a son." ⁷ Then Bilhah, Rachel's servant-girl, became pregnant again and gave Jacob a second son. ⁸ Rachel named him Naphtali (meaning "Wrestling"), for she said, "I am in a fierce contest with my sister and I am winning!"

⁹ Meanwhile, when Leah realized that she wasn't getting pregnant anymore, she gave her servant-girl Zilpah to Jacob, to be his wife, ¹⁰ and soon Zilpah presented him with a son. ¹¹ Leah named him Gad (meaning "My luck has turned!").

¹² Then Zilpah produced a second son, ¹³ and Leah named him Asher (meaning "Happy"), for she said, "What joy is mine! The other women will think me blessed indeed!"

¹⁴ One day during the wheat harvest, Reuben found some mandrakesᵇ growing in a field and brought them to his mother Leah. Rachel begged Leah to give some of them to her.

¹⁵ But Leah angrily replied, "Wasn't it enough to steal my husband? And now will you steal my son's mandrakes too?"

Rachel said sadly, "He will sleep with you tonight because of the mandrakes."

¹⁶ That evening as Jacob was coming home from the fields, Leah went out to meet him. "You must sleep with me tonight!" she said; "for I am hiring you with some mandrakes my son has found!" So he did. ¹⁷ And

God answered her prayers and she became pregnant again, and gave birth to her fifth son. ¹⁸ She named him Issachar (meaning "Wages"), for she said, "God has repaid me for giving my slave-girl to my husband." ¹⁹ Then once again she became pregnant, with a sixth son. ²⁰ She named him Zebulun (meaning "Gifts"), for she said, "God has given me good gifts for my husband. Now he will honor me, for I have given him six sons." ²¹ Afterwards she gave birth to a daughter and named her Dinah.

²² Then God remembered about Rachel's plight, and answered her prayers by giving her a child. ²³,²⁴ For she became pregnant and gave birth to a son. "God has removed the dark slur against my name," she said. And she named him Joseph (meaning "May I also have another!"), for she said, "May Jehovah give me another son."

²⁵ Soon after the birth of Joseph to Rachel, Jacob said to Laban, "I want to go back home. ²⁶ Let me take my wives and children—for I earned them from you —and be gone, for you know how fully I have paid for them with my service to you."

²⁷ "Please don't leave me," Laban replied, "for a fortune-teller that I consultedᶜ told me that the many blessings I've been enjoying are all because of your being here. ²⁸ How much of a raise do you need to get you to stay? Whatever it is, I'll pay it."

²⁹ Jacob replied, "You know how faithfully I've served you through these many years, and how your flocks and herds have grown. ³⁰ For it was little indeed you had before I came, and your wealth has increased enormously; Jehovah has blessed you from everything I do! But now, what about me? When should I provide for my own family?"

³¹,³² "What wages do you want?" Laban asked again.

Jacob replied, "If you will do one thing, I'll go back to work for you. Let me go out among your flocks today and remove all the goats that are speckled or spotted, and all the black sheep. Give them to me as my

---

a The meaning is not of the actual Hebrew name, but of a Hebrew word sounding like the name. The name given is a Hebrew pun. An example in English might be, "Because of the large hospital bill the child was named 'Bill'!"   b A leafy plant eaten by peasant women in the belief that this would aid them in becoming pregnant.   c Literally, "I have learned by divination."

wages. ³³ Then if you ever find any white goats or sheep in my flock, you will know that I have stolen them from you!"

³⁴ "All right!" Laban replied. "It shall be as you have said!"

³⁵,³⁶ So that very day Laban went out and formed a flock for Jacob of all the male goats that were ringed and spotted, and the females that were speckled and spotted with any white patches, and all of the black sheep. He gave them to Jacob's sons to take them three days' distance, and Jacob stayed and cared for Laban's flock. ³⁷ Then Jacob took fresh shoots from poplar, almond, and plane trees, and peeled white streaks in them, ³⁸ and placed these rods beside the watering troughs so that the flocks would see them when they came to drink; for that is when they mated. ³⁹,⁴⁰ So the flocks mated before the white-streaked rods, and their offspring were streaked and spotted, and Jacob added them to his flock. Then he divided out the ewes from Laban's flock and segregated them from the rams, and let them mate only with Jacob's black rams. Thus he built his flocks from Laban's. ⁴¹ Moreover, he watched for the stronger animals to mate, and placed the peeled branches before them, ⁴² but didn't with the feebler ones. So the less healthy lambs were Laban's and the stronger ones were Jacob's! ⁴³ As a result, Jacob's flocks increased rapidly and he became very wealthy, with many servants, camels, and donkeys.

31 BUT JACOB LEARNED that Laban's sons were grumbling, "He owes everything he owns to our father. All his wealth is at our father's expense." ² Soon Jacob noticed a considerable cooling in Laban's attitude towards him.

³ Jehovah now spoke to Jacob and told him, "Return to the land of your fathers, and to your relatives there; and I will be with you."

⁴ So one day Jacob sent for Rachel and Leah to come out to the field where he was with the flocks, ⁵ to talk things over with them.

"Your father has turned against me," he told them, "and now the God of my fathers has come and spoken to me. ⁶ You know how hard I've worked for your father, ⁷ but he has been completely unscrupulous and has broken his wage contract with me again and again and again. But God has not permitted him to do me any harm! ⁸ For if he said the speckled animals would be mine, then all the flock produced speckled; and when he changed and said I could have the streaked ones, then all the lambs were streaked! ⁹ In this way God has made me wealthy at your father's expense.

¹⁰ "And at the mating season, I had a dream, and saw that the he-goats mating with the flock were streaked, speckled, and mottled. ¹¹ Then, in my dream, the Angel of God called to me ¹² and told me that I should mate the white^a nanny goats with streaked, speckled, and mottled he-goats. 'For I have seen all that Laban has done to you,' the Angel said. ¹³ 'I am the God you met at Bethel,' he continued, 'the place where you anointed the pillar and made a vow to serve me. Now leave this country and return to the land of your birth.' "

¹⁴ Rachel and Leah replied, "That's fine with us! There's nothing for us here—none of our father's wealth will come to us anyway! ¹⁵ He has reduced our rights to those of foreign women; he sold us, and what he received for us has disappeared. ¹⁶ The riches God has given you from our father were legally ours and our children's to begin with! So go ahead and do whatever God has told you to."

¹⁷⁻²⁰ So one day while Laban was out shearing sheep, Jacob set his wives and sons on camels, and fled without telling Laban his intentions. He drove the flocks before him—Jacob's flocks he had gotten there at Paddan-aram—and took everything he owned and started out to return to his father Isaac in the land of Canaan. ²¹ So he fled with all of his possessions (and Rachel stole her father's household gods and took them with her) and crossed the Euphrates River and headed for the territory of Gilead. ²² Laban didn't learn of their flight for three days. ²³ Then, taking several men with him, he set out in hot pursuit and caught up with them seven days later, at

a Implied. Literally, "notice that all the mating males are speckled, streaked, and mottled."

Mount Gilead. ²⁴ That night God appeared to Laban in a dream. "Watch out what you say to Jacob," he was told. "Don't give him your blessing and don't curse him." ²⁵ Laban finally caught up with Jacob as he was camped at the top of a ridge; Laban, meanwhile, camped below him in the mountains.

²⁶ "What do you mean by sneaking off like this?" Laban demanded. "Are my daughters prisoners, captured in a battle, that you have rushed them away like this? ²⁷ Why didn't you give me a chance to have a farewell party, with singing and orchestra and harp? ²⁸ Why didn't you let me kiss my grandchildren and tell them good-bye? This is a strange way to act. ²⁹ I could crush you, but the God of your father appeared to me last night and told me, 'Be careful not to be too hard on Jacob!' ³⁰ But see here—though you feel you must go, and long so intensely for your childhood home—why have you stolen my idols?"

³¹ "I sneaked away because I was afraid," Jacob answered. "I said to myself, 'He'll take his daughters from me by force.' ³² But as for your household idols, a curse upon anyone who took them. Let him die! If you find a single thing we've stolen from you, I swear before all these men, I'll give it back without question." For Jacob didn't know that Rachel had taken them.

³³ Laban went first into Jacob's tent to search there, then into Leah's, and then searched the two tents of the concubines, but didn't find them. Finally he went into Rachel's tent. ³⁴ Rachel, remember, was the one who had stolen the idols; she had stuffed them into her camel saddle and now was sitting on them! So although Laban searched the tents thoroughly, he didn't find them.

³⁵ "Forgive my not getting up, father," Rachel explained, "but I'm pregnant."ᵇ

³⁶,³⁷ Now Jacob got mad at Laban. "What did you find?" he demanded. "What is my crime? You have come rushing after me as though you were chasing a criminal and have searched through everything.

Now put everything I stole out here in front of us, before your men and mine, for all to see and to decide whose it is! ³⁸ Twenty years I've been with you, and all that time I cared for your ewes and nanny goats so that they produced healthy offspring, and I never touched one ram of yours for food. ³⁹ If any were attacked and killed by wild animals, did I show them to you and ask you to reduce the count of your flock? No, I took the loss. You made me pay for every animal stolen from the flocks, whether I could help it or not.ᶜ ⁴⁰ I worked for you through the scorching heat of the day, and through the cold and sleepless nights. ⁴¹ Yes, twenty years—fourteen of them earning your two daughters, and six years to get the flock! And you have reduced my wages ten times! ⁴² In fact, except for the grace of God—the God of my grandfather Abraham, even the glorious God of Isaac, my father—you would have sent me off without a penny to my name. But God has seen your cruelty and my hard work, and that is why he appeared to you last night."

⁴³ Laban replied, "These women are my daughters, and these children are mine, and these flocks and all that you have—all are mine. So how could I harm my own daughters and grandchildren? ⁴⁴ Come now and we will sign a peace pact, you and I, and will live by its terms."

⁴⁵ So Jacob took a stone and set it up as a monument, ⁴⁶ and told his men to gather stones and make a heap, and Jacob and Laban ate together beside the pile of rocks. ⁴⁷,⁴⁸ They named it "The Witness Pile" —"Jegar-sahadutha," in Laban's language, and "Galeed" in Jacob's.

"This pile of stones will stand as a witness against us [if either of us trespasses across this lineᵈ]," Laban said. ⁴⁹ So it was also called "The Watchtower" (Mizpah). For Laban said, "May the Lord see to it that we keep this bargain when we are out of each other's sight. ⁵⁰ And if you are harsh to my daughters, or take other wives, I won't know, but God will see it. ⁵¹,⁵² This heap," Laban continued, "stands between

---

b Implied. Literally, "The manner of women is upon me." She was pregnant with Benjamin, but nevertheless may have been falsely claiming her menstrual period, which, under the later Mosaic law, caused ceremonial defilement of all that was sat upon. See Leviticus 15.   c Literally, "stolen by day or by night."
d Implied.

us as a witness of our vows that I will not cross this line to attack you and you will not cross it to attack me. [53] I call upon the God of Abraham and Nahor, and of their father, to destroy either one of us who does." So Jacob took oath before the mighty God of his father Isaac, to respect the boundary line. [54] Then Jacob presented a sacrifice to God there at the top of the mountain, and invited his companions to a feast, and afterwards spent the night with them on the mountain. [55] Laban was up early the next morning and kissed his daughters and grandchildren, and blessed them, and returned home.

32 SO JACOB AND his household[a] started on again. And the angels of God came to meet him. When he saw them he exclaimed, "God lives here!" So he named the place "God's territory!"[b]

[3] Jacob now sent messengers to his brother Esau in Edom, in the land of Seir, [4] with this message: "Hello from Jacob! I have been living with Uncle Laban until recently, [5] and now I own oxen, donkeys, sheep, and many servants, both men and women. I have sent these messengers to inform you of my coming, hoping that you will be friendly to us."

[6] The messengers returned with the news that Esau was on the way to meet Jacob—with an army of 400 men! [7] Jacob was frantic with fear. He divided his household, along with the flocks and herds and camels, into two groups; [8] for he said, "If Esau attacks one group, perhaps the other can escape."

[9] Then Jacob prayed, "O God of Abraham my grandfather, and of my father Isaac—O Jehovah who told me to return to the land of my relatives, and said that you would do me good— [10] I am not worthy of the least of all your loving kindnesses shown me again and again just as you promised me. For when I left home[c] I owned nothing except a walking stick! And now I am two armies! [11] O Lord, please deliver me from destruction at the hand of my brother Esau, for I am frightened—terribly afraid that he is coming to kill me and these mothers and

my children. [12] But you promised to do me good, and to multiply my descendants until they become as the sands along the shores—too many to count."

[13,14,15] Jacob stayed where he was for the night, and prepared a present for his brother Esau:

> 200 nanny goats,
> 20 billy goats,
> 200 ewes,
> 20 rams,
> 30 milk camels, with their colts,
> 40 cows,
> 10 bulls,
> 20 female donkeys,
> 10 male donkeys.

[16] He instructed his servants to drive them on ahead, each group of animals by itself, separated by a distance between. [17] He told the men driving the first group that when they met Esau and he asked, "Where are you going? Whose servants are you? Whose animals are these?"— [18] they should reply: "These belong to your servant Jacob. They are a present for his master Esau! He is coming right behind us!"

[19] Jacob gave the same instructions to each driver, with the same message. [20] Jacob's strategy was to appease Esau with the presents before meeting him face to face! "Perhaps," Jacob hoped, "he will be friendly to us." [21] So the presents were sent on ahead, and Jacob spent that night in the camp.

[22,23,24] But during the night he got up and wakened[a] his two wives and his two concubines and eleven children, and took them across the Jordan River at the Jabbok ford, then returned again to the camp and was there alone; and a Man wrestled with him until dawn. [25] And when the Man saw that he couldn't win the match, he struck Jacob's hip, and knocked it out of joint at the socket.

[26] Then the Man said, "Let me go, for it is dawn."

But Jacob panted, "I will not let you go until you bless me."

[27] "What is your name?" the Man asked.

"Jacob," was the reply.

[28] "It isn't anymore!" the Man told him.

---

a Implied.   b Literally, "Two encampments."   c Literally, "passed over this Jordan."

"It is Israel—one who has power with God. Because you have been strong with God, you shall prevail with men."
²⁹ "What is *your* name?" Jacob asked him. "No, you mustn't ask," the Man told him. And he blessed him there.
³⁰ Jacob named the place "Peniel" ("The Face of God"), for he said, "I have seen God face to face, and yet my life is spared."
³¹ The sun rose as he started on, and he was limping because of his hip. ³² (That is why the people of Israel still do not eat the sciatic muscle where it attaches to the hip.)

33 THEN, FAR IN the distance, Jacob saw Esau coming with his 400 men. ² Jacob now arranged his family into a column, with his two concubines and their children at the head, Leah and her children next, and Rachel and Joseph last. ³ Then Jacob went on ahead. As he approached his brother he bowed low seven times before him. ⁴ And then Esau ran to meet him and embraced him affectionately and kissed him; and both of them were in tears!
⁵ Then Esau looked at the women and children and asked, "Who are these people with you?"
"My children," Jacob replied. ⁶ Then the concubines came forward with their children, and bowed low before him. ⁷ Next came Leah with her children, and bowed, and finally Rachel and Joseph came and made their bows.
⁸ "And what were all the flocks and herds I met as I came?" Esau asked.
And Jacob replied, "They are my gifts, to curry your favor!"
⁹ "Brother, I have plenty," Esau laughed. "Keep what you have."
¹⁰ "No, but please accept them," Jacob said, "for what a relief it is to see your friendly smile! I was as frightened of you as though approaching God!ᵃ ¹¹ Please take my gifts. For God has been very generous to me and I have enough." So Jacob insisted, and finally Esau accepted them.
¹² "Well, let's be going," Esau said. "My men and I will stay with you and lead the way."

¹³ But Jacob replied, "As you can see,ᵇ some of the children are small, and the flocks and herds have their young, and if they are driven too hard, they will die. ¹⁴ So you go on ahead of us and we'll follow at our own pace and meet you at Seir."
¹⁵ "Well," Esau said, "at least let me leave you some of my men to assist you and be your guides."
"No," Jacob insisted, "we'll get along just fine. Please do as I suggest."
¹⁶ So Esau started back to Seir that same day. ¹⁷ Meanwhile Jacob and his household went as far as Succoth. There he built himself a camp, with pens for his flocks and herds. (That is why the place is called Succoth, meaning "huts.") ¹⁸ Then they arrived safely at Shechem, in Canaan, and camped outside the city. ¹⁹ (He bought the land he camped on from the family of Hamor, Shechem's father, for 100 pieces of silver. ²⁰ And there he erected an altar and called it "El-Elohe-Israel," "The Altar to the God of Israel.")

34 ONE DAY DINAH, Leah's daughter, went out to visit some of the neighborhood girls, ² but when Shechem, son of King Hamor the Hivite, saw her, he took her and raped her. ³ He fell deeply in love with her, and tried to win her affection.
⁴ Then he spoke to his father about it. "Get this girl for me," he demanded. "I want to marry her."
⁵ Word soon reached Jacob of what had happened, but his sons were out in the fields herding cattle, so he did nothing until their return. ⁶,⁷ Meanwhile King Hamor, Shechem's father, went to talk with Jacob, arriving just as Jacob's sons came in from the fields, too shocked and angry to overlook the insult, for it was an outrage against all of them.
⁸ Hamor told Jacob, "My son Shechem is truly in love with your daughter, and longs for her to be his wife. Please let him marry her. ⁹,¹⁰ Moreover, we invite you folks to live here among us and to let your daughters marry our sons, and we will give our daughters as wives for your young men. And you shall live among us wherever you

---

a Literally, "forasmuch as I have seen your face as one sees the face of God."   b Implied.

wish and carry on your business among us and become rich!"

[11] Then Shechem addressed Dinah's father and brothers. "Please be kind to me and let me have her as my wife," he begged. "I will give whatever you require. [12] No matter what dowry or gift you demand, I will pay it—only give me the girl as my wife."

[13] Her brothers then lied to Shechem and Hamor, acting dishonorably because of what Shechem had done to their sister. [14] They said, "We couldn't possibly. For you are not circumcised. It would be a disgrace for her to marry such a man. [15] I'll tell you what we'll do—if every man of you will be circumcised, [16] then we will intermarry with you and live here and unite with you to become one people. [17] Otherwise we will take her and be on our way."

[18,19] Hamor and Shechem gladly agreed, and lost no time in acting upon this request, for Shechem was very much in love with Dinah, and could, he felt sure, sell the idea to the other men of the city—for he was highly respected and very popular. [20] So Hamor and Shechem appeared before the city council[a] and presented their request.

[21] "Those men are our friends," they said. "Let's invite them to live here among us and ply their trade. For the land is large enough to hold them, and we can intermarry with them. [22] But they will only consider staying here on one condition—that every one of us men be circumcised, the same as they are. [23] But if we do this, then all they have will become ours and the land will be enriched. Come on, let's agree to this so that they will settle here among us."

[24] So all the men agreed, and all were circumcised. [25] But three days later, when their wounds were sore and sensitive to every move they made, two of Dinah's brothers, Simeon and Levi, took their swords, entered the city without opposition, and slaughtered every man there, [26] including Hamor and Shechem. They rescued Dinah from Shechem's house and returned to their camp again. [27] Then all of Jacob's sons went over and plundered the city because their sister had been dishonored there. [28] They confiscated all the flocks and herds and donkeys—everything they could lay their hands on, both inside the city and outside in the fields, [29] and took all the women and children, and wealth of every kind.

[30] Then Jacob said to Levi and Simeon, "You have made me stink among all the people of this land—all the Canaanites and Perizzites. We are so few that they will come and crush us, and we will all be killed."

[31] "Should he treat our sister like a prostitute?" they retorted.

35 "MOVE ON TO Bethel now, and settle there," God said to Jacob, "and build an altar to worship the God who appeared to you when you fled from your brother Esau."

[2] So Jacob instructed all those in his household to destroy the idols they had brought with them, and to wash themselves and to put on fresh clothing. [3] "For we are going to Bethel," he told them, "and I will build an altar there to the God who answered my prayers in the day of my distress, and was with me on my journey."

[4] So they gave Jacob all their idols and their earrings, and he buried them beneath the oak tree near Shechem. [5] Then they started on again. And the terror of God was upon all the cities they journeyed through, so that they were not attacked. [6] Finally they arrived at Luz (also called Bethel), in Canaan. [7] And Jacob erected an altar there and named it "The altar to the God who met me here at Bethel"[a] because it was there at Bethel that God appeared to him when he was fleeing from Esau.

[8] Soon[b] after this, Rebekah's old nurse Deborah died and was buried beneath the oak tree in the valley below Bethel. And ever after it was called "The Oak of Weeping."

[9] Upon Jacob's arrival at Bethel, en route from Paddan-aram, God appeared to him once again and blessed him. [10] And God said to him, "You shall no longer be called Jacob ('Grabber'), but Israel ('One who prevails with God'). [11] I am God Almighty," the Lord said to him, "and I will cause you

---

a Literally, "came into the gate of their city."   35a Literally, "The God of Bethel."   b Implied.

to be fertile and to multiply and to become a great nation, yes, many nations; many kings shall be among your descendants. [12] And I will pass on to you the land I gave to Abraham and Isaac. Yes, I will give it to you and to your descendants."

[13,14] Afterwards Jacob built a stone pillar at the place where God had appeared to him; and he poured wine over it as an offering to God, and then anointed the pillar with olive oil. [15] Jacob named the spot Bethel ("House of God"), because God had spoken to him there.

[16] Leaving Bethel, he and his household traveled on toward Ephrath (Bethlehem). But Rachel's pains of childbirth began while they were still a long way away. [17] After a very hard delivery, the midwife finally exclaimed, "Wonderful—another boy!" [18] And with Rachel's last breath (for she died) she named him "Ben-oni" ("Son of my sorrow"); but his father called him "Benjamin" ("Son of my right hand").

[19] So Rachel died, and was buried near the road to Ephrath (also called Bethlehem). [20] And Jacob set up a monument of stones upon her grave, and it is there to this day.

[21] Then Israel journeyed on and camped beyond the Tower of Eder. [22] It was while he was there that Reuben slept with Bilhah, his father's concubine, and someone told Israel about it.

Here are the names of the twelve sons of Jacob:

[23] The sons of Leah:

Reuben, Jacob's oldest child, Simeon, Levi, Judah, Issachar, Zebulun.

[24] The sons of Rachel:

Joseph, Benjamin.

[25] The sons of Bilhah, Rachel's servant-girl:

Dan, Naphtali.

[26] The sons of Zilpah, Leah's servant-girl:

Gad, Asher.

All these were born to him at Paddan-aram.

[27] So Jacob came at last to Isaac his father at Mamre in Kiriath-arba (now called Hebron), where Abraham too had lived. [28,29] Isaac died soon afterwards, at the ripe old age of 180. And his sons Esau and Jacob buried him.

36 HERE IS A list of the descendants of Esau (also called Edom):

[2,3] Esau married three local girls from Canaan:

Adah (daughter of Elon the Hethite),

Oholibamah (daughter of Anah and granddaughter of Zibeon the Hivite),

Basemath (his cousin[a]—she was a daughter of Ishmael—the sister of Nebaioth).

[4] Esau and Adah had a son named Eliphaz. Esau and Basemath had a son named Reuel.

[5] Esau and Oholibamah had sons named Jeush, Jalam, and Korah. All these sons were born to Esau in the land of Canaan.

[6,7,8] Then Esau took his wives, children, household servants, cattle and flocks—all the wealth he had gained in the land of Canaan—and moved away from his brother Jacob to Mount Seir. (For there was not land enough to support them both because of all their cattle.)

[9] Here are the names of Esau's descendants, the Edomites, born to him in Mount Seir:

[10,11,12] Descended from his wife Adah, born to her son Eliphaz were:

Teman, Omar, Zepho, Gatam, Kenaz, Amalek (born to Timna, Eliphaz' concubine).

[13,14b] Esau also had grandchildren from his wife Basemath. Born to her son Reuel were:

Nahath, Zerah, Shammah, Mizzah.

[15,16] Esau's grandchildren[c] became the heads of clans, as listed here:

The clan of Teman,
The clan of Omar,
The clan of Zepho,
The clan of Kenaz,
The clan of Korah,
The clan of Gatam,

---

a Implied. Literally, "the daughter of Ishmael." 5.   c Implied.

b Verse 14 is a repetition of the names listed in verse

The clan of Amalek.

The above clans were the descendants of Eliphaz, the oldest son of Esau and Adah.

[17] The following clans were the descendants of Reuel, born to Esau and his wife Basemath while they lived in Canaan:
The clan of Nahath,
The clan of Zerah,
The clan of Shammah,
The clan of Mizzah.

[18,19] And these are the clans named after the sons of Esau and his wife Oholibamah (daughter of Anah):
The clan of Jeush,
The clan of Jalam,
The clan of Korah.

[20,21] These are the names of the tribes that descended from Seir, the Horite—one of the native families of the land of Seir:
The tribe of Lotan,
The tribe of Shobal,
The tribe of Zibeon,
The tribe of Anah,
The tribe of Dishon,
The tribe of Ezer,
The tribe of Dishan.

[22] The children of Lotan (the son of Seir) were Hori and Heman. (Lotan had a sister, Timna.)

[23] The children of Shobal:
Alvan, Manahath, Ebal,
Shepho, Onam.

[24] The children of Zibeon:
Aiah,
Anah. (This is the boy who discovered a hot springs in the wasteland while he was grazing his father's donkeys.)

[25] The children of Anah:
Dishon, Oholibamah.

[26] The children of Dishon:
Hemdan, Eshban,
Ithran, Cheran.

[27] The children of Ezer:
Bilhan, Zaavan, Akan.

[28,29,30d] The children of Dishan:
Uz, Aran.

[31-39] These are the names of the kings of Edom (before Israel had her first king):
King Bela (son of Beor), from Din-habah in Edom.
Succeeded[e] by: King Jobab (son of Zerah), from the city[f] of Bozrah.
Succeeded by: King Husham, from the land of the Temanites.
Succeeded by: King Hadad (son of Bedad), the leader of the forces that defeated the army of Midian when it invaded Moab. His city was Avith.
Succeeded by: King Samlah, from Masrekah.
Succeeded by: King Shaul, from Rehoboth-by-the-River.
Succeeded by: King Baal-hanan (son of Achbor).
Succeeded by: King Hadad, from the city of Pau.
King Hadad's wife was Mehetabel, daughter of Matred and granddaughter of Mezahab.

[40-43] Here are the names of the sub-tribes of Esau, living in the localities named after themselves:
The clan of Timna,
The clan of Alvah,
The clan of Jetheth,
The clan of Oholibamah,
The clan of Elah,
The clan of Pinon,
The clan of Kenaz,
The clan of Teman,
The clan of Mibzar,
The clan of Magdiel,
The clan of Iram.

These, then, are the names of the sub-tribes of Edom, each giving its name to the area it occupied. (All were Edomites, descendants of Esau.)

37 SO JACOB SETTLED again in the land of Canaan, where his father had lived. [2] Jacob's son Joseph was now seventeen years old. His job, along with his half-brothers, the sons of his father's wives Bilhah and Zilpah, was to shepherd his father's flocks. But Joseph reported to his father some of the bad things they were doing. [3] Now as it happened, Israel loved Joseph more than any of his other children, because

---

d Verses 29 and 30 repeat the names listed in verses 20, 21. by . . ."   f Implied.

e More literally, "succeeded at his death

Joseph was born to him in his old age. So one day Jacob gave him a special gift—a brightly-colored coat.[a] [4] His brothers of course noticed their father's partiality, and consequently hated Joseph; they couldn't say a kind word to him. [5] One night Joseph had a dream and promptly reported the details to his brothers, causing even deeper hatred.

[6] "Listen to this," he proudly announced. [7] "We were out in the field binding sheaves, and my sheaf stood up, and your sheaves all gathered around it and bowed low before it!"

[8] "So you want to be our king, do you?" his brothers derided. And they hated him both for the dream and for his cocky attitude.

[9] Then he had another dream and told it to his brothers. "Listen to my latest dream," he boasted. "The sun, moon, and eleven stars bowed low before me!" [10] This time he told his father as well as his brothers; but his father rebuked him. "What is this?" he asked. "Shall I indeed, and your mother and brothers come and bow before you?" [11] His brothers were fit to be tied concerning this affair, but his father gave it quite a bit of thought and wondered what it all meant.

[12] One day Joseph's brothers took their father's flocks to Shechem to graze them there. [13,14] A few days later Israel called for Joseph, and told him, "Your brothers are over in Shechem grazing the flocks. Go and see how they are getting along, and how it is with the flocks, and bring me word."

"Very good," Joseph replied. So he traveled to Shechem from his home at Hebron Valley. [15] A man noticed him wandering in the fields.

"Who are you looking for?" he asked.

[16] "For my brothers and their flocks," Joseph replied. "Have you seen them?"

[17] "Yes," the man told him, "they are no longer here. I heard your brothers say they were going to Dothan." So Joseph followed them to Dothan and found them there. [18] But when they saw him coming, recognizing him in the distance, they decided to kill him!

[19,20] "Here comes that master-dreamer," they exclaimed. "Come on, let's kill him and toss him into a well and tell father that a wild animal has eaten him. Then we'll see what will become of all his dreams!"

[21,22] But Reuben hoped to spare Joseph's life. "Let's not kill him," he said; "we'll shed no blood—let's throw him alive into this well here; that way he'll die without our touching him!" (Reuben was planning to get him out later and return him to his father.) [23] So when Joseph got there, they pulled off his brightly-colored robe, [24] and threw him into an empty well—there was no water in it. [25] Then they sat down for supper. Suddenly they noticed a string of camels coming towards them in the distance, probably Ishmaelite traders who were taking gum, spices, and herbs from Gilead to Egypt.

[26,27] "Look there," Judah said to the others. "Here come some Ishmaelites. Let's sell Joseph to them! Why kill him and have a guilty conscience? Let's not be responsible for his death, for, after all, he is our brother!" And his brothers agreed. [28] So when the traders[b] came by, his brothers pulled Joseph out of the well and sold him to them for twenty pieces of silver, and they took him along to Egypt. [29] Some time later, Reuben (who was away when the traders came by)[c] returned to get Joseph out of the well. When Joseph wasn't there, he ripped at his clothes in anguish and frustration. [30] "The child is gone; and I, where shall I go now?" he wept to his brothers. [31] Then the brothers killed a goat and spattered its blood on Joseph's coat, [32] and took the coat to their father and asked him to identify it.

"We found this in the field," they told him. "Is it Joseph's coat or not?" [33] Their father recognized it at once.

"Yes," he sobbed, "it is my son's coat. A wild animal has eaten him. Joseph is without doubt torn in pieces."

[34] Then Israel tore his garments and put on sackcloth and mourned for his son in deepest mourning for many weeks. [35] His family all tried to comfort him, but it was

---

a More literally, "an ornamented tunic," or "long-sleeved tunic."　　b Literally, "Midianites."
c Implied.

no use.

"I will die in mourning for my son," he would say, and then break down and cry.

[36] Meanwhile, in Egypt, the traders sold Joseph to Potiphar, an officer of the Pharaoh—the king of Egypt. Potiphar was captain of the palace guard, the chief executioner.

38 ABOUT THIS TIME, Judah left home and moved to Adullam and lived there with a man named Hirah. [2] There he met and married a Canaanite girl—the daughter of Shua. [3,4,5] They lived at Chezib and had three sons, Er, Onan, and Shelah. These names were given to them by their mother, except for Er, who was named by his father.

[6] When his oldest son Er grew up, Judah arranged for him to marry a girl named Tamar. [7] But Er was a wicked man, and so the Lord killed him.

[8] Then Judah said to Er's brother, Onan, "You must marry Tamar, as our law requires of a dead man's brother; so that her sons from you will be your brother's heirs."

[9] But Onan was not willing to have a child who would not be counted as his own, and so, although he married her,[a] whenever he went in to sleep with her, he spilled the sperm on the bed[b] to prevent her from having a baby which would be his brother's. [10] So far as the Lord was concerned, it was very wrong of him [to deny a child to his deceased brother[a]], so he killed him, too. [11] Then Judah told Tamar, his daughter-in-law, not to marry again at that time, but to return to her childhood home and to her parents, and to remain a widow there until his youngest son Shelah was old enough to marry her. (But he didn't really intend for Shelah to do this, for fear God would kill him, too, just as he had his two brothers.) So Tamar went home to her parents.

[12] In the process of time Judah's wife died. After the time of mourning was over, Judah and his friend Hirah, the Adullamite, went to Timnah to supervise the shearing of his sheep. [13] When someone told Tamar that her father-in-law had left for the sheep-shearing at Timnah, [14] and realizing by now

that she was not going to be permitted to marry Shelah, though he was fully grown, she laid aside her widow's clothing and covered herself with a veil to disguise herself, and sat beside the road at the entrance to the village of Enaim, which is on the way to Timnah. [15] Judah noticed her as he went by and thought she was a prostitute, since her face was veiled. [16] So he stopped and propositioned her to sleep with him, not realizing of course that she was his own daughter-in-law.

"How much will you pay me?" she asked.

[17] "I'll send you a young goat from my flock," he promised.

"What pledge will you give me, so that I can be sure you will send it?" she asked.

[18] "Well, what do you want?" he inquired.

"Your identification seal and your walking stick," she replied. So he gave them to her and she let him come and sleep with her; and she became pregnant as a result. [19] Afterwards she resumed wearing her widow's clothing as usual. [20] Judah asked his friend Hirah the Adullamite to take the young goat back to her, and to pick up the pledges he had given her, but Hirah couldn't find her!

[21] So he asked around of the men of the city, "Where does the prostitute live who was soliciting out beside the road at the entrance of the village?"

"But we've never had a public prostitute here," they replied. [22] So he returned to Judah and told him he couldn't find her anywhere, and what the men of the place had told him.

[23] "Then let her keep them!" Judah exclaimed. "We tried our best. We'd be the laughingstock of the town to go back again." [24] About three months later word reached Judah that Tamar, his daughter-in-law, was pregnant, obviously as a result of prostitution.

"Bring her out and burn her," Judah shouted.

[25] But as they were taking her out to kill her she sent this message to her father-in-law: "The man who owns this identification

---

a Implied.   b Literally, "spilled it on the ground."

seal and walking stick is the father of my child. Do you recognize them?"

²⁶ Judah admitted that they were his and said, "She is more in the right than I am, because I refused to keep my promise to give her to my son Shelah." But he did not marry her.

²⁷ In due season the time of her delivery arrived and she had twin sons. ²⁸ As they were being born, the midwife tied a scarlet thread around the wrist of the child who appeared first, ²⁹ but he drew back his hand and the other baby was actually the first to be born. "Where did *you* come from!" she exclaimed. And ever after he was called Perez (meaning "Bursting Out"). ³⁰ Then, soon afterwards, the baby with the scarlet thread on his wrist was born, and he was named Zerah.

39 WHEN JOSEPH ARRIVED in Egypt as a captive of the Ishmaelite traders, he was purchased from them by Potiphar, a member of the personal staff of Pharaoh, the king of Egypt. Now this man Potiphar was the captain of the king's bodyguard and his chief executioner. ² The Lord greatly blessed Joseph there in the home of his master, so that everything he did succeeded. ³ Potiphar noticed this and realized that the Lord was with Joseph in a very special way. ⁴ So Joseph naturally became quite a favorite with him. Soon he was put in charge of the administration of Potiphar's household, and all of his business affairs. ⁵ At once the Lord began blessing Potiphar for Joseph's sake. All his household affairs began to run smoothly, his crops flourished and his flocks multiplied. ⁶ So Potiphar gave Joseph the complete administrative responsibility over everything he owned. He hadn't a worry in the world with Joseph there, except to decide what he wanted to eat! Joseph, by the way, was a very handsome young man.

⁷ One day at about this time Potiphar's wife began making eyes at Joseph, and suggested that he come and sleep with her.

⁸ Joseph refused. "Look," he told her, "my master trusts me with everything in the entire household; ⁹ he himself has no more authority here than I have! He has held back nothing from me except you yourself because you are his wife. How can I do such a wicked thing as this? It would be a great sin against God."

¹⁰ But she kept on with her suggestions day after day, even though he refused to listen, and kept out of her way as much as possible. ¹¹ Then one day as he was in the house going about his work—as it happened, no one else was around at the time— ¹² she came and grabbed him by the sleeveª demanding, "Sleep with me." He tore himself away, but as he did, his jacketª slipped off and she was left holding it as he fled from the house. ¹³ When she saw that she had his jacket, and that he had fled, ¹⁴,¹⁵ she began screaming; and when the other men around the place came running in to see what had happened, she was crying hysterically. "My husband had to bring in this Hebrew slave to insult us!" she sobbed. "He tried to rape me, but when I screamed, he ran, and forgot to take his jacket."

¹⁶ She kept the jacket, and when her husband came home that night, ¹⁷ she told him her story.

"That Hebrew slave you've had around here tried to rape me, ¹⁸ and I was only saved by my screams. He fled, leaving his jacket behind!"

¹⁹ Well, when her husband heard his wife's story, he was furious. ²⁰ He threw Joseph into prison, where the king's prisoners were kept in chains. ²¹ But the Lord was with Joseph there, too, and was kind to him by granting him favor with the chief jailer. ²² In fact, the jailer soon handed over the entire prison administration to Joseph, so that all the other prisoners were responsible to him. ²³ The chief jailer had no more worries after that, for Joseph took care of everything, and the Lord was with him so that everything ran smoothly and well.

40 SOME TIME LATER it so happened that the king of Egypt became angry with his chief baker and his wine taster, so he jailed them both in the prison where Joseph was, in the castle of Potiphar, the captain of the guard, who was the chief executioner. ⁴ They remained under arrest there for quite

---

a The Hebrew word is not specific.

some time, and Potiphar assigned Joseph to wait on them. ⁵ One night each of them had a dream. ⁶ The next morning Joseph noticed that they looked dejected and sad.

⁷ "What in the world is the matter?" he asked.

⁸ And they replied, "We both had dreams last night, but there is no one here to tell us what they mean."

"Interpreting dreams is God's business," Joseph replied. "Tell me what you saw."

⁹,¹⁰ The wine taster told his dream first. "In my dream," he said, "I saw a vine with three branches that began to bud and blossom, and soon there were clusters of ripe grapes. ¹¹ I was holding Pharaoh's wine cup in my hand, so I took the grapes and squeezed the juice into it, and gave it to him to drink."

¹² "I know what the dream means," Joseph said. "The three branches mean three days! ¹³ Within three days Pharaoh is going to take you out of prison and give you back your job as his wine taster. ¹⁴ And please have some pity on me when you are back in his favor, and mention me to Pharaoh, and ask him to let me out of here. ¹⁵ For I was kidnapped from my homeland among the Hebrews, and now this—here I am in jail when I did nothing to deserve it."

¹⁶ When the chief baker saw that the first dream had such a good meaning, he told his dream to Joseph, too.

"In my dream," he said, "there were three baskets of pastries on my head. ¹⁷ In the top basket were all kinds of bakery goods for Pharaoh, but the birds came and ate them."

¹⁸,¹⁹ "The three baskets mean three days," Joseph told him. "Three days from now Pharaoh will take off your head and impale your body on a pole, and the birds will come and pick off your flesh!"

²⁰ Pharaoh's birthday came three days later, and he held a party for all of his officials and household staff. He sent for his wine taster and chief baker, and they were brought to him from the prison. ²¹ Then he restored the wine taster to his former position; ²² but he sentenced the chief baker to be impaled, just as Joseph had predicted. ²³ Pharaoh's wine taster, however, promptly forgot all about Joseph, never giving him a thought.

41 ONE NIGHT TWO years later, Pharaoh dreamed that he was standing on the bank of the Nile River, ² when suddenly, seven sleek, fat cows came up out of the river and began grazing in the grass. ³ Then seven other cows came up from the river, but they were very skinny and all their ribs stood out. They went over and stood beside the fat cows. ⁴ Then the skinny cows ate the fat ones! At which point, Pharaoh woke up!

⁵ Soon he fell asleep again and had a second dream. This time he saw seven heads of grain on one stalk, with every kernel well formed and plump. ⁶ Then, suddenly, seven more heads appeared on the stalk, but these were shriveled and withered by the east wind. ⁷ And these thin heads swallowed up the seven plump, well-formed heads! Then Pharaoh woke up again and realized it was all a dream. ⁸ Next morning, as he thought about it, he became very concerned as to what the dreams might mean; he called for all the magicians and sages of Egypt and told them about it, but not one of them could suggest what his dreams meant. ⁹ Then the king's wine taster spoke up.

"Today I remember my sin!" he said. ¹⁰ "Some time ago when you were angry with a couple of us and put me and the chief baker in jail in the castle of the captain of the guard, ¹¹ the chief baker and I each had a dream one night. ¹² We told the dreams to a young Hebrew fellow there who was a slave of the captain of the guard, and he told us what our dreams meant. ¹³ And everything happened just as he said: I was restored to my position of wine taster, and the chief baker was executed, and impaled on a pole."

¹⁴ Pharaoh sent at once for Joseph. He was brought hastily from the dungeon, and after a quick shave and change of clothes, came in before Pharaoh.

¹⁵ "I had a dream last night," Pharaoh told him, "and none of these men can tell me what it means. But I have heard that you can interpret dreams, and that is why I have called for you."

¹⁶ "I can't do it by myself," Joseph replied, "but God will tell you what it

means!"

¹⁷ So Pharaoh told him the dream. "I was standing upon the bank of the Nile River," he said, ¹⁸ "when suddenly, seven fat, healthy-looking cows came up out of the river and began grazing along the river bank. ¹⁹ But then seven other cows came up from the river, very skinny and bony—in fact, I've never seen such poor-looking specimens in all the land of Egypt. ²⁰ And these skinny cattle ate up the seven fat ones that had come out first, ²¹ and afterwards they were still as skinny as before! Then I woke up.

²² "A little later I had another dream. This time there were seven heads of grain on one stalk, and all seven heads were plump and full. ²³ Then, out of the same stalk, came seven withered, thin heads. ²⁴ And the thin heads swallowed up the fat ones! I told all this to my magicians, but not one of them could tell me the meaning."

²⁵ "Both dreams mean the same thing," Joseph told Pharaoh. "God was telling you what he is going to do here in the land of Egypt. ²⁶ The seven fat cows (and also the seven fat, well-formed heads of grain) mean that there are seven years of prosperity ahead. ²⁷ The seven skinny cows (and also the seven thin and withered heads of grain) indicate that there will be seven years of famine following the seven years of prosperity.

²⁸ "So God has showed you what he is about to do: ²⁹ The next seven years will be a period of great prosperity throughout all the land of Egypt; ³⁰ but afterwards there will be seven years of famine so great that all the prosperity will be forgotten and wiped out; famine will consume the land. ³¹ The famine will be so terrible that even the memory of the good years will be erased. ³² The double dream gives double impact, showing that what I have told you is certainly going to happen, for God has decreed it, and it is going to happen soon. ³³ My suggestion is that you find the wisest man in Egypt and put him in charge of administering a nation-wide farm program. ^{34,35} Let Pharaoh divide Egypt into five ad-ministrative districts,^a and let the officials of these districts gather into the royal store-houses all the excess crops of the next seven years, ³⁶ so that there will be enough to eat when the seven years of famine come. Otherwise, disaster will surely strike."

³⁷ Joseph's suggestions were well received by Pharaoh and his assistants. ³⁸ As they discussed who should be appointed for the job, Pharaoh said, "Who could do it better than Joseph? For he is a man who is obviously filled with the Spirit of God." ³⁹ Turning to Joseph, Pharaoh said to him, "Since God has revealed the meaning of the dreams to you, you are the wisest man in the country! ⁴⁰ I am hereby appointing you to be in charge of this entire project. What you say goes, throughout all the land of Egypt. I alone will outrank you."

^{41,42} Then Pharaoh placed his own signet ring on Joseph's finger as a token of his authority, and dressed him in beautiful clothing and placed the royal golden chain about his neck and declared, "See, I have placed you in charge of all the land of Egypt."

⁴³ Pharaoh also gave Joseph the chariot of his second-in-command, and wherever he went the shout arose, "Kneel down!" ⁴⁴ And Pharaoh declared to Joseph, "I, the king of Egypt, swear that you shall have complete charge over all the land of Egypt."

⁴⁵ Pharaoh gave him a name meaning "He has the god-like power of life and death!"^b And he gave him a wife, a girl named Asenath, daughter of Potiphera, priest of Heliopolis.^c So Joseph became famous throughout the land of Egypt. ⁴⁶ He was thirty years old as he entered the service of the king. Joseph went out from the presence of Pharaoh, and began traveling all across the land.

⁴⁷ And sure enough, for the next seven years there were bumper crops everywhere. ⁴⁸ During those years, Joseph requisitioned for the government a portion of all the crops grown throughout Egypt, storing them in nearby cities. ⁴⁹ After seven years of this, the granaries were full to overflowing, and there was so much that no one kept track of the

a Or, "Let Pharaoh appoint officials to collect a fifth of all the crops . . ."   b Or, "God (or Pharaoh) says 'He is living.' "   c Joseph thus married into a family of high nobility, his father-in-law being a major priest-politician of the time.

amount.

⁵⁰ During this time before the arrival of the first of the famine years, two sons were born to Joseph by Asenath, the daughter of Potiphera, priest of the sun god Re of Heliopolis. ⁵¹ Joseph named his oldest son Manasseh (meaning "Made to Forget"—what he meant was that God had made up to him for all the anguish of his youth, and for the loss of his father's home). ⁵² The second boy was named Ephraim (meaning "Fruitful"—"For God has made me fruitful in this land of my slavery," he said).

⁵³ So at last the seven years of plenty came to an end. ⁵⁴ Then the seven years of famine began, just as Joseph had predicted. There were crop failures in all the surrounding countries too, but in Egypt there was plenty of grain in the storehouses. ⁵⁵ The people began to starve. They pleaded with Pharaoh for food, and he sent them to Joseph. "Do whatever he tells you to," he instructed them.

⁵⁶,⁵⁷ So now, with severe famine all over the world, Joseph opened up the storehouses and sold grain to the Egyptians and to those from other lands who came to Egypt to buy grain from Joseph.

42 WHEN JACOB HEARD that there was grain available in Egypt he said to his sons, "Why are you standing around looking at one another? ² I have heard that there is grain available in Egypt. Go down and buy some for us before we all starve to death."

³ So Joseph's ten older[a] brothers went down to Egypt to buy grain. ⁴ However, Jacob wouldn't let Joseph's younger brother Benjamin go with them, for fear some harm might happen to him [as it had to his brother Joseph[a]]. ⁵ So it was that Israel's sons arrived in Egypt along with many others from many lands to buy food, for the famine was as severe in Canaan as it was everywhere else. ⁶ Since Joseph was governor of all Egypt, and in charge of the sale of the grain, it was to him that his brothers came, and bowed low before him, with their faces to the earth. ⁷ Joseph recognized them instantly, but pretended he didn't.

"Where are you from?" he demanded roughly.

"From the land of Canaan," they replied. "We have come to buy grain."

⁸,⁹ Then Joseph remembered the dreams of long ago! But he said to them, "You are spies. You have come to see how destitute the famine has made our land."

¹⁰ "No, no," they exclaimed. "We have come to buy food. ¹¹ We are all brothers and honest men, sir! We are not spies!"

¹² "Yes, you are," he insisted. "You have come to see how weak we are."

¹³ "Sir," they said, "there are twelve of us brothers, and our father is in the land of Canaan. Our youngest brother is there with our father, and one of our brothers is dead."

¹⁴ "So?" Joseph asked. "What does that prove?[b] You are spies. ¹⁵ This is the way I will test your story: I swear by the life of Pharaoh that you are not going to leave Egypt until this youngest brother comes here. ¹⁶ One of you go and get your brother! I'll keep the rest of you here, bound in prison. Then we'll find out whether your story is true or not. If it turns out that you don't have a younger brother, then I'll know you are spies."

¹⁷ So he threw them all into jail for three days.

¹⁸ The third day Joseph said to them, "I am a God-fearing man and I'm going to give you an opportunity to prove yourselves. ¹⁹ I'm going to take a chance that you are honorable:[c] only one of you shall remain in chains in jail, and the rest of you may go on home with grain for your families; ²⁰ but bring your youngest brother back to me. In this way I will know whether you are telling me the truth; and if you are, I will spare you." To this they agreed.

²¹ Speaking among themselves, they said, "This has all happened because of what we did to Joseph long ago. We saw his terror and anguish and heard his pleadings, but we wouldn't listen."

²² "Didn't I tell you not to do it?" Reuben asked. "But you wouldn't listen. And now we are going to die because we murdered him."

²³ Of course they didn't know that Jo-

---

a Implied.   b Literally, "It is as I said: you are spies."   c Literally, "If you are forthright men."

seph understood them as he was standing there, for he had been speaking to them through an interpreter. ²⁴ Now he left the room and found a place where he could weep. Returning, he selected Simeon from among them and had him bound before their eyes. ²⁵ Joseph then ordered his servants to fill the men's sacks with grain, but also gave secret instructions to put each brother's payment at the top of his sack! He also gave them provisions for their journey. ²⁶ So they loaded up their donkeys with the grain and started for home. ²⁷ But when they stopped for the night and one of them opened his sack to get some grain to feed the donkeys, there was his money in the mouth of the sack!

²⁸ "Look," he exclaimed to his brothers, "my money is here in my sack." They were filled with terror. Trembling, they exclaimed to each other, "What is this that God has done to us?" ²⁹ So they came to their father Jacob in the land of Canaan and told him all that had happened.

³⁰ "The king's chief assistant spoke very roughly to us," they told him, "and took us for spies. ³¹ 'No, no,' we said, 'we are honest men, not spies. ³² We are twelve brothers, sons of one father; one is dead, and the youngest is with our father in the land of Canaan.' ³³ Then the man told us, 'This is the way I will find out if you are what you claim to be. Leave one of your brothers here with me and take grain for your families and go on home, ³⁴ but bring your youngest brother back to me. Then I shall know whether you are spies or honest men; if you prove to be what you say, then I will give you back your brother and you can come as often as you like to purchase grain.' "

³⁵ As they emptied out the sacks, there at the top of each was the money paid for the grain! Terror gripped them, as it did their father.

³⁶ Then Jacob exclaimed, "You have bereaved me of my children—Joseph didn't come back, Simeon is gone, and now you want to take Benjamin too! Everything has been against me."

³⁷ Then Reuben said to his father, "Kill my two sons if I don't bring Benjamin back to you. I'll be responsible for him."

³⁸ But Jacob replied, "My son shall not go down with you, for his brother Joseph is dead and he alone is left of his mother's children. If anything should happen to him, I would die."

43 BUT THERE WAS no relief from the terrible famine throughout the land. ² When the grain they had brought from Egypt was almost gone, their father said to them, "Go again and buy us a little food." ³,⁴,⁵ But Judah told him, "The man wasn't fooling one bit when he said, 'Don't ever come back again unless your brother is with you.' We cannot go unless you let Benjamin go with us."

⁶ "Why did you ever tell him you had another brother?" Israel moaned. "Why did you have to treat me like that?"

⁷ "But the man specifically asked us about our family," they told him. "He wanted to know whether our father was still living and he asked us if we had another brother, so we told him. How could we know that he was going to say, 'Bring me your brother'?"

⁸ Judah said to his father, "Send the lad with me and we will be on our way; otherwise we will all die of starvation—and not only we, but you and all our little ones. ⁹ I guarantee his safety. If I don't bring him back to you, then let me bear the blame forever. ¹⁰ For we could have gone and returned by this time if you had let him come."

¹¹ So their father Israel finally said to them, "If it can't be avoided, then at least do this. Load your donkeys with the best products of the land. Take them to the man as gifts—balm, honey, spices, myrrh, pistachio nuts, and almonds. ¹² Take double money so that you can pay back what was in the mouths of your sacks, as it was probably someone's mistake, ¹³ and take your brother and go. ¹⁴ May God Almighty give you mercy before the man, so that he will release Simeon and return Benjamin. And if I must bear the anguish of their deaths, then so be it."

¹⁵ So they took the gifts and double money and went to Egypt, and stood before Joseph. ¹⁶ When Joseph saw that Benjamin was with them he said to the manager of his household, "These men will eat with me

this noon. Take them home and prepare a big feast." ¹⁷ So the man did as he was told and took them to Joseph's palace. ¹⁸ They were badly frightened when they saw where they were being taken.

"It's because of the money returned to us in our sacks," they said. "He wants to pretend we stole it and seize us as slaves, with our donkeys."

¹⁹ As they arrived at the entrance to the palace, they went over to Joseph's household manager, ²⁰ and said to him, "O sir, after our first trip to Egypt to buy food, ²¹ as we were returning home, we stopped for the night and opened our sacks, and the money was there that we had paid for the grain. Here it is; we have brought it back again, ²² along with additional money to buy more grain. We have no idea how the money got into our sacks."

²³ "Don't worry about it," the household manager told them; "your God, even the God of your fathers, must have put it there, for we collected your money all right."

Then he released Simeon and brought him out to them. ²⁴ They were then conducted into the palace and given water to refresh their feet; and their donkeys were fed. ²⁵ Then they got their presents ready for Joseph's arrival at noon, for they were told that they would be eating there. ²⁶ When Joseph came home they gave him their presents, bowing low before him.

²⁷ He asked how they had been getting along. "And how is your father—the old man you spoke about? Is he still alive?"

²⁸ "Yes," they replied. "He is alive and well." Then again they bowed before him.

²⁹ Looking at his brother[a] Benjamin, he asked, "Is this your youngest brother, the one you told me about? How are you, my son? God be gracious to you." ³⁰ Then Joseph made a hasty exit, for he was overcome with love for his brother and had to go out and cry. Going into his bedroom, he wept there. ³¹ Then he washed his face and came out, keeping himself under control. "Let's eat," he said.

³² Joseph ate by himself, his brothers were served at a separate table, and the Egyptians at still another; for Egyptians despise Hebrews and never eat with them. ³³ He told each of them where to sit, and seated them in the order of their ages, from the oldest to the youngest, much to their amazement! ³⁴ Their food was served to them from his own table. He gave the largest serving to Benjamin—five times as much as to any of the others! They had a wonderful time bantering back and forth, and the wine flowed freely!

44 WHEN HIS BROTHERS were ready to leave,[a] Joseph ordered his household manager to fill each of their sacks with as much grain as they could carry—and to put into the mouth of each man's sack the money he had paid! ² He was also told to put Joseph's own silver cup at the top of Benjamin's sack, along with the grain money. So the household manager did as he was told. ³ The brothers were up at dawn and on their way with their loaded donkeys.

⁴ But when they were barely out of the city, Joseph said to his household manager, "Chase after them and stop them and ask them why they are acting like this when their benefactor has been so kind to them? ⁵ Ask them, 'What do you mean by stealing my lord's personal silver drinking cup, which he uses for fortune telling? What a wicked thing you have done!' " ⁶ So he caught up with them and spoke to them along the lines he had been instructed.

⁷ "What in the world are you talking about?" they demanded. "What kind of people do you think we are, that you accuse us of such a terrible thing as that? ⁸ Didn't we bring back the money we found in the mouth of our sacks? Why would we steal silver or gold from your master's house? ⁹ If you find his cup with any one of us, let that one die. And all the rest of us will be slaves forever to your master."

¹⁰ "Fair enough," the man replied, "except that only the one who stole it will be a slave, and the rest of you can go free."

¹¹ They quickly took down their sacks from the backs of their donkeys and opened them. ¹² He began searching the oldest brother's sack, going on down the line to the youngest. And the cup was found in Ben-

---

a Literally, "his brother Benjamin, his mother's son."   44a Implied.

jamin's! [13] They ripped their clothing in despair, loaded the donkeys again, and returned to the city. [14] Joseph was still home when Judah and his brothers arrived, and they fell to the ground before him.

[15] "What were you trying to do?" Joseph demanded. "Didn't you know such a man as I would know who stole it?"

[16] And Judah said, "Oh, what shall we say to my lord? How can we plead? How can we prove our innocence? God is punishing us for our sins. Sir, we have all returned to be your slaves, both we and he in whose sack the cup was found."

[17] "No," Joseph said. "Only the man who stole the cup, he shall be my slave. The rest of you can go on home to your father."

[18] Then Judah stepped forward and said, "O sir, let me say just this one word to you. Be patient with me for a moment, for I know you can doom me in an instant, as though you were Pharaoh himself.

[19] "Sir, you asked us if we had a father or a brother, [20] and we said, 'Yes, we have a father, an old man, and a child of his old age, a little one. And his brother is dead, and he alone is left of his mother's children, and his father loves him very much.' [21] And you said to us, 'Bring him here so that I can see him.' [22] But we said to you, 'Sir, the lad cannot leave his father, for his father would die.' [23] But you told us, 'Don't come back here unless your youngest brother is with you.' [24] So we returned to our father and told him what you had said. [25] And when he said, 'Go back again and buy us a little food,' [26] we replied, 'We can't, unless you let our youngest brother go with us. Only then may we come.'

[27] "Then my father said to us, 'You know that my wife had two sons, [28] and that one of them went away and never returned—doubtless torn to pieces by some wild animal; I have never seen him since. [29] And if you take away his brother from me also, and any harm befalls him, I shall die with sorrow.' [30] And now, sir, if I go back to my father and the lad is not with us—seeing that our father's life is bound up in the lad's life— [31] when he sees that the boy is not with us, our father will die; and we will be responsible for bringing down his gray hairs with sorrow to the grave. [32] Sir, I pledged

my father that I would take care of the lad. I told him, 'If I don't bring him back to you, I shall bear the blame forever.' [33] Please sir, let me stay here as a slave instead of the lad, and let the lad return with his brothers. [34] For how shall I return to my father if the lad is not with me? I cannot bear to see what this would do to him."

45 JOSEPH COULD STAND it no longer. "Out, all of you," he cried out to his attendants, and he was left alone with his brothers. [2] Then he wept aloud. His sobs could be heard throughout the palace, and the news was quickly carried to Pharaoh's palace.

[3] "I am Joseph!" he said to his brothers. "Is my father still alive?" But his brothers couldn't say a word, they were so stunned with surprise.

[4] "Come over here," he said. So they came closer. And he said again, "I am Joseph, your brother whom you sold into Egypt! [5] But don't be angry with yourselves that you did this to me, for God did it! He sent me here ahead of you to preserve your lives. [6] These two years of famine will grow to seven, during which there will be neither plowing nor harvest. [7] God has sent me here to keep you and your families alive, so that you will become a great nation. [8] Yes, it was God who sent me here, not you! And he has made me a counselor to Pharaoh, and manager of this entire nation, ruler of all the land of Egypt.

[9] "Hurry, return to my father and tell him, 'Your son Joseph says, "God has made me chief of all the land of Egypt. Come down to me right away! [10] You shall live in the land of Goshen so that you can be near me with all your children, your grandchildren, your flocks and herds, and all that you have. [11,12] I will take care of you there" ' (you men are witnesses of my promise, and my brother Benjamin has heard me say it) ' "for there are still five years of famine ahead of us. Otherwise you will come to utter poverty along with all your household." ' [13] Tell our father about all my power here in Egypt, and how everyone obeys me. And bring him to me quickly."

[14] Then, weeping with joy, he embraced Benjamin and Benjamin began weeping

too. [15] And he did the same with each of his brothers, who finally found their tongues! [16] The news soon reached Pharaoh—"Joseph's brothers have come"; and Pharaoh was very happy to hear it, as were his officials.

[17] Then Pharaoh said to Joseph, "Tell your brothers to load their pack animals and return quickly to their homes in Canaan, [18] and to bring your father and all of your families and come here to Egypt to live. Tell them, 'Pharaoh will assign to you the very best territory in the land of Egypt. You shall live off the fat of the land!' [19] And tell your brothers to take wagons from Egypt to carry their wives and little ones, and to bring your father here. [20] Don't worry about your property, for the best of all the land of Egypt is yours."

[21] So Joseph gave them wagons, as Pharaoh had commanded, and provisions for the journey, [22] and he gave each of them new clothes—but to Benjamin he gave five changes of clothes and three hundred pieces of silver! [23] He sent his father ten donkeyloads of the good things of Egypt, and ten donkeys loaded with grain and all kinds of other food, to eat on his journey. [24] So he sent his brothers off.

"Don't quarrel along the way!" was his parting shot! [25] And leaving, they returned to the land of Canaan, to Jacob their father.

[26] "Joseph is alive," they shouted to him. "And he is ruler over all the land of Egypt!" But Jacob's heart was like a stone; he couldn't take it in. [27] But when they had given him Joseph's messages, and when he saw the wagons filled with food that Joseph had sent him, his spirit revived.

[28] And he said, "It must be true! Joseph my son is alive! I will go and see him before I die."

46 SO ISRAEL SET out with all his possessions, and came to Beer-sheba, and offered sacrifices there to the God of his father Isaac. [2] During the night God spoke to him in a vision.

"Jacob! Jacob!" he called.

"Yes?" Jacob answered.

[3,4] "I am God," the voice replied, "the God of your father. Don't be afraid to go down to Egypt, for I will see to it that you become a great nation there. And I will go down with you into Egypt and I will bring your descendants back again; but you shall die in Egypt with Joseph at your side."

[5] So Jacob left Beer-sheba, and his sons brought him to Egypt, along with their little ones and their wives, in the wagons Pharaoh had provided for them. [6] They brought their livestock too, and all their belongings accumulated in the land of Canaan, and came to Egypt—Jacob and all his children, [7] sons and daughters, grandsons and granddaughters—all his loved ones.

[8-14] Here are the names of his sons and grandchildren who went with him into Egypt:

> Reuben, his oldest son;
> Reuben's sons: Hanoch, Pallu, Hezron, and Carmi.
> Simeon and his sons: Jemuel, Jamin, Ohad, Jachin, Zohar, and Shaul (Shaul's mother was a girl from Canaan).
> Levi and his sons: Gershon, Kohath, Merari.
> Judah and his sons: Er, Onan, Shelah, Perez, Zerah (however, Er and Onan died while still in Canaan, before Israel went to Egypt).
> The sons of Perez were Hezron and Hamul.
> Issachar and his sons: Tola, Puvah, Iob, Shimron.
> Zebulun and his sons: Sered, Elon, Jahleel.

[15] So these descendants of Jacob and Leah, not including their daughter Dinah, born to Jacob in Paddan-aram, were thirty-three in all.

[16,17] Also accompanying him were:

> Gad and his sons: Ziphion, Haggi, Shuni,
> Ezbon, Eri, Arodi, and Areli.
> Asher and his sons: Imnah, Ishvah, Ishvi,
> Beriah, and a sister, Serah.
> Beriah's sons were Heber and Malchiel.

[18] These sixteen persons were the sons of Jacob and Zilpah, the slave-girl given to Leah by her father, Laban.

[19-22] Also in the total of Jacob's

household were these fourteen sons and descendants of Jacob and Rachel:

Joseph and Benjamin;

Joseph's sons, born in the land of Egypt, were Manasseh and Ephraim (their mother was Asenath, the daughter of Potiphera, priest of Heliopolis);

Benjamin's sons: Bela, Becher, Ashbel, Gera, Naaman, Ehi, Rosh, Muppim, Huppim, and Ard.

²³,²⁴,²⁵ Also in the group were these seven sons and descendants of Jacob and Bilhah, the slave-girl given to Rachel by her father, Laban:

Dan and his son: Hushim.

Naphtali and his sons: Jahzeel, Guni, Jezer, and Shillem.

²⁶ So the total number of those going to Egypt, of his own descendants, not counting the wives of Jacob's sons, was sixty-six. ²⁷ With Joseph's two sons included, this total of Jacob's household there in Egypt totaled seventy.

²⁸ Jacob sent Judah on ahead to tell Joseph that they were on the way, and would soon arrive in Goshen—which they did. ²⁹ Joseph jumped into his chariot and journeyed to Goshen to meet his father and they fell into each other's arms and wept a long while.

³⁰ Then Israel said to Joseph, "Now let me die, for I have seen you again and know you are alive."

³¹ And Joseph said to his brothers and to all their households, "I'll go and tell Pharaoh that you are here, and that you have come from the land of Canaan to join me. ³² And I will tell him, 'These men are shepherds. They have brought with them their flocks and herds and everything they own.' ³³ So when Pharaoh calls for you and asks you about your occupation, ³⁴ tell him, 'We have been shepherds from our youth, as our fathers have been for many generations.' When you tell him this, he will let you live here in the land of Goshen." For shepherds were despised and hated in other parts of Egypt.

47 UPON THEIR ARRIVAL, Joseph went in to see Pharaoh.

"My father and my brothers are here from Canaan," he reported, "with all their flocks and herds and possessions. They wish to settle in the land of Goshen."

² He took five of his brothers with him, and presented them to Pharaoh. ³ Pharaoh asked them, "What is your occupation?"

And they replied, "We are shepherds like our ancestors. ⁴ We have come to live here in Egypt, for there is no pasture for our flocks in Canaan—the famine is very bitter there. We request permission to live in the land of Goshen."

⁵,⁶ And Pharaoh said to Joseph, "Choose anywhere you like for them to live. Give them the best land of Egypt. The land of Goshen will be fine. And if any of them are capable, put them in charge of my flocks, too."

⁷ Then Joseph brought his father Jacob to Pharaoh. And Jacob blessed Pharaoh.

⁸ "How old are you?" Pharaoh asked him.

⁹ Jacob replied, "I have lived 130 long, hard years, and I am not nearly as old as many of my ancestors." ¹⁰ Then Jacob blessed Pharaoh again before he left.

¹¹ So Joseph assigned the best land of Egypt—the land of Rameses—to his father and brothers, just as Pharaoh had commanded. ¹² And Joseph furnished food to them in accordance with the number of their dependents. ¹³ The famine became worse and worse, so that all the land of Egypt and Canaan were starving. ¹⁴ Joseph collected all the money in Egypt and Canaan in exchange for grain, and he brought the money to Pharaoh's treasure-houses. ¹⁵ When the people were out of money, they came to Joseph crying again for food.

"Our money is gone," they said, "but give us bread; for why should we die?"

¹⁶ "Well then," Joseph replied, "give me your livestock. I will trade you food in exchange."

¹⁷ So they brought their cattle to Joseph in exchange for food. Soon all the horses, flocks, herds, and donkeys of Egypt were in Pharaoh's possession.

¹⁸ The next year they came again and said, "Our money is gone, and our cattle are yours, and there is nothing left but our bod-

ies and land. ¹⁹ Why should we die? Buy us and our land and we will be serfs to Pharaoh. We will trade ourselves for food, then we will live, and the land won't be abandoned."

²⁰ So Joseph bought all the land of Egypt for Pharaoh; all the Egyptians sold him their fields because the famine was so severe. And the land became Pharaoh's. ²¹ Thus all the people of Egypt became Pharaoh's serfs. ²² The only land he didn't buy was that belonging to the priests, for they were assigned food from Pharaoh and didn't need to sell.

²³ Then Joseph said to the people, "See, I have bought you and your land for Pharaoh. Here is grain. Go and sow the land. ²⁴ And when you harvest it, a fifth of everything you get belongs to Pharaoh. Keep four parts for yourselves to be used for next year's seed, and as food for yourselves and for your households and little ones."

²⁵ "You have saved our lives," they said. "We will gladly be the serfs of Pharaoh."

²⁶ So Joseph made it a law throughout the land of Egypt—and it is still the law—that Pharaoh should have as his tax twenty percent of all the crops except those produced on the land owned by the temples.

²⁷ So Israel lived in the land of Goshen in Egypt, and soon the people of Israel began to prosper, and there was a veritable population explosion among them. ²⁸ Jacob lived seventeen years after his arrival, so that he was 147 years old at the time of his death. ²⁹ As the time drew near for him to die, he called for his son Joseph and said to him, "Swear to me most solemnly that you will honor this, my last request: do not bury me in Egypt. ³⁰ But when I am dead, take me out of Egypt and bury me beside my ancestors." And Joseph promised. ³¹ "Swear that you will do it," Jacob insisted. And Joseph did. Soon afterwards Jacob took to his bed.

48 ONE DAY NOT long after this, word came to Joseph that his father was failing rapidly. So, taking with him his two sons, Manasseh and Ephraim, he went to visit him. ² When Jacob heard that Joseph had arrived, he gathered his strength and sat up in the bed to greet him, ³ and said to him,

"God Almighty appeared to me at Luz in the land of Canaan and blessed me, ⁴ and said to me, 'I will make you a great nation and I will give this land of Canaan to you and to your children's children, for an everlasting possession.' ⁵ And now, as to these two sons of yours, Ephraim and Manasseh, born here in the land of Egypt before I arrived, I am adopting them as my own, and they will inherit from me just as Reuben and Simeon will. ⁶ But any other children born to you shall be your own, and shall inherit Ephraim's and Manasseh's portion from you. ⁷ For your mother Rachel died after only two children^a when I came from Paddan-aram, as we were just a short distance from Ephrath, and I buried her beside the road to Bethlehem." ⁸ Then Israel looked over at the two boys. "Are these the ones?" he asked.

⁹ "Yes," Joseph told him, "these are my sons whom God has given me here in Egypt."

And Israel said, "Bring them over to me and I will bless them."

¹⁰ Israel was half blind with age, so that he could hardly see. So Joseph brought the boys close to him and he kissed and embraced them.

¹¹ And Israel said to Joseph, "I never thought that I would see you again, but now God has let me see your children too."

^{12,13} Joseph took the boys by the hand, bowed deeply to him, and led the boys to their grandfather's knees—Ephraim at Israel's left hand and Manasseh at his right. ¹⁴ But Israel crossed his arms as he stretched them out to lay his hands upon the boys' heads, so that his right hand was upon the head of Ephraim, the younger boy, and his left hand was upon the head of Manasseh, the older. He did this purposely.

¹⁵ Then he blessed Joseph with this blessing: "May God, the God of my fathers Abraham and Isaac, the God who has shepherded me all my life, wonderfully bless these boys. ¹⁶ He is the Angel who has

---

a Implied.

kept me from all harm. May these boys be an honor to my name and to the names of my fathers Abraham and Isaac; and may they become a mighty nation."

[17] But Joseph was upset and displeased when he saw that his father had laid his right hand on Ephraim's head; so he lifted it to place it on Manasseh's head instead.

[18] "No, father," he said. "You've got your right hand on the wrong head! This one over here is the older. Put your right hand on him!"

[19] But his father refused. "I know what I'm doing, my son," he said. "Manasseh too shall become a great nation, but his younger brother shall become even greater."

[20] So Jacob blessed the boys that day with this blessing: "May the people of Israel bless each other by saying, 'God make you as prosperous as Ephraim and Manasseh.' " (Note that he put Ephraim before Manasseh.)

[21] Then Israel said to Joseph, "I am about to die, but God will be with you and will bring you again to Canaan, the land of your fathers. [22] And I have given the choice land of Shekem to you instead of to your brothers, as your portion of that land which I took from the Amorites with my sword and with my bow."

49 THEN JACOB CALLED together all his sons and said, "Gather around me and I will tell you what is going to happen to you in the days to come. [2] Listen to me, O sons of Jacob; listen to Israel your father.

[3] "Reuben, you are my oldest son, the child of my vigorous youth. You are the head of the list in rank and in honor. [4] But you are unruly as the wild waves of the sea, and you shall be first no longer. I am demoting you, for you slept with one of my wives and thus dishonored me.

[5] "Simeon and Levi are two of a kind. They are men of violence and injustice. [6] O my soul, stay away from them. May I never be a party to their wicked plans. For in their anger they murdered a man, and maimed oxen just for fun. [7] Cursed be their anger, for it is fierce and cruel. Therefore, I will scatter their descendants throughout Israel.[a]

[8] "Judah, your brothers shall praise you. You shall destroy your enemies. Your father's sons shall bow before you. [9] Judah is a young lion that has finished eating its prey. He has settled down as a lion—who will dare to rouse him? [10] The scepter shall not depart from Judah until Shiloh[b] comes, whom all people shall obey. [11] He has chained his steed to the choicest vine, and washed his clothes in wine.[c] [12] His eyes are darker than wine and his teeth are whiter than milk.

[13] "Zebulun shall dwell on the shores of the sea and shall be a harbor for ships, with his borders extending to Sidon.

[14] "Issachar is a strong beast of burden resting among the saddle bags. [15] When he saw how good the countryside was, how pleasant the land, he willingly bent his shoulder to the task and served his masters with vigor.

[16] "Dan shall govern his people like any other tribe in Israel. [17] He shall be a serpent in the path that bites the horses' heels, so that the rider falls off. [18] I trust in your salvation, Lord.

[19] "A marauding band shall stamp upon Gad, but he shall rob and pursue them!

[20] "Asher shall produce rich foods, fit for kings!

[21] "Naphtali is a deer let loose, producing lovely fawns.

[22] "Joseph is a fruitful tree beside a fountain. His branches shade the wall. [23] He has been severely injured by those who shot at him and persecuted him, [24] but their weapons were shattered by the Mighty One of Jacob, the Shepherd, the Rock of Israel. [25] May the God of your fathers, the Almighty, bless you with blessings of heaven above and of the earth beneath—blessings of the breasts and of the womb, [26] blessings of the grain and flowers, blessings reaching to the utmost bounds of the everlasting hills. These shall be the blessings upon the head of Joseph who was exiled from his brothers.

[27] "Benjamin is a wolf that prowls. He

---

a That is, the tribes of Simeon and Levi were not given land holdings, as were their brother-tribes.
b Which means, "he to whom it belongs."   c Showing wealth and extravagance.

devours his enemies in the morning, and in the evening divides the spoil." [28] So these are the blessings that Israel their father blessed his twelve sons with.

[29,30] Then he told them, "Soon I will die. You must bury me with my fathers in the land of Canaan, in the cave in the field of Mach-pelah, facing Mamre—the field Abraham bought from Ephron the Hethite for a burial ground. [31] There they buried Abraham and Sarah his wife; there they buried Isaac and Rebekah his wife; and there I buried Leah. [32] It is the cave which my grandfather Abraham purchased from the sons of Heth." [33] Then, when Jacob had finished his prophecies to his sons, he lay back in the bed, breathed his last, and died.

50 JOSEPH THREW HIMSELF upon his father's body and wept over him and kissed him. [2] Afterwards he commanded his morticians to embalm the body. [3] The embalming process required forty days, with a period of national mourning of seventy days. [4] Then, when at last the mourning was over, Joseph approached Pharaoh's staff and requested them to speak to Pharaoh on his behalf.

[5] "Tell his majesty," he requested them, "that Joseph's father made Joseph swear to take his body back to the land of Canaan, to bury him there. Ask his majesty to permit me to go and bury my father; assure him that I will return promptly."

[6] Pharaoh agreed. "Go and bury your father, as you promised," he said.

[7] So Joseph went, and a great number of Pharaoh's counselors and assistants—all the senior officers of the land, [8] as well as all of Joseph's people—his brothers and their families. But they left their little children and flocks and herds in the land of Goshen. [9] So a very great number of chariots, cavalry, and people accompanied Joseph.

[10] When they arrived at Atad[a] (meaning "Threshing Place of Brambles"), beyond the Jordan River, they held a very great and solemn funeral service, with a seven-day period of lamentation for Joseph's father. [11] The local residents, the Canaanites, re-named the place Abel-mizraim (meaning "Egyptian Mourners") for they said, "It is a place of very deep mourning by these Egyptians." [12,13] So his sons did as Israel commanded them, and carried his body into the land of Canaan and buried it there in the cave of Mach-pelah—the cave Abraham had bought in the field of Ephron the Hethite, close to Mamre.

[14] Then Joseph returned to Egypt with his brothers and all who had accompanied him to the funeral of his father. [15] But now that their father was dead, Joseph's brothers were frightened.

"Now Joseph will pay us back for all the evil we did to him," they said. [16,17] So they sent him this message: "Before he died, your father instructed us to tell you to forgive us for the great evil we did to you. We servants of the God of your father beg you to forgive us." When Joseph read the message, he broke down and cried.

[18] Then his brothers came and fell down before him and said, "We are your slaves."

[19] But Joseph told them, "Don't be afraid of me. Am I God, to judge and punish you? [20] As far as I am concerned, God turned into good what you meant for evil, for he brought me to this high position I have today so that I could save the lives of many people. [21] No, don't be afraid. Indeed, I myself will take care of you and your families." And he spoke very kindly to them, reassuring them.

[22] So Joseph and his brothers and their families continued to live in Egypt. Joseph was 110 years old when he died. [23] He lived to see the birth of his son Ephraim's children, and the children of Machir, Manasseh's son, who played at his feet.

[24] "Soon I will die," Joseph told his brothers, "but God will surely come and get you, and bring you out of this land of Egypt and take you back to the land he promised to the descendants of Abraham, Isaac and Jacob." [25] Then Joseph made his brothers promise with an oath that they would take his body back with them when they returned to Canaan. [26] So Joseph died at the age of 110, and they embalmed him, and his body was placed in a coffin in Egypt.

---

a Located just west of the Jordan River, near Jericho.

Let My People Go!

Wallowitch

Ghettos, Iron Curtains, and concentration camps—the names are new, but the ideas are as old as the pharaohs of Egypt's 19th Dynasty. Jews were hated, penned into one district called Goshen, and eventually brutalized as slaves in the first of many anti-Semitic outrages in history.

They escaped any ancient version of gas ovens, however, through the startling leadership of Moses. God took 80 years getting him ready; then, within weeks, he had called down upon the Nile valley an eerie parade of disasters and led two million Hebrews toward "the promised land."

Even after more than four centuries in Egypt, the huge caravan did not make a beeline for Palestine. It swerved southeast instead, deep into the Sinai Peninsula to a mysterious mountain where, for the next year, God dictated his laws and the details of worship at his holy tabernacle. The exhilaration of freedom wore off, and in its place came responsibility which the ex-slaves could not always handle.

EXODUS

1 THIS IS THE list of the sons of Jacob who accompanied him to Egypt, with their families:

Reuben, Simeon, Levi,
Judah, Issachar, Zebulun,
Benjamin, Dan, Naphtali,
Gad, Asher.

⁵ So the total number who went with him was seventy (for Joseph was already there). ⁶ In due season Joseph and each of his brothers died, ending that generation. ⁷ Meanwhile, their descendants were very fertile, increasing rapidly in numbers; there was a veritable population explosion so that they soon became a large nation, and they filled the land of Goshen.

⁸ Then, eventually,ᵃ a new king came to the throne of Egypt who felt no obligationᵇ to the descendants of Joseph.

⁹ He told his people, "These Israelis are becoming dangerous to us because there are so many of them. ¹⁰ Let's figure out a way to put an end to this. If we don't, and war breaks out, they will join our enemies and fight against us and escape out of the country."

¹¹ So the Egyptians made slaves of them and put brutal taskmasters over them to wear them down under heavy burdens while building the store-cities Pithom and Raamses. ¹² But the more the Egyptians mistreated and oppressed them, the more the Israelis seemed to multiply! The Egyptians became alarmed, ¹³,¹⁴ and made the Hebrew slavery more bitter still, forcing them to toil long and hard in the fields and to carry heavy loads of mortar and brick.

¹⁵,¹⁶ Then Pharaoh, the king of Egypt, instructed the Hebrew midwives (their names were Shiphrah and Puah) to kill all Hebrew boys as soon as they were born, but to let the girls live. ¹⁷ But the midwives feared God and didn't obey the king—they let the boys live too.

¹⁸ The king summoned them before him and demanded, "Why have you disobeyed my command and let the baby boys live?"

¹⁹ "Sir," they told him, "the Hebrew women have their babies so quickly that we can't get there in time! They are not slow like the Egyptian women!"

²⁰ And God blessed the midwives. So the people of Israel continued to multiply and to become a mighty nation. ²¹ And because the midwives revered God, he gave them children of their own. ²² Then Pharaoh commanded all of his people to throw the newborn Hebrew boys into the Nile River. But the girls, he said, could live.

2 THERE WERE AT this time a Hebrew fellow and girl of the tribe of Levi who married and had a family, and a baby son was born to them. When the baby's mother saw that he was an unusually beautiful baby, she hid him at home for three months. ³ Then, when she could no longer hide him, she made a little boat from papyrus reeds, waterproofed it with tar, put the baby in it, and laid it among the reeds along the river's edge. ⁴ The baby's sister watched from a distance to see what would happen to him.

⁵ Well, this is what happened: A princess, one of Pharaoh's daughters, came down to bathe in the river, and as she and her maids were walking along the river bank, she spied the little boat among the reeds and sent one of the maids to bring it to her. ⁶ When she opened it, there was a baby! And he was crying. This touched her heart. "He must be one of the Hebrew children!" she said.

⁷ Then the baby's sister approached the princess and asked her, "Shall I go and find one of the Hebrew women to nurse the baby for you?"

⁸ "Yes, do!" the princess replied. So the little girl rushed home and called her mother!

⁹ "Take this child home and nurse him for me," the princess instructed the baby's mother, "and I will pay you well!" So she took him home and nursed him.

¹⁰ Later, when he was older, she brought

ᵃ Implied. This incident occurred about four hundred years after Joseph's death. ᵇ Literally, "who did not know Joseph."

him back to the princess and he became her son. She named him Moses (meaning[a] "to draw out") because she had drawn him out of the water.

[11] One day, many years later[b] when Moses had grown up and become a man, he went out to visit his fellow Hebrews and saw the terrible conditions they were under. During his visit he saw an Egyptian knock a Hebrew to the ground—one of his own Hebrew brothers! [12] Moses looked this way and that to be sure no one was watching, then killed the Egyptian and hid his body in the sand.

[13] The next day as he was out visiting among the Hebrews again, he saw two of them fighting. "What are you doing, hitting your own Hebrew brother like that?" he said to the one in the wrong.

[14] "And who are you?" the man demanded. "I suppose you think you are *our* prince and judge! And do you plan to kill me as you did that Egyptian yesterday?" When Moses realized that his deed was known, he was frightened. [15] And sure enough, when Pharaoh heard about it he ordered Moses arrested and executed. But Moses ran away into the land of Midian. As he was sitting there beside a well, [16] seven girls who were daughters of the priest of Midian came to draw water and fill the water troughs for their father's flocks. [17] But the shepherds chased the girls away. Moses then came to their aid and rescued them from the shepherds and watered their flocks.

[18] When they returned to their father Reuel he asked, "How did you get the flocks watered so quickly today?"

[19] "An Egyptian defended us against the shepherds," they told him; "he drew water for us and watered the flocks."

[20] "Well, where is he?" their father demanded. "Did you just leave him there? Invite him home for supper."

[21] Moses eventually decided to accept Reuel's invitation to live with them, and Reuel gave him one of the girls, Zipporah, as his wife. [22] They had a baby named Gershom (meaning "foreigner"), for he said, "I am a stranger in a foreign land."

[23] Several years later the king of Egypt died. The Israelis were groaning beneath their burdens, in deep trouble because of their slavery, and weeping bitterly before the Lord. He heard their cries from heaven, [24] and remembered his promise to Abraham, Isaac, and Jacob [to bring their descendants back into the land of Canaan[b]]. [25] Looking down upon them, he knew that the time had come for their rescue.[c]

3 ONE DAY AS Moses was tending the flock of his father-in-law Jethro,[a] the priest of Midian, out at the edge of the desert near Horeb, the mountain of God, [2] suddenly the Angel of Jehovah appeared to him as a flame of fire in a bush. When Moses saw that the bush was on fire and that it didn't burn up, [3,4] he went over to investigate. Then God called out to him,

"Moses! Moses!"

"Who is it?" Moses asked.

[5] "Don't come any closer," God told him. "Take off your shoes, for you are standing on holy ground. [6] I am the God of your fathers—the God of Abraham, Isaac, and Jacob." (Moses covered his face with his hands, for he was afraid to look at God.)

[7] Then the Lord told him, "I have seen the deep sorrows of my people in Egypt, and have heard their pleas for freedom from their harsh taskmasters. [8] I have come to deliver them from the Egyptians and to take them out of Egypt into a good land, a large land, a land 'flowing with milk and honey'—the land where the Canaanites, Hittites, Amorites, Perizzites, Hivites, and Jebusites live. [9] Yes, the wail of the people of Israel has risen to me in heaven, and I have seen the heavy tasks the Egyptians have oppressed them with. [10] Now I am going to send you to Pharaoh, to demand that he let you lead my people out of Egypt."

[11] "But I'm not the person for a job like that!" Moses exclaimed.

[12] Then God told him, "I will certainly be with you, and this is the proof that I am the one who is sending you: When you have

---

a The name Moses sounds like another Hebrew word meaning "to draw out."   b Implied
c Literally, "knew their condition."   3a Moses' father-in-law goes under two names in these chapters, Jethro and Reuel.

led the people out of Egypt, you shall worship God here upon this mountain!"

¹³ But Moses asked, "If I go to the people of Israel and tell them that their fathers' God has sent me, they will ask, 'Which God are you talking about?' What shall I tell them?"

¹⁴ "'The Sovereign God,'"ᵇ was the reply. "Just say, 'I Am has sent me!' ¹⁵ Yes, tell them, 'Jehovah,ᶜ the God of your ancestors Abraham, Isaac, and Jacob, has sent me to you.' (This is my eternal name, to be used throughout all generations.)

¹⁶ "Call together all the elders of Israel," God instructed him, "and tell them about Jehovah appearing to you here in this burning bush and that he said to you, 'I have visited my people, and have seen what is happening to them there in Egypt. ¹⁷ I promise to rescue them from the drudgery and humiliation they are undergoing, and to take them to the land now occupied by the Canaanites, Hittites, Amorites, Perizzites, Hivites, and Jebusites, a land "flowing with milk and honey." ' ¹⁸ The elders of the people of Israel will accept your message. They must go with you to the king of Egypt and tell him, 'Jehovah, the God of the Hebrews, has met with us and instructed us to go three days' journey into the desert to sacrifice to him. Give us your permission.'

¹⁹ "But I know that the king of Egypt will not let you go except under heavy pressure. ²⁰ So I will give him all the pressure he needs! I will destroy Egypt with my miracles, and then at last he will let you go. ²¹ And I will see to it that the Egyptians load you down with gifts when you leave, so that you will by no means go out empty-handed! ²² Every woman will ask for jewels, silver, gold, and the finest of clothes from her Egyptian master's wife and neighbors. You will clothe your sons and daughters with the best of Egypt!"

4 BUT MOSES SAID, "They won't believe me! They won't do what *I* tell them to. They'll say, 'Jehovah never appeared to you!' "

² "What do you have there in your hand?" the Lord asked him.

And he replied, "A shepherd's rod."

³ "Throw it down on the ground," the Lord told him. So he threw it down—and it became a serpent, and Moses ran from it! ⁴ Then the Lord told him, "Grab it by the tail!" He did, and it became a rod in his hand again!

⁵ "Do that and they will believe you!" the Lord told him. "Then they will realize that Jehovah, the God of their ancestors Abraham, Isaac, and Jacob, has really appeared to you. ⁶ Now reach your hand inside your robe, next to your chest." And when he did, and took it out again, it was white with leprosy! ⁷ "Now put it in again," Jehovah said. And when he did, and took it out again, it was normal, just as before!

⁸ "If they don't believe the first miracle, they will the second," the Lord said, ⁹ "and if they don't accept you after these two signs, then take water from the Nile River and pour it upon the dry land, and it will turn to blood."

¹⁰ But Moses pleaded, "O Lord, I'm just not a good speaker. I never have been, and I'm not now, even after you have spoken to me, for I have a speech impediment."ᵃ

¹¹ "Who makes mouths?" Jehovah asked him. "Isn't it I, the Lord? Who makes a man so that he can speak or not speak, see or not see, hear or not hear? ¹² Now go ahead and do as I tell you, for I will help you to speak well, and I will tell you what to say."

¹³ But Moses said, "Lord, please! Send someone else."

¹⁴ Then the Lord became angry. "All right," he said, "your brother Aaronᵇ is a good speaker. And he is coming here to look for you, and will be very happy when he finds you. ¹⁵ So I will tell you what to tell him, and I will help both of you to speak well, and I will tell you what to do. ¹⁶ He will be your spokesman to the people. And you will be as God to him, telling him what to say. ¹⁷ And be sure to take your rod along so that you can perform the miracles I have

---

b Or, "the Living God." Literally, "I am what I am," or, "I will be what I will be."   c Properly the name should be pronounced "Yahweh," as it is spelled in many modern versions. In this paraphrase "Yahweh" is translated either "Jehovah" or "Lord."   4a Literally, "my speech is slow and halting."
b Literally, "your brother the Levite."

shown you."

[18] Moses returned home and talked it over with Jethro, his father-in-law. "With your permission," Moses said, "I will go back to Egypt and visit my relatives. I don't even know whether they are still alive."

"Go with my blessing," Jethro replied.

[19] Before Moses left Midian, Jehovah said to him, "Don't be afraid to return to Egypt, for all those who wanted to kill you are dead."

[20] So Moses took his wife and sons and put them on a donkey, and returned to the land of Egypt, holding tightly to the "rod of God"!

[21] Jehovah told him, "When you arrive back in Egypt you are to go to Pharaoh and do the miracles I have shown you, but I will make him stubborn so that he will not let the people go. [22] Then you are to tell him, 'Jehovah says, "Israel is my eldest son, [23] and I have commanded you to let him go away and worship me, but you have refused: and now see, I will slay your eldest son." ' "

[24] As Moses and his family were traveling along and had stopped for the night, Jehovah appeared to Moses and threatened to kill him. [25,26] Then Zipporah his wife took a flint knife and cut off the foreskin of her young son's penis, and threw it against Moses' feet, remarking disgustedly, "What a blood-smeared husband you've turned out to be!"

Then God let him alone.

[27] Now Jehovah said to Aaron, "Go into the wilderness to meet Moses." So Aaron traveled to Mount Horeb, the mountain of God, and met Moses there, and they greeted each other warmly. [28] Moses told Aaron what God had said they must do, and what they were to say, and told him about the miracles they must do before Pharaoh.

[29] So Moses and Aaron returned to Egypt and summoned the elders of the people of Israel to a council meeting. [30] Aaron told them what Jehovah had said to Moses, and Moses performed the miracles as they watched. [31] Then the elders believed that God had sent them, and when they heard that Jehovah had visited them and had seen their sorrows, and had decided to rescue them, they all rejoiced and bowed their heads and worshiped.

5 AFTER THIS PRESENTATION to the elders, Moses and Aaron went to see Pharaoh. They told him, "We bring you a message from Jehovah, the God of Israel. He says, 'Let my people go, for they must make a holy pilgrimage out into the wilderness, for a religious feast, to worship me there.' "

[2] "Is that so?" retorted Pharaoh. "And who is Jehovah, that I should listen to him, and let Israel go? I don't know Jehovah and I will not let Israel go."

[3] But Aaron and Moses persisted. "The God of the Hebrews has met with us," they declared. "We must take a three days' trip into the wilderness and sacrifice there to Jehovah our God; if we don't obey him, we face death by plague or sword."

[4,5] "Who do you think you are," Pharaoh shouted, "distracting the people from their work? Get back to your jobs!" [6] That same day Pharaoh sent this order to the taskmasters and officers he had set over the people of Israel: [7,8] "Don't give the people any more straw for making bricks! However, don't reduce their production quotas by a single brick, for they obviously don't have enough to do or else they wouldn't be talking about going out into the wilderness and sacrificing to their God. [9] Load them with work and make them sweat; that will teach them to listen to Moses' and Aaron's lies!"

[10,11] So the taskmasters and officers informed the people: "Pharaoh has given orders to furnish you with no more straw. Go and find it wherever you can; but you must produce just as many bricks as before!" [12] So the people scattered everywhere to gather straw.

[13] The taskmasters were brutal. "Fulfill your daily quota just as before," they kept demanding. [14] Then they whipped the Israeli work-crew bosses. "Why haven't you fulfilled your quotas either yesterday or today?" they roared.

[15] These foremen went to Pharaoh and pleaded with him. "Don't treat us like this," they begged. [16] "We are given no straw and told to make as many bricks as before, and we are beaten for something that isn't our fault—it is the fault of your taskmasters for

making such unreasonable demands."

¹⁷ But Pharaoh replied, "You don't have enough work, or else you wouldn't be saying, 'Let us go and sacrifice to Jehovah.' ¹⁸ Get back to work. No straw will be given you, and you must deliver the regular quota of bricks."

¹⁹ Then the foremen saw that they were indeed in a bad situation. ²⁰ When they met Moses and Aaron waiting for them outside the palace, as they came out from their meeting with Pharaoh, ²¹ they swore at them. "May God judge you for making us stink before Pharaoh and his people," they said, "and for giving them an excuse to kill us."

²² Then Moses went back to the Lord. "Lord," he protested, "how can you mistreat your own people like this? Why did you ever send me, if you were going to do this to them? ²³ Ever since I gave Pharaoh your message, he has only been more and more brutal to them, and you have not delivered them at all!"

6 "NOW YOU WILL see what I shall do to Pharaoh," the Lord told Moses. "For he must be forced to let my people go; he will not only let them go, but will *drive them out of his land!* ^{2,3} I am Jehovah, the Almighty God who appeared to Abraham, Isaac, and Jacob—though I did not reveal my name, Jehovah, to them. ⁴ And I entered into a solemn covenant with them; under its terms I promised to give them and their descendants the land of Canaan where they were living. ⁵ And now I have heard the groanings of the people of Israel, in slavery now to the Egyptians, and I remember my promise.

⁶ "Therefore tell the descendants of Israel that I will use my mighty power and perform great miracles to deliver them from slavery, and make them free. ⁷ And I will accept them as my people and be their God. And they shall know that I am Jehovah their God who has rescued them from the Egyptians. ^{8,9} I will bring them into the land I promised to give to Abraham, Isaac, and Jacob. It shall belong to my people."

So Moses told the people what God had said, but they wouldn't listen any more because they were too dispirited after the tragic consequence of what he had said before.^a

¹⁰ Now the Lord spoke to Moses again and told him, ¹¹ "Go back again to Pharaoh and tell him that he *must* let the people of Israel go."

¹² "But look," Moses objected, "my own people won't even listen to me any more; how can I expect Pharaoh to? I'm no orator!"

¹³ Then the Lord ordered Moses and Aaron to return to the people of Israel and to Pharaoh, king of Egypt, demanding that the people be permitted to leave.

¹⁴ These are the names of the heads of the clans of the various tribes of Israel:

The sons of Reuben, Israel's oldest son:
    Hanoch, Pallu,
    Hezron, Carmi.

¹⁵ The heads of the clans of the tribe of Simeon:
    Jemuel, Jamin, Ohad,
    Jachin, Zohar,
    Shaul (whose mother was a Canaanite).

¹⁶ These are the names of the heads of the clans of the tribe of Levi, in the order of their ages:^b
    Gershon, Kohath, Merari.
    (Levi lived 137 years.)

¹⁷ The sons of Gershon were:
    Libni, Shime-i,
    (and their clans).

¹⁸ The sons of Kohath:
    Amram, Izhar,
    Hebron, Uzziel.
    (Kohath lived 133 years.)

¹⁹ The sons of Merari:
    Mahli, Mushi.

The above are the families of the Levites, listed according to their ages.^c

²⁰ And Amram^d married Jochebed, his father's sister; and Aaron and Moses were their sons.

Amram lived to the age of 137.

²¹ The sons of Izhar:
    Korah, Nepheg, Zichri.

---

a Literally, "because of their broken spirit and the cruel bondage."   b Literally, "according to their generations."   c Literally, "according to their generations."   d See verse 18.

²² The sons of Uzziel:
Misha-el, Elzaphan, Sithri.
²³ Aaron married Elisheba, the daughter of Amminadab and sister of Nahshon. Their children were:
Nadab, Abihu,
Eleazar, Ithamar.
²⁴ The sons of Korah:
Assir, Elkanah, Abiasaph.
These are the families within the clan of Korah.

²⁵ Aaron's son Eleazar married one of the daughters of Puti-el, and Phinehas was one of his children. These are all the names of the heads of the clans of the Levites, and the families within the clans.

²⁶ Aaron and Moses, included in that list, are the same Aaron and Moses to whom Jehovah said, "Lead all the people of Israel out of the land of Egypt," ²⁷ and who went to Pharaoh to ask permission to lead the people from the land, ²⁸,²⁹ and to whom the Lord said, "I am Jehovah. Go in and give Pharaoh the message I have given you."

³⁰ This is that Moses who argued with the Lord, "I can't do it; I'm no speaker—why should Pharaoh listen to *me?*"

7 THEN THE LORD said to Moses, "See, I have appointed you as my ambassador to Pharaoh, and your brother Aaron shall be your spokesman. ² Tell Aaron everything I say to you, and he will announce it to Pharaoh, demanding that the people of Israel be allowed to leave Egypt. ³ But I will cause Pharaoh to stubbornly refuse, and I will multiply my miracles in the land of Egypt. ⁴ Yet even then Pharaoh won't listen to you; so I will crush Egypt with a final major disaster and then lead my people out. ⁵ The Egyptians will find out that I am indeed God when I show them my power and force them to let my people go."

⁶ So Moses and Aaron did as the Lord commanded them. ⁷ Moses was eighty years old and Aaron eighty-three at this time of their confrontation with Pharaoh.

⁸ Then the Lord said to Moses and Aaron, ⁹ "Pharaoh will demand that you show him a miracle to prove that God has sent you; when he does, Aaron is to throw down his rod, and it will become a serpent."

¹⁰ So Moses and Aaron went in to see Pharaoh, and performed the miracle, as Jehovah had instructed them—Aaron threw down his rod before Pharaoh and his court, and it became a serpent. ¹¹ Then Pharaoh called in his sorcerers—the magicians of Egypt—and they were able to do the same thing with their magical arts! ¹² Their rods became serpents, too! But Aaron's serpent swallowed their serpents! ¹³ Pharaoh's heart was still hard and stubborn, and he wouldn't listen, just as the Lord had predicted. ¹⁴ The Lord pointed this out to Moses, that Pharaoh's heart had been unmoved, and that he would continue to refuse to let the people go.

¹⁵ "Nevertheless," the Lord said, "go back to Pharaoh in the morning, to be there as he goes down to the river. Stand beside the river bank and meet him there, holding in your hand the rod that turned into a serpent. ¹⁶ Say to him, 'Jehovah, the God of the Hebrews, has sent me back to demand that you let his people go to worship him in the wilderness. You wouldn't listen before, ¹⁷ and now the Lord says this: "You are going to find out that I am God. For I have instructed Moses to hit the water of the Nile with his rod, and the river will turn to blood! ¹⁸ The fish will die and the river will stink, so that the Egyptians will be unwilling to drink it." ' "

¹⁹ Then the Lord instructed Moses: "Tell Aaron to point his rod toward the waters of Egypt: all its rivers, canals, marshes, and reservoirs, and even the water stored in bowls and pots in the homes will turn to blood."

²⁰ So Moses and Aaron did as the Lord commanded them. As Pharaoh and all of his officials watched, Aaron hit the surface of the Nile with the rod, and the river turned to blood. ²¹ The fish died and the water became so foul that the Egyptians couldn't drink it; and there was blood throughout the land of Egypt. ²² But then the magicians of Egypt used their secret arts and they, too, turned water into blood; so Pharaoh's heart remained hard and stubborn, and he wouldn't listen to Moses and Aaron, just as the Lord had predicted, ²³ and he returned to his palace, unimpressed. ²⁴ Then the Egyptians dug wells along the river bank to get drinking water,

for they couldn't drink from the river.
²⁵ The following week
(*continued in next chapter*)

8 THE LORD SAID to Moses, "Go in again to Pharaoh and tell him, 'Jehovah says, "Let my people go and worship me. ² If you refuse, I will send vast hordes of frogs across your land from one border to the other. ³,⁴ The Nile River will swarm with them, and they will come out into your houses, even into your bedrooms and right into your beds! Every home in Egypt will be filled with them. They will fill your ovens and your kneading bowls; you and your people will be immersed in them!" ' "

⁵ Then the Lord said to Moses, "Instruct Aaron to point the rod toward all the rivers, streams, and pools of Egypt, so that there will be frogs in every corner of the land." ⁶ Aaron did, and frogs covered the nation. ⁷ But the magicians did the same with their secret arts, and they, too, caused frogs to come up upon the land.

⁸ Then Pharaoh summoned Moses and Aaron and begged, "Plead with God to take the frogs away, and I will let the people go and sacrifice to him."

⁹ "Be so kind as to tell me when you want them to go," Moses said, "and I will pray that the frogs will die at the time you specify, everywhere except in the river."

¹⁰ "Do it tomorrow," Pharaoh said.

"All right," Moses replied, "it shall be as you have said; then you will know that there is no one like the Lord our God. ¹¹ All the frogs will be destroyed, except those in the river."

¹² So Moses and Aaron went out from the presence of Pharaoh, and Moses pleaded with the Lord concerning the frogs he had sent. ¹³ And the Lord did as Moses promised—dead frogs covered the countryside and filled the nation's homes. ¹⁴ They were piled into great heaps, making a terrible stench throughout the land. ¹⁵ But when Pharaoh saw that the frogs were gone, he hardened his heart and refused to let the people go, just as the Lord had predicted.

¹⁶ Then the Lord said to Moses, "Tell Aaron to strike the dust with his rod, and it will become lice, throughout all the land of Egypt." ¹⁷ So Moses and Aaron did as God commanded, and suddenly lice infested the entire nation, covering the Egyptians and their animals. ¹⁸ Then the magicians tried to do the same thing with their secret arts, but this time they failed.

¹⁹ "This is the finger of God," they exclaimed to Pharaoh. But Pharaoh's heart was hard and stubborn, and he wouldn't listen to them, just as the Lord had predicted.

²⁰ Next the Lord told Moses, "Get up early in the morning and meet Pharaoh as he comes out to the river to bathe, and say to him, 'Jehovah says, "Let my people go and worship me. ²¹ If you refuse I will send swarms of flies throughout Egypt. Your homes will be filled with them and the ground will be covered with them. ²² But it will be very different in the land of Goshen where the Israelis live. No flies will be there; thus you will know that I am the Lord God of all the earth, ²³ for I will make a distinction between your people and my people. All this will happen tomorrow." ' "

²⁴ And Jehovah did as he had said, so that there were terrible swarms of flies in Pharaoh's palace and in every home in Egypt.

²⁵ Pharaoh hastily summoned Moses and Aaron and said, "All right, go ahead and sacrifice to your God, but do it here in the land. Don't go out into the wilderness."

²⁶ But Moses replied, "That won't do! Our sacrifices to God are hated by the Egyptians, and if we do this right here before their eyes, they will kill us. ²⁷ We must take a three-day trip into the wilderness and sacrifice there to Jehovah our God, as he commanded us."

²⁸ "All right, go ahead," Pharaoh replied, "but don't go too far away. Now, hurry and plead with God for me."

²⁹ "Yes," Moses said, "I will ask him to cause the swarms of flies to disappear. But I am warning you that you must never again lie to us by promising to let the people go and then changing your mind."

³⁰ So Moses went out from Pharaoh and asked the Lord to get rid of the flies. ³¹,³² And the Lord did as Moses asked and caused the swarms to disappear, so that not one remained. But Pharaoh hardened his heart again and did not let the people go!

9 "GO BACK TO Pharaoh," the Lord commanded Moses, "and tell him, 'Jehovah, the God of the Hebrews, demands that you let his people go to sacrifice to him. ² If you refuse, ³ the power of God will send a deadly plague to destroy your cattle, horses, donkeys, camels, flocks, and herds. ⁴ But the plague will affect only the cattle of Egypt; none of the Israeli herds and flocks will even be touched!' "

⁵ The Lord announced that the plague would begin the very next day, ⁶ and it did. The next morning all the cattle of the Egyptians began dying, but not one of the Israeli herds was even sick. ⁷ Pharaoh sent to see whether it was true that none of the Israeli cattle were dead, yet when he found out that it was so, even then his mind remained unchanged and he refused to let the people go.

⁸ Then Jehovah said to Moses and Aaron, "Take ashes from the kiln. Moses, toss it into the sky as Pharaoh watches. ⁹ It will spread like fine dust over all the land of Egypt and cause boils to break out upon people and animals alike, throughout the land."

¹⁰ So they took ashes from the kiln and went to Pharaoh; as he watched, Moses tossed it toward the sky, and it became boils that broke out on men and animals alike throughout all Egypt. ¹¹ And the magicians couldn't stand before Moses because of the boils, for the boils appeared upon them too. ¹² But Jehovah hardened Pharaoh in his stubbornness, so that he refused to listen, just as the Lord had predicted to Moses.

¹³ Then the Lord said to Moses, "Get up early in the morning and stand before Pharaoh and tell him, 'Jehovah the God of the Hebrews says, "Let my people go to worship me. ¹⁴ This time I am going to send a plague that will really speak to you and to your servants and to all the Egyptian people, and prove to you there is no other God in all the earth. ¹⁵ I could have killed you all by now, ¹⁶ but I didn't, for I wanted to demonstrate my power to you and to all the earth. ¹⁷ So you still think you are so great, do you, and defy my power, and refuse to let my people go? ¹⁸ Well, tomorrow about this time I will send a hailstorm across the nation such as there has never been since Egypt was founded! ¹⁹ Quick!

Bring in your cattle from the fields, for every man and animal left out in the fields will die beneath the hail!" ' "

²⁰ Some of the Egyptians, terrified by this threat, brought their cattle and slaves in from the fields; ²¹ but those who had no regard for the word of Jehovah left them out in the storm.

²² Then Jehovah said to Moses, "Point your hand toward heaven and cause the hail to fall throughout all Egypt, upon the people, animals, and trees."

²³ So Moses held out his hand, and the Lord sent thunder and hail and lightning. ²⁴ It was terrible beyond description. Never in all the history of Egypt had there been a storm like that. ²⁵ All Egypt lay in ruins. Everything left in the fields, men and animals alike, was killed, and the trees were shattered and the crops were destroyed. ²⁶ The only spot in all Egypt without hail that day was the land of Goshen where the people of Israel lived.

²⁷ Then Pharaoh sent for Moses and Aaron. "I finally see my fault," he confessed. "Jehovah is right, and I and my people have been wrong all along. ²⁸ Beg God to end this terrifying thunder and hail, and I will let you go at once."

²⁹ "All right," Moses replied, "as soon as I have left the city I will spread out my hands to the Lord, and the thunder and hail will stop. This will prove to you that the earth is controlled by Jehovah. ³⁰ But as for you and your officials, I know that even yet you will not obey him." ³¹ All the flax and barley were knocked down and destroyed (for the barley was ripe, and the flax was in bloom), ³² but the wheat and the emmer were not destroyed, for they were not yet out of the ground.

³³ So Moses left Pharaoh and went out of the city and lifted his hands to heaven to the Lord, and the thunder and hail stopped, and the rain ceased pouring down. ³⁴ When Pharaoh saw this, he and his officials sinned yet more by their stubborn refusal to do what they had promised; ³⁵ so Pharaoh refused to let the people leave, just as the Lord had predicted to Moses.

10 THEN THE LORD said to Moses, "Go back again and make your demand upon Pharaoh; but I have hardened him and his officials, so that I can do more miracles demonstrating my power. ² What stories you can tell your children and grandchildren about the incredible things I am doing in Egypt! Tell them what fools I made of the Egyptians, and how I proved to you that I am Jehovah."

³ So Moses and Aaron requested another audience with Pharaoh and told him: "Jehovah, the God of the Hebrews, asks, 'How long will you refuse to submit to me? Let my people go so they can worship me. ⁴,⁵ If you refuse, tomorrow I will cover the entire nation with a thick layer of locusts so that you won't even be able to see the ground, and they will finish destroying everything that escaped the hail. ⁶ They will fill your palace, and the homes of your officials, and all the houses of Egypt. Never in the history of Egypt has there been a plague like this will be!' " Then Moses stalked out.

⁷ The court officials now came to Pharaoh and asked him, "Are you going to destroy us completely? Don't you know even yet that all Egypt lies in ruins? Let the *men* go and serve Jehovah their God!"

⁸ So Moses and Aaron were brought back to Pharaoh. "All right, go and serve Jehovah your God!" he said. "But just who is it you want to go?"

⁹ "We will go with our sons and daughters, flocks and herds," Moses replied. "We will take everything with us; for we must all join in the holy pilgrimage."

¹⁰ "In the name of God I will not let you take your little ones!" Pharaoh retorted. "I can see your plot! ¹¹ Never! You that are men, go and serve Jehovah, for that is what you asked for." And they were driven out from Pharaoh's presence.

¹² Then the Lord said to Moses, "Hold out your hand over the land of Egypt to bring locusts—they will cover the land and eat everything the hail has left."

¹³ So Moses lifted his rod and Jehovah caused an east wind to blow all that day and night; and when it was morning, the east wind had brought the locusts. ¹⁴ And the locusts covered the land of Egypt from border to border; it was the worst locust plague in all Egyptian history; and there will never again be another like it. ¹⁵ For the locusts covered the face of the earth and blotted out the sun so that the land was darkened; and they ate every bit of vegetation the hail had left; there remained not one green thing—not a tree, not a plant throughout all the land of Egypt.

¹⁶ Then Pharaoh sent an urgent call for Moses and Aaron and said to them, "I confess my sin against Jehovah your God and against you. ¹⁷ Forgive my sin only this once, and beg Jehovah your God to take away this death. I promise not to refuse afterwards to let you go."

¹⁸ So Moses went out from Pharaoh and entreated the Lord, ¹⁹ and he sent a very strong west wind that blew the locusts out into the Red Sea, so that there remained not one locust in all the land of Egypt! ²⁰ But the Lord hardened Pharaoh's heart and he did not let the people go.

²¹ Then Jehovah said to Moses, "Lift your hands to heaven, and darkness without a ray of light will descend upon the land of Egypt." ²² So Moses did, and there was thick darkness over all the land for three days. ²³ During all that time the people scarcely moved—but all the people of Israel had light as usual.

²⁴ Then Pharaoh called for Moses and said, "Go and worship Jehovah—but let your flocks and herds stay here; you can even take your children with you."

²⁵ "No," Moses said, "we must take our flocks and herds for sacrifices and burnt offerings to Jehovah our God. ²⁶ Not a hoof shall be left behind; for we must have sacrifices for the Lord our God, and we do not know what he will choose until we get there."

²⁷ So the Lord hardened Pharaoh's heart and he would not let them go.

²⁸ "Get out of here and don't let me ever see you again," Pharaoh shouted at Moses. "The day you do, you shall die."

²⁹ "Very well," Moses replied. "I will never see you again."

11 THEN THE LORD said to Moses, "I will send just one more disaster on Pharaoh and his land, and after that he will let you go; in fact, he will be so anxious to get rid of you that he will practically throw you out of the country. ² Tell all the men

and women of Israel to prepare to ask their Egyptian neighbors for costly gold and silver jewelry."

3 (For God caused the Egyptians to be very favorable to the people of Israel, and Moses was a very great man in the land of Egypt and was revered by Pharaoh's officials and the Egyptian people alike.)

4 Now Moses announced to Pharaoh,[a] "Jehovah says, 'About midnight I will pass through Egypt. 5 And all the oldest sons shall die in every family in Egypt, from the oldest child of Pharaoh, heir to his throne, to the oldest child of his lowliest slave; and even the firstborn of the animals. 6 The wail of death will resound throughout the entire land of Egypt; never before has there been such anguish, and it will never be again.

7 " 'But not a dog shall move his tongue against any of the people of Israel, nor shall any of their animals die. Then you will know that Jehovah makes a distinction between Egyptians and Israelis.' 8 All these officials of yours will come running to me, bowing low and begging, 'Please leave at once, and take all your people with you.' Only then will I go!" Then, red-faced with anger, Moses stomped from the palace.[b]

9 The Lord had told Moses, "Pharaoh won't listen, and this will give me the opportunity of doing mighty miracles to demonstrate my power." 10 So, although Moses and Aaron did these miracles right before Pharaoh's eyes, the Lord hardened his heart so that he wouldn't let the people leave the land.

12 THEN THE LORD said to Moses and Aaron, 2 "From now on, this month will be the first and most important month of the Jewish calendar. 3,4 Annually, on the tenth day of this month (announce this to all the people of Israel) each family shall get a lamb[a] (or, if a family is small, let it share the lamb with another small family in the neighborhood; whether to share in this way depends on the size of the families). 5 This animal shall be a year-old male, either a sheep or a goat, without any defects.

6 "On the evening of the fourteenth day of this month, all these lambs shall be killed, 7 and their blood shall be placed on the two side-frames of the door of every home and on the panel above the door. Use the blood of the lamb eaten in that home. 8 Everyone shall eat roast lamb that night, with unleavened bread and bitter herbs. 9 The meat must not be eaten raw or boiled, but roasted, including the head, legs, heart, and liver.[b] 10 Don't eat any of it the next day; if all is not eaten that night, burn what is left.

11 "Eat it with your traveling clothes on, prepared for a long journey, wearing your walking shoes and carrying your walking sticks in your hands; eat it hurriedly. This observance shall be called the Lord's Passover. 12 For I will pass through the land of Egypt tonight and kill all the oldest sons and firstborn male animals in all the land of Egypt, and execute judgment upon all the gods of Egypt—for I am Jehovah. 13 The blood you have placed on the doorposts will be proof that you obey me, and when I see the blood I will pass over you and I will not destroy your firstborn children when I smite the land of Egypt.

14 "You shall celebrate this event each year (this is a permanent law) to remind you of this fatal night. 15 The celebration shall last seven days. For that entire period you are to eat only bread made without yeast. Anyone who disobeys this rule at any time during the seven days of the celebration shall be excommunicated from Israel. 16 On the first day of the celebration, and again on the seventh day, there will be special religious services for the entire congregation, and no work of any kind may be done on those days except the preparation of food.

17 "This annual 'Celebration with Unleavened Bread' will cause you always to remember today as the day when I brought you out of the land of Egypt; so it is a law that you must celebrate this day annually, generation after generation. 18 Only bread without yeast may be eaten from the evening of the fourteenth day of the month until the evening of the twenty-first day of the month. 19 For these seven days there must be no trace of yeast in your homes;

---

a Implied.   b Literally, "he went out from Pharaoh."   12a The Hebrew word here translated "lamb" can also mean "kid"—a baby goat.   b Literally, "inner parts."

during that time anyone who eats anything that has yeast in it shall be excommunicated from the congregation of Israel. These same rules apply to foreigners who are living among you just as much as to those born in the land. ²⁰ Again I repeat, during those days you must not eat anything made with yeast; serve only yeastless bread."

²¹ Then Moses called for all the elders of Israel and said to them, "Go and get lambs from your flocks, a lamb for one or more families depending upon the number of persons in the families, and kill the lamb so that God will pass over you and not destroy you. ²² Drain the lamb's blood into a basin, and then take a cluster of hyssop branches and dip them into the lamb's blood, and strike the hyssop against the lintel above the door and against the two side panels, so that there will be blood upon them, and none of you shall go outside all night.

²³ "For Jehovah will pass through the land and kill the Egyptians; but when he sees the blood upon the panel at the top of the door and on the two side pieces, he will pass over^c that home and not permit the Destroyer to enter and kill your firstborn. ²⁴ And remember, this is a permanent law for you and your posterity. ²⁵ And when you come into the land that the Lord will give you, just as he promised, and when you are celebrating the Passover, ²⁶ and your children ask, 'What does all this mean? What is this ceremony about?' ²⁷ you will reply, 'It is the celebration of Jehovah's passing over us, for he passed over the homes of the people of Israel, though he killed the Egyptians; he passed over our houses and did not come in to destroy us.'" And all the people bowed their heads and worshiped.

²⁸ So the people of Israel did as Moses and Aaron had commanded. ²⁹ And that night, at midnight, Jehovah killed all the firstborn sons in the land of Egypt, from Pharaoh's oldest son to the oldest son of the captive in the dungeon; also all the firstborn of the cattle. ³⁰ Then Pharaoh and his officials and all the people of Egypt got up in the night; and there was bitter crying throughout all the land of Egypt, for there was not a house where there was not one dead.

³¹ And Pharaoh summoned Moses and Aaron during the night and said, "Leave us; please go away, all of you; go and serve Jehovah as you said. ³² Take your flocks and herds and be gone; and oh, give me a blessing^d as you go." ³³ And the Egyptians were urgent upon the people of Israel, to get them out of the land as quickly as possible. For they said, "We are as good as dead."

³⁴ The Israelis took with them their bread dough without yeast, and bound their kneading troughs into their spare clothes, and carried them on their shoulders. ³⁵ And the people of Israel did as Moses said and asked the Egyptians for silver and gold jewelry, and for clothing. ³⁶ And the Lord gave the Israelis favor with the Egyptians, so that they gave them whatever they wanted. And the Egyptians were practically stripped of everything they owned!

³⁷ That night the people of Israel left Rameses and started for Succoth; there were six hundred thousand of them, besides all the women and children, going on foot. ³⁸ People of various sorts^e went with them; and there were flocks and herds—a vast exodus of cattle. ³⁹ When they stopped to eat, they baked bread from the yeastless dough they had brought along. It was yeastless because the people were pushed out of Egypt and didn't have time to wait for bread to rise to take with them on the trip.

⁴⁰,⁴¹ The sons of Jacob and their descendants had lived in Egypt 430 years, and it was on the last day of the 430th year that all of Jehovah's people left the land. ⁴² This night was selected by the Lord to bring his people out from the land of Egypt; so the same night was selected as the date of the annual celebration of God's deliverance.

⁴³ Then Jehovah said to Moses and Aaron, "These are the rules concerning the observance of the Passover. No foreigners shall eat the lamb, ⁴⁴ but any slave who has been purchased may eat it if he has been circumcised. ⁴⁵ A hired servant or a visiting foreigner may not eat of it. ⁴⁶ You shall, all of you who eat each lamb, eat it together

---

c Or, "He will pause at the door of that home and not permit the Destroyer to enter . . . ."
d Or, "say farewell to me forever!"   e Literally, "a mixed multitude." The meaning is not clear.

in one house, and not carry it outside; and you shall not break any of its bones. ⁴⁷ All the congregation of Israel shall observe this memorial at the same time.

⁴⁸ "As to foreigners, if they are living with you and want to observe the Passover with you, let all the males be circumcised, and then they may come and celebrate with you—then they shall be just as though they had been born among you; but no uncircumcised person shall ever eat the lamb. ⁴⁹ The same law applies to those born in Israel and to foreigners living among you."

⁵⁰ So the people of Israel followed all of Jehovah's instructions to Moses and Aaron. ⁵¹ That very day the Lord brought out the people of Israel from the land of Egypt, wave after wave of them crossing the border.ᶠ

13 THE LORD INSTRUCTED Moses, "Dedicate to me all of the firstborn sonsª of Israel, and every firstborn male animal; they are mine!"

³ Then Moses said to the people, "This is a day to remember forever—the day of leaving Egypt and your slavery; for the Lord has brought you out with mighty miracles. Now remember, during the annual celebration of this event you are to use no yeast; don't even have any in your homes. ⁴·⁵ Mark this day of your exodus, at the end of Marchᵇ each year, when Jehovah brings you into the land of the Canaanites, Hittites, Amorites, Hivites, and Jebusites—the land he promised your fathers, a land 'flowing with milk and honey.' ⁶·⁷ For seven days you shall eat only bread without yeast, and there must be no yeast in your homes, or anywhere within the borders of your land! Then, on the seventh day, a great feast to the Lord shall be held.

⁸ "During those celebration days each year you must explain to your children why you are celebrating—it is a celebration of what the Lord did for you when you left Egypt. ⁹ This annual memorial week will brand you as his own unique people, just as though he had branded his mark of ownership upon your hands or your forehead.

¹⁰ "So celebrate the event annually in late March.ᶜ ¹¹ And remember, when the Lord brings you into the land he promised to your ancestors long ago, where the Canaanites are now living, ¹² all firstborn sons and firstborn male animals belong to the Lord, and you shall give them to him. ¹³ A firstborn donkey may be purchased back from the Lord in exchange for a lamb or baby goat; but if you decide not to trade, the donkey shall be killed. However, you *must* buy back your firstborn sons.

¹⁴ "And in the future, when your children ask you, 'What is this all about?' you shall tell them, 'With mighty miracles Jehovah brought us out of Egypt from our slavery. ¹⁵ Pharaoh wouldn't let us go, so Jehovah killed all the firstborn males throughout the land of Egypt, both of men and animals; that is why we now give all the firstborn males to the Lord—except that all the eldest sons are always bought back.' ¹⁶ Again I say, this celebration shall identify you as God's people, just as much as if his brand of ownership were placed upon your foreheads. It is a reminder that the Lord brought us out of Egypt with great power."

¹⁷·¹⁸ So at last Pharaoh let the people go.

God did not lead them through the land of the Philistines, although that was the most direct route from Egypt to the Promised Land. The reason was that God felt the people might become discouraged by having to fight their way through, even though they had left Egypt armed; he thought they might return to Egypt. Instead, God led them along a route through the Red Sea wilderness.

¹⁹ Moses took the bones of Joseph with them, for Joseph had made the sons of Israel vow before God that they would take his bones with them when God led them out of Egypt—as he was sure God would.

²⁰ Leaving Succoth, they camped in Etham at the edge of the wilderness. ²¹ The Lord guided them by a pillar of cloud during the daytime, and by a pillar of fire at night. So they could travel either by day or night. ²² The cloud and fire were never out of sight.

---

f Or, ". . . from the land of Egypt, all of the communities of them."   13a Literally, "all the firstborn."
b Literally, "the tenth day of Abib."   c Literally, "in its season from year to year."

14 JEHOVAH NOW INSTRUCTED Moses, [2] "Tell the people to turn toward Piha-hiroth between Migdol and the sea, opposite Baal-zephon, and to camp there along the shore. [3] For Pharaoh will think, 'Those Israelites are trapped now, between the desert and the sea!' [4] And once again I will harden Pharaoh's heart and he will chase after you. I have planned this to gain great honor and glory over Pharaoh and all his armies, and the Egyptians shall know that I am the Lord."

So they camped where they were told.

[5] When word reached the king of Egypt that the Israelis were not planning to return to Egypt after three days, but to keep on going, Pharaoh and his staff became bold again. "What is this we have done, letting all these slaves get away?" they asked. [6] So Pharaoh led the chase in his chariot, [7] followed by the pick of Egypt's chariot corps—600 chariots in all—and other chariots driven by Egyptian officers. [8] He pursued the people of Israel, for they had taken much of the wealth of Egypt with them. [9] Pharaoh's entire cavalry—horses, chariots, and charioteers—was used in the chase; and the Egyptian army overtook the people of Israel as they were camped beside the shore near Piha-hiroth, across from Baal-zephon.

[10] As the Egyptian army approached, the people of Israel saw them far in the distance, speeding after them, and they were terribly frightened, and cried out to the Lord to help them.

[11] And they turned against Moses, whining, "Have you brought us out here to die in the desert because there were not enough graves for us in Egypt? Why did you make us leave Egypt? [12] Isn't this what we told you, while we were slaves, to leave us alone? We said it would be better to be slaves to the Egyptians than dead in the wilderness."

[13] But Moses told the people, "Don't be afraid. Just stand where you are and watch, and you will see the wonderful way the Lord will rescue you today. The Egyptians you are looking at—you will never see them again. [14] The Lord will fight for you, and you won't need to lift a finger!"[a]

[15] Then the Lord said to Moses, "Quit praying and get the people moving! Forward, march! [16] Use your rod—hold it out over the water, and the sea will open up a path before you, and all the people of Israel shall walk through on dry ground! [17] I will harden the hearts of the Egyptians and they will go in after you and you will see the honor I will get in defeating Pharaoh and all his armies, chariots, and horsemen. [18] And all Egypt shall know that I am Jehovah."

[19] Then the Angel of God, who was leading the people of Israel, moved the cloud around behind them, [20] and it stood between the people of Israel and the Egyptians. And that night, as it changed to a pillar of fire, it gave darkness to the Egyptians but light to the people of Israel! So the Egyptians couldn't find the Israelis!

[21] Meanwhile, Moses stretched his rod over the sea, and the Lord opened up a path through the sea, with walls of water on each side; and a strong east wind blew all that night, drying the sea bottom. [22] So the people of Israel walked through the sea on dry ground! [23] Then the Egyptians followed them between the walls of water along the bottom of the sea—all of Pharaoh's horses, chariots, and horsemen. [24] But in the early morning Jehovah looked down from the cloud of fire upon the array of the Egyptians, and began to harass them. [25] Their chariot wheels began coming off, so that their chariots scraped along the dry ground. "Let's get out of here," the Egyptians yelled. "Jehovah is fighting for them and against us."

[26] When all the Israelites were on the other side,[b] the Lord said to Moses, "Stretch out your hand again over the sea, so that the waters will come back over the Egyptians and their chariots and horsemen." [27] Moses did, and the sea returned to normal beneath the morning light. The Egyptians tried to flee, but the Lord drowned them in the sea. [28] The water covered the path and the chariots and horsemen. And of all the army of Pharaoh that chased after Israel through the sea, not one remained alive.

---

a Or, "you will be speechless with amazement!"   b Implied.

²⁹ The people of Israel had walked through on dry land, and the waters had been walled up on either side of them. ³⁰ Thus Jehovah saved Israel that day from the Egyptians; and the people of Israel saw the Egyptians dead, washed up on the seashore. ³¹ When the people of Israel saw the mighty miracle the Lord had done for them against the Egyptians, they were afraid and revered the Lord, and believed in him and in his servant Moses.

15 THEN MOSES AND the people of Israel sang this song to the Lord:

I will sing to the Lord, for he has triumphed gloriously;
He has thrown both horse and rider into the sea.
² The Lord is my strength, my song, and my salvation.
He is my God, and I will praise him.
He is my father's God—I will exalt him.
³ The Lord is a warrior—
Yes, Jehovah is his name.
⁴ He has overthrown Pharaoh's chariots and armies,
Drowning them in the sea.
The famous Egyptian captains are dead beneath the waves.
⁵ The water covers them.
They went down into the depths like a stone.
⁶ Your right hand, O Lord, is glorious in power;
It dashes the enemy to pieces.
⁷ In the greatness of your majesty
You overthrew all those who rose against you.
You sent forth your anger, and it consumed them as fire consumes straw.
⁸ At the blast of your breath
The waters divided!
They stood as solid walls to hold the seas apart.
⁹ The enemy said, "I will chase after them,
Catch up with them, destroy them.
I will cut them apart with my sword
And divide the captured booty."
¹⁰ But God blew with his wind, and the sea covered them.

They sank as lead in the mighty waters.
¹¹ Who else is like the Lord among the gods?
Who is glorious in holiness like him?
Who is so awesome in splendor,
A wonder-working God?
¹² You reached out your hand and the earth swallowed them.
¹³ You have led the people you redeemed.
But in your lovingkindness
You have guided them wonderfully
To your holy land.
¹⁴ The nations heard what happened, and they trembled.
Fear has gripped the people of Philistia.
¹⁵ The leaders of Edom are appalled,
The mighty men of Moab tremble;
All the people of Canaan melt with fear.
¹⁶ Terror and dread have overcome them.
O Lord, because of your great power they won't attack us!
Your people whom you purchased
Will pass by them in safety.
¹⁷ You will bring them in and plant them on your mountain,
Your own homeland, Lord—
The sanctuary you made for them to live in.
¹⁸ Jehovah shall reign forever and forever.
¹⁹ The horses of Pharaoh, his horsemen, and his chariots
Tried to follow through the sea;
But the Lord let down the walls of water on them
While the people of Israel walked through on dry land.

²⁰ Then Miriam the prophetess, the sister of Aaron, took a timbrel and led the women in dances. ²¹ And Miriam sang this song:

Sing to the Lord, for he has triumphed gloriously.
The horse and rider have been drowned in the sea.

²² Then Moses led the people of Israel on from the Red Sea, and they moved out into the wilderness of Shur and were there three

days without water. ²³ Arriving at Marah, they couldn't drink the water because it was bitter (that is why the place was called Marah, meaning "bitter").

²⁴ Then the people turned against Moses. "Must we die of thirst?" they demanded.

²⁵ Moses pleaded with the Lord to help them, and the Lord showed him a tree to throw into the water, and the water became sweet.

It was there at Marah that the Lord laid before them the following conditions, to test their commitment to him: ²⁶ "If you will listen to the voice of the Lord your God, and obey it, and do what is right, then I will not make you suffer the diseases I sent on the Egyptians, for I am the Lord who heals you." ²⁷ And they came to Elim where there were twelve springs and seventy palm trees; and they camped there beside the springs.

16 NOW THEY LEFT Elim and journeyed on into the Sihn Wilderness, between Elim and Mt. Sinai, arriving there on the fifteenth day of the second month after leaving Egypt. ² There too, the people spoke bitterly against Moses and Aaron.

³ "Oh, that we were back in Egypt," they moaned, "and that the Lord had killed us there! For there we had plenty to eat. But now you have brought us into this wilderness to kill us with starvation."

⁴ Then the Lord said to Moses, "Look, I'm going to rain down food from heaven for them. Everyone can go out each day and gather as much food as he needs. And I will test them in this, to see whether they will follow my instructions or not. ⁵ Tell them to gather twice as much as usual on the sixth day of each week."

⁶ Then Moses and Aaron called a meeting of all the people of Israel and told them, "This evening you will realize that it was the Lord who brought you out of the land of Egypt. ⁷,⁸,⁹ In the morning you will see more of his glory; for he has heard your complaints against him (for you aren't really complaining against *us*—who are *we?*). The Lord will give you meat to eat in the evening, and bread in the morning. Come now before Jehovah, and hear his reply to your complaints."

¹⁰ So Aaron called them together and suddenly, out toward the wilderness, from within the guiding cloud, there appeared the awesome glory of Jehovah.

¹¹,¹² And Jehovah said to Moses, "I have heard their complaints. Tell them, 'In the evening you will have meat and in the morning you will be stuffed with bread, and you shall know that I am Jehovah your God.' "

¹³ That evening vast numbers of quail arrived and covered the camp, and in the morning the desert all around the camp was wet with dew; ¹⁴ and when the dew disappeared later in the morning it left tiny flakes of something as small as hoarfrost on the ground. ¹⁵ When the people of Israel saw it they asked each other, "What is it?"

And Moses told them, "It is the food Jehovah has given you to eat. ¹⁶ Jehovah has said for everyone to gather as much as is needed for his household—about three quarts[a] for each person in his home."

¹⁷ So the people of Israel went out and gathered it. ¹⁸ And when they poured it into a three-quart measure, there was just enough for everyone—three quarts apiece; those who gathered a lot had nothing left over and those who gathered little had no lack! Each home had just enough.

¹⁹ And Moses told them, "Don't leave it overnight."

²⁰ But of course some of them wouldn't listen, and left it until morning; and when they looked, it was full of maggots and had a terrible odor; and Moses was very angry with them. ²¹ So they gathered the food morning by morning, each home according to its need; and when the sun became hot upon the ground, the food melted and disappeared. ²² On the sixth day they gathered twice as much as usual, six quarts instead of three; then the leaders of the people came and asked Moses why this had been commanded them.

²³ And he told them, "Because the Lord has appointed tomorrow as a day of seriousness and rest, a holy Sabbath to the Lord when we must refrain from doing our daily tasks. So cook as much as you want to to-

---

a Literally, "an omer." The exact measure is not known.

day, and keep what is left overnight."
²⁴ And the next morning the food was
wholesome and good, without maggots or
odor. ²⁵ Moses said, "This is your food for
today, for today is the Sabbath to Jehovah
and there will be no food on the ground
today. ²⁶ Gather the food for six days, but
the seventh is a Sabbath, and there will be
none there for you on that day."

²⁷ But some of the people went out
anyway to gather food, even though it was
the Sabbath, but there wasn't any.

²⁸,²⁹ "How long will these people refuse
to obey?" the Lord asked Moses. "Don't
they realize that I am giving them twice as
much on the sixth day, so that there will be
enough for two days? For the Lord has
given you the seventh day as a day of Sabbath rest; stay in your tents and don't go out
to pick up food from the ground that day."
³⁰ So the people rested on the seventh day.

³¹ And the food became known as
"manna" (meaning "What is it?"); it was
white, like coriander seed, and flat, and
tasted like honey bread.

³² Then Moses gave them this further instruction from the Lord: they were to take
three quarts of it to be kept as a museum
specimen forever, so that later generations
could see the bread the Lord had fed them
with in the wilderness, when he brought
them from Egypt. ³³ Moses told Aaron to
get a container and put three quarts of
manna in it and to keep it in a sacred place
from generation to generation. ³⁴ Aaron did
this, just as the Lord had instructed Moses,
and eventually it was kept in the Ark in the
Tabernacle.

³⁵ So the people of Israel ate the manna
forty years until they arrived in the land of
Canaan, where there were crops to eat.
³⁶ The omer—the container used to measure
the manna—held about three quarts; it is
approximately a tenth of a bushel.

17 NOW, AT GOD'S command, the people
of Israel left the Sihn desert, going by
easy stages to Rephidim. But upon arrival,
there was no water!

² So once more the people growled and
complained to Moses. "Give us water!"
they wailed.

"Quiet!" Moses commanded. "Are you
trying to test God's patience with you?"

³ But, tormented by thirst, they cried
out, "Why did you ever take us out of
Egypt? Why did you bring us here to die,
with our children and cattle too?"

⁴ Then Moses pleaded with Jehovah.
"What shall I do? For they are almost ready
to stone me."

⁵,⁶ Then Jehovah said to Moses, "Take
the elders of Israel with you and lead the
people out to Mt. Horeb. I will meet you
there at the rock. Strike it with your rodᵃ
—the same one you struck the Nile with
—and water will come pouring out, enough
for everyone!" Moses did as he was told,
and the water gushed out! ⁷ Moses named
the place Massah (meaning "tempting Jehovah to slay us"), and sometimes they referred to it as Meribah (meaning
"argument" and "strife!")—for it was there
that the people of Israel argued against God
and tempted him to slayᵃ them by saying,
"Is Jehovah going to take care of us or not?"

⁸ But now the warriors of Amalek came
to fight against the people of Israel at Rephidim. ⁹ Moses instructed Joshua to issue
a call to arms to the Israelites, to fight the
army of Amalek.

"Tomorrow," Moses told him, "I will
stand at the top of the hill, with the rod of
God in my hand!"

¹⁰ So Joshua and his men went out to
fight the army of Amalek. Meanwhile
Moses, Aaron, and Hurᵇ went to the top of
the hill. ¹¹ And as long as Moses held up the
rod in his hands, Israel was winning; but
whenever he rested his arms at his sides, the
soldiers of Amalek were winning. ¹² Moses'
arms finally became too tired to hold up the
rod any longer; so Aaron and Hur rolled a
stone for him to sit on, and they stood on
each side, holding up his hands until sunset.
¹³ As a result, Joshua and his troops crushed
the army of Amalek, putting them to the
sword.

¹⁴ Then the Lord instructed Moses,
"Write this into a permanent record, to be

---

a Implied.   b Hur was a man of Judah, of the family of Hezron, house of Caleb (1 Chronicles 2:18,19).
He was the grandfather of Bezalel (Exodus 31:1,2).

remembered forever, and announce to Joshua that I will utterly blot out every trace of Amalek." [15,16] Moses built an altar there and called it "Jehovah-nissi" (meaning "Jehovah is my flag").

"Raise the banner of the Lord!" Moses said. "For the Lord will be at war with Amalek generation after generation."

18 WORD SOON REACHED Jethro, Moses' father-in-law, the priest of Midian, about all the wonderful things God had done for his people and for Moses, and how the Lord had brought them out of Egypt. [2] Then Jethro took Moses' wife, Zipporah, to him (for he had sent her home), [3] along with Moses' two sons, Gershom (meaning "foreigner," for Moses said when he was born, "I have been wandering in a foreign land") [4] and Eliezer (meaning "God is my help," for Moses said at his birth, "The God of my fathers was my helper, and delivered me from the sword of Pharaoh"). [5,6] They arrived while Moses and the people were camped at Mt. Sinai.[a]

"Jethro, your father-in-law, has come to visit you," Moses was told, "and he has brought your wife and your two sons."

[7] Moses went out to meet his father-in-law and greeted him warmly; they asked about each other's health and then went into Moses' tent to talk further. [8] Moses related to his father-in-law all that had been happening and what the Lord had done to Pharaoh and the Egyptians in order to deliver Israel, and all the problems there had been along the way, and how the Lord had delivered his people from all of them. [9] Jethro was very happy about everything the Lord had done for Israel, and about his bringing them out of Egypt.

[10] "Bless the Lord," Jethro said, "for he has saved you from the Egyptians and from Pharaoh, and has rescued Israel. [11] I know now that the Lord is greater than any other god because he delivered his people from the proud and cruel Egyptians."

[12] Jethro offered sacrifices[b] to God, and afterwards Aaron and the leaders of Israel came to meet Jethro, and they all ate the sacrificial meal together before the Lord.

[13] The next day Moses sat as usual to hear the people's complaints against each other, from morning to evening.

[14] When Moses' father-in-law saw how much time this was taking, he said, "Why are you trying to do all this alone, with people standing here all day long to get your help?"

[15,16] "Well, because the people come to me with their disputes, to ask for God's decisions," Moses told him. "I am their judge, deciding who is right and who is wrong, and instructing them in God's ways. I apply the laws of God to their particular disputes."

[17] "It's not right!" his father-in-law exclaimed. [18] "You're going to wear yourself out—and if you do, what will happen to the people? Moses, this job is too heavy a burden for you to try to handle all by yourself. [19,20] Now listen, and let me give you a word of advice, and God will bless you: Be these people's lawyer—their representative before God—bringing him their questions to decide; you will tell them his decisions, teaching them God's laws, and showing them the principles of godly living.

[21] "Find some capable, godly, honest men who hate bribes, and appoint them as judges, one judge for each 1000 people; he in turn will have ten judges under him, each in charge of a hundred; and under each of them will be two judges, each responsible for the affairs of fifty people; and each of these will have five judges beneath him, each counseling ten persons. [22] Let these men be responsible to serve the people with justice at all times. Anything that is too important or complicated can be brought to you. But the smaller matters they can take care of themselves. That way it will be easier for you because you will share the burden with them. [23] If you follow this advice, and if the Lord agrees, you will be able to endure the pressures, and there will be peace and harmony in the camp."

[24] Moses listened to his father-in-law's advice, and followed this suggestion. [25] He chose able men from all over Israel and

---

a Or, "Mt. Horeb." Literally, "the mountain of God." God."

b Literally, "a burnt offering and sacrifices for

made them judges over the people—thousands, hundreds, fifties, and tens. ²⁶ They were constantly available to administer justice. They brought the hard cases to Moses but judged the smaller matters themselves.

²⁷ Soon afterwards Moses let his father-in-law return to his own land.

19 THE ISRAELIS ARRIVED in the Sinai peninsula three months after the night of their departure from Egypt. ²,³ After breaking camp at Rephidim, they came to the base of Mt. Sinai and set up camp there. Moses climbed the rugged mountain to meet with God, and from somewhere in the mountain God called to him and said,

"Give these instructions to the people of Israel. Tell them, ⁴ 'You have seen what I did to the Egyptians, and how I brought you to myself as though on eagle's wings. ⁵ Now if you will obey me and keep your part of my contract with you, you shall be my own little flock from among all the nations of the earth; for all the earth is mine. ⁶ And you shall be a kingdom of priests to God, a holy nation.' "

⁷ Moses returned from the mountain and called together the leaders of the people and told them what the Lord had said.

⁸ They all responded in unison, "We will certainly do everything he asks of us." Moses reported the words of the people to the Lord.

⁹ Then he said to Moses, "I am going to come to you in the form of a dark cloud, so that the people themselves can hear me when I talk with you, and then they will always believe you. ¹⁰ Go down now and see that the people are ready for my visit. Sanctify them today and tomorrow, and have them wash their clothes. ¹¹ Then, the day after tomorrow, I will come down upon Mt. Sinai as all the people watch. ¹² Set boundary lines the people may not pass, and tell them, 'Beware! Do not go up into the mountain, or even touch its boundaries; whoever does shall die— ¹³ no hand shall touch him, but he shall be stoned or shot to death with arrows, whether man or animal.' Stay away from the mountain entirely until you hear a ram's horn sounding one long blast; then gather at the foot of the mountain!"

¹⁴ So Moses went down to the people and sanctified them and they washed their clothing.

¹⁵ He told them, "Get ready for God's appearance two days from now, and do not have sexual intercourse with your wives."

¹⁶ On the morning of the third day there was a terrific thunder and lightning storm, and a huge cloud came down upon the mountain, and there was a long, loud blast as from a ram's horn; and all the people trembled. ¹⁷ Moses led them out from the camp to meet God, and they stood at the foot of the mountain. ¹⁸ All Mt. Sinai was covered with smoke because Jehovah descended upon it in the form of fire; the smoke billowed into the sky as from a furnace, and the whole mountain shook with a violent earthquake. ¹⁹ As the trumpet blast grew louder and louder, Moses spoke and God thundered his reply. ²⁰ So the Lord came down upon the top of Mt. Sinai and called Moses up to the top of the mountain, and Moses ascended to God.

²¹ But the Lord told Moses, "Go back down and warn the people not to cross the boundaries. They must not come up here to try to see God, for they will die. ²² Even the priests on duty[a] must sanctify themselves, lest Jehovah destroy them."

²³ "But the people won't come up into the mountain!" Moses protested. "You told them not to! You told me to set boundaries around the mountain, and to declare it off limits because it is reserved for God."

²⁴ But Jehovah said, "Go on down, and bring Aaron back with you, and don't let the priests and the people break across the boundaries to try to come up here, or I will destroy them."

²⁵ So Moses went down to the people and told them what God had said.

20 THEN GOD ISSUED this edict:
² "I am Jehovah your God who liberated you from your slavery in Egypt.

³ "You may worship no other god than me.

⁴ "You shall not make yourselves any idols: any images resembling animals, birds,

---

a Literally, "The priests who come near to Jehovah."

or fish.[a] [5] You must never bow to an image or worship it in any way; for I, the Lord your God, am very possessive. I will not share your affection with any other god!

"And when I punish people for their sins, the punishment continues upon the children, grandchildren, and great-grandchildren of those who hate me; [6] but I lavish my love upon thousands of those who love me and obey my commandments.

[7] "You shall not use the name of Jehovah your God irreverently,[b] nor use it to swear to a falsehood. You will not escape punishment if you do.

[8] "Remember to observe the Sabbath as a holy day. [9] Six days a week are for your daily duties and your regular work, [10] but the seventh day is a day of Sabbath rest before the Lord your God. On that day you are to do no work of any kind, nor shall your son, daughter, or slaves—whether men or women—or your cattle or your house guests. [11] For in six days the Lord made the heaven, earth, and sea, and everything in them, and rested the seventh day; so he blessed the Sabbath day and set it aside for rest.[c]

[12] "Honor your father and mother, that you may have a long, good life in the land the Lord your God will give you.

[13] "You must not murder.

[14] "You must not commit adultery.

[15] "You must not steal.

[16] "You must not lie.[d]

[17] "You must not be envious of your neighbor's house, or want to sleep with his wife, or want to own his slaves, oxen, donkeys, or anything else he has."

[18] All the people saw the lightning and the smoke billowing from the mountain, and heard the thunder and the long, frightening trumpet blast; and they stood at a distance, shaking with fear.

[19] They said to Moses, "You tell us what God says and we will obey, but don't let God speak directly to us, or it will kill us."

[20] "Don't be afraid," Moses told them, "for God has come in this way to show you his awesome power, so that from now on you will be afraid to sin against him!"

[21] As the people stood in the distance, Moses entered into the deep darkness where God was.

[22] And the Lord told Moses to be his spokesman to the people of Israel. "You are witnesses to the fact that I have made known my will to you from heaven. [23] Remember, you must not make or worship idols made of silver or gold or of anything else!

[24] "The altars you make for me must be simple altars of earth. Offer upon them your sacrifices to me—your burnt offerings and peace offerings of sheep and oxen. Build altars only where I tell you to, and I will come and bless you there. [25] You may also build altars from stone, but if you do, then use only uncut stones and boulders. Don't chip or shape the stones with a tool, for that would make them unfit for my altar. [26] And don't make steps for the altar, or someone might look up beneath the skirts of your clothing and see your nakedness.

21 "HERE ARE OTHER laws you must obey:

[2] "If you buy[a] a Hebrew slave, he shall serve only six years and be freed in the seventh year, and need pay nothing to regain his freedom.

[3] "If he sold himself as a slave before he married, then if he married afterwards, only he shall be freed; but if he was married before he became a slave, then his wife shall be freed with him at the same time. [4] But if his master gave him a wife while he was a slave, and they have sons or daughters, the wife and children shall still belong to the master, and he shall go out by himself free.

[5] "But if the man shall plainly declare, 'I prefer my master, my wife, and my children, and I would rather not go free,' [6] then his master shall bring him before the judges and shall publicly bore his ear with an awl, and after that he will be a slave forever.

[7] "If a man sells his daughter as a slave, she shall not be freed at the end of six years as the men are. [8] If she does not please the man who bought her, then he shall let her be bought back again; but he has no power

---

a Literally, "of anything in heaven or earth or in the sea."   b Or, "use the name of the Lord your God to swear falsely."   c Or, "hallowed it."   d Or, "You must not give false testimony in court."
21a That is, "If he owes you money and defaults on the payment, and thus becomes your slave."

to sell her to foreigners, since he has wronged her by no longer wanting her after marrying her. ⁹ And if he arranges an engagement between a Hebrew slave-girl and his son, then he may no longer treat her as a slave-girl, but must treat her as a daughter. ¹⁰ If he himself marries her and then takes another wife, he may not reduce her food or clothing, or fail to sleep with her as his wife. ¹¹ If he fails in any of these three things, then she may leave freely without any payment.

¹² "Anyone who hits a man so hard that he dies shall surely be put to death. ¹³ But if it is accidental—an act of God—and not intentional, then I will appoint a place where he can run and get protection. ¹⁴ However, if a man deliberately attacks another, intending to kill him, drag him even from my altar, and kill him.

¹⁵ "Anyone who strikes his father or mother shall surely be put to death.

¹⁶ "A kidnapper must be killed, whether he is caught in possession of his victim or has already sold him as a slave.

¹⁷ "Anyone who reviles or curses his mother or father shall surely be put to death.

¹⁸ "If two men are fighting, and one hits the other with a stone or with his fist and injures him so that he must be confined to bed, but doesn't die, ¹⁹ if later he is able to walk again, even with a limp,ᵇ the man who hit him will be innocent except that he must pay for the loss of his time until he is thoroughly healed, and pay any medical expenses.

²⁰ "If a man beats his slave to death—whether the slave is male or female—that man shall surely be punished. ²¹ However, if the slave does not die for a couple of days, then the man shall not be punished—for the slave is his property.

²² "If two men are fighting, and in the process hurt a pregnant woman so that she has a miscarriage, but she lives, then the man who injured her shall be fined whatever amount the woman's husband shall demand, and as the judges approve. ²³ But if any harm comes to the woman and she dies,

he shall be executed.

²⁴ "If her eye is injured, injure his; if her tooth is knocked out, knock out his; and so on—hand for hand, foot for foot, ²⁵ burn for burn, wound for wound, lash for lash.

²⁶ "If a man hits his slave in the eye, whether man or woman, and the eye is blinded, then the slave shall go free because of his eye. ²⁷ And if a master knocks out his slave's tooth, he shall let him go free to pay for the tooth.

²⁸ "If an ox gores a man or woman to death, the ox shall be stoned and its flesh not eaten, but the owner shall not be held—²⁹ unless the ox was known to gore people in the past, and the owner had been notified and still the ox was not kept under control; in that case, if it kills someone, the ox shall be stoned and the owner also shall be killed. ³⁰ But the dead man's relatives may accept a fine instead, if they wish. The judges will determine the amount.ᶜ

³¹ "The same law holds if the ox gores a boy or a girl. ³² But if the ox gores a slave, whether male or female, the slave's master shall be given thirty pieces of silver, and the ox shall be stoned.

³³ "If a man digs a well and doesn't cover it, and an ox or a donkey falls into it, ³⁴ the owner of the well shall pay full damages to the owner of the animal, and the dead animal shall belong to him.

³⁵ "If a man's ox injures another, and it dies, then the two owners shall sell the live ox and divide the price between them—and each shall also own half of the dead ox. ³⁶ But if the ox was known from past experience to gore, and its owner has not kept it under control, then there will not be a division of the income; but the owner of the living ox shall pay in full for the dead ox, and the dead one shall be his.

22 "IF A MAN steals an ox or sheep and then kills or sells it, he shall pay a fine of five to one—five oxen shall be returned for each stolen ox. For sheep, the fine shall be four to one—four sheep returned for each sheep stolen.

² "If a thief is caught in the act of break-

---

b Literally, "if he walks abroad with his staff."   c Literally, verse 30 reads: "But if a ransom is laid upon him, then he shall give for the redemption of his life whatever is laid upon him."

ing into a house and is killed, the one who killed him is not guilty. ³ But if it happens in the daylight, it must be presumed to be murder and the man who kills him is guilty.

"If a thief is captured, he must make full restitution; if he can't, then he must be sold as a slave for his debt.

⁴ "If he is caught in the act of stealing a live ox or donkey or sheep or whatever it is, he shall pay double value as his fine.

⁵ "If someone deliberately lets his animal loose and it gets into another man's vineyard; or if he turns it into another man's field to graze, he must pay for all damages by giving the owner of the field or vineyard an equal amount of the best of his own crop.

⁶ "If the field is being burned off and the fire gets out of control and goes into another field so that the shocks of grain, or the standing grain, are destroyed, the one who started the fire shall make full restitution.

⁷ "If someone gives money or goods to anyone to keep for him, and it is stolen, the thief shall pay double if he is found. ⁸ But if no thief is found, then the man to whom the valuables were entrusted shall be brought before God to determine whether or not he himself has stolen his neighbor's property.

⁹ "In every case in which an ox, donkey, sheep, clothing, or anything else is lost, and the owner believes he has found it in the possession of someone else who denies it, both parties to the dispute shall come before God for a decision, and the one whom God declares guilty shall pay double to the other.

¹⁰ "If a man asks his neighbor to keep a donkey, ox, sheep, or any other animal for him, and it dies, or is hurt, or gets away, and there is no eyewitness to report just what happened to it, ¹¹ then the neighbor must take an oath that he has not stolen it, and the owner must accept his word, and no restitution shall be made for it. ¹² But if the animal or property has been stolen, the neighbor caring for it must repay the owner. ¹³ If it was attacked by some wild animal, he shall bring the torn carcass to confirm the fact, and shall not be required to make restitution.

¹⁴ "If a man borrows an animal (or anything else) from a neighbor, and it is injured or killed, and the owner is not there at the time, then the man who borrowed it must pay for it. ¹⁵ But if the owner is there, he need not pay; and if it was rented, then he need not pay, because this possibility was included in the original rental fee.

¹⁶ "If a man seduces a girlᵃ who is not engaged to anyone, and sleeps with her, he must pay the usual dowryᵇ and accept her as his wife. ¹⁷ But if her father utterly refuses to let her marry him, then he shall pay the money anyway.

¹⁸ "A sorceress shall be put to death.

¹⁹ "Anyone having sexual relations with an animal shall certainly be executed.

²⁰ "Anyone sacrificing to any other god than Jehovah shall be executed.ᶜ

²¹ "You must not oppress a stranger in any way; remember, you yourselves were foreigners in the land of Egypt.

²² "You must not exploit widows or orphans; ²³ if you do so in any way, and they cry to me for my help, I will surely give it. ²⁴ And my anger shall flame out against you, and I will kill you with enemy armies, so that your wives will be widows and your children fatherless.

²⁵ "If you lend money to a needy fellow-Hebrew, you are not to handle the transaction in an ordinary way, with interest. ²⁶ If you take his clothing as a pledge of his repayment, you must let him have it back at night. ²⁷ For it is probably his only warmth; how can he sleep without it? If you don't return it, and he cries to me for help, I will hear and be very gracious to him [at your expenseᵈ], for I am very compassionate.

²⁸ "You shall not blaspheme God, nor curse government officials—your judges and your rulers.

²⁹ "You must be prompt in giving me the tithe of your crops and your wine, and the redemption payment for your oldest son.

³⁰ "As to the firstborn of the oxen and the sheep, give it to me on the eighth day, after leaving it with its mother for seven days.

---

a Literally, "a virgin."   b More literally, "customary marriage present from a bridegroom to the bride's parents."   c Literally, "shall be utterly destroyed."   d Implied.

[31] "And since you yourselves are holy—my special people—do not eat any animal that has been attacked and killed by a wild animal. Leave its carcass for the dogs to eat.

23 "DO NOT PASS along untrue reports. Do not cooperate with an evil man by affirming on the witness stand something you know is false.

[2,3] "Don't join mobs intent on evil. When on the witness stand, don't be swayed in your testimony by the mood of the majority present, and do not slant your testimony in favor of a man just because he is poor.

[4] "If you come upon an enemy's ox or donkey that has strayed away, you must take it back to its owner. [5] If you see your enemy trying to get his donkey onto its feet beneath a heavy load, you must not go on by, but must help him.

[6] "A man's poverty is no excuse for twisting justice against him.

[7] "Keep far away from falsely charging anyone with evil; never let an innocent person be put to death. I will not stand for this.[a]

[8] "Take no bribes, for a bribe makes you unaware of what you clearly see! A bribe hurts the cause of the person who is right.

[9] "Do not oppress foreigners; you know what it's like to be a foreigner; remember your own experience in the land of Egypt.

[10] "Sow and reap your crops for six years, [11] but let the land rest and lie fallow during the seventh year, and let the poor among the people harvest any volunteer crop that may come up; leave the rest for the animals to enjoy. The same rule applies to your vineyards and your olive groves.

[12] "Work six days only, and rest the seventh; this is to give your oxen and donkeys a rest, as well as the people of your household—your slaves and visitors.

[13] "Be sure to obey all of these instructions; and remember—never mention the name of any other god.[b]

[14] "There are three annual religious pilgrimages you must make.[c]

[15] "The first is the Pilgrimage of Unleavened Bread, when for seven days you are not to eat bread with yeast, just as I commanded you before. This celebration is to be an annual event at the regular time in March, the month you left Egypt; everyone must bring me a sacrifice at that time. [16] Then there is the Harvest Pilgrimage, when you must bring to me the first of your crops. And, finally, the Pilgrimage of Ingathering at the end of the harvest season. [17] At these three times each year, every man in Israel shall appear before the Lord God.

[18] "No sacrificial blood shall be offered with leavened bread; no sacrificial fat shall be left unoffered until the next morning.

[19] "As you reap each of your crops, bring me the choicest sample of the first day's harvest; it shall be offered[d] to the Lord your God.

"Do not boil a young goat in its mother's milk.

[20] "See, I am sending an Angel before you to lead you safely to the land I have prepared for you. [21] Reverence him and obey all of his instructions; do not rebel against him, for he will not pardon your transgression; he is my representative[e]—he bears my name. [22] But if you are careful to obey him, following all my instructions, then I will be an enemy to your enemies. [23] For my Angel shall go before you and bring you into the land of the Amorites, Hittites, Perizzites, Canaanites, Hivites, and Jebusites, to live there. And I will destroy these people before you.

[24] "You must not worship the gods of these other nations, nor sacrifice to them in any way, and you must not follow the evil example of these heathen people; you must utterly conquer them and break down their shameful idols.

[25] "You shall serve the Lord your God only; then I will bless you with food and with water, and I will take away sickness from among you. [26] There will be no miscarriages nor barrenness throughout your land, and you will live out the full quota of the days of your life.

[27] "The terror of the Lord shall fall upon all the people whose land you invade, and

---

a Literally, "I will not acquit the wicked."　　　b In prayer, or in taking an oath.　　　c Or, "feasts you must celebrate."　　　d Literally, "you shall bring [it] into the house of Jehovah thy God."　　　e Literally, "my name is in him."

they will flee before you; [28] and I will send hornets to drive out the Hivites, Canaanites, and Hittites from before you. [29] I will not do it all in one year, for the land would become a wilderness, and the wild animals would become too many to control. [30] But I will drive them out a little at a time, until your population has increased enough to fill the land. [31] And I will set your enlarged boundaries from the Red Sea to the Philistine coast, and from the southern deserts as far as the Euphrates River; and I will cause you to defeat the people now living in the land, and you will drive them out ahead of you.

[32] "You must make no covenant with them, nor have anything to do with their gods. [33] Don't let them live among you! For I know that they will infect you with their sin of worshiping false gods, and that would be an utter disaster to you."

24 THE LORD NOW instructed Moses, "Come up here with Aaron, Nadab, Abihu, and seventy of the elders of Israel. All of you except Moses are to worship at a distance. [2] Moses alone shall come near to the Lord; and remember, none of the ordinary people are permitted to come up into the mountain at all."

[3] Then Moses announced to the people all the laws and regulations God had given him; and the people answered in unison, "We will obey them all."

[4] Moses wrote down the laws; and early the next morning he built an altar at the foot of the mountain, with twelve pillars around the altar because there were twelve tribes of Israel. [5] Then he sent some of the young men to sacrifice the burnt offerings and peace offerings to the Lord. [6] Moses took half of the blood of these animals, and drew it off into basins. The other half he splashed against the altar.

[7] And he read to the people the Book he had written—the Book of the Covenant —containing God's directions and laws. And the people said again, "We solemnly promise to obey every one of these rules."

[8] Then Moses threw the blood from the basins towards the people and said, "This blood confirms and seals the covenant the Lord has made with you in giving you these laws."

[9] Then Moses, Aaron, Nadab, Abihu, and seventy of the elders of Israel went up into the mountain. [10] And they saw the God of Israel; under his feet there seemed to be a pavement of brilliant sapphire stones, as clear as the heavens.

[11] Yet, even though the elders saw God, he did not destroy them; and they had a meal together before the Lord.

[12] And the Lord said to Moses, "Come up to me into the mountain, and remain until I give you the laws and commandments I have written on tablets of stone, so that you can teach the people from them." [13] So Moses and Joshua, his assistant, went up into the mountain of God.

[14] He told the elders, "Stay here and wait for us until we come back; if there are any problems while I am gone, consult with Aaron and Hur."

[15] Then Moses went up the mountain and disappeared into the cloud at the top. [16] And the glory of the Lord rested upon Mt. Sinai and the cloud covered it six days; the seventh day he called to Moses from the cloud. [17] Those at the bottom of the mountain saw the awesome sight: the glory of the Lord on the mountain top looked like a raging fire. [18] And Moses disappeared into the cloud-covered mountain top, and was there for forty days and forty nights.

25 JEHOVAH SAID TO Moses, "Tell the people of Israel that everyone who wants to may bring me an offering from this list:

> Gold, silver, bronze, blue cloth,
> purple cloth, scarlet cloth,
> fine-twined linen, goat's hair,
> red-dyed ram's skins, goat-skins,
> acacia wood, olive oil for the
> lamps, spices for the anointing
> oil and for the fragrant incense,
> onyx stones, stones to be set in
> the ephod and in the
> breastplate.

[8] For I want the people of Israel to make me a sacred Temple where I can live among them.

[9] "This home of mine shall be a tent pavilion—a Tabernacle. I will give you a drawing of the construction plan, and the

details of each furnishing.

¹⁰ "Using acacia wood, make an Ark 3¾ feet long, 2¼ feet wide, and 2¼ feet high. ¹¹ Overlay it inside and outside with pure gold, with a molding of gold all around it. ¹² Cast four rings of gold for it and attach them to the four lower corners, two rings on each side. ¹³,¹⁴ Make poles from acacia wood overlaid with gold, and fit the poles into the rings at the sides of the Ark, to carry it. ¹⁵ These carrying poles shall never be taken from the rings, but are to be left there permanently. ¹⁶ When the Ark is finished, place inside it the tablets of stone I will give you, with the Ten Commandments engraved on them.ª

¹⁷ "And make a lid of pure gold, 3¾ feet long and 2¼ feet wide. This is the place of mercy for your sins.ᵇ ¹⁸ Then make images of angels,ᶜ using beaten gold, and place them at the two ends of the lid of the Ark. ¹⁹ They shall be one piece with the mercy place, one at each end. ²⁰ The cherubim—the angels—shall be facing each other, looking down upon the place of mercy, and shall have wings spread out above the gold lid. ²¹ Install the lid upon the Ark, and place within the Ark the tablets of stone I shall give you. ²² And I will meet with you there and talk with you from above the place of mercy between the cherubim; and the Ark will contain the laws of my covenant. There I will tell you my commandments for the people of Israel.

²³ "Then make a table of acacia wood three feet long, 1½ feet wide, and 2¼ feet high. ²⁴ Overlay it with pure gold, and run a rib of gold around it. ²⁵ Put a molding four inches wide around the edge of the top, and a gold ridge along the molding, all around. ²⁶,²⁷ Make four golden rings and put the rings at the outside corner of the four legs, close to the top; these are rings for the poles that will be used to carry the table. ²⁸ Make the poles from acacia wood overlaid with gold. ²⁹ And make golden dishes, spoons, pitchers, and flagons; ³⁰ and always keep the special Bread of the Presence on the table before me.

³¹ "Make a lampstand of pure, beaten gold. The entire lampstand and its decorations shall be one piece—the base, shaft, lamps, and blossoms. ³²,³³ It will have three branches going out from each side of the center shaft, each branch decorated with three almond flowers. ³⁴,³⁵ The central shaft itself will be decorated with four almond flowers—one placed between each set of branches; also, there will be one flower above the top set of branches and one below the bottom set. ³⁶ These decorations and branches and the shaft are all to be one piece of pure, beaten gold. ³⁷ Then make seven lamps for the lampstand, and set them so that they reflect their light forward. ³⁸ The snuffers and trays are to be made of pure gold. ³⁹ You will need about 107ᵈ pounds of pure gold for the lampstand and its accessories.

⁴⁰ "Be sure that everything you make follows the pattern I am showing you here on the mountain.

26 "MAKE THE TABERNACLE-TENT from ten colored sheets of fine-twined linen, forty-two feet long and six feet wide, dyed blue, purple, and scarlet, with cherubim embroidered on them. ³ Join five sheets end to end for each side of the tent, forming two long pieces, one for each side. ⁴,⁵ Use loops at the edges to join these two long pieces together side by side. There are to be fifty loops on each side, opposite each other. ⁶ Then make fifty golden clasps to fasten the loops together, so that the Tabernacle, the dwelling place of God, becomes a single unit.

⁷,⁸ "The roof of the Tabernacle is made of goat's hair tarpaulins. There are to be eleven of these tarpaulins, each forty-five feet across and six feet wide. ⁹ Connect five of these tarpaulins into one wide section; and use the other six for another wide section. (The sixth tarpaulin will hang down to form a curtain across the front of the sacred tent.) ¹⁰,¹¹ Use fifty loops along the edges of each of these two wide pieces, to join them together with fifty bronze clasps. Thus the two widths become one. ¹² There will be a 1½-foot length of this roof-cover-

---

a Implied. Literally, "Put into the Ark the Testimony which I shall give you."   b Literally, "mercy seat" or "place of making propitiation."   c Literally, "cherubim." We are not told what they looked like. d Literally, "a [gold] talent." The exact weight is not known.

ing hanging down from the back of the tent, [13] and a 1½-foot length at the front. [14] On top of these blankets is placed a layer of rams' skins, dyed red, and over them a top layer of goatskins. This completes the roof-covering.

[15,16] "The framework of the sacred tent shall be made from acacia wood, each frame-piece being fifteen feet high and 2¼ feet wide, standing upright, [17] with grooves on each side to mortise into the next upright piece. [18,19] Twenty of these frames will form the south side of the sacred tent, with forty silver bases for the frames to fit into—two bases under each piece of the frame. [20] On the north side there will also be twenty of these frames, [21] with their forty silver bases, two bases for each frame, one under each edge. [22] On the west side there will be six frames, [23] and two frames at each corner. [24] These corner frames will be connected at the bottom and top with clasps. [25] So, in all, there will be eight frames on that end of the building with sixteen silver bases for the frames—two bases under each frame.

[26,27] "Make bars of acacia wood to run across the frames, five bars on each side of the Tabernacle. Also five bars for the rear of the building, facing westward. [28] The middle bar, halfway up the frames, runs all the way from end to end of the Tabernacle. [29] Overlay the frames with gold, and make gold rings to hold the bars; and also overlay the bars with gold. [30] Set up this Tabernacle-tent in the manner I showed you in the mountain.

[31] "[Inside the Tabernacle[a]], make a veil from blue, purple, and scarlet cloth, the fine-twined linen, with cherubim embroidered into the cloth. [32] Hang this upon four acacia pillars overlaid with gold, with four golden hooks. The pillars are to rest in four silver bases. [33] Hang the curtain from the hooks. Behind this curtain place the Ark containing the stone tablets engraved with God's laws. The curtain will separate the Holy Place and the Most Holy Place.

[34] "Now install the mercy place—the golden lid of the Ark—in the Most Holy Place. [35] Place the table and lampstand across the room from each other on the outer side of the veil. The lampstand will be on the south side of the Holy Place and the table on the north side.

[36] "As a screen for the door of the sacred tent, make another curtain from skillfully embroidered blue, purple, and scarlet fine-twined linen. [37] Hang up this curtain on five acacia wood posts, overlaid with gold, with hooks of gold, and a bronze socket for each pillar.

27 "USING ACACIA WOOD, make a square altar 7½ feet wide, and three feet high. [2] Make horns for the four corners of the altar, attach them firmly, and overlay everything with bronze. [3] The ash buckets, shovels, basins, carcass-hooks, and fire pans are all to be made of bronze. [4] Make a bronze grating, with a metal ring at each corner, [5] and fit the grating halfway down into the fire box, resting it upon the ledge built there. [6] For moving the altar, make poles from acacia wood overlaid with bronze. [7] To carry it, put the poles into the rings at each side of the altar. [8] The altar is to be hollow, made from planks, just as was shown you on the mountain.

[9,10] "Then make a courtyard for the Tabernacle, enclosed with curtains made from fine-twined linen. On the south side the curtains will stretch for 150 feet, and be held up by twenty posts, fitting into twenty bronze post holders. The curtains will be held up with silver hooks attached to silver rods, attached to the posts. [11] It will be the same on the north side of the court—150 feet of curtains held up by twenty posts fitted into bronze sockets, with silver hooks and rods. [12] The west side of the court will be seventy-five feet wide, with ten posts and ten sockets. [13] The east side will also be seventy-five feet. [14,15] On each side of the entrance there will be 22½ feet of curtain, held up by three posts imbedded in three sockets.

[16] "The entrance to the court will be a thirty-foot-wide curtain, made of beautifully embroidered blue, purple, and scarlet fine-twined linen, and attached to four posts imbedded in their four sockets. [17] All the posts around the court are to be connected

---

a Implied.

by silver rods, using silver hooks, the posts being imbedded in solid bronze bases. ¹⁸ So the entire court will be 150 feet long, and 75 feet wide, with curtain walls 7½ feet high, made from fine-twined linen.

¹⁹ "All utensils used in the work of the Tabernacle, including all the pins and pegs for hanging the utensils on the walls, will be made of bronze.

²⁰ "Instruct the people of Israel to bring you pure olive oil to use in the lamps of the Tabernacle, to burn there continually. ²¹ Aaron and his sons shall place this eternal flame in the outer holy room, tending it day and night before the Lord, so that it never goes out. This is a permanent rule for the people of Israel.

28 "CONSECRATE AARON YOUR brother, and his sons Nadab, Abihu, Eleazer, and Ithamar, to be priests, to minister to me. ² Make special clothes for Aaron, to indicate his separation to God—beautiful garments that will lend dignity to his work. ³ Instruct those to whom I have given special skill as tailors to make the garments that will set him apart from others, so that he may minister to me in the priest's office. ⁴ This is the wardrobe they shall make: a chestpiece, an ephod,ᵃ a robe, a checkered tunic, a turban, and a sash. They shall also make special garments for Aaron's sons.

⁵,⁶ "The ephod shall be made by the most skilled of the workmen, using blue, purple, and scarlet threads of fine-twined linen. ⁷ It will consist of two pieces, front and back, joined at the shoulders. ⁸ And the sash shall be made of the same material—threads of gold, blue, purple, and scarlet fine-twined linen. ⁹ Take two onyx stones, and engrave on them the names of the tribes of Israel. ¹⁰ Six names shall be on each stone, so that all the tribes are named in the order of their births. ¹¹ When engraving these names, use the same technique as in making a seal; and mount the stones in gold settings. ¹² Fasten the two stones upon the shoulders of the ephod, as memorial stones for the people of Israel: Aaron will carry their names before the Lord as a constant reminder. ¹³,¹⁴ Two

chains of pure, twisted gold shall be made and attached to golden clasps on the shoulder of the ephod.

¹⁵ "Then, using the most careful workmanship, make a chestpiece to be used as God's oracle; use the same gold, blue, purple, and scarlet threads of fine-twined linen as you did in the ephod. ¹⁶ This chestpiece is to be of two folds of cloth, forming a pouch. ¹⁷ Attach to it four rows of stones: A ruby, a topaz, and an emerald shall be in the first row. ¹⁸ The second row will be an emerald, a sapphire, and a diamond. ¹⁹ The third row will be an amber, an agate, and an amethyst. ²⁰ The fourth row will be an onyx, a beryl, and a jasper—all set in gold settings. ²¹ Each stone will represent one of the tribes of Israel and the name of that tribe will be engraved upon it like a seal.

²²,²³,²⁴ "Attach the top of the chestpiece to the ephod by means of two twisted cords of pure gold. One end of each cord is attached to golden rings placed at the outer top edge of the chestpiece. ²⁵ The other ends of the two cords are attached to the front edges of the two settings of the onyx stones on the shoulder of the ephod. ²⁶ Then make two more golden rings and place them on the two lower, inside edges of the chestpiece; ²⁷ also make two other golden rings for the bottom front edge of the ephod at the sash. ²⁸ Now attach the bottom of the chestpiece to the bottom rings of the ephod by means of blue ribbons; this will prevent the chestpiece from coming loose from the ephod. ²⁹ In this way Aaron shall carry the names of the tribes of Israel on the chestpiece over his heart (it is God's oracle) when he goes in to the Holy Place; thus Jehovah will be reminded of them continually. ³⁰,³¹ Insert into the pocket of the chestpiece the Urim and Thummim,ᵇ to be carried over Aaron's heart when he goes in before Jehovah. Thus Aaron shall always be carrying the oracle over his heart when he goes in before the Lord.

"The ephod shall be made of blue cloth, ³² with an opening for Aaron's head. It shall have a woven band around this opening, just as on the neck of a coat of mail, so that

a Apparently a sort of sleeveless tunic reaching from the shoulders to below the knees.   b What these looked like has been lost in antiquity. Possibly they were two stones that were marked in some way and used by the High Priest to determine God's "yes" or "no" on urgent matters.

it will not fray. [33,34] The bottom edge of the ephod shall be embroidered with blue, purple, and scarlet pomegranates, alternated with gold bells. [35] Aaron shall wear the ephod whenever he goes in to minister to the Lord; the bells will tinkle as he goes in and out of the presence of the Lord in the Holy Place, so that he will not die.

[36] "Next, make a plate of pure gold and engrave on it, just as you would upon a seal, 'Consecrated to Jehovah.' [37,38] This plate is to be attached by means of a blue ribbon to the front of Aaron's turban. In this way Aaron will be wearing it upon his forehead, and thus bear the guilt connected with any errors regarding the offerings of the people of Israel. It shall always be worn when he goes into the presence of the Lord, so that the people will be accepted and forgiven.

[39] "Weave Aaron's tunic from fine-twined linen, using a checkerboard pattern; make the turban, too, of this linen; and make him an embroidered sash.

[40] "Then, for Aaron's sons, make robes, sashes, and turbans to give them honor and respect. [41] Clothe Aaron and his sons with these garments, and then dedicate these men to their ministry by anointing their heads with olive oil, thus sanctifying them as the priests, my ministers. [42] Also make linen undershorts for them, to be worn beneath their robes next to their bodies, reaching from hips to knees. [43] These are to be worn whenever Aaron and his sons go into the Tabernacle or to the altar in the Holy Place, lest they be guilty and die. This is a permanent ordinance for Aaron and his sons.

29 "THIS IS THE ceremony for the dedication of Aaron and his sons as priests: get a young bull and two rams with no defects, [2] and bread made without yeast, and thin sheets of sweetened bread mingled with oil, and unleavened wafers with oil poured over them. (The various kinds of bread shall be made with finely ground wheat flour.) [3,4] Place the bread in a basket and bring it to the entrance of the Tabernacle, along with the young bull and the two rams.

"Bathe Aaron and his sons there at the entrance. [5] Then put Aaron's robe on him, and the tunic, ephod, chestpiece, and sash,

[6] and place on his head the turban with the golden plate. [7] Then take the anointing oil and pour it upon his head. [8] Next, dress his sons in their robes, [9] with their woven sashes, and place caps on their heads. They will then be priests forever; thus you shall consecrate Aaron and his sons.

[10] "Then bring the young bull to the Tabernacle, and Aaron and his sons shall lay their hands upon its head; [11] and you shall kill it before the Lord, at the entrance of the Tabernacle. [12] Place its blood upon the horns of the altar, smearing it on with your finger, and pour the rest at the base of the altar. [13] Then take all the fat that covers the inner parts, also the gall bladder and two kidneys, and the fat on them, and burn them upon the altar. [14] Then take the body, including the skin and the dung, outside the camp and burn it as a sin offering.

[15,16] "Next, Aaron and his sons shall lay their hands upon the head of one of the rams as it is killed. Its blood shall also be collected and sprinkled upon the altar. [17] Cut up the ram and wash off the entrails and the legs; place them with the head and the other pieces of the body, [18] and burn it all upon the altar; it is a burnt offering to the Lord, and very pleasant to him.

[19,20] "Now take the other ram, and Aaron and his sons shall lay their hands upon its head as it is killed. Collect the blood and place some of it upon the tip of the right ear of Aaron and his sons, and upon their right thumbs and the big toes of their right feet; sprinkle the rest of the blood over the altar. [21] Then scrape off some of the blood from the altar and mix it with some of the anointing oil and sprinkle it upon Aaron and his sons and upon their clothes; and they and their clothing shall be sanctified to the Lord.

[22] "Then take the fat of the ram, including the fat tail and the fat that covers the insides, also the gall bladder and the two kidneys and the fat surrounding them, and the right thigh—for this is the ram for ordination of Aaron and his sons— [23] and one loaf of bread, one cake of shortening bread, and one wafer from the basket of unleavened bread that was placed before the Lord: [24] Place these in the hands of Aaron and his sons, to wave them in a gesture of offering

to the Lord. ²⁵ Afterwards, take them from their hands and burn them on the altar as a fragrant burnt offering to him. ²⁶ Then take the breast of Aaron's ordination ram and wave it before the Lord in a gesture of offering; afterwards, keep it for yourself.

²⁷ "Give the breast and thigh of the consecration ram ²⁸ to Aaron and his sons. The people of Israel must always contribute this portion of their sacrifices—whether peace offerings or thanksgiving offerings—as their contribution to the Lord.

²⁹ "These sacred garments of Aaron shall be preserved for the consecration of his son who succeeds him, from generation to generation, for his anointing ceremony. ³⁰ Whoever is the next High Priest after Aaron shall wear these clothes for seven days before beginning to minister in the Tabernacle and the Holy Place.

³¹ "Take the ram of consecration—the ram used in the ordination ceremony—and boil its meat in a sacred area. ³² Aaron and his sons shall eat the meat, also the bread in the basket, at the door of the Tabernacle. ³³ They alone shall eat those items used in their atonement (that is, in their consecration ceremony). The ordinary people shall not eat them, for these things are set apart and holy. ³⁴ If any of the meat or bread remains until the morning, burn it; it shall not be eaten, for it is holy.

³⁵ "This, then, is the way you shall ordain Aaron and his sons to their offices. This ordination shall go on for seven days. ³⁶ Every day you shall sacrifice a young bull as a sin offering for atonement; afterwards,ᵃ purge the altar by making atonement for it; pour olive oil upon it to sanctify it. ³⁷ Make atonement for the altar and consecrate it to God every day for seven days. After this the altar shall be exceedingly holy, so that whatever touches it shall be set apart for God.ᵇ

³⁸ "Each day offer two yearling lambs upon the altar, ³⁹ one in the morning and the other in the evening. ⁴⁰ With one of them offer three quarts of finely ground flour mixed with 2½ pints of oil, pressed from olives; also 2½ pints of wine, as a libation.

⁴¹ Offer the other lamb in the evening, along with flour and the wine libation as in the morning, for a fragrant burnt offering to the Lord.

⁴² "This shall be a perpetual daily offering at the door of the Tabernacle before the Lord, where I will meet with you and speak with you. ⁴³ And I will meet with the people of Israel there, and the Tabernacle shall be sanctified by my glory. ⁴⁴ Yes, I will sanctify the Tabernacle and the altar and Aaron and his sons who are my ministers, the priests. ⁴⁵ And I will live among the people of Israel and be their God, ⁴⁶ and they shall know that I am the Lord their God. I brought them out of Egypt so that I could live among them. I am Jehovah their God.

30 "THEN MAKE A small altar for burning incense. It shall be made from acacia wood. ² It is to be eighteen inches square and three feet high, with horns carved from the wood of the altar—they are not to be merely separate parts that are attached. ³ Overlay the top, sides, and horns of the altar with pure gold, and run a gold molding around the entire altar. ⁴ Beneath the molding, on each of two sides, construct two gold rings to hold the carrying poles. ⁵ The poles are to be made of acacia wood overlaid with gold. ⁶ Place the altar just outside the veil, near the place of mercy that is above the Ark containing the Ten Commandments. I will meet with you there.

⁷ "Every morning when Aaron trims the lamps, he shall burn sweet spices on the altar, ⁸ and each evening when he lights the lamps he shall burn the incense before the Lord, and this shall go on from generation to generation. ⁹ Offer no unauthorized incense, burnt offerings, meal offerings, or drink offerings.

¹⁰ "Once a year Aaron must sanctifyᵃ the altar, smearingᵇ upon its horns the blood of the sin offering for atonement. This shall be a regular, annual event from generation to generation, for this is the Lord's supremely holy altar."

¹¹,¹² And Jehovah said to Moses, "Whenever you take a census of the people of Is-

rael, each man who is numbered shall give a ransom to the Lord for his soul, so that there will be no plague among the people when you number them. [13] His payment shall be half a dollar.[c] [14] All who have reached their twentieth birthday shall give this offering. [15] The rich shall not give more and the poor shall not give less, for it is an offering to the Lord to make atonement for yourselves. [16] Use this money for the care of the Tabernacle; it is to bring you, the people of Israel, to the Lord's attention, and to make atonement for you."

[17,18] And the Lord said to Moses, "Make a bronze basin with a bronze pedestal. Put it between the Tabernacle and the altar, and fill it with water. [19] Aaron and his sons shall wash their hands and feet there, [20] when they go into the Tabernacle to appear before the Lord, or when they approach the altar to burn offerings to the Lord. They must always wash before doing so, or they will die. [21] These are instructions to Aaron and his sons from generation to generation."

[22,23] Then the Lord told Moses to collect the choicest of spices—eighteen pounds[d] of pure myrrh; half as much of cinnamon and of sweet cane; [24] the same amount of cassia as of myrrh; and 1½ gallons of olive oil. [25] The Lord instructed skilled perfume-makers to compound all this into a holy anointing oil.

[26,27] "Use this," he said, "to anoint the Tabernacle, the Ark, the table and all its instruments, the lampstand and all its utensils, the incense altar, [28] the burnt offering altar with all its instruments, and the wash-basin and its pedestal. [29] Sanctify them, to make them holy; whatever touches them shall become holy.[e] [30] Use it to anoint Aaron and his sons, sanctifying them so that they can minister to me as priests. [31] And say to the people of Israel, 'This shall always be my holy anointing oil. [32] It must never be poured upon an ordinary person, and you shall never make any of it yourselves, for it is holy, and it shall be treated by you as holy. [33] Anyone who compounds any incense like it or puts any of it upon someone who is not a priest shall be excom-

municated.' "

[34] These were the Lord's directions to Moses concerning the incense: "Use sweet spices—stacte, onycha, galbanum, and pure frankincense, weighing out the same amounts of each, [35] using the usual techniques of the incensemaker, and seasoning it with salt; it shall be a pure and holy incense. [36] Beat some of it very fine and put some of it in front of the Ark where I meet with you in the Tabernacle; this incense is most holy. [37] Never make it for yourselves, for it is reserved for the Lord and you must treat it as holy. [38] Anyone making it for himself shall be excommunicated."

31 THE LORD ALSO said to Moses, "See, I have appointed Bezalel (son of Uri, and grandson of Hur, of the tribe of Judah), [3] and have filled him with the Spirit of God, giving him great wisdom, ability, and skill in constructing the Tabernacle and everything it contains. [4] He is highly capable as an artistic designer of objects made of gold, silver, and bronze. [5] He is skilled, too, as a jeweler and in carving wood.

[6] "And I have appointed Oholiab (son of Ahisamach of the tribe of Dan) to be his assistant; moreover, I have given special skill to all who are known as experts, so that they can make all the things I have instructed you to make: [7] the Tabernacle; the Ark with the place of mercy upon it; all the furnishings of the Tabernacle; [8] the table and its instruments; the pure gold lampstand with its instruments; the altar of incense; [9] the burnt offering altar with its instruments; the laver and its pedestal; [10] the beautifully made, holy garments for Aaron the priest, and the garments for his sons, so that they can minister as priests; [11] the anointing oil; and the sweet-spice incense for the Holy Place. They are to follow exactly the directions I gave you."

[12,13] The Lord then gave these further instructions to Moses: "Tell the people of Israel to rest on my Sabbath day, for the Sabbath is a reminder of the covenant between me and you forever; it helps you to remember that I am Jehovah who makes

---

c Literally, "half a shekel after the shekel of the sanctuary [the shekel is twenty gerahs], half a shekel for an offering to Jehovah."   d Literally, "five hundred shekels." The exact weight cannot be ascertained.
e Or, "shall be set apart for God," or, "only what is holy may touch them."

you holy. [14,15] Yes, rest on the Sabbath, for it is holy. Anyone who does not obey this command must die; anyone who does any work on that day shall be killed. [16] Work six days only, for the seventh day is a special day of solemn rest, holy to the Lord. This law is a perpetual covenant and obligation for the people of Israel. [17] It is an eternal symbol of the covenant between me and the people of Israel. For in six days the Lord made heaven and earth, and rested on the seventh day, and was refreshed."

[18] Then, as God finished speaking with Moses on Mount Sinai, he gave him the two tablets of stone on which the Ten Commandments were written with the finger of God.

32 WHEN MOSES DIDN'T come back down the mountain right away, the people went to Aaron. "Look," they said, "make us a god to lead us, for this fellow Moses who brought us here from Egypt has disappeared; something must have happened to him."

[2,3] "Give me your golden earrings," Aaron replied.

So they all did—men and women, boys and girls. [4] Aaron melted the gold, then molded and tooled it into the form of a calf. The people exclaimed, "O Israel, this is the god that brought you out of Egypt!"

[5] When Aaron saw how happy the people were about it, he built an altar before the calf and announced, "Tomorrow there will be a feast to Jehovah!"

[6] So they were up early the next morning and began offering burnt offerings and peace offerings to the calf-idol; afterwards they sat down to feast and drink at a wild party, followed by sexual immorality.

[7] Then the Lord told Moses, "Quick! Go on down, for your people that you brought from Egypt have defiled themselves, [8] and have quickly abandoned all my laws. They have molded themselves a calf, and worshiped it, and sacrificed to it, and said, 'This is your god, O Israel, that brought you out of Egypt.'"

[9] Then the Lord said, "I have seen what a stubborn, rebellious lot these people are. [10] Now let me alone and my anger shall blaze out against them and destroy them all; and I will make you, Moses, into a great nation instead of them."

[11] But Moses begged God not to do it. "Lord," he pleaded, "why is your anger so hot against your own people whom you brought from the land of Egypt with such great power and mighty miracles? [12] Do you want the Egyptians to say, 'God tricked them into coming to the mountains so that he could slay them, destroying them from off the face of the earth'? Turn back from your fierce wrath. Turn away from this terrible evil you are planning against your people! [13] Remember your promise to your servants—to Abraham, Isaac, and Israel. For you swore by your own self, 'I will multiply your posterity as the stars of heaven, and I will give them all of this land I have promised to your descendants, and they shall inherit it forever.'"

[14] So the Lord changed his mind and spared them. [15] Then Moses went down the mountain, holding in his hands the Ten Commandments written on both sides of two stone tablets. [16] (God himself had written the commandments on the tablets.)

[17] When Joshua heard the noise below them, of all the people shouting, he exclaimed to Moses, "It sounds as if they are preparing for war!"

[18] But Moses replied, "No, it's not a cry of victory or defeat, but singing."

[19] When they came near the camp, Moses saw the calf and the dancing, and in terrible anger he threw the tablets to the ground and they lay broken at the foot of the mountain. [20] He took the calf and melted it in the fire, and when the metal cooled, he ground it into powder and spread it upon the water and made the people drink it.

[21] Then he turned to Aaron. "What in the world did the people do to you," he demanded, "to make you bring such a terrible sin upon them?"

[22] "Don't get so upset," Aaron replied. "You know these people and what a wicked bunch they are. [23] They said to me, 'Make us a god to lead us, for something has happened to this fellow Moses who led us out of Egypt.' [24] Well, I told them, 'Bring me your gold earrings.' So they brought them to me and I threw them into the fire, and

. . . well . . . this calf came out!"

²⁵ When Moses saw that the people had been committing adultery—at Aaron's encouragement, and much to the amusement of their enemies— ²⁶ he stood at the camp entrance and shouted, "All of you who are on the Lord's side, come over here and join me." And all the Levites came.

²⁷ He told them, "Jehovah the God of Israel says, 'Get your swords and go back and forth from one end of the camp to the other and kill even your brothers, friends, and neighbors.' " ²⁸ So they did, and about three thousand men died that day.

²⁹ Then Moses told the Levites, "Today you have ordained yourselves for the service of the Lord, for you obeyed him even though it meant killing your own sons and brothers; now he will give you a great blessing."

³⁰ The next day Moses said to the people, "You have sinned a great sin, but I will return to the Lord on the mountain—perhaps I will be able to obtain his forgiveness for you."

³¹ So Moses returned to the Lord and said, "Oh, these people have sinned a great sin, and have made themselves gods of gold. ³² Yet now if you will only forgive their sin —and if not, then blot *me* out of the book you have written."ᵃ

³³ And the Lord replied to Moses, "Whoever has sinned against me will be blotted out of my book. ³⁴ And now go, lead the people to the place I told you about, and I assure you that my Angel shall travel on ahead of you; however, when I come to visit these people, I will punish them for their sins."

³⁵ And the Lord sent a great plague upon the people because they had worshiped Aaron's calf.

33 THE LORD SAID to Moses, "Lead these people you brought from Egypt to the land I promised Abraham, Isaac, and Jacob; for I said, 'I will give this land to your descendants.' ² I will send an Angel before you to drive out the Canaanites, Amorites, Hittites, Perizzites, Hivites, and Jebusites. ³ It is a land 'flowing with milk and honey'; but I will not travel among you, for you are a stubborn, unruly people, and I would be tempted to destroy you along the way."

⁴ When the people heard these stern words, they went into mourning and stripped themselves of their jewelry and ornaments.

⁵ For the Lord had told Moses to tell them, "You are an unruly, stubborn people. If I were there among you for even a moment, I would exterminate you. Remove your jewelry and ornaments until I decide what to do with you." ⁶ So, after that, they wore no jewelry.

⁷ Moses always erected the sacred tent (the "Tent for Meeting with God," he called it) far outside the camp, and everyone who wanted to consult with Jehovah went out there.

⁸ Whenever Moses went to the Tabernacle, all the people would rise and stand in their tent doors watching until he reached its entrance. ⁹ As he entered, the pillar of cloud would come down and stand at the door while the Lord spoke with Moses. ¹⁰ Then all the people worshiped from their tent doors, bowing low to the pillar of cloud. ¹¹ Inside the tent the Lord spoke to Moses face to face, as a man speaks to his friend. Afterwards Moses would return to the camp, but the young man who assisted him, Joshua (son of Nun), stayed behind in the Tabernacle.

¹² Moses talked there with the Lord and said to him, "You have been telling me, 'Take these people to the Promised Land,' but you haven't told me whom you will send with me. You say you are my friend,ᵃ and that I have found favor before you; ¹³ please, if this is really so, guide me clearly along the way you want me to travelᵇ so that I will understand you and walk acceptably before you. For don't forget that this nation is your people."

¹⁴ And the Lord replied, "I myself will go with you and give you success."

¹⁵ For Moses had said, "If you aren't going with us, don't let us move a step from

---

a Or, "then kill me instead of them."   33a Literally, "You have said you know me by name."
b Or, "show me your ways," or, "show me your majesty."

this place. [16] If you don't go with us, who will ever know that I and my people have found favor with you, and that we are different from any other people upon the face of the earth?"

[17] And the Lord had replied to Moses, "Yes, I will do what you have asked, for you have certainly found favor with me, and you are my friend."[c]

[18] Then Moses asked to see God's glory.

[19] The Lord replied, "I will make my goodness pass before you, and I will announce to you the meaning of my name[d] Jehovah, the Lord. I show kindness and mercy to anyone I want to. [20] But you may not see the glory of my face, for man may not see me and live. [21] However, stand here on this rock beside me. [22] And when my glory goes by, I will put you in the cleft of the rock and cover you with my hand until I have passed. [23] Then I will remove my hand and you shall see my back, but not my face."

34 THE LORD TOLD Moses, "Prepare two stone tablets like the first ones and I will write upon them the same commands that were on the tablets you broke. [2] Be ready in the morning to come up into Mount Sinai and present yourself to me on the top of the mountain. [3] No one shall come with you and no one must be anywhere on the mountain. Do not let the flocks or herds feed close to the mountain."

[4] So Moses took two tablets of stone like the first ones, and was up early and climbed Mount Sinai, as the Lord had told him to, taking the two stone tablets in his hands.

[5,6] Then the Lord descended in the form of a pillar of cloud and stood there with him, and passed in front of him and announced the meaning of his name.[a] "I am Jehovah, the merciful and gracious God," he said, "slow to anger and rich in steadfast love and truth. [7] I, Jehovah, show this steadfast love to many thousands by forgiving their sins;[b] or else[c] I refuse to clear the guilty, and require that a father's sins be

punished in the sons and grandsons, and even later generations."

[8] Moses fell down before the Lord and worshiped. [9] And he said, "If it is true that I have found favor in your sight, O Lord, then please go with us to the Promised Land; yes, it is an unruly, stubborn people, but pardon our iniquity and our sins, and accept us as your own."

[10] The Lord replied, "All right, this is the contract I am going to make with you. I will do miracles such as have never been done before anywhere in all the earth, and all the people of Israel shall see the power of the Lord—the terrible power I will display through you. [11] Your part of the agreement is to obey all of my commandments; then I will drive out from before you the Amorites, Canaanites, Hittites, Perizzites, Hivites, and Jebusites.

[12] "Be very, very careful never to compromise with the people there in the land where you are going, for if you do, you will soon be following their evil ways. [13] Instead, you must break down their heathen altars, smash the obelisks they worship, and cut down their shameful idols.[d] [14] For you must worship no other gods, but only Jehovah, for he is a God who claims absolute loyalty and exclusive devotion.

[15] "No, do not make a peace treaty of any kind with the people living in the land, for they are spiritual prostitutes, committing adultery against me[e] by sacrificing to their gods. If you become friendly with them and one of them invites you to go with him and worship his idol, you are apt to do it. [16] And you would accept their daughters, who worship other gods, as wives for your sons —and then your sons would commit adultery against me by worshiping their wives' gods. [17] You must have nothing to do with idols.

[18] "Be sure to celebrate the Feast of Unleavened Bread for seven days, just as I instructed you, at the dates appointed each year in March; that was the month you left Egypt.

---

c Literally, "I know you by name."   d Literally, "I will proclaim before you my name." His name, Jehovah, means "I will be what I will be." See Exodus 3:14.   34a Literally, "proclaimed the name of Jehovah."
b Literally, "forgiving iniquity and transgression and sin."   c Implied.   d Literally, "Asherim." These were carved statues of male and female genital organs.   e Literally, "they play the harlot worshiping their gods."

¹⁹ "Every firstborn male[f] is mine—cattle, sheep, and goats. ²⁰ The firstborn colt of a donkey may be redeemed by giving a lamb in its place. If you decide not to redeem it, then its neck must be broken. But your sons must all be redeemed. And no one shall appear before me without a gift.

²¹ "Even during plowing and harvest times, work only six days, and rest on the seventh.

²² "And you must remember to celebrate these three annual religious festivals: the Festival of Weeks, the Festival of the First Wheat, and the Harvest Festival. ²³ On each of these three occasions all the men and boys of Israel shall appear before the Lord. ²⁴ No one will attack and conquer your land when you go up to appear before the Lord your God those three times each year. For I will drive out the nations from before you and enlarge your boundaries.

²⁵ "You must not use leavened bread with your sacrifices to me, and none of the meat of the Passover lamb may be kept over until the following morning. ²⁶ And you must bring the best of the first of each year's crop to the Tabernacle of the Lord your God. You must not cook a young goat in its mother's milk."

²⁷ And the Lord said to Moses, "Write down these[g] laws that I have given you, for they represent the terms of my covenant with you and with Israel."

²⁸ Moses was up on the mountain with the Lord for forty days and forty nights, and in all that time he neither ate nor drank. At that time God[h] wrote out the Covenant—the Ten Commandments—on the stone tablets. ²⁹ Moses didn't realize as he came back down the mountain with the tablets that his face glowed from being in the presence of God. ³⁰ Because of this radiance upon his face, Aaron and the people of Israel were afraid to come near him.

³¹ But Moses called them over to him, and Aaron and the leaders of the congregation came and talked with him. ³² Afterwards, all the people came to him, and he gave them the commandments the Lord had given him upon the mountain. ³³ When Moses had finished speaking with them, he put a veil over his face;[i] ³⁴ but whenever he went into the Tabernacle to speak with the Lord, he removed the veil until he came out again; then he would pass on to the people whatever instructions God had given him, ³⁵ and the people would see his face aglow. Afterwards he would put the veil on again until he returned to speak with God.

35 NOW MOSES CALLED a meeting of all the people and told them, "These are the laws of Jehovah you must obey.

² "Work six days only; the seventh day is a day of solemn rest, a holy day to be used to worship Jehovah; anyone working on that day must die. ³ Don't even light the fires in your homes that day."

⁴ Then Moses said to all the people, "This is what the Lord has commanded: ⁵⁻⁹ All of you who wish to, all those with generous hearts, may bring these offerings to Jehovah:

Gold, silver, and bronze;
Blue, purple, and scarlet cloth, made of fine-twined linen or of goat's hair;
Tanned rams' skins and specially treated goatskins;
Acacia wood;
Olive oil for the lamps;
Spices for the anointing oil and for the incense;
Onyx stones and stones to be used for the ephod and chestpiece.

¹⁰⁻¹⁹ "Come, all of you who are skilled craftsmen having special talents, and construct what God has commanded us:

The Tabernacle tent, and its coverings, clasps, frames, bars, pillars, and bases;
The Ark and its poles;
The place of mercy;
The veil to enclose the Holy Place;
The table, its carrying poles, and all of its utensils;
The Bread of the Presence;
Lamp holders, with lamps and oil;
The incense altar and its carrying poles;

---

f Literally, "all that opens the womb."   g That is, the preceding laws in verses 12–26.
h Implied. See Exodus 34:1, Deuteronomy 10:1–4.   i So that the people would not see the glory fade. See
2 Corinthians 3:13.

The anointing oil and sweet incense;
The curtain for the door of the Tabernacle;
The altar for the burnt offerings;
The bronze grating of the altar, and its carrying poles and utensils;
The basin with its pedestal;
The drapes for the walls of the court;
The pillars and their bases;
Drapes for the entrance to the court;
The posts of the Tabernacle court, and their cords;
The beautiful clothing for the priests, to be used when ministering in the Holy Place;
The holy garments for Aaron the priest, and for his sons."

²⁰ So all the people went to their tents to prepare their gifts. ²¹ Those whose hearts were stirred by God's Spirit returned with their offerings of materials for the Tabernacle, its equipment, and for the holy garments. ²² Both men and women came, all who were willing-hearted. They brought to the Lord their offerings of gold, jewelry—earrings, rings from their fingers, necklaces—and gold objects of every kind. ²³ Others brought blue, purple, and scarlet cloth made from the fine-twined linen or goats' hair; and ram skins dyed red, and specially treated goatskins. ²⁴ Others brought silver and bronze as their offering to the Lord; and some brought the acacia wood needed in the construction.

²⁵ The women skilled in sewing and spinning prepared blue, purple, and scarlet thread and cloth, and fine-twined linen, and brought them in. ²⁶ Some other women gladly used their special skill to spin the goats' hair into cloth. ²⁷ The leaders brought onyx stones to be used for the ephod and the chestpiece; ²⁸ and spices, and oil—for the light, and for compounding the anointing oil and the sweet incense. ²⁹ So the people of Israel—every man and woman who wanted to assist in the work given to them by the Lord's command to Moses—brought their freewill offerings to him.

³⁰,³¹ And Moses told them, "Jehovah has specifically appointed Bezalel (the son of Uri and grandson of Hur of the tribe of Judah) as general superintendent of the project. ³² He will be able to create beautiful workmanship from gold, silver, and bronze; ³³ he can cut and set stones like a jeweler, and can do beautiful carving; in fact, he has every needed skill. ³⁴ And God has made him and Oholiab gifted teachers of their skills to others. (Oholiab is the son of Ahisamach, of the tribe of Dan.) ³⁵ God has filled them both with unusual skills as jewelers, carpenters, embroidery designers in blue, purple, and scarlet on linen backgrounds, and as weavers—they excel in all the crafts we will be needing in the work.

36 "ALL THE OTHER craftsmen with God-given abilities are to assist Bezalel and Oholiab in constructing and furnishing the Tabernacle." So Moses told Bezalel and Oholiab and all others who felt called to the work to begin. ³ Moses gave them the materials donated by the people and additional gifts were received each morning.

⁴⁻⁷ But finally the workmen all left their task to meet with Moses and told him, "We have more than enough materials on hand now to complete the job!" So Moses sent a message throughout the camp announcing that no more donations were needed. Then at last the people were restrained from bringing more!

⁸,⁹ The skilled weavers first made ten sheets from finely-twined blue, purple, and scarlet linen, with cherubim skillfully embroidered upon them. ¹⁰ Five of these sheets were attached end to end, then five others similarly attached, forming two long roofsheets. ¹¹,¹² Fifty blue ribbons were looped along the edges of these two long sheets, each loop being opposite its mate on the other long sheet. ¹³ Then fifty clasps of gold were made to connect the loops, thus tying the two long sheets together to form the ceiling of the Tabernacle.

¹⁴,¹⁵ Above the ceiling was a second layer formed by eleven draperies made of goats' hair (uniformly forty-five feet long and six feet wide). ¹⁶ Bezalel coupled five of these draperies together to make one long piece, and six others to make another long piece. ¹⁷ Then he made fifty loops along the end of each, ¹⁸ and fifty small bronze clasps to couple the loops so that the draperies were firmly attached to each other.

¹⁹ The top layer of the roof was made of

rams' skins, dyed red, and tanned goat skins.

²⁰ For the sides of the Tabernacle he used frames of acacia wood standing on end. ²¹ The height of each frame was fifteen feet and the width 2¼ feet. ²² Each frame had two clasps joining it to the next. ²³ There were twenty frames on the south side, ²⁴ with the bottoms fitting into forty silver bases. Each frame was connected to its base by two clasps. ²⁵,²⁶ There were also twenty frames on the north side of the Tabernacle, with forty silver bases, two for each frame. ²⁷ The west side of the Tabernacle, which was its rear, was made from six frames, ²⁸ plus another at each corner. ²⁹ These frames, including those at the corners, were linked to each other at both top and bottom by rings. ³⁰ So, on the west side, there were a total of eight frames with sixteen silver bases beneath them, two for each frame.

³¹,³² Then he made five sets of bars from acacia wood to tie the frames together along the sides, five for each side of the Tabernacle. ³³ The middle bar of the five was halfway up the frames, along each side, running from one end to the other. ³⁴ The frames and bars were all overlaid with gold, and the rings were pure gold.

³⁵ The blue, purple, and scarlet inner[a] veil was made from woven linen, with cherubim skillfully embroidered into it. ³⁶ The veil was then attached to four gold hooks set into four posts of acacia wood, overlaid with gold and set into four silver bases.

³⁷ Then he made a drapery for the entrance to the Tabernacle; it was woven from finespun linen, embroidered with blue, purple, and scarlet. ³⁸ This drapery was connected by five hooks to five posts. The posts and their capitals and rods were overlaid with gold; their five bases were molded from bronze.

37 NEXT BEZALEL MADE the Ark. This was constructed of acacia wood and was 3¾ feet long, 2¼ feet wide, and 2¼ feet high. ² It was plated with pure gold inside and out, and had a molding of gold all the way around the sides. ³ There were four golden rings fastened into its four feet, two rings at each end. ⁴ Then he made poles from acacia wood, and overlaid them with gold, ⁵ and put the poles into the rings at the sides of the Ark, to carry it.

⁶ Then, from pure gold, he made a lid called "the place of mercy"; it was 3¾ feet long and 2¼ feet wide. ⁷ He made two cherubim of beaten gold and placed them at the two ends of the golden lid. ⁸ They were molded so that they were actually a part of the golden lid—it was all one piece. ⁹ The cherubim faced each other, with outstretched wings that overshadowed the place of mercy, looking down upon it.

¹⁰ Then he made a table, using acacia wood, three feet long, 1½ feet wide and 2¼ feet high. ¹¹ It was overlaid with pure gold, with a golden molding all around the edge. ¹² A rim four inches high was constructed around the edges of the table, with a gold molding along the rim. ¹³ Then he cast four rings of gold and placed them into the four table legs, ¹⁴ close to the molding, to hold the carrying poles in place. ¹⁵,¹⁶ Next, using pure gold, he made the bowls, flagons, dishes, and spoons to be placed upon this table.

¹⁷ Then he made the lampstand, again using pure, beaten gold. Its base, shaft, lamp-holders, and decorations of almond flowers were all of one piece. ¹⁸ The lampstand had six branches, three from each side. ¹⁹ Each of the branches was decorated with identical carvings of blossoms. ²⁰,²¹ The main stem of the lampstand was similarly decorated with almond blossoms, a flower on the stem beneath each pair of branches; also a flower below the bottom pair and above the top pair, four in all. ²² The decorations and branches were all one piece of pure, beaten gold. ²³,²⁴ Then he made the seven lamps at the ends of the branches, the snuffers, and the ashtrays, all of pure gold. The entire lampstand weighed 107 pounds, all pure gold.

²⁵ The incense altar was made of acacia wood. It was eighteen inches square and three feet high, with its corner-horns made as part of the altar so that it was all one piece. ²⁶ He overlaid it all with pure gold

---

a Implied.

and ran a gold molding around the edge. [27] Two gold rings were placed on each side, beneath this molding, to hold the carrying poles. [28] The carrying poles were gold-plated acacia wood.

[29] Then, from sweet spices, he made the sacred oil for anointing the priests, and the pure incense, using the techniques of the most skilled perfumers.

38 THE BURNT-OFFERING ALTAR was also constructed of acacia wood; it was 7½ feet square at the top, and 4½ feet high. [2] There were four horns at the four corners, all of one piece with the rest. This altar was overlaid with bronze. [3] Then he made bronze utensils to be used with the altar—the pots, shovels, basins, meat hooks, and fire pans. [4] Next he made a bronze grating that rested upon a ledge about halfway up [in the fire box[a]]. [5] Four rings were cast for each side of the grating, to insert the carrying poles. [6] The carrying poles themselves were made of acacia wood, overlaid with bronze. [7] The carrying poles were inserted into the rings at the side of the altar. The altar was hollow, with plank siding.

[8] The bronze washbasin and its bronze pedestal were cast from the solid bronze mirrors donated by the women who assembled at the entrance to the Tabernacle.

[9] Then he constructed the courtyard. The south wall was 150 feet long; it consisted of drapes woven from fine-twined linen thread. [10] There were twenty posts to hold drapes, with bases of bronze and with silver hooks and rods. [11] The north wall was also 150 feet long, with twenty bronze posts and bases and with silver hooks and rods. [12] The west side was seventy-five feet wide; the walls were made from drapes supported by ten posts and bases, and with silver hooks and rods. [13] The east side was also seventy-five feet wide.

[14,15] The drapes at either side of the entrance were 22½ feet wide, each with three posts and three bases. [16] All the drapes making up the walls of the court were woven of fine-twined linen. [17] Each post had a bronze base, and all the hooks and rods were silver; the tops of the posts were overlaid with silver, and the rods to hold up the drapes were solid silver.

[18] The drapery covering the entrance to the court was made of fine-twined linen, beautifully embroidered with blue, purple, and scarlet thread.

It was thirty feet long and 7½ feet wide, just the same as the drapes composing the walls of the court. [19] It was supported by four posts, with four bronze bases, and with silver hooks and rods; the tops of the posts were also silver.

[20] All the nails used in constructing the Tabernacle and court were bronze.

[21] This summarizes the various steps in building the Tabernacle to house the Ark, so that the Levites could carry on their ministry. All was done in the order designated by Moses and was supervised by Ithamar, son of Aaron the priest. [22] Bezalel (son of Uri and grandson of Hur, of the tribe of Judah) was the master craftsman, [23] assisted by Oholiab (son of Ahisamach of the tribe of Dan); he too was a skilled craftsman and also an expert at engraving, weaving, and at embroidering blue, purple, and scarlet threads into fine linen cloth.

[24] The people brought gifts of 3,140 pounds of gold, all of which was used throughout the Tabernacle.

[25,26] The amount of silver used was 9,575 pounds, which came from the fifty-cent head tax collected from all those registered in the census who were twenty years old or older, a total of 603,550 men. [27] The bases for the frames of the sanctuary walls and for the posts supporting the veil required 9,500 pounds of silver, ninety-five pounds[b] for each socket. [28] The silver left over was used for the posts and to overlay their tops, and for the rods and hooks.

[29] The people brought 7,540 pounds of bronze, which was used for casting the bases for the posts at the entrance to the Tabernacle, and for the bronze altar, the bronze grating, the altar utensils, the bases for the posts supporting the drapes enclosing the court, and for all the nails used in the construction of the Tabernacle and the court.

a Implied.   b Literally, "a [silver] talent." The exact weight cannot be ascertained.

39 THEN, FOR THE priests, the people made beautiful garments of blue, purple, and scarlet cloth—garments to be used while ministering in the Holy Place. This same cloth was used for Aaron's sacred garments, in accordance with the Lord's instructions to Moses. [2] The ephod was made from this cloth too, woven from fine-twined linen thread. [3] Bezalel beat gold into thin plates and cut it into wire threads, to work into the blue, purple, and scarlet linen; it was a skillful and beautiful piece of workmanship when finished.

[4,5] The ephod was held together by shoulder straps at the top, and was tied down by an elaborate one-piece woven sash made of the same gold, blue, purple, and scarlet cloth cut from fine-twined linen thread, just as God had directed Moses. [6,7] The [two[a]] onyx stones, attached to the [two[a]] shoulder straps of the ephod, were set in gold, and the stones were engraved with the names of the tribes of Israel, just as initials are engraved upon a ring. These stones were reminders to Jehovah concerning the people of Israel;[b] all this was done in accordance with the Lord's instructions to Moses.

[8] The chestpiece was a beautiful piece of work, just like the ephod, made from the finest gold, blue, purple, and scarlet linen. [9] It was a piece nine inches square, doubled over to form a pouch; [10] there were four rows of stones across it. In the first row were a sardius, a topaz, and a carbuncle; [11] in the second row were an emerald, a sapphire, and a diamond. [12] In the third row were a jacinth, an agate, and an amethyst. [13] In the fourth row, a beryl, an onyx, and a jasper —all set in gold filigree. [14] The stones were engraved like a seal, with the names of the twelve tribes of Israel.

[15-18] [To attach the chestpiece to the ephod[a]], a gold ring was placed at the top of each shoulder strap of the ephod, and from these gold rings, two strands of twined gold attached to gold clasps on the top corners of the chestpiece. [19] Two gold rings were also set at the lower edge of the chestpiece, on the under side, next to the ephod. [20] Two other gold rings were placed low on the shoulder straps of the ephod, close to where the ephod joined its beautifully woven sash. [21] The chestpiece was held securely above the beautifully woven sash of the ephod by tying the rings of the chestpiece to the rings of the ephod, with a blue ribbon.

All this was commanded to Moses by the Lord.

[22] The main part of the ephod was woven, all of blue, [23] and there was a hole at the center just as in a coat of mail, for the head to go through, reinforced around the edge so that it would not tear. [24] Pomegranates were attached to the bottom edge of the robe; these were made of linen cloth, embroidered[a] with blue, purple, and scarlet. [25,26] Bells of pure gold were placed between the pomegranates along the bottom edge of the skirt, with bells and pomegranates alternating all around the edge. This robe was worn when Aaron ministered to the Lord, just as the Lord had commanded Moses.

[27] Robes were now made for Aaron and his sons from fine-twined linen thread. [28,29] The chestpiece, the beautiful turbans, and the caps and the underclothes were all made of this linen, and the linen belt was beautifully embroidered with blue, purple, and scarlet threads, just as Jehovah had commanded Moses. [30] Finally they made the holy plate of pure gold to wear on the front of the turban, engraved with the words, "Consecrated to Jehovah." [31] It was tied to the turban with a blue cord, just as the Lord had instructed.

[32] And so at last the Tabernacle was finished, following all of the Lord's instructions to Moses.

[33-40] Then they brought the entire Tabernacle to Moses:

Furniture; clasps; frames; bars;

Posts; bases; layers of covering for the roof and sides—the rams' skins dyed red, the specially tanned goat skins, and the entrance drape; the Ark with the Ten Commandments in it;

The carrying poles;

The place of mercy;

The table and all its utensils;

---

a Implied.   b Literally, "to be stones of memorial for the children of Israel."

The Bread of the Presence;
The pure [gold[c]] lampstand with its
  lamps, utensils, and oil;
The golden altar;
The anointing oil;
The sweet incense;
The curtain-door of the Tabernacle;
The bronze altar;
The bronze grating;
The poles and the utensils;
The washbasin and its base;
The drapes for the walls of the court
  and the posts holding them up;
The bases and the drapes at the gate
  of the court;
The cords and nails;
All the utensils used there in the
  work of the Tabernacle.

[41] They also brought for his inspection
the beautifully tailored garments to be worn
while ministering in the Holy Place, and the
holy garments for Aaron the priest and
those for his sons, to be worn when on duty.

[42] So the people of Israel followed all the
Lord's instructions to Moses. [43] And Moses
inspected all their work and blessed them
because it was all as the Lord had instructed
him.

40 THE LORD NOW said to Moses, [2] "Put
together the Tabernacle on the first
day of the first month. [3] In it, place the Ark
containing the Ten Commandments; and
install the veil to enclose the Ark within the
Holy of Holies. [4] Then bring in the table and
place the utensils on it, and bring in the
lampstand and light the lamps.

[5] "Place the golden altar for the incense
in front of the Ark. Set up the drapes at the
entrance of the Tabernacle, [6] and place the
altar for burnt offerings in front of the entrance. [7] Set the washbasin between the
Tabernacle-tent and the altar, and fill it
with water. [8] Then make the courtyard
around the outside of the tent, and hang the
curtain-door at the entrance to the courtyard.

[9] "Take the anointing oil and sprinkle it
here and there upon the Tabernacle and everything in it, upon all of its utensils and
parts, and all the furniture, to hallow it; and

it shall become holy. [10] Sprinkle the anointing oil upon the altar of burnt offering and
its utensils, sanctifying it; for the altar shall
then become most holy. [11] Then anoint the
washbasin and its pedestal, sanctifying it.

[12] "Now bring Aaron and his sons to the
entrance of the Tabernacle and wash them
with water; [13] and clothe Aaron with the
holy garments and anoint him, sanctifying
him to minister to me as a priest. [14] Then
bring his sons and put their robes upon
them, [15] and anoint them as you did their
father, that they may minister to me as
priests; their anointing shall be permanent
from generation to generation: all their children and children's children shall forever be
my priests."

[16] So Moses proceeded to do all as the
Lord had commanded him. [17] On the first
day of the first month, in the second year,
the Tabernacle was put together. [18] Moses
erected it by setting its frames into their
bases and attaching the bars. [19] Then he
spread the coverings over the framework,
and put on the top layers, just as the Lord
had commanded him.

[20] Inside the Ark he placed the stones
with the Ten Commandments engraved on
them, and attached the carrying poles to the
Ark and installed the golden lid, the place
of mercy. [21] Then he brought the Ark into
the Tabernacle and set up the veil to screen
it, just as the Lord had commanded.

[22] Next he placed the table at the north
side of the room outside the veil, [23] and set
the Bread of the Presence upon the table
before the Lord, just as the Lord had commanded.

[24] And he placed the lampstand next to
the table, on the south side of the Tabernacle. [25] Then he lighted the lamps before
the Lord, following all the instructions,
[26] and placed the golden altar in the Tabernacle next to the veil, [27] and burned upon
it the incense made from sweet spices, just
as the Lord had commanded.

[28] He attached the curtain at the entrance of the Tabernacle, [29] and placed the
outside altar for the burnt offerings near the
entrance, and offered upon it a burnt offering and a meal offering, just as the Lord had

---

c Implied.

commanded him.

³⁰ Next he placed the washbasin between the tent and the altar, and filled it with water so that the priests could use it for washing. ³¹ Moses and Aaron and Aaron's sons washed their hands and feet there. ³² Whenever they walked past the altar to enter the Tabernacle, they stopped and washed, just as the Lord had commanded Moses.

³³ Then he erected the enclosure surrounding the tent and the altar, and set up the curtain-door at the entrance of the enclosure. So at last Moses finished the work.

³⁴ Then the cloud covered the Tabernacle and the glory of the Lord filled it. ³⁵ Moses was not able to enter because the cloud was standing there, and the glory of the Lord filled the Tabernacle. ³⁶ Whenever the cloud lifted and moved, the people of Israel journeyed onward, following it. ³⁷ But if the cloud stayed, they stayed until it moved. ³⁸ The cloud rested upon the Tabernacle during the daytime, and at night there was fire in the cloud so that all the people of Israel could see it.

This continued throughout all their journeys.

Rick Kotter

Welcome to the Halls of Learning!

A newcomer at a state university fraternity gets his initiation—he's lashed to a telephone pole and swabbed with oil, honey, butter, mustard and grease. Then comes the final coat: feathers.

It's all part of the pageantry of American college culture in the twentieth century. It may look senseless to non-fraternity types—but for now, that's the way it's done on some campuses.

The pageantry, the ritual outlined here in Leviticus (in *minute* detail) may seem odd, exacting, or even perplexing—but that's the way God wanted it done. He wasn't playing jokes on his people; he was simply being particular about how he should be worshiped by a nation called to a special purpose.

The rules about sanitation and food may sound picky, but actually they make lots of sense. In fact, Leviticus shows more awareness of germs and health care than existed in any other ancient culture.

Named for the priestly tribe of Levi, the book tells everything you needed to know about offerings, feasts, vows, holidays, quarantines. If you're perceptive, you may see some interesting symbolism here.

LEVITICUS

1 THE LORD NOW spoke to Moses from the Tabernacle, [2,3] and commanded him to give the following instructions to the people of Israel: "When you sacrifice to the Lord, use animals from your herds and flocks.

"If your sacrifice is to be an ox given as a burnt offering, use only a bull with no physical defects. Bring the animal to the entrance of the Tabernacle where the priests will accept your gift for the Lord. [4] The person bringing it is to lay his hand upon its head, and it then becomes his substitute: the death of the animal will be accepted by God instead of the death of the man who brings it, as the penalty for his sins.[a] [5] The man shall then kill the animal there before the Lord, and Aaron's sons, the priests, will present the blood before the Lord, sprinkling it upon all sides of the altar at the entrance of the Tabernacle. [6,7] Then the priests will skin the animal[b] and quarter it, and build a wood fire upon the altar, [8] and put the sections of the animal and its head and fat upon the wood. [9] The internal organs and the legs are to be washed, then the priests will burn them upon the altar, and they will be an acceptable burnt offering with which the Lord is pleased.[c]

[10] "If the animal used as a burnt offering is a sheep or a goat, it too must be a male, and without any blemishes. [11] The man who brings it will kill it before the Lord on the north side of the altar, and Aaron's sons, the priests, will sprinkle its blood back and forth upon the altar. [12] Then the man will quarter it, and the priests will lay the pieces, with the head and the fat, on top of the wood on the altar. [13] But the internal organs and the legs shall first be washed with water. Then the priests shall burn it all upon the altar as an offering to the Lord; for burnt offerings give much pleasure to the Lord.

[14] "If anyone wishes to use a bird as his burnt offering, he may choose either turtle-doves or young pigeons. [15,16,17] A priest will take the bird to the altar and wring off its head, and the blood shall be drained out at the side of the altar. Then the priest will remove the crop and the feathers and throw them on the east side of the altar with the ashes. Then, grasping it by the wings, he shall tear it apart, but not completely. And the priest shall burn it upon the altar, and the Lord will have pleasure in this sacrifice.[d]

2 "ANYONE WHO WISHES to sacrifice a grain offering to the Lord is to bring fine

---

a Literally, "to make atonement for him." b Literally, "he . . . shall skin . . ." c Literally, "it will be a sweet savor unto the Lord." d Literally, "it will be a sweet savor unto the Lord."

flour and is to pour olive oil and incense upon it. [2] Then he is to take a handful, representing the entire amount,[a] to one of the priests to burn, and the Lord will be fully pleased. [3] The remainder of the flour is to be given to Aaron and his sons as their food; but all of it is counted as a holy burnt offering to the Lord.

[4] "If bread baked in the oven is brought as an offering to the Lord, it must be made from finely ground flour, baked with olive oil but without yeast. Wafers made without yeast and spread with olive oil may also be used as an offering. [5] If the offering is something from the griddle, it shall be made of finely ground flour without yeast, and mingled with olive oil. [6] Break it into pieces and pour oil upon it—it is a form of grain offering. [7] If your offering is cooked in a pan, it too shall be made of fine flour mixed with olive oil.

[8] "However it is prepared—whether baked, fried, or grilled—you are to bring this grain offering to the priest and he shall take it to the altar to present it to the Lord. [9] "The priests are to burn only a representative portion[b] of the offering, but all of it will be fully appreciated by the Lord. [10] The remainder belongs to the priests for their own use, but it is all counted as a holy burnt offering to the Lord.

[11] "Use no yeast with your offerings of flour; for no yeast or honey is permitted in burnt offerings to the Lord. [12] You may offer yeast bread and honey as thanksgiving offerings at harvest time, but not as burnt offerings.[c]

[13] "Every offering must be seasoned with salt,[d] because the salt is a reminder of God's covenant.

[14] "If you are offering from the first of your harvest, remove the kernels from a fresh ear, crush and roast them, then offer them to the Lord. [15] Put olive oil and incense on the offering, for it is a grain offering. [16] Then the priests shall burn part of the bruised grain mixed with oil and all of the incense as a representative portion before the Lord.

3 "WHEN ANYONE WANTS to give an offering of thanksgiving to the Lord, he may use either a bull or a cow, but the animal must be entirely without defect if it is to be offered to the Lord! [2] The man who brings the animal shall lay his hand upon its head and kill it at the door of the Tabernacle. Then Aaron's sons shall throw the blood against the sides of the altar, [3,4,5] and shall burn before the Lord the fat that covers the inward parts, the two kidneys and the loin-fat on them, and the gall bladder. And it will give the Lord much pleasure.

[6] "If a goat or sheep is used as a thank-offering to the Lord, it must have no defect and may be either a male or female—ram or ewe, billy goat or nanny goat.

[7,8] "If it is a lamb, the man who brings it shall lay his hand upon its head and kill it at the entrance of the Tabernacle; the priests shall throw the blood against the sides of the altar, [9,10,11] and shall offer upon the altar the fat, the tail removed close to the backbone, the fat covering the internal organs, the two kidneys with the loin-fat on them, and the gall bladder, as a burnt offering to the Lord.

[12] "If anyone brings a goat as his offering to the Lord, [13] he shall lay his hand upon its head and kill it at the entrance of the Tabernacle. The priest shall throw its blood against the sides of the altar, [14] and shall offer upon the altar, as a burnt offering to the Lord, the fat which covers the insides, [15,16] the two kidneys and the loin-fat on them, and the gall bladder. This burnt offering is very pleasing to the Lord. All the fat is Jehovah's. [17] This is a permanent law throughout your land, that you shall eat neither fat nor blood."

4 THEN THE LORD gave these further instructions to Moses:

[2] "Tell the people of Israel that these are the laws concerning anyone who unintentionally breaks any of my commandments. [3] If a priest sins unintentionally, and so brings guilt upon the people, he must offer a young bull without defect as a sin offering

---

a Literally, "shall burn the memorial portion thereof upon the altar, an offering made by fire."
b Literally, "the memorial."   c Literally, "but not for a sweet savor on the altar."   d In many of the languages of the ancient Near East, the word "salt" is a homonym of the word "good." It was used symbolically for "goodness" in making covenants.

to the Lord. [4] He shall bring it to the door of the Tabernacle, and shall lay his hand upon its head and kill it there before Jehovah. [5] Then the priest shall take the animal's blood into the Tabernacle, [6] and shall dip his finger in the blood and sprinkle it seven times before the Lord in front of the veil that bars the way to the Holy of Holies. [7] Then the priest shall put some of the blood upon the horns of the incense altar before the Lord in the Tabernacle; the remainder of the blood shall be poured out at the base of the altar for burnt offerings, at the entrance to the Tabernacle. [8] Then he shall take all the fat on the entrails, [9] the two kidneys and the loin-fat on them, and the gall bladder, [10] and shall burn them on the altar of burnt offering, just as in the case of a bull or cow sacrificed as a thank-offering. [11,12] But the remainder of the young bull— the skin, meat, head, legs, internal organs, and intestines—shall be carried to a ceremonially clean place outside the camp—a place where the ashes are brought from the altar—and burned there on a wood fire.

[13] "If the entire nation of Israel sins without realizing it, and does something that Jehovah has said not to do, all the people are guilty. [14] When they realize it, they shall offer a young bull for a sin offering, bringing it to the Tabernacle [15] where the leaders[a] of the nation shall lay their hands upon the animal's head and kill it before the Lord. [16] Then the priest shall bring its blood into the Tabernacle, [17] and shall dip his finger in the blood and sprinkle it seven times before the Lord, in front of the veil. [18] Then he shall put blood upon the horns of the altar there in the Tabernacle before the Lord, and all the remainder of the blood shall be poured out at the base of the burnt offering altar, at the entrance to the Tabernacle. [19] All the fat shall be removed and burned upon the altar. [20] He shall follow the same procedure as for a sin offering; in this way the priest shall make atonement for the nation, and everyone will be forgiven. [21] The priest shall then cart the young bull outside the camp and burn it there, just as though it were a sin offering for an individual, only this time it is a sin offering for the entire nation.

[22] "If one of the leaders sins without realizing it and is guilty of disobeying one of God's laws, [23] as soon as it is called to his attention he must bring as his sacrifice a billy goat without any physical defect. [24] He shall lay his hand upon its head and kill it at the place where the burnt offerings are killed, and present it to the Lord. This is his sin offering. [25] Then the priest shall take some of the blood of this sin offering and place it with his finger upon the horns of the altar of burnt offerings, and the rest of the blood shall be poured out at the base of the altar. [26] All the fat shall be burned upon the altar, just as if it were the fat of the sacrifice of a thank-offering;[b] thus the priest shall make atonement for the leader concerning his sin, and he shall be forgiven.

[27] "If any one of the common people sins and doesn't realize it, he is guilty. [28] But as soon as he does realize it, he is to bring as his sacrifice a nanny goat without defect to atone for his sin. [29] He shall bring it to the place where the animals for burnt offerings are killed, and there lay his hand upon the head of the sin offering and kill it. [30] And the priest shall take some of the blood with his finger and smear it upon the horns of the burnt offering altar. Then the priest shall pour out the remainder of the blood at the base of the altar. [31] All the fat shall be taken off, just as in the procedure for the thank-offering[b] sacrifice, and the priest shall burn it upon the altar; and the Lord will appreciate it. Thus the priest shall make atonement for that man, and he shall be forgiven.

[32] "However, if he chooses to bring a lamb as his sin offering, it must be a female without physical defect. [33] He shall bring it to the place where the burnt offerings are killed, and lay his hand upon its head and kill it there as a sin offering. [34] The priest shall take some of the blood with his finger and smear it upon the horns of the burnt offering altar, and all the rest of the blood shall be poured out at the base of the altar. [35] The fat shall be used just as in the case of a thank-offering[b] lamb—the priest shall burn the fat on the altar as in any other

---

a Literally, "elders."   b Literally, "peace offering."

sacrifice made to Jehovah by fire; and the priest shall make atonement for the man, and his sin shall be forgiven.

5 "ANYONE REFUSING TO give testimony concerning what he knows about a crime is guilty.

2 "Anyone touching anything ceremonially unclean—such as the dead body of an animal forbidden for food, wild or domesticated, or the dead body of some forbidden insect—is guilty, even though he wasn't aware of touching it. 3 Or if he touches human discharge of any kind, he becomes guilty as soon as he realizes that he has touched it.

4 "If anyone makes a rash vow, whether the vow is good or bad, when he realizes what a foolish vow he has taken, he is guilty.

5 "In any of these cases, he shall confess his sin 6 and bring his guilt offering to the Lord, a female lamb or goat, and the priest shall make atonement for him, and he shall be freed from his sin, and need not fulfill the vow.[a]

7 "If he is too poor to bring a lamb to the Lord, then he shall bring two turtledoves or two young pigeons as his guilt offering; one of the birds shall be his sin offering and the other his burnt offering. 8 The priest shall offer as the sin sacrifice whichever bird is handed to him first, wringing its neck, but not severing its head from its body. 9 Then he shall sprinkle some of the blood at the side of the altar and the rest shall be drained out at the base of the altar; this is the sin offering. 10 He shall offer the second bird as a burnt offering, following the customary procedures that have been set forth; so the priest shall make atonement for him concerning his sin and he shall be forgiven.

11 "If he is too poor to bring turtledoves or young pigeons as his sin offering, then he shall bring a tenth of a bushel of fine flour. He must not mix it with olive oil or put any incense on it, because it is a sin offering. 12 He shall bring it to the priest and the priest shall take out a handful as a representative portion, and burn it on the altar just as any other offering to Jehovah made

by fire; this shall be his sin offering. 13 In this way the priest shall make atonement for him for any sin of this kind, and he shall be forgiven. The rest of the flour shall belong to the priest, just as was the case with the grain offering."

14 And the Lord said to Moses, 15 "If anyone sins by unintentionally defiling what is holy, then he shall bring a ram without defect, worth whatever fine[b] you charge against him, as his guilt offering to the Lord. 16 And he shall make restitution for the holy thing he has spoiled, or the tithe omitted,[c] by paying for the loss, plus a twenty percent penalty; he shall bring it to the priest, and the priest shall make atonement for him with the ram of the guilt offering, and he shall be forgiven.

17,18 "Anyone who disobeys some law of God without realizing it is guilty anyway, and must bring his sacrifice of a value determined by Moses. This sacrifice shall be a ram without blemish taken to the priest as a guilt offering; with it the priest shall make atonement for him, so that he will be forgiven for whatever it is he has done without realizing it. 19 It must be offered as a guilt offering, for he is certainly guilty before the Lord."

6 AND THE LORD said to Moses, 2 "If anyone sins against me by refusing to return a deposit on something borrowed or rented, or by refusing to return something entrusted to him, or by robbery, or by oppressing his neighbor, 3 or by finding a lost article and lying about it, swearing that he doesn't have it— 4,5 on the day he is found guilty of any such sin, he shall restore what he took, adding a twenty percent fine, and give it to the one he has harmed; and on the same day he shall bring his guilt offering to the Tabernacle. 6 His guilt offering shall be a ram without defect, and must be worth whatever value you demand. He shall bring it to the priest, 7 and the priest shall make atonement for him before the Lord, and he shall be forgiven."

8 Then the Lord said to Moses, 9 *"Give Aaron and his sons these regulations con-*

---

a Implied.   b Literally, "using the standard of the shekel of the sanctuary."   c Implied in remainder of the verse.

cerning the burnt offering:

"The burnt offering shall be left upon the hearth of the altar all night, with the altar fire kept burning. [10] (The next morning) the priest shall put on his linen undergarments and his linen outer garments and clean out the ashes of the burnt offering and put them beside the altar. [11] Then he shall change his clothes and carry the ashes outside the camp to a place that is ceremonially clean. [12] Meanwhile, the fire on the altar must be kept burning—it must not go out. The priest shall put on fresh wood each morning, and lay the daily burnt offering on it, and burn the fat of the daily peace offering. [13] The fire must be kept burning upon the altar continually. It must never go out.

[14] *"These are the regulations concerning the grain offering:*

"Aaron's sons shall stand in front of the altar to offer it before the Lord. [15] The priest shall then take out a handful of the finely ground flour with the olive oil and the incense mixed into it, and burn it upon the altar as a representative portion for the Lord; and it will be received with pleasure by the Lord. [16] After taking out this handful, the remainder of the flour will belong to Aaron and his sons for their food; it shall be eaten without yeast in the courtyard of the Tabernacle. [17] (Stress this instruction, that if it is baked it must be without yeast.) I have given to the priests this part of the burnt offerings made to me. However, all of it is most holy, just as is the entire sin offering and the entire guilt offering. [18] It may be eaten by any male descendant of Aaron, any priest, generation after generation. But only[a] the priests may eat these offerings made by fire to the Lord."

[19,20] And Jehovah said to Moses, "On the day Aaron and his sons are anointed and inducted into the priesthood, they shall bring to the Lord a regular grain offering—a tenth of a bushel of fine flour, half to be offered in the morning and half in the evening. [21] It shall be cooked on a griddle, using olive oil, and should be well cooked, then brought to the Lord as an offering that pleases him very much. [22,23] As the sons of the priests replace their fathers, they shall

be inducted into office by offering this same sacrifice on the day of their anointing. This is a perpetual law. These offerings shall be entirely burned up before the Lord; none of it shall be eaten."

[24] Then the Lord said to Moses, [25] *"Tell Aaron and his sons that these are the instructions concerning the sin offering:*

"This sacrifice is most holy, and shall be killed before the Lord at the place where the burnt offerings are killed. [26] The priest who performs the ceremony shall eat it in the courtyard of the Tabernacle. [27] Only those who are sanctified—the priests—may touch this meat; if any blood sprinkles onto their clothing, it must be washed in a holy place. [28] Then the clay pot in which the clothing is boiled shall be broken; or if a bronze kettle is used, it must be scoured and rinsed out thoroughly. [29] Every male among the priests may eat this offering, but only they, for it is most holy. [30] No sin offering may be eaten by the priests if any of its blood is taken into the Tabernacle, to make atonement in the Holy Place. That carcass must be entirely burned with fire before the Lord.

7 "HERE ARE THE *instructions concerning the most holy offering for guilt:*

[2] "The sacrificial animal shall be killed at the place where the burnt offering sacrifices are slain, and its blood shall be sprinkled back and forth upon the altar. [3] The priest will offer upon the altar all its fat, including the tail, the fat that covers the insides, [4] the two kidneys and the loin-fat, and the gall bladder—all shall be set aside for sacrificing. [5] The priests will burn them upon the altar as a guilt offering to the Lord. [6] Only males among the priests may then eat the carcass, and it must be eaten in a holy place, for this is a most holy sacrifice.

[7] "The same instructions apply to both the sin offering and the guilt offering—the carcass shall be given to the priest who is in charge of the atonement ceremony, for his food. [8] (When the offering is a burnt sacrifice, the priest who is in charge shall also be given the animal's hide.) [9] The priests who present the people's grain offerings to the Lord shall be given whatever

---

a Literally, "(only) whoever is holy may touch them," or "whoever touches them shall become holy."

remains of the sacrifice after the ceremony is completed. This rule applies whether the sacrifice is baked, fried, or grilled. [10] All other grain offerings, whether mixed with olive oil or dry, are the common property of all sons of Aaron.

[11] *"Here are the instructions concerning the sacrifices given to the Lord as special peace offerings:*

[12] "If it is an offering of thanksgiving, unleavened short bread[a] shall be included with the sacrifice, along with unleavened wafers spread with olive oil and loaves from a batter of flour mixed with olive oil. [13] This thanksgiving peace offering shall be accompanied with loaves of leavened bread. [14] Part of this sacrifice shall be presented to the Lord by a gesture of waving it before the altar, then it shall be given to the assisting priest, the one who sprinkles the blood of the animal presented for the sacrifice. [15] After the animal has been sacrificed and presented to the Lord as a peace offering to show special appreciation and thanksgiving to him, its meat is to be eaten that same day, and none left to be eaten the next day.

[16] "However, if someone brings a sacrifice that is not for thanksgiving, but is because of a vow or is simply a voluntary offering to the Lord, any portion of the sacrifice that is not eaten the day it is sacrificed may be eaten the next day. [17,18] But anything left over until the third day shall be burned. For if any of it is eaten on the third day, the Lord will not accept it; it will have no value as a sacrifice, and there will be no credit to the one who brought it to be offered; and the priest who eats it shall be guilty, for it is detestable to the Lord, and the person who eats it must answer for his sin.

[19] "Any meat that comes into contact with anything that is ceremonially unclean shall not be eaten, but burned; and as for the meat that may be eaten, it may be eaten only by a person who is ceremonially clean. [20] Any priest who is ceremonially unclean but eats the thanksgiving offering anyway, shall be cut off from his people, for he has defiled what is sacred.[b] [21] Anyone who touches anything that is ceremonially unclean, whether it is uncleanness from man

or beast, and then eats the peace offering, shall be cut off from his people, for he has defiled what is holy."

[22] Then the Lord said to Moses, [23] "Tell the people of Israel never to eat fat, whether from oxen, sheep, or goats. [24] The fat of an animal that dies of disease, or is attacked and killed by wild animals, may be used for other purposes, but never eaten. [25] Anyone who eats fat from an offering sacrificed by fire to the Lord shall be outlawed from his people.

[26,27] "Never eat blood, whether of birds or animals. Anyone who does shall be excommunicated from his people."

[28] And the Lord said to Moses, [29] "Tell the people of Israel that anyone bringing a thanksgiving offering to the Lord must bring it personally with his own hands. [30] He shall bring the offering of the fat and breast, which is to be presented to the Lord by waving it before the altar. [31] Then the priest shall burn the fat upon the altar, but the breast shall belong to Aaron and his sons, [32,33] while the right thigh shall be given to the officiating priest. [34] For I have designated the breast and thigh as donations from the people of Israel to the sons of Aaron. Aaron and his sons must always be given this portion of the sacrifice. [35] This is their pay! It is to be set apart from the burnt offerings, and given to all who have been appointed to minister to the Lord as priests—to Aaron and to his sons. [36] For on the day the Lord anointed them, he commanded that the people of Israel give these portions to them; it is their right forever throughout all their generations."

[37] These were the instructions concerning the burnt offering, grain offering, sin offering, and guilt offering, and concerning the consecration offering and the peace offering; [38] these instructions were given to Moses by the Lord on Mount Sinai, to be passed on to the people of Israel so that they would know how to offer their sacrifices to God in the Sinai desert.

8 THE LORD SAID to Moses, "Now bring Aaron and his sons to the entrance of the Tabernacle, together with their gar-

---

a Literally, "unleavened loaves mingled with oil." b Literally, "it pertains unto Jehovah."

ments, the anointing oil, the young bull for the sin offering, the two rams, and the basket of bread made without yeast; and summon all Israel to a meeting there."

⁴ So all the people assembled, ⁵ and Moses said to them, "What I am now going to do has been commanded by Jehovah."

⁶ Then he took Aaron and his sons and washed them with water, ⁷ and he clothed Aaron with the special coat, sash, robe, and the ephod-jacket with its beautifully woven belt. ⁸ Then he put on him the chestpiece and deposited the Urim and the Thummimᵃ inside its pouch; ⁹ and placed on Aaron's head the turban with the sacred golden plate at its front—the holy crown —as the Lord had commanded Moses.

¹⁰ Then Moses took the anointing oil and sprinkled it upon the Tabernacle itself and on each item in it, sanctifying them. ¹¹ When he came to the altar he sprinkled it seven times, and also sprinkled the utensils of the altar and the washbasin and its pedestal, to sanctify them. ¹² Then he poured the anointing oil upon Aaron's head, thus setting him apart for his work. ¹³ Next Moses placed the robes on Aaron's sons, with the belts and caps, as the Lord had commanded him.

¹⁴ Then he took the young bull for the sin offering, and Aaron and his sons laid their hands upon its head ¹⁵,¹⁶ as Moses killed it. He smeared some of the blood with his finger upon the four horns of the altar, and upon the altar itself, to sanctify it, and poured out the rest of the blood at the base of the altar; thus he sanctified the altar, making atonement for it. He took all the fat covering the entrails, the fatty mass above the liver, and the two kidneys and their fat, and burned them all on the altar. ¹⁷ The carcass of the young bull, with its hide and dung, was burned outside the camp, as the Lord had commanded Moses.

¹⁸ Then he presented to the Lord the ram for the burnt offering. Aaron and his sons laid their hands upon its head, ¹⁹ and Moses killed it and sprinkled the blood back and forth upon the altar. ²⁰ Next he quartered the ram and burned the pieces, the head and

the fat. ²¹ He then washed the insides and the legs with water, and burned them upon the altar, so that the entire ram was consumed before the Lord; it was a burnt offering that pleased the Lord very much, for Jehovah's directions to Moses were followed in every detail.

²² Then Moses presented the other ram, the ram of consecration; Aaron and his sons laid their hands upon its head. ²³ Moses killed it and took some of its blood and smeared it upon the lobe of Aaron's right ear and the thumb of his right hand and upon the big toe of his right foot. ²⁴ Next he smeared some of the blood upon Aaron's sons—upon the lobes of their right ears, upon their right thumbs, and upon the big toes of their right feet. The rest of the blood he sprinkled back and forth upon the altar.ᵇ

²⁵ Then he took the fat, the tail, the fat upon the inner organs, the gall bladder, the two kidneys with their fat, and the right shoulder, ²⁶ and placed on top of these one unleavened wafer, one wafer spread with olive oil, and a slice of bread, all taken from the basket which had been placed there before the Lord. ²⁷ All this was placed in the hands of Aaron and his sons to present to the Lord by a gesture of waving them before the altar. ²⁸ Moses then took it all back from them and burned it upon the altar, along with the burnt offeringᶜ to the Lord; and Jehovah was pleased by the offering. ²⁹ Now Moses took the breast and presented it to the Lord by waving it before the altar; this was Moses' portion of the ram of consecration, just as the Lord had instructed him.

³⁰ Next he took some of the anointing oil and some of the blood that had been sprinkled upon the altar, and sprinkled it upon Aaron and upon his clothes and upon his sons and upon their clothes, thus consecrating to the Lord's use Aaron and his sons and their clothes.

³¹ Then Moses said to Aaron and his sons, "Boil the meat at the entrance of the Tabernacle, and eat it along with the bread that is in the basket of consecration, just as I instructed you to do. ³² Anything left of

a Apparently a kind of sacred lot used to determine the Lord's will by simple "Yes" or "No" alternatives.
b Literally, "Moses threw the blood upon the altar round about."   c Literally, "upon the burnt offering."

the meat and bread must be burned."

[33] Next he told them not to leave the Tabernacle entrance for seven days, after which time their consecration would be completed—for it takes seven days. [34] Then Moses stated again that all he had done that day had been commanded by the Lord in order to make atonement for them. [35] And again he warned Aaron and his sons to stay at the entrance of the Tabernacle day and night for seven days. "If you leave," he told them, "you will die—this is what the Lord has said."

[36] So Aaron and his sons did all that the Lord had commanded Moses.

9 ON THE EIGHTH day (of the consecration ceremonies), Moses summoned Aaron and Aaron's sons and the elders of Israel, [2] and told Aaron to take a bull calf from the herd for a sin offering, and a ram without bodily defect for a burnt offering, and to offer them before the Lord.

[3] "And tell the people of Israel," Moses instructed, "to select a male goat for their sin offering, also a yearling calf and a yearling lamb, all without bodily defect, for their burnt offering. [4] In addition, the people are to bring to the Lord a peace offering sacrifice—an ox and a ram, and a grain offering—flour mingled with olive oil. For today," Moses said, "Jehovah will appear to them."

[5] So they brought all these things to the entrance of the Tabernacle, as Moses had commanded, and the people came and stood there before the Lord.

[6] Moses told them, "When you have followed the Lord's instructions, his glory will appear to you."

[7] Moses then told Aaron to proceed to the altar and to offer the sin offering and the burnt offering, making atonement for himself first, and then for the people, as the Lord had commanded. [8] So Aaron went up to the altar and killed the calf as a sacrifice for his own sin; [9] his sons caught the blood for him, and he dipped his finger in it and smeared it upon the horns of the altar, and poured out the rest at the base of the altar. [10] Then he burned upon the altar the fat,

kidneys, and gall bladder from this sin offering, as the Lord had commanded Moses, [11] but he burned the meat and hide outside the camp.

[12] Next he killed the burnt offering animal, and his sons caught the blood and he sprinkled it back and forth upon the altar; [13] they brought the animal to him piece by piece, including the head, and he burned each part upon the altar. [14] Then he washed the insides and the legs, and offered these also upon the altar as a burnt offering.

[15] Next he sacrificed the people's offering; he killed the goat and offered it in just the same way as he had the sin offering for himself.[a] [16] Thus he sacrificed their burnt offering to the Lord, in accordance with the instructions God had given.

[17] Then he presented the grain offering, taking a handful and burning it upon the altar in addition to the regular morning offering.

[18] Next he killed the ox and ram—the people's peace offering sacrifice; and Aaron's sons brought the blood to him and he sprinkled it back and forth upon the altar. [19] Then he collected the fat of the ox and the ram—the fat from their tails and the fat covering the inner organs—and the kidneys and gall bladders. [20] The fat was placed upon the breasts of these animals, and Aaron burned it upon the altar; [21] but he waved the breasts and right shoulders slowly before the Lord as a gesture of offering it to him, just as Moses had commanded.

[22] Then, with hands spread out towards the people, Aaron blessed them and came down from the altar. [23] Moses and Aaron went into the Tabernacle, and when they came out again they blessed the people; and the glory of the Lord appeared to the whole assembly. [24] Then fire came from the Lord and consumed the burnt offering and fat on the altar; and when the people saw it, they all shouted and fell flat upon the ground before the Lord.

10 BUT NADAB AND Abihu, the sons of Aaron, placed unholy fire in their censers, laid incense on the fire, and offered

a See verses 8–11.

the incense before the Lord[a]—contrary to what the Lord had just commanded them! [2] So fire blazed forth from the presence of the Lord and destroyed them.

[3] Then Moses said to Aaron, "This is what the Lord meant when he said, 'I will show myself holy among those who approach me, and I will be glorified before all the people.'" And Aaron was speechless.

[4] Then Moses called for Misha-el and El-zaphon, Aaron's cousins, the sons of Uzziel, and told them, "Go and get the charred bodies from before the Tabernacle, and carry them outside the camp."

[5] So they went over and got them, and carried them out in their coats as Moses had told them to.

[6] Then Moses said to Aaron and his sons Eleazar and Ithamar, "Do not mourn—do not let your hair hang loose as a sign of your mourning, and do not tear your clothes. If you do, God will strike you dead too, and his wrath will come upon all the people of Israel. But the rest of the people of Israel may lament the death of Nadab and Abihu, and mourn because of the terrible fire the Lord has sent. [7] But you are not to leave the Tabernacle under penalty of death, for the anointing oil of Jehovah is upon you." And they did as Moses commanded.

[8,9] Now the Lord instructed Aaron, "Never drink wine or strong drink when you go into the Tabernacle, lest you die; and this rule applies to your sons and to all your descendants from generation to generation. [10] Your duties will be to arbitrate for the people, to teach them the difference between what is holy and what is ordinary, what is pure and what is impure; [11] and to teach them all the laws Jehovah has given through Moses."

[12] Then Moses said to Aaron and to his sons who were left, Eleazar and Ithamar, "Take the grain offering—the food that remains after the handful has been offered to the Lord by burning it on the altar—make sure there is no leaven in it, and eat it beside the altar. The offering is most holy; [13] therefore you must eat it in the sanctuary, in a holy place. It belongs to you and to your sons, from the offerings to Jehovah made by fire; for so I am commanded. [14] But the breast and the thigh, which have been offered to the Lord by the gesture of waving it before him, may be eaten in any holy place. It belongs to you and to your sons and daughters for your food. It is your portion of the peace offering sacrifices of the people of Israel.

[15] The people are to bring the thigh that was set aside, along with the breast that was offered when the fat was burned, and they shall be presented before the Lord by the gesture of waving them. And afterwards they shall belong to you and your family, for the Lord has commanded this."

[16] Then Moses searched everywhere for the goat of the sin offering and discovered that it had been burned! He was very angry about this with Eleazar and Ithamar, the remaining sons of Aaron.

[17] "Why haven't you eaten the sin offering in the sanctuary, since it is most holy, and God has given it to you to take away the iniquity and guilt of the people, to make atonement for them before the Lord?" he demanded. [18] "Since its blood was not taken inside the sanctuary, you should certainly have eaten it there, as I ordered you."

[19] But Aaron interceded with Moses. "They offered their sin offering and burnt offering before the Lord," he said, "but if I had eaten the sin offering on such a day as this, would it have pleased the Lord?" [20] And when Moses heard that, he was satisfied.

11 THEN THE LORD said to Moses and Aaron,

[2,3] "Tell the people of Israel that the animals which may be used for food include any animal with cloven hooves which chews its cud. [4-7] This means that the following may *not* be eaten:

The camel (it chews the cud but does not have cloven hooves);

The coney, or rock badger (because although it chews the cud, it does not have cloven hooves);

The hare (because although it chews the cud, it does not have cloven hooves);

---

a Or, "placed fire in their censers . . . and offered unholy fire . . ." Their fatal error is not clearly identified.

The swine (because although it has cloven hooves, it does not chew the cud).

⁸ You may not eat their meat or even touch their dead bodies; they are forbidden foods for you.

⁹ "As to fish, you may eat whatever has fins and scales, whether taken from rivers or from the sea; ¹⁰ but all other water creatures are strictly forbidden to you. ¹¹ You mustn't eat their meat or even touch their dead bodies. ¹² I'll repeat it again—any water creature that does not have fins or scales is forbidden to you.

¹³⁻¹⁹ "Among the birds, these are the ones you may *not* eat:

The eagle, the metire, the osprey,
The falcon (all kinds), the kite,
The raven (all kinds), the ostrich,
The nighthawk, the seagull,
The hawk (all kinds), the owl,
The cormorant, the ibis,
The marsh hen,
The pelican,
The vulture, the stork,
The heron (all kinds),
The hoopoe, the bat.

²⁰ "Flying insects with four legs must not be eaten, ²¹,²² with the exception of those that jump; locusts of all varieties—ordinary locusts, bald locusts, crickets, and grasshoppers—may be eaten. ²³ All other things that fly and have four feet are forbidden to you.

²⁴ "Anyone touching their dead bodies shall be defiled until the evening, ²⁵ and must wash his clothes immediately. He must also quarantine himself until nightfall, as being ceremonially defiled.

²⁶ "You are also defiled by touching any animal with only semi-parted hoofs, or any animal that does not chew the cud. ²⁷ Any animal that walks on paws is forbidden to you as food. Anyone touching the dead body of such an animal shall be defiled until evening. ²⁸ Anyone carrying away the carcass shall wash his clothes and be ceremonially defiled until evening; for it is forbidden to you.

²⁹,³⁰ "These are the forbidden small animals which scurry about your feet or crawl upon the ground:

The mole, the rat,

The great lizard, the gecko,
The mouse, the lizard,
The snail, the chameleon.

³¹ Anyone touching their dead bodies shall be defiled until evening, ³² and anything upon which the carcass falls shall be defiled—any article of wood, or of clothing, a rug, or a sack; anything it touches must be put into water, and is defiled until evening. After that it may be used again. ³³ If it falls into a pottery bowl, anything in the bowl is defiled, and you shall smash the bowl. ³⁴ If the water used to cleanse the defiled article touches any food, all of it is defiled. Any drink which is in the defiled bowl is also contaminated.

³⁵ "If the dead body of such an animal touches any clay oven, it is defiled and must be smashed. ³⁶ If the body falls into a spring or cistern where there is water, that water is not defiled; yet anyone who pulls out the carcass is defiled. ³⁷ And if the carcass touches grain to be sown in the field, it is not contaminated; ³⁸ but if the seeds are wet and the carcass falls upon it, the seed is defiled.

³⁹ "If an animal which you are permitted to eat dies of disease, anyone touching the carcass shall be defiled until evening. ⁴⁰ Also, anyone eating its meat or carrying away its carcass shall wash his clothes and be defiled until evening.

⁴¹,⁴² "Animals that crawl shall not be eaten. This includes all reptiles that slither along upon their bellies as well as those that have legs. No crawling thing with many feet may be eaten, for it is defiled. ⁴³ Do not defile yourselves by touching it.

⁴⁴ "I am the Lord your God. Keep yourselves pure concerning these things, and be holy, for I am holy; therefore do not defile yourselves by touching any of these things that crawl upon the earth. ⁴⁵ For I am the Lord who brought you out of the land of Egypt to be your God. You must therefore be holy, for I am holy." ⁴⁶ These are the laws concerning animals, birds, and whatever swims in the water or crawls upon the ground. ⁴⁷ These are the distinctions between what is ceremonially clean and may be eaten, and what is ceremonially defiled and may not be eaten, among all animal life upon the earth.

12 THE LORD TOLD Moses to give these instructions to the people of Israel:

[2] "When a baby boy is born, the mother shall be ceremonially defiled for seven days, and under the same restrictions as during her monthly periods. [3] On the eighth day, her son must be circumcised. [4] Then, for the next thirty-three days, while she is recovering from her ceremonial impurity, she must not touch anything sacred, nor enter the Tabernacle.

[5] "When a baby girl is born, the mother's ceremonial impurity shall last two weeks, during which time she will be under the same restrictions as during menstruation. Then for a further sixty-six days she shall continue her recovery.[a]

[6] "When these days of purification are ended (the following instructions are applicable whether her baby is a boy or girl), she must bring a yearling lamb as a burnt offering, and a young pigeon or a turtledove for a sin offering.

She must take them to the door of the Tabernacle to the priest; [7] and the priest will offer them before the Lord and make atonement for her; then she will be ceremonially clean again after her bleeding at childbirth.

"These then, are the procedures after childbirth. [8] But if she is too poor to bring a lamb, then she must bring two turtledoves or two young pigeons. One will be for a burnt offering and the other for a sin offering. The priest will make atonement for her with these, so that she will be ceremonially pure again."

13 THE LORD SAID to Moses and Aaron, "If anyone notices a swelling in his skin, or a scab or boil or pimple with transparent skin, leprosy is to be suspected. He must be brought to Aaron the priest or to one of his sons [3] for the spot to be examined. If the hair in this spot turns white, and if the spot looks to be more than skin-deep, it is leprosy, and the priest must declare him a leper.[a]

[4] "But if the white spot in the skin does not seem to be deeper than the skin, and the hair in the spot has not turned white, the priest shall quarantine him for seven days.

[5] At the end of that time, on the seventh day, the priest will examine him again, and if the spot has not changed and has not spread in the skin, then the priest must quarantine him seven days more. [6] Again on the seventh day the priest will examine him, and if the marks of the disease have become fainter and have not spread, then the priest shall pronounce him cured; it was only a scab, and the man need only wash his clothes and everything will be normal again. [7] But if the spot spreads in the skin after he has come to the priest to be examined, he must come back to the priest again, [8] and the priest shall look again, and if the spot has spread, then the priest must pronounce him a leper.

[9,10] "When anyone suspected of having leprosy is brought to the priest, the priest is to look to see if there is a white swelling in the skin with white hairs in the spot, and an ulcer developing. [11] If he finds these symptoms, it is an established case of leprosy, and the priest must pronounce him defiled. The man is not to be quarantined for further observation, for he is definitely diseased. [12] But if the priest sees that the leprosy has erupted and spread all over his body from head to foot wherever he looks, [13] then the priest shall pronounce him cured of leprosy, for it has all turned white; he is cured. [14,15] But if there is raw flesh anywhere, the man shall be declared a leper. It is proved by the raw flesh. [16,17] But if the raw flesh later changes to white, the leper will return to the priest to be examined again. If the spot has indeed turned completely white, then the priest will pronounce him cured.

[18] "In the case of a man who has a boil in his skin which heals, [19] but which leaves a white swelling or a bright spot, sort of reddish white, the man must go to the priest for examination. [20] If the priest sees that the trouble seems to be down under the skin, and if the hair at the spot has turned white, then the priest shall declare him defiled, for leprosy has broken out from the boil. [21] But if the priest sees that there are no white hairs in this spot, and the spot does not appear to be deeper than the skin, and if the

---

a Literally, "shall continue in her blood of purification."   13a Literally, "shall declare him unclean."

color is gray, then the priest shall quarantine him for seven days. ²² If during that time the spot spreads, the priest must declare him a leper. ²³ But if the bright spot grows no larger and does not spread, it is merely the scar from the boil, and the priest shall declare that all is well.

²⁴ "If a man is burned in some way, and the burned place becomes bright reddish-white or white, ²⁵ then the priest must examine the spot. If the hair in the bright spot turns white, and the problem seems to be more than skin-deep, it is leprosy that has broken out from the burn, and the priest must pronounce him a leper.ᵇ ²⁶ But if the priest sees that there are no white hairs in the bright spot, and the brightness appears to be no deeper than the skin and is fading, the priest shall quarantine him for seven days, ²⁷ and examine him again the seventh day. If the spot spreads in the skin, the priest must pronounce him a leper.ᵇ ²⁸ But if the bright spot does not move or spread in the skin, and is fading, it is simply a scar from the burn, and the priest shall declare that he does not have leprosy.

²⁹,³⁰ "If a man or woman has a sore on the head or chin, the priest must examine him; if the infection seems to be below the skin and yellow hair is found in the sore, the priest must pronounce him a leper. ³¹ But if the priest's examination reveals that the spot seems to be only in the skin and that there is black hair in it, then he shall be quarantined for seven days, ³² and examined again on the seventh day. If the spot has not spread and no yellow hair has appeared, and if the infection does not seem to be deeper than the skin, ³³ he shall shave off all the hair around the spot (but not on the spot itself) and the priest shall quarantine him for another seven days. ³⁴ He shall be examined again on the seventh day, and if the spot has not spread, and it appears to be no deeper than the skin, the priest shall pronounce him well, and after washing his clothes, he is free.ᶜ ³⁵ But if, later on, this spot begins to spread, ³⁶ then the priest must examine him again and, without waiting to see if any yellow hair develops, declare him

a leper. ³⁷ But if it appears that the spreading has stopped and black hairs are found in the spot, then he is healed and is not a leper, and the priest shall declare him healed.

³⁸ "If a man or a woman has white, transparent areas in the skin, ³⁹ but these spots are growing dimmer, this is not leprosy, but an ordinary infection that has broken out in the skin.

⁴⁰ "If a man's hair is gone, this does not make him a leper even though he is bald! ⁴¹ If the hair is gone from the front part of his head, he simply has a bald forehead, but this is not leprosy. ⁴² However, if in the baldness there is a reddish white spot, it may be leprosy breaking out. ⁴³ In that case the priest shall examine him, and if there is a reddish white lump that looks like leprosy, ⁴⁴ then he is a leper, and the priest must pronounce him such.

⁴⁵ "Anyone who is discovered to have leprosy must tear his clothes and let his hair grow in wild disarray, and cover his upper lip and call out as he goes, "I am a leper, I am a leper."ᵈ ⁴⁶ As long as the disease lasts, he is defiled and must live outside the camp.

⁴⁷,⁴⁸ "If leprosy is suspected in a woolen or linen garment or fabric, or in a piece of leather or leather-work, ⁴⁹ and there is a greenish or a reddish spot in it, it is probably leprosy, and must be taken to the priest to be examined. ⁵⁰ The priest will put it away for seven days ⁵¹ and look at it again on the seventh day. If the spot has spread, it is a contagious leprosy, ⁵² and he must burn the clothing, fabric, linen or woolen covering, or leather article, for it is contagious and must be destroyed by fire.

⁵³ "But if when he examines it again on the seventh day the spot has not spread, ⁵⁴ the priest shall order the suspected article to be washed, then isolated for seven more days. ⁵⁵ If after that time the spot has not changed its color, even though it has not spread, it is leprosy and shall be burned, for the article is infected through and through.ᵉ ⁵⁶ But if the priest sees that the spot has faded after the washing, then he

---

b Literally, "pronounce him unclean."   c Literally, "he is clean."   d Literally, "Unclean, unclean."
e Literally, "whether the bareness be within or without" or, "whether it be bald in the head thereof or in the forehead thereof."

shall cut it out from the garment or leather goods or whatever it is in. [57] However, if it then reappears, it is leprosy and he must burn it. [58] But if after washing it there is no further trouble, it can be put back into service after another washing."

[59] These are the regulations concerning leprosy in a garment or anything made of skin or leather, indicating whether to pronounce it leprous or not.

14 AND THE LORD gave Moses these regulations concerning a person whose leprosy disappears:

[3] "The priest shall go out of the camp to examine him. If the priest sees that the leprosy is gone, [4] he shall require two living birds of a kind permitted for food, and shall take some cedar wood, a scarlet string, and some hyssop branches, to be used for the purification ceremony of the one who is healed. [5] The priest shall then order one of the birds killed in an earthenware pot held above running water. [6] The other bird, still living, shall be dipped in the blood, along with the cedar wood, the scarlet thread, and the hyssop branch. [7] Then the priest shall sprinkle the blood seven times upon the man cured of his leprosy, and the priest shall pronounce him cured, and shall let the living bird fly into the open field.

[8] "Then the man who is cured shall wash his clothes, shave off all his hair, and bathe himself, and return to live inside the camp; however, he must stay outside his tent for seven days. [9] The seventh day he shall again shave all the hair from his head, beard, and eyebrows, and wash his clothes and bathe, and shall then be declared fully cured of his leprosy.

[10] "The next day, the eighth day, he shall take two male lambs without physical defect, one yearling ewe-lamb without physical defect, ten quarts of finely ground flour mixed with olive oil, and a pint of olive oil; [11] then the priest who examines him shall place the man and his offerings before the Lord at the entrance of the Tabernacle. [12] The priest shall take one of the lambs and the pint of olive oil and offer them to the Lord as a guilt offering by the gesture of waving them before the altar. [13] Then he shall kill the lamb at the place where sin offerings and burnt offerings are killed, there at the Tabernacle; this guilt offering shall then be given to the priest for food, as in the case of a sin offering. It is a most holy offering. [14] The priest shall take the blood from this guilt offering and smear some of it upon the tip of the right ear of the man being cleansed, and upon the thumb of his right hand, and upon the big toe of his right foot.

[15] "Then the priest shall take the olive oil and pour it into the palm of his left hand, [16] and dip his right finger into it, and sprinkle it with his finger seven times before the Lord. [17] Some of the oil remaining in his left hand shall then be placed by the priest upon the tip of the man's right ear and the thumb of his right hand and the big toe of his right foot—just as he did with the blood of the guilt offering. [18] The remainder of the oil in his hand shall be used to anoint the man's head. Thus the priest shall make atonement for him before the Lord.

[19] "Then the priest must offer the sin offering and again[a] perform the rite of atonement for the person being cleansed from his leprosy; and afterwards the priest shall kill the burnt offering, [20] and offer it along with the grain offering upon the altar, making atonement for the man, who shall then be pronounced finally cleansed.

[21] "If he is so poor that he cannot afford two lambs, then he shall bring only one, a male lamb for the guilt offering, to be presented to the Lord in the rite of atonement by waving it before the altar; and only three quarts of fine white flour, mixed with olive oil, for a grain offering, and a pint of olive oil. [22] "He shall also bring two turtledoves or two young pigeons—whichever he is able to afford—and use one of the pair for a sin offering and the other for a burnt offering. [23] He shall bring them to the priest at the entrance of the Tabernacle on the eighth day, for his ceremony of cleansing before the Lord. [24] The priest shall take the lamb for the guilt offering, and the pint of oil, and wave them before the altar as a gesture of

---

a Implied.

102

offering to the Lord. ²⁵ Then he shall kill the lamb for the guilt offering and smear some of its blood upon the tip of the man's right ear—the man on whose behalf the ceremony is being performed—and upon the thumb of his right hand and on the big toe of his right foot.

²⁶ "The priest shall then pour the olive oil into the palm of his own left hand, ²⁷ and with his right finger he is to sprinkle some of it seven times before the Lord. ²⁸ Then he must put some of the olive oil from his hand upon the tip of the man's right ear, and upon the thumb of his right hand, and upon the big toe of his right foot, just as he did with the blood of the guilt offering. ²⁹ The remaining oil in his hand shall be placed upon the head of the man being cleansed, to make atonement for him before the Lord.

³⁰ "Then he must offer the two turtledoves or two young pigeons (whichever pair he is able to afford). ³¹ One of the pair is for a sin offering and the other for a burnt offering, to be sacrificed along with the grain offering; and the priest shall make atonement for the man before the Lord."

³² These, then, are the laws concerning those who are cleansed of leprosy but are not able to bring the sacrifices normally required for the ceremony of cleansing.

³³,³⁴ Then the Lord said to Moses and Aaron, "When you arrive in the land of Canaan which I have given you, and I place leprosy in some house there, ³⁵ then the owner of the house shall come and report to the priest, 'It seems to me that there may be leprosy in my house!'

³⁶ "The priest shall order the house to be emptied before he examines it, so that everything in the house will not be declared contaminated if he decides that there is leprosy there. ³⁷ If he finds greenish or reddish streaks in the walls of the house which seem to be beneath the surface of the wall, ³⁸ he shall close up the house for seven days, ³⁹ and return the seventh day to look at it again. If the spots have spread in the wall, ⁴⁰ then the priest shall order the removal of the spotted section of wall, and the material must be thrown into a defiled place outside the city. ⁴¹ Then he shall order the inside

walls of the house scraped thoroughly, and the scrapings dumped in a defiled place outside the city. ⁴² Other stones shall be brought to replace those that have been removed, new mortar used, and the house replastered.

⁴³ "But if the spots appear again, ⁴⁴ the priest shall come again and look, and if he sees that the spots have spread, it is leprosy, and the house is defiled. ⁴⁵ Then he shall order the destruction of the house—all its stones, timbers, and mortar shall be carried out of the city to a defiled place. ⁴⁶ Anyone entering the house while it is closed shall be defiled until evening. ⁴⁷ Anyone who lies down or eats in the house shall wash his clothing.

⁴⁸ "But if, when the priest comes again to look, the spots have not reappeared after the fresh plastering, then he will pronounce the house cleansed, and declare the leprosy gone. ⁴⁹ He shall also perform the ceremony of cleansing, using two birds, cedar wood, scarlet thread, and hyssop branches. ⁵⁰ He shall kill one of the birds over fresh water in an earthenware bowl, ⁵¹,⁵² and dip the cedar wood, hyssop branch, and scarlet thread, as well as the living bird, into the blood of the bird that was killed over the fresh water, and shall sprinkle the house seven times. In this way the house shall be cleansed. ⁵³ Then he shall let the live bird fly away into an open field outside the city. This is the method for making atonement for the house and cleansing it."

⁵⁴ These, then, are the laws concerning the various places where leprosy may appear: ⁵⁵ in a garment or in a house, ⁵⁶ or in any swelling in one's skin, or a scab from a burn, or a bright spot. ⁵⁷ In this way you will know whether or not it is actually leprosy. That is why these laws are given.

15 THE LORD TOLD Moses and Aaron to give the people of Israel these further instructions:

"Any man who has a genital discharge* is ceremonially defiled. ³ This applies not only while the discharge is active, but also for a time after it heals. ⁴ Any bed he lies on and anything he sits on is contaminated;

---

a Literally, "an issue out of his flesh."

[5] so anyone touching the man's bed is ceremonially defiled until evening, and must wash his clothes and bathe himself. [6] Anyone sitting on a seat the man has sat upon while defiled is himself ceremonially unclean until evening, and must wash his clothes and bathe himself. [7] The same instructions apply to anyone touching him. [8] Anyone he spits on is ceremonially unclean until evening, and must wash his clothes and bathe himself. [9] Any saddle he rides on is defiled. [10] Anyone touching or carrying anything else that was beneath him shall be defiled until evening, and must wash his clothes and bathe himself. [11] If the defiled man touches anyone without first rinsing his hands, that person must wash his clothes and bathe himself and be defiled until evening. [12] Any earthen pot touched by the defiled man must be broken, and every wooden utensil must be rinsed in water.

[13] "When the discharge stops, he shall begin a seven-day cleansing ceremony by washing his clothes and bathing in running water. [14] On the eighth day he shall take two turtledoves or two young pigeons and come before the Lord at the entrance of the Tabernacle, and give them to the priest. [15] The priest shall sacrifice them there, one for a sin offering and the other for a burnt offering; thus the priest shall make atonement before the Lord for the man because of his discharge.

[16] "Whenever a man's semen goes out from him, he shall take a complete bath and be unclean until the evening. [17] Any clothing or bedding the semen spills on must be washed and remain ceremonially defiled until evening. [18] After sexual intercourse, the woman as well as the man must bathe, and they are ceremonially defiled until the next evening.

[19] "Whenever a woman menstruates, she shall be in a state of ceremonial defilement for seven days afterwards, and during that time anyone touching her shall be defiled until evening. [20] Anything she lies on or sits on during that time shall be defiled. [21,22,23] Anyone touching her bed or anything she sits upon shall wash his clothes and bathe himself and be ceremonially defiled until evening. [24] A man having sexual intercourse with her during this time is ceremonially defiled for seven days, and every bed he lies upon shall be defiled.

[25] "If the menstrual flow continues after the normal time, or at some irregular time during the month, the same rules apply as indicated above, [26] so that anything she lies upon during that time is defiled, just as it would be during her normal menstrual period, and everything she sits on is in a similar state of defilement. [27] Anyone touching her bed or anything she sits on shall be defiled, and shall wash his clothes and bathe and be defiled until evening. [28] Seven days after the menstruating stops, she is no longer ceremonially defiled.

[29] "On the eighth day, she shall take two turtledoves or two young pigeons and bring them to the priest at the entrance of the Tabernacle, [30] and the priest shall offer one for a sin offering and the other for a burnt offering, and make atonement for her before the Lord, for her menstrual defilement. [31] In this way you shall cleanse the people of Israel from their defilement, lest they die because of defiling my Tabernacle that is among them."

[32] This, then, is the law for the man who is defiled by a genital disease[b] or by a seminal emission; [33] and for a woman's menstrual period; and for anyone who has sexual intercourse with her while she is in her period of defilement afterwards.

16 AFTER AARON'S TWO sons died before the Lord, the Lord said to Moses, "Warn your brother Aaron not to enter into the Holy Place behind the veil, where the Ark and the place of mercy are, just whenever he chooses. The penalty for intrusion is death. For I myself am present in the cloud above the place of mercy.

[3] "Here are the conditions for his entering there: He must bring a young bull for a sin offering, and a ram for a burnt offering. [4] He must bathe himself and put on the sacred linen coat, shorts, belt, and turban. [5] The people of Israel shall then bring him two male goats for their sin offering, and a ram for their burnt offering. [6] First he shall

---

b Literally, "has an issue."

present to the Lord the young bull as a sin offering for himself, making atonement for himself and his family. [7] Then he shall bring the two goats before the Lord at the entrance of the Tabernacle, [8] and cast lots to determine which is the Lord's and which is to be sent away.[a] [9] The goat allotted to the Lord shall then be sacrificed by Aaron as a sin offering. [10] The other goat shall be kept alive and placed before the Lord. The rite of atonement shall be performed over it, and it shall then be sent out into the desert as a scapegoat.[a]

[11] "After Aaron has sacrificed the young bull as a sin offering for himself and his family, [12] he shall take a censer full of live coals from the altar of the Lord, and fill his hands with sweet incense beaten into fine powder, and bring it inside the veil. [13] There before the Lord he shall put the incense upon the coals, so that a cloud of incense will cover the mercy place above the Ark (containing the stone tablets of the Ten Commandments); thus he will not die. [14] And he shall bring some of the blood of the young bull and sprinkle it with his finger upon the east side of the mercy place, and then seven times in front of it.

[15] "Then he must go out[b] and sacrifice the people's sin offering goat, and bring its blood within the veil, and sprinkle it upon the place of mercy and in front of it, just as he did with the blood of the young bull. [16] Thus he shall make atonement for the holy place because it is defiled by the sins of the people of Israel, and for the Tabernacle, located right among them and surrounded by their defilement. [17] Not another soul shall be inside the Tabernacle when Aaron enters to make atonement in the Holy Place—not until after he comes out again and has made atonement for himself and his household and for all the people of Israel. [18] Then he shall go out to the altar before the Lord and make atonement for it. He must smear the blood of the young bull and the goat on the horns of the altar, [19] and sprinkle blood upon the altar seven times with his finger, thus cleansing it from the sinfulness of Israel, and making it holy.[c]

[20] "When he has completed the rite of atonement for the Holy Place, the entire Tabernacle, and the altar, he shall bring the live goat and, [21] laying both hands upon its head, confess over it all the sins of the people of Israel. He shall lay all their sins upon the head of the goat and send it into the desert, led by a man appointed for the task. [22] So the goat shall carry all the sins of the people into a land where no one lives,[d] and the man shall let it loose in the wilderness.

[23] "Then Aaron shall go into the Tabernacle again and take off the linen garments he wore when he went behind the veil, and leave them there in the Tabernacle. [24] Then he shall bathe in a sacred place, put on his clothes again, and go out and sacrifice his own burnt offering and the burnt offering for the people, making atonement for himself and for them. [25] He shall also burn upon the altar the fat for the sin offering.

[26] "(The man who took the goat out into the desert[a] shall afterwards wash his clothes and bathe himself and then come back into the camp.) [27] And the young bull and the goat used for the sin offering (their blood was taken into the Holy Place by Aaron, to make atonement) shall be carried outside the camp and burned, including the hides and internal organs. [28] Afterwards, the person doing the burning shall wash his clothes and bathe himself and then return to camp.

[29,30] "This is a permanent law: You must do no work on the twenty-fifth day of September[e], but must spend the day in self-examination and humility. This applies whether you are born in the land or are a foreigner living among the people of Israel; for this is the day commemorating the atonement, cleansing you in the Lord's eyes from all of your sins. [31] It is a Sabbath of solemn rest for you, and you shall spend the day in quiet humility;[f] this is a permanent law. [32] This ceremony, in later generations, shall be performed by the anointed High Priest, consecrated in place of his ancestor Aaron; he shall be the one to put on the holy linen garments, [33] and make atonement for the holy sanctuary, the Tabernacle, the altar, the priests, and the people. [34] This shall

a Literally, "for Azazel" or "for removal."   b Implied.   c Literally, "hallowing it."
d Literally, "a solitary land."   e Literally, "on the tenth day of the seventh month" of the Hebrew calendar.
f Or, "in fasting."

105

be an everlasting law for you, to make atonement for the people of Israel once each year, because of their sins."

[35] And Aaron followed all these instructions that the Lord gave to Moses.

17 THE LORD GAVE to Moses these additional instructions for Aaron and the priests and for all the people of Israel:

[3,4] "Any Israelite who sacrifices[a] an ox, lamb, or goat anywhere except at the Tabernacle is guilty of murder and shall be excommunicated from his nation. [5] The purpose of this law is to stop the people of Israel from sacrificing in the open fields, and to cause them to bring their sacrifices to the priest at the entrance of the Tabernacle, and to burn the fat as a savor the Lord will appreciate and enjoy— [6] for in this way the priest will be able to sprinkle the blood upon the altar of the Lord at the entrance of the Tabernacle, and to burn the fat as a savor the Lord will appreciate and enjoy— [7] instead of the people's sacrificing to evil spirits[b] out in the fields. This shall be a permanent law for you, from generation to generation. [8,9] I repeat: Anyone, whether an Israelite or a foreigner living among you who offers a burnt offering or a sacrifice anywhere other than at the entrance of the Tabernacle, where it will be sacrificed to the Lord, shall be excommunicated.

[10] "And I will turn my face against anyone, whether an Israelite or a foreigner living among you, who eats blood in any form. I will excommunicate him from his people. [11] For the life of the flesh is in the blood, and I have given you the blood to sprinkle upon the altar as an atonement for your souls; it is the blood that makes atonement, because it is the life.[c] [12] That is the reasoning behind my decree to the people of Israel, that neither they, nor any foreigner living among them, may eat blood. [13] Anyone, whether an Israelite or a foreigner living among you, who goes hunting and kills an animal or bird of a kind permitted for food, must pour out the blood and cover it with dust, [14] for the blood is the life. That is why I told the people of Israel never to eat it, for the life of every bird and animal[d] is its blood. Therefore, anyone who eats blood must be excommunicated.

[15] "And anyone—native born or foreigner—who eats the dead body of an animal that dies of itself, or is torn by wild animals, must wash his clothes and bathe himself and be defiled until evening; after that he shall be declared cleansed. [16] But if he does not wash his clothes and bathe, he shall suffer the consequence."

18 THE LORD THEN told Moses to tell the people of Israel,

"I am Jehovah your God, [3] so don't act like heathen—like the people of Egypt where you lived so long, or the people of Canaan where I am going to take you. [4,5] You must obey only my laws, and you must carry them out in detail, for I am the Lord your God. If you obey them you shall live.[a] I am the Lord.

[6] "None of you shall marry[b] a near relative, for I am the Lord. [7] A girl may not marry her father; nor a son his mother, [8] nor any other of his father's wives, [9] nor his sister or half-sister, whether the daughter of his father or his mother, whether born in the same house or elsewhere.

[10] "You shall not marry your granddaughter—the daughter of either your son or your daughter—for she is a close relative.[c] [11] You may not marry a half-sister —your father's wife's daughter; [12] nor your aunt—your father's sister—because she is so closely related to your father; [13] nor your aunt—your mother's sister—because she is a close relative of your mother; [14] nor your aunt—the wife of your father's brother.[d]

[15] "You may not marry your daughter-in-law—your son's wife; [16] nor your brother's wife, for she is your brother's.[e] [17] You may not marry both a woman and her daughter or granddaughter, for they are

---

a Literally, "slaughters."   b Literally, "hairy ones."   c Implied.   d Literally, "every creature."
18a Literally, "shall live in them" or "shall live by them."   b Literally, "uncover the nakedness of," that is, "have sexual intercourse with."   c Literally, "for theirs is your own nakedness."   d This prohibition applied not only while her husband lived, but also after his death.   e Except when the brother died and left no heir, in which case his wife was left to a brother to beget children from her to carry on the name and inheritance of the deceased. See Deuteronomy 25:5.

near relatives, and to do so is horrible wickedness. ¹⁸ You shall not marry two sisters, for they will be rivals. However, if your wife dies, then it is all right to marry her sister.

¹⁹ "There must be no sexual relationship with a woman who is menstruating; ²⁰ nor with anyone else's wife, to defile yourself with her.

²¹ "You shall not give any of your children to Molech, burning them upon his altar; never profane the name of your God, for I am Jehovah.

²² "Homosexuality is absolutely forbidden, for it is an enormous sin. ²³ A man shall have no sexual intercourse with any female animal, thus defiling himself; and a woman must never give herself to a male animal, to mate with it; this is a terrible perversion.

²⁴ "Do not defile yourselves in any of these ways, for these are the things the heathen do; and because they do them I am going to cast them out from the land into which you are going. ²⁵ That entire country is defiled with this kind of activity; that is why I am punishing the people living there, and will throw them out of the land.^f ²⁶ You must strictly obey all of my laws and ordinances, and you must not do any of these abominable things; these laws apply both to you who are born in the nation of Israel and to foreigners living among you.

²⁷ "Yes, all these abominations have been done continually by the people of the land where I am taking you, and the land is defiled. ²⁸ Do not do these things or I will throw you out of the land, just as I will throw out^g the nations that live there now. ^{29,30} Whoever does any of these terrible deeds shall be excommunicated from this nation. So be very sure to obey my laws, and do not practice any of these horrible customs. Do not defile yourselves with the evil deeds of those living in the land where you are going. For I am Jehovah your God."

19 THE LORD ALSO told Moses to tell the people of Israel, "You must be holy because I, the Lord your God, am holy. You must respect your mothers and fathers,

and obey my Sabbath law, for I am the Lord your God. ^{3,4} Do not make or worship idols, for I am Jehovah your God.

⁵ "When you sacrifice a peace offering to the Lord, offer it correctly so that it will be accepted: ⁶ Eat it the same day you offer it, or the next day at the latest; any remaining until the third day must be burned. ⁷ For any of it eaten on the third day is repulsive to me, and will not be accepted. ⁸ If you eat it on the third day you are guilty, for you profane the holiness of Jehovah, and you shall be excommunicated from Jehovah's people.

⁹ "When you harvest your crops, don't reap the corners of your fields, and don't pick up stray grains of wheat from the ground. ¹⁰ It is the same with your grape crop—don't strip every last piece of fruit from the vines, and don't pick up the grapes that fall to the ground. Leave them for the poor and for those traveling through, for I am Jehovah your God.

¹¹ "You must not steal nor lie nor defraud. ¹² You must not swear to a falsehood, thus bringing reproach upon the name of your God, for I am Jehovah.

¹³ "You shall not rob nor oppress anyone, and you shall pay your hired workers promptly. If something is due them, don't even keep it overnight.

¹⁴ "You must not curse the deaf nor trip up a blind man as he walks. Fear your God; I am Jehovah!

¹⁵ "Judges must always be just in their sentences, not noticing whether a person is poor or rich; they must always be perfectly fair.

¹⁶ "Don't gossip. Don't falsely accuse your neighbor of some crime,^a for I am Jehovah.

¹⁷ "Don't hate your brother. Rebuke anyone who sins; don't let him get away with it, or you will be equally guilty. ¹⁸ Don't seek vengeance. Don't bear a grudge; but love your neighbor as yourself, for I am Jehovah.

¹⁹ "Obey my laws: Do not mate your cattle with a different kind; don't sow your field with two kinds of seed; don't wear clothes

---

f Literally, "the land vomits out her inhabitants." as it vomited out . . ."　　**19a** Literally, "neither shall you stand against the blood of your neighbor."

g Literally, "that the land vomit not you out also . . .

made of half wool and half linen.

²⁰ "If a man seduces a slave[b] girl who is engaged to be married, they shall be tried in a court but not put to death, because she is not free. ²¹ The man involved shall bring his guilt offering to the Lord at the entrance of the Tabernacle; the offering shall be a ram. ²² The priest shall make atonement with the ram for the sin the man has committed, and it shall be forgiven him.

²³ "When you enter the land and have planted all kinds of fruit trees, do not eat the first three crops, for they are considered ceremonially defiled.[c] ²⁴ And the fourth year the entire crop shall be devoted to the Lord, and shall be given to the Lord in praise to him. ²⁵ Finally, in the fifth year, the crop is yours.

²⁶ "I am Jehovah your God! You must not eat meat with undrained blood; nor use fortune telling or witchcraft.

²⁷ "You must not trim off your hair on your temples or clip the edges of your beard, as the heathen do.[d] ²⁸ You shall not cut yourselves nor put tattoo marks upon yourselves in connection with funeral rites; I am the Lord.

²⁹ "Do not violate your daughter's sanctity by making her a prostitute, lest the land become full of enormous wickedness.

³⁰ "Keep my Sabbath laws and reverence my Tabernacle, for I am the Lord.

³¹ "Do not defile yourselves by consulting mediums and wizards, for I am Jehovah your God.

³² "You shall give due honor and respect to the elderly, in the fear of God. I am Jehovah.

³³ "Do not take advantage of foreigners in your land; do not wrong them. ³⁴ They must be treated like any other citizen; love them as yourself, for remember that you too were foreigners in the land of Egypt. I am Jehovah your God.

³⁵,³⁶ "You must be impartial in judgment. Use accurate measurements—lengths, weights, and volumes—and give full measure, for I am Jehovah your God who brought you from the land of Egypt. ³⁷ You must heed all of my commandments and ordinances, carefully obeying them, for I am Jehovah."

20 THE LORD GAVE Moses these further instructions for the people of Israel: "Anyone—whether an Israelite or a foreigner living among you—who sacrifices his child as a burnt offering to Molech shall without fail be stoned by his peers. ³ And I myself will turn against that man and cut him off from all his people, because he has given his child to Molech, thus making my Tabernacle[a] unfit for me to live in, and insulting my holy name. ⁴ And if the people of the land pretend they do not know what the man has done, and refuse to put him to death, ⁵ then I myself will set my face against that man and his family and cut him off, along with all others who turn to other gods than me.

⁶ "I will set my face against anyone who consults mediums and wizards instead of me and I will cut that person off from his people. ⁷ So sanctify yourselves and be holy, for I am the Lord your God. ⁸ You must obey all of my commandments, for I am the Lord who sanctifies you.

⁹ "Anyone who curses his father or mother shall surely be put to death—for he has cursed his own flesh and blood.

¹⁰ "If a man commits adultery with another man's wife, both the man and woman shall be put to death. ¹¹ If a man sleeps with his father's wife, he has defiled what is his father's; both the man and the woman must die, for it is their own fault. ¹² And if a man has sexual intercourse with his daughter-in-law, both shall be executed: they have brought it upon themselves by defiling each other. ¹³ The penalty for homosexual acts is death to both parties. They have brought it upon themselves. ¹⁴ If a man has sexual intercourse with a woman and with her mother, it is a great evil. All three shall be burned alive to wipe out wickedness from among you.

¹⁵ "If a man has sexual intercourse with an animal, he shall be executed and the animal killed. ¹⁶ If a woman has sexual intercourse with an animal, kill the woman and

---

b Literally, "not yet redeemed, nor given her freedom."   c Literally, "you shall count the fruit thereof as their uncircumcision."   d Implied.   20a Literally, "my sanctuary . . ."

the animal, for they deserve their punishment.[b]

[17] "If a man has sexual intercourse with his sister, whether the daughter of his father or of his mother, it is a shameful thing, and they shall publicly be cut off from the people of Israel. He shall bear his guilt. [18] If a man has sexual intercourse with a woman during her period of menstruation, both shall be excommunicated, for he has uncovered her uncleanness.

[19] "Sexual intercourse is outlawed between a man and his maiden aunt—whether the sister of his mother or of his father—for they are near of kin; they shall bear their guilt. [20] If a man has intercourse with his uncle's widow,[c] he has taken what belongs to his uncle; their punishment is that they shall bear their sin and die childless. [21] If a man marries his brother's widow,[d] this is impurity; for he has taken what belongs to his brother, and they shall be childless.

[22] "You must obey all of my laws and ordinances so that I will not throw you out of your new land.[e] [23] You must not follow the customs of the nations I cast out before you, for they do all these things I have warned you against; that is the reason I abhor them. [24] I have promised you their land; I will give it to you to possess it. It is a land 'flowing with milk and honey.' I am the Lord your God who has made a distinction between you and the people of other nations.

[25] "You shall therefore make a distinction between the birds and animals I have given you permission to eat and those you may not eat. You shall not contaminate yourselves and make yourselves hateful to me by eating any animal or bird which I have forbidden, though the land teem with them. [26] You shall be holy to me, for I the Lord am holy, and I have set you apart from all other peoples, to be mine.

[27] "A medium or a wizard—whether man or woman—shall surely be stoned to death. They have caused their own doom."

21 THE LORD SAID to Moses: "Tell the priests never to defile themselves by touching a dead person, [2,3] unless it is a near relative—a mother, father, son, daughter, brother, or unmarried[a] sister for whom he has special responsibility since she has no husband. [4] For the priest is a leader among his people and he may not ceremonially defile himself as an ordinary person can.

[5] "The priests shall not clip bald spots in their hair or beards, nor cut their flesh. [6] They shall be holy unto their God, and shall not dishonor and profane his name; otherwise they will be unfit to make food offerings by fire to the Lord their God. [7] A priest shall not marry a prostitute, nor a woman of another tribe, and he shall not marry a divorced woman, for he is a holy man of God. [8] The priest is set apart to offer the sacrifices of your God; he is holy, for I, the Lord who sanctifies you, am holy. [9] The daughter of any priest who becomes a prostitute, thus violating her father's holiness as well as her own, shall be burned alive.

[10] "The High Priest—anointed with the special anointing oil and wearing the special garments—must not let his hair hang loose in mourning, nor tear his clothing, [11] nor be in the presence of any dead person—not even his father or mother.[b] [12] He shall not leave the sanctuary [when on duty[c]], nor treat my Tabernacle like an ordinary house, for the consecration of the anointing oil of his God is upon him; I am Jehovah. [13] He must marry a virgin. [14,15] He may not marry a widow, nor a woman who is divorced, nor a prostitute. She must be a virgin from his own tribe, for he must not be the father of children of mixed blood—half priestly and half ordinary."[d]

[16,17] And the Lord said to Moses, "Tell Aaron that any of his descendants from generation to generation who have any bodily defect may not offer the sacrifices to God. [18] For instance, if a man is blind or lame, or has a broken nose or any extra fingers or toes, [19] or has a broken foot or hand, [20] or has a humped back, or is a dwarf,

---

b Literally, "their blood shall be upon them."   c Literally, "his uncle's wife."   d Literally, "his brother's wife." However such a marriage was required if she had no children. See Deuteronomy 25:5.
e Literally, "that the land I give you will not vomit you out again."   21a Literally, "a virgin."
b Note that this rule applied to the High Priest, while the contrary instructions in verse 1 applied to ordinary priests.   c Implied.   d Literally, "he must not profane his offspring among his people."

or has a defect in his eye, or has pimples or scabby skin, or has imperfect testicles— [21] although he is a descendant of Aaron—he is not permitted to offer the fire sacrifices to the Lord because of his physical defect. [22] However, he shall be fed with the food of the priests from the offerings sacrificed to God, both from the holy and most holy offerings. [23] But he shall not go in behind the veil, nor come near the altar, because of the physical defect; this would defile my sanctuary, for it is Jehovah who sanctifies it."

[24] So Moses gave these instructions to Aaron and his sons and to all the people of Israel.

22 THE LORD TOLD Moses, "Instruct Aaron and his sons to be very careful not to defile my holy name by desecrating the people's sacred gifts; for I am Jehovah. [3] From now on and forever, if a priest who is ceremonially defiled sacrifices the animals brought by the people or handles the gifts dedicated to Jehovah, he shall be discharged from the priesthood. For I am Jehovah!

[4] "No priest who is a leper or who has a running sore may eat the holy sacrifices until healed. And any priest who touches a dead person, or who is defiled by a seminal emission, [5] or who touches any reptile or other forbidden thing, or who touches anyone who is ceremonially defiled for any reason— [6] that priest shall be defiled until evening, and shall not eat of the holy sacrifices until after he has bathed that evening. [7] When the sun is down, then he shall be purified again and may eat the holy food, for it is his source of life. [8] He may not eat any animal that dies of itself or is torn by wild animals, for this will defile him. I am Jehovah. [9] Warn the priests to follow these instructions carefully, lest they be declared guilty and die for violating these rules. I am the Lord who sanctifies them.

[10] "No one may eat of the holy sacrifices unless he is a priest; no one visiting the priest, for instance, nor a hired servant, may eat this food. [11] However, there is one exception—if the priest buys a slave with his own money, that slave may eat it, and any slave

children born in his household may eat it. [12] If a priest's daughter is married outside the tribe, she may not eat the sacred offerings.[a] [13] But if she is a widow or divorced and has no son to support her, and has returned home to her father's household, she may eat of her father's food again. But otherwise, no one who is not in the priestly families may eat this food.

[14] "If someone should eat of the holy sacrifices without realizing it, he shall return to the priest the amount he has used, with twenty per cent added; [15] for the holy sacrifices brought by the people of Israel must not be defiled by being eaten by unauthorized persons, for these sacrifices have been offered to the Lord. [16] Anyone who violates this law is guilty and is in great danger because he has eaten the sacred offerings; for I am Jehovah who sanctifies the offerings."

[17,18] And the Lord said to Moses, "Tell Aaron and his sons and all the people of Israel that if an Israelite or other person living among you offers a burnt offering sacrifice to the Lord—whether it is to fulfill a promise or is a spontaneous free will offering— [19] it will only be acceptable to the Lord if it is a male animal without defect; it must be a young bull or a sheep or a goat. [20] Anything that has a defect must not be offered, for it will not be accepted.

[21] "Anyone sacrificing a peace offering to the Lord from the herd or flock, whether to fulfill a vow or as a voluntary offering, must sacrifice an animal that has no defect, or it will not be accepted: [22] An animal that is blind or disabled or mutilated, or which has sores or itch or any other skin disease, must not be offered to the Lord; it is not a fit burnt offering for the altar of the Lord. [23] If the young bull or lamb presented to the Lord has anything superfluous or lacking in its body parts, it may be offered as a free will offering, but not for a vow. [24] An animal that has injured genitals—crushed or castrated—shall not be offered to the Lord at any time. [25] This restriction applies to the sacrifices made by foreigners among you as well as those made by yourselves, for no defective animal is acceptable for this sacrifice."

---

a Literally, "the elevation of the holy things."

²⁶,²⁷ And the Lord said to Moses, "When a bullock, sheep, or goat is born, it shall be left with its mother for seven days, but from the eighth day onward it is acceptable as a sacrifice by fire to the Lord. ²⁸ You shall not slaughter a mother animal and her offspring the same day, whether she is a cow or ewe. ²⁹,³⁰ When you offer the Lord a sacrifice of thanksgiving, you must do it in the right way, eating the sacrificial animal the same day it is slain. Leave none of it for the following day. I am the Lord.

³¹ "You must keep all of my commandments, for I am the Lord. ³²,³³ You must not treat me as common and ordinary. Revere me and hallow me, for I, the Lord, made you holy to myself and rescued you from Egypt to be my own people! I am Jehovah!"

23 THE LORD SAID to Moses, "Announce to the people of Israel that they are to celebrate several annual festivals of the Lord—times when all Israel will assemble and worship me. ³ (These are in addition to your Sabbaths^a—the seventh day of every week—which are always days of solemn rest in every home, times for assembling to worship, and for resting from the normal business of the week.) ⁴ These are the holy festivals which are to be observed each year:

⁵ *"The Passover of the Lord:* This is to be celebrated at the end of March.^b

⁶ *"The Festival of Unleavened Bread:* This is to be celebrated beginning the day following the Passover. ⁷ On the first day of this festival, you shall gather the people for worship, and all ordinary work shall cease.^c ⁸ You shall do the same on the seventh day of the festival. On each of the intervening days you shall make an offering by fire to the Lord.

⁹,¹⁰,¹¹ *"The Festival of First Fruits:* When you arrive in the land I will give you and reap your first harvest, bring the first sheaf of the harvest to the priest on the day after the Sabbath. He shall wave it before the Lord in a gesture of offering, and it will be accepted by the Lord as your gift. ¹² That same day you shall sacrifice to the Lord a male yearling lamb without defect as a burnt offering. ¹³ A grain offering shall accompany it, consisting of a fifth of a bushel of finely ground flour mixed with olive oil, to be offered by fire to the Lord; this will be very pleasant to him. Also offer a drink offering consisting of three pints of wine. ¹⁴ Until this is done you must not eat any of the harvest for yourselves—neither fresh kernels nor bread nor parched grain. This is a permanent law throughout your nation.

¹⁵,¹⁶ *"The Festival of Pentecost:* Fifty days later you shall bring to the Lord an offering of a sample of the new grain of your later crops. ¹⁷ This shall consist of two loaves of bread from your homes to be waved before the Lord in a gesture of offering. Bake this bread from a fifth of a bushel of fine flour containing yeast. It is an offering to the Lord of the first sampling of your later crops.^d ¹⁸ Along with the bread and the wine, you shall sacrifice as burnt offerings to the Lord seven yearling lambs without defects, one young bull, and two rams. All are fire offerings, very acceptable to Jehovah.^e ¹⁹ And you shall offer one male goat for a sin offering, and two male yearling lambs for a peace offering.

²⁰ "The priests shall wave these offerings before the Lord along with the loaves representing the first sampling of your later crops. They are holy to the Lord, and will be given to the priests as food. ²¹ That day shall be announced as a time of sacred convocation of all the people; don't do any work that day. This is a law to be honored from generation to generation. ²² (When you reap your harvests, you must not thoroughly reap all the corners of the fields, nor pick up the fallen grain; leave it for the poor and for foreigners living among you who have no land of their own; I am Jehovah your God!)

²³,²⁴ *"The Festival of Trumpets:* Mid-September^f is a solemn time for all the people to meet together for worship; it is a time of remembrance, and is to be announced by loud blowing of trumpets. ²⁵ Don't do any work on the day of the celebration, but offer a sacrifice by fire to the Lord.

²⁶,²⁷ *"The Day of Atonement* follows nine

---

a Implied.   b Literally, "on the fourteenth day of the first month" (of the Hebrew calendar).
c Literally, "you shall do no hard work."   d Literally, "as first fruits to the Lord."   e Literally, "of a sweet odor to the Lord."   f Literally, "the first day of the seventh month" (of the Hebrew calendar).

days later:[g] All the people are to come together before the Lord, saddened by their sin; and they shall offer sacrifices by fire to the Lord. [28] Don't do any work that day, for it is a special day for making atonement before the Lord your God. [29] Anyone who does not spend the day in repentance and sorrow for sin shall be excommunicated from his people. [30,31] And I will put to death anyone who does any kind of work that day. This is a law of Israel from generation to generation. [32] For this is a Sabbath of solemn rest, and in it you shall humble your souls and be filled with remorse; this time for atonement begins on the previous evening and goes on until the next evening.

[33,34] *"The Festival of Tabernacles:* Five days later, on the last day of September,[h] is the Festival of Shelters[i] to be celebrated before the Lord for seven days. [35] On the first day there will be a sacred assembly of all the people; don't do any hard work that day. [36] On each of the seven days of the festival you are to sacrifice an offering by fire to the Lord. The eighth day requires another sacred convocation of all the people, at which time there will again be an offering by fire to the Lord. It is a joyous celebration, and no heavy work is permitted.

[37] "(These, then, are the regular annual festivals—sacred convocations of all people—when offerings to the Lord are to be made by fire. [38] These annual festivals are in addition to your regular weekly days of holy rest. The sacrifices made during the festivals are to be in addition to your regular giving and normal fulfillment of your vows.)

[39] "This last day of September, at the end of your harvesting, is the time to celebrate this seven-day festival before the Lord. Remember that the first and last days of the festival are days of solemn rest. [40] On the first day, take boughs of fruit trees laden with fruit, and palm fronds, and the boughs of leafy trees—such as willows that grow by the brooks—and [build shelters with them[j]], rejoicing before the Lord your God for seven days. [41] This seven-day annual feast is a law from generation to generation.

[42] During those seven days, all of you who are native Israelites are to live in these shelters. [43] The purpose of this is to remind the people of Israel, generation after generation, that I rescued you from Egypt, and caused you to live in shelters. I am Jehovah your God."

[44] So Moses announced these annual festivals of the Lord to the people of Israel.

24 THE LORD SAID to Moses, "Tell the people of Israel to bring you pure olive oil for an eternal flame [3,4] in the lampstand of pure gold which stands outside the veil that secludes the Holy of Holies. Each morning and evening Aaron shall supply it with fresh oil and trim the wicks. It will be an eternal flame before the Lord from generation to generation.

[5-8] "Every Sabbath day the High Priest shall place twelve loaves of bread in two rows upon the golden table that stands before the Lord. These loaves shall be baked from finely ground flour, using a fifth of a bushel for each. Pure frankincense shall be sprinkled along each row. This will be a memorial offering made by fire to the Lord, in memory of his everlasting covenant with the people of Israel. [9] The bread shall be eaten by Aaron and his sons, in a place set apart for the purpose. For these are offerings made by fire to the Lord under a permanent law of God, and are most holy."

[10] Out in the camp one day, a young man whose mother was an Israelite and whose father was an Egyptian, got into a fight with one of the men of Israel. [11] During the fight the Egyptian man's son[a] cursed God,[b] and was brought to Moses for judgment. (His mother's name was Shelomith, daughter of Dibri of the tribe of Dan.) [12] He was put in jail until the Lord would indicate what to do with him.

[13,14] And the Lord said to Moses, "Take him outside the camp and tell all who heard him to lay their hands upon his head; then all the people are to execute him by stoning. [15,16] And tell the people of Israel that anyone who curses his God must pay the penalty: he must die. All the congregation shall

---

g Literally, "on the tenth day of the seventh month" (of the Hebrew calendar).   h Literally, "on the fifteenth day of the seventh month" (of the Hebrew calendar).   i Or, "Feast of Tabernacles."
j Implied.   24a Literally, "the Israelite woman's son."   b Literally, "blasphemed the Name."

stone him; this law applies to the foreigner as well as to the Israelite who blasphemes the name of Jehovah. He must die.

[17] "Also, all murderers must be executed. [18] Anyone who kills an animal [that isn't his[c]] shall replace it.[d] [19] The penalty for injuring anyone is to be injured in exactly the same way: [20] fracture for fracture, eye for eye, tooth for tooth. Whatever anyone does to another shall be done to him.

[21] "To repeat, whoever kills an animal must replace it, and whoever kills a man must die. [22] You shall have the same law for the foreigner as for the home-born citizen, for I am Jehovah your God."

[23] So they took the youth out of the camp and stoned him until he died, as Jehovah had commanded Moses.

25 WHILE MOSES WAS on Mount Sinai, the Lord gave him these instructions for the people of Israel:

"When you come into the land I am going to give you, you must let the land rest before the Lord every seventh year. [3] For six years you may sow your field and prune your vineyards and harvest your crops, [4] but during the seventh year the land is to lie fallow before the Lord, uncultivated. Don't sow your crops and don't prune your vineyards during that entire year. [5] Don't even reap for yourself the volunteer crops that come up, and don't gather the grapes for yourself; for it is a year of rest for the land. [6,7] Any crops that do grow that year shall be free to all—for you, your servants, your slaves, and any foreigners living among you. Cattle and wild animals alike shall be allowed to graze there.

[8] "Every fiftieth year, [9] on the Day of Atonement,[a] let the trumpets blow loud and long throughout the land. [10] For the fiftieth year shall be holy, a time to proclaim liberty throughout the land to all enslaved debtors, and a time for the canceling of all public and private debts. It shall be a year when all the family estates sold to others shall be returned to the original owners or their heirs.

[11] "What a happy year it will be! In it you shall not sow, nor gather crops nor grapes;

[12] for it is a holy Year of Jubilee for you. That year your food shall be the volunteer crops that grow wild in the fields. [13] Yes, during the Year of Jubilee everyone shall return home to his original family possession; if he has sold it, it shall be his again! [14,15,16] Because of this, if the land is sold or bought during the preceding forty-nine years, a fair price shall be arrived at by counting the number of years until the Jubilee. If the Jubilee is many years away, the price will be high; if few years, the price will be low; for what you are really doing is selling the number of crops the new owner will get from the land before it is returned to you.

[17,18] "You must fear your God and not overcharge! For I am Jehovah. Obey my laws if you want to live safely in the land. [19] When you obey, the land will yield bumper crops and you can eat your fill in safety. [20] But you will ask, 'What shall we eat the seventh year, since we are not allowed to plant or harvest crops that year?' [21,22] The answer is, 'I will bless you with bumper crops the sixth year that will last you until the crops of the eighth year are harvested!' [23] And remember, the land is mine, so you may not sell it permanently. You are merely my tenants and sharecroppers!

[24] "In every contract of sale there must be a stipulation that the land can be redeemed at any time by the seller. [25] If anyone becomes poor and sells some of his land, then his nearest relatives may redeem it. [26] If there is no one else to redeem it, and he himself gets together enough money, [27] then he may always buy it back at a price proportionate to the number of harvests until the Jubilee, and the owner must accept the money and return the land to him. [28] But if the original owner is not able to redeem it, then it shall belong to the new owner until the Year of Jubilee; but at the Jubilee year it must be returned again.

[29] "If a man sells a house in the city,[b] he has up to one year to redeem it, with full right of redemption during that time. [30] But if it is not redeemed within the year, then

---

c Implied.   d Literally, "shall make it good, life for life."   25a Literally, "the tenth day of the seventh month" (of the Hebrew calendar).   b Literally, "in a walled city."

it will belong permanently to the new owner —it does not return to the original owner in the Year of Jubilee. ³¹ But village houses—a village is a settlement without fortifying walls around it—are like farmland, redeemable at any time, and are always returned to the original owner in the Year of Jubilee.

³² "There is one exception: The homes of the Levites, even though in walled cities, may be redeemed at any time, ³³ and must be returned to the original owners in the Year of Jubilee; for the Levites will not be given farmland like the other tribes, but will receive only houses in their cities, and the surrounding fields.^c ³⁴ The Levites are not permitted to sell the fields of common land surrounding their cities, for these are their permanent possession, and they must belong to no one else.

³⁵ "If your brother becomes poor, you are responsible to help him; invite him to live with you as a guest in your home. ³⁶ Fear your God and let your brother live with you; and don't charge him interest on the money you lend him. ³⁷ Remember—no interest; and give him what he needs, at your cost: don't try to make a profit! ³⁸ For I, the Lord your God, brought you out of the land of Egypt to *give* you the land of Canaan, and to be your God.

³⁹ "If a fellow Israelite becomes poor and sells himself to you, you must not treat him as an ordinary slave, ⁴⁰ but rather as a hired servant or as a guest; and he shall serve you only until the Year of Jubilee. ⁴¹ At that time he can leave with his children, and return to his own family and possessions. ⁴² For I brought you from the land of Egypt, and you are my servants; so you may not be sold as ordinary slaves, ⁴³ or treated harshly; fear your God.

⁴⁴ "However, you may purchase slaves from the foreign nations living around you, ⁴⁵ and you may purchase the children of the foreigners living among you, even though they have been born in your land. ⁴⁶ They will be permanent slaves for you to pass on to your children after you; but your brothers, the people of Israel, shall not be treated so.

⁴⁷ "If a foreigner living among you becomes rich, and an Israelite becomes poor and sells himself to the foreigner or to the foreigner's family, ⁴⁸ he may be redeemed by one of his brothers, ⁴⁹ his uncle, nephew, or anyone else who is a near relative. He may also redeem himself if he can find the money. ⁵⁰ The price of his freedom shall be in proportion to the number of years left before the Year of Jubilee—whatever it would cost to hire a servant for that number of years. ⁵¹ If there are still many years until the Jubilee, he shall pay almost the amount he received when he sold himself; ⁵² if the years have passed and only a few remain until the Jubilee, then he will repay only a small part of the amount he received when he sold himself. ⁵³ If he sells himself to a foreigner, the foreigner must treat him as a hired servant rather than as a slave or as property. ⁵⁴ If he has not been redeemed by the time the Year of Jubilee arrives, then he and his children shall be freed at that time. ⁵⁵ For the people of Israel are *my* servants; I brought them from the land of Egypt; I am the Lord your God.

26 "YOU MUST HAVE no idols; you must never worship carved images, obelisks, or shaped stones, for I am the Lord your God. ² You must obey my Sabbath laws of rest, and reverence my Tabernacle, for I am the Lord.

³ "If you obey all of my commandments, ^{4,5} I will give you regular rains, and the land will yield bumper crops, and the trees will be loaded with fruit long after the normal time!^a And grapes will still be ripening when sowing time comes again. You shall eat your fill, and live safely in the land, ⁶ for I will give you peace, and you will go to sleep without fear. I will chase away the dangerous animals. ⁷ You will chase your enemies; they will die beneath your swords. ⁸ Five of you will chase a hundred, and a hundred of you, ten thousand! You will defeat all of your enemies. ⁹ I will look after you, and multiply you, and fulfill my covenant with you. ¹⁰ You will have such a surplus of crops that you won't know what to do with them when the new harvest is

---

c Implied.   26a Literally, "until the grape harvest."

ready! [11] And I will live among you, and not despise you. [12] I will walk among you and be your God, and you shall be my people. [13] For I am the Lord your God who brought you out of the land of Egypt, with the intention that you be slaves no longer; I have broken your chains and will make you walk with dignity.[b]

[14] "But if you will not listen to me or obey me, [15] but reject my laws, [16] this is what I will do to you: I will punish you with sudden terrors and panic, and with tuberculosis and burning fever; your eyes shall be consumed and your life shall ebb away; you will sow your crops in vain, for your enemies will eat them. [17] I will set my face against you and you will flee before your attackers; those who hate you will rule you; you will even run when no one is chasing you!

[18] "And if you still disobey me, I will punish you seven times more severely for your sins. [19] I will break your proud power and make your heavens as iron, and your earth as bronze. [20] Your strength shall be spent in vain; for your land shall not yield its crops, nor your trees their fruit.

[21] "And if even then you will not obey me and listen to me, I will send you seven times more plagues because of your sins. [22] I will send wild animals to kill your children and destroy your cattle and reduce your numbers so that your roads will be deserted.

[23] "And if even this will not reform you, but you continue to walk against my wishes, [24] then I will walk against your wishes, and I, even I, will personally smite you seven times for your sin. [25] I will revenge the breaking of my covenant by bringing war against you. You will flee to your cities, and I will send a plague among you there; and you will be conquered by your enemies. [26] I will destroy your food supply so that one oven will be large enough to bake all the bread available for ten entire families; and you will still be hungry after your pittance has been doled out to you.

[27] "And if you still won't listen to me or obey me, [28] then I will let loose my great anger and send you seven times greater punishment for your sins. [29] You shall eat your own sons and daughters, [30] and I will destroy the altars on the hills where you worship your idols, and I will cut down your incense altars, leaving your dead bodies to rot among your idols; and I will abhor you. [31] I will make your cities desolate, and destroy your places of worship, and will not respond to your incense offerings. [32] Yes, I will desolate your land; your enemies shall live in it, utterly amazed at what I have done to you.

[33] "I will scatter you out among the nations, destroying you with war as you go. Your land shall be desolate and your cities destroyed. [34,35] Then at last the land will rest and make up for the many years you refused to let it lie idle; for it will lie desolate all the years that you are captives in enemy lands. Yes, then the land will rest and enjoy its Sabbaths! It will make up for the rest you didn't give it every seventh year when you lived upon it.

[36] "And for those who are left alive, I will cause them to be dragged away to distant lands as prisoners of war, and slaves. There they will live in constant fear. The sound of a leaf driven in the wind will send them fleeing as though chased by a man with a sword; they shall fall when no one is pursuing them. [37] Yes, though none pursue they shall stumble over each other in flight, as though fleeing in battle, with no power to stand before their enemies. [38] You shall perish among the nations and be destroyed among your enemies. [39] Those left shall pine away in enemy lands because of their sins, the same sins as those of their fathers.

[40,41] "But at last they shall confess their sins and their fathers' sins of treachery against me. (Because they were against me, I was against them, and brought them into the land of their enemies.) When at last their evil hearts are humbled and they accept the punishment I send them for their sins, [42] then I will remember again my promises to Abraham, Isaac, and Jacob, and I will remember the land (and its desolation). [43] For the land shall enjoy its Sabbaths as it lies desolate. But then at last they shall accept their punishment for rejecting my laws and for despising my rule. [44] But

---

b Literally, "and made you go upright."

despite all they have done, I will not utterly destroy them and my covenant with them, for I am Jehovah their God. ⁴⁵ For their sakes I will remember my promises to their ancestors, to be their God. For I brought their forefathers out of Egypt as all the nations watched in wonder. I am Jehovah."

⁴⁶ These were the laws, ordinances, and instructions that Jehovah gave to the people of Israel, through Moses, on Mount Sinai.

27 THE LORD SAID to Moses, "Tell the people of Israel that when a person makes a special vow to give himself to the Lord, he shall give these payments instead: ³ A man from the age of twenty to sixty shall pay twenty-five dollars;ᵃ ⁴ a woman from the age of twenty to sixty shall pay fifteen dollars; ⁵ a boy from five to twenty shall pay ten dollars; a girl, five dollars. ⁶ A boy one month to five years old shall have paid for him two and a half dollars; a girl, one and a half dollars. ⁷ A man over sixty shall pay seven and a half dollars; a woman, five dollars. ⁸ But if the person is too poor to pay this amount, he shall be brought to the priest and the priest shall talk it over with him, and he shall pay as the priest shall decide.

⁹ "But if it is an animal that is vowed to be given to the Lord as a sacrifice, it must be given. ¹⁰ The vow may not be changed; the donor may neither change his mind about giving it to the Lord, nor substitute good for bad or bad for good; if he does, both the first and the second shall belong to the Lord! ¹¹,¹² But if the animal given to the Lord is not a kind that is permitted as a sacrifice, the owner shall bring it to the priest to value it, and he shall be told how much to pay instead. ¹³ If the animal is a kind that may be offered as a sacrifice,ᵇ but the man wants to redeem it, then he shall pay twenty percent more than the value set by the priest.

¹⁴,¹⁵ "If someone donates his home to the Lord and then wishes to redeem it, the priest will decide its value and the man shall pay that amount plus twenty percent, and

the house will be his again.

¹⁶ "If a man dedicates any part of his field to the Lord, value it in proportion to its size, as indicated by the amount of seed required to sow it. A section of land that requires ten bushels of barley seed for sowing is valued at twenty-five dollars. ¹⁷ If a man dedicates his field in the Year of Jubilee, then the whole estimate shall stand; ¹⁸ but if it is after the Year of Jubilee, then the value shall be in proportion to the number of years remaining until the next Year of Jubilee. ¹⁹ If the man decides to redeem the field, he shall pay twenty percent in addition to the priest's valuation, and the field will be his again. ²⁰ But if he decides not to redeem the field, or if he has sold the field to someone else [and has given to the Lord his rights to it at the Year of Jubileeᵇ], it shall not be returned to him again. ²¹ When it is freed in the Year of Jubilee, it shall belong to the Lord as a field devoted to him, and it shall be given to the priests.

²² "If a man dedicates to the Lord a field he has bought, but which is not part of his family possession, ²³ the priest shall estimate the value until the Year of Jubilee, and he shall immediately give that estimated value to the Lord, ²⁴ and in the Year of Jubilee the field shall return to the original owner from whom it was bought. ²⁵ All the valuations shall be stated in standard money.ᶜ

²⁶ "You may not dedicate to the Lord the firstborn of any ox or sheep, for it is already his. ²⁷ But if it is the firstborn of an animal that cannot be sacrificed because it is not on the list of those acceptable to the Lord, then the owner shall pay the priest's estimate of its worth, plus twenty percent; or if the owner does not redeem it, the priest may sell it to someone else. ²⁸ However, anything utterly devoted to the Lord—people, animals, or inherited fields—shall not be sold or redeemed, for they are most holy to the Lord. ²⁹ No one sentenced by the courts to die may pay a fine instead; he shall surely be put to death.ᵈ

³⁰ "A tenth of the produce of the land, whether grain or fruit, is the Lord's, and is

---

a Note: The actual value by today's standards is uncertain. The above figures are approximate.
b Implied.   c Literally, "and all your estimations shall be according to the shekel of the sanctuary: twenty gerahs shall be the shekel."   d Literally, "no one who is under the ban of God to be put to death, may be ransomed."

holy. [31] If anyone wants to buy back this fruit or grain, he must add a fifth to its value. [32] And the Lord owns every tenth animal of your herds and flocks and other domestic animals, as they pass by for counting. [33] The tenth given to the Lord shall not be selected on the basis of whether it is good or bad, and there shall be no substitutions; for if there is any change made, then both the original and the substitution shall belong to the Lord, and may not be bought back!"

[34] These are the commandments the Lord gave to Moses for the people of Israel on Mount Sinai.

Sticking It Out

Like most teenagers who work part-time, Steve Henry and Elesia Jackson have "service jobs", the category of work which pays the least and often brings on the most headaches. Steve has to tactfully dodge irate customers and sometimes even flying hotdogs from them! Life behind the dry cleaning counter holds its own excitement as Elesia can testify. Like the day the lady customer threw her repaired dress on the floor, and jumped up and down in sheer exasperation.

Most days aren't that exciting, though. Part-time work—in cleaners, meat markets, hamburger stands or gas stations—can be a lot of drudgery. How can you add zip to the dull parts of life? The book of Numbers shows how *not* to respond to drudgery.

The book of Numbers (so called because it includes two censuses) is a classic example of how to do yourself in by ignoring God's way.

The Israelites' job was clear: obey God's laws and he would lead them on a relatively brief, 200-mile journey through the desert. When the Israelis moved out from Mount Sinai (Chapter 10), they could never have guessed all the hazards ahead: hostile enemies, hunger, hassles among themselves, pagan temptations, the ever-growing fatigue of desert travel.

Worse yet, when they reached their destination, the majority decided they didn't like it ... and so a trip of no more than 200 miles ended up taking 38 years!

NUMBERS

1 IT WAS ON the fifteenth day of April[a] of the second year after the Israelis left Egypt that the Lord issued the following instructions to Moses. (He was in the Tabernacle at the camp of Israel on the Sinai peninsula at the time.)

[2-15] "Take a census of all the men twenty years old and older who are able to go to war, indicating their tribe and family. You and Aaron are to direct the project, assisted by leaders from each tribe:"

Tribe	Leader
Reuben	Elizur (son of Shedeur)
Simeon	Shelumi-el (son of Zuri-shaddai)
Judah	Nahshon (son of Amminadab)
Issachar	Nethanel (son of Zuar)
Zebulun	Eliab (son of Helon)
Ephraim (son of Joseph)	Elishama (son of Ammihud)
Manasseh (son of Joseph)	Gamaliel (son of Pedahzur)
Benjamin	Abidan (son of Gideoni)
Dan	Ahiezer (son of Ammishaddai)
Asher	Pagiel (son of Ochran)
Gad	Eliasaph (son of Deuel)
Naphtali	Ahira (son of Enan)

[16] These were the tribal leaders elected from among the people.

[17,18,19] On the same day[b] Moses and Aaron and the above-named leaders summoned all the men of Israel who were twenty years old or older to come and register, each man indicating his tribe and family, as the Lord had commanded Moses.[c] [20-46] Here is the final tabulation:

Tribe	Total
Reuben (the oldest son of Jacob)	46,500
Simeon	59,300
Gad	45,650
Judah	74,600
Issachar	54,400
Zebulun	57,400
Joseph: Ephraim (son of Joseph)	40,500
Joseph: Manasseh (son of Joseph)	32,200
Benjamin	35,400
Dan	62,700
Asher	41,500
Naphtali	53,400
Grand Total:	603,550

[47,48,49] This total does not include the Levites, for the Lord had said to Moses, "Exempt the entire tribe of Levi from the draft, and do not include their number in the census. [50] For the Levites are assigned for the work connected with the Tabernacle and its transportation. They are to live near the Tabernacle, [51] and whenever the Tabernacle is moved, the Levites are to take it down and set it up again; anyone else touching it shall be executed. [52] Each tribe of Israel shall have a separate camping area with its own flag. [53] The Levites' tents shall be clustered around the Tabernacle as a wall between the people of Israel and God's

---

a Literally, "on the first day of the second month" (of the Jewish calendar).   b Literally, "on the first day of the second month" (of the Jewish calendar).   c Added in the Hebrew text is this sentence: "So he numbered them in the wilderness of Sinai."

wrath—to protect them from his fierce anger against their sins."

54 So all these instructions of the Lord to Moses were put into effect.

2 THE LORD GAVE these further instructions to Moses and Aaron: "Each tribe will have its own tent area, with its flagpole and tribal banner; and at the center of these tribal compounds will be the Tabernacle."
3-31 Here are the tribal locations:[a]

Tribe:	Leader:	Location:	Census:
Judah	Nahshon (son of Amminadab)	East side of the Tabernacle	74,600
Issachar	Nethanel (son of Zuar)	Next to Judah	54,400
Zebulun	Eliab (son of Helon)	Next to Issachar	57,400

So the total of all those on Judah's side of the camp was 186,400. These three tribes led the way whenever the Israelites traveled to a new campsite.

Reuben	Elizur (son of Shedeur)	South side of the Tabernacle	46,500
Simeon	Shelumi-el (son of Zurishaddai)	Next to Reuben	59,300
Gad	Eliasaph (son of Reuel[b])	Next to Simeon	45,650

So the total of the Reuben side of the camp was 151,450. These three tribes were next in line whenever the Israelis traveled.

Next in the line of march was the Tabernacle, with the Levites. When traveling, each tribe stayed together under its own flag, just as each was separate from the others in camp.

Ephraim	Elishama (son of Ammihud)	West side of Tabernacle	40,500
Manasseh	Gamaliel (son of Pedahzur)	Next to Ephraim	32,200
Benjamin	Abidan (son of Gideoni)	Next to Manasseh	35,400

So the total on the Ephraim side of the camp was 108,100, and they were next in the line of march.

Dan	Ahiezer (son of Ammishaddai)	North side of Tabernacle	62,700
Asher	Pagiel (son of Ochran)	Next to Dan	41,500
Naphtali	Ahira (son of Enan)	Next to Asher	53,400

So the total on Dan's side of the camp was 157,600. They brought up the rear whenever Israel traveled. 32,33 In summary, the armies of Israel totaled 603,550 (not including the Levites, who were exempted by Jehovah's commandment to Moses). 34 So the people of Israel set up their camps, each tribe under its own banner, in the locations indicated by the Lord to Moses.

3 AT THE TIME when the Lord spoke to Moses on Mount Sinai, 2 Aaron's[a] sons were:

> Nadab (his oldest), Abihu, Eleazar, Ithamar.

3 All were anointed as priests and set apart to minister at the Tabernacle. 4 But Nadab and Abihu died before the Lord in the wilderness of Sinai when they used unholy fire. And since they had no children, this left only Eleazar and Ithamar to assist their father Aaron.

5 Then the Lord said to Moses, 6 "Summon the tribe of Levi and present them to Aaron as his assistants. 7,8,9 They will follow his instructions and perform the sacred duties at the Tabernacle on behalf of all the people of Israel. For they are assigned to him as representatives of all the people of Israel. They are in charge of all the furnishings and maintenance of the Tabernacle. 10 However, only Aaron and his sons may carry out the duties of the priesthood; anyone else who presumes to assume this office shall be executed."

11,12 And the Lord said to Moses, "I have accepted the Levites in substitution for all the oldest sons of the people of Israel. The Levites are mine 13 in exchange for all the

---

a Implied.　　b Deuel in chapter 1.　　3a Literally, "these are the generations of Aaron and Moses."

oldest sons. From the day I killed all the oldest sons of the Egyptians, I took for myself all the firstborn in Israel of both men and animals! They are mine; I am Jehovah."

[14,15] The Lord now spoke again to Moses at the Sinai peninsula, telling him, "Take a census of the tribe of Levi, indicating each person's clan; count every male down to one month old." [16-24] So Moses did:

Levi's son	Levi's grand-sons	Census	Leader	Camp Location
Gershon	(clan names) Libni Shime-i	7,500	Elisaph (son of Lael)	West side of Tabernacle

[25-30] *Responsibilities:*

The responsibility of these two clans of Levites was the care of the Tabernacle: its coverings, its entry drapes, the drapes covering the fence surrounding the courtyard, the screen at the entrance of the courtyard surrounding the Tabernacle, the altar, and all the ropes used in tying the Tabernacle together.

Levi's son	Levi's grand-sons	Census	Leader	Camp Location
Kohath	(clan names) Amram Izhar Hebron Uzziel	8,600	Eliza-phan (son of Uzziel)	South-side of the Tabernacle

[31-35] *Responsibilities:*

The responsibility of these four clans of Levites was the care of the Ark, the table, the lampstand, the altars, the various utensils used in the Tabernacle, the veil, and any repairs needed on any of these items. (Note: Eleazar, Aaron's son, shall be the chief administrator over the leaders of the Levites, with special responsibility for the oversight of the sanctuary.)

Levi's son	Levi's grand-sons	Census	Leader	Camp Location
Merari	(clan names) Mahli Mushi	6,200	Zuriel (son of Abihail)	North side of Tabernacle

[36,37] *Responsibilities:*

The responsibility of these two clans was the care of the frames of the Tabernacle building; the posts; the bases for the posts, and all of the equipment needed for their use; the posts around the courtyard and their bases, pegs, and ropes.

[38] The area east of the Tabernacle was reserved for the tents of Moses and of Aaron and his sons, who had the final responsibility for the Tabernacle on behalf of the people of Israel. (Anyone who was not a priest or Levite, but came into the Tabernacle, was to be executed.)

[39] So all the Levites, as numbered by Moses and Aaron at the command of the Lord, were 22,000 males a month old and older.

[40] Then the Lord said to Moses, "Now take a census of all the eldest sons in Israel who are a month old and older, and register each name. [41] The Levites shall be mine (I am Jehovah) as substitutes for the eldest sons of Israel; and the Levites' cattle are mine as substitutes for the firstborn cattle of the whole nation."

[42] So Moses took a census of the eldest sons of the people of Israel, as the Lord had commanded, [43] and found the total number of eldest sons a month old and older to be 22,273.

[44] Now the Lord said to Moses, [45] "Give me the Levites instead of the eldest sons of the people of Israel; and give me the cattle of the Levites instead of the firstborn cattle of the people of Israel; yes, the Levites shall be mine; I am Jehovah. [46] To redeem the 273 eldest sons in excess of the number of Levites, [47,48] pay five dollars[b] for each one to Aaron and his sons."

[49] So Moses received redemption money for the 273 eldest sons of Israel who were in excess of the number of Levites. (All the others were redeemed because the Levites had been given to the Lord in their place.) [50] The money collected came to a total of $1,365.[c] [51] And Moses gave it to Aaron and his sons as the Lord had commanded.

4 THEN THE LORD said to Moses and Aaron, "Take a census of the Kohath

b Literally, "five shekels apiece by the polls; after the shekel of the sanctuary shalt thou take them. (The shekel is twenty gerahs.)" c Literally, "1,365 shekels after the shekel of the sanctuary."

division of the Levite tribe. ³ This census will be of all males from ages thirty to fifty who are able to work in the Tabernacle. ⁴ These are their sacred duties:

⁵ "When the camp moves, Aaron and his sons will enter the Tabernacle first and take down the veil and cover the Ark with it. ⁶ Then they will cover the veil with goatskin leather, cover the goatskins with a blue cloth, and place the carrying poles of the Ark in their rings.

⁷ "Next they must spread a blue cloth over the table where the Bread of the Presence is displayed, and place the dishes, spoons, bowls, cups, and the Bread upon the cloth. ⁸ They will spread a scarlet cloth over that, and finally a covering of goatskin leather on top of the scarlet cloth. Then they shall insert the carrying poles into the table.

⁹ "Next they must cover with a blue cloth the lampstand, the lamps, snuffers, trays, and the reservoir of olive oil. ¹⁰ This entire group of objects shall then be covered with goatskin leather, and the bundle shall be placed upon a carrying frame.

¹¹ "They must then spread a blue cloth over the gold altar, cover it with a covering of goatskin leather, and insert the carrying poles into the altar. ¹² All of the remaining utensils of the Tabernacle are to be wrapped in a blue cloth, covered with goatskin leather, and placed on the carrying frame.

¹³ "The ashes are to be removed from the altar, and the altar shall be covered with a purple cloth. ¹⁴ All of the altar utensils are to be placed upon the cloth—the firepans, hooks, shovels, basins, and other containers —and a cover of goatskin leather will be spread over them. Finally, the carrying poles are to be put in place. ¹⁵ When Aaron and his sons have finished packing the sanctuary and all the utensils, the clan of Kohath shall come and carry the units to wherever the camp is traveling; but they must not touch the holy items, lest they die. This, then, is the sacred work of the sons of Kohath.

¹⁶ "Aaron's son Eleazar shall be responsible for the oil for the light, the sweet incense, the daily grain offering, and the anointing oil—in fact, the supervision of the entire Tabernacle and everything in it will be his responsibility."

¹⁷,¹⁸,¹⁹ Then the Lord said to Moses and Aaron, "Don't let the families of Kohath destroy themselves! This is what you must do so that they will not die when they carry the most holy things: Aaron and his sons shall go in with them and point out what each is to carry. ²⁰ Otherwise they must never enter the sanctuary for even a moment, lest they look at the sacred objects there and die."

²¹,²²,²³ And the Lord said to Moses, "Take a census of the Gershonite division of the tribe of Levi, all of the men between the ages of thirty and fifty who are eligible for the sacred work of the Tabernacle. ²⁴ These will be their duties:

²⁵ "They will carry the curtains of the Tabernacle, the Tabernacle itself with its coverings, the goatskin leather roof, and the curtain for the Tabernacle entrance. ²⁶ They are also to carry the drapes covering the courtyard fence, and the curtain across the entrance to the courtyard that surrounds the altar and the Tabernacle. They will also carry the altar, the ropes, and all of the accessories. They are fully responsible for the transportation of these items. ²⁷ Aaron or any of his sons may assign the Gershonites' tasks to them, ²⁸ but the Gershonites will be directly responsible to Aaron's son Ithamar.

²⁹ "Now take a census of the Merari division of the Levite tribe, all of the men from thirty to fifty who are eligible for the Tabernacle service. ³⁰,³¹ When the Tabernacle is moved, they are to carry the frames of the Tabernacle, the bars, the bases, ³² the frames for the courtyard fence with their bases, pegs, cords, and everything else connected with their use and repair.

"Assign duties to each man by name. ³³ The Merari division will also report to Aaron's son Ithamar."

³⁴ So Moses and Aaron and the other leaders took a census of the Kohath division, ³⁵ including all of the men thirty to fifty years of age who were eligible for the Tabernacle service, ³⁶ and found that the total number was 2,750. ³⁷ All this was done to carry out the Lord's instructions to Moses. ³⁸⁻⁴¹ A similar census of the Gershon division totaled 2,630. ⁴²⁻⁴⁵ And of the Merari

division, 3,200. ⁴⁶,⁴⁷,⁴⁸ Thus Moses and Aaron and the leaders of Israel found that the total of all the Levites who were thirty to fifty years old and who were eligible for the Tabernacle service and transportation, was 8,580. ⁴⁹ This census was taken in response to the Lord's instructions to Moses.

5 THESE ARE FURTHER instructions from the Lord to Moses: "Inform the people of Israel that they must expel all lepers from the camp, and all who have open sores, or who have been defiled by touching a dead person. ³ This applies to men and women alike. Remove them so that they will not defile the camp where I live among you." ⁴ These instructions were put into effect.

⁵,⁶ Then the Lord said to Moses, "Tell the people of Israel that when anyone, man or woman, betrays the Lord by betraying a trust, it is sin. ⁷ He must confess his sin and make full repayment for what he has stolen,ᵃ adding twenty percent and returning it to the person he took it from. ⁸ But if the person he wronged is dead,ᵇ and there is no near relative to whom the payment can be made, it must be given to the priest, along with a lamb for atonement. ⁹,¹⁰ When the people of Israel bring a gift to the Lord it shall go to the priests."

¹¹,¹² And the Lord said to Moses, "Tell the people of Israel that if a man's wife commits adultery, ¹³ but there is no proof, there being no witness, ¹⁴ and he is jealous and suspicious, ¹⁵ the man shall bring his wife to the priest with an offering for her of a tenth of a bushel of barley meal without oil or frankincense mingled with it—for it is a suspicion offering—to bring out the truthᶜ as to whether or not she is guilty.

¹⁶ "The priest shall bring her before the Lord, ¹⁷ and take holy water in a clay jar and mix into it dust from the floor of the Tabernacle. ¹⁸ He shall unbind her hair and place the suspicion offering in her hands to determine whether or not her husband's suspicions are justified. The priest shall stand before her holding the jar of bitter water that brings a curse. ¹⁹ He shall require her to swear that she is innocent, and then he shall say to her, 'If no man has slept with you except your husband, be free from the effects of this bitter water that causes the curse. ²⁰ But if you have committed adultery, ²¹,²² then Jehovah shall make you a curse among your people, for he will make your thigh rot away and your body swell.' And the woman shall be required to say, 'Yes, let it be so.' ²³ Then the priest shall write these curses in a book and wash them off into the bitter water. ²⁴ (When he requires the woman to drink the water, it becomes bitter within her [if she is guiltyᵈ].)

²⁵ "Then the priest shall take the suspicion offering from the woman's hand and wave it before Jehovah, and carry it to the altar. ²⁶ He shall take a handful, representing all of it, and burn the handful upon the altar, and then require the woman to drink the water. ²⁷ If she has been defiled, having committed adultery against her husband, the water will become bitter within her, and her body will swell and her thigh will rot, and she shall be a curse among her people. ²⁸ But if she is pure and has not committed adultery, she shall be unharmed and will soon become pregnant.

²⁹ "This, then, is the law concerning a wayward wife—or a husband's suspicions against his wife— ³⁰ to determine whether or not she has been unfaithful to him. He shall bring her before the Lord and the priest shall handle the situation as outlined above. ³¹ Her husband shall not be brought to trial for causing her horrible disease, for she is responsible."

6 THE LORD GAVE Moses these further instructions for the people of Israel: "When either a man or a woman takes the special vow of a Nazirite, consecrating himself to the Lord in a special way, ³,⁴ he must not thereafter, during the entire period of his special consecration to the Lord, taste strong drink or wine or even fresh wine, grape juice, grapes, or raisins! He may eat nothing that comes from grape vines, not even the seeds or skins!

⁵ "Throughout that time he must never

---

a Literally, "for his wrong."   b Implied.   c Literally, "an offering for remembrance."
d Implied.

cut his hair, for he is holy and consecrated to the Lord; that is why he must let his hair grow.

⁶,⁷ "And he may not go near any dead body during the entire period of his vow, even if it is the body of his father, mother, brother, or sister; for his vow of consecration remains in effect, ⁸ and he is consecrated to the Lord throughout the entire period. ⁹ If he is defiled by having someone fall dead beside him, then seven days later he shall shave his defiled head; he will then be cleansed from the contamination of being in the presence of death. ¹⁰ The next day, the eighth day, he must bring two turtledoves or two young pigeons to the priest at the entrance of the Tabernacle. ¹¹ The priest shall offer one of the birds for a sin offering, and the other for a burnt offering, and make atonement for his defilement. And he must renew his vows that day and let his hair begin to grow again. ¹² The days of his vow that were fulfilled before his defilement no longer count. He must begin all over again with a new vow, and must bring a male lamb a year old for a guilt offering.

¹³ "At the conclusion of the period of his vow of separation to the Lord, he must go to the entrance of the Tabernacle ¹⁴ and offer a burnt sacrifice to the Lord, a year-old lamb without defect. He must also offer a sin offering, a yearling ewe lamb without defect; a peace offering, a ram without defect; ¹⁵ a basket of bread made without yeast; pancakes made of fine flour mixed with olive oil; unleavened wafers spread with oil; and the accompanying grain offering and drink offerings. ¹⁶ The priest shall present these offerings before the Lord: first the sin offering and the burnt offering; ¹⁷ then the ram for a peace offering, along with the basket of bread made without yeast; and finally the grain offering along with the drink offering.

¹⁸ "Then the Nazirite shall shave his long hair—the sign of his vow of separation. This shall be done at the entrance of the Tabernacle, after which the hair shall be put in the fire under the peace offering sacrifice. ¹⁹ After the man's head has been shaved, the priest shall take the roasted shoulder of the lamb, one of the pancakes (made without yeast), and one of the wafers (also made without yeast), and put them all into the man's hands. ²⁰ The priest shall then wave it all back and forth before the Lord in a gesture of offering; all of it is a holy portion for the priest, as are the rib piece and shoulder that were waved before the Lord. After that the Nazirite may again drink wine, for he is freed from his vow.

²¹ "These are the regulations concerning a Nazirite and his sacrifices at the conclusion of his period of special dedication. In addition to these sacrifices he must bring any further offering he promised at the time he took his vow to become a Nazirite."

²²,²³ Now the Lord said to Moses, "Tell Aaron and his sons that they are to give this special blessing to the people of Israel: ²⁴,²⁵,²⁶ 'May the Lord bless and protect you; may the Lord's face radiate with joy because of you; may he be gracious to you, show you his favor, and give you his peace.' ²⁷ This is how Aaron and his sons shall call down my blessings[a] upon the people of Israel; and I myself will personally bless them."

7 MOSES ANOINTED AND sanctified each part of the Tabernacle, including the altar and its utensils, on the day he finished setting it up. ² Then the leaders of Israel— the chiefs of the tribes, the men who had organized the census—brought their offerings. ³ They brought six covered wagons, each drawn by two oxen—a wagon for every two leaders and an ox for each one; and they presented them to the Lord in front of the Tabernacle.

⁴,⁵ "Accept their gifts," the Lord told Moses, "and use these wagons for the work of the Tabernacle. Give them to the Levites for whatever needs they may have."

⁶ So Moses presented the wagons and the oxen to the Levites. ⁷ Two wagons and four oxen were given to the Gershon division for their use, ⁸ and four wagons and eight oxen were given to the Merari division, which was under the leadership of Ithamar, Aaron's son. ⁹ None of the wagons or teams was given to the Kohath division, for they were

---

a Literally, "shall put my name upon the people of Israel."

required to carry their portion of the Tabernacle upon their shoulders.

[10] The leaders also presented dedication gifts on the day the altar was anointed, placing them before the altar. [11] The Lord said to Moses, "Let each of them bring his gift on a different day for the dedication of the altar."

[12] So Nahshon, the son of Amminadab of the tribe of Judah, brought his gift the first day. [13] It consisted of a silver platter weighing two pounds and a silver bowl of about one pound, both filled with grain offerings of fine flour mixed with oil. [14] He also brought a tiny[a] gold box of incense which weighed only about six ounces. [15] He brought a young bull, a ram, and a male yearling lamb as burnt offerings; [16] a male goat for a sin offering; [17] and for the peace offerings two oxen, five rams, five male goats, and five male yearling lambs.

[18-23] The next day Nethanel, the son of Zuar, chief of the tribe of Issachar, brought his gifts and offerings. They were exactly the same as Nahshon had presented on the previous day.[b]

[24-29] On the third day Eliab, the son of Helon, chief of the tribe of Zebulun, came with his offerings—the same as those presented on the previous days.[b]

[30-35] On the fourth day the gifts were presented by Elizur, son of Shedeur, chief of the tribe of Reuben; his gifts and offerings were the same as those given on the previous days.[b]

[36-41] On the fifth day came Shelumi-el, the son of Zuri-shaddai, chief of the tribe of Simeon, with the same gifts.[b]

[42-47] The next day it was Eliasaph's turn, son of Deuel, chief of the tribe of Gad. He, too, offered the same gifts and sacrifices.[b]

[48-53] On the seventh day, Elishama, the son of Ammihud, chief of the tribe of Ephraim, brought his gifts, the same as those presented on the previous days.[b]

[54-59] Gamaliel, son of Pedahzur, prince of the tribe of Manasseh, came the eighth day with the same offerings.[b]

[60-65] On the ninth day it was Abidan the son of Gideoni, chief of the tribe of Benjamin, with his gifts, the same as those offered by the others.[b]

[66-71] Ahiezer, the son of Ammishaddai, brought his gifts on the tenth day. He was the chief of the tribe of Dan and his offerings were the same as those on the previous days.[b]

[72-77] Pagiel, son of Ochran, chief of the tribe of Asher, brought his gifts on the eleventh day—the same gifts and offerings as the others.[b]

[78-83] On the twelfth day came Ahira, son of Enan, chief of the tribe of Naphtali, with his offerings; they were identical to those brought by the others.[b]

[84,85,86] So, beginning the day the altar was anointed, it was dedicated by these gifts from the chiefs of the tribes of Israel. Their combined offerings were as follows:

12 silver platters (each weighing about two pounds);

12 silver bowls (each weighing about one pound); (so the total weight of the silver was about thirty-six pounds);

12 golden trays (the trays weighing about four ounces apiece); (so the total weight of gold was about three pounds).

[87] For the burnt offerings they brought:
12 bulls, 12 rams,
12 yearling male goats (with the grain offerings that accompanied them).

For sin offerings they brought:
12 male goats.

[88] For the peace offerings they brought:
24 young bulls,
60 rams, 60 male goats,
60 male lambs a year old.

[89] When Moses went into the Tabernacle to speak with God, he heard the Voice speaking to him from above the place of mercy over the Ark, the spot between the two cherubim.

8 THE LORD SAID to Moses, [2] "Tell Aaron that when he lights the seven lamps in the lampstand, he is to set them so that they will throw their light forward."

[3] So Aaron did this. [4] The lampstand, including the floral decorations on the base and branches, was made entirely of beaten

---

a Implied.   b The original text repeats the lists of the offerings recorded in verses 13 to 17.

gold. It was constructed according to the exact design the Lord had shown Moses.

^{5,6} Then the Lord said to Moses, "Now set apart the Levites from the other people of Israel. ⁷ Do this by sprinkling water of purification upon them, then having them shave their entire bodies and wash their clothing and themselves. ⁸ Have them bring a young bull and a grain offering of fine flour mingled with oil, along with another young bull for a sin offering. ⁹ Then bring the Levites to the door of the Tabernacle as all the people watch. ¹⁰ There the leaders[a] of the tribes shall lay their hands upon them, ¹¹ and Aaron, with a gesture of offering, shall present them to the Lord as a gift from the entire nation of Israel. The Levites will represent all the people in serving the Lord.

¹² "Next, the Levite leaders[a] shall lay their hands upon the heads of the young bulls and offer them before the Lord; one for a sin offering and the other for a burnt offering, to make atonement for the Levites. ¹³ Then the Levites are to be presented to Aaron and his sons, just as any other gift to the Lord is given to the priests! ¹⁴ In this way you will dedicate the Levites from among the rest of the people of Israel, and the Levites shall be mine. ¹⁵ After you have sanctified them and presented them in this way, they shall go in and out of the Tabernacle to do their work.

¹⁶ "They are mine from among all the people of Israel, and I have accepted them in place of all the firstborn children of the Israelites: I have taken the Levites as their substitutes. ¹⁷ For all the firstborn among the people of Israel are mine, both men and animals; I claimed them for myself the night I killed all the firstborn Egyptians. ¹⁸ Yes, I have accepted the Levites in place of all the eldest sons of Israel. ¹⁹ And I will give the Levites as a gift to Aaron and his sons. The Levites will carry out the sacred duties required of the people of Israel in the Tabernacle, and will offer the people's sacrifices, making atonement for them. There will be no plague among the Israelites—as there would be if the ordinary people entered the Tabernacle."

²⁰ So Moses and Aaron and all the people of Israel dedicated the Levites, carefully following Jehovah's instructions to Moses. ²¹ The Levites purified themselves and washed their clothes, and Aaron presented them to the Lord in a gesture of offering. He then performed the rite of atonement over them to purify them. ²² After that they went into the Tabernacle as assistants to Aaron and his sons; everything was done just as the Lord had commanded Moses.

^{23,24} The Lord also instructed Moses, "The Levites are to begin serving in the Tabernacle at the age of twenty-five, and are to retire at the age of fifty. ^{25,26} After retirement they can assist with various light duties in the Tabernacle, but will have no regular responsibilities."

9 JEHOVAH GAVE THESE instructions to Moses while he and the rest of the Israelis were on the Sinai peninsula, during the first month of the second year after leaving Egypt: ^{2,3} "The people of Israel must celebrate the Passover annually on the fourteenth day of this first month,[a] beginning in the evening. Be sure to follow all of my instructions concerning this celebration."

^{4,5} So Moses announced that the Passover celebration would begin on the evening of the fourteenth, there in the Sinai peninsula, just as the Lord had commanded. ^{6,7} But as it happened, some of the men had just attended a funeral, and were ceremonially defiled by having touched the dead, so they couldn't eat the Passover lamb that night. They came to Moses and Aaron and explained their problem and protested at being forbidden from offering their sacrifice to the Lord at the time he had appointed.

⁸ Moses said he would ask the Lord about it, ⁹ and this was God's reply:

¹⁰ "If any of the people of Israel, now or in the generations to come, are defiled at Passover time because of touching a dead body, or if they are on a journey and cannot be present, they may still celebrate the Passover, but one month later, ¹¹ on the four-

---

a Implied.   9a Note: The 14th day of the first month of the Hebrew calendar corresponds approximately to our first day of April.

teenth day of the *second* month, beginning in the evening. They are to eat the lamb at that time, with unleavened bread and bitter herbs. [12] They must not leave any of it until the next morning, and must not break a bone of it, and must follow all the regular instructions concerning the Passover.

[13] "But anyone who is not defiled, and anyone who is not away on a trip, and yet refuses to celebrate the Passover at the regular time, shall be excommunicated from the people of Israel for refusing to sacrifice to Jehovah at the proper time; he must bear his guilt. [14] And if a foreigner is living among you and wants to celebrate the Passover to the Lord, he shall follow all these same instructions. There is one law for all."

[15] On the day the Tabernacle was raised, the Cloud covered it; and that evening the Cloud changed to the appearance of fire, and stayed that way throughout the night. [16] It was always so—the daytime Cloud changing to the appearance of fire at night. [17] When the Cloud lifted, the people of Israel moved on to wherever it stopped, and camped there. [18] In this way they journeyed at the command of the Lord and stopped where he told them to, then remained there as long as the Cloud stayed. [19] If it stayed a long time, then they stayed a long time. But if it stayed only a few days, then they remained only a few days; for so the Lord had instructed them. [20,21] Sometimes the fire-cloud stayed only during the night and moved on the next morning. But day or night, when it moved, the people broke camp and followed. [22] If the Cloud stayed above the Tabernacle two days, a month, or a year, that is how long the people of Israel stayed; but as soon as it moved, they moved. [23] So it was that they camped or traveled at the commandment of the Lord; and whatever the Lord told Moses they should do, they did.

10 NOW THE LORD said to Moses, "Make two trumpets of beaten silver to be used for summoning the people to assemble and for signaling the breaking of camp. [3] When both trumpets are blown, the people will know that they are to gather at the entrance of the Tabernacle. [4] But if only one is blown, then only the chiefs of the tribes of Israel shall come to you.

[5,6,7] "Different trumpet blasts will be necessary to distinguish between the summons to assemble and the signal to break camp and move onward.[a] When the travel signal is blown, the tribes camped on the east side of the Tabernacle shall leave first; at the second signal, the tribes on the south shall go. [8] Only the priests are permitted to blow the trumpets. This is a permanent instruction to be followed from generation to generation.

[9] "When you arrive in the Promised Land and go to war against your enemies, God will hear you and save you from your enemies when you sound the alarm with these trumpets. [10] Use the trumpets in times of gladness, too, blowing them at your annual festivals and at the beginning of each month to rejoice over your burnt offerings and peace offerings. And God will be reminded of his covenant with you. For I am Jehovah, your God."

[11] The Cloud lifted from the Tabernacle on the twentieth day of the second month[b] of the second year of Israel's leaving Egypt; [12] so the Israelites left the Sinai wilderness, and followed the Cloud until it stopped in the wilderness of Paran. [13] This was their first journey after having received the Lord's travel instructions to Moses.

[14] At the head of the march was the tribe of Judah grouped behind its flag, and led by Nahshon, the son of Amminadab. [15] Next came the tribe of Issachar, led by Nethanel, the son of Zuar, [16] and the tribe of Zebulun, led by Eliab, the son of Helon.

[17] The Tabernacle was taken down and the men of the Gershon and Merari divisions of the tribe of Levi were next in the line of march, carrying the Tabernacle upon their shoulders. [18] Then came the flag of the camp of Reuben, with Elizur the son of Shedeur leading his people. [19] Next was the tribe of Simeon headed by Shelumi-el, the son of Zuri-shaddai; [20] and the tribe of Gad led by Eliasaph, the son of Deuel.

---

a More literally, verse 7 reads: "But when the Assembly is to be gathered together, you shall blow but you shall not sound the alarm."   b Note: This was approximately May 5.

²¹ Next came the Kohathites carrying the items from the inner sanctuary. (The Tabernacle was already erected in its new location by the time they arrived.) ²² Next in line was the tribe of Ephraim behind its flag, led by Elishama, the son of Ammihud; ²³ and the tribe of Manasseh led by Gamaliel the son of Pedahzur; ²⁴ and the tribe of Benjamin, led by Abidan the son of Gideoni. ²⁵ Last of all were the tribes headed by the flag of the tribe of Dan under the leadership of Ahiezer, the son of Ammishaddai; ²⁶ the tribe of Asher, led by Pagiel, the son of Ochran; ²⁷ and the tribe of Naphtali, led by Ahira, the son of Enan. ²⁸ That was the order in which the tribes traveled.

²⁹ One day Moses said to his brother-in-law Hobab (son of Reuel, the Midianite), "At last we are on our way to the Promised Land. Come with us and we will do you good; for the Lord has given wonderful promises to Israel!"

³⁰ But his brother-in-law replied, "No, I must return to my own land and kinfolk."

³¹ "Stay with us," Moses pleaded, "for you know the ways of the wilderness and will be a great help to us.ᶜ ³² If you come, you will share in all the good things the Lord does for us."

³³ They traveled for three days after leaving Mount Sinai,ᵈ with the Ark at the front of the column to choose a place for them to stop. ³⁴ It was daytime when they left, with the Cloud moving along ahead of them as they began their march. ³⁵ As the Ark was carried forward, Moses cried out, "Arise, O Lord, and scatter your enemies; let them flee before you." ³⁶ And when the Ark was set down he said, "Return, O Lord, to the millions of Israel."

11 THE PEOPLE WERE soon complaining about all their misfortunes, and the Lord heard them. His anger flared out against them because of their complaints, so the fire of the Lord began destroying those at the far end of the camp. ² They screamed to Moses for help, and when he prayed for them the fire stopped. ³ Ever after, the area was known as "The Place of Burning,"ᵃ be-cause the fire from the Lord burned among them there.

⁴,⁵ Then the Egyptians who had come with them began to long for the good things of Egypt. This added to the discontent of the people of Israel and they wept, "Oh, for a few bites of meat! Oh, that we had some of the delicious fish we enjoyed so much in Egypt, and the wonderful cucumbers and melons, leeks, onions, and garlic! ⁶ But now our strength is gone, and day after day we have to face this manna!"

⁷ The manna was about the size of coriander seed, and looked like droplets of gum from the bark of a tree. ⁸ The people gathered it from the ground and crushed it into flour or pounded it in mortars, boiled it, and then made pancakes from it—they tasted like pancakes fried in vegetable oil.ᵇ ⁹ The manna fell with the dew during the night.

¹⁰ Moses heard all the families standing around their tent doors weeping, and the anger of the Lord grew hot; Moses too was highly displeased.

¹¹ Moses said to the Lord, "Why pick on me, to give me the burden of a people like this? ¹² Are they *my* children? Am I their father? Is that why you have given me the job of nursing them along like babies until we get to the land you promised their ancestors? ¹³ Where am I supposed to get meat for all these people? For they weep to me saying, 'Give us meat!' ¹⁴ I can't carry this nation by myself! The load is far too heavy! ¹⁵ If you are going to treat me like this, please kill me right now; it will be a kindness! Let me out of this impossible situation!"

¹⁶ Then the Lord said to Moses, "Summon before me seventy of the leaders of Israel; bring them to the Tabernacle, to stand there with you. ¹⁷ I will come down and talk with you there and I will take of the Spirit which is on you and will put it upon them also; they shall bear the burden of the people along with you, so that you will not have the task alone.

¹⁸ "And tell the people to purify themselves, for tomorrow they shall have meat

---

c Literally, "you know how we are to encamp in the wilderness, and you will serve as eyes for us."
d Literally, "the mount of Jehovah."   11a Literally, "Taberah."   b Literally, "olive oil."

to eat. Tell them, 'The Lord has heard your tearful complaints about all you left behind in Egypt, and he is going to give you meat. You shall eat it, [19,20] not for just a day or two, or five or ten or even twenty! For one whole month you will have meat until you vomit it from your noses; for you have rejected the Lord who is here among you, and you have wept for Egypt.' "

[21] But Moses said, "There are 600,000 men alone [besides all the women and children[c]], and yet you promise them meat for a whole month! [22] If we butcher all our flocks and herds it won't be enough! We would have to catch every fish in the ocean to fulfill your promise!"

[23] Then the Lord said to Moses, "When did I become weak? Now you shall see whether my word comes true or not!"

[24] So Moses left the Tabernacle and reported Jehovah's words to the people; and he gathered the seventy elders and placed them around the Tabernacle. [25] And the Lord came down in the Cloud and talked with Moses, and the Lord took of the Spirit that was upon Moses and put it upon the seventy elders; and when the Spirit rested upon them, they prophesied for some time.

[26] But two of the seventy—Eldad and Medad—were still in the camp, and when the Spirit rested upon them, they prophesied there. [27] Some young men ran and told Moses what was happening, [28] and Joshua (the son of Nun), one of Moses' personally chosen assistants, protested, "Sir, make them stop!"

[29] But Moses replied, "Are you jealous for my sake? I only wish that all of the Lord's people were prophets, and that the Lord would put his Spirit upon them all!" [30] Then Moses returned to the camp with the elders of Israel.

[31] The Lord sent a wind that brought quail from the sea, and let them fall into the camp and all around it! As far as one could walk in a day in any direction, there were quail flying three or four feet above the ground.[d] [32] So the people caught and killed quail all that day and through the night and all the next day too! The least anyone gathered was 100 bushels! Quail were spread out all around[e] the camp. [33] But as everyone began eating the meat, the anger of the Lord rose against the people and he killed large numbers of them with a plague. [34] So the name of that place was called, "The Place of the Graves Caused by Lust,"[f] because they buried the people there who had lusted for meat and for Egypt. [35] And from that place they journeyed to Hazeroth, where they stayed awhile.

12 ONE DAY MIRIAM and Aaron were criticizing Moses because his wife was a Cushite[a] woman, [2] and they said, "Has the Lord spoken only through Moses? Hasn't he spoken through us, too?"

But the Lord heard them. [3,4] Immediately he summoned Moses, Aaron, and Miriam to the Tabernacle: "Come here, you three," he commanded. So they stood before the Lord. (Now Moses was the humblest man on earth.)

[5] Then the Lord descended in the Cloud and stood at the entrance of the Tabernacle. "Aaron and Miriam, step forward," he commanded; and they did. [6] And the Lord said to them, "Even with a prophet, I would communicate by visions and dreams; [7,8] but that is not how I communicate with my servant Moses. He is completely at home in my house! With him I speak face to face! And he shall see the very form of God! Why then were you not afraid to criticize him?"

[9] Then the anger of the Lord grew hot against them, and he departed. [10] As the Cloud moved from above the Tabernacle, Miriam suddenly became white with leprosy. When Aaron saw what had happened, [11] he cried out to Moses, "Oh, sir, do not punish us for this sin; we were fools to do such a thing. [12] Don't let her be as one dead, whose body is half rotted away at birth."

[13] And Moses cried out to the Lord,

---

c Implied.   d Or, "The ground was covered with them, three feet thick!"   e To cure them by drying.
f Literally, "Kibroth-hattaavah."   12 a Literally, "because of the Cushite woman he had married." Apparently they were referring to his wife Zipporah, the Midianite daughter of Reuel (Exodus 2:21); for the land of Midian from which she came was sometimes called Cush. But areas of Ethiopia and Babylon were also known as Cush, so it is possible that the reference is to a second wife of Moses. It is indeterminate from the text as to whether the criticism was because she was a Gentile or (if she was a Cushite from Ethiopia) because of her color.

"Heal her, O God, I beg you!"

[14] And the Lord said to Moses, "If her father had but spit in her face she would be defiled seven days. Let her be confined outside the camp for seven days, and after that she can come back again."

[15] So Miriam was excluded from the camp for seven days, and the people waited until she was brought back in before they traveled again. [16] Afterwards they left Hazeroth and camped in the wilderness of Paran.

13 JEHOVAH NOW INSTRUCTED Moses, [2] "Send spies into the land of Canaan—the land I am giving to Israel; send one leader from each tribe."

[3-15] (The Israelis were camped in the wilderness of Paran at the time.) Moses did as the Lord had commanded and sent these twelve tribal leaders:

> Shammu-a, son of Zaccur, from the tribe of Reuben;
>
> Shaphat, son of Hori, from the tribe of Simeon;
>
> Caleb, son of Jephunneh, from the tribe of Judah;
>
> Igal, son of Joseph, from the tribe of Issachar;
>
> Hoshea,[a] son of Nun, from the half-tribe of Ephraim;
>
> Palti, son of Raphu, from the tribe of Benjamin;
>
> Gaddiel, son of Sodi, from the tribe of Zebulun;
>
> Gaddi, son of Susi, from the tribe of Joseph (actually, the half-tribe of Manasseh);
>
> Ammiel, son of Gemalli, from the tribe of Dan;
>
> Sethur, son of Michael, from the tribe of Asher;
>
> Nahbi, son of Vophsi, from the tribe of Naphtali;
>
> Geuel, son of Machi, from the tribe of Gad.

[16] It was at this time that Moses changed Hoshea's name to Joshua.[b]

[17] Moses sent them out with these instructions: "Go northward into the hill country of the Negeb, [18] and see what the land is like; see also what the people are like who live there, whether they are strong or weak, many or few; [19] and whether the land is fertile or not; and what cities there are, and whether they are villages or are fortified; [20] whether the land is rich or poor, and whether there are many trees. Don't be afraid, and bring back some samples of the crops you see." (The first of the grapes were being harvested at that time.)

[21] So they spied out the land all the way from the wilderness of Zin to Rehob near Hamath. [22] Going northward, they passed first through the Negeb and arrived at Hebron. There they saw the Ahimanites, Sheshites, and Talmites, all families descended from Anak. (By the way, Hebron was very ancient, having been founded seven years before Tanis[c] in Egypt). [23] Then they came to what is now known as the Valley of Eshcol where they cut down a single cluster of grapes so large that it took two of them to carry it on a pole between them! They also took some samples of the pomegranates and figs. [24] The Israelis named the valley "Eshcol" at that time (meaning "Cluster") because of the cluster of grapes they found!

[25] Forty days later they returned from their tour. [26] They made their report to Moses, Aaron, and all the people of Israel in the wilderness of Paran at Kadesh, and they showed the fruit they had brought with them.

[27] This was their report: "We arrived in the land you sent us to see, and it is indeed a magnificent country—a land 'flowing with milk and honey.' Here is some fruit we have brought as proof. [28] But the people living there are powerful, and their cities are fortified and very large; and what's more, we saw Anakim giants there! [29] The Amalekites live in the south, while in the hill country there are the Hittites, Jebusites, and Amorites; down along the coast of the Mediterranean Sea and in the Jordan River valley are the Canaanites."

[30] But Caleb reassured the people as they stood before Moses. "Let us go up at once and possess it," he said, "for we are well

---

a Or, "Joshua." See verse 16.   b "Hoshea" means "salvation"; "Joshua" means "Jehovah is salvation." Joshua is the same name in Hebrew as the Greek name "Jesus."   c Tanis (or Zoan, as it was pronounced in ancient times) was founded about 1720 B.C.

able to conquer it!"

[31] "Not against people as strong as they are!" the other spies said. "They would crush us!"

[32] So the majority report of the spies was negative: "The land is full of warriors, the people are powerfully built, [33] and we saw some of the Anakim there, descendants of the ancient race of giants. We felt like grasshoppers before them, they were so tall!"

14 THEN ALL THE people began weeping aloud, and they carried on all night. [2] Their voices rose in a great chorus of complaint against Moses and Aaron.

"We wish we had died in Egypt," they wailed, "or even here in the wilderness, [3] rather than be taken into this country ahead of us. Jehovah will kill us there, and our wives and little ones will become slaves. Let's get out of here and return to Egypt!" [4] The idea swept the camp. "Let's elect a leader to take us back to Egypt!" they shouted.

[5] Then Moses and Aaron fell face downward on the ground before the people of Israel; [6] two of the spies, Joshua (the son of Nun), and Caleb (the son of Jephunneh), ripped their clothing [7] and said to all the people, "It is a wonderful country ahead, [8] and the Lord loves us. He will bring us safely into the land and give it to us. It is *very* fertile, a land 'flowing with milk and honey'! [9] Oh, do not rebel against the Lord, and do not fear the people of the land. For they are but bread for us to eat! The Lord is with us and he has removed his protection from them! Don't be afraid of them!"

[10,11] But the only response of the people was to talk of stoning them. Then the glory of the Lord appeared, and the Lord said to Moses, "How long will these people despise me? Will they *never* believe me, even after all the miracles I have done among them? [12] I will disinherit them and destroy them with a plague, and I will make you into a nation far greater and mightier than they are!"

[13] "But what will the Egyptians think when they hear about it?" Moses pleaded with the Lord. "They know full well the power you displayed in rescuing your people. [14] They have told this to the inhabitants of this land, who are well aware that you are with Israel and that you talk with her face to face. They see the pillar of cloud and fire standing above us, and they know that you lead and protect us day and night. [15] Now if you kill all your people, the nations that have heard your fame will say, [16] 'The Lord had to kill them because he wasn't able to take care of them in the wilderness. He wasn't strong enough to bring them into the land he swore he would give them.'

[17,18] "Oh, please, show the great power [of your patience[a]] by forgiving our sins and showing us your steadfast love. Forgive us, even though you have said that you don't let sin go unpunished, and that you punish the father's fault in the children to the third and fourth generation. [19] Oh, I plead with you, pardon the sins of this people because of your magnificent, steadfast love, just as you have forgiven them all the time from when we left Egypt until now."

[20,21] Then the Lord said, "All right, I will pardon them as you have requested. But I vow by my own name that just as it is true that all the earth shall be filled with the glory of the Lord, [22] so it is true that not one of the men who has seen my glory and the miracles I did both in Egypt and in the wilderness—and ten times refused to trust me and obey me— [23] shall even see the land I promised to this people's ancestors. [24] But my servant Caleb is a different kind of man—he has obeyed me fully. I will bring him into the land he entered as a spy, and his descendants shall have their full share in it. [25] But now, since the people of Israel are so afraid of the Amalekites and the Canaanites living in the valleys, tomorrow you must turn back into the wilderness in the direction of the Red Sea."

[26,27] Then the Lord added to Moses and to Aaron, "How long will these wicked people complain about me? For I have heard all that they have been saying. [28] Tell them, 'The Lord vows to do to you what you feared: [29] You will all die here in this wilderness! Not a single one of you twenty years

---

a Implied.

old and older, who has complained against me, [30] shall enter the Promised Land. Only Caleb (son of Jephunneh) and Joshua (son of Nun) are permitted to enter it.

[31] " 'You said your children would become slaves of the people of the land. Well, instead I will bring *them* safely into the land and they shall inherit what you have despised. [32] But as for you, your dead bodies shall fall in this wilderness. [33] You must wander in the desert like nomads for forty years. In this way you will pay for your faithlessness, until the last of you lies dead in the desert.

[34,35] " 'Since the spies were in the land for forty days, you must wander in the wilderness for forty years—a year for each day, bearing the burden of your sins. I will teach you what it means to reject me. I, Jehovah, have spoken. Every one of you who has conspired against me shall die here in this wilderness.' "

[36,37,38] Then the ten spies who had incited the rebellion against Jehovah by striking fear into the hearts of the people were struck dead before the Lord. Of all the spies, only Joshua and Caleb remained alive. [39] What sorrow there was throughout the camp when Moses reported God's words to the people!

[40] They were up early the next morning, and started towards the Promised Land.

"Here we are!" they said. "We realize that we have sinned, but now we are ready to go on into the land the Lord has promised us."

[41] But Moses said, "It's too late. Now you are disobeying the Lord's orders to return to the wilderness. [42] Don't go ahead with your plan or you will be crushed by your enemies, for the Lord is not with you. [43] Don't you remember? The Amalekites and the Canaanites are there! You have deserted the Lord, and now he will desert you."

[44] But they went ahead into the hill country, despite the fact that neither the Ark nor Moses left the camp. [45] Then the Amalekites and the Canaanites who lived in the hills came down and attacked them and chased them to Hormah.

15 THE LORD TOLD Moses to give these instructions to the people of Israel: "When your children finally live in the land I am going to give them, [3,4] and they want to please the Lord with a burnt offering or any other offering by fire, their sacrifice must be an animal from their flocks of sheep and goats, or from their herds of cattle. Each sacrifice—whether an ordinary one, or a sacrifice to fulfill a vow, or a free-will offering, or a special sacrifice at any of the annual festivals—must be accompanied by a grain offering. If a lamb is being sacrificed, use three quarts of fine flour mixed with three pints of oil, [5] accompanied by three pints of wine for a drink offering.

[6] "If the sacrifice is a ram, use six quarts of fine flour mixed with four pints of oil, [7] and four pints of wine for a drink offering. This will be a sacrifice that is a pleasing fragrance to the Lord.

[8,9] "If the sacrifice is a young bull, then the grain offering accompanying it must consist of nine quarts of fine flour mixed with three quarts of oil, [10] plus three quarts of wine for the drink offering. This shall be offered by fire as a pleasing fragrance to the Lord.

[11,12] "These are the instructions for what is to accompany each sacrificial bull, ram, lamb, or young goat. [13,14] These instructions apply both to native-born Israelis and to foreigners living among you who want to please the Lord with sacrifices offered by fire; [15,16] for there is the same law for all, native-born or foreigner, and this shall be true forever from generation to generation; all are equal before the Lord.[a] Yes, one law for all!"

[17,18] The Lord also said to Moses at this time, "Instruct the people of Israel that when they arrive in the land that I am going to give them, [19,20,21] they must present to the Lord a sample of each year's new crops by making a loaf, using coarse flour from the first grain that is cut each year. This loaf must be waved back and forth before the altar in a gesture of offering to the Lord. It is an annual offering from your threshing floor, and must be observed from generation to generation.

---

a Literally, "as you are, so shall the foreigner be before Jehovah."

²² "If by mistake you or future generations fail to carry out all of these regulations which the Lord has given you over the years through Moses, ²³,²⁴ then when the people realize their error, they must offer one young bull for a burnt offering. It will be a pleasant odor before the Lord, and must be offered along with the usual grain offering and drink offering, and one male goat for a sin offering. ²⁵ And the priest shall make atonement for all of the people of Israel and they shall be forgiven; for it was an error, and they have corrected it with their sacrifice made by fire before the Lord, and by their sin offering. ²⁶ All the people shall be forgiven, including the foreigners living among them, for the entire population is involved in such error and forgiveness.

²⁷ "If the error is made by a single individual, then he shall sacrifice a one-year-old female goat for a sin offering, ²⁸ and the priest shall make atonement for him before the Lord, and he shall be forgiven. ²⁹ This same law applies to individual foreigners who are living among you.

³⁰ "But anyone who deliberately makes the 'mistake,' whether he is a native Israeli or a foreigner, is blaspheming Jehovah, and shall be cut off from among his people. ³¹ For he has despised the commandment of the Lord and deliberately failed to obey his law; he must be executed,ᵇ and die in his sin."

³² One day while the people of Israel were in the wilderness, one of them was caught gathering wood on the Sabbath day. ³³ He was arrested and taken before Moses and Aaron and the other judges.ᶜ ³⁴ They jailed him until they could find out the Lord's mind concerning him. ³⁵ Then the Lord said to Moses, "The man must die—all the people shall stone him to death outside the camp."

³⁶ So they took him outside the camp and killed him as the Lord had commanded.

³⁷,³⁸ The Lord said to Moses, "Tell the people of Israel to make tassels for the hems of their clothes (this is a permanent regulation from generation to generation) and to attach the tassels to their clothes with a blue cord. ³⁹ The purpose of this regulation is to remind you, whenever you notice the tassels, of the commandments of the Lord, and that you are to obey his laws instead of following your own desires and going your own ways, as you used to do in serving other gods. ⁴⁰ It will remind you to be holy to your God. ⁴¹ For I am Jehovah your God who brought you out of the land of Egypt; yes, I am the Lord, your God."

16 ONE DAY KORAH (son of Izhar, grandson of Kohath, and a descendant of Levi) conspired with Dathan and Abiram (the sons of Eliab) and On (the son of Peleth), all three from the tribe of Reuben, ² to incite a rebellion against Moses. Two hundred and fifty popular leaders, all members of the Assembly, were involved.

³ They went to Moses and Aaron and said, "We have had enough of your presumption; you are no better than anyone else; everyone in Israel has been chosen of the Lord, and he is with all of us. What right do you have to put yourselves forward, claiming that we must obey you, and acting as though you were greater than anyone else among all these people of the Lord?"

⁴ When Moses heard what they were saying he fell face downward to the ground. ⁵ Then he said to Korah and to those who were with him, "In the morning the Lord will show you who are his, and who is holy, and whom he has chosen as his priest. ⁶,⁷ Do this: You, Korah, and all those with you, take censers tomorrow and light them, and put incense upon them before the Lord, and we will find out whom the Lord has chosen.ᵃ You are the presumptuous ones, you sons of Levi."

⁸,⁹ Then Moses spoke again to Korah: "Does it seem a small thing to you that the God of Israel has chosen you from among all the people of Israel to be near to himself as you work in the Tabernacle of Jehovah, and to stand before the people to minister to them? ¹⁰ Is it nothing to you that he has given this task to only you Levites? And now are you demanding the priesthood also? ¹¹,¹² That is what you are really after!

---

b Literally, "that soul shall be utterly cut off; his iniquity shall be upon him."   c Literally, "to all the congregation."   **16a** Literally, "whom Jehovah chooses to be the holy one."

That is why you are revolting against Jehovah. And what has Aaron done, that you are dissatisfied with him?" Then Moses summoned Dathan and Abiram (the sons of Eliab), but they refused to come. [13] "Is it a small thing," they mimicked,[b] "that you brought us out of lovely Egypt to kill us here in this terrible wilderness, and that now you want to make yourself our king? [14] What's more, you haven't brought us into the wonderful country you promised, nor given us fields and vineyards. Whom are you trying to fool? We refuse to come."

[15] Then Moses was very angry and said to the Lord, "Do not accept their sacrifices! I have never stolen so much as a donkey from them, and have not hurt one of them." [16] And Moses said to Korah, "Come here tomorrow before the Lord with all your friends; Aaron will be here too. [17] Be sure to bring your censers with incense on them; a censer for each man, 250 in all; and Aaron will also be here with his." [18] So they did. They came with their censers and lit them and placed the incense on them, and stood at the entrance of the Tabernacle with Moses and Aaron. [19] Meanwhile, Korah had stirred up the entire nation against Moses and Aaron, and they all assembled to watch. Then the glory of Jehovah appeared to all the people, [20] and Jehovah said to Moses and Aaron, [21] "Get away from these people so that I may instantly destroy them."

[22] But Moses and Aaron fell face downward to the ground before the Lord. "O God, the God of all mankind," they pleaded, "must you be angry with all the people when one man sins?"

[23,24] And the Lord said to Moses, "Then tell the people to get away from the tents of Korah, Dathan, and Abiram."

[25] So Moses rushed over to the tents of Dathan and Abiram, followed closely by the 250 Israeli leaders. [26] "Quick!" he told the people, "get away from the tents of these wicked men, and don't touch anything that belongs to them, lest you be included in their sins [and be destroyed with them[c]]."

[27] So all the people stood back from the tents of Korah, Dathan, and Abiram. And Dathan and Abiram came out and stood at the entrances of their tents with their wives and sons and little ones.

[28] And Moses said, "By this you shall know that Jehovah has sent me to do all these things that I have done—for I have not done them on my own. [29] If these men die a natural death or from some ordinary accident or disease, then Jehovah has not sent me. [30] But if the Lord does a miracle and the ground opens up and swallows them and everything that belongs to them, and they go down alive into Sheol, then you will know that these men have despised the Lord."

[31] He had hardly finished speaking the words when the ground suddenly split open beneath them, [32] and a great fissure swallowed them up, along with their tents and families and the friends who were standing with them, and everything they owned. [33] So they went down alive into Sheol and the earth closed upon them, and they perished. [34] All of the people of Israel fled at their screams, fearing that the earth would swallow them too. [35] Then fire came forth from Jehovah and burned up the 250 men who were offering incense.

[36,37] And the Lord said to Moses, "Tell Eleazar the son of Aaron the priest to pull those censers from the fire; for they are holy, dedicated to the Lord. He must also scatter the burning incense [38] from the censers of these men who have sinned at the cost of their lives. He shall then beat the metal into a sheet as a covering for the altar, for these censers are holy because they were used before the Lord; and the altar sheet shall be a reminder to the people of Israel."

[39] So Eleazar the priest took the 250 bronze censers and beat them out into a sheet of metal to cover the altar, [40] to be a reminder to the people of Israel that no unauthorized person—no one who is not a descendant of Aaron—may come before the Lord to burn incense, lest the same thing happen to him as happened to Korah and his associates. Thus the Lord's directions to Moses were carried out.

[41] But the very next morning all the peo-

---

b Literally, "said."   c Implied.

ple began muttering again against Moses and Aaron, saying, "You have killed the Lord's people."

[42] Soon a great, sullen mob formed; suddenly, as they looked toward the Tabernacle, the Cloud appeared and the awesome glory of the Lord was seen. [43,44] Moses and Aaron came and stood at the entrance of the Tabernacle, and the Lord said to Moses, [45] "Get away from these people so that I can instantly destroy them." But Moses and Aaron fell face downward to the earth before the Lord.

[46] And Moses said to Aaron, "Quick, take a censer and place fire in it from the altar; lay incense on it, and carry it quickly among the people and make atonement for them; for God's anger has gone out among them—the plague has already begun."

[47] Aaron did as Moses had told him to, and ran among the people, for the plague had indeed already begun; and he put on the incense and made atonement for them. [48] And he stood between the living and the dead, and the plague was stopped, [49] but not before 14,700 people had died (in addition to those who had died the previous day with Korah). [50] Then Aaron returned to Moses at the entrance of the Tabernacle; and so the plague was stopped.

17 THEN THE LORD said to Moses, "Tell the people of Israel that each of their tribal chiefs is to bring you a wooden rod with his name inscribed upon it. Aaron's name is to be on the rod of the tribe of Levi. [4] Put these rods in the inner room of the Tabernacle where I meet with you, in front of the Ark. [5] I will use these rods to identify the man I have chosen: for buds will grow on his rod! Then at last this murmuring and complaining against you will stop!"

[6] So Moses gave the instructions to the people, and each of the twelve chiefs (including Aaron) brought him a rod. [7] He put them before the Lord in the inner room of the Tabernacle, [8] and when he went in the next day, he found that Aaron's rod, representing the tribe of Levi, had budded and was blossoming, and had ripe almonds hanging from it!

[9] When Moses brought them out to show the others, they stared in disbelief! Then each man except Aaron claimed his rod. [10] The Lord told Moses to place Aaron's rod permanently beside the Ark as a reminder of this rebellion. He was to [bring it out and show it to the people again[a]] if there were any further complaints about Aaron's authority; this would ward off further catastrophe to the people. [11] So Moses did as the Lord commanded him.

[12,13] But the people of Israel only grumbled the more. "We are as good as dead," they whined. "Everyone who even comes close to the Tabernacle dies. Must we all perish?"

18 THE LORD NOW spoke to Aaron: "You and your sons and your family are responsible for any desecration of the sanctuary," he said, "and will be held liable for any impropriety in your priestly work. [2,3] Your kinsmen, the tribe of Levi, are your assistants; but only you and your sons may perform the sacred duties in the Tabernacle itself. The Levites must be careful not to touch any of the sacred articles or the altar, lest I destroy both them and you. [4] No one who is not a member of the tribe of Levi shall assist you in any way. [5] Remember, only the priests are to perform the sacred duties within the sanctuary and at the altar. If you follow these instructions the wrath of God will never again fall upon any of the people of Israel for violating this law. [6] I say it again—your kinsmen the Levites are your assistants for the work of the Tabernacle. They are a gift to you from the Lord. [7] But you and your sons, the priests, shall personally handle all the sacred service, including the altar and all that is within the veil, for the priesthood is your special gift of service. Anyone else who attempts to perform these duties shall die."

[8] The Lord gave these further instructions to Aaron: "I have given the priests all the gifts which are brought to the Lord by the people; all these offerings presented to the Lord by the gesture of waving them before the altar belong to you and your sons, by permanent law. [9] The grain offer-

---

a Implied.

ings, the sin offerings, and the guilt offerings are yours, except for the sample presented to the Lord by burning upon the altar. All these are most holy offerings. [10] They are to be eaten only in a most holy place, and only by males. [11] All other gifts presented to me by the gesture of waving them before the altar are for you and your families, sons and daughters alike. For all the members of your families may eat these unless anyone is ceremonially impure at the time.

[12] "Yours also are the first-of-the-harvest gifts the people bring as offerings to the Lord—the best of the olive oil, wine, grain, [13] and every other crop. Your families may eat these unless they are ceremonially defiled at the time. [14,15] So everything that is dedicated to the Lord shall be yours, including the firstborn sons of the people of Israel, and the firstborn of their animals. [16] However, you may never accept the firstborn sons, nor the firstborn of any animals that I do not permit for food. Instead, there must be a payment of two and a half dollars made for each firstborn child. It is to be brought when he is one month old.

[17] "However, the firstborn of cows, sheep, or goats may not be bought back; they must be sacrificed to the Lord.[a] Their blood is to be sprinkled upon the altar, and their fat shall be burned as a fire offering; it is very pleasant to the Lord. [18] The meat of these animals shall be yours, including the breast and right thigh that are presented to the Lord by the gesture of waving before the altar. [19] Yes, I have given to you all of these 'wave offerings' brought by the people of Israel to the Lord; they are for you and your families as food; this is a permanent contract[b] between the Lord and you and your descendants.

[20] "You priests may own no property, nor have any other income, for I am all that you need. [21] As for the tribe of Levi, your relatives, they shall be paid for their service with the tithes from the entire land of Israel.

[22] "From now on, Israelites other than the priests and Levites shall not enter the sanctuary, lest they be judged guilty and die. [23] Only the Levites shall do the work there, and they shall be guilty if they fail.

This is a permanent law among you, that the Levites shall own no property in Israel, [24] for the people's tithes, offered to the Lord by the gesture of waving before the altar, shall belong to the Levites; these are their inheritance, and so they have no need for property."

[25,26] The Lord also said to Moses, "Tell the Levites to give to the Lord a tenth of the tithes they receive—a tithe of the tithe, to be presented to the Lord by the gesture of waving before the altar. [27] The Lord will consider this as your first-of-the-harvest offering to him of grain and wine, as though it were from your own property. [28,29] This tithe of the tithe shall be selected from the choicest part of the tithes you receive as the Lord's portion, and shall be given to Aaron the priest. [30] It shall be credited to you just as though it were from your own threshing floor and wine press. [31] Aaron and his sons and their families may eat it in their homes or anywhere they wish, for it is their compensation for their service in the Tabernacle. [32] You Levites will not be held guilty for accepting the Lord's tithes if you then give the best tenth to the priests. But beware that you do not treat the holy gifts of the people of Israel as though they were common, lest you die."

19 THE LORD SAID to Moses and Aaron, "Here is another of my laws:

"Tell the people of Israel to bring you a red heifer without defect, one that has never been yoked. Give her to Eleazar the priest and he shall take her outside the camp and someone shall kill her as he watches. [4] Eleazar shall take some of her blood upon his finger and sprinkle it seven times towards the front of the Tabernacle. [5] Then someone shall burn the heifer as he watches—her hide, meat, blood, and dung. [6] Eleazar shall take cedar wood and hyssop branches and scarlet thread, and throw them into the burning pile.

[7] "Then he must wash his clothes, and bathe, and afterwards return to the camp and be ceremonially defiled until the evening. [8] And the one who burns the animal must wash his clothes, and bathe, and he

---

a Literally, "they are holy."   b Literally, "a covenant of salt."

too shall be defiled until evening. ⁹ Then someone who is not ceremonially defiled shall gather up the ashes of the heifer and place them in some purified place outside the camp, where they shall be kept for the people of Israel as a source of water for the purification ceremonies, for removal of sin. ¹⁰ And the one who gathers up the ashes of the heifer must wash his clothes and be defiled until evening; this is a permanent law for the benefit of the people of Israel and any foreigners living among them.

¹¹ "Anyone who touches a dead human body shall be defiled for seven days, ¹² and must purify himself the third and seventh days with water [run through the ashes of the red heifer[a]]; then he will be purified; but if he does not do this on the third day, he will continue to be defiled even after the seventh day. ¹³ Anyone who touches a dead person and does not purify himself in the manner specified, has defiled the Tabernacle of the Lord, and shall be excommunicated from Israel. The cleansing water was not sprinkled upon him, so the defilement continues.

¹⁴ "When a man dies in a tent, these are the various regulations: Everyone who enters the tent, and those who are in it at the time, shall be defiled seven days. ¹⁵ Any container in the tent without a lid over it is defiled.

¹⁶ "If someone out in a field touches the corpse of someone who has been killed in battle, or who has died in any other way, or if he even touches a bone or a grave, he shall be defiled seven days. ¹⁷ To become purified again, ashes from the red heifer sin offering[b] are to be added to spring water in a kettle. ¹⁸ Then a person who is not defiled shall take hyssop branches and dip them into the water and sprinkle the water upon the tent and upon all the pots and pans in the tent, and upon anyone who has been defiled by being in the tent, or by touching a bone, or touching someone who has been killed or is otherwise dead, or has touched a grave. ¹⁹ This shall take place on the third and seventh days; then the defiled person must wash his clothes and bathe himself,

and that evening he will be out from under the defilement.

²⁰ "But anyone who is defiled and doesn't purify himself shall be excommunicated, for he has defiled the sanctuary of the Lord, and the water to cleanse him has not been sprinkled upon him; so he remains defiled. ²¹ This is a permanent law. The man who sprinkles the water must afterwards wash his clothes; and anyone touching the water shall be defiled until evening. ²² And anything a defiled person touches shall be defiled until evening."

20 THE PEOPLE OF Israel arrived in the wilderness of Zin in April[a] and camped at Kadesh, where Miriam died and was buried. ² There was not enough water to drink at that place, so the people again rebelled against Moses and Aaron. A great mob formed, ³ and they held a protest meeting.

"Would that we too had died with our dear brothers the Lord killed!" they shouted at Moses. ⁴ "You have deliberately brought us into this wilderness to get rid of us, along with our flocks and herds. ⁵ Why did you ever make us leave Egypt and bring us here to this evil place? Where is the fertile land of wonderful crops—the figs, vines, and pomegranates you told us about? Why, there isn't even water enough to drink!"

⁶ Moses and Aaron turned away and went to the entrance of the Tabernacle, where they fell face downward before the Lord; and the glory of Jehovah appeared to them.

⁷ And he said to Moses, ⁸ "Get Aaron's[b] rod; then you and Aaron must summon the people. As they watch, speak to that rock over there and tell it to pour out its water! You will give them water from a rock, enough for all the people and all their cattle!"

⁹ So Moses did as instructed. He took the rod from the place where it was kept before the Lord; ¹⁰ then Moses and Aaron summoned the people to come and gather at the rock; and he said to them, "Listen, you rebels! Must we bring you water from this

---

a Implied. See verse 17.   b Literally, "ashes of the burnt sin offering."   20 a Literally, "the first month."
b Literally, "get the rod."

138

rock?"

¹¹ Then Moses lifted the rod and struck the rock twice, and water gushed out; and the people and their cattle drank.

¹² But the Lord said to Moses and Aaron, "Because you did not believe me[c] and did not sanctify me in the eyes of the people of Israel, you shall not bring them into the land I have promised them!"

¹³ This place was named Meribah (meaning "Rebel Waters"), because it was where the people of Israel fought against Jehovah, and where he showed himself to be holy before them.

¹⁴ While Moses was at Kadesh he sent messengers to the king of Edom: "We are the descendants of your brother[d] Israel," he declared. "You know our sad history, ¹⁵ how our ancestors went down to visit Egypt and stayed there so long, and became slaves of the Egyptians. ¹⁶ But when we cried to the Lord he heard us and sent an Angel who brought us out of Egypt, and now we are here at Kadesh, encamped on the borders of your land. ¹⁷ Please let us pass through your country. We will be careful not to go through your planted fields, nor through your vineyards; we won't even drink water from your wells, but will stay on the main road and not leave it until we have crossed your border on the other side."

¹⁸ But the king of Edom said, "Stay out! If you attempt to enter my land I will meet you with an army!"

¹⁹ "But, sir," protested the Israeli ambassadors, "we will stay on the main road and will not even drink your water unless we pay whatever you demand for it. We only want to pass through, and nothing else."

²⁰ But the king of Edom was adamant. "Stay out!" he warned, and, mobilizing his army, he marched to the frontier with a great force. ²¹,²² Because Edom refused to allow Israel to pass through their country, Israel turned back and journeyed from Kadesh to Mount Hor.

²³ Then the Lord said to Moses and Aaron at the border of the land of Edom, ²⁴ "The time has come for Aaron to die—for he shall not enter the land I have given the people of Israel, for the two of you rebelled against my instructions concerning the water at Meribah. ²⁵ Now take Aaron and his son Eleazar and lead them up onto Mount Hor. ²⁶ There you shall remove Aaron's priestly garments from him and put them on Eleazar his son; and Aaron shall die there."

²⁷ So Moses did as the Lord commanded him. The three[e] of them went up together into Mount Hor as all the people watched. ²⁸ When they reached the summit, Moses removed the priestly garments from Aaron and put them on his son Eleazar; and Aaron died on the top of the mountain. Moses and Eleazar returned, ²⁹ and when the people were informed of Aaron's death, they mourned for him for thirty days.

21 WHEN THE KING of Arad heard that the Israelis were approaching (for they were traveling the same route as the spies), he mobilized his army and attacked Israel, taking some of the men as prisoners. ² Then the people of Israel vowed to the Lord that if he would help them conquer the king of Arad and his people, they would completely annihilate all the cities of that area. ³ The Lord heeded their request and defeated the Canaanites; and the Israelis completely destroyed them and their cities. The name of the region was thereafter called Hormah (meaning "Utterly Destroyed").

⁴ Then the people of Israel returned to Mount Hor, and from there continued southward along the road to the Red Sea in order to go around the land of Edom. The people were very discouraged; ⁵ they began to murmur against God and to complain against Moses. "Why have you brought us out of Egypt to die here in the wilderness?" they whined. "There is nothing to eat here, and nothing to drink, and we hate this insipid manna."

⁶ So the Lord sent poisonous snakes among them to punish them, and many of them were bitten and died.

⁷ Then the people came to Moses and cried out, "We have sinned, for we have

---

c Literally, "did not sanctify me." The Lord had said to *speak* to the rock. Moses *struck* it, not once, but *twice.*
d The people of Edom were descended from Esau, while the people of Israel were descended from his brother Jacob, whose name was later changed to Israel.   e Implied.

spoken against Jehovah and against you. Pray to him to take away the snakes." Moses prayed for the people.

[8] Then the Lord told him, "Make a bronze replica[a] of one of these snakes and attach it to the top of a pole; anyone who is bitten shall live if he simply looks at it!"

[9] So Moses made the replica, and whenever anyone who had been bitten looked at the bronze snake, he recovered!

[10] Israel journeyed next to Oboth and camped there. [11] Then they went on to Iye-abarim, in the wilderness, a short distance east of Moab, [12] and from there they traveled to the valley of the brook Zared and set up camp. [13] Then they moved to the far side of the Arnon River, near the borders of the Amorites. (The Arnon River is the boundary line between the Moabites and the Amorites. [14] This fact is mentioned in *The Book of the Wars of Jehovah,* where it is stated that the valley of the Arnon River, and the city of Waheb, [15] lie between the Amorites and the people of Moab.)

[16] Then Israel traveled to Beer (meaning "A Well"). This is the place where the Lord told Moses, "Summon the people, and I will give them water." [17,18] What happened is described in this song that the people sang:

Spring up, O well!
Sing of the water!
This is a well
The leaders dug.
It was hollowed
With their staves
And shovels.

Then they left the desert and proceeded on through Mattanah, [19] Nahaliel, and Bamoth; [20] then to the valley in the plateau of Moab, which overlooks the desert with Mount Pisgah in the distance. [21] Israel now sent ambassadors to King Sihon of the Amorites.

[22] "Let us travel through your land," they requested. "We will not leave the road until we have passed beyond your borders. We won't trample your fields or touch your vineyards or drink your water."

[23] But King Sihon refused. Instead he mobilized his army and attacked Israel in the wilderness, battling them at Jahaz. [24] But Israel slaughtered them and occupied their land from the Arnon River to the Jabbok River, as far as the borders of the Ammonites; but they were stopped there by the rugged terrain.[b]

[25,26] So Israel captured all the cities of the Amorites and lived in them, including the city of Heshbon, which had been King Sihon's capital. [27-30] The ancient poets had referred to King Sihon in this poem:

Come to Heshbon,
King Sihon's capital,
For a fire has flamed forth
And devoured
The city of Ar in Moab,
On the heights of the Arnon River.
Woe to Moab!
You are finished,
O people of Chemosh;
His sons have fled,
And his daughters are captured
By King Sihon of the Amorites.
He has destroyed
The little children
And the men and women
As far as Dibon, Nophah, and Medeba.

[31,32] While Israel was there in the Amorite country, Moses sent spies to look over the Jazer area; he followed up with an armed attack, capturing all of the towns and driving out the Amorites. [33] They next turned their attention to the city of Bashan, but King Og of Bashan met them with his army at Edre-i. [34] The Lord told Moses not to fear—that the enemy was already conquered! "The same thing will happen to King Og as happened to King Sihon at Heshbon," the Lord assured him. [35] And sure enough, Israel was victorious and killed King Og, his sons, and his subjects, so that not a single survivor remained; and Israel occupied the land.

22 THE PEOPLE OF Israel now traveled to the plains of Moab and camped east of the Jordan River opposite Jericho. [2,3] When King Balak of Moab (the son of Zippor) realized how many of them there

---

a Literally, "Make a fiery serpent."   b Literally, "For the border of the children of Ammon was strong." Deuteronomy 2:19 indicates that God had promised the land of the Ammonites to the descendants of Lot.

were, and when he learned what they had done to the Amorites, he and his people were terrified. ⁴ They quickly consulted with the leaders of Midian.

"This mob will eat us like an ox eats grass," they exclaimed.

So King Balak ⁵,⁶ sent messengers to Balaam (son of Beor) who was living in his native land of Pethor, near the Euphrates River. He begged Balaam to come and help him.

"A vast horde of people has arrived from Egypt, and they cover the face of the earth and are headed toward me," he frantically explained. "Please come and curse them for me, so that I can drive them out of my land; for I know what fantastic blessings fall on those whom you bless, and I also know that those whom you curse are doomed."

⁷ The messengers he sent were some of the top leaders of Moab and Midian. They went to Balaam with money in hand, and urgently explained to him what Balak wanted.

⁸ "Stay here overnight," Balaam said, "and I'll tell you in the morning whatever the Lord directs me to say." So they did.

⁹ That night God came to Balaam and asked him, "Who are these men?"

¹⁰ "They have come from King Balak of Moab," he replied. ¹¹ "The king says that a vast horde of people from Egypt has arrived at his border, and he wants me to go at once and curse them, in the hope that he can battle them successfully."

¹² "Don't do it!" God told him. "You are not to curse them, for I have blessed them!"

¹³ The next morning Balaam told the men, "Go on home! The Lord won't let me do it."

¹⁴ So King Balak's ambassadors returned without him and reported his refusal. ¹⁵ Balak tried again. This time he sent a larger number of even more distinguished ambassadors than the former group. ¹⁶,¹⁷ They came to Balaam with this message:

"King Balak pleads with you to come. He promises you great honors plus any payment you ask. Name your own figure! Only come and curse these people for us."

¹⁸ But Balaam replied, "If he were to give me a palace filled with silver and gold, I could do nothing contrary to the command of the Lord my God. ¹⁹ However, stay here tonight so that I can find out whether the Lord will add anything to what he said before."

²⁰ That night God told Balaam, "Get up and go with these men, but be sure to say only what I tell you to."

²¹ So the next morning he saddled his donkey and started off with them. ²²,²³ But God was angry about Balaam's eager attitude,ᵃ so he sent an angel to stand in the road to kill him. As Balaam and two servants were riding along, Balaam's donkey suddenly saw the angel of the Lord standing in the road with a drawn sword. She bolted off the road into a field, but Balaam beat her back onto the road. ²⁴ Now the angel of the Lord stood at a place where the road went between two vineyard walls. ²⁵ When the donkey saw him standing there, she squirmed past by pressing against the wall, crushing Balaam's foot in the process. So he beat her again. ²⁶ Then the angel of the Lord moved farther down the road and stood in a place so narrow that the donkey couldn't get by at all. ²⁷ So she lay down in the road! In a great fit of temper Balaam beat her again with his staff.

²⁸ Then the Lord caused the donkey to speak! "What have I done that deserves your beating me these three times?" she asked.

²⁹ "Because you have made me look like a fool!" Balaam shouted. "I wish I had a sword with me, for I would kill you."

³⁰ "Have I ever done anything like this before in my entire life?" the donkey asked.

"No," he admitted.

³¹ Then the Lord opened Balaam's eyes and he saw the angel standing in the road way with drawn sword, and he fell flat on the ground before him.

³² "Why did you beat your donkey those three times?" the angel demanded. "I have come to stop you because you are headed for destruction. ³³ Three times the donkey saw me and shied away from me; otherwise I would certainly have killed you by now, and spared her."

---

a Literally, "God was angry because he went."

³⁴ Then Balaam confessed, "I have sinned. I didn't realize you were there. I will go back home if you don't want me to go on."

³⁵ But the angel told him, "Go with the men, but say only what I tell you to say." So Balaam went on with them. ³⁶ When King Balak heard that Balaam was on the way, he left the capital and went out to meet him at the Arnon River, at the border of his land.

³⁷ "Why did you delay so long?" he asked Balaam. "Didn't you believe me when I said I would give you great honors?"

³⁸ Balaam replied, "I have come, but I have no power to say anything except what God tells me to say; and that is what I shall speak." ³⁹ Balaam accompanied the king to Kiriathhuzoth, ⁴⁰ where King Balak sacrificed oxen and sheep, and gave animals to Balaam and the ambassadors for their sacrifices. ⁴¹ The next morning Balak took Balaam to the top of Mount Bamoth-baal, from which he could see the people of Israel spread out before him.

23 BALAAM SAID TO the king, "Build seven altars here, and prepare seven young bulls and seven rams for sacrifice."

² Balak followed his instructions, and a young bull and a ram were sacrificed on each altar.

³,⁴ Then Balaam said to the king, "Stand here by your burnt offerings and I will see if the Lord will meet me; and I will tell you what he says to me." So he went up to a barren height, and God met him there. Balaam told the Lord, "I have prepared seven altars, and have sacrificed a young bull and a ram on each." ⁵ Then the Lord gave Balaam a message for King Balak.

⁶ When Balaam returned, the king was standing beside the burnt offerings with all the princes of Moab. ⁷⁻¹⁰ This was Balaam's message:

"King Balak, king of Moab, has brought me
From the land of Aram,
From the eastern mountains.
'Come,' he told me, 'curse Jacob for me!
Let your anger rise on Israel.'
But how can I curse
What God has not cursed?
How can I denounce
A people God has not denounced?
I see them from the cliff tops,
I watch them from the hills.
They live alone,
And prefer to remain distinct
From every other nation.
They are as numerous as dust!
They are beyond numbering.
If only I could die as happy as an Israelite!
Oh, that my end might be like theirs!"

¹¹ "What have you done to me?" demanded King Balak. "I told you to curse my enemies, and now you have blessed them!"

¹² But Balaam replied, "Can I say anything except what Jehovah tells me to?"

¹³ Then Balak told him, "Come with me to another place; there you will see only a portion of the nation of Israel. Curse at least that many!"

¹⁴ So King Balak took Balaam into the fields of Zophim at the top of Mount Pisgah, and built seven altars there; and he offered up a young bull and a ram on each altar.

¹⁵ Then Balaam said to the king, "Stand here by your burnt offering while I go to meet the Lord." ¹⁶ And the Lord met Balaam and told him what to say. ¹⁷ So he returned to where the king and the princes of Moab were standing beside their burnt offerings.

"What has Jehovah said?" the king eagerly inquired.

¹⁸⁻²⁴ And he replied,

"Rise up, Balak, and hear:
Listen to me, you son of Zippor.
God is not a man, that he should lie;
He doesn't change his mind like humans do.
Has he ever promised,
Without doing what he said?
Look! I have received a command to bless them,
For God has blessed them,
And I cannot reverse it!
He has not seen sin in Jacob.
He will not trouble Israel!
Jehovah their God is with them.
He is their king!

God has brought them out of Egypt.
Israel has the strength of a wild ox.
No curse can be placed on Jacob,
And no magic shall be done against
   him.
For now it shall be said of Israel,
'What wonders God has done for
   them!'
These people rise up as a lion;
They shall not lie down
Until they have eaten what they cap-
   ture
And have drunk the blood of the
   slain!"

²⁵ "If you aren't going to curse them, at least don't *bless* them!" the king exclaimed to Balaam.

²⁶ But Balaam replied, "Didn't I tell you that I must say whatever Jehovah tells me to?"

²⁷ Then the king said to Balaam, "I will take you to yet another place. Perhaps it will please God to let you curse them from there."

²⁸ So King Balak took Balaam to the top of Mount Peor, overlooking the desert. ²⁹ Balaam again told the king to build seven altars, and to prepare seven young bulls and seven rams for the sacrifice. ³⁰ The king did as Balaam said, and offered a young bull and ram on every altar.

24 BALAAM REALIZED BY now that Jehovah planned to bless Israel, so he didn't even go to meet the Lord as he had earlier. Instead, he went at once and looked out toward the camp of Israel ² which stretched away across the plains, divided by tribal areas.

Then the Spirit of God came upon him, ³⁻⁹ and he spoke this prophecy concerning them:

"Balaam the son of Beor says that
The man whose eyes are open says,
'I have listened to the word of God,
I have seen what God Almighty
   showed me;
I fell, and my eyes were opened:
Oh, the joys awaiting Israel,
Joys in the homes of Jacob.
I see them spread before me as green
   valleys,
And fruitful gardens by the riverside;

As aloes planted by the Lord himself;
As cedar trees beside the waters.
They shall be blessed with an abun-
   dance of water,
And they shall live in many places.
Their king will be greater than Agag;
Their kingdom is exalted.
God has brought them from Egypt.
Israel has the strength of a wild ox,
And shall eat up the nations that op-
   pose him;
He shall break their bones in pieces,
And shall shoot them with many ar-
   rows.
Israel sleeps as a lion or a lioness—
Who dares arouse him?
Blessed is everyone who blesses you,
   O Israel,
And curses shall fall upon everyone
   who curses you.' "

¹⁰ King Balak was livid with rage by now. Striking his hands together in anger and disgust he shouted, "I called you to curse my enemies and instead you have blessed them three times. ¹¹ Get out of here! Go back home! I had planned to promote you to great honor, but Jehovah has kept you from it!"

¹² Balaam replied, "Didn't I tell your messengers ¹³ that even if you gave me a palace filled with silver and gold, I could not go beyond the words of Jehovah, and could not say a word of my own? I said that I would say only what Jehovah says! ¹⁴ Yes, I shall return now to my own people. But first, let me tell you what the Israelites are going to do to your people!"

¹⁵⁻¹⁹ So he spoke this prophecy to him:

"Balaam the son of Beor is the man
   Whose eyes are open!
He hears the words of God
And has knowledge from the Most
   High;
He sees what Almighty God has
   shown him;
He fell, and his eyes were opened:
I see in the future of Israel,
Far down the distant trail,
That there shall come a star from
   Jacob!
This ruler of Israel
Shall smite the people of Moab,
And destroy the sons of Sheth.

Israel shall possess all Edom and Seir.
They shall overcome their enemies.
Jacob shall arise in power
And shall destroy many cities."

[20] Then Balaam looked over at the homes of the people of Amalek and prophesied:

"Amalek was the first of the nations,
But its destiny is destruction!"

[21,22] Then he looked over at the Kenites:

"Yes, you are strongly situated,
Your nest is set in the rocks!
But the Kenites shall be destroyed,
And the mighty army of the king of Assyria shall deport you from this land!"

[23,24] He concluded his prophecies by saying:

"Alas, who can live when God does this?
Ships shall come from the coasts of Cyprus,
And shall oppress both Eber and Assyria.
They too must be destroyed."

[25] So Balaam and Balak returned to their homes.[a]

25 WHILE ISRAEL WAS camped at Acacia, some of the young men began going to wild parties with the local Moabite girls. [2] These girls also invited them to attend the sacrifices to their gods, and soon the men were not only attending the feasts, but also bowing down and worshiping the idols. [3] Before long all Israel was joining freely in the worship of Baal, the god of Moab; and the anger of the Lord was hot against his people.

[4] He issued the following command to Moses:

"Execute all the tribal leaders of Israel. Hang them up before the Lord in broad daylight, so that his fierce anger will turn away from the people."

[5] So Moses ordered the judges to execute all who had worshiped Baal.

[6] But one of the Israeli men insolently brought a Midianite girl into the camp, right before the eyes of Moses and all the people, as they were weeping at the door of the Tabernacle. [7] When Phinehas (son of Eleazar and grandson of Aaron the priest) saw this, he jumped up, grabbed a spear, [8] and rushed after the man into his tent, where he had taken the girl. He thrust the spear all the way through the man's body and into her stomach. So the plague was stopped, [9] but only after 24,000 people had already died.

[10,11] Then the Lord said to Moses, "Phinehas (son of Eleazar and grandson of Aaron the priest) has turned away my anger, for he was as angry as I, concerning my honor; so I have stopped destroying all Israel as I had intended. [12,13] Now because of what he has done—because of his zeal for his God, and because he has made atonement for the people of Israel by what he did—I promise that he and his descendants shall be priests forever."

[14] The name of the man who was killed with the Midianite girl was Zimri, son of Salu, a leader of the tribe of Simeon. [15] The girl's name was Cozbi, daughter of Zur, a Midianite prince.

[16,17] Then the Lord said to Moses, "Destroy the Midianites, [18] for they are destroying you with their wiles. They are causing you to worship Baal, and they are leading you astray, as you have just seen by the death of Cozbi."

26 AFTER THE PLAGUE had ended, Jehovah said to Moses and to Eleazar (son of Aaron the priest), [2] "Take a census of all the men of Israel who are twenty years old or older, to find out how many of each tribe and clan are able to go to war."

[3,4] So Moses and Eleazar issued census instructions to the leaders of Israel. (The entire nation was camped in the plains of Moab beside the Jordan River, opposite Jericho.) Here are the results of the census:

[5-11] *The tribe of Reuben:* 43,730.

(Reuben was Israel's eldest son.) In this tribe were the following clans, named after Reuben's sons:

The Hanochites, named after their

---

a But not before Balaam gave insidious advice that brought about the situation described in Numbers 25:1–3. See Numbers 31:16.

ancestor Hanoch.

The Palluites, named after their ancestor Pallu.

(In the sub-clan of Eliab—who was one of the sons of Pallu— were the families of Nemu-el, Abiram, and Dathan. This Dathan and Abiram were the two leaders who conspired with Korah against Moses and Aaron, and in fact challenged the very authority of God! But the earth opened and swallowed them; and 250 men were destroyed by fire from the Lord that day, as a warning to the entire nation.)

The Hezronites, named after their ancestor Hezron.

The Carmites, named after their ancestor Carmi.

¹²⁻¹⁴ *The tribe of Simeon:* 22,200.

In this tribe were the following clans, founded by Simeon's sons:

The Nemu-elites, named after their ancestor Nemu-el.

The Jaminites, named after their ancestor Jamin.

The Jachinites, named after their ancestor Jachin.

The Zerahites, named after their ancestor Zerah.

The Shaulites, named after their ancestor Shaul.

¹⁵⁻¹⁸ *The tribe of Gad:* 40,500.

In this tribe were the following clans founded by the sons of Gad:

The Zephonites, named after their ancestor Zephon.

The Haggites, named after their ancestor Haggi.

The Shunites, named after their ancestor Shuni.

The Oznites, named after their ancestor Ozni.

The Erites, named after their ancestor Eri.

The Arodites, named after their ancestor Arod.

The Arelites, named after their ancestor Areli.

¹⁹⁻²² *The tribe of Judah:* 76,500.

In this tribe were the following clans named after the sons of Judah—but not including Er and Onan who died in the land of Canaan:

The Shelanites, named after their ancestor Shelah.

The Perezites, named after their ancestor Perez.

The Zerahites, named after their ancestor Zerah.

This census also included the subclans of Perez:

The Hezronites, named after their ancestor Hezron.

The Hamulites, named after their ancestor Hamul.

²³⁻²⁵ *The tribe of Issachar:* 64,300.

In this tribe were the following clans named after the sons of Issachar:

The Tolaites, named after their ancestor Tola.

The Punites, named after their ancestor Puvah.

The Jashubites, named after their ancestor Jashub.

The Shimronites, named after their ancestor Shimron.

²⁶,²⁷ *The tribe of Zebulun:* 60,500.

In this tribe were the following clans named after the sons of Zebulun:

The Seredites, named after their ancestor Sered.

The Elonites, named after their ancestor Elon.

The Jahleelites, named after their ancestor Jahleel.

²⁸⁻³⁷ *The tribe of Joseph:* 32,500 *in the halftribe of Ephraim; and* 52,700 *in the halftribe of Manasseh.*

In the half-tribe of Manasseh was the following clan of Machirites, named after their ancestor Machir.

The sub-clan of the Machirites was the Gileadites, named after their ancestor Gilead.

The tribes of the Gileadites:

The Jezerites, named after their ancestor Jezer.

The Helekites, named after their ancestor Helek.

The Asrielites, named after their ancestor Asriel.

The Shechemites, named after their ancestor Shechem.

The Shemidaites, named after

their ancestor Shemida.

The Hepherites, named after their ancestor Hepher. (Hepher's son, Zelophehad, had no sons. Here are the names of his daughters: Mahlah, Noah, Hoglah, Milcah, Tirzah.

The 32,500 registered in the half-tribe of Ephraim included the following clans, named after the sons of Ephraim:

The Shuthelahites, named after their ancestor Shuthelah. (A sub-clan of the Shuthelahites was the Eranites, named after their ancestor Eran, a son of Shuthelah.)

The Becherites, named after their ancestor Becher.

The Tahanites, named after their ancestor Tahan.

³⁸⁻⁴¹ *The tribe of Benjamin:* 45,600.

In this tribe were the following clans named after the sons of Benjamin:

The Bela-ites, named after their ancestor Bela.

Sub-clans named after sons of Bela were:

The Ardites, named after their ancestor Ard.

The Naamites, named after their ancestor Naaman.

The Ashbelites, named after their ancestor Ashbel.

The Ahiramites, named after their ancestor Ahiram.

The Shuphamites, named after their ancestor Shephupham.

The Huphamites, named after their ancestor Hupham.

⁴²,⁴³ *The tribe of Dan:* 64,400.

In this tribe was the clan of the Shuhamites, named after Shuham, the son of Dan. ⁴⁴⁻⁴⁷ *The tribe of Asher:* 53,400.

In this tribe were the following clans named after the sons of Asher:

The Imnites, named after their ancestor Imnah.

The Ishvites, named after their ancestor Ishvi.

The Beriites, named after their ancestor Beriah.

Sub-clans named after the sons of Beriah were:

The Heberites, named after their ancestor Heber.

The Malchi-elites, named after their ancestor Malchi-el.

Asher also had a daughter named Serah.

⁴⁸⁻⁵⁰ *The tribe of Naphtali:* 45,400.

In this tribe were the following clans, named after the sons of Naphtali:

The Jahzeelites, named after their ancestor Jahzeel.

The Gunites, named after their ancestor Guni.

The Jezerites, named after their ancestor Jezer.

The Shillemites, named after their ancestor Shillem.

⁵¹ So the total number of the draftable men throughout Israel was 601,730.

⁵²,⁵³ Then the Lord told Moses to divide the land among the tribes in proportion to their population, as indicated by the census— ⁵⁴ the larger tribes to be given more land, the smaller tribes less land.

⁵⁵,⁵⁶ "Let the representatives of the larger tribes have a lottery, drawing for the larger sections," the Lord instructed, "and let the smaller tribes draw for the smaller sections."

⁵⁷ These are the clans of the Levites numbered in the census:

The Gershonites, named after their ancestor Gershon.

The Kohathites, named after their ancestor Kohath.

The Merarites, named after their ancestor Merari.

⁵⁸,⁵⁹ These are the families of the tribe of Levi:

The Libnites, the Hebronites, The Mahlites, the Mushites, The Korahites.

While Levi was in Egypt, a daughter, Jochebed, was born to him and she became the wife of Amram, son of Kohath. They were the parents of Aaron, Moses, and Miriam. ⁶⁰ To Aaron were born Nadab, Abihu, Eleazar, and Ithamar. ⁶¹ But Nadab and Abihu died when they offered unholy fire before the Lord.

⁶² *The total number of Levites in the census* was 23,000, counting all the males a month old and upward. But the Levites were not included in the total census figure

of the people of Israel, for the Levites were given no land when it was divided among the tribes. [63] So these are the census figures as prepared by Moses and Eleazar the priest, in the plains of Moab beside the Jordan River, across from Jericho. [64,65] Not one person in this entire census had been counted[a] in the previous census taken in the wilderness of Sinai! For all who had been counted then had died, as the Lord had decreed when he said of them, "They shall die in the wilderness." The only exceptions were Caleb (son of Jephunneh) and Joshua (son of Nun).

27 ONE DAY THE daughters of Zelophehad came to the entrance of the Tabernacle to give a petition to Moses, Eleazar the priest, the tribal leaders, and others who were there. These women were of the half-tribe of Manasseh (a son of Joseph). Their ancestor was Machir, son of Manasseh. Manasseh's son Gilead was their great-grandfather, his son Hepher was their grandfather, and his son Zelophehad was their father.

[3,4] "Our father died in the wilderness," they said, "and he was not one of those who perished in Korah's revolt against the Lord —it was a natural death, but he had no sons. Why should the name of our father disappear just because he had no son? We feel that we should be given property along with our father's brothers."

[5] So Moses brought their case before the Lord.

[6,7] And the Lord replied to Moses, "The daughters of Zelophehad are correct. Give them land along with their uncles; give them the property that would have been given to their father if he had lived. [8] Moreover, this is a general law among you, that if a man dies and has no sons, then his inheritance shall be passed on to his daughters. [9] And if he has no daughter, it shall belong to his brothers. [10] And if he has no brother, then it shall go to his uncles. [11] But if he has no uncles, then it shall go to the nearest relative."

[12] One day the Lord said to Moses, "Go up into Mount Abarim and look across the river to the land I have given to the people of Israel. [13] After you have seen it, you shall die as Aaron your brother did, [14] for you rebelled against my instructions in the wilderness of Zin. When the people of Israel rebelled, you did not glorify me[a] before them by following my instructions to order water to come out of the rock." He was referring to the incident at the waters of Meribah ("Place of Strife") in Kadesh, in the wilderness of Zin.

[15] Then Moses said to the Lord, [16] "O Jehovah, the God of the spirits of all mankind, [before I am taken away[a]] please appoint a new leader for the people, [17] a man who will lead them into battle and care for them, so that the people of the Lord will not be as sheep without a shepherd."

[18] The Lord replied, "Go and get Joshua (son of Nun), who has the Spirit in him, [19] and take him to Eleazar the priest, and as all the people watch, charge him with the responsibility of leading the people. [20] Publicly give him your authority so that all the people of Israel will obey him. [21] He shall be the one to consult with Eleazar the priest in order to get directions from the Lord. The Lord will speak to Eleazar through the use of the Urim, and Eleazar will pass on these instructions to Joshua and the people. In this way the Lord will continue to give them guidance."

[22] So Moses did as Jehovah commanded, and took Joshua to Eleazar the priest. As the people watched, [23] Moses laid his hands upon him and dedicated him to his responsibilities, as the Lord had commanded.

28 THE LORD GAVE Moses these instructions to give to the people of Israel: "The offerings which you burn on the altar for me are my food, and are a pleasure to me; so see to it that they are brought regularly and are offered as I have instructed you.

[3] "When you make offerings by fire, you shall use yearling male lambs—each without defect. Two of them shall be offered each day as a regular burnt offering. [4] One

---

a Forty years earlier, at the time of the first census, they had been under twenty years of age, and so were not counted. All who at that time were older than twenty years of age were now dead.　　27a Implied.

lamb shall be sacrificed in the morning, the other in the evening. [5] With them shall be offered a grain offering of three quarts of finely ground flour mixed with three pints of oil. [6] This is the burnt offering ordained at Mount Sinai, to be regularly offered as a fragrant odor, an offering made by fire to the Lord. [7] Along with it shall be the drink offering, consisting of three pints of strong wine with each lamb, poured out in the holy place before the Lord. [8] Offer the second lamb in the evening with the same grain offering and drink offering. It too is a fragrant odor to the Lord, an offering made by fire.

[9,10] "On the Sabbath day, sacrifice two yearling male lambs—both without defect —in addition to the regular offerings. They are to be accompanied by a grain offering of six quarts of fine flour mixed with oil, and the usual drink offering.

[11] "Also, on the first day of each month there shall be an extra burnt offering to the Lord of two young bulls, one ram, and seven male yearling lambs—all without defect. [12] Accompany them with nine quarts of finely ground flour mixed with oil as a grain offering with each bull; and six quarts of finely ground flour mixed with oil as a grain offering for the ram; [13] and for each lamb, three quarts of finely ground flour mixed with oil for a grain offering. This burnt offering shall be presented by fire, and will please the Lord very much. [14] Along with each sacrifice shall be a drink offering —six pints of wine with each bull, four pints for a ram, and three pints for a lamb. This, then, will be the burnt offering each month throughout the year.

[15] "Also on the first day of each month you shall offer one male goat for a sin offering to the Lord. This is in addition to the regular daily burnt offering and its drink offering.

[16] "On the fourteenth day of the first month of each year, you shall celebrate the Passover—[when the death angel passed over the oldest sons of the Israelites in Egypt, leaving them unharmed[a]]. [17] On the following day, a great, joyous seven-day festival will begin, but no leavened bread shall

be served. [18] On the first day of the festival a holy assembly of all the people shall be called, and no hard work shall be done on that day. [19] You shall offer as burnt sacrifices to the Lord two young bulls, one ram, and seven yearling male lambs—all without defect. [20,21] With each bull there shall be a grain offering of nine quarts of fine flour mixed with oil; with the ram there shall be six quarts; and with each of the seven lambs there shall be three quarts of fine flour. [22] You must also offer a male goat as a sin offering, to make atonement for yourselves. [23] These offerings shall be in addition to the usual daily sacrifices. [24] This same sacrifice shall be offered on each of the seven days of the feast; they will be very pleasant to the Lord. [25] On the seventh day there shall again be a holy and solemn assembly of all the people, and during that day you may do no hard work.

[26] "On the Day of First-fruits (also called the Festival of Weeks, or Pentecost), there must be a special, solemn assembly of all the people to celebrate the new harvest. On that day you are to present the first of the new crop of grain as a grain offering to the Lord; there is to be no hard work by anyone on that day. [27] A special burnt offering, very pleasant to the Lord, shall be offered that day. It shall consist of two young bulls, one ram, and seven yearling male lambs. [28,29] These shall be accompanied by your grain offering of nine quarts of fine flour mixed with oil with each bull, six quarts with the ram, and three quarts with each of the seven lambs. [30] Also offer one male goat to make atonement for yourselves. [31] These special offerings are in addition to the regular daily burnt offerings and grain offerings and drink offerings. Make sure that the animals you sacrifice are without defect.

29   THE FESTIVAL OF Trumpets shall be celebrated on the fifteenth day of September[a] each year; there shall be a solemn assembly of all the people on that day, and no hard work may be done. [2] On that day you shall offer a burnt sacrifice consisting of one young bull, one ram, and seven yearling male lambs—all without defect. These

---

a Implied.   29a Literally, "upon the first day of the seventh month" (of the Hebrew calendar).

are sacrifices which the Lord will appreciate and enjoy. [3,4] A grain offering of nine quarts of fine flour mingled with oil shall be offered with the bull, six quarts with the ram, and three quarts with each of the seven lambs. [5] In addition, there shall be a male goat sacrificed as a sin offering, to make atonement for you. [6] These special sacrifices are in addition to the regular monthly burnt offering for that day,[b] and also in addition to the regular daily burnt sacrifices, which are to be offered with the respective grain offerings and drink offerings, as specified by the ordinances governing them.

[7] "Ten days later[c] another convocation of all the people shall be held. This will be a day of solemn humility before the Lord, and no work of any kind may be done. [8] On that day you shall offer a burnt sacrifice to the Lord—it will be very pleasant to him —of one young bull, one ram, seven yearling male lambs—each without defect— [9,10] and their accompanying grain offerings. Nine quarts of fine flour mixed with oil are to be offered with the bull; six with the ram; and three with each of the seven lambs. [11] You are also to sacrifice one male goat for a sin offering. This is in addition to the sin offering of the Day of Atonement [offered annually on that day[d]], and in addition to the regular daily burnt sacrifices, grain offerings, and drink offerings.

[12] "Five days later[e] there shall be yet another assembly of all the people, and on that day no hard work shall be done; it is the beginning of a seven-day festival before the Lord. [13] Your special burnt sacrifice that day, which will give much pleasure to the Lord, shall be thirteen young bulls, two rams, and fourteen male yearling lambs —each without defect— [14] accompanied by the usual grain offerings—nine quarts of fine flour mingled with oil for each of the thirteen young bulls; six quarts for each of the two rams; [15] and three quarts for each of the fourteen lambs. [16] There must also be a male goat sacrificed for a sin offering, in addition to the regular daily burnt sacrifice with its accompanying grain offerings and drink offerings.

[17] "On the second day of this seven-day festival you shall sacrifice twelve young bulls, two rams, and fourteen male yearling lambs—each without defect— [18] accompanied by the usual grain offerings and drink offerings. [19] Also, in addition to the regular daily burnt sacrifice, you are to sacrifice a male goat with its accompanying grain offering and drink offering for a sin offering.

[20] "On the third day of the festival, offer eleven young bulls, two rams, fourteen male yearling lambs—each without defect— [21] and the usual grain offering and drink offering with each sacrifice. [22] And in addition to the regular daily burnt sacrifices, sacrifice a male goat for a sin offering, with its accompanying grain offering and drink offering.

[23] "On the fourth day of the festival, you are to sacrifice ten young bulls, two rams, and fourteen male yearling lambs—each without defect— [24] each with its accompanying grain offering and drink offering; [25] also a male goat as a sin offering (along with the usual grain and drink offerings) in addition to the regular daily sacrifices.

[26,27] "On the fifth day of the festival, sacrifice nine young bulls, two rams, and fourteen male yearling lambs—each without defect—accompanied by the usual grain offerings and drink offerings; [28] also sacrifice a male goat with the usual grain and drink offerings, as a special sin offering, in addition to the usual daily sacrifices.

[29] "On the sixth day of the festival, you must sacrifice eight young bulls, two rams, and fourteen male yearling lambs—each without defect— [30] along with their usual grain and drink offerings. [31] In addition to the usual daily sacrifices, sacrifice a male goat and the usual grain and drink offerings as a sin offering.

[32] "On the seventh day of the festival, sacrifice seven young bulls, two rams, and fourteen male yearling lambs—each without defect— [33] each with its customary grain and drink offerings; [34] also sacrifice an extra sin offering of one male goat, with the usual grain and drink offerings, in addition to the

b Literally, "burnt offerings of the new moon." the Hebrew calendar).   d Implied.   c Literally, "on the tenth day of the seventh month" (of e Literally, "on the fifteenth day of the seventh month" (of the Hebrew calendar).

regular daily sacrifices.

³⁵ "On the eighth day summon the people to another solemn assembly; you must do no hard work that day. ³⁶ Sacrifice a burnt offering—they are very pleasant to the Lord—of one young bull, one ram, seven male yearling lambs—each without defect—³⁷ and the customary grain and drink offerings. ³⁸ Sacrifice also one male goat with the usual grain and drink offerings for a sin offering, in addition to the regular daily sacrifices. ³⁹ These offerings are compulsory at the times of your annual feasts, and are in addition to sacrifices and offerings you present in connection with vows, or as free-will offerings, burnt sacrifices, grain offerings, drink offerings, or peace offerings."

⁴⁰ So Moses gave all of these instructions to the people of Israel.

30 NOW MOSES SUMMONED the leaders of the tribes and told them, "The Lord has commanded that when anyone makes a promise to the Lord, either to do something or to quit doing something, that vow must not be broken: the person making the vow must do exactly as he has promised.

³ "If a woman promises the Lord to do or not do something, and she is still a girl at home in her father's home, ⁴ and her father hears that she has made a vow with penalties, but says nothing, then her vow shall stand. ⁵ But if her father refuses to let her make the vow, or feels that the penalties she has agreed to are too harsh, then her promise will automatically become invalid. Her father must state his disagreement on the first day he hears about it; and then Jehovah will forgive her because her father would not let her do it.

⁶ "If she takes a vow or makes a foolish pledge, and later marries, ⁷ and her husband learns of her vow and says nothing on the day he hears of it, her vow shall stand. ⁸ But if her husband refuses to accept her vow or foolish pledge, his disagreement makes it void, and Jehovah will forgive her.

⁹ "But if the woman is a widow or is divorced, she must fulfill her vow.

¹⁰ "If she is married and living in her husband's home when she makes the vow, ¹¹ and her husband hears of it and does nothing, the vow shall stand; ¹² but if he refuses to allow it on the first day he hears of it, her vow is void and Jehovah will forgive her. ¹³ So her husband may either confirm or nullify her vow, ¹⁴ but if he says nothing for a day, then he has already agreed to it. ¹⁵ If he waits more than a day and then refuses to permit the vow, whatever penalties to which she agreed shall come upon him—he shall be responsible."

¹⁶ These, then, are the commandments the Lord gave Moses concerning relationships between a man and his wife and between a father and his daughter who is living at home.

31 THEN THE LORD said to Moses, "Take vengeance on the Midianites for leading you into idolatry, and then you must die."

³ Moses said to the people, "Some of you must take arms to wage Jehovah's war against Midian. ⁴,⁵ Conscript 1,000 men from each tribe." So this was done; and out of the many thousands of Israel, 12,000 armed men were sent to battle by Moses. ⁶ Phinehas (son of Eleazar the priest) led them into battle, accompanied by the Ark,ᵃ with trumpets blaring. ⁷ And every man of Midian was killed in battle! ⁸ Among those killed were all five of the Midianite kings—Evi, Rekem, Zur, Hur, and Reba. Balaam, the son of Beor, was also killed.

⁹,¹⁰,¹¹ Then the Israeli army took as captives all the women and children, and seized the cattle and flocks and a lot of miscellaneous booty. All of the cities, towns, and villages of Midian were then burned. ¹² The captives and other spoils of war were brought to Moses and Eleazar the priest, and to the rest of the people of Israel who were camped on the plains of Moab beside the Jordan River, across from Jericho. ¹³ Moses and Eleazar the priest and all the leaders of the people went out to meet the victorious army, ¹⁴ but Moses was very angry with the army officers and battalion leaders.

¹⁵ "Why have you let all the women

---

a Literally, "with the vessels of the sanctuary."

live?" he demanded. [16] "These are the very ones who followed Balaam's advice and caused the people of Israel to worship idols on Mount Peor, and they are the cause of the plague that destroyed us. [17] Now kill all the boys and all the women who have had sexual intercourse. [18] Only the little girls may live; you may keep them for yourselves. [19] Now stay outside of the camp for seven days, all of you who have killed anyone or touched a dead body. Then purify yourselves and your captives on the third and seventh days. [20] Remember also to purify all your garments and everything made of leather, goat's hair, or wood."

[21] Then Eleazar the priest said to the men who were in the battle, "This is the commandment Jehovah has given Moses: [22] 'Anything that will stand heat—such as gold, silver, bronze, iron, tin, or lead— [23] shall be passed through fire in order to be made ceremonially pure; it must then be further purified with the purification water. But anything that won't stand heat shall be purified by the water alone.' [24] On the seventh day you must wash your clothes and be purified, and then you may come back into the camp."

[25] And the Lord said to Moses, [26] "You and Eleazar the priest and the leaders of the tribes are to make a list of all the booty, including the people and animals; [27] then divide it into two parts. Half of it is for the men who were in the battle, and the other half is to be given to the people of Israel. [28] But first, the Lord gets a share of all the captives, oxen, donkeys, and flocks kept by the army. His share is one out of every five hundred. [29] Give this share to Eleazar the priest to be presented to the Lord by the gesture of waving before the altar. [30] Also levy a two percent tribute of all the captives, flocks, and cattle that are given to the people of Israel. Present this to the Levites in charge of the Tabernacle, for it is the Lord's portion."

[31] So Moses and Eleazar the priest did as the Lord commanded. [32-35] The total booty (besides the jewelry, clothing, etc., which the soldiers kept for themselves) was 675,000 sheep; 72,000 oxen; 61,000 donkeys; and 32,000 young girls.

[36-40] So the half given to the army totaled:

337,500 sheep (of which 675 were given to the Lord);

36,000 oxen (of which 72 were given to the Lord);

30,500 donkeys (of which 61 were given to the Lord);

16,000 girls (of whom 32 went to the Levites).[b]

[41] All of the Lord's portion was given to Eleazar the priest, as the Lord had directed Moses.

[42-46] The half of the booty assigned to the people of Israel—Moses had separated it from the half belonging to the warriors —amounted to:

337,500 sheep,

36,000 oxen,

30,500 donkeys, and

16,000 girls

[47] In accordance with the Lord's directions, Moses gave two percent of these to the Levites.

[48,49] Then the officers and battalion leaders came to Moses and said, "We have accounted for all the men who went out to battle, and not one of us is missing! [50] So we have brought a special thank-offering to the Lord from our booty—gold jewelry, bracelets, anklets, rings, earrings, and necklaces. This is to make atonement for our souls before the Lord."

[51,52] Moses and Eleazar the priest received this special offering from the captains and battalion leaders and company commanders, and found its total value to be more than $300,000. [53] (The soldiers had also kept personal booty for themselves.) [54] The offering was taken into the Tabernacle and kept there before the Lord as a memorial of the people of Israel.

32 WHEN ISRAEL ARRIVED in the land of Jazar and Gilead, the tribes of Reuben and Gad (who had large flocks of sheep) noticed what wonderful sheep country it was. [2] So they came to Moses and Eleazar the priest and the other tribal leaders and said, [3,4] "The Lord has used Israel to destroy the population of this whole coun-

---

b Literally, "were the Lord's portion."

tryside—Ataroth, Dibon, Jazer, Nimrah, Heshbon, Elealeh, Sebam, Nebo, and Beon. And it is all wonderful sheep country, ideal for our flocks. ⁵ Please let us have this land as our portion instead of the land on the other side of the Jordan River."

⁶ "You mean you want to sit here while your brothers go across and do all the fighting?" Moses demanded. ⁷ "Are you trying to discourage the rest of the people from going across to the land that the Lord has given them? ⁸ This is the same kind of thing your fathers did! I sent them from Kadesh-barnea to spy out the land, ⁹ but when they finished their survey and returned from the valley of Eshcol, they discouraged the people from going on into the Promised Land. ¹⁰,¹¹ And the Lord's anger was hot against them, and he swore that of all those he had rescued from Egypt, no one over twenty years of age would ever see the land he promised Abraham, Isaac, and Jacob, for they had refused to do what he wanted them to. ¹² The only exceptions were Caleb (son of Jephunneh the Kenizzite) and Joshua (son of Nun)—for they wholeheartedly followed the Lord and urged the people to go on into the Promised Land.

¹³ "The Lord made us wander back and forth in the wilderness for forty years until all that evil generation died. ¹⁴ But here you are, a brood of sinners doing exactly the same thing! Only there are more of you, so Jehovah's anger against Israel will be even fiercer this time. ¹⁵ If you turn away from God like this, he will make the people stay even longer in the wilderness, and you will be responsible for destroying his people and bringing disaster to this entire nation!"

¹⁶ "Not at all!" they explained. "We will build sheepfolds for our flocks and cities for our little ones, ¹⁷ but we ourselves will go over armed, ahead of the rest of the people of Israel, until we have brought them safely to their inheritance. But first we will need to build walled cities here for our families, to keep them safe from attack by the local inhabitants. ¹⁸ We will not settle down here until all the people of Israel have received their inheritance. ¹⁹ We don't want land on the other side of the Jordan; we would rather have it on this side, on the east."

²⁰ Then Moses said, "All right, if you will do what you have said and arm yourselves for Jehovah's war, ²¹ and keep your troops across the Jordan until the Lord has driven out his enemies, ²² then, when the land is finally subdued before the Lord, you may return. Then you will have discharged your duty to the Lord and to the rest of the people of Israel. And the land on the eastern side shall be your possession from the Lord. ²³ But if you don't do as you have said, then you will have sinned against the Lord, and you may be sure that your sin will catch up with you. ²⁴ Go ahead and build cities for your families and sheepfolds for your sheep, and do all you have said."

²⁵ "We will follow your instructions exactly," the people of Gad and Reuben replied. ²⁶ "Our children, wives, flocks, and cattle shall stay here in the cities of Gilead. ²⁷ But all of us who are conscripted will go over to battle for the Lord, just as you have said."

²⁸ So Moses gave his approval by saying to Eleazar, Joshua, and the tribal leaders of Israel, ²⁹ "If all the men of the tribes of Gad and Reuben who are conscripted for the Lord's battles go with you over Jordan, then, when the land is conquered, you must give them the land of Gilead; ³⁰ but if they refuse, then they must accept land among the rest of you in the land of Canaan."

³¹ The tribes of Gad and Reuben said again, "As the Lord has commanded, so we will do— ³² we will follow the Lord fully armed into Canaan, but our own land shall be here on this side of the Jordan."

³³ So Moses assigned the territory of King Sihon of the Amorites, and of King Og of Bashan—all the land and cities—to the tribes of Gad, Reuben, and the half-tribe of Manasseh (son of Joseph).

³⁴,³⁵,³⁶ The people of Gad built these cities:

> Dibon, Ataroth, Aroer,
> Atroth-shophan, Jazer,
> Jogbehah, Beth-nimrah,
> Beth-haran.

They were all fortified cities with sheepfolds.

³⁷,³⁸ The children of Reuben built the following cities:

> Heshbon, Elealeh,
> Kiriathaim, Nebo,

Baal-meon, Sibmah.
(The Israelites later changed the names of some of these cities they had conquered and rebuilt.)

³⁹ Then the clan of Machir of the tribe of Manasseh went to Gilead and conquered it, and drove out the Amorites who were living there. ⁴⁰ So Moses gave Gilead to the Machirites, and they lived there. ⁴¹ The men of Jair, another clan of the tribe of Manasseh, occupied many of the towns in Gilead, and changed the name of their area to Havroth-jair. ⁴² Meanwhile, a man named Nobah led an army[a] to Kenath and its surrounding villages, and occupied them, and he called the area Nobah, after his own name.

33 THIS IS THE itinerary of the nation of Israel from the time Moses and Aaron led them out of Egypt. ² Moses had written down their movements as the Lord had instructed him. ^{3,4} They left the city of Rameses, Egypt, on the first day of April,[a] the day after the night of the Passover. They left proudly, hurried along by the Egyptians who were burying all their eldest sons, killed by the Lord the night before. The Lord had certainly defeated all the gods of Egypt that night!

^{5,6} After leaving Rameses, they stayed in Succoth, Etham (at the edge of the wilderness), and ⁷ Pihahiroth (near Baal-zephon, where they camped at the foot of Mount Migdol). ⁸ From there they went through the middle of the Red Sea and on for three days into the Etham wilderness, camping at Marah.

⁹ Leaving Marah, they came to Elim, where there are twelve springs of water and seventy palm trees; they stayed there for quite a long time.

¹⁰ Leaving Elim, they camped beside the Red Sea, ¹¹ and then in the wilderness of Sihn.

¹² Next was Dophkah, ¹³ and then Alush; ¹⁴ then on to Rephidim (where there was no water for the people to drink).

¹⁵⁻³⁷ From Rephidim they went to the wilderness of Sinai; from the wilderness of Sinai to Kibroth-hattaavah;
From Kibroth-hattaavah to Hazeroth;
From Hazeroth to Rithmah;
From Rithmah to Rimmon-parez;
From Rimmon-parez to Libnah;
From Libnah to Rissah;
From Rissah to Kehelathah;
From Kehelathah to Mount Shepher;
From Mount Shepher to Haradah;
From Haradah to Makheloth;
From Makheloth to Tahath;
From Tahath to Terah;
From Terah to Mithkah;
From Mithkah to Hashmonah;
From Hashmonah to Moseroth;
From Moseroth to Bene-jaakan;
From Bene-jaakan to Hor-haggidgad;
From Hor-haggidgad to Jotbathah;
From Jotbathah to Abronah;
From Abronah to Ezion-geber;
From Ezion-geber to Kadesh (in the wilderness of Zin);
From Kadesh to Mount Hor (at the edge of the land of Edom).

^{38,39} While they were at the foot of Mount Hor, Aaron the priest was directed by the Lord to go up into the mountain, and there he died. This occurred during the fortieth year after the people of Israel had left Egypt. The date of his death was July 15,[b] when he was 123 years old.

⁴⁰ It was then that the Canaanite king of Arad, who lived in the Negeb, in the land of Canaan, heard that the people of Israel were approaching his land. ⁴¹ After dealing with him, the Israelis journeyed from Mount Hor and camped in Zalmonah, ⁴² then at Punon, ⁴³ then at Oboth, ⁴⁴ then Iyeabarim (at the border of Moab). ⁴⁵ From there they went to Dibon-gad, ⁴⁶ and then to Almon-diblathaim, ⁴⁷ and on into the mountains of Abarim, near Mount Nebo, ⁴⁸ and finally to the plains of Moab beside the river Jordan, opposite Jericho. ⁴⁹ While in that area they camped at various places along the Jordan River, from Beth-jeshimoth as far as Abel-shittim, on the plains of Moab.

---

a Implied.   33 a Literally, "on the fifteenth day of the first month" (of the Hebrew calendar).
b Literally, "the first day of the fifth month" (of the Hebrew calendar).

⁵⁰,⁵¹ It was while they were camped there that the Lord told Moses to tell the people of Israel, "When you pass across the Jordan River into the land of Canaan, ⁵² you must drive out all the people living there and destroy all their idols—their carved stones, molten images, and the open-air sanctuaries in the hills where they worship their idols. ⁵³ I have given the land to you; take it and live there. ⁵⁴ You will be given land in proportion to the size of your tribes. The larger sections of land will be divided by lot among the larger tribes, and the smaller sections will be allotted to the smaller tribes. ⁵⁵ But if you refuse to drive out the people living there, those who remain will be as cinders in your eyes and thorns in your sides. ⁵⁶ And I will destroy you as I had planned for you to destroy them."

34 THE LORD TOLD Moses to tell the people of Israel, "When they come into the land of Canaan (I am giving you the entire land as your homeland), ³ "the southern portion of the country will be the wilderness of Zin, along the edge of Edom. The southern boundary will begin at the Dead Sea, ⁴ and will continue south past Scorpion Passᵃ in the direction of Zin. Its southernmost point will be Kadesh-barnea, from which it will go to Hazaraddar, and on to Azmon. ⁵ From Azmon the boundary will follow the Wadi-el-Arishᵇ down to the Mediterranean Sea.

⁶ "Your western boundary will be the coastline of the Mediterranean Sea.

⁷,⁸,⁹ "Your northern border will begin at the Mediterranean Sea and will proceed eastward to Mount Hor, then to Lebo-Hamath, and on through Zedad and Ziphron to Hazar-enan.

¹⁰,¹¹ "The eastern border will be from Hazar-enan south to Shepham, then on to Riblah at the east side of Ain. From there it will make a large half-circle, first going south and then westward until it touches the southernmost tip of the Sea of Galilee, ¹² and then along the Jordan River, ending at the Dead Sea."

¹³ "This is the territory you are to apportion among yourselves by lot," Moses said.

"It is to be divided up among the nine and one-half tribes, ¹⁴,¹⁵ for the tribes of Reuben and Gad and the half-tribe of Manasseh have already been assigned land on the east side of the Jordan, opposite Jericho."

¹⁶⁻²⁸ And the Lord said to Moses, "These are the names of the men I have appointed to handle the dividing up of the land: Eleazar the priest, Joshua (son of Nun), and one leader from each tribe, as listed below:

Tribe	Leader
Judah	Caleb (son of Jephunneh)
Simeon	Shemuel (son of Ammihud)
Benjamin	Elidad (son of Chislon)
Dan	Bukki (son of Jogli)
Manasseh	Hanniel (son of Ephod)
Ephraim	Kemuel (son of Shiphtan)
Zebulun	Elizaphan (son of Parnach)
Issachar	Paltiel (son of Azzan)
Asher	Ahihud (son of Shelomi)
Naphtali	Pedahel (son of Ammihud)

²⁹ These are the names of the men I have appointed to oversee the dividing of the land among the tribes."

35 WHILE ISRAEL WAS camped beside the Jordan on the plains of Moab, opposite Jericho, the Lord said to Moses,

² "Instruct the people of Israel to give to the Levites as their inheritance certain cities and surrounding pasture lands. ³ These cities are for their homes, and the surrounding lands for their cattle, flocks, and other livestock. ⁴ Their pasturelands shall extend outward from the city walls for 1500 feet in each direction. ⁵ Thus there will be 3000 feet between the boundaries, with the city in the center.

⁶ "You shall give the Levites the six Cities of Refuge where a person who has accidentally killed someone can run and be safe, and forty-two other cities besides. ⁷ In all, there shall be forty-eight cities with the surrounding pastureland given to the Levites. ⁸ These cities shall be in various parts of the nation; the larger tribes with many cities will give several to the Levites, while the smaller tribes will give fewer."

⁹,¹⁰ And the Lord said to Moses, "Tell the people that when they arrive in the land,

---

a Literally, "ascent of Akrabbim."   b Literally, "the brook of Egypt."

¹¹ Cities of Refuge shall be designated for anyone to flee into if he has killed someone accidentally. ¹² These Cities will be places of protection from the dead man's relatives who want to avenge his death; for the slayer must not be killed unless a fair trial establishes his guilt. ¹³,¹⁴ Three of these six Cities of Refuge are to be located in the land of Canaan, and three on the east side of the Jordan River. ¹⁵ These are not only for the protection of Israelites, but also for foreigners and travelers.

¹⁶ "But if someone is struck and killed by a piece of iron, it must be presumed to be murder, and the murderer must be executed. ¹⁷ Or if the slain man was struck down with a large stone, it is murder, and the murderer shall die. ¹⁸ The same is true if he is killed with a wooden weapon. ¹⁹ The avenger of his death shall personally kill the murderer when he meets him. ²⁰ So, if anyone kills another out of hatred by throwing something at him, or ambushing him, ²¹ or angrily striking him with his fist so that he dies, he is a murderer; and the murderer shall be executed by the avenger.

²²,²³ "But if it is an accident—a case in which something is thrown unintentionally, or in which a stone is thrown without anger, without realizing it will hit anyone, and without wanting to harm an enemy—yet the man dies, ²⁴ then the people shall judge whether or not it was an accident, and whether or not to hand the killer over to the avenger of the dead man. ²⁵ If it is decided that it was accidental, then the people shall save the killer from the avenger; the killer shall be permitted to stay in the City of Refuge; and he must live there until the death of the High Priest.

²⁶ "If the slayer leaves the City, ²⁷ and the avenger finds him outside and kills him, it is not murder, ²⁸ for the man should have stayed inside the City until the death of the High Priest. But after the death of the High Priest, the man may return to his own land and home. ²⁹ These are permanent laws for all Israel from generation to generation.

³⁰ "All murderers must be executed, but only if there is more than one witness; no man shall die with only one person testifying against him. ³¹ Whenever anyone is judged guilty of murder, he must die—no

ransom may be accepted for him. ³² Nor may a payment be accepted from a refugee in a City of Refuge, permitting him to return to his home before the death of the High Priest. ³³ In this way the land will not be polluted, for murder pollutes the land, and no atonement can be made for murder except by the execution of the murderer. ³⁴ You shall not defile the land where you are going to live, for I, Jehovah, will be living there."

36 THEN THE HEADS of the sub-clan of Gilead (of the clan of Machir, of the tribe of Manasseh, one of the sons of Joseph) came to Moses and the leaders of Israel with a petition: "The Lord instructed you to divide the land by lot among the people of Israel," they reminded Moses, "and to give the inheritance of our brother Zelophehad to his daughters. ³ But if they marry into another tribe, their land will go with them to the tribe into which they marry. In this way the total area of our tribe will be reduced, ⁴ and will not be returned at the Year of Jubilee."

⁵ Then Moses replied publicly, giving them these instructions from the Lord: "The men of the tribe of Joseph have a proper complaint. ⁶ This is what the Lord has further commanded concerning the daughters of Zelophehad: 'Let them be married to anyone they like, so long as it is within their own tribe. ⁷ In this way none of the land of the tribe will shift to any other tribe, for the inheritance of every tribe is to remain permanently as it was first allotted. ⁸ The girls throughout the tribes of Israel who are heiresses must marry within their own tribe, so that their land won't leave the tribe. ⁹ In this way no inheritance shall move from one tribe to another.' "

¹⁰ The daughters of Zelophehad did as the Lord commanded Moses. ¹¹,¹² These girls, Mahlah, Tirzah, Hoglah, Milcah, and Noah, were married to men in their own tribe of Manasseh (son of Joseph); so their inheritance remained in their tribe.

¹³ These are the commandments and ordinances which the Lord gave to the people of Israel through Moses, while they were camped on the plains of Moab beside the Jordan River, across from Jericho.

People Listen to Charlie

In the tiny town of Bartow, Fla., lives an old man who spends his days rocking on the porch of a beat-up candy store. Not what you'd call newsworthy. Yet each year, the members of the media, armed with cameras, take the hot, sandy road to Bartow to visit Charlie Smith. The reason? During the Bicentennial year, he celebrated another birthday— Charlie turned 134, making him the oldest living American of this century.

Charlie can prove his age: a bill of sale validates his purchase into slavery at age 12 in 1855. A group

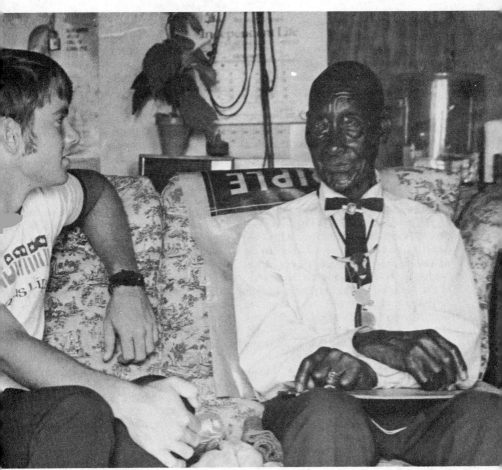

Wally Clark

of teenagers who went to visit him on assignment for CAMPUS LIFE Magazine heard an earful— firsthand tales about Billy the Kid and Jessie James. He also recalls how he was lured onto a slave ship by a fake tree rigged up to look like it was growing fritters. Charlie said on a national TV special, "When I talk about slavery, everybody listens. 'Cause I'm the only one still around who knows what it was like!"

Old people have a way of making you listen. Their broader world throws new light on things. That's why the Israelites listened to Moses' sermons as recorded in Deuteronomy. He was a spry 120 then. He'd seen the courts of Pharoah and had out-survived thousands of Israelites. Moses was worth listening to, especially since God had chosen him as his special mouthpiece.

Deuteronomy is Moses' swan song, his summary of God's way and his startling predictions of what would happen to Israel. You won't find a feeble mind here; Moses spoke eloquently and forcefully. Then, he quietly turned the future over to Joshua and the younger generation.

DEUTERONOMY

1 THIS BOOK RECORDS Moses' address to the people of Israel when they were camped in the valley of the Arabah in the wilderness of Moab, east of the Jordan River. (Cities in the area included Suph, Paran, Tophel, Laban, Hazeroth, and Dizahab.) The speech was given on February 15,[a] forty years after the people of Israel left Mount Horeb—though it takes only eleven days to travel by foot from Mount Horeb to Kadesh-barnea,[b] going by way of Mount Seir! At the time of this address, King Sihon of the Amorites had already been defeated at Heshbon, and King Og of Bashan had been defeated at Ashtaroth, near Edre-i. Here, then, is Moses' address to Israel, stating all the laws God had commanded him to pass on to them:

[6] "It was forty years ago, at Mount Horeb, that Jehovah our God told us, 'You have stayed here long enough. [7] Now go and occupy the hill country of the Amorites, the valley of the Arabah, and the Negeb, and all the land of Canaan and Lebanon—the entire area from the shores of the Mediterranean Sea to the Euphrates River. [8] I am giving all of it to you! Go in and possess it, for it is the land the Lord promised to your ancestors Abraham, Isaac, and Jacob, and all of their descendants.'

[9] "At that time I told the people, 'I need help! You are a great burden for me to carry all by myself, [10] for the Lord has multiplied you like stars! [11] And may he multiply you a thousand times more, and bless you as he promised, [12] but what can one man do to settle all your quarrels and problems? [13] So choose some men from each tribe who are wise, experienced, and understanding, and I will appoint them as your leaders.'

[14] "They agreed to this; [15] I took the men they selected, some from every tribe, and appointed them as administrative assistants in charge of thousands, hundreds, fifties, and tens to decide their quarrels and assist them in every way. [16] I instructed them to be perfectly fair at all times, even to foreigners! [17] 'When giving your decisions,' I told them, 'never favor a man because he is rich; be fair to great and small alike. Don't fear their displeasure, for you are judging in the place of God. Bring me any cases too difficult for you, and I will handle them.' [18] And I gave them other instructions at that time, also.

[19,20,21] "Then we left Mount Horeb and traveled through the great and terrible desert, finally arriving among the Amorite hills to which the Lord our God had directed us. We were then at Kadesh-barnea [on the border of the Promised Land[c]] and I said to the people, 'The Lord God has given us this land. Go and possess it as he told us to. Don't be afraid! Don't even doubt!'

[22] "But they replied, 'First let's send out spies to discover the best route of entry, and to decide which cities we should capture first.'

[23] "This seemed like a good idea, so I chose twelve spies, one from each tribe. [24,25] They crossed into the hills and came to the Valley of Eshcol, and returned with samples of the local fruit. One look was enough to convince us that it was indeed a good land the Lord our God had given us. [26] But the people refused to go in, and rebelled against the Lord's command.

[27] "They murmured and complained in their tents and said, 'The Lord must hate us, bringing us here from Egypt to be slaughtered by these Amorites. [28] What are we getting into? Our brothers who spied out the land have frightened us with their report. They say that the people of the land are tall and powerful, and that the walls of their cities rise high into the sky! They have even seen giants there—the descendants of the Anakim!'

---

a Literally, "the first day of the eleventh month" (of the Hebrew calendar). b Kadesh-barnea was at the southern edge of the Promised Land. c Implied.

29 "But I said to them, 'Don't be afraid! 30 The Lord God is your leader, and he will fight for you with his mighty miracles, just as you saw him do in Egypt. 31 And you know how he has cared for you again and again here in the wilderness, just as a father cares for his child!' 32 But nothing I said did any good.

"They refused to believe the Lord our God 33 who had led them all the way, and had selected the best places for them to camp, and had guided them by a pillar of fire at night and a pillar of cloud during the day.

34,35 "Well, the Lord heard their complaining and was very angry. He vowed that not one person in that entire generation would live to see the good land he had promised their fathers, 36 except Caleb (the son of Jephunneh), who, because he had wholly followed the Lord, would receive as his personal inheritance some of the land he had walked over.

37 "And the Lord was even angry with me because of them and said to me, 'You shall not enter the Promised Land! 38 Instead, your assistant, Joshua (the son of Nun), shall lead the people. Encourage him as he prepares to take over the leadership. 39 I will give the land to the children they said would die in the wilderness. 40 But as for you of the older generation, turn around now and go on back across the desert toward the Red Sea.'

41 "Then they confessed, 'We have sinned! We will go into the land and fight for it as the Lord our God has told us to.' So they strapped on their weapons and thought it would be easy to conquer the whole area.

42 "But the Lord said to me, 'Tell them not to do it, for I will not go with them; they will be struck down before their enemies.'

43 "I told them, but they wouldn't listen. Instead, they rebelled again against the Lord's commandment and went on up into the hill country to fight. 44 But the Amorites who lived there came out against them, and chased them like bees and killed them from Seir to Hormah. 45 Then they returned and wept before the Lord, but he wouldn't listen. 46 So they stayed there at Kadesh for a long time.

2 "THEN WE TURNED back across the wilderness toward the Red Sea, for so the Lord had instructed me. For many years we wandered around in the area of Mount Seir. 2 Then at last the Lord said, 3 " 'You have stayed here long enough. Turn northward. 4 Inform the people that they will be passing through the country belonging to their brothers the Edomites, the descendants of Esau who live in Seir; the Edomites will be nervous, so be careful. 5 Don't start a fight! For I have given them all the Mount Seir hill country as their permanent possession, and I will not give you even a tiny piece of their land. 6 Pay them for whatever food or water you use. 7 The Lord your God has watched over you and blessed you every step of the way for all these forty years as you have wandered around in this great wilderness; and you have lacked nothing in all that time.'

8 "So we passed through Edom where our brothers lived, crossing the Arabah Road that goes south to Elath and Ezi-on-geber, and traveling northward toward the Moab desert.

9 "Then the Lord warned us, 'Don't attack the Moabites either, for I will not give you any of their land; I have given it to the descendants of Lot.'

10 "(The Emim used to live in that area, a very large tribe, tall as the giants of Anakim; 11 both the Emim and the Anakim are often referred to as the Rephaim, but the Moabites call them Emim. 12 In earlier days the Horites lived in Seir, but they were driven out and displaced by the Edomites, the descendants of Esau, just as Israel would displace the peoples of Canaan, whose land had been assigned to Israel by the Lord.)

13 " 'Now cross Zered Brook,' the Lord said; and we did.

14,15 "So it took us thirty-eight years to finally get across Zered Brook from Kadesh! For the Lord had decreed that this could not happen until all the men, who thirty-eight years earlier were old enough to bear arms, had died. Yes, the hand of the Lord was against them until finally all were dead.

16,17 Then at last the Lord said to me, 18 " 'Today Israel shall cross the borders of Moab at Ar, 19 into the land of the Ammonites. But do not attack them, for I will not give you any of their land. I have given it to the descendants of Lot.'

²⁰ "(That area, too, used to be inhabited by the Rephaim, called 'Zamzummim' by the Ammonites. ²¹ They were a large and powerful tribe, as tall as the Anakim; but Jehovah destroyed them as the Ammonites came in, and the Ammonites lived there in their place. ²² The Lord had similarly helped the descendants of Esau at Mount Seir, for he destroyed the Horites who were living there before them. ²³ Another similar situation occurred when the people of Caphtor invaded and destroyed the tribe of Avvim living in villages scattered across the countryside as far away as Gaza.)

²⁴ "Then the Lord said, 'Cross the Arnon River into the land of King Sihon the Amorite, king of Heshbon. War against him and begin to take possession of his land. ²⁵ Beginning today I will make people throughout the whole earth tremble with fear because of you, and dread your arrival.'

²⁶ "Then from the wilderness of Kedemoth I sent ambassadors to King Sihon of Heshbon with a proposal of peace. ²⁷ 'Let us pass through your land,' we said. 'We will stay on the main road and won't turn off into the fields on either side. ²⁸ We will not steal food as we go, but will purchase every bite we eat and everything we drink; all we want is permission to pass through. ²⁹ The Edomites at Seir allowed us to go through their country, and so did the Moabites, whose capital is at Ar. We are on our way across the Jordan into the land the Lord our God has given us.'

³⁰ "But King Sihon refused because Jehovah your God made him obstinate, so that he could destroy Sihon by the hands of Israel, as has now been done.

³¹ "Then the Lord said to me, 'I have begun to give you the land of King Sihon; when you possess it, it shall belong to Israel forever.'

³² "King Sihon then declared war on us and mobilized his forces at Jahaz. ³³,³⁴ But the Lord our God crushed him, and we conquered all his cities, and utterly destroyed everything, including the women and babies. We left nothing alive ³⁵,³⁶ except the cattle, which we took as our reward, along

with the booty gained from ransacking the cities we had taken. We conquered everything from Aroer to Gilead—from the edge of the Arnon River valley, and including all the cities in the valley. Not one city was too strong for us, for the Lord our God gave all of them to us. ³⁷ However, we stayed away from the people of Ammon and from the Jabbok River and the hill country cities, the places Jehovah our God had forbidden us to enter.

3 "NEXT WE TURNED toward King Og's land of Bashan. He immediately mobilized his army and attacked us at Edre-i. But the Lord told me not to be afraid of him. 'All his people and his land are yours,' the Lord told me. 'You will do to him as you did to King Sihon of the Amorites, at Heshbon.' ³ So the Lord helped us fight against King Og and his people, and we killed them all. ⁴ We conquered all sixty of his cities, the entire Argob region of Bashan. ⁵ These were well-fortified cities with high walls and barred gates. Of course we also took all of the unwalled towns. ⁶ We utterly destroyed the kingdom of Bashan just as we had destroyed King Sihon's kingdom at Heshbon, killing the entire population—men, women, and children alike. ⁷ But we kept the cattle and loot for ourselves.

⁸ "We now possessed all the land of the two kings of the Amorites east of the Jordan River—all the land from the valley of the Arnon to Mount Hermon. ⁹ (The Sidonians called Mount Hermon 'Sirion,' while the Amorites called it 'Senir.') ¹⁰ We had now conquered all the cities on the plateau, and all of Gilead and Bashan as far as the cities of Salecah and Edre-i.

¹¹ "Incidentally, King Og of Bashan was the last of the giant Rephaim. His iron bedstead is kept in a museum at Rabbah, one of the cities of the Ammonites, and measures thirteen and a half feet long by six feet wide.

¹² "At that time I gave the conquered land to the tribes of Reuben, Gad, and the half-tribe of Manasseh. To the tribes of Reuben and Gad I gave the area beginning at Aroer on the Arnon River, plus half of Mount Gilead, including its cities. ¹³ The half-tribe of Manasseh received the remain-

der of Gilead and all of the former kingdom of King Og, the Argob region. (Bashan is sometimes called 'The Land of the Rephaim.') [14] The clan of Jair, of the tribe of Manasseh, took over the whole Argob region (Bashan) to the borders of the Geshurites and Ma-acthites. They renamed their country after themselves, calling it Havvoth-jair (meaning 'Jair's Villages') as it is still known today. [15] Then I gave Gilead to the clan of Machir. [16] The tribes of Reuben and Gad received the area extending from the Jabbok River in Gilead (which was the Ammonite frontier) to the middle of the valley of the Arnon River. [17] They also received the Arabah (or, wasteland), bounded by the Jordan River on the west, from Chinnereth to Mount Pisgah and the Salt Sea (also called the Sea of the Arabah).

[18] "At that time I reminded the tribes of Reuben and Gad and the half-tribe of Manasseh, that although the Lord had given them the land, they could not begin settling down until their armed men led the other tribes across the Jordan to the land the Lord was giving them.

[19] " 'But your wives and children,' I told them, 'may live here in the cities the Lord has given you, caring for your many cattle [20] until you return after the Lord has given victory to the other tribes, too. When they conquer the land the Lord your God has given them across the Jordan River, then you may return here to your own land.'

[21] "Then I said to Joshua, 'You have seen what the Lord your God has done to those two kings. You will do the same to all the kingdoms on the other side of the Jordan. [22] Don't be afraid of the nations there, for the Lord your God will fight for you.'

[23,24,25] "At that time I made this plea to God: 'O Lord God, please let me cross over into the Promised Land—the good land beyond the Jordan River with its rolling hills—and Lebanon. I want to see the result of all the greatness and power you have been showing us; for what God in all of heaven or earth can do what you have done for us?'

[26] "But the Lord was angry with me because of you, and would not let me cross over. 'Speak of it no more,' he ordered, [27] 'but go to the top of Mount Pisgah where you can look out in every direction, and there you will see the land in the distance. But you shall not cross the Jordan River. [28] Commission Joshua to replace you, and then encourage him, for he shall lead the people across to conquer the land you will see from the mountain top.'

[29] "So we remained in the valley near Beth-peor.

4 "AND NOW, O Israel, listen carefully to these laws I teach you, and obey them if you want to live and enter into and possess the land given you by the Lord God of your ancestors. [2] Do not add other laws or subtract from these; just obey them, for they are from the Lord your God. [3] You have seen what the Lord did to you at Baalpeor, where he destroyed many people for worshiping idols. [4] But all of you who were faithful to the Lord your God are still alive today.

[5] "These are the laws for you to obey when you arrive in the land where you will live. They are from the Lord our God. He has given them to me to pass on to you. [6] If you obey them they will give you a reputation for wisdom and intelligence. When the surrounding nations hear these laws they will exclaim, 'What other nation is as wise and prudent as Israel!' [7] For what other nation, great or small, has God among them, as the Lord our God is here among us whenever we call upon him? [8] And what nation, no matter how great, has laws as fair as these I am giving you today?

[9] "But watch out! Be very careful never to forget what you have seen God doing for you. May his miracles have a deep and permanent effect upon your lives! Tell your children and your grandchildren about the glorious miracles he did. [10] Tell them especially about the day you stood before the Lord at Mount Horeb, and he told me, 'Summon the people before me and I will instruct them, so that they will learn always to reverence me, and so that they can teach my laws to their children.' [11] You stood at the foot of the mountain, and the mountain burned with fire; flames shot far into the sky, surrounded by black clouds and deep darkness. [12] And the Lord spoke to you from the fire; you heard his words but didn't

see him. [13] He proclaimed the laws you must obey—the Ten Commandments—and wrote them on two stone tablets. [14] Yes, it was at that time that the Lord commanded me to issue the laws you must obey when you arrive in the Promised Land.

[15] "But beware! You didn't see the form of God that day as he spoke to you from the fire at Mount Horeb, [16,17] so do not defile yourselves by trying to make a statue of God—an idol in any form, whether of a man, woman, animal, bird, [18] a small animal that runs along the ground, or a fish. [19] And do not look up into the sky to worship the sun, moon, or stars. The Lord may permit other nations to get away with this, but not you. [20] The Lord has rescued you from prison—Egypt—to be his special people, his own inheritance; this is what you are today. [21,22] But he was angry with me because of you; he vowed that I could not go over the Jordan River into the good land he has given you as your inheritance. I must die here on this side of the river. [23] Beware lest you break the contract the Lord your God has made with you! You will break it if you make any idols, for the Lord your God has utterly forbidden this. [24] He is a devouring fire, a jealous God.

[25] "In the future, when your children and grandchildren are born and you have been in the land a long time, and you have defiled yourselves by making idols, and the Lord your God is very angry because of your sin, [26] heaven and earth are witnesses that you shall be quickly destroyed from the land. Soon, now, you will cross the Jordan River and conquer that land. But your days there will be brief; you will then be utterly destroyed. [27] Jehovah will scatter you among the nations, and you will be but few in number. [28] There, far away, you will worship idols made from wood and stone, idols that neither see nor hear nor eat nor smell.

[29] "But you will also begin to search again for Jehovah your God, and you shall find him when you search for him with all your hearts and souls. [30] When those bitter days have come upon you in the latter times, you will finally return to the Lord your God and listen to what he tells you. [31] For the Lord your God is merciful—he will not abandon you nor destroy you nor

forget the promises he has made to your ancestors.

[32] "In all history, going back to the time when God created man upon the earth, search from one end of the heavens to the other to see if you can find anything like this: [33] An entire nation heard the voice of God speaking to it from fire, as you did, and lived! [34] Where else will you ever find another example of God's removing a nation from its slavery by sending terrible plagues, mighty miracles, war, and terror? Yet that is what the Lord your God did for you in Egypt, right before your very eyes. [35] He did these things so you would realize that Jehovah is God, and that there is no one else like him. [36] He let you hear his voice instructing you from heaven, and he let you see his great pillar of fire upon the earth; you even heard his words from the center of the fire.

[37] "It was because he loved your ancestors and chose to bless their descendants that he personally brought you out from Egypt with a great display of power. [38] He drove away other nations greater by far than you, and gave you their land as an inheritance, as it is today. [39] This is your wonderful thought for the day: Jehovah is God both in heaven and down here upon the earth; and there is no God other than him! [40] You must obey these laws that I will tell you today, so that all will be well with you and your children, and so that you will live forever in the land the Lord your God is giving you."

[41] Then Moses instructed the people of Israel to set apart three cities east of the Jordan River, [42] where anyone who accidentally killed someone could flee for safety. [43] These cities were Bezer, on the plateau in the wilderness, for the tribe of Reuben; Ramoth, in Gilead, for the tribe of Gad; and Golan, in Bashan, for the tribe of Manasseh.

[44,45,46] Listed below are the laws Moses issued to the people of Israel when they left Egypt, and as they were camped east of the Jordan River near the city of Beth-peor. (This was the land formerly occupied by the Amorites under King Sihon, whose capital was Heshbon; he and his people were destroyed by Moses and the Israelis. [47] Israel conquered his land and that of King Og of Bashan—they were two Amorite kings east of the Jordan. ⁴⁸ Israel also conquered all the area from Aroer at the edge of the Arnon River valley to Mount Sirion, or Mount Hermon, as it is sometimes called; ⁴⁹ and all the Arabah east of the Jordan River over to the Salt Sea, below the slopes of Mount Pisgah.)

5 MOSES CONTINUED SPEAKING to the people of Israel and said, "Listen carefully now to all these laws God has given you; learn them, and be sure to obey them! ²,³ "The Lord our God made a contract with you at Mount Horeb—*not with your ancestors, but with you who are here alive today.* ⁴ He spoke with you face to face from the center of the fire, there at the mountain. ⁵ I stood as an intermediary between you and Jehovah, for you were afraid of the fire and did not go up to him on the mountain. He spoke to me and I passed on his laws to you. This is what he said:

⁶ " 'I am Jehovah your God who rescued you from slavery in Egypt.

⁷ " 'Never worship any god but me.

⁸ " 'Never make idols; don't worship images, whether of birds, animals, or fish. ⁹,¹⁰ You shall not bow down to any images nor worship them in any way, for I am the Lord your God. I am a jealous God, and I will bring the curse of a father's sins upon even the third and fourth generation of the children of those who hate me; but I will show kindness to a thousand generations of those who love me and keep my commandments.

¹¹ " 'You must never use my name to make a vow you don't intend to keep.ᵃ I will not overlook that.

¹² " 'Keep the Sabbath day holy. This is my command. ¹³ Work the other six days, ¹⁴ but the seventh day is the Sabbath of the Lord your God; no work shall be done that day by you or by any of your household —your sons, daughters, servants, oxen, donkeys, or cattle; even foreigners living among you must obey this law. Everybody must rest as you do. ¹⁵ Why should you keep the Sabbath? It is because you were slaves in Egypt, and the Lord your God brought you out with a great display of miracles.

¹⁶ " 'Honor your father and mother (remember, this is a commandment of the Lord your God); if you do so, you shall have a long, prosperous life in the land he is giving you.

¹⁷ " 'You must not murder.

¹⁸ " 'You must not commit adultery.

¹⁹ " 'You must not steal.

²⁰ " 'You must not tell lies.

²¹ " 'You must not burn with desire for another man's wife, nor envy him for his home, land, servants, oxen, donkeys, nor anything else he owns.'

²² "The Lord has given these laws to each one of you from the heart of the fire, surrounded by the clouds and thick darkness that engulfed Mount Sinai. Those were the only commandments he gave you at that time,ᵇ and he wrote them out on two stone tablets and gave them to me. ²³ But when you heard the loud voice from the darkness, and saw the terrible fire at the top of the mountain, all your tribal leaders came to me ²⁴ and pleaded, 'Today the Lord our God has shown us his glory and greatness; we have even heard his voice from the heart of the fire. Now we know that a man may speak to God and not die; ²⁵ but we will surely die if he speaks to us again. This awesome fire will consume us. ²⁶,²⁷ What man can hear, as we have, the voice of the living God speaking from the heart of fire, and live? You go and listen to all that God says, then come and tell us, and we will listen and obey.'

²⁸ "And the Lord agreed to your request, and said to me, 'I have heard what the people have said to you, and I agree. ²⁹ Oh, that they would always have such a heart for me, wanting to obey my commandments. Then all would go well with them in the future, and with their children throughout all generations! ³⁰ Go and tell them to return to their tents. ³¹ Then you come back and stand here beside me, and I will give you all my commandments, and you shall teach them to the people; and they will obey them in the land I am giving to them.' "

³² So Moses told the people, "You must

---

a Literally, "You must not utter the name of the Lord your God to misuse it."   b Literally, "and he added no more."

obey all the commandments of the Lord your God, following his directions in every detail, going the whole way he has laid out for you; [33] only then will you live long and prosperous lives in the land you are to enter and possess.

6 "THE LORD YOUR God told me to give you all these commandments which you are to obey in the land you will soon be entering, where you will live. [2] The purpose of these laws is to cause you, your sons, and your grandsons to reverence the Lord your God by obeying all of his instructions as long as you live; if you do, you will have long, prosperous years ahead of you. [3] Therefore, O Israel, listen closely to each command and be careful to obey it, so that all will go well with you, and so that you will have many children. If you obey these commands you will become a great nation in a glorious land 'flowing with milk and honey,' even as the God of your fathers promised you.

[4] "O Israel, listen: Jehovah is our God, Jehovah alone. [5] You must love him with *all* your heart, soul, and might. [6] And you must think constantly about these commandments I am giving you today. [7] You must teach them to your children and talk about them when you are at home or out for a walk; at bedtime and the first thing in the morning. [8] Tie them on your finger, wear them on your forehead, [9] and write them on the doorposts of your house!

[10,11,12] "When the Lord your God has brought you into the land he promised your ancestors, Abraham, Isaac, and Jacob, and when he has given you great cities full of good things—cities you didn't build, wells you didn't dig, and vineyards and olive trees you didn't plant—and when you have eaten until you can hold no more, then beware lest you forget the Lord who brought you out of the land of Egypt, the land of slavery. [13] When you are full, don't forget to be reverent to him and to serve him and to use *his* name alone to endorse your promises.

[14] "You must not worship the gods of the neighboring nations, [15] for Jehovah your God who lives among you is a jealous God, and his anger may rise quickly against you, and wipe you off the face of the earth. [16] You must not provoke him and try his patience as you did when you complained against him at Massah. [17] You must actively obey him in everything he commands. [18] Only then will you be doing what is right and good in the Lord's eyes. If you obey him, all will go well for you, and you will be able to go in and possess the good land which the Lord promised your ancestors. [19] You will also be able to throw out all the enemies living in your land, as the Lord agreed to help you do.

[20] "In the years to come when your son asks you, 'What is the purpose of these laws which the Lord our God has given us?' [21] you must tell him, 'We were Pharaoh's slaves in Egypt, and the Lord brought us out of Egypt with great power [22] and mighty miracles—with terrible blows against Egypt and Pharaoh and all his people. We saw it all with our own eyes. [23] He brought us out of Egypt so that he could give us this land he had promised to our ancestors. [24] And he has commanded us to obey all of these laws and to reverence him so that he can preserve us alive as he has until now. [25] For it always goes well with us when we obey all the laws of the Lord our God.'

7 "WHEN THE LORD brings you into the Promised Land, as he soon will, he will destroy the following seven nations, all greater and mightier than you are:

The Hittites, the Girgashites,
The Amorites, the Canaanites,
The Perizzites, the Hivites,
The Jebusites.

[2] When the Lord your God delivers them over to you to be destroyed, do a complete job of it—don't make any treaties or show them mercy; utterly wipe them out. [3] Do not intermarry with them, nor let your sons and daughters marry their sons and daughters. [4] That would surely result in your young people's beginning to worship their gods. Then the anger of the Lord would be hot against you and he would surely destroy you.

[5] "You must break down the heathen altars and shatter the obelisks and cut up the shameful images and burn the idols. [6] For you are a holy people, dedicated to the Lord your God. He has chosen you from all the

people on the face of the whole earth to be his own chosen ones. [7] He didn't choose you and pour out his love upon you because you were a larger nation than any other, for you were the smallest of all! [8] It was just because he loves you, and because he kept his promise to your ancestors. That is why he brought you out of slavery in Egypt with such amazing power and mighty miracles.

[9] "Understand, therefore, that the Lord your God is the faithful God who for a thousand generations keeps his promises and constantly loves those who love him and who obey his commands. [10] But those who hate him shall be punished publicly and destroyed. He will deal with them personally. [11] Therefore, obey all these commandments I am giving you today. [12] Because of your obedience, the Lord your God will keep his part of the contract which, in his tender love, he made with your fathers. [13] And he will love you and bless you and make you into a great nation. He will make you fertile and give fertility to your ground and to your animals, so that you will have large crops of grain, grapes, and olives, and great flocks of cattle, sheep, and goats when you arrive in the land he promised your fathers to give you. [14] You will be blessed above all the nations of the earth; not one of you, whether male or female, shall be barren, not even your cattle. [15] And the Lord will take away all your sickness and will not let you suffer any of the diseases of Egypt you remember so well; he will give them all to your enemies!

[16] "You must destroy all the nations which the Lord your God delivers into your hands. Have no pity, and do not worship their gods; if you do, it will be a sad day for you. [17] Perhaps you will think to yourself, 'How can we ever conquer these nations that are so much more powerful than we are?' [18] But don't be afraid of them! Just remember what the Lord your God did to Pharaoh and to all the land of Egypt. [19] Do you remember the terrors the Lord sent upon them—your parents saw it with their own eyes—and the mighty miracles and wonders, and the power and strength of Almighty God which he used to bring you out of Egypt? Well, the Lord your God will use this same might against the people you fear.

[20] Moreover, the Lord your God will send hornets to drive out those who hide from you!

[21] "No, do not be afraid of those nations, for the Lord your God is among you, and he is a great and awesome God. [22] He will cast them out a little at a time; he will not do it all at once, for if he did, the wild animals would multiply too quickly and become dangerous. [23] He will do it gradually, and you will move in against those nations and destroy them. [24] He will deliver their kings into your hands, and you will erase their names from the face of the earth. No one will be able to stand against you.

[25] "Burn their idols and do not touch the silver or gold they are made of. Do not take it or it will be a snare to you, for it is horrible to the Lord your God. [26] Do not bring an idol into your home and worship it, for then your doom is sealed. Utterly detest it, for it is a cursed thing.

8 "YOU MUST OBEY all the commandments I give you today. If you do, you will not only live, you will multiply and will go in and take over the land promised to your fathers by the Lord. [2] Do you remember how the Lord led you through the wilderness for all those forty years, humbling you and testing you to find out how you would respond, and whether or not you would really obey him? [3] Yes, he humbled you by letting you go hungry and then feeding you with manna, a food previously unknown to both you and your ancestors. He did it to help you realize that food isn't everything, and that real life comes by obeying every command of God. [4] For all these forty years your clothes haven't grown old, and your feet haven't been blistered or swollen. [5] So you should realize that, as a man punishes his son, the Lord punishes you to help you.

[6] "Obey the laws of the Lord your God. Walk in his ways and fear him. [7] For the Lord your God is bringing you into a good land of brooks, pools, gushing springs, valleys, and hills; [8] it is a land of wheat and barley, of grape vines, fig trees, pomegranates, olives, and honey; [9] it is a land where food is plentiful, and nothing is lacking; it is a land where iron is as common as

stone, and copper is abundant in the hills. [10] When you have eaten your fill, bless the Lord your God for the good land he has given you.

[11] "But that is the time to be careful! Beware that in your plenty[a] you don't forget the Lord your God and begin to disobey him. [12,13] For when you have become full and prosperous and have built fine homes to live in, and when your flocks and herds have become very large, and your silver and gold have multiplied, [14] that is the time to watch out that you don't become proud, and forget the Lord your God who brought you out of your slavery in the land of Egypt. [15] Beware that you don't forget the God who led you through the great and terrible wilderness with the dangerous snakes and scorpions, where it was so hot and dry. He gave you water from the rock! [16] He fed you with manna in the wilderness (it was a kind of bread unknown before) so that you would become humble and so that your trust in him would grow, and he could do you good. [17] He did it so that you would never feel that it was your own power and might that made you wealthy. [18] Always remember that it is the Lord your God who gives you power to become rich, and he does it to fulfill his promise to your ancestors.

[19] "But if you forget about the Lord your God and worship other gods instead, and follow evil ways, you shall certainly perish, [20] just as the Lord has caused other nations in the past to perish. That will be your fate, too, if you don't obey the Lord your God.

9 "O ISRAEL, LISTEN! Today you are to cross the Jordan River and begin to dispossess the nations on the other side. Those nations are much greater and more powerful than you are! They live in high walled cities. Among them are the famed Anak giants, against whom none can stand! [3] But the Lord your God will go before you as a devouring fire to destroy them, so that you will quickly conquer them and drive them out.

[4] "Then, when the Lord has done this for you, don't say to yourselves, 'The Lord has helped us because we are so good!' No, it is because of the wickedness of the other nations that he is doing it. [5] It is not at all because you are such fine, upright people that the Lord will drive them out from before you! I say it again, it is only because of the wickedness of the other nations, and because of his promises to your ancestors, Abraham, Isaac, and Jacob, that he will do it. [6] I say it yet again: *Jehovah your God is not giving you this good land because you are good, for you are not*—you are a wicked, stubborn people.

[7] "Don't you remember (oh, never forget it!) how continually angry you made the Lord your God out in the wilderness, from the day you left Egypt until now? For all this time you have constantly rebelled against him.

[8] "Don't you remember how angry you made him at Mount Horeb? He was ready to destroy you. [9] I was on the mountain at the time, receiving the contract which Jehovah had made with you—the stone tablets with the laws inscribed upon them. I was there for forty days and forty nights, and all that time I ate nothing. I didn't even take a drink of water. [10,11] At the end of those forty days and nights the Lord gave me the contract, the tablets on which he had written the commandments he had spoken from the fire-covered mountain while the people had watched below. [12] He told me to go down quickly because the people I had led out of Egypt had defiled themselves, quickly turning away from the laws of God, and had made an idol from molten metal.

[13,14] " 'Let me alone that I may destroy this evil, stubborn people!' the Lord told me, 'and I will blot out their name from under heaven, and I will make a mighty nation of you, mightier and greater than they are.'

[15] "I came down from the burning mountain, holding in my hands the two tablets inscribed with the laws of God. [16] There below me I could see the calf you had made in your terrible sin against the Lord your God. How quickly you turned away from him! [17] I lifted the tablets high above my head and dashed them to the ground! I smashed them before your eyes! [18] Then, for

---

a Implied.

another forty days and nights I lay before the Lord, neither eating bread nor drinking water, for you had done what the Lord hated most, thus provoking him to great anger. ¹⁹ How I feared for you—for the Lord was ready to destroy you. But that time, too, he listened to me. ²⁰ Aaron was in great danger because the Lord was so angry with him; but I prayed, and the Lord spared him. ²¹ I took your sin—the calf you had made—and burned it and ground it into fine dust, and threw it into the stream that cascaded out of the mountain.

²² "Again at Taberah and once again at Massah you angered the Lord, and yet again at Kibroth-hattaavah. ²³ At Kadesh-barnea, when the Lord told you to enter the land he had given you, you rebelled and wouldn't believe that he would help you; you refused to obey him. ²⁴ Yes, you have been rebellious against the Lord from the first day I knew you. ²⁵ That is why I fell down before him for forty days and nights when the Lord was ready to destroy you.

²⁶ "I prayed to him, 'O Lord God, don't destroy your own people. They are your inheritance saved from Egypt by your mighty power and glorious strength. ²⁷ Don't notice the rebellion and stubbornness of these people, but remember instead your promises to your servants Abraham, Isaac, and Jacob. Oh, please overlook the awful wickedness and sin of these people. ²⁸ For if you destroy them the Egyptians will say, "It is because the Lord wasn't able to bring them to the land he promised them," or "He destroyed them because he hated them: he brought them into the wilderness to slay them." ²⁹ They are your people and your inheritance which you brought from Egypt by your great power and your mighty arm.'

10 "AT THAT TIME the Lord told me to cut two more stone tablets like the first ones, and to make a wooden Ark to keep them in, and to return to God on the mountain. ² He said he would rewrite on the tablets the same commandments that were on the tablets I had smashed, and that I should place them in the Ark. ³ So I made an Ark of acacia wood and hewed out two stone tablets like the first two, and took the tablets up on the mountain to God. ⁴ He again wrote the Ten Commandments on them and gave them to me. (They were the same commandments he had given you from the heart of the fire on the mountain as you all watched below.) ⁵ Then I came down and placed the tablets in the Ark I had made, where they are to this day, just as the Lord commanded me.

⁶ "The people of Israel then journeyed from Be-eroth of Bene-jaakan to Moserah, where Aaron died and was buried. His son Eleazar became the next priest.

⁷ "Then they journeyed to Gudgodah, and from there to Jotbathah, a land of brooks and water. ⁸ It was there that Jehovah set apart the tribe of Levi to carry the Ark containing the Ten Commandments of Jehovah, and to stand before the Lord and to do his work and to bless his name, just as is done today. ⁹ (That is why the tribe of Levi does not have a portion of land reserved for it in the Promised Land, as their brother tribes do; for as the Lord told them, he himself is their inheritance.)

¹⁰ "As I said before, I stayed on the mountain before the Lord for forty days and nights the second time, just as I had the first, and the Lord again yielded to my pleas and didn't destroy you.

¹¹ "But he said to me, 'Arise and lead the people to the land I promised their fathers. It is time to go in and possess it.'

¹²,¹³ "And now, Israel, what does the Lord your God require of you except to listen carefully to all he says to you, and to obey for your own good the commandments I am giving you today, and to love him, and to worship him with all your hearts and souls? ¹⁴ Earth and highest heaven belong to the Lord your God. ¹⁵ And yet he rejoiced in your fathers and loved them so much that he chose you, their children, to be above every other nation, as is evident today. ¹⁶ Therefore, cleanse your sinful hearts and stop your stubbornness.

¹⁷ "Jehovah your God is God of gods and Lord of lords. He is the great and mighty God, the God of terror who shows no partiality and takes no bribes. ¹⁸ He gives justice to the fatherless and widows. He loves foreigners and gives them food and clothing. ¹⁹ (You too must love foreigners, for

you yourselves were foreigners in the land of Egypt.) [20] You must fear the Lord your God and worship him and cling to him and take oaths by his name alone. [21] He is your praise and he is your God, the one who has done mighty miracles you yourselves have seen. [22] When your ancestors went down into Egypt there were only seventy of them, but now the Lord your God has made you as many as the stars in the sky!

11 "YOU MUST LOVE the Lord your God and obey every one of his commands. [2] Listen! I am not talking now to your children who have never experienced the Lord's punishments or seen his greatness and his awesome power. [3] They weren't there to see the miracles he did in Egypt against Pharaoh and all his land. [4] They didn't see what God did to the armies of Egypt and to their horses and chariots—how he drowned them in the Red Sea as they were chasing you, and how the Lord has kept them powerless against you until this very day! [5] They didn't see how the Lord cared for you time and again through all the years you were wandering in the wilderness, until your arrival here. [6] They weren't there when Dathan and Abiram (the sons of Eliab, descendants[a] of Reuben) sinned, and the earth opened up and swallowed them, with their households and tents and all their belongings, as all Israel watched!

[7] "But *you* have seen these mighty miracles! [8] How carefully, then, you should obey these commandments I am going to give you today, so that you may have the strength to go in and possess the land you are about to enter. [9] If you obey the commandments, you will have a long and good life in the land the Lord promised to your ancestors and to you, their descendants—a wonderful land 'flowing with milk and honey'! [10] For the land you are about to enter and possess is not like the land of Egypt where you have come from, where irrigation is necessary. [11] It is a land of hills and valleys with plenty of rain— [12] a land that the Lord your God personally cares for! His eyes are always upon it, day after day throughout the year!

[13] "And if you will carefully obey all of his commandments that I am going to give you today, and if you will love the Lord your God with all your hearts and souls, and will worship him, [14] then he will continue to send both the early and late rains that will produce wonderful crops of grain, grapes for your wine, and olive oil. [15] He will give you lush pastureland for your cattle to graze in, and you yourselves shall have plenty to eat and be fully content.

[16] "But beware that your hearts do not turn from God to worship other gods. [17] For if you do, the anger of the Lord will be hot against you, and he will shut the heavens—there will be no rain and no harvest, and you will quickly perish from the good land the Lord has given you. [18] So keep these commandments carefully in mind. Tie them to your hand to remind you to obey them, and tie them to your forehead between your eyes! [19] Teach them to your children. Talk about them when you are sitting at home, when you are out walking, at bedtime, and before breakfast! [20] Write them upon the doors of your houses and upon your gates, [21] so that as long as there is sky above the earth, you and your children will enjoy the good life awaiting you in the land the Lord has promised you.[b]

[22] "If you carefully obey all the commandments I give you, loving the Lord your God, walking in all his ways, and clinging to him, [23] then the Lord will drive out all the nations in your land, no matter how much greater and stronger than you they might be. [24] Wherever you go, the land is yours. Your frontiers will stretch from the southern Negeb to Lebanon, and from the Euphrates River to the Mediterranean Sea. [25] No one will be able to stand against you, for the Lord your God will send fear and dread ahead of you wherever you go, just as he has promised.

[26] "I am giving you the choice today between God's blessing or God's curse! [27] There will be blessing if you obey the commandments of the Lord your God which I am giving you today, [28] and a curse if you refuse them and worship the gods of these other nations. [29] When the Lord your

---

a Literally, "sons."   b Literally, "your fathers."

God brings you into the land to possess it, a blessing shall be proclaimed from Mount Gerizim, and a curse from Mount Ebal! ³⁰ (Gerizim and Ebal are mountains west of the Jordan River, where the Canaanites live, in the wasteland near Gilgal, where the oaks of Moreh are.)) ³¹ For you are to cross the Jordan and live in the land the Lord is giving you. ³² But you must obey all the laws I am giving you today.

12 "THESE ARE THE laws you must obey when you arrive in the land which Jehovah, the God of your fathers, has given you forever:

² "You must destroy all the heathen altars wherever you find them—high in the mountains, up in the hills, or under the trees. ³ Break the altars, smash the obelisks, burn the shameful images, cut down the metal idols, and leave nothing even to remind you of them!

⁴,⁵ "You must not make sacrifices to your God just anywhere, as the heathen sacrifice to their gods. Rather, you must build a sanctuary for him at a place he himself will select as his home. ⁶ There you shall bring to the Lord your burnt offerings and other sacrifices—your tithes, your offerings presented by the gesture of waving before the altar, your offerings to fulfill your vows, your free-will offerings, and your offerings of the firstborn animals of your flocks and herds. ⁷ There you and your families shall feast before the Lord your God, and shall rejoice in all he has done for you.

⁸ "You will no longer go your own way as you do now, everyone doing whatever he thinks is right; ⁹ (for these laws don't go into effect until you arrive in the place of rest the Lord will give to you). ¹⁰ But when you cross the Jordan River and live in the Promised Land, and the Lord gives you rest and keeps you safe from all your enemies, ¹¹ then you must bring all your burnt sacrifices and other offerings to his sanctuary, the place he will choose as his home. ¹² You shall rejoice there before the Lord with your sons and daughters and servants; and remember to invite the Levites to feast with you, for they have no land of their own.

¹³ "You are not to sacrifice your burnt offerings just anywhere; ¹⁴ you may only do so in the place the Lord will choose. He will pick a place in the territory allotted to one of the tribes. Only there may you offer your sacrifices and bring your offerings. ¹⁵ However, the meat you eat may be butchered anywhere, just as you do now with gazelle and deer. Eat as much of this meat as you wish and as often as you are able to obtain it, because the Lord has prospered you. Those who are ceremonially defiled may eat it, too. ¹⁶ The only restriction is that you are not to eat the blood—pour it out on the ground, like water.

¹⁷ "But none of the offerings may be eaten at home. Neither the tithe of your grain and new wine and olive oil, nor the firstborn of your flocks and herds, nor anything you have vowed to give the Lord, nor your freewill offerings, nor the offerings to be presented to the Lord by waving them before his altar. ¹⁸ All these must be brought to the central altar where you, your children, and the Levites shall eat them before the Lord your God. He will tell you where this altar must be located. Rejoice before the Lord your God in everything you do. ¹⁹ (By the way, be very careful not to forget about the Levites. Share with them.)

²⁰⁻²³ "If, when the Lord enlarges your borders, the central altar is too far away from you, then your flocks and herds may be butchered on your own farms, just as you do now with gazelle and deer. And even persons who are ceremonially defiled may eat them. The only restriction is never to eat the blood, for the blood is the life, and you shall not eat the life with the meat. ²⁴,²⁵ Instead, pour the blood out upon the earth. If you do, all will be well with you and your children. ²⁶,²⁷ Only your gifts to the Lord, and the offerings you have promised in your vows, and your burnt offerings need be taken to the central altar. These may only be sacrificed upon the altar of the Lord your God. The blood will be poured out upon the altar, and you will eat the meat.

²⁸ "Be careful to obey all of these commandments. If you do what is right in the eyes of the Lord your God, all will go well with you and your children forever. ²⁹ When he destroys the nations in the land where you will live, ³⁰ don't follow their example in worshiping their gods. Do not ask, 'How

do these nations worship their gods?' and then go and worship as they do! [31] You must not insult the Lord your God like that! These nations have done horrible things that he hates, all in the name of their religion. They have even roasted their sons and daughters before their gods. [32] Obey all the commandments I give you. Do not add to or subtract from them.

13 "IF THERE IS a prophet among you, or one who claims to foretell the future by dreams, [2] and if his predictions come true but he says, 'Come, let us worship the gods of the other nations,' [3] don't listen to him. For the Lord is testing you to find out whether or not you really love him with all your heart and soul. [4] You must *never* worship any God but Jehovah; obey only his commands and cling to him.

[5] "The prophet who tries to lead you astray must be executed, for he has attempted to foment rebellion against the Lord your God who brought you out of slavery in the land of Egypt. By executing him you will clear out the evil from among you. [6,7] If your nearest relative or closest friend, even a brother, son, daughter, or beloved wife whispers to you to come and worship these foreign gods, [8] do not consent nor listen, and have no pity: Do not spare that person from the penalty; don't conceal his horrible suggestion. [9] Execute him! Your own hand shall be the first upon him to put him to death, then the hands of all the people. [10] Stone him to death because he has tried to draw you away from the Lord your God who brought you from the land of Egypt, the place of slavery. [11] Then all Israel will hear about his evil deed, and will fear such wickedness as this among you.

[12,13,14] "If you ever hear it said about one of the cities of Israel that some worthless rabble have led their fellow citizens astray with the suggestion that they worship foreign gods, first check the facts to see if the rumor is true. If you find that it is, that it is certain that such a horrible thing is happening among you in one of the cities the Lord has given you, [15] you must without fail declare war against that city and utterly destroy all of its inhabitants, and even all of the cattle. [16] Afterwards you must pile all the booty into the middle of the street and burn it, then put the entire city to the torch, as a burnt offering to Jehovah your God. That city shall forever remain a lifeless mound and may never be rebuilt. [17] Keep none of the booty! Then the Lord will turn from his fierce anger and be merciful to you, and have compassion upon you, and make you a great nation just as he promised your ancestors. [18] Of course, the Lord your God will be merciful only if you have been obedient to him and to his commandments which I am giving you today, and if you have been doing that which is right in the eyes of the Lord.

14 "SINCE YOU ARE the people of God, never cut yourselves [as the heathen do when they worship their idols[a]] nor shave the front halves of your heads for funerals. [2] You belong exclusively to the Lord your God, and he has chosen you to be his own possession, more so than any other nation on the face of the earth.

[3,4,5] "You are not to eat any animal I have declared to be ceremonially defiled. These are the animals you may eat:

The ox, the sheep, the goat,
The deer, the gazelle, the roebuck,
The wild goat, the ibex,
The antelope, and the mountain sheep.

[6] "Any animal that has cloven hooves and chews the cud may be eaten, [7] but if the animal doesn't have both, it may not be eaten. So you may not eat the camel, the hare, or the coney.

"They chew the cud but do not have cloven hooves. [8] Pigs may not be eaten because, although they have cloven hooves, they don't chew the cud. You may not even touch the dead bodies of such animals.

[9] "Only sea animals with fins and scales may be eaten; [10] all other kinds are ceremonially defiled.

[11-18] "You may eat any bird except the following:

The eagle, the vulture,
The osprey, the buzzard,

---

a Implied.

The falcon (any variety),
The raven (any variety),
The ostrich, the nighthawk,
The sea gull, the hawk (any variety),
The screech owl, the great owl,
The horned owl, the pelican,
The vulture, the cormorant,
The stork, the heron (any variety),
The hoopoe, the bat.

19,20 "With certain exceptions,[b] winged insects are a defilement to you and may not be eaten.

21 "Don't eat anything that has died a natural death. However, a foreigner among you may eat it. You may give it or sell it to him, but don't eat it yourself, for you are holy to the Lord your God.

"You must not boil a young goat in its mother's milk.

22 "You must tithe all of your crops every year. 23 Bring this tithe to eat before the Lord your God at the place he shall choose as his sanctuary; this applies to your tithes of grain, new wine, olive oil, and the firstborn of your flocks and herds. The purpose of tithing is to teach you always to put God first in your lives. 24 If the place the Lord chooses for his sanctuary is so far away that it isn't convenient to carry your tithes to that place, 25 then you may sell the tithe portion of your crops and herds and take the money to the Lord's sanctuary. 26 When you arrive, use the money to buy an ox, a sheep, some wine, or some strong drink, to feast there before the Lord your God, and to rejoice with your household.

27 "Don't forget to share your income with the Levites in your community, for they have no property or crops as you do.

28 "Every third year you are to use your entire tithe for local welfare programs: 29 Give it to the Levites who have no inheritance among you, or to foreigners, or to widows and orphans within your city, so that they can eat and be satisfied; and then Jehovah your God will bless you and your work.

15 "AT THE END of every seventh year there is to be a canceling of all debts! 2 Every creditor shall write "Paid in full" on any promissory note he holds against a fellow Israelite, for the Lord has released everyone from his obligation. 3 (This release does not apply to foreigners.) 4,5 No one will become poor because of this, for the Lord will greatly bless you in the land he is giving you if you obey this command. The only prerequisite for his blessing is that you carefully heed all the commands of the Lord your God that I am giving you today. 6 He will bless you as he has promised. You shall lend money to many nations but will never need to borrow! You shall rule many nations, but they shall not rule over you!

7 "But if, when you arrive in the land the Lord will give you, there are any among you who are poor, you must not shut your heart or hand against them; 8 you must lend them as much as they need. 9 Beware! Don't refuse a loan because the year of debt cancellation is close at hand! If you refuse to make the loan and the needy man cries out to the Lord, it will be counted against you as a sin. 10 You must lend him what he needs, and don't moan about it either! For the Lord will prosper you in everything you do because of this! 11 There will always be some among you who are poor; that is why this commandment is necessary. You must lend to them liberally.

12 "If you buy a Hebrew slave, whether a man or woman, you must free him at the end of the sixth year you have owned him, 13 and don't send him away empty-handed! 14 Give him a large farewell present from your flock, your olive press, and your wine press. Share with him in proportion as the Lord your God has blessed you. 15 Remember that you were slaves in the land of Egypt and the Lord your God rescued you! That is why I am giving you this command.

16 "But if your Hebrew slave doesn't want to leave—if he says he loves you and enjoys your pleasant home and gets along well with you— 17 then take an awl and pierce his ear into the door, and after that he shall be your slave forever. Do the same with your women slaves. 18 But when you free a slave you must not feel bad, for remember that for six years he has cost you less than half the price of a hired hand! And

b See Leviticus 11:20–23.

the Lord your God will prosper all you do because you have released him!

[19] "You shall set aside for God all the firstborn males from your flocks and herds. Do not use the firstborn of your herds to work your fields, and do not shear the firstborn of your flocks of sheep and goats. [20] Instead, you and your family shall eat these animals before the Lord your God each year at his sanctuary. [21] However, if this firstborn animal has any defect such as being lame or blind, or if anything else is wrong with it, you shall not sacrifice it. [22] Instead, use it for food for your family at home. Anyone, even if ceremonially defiled at the time, may eat it, just as anyone may eat a gazelle or deer. [23] But don't eat the blood; pour it out upon the ground like water.

16 "ALWAYS REMEMBER TO celebrate the Passover during the month of April,[a] for that was when Jehovah your God brought you out of Egypt by night. [2] Your Passover sacrifice shall be either a lamb or an ox, sacrificed to the Lord your God at his sanctuary. [3] Eat the sacrifice with unleavened bread. Eat unleavened bread for seven days as a reminder of the bread you ate as you escaped from Egypt. This is to remind you that you left Egypt in such a hurry that there was no time for the bread to rise.[b] Remember that day all the rest of your lives! [4] For seven days no trace of yeast shall be in your homes, and none of the Passover lamb shall be left until the next morning.

[5] "The Passover is not to be eaten in your homes. [6] It must be eaten at the place the Lord shall choose as his sanctuary. Sacrifice it there on the anniversary evening just as the sun goes down. [7] Roast the lamb and eat it, then start back to your homes the next morning. [8] For the following six days you shall eat no bread made with yeast. On the seventh day there shall be a quiet gathering of the people of each city before the Lord your God. Don't do any work that day.

[9] "Seven weeks after the harvest begins, [10] there shall be another festival before the Lord your God called the Festival of Weeks. At that time bring to him a free-will offering proportionate in size to his blessing upon you as judged by the amount of your harvest. [11] It is a time to rejoice before the Lord with your family and household. And don't forget to include the local Levites, foreigners, widows, and orphans. Invite them to accompany you to the celebration at the sanctuary. [12] Remember! You were a slave in Egypt, so be sure to carry out this command.

[13] "Another celebration, the Festival of Shelters, must be observed for seven days at the end of the harvest season, after the grain is threshed and the grapes have been pressed. [14] This will be a happy time of rejoicing together with your family and servants. And don't forget to include the Levites, foreigners, orphans, and widows of your town.

[15] "This feast will be held at the sanctuary, which will be located at the place the Lord will designate. It is a time of deep thanksgiving to the Lord for blessing you with a good harvest and in so many other ways; it shall be a time of great joy.

[16] "Every man in Israel shall appear before the Lord your God three times a year at the sanctuary for these festivals:

The Festival of Unleavened Bread,
The Festival of Weeks,
The Festival of Shelters.

"On each of these occasions bring a gift to the Lord. [17] Give as you are able, according as the Lord has blessed you.

[18] "Appoint judges and administrative officials for all the cities the Lord your God is giving you. They will administer justice in every part of the land. [19] Never twist justice to benefit a rich man, and never accept bribes. For bribes blind the eyes of the wisest and corrupt their decisions. [20] Justice must prevail.

"That is the only way you will be successful in the land which the Lord your God is giving you.

[21] "Never, under any circumstances, are you to erect shameful images beside the altar of the Lord your God. [22] And never set up an obelisk, for the Lord hates them!

---

a Literally, "Abib"—the first month of the Hebrew calendar.
b Literally, "For you left Egypt in hurried flight."

17 "NEVER SACRIFICE A sick or defective ox or sheep to the Lord your God. He doesn't feel honored by such gifts!

2,3 "If anyone, whether man or woman, in any village throughout your land violates your covenant with God by worshiping other gods, the sun, moon, or stars—which I have strictly forbidden— 4 first check the rumor very carefully; if there is no doubt it is true, 5 then that man or woman shall be taken outside the city and shall be stoned to death. 6 However, never put a man to death on the testimony of only one witness; there must be at least two or three. 7 The witnesses shall throw the first stones, and then all the people shall join in. In this way you will purge all evil from among you.

8 "If a case arises that is too hard for you to decide—for instance, whether someone is guilty of murder when there is insufficient evidence, or whether someone's rights have been violated—you shall take the case to the sanctuary of the Lord your God, 9 to the priests and Levites, and the chief judge on duty at the time will make the decision. 10 His decision is without appeal and is to be followed to the letter. 11 The sentence he imposes is to be fully executed. 12 If the defendant refuses to accept the decision of the priest or judge appointed by God for this purpose, the penalty is death. Such sinners must be purged from Israel. 13 Then everyone will hear about what happened to the man who refused God's verdict, and they will be afraid to defy the court's judgment a second time.

14 "When you arrive in the land the Lord your God will give you, and have conquered it, and begin to think, 'We ought to have a king like the other nations around us'— 15 be sure that you select as king the man the Lord your God shall choose. He must be an Israelite, not a foreigner. 16 Be sure that he doesn't build up a large stable of horses for himself, nor send his men to Egypt to raise horses for him there, for the Lord has told you, 'Never return to Egypt again.' 17 He must not have too many wives, lest his heart be turned away from the Lord, neither shall he be excessively rich.

18 "And when he has been crowned and sits upon his throne as king, then he must copy these laws from the book kept by the Levite-priests. 19 That copy of the laws shall be his constant companion. He must read from it every day of his life so that he will learn to respect the Lord his God by obeying all of his commands. 20 This regular reading of God's laws will prevent him from feeling that he is better than his fellow citizens. It will also prevent him from turning away from God's laws in the slightest respect, and will ensure his having a long, good reign. His sons will then follow him upon the throne.

18 "REMEMBER THAT THE priests and all the other members of the Levite tribe will not be given property like the other tribes. So the priests and Levites are to be supported by the sacrifices brought to the altar of the Lord and by the other offerings the people bring to him. 2 They don't need to own property, for the Lord is their property! That is what he promised them! 3 The shoulder, the cheeks, and the stomach of every ox or sheep brought for sacrifice must be given to the priests. 4 In addition, the priests shall receive the harvest samples brought in thanksgiving to the Lord—the first of the grain, the new wine, the olive oil, and of the fleece at shearing time. 5 For the Lord your God has chosen the tribe of Levi, of all the tribes, to minister to the Lord from generation to generation.

6,7 "Any Levite, no matter where he lives in the land of Israel, has the right to come to the sanctuary at any time and minister in the name of the Lord, just like his brother Levites who work there regularly. 8 He shall be given his share of the sacrifices and offerings as his right, not just if he is in need.

9 "When you arrive in the Promised Land you must be very careful lest you be corrupted by the horrible customs of the nations now living there. 10 For example, any Israeli who presents his child to be burned to death as a sacrifice to heathen gods, must be killed.a No Israeli may practice black magic, or call on the evil spirits for aid, or be a fortune teller, 11 or be a serpent charmer, medium, or wizard, or call

---

a Implied.

forth the spirits of the dead. ¹² Anyone doing these things is an object of horror and disgust to the Lord, and it is because the nations do these things that the Lord your God will displace them. ¹³ You must walk blamelessly before the Lord your God. ¹⁴ The nations you replace all do these evil things, but the Lord your God will not permit you to do such things.

¹⁵ "Instead, he will raise up for you a Prophet like me, an Israeli, a man to whom you must listen and whom you must obey. ¹⁶ For this is what you yourselves begged of God at Mount Horeb. There at the foot of the mountain you begged that you might not have to listen to the terrifying voice of God again, or see the awesome fire on the mountain, lest you die.

¹⁷ " 'All right,' the Lord said to me, 'I will do as they have requested. ¹⁸ I will raise up from among them a Prophet, an Israeli like you. I will tell him what to say, and he shall be my spokesman to the people. ¹⁹ I will personally deal with anyone who will not listen to him and heed his messages from me. ²⁰ But any prophet who falsely claims that his message is from me, shall die. And any prophet who claims to give a message from other gods must die.' ²¹ If you wonder, 'How shall we know whether the prophecy is from the Lord or not?' ²² this is the way to know: If the thing he prophesies doesn't happen, it is not the Lord who has given him the message; he has made it up himself. You have nothing to fear from him.

19 "WHEN THE LORD your God has destroyed the nations you will displace, and when you are living in their cities and homes, ²,³ you must set apart three Cities of Refuge so that anyone who accidentally kills someone may flee to safety. Divide the country into three districts, with one of these cities in each district; and keep the roads to these cities in good repair.

⁴ "Here is an example of the purpose of these cities: ⁵ If a man goes into the forest with his neighbor to chop wood, and the axe head flies off the handle and kills the man's neighbor, he may flee to one of those cities and be safe. ⁶,⁷ Anyone seeking to avenge the death will not be able to. These cities must be scattered so that one of them will be reasonably close to everyone; otherwise the angry avenger might catch and kill the innocent slayer, even though he should not have died since he had not killed deliberately.

⁸ "If the Lord enlarges your boundaries as he promised your ancestors, and gives you all the land he promised ⁹ (whether he does this depends on your obedience to all these commandments I am giving you today—loving the Lord your God and walking his paths), then you must designate three additional Cities of Refuge. ¹⁰ In this way you will be able to avoid the death of innocent people, and you will not be held responsible for unjustified bloodshed.

¹¹ "But if anyone hates his neighbor and springs out of hiding and kills him, and then flees into one of the Cities of Refuge, ¹² the elders of his home town shall send for him and shall bring him home and deliver him over to the dead man's avenger, to kill him. ¹³ Don't pity him! Purge all murderers from Israel! Only then will all go well with you.

¹⁴ "When you arrive in the land the Lord your God is giving you, remember that you must never steal a man's land by moving the boundary marker.

¹⁵ "Never convict anyone on the testimony of one witness. There must be at least two, and three is even better. ¹⁶ If anyone gives false witness, claiming he has seen someone do wrong when he hasn't, ¹⁷ both men shall be brought before the priests and judges on duty before the Lord at the time. ¹⁸ They must be closely questioned, and if the witness is lying, ¹⁹ his penalty shall be the punishment he thought the other man would get. In this way you will purge out evil from among you. ²⁰ Then those who hear about it will be afraid to tell lies on the witness stand. ²¹ You shall not show pity to a false witness. Life for life, eye for eye, tooth for tooth, hand for hand, foot for foot; this is your rule in such cases.

20 "WHEN YOU GO to war and see before you vast numbers of horses and chariots, an army far greater than yours, don't be frightened! The Lord your God is with you—the same God who brought you safely out of Egypt! ² Before you begin the battle,

a priest shall stand before the Israeli army and say,

³ " 'Listen to me, all you men of Israel! Don't be afraid as you go out to fight today! ⁴ For the Lord your God is going with you! He will fight for you against your enemies, and he will give you the victory!'

⁵ "Then the officers of the army shall address the men in this manner: 'Has anyone just built a new house, but not yet dedicated it? If so, go home! For you might be killed in the battle, and someone else would dedicate it! ⁶ Has anyone just planted a vineyard but not yet eaten any of its fruit? If so, go home! You might die in battle and someone else would eat it! ⁷ Has anyone just become engaged? Well, go home and get married! For you might die in the battle, and someone else would marry your fiancée. ⁸ And now, is anyone afraid? If you are, go home before you frighten the rest of us!' ⁹ When the officers have finished saying this to their men, they will announce the names of the battalion leaders.

¹⁰ "As you approach a city to fight against it, first offer it a truce. ¹¹ If it accepts the truce and opens its gates to you, then all its people shall become your servants. ¹² But if it refuses and won't make peace with you, you must besiege it. ¹³ When the Lord your God has given it to you, kill every male in the city; ¹⁴ but you may keep for yourselves all the women, children, cattle, and booty. ¹⁵ These instructions apply only to distant cities, not to those in the Promised Landᵃ itself.

¹⁶ "For in the cities within the boundaries of the Promised Land you are to save no one; destroy every living thing. ¹⁷ Utterly destroy the Hittites, the Amorites, the Canaanites, the Perizzites, the Hivites, and the Jebusites. This is the commandment of the Lord your God. ¹⁸ The purpose of this command is to prevent the people of the land from luring you into idol worship and into participation in their loathsome customs, thus sinning deeply against the Lord your God.

¹⁹ "When you besiege a city, don't destroy the fruit trees. Eat all the fruit you wish; just don't cut down the trees. They aren't enemies who need to be slaughtered! ²⁰ But you may cut down trees that aren't valuable for food. Use them for the siege [to make ladders, portable towers, and battering ramsᵇ].

21 "IF, WHEN YOU arrive in the Promised Land, a murder victim is found lying in a field and no one has seen the murder, ² the elders and judges shall measure from the body to the nearest city. ³ Then the elders of that city shall take a heifer that has never been yoked, ⁴ and lead it to a valley where there is running water—a valley neither plowed nor sowed—and there break its neck.

⁵ "Then the priests shall come (for the Lord your God has chosen them to minister before him and to pronounce his blessings and decide lawsuits and punishments), ⁶ and shall wash their hands over the heifer, ⁷ and say, 'Our hands have not shed this blood, neither have our eyes seen it. ⁸ O Lord, forgive your people Israel whom you have redeemed, and do not charge them with murdering an innocent man. Forgive us the guilt of this man's blood.' ⁹ In this way you will put away the guilt from among you by following the Lord's directions.

¹⁰ "When you go to war and the Lord your God delivers your enemies to you, ¹¹ and you see among the captives a beautiful girl you want as your wife, ¹² take her home with you. She must shave her head and pare her nails ¹³ and change her clothing, laying aside that which she was wearing when she was captured, then remain in your home in mourning for her father and mother for a full month. After that you may marry her. ¹⁴ However, if after marrying her you decide you don't like her, you must let her go free—you may not sell her or treat her as a slave, for you have humiliated her.

¹⁵ "If a man has two wives but loves one and not the other, and both have borne him children, and the mother of his oldest son is the wife he doesn't love, ¹⁶ he may not give a larger inheritance to his younger son, the son of the wife he loves. ¹⁷ He must give the customary double portion to his oldest son, who is the beginning of his strength and

a Literally, "which are not of the cities of these nations."　　b Implied.

who owns the rights of a firstborn son, even though he is the son of the wife his father doesn't love.

[18] "If a man has a stubborn, rebellious son who will not obey his father or mother, even though they punish him, [19] then his father and mother shall take him before the elders of the city [20] and declare, 'This son of ours is stubborn and rebellious and won't obey; he is a worthless drunkard.' [21] Then the men of the city shall stone him to death. In this way you shall put away this evil from among you, and all the young men of Israel will hear about what happened and will be afraid.

[22] "If a man has committed a crime worthy of death, and is executed and then hanged on a tree, [23] his body shall not remain on the tree overnight. You must bury him the same day, for anyone hanging on a tree is cursed of God. Don't defile the land the Lord your God has given you.

22 "IF YOU SEE someone's ox or sheep wandering away, don't pretend you didn't see it; take it back to its owner. [2] If you don't know who the owner is, take it to your farm and keep it there until the owner comes looking for it, and then give it to him. [3] The same applies to donkeys, clothing, or anything else you find. Keep it for its owner.

[4] "If you see someone trying to get an ox or donkey onto its feet when it has slipped beneath its load,[a] don't look the other way. Go and help!

[5] "A woman must not wear men's clothing, and a man must not wear women's clothing. This is abhorrent to the Lord your God.

[6] "If a bird's nest is lying on the ground, or if you spy one in a tree, and there are young ones or eggs in it with the mother sitting in the nest, don't take the mother with the young. [7] Let her go, and take only the young. The Lord will bless you for it.

[8] "Every new house must have a guardrail around the edge of the flat rooftop to prevent anyone from falling off and bringing guilt to both the house and its owner.

[9] "Do not sow other crops in the rows of your vineyard. If you do, both the crops and the grapes shall be confiscated by the priests.[b]

[10] "Don't plow with an ox and a donkey harnessed together.

[11] "Don't wear clothing woven from two kinds of thread: for instance, wool and linen.

[12] "You must sew tassels on the four corners of your cloaks.

[13,14] "If a man marries a girl, then after sleeping with her accuses her of having had premarital intercourse with another man, saying, 'She was not a virgin when I married her,' [15] then the girl's father and mother shall bring the proof of her virginity to the city judges.

[16] "Her father shall tell them, 'I gave my daughter to this man to be his wife, and now he despises her, [17,18] and has accused her of shameful things, claiming that she was not a virgin when she married; yet here is the proof.' And they shall spread the garment before the judges. The judges shall sentence the man to be whipped, [19] and fine him one hundred dollars[c] to be given to the girl's father, for he has falsely accused a virgin of Israel. She shall remain his wife and he may never divorce her. [20] But if the man's accusations are true, and she was not a virgin, [21] the judges shall take the girl to the door of her father's home where the men of the city shall stone her to death. She has defiled Israel by flagrant crime, being a prostitute while living at home with her parents; and such evil must be cleansed from among you.

[22] "If a man is discovered committing adultery, both he and the other man's wife must be killed; in this way evil will be cleansed from Israel. [23,24] If a girl who is engaged is seduced within the walls of a city, both she and the man who seduced her shall be taken outside the gates and stoned to death—the girl because she didn't scream for help, and the man because he has violated the virginity of another man's fiancée. [25,26,27] In this way you will reduce crime among you. But if this deed takes place out in the country, only the man shall die. The

---

a Implied.   b Literally, "Lest the fulness of the fruit be consecrated."   c Literally, "a hundred shekels of silver." The exact value cannot be determined.

girl is as innocent as a murder victim; for it must be assumed that she screamed, but there was no one to hear and rescue her out in the field. [28,29] If a man rapes a girl who is not engaged, and is caught in the act, he must pay a fine[d] to the girl's father and marry her; he may never divorce her. [30] A man shall not sleep with his father's widow[e] since she belonged to his father.

23 "IF A MAN'S testicles are crushed or his penis cut off, he shall not enter the sanctuary. [2] A bastard may not enter the sanctuary, nor any of his descendants for ten generations.

[3] "No Ammonite or Moabite may ever enter the sanctuary, even after the tenth generation. [4] The reason for this law is that these nations did not welcome you with food and water when you came out of Egypt; they even tried to hire Balaam, the son of Beor from Pethor, Mesopotamia, to curse you. [5] But the Lord wouldn't listen to Balaam; instead, he turned the intended curse into a blessing for you, because the Lord loves you. [6] You must never, as long as you live, try to help the Ammonites or the Moabites in any way. [7] But don't look down on the Edomites and the Egyptians; the Edomites are your brothers and you lived among the Egyptians. [8] The grandchildren of the Egyptians who came with you from Egypt may enter the sanctuary of the Lord.

[9,10] "When you are at war, the men in the camps must stay away from all evil. Any man who becomes ceremonially defiled because of a seminal emission during the night must leave the camp, [11] and stay outside until the evening; then he shall bathe himself and return at sunset. [12] The toilet area shall be outside the camp. [13] Each man must have a spade as part of his equipment; after every bowel movement he must dig a hole with the spade and cover the excrement. [14] The camp must be holy, for the Lord walks among you to protect you and to cause your enemies to fall before you; and the Lord does not want to see anything indecent lest he turn away from you.

[15,16] "If a slave escapes from his master, you must not force him to return; let him live among you in whatever town he shall choose, and do not oppress him.

[17,18] "No prostitutes are permitted in Israel, either men or women; you must not bring to the Lord any offering from the earnings of a prostitute or a homosexual, for both are detestable to the Lord your God.

[19] "Don't demand interest on loans you make to a brother Israelite, whether it is in the form of money, food, or anything else. [20] You may take interest from a foreigner, but not from an Israeli. For if you take interest from a brother, an Israeli, the Lord your God won't bless you when you arrive in the Promised Land.

[21] "When you make a vow to the Lord, be prompt in doing whatever it is you promised him, for the Lord demands that you promptly fulfill your vows; it is a sin if you don't. [22] (But it is not a sin if you refrain from vowing!) [23] Once you make the vow, you must be careful to do as you have said, for it was your own choice, and you have vowed to the Lord your God.

[24] "You may eat your fill of the grapes from another man's vineyard, but do not take any away in a container. [25] It is the same with someone else's grain—you may eat a few handfuls of it, but don't use a sickle.

24 "IF A MAN doesn't like something about his wife, he may write a letter stating that he has divorced her, give her the letter, and send her away. [2] If she then remarries, [3] and the second husband also divorces her, or dies, [4] the former husband may not marry her again, for she has been defiled; this would bring guilt upon the land the Lord your God is giving you.

[5] "A newly married man is not to be drafted into the army nor given any other special responsibilities; for a year he shall be free to be at home, happy with his wife.

[6] "It is illegal to take a millstone as a pledge, for it is a tool by which its owner gains his livelihood. [7] If anyone kidnaps a brother Israelite, and treats him as a slave

---

d Literally, "shall pay her father fifty of silver." e Literally, "his father's wife." The general law against adultery protected her and his other wives while their husband was living.

or sells him, the kidnapper must die, in order to purge the evil from among you.

[8] "Be very careful to follow the instructions of the priest in cases of leprosy, for I have given him rules and guidelines you must obey to the letter: [9] Remember what the Lord your God did to Miriam as you were coming from Egypt.

[10] "If you lend anything to another man, you must not enter his house to get his security. [11] Stand outside! The owner will bring it out to you. [12,13] If the man is poor and gives you his cloak as security, you are not to sleep in it. Take it back to him at sundown so that he can use it through the night and bless you; and the Lord your God will count it as righteousness for you.

[14,15] "Never oppress a poor hired man, whether a fellow Israelite or a foreigner living in your town. Pay him his wage each day before sunset, for since he is poor he needs it right away; otherwise he may cry out to the Lord against you and it would be counted as a sin against you.

[16] "Fathers shall not be put to death for the sins of their sons nor the sons for the sins of their fathers; every man worthy of death shall be executed for his own crime.

[17] "Justice must be given to migrants and orphans and you must never accept a widow's garment in pledge of her debt. [18] Always remember that you were slaves in Egypt, and that the Lord your God rescued you; that is why I have given you this command. [19] If, when reaping your harvest, you forget to bring in a sheaf from the field, don't go back after it. Leave it for the migrants, orphans, and widows; then the Lord your God will bless and prosper all you do. [20] When you beat the olives from your olive trees, don't go over the boughs twice; leave anything remaining for the migrants, orphans, and widows. [21] It is the same for the grapes in your vineyard; don't glean the vines after they are picked, but leave what's left for those in need. [22] Remember that you were slaves in the land of Egypt—that is why I am giving you this command.

25 "IF A MAN is guilty of a crime, and the penalty is a beating, the judge shall command him to lie down and be beaten in his presence with up to forty stripes in proportion to the seriousness of the crime; but no more than forty stripes may be given lest the punishment seem too severe, and your brother be degraded in your eyes.

[4] "Don't muzzle an ox as it treads out the grain.

[5] "If a man's brother dies without a son, his widow must not marry outside the family; instead, her husband's brother must marry her and sleep with her. [6] The first son she bears to him shall be counted as the son of the dead brother, so that his name will not be forgotten. [7] But if the dead man's brother refuses to do his duty in this matter, refusing to marry the widow, then she shall go to the city elders and say to them, 'My husband's brother refuses to let his brother's name continue—he refuses to marry me.' [8] The elders of the city will then summon him and talk it over with him, and if he still refuses, [9] the widow shall walk over to him in the presence of the elders, pull his sandal from his foot and spit in his face. She shall then say, 'This is what happens to a man who refuses to build his brother's house.' [10] And ever afterwards his house shall be referred to as 'the home of the man who had his sandal pulled off!'

[11] "If two men are fighting and the wife of one intervenes to help her husband by grabbing the testicles of the other man, [12] her hand shall be cut off without pity.

[13,14,15] "In all your transactions you must use accurate scales and honest measurements, so that you will have a long, good life in the land the Lord your God is giving you. [16] All who cheat with unjust weights and measurements are detestable to the Lord your God.

[17] "You must never forget what the people of Amalek did to you as you came from Egypt. [18] Remember that they fought with you and struck down those who were faint and weary and lagging behind, with no respect or fear of God. [19] Therefore, when the Lord your God has given you rest from all your enemies in the Promised Land, you are utterly to destroy the name of Amalek from under heaven. Never forget this.

26 "WHEN YOU ARRIVE in the land and have conquered it and are living there, [2,3] you must present to the Lord at his sanc-

tuary the first sample from each annual[a] harvest. Bring it in a basket and hand it to the priest on duty and say to him, 'This gift is my acknowledgment that the Lord my God has brought me to the land he promised our ancestors.' [4] The priest will then take the basket from your hand and set it before the altar. [5] You shall then say before the Lord your God, 'My ancestors were migrant Arameans who went to Egypt for refuge. They were few in number, but in Egypt they became a mighty nation. [6,7] The Egyptians mistreated us and we cried to the Lord God. He heard us and saw our hardship, toil, and oppression, [8] and brought us out of Egypt with mighty miracles and a powerful hand. He did great and awesome miracles before the Egyptians, [9] and has brought us to this place and given us this land "flowing with milk and honey!" [10] And now, O Lord, see, I have brought you a token of the first of the crops from the ground you have given me.' Then place the samples before the Lord your God, and worship him. [11] Afterwards, go and feast on all the good things he has given you. Celebrate with your family and with any Levites or migrants living among you.

[12] "Every third year is a year of special tithing. That year you are to give all your tithes to the Levites, migrants, orphans, and widows, so that they will be well fed. [13] Then you shall declare before the Lord your God, 'I have given all of my tithes to the Levites, the migrants, the orphans, and the widows, just as you commanded me; I have not violated or forgotten any of your rules. [14] I have not touched the tithe while I was ceremonially defiled (for instance, while I was in mourning), nor have I offered any of it to the dead. I have obeyed the Lord my God and have done everything you commanded me. [15] Look down from your holy home in heaven and bless your people and the land you have given us, as you promised our ancestors; make it a land "flowing with milk and honey"!'

[16] "You must wholeheartedly obey all of these commandments and ordinances which the Lord your God is giving you to-day. [17] You have declared today that he is your God, and you have promised to obey and keep his laws and ordinances, and to heed all he tells you to do. [18] And the Lord has declared today that you are his very own people, just as he promised, and that you must obey all of his laws. [19] If you do, he will make you greater than any other nation, allowing you to receive praise, honor, and renown; but to attain this honor and renown you must be a holy people to the Lord your God, as he requires."

27 THEN MOSES AND the elders of Israel gave the people these further instructions to obey:[a]

[2,3,4] "When you cross the Jordan River and go into the Promised Land—a land 'flowing with milk and honey'—take out boulders from the river bottom and immediately pile them into a monument on the other side, at Mount Ebal. Face the stones with a coating of lime[b] and then write the laws of God in the lime. [5,6] And build an altar there to the Lord your God. Use uncut boulders, and on the altar offer burnt offerings to the Lord your God. [7] Sacrifice peace offerings upon it also, and feast there with great joy before the Lord your God. [8] Write all of these laws plainly [upon the monument[c]]."

[9] Then Moses and the Levite-priests addressed all Israel as follows: "O Israel, listen! Today you have become the people of the Lord your God, [10] so today you must begin to obey all of these commandments I have given you."

[11] That same day Moses gave this charge to the people:

[12] "When you cross into the Promised Land, the tribes of Simeon, Levi, Judah, Issachar, Joseph, and Benjamin shall stand upon Mount Gerizim to proclaim a blessing, [13] and the tribes of Reuben, Gad, Asher, Zebulun, Dan, and Naphtali shall stand upon Mount Ebal to proclaim a curse. [14] Then the Levites standing between[d] them shall shout to all Israel,

[15] " 'The curse of God be upon anyone who makes and worships an idol, even in

---

a Implied.   27a Literally, "Keep all the commandments I enjoin on you today."   b Literally, "Plaster them with plaster."   c Implied. See verses 1-4.   d Implied.

secret, whether carved of wood or made from molten metal—for these handmade gods are hated by the Lord.' And all the people shall reply, 'Amen.'

¹⁶ " 'Cursed is anyone who despises his father or mother.' And all the people shall reply, 'Amen.'

¹⁷ " 'Cursed is he who moves the boundary marker between his land and his neighbor's.' And all the people shall reply, 'Amen.'

¹⁸ " 'Cursed is he who takes advantage of a blind man.' And all the people shall reply, 'Amen.'

¹⁹ " 'Cursed is he who is unjust to the foreigner, the orphan, and the widow.' And all the people shall reply, 'Amen.'

²⁰ " 'Cursed is he who commits adultery with one of his father's wives, for she belongs to his father.' And all the people shall reply, 'Amen.'

²¹ " 'Cursed is he who has sexual intercourse with an animal.' And all the people shall reply, 'Amen.'

²² " 'Cursed is he who has sexual intercourse with his sister, whether she be a full sister or a half-sister.' And all the people shall reply, 'Amen.'

²³ " 'Cursed is he who has sexual intercourse with his widowedᶜ mother-in-law.' And all the people shall reply, 'Amen.'

²⁴ " 'Cursed is he who secretly slays another.' And all the people shall reply, 'Amen.'

²⁵ " 'Cursed is he who accepts a bribe to kill an innocent person.' And all the people shall reply, 'Amen.'

²⁶ " 'Cursed is anyone who does not obey these laws.' And all the people shall reply, 'Amen.'

28 "IF YOU FULLY obey all of these commandments of the Lord your God, the laws I am declaring to you today, God will transform you into the greatest nation in the world. ²⁻⁶ These are the blessings that will come upon you:

> Blessings in the city,
> Blessings in the field;
> Many children,
> Ample crops,

> Large flocks and herds;
> Blessings of fruit and bread;
> Blessings when you come in,
> Blessings when you go out.

⁷ "The Lord will defeat your enemies before you; they will march out together against you but scatter before you in seven directions! ⁸ The Lord will bless you with good crops and healthy cattle, and prosper everything you do when you arrive in the land the Lord your God is giving you. ⁹ He will change you into a holy people dedicated to himself; this he has promised to do if you will only obey him and walk in his ways. ¹⁰ All the nations in the world shall see that you belong to the Lord, and they will stand in awe.

¹¹ "The Lord will give you an abundance of good things in the land, just as he promised: many children, many cattle, and abundant crops. ¹² He will open to you his wonderful treasury of rain in the heavens, to give you fine crops every season. He will bless everything you do; and you shall lend to many nations, but shall not borrow from them. ¹³ If you will only listen and obey the commandments of the Lord your God that I am giving you today, he will make you the head and not the tail, and you shall always have the upper hand. ¹⁴ But each of these blessings depends on your not turning aside in any way from the laws I have given you; and you must never worship other gods.

¹⁵⁻¹⁹ "If you won't listen to the Lord your God and won't obey these laws I am giving you today, then all of these curses shall come upon you:

> Curses in the city;
> Curses in the fields;
> Curses on your fruit and bread;
> The curse of barren wombs;
> Curses upon your crops;
> Curses upon the fertility of your cattle and flocks;
> Curses when you come in;
> Curses when you go out.

²⁰ "For the Lord himself will send his personal curse upon you. You will be confused and a failure in everything you do, until at last you are destroyed because of the

---

c Implied. If she were still married, no special law would be needed to prohibit adultery.

sin of forsaking him. [21] He will send disease among you until you are destroyed from the face of the land which you are about to enter and possess. [22] He will send tuberculosis, fever, infections, plague, and war. He will blight your crops, covering them with mildew. All these devastations shall pursue you until you perish.

[23] "The heavens above you will be as unyielding as bronze, and the earth beneath will be as iron. [24] The land will become as dry as dust for lack of rain, and dust storms shall destroy you.

[25] "The Lord will cause you to be defeated by your enemies. You will march out to battle gloriously, but flee before your enemies in utter confusion; and you will be tossed to and fro among all the nations of the earth. [26] Your dead bodies will be food to the birds and wild animals, and no one will be there to chase them away.

[27] "He will send upon you Egyptian boils, tumors, scurvy, and itch, for none of which will there be a remedy. [28] He will send madness, blindness, fear, and panic upon you. [29] You shall grope in the bright sunlight just as the blind man gropes in darkness. You shall not prosper in anything you do; you will be oppressed and robbed continually, and nothing will save you.

[30] "Someone else will marry your fiancée; someone else will live in the house you build; someone else will eat the fruit of the vineyard you plant. [31] Your oxen shall be butchered before your eyes, but you won't get a single bite of the meat. Your donkeys will be driven away as you watch, and will never return to you again. Your sheep will be given to your enemies. And there will be no one to protect you. [32] You will watch as your sons and daughters are taken away as slaves. Your heart will break with longing for them, but you will not be able to help them. [33] A foreign nation you have not even heard of will eat the crops you will have worked so hard to grow. You will always be oppressed and crushed. [34] You will go mad because of all the tragedy you see around you. [35] The Lord will cover you with boils from head to foot.

[36] "He will exile you and the king you will choose, to a nation to whom neither you nor your ancestors gave a second thought; and while in exile you shall worship gods of wood and stone! [37] You will become an object of horror, a proverb and a byword among all the nations, for the Lord will thrust you away.

[38] "You will sow much but reap little, for the locusts will eat your crops. [39] You will plant vineyards and care for them, but you won't eat the grapes or drink the wine, for worms will destroy the vines. [40] Olive trees will be growing everywhere, but there won't be enough olive oil to anoint yourselves! For the trees will drop their fruit before it is matured. [41] Your sons and daughters will be snatched away from you as slaves. [42] The locusts shall destroy your trees and vines. [43] Foreigners living among you shall become richer and richer while you become poorer and poorer. [44] They shall lend to you, not you to them! They shall be the head and you shall be the tail!

[45] "All these curses shall pursue and overtake you until you are destroyed—all because you refuse to listen to the Lord your God. [46] These horrors shall befall you and your descendants as a warning: [47,48] You will become slaves to your enemies because of your failure to praise God for all that he has given you. The Lord will send your enemies against you, and you will be hungry, thirsty, naked, and in want of everything. A yoke of iron shall be placed around your neck until you are destroyed!

[49] "The Lord will bring a distant nation against you, swooping down upon you like an eagle; a nation whose language you don't understand— [50] a nation of fierce and angry men who will have no mercy upon young or old. [51] They will eat you out of house and home until your cattle and crops are gone. Your grain, new wine, olive oil, calves, and lambs will all disappear. [52] That nation will lay siege to your cities and knock down your highest walls—the walls you will trust to protect you. [53] You will even eat the flesh of your own sons and daughters in the terrible days of siege that lie ahead. [54] The most tenderhearted man among you will be utterly callous toward his own brother and his beloved wife and his children who are still alive. [55] He will refuse to give them a share of the flesh he is devouring—the flesh of his own children—because he is starving in the

midst of the siege of your cities. [56,57] The most tender and delicate woman among you—the one who would not so much as touch her feet to the ground—will refuse to share with her beloved husband, son, and daughter. She will hide from them the afterbirth and the new baby she has borne, so that she herself can eat them: so terrible will be the hunger during the siege and the awful distress caused by your enemies at your gates.

[58,59] "If you refuse to obey all the laws written in this book, thus refusing reverence to the glorious and fearful name of Jehovah your God, then Jehovah will send perpetual plagues upon you and upon your children. [60] He will bring upon you all the diseases of Egypt which you feared so much, and they shall plague the land. [61] And that is not all! The Lord will bring upon you every sickness and plague there is, even those not mentioned in this book, until you are destroyed. [62] There will be few of you left, though before you were as numerous as stars. All this if you do not listen to the Lord your God.

[63] "Just as the Lord has rejoiced over you and has done such wonderful things for you and has multiplied you, so the Lord at that time will rejoice in destroying you; and you shall disappear from the land. [64] For the Lord will scatter you among all the nations from one end of the earth to the other. There you will worship heathen gods that neither you nor your ancestors have known, gods made of wood and stone! [65] There among those nations you shall find no rest, but the Lord will give you trembling hearts, darkness, and bodies wasted from sorrow and fear. [66] Your lives will hang in doubt. You will live night and day in fear, and will have no reason to believe that you will see the morning light. [67] In the morning you will say, 'Oh, that night were here!' And in the evening you will say, 'Oh, that morning were here!' You will say this because of the awesome horrors surrounding you. [68] Then the Lord will send you back to Egypt in ships, a journey I promised you would never need to make again; and there you will offer to sell yourselves to your enemies as slaves—but no one will even want to buy you."

29 IT WAS ON the plains of Moab that Moses restated the covenant which the Lord had made with the people of Israel at Mount Horeb. [2,3] He summoned all Israel before him and told them,

"You have seen with your own eyes the great plagues and mighty miracles that the Lord brought upon Pharaoh and his people in the land of Egypt. [4] But even yet the Lord hasn't given you hearts that understand or eyes that see or ears that hear! [5] For forty years God has led you through the wilderness, yet your clothes haven't become old, and your shoes haven't worn out! [6] The reason he hasn't let you settle down to grow grain for bread or grapes for wine and strong drink, is so that you would realize that it is the Lord your God who has been caring for you.

[7] "When we came here, King Sihon of Heshbon and King Og of Bashan came out against us in battle, but we destroyed them, [8] and took their land and gave it to the tribes of Reuben and Gad and to the half-tribe of Manasseh as their inheritance. [9] Therefore, obey the terms of this covenant so that you will prosper in everything you do. [10] All of you—your leaders, the people, your judges, and your administrative officers—are standing today before the Lord your God, [11] along with your little ones and your wives and the foreigners that are among you— those who chop your wood and carry your water. [12] You are standing here to enter into a contract with Jehovah your God, a contract he is making with you today. [13] He wants to confirm you today as his people, and to confirm that he is your God, just as he promised your ancestors, Abraham, Isaac, and Jacob. [14,15] This contract is not with you alone as you stand before him today, but with all future generations of Israel as well.

[16] "Surely you remember how we lived in the land of Egypt, and how as we left, we came safely through the territory of enemy nations. [17] And you have seen their heathen idols made of wood, stone, silver, and gold. [18] The day that any of you—man or woman, family or tribe of Israel—begins to turn away from the Lord our God and desires to worship these gods of other nations, that day a root will be planted that will grow

bitter and poisonous fruit.

¹⁹ "Let no one blithely think, when he hears the warnings of this curse, 'I shall prosper even though I walk in my own stubborn way!' ²⁰ For the Lord will not pardon! His anger and jealousy will be hot against that man. And all the curses written in this book shall lie heavily upon him, and the Lord will blot out his name from under heaven. ²¹ The Lord will separate that man from all the tribes of Israel, to pour out upon him all the curses (which are recorded in this book) that befall those who break this contract. ²² Then your children and the generations to come and the foreigners that pass by from distant lands shall see the devastation of the land and the diseases the Lord will have sent upon it. ²³ They will see that the whole land is alkali and salt, a burned over wasteland, unsown, without crops, without a shred of vegetation—just like Sodom and Gomorrah and Admah and Zeboiim, destroyed by the Lord in his anger.

²⁴ " 'Why has the Lord done this to his land?' the nations will ask. 'Why was he so angry?'

²⁵ "And they will be told, 'Because the people of the land broke the contract made with them by Jehovah, the God of their ancestors, when he brought them out of the land of Egypt. ²⁶ For they worshiped other gods, violating his express command. ²⁷ That is why the anger of the Lord was hot against this land, so that all his curses (which are recorded in this book) broke forth upon them. ²⁸ In great anger the Lord rooted them out of their land and threw them away into another land, where they still live today!'

²⁹ "There are secrets the Lord your God has not revealed to us, but these words which he has revealed are for us and our children to obey forever.

30 "WHEN ALL THESE things have happened to you—the blessings and the curses I have listed—you will meditate upon them as you are living among the nations where the Lord your God will have driven you. ² If at that time you want to return to the Lord your God, and you and your children have begun wholeheartedly to

obey all of the commandments I have given you today, ³ then the Lord your God will rescue you from your captivity! He will have mercy upon you and come and gather you out of all the nations where he will have scattered you. ⁴ Though you are at the ends of the earth, he will go and find you and bring you back again ⁵ to the land of your ancestors. You shall possess the land again, and he will do you good and bless you even more than he did your ancestors! ⁶ He will cleanse your hearts and the hearts of your children and of your children's children so that you will love the Lord your God with all your hearts and souls, and Israel shall come alive again!

⁷,⁸ "If you return to the Lord and obey all the commandments that I command you today, the Lord your God will take his curses and turn them against your enemies —against those who hate you and persecute you. ⁹ The Lord your God will prosper everything you do and give you many children and much cattle and wonderful crops; for the Lord will again rejoice over you as he did over your fathers. ¹⁰ He will rejoice if you but obey the commandments written in this book of the law, and if you turn to the Lord your God with all your hearts and souls. ¹¹ Obeying these commandments is not something beyond your strength and reach; ¹² for these laws are not in the far heavens, so distant that you can't hear and obey them, and with no one to bring them down to you; ¹³ nor are they beyond the ocean, so far that no one can bring you their message; ¹⁴ but they are very close at hand —in your hearts and on your lips—so that you can obey them.

¹⁵ "Look, today I have set before you life and death, depending on whether you obey or disobey. ¹⁶ I have commanded you today to love the Lord your God and to follow his paths and to keep his laws, so that you will live and become a great nation, and so that the Lord your God will bless you and the land you are about to possess. ¹⁷ But if your hearts turn away and you won't listen—if you are drawn away to worship other gods— ¹⁸ then I declare to you this day that you shall surely perish; you will not have a long, good life in the land you are going in to possess.

¹⁹ "I call heaven and earth to witness against you that today I have set before you life or death, blessing or curse. Oh, that you would choose life; that you and your children might live! ²⁰ Choose to love the Lord your God and to obey him and to cling to him, for he is your life and the length of your days. You will then be able to live safely in the land the Lord promised your ancestors, Abraham, Isaac, and Jacob."

31 AFTER MOSES HAD said all these things to the people of Israel, ² he told them, "I am now 120 years old! I am no longer able to lead you,ᵃ for the Lord has told me that I shall not cross the Jordan River. ³ But the Lord himself will lead you, and will destroy the nations living there, and you shall overcome them. Joshua is your new commander, as the Lord has instructed. ⁴ The Lord will destroy the nations living in the land, just as he destroyed Sihon and Og, the kings of the Amorites. ⁵ The Lord will deliver over to you the people living there, and you shall destroy them as I have commanded you. ⁶ Be strong! Be courageous! Do not be afraid of them! For the Lord your God will be with you. He will neither fail you nor forsake you."

⁷ Then Moses called for Joshua and said to him, as all Israel watched, "Be strong! Be courageous! For you shall lead these people into the land promised by the Lord to their ancestors; see to it that they conquer it. ⁸ Don't be afraid, for the Lord will go before you and will be with you; he will not fail nor forsake you."

⁹ Then Moses wrote out the laws he had already delivered to the people and gave them to the priests, the sons of Levi, who carried the Ark containing the Ten Commandments of the Lord. Moses also gave copies of the laws to the elders of Israel. ¹⁰,¹¹ The Lord commanded that these laws be read to all the people at the end of every seventh year—the Year of Release—at the Festival of Tabernacles, when all Israel would assemble before the Lord at the sanctuary. ¹² "Call them all together," the Lord instructed, "—men, women, children, and

foreigners living among you—to hear the laws of God and to learn his will, so that you will reverence the Lord your God and obey his laws. ¹³ Do this so that your little children who have not known these laws will hear them and learn how to revere the Lord your God as long as you live in the Promised Land."

¹⁴ Then the Lord said to Moses, "The time has come when you must die. Summon Joshua and come into the Tabernacle where I can give him his instructions." So Moses and Joshua came and stood before the Lord.

¹⁵ He appeared to them in a great cloud at the Tabernacle entrance, ¹⁶ and said to Moses, "You shall die and join your ancestors. After you are gone, these people will begin worshiping foreign gods in the Promised Land. They will forget about me and break the contract I have made with them. ¹⁷ Then my anger will flame out against them and I will abandon them, hiding my face from them, and they shall be destroyed. Terrible trouble will come upon them, so that they will say, 'God is no longer among us!' ¹⁸ I will turn away from them because of their sins in worshiping other gods.

¹⁹ "Now write down the words of this song, and teach it to the people of Israel as my warning to them. ²⁰ When I have brought them into the land I promised their ancestors—a land 'flowing with milk and honey'—and when they have become fat and prosperous, and worship other gods and despise me and break my contract, ²¹ and great disasters come upon them, then this song will remind them of the reason for their woes. (For this song will live from generation to generation.) I know now, even before they enter the land, what these people are like."

²² So, on that very day, Moses wrote down the words of the song and taught it to the Israelites. ²³ Then he charged Joshua (son of Nun) to be strong and courageous, and said to him, "You must bring the people of Israel into the land the Lord promised them; for the Lord says, 'I will be with you.'"

²⁴ When Moses had finished writing down all the laws that are recorded in this

a Literally, "I am no longer able to go out and come in."

book, [25] he instructed the Levites who carried the Ark containing the Ten Commandments [26] to put this book of the law beside the Ark, as a solemn warning to the people of Israel.

[27] "For I know how rebellious and stubborn you are," Moses told them. "If even today, while I am still here with you, you are defiant rebels against the Lord, how much more rebellious will you be after my death! [28] Now summon all the elders and officers of your tribes so that I can speak to them, and call heaven and earth to witness against them. [29] I know that after my death you will utterly defile yourselves and turn away from God and his commands; and in the days to come evil will crush you for you will do what the Lord says is evil, making him very angry."

[30] So Moses recited this entire song to the whole assembly of Israel:

32 "LISTEN, O HEAVENS and earth!
Listen to what I say!
[2] My words shall fall upon you
Like the gentle rain and dew,
Like rain upon the tender grass,
Like showers on the hillside.
[3] I will proclaim the greatness of the Lord.
How glorious he is!
[4] He is the Rock. His work is perfect.
Everything he does is just and fair.
He is faithful, without sin.
[5] But Israel has become corrupt,
Smeared with sin. They are no longer his;
They are a stubborn, twisted generation.
[6] Is this the way you treat Jehovah?
O foolish people,
Is not God your Father?
Has he not created you?
Has he not established you and made you strong?
[7] Remember the days of long ago!
(Ask your father and the aged men;
They will tell you all about it.)
[8] When God divided up the world among the nations,
He gave each of them a supervising angel!
[9] But he appointed none for Israel;
For Israel was God's own personal possession!
[10] God protected them in the howling wilderness
As though they were the apple of his eye.
[11] He spreads his wings over them,
Even as an eagle overspreads her young.
She carries them upon her wings—
As does the Lord his people!
[12] When the Lord alone was leading them,
And they lived without foreign gods,
[13] God gave them fertile hilltops,
Rolling, fertile fields,
Honey from the rock,
And olive oil from stony ground![a]
[14] He gave them milk and meat—
Choice Bashan rams, and goats—
And the finest of the wheat;
They drank the sparkling wine.
[15] But Israel[b] was soon overfed;
Yes, fat and bloated;
Then, in plenty, they forsook their God.
They shrugged away the Rock of their salvation.
[16] Israel began to follow foreign gods,
And Jehovah was very angry;
He was jealous of his people.
[17] They sacrificed to heathen gods,
To new gods never before worshiped.
[18] They spurned the Rock who had made them,
Forgetting it was God who had given them birth.
[19] God saw what they were doing,
And detested them!
His sons and daughters were insulting him.
[20] He said, 'I will abandon them;
See what happens to them then!
For they are a stubborn, faithless generation.
[21] They have made me very jealous of their idols,
Which are not gods at all.
Now I, in turn, will make them

---

a Or, "oil from flinty rocks."　　　b Literally, "Jeshurun."

jealous
By giving my affections
To the foolish Gentile nations of the
world.
²² For my anger has kindled a fire
That burns to the depths of the un-
derworld,
Consuming the earth and all of its
crops,
And setting its mountains on fire.
²³ I will heap evils upon them
And shoot them down with my ar-
rows.
²⁴ I will waste them with hunger,
Burning fever, and fatal disease.
I will devour them! I will set wild
beasts upon them,
To rip them apart with their teeth;
And deadly serpents
Crawling in the dust.
²⁵ Outside, the enemies' sword—
Inside, the plague[c]—
Shall terrorize young men and girls
alike;
The baby nursing at the breast,
And aged men.
²⁶ I had decided to scatter them to
distant lands,
So that even the memory of them
Would disappear.
²⁷ But then I thought,
'My enemies will boast,
"Israel is destroyed by our own
might;
It was not the Lord
Who did it!"'
²⁸ Israel is a stupid nation;
Foolish, without understanding.
²⁹ Oh, that they were wise!
Oh, that they could understand!
Oh, that they would know what they
are getting into!
³⁰ How could one single enemy chase
a thousand of them,
And two put ten thousand to flight,
Unless their Rock had abandoned
them,
Unless the Lord had destroyed them?
³¹ But the rock of other nations
Is not like our Rock;
Prayers to their gods are valueless.

³² They act like men of Sodom and
Gomorrah:
Their deeds[d] are bitter with poison;
³³ They drink the wine of serpent
venom.
³⁴ But Israel[c] is my special people,
Sealed as jewels within my treasury.
³⁵ Vengeance is mine,
And I decree the punishment of all
her enemies:
Their doom is sealed.
³⁶ The Lord will see his people
righted,
And will have compassion on them
when they slip.
He will watch their power ebb away,
Both slave and free.
³⁷ Then God will ask,
'Where are their gods—
The rocks they claimed to be their
refuge?
³⁸ Where are these gods now,
To whom they sacrificed their fat and
wine?
Let those gods arise,
And help them!
³⁹ Don't you see that I alone am God?
I kill and make live.
I wound and heal—
No one delivers from my power.
⁴⁰,⁴¹ I raise my hand to heaven
And vow by my existence,
That I will whet the lightning of my
sword!
And hurl my punishments upon my
enemies!
My arrows shall be drunk with blood!
My sword devours the flesh and
blood
Of all the slain and captives.
The heads of the enemy
Are gory with blood.'
Praise his people,
O Gentile nations,
For he will avenge his people,
Taking vengeance on his enemies,
Purifying his land
And his people."
⁴⁴,⁴⁵ When Moses and Joshua had recited
all the words of this song to the people,
⁴⁶ Moses made these comments:

---

c Implied.   d Literally, "grapes."

"Meditate upon all the laws I have given you today, and pass them on to your children. ⁴⁷ These laws are not mere words—they are your life! Through obeying them you will live long, plentiful lives in the land you are going to possess across the Jordan River."

⁴⁸ That same day, the Lord said to Moses, ⁴⁹ "Go to Mount Nebo in the Abarim mountains, in the land of Moab across from Jericho. Climb to its heights, and look out across the land of Canaan, the land I am giving to the people of Israel. ⁵⁰ After you see the land you must die and join your ancestors, just as Aaron your brother died in Mount Hor and joined them. ⁵¹ For you dishonored me among the people of Israel at the springs of Meribath-kadesh, in the wilderness of Zin. ⁵² You will see spread out before you the land I am giving the people of Israel, but you will not enter it."

33 THIS IS THE blessing that Moses, the man of God, gave to the people of Israel before his death:

² "The Lord came to us at Mount Sinai,
And dawned upon us from Mount Seir;
He shone from Mount Paran,
Surrounded by ten thousands of holy angels,ᵃ
And with flaming fire at his right hand.
³ How he loves his people—
His holy ones are in his hands.
They followed in your steps, O Lord.
They have received their directions from you.
⁴ The laws I have given
Are your precious possession.
⁵ The Lord became king in Jerusalem,
Elected by a convocation of the leaders of the tribes!
⁶ Let Reuben live forever
And may his tribe increase!"

⁷ And Moses said of Judah:
"O Lord, hear the cry of Judah
And unite him with Israel;
Fight for him against his enemies."

⁸ Then Moses said concerning the tribe of Levi:
"Give to godly Levi
Your Urim and your Thummim.
You tested Levi at Massah and at Meribah;
⁹ He obeyed your instructions
[and destroyed many sinnersᵇ],
Even his own children, brothers, fathers, and mothers.
¹⁰ The Levites shall teach God's laws to Israel
And shall work before you at the incense altar
And the altar of burnt offering.
¹¹ O Lord, prosper the Levites
And accept the work they do for you.
Crush those who are their enemies;
Don't let them rise again."

¹² Concerning the tribe of Benjamin, Moses said:
"He is beloved of God
And lives in safety beside him.
God surrounds him with his loving care,
And preserves him from every harm."

¹³ Concerning the tribe of Joseph, he said:
"May his land be blessed by God
With the choicest gifts of heaven
And of the earth that lies below.
¹⁴ May he be blessed
With the best of what the sun makes grow;
Growing richly month by month,
¹⁵ With the finest of mountain crops
And of the everlasting hills.
¹⁶ May he be blessed with the best gifts
Of the earth and its fullness,
And with the favor of God who appeared
In the burning bush.
Let all these blessings come upon Joseph,
The prince among his brothers.
¹⁷ He is a young bull in strength and splendor,
With the strong horns of a wild ox
To push against the nations every-

---

a Literally, "holy ones."　　　b Implied.

where;
This is my blessing on the multitudes
of Ephraim
And the thousands of Manasseh."

¹⁸ Of the tribe of Zebulun, Moses said:
"Rejoice, O Zebulun, you outdoors-
men,
And Issachar, you lovers of your
tents;
¹⁹ They shall summon the people
To celebrate their sacrifices with
them.
Lo, they taste the riches of the sea
And the treasures of the sand."

²⁰ Concerning the tribe of Gad, Moses
said:
"A blessing upon those who help
Gad.
He crouches like a lion,
With savage arm and face and head.
²¹ He chose the best of the land for
himself
Because it is reserved for a leader.
He led the people
Because he carried out God's penal-
ties for Israel."

²² Of the tribe of Dan, Moses said:
"Dan is like a lion's cub
Leaping out from Bashan."

²³ Of the tribe of Naphtali, Moses said:
"O Naphtali, you are satisfied
With all the blessings of the Lord;
The Mediterranean coast and the
Negeb
Are your home."

²⁴ Of the tribe of Asher:
"Asher is a favorite son,
Esteemed above his brothers;
He bathes his feet in soothing olive
oil.
²⁵ May you be protected with strong
bolts
Of iron and bronze,
And may your strength match the
length of your days!
²⁶ There is none like the God of
Jerusalem—
He descends from the heavens
In majestic splendor to help you.
²⁷ The eternal God is your Refuge,
And underneath are the everlasting
arms.
He thrusts out your enemies before

you;
It is he who cries, 'Destroy them!'
²⁸ So Israel dwells safely,
Prospering in a land of corn and
wine,
While the gentle rains descend from
heaven.
²⁹ What blessings are yours, O Israel!
Who else has been saved by the Lord?
He is your shield and your helper!
He is your excellent sword!
Your enemies shall bow low before
you,
And you shall trample on their
backs!"

34 THEN MOSES CLIMBED from the plains of Moab to Pisgah Peak in Mount Nebo, across from Jericho. And the Lord pointed out to him the Promised Land, as they gazed out across Gilead as far as Dan: ² "There is Naphtali; and there is Ephraim and Manasseh; and across there, Judah, extending to the Mediterranean Sea; ³ there is the Negeb; and the Jordan Valley; and Jericho, the city of palm trees; and Zoar," the Lord told him.

⁴ "It is the Promised Land," the Lord told Moses. "I promised Abraham, Isaac, and Jacob that I would give it to their descendants. Now you have seen it, but you will not enter it."

⁵ So Moses, the disciple of the Lord, died in the land of Moab as the Lord had said. ⁶ The Lord buried him in a valley near Beth-Peor in Moab, but no one knows the exact place.

⁷ Moses was 120 years old when he died, yet his eyesight was perfect and he was as strong as a young man. ⁸ The people of Israel mourned for him for thirty days on the plains of Moab.

⁹ Joshua (son of Nun) was full of the spirit of wisdom, for Moses had laid his hands upon him; so the people of Israel obeyed him, and followed the commandments that the Lord had given to Moses.

¹⁰ There has never been another prophet like Moses, for the Lord talked to him face to face. ¹¹,¹² And at God's command he performed amazing miracles which have never been equaled.

He did great and terrifying wonders before Pharaoh and his entire court in Egypt, and before the people of Israel in the wilderness.

In 1970 Tom Dempsey, born without a right hand and only half a foot, kicked the NFL's longest field goal–63 yards–with a specially-made shoe.

Ron Santo starred for the Cubs and White Sox despite diabetes.

Babe Didrickson Zaharias bounded back from two near-fatal cancer operations to win golf's National Open.

Celebrating Victory

Sports heroes are among our favorite legends. The athletes pictured overcame tremendous handicaps to notch their names in sports history. Mildred "Babe" Didrickson, for example, has been called the greatest woman athlete of all time. The first time she tossed a javelin at a meet, she broke a world's record! Her career as a championship golfer seemed ruined when she was struck down with cancer. Eighteen months later Babe captured the woman's golf title.

All these champions shared common traits. They set a goal and, despite failures along the way, each persevered and reached it. They were absolutely committed.

Joshua tells the story of an army which had a clear goal from God. God wanted idol-worshipping nations driven out of the land he had promised the Israelites. Joshua's disciplined troops took on the goal. Following God's instructions, they tasted sweet victory. But whenever they took matters into their own hands, relying on their own strength, they failed miserably.

JOSHUA

1 AFTER THE DEATH of Moses, the Lord's disciple, God spoke to Moses' assistant, whose name was Joshua (the son of Nun), and said to him,

2 "Now that my disciple is dead, [you are the new leader of Israel[a]]. Lead my people across the Jordan River into the Promised Land. 3 I say to you what I said to Moses: 'Wherever you go will be part of the land of Israel— 4 all the way from Negeb desert in the south to the Lebanon mountains in the north, and from the Mediterranean Sea in the west to the Euphrates River in the east, including all the land of the Hittites.' 5 No one will be able to oppose you as long as you live, for I will be with you just as I was with Moses; I will not abandon you or fail to help you.

6 "Be strong and brave, for you will be a successful leader of my people; and they shall conquer all the land I promised to their ancestors. 7 You need only to be strong and courageous and to obey to the letter every law Moses gave you, for if you are careful to obey every one of them you will be successful in everything you do. 8 Constantly remind the people about these laws, and you yourself must think about them every day and every night so that you will be sure to obey all of them. For only then will you succeed. 9 Yes, be bold and strong! Banish fear and doubt! For remember, the Lord your God is with you wherever you go."

10,11 Then Joshua issued instructions to the leaders of Israel to tell the people to get ready to cross the Jordan River. "In three days we will go across and conquer and live in the land which God has given us!" he told them.

12,13 Then he summoned the leaders of the tribes of Reuben, Gad, and the half-tribe of Manasseh and reminded them of their agreement with Moses: "The Lord your God has given you a homeland here on the east side of the Jordan River," Moses had told them, 14 "so your wives and children and cattle may remain here, but your troops, fully armed, must lead the other tribes across the Jordan River to help them conquer their territory on the other side; 15 stay with them until they complete the conquest. Only then may you settle down here on the east side of the Jordan."

16 To this they fully agreed, and pledged themselves to obey Joshua as their commander-in-chief.

17,18 "We will obey you just as we obeyed Moses," they assured him, "and may the Lord your God be with you as he was with Moses. If anyone, no matter who, rebels against your commands, he shall die. So lead on with courage and strength!"

2 THEN JOSHUA SENT two spies from the Israeli camp at Acacia to cross the river and check out the situation on the other side, especially at Jericho. They arrived at an inn operated by a woman named Rahab, who was a prostitute. They were planning to spend the night there, 2 but someone informed the king of Jericho that two Israelis who were suspected of being spies had arrived in the city that evening. 3 He dispatched a police squadron to Rahab's home, demanding that she surrender them.

"They are spies," he explained. "They have been sent by the Israeli leaders to discover the best way to attack us."

4 But she had hidden them, so she told the officer in charge, "The men were here earlier, but I didn't know they were spies. 5 They left the city at dusk as the city gates were about to close, and I don't know where they went. If you hurry you can probably catch up with them!"

---

a Implied.

[6] But actually she had taken them up to the roof and hidden them beneath piles of flax that were drying there. [7] So the constable and his men went all the way to the Jordan River looking for them; meanwhile, the city gates were kept shut. [8] Rahab went up to talk to the men before they retired for the night.

[9] "I know perfectly well that your God is going to give my country to you," she told them. "We are all afraid of you; everyone is terrified if the word *Israel* is even mentioned. [10] For we have heard how the Lord made a path through the Red Sea for you when you left Egypt! And we know what you did to Sihon and Og, the two Amorite kings east of the Jordan, and how you ruined their land and completely destroyed their people. [11] No wonder we are afraid of you! No one has any fight left in him after hearing things like that, for your God is the supreme God of heaven, not just an ordinary god. [12,13] Now I beg for this one thing: Swear to me by the sacred name of your God that when Jericho is conquered you will let me live, along with my father and mother, my brothers and sisters, and all their families. This is only fair after the way I have helped you."

[14] The men agreed. "If you won't betray us, we'll see to it that you and your family aren't harmed," they promised. [15] "We'll defend you with our lives." Then, since her house was on top of the city wall, she let them down by a rope from a window.

[16] "Escape to the mountains," she told them. "Hide there for three days until the men who are searching for you have returned; then go on your way."

[17,18] But before they left, the men had said to her, "We cannot be responsible for what happens to you unless this rope is hanging from this window and unless all your relatives—your father, mother, brothers, and anyone else—are here inside the house. [19] If they go out into the street we assume no responsibility whatsoever; but we swear that no one inside this house will be killed or injured. [20] However, if you betray us, then this oath will no longer bind us in any way."

[21] "I accept your terms," she replied. And she left the scarlet rope hanging from the window. [22] The spies went up into the mountains and stayed there three days, until the men who were chasing them had returned to the city after searching everywhere along the road without success. [23] Then the two spies came down from the mountain and crossed the river and reported to Joshua all that had happened to them.

[24] "The Lord will certainly give us the entire land," they said, "for all the people over there are scared to death of us."

3 EARLY THE NEXT morning Joshua and all the people of Israel left Acacia, and arrived that evening at the banks of the Jordan River, where they camped for a few days before crossing.

[2,3,4] On the third day, officers went through the camp giving these instructions: "When you see the priests carrying the Ark of God,[a] follow them. You have never before been where we are going now, so they will guide you. However, stay about a half mile behind, with a clear space between you and the Ark; be sure that you don't get any closer."

[5] Then Joshua told the people to perform the purification ceremony for themselves. "For tomorrow," he said, "the Lord will do a great miracle."

[6] In the morning Joshua ordered the priests, "Take up the Ark and lead us across the river!" And so they started out.

[7] "Today," the Lord told Joshua, "I will give you great honor, so that all Israel will know that I am with you just as I was with Moses. [8] Instruct the priests who are carrying the Ark to stop at the edge of the river."

[9] Then Joshua summoned all the people and told them, "Come and listen to what the Lord your God has said. [10] Today you are going to know for sure that the living God is among you and that he will, without fail, drive out the Canaanites, Hittites, Hivites, Perizzites, Girgashites, Amorites, and Jebusites—all the people who now live in the land you will soon occupy. [11] Think of it! The Ark of God, who is Lord of the

---

a Literally, "the Ark of the covenant of the Lord."

whole earth, will lead you across the river! [12] "Now select twelve men, one from each tribe, for a special task.[b] [13,14] When the priests who are carrying the Ark touch the water with their feet, the river will stop flowing as though held back by a dam, and will pile up as though against an invisible wall!" Now it was the harvest season and the Jordan was overflowing all its banks; but as the people set out to cross the river and as the feet of the priests who were carrying the Ark touched the water at the river's edge, [15,16] suddenly, far up the river at the city of Adam, near Zarethan, the water began piling up as though against a dam! And the water below that point flowed on to the Salt Sea until the riverbed was empty. Then all the people crossed at a spot where the river was close to the city of Jericho, [17] and the priests who were carrying the Ark stood on dry ground in the middle of the Jordan and waited as all the people passed by.

4 WHEN ALL THE people were safely across, the Lord said to Joshua, [2,3] "Tell the twelve men chosen for a special task, one from each tribe, each to take a stone from where the priests are standing in the middle of the Jordan, and to carry them out and pile them up as a monument at the place where you camp tonight."

[4] So Joshua summoned the twelve men, [5] and told them, "Go out into the middle of the Jordan where the Ark is. Each of you is to carry out a stone on your shoulder—twelve stones in all, one for each of the twelve tribes. [6] We will use them to build a monument so that in the future, when your children ask, 'What is this monument for?' [7] you can tell them, 'It is to remind us that the Jordan River stopped flowing when the Ark of God went across!' The monument will be a permanent reminder to the people of Israel of this amazing miracle."

[8] So the men did as Joshua told them. They took twelve stones from the middle of the Jordan river—one for each tribe, just as the Lord had commanded Joshua. They carried them to the place where they were

camped for the night and constructed a monument there. [9] Joshua also built another monument of twelve stones in the middle of the river, at the place where the priests were standing; and it is there to this day. [10] The priests who were carrying the Ark stood in the middle of the river until all these instructions of the Lord, which had been given to Joshua by Moses, had been carried out. Meanwhile, the people had hurried across the riverbed, [11] and when everyone was over, the people watched the priests carry the Ark up out of the river.

[12,13] The troops of Reuben, Gad, and the half-tribe of Manasseh—fully armed as Moses had instructed, and forty thousand strong—led the other tribes of the Lord's army across to the plains of Jericho.

[14] It was a tremendous day for Joshua! The Lord made him great in the eyes of all the people of Israel, and they revered him as much as they had Moses, and respected him deeply all the rest of his life. [15,16] For it was Joshua who, at the Lord's command, issued the orders to the priests carrying the Ark.

"Come up from the riverbed," the Lord now told him to command them.

[17] So Joshua issued the order. [18] And as soon as the priests came out, the water poured down again as usual and overflowed the banks of the river as before! [19] This miracle occurred on the 25th of March.[a] That day the entire nation crossed the Jordan River and camped in Gilgal at the eastern edge of the city of Jericho; [20] and there the twelve stones from the Jordan were piled up as a monument.

[21] Then Joshua explained again the purpose of the stones: "In the future," he said, "when your children ask you why these stones are here and what they mean, [22] you are to tell them that these stones are a reminder of this amazing miracle—that the nation of Israel crossed the Jordan River on dry ground! [23] Tell them how the Lord our God dried up the river right before our eyes, and then kept it dry until we were all across! It is the same thing the Lord did forty years ago[b] at the Red Sea! [24] He did this so that

---

b Their duties are explained in chapter 4, verses 2–7. the Jewish calendar).   b Implied.

4a Literally, "The tenth day of the first month" (of

all the nations of the earth will realize that Jehovah is the mighty God, and so that all of you will worship him forever."

5 WHEN THE NATIONS west of the Jordan River—the Amorites and Canaanites who lived along the Mediterranean coast— heard that the Lord had dried up the Jordan River so the people of Israel could cross, their courage melted away completely and they were paralyzed with fear.

2,3 The Lord then told Joshua to set aside a day to circumcise the entire male population of Israel. (It was the second time in Israel's history that this was done.) The Lord instructed them to manufacture flint knives for this purpose. The place where the circumcision rite took place was named "The Hill of the Foreskins." 4,5 The reason for this second circumcision ceremony was that although when Israel left Egypt all of the men who had been old enough to bear arms had been circumcised, that entire generation had died during the years in the wilderness, and none of the boys born since that time had been circumcised. 6 For the nation of Israel had traveled back and forth across the wilderness for forty years until all the men who had been old enough to bear arms when they left Egypt were dead; they had not obeyed the Lord, and he vowed that he wouldn't let them enter the land he had promised to Israel—a land that "flowed with milk and honey." 7 So now Joshua circumcised their children—the men who had grown up to take their fathers' places.

8,9 And the Lord said to Joshua, "Today I have ended your shame of not being circumcised."[a] So the place where this was done was called Gilgal (meaning, "to end"[b]), and is still called that today. After the ceremony the entire nation rested in camp until the raw flesh of their wounds had been healed.

10 While they were camped at Gilgal on the plains of Jericho, they celebrated the Passover during the evening of the 14th day of the month. 11,12 The next day they began to eat from the gardens and grain fields which they invaded, and they made unleav-

ened bread. The following day no manna fell, and it was never seen again! So from that time on they lived on the crops of Canaan.

13 As Joshua was sizing up the city of Jericho, a man appeared nearby with a drawn sword. Joshua strode over to him and demanded, "Are you friend or foe?"

14 "I am the Commander-in-Chief of the Lord's army," he replied.

Joshua fell to the ground before him and worshiped him and said, "Give me your commands."

15 "Take off your shoes," the Commander told him, "for this is holy ground." And Joshua did.

6 THE GATES OF Jericho were kept tightly shut because the people were afraid of the Israelis; no one was allowed to go in or out.

2 But the Lord said to Joshua, "Jericho and its king and all its mighty warriors are already defeated, for I have given them to you! 3,4 Your entire army is to walk around the city once a day for six days, followed by seven priests walking ahead of the Ark, each carrying a trumpet made from a ram's horn. On the seventh day you are to walk around the city seven times, with the priests blowing their trumpets. 5 Then, when they give one long, loud blast, all the people are to give a mighty shout and the walls of the city will fall down; then move in upon the city from every direction."

6-9 So Joshua summoned the priests and gave them their instructions: the armed men would lead the procession followed by seven priests blowing continually on their trumpets. Behind them would come the priests carrying the Ark, followed by a rearguard.

10 "Let there be complete silence except for the trumpets," Joshua commanded. "Not a single word from any of you until I tell you to shout; then *shout!*"

11 The Ark was carried around the city once that day, after which everyone returned to the camp again and spent the night there. 12,13,14 At dawn the next morning they went around again, and returned again

---

a Literally, "the shame of Egypt."   b Literally, "to roll" (away).

to the camp. They followed this pattern for six days. [15] At dawn of the seventh day they started out again, but this time they went around the city not once, but seven times. [16] The seventh time, as the priests blew a long, loud trumpet blast, Joshua yelled to the people, *"Shout!* The Lord has given us the city!"

[17] (He had told them previously, "Kill everyone except Rahab the prostitute and anyone in her house, for she protected our spies. [18] Don't take any loot, for everything is to be destroyed. If it isn't, disaster will fall upon the entire nation of Israel. [19] But all the silver and gold and the utensils of bronze and iron will be dedicated to the Lord, and must be brought into his treasury.")

[20] So when the people heard the trumpet blast, they shouted as loud as they could. And suddenly the walls of Jericho crumbled and fell before them, and the people of Israel poured into the city from every side and captured it! [21] They destroyed everything in it—men and women, young and old; oxen; sheep; donkeys—everything.

[22] Then Joshua said to the two spies, "Keep your promise. Go and rescue the prostitute and everyone with her."

[23] The young men found her and rescued her, along with her father, mother, brothers, and other relatives who were with her. Arrangements were made for them to live outside the camp of Israel. [24] Then the Israelis burned the city and everything in it except that the silver and gold and the bronze and iron utensils were kept for the Lord's treasury. [25] Thus Joshua saved Rahab the prostitute and her relatives who were with her in the house, and they still live among the Israelites because she hid the spies sent to Jericho by Joshua.

[26] Then Joshua declared a terrible curse upon anyone who might rebuild Jericho, warning that when the foundation was laid, the builder's oldest son would die, and when the gates were set up, his youngest son would die.[a]

[27] So the Lord was with Joshua, and his name became famous everywhere.

7 BUT THERE WAS sin among the Israelis. God's command to destroy everything except that which was reserved for the Lord's treasury was disobeyed. For Achan (the son of Carmi, grandson of Zabdi, and great-grandson of Zerah, of the tribe of Judah) took some loot for himself, and the Lord was very angry with the entire nation of Israel because of this.

[2] Soon after Jericho's defeat, Joshua sent some of his men to spy on the city of Ai, east of Bethel.

[3] Upon their return they told Joshua, "It's a small city and it won't take more than two or three thousand of us to destroy it; there's no point in all of us going there."

[4] So approximately three thousand soldiers were sent—and they were soundly defeated. [5] About thirty-six of the Israelis were killed during the attack, and many others died while being chased by the men of Ai as far as the quarries. The Israeli army was paralyzed with fear at this turn of events. [6] Joshua and the elders of Israel tore their clothing and lay prostrate before the Ark of the Lord until evening, with dust on their heads.

[7] Joshua cried out to the Lord, "O Jehovah, why have you brought us over the Jordan River if you are going to let the Amorites kill us? Why weren't we content with what we had? Why didn't we stay on the other side? [8] O Lord, what am I to do now that Israel has fled from her enemies! [9] For when the Canaanites and the other nearby nations hear about it, they will surround us and attack us and wipe us out. And then what will happen to the honor of your great name?"

[10,11] But the Lord said to Joshua, "Get up off your face! Israel has sinned and disobeyed my commandment and has taken loot when I said it was not to be taken; and they have not only taken it, they have lied about it and have hidden it among their belongings. [12] That is why the people of Israel are being defeated. That is why your men are running from their enemies—for they are cursed.[a] I will not stay with you any longer unless you completely rid your-

---

a See 1 Kings 16:34 for the fulfillment of this curse.
be totally destroyed" or else become totally God's.

7a Literally, they have become "something which must

194

selves of this sin.

[13] "Get up! Tell the people, 'Each of you must undergo purification rites in preparation for tomorrow, for the Lord your God of Israel says that someone has stolen from him, and you cannot defeat your enemies until you deal with this sin. [14] In the morning you must come by tribes, and the Lord will point out the tribe to which the guilty man belongs. And that tribe must come by its clans and the Lord will point out the guilty clan; and the clan must come by its families, and then each member of the guilty family must come one by one. [15] And the one who has stolen that which belongs to the Lord shall be burned with fire, along with everything he has, for he has violated the covenant of the Lord and has brought calamity upon all of Israel.'"

[16] So, early the next morning, Joshua brought the tribes of Israel before the Lord, and the tribe of Judah was indicated. [17] Then he brought the clans of Judah, and the clan of Zerah was singled out. Then the families of that clan were brought before the Lord and the family of Zabdi was indicated. [18] Zabdi's family was brought man by man, and his grandson Achan was found to be the guilty one.

[19] Joshua said to Achan, "My son, give glory to the God of Israel and make your confession. Tell me what you have done."

[20] Achan replied, "I have sinned against the Lord, the God of Israel. [21] For I saw a beautiful robe imported from Babylon, and some silver worth $200, and a bar of gold worth $500. I wanted them so much that I took them, and they are hidden in the ground beneath my tent, with the silver buried deeper than the rest."

[22] So Joshua sent some men to search for the loot. They ran to the tent and found the stolen goods hidden there just as Achan had said, with the silver buried beneath the rest. [23] They brought it all to Joshua and laid it on the ground in front of him. [24] Then Joshua and all the Israelites took Achan, the silver, the robe, the wedge of gold, his sons, his daughters, his oxen, donkeys, sheep, his tent, and everything he had, and brought them to the valley of Achor.

[25] Then Joshua said to Achan, "Why have you brought calamity upon us? The Lord will now bring calamity upon you."

And the men of Israel stoned them to death and burned their bodies, [26] and piled a great heap of stones upon them. The stones are still there to this day, and even today that place is called "The Valley of Calamity." And so the fierce anger of the Lord was ended.

8 THEN THE LORD said to Joshua, "Don't be afraid or discouraged; take the entire army and go to Ai, for it is now yours to conquer. I have given the king of Ai and all of his people to you. [2] You shall do to them as you did to Jericho and her king; but this time you may keep the loot and the cattle for yourselves. Set an ambush behind the city."

[3,4] Before the main army left for Ai, Joshua sent thirty thousand of his bravest troops to hide in ambush close behind the city, alert for action.

[5] "This is the plan," he explained to them. "When our main army attacks, the men of Ai will come out to fight as they did before, and we will run away. [6] We will let them chase us until they have all left the city; for they will say, 'The Israelis are running away again just as they did before!' [7] Then you will jump up from your ambush and enter the city, for the Lord will give it to you. [8] Set the city on fire, as the Lord has commanded. You now have your instructions."

[9] So they left that night and lay in ambush between Bethel and the west side of Ai; but Joshua and the rest of the army remained in the camp at Jericho. [10] Early the next morning Joshua roused his men and started toward Ai, accompanied by the elders of Israel, [11,12,13] and stopped at the edge of a valley north of the city. That night Joshua sent another five thousand men to join the troops in ambush on the west side of the city.[a] He himself spent the night in the valley.

[14] The King of Ai, seeing the Israelis

---

a These were evidently additional to the thirty thousand men already hiding there. Perhaps the additional five thousand were to intercept the forces expected from Bethel (verse 17)

across the valley, went out early the next morning and attacked at the Plain of Arabah. But of course he didn't realize that there was an ambush behind the city. [15] Joshua and the Israeli army fled across the wilderness as though badly beaten, [16] and all the soldiers in the city were called out to chase after them; so the city was left defenseless; [17] there was not a soldier left in Ai or Bethel and the city gates were left wide open.

[18] Then the Lord said to Joshua, "Point your spear toward Ai, for I will give you the city." Joshua did. [19] And when the men in ambush saw his signal, they jumped up and poured into the city and set it on fire. [20,21] When the men of Ai looked behind them, smoke from the city was filling the sky, and they had nowhere to go. When Joshua and the troops who were with him saw the smoke, they knew that their men who had been in ambush were inside the city, so they turned upon their pursuers and began killing them. [22] Then the Israelis who were inside the city came out and began destroying the enemy from the rear. So the men of Ai were caught in a trap and all of them died; not one man survived or escaped, [23] except for the king of Ai, who was captured and brought to Joshua.

[24] When the army of Israel had finished slaughtering all the men outside the city, they went back and finished off everyone left inside. [25] So the entire population of Ai, twelve thousand in all, was wiped out that day. [26] For Joshua kept his spear pointed toward Ai until the last person was dead. [27] Only the cattle and the loot were not destroyed, for the armies of Israel kept these for themselves. (The Lord had told Joshua they could.) [28] So Ai became a desolate mound of refuse, as it still is today.

[29] Joshua hanged the king of Ai on a tree until evening, but as the sun was going down, he took down the body and threw it in front of the city gate. There he piled a great heap of stones over it, which can still be seen.

[30] Then Joshua built an altar to the Lord God of Israel at Mount Ebal, [31] as Moses had commanded[b] in the book of his laws:

"Make me an altar of boulders that have neither been broken nor carved," the Lord had said concerning Mount Ebal. Then the priests offered burnt sacrifices and peace offerings to the Lord on the altar. [32] And as the people of Israel watched, Joshua carved upon the stones of the altar each of the Ten Commandments.[c]

[33] Then all the people of Israel—including the elders, officers, judges, and the foreigners living among them—divided into two groups, half of them standing at the foot of Mount Gerizim and half at the foot of Mount Ebal. Between them stood the priests with the Ark, ready to pronounce their blessing. (This was all done in accordance with the instructions given long before by Moses.) [34] Joshua then read to them all of the statements of blessing and curses that Moses had written in the book of God's laws. [35] Every commandment Moses had ever given was read before the entire assembly, including the women and children and the foreigners who lived among the Israelis.

[9] WHEN THE KINGS of the surrounding area heard what had happened to Jericho, they quickly combined their armies to fight for their lives against Joshua and the Israelis. These were the kings of the nations west of the Jordan River, along the shores of the Mediterranean as far north as the Lebanon mountains—the Hittites, Amorites, Canaanites, Perizzites, Hivites, and Jebusites.

[3,4,5] But when the people of Gibeon heard what had happened to Jericho and Ai, they resorted to trickery to save themselves. They sent ambassadors to Joshua wearing worn-out clothing, as though from a long journey, with patched shoes, weatherworn saddlebags on their donkeys, old, patched wineskins and dry, moldy bread. [6] When they arrived at the camp of Israel at Gilgal, they told Joshua and the men of Israel, "We have come from a distant land to ask for a peace treaty with you."

[7] The Israelis replied to these Hivites, "How do we know you don't live nearby? For if you do, we cannot make a treaty with you."

---

b See Deuteronomy 27:2–8.   c Literally, "the law of Moses."

⁸ They replied, "We will be your slaves." "But who are you?" Joshua demanded. "Where do you come from?"

⁹ And they told him, "We are from a very distant country; we have heard of the might of the Lord your God and of all that he did in Egypt, ¹⁰ and what you did to the two kings of the Amorites—Sihon, king of Heshbon, and Og, king of Bashan. ¹¹ So our elders and our people instructed us, 'Prepare for a long journey; go to the people of Israel and declare our nation to be their servants, and ask for peace.' ¹² This bread was hot from the ovens when we left, but now as you see, it is dry and moldy; ¹³ these wineskins were new, but now they are old and cracked; our clothing and shoes have become worn out from our long, hard trip."

¹⁴,¹⁵ Joshua and the other leaders finally believed them. They did not bother to ask the Lord, but went ahead and signed a peace treaty. And the leaders of Israel ratified the agreement with a binding oath.

¹⁶ Three days later the facts came out—these men were close neighbors. ¹⁷ The Israeli army set out at once to investigate, and reached their cities in three days. (The names of the cities were Gibeon, Chephirah, Be-eroth, and Kiriath-jearim.) ¹⁸ But the cities were not harmed because of the vow which the leaders of Israel had made before the Lord God. The people of Israel were angry with their leaders because of the peace treaty.

¹⁹ But the leaders replied, "We have sworn before the Lord God of Israel that we will not touch them, and we won't. ²⁰ We must let them live, for if we break our oath the wrath of Jehovah will be upon us."

²¹ So they became servants of the Israelis, chopping their wood and carrying their water.

²² Joshua summoned their leaders and demanded, "Why have you lied to us by saying that you lived in a distant land, when you were actually living right here among us? ²³ Now a curse shall be upon you! From this moment you must always furnish us with servants to chop wood and carry water for the service of our God."

²⁴ They replied, "We did it because we were told that Jehovah instructed his disciple Moses to conquer this entire land and destroy all the people living in it. So we feared for our lives because of you; that is why we have done it. ²⁵ But now we are in your hands; you may do with us as you wish."

²⁶ So Joshua would not allow the people of Israel to kill them, ²⁷ but they became wood-choppers and water-carriers for the people of Israel and for the altar of the Lord—wherever it would be built (for the Lord hadn't yet told them where to build it). This arrangement is still in force at the time of this writing.

10 WHEN ADONI-ZEDEK, THE king of Jerusalem, heard how Joshua had captured and destroyed Ai and had killed its king, the same as he had done at Jericho, and how the people of Gibeon had made peace with Israel and were now their allies, ² he was very frightened. For Gibeon was a great city—as great as the royal cities and much larger than Ai—and its men were known as hard fighters. ³ So King Adoni-zedek of Jerusalem sent messengers to several other kings:

> King Hoham of Hebron,
> King Piram of Jarmuth,
> King Japhia of Lachish,
> King Debir of Eglon.

⁴ "Come and help me destroy Gibeon," he urged them, "for they have made peace with Joshua and the people of Israel."

⁵ So these five Amorite kings combined their armies for a united attack on Gibeon. ⁶ The men of Gibeon hurriedly sent messengers to Joshua at Gilgal.

"Come and help your servants!" they demanded. "Come quickly and save us! For all the kings of the Amorites who live in the hills are here with their armies."

⁷ So Joshua and the Israeli army left Gilgal and went to rescue Gibeon.

⁸ "Don't be afraid of them," the Lord said to Joshua, "for they are already defeated! I have given them to you to destroy. Not a single one of them will be able to stand up to you."

⁹ Joshua traveled all night from Gilgal and took the enemy armies by surprise. ¹⁰ Then the Lord threw them into a panic so that the army of Israel slaughtered great numbers of them at Gibeon and chased the

others all the way to Beth-horon and Aze-kah and Makkedah, killing them along the way. [11] And as the enemy was racing down the hill to Beth-horon, the Lord destroyed them with a great hailstorm that continued all the way to Azekah; in fact, more men died from the hail than by the swords of the Israelis.

[12] As the men of Israel were pursuing and harassing the foe, Joshua prayed aloud, "Let the sun stand still over Gibeon, and let the moon stand in its place over the valley of Aijalon!"

[13] And the sun and the moon didn't move until the Israeli army had finished the destruction of its enemies! This is described in greater detail in *The Book of Jashar.* So the sun stopped in the heavens and stayed there for almost twenty-four hours! [14] There had never been such a day before, and there has never been another since, when the Lord stopped the sun and moon—all because of the prayer of one man. But the Lord was fighting for Israel. [15] (Afterwards Joshua and the Israeli army returned to Gilgal.)

[16] During the battle the five kings escaped and hid in a cave at Makkedah. [17] When the news was brought to Joshua that they had been found, [18] he issued a command that a great stone be rolled against the mouth of the cave and that guards be placed there to keep the kings inside.

[19] Then Joshua commanded the rest of the army, "Go on chasing the enemy and cut them down from the rear. Don't let them get back to their cities, for the Lord will help you to completely destroy them."

[20] So Joshua and the Israeli army continued the slaughter and wiped out the five armies except for a tiny remnant that managed to reach their fortified cities. [21] Then the Israelis returned to their camp at Makkedah without having lost a single man! And after that no one dared to attack Israel.

[22,23] Joshua now instructed his men to remove the stone from the mouth of the cave and to bring out the five kings—of Jerusalem, Hebron, Jarmuth, Lachish, and Eglon. [24] Joshua told the captains of his army to put their feet on the kings' necks.

[25] "Don't ever be afraid or discouraged," Joshua said to his men. "Be strong and courageous, for the Lord is going to do this to all of your enemies."

[26] With that, Joshua plunged his sword into each of the five kings, killing them. He then hanged them on five trees until evening.

[27] As the sun was going down, Joshua instructed that their bodies be taken down and thrown into the cave where they had been hiding; and a great pile of stones was placed at the mouth of the cave. (The pile is still there today.)

[28] On that same day Joshua destroyed the city of Makkedah and killed its king and everyone in it. Not one person in the entire city was left alive. [29] Then the Israelis went to Libnah. [30] There, too, the Lord gave them the city and its king. Every last person was slaughtered, just as at Jericho.

[31] From Libnah they went to Lachish and attacked it. [32] And the Lord gave it to them on the second day; here, too, the entire population was slaughtered, just as at Libnah.

[33] During the attack on Lachish, King Horam of Gezer arrived with his army to try to help defend the city, but Joshua's men killed him and destroyed his entire army.

[34,35] The Israeli army then captured Eglon on the first day and, as at Lachish, they killed everyone in the city. [36] After leaving Eglon they went to Hebron, [37] and captured it and all of its surrounding villages, slaughtering the entire population. Not one person was left alive. [38] Then they turned back to Debir, [39] which they quickly captured with all of its outlying villages. And they killed everyone just as they had at Libnah.

[40] So Joshua and his army conquered the whole country—the nations and kings of the hill country, the Negeb, the lowlands, and the mountain slopes. They destroyed everyone in the land, just as the Lord God of Israel had commanded, [41] slaughtering them from Kadesh-barnea to Gaza, and from Goshen to Gibeon. [42] This was all accomplished in one campaign, for the Lord God of Israel was fighting for his people. [43] Then Joshua and his army returned to their camp at Gilgal.

11 WHEN KING JABIN of Hazor heard what had happened, he sent urgent messages to the following kings:

King Jobab of Madon;
The king of Shimron;
The king of Achshaph;
All the kings of the northern hill country;
The kings in the Arabah, south of Chinneroth;
Those in the lowland;
The kings in the mountain areas of Dor, on the west;
The kings of Canaan, both east and west;
The kings of the Amorites;
The kings of the Hittites;
The kings of the Perizzites;
The kings in the Jebusite hill country;
The Hivite kings in the cities on the slopes of Mount Hermon, in the land of Mizpah.

⁴ All these kings responded by mobilizing their armies, and uniting to crush Israel. Their combined troops, along with a vast array of horses and chariots, covered the landscape around the Springs of Merom as far as one could see; ⁵ for they established their camp at the Springs of Merom.

⁶ But the Lord said to Joshua, "Don't be afraid of them, for by this time tomorrow they will all be dead! Hamstring their horses and burn their chariots." ⁷ Joshua and his troops arrived suddenly at the Springs of Merom and attacked. ⁸ And the Lord gave all that vast army to the Israelis, who chased them as far as Great Sidon and a place called the Salt Pits, and eastward into the valley of Mizpah; so not one enemy troop survived the battle. ⁹ Then Joshua and his men did as the Lord had instructed, for they hamstrung the horses and burned all the chariots.

¹⁰ On the way back, Joshua captured Hazor and killed its king. (Hazor had at one time been the capital of the federation of all those kingdoms.) ¹¹ Every person there was killed and the city was burned.

¹² Then he attacked and destroyed all the other cities of those kings. All the people were slaughtered, just as Moses had commanded long before. ¹³ (However, Joshua did not burn any of the cities built on mounds except for Hazor.) ¹⁴ All the loot and cattle of the ravaged cities were taken by the Israelis for themselves, but they killed all the people. ¹⁵ For so the Lord had commanded his disciple Moses; and Moses had passed the commandment on to Joshua, who did as he had been told: he carefully obeyed all of the Lord's instructions to Moses.

¹⁶ So Joshua conquered the entire land— the hill country, the Negeb, the land of Goshen, the lowlands, the Arabah, and the hills and lowlands of Israel. ¹⁷ The Israeli territory now extended all the way from Mount Halak, near Seir, to Baal-gad in the valley of Lebanon, at the foot of Mount Hermon. And Joshua killed all the kings of those territories. ¹⁸ It took seven years[a] of war to accomplish all of this. ¹⁹ None of the cities was given a peace treaty except the Hivites of Gibeon; all of the others were destroyed. ²⁰ For the Lord made the enemy kings want to fight the Israelis instead of asking for peace; so they were mercilessly killed, as the Lord had commanded Moses.

²¹ During this period Joshua routed all of the giants—the descendants of Anak who lived in the hill country in Hebron, Debir, Anab, Judah, and Israel; he killed them all and completely destroyed their cities. ²² None was left in all the land of Israel, though some still remained in Gaza, Gath, and Ashdod.

²³ So Joshua took the entire land just as the Lord had instructed Moses; and he gave it to the people of Israel as their inheritance, dividing the land among the tribes. So the land finally rested from its war.

12 HERE IS THE list of the kings on the east side of the Jordan River whose cities were destroyed by the Israelis: (The area involved stretched all the way from the valley of the Arnon River to Mount Hermon, including the cities of the eastern desert.)

² King Sihon of the Amorites, who lived in Heshbon. His kingdom extended from Aroer, on the edge of the Arnon Valley, and

---

a Implied in other text. Literally, "a long time."

from the middle of the valley of the Arnon River to the Jabbok River, which is the boundary of the Ammonites. This includes half of the present area of Gilead, which lies north of the Jabbok River. ³ Sihon also controlled the Jordan River valley as far north as the western shores of the Lake of Galilee; and as far south as the Salt Sea and the slopes of Mount Pisgah.

⁴ King Og of Bashan, the last of the Rephaim, who lived at Ashtaroth and Edre-i: ⁵ He ruled a territory stretching from Mount Hermon in the north to Salecah on Mount Bashan in the east, and on the west, extending to the boundary of the kingdoms of Geshur and Ma-acah. His kingdom also stretched south to include the northern half of Gilead where the boundary touched the border of the kingdom of Sihon, king of Heshbon. ⁶ Moses and the people of Israel had destroyed these people, and Moses gave the land to the tribes of Reuben and the half-tribe of Manasseh.

⁷ Here is a list of the kings destroyed by Joshua and the armies of Israel on the west side of the Jordan. (This land which lay between Baal-gad in the Valley of Lebanon and Mount Halak, west of Mount Seir, was allotted by Joshua to the other tribes of Israel. ⁸⁻²⁴ The area included the hill country, the lowlands, the Arabah, the mountain slopes, the Judean Desert, and the Negeb. The people who lived there were the Hittites, the Amorites, the Canaanites, the Perizzites, the Hivites, and the Jebusites):

The king of Jericho;
The king of Ai, near Bethel;
The king of Jerusalem;
The king of Hebron;
The king of Jarmuth;
The king of Lachish;
The king of Eglon;
The king of Gezer;
The king of Debir;
The king of Geder;
The king of Hormah;
The king of Arad;
The king of Libnah;
The king of Adullam;
The king of Makkedah;
The king of Bethel;

The king of Tappu-ah;
The king of Hepher;
The king of Aphek;
The king of Lasharon;
The king of Madon;
The king of Hazor;
The king of Shimron-meron;
The king of Achshaph;
The king of Taanach;
The king of Megiddo;
The king of Kedesh;
The king of Jokne-am, in Carmel;
The king of Dor in the city of Naphathdor;
The king of Goiim in Gilgal;
The king of Tirzah.

So in all, thirty-one kings and their cities were destroyed.

13 JOSHUA WAS NOW an old man. "You are growing old," the Lord said to him, "and there are still many nations to be conquered. ²⁻⁷ Here is a list of the areas still to be occupied:

All the land of the Philistines;
The land of the Geshurites;
The territory now belonging to the Canaanites from the brook of Egypt to the southern boundary of Ekron;
Five cities of the Philistines:
Gaza,
Ashdod,
Ashkelon,
Gath,
Ekron;
The land of the Avvim in the south;
In the north,ᵃ all the land of the Canaanites, including Me-arah (which belongs to the Sidonians), stretching northwardᵃ to Aphek at the boundary of the Amorites;
The land of the Gebalites on the coastᵃ and all of the Lebanon mountain area from Baal-gad beneath Mount Hermon in the south to the entrance of Hamath in the north;
All the hill country from Lebanon to Misrephoth-maim, including all the land of the Sidonians.

a Implied.

I am ready to drive these people out from before the nation of Israel, so include all this territory when you divide the land among the nine tribes and the half-tribe of Manasseh as I have commanded you."

⁸ The other half of the tribe of Manasseh, and the tribes of Reuben and Gad, had already received their inheritance on the east side of the Jordan, for Moses had previously assigned this land to them. ⁹ Their territory ran from Aroer, on the edge of the valley of the Arnon River, included the city in the valley, and crossed the tableland of Medeba to Dibon; ¹⁰ it also included all the cities of King Sihon of the Amorites, who reigned in Heshbon, and extended as far as the borders of Ammon. ¹¹ It included Gilead; the territory of the Geshurites and the Maacathites; all of Mount Hermon; Mount Bashan with its city of Salecah; ¹² and all the territory of King Og of Bashan, who had reigned in Ashtaroth and Edre-i. (He was the last of the Rephaim, for Moses had attacked them and driven them out. ¹³ However, the people of Israel had not driven out the Geshurites or the Ma-acathites, who still live there among the Israelites to this day.)

¹⁴ The Territorial Assignments

The Land Given to the Tribe of Levi:

Moses hadn't assigned any land to the tribe of Levi: instead, they were given the offerings brought to the Lord.

¹⁵ *The Land Given to the Tribe of Reuben:*

Fitting the size of its territory to its size of population,ᵇ Moses had assigned the following area to the tribe of Reuben: ¹⁶ Their land extended from Aroer on the edge of the valley of the Arnon River, past the city of Arnon in the middle of the valley, to beyond the tableland near Medeba. ¹⁷ It included Heshbon and the other cities on the plain— Dibon, Bamoth-baal, Beth-baal-meon, ¹⁸ Jahaz, Kedemoth, Mepha-ath, ¹⁹ Kiriathaim, Sibmah, Zereth-shahar on the mountain above the valley, ²⁰ Beth-peor, Beth-jeshimoth, and the slopes of Mount Pisgah.

²¹ The land of Reuben also included the cities of the tableland and the kingdom of Sihon. Sihon was the king who had lived in Heshbon and was killed by Moses along with the other chiefs of Midian—Evi, Rekem, Zur, Hur, and Reba. ²² The people of Israel also killed Balaam the magician, the son of Beor. ²³ The Jordan River was the western boundary of the tribe of Reuben.

²⁴ *The Land Given to the Tribe of Gad:*

Moses also assigned land to the tribe of Gad in proportion to its population.ᵇ ²⁵ This territory included Jazer, all the cities of Gilead and half of the land of Ammon as far as Aroer near Rabbah. ²⁶ It also extended from Heshbon to Ramath-mizpeh and Betonim, and from Mahanaim to Lodebar. ²⁷,²⁸ In the valley were Beth-haram, and Beth-nimrah, Succoth, Zaphon, and the rest of the kingdom of King Sihon of Heshbon. The Jordan River was the western border, extending as far as the Lake of Galilee; then the border turned east from the Jordan River.

²⁹ *The Land Given to the Half-Tribe of Manasseh:*

Moses had assigned the following territory to the half-tribe of Manasseh in proportion to its needs:ᵇ ³⁰ Their territory extended north from Mahanaim, included all of Bashan, the former kingdom of King Og, and the sixty cities of Jair in Bashan. ³¹ Half of Gilead and King Og's royal cities of Ashtaroth and Edre-i were given to half of the clan Machir, who was Manasseh's son.

³² That was how Moses divided the land east of the Jordan River where the people were camped at that time across from Jericho. ³³ But Moses had given no land to the tribe of Levi for, as he had explained to them, the Lord God was their inheritance. He was all they needed. He would take care of them in other ways.

14 THE CONQUERED LANDS of Canaan were allotted to the remaining nine and a half tribes of Israel. The decision as to which tribe would receive which area was decided by throwing dice before the Lord, and he caused them to turn up in the ways he wanted.ᵃ Eleazar the priest, Joshua, and the tribal leaders supervised the lottery.

³,⁴ (Moses had already given land to the

ᵇ Literally, "according to its families."   14a Literally, "by lot."

two and a half tribes on the east side of the Jordan River. The tribe of Joseph had become two separate tribes, Manasseh and Ephraim, and the Levites were given no land at all, except cities in which to live and the surrounding pasturelands for their cattle. ⁵ So the distribution of the land was in strict accordance with the Lord's directions to Moses.)

⁶ *The Land Given to Caleb:*

A delegation from the tribe of Judah, led by Caleb, came to Joshua in Gilgal.

"Remember what the Lord said to Moses about you and me when we were at Kadesh-barnea?" Caleb asked Joshua. ⁷ "I was forty years old at the time, and Moses had sent us from Kadesh-barnea to spy out the land of Canaan. I reported what I felt was the truth, ⁸ but our brothers who went with us frightened the people and discouraged them from entering the Promised Land. But since I had followed the Lord my God,. ⁹ Moses told me, 'The section of Canaan you were just in shall belong to you and your descendants forever.'

¹⁰ "Now, as you see, from that time until now the Lord has kept me alive and well for all these forty-five years since crisscrossing the wilderness, and today I am eighty-five years old. ¹¹ I am as strong now as I was when Moses sent us on that journey, and I can still travel and fight as well as I could then! ¹² So I'm asking that you give me the hill country which the Lord promised me. You will remember that as spies we found the Anakim living there in great, walled cities, but if the Lord is with me I shall drive them out of the land."

¹³,¹⁴ So Joshua blessed him and gave him Hebron as a permanent inheritance because he had followed the Lord God of Israel. ¹⁵ (Before that time Hebron had been called Kiriath-arba, after a great hero of the Anakim.)

And there was no resistance from the local populations as the Israelis resettled the land.

15 THE LAND GIVEN *to the Tribe of Judah* (as assigned by sacred lot):

Judah's southern boundary began at the northern border of Edom, crossed the Wilderness of Zin, and ended at the northern edge of the Negeb. ²,³,⁴ More specifically, this boundary began at the south bay of the Salt Sea, ran along the road going south of Mount Akrabbim, on into the Wilderness of Zin to Hezron (south of Kadesh-barnea), and then up through Karka and Azmon, until it finally reached the Brook of Egypt, and along that to the Mediterranean Sea.

⁵ The eastern boundary extended along the Salt Sea to the mouth of the Jordan River.

The northern boundary began at the bay where the Jordan River empties into the Salt Sea, ⁶ crossed to Beth-hoglah, then proceeded north of Beth-arabah to the stone of Bohan (son of Reuben). ⁷ From that point it went through the Valley of Achor to Debir, where it turned northwest toward Gilgal, opposite the slopes of Adummim on the south side of the valley. From there the border extended to the springs at En-shemesh and on to En-rogel. ⁸ The boundary then passed through the Valley of Hinnom, along the southern shoulder of Jebus (where the city of Jerusalem is located), then west to the top of the mountain above the Valley of Hinnom and on up to the northern end of the Valley of Rephaim. ⁹ From there the border extended from the top of the mountain to the spring of Nephtoah, and from there to the cities of Mount Ephron before it turned northward to circle around Baalah (which is another name for Kiriath-jearim). ¹⁰,¹¹ Then the border circled west of Baalah to Mount Seir, passed along to the town of Chesalon on the northern shoulder of Mount Jearim, and went down to Beth-shemesh. Turning northwest again, the boundary line proceeded past the south of Timnah to the shoulder of the hill north of Ekron, where it bent to the left, passing south of Shikkeron and Mount Baalah. Turning again to the north, it passed Jabneel and ended at the Mediterranean Sea.

¹² The western border was the shoreline of the Mediterranean.

¹³ *The Land Given to Caleb:*

The Lord instructed Joshua to assign some of Judah's territory to Caleb (son of Jephunneh), so he was given the city of Arba (also called Hebron), which had been named after Anak's father. ¹⁴ Caleb drove out the descendants of the three sons of Anak: Talmai, Sheshai, and Ahiman. ¹⁵ Then he fought against the people living in the city of Debir (formerly called Kiriath-sepher).

¹⁶ Caleb said that he would give his daughter Achsah to be the wife of anyone who would go and capture Kiriath-sepher. ¹⁷ Othni-el (son of Kenaz), Caleb's nephew, was the one who conquered it, so Achsah became Othni-el's wife. ^{18,19} As she was leaving with him, she urged him to ask her father for an additional field as a wedding present.^a She got off her donkey to speak to Caleb about this.

"What is it? What can I do for you?" he asked.

And she replied, "Give me another present! For the land you gave me is a desert. Give us some springs, too!" Then he gave her the upper and lower springs.

²⁰ So this was the assignment of land to the tribe of Judah:

²¹⁻³² The cities of Judah which were situated along the borders of Edom in the Negeb, namely:

> Kabzeel, Eder, Jagur, Kinah,
> Dimonah, Adadah, Kedesh, Hazor,
> Ithnan, Ziph, Telem, Be-aloth,
> Hazor-hadattah, Keri-oth-hezron
> (or, Hazor), Amam, Shema,
> Moladah, Hazar-gaddah, Heshmon,
> Beth-pelet, Hazar-shual,
> Beer-sheba, Biziothiah, Baalah, Iim,
> Ezem, Eltolad, Chesil, Hormah,
> Ziklag, Madmannah, Sansannah,
> Lebaoth, Shilhim, Ain, and
> Rimmon.

In all, there were twenty-nine of these cities with their surrounding villages.

³³⁻³⁶ The following cities situated in the lowlands were also given to Judah:

> Eshtaol, Zorah, Ashnah, Zanoah,
> En-gannim, Tappu-ah, Enam,
> Jarmuth, Adullam, Socoh, Azekah,
> Sha-araim, Adithaim, Gederah, and
> Gederothaim.

In all, there were fourteen of these cities with their surrounding villages.

³⁷⁻⁴⁴ The tribe of Judah also inherited twenty-five other cities with their villages:^b

> Zenan, Hadashah, Migdal-gad,
> Dilean, Mizpeh, Jokthe-el, Lachish,
> Bozkath, Eglon, Cabbon, Lahmam,
> Chitlish, Gederoth, Beth-dagon,
> Naamah, Makkedah, Libnah,
> Ether, Ashan, Iphtah, Ashnah,
> Nezib, Keilah, Achzib, and
> Mareshah.

⁴⁵ The territory of the tribe of Judah also included all the towns and villages of Ekron. ⁴⁶ From Ekron the boundary extended to the Mediterranean, and included the cities along the borders of Ashdod with their nearby villages; ⁴⁷ also the city of Ashdod with its villages, and Gaza with its villages as far as the Brook of Egypt; also the entire Mediterranean coast from the mouth of the Brook of Egypt on the south, to Tyre on the north.

⁴⁸⁻⁶² Judah also received these forty-four^c cities in the hill country with their surrounding villages:

> Shamir, Jattir, Socoh, Dannah,
> Kiriath-sannah (or, Debir), Anab,
> Eshtemoh, Anim, Goshen, Holon,
> Giloh, Arab, Dumah, Eshan,
> Janim, Beth-tappu-ah, Aphekah,
> Humtah, Kiriath-arba (or, Hebron),
> Zior, Maon, Carmel, Ziph, Juttah,
> Jezreel, Jokde-am, Zanoah, Kain,
> Gibe-ah, Timnah, Halhul, Beth-zur,
> Gedor, Maarath, Beth-anoth,
> Eltekon, Kiriath-baal (also known
> as Kiriath-jearim), Rabbah,
> Beth-arabah, Middin, Secacah,
> Nibshan, The City of Salt, and
> En-gedi.

⁶³ But the tribe of Judah could not drive out the Jebusites who lived in the city of Jerusalem, so the Jebusites live there among the people of Judah to this day.

16 THE SOUTHERN BOUNDARY *of the Tribes of Joseph* (Ephraim and the half-tribe of Manasseh):

This boundary extended from the Jordan River at Jericho through the wilderness and the hill country to Bethel. It then went from Bethel to Luz, then on to Ataroth, in

---

a Implied.   b Implied. See verses 41 and 44.   c Implied in verses 51, 54, 57, 59, 60, and 62, where the original text indicates sub-totals of the number of cities assigned to Judah.

the territory of the Archites; and west to the border of the Japhletites as far as Lower Beth-horon, then to Gezer and on over to the Mediterranean.

⁵,⁶ *The Land Given to the Tribe of Ephraim*: The eastern boundary began at Ataroth-addar. From there it ran to Upper Beth-horon, then on to the Mediterranean Sea. The northern boundary began at the Sea, ran east past Michmethath, then continued on past Taanath-shiloh and Janoah. ⁷ From Janoah it turned southward to Ataroth and Naarah, and touched Jericho, and ended at the Jordan River. ⁸ [The western half of the northern boundaryᵃ] went from Tappu-ah, and followed along Kanah Brook to the Mediterranean Sea. ⁹ Ephraim was also given some of the cities in the territory of the half-tribe of Manasseh. ¹⁰ The Canaanites living in Gezer were never driven out, so they still live as slaves among the people of Ephraim.

17 THE LAND GIVEN *to the Half-tribe of Manasseh* (Joseph's oldest son): The clan of Machir (Manasseh's oldest son who was the father of Gilead) had already been given the land of Gilead and Bashan [on the east side of the Jordan Riverᵃ], for they were great warriors. ² So now, land on the west side of the Jordanᵃ was given to the clans of Abiezer, Helek, Asri-el, Shechem, Shemida, and Hepher.

³ However, Hepher's son Zelophehad (grandson of Gilead, great-grandson of Machir, and great-great-grandson of Manasseh) had no sons. He had only five daughters whose names were Mahlah, Noah, Hoglah, Milcah, and Tirzah. ⁴ These women came to Eleazar the priest and to Joshua and the Israeli leaders and reminded them,

"The Lord told Moses that we were to receive as much property as the men of our tribe."ᵇ

⁵,⁶ So, as the Lord had commanded through Moses, these five women were given an inheritance along with their five great-uncles, and the total inheritance came to ten sections of land (in addition to the land of Gilead and Bashan across the Jor-

dan River).

⁷ The northern boundary of the tribe of Manasseh extended southward from the border of Asher to Michmethath, which is east of Shechem. On the south the boundary went from Michmethath to the Spring of Tappu-ah. ⁸ (The land of Tappu-ah belonged to Manasseh, but the city of Tappu-ah, on the border of Manasseh's land, belonged to the tribe of Ephraim.) ⁹ From the spring of Tappu-ah the border of Manasseh followed the north bank of the Brook of Kanah to the Mediterranean Sea. (Several cities south of the brook belonged to the tribe of Ephraim, though they were located in Manasseh's territory.) ¹⁰ The land south of the brook and as far west as the Mediterranean Sea was assigned to Ephraim, and the land north of the brook and east of the sea went to Manasseh. Manasseh's northern boundary was the territory of Asher and the eastern boundary was the territory of Issachar.

¹¹ The half-tribe of Manasseh was also given the following cities which were situated in the areas assigned to Issachar and Asher: Beth-shean, Ible-am, Dor, En-dor, Taanach, Megiddo (where there are the three cliffs), with their respective villages. ¹² But since the descendants of Manasseh could not drive out the people who lived in those cities, the Canaanites remained. ¹³ Later on, however, when the Israelis became strong enough, they forced the Canaanites to work as slaves.

¹⁴ Then the two tribes of Joseph came to Joshua and asked, "Why have you given us only one portion of land when the Lord has given us such large populations?"

¹⁵ "If the hill country of Ephraim is not large enough for you," Joshua replied, "and if you are able to do it, you may clear out the forest land where the Perizzites and Rephaim live."

¹⁶,¹⁷,¹⁸ "Fine," said the tribes of Joseph, "for the Canaanites in the lowlands around Beth-shean and the Valley of Jezreel have iron chariots and are too strong for us."

"Then you shall have the mountain forests," Joshua replied, "and since you are such a large, strong tribe you will surely be

---

a Implied.   17a Implied.   b See Numbers 27:5–7.

able to clear it all and live there. And I'm sure you can drive out the Canaanites from the valleys, too, even though they are strong and have iron chariots."

18 AFTER THE CONQUEST—although seven of the tribes of Israel had not yet entered and conquered the land God had given them—all Israel gathered at Shiloh to set up the Tabernacle.

³ Then Joshua asked them, "How long are you going to wait before clearing out the people living in the land which the Lord your God has given to you? ⁴ Select three men from each tribe and I will send them to scout the unconquered territory and bring back a report of its size and natural divisions so that I can divide it for you. ⁵,⁶ The scouts will map it into seven sections, and then I will throw the sacred dice to decide which section will be assigned to each tribe. ⁷ However, remember that the Levites won't receive any land; they are priests of the Lord. That is their wonderful heritage. And of course the tribes of Gad and Reuben and the half-tribe of Manasseh won't receive any more, for they already have land on the east side of the Jordan where Moses promised them that they could settle."

⁸ So the scouts went out to map the country and to bring back their report to Joshua. Then the Lord could assign the sections of land to the tribes by the throw of the sacred dice. ⁹ The men did as they were told and divided the entire territory into seven sections, listing the cities in each section. Then they returned to Joshua and the camp at Shiloh. ¹⁰ There at the Tabernacle at Shiloh the Lord showed Joshua by the sacred lottery which tribe should have each section:

¹¹ *The Land Given to the Tribe of Benjamin:*

The section of land assigned to the families of the tribe of Benjamin lay between the territory previously assigned to the tribes of Judah and Joseph.

¹² The northern boundary began at the Jordan River, went north of Jericho, then west through the hill country and the Wil-

derness of Beth-aven. ¹³ From there the boundary went south to Luz (also called Bethel) and proceeded down to Ataroth-addar in the hill country south of Lower Beth-horon. ¹⁴ There the border turned south, passing the mountain near Beth-horon and ending at the village of Kiriath-baal (sometimes called Kiriath-jearim), one of the cities of the tribe of Judah. This was the western boundary.

¹⁵ The southern border ran from the edge of Kiriath-baal, over Mount Ephron to the spring of Naphtoah, ¹⁶ and down to the base of the mountain beside the valley of Hinnom, north of the valley of Rephaim. From there it continued across the valley of Hinnom, crossed south of the old city of Jerusalemᵃ where the Jebusites lived, and continued down to En-rogel. ¹⁷ From En-rogel the boundary proceeded northeast to En-shemesh and on to Geliloth (which is opposite the slope of Adummim). Then it went down to the Stone of Bohan (who was a son of Reuben), ¹⁸ where it passed along the north edge of the Arabah. The border then went down into the Arabah, ¹⁹ ran south past Beth-hoglah, and ended at the north bay of the Salt Sea—which is the southern end of the Jordan River.

²⁰ The eastern border was the Jordan River. This was the land assigned to the tribe of Benjamin. ²¹⁻²⁸ These twenty-sixᵇ cities were included in the land given to the tribe of Benjamin:

> Jericho, Beth-hoglah, Emek-keziz, Beth-arabah, Zimaraim, Bethel, Avvim, Parah, Ophrah, Chephar-ammoni, Ophni, Geba, Gibeon, Ramah, Be-eroth, Mizpeh, Chephirah, Mozah, Rekem, Irpeel, Taralah, Zela, Ha-eleph, Jebus (or, Jerusalem), Gibe-ah, and Kiriath-jearim.

All of these cities and their surrounding villages were given to the tribe of Benjamin.

19 THE LAND GIVEN *to the Tribe of Simeon:*

The tribe of Simeon received the next assignment of land—including part of the land previously assigned to Judah. ²⁻⁷ Their

---

a Implied.   b Implied in verses 24 and 28, where the original manuscript indicates sub-totals.

inheritance included these seventeen[a] cities with their respective villages:

Beer-sheba, Sheba, Moladah,
Hazar-shual, Balah, Ezem, Eltolad,
Bethul, Hormah, Ziklag,
Beth-marcaboth, Hazar-susah,
Beth-lebaoth, Sharuhen,
En-rimmon, Ether, and Ashan.

[8] The cities as far south as Baalath-beer (also known as Ramah-in-the-Negeb) were also given to the tribe of Simeon. [9] So the Simeon tribe's inheritance came from what had earlier been given to Judah, for Judah's section had been too large for them.

[10] *The Land Given to the Tribe of Zebulun:*

The third tribe to receive its assignment of land was Zebulun. Its boundary started on the south side of Sarid. [11] From there it circled to the west, going near Mareal and Dabbesheth until it reached the brook east of Jeokne-am. [12] In the other direction, the boundary line went east to the border of Chisloth-tabor, and from there to Daberath and Japhia; [13] then it continued east of Gath-hepher, Ethkazin, and Rimmon and turned toward Neah. [14] The northern boundary of Zebulun passed Hannathon and ended at the Valley of Iphtahel. [15,16] The cities in these areas, besides those already mentioned,[b] included Kattath, Nahalal, Shimron, Idalah, Bethlehem, and each of their surrounding villages. Altogether there were twelve of these cities.

[17-23] *The Land Given to the Tribe of Issachar:*

The fourth tribe to be assigned its land was Issachar. Its boundaries included the following cities:

Jezreel, Chesulloth, Shunem,
Hapharaim, Shion, Anaharath,
Rabbith, Kishion, Ebez, Remeth,
En-gannim, En-haddah,
Beth-pazzez, Tabor, Shahazumah,
and Beth-shemesh—

sixteen cities in all, each with its surrounding villages. The boundary of Issachar ended at the Jordan River.

[24,25,26] *The Land Given to the Tribe of Asher:*

The fifth tribe to be assigned its land was Asher. The boundaries included these cities:

Helkath, Hali, Beten, Achshaph,
Allammelech, Amad, and Mishal.

The boundary on the west side went from Carmel to Shihor-libnath, [27] turned east toward Beth-dagon, and ran as far as Zebulun in the Valley of Iphtahel, running north of Beth-emek and Neiel. It then passed to the east of Kabul, [28] Ebron, Rehob, Hammon, Kanah, and Greater Sidon. [29] Then the boundary turned toward Ramah and the fortified city of Tyre and came to the Mediterranean Sea at Hosah. The territory also included Mahalab, Achzib, [30,31] Ummah, Aphek, and Rehob—an overall total of twenty-two cities and their surrounding villages.

[32] *The Land Given to the Tribe of Naphtali:*

The sixth tribe to receive its assignment was the tribe of Naphtali. [33] Its boundary began at Judah, at the oak in Zaanannim, and extended across to Adami-nekeb, Jabneel, and Lakkum, ending at the Jordan River. [34] The western boundary began near Heleph and ran past Aznoth-tabor, then to Hukkok, and coincided with the Zebulun boundary in the south, and with the boundary of Asher on the west, and with the Jordan River at the east. [35-39] The fortified cities included in this territory were:

Ziddim, Zer, Hammath, Rakkath,
Chinnereth, Adamah, Ramah,
Hazor, Kedesh, Edre-i, Enhazor,
Yiron, Migdal-el, Horem,
Beth-anath, and Beth-shemesh.

So altogether the territory included nineteen cities with their surrounding villages.

[40] *The Land Given to the Tribe of Dan:*

The last tribe to be assigned its land was Dan. [41-46] The cities within its area included:

Zorah, Eshta-ol, Ir-shemesh,
Sha-alabbin, Aijalon, Ithlah, Elon,
Timnah, Ekron, Eltekeh,
Gibbethon, Baalath, Jehud,
Bene-berak, Gath-rimmon,
Me-jarkon, and Rakkon, also the
territory near Joppa.

---

a Totaled from verses 6 and 7 of the original manuscript, where sub-totals are indicated.
b Implied.

47,48 But some of this territory proved impossible to conquer, so the tribe of Dan captured the city of Leshem, slaughtered its people, and lived there; and they called the city "Dan," naming it after their ancestor.

49 So all the land was divided among the tribes, with the boundaries indicated; and the nation of Israel gave a special piece of land to Joshua, **50** for the Lord had said that he could have any city he wanted. He chose Timnath-serah in the hill country of Ephraim; he rebuilt it and lived there. **51** Eleazar the priest, Joshua, and the leaders of the tribes of Israel supervised the sacred lottery to divide the land among the tribes. This was done in the Lord's presence at the entrance of the Tabernacle at Shiloh.

20 THE LORD SAID to Joshua, **2** "Tell the people of Israel to designate now the Cities of Refuge, as I instructed Moses.[a] **3** If a man is guilty of killing someone unintentionally, he can run to one of these cities and be protected from the relatives of the dead man, who may try to kill him in revenge. **4** When the innocent killer reaches any of these cities, he will meet with the city council and explain what happened, and they must let him come in and must give him a place to live among them. **5** If a relative of the dead man comes to kill him in revenge, the innocent slayer must not be released to them, for the death was accidental. **6** The man who caused the accidental death must stay in that city until he has been tried by the judges, and must live there until the death of the High Priest who was in office at the time of the accident. But then he is free to return to his own city and home."

7 The cities chosen as Cities of Refuge were Kedesh of Galilee in the hill country of Naphtali; Shechem, in the hill country of Ephraim; and Kiriath-arba (also known as Hebron) in the hill country of Judah. **8** The Lord also instructed that three cities be set aside for this purpose on the east side of the Jordan River, across from Jericho. They were Bezer, in the wilderness of the land of the tribe of Reuben; Ramoth of Gilead, in the territory of the tribe of Gad; and Golan of Bashan, in the land of the tribe of Manasseh. **9** These Cities of Refuge were for foreigners living in Israel as well as for the Israelis themselves, so that anyone who accidentally killed another man could run to that place for a trial, and not be killed in revenge.

21 THEN THE LEADERS of the tribe of Levi came to Shiloh to consult with Eleazar the priest and with Joshua and the leaders of the various tribes.

2 "The Lord instructed Moses to give cities to us Levites for our homes, and pastureland for our cattle," they said.

3 So they were given some of the recently conquered cities with their pasturelands. **4** Thirteen of these cities had been assigned originally to the tribes of Judah, Simeon, and Benjamin. These were given to some of the priests of the Kohath division (of the tribe of Levi, descendants of Aaron). **5** The other families of the Kohath division were given ten cities from the territories of Ephraim, Dan, and the half-tribe of Manasseh. **6** The Gershon division received thirteen cities, selected by sacred lot in the area of Bashan. These cities were given by the tribes of Issachar, Asher, Naphtali, and the half-tribe of Manasseh. **7** The Merari division received twelve cities from the tribes of Reuben, Gad, and Zebulun. **8** So the Lord's command to Moses was obeyed, and the cities and pasturelands were assigned by the toss of the sacred dice.

9-16 First to receive their assignment were the priests—the descendants of Aaron, who was a member of the Kohath division of the Levites. The tribes of Judah and Simeon gave them the nine[a] cities listed below, with their surrounding pasturelands:

Hebron, in the Judean hills, as a City of Refuge—it was also called Kiriath-arba (Arba was the father of Anak)—although the fields beyond the city and the surrounding villages were given to Caleb, the son of Jephunneh;

Libnah, Jattir, Eshtemoa, Holon, Debir, Ain, Juttah, and

---

a See Numbers 35 and 1 Chronicles 6.   21a Implied in verse 16, where a sub-total is indicated in the original text.

Beth-shemesh.

^{17,18} The tribe of Benjamin gave them these four cities and their pasturelands:

Gibeon, Gaba, Anathoth, and Almon.

¹⁹ So in all, thirteen cities were given to the priests—the descendants of Aaron.

^{20,21,22} The other families of the Kohath division received four^b cities and pasturelands from the tribe of Ephraim:

Shechem (a City of Refuge), Gezer, Kibza-im, and Beth-horon.

^{23,24} The following four cities and pasturelands were given by the tribe of Dan:

Elteke, Gibbethon, Aijalon, and Gath-rimmon.

²⁵ The half-tribe of Manasseh gave the cities of Taanach and Gath-rimmon with their surrounding pasturelands. ²⁶ So the total number of cities and pasturelands given to the remainder of the Kohath division was ten.

²⁷ The descendants of Gershon, another division of the Levites, received two cities and pasturelands from the half-tribe of Manasseh:

Golan, in Bashan (a City of Refuge), and Be-eshterah.

^{28,29} The tribe of Issachar gave four cities:

Kishion, Daberath, Jarmuth, and Engannim.

^{30,31} The tribe of Asher gave four cities and pasturelands:

Mishal, Abdon, Helkath, and Rehob.

³² The tribe of Naphtali gave:

Kedesh, in Galilee (a City of Refuge), Hammoth-dor, and Kartan.

³³ So thirteen cities with their pasturelands were assigned to the division of Gershon.

^{34,35} The remainder of the Levites—the Merari division—were given four cities by the tribe of Zebulun:

Jokne-am, Kartah, Dimnah, and Nahalal.

^{36,37} Reuben gave them:

Bezer, Jahaz, Kedemoth, and Mepha-ath.

^{38,39} Gad gave them four cities with pasturelands:

Ramoth (a City of Refuge), Mahanaim, Heshbon, and Jazer.

⁴⁰ So the Merari division of the Levites was given twelve cities in all.

^{41,42} The total number of cities and pasturelands given to the Levites came to forty-eight.

⁴³ So in this way the Lord gave to Israel all the land he had promised to their ancestors, and they went in and conquered it and lived there. ⁴⁴ And the Lord gave them peace, just as he had promised, and no one could stand against them; the Lord helped them destroy all their enemies. ⁴⁵ Every good thing the Lord had promised them came true.

22 JOSHUA NOW CALLED together the troops from the tribes of Reuben, Gad, and the half-tribe of Manasseh, ^{2,3} and addressed them as follows:

"You have done as the Lord's disciple Moses commanded you, and have obeyed every order I have given you—every order of the Lord your God. You have not deserted your brother tribes, even though the campaign has lasted for such a long time. ⁴ And now the Lord our God has given us success and rest as he promised he would. So go home now to the land given you by the Lord's servant Moses, on the other side of the Jordan River. ⁵ Be sure to continue to obey all of the commandments Moses gave you. Love the Lord and follow his plan for your lives. Cling to him and serve him enthusiastically."

⁶ So Joshua blessed them and sent them home. ^{7,8} (Moses had assigned the land of Bashan to the half-tribe of Manasseh, although the other half of the tribe was given land on the west side of the Jordan.) As Joshua sent away these troops, he blessed them and told them to share their great wealth with their relatives back home—their booty of cattle, silver, gold, bronze, iron, and clothing.

⁹ So the troops of Reuben, Gad, and the half-tribe of Manasseh left the army of Israel at Shiloh in Canaan and crossed the Jordan River to their own homeland of

---

b Implied in verse 22, where the total appears in the text.

Gilead. ¹⁰ Before they went across, while they were still in Canaan, they built a large monument for everyone to see, in the shape of an altar.

¹¹ But when the rest of Israel heard about what they had done, ¹² they mustered an army at Shiloh and prepared to go to war against their brother tribes. ¹³ First, however, they sent a delegation led by Phinehas, the son of Eleazar the priest. They crossed the river and talked to the tribes of Reuben, Gad, and Manasseh. ¹⁴ In this delegation were ten high officials of Israel, one from each of the ten tribes, and each a clan leader. ¹⁵ When they arrived in the land of Gilead they said to the tribes of Reuben, Gad, and the half-tribe of Manasseh,

¹⁶ "The whole congregation of the Lord demands to know why you are sinning against the God of Israel by turning away from him and building an altar of rebellion against the Lord. ¹⁷,¹⁸ Was our guilt at Peor—from which we have not even yet been cleansed despite the plague that tormented us—so little that you must rebel again? For you know that if you rebel today the Lord will be angry with all of us tomorrow. ¹⁹ If you need the altar because your land is defiled, then join us on our side of the river where the Lord lives among us in his Tabernacle, and we will share our land with you. But do not rebel against the Lord by building another altar in addition to the only true altar of our God. ²⁰ Don't you remember that when Achan, the son of Zerah, sinned against the Lord, the entire nation was punished in addition to the one man who had sinned?"

²¹ This was the reply of the people of Reuben, Gad, and the half-tribe of Manasseh to these high officials:

²²,²³ "We swear by Jehovah, the God of gods, that we have not built the altar in rebellion against the Lord. He knows (and let all Israel know it too) that we have not built the altar to sacrifice burnt offerings or grain offerings or peace offerings—may the curse of God be on us if we did. ²⁴,²⁵ We have done it because we love the Lord and because we fear that in the future your children will say to ours, 'What right do you have to worship the Lord God of Israel? The Lord has placed the Jordan River as a barrier between our people and your people! You have no part in the Lord.' And your children may make our children stop worshiping him. ²⁶,²⁷ So we decided to build the altar as a symbol to show our children and your children that we, too, may worship the Lord with our burnt offerings and peace offerings and sacrifices, and your children will not be able to say to ours, 'You have no part in the Lord our God.' ²⁸ If they say this, our children can reply, 'Look at the altar of the Lord which our fathers made, patterned after the altar of Jehovah. It is not for burnt offerings or sacrifices but is a symbol of the relationship with God that both of us have.' ²⁹ Far be it from us to turn away from the Lord or to rebel against him by building our own altar for burnt offerings, grain offerings, or sacrifices. Only the altar in front of the Tabernacle may be used for that."

³⁰ When Phinehas the priest and the high officials heard this from the tribes of Reuben, Gad, and Manasseh, they were very happy.

³¹ Phinehas replied to them, "Today we know that the Lord is among us because you have not sinned against the Lord as we thought; instead, you have saved us from destruction!"

³² Then Phinehas and the ten ambassadors went back to the people of Israel and told them what had happened, ³³ and all Israel rejoiced and praised God and spoke no more of war against Reuben and Gad. ³⁴ The people of Reuben and Gad named the altar "The Altar of Witness," for they said, "It is a witness between us and them that Jehovah is our God, too."

23 LONG AFTER THIS, when the Lord had given success to the people of Israel against their enemies and when Joshua was very old, ² he called for the leaders of Israel—the elders, judges, and officers—and said to them, "I am an old man now, ³ and you have seen all that the Lord your God has done for you during my lifetime. He has fought for you against your enemies and has given you their land. ⁴,⁵ And I have divided to you the land of the nations yet unconquered as well as the land of those you have already destroyed. All the land from the

Jordan River to the Mediterranean Sea shall be yours, for the Lord your God will drive out all the people living there now, and you will live there instead, just as he has promised you.

⁶ "But be very sure to follow all the instructions written in the book of the laws of Moses; do not deviate from them the least little bit. ⁷ Be sure that you do not mix with the heathen people still remaining in the land; do not even mention the names of their gods, much less swear by them or worship them. ⁸ But follow the Lord your God just as you have until now. ⁹ He has driven out great, strong nations from before you, and no one has been able to defeat you. ¹⁰ Each one of you has put to flight a thousand of the enemy, for the Lord your God fights for you, just as he has promised. ¹¹ So be very careful to keep on loving him.

¹² "If you don't, and if you begin to intermarry with the nations around you, ¹³ then know for a certainty that the Lord your God will no longer chase those nations from your land. Instead, they will be a snare and a trap to you, a pain in your side and a thorn in your eyes, and you will disappear from this good land which the Lord your God has given you.

¹⁴ "Soon I will be going the way of all the earth—I am going to die.

"You know very well that God's promises to you have all come true. ¹⁵,¹⁶ But as certainly as the Lord has given you the good things he promised, just as certainly he will bring evil upon you if you disobey him. For if you worship other gods he will completely wipe you out from this good land which the Lord has given you. His anger will rise hot against you, and you will quickly perish."

24 THEN JOSHUA SUMMONED all the people of Israel to him at Shechem, along with their leaders—the elders, officers, and judges. So they came and presented themselves before God.

² Then Joshua addressed them as follows: "The Lord God of Israel says, 'Your ancestors, including Terah the father of Abraham and Nahor, lived east of the Euphrates River; and they worshiped other gods. ³ But I took your father Abraham from that land across the river and led him into the land of Canaan and gave him many descendants through Isaac his son. ⁴ Isaac's children, whom I gave him, were Jacob and Esau. To Esau I gave the area around Mount Seir while Jacob and his children went into Egypt.

⁵ "'Then I sent Moses and Aaron to bring terrible plagues upon Egypt; and afterwards I brought my people out as free men. ⁶ But when they arrived at the Red Sea, the Egyptians chased after them with chariots and cavalry. ⁷ Then Israel cried out to me and I put darkness between them and the Egyptians; and I brought the sea crashing in upon the Egyptians, drowning them. You saw what I did. Then Israel lived in the wilderness for many years.

⁸ "'Finally I brought you into the land of the Amorites on the other side of the Jordan; and they fought against you, but I destroyed them and gave you their land. ⁹ Then King Balak of Moab started a war against Israel, and he asked Balaam, the son of Beor, to curse you. ¹⁰ But I wouldn't listen to him. Instead I made him bless you; and so I delivered Israel from him.

¹¹ "'Then you crossed the Jordan River and came to Jericho. The men of Jericho fought against you, and so did many others—the Perizzites, the Canaanites, the Hittites, the Girgashites, the Hivites, and the Jebusites. Each in turn fought against you but I destroyed them all. ¹² And I sent hornets ahead of you to drive out the two kings of the Amorites and their people. It was not your swords or bows that brought you victory! ¹³ I gave you land you had not worked for and cities you did not build— these cities where you are now living. I gave you vineyards and olive groves for food, though you did not plant them.'

¹⁴ "So revere Jehovah and serve him in sincerity and truth. Put away forever the idols which your ancestors worshiped when they lived beyond the Euphrates River and in Egypt. Worship the Lord alone. ¹⁵ But if you are unwilling to obey the Lord, then decide today whom you will obey. Will it be the gods of your ancestors beyond the Euphrates or the gods of the Amorites here in this land? But as for me and my family, we will serve the Lord."

¹⁶ And the people replied, "We would

never forsake the Lord and worship other gods! [17] For the Lord our God is the one who rescued our fathers from their slavery in the land of Egypt. He is the God who did mighty miracles before the eyes of Israel, as we traveled through the wilderness, and preserved us from our enemies when we passed through their land. [18] It was the Lord who drove out the Amorites and the other nations living here in the land. Yes, we choose the Lord, for he alone is our God."

[19] But Joshua replied to the people, "You can't worship the Lord God, for he is holy and jealous; he will not forgive your rebellion and sins. [20] If you forsake him and worship other gods, he will turn upon you and destroy you, even though he has taken care of you for such a long time."

[21] But the people answered, "We choose the Lord!"

[22] "You have heard yourselves say it," Joshua said—"you have chosen to obey the Lord."

"Yes," they replied, "we are witnesses."

[23] "All right," he said, "then you must destroy all the idols you now own, and you must obey the Lord God of Israel."

[24] The people replied to Joshua, "Yes, we will worship and obey the Lord alone."

[25] So Joshua made a covenant with them that day at Shechem, committing them to a permanent and binding contract between themselves and God. [26] Joshua recorded the people's reply in the book of the laws of God, and took a huge stone as a reminder and rolled it beneath the oak tree that was beside the Tabernacle.

[27] Then Joshua said to all the people, "This stone has heard everything the Lord said, so it will be a witness to testify against you if you go back on your word."

[28] Then Joshua sent the people away to their own sections of the country.

[29] Soon after this he died at the age of 110. [30] He was buried on his own estate at Timnath-serah, in the hill country of Ephraim, on the north side of the mountains of Gaash.

[31] Israel obeyed the Lord throughout the lifetimes of Joshua and the other old men who had personally witnessed the amazing deeds which the Lord had done for Israel.

[32] The bones of Joseph, which the people of Israel had brought with them when they left Egypt, were buried in Shechem, in the parcel of ground which Jacob had bought for $200 from the sons of Hamor. (The land was located in the territory assigned to the tribes of Joseph.)

[33] Eleazar, the son of Aaron, also died; he was buried in the hill country of Ephraim, at Gibe-ah, the city which had been given to his son Phinehas.

Screamin' Machine

Get up enough nerve ... say good-bye to your stomach ... and squeeze your eyes shut only on the way down. No matter what the fancy name, a roller coaster still goes up and then goes down (with a few sideway turns thrown in)— with or without your cooperation.

The book of Judges is the story of Joshua's once-powerful nation on a spiritual coaster ride—at least six trips down into sin followed by invasion and conquest, and a string of courageous judges who would take charge and lead the people back up to God and independence. Guerrilla fighter Ehud, a tough woman named Deborah, self-conscious Gideon, maverick Jephthah, and even playboy Samson were used by God over a 175-year period to bail out the wayward Israelis. The last five chapters of the book are samples of the religious rackets and sexual perversions of the times. It's a rather grim record of what happened when "everyone did whatever he wanted to—whatever seemed right in his own eyes" (17:6).

JUDGES

1 AFTER JOSHUA DIED, the nation of Israel went to the Lord to receive his instructions.

"Which of our tribes should be the first to go to war against the Canaanites?" they inquired.

² God's answer came, "Judah. And I will give them a great victory."

³ The leaders of the tribe of Judah, however, asked help from the tribe of Simeon. "Join us in clearing out the people living in the territory allotted to us," they said, "and then we will help you conquer yours." So the army of Simeon went with the army of Judah. ⁴,⁵,⁶ And the Lord helped them defeat the Canaanites and Perizzites, so that ten thousand of the enemy were slain at Bezek. King Adoni-bezek escaped, but the Israeli army soon captured him and cut off his thumbs and big toes.

⁷ "I have treated seventy kings in this same manner and have fed them the scraps under my table!" King Adoni-bezek said. "Now God has paid me back." He was taken to Jerusalem, and died there.

⁸ (Judah had conquered Jerusalem, and massacred its people, setting the city on fire.) ⁹ Afterward the army of Judah fought the Canaanites in the hill country and in the Negeb, as well as on the coastal plains.

[10] Then Judah marched against the Canaanites in Hebron (formerly called Kiriath-arba), destroying the cities of Sheshai, Ahiman, and Talmai. [11] Later they attacked the city of Debir (formerly called Kiriath-sepher).

[12] "Who will lead the attack against Debir?" Caleb challenged them. "Whoever conquers it shall have my daughter Achsah as his wife!"

[13] Caleb's nephew, Othni-el, son of his younger brother Kenaz, volunteered to lead the attack; and he conquered the city and won Achsah as his bride. [14] As they were leaving for their new home,[a] she urged him to ask her father for an additional[b] piece of land. She dismounted from her donkey to speak to Caleb about it.

"What do you wish?" he asked.

[15] And she replied, "You have been kind enough to give me land in the Negeb, but please give us springs of water too."

So Caleb gave her the upper and lower springs.

[16] When the tribe of Judah moved into its new land in the Negeb wilderness south of Arad, the descendants of Moses' father-in-law—members of the Kenite tribe—accompanied them. They left their homes in Jericho, "The City of Palm Trees," and the two tribes lived together after that. [17] Afterwards the army of Judah joined Simeon's and they fought the Canaanites at the city of Zephath and massacred all its people. So now the city is named Hormah (meaning, "massacred"). [18] The army of Judah also conquered the cities of Gaza, Ashkelon, and Ekron, with their surrounding villages. [19] The Lord helped the tribe of Judah exterminate the people of the hill country, though they failed in their attempt to conquer the people of the valley, who had iron chariots.

[20] The city of Hebron was given to Caleb as the Lord had promised; so Caleb drove out the inhabitants of the city; they were descendants of the three sons of Anak. [21] The tribe of Benjamin failed to exterminate the Jebusites living in Jerusalem, so they still live there today, mingled with the Israelis.

[22,23] As for the tribe of Joseph, they attacked the city of Bethel, formerly known as Luz, and the Lord was with them. First they sent scouts, [24] who captured a man coming out of the city. They offered to spare his life and that of his family if he would show them the entrance passage through the wall.[c] [25] So he showed them how to get in, and they massacred the entire population except for this man and his family. [26] Later the man moved to Syria and founded a city there, naming it Luz, too, as it is still known today.

[27] The tribe of Manasseh failed to drive out the people living in Beth-shean, Taanach, Dor, Ibleam, Megiddo, with their surrounding towns; so the Canaanites stayed there. [28] In later years when the Israelis were stronger they put the Canaanites to work as slaves, but never did force them to leave the country. [29] This was also true of the Canaanites living in Gezer; they still live among the tribe of Ephraim.

[30] And the tribe of Zebulun did not massacre the people of Kitron or Nahalol, but made them their slaves; [31,32] nor did the tribe of Asher drive out the residents of Acco, Sidon, Ahlab, Achzib, Helbah, Aphik, or Rehob; so the Israelis still live among the Canaanites, who were the original people of that land. [33] And the tribe of Naphtali did not drive out the people of Beth-shemesh or of Beth-anath, so these people continue to live among them as servants.

[34] As for the tribe of Dan, the Amorites forced them into the hill country and wouldn't let them come down into the valley; [35] but when the Amorites later spread into Mount Heres, Aijalon, and Sha-albim, the tribe of Joseph conquered them and made them their slaves. [36] The boundary of the Amorites begins at the ascent of Scorpion Pass, runs to a spot called The Rock, and continues upward from there.

2 ONE DAY THE Angel of the Lord arrived at Bochim, coming from Gilgal, and announced to the people of Israel, "I brought you out of Egypt into this land which I

---

a Literally, "when she came to him."   b Implied.   c Literally, "the way into the city." Obviously this does not mean via the city gates.

promised to your ancestors, and I said that I would never break my covenant with you, ² if you, on your part, would make no peace treaties with the people living in this land; I told you to destroy their heathen altars. Why have you not obeyed? ³ And now since you have broken the contract, it is no longer in effect, and I no longer promise to destroy the nations living in your land; rather, they shall be thorns in your sides, and their gods will be a constant temptation to you."

⁴ The people broke into tears as the Angel finished speaking; ⁵ so the name of that place was called "Bochim" (meaning, "the place where people wept"). Then they offered sacrifices to the Lord.

⁶ When Joshua finally disbanded the armies of Israel, the tribes moved into their new territories and took possession of the land. ⁷⁻⁹ Joshua, the man of God, died at the age of 110, and was buried at the edge of his property in Timnath-heres, in the hill country of Ephraim, north of Mount Gaash. The people had remained true to the Lord throughout Joshua's lifetime, and as long afterward as the old men of his generation were still living—those who had seen the mighty miracles the Lord had done for Israel.

¹⁰ But finally all that generation died; and the next generation did not worship Jehovah as their God, and did not care about the mighty miracles he had done for Israel. ¹¹ They did many things which the Lord had expressly forbidden, including the worshiping of heathen gods. ¹²⁻¹⁴ They abandoned Jehovah, the God loved and worshiped by their ancestors—the God who had brought them out of Egypt. Instead, they were worshiping and bowing low before the idols of the neighboring nations. So the anger of the Lord flamed out against all Israel. He left them to the mercy of their enemies, for they had departed from Jehovah and were worshiping Baal and the Ashtaroth idols.

¹⁵ So now when the nation of Israel went out to battle against its enemies, the Lord blocked their path. He had warned them about this, and in fact had vowed that he would do it. But when the people were in this terrible plight, ¹⁶ the Lord raised up judges to save them from their enemies. ¹⁷ Yet even then Israel would not listen to the judges, but broke faith with Jehovah by worshiping other gods instead. How quickly they turned away from the true faith of their ancestors, for they refused to obey God's commands. ¹⁸ Each judge rescued the people of Israel from their enemies throughout his lifetime, for the Lord was moved to pity by the groaning of his people under their crushing oppressions; so he helped them as long as that judge lived. ¹⁹ But when the judge died, the people turned from doing right and behaved even worse than their ancestors had. They prayed to heathen gods again, throwing themselves to the ground in humble worship. They stubbornly returned to the evil customs of the nations around them.

²⁰ Then the anger of the Lord would flame out against Israel again. He declared, "Because these people have violated the treaty I made with their ancestors, ²¹ I will no longer drive out the nations left unconquered by Joshua when he died. ²² Instead, I will use these nations to test my people, to see whether or not they will obey the Lord as their ancestors did."

²³ So the Lord left those nations in the land and did not drive them out, nor let Israel destroy them.

3 HERE IS A list of the nations the Lord left in the land to test the new generation of Israel who had not experienced the wars of Canaan. For God wanted to give opportunity to the youth of Israel to exercise faith[a] and obedience[a] in conquering their enemies:[b]

The Philistines (five cities),
The Canaanites,
The Sidonians,
The Hivites living in Mount Lebanon, from Baal-hermon to the entrance of Hamath.

⁴ These people were a test to the new generation of Israel, to see whether they would obey the commandments the Lord had

---

a Implied in chapter 2, verse 22; and chapter 3, verse 4. might know war . . ."

b Literally, "that . . . the people of Israel . . .

given to them through Moses.

⁵ So Israel lived among the Canaanites, Hittites, Hivites, Perizzites, Amorites, and Jebusites. ⁶ But instead of destroying them, the people of Israel intermarried with them. The young men of Israel took their girls as wives, and the Israeli girls married their men. And soon Israel was worshiping their gods. ⁷ So the people of Israel were very evil in God's sight, for they turned against Jehovah their God and worshiped Baal and the Asheroth idols.

⁸ Then the anger of the Lord flamed out against Israel, and he let King Cushan-rishathaim of eastern Syria conquer them. They were under his rule for eight years. ⁹ But when Israel cried out to the Lord, he gave them Caleb's nephew, Othni-el (son of Kenaz, Caleb's younger brother) to save them. ¹⁰ The Spirit of the Lord took control of him and he reformed and purged Israel so that when he led the forces of Israel against the army of King Cushan-rishathaim, the Lord helped Israel conquer him completely.

¹¹ Then, for forty years under Othni-el, there was peace in the land. But when Othni-el died, ¹² the people of Israel turned once again to their sinful ways, so God helped King Eglon of Moab to conquer part of Israel at that time. ¹³ Allied with him were the armies of the Ammonites and the Amalekites. These forces defeated the Israelis and took possession of Jericho, often called "The City of Palm Trees." ¹⁴ For the next eighteen years the people of Israel were required to pay crushing taxes to King Eglon.

¹⁵ But when they cried to the Lord, he sent them a savior, Ehud (son of Gera, a Benjaminite), who was left-handed. Ehud was the man chosen to carry Israel's annual tax money to the Moabite capital. ¹⁶ Before he went on this journey he made himself a double-edged dagger eighteen inches long and hid it in his clothing, strapped against his right thigh. ¹⁷⋅¹⁸⋅¹⁹ After delivering the money to King Eglon (who, by the way, was very fat!) he started home again. But outside the city, at the quarries of Gilgal, he sent his companions on and returned alone to the king.

"I have a secret message for you," he told him.

The king immediately dismissed all those who were with him so that he could have a private interview. ²⁰ Ehud walked over to him as he was sitting in a cool upstairs room and said to him, "It is a message from God!"

King Eglon stood up at once to receive it, ²¹ whereupon Ehud reached beneath his robe with his strong left hand, pulled out the double-bladed dagger strapped against his right thigh, and plunged it deep into the king's belly. ²²⋅²³ The hilt of the dagger disappeared beneath the flesh, and the fat closed over it as the entrails oozed out. Leaving the dagger there, Ehud locked the doors behind him and escaped across an upstairs porch.

²⁴ When the king's servants returned and saw that the doors were locked, they waited, thinking that perhaps he was using the bathroom. ²⁵ But when, after a long time, he still didn't come out, they became concerned and got a key. And when they opened the door, they found their master dead on the floor.

²⁶ Meanwhile Ehud had escaped past the quarries to Se-irah. ²⁷ When he arrived in the hill country of Ephraim, he blew a trumpet as a call to arms and mustered an army under his own command.

²⁸ "Follow me," he told them, "for the Lord has put your enemies, the Moabites, at your mercy!"

The army then proceeded to seize the fords of the Jordan River near Moab, preventing anyone from crossing. ²⁹ Then they attacked the Moabites and killed about ten thousand of the strongest and most skillful of their fighting men, letting not one escape. ³⁰ So Moab was conquered by Israel that day, and the land was at peace for the next eighty years.

³¹ The next judge after Ehud was Shamgar (son of Anath). He once killed six hundred Philistines with an ox goad, thereby saving Israel from disaster.

4 AFTER EHUD'S DEATH the people of Israel again sinned against the Lord, ²⋅³ so the Lord let them be conquered by King Jabin of Hazor, in Canaan. The commander-in-chief of his army was Sisera, who lived

in Harosheth-ha-goiim. He had nine hundred iron chariots, and made life unbearable for the Israelis for twenty years. But finally they begged the Lord for help.

⁴ Israel's leader at that time, the one who was responsible for bringing the people back to God, was Deborah, a prophetess, the wife of Lappidoth. ⁵ She held court at a place now called "Deborah's Palm Tree," between Ramah and Bethel, in the hill country of Ephraim; and the Israelites came to her to decide their disputes.ᵃ

⁶ One day she summoned Barak (son of Abinoam), who lived in Kedesh, in the land of Naphtali, and said to him, "The Lord God of Israel has commanded you to mobilize ten thousand men from the tribes of Naphtali and Zebulun. Lead them to Mount Tabor, ⁷ to fight King Jabin's mighty army with all his chariots, under General Sisera's command. The Lord says, 'I will draw them to the Kishon River, and you will defeat them there.' "

⁸ "I'll go, but only if you go with me!" Barak told her.

⁹ "All right," she replied, "I'll go with you; but I'm warning you now that the honor of conquering Sisera will go to a woman instead of to you!" So she went with him to Kedesh.

¹⁰ When Barak summoned the men of Zebulun and Naphtali to mobilize at Kedesh, ten thousand men volunteered. And Deborah marched with them. ¹¹ (Heber, the Kenite—the Kenites were the descendants of Moses' father-in-law Hobab—had moved away from the rest of his clan, and had been living in various places as far away as the Oak of Za-anannim, near Kedesh.) ¹² When General Sisera was told that Barak and his army were camped at Mount Tabor, ¹³ he mobilized his entire army, including the nine hundred iron chariots, and marched from Harosheth-ha-goiim to the Kishon River.

¹⁴ Then Deborah said to Barak, "Now is the time for action! The Lord leads on! He has already delivered Sisera into your hand!"

So Barak led his ten thousand men down the slopes of Mount Tabor into battle.

¹⁵ Then the Lord threw the enemy into a panic, both the soldiers and the charioteers, and Sisera leaped from his chariot and escaped on foot. ¹⁶ Barak and his men chased the enemy and the chariots as far as Harosheth-ha-goiim, until all of Sisera's army was destroyed; not one man was left alive. ¹⁷ Meanwhile, Sisera had escaped to the tent of Jael, the wife of Heber the Kenite, for there was a mutual-assistance agreement between King Jabin of Hazor and the clan of Heber.

¹⁸ Jael went out to meet Sisera and said to him, "Come into my tent, sir. You will be safe here in our protection. Don't be afraid." So he went into her tent and she covered him with a blanket.

¹⁹ "Please give me some water," he said, "for I am very thirsty." So she gave him some milk and covered him again.

²⁰ "Stand in the door of the tent," he told her, "and if anyone comes by, looking for me, tell them that no one is here."

²¹ Then Jael took a sharp tent peg and a hammer and, quietly creeping up to him as he slept, she drove the peg through his temples and into the ground; and so he died, for he was fast asleep from weariness.

²² When Barak came by looking for Sisera, Jael went out to meet him and said, "Come, and I will show you the man you are looking for."

So he followed her into the tent and found Sisera lying there dead, with the tent peg through his temples. ²³ So that day the Lord used Israel to subdue King Jabin of Canaan. ²⁴ And from that time on Israel became stronger and stronger against King Jabin, until he and all his people were destroyed.

5 THEN DEBORAH AND Barak sang this song about the wonderful victory:

² "Praise the Lord!
Israel's leaders bravely led;
The people gladly followed!
Yes, bless the Lord!
³ Listen, O you kings and princes,
For I shall sing about the Lord,
The God of Israel.
⁴ When you led us out from Seir,

ᵃ Or, "to listen to her speak to them about God."

Out across the fields of Edom,
The earth trembled
And the sky poured down its rain.
⁵ Yes, even Mount Sinai quaked
At the presence of the God of Israel!
⁶ In the days of Shamgar and of Jael,
The main roads were deserted.
Travelers used the narrow, crooked
side paths.
⁷ Israel's population dwindled,
Until Deborah became a mother to
Israel.
⁸ When Israel chose new gods,
Everything collapsed.
Our masters would not let us have
A shield or spear.
Among forty thousand men of Israel,
Not a weapon could be found!
⁹ How I rejoice
In the leaders of Israel
Who offered themselves so willingly!
Praise the Lord!
¹⁰ Let all Israel, rich and poor,
Join in his praises—
Those who ride on white donkeys
And sit on rich carpets,
And those who are poor and must
walk.
¹¹ The village musicians
Gather at the village well
To sing of the triumphs of the Lord.
Again and again they sing the ballad
Of how the Lord saved Israel
With an army of peasants!
The people of the Lord
Marched through the gates!
¹² Awake, O Deborah, and sing!
Arise, O Barak!
O son of Abino-am, lead away your
captives!
¹³·¹⁴ Down from Mount Tabor
marched the noble remnant.
The people of the Lord
Marched down against great odds.
They came from Ephraim and Benja-
min,
From Machir and from Zebulun.
¹⁵ Down into the valley
Went the princes of Issachar
With Deborah and Barak.
At God's command they rushed into
the valley.
(But the tribe of Reuben

didn't go.
¹⁶ Why did you sit at home among the
sheepfolds,
Playing your shepherd pipes?
Yes, the tribe of Reuben has an
uneasy conscience.
¹⁷ Why did Gilead remain across the
Jordan,
And why did Dan remain with his
ships?
And why did Asher sit unmoved
Upon the seashore,
At ease beside his harbors?)
¹⁸ But the tribes of Zebulun and
Naphtali
Dared to die upon the fields of battle.
¹⁹ The kings of Canaan fought in Taa-
nach
By Megiddo's springs,
But did not win the victory.
²⁰ The very stars of heaven
Fought Sisera.
²¹ The rushing Kishon River
Swept them away.
March on, my soul, with strength!
²² Hear the stamping
Of the horsehoofs of the enemy!
See the prancing of his steeds!
²³ But the Angel of Jehovah
Put a curse on Meroz.
'Curse them bitterly,' he said,
'Because they did not come to help
the Lord
Against his enemies.'
²⁴ Blessed be Jael,
The wife of Heber the Kenite—
Yes, may she be blessed
Above all women who live in tents.
²⁵ He asked for water
And she gave him milk in a beautiful
cup!
²⁶ Then she took a tent pin and a
workman's hammer
And pierced Sisera's temples,
Crushing his head.
She pounded the tent pin through his
head,
²⁷ And he lay at her feet,
Dead.
²⁸ The mother of Sisera watched
through the window
For his return.
'Why is his chariot so long in

coming?
Why don't we hear the sound of the
  wheels?'
²⁹ But her ladies-in-waiting—and she
  herself—replied,
³⁰ 'There is much loot to be divided,
And it takes time.
Each man receives a girl or two;
And Sisera will get gorgeous robes,
And he will bring home
Many gifts for me.'
³¹ O Lord, may all your enemies
Perish as Sisera did,
But may those who love the Lord
Shine as the sun!"

After that there was peace in the land for
forty years.

6 THEN THE PEOPLE of Israel began once
  again to worship other gods, and once
again the Lord let their enemies harass
them. This time it was by the people of
Midian, for seven years. ² The Midianites
were so cruel that the Israelis took to the
mountains, living in caves and dens.
³,⁴ When they planted their seed, marauders
from Midian, Amalek, and other neighboring nations came and destroyed their crops
and plundered the countryside as far away
as Gaza, leaving nothing to eat, and taking
away all their sheep, oxen, and donkeys.
⁵ These enemy hordes arrived on droves of
camels too numerous to count and stayed
until the land was completely stripped and
devastated. ⁶,⁷ So Israel was reduced to ab-
ject poverty because of the Midianites.
Then at last the people of Israel began to
cry out to the Lord for help.

⁸ However, the Lord's reply through the
prophet he sent to them was this: "The
Lord God of Israel brought you out of slavery in Egypt, ⁹ and rescued you from the
Egyptians and from all who were cruel to
you, and drove out your enemies from
before you, and gave you their land. ¹⁰ He
told you that he is the Lord your God, and
that you must not worship the gods of the
Amorites who live around you on every
side. But you have not listened to him."

¹¹ But one day the Angel of the Lord

came and sat beneath the oak tree at
Ophrah, on the farm of Joash the Abiezrite.
Joash's son, Gideon, had been threshing
wheat by hand in the bottom of a grape
press—a pit where grapes were pressed to
make wine—for he was hiding from the
Midianites.

¹² The Angel of the Lord appeared to
him and said, "Mighty soldier, the Lord is
with you!"

¹³ "Stranger," Gideon replied, "if the
Lord is with us, why has all this happened
to us? And where are all the miracles our
ancestors have told us about—such as when
God brought them out of Egypt? Now the
Lord has thrown us away and has let the
Midianites completely ruin us."

¹⁴ Then the Lord turned to him and said,
"I will make you strong! Go and save Israel
from the Midianites! I am sending you!"

¹⁵ But Gideon replied, "Sir, how can *I*
save Israel? My family is the poorest in the
whole tribe of Manasseh, and I am the least
thought of in the entire family!"

¹⁶ Whereupon the Lord said to him, "But
I, Jehovah,ᵃ will be with you! And you shall
quickly destroy the Midianite hordes!"

¹⁷ Gideon replied, "If it is really true that
you are going to help me like that, then do
some miracle to prove it! Prove that it is
really Jehovah who is talking to me! ¹⁸ But
stay here until I go and get a present for
you."

"All right," the Angel agreed. "I'll stay
here until you return."

¹⁹ Gideon hurried home and roasted a
young goat, and baked some unleavened
bread from a bushel of flour. Then, carrying
the meat in a basket and broth in a pot, he
took it out to the Angel, who was beneath
the oak tree, and presented it to him.

²⁰ The Angel said to him, "Place the
meat and the bread upon that rock over
there, and pour the broth over it."

When Gideon had followed these instructions, ²¹ the Angel touched the meat
and bread with his staff, and fire flamed up
from the rock and consumed them! And
suddenly the Angel was gone!

²² When Gideon realized that it had in-

---

a Literally, "I Am will be with you." The same name is used here as in Exodus 3:14. God is telling Gideon
that the same one who appeared to Moses and rescued Israel from Egypt (much on Gideon's mind: see verse
13) will now do it again, rescuing Israel from Midian.

deed been the Angel of the Lord, he cried out, "Alas, O Lord God, for I have seen the Angel of the Lord face to face!" [23] "It's all right," the Lord replied. "Don't be afraid! You shall not die."

[24] And Gideon built an altar there and named it "The Altar of Peace with Jehovah." (The altar is still there in Ophrah in the land of the Abiezrites.) [25] That night the Lord told Gideon to hitch his father's best ox to the family altar of Baal, and pull it down, and to cut down the wooden idol of the goddess Asherah that stood nearby.

[26] "Replace it with an altar for the Lord your God, built here on this hill, laying the stones carefully. Then sacrifice the ox as a burnt offering to the Lord, using the wooden idol as wood for the fire on the altar."

[27] So Gideon took ten of his servants and did as the Lord had commanded. But he did it at night for fear of the other members of his father's household, and for fear of the men of the city; for he knew what would happen if they found out who did it! [28] Early the next morning, as the city began to stir, someone discovered that the altar of Baal was knocked apart, the idol beside it was gone, and a new altar had been built instead, with the remains of a sacrifice on it.

[29] "Who did this?" everyone demanded. Finally they learned that it was Gideon, the son of Joash.

[30] "Bring out your son," they shouted to Joash. "He must die for insulting the altar of Baal, and for cutting down the Asherah idol."

[31] But Joash retorted to the whole mob, "Does Baal need *your* help? What an insult to a god! You are the ones who should die for insulting Baal! If Baal is really a god, let him take care of himself and destroy the one who broke apart his altar!"

[32] From then on Gideon was called "Jerubbaal," a nickname meaning "Let Baal take care of himself!"[b]

[33] Soon afterward the armies of Midian, Amalek, and other neighboring nations united in one vast alliance against Israel. They crossed the Jordan and camped in the valley of Jezreel. [34] Then the Spirit of the Lord came upon Gideon, and he blew a trumpet as a call to arms, and the men of Abiezer came to him. [35] He also sent messengers throughout Manasseh, Asher, Zebulun, and Naphtali, summoning their fighting forces, and all of them responded.

[36] Then Gideon said to God, "If you are really going to use me to save Israel as you promised, [37] prove it to me in this way: I'll put some wool on the threshing floor tonight, and if, in the morning, the fleece is wet and the ground is dry, I will know you are going to help me!"

[38] And it happened just that way! When he got up the next morning he pressed the fleece together and wrung out a whole bowlful of water!

[39] Then Gideon said to the Lord, "Please don't be angry with me, but let me make one more test: this time let the fleece remain dry while the ground around it is wet!"

[40] So the Lord did as he asked; that night the fleece stayed dry, but the ground was covered with dew!

7 JERUBBAAL (THAT IS, Gideon—his other name) and his army got an early start and went as far as the spring of Harod. The armies of Midian were camped north of them, down in the valley beside the hill of Moreh.

[2] The Lord then said to Gideon, "There are too many of you! I can't let all of you fight the Midianites, for then the people of Israel will boast to me that they saved themselves by their own strength! [3] Send home any of your men who are timid and frightened."

So twenty-two thousand of them left, and only ten thousand remained who were willing to fight.

[4] But the Lord told Gideon, "There are still too many! Bring them down to the spring and I'll show you which ones shall go with you and which ones shall not."

[5,6] So Gideon assembled them at the water. There the Lord told him, "Divide them into two groups decided by the way they drink. In Group 1 will be all the men who cup the water in their hands to get it to their mouths and lap it like dogs. In Group 2 will

---

b Literally, "Let Baal bring charges," or, used mockingly, "Let Baal be honored!"

be those who kneel, with their mouths in the stream."

Only three hundred of the men drank from their hands; all the others drank with their mouths to the stream.

[7] "I'll conquer the Midianites with these three hundred!" the Lord told Gideon. "Send all the others home!"

[8,9] So after Gideon had collected all the clay jars and trumpets they had among them, he sent them home, leaving only three hundred men with him.

During the night, with the Midianites camped in the valley just below, the Lord said to Gideon, "Get up! Take your troops and attack the Midianites, for I will cause you to defeat them! [10] But if you are afraid, first go down to the camp alone—take along your servant Purah if you like— [11] and listen to what they are saying down there! You will be greatly encouraged and be eager to attack!"

So he took Purah and crept down through the darkness to the outposts of the enemy camp. [12,13] The vast armies of Midian, Amalek, and the other nations of the East were crowded across the valley like locusts—yes, like the sand upon the seashore—and there were too many camels even to count! Gideon crept up to one of the tents just as a man inside had wakened from a nightmare and was telling his tent-mate about it.

"I had this strange dream," he was saying, "and there was this huge loaf of barley bread that came tumbling down into our camp. It hit our tent and knocked it flat!"

[14] The other soldier replied, "Your dream can mean only one thing! Gideon, the son of Joash, the Israeli, is going to come and massacre all the allied forces of Midian!"

[15] When Gideon heard the dream and the interpretation, all he could do was just stand there worshiping God! Then he returned to his men and shouted, "Get up! For the Lord is going to use you to conquer all the vast armies of Midian!"

[16] He divided the three hundred men into three groups and gave each man a trumpet and a clay jar with a torch in it. [17] Then he explained his plan.

"When we arrive at the outer guardposts of the camp," he told them, "do just as I do. [18] As soon as I and the men in my group blow our trumpets, you blow yours on all sides of the camp and shout, 'We fight for God and for Gideon!' "

[19,20] It was just after midnight and the change of guards when Gideon and the hundred men with him crept to the outer edge of the camp of Midian.

Suddenly they blew their trumpets and broke their clay jars so that their torches blazed into the night. Then the other two hundred of his men did the same, blowing the trumpets in their right hands, and holding the flaming torches in their left hands, all yelling, "For the Lord and for Gideon!"

[21] Then they just stood and watched as the whole vast enemy army began rushing around in a panic, shouting and running away. [22] For in the confusion the Lord caused the enemy troops to begin fighting and killing each other from one end of the camp to the other, and they fled into the night to places as far away as Beth-shittah near Zererah, and to the border of Abel-meholah near Tabbath.

[23] Then Gideon sent for the troops of Naphtali, Asher, and Manasseh and told them to come and chase and destroy the fleeing army of Midian. [24] Gideon also sent messengers throughout the hill country of Ephraim summoning troops who seized the fords of the Jordan River at Beth-barah, thus preventing the Midianites from escaping by going across. [25] Oreb and Zeeb, the two generals of Midian, were captured. Oreb was killed at the rock now known by his name, and Zeeb at the winepress of Zeeb, as it is now called; and the Israelis took the heads of Oreb and Zeeb across the Jordan to Gideon.

8 BUT THE TRIBAL leaders of Ephraim were violently angry with Gideon.

"Why didn't you send for us when you first went out to fight the Midianites?" they demanded.

[2,3] But Gideon replied, "God let you capture Oreb and Zeeb, the generals of the army of Midian! What have I done in comparison with that? Your actions at the end of the battle were more important than ours

at the beginning!"[a] So they calmed down.

[4] Gideon now crossed the Jordan River with his three hundred men. They were very tired, but still chasing the enemy. [5] He asked the men of Succoth for food. "We are weary from chasing after Zebah and Zalmunna, the kings of Midian," he said.

[6] But the leaders of Succoth replied, "You haven't caught them yet! If we feed you and you fail, they'll return and destroy us."[b]

[7] Then Gideon warned them, "When the Lord has delivered them to us, I will return and tear your flesh with the thorns and briars of the wilderness."

[8] Then he went up to Penuel and asked for food there, but got the same answer. [9] And he said to them also, "When this is all over, I will return and break down this tower."

[10] By this time King Zebah and King Zalmunna with a remnant of fifteen thousand troops were in Karkor. That was all that was left of the allied armies of the east; for one hundred twenty thousand had already been killed. [11] Then Gideon circled around by the caravan route east of Nobah and Jogbehah, striking at the Midianite army in surprise raids. [12] The two kings fled, but Gideon chased and captured them, routing their entire force. [13] Later, Gideon returned by way of Heres Pass. [14] There he captured a young fellow from Succoth and demanded that he write down the names of all the seventy-seven political and religious leaders of the city.

[15] He then returned to Succoth. "You taunted me that I would never catch King Zebah and King Zalmunna, and you refused to give us food when we were tired and hungry," he said. "Well, here they are!" [16] Then he took the leaders of the city and scraped them to death[c] with thorns and briars. [17] He also went to Penuel and knocked down the city tower and killed the entire male population.

[18] Then Gideon asked King Zebah and King Zalmunna, "The men you killed at Tabor—what were they like?"

They replied, "They were dressed just like you—like sons of kings!"

[19] "They must have been my brothers!" Gideon exclaimed. "I swear that if you hadn't killed them I wouldn't kill you."

[20] Then, turning to Jether, his oldest son, he instructed him to kill them. But the boy was only a lad and was afraid to.

[21] Then Zebah and Zalmunna said to Gideon, "You do it; we'd rather be killed by a man!"[d] So Gideon killed them and took the ornaments from their camels' necks.

[22] Now the men of Israel said to Gideon, "Be our king! You and your sons and all your descendants shall be our rulers, for you have saved us from Midian."

[23,24] But Gideon replied, "I will not be your king, nor shall my son; the Lord is your King! However, I have one request. Give me all the earrings collected from your fallen foes,"—for the troops of Midian, being Ishmaelites, all wore golden earrings.

[25] "Gladly!" they replied, and spread out a sheet for everyone to throw in the gold earrings he had gathered. [26] Their value was estimated at $25,000, not including the crescents and pendants or the royal clothing of the kings, or the chains around the camels' necks. [27] Gideon made an ephod[e] from the gold and put it in Ophrah, his home town. But all Israel soon began worshiping it, so it became an evil deed that Gideon and his family did.

[28] That is the true account of how Midian was subdued by Israel. Midian never recovered, and the land was at peace for forty years—all during Gideon's lifetime. [29] He returned home, [30] and eventually had seventy sons, for he married many wives. [31] He also had a concubine in Shechem, who presented him with a son named Abimelech. [32] Gideon finally died, an old, old man, and was buried in the sepulcher of his father Joash in Ophrah, in the land of the Abiezrites.

[33] But as soon as Gideon was dead, the Israelis began to worship the idols Baal and

---

a More literally, "Are not the last grapes of Ephraim better than the entire crop of Abiezer?"
b Literally, "are Zebah and Zalmunna already in your hand . . . ?"   c Literally, "he taught the men of Succoth."   d Literally, "For as the man is, so is his strength." Perhaps the meaning is, "A quick death is less painful."   e An ephod was usually a linen pouch worn by priests on their chests. In this case the ephod evidently was highly decorated with gold, and probably, because of its weight, hung upon a wall.

Baal-berith. [34] They no longer considered the Lord as their God, though he had rescued them from all their enemies on every side. [35] Nor did they show any kindness to the family of Gideon despite all he had done for them.

9 ONE DAY GIDEON'S son Abimelech visited his uncles—his mother's brothers —in Shechem.

[2] "Go and talk to the leaders of Shechem," he requested, "and ask them whether they want to be ruled by seventy kings—Gideon's seventy sons—or by one man—meaning me, your own flesh and blood!"[a]

[3] So his uncles went to the leaders of the city and proposed Abimelech's scheme; and they decided that since his mother was a native of their town they would go along with it. [4] They gave him money from the temple offerings of the idol Baal-berith, which he used to hire some worthless loafers who agreed to do whatever he told them to. [5] He took them to his father's home at Ophrah and there, upon one stone, they slaughtered all seventy of his half-brothers, except for the youngest, Jotham, who escaped and hid. [6] Then the citizens of Shechem and Beth-millo called a meeting under the oak beside the garrison at Shechem, and Abimelech was acclaimed king of Israel.

[7] When Jotham heard about this, he stood at the top of Mount Gerizim and shouted across to the men of Shechem, "If you want God's blessing, listen to me! [8] Once upon a time the trees decided to elect a king. First they asked the olive tree, [9] but it refused.

" 'Should I quit producing the olive oil that blesses God and man, just to wave to and fro over the other trees?' it asked.

[10] "Then they said to the fig tree, 'You be our king!'

[11] "But the fig tree also refused. 'Should I quit producing sweetness and fruit just to lift my head above all the other trees?' it asked.

[12] "Then they said to the grapevine, 'You reign over us!'

[13] "But the grapevine replied, 'Shall I quit producing the wine that cheers both God and man, just to be mightier than all the other trees?'

[14] "Then all the trees finally turned to the thorn bush. 'You be our king!' they exclaimed.

[15] "And the thorn bush replied, 'If you really want me, come and humble yourselves beneath my shade! If you refuse, let fire flame forth from me and burn down the great cedars of Lebanon!'

[16] "Now make sure that you have done the right thing in making Abimelech your king, that you have done right by Gideon and all of his descendants. [17] For my father fought for you and risked his life and delivered you from the Midianites, [18] yet you have revolted against him and killed his seventy sons upon one stone. And now you have chosen his slave girl's son, Abimelech, to be your king just because he is your relative. [19] If you are sure that you have done right by Gideon and his descendants, then may you and Abimelech have a long and happy life together. [20] But if you have not been fair to Gideon, then may Abimelech destroy the citizens of Shechem and Beth-millo; and may they destroy Abimelech!"

[21] Then Jotham escaped and lived in Beer for fear of his brother Abimelech.

[22, 23] Three years later God stirred up trouble between King Abimelech and the citizens of Shechem, and they revolted. [24] In the events that followed, both Abimelech and the citizens of Shechem who aided him in butchering Gideon's seventy sons were given their just punishment for these murders. [25] For the men of Shechem set an ambush for Abimelech along the trail at the top of the mountain. (While they were waiting for him to come along, they robbed everyone else who passed that way.) But someone warned Abimelech about their plot. [26] At that time Gaal (the son of Ebed) moved to Shechem with his brothers, and he became one of the leading citizens. [27] During the harvest feast at Shechem that year, held in the temple of the local god, the wine flowed freely and everyone began curs-

a Of all of Gideon's wives, only Abimelech's mother was from Shechem (Judges 8:30–31), so Abimelech felt close kinship there.

ing Abimelech.

28 "Who is Abimelech," Gaal shouted, "and why should he be our king? Why should we be his servants? He and his friend Zebul should be *our* servants. Down with Abimelech! 29 Make me your king and you'll soon see what happens to Abimelech! I'll tell Abimelech, 'Get up an army and come on out and fight!' "

30 But when Zebul, the mayor of the city, heard what Gaal was saying, he was furious. 31 He sent messengers to Abimelech in Arumah telling him, "Gaal, son of Ebed, and his relatives have come to live in Shechem, and now they are arousing the city to rebellion against you. 32 Come by night with an army and hide out in the fields; 33 and in the morning, as soon as it is daylight, storm the city. When he and those who are with him come out against you, you can do with them as you wish!"

34 So Abimelech and his men marched through the night and split into four groups, stationing themselves around the city. 35 The next morning as Gaal sat at the city gates, discussing various issues with the local leaders, Abimelech and his men began their march upon the city.

36 When Gaal saw them, he exclaimed to Zebul, "Look over at that mountain! Doesn't it look like people coming down?"

"No!" Zebul said. "You're just seeing shadows that look like men!"

37 "No, look over there," Gaal said. "I'm sure I see people coming towards us. And look! There are others coming along the road past the oak of Meonenim!"

38 Then Zebul turned on him triumphantly. "Now where is that big mouth of yours?" he demanded. "Who was it who said, 'Who is Abimelech, and why should he be our king?' The men you taunted and cursed are right outside the city! Go on out and fight!"

39 So Gaal led the men of Shechem into the battle and fought with Abimelech, 40 but was defeated, and many of the men of Shechem were left wounded all the way to the city gate. 41 Abimelech was living at Arumah at this time, and Zebul drove Gaal and his relatives out of Shechem, and wouldn't let them live there any longer.

42 The next day the men of Shechem went out to battle again. However, someone had told Abimelech about their plans, 43 so he had divided his men into three groups hiding in the fields. And when the men of the city went out to attack, he and his men jumped up from their hiding places and began killing them. 44 Abimelech stormed the city gate to keep the men of Shechem from getting back in, while his other two groups cut them down in the fields. 45 The battle went on all day before Abimelech finally captured the city, killed its people, and leveled it to the ground. 46 The people at the nearby town of Migdal saw what was happening and took refuge in the fort next to the temple of Baal-berith.

47,48 When Abimelech learned of this, he led his forces to Mount Zalmon where he began chopping a bundle of firewood, and placed it upon his shoulder. "Do as I have done," he told his men. 49 So each of them quickly cut a bundle and carried it back to the town where, following Abimelech's example, the bundles were piled against the walls of the fort and set on fire. So all the people inside died, about a thousand men and women.

50 Abimelech next attacked the city of Thebez, and captured it. 51 However, there was a fort inside the city and the entire population fled into it, barricaded the gates, and climbed to the top of the roof to watch. 52 But as Abimelech was preparing to burn it, 53 a woman on the roof threw down a millstone. It landed on Abimelech's head, crushing his skull.

54 "Kill me!" he groaned to his youthful armor bearer. "Never let it be said that a woman killed Abimelech!"

So the young man pierced him with his sword, and he died. 55 When his men saw that he was dead, they disbanded and returned to their homes. 56,57 Thus God punished both Abimelech and the men of Shechem for their sin of murdering Gideon's seventy sons. So the curse of Jotham, Gideon's son, came true.

10 AFTER ABIMELECH'S DEATH, the next judge of Israel was Tola (son of Puah and grandson of Dodo). He was from the tribe of Issachar, but lived in the city of Shamir in the hill country of Ephraim. 2 He

was Israel's judge for twenty-three years. When he died, he was buried in Shamir, [3] and was succeeded by Jair, a man from Gilead, who judged Israel for twenty-two years. [4] His thirty sons rode around together on thirty donkeys, and they owned thirty cities in the land of Gilead which are still called "The Cities of Jair." [5] When Jair died he was buried in Kamon.

[6] Then the people of Israel turned away from the Lord again, and worshiped the heathen gods Baal and Ashtaroth, and the gods of Syria, Sidon, Moab, Ammon and Philistia. Not only this, but they no longer worshiped Jehovah at all. [7,8] This made Jehovah very angry with his people, so he immediately permitted the Philistines and the Ammonites to begin tormenting them. These attacks took place east of the Jordan River in the land of the Amorites (that is, in Gilead), [9] and also in Judah, Benjamin, and Ephraim. For the Ammonites crossed the Jordan to attack the Israelis. This went on for eighteen years. [10] Finally the Israelis turned to Jehovah again and begged him to save them.

"We have sinned against you and have forsaken you as our God and have worshiped idols," they confessed.

[11] But the Lord replied, "Didn't I save you from the Egyptians, the Amorites, the Ammonites, the Philistines, [12] the Sidonians, the Amalekites, and the Maonites? Has there ever been a time when you cried out to me that I haven't rescued you? [13] Yet you continue to abandon me and to worship other gods. So go away; I won't save you any more. [14] Go and cry to the new gods you have chosen! Let them save you in your hour of distress!"

[15] But they pleaded with him again and said, "We have sinned. Punish us in any way you think best, only save us once more from our enemies."

[16] Then they destroyed their foreign gods and worshiped only the Lord; and he was grieved by their misery. [17] The armies of Ammon were mobilized in Gilead at that time, preparing to attack Israel's army at Mizpah.

[18] "Who will lead our forces against the Ammonites?" the leaders of Gilead asked each other. "Whoever volunteers shall be our king!"

11 NOW JEPHTHAH WAS a great warrior from the land of Gilead, but his mother was a prostitute. His father (whose name was Gilead) had several other sons by his legitimate wife, and when these half brothers grew up, they chased Jephthah out of the country.

"You son of a whore!" they said. "You'll not get any of our father's estate."

[3] So Jephthah fled from his father's home and lived in the land of Tob. Soon he had quite a band of malcontents as his followers, living off the land as bandits. [4] It was about this time that the Ammonites began their war against Israel. [5] The leaders of Gilead sent for Jephthah, [6] begging him to come and lead their army against the Ammonites.

[7] But Jephthah said to them, "Why do you come to me when you hate me and have driven me out of my father's house? Why come now when you're in trouble?"

[8] "Because we need you," they replied. "If you will be our commander-in-chief against the Ammonites, we will make you the king of Gilead."

[9] "Sure!" Jephthah exclaimed. "Do you expect me to believe that?"

[10] "We swear it," they replied. "We promise with a solemn oath."

[11] So Jephthah accepted the commission and was made commander-in-chief and king. The contract was ratified before the Lord in Mizpah at a general assembly of all the people. [12] Then Jephthah sent messengers to the king of Ammon, demanding to know why Israel was being attacked. [13] The king of Ammon replied that the land belonged to the people of Ammon; it had been stolen from them, he said, when the Israelis came from Egypt; the whole territory from the Arnon River to the Jabbok and the Jordan was his, he claimed.

"Give us back our land peaceably," he demanded.

[14,15] Jephthah replied, "Israel did not steal the land. [16] What happened was this: When the people of Israel arrived at Kadesh, on their journey from Egypt after crossing the Red Sea, [17] they sent a message to the king of Edom asking permission to pass through his land. But their petition was

denied. Then they asked the king of Moab for similar permission. It was the same story there, so the people of Israel stayed in Kadesh.

¹⁸ "Finally they went around Edom and Moab through the wilderness, and traveled along the eastern border until at last they arrived beyond the boundary of Moab at the Arnon River; but they never once crossed into Moab. ¹⁹ Then Israel sent messengers to King Sihon of the Amorites, who lived in Heshbon, and asked permission to cross through his land to get to their destination. ²⁰ But King Sihon didn't trust Israel, so he mobilized an army at Jahaz and attacked them. ²¹,²² But the Lord our God helped Israel defeat King Sihon and all your people, so Israel took over all of your land from the Arnon River to the Jabbok, and from the wilderness to the Jordan River.

²³ "So you see, it was the Lord God of Israel who took away the land from the Amorites and gave it to Israel. Why, then, should we return it to you? ²⁴ You keep whatever your god Chemosh gives you, and we will keep whatever Jehovah our God gives us! ²⁵ And besides, just who do you think you are? Are you better than King Balak, the king of Moab? Did he try to recover his land after Israel defeated him? No, of course not. ²⁶ But now after three hundred years you make an issue of this! Israel has been living here for all that time, spread across the land from Heshbon to Aroer, and all along the Arnon River. Why have you made no effort to recover it before now? ²⁷ No, I have not sinned against you; rather, you have wronged me by coming to war against me; but Jehovah the Judge will soon show which of us is right—Israel or Ammon."

²⁸ But the king of Ammon paid no attention to Jephthah's message.

²⁹ At that time the Spirit of the Lord came upon Jephthah and he led his army across the land of Gilead and Manasseh, past Mizpah in Gilead, and attacked the army of Ammon. ³⁰,³¹ Meanwhile Jephthah had vowed to the Lord that if God would help Israel conquer the Ammonites, then when he returned home in peace, the first person coming out of his house to meet him would be sacrificed as a burnt offering to the Lord!

³² So Jephthah led his army against the Ammonites, and the Lord gave him the victory. ³³ He destroyed the Ammonites with a terrible slaughter all the way from Aroer to Minnith, including twenty cities, and as far away as Vineyard Meadow. Thus the Ammonites were subdued by the people of Israel.

³⁴ When Jephthah returned home his daughter—his only child—ran out to meet him, playing on a tambourine and dancing for joy. ³⁵ When he saw her he tore his clothes in anguish.

"Alas, my daughter!" he cried out. "You have brought me to the dust. For I have made a vow to the Lord and I cannot take it back."

³⁶ And she said, "Father, you must do whatever you promised the Lord, for he has given you a great victory over your enemies, the Ammonites. ³⁷ But first let me go up into the hills and roam with my girl friends for two months, weeping because I'll never marry."

³⁸ "Yes," he said. "Go."

And so she did, bewailing her fate with her friends for two months. ³⁹ Then she returned to her father, who did as he had vowed. So she was never married.ᵃ And after that it became a custom in Israel, ⁴⁰ that the young girls went away for four days each year to lament the fate of Jephthah's daughter.

12 THEN THE TRIBE of Ephraim mobilized its army at Zaphon and sent this message to Jephthah: "Why didn't you call for us to help you fight against Ammon? We are going to burn down your house, with you in it!"

² "I summoned you, but you refused to come!" Jephthah retorted. "You failed to help us in our time of need, ³ so I risked my life and went to battle without you, and the Lord helped me to conquer the enemy. Is that anything for you to fight us about?"

⁴ Then Jephthah, furious at the taunt of Ephraim that the men of Gilead were mere

---

a It is not clear whether he killed her or satisfied his vow by consecrating her to perpetual virginity.

outcasts[a] and the scum of the earth, mobilized his army and attacked the army of Ephraim. [5] He captured the fords of the Jordan behind the army of Ephraim, and whenever a fugitive from Ephraim tried to cross the river, the Gilead guards challenged him.

"Are you a member of the tribe of Ephraim?" they asked. If the man replied that he was not, [6] then they demanded, "Say 'Shibboleth.' " But if he couldn't pronounce the H and said, "Sibboleth" instead of "Shibboleth," he was dragged away and killed. So forty-two thousand people of Ephraim died there at that time.

[7] Jephthah was Israel's judge for six years. At his death he was buried in one of the cities of Gilead.

[8] The next judge was Ibzan, who lived in Bethlehem. [9,10] He had thirty sons and thirty daughters. He married his daughters to men outside his clan, and brought in thirty girls to marry his sons. He judged Israel for seven years before he died, and was buried at Bethlehem.

[11,12] The next judge was Elon from Zebulun. He judged Israel for ten years and was buried at Aijalon in Zebulun.

[13] Next was Abdon (son of Hillel) from Pirathon. [14] He had forty sons and thirty grandsons, who rode on seventy donkeys. He was Israel's judge for eight years. [15] Then he died and was buried in Pirathon, in Ephraim, in the hill country of the Amalekites.

13 ONCE AGAIN ISRAEL sinned by worshiping other gods, so the Lord let them be conquered by the Philistines, who kept them in subjection for forty years. [2,3] Then one day the Angel of the Lord appeared to the wife of Manoah, of the tribe of Dan, who lived in the city of Zorah. She had no children, but the Angel said to her, "Even though you have been barren so long, you will soon conceive and have a son! [4] Don't drink any wine or beer, and don't eat any food that isn't kosher. [5] Your son's hair must never be cut, for he shall be a Nazirite, a special servant of God from the time of his birth; and he will begin to rescue Israel from the Philistines."

[6] The woman ran and told her husband, "A man from God appeared to me and I think he must be the Angel of the Lord, for he was almost too glorious to look at. I didn't ask where he was from, and he didn't tell me his name, [7] but he told me, 'You are going to have a baby boy!' And he told me not to drink any wine or beer, and not to eat food that isn't kosher, for the baby is going to be a Nazirite—he will be dedicated to God from the moment of his birth until the day of his death!"

[8] Then Manoah prayed, "O Lord, please let the man from God come back to us again and give us more instructions about the child you are going to give us." [9] The Lord answered his prayer, and the Angel of God appeared once again to his wife as she was sitting in the field. But again she was alone—Manoah was not with her— [10] so she quickly ran and found her husband and told him, "The same man is here again!"

[11] Manoah ran back with his wife and asked, "Are you the man who talked to my wife the other day?"

"Yes," he replied, "I am."

[12] So Manoah asked him, "Can you give us any special instructions about how we should raise the baby after he is born?"

[13,14] And the Angel replied, "Be sure that your wife follows the instructions I gave her. She must not eat grapes or raisins, or drink any wine or beer, or eat anything that isn't kosher."

[15] Then Manoah said to the Angel, "Please stay here until we can get you something to eat."

[16] "I'll stay," the Angel replied, "but I'll not eat anything. However, if you wish to bring something, bring an offering to sacrifice to the Lord." (Manoah didn't yet realize that he was the Angel of the Lord.)

[17] Then Manoah asked him for his name. "When all this comes true and the baby is born," he said to the Angel, "we will certainly want to tell everyone that you predicted it!"

[18] "Don't even ask my name," the Angel replied, "for it is a secret."

[19] Then Manoah took a young goat and

---

a Literally, "fugitives of Ephraim . . ."

a grain offering and offered it as a sacrifice to the Lord; and the Angel did a strange and wonderful thing, [20] for as the flames from the altar were leaping up toward the sky, and as Manoah and his wife watched, the Angel ascended in the fire! Manoah and his wife fell face downward to the ground, [21] and that was the last they ever saw of him. It was then that Manoah finally realized that it had been the Angel of the Lord.

[22] "We will die," Manoah cried out to his wife, "for we have seen God!"

[23] But his wife said, "If the Lord were going to kill us he wouldn't have accepted our burnt offerings and wouldn't have appeared to us and told us this wonderful thing and done these miracles."

[24] When her son was born they named him Samson, and the Lord blessed him as he grew up. [25] And the Spirit of the Lord began to excite him whenever he visited the parade grounds of the army of the tribe of Dan, located between the cities of Zorah and Eshta-ol.

14 ONE DAY WHEN Samson was in Timnah, he noticed a certain Philistine girl, [2] and when he got home he told his father and mother that he wanted to marry her. [3] They objected strenuously.

"Why don't you marry a Jewish girl?" they asked. "Why must you go and get a wife from these heathen Philistines? Isn't there one girl among all the people of Israel you could marry?"

But Samson told his father, "She is the one I want. Get her for me."

[4] His father and mother didn't realize that the Lord was behind the request, for God was setting a trap for the Philistines, who at that time were the rulers of Israel.

[5] As Samson and his parents were going to Timnah, a young lion attacked Samson in the vineyards on the outskirts of the town. [6] At that moment the Spirit of the Lord came mightily upon him and since he had no weapon, he ripped the lion's jaws apart, and did it as easily as though it were a young goat! But he didn't tell his father or mother about it. [7] Upon arriving at Timnah he talked with the girl and found her

to be just what he wanted, so the arrangements were made.[a]

[8] When he returned for the wedding, he turned off the path to look at the carcass of the lion. And he found a swarm of bees in it, and some honey! [9] He took some of the honey with him, eating as he went, and gave some of it to his father and mother. But he didn't tell them where he had gotten it.

[10,11] As his father was making final arrangements for the marriage, Samson threw a party for thirty young men of the village, as was the custom of the day. [12] When Samson asked if they would like to hear a riddle, they replied that they would.

"If you solve my riddle during these seven days of the celebration," he said, "I'll give you thirty plain robes and thirty fancy robes. [13] But if you can't solve it, then you must give the robes to me!"

"All right," they agreed, "let's hear it."

[14] This was his riddle: "Food came out of the eater, and sweetness from the strong!" Three days later they were still trying to figure it out.

[15] On the fourth day they said to his new wife, "Get the answer from your husband, or we'll burn down your father's house with you in it. Were we invited to this party just to make us poor?"

[16] So Samson's wife broke down in tears before him and said, "You don't love me at all; you hate me, for you have told a riddle to my people and haven't told me the answer!"

"I haven't even told it to my father or mother; why should I tell you?" he replied.

[17] So she cried whenever she was with him and kept it up for the remainder of the celebration. At last, on the seventh day, he told her the answer and she, of course, gave the answer to the young men. [18] So before sunset of the seventh day they gave him their reply.

"What is sweeter than honey?" they asked, "and what is stronger than a lion?"

"If you hadn't plowed with my heifer, you wouldn't have found the answer to my riddle!" he retorted.

[19] Then the Spirit of the Lord came upon him and he went to the city of Ashkelon,

---

a Implied.

killed thirty men, took their clothing, and gave it to the young men who had told him the answer to his riddle. But he was furious about it and abandoned his wife and went back home to live with his father and mother. ²⁰ So his wife was married instead to the fellow who had been best man at Samson's wedding.

15 LATER ON, DURING the wheat harvest, Samson took a young goat as a present to his wife, intending to sleep with her; but her father wouldn't let him in.

² "I really thought you hated her," he explained, "so I married her to your best man. But look, her sister is prettier than she is. Marry her instead."

³ Samson was furious. "You can't blame me for whatever happens now," he shouted.

⁴ So he went out and caught three hundred foxes and tied their tails together in pairs, with a torch between each pair. ⁵ Then he lit the torches and let the foxes run through the fields of the Philistines, burning the grain to the ground along with all the sheaves and shocks of grain, and destroying the olive trees.

⁶ "Who did this?" the Philistines demanded.

"Samson," was the reply, "because his wife's father gave her to another man." So the Philistines came and got the girl and her father and burned them alive.

⁷ "Now my vengeance will strike again!" Samson vowed. ⁸ So he attacked them with great fury and killed many of them. Then he went to live in a cave in the rock of Etam. ⁹ The Philistines in turn sent a huge posse into Judah and raided Lehi.

¹⁰ "Why have you come here?" the men of Judah asked.

And the Philistines replied, "To capture Samson and do to him as he has done to us."

¹¹ So three thousand men of Judah went down to get Samson at the cave in the rock of Etam.

"What are you doing to us?" they demanded of him. "Don't you realize that the Philistines are our rulers?"

But Samson replied, "I only paid them back for what they did to me."

¹²·¹³ "We have come to capture you and take you to the Philistines," the men of Judah told him.

"All right," Samson said, "but promise me that you won't kill me yourselves."

"No," they replied, "we won't do that."

So they tied him with two new ropes and led him away. ¹⁴ As Samson and his captors arrived at Lehi, the Philistines shouted with glee; but then the strength of the Lord came upon Samson, and the ropes with which he was tied snapped like thread and fell from his wrists! ¹⁵ Then he picked up a donkey's jawbone that was lying on the ground and killed a thousand Philistines with it. ¹⁶·¹⁷ Tossing away the jawbone, he remarked,

> "Heaps upon heaps,
> All with a donkey's jaw!
> I've killed a thousand men,
> All with a donkey's jaw!"

(The place has been called "Jawbone Hill" ever since.)

¹⁸ But now he was very thirsty and he prayed to the Lord and said, "You have given Israel such a wonderful deliverance through me today! Must I now die of thirst, and fall to the mercy of these heathen?" ¹⁹ So the Lord caused water to gush out from a hollow in the ground and Samson's spirit was revived as he drank. Then he named the place "The Spring of the Man Who Prayed," and the spring is still there today.

²⁰ Samson was Israel's judge for the next twenty years, but the Philistines still controlled the land.

16 ONE DAY SAMSON went to the Philistine city of Gaza and spent the night with a prostitute. ² Word soon spread that he had been seen in the city, so the police were alerted and many men of the city lay in wait all night at the city gate to capture him if he tried to leave.

"In the morning," they thought, "when there is enough light, we'll find him and kill him."

³ Samson stayed in bed with the girl until midnight, then went out to the city gates and lifted them, with the two gateposts, right out of the ground. He put them on his shoulders and carried them to the top of the mountain across from Hebron!

⁴ Later on he fell in love with a girl

named Delilah over in the valley of Sorek.
[5] The five heads of the Philistine nation went personally to her and demanded that she find out from Samson what made him so strong, so that they would know how to overpower and subdue him and put him in chains.

"Each of us will give you a thousand dollars for this job," they promised.

[6] So Delilah begged Samson to tell her his secret. *"Please* tell me, Samson, why you are so strong," she pleaded. "I don't think anyone could ever capture you!"

[7] "Well," Samson replied, "if I were tied with seven raw-leather bowstrings, I would become as weak as anyone else."

[8] So they brought her the seven bowstrings, and while he slept[a] she tied him with them. [9] Some men were hiding in the next room, so as soon as she had tied him up she exclaimed,

"Samson! The Philistines are here!"

Then he snapped the bowstrings like cotton thread,[b] and so his secret was not discovered.

[10] Afterward Delilah said to him, "You are making fun of me! You told me a lie! *Please* tell me how you can be captured!"

[11] "Well," he said, "if I am tied with brand new ropes which have never been used, I will be as weak as other men."

[12] So that time, as he slept,[c] Delilah took new ropes and tied him with them. The men were hiding in the next room, as before. Again Delilah exclaimed,

"Samson! The Philistines have come to capture you!"

But he broke the ropes from his arms like spiderwebs!

[13] "You have mocked me again, and told me more lies!" Delilah complained. "Now tell me how you can *really* be captured."

"Well," he said, "if you weave my hair into your loom . . . !"

[14] So while he slept, she did just that and then screamed, "The Philistines have come, Samson!" And he woke up and yanked his hair away, breaking the loom.

[15] "How can you say you love me when you don't confide in me?" she whined.

"You've made fun of me three times now, and you still haven't told me what makes you so strong!"

[16,17] She nagged at him every day until he couldn't stand it any longer and finally told her his secret.

"My hair has never been cut," he confessed, "for I've been a Nazirite to God since before my birth. If my hair were cut, my strength would leave me, and I would become as weak as anyone else."

[18] Delilah realized that he had finally told her the truth, so she sent for the five Philistine leaders.

"Come just this once more," she said, "for this time he has told me everything."

So they brought the money with them. [19] She lulled him to sleep with his head in her lap, and they brought in a barber and cut off his hair. Delilah began to hit him, but she could see that his strength was leaving him.

[20] Then she screamed, "The Philistines are here to capture you, Samson!" And he woke up and thought, "I will do as before; I'll just shake myself free." But he didn't realize that the Lord had left him. [21] So the Philistines captured him and gouged out his eyes and took him to Gaza, where he was bound with bronze chains and made to grind grain in the prison. [22] But before long his hair began to grow again.

[23,24] The Philistine leaders declared a great festival to celebrate the capture of Samson. The people made sacrifices to their god Dagon and excitedly praised him.

"Our god has delivered our enemy Samson to us!" they gloated as they saw him there in chains. "The scourge of our nation who killed so many of us is now in our power!" [25,26] Half drunk by now, the people demanded, "Bring out Samson so we can have some fun with him!"

So he was brought from the prison and made to stand at the center of the temple, between the two pillars supporting the roof. Samson said to the boy who was leading him by the hand, "Place my hands against the two pillars. I want to rest against them."

[27] By then the temple was completely

---

a Implied in verse 14.   b Literally, "like a string of tow snaps when it touches the fire."
c Implied.

filled with people. The five Philistine leaders were there as well as three thousand people in the balconies[d] who were watching Samson and making fun of him.

[28] Then Samson prayed to the Lord and said, "O Lord Jehovah, remember me again—please strengthen me one more time, so that I may pay back the Philistines for the loss of at least one of my eyes."

[29] Then Samson pushed against the pillars with all his might.

[30] "Let me die with the Philistines," he prayed.

And the temple crashed down upon the Philistine leaders and all the people. So those he killed at the moment of his death were more than those he had killed during his entire lifetime. [31] Later, his brothers and other relatives came down to get his body, and they brought him back home and buried him between Zorah and Eshta-ol, where his father, Manoah, was buried. He had judged Israel for twenty years.

17 IN THE HILL country of Ephraim lived a man named Micah.

[2] One day he said to his mother, "That thousand dollars you thought was stolen from you, and you were cursing about—well, I stole it!"

"God bless you for confessing it," his mother replied. [3] So he returned the money to her.

"I am going to give it to the Lord as a credit for your account," she declared. "I'll have an idol carved for you and plate it with the silver."

[4,5] So his mother took a fifth of it to a silversmith, and the idol he made from it was placed in Micah's shrine. Micah had many idols in his collection, also an ephod and some teraphim, and he installed one of his sons as the priest. [6] (For in those days Israel had no king, so everyone did whatever he wanted to—whatever seemed right in his own eyes.)

[7,8] One day a young priest[a] from the town of Bethlehem, in Judah, arrived in that area of Ephraim, looking for a good place to live. He happened to stop at Micah's house as he was traveling through.

[9] "Where are you from?" Micah asked him.

And he replied, "I am a priest[a] from Bethlehem, in Judah, and I am looking for a place to live."

[10,11] "Well, stay here with me," Micah said, "and you can be my priest. I will give you ten dollars a year plus a new suit and your board and room." The young man agreed to this, and became as one of Micah's sons. [12] So Micah consecrated him as his personal priest.

[13] "I know the Lord will really bless me now," Micah exclaimed, "because now I have a genuine priest working for me!"[b]

18 AS HAS ALREADY been stated, there was no king in Israel at that time. The tribe of Dan was trying to find a place to settle, for they had not yet driven out the people living in the land assigned to them. [2] So the men of Dan chose five army heroes from the cities of Zorah and Eshta-ol as scouts to go and spy out the land they were supposed to settle in. Arriving in hill country of Ephraim, they stayed at Micah's home. [3] Noticing the young Levite's accent, they took him aside and asked him, "What are you doing here? Why did you come?" [4] He told them about his contract with Micah, and that he was his personal priest.

[5] "Well, then," they said, "ask God whether or not our trip will be successful."

[6] "Yes," the priest replied, "all is well. The Lord is taking care of you."

[7] So the five men went on to the town of Laish, and noticed how secure everyone felt. Their manner of life was Phoenician, and they were wealthy. They lived quietly, and were unprepared for an attack, for there were no tribes in the area strong enough to try it. They lived a great distance from their relatives in Sidon, and had little or no contact with the nearby villages. [8] So the spies returned to their people in Zorah and Eshta-ol.

"What about it?" they were asked. "What did you find?"

[9,10] And the men replied, "Let's attack! We have seen the land and it is ours for the taking—a broad, fertile, wonderful

---

d Literally, "on the roof."   17a Literally, "a Levite."   b Literally, "a Levite as a priest."

place—a real paradise. The people aren't even prepared to defend themselves! Come on, let's go! For God has given it to us!"

¹¹ So six hundred armed troops of the tribe of Dan set out from Zorah and Eshtaol. ¹² They camped first at a place west of Kiriath-jearim in Judah (which is still called "The Camp of Dan"), ¹³ then they went on up into the hill country of Ephraim.

As they passed the home of Micah, ¹⁴ the five spies told the others. "There is a shrine in there with an ephod, some teraphim, and many plated idols. It's obvious what we ought to do!"

¹⁵·¹⁶ So the five men went over to the house and with all of the armed men standing just outside the gate, they talked to the young priest, and asked him how he was getting along. ¹⁷ Then the five spies entered the shrine and took the idols, the ephod, and the teraphim.

¹⁸ "What are you doing?" the young priest demanded when he saw them carrying them out.

¹⁹ "Be quiet and come with us," they said. "Be a priest to all of us. Isn't it better for you to be a priest to a whole tribe in Israel instead of just to one man in his private home?"

²⁰ The young priest was then quite happy to go with them, and he took along the ephod, the teraphim, and the idols. ²¹ They started on their way again, placing their children, cattle, and household goods at the front of the column. ²² When they were quite a distance from Micah's home, Micah and some of his neighbors came chasing after them, ²³ yelling at them to stop.

"What do you want, chasing after us like this?" the men of Dan demanded.

²⁴ "What do you mean, 'What do I want'!" Micah retorted. "You've taken away all my gods and my priest, and I have nothing left!"

²⁵ "Be careful how you talk, mister," the men of Dan replied. "Somebody's apt to get angry and kill every one of you."

²⁶ So the men of Dan kept going. When Micah saw that there were too many of them for him to handle, he turned back home.

²⁷ Then, with Micah's idols and the priest, the men of Dan arrived at the city of Laish. There weren't even any guards, so they went in and slaughtered all the people and burned the city to the ground. ²⁸ There was no one to help the inhabitants, for they were too far away from Sidon, and they had no local allies, for they had no dealings with anyone. This happened in the valley next to Beth-rehob. Then the people of the tribe of Dan rebuilt the city and lived there. ²⁹ The city was named "Dan" after their ancestor, Israel's son, but it had originally been called Laish.

³⁰ Then they set up the idols and appointed a man named Jonathan (son of Gershom and grandson of Moses!) and his sons as their priests. This family continued as priests until the city was finally conquered by its enemies. ³¹ So Micah's idols were worshiped by the tribe of Dan as long as the Tabernacle remained at Shiloh.

19 AT THIS TIME before Israel had a king, there was a man of the tribe of Levi living on the far side of the hill country of Ephraim, who brought home a girl from Bethlehem in Judah to be his concubine. ² But she became angry with him and ran away, and returned to her father's home in Bethlehem, and was there about four months. ³ Then her husband, taking along a servant and an extra donkey, went to see her to try to win her back again. When he arrived at her home, she let him in and introduced him to her father, who was delighted to meet him. ⁴ Her father urged him to stay awhile, so he stayed three days, and they all had a very pleasant time.

⁵ On the fourth day they were up early, ready to leave, but the girl's father insisted on their having breakfast first. ⁶ Then he pleaded with him to stay one more day, as they were having such a good time. ⁷ At first the man refused, but his father-in-law kept urging him until finally he gave in. ⁸ The next morning they were up early again, and again the girl's father pleaded, "Stay just today and leave sometime this evening." So they had another day of feasting.

⁹ That afternoon as he and his wife and servant were preparing to leave, his father-in-law said, "Look, it's getting late. Stay just tonight, and we will have a pleasant evening together and tomorrow you can get

up early and be on your way."

¹⁰ But this time the man was adamant, so they left, getting as far as Jerusalem (also called Jebus) before dark.

¹¹ His servant said to him, "It's getting too late to travel; let's stay here tonight."

¹².¹³ "No," his master said, "we can't stay in this heathen city where there are no Israelites—we will go on to Gibe-ah, or possibly Ramah."

¹⁴ So they went on. The sun was setting just as they came to Gibe-ah, a village of the tribe of Benjamin, ¹⁵ so they went there for the night. But as no one invited them in, they camped in the village square. ¹⁶ Just then an old man came by on his way home from his work in the fields. (He was originally from the hill country of Ephraim, but was living now in Gibe-ah, even though it was in the territory of Benjamin.) ¹⁷ When he saw the travelers camped in the square, he asked them where they were from, and where they were going.

¹⁸ "We're on the way home from Bethlehem, in Judah," the man replied. "I live on the far edge of the Ephraim hill country, near Shiloh. But no one has taken us in for the night, ¹⁹ even though we have fodder for our donkeys, and plenty of food and wine for ourselves."

²⁰ "Don't worry," the old man said, "be my guests; for you mustn't stay here in the square. It's too dangerous."

²¹ So he took them home with him. He fed their donkeys while they rested, and afterward they had supper together. ²² Just as they were beginning to warm to the occasion, a gang of sex perverts gathered around the house and began beating at the door and yelling at the old man to bring out the man who was staying with him, so they could rape him. ²³ The old man stepped outside to talk to them.

"No, my brothers, don't do such a dastardly act," he begged, "for he is my guest. ²⁴ Here, take my virgin daughter and this man's wife. I'll bring them out and you can do whatever you like to them—but don't do such a thing to this man."

²⁵ But they wouldn't listen to him. Then the girl's husband pushed her out to them, and they abused her all night, taking turns raping her until morning. Finally, just at dawn, they let her go. ²⁶ She fell down at the door of the house and lay there until it was light. ²⁷ When her husband opened the door to be on his way, he found her there, fallen down in front of the door with her hands digging into the threshold.

²⁸ "Well, come on," he said. "Let's get going."

But there was no answer, for she was dead; so he threw her across the donkey's back and took her home. ²⁹ When he got there he took a knife and cut her body into twelve parts and sent one piece to each tribe of Israel. ³⁰ Then the entire nation was roused to action against the men of Benjamin because of this awful deed.

"There hasn't been such a horrible crime since Israel left Egypt," everyone said. "We've got to do something about it."

20 THEN THE ENTIRE nation of Israel sent their leaders and 450,000 troops to assemble with one mind before the Lord at Mizpah. They came from as far away as Dan and Beersheba, and everywhere between, and from across the Jordan in the land of Gilead. ³ (Word of the mobilization of the Israeli forces at Mizpah soon reached the land of Benjamin.) The chiefs of Israel now called for the murdered woman's husband and asked him just what had happened.

⁴ "We arrived one evening at Gibe-ah, a village in Benjamin," he began. ⁵ "That night the men of Gibe-ah surrounded the house, planning to kill me, and they raped my wife until she was dead. ⁶ So I cut her body into twelve pieces and sent the pieces throughout the land of Israel, for these men have committed a terrible crime. ⁷ Now then, sons of Israel, express your mind and give me your counsel!"

⁸.⁹.¹⁰ And as one man they replied, "Not one of us will return home until we have punished the village of Gibe-ah. A tenth of the army will be selected by lot as a supply line to bring us food, and the rest of us will destroy Gibe-ah for this horrible deed."

¹¹ So the whole nation united in this task.

¹² Then messengers were sent to the tribe of Benjamin, asking, "Did you know about the terrible thing that was done among you? ¹³ Give up these evil men from the city of

Gibe-ah so that we can execute them and purge Israel of her evil." But the people of Benjamin wouldn't listen. [14.15] Instead, twenty-six thousand of them arrived in Gibe-ah to join the seven hundred local men in their defense against the rest of Israel. [16] (Among all these there were seven hundred men who were left-handed sharp-shooters. They could hit a target within a hair's breadth, never missing!) [17] The army of Israel, not counting the men of Benjamin, numbered 400,000 men.

[18] Before the battle the Israeli army went to Bethel first to ask counsel from God. "Which tribe shall lead us against the people of Benjamin?" they asked.

And the Lord replied, "Judah shall go first."

[19.20] So the entire army left early the next morning to go to Gibe-ah, to attack the men of Benjamin. [21] But the men defending the village stormed out and killed twenty-two thousand Israelis that day. [22.23.24] Then the Israeli army wept before the Lord until evening and asked him, "Shall we fight further against our brother Benjamin?"

And the Lord said, "Yes." So the men of Israel took courage and went out again the next day to fight at the same place. [25] And that day they lost another eighteen thousand men, all experienced swordsmen.

[26] Then the entire army went up to Bethel and wept before the Lord and fasted until evening, offering burnt sacrifices and peace offerings. [27.28] (The Ark of God was in Bethel in those days. Phinehas, the son of Eleazar and grandson of Aaron, was the priest.)

The men of Israel asked the Lord, "Shall we go out again and fight against our brother Benjamin, or shall we stop?"

And the Lord said, "Go, for tomorrow I will see to it that you defeat the men of Benjamin."

[29] So the Israeli army set an ambush all around the village, [30] and went out again on the third day and set themselves in their usual battle formation. [31] When the army of Benjamin came out of the town to attack, the Israeli forces retreated and Benjamin was drawn away from the town as they chased after Israel. And as they had done previously, Benjamin began to kill the men

of Israel along the roadway running between Bethel and Gibe-ah, so that about thirty of them died.

[32] Then the army of Benjamin shouted, "We're defeating them again!" But the armies of Israel had agreed in advance to run away so that the army of Benjamin would chase them and be drawn away from the town. [33] But when the main army of Israel reached Baal-tamar, it turned and attacked, and the ten thousand men in ambush west of Geba jumped up from where they were, [34] and advanced against the rear of the army of Benjamin, who still didn't realize the impending disaster. [35-39] So the Lord helped Israel defeat Benjamin, and the Israeli army killed 25,100 men of Benjamin that day, leaving but a tiny remnant of their forces.

Summary of the Battle:

The army of Israel retreated from the men of Benjamin in order to give the ambush more room for maneuvering. When the men of Benjamin had killed about thirty of the Israelis, they were confident of a massive slaughter just as on the previous days. But then the men in ambush rushed into the village and slaughtered everyone in it, and set it on fire. The great cloud of smoke pouring into the sky was the signal for the Israeli army to turn around and attack the army of Benjamin, [40.41] who now looked behind them and were terrified to discover that their city was on fire, and that they were in serious trouble. [42] So they ran toward the wilderness, but the Israelis chased after them, and the men who had set the ambush came out and joined the slaughter from the rear. [43] They encircled the army of Benjamin east of Gibe-ah, and killed most of them there. [44] Eighteen thousand of the Benjamin troops died in that day's battle. [45] The rest of the army fled into the wilderness toward the rock of Rimmon, but five thousand were killed along the way, and two thousand more near Gidom.

[46.47] So the tribe of Benjamin lost twenty-five thousand brave warriors that day, leaving only six hundred men who escaped to the rock of Rimmon, where they lived for four months. [48] Then the Israeli army returned and slaughtered the entire population of the tribe of Benjamin—men, women, children, and cattle—and burned down every city and village in the entire land.

21 THE LEADERS OF Israel had vowed at Mizpah never to let their daughters marry a man from the tribe of Benjamin. [2] And now the Israeli leaders met at Bethel and sat before God until evening, weeping bitterly.

[3] "O Lord God of Israel," they cried out, "why has this happened, that now one of our tribes is missing?"

[4] The next morning they were up early and built an altar, and offered sacrifices and peace offerings on it. [5] And they said among themselves, "Was any tribe of Israel not represented when we held our council before the Lord at Mizpah?" For at that time it was agreed by solemn oath that anyone who refused to come must die. [6] There was deep sadness throughout all Israel for the loss of their brother tribe, Benjamin.

"Gone," they kept saying to themselves, "gone—an entire tribe of Israel has been cut off, and is gone. [7] And how shall we get wives for the few who remain, since we have sworn by the Lord that we will not give them our daughters?"

[8.9] Then they thought again of their oath to kill anyone who refused to come to Mizpah, and discovered that no one had attended from Jabesh-gilead. [10.11.12] So they sent twelve thousand of their best soldiers to destroy the people of Jabesh-gilead. All the men, married women, and children were slain, but the young virgins of marriageable age were saved. There were four hundred of these, and they were brought to the camp at Shiloh.

[13] Then Israel sent a peace delegation to the little remnant of the men of Benjamin at Rimmon Rock. [14] The four hundred girls were given to them as wives, and they returned to their homes; but there were not enough of these girls for all of them. [15] (What a sad time it was in Israel in those days, because the Lord had made a breach in the tribes of Israel.)

[16] "What shall we do for wives for the others, since all the women of the tribe of Benjamin are dead?" the leaders of Israel asked. [17] "There must be some way to get wives for them, so that an entire tribe of Israel will not be lost forever. [18] But we can't give them our own daughters. We have sworn with a solemn oath that anyone who does this shall be cursed of God."

[19] Suddenly someone thought of the annual religious festival held in the fields of Shiloh, between Lebonah and Bethel, along the east side of the road that goes from Bethel to Shechem.

[20] They told the men of Benjamin who still needed wives, "Go and hide in the vineyards, [21] and when the girls of Shiloh come out for their dances, rush out and catch them and take them home with you to be your wives! [22] And when their fathers and brothers come to us in protest, we will tell them, 'Please be understanding and let them have your daughters, for we didn't find enough wives for them when we destroyed Jabesh-gilead, and you couldn't have given your daughters to them without being guilty.' "

[23] So the men of Benjamin did as they were told and kidnapped the girls who took part in the celebration, and carried them off to their own land. Then they rebuilt their cities and lived in them. [24] So the people of Israel returned to their homes.

[25] (There was no king in Israel in those days, and every man did whatever he thought was right.)

What Next?

Sue may look like any other Midwestern college student—no one would guess that she has already fought off three attacks of arthritis. Arthritis? The crippling disease that usually swells the joints of only the elderly hit her first as a 15-year-old sophomore in high school. After Sue spent weeks in bed, the pain left, only to return the next year, and the next.

Since then, she's been fine, although doctors won't guarantee the future. She, like Ruth in the following short book, goes on living a normal life, trusting God and hoping that suffering will not come again.

In Ruth's case, it didn't—the pain of losing her first husband and leaving her country was pushed far into the past as a whole new life developed for her in Bethlehem. This amazing story of God's guidance through circumstances says a lot to people like Sue and the rest of us who wonder about our future.

RUTH

1 LONG AGO WHEN judges ruled in Israel, a man named Elimelech, from Bethlehem,[a] left the country because of a famine and moved to the land of Moab. With him were his wife, Naomi, and his two sons, Mahlon and Chilion. [3] During the time of their residence there, Elimelech died and Naomi was left with her two sons.

[4,5] These young men, Mahlon and Chilion, married girls of Moab, Orpah and Ruth. But later, both men died, so that Naomi was left alone, without her husband or sons. [6,7] She decided to return to Israel with her daughters-in-law, for she had heard that the Lord had blessed his people by giving them good crops again.

[8] But after they had begun their homeward journey, she changed her mind and said to her two daughters-in-law, "Why don't you return to your parents' homes instead of coming with me? And may the Lord reward you for your faithfulness to your husbands and to me. [9] And may he bless you with another happy marriage." Then she kissed them and they all broke down and cried.

[10] "No," they said. "We want to go with you to your people."

[11] But Naomi replied, "It is better for you to return to your own people. Do I have younger sons who could grow up to be your husbands?[b] [12] No, my daughters, return to your parents' homes, for I am too old to have a husband. And even if that were possible, and I became pregnant tonight, and bore sons, [13] would you wait for them to grow up? No, of course not, my daughters; oh, how I grieve for you that the Lord has punished me in a way that injures you."

[14] And again they cried together, and Orpah kissed her mother-in-law good-bye, and returned to her childhood home; but Ruth insisted on staying with Naomi.

[15] "See," Naomi said to her, "your sister-in-law has gone back to her people and to her gods; you should do the same."

[16] But Ruth replied, "Don't make me leave you, for I want to go wherever you go, and to live wherever you live; your people shall be my people, and your God shall be my God; [17] I want to die where you die, and be buried there. May the Lord do terrible things to me if I allow anything but death to separate us."

[18] And when Naomi saw that Ruth had made up her mind and could not be persuaded otherwise, she stopped urging her. [19] So they both came to Bethlehem and the entire village was stirred by their arrival.

"Is it really Naomi?" the women asked.

[20] But she told them, "Don't call me Naomi. Call me Mara," (Naomi means "pleasant"; Mara means "bitter") "for Almighty God has dealt me bitter blows. [21] I went out full and the Lord has brought me home empty; why should you call me Naomi when the Lord has turned his back on me and sent such calamity!"

[22] (Their return from Moab and arrival in Bethlehem was at the beginning of the barley harvest.)

2 NOW NAOMI HAD an in-law there in Bethlehem who was a very wealthy man. His name was Boaz.

[2] One day Ruth said to Naomi, "Perhaps I can go out into the fields of some kind man to glean the free grain[a] behind his reapers."

And Naomi said, "All right, dear daughter. Go ahead."

[3] So she did. And as it happened, the field where she found herself belonged to Boaz, this relative of Naomi's husband.

[4,5] Boaz arrived from the city while she was there. After exchanging greetings with the reapers he said to his foreman, "Hey, who's that girl over there?"

[6] And the foreman replied, "It's that girl from the land of Moab who came back with Naomi. [7] She asked me this morning if she could pick up the grains dropped by the reapers, and she has been at it ever since except for a few minutes' rest over there in the shade."

---

a Literally, "They were Ephrathites from Bethlehem in Judah." b This refers to the custom of the day. Parents kept a widowed daughter-in-law in the family by marrying her off to a younger brother of her former husband. See Deuteronomy 25:5–10. 2a See Leviticus 19:9 and Deuteronomy 24:19.

8,9 Boaz went over and talked to her. "Listen, my child," he said to her. "Stay right here with us to glean; don't think of going to any other fields. Stay right behind my women workers; I have warned the young men not to bother you; when you are thirsty, go and help yourself to the water."

10,11 She thanked him warmly. "How can you be so kind to me?" she asked. "You must know I am only a foreigner."

"Yes, I know," Boaz replied, "and I also know about all the love and kindness you have shown your mother-in-law since the death of your husband, and how you left your father and mother in your own land and have come here to live among strangers. 12 May the Lord God of Israel, under whose wings you have come to take refuge, bless you for it."

13 "Oh, thank you, sir," she replied. "You are so good to me, and I'm not even one of your workers!"

14 At lunch time Boaz called to her, "Come and eat with us."

So she sat with his reapers and he gave her food,b more than she could eat. 15 And when she went back to work again, Boaz told his young men to let her glean right among the sheaves without stopping her, 16 and to snap off some heads of barley and drop them on purpose for her to glean, and not to make any remarks. 17 So she worked there all day, and in the evening when she had beaten out the barley she had gleaned, it came to a whole bushel! 18 She carried it back into the city and gave it to her mother-in-law, with what was left of her lunch.

19 "So much!" Naomi exclaimed. "Where in the world did you glean today? Praise the Lord for whoever was so kind to you." So Ruth told her mother-in-law all about it, and mentioned that the owner of the field was Boaz.

20 "Praise the Lord for a man like that! God has continued his kindness to us as well as to your dead husband!" Naomi cried excitedly. "Why, that man is one of our closest relatives!"c

21 "Well," Ruth told her, "he said to come back and stay close behind his reapers until the entire field is harvested."

22 "This is wonderful!" Naomi exclaimed. "Do as he has said. Stay with his girls right through the whole harvest; you will be safer there than in any other field!"

23 So Ruth did, and gleaned with them until the end of the barley harvest, and then the wheat harvest, too.

3 ONE DAY NAOMI said to Ruth, "My dear, isn't it time that I try to find a husband for you, and get you happily married again? 2 The man I'm thinking of is Boaz! He has been so kind to us, and is a close relative. I happen to know that he will be winnowing barley tonight out on the threshing-floor. 3 Now do what I tell you— bathe and put on some perfume and some nice clothes and go on down to the threshing-floor, but don't let him see you until he has finished his supper. 4 Notice where he lies down to sleep; then go and lift the cover off his feet and lie down there, and he will tell you what to do concerning marriage."

5 And Ruth replied, "All right. I'll do whatever you say."

6,7 So she went down to the threshing-floor that night and followed her mother-in-law's instructions. After Boaz had finished a good meal, he lay down very contentedly beside a heap of grain and went to sleep. Then Ruth came quietly and lifted the covering off his feet and lay there. 8 Suddenly, around midnight, he wakened and sat up, startled. There was a woman lying at his feet!

9 "Who are you?" he demanded.

"It's I, sir—Ruth," she replied. "Make me your wife according to God's law, for you are my close relative."

10 "Thank God for a girl like you!" he exclaimed. "For you are being even kinder to Naomi now than before. Naturally you'd prefer a younger man, even though poor. But you have put aside your personal desires [so that you can give Naomi an heir by marrying mea]. 11 Now don't worry about a thing, my child; I'll handle all the details, for everyone knows what a wonderful person you are. 12 But there is one prob-

---

b Literally, "ate the parched grain and dipped her morsels of food in the wine." c Literally, "a near relative, one of our redeemers." 3a Implied.

lem. It's true that I am a close relative, but there is someone else who is more closely related to you than I am. [13] Stay here tonight, and in the morning I'll talk to him, and if he will marry you, fine; let him do his duty; but if he won't, then I will, I swear by Jehovah; lie down until the morning."

[14] So she lay at his feet until the morning and was up early, before daybreak, for he had said to her, "Don't let it be known that a woman was here at the threshing-floor."

[15-18] "Bring your shawl," he told her. Then he tied up a bushel and a half of barley in it as a present for her mother-in-law, and laid it on her back. Then she returned to the city.

"Well, what happened, dear?" Naomi asked her when she arrived home. She told Naomi everything and gave her the barley from Boaz, and mentioned his remark that she mustn't go home without a present.

Then Naomi said to her, "Just be patient until we hear what happens, for Boaz won't rest until he has followed through on this. He'll settle it today."

4 SO BOAZ WENT down to the market place[a] and found the relative he had mentioned.

"Say, come over here," he called to him. "I want to talk to you a minute."

So they sat down together. [2] Then Boaz called for ten of the chief men of the village, and asked them to sit as witnesses.

[3] Boaz said to his relative, "You know Naomi, who came back to us from Moab. She is selling our brother Elimelech's property. [4] I felt that I should speak to you about it so that you can buy it if you wish, with these respected men as witnesses. If you want it,[b] let me know right away, for if you don't take it, I will. You have the first right to purchase it and I am next."

The man replied, "All right, I'll buy it."

[5] Then Boaz told him, "Your purchase of the land from Naomi requires your marriage to Ruth so that she can have children to carry on her husband's name, and to inherit the land."

[6] "Then I can't do it," the man replied.

"For her son would become an heir to my property, too;[c] you buy it."

[7] In those days it was the custom in Israel for a man transferring a right of purchase to pull off his sandal and hand it to the other party; this publicly validated the transaction. [8] So, as the man said to Boaz, "You buy it for yourself," he drew off his sandal.

[9] Then Boaz said to the witnesses and to the crowd standing around, "You have seen that today I have bought all the property of Elimelech, Chilion, and Mahlon, from Naomi, [10] and that with it I have purchased Ruth the Moabitess, the widow of Mahlon, to be my wife, so that she can have a son to carry on the family name of her dead husband."

[11] And all the people standing there, and the witnesses replied, "We are witnesses. May the Lord make this woman, who has now come into your home, as fertile as Rachel and Leah, from whom all the nation of Israel descended! May you be a great and successful man in Bethlehem, [12] and may the descendants the Lord will give you from this young woman be as numerous and honorable as those of our ancestor Perez, the son of Tamar and Judah."

[13] So Boaz married Ruth, and when he slept with her, the Lord gave her a son.

[14] And the women of the city said to Naomi, "Bless the Lord who has given you this little grandson; may he be famous in Israel. [15] May he restore your youth and take care of you in your old age; for he is the son of your daughter-in-law who loves you so much, and who has been kinder to you than seven sons!"

[16,17] Naomi took care of the baby, and the neighbor women said, "Now at last Naomi has a son again!"

And they named him Obed. He was the father of Jesse and grandfather of King David.

[18-22] This is the family tree of Boaz, beginning with his ancestor Perez:

Perez, Hezron, Ram, Amminadab, Nashon, Salmon, Boaz, Obed, Jesse, David.

---

a Literally, "the gate" of the city, where legal affairs were usually transacted.　　b Literally, "if you want to redeem it."　　c Or, "that would ruin my own inheritance," i.e., complicate his estate for the children he already had.

Young Men on the Move

Run all the way across America? That's right. Tony and Joel Ahlstrom were the first U.S. amateurs to do it. They had two messages to spread—a warning against pollution, and the story of their personal faith in Christ.

Running in the cool hours of the morning, they covered 30 miles a day. The rest of the day they held news conferences, talked with local officials, and spoke to crowds about their faith. It took all summer, and they had to survive 115° heat, snakes sunning on desert roads and angry motorists. But, 2,950

miles later, they splashed in the Atlantic Ocean.

And people listened to them. The same way people listened to the young men who stepped out and changed Israel's future: Samuel ("the Lord was with him and people listened carefully to his advice," 3:19); Saul ("he stood head and shoulders above anyone else," 10:23—and then he blew it); David (he "continued to succeed in everything he undertook," 18:14). At the end of the 100-plus years covered in these two books, Israel had never been stronger.

Who says one person—or two or more—can't make a difference?

1 SAMUEL

1 THIS IS THE story of Elkanah, a man of the tribe of Ephraim who lived in Ramathaim-zophim, in the hills of Ephraim. His father's name was Jeroham,
His grandfather was Elihu,
His great-grandfather was Tohu,
His great-great-grandfather was Zuph.

² He had two wives, Hannah and Peninnah. Peninnah had some children, but Hannah didn't.

³ Each year Elkanah and his families journeyed to the Tabernacle at Shiloh to worship the Lord of the heavens and to sacrifice to him. (The priests on duty at that time were the two sons of Eli—Hophni and Phinehas.) ⁴ On the day he presented his sacrifice, Elkanah would celebrate the happy occasion by giving presents to Peninnah and her children; ⁵ but although he loved Hannah very much, he could give her only one present, for the Lord had sealed her womb; so she had no children to give presents to. ⁶ Peninnah made matters worse by taunting Hannah because of her barrenness. ⁷ Every year it was the same—Peninnah scoffing and laughing at her as they went to Shiloh, making her cry so much she couldn't eat.

⁸ "What's the matter, Hannah?" Elkanah would exclaim. "Why aren't you eating? Why make such a fuss over having no children? Isn't having me better than having ten sons?"

⁹ One evening after supper, when they were at Shiloh, Hannah went over to the Tabernacle. Eli the priest was sitting at his customary place beside the entrance. ¹⁰ She was in deep anguish and was crying bitterly as she prayed to the Lord.

¹¹ And she made this vow: "O Lord of heaven, if you will look down upon my sorrow and answer my prayer and give me a son, then I will give him back to you, and he'll be yours for his entire lifetime, and his hair shall never be cut."ᵃ

¹²,¹³ Eli noticed her mouth moving as she was praying silently and, hearing no sound, thought she had been drinking.

¹⁴ "Must you come here drunk?" he demanded. "Throw away your bottle."

¹⁵,¹⁶ "Oh, no, sir!" she replied, "I'm not drunk! But I am very sad and I was pouring out my heart to the Lord. Please don't think that I am just some drunken bum!"

¹⁷ "In that case," Eli said, "cheer up! May the Lord of Israel grant you your petition, whatever it is!"

¹⁸ "Oh, thank you, sir!" she exclaimed, and went happily back, and began to take her meals again.

¹⁹,²⁰ The entire family was up early the next morning and went to the Tabernacle to worship the Lord once more. Then they returned home to Ramah, and when Elkanah slept with Hannah, the Lord remembered her petition; in the process of time, a baby boy was born to her. She named him Samuel (meaningᵇ "asked of God") because, as she said, "I asked the Lord for him."

²¹,²² The next year Elkanah and Peninnah and her children went on the annual trip to the Tabernacle without Hannah, for she told her husband, "Wait until the baby is weaned, and then I will take him to the Tabernacle and leave him there."

²³ "Well, whatever you think best," Elkanah agreed. "May the Lord's will be done."

So she stayed home until the baby was weaned. ²⁴ Then, though he was still so small, they took him to the Tabernacle in Shiloh, along with a three-year-old bull for the sacrifice, and a bushel of flour and some wine. ²⁵ After the sacrifice they took the child to Eli.

²⁶ "Sir, do you remember me?" Hannah asked him. "I am the woman who stood here that time praying to the Lord! ²⁷ I asked him to give me this child, and he has given me my request; ²⁸ and now I am giving him to the Lord for as long as he lives." So she left him there at the Tabernacle for the

---

a This was an approved custom for those who were wholly dedicated to God. The word Samuel in Hebrew sounds like the word "to ask." b This was a play on words.

Lord to use.

2 THIS WAS HANNAH'S prayer:
"How I rejoice in the Lord!
How he has blessed me!
Now I have an answer for my ene-
mies,
For the Lord has solved my problem.
How I rejoice!
[2] No one is as holy as the Lord!
There is no other God,
Nor any Rock like our God.
[3] Quit acting so proud and arrogant!
The Lord knows what you have
done,
And he will judge your deeds.
[4] Those who were mighty are mighty
no more!
Those who were weak are now
strong.
[5] Those who were well are now starv-
ing;
Those who were starving are fed.
The barren woman now has seven
children;
She with many children has no more!
[6] The Lord kills,
The Lord gives life.
[7] Some he causes to be poor
And others to be rich.
He cuts one down
And lifts another up.
[8] He lifts the poor from the dust—
Yes, from a pile of ashes—
And treats them as princes
Sitting in the seats of honor.
For all the earth is the Lord's
And he has set the world in order.
[9] He will protect his godly ones,
But the wicked shall be silenced in
darkness.
No one shall succeed by strength
alone.
[10] Those who fight against the Lord
shall be broken;
He thunders against them from
heaven.
He judges throughout the earth.
He gives mighty strength to his King,
And gives great glory to his anointed
one."

[11] So they returned home to Ramah without Samuel; and the child became the Lord's helper, for he assisted Eli the priest.

[12] Now the sons of Eli were evil men who didn't love the Lord. [13,14] It was their regular practice to send out a servant whenever anyone was offering a sacrifice, and while the flesh of the sacrificed animal was boiling, the servant would put a three-pronged fleshhook into the pot and demand that whatever it brought up be given to Eli's sons. They treated all of the Israelites in this way when they came to Shiloh to worship. [15] Sometimes the servant would come even before the rite of burning the fat on the altar had been performed, and he would demand raw meat before it was boiled, so that it could be used for roasting.

[16] If the man offering the sacrifice replied, "Take as much as you want, but the fat must first be burned," [as the law requires[a]], then the servant would say,

"No, give it to me now or I'll take it by force."

[17] So the sin of these young men was very great in the eyes of the Lord; for they treated the people's offerings to the Lord with contempt.

[18] Samuel, though only a child, was the Lord's helper and wore a little linen robe just like the priest's.[b] [19] Each year his mother made a little coat for him and brought it to him when she came with her husband for the sacrifice. [20] Before they returned home Eli would bless Elkanah and Hannah and ask God to give them other children to take the place of this one they had given to the Lord. [21] And the Lord gave Hannah three sons and two daughters. Meanwhile Samuel grew up in the service of the Lord.

[22] Eli was now very old, but he was aware of what was going on around him. He knew, for instance, that his sons were seducing the young women who assisted at the entrance to the Tabernacle.

[23,24,25] "I have been hearing terrible reports from the Lord's people about what you are doing," Eli told his sons. "It is an awful thing to make the Lord's people sin. Ordinary sin receives heavy punishment,

---

a Implied.   b Literally, "wore a linen ephod."

but how much more this sin of yours which has been committed against the Lord?" But they wouldn't listen to their father, for the Lord was already planning to kill them.

²⁶ Little Samuel was growing in two ways—he was getting taller, and he was becoming everyone's favorite (and he was a favorite of the Lord's, too!).

²⁷ One day a prophet^c came to Eli and gave him this message from the Lord: "Didn't I demonstrate my power when the people of Israel were slaves in Egypt? ²⁸ Didn't I choose your ancestor Levi from among all his brothers to be my priest, and to sacrifice upon my altar, and to burn incense, and to wear a priestly robe^d as he served me? And didn't I assign the sacrificial offerings to you priests? ²⁹ Then why are you so greedy for all the other offerings which are brought to me? Why have you honored your sons more than me—for you and they have become fat from the best of the offerings of my people!

³⁰ "Therefore, I, the Lord God of Israel, declare that although I promised that your branch of the tribe of Levi could always be my priests, it is ridiculous to think that what you are doing can continue. I will honor only those who honor me, and I will despise those who despise me. ³¹ I will put an end to your family, so that it will no longer serve as priests. Every member will die before his time. None shall live to be old. ³² You will envy the prosperity I will give my people, but you and your family will be in distress and need. Not one of them will live out his days. ³³ Those who are left alive will live in sadness and grief; and their children shall die by the sword. ³⁴ And to prove that what I have said will come true, I will cause your two sons, Hophni and Phinehas, to die on the same day!

³⁵ "Then I will raise up a faithful priest who will serve me and do whatever I tell him to do. I will bless his descendants, and his family shall be priests to my kings forever. ³⁶ Then all of your descendants shall bow before him, begging for money and food. 'Please,' they will say, 'give me a job among the priests so that I will have enough to eat.' "

3 MEANWHILE LITTLE SAMUEL was helping the Lord by assisting Eli. Messages from the Lord were very rare in those days, ²,³ but one night after Eli had gone to bed (he was almost blind with age by now), and Samuel was sleeping in the Temple near the Ark, ⁴,⁵ the Lord called out, "Samuel! Samuel!"

"Yes?" Samuel replied. "What is it?" He jumped up and ran to Eli. "Here I am. What do you want?" he asked.

"I didn't call you," Eli said. "Go on back to bed." So he did. ⁶ Then the Lord called again, "Samuel!" And again Samuel jumped up and ran to Eli.

"Yes?" he asked. "What do you need?"

"No, I didn't call you, my son," Eli said. "Go on back to bed."

⁷ (Samuel had never had a message from Jehovah before.^a) ⁸ So now the Lord called the third time, and once more Samuel jumped up and ran to Eli.

"Yes?" he asked. "What do you need?"

Then Eli realized it was the Lord who had spoken to the child. ⁹ So he said to Samuel, "Go and lie down again, and if he calls again, say, 'Yes, Lord, I'm listening.' " So Samuel went back to bed.

¹⁰ And the Lord came and called as before, "Samuel! Samuel!"

And Samuel replied, "Yes, I'm listening."

¹¹ Then the Lord said to Samuel, "I am going to do a shocking thing in Israel. ¹² I am going to do all of the dreadful things I warned Eli about. ¹³ I have continually threatened him and his entire family with punishment because his sons are blaspheming God, and he doesn't stop them. ¹⁴ So I have vowed that the sins of Eli and of his sons shall never be forgiven by sacrifices and offerings."

¹⁵ Samuel stayed in bed until morning, then opened the doors of the Temple as usual, for he was afraid to tell Eli what the Lord had said to him. ¹⁶,¹⁷ But Eli called him.

"My son," he said, "what did the Lord say to you? Tell me everything. And may God punish you if you hide anything from me!"

---

c Literally, "man of God."   d Literally, "wear an ephod."   3a Literally, "did not yet know Jehovah."

¹⁸ So Samuel told him what the Lord had said.

"It is the Lord's will," Eli replied; "let him do what he thinks best."

¹⁹ As Samuel grew, the Lord was with him and people listened carefully to his advice. ²⁰ And all Israel from Dan to Beersheba knew that Samuel was going to be a prophet of the Lord. ²¹,⁴:¹ Then the Lord began to give messages to him there at the Tabernacle in Shiloh, and he passed them on to the people of Israel.

4 AT THAT TIME Israel was at war with the Philistines. The Israeli army was camped near Ebenezer, the Philistines at Aphek. ² And the Philistines defeated Israel, killing four thousand of them. ³ After the battle was over, the army of Israel returned to their camp and their leaders discussed why the Lord had let them be defeated.

"Let's bring the Ark here from Shiloh," they said. "If we carry it into battle with us, the Lord will be among us and he will surely save us from our enemies."

⁴ So they sent for the Ark of the Lord of heaven who is enthroned above the angels. Hophni and Phinehas, the sons of Eli, accompanied it into the battle. ⁵ When the Israelis saw the Ark coming, their shout of joy was so loud that it almost made the ground shake!

⁶ "What's going on?" the Philistines asked. "What's all the shouting about over in the camp of the Hebrews?"

When they were told it was because the Ark of the Lord had arrived, ⁷ they panicked.

"God has come into their camp!" they cried out. "Woe upon us, for we have never had to face anything like this before! ⁸ Who can save us from these mighty gods of Israel? They are the same gods who destroyed the Egyptians with plagues when Israel was in the wilderness. ⁹ Fight as you never have before, O Philistines, or we will become their slaves just as they have been ours."

¹⁰ So the Philistines fought desperately and Israel was defeated again. Thirty thousand men of Israel died that day and the remainder fled to their tents. ¹¹ And the Ark of God was captured and Hophni and Phinehas were killed.

¹² A man from the tribe of Benjamin ran from the battle and arrived at Shiloh the same day with his clothes torn and dirt on his head.ᵃ ¹³ Eli was waiting beside the road to hear the news of the battle, for his heart trembled for the safety of the Ark of God. As the messenger from the battlefront arrived and told what had happened, a great cry arose throughout the city.

¹⁴ "What is all the noise about?" Eli asked. And the messenger rushed over to Eli and told him what had happened. ¹⁵ (Eli was ninety-eight years old and was blind.)

¹⁶ "I have just come from the battle—I was there today," he told Eli, ¹⁷ "and Israel has been defeated and thousands of the Israeli troops are dead on the battlefield. Hophni and Phinehas were killed too, and the Ark has been captured."

¹⁸ When the messenger mentioned what had happened to the Ark, Eli fell backward from his seat beside the gate and his neck was broken by the fall and he died (for he was old and fat). He had judged Israel for forty years.

¹⁹ When Eli's daughter-in-law, Phinehas's wife, who was pregnant, heard that the Ark had been captured and that her husband and father-in-law were dead, her labor pains suddenly began. ²⁰ Just before she died, the women who were attending her told her that everything was all right and that the baby was a boy. But she did not reply or respond in any way. ²¹,²² Then she murmured, "Name the child 'Ichabod,' for Israel's glory is gone." (Ichabod means "there is no glory." She named him this because the Ark of God had been captured and because her husband and her father-in-law were dead.)

5 THE PHILISTINES TOOK the captured Ark of God from the battleground at Ebenezer to the temple of their idol Dagon in the city of Ashdod. ³ But when the local citizens went to see it the next morning, Dagon had fallen with his face to the ground before the Ark of Jehovah! They set

---

a This was a common expression of grief in that day.

him up again, ⁴ but the next morning the same thing had happened—the idol had fallen face down before the Ark of the Lord again. This time his head and hands had been cut off and were lying in the doorway; only the trunk of his body was left intact. ⁵ (That is why to this day neither the priests of Dagon nor his worshipers will walk on the threshold of the temple of Dagon in Ashdod.)

⁶ Then the Lord began to destroy the people of Ashdod and the nearby villages with a plague of boils. ⁷ When the people realized what was happening, they exclaimed, "We can't keep the Ark of the God of Israel here any longer. We will all perish along with our god Dagon."

⁸ So they called a conference of the mayors of the five cities of the Philistines to decide how to dispose of the Ark. The decision was to take it to Gath. ⁹ But when the Ark arrived at Gath, the Lord began destroying its people, young and old, with the plague, and there was a great panic. ¹⁰ So they sent the Ark to Ekron, but when the people of Ekron saw it coming they cried out, "They are bringing the Ark of the God of Israel here to kill us too!"

¹¹ So they summoned the mayors again and begged them to send the Ark back to its own country, lest the entire city die. For the plague had already begun and great fear was sweeping across the city. ¹² Those who didn't die were deathly ill; and there was weeping everywhere.

6 THE ARK REMAINED in the Philistine country for seven months in all. ² Then the Philistines called for their priests and diviners and asked them, "What shall we do about the Ark of God? What sort of gift shall we send with it when we return it to its own land?"

³ "Yes, send it back with a gift," they were told. "Send a guilt offering so that the plague will stop. Then, if it doesn't, you will know God didn't send the plague upon you after all."

⁴,⁵ "What guilt offering shall we send?" they asked.

And they were told, "Send five gold models of the tumor caused by the plague, and five gold models of the rats that have ravaged the whole land—the capital cities and villages alike. If you send these gifts and then praise the God of Israel, perhaps he will stop persecuting you and your god. ⁶ Don't be stubborn and rebellious as Pharaoh and the Egyptians were. They wouldn't let Israel go until God had destroyed them with dreadful plagues. ⁷ Now build a new cart and hitch to it two cows that have just had calves—cows that never before have been yoked—and shut their calves away from them in the barn. ⁸ Place the Ark of God on the cart beside a chest containing the gold models of the rats and tumors, and let the cows go wherever they want to. ⁹ If they cross the border of our land and go into Beth-shemesh, then you will know that it was God who brought this great evil upon us; if they don't, [but return to their calves,ᵃ] then we will know that the plague was simply a coincidence and was not sent by God at all."

¹⁰ So these instructions were carried out. Two fresh cows were hitched to the cart and their calves were shut up in the barn. ¹¹ Then the Ark of the Lord and the chest containing the gold rats and tumors were placed upon the cart. ¹² And sure enough, the cows went straight along the road toward Beth-shemesh, lowing as they went; and the Philistine mayors followed them as far as the border of Beth-shemesh. ¹³ The people of Beth-shemesh were reaping wheat in the valley, and when they saw the Ark they went wild with joy!

¹⁴ The cart came into the field of a man named Joshua and stopped beside a large rock. So the people broke up the wood of the cart for a fire and killed the cows and sacrificed them to the Lord as a burnt offering. ¹⁵ Several men of the tribe of Levi lifted the Ark and the chest containing the golden rats and tumors from the cart and laid them on the rock. And many burnt offerings and sacrifices were offered to the Lord that day by the men of Beth-shemesh.

¹⁶ After the five Philistine mayors had watched for awhile, they returned to Ekron that same day. ¹⁷ The five gold models of

---

a Implied.

tumors which had been sent by the Philistines as a guilt offering to the Lord were gifts from the mayors of the capital cities, Ashdod, Gaza, Ashkelon, Gath, and Ekron. [18] The gold rats were to placate God for the other Philistine cities, both the fortified cities and the country villages controlled by the five capitals. (By the way, that large rock at Beth-shemesh can still be seen in the field of Joshua.) [19] But the Lord killed seventy of the men of Beth-shemesh because they looked into the Ark. And the people mourned because of the many people whom the Lord had killed.

[20] "Who is able to stand before Jehovah, this holy God?" they cried out. "Where can we send the Ark from here?"

[21] So they sent messengers to the people at Kiriath-jearim and told them that the Philistines had brought back the Ark of the Lord.

"Come and get it!" they begged.

7 SO THE MEN of Kiriath-jearim came and took the Ark to the hillside home of Abinadab; and installed his son Eleazar to be in charge of it. [2] The Ark remained there for twenty years, and during that time all Israel was in sorrow because the Lord had seemingly abandoned them.

[3] At that time Samuel said to them, "If you are really serious about wanting to return to the Lord, get rid of your foreign gods and your Ashtaroth idols. Determine to obey only the Lord; then he will rescue you from the Philistines."

[4] So they destroyed their idols of Baal and Ashtaroth and worshiped only the Lord.

[5] Then Samuel told them, "Come to Mizpah, all of you, and I will pray to the Lord for you."

[6] So they gathered there and, in a great ceremony, drew water from the well and poured it out before the Lord. They also went without food all day as a sign of sorrow for their sins. So it was at Mizpah that Samuel became Israel's judge.

[7] When the Philistine leaders heard about the great crowds at Mizpah, they mobilized their army and advanced. The Israelis were badly frightened when they learned that the Philistines were approaching.

[8] "Plead with God to save us!" they begged Samuel.

[9] So Samuel took a suckling lamb and offered it to the Lord as a whole burnt offering and pleaded with him to help Israel. And the Lord responded. [10] Just as Samuel was sacrificing the burnt offering, the Philistines arrived for battle, but the Lord spoke with a mighty voice of thunder from heaven, and they were thrown into confusion, and the Israelis routed them, [11] and chased them from Mizpah to Beth-car, killing them all along the way. [12] Samuel then took a stone and placed it between Mizpah and Jeshanah and named it Ebenezer (meaning, "the Stone of Help"), for he said, "The Lord has certainly helped us!" [13] So the Philistines were subdued and didn't invade Israel again at that time, because the Lord was against them throughout the remainder of Samuel's lifetime. [14] The Israeli cities between Ekron and Gath, which had been conquered by the Philistines, were now returned to Israel, for the Israeli army rescued them from their Philistine captors. And there was peace between Israel and the Amorites in those days.

[15] Samuel continued as Israel's judge for the remainder of his life. [16] He rode circuit annually, setting up his court first at Bethel, then Gilgal, and then Mizpah, and cases of dispute were brought to him in each of those three cities from all the surrounding territory. [17] Then he would come back to Ramah, for his home was there, and he would hear cases there, too. And he built an altar to the Lord at Ramah.

8 IN HIS OLD age, Samuel retired and appointed his sons as judges in his place. [2] Joel and Abijah, his oldest sons, held court in Beer-sheba; [3] but they were not like their father, for they were greedy for money. They accepted bribes and were very corrupt in the administration of justice. [4] Finally the leaders of Israel met in Ramah to discuss the matter with Samuel. [5] They told him that since his retirement things hadn't been the same, for his sons were not good men.

"Give us a king like all the other nations have," they pleaded.

[6] Samuel was terribly upset and went to

the Lord for advice.

⁷ "Do as they say," the Lord replied, "for I am the one they are rejecting, not you—they don't want me to be their king any longer. ⁸ Ever since I brought them from Egypt they have continually forsaken me and followed other gods. And now they are giving you the same treatment. ⁹ Do as they ask, but warn them about what it will be like to have a king!"

¹⁰ So Samuel told the people what the Lord had said:

¹¹ "If you insist on having a king, he will conscript your sons and make them run before his chariots; ¹² some will be made to lead his troops into battle, while others will be slave laborers; they will be forced to plow in the royal fields, and harvest his crops without pay; and make his weapons and chariot equipment. ¹³ He will take your daughters from you and force them to cook and bake and make perfumes for him. ¹⁴ He will take away the best of your fields and vineyards and olive groves and give them to his friends. ¹⁵ He will take a tenth of your harvest and distribute it to his favorites. ¹⁶ He will demand your slaves and the finest of your youth and will use your animals for his personal gain. ¹⁷ He will demand a tenth of your flocks, and you shall be his slaves. ¹⁸ You will shed bitter tears because of this king you are demanding, but the Lord will not help you."

¹⁹ But the people refused to listen to Samuel's warning.

"Even so, we still want a king," they said, ²⁰ "for we want to be like the nations around us. He will govern us and lead us to battle."

²¹ So Samuel told the Lord what the people had said, ²² and the Lord replied again, "Then do as they say and give them a king."

So Samuel agreed and sent the men home again.

9 KISH WAS A rich, influential man from the tribe of Benjamin. He was the son of Abiel, grandson of Zeror, great-grandson of Becorath, and great-great-grandson of Aphiah. ² His son Saul was the most handsome man in Israel. And he was head and shoulders taller than anyone else in the land!

³ One day Kish's donkeys strayed away, so he sent Saul and a servant to look for them. ⁴ They traveled all through the hill country of Ephraim, the land of Shalisha, the Shaalim area, and the entire land of Benjamin, but couldn't find them anywhere. ⁵ Finally, after searching in the land of Zuph, Saul said to the servant, "Let's go home; by now my father will be more worried about us than about the donkeys!"

⁶ But the servant said, "I've just thought of something! There is a prophet who lives here in this city; he is held in high honor by all the people because everything he says comes true; let's go and find him and perhaps he can tell us where the donkeys are."

⁷ "But we don't have anything to pay him with," Saul replied. "Even our food is gone and we don't have a thing to give him."

⁸ "Well," the servant said, "I have a dollar! We can at least offer it to him and see what happens!"

⁹,¹⁰,¹¹ "All right," Saul agreed, "let's try it!"

So they started into the city where the prophet lived. As they were climbing a hill toward the city, they saw some young girls going out to draw water and asked them if they knew whether the seer was in town. (In those days prophets were called seers. "Let's go and ask the seer," people would say, rather than, "Let's go and ask the prophet," as we would say now.)

¹²,¹³ "Yes," they replied, "stay right on this road. He lives just inside the city gates. He has just arrived back from a trip to take part in a public sacrifice up on the hill. So hurry, because he'll probably be leaving about the time you get there; the guests can't eat until he arrives and blesses the food."

¹⁴ So they went into the city, and as they were entering the gates they saw Samuel coming out toward them to go up the hill. ¹⁵ The Lord had told Samuel the previous day,

¹⁶ "About this time tomorrow I will send you a man from the land of Benjamin. You are to anoint him as the leader of my people. He will save them from the Philistines, for I have looked down on them in mercy and have heard their cry."

¹⁷ When Samuel saw Saul the Lord said, "That's the man I told you about! He will rule my people."

¹⁸ Just then Saul approached Samuel and asked, "Can you please tell me where the seer's house is?"

¹⁹ "I am the seer!" Samuel replied. "Go on up the hill ahead of me and we'll eat together; in the morning I will tell you what you want to know and send you on your way. ²⁰ And don't worry about those donkeys that were lost three days ago, for they have been found. And anyway, you own all the wealth of Israel now!"

²¹ "Pardon me, sir," Saul replied. "I'm from the tribe of Benjamin, the smallest in Israel, and my family is the least important of all the families of the tribe! You must have the wrong man!"

²² Then Samuel took Saul and his servant into the great hall and placed them at the head of the table, honoring them above the thirty special guests. ²³ Samuel then instructed the chef to bring Saul the choicest cut of meat, the piece that had been set aside for the guest of honor. ²⁴ So the chef brought it in and placed it before Saul.

"Go ahead and eat it," Samuel said, "for I was saving it for you, even before I invited these others!"

So Saul ate with Samuel. ²⁵ After the feast, when they had returned to the city, Samuel took Saul up to the porch on the roof and talked with him there. ²⁶,²⁷ At daybreak the next morning, Samuel called up to him, "Get up; it's time you were on your way!"

So Saul got up and Samuel accompanied him to the edge of the city. When they reached the city walls Samuel told Saul to send the servant on ahead. Then he told him, "I have received a special message for you from the Lord."

10 THEN SAMUEL TOOK a flask of olive oil and poured it over Saul's head and kissed him on the cheek and said,

"I am doing this because the Lord has appointed you to be the king of his people, Israel! ² When you leave me, you will see two men beside Rachel's tomb at Zelzah, in the land of Benjamin; they will tell you that the donkeys have been found and that your father is worried about you and is asking, 'How am I to find my son?' ³ And when you get to the oak of Tabor you will see three men coming toward you who are on their way to worship God at the altar at Bethel; one will be carrying three young goats, another will have three loaves of bread, and the third will have a bottle of wine. ⁴ They will greet you and offer you two of the loaves, which you are to accept. ⁵ After that you will come to Gibeath-elohim, also known as "God's Hill," where the garrison of the Philistines is. As you arrive there you will meet a band of prophets coming down the hill playing a psaltery, a timbrel, a flute, and a harp, and prophesying as they come.

⁶ "At that time the Spirit of the Lord will come mightily upon you, and you will prophesy with them and you will feel and act like a different person. ⁷ From that time on your decisions should be based on whatever seems best under the circumstances, for the Lord will guide you. ⁸ Go to Gilgal and wait there seven days for me, for I will be coming to sacrifice burnt offerings and peace offerings. I will give you further instructions when I arrive."

⁹ As Saul said good-bye and started to go, God gave him a new attitude, and all of Samuel's prophecies came true that day. ¹⁰ When Saul and the servant arrived at the Hill of God they saw the prophets coming toward them, and the Spirit of God came upon him, and he too began to prophesy. ¹¹ When his friends heard about it, they exclaimed, "What? Saul a prophet?" ¹² And one of the neighbors added, "With a father like his?" So that is the origin of the proverb, "Is Saul a prophet, too?"ᵃ

¹³ When Saul had finished prophesying he climbed the hill to the altar.

¹⁴ "Where in the world did you go?" Saul's uncle asked him.

And Saul replied, "We went to look for the donkeys, but we couldn't find them; so we went to the prophet Samuel to ask him where they were."

---

a This was an expression of surprise concerning worldly Saul becoming religious, equivalent to our "He got religion."

¹⁵ "Oh? And what did he say?" his uncle asked.

¹⁶ "He said the donkeys had been found!" Saul replied. (But he didn't tell him that he had been anointed as king!)

¹⁷ Samuel now called a convocation of all Israel at Mizpah, ¹⁸,¹⁹ and gave them this message from the Lord God: "I brought you from Egypt and rescued you from the Egyptians and from all of the nations that were torturing you. But although I have done so much for you, you have rejected me and have said, 'We want a king instead!' All right, then, present yourselves before the Lord by tribes and clans."

²⁰ So Samuel called the tribal leaders together before the Lord, and the tribe of Benjamin was chosen by sacred lot. ²¹ Then he brought each family of the tribe of Benjamin before the Lord, and the family of the Matrites was chosen. And finally, the sacred lot selected Saul, the son of Kish. But when they looked for him, he had disappeared!

²² So they asked the Lord, "Where is he? Is he here among us?"

And the Lord replied, "He is hiding in the baggage."

²³ So they found him and brought him out, and he stood head and shoulders above anyone else.

²⁴ Then Samuel said to all the people, "This is the man the Lord has chosen as your king. There isn't his equal in all of Israel!"

And all the people shouted, "Long live the king!"

²⁵ Then Samuel told the people again what the rights and duties of a king were; he wrote them in a book and put it in a special place before the Lord. Then Samuel sent the people home again.

²⁶ When Saul returned to his home at Gibe-ah, a band of men whose hearts the Lord had touched became his constant companions. ²⁷ There were, however, some bums and loafers who exclaimed, "How can this man save us?" And they despised him and refused to bring him presents, but he took no notice.

11 AT THIS TIME Nahash led the army of the Ammonites against the Israeli city of Jabesh-gilead. But the citizens of Jabesh asked for peace. "Leave us alone and we will be your servants," they pleaded.

² "All right," Nahash said, "but only on one condition: I will gouge out the right eye of every one of you as a disgrace upon all Israel!"

³ "Give us seven days to see if we can get some help!" replied the elders of Jabesh. "If none of our brothers will come and save us, we will agree to your terms."

⁴ When a messenger came to Gibe-ah, Saul's home town, and told the people about their plight, everyone broke into tears.

⁵ Saul was plowing in the field, and when he returned to town he asked, "What's the matter? Why is everyone crying?"

So they told him about the message from Jabesh. ⁶ Then the Spirit of God came strongly upon Saul and he became very angry. ⁷ He took two oxen and cut them into pieces and sent messengers to carry them throughout all Israel.

"This is what will happen to the oxen of anyone who refuses to follow Saul and Samuel to battle!" he announced. And God caused the people to be afraid of Saul's anger, and they came to him as one man. ⁸ He counted them in Bezek and found that there were three hundred thousand of them in addition to thirty thousand from Judah.

⁹ So he sent the messengers back to Jabesh-gilead to say, "We will rescue you before tomorrow noon!" What joy there was throughout the city when that message arrived!

¹⁰ The men of Jabesh then told their enemies, "We surrender. Tomorrow we will come out to you and you can do to us as you wish."

¹¹ But early the next morning Saul arrived, having divided his army into three detachments, and launched a surprise attack against the Ammonites and slaughtered them all morning. The remnant of their army was so badly scattered that no two of them were left together.

¹² Then the people exclaimed to Samuel, "Where are those men who said that Saul shouldn't be our king? Bring them here and we will kill them!"

¹³ But Saul replied, "No one will be executed today; for today the Lord has

rescued Israel!"

¹⁴ Then Samuel said to the people, "Come, let us all go to Gilgal and reconfirm Saul as our king."

¹⁵ So they went to Gilgal and in a solemn ceremony before the Lord they crowned him king. Then they offered peace offerings to the Lord, and Saul and all Israel were very happy.

12 THEN SAMUEL ADDRESSED the people again:

"Look," he said, "I have done as you asked. I have given you a king. ² I have selected him ahead of my own sons and now I stand here, an old, grey-haired man who has been in public service from the time he was a lad. ³ Now tell me as I stand before the Lord and before his anointed king— whose ox or donkey have I stolen? Have I ever defrauded you? Have I ever oppressed you? Have I ever taken a bribe? Tell me and I will make right whatever I have done wrong."

⁴ "No," they replied, "you have never defrauded or oppressed us in any way and you have never taken even one single bribe."

⁵ "The Lord and his anointed king are my witnesses," Samuel declared, "that you can never accuse me of robbing you."

"Yes, it is true," they replied.

⁶ "It was the Lord who appointed Moses and Aaron," Samuel continued. "He brought your ancestors out of the land of Egypt.

⁷ "Now stand here quietly before the Lord as I remind you of all the good things he has done for you and for your ancestors:

⁸ "When the Israelites were in Egypt and cried out to the Lord, he sent Moses and Aaron to bring them into this land. ⁹ But they soon forgot about the Lord their God, so he let them be conquered by Sisera, the general of King Hazor's army, and by the Philistines and the king of Moab.

¹⁰ "Then they cried to the Lord again and confessed that they had sinned by turning away from him and worshiping the Baal and Ashtaroth idols. And they pleaded, 'We will worship you and you alone if you will only rescue us from our enemies.' ¹¹ Then the Lord sent Gideon, Barak, Jephthah,

and Samuel to save you, and you lived in safety.

¹² "But when you were afraid of Nahash, the king of Ammon, you came to me and said that you wanted a king to reign over you. But the Lord your God was already your King, for he has always been your King. ¹³ All right, here is the king you have chosen. Look him over. You have asked for him, and the Lord has answered your request.

¹⁴ "Now if you will fear and worship the Lord and listen to his commandments and not rebel against the Lord, and if both you and your king follow the Lord your God, then all will be well. ¹⁵ But if you rebel against the Lord's commandments and refuse to listen to him, then his hand will be as heavy upon you as it was upon your ancestors.

¹⁶ "Now watch as the Lord does great miracles. ¹⁷ You know that it does not rain at this time of the year, during the wheat harvest; I will pray for the Lord to send thunder and rain today, so that you will realize the extent of your wickedness in asking for a king!"

¹⁸ So Samuel called to the Lord, and the Lord sent thunder and rain; and all the people were very much afraid of the Lord and of Samuel.

¹⁹ "Pray for us lest we die!" they cried out to Samuel. "For now we have added to all our other sins by asking for a king."

²⁰ "Don't be frightened," Samuel reassured them. "You have certainly done wrong, but make sure now that you worship the Lord with true enthusiasm, and that you don't turn your back on him in any way. ²¹ Other gods can't help you. ²² The Lord will not abandon his chosen people, for that would dishonor his great name. He made you a special nation for himself—just because he wanted to!

²³ "As for me, far be it from me that I should sin against the Lord by ending my prayers for you; and I will continue to teach you those things which are good and right.

²⁴ "Trust the Lord and sincerely worship him; think of all the tremendous things he has done for you. ²⁵ But if you continue to sin, you and your king will be destroyed."

13 BY THIS TIME Saul had reigned for one year.[a] In the second year of his reign, [2] he selected three thousand special troops and took two thousand of them with him to Michmash and Mount Bethel while the other thousand remained with Jonathan, Saul's son, in Gibe-ah in the land of Benjamin. The rest of the army was sent home. [3,4] Then Jonathan attacked and destroyed the garrison of the Philistines at Geba. The news spread quickly throughout the land of the Philistines, and Saul sounded the call to arms throughout Israel. He announced that he had destroyed the Philistine garrison and warned his troops that they stank to high heaven as far as the Philistines were concerned. So the entire Israeli army mobilized again and joined at Gilgal. [5] The Philistines recruited a mighty army of three thousand chariots, six thousand horsemen, and so many soldiers that they were as thick as sand along the seashore; and they camped at Michmash east of Beth-aven.

[6] When the men of Israel saw the vast mass of enemy troops, they lost their nerve entirely and tried to hide in caves, thickets, coverts, among the rocks, and even in tombs and cisterns. [7] Some of them crossed the Jordan River and escaped to the land of Gad and Gilead. Meanwhile, Saul stayed at Gilgal, and those who were with him trembled with fear at what awaited them. [8] Samuel had told Saul earlier to wait seven days for his arrival, but when he still didn't come, and Saul's troops were rapidly slipping away, [9] he decided to sacrifice the burnt offering and the peace offerings himself. [10] But just as he was finishing, Samuel arrived. Saul went out to meet him and to receive his blessing, [11] but Samuel said, "What is this you have done?"

"Well," Saul replied, "when I saw that my men were scattering from me, and that you hadn't arrived by the time you said you would, and that the Philistines were at Michmash, ready for battle, [12] I said, 'The Philistines are ready to march against us and I haven't even asked for the Lord's help!' So I reluctantly offered the burnt offering without waiting for you to arrive."

[13] "You fool!" Samuel exclaimed. "You have disobeyed the commandment of the Lord your God. He was planning to make you and your descendants kings of Israel forever, [14] but now your dynasty must end; for the Lord wants a man who will obey him. And he has discovered the man he wants and has already appointed him as king over his people; for you have not obeyed the Lord's commandment."

[15] Samuel then left Gilgal and went to Gibe-ah in the land of Benjamin.

When Saul counted the soldiers who were still with him, he found that there were only about six hundred left! [16] Saul and Jonathan and these six hundred men set up their camp in Geba in the land of Benjamin; but the Philistines stayed at Michmash. [17] Three companies of raiders soon left the camp of the Philistines; one went toward Ophrah in the land of Shual, [18] another went to Beth-horon, and the third moved toward the border above the valley of Zeboim near the desert.

[19] There were no blacksmiths at all in the land of Israel in those days, for the Philistines wouldn't allow them for fear of their making swords and spears for the Hebrews. [20] So whenever the Israelites needed to sharpen their plowshares, discs, axes, or sickles, they had to take them to a Philistine blacksmith. [21] (The schedule of charges was as follows:

> For sharpening a plow point, 60¢
> For sharpening a disc, 60¢
> For sharpening an axe, 30¢
> For sharpening a sickle, 30¢
> For sharpening an ox goad, 30¢)

[22] So there was not a single sword or spear in the entire "army" of Israel that day, except for Saul's and Jonathan's. [23] The mountain pass at Michmash had meanwhile been secured by a contingent of the Philistine army.

14 A DAY OR so later, Prince Jonathan said to his young bodyguard, "Come on, let's cross the valley to the garrison of the Philistines." But he didn't tell his father that he was leaving.

---

a The Hebrew, from which the numbers have evidently dropped out in copying, reads: "Saul was . . . years old when he began to reign, and he reigned . . . and two years over Israel."

[2] Saul and his six hundred men were camped at the edge of Gibe-ah, around the pomegranate tree at Migron. [3] Among his men was Ahijah the priest (the son of Ahitub, Ichabod's brother; Ahitub was the grandson of Phinehas and the great-grandson of Eli, the priest of the Lord in Shiloh).

No one realized that Jonathan had gone. [4] To reach the Philistine garrison, Jonathan had to go over a narrow pass between two rocky crags which had been named Bozez and Seneh. [5] The crag on the north was in front of Michmash and the southern one was in front of Geba.

[6] "Yes, let's go across to those heathen," Jonathan had said to his bodyguard. "Perhaps the Lord will do a miracle for us. For it makes no difference to him how many enemy troops there are!"

[7] "Fine!" the youth replied. "Do as you think best; I'm with you heart and soul, whatever you decide."

[8] "All right, then this is what we'll do," Jonathan told him. [9] "When they see us, if they say, 'Stay where you are or we'll kill you!' then we will stop and wait for them. [10] But if they say, 'Come on up and fight!' then we will do just that; for it will be God's signal that he will help us defeat them!"

[11] When the Philistines saw them coming they shouted, "Look! The Israelis are crawling out of their holes!" [12] Then they shouted to Jonathan, "Come on up here and we'll show you how to fight!"

"Come on, climb right behind me," Jonathan exclaimed to his bodyguard, "for the Lord will help us defeat them!"

[13] So they clambered up on their hands and knees, and the Philistines fell back as Jonathan and the lad killed them right and left, [14] about twenty men in all, and their bodies were scattered over about half an acre of land. [15] Suddenly panic broke out throughout the entire Philistine army, and even among the raiders. And just then there was a great earthquake, increasing the terror.

[16] Saul's lookouts in Gibe-ah saw a strange sight—the vast army of the Philistines began to melt away in all directions.

[17] "Find out who isn't here," Saul ordered. And when they had checked, they found that Jonathan and his bodyguard were gone. [18] "Bring the Ark of God," Saul shouted to Ahijah. (For the Ark was among the people of Israel at that time.) [19] But while Saul was talking to the priest, the shouting and the tumult in the camp of the Philistines grew louder and louder. "Quick! What does God say?" Saul demanded.

[20] Then Saul and his six hundred men rushed out to the battle and found the Philistines killing each other, and there was terrible confusion everywhere. [21] And now the Hebrews who had been drafted into the Philistine army revolted and joined with the Israelis. [22] Finally even the men hiding in the hills joined the chase when they saw that the Philistines were running away. [23] So the Lord saved Israel that day, and the battle continued out beyond Beth-aven.

[24,25] Saul had declared, "A curse upon anyone who eats anything before evening —before I have full revenge on my enemies." So no one ate anything all day, even though they found honeycomb on the ground in the forest, [26] for they all feared Saul's curse. [27] Jonathan, however, had not heard his father's command; so he dipped a stick into a honeycomb, and when he had eaten the honey he felt much better. [28] Then someone told him that his father had laid a curse upon anyone who ate food that day, and everyone was weary and faint as a result.

[29] "That's ridiculous!" Jonathan exclaimed. "A command like that only hurts us. See how much better I feel now that I have eaten this little bit of honey. [30] If the people had been allowed to eat freely from the food they found among our enemies, think how many more we could have slaughtered!"

[31] But hungry as they were, they chased and killed the Philistines all day from Michmash to Aijalon, growing more and more faint. [32] That evening[a] they flew upon the spoils of battle and butchered the sheep, oxen, and calves, and ate the raw, bloody meat. [33] Someone reported to Saul what was happening, that the people were sinning against the Lord by eating blood.

a Implied.

"That is very wrong," Saul said. "Roll a great stone over here, [34] and go out among the troops and tell them to bring the oxen and sheep here to kill and drain them, and not to sin against the Lord by eating the blood." So that is what they did.

[35] And Saul built an altar to the Lord—his first.

[36] Afterwards Saul said, "Let's chase the Philistines all night and destroy every last one of them."

"Fine!" his men replied. "Do as you think best."

But the priest said, "Let's ask God first."

[37] So Saul asked God, "Shall we go after the Philistines? Will you help us defeat them?" But the Lord made no reply all night.

[38] Then Saul said to the leaders, "Something's wrong![b] We must find out what sin was committed today. [39] I vow by the name of the God who saved Israel that though the sinner be my own son Jonathan, he shall surely die!" But no one would tell him what the trouble was.

[40] Then Saul proposed, "Jonathan and I will stand over here, and all of you stand over there." And the people agreed.

[41] Then Saul said, "O Lord God of Israel, why haven't you answered my question? What is wrong? Are Jonathan and I guilty, or is the sin among the others? O Lord God, show us who is guilty." And Jonathan and Saul were chosen by sacred lot as the guilty ones, and the people were declared innocent.

[42] Then Saul said, "Now draw lots between me and Jonathan." And Jonathan was chosen as the guilty one.

[43] "Tell me what you've done," Saul demanded of Jonathan.

"I tasted a little honey," Jonathan admitted. "It was only a little bit on the end of a stick; but now I must die."

[44] "Yes, Jonathan," Saul said, "you must die; may God strike me dead if you are not executed for this."

[45] But the troops retorted, "Jonathan, who saved Israel today, shall die? Far from it! We vow by the life of God that not one hair on his head will be touched, for he has been used of God to do a mighty miracle today." So the people rescued Jonathan.

[46] Then Saul called back the army, and the Philistines returned home. [47] And now, since he was securely in the saddle as king of Israel, Saul sent the Israeli army out in every direction against Moab, Ammon, Edom, the kings of Zobah, and the Philistines. And wherever he turned, he was successful. [48] He did great deeds and conquered the Amalekites and saved Israel from all those who had been their conquerors.

[49] Saul had three sons, Jonathan, Ishvi, and Malchishua; and two daughters, Merab and Michal. [50,51] Saul's wife was Ahino-am, the daughter of Ahima-az. And the general-in-chief of his army was his cousin Abner, his uncle Ner's son. (Abner's father, Ner, and Saul's father, Kish, were brothers; both were the sons of Abiel.)

[52] The Israelis fought constantly with the Philistines throughout Saul's lifetime. And whenever Saul saw any brave, strong young man, he conscripted him into his army.

15 ONE DAY SAMUEL said to Saul, "I crowned you king of Israel because God told me to. Now be sure that you obey him. [2] Here is his commandment to you: 'I have decided to settle accounts with the nation of Amalek for refusing to allow my people to cross their territory when Israel came from Egypt. [3] Now go and completely destroy the entire Amalek nation—men, women, babies, little children, oxen, sheep, camels, and donkeys.'"

[4] So Saul mobilized his army at Telaim. There were two hundred thousand troops in addition to ten thousand men from Judah. [5] The Amalekites were camped in the valley below them. [6] Saul sent a message to the Kenites, telling them to get out from among the Amalekites or else die with them. "For you were kind to the people of Israel when they came out of the land of Egypt," he explained. So the Kenites packed up and left.

[7] Then Saul butchered the Amalekites from Havilah all the way to Shur, east of Egypt. [8] He captured Agag, the king of the Amalekites, but killed everyone else.

b Implied.

⁹ However, Saul and his men kept the best of the sheep and oxen and the fattest of the lambs—everything, in fact, that appealed to them. They destroyed only what was worthless or of poor quality. ¹⁰ Then the Lord said to Samuel,

¹¹ "I am sorry that I ever made Saul king, for he has again refused to obey me."

Samuel was so deeply moved when he heard what God was saying, that he cried to the Lord all night. ¹² Early the next morning he went out to find Saul. Someone said that he had gone to Mount Carmel to erect a monument to himself, and had then gone on to Gilgal. ¹³ When Samuel finally found him, Saul greeted him cheerfully.

"Hello there," he said. "Well, I have carried out the Lord's command!"

¹⁴ "Then what was all the bleating of sheep and lowing of oxen I heard?" Samuel demanded.

¹⁵ "It's true that the army spared the best of the sheep and oxen," Saul admitted, "but they are going to sacrifice them to the Lord your God; and we have destroyed everything else."

¹⁶ Then Samuel said to Saul, "Stop! Listen to what the Lord told me last night!"

"What was it?" Saul asked.

¹⁷ And Samuel told him, "When you didn't think much of yourself, God made you king of Israel. ¹⁸ And he sent you on an errand and told you, 'Go and completely destroy the sinners, the Amalekites, until they are all dead.' ¹⁹ Then why didn't you obey the Lord? Why did you rush for the loot and do exactly what God said not to?"

²⁰ "But I *have* obeyed the Lord," Saul insisted. "I did what he told me to; and I brought King Agag but killed everyone else. ²¹ And it was only when my troops demanded it that I let them keep the best of the sheep and oxen and loot to sacrifice to the Lord."

²² Samuel replied, "Has the Lord as much pleasure in your burnt offerings and sacrifices as in your obedience? Obedience is far better than sacrifice. He is much more interested in your listening to him than in your offering the fat of rams to him. ²³ For rebellion is as bad as the sin of witchcraft, and stubbornness is as bad as worshiping idols. And now because you have rejected the word of Jehovah, he has rejected you from being king."

²⁴ "I have sinned," Saul finally admitted. "Yes, I have disobeyed your instructions and the command of the Lord, for I was afraid of the people and did what they demanded. ²⁵ Oh, please pardon my sin now and go with me to worship the Lord."

²⁶ But Samuel replied, "It's no use! Since you have rejected the commandment of the Lord, he has rejected you from being king of Israel."

²⁷ As Samuel turned to go, Saul grabbed at him to try to hold him back, and tore his robe.

²⁸ And Samuel said to him, "See? The Lord has torn the kingdom of Israel from you today and has given it to a countryman of yours who is better than you are. ²⁹ And he who is the glory of Israel is not lying, nor will he change his mind, for he is not a man!"

³⁰ Then Saul pleaded again, "I have sinned; but oh, at least honor me before the leaders and before my people by going with me to worship the Lord your God."

³¹ So Samuel finally agreed and went with him. ³² Then Samuel said, "Bring King Agag to me." Agag arrived all full of smiles, for he thought, "Surely the worst is over and I have been spared!" ³³ But Samuel said, "As your sword has killed the sons of many mothers, now your mother shall be childless." And Samuel chopped him in pieces before the Lord at Gilgal. ³⁴ Then Samuel went home to Ramah, and Saul returned to Gibe-ah. ³⁵ Samuel never saw Saul again, but he mourned constantly for him; and the Lord was sorry that he had ever made Saul king of Israel.

16 FINALLY THE LORD said to Samuel, "You have mourned long enough for Saul, for I have rejected him as king of Israel. Now take a vial of olive oil and go to Bethlehem and find a man named Jesse, for I have selected one of his sons to be the new king."

² But Samuel asked, "How can I do that? If Saul hears about it, he will kill me."

"Take a heifer with you," the Lord replied, "and say that you have come to make a sacrifice to the Lord. ³ Then call Jesse to the sacrifice and I will show you which of his sons to anoint."

⁴ So Samuel did as the Lord had told him to. When he arrived at Bethlehem, the elders of the city came trembling to meet him. "What is wrong?" they asked. "Why have you come?"

⁵ But he replied, "All is well. I have come to sacrifice to the Lord. Purify yourselves and come with me to the sacrifice."

And he performed the purification rite on Jesse and his sons, and invited them too. ⁶ When they arrived, Samuel took one look at Eliab and thought, "Surely this is the man the Lord has chosen!"

⁷ But the Lord said to Samuel, "Don't judge by a man's face or height, for this is not the one. I don't make decisions the way you do! Men judge by outward appearance, but I look at a man's thoughts and intentions."

⁸ Then Jesse told his son Abinadab to step forward and walk in front of Samuel. But the Lord said, "This is not the right man either."

⁹ Next Jesse summoned Shammah, but the Lord said, "No, this is not the one." In the same way all seven of his sons presented themselves to Samuel and were rejected.

¹⁰,¹¹ "The Lord has not chosen any of them," Samuel told Jesse. "Are these all there are?"

"Well, there is the youngest," Jesse replied. "But he's out in the fields watching the sheep."

"Send for him at once," Samuel said, "for we will not sit down to eat until he arrives."

¹² So Jesse sent for him. He was a fine looking boy, ruddy-faced, and with pleasant eyes. And the Lord said, "This is the one; anoint him."

¹³ So as David stood there among his brothers, Samuel took the olive oil he had brought and poured it upon David's head; and the Spirit of Jehovah came upon him and gave him great power from that day onward. Then Samuel returned to Ramah.

¹⁴ But the Spirit of the Lord had left Saul, and instead, the Lord had sent a tormenting spirit that filled him with depression and fear. ¹⁵,¹⁶ Some of Saul's aides suggested a cure.

"We'll find a good harpist to play for you whenever the tormenting spirit is bothering you," they said. "The harp music will quiet you and you'll soon be well again."

¹⁷ "All right," Saul said. "Find me a harpist."

¹⁸ One of them said he knew a young fellow in Bethlehem, the son of a man named Jesse, who was not only a talented harp player, but was handsome, brave, and strong, and had good, solid judgment. "What's more," he added, "the Lord is with him."

¹⁹ So Saul sent messengers to Jesse, asking that he send his son David the shepherd. ²⁰ Jesse responded by sending not only David but a young goat and a donkey carrying a load of food and wine. ²¹ From the instant he saw David, Saul admired and loved him; and David became his bodyguard.

²² Then Saul wrote to Jesse, "Please let David join my staff, for I am very fond of him."

²³ And whenever the tormenting spirit from God troubled Saul, David would play the harp and Saul would feel better, and the evil spirit would go away.

17 THE PHILISTINES NOW mustered their army for battle and camped between Socoh in Judah and Azekah in Ephes-dammim. ² Saul countered with a buildup of forces at Elah Valley. ³ So the Philistines and Israelis faced each other on opposite hills, with the valley between them.

⁴⁻⁷ Then Goliath, a Philistine champion from Gath, came out of the Philistine ranks to face the forces of Israel. He was a giant of a man, measuring over nine feet tall! He wore a bronze helmet, a two-hundred-pound coat of mail, bronze leggings, and carried a bronze javelin several inches thick, tipped with a twenty-five-pound iron spearhead, and his armor bearer walked ahead of him with a huge shield.

⁸ He stood and shouted across to the Israelis, "Do you need a whole army to settle this? I will represent the Philistines, and you choose someone to represent you, and we will settle this in single combat! ⁹ If your man is able to kill me, then we will be your slaves. But if I kill him, then you must be our slaves! ¹⁰ I defy the armies of Israel!

Send me a man who will fight with me!"

[11] When Saul[a] and the Israeli army heard this, they were dismayed and frightened. [12] David (the son of aging Jesse, a member of the tribe of Judah who lived in Bethlehem-Judah) had seven older brothers. [13] The three oldest—Eliab, Abinadab, and Shammah—had already volunteered for Saul's army to fight the Philistines. [14,15] David was the youngest son, and was on Saul's staff on a part-time basis. He went back and forth to Bethlehem to help his father with the sheep. [16] For forty days, twice a day, morning and evening the Philistine giant strutted before the armies of Israel.

[17] One day Jesse said to David, "Take this bushel of roasted grain and these ten loaves of bread to your brothers. [18] Give this cheese to their captain and see how the boys are getting along; and bring us back a letter[b] from them!"

[19] (Saul and the Israeli army were camped at the valley of Elah.)

[20] So David left the sheep with another shepherd and took off early the next morning with the gifts. He arrived at the outskirts of the camp just as the Israeli army was leaving for the battlefield with shouts and battle cries. [21] Soon the Israeli and Philistine forces stood facing each other, army against army. [22] David left his luggage with a baggage officer and hurried out to the ranks to find his brothers. [23] As he was talking with them, he saw Goliath the giant step out from the Philistine troops and shout his challenge to the army of Israel. [24] As soon as they saw him the Israeli army began to run away in fright.

[25] "Have you seen the giant?" the soldiers were asking. "He has insulted the entire army of Israel. And have you heard about the huge reward the king has offered to anyone who kills him? And the king will give him one of his daughters for a wife, and his whole family will be exempted from paying taxes!"

[26] David talked to some others standing there to verify the report. "What will a man get for killing this Philistine and ending his insults to Israel?" he asked them. "Who is

this heathen Philistine, anyway, that he is allowed to defy the armies of the living God?" [27] And he received the same reply as before.

[28] But when David's oldest brother, Eliab, heard David talking like that, he was angry. "What are you doing around here, anyway?" he demanded. "What about the sheep you're supposed to be taking care of? I know what a cocky brat you are; you just want to see the battle!"

[29] "What have I done now?" David replied. "I was only asking a question!"

[30] And he walked over to some others and asked them the same thing and received the same answer. [31] When it was finally realized what David meant, someone told King Saul, and the king sent for him.

[32] "Don't worry about a thing," David told him. "I'll take care of this Philistine!"

[33] "Don't be ridiculous!" Saul replied. "How can a kid like you fight with a man like him? You are only a boy and he has been in the army *since* he was a boy!"

[34] But David persisted. "When I am taking care of my father's sheep," he said, "and a lion or a bear comes and grabs a lamb from the flock, [35] I go after it with a club and take the lamb from its mouth. If it turns on me I catch it by the jaw and club it to death. [36] I have done this to both lions and bears, and I'll do it to this heathen Philistine too, for he has defied the armies of the living God! [37] The Lord who saved me from the claws and teeth of the lion and the bear will save me from this Philistine!"

Saul finally consented, "All right, go ahead," he said, "and may the Lord be with you!"

[38,39] Then Saul gave David his own armor—a bronze helmet and a coat of mail. David put it on, strapped the sword over it, and took a step or two to see what it was like, for he had never worn such things before. "I can hardly move!" he exclaimed, and took them off again. [40] Then he picked up five smooth stones from a stream and put them in his shepherd's bag and, armed only with his shepherd's staff and sling, started across to Goliath. [41,42] Goliath walked out

---

a Probably King Saul was especially worried, for he was the tallest of the Israelites, and was obviously the best match!   b Literally, "take their pledge."

towards David with his shield bearer ahead of him, sneering in contempt at this nice little red-cheeked boy!

⁴³ "Am I a dog," he roared at David, "that you come at me with a stick?" And he cursed David by the names of his gods. ⁴⁴ "Come over here and I'll give your flesh to the birds and wild animals," Goliath yelled.

⁴⁵ David shouted in reply, "You come to me with a sword and a spear, but I come to you in the name of the Lord of the armies of heaven and of Israel—the very God whom you have defied. ⁴⁶ Today the Lord will conquer you and I will kill you and cut off your head; and then I will give the dead bodies of *your* men to the birds and wild animals, and the whole world will know that there is a God in Israel! ⁴⁷ And Israel will learn that the Lord does not depend on weapons to fulfill his plans—he works without regard to human means! He will give you to us!"

⁴⁸,⁴⁹ As Goliath approached, David ran out to meet him and, reaching into his shepherd's bag, took out a stone, hurled it from his sling, and hit the Philistine in the forehead. The stone sank in, and the man fell on his face to the ground. ⁵⁰,⁵¹ So David conquered the Philistine giant with a sling and a stone. Since he had no sword, he ran over and pulled Goliath's from its sheath and killed him with it, and then cut off his head. When the Philistines saw that their champion was dead, they turned and ran.

⁵² Then the Israelis gave a great shout of triumph and rushed after the Philistines, chasing them as far as Gath and the gates of Ekron. The bodies of the dead and wounded Philistines were strewn all along the road to Shaaraim. ⁵³ Then the Israeli army returned and plundered the deserted Philistine camp.

⁵⁴ (Later David took Goliath's head to Jerusalem, but stored his armor in his tent.) ⁵⁵ As Saul was watching David go out to fight Goliath, he asked Abner, the general of his army, "Abner, what sort of family does this young fellow come from?"ᶜ

"I really don't know," Abner said.

⁵⁶ "Well, find out!" the king told him.

⁵⁷ After David had killed Goliath, Abner brought him to Saul with the Philistine's head still in his hand.

⁵⁸ "Tell me about your father, my boy," Saul said.

And David replied, "His name is Jesse and we live in Bethlehem."

18 AFTER KING SAUL had finished his conversation with David, David met Jonathan, the king's son, and there was an immediate bond of love between them. Jonathan swore to be his blood brother, ⁴ and sealed the pact by giving him his robe, sword, bow, and belt.

King Saul now kept David at Jerusalem and wouldn't let him return home any more. ⁵ He was Saul's special assistant, and he always carried out his assignments successfully. So Saul made him commander of his troops, an appointment which was applauded by the army and general public alike. ⁶ But something had happened when the victorious Israeli army was returning home after David had killed Goliath. Women came out from all the towns along the way to celebrate and to cheer for King Saul, and were singing and dancing for joy with tambourines and cymbals.

⁷ However, this was their song: "Saul has slain his thousands, and David his ten thousands!"

⁸ Of course Saul was very angry. "What's this?" he said to himself. "They credit David with ten thousands and me with only thousands. Next they'll be making him their king!"

⁹ So from that time on King Saul kept a jealous watch on David. ¹⁰ The very next day, in fact, a tormenting spirit from God overwhelmed Saul, and he began to rave like a madman. David began to soothe him by playing the harp, as he did whenever this happened. But Saul, who was fiddling with his spear, ¹¹,¹² suddenly hurled it at David, intending to pin him to the wall. But David jumped aside and escaped. This happened another time, too, for Saul was afraid of him and jealous because the Lord had left him

---

c Literally, "Whose son is this?" Since David was, if successful, scheduled to marry Saul's daughter, Saul wanted to know more about his family! The other explanation of this confusing passage is that Saul's unstable mental condition caused forgetfulness, so that he didn't recognize David.

and was now with David. [13] Finally Saul banned him from his presence and demoted him to the rank of captain. But the controversy put David more than ever in the public eye. [14] David continued to succeed in everything he undertook, for the Lord was with him. [15,16] When King Saul saw this, he became even more afraid of him; but all Israel and Judah loved him, for he was as one of them.

[17] One day Saul said to David, "I am ready to give you my oldest daughter Merab as your wife. But first you must prove yourself to be a real soldier by fighting the Lord's battles." For Saul thought to himself, "I'll send him out against the Philistines and let them kill him rather than doing it myself."

[18] "Who am I that I should be the king's son-in-law?" David exclaimed. "My father's family is nothing!"

[19] But when the time arrived for the wedding, Saul married her to Adriel, a man from Meholath, instead. [20] In the meantime Saul's daughter Michal had fallen in love with David, and Saul was delighted when he heard about it.

[21] "Here's another opportunity to see him killed by the Philistines!" Saul said to himself. But to David he said, "You can be my son-in-law after all, for I will give you my youngest daughter."

[22] Then Saul instructed his men to say confidentially to David that the king really liked him a lot, and that they all loved him and thought he should accept the king's proposition and become his son-in-law.

[23] But David replied, "How can a poor man like me from an unknown family find enough dowry to marry the daughter of a king?"

[24] When Saul's men reported this back to him, [25] he told them, "Tell David that the only dowry I need is one hundred dead Philistines![a] Vengeance on my enemies is all I want." But what Saul had in mind was that David would be killed in the fight.

[26] David was delighted to accept the offer. So, before the time limit expired, [27] he and his men went out and killed two hundred Philistines and presented their foreskins to King Saul. So Saul gave Michal to him.

[28] When the king realized how much the Lord was with David and how immensely popular he was with all the people, [29] he became even more afraid of him, and grew to hate him more with every passing day. [30] Whenever the Philistine army attacked, David was more successful against them than all the rest of Saul's officers. So David's name became very famous throughout the land.

19 SAUL NOW URGED his aides and his son Jonathan to assassinate David. But Jonathan, because of his close friendship with David, [2] told him what his father was planning. "Tomorrow morning," he warned him, "you must find a hiding place out in the fields. [3] I'll ask my father to go out there with me, and I'll talk to him about you; then I'll tell you everything I can find out."

[4] The next morning[a] as Jonathan and his father were talking together, he spoke well of David and begged him not to be against David.

"He's never done anything to harm you," Jonathan pleaded. "He has always helped you in any way he could. [5] Have you forgotten about the time he risked his life to kill Goliath, and how the Lord brought a great victory to Israel as a result? You were certainly happy about it then. Why should you now murder an innocent man by killing him? There is no reason for it at all!"

[6] Finally Saul agreed, and vowed, "As the Lord lives, he shall not be killed."

[7] Afterwards Jonathan called David and told him what had happened. Then he took David to Saul and everything was as it had been before. [8] War broke out shortly after that and David led his troops against the Philistines and slaughtered many of them, and put to flight their entire army.

[9,10] But one day as Saul was sitting at home, listening to David playing the harp, suddenly the tormenting spirit from the Lord attacked him. He had his spear in his hand, and hurled it at David in an attempt

---

a Literally, "one hundred foreskins of the Philistines."   19 a Implied.

to kill him. But David dodged out of the way and fled into the night, leaving the spear imbedded in the timber of the wall. ¹¹ Saul sent troops to watch David's house and kill him when he came out in the morning.

"If you don't get away tonight," Michal warned him, "you'll be dead by morning." ¹² So she helped him get down to the ground through a window. ¹³ Then she took an idolᵇ and put it in his bed, and covered it with blankets, with its head on a pillow of goat's hair. ¹⁴ When the soldiers came to arrest David and take him to Saul,ᶜ she told them he was sick and couldn't get out of bed. ¹⁵ Saul said to bring him in his bed, then, so that he could kill him. ¹⁶ But when they came to carry him out, they discovered that it was only an idol!

¹⁷ "Why have you deceived me and let my enemy escape?" Saul demanded of Michal.

"I had to," Michal replied. "He threatened to kill me if I didn't help him."

¹⁸ In that way David got away and went to Ramah to see Samuel, and told him all that Saul had done to him. So Samuel took David with him to live at Naioth. ¹⁹ When the report reached Saul that David was at Naioth in Ramah, ²⁰ he sent soldiers to capture him; but when they arrived and saw Samuel and the other prophets prophesying, the Spirit of God came upon them and they also began to prophesy. ²¹ When Saul heard what had happened, he sent other soldiers, but they too prophesied! The same thing happened a third time! ²² Then Saul himself went to Ramah and arrived at the great well in Secu.

"Where are Samuel and David?" he demanded.

Someone told him they were at Naioth. ²³ But on the way to Naioth the Spirit of God came upon Saul, and he too began to prophesy! ²⁴ He tore off his clothes and lay naked all day and all night, prophesying with Samuel's prophets. Saul's men were incredulous!

"What!" they exclaimed. "Is Saul a prophet, too?"ᵈ

20 DAVID NOW FLED from Naioth in Ramah, and found Jonathan.

"What have I done?" he exclaimed. "Why is your father so determined to kill me?"

² "That's not true!" Jonathan protested. "I'm sure he's not planning any such thing, for he always tells me everything he's going to do, even little things, and I know he wouldn't hide something like this from me. It just isn't so."

³ "Of course you don't know about it!" David fumed. "Your father knows perfectly well about our friendship, so he has said to himself, 'I'll not tell Jonathan—why should I hurt him?' But the truth is that I am only a step away from death! I swear it by the Lord and by your own soul!"

⁴ "Tell me what I can do," Jonathan begged.

⁵ And David replied, "Tomorrow is the beginning of the celebration of the new moon. Always before, I've been with your father for this occasion, but tomorrow I'll hide in the field and stay there until the evening of the third day. ⁶ If your father asks where I am, tell him that I asked permission to go home to Bethlehem for an annual family reunion. ⁷ If he says, 'Fine!' then I'll know that all is well. But if he is angry, then I'll know that he is planning to kill me. ⁸ Do this for me as my sworn brother. Or else kill me yourself if I have sinned against your father, but don't betray me to him!"

⁹ "Of course not!" Jonathan exclaimed. "Look, wouldn't I say so if I knew that my father was planning to kill you?"

¹⁰ Then David asked, "How will I know whether or not your father is angry?"

¹¹ "Come out to the field with me," Jonathan replied. And they went out there together.

¹² Then Jonathan told David, "I promise by the Lord God of Israel that about this time tomorrow, or the next day at the latest, I will talk to my father about you and let you know at once how he feels about you. ¹³ If he is angry and wants you killed, then may the Lord kill me if I don't tell you, so

---

b Literally, "teraphim."   c Implied.
prophets?' " (See 1 Samuel 10:10–12.)

d Implied. Literally, "hence it is said, 'Is Saul also among the

261

you can escape and live. May the Lord be with you as he used to be with my father. ¹⁴ And remember, you must demonstrate the love and kindness of the Lord not only to me during my own lifetime, ¹⁵ but also to my children after the Lord has destroyed all of your enemies."

¹⁶ So Jonathan made a covenant with the family of David, and David swore to it with a terrible curse against himself and his descendants, should he be unfaithful to his promise. ¹⁷ But Jonathan made David swear to it again, this time by his love for him, for he loved him as much as he loved himself.

¹⁸ Then Jonathan said, "Yes, they will miss you tomorrow when your place at the table is empty. ¹⁹ By the day after tomorrow, everyone will be asking about you, so be at the hideout where you were before, over by the stone pile. ²⁰ I will come out and shoot three arrows in front of the pile as though I were shooting at a target. ²¹ Then I'll send a lad to bring the arrows back. If you hear me tell him, 'They're on this side,' then you will know that all is well and that there is no trouble. ²² But if I tell him, 'Go farther— the arrows are still ahead of you,' then it will mean that you must leave immediately. ²³ And may the Lord make us keep our promises to each other, for he has witnessed them."ᵃ

²⁴·²⁵ So David hid himself in the field.

When the new moon celebration began, the king sat down to eat at his usual place against the wall. Jonathan sat opposite him and Abner was sitting beside Saul, but David's place was empty. ²⁶ Saul didn't say anything about it that day, for he supposed that something had happened so that David was ceremonially impure. Yes, surely that must be it! ²⁷ But when his place was still empty the next day, Saul asked Jonathan, "Why hasn't David been here for dinner either yesterday or today?"

²⁸·²⁹ "He asked me if he could go to Bethlehem to take part in a family celebration," Jonathan replied. "His brother demanded that he be there, so I told him to go ahead."

³⁰ Saul boiled with rage. "You fool!"ᵇ he yelled at him. "Do you think I don't know

that you want this son of a nobodyᶜ to be king in your place, shaming yourself and your mother? ³¹ As long as that fellow is alive, you'll never be king. Now go and get him so I can kill him!"

³² "But what has he done?" Jonathan demanded. "Why should he be put to death?"

³³ Then Saul hurled his spear at Jonathan, intending to kill him; so at last Jonathan realized that his father really meant it when he said that David must die. ³⁴ Jonathan left the table in fierce anger and refused to eat all that day, for he was hurt by his father's shameful behavior toward David.

³⁵ The next morning, as agreed, Jonathan went out into the field and took a young boy with him to gather his arrows.

³⁶ "Start running," he told the boy, "so that you can find the arrows as I shoot them." So the boy ran and Jonathan shot an arrow beyond him. ³⁷ When the boy had almost reached the arrow, Jonathan shouted, "The arrow is still ahead of you. ³⁸ Hurry, hurry, don't wait." So the boy quickly gathered up the arrows and ran back to his master. ³⁹ He, of course, didn't understand what Jonathan meant; only Jonathan and David knew. ⁴⁰ Then Jonathan gave his bow and arrows to the boy and told him to take them back to the city.

⁴¹ As soon as he was gone, David came out from where he had been hiding near the south edge of the field and they sadly shook hands, tears running down their cheeks until David could weep no more.ᵈ ⁴² At last Jonathan said to David, "Cheer up, for we have entrusted each other and each other's children into God's hands forever." So they parted, David going away and Jonathan returning to the city.

21 DAVID WENT TO the city of Nob to see Ahimelech, the priest. Ahimelech trembled when he saw him.

"Why are you alone?" he asked. "Why is no one with you?"

² "The king has sent me on a private matter," David lied. "He told me not to tell anybody why I am here. I have told my men where to meet me later. ³ Now, what is there

---

a Literally, "The Lord is our mediator forever."
c Literally, "son of Jesse."   d Literally,   "David . . . bowed himself three times and they kissed each other and wept until David exceeded."

b Literally, "son of a perverse, rebellious woman."

to eat? Give me five loaves of bread, or anything else you can."

⁴ "We don't have any regular bread," the priest replied, "but there is the holy bread, which I guess you can have if only your young men have not slept with any women for awhile."

⁵ "Rest assured," David replied. "I never let my men run wild when they are on an expedition, and since they stay clean even on ordinary trips, how much more so on this one!"

⁶ So, since there was no other food available, the priest gave him the holy bread—the Bread of the Presence that was placed before the Lord in the Tabernacle. It had just been replaced that day with fresh bread.

⁷ (Incidentally, Doeg the Edomite, Saul's chief herdsman, was there at that time for ceremonial purification.ᵃ)

⁸ David asked Ahimelech if he had a spear or sword he could use. "The king's business required such haste, and I left in such a rush that I came away without a weapon!" David explained.

⁹ "Well," the priest replied, "I have the sword of Goliath, the Philistine—the fellow you killed in the valley of Elah. It is wrapped in a cloth in the clothes closet.ᵇ Take that if you want it, for there is nothing else here."

"Just the thing!" David replied. "Give it to me!"

¹⁰ Then David hurried on, for he was fearful of Saul, and went to King Achish of Gath. ¹¹ But Achish's officers weren't happy about his being there. "Isn't he the top leader of Israel?" they asked.

"Isn't he the one the people honor at their dances, singing, 'Saul has slain his thousands and David his ten thousands'?"

¹² David heard these comments and was afraid of what King Achish might do to him, ¹³ so he pretended to be insane! He scratched on doors and let his spittle flow down his beard, ¹⁴·¹⁵ until finally King Achish said to his men,

"Must you bring me a madman? We already have enough of them around here! Should such a fellow as this be my guest?"

22 SO DAVID LEFT Gath and escaped to the cave of Adullam, where his brothers and other relatives soon joined him. ² Then others began coming—those who were in any kind of trouble, such as being in debt, or merely discontented—until David was the leader of about four hundred men.

³ (Later David went to Mizpeh in Moab to ask permission of the king for his father and mother to live there under royal protection until David knew what God was going to do for him. ⁴ They stayed in Moab during the entire period when David was living in the cave.)

⁵ One day the prophet Gad told David to leave the cave and return to the land of Judah. So David went to the forest of Hereth. ⁶ The news of his arrival in Judah soon reached Saul. He was in Gibe-ah at the time, sitting beneath an oak tree playing with his spear, surrounded by his officers.

⁷ "Listen here, you men of Benjamin!" Saul exclaimed when he heard the news. "Has David promised you fields and vineyards and commissions in his army? ⁸ Is that why you are against me? For not one of you has ever told me that my own son is on David's side. You're not even sorry for me. Think of it! My own son—encouraging David to come and kill me!"

⁹·¹⁰ Then Doeg the Edomite, who was standing there with Saul's men, spoke up. "When I was at Nob," he said, "I saw David talking to Ahimelech the priest. Ahimelech consulted the Lord to find out what David should do, and then gave him food and the sword of Goliath the Philistine."

¹¹·¹² King Saul immediately summoned Ahimelech and all his family and all the other priests at Nob. When they arrived Saul shouted at him, "Listen to me, you son of Ahitub!"

"What is it?" quavered Ahimelech.

¹³ "Why have you and David conspired against me?" Saul demanded. "Why did you give him food and a sword and talk to God for him? Why did you encourage him to revolt against me and to come here and attack me?"

¹⁴ "But sir," Ahimelech replied, "is there

---

a Literally, "detained before the Lord."   b Literally, "behind the ephod."

anyone among all your servants who is as faithful as David your son-in-law? Why, he is the captain of your bodyguard and a highly honored member of your own household! [15] This was certainly not the first time I had consulted God for him! It's unfair for you to accuse me and my family in this matter, for we knew nothing of any plot against you."

[16] "You shall die, Ahimelech, along with your entire family!" the king shouted. [17] He ordered his bodyguards, "Kill these priests, for they are allies and conspirators with David; they knew he was running away from me, but they didn't tell me!"

But the soldiers refused to harm the clergy.

[18] Then the king said to Doeg, "You do it."

So Doeg turned on them and killed them, eighty-five priests in all, all wearing their priestly robes. [19] Then he went to Nob, the city of the priests, and killed the priests' families—men, women, children, and babies, and also all the oxen, donkeys, and sheep. [20] Only Abiathar, one of the sons of Ahimelech, escaped and fled to David.

[21] When he told him what Saul had done, [22] David exclaimed, "I knew it! When I saw Doeg there, I knew he would tell Saul. Now I have caused the death of all of your father's family. [23] Stay here with me, and I'll protect you with my own life. Any harm to you will be over my dead body."

23 ONE DAY NEWS came to David that the Philistines were at Keilah robbing the threshing floors.

[2] David asked the Lord, "Shall I go and attack them?"

"Yes, go and save Keilah," the Lord told him.

[3] But David's men said, "We're afraid even here in Judah; we certainly don't want to go to Keilah to fight the whole Philistine army!"

[4] David asked the Lord again, and the Lord again replied, "Go down to Keilah, for I will help you conquer the Philistines."

[5] They went to Keilah and slaughtered the Philistines and confiscated their cattle, and so the people of Keilah were saved.

[6] (Abiathar the priest went to Keilah with David, taking his ephod with him to get answers for David from the Lord.) [7] Saul soon learned that David was at Keilah.

"Good!" he exclaimed. "We've got him now! God has delivered him to me, for he has trapped himself in a walled city!"

[8] So Saul mobilized his entire army to march to Keilah and besiege David and his men. [9] But David learned of Saul's plan and told Abiathar the priest to bring the ephod and to ask the Lord what he should do.

[10] "O Lord God of Israel," David said, "I have heard that Saul is planning to come and destroy Keilah because I am here. [11] Will the men of Keilah surrender me to him? And will Saul actually come, as I have heard? O Lord God of Israel, please tell me."

And the Lord said, "He will come."

[12] "And will these men of Keilah betray me to Saul?" David persisted.

And the Lord replied, "Yes, they will betray you."

[13] So David and his men—about six hundred of them now—left Keilah and began roaming the countryside. Word soon reached Saul that David had escaped, so he didn't go there after all. [14,15] David now lived in the wilderness caves in the hill country of Ziph. One day near Horesh he received the news that Saul was on the way to Ziph to search for him and kill him. Saul hunted him day after day, but the Lord didn't let him find him.

[16] (Prince Jonathan now went to find David; he met him at Horesh and encouraged him in his faith in God.

[17] "Don't be afraid," Jonathan reassured him. "My father will never find you! You are going to be the king of Israel and I will be next to you, as my father is well aware." [18] So the two of them renewed their pact of friendship; and David stayed at Horesh while Jonathan returned home.)

[19] But now the men of Ziph went to Saul in Gibe-ah and betrayed David to him.

"We know where he is hiding," they said. "He is in the caves of Horesh on Hachilah Hill, down in the southern part of the wilderness. [20] Come on down, sir, and we will catch him for you and your fondest wish will be fulfilled!"

[21] "Well, praise the Lord!" Saul said. "At

last someone has had pity on me! ²² Go and check again to be sure of where he is staying and who has seen him there, for I know that he is very crafty. ²³ Discover his hiding places and then come back and give me a more definite report. Then I'll go with you. And if he is in the area at all, I'll find him if I have to search every inch of the entire land!"

²⁴˒²⁵ So the men of Ziph returned home. But when David heard that Saul was on his way to Ziph, he and his men went even further into the wilderness of Maon in the south of the desert. But Saul followed them there. ²⁶ He and David were now on opposite sides of a mountain. As Saul and his men began to close in, David tried his best to escape, but it was no use. ²⁷ But just then a message reached Saul that the Philistines were raiding Israel again, ²⁸ so Saul quit the chase and returned to fight the Philistines. Ever since that time the place where David was camped has been called, "The Rock of Escape!" ²⁹ David then went to live in the caves of Engedi.

24 AFTER SAUL'S RETURN from his battle with the Philistines, he was told that David had gone into the wilderness of Engedi; ² so he took three thousand special troops and went to search for him among the rocks and wild goats of the desert. ³ At the place where the road passes some sheepfolds, Saul went into a cave to go to the bathroom, but as it happened, David and his men were hiding in the cave!

⁴ "Now's your time!" David's men whispered to him. "Today is the day the Lord was talking about when he said, 'I will certainly put Saul into your power, to do with as you wish'!" Then David crept forward and quietly slit off the bottom of Saul's robe! ⁵ But then his conscience began bothering him.

⁶ "I shouldn't have done it," he said to his men. "It is a serious sin to attack God's chosen king in any way."

⁷˒⁸ These words of David persuaded his men not to kill Saul.

After Saul had left the cave and gone on his way, David came out and shouted after him, "My lord the king!" And when Saul looked around, David bowed low before

him.

⁹˒¹⁰ Then he shouted to Saul, "Why do you listen to the people who say that I am trying to harm you? This very day you have seen that it isn't true. The Lord placed you at my mercy back there in the cave and some of my men told me to kill you, but I spared you. For I said, 'I will never harm him—he is the Lord's chosen king.' ¹¹ See what I have in my hand? It is the hem of your robe! I cut it off, but I didn't kill you! Doesn't this convince you that I am not trying to harm you and that I have not sinned against you, even though you have been hunting for my life?

¹² "The Lord will decide between us. Perhaps he will kill you for what you are trying to do to me, but I will never harm you. ¹³ As that old proverb says, 'Wicked is as wicked does,' but despite your wickedness, I'll not touch you. ¹⁴ And who is the king of Israel trying to catch, anyway? Should he spend his time chasing one who is as worthless as a dead dog or a flea? ¹⁵ May the Lord judge as to which of us is right and punish whichever one of us is guilty. He is my lawyer and defender, and he will rescue me from your power!"

¹⁶ Saul called back, "Is it really you, my son David?" Then he began to cry. ¹⁷ And he said to David, "You are a better man than I am, for you have repaid me good for evil. ¹⁸ Yes, you have been wonderfully kind to me today, for when the Lord delivered me into your hand, you didn't kill me. ¹⁹ Who else in all the world would let his enemy get away when he had him in his power? May the Lord reward you well for the kindness you have shown me today. ²⁰ And now I realize that you are surely going to be king, and Israel shall be yours to rule. ²¹ Oh, swear to me by the Lord that when that happens you will not kill my family and destroy my line of descendants!"

²² So David promised, and Saul went home, but David and his men went back to their cave.

25 SHORTLY AFTERWARDS, SAMUEL died and all Israel gathered for his funeral and buried him in his family plot at Ramah.

Meanwhile David went down to the wilderness of Paran. [2] A wealthy man from Maon owned a sheep ranch there, near the village of Carmel. He had three thousand sheep and a thousand goats, and was at his ranch at this time for the sheep shearing. [3] His name was Nabal and his wife, a beautiful and very intelligent woman, was named Abigail. But the man, who was a descendant of Caleb, was uncouth, churlish, stubborn, and ill-mannered.

[4] When David heard that Nabal was shearing his sheep, [5] he sent ten of his young men to Carmel to give him this message: [6] "May God prosper you and your family and multiply everything you own. [7] I am told that you are shearing your sheep and goats. While your shepherds have lived among us, we have never harmed them, nor stolen anything from them the whole time they have been in Carmel. [8] Ask your young men and they will tell you whether or not this is true. Now I have sent my men to ask for a little contribution from you, for we have come at a happy time of holiday. Please give us a present of whatever is at hand."

[9] The young men gave David's message to Nabal and waited for his reply.

[10] "Who is this fellow David?" he asked. "Who does this son of Jesse think he is? There are lots of servants these days who run away from their masters. [11] Should I take my bread and my water and my meat that I've slaughtered for my shearers and give it to a gang who suddenly appear from nowhere?"[a]

[12] So David's messengers returned and told him what Nabal had said.

[13] "Get your swords!" was David's reply as he strapped on his own. Four hundred of them started off with David and two hundred remained behind to guard their gear.

[14] Meanwhile, one of Nabal's men went and told Abigail, "David sent men from the wilderness to talk to our master, but he insulted them and railed at them. [15,16] But David's men were very good to us and we never suffered any harm from them; in fact, day and night they were like a wall of protection to us and the sheep, and nothing was stolen from us the whole time they were with us.

[17] You'd better think fast, for there is going to be trouble for our master and his whole family—he's such a stubborn lout that no one can even talk to him!"

[18] Then Abigail hurriedly took two hundred loaves of bread, two barrels of wine, five dressed sheep, two bushels of roasted grain, one hundred raisin cakes, and two hundred fig cakes, and packed them onto donkeys.

[19] "Go on ahead," she said to her young men, "and I will follow." But she didn't tell her husband what she was doing. [20] As she was riding down the trail on her donkey, she met David coming towards her.

[21] David had been saying to himself, "A lot of good it did us to help this fellow. We protected his flocks in the wilderness so that not one thing was lost or stolen, but he has repaid me bad for good. All that I get for my trouble is insults. [22] May God curse me if even one of his men remains alive by tomorrow morning!"

[23] When Abigail saw David, she quickly dismounted and bowed low before him.

[24] "I accept all blame in this matter, my lord," she said. "Please listen to what I want to say. [25] Nabal is a bad-tempered boor, but please don't pay any attention to what he said. He is a fool—just like his name means. But I didn't see the messengers you sent. [26] Sir, since the Lord has kept you from murdering and taking vengeance into your own hands, I pray by the life of God, and by your own life too, that all your enemies shall be as cursed as Nabal is. [27] And now, here is a present I have brought to you and your young men. [28] Forgive me for my boldness in coming out here. The Lord will surely reward you with eternal royalty for your descendants, for you are fighting his battles; and you will never do wrong throughout your entire life. [29] Even when you are chased by those who seek your life, you are safe in the care of the Lord your God, just as though you were safe inside his purse! But the lives of your enemies shall disappear like stones from a sling! [30,31] When the Lord has done all the good things he promised you and has made you king of Israel, you won't want the conscience of a

---

a Literally, "to men who come from God knows where."

murderer who took the law into his own hands! And when the Lord has done these great things for you, please remember me!" [32] David replied to Abigail, "Bless the Lord God of Israel who has sent you to meet me today! [33] Thank God for your good sense! Bless you for keeping me from murdering the man and carrying out vengeance with my own hands. [34] For I swear by the Lord, the God of Israel who has kept me from hurting you, that if you had not come out to meet me, not one of Nabal's men would be alive tomorrow morning."

[35] Then David accepted her gifts and told her to return home without fear, for he would not kill her husband. [36] When she arrived home she found that Nabal had thrown a big party. He was roaring drunk, so she didn't tell him anything about her meeting with David until the next morning. [37,38] By that time he was sober, and when his wife told him what had happened, he had a stroke and lay paralyzed[b] for about ten days, then died, for the Lord killed him.

[39] When David heard that Nabal was dead, he said, "Praise the Lord! God has paid back Nabal and kept me from doing it myself; he has received his punishment for his sin."

Then David wasted no time in sending messengers to Abigail to ask her to become his wife. [40] When the messengers arrived at Carmel and told her why they had come, [41] she readily agreed to his request. [42] Quickly getting ready, she took along five of her serving girls as attendants, mounted her donkey, and followed the men back to David. So she became his wife.

[43] David also married Ahino-am from Jezreel. [44] King Saul, meanwhile, had forced David's wife Michal, Saul's daughter, to marry a man from Gallim named Palti (the son of Laish).

26 NOW THE MEN from Ziph came back to Saul at Gibe-ah to tell him that David had returned to the wilderness and was hiding on Hachilah Hill. [2] So Saul took his elite corps of three thousand troops and went to hunt him down. [3,4] Saul camped along the road at the edge of the wilderness where David was hiding, but David knew of Saul's arrival and sent out spies to watch his movements.

[5,6,7] David slipped over to Saul's camp one night to look around. King Saul and General Abner were sleeping inside a ring formed by the slumbering soldiers.

"Any volunteers to go down there with me?" David asked Ahimelech (the Hittite) and Abishai (Joab's brother and the son of Zeruiah).

"I'll go with you," Abishai replied. So David and Abishai went to Saul's camp and found him asleep, with his spear in the ground beside his head.

[8] "God has put your enemy within your power this time for sure," Abishai whispered to David. "Let me go and put that spear through him. I'll pin him to the earth with it—I'll not need to strike a second time!"

[9] "No," David said. "Don't kill him, for who can remain innocent after attacking the Lord's chosen king? [10] Surely God will strike him down some day, or he will die in battle or of old age. [11] But God forbid that I should kill the man he has chosen to be king! But I'll tell you what—we'll take his spear and his jug of water and then get out of here!"

[12] So David took the spear and jug of water, and they got away without anyone seeing them or even waking up, because the Lord had put them sound asleep. [13] They climbed the mountain slope opposite the camp until they were at a safe distance.

[14] Then David shouted down to Abner and Saul, "Wake up, Abner!"

"Who is it?" Abner demanded.

[15] "Well, Abner, you're a great fellow, aren't you?" David taunted. "Where in all Israel is there anyone as wonderful? So why haven't you guarded your master the king when someone came to kill him? [16] This isn't good at all! I swear by the Lord that you ought to die for your carelessness. Where is the king's spear and the jug of water that was beside his head? Look and see!"

[17,18] Saul recognized David's voice and said, "Is that you, my son David?"

---

b Literally, "his heart died within him and he became as stone."

And David replied, "Yes, sir, it is. Why are you chasing me? What have I done? What is my crime? [19] If the Lord has stirred you up against me, then let him accept my peace offering. But if this is simply the scheme of a man, then may he be cursed by God. For you have driven me out of my home so that I can't be with the Lord's people, and you have sent me away to worship heathen gods. [20] Must I die on foreign soil, far from the presence of Jehovah? Why should the king of Israel come out to hunt my life like a partridge on the mountains?"

[21] Then Saul confessed, "I have done wrong. Come back home, my son, and I'll no longer try to harm you; for you saved my life today. I have been a fool, and very, very wrong."

[22] "Here is your spear, sir," David replied. "Let one of your young men come over and get it. [23] The Lord gives his own reward for doing good and for being loyal, and I refused to kill you even when the Lord placed you in my power. [24] Now may the Lord save my life, even as I have saved yours today. May he rescue me from all my troubles."

[25] And Saul said to David, "Blessings on you, my son David. You shall do heroic deeds and be a great conqueror."

Then David went away and Saul returned home.

27 BUT DAVID KEPT thinking to himself, "Some day Saul is going to get me. I'll try my luck among the Philistines until Saul gives up and quits hunting for me; then I will finally be safe again."

[2,3] So David took his six hundred men and their families to live at Gath under the protection of King Achish. He had his two wives with him—Ahino-am of Jezreel and Abigail of Carmel, Nabal's widow. [4] Word soon reached Saul that David had fled to Gath, so he quit hunting for him.

[5] One day David said to Achish, "My lord, if it is all right with you, we would rather live in one of the country towns instead of here in the royal city."

[6] So Achish gave him Ziklag (which still belongs to the kings of Judah to this day), [7] and they lived there among the Philistines for a year and four months. [8] He and his men spent their time raiding the Geshurites, the Girzites, and the Amalekites—people who had lived near Shur along the road to Egypt ever since ancient times. [9] They didn't leave one person alive in the villages they hit, and took for themselves the sheep, oxen, donkeys, camels, and clothing before returning to their homes.

[10] "Where did you make your raid today?" Achish would ask.

And David would reply, "Against the south of Judah and the people of Jerahmeel and the Kenites."

[11] No one was left alive to come to Gath and tell where he had really been. This happened again and again while he was living among the Philistines. [12] Achish believed David and thought that the people of Israel must hate him bitterly by now. "Now he will have to stay here and serve me forever!" the king thought.

28 ABOUT THAT TIME the Philistines mustered their armies for another war with Israel.

"Come and help us fight," King Achish said to David and his men.

[2] "Good," David agreed. "You will soon see what a help we can be to you."

"If you are, you shall be my personal bodyguard for life," Achish told him.

[3] (Meanwhile, Samuel had died and all Israel had mourned for him. He was buried in Ramah, his home town. King Saul had banned all mediums and wizards from the land of Israel.)

[4] The Philistines set up their camp at Shunem, and Saul and the armies of Israel were at Gilboa. [5,6] When Saul saw the vast army of the Philistines, he was frantic with fear and asked the Lord what he should do. But the Lord refused to answer him, either by dreams, or by Urim,[a] or by the prophets. [7,8] Saul then instructed his aides to try to find a medium so that he could ask her what to do, and they found one at Endor. Saul disguised himself by wearing ordinary

---

a The Urim and Thummim were holy instruments which were used as lots in determining the will of God. See Exodus 28:30.

clothing instead of his royal robes. He went to the woman's home at night, accompanied by two of his men.

"I've got to talk to a dead man," he pleaded. "Will you bring his spirit up?"

⁹ "Are you trying to get me killed?" the woman demanded. "You know that Saul has had all of the mediums and fortune-tellers executed. You are spying on me."

¹⁰ But Saul took a solemn oath that he wouldn't betray her.

¹¹ Finally the woman said, "Well, whom do you want me to bring up?"

"Bring me Samuel," Saul replied.

¹² When the woman saw Samuel, she screamed, "You've deceived me! You are Saul!"

¹³ "Don't be frightened!" the king told her. "What do you see?"

"I see a specter coming up out of the earth," she said.

¹⁴ "What does he look like?"

"He is an old man wrapped in a robe." Saul realized that it was Samuel and bowed low before him.

¹⁵ "Why have you disturbed me by bringing me back?" Samuel asked Saul.

"Because I am in deep trouble," he replied. "The Philistines are at war with us, and God has left me and won't reply by prophets or dreams; so I have called for you to ask you what to do."

¹⁶ But Samuel replied, "Why ask me if the Lord has left you and has become your enemy? ¹⁷ He has done just as he said he would and has taken the kingdom from you and given it to your rival, David. ¹⁸ All this has come upon you because you did not obey the Lord's instructions when he was so angry with Amalek. ¹⁹ What's more, the entire Israeli army will be routed and destroyed by the Philistines tomorrow, and you and your sons will be here with me."

²⁰ Saul now fell full length upon the ground, paralyzed with fright because of Samuel's words. He was also faint with hunger, for he had eaten nothing all day. ²¹ When the woman saw how distraught he was, she said, "Sir, I obeyed your command at the risk of my life. ²² Now do what I say, and let me give you something to eat so you'll regain your strength for the trip back."

²³ But he refused. The men who were with him added their pleas to that of the woman until he finally yielded and got up and sat on the bed. ²⁴ The woman had been fattening a calf, so she hurried out and killed it and kneaded dough and baked unleavened bread. ²⁵ She brought the meal to the king and his men, and they ate it. Then they went out into the night.

29 THE PHILISTINE ARMY now mobilized at Aphek, and the Israelis camped at the springs in Jezreel. ² As the Philistine captains were leading out their troops by battalions and companies, David and his men marched at the rear with King Achish.

³ But the Philistine commanders demanded, "What are these Israelis doing here?"

And King Achish told them, "This is David, the runaway servant of King Saul of Israel. He's been with me for years, and I've never found one fault in him since he arrived."

⁴ But the Philistine leaders were angry. "Send them back!" they demanded. "They aren't going into the battle with us—they'll turn against us. Is there any better way for him to reconcile himself with his master than by turning against us in the battle? ⁵ This is the same man the women of Israel sang about in their dances: 'Saul has slain his thousands and David his ten thousands!'"

⁶ So Achish finally summoned David and his men.

"I swear by the Lord," he told them, "you are some of the finest men I've ever met, and I think you should go with us, but my commanders say no. ⁷ Please don't upset them, but go back quietly."

⁸ "What have I done to deserve this treatment?" David demanded. "Why can't I fight your enemies?"

⁹ But Achish insisted, "As far as I'm concerned, you're as perfect as an angel of God. But my commanders are afraid to have you with them in the battle. ¹⁰ Now get up early in the morning and leave as soon as it is light."

¹¹ So David headed back into the land of the Philistines while the Philistine army went on to Jezreel.

30 THREE DAYS LATER, when David and his men arrived home at their city of Ziklag, they found that the Amalekites had raided the city and burned it to the ground, ² carrying off all the women and children. ³ As David and his men looked at the ruins and realized what had happened to their families, ⁴ they wept until they could weep no more. ⁵ (David's two wives, Ahino-am and Abigail, were among those who had been captured.) ⁶ David was seriously worried, for in their bitter grief for their children, his men began talking of killing him. But David took strength from the Lord.

⁷ Then he said to Abiathar the priest, "Bring me the ephod!" So Abiathar brought it.

⁸ David asked the Lord, "Shall I chase them? Will I catch them?"

And the Lord told him, "Yes, go after them; you will recover everything that was taken from you!"

⁹,¹⁰ So David and his six hundred men set out after the Amalekites. When they reached Besor Brook, two hundred of the men were too exhausted to cross, but the other four hundred kept going. ¹¹,¹² Along the way they found an Egyptian youth in a field and brought him to David. He had not had anything to eat or drink for three days and nights, so they gave him part of a fig cake, two clusters of raisins, and some water, and his strength soon returned.

¹³ "Who are you and where do you come from?" David asked him.

"I am an Egyptian—the servant of an Amalekite," he replied. "My master left me behind three days ago because I was sick. ¹⁴ We were on our way back from raiding the Cherethites in the Negeb, and had raided the south of Judah and the land of Caleb, and had burned Ziklag."

¹⁵ "Can you tell me where they went?" David asked.

The young man replied, "If you swear by God's name that you will not kill me or give me back to my master, then I will guide you to them."

¹⁶ So he led them to the Amalekite encampment. They were spread out across the fields, eating and drinking and dancing with joy because of the vast amount of loot they had taken from the Philistines and from the men of Judah. ¹⁷ David and his men rushed in among them and slaughtered them all that night and the entire next day until evening. No one escaped except four hundred young men who fled on camels. ¹⁸,¹⁹ David got back everything they had taken. The men recovered their families and all of their belongings, and David rescued his two wives. ²⁰ His troops rounded up all the flocks and herds and drove them on ahead of them. "These are all yours personally, as your reward!" they told David.

²¹ When they reached Besor Brook and the two hundred men who had been too exhausted to go on, David greeted them joyfully. ²² But some of the ruffians among David's men declared, "They didn't go with us, so they can't have any of the loot. Give them their wives and their children and tell them to be gone."

²³ But David said, "No, my brothers! The Lord has kept us safe and helped us defeat the enemy. ²⁴ Do you think that anyone will listen to you when you talk like this? We share and share alike—those who go to battle and those who guard the equipment."

²⁵ From then on David made this a law for all Israel, and it is still followed.

²⁶ When he arrived at Ziklag, he sent part of the loot to the elders of Judah. "Here is a present for you, taken from the Lord's enemies," he wrote them. ²⁷⁻³¹ The gifts were sent to the elders in the following cities where David and his men had been:

Bethel, South Ramoth, Jattir,
Aroer, Siphmoth, Eshtemoa, Racal,
the cities of the Jerahmeelites, the
cities of the Kenites, Hormah,
Borashan, Athach, Hebron.

31 MEANWHILE THE PHILISTINES had begun the battle against Israel, and the Israelis fled from them and were slaughtered wholesale on Mount Gilboa. ² The Philistines closed in on Saul, and killed his sons Jonathan, Abinidab, and Malchishua. ³,⁴ Then the archers overtook Saul and wounded him badly. He groaned to his armor bearer, "Kill me with your sword before these heathen Philistines capture me and torture me." But his armor bearer was afraid to, so Saul took his own sword and fell upon the point of the blade, and it pierced him through. ⁵ When his armor bearer saw that he was dead, he also fell upon his sword and died with him. ⁶ So Saul, his armor bearer, his three sons, and his troops died together that same day.

⁷ When the Israelis on the other side of the valley and beyond the Jordan heard that their comrades had fled and that Saul and his sons were dead, they abandoned their cities; and the Philistines lived in them.

⁸ The next day when the Philistines went out to strip the dead, they found the bodies of Saul and his three sons on Mount Gilboa. ⁹ They cut off Saul's head and stripped off his armor and sent the wonderful news of Saul's death to their idols and to the people throughout their land.

¹⁰ His armor was placed in the temple of Ashtaroth, and his body was fastened to the wall of Beth-shan.

¹¹ But when the people of Jabesh-gilead heard what the Philistines had done, ¹² warriors from that town traveled all night to Beth-shan and took down the bodies of Saul and his sons from the wall and brought them to Jabesh, where they cremated them. ¹³ Then they buried their remains beneath the oak tree at Jabesh and fasted for seven days.

---

2 SAMUEL

1 SAUL WAS DEAD and David had returned to Ziklag after slaughtering the Amalekites. Three days later a man arrived from the Israeli army with his clothes torn and with dirt on his head as a sign of mourning. He fell to the ground before David in deep respect.

³ "Where do you come from?" David asked.

"From the Israeli army," he replied.

⁴ "What happened?" David demanded. "Tell me how the battle went."

And the man replied, "Our entire army fled. Thousands of men are dead and wounded on the field, and Saul and his son Jonathan have been killed."

⁵ "How do you know they are dead?"

⁶ "Because I was on Mount Gilboa and saw Saul leaning against his spear with the enemy chariots closing in upon him. ⁷ When he saw me he cried out for me to come to him.

⁸ " 'Who are you?' he asked.

" 'An Amalekite,' I replied.

⁹ " 'Come and put me out of my misery,' he begged, 'for I am in terrible pain but life lingers on.'

¹⁰ "So I killed him, for I knew he couldn't live.ᵃ Then I took his crown and one of his bracelets to bring to you, my lord."

¹¹ David and his men tore their clothes in sorrow when they heard the news. ¹² They mourned and wept and fasted all day for Saul and his son Jonathan, and for the Lord's people, and for the men of Israel who had died that day.

¹³ Then David said to the young man who had brought the news, "Where are you from?"

And he replied, "I am an Amalekite."

¹⁴ "Why did you kill God's chosen king?" David demanded.

¹⁵ Then he said to one of his young men, "Kill him!" So he ran him through with his sword and he died.

¹⁶ "You die self-condemned," David said, "for you yourself confessed that you killed God's appointed king."

¹⁷,¹⁸ Then David composed a dirge for Saul and Jonathan and afterward commanded that it be sung throughout Israel. It is quoted here from the book, *Heroic Ballads.*

¹⁹ O Israel, your pride and joy lies
   dead upon the hills;
Mighty heroes have fallen.
²⁰ Don't tell the Philistines, lest they
   rejoice.
Hide it from the cities of Gath and

---

a He was evidently lying. See 1 Samuel 31:3, 4 for the true account. Probably he had found Saul dead upon the field and thought David would reward him for killing his rival.

Ashkelon,
Lest the heathen nations laugh in triumph.
²¹ O Mount Gilboa,
Let there be no dew nor rain upon you,
Let no crops of grain grow on your slopes.ᵇ
For there the mighty Saul has died;
He is God's appointed king no more.
²² Both Saul and Jonathan slew their strongest foes,
And did not return from battle empty-handed.
²³ How much they were loved, how wonderful they were—
Both Saul and Jonathan!
They were together in life and in death.
They were swifter than eagles, stronger than lions.
²⁴ But now, O women of Israel, weep for Saul;
He enriched you
With fine clothing and golden ornaments.
²⁵ These mighty heroes have fallen in the midst of the battle.
Jonathan is slain upon the hills.
²⁶ How I weep for you, my brother Jonathan;
How much I loved you!
And your love for me was deeper
Than the love of women!
²⁷ The mighty ones have fallen,
Stripped of their weapons, and dead.

2 DAVID THEN ASKED the Lord, "Shall I move back to Judah?"
And the Lord replied, "Yes."
"Which city shall I go to?"
And the Lord replied, "Hebron."

² So David and his wives—Ahino-am from Jezreel and Abigail the widow of Nabal from Carmel— ³ and his men and their families all moved to Hebron. ⁴ Then the leaders of Judah came to David and crowned him king of the Judean confederacy.

When David heard that the men of Jabesh-gilead had buried Saul, ⁵ he sent them this message: "May the Lord bless you for being so loyal to your king and giving him a decent burial. ⁶ May the Lord be loyal to you in return, and reward you with many demonstrations of his love! And I too will be kind to you because of what you have done. ⁷ And now I ask you to be my strong and loyal subjects, now that Saul is dead. Be like the tribe of Judah who have appointed me as their new king."

⁸ But Abner, Saul's commander-in-chief, had gone to Mahanaim to crown Saul's son Ish-bosheth as king. ⁹ His territory included Gilead, Ashuri, Jezreel, Ephraim, the tribe of Benjamin, and all the rest of Israel. ¹⁰,¹¹ Ish-bosheth was forty years old at the time. He reigned in Mahanaim for two years; meanwhile, David was reigning in Hebron as king of the Judean confederacy for seven and one-half years.

¹² One day General Abner led some of Ish-bosheth's troops to Gibeon from Mahanaim, ¹³ and General Joab (the son of Zeruiah) led David's troops out to meet them. They met at the pool of Gibeon, where they sat facing each other on opposite sides of the pool. ¹⁴ Then Abner suggested to Joab, "Let's watch some sword play between our young men!"

Joab agreed, ¹⁵ so twelve men were chosen from each side to fight in mortal combat. ¹⁶ Each one grabbed his opponent by the hair and thrust his sword into the other's side, so that all of them died. The place has been known ever since as Sword Field.

¹⁷ The two armies then began to fight each other, and by the end of the day Abner and the men of Israel had been defeated by Joabᵃ and the forces of David. ¹⁸ Joab's brothers, Abishai and Asahel, were also in the battle. Asahel could run like a deer, ¹⁹ and he began chasing Abner. He wouldn't stop for anything, but kept on, singlemindedly, after Abner alone.

²⁰ When Abner looked behind and saw him coming, he called out to him, "Is that you, Asahel?"

"Yes," he called back, "it is."

²¹ "Go after someone else!" Abner warned. But Asahel refused and kept on

---

b The text is uncertain in the original manuscripts.   2a Implied.

coming.

²² Again Abner shouted to him, "Get away from here. I could never face your brother Joab if I have to kill you!"

²³ But he refused to turn away, so Abner pierced him through the belly with the butt end of his spear. It went right through his body and came out his back. He stumbled to the ground and died there, and everyone stopped when they came to the place where he lay.

²⁴ Now Joab and Abishai set out after Abner. The sun was just going down as they arrived at Ammah Hill near Giah, along the road into the Gibeon desert. ²⁵ Abner's troops from the tribe of Benjamin regrouped there at the top of the hill, ²⁶ and Abner shouted down to Joab, "Must our swords continue to kill each other forever? How long will it be before you call off your people from chasing their brothers?"

²⁷ Joab shouted back, "I swear by God that even if you hadn't spoken, we would all have gone home tomorrow morning." ²⁸ Then he blew his trumpet and his men stopped chasing the troops of Israel.

²⁹ That night Abner and his men retreated across the Jordan Valley, crossed the river, and traveled all the next morning until they arrived at Mahanaim. ³⁰ Joab and the men who were with him returned home too, and when he counted his casualties, he learned that only nineteen men were missing, in addition to Asahel. ³¹ But three hundred and sixty of Abner's men (all from the tribe of Benjamin) were dead. ³² Joab and his men took Asahel's body to Bethlehem and buried him beside his father; then they traveled all night and reached Hebron at daybreak.

3 THAT WAS THE beginning of a long war between the followers of Saul and of David. David's position now became stronger and stronger, while Saul's dynasty became weaker and weaker.

² Several sons were born to David while he was at Hebron. The oldest was Amnon, born to his wife Ahino-am. ³ His second son, Chileab, was born to Abigail, the widow of Nabal of Carmel. The third was Absalom, born to Maacah, the daughter of King Talmai of Geshur. ⁴ The fourth was Adonijah, who was born to Haggith. Then Shephatiah was born to Abital, and ⁵ Ithream was born to Eglah.

⁶ As the war went on, Abner became a very powerful political leader among the followers of Saul. ⁷ He took advantage of his position by sleeping with one of Saul's concubines, a girl named Rizpah. But when Ish-bosheth accused Abner of this, ⁸ Abner was furious.

"Am I a Judean dog to be kicked around like this?" he shouted. "After all I have done for you and for your father by not betraying you to David, is this my reward —to find fault with me about some woman? ⁹,¹⁰ May God curse me if I don't do everything I can to take away the entire kingdom from you, all the way from Dan to Beersheba, and give it to David, just as the Lord predicted."

¹¹ Ish-bosheth made no reply, for he was afraid of Abner.

¹² Then Abner sent messengers to David to discuss a deal—to surrender the kingdom of Israel to him in exchange for becoming commander-in-chief of the combined armies of Israel and Judah.

¹³ "All right," David replied, "but I will not negotiate with you unless you bring me my wife Michal, Saul's daughter." ¹⁴ David then sent this message to Ish-bosheth: "Give me back my wife Michal, for I bought her with the lives of one hundred Philistines."

¹⁵ So Ish-bosheth took her away from her husband Palti.ᵃ ¹⁶ He followed along behind her as far as Behurim, weeping as he went. Then Abner told him, "Go on home now." So he returned.

¹⁷ Meanwhile, Abner consulted with the leaders of Israel and reminded them that for a long time they had wanted David as their king.

¹⁸ "Now is the time!" he told them. "For the Lord has said, 'It is David by whom I will save my people from the Philistines and from all their other enemies.' "

¹⁹ Abner also talked to the leaders of the tribe of Benjamin; then he went to Hebron

a See 1 Samuel 25:44.

and reported to David his progress with the people of Israel and Benjamin. [20] Twenty men accompanied him, and David entertained them with a feast.

[21] As Abner left, he promised David, "When I get back I will call a convention of all the people of Israel, and they will elect you as their king, as you've so long desired." So David let Abner return in safety.

[22] But just after Abner left, Joab and some of David's troops returned from a raid, bringing much loot with them. [23] When Joab was told that Abner had just been there visiting the king and had been sent away in peace, [24,25] he rushed to the king, demanding, "What have you done? What do you mean by letting him get away? You know perfectly well that he came to spy on us and that he plans to return and attack us!"

[26] Then Joab sent messengers to catch up with Abner and tell him to come back. They found him at the well of Sirah and he returned with them; but David knew nothing about it. [27] When Abner arrived at Hebron, Joab took him aside at the city gate as if to speak with him privately; but then he pulled out a dagger and killed him in revenge for the death of his brother Asahel.

[28] When David heard about it he declared, "I vow by the Lord that I and my people are innocent of this crime against Abner. [29] Joab and his family are the guilty ones. May each of his children be victims of cancer, or be lepers, or be sterile, or die of starvation, or be killed by the sword!"

[30] So Joab and his brother Abishai killed Abner because of the death of their brother Asahel at the battle of Gibeon.

[31] Then David said to Joab and to all those who were with him, "Go into deep mourning for Abner." And King David accompanied the bier to the cemetery. [32] They buried Abner in Hebron. And the king and all the people wept at the graveside.

[33,34] "Should Abner have died like a fool?" the king lamented.

"Your hands were not bound,
Your feet were not tied—
You were murdered—
The victim of a wicked plot."

And all the people wept again for him. [35,36] David had refused to eat anything the day of the funeral, and now everyone begged him to take a bite of supper. But David vowed that he would eat nothing until sundown. This pleased his people, just as everything else he did pleased them! [37] Thus the whole nation, both Judah and Israel, understood from David's actions that he was in no way responsible for Abner's death.

[38] And David said to his people, "A great leader and a great man has fallen today in Israel; [39] and even though I am God's chosen king, I can do nothing with these two sons of Zeruiah. May the Lord repay wicked men for their wicked deeds."

4 WHEN KING ISH-BOSHETH heard about Abner's death at Hebron, he was paralyzed with fear, and his people too were badly frightened. [2,3] The command of the Israeli troops then fell to two brothers, Baanah and Rechab, who were captains of King Ish-bosheth's raiding bands. They were the sons of Rimmon, who was from Be-eroth in Benjamin. (People from Be-eroth are counted as Benjaminites even though they fled to Gittaim,[a] where they now live.)

[4] (There was a little lame grandson of King Saul's named Mephibosheth, who was the son of Prince Jonathan. He was five years old at the time Saul and Jonathan were killed at the battle of Jezreel. When the news of the outcome of the battle reached the capital, the child's nurse grabbed him and fled, but she fell and dropped him as she was running, and he became lame.)

[5] Rechab and Baanah arrived at King Ish-bosheth's home one noon as he was taking a nap. [6,7] They walked into the kitchen as though to get a sack of wheat, but then sneaked into his bedroom and murdered him and cut off his head. Taking his head with them, they fled across the desert that night and escaped. [8] They presented the head to David at Hebron.

"Look!" they exclaimed. "Here is the head of Ish-bosheth, the son of your enemy Saul who tried to kill you. Today the Lord has given you revenge upon Saul and upon

---

a Gittaim is not in Benjamin.

his entire family!"

⁹ But David replied, "I swear by the Lord who saved me from my enemies, ¹⁰ that when someone told me, 'Saul is dead,' thinking he was bringing me good news, I killed him; that is how I rewarded him for his 'glad tidings.' ¹¹ And how much more shall I do to wicked men who kill a good man in his own house and on his bed! Shall I not demand your lives?"

¹² So David ordered his young men to kill them, and they did. They cut off their hands and feet and hanged their bodies beside the pool in Hebron. And they took Ishbosheth's head and buried it in Abner's tomb in Hebron.

5 THEN REPRESENTATIVES OF all the tribes of Israel came to David at Hebron and gave him their pledge of loyalty.

"We are your blood brothers," they said. ² "And even when Saul was our king you were our real leader. The Lord has said that you should be the shepherd and leader of his people."

³ So David made a contract before the Lord with the leaders of Israel there at Hebron, and they crowned him king of Israel. ⁴,⁵ (He had already been the king of Judah for seven years, since the age of thirty. He then ruled thirty-three years in Jerusalem as king of both Israel and Judah; so he reigned for forty years altogether.)

⁶ David now led his troops to Jerusalem to fight against the Jebusites who lived there.

"You'll never come in here," they told him. "Even the blind and lame could keep you out!" For they thought they were safe. ⁷ But David and his troops defeated them and captured the stronghold of Zion, now called the City of David.

⁸ When the insulting message from the defenders of the city reached David, he told his troops, "Go up through the water tunnel into the city and destroy those 'lame' and 'blind' Jebusites. How I hate them." (That is the origin of the saying, "Even the blind and the lame could conquer you!")

⁹ So David made the stronghold of Zion (also called the City of David) his headquarters. Then, beginning at the old Millo section of the city, he built northward toward the present city center. ¹⁰ So David became greater and greater, for the Lord God of heaven was with him.

¹¹ Then King Hiram of Tyre sent cedar lumber, carpenters, and masons to build a palace for David. ¹² David now realized why the Lord had made him the king and blessed his kingdom so greatly—it was because God wanted to pour out his kindness on Israel, his chosen people.

¹³ After moving from Hebron to Jerusalem, David married additional wives and concubines, and had many sons and daughters. ¹⁴,¹⁵,¹⁶ These are his children who were born at Jerusalem:

Shammu-a, Shobab, Nathan, Solomon, Ibhar, Elishu-a, Nepheg, Japhia, Elishama, Eliada, Eliphelet.

¹⁷ When the Philistines heard that David had been crowned king of Israel, they tried to capture him; but David was told that they were coming and went into the stronghold. ¹⁸ The Philistines arrived and spread out across the valley of Rephaim.

¹⁹ Then David asked the Lord, "Shall I go out and fight against them? Will you defeat them for me?"

And the Lord replied, "Yes, go ahead, for I will give them to you."

²⁰ So David went out and fought with them at Baal-perazim, and defeated them. "The Lord did it!" he exclaimed. "He burst through my enemies like a raging flood." So he named the place "Bursting." ²¹ At that time David and his troops confiscated many idols which had been abandoned by the Philistines. ²² But the Philistines returned and again spread out across the valley of Rephaim.

²³ When David asked the Lord what to do, he replied, "Don't make a frontal attack. Go behind them and come out by the balsam trees. ²⁴ When you hear a sound like marching feet in the tops of the balsam trees, attack! For it will signify that the Lord has prepared the way for you and will destroy them."

²⁵ So David did as the Lord had instructed him and destroyed the Philistines all the way from Geba to Gezer.

6 THEN DAVID MOBILIZED thirty thousand special troops and led them to

Baal-judah to bring home the Ark of the Lord of heaven enthroned above the cherubim. [3] The Ark was placed upon a new cart and taken from the hillside home of Abinadab. It was driven by Abinadab's sons, Uzzah and Ahio. [4] Ahio was walking in front, [5] and was followed by David and the other leaders of Israel, who were joyously waving branches of juniper trees and playing every sort of musical instrument before the Lord —lyres, harps, tambourines, castanets, and cymbals.

[6] But when they arrived at the threshing floor of Nacon, the oxen stumbled and Uzzah put out his hand to steady the Ark. [7] Then the anger of the Lord flared out against Uzzah and he killed him for doing this, so he died there beside the Ark. [8] David was angry at what the Lord had done, and named the spot "The Place of Wrath upon Uzzah" (which it is still called to this day).

[9] David was now afraid of the Lord and asked, "How can I ever bring the Ark home?" [10] So he decided against taking it into the City of David, but carried it instead to the home of Obed-edom, who had come from Gath. [11] It remained there for three months, and the Lord blessed Obed-edom and all his household.

[12] When David heard this, he brought the Ark to the City of David with a great celebration. [13] After the men who were carrying it had gone six paces, they stopped and waited so that he could sacrifice an ox and a fat lamb. [14] And David danced before the Lord with all his might, and was wearing priests' clothing.[a] [15] So Israel brought home the Ark of the Lord with much shouting and blowing of trumpets.

[16] (But as the procession came into the city, Michal, Saul's daughter, watched from a window and saw King David leaping and dancing before the Lord; and she was filled with contempt for him.)

[17] The Ark was placed inside the tent which David had prepared for it; and he sacrificed burnt offerings and peace offerings to the Lord. [18] Then he blessed the people in the name of the Lord of heaven, [19] and gave a present to everyone—men and women alike—of a loaf of bread, some wine,

and a cake of raisins. When it was all over, and everyone had gone home, [20] David returned to bless his family.

But Michal came out to meet him and exclaimed in disgust, "How glorious the king of Israel looked today! He exposed himself to the girls along the street like a common pervert!"

[21] David retorted, "I was dancing before the Lord who chose me above your father and his family and who appointed me as leader of Israel, the people of the Lord! So I am willing to act like a fool in order to show my joy in the Lord. [22] Yes, and I am willing to look even more foolish than this, but I will be respected by the girls of whom you spoke!"

[23] So Michal was childless throughout her life.

7 WHEN THE LORD finally sent peace upon the land, and Israel was no longer at war with the surrounding nations, [2] David said to Nathan the prophet, "Look! Here I am living in this beautiful cedar palace while the Ark of God is out in a tent!"

[3] "Go ahead with what you have in mind," Nathan replied, "for the Lord is with you."

[4] But that night the Lord said to Nathan, [5] "Tell my servant David not to do it![a] [6] For I have never lived in a temple. My home has been a tent ever since the time I brought Israel out of Egypt. [7] And I have never once complained to Israel's leaders, the shepherds of my people. Have I ever asked them, 'Why haven't you built me a beautiful cedar temple?'

[8] "Now go and give this message to David from the Lord of heaven: 'I chose you to be the leader of my people Israel when you were a mere shepherd, tending your sheep in the pastureland. [9] I have been with you wherever you have gone and have destroyed your enemies. And I will make your name greater yet, so that you will be one of the most famous men in the world! [10,11] I have selected a homeland for my people from which they will never have to move. It will be their own land where the heathen nations won't bother them as they did when

---

a Literally, "David was girded with a linen ephod."   7a Literally, "Shall you build me a house to dwell in?"

the judges ruled my people. There will be no more wars against you; and your descendants shall rule this land for generations to come! ¹² For when you die, I will put one of your sons upon your throne and I will make his kingdom strong. ¹³ He is the one who shall build me a temple. And I will continue his kingdom into eternity. ¹⁴ I will be his father and he shall be my son. If he sins, I will use other nations to punish him, ¹⁵ but my love and kindness shall not leave him as I took it from Saul, your predecessor. ¹⁶ Your family shall rule my kingdom forever.' "

¹⁷ So Nathan went back to David and told him everything the Lord had said.

¹⁸ Then David went into the Tabernacle and sat before the Lord and prayed, "O Lord God, why have you showered your blessings on such an insignificant person as I am? ¹⁹ And now, in addition to everything else, you speak of giving me an eternal dynasty! Such generosity is far beyond any human standard! Oh, Lord God! ²⁰ What can I say? For you know what I am like! ²¹ You are doing all these things just because you promised to and because you want to! ²² How great you are, Lord God! We have never heard of any other god like you. And there is no other god. ²³ What other nation in all the earth has received such blessings as Israel, your people? For you have rescued your chosen nation in order to bring glory to your name. You have done great miracles to destroy Egypt and its gods. ²⁴ You chose Israel to be your people forever, and you became our God.

²⁵ "And now, Lord God, do as you have promised concerning me and my family. ²⁶ And may you be eternally honored when you have established Israel as your people and have established my dynasty before you. ²⁷ For you have revealed to me, O Lord of heaven, God of Israel, that I am the first of a dynasty which will rule your people forever; that is why I have been bold enough to pray this prayer of acceptance. ²⁸ For you are indeed God, and your words are truth; and you have promised me these good things— ²⁹ so do as you have promised! Bless me and my family forever! May our dynasty continue on and on before you; for you, Lord God, have promised it.

8 AFTER THIS DAVID subdued and humbled the Philistines by conquering Gath, their largest city. ² He also devastated the land of Moab. He divided his victims by making them lie down side by side in rows. Two-thirds of each row, as measured with a tape, were butchered, and one-third were spared to become David's servants—they paid him tribute each year.

³ He also destroyed the forces of King Hadadezer (son of Rehob) of Zobah in a battle at the Euphrates River, for Hadadezer had attempted to regain his power. ⁴ David captured seventeen hundred cavalry and twenty thousand infantry; then he lamed all of the chariot horses except for one hundred teams. ⁵ He also slaughtered twenty-two thousand Syrians from Damascus when they came to help Hadadezer. ⁶ David placed several army garrisons in Damascus, and the Syrians became David's subjects and brought him annual tribute money. So the Lord gave him victories wherever he turned. ⁷ David brought the gold shields to Jerusalem which King Hadadezer's officers had used. ⁸ He also carried back to Jerusalem a very large amount of bronze from Hadadezer's cities of Betah and Berothai.

⁹ When King Toi of Hamath heard about David's victory over the army of Hadadezer, ¹⁰ he sent his son Joram to congratulate him, for Hadadezer and Toi were enemies. He gave David presents made from silver, gold, and bronze. ¹¹,¹² David dedicated all of these to the Lord, along with the silver and gold he had taken from Syria, Moab, Ammon, the Philistines, Amalek, and King Hadadezer.

¹³ So David became very famous. After his return he destroyed eighteen thousand Edomites[a] at the Valley of Salt, ¹⁴ and then placed garrisons throughout Edom, so that the entire nation was forced to pay tribute to Israel—another example of the way the Lord made him victorious wherever he went.

¹⁵ David reigned with justice over Israel

---

a Literally, "Syrians."

and was fair to everyone. [16] The general of his army was Joab (son of Zeruiah), and his secretary of state was Jehoshaphat (son of Ahilud). [17] Zadok (son of Ahitub) and Ahimelech (son of Abiathar) were the High Priests, and Seraiah was the king's private secretary. [18] Benaiah (son of Jehoiada) was captain of his bodyguard,[b] and David's sons were his assistants.[c]

9 ONE DAY DAVID began wondering if any of Saul's family was still living, for he wanted to be kind to them, as he had promised Prince Jonathan. [2] He heard about a man named Ziba who had been one of Saul's servants, and summoned him.

"Are you Ziba?" the king asked.

"Yes, sir, I am," he replied.

[3] The king then asked him, "Is anyone left from Saul's family? If so, I want to fulfill a sacred vow by being kind to him."

"Yes," Ziba replied, "Jonathan's lame son is still alive."

[4] "Where is he?" the king asked.

"In Lo-debar," Ziba told him. "At the home of Machir."

[5,6] So King David sent for Mephibosheth —Jonathan's son and Saul's grandson. Mephibosheth arrived in great fear and greeted the king in deep humility, bowing low before him.

[7] But David said, "Don't be afraid! I've asked you to come so that I can be kind to you because of my vow to your father Jonathan. I will restore to you all the land of your grandfather Saul, and you shall live here at the palace!"

[8] Mephibosheth fell to the ground before the king. "Should the king show kindness to a dead dog like me?" he exclaimed.

[9] Then the king summoned Saul's servant Ziba. "I have given your master's grandson everything that belonged to Saul and his family," he said. [10,11] "You and your sons and servants are to farm the land for him, to produce food for his family; but he will live here with me."

Ziba, who had fifteen sons and twenty servants, replied, "Sir, I will do all that you have commanded."

And from that time on, Mephibosheth ate regularly with King David, as though he were one of his own sons. [12] Mephibosheth had a young son, Mica. All the household of Ziba became Mephibosheth's servants, [13] but Mephibosheth (who was lame in both feet) moved to Jerusalem to live at the palace.

10 SOME TIME AFTER this the Ammonite king died and his son Hanun replaced him.

[2] "I am going to show special respect for him," David said, "because his father Nahash was always so loyal and kind to me." So David sent ambassadors to express regrets to Hanun about his father's death.

[3] But Hanun's officers told him, "These men aren't here to honor your father! David has sent them to spy out the city before attacking it!"

[4] So Hanun took David's men and shaved off half their beards and cut their robes off at the buttocks and sent them home half naked. [5] When David heard what had happened he told them to stay at Jericho until their beards grew out; for the men were very embarrassed over their appearance.

[6] Now the people of Ammon realized how seriously they had angered David, so they hired twenty thousand Syrian mercenaries from the lands of Rehob and Zobah, one thousand from the king of Maacah, and ten thousand from the land of Tob. [7,8] When David heard about this, he sent Joab and the entire Israeli army to attack them. The Ammonites defended the gates of their city while the Syrians from Zobah, Rehob, Tob, and Maacah fought in the fields. [9] When Joab realized that he would have to fight on two fronts, he selected the best fighters in his army, placed them under his personal command, and took them out to fight the Syrians in the fields. [10] He left the rest of the army to his brother Abishai, who was to attack the city.

[11] "If I need assistance against the Syrians, come out and help me," Joab instructed him. "And if the Ammonites are too strong for you, I will come and help you. [12] Courage! We must really act like

---

b Literally, "the Cherethites and Pelethites."   c Literally, "were priests." See 1 Chronicles 18:17.

men today if we are going to save our people and the cities of our God. May the Lord's will be done."

[13] And when Joab and his troops attacked, the Syrians began to run away. [14] Then, when the Ammonites saw the Syrians running, they ran too, and retreated into the city. Afterwards Joab returned to Jerusalem. [15,16] The Syrians now realized that they were no match for Israel. So when they regrouped, they were joined by additional Syrian troops summoned by Hadadezer from the other side of the Euphrates River. These troops arrived at Helam under the command of Shobach, the commander-in-chief of all of Hadadezer's forces.

[17] When David heard what was happening, he personally led the Israeli army to Helam, where the Syrians attacked him. [18] But again the Syrians fled from the Israelis, this time leaving seven hundred charioteers dead on the field, also forty thousand cavalrymen, including General Shobach. [19] When Hadadezer's allies saw that the Syrians had been defeated, they surrendered to David and became his servants. And the Syrians were afraid to help the Ammonites anymore after that.

11 IN THE SPRING of the following year, at the time when wars begin, David sent Joab and the Israeli army to destroy the Ammonites. They began by laying siege to the city of Rabbah. But David stayed in Jerusalem.

[2] One night he couldn't get to sleep[a] and went for a stroll on the roof of the palace. As he looked out over the city, he noticed a woman of unusual beauty taking her evening bath. [3] He sent to find out who she was and was told that she was Bath-sheba, the daughter of Eliam and the wife of Uriah. [4] Then David sent for her and when she came he slept with her. (She had just completed the purification rites after menstruation.) Then she returned home. [5] When she found that he had gotten her pregnant she sent a message to inform him.

[6] So David dispatched a memo to Joab: "Send me Uriah the Hittite." [7] When he arrived, David asked him how Joab and the army were getting along and how the war was prospering. [8] Then he told him to go home and relax, and he sent a present to him at his home. [9] But Uriah didn't go there. He stayed that night at the gateway of the palace with the other servants of the king.

[10] When David heard what Uriah had done, he summoned him and asked him, "What's the matter with you? Why didn't you go home to your wife last night after being away for so long?"

[11] Uriah replied, "The Ark and the armies and the general and his officers are camping out in open fields, and should I go home to wine and dine and sleep with my wife? I swear that I will never be guilty of acting like that."

[12] "Well, stay here tonight," David told him, "and tomorrow you may return to the army."

So Uriah stayed around the palace. [13] David invited him to dinner and got him drunk; but even so he didn't go home that night, but again he slept at the entry to the palace.

[14] Finally the next morning David wrote a letter to Joab and gave it to Uriah to deliver. [15] The letter instructed Joab to put Uriah at the front of the hottest part of the battle—and then pull back and leave him there to die! [16] So Joab assigned Uriah to a spot close to the besieged city where he knew that the enemies' best men were fighting; [17] and Uriah was killed along with several other Israeli soldiers.

[18] When Joab sent a report to David of how the battle was going, [19,20,21] he told his messenger, "If the king is angry and asks, 'Why did the troops go so close to the city? Didn't they know there would be shooting from the walls? Wasn't Abimelech killed at Thebez by a woman who threw down a millstone on him?'—then tell him, 'Uriah was killed, too.' "

[22] So the messenger arrived at Jerusalem, and gave the report to David.

[23] "The enemy came out against us," he said, "and as we chased them back to the city gates, [24] the men on the wall attacked

---

a Literally, "arose from his bed."

us; and some of our men were killed, and Uriah the Hittite is dead too."

²⁵ "Well, tell Joab not to be discouraged," David said. "The sword kills one as well as another!ᵇ Fight harder next time, and conquer the city; tell him he is doing well."

²⁶ When Bath-sheba heard that her husband was dead, she mourned for him; ²⁷ then, when the period of mourning was over, David sent for her and brought her to the palace and she became one of his wives; and she gave birth to his son. But the Lord was very displeased with what David had done.

12 SO THE LORD sent the prophet Nathan to tell David this story:

"There were two men in a certain city, one very rich, owning many flocks of sheep and herds of goats; ³ and the other very poor, owning nothing but a little lamb he had managed to buy. It was his children's pet and he fed it from his own plate and let it drink from his own cup; he cuddled it in his arms like a baby daughter. ⁴ Recently a guest arrived at the home of the rich man. But instead of killing a lamb from his own flocks for food for the traveler, he took the poor man's lamb and roasted it and served it."

⁵ David was furious. "I swear by the living God," he vowed, "any man who would do a thing like that should be put to death; ⁶ he shall repay four lambs to the poor man for the one he stole, and for having no pity."

⁷ Then Nathan said to David, "*You* are that rich man! The Lord God of Israel says, 'I made you king of Israel and saved you from the power of Saul. ⁸ I gave you his palace and his wives and the kingdoms of Israel and Judah; and if that had not been enough, I would have given you much, much more. ⁹ Why, then, have you despised the laws of God and done this horrible deed? For you have murdered Uriah and stolen his wife. ¹⁰ Therefore murder shall be a constant threat in your family from this time on, because you have insulted me by taking Uriah's wife. ¹¹ I vow that because of what you have done I will cause your own

household to rebel against you. I will give your wives to another man, and he will go to bed with them in public view.ᵃ ¹² You did it secretly, but I will do this to you openly, in the sight of all Israel.' "

¹³ "I have sinned against the Lord," David confessed to Nathan.

Then Nathan replied, "Yes, but the Lord has forgiven you, and you won't die for this sin. ¹⁴ But you have given great opportunity to the enemies of the Lord to despise and blaspheme him, so your child shall die."

¹⁵ Then Nathan returned to his home. And the Lord made Bath-sheba's baby deathly sick. ¹⁶ David begged him to spare the child, and went without food and lay all night before the Lord on the bare earth. ¹⁷ The leaders of the nation pleaded with him to get up and eat with them, but he refused. ¹⁸ Then, on the seventh day, the baby died. David's aides were afraid to tell him.

"He was so broken up about the baby being sick," they said, "what will he do to himself when we tell him the child is dead?"

¹⁹ But when David saw them whispering, he realized what had happened.

"Is the baby dead?" he asked.

"Yes," they replied, "he is." ²⁰ Then David got up off the ground, washed himself, brushed his hair, changed his clothes, and went into the Tabernacle and worshiped the Lord. Then he returned to the palace and ate. ²¹ His aides were amazed.

"We don't understand you," they told him. "While the baby was still living, you wept and refused to eat; but now that the baby is dead, you have stopped your mourning and are eating again."

²² David replied, "I fasted and wept while the child was alive, for I said, 'Perhaps the Lord will be gracious to me and let the child live.' ²³ But why should I fast when he is dead? Can I bring him back again? I shall go to him, but he shall not return to me."

²⁴ Then David comforted Bath-sheba; and when he slept with her, she conceived and gave birth to a son and named him Solomon. And the Lord loved the baby,

---

b Literally, "the sword devours now one and now another."   12a Literally, "under this sun."

[25] and sent congratulations[b] and blessings through Nathan the prophet. David nicknamed the baby Jedidiah (meaning, "Beloved of Jehovah") because of the Lord's interest.[c]

[26,27] Meanwhile Joab and the Israeli army were successfully ending their siege of Rabbah the capital of Ammon. Joab sent messengers to tell David, "Rabbah and its beautiful harbor are ours![d] [28] Now bring the rest of the army and finish the job, so that you will get the credit for the victory instead of me."

[29,30] So David led his army to Rabbah and captured it. Tremendous amounts of loot were carried back to Jerusalem, and David took the king of Rabbah's crown—a $50,000 treasure made from solid gold set with gems—and placed it on his own head. [31] He made slaves of the people of the city and made them labor with saws, picks, and axes and work in the brick kilns;[e] that is the way he treated all of the cities of the Ammonites. Then David and the army returned to Jerusalem.

13 PRINCE ABSALOM, DAVID'S son, had a beautiful sister named Tamar. And Prince Amnon (her half brother) fell desperately in love with her. [2] Amnon became so tormented by his love for her that he became ill. He had no way of talking to her, for the girls and young men were kept strictly apart.[a] [3] But Amnon had a very crafty friend—his cousin Jonadab (the son of David's brother Shime-ah).

[4] One day Jonadab said to Amnon, "What's the trouble? Why should the son of a king look so haggard morning after morning?"

So Amnon told him, "I am in love with Tamar, my half sister."

[5] "Well," Jonadab said, "I'll tell you what to do. Go back to bed and pretend you are sick; when your father comes to see you, ask him to let Tamar come and prepare some food for you. Tell him you'll feel better if she feeds you."

[6] So Amnon did. And when the king came to see him, Amnon asked him for this favor—that his sister Tamar be permitted to come and cook a little something for him to eat. [7] David agreed, and sent word to Tamar to go to Amnon's quarters and prepare some food for him. [8] So she did, and went into his bedroom so that he could watch her mix some dough; then she baked some special bread for him. [9] But when she set the serving tray before him, he refused to eat!

"Everyone get out of here," he told his servants; so they all left the apartment.

[10] Then he said to Tamar, "Now bring me the food again here in my bedroom and feed it to me." So Tamar took it to him. [11] But as she was standing there before him, he grabbed her and demanded, "Come to bed with me, my darling."

[12] "Oh, Amnon," she cried. "Don't be foolish! Don't do this to me! You know what a serious crime it is in Israel.[b] [13] Where could I go in my shame? And you would be called one of the greatest fools in Israel. Please, just speak to the king about it, for he will let you marry me."

[14] But he wouldn't listen to her; and since he was stronger than she, he forced her. [15] Then suddenly his love turned to hate, and now he hated her more than he had loved her.

"Get out of here!" he snarled at her.

[16] "No, no!" she cried. "To reject me now is a greater crime than the other you did to me."

But he wouldn't listen to her. [17,18] He shouted for his valet and demanded, "Throw this woman out and lock the door behind her."

So he put her out. She was wearing a long robe with sleeves, as was the custom in those days for virgin daughters of the king. [19] Now she tore the robe and put ashes on her head and with her head in her hands went away crying.

[20] Her brother Absalom asked her, "Is it true that Amnon raped you? Don't be so upset, since it's all in the family anyway. It's not anything to worry about!"

---

b Literally, "Jehovah sent word by Nathan the prophet." c Literally, "because of the Lord."
d "I have taken the City of Waters." e Or, "killed them with saws and iron harrows, and in brick kilns."
13 a Literally, "for she was a virgin, and it seemed impossible to Amnon to do anything to her."
b Literally, "No such thing ought to be done in Israel; do not this folly."

So Tamar lived as a desolate woman in her brother Absalom's quarters.

²¹⁻²⁴ When King David heard what had happened, he was very angry, but Absalom said nothing one way or the other about this to Amnon. However, he hated him with a deep hatred because of what he had done to his sister. Then, two years later, when Absalom's sheep were being sheared at Baal-hazor in Ephraim, Absalom invited his father and all his brothers to come to a feast to celebrate the occasion.

²⁵ The king replied, "No, my boy; if we all came, we would be too much of a burden on you."

Absalom pressed him, but he wouldn't come, though he sent his thanks.

²⁶ "Well, then," Absalom said, "if you can't come, how about sending my brother Amnon instead?"

"Why Amnon?" the king asked.

²⁷ Absalom kept on urging the matter until finally the king agreed, and let all of his sons attend, including Amnon.

²⁸ Absalom told his men, "Wait until Amnon gets drunk, then, at my signal, kill him! Don't be afraid. I'm the one who gives the orders around here, and this is a command. Take courage and do it!"

²⁹,³⁰ So they murdered Amnon. Then the other sons of the king jumped on their mules and fled. As they were on the way back to Jerusalem, the report reached David: "Absalom has killed all of your sons, and not one is left alive!"

³¹ The king jumped up, ripped off his robe, and fell prostrate to the ground. His aides also tore their clothes in horror and sorrow.

³²,³³ But just then Jonadab (the son of David's brother Shime-ah) arrived and said, "No, not all have been killed! It was only Amnon! Absalom has been plotting this ever since Amnon raped Tamar. No, no! Your sons aren't all dead! It was only Amnon."

³⁴ (Absalom got away.) Now the watchman on the Jerusalem wall saw a great crowd coming toward the city along the road at the side of the hill.

³⁵ "See!" Jonadab told the king. "There they are now! Your sons are coming, just as I said."

³⁶ They soon arrived, weeping and sobbing, and the king and his officials wept with them. ³⁷,³⁸,³⁹ Absalom fled to King Talmai of Geshur^c (the son of Ammihud) and stayed there three years. Meanwhile David, now reconciled to Amnon's death, longed day after day for fellowship with his son Absalom.

14 WHEN GENERAL JOAB realized how much the king was longing to see Absalom, ²,³ he sent for a woman of Tekoa who had a reputation for great wisdom and told her to ask for an appointment with the king. He told her what to say to him.

"Pretend you are in mourning," Joab instructed her. "Wear mourning clothes, and dishevel your hair as though you have been in deep sorrow for a long time."

⁴ When the woman approached the king, she fell face downward on the floor in front of him, and cried out, "O king! Help me!"

⁵,⁶ "What's the trouble?" he asked.

"I am a widow," she replied, "and my two sons had a fight out in the field, and since no one was there to part them, one of them was killed. ⁷ Now the rest of the family is demanding that I surrender my other son to them to be executed for murdering his brother. But if I do that, I will have no one left, and my husband's name will be destroyed from the face of the earth."

⁸ "Leave it with me," the king told her, "I'll see to it that no one touches him."

⁹ "Oh, thank you, my lord," she replied. "And I'll take the responsibility if you are criticized for helping me like this."

¹⁰ "Don't worry about that!" the king replied. "If anyone objects, bring him to me; I can assure you he will never complain again!"

¹¹ Then she said, "Please swear to me by God that you won't let anyone harm my son. I want no more bloodshed."

"I vow by God," he replied, "that not a hair of your son's head shall be disturbed!"

¹² "Please let me ask one more thing of you!" she said.

---

c King Talmai was his grandfather—his mother's father.

"Go ahead," he replied. "Speak!"

¹³ "Why don't you do as much for all the people of God as you have promised to do for me?" she asked. "You have convicted yourself in making this decision, because you have refused to bring home your own banished son. ¹⁴ All of us must die eventually; our lives are like water that is poured out on the ground—it can't be gathered up again. But God will bless you with a longer life if you will find a way to bring your son back from his exile.ᵃ ¹⁵·¹⁶ But I have come to plead with you for my son because my life and my son's life have been threatened, and I said to myself, 'Perhaps the king will listen to me and rescue us from those who would end our existence in Israel. ¹⁷ Yes, the king will give us peace again.' I know that you are like the angel of God and can discern good from evil. May God be with you."

¹⁸ "I want to know one thing," the king replied.

"Yes, my lord?" she asked.

¹⁹ "Did Joab send you here?"

And the woman replied, "How can I deny it? Yes, Joab sent me and told me what to say. ²⁰ He did it in order to place the matter before you in a different light. But you are as wise as an angel of God, and you know everything that happens!"

²¹ So the king sent for Joab and told him, "All right, go and bring back Absalom."

²² Joab fell to the ground before the king and blessed him and said, "At last I know that you like me! For you have granted me this request!"

²³ Then Joab went to Geshur and brought Absalom back to Jerusalem.

²⁴ "He may go to his own quarters," the king ordered, "but he must never come here. I refuse to see him."

²⁵ Now no one in Israel was such a handsome specimen of manhood as Absalom, and no one else received such praise. ²⁶ He cut his hair only once a year—and then only because it weighed three pounds and was too much of a load to carry around! ²⁷ He had three sons and one daughter, Tamar, who was a very beautiful girl.

²⁸ After Absalom had been in Jerusalem for two years and had not yet seen the king, ²⁹ he sent for Joab to ask him to intercede for him; but Joab wouldn't come. Absalom sent for him again, but again he refused to come.

³⁰ So Absalom said to his servants, "Go and set fire to that barley field of Joab's next to mine," and they did.

³¹ Then Joab came to Absalom and demanded, "Why did your servants set my field on fire?"

³² And Absalom replied, "Because I wanted you to ask the king why he brought me back from Geshur if he didn't intend to see me. I might as well have stayed there. Let me have an interview with the king; then if he finds that I am guilty of murder, let him execute me."

³³ So Joab told the king what Absalom had said. Then at last David summoned Absalom, and he came and bowed low before the king, and David kissed him.

15 ABSALOM THEN BOUGHT a magnificent chariot and chariot horses, and hired fifty footmen to run ahead of him. ² He got up early every morning and went out to the gate of the city; and when anyone came to bring a case to the king for trial, Absalom called him over and expressed interest in his problem.

³ He would say, "I can see that you are right in this matter; it's unfortunate that the king doesn't have anyone to assist him in hearing these cases. ⁴ I surely wish I were the judge; then anyone with a lawsuit could come to me, and I would give him justice!"

⁵ And when anyone came to bow to him, Absalom wouldn't let him, but shook his hand instead!ᵃ ⁶ So in this way Absalom stole the hearts of all the people of Israel.

⁷·⁸ After four years, Absalom said to the king, "Let me go to Hebron to sacrifice to the Lord in fulfillment of a vow I made to him while I was at Geshur—that if he would bring me back to Jerusalem, I would sacrifice to him."

⁹ "All right," the king told him, "go and fulfill your vow."

---

a Or, "God does not sweep life away, but has made provision to bring back those he banishes, so that they will not be forever exiles."   15a Literally, "took hold of him and kissed him."

So Absalom went to Hebron.[b] [10] But while he was there, he sent spies to every part of Israel to incite rebellion against the king. "As soon as you hear the trumpets," his message read, "you will know that Absalom has been crowned in Hebron." [11] He took two hundred men from Jerusalem with him as guests, but they knew nothing of his intentions. [12] While he was offering the sacrifice, he sent for Ahithophel, one of David's counselors who lived in Giloh. Ahithophel declared for Absalom, as did more and more others. So the conspiracy became very strong.

[13] A messenger soon arrived in Jerusalem to tell King David, "All Israel has joined Absalom in a conspiracy against you!"

[14] "Then we must flee at once or it will be too late!" was David's instant response to his men. "If we get out of the city before he arrives, both we and the city of Jerusalem will be saved."

[15] "We are with you," his aides replied. "Do as you think best."

[16] So the king and his household set out at once. He left no one behind except ten of his young wives to keep the palace in order. [17,18] David paused at the edge of the city to let his troops move past him to lead the way—six hundred Gittites who had come with him from Gath, and the Cherethites and Pelethites.

[19,20] But suddenly the king turned to Ittai, the captain of the six hundred Gittites, and said to him, "What are you doing here? Go on back with your men to Jerusalem, to your king, for you are a guest in Israel, a foreigner in exile. It seems but yesterday that you arrived, and now today should I force you to wander with us, who knows where? Go on back and take your troops with you, and may the Lord be merciful to you."

[21] But Ittai replied, "I vow by God and by your own life that wherever you go, I will go, no matter what happens—whether it means life or death."

[22] So David replied, "All right, come with us." Then Ittai and his six hundred men and their families went along.

[23] There was deep sadness throughout the city as the king and his retinue passed by, crossed Kidron Brook, and went out into the country. [24] Abiathar and Zadok and the Levites took the Ark of the Covenant of God and set it down beside the road until everyone had passed. [25,26] Then, following David's instructions, Zadok took the Ark back into the city. "If the Lord sees fit," David said, "he will bring me back to see the Ark and the Tabernacle again. But if he is through with me, well, let him do what seems best to him."

[27] Then the king told Zadok, "Look, here is my plan. Return quietly to the city with your son Ahima-az and Abiathar's son Jonathan. [28] I will stop at the ford of the Jordan River and wait there for a message from you. Let me know what happens in Jerusalem before I disappear into the wilderness."

[29] So Zadok and Abiathar carried the Ark of God back into the city and stayed there.

[30] David walked up the road that led to the Mount of Olives, weeping as he went. His head was covered and his feet were bare as a sign of mourning. And the people who were with him covered their heads and wept as they climbed the mountain. [31] When someone told David that Ahithophel, his advisor, was backing Absalom, David prayed, "O Lord, please make Ahithophel give Absalom foolish advice!" [32] As they reached the spot at the top of the Mount of Olives where people worshiped God, David found Hushai the Archite waiting for him with torn clothing and earth upon his head.

[33,34] But David told him, "If you go with me, you will only be a burden; return to Jerusalem and tell Absalom, 'I will counsel you as I did your father.' Then you can frustrate and counter Ahithophel's advice. [35,36] Zadok and Abiathar, the priests, are there. Tell them the plans that are being made to capture me, and they will send their sons Ahima-az and Jonathan to find me and tell me what is going on."

[37] So David's friend Hushai returned to

---

b Hebron was King David's first capital, and it was also Absalom's home town, its people doubtless very proud of him.

the city, getting there just as Absalom arrived.

16 DAVID WAS JUST past the top of the hill when Ziba, the manager of Mephibosheth's household, caught up with him. He was leading two donkeys loaded with two hundred loaves of bread, one hundred clusters of raisins, one hundred bunches of grapes, and a small barrel of wine.

² "What are these for?" the king asked Ziba.

And Ziba replied, "The donkeys are for your people to ride on, and the bread and summer fruit are for the young men to eat; the wine is to be taken with you into the wilderness for any who become faint."

³ "And where is Mephibosheth?" the king asked him.

"He stayed at Jerusalem," Ziba replied. "He said, 'Now I'll get to be king! Today I will get back the kingdom of my father, Saul.'ᵃ

⁴ "In that case," the king told Ziba, "I give you everything he owns."

"Thank you, thank you, sir," Ziba replied.

⁵ As David and his party passed Bahurim, a man came out of the village cursing them. It was Shime-i, the son of Gera, a member of Saul's family. ⁶ He threw stones at the king and the king's officers and all the mighty warriors who surrounded them!

⁷·⁸ "Get out of here, you murderer, you scoundrel!" he shouted at David. "The Lord is paying you back for murdering King Saul and his family; you stole his throne and now the Lord has given it to your son Absalom! At last you will taste some of your own medicine, you murderer!"

⁹ "Why should this dead dog curse my lord the king?" Abishai demanded. "Let me go over and strike off his head!"

¹⁰ "No!" the king said. "If the Lord has told him to curse me, who am I to say no? ¹¹ My own son is trying to kill me, and this Benjaminite is merely cursing me. Let him alone, for no doubt the Lord has told him to do it. ¹² And perhaps the Lord will see

that I am being wronged and will bless me because of these curses."

¹³ So David and his men continued on, and Shime-i kept pace with them on a nearby hillside, cursing as he went and throwing stones at David and tossing dust into the air. ¹⁴ The king and all those who were with him were weary by the time they reached Bahurim, so they stayed there awhile and rested.

¹⁵ Meanwhile, Absalom and his men arrived at Jerusalem, accompanied by Ahithophel. ¹⁶ When David's friend, Hushai the Archite, arrived, he went immediately to see Absalom.

"Long live the king!" he exclaimed. "Long live the king!"

¹⁷ "Is this the way to treat your friend David?" Absalom asked him. "Why aren't you with him?"

¹⁸ "Because I work for the man who is chosen by the Lord and by Israel," Hushai replied. ¹⁹ "And anyway, why shouldn't I? I helped your father and now I will help you!"

²⁰ Then Absalom turned to Ahithophel and asked him, "What shall I do next?"

²¹ Ahithophel told him, "Go and sleep with your father's wives, for he has left them here to keep the house. Then all Israel will know that you have insulted him beyond the possibility of reconciliation, and they will all close ranks behind you."ᵇ

²² So a tent was erected on the roof of the palace where everybody could see it, and Absalom went into the tent to lie with his father's wives. ²³ (Absalom did whatever Ahithophel told him to, just as David had; for every word Ahithophel spoke was as wise as though it had come directly from the mouth of God.)

17 "NOW," AHITHOPHEL SAID, "give me twelve thousand men to start out after David tonight. ²·³ I will come upon him while he is weary and discouraged, and he and his troops will be thrown into a panic and everyone will run away; and I will kill only the king, and let all those who are with him live, and restore them to you."

---

a Saul was Mephibosheth's grandfather.

b Literally, "the hands of all who are with you will be strengthened."

⁴ Absalom and all the elders of Israel approved of the plan, ⁵ but Absalom said, "Ask Hushai the Archite what he thinks about this."

⁶ When Hushai arrived, Absalom told him what Ahithophel had said.

"What is your opinion?" Absalom asked him. "Should we follow Ahithophel's advice? If not, speak up."

⁷ "Well," Hushai replied, "this time I think Ahithophel has made a mistake. ⁸ You know your father and his men; they are mighty warriors and are probably as upset as a mother bear who has been robbed of her cubs. And your father is an old soldier and isn't going to be spending the night among the troops; ⁹ he has probably already hidden in some pit or cave. And when he comes out and attacks and a few of your men fall, there will be panic among your troops and everyone will start shouting that your men are being slaughtered. ¹⁰ Then even the bravest of them, though they have hearts of lions, will be paralyzed with fear; for all Israel knows what a mighty man your father is and how courageous his soldiers are.

¹¹ "What I suggest is that you mobilize the entire army of Israel, bringing them from as far away as Dan and Beer-sheba, so that you will have a huge force. And I think that you should personally lead the troops. ¹² Then when we find him we can destroy his entire army so that not one of them is left alive. ¹³ And if David has escaped into some city, you will have the entire army of Israel there at your command, and we can take ropes and drag the walls of the city into the nearest valley until every stone is torn down."

¹⁴ Then Absalom and all the men of Israel said, "Hushai's advice is better than Ahithophel's." For the Lord had arranged to defeat the counsel of Ahithophel, which really was the better plan, so that he could bring disaster upon Absalom! ¹⁵ Then Hushai reported to Zadok and Abiathar, the priests, what Ahithophel had said and what he himself had suggested instead.

¹⁶ "Quick!" he told them. "Find David and urge him not to stay at the ford of the Jordan River tonight. He must go across at once into the wilderness beyond; otherwise he will die, and his entire army with him."

¹⁷ Jonathan and Ahima-az had been staying at En-rogel so as not to be seen entering and leaving the city. Arrangements had been made for a servant girl to carry to them the messages they were to take to King David. ¹⁸ But a boy saw them leaving En-rogel to go to David, and he told Absalom about it. Meanwhile, they escaped to Bahurim where a man hid them inside a well in his backyard. ¹⁹ The man's wife put a cloth over the top of the well with grain on it to dry in the sun; so no one suspected they were there.

²⁰ When Absalom's men arrived and asked her if she had seen Ahima-az and Jonathan, she said they had crossed the brook and were gone. They looked for them without success and returned to Jerusalem. ²¹ Then the two men crawled out of the well and hurried on to King David. "Quick!" they told him, "cross the Jordan tonight!" And they told him how Ahithophel had advised that he be captured and killed. ²² So David and all the people with him went across during the night and were all on the other bank before dawn.

²³ Meanwhile, Ahithophel—publicly disgraced when Absalom refused his advice—saddled his donkey, went to his home town, set his affairs in order, and hanged himself; so he died and was buried beside his father.

²⁴ David soon arrived at Mahanaim. Meanwhile, Absalom had mobilized the entire army of Israel and was leading them across the Jordan River. ²⁵ Absalom had appointed Amasa as general of the army, replacing Joab. (Amasa was Joab's second cousin; his father was Ithra, an Ishmaelite, and his mother was Abigal, the daughter of Nahash, who was the sister of Joab's mother Zeruiah.) ²⁶ Absalom and the Israeli army now camped in the land of Gilead.

²⁷ When David arrived at Mahanaim, he was warmly greeted by Shobi (son of Nahash of Rabbah, an Ammonite) and Machir (son of Ammiel of Lodebar) and Barzillai (a Gileadite of Rogelim). ²⁸⁻²⁹ They brought him and those who were with him mats to sleep on, cooking pots, serving bowls, wheat and barley flour, parched grain, beans, lentils, honey, butter, and cheese. For they said, "You must be very tired and hungry

and thirsty after your long march through the wilderness."

18 DAVID NOW APPOINTED regimental colonels and company commanders over his troops. [2] A third were placed under Joab's brother, Abishai (the son of Zeruiah); and a third under Ittai, the Gittite. The king planned to lead the army himself, but his men objected strongly.

[3] "You mustn't do it," they said, "for if we have to turn and run, and half of us die, it will make no difference to them—they will be looking only for you. You are worth ten thousand of us, and it is better that you stay here in the city and send us help if we need it."

[4] "Well, whatever you think best," the king finally replied. So he stood at the gate of the city as all the troops passed by.

[5] And the king commanded Joab, Abishai, and Ittai, "For my sake, deal gently with young Absalom." And all the troops heard the king give them this charge.

[6] So the battle began in the forest of Ephraim, [7] and the Israeli troops were beaten back by David's men. There was a great slaughter and twenty thousand men laid down their lives that day. [8] The battle raged all across the countryside, and more men disappeared in the forest than were killed. [9] During the battle Absalom came upon some of David's men and as he fled[a] on his mule, it went beneath the thick boughs of a great oak tree, and his hair caught in the branches. His mule went on, leaving him dangling in the air. [10] One of David's men saw him and told Joab.

[11] "What? You saw him there and didn't kill him?" Joab demanded. "I would have rewarded you handsomely and made you a commissioned officer."[b]

[12] "For a million dollars I wouldn't do it," the man replied. "We all heard the king say to you and Abishai and Ittai, 'For my sake, please don't harm young Absalom.' [13] And if I had betrayed the king by killing his son (and the king would certainly find out who did it), you yourself would be the first to accuse me."

[14] "Enough of this nonsense," Joab said. Then he took three daggers and plunged them into the heart of Absalom as he dangled alive from the oak. [15] Ten of Joab's young armor bearers then surrounded Absalom and finished him off. [16] Then Joab blew the trumpet, and his men returned from chasing the army of Israel. [17] They threw Absalom's body into a deep pit in the forest and piled a great heap of stones over it. And the army of Israel fled to their homes.

[18] (Absalom had built a monument to himself in the King's Valley, for he said, "I have no sons to carry on my name." He called it "Absalom's Monument," as it is still known today.)

[19] Then Zadok's son Ahima-az said, "Let me run to King David with the good news that the Lord has saved him from his enemy Absalom."

[20] "No," Joab told him, "it wouldn't be good news to the king that his son is dead. You can be my messenger some other time."

[21] Then Joab said to a man from Cush, "Go tell the king what you have seen." The man bowed and ran off.

[22] But Ahima-az pleaded with Joab, "Please let me go, too."

"No, we don't need you now, my boy." Joab replied. "There is no further news to send."

[23] "Yes, but let me go anyway," he begged.

And Joab finally said, "All right, go ahead." Then Ahima-az took a short cut across the plain and got there ahead of the man from Cush. [24] David was sitting at the gate of the city. When the watchman climbed the stairs to his post at the top of the wall, he saw a lone man running towards them.

[25] He shouted the news down to David, and the king replied, "If he is alone, he has news."

As the messenger came closer, [26] the watchman saw another man running towards them. He shouted down, "Here comes another one."

---

a Implied.   b Literally, "Given you ten pieces of silver and a belt." There is no way of knowing the value of the silver. The belt was probably that worn by a commissioned officer.

And the king replied, "He will have more news."

²⁷ "The first man looks like Ahima-az, the son of Zadok," the watchman said.

"He is a good man and comes with good news," the king replied.

²⁸ Then Ahima-az cried out to the king, "All is well!" He bowed low with his face to the ground and said, "Blesssed be the Lord your God who has destroyed the rebels who dared to stand against you."

²⁹ "What of young Absalom?" the king demanded. "Is he all right?"

"When Joab told me to come, there was a lot of shouting; but I didn't know what was happening,"ᶜ Ahima-az answered.

³⁰ "Wait here," the king told him. So Ahima-az stepped aside.

³¹ Then the man from Cush arrived and said, "I have good news for my lord the king. Today Jehovah has rescued you from all those who rebelled against you."

³² "What about young Absalom? Is he all right?" the king demanded.

And the man replied, "May all of your enemies be as that young man is!"

³³ Then the king broke into tears, and went up to his room over the gate, crying as he went. "O my son Absalom, my son, my son Absalom. If only I could have died for you! O Absalom, my son, my son."

19 WORD SOON REACHED Joab that the king was weeping and mourning for Absalom. ² As the people heard of the king's deep grief for his son, the joy of that day's wonderful victory was turned into deep sadness. ³ The entire army crept back into the city as though they were ashamed and had been beaten in battle.

⁴ The king covered his face with his hands and kept on weeping, "O my son Absalom! O Absalom my son, my son!"

⁵ Then Joab went to the king's room and said to him, "We saved your life today and the lives of your sons, your daughters, your wives and concubines; and yet you act like this, making us feel ashamed, as though we had done something wrong. ⁶ You seem to love those who hate you, and hate those who love you. Apparently we don't mean anything to you; if Absalom had lived and all of us had died, you would be happy. ⁷ Now go out there and congratulate the troops, for I swear by Jehovah that if you don't, not a single one of them will remain here during the night; then you will be worse off than you have ever been in your entire life."

⁸,⁹,¹⁰ So the king went out and sat at the city gates, and as the news spread throughout the city that he was there, everyone went to him.

Meanwhile, there was much discussion and argument going on all across the nation: "Why aren't we talking about bringing the king back?" was the great topic everywhere. "For he saved us from our enemies, the Philistines; and Absalom, whom we made our king instead, chased him out of the country, but now Absalom is dead. Let's ask David to return and be our king again."

¹¹,¹² Then David sent Zadok and Abiathar the priests to say to the elders of Judah, "Why are you the last ones to reinstate the king? For all Israel is ready, and only you are holding out. Yet you are my own brothers, my own tribe, my own flesh and blood!"

¹³ And he told them to tell Amasa, "Since you are my nephew, may God strike me dead if I do not appoint you as commander-in-chief of my army in place of Joab." ¹⁴ Then Amasa convinced all the leaders of Judah, and they responded as one man. They sent word to the king, "Return to us and bring back all those who are with you."

¹⁵ So the king started back to Jerusalem. And when he arrived at the Jordan River, it seemed as if everyone in Judah had come to Gilgal to meet him and escort him across the river! ¹⁶ Then Shime-i (the son of Gera the Benjaminite), the man from Bahurim, hurried across with the men of Judah to welcome King David. ¹⁷ A thousand men from the tribe of Benjamin were with him, including Ziba, the servant of Saul, and Ziba's fifteen sons and twenty servants; they rushed down to the Jordan to arrive ahead of the king. ¹⁸ They all worked hard ferrying the king's household and troops across, and helped them in every way they could.

---

c Ahima-az apparently was afraid to tell the king what actually had happened.

As the king was crossing, Shime-i fell down before him, [19] and pleaded, "My lord the king, please forgive me and forget the terrible thing I did when you left Jerusalem; [20] for I know very well how much I sinned. That is why I have come here today, the very first person in all the tribe of Joseph to greet you."

[21] Abishai asked, "Shall not Shime-i die, for he cursed the Lord's chosen king!"

[22] "Don't talk to me like that!" David exclaimed. "This is not a day for execution but for celebration! I am once more king of Israel!"

[23] Then, turning to Shime-i, he vowed, "Your life is spared."

[24,25] Now Mephibosheth, Saul's grandson, arrived from Jerusalem to meet the king. He had not washed his feet or clothes nor trimmed his beard since the day the king left Jerusalem.

"Why didn't you come with me, Mephibosheth?" the king asked him.

[26] And he replied, "My lord, O king, my servant Ziba deceived me. I told him, 'Saddle my donkey so that I can go with the king.' For as you know I am lame. [27] But Ziba has slandered me by saying that I refused to come.[a] But I know that you are as an angel of God, so do what you think best. [28] I and all my relatives could expect only death from you, but instead you have honored me among all those who eat at your own table! So how can I complain?"

[29] "All right," David replied. "My decision is that you and Ziba will divide the land equally between you."

[30] "Give him all of it," Mephibosheth said. "I am content just to have you back again!"

[31,32] Barzillai, who had fed the king and his army during their exile in Mahanaim, arrived from Rogelim to conduct the king across the river. He was very old now, about eighty, and very wealthy.

[33] "Come across with me and live in Jerusalem," the king said to Barzillai. "I will take care of you there."

[34] "No," he replied, "I am far too old for that. [35] I am eighty years old today, and life

has lost its excitement.[b] Food and wine are no longer tasty, and entertainment is not much fun; I would only be a burden to my lord the king. [36] Just to go across the river with you is all the honor I need! [37] Then let me return again to die in my own city, where my father and mother are buried. But here is Chimham.[c] Let him go with you and receive whatever good things you want to give him."

[38] "Good," the king agreed. "Chimham shall go with me, and I will do for him whatever I would have done for you."

[39] So all the people crossed the Jordan with the king; and after David had kissed and blessed Barzillai, he returned home. [40] The king then went on to Gilgal, taking Chimham with him. And most of Judah and half of Israel were there to greet him. [41] But the men of Israel complained to the king because only men from Judah had ferried him and his household across the Jordan.

[42] "Why not?" the men of Judah replied. "The king is one of our own tribe. Why should this make you angry? We have charged him nothing—he hasn't fed us or given us gifts!"

[43] "But there are ten tribes in Israel," the others replied, "so we have ten times as much right in the king as you do; why didn't you invite the rest of us? And, remember, we were the first to speak of bringing him back to be our king again."

The argument continued back and forth, and the men of Judah were very rough in their replies.

20 THEN A HOT-HEAD whose name was Sheba (son of Bichri, a Benjaminite) blew a trumpet and yelled, "We want nothing to do with David. Come on, you men of Israel, let's get out of here. He's not our king!"

[2] So all except Judah and Benjamin turned around and deserted David and followed Sheba! But the men of Judah stayed with their king, accompanying him from the Jordan to Jerusalem. [3] When he arrived at his palace in Jerusalem, the king in-

---

a Implied.   b Literally, "can I discern between good and bad?"   c According to Josephus, Chimham was Barzillai's son.

structed that his ten wives he had left to keep house should be placed in seclusion. Their needs were to be cared for, he said, but he would no longer sleep with them as his wives. So they remained in virtual widowhood until their deaths.

⁴ Then the king instructed Amasa to mobilize the army of Judah within three days and to report back at that time. ⁵ So Amasa went out to notify the troops, but it took him longer than the three days he had been given.

⁶ Then David said to Abishai, "That fellow Sheba is going to hurt us more than Absalom did. Quick, take my bodyguard and chase after him before he gets into a fortified city where we can't reach him."

⁷ So Abishai and Joab set out after Sheba with an elite guard from Joab's army and the king's own bodyguard. ⁸,⁹,¹⁰ As they arrived at the great stone in Gibeon, they came face to face with Amasa. Joab was wearing his uniform with a dagger strapped to his side. As he stepped forward to greet Amasa, he stealthily slipped the dagger from its sheath. "I'm glad to see you, my brother," Joab said, and took him by the beard with his right hand as though to kiss him. Amasa didn't notice the dagger in his left hand, and Joab stabbed him in the stomach with it, so that his bowels gushed out onto the ground. He did not need to strike again, and he died there. Joab and his brother Abishai left him lying there and continued after Sheba.

¹¹ One of Joab's young officers shouted to Amasa's troops, "If you are for David, come and follow Joab."

¹² But Amasa lay in his blood in the middle of the road, and when Joab's young officers saw that a crowd was gathering around to stare at him, they dragged him off the road into a field and threw a garment over him. ¹³ With the body out of the way, everyone went on with Joab to capture Sheba.

¹⁴ Meanwhile Sheba had traveled across Israel to mobilize his own clan of Bichri at the city of Abel in Beth-maacah. ¹⁵ When Joab's forces arrived, they besieged Abel and built a mound to the top of the city wall and began battering it down.

¹⁶ But a wise woman in the city called out to Joab, "Listen to me, Joab. Come over here so I can talk to you."

¹⁷ As he approached, the woman asked, "Are you Joab?"

And he replied, "I am."

¹⁸ So she told him, "There used to be a saying, 'If you want to settle an argument, ask advice at Abel.' For we always give wise counsel. ¹⁹ You are destroying an ancient, peace-loving city, loyal to Israel. Should you destroy what is the Lord's?"

²⁰ And Joab replied, "That isn't it at all. ²¹ All I want is a man named Sheba from the hill country of Ephraim, who has revolted against King David. If you will deliver him to me, we will leave the city in peace."

"All right," the woman replied, "we will throw his head over the wall to you."

²² Then the woman went to the people with her wise advice, and they cut off Sheba's head and threw it out to Joab. And he blew the trumpet and called his troops back from the attack, and they returned to the king at Jerusalem.

²³ Joab was commander-in-chief of the army, and Benaiah was in charge of the king's bodyguard.ᵃ ²⁴ Adoram was in charge of the forced labor battalions, and Jehoshaphat was the historian who kept the records. ²⁵ Sheva was the secretary, and Zadok and Abiathar were the chief priests. ²⁶ Ira the Jairite was David's personal chaplain.

21 THERE WAS A famine during David's reign that lasted year after year for three years, and David spent much time in prayer about it. Then the Lord said, "The famine is because of the guilt of Saul and his family, for they murdered the Gibeonites."

² So King David summoned the Gibeonites. They were not part of Israel, but were what was left of the nation of the Amorites. Israel had sworn not to kill them; but Saul, in his nationalistic zeal, had tried to wipe them out.

³ David asked them, "What can I do for you, to rid ourselves of this guilt and to induce you to ask God to bless us?"

---

a Literally, "the Cherethites and Pelethites."

⁴ "Well, money won't do it," the Gibeonites replied, "and we don't want to see Israelites executed in revenge."

"What can I do, then?" David asked. "Just tell me and I will do it for you."

⁵,⁶ "Well, then," they replied, "give us seven of Saul's sons—the sons of the man who did his best to destroy us. We will hang them before the Lord in Gibeon, the city of King Saul."

"All right," the king said, "I will do it." ⁷ He spared Jonathan's son Mephibosheth, who was Saul's grandson, because of the oath between himself and Jonathan. ⁸ But he gave them the two sons of Rizpah—Armoni and Mephibosheth—who were grandsons of Saul by his wife Aiah. He also gave them the five adopted sons of Michal that she brought up for Saul's daughter Merab, the wife of Adri-el. ⁹ The men of Gibeon impaled them in the mountain before the Lord. So all seven of them died together at the beginning of the barley harvest.

¹⁰ Then Rizpah, the mother of two of the men,ᵃ spread sackcloth upon a rock and stayed there through the entire harvest seasonᵇ to prevent the vultures from tearing at their bodies during the day and the wild animals from eating them at night. ¹¹ When David learned what she had done, ¹²,¹³,¹⁴ he arranged for the men's bones to be buried in the grave of Saul's father, Kish. At the same time he sent a request to the men of Jabesh-gilead, asking them to bring him the bones of Saul and Jonathan. They had stolen their bodies from the public square at Beth-shan where the Philistines had impaled them after they had died in battle on Mount Gilboa. So their bones were brought to him. Then at last God answered prayer and ended the famine.

¹⁵ Once when the Philistines were at war with Israel, and David and his men were in the thick of the battle, David became weak and exhausted. ¹⁶ Ishbi-benob, a giant whose speartip weighed more than twelve pounds and who was sporting a new suit of armor, closed in on David and was about to kill him. ¹⁷ But Abishai the son of Zer-uiah came to his rescue and killed the Philistine. After that David's men declared, "You are not going out to battle again! Why should we risk snuffing out the light of Israel?"

¹⁸ Later, during a war with the Philistines at Gob, Sibbecai the Hushathite killed Saph, another giant. ¹⁹ At still another time and at the same place, Elhanan killed the brother of Goliath the Gittite,ᶜ whose spearhandle was as huge as a weaver's beam! ²⁰,²¹ And once when the Philistines and the Israelis were fighting at Gath, a giant with six fingers on each hand and six toes on each foot defied Israel, and David's nephew Jonathan—the son of David's brother Shime-i—killed him. ²² These four were from the tribe of giants in Gath, and were killed by David's troops.

22 DAVID SANG THIS song to the Lord after he had rescued him from Saul and from all his other enemies:

² "Jehovah is my rock,
My fortress and my Savior.
³ I will hide in God,
Who is my rock and my refuge.
He is my shield
And my salvation,
My refuge and high tower.
Thank you, O my Savior,
For saving me from all my enemies.
⁴ I will call upon the Lord,
Who is worthy to be praised;
He will save me from all my enemies.
⁵ The waves of death surrounded me;
Floods of evil burst upon me;
⁶ I was trapped, and bound
By hell and death;
⁷ But I called upon the Lord in my distress,
And he heard me from his Temple.
My cry reached his ears.
⁸ Then the earth shook and trembled;
The foundations of the heavens quaked
Because of his wrath.
⁹ Smoke poured from his nostrils;
Fire leaped from his mouth
And burned up all before him,

a Implied.   b The harvest lasted six months, from April until October.   c Literally, "slew Goliath of Gath." (See 1 Chronicles 20:5.)

Setting fire to the world.[a]

¹⁰ He bent the heavens down and
came to earth;
He walked upon dark clouds.

¹¹ He rode upon the glorious—
On the wings of the wind.

¹² Darkness surrounded him,
And clouds were thick around him;

¹³ The earth was radiant with his
brightness.

¹⁴ The Lord thundered from heaven;
The God above all gods gave out a
mighty shout.

¹⁵ He shot forth his arrows of lightning
And routed his enemies.

¹⁶ By the blast of his breath
Was the sea split in two.
The bottom of the sea appeared.

¹⁷ From above, he rescued me.
He drew me out from the waters;

¹⁸ He saved me from powerful enemies,
From those who hated me
And from those who were too strong
for me.

¹⁹ They came upon me
In the day of my calamity,
But the Lord was my salvation.

²⁰ He set me free and rescued me,
For I was his delight.

²¹ The Lord rewarded me for my
goodness,
For my hands were clean;

²² And I have not departed from my
God.

²³ I knew his laws,
And I obeyed them.

²⁴ I was perfect in obedience
And kept myself from sin.

²⁵ That is why the Lord has done so
much for me,
For he sees that I am clean.

²⁶ You are merciful to the merciful;
You show your perfections
To the blameless.

²⁷ To those who are pure,
You show yourself pure;
But you destroy those who are evil.

²⁸ You will save those in trouble,
But you bring down the haughty;

For you watch their every move.

²⁹ O Lord, you are my light!
You make my darkness bright.

³⁰ By your power I can crush an
army;
By your strength I leap over a wall.

³¹ As for God, his way is perfect;
The word of the Lord is true.
He shields all who hide behind him.

³² Our Lord alone is God;
We have no other Savior.[b]

³³ God is my strong fortress;
He has made me safe.

³⁴ He causes the good to walk a steady
tread
Like mountain goats upon the rocks.

³⁵ He gives me skill in war
And strength to bend a bow of
bronze.

³⁶ You have given me the shield of
your salvation;
Your gentleness has made me great.

³⁷ You have made wide steps for my
feet,
To keep them from slipping.

³⁸ I have chased my enemies
And destroyed them.
I did not stop till all were gone.

³⁹ I have destroyed them
So that none can rise again.
They have fallen beneath my feet.

⁴⁰ For you have given me strength for
the battle
And have caused me to subdue
All those who rose against me.

⁴¹ You have made my enemies
Turn and run away;
I have destroyed them all.

⁴² They looked in vain for help;
They cried to God,
But he refused to answer.

⁴³ I beat them into dust;
I crushed and scattered them
Like dust along the streets.

⁴⁴ You have preserved me
From the rebels of my people;
You have preserved me
As the head of the nations.
Foreigners shall serve me

⁴⁵ And shall quickly submit to me
When they hear of my power.

---

a Literally, "coals were kindled by it."   b Literally, "Who is a rock save our God?"

⁴⁶ They shall lose heart
And come, trembling,
From their hiding places.
⁴⁷ The Lord lives.
Blessed be my Rock.
Praise to him—
The Rock of my salvation.
⁴⁸ Blessed be God
Who destroys those who oppose me
⁴⁹ And rescues me from my enemies.
Yes, you hold me safe above their
    heads.
You deliver me from violence.
⁵⁰ No wonder I give thanks to you, O
    Lord, among the nations,
And sing praises to your name.
⁵¹ He gives wonderful deliverance to
    his king,
And shows mercy to his anointed—
To David and his family,
Forever."

23 THESE ARE THE last words of David:
"David, the son of Jesse, speaks.
David, the man to whom God gave
    such wonderful success;
David, the anointed of the God of
    Jacob;
David, sweet psalmist of Israel:
² The Spirit of the Lord spoke by me,
And his word was on my tongue.
³ The Rock of Israel said to me:
'One shall come who rules right-
    eously,
Who rules in the fear of God.
⁴ He shall be as the light of the morn-
    ing;
A cloudless sunrise
When the tender grass
Springs forth upon the earth;
As sunshine after rain.'
⁵ And it is my family
He has chosen!
Yes, God has made
An everlasting covenant with me;
His agreement is eternal, final, sealed.
He will constantly look after
My safety and success.ᵃ
⁶ But the godless are as thorns to be
    thrown away,
For they tear the hand that touches

them.
⁷ One must be armed to chop them
    down;
They shall be burned."
⁸ These are the names of the Top
Three—the most heroic men in David's
army: the first was Josheb-basshebeth from
Tah-chemon, known also as Adino, the Ez-
nite. He once killed eight hundred men in
one battle.
⁹ Next in rank was Eleazar, the son of
Dodo and grandson of Ahohi. He was one
of the three men who, with David, held
back the Philistines that time when the rest
of the Israeli army fled. ¹⁰ He killed the Philistines until his hand was too tired to hold
his sword; and the Lord gave him a great
victory. (The rest of the army did not return
until it was time to collect the loot!)
¹¹,¹² After him was Shammah, the son of
Agee from Harar. Once during a Philistine
attack, when all his men deserted him and
fled, he stood alone at the center of a field
of lentils and beat back the Philistines; and
God gave him a great victory.
¹³ One time when David was living in the
cave of Adullam and the invading Philistines were at the valley of Rephaim, three
of The Thirty—the top-ranking officers of
the Israeli army—went down at harvest
time to visit him. ¹⁴ David was in the stronghold at the time, for Philistine marauders
had occupied the nearby city of Bethlehem.
¹⁵ David remarked, "How thirsty I am
for some of that good water in the city
well!" (The well was near the city gate.)
¹⁶ So the three men broke through the
Philistine ranks and drew water from the
well and brought it to David. But he refused
to drink it! Instead, he poured it out before
the Lord.
¹⁷ "No, my God," he exclaimed, "I cannot do it! This is the blood of these men who
have risked their lives."
¹⁸,¹⁹ Of those three men, Abishai, the
brother of Joab (son of Zeruiah), was the
greatest. Once he took on three hundred of
the enemy singlehanded and killed them all.
It was by such feats that he earned a reputation equal to The Three, though he was not
actually one of them. But he was the great-

---

a Literally, "He will cause my help and my desire to sprout."

est of The Thirty—the top-ranking officers of the army—and was their leader.

²⁰ There was also Benaiah (son of Jehoiada), a heroic soldier from Kabzeel. Benaiah killed two giants,ᵇ sons of Ariel of Moab. Another time he went down into a pit and, despite the slippery snow on the ground, took on a lion that was caught there and killed it. ²¹ Another time, armed only with a staff, he killed an Egyptian warrior who was armed with a spear; he wrenched the spear from the Egyptian's hand and killed him with it. ²² These were some of the deeds that gave Benaiah almost as much renown as the Top Three. ²³ He was one of the greatest of The Thirty, but was not actually one of the Top Three. And David made him chief of his bodyguard.

²⁴⁻³⁹ Asahel, the brother of Joab, was also one of The Thirty. Others were:

Elhanan (son of Dodo) from Bethlehem;

Shammah from Harod:

Elika from Harod;

Helez from Palti;

Ira (son of Ikkesh) from Tekoa;

Abi-ezer from Anathoth;

Mebunnai from Hushath;

Zalmon from Ahoh;

Maharai from Netophah;

Heleb (son of Baanah) from Netophah;

Ittai (son of Ribai) from Gibe-ah, of the tribe of Benjamin;

Benaiah of Pirathon;

Hiddai from the brooks of Gaash;

Abi-albon from Arbath;

Azmaveth from Bahurim;

Eliahba from Sha-albon;

The sons of Jashen;

Jonathan;

Shammah from Harar;

Ahiam (the son of Sharar) from Harar;

Eliphelet (son of Ahasbai) from Maacah;

Eliam (the son of Ahithophel) from Gilo;

Hezro from Carmel;

Paarai from Arba;

Igal (son of Nathan) from Zobah;

Bani from Gad;

Zelek from Ammon;

Naharai from Be-eroth, the armor bearer of Joab (son of Zeruiah);

Ira from Ithra;

Gareb from Ithra;

Uriah the Hittite—thirty-sevenᶜ in all.

24 ONCE AGAIN THE anger of the Lord flared against Israel, and David was moved to harm them by taking a national census.

² The king said to Joab, commander-in-chief of his army, "Take a census of all the people from one end of the nation to the other, so that I will know how many of them there are."

³ But Joab replied, "God grant that you will live to see the day when there will be a hundred times as many people in your kingdom as there are now! But you have no right to rejoice in their strength."ᵃ

⁴ But the king's command overcame Joab's remonstrance; so Joab and the other army officers went out to count the people of Israel. ⁵ First they crossed the Jordan and camped at Aroer, south of the city that lies in the middle of the valley of Gad, near Jazer; ⁶ then they went to Gilead in the land of Tahtim-hodshi and to Dan-jaan and around to Sidon; ⁷ and then to the stronghold of Tyre, and all the cities of the Hivites and Canaanites, and south to Judah as far as Beer-sheba. ⁸ Having gone through the entire land, they completed their task in nine months and twenty days. ⁹ And Joab reported the number of the people to the king—800,000 men of conscription age in Israel, and 500,000 in Judah.

¹⁰ But after he had taken the census, David's conscience began to bother him, and he said to the Lord, "What I did was very wrong. Please forgive this foolish wickedness of mine."

¹¹ The next morning the word of the Lord came to the prophet Gad, who was David's contact with God.

The Lord said to Gad, ¹² "Tell David

---

b The meaning of the Hebrew wording is uncertain.   c The Thirty, plus the Top Three, plus Generals Joab, Abishai, Asahel, and Benaiah. Apparently new names were elected to this hall of fame to replace those who died.   24a Literally, "But why does my lord the king delight in this thing?"

that I will give him three choices."

[13] So Gad came to David and asked him, "Will you choose seven years of famine across the land, or to flee for three months before your enemies, or to submit to three days of plague? Think this over and let me know what answer to give to God."

[14] "This is a hard decision," David replied, "but it is better to fall into the hand of the Lord (for his mercy is great) than into the hands of men."

[15] So the Lord sent a plague upon Israel that morning, and it lasted for three days; and seventy thousand men died throughout the nation. [16] But as the death angel was preparing to destroy Jerusalem, the Lord was sorry for what was happening and told him to stop. He was by the threshing floor of Araunah the Jebusite at the time.

[17] When David saw the angel, he said to the Lord, "Look, I am the one who has sinned! What have these sheep done? Let your anger be only against me and my family."

[18] That day Gad came to David and said to him, "Go and build an altar to the Lord on the threshing floor of Araunah the Jebusite." [19] So David went to do what the Lord had commanded him. [20] When Araunah saw the king and his men coming towards him, he came forward and fell flat on the ground with his face in the dust.

[21] "Why have you come?" Araunah asked.

And David replied, "To buy your threshing floor, so that I can build an altar to the Lord, and he will stop the plague."

[22] "Use anything you like," Araunah told the king. "Here are oxen for the burnt offering, and you can use the threshing instruments and ox yokes for wood to build a fire on the altar. [23] I will give it all to you, and may the Lord God accept your sacrifice."

[24] But the king said to Araunah, "No, I will not have it as a gift. I will buy it, for I don't want to offer to the Lord my God burnt offerings that have cost me nothing."

So David paid him[b] for the threshing floor and the oxen. [25] And David built an altar there to the Lord and offered burnt offerings and peace offerings. And the Lord answered his prayer, and the plague was stopped.

---

b Literally, "paid him fifty shekels of silver."

QB= Quick Brains

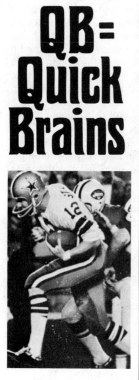

A good quarterback needs more than just a deadly throwing arm. He must read enemy defenses, choose offensive plays, make all the right moves, and keep a cool head through the pass rushes. That's what great quarterbacking is all about.

The political quarterbacks who ruled after David were not always as tough under pressure as their ancestor. David's grandson, Rehoboam, took a hard line on the draft and taxes, and promptly split the nation in two—"Judah" (two tribes) and "Israel" (ten tribes). Together, 1 and 2 Kings cover more than four centuries of leaders, a few of them godly and successful, but more of them off on their own ego-trips which left God out of their plan.

Tough prophets like Elijah and Elisha sometimes succeeded at pounding sense into royal heads, but by 587 B.C. the Assyrians and Babylonians had combined to force-march the Israelis away from their homes and to devastate the splendid capital of David and Solomon. Then, as now, it all depended upon who was listening to God and who was ignoring him.

The Christian Athlete

1 KINGS

1 IN HIS OLD age King David was confined to his bed; but no matter how many blankets were heaped upon him, he was always cold.

[2] "The cure for this," his aides told him, "is to find a young virgin to be your concubine and nurse. She will lie in your arms and keep you warm."

[3,4] So they searched the country from one end to the other to find the most beautiful girl in all the land. Abishag, from Shunam, was finally selected. They brought her to the king and she lay in his arms to warm him (but he had no sexual relations with her).

[5] At about that time, David's son[a] Adonijah (his mother was Haggith) decided to crown himself king in place of his aged father. So he hired chariots and drivers and recruited fifty men to run down the streets before him as royal footmen. [6] Now his father, King David, had never disciplined him at any time—not so much as by a single scolding! He was a very handsome man, and was Absalom's younger brother. [7] He took General Joab and Abiathar the priest into his confidence, and they agreed to help him become king. [8] But among those who remained loyal to King David and refused to endorse Adonijah were the priests Zadok and Benaiah, the prophet Nathan, Shime-i, Rei, and David's army chiefs.

[9] Adonijah went to En-rogel where he sacrificed sheep, oxen, and fat young goats at the Serpent's Stone. Then he summoned

a Implied.

all of his brothers—the other sons of King David—and all the royal officials of Judah, requesting that they come to his coronation. ¹⁰ But he didn't invite Nathan the prophet, Benaiah, the loyal army officers, or his brother Solomon.

¹¹ Then Nathan the prophet went to Bath-sheba, Solomon's mother, and asked her, "Do you realize that Haggith's son, Adonijah, is now the king and that our lord David doesn't even know about it? ¹² If you want to save your own life and the life of your son Solomon—do exactly as I say! ¹³ Go at once to King David and ask him, 'My lord, didn't you promise me that my son Solomon would be the next king and would sit upon your throne? Then why is Adonijah reigning?' ¹⁴ And while you are still talking with him, I'll come and confirm everything you've said."

¹⁵ So Bath-sheba went into the king's bedroom. He was an old, old man now, and Abishag was caring for him. ¹⁶ Bath-sheba bowed low before him.

"What do you want?" he asked her.

¹⁷ She replied, "My lord, you vowed to me by the Lord your God that my son Solomon would be the next king and would sit upon your throne. ¹⁸ But instead, Adonijah is the new king, and you don't even know about it. ¹⁹ He has celebrated his coronation by sacrificing oxen, fat goats, and many sheep and has invited all your sons and Abiathar the priest and General Joab. But he didn't invite Solomon. ²⁰ And now, my lord the king, all Israel is waiting for your decision as to whether Adonijah is the one you have chosen to succeed you. ²¹ If you don't act, my son Solomon and I will be arrested and executed as criminals as soon as you are dead."

²²,²³ While she was speaking, the king's aides told him, "Nathan the prophet is here to see you."

Nathan came in and bowed low before the king, ²⁴ and asked, "My lord, have you appointed Adonijah to be the next king? Is he the one you have selected to sit upon your throne? ²⁵ Today he celebrated his coronation by sacrificing oxen and fat goats and many sheep, and has invited your sons

to attend the festivities. He also invited General Joab and Abiathar the priest; and they are feasting and drinking with him and shouting, 'Long live King Adonijah!' ²⁶ But Zadok the priest and Benaiah and Solomon and I weren't invited. ²⁷ Has this been done with your knowledge? For you haven't said a word as to which of your sons you have chosen to be the next king."

²⁸ "Call Bath-sheba," David said. So she came back in and stood before the king.

²⁹ And the king vowed, "As the Lord lives who has rescued me from every danger, ³⁰ I decree that your son Solomon shall be the next king and shall sit upon my throne, just as I swore to you before by the Lord God of Israel."

³¹ Then Bath-sheba bowed low before him again[b] and exclaimed, "Oh, thank you, sir. May my lord the king live forever!"

³² "Call Zadok the priest," the king ordered, "and Nathan the prophet, and Benaiah."

When they arrived, ³³ he said to them, "Take Solomon and my officers to Gihon. Solomon is to ride on my personal mule, ³⁴ and Zadok the priest and Nathan the prophet are to anoint him there as king of Israel. Then blow the trumpets and shout, 'Long live King Solomon!' ³⁵ When you bring him back here, place him upon my throne as the new king; for I have appointed him king of Israel and Judah."

³⁶ "Amen! Praise God!" replied Benaiah, and added, ³⁷ "May the Lord be with Solomon as he has been with you, and may God make Solomon's reign even greater than yours!"

³⁸ So Zadok the priest, Nathan the prophet, Benaiah, and David's bodyguard took Solomon to Gihon, riding on King David's own mule. ³⁹ At Gihon, Zadok took a flask of sacred oil from the Tabernacle and poured it over Solomon; and the trumpets were blown and all the people shouted, "Long live King Solomon!"

⁴⁰ Then they all returned with him to Jerusalem. making a joyous and noisy celebration all along the way. ⁴¹ Adonijah and his guests heard the commotion and shouting just as they were finishing their banquet.

---

b Literally, "did reverence to the king."

"What's going on?" Joab demanded. "Why is the city in such an uproar?"

⁴² And while he was still speaking, Jonathan, the son of Abiathar the priest, rushed in.

"Come in," Adonijah said to him, "for you are a good man; you must have good news."

⁴³ "Our lord King David has declared Solomon as king!" Jonathan shouted. ⁴⁴,⁴⁵ "The king sent him to Gihon with Zadok the priest and Nathan the prophet and Benaiah, protected by the king's own bodyguard; and he rode on the king's own mule. And Zadok and Nathan have anointed him as the new king! They have just returned, and the whole city is celebrating and rejoicing. That's what all the noise is. ⁴⁶,⁴⁷ Solomon is sitting on the throne, and all the people are congratulating King David, saying, 'May God bless you even more through Solomon than he has blessed you personally! May God make Solomon's reign even greater than yours!' And the king is lying in bed, acknowledging their blessings. ⁴⁸ He is saying, 'Blessed be the Lord God of Israel who has selected one of my sons to sit upon my throne while I am still alive to see it.'"

⁴⁹,⁵⁰ Then Adonijah and his guests jumped up from the banquet table and fled in panic; for they were fearful for their lives. Adonijah rushed into the Tabernacle and caught hold of the horns of the sacred altar. ⁵¹ When word reached Solomon that Adonijah was claiming sanctuary in the Tabernacle, and pleading for clemency, ⁵² Solomon replied, "If he behaves himself, he will not be harmed; but if he does not, he shall die." ⁵³ So King Solomon summoned him, and they brought him down from the altar. He came to bow low before the king; and then Solomon curtly dismissed him.

"Go on home," he said.

2 AS THE TIME of King David's death approached, he gave this charge to his son Solomon:

² "I am going where every man on earth must some day go. I am counting on you to be a strong and worthy successor. ³ Obey the laws of God and follow all his ways; keep each of his commands written in the law of Moses so that you will prosper in everything you do, wherever you turn. ⁴ If you do this, then the Lord will fulfill the promise he gave me, that if my children and their descendants watch their step and are faithful to God, one of them shall always be the king of Israel—my dynasty will never end.

⁵ "Now listen to my instructions. You know that Joab murdered my two generals, Abner and Amasa. He pretended that it was an act of war, but it was done in a time of peace. ⁶ You are a wise man and will know what to do—don't let him die in peace. ⁷ But be kind to the sons of Barzillai the Gileadite. Make them permanent guests of the king, for they took care of me when I fled from your brother Absalom. ⁸ And do you remember Shime-i, the son of Gera the Benjaminite from Bahurim? He cursed me with a terrible curse as I was going to Mahanaim; but when he came down to meet me at the Jordan River I promised I wouldn't kill him. ⁹ But that promise doesn't bind you! You are a wise man, and you will know how to arrange a bloody death for him."

¹⁰ Then David died and was buried in Jerusalem. ¹¹ He had reigned over Israel for forty years, seven of them in Hebron and thirty-three in Jerusalem. ¹² And Solomon became the new king, replacing his father David; and his kingdom prospered.

¹³ One day Adonijah the son of Haggith came to see Solomon's mother, Bath-sheba.

"Have you come to make trouble?" she asked him.

"No," he replied, "I come in peace. ¹⁴ As a matter of fact, I have a favor to ask of you."

"What is it?" she asked.

¹⁵ "Everything was going well for me," he said, "and the kingdom was mine: everyone expected me to be the next king. But the tables are turned, and everything went to my brother instead; for that is the way the Lord wanted it. ¹⁶ But now I have just a small favor to ask of you; please don't turn me down."

"What is it?" she asked.

¹⁷ He replied, "Speak to King Solomon on my behalf (for I know he will do anything you request) and ask him to give me Abishag, the Shunammite, as my wife."

[18] "All right," Bath-sheba replied, "I'll ask him."

[19] So she went to ask the favor of King Solomon. The king stood up from his throne as she entered and bowed low to her. He ordered that a throne for his mother be placed beside his; so she sat at his right hand.

[20] "I have one small request to make of you," she said. "I hope you won't turn me down."

"What is it, my mother?" he asked. "You know I won't refuse you."

[21] "Then let your brother Adonijah marry Abishag," she replied.

[22] "Are you crazy?" he asked her. "If I were to give him Abishag, I would be giving him the kingdom too! For he is my older brother! He and Abiathar the priest and General Joab would take over!" [23,24] Then King Solomon swore with a great oath, "May God strike me dead if Adonijah does not die this very day for this plot against me! I swear it by the living God who has given me the throne of my father David and this kingdom he promised me."

[25] So King Solomon sent Benaiah to execute him, and he killed him with a sword.

[26] Then the king said to Abiathar the priest, "Go back to your home in Anathoth. You should be killed, too, but I won't do it now. For you carried the Ark of the Lord during my father's reign, and you suffered right along with him in all of his troubles."

[27] So Solomon forced Abiathar to give up his position as the priest of the Lord, thereby fulfilling the decree of Jehovah at Shiloh concerning the descendants of Eli.[a]

[28] When Joab heard about Adonijah's death (Joab had joined Adonijah's revolt, though not Absalom's) he ran to the Tabernacle for sanctuary and caught hold of the horns of the altar. [29] When news of this reached King Solomon, he sent Benaiah to execute him.

[30] Benaiah went into the Tabernacle and said to Joab, "The king says to come out!"

"No," he said, "I'll die here."

So Benaiah returned to the king for further instructions.

[31] "Do as he says," the king replied.

"Kill him there beside the altar and bury him. This will remove the guilt of his senseless murders from me and from my father's family. [32] Then Jehovah will hold him personally responsible for the murders of two men who were better than he. For my father was no party to the deaths of General Abner, commander-in-chief of the army of Israel, and General Amasa, commander-in-chief of the army of Judah. [33] May Joab and his descendants be forever guilty of these murders, and may the Lord declare David and his descendants guiltless concerning their deaths."

[34] So Benaiah returned to the Tabernacle and killed Joab; and he was buried beside his house in the desert.

[35] Then the king appointed Benaiah as commander-in-chief, and Zadok as priest instead of Abiathar.

[36,37] The king now sent for Shime-i and told him, "Build a house here in Jerusalem, and don't step outside the city on pain of death. The moment you go beyond Kidron Brook, you die; and it will be your own fault."

[38] "All right," Shime-i replied, "whatever you say." So he lived in Jerusalem for a long time.

[39] But three years later two of Shime-i's slaves escaped to King Achish of Gath. When Shime-i learned where they were, [40] he saddled a donkey and went to Gath to visit the king. And when he had found his slaves, he took them back to Jerusalem.

[41] When Solomon heard that Shime-i had left Jerusalem and had gone to Gath and returned, [42] he sent for him and demanded, "Didn't I command you in the name of God to stay in Jerusalem or die? You replied, 'Very well, I will do as you say.' [43] Then why have you not kept your agreement and obeyed my commandment? [44] And what about all the wicked things you did to my father, King David? May the Lord take revenge on you, [45] but may I receive God's rich blessings, and may one of David's descendants always sit upon this throne."

[46] Then, at the king's command, Benaiah took Shime-i outside and killed him.

---

a See 1 Samuel 2:31-35.

So Solomon's grip upon the kingdom became secure.

3 SOLOMON MADE AN alliance with Pharaoh, the king of Egypt, and married one of his daughters. He brought her to Jerusalem to live in the City of David until he could finish building his palace and the Temple and the wall around the city.

² At that time the people of Israel sacrificed their offerings on altars in the hills, for the Temple of the Lord hadn't yet been built.

³ (Solomon loved the Lord and followed all of his father David's instructions except that he continued to sacrifice in the hills and to offer incense there.) ⁴ The most famous of the hilltop altars was at Gibeon and now the king went there and sacrificed one thousand burnt offerings! ⁵ The Lord appeared to him in a dream that night and told him to ask for anything he wanted, and it would be given to him!

⁶ Solomon replied, "You were wonderfully kind to my father David because he was honest and true and faithful to you, and obeyed your commands. And you have continued your kindness to him by giving him a son to succeed him. ⁷ O Lord my God, now you have made me the king instead of my father David, but I am as a little child who doesn't know his way around. ⁸ And here I am among your own chosen people, a nation so great that there are almost too many people to count! ⁹ Give me an understanding mind so that I can govern your people well and know the difference between what is right and what is wrong. For who by himself is able to carry such a heavy responsibility?"

¹⁰ The Lord was pleased with his reply and was glad that Solomon had asked for wisdom. ¹¹ So he replied, "Because you have asked for wisdom in governing my people, and haven't asked for a long life or riches for yourself, or the defeat of your enemies— ¹² yes, I'll give you what you asked for! I will give you a wiser mind than anyone else has ever had or ever will have! ¹³ And I will also give you what you didn't ask for—riches and honor! And no one in all the world will be as rich and famous as you for the rest of your life! ¹⁴ And I will give you a long life

if you follow me and obey my laws as your father David did."

¹⁵ Then Solomon woke up and realized it had been a dream. He returned to Jerusalem and went into the Tabernacle. And as he stood before the Ark of the Covenant of the Lord, he sacrificed burnt offerings and peace offerings. Then he invited all of his officials to a great banquet.

¹⁶ Soon afterwards two young prostitutes came to the king to have an argument settled.

¹⁷,¹⁸ "Sir," one of them began, "we live in the same house, just the two of us, and recently I had a baby. When it was three days old, this woman's baby was born too. ¹⁹ But her baby died during the night when she rolled over on it in her sleep and smothered it. ²⁰ Then she got up in the night and took my son from beside me while I was asleep, and laid her dead child in my arms and took mine to sleep beside her. ²¹ And in the morning when I tried to feed my baby it was dead! But when it became light outside, I saw that it wasn't my son at all."

²² Then the other woman interrupted, "It certainly was her son, and the living child is mine."

"No," the first woman said, "the dead one is yours and the living one is mine." And so they argued back and forth before the king.

²³ Then the king said, "Let's get the facts straight: both of you claim the living child, and each says that the dead child belongs to the other. ²⁴ All right, bring me a sword." So a sword was brought to the king. ²⁵ Then he said, "Divide the living child in two and give half to each of these women!"

²⁶ Then the woman who really was the mother of the child, and who loved him very much, cried out, "Oh, no, sir! Give her the child—don't kill him!"

But the other woman said, "All right, it will be neither yours nor mine; divide it between us!"

²⁷ Then the king said, "Give the baby to the woman who wants him to live, for she is the mother!"

²⁸ Word of the king's decision spread quickly throughout the entire nation, and all the people were awed as they realized the great wisdom God had given him.

4 HERE IS A list of King Solomon's cabinet members:

Azariah (son of Zadok) was the High Priest;

Elihoreph and Ahijah (sons of Shisha) were secretaries;

Jehoshaphat (son of Ahilud) was the official historian and in charge of the archives;

Benaiah (son of Jehoiada) was commander-in-chief of the army;

Zadok and Abiathar were priests;

Azariah (son of Nathan) was secretary of state;

Zabud (son of Nathan) was the king's personal priest and special friend;

Ahishar was manager of palace affairs;

Adoniram (son of Abda) was superintendent of public works.

⁷ There were also twelve officials of Solomon's court—one man from each tribe—responsible for requisitioning food from the people for the king's household. Each of them arranged provisions for one month of the year.

⁸⁻¹⁹ The names of these twelve officers were:

Ben-hur, whose area for this taxation was the hill country of Ephraim;

Ben-deker, whose area was Makaz, Sha-albim, Beth-shemesh, and Elon-beth-hanan;

Ben-hesed, whose area was Arubboth, including Socoh and all the land of Hepher;

Ben-abinadab (who married Solomon's daughter, the princess Taphath), whose area was the highlands of Dor;

Baana (son of Ahilud), whose area was Taanach and Megiddo, all of Beth-shean near Zarethan below Jezreel, and all the territory from Beth-shean to Abel-meholah and over to Jokmeam;

Ben-geber, whose area was Ramoth-gilead, including the villages of Jair (the son of Manasseh) in Gilead; and the region of Argob in Bashan, including sixty walled cities with bronze gates;

Ahinadab (the son of Iddo), whose area was Mahanaim;

Ahima-az (who married Princess Basemath, another of Solomon's daughters), whose area was Naphtali;

Baana (son of Hushai), whose areas were Asher and Bealoth;

Jehoshaphat (son of Paruah), whose area was Issachar;

Shime-i (son of Ela), whose area was Benjamin;

Geber (son of Uri), whose area was Gilead, including the territories of King Sihon of the Amorites and King Og of Bashan.

A general manager supervised these officials and their work.

²⁰ Israel and Judah were a wealthy, populous, contented nation at this time. ²¹ King Solomon ruled the whole area from the Euphrates River to the land of the Philistines, and down to the borders of Egypt. The conquered peoples of those lands sent taxes to Solomon and continued to serve him throughout his lifetime.

²² The daily food requirements for the palace were 195 bushels of fine flour, 390 bushels of meal, ²³ 10 oxen from the fattening pens, 20 pasture-fed cattle, 100 sheep, and, from time to time, deer, gazelles, roebucks, and plump fowl.

²⁴ His dominion extended over all the kingdoms west of the Euphrates River, from Tiphsah to Gaza. And there was peace throughout the land.

²⁵ Throughout the lifetime of Solomon, all of Judah and Israel lived in peace and safety; and each family had its own home and garden.

²⁶ Solomon owned forty thousand chariot horses and employed twelve thousand charioteers. ²⁷ Each month the tax officials provided food for King Solomon and his court; ²⁸ also the barley and straw for the royal horses in the stables.

²⁹ God gave Solomon great wisdom and understanding, and a mind with broad interests. ³⁰ In fact, his wisdom excelled that of any of the wise men of the East, including those in Egypt. ³¹ He was wiser than Ethan the Ezrahite and Heman, Calcol, and Darda, the sons of Mahol; and he was famous among all the surrounding nations.

[32] He was the author of 3,000 proverbs and wrote 1,005 songs. [33] He was a great naturalist, with interest in animals, birds, snakes, fish, and trees—from the great cedars of Lebanon down to the tiny hyssop which grows in cracks in the wall. [34] And kings from many lands sent their ambassadors to him for his advice.

5 KING HIRAM OF Tyre had always been a great admirer of David, so when he learned that David's son Solomon was the new king of Israel, he sent ambassadors to extend congratulations and good wishes. [2,3] Solomon replied with a proposal about the Temple of the Lord he wanted to build. His father David, Solomon pointed out to Hiram, had not been able to build it because of the numerous wars going on, and he had been waiting for the Lord to give him peace.

[4] "But now," Solomon said to Hiram, "the Lord my God has given Israel peace on every side; I have no foreign enemies or internal rebellions. [5] So I am planning to build a Temple for the Lord my God, just as he instructed my father that I should do. For the Lord told him, 'Your son, whom I will place upon your throne, shall build me a Temple.' [6] Now please assist me with this project. Send your woodsmen to the mountains of Lebanon to cut cedar timber for me, and I will send my men to work beside them, and I will pay your men whatever wages you ask; for as you know, no one in Israel can cut timber like you Sidonians!"

[7] Hiram was very pleased with the message from Solomon. "Praise God for giving David a wise son to be king of the great nation of Israel," he said. [8] Then he sent this reply to Solomon: "I have received your message and I will do as you have asked concerning the timber. I can supply both cedar and cypress. [9] My men will bring the logs from the Lebanon mountains to the Mediterranean Sea and build them into rafts. We will float them along the coast to wherever you need them; then we will break the rafts apart and deliver the timber to you. You can pay me with food for my household."

[10] So Hiram produced for Solomon as much cedar and cypress timber as he desired, [11] and in return Solomon sent him an annual payment of 125,000 bushels of wheat for his household and 96 gallons of pure olive oil. [12] So the Lord gave great wisdom to Solomon just as he had promised. And Hiram and Solomon made a formal alliance of peace.

[13] Then Solomon drafted thirty thousand laborers from all over Israel, [14] and rotated them to Lebanon, ten thousand a month, so that each man was a month in Lebanon and two months at home. Adoniram was the general superintendent of this labor camp. [15] Solomon also had seventy thousand additional laborers, eighty thousand stonecutters in the hill country, [16] and thirty-three hundred foremen. [17] The stonecutters quarried and shaped huge blocks of stone—a very expensive job—for the foundation of the Temple. [18] Men from Gebal helped Solomon's and Hiram's builders in cutting the timber and making the boards, and in preparing the stone for the Temple.

6 IT WAS IN the spring of the fourth year of Solomon's reign that he began the actual construction of the Temple. (This was 480 years after the people of Israel left their slavery in Egypt.) [2] The Temple was ninety feet long, thirty feet wide, and forty-five feet high. [3] All along the front of the Temple was a porch thirty feet long and fifteen feet deep. [4] Narrow windows were used throughout.

[5] An annex of rooms was built along the full length of both sides of the Temple against the outer walls. [6] These rooms were three stories high. the lower floor being 7½ feet wide, the second floor 9 feet wide, and the upper floor 10½ feet wide. The rooms were connected to the walls of the Temple by beams resting on blocks built out from the wall—so the beams were not inserted into the walls themselves.

[7] The stones used in the construction of the Temple were prefinished at the quarry, so the entire structure was built without the sound of hammer, axe, or any other tool at the building site.

[8] The bottom floor of the side rooms was entered from the right side of the Temple, and there were winding stairs going up to the second floor; another flight of stairs led from the second to the third. [9] After com-

pleting the Temple, Solomon paneled it all, including the beams and pillars, with cedar. [10] As already stated, there was an annex on each side of the building, attached to the Temple walls by cedar timbers. Each story of the annex was 7½ feet high.

[11,12] Then the Lord sent this message to Solomon concerning the Temple he was building: "If you do as I tell you to and follow all of my commandments and instructions, I will do what I told your father David I would do: [13] I will live among the people of Israel and never forsake them."

[14] At last the Temple was finished. [15] The entire inside, from floor to ceiling, was paneled with cedar, and the floors were made of cypress boards. [16] The thirty-foot inner room at the far end of the Temple—the Most Holy Place—was also paneled from the floor to the ceiling with cedar boards. [17] The remainder of the Temple—other than the Most Holy Place—was sixty feet long. [18] Throughout the Temple the cedar paneling laid over the stone walls was carved with designs of rosebuds and open flowers.

[19] The inner room was where the Ark of the Covenant of the Lord was placed. [20] This inner sanctuary was thirty feet long, thirty feet wide, and thirty feet high. Its walls and ceiling were overlaid with pure gold, and Solomon made a cedar-wood altar for this room. [21,22] Then he overlaid the interior of the remainder of the Temple—including the cedar altar—with pure gold; and he made gold chains to protect the entrance to the Most Holy Place.

[23-28] Within the inner sanctuary Solomon placed two statues of angels[a] made from olive wood, each fifteen feet high. They were placed so that their outspread wings reached from wall to wall, while their inner wings touched each other at the center of the room; each wing was 7½ feet long, so each angel measured fifteen feet from wing tip to wing tip. The two angels were identical in all dimensions, and each was overlaid with gold.

[29] Figures of angels, palm trees, and open flowers were carved on all the walls of both rooms of the Temple, [30] and the floor of both rooms was overlaid with gold.

[31] The doorway to the inner sanctuary was a five-sided opening, [32] and its two olive-wood doors were carved with cherubim, palm trees, and open flowers, all overlaid with gold.

[33] Then he made square doorposts of olive wood for the entrance to the Temple. [34] There were two folding doors of cypress wood, and each door was hinged to fold back upon itself. [35] Angels, palm trees, and open flowers were carved on these doors and carefully overlaid with gold.

[36] The wall of the inner court had three layers of hewn stone and one layer of cedar beams.

[37] The foundation of the Temple was laid in the month of May in the fourth year of Solomon's reign, [38] and the entire building was completed in every detail in November of the eleventh year of his reign. So it took seven years to build.

7 THEN SOLOMON BUILT his own palace, which took thirteen years to construct.

[2] One of the rooms in the palace was called the Hall of the Forest of Lebanon. It was huge—measuring 150 feet long, 75 feet wide, and 45 feet high. The great cedar ceiling beams rested upon four rows of cedar pillars. [3,4] There were forty-five windows in the hall, set in three tiers, one tier above the other, five to a tier, facing each other from three walls. [5] Each of the doorways and windows had a square frame.

[6] Another room was called the Hall of Pillars. It was seventy-five feet long and forty-five feet wide, with a porch in front covered by a canopy which was supported by pillars.

[7] There was also the Throne Room or Judgment Hall, where Solomon sat to hear legal matters; it was paneled with cedar from the floor to the rafters.

[8] His cedar-paneled living quarters surrounded a courtyard behind this hall. (He designed similar living quarters, the same size, in the palace which he built for Pharaoh's daughter—one of his wives.) [9] These buildings were constructed entirely from huge, expensive stones, cut to measure. [10] The foundation stones were twelve to

---

a Literally, "he made two cherubim."

fifteen feet across. [11] The huge stones in the walls were also cut to measure, and were topped with cedar beams. [12] The Great Court had three courses of hewn stone in its walls, topped with cedar beams, just like the inner court of the Temple and the porch of the palace.

[13] King Solomon then asked for a man named Hiram to come from Tyre, for he was a skilled craftsman in bronze work. [14] He was half Jewish, being the son of a widow of the tribe of Naphtali, and his father had been a foundry worker from Tyre. So he came to work for King Solomon.

[15] He cast two hollow bronze pillars, each twenty-seven feet high and eighteen feet around, with four-inch-thick walls. [16-22] At the tops of the pillars he made two lily-shaped capitals of molten bronze, each 7½ feet high, and 6 feet wide. Each capital was decorated with seven sets of bronze, chain-designed lattices and four hundred pomegranates in two rows. Hiram set these pillars at the entrance of the Temple. The one on the south was named the Jachin Pillar, and the one on the north, the Boaz Pillar.[a]

[23] Then Hiram cast a round bronze tank, 7½ feet high and 15 feet from brim to brim; 45 feet in circumference. [24] On the underside of the rim were two rows of ornaments an inch or two apart,[b] which were cast along with the tank. [25] It rested on twelve bronze[c] oxen standing tail to tail, three facing north, three west, three south, and three east. [26] The sides of the tank were four inches thick; its brim was shaped like a goblet, and it had a twelve thousand gallon capacity.

[27-30] Then he made ten four-wheeled movable stands, each 6 feet square and 4½ feet high. They were constructed with undercarriages braced with square[d] crosspieces. These crosspieces were decorated with carved lions, oxen, and angels. Above and below the lions and oxen were wreath decorations. Each of these movable stands had four bronze wheels and bronze axles, and at each corner of the stands were supporting posts made of bronze and decorated with wreaths on each side. [31] The top of each stand was a round piece 1½ feet high. Its center was concave, 2¼ feet deep, decorated on the outside with wreaths. Its panels were square, not round.

[32] The stands rode on four wheels which were connected to axles that had been cast as part of the stands. The wheels were twenty-seven inches high, [33] and were similar to chariot wheels. All the parts of the stands were cast from molten bronze, including the axles, spokes, rims, and hubs. [34] There were supports at each of the four corners of the stands, and these, too, were cast with the stands. [35] A nine-inch rim surrounded the tip of each stand, banded with lugs. All was cast as one unit with the stand. [36] Cherubim, lions, and palm trees surrounded by wreaths were engraved on the borders of the band wherever there was room. [37] All ten stands were the same size and were made alike, for each was cast from the same mold.

[38] Then he made ten brass vats, and placed them on the stands. Each vat was six feet square and contained 240 gallons of water. [39] Five of these vats were arranged on the left and five on the right-hand side of the room. The tank was in the southeast corner, on the right-hand side of the room. [40] Hiram also made the necessary pots, shovels, and basins and at last completed the work in the Temple of the Lord which had been assigned to him by King Solomon.

[41-46] Here is a list of the items he made:
Two pillars;
A capital at the top of each pillar;
Latticework covering the bases of the capitals of each pillar;
Four hundred pomegranates in two rows on the latticework, to cover the bases of the two capitals;
Ten movable stands holding ten vats;
One large tank and twelve oxen supporting it;
Pots;
Shovels;
Basins.

All these items were made of burnished bronze, and were cast at the plains of the

---

a Jachin means "to establish," and Boaz means "strength."
c Implied.   d Implied in verse 31.

b Literally, "ten in a cubit."

Jordan River between Succoth and Zarethan. ⁴⁷ The total weight of these pieces was not known because they were too heavy to weigh!

⁴⁸ All the utensils and furniture used in the Temple were made of solid gold. This included the altar, the table where the Bread of the Presence of God was displayed, ⁴⁹ the lampstands (five on the right-hand side and five on the left, in front of the Most Holy Place), the flowers, lamps, tongs, ⁵⁰ cups, snuffers, basins, spoons, firepans, the hinges of the doors to the Most Holy Place, and the main entrance doors of the Temple. Each of these was made of solid gold.

⁵¹ When the Temple was finally finished, Solomon took into the treasury of the Temple the silver, the gold, and all the vessels dedicated for that purpose by his father David.

8 THEN SOLOMON CALLED a convocation at Jerusalem of all the leaders of Israel—the heads of the tribes and clans—to observe the transferring of the Ark of the Covenant of the Lord from the Tabernacle in Zion, the City of David, to the Temple. ² This celebration occurred at the time of the Tabernacle Festival in the month of October. ³,⁴ During the festivities the priests carried the Ark to the Temple, along with all the sacred vessels which had previously been in the Tabernacle. ⁵ King Solomon and all the people gathered before the Ark, sacrificing uncounted sheep and oxen.

⁶ Then the priests took the Ark into the inner sanctuary of the Temple—the Most Holy Place—and placed it under the wings of the angels. ⁷ The angels had been constructed in such a manner that their wings spread out over the spot where the Ark would be placed; so now their wings overshadowed the Ark and its carrying poles. ⁸ The poles were so long that they stuck out past the angels and could be seen from the next room, but not from the outer court; and they remain there to this day. ⁹ There was nothing in the Ark at that time except the two stone tablets which Moses had placed there at Mount Horeb at the time the Lord made his covenant with the people of Israel after they left Egypt.

¹⁰ *Look! As the priests are returning from the inner sanctuary, a bright cloud fills the Temple!* ¹¹ *The priests have to go outside because the glory of the Lord is filling the entire building!*

¹²,¹³ Now King Solomon prayed this invocation:

"The Lord has said that he would live in the thick darkness;
But, O Lord, I have built you a lovely home on earth, a place for you to live forever."

¹⁴ Then the king turned around and faced the people as they stood before him, and blessed them.

¹⁵ "Blessed be the Lord God of Israel," he said, "who has done today what he promised my father David: ¹⁶ for he said to him, 'When I brought my people from Egypt, I didn't appoint a place for my Temple, but I appointed a man to be my people's leader.' ¹⁷ This man was my father, David. He wanted to build a Temple for the Lord God of Israel, ¹⁸ but the Lord told him not to. 'I am glad you want to do it,' he said, ¹⁹ 'but your son is the one who shall build my Temple.' ²⁰ And now the Lord has done what he promised; for I have followed my father as king of Israel, and now this Temple has been built for the Lord God of Israel. ²¹ And I have prepared a place in the Temple for the Ark which contains the covenant made by the Lord with our fathers, at the time that he brought them out of the land of Egypt."

²²,²³ Then, as all the people watched, Solomon stood before the altar of the Lord with his hands spread out towards heaven and said, "O Lord God of Israel, there is no god like you in heaven or earth, for you are loving and kind and you keep your promises to your people if they do their best to do your will. ²⁴ Today you have fulfilled your promise to my father David, who was your servant; ²⁵ and now, O Lord God of Israel, fulfill your further promise to him: that if his descendants follow your ways and try to do your will as he did, one of them shall always sit upon the throne of Israel. ²⁶ Yes, O God of Israel, fulfill this promise too.

²⁷ "But is it possible that God would really live on earth? Why, even the skies and

the highest heavens cannot contain you, much less this Temple I have built! [28] And yet, O Lord my God, you have heard and answered my request: [29] Please watch over this Temple night and day—this place you have promised to live in—and as I face toward the Temple and pray, whether by night or by day, please listen to me and answer my requests. [30] Listen to every plea of the people of Israel whenever they face this place to pray; yes, hear in heaven where you live, and when you hear, forgive.

[31] "If a man is accused of doing something wrong and then, standing here before your altar, swears that he didn't do it, [32] hear him in heaven and do what is right; judge whether or not he did it.

[33,34] "And when your people sin and their enemies defeat them, hear them from heaven and forgive them if they turn to you again and confess that you are their God. Bring them back again to this land which you have given to their fathers.

[35,36] "And when the skies are shut up and there is no rain because of their sin, hear them from heaven and forgive them when they pray toward this place and confess your name. And after you have punished them, help them to follow the good ways in which they should walk, and send rain upon the land which you have given your people.

[37] "If there is a famine in the land caused by plant disease or locusts or caterpillers, or if Israel's enemies besiege one of her cities, or if the people are struck by an epidemic or plague—or whatever the problem is— [38] then when the people realize their sin and pray toward this Temple, [39] hear them from heaven and forgive and answer all who have made an honest confession; for you know each heart. [40] In this way they will always learn to reverence you as they continue to live in this land which you have given their fathers.

[41,42] "And when foreigners hear of your great name and come from distant lands to worship you (for they shall hear of your great name and mighty miracles) and pray toward this Temple, [43] hear them from heaven and answer their prayers. And all the nations of the earth will know and fear your name just as your own people Israel do; and all the earth will know that this is your Temple.

[44] "When you send your people out to battle against their enemies and they pray to you, looking toward your chosen city of Jerusalem and toward this Temple which I have built for your name, [45] hear their prayer and help them.

[46] "If they sin against you (and who doesn't?) and you become angry with them and let their enemies lead them away as captives to some foreign land, whether far or near, [47] and they come to their senses and turn to you and cry to you saying, 'We have sinned, we have done wrong'; [48] if they honestly return to you and pray toward this land which you have given their fathers, and toward this city of Jerusalem which you have chosen, and toward this Temple, which I have built for your name, [49] hear their prayers and pleadings from heaven where you live, and come to their assistance.

[50] "Forgive your people for all of their evil deeds, and make their captors merciful to them; [51] for they are your people—your inheritance that you brought out from the Egyptian furnace. [52] May your eyes be open and your ears listening to their pleas. O Lord, hear and answer them whenever they cry out to you, [53] for when you brought our fathers out of the land of Egypt, you told your servant Moses that you had chosen Israel from among all the nations of the earth to be your own special people."

[54,55] Solomon had been kneeling with his hands outstretched toward heaven. As he finished this prayer, he rose from before the altar of Jehovah and cried out this blessing upon all the people of Israel:

[56] "Blessed be the Lord who has fulfilled his promise and given rest to his people Israel; not one word has failed of all the wonderful promises proclaimed by his servant Moses. [57] May the Lord our God be with us as he was with our fathers; may he never forsake us. [58] May he give us the desire to do his will in everything, and to obey all the commandments and instructions he has given our ancestors. [59] And may these words of my prayer be constantly before him day and night, so that he helps me and all of Israel in accordance with our daily needs. [60] May people all over the earth know

that the Lord is God, and that there is no other god at all. [61] O my people, may you live good and perfect lives before the Lord our God; may you always obey his laws and commandments, just as you are doing today."

[62,63] Then the king and all the people dedicated the Temple by sacrificing peace offerings to the Lord—a total of 22,000 oxen and 120,000 sheep and goats! [64] As a temporary measure the king sanctified the court in front of the Temple for the burnt offerings, grain offerings, and the fat of the peace offerings: for the bronze altar was too small to handle so much. [65] The celebration lasted for fourteen days, and a great crowd came from one end of the land to the other. [66] Afterwards Solomon sent the people home, happy for all the goodness that the Lord had shown to his servant David and to his people Israel. And they blessed the king.

9 WHEN SOLOMON HAD finished building the Temple and the palace and all the other buildings he had always wanted, [2,3] the Lord appeared to him the second time (the first time had been at Gibeon) and said to him,

"I have heard your prayer. I have hallowed this Temple which you have built and have put my name here forever. I will constantly watch over it and rejoice in it. [4] And if you live in honesty and truth as your father David did, always obeying me, [5] then I will cause your descendants to be the kings of Israel forever, just as I promised your father David when I told him, 'One of your sons shall always be upon the throne of Israel.'

[6] "However, if you or your children turn away from me and worship other gods and do not obey my laws, [7] then I will take away the people of Israel from this land which I have given them. I will take them from this Temple which I have hallowed for my name and I will cast them out of my sight; and Israel will become a joke to the nations and an example and proverb of sudden disaster. [8] This Temple will become a heap of ruins, and everyone passing by will be amazed and will whistle with astonishment, asking, 'Why has the Lord done such things to this land and this Temple?' [9] And the answer will be, 'The people of Israel abandoned the Lord their God who brought them out of the land of Egypt; they worshiped other gods instead. That is why the Lord has brought this evil upon them.' "

[10] At the end of the twenty years during which Solomon built the Temple and the palace, [11,12] he gave twenty cities in the land of Galilee to King Hiram of Tyre as payment for all the cedar and cypress lumber and gold he had furnished for the construction of the palace and Temple. Hiram came from Tyre to see the cities, but he wasn't at all pleased with them.

[13] "What sort of deal is this, my brother?" he asked. "These cities are a wasteland!" (And they are still known as "The Wasteland" today.) [14] For Hiram had sent gold to Solomon valued at $3,500,000!

[15] Solomon had conscripted forced labor to build the Temple, his palace, Fort Millo, the wall of Jerusalem, and the cities of Hazor, Megiddo, and Gezer. [16] Gezer was the city the king of Egypt conquered and burned, killing the Israeli population; later he had given the city to his daughter as dowry—she was one of Solomon's wives. [17,18] So now Solomon rebuilt Gezer along with Lower Beth-horon, Baalath, and Tamar, a desert city. [19] He also built cities for grain storage, cities in which to keep his chariots, cities for homes for his cavalry and chariot drivers, and resort cities near Jerusalem and in the Lebanon mountains and elsewhere throughout the land.

[20,21] Solomon conscripted his labor forces from those who survived in the nations he conquered—the Amorites, Hittites, Perizzites, Hivites, and Jebusites. For the people of Israel had not been able to wipe them out completely at the time of the invasion and conquest of Israel, and they continue as slaves even today. [22] Solomon didn't conscript any Israelis for this work, although they became soldiers, officials, army officers, chariot commanders, and cavalrymen. [23] And there were 550 men of Israel who were overseers of the labor forces.

Miscellaneous Notes:

[24] King Solomon moved Pharaoh's daughter from the City of David—the old sector of Jerusalem—to the new quarters he

had built for her in the palace. Then he built Fort Millo.

²⁵ After the Temple was completed, Solomon offered burnt offerings and peace offerings three times a year on the altar he had built. And he also burned incense upon it.

²⁶ King Solomon had a shipyard in Ezion-geber near Eloth on the Red Sea in the land of Edom, where he built a fleet of ships.

²⁷,²⁸ King Hiram supplied experienced sailors to accompany Solomon's crews. They used to run back and forth from Ophir, bringing gold to King Solomon, the total value of which was more than $12,000,000.

10 WHEN THE QUEEN of Sheba heard how wonderfully the Lord had blessed Solomon with wisdom,ᵃ she decided to test him with some hard questions. ² She arrived in Jerusalem with a long train of camels carrying spices, gold, and jewels; and she told him all her problems. ³ Solomon answered all her questions; nothing was too difficult for him, for the Lord gave him the right answers every time.ᵇ ⁴ She soon realized that everything she had ever heard about his great wisdom was true. She also saw the beautiful palace he had built, ⁵ and when she saw the wonderful foods on his table, the great number of servants and aides who stood around in splendid uniforms, his cupbearers, and the many offerings he sacrificed by fire to the Lord—well, there was no more spirit in her!

⁶ She exclaimed to him, "Everything I heard in my own country about your wisdom and about the wonderful things going on here is all true. ⁷ I didn't believe it until I came, but now I have seen it for myself! And really! The half had not been told me! Your wisdom and prosperity are far greater than anything I've ever heard of! ⁸ Your people are happy and your palace aides are content—but how could it be otherwise, for they stand here day after day listening to your wisdom! ⁹ Blessed be the Lord your God who chose you and set you on the throne of Israel. How the Lord must love Israel—for he gave you to them as their king! And you give your people a just, good government!"

¹⁰ Then she gave the king a gift of $3,500,000 in gold, along with a huge quantity of spices and precious gems; in fact, it was the largest single gift of spices King Solomon had ever received.

¹¹ (And when King Hiram's ships brought gold to Solomon from Ophir, they also brought along a great supply of algum trees and gems. ¹² Solomon used the algum wood to make pillars for the Temple and the palace, and for harps and harpsichords for his choirs. Never before or since has there been such a supply of beautiful wood.)

¹³ In exchange for the gifts from the queen of Sheba, King Solomon gave her everything she asked him for, besides the presents he had already planned. Then she and her servants returned to their own land.

¹⁴ Each year Solomon received gold worth about $20,000,000, ¹⁵ besides sales taxes and profits from trade with the kings of Arabia and the other surrounding territories. ¹⁶,¹⁷ Solomon had some of the gold beaten into two hundred pieces of armor (gold worth $6,000 went into each piece) and three hundred shields ($1,800 worth of gold in each). And he kept them in his palace in the Hall of the Forest of Lebanon.

¹⁸ He also made a huge ivory throne and overlaid it with pure gold. ¹⁹ It had six steps and a rounded back, with arm rests; and a lion standing on each side. ²⁰ And there were two lions on each step—twelve in all. There was no other throne in all the world so splendid as that one.

²¹ All of King Solomon's cups were of solid gold, and in the Hall of the Forest of Lebanon his entire dining service was made of solid gold. (Silver wasn't used because it wasn't considered to be of much value!)

²² King Solomon's merchant fleet was in partnership with King Hiram's, and once every three years a great load of gold, silver, ivory, apes, and peacocks arrived at the Israeli ports.

²³ So King Solomon was richer and wiser

---

a Literally, "heard of the fame of Solomon concerning the name of the Lord." b Literally, "there was nothing hidden from the king which he could not explain to her."

than all the kings of the earth. [24] Great men from many lands came to interview him and listen to his God-given wisdom. [25] They brought him annual tribute of silver and gold dishes, beautiful cloth, myrrh, spices, horses, and mules.

[26] Solomon built up a great stable of horses with a vast number of chariots and cavalry—1,400 chariots in all, and 12,000 cavalrymen who lived in the chariot cities and with the king at Jerusalem. [27] Silver was as common as stones in Jerusalem in those days, and cedar was of no greater value than the common sycamore! [28] Solomon's horses were brought to him from Egypt and southern Turkey, where his agents purchased them at wholesale prices. [29] An Egyptian chariot delivered to Jerusalem cost $400, and the horses were valued at $150 each. Many of these were then resold to the Hittite and Syrian kings.

11 KING SOLOMON MARRIED many other girls besides the Egyptian princess. Many of them came from nations where idols were worshiped[a]—Moab, Ammon, Edom, Sidon, and from the Hittites— [2] even though the Lord had clearly instructed his people not to marry into those nations, because the women they married would get them started worshiping their gods. Yet Solomon did it anyway. [3] He had seven hundred wives and three hundred concubines; and sure enough, they turned his heart away from the Lord, [4] especially in his old age. They encouraged him to worship their gods instead of trusting completely in the Lord as his father David had done. [5] Solomon worshiped Ashtoreth, the goddess of the Sidonians, and Milcom, the horrible god of the Ammonites. [6] Thus Solomon did what was clearly wrong and refused to follow the Lord as his father David did. [7] He even built a temple on the Mount of Olives, across the valley from Jerusalem, for Chemosh, the depraved god of Moab, and another for Molech, the utterly vile god of the Ammonites. [8] Solomon built temples for these foreign wives to use for burning incense and sacrificing to their gods.

[9,10] Jehovah was very angry with Solomon about this, for now Solomon was no longer interested in the Lord God of Israel who had appeared to him twice to warn him specifically against worshiping other gods. But he hadn't listened, [11] so now the Lord said to him, "Since you have not kept our agreement and have not obeyed my laws, I will tear the kingdom away from you and your family and give it to someone else. [12,13] However, for the sake of your father David, I won't do this while you are still alive. I will take the kingdom away from your son. And even so I will let him be king of one tribe, for David's sake and for the sake of Jerusalem, my chosen city."

[14] So the Lord caused Hadad the Edomite to grow in power. And Solomon became apprehensive, for Hadad was a member of the royal family of Edom. [15] Years before, when David had been in Edom with Joab to arrange for the burial of some Israeli soldiers who had died in battle, the Israeli army had killed nearly every male in the entire country. [16,17,18] It took six months to accomplish this, but they finally killed all except Hadad and a few royal officials who took him to Egypt (he was a very small child at the time). They slipped out of Midian and went to Paran, where others joined them and accompanied them to Egypt, and Pharaoh had given them homes and food.

[19] Hadad became one of Pharaoh's closest friends, and he gave him a wife—the sister of Queen Tahpenes. [20] She presented him with a son, Genubath, who was brought up in Pharaoh's palace among Pharaoh's own sons. [21] When Hadad, there in Egypt, heard that David and Joab were both dead, he asked Pharaoh for permission to return to Edom.

[22] "Why?" Pharaoh asked him. "What do you lack here? How have we disappointed you?"

"Everything is wonderful," he replied, "but even so, I'd like to go back home."

[23] Another of Solomon's enemies whom God raised to power was Rezon, one of the officials of King Hadad-ezer of Zobah who had deserted his post and fled the country. [24] He had become the leader of a gang of

a Implied.

bandits—men who fled with him to Damascus (where he later became king) when David destroyed Zobah. [25] During Solomon's entire lifetime, Rezon and Hadad were his enemies, for they hated Israel intensely.

[26] Another rebel leader was Jeroboam (the son of Nebat), who came from the city of Zeredah in Ephraim; his mother was Zeruah, a widow. [27,28] Here is the story back of his rebellion: Solomon was rebuilding Fort Millo, repairing the walls of this city his father had built. Jeroboam was very able, and when Solomon saw how industrious he was, he put him in charge of his labor battalions from the tribe of Joseph.

[29] One day as Jeroboam was leaving Jerusalem, the prophet Ahijah from Shiloh (who had put on a new robe for the occasion) met him and called him aside to talk to him. And as the two of them were alone in the field, [30] Ahijah tore his new robe into twelve parts, [31] and said to Jeroboam, "Take ten of these pieces, for the Lord God of Israel says, 'I will tear the kingdom from the hand of Solomon and give ten of the tribes to you! [32] But I will leave him one tribe[b] for the sake of my servant David and for the sake of Jerusalem, which I have chosen above all the other cities of Israel. [33] For Solomon has forsaken me and worships Ashtoreth, the goddess of the Sidonians; and Chemosh, the god of Moab; and Milcom, the god of the Ammonites. He has not followed my paths and has not done what I consider right; he has not kept my laws and instructions as his father David did. [34] I will not take the kingdom from him now, however; for the sake of my servant David, my chosen one who obeyed my commandments, I will let Solomon reign for the rest of his life.

[35] " 'But I will take away the kingdom from his son and give ten of the tribes to you. [36] His son shall have the other one so that the descendants of David will continue to reign in Jerusalem, the city I have chosen to be the place for my name to be enshrined. [37] And I will place you on the throne of Israel, and give you absolute power. [38] If you listen to what I tell you and walk in my path and do whatever I consider right,

obeying my commandments as my servant David did, then I will bless you; and your descendants shall rule Israel forever. (I once made this same promise to David. [39] But because of Solomon's sin I will punish the descendants of David—though not forever.)' "

[40] Solomon tried to kill Jeroboam, but he fled to King Shishak of Egypt and stayed there until the death of Solomon.

[41] The rest of what Solomon did and said is written in the book *The Acts of Solomon.* [42] He ruled in Jerusalem for forty years, [43] and then died and was buried in the city of his father David; and his son Rehoboam reigned in his place.

12 REHOBOAM'S INAUGURATION WAS at Shechem, and all Israel came for the coronation ceremony. [2,3,4] Jeroboam, who was still in Egypt where he had fled from King Solomon, heard about the plans from his friends. They urged him to attend, so he joined the rest of Israel at Shechem, and was the ringleader in getting the people to make certain demands upon Rehoboam.

"Your father was a hard master," they told Rehoboam. "We don't want you as our king unless you promise to treat us better than he did."

[5] "Give me three days to think this over," Rehoboam replied. "Come back then for my answer." So the people left.

[6] Rehoboam talked it over with the old men who had counseled his father Solomon.

"What do you think I should do?" he asked them.

[7] And they replied, "If you give them a pleasant reply and agree to be good to them and serve them well, you can be their king forever."

[8] But Rehoboam refused the old men's counsel and called in the young men with whom he had grown up.

[9] "What do you think I should do?" he asked them.

[10] And the young men replied, "Tell them, 'If you think my father was hard on you, well, I'll be harder! [11] Yes, my father was harsh, but I'll be even harsher! My father used whips on you, but I'll use scor-

b Of the twelve tribes, Judah and Benjamin were left to Solomon's son.

pions!' "

¹² So when Jeroboam and the people returned three days later, ¹³,¹⁴ the new king answered them roughly. He ignored the old men's advice and followed that of the young men; ¹⁵ so the king refused the people's demands. (But the Lord's hand was in it—he caused the new king to do this in order to fulfill his promise to Jeroboam, made through Ahijah, the prophet from Shiloh.)

¹⁶,¹⁷ When the people realized that the king meant what he said and was refusing to listen to them, they began shouting, "Down with David and all his relatives! Let's go home! Let Rehoboam be king of his own family!"

And they all deserted him except for the tribe of Judah, who remained loyal and accepted Rehoboam as their king. ¹⁸ When King Rehoboam sent Adoram (who was in charge of the draft) to conscript men from the other tribes, a great mob stoned him to death. But King Rehoboam escaped by chariot and fled to Jerusalem. ¹⁹ And Israel has been in rebellion against the dynasty of David to this day.

²⁰ When the people of Israel learned of Jeroboam's return from Egypt, he was asked to come before an open meeting of all the people; and there he was made king of Israel. Only the tribe of Judah[a] continued under the kingship of the family of David.

²¹ When King Rehoboam arrived in Jerusalem, he summoned his army—all the able-bodied men of Judah and Benjamin: 180,000 special troops—to force the rest of Israel to acknowledge him as their king. ²² But God sent this message to Shemaiah, the prophet:

²³,²⁴ "Tell Rehoboam the son of Solomon, king of Judah, and all the people of Judah and Benjamin that they must not fight against their brothers, the people of Israel. Tell them to disband and go home, for what has happened to Rehoboam is according to my wish." So the army went home as the Lord had commanded.

²⁵ Jeroboam now built the city of Shechem in the hill country of Ephraim, and it became his capital. Later he built Penuel.

²⁶ Jeroboam thought, "Unless I'm careful, the people will want a descendant of David as their king. ²⁷ When they go to Jerusalem to offer sacrifices at the Temple, they will become friendly with King Rehoboam; then they will kill me and ask him to be their king instead."

²⁸ So on the advice of his counselors, the king had two gold calf-idols made and told the people, "It's too much trouble to go to Jerusalem to worship; from now on these will be your gods—they rescued you from your captivity in Egypt!"

²⁹ One of these calf-idols was placed in Bethel and the other in Dan. ³⁰ This was of course a great sin, for the people worshiped them. ³¹ He also made shrines on the hills and ordained priests from the rank and file of the people—even those who were not from the priest-tribe of Levi. ³²,³³ Jeroboam also announced that the annual Tabernacle Festival would be held at Bethel on the first of November[b] (a date he decided upon himself), similar to the annual festival at Jerusalem; he himself offered sacrifices upon the altar to the calves at Bethel, and burned incense to them. And it was there at Bethel that he ordained priests for the shrines on the hills.

13 AS JEROBOAM APPROACHED the altar to burn incense to the golden calf-idol, a prophet of the Lord from Judah walked up to him. ² Then, at the Lord's command, the prophet shouted, "O altar, the Lord says that a child named Josiah shall be born into the family line of David, and he shall sacrifice upon you the priests from the shrines on the hills who come here to burn incense; and men's bones shall be burned upon you."

³ Then he gave this proof that his message was from the Lord: "This altar will split apart, and the ashes on it will spill to the ground."

⁴ The king was very angry with the prophet for saying this. He shouted to his guards, "Arrest that man!" and shook his fist at him. Instantly the king's arm became paralyzed in that position; he couldn't pull

---

a Judah and Benjamin were sometimes (as in this instance) counted together as one tribe.
b Literally, "on the fifteenth day of the eighth month" of the Hebrew calendar. This was a month later than the annual celebration in Jerusalem, which God had ordained.

it back again! [5] At the same moment a wide crack appeared in the altar and the ashes poured out, just as the prophet had said would happen. For this was the prophet's proof that God had been speaking through him.

[6] "Oh, please, please," the king cried out to the prophet, "beg the Lord your God to restore my arm again."

So he prayed to the Lord, and the king's arm became normal again.

[7] Then the king said to the prophet, "Come to the palace with me and rest awhile and have some food; and I'll give you a reward because you healed my arm."

[8] But the prophet said to the king, "Even if you gave me half your palace, I wouldn't go into it; nor would I eat or drink even water in this place! [9] For the Lord has given me strict orders not to eat anything or drink any water while I'm here, and not to return to Judah by the road I came on."

[10] So he went back another way.

[11] As it happened, there was an old prophet living in Bethel, and his sons went home and told him what the prophet from Judah had done and what he had said to the king.

[12] "Which way did he go?" the old prophet asked. So they told him.

[13] "Quick, saddle the donkey," the old man said. And when they had saddled the donkey for him, [14] he rode after the prophet and found him sitting under an oak tree.

"Are you the prophet who came from Judah?" he asked him.

"Yes," he replied, "I am."

[15] Then the old man said to the prophet, "Come home with me and eat."

[16,17] "No," he replied, "I can't; for I am not allowed to eat anything or to drink any water at Bethel. The Lord strictly warned me against it; and he also told me not to return home by the same road I came on."

[18] But the old man said, "I am a prophet too, just as you are; and an angel gave me a message from the Lord. I am to take you home with me and give you food and water."

But the old man was lying to him. [19] So they went back together, and the prophet ate some food and drank some water at the old man's home.

[20] Then, suddenly, while they were sitting at the table, a message from the Lord came to the old man, [21,22] and he shouted at the prophet from Judah, "The Lord says that because you have been disobedient to his clear command, and have come here, and have eaten and drunk water in the place he told you not to, therefore your body shall not be buried in the grave of your fathers."

[23] After finishing the meal, the old man saddled the prophet's donkey, [24,25] and the prophet started off again. But as he was traveling along, a lion came out and killed him. His body lay there on the road, with the donkey and the lion standing beside it. Those who came by and saw the body lying in the road and the lion standing quietly beside it, reported it in Bethel where the old prophet lived.

[26] When he heard what had happened he exclaimed, "It is the prophet who disobeyed the Lord's command; the Lord fulfilled his warning by causing the lion to kill him."

[27] Then he said to his sons, "Saddle my donkey!" And they did.

[28] He found the prophet's body lying in the road; and the donkey and lion were still standing there beside it, for the lion had not eaten the body nor attacked the donkey.

[29] So the prophet laid the body upon the donkey and took it back to the city to mourn over it and bury it.

[30] He laid the body in his own grave, exclaiming, "Alas, my brother!"

[31] Afterwards he said to his sons, "When I die, bury me in the grave where the prophet is buried. Lay my bones beside his bones. [32] For the Lord told him to shout against the altar in Bethel, and his curse against the shrines in the cities of Samaria shall surely be fulfilled."

[33] Despite the prophet's warning, Jeroboam did not turn away from his evil ways; instead, he made more priests than ever from the common people, to offer sacrifices to idols in the shrines on the hills. Anyone who wanted to could be a priest. [34] This was a great sin, and resulted in the destruction of Jeroboam's kingdom and the death of all of his family.

14 JEROBOAM'S SON ABIJAH now became very sick. [2] Jeroboam told his wife,

"Disguise yourself so that no one will recognize you as the queen, and go to Ahijah the prophet at Shiloh—the man who told me that I would become king. ³ Take him a gift of ten loaves of bread, some fig bars, and a jar of honey and ask him whether the boy will recover."

⁴ So his wife went to Ahijah's home at Shiloh. He was an old man now, and could no longer see. ⁵ But the Lord told him that the queen, pretending to be someone else, would come to ask about her son, for he was very sick. And the Lord told him what to tell her.

⁶ So when Ahijah heard her at the door, he called out, "Come in, wife of Jeroboam! Why are you pretending to be someone else?" Then he told her, "I have sad news for you. ⁷ Give your husband this message from the Lord God of Israel: 'I promoted you from the ranks of the common people and made you king of Israel. ⁸ I ripped the kingdom away from the family of David and gave it to you, but you have not obeyed my commandments as my servant David did. His heart's desire was always to obey me and to do whatever I wanted him to. ⁹ But you have done more evil than all the other kings before you; you have made other gods and have made me furious with your gold calves. And since you have refused to acknowledge me, ¹⁰ I will bring disaster upon your home and will destroy all of your sons—this boy who is sick and all those who are well.ᵃ I will sweep away your family as a stable hand shovels out manure. ¹¹ I vow that those of your family who die in the city shall be eaten by dogs, and those who die in the field shall be eaten by birds.'"

¹² Then Ahijah said to Jeroboam's wife, "Go on home, and when you step into the city, the child will die. ¹³ All of Israel will mourn for him and bury him, but he is the only member of your family who will come to a quiet end. For this child is the only good thing which the Lord God of Israel sees in the entire family of Jeroboam. ¹⁴ And the Lord will raise up a king over Israel who will destroy the family of Jeroboam. ¹⁵ Then the Lord will shake Israel like a reed whipped about in a stream; he will uproot the people of Israel from this good land of their fathers and scatter them beyond the Euphrates River, for they have angered the Lord by worshiping idol-gods. ¹⁶ He will abandon Israel because Jeroboam sinned and made all of Israel sin along with him."

¹⁷ So Jeroboam's wife returned to Tirzah; and the child died just as she walked through the door of her home. ¹⁸ And there was mourning for him throughout the land, just as the Lord had predicted through Ahijah.

¹⁹ The rest of Jeroboam's activities—his wars and the other events of his reign—are recorded in *The Annals of the Kings of Israel.* ²⁰ Jeroboam reigned twenty-two years, and when he died, his son Nadab took the throne.

²¹ Meanwhile, Rehoboam the son of Solomon was king in Judah. He was forty-one years old when he began to reign, and he was on the throne seventeen years in Jerusalem, the city which, among all the cities of Israel, the Lord had chosen to live in. (Rehoboam's mother was Naamah, an Ammonite woman.) ²² During his reign the people of Judah, like those in Israel, did wrong and angered the Lord with their sin, for it was even worse than that of their ancestors. ²³ They built shrines and obelisks and idols on every high hill and under every green tree. ²⁴ There was homosexuality throughout the land, and the people of Judah became as depraved as the heathen nations which the Lord drove out to make room for his people.

²⁵ In the fifth year of Rehoboam's reign, King Shishak of Egypt attacked and conquered Jerusalem. ²⁶ He ransacked the Temple and the palace and stole everything, including all the gold shields Solomon had made. ²⁷ Afterwards Rehoboam made bronze shields as substitutes, and the palace guards used these instead. ²⁸ Whenever the king went to the Temple, the guards paraded before him and then took the shields back to the guard chamber.

²⁹ The other events in Rehoboam's reign are written in *The Annals of the Kings of Judah.* ³⁰ There was constant war between

---

a Literally, "every male, both bond and free."

Rehoboam and Jeroboam. [31] When Rehoboam died—his mother was Naamah the Ammonitess—he was buried among his ancestors in Jerusalem, and his son Abijam took the throne.

15 ABIJAM BEGAN HIS three-year reign as king of Judah in Jerusalem during the eighteenth year of Jeroboam's reign in Israel. (Abijam's mother was Maacah, the daughter of Abishalom.) [3] He was as great a sinner as his father was, and his heart was not right with God, as King David's was. [4] But despite Abijam's sin, the Lord remembered David's love[a] and did not end the line of David's royal descendants. [5] For David had obeyed God during his entire life except for the affair concerning Uriah the Hittite. [6] During Abijam's reign there was constant war between Israel and Judah.[b] [7] The rest of Abijam's history is recorded in *The Annals of the Kings of Judah.* [8] When he died he was buried in Jerusalem, and his son Asa reigned in his place.

[9] Asa became king of Judah, in Jerusalem, in the twentieth year of the reign of Jeroboam over Israel, [10] and reigned forty-one years. (His grandmother was Maacah, the daughter of Abishalom.) [11] He pleased the Lord like his ancestor King David. [12] He executed the male prostitutes and removed all the idols his father had made. [13] He deposed his grandmother Maacah as queen-mother because she had made an idol—which he cut down and burned at Kidron Brook. [14] However, the shrines on the hills were not removed, for Asa did not realize that these were wrong.[c] [15] He made permanent exhibits in the Temple of the bronze shields his grandfather had dedicated,[d] along with the silver and gold vessels he himself had donated.

[16] There was lifelong war between King Asa of Judah and King Baasha of Israel. [17] King Baasha built the fortress city of Ramah in an attempt to cut off all trade with Jerusalem. [18] Then Asa took all the silver and gold left in the Temple treasury and all the treasures of the palace, and gave them to his officials to take to Damascus, to King Ben-hadad of Syria, with this message:

[19] "Let us be allies just as our fathers were. I am sending you a present of gold and silver. Now break your alliance with King Baasha of Israel so that he will leave me alone."

[20] Ben-hadad agreed and sent his armies against some of the cities of Israel; and he destroyed Ijon, Dan, Abel-beth-maacah, all of Chinneroth, and all the cities in the land of Naphtali. [21] When Baasha received word of the attack, he discontinued building the city of Ramah and returned to Tirzah. [22] Then King Asa made a proclamation to all Judah, asking every able-bodied man to help demolish Ramah and haul away its stones and timbers. And King Asa used these materials to build the city of Geba in Benjamin and the city of Mizpah.

[23] The rest of Asa's biography—his conquests and deeds and the names of the cities he built—is found in *The Annals of the Kings of Judah.* In his old age his feet became diseased, [24] and when he died he was buried in the royal cemetery in Jerusalem. Then his son Jehoshaphat became the new king of Judah.

[25] Meanwhile, over in Israel, Nadab the son of Jeroboam had become king. He reigned two years, beginning in the second year of the reign of King Asa of Judah. [26] But he was not a good king; like his father, he worshiped many idols and led all of Israel into sin.

[27] Then Baasha (the son of Ahijah, from the tribe of Issachar) plotted against him and assassinated him while he was with the Israeli army laying siege to the Philistine city of Gibbethon. [28] So Baasha replaced Nadab as the king of Israel in Tirzah, during the third year of the reign of King Asa of Judah. [29] He immediately killed all of the descendants of King Jeroboam, so that not one of the royal family was left, just as the Lord had said would happen when he spoke through Ahijah, the prophet from Shiloh. [30] This was done because Jeroboam had angered the Lord God of Israel by sinning and leading the rest of Israel into sin.

---

a Literally, "for David's sake."   b Literally, "between Rehoboam and Jeroboam."   c Literally, "nevertheless, the heart of Asa was perfect toward Jehovah all his days."   d Literally, "the dedicated objects of his grandfather." See 1 Kings 14:27.

[31] Further details of Baasha's reign are recorded in *The Annals of the Kings of Israel.* [32,33] There was continuous warfare between King Asa of Judah and King Baasha of Israel. Baasha reigned for twenty-four years, [34] but all that time he continually disobeyed the Lord. He followed the evil paths of Jeroboam, for he led the people of Israel into the sin of worshiping idols.

16 A MESSAGE OF condemnation from the Lord was delivered to King Baasha at this time by the prophet Jehu: [2] "I lifted you out of the dust," the message said, "to make you king of my people Israel; but you have walked in the evil paths of Jeroboam. You have made my people sin, and I am angry! [3] So now I will destroy you and your family, just as I did the descendants of Jeroboam. [4-7] Those of your family who die in the city will be eaten by dogs, and those who die in the fields will be eaten by the birds."

The message was sent to Baasha and his family because he had angered the Lord by all his evil deeds. He was as evil as Jeroboam despite the fact that the Lord had destroyed all of Jeroboam's descendants for their sins.

The rest of Baasha's biography—his deeds and conquests—are written in *The Annals of the Kings of Israel.*

[8] Elah, Baasha's son, began reigning during the twenty-sixth year of the reign of King Asa of Judah, but he reigned only two years. [9] Then General Zimri, who had charge of half the royal chariot troops, plotted against him. One day King Elah was half drunk at the home of Arza, the superintendent of the palace, in the capital city of Tirzah. [10] Zimri simply walked in and struck him down and killed him. (This occurred during the twenty-seventh year of the reign of King Asa of Judah.) Then Zimri declared himself to be the new king of Israel.

[11] He immediately killed the entire royal family—leaving not a single male child. He even destroyed distant relatives and friends. [12] This destruction of the descendants of Baasha was in line with what the Lord had predicted through the prophet Jehu. [13] The tragedy occurred because of the sins of Baasha and his son Elah; for they had led Israel into worshiping idols and the Lord was very angry about it. [14] The rest of the history of Elah's reign is written in *The Annals of the Kings of Israel.*

[15,16] But Zimri lasted only seven days; for when the army of Israel, which was then engaged in attacking the Philistine city of Gibbethon, heard that Zimri had assassinated the king, they decided on General Omri, commander-in-chief of the army, as their new ruler. [17] So Omri led the army of Gibbethon to besiege Tirzah, Israel's capital. [18] When Zimri saw that the city had been taken, he went into the palace and burned it over him and died in the flames. [19] For he, too, had sinned like Jeroboam; he had worshiped idols and had led the people of Israel to sin with him. [20] The rest of the story of Zimri and his treason are written in *The Annals of the Kings of Israel.*

[21] But now the kingdom of Israel was split in two; half the people were loyal to General Omri, and the other half followed Tibni, the son of Ginath. [22] But General Omri won and Tibni was killed; so Omri reigned without opposition.

[23] King Asa of Judah had been on the throne thirty-one years when Omri began his reign over Israel, which lasted twelve years, six of them in Tirzah. [24] Then Omri bought the hill now known as Samaria from its owner, Shemer, for $4,000 and built a city on it, calling it Samaria in honor of Shemer. [25] But Omri was worse than any of the kings before him; [26] he worshiped idols as Jeroboam had, and led Israel into this same sin. So God was very angry. [27] The rest of Omri's history is recorded in *The Annals of the Kings of Israel.* [28] When Omri died he was buried in Samaria, and his son Ahab became king in his place.

[29] King Asa of Judah had been on the throne thirty-eight years when Ahab became the king of Israel; and Ahab reigned for twenty-two years. [30] But he was even more wicked than his father Omri; he was worse than any other king of Israel! [31] And as though that were not enough, he married Jezebel, the daughter of King Ethbaal of the Sidonians, and then began worshiping Baal. [32] First he built a temple and an altar for Baal in Samaria. [33] Then he made other

idols and did more to anger the Lord God of Israel than any of the other kings of Israel before him.

³⁴ (It was during his reign that Hiel, a man from Bethel, rebuilt Jericho. When he laid the foundations, his oldest son, Abiram, died; and when he finally completed it by setting up the gates, his youngest son, Segub, died. For this was the Lord's curse upon Jericho[a] as declared by Joshua, the son of Nun.)

17 THEN ELIJAH, THE prophet[a] from Tishbe in Gilead, told King Ahab, "As surely as the Lord God of Israel lives — the God whom I worship and serve—there won't be any dew or rain for several years until I say the word!"

² Then the Lord said to Elijah, ³ "Go to the east and hide by Cherith Brook at a place east of where it enters the Jordan River. ⁴ Drink from the brook and eat what the ravens bring you, for I have commanded them to feed you."

⁵ So he did as the Lord had told him to, and camped beside the brook. ⁶ The ravens brought him bread and meat each morning and evening, and he drank from the brook. ⁷ But after awhile the brook dried up, for there was no rainfall anywhere in the land.

⁸,⁹ Then the Lord said to him, "Go and live in the village of Zarephath, near the city of Sidon. There is a widow there who will feed you. I have given her my instructions."

¹⁰ So he went to Zarephath. As he arrived at the gates of the city he saw a widow gathering sticks; and he asked her for a cup of water.

¹¹ As she was going to get it, he called to her, "Bring me a bite of bread, too."

¹² But she said, "I swear by the Lord your God that I haven't a single piece of bread in the house. And I have only a handful of flour left and a little cooking oil in the bottom of the jar. I was just gathering a few sticks to cook this last meal, and then my son and I must die of starvation."

¹³ But Elijah said to her, "Don't be afraid! Go ahead and cook that 'last meal,' but bake me a little loaf of bread first; and afterwards there will still be enough food for you and your son. ¹⁴ For the Lord God of Israel says that there will always be plenty of flour and oil left in your containers until the time when the Lord sends rain, and the crops grow again!"

¹⁵ So she did as Elijah said, and she and Elijah and her son continued to eat from her supply of flour and oil as long as it was needed. ¹⁶ For no matter how much they used, there was always plenty left in the containers, just as the Lord had promised through Elijah!

¹⁷ But one day the woman's son became sick and died.

¹⁸ "O man of God," she cried, "what have you done to me? Have you come here to punish my sins by killing my son?"

¹⁹ "Give him to me," Elijah replied. And he took the boy's body from her and carried it upstairs to the guest room where he lived, and laid the body on his bed, ²⁰ and then cried out to the Lord, "O Lord my God, why have you killed the son of this widow with whom I am staying?"

²¹ And he stretched himself upon the child three times, and cried out to the Lord, "O Lord my God, please let this child's spirit return to him."

²² And the Lord heard Elijah's prayer; and the spirit of the child returned, and he became alive again! ²³ Then Elijah took him downstairs and gave him to his mother.

"See! He's alive!" he beamed.

²⁴ "Now I know for sure that you are a prophet," she told him afterward,[a] "and that whatever you say is from the Lord!"

18 IT WAS THREE years later that the Lord said to Elijah, "Go and tell King Ahab that I will soon send rain again!"

² So Elijah went to tell him. Meanwhile the famine had become very severe in Samaria.

³,⁴ The man in charge of Ahab's household affairs was Obadiah, who was a devoted follower of the Lord. Once when Queen Jezebel had tried to kill all of the Lord's prophets, Obadiah had hidden one hundred of them in two caves—fifty in each —and had fed them with bread and water.

⁵ That same day, while Elijah was on the

---

a See Joshua 6:26.   17a Implied.

way to see King Ahab,[a] the king said to
Obadiah, "We must check every stream and
brook to see if we can find enough grass to
save at least some of my horses and mules.
You go one way and I'll go the other, and
we will search the entire land."

⁶ So they did, each going alone. ⁷ Suddenly Obadiah saw Elijah coming toward
him! Obadiah recognized him at once and
fell to the ground before him.

"Is it really you, my lord Elijah?" he
asked.

⁸ "Yes, it is," Elijah replied. "Now go
and tell the king I am here."

⁹ "Oh, sir," Obadiah protested, "what
harm have I done to you that you are sending me to my death? ¹⁰ For I swear by God
that the king has searched every nation and
kingdom on earth from end to end to find
you. And each time when he was told 'Elijah isn't here,' King Ahab forced the king
of that nation to swear to the truth of his
claim. ¹¹ And now you say, 'Go and tell him
Elijah is here'! ¹² But as soon as I leave you,
the Spirit of the Lord will carry you away,
who knows where, and when Ahab comes
and can't find you, he will kill me; yet I have
been a true servant of the Lord all my life.
¹³ Has no one told you about the time when
Queen Jezebel was trying to kill the Lord's
prophets, and I hid a hundred of them in
two caves and fed them with bread and water? ¹⁴ And now you say, 'Go tell the king
that Elijah is here'! Sir, if I do that, I'm
dead!"

¹⁵ But Elijah said, "I swear by the Lord
God of the armies of heaven, in whose pres-
ence I stand, that I will present myself to
Ahab today."

¹⁶ So Obadiah went to tell Ahab that Elijah had come; and Ahab went out to meet
him.

¹⁷ "So it's you, is it?—the man who
brought this disaster upon Israel!" Ahab exclaimed when he saw him.

¹⁸ "You're talking about yourself," Elijah answered. "For you and your family
have refused to obey the Lord, and have
worshiped Baal instead. ¹⁹ Now bring all the
people of Israel to Mount Carmel, with all
450 prophets of Baal and the 400 prophets

of Asherah who are supported by Jezebel."

²⁰ So Ahab summoned all the people and
the prophets to Mount Carmel.

²¹ Then Elijah talked to them. "How
long are you going to waver between two
opinions?" he asked the people. "If the
Lord is God, *follow* him! But if Baal is God,
then follow *him!*"

²² Then Elijah spoke again. "I am the
only prophet of the Lord who is left," he
told them, "but Baal has 450 prophets.
²³ Now bring two young bulls. The prophets
of Baal may choose whichever one they
wish and cut it into pieces and lay it on the
wood of their altar, but without putting any
fire under the wood; and I will prepare the
other young bull and lay it on the wood on
the Lord's altar, with no fire under it.
²⁴ Then pray to your god, and I will pray to
the Lord; and the god who answers by sending fire to light the wood is the true God!"
And all the people agreed to this test.

²⁵ Then Elijah turned to the prophets of
Baal. "You first," he said, "for there are
many of you; choose one of the bulls and
prepare it and call to your god; but don't
put any fire under the wood."

²⁶ So they prepared one of the young
bulls and placed it on the altar; and they
called to Baal all morning, shouting, "O
Baal, hear us!" But there was no reply of
any kind. Then they began to dance around
the altar. ²⁷ About noontime, Elijah began
mocking them.

"You'll have to shout louder than that,"
he scoffed, "to catch the attention of your
god! Perhaps he is talking to someone, or
is out sitting on the toilet, or maybe he is
away on a trip, or is asleep and needs to be
wakened!"

²⁸ So they shouted louder and, as was
their custom, cut themselves with knives
and swords until the blood gushed out.
²⁹ They raved all afternoon until the time of
the evening sacrifice, but there was no reply,
no voice, no answer.

³⁰ Then Elijah called to the people,
"Come over here."

And they all crowded around him as he
repaired the altar of the Lord which had
been torn down. ³¹ He took twelve stones,

---

a Implied.

one to represent each of the tribes of Israel,[b] [32] and used the stones to rebuild the Lord's altar. Then he dug a trench about three feet wide[c] around the altar. [33] He piled wood upon the altar and cut the young bull into pieces and laid the pieces on the wood.

"Fill four barrels with water," he said, "and pour the water over the carcass and the wood."

After they had done this he said, [34] "Do it again." And they did.

"Now, do it once more!" And they did; [35] and the water ran off the altar and filled the trench.

[36] At the customary time for offering the evening sacrifice, Elijah walked up to the altar and prayed, "O Lord God of Abraham, Isaac, and Israel, prove today that you are the God of Israel and that I am your servant; prove that I have done all this at your command. [37] O Lord, answer me! Answer me so these people will know that you are God and that you have brought them back to yourself."

[38] Then, suddenly, fire flashed down from heaven and burned up the young bull, the wood, the stones, the dust, and even evaporated all the water in the ditch!

[39] And when the people saw it, they fell to their faces upon the ground shouting, "Jehovah is God! Jehovah is God!"

[40] Then Elijah told them to grab the prophets of Baal. "Don't let a single one escape," he commanded.

So they seized them all, and Elijah took them to Kishon Brook and killed them there.

[41] Then Elijah said to Ahab, "Go and enjoy a good meal! For I hear a mighty rainstorm coming!"

[42] So Ahab prepared a feast. But Elijah climbed to the top of Mount Carmel and got down on his knees, with his face between his knees, [43] and said to his servant, "Go and look out toward the sea."

He did, but returned to Elijah and told him, "I didn't see anything."

Then Elijah told him, "Go again, and again, and again, seven times!"

[44] Finally, the seventh time, his servant told him, "I saw a little cloud about the size of a man's hand rising from the sea."

Then Elijah shouted, "Hurry to Ahab and tell him to get into his chariot and get down the mountain, or he'll be stopped by the rain!"

[45] And sure enough, the sky was soon black with clouds, and a heavy wind brought a terrific rainstorm. Ahab left hastily for Jezreel, [46] and the Lord gave special strength to Elijah so that he was able to run ahead of Ahab's chariot to the entrance of the city!

19 WHEN AHAB TOLD Queen Jezebel what Elijah had done, and that he had slaughtered the prophets of Baal, [2] she sent this message to Elijah: "You killed my prophets, and now I swear by the gods that I am going to kill you by this time tomorrow night."

[3] So Elijah fled for his life; he went to Beer-sheba, a city of Judah, and left his servant there. [4] Then he went on alone into the wilderness, traveling all day, and sat down under a broom bush and prayed that he might die.

"I've had enough," he told the Lord. "Take away my life. I've got to die sometime, and it might as well be now."[a]

[5] Then he lay down and slept beneath the broom bush. But as he was sleeping, an angel touched him and told him to get up and eat! [6] He looked around and saw some bread baking on hot stones, and a jar of water! So he ate and drank and lay down again.

[7] Then the angel of the Lord came again and touched him and said, "Get up and eat some more, for there is a long journey ahead of you."

[8] So he got up and ate and drank, and the food gave him enough strength to travel forty days and forty nights to Mount Horeb, the mountain of God, [9] where he lived in a cave.

But the Lord said to him, "What are you doing here, Elijah?"

[10] He replied, "I have worked very hard for the Lord God of the heavens; but the people of Israel have broken their covenant

---

b Literally, "each of the tribes of the sons of Jacob to whom the Lord had said, 'Israel shall be your name.'"
c Literally, "as great as would contain two measures of seed." 19a Literally, "I am no better than my fathers."

with you and torn down your altars and killed your prophets, and only I am left; and now they are trying to kill me, too."

[11] "Go out and stand before me on the mountain," the Lord told him. And as Elijah stood there the Lord passed by, and a mighty windstorm hit the mountain; it was such a terrible blast that the rocks were torn loose, but the Lord was not in the wind. After the wind, there was an earthquake, but the Lord was not in the earthquake. [12] And after the earthquake, there was a fire, but the Lord was not in the fire. And after the fire, there was the sound of a gentle whisper. [13] When Elijah heard it, he wrapped his face in his scarf and went out and stood at the entrance of the cave.

And a voice said, "Why are you here, Elijah?"

[14] He replied again, "I have been working very hard for the Lord God of the armies of heaven, but the people have broken their covenant and have torn down your altars; they have killed every one of your prophets except me; and now they are trying to kill me, too."

[15] Then the Lord told him, "Go back by the desert road to Damascus, and when you arrive, anoint Hazael to be king of Syria. [16] Then anoint Jehu (son of Nimshi) to be king of Israel, and anoint Elisha (the son of Shaphat of Abel-meholah) to replace you as my prophet. [17] Anyone who escapes from Hazael shall be killed by Jehu, and those who escape Jehu shall be killed by Elisha! [18] And incidentally, there are 7,000 men in Israel who have never bowed to Baal nor kissed him!"

[19] So Elijah went and found Elisha who was plowing a field with eleven other teams ahead of him; he was at the end of the line with the last team. Elijah went over to him and threw his coat across his shoulders and walked away again.[b]

[20] Elisha left the oxen standing there and ran after Elijah and said to him, "First let me go and say good-bye to my father and mother, and then I'll go with you!"

Elijah replied, "Go on back! Why all the excitement?"

[21] Elisha then returned to his oxen, killed them, and used wood from the plow to build a fire to roast their flesh. He passed around the meat to the other plowmen, and they all had a great feast. Then he went with Elijah, as his assistant.

20 KING BEN-HADAD OF Syria now mobilized his army and, with thirty-two allied nations and their hordes of chariots and horses, besieged Samaria, the Israeli capital. [2,3] He sent this message into the city to King Ahab of Israel: "Your silver and gold are mine, as are your prettiest wives and the best of your children!"

[4] "All right, my lord," Ahab replied. "All that I have is yours!"

[5,6] Soon Ben-hadad's messengers returned again with another message: "You must not only give me your silver, gold, wives, and children, but about this time tomorrow I will send my men to search your palace and the homes of your people, and they will take away whatever they like!"

[7] Then Ahab summoned his advisors. "Look what this man is doing," he complained to them. "He is stirring up trouble despite the fact that I have already told him he could have my wives and children and silver and gold, just as he demanded."

[8] "Don't give him anything more," the elders advised.

[9] So he told the messengers from Ben-hadad, "Tell my lord the king, 'I will give you everything you asked for the first time, but your men may not search the palace and the homes of the people.' "[a] So the messengers returned to Ben-hadad.

[10] Then the Syrian king sent this message to Ahab: "May the gods do more to me than I am going to do to you if I don't turn Samaria into handfuls of dust!"

[11] The king of Israel retorted, "Don't count your chickens before they hatch!"

[12] This reply of Ahab's reached Ben-hadad and the other kings as they were drinking in their tents.

"Prepare to attack!" Ben-hadad commanded his officers.

[13] Then a prophet came to see King Ahab and gave him this message from the Lord: "Do you see all these enemy forces?

---

b Implied.   20 a Literally, "this thing I cannot do."

I will deliver them all to you today. Then at last you will know that I am the Lord."

¹⁴ Ahab asked, "How will he do it?"

And the prophet replied, "The Lord says, 'By the troops from the provinces.' "

"Shall we attack first?" Ahab asked.

"Yes," the prophet answered.

¹⁵ So he mustered the troops from the provinces, 232 of them, then the rest of his army of 7,000 men. ¹⁶ About noontime, as Ben-hadad and the thirty-two allied kings were still drinking themselves drunk, the first of Ahab's troops marched out of the city.

¹⁷ As they approached, Ben-hadad's scouts reported to him, "Some troops are coming!"

¹⁸ "Take them alive," Ben-hadad commanded, "whether they have come for truce or for war."

¹⁹ By now Ahab's entire army had joined the attack. ²⁰ Each one killed a Syrian soldier, and suddenly the entire Syrian army panicked and fled. The Israelis chased them, but King Ben-hadad and a few others escaped on horses. ²¹ However, the great bulk of the horses and chariots were captured, and most of the Syrian army was killed in a great slaughter.

²² Then the prophet approached King Ahab and said, "Get ready for another attack by the king of Syria."

²³ For after their defeat, Ben-hadad's officers said to him, "The Israeli God is a god of the hills; that is why they won. But we can beat them easily on the plains. ²⁴ Only this time replace the kings with generals! ²⁵ Recruit another army like the one you lost; give us the same number of horses, chariots, and men, and we will fight against them in the plains; there's not a shadow of a doubt that we will beat them." So King Ben-hadad did as they suggested. ²⁶ The following year he called up the Syrian army and marched out against Israel again, this time at Aphek. ²⁷ Israel then mustered its army, set up supply lines, and moved into the battle; but the Israeli army looked like two little flocks of baby goats in comparison to the vast Syrian forces that filled the countryside!

²⁸ Then a prophet went to the king of Israel with this message from the Lord: "Because the Syrians have declared, 'The Lord is a God of the hills and not of the plains,' I will help you defeat this vast army, and you shall know that I am indeed the Lord."

²⁹ The two armies camped opposite each other for seven days, and on the seventh day the battle began. And the Israelis killed 100,000 Syrian infantrymen that first day. ³⁰ The rest fled behind the walls of Aphek, but the wall fell on them and killed another 27,000. Ben-hadad fled into the city and hid in the inner room of one of the houses.

³¹ "Sir," his officers said to him, "we have heard that the kings of Israel are very merciful. Let us wear sackcloth and put ropes on our heads and go out to King Ahab to see if he will let you live."

³² So they went to the king of Israel and begged, "Your servant Ben-hadad pleads, 'Let me live!' "

"Oh, is he still alive?" the king of Israel asked. "He is my brother!"

³³ The men were quick to grab this straw of hope and hurried to clinch the matter by exclaiming, "Yes, your brother Ben-hadad!"

"Go and get him," the king of Israel told them. And when Ben-hadad arrived, he invited him up into his chariot!

³⁴ Ben-hadad told him, "I will restore the cities my father took from your father, and you may establish trading posts in Damascus, as my father did in Samaria."

³⁵ Meanwhile, the Lord instructed one of the prophets to say to another man, "Strike me with your sword!" But the man refused.

³⁶ Then the prophet told him, "Because you have not obeyed the voice of the Lord, a lion shall kill you as soon as you leave me." And sure enough, as he turned to go a lion attacked and killed him.

³⁷ Then the prophet turned to another man and said, "Strike me with your sword." And he did, wounding him.

³⁸ The prophet waited for the king beside the road, having placed a bandage over his eyes to disguise himself.

³⁹ As the king passed by, the prophet called out to him, "Sir, I was in the battle, and a man brought me a prisoner and said, 'Keep this man; if he gets away, you must die, ⁴⁰ or else pay me $2,000!' But while I

was busy doing something else, the prisoner disappeared!"

"Well, it's your own fault," the king replied. "You'll have to pay."

⁴¹ Then the prophet yanked off the bandage from his eyes, and the king recognized him as one of the prophets. ⁴² Then the prophet told him, "The Lord says, 'Because you have spared the man I said must die, now you must die in his place, and your people shall perish instead of his.' "

⁴³ So the king of Israel went home to Samaria angry and sullen.

21 NABOTH, A MAN from Jezreel, had a vineyard on the outskirts of the city near King Ahab's palace. ² One day the king talked to him about selling him this land.

"I want it for a garden," the king explained, "because it's so convenient to the palace." He offered cash or, if Naboth preferred, a piece of better land in trade.

³ But Naboth replied, "Not on your life! That land has been in my family for generations."

⁴ So Ahab went back to the palace angry and sullen. He refused to eat and went to bed with his face to the wall!

⁵ "What in the world is the matter?" his wife, Jezebel, asked him. "Why aren't you eating? What has made you so upset and angry?"

⁶ "I asked Naboth to sell me his vineyard, or to trade it, and he refused!" Ahab told her.

⁷ "Are you the king of Israel or not?" Jezebel demanded. "Get up and eat and don't worry about it. I'll get you Naboth's vineyard!"

⁸ So she wrote letters in Ahab's name, sealed them with his seal, and addressed them to the civic leaders of Jezreel, where Naboth lived. ⁹ In her letter she commanded: "Call the citizens together for fasting and prayer.ᵃ Then summon Naboth, ¹⁰ and find two scoundrels who will accuse him of cursing God and the king. Then take him out and execute him."

¹¹ The city fathers followed the queen's instructions. ¹² They called the meeting and put Naboth on trial. ¹³ Then two men who had no conscience accused him of cursing God and the king; and he was dragged outside the city and stoned to death. ¹⁴ The city officials then sent word to Jezebel that Naboth was dead.

¹⁵ When Jezebel heard the news, she said to Ahab, "You know the vineyard Naboth wouldn't sell you? Well, you can have it now! He's dead!"

¹⁶ So Ahab went down to the vineyard to claim it.

¹⁷ But the Lord said to Elijah, ¹⁸ "Go to Samaria to meet King Ahab. He will be at Naboth's vineyard, taking possession of it. ¹⁹ Give him this message from me: 'Isn't killing Naboth bad enough? Must you rob him, too? Because you have done this, dogs shall lick your blood outside the city just as they licked the blood of Naboth!' "

²⁰ "So my enemy has found me!" Ahab exclaimed to Elijah.

"Yes," Elijah answered, "I have come to place God's curse upon you because you have sold yourself to the devil.ᵇ ²¹ The Lord is going to bring great harm to you and sweep you away; he will not let a single one of your male descendants survive! ²² He is going to destroy your family as he did the family of King Jeroboam and the family of King Baasha, for you have made him very angry and have led all of Israel into sin. ²³ The Lord has also told me that the dogs of Jezreel shall tear apart the body of your wife, Jezebel. ²⁴ The members of your family who die in the city shall be eaten by dogs and those who die in the country shall be eaten by vultures."

²⁵ No one else was so completely sold out to the devil as Ahab, for his wife Jezebel encouraged him to do every sort of evil. ²⁶ He was especially guilty because he worshiped idols just as the Amorites did—the people whom the Lord had chased out of the land to make room for the people of Israel. ²⁷ When Ahab heard these prophecies, he tore his clothing, put on rags, fasted, slept in sackcloth, and went about in deep humility.

²⁸ Then another message came to Elijah:

---

a This inquiry was perhaps ostensibly to discover whose sins had caused the famine.   b Literally, "I have found you because you have sold yourself to that which is evil in the sight of the Lord."

[29] "Do you see how Ahab has humbled himself before me? Because he has done this, I will not do what I promised during his lifetime; it will happen to his sons; I will destroy his descendants."

22 FOR THREE YEARS there was no war between Syria and Israel. [2] But during the third year, while King Jehoshaphat of Judah was visiting King Ahab of Israel, [3] Ahab said to his officials, "Do you realize that the Syrians are still occupying our city of Ramoth-gilead? And we're sitting here without doing a thing about it!"

[4] Then he turned to Jehoshaphat and asked him, "Will you send your army with mine to recover Ramoth-gilead?"

And King Jehoshaphat of Judah replied, "Of course! You and I are brothers; my people are yours to command, and my horses are at your service. [5] But," he added, "we should ask the Lord first, to be sure of what he wants us to do."

[6] So King Ahab summoned his four hundred heathen[a] prophets and asked them, "Shall I attack Ramoth-gilead, or not?"

And they all said, "Yes, go ahead, for God will help you conquer it."

[7] But Jehoshaphat asked, "Isn't there a prophet of the Lord here? I'd like to ask him, too."

[8] "Well, there's one," King Ahab replied, "but I hate him, for he never prophesies anything good. He always has something gloomy to say. His name is Micaiah, the son of Imlah."

"Oh, come now!" Jehoshaphat replied. "Don't talk like that!"

[9] So King Ahab called to one of his aides, "Go get Micaiah. Hurry!"

[10] Meanwhile, all the prophets continued prophesying before the two kings, who were dressed in their royal robes and were sitting on thrones placed on the threshing floor near the city gate. [11] One of the prophets, Zedekiah (son of Chenaanah), made some iron horns and declared, "The Lord promises that you will push the Syrians around with these horns until they are destroyed."

[12] And all the others agreed. "Go ahead and attack Ramoth-gilead," they said, "for the Lord will cause you to triumph!"

[13] The messenger who went to get Micaiah told him what the other prophets were saying, and urged him to say the same thing.

[14] But Micaiah told him, "This I vow, that I will say only what the Lord tells me to!"

[15] When he arrived, the king asked him, "Micaiah, shall we attack Ramoth-gilead, or not?"

"Why, of course! Go right ahead!" Micaiah told him. "You will have a great victory, for the Lord will cause you to conquer!"

[16] "How many times must I tell you to speak only what the Lord tells you to?" the king demanded.

[17] Then Micaiah told him, "I saw all Israel scattered upon the mountains as sheep without a shepherd. And the Lord said, 'Their king is dead; send them to their homes.'"

[18] Turning to Jehoshaphat, Ahab complained, "Didn't I tell you this would happen? He *never* tells me anything good. It's *always* bad."

[19] Then Micaiah said, "Listen to this further word from the Lord. I saw the Lord sitting on his throne, and the armies of heaven stood around him.

[20] "Then the Lord said, 'Who will entice Ahab to go and die at Ramoth-gilead?'

"Various suggestions were made, until one angel approached the Lord and said, 'I'll do it!'

[22] "'How?' the Lord asked.

"And he replied, 'I will go as a lying spirit in the mouths of all his prophets.'

"And the Lord said, 'That will do it; you will succeed. Go ahead.'

[23] "Don't you see? The Lord has put a lying spirit in the mouths of all these prophets, but the fact of the matter is that the Lord has decreed disaster upon you."

[24] Then Zedekiah (son of Chenaanah) walked over and slapped Micaiah on the face.

"When did the Spirit of the Lord leave

---

a Implied. These were evidently the 400 Asherah priests left alive by Elijah at Carmel, though the 450 prophets of Baal were slain. See 1 Kings 18:19 and 40.

me and speak to you?" he demanded.

²⁵ And Micaiah replied, "You will have the answer to your question when you find yourself hiding in an inner room."

²⁶ Then King Ahab ordered Micaiah's arrest.

"Take him to Amon, the mayor of the city, and to my son Joash. ²⁷ Tell them, 'The king says to put this fellow in jail and feed him with bread and water—and only enough to keep him alive[b]—until I return in peace.' "

²⁸ "If you return in peace," Micaiah replied, "it will prove that the Lord has not spoken through me." Then he turned to the people standing nearby and said, "Take note of what I've said."

²⁹ So King Ahab of Israel and King Jehoshaphat of Judah led their armies to Ramoth-gilead.

³⁰ Ahab said to Jehoshaphat, "You wear your royal robes, but I'll not wear mine!"

So Ahab went into the battle disguised in an ordinary soldier's uniform. ³¹ For the king of Syria had commanded his thirty-two chariot captains to fight no one except King Ahab himself. ³²,³³ When they saw King Jehoshaphat in his royal robes, they thought, "That's the man we're after." So they wheeled around to attack him. But when Jehoshaphat shouted out to identify himself,[c] they turned back! ³⁴ However, someone shot an arrow at random and it struck King Ahab between the joints of his armor.

"Take me out of the battle, for I am badly wounded," he groaned to his chariot driver.

³⁵ The battle became more and more intense as the day wore on, and King Ahab went back in, propped up in his chariot with the blood from his wound running down onto the floorboards. Finally, toward evening, he died. ³⁶,³⁷ Just as the sun was going down the cry ran through his troops. "It's all over—return home! The king is dead!"

And his body was taken to Samaria and buried there. ³⁸ When his chariot and armor were washed beside the pool of Samaria, where the prostitutes bathed, dogs came and licked the king's blood just as the Lord had said would happen.

³⁹ The rest of Ahab's history—including the story of the ivory palace and the cities he built—is written in *The Annals of the Kings of Israel.* ⁴⁰ So Ahab was buried among his ancestors, and Ahaziah his son became the new king of Israel.

⁴¹ Meanwhile, over in Judah, Jehoshaphat the son of Asa had become king during the fourth year of the reign of King Ahab of Israel. ⁴² Jehoshaphat was thirty-five years old when he ascended the throne, and he reigned in Jerusalem for twenty-five years. His mother was Azubah, the daughter of Shilhi. ⁴³ He did as his father Asa had done, obeying the Lord in all but one thing: he did not destroy the shrines on the hills, so the people sacrificed and burned incense there. ⁴⁴ He also made peace with Ahab, the king of Israel. ⁴⁵ The rest of the deeds of Jehoshaphat and his heroic achievements and his wars are described in *The Annals of the Kings of Judah.*

⁴⁶ He also closed all the houses of male prostitution that still continued from the days of his father Asa. ⁴⁷ (There was no king in Edom at that time, only a deputy.)

⁴⁸ King Jehoshaphat built great freighters to sail to Ophir for gold; but they never arrived, for they were wrecked at Eziongeber. ⁴⁹ Ahaziah, King Ahab's son and successor, had proposed to Jehoshaphat that his men go too, but Jehoshaphat had refused the offer.

⁵⁰ When King Jehoshaphat died he was buried with his ancestors in Jerusalem, the city of his forefather David; and his son Jehoram took the throne. ⁵¹ It was during the seventeenth year of the reign of King Jehoshaphat of Judah that Ahaziah, Ahab's son, began to reign over Israel in Samaria; and he reigned two years. ⁵²,⁵³ But he was not a good king, for he followed in the footsteps of his father and mother and of Jeroboam, who had led Israel into the sin of worshiping idols. So Ahaziah made the Lord God of Israel very angry.

---

b Literally, "as though the city were under siege."   c Implied.

2 KINGS

1 AFTER KING AHAB'S death the nation of Moab declared its independence and refused to pay tribute to Israel any longer. [2] Israel's new king, Ahaziah, had fallen off the upstairs porch of his palace at Samaria and was seriously injured. He sent messengers to the temple of the god Baal-zebub at Ekron to ask whether he would recover.

[3] But an angel of the Lord told Elijah the prophet,[a] "Go and meet the messengers and ask them, 'Is it true that there is no God in Israel? Is that why you are going to Baal-zebub, the god of Ekron, to ask whether the king will get well? [4,5] Because King Ahaziah has done this, the Lord says that he will never leave the bed he is lying on; he will surely die.'"

When Elijah told the messengers this, they returned immediately to the king.

"Why have you returned so soon?" he asked them.

[6] "A man came up to us," they said, "and told us to go back to the king and tell him, 'The Lord wants to know why you are asking questions of Baal-zebub, the god of Ekron. Is it because there is no God in Israel? Now, since you have done this, you will not leave the bed you are lying on; you will surely die.'"

[7] "Who was this fellow?" the king demanded. "What did he look like?"

[8] "He was a hairy man," they replied, "with a wide leather belt."

"It was Elijah the prophet!" the king exclaimed. [9] Then he sent an army captain with fifty soldiers to arrest him. They found him sitting on top of a hill. The captain said to him, "O man of God, the king has commanded you to come along with us."

[10] But Elijah replied, "If I am a man of God, let fire come down from heaven and destroy you and your fifty men!" Then lightning struck them and killed them all!

[11] So the king sent another captain with fifty men to demand, "O man of God, the king says that you must come down right away."

[12] Elijah replied, "If I am a man of God, let fire come down from heaven and destroy you and your fifty men." And again the fire from God burned them up.

[13] Once more the king sent fifty men, but this time the captain fell to his knees before Elijah and pleaded with him, "O man of God, please spare my life and the lives of these, your fifty servants. [14] Have mercy on us! Don't destroy us as you did the others."

[15] Then the angel of the Lord said to Elijah, "Don't be afraid. Go with him." So Elijah went to the king.

[16] "Why did you send messengers to Baal-zebub, the god of Ekron, to ask about your sickness?" Elijah demanded. "Is it because there is no God in Israel to ask? Because you have done this, you shall not leave this bed; you will surely die."

[17] So Ahaziah died as the Lord had predicted through Elijah, and his brother Jehoram became the new king—for Ahaziah did not have a son to succeed him. This occurred in the second year of the reign of King Jehoram (son of Jehoshaphat) of Judah. [18] The rest of the history of Ahaziah's reign is recorded in *The Annals of the Kings of Israel.*

2 NOW THE TIME came for the Lord to take Elijah to heaven—by means of a whirlwind! Elijah said to Elisha as they left Gilgal, "Stay here, for the Lord has told me to go to Bethel."

But Elisha replied, "I swear to God that I won't leave you!"

So they went on together to Bethel. [3] There the young prophets of Bethel Seminary came out to meet them and asked Elisha, "Did you know that the Lord is going to take Elijah away from you today?"

"Quiet!" Elisha snapped. "Of course I know it."

[4] Then Elijah said to Elisha, "Please stay here in Bethel, for the Lord has sent me to Jericho."

But Elisha replied again, "I swear to God that I won't leave you." So they went

---

a Literally, "Elijah the Tishbite."

on together to Jericho.

⁵ Then the students at Jericho Seminary came to Elisha and asked him, "Do you know that the Lord is going to take away your master today?"

"Will you please be quiet?" he commanded. "Of course I know it!"

⁶,⁷ Then Elijah said to Elisha, "Please stay here, for the Lord has sent me to the Jordan River."

But Elisha replied as before, "I swear to God that I won't leave you."

So they went on together and stood beside the Jordan River as fifty of the young prophets watched from a distance. ⁸ Then Elijah folded his cloak together and struck the water with it; and the river divided and they went across on dry ground!

⁹ When they arrived on the other side Elijah said to Elisha, "What wish shall I grant you before I am taken away?"

And Elisha replied, "Please grant me twice as much prophetic power as you have had."

¹⁰ "You have asked a hard thing," Elijah replied. "If you see me when I am taken from you, then you will get your request. But if not, then you won't."

¹¹ As they were walking along, talking, suddenly a chariot of fire, drawn by horses of fire, appeared and drove between them, separating them, and Elijah was carried by a whirlwind into heaven.

¹² Elisha saw it and cried out, "My father! My father! The Chariot of Israel and the charioteers!"

As they disappeared from sight he tore his robe. ¹³,¹⁴ Then he picked up Elijah's cloak and returned to the bank of the Jordan River, and struck the water with it.

"Where is the Lord God of Elijah?" he cried out. And the water parted and Elisha went across!

¹⁵ When the young prophets of Jericho saw what had happened, they exclaimed, "The spirit of Elijah rests upon Elisha!" And they went to meet him and greeted him respectfully.

¹⁶ "Sir," they said, "just say the word and fifty of our best athletes will search the wilderness for your master; perhaps the Spirit of the Lord has left him on some mountain or in some ravine."

"No," Elisha said, "don't bother."

¹⁷ But they kept urging until he was embarrassed, and finally said, "All right, go ahead." Then fifty men searched for three days, but didn't find him.

¹⁸ Elisha was still at Jericho when they returned. "Didn't I tell you not to go?" he growled.

¹⁹ Now a delegation of the city officials of Jericho visited Elisha. "We have a problem," they told him. "This city is located in beautiful natural surroundings, as you can see; but the water is bad, and causes our women to have miscarriages."ᵃ

²⁰ "Well," he said, "bring me a new bowl filled with salt." So they brought it to him.

²¹ Then he went out to the city well and threw the salt in and declared, "The Lord has healed these waters. They shall no longer cause death or miscarriage."

²² And sure enough! The water was purified, just as Elisha had said.

²³ From Jericho he went to Bethel. As he was walking along the road, some young boys from the city began mocking and making fun of him because of his bald head. ²⁴ He turned around and cursed them in the name of the Lord; and two female bears came out of the woods and killed forty-two of them. ²⁵ Then he went to Mount Carmel and finally returned to Samaria.

3 AHAB'S SON JEHORAM began his reign over Israel during the eighteenth year of the reign of King Jehoshaphatᵃ of Judah; and he reigned twelve years. His capital was Samaria. ² He was a very evil man, but not as wicked as his father and mother had been, for he at least tore down the pillar to Baal that his father had made. ³ Nevertheless he still clung to the great sin of Jeroboam (the son of Nebat), who had led the people of Israel into the worship of idols.

⁴ King Mesha of Moab and his people were sheep ranchers. They paid Israel an annual tribute of 100,000 lambs and the wool of 100,000 rams; ⁵ but after Ahab's

---

a Implied in verse 21. Literally, "the land is unfruitful."   3a Chapter 1, verse 17, says King Jehoram was the king of Judah at this time. Possibly there was a co-regency.

death, the king of Moab rebelled against Israel. ⁶,⁷,⁸ So King Jehoram mustered the Israeli army and sent this message to King Jehoshaphat of Judah:

"The king of Moab has rebelled against me. Will you help me fight him?"

"Of course I will," Jehoshaphat replied. "My people and horses are yours to command. What are your battle plans?"

"We'll attack from the wilderness of Edom," Jehoram replied.

⁹ So their two armies, now joined also by troops from Edom, moved along a roundabout route through the wilderness for seven days; but there was no water for the men or their pack animals.

¹⁰ "Oh, what shall we do?" the king of Israel cried out. "The Lord has brought us here to let the king of Moab defeat us."

¹¹ But Jehoshaphat, the king of Judah, asked, "Isn't there a prophet of the Lord with us? If so, we can find out what to do!"

"Elisha is here," one of the king of Israel's officers replied. Then he added, "He was Elijah's assistant."

¹² "Fine," Jehoshaphat said. "He's just the man we want."ᵇ So the kings of Israel, Judah, and Edom went to consult Elisha.

¹³ "I want no part of you," Elisha snarled at King Jehoram of Israel. "Go to the false prophets of your father and mother!"

But King Jehoram replied, "No! For it is the Lord who has called us here to be destroyed by the king of Moab!"

¹⁴ "I swear by the Lord God that I wouldn't bother with you except for the presence of King Jehoshaphat of Judah," Elisha replied. ¹⁵ "Now bring me someone to play the lute." And as the lute was played, the message of the Lord came to Elisha:

¹⁶ "The Lord says to fill this dry valley with trenches to hold the water he will send. ¹⁷ You won't see wind nor rain, but this valley will be filled with water, and you will have plenty for yourselves and for your animals! ¹⁸ But this is only the beginning, for the Lord will make you victorious over the army of Moab! ¹⁹ You will conquer the best of their cities—even those that are fortified —and ruin all the good land with stones."

²⁰ And sure enough, the next day at about the time when the morning sacrifice was offered—look! Water! It was flowing from the direction of Edom, and soon there was water everywhere.

²¹ Meanwhile, when the people of Moab heard about the three armies marching against them, they mobilized every man who could fight, old and young, and stationed themselves along their frontier. ²² But early the next morning the sun looked red as it shone across the water!

²³ "Blood!" they exclaimed. "The three armies have attacked and killed each other! Let's go and collect the loot!"

²⁴ But when they arrived at the Israeli camp, the army of Israel rushed out and began killing them; and the army of Moab fled. Then the men of Israel moved forward into the land of Moab, destroying everything as they went. ²⁵ They destroyed the cities, threw stones on every good piece of land, stopped up the wells, and felled the fruit trees; finally, only Fort Kir-hareseth was left, but even that finally fell to them.ᶜ

²⁶ When the king of Moab saw that the battle had been lost, he led 700 of his swordsmen in a last desperate attempt to break through to the king of Edom; but he failed. ²⁷ Then he took his oldest son, who was to have been the next king, and to the horror of the Israeli army, killed him and sacrificed him as a burnt offering upon the wall. So the army of Israel turned back in disgust to their own land.

4 ONE DAY THE wife of one of the seminary students came to Elisha to tell him of her husband's death. He was a man who had loved God, she said. But he had owed some money when he died, and now the creditor was demanding it back. If she didn't pay, he said he would take her two sons as his slaves.

² "What shall I do?" Elisha asked. "How much food do you have in the house?"

"Nothing at all, except a jar of olive oil," she replied.

³ "Then borrow many pots and pans from your friends and neighbors!" he in-

---

b Literally, "the word of the Lord is with him."   c Literally, "the slingers surrounded and conquered it."

structed. ⁴ "Go into your house with your sons and shut the door behind you. Then pour olive oil from your jar into the pots and pans, setting them aside as they are filled!"

⁵ So she did. Her sons brought the pots and pans to her, and she filled one after another! ⁶ Soon every container was full to the brim!

"Bring me another jar," she said to her sons.

"There aren't any more!" they told her. And then the oil stopped flowing!

⁷ When she told the prophet what had happened, he said to her, "Go and sell the oil and pay your debt, and there will be enough money left for you and your sons to live on!"

⁸ One day Elisha went to Shunem. A prominent woman of the city invited him in to eat, and afterwards, whenever he passed that way, he stopped for dinner.

⁹ She said to her husband, "I'm sure this man who stops in from time to time is a holy prophet. ¹⁰ Let's make a little room for him on the roof; we can put in a bed, a table, a chair, and a lamp, and he will have a place to stay whenever he comes by."

¹¹,¹² Once when he was resting in the room he said to his servant Gehazi, "Tell the woman I want to speak to her."

When she came, ¹³ he said to Gehazi, "Tell her that we appreciate her kindness to us. Now ask her what we can do for her. Does she want me to put in a good word for her to the king or to the general of the army?"

"No," she replied, "I am perfectly content."

¹⁴ "What can we do for her?" he asked Gehazi afterwards.

He suggested, "She doesn't have a son, and her husband is an old man."

¹⁵,¹⁶ "Call her back again," Elisha told him.

When she returned, he talked to her as she stood in the doorway. "Next year at about this time you shall have a son!"

"O man of God," she exclaimed, "don't lie to me like that!"

¹⁷ But it was true; the woman soon conceived and had a baby boy the following year, just as Elisha had predicted.

¹⁸ One day when her child was older, he went out to visit his father, who was working with the reapers. ¹⁹ He complained about a headache, and soon was moaning in pain. His father said to one of the servants, "Carry him home to his mother."

²⁰ So he took him home, and his mother held him on her lap; but around noontime he died. ²¹ She carried him up to the bed of the prophet and shut the door; ²² then she sent a message to her husband: "Send one of the servants and a donkey so that I can hurry to the prophet and come right back."

²³ "Why today?" he asked. "This isn't a religious holiday."

But she said, "It's important. I must go."

²⁴ So she saddled the donkey and said to the servant, "Hurry! Don't slow down for my comfort unless I tell you to."

²⁵ As she approached Mount Carmel, Elisha saw her in the distance and said to Gehazi, "Look, that woman from Shunem is coming. ²⁶ Run and meet her and ask her what the trouble is. See if her husband is all right and if the child is well."

"Yes," she told Gehazi, "everything is fine."

²⁷ But when she came to Elisha at the mountain she fell to the ground before him and caught hold of his feet. Gehazi began to push her away, but the prophet said, "Let her alone; something is deeply troubling her and the Lord hasn't told me what it is."

²⁸ Then she said, "It was you who said I'd have a son. And I begged you not to lie to me!"

²⁹ Then he said to Gehazi, "Quick, take my staff! Don't talk to anyone along the way. Hurry! Lay the staff upon the child's face."

³⁰ But the boy's mother said, "I swear to God that I won't go home without you." So Elisha returned with her.

³¹ Gehazi went on ahead and laid the staff upon the child's face, but nothing happened. There was no sign of life. He returned to meet Elisha and told him, "The child is still dead."

³² When Elisha arrived, the child was indeed dead, lying there upon the prophet's bed. ³³ He went in and shut the door behind him and prayed to the Lord. ³⁴ Then he lay

upon the child's body, placing his mouth upon the child's mouth, and his eyes upon the child's eyes, and his hands upon the child's hands. And the child's body began to grow warm again! [35] Then the prophet went down and walked back and forth in the house a few times; returning upstairs, he stretched himself again upon the child. This time the little boy sneezed seven times and opened his eyes!

[36] Then the prophet summoned Gehazi. "Call her!" he said. And when she came in, he said, "Here's your son!"

[37] She fell to the floor at his feet and then picked up her son and went out.

[38] Elisha now returned to Gilgal, but there was a famine in the land. One day as he was teaching the young prophets, he said to Gehazi, "Make some stew for supper for these men."

[39] One of the young men went out into the field to gather vegetables and came back with some wild gourds. He shredded them and put them into a kettle without realizing that they were poisonous. [40] But after the men had eaten a bite or two they cried out, "Oh, sir, there's poison in this stew!"

[41] "Bring me some meal," Elisha said. He threw it into the kettle and said, "Now it's all right! Go ahead and eat!" And then it didn't harm them.

[42] One day a man from Baal-shalishah brought Elisha a sack of fresh corn[a] and twenty individual loaves of barley bread made from the first grain of his harvest. Elisha told Gehazi to use it to feed the young prophets.

[43] "What?" Gehazi exclaimed. "Feed one hundred men with only this?"

But Elisha said, "Go ahead, for the Lord says there will be plenty for all, and some will even be left over!"

[44] And sure enough, there was, just as the Lord had said!

5 THE KING OF Syria had high admiration for Naaman, the commander-in-chief of his army, for he had led his troops to many glorious victories. So he was a great hero, but he was a leper. [2] Bands of Syrians had invaded the land of Israel and among their captives was a little girl who had been given to Naaman's wife as a maid.

[3] One day the little girl said to her mistress, "I wish my master would go to see the prophet in Samaria. He would heal him of his leprosy!"

[4] Naaman told the king what the little girl had said.

[5] "Go and visit the prophet," the king told him. "I will send a letter of introduction for you to carry to the king of Israel."

So Naaman started out, taking gifts of $20,000 in silver, $60,000 in gold, and ten suits of clothing. [6] The letter to the king of Israel said: "The man bringing this letter is my servant Naaman; I want you to heal him of his leprosy."

[7] When the king of Israel read it, he tore his clothes and said, "This man sends me a leper to heal! Am I God, that I can kill and give life? He is only trying to get an excuse to invade us again."

[8] But when Elisha the prophet heard about the king of Israel's plight, he sent this message to him: "Why are you so upset? Send Naaman to me, and he will learn that there is a true prophet of God here in Israel."

[9] So Naaman arrived with his horses and chariots and stood at the door of Elisha's home. [10] Elisha sent a messenger out to tell him to go and wash in the Jordan River seven times and he would be healed of every trace of his leprosy! [11] But Naaman was angry and stalked away.

"Look," he said, "I thought at least he would come out and talk to me! I expected him to wave his hand over the leprosy and call upon the name of the Lord his God, and heal me! [12] Aren't the Abana River and Pharpar River of Damascus better than all the rivers of Israel put together? If it's rivers I need, I'll wash at home and get rid of my leprosy." So he went away in a rage.

[13] But his officers tried to reason with him and said, "If the prophet had told you to do some great thing, wouldn't you have done it? So you should certainly obey him when he says simply to go and wash and be cured!"

[14] So Naaman went down to the Jordan

---

a Literally, "fresh grain."

River and dipped himself seven times, as the prophet had told him to. And his flesh became as healthy as a little child's, and he was healed! [15] Then he and his entire party went back to find the prophet; they stood humbly before him and Naaman said, "I know at last that there is no God in all the world except in Israel; now please accept my gifts."

[16] But Elisha replied, "I swear by Jehovah my God that I will not accept them."

Naaman urged him to take them, but he absolutely refused. [17] "Well," Naaman said, "all right. But please give me two muleloads of earth to take back with me, for from now on I will never again offer any burnt offerings or sacrifices to any other God except the Lord.[a] [18] However, may the Lord pardon me this one thing—when my master the king goes into the temple of the god Rimmon to worship there and leans on my arm, may the Lord pardon me when I bow too."

[19] "All right," Elisha said. So Naaman started home again.

[20] But Gehazi, Elisha's servant, said to himself, "My master shouldn't have let this fellow get away without taking his gifts. I will chase after him and get something from him."

[21] So Gehazi caught up with him. When Naaman saw him coming, he jumped down from his chariot and ran to meet him.

"Is everything all right?" he asked.

[22] "Yes," he said, "but my master has sent me to tell you that two young prophets from the hills of Ephraim have just arrived, and he would like $2,000 in silver and two suits to give to them."

[23] "Take $4,000," Naaman insisted. He gave him two expensive robes, tied up the money in two bags, and gave them to two of his servants to carry back with Gehazi. [24] But when they arrived at the hill where Elisha lived,[b] Gehazi took the bags from the servants and sent the men back. Then he hid the money in his house.

[25] When he went in to his master, Elisha asked him, "Where have you been, Gehazi?"

"I haven't been anywhere," he replied.

[26] But Elisha asked him, "Don't you realize that I was there in thought when Naaman stepped down from his chariot to meet you? Is this the time to receive money and clothing and olive farms and vineyards and sheep and oxen and servants? [27] Because you have done this, Naaman's leprosy shall be upon you and upon your children and your children's children forever."

And Gehazi walked from the room a leper, his skin as white as snow.

6 ONE DAY THE seminary students came to Elisha and told him, "As you can see, our dormitory is too small. Tell us, as our president, whether we can build a new one down beside the Jordan River, where there are plenty of logs."

"All right," he told them, "go ahead."

[3] "Please, sir, come with us," someone suggested.

"I will," he said.

[4] When they arrived at the Jordan, they began cutting down trees; [5] but as one of them was chopping, his axhead fell into the river.

"Oh, sir," he cried, "it was borrowed!"

[6] "Where did it fall?" the prophet asked. The youth showed him the place, and Elisha cut a stick and threw it into the water; and the axhead rose to the surface and floated! [7] "Grab it," Elisha said to him; and he did.

[8] Once when the king of Syria was at war with Israel, he said to his officers, "We will mobilize our forces at ____" (naming the place).

[9] Immediately Elisha warned the king of Israel, "Don't go near ____" (naming the same place) "for the Syrians are planning to mobilize their troops there!"

[10] The king sent a scout to see if Elisha was right, and sure enough, he had saved him from disaster. This happened several times.

[11] The king of Syria was puzzled. He called together his officers and demanded, "Which of you is the traitor? Who has been informing the king of Israel about my plans?"

---

a Thus even in a foreign land he could worship Jehovah on Israel's soil.　　b Implied.

[12] "It's not us, sir," one of the officers replied. "Elisha, the prophet, tells the king of Israel even the words you speak in the privacy of your bedroom!"

[13] "Go and find out where he is, and we'll send troops to seize him," the king exclaimed.

And the report came back, "Elisha is at Dothan."

[14] So one night the king of Syria sent a great army with many chariots and horses to surround the city. [15] When the prophet's servant got up early the next morning and went outside, there were troops, horses, and chariots everywhere.

"Alas, my master, what shall we do now?" he cried out to Elisha.

[16] "Don't be afraid!" Elisha told him. "For our army is bigger than theirs!"

[17] Then Elisha prayed, "Lord, open his eyes and let him see!" And the Lord opened the young man's eyes so that he could see horses of fire and chariots of fire everywhere upon the mountain!

[18] As the Syrian army advanced upon them, Elisha prayed, "Lord, please make them blind." And he did.

[19] Then Elisha went out and told them, "You've come the wrong way! This isn't the right city! Follow me and I will take you to the man you're looking for." And he led them to Samaria!

[20] As soon as they arrived Elisha prayed, "Lord, now open their eyes and let them see." And the Lord did, and they discovered that they were in Samaria, the capital city of Israel!

[21] When the king of Israel saw them, he shouted to Elisha, "Oh, sir, shall I kill them? Shall I kill them?"

[22] "Of course not!" Elisha told him. "Do we kill prisoners of war? Give them food and drink and send them home again."

[23] So the king made a great feast for them, and then sent them home to their king. And after that the Syrian raiders stayed away from the land of Israel.

[24] Later on, however, King Ben-hadad of Syria mustered his entire army and besieged Samaria. [25] As a result there was a great famine in the city, and after a long while even a donkey's head sold for fifty dollars and a pint of dove's dung brought three dollars!

[26-30] One day as the king of Israel was walking along the wall of the city, a woman called to him, "Help, my lord the king!"

"If the Lord doesn't help you, what can I do?" he retorted. "I have neither food nor wine to give you. However, what's the matter?"

She replied, "This woman proposed that we eat my son one day and her son the next. So we boiled my son and ate him, but the next day when I said, 'Kill your son so we can eat him,' she hid him."

When the king heard this he tore his clothes. (The people watching noticed through the rip he tore in them that he was wearing an inner robe made of sackcloth next to his flesh.)

[31] "May God kill me if I don't execute Elisha this very day," the king vowed.

[32] Elisha was sitting in his house at a meeting with the elders of Israel when the king sent a messenger to summon him. But before the messenger arrived Elisha said to the elders, "This murderer has sent a man to kill me. When he arrives, shut the door and keep him out, for his master will soon follow him."

[33] While Elisha was still saying this, the messenger arrived [followed by the king[a]].

"The Lord has caused this mess," the king stormed. "Why should I expect any help from him?"

7 ELISHA REPLIED, "THE Lord says that by this time tomorrow two gallons of flour or four gallons of barley grain will be sold in the markets of Samaria for a dollar!"

[2] The officer assisting the king said, "That couldn't happen if the Lord made windows in the sky!"

But Elisha replied, "You will see it happen, but you won't be able to buy any of it!"

[3] Now there were four lepers sitting outside the city gates.

"Why sit here until we die?" they asked each other. [4] "We will starve if we stay here and we will starve if we go back into the city; so we might as well go out and surren-

---

a Implied.

der to the Syrian army. If they let us live, so much the better; but if they kill us, we would have died anyway."

⁵ So that evening they went out to the camp of the Syrians, but there was no one there! ⁶ (For the Lord had made the whole Syrian army hear the clatter of speeding chariots and a loud galloping of horses and the sounds of a great army approaching. "The king of Israel has hired the Hittites and Egyptians to attack us," they cried out. ⁷ So they panicked and fled into the night, abandoning their tents, horses, donkeys, and everything else.)

⁸ When the lepers arrived at the edge of the camp they went into one tent after another, eating, drinking wine, and carrying out silver and gold and clothing and hiding it. ⁹ Finally they said to each other, "This isn't right. This is wonderful news, and we aren't sharing it with anyone! Even if we wait until morning, some terrible calamity will certainly fall upon us; come on, let's go back and tell the people at the palace."

¹⁰ So they went back to the city and told the watchmen what had happened—they had gone out to the Syrian camp and no one was there! The horses and donkeys were tethered and the tents were all in order, but there was not a soul around. ¹¹ Then the watchmen shouted the news to those in the palace.

¹² The king got out of bed and told his officers, "I know what has happened. The Syrians know we are starving, so they have left their camp and have hidden in the fields, thinking that we will be lured out of the city. Then they will attack us and make slaves of us and get in."

¹³ One of his officers replied, "We'd better send out scouts to see. Let them take five of the remaining horses—if something happens to the animals it won't be any greater loss than if they stay here and die with the rest of us!"

¹⁴ Four chariot-horses were found and the king sent out two charioteers to see where the Syrians had gone. ¹⁵ They followed a trail of clothing and equipment all the way to the Jordan River—thrown away by the Syrians in their haste. The scouts returned and told the king, ¹⁶ and the people of Samaria rushed out and plundered the camp of the Syrians. So it was true that two gallons of flour and four gallons of barley were sold that day for one dollar, just as the Lord had said!

¹⁷ The king appointed his special assistant to control the traffic at the gate, but he was knocked down and trampled and killed as the people rushed out. This is what Elisha had predicted on the previous day when the king had come to arrest him, ¹⁸ and the prophet had told the king that flour and barley would sell for so little on the following day.

¹⁹ The king's officer had replied, "That couldn't happen even if the Lord opened the windows of heaven!"

And the prophet had said, "You will see it happen, but you won't be able to buy any of it!"

²⁰ And he couldn't, for the people trampled him to death at the gate!

8 ELISHA HAD TOLD the woman whose son he had brought back to life, "Take your family and move to some other country, for the Lord has called down a famine on Israel that will last for seven years."

² So the woman took her family and lived in the land of the Philistines for seven years. ³ After the famine ended, she returned to the land of Israel and went to see the king about getting back her house and land. ⁴ Just as she came in, the king was talking with Gehazi, Elisha's servant, and saying, "Tell me some stories of the great things Elisha has done." ⁵ And Gehazi was telling the king about the time when Elisha brought a little boy back to life. At that very moment, the mother of the boy walked in!

"Oh, sir!" Gehazi exclaimed. "Here is the woman now, and this is her son—the very one Elisha brought back to life!"

⁶ "Is this true?" the king asked her. And she told him that it was. So he directed one of his officials to see to it that everything she had owned was restored to her, plus the value of any crops that had been harvested during her absence.

⁷ Afterwards Elisha went to Damascus (the capital of Syria), where King Benhadad lay sick. Someone told the king that the prophet had come.

^{8.9} When the king heard the news, he said to Hazael, "Take a present to the man of God and tell him to ask the Lord whether I will get well again."

So Hazael took forty camel-loads of the best produce of the land as presents for Elisha and said to him, "Your son Ben-hadad, the king of Syria, has sent me to ask you whether he will recover."

¹⁰ And Elisha replied, "Tell him, 'Yes.' But the Lord has shown me that he will surely die!"

¹¹ Elisha stared at Hazael until he became embarrassed, and then Elisha started crying.

¹² "What's the matter, sir?" Hazael asked him.

Elisha replied, "I know the terrible things you will do to the people of Israel: you will burn their forts, kill the young men, dash their babies against the rocks, and rip open the bellies of the pregnant women!"

¹³ "Am I a dog?" Hazael asked him. "I would *never* do that sort of thing."

But Elisha replied, "The Lord has shown me that you are going to be the king of Syria."

¹⁴ When Hazael went back, the king asked him, "What did he tell you?"

And Hazael replied, "He told me that you would recover."

¹⁵ But the next day Hazael took a blanket and dipped it in water and held it over the king's face until he smothered to death. And Hazael became king instead.

¹⁶ King Jehoram, the son of King Jehoshaphat of Judah, began his reign during the fifth year of the reign of King Joram of Israel, the son of Ahab. ¹⁷ Jehoram was thirty-two years old when he became king, and he reigned in Jerusalem for eight years. ¹⁸ But he was as wicked as Ahab and the other kings of Israel; he even married one of Ahab's daughters. ¹⁹ Nevertheless, because God had promised his servant David that he would watch over and guide his descendants, he did not destroy Judah.

²⁰ During Jehoram's reign, the people in Edom revolted from Judah and appointed their own king. ²¹ King Jehoram^a tried un-successfully to crush the rebellion: he crossed the Jordan River and attacked the city of Zair, but was quickly surrounded by the army of Edom. Under cover of night he broke through their ranks, but his army deserted him and fled. ²² So Edom has maintained its independence to this day. Libnah also rebelled at that time.

²³ The rest of the history of King Joram is written in *The Annals of the Kings of Judah.* ^{24.25} He died and was buried in the royal cemetery in the City of David—the old section of Jerusalem.

Then his son Ahaziah^b became the new king during the twelfth year of the reign of King Joram of Israel, the son of Ahab. ²⁶ Ahaziah was twenty-two years old when he began to reign but he reigned only one year, in Jerusalem. His mother was Athaliah, the granddaughter of King Omri of Israel. ²⁷ He was an evil king, just as all of King Ahab's descendants were—for he was related to Ahab by marriage.

²⁸ He joined King Joram of Israel (son of Ahab) in his war against Hazael, the king of Syria, at Ramoth-gilead. King Joram was wounded in the battle, ²⁹ so he went to Jezreel to rest and recover from his wounds. While he was there, King Ahaziah of Judah (son of Jehoram) came to visit him.

9 MEANWHILE ELISHA HAD summoned one of the young prophets.

"Get ready to go to Ramoth-gilead," he told him. "Take this vial of oil with you, ² and find Jehu (the son of Jehoshaphat, the son of Nimshi). Call him into a private room away from his friends, ³ and pour the oil over his head. Tell him that the Lord has anointed him to be the king of Israel; then run for your life!"

⁴ So the young prophet did as he was told. When he arrived in Ramoth-gilead, ⁵ he found Jehu sitting around with the other army officers.

"I have a message for you, sir," he said.

"For which one of us?" Jehu asked.

"For you," he replied.

⁶ So Jehu left the others and went into the house, and the young man poured the oil over his head and said, "The Lord God

---

a Literally, "Joram." b Ahaziah is an alternate form of the name Jehoshaz.

of Israel says, 'I anoint you king of the Lord's people, Israel. [7] You are to destroy the family of Ahab; you will avenge the murder of my prophets and of all my other people who were killed by Jezebel. [8] The entire family of Ahab must be wiped out —every male, no matter who. [9] I will destroy the family of Ahab as I destroyed the families of Jeroboam (son of Nebat) and of Baasha (son of Ahijah). [10] Dogs shall eat Ahab's wife Jezebel at Jezreel, and no one will bury her.' "

Then he opened the door and ran.

[11] Jehu went back to his friends and one of them asked him, "What did that crazy fellow want? Is everything all right?"

"You know very well who he was and what he wanted," Jehu replied.

[12] "No, we don't," they said. "Tell us."

So he told them what the man had said and that he had been anointed king of Israel!

[13] They quickly carpeted the bare steps with their coats and blew a trumpet, shouting, "Jehu is king!"

[14] That is how Jehu (son of Jehoshaphat, son of Nimshi) rebelled against King Joram. (King Joram had been with the army at Ramoth-gilead, defending Israel against the forces of King Hazael of Syria. [15] But he had returned to Jezreel to recover from his wounds.)

"Since you want me to be king," Jehu told the men who were with him, "don't let anyone escape to Jezreel to report what we have done."

[16] Then Jehu jumped into a chariot and rode to Jezreel himself to find King Joram, who was lying there wounded. (King Ahaziah of Judah was there too, for he had gone to visit him.) [17] The watchman on the Tower of Jezreel saw Jehu and his company approaching and shouted, "Someone is coming."

"Send out a rider and find out if he is friend or foe," King Joram shouted back. [18] So a soldier rode out to meet Jehu.

"The king wants to know whether you are friend or foe," he demanded. "Do you come in peace?"

Jehu replied, "What do you know about peace? Get behind me!"

The watchman called out to the king that the messenger had met them but was not returning. [19] So the king sent out a second rider. He rode up to them and demanded in the name of the king to know whether their intentions were friendly or not.

Jehu answered, "What do you know about friendliness? Get behind me!"

[20] "He isn't returning either!" the watchman exclaimed. "It must be Jehu, for he is driving so furiously."

[21] "Quick! Get my chariot ready!" King Joram commanded.

Then he and King Ahaziah of Judah rode out to meet Jehu. They met him at the field of Naboth, [22] and King Joram demanded, "Do you come as a friend, Jehu?"

Jehu replied, "How can there be friendship as long as the evils of your mother Jezebel are all around us?"

[23] Then King Joram reined the chariot-horses around and fled, shouting to King Ahaziah, "There is treachery, Ahaziah! Treason!"

[24] Then Jehu drew his bow with his full strength and shot Joram between the shoulders; and the arrow pierced his heart, and he sank down dead in his chariot.

[25] Jehu said to Bidkar, his assistant, "Throw him into the field of Naboth, for once when you and I were riding along behind his father Ahab, the Lord revealed this prophecy to me: [26] 'I will repay him here on Naboth's property for the murder of Naboth and his sons.' So throw him out on Naboth's field, just as the Lord said."

[27] Meanwhile, King Ahaziah of Judah had fled along the road to Beth-haggan. Jehu rode after him, shouting, "Shoot him, too."

So they shot him in his chariot at the place where the road climbs to Gur, near Ibleam. He was able to go on as far as Megiddo, but died there. [28] His officials took him by chariot to Jerusalem where they buried him in the royal cemetery. [29] (Ahaziah's reign over Judah had begun in the twelfth[a] year of the reign of King Joram of Israel.)

---

a Implied in 2 Kings 8:25. Literally, "eleventh."

³⁰ When Jezebel heard that Jehu had come to Jezreel, she painted her eyelids and fixed her hair and sat at a window. ³¹ When Jehu entered the gate of the palace, she shouted at him, "How are you today, you murderer! You son of a Zimri who murdered his master!"

³² He looked up and saw her at the window and shouted, "Who is on my side?" And two or three eunuchs looked out at him.

³³ "Throw her down!" he yelled.

So they threw her out the window, and her blood spattered against the wall and on the horses; and she was trampled by the horses' hoofs.

³⁴ Then Jehu went into the palace for lunch. Afterwards he said, "Someone go and bury this cursed woman, for she is the daughter of a king."

³⁵ But when they went out to bury her, they found only her skull, her feet, and her hands.

³⁶ When they returned and told him, he remarked, "That is just what the Lord said would happen. He told Elijah the prophet that dogs would eat her flesh and that her body would be scattered like manure upon the field, so that no one could tell whose it was."

10 THEN JEHU WROTE a letter to the city council of Samaria and to the guardians of Ahab's seventy sons—all of whom were living there.

²,³ "Upon receipt of this letter, select the best one of Ahab's sons to be your king, and prepare to fight for his throne. For you have chariots and horses and a fortified city and an armory."

⁴ But they were too frightened to do it. "Two kings couldn't stand against this man! What can we do?" they said.

⁵ So the manager of palace affairs and the city manager, together with the city council and the guardians of Ahab's sons, sent him this message:

"Jehu, we are your servants and will do anything you tell us to. We have decided that you should be our king instead of one of Ahab's sons."

⁶ Jehu responded with this message: "If you are on my side and are going to obey me, bring the heads of your master's sons to me at Jezreel at about this time tomorrow."

(These seventy sons of King Ahab were living in the homes of the chief men of the city, where they had been raised since childhood.) ⁷ When the letter arrived, all seventy of them were murdered, and their heads were packed into baskets and presented to Jehu at Jezreel. ⁸ When a messenger told Jehu that the heads of the king's sons had arrived, he said to pile them in two heaps at the entrance of the city gate, and to leave them there until the next morning.

⁹,¹⁰ In the morning he went out and spoke to the crowd that had gathered around them. "You aren't to blame," he told them. "I conspired against my master and killed him, but I didn't kill his sons! The Lord has done that, for everything he says comes true. He declared through his servant Elijah that this would happen to Ahab's descendants."

¹¹ Jehu then killed all the rest of the members of the family of Ahab who were in Jezreel, as well as all of his important officials, personal friends, and private chaplains. Finally, no one was left who had been close to him in any way.ᵃ ¹² Then he set out for Samaria, and stayed overnight at a shepherd's inn along the way. ¹³ While he was there he met the brothers of King Ahaziah of Judah.

"Who are you?" he asked them.

And they replied, "We are brothersᵇ of King Ahaziah. We are going to Samaria to visit the sons of King Ahab and of the Queen Mother, Jezebel."

¹⁴ "Grab them!" Jehu shouted to his men. And he took them out to the cistern and killed all forty-two of them.

¹⁵ As he left the inn, he met Jehonadab, the son of Rechab, who was coming to meet him. After they had greeted each other, Jehu said to him, "Are you as loyal to me as I am to you?"

"Yes," Jehonadab replied.

---

a Apparently Jehu in his zeal exceeded the Lord's command in this bloodbath, for he was blamed for it by the prophet Hosea (1:4).   b Literally, "kinsmen."

"Then give me your hand," Jehu said, and he helped him into the royal chariot. [16] "Now come along with me," Jehu said, "and see how much I have done for the Lord." So Jehonadab rode along with him. [17] When he arrived in Samaria he butchered all of Ahab's friends and relatives, just as Elijah, speaking for the Lord, had predicted.

Then Jehu called a meeting of all the people of the city and said to them, "Ahab hardly worshiped Baal at all in comparison to the way I am going to! [18,19] Summon all the prophets and priests of Baal, and call together all his worshipers. See to it that every one of them comes, for we worshipers of Baal are going to have a great celebration to praise him. Any of Baal's worshipers who don't come will be put to death."

But Jehu's plan was to exterminate them. [20,21] He sent messengers throughout all Israel summoning those who worshiped Baal; and they all came and filled the temple of Baal from one end to the other. [22] He instructed the head of the robing room, "Be sure that every worshiper wears one of the special robes."

[23] Then Jehu and Jehonadab (son of Rechab) went into the temple to address the people: "Check to be sure that only those who worship Baal are here; don't let anyone in who worships the Lord!"

[24] As the priests of Baal began offering sacrifices and burnt offerings, Jehu surrounded the building with eighty of his men and told them, "If you let anyone escape, you'll pay for it with your own life."

[25] As soon as he had finished sacrificing the burnt offering, Jehu went out and told his officers and men, "Go in and kill the whole bunch of them. Don't let a single one escape."

So they slaughtered them all and dragged their bodies outside. Then Jehu's men went into the inner temple, [26] dragged out the pillar used for the worship of Baal, and burned it. [27] They wrecked the temple and converted it into a public toilet, which it still is today. [28] Thus Jehu destroyed every trace of Baal from Israel. [29] However, he didn't destroy the golden calves at Bethel and Dan—this was the great sin of Jeroboam (son of Nebat), for it resulted in all Israel sinning.

[30] Afterwards the Lord said to Jehu, "You have done well in following my instructions to destroy the dynasty of Ahab. Because of this I will cause your son, your grandson, and your great-grandson to be the kings of Israel."

[31] But Jehu didn't follow the Lord God of Israel with all his heart, for he continued to worship Jeroboam's gold calves that had been the cause of such great sin in Israel.

[32,33] At about that time the Lord began to whittle down the size of Israel. King Hazael conquered several sections of the country east of the Jordan River, as well as all of Gilead, Gad, and Reuben; he also conquered parts of Manasseh from the Aroer River in the valley of the Arnon as far as Gilead and Bashan.

[34] The rest of Jehu's activities are recorded in *The Annals of the Kings of Israel.* [35] When Jehu died, he was buried in Samaria; and his son Jehoahaz became the new king. [36] In all, Jehu reigned as king of Israel, in Samaria, for twenty-eight years.

11 WHEN ATHALIAH, THE mother of King Ahaziah of Judah, learned that her son was dead, she killed all of his children, [2,3] except for his year-old[a] son Joash. Joash was rescued by his Aunt Jehosheba, who was a sister of King Ahaziah (for she was a daughter of King Jehoram, Ahaziah's father). She stole him away from among the rest of the king's children who were waiting to be slain, and hid him and his nurse in a storeroom of the Temple.[b] They lived there for six years while Athaliah reigned as queen.

[4] In the seventh year of Queen Athaliah's reign, Jehoiada the priest[a] summoned the officers of the palace guard and the queen's bodyguard. He met them in the Temple, swore them to secrecy, and showed them the king's son.

[5] Then he gave them their instructions: "A third of those who are on duty on the

---

a Implied.   b This arrangement was practical because Jehosheba was the wife of Jehoiada the High Priest.

Sabbath are to guard the palace. [6,7,8] The other two-thirds shall stand guard at the Temple; surround the king, weapons in hand, and kill anyone who tries to break through. Stay with the king at all times."

[9] So the officers followed Jehoiada's instructions. They brought to Jehoiada the men who were going off duty on the Sabbath and those who were coming on duty, [10] and he armed them from the supply of spears and shields in the Temple that had belonged to King David. [11] The guards, with weapons ready, stood across the front of the sanctuary, and surrounded the altar, which was near Joash's hideaway.

[12] Then Jehoiada brought out the young prince and put the crown upon his head and gave him a copy of the Ten Commandments, and anointed him as king. Then everyone clapped and shouted, "Long live the king!"

[13,14] When Athaliah heard all the noise, she ran into the Temple and saw the new king standing beside the pillar, as was the custom at times of coronation, surrounded by her bodyguard and many trumpeters; and everyone was rejoicing and blowing trumpets.

"Treason! Treason!" she screamed, and began to tear her clothes.

[15] "Get her out of here," shouted Jehoiada to the officers of the guard. "Don't kill her here in the Temple. But kill anyone who tries to come to her rescue."

[16] So they dragged her to the palace stables and killed her there.

[17] Jehoiada made a treaty between the Lord, the king, and the people, that they would be the Lord's people. He also made a contract between the king and the people. [18] Everyone went over to the temple of Baal and tore it down, breaking the altars and images and killing Mattan, the priest of Baal, in front of the altar. And Jehoiada set guards at the Temple of the Lord. [19] Then he and the officers and the guard and all the people led the king from the Temple, past the guardhouse, and into the palace. And he sat upon the king's throne.

[20] So everyone was happy, and the city settled back into quietness after Athaliah's death. [21] Joash was seven years old when he became king.

12 IT WAS SEVEN years after Jehu had become the king of Israel that Joash became king of Judah. He reigned in Jerusalem for forty years. (His mother was Zibiah, from Beer-sheba.) [2] All his life Joash did what was right because Jehoiada the High Priest instructed him. [3] Yet even so he didn't destroy the shrines on the hills—the people still sacrificed and burned incense there.

[4,5] One day King Joash said to Jehoiada, "The Temple building needs repairing. Whenever anyone brings a contribution to the Lord, whether it is a regular assessment or some special gift, use it to pay for whatever repairs are needed."

[6] But in the twenty-third year of his reign the Temple was still in disrepair. [7] So Joash called for Jehoiada and the other priests and asked them, "Why haven't you done anything about the Temple? Now don't use any more money for your own needs; from now on it must all be spent on getting the Temple into good condition."

[8] So the priests agreed to set up a special repair fund that would not go through their hands, lest it be diverted to care for their personal needs. [9] Jehoiada the priest bored a hole in the lid of a large chest and set it on the right-hand side of the altar at the Temple entrance. The doorkeepers put all of the people's contributions into it. [10] Whenever the chest became full, the king's financial secretary and the High Priest counted it, put it into bags, [11,12] and gave it to the construction superintendents to pay the carpenters, stonemasons, quarrymen, timber dealers, and stone merchants, and to buy the other materials needed to repair the Temple of the Lord. [13,14] It was not used to buy silver cups, gold snuffers, bowls, trumpets, or similar articles, but only for repairs to the building. [15] No accounting was required from the construction superintendents, for they were honest and faithful men. [16] However, the money that was contributed for guilt offerings and sin offerings was given to the priests for their own use. It was not put into the chest.

[17] About this time, King Hazael of Syria went to war against Gath and captured it; then he moved on toward Jerusalem to attack it. [18] King Joash took all the sacred

objects that his ancestors—Jehoshaphat, Jehoram, and Ahaziah, the kings of Judah—had dedicated, along with what he himself had dedicated, and all the gold in the treasuries of the Temple and the palace, and sent it to Hazael. So Hazael called off the attack. [19] The rest of the history of Joash is recorded in *The Annals of the Kings of Judah.* [20] But his officers plotted against him and assassinated him in his royal residence at Millo on the road to Silla. [21] The assassins were Jozachar, the son of Shimeath, and Jehozabad, the son of Shomer—both trusted aides.[a] He was buried in the royal cemetery in Jerusalem, and his son Amaziah became the new king.

13 JEHOAHAZ (THE SON of Jehu) began a seventeen-year reign over Israel during the twenty-third year of the reign of King Joash of Judah. [2] But he was an evil king, and he followed the wicked paths of Jeroboam, who had caused Israel to sin. [3] So the Lord was very angry with Israel, and he continually allowed King Hazael of Syria and his son Ben-hadad to conquer them. [4] But Jehoahaz prayed for the Lord's help, and the Lord listened to him; for the Lord saw how terribly the king of Syria was oppressing Israel. [5] So the Lord raised up leaders among the Israelis to rescue them from the tyranny of the Syrians; and then Israel lived in safety again as they had in former days. [6] But they continued to sin, following the evil ways of Jeroboam; and they continued to worship the goddess Asherah at Samaria. [7] Finally the Lord reduced Jehoahaz's army to fifty mounted troops, ten chariots, and ten thousand infantry; for the king of Syria had destroyed the others as though they were dust beneath his feet. [8] The rest of the history of Jehoahaz is recorded in *The Annals of the Kings of Israel.* [9,10] Jehoahaz died and was buried in Samaria, and his son Joash reigned in Samaria for sixteen years. He came to the throne in the thirty-seventh year of the reign of King Joash of Judah. [11] But he was an evil man, for, like Jeroboam, he encouraged the people to worship idols and led them into sin. [12] The rest of the history of the reign of Joash, including his wars against King Amaziah of Judah, are written in *The Annals of the Kings of Israel.* [13] Joash died and was buried in Samaria with the other kings of Israel; and Jeroboam II became the new king.

[14] When Elisha was in his last illness, King Joash visited him and wept over him. "My father! My father! You are the strength of Israel!"[a] he cried.

[15] Elisha told him, "Get a bow and some arrows," and he did.

[16,17] "Open that eastern window," he instructed.

Then he told the king to put his hand upon the bow, and Elisha laid his own hands upon the king's hands.

"Shoot!" Elisha commanded, and he did.

Then Elisha proclaimed, "This is the Lord's arrow, full of victory over Syria; for you will completely conquer the Syrians at Aphek. [18] Now pick up the other arrows and strike them against the floor."

So the king picked them up and struck the floor three times. [19] But the prophet was angry with him. "You should have struck the floor five or six times," he exclaimed, "for then you would have beaten Syria until they were entirely destroyed; now you will be victorious only three times."

[20,21] So Elisha died and was buried.

In those days bandit gangs of Moabites used to invade the land each spring. Once some men who were burying a friend spied these marauders so they hastily threw his body into the tomb of Elisha. And as soon as the body touched Elisha's bones, the dead man revived and jumped to his feet.

[22] King Hazael of Syria had oppressed Israel during the entire reign of King Jehoahaz. [23] But the Lord was gracious to the people of Israel, and they were not totally destroyed. For God pitied them, and also he was honoring his contract with Abraham, Isaac, and Jacob. And this is still true. [24] Then King Hazael of Syria died, and his son Ben-hadad reigned in his place. [25] King Joash of Israel[b] (the son of Jehoa-

---

a Literally, "his servants."   13a Literally, "The chariots of Israel and its horsemen!"   b Implied.

haz) was successful on three occasions in reconquering the cities that his father had lost to Ben-hadad.

14 DURING THE SECOND year of the reign of King Joash of Israel, King Amaziah began his reign over Judah. ² Amaziah was twenty-five years old at the time, and he reigned in Jerusalem for twenty-nine years. (His mother was Jeho-addin, a native of Jerusalem.) ³ He was a good king in the Lord's sight, though not quite like his ancestor David; but he was as good a king as his father Joash. ⁴ However, he didn't destroy the shrines on the hills, so the people still sacrificed and burned incense there.

⁵ As soon as he had a firm grip on the kingdom, he killed the men who had assassinated his father; ⁶ but he didn't kill their children, for the Lord had commanded through the law of Moses that fathers shall not be killed for their children, nor children for the sins of their fathers: everyone must pay the penalty for his own sins. ⁷ Once Amaziah killed ten thousand Edomites in Salt Valley; he also conquered Sela and changed its name to Jokthe-el, as it is called to this day.

⁸ One day he sent a message to King Joash of Israel (the son of Jehoahaz and the grandson of Jehu), daring him to mobilize his army and come out and fight. ⁹ But King Joash replied, "The thistle of Lebanon demanded of the mighty cedar tree, 'Give your daughter to be a wife for my son.' But just then a wild animal passed by and stepped on the thistle and trod it into the ground! ¹⁰ You have destroyed Edom and are very proud about it; but my advice to you is, be content with your glory and stay home! Why provoke disaster for both yourself and Judah?"

¹¹ But Amaziah refused to listen, so King Joash of Israel mustered his army. The battle began at Beth-shemesh, one of the cities of Judah, ¹² and Judah was defeated and the army fled home. ¹³ King Amaziah was captured, and the army of Israel marched on Jerusalem and broke down its wall from the Gate of Ephraim to the Corner Gate, a distance of about six hundred feet. ¹⁴ King Joash took many hostages and all the gold and silver from the Temple and palace treasury, also the gold cups. Then he returned to Samaria.

¹⁵ The rest of the history of Joash and his war with King Amaziah of Judah are recorded in *The Annals of the Kings of Israel.* ¹⁶ When Joash died, he was buried in Samaria with the other kings of Israel. And his son Jeroboam became the new king.

¹⁷ Amaziah lived fifteen years longer than Joash, ¹⁸ and the rest of his biography is recorded in *The Annals of the Kings of Judah.* ¹⁹ There was a plot against his life in Jerusalem, and he fled to Lachish; but his enemies sent assassins and killed him there. ²⁰ His body was returned on horses, and he was buried in the royal cemetery, in the City of David section of Jerusalem.

²¹ Then his son Azariah[a] became the new king at the age of sixteen. ²² After his father's death he built Elath and restored it to Judah.

²³ Meanwhile, over in Israel, Jeroboam II had become king during the fifteenth year of the reign of King Amaziah of Judah. Jeroboam's reign lasted forty-one years. ²⁴ But he was as evil as Jeroboam I (the son of Nebat), who had led Israel into the sin of worshiping idols. ²⁵ Jeroboam II recovered the lost territories of Israel between Hamath and the Dead Sea, just as the Lord God of Israel had predicted through Jonah (son of Amittai) the prophet from Gath-hepher. ²⁶ For the Lord saw the bitter plight of Israel—she had no one to help her. ²⁷ And he had not said that he would blot out the name of Israel, so he used King Jeroboam II to save her.

²⁸ The rest of Jeroboam's biography—all that he did, and his great power, and his wars, and how he recovered Damascus and Hamath (which had been captured by Judah)—is recorded in *The Annals of the Kings of Israel.* ²⁹ When Jeroboam II died he was buried with the other kings of Israel, and his son Zechariah became the new king of Israel.

15 NEW KING OF Judah: Azariah[a] Name of his father: Amaziah, the

---

a Also known as "Uzziah."   15 a Also called Uzziah.

former king
Name of his mother: Jecoliah of
Jerusalem
Length of his reign: 52 years, in
Jerusalem
His age at the beginning of his reign:
16 years old
Reigning in Israel at this time: King
Jeroboam, who had been the king
there for 27 years.

[3] Azariah was a good king, and he pleased the Lord just as his father Amaziah had. [4] But like his predecessors, he didn't destroy the shrines on the hills where the people sacrificed and burned incense. [5] Because of this[b] the Lord struck him with leprosy, which lasted until the day of his death; so he lived in a house by himself. And his son Jotham was the acting king. [6] The rest of the history of Azariah is recorded in *The Annals of the Kings of Judah.* [7] When Azariah died, he was buried with his ancestors in the City of David, and his son Jotham became king.

[8] New king of Israel: Zechariah
Name of his father: Jeroboam
Length of reign: 6 months
Reigning in Judah at that time: King
Azariah, who had been the king
there for 38 years

[9] But Zechariah was an evil king in the Lord's opinion, just like his ancestors. Like Jeroboam I (the son of Nebat), he encouraged Israel in the sin of worshiping idols. [10] Then Shallum (the son of Jabesh) conspired against him and assassinated him at Ibleam and took the crown himself. [11] The rest of the history of Zechariah's reign is found in *The Annals of the Kings of Israel.* [12] (So the Lord's statement to Jehu came true, that Jehu's son, grandson, and great-grandson would be kings of Israel[c].)

[13] New king of Israel: Shallum
Father's name: Jabesh
Length of reign: 1 month
Reigning in Judah at that time: King
Uzziah, who had been the king
there for 39 years

[14] One month after Shallum became king, Menahem (the son of Gadi) came to Samaria from Tirzah and assassinated him

and took the throne. [15] Additional details about King Shallum and his conspiracy[d] are recorded in *The Annals of the Kings of Israel.*

[16] Menahem destroyed the city of Tappuah and the surrounding countryside, for its citizens refused to accept him as their king; he killed the entire population and ripped open the pregnant women.

[17] Name of new king of Israel: Menahem
Length of reign: 10 years, in Samaria
Concurrent with: King Azariah of
Judah who had been the king
there for 39 years

[18] But Menahem was an evil king. He worshiped idols, as King Jeroboam I had done so long before, and he led the people of Israel into grievous sin. [19,20] Then King Pul of Assyria invaded the land; but King Menahem bought him off with a gift of $2,000,000, so he turned around and returned home. Menahem extorted the money from the rich, assessing each one $2,000 in the form of a special tax. [21] The rest of the history of King Menahem is written in *The Annals of the Kings of Israel.* [22] When he died, his son Pekahiah became the new king.

[23] Name of new king of Israel: Pekahiah
Father's name: King Menahem
Length of reign: 2 years, in Samaria
Concurrent with: King Azariah of
Judah, who had been the king
there for 50 years

[24] But Pekahiah was an evil king, and he continued the idol-worship begun by Jeroboam I (son of Nebat) who led Israel down that evil trail.

[25] Then Pekah (son of Remaliah), the commanding general of his army, conspired against him with fifty men from Gilead, and assassinated him in the palace at Samaria (Argob and Arieh were also slain in the revolt). So Pekah became the new king. [26] The rest of the history of King Pekahiah is recorded in *The Annals of the Kings of Israel.*

[27] New king of Israel: Pekah
Father's name: Remaliah

---

b Implied.   c See 2 Kings 10:30.   d See verse 10.

Length of reign: 20 years, in Samaria
Concurrent with: King Azariah of Judah, who had been the king there for 52 years
[28] Pekah, too, was an evil king, and he continued in the example of Jeroboam I (son of Nebat), who led all of Israel into the sin of worshiping idols. [29] It was during his reign that King Tiglath-pileser[e] led an attack against Israel. He captured the cities of Ijon, Abel-beth-maacah, Janoah, Kedesh, Hazor, Gilead, Galilee, and all the land of Naphtali; and he took the people away to Assyria as captives. [30] Then Hoshea (the son of Elah) plotted against Pekah and assassinated him; and he took the throne for himself.

New king of Israel: Hoshea
Concurrent with: Jotham (son of Uzziah) king of Judah, who had been the king there for 20 years
[31] The rest of the history of Pekah's reign is recorded in *The Annals of the Kings of Israel.*

[32,33] New king of Judah: Jotham
Father's name: King Uzziah
His age when he became king: 25 years old
Duration of his reign: 16 years, in Jerusalem
Mother's name: Jerusha (daughter of Zadok)
Reigning in Israel at this time: Pekah (son of Remaliah), who had been the king there for 2 years
[34,35] Generally speaking, Jotham was a good king. Like his father Uzziah,[f] he followed the Lord. But he didn't destroy the shrines on the hills where the people sacrificed and burned incense. It was during King Jotham's reign that the upper gate of the Temple of the Lord was built. [36] The rest of Jotham's history is written in *The Annals of the Kings of Judah.* [37] In those days the Lord caused King Rezin of Syria and King Pekah of Israel to attack Judah. [38] When Jotham died he was buried with the other kings of Judah in the royal cemetery, in the City of David section of Jerusalem. Then his son Ahaz became the new king.

16 NEW KING OF Judah: Ahaz
Father's name: Jotham
Age: 20 years old
Duration of reign: 16 years, in Jerusalem
Character of his reign: evil
Reigning in Israel at this time: King Pekah (son of Remaliah) who had been the king there for 17 years
[2] But he did not follow the Lord as his ancestor David had; [3] he was as wicked as the kings of Israel. He even killed his own son by offering him as a burnt sacrifice to the gods, following the heathen customs of the nations around Judah—nations which the Lord destroyed when the people of Israel entered the land. [4] He also sacrificed and burned incense at the shrines on the hills and at the numerous altars in the groves of trees.

[5] Then King Rezin of Syria and King Pekah (son of Remaliah) of Israel declared war on Ahaz and besieged Jerusalem; but they did not conquer it. [6] However, at that time King Rezin of Syria recovered the city of Elath for Syria; he drove out the Jews and sent Syrians to live there, as they do to this day. [7] King Ahaz sent a messenger to King Tiglath-pileser of Assyria, begging him to help him fight the attacking armies of Syria and Israel.[8] [8] Ahaz took the silver and gold from the Temple and from the royal vaults and sent it as a payment to the Assyrian king. [9] So the Assyrians attacked Damascus, the capital of Syria. They took away the population of the city as captives, resettling them in Kir, and King Rezin of Syria was killed.

[10] King Ahaz now went to Damascus to meet with King Tiglath-pileser, and while he was there he noticed an unusual altar in a heathen temple.[b] He jotted down its dimensions and made a sketch and sent it back to Uriah the priest with a detailed description. [11,12] Uriah built one just like it by following these directions and had it ready for the king, who, upon his return from Damascus, inaugurated it with an offering. [13] The king presented a burnt offering and a grain offering, poured a drink offering

e Also called Pul, in verse 19 above. f Also called Azariah. 16a Literally, "saying, 'I am your servant and your son. Come and rescue me.'" b Literally, "he saw the altar that was at Damascus."

over it, and sprinkled the blood of peace offerings upon it. [14] Then he removed the old bronze altar from the front of the Temple (it had stood between the Temple entrance and the new altar), and placed it on the north side of the new altar. [15] He instructed Uriah the priest to use the new altar for the sacrifices of burnt offering, the evening grain offering, the king's burnt offering and grain offering, and the offerings of the people, including their drink offerings. The blood from the burnt offerings and sacrifices was also to be sprinkled over the new altar. So the old altar was used only for purposes of divination.

"The old bronze altar," he said, "will be only for my personal use."

[16] Uriah the priest did as King Ahaz instructed him. [17] Then the king dismantled the wheeled stands in the Temple, removed their crosspieces and the water vats they supported, and removed the great tank from the backs of the bronze oxen and placed it upon the stone pavement. [18] In deference to the king of Assyria he also removed the festive passageway he had constructed between the palace and the Temple.[c]

[19] The rest of the history of the reign of King Ahaz is recorded in *The Annals of the Kings of Judah*. [20] When Ahaz died he was buried in the royal cemetery, in the City of David sector of Jerusalem, and his son Hezekiah became the new king.

17 NEW KING OF Israel: Hoshea
Father's name: Elah
Length of his reign: 9 years, in Samaria
Character of his reign: evil—but not as bad as some of the other kings of Israel
Reigning in Judah at this time: King Ahaz, who had been the king there for 12 years

[3] King Shalmaneser of Assyria attacked and defeated King Hoshea, so Israel had to pay heavy annual taxes to Assyria. [4] Then Hoshea conspired against the king of Assyria by asking King So of Egypt to help him shake free of Assyria's power, but this treachery was discovered. At the same time he refused to pay the annual tribute to Assyria. So the king of Assyria put him in prison and in chains for his rebellion.

[5] Now the land of Israel was filled with Assyrian troops for three years besieging Samaria, the capital city of Israel. [6] Finally, in the ninth year of King Hoshea's reign, Samaria fell and the people of Israel were exiled to Assyria. They were placed in colonies in the city of Halah and along the banks of the Habor River in Gozan, and among the cities of the Medes.

[7] This disaster came upon the nation of Israel because the people worshiped other gods, thus sinning against the Lord their God who had brought them safely out of their slavery in Egypt. [8] They had followed the evil customs of the nations which the Lord had cast out from before them. [9] The people of Israel had also secretly done many things that were wrong, and they had built altars to other gods throughout the land.[a] [10] They had placed obelisks and idols at the top of every hill and under every green tree; [11] and they had burned incense to the gods of the very nations which the Lord had cleared out of the land when Israel came in. So the people of Israel had done many evil things, and the Lord was very angry. [12] Yes, they worshiped idols, despite the Lord's specific and repeated warnings.

[13] Again and again the Lord had sent prophets to warn both Israel and Judah to turn from their evil ways; he had warned them to obey his commandments which he had given to their ancestors through these prophets, [14] but Israel wouldn't listen. The people were as stubborn as their ancestors and refused to believe in the Lord their God. [15] They rejected his laws and the covenant he had made with their ancestors, and despised all his warnings. In their foolishness they worshiped heathen idols despite the Lord's stern warnings. [16] They defied all the commandments of the Lord their God and made two calves from molten gold. They made detestable, shameful idols and worshiped Baal and the sun, moon, and stars. [17] They even burned their own sons and daughters to death on the altars of Mo-

c The Hebrew is unclear.   17a Literally, "built them high places in all their cities."

lech;[b] they consulted fortune-tellers and used magic and sold themselves to evil. So the Lord was very angry. [18] He swept them from his sight until only the tribe of Judah remained in the land.

[19] But even Judah refused to obey the commandments of the Lord their God; they too walked in the same evil paths as Israel had. [20] So the Lord rejected all the descendants of Jacob.[c] He punished them by delivering them to their attackers until they were destroyed. [21] For Israel split off from the kingdom of David and chose Jeroboam I (the son of Nebat) as its king. Then Jeroboam drew Israel away from following the Lord. He made them sin a great sin, [22] and the people of Israel never quit doing the evil things that Jeroboam led them into, [23] until the Lord finally swept them away, just as all his prophets had warned would happen. So Israel was carried off to the land of Assyria where they remain to this day.

[24] And the king of Assyria transported colonies of people from Babylon, Cuthah, Avva, Hamath, and Sepharvaim and resettled them in the cities of Samaria, replacing the people of Israel. So the Assyrians took over Samaria and the other cities of Israel. [25] But since these Assyrian colonists did not worship the Lord when they first arrived, the Lord sent lions among them to kill some of them.

[26] Then they sent a message to the king of Assyria: "We colonists here in Israel don't know the laws of the god of the land, and he has sent lions among us to destroy us because we have not worshiped him." [27,28] The king of Assyria then decreed that one of the exiled priests from Samaria should return to Israel and teach the new residents the laws of the god of the land. So one of them returned to Bethel and taught the colonists from Babylon how to worship the Lord.

[29] But these foreigners also worshiped their own gods. They placed them in the shrines on the hills near their cities. [30] Those from Babylon worshiped idols of their god Succoth-benoth; those from Cuth worshiped their god Nergal; and the men of Hamath worshiped Ashima. [31] The gods Nibhaz and Tartak were worshiped by the Avvites, and the people from Sephar even burned their own children on the altars of their gods Adrammelech and Anammelech.

[32] They also worshiped the Lord, and they appointed from among themselves priests to sacrifice to the Lord on the hilltop altars. [33] But they continued to follow the religious customs of the nations from which they came. [34] And this is still going on among them today—they follow their former practices instead of truly worshiping the Lord or obeying the laws he gave to the descendants of Jacob (whose name was later changed to Israel). [35,36] For the Lord had made a contract with them—that they were never to worship or make sacrifices to any heathen gods. They were to worship only the Lord who had brought them out of the land of Egypt with such tremendous miracles and power. [37] The descendants of Jacob were to obey all of God's laws and *never worship other gods.*

[38] For God had said, *"You must never forget the covenant I made with you; never worship other gods.* [39] *You must worship only the Lord; he will save you from all your enemies."*

[40] But Israel didn't listen, and the people continued to worship other gods. [41] These colonists from Babylon worshiped the Lord, yes—but they also worshiped their idols. And to this day their descendants do the same thing.

18 NEW KING OF Judah: Hezekiah
Father's name: Ahaz
Length of his reign: 29 years, in Jerusalem
His age at the beginning of his reign: 25 years old
His mother's name: Abi (daughter of Zechariah)
Character of his reign: good (similar to that of his ancestor David).
Reigning in Israel at this time: King Hoshea (son of Elah), who had been the king there for 3 years

[4] He removed the shrines on the hills, broke down the obelisks, knocked down the shameful idols of Asherah, and broke up the

---

b Literally, "as offerings."   c Literally, "descendants of Israel."

bronze serpent that Moses had made, because the people of Israel had begun to worship it by burning incense to it; even though, as King Hezekiah[a] pointed out to them, it was merely a piece of bronze. [5] He trusted very strongly in the Lord God of Israel. In fact, none of the kings before or after him were as close to God as he was. [6] For he followed the Lord in everything, and carefully obeyed all of God's commands to Moses. [7] So the Lord was with him and prospered everything he did. Then he rebelled against the king of Assyria and refused to pay tribute any longer. [8] He also conquered the Philistines as far distant as Gaza and its suburbs, destroying cities both large and small.[b]

[9] It was during the fourth year of his reign (which was the seventh year of the reign of King Hoshea in Israel) that King Shalmaneser of Assyria attacked Israel and began a siege on the city of Samaria. [10] Three years later (during the sixth year of the reign of King Hezekiah and the ninth year of the reign of King Hoshea of Israel) Samaria fell. [11] It was at that time that the king of Assyria transported the Israelis to Assyria and put them in colonies in the city of Halath and along the banks of the Habor River in Gozan, and in the cities of the Medes. [12] For they had refused to listen to the Lord their God or to do what he wanted them to do. Instead, they had transgressed his covenant and disobeyed all the laws given to them by Moses the servant of the Lord.

[13] Later, during the fourteenth year of the reign of King Hezekiah, King Sennacherib of Assyria besieged and captured all the fortified cities of Judah. [14] King Hezekiah sued for peace and sent this message to the king of Assyria at Lachish: "I have done wrong. I will pay whatever tribute you demand if you will only go away." The king of Assyria then demanded a settlement of $1,500,000. [15] To gather this amount, King Hezekiah used all the silver stored in the Temple and in the palace treasury. [16] He even stripped off the gold from the Temple doors, and from the doorposts he had overlaid with gold, and gave it all

to the Assyrian king.

[17] Nevertheless the king of Assyria sent his field marshal, his chief treasurer, and his chief of staff from Lachish with a great army; and they camped along the highway beside the field where cloth was bleached, near the conduit of the upper pool. [18] They demanded that King Hezekiah come out to speak to them, but instead he sent a truce delegation of the following men: Eliakam, his business manager; Shebnah, his secretary; and Joah, his royal historian.

[19] Then the Assyrian general sent this message to King Hezekiah: "The great King of Assyria says, 'No one can save you from my power! [20,21] You need more than mere promises of help before rebelling against me. But which of your allies will give you more than words? Egypt? If you lean on Egypt, you will find her to be a stick that breaks beneath your weight and pierces your hand. The Egyptian Pharaoh is totally unreliable! [22] And if you say, "We're trusting the Lord to rescue us"—just remember that he is the very one whose hilltop altars you've destroyed. For you require everyone to worship at the altar in Jerusalem!' [23] I'll tell you what: Make a bet with my master, the king of Assyria! If you have two thousand men left who can ride horses, we'll furnish the horses! [24] And with an army as small as yours,[c] you are no threat to even the least lieutenant in charge of the smallest contingent in my master's army. Even if Egypt supplies you with horses and chariots, it will do no good. [25] And do you think we have come here on our own? No! The Lord sent us and told us, 'Go and destroy this nation!' "

[26] Then Eliakim, Shebnah, and Joah said to them, "Please speak in Aramaic, for we understand it. Don't use Hebrew, for the people standing on the walls will hear you."

[27] But the Assyrian general replied, "Has my master sent me to speak only to you and to your master? Hasn't he sent me to the people on the walls too? For they are doomed with you to eat their own excrement and drink their own urine!"

[28] Then the Assyrian ambassador shouted in Hebrew to the people on the

---

a Implied.   b Literally, "from the tower of the watchman to the fortified cities."   c Implied.

wall, "Listen to the great king of Assyria! [29] 'Don't let King Hezekiah fool you. He will never be able to save you from my power. [30] Don't let him fool you into trusting in the Lord to rescue you. [31,32] Don't listen to King Hezekiah. Surrender! You can live in peace here in your own land until I take you to another land just like this one—with plentiful crops, grain, wine, olive trees, and honey. All of this instead of death! Don't listen to King Hezekiah when he tries to persuade you that the Lord will deliver you. [33] Have any of the gods of the other nations ever delivered their people from the king of Assyria? [34] What happened to the gods of Hamath, Arpad, Sepharvaim, Hena, and Ivvah? Did they rescue Samaria? [35] What god has ever been able to save any nation from my power? So what makes you think the Lord can save Jerusalem?' "

[36] But the people on the wall remained silent, for the king had instructed them to say nothing. [37] Then Eliakim (son of Hilkiah) the business manager, and Shebnah the king's secretary, and Joah (son of Asaph) the historian went to King Hezekiah with their clothes torn and told him what the Assyrian general had said.

19 WHEN KING HEZEKIAH heard their report he tore his clothes and put on sackcloth and went into the Temple to pray. [2] Then he told Eliakim, Shebnah, and some of the older priests to clothe themselves in sackcloth and to go to Isaiah (son of Amoz), the prophet, with this message:

[3] "King Hezekiah says, 'This is a day of trouble, insult, and dishonor. It is as when a child is ready to be born, but the mother has no strength to deliver it. [4] Yet perhaps the Lord your God has heard the Assyrian general defying the living God, and will rebuke him. Oh, pray for the few of us who are left.' "

[5,6] Isaiah replied, "The Lord says, 'Tell your master not to be troubled by the sneers these Assyrians have made against me.' [7] For the king of Assyria will receive bad news from home and will decide to return; and the Lord will see to it that he is killed when he arrives there."

[8] Then the Assyrian general returned to his king at Libnah (for he received word that he had left Lachish). [9] Soon afterwards news reached the king that King Tirhakah of Ethiopia was coming to attack him. Before leaving to meet the attack, he sent back this message to King Hezekiah:

[10] "Don't be fooled by that god you trust in. Don't believe it when he says that I won't conquer Jerusalem. [11] You know perfectly well what the kings of Assyria have done wherever they have gone; they have completely destroyed everything. Why would you be any different? [12] Have the gods of the other nations delivered them—such nations as Gozan, Haran, Rezeph, and Eden in the land of Telassar? The former kings of Assyria destroyed them all! [13] What happened to the king of Hamoth and the king of Arpad? What happened to the kings of Sepharvaim, Hena, and Ivvah?"

[14] Hezekiah took the letter from the messengers, read it, and went over to the Temple and spread it out before the Lord. [15] Then he prayed this prayer:

"O Lord God of Israel, sitting on your throne high above the angels,[a] you alone are the God of all the kingdoms of the earth. You created the heavens and the earth. [16] Bend low, O Lord, and listen. Open your eyes, O Lord, and see. Listen to this man's defiance of the living God. [17] Lord, it is true that the kings of Assyria have destroyed all those nations, [18] and have burned their idol-gods. But they weren't gods at all; they were destroyed because they were only things that men had made of wood and stone. [19] O Lord our God, we plead with you to save us from his power; then all the kingdoms of the earth will know that you alone are God."

[20] Then Isaiah sent this message to Hezekiah: "The Lord God of Israel says, 'I have heard you! [21] And this is my reply to King Sennacherib: The virgin daughter of Zion isn't afraid of you! The daughter of Jerusalem scorns and mocks at you. [22] Whom have you defied and blasphemed? And toward whom have you felt so cocky? It is the Holy One of Israel!

[23] " 'You have boasted, "My chariots

---

a Literally, "cherubim."

have conquered the highest mountains, yes, the peaks of Lebanon. I have cut down the tallest cedars and choicest cypress trees and have conquered the farthest borders. ²⁴ I have been refreshed at many conquered wells, and I destroyed the strength of Egypt just by walking by!"

²⁵ " 'Why haven't you realized long before this that it is I, the Lord, who lets you do these things? I decreed your conquest of all those fortified cities! ²⁶ So of course the nations you conquered had no power against you! They were like grass shriveling beneath the hot sun, and like grain blighted before it is half grown. ²⁷ I know everything about you. I know all your plans and where you are going next; and I also know the evil things you have said about me. ²⁸ And because of your arrogance against me I am going to put a hook in your nose and a bridle in your mouth and turn you back on the road by which you came. ²⁹ And this is the proof that I will do as I have promised: This year my people will eat the volunteer wheat, and use it as seed for next year's crop; and in the third year they will have a bountiful harvest.

³⁰ " 'O my people Judah, those of you who have escaped the ravages of the siege shall become a great nation again; you shall be rooted deeply in the soil and bear fruit for God. ³¹ A remnant of my people shall become strong in Jerusalem. The Lord is eager to cause this to happen.

³² " 'And my command concerning the king of Assyria is that he shall not enter this city. He shall not stand before it with a shield, nor build a ramp against its wall, nor even shoot an arrow into it. ³³ He shall return by the road he came, ³⁴ for I will defend and save this city for the sake of my own name and for the sake of my servant David.' "

³⁵ That very night the angel of the Lord killed 185,000 Assyrian troops, and dead bodies were seen all across the landscape in the morning.

³⁶ Then King Sennacherib returned to Nineveh; ³⁷ and as he was worshiping in the temple of his god Nisroch, his sons Adram-

melech and Sharezer killed him. They escaped into eastern Turkey—the land of Ararat—and his son Esarhaddon became the new king.

20 HEZEKIAH NOW BECAME deathly sick, and Isaiah the prophet went to visit him.

"Set your affairs in order and prepare to die," Isaiah told him. "The Lord says you won't recover."

² Hezekiah turned his face to the wall.

³ "O Lord," he pleaded, "remember how I've always tried to obey you and to please you in everything I do . . . ." Then he broke down and cried.

⁴ So before Isaiah had left the courtyard, the Lord spoke to him again.

⁵ "Go back to Hezekiah, the leader of my people, and tell him that the Lord God of his ancestor David has heard his prayer and seen his tears. I will heal him, and three days from now he will be out of bed and at the Temple! ⁶ I will add fifteen years to his life and save him and this city from the king of Assyria. And it will all be done for the glory of my own name and for the sake of my servant David."

⁷ Isaiah then instructed Hezekiah to boil some dried figs and to make a paste of them and spread it on the boil. And he recovered!

⁸ Meanwhile, King Hezekiah had said to Isaiah, "Do a miracle to prove to me that the Lord will heal me and that I will be able to go to the Temple again three days from now."

⁹ "All right, the Lord will give you a proof," Isaiah told him. "Do you want the shadow on the sundial to go forward ten points or backward ten points?"

¹⁰ "The shadow always moves forward," Hezekiah replied; "make it go backward."

¹¹ So Isaiah asked the Lord to do this, and he caused the shadow to move ten points backward on the sundial of Ahaz!^a

¹² At that time Merodach-baladan (the son of King Baladan of Babylon) sent ambassadors with greetings and a present to Hezekiah, for he had learned of his sickness. ¹³ Hezekiah welcomed them and showed

---

a Or, "on the steps of Ahaz." Egyptian sundials in this period were made in the form of miniature staircases, so that the shadow moved up and down the steps.

them all his treasures—the silver, gold, spices, aromatic oils, the armory—everything. [14] Then Isaiah went to King Hezekiah and asked him, "What did these men want? Where are they from?"

"From far away in Babylon," Hezekiah replied.

[15] "What have they seen in your palace?" Isaiah asked.

And Hezekiah replied, "Everything. I showed them all my treasures."

[16] Then Isaiah said to Hezekiah, "Listen to the word of the Lord: [17] The time will come when everything in this palace shall be carried to Babylon. All the treasures of your ancestors will be taken—nothing shall be left. [18] Some of your own sons will be taken away and made into eunuchs who will serve in the palace of the king of Babylon."

[19] "All right," Hezekiah replied, "if this is what the Lord wants, it is good." But he was really thinking, "At least there will be peace and security during the remainder of my own life!"

[20] The rest of the history of Hezekiah and his great deeds—including the pool and conduit he made and how he brought water into the city—are recorded in *The Annals of the Kings of Judah.* [21] When he died, his son Manasseh became the new king.

21 NEW KING OF Judah: Manasseh
His age at beginning of his reign: 12 years
Length of his reign: 55 years, in Jerusalem
Name of his mother: Hephzibah
Character of his reign: evil. He did the same things the nations had done that were thrown out of the land to make room for the people of Israel
[3,4,5] He rebuilt the hilltop shrines which his father Hezekiah had destroyed. He built altars for Baal and made a shameful Asherah idol, just as Ahab the king of Israel had done. Heathen altars to the sun god, moon god, and the gods of the stars were placed even in the Temple of the Lord—in the very city and building which the Lord had selected to honor his own name. [6] And he sacrificed one of his sons as a burnt offering on a heathen altar. He practiced black magic and used fortune-telling, and patronized mediums and wizards. So the Lord was very angry, for Manasseh was an evil man, in God's opinion. [7] Manasseh even set up a shameful Asherah-idol in the Temple—the very place which the Lord had spoken to David and Solomon about when he said, "I will place my name forever in this Temple, and in Jerusalem—the city I have chosen from among all the cities of the tribes of Israel. [8] If the people of Israel will only follow the instructions I gave them through Moses, I will never again expel them from this land of their fathers."

[9] But the people did not listen to the Lord, and Manasseh enticed them to do even more evil than the surrounding nations had done, even though Jehovah had destroyed those nations for their evil ways when the people of Israel entered the land.

[10] Then the Lord declared through the prophets,

[11] "Because King Manasseh has done these evil things and is even more wicked than the Amorites who were in this land long ago, and because he has led the people of Judah into idolatry: [12] I will bring such evil upon Jerusalem and Judah that the ears of those who hear about it will tingle with horror. [13] I will cause the kings of Israel to conquer Jerusalem, and I will wipe Jerusalem as a man wipes a dish and turns it upside down to dry. [14] Then I will reject even those few of my people who are left, and I will hand them over to their enemies. [15] For they have done great evil and have angered me ever since I brought their ancestors from Egypt."

[16] In addition to the idolatry which God hated and into which Manasseh led the people of Judah, he murdered great numbers of innocent people. And Jerusalem was filled from one end to the other with the bodies of his victims.

[17] The rest of the history of Manasseh's sinful reign is recorded in *The Annals of the Kings of Judah.* [18] When he died he was buried in the garden of his palace at Uzza, and his son Amon became the new king.

[19,20] Name of the new king of Judah: Amon
His age at the beginning of his reign:

22 years old

Length of his reign: 2 years, in Jerusalem

His mother's name: Meshullemeth (daughter of Haruz, of Jotbah)

Character of his reign: evil

²¹ He did all the evil things his father had done: he worshiped the same idols, ²² and turned his back on the Lord God of his ancestors. He refused to listen to God's instructions. ²³ But his aides conspired against him and killed him in the palace. ²⁴ Then a posse of civilians killed all the assassins and placed Amon's son Josiah upon the throne. ²⁵ The rest of Amon's biography is recorded in *The Annals of the Kings of Judah.* ²⁶ He was buried in a crypt in the garden of Uzza, and his son Josiah became the new king.

22 NEW KING OF Judah: Josiah

His age at the beginning of his reign: 8 years old

Duration of his reign: 31 years in Jerusalem

Name of his mother: Jedidah (daughter of Adaiah of Bozkath)

Character of his reign: good; for he followed in the steps of his ancestor King David, obeying the Lord completely

³·⁴ In the eighteenth year of his reign, King Josiah sent his secretary Shaphan (son of Azaliah, son of Meshullam) to the Temple to give instruction to Hilkiah, the High Priest:

"Collect the money given to the priests at the door of the Temple when the people come to worship. ⁵·⁶ Give this money to the building superintendents so that they can hire carpenters and masons to repair the Temple, and to buy lumber and stone."

⁷ (The building superintendents were not required to keep account of their expenditures, for they were honest men.)

⁸ One day Hilkiah the High Priest went to Shaphan the secretary and exclaimed, "I have discovered a scroll in the Temple, with God's laws written on it!"

He gave the scroll to Shaphan to read. ⁹·¹⁰ When Shaphan reported to the king about the progress of the repairs at the Temple, he also mentioned the scroll found by Hilkiah. Then Shaphan read it to the king.

¹¹ When the king heard what was written in it, he tore his clothes in terror. ¹²·¹³ He commanded Hilkiah the priest, and Shaphan, and Asaiah, the king's assistant, and Ahikam (Shaphan's son), and Achbor (Michaiah's son) to ask the Lord, "What shall we do? For we have not been following the instructions of this book: you must be very angry with us, for neither we nor our ancestors have followed your commands."

¹⁴ So Hilkiah the priest, and Ahikam, and Achbor, and Shaphan, and Asaiah went to the Mishneh section of Jerusalem to find Huldah the prophetess. (She was the wife of Shallum—son of Tikvah, son of Harhas—who was in charge of the palace tailor shop.) ¹⁵·¹⁶ She gave them this message from the Lord God of Israel:

"Tell the man who sent you to me, that I am going to destroy this city and its people, just as I stated in that book you read. ¹⁷ For the people of Judah have thrown me aside and have worshiped other gods and have made me very angry; and my anger can't be stopped. ¹⁸·¹⁹ But because you were sorry and concerned and humbled yourself before the Lord when you read the book and its warnings that this land would be cursed and become desolate, and because you have torn your clothing and wept before me in contrition, I will listen to your plea. ²⁰ The death of this nation will not occur until after you die—you will not see the evil which I will bring upon this place."

So they took the message to the king.

23 THEN THE KING sent for the elders and other leaders of Judah and Jerusalem to go to the Temple with him. So all the priests and prophets and the people, small and great, of Jerusalem and Judah gathered there at the Temple so that the king could read to them the entire book of God's laws which had been discovered in the Temple. ³ He stood beside the pillar in front of the people, and he and they made a solemn promise to the Lord to obey him at all times and to do everything the book commanded.

⁴ Then the king instructed Hilkiah the High Priest and the rest of the priests and the guards of the Temple to destroy all the equipment used in the worship of Baal, Asherah, and the sun, moon, and stars. The

king had it all burned in the fields of the Kidron Valley outside Jerusalem, and he carried the ashes to Bethel. [5] He killed the heathen priests who had been appointed by the previous kings of Judah, for they had burned incense in the shrines on the hills throughout Judah and even in Jerusalem. They had also offered incense to Baal and to the sun, moon, stars, and planets. [6] He removed the shameful idol of Asherah from the Temple and took it outside Jerusalem to Kidron Brook; there he burned it and beat it to dust and threw the dust on the graves of the common people. [7] He also tore down the houses of male prostitution around the Temple, where the women wove robes for the Asherah-idol.

[8] He brought back to Jerusalem the priests of the Lord, who were living in other cities of Judah, and tore down all the shrines on the hills where they had burned incense, even those as far away as Geba and Beersheba. He also destroyed the shrines at the entrance of the palace of Joshua, the former mayor of Jerusalem, located on the left side as one enters the city gate. [9] However, these priests[a] did not serve at the altar of the Lord in Jerusalem, even though they ate with the other priests.

[10] Then the king destroyed the altar of Topheth in the Valley of the Sons of Hinnom, so that no one could ever again use it to burn his son or daughter to death as a sacrifice to Molech. [11] He tore down the statues of horses and chariots located near the entrance of the Temple, next to the quarters of Nathan-melech the eunuch. These had been dedicated by former kings of Judah to the sun god. [12] Then he tore down the altars which the kings of Judah had built on the palace roof above the Ahaz Room. He also destroyed the altars which Manasseh had built in the two courts of the Temple; he smashed them to bits and scattered the pieces in Kidron Valley.

[13] Next he removed the shrines on the hills east of Jerusalem and south of Destruction Mountain. (Solomon had built these shrines for Ashtoreth, the evil goddess of the Sidonians; and for Chemosh, the evil god of Moab; and for Milcom, the evil god of the Ammonites.) [14] He smashed the obelisks and cut down the shameful idols of Asherah; then he defiled these places by scattering human bones over them. [15] He also tore down the altar and shrine at Bethel which Jeroboam I had made when he led Israel into sin. He crushed the stones to dust and burned the shameful idol of Asherah.

[16] As Josiah was looking around, he noticed several graves in the side of the mountain. He ordered his men to bring out the bones in them and to burn them there upon the altar at Bethel to defile it, just as the Lord's prophet had declared would happen to Jeroboam's altar.[b]

[17] "What is that monument over there?" he asked.

And the men of the city told him, "It is the grave of the prophet who came from Judah and proclaimed that what you have just done would happen here at the altar at Bethel!"

[18] So King Josiah replied, "Leave it alone. Don't disturb his bones."

So they didn't burn his bones or those of the prophet from Samaria.[c]

[19] Josiah demolished the shrines on the hills in all of Samaria. They had been built by the various kings of Israel and had made the Lord very angry. But now he crushed them into dust, just as he had done at Bethel. [20] He executed the priests of the heathen shrines upon their own altars, and he burned human bones upon the altars to defile them. Finally he returned to Jerusalem.

[21] The king then issued orders for his people to observe the Passover ceremonies as recorded by the Lord their God in *The Book of the Covenant.* [22] There had not been a Passover celebration like that since the days of the judges of Israel, and there was never another like it in all the years of the kings of Israel and Judah. [23] This Passover was in the eighteenth year of the reign of King Josiah, and it was celebrated in Jerusalem.

[24] Josiah also exterminated the mediums and wizards, and every kind of idol worship, both in Jerusalem and throughout the land. For Josiah wanted to follow all the

---

a Literally, "the priests of the high places."   b See 1 Kings 13:20.   c See 1 Kings 13:31, 32.

laws which were written in the book that Hilkiah the priest had found in the Temple. ²⁵ There was no other king who so completely turned to the Lord and followed all the laws of Moses; and no king since the time of Josiah has approached his record of obedience.

²⁶ But the Lord still did not hold back his great anger against Judah, caused by the evils of King Manasseh. ²⁷ For the Lord had said, "I will destroy Judah just as I have destroyed Israel; and I will discard my chosen city of Jerusalem and the Temple that I said was mine."

²⁸ The rest of the biography of Josiah is written in *The Annals of the Kings of Judah.* ²⁹ In those days King Neco of Egypt attacked the king of Assyria at the Euphrates River, and King Josiah went to assist him; but King Neco killed Josiah at Megiddo when he saw him. ³⁰ His officers took his body back in a chariot from Megiddo to Jerusalem and buried him in the grave he had selected. And his son Jehoahaz was chosen by the nation as its new king.

³¹,³² New king of Judah: Jehoahaz

His age when he became king: 23 years old

Length of his reign: 3 months, in Jerusalem

His mother's name: Hamutal (the daughter of Jeremiah of Libnah)

Character of his reign: evil, like the other kings who had preceded him

³³ Pharaoh-Neco jailed him at Riblah in Hamath to prevent his reigning in Jerusalem, and he levied a tax against Judah totaling $230,000. ³⁴ The Egyptian king then chose Eliakim, another of Josiah's sons, to reign in Jerusalem; and he changed his name to Jehoiakim. Then he took King Jehoahaz to Egypt, where he died. ³⁵ Jehoiakim taxed the people to get the money that the Pharaoh had demanded.

³⁶,³⁷ New king of Judah: Jehoiakim

His age when he became king: 25 years old

Length of his reign: 11 years, in Jerusalem

His mother's name: Zebidah (daughter of Pedaiah of Rumah)

Character of his reign: evil, like the other kings preceding him

24 DURING THE REIGN of King Jehoiakim, King Nebuchadnezzar of Babylon attacked Jerusalem. Jehoiakim surrendered and paid him tribute for three years, but then rebelled. ² And the Lord sent bands of Chaldeans, Syrians, Moabites, and Ammonites against Judah in order to destroy the nation, just as the Lord had warned through his prophets that he would. ³,⁴ It is clear that these disasters befell Judah at the direct command of the Lord. He had decided to wipe Judah out of his sight because of the many sins of Manasseh, for he had filled Jerusalem with blood, and the Lord would not pardon it.

⁵ The rest of the history of the life of Jehoiakim is recorded in *The Annals of the Kings of Judah.* ⁶ When he died, his son Jehoiachin became the new king. ⁷ (The Egyptian Pharaoh never returned after that, for the king of Babylon occupied the entire area claimed by Egypt—all of Judah from the Brook of Egypt to the Euphrates River.)

⁸,⁹ New king of Judah, Jehoiachin

His age at the beginning of his reign: 18 years old

Length of his reign: 3 months, in Jerusalem

Name of his mother: Nehushta (daughter of Elnathan, a citizen of Jerusalem)

¹⁰ During his reign the armies of King Nebuchadnezzar of Babylon besieged the city of Jerusalem. ¹¹ Nebuchadnezzar himself arrived during the siege, ¹² and King Jehoiachin, all of his officials, and the queen mother surrendered to him. The surrender was accepted, and Jehoiachin was imprisoned in Babylon during the eighth year of Nebuchadnezzar's reign.

¹³ The Babylonians carried home all the treasures from the Temple and the royal palace; and they cut apart all the gold bowls which King Solomon of Israel had placed in the Temple at the Lord's directions. ¹⁴ King Nebuchadnezzar took ten thousand captives from Jerusalem, including all the princes and the best of the soldiers, craftsmen, and smiths. So only the poorest and least skilled people were left in the land. ¹⁵ Nebuchadnezzar took King Jehoiachin,

his wives and officials, and the queen mother, to Babylon. [16] He also took seven thousand of the best troops and one thousand craftsmen and smiths, all of whom were strong and fit for war. [17] Then the king of Babylon appointed King Jehoiachin's great-uncle,[a] Mattaniah, to be the next king; and he changed his name to Zedekiah.

[18,19] New king of Judah: Zedekiah

His age when he became king: 21 years old

Length of his reign: 11 years, in Jerusalem

His mother's name: Hamutal (daughter of Jeremiah of Libnah)

Character of his reign: evil, like that of Jehoiakim

[20] So the Lord finally, in his anger, destroyed the people of Jerusalem and Judah. But now King Zedekiah rebelled against the king of Babylon.

25 THEN KING NEBUCHADNEZZAR of Babylon mobilized his entire army and laid siege to Jerusalem, arriving on March 25 of the ninth year of the reign of King Zedekiah of Judah. [2] The siege continued into the eleventh year of his reign.

[3] The last food in the city was eaten on July 24, [4,5] and that night the king and his troops made a hole in the inner wall and fled out toward the Arabah through a gate that lay between the double walls near the king's garden. The Babylonian troops surrounding the city took out after him and captured him in the plains of Jericho, and all his men scattered. [6] He was taken to Riblah, where he was tried and sentenced before the king of Babylon. [7] He was forced to watch as his sons were killed before his eyes; then his eyes were put out and he was bound with chains and taken away to Babylon.

[8] General Nebuzaradan, the captain of the royal bodyguard, arrived at Jerusalem from Babylon on July 22 of the nineteenth year of the reign of King Nebuchadnezzar. [9] He burned down the Temple, the palace, and all the other houses of any worth. [10] He then supervised the Babylonian army in tearing down the walls of Jerusalem. [11] The remainder of the people in the city and the Jewish deserters who had declared their allegiance to the king of Babylon were all taken as exiles to Babylon. [12] But the poorest of the people were left to farm the land.

[13] The Babylonians broke up the bronze pillars of the Temple and the bronze tank and its bases and carried all the bronze to Babylon. [14,15] They also took all the pots, shovels, firepans, snuffers, spoons, and other bronze instruments used for the sacrifices. The gold and silver bowls, with all the rest of the gold and silver, were melted down to bullion. [16] It was impossible to estimate the weight of the two pillars and the great tank and its bases—all made for the Temple by King Solomon—because they were so heavy. [17] Each pillar was twenty-seven feet high, with an intricate bronze network of pomegranates decorating the 4½-foot capitals at the tops of the pillars.

[18] The general took Seraiah, the chief priest, his assistant Zephaniah, and the three Temple guards to Babylon as captives. [19] A commander of the army of Judah, the chief recruiting officer, five of the king's counselors, and sixty farmers, all of whom were discovered hiding in the city, [20] were taken by General Nebuzaradan to the king of Babylon at Riblah, [21] where they were put to the sword and died.

So Judah was exiled from its land.

[22] Then King Nebuchadnezzar appointed Gedaliah (the son of Ahikam and grandson of Shaphan) as governor over the people left in Judah. [23] When the Israeli guerrilla forces learned that the king of Babylon had appointed Gedaliah as governor, some of these underground leaders and their men joined him at Mizpah. These included Ishmael, the son of Nethaniah; Johanan, the son of Kareah; Seraiah, the son of Tanhumeth the Netophathite; and Jaazaniah, son of Maachathite, and their men. [24] Gedaliah vowed that if they would give themselves up and submit to the Babylonians, they would be allowed to live in the land and would not be exiled. [25] But seven months later, Ishmael, who was a member of the royal line, went to Mizpah with ten men and killed Gedaliah and his court—both the Jews and the Babylonians.

---

a Implied in 23:31 and 24:18.

²⁶ Then all the men of Judah and the guerrilla leaders fled in panic to Egypt, for they were afraid of what the Babylonians would do to them.

²⁷ King Jehoiachin was released from prison on the twenty-seventh day of the last month of the thirty-seventh year of his captivity.

This occurred during the first year of the reign of King Evil-merodach of Babylon. ²⁸ He treated Jehoiachin kindly and gave him preferential treatment over all the other kings who were being held as prisoners in Babylon. ²⁹ Jehoiachin was given civilian clothing to replace his prison garb, and for as long as he lived, he ate regularly at the king's table. ³⁰ The king also gave him a daily cash allowance for the rest of his life.

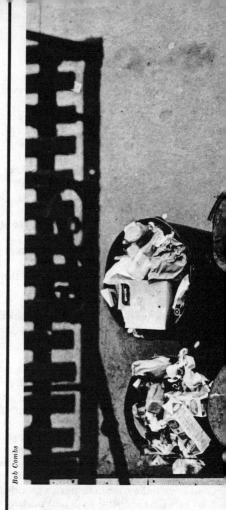

Bob Combs

View from the Top

God must get slightly sick staring down into our cruddy world—especially when he thinks of the beautiful start he gave us back in Eden. The two books of Chronicles are a God's-eye view of the people on planet Earth—his people—slowly disintegrating.

1 Chronicles (once you get past the opening chapters of genealogical records) is a rerun of the reign of King David, first told in 2 Samuel. Some of the uglier parts (the Bath-sheba affair, Absalom's attempted coup) are omitted — maybe because God considered them forgiven and forgotten.

2 Chronicles is a rerun of 1 and 2 Kings, but only the Judah-half of the story. If you want to know what God thought about the successors of David, read 2 Chronicles. For example:

* Rehoboam — "he never did decide really to please the Lord" (12:14).
* Abijah—"God gave his kingdom peace" (14:5).
* Uzziah—"As long as the king followed the paths of God, he prospered, for God blessed him" (26:5).

God's way of looking at things —we need all of that we can get.

1 CHRONICLES

1 THESE ARE THE earliest generations of mankind:[a]

> Adam, Seth, Enosh, Kenan,
> Mahalalel, Jared, Enoch,
> Methuselah, Lamech, Noah, **Shem,**
> **Ham,** and **Japheth.**[b]

5-9 The sons of *Japheth*[c] were:

> **Gomer,** Magog, Madai, **Javan,**
> Tubal, Meshech, and Tiras.

The sons of *Gomer:*

> Ashkenaz, Diphath, and Togarmah.

The sons of *Javan:*

> Elishah, Tarshish, Kittim, and
> Rodanim.

The sons of *Ham:*

> **Cush, Misream, Canaan,** and **Put.**

The sons of *Cush* were:

> Seba, Havilah, Sabta, Raama, and
> Sabteca.

The sons of Raama were Sheba and Dedan.

10 Another of the sons of *Cush* was Nimrod, who became a great hero.

11,12 The clans named after the sons of *Misream* were:

> the Ludim, the Anamim, the
> Lehabim, the Naphtuhim, the
> Pathrusim, the Caphtorim, and the
> Casluhim (the ancestors of the
> Philistines).

13-16 Among *Canaan's* sons were:

> Sidon (his firstborn) and Heth.

Canaan was also the ancestor of the Jebusites, Amorites, Girgashites, Hivites, Arkites, Sinites, Arvadites, Zemarites, and Hamathites.

17 The sons of *Shem:*

> Elam, Asshur, **Arpachshad,** Lud,
> Aram, Uz, Hul, Gether,
> and Meshech.

18 *Arpachshad's* son was **Shelah,** and *Shelah's* son was **Eber.**

19 *Eber* had two sons: Peleg (which means "Divided," for it was during his lifetime that the people of the earth were divided into different language groups), and Joktan.

20-23 The sons of Joktan:

> Almodad, Sheleph, Hazarmaveth,
> Jerah, Hadoram, Uzal, Diklah,
> Ebal, Abima-el, Sheba, Ophir,
> Havilah, and Jobab.

24-27 So the son[d] of *Shem* was Arpachshad, the son of Arpachshad was Shelah,

> The son of Shelah was Eber,
> The son of Eber was Peleg,
> The son of Peleg was Reu,
> The son of Reu was Serug,
> The son of Serug was Nahor,
> The son of Nahor was Terah,
> The son of Terah was Abram (later
> known as Abraham).

28-31 Abraham's sons were **Isaac** and **Ishmael.**

The sons of *Ishmael:*

> Nabaioth (the oldest), Kedar,
> Adbeel, Mibsam, Mishma, Dumah,

---

a Implied.   b The names in bold face type are referred to in the following verse or verses. The use of bold type or italic type does not mean that these persons were more important; it is simply a way of easier identification of ancestors and descendants.   c Italic means that the name has previously appeared in bold face type.   d Or, "descendant." The subsequent usage of the word "son" could also be interpreted "descendant."

Massa, Hadad, Tema, Jetur,
Naphish, and Kedemah.

³² Abraham also had sons by his concubine Keturah:

Zimram, **Jokshan,** Medan, **Midian,**
Ishbak, and Shuah.

Jokshan's sons were Sheba and Dedan.

³³ The sons of *Midian:*

Ephah, Epher, Hanoch, Abida, and
Eldaah. These were the descendants
of Abraham by his concubine
Keturah.

³⁴ Abraham's son *Isaac* had two sons,
Esau and Israel.

³⁵ The sons of *Esau:*

Eliphaz, Reuel, Jeush, Jalam, and
Korah.

³⁶ The sons of *Eliphaz:*

Teman, Omar, Zephi, Gatam,
Kenaz, Timna, and Amalek.

³⁷ The sons of *Reuel:*

Nahath, Zerah, Shammah, and
Mizzah.

³⁸,³⁹ The sons of *Esau*ᵉ also included **Lotan, Shobal, Zibeon,** Anah, Dishon, **Ezer,** and **Dishan;** and Esau's daughter was named Timna.

Lotan's sons: Hori and Homam.

⁴⁰ The sons of *Shobal:* Alian, Manahath, Ebal, Shephi, and Onam.

Zibeon's sons were Aiah and **Anah.**

⁴¹ *Anah's* son was **Dishon:**

The sons of *Dishon:* Hamran,
Eshban, Ithran, and Cheran.

⁴² The sons of *Ezer:* Bilhan, Zaavan, and Jaakan.

Dishan's sons were Uz and Aran.

⁴³ Here is a list of the names of the kings of Edom who reigned before the kingdom of Israel began:

Bela (the son of Beor), who lived in the city of Dinhabah.

⁴⁴ When Bela died, Jobab the son of Zerah from Bozrah became the new king.

⁴⁵ When Jobab died, Husham from the country of the Temanites became the king.

⁴⁶ When Husham died, Hadad the son of Bedad—the one who destroyed the army of Midian in the fields of Moab—became king and ruled from the city of Avith.

⁴⁷ When Hadad died, Samlah from the city of Masrekah came to the throne.

⁴⁸ When Samlah died, Shaul from the river town of Rehoboth became the new king.

⁴⁹ When Shaul died, Baal-hanan the son of Achbor became king.

⁵⁰ When Baal-hanan died, Hadad became king and ruled from the city of Pai (his wife was Mehetabel, the daughter of Matred and granddaughter of Mezahab).

⁵¹⁻⁵⁴ At the time of Hadad's death, the kings of Edom were:

Chief Timna, Chief Aliah, Chief
Jetheth, Chief Oholibamah, Chief
Elah, Chief Pinon, Chief Kenaz,
Chief Teman, Chief Mibzar, Chief
Magdi-el, Chief Iram.

2 THE SONS OF Israel were:

Reuben, Simeon, Levi, Judah,
Issachar, Zebulun, Dan, Joseph,
Benjamin, Naphtali, Gad, Asher.

³ Judah had three sons by Bath-shua, a girl from Canaan: **Er,** Onan, and Shelah. But the oldest son, *Er,* was so wicked that the Lord killed him.

⁴ Then Er's widow, Tamar, and her father-in-law, Judah, became the parents of twin sons, **Perez** and **Zerah.** So Judah had five sons.

⁵ The sons of *Perez* were **Hezron** and Hamul.

⁶ The sons of *Zerah* were:

Zimri, **Ethan,** Heman,
Calcol, and Dara.

⁷ (Achan, the son of Carmi, was the man who robbed God and was such a troublemaker for his nation.)

⁸ *Ethan's* son was Azariah.

⁹ The sons of *Hezron* were Jerahmeel, Ram, and Chelubai.

¹⁰ Ram was the father of Amminadab, and Amminadab was the father of Nahshon, a leader of Israel.

¹¹ Nahshon was the father of Salma, and Salma was the father of Boaz.

¹² Boaz was the father of Obed, and Obed was the father of Jesse.

¹³ *Jesse's* first son was Eliab, his second was Abinadab, his third was Shimea, ¹⁴ his fourth was Nethanel, his fifth was Raddai,

---

e Or, "Seir."

¹⁵ his sixth was Ozem, and his seventh was David. ¹⁶ He also had two girls (by the same wife) named **Zeruiah** and **Abigail**.

Zeruiah's sons were Abishai, Joab, and Asahel.

¹⁷ *Abigail,* whose husband was Jether from the land of Ishmael, had a son named Amasa.

¹⁸ Caleb (the son of **Hezron**) had two wives, **Azubah** and Jerioth. These are the children of *Azubah:*

Jesher, Shobab, and Ardon.

¹⁹ After Azubah's death, Caleb married Ephrath, who presented him with a son, **Hur.**

²⁰ *Hur's* son was **Uri,** and *Uri's* son was Bezalel.

²¹ **Hezron** married Machir's daughter at the age of sixty, and she presented him with a son, **Segub.** (Machir was also the father of Gilead.)

²² *Segub* was the father of Jair, who ruled[a] twenty-three cities in the land of Gilead. ²³ But Geshur and Aram wrested these cities from him and also took Kenath and its sixty surrounding villages.

²⁴ Soon after his father *Hezron's* death, Caleb married Ephrathah, his father's widow, and she gave birth to Ashhur, the father of Tekoa.

²⁵ These are the sons of **Jerahmeel** (the oldest son of *Hezron*):

Ram (the oldest), Bunah, Oren, Ozem, and Ahijah.

²⁶ *Jerahmeel's* second wife Atarah was the mother of **Onam.**

²⁷ The sons of *Ram:*

Maaz, Jamin, and Eker.

²⁸ *Onam's* sons were **Shammai** and Jada. *Shammai's* sons were **Nadab** and **Abishur.**

²⁹ The sons of *Abishur* and his wife Abihail were Ahban and Molid.

³⁰ *Nadab's* sons were **Seled** and **Appa-im.** *Seled* died without children, ³¹ but *Appa-im* had a son named **Ishi;** *Ishi's* son was **Sheshan;** and *Sheshan's* son was Ahlai.

³² *Shammai's* brother Jada had two sons, **Jether** and **Jonathan.** *Jether* died without children, ³³ but *Jonathan* had two sons named Peleth and Zaza.

³⁴,³⁵ *Sheshan*[b] had no sons, although he had several daughters. He gave one of his daughters to be the wife of Jarha, his Egyptian servant. And they had a son whom they named **Attai.**

³⁶ **Attai**'s son was Nathan; Nathan's son was Zabad; ³⁷ Zabad's son was Ephlal; Ephlal's son was Obed; ³⁸ Obed's son was Jehu; Jehu's son was Azariah; ³⁹ Azariah's son was Helez; Helez's son was Ele-asah; ⁴⁰ Eleasah's son was Sismai; Sismai's son was Shallum; ⁴¹ Shallum's son was Jekamiah; Jekamiah's son was Elishama.

⁴² The oldest son of **Caleb** (Jerahmeel's brother) was Mesha; he was the father of Ziph, who was father of Mareshah, who was the father of **Hebron.**

⁴³ The sons of *Hebron:* Korah, Tappuah, **Rekem,** and **Shema.**

⁴⁴ **Shema** was the father of Raham, who was the father of Jorke-am.

Rekem was the father of **Shammai.**

⁴⁵ *Shammai's* son was Maon, the father of Bethzur.

⁴⁶ *Caleb's* concubine Ephah bore him **Haran,** Moza, and Gazez; *Haran* had a son named Gazez.

⁴⁷ The sons of Jahdai:

Regem, Jotham, Geshan, Pelet, Ephah, and Shaaph.

⁴⁸,⁴⁹ Another of *Caleb's* concubines, Maacah, bore him Sheber, Tirhanah, Shaaph (the father of Madmannah), and Sheva (the father of Machbenah and of Gibe-a). *Caleb* also had a daughter, whose name was Achsah.

⁵⁰ The sons of Hur (who was the oldest son of *Caleb*[c] and Ephrathah) were **Shobal** (the father of Kiriath-jearim), ⁵¹ **Salma** (the father of Bethlehem), and Hareph (the father of Beth-gader).

⁵² **Shobal's** sons included **Kiriath-jearim** and Haroeh, the ancestor of half of the Menuhoth tribe.

⁵³ The families of *Kiriath-jearim* were the Ithrites, the Puthites, the Shumathites, and the Mishraites (from whom descended the Zorathites and Eshtaolites).

⁵⁴ The descendants of Salma were his son Bethlehem, the Netophathites, Atroth-beth-joab, half the Manahathites, and the

---

a Literally, "had."   b Apparently a different Sheshan than in verse 31.   c Implied in 2:24.

Zorites; [55] they also included the families of the writers living at Jabez—the Tirathites, Shime-athites, and Sucathites. All these are Kenites who descended from Hammath, the founder of the family of Rechab.

3 KING DAVID'S OLDEST son was Amnon, who was born to his wife, Ahino-am of Jezreel.

The second was Daniel, whose mother was Abigail from Carmel.

[2] The third was Absalom, the son of his wife Maacah, who was the daughter of King Talmai of Geshur.

The fourth was Adonijah, the son of Haggith.

[3] The fifth was Shephatiah, the son of Abital.

The sixth was Ithream, the son of his wife Eglah.

[4] These six were born to him in Hebron, where he reigned seven and one-half years. Then he moved the capital to Jerusalem, where he reigned another thirty-three years.

[5] While he was in Jerusalem, his wife Bathsheba[a] (the daughter of Ammi-el) became the mother of his sons Shime-a, Shobab, Nathan, and **Solomon.**

[6-8] David also had nine other sons: Ibhar, Elishama, Eliphelet, Nogah, Nepheg, Japhia, Elishama, Eliada, and Eliphelet.

[9] (This list does not include the sons of his concubines.) David also had a daughter Tamar.

[10-14] These are the descendants of King *Solomon:*

Rehoboam, Abijah, Asa, Jehoshaphat, Joram,[b] Ahaziah, Joash, Amaziah, Azariah,[c] Jotham, Ahaz, Hezekiah, Manasseh, Amon, **Josiah.**

[15] The sons of *Josiah* were: Johanan,[d] **Jehoiakim,** Zedekiah, Shallum.

[16] The sons of *Jehoiakim:*[e] **Jeconiah,** Zedekiah.

[17,18] These are the sons who were born to King *Jeconiah* during the years that he was under house arrest:

She-altiel, Malchiram, **Pedaiah,** Shenazzar, Jekamiah, Hoshama, Nedabiah.

[19,20] *Pedaiah* was the father of **Zerubbabel** and Shime-i.

Zerubbabel's children were: Meshullam, **Hananiah,** Hashubah, Ohel, Berechiah, Hasadiah, Jushab-hesed, Shelomith (a daughter).

[21,22] *Hananiah's* sons were Pelatiah and Jeshaiah;

Jeshaiah's son was Rephaiah;

Rephaiah's son was Arnan;

Arnan's son was Obadiah;

Obadiah's son was Shecaniah.

Shecaniah's son was Shemaiah;

Shemaiah had six sons, including Hattush, Igal, Bariah, **Neariah,** and Shaphat.

[23] *Neariah* had three sons: **Eli-o-enai,** Hizkiah, Azrikam.

[24] *Eli-o-enai* had seven sons: Hodaviah, Eliashib, Pelaiah, Akkub, Johanan, Delaiah, Anani.

4 THESE ARE THE sons of Judah: Perez, Hezron, Carmi, Hur, **Shobal.**

[2] *Shobal's* son Re-aiah was the father of Jahath, the ancestor of Ahumai and Lahad. These were known as the Zorathite clans.

[3-4] The descendants of Etam: Jezreel, Ishma, Idbash, Hazzelelponi (his daughter), Penuel (the ancestor of Gedor), Ezer (the ancestor of Hushah), The son of Hur, the oldest son of Ephrathah, who was the father of Bethlehem.

[5] Ashhur, the father of Tekoa, had two wives—**Helah,** and **Naarah.**

[6] *Naarah* bore him Ahuzzam, Hepher, Temeni, and Haahashtari; [7] and *Helah* bore him Zereth, Izhar, and Ethnan.

[8] Koz was the father of Anub and Zobebah; he was also the ancestor of the clan named after Aharhel, the son of Harum.

[9] Jabez was more distinguished than any of his brothers. His mother named him Jabez because she had such a hard time at his

---

a Literally, "Bath-shua."   b Or, "Jehoram."   c Or, "Uzziah."   d Or, "Jehoahaz" (see 2 Kings 23:30 f.).   e Also known as Jehoiachin or Coniah.

birth (Jabez means[a] "Distress").

[10] He was the one who prayed to the God of Israel, "Oh, that you would wonderfully bless me and help me in my work; please be with me in all that I do, and keep me from all evil and disaster!" And God granted him his request.

[11,12] The descendants of Recah were:

Chelub (the brother of Shuhah), whose son was Mahir, the father of **Eshton;**

Eshton was the father of Bethrapha, Paseah, and Tehinnah;

Tehinnah was the father of Irnahash.

[13] The sons of Kenaz were **Othni-el** and **Seraiah.**

Othni-el's sons were Hathath and **Meonothai;**

[14] *Meonothai* was the father of Ophrah;

Seraiah was the father of Joab, the ancestor of the inhabitants of Craftsman Valley (called that because many craftsmen lived there).

[15] The sons of Caleb (the son of Jephunneh):

Iru, **Elah,** Naam.

The sons of *Elah* included Kenaz.

[16] Jehallelel's sons were:

Ziph, Ziphah, Tiri-a, Asarel.

[17] Ezrah's sons were:

Jether, **Mered,** Epher, Jalon.

Mered married Bithi-ah, an Egyptian princess. She was the mother of Miriam, Shammai, and Ishbah—an ancestor of **Eshtemoa.**

[18] *Eshtemoa's* wife was a Jewess; she was the mother of Jered, Heber, and Jekuthiel, who were, respectively, the ancestors of the Gedorites, Socoites, and Zanoahites.

[19] Hodiah's wife was the sister of Naham. One of her sons was the father of Keilah the Garmite, and another was the father of Eshtemoa the Maacathite.

[20] The sons of Shimon:

Amnon, Rinnah, Ben-hanan, Tilon.

The sons of Ishi:

Zoheth, Ben-zoheth.

[21-22] The sons of Shelah (the son of Judah):

Er (the father of Lecah),

Laadah (the father of Mareshah),

The families of the linen workers who worked at Beth-ashbea,

Jokim,

The clans of Cozeba,

Joash,

Saraph (who was a ruler in Moab before he returned to Lehem).

These names all come from very ancient records.

[23] These clans were noted for their pottery, gardening, and planting; they all worked for the king:

[24] The sons of Simeon:

Nemu-el, Jamin, Jarib, Zerah, **Shaul.**

[25] *Shaul's* son was Shallum, his grandson was Mibsam, and his great-grandson was **Mishma.**

[26] *Mishma's* sons included Hammu-el (the father of Zaccur and grandfather of **Shime-i**).

[27] *Shime-i* had sixteen sons and six daughters, but none of his brothers had large families—they all had fewer children than was normal in Judah.

[28] They lived at Beer-sheba, Moladah, Hazar-shual, [29] Bilhah, Ezem, Tolad, [30] Bethuel, Hormah, Ziklag, [31] Beth-marcaboth, Hazar-susim, Beth-biri, and Shaaraim. These cities were under their control until the time of David.

[32,33] Their descendants also lived in or near Etam, Ain, Rimmon, Tochen, and Ashan; some were as far away as Baal. (These facts are recorded in their genealogies.)

[34-39] These are the names of some of the princes of wealthy clans who traveled to the east side of Gedor Valley in search of pasture for their flocks:

Meshobab, Jamlech, Joshah, Joel, Jehu, Eli-o-enai, Ja-akobah, Jeshohaiah, Asaiah, Adi-el, Jesimi-el, Benaiah, Ziza (the son of Shiphi, son of Allon, son of Jedaiah, son of Shimri, son of Shemaiah).

[40,41] They found good pastures, and everything was quiet and peaceful; but the land belonged to the descendants of Ham.

---

a A play on words. *Jabez* sounds like *ozeb,* the Hebrew word meaning "distress."

So during the reign of King Hezekiah of Judah these princes invaded the land and struck down the tents and houses of the descendants of Ham; they killed the inhabitants of the land and took possession of it for themselves.

[42] Later, five hundred of these invaders from the tribe of Simeon went to Mount Seir. (Their leaders were Pelatiah, Ne-ariah, Rephaiah, and Uzziel—all sons of Ishi.) [43] There they destroyed the few surviving members of the tribe of Amalek. And they have lived there ever since.

5 THE OLDEST SON of Israel was Reuben, but since he dishonored his father by sleeping with one of his father's wives, his birthright was given to his half brother, Joseph. So the official genealogy doesn't name Reuben as the oldest son.

[2] Although Joseph received the birthright, yet Judah was a powerful and influential tribe in Israel, and from Judah came a Prince.

[3] The sons of Reuben, Israel's son, were: Hanoch, Pallu, Hezron, Carmi.

[4] Joel's descendants were his son Shemaiah, his grandson Gog, and his great-grandson **Shime-i.**

[5] *Shime-i's* son was Micah; his grandson was Reaiah; and his great-grandson was **Baal.**

[6] *Baal's* son was Beerah. He was a prince of the tribe of Reuben and was taken into captivity by King Tilgath-pilneser of Assyria.

[7,8] His relatives became heads of clans and were included in the official genealogy:

Je-iel, Zechariah,
Bela (the son of Azaz, grandson of Shema, and great-grandson of **Joel).**

These Reubenites[a] lived in Aroer and as far distant as Mount Nebo and Baal-meon.

[9] Joel was a cattle man, and he pastured his animals eastward to the edge of the desert and to the Euphrates River, for there were many cattle in the land of Gilead.

[10] During the reign of King Saul, the men of Reuben defeated the Hagrites in war and moved into their tents on the eastern edge of Gilead. [11] Across from them, in the land of Bashan, lived the descendants of Gad, who were spread as far as Salecah.

[12] Joel was the greatest and was followed by Shapham, also Janai and Shaphat. [13] Their relatives, the heads of the seven clans, were Michael, Meshullam, Sheba, Jorai, Jacan, Zia, and Eber.

[14] The descendants of Buz, in the order of their generations, were:

Jahdo, Jeshishai, Michael, Gilead,
Jaroah, Huri, Abihail.

[15] Ahi, the son of Abdi-el and grandson of Guni, was the leader of the clan. [16] The clan lived in and around Gilead (in the land of Bashan) and throughout the entire pasture country of Sharon. [17] All were included in the official genealogy at the time of King Jotham of Judah and King Jeroboam of Israel.

[18] There were 44,760 armed, trained, and brave troops in the army of Reuben, Gad, and the half-tribe of Manasseh. [19] They declared war on the Hagrites, the Jeturites, the Naphishites, and the Nodabites. [20] They cried out to God to help them, and he did, for they trusted in him. So the Hagrites and all their allies were defeated. [21] The booty included 50,000 camels, 250,000 sheep, 2,000 donkeys, and 100,000 captives. [22] A great number of the enemy also died in the battle, for God was fighting against them. So the Reubenites lived in the territory of the Hagrites until the time of the exile.

[23] The half-tribe of Manasseh spread through the land from Bashan to Baal-hermon, Senir, and Mount Hermon. They too were very numerous.

[24] The chiefs of their clans were the following:

Epher, Ishi, Eliel, Azri-el,
Jeremiah, Hodaviah, Jahdi-el.

Each of these men had a great reputation as a warrior and leader. [25] But they were not true to the God of their fathers; instead they worshiped the idols of the people whom God had destroyed. [26] So God caused King Pul of Assyria (also known as Tilgath-pilneser III) to invade the land and deport the men of Reuben, Gad, and the half-tribe of Manasseh. They took them to Halah, Ha-

---

a Implied in 5:1.

bor, Hara, and the Gozan River, where they remain to this day.

6 THESE ARE THE names of the sons of Levi:

Gershom, Kohath, Merari.

[2] *Kohath's* sons were:

Amram, Izhar, Hebron, Uzziel.

[3] *Amram's* descendants included:

Aaron, Moses, Miriam.

Aaron's sons were:

Nadab, Abihu, Eleazar, Ithamar.

[4-15] The oldest sons of the successive generations of Aaron were as follows:[a]

Eleazar, the father of

Phinehas, the father of

Abishua, the father of

Bukki, the father of

Uzzi, the father of

Zerahiah, the father of

Meraioth, the father of

Amariah, the father of

Ahitub, the father of

Zadok, the father of

Ahima-az, the father of

Azariah, the father of

Johanan, the father of

Azariah (the High Priest in Solomon's Temple at Jerusalem), the father of

Amariah, the father of

Ahitub, the father of

Zadok, the father of

Shallum, the father of

Hilkiah, the father of

Azariah, the father of

Seraiah, the father of

Jehozadak (who went into exile when the Lord sent the people of Judah and Jerusalem into captivity under Nebuchadnezzar).

[16] As previously stated,[b] the sons of Levi were:

Gershom, Kohath, Merari.

[17] The sons of *Gershom* were:

Libni, Shime-i.

[18] The sons of *Kohath* were:

Amram, Izhar, Hebron, Uzziel.

[19,20,21] The sons of *Merari* were:

Mahli, Mushi.

The subclans of the Levites were:

In the Gershom clan:

Libni, Jahath, Zimmah, Joah, Iddo, Zerah, Jeatherai.

[22,23,24] In the Kohath clan:

Amminadab, Korah, Assir,

Elkanah, Ebiasaph, Assir, Tahath, Uriel, Uzziah, Shaul.

[25,26,27] The subclan of *Elkanah* was further divided into the families of his sons:

Amasai, Ahimoth, Elkanah,

Zophai, Nahath, Eliab,

Jeroham, Elkanah.

[28] The families of the subclan of Samuel were headed by Samuel's sons:

Joel, the oldest;

Abijah, the second.

[29,30] The subclans of the clan of Merari were headed by his sons:

Mahli, Libni, Shime-i, Uzzah,

Shime-a, Haggiah, Asaiah.

[31] King David appointed songleaders and choirs to praise God in the Tabernacle after he had placed the Ark in it. [32] Then, when Solomon built the Temple at Jerusalem, the choirs carried on their work there.

[33-38] These are the names and ancestries[a] of choir leaders: Heman the Cantor was from the clan of Kohath; his genealogy was traced back through:

Joel, Samuel, Elkanah III,

Jeroham, Eliel, Toah, Zuph,

Elkanah II, Mahath, Amasai,

Elkanah I, Joel, Azariah,

Zephaniah, Tahath, Assir,

Ebiasaph, Korah, Izhar, Kohath,

Levi, Israel.

[39-43] Heman's assistant[c] was his colleague Asaph, whose genealogy was traced back through:

Berechiah, Shime-a, Michael,

Ba-aseiah, Malchijah, Ethni, Zerah,

Adaiah, Ethan, Zimmah, Shime-i,

Jahath, Gershom, Levi.

[44-47] Heman's second assistant was Ethan, a representative from the clan of Merari, who stood on his left. Merari's ancestry was traced back through:

Kishi, Abdi, Malluch, Hashabiah,

Amaziah, Hilkiah, Amzi, Bani,

Shemer, Mahli, Mushi, Merari,

Levi.

---

a Implied.   b Implied in 6:1.   c Literally, "brother," or "kinsman."

⁴⁸ Their relatives—all the other Levites—were appointed to various other tasks in the Tabernacle. ⁴⁹ But only Aaron and his descendants were the priests. Their duties included sacrificing burnt offerings and incense, handling all the tasks relating to the inner sanctuary—the Holy of Holies —and the tasks relating to the annual Day of Atonement for Israel. They saw to it that all the details commanded by Moses the servant of God were strictly followed.

⁵⁰⁻⁵³ The descendants of Aaron were:
Eleazar, Phinehas, Abishua,
Bukki, Uzzi, Zerahiah,
Meraioth, Amariah, Ahitub,
Zadok, Ahima-az.

⁵⁴ This is a record of the cities and land assigned by lot to the descendants of Aaron, all of whom were members of the Kohath clan:

⁵⁵,⁵⁶,⁵⁷ Hebron and its surrounding pasturelands in Judah (although the fields and suburbs were given to Caleb the son of Jephunneh), ⁵⁸,⁵⁹ and the following Cities of Refuge with their surrounding pasturelands:
Libnah, Jattir, Eshtemoa, Hilen,
Debir, Ashan, Beth-shemesh.

⁶⁰ Thirteen other cities with surrounding pastures—including Geba, Alemeth, and Anathoth—were given to the priests by the tribe of Benjamin. ⁶¹ Lots were then drawn to assign land to the remaining descendants of Kohath, and they received ten cities in the territory of the half-tribe of Manasseh.

⁶² The subclans of the Gershom clan received by lot thirteen cities in the Bashan area from the tribes of Issachar, Asher, Naphtali, and Manasseh.

⁶³ The subclans of Merari received by lot twelve cities from the tribes of Reuben, Gad, and Zebulun.

⁶⁴,⁶⁵ Cities and pasturelands were also assigned by lot to the Levites (and then renamed) from the tribes of Judah, Simeon, and Benjamin.

⁶⁶⁻⁶⁹ The tribe of Ephraim gave these Cities of Refuge with the surrounding pasturelands to the subclans of Kohath:
Shechem, in Mount Ephraim;
Gezer; Jokme-am; Beth-horon;
Aijalon; Gath-rimmon.

⁷⁰ The following Cities of Refuge and their pasturelands were given to the subclans of the Kohathites by the half-tribe of Manasseh:
Aner, Bile-am.

⁷¹ Cities of Refuge and pastureland given to the clan of Gershom by the half-tribe of Manasseh were:
Golan, in Bashan; Ashtaroth.

⁷² The tribe of Issachar gave them Kedesh, Daberath, ⁷³ Ramoth, and Anem, and the surrounding pastureland of each.

⁷⁴ The tribe of Asher gave them Abdon, Mashal, ⁷⁵ Hukok, and Rehob, with their pasturelands.

⁷⁶ The tribe of Naphtali gave them Kedesh in Galilee, Hammon, and Kiriathaim with pasturelands.

⁷⁷ The tribe of Zebulun gave Rimmono and Tabor to the Merari clan as Cities of Refuge.

⁷⁸,⁷⁹ And across the Jordan River, opposite Jericho, the tribe of Reuben gave them Bezer (a desert town), Jahzah, Kedemoth and Mepha-ath, along with their pasturelands.

⁸⁰ The tribe of Gad gave them Ramoth in Gilead, Mahanaim, ⁸¹ Heshbon, and Jazer, each with their surrounding pasturelands.

7 THE SONS OF Issachar:
Tola, Puah, Jashub, Shimron.

² The sons of *Tola,* each of whom was the head of a subclan:
Uzzi, Rephaiah, Jeri-el, Jahmai,
Ibsam, Shemuel.

At the time of King David, the total number of men of war from these families totaled 22,600.

³ Uzzi's son was Izrahiah among whose five sons were Michael, Obadiah, Joel, and Isshiah, all chiefs of subclans. ⁴ Their descendants, at the time of King David, numbered 36,000 troops; for all five of them had several wives and many sons. ⁵ The total number of men available for military service from all the clans of the tribe of Issachar numbered 87,000 stouthearted warriors, all included in the official genealogy.

⁶ The sons of Benjamin were:
Bela, Becher, Jedia-el.

⁷ The sons of *Bela:*
Ezbon, Uzzi, Uzziel, Jerimoth, Iri.

These five mighty warriors were chiefs of subclans and were the leaders of 22,034 troops (all of whom were recorded in the official genealogies).

⁸ The sons of *Becher* were:
Zemirah, Joash, Eliezer, Eli-o-enai, Omri, Jeremoth, Abijah, Anathoth, Alemeth.

⁹ At the time of David there were 22,200 mighty warriors among their descendants; and they were led by their clan chiefs.

¹⁰ The son of *Jedia-el* was **Bilhan.**
The sons of *Bilhan* were:
Jeush, Benjamin, Ehud, Chenaanah, Zethan, Tarshish, Ahishahar.

¹¹ They were the chiefs of the subclans of *Jedia-el,* and their descendants included 17,200 warriors at the time of King David.

¹² The sons of Ir were Shuppim and Huppim. Hushim was one of the sons of Aher.

¹³ The sons of Naphtali (descendants of Jacob's wifeᵃ Bilhah) were:
Jahzi-el, Guni, Jezer, Shallum.

¹⁴ The sons of Manasseh, born to his Aramaean concubine, were Asri-el and **Machir** (who became the father of Gilead).

¹⁵ It was Machir who found wives for Huppim and Shuppim.ᵇ Machir's sister was Maacah. Another descendant was Zelophehad, who had onlyᶜ daughters.

¹⁶ Machir's wife, also named Maacah, bore him a son whom she named Peresh; his brother's name was Sheresh, and he had sons named Ulam and Rakem.

¹⁷ Ulam's son was Bedan. So these were the sons of Gilead, the grandsons of Machir, and the great-grandsons of Manasseh.

¹⁸ Hammolecheth, Machir's sister, bore Ishhod, Abiezer, and Mahlah.

¹⁹ The sons of Shemida were Ahian, Shechem, Likhi, and Aniam.

²⁰,²¹ The sons of Ephraim:
Shuthelah, Bered, Tahath, Eleadah, Tahath, Zabad, Shuthelah,
Ezer, Ele-ad.

Ele-ad and *Ezer* attempted to rustle cattle at Gath, but they were killed by the local farmers. ²² Their father Ephraim mourned for them a long time, and his brothers tried to comfort him. ²³ Afterwards, his wife conceived and bore a son whom he called Beriah (meaning "a tragedy") because of what had happened.

²⁴ Ephraim's daughter's name was Sheerah. She built Lower and Upper Beth-horon and Uzzen-sheerah.

²⁵,²⁶,²⁷ This is Ephraim's line of descent:
Rephah, the father of
Resheph, the father of
Telah, the father of
Tahan, the father of
Ladan, the father of
Ammihud, the father of
Elishama, the father of
Nun, the father of
Joshua.

²⁸ They lived in an area bounded on one side by Bethel and its surrounding towns, on the east by Naaran, on the west by Gezer and its villages, and finally by Shechem and its surrounding villages as far as Ayyah and its towns.

²⁹ The tribe of Manasseh, descendants of Joseph the son of Israel, controlled the following cities and their surrounding areas: Beth-shean, Taanach, Megiddo, and Dor.

³⁰ The children of Asher:
Imnah, Ishvah, Ishvi, **Beriah,** Serah (their sister).

³¹ The sons of *Beriah* were:
Heber, Malchi-el (the father of Birzaith).

³² *Heber's* children were:
Japhlet, Shomer, Hotham, Shua (their sister).

³³ *Japhlet's* sons were:
Pasach, Bimhal, Ashvath.

³⁴ His brother *Shomer's*ᵈ sons were:
Rohgah, Jehubbah, Aram.

³⁵ The sons of his brother *Hotham*ᵉ were:
Zophah, Imna, Shelesh, Amal.

³⁶,³⁷ The sons of *Zophah* were:
Suah, Harnepher, Shual, Beri, Imrah, Bezer, Hod, Shamma, Shilshah, **Ithran,** Be-era.

³⁸ The sons of *Ithran*ᶠ were:
Jephunneh, Pispa, Ara.

³⁹ The sons of Ulla were:
Arah, Hanniel, Rizia.

---

a Implied.   b See verse 12.   c Implied. See Numbers 26:33.   d Or, "Shemer "
e Literally, "Helem."   f Literally, "Jether."

⁴⁰ These descendants of Asher were heads of subclans and were all skilled warriors and chiefs. Their descendants in the official genealogy numbered 36,000 men of war.

8 THE SONS OF Benjamin, according to age, were:
Bela, the first,
Ashbel, the second,
Aharah, the third,
Nohah, the fourth,
Rapha, the fifth.
³,⁴,⁵ The sons of *Bela* were:
Addar, Gera, Abihud, Abishua,
Naaman, Ahoah, Gera,
Shephuphan, Huram.
⁶,⁷ The sons of Ehud, chiefs of the subclans living at Geba, were captured in war and exiled to Manahath. They were:
Naaman, Ahijah,
Gera (also called Heglam), the father of Uzza and Ahihud.
⁸,⁹,¹⁰ Shaharaim divorced his wives **Hushim** and Baara, but he had children in the land of Moab by Hodesh, his new wife:
Jobab, Zibia, Mesha, Malcam,
Jeuz, Sachia, Mirmah.
These sons all became chiefs of subclans.
¹¹ His wife *Hushim* had borne him Abitub and **Elpaal**.
¹² The sons of *Elpaal* were:
Eber, Misham,
Shemed (who built Ono and Lod and their surrounding villages).
¹³ His other sons were **Beriah** and Shema, chiefs of subclans living in Aijalon; they chased out the inhabitants of Gath.
¹⁴ *Elpaal's* sons also included:
Ahio, **Shashak**, Jeremoth.
¹⁵,¹⁶ The sons of *Beriah* were:
Zebadiah, Arad, Eder, Michael,
Ishpah, Joha.
¹⁷,¹⁸ The sons of *Elpaal* also included:
Zebadiah, Meshullam, Hizki,
Heber, Ishmerai, Izliah, Jobab.
¹⁹,²⁰,²¹ The sons of *Shime-i* were:
Jakim, Zichri, Zabdi, Eli-enai,
Zille-thai, Eliel, Adaiah, Beraiah,
Shimrath.
²²⁻²⁵ The sons of *Shashak* were:

Ishpan, Eber, Eliel, Abdon, Zichri,
Hanan, Hananiah, Elam,
Anthothijah, Iphdeiah, Penuel.
²⁶,²⁷ The sons of Jeroham were:
Shamsherai, Shehariah, Athaliah,
Jaareshiah, Elijah, Zichri.
²⁸ These were the chiefs of the subclans living at Jerusalem.
²⁹ Je-iel, the father of Gibeon, lived at Gibeon; and his wife's name was Maacah.
³⁰,³¹,³² His oldest son was named Abdon, followed by:
Zur, Kish, Baal, Nadab, Gedor,
Ahio, Zecher, Mikloth who was the father of Shimeah.
All of these families lived together near Jerusalem.
³³ Ner was the father of Kish, and Kish was the father of Saul;
Saul's sons included:
Jonathan, Malchishua, Abinadab,
Eshbaal.
³⁴ The son of *Jonathan* was Mephibosheth;[a]
The son of Mephibosheth[a] was Micah.
³⁵ The sons of Micah:
Pithon, Melech, Tarea, Ahaz.
³⁶ Ahaz was the father of Jehoaddah,
Jehoaddah was the father of:
Alemeth, Azmaveth, Zimri.
Zimri's son was Moza.
³⁷ Moza was the father of Bine-a, whose sons were:
Raphah, Eleasah, Azel.
³⁸ Azel had six sons:
Azrikam, Bocheru, Ishmael,
She-ariah, Obadiah, Hanan.
³⁹ Azel's brother Eshek had three sons:
Ulam, the first,
Jeush, the second,
Eliphelet, the third.
⁴⁰ *Ulam's* sons were prominent warriors who were expert marksmen with their bows. These men had 150 sons and grandsons, and they were all from the tribe of Benjamin.

9 THE FAMILY TREE of every person in Israel was carefully recorded in *The Annals of the Kings of Israel*.
Judah was exiled to Babylon because the

---

a Or, "Merib-baal."

people worshiped idols.

² The first to return and live again in their former cities were families from the tribes of Israel, and also the priests, the Levites, and the Temple assistants.

³ Then some families from the tribes of Judah, Benjamin, Ephraim, and Manasseh arrived in Jerusalem:

⁴ One family was that of Uthai (the son of Ammihud, son of Omri, son of Imri, son of Bani) of the clan of Perez (son of Judah).

⁵ The Shilonites were another family to return, including Asaiah (Shilon's oldest son) and his sons; ⁶ there were also the sons of Zerah, including Jeuel and his relatives: 690 in all.

⁷,⁸ Among the members of the tribe of Benjamin who returned were these:

> Sallu (the son of Meshullam, the son of Hodaviah, the son of Hassenuah);
>
> Ibneiah (the son of Jeroham);
>
> Elah (the son of Uzzi, the son of Michri);
>
> Meshullam (the son of Shephatiah, the son of Reuel, the son of Ibnijah).

⁹ These men were all chiefs of subclans. A total of 956 Benjaminites returned.

¹⁰,¹¹ The priests who returned were:

> Jedaiah, Jehoiarib, Jachin,
>
> Azariah (the son of Hilkiah, son of Meshullam, son of Zadok, son of Meraioth, son of Ahitub). He was the chief custodian of the Temple.

¹² Another of the returning priests was Adaiah (son of Jeroham, son of Pashhur, son of Malchijah).

Another priest was Maasai (son of Adiel, son of Jahzerah, son of Meshullam, son of Meshillemith, son of Immer).

¹³ In all, 1,760 priests returned.

¹⁴ Among the Levites who returned was Shemaiah (son of Hasshub, son of Azrikam, son of Hashabiah, who was a descendant of Merari).

¹⁵,¹⁶ Other Levites who returned included:

> Bakbakkar, Heresh, Galal,
>
> Mattaniah (the son of Mica, who was the son of Zichri, who was the son

of Asaph).

> Obadiah (the son of Shemaiah, son of Galal, son of Jeduthun).
>
> Berechiah (the son of Asa, son of Elkanah, who lived in the area of the Netophathites).

¹⁷,¹⁸ The gatekeepers were Shallum (the chief gatekeeper), Akkub, Talmon, and Ahiman—all Levites. They are still responsible for the eastern royal gate. ¹⁹ Shallum's ancestry went back through Kore and Ebiasaph to Korah. He and his close relatives the Korahites were in charge of the sacrifices and the protection of the sanctuary, just as their ancestors had supervised and guarded the Tabernacle. ²⁰ Phinehas, the son of Eleazar, was the first director of this division in ancient times. And the Lord was with him.

²¹ At that time Zechariah, the son of Meshelemiah, had been responsible for the protection of the entrance to the Tabernacle. ²² There were 212 doorkeepers in those days. They were chosen from their villages on the basis of their genealogies, and they were appointed by David and Samuel because of their reliability. ²³ They and their descendants were in charge of the Lord's Tabernacle. ²⁴ They were assigned to each of the four sides: east, west, north, and south. ²⁵ And their relatives in the villages were assigned to them from time to time, for seven days at a time.

²⁶ The four head gatekeepers, all Levites, were in an office of great trust, for they were responsible for the rooms and treasuries in the Tabernacle of God. ²⁷ Because of their important positions they lived near the Tabernacle, and they opened the gates each morning. ²⁸ Some of them were assigned to care for the various vessels used in the sacrifices and worship; they checked them in and out to avoid loss. ²⁹ Others were responsible for the furniture, the items in the sanctuary, and the supplies such as fine flour, wine, incense, and spices.

³⁰ Other priests prepared the spices and incense.

³¹ And Mattithiah (a Levite and the oldest son of Shallum the Korahite) was entrusted with making the flat cakes for grain offerings.

³² Some members of the Kohath clan

were in charge of the preparation of the special bread[a] each Sabbath. [33,34] The cantors were all prominent Levites. They lived in Jerusalem at the Temple and were on duty at all hours. They were free from other responsibilities and were selected by their genealogies. [35,36,37] Jeiel (whose wife was Maacah) lived in Gibeon. He had many[b] sons, including:

Gibeon, Abdon (the oldest), Zur, Kish, Baal, **Ner**, Nadab, Gedor, Ahio, Zechariah, Mikloth.

[38] Mikloth lived with his son Shime-am in Jerusalem near his relatives.

[39] Ner was the father of Kish, Kish was the father of Saul, Saul was the father of Jonathan, Malchishua, Abinadab, and Eshbaal.

[40] Jonathan was the father of Mephibosheth;[c]

Mephibosheth[c] was the father of Micah; [41] Micah was the father of Pithon, Melech, Tahre-a, and Ahaz;

[42] Ahaz was the father of Jarah; Jarah was the father of Alemeth, Azmaveth, and Zimri;

Zimri was the father of Moza.

[43] Moza was the father of Bine-a, Rephaiah, Eleasah, and Azel.

[44] Azel had six sons:

Azrikam, Bocheru, Ishmael, She-ariah, Obadiah, Hanan.

10[a] THE PHILISTINES ATTACKED and defeated the Israeli troops, who turned and fled and were slaughtered on the slopes of Mount Gilboa. [2] They caught up with Saul and his three sons, Jonathan, Abinadab, and Malchishua, and killed them all. [3] Saul had been hard pressed with heavy fighting all around him, when the Philistine archers shot and wounded him.

[4] He cried out to his bodyguard, "Quick, kill me with your sword before these uncircumcised heathen capture and torture me."

But the man was afraid to do it, so Saul took his own sword and fell against its point; and it pierced his body. [5] Then his bodyguard, seeing that Saul was dead, killed

himself in the same way. [6] So Saul and his three sons died together; the entire family was wiped out in one day.

[7] When the Israelis in the valley below the mountain heard that their troops had been routed and that Saul and his sons were dead, they abandoned their cities and fled. And the Philistines came and lived in them. [8] When the Philistines went back the next day to strip the bodies of the men killed in action and to gather the booty from the battlefield, they found the bodies of Saul and his sons. [9] So they stripped off Saul's armor and cut off his head; then they displayed them throughout the nation and celebrated the wonderful news before their idols. [10] They fastened his armor to the walls of the Temple of the Gods and nailed his head to the wall of Dagon's temple.

[11] But when the people of Jabesh-gilead heard what the Philistines had done to Saul, [12] their heroic warriors went out to the battlefield[b] and brought back his body and the bodies of his three sons. Then they buried them beneath the oak tree at Jabesh and mourned and fasted for seven days.

[13] Saul died for his disobedience to the Lord and because he had consulted a medium,[c] [14] and did not ask the Lord for guidance. So the Lord killed him and gave the kingdom to David, the son of Jesse.

11 THEN THE LEADERS of Israel went to David at Hebron and told him, "We are your relatives,[a] [2] and even when Saul was king, you were the one who led our armies to battle and brought them safely back again. And the Lord your God has told you, 'You shall be the shepherd of my people Israel. You shall be their king.' "

[3] So David made a contract with them before the Lord, and they anointed him as king of Israel, just as the Lord had told Samuel. [4] Then David and the leaders went to Jerusalem (or Jebus, as it used to be called) where the Jebusites—the original inhabitants of the land—lived. [5,6] But the people of Jebus refused to let them enter the city. So David captured the fortress of Zion, later called the City of David, and said to

---

a Literally, "showbread."   b Implied.   c Or, "Merib-baal."   10a The remainder of 1 Chronicles deals with events preceding chapter 9.   b Implied.   c See 1 Samuel 28.   11a Literally, "your bone and flesh."

his men, "The first man to kill a Jebusite shall be made commander-in-chief!" Joab, the son of Zeruiah, was the first, so he became the general of David's army. [7] David lived in the fortress and that is why that area of Jerusalem is called the City of David. [8] He extended the city out around the fortress while Joab rebuilt the rest of Jerusalem. [9] And David became more and more famous and powerful, for the Lord of the heavens was with him.

[10] These are the names of some of the bravest of David's warriors (who also encouraged the leaders of Israel to make David their king, as the Lord had said would happen):

[11] Jashobeam (the son of a man from Hachmon) was the leader of The Top Three—the three greatest heroes among David's men. He once killed 300 men with his spear.

[12] The second of The Top Three was Eleazar, the son of Dodo, a member of the subclan of Ahoh. [13] He was with David in the battle against the Philistines at Pasdammim. The Israeli army was in a barley field and had begun to run away, [14] but he held his ground in the middle of the field, and recovered it and slaughtered the Philistines; and the Lord saved them with a great victory.

[15] Another time, three of The Thirty[b] went to David while he was hiding in the cave of Adullam. The Philistines were camped in the Valley of Rephaim, [16] and David was in the stronghold at the time; an outpost of the Philistines had occupied Bethlehem. [17] David wanted a drink from the Bethlehem well beside the gate, and when he mentioned this to his men, [18,19] these three broke through to the Philistine camp, drew some water from the well, and brought it back to David. But he refused to drink it! Instead he poured it out as an offering to the Lord and said, "God forbid that I should drink it! It is the very blood of these men who risked their lives to get it."

[20] Abishai, Joab's brother, was commander of The Thirty. He had gained his place among The Thirty by killing 300 men at one time with his spear. [21] He was the chief and the most famous of The Thirty, but he was not as great as The Three.

[22] Benaiah, whose father was a mighty warrior from Kabzeel, killed the two famous giants[c] from Moab. He also killed a lion in a slippery pit when there was snow on the ground. [23] Once he killed an Egyptian who was seven and one-half feet tall, whose spear was as thick as a weaver's beam. But Benaiah went up to him with only a club in his hand and pulled the spear away from him and used it to kill him. [24,25] He was nearly as great as The Three, and he was very famous among The Thirty. David made him captain of his bodyguard.

[26-47] Other famous warriors among David's men were:

Asahel (Joab's brother);
Elhanan, the son of Dodo from Bethlehem;
Shammoth from Harod;
Helez from Pelon;
Ira (son of Ikkesh) from Tekoa;
Abi-ezer from Anathoth;
Sibbecai from Hushath;
Ilai from Ahoh;
Maharai from Netophah;
Heled (son of Baanah) from Netophah;
Ithai (son of Ribai) a Benjaminite from Gibe-ah;
Benaiah from Pirathon;
Hurai from near the brooks of Gaash;
Abiel from Arbath;
Azmaveth from Baharum;
Eliahba from Sha-albon;
The sons[d] of Hashem from Gizon;
Jonathan (son of Shagee) from Harar;
Ahiam (son of Sacher) from Harar;
Eliphal (son of Ur);
Hepher from Mecherath;
Ahijah from Pelon;
Hezro from Carmel;
Naarai (son of Ezbai);
Joel (brother of Nathan);
Mibhar (son of Hagri);
Zelek from Ammon;

---

b "The Thirty" were the highest-ranking officers in the army. term is uncertain.   d Implied in 2 Samuel 23:30.   c Literally, "ariels." The meaning of the

Naharai from Be-eroth—he was General Joab's armor bearer;
Ira from Ithra;
Gareb from Ithra;
Uriah the Hittite;
Zabad (son of Ahlai);
Adina (son of Shiza) from the tribe of Reuben—he was among the thirty-one leaders of the tribe of Reuben;
Hanan (son of Maacah);
Joshaphat from Mithna;
Uzzia from Ashterath;
Shama and Je-iel (sons of Hotham) from Aroer;
Jedia-el (son of Shimri);
Joha (his brother) from Tiza;
Eliel from Mahavi;
Jeribai and Joshaviah (sons of Elnaam);
Ithmah from Moab;
Eliel; Obed; Ja-asiel from Mezoba.

12 THESE ARE THE names of the famous warriors who joined David at Ziklag while he was hiding from King Saul.[a] 2 All of them were expert archers and slingers, and they could use their left hands as readily as their right! Like King Saul, they were all of the tribe of Benjamin.

3-7 Their chief was Ahi-ezer, son of Shemaah from Gibe-ah. The others were:
His brother Joash; Jezi-el and Pelet, sons of Azmaveth; Beracah; Jehu from Anathoth; Ishmaiah from Gibeon (a brave warrior rated as high or higher than The Thirty); Jeremiah; Jahaziel; Johanan; Jozabad from Gederah; Eluzai; Jerimoth; Bealiah; Shemariah; Shephatiah from Haruph; Elkanah, Isshiah, Azarel, Jo-ezer, Jashobe-am—all Korahites; Jo-elah and Zebadiah (sons of Jeroham from Gedor).

8-13 Great and brave warriors from the tribe of Gad also went to David in the wilderness. They were experts with both shield and spear and were "lion-faced men, swift as deer upon the mountains."
Ezer was the chief;

Obadiah was second in command;
Eliab was third in command;
Mishmannah was fourth in command;
Jeremiah was fifth in command;
Attai was sixth in command;
Eliel was seventh in command;
Johanan was eighth in command;
Elzabad was ninth in command;
Jeremiah was tenth in command;
Machbannai was eleventh in command.

14 These men were army officers; the weakest was worth a hundred normal troops, and the greatest was worth a thousand! 15 They crossed the Jordan River during its seasonal flooding and conquered the lowlands on both the east and west banks.

16 Others came to David from Benjamin and Judah. 17 David went out to meet them and said, "If you have come to help me, we are friends; but if you have come to betray me to my enemies when I am innocent, then may the God of our fathers see and judge you."

18 Then the Holy Spirit came upon them, and Amasai, a leader of The Thirty, replied,
"We are yours, David;
We are on your side, son of Jesse.
Peace, peace be unto you,
And peace to all who aid you;
For your God is with you."
So David let them join him, and he made them captains of his army.

19 Some men from Manasseh deserted the Israeli army and joined David just as he was going into battle with the Philistines against King Saul. But as it turned out, the Philistine generals refused to let David and his men go with them. After much discussion they sent them back, for they were afraid that David and his men would imperil them by deserting to King Saul.

20 Here is a list of the men from Manasseh who deserted to David as he was en route to Ziklag:
Adnah, Jozabad, Jedia-el, Michael, Jozabad, Elihu, Zillethai.
Each was a high-ranking officer of Manasseh's troops. 21 They were brave and able warriors, and they assisted David when

a Literally, "the son of Kish."

he fought against the Amalek raiders at Ziklag.^b

²² More men joined David almost every day until he had a tremendous army—the army of God. ²³ Here is the registry of recruits who joined David at Hebron. They were all anxious to see David become king instead of Saul, just as the Lord had said would happen.

²⁴⁻³⁷ From Judah, 6,800 troops armed with shields and spears.

From the tribe of Simeon, 7,100 outstanding warriors.

From the Levites, 4,600.

From the priests—descendants of Aaron—there were 3,700 troops under the command of Zadok, a young man of unusual courage, and Jehoiada. (He and twenty-two members of his family were officers of the fighting priests.)

From the tribe of Benjamin, the same tribe Saul was from, there were 3,000. (Most of that tribe retained its allegiance to Saul.)

From the tribe of Ephraim, 20,800 mighty warriors, each famous in his respective clan.

From the half-tribe of Manasseh, 18,000 were sent for the express purpose of helping David become king.

From the tribe of Issachar there were 200 leaders of the tribe with their relatives—all men who understood the temper of the times and knew the best course for Israel to take.

From the tribe of Zebulun there were 50,000 trained warriors; they were fully armed and totally loyal to David.

From Naphtali there were 1,000 officers and 37,000 troops equipped with shields and spears.

From the tribe of Dan there were 28,600 troops, all of them prepared for war.

From the tribe of Asher, there were 40,000 trained and ready troops.

From the other side of the Jordan River—where the tribes of Reuben and Gad and the half-tribe of Manasseh lived—there were 120,000 troops equipped with every kind of weapon.

³⁸ All these men came in battle array to Hebron with the single purpose of making David the king of Israel. In fact, all of Israel was ready for this change. ³⁹ They feasted and drank with David for three days, for preparations had been made for their arrival. ⁴⁰ People from nearby and from as far away as Issachar, Zebulun, and Naphtali brought food on donkeys, camels, mules, and oxen. Vast supplies of flour, fig cakes, raisins, wine, oil, cattle, and sheep were brought to the celebration, for joy had spread throughout the land.

13 AFTER DAVID HAD consulted with all of his army officers, ² he addressed the assembled men of Israel as follows:

"Since you think that I should be your king, and since the Lord our God has given his approval, let us send messages to our brothers throughout the land of Israel, including the priests and Levites, inviting them to come and join us. ³ And let us bring back the Ark of our God, for we have been neglecting it ever since Saul became king."

⁴ There was unanimous consent, for everyone agreed with him. ⁵ So David summoned the people of Israel from all across the nation^a so that they could be present when the Ark of God was brought from Kiriath-jearim.

⁶ Then David and all Israel went to Baalah (i.e., Kiriath-jearim) in Judah to bring back the Ark of the Lord God enthroned above the angels.^b ⁷ It was taken from the house of Abinadab on a new cart. Uzza and Ahio drove the oxen. ⁸ Then David and all the people danced before the Lord with great enthusiasm, accompanied by singing and by zithers, harps, tambourines, cymbals, and trumpets. ⁹ But as they arrived at the threshing-floor of Chidon, the oxen stumbled and Uzza reached out his hand to steady the Ark. ¹⁰ Then the anger of the

---

b Implied.   13a Literally, "from Shihor—the Brook of Egypt—to the entrance of Hamath."
b Literally, "above the cherubim."

Lord blazed out against Uzza, and killed him because he had touched the Ark. And so he died there before God. [11] David was angry at the Lord for what he had done to Uzza, and he named the place "The Outbreak Against Uzza." And it is still called that today.

[12] Now David was afraid of God and asked, "How shall I ever get the Ark of God home?"

[13] Finally he decided to take it to the home of Obed-edom the Gittite instead of bringing it to the City of David. [14] The Ark remained there with the family of Obed-edom for three months, and the Lord blessed him and his family.

14 KING HIRAM OF Tyre sent masons and carpenters to help build David's palace and he supplied him with much cedar lumber. [2] David now realized why the Lord had made him king and why he had made his kingdom so great; it was for a special reason—to give joy to God's people!

[3] After David moved to Jerusalem, he married additional wives and became the father of many sons and daughters.

[4-7] These are the names of the sons born to him in Jerusalem:

Shammua, Shobab, Nathan,
Solomon, Ibhar, Elishu-a, Elpelet,
Nogah, Nepheg, Japhia, Elishama,
Beeliada, Eliphelet.

[8] When the Philistines heard that David was Israel's new king, they mobilized their forces to capture him. But David learned that they were on the way, so he called together his army. [9] The Philistines were raiding the Valley of Rephaim, [10] and David asked the Lord, "If I go out and fight them, will you give me the victory?"

And the Lord replied, "Yes, I will."

[11] So he attacked them at Baal-perazim and wiped them out. He exulted, "God has used me to sweep away my enemies like water bursting through a dam!" That is why the place has been known as Baal-perazim ever since (meaning, "The Place of Breaking Through").

[12] After the battle the Israelis picked up many idols left by the Philistines, but David ordered them burned.

[13] Later the Philistines raided the valley again, [14] and again David asked God what to do.

The Lord replied, "Go around by the mulberry trees and attack from there. [15] When you hear a sound like marching in the tops of the mulberry trees, that is your signal to attack, for God will go before you and destroy the enemy."

[16] So David did as the Lord commanded him; and he cut down the army of the Philistines all the way from Gibeon to Gezer. [17] David's fame spread everywhere, and the Lord caused all the nations to fear him.

15 DAVID NOW BUILT several palaces for himself in Jerusalem, and he also built a new Tabernacle to house the Ark of God, [2] and issued these instructions: [When we transfer the Ark to its new home[a]], no one except the Levites may carry it, for God has chosen them for this purpose; they are to minister to him forever."

[3] Then David summoned all Israel to Jerusalem to celebrate the bringing of the Ark into the new Tabernacle. [4-10] These were the priests and Levites present:

120 from the clan of Kohath; with
Uriel as their leader;
220 from the clan of Merari; with
Asaiah as their leader;
130 from the clan of Gershom; with
Joel as their leader;
200 from the subclan of Elizaphan;
with Shemaiah as their leader;
80 from the subclan of Hebron; with
Eliel as their leader;
112 from the subclan of Uzziel; with
Amminadab as their leader.

[11] Then David called for Zadok and Abiathar, the High Priests, and for the Levite leaders: Uriel, Asaiah, Joel, Shemaiah, Eliel, and Amminadab.

[12] "You are the leaders of the clans of the Levites," he told them. "Now sanctify yourselves with all your brothers so that you may bring the Ark of Jehovah, the God of Israel, to the place I have prepared for it. [13] The Lord destroyed us before because we handled the matter improperly—you were

---

a Implied.

not carrying it."

¹⁴ So the priests and the Levites underwent the ceremonies of sanctification in preparation for bringing home the Ark of Jehovah, the God of Israel. ¹⁵ Then the Levites carried the Ark on their shoulders with its carrying poles, just as the Lord had instructed Moses.

¹⁶ King David also ordered the Levite leaders to organize the singers into an orchestra, and they played loudly and joyously upon psaltries, harps, and cymbals. ¹⁷ Heman (son of Joel), Asaph (son of Berechiah), and Ethan (son of Kushaiah) from the clan of Merari were the heads of the musicians.

¹⁸ The following men were chosen as their assistants:

Zechariah, Ja-aziel, Shemiramoth,
Jehiel, Unni, Eliab, Benaiah,
Ma-asseiah, Mattithiah, Eliphelehu,
Mikneiah, Obed-edom and Je-iel,
the door keepers.

¹⁹ Heman, Asaph, and Ethan were chosen to sound the bronze cymbals; ²⁰ and Zechariah, Azi-el, Shemiramoth, Jehiel, Unni, Eliab, Ma-aseiah, and Benaiah comprised an octet accompanied by harps.ᵇ ²¹ Mattithiah, Eliphelehu, Mikneiah, Obed-edom, Je-iel, and Azaziah were the harpists.ᶜ ²² The song leader was Chenaniah, the chief of the Levites, who was selected for his skill. ²³ Berechiah and Elkanah were guards for the Ark. ²⁴ Shebaniah, Joshaphat, Nethanel, Amasai, Zechariah, Benaiah, and Eliezer—all of whom were priests—formed a bugle corps to march at the head of the procession. And Obed-edom and Jehiah guarded the Ark.

²⁵ Then David and the elders of Israel and the high officers of the army went with great joy to the home of Obed-edom to take the Ark to Jerusalem. ²⁶ And because God didn't destroy the Levites who were carrying the Ark, they sacrificed seven bulls and seven lambs. ²⁷ David, the Levites carrying the Ark, the singers, and Chenaniah the song leader were all dressed in linen robes. David also wore a linen ephod. ²⁸ So the leaders of Israel took the Ark to Jerusalem with shouts of joy, the blowing of horns and trumpets, the crashing of cymbals, and loud playing on the harps and zithers.

²⁹ (But as the Ark arrived in Jerusalem, David's wife Michal, the daughter of King Saul, felt a deep disgust for David as she watched from the window and saw him dancing like a madman.)

16 SO THE ARK of God was brought into the Tabernacle. David had prepared for it, and the leaders of Israel sacrificed burnt offerings and peace offerings before God. ² At the conclusion of these offerings David blessed the people in the name of the Lord; ³ then he gave every person presentᵃ (men and women alike) a loaf of bread, some wine, and a cake of raisins.

⁴ He appointed certain of the Levites to minister before the Ark by giving constant praise and thanks to the Lord God of Israel and by asking for his blessings upon his people. These are the names of those given this assignment: ⁵ Asaph, the leader of this detail, sounded the cymbals. His associates were Zechariah, Je-iel, Shemiramoth, Jehiel, Mattithiah, Eliab, Benaiah, Obed-edom, and Je-iel; they played the harps and zithers. ⁶ The priests Benaiah and Jahaziel played their trumpets regularly before the Ark.

⁷ At that time David began the custom of using choirs in the Tabernacle to sing thanksgiving to the Lord. Asaph was the director of this choral group of priests.

⁸ "Oh, give thanks to the Lord and
        pray to him," they sang.
"Tell the peoples of the world
About his mighty doings.
⁹ Sing to him; yes, sing his praises
And tell of his marvelous works.
¹⁰ Glory in his holy name;
Let all rejoice who seek the Lord.
¹¹ Seek the Lord; yes, seek his
        strength
And seek his face untiringly.
¹²,¹³ O descendants of his servant
        Abraham,
O chosen sons of Jacob,
Remember his mighty miracles

---

b Literally, "set to Alamoth." The meaning of the term is uncertain. (or harps) set to the Sheminith." The meaning is uncertain.

c Literally, "were to lead with zithers 16a Literally, "to each Israelite."

And his marvelous miracles
And his authority:
¹⁴ He is the Lord our God!
His authority is seen throughout the earth.
¹⁵ Remember his covenant forever—
The words he commanded
To a thousand generations:
¹⁶ His agreement with Abraham,
And his oath to Isaac,
¹⁷ And his confirmation to Jacob.
He promised Israel
With an everlasting promise:
¹⁸ 'I will give you the land of Canaan
As your inheritance.'
¹⁹ When Israel was few in number
—oh, so few—
And merely strangers in the Promised Land;
²⁰ When they wandered from country to country,
From one kingdom to another—
²¹ God didn't let anyone harm them.
Even kings were killed who sought to hurt them.
²² 'Don't harm my chosen people,' he declared.
'These are my prophets—touch them not.'
²³ Sing to the Lord, O earth,
Declare each day that he is the one who saves!
²⁴ Show his glory to the nations!
Tell everyone about his miracles.
²⁵ For the Lord is great, and should be highly praised;
He is to be held in awe above all gods.
²⁶ The other so-called gods are demons,
But the Lord made the heavens.
²⁷ Majesty and honor march before him,
Strength and gladness walk beside him.
²⁸ O people of all nations of the earth,
Ascribe great strength and glory to his name!
²⁹ Yes, ascribe to the Lord
The glory due his name!
Bring an offering and come before him;

Worship the Lord when clothed with holiness!
³⁰ Tremble before him, all the earth!
The world stands unmoved.
³¹ Let the heavens be glad, the earth rejoice;
Let all the nations say, 'It is the Lord who reigns.'
³² Let the vast seas roar,
Let the countryside and everything in it rejoice!
³³ Let the trees in the woods sing for joy before the Lord,
For he comes to judge the earth.
³⁴ Oh, give thanks to the Lord, for he is good;
His love and his kindness go on forever.
³⁵ Cry out to him, 'Oh, save us, God of our salvation;
Bring us safely back from among the nations.
Then we will thank your holy name,
And triumph in your praise.'
³⁶ Blessed be Jehovah, God of Israel,
Forever and forevermore."
And all the people shouted "Amen!" and praised the Lord.

³⁷ David arranged for Asaph and his fellow Levites to minister regularly at the Tabernacle,ᵇ doing each day whatever needed to be done. ³⁸ This group included Obed-edom (the son of Jeduthun), Hosah and sixty-eight of their colleagues as guards. ³⁹ Meanwhile the old Tabernacle of the Lord on the hill of Gibeon continued to be active. David left Zadok the priest and his fellow-priests to minister to the Lord there. ⁴⁰ They sacrificed burnt offerings to the Lord each morning and evening upon the altar set aside for that purpose, just as the Lord had commanded Israel. ⁴¹ David also appointed Heman, Jeduthun, and several others who were chosen by name to give thanks to the Lord for his constant love and mercy. ⁴² They used their trumpets and cymbals to accompany the singers with loud praises to God. And Jeduthun's sons were appointed as guards.

⁴³ At last the celebration ended and the people returned to their homes, and David

b Literally, "before the Ark of the Covenant of the Lord."

returned to bless his own household.

17 AFTER DAVID HAD been living in his new palace for some time he said to Nathan the prophet, "Look! I'm living here in a cedar-paneled home while the Ark of the Covenant of God is out there in a tent!"

² And Nathan replied, "Carry out your plan in every detail, for it is the will of the Lord."

³ But that same night God said to Nathan, ⁴ "Go and give my servant David this message: 'You are not to build my temple! ⁵ I've gone from tent to tent as my home from the time I brought Israel out of Egypt. ⁶ In all that time I never suggested to any of the leaders of Israel—the shepherds I appointed to care for my people—that they should build me a cedar-lined temple.'

⁷ "Tell my servant David, 'The Lord of heaven says to you, I took you from being a shepherd and made you the king of my people. ⁸ And I have been with you everywhere you've gone; I have destroyed your enemies, and I will make your name as great as the greatest of the earth. ⁹ And I will give a permanent home to my people Israel, and will plant them in their land. They will not be disturbed again; the wicked nations won't conquer them as they did before, ¹⁰ when the judges ruled them. I will subdue all of your enemies. And I now declare that I will cause your descendants to be kings of Israel just as you are.

¹¹ " 'When your time here on earth is over and you die, I will place one of your sons upon your throne; and I will make his kingdom strong. ¹² He is the one who shall build me a temple, and I will establish his royal line of descent forever. ¹³ I will be his father, and he shall be my son; I will never remove my mercy and love from him as I did from Saul. ¹⁴ I will place him over my people and over the kingdom of Israel forever—and his descendants will always be kings.' "

¹⁵ So Nathan told King David everything the Lord had said.

¹⁶ Then King David went in and sat before the Lord and said, "Who am I, O Lord God, and what is my family that you have given me all this? ¹⁷ For all the great things you have already done for me are nothing in comparison to what you have promised to do in the future! For now, O Lord God, you are speaking of future generations of my children being kings too! You speak as though I were someone very great. ¹⁸ What else can I say? You know that I am but a dog, yet you have decided to honor me! ¹⁹ O Lord, you have given me these wonderful promises just because you want to be kind to me, because of your own great heart. ²⁰ O Lord, there is no one like you—there is no other God. In fact, we have never even heard of another god like you!

²¹ "And what other nation in all the earth is like Israel? You have made a unique nation and have redeemed it from Egypt so that the people could be your people. And you made a great name for yourself when you did glorious miracles in driving out the nations from before your people. ²² You have declared that your people Israel belong to you forever, and you have become their God.

²³ "And now I accept your promise, Lord, that I and my children will always rule this nation. ²⁴ And may this bring eternal honor to your name as everyone realizes that you always do what you say. They will exclaim, 'The Lord of heaven is indeed the God of Israel!' And Israel shall always be ruled by my children and their posterity! ²⁵ Now I have the courage to pray to you, for you have revealed this to me. ²⁶ God himself has promised this good thing to me! ²⁷ May this blessing rest upon my children forever, for when you grant a blessing, Lord, it is an eternal blessing!"

18 DAVID FINALLY SUBDUED the Philistines and conquered Gath and its surrounding towns. ² He also conquered Moab and required its people to send him a large sum of money every year. ³ He conquered the dominion of King Hadadezer of Zobah (as far as Hamath) at the time Hadadezer went to tighten his grip along the Euphrates River. ⁴ David captured a thousand of his chariots, seven thousand cavalry, and twenty thousand troops. He crippled all the chariot teams except a hundred that he kept for his own use.

⁵ When the Syrians arrived from Damascus to help King Hadadezer, David killed

twenty-two thousand of them; ⁶ then he placed a garrison of his troops in Damascus, the Syrian capital. So the Syrians, too, were forced to send him large amounts of money every year. And the Lord gave David victory everywhere he went. ⁷ He brought the gold shields of King Hadadezer's officers to Jerusalem, ⁸ as well as a great amount of bronze from Hadadezer's cities of Tibhath and Cun. (King Solomon later melted the bronze and used it for the Temple. He molded it into the bronze tank, the pillars, and the instruments used in offering sacrifices on the altar.)

⁹ When King Tou of Hamath learned that King David had destroyed Hadadezer's army, ¹⁰ he sent his son Hadoram to greet and congratulate King David on his success and to present him with many gifts of gold, silver, and bronze, seeking an alliance. For Hadadezer and Tou had been enemies and there had been many wars between them. ¹¹ King David dedicated these gifts to the Lord, as he did the silver and gold he took from the nations of Edom, Moab, Ammon, Amalek, and the Philistines.

¹² Abishai (son of Zeruiah) then destroyed eighteen thousand Edomites in the Valley of Salt. ¹³ He put garrisons in Edom and forced the Edomites to pay large sums of money annually to David. This is just another example of how the Lord gave David victory after victory. ¹⁴ David reigned over all of Israel and was a just ruler.

¹⁵ Joab (son of Zeruiah) was commander-in-chief of the army; Jehoshaphat (son of Ahilud) was the historian; ¹⁶ Zadok (son of Ahitub) and Ahimelech (son of Abiathar) were the head priests; Shavsha was the king's special assistant;[a] ¹⁷ Benaiah (son of Jehoiada) was in charge of the king's bodyguard—the Cherethites and Pelethites —and David's sons were his chief aides.

19 WHEN KING NAHASH of Ammon died, his son Hanun became the new king.

²,³ Then David declared, "I am going to show friendship to Hanun because of all the kind things his father did for me."

So David sent a message of sympathy to Hanun for the death of his father. But when David's ambassadors arrived, King Hanun's counselors warned him, "Don't fool yourself that David has sent these men to honor your father! They are here to spy out the land so that they can come in and conquer it!"

⁴ So King Hanun insulted King David's ambassadors by shaving their beards and cutting their robes off at the middle to expose their buttocks; then he sent them back to David in shame. ⁵ When David heard what had happened, he sent a message to his embarrassed emissaries, telling them to stay at Jericho until their beards had grown out again. ⁶ When King Hanun realized his mistake he sent $2,000,000[a] to enlist mercenary troops, chariots, and cavalry from Mesopotamia, Aram-maacah, and Zobah. ⁷ He hired thirty-two thousand chariots, as well as the support of the king of Maacah and his entire army. These forces camped at Medeba where they were joined by the troops King Hanun had recruited from his cities.

⁸ When David learned of this, he sent Joab and the mightiest warriors of Israel. ⁹ The army of Ammon went out to meet them and began the battle at the gates of the city of Medeba. Meanwhile, the mercenary forces were out in the field. ¹⁰ When Joab realized that the enemy forces were both in front and behind him, he divided his army and sent one group to engage the Syrians. ¹¹ The other group, under the command of his brother Abishai, moved against the Ammonites.

¹² "If the Syrians are too strong for me, come and help me," Joab told his brother; "and if the Ammonites are too strong for you, I'll come and help you. ¹³ Be courageous and let us act like men to save our people and the cities of our God. And may the Lord do what is best."

¹⁴ So Joab and his troops attacked the Syrians, and the Syrians turned and fled. ¹⁵ When the Ammonites, under attack by Abishai's troops, saw that the Syrians were

---

a Literally, "secretary" or "scribe."   **19**a Literally, "a thousand talents of silver," approximately 800,000 pounds sterling at current value.

retreating, they fled into the city. Then Joab returned to Jerusalem.

¹⁶ After their defeat, the Syrians summoned additional troops from east of the Euphrates River, led personally by Shophach, King Hadadezer's commander-in-chief. ¹⁷,¹⁸ When this news reached David, he mobilized all Israel, crossed the Jordan River, and engaged the enemy troops in battle. But the Syrians again fled from David, and he killed seven thousand charioteers and forty thousand of their troops. He also killed Shophach, the commander-in-chief of the Syrian army. ¹⁹ Then King Hadadezer's troops surrendered to King David and became his subjects. And never again did the Syrians aid the Ammonites in their battles.

20 THE FOLLOWING SPRING (spring was the season when wars usually began) Joab led the Israeli army in successful attacks against the cities and villages of the people of Ammon. After destroying them, he laid siege to Rabbah and conquered it. Meanwhile, David had stayed in Jerusalem. ² When David arrived on the scene, he removed the crown from the head of King Milcomᵃ of Rabbah and placed it upon his own head. It was made of gold inlaid with gems and weighed seventy-five pounds! David also took great amounts of plunder from the city. ³ He drove the people from the city and set them to work with saws, iron picks, and axes,ᵇ as was his custom with all the conquered Ammonite peoples. Then David and all his army returned to Jerusalem.

⁴ The next war was against the Philistines again, at Gezer. But Sibbecai, a man from Hushath, killed one of the sons of the giant, Sippai, and so the Philistines surrendered. ⁵ During another war with the Philistines, Elhanan (the son of Jair) killed Lahmi, the brother of Goliath the giant; the handle of his spear was like a weaver's beam! ⁶,⁷ During another battle, at Gath, a giant with six fingers on each hand and six toes on each foot (his father was also a giant) defied and taunted Israel; but he was killed by David's nephew Jonathan, the son of David's brother Shimea. ⁸ These giants were descendants of the giants of Gath, and they were killed by David and his soldiers.

21 THEN SATAN BROUGHT disaster upon Israel, for he made David decide to take a census.

² "Take a complete census throughout the landᵃ and bring me the totals," he told Joab and the other leaders.

³ But Joab objected. "If the Lord were to multiply his people a hundred times, would they not all be yours? So why are you asking us to do this? Why must you cause Israel to sin?"

⁴ But the king won the argument, and Joab did as he was told; he traveled all through Israel and returned to Jerusalem. ⁵ The total population figure which he gave came to 1,100,000 men of military age in Israel and 470,000 in Judah. ⁶ But he didn't include the tribes of Levi and Benjamin in his figures because he was so distressed at what the king had made him do. ⁷ And God, too, was displeased with the census and punished Israel for it.

⁸ But David said to God, "I am the one who has sinned. Please forgive me, for I realize now how wrong I was to do this."

⁹ Then the Lord said to Gad, David's personal prophet, ¹⁰,¹¹ "Go and tell David, 'The Lord has offered you three choices. Which will you choose? ¹² You may have three years of famine, or three months of destruction by the enemies of Israel, or three days of deadly plague as the angel of the Lord brings destruction to the land. Think it over and let me know what answer to return to the one who sent me.' "

¹³ "This is a terrible decision to make," David replied, "but let me fall into the hands of the Lord rather than into the power of men, for God's mercies are very great."

¹⁴ So the Lord sent a plague upon Israel and 70,000 men died as a result. ¹⁵ During the plague God sent an angel to destroy Jerusalem; but then he felt such compassion that he changed his mind and commanded the destroying angel, "Stop! It is enough!" (The angel of the Lord was standing at the

---

a Implied; see 1 Kings 11:5.   b Literally, "he conducted them to the saw." Whether this means that he made them labor with saws or that he sawed them to pieces is uncertain.   21a Literally, "from Beer-sheba to Dan."

time by the threshing-floor of Ornan the Jebusite.) ¹⁶ When David saw the angel of the Lord standing between heaven and earth with his sword drawn, pointing toward Jerusalem, he and the elders of Israel clothed themselves in sackcloth and fell to the ground before the Lord.

¹⁷ And David said to God, "I am the one who sinned by ordering the census. But what have these sheep done? O Lord my God, destroy me and my family, but do not destroy your people."

¹⁸ Then the angel of the Lord told Gad to instruct David to build an altar to the Lord at the threshing-floor of Ornan the Jebusite. ¹⁹,²⁰ So David went to see Ornan, who was threshing wheat at the time. Ornan saw the angel as he turned, and his four sons ran and hid. ²¹ Then Ornan saw the king approaching. So he left the threshing-floor and bowed to the ground before King David.

²² David said to Ornan, "Let me buy this threshing-floor from you at its full price; then I will build an altar to the Lord and the plague will stop."

²³ "Take it, my lord, and use it as you wish," Ornan said to David. "Take the oxen, too, for burnt offerings; use the threshing instruments for wood for the fire and use the wheat for the grain offering. I give it all to you."

²⁴ "No," the king replied, "I will buy it for the full price; I cannot take what is yours and give it to the Lord. I will not offer a burnt offering that has cost me nothing!"

²⁵ So David paid Ornan $4,300 in gold,ᵇ ²⁶ and built an altar to the Lord there, and sacrificed burnt offerings and peace offerings upon it; and he called out to the Lord, who answered by sending down fire from heaven to burn up the offering on the altar. ²⁷ Then the Lord commanded the angel to put back his sword into its sheath; ²⁸ and when David saw that the Lord had answered his plea, he sacrificed to him again. ²⁹ The Tabernacle and altar made by Moses in the wilderness were on the hill of Gibeon, ³⁰ but David didn't have time to go there to plead before the Lord, for he was terrified by the drawn sword of the angel of Jehovah.

22 THEN DAVID SAID, "Right here at Ornan's threshing-floor is the place where I'll build the Temple of the Lord and construct the altar for Israel's burnt offering!"

² David now drafted all the resident aliens in Israel to prepare blocks of squared stone for the Temple. ³ They also manufactured iron into the great quantity of nails needed for the doors in the gates and for the clamps; and they smelted so much bronze that it was too much to weigh. ⁴ The men of Tyre and Sidon brought great rafts of cedar logs to David.

⁵ "Solomon my son is young and tender," David said, "and the Temple of the Lord must be a marvelous structure, famous and glorious throughout the world; so I will begin the preparations for it now."

So David collected the construction materials before his death. ⁶ He now commanded his son Solomon to build a temple for the Lord God of Israel.

⁷ "I wanted to build it myself," David told him, ⁸ "but the Lord said not to do it. 'You have killed too many men in great wars,' he told me. 'You have reddened the ground before me with blood: so you are not to build my Temple. ⁹ But I will give you a son,' he told me, 'who will be a man of peace, for I will give him peace with his enemies in the surrounding lands. His name shall be Solomon (meaning "Peaceful"), and I will give peace and quietness to Israel during his reign. ¹⁰ He shall build my temple, and he shall be as my own son and I will be his father; and I will cause his sons and his descendants to reign over every generation of Israel.'

¹¹ "So now, my son, may the Lord be with you and prosper you as you do what he told you to do and build the Temple of the Lord. ¹² And may the Lord give you the good judgment to follow all his laws when he makes you king of Israel. ¹³ For if you carefully obey the rules and regulations which he gave to Israel through Moses, you will prosper. Be strong and courageous, fearless and enthusiastic!

¹⁴ "By hard work I have collected $3,000,000,000 worth of gold bullion,

---

ᵇ Literally, "six hundred shekels of gold by weight."

$2,000,000 worth of silver,[a] and so much iron and bronze that I haven't even weighed it; I have also gathered timber and stone for the walls. This is at least a beginning, something with which to start. [15] And you have many skilled stonemasons and carpenters and craftsmen of every kind. [16] They are expert gold and silver smiths and bronze and iron workers. So get to work, and may the Lord be with you!"

[17] Then David ordered all the leaders of Israel to assist his son in this project. [18] "The Lord your God is with you," he declared. "He has given you peace with the surrounding nations, for I have conquered them in the name of the Lord and for his people. [19] Now try with every fiber of your being to obey the Lord your God, and you will soon be bringing the Ark and the other holy articles of worship into the Temple of the Lord!"

23 BY THIS TIME David was an old, old man, so he stepped down from the throne and appointed his son Solomon as the new king of Israel. [2] He summoned all the political and religious leaders of Israel for the coronation ceremony. [3] At this time a census was taken of the men of the tribe of Levi who were thirty years or older. The total came to 38,000.

[4,5] "Twenty-four thousand of them will supervise the work at the Temple," David instructed, "six thousand are to be bailiffs and judges, four thousand will be temple guards, and four thousand will praise the Lord with the musical instruments I have made."

[6] Then David divided them into three main divisions named after the sons of Levi—the **Gershom** division, the **Kohath** division and the **Merari** division.

[7] Subdivisions of the *Gershom* corps were named after his sons **Ladan** and **Shime-i.** [8,9] These subdivisions were still further divided into six groups named after the sons of *Ladan:* Jehiel the leader, Zetham, Joel; and the sons of *Shime-i*[a]—Shelomoth, Haziel, and Haran.

[10,11] The subclans of *Shime-i* were named

after his four sons: Jahath was greatest, Zizah[b] was next, and Jeush and Beriah were combined into a single subclan because neither had many sons.

[12] The division of Kohath was subdivided into four groups named after his sons **Amram, Izhar, Hebron,** and **Uzziel.**

[13] *Amram* was the ancestor of Aaron and Moses.[c] Aaron and his sons were set apart for the holy service of sacrificing the people's offerings to the Lord. He served the Lord constantly and pronounced blessings in his name at all times.

[14,15] As for Moses, the man of God, his sons **Gershom** and **Eliezer** were included with the tribe of Levi. [16] *Gershom's* sons were led by Shebuel, [17] and *Eliezer's* only son, Rehabiah, was the leader of his clan, for he had many children.

[18] The sons of *Izhar* were led by Shelomith.

[19] The sons of *Hebron* were led by Jeriah. Amariah was second in command, Jahaziel was third, and Jekameam was fourth.

[20] The sons of *Uzziel* were led by Micah, and Isshiah was the second in command.

[21] The sons of *Merari* were **Mahli** and **Mushi.** The sons of *Mahli* were **Eleazar** and Kish. [22] *Eleazar* died without any sons, and his daughters were married to their cousins, the sons of *Kish.* [23] *Mushi's* sons were Mahli, Eder, and Jeremoth.

[24] In the census, all the men of Levi who were twenty years old or older were classified under the names of these clans and subclans; and they were all assigned to the ministry at the Temple. [25] For David said, "The Lord God of Israel has given us peace, and he will always live in Jerusalem. [26] Now the Levites will no longer need to carry the Tabernacle and its instruments from place to place."

[27] (This census of the tribe of Levi was one of the last things David did before his death.) [28] The work of the Levites was to assist the priests—the descendants of Aaron—in the sacrifices at the Temple; they also did the custodial work and helped perform the ceremonies of purification. [29] They provided the Bread of the Presence, the

---

a Literally, "a hundred thousand talents of gold" and "a million talents of silver."   23 a Probably not the same Shime-i as in verse 7.   b Or "Zina."   c Literally, "the sons of Amram: Aaron and Moses."

flour for the grain offerings, and the wafers made without yeast (either fried or mixed with olive oil); they also checked all the weights and measures. [30] Each morning and evening they stood before the Lord to sing thanks and praise to him. [31] They assisted in the special sacrifices of burnt offerings, the Sabbath sacrifices, the new moon celebrations, and at all the festivals. There were always as many Levites present as were required for the occasion. [32] And they took care of the Tabernacle and the Temple and assisted the priests in whatever way they were needed.

24 THE PRIESTS (THE descendants of Aaron) were placed into two divisions named after Aaron's sons, **Eleazar** and **Ithamar.**

Nadab and Abihu were also sons of Aaron, but they died before their father did and had no children; so only Eleazar and Ithamar were left to carry on. [3] David consulted with Zadok, who represented the Eleazar clan, and with Ahimelech, who represented the Ithamar clan; then he divided Aaron's descendants into many groups to serve at various times. [4] *Eleazar's* descendants were divided into sixteen groups and *Ithamar's* into eight (for there was more leadership ability among the descendants of Eleazar).

[5] All tasks were assigned to the various groups by coin-toss[a] so that there would be no preference, for there were many famous men and high officials of the Temple in each division. [6] Shemaiah, a Levite and the son of Nethanel, acted as recording secretary and wrote down the names and assignments in the presence of the king and of these leaders: Zadok the priest, Ahimelech the son of Abiathar, and the heads of the priests and Levites. Two groups from the division of Eleazar and one from the division of Ithamar were assigned to each task.

[7-18] The work was assigned (by coin-toss) in this order:

First, the group led by Jehoiarib;
Second, the group led by Jedaiah;
Third, the group led by Harim;
Fourth, the group led by Se-orim;

Fifth, the group led by Malchijah;
Sixth, the group led by Mijamin;
Seventh, the group led by Hakkoz;
Eighth, the group led by Ahijah;
Ninth, the group led by Jeshua;
Tenth, the group led by Shecaniah;
Eleventh, the group led by Eliashib;
Twelfth, the group led by Jakim;
Thirteenth, the group led by Huppah;
Fourteenth, the group led by Jeshebe-ab;
Fifteenth, the group led by Bilgah;
Sixteenth, the group led by Immer;
Seventeenth, the group led by Hezir;
Eighteenth, the group led by Happizzez;
Nineteenth, the group led by Pethahiah;
Twentieth, the group led by Jehezkel;
Twenty-first, the group led by Jachin;
Twenty-second, the group led by Gamul;
Twenty-third, the group led by Delaiah;
Twenty-fourth, the group led by Maaziah.

[19] Each group carried out the Temple duties as originally assigned by God through their ancestor Aaron.

[20] These were the other descendants of Levi: Amram; his descendant Shuba-el; and Shuba-el's descendant Jehdeiah; [21] the Rehabiah group, led by his oldest son Isshiah; [22] the Izhar group, consisting of Shelamoth and his descendant Jahath. [23] The Hebron group:

Jeriah, Hebron's oldest son;
Amariah, his second son;
Jahaziel, his third son;
Jekameam, his fourth son.

[24,25] The Uzziel group was led by his son Micah and his grandsons Shamir and Isshiah, and by Isshiah's son Zechariah.

[26,27] The Merari group was led by his sons: **Mahli** and **Mushi.** (Ja-aziah's group, led by his son Beno, included his brothers Shoham, Zaccur, and Ibri.) [28] *Mahli's* descendants were Eleazar, who had no sons, [29] and Kish, among whose sons was Jerahmeel. [30] The sons of *Mushi* were Mahli,

Eder, and Jerimoth.

These were the descendants of Levi in their various clans. [31] Like the descendants of Aaron, they were assigned to their duties by coin-toss without distinction as to age or rank. It was done in the presence of King David, Zadok, Ahimelech, and the leaders of the priests and the Levites.

25 DAVID AND THE officials of the Tabernacle then appointed men to prophesy to the accompaniment of zithers, harps, and cymbals. These men were from the groups of Asaph, Heman, and Jeduthun. Here is a list of their names and their work:

[2] Under the leadership of Asaph, the king's private prophet, were his sons Zaccur, Joseph, Nethaniah, and Asharelah.

[3] Under Jeduthun, who led in giving thanks and praising the Lord (while accompanied by the zither), were his six sons: Gedaliah, Zeri, Jeshaiah, Shime-i, Hashabiah, and Mattithiah.

[4,5] Under the direction of Heman, the king's private chaplain, were his sons: Bukkiah, Mattaniah, Uzziel, Shebuel, Jerimoth, Hananiah, Hanani, Eliathah, Geddalti, Romamti-ezer, Joshbekashah, Mallothi, Hothir, and Mahazi-oth. (For God had honored him with fourteen sons and three daughters.) [6,7] Their music ministry included the playing of cymbals, harps, and zithers; all were under the direction of their father as they performed this ministry in the Tabernacle.

Asaph, Jeduthun, and Heman reported directly to the king. They and their families were all trained in singing praises to the Lord; each one—288 of them in all—was a master musician. [8] The singers were appointed to their particular term of service by coin-toss, without regard to age or reputation.

[9-31] The first toss indicated Joseph of the Asaph clan;

The second, Gedaliah, along with twelve of his sons and brothers;

The third, Zaccur and twelve of his sons and brothers;

The fourth, Izri and twelve of his sons and brothers;

Fifth, Nethaniah and twelve of his sons and brothers;

Sixth, Bukkiah and twelve of his sons and brothers;

Seventh, Jesharelah and twelve of his sons and brothers;

Eighth, Jeshaiah and twelve of his sons and brothers;

Ninth, Mattaniah and twelve of his sons and brothers;

Tenth, Shime-i and twelve of his sons and brothers;

Eleventh, Azarel and twelve of his sons and brothers;

Twelfth, Hashabiah and twelve of his sons and brothers;

Thirteenth, Shuba-el and twelve of his sons and brothers;

Fourteenth, Mattithiah and twelve of his sons and brothers;

Fifteenth, Jeremoth and twelve of his sons and brothers;

Sixteenth, Hananiah and twelve of his sons and brothers;

Seventeenth, Joshbekasha and twelve of his sons and brothers;

Eighteenth, Hanani and twelve of his sons and brothers;

Nineteenth, Mallothi and twelve of his sons and brothers;

Twentieth, Eliathah and twelve of his sons and brothers;

Twenty-first, Hothir and twelve of his sons and brothers;

Twenty-second, Giddalti and twelve of his sons and brothers;

Twenty-third, Mahazi-oth and twelve of his sons and brothers;

Twenty-fourth, Romamti-ezer and twelve of his sons and brothers.

26 THE TEMPLE GUARDS were from the Asaph division of the Korah clan. The captain of the guard was Meshelemiah, the son of Kore.

[2,3] His sergeants were his sons:
Zechariah (the oldest),
Jedia-el (the second),
Zebadiah (the third),
Jathni-el (the fourth),
Elam (the fifth),
Jeho-hanan (the sixth),
Elie-ho-enai (the seventh).

[4,5] The sons of Obed-edom were also appointed as Temple guards:

Shemaiah (the oldest),
Jehozabad (the second),
Joah (the third),
Sacar (the fourth),
Nethanel (the fifth),
Ammi-el (the sixth),
Issachar (the seventh),
Pe-ullethai (the eighth).
What a blessing God gave him with all those sons!

⁶,⁷ Shemaiah's sons were all outstanding men, and had positions of great authority in their clan. Their names were:

Othni, Repha-el,
Obed, Elzabad.

Their brave brothers, Elihu and Sema-chiah, were also very able men.

⁸ All of these sons and grandsons of Obed-edom—all sixty-two of them—were outstanding men who were particularly well qualified for their work. ⁹ Meshelemiah's eighteen sons and brothers, too, were real leaders. ¹⁰ Hosah, one of the Merari group, appointed Shimri as the leader among his sons, though he was not the oldest. ¹¹ The names of some of his other sons were:

Hilkiah, the second;
Tebaliah, the third;
Zechariah, the fourth.

Hosah's sons and brothers numbered thirteen in all.

¹² The divisions of the Temple guards were named after the leaders. Like the other Levites, they were responsible to minister at the Temple. ¹³ They were assigned guard duty at the various gates without regard to the reputation of their families, for it was all done by coin-toss. ¹⁴,¹⁵ The responsibility of the east gate went to Shelemiah and his group; of the north gate to his son Zecha-riah, a man of unusual wisdom; of the south gate to Obed-edom and his group (his sons were given charge of the storehouses); ¹⁶ of the west gate and the Shallecheth Gate on the upper road, to Shuppim and Hosah. ¹⁷ Six guards were assigned daily to the east gate, four to the north gate, four to the south gate, and two to each of the store-houses. ¹⁸ Six guards were assigned each day to the west gate, four to the upper road, and two to the nearby areas. ¹⁹ The Temple

guards were chosen from the clans of Korah and Merari.

²⁰,²¹,²² Other Levites, led by Ahijah, were given the care of the gifts brought to the Lord and placed in the Temple treasury. These men of the Ladan subclan from the clan of Gershom included Zetham and Joel, the sons of Jehieli. ²³,²⁴ Shebuel, son of Ger-shom and grandson of Moses, was the chief officer of the treasury. He was in charge of the divisions named after Amram, Izhar, Hebron, and Uzziel.

²⁵ The line of descendants from Eliezer went through Rehabiah, Jesha-iah, Joram, Zichri, and Shelomoth. ²⁶ Shelomoth and his brothers were appointed to care for the gifts given to the Lord by King David and the other leaders of the nation such as the officers and generals of the army. ²⁷ For these men dedicated their war loot to sup-port the operating expenses of the Temple. ²⁸ Shelomoth and his brothers were also re-sponsible for the care of the items dedicated to the Lord by Samuel the prophet, Saul the son of Kish, Abner the son of Ner, Joab the son of Zeruiah, and anyone else of distinc-tionᵃ who brought gifts to the Lord.

²⁹ Chenaniah and his sons (from the sub-clan of Izhar) were appointed public ad-ministrators and judges. ³⁰ Hashabiah and 1,700 of his clansmen from Hebron, all out-standing men, were placed in charge of the territory of Israel west of the Jordan River; they were responsible for the religious af-fairs and public administration of that area. ³¹,³² Twenty-seven hundred outstanding men of the clan of the Hebronites, under the supervision of Jerijah, were appointed to control the religious and public affairs of the tribes of Reuben, Gad, and the half-tribe of Manasseh. These men, all of whom had ex-cellent qualifications, were appointed on the basis of their ancestry and ability at Jazer in Gilead in the fortieth year of King Da-vid's reign.

27 THE ISRAELI ARMY was divided into twelve regiments, each with 24,000 troops, including officers and administrative staff. These units were called up for active duty one month each year. Here is the list

---

ᵃ Implied.

of the units and their regimental commanders:

2,3 The commander of the First Division was Jashobeam. He had charge of 24,000 troops who were on duty the first month of each year.

4 The commander of the Second Division was Dodai (a descendant of Ahohi). He had charge of 24,000 troops who were on duty the second month of each year. Mikloth was his executive officer.

5,6 The commander of the Third Division was Benaiah. His 24,000 men were on duty the third month of each year. (He was the son of Jehoiada the High Priest, and was the chief of the thirty highest-ranking officers in David's army.) His son Ammizabad succeeded him as division commander.

7 The commander of the Fourth Division was Asahel (the brother of Joab), who was later replaced by his son Zebadiah. He had 24,000 men on duty the fourth month of each year.

8 The commander of the Fifth Division was Shamuth from Izrah, with 24,000 men on duty the fifth month of each year.

9 The commander of the Sixth Division was Ira, the son of Ikkesh from Tekoa; he had 24,000 men on duty the sixth month of each year.

10 The commander of the Seventh Division was Helez from Pelona in Ephraim, with 24,000 men on duty the seventh month of each year.

11 The commander of the Eighth Division was Sibbecai of the Hushite subclan from Zerah, who had 24,000 men on duty the eighth month of each year.

12 The commander of the Ninth Division was Abi-ezer (from Anathoth in the tribe of Benjamin), who commanded 24,000 troops during the ninth month of each year.

13 The commander of the Tenth Division was Maharai from Netophah in Zerah, with 24,000 men on duty the tenth month of each year.

14 The commander of the Eleventh Division was Benaiah from Pirathon in Ephraim, with 24,000 men on duty during the eleventh month of each year.

15 The commander of the Twelfth Division was Heldai from Netophah in the area of Othni-el, who commanded 24,000 men on duty during the twelfth month of each year.

16-22 The top political officers of the tribes of Israel were as follows:

> Over Reuben, Eliezer (son of Zichri);
> Over Simeon, Shephatiah (son of Maacah);
> Over Levi, Hashabiah (son of Kemuel);
> Over the descendants of Aaron, Zadok;
> Over Judah, Elihu (a brother of King David);
> Over Issachar, Omri (son of Michael);
> Over Zebulun, Ishmaiah (son of Obadiah);
> Over Naphtali, Jeremoth (son of Azriel);
> Over Ephraim, Hoshea (son of Azaziah);
> Over the half-tribe of Manasseh, Joel (son of Pedaiah);
> Over the other half of Manasseh, in Gilead, Iddo (son of Zechariah);
> Over Benjamin, Ja-asiel (son of Abner);
> Over Dan, Azarel (son of Jeroham).

23 When David took his census he didn't include the twenty-year-olds, or those younger, for the Lord had promised a population explosion for his people.a 24 Joab began the census, but he never finished it, for the anger of God broke out upon Israel; the final total was never put into the annals of King David.

25 Azmaveth (son of Adi-el) was the chief financial officer in charge of the palace treasuries, and Jonathan (son of Uzziah) was chief of the regional treasuries throughout the cities, villages, and fortresses of Israel.

26 Ezri (son of Chelub) was manager of the laborers on the king's estates. 27 And Shime-i from Ramath had the oversight of the king's vineyards; and Zabdi from Shiphma was responsible for his wine production and storage. 28 Baal-hanan from Gedera was responsible for the king's olive

---

a Literally, "the Lord had said he would increase Israel like to the stars of heaven."

yards and sycamore trees in the lowlands bordering Philistine territory, while Joash had charge of the supplies of olive oil.

²⁹ Shitrai from Sharon was in charge of the cattle on the Plains of Sharon, and Shaphat (son of Adlai) had charge of those in the valleys. ³⁰ Obil, from the territory of Ishmael, had charge of the camels, and Jehdeiah from Meronoth had charge of the donkeys. ³¹ The sheep were under the care of Jaziz the Hagrite. These men were King David's overseers.

³² The attendant to the king's sons was Jonathan, David's uncle, a wise counselor and an educated man.ᵇ Jehiel (the son of Hachmoni) was their tutor.

³³ Ahithophel was the king's official counselor and Hushai the Archite was his personal advisor. ³⁴ Ahithophel was assisted by Jehoiada (the son of Benaiah) and by Abiathar. Joab was commander-in-chief of the Israeli army.

28 DAVID NOW SUMMONED all of his officials to Jerusalem—the political leaders, the commanders of the twelve army divisions, the other army officers, those in charge of his property and livestock and all the other men of authority in his kingdom. ² He rose and stood before them and addressed them as follows:

"My brothers and my people! It was my desire to build a temple in which the Ark of the Covenant of the Lord could rest—a place for our God to live in.ᵃ I have now collected everything that is necessary for the building, ³ but God has told me, 'You are not to build my temple, for you are a warrior and have shed much blood.'

⁴ "Nevertheless, the Lord God of Israel has chosen me from among all my father's family to begin a dynasty that will rule Israel forever; he has chosen the tribe of Judah, and from among the families of Judah, my father's family; and from among his sons, the Lord took pleasure in me and has made me king over all Israel. ⁵ And from among my sons—the Lord has given me many children—he has chosen Solomon to succeed me on the throne of his Kingdom

of Israel. ⁶ He has told me, 'Your son Solomon shall build my temple; for I have chosen him as my son and I will be his father. ⁷ And if he continues to obey my commandments and instructions as he has until now, I will make his kingdom last forever.' "

⁸ Then David turned to Solomon and said:ᵇ

"Here before the leaders of Israel, the people of God, and in the sight of our God, I am instructing you to search out every commandment of the Lord so that you may continue to rule this good land and leave it to your children to rule forever. ⁹ Solomon, my son, get to know the God of your fathers. Worship and serve him with a clean heart and a willing mind, for the Lord sees every heart and understands and knows every thought. If you seek him, you will find him; but if you forsake him, he will permanently throw you aside. ¹⁰ So be very careful, for the Lord has chosen you to build his holy temple. Be strong and do as he commands."

¹¹ Then David gave Solomon the blueprint of the Temple and its surroundings—the treasuries, the upstairs rooms, the inside rooms, and the sanctuary for the place of mercy. ¹² He also gave Solomon his plans for the outer court, the outside rooms, the Temple storage areas, and the treasuries for the gifts dedicated by famous persons. For the Holy Spirit had given David all these plans.ᶜ ¹³ The king also passed on to Solomon the instructions concerning the work of the various groups of priests and Levites; and he gave specifications for each item in the Temple which was to be used for worship and sacrifice.

¹⁴ David weighed out enough gold and silver to make these various items, ¹⁵ as well as the specific amount of gold needed for the lampstands and lamps. He also weighed out enough silver for the silver candlesticks and lamps, each according to its use. ¹⁶ He weighed out the gold for the table on which the Bread of the Presence would be placed and for the other gold tables, and he weighed the silver for the silver tables.

---

b Literally, "a scribe."　　**28** a Literally, "a footstool."　　b Implied.　　c Or, "and the other plans he had in mind." The word in the Hebrew for "spirit" can be interpreted either way.

¹⁷ Then he weighed out the gold for the solid gold hooks used in handling the sacrificial meat and for the basins, cups, and bowls of gold and silver. ¹⁸ Finally, he weighed out the refined gold for the altar of incense and for the gold angels whose wings were stretched over the Ark of the Covenant of the Lord.

¹⁹ "Every part of this blueprint," David told Solomon, "was given to me in writing from the hand of the Lord." ²⁰ Then he continued, "Be strong and courageous and get to work. Don't be frightened by the size of the task, for the Lord my God is with you; he will not forsake you. He will see to it that everything is finished correctly. ²¹ And these various groups of priests and Levites will serve in the Temple. Others with skills of every kind will volunteer, and the army and the entire nation are at your command."

29 THEN KING DAVID turned to the entire assembly and said: "My son Solomon, whom God has chosen to be the next king of Israel, is still young and inexperienced, and the work ahead of him is enormous; for the temple he will build is not just another building—it is for the Lord God himself! ² Using every resource at my command, I have gathered as much as I could for building it—enough gold, silver, bronze, iron, wood, and great quantities of onyx, other precious stones, costly jewels, and marble. ³ And now, because of my devotion to the Temple of God, I am giving all of my own private treasures to aid in the construction. This is in addition to the building materials I have already collected. ⁴,⁵ These personal contributions consist of $85,000,000 worth of gold from Ophir and $20,000,000 worth of purest silver to be used for overlaying the walls of the buildings. This will be used for the articles made of gold and silver and for the artistic decorations. Now then, who will follow my example? Who will give himself and all that he has to the Lord?"

⁶,⁷ Then the clan leaders, the heads of the tribes, the army officers, and the administrative officers of the king pledged $145,000,000 in gold; $50,000 in foreign currency; $30,000,000 in silver; 800 tons of bronze; and 4,600 tons of iron. ⁸ They also contributed great amounts of jewelry, which were deposited at the Temple treasury with Jehiel (a descendant of Gershom). ⁹ Everyone was excited and happy for this opportunity of service, and King David was moved with deep joy.

¹⁰ While still in the presence of the whole assembly, David expressed his praises to the Lord: "O Lord God of our father Israel, praise your name for ever and ever! ¹¹ Yours is the mighty power and glory and victory and majesty. Everything in the heavens and earth is yours, O Lord, and this is your kingdom. We adore you as being in control of everything. ¹² Riches and honor come from you alone, and you are the Ruler of all mankind; your hand controls power and might, and it is at your discretion that men are made great and given strength. ¹³ O our God, we thank you and praise your glorious name, ¹⁴ but who am I and who are my people that we should be permitted to give anything to you? Everything we have has come from you, and we only give you what is yours already! ¹⁵ For we are here for but a moment, strangers in the land as our fathers were before us; our days on earth are like a shadow, gone so soon, without a trace. ¹⁶ O Lord our God, all of this material that we have gathered to build a temple for your holy name comes from you! It all belongs to you! ¹⁷ I know, my God, that you test men to see if they are good; for you enjoy good men. I have done all this with good motives, and I have watched your people offer their gifts willingly and joyously.

¹⁸ "O Lord God of our fathers: Abraham, Isaac, and Israel! Make your people always want to obey you, and see to it that their love for you never changes. ¹⁹ Give my son Solomon a good heart toward God, so that he will want to obey you in the smallest detail, and will look forward eagerly to finishing the building of your temple, for which I have made all of these preparations."

²⁰ Then David said to all the people, "Give praise to the Lord your God!" And they did, bowing low before the Lord and the king.

²¹ The next day they brought a thousand young bulls, a thousand rams, and a thousand lambs as burnt offerings to the Lord;

they also offered drink offerings and many other sacrifices on behalf of all Israel. [22] Then they feasted and drank before the Lord with great joy.

And again[a] they crowned King David's son Solomon as their king. They anointed him before the Lord as their leader, and they anointed Zadok as their priest. [23] So God appointed Solomon to take the throne of his father David; and he prospered greatly, and all Israel obeyed him. [24] The national leaders, the army officers, and his brothers all pledged their allegiance to King Solomon. [25] And the Lord gave him great popularity with all the people of Israel, and he amassed even greater wealth and honor than his father.

[26,27] David was king of the land of Israel for forty years; seven of them during his reign in Hebron and thirty-three in Jerusalem. [28] He died at an old age, wealthy and honored; and his son Solomon reigned in his place. [29] Detailed biographies of King David have been written in the history of Samuel the prophet, the history written by Nathan the prophet, and in the history written by the prophet Gad. [30] These accounts tell of his reign and of his might and all that happened to him and to Israel and to the kings of the nearby nations.

2 CHRONICLES

1 KING DAVID'S SON Solomon was now the undisputed ruler of Israel, for the Lord his God had made him a powerful monarch. [2,3] He summoned all the army officers and judges to Gibeon[a] as well as all the political and religious leaders of Israel. He led them up to the hill to the old[b] Tabernacle constructed by Moses, the Lord's assistant, while he was in the wilderness. [4] (There was a later Tabernacle in Jerusalem, built by King David for the Ark of God when he removed it from Kiriath-jearim.) [5,6] The bronze altar made by Bezalel (son of Uri, son of Hur) still stood in front of the old Tabernacle, and now Solomon and those he had invited assembled themselves before it, as he sacrificed upon it 1,000 burnt offerings to the Lord.

[7] That night God appeared to Solomon and told him, "Ask me for anything, and I will give it to you!"

[8] Solomon replied, "O God, you have been so kind and good to my father David, and now you have given me the kingdom— [9] this is all I want! For you have fulfilled your promise to David my father and have made me king over a nation as full of people as the earth is full of dust! [10] Now give me wisdom and knowledge to rule them properly, for who is able to govern by himself such a great nation as this one of yours?"

[11] God replied, "Because your greatest desire is to help your people, and you haven't asked for personal wealth and honor, and you haven't asked me to curse your enemies, and you haven't asked for a long life, but for wisdom and knowledge to properly guide my people— [12] yes, I am giving you the wisdom and knowledge you asked for! And I am also giving you such riches, wealth, and honor as no other king has ever had before you! And there will never again be so great a king in all the world!"

[13] Solomon then left the Tabernacle, returned down the hill, and went back to Jerusalem to rule Israel. [14] He built up a huge force of 1,400 chariots and recruited 12,000 cavalry to guard the cities where the chariots were garaged, though some, of course, were stationed at Jerusalem near the king. [15] During Solomon's reign, silver and gold were as plentiful in Jerusalem as rocks on the road! And expensive cedar lumber was used like common sycamore! [16] Solomon sent horse-traders to Egypt to purchase entire herds at wholesale prices. [17] At that time Egyptian chariots sold for $400

---

a Or, "and they installed him as co-regent" (with King David).　　1a Implied.　　b Moses had built the Tabernacle 500 years before the reign of King Solomon.

each and horses for $100, delivered at Jerusalem. Many of these were then resold to the kings of the Hittites and Syria.

2 SOLOMON NOW DECIDED that the time had come to build a temple for the Lord and a palace for himself. ² This required a force of 70,000 laborers, 80,000 stonecutters in the hills, and 3,600 foremen. ³ Solomon sent an ambassador to King Hiram at Tyre, requesting shipments of cedar lumber such as Hiram had supplied to David when he was building his palace.

⁴ "I am about to build a temple for the Lord my God," Solomon told Hiram. "It will be a place where I can burn incense and sweet spices before God, and display the special sacrificial bread,ᵃ and sacrifice burnt offerings each morning and evening, and on the Sabbaths, and at the new moon celebration and other regular festivals of the Lord our God. For God wants Israel always to celebrate these special occasions. ⁵ It is going to be a wonderful temple because he is a great God, greater than any other. ⁶ But who can ever build him a worthy home? Not even the highest heaven would be beautiful enough! And who am I to be allowed to build a temple for God? But it will be a place to worshipᵇ him.

⁷ "So send me skilled craftsmen—goldsmiths and silversmiths, brass and iron workers; and send me weavers to make purple, crimson, and blue cloth; and skilled engravers to work beside the craftsmen of Judah and Jerusalem who were selected by my father David. ⁸ Also send me cedar trees, fir trees, and algum trees from the Forests of Lebanon, for your men are without equal as lumbermen, and I will send my men to help them. ⁹ An immense amount of lumber will be needed, for the temple I am going to build will be huge and incredibly beautiful. ¹⁰ As to the financial arrangements, I will pay your men 20,000 sacks of crushed wheat, 20,000 barrels of barley, 20,000 barrels of wine, and 20,000 barrels of olive oil."

¹¹ King Hiram replied to King Solomon: "It is because the Lord loves his people that he has made you their king! ¹² Blessed be the Lord God of Israel who made the heavens and the earth and who has given to David such a wise, intelligent, and understanding son to build God's Temple, and a royal palace for himself.

¹³ "I am sending you a master craftsman—my famous Huramabi! He is a brilliant man, ¹⁴ the son of a Jewish woman from Dan in Israel; his father is from here in Tyre. He is a skillful goldsmith and silversmith, and also does exquisite work with brass and iron, and knows all about stonework, carpentry, and weaving; and he is an expert in the dying of purple and blue linen and crimson cloth. He is an engraver besides, and an inventor! He will work with your craftsmen and those appointed by my lord David, your father. ¹⁵ So send along the wheat, barley, olive oil, and wine you mentioned, ¹⁶ and we will begin cutting wood from the Lebanon mountains, as much as you need, and bring it to you in log floats across the sea to Joppa, and from there you can take them inland to Jerusalem."

¹⁷ Solomon now took a census of all foreigners in the country (just as his father David had done) and found that there were 153,600 of them. ¹⁸ He indentured 70,000 as common laborers, 80,000 as loggers and 3,600 as foremen.

3 FINALLY THE ACTUAL construction of the Temple began. Its location was in Jerusalem at the top of Mount Moriah, where the Lord had appeared to Solomon's father, King David, and where the threshing-floor of Ornan the Jebusite had been. David had selected it as the site for the Temple. ² The actual construction began on the seventeenth day of April in the fourth year of King Solomon's reign.

³ The foundation was ninety feet long and thirty feet wide. ⁴ A covered porch ran along the entire thirty-foot width of the house, with the inner walls and ceiling overlaid with pure gold! The roof was 180 feet high.

⁵ The main part of the Temple was paneled with cypress wood, plated with pure gold, and engraved with palm trees and chains. ⁶ Beautiful jewels were inlaid into

---

a Literally, "The Bread of the Presence."   b Literally, "a place to burn incense before him."

the walls to add to the beauty; the gold, by the way, was of the best, from Parvaim. [7] All the walls, beams, doors, and thresholds throughout the Temple were plated with gold, with angels engraved on the walls.

[8] Within the Temple, at one end, was the most sacred room—the Holy of Holies—thirty feet square. This too was overlaid with the finest gold, valued at $18,000,000. [9] Twenty-six-ounce gold nails were used. The upper rooms were also plated with gold.

[10] Within the innermost room, the Holy of Holies, Solomon placed two sculptured statues of angels, and plated them with gold. [11,12,13] They stood on the floor facing the outer room, with wings stretched wingtip to wingtip across the room, from wall to wall.[a] [14] Across the entrance to this room he placed a veil of blue and crimson finespun linen, decorated with angels.

[15] At the front of the Temple were two pillars 52½ feet high, topped by a 7½-foot capital flaring out to the roof. [16] He made chains[b] and placed them on top of the pillars, with 100 pomegranates attached to the chains. [17] Then he set up the pillars at the front of the Temple, one on the right and the other on the left. And he gave them names: Jachin (the one on the right), and Boaz (the one on the left).

4 HE ALSO MADE a bronze altar thirty feet long, thirty feet wide, and fifteen feet high. [2] Then he forged a huge round tank fifteen feet across from rim to rim. The rim stood 7½ feet above the floor, and was forty-five feet around. [3] This tank was set on the backs of two rows of metal oxen. The tank and oxen were cast as one piece. [4] There were twelve of these oxen standing tail to tail, three facing north, three west, three south, and three east. [5] The walls of the tank were five inches thick, flaring out like the cup of a lily. It held 3,000 barrels of water.

[6] He also constructed ten vats for water to wash the offerings, five to the right of the huge tank and five to the left. The priests used the tank, and not the vats, for their own washing.

[7] Carefully following God's instructions, he then cast ten gold lampstands and placed them in the Temple, five against each wall; [8] he also built ten tables and placed five against each wall on the right and left. And he molded 100 solid gold bowls. [9] Then he constructed a court for the priests, also the public court, and overlaid the doors of these courts with bronze. [10] The huge tank was in the southeast corner of the outer room of the Temple. [11] Huramabi also made the necessary pots, shovels, and basins for use in connection with the sacrifices.

So at last he completed the work assigned to him by King Solomon:

[12-16] The construction of the two pillars,

The two flared capitals on the tops of the pillars,

The two sets of chains on the capitals,

The 400 pomegranates hanging from the two sets of chains on the capitals,

The bases for the vats, and the vats themselves,

The huge tank and the twelve oxen under it,

The pots, shovels, and fleshhooks.

This skillful craftsman, Huramabi, made all of the above-mentioned items for King Solomon, using polished bronze. [17,18] The king did the casting at the claybanks of the Jordan valley between Succoth and Zeredah. Great quantities of bronze were used, too heavy to weigh.

[19] But in the Temple only gold was used. For Solomon commanded that all of the utensils, the altar, and the table for the Bread of the Presence must be made of gold; [20] also the lamps and lampstands, [21] the floral decorations, tongs, [22] lamp snuffers, basins, spoons, and firepans—all were made of pure gold. Even the doorway of the Temple, the main door, and the inner doors to the Holy of Holies were of gold.

5 SO THE TEMPLE was finally finished. Then Solomon brought in the gifts dedicated to the Lord by his father, King David. They were stored in the Temple treasuries. [2] Solomon now summoned to Jerusalem

---

a Literally, "one wing of a cherub, five cubits long."   b Literally, "chains in the Holy of Holies, and . . . ."

all of the leaders of Israel—the heads of the tribes and clans—for the ceremony of transferring the Ark from the [Tabernacle in the[a]] City of David, also known as Zion, [to its new home in the Temple[a]]. [3] This celebration took place in October at the annual Festival of Tabernacles. [4,5] As the leaders of Israel watched, the Levites lifted the Ark and carried it out of the Tabernacle, along with all the other sacred vessels. [6] King Solomon and the others sacrificed sheep and oxen before the Ark in such numbers that no one tried to keep count!

[7,8] Then the priests carried the Ark into the inner room of the Temple—the Holy of Holies—and placed it beneath the angels' wings; their wings spread over the Ark and its carrying poles. [9] These carrying poles were so long that their ends could be seen from the outer room, but not from the outside doorway.

The Ark is still there at the time of this writing. [10] Nothing was in the Ark except the two stone tablets which Moses had put there at Mount Horeb, when the Lord made a covenant with the people of Israel as they were leaving Egypt.

[11,12] When the priests had undergone the purification rites for themselves, they all took part in the ceremonies without regard to their normal duties. And how the Levites were praising the Lord as the priests came out of the Holy of Holies! The singers were Asaph, Heman, Jeduthun and all their sons and brothers, dressed in finespun linen robes and standing at the east side of the altar. The choir was accompanied by 120 priests who were trumpeters, while others played the cymbals, lyres, and harps. [13,14] The band and chorus united as one to praise and thank the Lord; their selections were interspersed with trumpet obbligatos, the clashing of cymbals, and the loud playing of other musical instruments—all praising and thanking the Lord. Their theme was "He is so good! His lovingkindness lasts forever!"

And at that moment the glory of the Lord, coming as a bright cloud, filled the Temple so that the priests could not continue their work.

6 THIS IS THE prayer prayed by Solomon on that occasion:

"The Lord has said that he would live
    in the thick darkness,
But I have made a Temple for you,
    O Lord, to live in forever!"

[3] Then the king turned around to the people and they stood to receive his blessing:

[4] "Blessed be the Lord God of Israel," he said to them, "—the God who talked personally to my father David and has now fulfilled the promise he made to him. For he told him, [5,6] 'I have never before, since bringing my people from the land of Egypt, chosen a city anywhere in Israel as the location of my Temple where my name will be glorified; and never before have I chosen a king for my people Israel. But now I have chosen Jerusalem as that city, and David as that king.'

[7] "My father David wanted to build this Temple, [8] but the Lord said not to. It was good to have the desire, the Lord told him, [9] but he was not the one to build it: his son was chosen for that task. [10] And now the Lord has done what he promised, for I have become king in my father's place, and I have built the Temple for the Name of the Lord God of Israel, [11] and placed the Ark there. And in the Ark is the Covenant between the Lord and his people Israel."

[12,13] As he spoke, Solomon was standing before the people on a platform in the center of the outer court, in front of the altar of the Lord. The platform was made of bronze, 7½ feet square and 4½ feet high. Now, as all the people watched, he knelt down, reached out his arms toward heaven, and prayed this prayer:

[14] "O Lord God of Israel, there is no God like you in all of heaven and earth. You are the God who keeps his kind promises to all those who obey you, and who are anxious to do your will. [15] And you have kept your promise to my father David,[a] as is evident today. [16] And now, O God of Israel, carry out your further promise to him that 'your descendants shall always reign over Israel if they will obey my laws as you have.' [17] Yes, Lord God of Israel, please fulfill this

---

a Implied.   6a Literally, "David your servant."

promise too. [18] But will God really live upon the earth with men? Why, even the heaven and the heaven of heavens cannot contain you—how much less this Temple which I have built!

[19] "How I pray that you will heed my prayers, O Lord my God! Listen to my prayer that I am praying to you now! [20,21] Look down with favor day and night upon this Temple—upon this place where you have said that you would put your name. May you always hear and answer the prayers I will pray to you as I face toward this place. Listen to my prayers and to those of your people Israel when they pray toward this Temple; yes, hear us from heaven, and when you hear, forgive.

[22] "Whenever someone commits a crime, and is required to swear to his innocence before this altar, [23] then hear from heaven and punish him if he is lying, or else declare him innocent.

[24] "If your people Israel are destroyed before their enemies because they have sinned against you, and if they turn to you and call themselves your people, and pray to you here in this Temple, [25] then listen to them from heaven and forgive their sins and give them back this land you gave to their fathers.

[26] "When the skies are shut and there is no rain because of our sins, and then we pray toward this Temple and claim you as our God, and turn from our sins because you have punished us, [27] then listen from heaven and forgive the sins of your people, and teach them what is right; and send rain upon this land which you have given to your people as their own property.

[28] "If there is a famine in the land, or plagues, or crop disease, or attacks of locusts or caterpillars, or if your people's enemies are in the land besieging our cities—whatever the trouble is— [29] listen to every individual's prayer concerning his private sorrow, as well as all the public prayers. [30] Hear from heaven where you live, and forgive, and give each one whatever he deserves, for you know the hearts of all mankind. [31] Then they will reverence you forever, and will continually walk where you tell them to go.[b]

[32] "And when foreigners hear of your power, and come from distant lands to worship your great name, and to pray toward this Temple, [33] hear them from heaven where you live, and do what they request of you. Then all the peoples of the earth will hear of your fame and will reverence you, just as your people Israel do; and they too will know that this Temple I have built is truly yours.

[34] "If your people go out at your command to fight their enemies, and they pray toward this city of Jerusalem which you have chosen, and this Temple which I have built for your name, [35] then hear their prayers from heaven and give them success.

[36] "If they sin against you (and who has never sinned?) and you become angry with them, and you let their enemies defeat them and take them away as captives to some foreign nation near or far, [37,38] and if in that land of exile they turn to you again, and face toward this land you gave their fathers, and this city and your Temple I have built, and plead with you with all their hearts to forgive them, [39] then hear from heaven where you live and help them and forgive your people who have sinned against you.

[40] "Yes, O my God, be wide awake and attentive to all the prayers made to you in this place. [41] And now, O Lord God, arise and enter this resting place of yours where the Ark of your strength has been placed. Let your priests, O Lord God, be clothed with salvation, and let your saints rejoice in your kind deeds. [42] O Lord God, do not ignore me—do not turn your face away from me, your anointed one. Oh, remember your love for David and your kindness to him."

7 AS SOLOMON FINISHED praying, fire flashed down from heaven and burned up the sacrifices! And the glory of the Lord filled the Temple, so that the priests couldn't enter! [3] All the people had been watching and now they fell flat on the pavement, and worshiped and thanked the Lord.

"How good he is!" they exclaimed. "He is always so loving and kind."

---

b Or, "as long as they are living in this land which you gave to our fathers."

⁴,⁵ Then the king and all the people dedicated the Temple by sacrificing burnt offerings to the Lord. King Solomon's contribution for this purpose was 22,000 oxen and 120,000 sheep. ⁶ The priests were standing at their posts of duty, and the Levites were playing their thanksgiving song, "His Lovingkindness Is Forever," using the musical instruments that King David himself had made and had used to praise the Lord. Then, when the priests blew the trumpets, all the people stood again. ⁷ Solomon consecrated the inner court of the Temple for use that day as a place of sacrifice, for there were too many sacrifices for the bronze altar to accommodate.

⁸ For the next seven days, they celebrated the Tabernacle Festival, with large crowds coming in from all over Israel; they arrived from as far away as Hamath at one end of the country to the brook of Egypt at the other. ⁹ A final religious service was held on the eighth day. ¹⁰ Then, on October 7, he sent the people home, joyful and happy because the Lord had been so good to David and Solomon and to his people Israel.

¹¹ So Solomon finished building the Temple as well as his own palace. He completed what he had planned to do.

¹² One night the Lord appeared to Solomon and told him, "I have heard your prayer and have chosen this Temple as the place where I want you to sacrifice to me. ¹³ If I shut up the heavens so that there is no rain, or if I command the locust swarms to eat up all of your crops, or if I send an epidemic among you, ¹⁴ then if my people will humble themselves and pray, and search for me, and turn from their wicked ways, I will hear them from heaven and forgive their sins and heal their land. ¹⁵ I will listen, wide awake, to every prayer made in this place. ¹⁶ For I have chosen this Temple and sanctified it to be my home forever; my eyes and my heart shall always be here.

¹⁷ "As for yourself, if you follow me as your father David did, ¹⁸ then I will see to it that you and your descendants will always be the kings of Israel; ¹⁹ but if you don't follow me, if you refuse the laws I have given you, and worship idols, ²⁰ then I will destroy my people from this land of mine which I have given them, and this Temple shall be destroyed even though I have sanctified it for myself. Instead, I will make it a public horror and disgrace. ²¹ Instead of its being famous, all who pass by will be incredulous.

" 'Why has the Lord done such a terrible thing to this land and to this Temple?' they will ask.

²² "And the answer will be, 'Because his people abandoned the Lord God of their fathers, the God who brought them out of the land of Egypt, and they worshiped other gods instead. That is why he has done all this to them.' "

8 IT WAS NOW twenty years since Solomon had become king, and the great building projects of the Lord's Temple and his own royal palace were completed. ² He now turned his energies to rebuilding the cities which King Hiram of Tyre had given to him, and he relocated some of the people of Israel into them. ³ It was at this time, too, that Solomon fought against the city of Hamath-zobah and conquered it. ⁴ He built Tadmor in the desert, and built cities in Hamath as supply centers. ⁵ He fortified the cities of upper Beth-horon and lower Beth-horon, both being supply centers, building their walls and installing barred gates. ⁶ He also built Baalath and other supply centers at this time, and constructed cities where his chariots and horses were kept. He built to his heart's desire in Jerusalem and Lebanon and throughout the entire realm.

⁷,⁸ He began the practice that still continues of conscripting as slave laborers the Hittites, Amorites, Perizzites, Hivites, and Jebusites—the descendants of those nations which the Israelis had not completely wiped out. ⁹ However, he didn't make slaves of any of the Israeli citizens, but used them as soldiers, officers, charioteers, and cavalrymen; ¹⁰ also, two hundred fifty of them were government officials who administered all public affairs.

¹¹ Solomon now moved his wife (she was Pharaoh's daughter) from the City of David sector of Jerusalem to the new palace he had built for her. For he said, "She must not live in King David's palace, for the Ark of the Lord was there and it is holy ground."

¹² Then Solomon sacrificed burnt offerings to the Lord on the altar he had built in front of the porch of the Temple. ¹³ The number of sacrifices differed from day to day in accordance with the instructions Moses had given; there were extra sacrifices on the Sabbaths, on new moon festivals, and at the three annual festivals—the Passover celebration, the Festival of Weeks, and the Festival of Tabernacles. ¹⁴ In assigning the priests to their posts of duty he followed the organizational chart prepared by his father David; he also assigned the Levites to their work of praise and of helping the priests in each day's duties; and he assigned the gatekeepers to their gates. ¹⁵ Solomon did not deviate in any way from David's instructions concerning these matters and concerning the treasury personnel. ¹⁶ Thus Solomon successfully completed the construction of the Temple.

¹⁷,¹⁸ Then he went to the seaport towns of Ezion-geber and Eloth, in Edom, to launch a fleet presented to him by King Hiram. These ships, with King Hiram's experienced crews working alongside Solomon's men, went to Ophir and brought back $13,000,000 worth of gold to him!

9 WHEN THE QUEEN of Sheba heard of Solomon's fabled wisdom, she came to Jerusalem to test him with hard questions. A very great retinue of aides and servants accompanied her, including camel-loads of spices, gold, and jewels. ² And Solomon answered all her problems. Nothing was hidden from him; he could explain everything to her. ³ When she discovered how wise he really was, and how breathtaking the beauty of his palace, ⁴ and how wonderful the food at his tables, and how many servants and aides he had, and when she saw their spectacular uniforms and his stewards in full regalia, and saw the size of the men in his bodyguard, she could scarcely believe it! ⁵ Finally she exclaimed to the king, "Everything I heard about you in my own country is true! ⁶ I didn't believe it until I got here and saw it with my own eyes. Your wisdom is far greater than I could ever have imagined. ⁷ What a privilege for these men of yours to stand here and listen to you talk! ⁸ Blessed be the Lord your God! How he

must love Israel to give them a just king like you! He wants them to be a great, strong nation forever."

⁹ She gave the king a gift of over a million dollars in gold, and great quantities of spices of incomparable quality, and many, many jewels.

¹⁰ King Hiram's and King Solomon's crews brought gold from Ophir, also sandalwood and jewels. ¹¹ The king used the sandalwood to make terraced steps for the Temple and the palace, and to construct harps and lyres for the choir. Never before had there been such beautiful instruments in all the land of Judah.

¹² King Solomon gave the Queen of Sheba gifts of the same value as she had brought to him, plus everything else she asked for! Then she and her retinue returned to their own land.

¹³,¹⁴ Solomon received a billion dollars worth of gold each year from the kings of Arabia and many other lands that paid annual tribute to him. In addition, there was a trade balance from the exports of his merchants. ¹⁵ He used some of the gold to make 200 large shields, each worth $280,000, ¹⁶ and 300 smaller shields, each worth $140,000. The king placed these in the Forest of Lebanon Room in his palace. ¹⁷ He also made a huge ivory throne overlaid with pure gold. ¹⁸ It had six gold steps and a footstool of gold; also gold armrests, each flanked by a gold lion. ¹⁹ Gold lions also stood at each side of each step. No other throne in all the world could be compared with it! ²⁰ All of King Solomon's cups were solid gold, as were all the furnishings in the Forest of Lebanon Room. Silver was too cheap to count for much in those days! ²¹ Every three years the king sent his ships to Tarshish, using sailors supplied by King Hiram, to bring back gold, silver, ivory, apes, and peacocks.

²² So King Solomon was richer and wiser than any other king in all the earth. ²³ Kings from every nation came to visit him, and to hear the wisdom God had put into his heart. ²⁴ Each brought him annual tribute of silver and gold bowls, clothing, armor, spices, horses, and mules.

²⁵ In addition, Solomon had 4,000 stalls of horses and chariots, and 12,000 cavalry-

men stationed in the chariot cities, as well as in Jerusalem to protect the king. [26] He ruled over all kings and kingdoms from the Euphrates River to the land of the Philistines and as far away as the border of Egypt. [27] He made silver become as plentiful in Jerusalem as stones in the road! And cedar was used as though it were common sycamore. [28] Horses were brought to him from Egypt and other countries.

[29] The rest of Solomon's biography is written in the history of Nathan the prophet and in the prophecy of Ahijah the Shilonite, and also in the visions of Iddo the seer concerning Jeroboam the son of Nebat.

[30] So Solomon reigned in Jerusalem over all of Israel for forty years. [31] Then he died and was buried in Jerusalem, and his son Rehoboam became the new king.

10 ALL THE LEADERS of Israel came to Shechem for Rehoboam's coronation. [2,3] Meanwhile, friends of Jeroboam (son of Nebat) sent word to him of Solomon's death. He was in Egypt at the time, where he had gone to escape from King Solomon. He now quickly returned, and was present at the coronation, and led the people's demands on Rehoboam:

[4] "Your father was a hard master," they said. "Be easier on us than he was, and we will let you be our king!"

[5] Rehoboam told them to return in three days for his decision. [6] He discussed their demand with the old men who had counseled his father Solomon.

"What shall I tell them?" he asked.

[7] "If you want to be their king," they replied, "you will have to give them a favorable reply and treat them with kindness."

[8,9] But he rejected their advice and asked the opinion of the young men who had grown up with him. "What do you fellows think I should do?" he asked. "Shall I be easier on them than my father was?"

[10] "No!" they replied. "Tell them, 'If you think my father was hard on you, just wait and see what I'll be like!' Tell them, 'My little finger is thicker than my father's loins! [11] I am going to be tougher on you, not easier! My father used whips on you, but I'll

use scorpions!' "

[12] So when Jeroboam and the people returned in three days to hear King Rehoboam's decision, [13] he spoke roughly to them; for he refused the advice of the old men, [14] and followed the counsel of the younger ones.

"My father gave you heavy burdens but I will give you heavier!" he told them. "My father punished you with whips, but I will punish you with scorpions!"

[15] So the king turned down the people's demands. (God caused him to do it in order to fulfill his prediction[a] spoken to Jeroboam by Ahijah, the Shilonite.) [16] When the people realized what the king was saying they turned around and deserted him.

"Forget David and his dynasty!" they shouted angrily. "We'll get someone else to be our king. Let Rehoboam rule his own tribe of Judah! Let's go home!" So they did.

[17] The people of the tribe of Judah, however, remained loyal to Rehoboam. [18] Afterwards, when King Rehoboam sent Hadoram to draft forced labor from the other tribes of Israel, the people stoned him to death. When this news reached King Rehoboam he jumped into his chariot and fled to Jerusalem. [19] And Israel has refused to be ruled by a descendant of David to this day.

11 UPON ARRIVAL AT Jerusalem, Rehoboam mobilized the armies of Judah and Benjamin, 180,000 strong, and declared war against the rest of Israel in an attempt to reunite the kingdom.

[2] But the Lord told Shemaiah the prophet,

[3] "Go and say to King Rehoboam of Judah, Solomon's son, and to the people of Judah and of Benjamin:

[4] " 'The Lord says, Do not fight against your brothers. Go home, for I am behind their rebellion.' " So they obeyed the Lord and refused to fight against Jeroboam.

[5-10] Rehoboam stayed in Jerusalem and fortified these cities of Judah with walls and gates to protect himself:

Bethlehem, Etam, Tekoa,

_____

a See 1 Kings 11:30, 31.

Beth-zur, Soco, Adullam,
Gath, Mareshah, Ziph,
Adoraim, Lachish, Azekah,
Zorah, Aijalon, and Hebron.
[11] He also rebuilt and strengthened the forts, and manned them with companies of soldiers under their officers, and stored them with food, olive oil, and wine. [12] Shields and spears were placed in armories in every city as a further safety measure. For only Judah and Benjamin remained loyal to him.

[13,14] However, the priests and Levites from the other tribes now abandoned their homes and moved to Judah and Jerusalem, for King Jeroboam had fired them, telling them to stop being priests of the Lord. [15] He had appointed other priests instead who encouraged the people to worship idols instead of God, and to sacrifice to carved statues of goats and calves which he placed on the hills. [16] Laymen, too, from all over Israel began moving to Jerusalem where they could freely worship the Lord God of their fathers, and sacrifice to him. [17] This strengthened the kingdom of Judah, so King Rehoboam survived for three years without difficulty; for during those years there was an earnest effort to obey the Lord as King David and King Solomon had done.[a]

[18] Rehoboam married his cousin[b] Mahalath. She was the daughter of David's son Jerimoth and of Abihail, the daughter of David's brother Eliab. [19] Three sons were born from this marriage—Jeush, Shemariah, and Zaham.

[20] Later he married Maacah, the daughter of Absalom. The children she bore him were Abijah, Attai, Ziza, and Shelomith. [21] He loved Maacah more than any of his other wives and concubines (he had eighteen wives and sixty concubines—with twenty-eight sons and sixty daughters). [22] Maacah's son Abijah was his favorite, and he intended to make him the next king. [23] He very wisely scattered his other sons in the fortified cities throughout the land of Judah and Benjamin, and gave them large allowances and arranged for them to have several wives apiece.

12 BUT JUST WHEN Rehoboam was at the height of his popularity and power he abandoned the Lord, and the people followed him in this sin. [2] As a result, King Shishak of Egypt attacked Jerusalem in the fifth year of King Rehoboam's reign, [3] with twelve hundred chariots, sixty thousand cavalrymen and an unnumbered host of infantrymen—Egyptians, Libyans, Sukkiim, and Ethiopians. [4] He quickly conquered Judah's fortified cities and soon arrived at Jerusalem.

[5] The prophet Shemaiah now met with Rehoboam and the Judean leaders from every part of the nation (they had fled to Jerusalem for safety), and told them, "The Lord says, 'You have forsaken me, so I have forsaken you and abandoned you to Shishak.' "

[6] Then the king and the leaders of Israel confessed their sins and exclaimed, "The Lord is right in doing this to us!"

[7] And when the Lord saw them humble themselves he sent Shemaiah to tell them, "Because you have humbled yourselves, I will not completely destroy you; some will escape. I will not use Shishak to pour out my anger upon Jerusalem. [8] But you must pay annual tribute to him. Then you will realize how much better it is to serve me than to serve him!"

[9] So King Shishak of Egypt conquered Jerusalem and took away all the treasures of the Temple and of the palace, also all of Solomon's gold shields. [10] King Rehoboam replaced them with bronze shields and committed them to the care of the captain of his bodyguard. [11] Whenever the king went to the Temple, the guards would carry them, and afterwards return them to the armory. [12] When the king humbled himself, the Lord's anger was turned aside and he didn't send total destruction; in fact, even after Shishak's invasion, the economy of Judah remained strong.

[13] King Rehoboam reigned seventeen years in Jerusalem, the city God had chosen as his residence after considering all the other cities of Israel. He had become king at the age of forty-one, and his mother's name was Naamah the Ammonitess. [14] But

---

a Literally, "they walked in the way of David and Solomon."   b Implied.

he was an evil king, for he never did decide really to please the Lord. [15] The complete biography of Rehoboam is recorded in the histories written by Shemaiah the prophet and by Iddo the seer, and in *The Genealogical Register.*

There were continual wars between Rehoboam and Jeroboam. [16] When Rehoboam died he was buried in Jerusalem, and his son Abijah became the new king.

13 ABIJAH BECAME THE new king of Judah, in Jerusalem, in the eighteenth year of the reign of King Jeroboam of Israel. He lasted three years. His mother's name was Micaiah (daughter of Uriel of Gibeah).

Early in his reign war broke out between Judah and Israel. [3] Judah, led by King Abijah, fielded 400,000 seasoned warriors against twice as many Israeli troops—strong, courageous men led by King Jeroboam. [4] When the army of Judah arrived at Mount Zemaraim, in the hill country of Ephraim, King Abijah shouted to King Jeroboam and the Israeli army:

[5] "Listen! Don't you realize that the Lord God of Israel swore that David's descendants would always be the kings of Israel? [6] Your King Jeroboam is a mere servant of David's son, and was a traitor to his master. [7] Then a whole gang of worthless rebels joined him, defying Solomon's son Rehoboam, for he was young and frightened and couldn't stand up to them. [8] Do you really think you can defeat the kingdom of the Lord that is led by a descendant of David? Your army is twice as large as mine, but you are cursed with those gold calves you have with you, that Jeroboam made for you—he calls them your gods! [9] And you have driven away the priests of the Lord and the Levites, and have appointed heathen priests instead. Just like the people of other lands, you accept as priests anybody who comes along with a young bullock and seven rams for consecration. Anyone at all can be a priest of these no-gods of yours!

[10] "But as for us, the Lord is our God and we have not forsaken him. Only the descendants of Aaron are our priests, and the Levites alone may help them in their work. [11] They burn sacrifices to the Lord every morning and evening—burnt offerings and sweet incense; and they place the Bread of the Presence upon the holy table. The golden lampstand is lighted every night, for we are careful to follow the instructions of the Lord our God; but you have forsaken him. [12] So you see, God is with us; he is our Leader. His priests, trumpeting as they go, will lead us into battle against you. O people of Israel, do not fight against the Lord God of your fathers, for you will not succeed!"

[13,14] Meanwhile, Jeroboam had secretly sent part of his army around behind the men of Judah to ambush them; so Judah was surrounded, with the enemy before and behind them. Then they cried out to the Lord for mercy, and the priests blew the trumpets. [15,16] The men of Judah began to shout. And as they shouted, God used King Abijah and the men of Judah to turn the tide of battle against King Jeroboam and the army of Israel, [17] and they slaughtered 500,000 elite troops of Israel that day.

[18,19] So Judah, depending upon the Lord God of their fathers, defeated Israel, and chased King Jeroboam's troops, and captured some of his cities—Bethel, Jeshanah, Ephron, and their suburbs. [20] King Jeroboam of Israel never regained his power during Abijah's lifetime, and eventually the Lord struck him and he died.

[21] Meanwhile, King Abijah of Judah became very strong. He married fourteen wives and had twenty-two sons and sixteen daughters. [22] His complete biography and speeches are recorded in the prophet Iddo's *History of Judah.*

14 KING ABIJAH WAS buried in Jerusalem. Then his son Asa became the new king of Judah, and there was peace in the land for the first ten years of his reign, [2] for Asa was careful to obey the Lord his God. [3] He demolished the heathen altars on the hills, and broke down the obelisks, and chopped down the shameful Asherim-idols, [4] and demanded that the entire nation obey the commandments of the Lord God of their ancestors. [5] Also, he removed the sun-images from the hills, and the incense altars from every one of Judah's cities. That is why God gave his kingdom peace. [6] This

made it possible for him to build walled cities throughout Judah.

⁷ "Now is the time to do it, while the Lord is blessing us with peace because of our obedience to him," he told his people. "Let us build and fortify cities now, with walls, towers, gates, and bars." So they went ahead with these projects very successfully.

⁸ King Asa's Judean army was 300,000 strong, equipped with light shields and spears. His army of Benjaminites numbered 280,000, armed with large shields and bows. Both armies were composed of well-trained, brave men. ⁹,¹⁰ But now he was attacked by an army of 1,000,000 troops from Ethiopia with 300 chariots, under the leadership of General Zerah. They advanced to the city of Mareshah, in the valley of Zephathah, and King Asa sent his troops to meet them there.

¹¹ "O Lord," he cried out to God, "no one else can help us! Here we are, powerless against this mighty army. Oh, help us, Lord our God! For we trust in you alone to rescue us, and in your name we attack this vast horde. Don't let mere men defeat you!"

¹² Then the Lord defeated the Ethiopians, and Asa and the army of Judah triumphed as the Ethiopians fled. ¹³ They chased them as far as Gerar, and the entire Ethiopian army was wiped out so that not one man remained; for the Lord and his army destroyed them all. Then the army of Judah carried off vast quantities of plunder. ¹⁴ While they were at Gerar they attacked all the cities in that area, and terror from the Lord came upon the residents. As a result, additional vast quantities of plunder were collected from these cities too. ¹⁵ They not only plundered the cities, but destroyed the cattle tents and captured great herds of sheep and camels before finally returning to Jerusalem.

15 THEN THE SPIRIT of God came upon Azariah (son of Oded), ² and he went out to meet King Asa as he was returning from the battle.

"Listen to me, Asa! Listen, armies of Judah and Benjamin!" he shouted. "The Lord will stay with you as long as you stay with him! Whenever you look for him, you will find him. But if you forsake him, he will forsake you. ³ For a long time now, over in Israel, the people haven't worshiped the true God, and have not had a true priest to teach them. They have lived without God's laws. ⁴ But whenever they have turned again to the Lord God of Israel in their distress, and searched for him, he has helped them. ⁵ In their times of rebellion against God there was no peace. Problems troubled the nation on every hand. Crime was on the increase everywhere. ⁶ There were external wars, and internal fighting of city against city, for God was plaguing them with all sorts of trouble. ⁷ But you men of Judah, keep up the good work and don't get discouraged, for you will be rewarded."

⁸ When King Asa heard this message from God, he took courage and destroyed all the idols in the land of Judah and Benjamin, and in the cities he had captured in the hill country of Ephraim, and he rebuilt the altar of the Lord in front of the Temple.

⁹ Then he summoned all the people of Judah and Benjamin, and the immigrants from Israel (for many had come from the territories of Ephraim, Manasseh, and Simeon, in Israel, when they saw that the Lord God was with King Asa). ¹⁰ They all came to Jerusalem in June of the fifteenth year of King Asa's reign, ¹¹ and sacrificed to the Lord seven hundred oxen and seven thousand sheep—it was part of the plunder they had captured in the battle. ¹² Then they entered into a contract to worship only the Lord God of their fathers, ¹³ and agreed that anyone who refused to do this must die— whether old or young, man or woman. ¹⁴ They shouted out their oath of loyalty to God with trumpets blaring and horns sounding. ¹⁵ All were happy for this covenant with God, for they had entered into it with all their hearts and wills, and wanted him above everything else, and they found him! And he gave them peace throughout the nation.

¹⁶ King Asa even removed his mother Maacah from being the queen mother because she made an Asherah-idol; he cut down the idol and crushed and burned it at Kidron Brook. ¹⁷ Over in Israel the idol-temples were not removed. But here in Judah and Benjamin the heart of King Asa was perfect before God throughout his life-

time. [18] He brought back into the Temple the silver and gold bowls which he and his father had dedicated to the Lord. [19] So there was no more war until the thirty-fifth year of King Asa's reign.

16 IN THE THIRTY-SIXTH year of King Asa's reign, King Baasha of Israel declared war on him and built the fortress[a] of Ramah in order to control the road to Judah. [2] Asa's response was to take the silver and gold from the Temple and from the palace, and to send it to King Ben-hadad of Syria, at Damascus, with this message: [3] "Let us renew the mutual security pact that there was between your father and my father. See, here is silver and gold to induce you to break your alliance with King Baasha of Israel, so that he will leave me alone."

[4] Ben-hadad agreed to King Asa's request and mobilized his armies to attack Israel. They destroyed the cities of Ijon, Dan, Abel-maim and all of the supply centers in Naphtali. [5] As soon as King Baasha of Israel heard what was happening, he discontinued building Ramah and gave up his plan to attack Judah. [6] Then King Asa and the people of Judah went out to Ramah and carried away the building stones and timbers and used them to build Geba and Mizpah instead.

[7] About that time the prophet Hanani came to King Asa and told him, "Because you have put your trust in the king of Syria instead of in the Lord your God, the army of the king of Syria has escaped from you. [8] Don't you remember what happened to the Ethiopians and Libyans and their vast army, with all of their chariots and cavalrymen? But you relied then on the Lord, and he delivered them all into your hand. [9] For the eyes of the Lord search back and forth across the whole earth, looking for people whose hearts are perfect toward him, so that he can show his great power in helping them. What a fool you have been! From now on you shall have wars."

[10] Asa was so angry with the prophet for saying this that he threw him into jail. And Asa oppressed all the people at that time.

[11] The rest of the biography of Asa is written in *The Annals of the Kings of Israel and Judah.* [12] In the thirty-ninth year of his reign, Asa became seriously diseased in his feet but he didn't go to the Lord with the problem, but to the doctors. [13,14] So he died in the forty-first year of his reign, and was buried in his own vault that he had hewn out for himself in Jerusalem. He was laid on a bed perfumed with sweet spices and ointments, and his people made a very great burning of incense for him at his funeral.

17 THEN HIS SON Jehoshaphat became the king and mobilized for war against Israel. [2] He placed garrisons in all of the fortified cities of Judah, in various other places throughout the country, and in the cities of Ephraim that his father had conquered.

[3] The Lord was with Jehoshaphat because he followed in the good footsteps of his father's early years, and did not worship idols. [4] He obeyed the commandments of his father's God—quite unlike the people across the border in the land of Israel. [5] So the Lord strengthened his position as king of Judah. All the people of Judah cooperated by paying their taxes, so he became very wealthy as well as being very popular. [6] He boldly followed the paths of God —even knocking down the heathen altars on the hills, and destroying the Asherim idols.

[7,8,9] In the third year of his reign he began a nationwide religious education program. He sent out top government officials as teachers in all the cities of Judah. These men included Ben-hail, Obadiah, Zechariah, Nethanel, and Micaiah. He also used the Levites for this purpose, including Shemaiah, Nethaniah, Zebadiah, Asahel, Shemiramoth, Jehonathan, Adonijah, Tobijah, and Tobadonijah; also the priests, Elishama and Jehoram. They took copies of *The Book of the Law of the Lord* to all the cities of Judah, to teach the Scriptures to the people.

[10] Then the fear of the Lord fell upon all the surrounding kingdoms so that none of them declared war on King Jehoshaphat.

---

a Literally, "high places."

¹¹ Even some of the Philistines brought him presents and annual tribute, and the Arabs donated 7,700 rams and 7,700 male goats. ¹² So Jehoshaphat became very strong, and built fortresses and supply cities throughout Judah.

¹³ His public works program was also extensive, and he had a huge army stationed at Jerusalem, his capital. ¹⁴,¹⁵ Three hundred thousand Judean troops were there under General Adnah. Next in command was Jeho-hanan with an army of 280,000 men. ¹⁶ Next was Amasiah (son of Zichri), a man of unusual piety, with 200,000 troops. ¹⁷ Benjamin supplied 200,000 men equipped with bows and shields under the command of Eliada, a great general. ¹⁸ His second in command was Jehozabad, with 180,000 trained men. ¹⁹ These were the troops in Jerusalem in addition to those placed by the king in the fortified cities throughout the nation.

18 BUT RICH, POPULAR King Jehoshaphat of Judah made a marriage alliance [for his sonª] with [the daughter ofª] King Ahab of Israel. ² A few years later he went down to Samaria to visit King Ahab, and King Ahab gave a great party for him and his aides, butchering great numbers of sheep and oxen for the feast. Then he asked King Jehoshaphat to join forces with him against Ramoth-gilead.

³,⁴,⁵ "Why, of course!" King Jehoshaphat replied. "I'm with you all the way. My troops are at your command! However, let's check with the Lord first."

So King Ahab summoned 400 of his heathen prophets and asked them, "Shall we go to war with Ramoth-gilead or not?"

And they replied, "Go ahead, for God will give you a great victory!"

⁶,⁷ But Jehoshaphat wasn't satisfied. "Isn't there some prophet of the Lord around here too?" he asked. "I'd like to ask him the same question."

"Well," Ahab told him, "there is one, but I hate him, for he never prophesies anything but evil! His name is Micaiah (son of Imlah)."

"Oh, come now, don't talk like that!"

Jehoshaphat exclaimed. "Let's hear what he has to say."

⁸ So the king of Israel called one of his aides. "Quick! Go and get Micaiah (son of Imlah)," he ordered.

⁹ The two kings were sitting on thrones in full regalia at an open place near the Samaria gate, and all the "prophets" were prophesying before them. ¹⁰ One of them, Zedekiah (son of Chenaanah), made some iron horns for the occasion and proclaimed, "The Lord says you will gore the Syrians to death with these!"

¹¹ And all the others agreed. "Yes," they chorused, "go up to Ramoth-gilead and prosper, for the Lord will cause you to conquer."

¹² The man who went to get Micaiah told him what was happening, and what all the prophets were saying—that the war would end in triumph for the king.

"I hope you will agree with them and give the king a favorable reading," the man ventured.

¹³ But Micaiah replied, "I vow by God that whatever God says is what I will say."

¹⁴ When he arrived before the king, the king asked him, "Micaiah, shall we go to war against Ramoth-gilead or not?"

And Micaiah replied, "Sure, go ahead! It will be a glorious victory!"

¹⁵ "Look here," the king said sharply, "how many times must I tell you to speak nothing except what the Lord tells you to?"

¹⁶ Then Micaiah told him, "In my vision I saw all Israel scattered upon the mountain as sheep without a shepherd. And the Lord said, 'Their master has been killed. Send them home.' "

¹⁷ "Didn't I tell you?" the king of Israel exclaimed to Jehoshaphat. "He does it every time. He *never* prophesies *anything* but evil against me."

¹⁸ "Listen to what else the Lord has told me," Micaiah continued. "I saw him upon his throne surrounded by vast throngs of angels.

¹⁹,²⁰ "And the Lord said, 'Who can get King Ahab to go to battle against Ramoth-gilead and be killed there?'

"There were many suggestions, but fi-

a Implied in 21:6.

395

nally a spirit stepped forward before the Lord and said, 'I can do it!'

" 'How?' the Lord asked him.

²¹ "He replied, 'I will be a lying spirit in the mouth of all of the king's prophets!'

" 'It will work,' the Lord said; 'go and do it.'

²² "So you see, the Lord has put a lying spirit in the mouth of these prophets of yours, when actually he has determined just the opposite of what they are telling you!"

²³ Then Zedekiah (son of Chenaanah) walked up to Micaiah and slapped him across the face. "You liar!" he yelled. "When did the Spirit of the Lord leave me and enter you?"

²⁴ "You'll find out soon enough," Micaiah replied, "—when you are hiding in an inner room!"

²⁵ "Arrest this man and take him back to Governor Amon and to my son Joash," the king of Israel ordered. ²⁶ "Tell them, 'The king says to put this fellow in prison and feed him with bread and water until I return safely from the battle!' "

²⁷ Micaiah replied, "If you return safely, the Lord has not spoken through me." Then, turning to those around them, he remarked, "Take note of what I have said."

²⁸ So the king of Israel and the king of Judah led their armies to Ramoth-gilead.

²⁹ The king of Israel said to Jehoshaphat, "I'll disguise myself so that no one will recognize me, but you put on your royal robes!" So that is what they did.

³⁰ Now the king of Syria had issued these instructions to his charioteers: "Ignore everyone but the king of Israel!"

³¹ So when the Syrian charioteers saw King Jehoshaphat of Judah in his royal robes, they went for him, supposing that he was the man they were after. But Jehoshaphat cried out to the Lord to save him, and the Lord made the charioteers see their mistake and leave him. ³² For as soon as they realized he was not the king of Israel, they stopped chasing him. ³³ But one of the Syrian soldiers shot an arrow haphazardly at the Israeli troops, and it struck the king of Israel at the opening where the lower armor and the breastplate meet. "Get me out of here," he groaned to the driver of his chariot, "for I am badly wounded." ³⁴ The

battle grew hotter and hotter all that day, and King Ahab went back in, propped up in his chariot, to fight the Syrians, but just as the sun sank into the western skies, he died.

19 AS KING JEHOSHAPHAT of Judah returned home, uninjured, ² the prophet Jehu (son of Hanani) went out to meet him.

"Should you be helping the wicked, and loving those who hate the Lord?" he asked him. "Because of what you have done, God's wrath is upon you. ³ But there are some good things about you, in that you got rid of the shame-idols throughout the land, and you have tried to be faithful to God."

⁴ So Jehoshaphat made no more trips to Israel after that, but remained quietly at Jerusalem. Later he went out again among the people, traveling from Beer-sheba to the hill country of Ephraim to encourage them to worship the God of their ancestors. ⁵ He appointed judges throughout the nation in all the larger cities, ⁶ and instructed them: "Watch your step—I have not appointed you—God has; and he will stand beside you and help you give justice in each case that comes before you. ⁷ Be very much afraid to give any other decision than what God tells you to. For there must be no injustice among God's judges, no partiality, no taking of bribes."

⁸ Jehoshaphat set up courts in Jerusalem, too, with the Levites and priests and clan leaders and judges. ⁹ These were his instructions to them: "You are to act always in the fear of God, with honest hearts. ¹⁰ Whenever a case is referred to you by the judges out in the provinces, whether murder cases or other violations of the laws and ordinances of God, you are to clarify the evidence for them and help them to decide justly, lest the wrath of God come down upon you and them; if you do this, you will discharge your responsibility."

¹¹ Then he appointed Amariah, the High Priest, to be the court of final appeal in cases involving violation of sacred affairs; and Zebadiah (son of Ishmael), a ruler in Judah, as the court of final appeal in all civil cases; with the Levites as their assistants. "Be fearless in your stand for truth and honesty.

And may God use you to defend the innocent," was his final word to them.

20 LATER ON, THE armies of the kings of Moab, Ammon, and of the Meunites declared war on Jehoshaphat and the people of Judah. ² Word reached Jehoshaphat that "a vast army is marching against you from beyond the Salt Sea, from Syria. It is already at Hazazon-tamar" (also called Engedi). ³ Jehoshaphat was badly shaken by this news and determined to beg for help from the Lord; so he announced that all the people of Judah should go without food for a time, in penitence and intercession before God. ⁴ People from all across the nation came to Jerusalem to plead unitedly with him. ⁵ Jehoshaphat stood among them as they gathered at the new court of the Temple, and prayed this prayer:

⁶ "O Lord God of our fathers—the only God in all the heavens, the Ruler of all the kingdoms of the earth—you are so powerful, so mighty. Who can stand against you? ⁷ O our God, didn't you drive out the heathen who lived in this land when your people arrived? And didn't you give this land forever to the descendants of your friend Abraham? ⁸ Your people settled here and built this Temple for you, ⁹ truly believing that in a time like this—whenever we are faced with any calamity such as war, disease, or famine—we can stand here before this Temple and before you—for you are here in this Temple—and cry out to you to save us; and that you will hear us and rescue us.

¹⁰ "And now see what the armies of Ammon, Moab, and Mount Seir are doing. You wouldn't let our ancestors invade those nations when Israel left Egypt, so we went around and didn't destroy them. ¹¹ Now see how they reward us! For they have come to throw us out of your land which you have given us. ¹² O our God, won't you stop them? We have no way to protect ourselves against this mighty army. We don't know what to do, but we are looking to you."

¹³ As the people from every part of Judah stood before the Lord with their little ones, wives, and children, ¹⁴ the Spirit of the Lord came upon one of the men standing there—Jahaziel (son of Zechariah, son of Benaiah,

son of Je-iel, son of Mattaniah the Levite, who was one of the sons of Asaph).

¹⁵ "Listen to me, all you people of Judah and Jerusalem, and you, O king Jehoshaphat!" he exclaimed. "The Lord says, 'Don't be afraid! Don't be paralyzed by this mighty army! For the battle is not yours, but God's! ¹⁶ Tomorrow, go down and attack them! You will find them coming up the slopes of Ziz at the end of the valley that opens into the wilderness of Jeruel. ¹⁷ But you will not need to fight! Take your places; stand quietly and see the incredible rescue operation God will perform for you, O people of Judah and Jerusalem! Don't be afraid or discouraged! Go out there tomorrow, for the Lord is with you!' "

¹⁸ Then King Jehoshaphat fell to the ground with his face to the earth, and all the people of Judah and the people of Jerusalem did the same, worshiping the Lord. ¹⁹ Then the Levites of the Kohath clan and the Korah clan stood to praise the Lord God of Israel with songs of praise that rang out strong and clear.

²⁰ Early the next morning the army of Judah went out into the wilderness of Tekoa. On the way Jehoshaphat stopped and called them to attention. "Listen to me, O people of Judah and Jerusalem," he said. "Believe in the Lord your God, and you shall have success! Believe his prophets, and everything will be all right!"

²¹ After consultation with the leaders of the people, he determined that there should be a choir leading the march, clothed in sanctified garments and singing the song "His Lovingkindness Is Forever" as they walked along praising and thanking the Lord! ²² And at the moment they began to sing and to praise, the Lord caused the armies of Ammon, Moab, and Mount Seir to begin fighting among themselves, and they destroyed each other! ²³ For the Ammonites and Moabites turned against their allies from Mount Seir and killed every one of them. And when they had finished that job, they turned against each other! ²⁴ So, when the army of Judah arrived at the watchtower that looks out over the wilderness, as far as they could look there were dead bodies lying on the ground—not a single one of the enemy had escaped. ²⁵ King Je-

hoshaphat and his people went out to plunder the bodies and came away loaded with money, garments, and jewels stripped from the corpses—so much that it took them three days to cart it all away! ²⁶ On the fourth day they gathered in the Valley of Blessing, as it is called today, and how they praised the Lord!

²⁷ Then they returned to Jerusalem, with Jehoshaphat leading them, full of joy that the Lord had given them this marvelous rescue from their enemies. ²⁸ They marched into Jerusalem accompanied by a band of harps, lyres, and trumpets and proceeded to the Temple. ²⁹ And as had happened before, when the surrounding kingdoms heard that the Lord himself had fought against the enemies of Israel, the fear of God fell upon them. ³⁰ So Jehoshaphat's kingdom was quiet, for his God had given him rest.

³¹ A thumbnail sketch of King Jehoshaphat: He became king of Judah when he was thirty-five years old, and reigned twenty-five years, in Jerusalem. His mother's name was Azubah, the daughter of Shilhi. ³² He was a good king, just as his father Asa was. He continually tried to follow the Lord, ³³ with the exception that he did not destroy the idol shrines on the hills, nor had the people as yet really decided to follow the God of their ancestors.

³⁴ The details of Jehoshaphat's reign from first to last are written in the history of Jehu the son of Hanani, which is inserted in *The Annals of the Kings of Israel.*

³⁵ But at the close of his life, Jehoshaphat, king of Judah, went into partnership with Ahaziah, king of Israel, who was a very wicked man. ³⁶ They made ships in Ezion-geber to sail to Tarshish. ³⁷ Then Eliezer, son of Dodavahu from Mareshah, prophesied against Jehoshaphat, telling him, "Because you have allied yourself with King Ahaziah, the Lord has destroyed your work." So the ships met disaster and never arrived at Tarshish.

21 WHEN JEHOSHAPHAT DIED, he was buried in the cemetery of the kings in Jerusalem, and his son Jehoram became the new ruler of Judah. ² His brothers—other sons of Jehoshaphat—were Azariah, Jehiel, Zechariah, Azariah, Michael, and Shephatiah. ^{3,4} Their father had given each of them valuable gifts of money and jewels, also the ownership of some of the fortified cities of Judah. However, he gave the kingship to Jehoram because he was the oldest. But when Jehoram had become solidly established as king, he killed all of his brothers and many other leaders of Israel. ⁵ He was thirty-two years old when he began to reign, and he reigned eight years, in Jerusalem. ⁶ But he was as wicked as the kings who were over in Israel. Yes, as wicked as Ahab, for Jehoram had married one of the daughters of Ahab, and his whole life was one constant binge of doing evil. ⁷ However, the Lord was unwilling to end the dynasty of David, for he had made a covenant with David always to have one of his descendants upon the throne.

⁸ At that time the king of Edom revolted, declaring his independence of Judah. ⁹ Jehoram attacked him with his full army and with all of his chariots, marching by night, and almost^a managed to subdue him. ¹⁰ But to this day Edom has been successful in throwing off the yoke of Judah. Libnah revolted too, because Jehoram had turned away from the Lord God of his fathers. ¹¹ What's more, Jehoram constructed idol shrines in the mountains of Judah, and led the people of Jerusalem in worshiping idols; in fact, he compelled his people to worship them.

¹² Then Elijah the prophet wrote him this letter: "The Lord God of your ancestor David says that because you have not followed in the good ways of your father Jehoshaphat, nor the good ways of King Asa, ¹³ but you have been as evil as the kings over in Israel, and have made the people of Jerusalem and Judah worship idols just as in the times of King Ahab, and because you have killed your brothers who were better than you, ¹⁴ now the Lord will destroy your nation with a great plague. You, your children, your wives, and all that you have will be struck down. ¹⁵ You will be stricken with an intestinal disease and your bowels will rot away."

---

a Literally, "Jehoram . . . struck down the Edomites. . . . Nevertheless Edom . . . revolted. . . ."

[16] Then the Lord stirred up the Philistines and the Arabs living next to the Ethiopians to attack Jehoram. [17] They marched against Judah, broke across the border, and carried away everything of value in the king's palace, including his sons and his wives; only his youngest son, Jehoahaz, escaped.

[18] It was after this that Jehovah struck him down with the incurable bowel disease. [19] In the process of time, at the end of two years, his intestines came out and he died in terrible suffering. (The customary pomp and ceremony was omitted at his funeral.) [20] He was thirty-two years old when he began to reign and he reigned in Jerusalem eight years, and died unmourned. He was buried in Jerusalem, but not in the royal cemetery.

22 THEN THE PEOPLE of Jerusalem chose Ahaziah,[a] his youngest son, as their new king (for the marauding bands of Arabs had killed his older sons). [2] Ahaziah was twenty-two years old[b] when he began to reign, and he reigned one year, in Jerusalem. His mother's name was Athaliah, granddaughter of Omri. [3] He, too, walked in the evil ways of Ahab, for his mother encouraged him in doing wrong. [4] Yes, he was as evil as Ahab, for Ahab's family became his advisors after his father's death, and they led him on to ruin.

[5] Following their evil advice, Ahaziah made an alliance with King Jehoram of Israel (the son of Ahab), who was at war with King Hazael of Syria at Ramoth-gilead. Ahaziah led his army there to join the battle. King Jehoram of Israel was wounded, [6] and returned to Jezreel to recover. Ahaziah went to visit him, [7] but this turned out to be a fatal mistake; for God had decided to punish Ahaziah for his alliance with Jehoram. It was during this visit that Ahaziah went out with Jehoram to challenge Jehu (son of Nimshi), whom the Lord had appointed to end the dynasty of Ahab.

[8] While Jehu was hunting down and killing the family and friends of Ahab, he met King Ahaziah's nephews, the princes of Judah, and killed them. [9] As he and his men were searching for Ahaziah, they found him hiding in the city of Samaria, and brought him to Jehu, who killed him. Even so, Ahaziah was given a royal burial because he was the grandson of King Jehoshaphat—a man who enthusiastically served the Lord. None of his sons, however, except for Joash, lived to succeed him as king, [10] for their grandmother Athaliah killed them when she heard the news of her son Ahaziah's death.

[11] Joash was rescued by his Aunt Jehoshabeath, who was King Ahaziah's sister[c], and was hidden away in a storage room in the Temple. She was a daughter of King Jehoram, and the wife of Jehoiada the priest. [12] Joash remained hidden in the Temple for six years while Athaliah reigned as queen. He was cared for by his nurse and by his aunt and uncle.

23 IN THE SEVENTH year of the reign of Queen Athaliah, Jehoiada the priest got up his courage and took some of the army officers into his confidence: Azariah (son of Jeroham), Ishmael (son of Jehohanan), Azariah (son of Obed), Maaseiah (son of Adaiah), and Elishaphat (son of Zichri). [2,3] These men traveled out across the nation secretly, to tell the Levites and clan leaders about his plans and to summon them to Jerusalem. On arrival they swore allegiance to the young king, who was still in hiding at the Temple.

"At last the time has come for the king's son to reign!" Jehoiada exclaimed. "The Lord's promise—that a descendant of King David shall be our king—will be true again. [4] This is how we'll proceed: A third of you priests and Levites who come off duty on the Sabbath will stay at the entrance as guards. [5,6] Another third will go over to the palace, and a third will be at the Lower Gate. Everyone else must stay in the outer courts of the Temple, as required by God's laws. For only the priests and Levites on duty may enter the Temple itself, for they are sanctified. [7] You Levites, form a bodyguard for the king, weapons in hand, and kill any unauthorized person entering the

---

a Also called "Jehoahaz."   b Literally, "forty-two years old"; but see 2 Kings 8:26.
c Literally, "the king's daughter," i.e., King Jehoram's daughter, verse 11.

Temple. Stay right beside the king."

⁸ So all the arrangements were made. Each of the three leaders led a third of the priests arriving for duty that Sabbath, and a third of those whose week's work was done and were going off duty—for Jehoiada the chief priest didn't release them to go home. ⁹ Then Jehoiada issued spears and shields to all the army officers. These had once belonged to King David and were stored in the Temple. ¹⁰ These officers, fully armed, formed a line from one side to the other in front of the Temple and around the altar in the outer court. ¹¹ Then they brought out the little prince and placed the crown upon his head and handed him a copy of the law of God, and proclaimed him king.

A great shout went up, "Long live the king!" as Jehoiada and his sons anointed him.

¹² When Queen Athaliah heard all the noise and commotion, and the shouts of praise to the king, she rushed over to the Temple to see what was going on—and there stood the king by his pillar at the entrance, with the army officers and the trumpeters surrounding him, and people from all over the land rejoicing and blowing trumpets, and the singers singing, accompanied by an orchestra leading the people in a great psalm of praise.

Athaliah ripped her clothes and screamed, "Treason! Treason!"

¹³,¹⁴ "Take her out and kill her," Jehoiada the priest shouted to the army officers. "Don't do it here at the Temple. And kill anyone who tries to help her."

¹⁵,¹⁶,¹⁷ So the crowd opened up for them to take her out and they killed her at the palace stables.

Then Jehoiada made a solemn contract that he and the king and the people would be the Lord's. And all the people rushed over to the temple of Baal and knocked it down, and broke up the altars and knocked down the idols, and killed Mattan the priest of Baal before his altar. ¹⁸ Jehoiada now appointed the Levite priests as guards, and to sacrifice the burnt offering to the Lord as prescribed in the law of Moses. He made the identical assignments of the Levite clans that King David had. They sang with joy as they worked. ¹⁹ The guards at the Temple gates kept out everything that was not consecrated and all unauthorized personnel.

²⁰ Then the army officers, nobles, governors, and all the people escorted the king from the Temple, wending their way from the Upper Gate to the palace, and seated the king upon his throne. ²¹ So all the people of the land rejoiced, and the city was quiet and peaceful because Queen Athaliah was dead.

24 JOASH WAS SEVEN years old when he became king, and he reigned forty years, in Jerusalem. His mother's name was Zibiah, from Beer-sheba. ² Joash tried hard to please the Lord all during the lifetime of Jehoiada the priest. ³ Jehoiada arranged two marriages for him, and he had sons and daughters.

⁴ Later on, Joash decided to repair and recondition the Temple. ⁵ He summoned the priests and Levites and gave them these instructions:

"Go to all the cities of Judah and collect offerings for the building fund, so that we can maintain the Temple in good repair. Get at it right away. Don't delay." But the Levites took their time.

⁶ So the king called for Jehoiada, the High Priest, and asked him, "Why haven't you demanded that the Levites go out and collect the Temple taxes from the cities of Judah, and from Jerusalem? The tax law enacted by Moses the servant of the Lord must be enforced so that the Temple can be repaired."

⁷,⁸ (The followers of wicked Athaliah had ravaged the Temple, and everything dedicated to the worship of God had been removed to the temple of Baalam.) So now the king instructed that a chest be made and set outside the Temple gate. ⁹ Then a proclamation was sent to all the cities of Judah and throughout Jerusalem telling the people to bring to the Lord the tax that Moses the servant of God had assessed upon Israel. ¹⁰ And all the leaders and the people were glad, and brought the money and placed it in the chest until it was full.

¹¹ Then the Levites carried the chest to the king's accounting office where the recording secretary and the representative of the High Priest counted the money, and

took the chest back to the Temple again. This went on day after day, and money continued to pour in. ¹² The king and Jehoiada gave the money to the building superintendents, who hired masons and carpenters to restore the Temple; and to foundrymen who made articles of iron and brass. ¹³ So the work went forward, and finally the Temple was in much better condition than before. ¹⁴ When all was finished, the remaining money was brought to the king and Jehoiada, and it was agreed to use it for making the gold and silver spoons and bowls used for incense, and for making the instruments used in the sacrifices and offerings.

Burnt offerings were sacrificed continually during the lifetime of Jehoiada the priest. ¹⁵ He lived to a very old age, finally dying at 130. ¹⁶ He was buried in the City of David among the kings, because he had done so much good for Israel, for God, and for the Temple.

¹⁷,¹⁸ But after his death the leaders of Judah came to King Joash and induced him to abandon the Temple of the God of their ancestors, and to worship shame-idols instead! So the wrath of God came down upon Judah and Jerusalem again. ¹⁹ God sent prophets to bring them back to the Lord, but the people wouldn't listen.

²⁰ Then the Spirit of God came upon Zechariah, Jehoiada's son. He called a meeting of all the people. Standing before them upon a platform, he said to them, "God wants to know why you are disobeying his commandments. For when you do, everything you try fails. You have forsaken the Lord, and now he has forsaken you."

²¹ Then the leaders plotted to kill Zechariah, and finally King Joash himself ordered him executed in the court of the Temple. ²² That was how King Joash repaid Jehoiada for his love and loyalty—by killing his son. Zechariah's last words as he died were "Lord, see what they are doing and pay them back."

²³ A few months later the Syrian army arrived and conquered Judah and Jerusalem, killing all the leaders of the nation and sending back great quantities of booty to the king of Damascus. ²⁴ It was a great triumph for the tiny Syrian army, but the Lord let the great army of Judah be conquered by them because they had forsaken the Lord God of their ancestors. In that way God executed judgment upon Joash. ²⁵ When the Syrians left—leaving Joash severely wounded—his own officials decided to kill him for murdering the son of Jehoiada the priest. They assassinated him as he lay in bed, and buried him in the City of David, but not in the cemetery of the kings. ²⁶ The conspirators were Zabad, whose mother was Shime-ath, a woman from Ammon; and Jehozabad, whose mother was Shimrith, a woman from Moab.

²⁷ If you want to read about the sons of Joash, and the curses laid upon Joash, and about the restoration of the Temple, see *The Annals of the Kings.*

When Joash died, his son Amaziah became the new king.

25 AMAZIAH WAS TWENTY-FIVE years old when he became king, and he reigned twenty-nine years, in Jerusalem. His mother's name was Jeho-addan, a native of Jerusalem. ² He did what was right, but sometimes resented it! ³ When he was well established as the new king, he executed the men who had assassinated his father. ⁴ However, he didn't kill their children but followed the command of the Lord written in the law of Moses, that the fathers shall not die for the children's sins, nor the children for the father's sins. No, everyone must pay for his own sins.

⁵,⁶ Another thing Amaziah did was to organize the army, assigning leaders to each clan from Judah and Benjamin. Then he took a census and found that he had an army of 300,000 men twenty years old and older, all trained and highly skilled in the use of spear and sword. He also paid $200,000 to hire 100,000 experienced mercenaries from Israel.

⁷ But a prophet arrived with this message from the Lord: "Sir, do not hire troops from Israel, for the Lord is not with them. ⁸ If you let them go with your troops to battle, you will be defeated no matter how well you fight; for God has power to help or to frustrate."

⁹ "But the money!" Amaziah whined. "What shall I do about that?"

And the prophet replied, "The Lord is able to give you much more than this!"

¹⁰ So Amaziah sent them home again to Ephraim, which made them very angry and insulted. ¹¹ Then Amaziah took courage and led his army to the Valley of Salt, and there killed 10,000 men from Seir. ¹² Another 10,000 were taken alive to the top of a cliff and thrown over, so that they were crushed upon the rocks below.

¹³ Meanwhile, the army of Israel that had been sent home raided several of the cities of Judah in the vicinity of Beth-horon, toward Samaria, killing 3,000 people and carrying off great quantities of booty.

¹⁴ When King Amaziah returned from this slaughter of the Edomites, he brought with him idols taken from the people of Seir, and set them up as gods, and bowed before them, and burned incense to them! ¹⁵ This made the Lord very angry and he sent a prophet to demand, "Why have you worshiped gods who couldn't even save their own people from you?"

¹⁶ "Since when have I asked your advice?" the king retorted. "Be quiet now, before I have you killed."

The prophet left with this parting warning: "I know that God has determined to destroy you because you have worshiped these idols, and have not accepted my counsel."

¹⁷ King Amaziah of Judah now took the advice of his counselors and declared war on King Joash of Israel (son of Jehoahaz, grandson of Jehu).

¹⁸ King Joash replied with this parable: "Out in the Lebanon mountains a thistle demanded of a cedar tree, 'Give your daughter in marriage to my son.' Just then a wild animal came by and stepped on the thistle, crushing it! ¹⁹ You are very proud about your conquest of Edom, but my advice is to stay home and don't meddle with me, lest you and all Judah get badly hurt."

²⁰ But Amaziah wouldn't listen, for God was arranging to destroy him for worshiping the gods of Edom. ²¹ The armies met at Beth-shemesh, in Judah, ²² and Judah was defeated, and its army fled home. ²³ King Joash of Israel captured the defeated King Amaziah of Judah and took him as a prisoner to Jerusalem. Then King Joash ordered two hundred yards of the walls of Jerusalem dismantled, from the gate of Ephraim to the Corner Gate. ²⁴ He carried off all the treasures and golden bowls from the Temple, as well as the treasures from the palace; and he took hostages, including Obed-edom, and returned to Samaria.

²⁵ However, King Amaziah of Judah lived on for fifteen years after the death of King Joash of Israel. ²⁶ The complete biography of King Amaziah is written in *The Annals of the Kings of Judah and Israel.* ²⁷ This account includes a report of Amaziah's turning away from God, and how his people conspired against him in Jerusalem, and how he fled to Lachish—but they went after him and killed him there. ²⁸ And they brought him back on horses to Jerusalem and buried him in the royal cemetery.

26 THE PEOPLE OF Judah now crowned sixteen-year-old Uzziah as their new king. ² After his father's death, he rebuilt the city of Eloth and restored it to Judah. ³ In all, he reigned fifty-two years, in Jerusalem. His mother's name was Jecoliah, from Jerusalem. ⁴ He followed in the footsteps of his father Amaziah, and was, in general, a good king so far as the Lord's opinion of him was concerned.

⁵ While Zechariah was alive Uzziah was always eager to please God. Zechariah was a man who had special revelations from God. And as long as the king followed the paths of God, he prospered, for God blessed him. ⁶ He declared war on the Philistines and captured the city of Gath and broke down its walls, also those of Jabneh and Ashdod. Then he built new cities in the Ashdod area and in other parts of the Philistine country. ⁷ God helped him not only with his wars against the Philistines but also in his battles with the Arabs of Gurbaal and in his wars with the Meunites. ⁸ The Ammonites paid annual tribute to him, and his fame spread even to Egypt, for he was very powerful.

⁹ He built fortified towers in Jerusalem at the Corner Gate, and the Valley Gate, and at the turning of the wall. ¹⁰ He also constructed forts in the Negeb, and made many water reservoirs, for he had great herds of cattle out in the valleys and on the

plains. He was a man who loved the soil and had many farms and vineyards, both on the hillsides and in the fertile valleys.

¹¹ He organized his army into regiments to which men were drafted under quotas set by Je-iel, the secretary of the army, and his assistant, Ma-aseiah. The commander-in-chief was General Hananiah. ¹² Twenty-six hundred brave clan leaders commanded these regiments. ¹³ The army consisted of 307,500 men, all elite troops. ¹⁴ Uzziah issued to them shields, spears, helmets, coats of mail, bows, and slingstones. ¹⁵ And he produced engines of war manufactured in Jerusalem, invented by brilliant men to shoot arrows and huge stones from the towers and battlements. So he became very famous, for the Lord helped him wonderfully until he was very powerful.

¹⁶ But at that point he became proud —and corrupt. He sinned against the Lord his God by entering the forbidden sanctuary of the Temple and personally burning incense upon the altar. ¹⁷,¹⁸ Azariah the High Priest went in after him with eighty other priests, all brave men, and demanded that he get out.

"It is not for you, Uzziah, to burn incense," they declared. "That is the work of the priests alone, the sons of Aaron who are consecrated to this work. Get out, for you have trespassed, and the Lord is not going to honor you for this!"

¹⁹ Uzziah was furious, and refused to set down the incense burner he was holding. But look! Suddenly—leprosy appeared in his forehead! ²⁰ When Azariah and the others saw it, they rushed him out; in fact, he himself was as anxious to get out as they were to get him out, because the Lord had struck him.

²¹ So King Uzziah was a leper until the day of his death and lived in isolation, cut off from his people and from the Temple. His son Jotham became vice-regent, in charge of the king's affairs and of the judging of the people of the land.

²² The other details of Uzziah's reign from first to last are recorded by the prophet Isaiah (son of Amoz). ²³ When Uzziah died, he was buried in the royal cemetery even though he was a leper, and his son Jotham became the new king.

27 JOTHAM WAS TWENTY-FIVE years old at the time he became king, and he reigned sixteen years, in Jerusalem. His mother was Jerushah, daughter of Zadok. ² He followed the generally good example of his father Uzziah—who had, however, sinned by invading the Temple—but even so his people became very corrupt.

³ He built the Upper Gate of the Temple, and also did extensive rebuilding of the walls on the hill where the Temple was situated. ⁴ And he built cities in the hill country of Judah, and erected fortresses and towers on the wooded hills.

⁵ His war against the Ammonites was successful, so that for the next three years he received from them an annual tribute of $200,000 in silver, 10,000 sacks of wheat, and 10,000 sacks of barley. ⁶ King Jotham became powerful because he was careful to follow the path of the Lord his God.

⁷ The remainder of his history, including his wars and other activities, is written in *The Annals of the Kings of Israel and Judah.* ⁸ In summary, then, he was twenty-five years old when he began to reign and he reigned sixteen years, in Jerusalem. ⁹ When he died, he was buried in Jerusalem, and his son Ahaz became the new king.

28 AHAZ WAS TWENTY years old when he became king and he reigned sixteen years, in Jerusalem. But he was an evil king, unlike his ancestor King David. ² For he followed the example of the kings over in Israel and worshiped the idols of Baal. ³ He even went out to the Valley of Hinnom, and it was not just to burn incense to the idols, for he even sacrificed his own children in the fire, just like the heathen nations that were thrown out of the land by the Lord to make room for Israel. ⁴ Yes, he sacrificed and burned incense at the idol shrines on the hills and under every green tree.

⁵ That is why the Lord God allowed the king of Syria to defeat him and deport large numbers of his people to Damascus. The armies from Israel also slaughtered great numbers of his troops. ⁶ On a single day, Pekah, the son of Remaliah, killed 120,000 of his bravest soldiers because they had turned away from the Lord God of their fathers. ⁷ Then Zichri, a great warrior from

Ephraim, killed the king's son Ma-aseiah, and the king's administrator Azrikam, and the king's second-in-command Elkanah. [8] The armies from Israel also captured 200,000 Judean women and children, and tremendous amounts of booty which they took to Samaria.

[9] But Oded, a prophet of the Lord, was there in Samaria and he went out to meet the returning army.

"Look!" he exclaimed. "The Lord God of your fathers was angry with Judah and let you capture them, but you have butchered them without mercy, and all heaven is disturbed. [10] And now are you going to make slaves of these people from Judah and Jerusalem? What about your own sins against the Lord your God? [11] Listen to me and return these relatives of yours to their homes, for now the fierce anger of the Lord is upon *you.*"

[12] Some of the top leaders of Ephraim also added their opposition. These men were Azariah the son of Johanan, Berechiah the son of Meshillemoth, Jehizkiah the son of Shallum, and Amasa the son of Hadlai. [13] "You must not bring the captives here!" they declared. "If you do, the Lord will be angry, and this sin will be added to our many others. We are in enough trouble with God as it is."

[14] So the army officers turned over the captives and booty to the political leaders to decide what to do. [15] Then the four men already mentioned distributed captured stores of clothing to the women and children who needed it, and gave them shoes, food, and wine, and put those who were sick and old on donkeys, and took them back to their families in Jericho, the City of Palm Trees. Then their escorts returned to Samaria.

[16] About that time King Ahaz of Judah asked the king of Assyria to be his ally in his war against the armies of Edom. For Edom was invading Judah and capturing many people as slaves. [17,18] Meanwhile, the Philistines had invaded the lowland cities and the Negeb and had already captured Beth-shemesh, Aijalon, Gederoth, Soco, Timnah, and Gimzo with their surrounding villages, and were living there. [19] For the Lord brought Judah very low on account of the evil deeds of King Ahaz of Israel,[a] for he had destroyed the spiritual fiber of Judah and had been faithless to the Lord. [20] But when Tilgath-pilneser, king of Assyria, arrived, he caused trouble for King Ahaz instead of helping him. [21] So even though Ahaz had given him the Temple gold and the palace treasures, it did no good.

[22] In this time of deep trial, King Ahaz collapsed spiritually. [23] He sacrificed to the gods of the people of Damascus who had defeated him, for he felt that since these gods had helped the kings of Syria, they would help him too if he sacrificed to them. But instead, they were his ruin, and that of all his people. [24] The king took the gold bowls from the Temple and slashed them to pieces, and nailed the door of the Temple shut so that no one could worship there, and made altars to the heathen gods in every corner of Jerusalem. [25] And he did the same in every city of Judah, thus angering the Lord God of his fathers.

[26] The other details of his life and activities are recorded in *The Annals of the Kings of Judah and Israel.* [27] When King Ahaz died, he was buried in Jerusalem but not in the royal tombs, and his son Hezekiah became the new king.

29 HEZEKIAH WAS TWENTY-FIVE years old when he became the king of Judah, and he reigned twenty-nine years, in Jerusalem. His mother's name was Abijah, the daughter of Zechariah. [2] His reign was a good one in the Lord's opinion, just as his ancestor David's had been.

[3] In the very first month of the first year of his reign, he reopened the doors of the Temple and repaired them. [4,5] He summoned the priests and Levites to meet him at the open space east of the Temple, and addressed them thus:

"Listen to me, you Levites. Sanctify yourselves and sanctify the Temple of the Lord God of your ancestors—clean all the

---

a King Ahaz ruled two tribes of Israel—Judah and Benjamin—and so is referred to here in this unusual way as a king of Israel.

debris from the holy place. ⁶ For our fathers have committed a deep sin before the Lord our God; they abandoned the Lord and his Temple and turned their backs on it. ⁷ The doors have been shut tight, the perpetual flame has been put out, and the incense and burnt offerings have not been offered. ⁸ Therefore the wrath of the Lord has been upon Judah and Jerusalem. He has caused us to be objects of horror, amazement, and contempt, as you see us today. ⁹ Our fathers have been killed in war, and our sons and daughters and wives are in captivity because of this.

¹⁰ "But now I want to make a covenant with the Lord God of Israel so that his fierce anger will turn away from us. ¹¹ My children, don't neglect your duties any longer, for the Lord has chosen you to minister to him and to burn incense."

¹²,¹³,¹⁴ Then the Levites went into action:

From the Kohath clan, Mahath (son of Amasai) and Joel (son of Azariah);

From the Merari clan, Kish (son of Abdi) and Azariah (son of Jehallelel);

From the Gershon clan, Joah (son of Zimmah) and Eden (son of Joah).

From the Elizaphan clan, Shimri and Jeuel;

From the Asaph clan, Zechariah and Mattaniah;

From the Hemanite clan, Jehuel and Shime-i;

From the Jeduthun clan, Shemaiah and Uzziel.

¹⁵ They in turn summoned their fellow Levites and sanctified themselves, and began to clean up and sanctify the Temple, as the king (who was speaking for the Lord) had commanded them. ¹⁶ The priests cleaned up the inner room of the Temple, and brought out into the court all the filth and decay they found there. The Levites then carted it out to the brook Kidron. ¹⁷ This all began on the first day of April, and by the eighth day they had reached the outer court, which took eight days to clean up, so the entire job was completed in sixteen days.

¹⁸ Then they went back to the palace and reported to King Hezekiah, "We have com-pleted the cleansing of the Temple and of the altar of burnt offerings and of its accessories, also the table of the Bread of the Presence and its equipment. ¹⁹ What's more, we have recovered and sanctified all the utensils thrown away by King Ahaz when he closed the Temple. They are beside the altar of the Lord."

²⁰ Early the next morning, King Hezekiah went to the Temple with the city officials, ²¹ taking seven young bulls, seven rams, seven lambs, and seven male goats for a sin offering for the nation and for the Temple.

He instructed the priests, the sons of Aaron, to sacrifice them on the altar of the Lord. ²² So they killed the young bulls, and the priests took the blood and sprinkled it on the altar, and they killed the rams and sprinkled their blood upon the altar, and did the same with the lambs. ²³ The male goats for the sin offering were then brought before the king and his officials, who laid their hands upon them. ²⁴ Then the priests killed the animals and made a sin offering with their blood upon the altar, to make atonement for all Israel as the king had commanded—for the king had specified that the burnt offering and sin offering must be sacrificed for the entire nation.

²⁵,²⁶ He organized Levites at the Temple into an orchestral group, using cymbals, psalteries, and harps. This was in accordance with the directions of David and the prophets Gad and Nathan—who had received their instructions from the Lord. The priests formed a trumpet corps. ²⁷ Then Hezekiah ordered the burnt offering to be placed upon the altar, and as the sacrifice began, the instruments of music began to play the songs of the Lord, accompanied by the trumpets. ²⁸ Throughout the entire ceremony everyone worshiped the Lord as the singers sang and the trumpets blew. ²⁹ Afterwards the king and his aides bowed low before the Lord in worship. ³⁰ Then King Hezekiah ordered the Levites to sing before the Lord some of the psalms of David and of the prophet Asaph, which they gladly did, and bowed their heads and worshiped.

³¹ "The consecration ceremony is now ended," Hezekiah said. "Now bring your sacrifices and thank offerings." So the peo-

ple from every part of the nation brought their sacrifices and thank offerings, and those who wished to, brought burnt offerings too. [32,33] In all, there were 70 young bulls for burnt offerings, 100 rams, and 200 lambs. In addition, 600 oxen and 3,000 sheep were brought as holy gifts. [34] But there were too few priests to prepare the burnt offerings, so their brothers the Levites helped them until the work was finished —and until more priests had reported to work—for the Levites were much more ready to sanctify themselves than the priests were. [35] There was an abundance of burnt offerings, and the usual drink offering with each, and many peace offerings. So it was that the Temple was restored to service, and the sacrifices offered again. [36] And Hezekiah and all the people were very happy because of what God had accomplished so quickly.

30 KING HEZEKIAH NOW sent letters throughout all of Israel, Judah, Ephraim, and Manasseh, inviting everyone to come to the Temple at Jerusalem for the annual Passover celebration. [2,3] The king, his aides, and all the assembly of Jerusalem had voted to celebrate the Passover in May this time, rather than at the normal time in April, because not enough priests were sanctified at the earlier date, and there wasn't enough time to get notices out. [4] The king and his advisors were in complete agreement in this matter, [5] so they sent a Passover proclamation throughout Israel, from Dan to Beer-sheba, inviting everyone. They had not kept it in great numbers as prescribed.[a]

[6] "Come back to the Lord God of Abraham, Isaac, and Israel," the king's letter said, "so that he will return to us who have escaped from the power of the kings of Assyria. [7] Do not be like your fathers and brothers who sinned against the Lord God of their fathers and were destroyed. [8] Do not be stubborn, as they were, but yield yourselves to the Lord and come to his Temple which he has sanctified forever, and worship the Lord your God so that his fierce anger will turn away from you. [9] For if you turn to the Lord again, your brothers and your children will be treated mercifully by their captors, and they will be able to return to this land. For the Lord your God is full of kindness and mercy and will not continue to turn away his face from you if you return to him."

[10] So the messengers went from city to city throughout Ephraim and Manasseh and as far as Zebulun. But for the most part they were received with laughter and scorn! [11] However, some from the tribes of Asher, Manasseh, and Zebulun turned to God and came to Jerusalem. [12] But in Judah the entire nation felt a strong, God-given desire to obey the Lord's direction as commanded by the king and his officers. [13] And so it was that a very large crowd assembled at Jerusalem in the month of May for the Passover celebration. [14] They set to work and destroyed the heathen altars in Jerusalem, and knocked down all the incense altars, and threw them into Kidron Brook.

[15] On the first day of May the people killed their Passover lambs. Then the priests and Levites became ashamed of themselves for not taking a more active part, so they sanctified themselves and brought burnt offerings into the Temple. [16] They stood at their posts as instructed by the law of Moses the man of God; and the priests sprinkled the blood received from the Levites.

[17,18,19] Since many of the people arriving from Ephraim, Manasseh, Issachar, and Zebulun were ceremonially impure because they had not undergone the purification rites, the Levites killed their Passover lambs for them, to sanctify them. Then King Hezekiah prayed for them and they were permitted to eat the Passover anyway, even though this was contrary to God's rules. But Hezekiah said, "May the good Lord pardon everyone who determines to follow the Lord God of his fathers, even though he is not properly sanctified for the ceremony." [20] And the Lord listened to Hezekiah's prayer and did not destroy them.

[21] So the people of Israel celebrated the Passover at Jerusalem for seven days with great joy.

---

a Or, "The Passover had not been celebrated by the northern tribe of Israel for a long time; only a faithful few had been doing it in the proper way."

Meanwhile the Levites and priests praised the Lord with music and cymbals day after day. [22] (King Hezekiah spoke very appreciatively to the Levites of their excellent music.)

So, for seven days the observance continued, and peace offerings were sacrificed, and the people confessed their sins to the Lord God of their fathers. [23] The enthusiasm continued, so it was unanimously decided to continue the observance for another seven days. [24] King Hezekiah gave the people 1,000 young bulls for offerings, and 7,000 sheep; and the princes donated 1,000 young bulls and 10,000 sheep. And at this time another large group of priests stepped forward and sanctified themselves.

[25] Then the people of Judah, together with the priests, the Levites, the foreign residents, and the visitors from Israel, were filled with deep joy. [26] For Jerusalem hadn't seen a celebration like this one since the days of King David's son Solomon. [27] Then the priests and Levites stood and blessed the people, and the Lord heard their prayers from his holy temple in heaven.

31 AFTERWARDS A MASSIVE campaign against idol worship was begun. Those who were at Jerusalem for the Passover went out to the cities of Judah, Benjamin, Ephraim, and Manasseh and tore down the idol altars, the obelisks, shameimages, and other heathen centers of worship. Then the people who had come to the Passover from the northern tribes returned again to their own homes.

[2] Hezekiah now organized the priests and Levites into service corps to offer the burnt offerings and peace offerings, and to worship and give thanks and praise to the Lord. [3] He also made a personal contribution of animals for the daily morning and evening burnt offerings, as well as for the weekly Sabbath and monthly new moon festivals, and for the other annual feasts as required in the law of God.

[4] In addition, he required the people in Jerusalem to bring their tithes to the priests and Levites, so that they wouldn't need other employment but could apply themselves fully to their duties as required in the law of God. [5,6] The people responded immediately and generously with the first of their crops and grain, new wine, olive oil, money, and everything else—a tithe of all they owned, as required by law to be given to the Lord their God. Everything was laid out in great piles. The people who had moved to Judah from the northern tribes and the people of Judah living in the provinces also brought in the tithes of their cattle and sheep, and brought a tithe of the dedicated things to give to the Lord and piled them up in great heaps. [7,8] The first of these tithes arrived in June, and the piles continued to grow until October. When Hezekiah and his officials came and saw these huge piles, how they blessed the Lord and praised his people!

[9] "Where did all this come from?" Hezekiah asked the priests and Levites.

[10] And Azariah the High Priest from the clan of Zadok replied, "These are tithes! We have been eating from these stores of food for many weeks, but all this is left over, for the Lord has blessed his people."

[11] Hezekiah decided to prepare storerooms in the Temple. [12,13] All the dedicated supplies were brought into the Lord's house. Conaniah, the Levite, was put in charge, assisted by his brother Shime-i and the following aides:

Jehiel, Azaziah, Nahath, Asahel,
Jerimoth, Jozabad, Eliel,
Ismachiah, Mahath, Benaiah.

These appointments were made by King Hezekiah and Azariah the High Priest.

[14,15] Kore (son of Imnah, the Levite), who was the gatekeeper at the East Gate, was put in charge of distributing the offerings to the priests. His faithful assistants were Eden, Miniamin, Jeshua, Shemaiah, Amariah, and Shecaniah. They distributed the gifts to the clans of priests in their cities, dividing it to young and old alike. [16] However, the priests on duty at the Temple and their families[a] were supplied directly from there, so they were not included in this distribution. [17,18] The priests were listed in the genealogical register by clans, and the Levites twenty years old and older

---

a Literally, "males from three years old and upward."

were listed under the names of their work corps. A regular food allotment was given to all families of properly registered priests, for they had no other source of income because their time and energies were devoted to the service of the Temple. ¹⁹ One of the priests was appointed in each of the cities of the priests to issue food and other supplies to all priests in the area, and to all registered Levites.

²⁰ In this way King Hezekiah handled the distribution throughout all Judah, doing what was just and fair in the sight of the Lord his God. ²¹ He worked very hard to encourage respect for the Temple, the law, and godly living, and was very successful.

32 SOME TIME LATER, after this good work of King Hezekiah, King Sennacherib of Assyria invaded Judah and laid siege to the fortified cities, planning to place them under tribute. ² When it was clear that Sennacherib was intending to attack Jerusalem, ³ Hezekiah summoned his princes and officers for a council of war, and it was decided to plug the springs outside the city. ⁴ They organized a huge work crew to block them, and to cut off the brook running through the fields.

"Why should the king of Assyria come and find water?" they asked.

⁵ Then Hezekiah further strengthened his defenses by repairing the wall wherever it was broken down and by adding to the fortifications, and constructing a second wall outside it. He also reinforced Fort Millo in the City of David, and manufactured large numbers of weapons and shields. ⁶ He recruited an army and appointed officers and summoned them to the plains before the city, and encouraged them with this address:

⁷ "Be strong, be brave, and do not be afraid of the king of Assyria or his mighty army, for there is someone with us who is far greater than he is! ⁸ He has a great army, but they are all mere men, while we have the Lord our God to fight our battles for us!" This greatly encouraged them.

⁹ Then King Sennacherib of Assyria, while still besieging the city of Lachish, sent ambassadors with this message to King Hezekiah and the citizens of Jerusalem:

¹⁰ "King Sennacherib of Assyria asks, 'Do you think you can survive my siege of Jerusalem? ¹¹ King Hezekiah is trying to persuade you to commit suicide by staying there—to die by famine and thirst—while he promises that "the Lord our God will deliver us from the king of Assyria"! ¹² Don't you realize that Hezekiah is the very person who destroyed all the idols, and commanded Judah and Jerusalem to use only the one altar at the Temple, and to burn incense upon it alone? ¹³ Don't you realize that I and the other kings of Assyria before me have never yet failed to conquer a nation we attacked? The gods of those nations weren't able to do a thing to save their lands! ¹⁴ Name just one time when anyone, anywhere, was able to resist us successfully. What makes you think your God can do any better? ¹⁵ Don't let Hezekiah fool you! Don't believe him. I say it again—no god of any nation has ever yet been able to rescue his people from me or my ancestors; how much less your God!' " ¹⁶ Thus the ambassador mocked the Lord God and God's servant Hezekiah, heaping up insults.

¹⁷ King Sennacherib also sent letters scorning the Lord God of Israel.

"The gods of all the other nations failed to save their people from my hand, and the God of Hezekiah will fail, too," he wrote.

¹⁸ The messengers who brought the letters shouted threats in the Jewish language to the people gathered on the walls of the city, trying to frighten and dishearten them. ¹⁹ These messengers talked about the God of Jerusalem just as though he were one of the heathen gods—a handmade idol!

²⁰ Then King Hezekiah and Isaiah the prophet (son of Amoz) cried out in prayer to God in heaven, ²¹ and the Lord sent an angel who destroyed the Assyrian army with all its officers and generals! So Sennacherib returned home in deep shame to his own land. And when he arrived at the temple of his god, some of his own sons killed him there. ²² That is how the Lord saved Hezekiah and the people of Jerusalem. And now there was peace at last throughout his realm.

²³ From then on King Hezekiah became immensely respected among the surrounding nations, and many gifts for the Lord

arrived at Jerusalem, with valuable presents for King Hezekiah, too.

²⁴ But about that time Hezekiah became deathly sick, and he prayed to the Lord, and the Lord replied with a miracle. ²⁵ However, Hezekiah didn't respond with true thanksgiving and praise, for he had become proud, and so the anger of God was upon him and upon Judah and Jerusalem. ²⁶ But finally Hezekiah and the residents of Jerusalem humbled themselves, so the wrath of the Lord did not fall upon them during Hezekiah's lifetime.

²⁷ So Hezekiah became very wealthy and was highly honored. He had to construct special treasury buildings for his silver, gold, precious stones, and spices, and for his shields and gold bowls. ²⁸,²⁹ He also built many storehouses for his grain, new wine, and olive oil, with many stalls for his animals, and folds for the great flocks of sheep and goats he purchased; and he acquired many towns, for God had given him great wealth. ³⁰ He dammed up the Upper Spring of Gihon and brought the water down through an aqueduct to the west side of the City of David sector in Jerusalem. He prospered in everything he did.

³¹ However, when ambassadors arrived from Babylon to find out about the miracle of his being healed, God left him to himself in order to test him and to see what he was really like.

³² The rest of the story of Hezekiah and all of the good things he did are written in *The Book of Isaiah* (the prophet, the son of Amoz), and in *The Annals of the Kings of Judah and Israel.* ³³ When Hezekiah died he was buried in the royal hillside cemetery among the other kings, and all Judah and Jerusalem honored him at his death. Then his son Manasseh became the new king.

33 MANASSEH WAS ONLY twelve years old when he became king, and he reigned fifty-five years, in Jerusalem. ² But it was an evil reign, for he encouraged his people to worship the idols of the heathen nations destroyed by the Lord when the people of Israel entered the land. ³ He rebuilt the heathen altars his father Hezekiah had destroyed—the altars of Baal, and of the shame-images, and of the sun, moon,

and stars. ⁴,⁵ He even constructed heathen altars in both courts of the Temple of the Lord, for worshiping the sun, moon and stars—in the very place where the Lord had said that he would be honored forever. ⁶ And Manasseh sacrificed his own children as burnt offerings in the Valley of Hinnom. He consulted spirit-mediums, too, and fortune-tellers and sorcerers, and encouraged every sort of evil, making the Lord very angry.

⁷ Think of it! He placed an idol in the very Temple of God, where God had told David and his son Solomon, "I will be honored here in this Temple, and in Jerusalem—the city I have chosen to be honored forever above all the other cities of Israel. ⁸ And if you will only obey my commands—all the laws and instructions given to you by Moses—I won't ever again exile Israel from this land which I gave your ancestors."

⁹ But Manasseh encouraged the people of Judah and Jerusalem to do even more evil than the nations the Lord destroyed when Israel entered the land. ¹⁰ Warnings from the Lord were ignored by both Manasseh and his people. ¹¹ So God sent the Assyrian armies, and they seized him with hooks and bound him with bronze chains and carted him away to Babylon. ¹² Then at last he came to his senses and cried out humbly to God for help. ¹³ And the Lord listened, and answered his plea by returning him to Jerusalem and to his kingdom! At that point Manasseh finally realized that the Lord was really God!

¹⁴ It was after this that he rebuilt the outer wall of the City of David and the wall from west of the Spring of Gihon in the Kidron Valley, and then to the Fish Gate, and around Citadel Hill, where it was built very high. And he stationed his army generals in all of the fortified cities of Judah. ¹⁵ He also removed the foreign gods from the hills and took his idol from the Temple and tore down the altars he had built on the mountain where the Temple stood, and the altars that were in Jerusalem, and dumped them outside the city. ¹⁶ Then he rebuilt the altar of the Lord and offered sacrifices upon it—peace offerings and thanksgiving offerings—and demanded that the people of

Judah worship the Lord God of Israel. ¹⁷ However, the people still sacrificed upon the altars on the hills, but only to the Lord their God.

¹⁸ The rest of Manasseh's deeds, and his prayer to God, and God's reply through the prophets—this is all written in *The Annals of the Kings of Israel.* ¹⁹ His prayer, and the way God answered, and a frank account of his sins and errors, including a list of the locations where he built idols on the hills and set up shame-idols and graven images (this of course was before the great change in his attitude) is recorded in *The Annals of the Prophets.*

^{20,21} When Manasseh died he was buried beneath his own palace, and his son Amon became the new king. Amon was twenty-two years old when he began to reign in Jerusalem, but he lasted for only two years. ²² It was an evil reign like the early years of his father Manasseh; for Amon sacrificed to all the idols just as his father had. ²³ But he didn't change as his father did; instead he sinned more and more. ²⁴ At last his own officers assassinated him in his palace. ²⁵ But some public-spirited citizens killed all of those who assassinated him, and declared his son Josiah to be the new king.

34 JOSIAH WAS ONLY eight years old when he became king. He reigned thirty-one years, in Jerusalem. ² His was a good reign, as he carefully followed the good example of his ancestor King David. ³ For when he was sixteen years old, in the eighth year of his reign, he began to search for the God of his ancestor David; and four years later he began to clean up Judah and Jerusalem, destroying the heathen altars and the shame-idols on the hills. ⁴ He went out personally to watch as the altars of Baal were knocked apart, the obelisks above the altars chopped down, and the shame-idols ground into dust and scattered over the graves of those who had sacrificed to them. ⁵ Then he burned the bones of the heathen priests upon their own altars, feeling that this action would clear the people of Judah and Jerusalem from the guilt of their sin of idol-worship.

⁶ Then he went to the cities of Manasseh, Ephraim, and Simeon, even to distant Naphtali, and did the same thing there. ⁷ He broke down the heathen altars, ground to powder the shame-idols, and chopped down the obelisks. He did this everywhere throughout the whole land of Israel before returning to Jerusalem.

⁸ During the eighteenth year of his reign, after he had purged the land and cleaned up the situation at the Temple, he appointed Shaphan (son of Azaliah) and Ma-aseiah, governor of Jerusalem, and Joah (son of Joahaz), the city treasurer, to repair the Temple. ⁹ They set up a collection system for gifts for the Temple. The money was collected at the Temple gates by the Levites on guard duty there. Gifts were brought by the people coming from Manasseh, Ephraim, and other parts of the remnant of Israel, as well as from the people of Jerusalem. The money was taken to Hilkiah the High Priest for accounting, ^{10,11} and then used by the Levites to pay the carpenters and stonemasons, and to purchase building materials—stone building blocks, timber, lumber, and beams. He now rebuilt what earlier kings of Judah had torn down.

¹² The workmen were energetic under the leadership of Jahath and Obadiah, Levites of the subclan of Merari. Zechariah and Meshullam, of the subclan of Kohath, were the building superintendents. The Levites who were skilled musicians played background music while the work progressed. ¹³ Other Levites superintended the unskilled laborers who carried in the materials to the workmen. Still others assisted as accountants, supervisors, and carriers.

¹⁴ One day when Hilkiah, the High Priest, was at the Temple recording the money collected at the gates, he found an old scroll which turned out to be the laws of God as given to Moses!

^{15,16} "Look!" Hilkiah exclaimed to Shaphan, the king's secretary. "See what I have found in the Temple! These are the laws of God!" Hilkiah gave the scroll to Shaphan, and Shaphan took it to the king, along with his report that there was good progress being made in the reconstruction of the Temple.

¹⁷ "The money chests have been opened and counted, and the money has been put

into the hand of the overseers and workmen," he said to the king.

[18] Then he mentioned the scroll, and how Hilkiah had discovered it. So he read it to the king. [19] When the king heard what these laws required of God's people, he ripped his clothing in despair, and summoned Hilkiah, Ahikam (son of Shaphan), Abdon (son of Micah), Shaphan the treasurer, and Asaiah, the king's personal aide.

[21] "Go to the Temple and plead with the Lord for me!" the king told them. "Pray for all the remnant of Israel and Judah! For this scroll says that the reason the Lord's great anger has been poured out upon us is that our ancestors have not obeyed these laws that are written here."

[22] So the men went to Huldah the prophetess, the wife of Shallum (son of Tokhath, son of Hasrah). (Shallum was the king's tailor, living in the second ward.) When they told her of the king's trouble, [23] she replied, "The Lord God of Israel says, Tell the man who sent you,

[24] "'Yes, the Lord will destroy this city and its people. All the curses written in the scroll will come true. [25] For my people have forsaken me and have worshiped heathen gods, and I am very angry with them for their deeds. Therefore, my unquenchable wrath is poured out upon this place.'

[26] "But the Lord also says this to the king of Judah who sent you to ask me about this: Tell him, the Lord God of Israel says, [27] 'Because you are sorry and have humbled yourself before God when you heard my words against this city and its people, and have ripped your clothing in despair and wept before me—I have heard you, says the Lord, [28] and I will not send the promised evil upon this city and its people until after your death.'" So they brought back to the king this word from the Lord. [29] Then the king summoned all the elders of Judah and Jerusalem, [30] and the priests and Levites and all the people great and small, to accompany him to the Temple. There the king read the scroll to them—the covenant of God that was found in the Temple. [31] As the king stood before them, he made a pledge to the Lord to follow his commandments with all his heart and soul, and to do what was written in the scroll. [32] And he required

everyone in Jerusalem and Benjamin to subscribe to this pact with God, and all of them did.

[33] So Josiah removed all idols from the areas occupied by the Jews, and required all of them to worship Jehovah their God. And throughout the remainder of his lifetime they continued serving Jehovah, the God of their ancestors.

35 THEN JOSIAH ANNOUNCED that the Passover would be celebrated on the first day of April, in Jerusalem. The Passover lambs were slain that evening. [2] He also reestablished the priests in their duties, and encouraged them to begin their work at the Temple again. [3] He issued this order to the sanctified Levites, the religious teachers in Israel:

"Since the Ark is now in Solomon's Temple and you don't need to carry it back and forth upon your shoulders, spend your time ministering to the Lord and to his people. [4,5] Form yourselves into the traditional service corps of your ancestors, as first organized by King David of Israel and by his son Solomon. Each corps will assist particular clans of the people who bring in their offerings to the Temple. [6] Kill the Passover lambs and sanctify yourselves and prepare to assist the people who come. Follow all of the instructions of the Lord through Moses."

[7] Then the king contributed 30,000 lambs and young goats for the people's Passover offerings, and 3,000 young bulls. [8] The king's officials made willing contributions to the priests and Levites. Hilkiah, Zechariah, and Jehiel, the overseers of the Temple, gave the priests 2,600 sheep and goats, and 300 oxen as Passover offerings. [9] The Levite leaders—Conaniah, Shemaiah, and Nethanel, and his brothers Hashabiah, Je-iel, and Jozabad—gave 5,000 sheep and goats and 500 oxen to the Levites for their Passover offerings.

[10] When everything was organized, and the priests were standing in their places, and the Levites were formed into service corps as the king had instructed, [11] then the Levites killed the Passover lambs and presented the blood to the priests, who sprinkled it upon the altar as the Levites

removed the skins. [12] They piled up the carcasses for each tribe to present its own burnt sacrifices to the Lord, as it is written in the law of Moses. They did the same with the oxen. [13] Then, as directed by the laws of Moses, they roasted the Passover lambs and boiled the holy offerings in pots, kettles, and pans, and hurried them out to the people to eat. [14] Afterwards the Levites prepared a meal for themselves and for the priests, for they had been busy from morning till night offering the fat of the burnt offerings.

[15] The singers (the sons of Asaph) were in their places, following directions issued centuries earlier by King David, Asaph, Heman, and Jeduthun the king's prophet. The gatekeepers guarded the gates, and didn't need to leave their posts of duty, for their meals were brought to them by their Levite brothers. [16] The entire Passover ceremony was completed in that one day. All the burnt offerings were sacrificed upon the altar of the Lord, as Josiah had instructed.

[17] Everyone present in Jerusalem took part in the Passover observance, and this was followed by the Feast of Unleavened Bread for the next seven days. [18] Never since the time of Samuel the prophet had there been such a Passover—not one of the kings of Israel could vie with King Josiah in this respect, involving so many of the priests, Levites, and people from Jerusalem and from all parts of Judah, and from over in Israel. [19] This all happened in the eighteenth year of the reign of Josiah. [20] Afterwards King Neco of Egypt led his army [against the Assyrians[a]] at Carchemish on the Euphrates River, and Josiah declared war on him.

[21] But King Neco sent ambassadors to Josiah with this message: "I don't want a fight with you, O king of Judah! I have come only to fight the king of Assyria![b] Leave me alone! God has told me to hurry! Don't meddle with God or he will destroy you, for he is with me."

[22] But Josiah refused to turn back. Instead he led his army into the battle at the Valley of Megiddo. (He laid aside his royal robes so that the enemy wouldn't recognize him.) Josiah refused to believe that Neco's message was from God. [23] The enemy archers struck King Josiah with their arrows and fatally wounded him.

"Take me out of the battle," he exclaimed to his aides.

[24,25] So they lifted him out of his chariot and placed him in his second chariot and brought him back to Jerusalem where he died. He was buried there, in the royal cemetery. And all Judah and Jerusalem, including even Jeremiah the prophet, mourned for him, as did the Temple choirs. To this day they still sing sad songs about his death, for these songs of sorrow were recorded among the official lamentations.

[26] The other activities of Josiah, and his good deeds, and how he followed the laws of the Lord, [27] all are written in *The Annals of the Kings of Israel and Judah.*

36 JOSIAH'S SON JEHOAHAZ was selected as the new king. [2] He was twenty-three years old when he began to reign, but lasted only three months. [3] Then he was deposed by the king of Egypt, who demanded an annual tribute from Judah of $250,000.

[4] The king of Egypt now appointed Eliakim, the brother of Jehoahaz, as the new king of Judah. (Eliakim's name was changed to Jehoiakim.) Jehoahaz was taken to Egypt as a prisoner. [5] Jehoiakim was twenty-five years old when he became king, and he reigned eleven years, in Jerusalem; but his reign was an evil one. [6] Finally Nebuchadnezzar king of Babylon conquered Jerusalem, and took away the king in chains to Babylon. [7] Nebuchadnezzar also took some of the golden bowls and other items from the Temple, placing them in his own temple in Babylon. [8] The rest of the deeds of Jehoiakim, and all the evil he did, are written in *The Annals of the Kings of Judah;* and his son Jehoiachin became the new king.

[9] Jehoiachin was eight years old when he ascended the throne. But he lasted only three months and ten days, and it was an evil reign as far as the Lord was concerned. [10] The following spring he was summoned to Babylon by King Nebuchadnezzar.

---

a Implied. See 2 Kings 23:29.　　b Implied. Literally, "the power with which I am at war."

Many treasures from the Temple were taken away to Babylon at that time, and King Nebuchadnezzar appointed Jehoiachin's brother Zedekiah as the new king of Judah and Jerusalem.

[11] Zedekiah was twenty-one years old when he became king and he reigned eleven years, in Jerusalem. [12] His reign, too, was evil so far as the Lord was concerned, for he refused to take the counsel of Jeremiah the prophet, who gave him messages from the Lord. [13] He rebelled against King Nebuchadnezzar, even though he had taken an oath of loyalty. Zedekiah was a hard and stubborn man so far as obeying the Lord God of Israel was concerned, for he refused to follow him.

[14] All the important people of the nation, including the High Priests, worshiped the heathen idols of the surrounding nations, thus polluting the Temple of the Lord in Jerusalem. [15] Jehovah the God of their fathers sent his prophets again and again to warn them, for he had compassion on his people and on his Temple. [16] But the people mocked these messengers of God and despised their words, scoffing at the prophets until the anger of the Lord could no longer be restrained, and there was no longer any remedy.

[17] Then the Lord brought the king of Babylon against them and killed their young men, even going after them right into the Temple, and had no pity upon them, killing even young girls and old men. The Lord used the king of Babylon to destroy them completely. [18] He also took home with him all the items, great and small, used in the Temple, and treasures from both the Temple and the palace, and took with him all the royal princes. [19] Then his army burned the Temple and broke down the walls of Jerusalem and burned all the palaces and destroyed all the valuable Temple utensils. [20] Those who survived were taken away to Babylon as slaves to the king and his sons until the kingdom of Persia conquered Babylon.

[21] Thus the word of the Lord spoken through Jeremiah came true, that the land must rest for seventy years to make up for the years when the people refused to observe the Sabbath.

[22,23] But in the first year of King Cyrus of Persia, the Lord stirred up the spirit of Cyrus to make this proclamation throughout his kingdom, putting it into writing:

"All the kingdoms of the earth have been given to me by the Lord God of heaven, and he has instructed me to build him a Temple in Jerusalem, in the land of Judah. All among you who are the Lord's people, return to Israel for this task, and the Lord be with you."

This also fulfilled the prediction of Jeremiah the prophet.

Back Home!

Today, young Israelis swagger on Tel Aviv sidewalks (above) while Orthodox Jews stride towards Jerusalem's Wailing Wall (far right) and a young *kibbutznik* gives the signal that everything's looking up again in Palestine—the Jews are back home.

It's not the first time. In 539 B.C. the new Persian monarch Cyrus, having just conquered Babylon and inherited its captive Israelis, decreed that they could go back to their homeland, rebuild the Temple, and create a Jewish society once more. Ezra, a priest, helped lead the happy migration, and he opens his book with Cyrus' royal pronouncement. Ninety-four years later, Nehemiah gave up his post as royal butler to head for Jerusalem and lead the rebuilding of the city wall —even though it meant working around the clock for days on end. These two books tell the fulfilling of much prophecy—a dream coming true through the sweat and prayers of its dreamers.

EZRA

1 DURING THE FIRST year of the reign of King Cyrus of Persia, the Lord fulfilled Jeremiah's prophecy[a] by giving King Cyrus the desire to send this proclamation throughout his empire (he also put it into the permanent records of the realm):

[2] "Cyrus, king of Persia, hereby announces that Jehovah, the God of heaven who gave me my vast empire, has now given me the responsibility of building him a Temple in Jerusalem, in the land of Judah. [3] All Jews throughout the kingdom may now return to Jerusalem to rebuild this Temple of Jehovah, who is the God of Israel and of Jerusalem. May his blessings rest upon you. [4] Those Jews[b] who do not go should contribute toward the expenses of those who do, and also supply them with clothing, transportation, supplies for the journey, and a freewill offering for the Temple."

[5] Then God gave a great desire to the leaders of the tribes of Judah and Benjamin, and to the priests and Levites, to return to

a Jeremiah had predicted (in Jeremiah 25:12 and 29:10) that the Jews would remain in captivity to the Babylonians for seventy years.   b Implied.

Jerusalem at once to rebuild the Temple.
⁶ And all the Jewish exiles^c who chose to
remain in Persia gave them whatever assistance they could, as well as gifts for the Temple.

⁷ King Cyrus himself donated the gold
bowls and other valuable items which King
Nebuchadnezzar had taken from the Temple at Jerusalem and had placed in the temple of his own gods. ⁸ He instructed
Mithredath, the treasurer of Persia, to present these gifts to Shesh-bazzar, the leader
of the exiles returning to Judah.

⁹,¹⁰ The items Cyrus donated included:
   1,000 gold trays,
   1,000 silver trays,
   29 censers,
   30 bowls of solid gold,
   2,410 silver bowls (of various designs),
   1,000 miscellaneous items.
¹¹ In all there were 5,469 gold and silver
items turned over to Shesh-bazzar to take
back to Jerusalem.

2 HERE IS THE list of the Jewish exiles
   who now returned to Jerusalem and to
the other cities of Judah, from which their
parents^a had been deported to Babylon by
King Nebuchadnezzar.

   ² The leaders were:
   Zerubbabel, Jeshua, Nehemiah,
   Seraiah, Re-el-aiah, Mordecai,
   Bilshan, Mispar, Bigvai,
   Rehum, Baanah.

Here is a census of those who returned
(listed by subclans):
   ³⁻³⁵ From the subclan of Parosh,
   2,172;
   From the subclan of Shephatiah, 372;
   From the subclan of Arah, 775;
   From the subclan of Pahath-moab
   (the descendants of Jeshua and
   Joab), 2,812;
   From the subclan of Elam, 1,254;
   From the subclan of Zattu, 945;
   From the subclan of Zaccai, 760;
   From the subclan of Bani, 642;
   From the subclan of Bebai, 623;
   From the subclan of Azgad, 1,222;
   From the subclan of Adonikam, 666;

From the subclan of Bigvai, 2,056;
From the subclan of Adin, 454;
From the subclan of Ater (the descendants of Hezekiah), 98;
From the subclan of Bezai, 323;
From the subclan of Jorah, 112;
From the subclan of Hashum, 223;
From the subclan of Gibbar, 95;
From the subclan of Bethlehem, 123;
From the subclan of Netophah, 56;
From the subclan of Anathoth, 128;
From the subclan of Azmaveth, 42;
From the subclans of Kiriatharim,
   Chephirah, and Be-eroth, 743;
From the subclans of Ramah and
   Geba, 621;
From the subclan of Michmas, 122;
From the subclans of Bethel and Ai,
   223;
From the subclan of Nebo, 52;
From the subclan of Magbish, 156;
From the subclan of Elam, 1,254;
From the subclan of Harim, 320;
From the subclans of Lod, Hadid,
   and Ono, 725;
From the subclan of Jericho, 345;
From the subclan of Senaah, 3,630.
³⁶⁻³⁹ Here are the statistics concerning
the returning priests:
   From the families of Jedaiah of the
   subclan of Jeshua, 973;
   From the subclan of Immer, 1,052;
   From the subclan of Pashhur, 1,247;
   From the subclan of Harim, 1,017.
⁴⁰,⁴¹,⁴² Here are the statistics concerning
the Levites who returned:
   From the families of Jeshua and Kedmi-el of the subclan of Hodaviah,
   74;
   The choir members from the clan of
   Asaph, 128;
   From the descendants of the gatekeepers (the families of Shallum,
   Ater, Talmon, Akkub, Hatita,
   and Shobai), 139.
⁴³⁻⁵⁴ The following families of the Temple
assistants were represented:
   Ziha, Hasupha, Tabbaoth, Keros,
   Siaha, Padon, Lebanah, Hagabah,
   Akkub, Hagab, Shamlai, Hanan,
   Giddel, Gahar, Re-aiah, Rezin,

Nekoda, Gazzam, Uzza, Paseah,
Besai, Asnah, Me-unim, Nephisim,
Bakbuk, Hakupha, Harhur,
Bazluth, Mehida, Harsha, Barkos,
Sisera, Temah, Neziah, Hatipha.

⁵⁵,⁵⁶,⁵⁷ Those who made the trip also included the descendants of King Solomon's officials:

Sotai, Hassophereth, Peruda,
Jaalah, Darkon, Giddel,
Shephatiah, Hattil,
Pochereth-hazzebaim, Ami.

⁵⁸ The Temple assistants and the descendants of Solomon's officers numbered 392.

⁵⁹ Another group returned to Jerusalem at this time from the Persian cities of Tel-melah, Tel-harsha, Cherub, Addan, and Immer. However, they had lost their genealogies and could not prove that they were really Israelites. ⁶⁰ This group included the subclans of Delaiah, Tobiah, and Nekoda—a total of 652.

⁶¹ Three subclans of priests—Habaiah, Hakkoz, and Barzillai (he married one of the daughters of Barzillai the Gileadite and took her family name)—also returned to Jerusalem. ⁶²,⁶³ But they too had lost their genealogies, so the leaders refused to allow them to continue as priests; they would not even allow them to eat the priests' share of food from the sacrifices until the Urim and Thummim could be consulted, to find out from God whether they actually were descendants of priests or not.

⁶⁴,⁶⁵ So a total of 42,360 persons returned to Judah; in addition to 7,337 slaves and 200 choir members, both men and women. ⁶⁶,⁶⁷ They took with them 736 horses, 245 mules, 435 camels, and 6,720 donkeys.

⁶⁸ Some of the leaders were able to give generously toward the rebuilding of the Temple, ⁶⁹ and each gave as much as he could. The total value of their gifts amounted to $300,000 of gold, $170,000 of silver, and 100 robes for the priests.

⁷⁰ So the priests and Levites and some of the common people settled in Jerusalem and its nearby villages; and the singers, the gatekeepers, the Temple workers, and the rest of the people returned to the other cities

of Judah from which they had come.

3 DURING THE MONTH of September everyone who had returned to Judah came to Jerusalem from their homes in the other towns. Then Jeshua (son of Jozadak) with his fellow priests, and Zerubbabel (son of She-alti-el) and his clan, rebuilt the altar of the God of Israel; and sacrificed burnt offerings upon it, as instructed in the laws of Moses, the man of God. ³ The altar was rebuilt on its old site, and it was used immediately to sacrifice morning and evening burnt offerings to the Lord; for the people were fearful of attack.

⁴ And they celebrated the Feast of Tabernacles as prescribed in the laws of Moses, sacrificing the burnt offerings specified for each day of the feast. ⁵ They also offered the special sacrifices required for the Sabbaths, the new moon celebrations, and the other regular annual feasts of the Lord. Voluntary offerings of the people were also sacrificed. ⁶ It was on the fifteenth day of September[a] that the priests began sacrificing the burnt offerings to the Lord. (This was before they began building the foundation of the Temple.)

⁷ Then they hired masons and carpenters, and bought cedar logs from the people of Tyre and Sidon, paying for them with food, wine, and olive oil. The logs were brought down from the Lebanon mountains and floated along the coast of the Mediterranean Sea to Joppa, for King Cyrus had included this provision in his grant.

⁸ The actual construction of the Temple began in June of the second year of their arrival at Jerusalem. The work force was made up of all those who had returned, and they were under the direction of Zerubbabel (son of She-alti-el), Jeshua (son of Jozadak), and their fellow priests and the Levites. The Levites who were twenty years old or older were appointed to supervise the workmen. ⁹ The supervision of the entire project was given to Jeshua, Kadmi-el, Henadad, and their sons and relatives, all of whom were Levites.

¹⁰ When the builders completed the foundation of the Temple, the priests put on

---

a Literally, "the first day of the seventh month" of the Hebrew calendar.

their priestly robes and blew their trumpets; and the descendants of Asaph crashed their cymbals to praise the Lord in the manner ordained by King David. [11] They sang rounds of praise and thanks to God, singing this song: "He is good, and his love and mercy toward Israel will last forever." Then all the people gave a great shout, praising God because the foundation of the Temple had been laid.

[12] But many of the priests and Levites and other leaders—the old men who remembered Solomon's beautiful Temple—wept aloud, while others were shouting for joy! [13] So the shouting and the weeping mingled together in a loud commotion that could be heard from far away!

4 WHEN THE ENEMIES of Judah and Benjamin heard that the exiles had returned and were rebuilding the Temple, [2] they approached Zerubbabel and the other leaders and suggested, "Let us work with you, for we are just as interested in your God as you are; we have sacrificed to him ever since King Esar-haddon of Assyria brought us here."

[3] But Zerubbabel and Jeshua and the other Jewish leaders replied, "No, you may have no part in this work. The Temple of the God of Israel must be built by the Israelis, just as King Cyrus has commanded."

[4,5] Then the local residents tried to discourage and frighten them by sending agents to tell lies about them to King Cyrus. This went on during his entire reign and lasted until King Darius took the throne.

[6] And afterwards, when King Ahasuerus began to reign, they wrote him a letter of accusation against the people of Judah and Jerusalem, [7] and did the same thing during the reign of Ar-ta-xerxes. Bishlam, Mithredath, and Tabe-el and their associates wrote a letter to him in the Aramaic language, and it was translated to him. [8,9] Others who participated were Governor Rehum, Shimshai (a scribe), several judges and other local leaders, the Persians, the Babylonians, the men of Erech and Susa, [10] and men from several other nations. (They had been taken from their own lands by the great and noble Osnappar and relocated in Jerusalem, Samaria, and throughout the neighboring lands west of the Euphrates River.)

[11] Here is the text of the letter they sent to King Ar-ta-xerxes:

"Sir: Greetings from your loyal subjects west of the Euphrates River. [12] Please be informed that the Jews sent to Jerusalem from Babylon are rebuilding this historically rebellious and evil city; they have already rebuilt its walls and have repaired the foundations of the Temple. [13] But we wish you to know that if this city is rebuilt, it will be much to your disadvantage, for the Jews will then refuse to pay their taxes to you. [14] Since we are grateful to you as our patron, and we do not want to see you taken advantage of and dishonored in this way, we have decided to send you this information. [15] We suggest that you search the ancient records to discover what a rebellious city this has been in the past; in fact, it was destroyed because of its long history of sedition against the kings and countries who attempted to control it. [16] We wish to declare that if this city is rebuilt and the walls finished, you might as well forget about this part of your empire beyond the Euphrates, for it will be lost to you."

[17] Then the king made this reply to Governor Rehum and Shimshai the scribe, and to their companions living in Samaria and throughout the area west of the Euphrates River:

[18] "Gentlemen: Greetings! The letter you sent has been translated and read to me. [19] I have ordered a search made of the records and have indeed found that Jerusalem has in times past been a hotbed of insurrection against many kings; in fact, rebellion and sedition are normal there! [20] I find, moreover, that there have been some very great kings in Jerusalem who have ruled the entire land beyond the Euphrates River and have received vast tribute, custom, and toll. [21] Therefore, I command that these men must stop building the Temple until I have investigated the matter more thoroughly. [22] Do not delay, for we must not permit the situation to get out of control!"

[23] When this letter from King Ar-ta-xerxes was read to Rehum and Shimshai, they hurried to Jerusalem and forced the Jews to stop building. [24] So the work ended

until the second year of the reign of King Darius of Persia.

5 BUT THERE WERE prophets in Jerusalem and Judah at that time—Haggai, and Zechariah (the son of Iddo)—who brought messages from the God of Israel to Zerubbabel (son of She-alti-el) and Jeshua (son of Jozadak), encouraging them to begin building again! So they did and the prophets helped them.

³ But Tattenai, the governor of the lands west of the Euphrates, and Shethar-bozenai, and their companions soon arrived in Jerusalem and demanded, "Who gave you permission to rebuild this Temple and finish these walls?"

⁴ They also asked for a list of the names of all the men who were working on the Temple. ⁵ But because the Lord was overseeing the entire situation, our enemies did not force us to stop building, but let us continue while King Darius looked into the matter and returned his decision.

⁶ Following is the letter which governor Tattenai, Shethar-bozenai, and the other officials sent to King Darius:

⁷ "To King Darius:

"Greetings!

⁸ "We wish to inform you that we went to the construction site of the Temple of the great God of Judah. It is being built with huge stones, and timber is being laid in the city walls. The work is going forward with great energy and success. ⁹ We asked the leaders, 'Who has given you permission to do this?' ¹⁰ And we demanded their names so that we could notify you. ¹¹ Their answer was, 'We are the servants of the God of heaven and earth and we are rebuilding the Temple that was constructed here many centuries ago by a great king of Israel. ¹² But afterwards our ancestors angered the God of heaven, and he abandoned them and let King Nebuchadnezzar destroy this Temple and exile the people to Babylonia.'

¹³ "But they insist that King Cyrus of Babylon, during the first year of his reign, issued a decree that the Temple should be rebuilt, ¹⁴ and they say King Cyrus returned the gold and silver bowls which Nebuchad-

nezzar had taken from the Temple in Jerusalem and had placed in the temple of Babylon. They say these items were delivered into the safekeeping of a man named Shesh-bazzar, whom King Cyrus appointed as governor of Judah. ¹⁵ The king instructed him to return the bowls to Jerusalem and to let the Temple of God be built there as before. ¹⁶ So Shesh-bazzar came and laid the foundations of the Temple at Jerusalem; and the people have been working on it ever since, though it is not yet completed. ¹⁷ We request that you search in the royal library of Babylon to discover whether King Cyrus ever made such a decree; and then let us know your pleasure in this matter."

6 SO KING DARIUS issued orders that a search be made in the Babylonian archives, where documents were stored.

² Eventually the record was found in the palace at Ecbatana, in the province of Media. This is what it said:

³ "In this first year of the reign of King Cyrus, a decree has been sent out concerning the Temple of God at Jerusalem where the Jews offer sacrifices. It is to be rebuilt, and the foundations are to be strongly laid. The height will be ninety feet and the width will be ninety feet. ⁴ There will be three layers of huge stones in the foundation, topped with a layer of new timber. All expenses will be paid by the king. ⁵ And the gold and silver bowls which were taken from the Temple of God by Nebuchadnezzar shall be taken back to Jerusalem and put into the Temple as they were before."

⁶ So King Darius sent this message[a] to Governor Shethar-bozenai, and the other officials west of the Euphrates:

"Do not disturb the construction of the Temple. Let it be rebuilt on its former site, ⁷ and don't molest the governor of Judah and the other leaders in their work. ⁸ Moreover, I decree that you are to pay the full construction costs without delay from my taxes collected in your territory. ⁹ Give the priests in Jerusalem young bulls, rams, and

---

a Implied.

lambs for burnt offerings to the God of heaven; and give them wheat, wine, salt, and olive oil each day without fail. [10] Then they will be able to offer acceptable sacrifices to the God of heaven, and to pray for me and my sons. [11] Anyone who attempts to change this message in any way shall have the beams pulled from his house and built into a gallows on which he will be hanged;[b] and his house shall be reduced to a pile of rubble. [12] The God who has chosen the city of Jerusalem will destroy any king and any nation that alters this commandment and destroys this Temple. I, Darius, have issued this decree; let it be obeyed with all diligence."

[13] Governor Tattenai, Shethar-bozenai, and their companions complied at once with the command of King Darius.

[14] So the Jewish leaders continued in their work, and they were greatly encouraged by the preaching of the prophets Haggai and Zechariah (son of Iddo). The Temple was finally finished, as had been commanded by God and decreed by Cyrus, Darius, and Ar-ta-xerxes, the kings of Persia. [15] The completion date was February 18[c] in the sixth year of the reign of King Darius.

[16] The Temple was then dedicated with great joy by the priests, the Levites, and all the people. [17] During the dedication celebration 100 young bulls, 200 rams, and 400 lambs were sacrificed; and twelve male goats were presented as a sin offering for the twelve tribes of Israel. [18] Then the priests and Levites were divided into their various service corps, to do the work of God as instructed in the laws of Moses.

[19] The Passover was celebrated on the first day of April.[d] [20] For by that time many of the priests and Levites had consecrated themselves. [21,22] And some of the heathen people who had been relocated in Judah turned from their immoral customs and joined the Israelis in worshiping the Lord God. They, with the entire nation, ate the Passover feast and celebrated the Feast of Unleavened Bread for seven days. There was great joy throughout the land because the Lord had caused the king of Assyria to be generous to Israel and to assist in the construction of the Temple.

7 HERE IS THE genealogy of Ezra, who traveled from Babylon to Jerusalem[a] during the reign of King Ar-ta-xerxes of Persia:

Ezra was the son of Seriah;
Seriah was the son of Azariah;
Azariah was the son of Hilkiah;
Hilkiah was the son of Shallum;
Shallum was the son of Zadok;
Zadok was the son of Ahitub;
Ahitub was the son of Amariah;
Amariah was the son of Meraioth;
Meraioth was the son of Zerahiah;
Zerahiah was the son of Uzzi;
Uzzi was the son of Bukki;
Bukki was the son of Abishu-a;
Abishu-a was the son of Phinehas;
Phinehas was the son of Eleazar;
Eleazar was the son of Aaron, the chief priest.

[6] As a Jewish religious leader, Ezra was well versed in Jehovah's laws which Moses had given to the people of Israel. He asked to be allowed to return to Jerusalem, and the king granted his request; for the Lord his God was blessing him. [7,8,9] Many ordinary people as well as priests, Levites, singers, gatekeepers, and Temple workers traveled with him. They left Babylon in the middle of March in the seventh year of the reign of Ar-ta-xerxes and arrived at Jerusalem in the month of August; for the Lord gave them a good trip. [10] This was because Ezra had determined to study and obey the laws of the Lord and to become a Bible teacher, teaching those laws to the people of Israel.

[11] King Ar-ta-xerxes presented this letter to Ezra the priest, the student of God's commands:

[12] "From: Ar-ta-xerxes, the king of kings.

"To: Ezra, the priest, the teacher of the laws of the God of heaven.

[13] "I decree that any Jew in my realm, including the priests and Levites, may re-

---

b Literally, "impaled."   c Literally, "the third day of the month of Adar."   d Literally, "the fourteenth day of the first month" of the Hebrew calendar.   7a Implied.

turn to Jerusalem with you. ¹⁴ I and my Council of Seven hereby instruct you to take a copy of God's laws to Judah and Jerusalem and to send back a report of the religious progress being made there. ¹⁵ We also commission you to take with you to Jerusalem the silver and gold which we are presenting as an offering to the God of Israel. ¹⁶ Moreover, you are to collect voluntary Temple offerings of silver and gold from the Jews and their priests in all of the provinces of Babylon. ¹⁷ These funds are to be used primarily for the purchase of oxen, rams, lambs, grain offerings, and drink offerings, all of which will be offered upon the altar of your Temple when you arrive in Jerusalem. ¹⁸ The money that is left over may be used in whatever way you and your brothers feel is the will of your God. ¹⁹ And take with you the gold bowls and other items we are giving you for the Temple of your God at Jerusalem. ²⁰ If you run short of money for the construction of the Temple or for any similar needs, you may requisition funds from the royal treasury.

²¹ "I, Ar-ta-xerxes the king, send this decree to all the treasurers in the provinces west of the Euphrates River: 'You are to give Ezra whatever he requests of you (for he is a priest and teacher of the laws of the God of heaven), ²² up to $200,000 in silver; 1,225 bushels of wheat; 990 gallons of wine; any amount of salt; ²³ and whatever else the God of heaven demands for his Temple; for why should we risk God's wrath against the king and his sons? ²⁴ I also decree that no priest, Levite, choir member, gatekeeper, Temple attendant, or other worker in the Temple shall be required to pay taxes of any kind.'

²⁵ "And you, Ezra, are to use the wisdom God has given you to select and appoint judges and other officials to govern all the people west of the Euphrates River; if they are not familiar with the laws of your God, you are to teach them. ²⁶ Anyone refusing to obey the law of your God and the law of the king shall be punished immediately by death, banishment, confiscation of goods, or imprisonment."

²⁷ Well, praise the Lord God of our ancestors, who made the king want to beautify the Temple of the Lord in Jerusalem! ²⁸ And praise God for demonstrating such lovingkindness to me[b] by honoring me before the king and his Council of Seven and before all of his mighty princes! I was given great status because the Lord my God was with me; and I persuaded some of the leaders of Israel to return with me to Jerusalem.

8 THESE ARE THE names and genealogies of the leaders who accompanied me from Babylon during the reign of King Ar-ta-xerxes:

²⁻¹⁴ From the clan of Phinehas—Gershom;

From the clan of Ithamar—Daniel;

From the subclan of David of the clan of Shecaniah—Hattush;

From the clan of Parosh—Zechariah, and 150 other men;

From the clan of Pahath-moab —Eli-e-ho-enai (son of Zerahiah), and 200 other men;

From the clan of Shecaniah—the son of Jahaziel, and 300 other men;

From the clan of Adin—Ebed (son of Jonathan), and 50 other men;

From the clan of Elam—Jeshaiah (son of Athaliah), and 70 other men;

From the clan of Shephatiah— Zebadiah (son of Michael), and 80 other men;

From the clan of Joab—Obadiah (son of Jehiel), and 218 other men;

From the clan of Bani—Shelomith (son of Josiphiah), and 160 other men;

From the clan of Bebai—Zechariah (son of Bebai), and 28 other men;

From the clan of Azgad—Johanan (son of Hakkatan), and 110 other men;

From the clan of Adonikam —Eliphelet, Jeuel, Shemaiah, and 60 other men (they arrived at a later time);

From the clan of Bigvai—Uthai, Zaccur, and 70 other men.

---

b The speaker, as in the remainder of the book, is Ezra.

[15] We assembled at the Ahava River and camped there for three days while I went over the lists of the people and the priests who had arrived; and I found that not one Levite had volunteered! [16] So I sent for Eliezer, Ari-el, Shemaiah, Elnathan, Jarib, Elnathan, Nathan, Zechariah, and Meshullam, the Levite leaders; I also sent for Joiarib and Elnathan, who were very wise men. [17] I sent them to Iddo, the leader of the Jews at Casiphia, to ask him and his brothers and the Temple attendants to send us priests for the Temple of God at Jerusalem. [18] And God was good! He sent us an outstanding man named Sherebiah, along with eighteen of his sons and brothers; he was a very astute man and a descendant of Mahli, the son of Levi and grandson of Israel. [19] God also sent Hashabiah; and Jeshaiah (the son of Merari), with twenty of his sons and brothers; [20] and 220 Temple attendants. (The Temple attendants were assistants to the Levites—a job classification of Temple employees first instituted by King David.) These 220 men were all listed by name.

[21] Then I declared a fast while we were at the Ahava River so that we would humble ourselves before our God; and we prayed that he would give us a good journey and protect us, our children, and our goods as we traveled. [22] For I was ashamed to ask the king for soldiers and cavalry to accompany us and protect us from the enemies along the way. After all, we had told the king that our God would protect all those who worshiped him, and that disaster could come only to those who had forsaken him! [23] So we fasted and begged God to take care of us. And he did.

[24] I appointed twelve leaders of the priests—Sherebiah, Hashabiah, and ten other priests— [25] to be in charge of transporting the silver, gold, the golden bowls, and the other items which the king and his council and the leaders and people of Israel had presented to the Temple of God. [26,27] I weighed the money as I gave it to them and found it to total $1,300,000 in silver; $200,000 in silver utensils; $3,000,000 in gold; and twenty gold bowls worth a total of $5,000. There were also two beautiful pieces of brass which were as precious as gold. [28] I consecrated these men to the Lord, and then consecrated the treasures—the equipment and money and bowls which had been given as free-will offerings to the Lord God of our fathers.

[29] "Guard these treasures well!" I told them; "present them without a penny lost to the priests and the Levite leaders and the elders of Israel at Jerusalem, where they are to be placed in the treasury of the Temple."

[30] So the priests and the Levites accepted the responsibility of taking it to God's Temple in Jerusalem. [31] We broke camp at the Ahava River at the end of March[a] and started off to Jerusalem; and God protected us and saved us from enemies and bandits along the way. [32] So at last we arrived safely at Jerusalem.

[33] On the fourth day after our arrival the silver, gold, and other valuables were weighed in the Temple by Meremoth (the son of Uriah the priest), Eleazar (son of Phinehas), Jozabad (son of Jeshua), and Noadiah (son of Binnui)—all of whom were Levites. [34] A receipt was given for each item, and the weight of the gold and silver was noted.

[35] Then everyone in our party sacrificed burnt offerings to the God of Israel—twelve oxen for the nation of Israel; ninety-six rams; seventy-seven lambs; and twelve goats as a sin offering. [36] The king's decrees were delivered to his lieutenants and the governors of all the provinces west of the Euphrates River, and of course they then cooperated in the rebuilding of the Temple of God.

9 BUT THEN THE Jewish leaders came to tell me that many of the Jewish people and even some of the priests and Levites had taken up the horrible customs of the heathen people who lived in the land—the Canaanites, Hittites, Perizzites, Jebusites, Ammonites, Moabites, Egyptians, and Amorites. [2] The men of Israel had married girls from these heathen nations, and had taken them as wives for their sons. So the holy people of God were being polluted by these mixed marriages, and the political leaders

a Or, "the twelfth day of the first month" of the Hebrew calendar.

were some of the worst offenders.

³ When I heard this, I tore my clothing and pulled hair from my head and beard and sat down utterly baffled. ⁴ Then many who feared the God of Israel because of this sin of his people came and sat with me until the time of the evening burnt offering.

⁵ Finally I stood before the Lord in great embarrassment; then I fell to my knees and lifted my hands to the Lord, ⁶ and cried out, "O my God, I am ashamed; I blush to lift up my face to you, for our sins are piled higher than our heads and our guilt is as boundless as the heavens. ⁷ Our whole history has been one of sin; that is why we and our kings and our priests were slain by the heathen kings—we were captured, robbed, and disgraced, just as we are today. ⁸ But now we have been given a moment of peace, for you have permitted a few of us to return to Jerusalem from our exile. You have given us a moment of joy and new life in our slavery. ⁹ For we were slaves, but in your love and mercy you did not abandon us to slavery; instead you caused the kings of Persia to be favorable to us. They have even given us their assistance in rebuilding the Temple of our God and in giving us Jerusalem as a walled city in Judah.

¹⁰ "And now, O God, what can we say after all of this? For once again we have abandoned you and broken your laws! ¹¹ The prophets warned us that the land we would possess was totally defiled by the horrible practices of the people living there. From one end to the other it is filled with corruption. ¹² You told us not to let our daughters marry their sons, and not to let our sons marry their daughters, and not to help those nations in any way. You warned us that only if we followed this rule could we become a prosperous nation and forever leave that prosperity to our children as an inheritance. ¹³ And now, even after our punishment in exile because of our wickedness (and we have been punished far less than we deserved), and even though you have let some of us return, ¹⁴ we have broken your commandments again and intermarried with people who do these awful things. Surely your anger will destroy us now until

not even this little remnant escapes. ¹⁵ O Lord God of Israel, you are a just God; what hope can we have if you give us justice as we stand here before you in our wickedness?"

10 AS I LAY on the ground in front of the Temple, weeping and praying and making this confession, a large crowd of men, women, and children gathered around and cried with me.

² Then Shecaniah (the son of Jehiel of the clan of Elam) said to me, "We acknowledge our sin against our God, for we have married these heathen women. But there is hope for Israel in spite of this. ³ For we agree before our God to divorce our heathen wives and to send them away with our children; we will follow your commands, and the commands of the others who fear our God. We will obey the laws of God. ⁴ Take courage and tell us how to proceed in setting things straight, and we will fully cooperate."

⁵ So I stood up and demanded that the leaders of the priests and the Levites and all the people of Israel swear that they would do as Shecaniah had said; and they all agreed. ⁶ Then I went into the room of Jehohanan in the Temple and refused all food and drink; for I was mourning because of the sin of the returned exiles.

⁷,⁸ Then a proclamation was made throughout Judah and Jerusalem that everyone should appear at Jerusalem within three days and that the leaders and elders had decided that anyone who refused to come would be disinherited and excommunicated from Israel. ⁹ Within three days, on the fifth day of December,ᵃ all the men of Judah and Benjamin had arrived and were sitting in the open space before the Temple; and they were trembling because of the seriousness of the matter and because of the heavy rainfall. ¹⁰ Then I, Ezra the priest, arose and addressed them:

"You have sinned, for you have married heathen women; now we are even more deeply under God's condemnation than we were before. ¹¹ Confess your sin to the Lord God of your fathers and do what he de-

---

a Literally, "the twentieth day of the ninth month" of the Hebrew calendar.

mands: separate yourselves from the heathen people about you and from these women."

¹² Then all the men spoke up and said, "We will do what you have said. ¹³ But this isn't something that can be done in a day or two, for there are many of us involved in this sinful affair. And it is raining so hard that we can't stay out here much longer. ¹⁴ Let our leaders arrange trials for us. Everyone who has a heathen wife will come at the scheduled time with the elders and judges of his city; then each case will be decided and the situation will be cleared up and the fierce wrath of our God will be turned away from us."

¹⁵ Only Jonathan (son of Asahel), Jahzeiah (son of Tikvah), Meshullam, and Shabbethai the Levite opposed this course of action.

¹⁶⁻¹⁹ So this was the plan that was followed: Some of the clan leaders and I were designated as judges; we began our work on December 15, and finished by March 15.

Following is the list of priests who had married heathen wives (they vowed to divorce their wives and acknowledged their guilt by offering rams as sacrifices):

> Ma-aseiah, Eliezer,
> Jarib, Gedaliah.

²⁰ The sons of Immer:
> Hanani, Zebadiah.

²¹ The sons of Harim:
> Ma-aseiah, Elijah, Shemaiah,
> Jehiel, Uzziah.

²² The sons of Pashhur:
> Eli-o-enai, Ma-aseiah, Ishmael,
> Nethanel, Jozabad, Elasah.

²³ The Levites who were guilty:
> Jozabad, Shime-i,
> Kelaiah (also called Kelita),
> Petha-haiah, Judah, Eliezer.

²⁴ Of the singers, there was Eliashib. Of the gatekeepers, Shallum, Telem, and Uri.

²⁵ Here is the list of ordinary citizens who were declared guilty:

From the clan of Parosh:
> Ramiah, Izziah, Malchijah,
> Mijamin, Eleazar,
> Hashabiah, Benaiah.

²⁶ From the clan of Elam:
> Mattaniah, Zechariah, Jehiel,
> Abdi, Jeremoth, Elijah.

²⁷ From the clan of Zattu:
> Eli-o-enai, Eliashib, Mattaniah,
> Jeremoth, Zabad, Aziza.

²⁸ From the clan of Bebai:
> Jeho-hanan, Hananiah,
> Zabbai, Athlai.

²⁹ From the clan of Bani:
> Meshullam, Malluch, Adaiah,
> Jashub, Sheal, Jeremoth.

³⁰ From the clan of Pahath-moab:
> Adna, Chelal, Benaiah, Ma-aseiah,
> Mattaniah, Bezalel,
> Binnui, Manasseh.

³¹,³² From the clan of Harim:
> Eliezer, Isshijah, Malchijah,
> Shemaiah, Shime-on, Benjamin,
> Malluch, Shemariah.

³³ From the clan of Hashum:
> Mattenai, Matattah, Zabad,
> Eliphelet, Jeremai,
> Manasseh, Shime-i.

³⁴⁻⁴² From the clan of Bani:
> Ma-adai, Amram, Uel, Banaiah,
> Bedeiah, Cheluhi, Vaniah,
> Meremoth, Eliashib, Mattaniah,
> Mattenai, Jaasu, Bani, Binnui,
> Shime-i, Shelemiah, Nathan,
> Adaiah, Machnadebai, Shashai,
> Sharai, Azarel, Shelemiah,
> Shemariah, Shallum,
> Amariah, Joseph.

⁴³ From the clan of Nebo:
> Je-iel, Mattithiah, Zabad, Zebina,
> Jaddai, Joel, Benaiah.

⁴⁴ Each of these men had heathen wives, and many had children by these wives.

NEHEMIAH

1 THE AUTOBIOGRAPHY OF *Nehemiah, the son of Hecaliah:*

In December of the twentieth year of the reign of King Ar-ta-xerxes of Persia,[a] when I was at the palace at Shushan, [2] one of my fellow Jews named Hanani came to visit me with some men who had arrived from Judah. I took the opportunity to inquire about how things were going in Jerusalem.

"How are they getting along?" I asked. "—the Jews who returned to Jerusalem from their exile here?"

[3] "Well," they replied, "things are not good; the wall of Jerusalem is still torn down, and the gates are burned."

[4] When I heard this, I sat down and cried. In fact, I refused to eat for several days, for I spent the time in prayer to the God of heaven.

[5] "O Lord God," I cried out; "O great and awesome God who keeps his promises and is so loving and kind to those who love and obey him! Hear my prayer! [6,7] Listen carefully to what I say! Look down and see me praying night and day for your people Israel. I confess that we have sinned against you; yes, I and my people have committed the horrible sin of not obeying the commandments you gave us through your servant Moses. [8] Oh, please remember what you told Moses! You said,

" *'If you sin, I will scatter you among the nations;* [9] *but if you return to me and obey my laws, even though you are exiled to the farthest corners of the universe, I will bring you back to Jerusalem. For Jerusalem is the place in which I have chosen to live.'*

[10] "We are your servants, the people you rescued by your great power. [11] O Lord, please hear my prayer! Heed the prayers of those of us who delight to honor you. Please help me now as I go in and ask the king for a great favor—put it into his heart to be kind to me." (I was the king's cupbearer.)

2 ONE DAY IN April four months later, as I was serving the king his wine he asked me, "Why so sad? You aren't sick, are you?

You look like a man with deep troubles." (For until then I had always been cheerful when I was with him.) I was badly frightened, [3] but I replied, "Sir,[a] why shouldn't I be sad? For the city where my ancestors are buried is in ruins, and the gates have been burned down."

[4] "Well, what should be done?" the king asked.

With a quick prayer to the God of heaven, I replied, "If it please Your Majesty and if you look upon me with your royal favor, send me to Judah to rebuild the city of my fathers!"

[5,6] The king replied, with the queen sitting beside him, "How long will you be gone? When will you return?"

So it was agreed! And I set a time for my departure!

[7] Then I added this to my request: "If it please the king, give me letters to the governors west of the Euphrates River instructing them to let me travel through their countries on my way to Judah; [8] also a letter to Asaph, the manager of the king's forest, instructing him to give me timber for the beams and for the gates of the fortress near the Temple, and for the city walls, and for a house for myself."

And the king granted these requests, for God was being gracious to me.

[9] When I arrived in the provinces west of the Euphrates River, I delivered the king's letters to the governors there. (The king, I should add, had sent along army officers and troops to protect me!) [10] But when Sanballat (the Horonite) and Tobiah (an Ammonite who was a government official) heard of my arrival, they were very angry that anyone was interested in helping Israel.

[11,12] Three days after my arrival at Jerusalem I stole out during the night, taking only a few men with me; for I hadn't told a soul about the plans for Jerusalem which God had put into my heart. I was mounted on my donkey and the others were on foot, [13] and we went out through the Val-

---

a Implied.   2a Literally, "Let the king live forever."

ley Gate toward the Jackal's Well and over to the Dung Gate to see the broken walls and burned gates. [14,15] Then we went to the Fountain Gate and to the King's Pool, but my donkey couldn't get through the rubble. So we circled the city, and I followed the brook, inspecting the wall, and entered again at the Valley Gate.

[16] The city officials did not know I had been out there, or why, for as yet I had said nothing to anyone about my plans—not to the political or religious leaders, or even to those who would be doing the work.

[17] But now I told them, "You know full well the tragedy of our city; it lies in ruins and its gates are burned. Let us rebuild the wall of Jerusalem and rid ourselves of this disgrace!"

[18] Then I told them about the desire God had put into my heart, and of my conversation with the king, and the plan to which he had agreed.

They replied at once, "Good! Let's rebuild the wall!" And so the work began.

[19] But when Sanballat and Tobiah and Geshem the Arab heard of our plan, they scoffed and said, "What are you doing, rebelling against the king like this?"

[20] But I replied, "The God of heaven will help us, and we, his servants, will rebuild this wall; but you may have no part in this affair."

3 THEN ELIASHIB THE High Priest and the other priests rebuilt the wall as far as the Tower of the Hundred and the Tower of Hananel; then they rebuilt the Sheep Gate, hung its doors, and dedicated it. [2] Men from the city of Jericho worked next to them, and beyond them was the work crew led by Zaccur (son of Imri).

[3] The Fish Gate was built by the sons of Hassenaah; they did the whole thing—cut the beams, hung the doors, and made the bolts and bars. [4] Meremoth (son of Uriah, son of Hakkoz) repaired the next section of wall, and beyond him were Meshullam (son of Berechiah, son of Meshezabel) and Zadok (son of Baana). [5] Next were the men from Tekoa, but their leaders were lazy and didn't help.

[6] The Old Gate was repaired by Joiada (son of Paseah) and Meshullam (son of Besodeiah). They laid the beams, set up the doors, and installed the bolts and bars. [7] Next to them were Melatiah from Gibeon; Jadon from Meronoth; and men from Gibeon and Mizpah, who were citizens of the province. [8] Uzziel (son of Harhaiah) was a goldsmith by trade, but he too worked on the wall. Beyond him was Hananiah, a manufacturer of perfumes. Repairs were not needed from there to the Broad Wall.

[9] Rephaiah (son of Hur), the mayor of half of Jerusalem, was next down the wall from them. [10] Jedaiah (son of Harumaph) repaired the wall beside his own house, and next to him was Hattush (son of Hashabneiah). [11] Then came Malchijah (son of Harim) and Hasshub (son of Pahath-moab), who repaired the Furnace Tower in addition to a section of the wall. [12] Shallum (son of Hallohesh) and his daughters repaired the next section. He was the mayor of the other half of Jerusalem.

[13] The people from Zanoah, led by Hanun, built the Valley Gate, hung the doors, and installed the bolts and bars; then they repaired the 1,500 feet of wall to the Dung Gate.

[14] The Dung Gate was repaired by Malchijah (son of Rechab), the mayor of the Beth-haccherem area; and after building it, he hung the doors and installed the bolts and bars.

[15] Shallum (son of Colhozeh), the mayor of the Mizpah district, repaired the Fountain Gate. He rebuilt it, roofed it, hung its doors, and installed its locks and bars. Then he repaired the wall from the Pool of Siloam to the king's garden and the stairs that descend from the City of David section of Jerusalem. [16] Next to him was Nehemiah (son of Azbuk), the mayor of half the Beth-zur district; he built as far as the royal cemetery, the water reservoir, and the old Officers' Club building.[a] [17] Next was a group of Levites working under the supervision of Rehum (son of Bani). Then came Hashabiah, the mayor of half the Keilah district, who supervised the building of the wall in his own district. [18] Next down the line were

---

a Literally, "the house of the mighty men."

his clan brothers led by Bavvai (son of Henadad), the mayor of the other half of the Keilah district.

¹⁹ Next to them the workers were led by Ezer (son of Jeshua), the mayor of another part of Mizpah; they also worked on the section of wall across from the Armory, where the wall turns. ²⁰ Next to him was Baruch (son of Zabbai), who built from the turn in the wall to the home of Eliashib the High Priest. ²¹ Meremoth (son of Uriah, son of Hakkoz) built a section of the wall extending from a point opposite the door of Eliashib's house to the side of the house.

²² Then came the priests from the plains outside the city.ᵇ ²³ Benjamin, Hasshub, and Azariah (son of Ma-aseiah, son of Ananiah) repaired the sections next to their own houses. ²⁴ Next was Binnui (son of Henadad), who built the portion of the wall from Azariah's house to the corner. ²⁵ Palal (son of Uzai) carried on the work from the corner to the foundations of the upper tower of the king's castle beside the prison yard. Next was Pedaiah (son of Parosh).

²⁶ The Temple attendants living in Ophel repaired the wall as far as the East Water Gate and the Projecting Tower. ²⁷ Then came the Tekoites, who repaired the section opposite the Castle Tower and over to the wall of Ophel. ²⁸ The priests repaired the wall beyond the Horse Gate, each one doing the section immediately opposite his own house.

²⁹ Zadok (son of Immer) also rebuilt the wall next to his own house, and beyond him was Shemaiah (son of Shecaniah), the gatekeeper of the East Gate. ³⁰ Next was Hananiah (son of Shelemiah); Hanun (the sixth son of Zalaph); and Meshullam (son of Berechiah), who built next to his own house. ³¹ Malchijah, one of the goldsmiths, repaired as far as the Temple attendants' and merchants' Guild Hall, opposite the Muster Gate; then to the upper room at the corner. ³² The other goldsmiths and merchants completed the wall from that corner to the Sheep Gate.

4 SANBALLAT WAS VERY angry when he learned that we were rebuilding the

wall. He flew into a rage, and insulted and mocked us and laughed at us, and so did his friends and the Samaritan army officers. "What does this bunch of poor, feeble Jews think they are doing?" he scoffed. "Do they think they can build the wall in a day if they offer enough sacrifices? And look at those charred stones they are pulling out of the rubbish and using again!"

³ Tobiah, who was standing beside him, remarked, "If even a fox walked along the top of their wall, it would collapse!"

⁴ Then I prayed, "Hear us, O Lord God, for we are being mocked. May their scoffing fall back upon their own heads, and may they themselves become captives in a foreign land! ⁵ Do not ignore their sin. Do not blot it out, for they have despised you in despising us who are building your wall."

⁶ At last the wall was completed to half its original height around the entire city— for the workers worked hard.

⁷ But when Sanballat and Tobiah and the Arabians, Ammonites, and Ashdodites heard that the work was going right ahead and that the breaks in the wall were being repaired, they became furious. ⁸ They plotted to lead an army against Jerusalem to bring about riots and confusion. ⁹ But we prayed to our God and guarded the city day and night to protect ourselves.

¹⁰ Then some of the leaders began complaining that the workmen were becoming tired; and there was so much rubble to be removed that we could never get it done by ourselves. ¹¹ Meanwhile, our enemies were planning to swoop down upon us and kill us, thus ending our work. ¹² And whenever the workers who lived in the nearby cities went home for a visit, our enemies tried to talk them out of returning to Jerusalem. ¹³ So I placed armed guards from each family in the cleared spaces behind the walls.

¹⁴ Then as I looked over the situation, I called together the leaders and the people and said to them, "Don't be afraid! Remember the Lord who is great and glorious; fight for your friends, your families, and your homes!"

¹⁵ Our enemies learned that we knew of

---

b Implied.

their plot, and that God had exposed and frustrated their plan. Now we all returned to our work on the wall; [16] but from then on, only half worked while the other half stood guard behind them. [17] And the masons and laborers worked with weapons within easy reach beside them, [18] or with swords belted to their sides. The trumpeter stayed with me to sound the alarm.

[19] "The work is so spread out," I explained to them, "and we are separated so widely from each other, that when you hear the trumpet blow you must rush to where I am; and God will fight for us."

[20,21] We worked early and late, from sunrise to sunset; and half the men were always on guard. [22] I told everyone living outside the walls to move into Jerusalem so that their servants could go on guard duty as well as work during the day. [23] During this period none of us—I, nor my brothers, nor the servants, nor the guards who were with me—ever took off our clothes. And we carried our weapons with us at all times.

5 ABOUT THIS TIME there was a great outcry of protest from parents against some of the rich Jews who were profiteering on them. [2,3,4] What was happening was that families who ran out of money for food had to sell their children or mortgage their fields, vineyards, and homes to these rich men; and some couldn't even do that, for they already had borrowed to the limit to pay their taxes.

[5] "We are their brothers, and our children are just like theirs," the people protested. "Yet we must sell our children into slavery to get enough money to live. We have already sold some of our daughters, and we are helpless to redeem them, for our fields, too, are mortgaged to these men."

[6] I was very angry when I heard this; [7] so after thinking about it I spoke out against these rich government officials.

"What is this you are doing?" I demanded. "How dare you demand a mortgage as a condition for helping another Israelite?"

Then I called a public trial to deal with them.

[8] At the trial I shouted at them, "The rest of us are doing all we can to *help* our Jewish brothers who have returned from exile as slaves in distant lands, but you are forcing them right back into slavery again. How often must we redeem them?"

And they had nothing to say in their own defense.

[9] Then I pressed further. "What you are doing is very evil," I exclaimed. "Should you not walk in the fear of our God? Don't we have enough enemies among the nations around us who are trying to destroy us? [10] The rest of us are lending money and grain to our fellow-Jews without any interest. I beg you, gentlemen, stop this business of usury. [11] Restore their fields, vineyards, oliveyards, and homes to them this very day and drop your claims against them."

[12] So they agreed to do it and said that they would assist their brothers without requiring them to mortgage their lands and sell them their children. Then I summoned the priests and made these men formally vow to carry out their promises. [13] And I invoked the curse of God upon any of them who refused.[a]

"May God destroy your homes and livelihood if you fail to keep this promise," I declared.

And all the people shouted, "Amen," and praised the Lord. And the rich men did as they had promised.

[14] I would like to mention that for the entire twelve years that I was governor of Judah—from the twentieth until the thirty-second year of the reign of King Ar-ta-xerxes—my aides and I accepted no salaries or other assistance from the people of Israel. [15] This was quite a contrast to the former governors who had demanded food and wine and $100 a day in cash, and had put the population at the mercy of their aides, who tyrannized them; but I obeyed God and did not act that way. [16] I stayed at work on the wall and refused to speculate in land; I also required my officials to spend time on the wall. [17] All this despite the fact that I regularly fed 150 Jewish officials at my table, besides visitors from other countries! [18] The provisions required for each day were

a Literally, "then I shook out the lap of my gown . . ."

one ox, six fat sheep, and a large number of domestic fowls; and we needed a huge supply of all kinds of wines every ten days. Yet I refused to make a special levy against the people, for they were already having a difficult time. [19] O my God, please keep in mind all that I've done for these people and bless me for it.

6 WHEN SANBALLAT, TOBIAH, Geshem the Arab, and the rest of our enemies found out that we had almost completed the rebuilding of the wall—though we had not yet hung all the doors of the gates— [2] they sent me a message asking me to meet them in one of the villages in the Plain of Ono. But I realized they were plotting to kill me, [3] so I replied by sending back this message to them:

"I am doing a great work! Why should I stop to come and visit with you?"

[4] Four times they sent the same message, and each time I gave the same reply. [5,6] The fifth time, Sanballat's servant came with an open letter in his hand and this is what it said:

"Geshem tells me that everywhere he goes he hears that the Jews are planning to rebel, and that is why you are building the wall. He claims you plan to be their king— that is what is being said. [7] He also reports that you have appointed prophets to campaign for you at Jerusalem by saying, 'Look! Nehemiah is just the man we need!'

"You can be very sure that I am going to pass these interesting comments on to King Ar-ta-xerxes! I suggest that you come and talk it over with me—for that is the only way you can save yourself!"

[8] My reply was, "You know you are lying. There isn't one bit of truth to the whole story. [9] You're just trying to scare us into stopping our work." (O Lord God, please strengthen me!)

[10] A few days later I went to visit Shemaiah (son of Delaiah, who was the son of Mehetabel), for he said he was receiving a message from God.

"Let us hide in the Temple and bolt the door," he exclaimed, "for they are coming tonight to kill you."

[11] But I replied, "Should I, the governor, run away from danger? And if I go into the Temple, not being a priest, I would forfeit my life. No, I won't do it!"

[12,13] Then I realized that God had not spoken to him, but Tobiah and Sanballat had hired him to scare me and make me sin by fleeing to the Temple; and then they would be able to accuse me.

[14] "O my God," I prayed, "don't forget all the evil of Tobiah, Sanballat, No-adiah the prophetess, and all the other prophets who have tried to discourage me."

[15] The wall was finally finished in early September[a]—just fifty-two days after we had begun!

[16] When our enemies and the surrounding nations heard about it, they were frightened and humiliated, and they realized that the work had been done with the help of our God. [17] During those fifty-two days many letters went back and forth between Tobiah and the wealthy politicians of Judah. [18] For many in Judah had sworn allegiance to him because his father-in-law was Shecaniah (son of Arah) and because his son Jehohanan was married to the daughter of Meshullam (son of Berechiah). [19] They all told me what a wonderful man Tobiah was, and then they told him everything I had said; and Tobiah sent many threatening letters to frighten me.

7 AFTER THE WALL was finished and we had hung the doors in the gates and had appointed the gatekeepers, singers, and Levites, [2] I gave the responsibility of governing Jerusalem to my brother Hanani and to Hananiah, the commander of the fortress—a very faithful man who revered God more than most people do. [3] I issued instructions to them not to open the Jerusalem gates until well after sunrise, and to close and lock them while the guards were still on duty. I also directed that the guards be residents of Jerusalem, and that they must be on duty at regular times, and that each homeowner who lived near the wall must guard the section of wall next to his own home. [4] For the city was large, but the population was small; and only a few houses

---

a Or, "twenty-fifth day of the month Elul."

were scattered throughout the city.

⁵ Then the Lord told me to call together all the leaders of the city, along with the ordinary citizens, for registration. For I had found the record of the genealogies of those who had returned to Judah before, and this is what was written in it:

⁶ "The following is a list of the names of the Jews who returned to Judah after being exiled by King Nebuchadnezzar of Babylon.

⁷ "Their leaders were:
Zerubbabel, Jeshua, Nehemiah;
Azariah, Ra-amiah, Nahamani;
Mordecai, Bilshan, Mispereth;
Bigvai, Nehum, Baanah.

"The others who returned at that time were:

⁸⁻³⁸ From the subclan of Parosh, 2,172;
From the subclan of Shephatiah, 372;
From the subclan of Arah, 652;
From the families of Jeshua and Joab of the subclan of Pahath-moab, 2,818;
From the subclan of Elam, 1,254;
From the subclan of Zattu, 845;
From the subclan of Zaccai, 760;
From the subclan of Binnui, 648;
From the subclan of Bebai, 628;
From the subclan of Azgad, 2,322;
From the subclan of Adonikam, 667;
From the subclan of Bigvai, 2,067;
From the subclan of Adin, 655;
From the family of Hezekiah of the subclan of Ater, 98;
From the subclan of Hashum, 328;
From the subclan of Bezai, 324;
From the subclan of Hariph, 112;
From the subclan of Gibeon, 95;
From the subclans of Bethlehem and Netophah, 188;
From the subclan of Anathoth, 128;
From the subclan of Beth-azmaveth, 42;
From the subclans of Kiriath-jearim, Chephirah, and Be-eroth, 743;
From the subclans of Ramah and Geba, 621;
From the subclan of Michmas, 122;
From the subclans of Bethel and Ai, 123;
From the subclan of Nebo, 52;

From the subclan of Elam, 1,254;
From the subclan of Harim, 320;
From the subclan of Jericho, 345;
From the subclans of Lod, Hadid, and Ono, 721;
From the subclan of Sanaah, 3,930.

³⁹⁻⁴² "Here are the statistics concerning the returning priests:
From the family of Jeshua of the subclan of Jedaiah, 973;
From the subclan of Immer, 1,052;
From the subclan of Pashhur, 1,247;
From the subclan of Harim, 1,017.

⁴³,⁴⁴,⁴⁵ "Here are the statistics concerning the Levites:
From the family of Kadmi-el of the subclan of Hodevah of the clan of Jeshua, 74;
The choir members from the clan of Asaph, 148;
From the clans of Shallum, (all of whom were gatekeepers), 138.

⁴⁶⁻⁵⁶ "Of the Temple assistants, the following subclans were represented:
Ziha, Hasupha, Tabbaoth, Keros,
Sia, Padon, Lebana, Hagaba,
Shalmai, Hanan, Giddel, Gahar,
Re-aiah, Rezin, Nekoda,
Gazzam, Uzza, Paseah, Besai,
Asnah, Me-unim, Nephushesim,
Bakbuk, Hakupha, Harhur,
Bazlith, Mehida, Harsha,
Barkos, Sisera, Temah,
Neziah, Hatipha.

⁵⁷,⁵⁸,⁵⁹ "Following is a list of the descendants of Solomon's officials who returned to Judah:
Sotai, Sophereth, Perida,
Jaala, Darkon, Giddel,
Shephatiah, Hattil,
Pochereth-hazzebaim, Amon.

⁶⁰ "In all, the Temple assistants and the descendants of Solomon's officers numbered 392."

⁶¹ Another group returned to Jerusalem at that time from the Persian cities of Tel-melah, Tel-harsha, Cherub, Addon, and Immer. But they had lost their genealogies and could not prove their Jewish ancestry; ⁶² these were the subclans of Delaiah, Tobiah, and Nekoda—a total of 642.

⁶³ There were also several subclans of priests named after Habaiah, Hakkoz, and

Barzillai (he married one of the daughters of Barzillai the Gileadite and took her family name), [64,65] whose genealogies had been lost. So they were not allowed to continue as priests or even to receive the priests' share of food from the sacrifices until the Urim and Thummim had been consulted to find out from God whether or not they actually were descendants of priests.

[66] There was a total of 42,360 citizens who returned to Judah at that time; [67] also, 7,337 slaves and 245 choir members, both men and women. [68,69] They took with them 736 horses, 245 mules, 435 camels, and 6,720 donkeys.

[70] Some of their leaders gave gifts for the work. The governor gave $5,000 in gold, 50 golden bowls, and 530 sets of clothing for the priests. [71] The other leaders gave a total of $100,000 in gold and $77,000 in silver; [72] and the common people gave $100,000 in gold, $70,000 in silver, and sixty-seven sets of clothing for the priests.

[73] The priests, the Levites, the gatekeepers, the choir members, the Temple attendants, and the rest of the people now returned home to their own towns and villages throughout Judah. But during the month of September, they came back to Jerusalem.

8 NOW, IN MID-SEPTEMBER, all the people assembled at the plaza in front of the Water Gate and requested Ezra, their religious leader, to read to them the law of God which he had given to Moses.

So Ezra the priest brought out to them the scroll of Moses' laws. He stood on a wooden stand made especially for the occasion so that everyone could see him as he read. He faced the square in front of the Water Gate, and read from early morning until noon. Everyone stood up as he opened the scroll. And all who were old enough to understand paid close attention. To his right stood Mattithiah, Shema, Anaiah, Uriah, Hilkiah, and Ma-aseiah. To his left were Pedaiah, Misha-el, Malchijah, Hashum, Hash-baddenah, Zechariah, and Meshullam.

[6] Then Ezra blessed the Lord, the great God, and all the people said, "Amen," and lifted their hands toward heaven; then they bowed and worshiped the Lord with their faces toward the ground.

[7,8] As Ezra read from the scroll, Jeshua, Bani, Sherebiah, Jamin, Akkub, Shabbethai, Hodiah, Ma-aseiah, Kelita, Azariah, Jozabad, Hanan, Pelaiah, and the Levites went among the people[a] and explained the meaning of the passage that was being read. [9] All the people began sobbing when they heard the commands of the law.

Then Ezra the priest, and I as governor, and the Levites who were assisting me, said to them, "Don't cry on such a day as this! For today is a sacred day before the Lord your God— [10] it is a time to celebrate with a hearty meal, and to send presents to those in need, for the joy of the Lord is your strength. You must not be dejected and sad!"

[11] And the Levites, too, quieted the people, telling them, "That's right! Don't weep! For this is a day of holy joy, not of sadness."

[12] So the people went away to eat a festive meal and to send presents; it was a time of great and joyful celebration because they could hear and understand God's words.

[13] The next day the clan leaders and the priests and Levites met with Ezra to go over the law in greater detail. [14] As they studied it, they noted that Jehovah had told Moses that the people of Israel should live in tents during the Festival of Tabernacles to be held that month. [15] He had said also that a proclamation should be made throughout the cities of the land, especially in Jerusalem, telling the people to go to the hills to get branches from olive, myrtle, palm, and fig trees and to make huts in which to live for the duration of the feast.

[16] So the people went out and cut branches and used them to build huts on the roofs of their houses, or in their courtyards, or in the court of the Temple, or on the plaza beside the Water Gate, or at the Ephraim Gate Plaza. [17] They lived in these huts for the seven days of the feast, and everyone was filled with joy! (This procedure had not been carried out since the days

---

a Literally, "while the people remained in their places."

of Joshua.) [18] Ezra read from the scroll on each of the seven days of the feast, and on the eighth day there was a solemn closing service as required by the laws of Moses.

9 ON OCTOBER 10[a] the people returned for another observance; this time they fasted and clothed themselves with sackcloth and sprinkled dirt in their hair. And the Israelis separated themselves from all foreigners. [3] The laws of God were read aloud to them for two or three hours, and for several more hours they took turns confessing their own sins and those of their ancestors. And everyone worshiped the Lord their God. [4] Some of the Levites were on the platform praising the Lord God with songs of joy. These men were Jeshua, Kadmi-el, Bani, Shebaniah, Bunni, Sherebiah, Bani, and Chenani.

[5] Then the Levite leaders called out to the people, "Stand up and praise the Lord your God, for he lives from everlasting to everlasting. Praise his glorious name! It is far greater than we can think or say."

The leaders in this part of the service were Jeshua, Kadmi-el, Bani, Hashabneiah, Sherebiah, Hodiah, Shebaniah, and Pethahiah.

[6] Then Ezra prayed, "You alone are God. You have made the skies and the heavens, the earth and the seas, and everything in them. You preserve it all; and all the angels of heaven worship you.

[7] "You are the Lord God who chose Abram and brought him from Ur of the Chaldeans and renamed him Abraham. [8] When he was faithful to you, you made a contract with him to forever give him and his descendants the land of the Canaanites, Hittites, Amorites, Perizzites, Jebusites, and Girgashites; and now you have done what you promised, for you are always true to your word.

[9] "You saw the troubles and sorrows of our ancestors in Egypt, and you heard their cries from beside the Red Sea. [10] You displayed great miracles against Pharaoh and his people, for you knew how brutally the Egyptians were treating them; you have a glorious reputation because of those

never-to-be-forgotten deeds. [11] You divided the sea for your people so they could go through on dry land! And then you destroyed their enemies in the depths of the sea; they sank like stones beneath the mighty waters. [12] You led our ancestors by a pillar of cloud during the day and a pillar of fire at night so that they could find their way.

[13] "You came down upon Mount Sinai and spoke with them from heaven and gave them good laws and true commandments, [14] including the laws about the holy Sabbath; and you commanded them, through Moses your servant, to obey them all.

[15] "You gave them bread from heaven when they were hungry and water from the rock when they were thirsty. You commanded them to go in and conquer the land you had sworn to give them; [16] but our ancestors were a proud and stubborn lot, and they refused to listen to your commandments.

[17] "They refused to obey and didn't pay any attention to the miracles you did for them; instead, they rebelled and appointed a leader to take them back into slavery in Egypt! But you are a God of forgiveness, always ready to pardon, gracious and merciful, slow to become angry, and full of love and mercy; you didn't abandon them, [18] even though they made a calf-idol and proclaimed, 'This is our God! He brought us out of Egypt!' They sinned in so many ways, [19] but in your great mercy you didn't abandon them to die in the wilderness! The pillar of cloud led them forward day by day, and the pillar of fire showed them the way through the night. [20] You sent your good Spirit to instruct them, and you did not stop giving them bread from heaven or water for their thirst. [21] For forty years you sustained them in the wilderness; they lacked nothing in all that time. Their clothes didn't wear out and their feet didn't swell!

[22] "Then you helped them conquer great kingdoms and many nations, and you placed your people in every corner of the land; they completely took over the land of King Sihon of Heshbon and King Og of Bashan. [23] You caused a population explo-

---

a Literally, "the twenty-fourth day" of the Hebrew month.

sion among the Israelis and brought them into the land you had promised to their ancestors. [24] You subdued whole nations before them—even the kings and the people of the Canaanites were powerless! [25] Your people captured fortified cities and fertile land; they took over houses full of good things, with cisterns and vineyards and oliveyards and many, many fruit trees; so they ate and were full and enjoyed themselves in all your blessings.

[26] "But despite all this they were disobedient and rebelled against you. They threw away your law, killed the prophets who told them to return to you, and they did many other terrible things. [27] So you gave them to their enemies. But in their time of trouble they cried to you and you heard them from heaven, and in great mercy you sent them saviors who delivered them from their enemies. [28] But when all was going well, your people turned to sin again, and once more you let their enemies conquer them. Yet whenever your people returned to you and cried to you for help, once more you listened from heaven, and in your wonderful mercy delivered them! [29] You punished them in order to turn them toward your laws; but even though they should have obeyed them,[b] they were proud and wouldn't listen, and continued to sin. [30] You were patient with them for many years. You sent your prophets to warn them about their sins, but still they wouldn't listen. So once again you allowed the heathen nations to conquer them. [31] But in your great mercy you did not destroy them completely or abandon them forever. What a gracious and merciful God you are!

[32] "And now, O great and awesome God, you who keep your promises of love and kindness—do not let all the hardships we have gone through become as nothing to you. Great trouble has come upon us and upon our kings and princes and priests and prophets and ancestors from the days when the kings of Assyria first triumphed over us until now. [33] Every time you punished us you were being perfectly fair; we have sinned so greatly that you gave us only what we deserved. [34] Our kings, princes, priests,

and ancestors didn't obey your laws or listen to your warnings. [35] They did not worship you despite the wonderful things you did for them and the great goodness you showered upon them. You gave them a large, fat land, but they refused to turn from their wickedness.

[36] "So now we are slaves here in the land of plenty which you gave to our ancestors! Slaves among all this abundance! [37] The lush yield of this land passes into the hands of the kings whom you have allowed to conquer us because of our sins. They have power over our bodies and our cattle, and we serve them at their pleasure and are in great misery. [38] Because of all this, we again promise to serve the Lord! And we and our princes and Levites and priests put our names to this covenant."

10 I, NEHEMIAH THE governor, signed the covenant. The others who signed it were:

> Zedekiah, Seraiah, Azariah,
> Jeremiah, Pashhur, Amariah,
> Malchijah, Hattush, Shebaniah,
> Malluch, Harim, Meremoth,
> Obadiah, Daniel, Ginnethon,
> Baruch, Meshullam, Abijah,
> Mija-min, Ma-aziah, Bilgai,
> Shemaiah. (All those listed
> above were priests.)

[9-13] These were the Levites who signed:

> Jeshua (son of Azaniah), Binnui
> (son of Henadad), Kadmi-el,
> Shebaniah, Hodiah, Kelita,
> Pelaiah, Hanan, Mica, Rehob,
> Hashabiah, Zaccur, Sherebiah,
> Shebaniah, Hodiah,
> Bani, Beninu.

[14-27] The political leaders who signed:

> Parosh, Pahath-moab, Elam, Zattu,
> Bani, Bunni, Azgad, Bebai,
> Adonijah, Bigvai, Adin, Ater,
> Hezekiah, Azzur, Hodiah,
> Hashum, Bezai, Hariph,
> Anathoth, Nebai, Magpiash,
> Meshullam, Hezir, Meshezabel,
> Zadok, Jaddu-a, Pelatiah,
> Hanan, Anaiah, Hoshea,
> Hananiah, Hasshub, Hallohesh,

---

b Literally, "by the observance of which a man shall live."

Pilha, Shobek, Rehum,
Hashabnah, Ma-aseiah, Ahiah,
Hanan, Anan, Malluch,
Harim, Baanah.

²⁸ These men signed on behalf of the entire nation—for the common people; the priests; the Levites; the gatekeepers; the choir members; the Temple servants; and all the rest who, with their wives and sons and daughters who were old enough to understand, had separated themselves from the heathen people of the land in order to serve God. ²⁹ For we all heartily agreed to this oath and vowed to accept the curse of God unless we obeyed God's laws as issued by his servant Moses.

³⁰ We also agreed not to let our daughters marry non-Jewish men and not to let our sons marry non-Jewish girls.

³¹ We further agreed that if the heathen people in the land should bring any grain or other produce to be sold on the Sabbath or on any other holy day, we would refuse to buy it. And we agreed not to do any work every seventh year and to forgive and cancel the debts of our brother Jews.

³² We also agreed to charge ourselves annually with a Temple tax so that there would be enough money to care for the Temple of our God; ³³ for we needed supplies of the special Bread of the Presence, as well as grain offerings and burnt offerings for the Sabbaths, the new moon feasts, and the annual feasts. We also needed to purchase the other items necessary for the work of the Temple and for the atonement of Israel.

³⁴ Then we tossed a coin[a] to determine when—at regular times each year—the families of the priests, Levites, and leaders should supply the wood for the burnt offerings at the Temple as required in the law.

³⁵ We also agreed always to bring the first part of every crop to the Temple—whether it be a ground crop or from our fruit and olive trees.

³⁶ We agreed to give to God our oldest sons and the firstborn of all our cattle, herds, and flocks, just as the law requires; we presented them to the priests who minister in the Temple of our God. ³⁷ They stored the produce in the Temple of our God—the best of our grain crops, and other contributions, the first of our fruit, and the first of the new wine and olive oil. And we promised to bring to the Levites a tenth of everything our land produced, for the Levites were responsible to collect the tithes in all our rural towns. ³⁸ A priest—a descendant of Aaron—would be with the Levites as they received these tithes, and a tenth of all that was collected as tithes was delivered to the Temple and placed in the storage areas. ³⁹,⁴⁰ The people and the Levites were required by law to bring these offerings of grain, new wine, and olive oil to the Temple and place them in the sacred containers for use by the ministering priests, the gatekeepers, and the choir singers.

So we agreed together not to neglect the Temple of our God.

11 THE ISRAELI OFFICIALS were living in Jerusalem, the Holy City, at this time; but now a tenth of the people from the other cities and towns of Judah and Benjamin were selected by lot to live there too. ² Some who moved to Jerusalem at this time were volunteers, and they were highly honored.

³ Following is a list of the names of the provincial officials who came to Jerusalem (though most of the leaders, the priests, the Levites, the Temple assistants, and the descendants of Solomon's servants continued to live in their own homes in the various cities of Judah).

⁴,⁵,⁶ Leaders from the tribe of Judah:
Athaiah (son of Uzziah, son of Zechariah, son of Amariah, son of Shephatiah, son of Mahalelel, a descendant of Perez);
Ma-aseiah (son of Baruch, son of Col-hozeh, son of Hazaiah, son of Adaiah, son of Joiarib, son of Zechariah, son of the Shilonite).
These were the 468 stalwart descendants of Perez who lived in Jerusalem.
⁷,⁸,⁹ Leaders from the tribe of Benjamin:
Sallu (son of Meshullam, son of Joed, son of Pedaiah, son of Kolaiah, son of Ma-aseiah, son of Ithi-el,

---

a Literally, "cast lots," a form of dice.

son of Jeshaiah).

The 968 descendants of Gabbai and Sallai. Their chief was Joel, son of Zichri, who was assisted by Judah, son of Hassenu-ah.

¹⁰⁻¹⁴ Leaders from among the priests:
Jedaiah (son of Joiarib);
Jachin;
Seraiah (son of Hilkiah, son of Meshullam, son of Zadok, son of Meraioth, son of Ahitub the chief priest).

In all, there were 822 priests doing the work at the Temple under the leadership of these men. And there were 242 priests under the leadership of Adaiah (son of Jeroham, son of Pelaliah, son of Amzi, son of Zechariah, son of Pashhur, son of Malchijah).

There were also 128 stalwart men under the leadership of Amashsai (son of Azarel, son of Ahzai, son of Meshillemoth, son of Immer); who was assisted by Zabdiel (son of Haggedolim).

¹⁵,¹⁶,¹⁷ Levite leaders:
Shemaiah (son of Hasshub, son of Azrikam, son of Hashabiah, son of Bunni);
Shabbethai and Jozabad, who were in charge of the work outside the Temple;
Mattaniah (son of Mica, son of Zabdi, son of Asaph) was the one who began the thanksgiving services with prayer;
Bakbukiah and Abda (son of Shammua, son of Galal, son of Jeduthun) were his assistants.

¹⁸ In all, there were 284 Levites in Jerusalem. ¹⁹ There were also 172 gatekeepers, led by Akkub, Talmon, and others of their clan. ²⁰ The other priests, Levites, and people lived wherever their family inheritance was located. ²¹ However, the Temple workers (whose leaders were Ziha and Gishpa) all lived in Ophel.

²²,²³ The supervisor of the Levites in Jerusalem and of those serving at the Temple was Uzzi (son of Bani, son of Hashabiah, son of Mattaniah, son of Mica), a descendant of Asaph, whose clan became the Tabernacle singers. He was appointed by King David,ᵃ who also set the pay scale of the singers.

²⁴ Pethahiah (son of Meshezabel, a descendant of Zerah, a son of Judah) assisted in all matters of public administration.

²⁵⁻³⁰ Some of the towns where the people of Judah lived were:
Kiriath-arba, Dibon, Jekabzeel (and their surrounding villages),
Jeshua, Moladah, Beth-pelet,
Hazar-shual, Beer-sheba (and its surrounding villages), Ziklag,
Meconah and its villages,
En-rimmon, Zorah, Jarmuth,
Zanoah, Adullam (and their surrounding villages), Lachish and its nearby fields, Azekah and its towns.

So the people spread from Beer-sheba to the valley of Hinnom.

³¹⁻³⁵ The people of the tribe of Benjamin lived at:
Geba, Michmash, Aija, Bethel (and its surrounding villages),
Anathoth, Nob, Ananiah,
Hazor, Ramah, Gittaim, Hadid,
Zeboim, Neballat, Lod, Ono (the Valley of the Craftsmen).

³⁶ Some of the Levites who lived in Judah were sent to live with the tribe of Benjamin.

12 HERE IS A list of the priests who accompanied Zerubbabel (son of Shealtiel) and Jeshua:
Seraiah, Jeremiah, Ezra, Amariah,
Malluch, Hattush, Shecaniah,
Rehum, Meremoth, Iddo,
Ginnethoi, Abijah, Mijamin,
Ma-adiah, Bilgah, Shemaiah,
Joiarib, Jedaiah, Sallu, Amok,
Hilkiah, Jedaiah.

⁸ The Levites who went with them were:
Jeshua, Binnui, Kadmi-el,
Sherebiah, Judah,
Mattaniah—who was the one in charge of the thanksgiving service.

⁹ Bakbukiah and Unno, their fellow clansmen, helped them during the service.

---

a Literally, "There was a commandment from the king concerning them."

10,11 Jeshua was the father of Joiakim; Joiakim was the father of Eliashib; Eliashib was the father of Joiada; Joiada was the father of Jonathan; Jonathan was the father of Jaddu-a.

12-21 The following were the clan leaders of the priests who served under the High Priest Joiakim:

Meraiah, leader of the Seraiah clan;
Hananiah, leader of the Jeremiah clan;
Meshullam, leader of the Ezra clan;
Jehohanan, leader of the Amariah clan;
Jonathan, leader of the Malluchi clan;
Joseph, leader of the Shebaniah clan;
Adna, leader of the Harim clan;
Helkai, leader of the Meraioth clan;
Zechariah, leader of the Iddo clan;
Meshullam, leader of the Ginnethon clan;
Zichri, leader of the Abijah clan;
Piltai, leader of the Moadiah and Miniamin clans;
Shammu-a, leader of the Bilgah clan;
Jehonathan, leader of the Shemaiah clan;
Mattenai, leader of the Joiarib clan;
Uzzi, leader of the Jedaiah clan;
Kallai, leader of the Sallai clan;
Eber, leader of the Amok clan;
Hashabiah, leader of the Hilkiah clan;
Nethanel, leader of the Jedaiah clan.

22 A genealogical record of the heads of the clans of the priests and Levites was compiled during the reign of King Darius of Persia, in the days of Eliashib, Joiada, Johanan, and Jaddu-a—all of whom were Levites. 23 In *The Book of the Chronicles* the Levite names were recorded down to the days of Johanan, the son of Eliashib.

24 These were the chiefs of the Levites at that time:

Hashabiah, Sherebiah, and Jeshua (son of Kadmi-el).

Their fellow-clansmen helped them during the ceremonies of praise and thanksgiving, just as commanded by David, the man of God.

25 The gatekeepers who had charge of the collection centers at the gates were:

Mattaniah, Bakbukiah, Obadiah, Meshullam, Talmon, Akkub.

26 These were the men who were active in the time of Joiakim (son of Jeshua, son of Jozadak), and when I was the governor, and when Ezra was the priest and teacher of religion.

27 During the dedication of the new Jerusalem wall, all the Levites throughout the land came to Jerusalem to assist in the ceremonies and to take part in the joyous occasion with their thanksgiving, cymbals, psaltries, and harps. 28 The choir members also came to Jerusalem from the surrounding villages and from the villages of the Netophathites; 29 they also came from Beth-gilgal and the area of Geba and Azmaveth, for the singers had built their own villages as suburbs of Jerusalem. 30 The priests and Levites first dedicated themselves, then the people, the gates, and the wall.

31,32 I led the Judean leaders to the top of the wall and divided them into two long lines to walk in opposite directions along the top of the wall, giving thanks as they went. The group which went to the right toward the Dung Gate consisted of half of the leaders of Judah, 33 including Hoshaiah, Azariah, Ezra, Meshullam, 34 Judah, Benjamin, Shemaiah, and Jeremiah.

35,36 The priests who played the trumpets were Zechariah (son of Jonathan, son of Shemaiah, son of Mattaniah, son of Micaiah, son of Zaccur, son of Asaph),

Shemaiah, Azarel, Milalai,
Gilalai, Maai, Nethanel,
Judah, and Hanani.

(They used the original musical instruments of King David.) Ezra the priest led this procession. 37 When they arrived at the Fountain Gate they went straight ahead and climbed the stairs which go up beside the castle to the old City of David; then they went to the Water Gate on the east.

38 The other group, of which I was a member, went around the other way to meet them. We walked from the Tower of Furnaces to the Broad Wall, 39 then from the Ephraim Gate to the Old Gate, passed the Fish Gate and the Tower of Hananel, and went on to the gate of the Tower of the Hundred; then we continued on to the Sheep Gate and stopped at the Prison Gate.

⁴⁰,⁴¹ Both choirs then proceeded to the Temple. Those with me were joined by the trumpet-playing priests—
> Eliakim, Ma-aseiah, Miniamin,
> Micaiah, Eli-o-enai, Zechariah,
> and Hananiah,

⁴² and by the singers—
> Ma-aseiah, Shemaiah, Eleazar,
> Uzzi, Jehohanan, Malchijah,
> Elam and Ezer.

They sang loudly and clearly under the direction of Jezrahiah the choirmaster.

⁴³ Many sacrifices were offered on that joyous day, for God had given us cause for great joy. The women and children rejoiced too, and the joy of the people of Jerusalem was heard far away!

⁴⁴ On that day men were appointed to be in charge of the treasuries, the wave offerings, the tithes, and first-of-the-harvest offerings, and to collect these from the farms as decreed by the laws of Moses. These offerings were assigned to the priests and Levites, for the people of Judah appreciated the priests and Levites and their ministry. ⁴⁵ They also appreciated the work of the singers and gatekeepers, who assisted them in worshiping God and performing the purification ceremonies as required by the laws of David and his son Solomon. ⁴⁶ (It was in the days of David and Asaph that the custom began of having choir directors to lead the choirs in hymns of praise and thanks to God.) ⁴⁷ So now, in the days of Zerubbabel and Nehemiah, the people brought a daily supply of food for the members of the choir, the gatekeepers, and the Levites. The Levites, in turn, gave a portion of what they received to the priests.ᵃ

13 ON THAT SAME day, as the laws of Moses were being read, the people found a statement which said that the Ammonites and Moabites should never be permitted to worship at the Temple.ᵃ ² For they had not been friendly to the people of Israel. Instead, they had hired Balaam to curse them—although God turned the curse into a blessing. ³ When this rule was read, all the foreigners were immediately expelled from the assembly.

⁴ Before this had happened, Eliashib the priest, who had been appointed as custodian of the Temple storerooms and who was also a good friend of Tobiah, ⁵ had converted a storage room into a beautiful guest room for Tobiah. The room had previously been used for storing the grain offerings, frankincense, bowls, and tithes of grain, new wine, and olive oil. Moses had decreed that these offerings belonged to the Levites, the members of the choir, and the gatekeepers. (The wave offerings were for the priests.)

⁶ I was not in Jerusalem at the time, for I had returned to Babylon in the thirty-second year of the reign of King Ar-ta-xerxes (though I later received his permission to go back again to Jerusalem). ⁷ When I arrived back in Jerusalem and learned of this evil deed of Eliashib—that he had prepared a guest room in the Temple for Tobiah— ⁸ I was very upset and threw out all of his belongings from the room. ⁹ Then I demanded that the room be thoroughly cleaned, and I brought back the Temple bowls, the grain offerings, and frankincense.

¹⁰ I also learned that the Levites had not been given what was due them, so they and the choir singers who were supposed to conduct the worship services had returned to their farms. ¹¹ I immediately confronted the leaders and demanded, "Why has the Temple been forsaken?" Then I called all the Levites back again and restored them to their proper duties. ¹² And once more all the people of Judah began bringing their tithes of grain, new wine, and olive oil to the Temple treasury.

¹³ I put Shelemiah the priest, Zadok the scribe, and Pedaiah the Levite in charge of the administration of the storehouses; and I appointed Hanan (son of Zaccur, son of Mattaniah) as their assistant. These men had an excellent reputation, and their job was to make an honest distribution to their fellow-Levites.

¹⁴ O my God, remember this good deed and do not forget all that I have done for the Temple.

¹⁵ One day I was on a farm and saw some men treading winepresses on the Sabbath, hauling in sheaves, and loading their

---

a Literally, "to the descendants of Aaron the priest."   13a Deuteronomy 23:3–5.

donkeys with wine, grapes, figs, and all sorts of produce which they took that day into Jerusalem. So I opposed them publicly. [16] There were also some men from Tyre bringing in fish and all sorts of wares and selling them on the Sabbath to the people of Jerusalem.

[17] Then I asked the leaders of Judah, "Why are you profaning the Sabbath? [18] Wasn't it enough that your fathers did this sort of thing and brought the present evil days upon us and upon our city? And now you are bringing more wrath upon the people of Israel by permitting the Sabbath to be desecrated in this way."

[19] So from then on I commanded that the gates of the city be shut as darkness fell on Friday evenings and not be opened until the Sabbath had ended; and I sent some of my servants to guard the gates so that no merchandise could be brought in on the Sabbath day. [20] The merchants and tradesmen camped outside Jerusalem once or twice, [21] but I spoke sharply to them and said, "What are you doing out here, camping around the wall? If you do this again, I will arrest you." And that was the last time they came on the Sabbath.

[22] Then I commanded the Levites to purify themselves and to guard the gates in order to preserve the sanctity of the Sabbath. Remember this good deed, O my God! Have compassion upon me in accordance with your great goodness.

[23] About the same time I realized that some of the Jews had married women from Ashdod, Ammon, and Moab, [24] and that many of their children spoke in the language of Ashdod and couldn't speak the language of Judah at all. [25] So I argued with these parents and cursed them and punched a few of them and knocked them around and pulled out their hair; and they vowed before God that they would not let their children intermarry with non-Jews.

[26] "Wasn't this exactly King Solomon's problem?" I demanded. "There was no king who could compare with him, and God loved him and made him the king over all Israel; but even so he was led into idolatry by foreign women. [27] Do you think that we will let you get away with this sinful deed?"

[28] One of the sons of Jehoiada (the son of Eliashib the High Priest) was a son-in-law of Sanballat the Horonite, so I chased him out of the Temple. [29] Remember them, O my God, for they have defiled the priesthood and the promises and vows of the priests and Levites. [30] So I purged out the foreigners, and assigned tasks to the priests and Levites, making certain that each knew his work. [31] They supplied wood for the altar at the proper times and cared for the sacrifices and the first offerings of every harvest. Remember me, my God, with your kindness.

Rohn Engh

Irresistible Queen

There's nothing like quiet feminine power to get next to a man and change his mind! This exciting short story is how Queen Esther, the young Jewess, prevented an anti-Semitic bloodbath.

Her husband, here called Ahasuerus, was actually Xerxes the Great (486-465 B.C.)—that most extravagant Persian emperor who booted his first wife Vashti (chapter one) when she refused to promenade for his stag party, then roared off on a military campaign that swept across Asia Minor (modern Turkey) and into Greece before getting wiped out, and then returned to choose a new queen (chapter two). Like most oriental potentates, he was susceptible to the bright ideas of his court favorites, like why not kill all the Jews? That's when Esther decided to literally take her life in her hands and beg the king to save them.

ESTHER

1 IT WAS THE third year of the reign of King Ahasuerus, emperor of vast Media-Persia, with its 127 provinces stretching from India to Ethiopia. This was the year of the great celebration at Shushan Palace, to which the emperor invited all his governors, aides, and army officers, bringing them in from every part of Media-Persia for the occasion. ⁴ The celebration lasted six months, a tremendous display of the wealth and glory of his empire.

⁵ When it was all over, the king gave a special party for the palace servants and officials—janitors and cabinet officials alike—for seven days of revelry, held in the courtyard of the palace garden. ⁶ The decorations were green, white, and blue, fastened with purple ribbonsª tied to silver rings imbedded in marble pillars. Gold and silver benches stood on pavements of black, red, white, and yellow marble. ⁷ Drinks were served in golden goblets of many designs, and there was an abundance of royal wine, for the king was feeling very generous.

---

a Literally, "fastened with cords of fine linen and purple thread."

[8] The only restriction on the drinking was that no one should be compelled to take more than he wanted, but those who wished could have as much as they pleased. For the king had instructed his officers to let everyone decide this matter for himself.

[9] Queen Vashti gave a party for the women of the palace at the same time.

[10] On the final day, when the king was feeling high, half drunk from wine, he told the seven eunuchs who were his personal aides—Mehuman, Biztha, Harbona, Bigtha, Abagtha, Zethar, and Carkas— [11] to bring Queen Vashti to him with the royal crown upon her head so that all the men could gaze upon her beauty—for she was a very beautiful woman. [12] But when they conveyed the emperor's order to Queen Vashti, she refused to come. The king was furious, [13-15] but first consulted his lawyers, for he did nothing without their advice. They were men of wisdom who knew the temper of the times as well as Persian law and justice, and the king trusted their judgment. These men were Carshena, Shethar, Admatha, Tarshish, Meres, Marsena, and Memucan—seven high officials of Media-Persia. They were his personal friends as well as being the chief officers of the government.

"What shall we do about this situation?" he asked them. "What penalty does the law provide for a queen who refuses to obey the king's orders, properly sent through his aides?"

[16] Memucan answered for the others, "Queen Vashti has wronged not only the king but every official and citizen of your empire. [17] For women everywhere will begin to disobey their husbands when they learn what Queen Vashti has done. [18] And before this day is out, the wife of every one of us officials throughout your empire will hear what the queen did and will start talking to us husbands the same way, and there will be contempt and anger throughout your realm. [19] We suggest that, subject to your agreement, you issue a royal edict, a law of the Medes and Persians that can never be changed, that Queen Vashti be forever banished from your presence and that you

choose another queen more worthy than she. [20] When this decree is published throughout your great kingdom, husbands everywhere, whatever their rank, will be respected by their wives!"

[21] The king and all his aides thought this made good sense, so he followed Memucan's counsel, [22] and sent letters to all of his provinces, in all the local languages, stressing that every man should rule his home, and should assert his authority.

2 BUT AFTER KING Ahasuerus' anger had cooled, he began brooding over the loss of Vashti, realizing that he would never see her again.

[2] So his aides suggested, "Let us go and find the most beautiful girls in the empire and bring them to the king for his pleasure. [3] We will appoint agents in each province to select young lovelies for the royal harem. Hegai, the eunuch in charge, will see that they are given beauty treatments, [4] and after that, the girl who pleases you most shall be the queen instead of Vashti."

This suggestion naturally pleased the king very much, and he put the plan into immediate effect.

[5] Now there was a certain Jew at the palace named Mordecai (son of Jair, son of Shime-i, son of Kish, a Benjaminite). [6] He had been captured when Jerusalem was destroyed by King Nebuchadnezzar, and had been exiled to Babylon along with King Jeconiah of Judah and many others. [7] This man had a beautiful and lovely young cousin,[a] Hadassah (also called Esther), whose father and mother were dead, and whom he had adopted into his family and raised as his own daughter. [8] So now, as a result of the king's decree, Esther was brought to the king's harem at Shushan Palace, along with many other young girls. [9] Hegai, who was responsible for the harem, was very much impressed with her, and did his best to make her happy; he ordered a special menu for her, favored her for the beauty treatments, gave her seven girls from the palace as her maids, and gave her the most luxurious apartment in the harem. [10] Esther hadn't told anyone that she was a

---

a His uncle's daughter.

Jewess, for Mordecai had said not to. [11] He came daily to the court of the harem to ask about Esther and to find out what was happening to her.

[12,13,14] The instructions concerning these girls were that before being taken to the king's bed, each would be given six months of beauty treatments with oil of myrrh, followed by six months with special perfumes and ointments. Then, as each girl's turn came for spending the night with King Ahasuerus, she was given her choice of clothing or jewelry she wished, to enhance her beauty. She was taken to the king's apartment in the evening and the next morning returned to the second harem where the king's wives lived. There she was under the care of Shaashgaz, another of the king's eunuchs, and lived there the rest of her life, never seeing the king again unless he had especially enjoyed her, and called for her by name.

[15] When it was Esther's[b] turn to go to the king, she accepted the advice of Hegai, the eunuch in charge of the harem, dressing according to his instructions. And all the other girls exclaimed with delight when they saw her. [16] So Esther was taken to the palace of the king in January of the seventh year of his reign. [17] Well, the king loved Esther more than any of the other girls. He was so delighted with her that he set the royal crown on her head and declared her queen instead of Vashti. [18] To celebrate the occasion, he threw another big party for all his officials and servants, giving generous gifts to everyone and making grants to the provinces in the form of remission of taxes.

[19] Later, the king demanded a second bevy of beautiful girls.[c] By that time Mordecai had become a government official.

[20] Esther still hadn't told anyone she was a Jewess, for she was still following Mordecai's orders, just as she had in his home.

[21] One day, as Mordecai was on duty at the palace, two of the king's eunuchs, Bigthan and Teresh—who were guards at the palace gate—became angry at the king and plotted to assassinate him. [22] Mordecai heard about it and passed on the information to Queen Esther, who told the king, crediting Mordecai with the information. [23] An investigation was made, the two men found guilty, and impaled alive.[d] This was all duly recorded in the book of the history of King Ahasuerus' reign.

3 SOON AFTERWARDS KING Ahasuerus appointed Haman (son of Hammedatha the Agagite), as prime minister. He was the most powerful official in the empire next to the king himself. [2] Now all the king's officials bowed before him in deep reverence whenever he passed by, for so the king had commanded. But Mordecai refused to bow.

[3,4] "Why are you disobeying the king's commandment?" the others demanded day after day, but he still refused. Finally they spoke to Haman about it, to see whether Mordecai could get away with it because of his being a Jew, which was the excuse he had given them. [5,6] Haman was furious, but decided not to lay hands on Mordecai alone, but to move against all of Mordecai's people, the Jews, and destroy all of them throughout the whole kingdom of Ahasuerus. [7] The most propitious time for this action was determined by throwing dice. This was done in April of the twelfth year of the reign of Ahasuerus, and February of the following year was the date indicated.

[8] Haman now approached the king about the matter. "There is a certain race of people scattered through all the provinces of your kingdom," he began, "and their laws are different from those of any other nation, and they refuse to obey the king's laws; therefore, it is not in the king's interest to let them live. [9] If it please the king, issue a decree that they be destroyed, and I will pay $20,000,000 into the royal treasury for the expenses involved in this purge."

[10] The king agreed, confirming his decision by removing his ring from his finger and giving it to Haman,[a] telling him, [11] "Keep the money, but go ahead and do as you like with these people—whatever

---

b Literally, "Esther, the daughter of Abihail who was Mordecai's uncle, who had adopted her."
c Or, "When Esther and the other girls had been transferred to the second harem."   d Literally, "hanged on a tree." Possibly the meaning is that they were crucified.   3a Literally, "Haman, son of Hammedatha the Agagite."

you think best."

[12] Two or three weeks later,[b] Haman called in the king's secretaries and dictated letters to the governors and officials throughout the empire, to each province in its own languages and dialects; these letters were signed in the name of King Ahasuerus and sealed with his ring. [13] They were then sent by messengers into all the provinces of the empire, decreeing that the Jews—young and old, women and children—must all be killed on the 28th day of February of the following year, and their property given to those who killed them. [14] "A copy of this edict," the letter stated, "must be proclaimed as law in every province, and made known to all your people, so that they will be ready to do their duty on the appointed day." [15] The edict went out by the king's speediest couriers, after being first proclaimed in the city of Shushan. Then the king and Haman sat down for a drinking spree as the city fell into confusion and panic.

4 WHEN MORDECAI LEARNED what had been done, he tore his clothes and put on sackcloth and ashes, and went out into the city, crying with a loud and bitter wail. [2] Then he stood outside the gate of the palace, for no one was permitted to enter in mourning clothes. [3] And throughout all the provinces there was great mourning among the Jews, fasting, weeping, and despair at the king's decree; and many lay in sackcloth and ashes.

[4] When Esther's maids and eunuchs came and told her about Mordecai, she was deeply distressed and sent clothing to him to replace the sackcloth, but he refused it. [5] Then Esther sent for Hathach, one of the king's eunuchs who had been appointed as her attendant, and told him to go out to Mordecai and find out what the trouble was, and why he was acting like that. [6] So Hathach went out to the city square, and found Mordecai just outside the palace gates, [7] and heard the whole story from him; and about the $20,000,000 Haman had promised to pay into the king's treasury for the destruction of the Jews. [8] Mordecai also

gave Hathach a copy of the king's decree dooming all Jews, and told him to show it to Esther and to tell her what was happening, and that she should go to the king to plead for her people. [9] So Hathach returned to Esther with Mordecai's message. [10] Esther told Hathach to go back and say to Mordecai,

[11] "All the world knows that anyone, whether man or woman, who goes into the king's inner court without his summons is doomed to die unless the king holds out his golden scepter; and the king has not called for me to come to him in more than a month."

[12] So Hathach gave Esther's message to Mordecai.

[13] This was Mordecai's reply to Esther: "Do you think you will escape there in the palace, when all other Jews are killed? [14] If you keep quiet at a time like this, God will deliver the Jews from some other source, but you and your relatives will die; what's more, who can say but that God has brought you into the palace for just such a time as this?"

[15] Then Esther said to tell Mordecai:

[16] "Go and gather together all the Jews of Shushan and fast for me; do not eat or drink for three days, night or day; and I and my maids will do the same; and then, though it is strictly forbidden, I will go in to see the king; and if I perish, I perish."

[17] So Mordecai did as Esther told him to.

5 THREE DAYS LATER Esther put on her royal robes and entered the inner court just beyond the royal hall of the palace, where the king was sitting upon his royal throne. [2] And when he saw Queen Esther standing there in the inner court, he welcomed her, holding out the golden scepter to her. So Esther approached and touched its tip.

[3] Then the king asked her, "What do you wish, Queen Esther? What is your request? I will give it to you, even if it is half the kingdom!"

[4] And Esther replied, "If it please Your Majesty, I want you and Haman to come to a banquet I have prepared for you to-

---

b Literally, "Then, on the 13th day of the first month . . ."

day."

⁵ The king turned to his aides. "Tell Haman to hurry!" he said. So the king and Haman came to Esther's banquet.

⁶ During the wine course the king said to Esther, "Now tell me what you really want, and I will give it to you, even if it is half of the kingdom!"

⁷,⁸ Esther replied, "My request, my deepest wish, is that if Your Majesty loves me, and wants to grant my request, that you come again with Haman tomorrow to the banquet I shall prepare for you. And tomorrow I will explain what this is all about."

⁹ What a happy man was Haman as he left the banquet! But when he saw Mordecai there at the gate, not standing up or trembling before him, he was furious. ¹⁰ However, he restrained himself and went on home and gathered together his friends and Zeresh his wife, ¹¹ and boasted to them about his wealth, and his many children, and promotions the king had given him, and how he had become the greatest man in the kingdom next to the king himself.

¹² Then he delivered his final punch line: "Yes, and Esther the queen invited only me and the king himself to the banquet she prepared for us; and tomorrow we are invited again! ¹³ But yet," he added, "all this is nothing when I see Mordecai the Jew just sitting there in front of the king's gate, refusing to bow to me."

¹⁴ "Well," suggested Zeresh his wife and all his friends, "get ready a 75-foot-high gallows, and in the morning ask the king to let you hang Mordecai on it; and when this is done you can go on your merry way with the king to the banquet." This pleased Haman immensely and he ordered the gallows built.

6 THAT NIGHT THE king had trouble sleeping and decided to read awhile. He ordered the historical records of his kingdom from the library, and in them he came across the item telling how Mordecai had exposed the plot of Bigthana and Teresh, two of the king's eunuchs, watchmen at the palace gates, who had plotted to assassinate him.

³ "What reward did we ever give Mordecai for this?" the king asked.

His courtiers replied, "Nothing!"

⁴ "Who is on duty in the outer court?" the king inquired. Now, as it happened, Haman had just arrived in the outer court of the palace to ask the king to hang Mordecai from the gallows he was building.

⁵ So the courtiers replied to the king, "Haman is out there."

"Bring him in," the king ordered. ⁶ So Haman came in and the king said to him, "What should I do to honor a man who truly pleases me?"

Haman thought to himself, "Whom would he want to honor more than me?"
⁷,⁸ So he replied, "Bring out some of the royal robes the king himself has worn, and the king's own horse, and the royal crown, ⁹ and instruct one of the king's most noble princes to robe the man and to lead him through the streets on the king's own horse, shouting before him, 'This is the way the king honors those who truly please him!'"

¹⁰ "Excellent!" the king said to Haman. "Hurry and take these robes and my horse, and do just as you have said—to Mordecai the Jew, who works at the Chancellery. Follow every detail you have suggested."

¹¹ So Haman took the robes and put them on Mordecai and mounted him on the king's own steed, and led him through the streets of the city, shouting, "This is the way the king honors those he delights in."

¹² Afterwards Mordecai returned to his job, but Haman hurried home utterly humiliated. ¹³ When Haman told Zeresh his wife and all his friends what had happened, they said, "If Mordecai is a Jew, you will never succeed in your plans against him; to continue to oppose him will be fatal."

¹⁴ While they were still discussing it with him, the king's messengers arrived to conduct Haman quickly to the banquet Esther had prepared.

7 SO THE KING and Haman came to Esther's banquet. ² Again, during the wine course, the king asked her, "What is your petition, Queen Esther? What do you wish? Whatever it is, I will give it to you, even if it is half of my kingdom!"

³ And at last Queen Esther replied, "If I have won your favor, O king, and if it please Your Majesty, save my life and the

lives of my people. ⁴ For I and my people have been sold to those who will destroy us. We are doomed to destruction and slaughter. If we were only to be sold as slaves, perhaps I could remain quiet, though even then there would be incalculable damage to the king that no amount of money could begin to cover."

⁵ "What are you talking about?" King Ahasuerus demanded. "Who would dare touch you?"

⁶ Esther replied, "This wicked Haman is our enemy."

Then Haman grew pale with fright before the king and queen. ⁷ The king jumped to his feet and went out into the palace garden as Haman stood up to plead for his life to Queen Esther, for he knew that he was doomed. ⁸ In despair he fell upon the couch where Queen Esther was reclining, just as the king returned from the palace garden.

"Will he even rape the queen right here in the palace, before my very eyes?" the king roared. Instantly the death veil was placed over Haman's face.

⁹ Then Harbona, one of the king's aides, said, "Sir, Haman has just ordered a 75-foot gallows constructed, to hang Mordecai, the man who saved the king from assassination! It stands in Haman's courtyard."

"Hang Haman on it," the king ordered. ¹⁰ So they did, and the king's wrath was pacified.

8 ON THAT SAME day King Ahasuerus gave the estate of Haman, the Jews' enemy, to Queen Esther. Then Mordecai was brought before the king, for Esther had told the king that he was her cousin and foster father.ᵃ ² The king took off his ring—which he had taken back from Haman—and gave it to Mordecai, [appointing him Prime Ministerᵇ]; and Esther appointed Mordecai to be in charge of Haman's estate.

³ And now once more Esther came before the king, falling down at his feet and begging him with tears to stop Haman's plot against the Jews. ⁴ And again the king held out the golden scepter to Esther. So she arose and stood before him, ⁵ and said, "If it please Your Majesty, and if you love me, send out a decree reversing Haman's order to destroy the Jews throughout the king's provinces. ⁶ For how can I endure it, to see my people butchered and destroyed?"

⁷ Then King Ahasuerus said to Queen Esther and Mordecai the Jew, "I have given Esther the palace of Haman and he has been hanged upon the gallows because he tried to destroy you. ⁸ Now go ahead and send a message to the Jews, telling them whatever you want to in the king's name, and seal it with the king's ring, so that it can never be reversed.ᶜ"

⁹,¹⁰ Immediately the king's secretaries were called in—it was now the 23rd day of the month of July—and they wrote as Mordecai dictated—a decree to the Jews and to the officials, governors, and princes of all the provinces from India to Ethiopia, 127 in all; the decree was translated into the languages and dialects of all the people of the kingdom. Mordecai wrote in the name of King Ahasuerus and sealed the message with the king's ring and sent the letters by swift carriers—riders on camels, mules, and young dromedaries used in the king's service. ¹¹ This decree gave the Jews everywhere permission to unite in the defense of their lives and their families, to destroy all the forces opposed to them, and to take their property. ¹² The day chosen for this throughout all the provinces of King Ahasuerus was the 28th day of February!ᵈ ¹³ It further stated that a copy of this decree, which must be recognized everywhere as law, must be broadcast to all the people so that the Jews would be ready and prepared to overcome their enemies. ¹⁴ So the mail went out swiftly, carried by the king's couriers and speeded by the king's commandment. The same decree was also issued at Shushan Palace.

¹⁵ Then Mordecai put on the royal robes of blue and white and the great crown of

---

a Literally, "had made known how they were related." b Implied. c Haman's message, too, had been sealed with the king's ring and could not be reversed, even by the king. This was part of the famed "law of the Medes and Persians." Now the king is giving permission for whatever other decree Mordecai can devise that will offset the first, without actually canceling it. d This was the same day as was set by Haman for the extermination of the Jews.

gold, with an outer cloak of fine linen and purple, and went out from the presence of the king through the city streets filled with shouting people. [16] And the Jews had joy and gladness, and were honored everywhere. [17] And in every city and province, as the king's decree arrived, the Jews were filled with joy and had a great celebration and declared a holiday. And many of the people of the land pretended to be Jews, for they feared what the Jews might do to them.

9 SO ON THE 28th day of February, the day the two decrees of the king were to be put into effect—the day the Jews' enemies had hoped to vanquish them, though it turned out quite to the contrary—the Jews gathered in their cities throughout all the king's provinces to defend themselves against any who might try to harm them; but no one tried, for they were greatly feared. [3] And all the rulers of the provinces—the governors, officials, and aides—helped the Jews for fear of Mordecai; [4] for Mordecai was a mighty name in the king's palace and his fame was known throughout all the provinces, for he had become more and more powerful.

[5] But the Jews went ahead on that appointed day and slaughtered their enemies. [6] They even killed 500 men in Shushan. [7-10] They also killed the ten sons of Haman (son of Hammedatha), the Jews' enemy—

Parshandatha, Dalphon, Aspatha,
Poratha, Adalia, Aridatha,
Parmashta, Arisai,
Aridai, and Vaizatha.

But they did not try to take Haman's property.

[11] Late that evening, when the king was informed of the number of those slain in Shushan, [12] he called for Queen Esther. "The Jews have killed 500 men in Shushan alone," he exclaimed, "and also Haman's ten sons. If they have done that here, I wonder what has happened in the rest of the provinces! But now, what more do you want? It will be granted to you. Tell me and I will do it."

[13] And Esther said, "If it please Your Majesty, let the Jews who are here at Shushan do again tomorrow as they have done today, and let Haman's ten sons be hanged upon the gallows."

[14] So the king agreed, and the decree was announced at Shushan, and they hung up the bodies of Haman's ten sons. [15] Then the Jews at Shushan gathered together the next day also and killed 300 more men, though again they took no property.

[16] Meanwhile, the other Jews throughout the king's provinces had gathered together and stood for their lives and destroyed all their enemies, killing 75,000 of those who hated them; but they did not take their goods. [17] Throughout the provinces this was done on the 28th day of February, and the next day they rested, celebrating their victory with feasting and gladness. [18] But the Jews at Shushan went on killing their enemies the second day also, and rested the next day, with feasting and gladness. [19] And so it is that the Jews in the unwalled villages throughout Israel to this day have an annual celebration on the second day, when they rejoice and send gifts to each other.

[20] Mordecai wrote a history of all these events, and sent letters to the Jews near and far, throughout all the king's provinces, [21] encouraging them to declare an annual holiday on the last days of the month, [22] to celebrate with feasting, gladness, and the giving of gifts this historic day when the Jews were saved from their enemies, when their sorrow was turned to gladness and their mourning into happiness.

[23] So the Jews adopted Mordecai's suggestion and began this annual custom, [24,25] as a reminder of the time when Haman (son of Hammedatha the Agagite), the enemy of all the Jews, had plotted to destroy them at the time determined by a throw of the dice; and to remind them that when the matter came before the king, he issued a decree causing Haman's plot to boomerang, and he and his sons were hanged on the gallows. [26] That is why this celebration is called "Purim," because the word for "throwing dice" in Persian is "pur." [27] All the Jews throughout the realm agreed to inaugurate this tradition and to pass it on to their descendants and to all who became Jews; they declared they would never fail to celebrate these two days at the appointed time each year. [28] It would be an annual event from generation to generation,

celebrated by every family throughout the countryside and cities of the empire, so that the memory of what had happened would never perish from the Jewish race.

[29-31] Meanwhile, Queen Esther (daughter of Abihail and later adopted by Mordecai the Jew) had written a letter throwing her full support behind Mordecai's letter inaugurating his annual Feast of Purim. In addition, letters were sent to all the Jews throughout the 127 provinces of the kingdom of Ahasuerus with messages of good will, and encouragement to confirm these two days annually as the Feast of Purim, decreed by both Mordecai the Jew and by Queen Esther; indeed, the Jews themselves had decided upon this tradition as a remembrance of the time of their national fasting and prayer. [32] So the commandment of Esther confirmed these dates and it was recorded as law.

10 KING AHASUERUS NOT only laid tribute upon the mainland, but even on the islands of the sea. [2] His great deeds, and also the full account of the greatness of Mordecai and the honors given him by the king, are written in *The Book of the Chronicles of the Kings of Media and Persia.* [3] Mordecai the Jew was the Prime Minister, with authority next to that of King Ahasuerus himself. He was, of course, very great among the Jews, and respected by all his countrymen because he did his best for his people, and was a friend at court for all of them.

Fire & Pain

John R. Mahoney

In an early lap of the Indianap-
olis 500, Gordon Johncock (car
number seven, below,) roars over
the top of Mel Kenyon (helmet in
circle) as Mario Andretti (fore-
ground) goes into a spin to avoid
them. Kenyon had bounced off the
wall after hitting an oil slick.

That he was even in the race at
all was something of a miracle; several years earlier at the Langhorne
(Pa.) Speedway Mel was knocked
unconscious by an accident that
ruptured his fuel tanks. "Three
minutes in a burning car," he said

later, "will make anyone think seriously about God and death." With third-degree burns over 40 percent of his body, he spent the next four months in a hospital, and came out with only a stump of a left hand.

But he also emerged with something else: a faith in Christ, the result of some long talks with his wife. He found the courage to return to racing. His father and brother helped him design a custom glove with a metal socket which he could lace to his stump (above), then hook onto a steering wheel. Since then, Mel has finished fifth, third, and fourth at Indy.

When people get suddenly wiped out by disaster, how do they make a comeback? How do they answer the why-did-this-happen-to-me questions? That's what the book of Job is all about. It's something like a tape recording of devastated Job and four friends trying to figure out what's happened—and God speaking from heaven to put it all in perspective.

JOB

1 THERE LIVED IN the land of Uz a man named Job—a good[a] man who feared God and stayed away from evil. [2,3] He had a large family of seven sons and three daughters, and was immensely wealthy,[b] for he owned 7,000 sheep, 3,000 camels, 500 teams of oxen, 500 female donkeys, and employed many servants. He was, in fact, the richest cattleman in that entire area.

[4] Every year when each of Job's sons had a birthday, he invited his brothers and sisters to his home for a celebration. On these occasions they would eat and drink with great merriment. [5] When these birthday parties ended—and sometimes they lasted several days—Job would summon his children to him and sanctify them, getting up early in the morning and offering a burnt offering for each of them. For Job said, "Perhaps my sons have sinned and turned away from God[c] in their hearts." This was Job's regular practice.

[6] One day as the angels[d] came to present themselves before the Lord, Satan, the Accuser, came with them.

[7] "Where have you come from?" the Lord asked Satan.

And Satan replied, "From patroling the earth."

[8] Then the Lord asked Satan, "Have you noticed my servant Job? He is the finest man in all the earth—a good[b] man who fears God and will have nothing to do with evil."

[9] "Why shouldn't he, when you pay him so well?" Satan scoffed. [10] "You have always protected him and his home and his property from all harm. You have prospered everything he does—look how rich he is! No wonder he 'worships' you! [11] But just take away his wealth, and you'll see him curse you to your face!"

[12,13] And the Lord replied to Satan, "You may do anything you like with his wealth, but don't harm him physically."

So Satan went away; and sure enough,[b] not long afterwards when Job's sons and daughters were dining at the oldest brother's house, tragedy struck.

[14,15] A messenger rushed to Job's home with this news: "Your oxen were plowing, with the donkeys feeding beside them, when the Sabeans raided us, drove away the ani-

---

a Literally, "upright." b Implied. c Literally, "have cursed God." d Literally, "the sons of God."

449

mals and killed all the farmhands except me. I am the only one left."

¹⁶ While this messenger was still speaking, another arrived with more bad news: "The fire of God has fallen from heaven and burned up your sheep and all the herdsmen, and I alone have escaped to tell you."

¹⁷ Before this man finished, still another messenger rushed in: "Three bands of Chaldeans have driven off your camels and killed your servants, and I alone have escaped to tell you."

¹⁸ As he was still speaking, another arrived to say, "Your sons and daughters were feasting in their oldest brother's home, ¹⁹ when suddenly a mighty wind swept in from the desert, and engulfed the house so that the roof fell in on them and all are dead; and I alone escaped to tell you."

²⁰ Then Job stood up and tore his robe in grief[e] and fell down upon the ground before God. ²¹ "I came naked from my mother's womb," he said, "and I shall have nothing when I die. The Lord gave me everything I had, and they were his to take away. Blessed be the name of the Lord."

²² In all of this, Job did not sin or revile God.

2 NOW THE ANGELS[a] came again to present themselves before the Lord, and Satan with them.

² "Where have you come from?" the Lord asked Satan.

"From patroling the earth," Satan replied.

³ "Well, have you noticed my servant Job?" the Lord asked. "He is the finest man in all the earth—a good man who fears God and turns away from all evil. And he has kept his faith in me despite the fact that you persuaded me to let you harm him without any cause."

⁴,⁵ "Skin for skin," Satan replied. "A man will give anything to save his life. Touch his body with sickness and he will curse you to your face!"

⁶ "Do with him as you please," the Lord replied; "only spare his life."

⁷ So Satan went out from the presence of the Lord and struck Job with a terrible case of boils from head to foot. ⁸ Then Job took a broken piece of pottery to scrape himself, and sat among the ashes.

⁹ His wife said to him, "Are you still trying to be godly when God has done all this to you? Curse him and die."

¹⁰ But he replied, "You talk like some heathen woman. What? Shall we receive only pleasant things from the hand of God and never anything unpleasant?" So in all this Job said nothing wrong.

¹¹ When three of Job's friends heard of all the tragedy that had befallen him, they got in touch with each other and traveled from their homes to comfort and console him. Their names were Eliphaz the Temanite, Bildad the Shuhite, and Zophar the Naamathite. ¹² Job was so changed that they could scarcely recognize him. Wailing loudly in despair, they tore their robes and threw dust into the air and put earth on their heads to demonstrate their sorrow. ¹³ Then they sat upon the ground with him silently for seven days and nights, no one speaking a word; for they saw that his suffering was too great for words.

3 AT LAST JOB spoke, and cursed the day of his birth.

²,³ "Let the day of my birth be cursed," he said, "and the night when I was conceived. ⁴ Let that day be forever forgotten.[a] Let it be lost even to God, shrouded in eternal darkness. ⁵ Yes, let the darkness claim it for its own, and may a black cloud overshadow it. ⁶ May it be blotted off the calendar, never again to be counted among the days of the month of that year. ⁷ Let that night be bleak and joyless. ⁸ Let those who are experts at cursing curse it.[b] ⁹ Let the stars of the night disappear. Let it long for light, but never see it, never see the morning light. ¹⁰ Curse it for its failure to shut my mother's womb, for letting me be born to come to all this trouble.

¹¹ "Why didn't I die at birth? ¹² Why did the midwife let me live? Why did she nurse me at her breasts? ¹³ For if only I had died

---

e Literally, "tore his robe and shaved his head."   2a Literally, "sons of God."   3a Literally, "a day of darkness."   b Literally, "Let them who can curse the sea, who know how to rouse the sea monster, curse it."

at birth, then I would be quiet now, asleep and at rest, [14,15] along with prime ministers and kings with all their pomp, and wealthy princes whose castles are full of rich treasures. [16] Oh, to have been still-born!—to have never breathed or seen the light. [17] For there in death the wicked cease from troubling, and there the weary are at rest. [18] There even prisoners are at ease, with no brutal jailer to curse them. [19] Both rich and poor alike are there, and the slave is free at last from his master.

[20,21] "Oh, why should light and life be given to those in misery and bitterness, who long for death, and it won't come; who search for death as others search for food or money? [22] What blessed relief when at last they die! [23] Why is a man allowed to be born if God is only going to give him a hopeless life of uselessness and frustration? [24] I cannot eat for sighing; my groans pour out like water. [25] What I always feared has happened to me. [26] I was not fat and lazy, yet trouble struck me down."

4 A REPLY TO *Job from Eliphaz the Temanite:*

[2] "Will you let me say a word? For who could keep from speaking out? [3,4] In the past[a] you have told many a troubled soul to trust in God[b] and have encouraged those who are weak or falling, or lie crushed upon the ground or are tempted to despair. [5] But now, when trouble strikes, you faint and are broken.

[6] "At such a time as this should not trust in God still be your confidence? Shouldn't you believe that God will care for those who are good?[c] [7,8] Stop and think! Have you ever known a truly good and innocent person who was punished? Experience teaches that it is those who sow sin and trouble who harvest the same. [9] They die beneath the hand of God. [10] Though they are fierce as young lions, they shall all be broken and destroyed. [11] Like aged, helpless lions they shall starve, and all their children shall be scattered.

[12] "This truth was given me in secret, as though whispered in my ear. [13] It came in

a nighttime vision as others slept. [14] Suddenly, fear gripped me; I trembled and shook with terror, [15] as a spirit passed before my face—my hair stood up on end. [16] I felt the spirit's presence, but couldn't see it standing there. Then out of the dreadful silence came this voice:

[17] " 'Is mere man more just than God? More pure than his Creator?'

[18,19] "If God cannot trust his own messengers (for even angels make mistakes), how much less men made of dust, who are crushed to death as easily as moths! [20] They are alive in the morning, but by evening they are dead, gone forever with hardly a thought from anyone. [21] Their candle of life is snuffed out. They die and no one cares.

5 "THEY CRY FOR help but no one listens; they turn to their gods, but none gives them aid. [2] They die in helpless frustration, overcome by their own anger. [3] Those who turn from God may be successful for the moment, but then comes sudden disaster. [4] Their children are cheated, with no one to defend them. [5] Their harvests are stolen and their wealth slakes the thirst of many others, not themselves! [6] Misery comes upon them to punish them for sowing seeds of sin. [7] Mankind heads for sin and misery as predictably as flames shoot upwards from a fire.

[8] "My advice to you is this: Go to God and confess your sins[a] to him. [9] For he does wonderful miracles, marvels without number. [10] He sends the rain upon the earth to water the fields, [11] and gives prosperity to the poor and humble, and takes sufferers to safety.

[12] "He frustrates the plans of crafty men. [13] They are caught in their own traps; he thwarts their schemes. [14] They grope like blind men in the daylight; they see no better in the daytime than at night.

[15] "God saves the fatherless and the poor from the grasp of these oppressors. [16] And so at last the poor have hope, and the fangs of the wicked are broken.

[17] "How enviable the man whom God corrects! Oh, do not despise the chastening

---

a Implied.   b Literally, "Thou hast instructed many."   c Literally, "the integrity of your ways, your hope."   5a Literally, "I would seek God, and to God would I commit my cause."

of the Lord when you sin. [18] For though he wounds, he binds and heals again. [19] He will deliver you again and again, so that no evil can touch you.

[20] "He will keep you from death in famine, and from the power of the sword in time of war.

[21] "You will be safe from slander; no need to fear the future.

[22] "You shall laugh at war and famine; wild animals will leave you alone. [23] Dangerous animals will be at peace with you.

[24] "You need not worry about your home while you are gone; nothing shall be stolen from your barns.

[25] "Your sons shall become important men; your descendants shall be as numerous as grass! [26] You shall live a long, good life; like standing grain, you'll not be harvested until it's time! [27] I have found from experience that all of this is true. For your own good, listen to my counsel."

6 JOB'S REPLY:

[2] "Oh, that my sadness and troubles were weighed. [3] For they are heavier than the sand of a thousand seashores. That is why I spoke so rashly. [4] For the Lord has struck me down with his arrows; he has sent his poisoned arrows deep within my heart. All God's terrors are arrayed against me. [5,6,7] When wild donkeys bray, it is because their grass is gone; oxen do not low when they have food; a man complains when there is no salt in his food. And how tasteless is the uncooked white of an egg—my appetite is gone when I look at it; I gag at the thought of eating it!

[8,9] "Oh, that God would grant the thing I long for most—to die beneath his hand, and be freed from his painful grip. [10] This, at least, gives me comfort despite all the pain—that I have not denied the words of the holy God. [11] Oh, why does my strength sustain me? How can I be patient till I die? [12] Am I unfeeling, like stone? Is my flesh made of brass? [13] For I am utterly helpless, without any hope.

[14] "One should be kind to a fainting friend, but you have accused me without the slightest fear of God. [15-18] My brother, you have proved as unreliable as a brook; it floods when there is ice and snow, but in hot weather, disappears. The caravans turn aside to be refreshed, but there is nothing there to drink, and so they perish. [19-21] When caravans from Tema and from Sheba stop for water there, their hopes are dashed. And so my hopes in you are dashed—you turn away from me in terror and refuse to help. [22] But why? Have I ever asked you for one slightest thing? Have I begged you for a present? [23] Have I ever asked your help? [24] All I want is a reasonable answer—then I will keep quiet. Tell me, what have I done wrong?

[25,26] "It is wonderful to speak the truth, but your criticisms are not based on fact. Are you going to condemn me just because I impulsively cried out in desperation? [27] That would be like injuring a helpless orphan, or selling a friend. [28] Look at me! Would I lie to your face? [29] Stop assuming my guilt, for I am righteous. Don't be so unjust. [30] Don't I know the difference between right and wrong? Would I not admit it if I had sinned?

7 "HOW MANKIND MUST struggle. A man's life is long and hard, like that of a slave. [2] How he longs for the day to end. How he grinds on to the end of the week and his wages. [3] And so to me also have been allotted months of frustration, these long and weary nights. [4] When I go to bed I think, 'Oh, that it were morning,' and then I toss till dawn.

[5] "My skin is filled with worms and blackness. My flesh breaks open, full of pus. [6] My life flies by—day after hopeless day. [7] My life is but a breath, and nothing good is left. [8] You see me now, but not for long. Soon you'll look upon me dead. [9] As a cloud disperses and vanishes, so those who die shall go away forever— [10] gone forever from their family and their home—never to be seen again. [11] Ah, let me express my anguish. Let me be free to speak out of the bitterness of my soul.

[12] "O God, am I some monster, that you never let me alone? [13,14] Even when I try to forget my misery in sleep, you terrify with nightmares. [15] I would rather die of strangulation than go on and on like this. [16] I hate my life. Oh, let me alone for these few remaining days. [17] What is mere man that you

should spend your time persecuting him?
[18] Must you be his inquisitor every morning,
and test him every moment of the day?
[19] Why won't you let me alone—even long
enough to spit?

[20] "Has my sin harmed you, O God,
Watcher of mankind? Why have you made
me your target, and made my life so heavy
a burden to me? [21] Why not just pardon my
sin and take it all away? For all so soon I'll
lie down in the dust and die, and when you
look for me, I shall be gone."

8 **BILDAD THE SHUHITE** *replies to Job:*
[2] "How long will you go on like this,
Job, blowing words around like wind?
[3] Does God twist justice? [4] If your children
sinned against him, and he punished them,
[5] and you begged Almighty God for them—
[6] if you were pure and good, he would hear
your prayer, and answer you, and bless you
with a happy home. [7] And though you
started with little, you would end with
much.

[8] "Read the history books and see— [9] for
we were born but yesterday and know so
little; our days here on earth are as transient
as shadows. [10] But the wisdom of the past
will teach you. The experience of others will
speak to you, reminding you that [11-13] those
who forget God have no hope. They are like
rushes without any mire to grow in; or grass
without water to keep it alive. Suddenly it
begins to wither, even before it is cut. [14] A
man without God is trusting in a spider's
web. Everything he counts on will collapse.
[15] If he counts on his home for security, it
won't last. [16] At dawn he seems so strong
and virile, like a green plant; his branches
spread across the garden. [17] His roots are in
the stream, down among the stones. [18] But
when he disappears, he isn't even missed!
[19] That is all he can look forward to! And
others spring up from the earth to replace
him!

[20] "But look! God will not cast away a
good man, nor prosper evildoers. [21] He will
yet fill your mouth with laughter and your
lips with shouts of joy. [22] Those who hate
you shall be clothed with shame, and the
wicked destroyed."

9 JOB'S REPLY:
[2] "Sure, I know all that. You're not telling me anything new. But how can a man
be truly good in the eyes of God? [3] If God
decides to argue with him, can a man answer even one question of a thousand he
asks? [4] For God is so wise and so mighty.
Who has ever opposed him successfully?

[5] "Suddenly he moves the mountains,
overturning them in his anger. [6] He shakes
the earth to its foundations. [7] The sun won't
rise, the stars won't shine, if he commands
it so! [8] Only he has stretched the heavens out
and stalked along the seas. [9] He made the
Bear, Orion and the Pleiades, and the constellations of the southern Zodiac.

[10] "He does incredible miracles, too
many to count. [11] He passes by, invisible; he
moves along, but I don't see him go.
[12] When he sends death to snatch a man
away,[a] who can stop him? Who dares to ask
him, 'What are you doing?'

[13] "And God does not abate his anger.
The pride of man[b] collapses before him.
[14] And who am I that I should try to argue
with Almighty God, or even reason with
him? [15] Even if I were sinless I wouldn't say
a word. I would only plead for mercy.
[16] And even if my prayers were answered I
could scarce believe that he had heard my
cry. [17] For he is the one who destroys, and
multiplies my wounds without a cause.
[18] He will not let me breathe, but fills me
with bitter sorrows. [19] He alone is strong
and just.

[20] "But I? Am I righteous? My own
mouth says no. Even if I were perfect, God
would prove me wicked. [21] And even if I am
utterly innocent, I dare not think of it. I
despise what I am. [22] Innocent or evil, it is
all the same to him, for he destroys both
kinds. [23] He will laugh when calamity
crushes the innocent. [24] The whole earth is
in the hands of the wicked. God blinds the
eyes of the judges and lets them be unfair.
If not he, then who?

[25] "My life passes swiftly away, filled
with tragedy. [26] My years disappear like
swift ships, like the eagle that swoops upon
its prey.
[27] "If I decided to forget my complaints

---

a Literally, "he seizes."   b Or, "the helpers of Rahab."

against God, to end my sadness and be cheerful, ²⁸ then he would pour even greater sorrows upon me. For I know that you will not hold me innocent, O God, ²⁹ but will condemn me. So what's the use of trying? ³⁰ Even if I were to wash myself with purest water and cleanse my hands with lye to make them utterly clean, ³¹ even so you would plunge me into the ditch and mud; and even my clothing would be less filthy than you consider me to be!

³²,³³ "And I cannot defend myself, for you are no mere man as I am. If you were, then we could discuss it fairly, but there is no umpire between us, no middle man, no mediator to bring us together. ³⁴ Oh, let him stop beating me, so that I need no longer live in terror of his punishment. ³⁵ Then I could speak without fear to him, and tell him boldly that I am not guilty.

10 "I AM WEARY of living. Let me complain freely. I will speak in my sorrow and bitterness. ² I will say to God, 'Don't just condemn me—tell me *why* you are doing it. ³ Does it really seem right to you to oppress and despise me, a man you have made; and to send joy and prosperity to the wicked? ⁴⁻⁷ Are you unjustᵃ like men? Is your life so short that you must hound me for sins you know full well I've not committed? Is it because you know no one can save me from your hand?

⁸ " 'You have made me, and yet you destroy me. ⁹ Oh, please remember that I'm made of dust—will you change me back again to dust so soon? ¹⁰ You have already poured me from bottle to bottle like milk, and curdled me like cheese. ¹¹ You gave me skin and flesh and knit together bones and sinews. ¹² You gave me life and were so kind and loving to me, and I was preserved by your care.

¹³,¹⁴ " 'Yet all the time your real motive in making me was to destroy me if I sinned; and to refuse to forgive my iniquity. ¹⁵ Just the slightest wickedness, and I am done for. And if I'm good, that doesn't count. I am filled with frustration. ¹⁶ If I start to get up off the ground, you leap upon me like a lion and quickly finish me off. ¹⁷ Again and again

you witness against me and pour out an ever-increasing volume of wrath upon me and bring fresh armies against me.

¹⁸ " 'Why then did you even let me be born? Why didn't you let me die at birth? ¹⁹ Then I would have been spared this miserable existence. I would have gone directly from the womb to the grave. ²⁰,²¹ Can't you see how little time I have left? Oh, let me alone that I may have a little moment of comfort before I leave for the land of darkness and the shadow of death, never to return— ²² a land as dark as midnight, a land of the shadow of death where only confusion reigns, and where the brightest light is dark as midnight.' "

11 ZOPHAR THE NAAMATHITE *replies to Job:*

² "Shouldn't someone stem this torrent of words? Is a man proved right by all this talk? ³ Should I remain silent while you boast? When you mock God, shouldn't someone make you ashamed? ⁴ You claim you are pure in the eyes of God! ⁵ Oh, that God would speak and tell you what he thinks! ⁶ Oh, that he would make you truly see yourself, for he knows everything you've done. Listen! God is doubtless punishing you far less than you deserve!

⁷ "Do you know the mind and purposes of God? Will long searching make them known to you? Are you qualified to judge the Almighty? ⁸ He is as faultless as heaven is high—but who are you? His mind is fathomless—what can you know in comparison? ⁹ His Spirit is broader than the earth and wider than the sea. ¹⁰ If he rushes in and makes an arrest, and calls the court to order, who is going to stop him? ¹¹ For he knows perfectly all the faults and sins of mankind; he sees all sin without searching.

¹² "Mere man is as likely to be wise as a wild donkey's colt is likely to be born a man!

¹³,¹⁴ "Before you turn to God and stretch out your hands to him, get rid of your sins and leave all iniquity behind you. ¹⁵ Only then, without the spots of sin to defile you, can you walk steadily forward to God without fear. ¹⁶ Only then can you forget your

---

a Literally, "Have you the eyes of flesh?"

misery. It will all be in the past. [17] And your life will be cloudless; any darkness will be as bright as morning!

[18] "You will have courage because you will have hope. You take your time, and rest in safety. [19] You will lie down unafraid and many will look to you for help. [20] But the wicked shall find no way to escape; their only hope is death."

12 JOB'S REPLY: [2] "Yes, I realize you know everything! All wisdom will die with you! [3] Well, I know a few things myself—you are no better than I am. And who doesn't know these things you've been saying? [4] I, the man who begged God for help, and God answered him, have become a laughingstock to my neighbors. Yes, I, a righteous man, am now the man they scoff at. [5] Meanwhile, the rich mock those in trouble and are quick to despise all those in need. [6] For robbers prosper. Go ahead and provoke God—it makes no difference! He will supply your every need anyway!

[7,8,9] "Who doesn't know that the Lord does things like that? Ask the dumbest beast—he knows that it is so; ask the birds—they will tell you; or let the earth teach you, or the fish of the sea. [10] For the soul of every living thing is in the hand of God, and the breath of all mankind. [11] Just as my mouth can taste good food, so my mind tastes truth when I hear it. [12] And as you say, older men like me[a] are wise. They understand. [13] But true wisdom and power are God's. He alone knows what we should do; he understands.

[14] "And how great is his might! What he destroys can't be rebuilt. When he closes in on a man, there is no escape. [15] He withholds the rain, and the earth becomes a desert; he sends the storms, and floods the ground. [16] Yes, with him is strength and wisdom. Deceivers and deceived are both his slaves.

[17] "He makes fools of counselors and judges. [18] He reduces kings to slaves and frees their servants. [19] Priests are led away as slaves. He overthrows the mighty. [20] He takes away the voice of orators, and the insight of the elders. [21] He pours contempt upon princes, and weakens the strong. [22] He floods the darkness with light, even the dark shadow of death. [23] He raises up a nation and then destroys it. He makes it great, and then reduces it to nothing. [24,25] He takes away the understanding of presidents and kings, and leaves them wandering, lost and groping, without a guiding light.

13 "LOOK, I HAVE seen many instances such as you describe. I understand what you are saying. [2] I know as much as you do. I'm not stupid. [3] Oh, how I long to speak directly to the Almighty. I want to talk this over with God himself. [4] For you are misinterpreting the whole thing. You are doctors who don't know what they are doing. [5] Oh, please be quiet! That would be your highest wisdom.

[6] "Listen to me now, to my reasons for what I think, and to my pleadings.

[7] "Must you go on 'speaking for God' when he never once has said the things that you are putting in his mouth? [8] Does God want your help if you are going to twist the truth for him? [9] Be careful that he doesn't find out what you are doing! Or do you think you can fool God as well as men? [10] No, you will be in serious trouble with him if you use lies to try to help him out. [11] Doesn't his majesty strike terror to your heart? How can you do this thing? [12] These tremendous statements you have made have about as much value as ashes. Your defense of God is as fragile as a clay vase!

[13] "Be silent now and let me alone, that I may speak—and I am willing to face the consequences. [14] Yes, I will take my life in my hand and say what I really think. [15] God may kill me for saying this—in fact, I expect him to. Nevertheless I am going to argue my case with him.[a] [16] This at least will be in my favor, that I am not godless, to be rejected instantly from his presence. [17] Listen closely to what I am about to say. Hear me out.

[18] "This is my case: *I know that I am righteous.* [19] Who can argue with me over this? If you could prove me wrong I would stop defending myself and die.

---

a Implied.   13a Or, "Though he slay me, yet will I trust in him. I will argue my case before him."

20 "O God, there are two things I beg you not to do to me; only then will I be able to face you. 21 Don't abandon me. And don't terrify me with your awesome presence. 22 Call to me to come—how quickly I will answer! Or let me speak to you, and you reply. 23 Tell me, what have I done wrong? Help me! Point out my sin to me. 24 Why do you turn away from me? Why hand me over to my enemy? 25 Would you blame a leaf that is blown about by the wind? Will you chase dry, useless straws?

26 "You write bitter things against me and bring up all the follies of my youth. 27,28 You send me to prison and shut me in on every side. I am like a fallen, rotten tree, like a moth-eaten coat.

14 "HOW FRAIL IS man, how few his days, how full of trouble! 2 He blossoms for a moment like a flower—and withers; as the shadow of a passing cloud, he quickly disappears. 3 Must you be so harsh with frail men, and demand an accounting from them? 4 How can you demand purity in one born impure? 5 You have set mankind so brief a span of life—months is all you give him! Not one bit longer may he live. 6 So give him a little rest, won't you? Turn away your angry gaze and let him have a few moments of relief before he dies.

7 "For there is hope for a tree—if it's cut down it sprouts again, and grows tender, new branches. 8,9 Though its roots have grown old in the earth, and its stump decays, it may sprout and bud again at the touch of water, like a new seedling. 10 But when a man dies and is buried, where does his spirit go? 11,12 As water evaporates from a lake, as a river disappears in drought, so a man lies down for the last time, and does not rise again until the heavens are no more; he shall not awaken, nor be roused from his sleep. 13 Oh, that you would hide me with the dead, and forget me there until your anger ends; but mark your calendar to think of me again!

14 "If a man dies, shall he live again? This thought gives me hope, so that in all my anguish I eagerly await sweet death! 15 You would call and I would come, and you would reward all I do. 16 But now, instead, you give me so few steps upon the stage of life, and notice every mistake I make. 17 You bundle them all together as evidence against me.

18,19 "Mountains wear away and disappear. Water grinds the stones to sand. Torrents tear away the soil. So every hope of man is worn away. 20,21 Always you are against him, and then he passes off the scene. You make him old and wrinkled, then send him away. He never knows it if his sons are honored; or they may fail and face disaster, but he knows it not. 22 For him there is only sorrow and pain."

15 THE ANSWER OF *Eliphaz the Temanite:*

2 "You are supposed to be a wise man, and yet you give us all this foolish talk. You are nothing but a windbag. 3 It isn't right to speak so foolishly. What good do such words do? 4,5 Have you no fear of God? No reverence for him? Your sins are telling your mouth what to say! Your words are based on clever deception, 6 but why should I condemn you? Your own mouth does!

7,8 "Are you the wisest man alive? Were you born before the hills were made? Have you heard the secret counsel of God? Are you called into his counsel room? Do you have a monopoly on wisdom? 9 What do you know more than we do? What do you understand that we don't? 10 On our side are aged men much older than your father! 11 Is God's comfort too little for you? Is his gentleness too rough?

12 "What is this you are doing, getting carried away by your anger, with flashing eyes? 13 And you turn against God and say all these evil things against him. 14 What man in all the earth can be as pure and righteous as you claim to be? 15 Why, God doesn't even trust the angels! Even the heavens can't be absolutely pure compared with him! 16 How much less someone like you, who is corrupt and sinful, drinking in sin as a sponge soaks up water!

17-19 "Listen, and I will answer you from my own experience, confirmed by the experience of wise men who have been told this same thing from their fathers—our ancestors to whom alone the land was given—and they have passed this wisdom to us:

20 "A wicked man is always in trouble

throughout his life. ²¹ He is surrounded by terrors, and if there are good days they will soon be gone. ²² He dares not go out into the darkness, lest he be murdered. ²³,²⁴ He wanders around begging for food. He lives in fear, distress, and anguish. His enemies conquer him as a king defeats his foes. ²⁵,²⁶ Armed with his tin shield, he clenches his fist against God, defying the Almighty, stubbornly assaulting him.

²⁷,²⁸ "This wicked man is fat and rich, and has lived in conquered cities after killing off its citizens. ²⁹ But he will not continue to be rich, or to extend his possessions. ³⁰ No, darkness shall overtake him forever; the breath of God shall destroy him; the flames shall burn up all he has.

³¹ "Let him no longer trust in foolish riches;ᵃ let him no longer deceive himself, for the money he trusts in will be his only reward. ³² Before he dies, all this futility will become evident to him. For all he counted on will disappear, ³³ and fall to the ground like a withered grape.ᵇ How little will come of his hopes! ³⁴ For the godless are barren: they can produce nothing truly good. God's fire consumes them with all their possessions. ³⁵ The only thing they can 'conceive' is sin, and their hearts give birth only to wickedness."

16 JOB'S REPLY:
² "I have heard all this before. What miserable comforters all of you are. ³ Won't you ever stop your flow of foolish words? What have I said that makes you speak so endlessly? ⁴ But perhaps I'd sermonize the same as you—if you were I and I were you. I would spout off my criticisms against you and shake my head at you. ⁵ But no! I would speak in such a way that it would help you. I would try to take away your grief.

⁶ "But now my grief remains no matter how I defend myself; nor does it help if I refuse to speak. ⁷ For God has ground me down, and taken away my family. ⁸ O God, you have turned me to skin and bones—as a proof, they say, of my sins. ⁹ God hates me and angrily tears at my flesh; he has gnashed upon me with his teeth, and watched to snuff out any sign of life.

¹⁰ These 'comforters' have gaping jaws to swallow me; they slap my cheek. My enemies gather themselves against me. ¹¹ And God has delivered me over to sinners, into the hands of the wicked.

¹² "I was living quietly until he broke me apart. He has taken me by the neck and dashed me to pieces, then hung me up as his target. ¹³ His archers surround me, letting fly their arrows, so that the ground is wet from my wounds. ¹⁴ Again and again he attacks me, running upon me like a giant. ¹⁵ Here I sit in sackcloth; and have laid all hope in the dust. ¹⁶ My eyes are red with weeping and on my eyelids is the shadow of death.

¹⁷ "Yet I am innocent, and my prayer is pure. ¹⁸ O earth, do not conceal my blood. Let it protest on my behalf.

¹⁹ "Yet even now the Witness to my innocence is there in heaven; my Advocate is there on high. ²⁰ My friends scoff at me, but I pour out my tears to God, ²¹ pleading that he will listen as a man would listen to his neighbor. ²² For all so soon I must go down that road from which I shall never return.

17 "I AM SICK and near to death; the grave is ready to receive me. ² I am surrounded by mockers. I see them everywhere. ³,⁴ Will no one anywhere confirm my innocence? But you, O God, have kept them back from understanding this. Oh, do not let them triumph. ⁵ If they accept bribes to denounce their friends, their children shall go blind.

⁶ "He has made me a mockery among the people; they spit in my face. ⁷ My eyes are dim with weeping and I am but a shadow of my former self. ⁸ Fair-minded men are astonished when they see me.

"Yet, finally, the innocent shall come out on top, above the godless; ⁹ the righteous shall move onward and forward; those with pure hearts shall become stronger and stronger.

¹⁰ "As for you—all of you please go away; for I do not find a wise man among you. ¹¹ My good days are in the past. My hopes have disappeared. My heart's desires are broken. ¹² They say that night is day and

---

a Literally, "trust in vanity."　　　b Literally, "shall cast off his flower as the olive tree."

day is night; how they pervert the truth!

13,14 "If I die, I go out into darkness, and call the grave my father, and the worm my mother and my sister. 15 Where then is my hope? Can anyone find any? 16 No, my hope will go down with me to the grave. We shall rest together in the dust!"

18 THE FURTHER REPLY *of Bildad the Shuhite:*

2 "Who are you trying to fool? Speak some sense if you want us to answer! 3 Have we become like animals to you, stupid and dumb? 4 Just because you tear your clothes in anger, is this going to start an earthquake? Shall we all go and hide?

5 "The truth remains that if you do not prosper, it is because you are wicked. And your bright flame shall be put out. 6 There will be darkness in every home where there is wickedness.

7 "The confident stride of the wicked man will be shortened; he will realize his failing strength. 8,9 He walks into traps, and robbers will ambush him. 10 There is a booby-trap in every path he takes. 11 He has good cause for fear—his enemy is close behind him!

12 "His vigor is depleted by hunger; calamity stands ready to pounce upon him. 13 His skin is eaten by disease. Death shall devour him. 14 The wealth he trusted in shall reject him, and he shall be brought down to the King of Terrors. 15 His home shall disappear beneath a fiery barrage of brimstone. 16 He shall die from the roots up, and all his branches will be lopped off.

17 "All memory of his existence will perish from the earth; no one will remember him. 18 He will be driven out from the kingdom of light into darkness, and chased out of the world. 19 He will have neither son nor grandson left, nor any other relatives. 20 Old and young alike will be horrified by his fate. 21 Yes, that is what happens to sinners, to those rejecting God."

19 THE REPLY OF *Job:*

2 "How long are you going to trouble me, and try to break me with your words? 3 Ten times now you have declared I am a

sinner. Why aren't you ashamed to deal with me so harshly? 4 And if indeed I was wrong, you have yet to prove it. 5 You think yourselves so great? Then prove my guilt!

6 "The fact of the matter is that God has overthrown me and caught me in his net. 7 I scream for help and no one hears me. I shriek, but get no justice. 8 God has blocked my path and turned my light to darkness. 9 He has stripped me of my glory and removed the crown from my head. 10 He has broken me down on every side, and I am done for. He has destroyed all hope. 11 His fury burns against me; he counts me as an enemy. 12 He sends his troops to surround my tent.

13 "He has sent away my brothers, and my friends. 14 My relatives have failed me; my friends have all forsaken me. 15 Those living in my home, even my servants, regard me as a stranger. I am like a foreigner to them. 16 I call my servant, but he doesn't come; I even beg him! 17 My own wife and brothers refuse to recognize me. 18 Even young children despise me. When I stand to speak, they mock.

19 "My best friends abhor me. Those I loved have turned against me. 20 I am skin and bones and have escaped death by the skin of my teeth.

21 "Oh, my friends, pity me, for the angry hand of God has touched me. 22 Why must you persecute me as God does? Why aren't you satisfied with my anguish? 23,24 Oh, that I could write my plea with an iron pen in the rock forever.

25 "But as for me, I know that my Redeemer lives, and that he will stand upon the earth at last. 26 And I know that after this body has decayed, this body shall see God!a 27 Then he will be on *my* side! Yes, I shall see him, not as a stranger, but as a friend! What a glorious hope!

28 "How dare you go on persecuting me, as though I were proven guilty? 29 I warn you, you yourselves are in danger of punishment for your attitude."

20 THE SPEECH OF *Zophar the Naamathite:*

2 "I hasten to reply, for I have the answer

a Or, "then even without my flesh I shall see God."

for you. ³ You have tried to make me feel ashamed of myself for calling you a sinner, but my spirit won't let me stop.

⁴ "Don't you realize that ever since man was first placed upon the earth, ⁵ the triumph of the wicked has been short-lived, and the joy of the godless but for a moment? ⁶ Though the godless be proud as the heavens, and walk with his nose in the air, ⁷ yet he shall perish forever, cast away like his own dung. Those who knew him will wonder where he is gone. ⁸ He will fade like a dream. ⁹ Neither his friends nor his family will ever see him again.

¹⁰ "His children shall beg from the poor, their hard labor shall repay his debts. ¹¹ Though still a young man, his bones shall lie in the dust.

¹² "He enjoyed the taste of his wickedness, letting it melt in his mouth, ¹³ sipping it slowly, lest it disappear.

¹⁴ "But suddenly the food he has eaten turns sour within him. ¹⁵ He will vomit the plunder he gorged. God won't let him keep it down. ¹⁶ It is like poison and death to him. ¹⁷ He shall not enjoy the goods he stole; they will not be butter and honey to him after all. ¹⁸ His labors shall not be rewarded; wealth will give him no joy. ¹⁹ For he has oppressed the poor and foreclosed their homes; he will never recover. ²⁰ Though he was always greedy, now he has nothing; of all the things he dreamed of—none remain. ²¹ Because he stole at every opportunity, his prosperity shall not continue.

²² "He shall run into trouble at the peak of his powers; all the wicked shall destroy him. ²³ Just as he is about to fill his belly, God will rain down wrath upon him. ²⁴ He will be chased and struck down. ²⁵ The arrow is pulled from his body—and the glittering point comes out from his gall. The terrors of death are upon him.

²⁶ "His treasures will be lost in deepest darkness. A raging fire will devour his goods, consuming all he has left. ²⁷ The heavens will reveal his sins, and the earth will give testimony against him. ²⁸ His wealth will disappear beneath the wrath of God. ²⁹ This is what awaits the wicked man, for God prepares it for him."

21 JOB'S REPLY:
²,³ "Listen to me; let me speak, and afterwards, mock on.

⁴ "I am complaining about God,ª not man; no wonder my spirit is so troubled. ⁵ Look at me in horror, and lay your hand upon your mouth. ⁶ Even I am frightened when I see myself. Horror takes hold upon me and I shudder.

⁷ "The truth is that the wicked live on to a good old age, and become great and powerful. ⁸ They live to see their children grow to maturity around them, and their grandchildren, too. ⁹ Their homes are safe from every fear, and God does not punish them. ¹⁰ Their cattle are productive, ¹¹ they have many happy children, ¹²,¹³ they spend their time singing and dancing. They are wealthy and need deny themselves nothing; they are prosperous to the end. ¹⁴ All this despite the fact that they ordered God away and wanted no part of him and his ways.

¹⁵ " 'Who is Almighty God?' " they scoff. 'Why should we obey him? What good will it do us?'

¹⁶ "Look, everything the wicked touch has turned to gold! But I refuse even to deal with people like that. ¹⁷ Yet the wicked get away with it every time. They never have trouble, and God skips them when he distributes his sorrows and anger. ¹⁸ Are they driven before the wind like straw? Are they carried away by the storm? Not at all!

¹⁹ " 'Well,' you say, 'at least God will punish their children!' But I say that God should punish the man who sins, not his children! Let him feel the penalty himself. ²⁰ Yes, let him be destroyed for his iniquity. Let him drink deeply of the anger of the Almighty. ²¹ For when he is dead, then he will never again be able to enjoy his family.

²² "But who can rebuke God, the supreme Judge? ²³,²⁴ He destroys those who are healthy, wealthy, fat, and prosperous; ²⁵ God also destroys those in deep and grinding poverty who have never known anything good. ²⁶ Both alike are buried in the same dust, both eaten by the same worms.

²⁷ "I know what you are going to say— ²⁸ you will tell me of rich and wicked men

---

ª Implied.

who came to disaster because of their sins.
²⁹ But I reply, Ask anyone who has been
around and he can tell you the truth,
³⁰⁻³² that the evil man is usually spared in the
day of calamity, and allowed to escape. No
one rebukes him openly. No one repays him
for what he has done. And an honor guard
keeps watch at his grave. ³³ A great funeral
procession precedes and follows him as the
soft earth covers him. ³⁴ How can you comfort me when your whole premise is so
wrong?"

22 ANOTHER ADDRESS FROM *Eliphaz:*
² "Is mere man of any worth to God?
Even the wisest is of value only to himself!
³ Is it any pleasure to the Almighty if you
are righteous? Would it be any gain to him
if you were perfect? ⁴ Is it because you are
good that he is punishing you? ⁵ Not at all!
It is because of your wickedness! Your sins
are endless!

⁶ "For instance, you must have refused
to loan money to needy friends unless they
gave you all their clothing as a pledge—yes,
you must have stripped them to the bone.
⁷ You must have refused water to the
thirsty, and bread to the starving. ⁸ But no
doubt you gave men of importance anything
they wanted, and let the wealthy live wherever they chose. ⁹ You sent widows away
without helping them, and broke the arms
of orphans. ¹⁰,¹¹ That is why you are now
surrounded by traps and sudden fears, and
darkness and waves of horror.

¹² "God is so great—higher than the
heavens, higher than the stars. ¹³ But you
reply, 'That is why he can't see what I am
doing! How can he judge through the thick
darkness? ¹⁴ For thick clouds swirl about
him so that he cannot see us. He is way up
there, walking on the vault of heaven.'

¹⁵,¹⁶ "Don't you realize that those treading the ancient paths of sin are snatched
away in youth, and the foundations of their
lives washed out forever? ¹⁷ For they said to
God, 'Go away, God! What can you do for
us?' ¹⁸ (God forbid that I should say a thing
like that.) Yet they forgot that he had filled
their homes with good things. ¹⁹ And now
the righteous shall see them destroyed; the
innocent shall laugh the wicked to scorn.
²⁰ 'See,' they will say, 'the last of our ene-

mies have been destroyed in the fire.'

²¹ "Quit quarreling with God! Agree
with him and you will have peace at last!
His favor will surround you if you will only
admit that you were wrong. ²² Listen to his
instructions and store them in your heart.
²³ If you return to God and put right all the
wrong in your home, then you will be restored. ²⁴ If you give up your lust for money,
and throw your gold away, ²⁵ then the Almighty himself shall be your treasure; he
will be your precious silver!

²⁶ "Then you will delight yourself in the
Lord, and look up to God. ²⁷ You will pray
to him, and he will hear you, and you will
fulfill all your promises to him. ²⁸ Whatever
you wish will happen! And the light of
heaven will shine upon the road ahead of
you. ²⁹ If you are attacked and knocked
down, you will know that there is someone
who will lift you up again. Yes, he will save
the humble, ³⁰ and help even sinners by your
pure hands."

23 THE REPLY OF *Job:*
² "My complaint today is still a bitter
one, and my punishment far more severe
than my fault deserves. ³ Oh, that I knew
where to find God—that I could go to his
throne and talk with him there. ⁴,⁵ I would
tell him all about my side of this argument,
and listen to his reply, and understand what
he wants. ⁶ Would he merely overpower me
with his greatness? No, he would listen with
sympathy. ⁷ Fair and honest men could reason with him, and be acquitted by my
Judge.

⁸ "But I search in vain. I seek him here,
I seek him there, and cannot find him. ⁹ I
seek him in his workshop in the North, but
cannot find him there; nor can I find him
in the South; there, too, he hides himself.
¹⁰ But he knows every detail of what is happening to me; and when he has examined
me, he will pronounce me completely innocent—as pure as solid gold!

¹¹ "I have stayed in God's paths, following his steps. I have not turned aside. ¹² I
have not refused his commandments but
have enjoyed them more than my daily
food. ¹³ Nevertheless, his mind concerning
me remains unchanged, and who can turn
him from his purposes? Whatever he wants

to do, he does. [14] So he will do to me all he has planned, and there is more ahead.[a]

[15] "No wonder I am so terrified in his presence. When I think of it, terror grips me. [16,17] God has given me a fainting heart; he, the Almighty, has terrified me with darkness all around me, thick, impenetrable darkness everywhere.

24 "WHY DOESN'T GOD open the court and listen to my case? Why must the godly wait for him in vain? [2] For a crime wave has engulfed us—landmarks are moved, flocks of sheep are stolen, [3] and even the donkeys of the poor and fatherless are taken. Poor widows must surrender the little they have as a pledge to get a loan. [4] The needy are kicked aside; they must get out of the way. [5] Like the wild donkeys in the desert, the poor must spend all their time just getting barely enough to keep soul and body together. They are sent into the desert to search for food for their children. [6] They eat what they find that grows wild, and must even glean the vineyards of the wicked. [7] All night they lie naked in the cold, without clothing or covering. [8] They are wet with the showers of the mountains and live in caves for want of a home.

[9] "The wicked snatch fatherless children from their mother's breasts, and take a poor man's baby as a pledge before they will loan him any money or grain. [10] That is why they must go about naked, without clothing, and are forced to carry food while they are starving. [11] They are forced to press out the olive oil without tasting it, and to tread out the grape juice as they suffer from thirst. [12] The bones of the dying cry from the city; the wounded cry for help; yet God does not respond to their moaning.

[13] "The wicked rebel against the light and are not acquainted with the right and the good. [14,15] They are murderers who rise in the early dawn to kill the poor and needy; at night they are thieves and adulterers, waiting for the twilight 'when no one will see me,' they say. They mask their faces so no one will know them. [16] They break into houses at night and sleep in the daytime—they are not acquainted with the light.

[17] The black night is their morning; they ally themselves with the terrors of the darkness. [18] "But how quickly they disappear from the face of the earth. Everything they own is cursed. They leave no property for their children. [19] Death consumes sinners as drought and heat consume snow. [20] Even the sinner's own mother shall forget him. Worms shall feed sweetly on him. No one will remember him any more. For wicked men are broken like a tree in the storm. [21] For they have taken advantage of the childless who have no protecting sons. They refuse to help the needy widows.

[22,23] "Yet sometimes[a] it seems as though God preserves the rich by his power, and restores them to life when anyone else would die. God gives them confidence and strength, and helps them in many ways. [24] But though they are very great now, yet in a moment they shall be gone like all others, cut off like heads of grain. [25] Can anyone claim otherwise? Who can prove me a liar and claim that I am wrong?"

25 THE FURTHER REPLY *of Bildad the Shuhite:*

[2] "God is powerful and dreadful. He enforces peace in heaven. [3] Who is able to number his hosts of angels? And his light shines down on all the earth. [4] How can mere man stand before God and claim to be righteous? Who in all the earth can boast that he is clean? [5] God is so glorious that even the moon and stars are less than nothing as compared to him. [6] How much less is man, who is but a worm in his sight?"

26 JOB'S REPLY:

[2] "What wonderful helpers you all are! And how you have encouraged me in my great need! [3] How you have enlightened my stupidity! What wise things you have said! [4] How did you ever think of all these brilliant comments?

[5,6] "The dead stand naked, trembling before God in the place where they go. [7] God stretches out heaven over empty space, and hangs the earth upon nothing. [8] He wraps the rain in his thick clouds and the clouds are not split by the weight. [9] He

---

a Literally, "and many such things are with him."   24a Implied.

shrouds his throne with his clouds. [10] He sets a boundary for the ocean, yes, and a boundary for the day and for the night. [11] The pillars of heaven tremble at his rebuke. [12] And by his power the sea grows calm; he is skilled at crushing its pride! [13] The heavens are made beautiful by his Spirit;[a] he pierces the swiftly gliding serpent.

[14] "These are some of the minor things he does, merely a whisper of his power. Who then can withstand his thunder?"

27 JOB'S FINAL DEFENSE:

[2] "I vow by the living God, who has taken away my rights, even the Almighty God who has embittered my soul, [3] that as long as I live, while I have breath from God, [4] my lips shall speak no evil, my tongue shall speak no lies. [5] I will never, never agree that you are right; until I die I will vow my innocence. [6] I am *not* a sinner—I repeat it again and again. My conscience is clear for as long as I live. [7] Those who declare otherwise are my wicked enemies. They are evil men.

[8] "But what hope has the godless when God cuts him off and takes away his life? [9] Will God listen to his cry when trouble comes upon him? [10] For he does not delight himself in the Almighty or pay any attention to God except in times of crisis.

[11] "I will teach you about God— [12] but really, I don't need to, for you yourselves know as much about him as I do; yet you are saying all these useless things to me.

[13] "This is the fate awaiting the wicked from the hand of the Almighty: [14] If he has a multitude of children, it is so that they will die in war, or starve to death. [15] Those who survive shall be brought down to the grave by disease and plague, with no one to mourn them, not even their wives.

[16] "The evil man may accumulate money like dust, with closets jammed full of clothing— [17] yes, he may order them made by his tailor, but the innocent shall wear that clothing, and shall divide his silver among them. [18] Every house built by the wicked is as fragile as a spider web, as full of cracks as a leafy booth!

[19] "He goes to bed rich, but wakes up to find that all his wealth is gone. [20] Terror overwhelms him, and he is blown away in the storms of the night. [21] The east wind carries him away, and he is gone. It sweeps him into eternity. [22] For God shall hurl at him unsparingly. He longs to flee from God. [23] Everyone will cheer at his death, and boo him into eternity.

28 "MEN KNOW HOW to mine silver and refine gold, [2] to dig iron from the earth and melt copper from stone. [3,4] Men know how to put light into darkness so that a mine shaft can be sunk into the earth, and the earth searched and its deep secrets explored. Into the black rock, shadowed by death, men descend on ropes, swinging back and forth.

[5] "Men know how to obtain food from the surface of the earth, while underneath there is fire.

[6] "They know how to find sapphires and gold dust— [7] treasures that no bird of prey can see, no eagle's eye observe— [8] for they are deep within the mines. No wild animal has ever walked upon those treasures; no lion has set his paw there. [9] Men know how to tear apart flinty rocks and how to overturn the roots of mountains. [10] They drill tunnels in the rocks and lay bare precious stones. [11] They dam up streams of water and pan the gold.[a]

[12] "But though men can do all these things, they don't know where to find wisdom and understanding. [13] They not only don't know how to get it, but, in fact, it is not to be found among the living.

[14] " 'It's not here,' the oceans say; and the seas reply, 'Nor is it here.'

[15] "It cannot be bought for gold or silver, [16] nor for all the gold of Ophir or precious onyx stones or sapphires. [17] Wisdom is far more valuable than gold and glass. It cannot be bought for jewels mounted in fine gold. [18] Coral or crystal is worthless in trying to get it; its price is far above rubies. [19] Topaz from Ethiopia cannot purchase it, nor even the purest gold.

---

a Or, "the bars of heaven are afraid of him." See verse 11. things that are hidden."

28a Literally, "He brings forth to the light the

²⁰ "Then where can we get it? Where can it be found? ²¹ For it is hid from the eyes of all mankind; even the sharp-eyed birds in the sky cannot discover it.

²² "But Destruction and Death speak of knowing something about it! ²³,²⁴ And God surely knows where it is to be found, for he looks throughout the whole earth, under all the heavens. ²⁵ He makes the winds blow and sets the boundaries of the oceans. ²⁶ He makes the laws of the rain and a path for the lightning. ²⁷ He knows where wisdom is and declares it to all who will listen. He established it and examined it thoroughly. ²⁸ And this is what he says to all mankind: 'Look, to fear the Lord is true wisdom; to forsake evil is real understanding.' "

29 JOB CONTINUED:
² "Oh, for the years gone by when God took care of me, ³ when he lighted the way before me and I walked safely through the darkness; ⁴ yes, in my early years, when the friendship of God was felt in my home; ⁵ when the Almighty was still with me and my children were around me; ⁶ when my projects prospered, and even the rock poured out streams of olive oil to me!

⁷ "Those were the days when I went out to the city gate and took my place among the honored elders. ⁸ The young saw me and stepped aside, and even the aged rose and stood up in respect at my coming. ⁹ The princes stood in silence and laid their hands upon their mouths. ¹⁰ The highest officials of the city stood in quietness. ¹¹ All rejoiced in what I said. All who saw me spoke well of me.

¹² "For I, as an honest judge,ᵃ helped the poor in their need, and the fatherless who had no one to help them. ¹³ I helped those who were ready to perish and they blessed me. And I caused the widows' hearts to sing for joy. ¹⁴ All I did was just and honest, for righteousness was my clothing! ¹⁵ I served as eyes for the blind and feet for the lame. ¹⁶ I was as a father to the poor, and saw to it that even strangers received a fair trial. ¹⁷ I knocked out the fangs of the godless oppressors and made them drop their victims.

¹⁸ "I thought, 'Surely I shall die quietly in my nest after a long, good life.' ¹⁹ For everything I did prospered; the dew lay all night upon my fields and watered them. ²⁰ Fresh honors were constantly given me, and my abilities were constantly refreshed and renewed. ²¹ Everyone listened to me and valued my advice, and were silent until I spoke. ²² And after I spoke, they spoke no more, for my counsel satisfied them. ²³ They longed for me to speak as those in drought-time long for rain. They waited eagerly with open mouths. ²⁴ When they were discouraged, I smiled and that encouraged them, and lightened their spirits. ²⁵ I told them what they should do, and corrected them as their chief, or as a king instructs his army, and as one who comforts those who mourn.

30 "BUT NOW THOSE younger than I deride me—young men whose fathers are less than my dogs. ² Oh, they have strong backs all right, but they are useless, stupid fools. ³ They are gaunt with famine and have been cast out into deserts and the wastelands, desolate and gloomy. ⁴ They eat roots and leaves, ⁵ having been driven from civilization. Men shouted after them as after thieves. ⁶ So now they live in frightening ravines, and in caves, and among the rocks. ⁷ They sound like animals among the bushes, huddling together for shelter beneath the nettles. ⁸ These sons of theirs have also turned out to be fools, yes, children of no name, outcasts of civilization.

⁹ "And now I have become the subject of their ribald song! I am a joke among *them!* ¹⁰ *They* despise me and won't come near me, and don't mind spitting in my face. ¹¹ For God has placed my life in jeopardy. These young men, having humbled me, now cast off all restraint before me. ¹² This rabble trip me and lay traps in my path. ¹³ They block my road and do everything they can to hasten my calamity, knowing full well that I have no one to help me. ¹⁴ They come at me from all directions. They rush upon me when I am down.

¹⁵ "I live in terror now. They hold me in contempt and my prosperity has vanished

---

a Implied in verse 7.

as a cloud before a strong wind. [16] My heart is broken. Depression haunts my days. [17] My weary nights are filled with pain as though something were relentlessly gnawing at my bones. [18] All night long I toss and turn, and my garments bind about me. [19] God has thrown me into the mud. I have become as dust and ashes.

[20] "I cry to you, O God, but you don't answer me. I stand before you and you don't bother to look. [21] You have become cruel toward me, and persecute me with great power and effect. [22] You throw me into the whirlwind and dissolve me in the storm. [23] And I know that your purpose for me is death. [24] I expected my fall to be broken, just as one who falls stretches out his hand or cries for help in his calamity.

[25] "And did I not weep for those in trouble? Wasn't I deeply grieved for the needy? [26] I therefore looked for good to come. Evil came instead. I waited for the light. Darkness came. [27] My heart is troubled and restless. Waves of affliction have come upon me. [28,29] I am black, but not from sunburn. I stand up and cry to the assembly for help. [But I might as well save my breath,[a]] for I am considered a brother to jackals and a companion to ostriches. [30] My skin is black and peeling. My bones burn with fever. [31] The voice of joy and gladness has turned to mourning.

31 "I MADE A covenant with my eyes not to look with lust upon a girl. [2,3] I know full well that Almighty God above sends calamity on those who do. [4] He sees everything I do, and every step I take.

[5] "If I have lied and deceived— [6] but God knows that I am innocent— [7,8] or if I have stepped off God's pathway, or if my heart has lusted for what my eyes have seen, or if I am guilty of any other sin, then let someone else reap the crops I have sown and let all that I have planted be rooted out.

[9] "Or if I have longed for another man's wife, [10] then may I die, and may my wife be in another man's home, and someone else become her husband. [11] For lust is a shameful sin, a crime that should be punished. [12] It is a devastating fire that destroys to hell,

and would root out all I have planted.

[13] "If I have been unfair to my servants, [14] how could I face God? What could I say when he questioned me about it? [15] For God made me, and made my servant too. He created us both.

[16] "If I have hurt the poor or caused widows to weep, [17] or refused food to hungry orphans— [18] (but we have always cared for orphans in our home, treating them as our own children)— [19,20] or if I have seen anyone freezing and not given him clothing, or fleece from my sheep to keep him warm, [21] or if I have taken advantage of an orphan because I thought I could get away with it— [22] if I have done any of these things, then let my arm be torn from its socket! Let my shoulder be wrenched out of place! [23] Rather that than face the judgment sent by God; that I dread more than anything else. For if the majesty of God opposes me, what hope is there?

[24] "If I have put my trust in money, [25] if my happiness depends on wealth, [26] or if I have looked at the sun shining in the skies, or the moon walking down her silver pathway, [27] and my heart has been secretly enticed, and I have worshiped them by kissing my hand to them, [28] this, too, must be punished by the judges. For if I had done such things, it would mean that I denied the God of heaven.

[29] "If I have rejoiced at harm to an enemy— [30] (but actually I have never cursed anyone nor asked for revenge)— [31] or if any of my servants have ever gone hungry— [32] (actually I have never turned away even a stranger but have opened my doors to all)— [33] or if, like Adam, I have tried to hide my sins, [34] fearing the crowd and its contempt, so that I refused to acknowledge my sin and do not go out of my way to help others— [35] (oh, that there were someone who would listen to me and try to see my side of this argument. Look, I will sign my signature to my defense; now let the Almighty show me that I am wrong; let *him* approve the indictments made against me by my enemies. [36] I would treasure it like a crown. [37] Then I would tell him exactly what I have done and why, presenting my

---

a Implied.

defense as one he listens to).

[38,39] "Or if my land accuses me because I stole the fruit it bears, or if I have murdered its owners to get their land for myself, [40] then let thistles grow on that land instead of wheat, and weeds instead of barley."
Job's words are ended.

32 THE THREE MEN refused to reply further to Job because he kept insisting on his innocence.

[2] Then Elihu (son of Barachel, the Buzite, of the Clan of Ram) became angry because Job refused to admit he had sinned and to acknowledge that God had just cause for punishing him. [3] But he was also angry with Job's three friends because they had been unable to answer Job's arguments and yet had condemned him. [4] Elihu had waited until now to speak because the others were older than he.

[5] But when he saw that they had no further reply, he spoke out angrily, [6] and said, "I am young and you are old, so I held back and did not dare to tell you what I think, [7] for those who are older are said to be wiser; [8,9] but it is not mere age that makes men wise. Rather, it is the spirit in a man, the breath of the Almighty which makes him intelligent. [10] So listen to me awhile and let me express my opinion.

[11,12] "I have waited all this time, listening very carefully to your arguments, but not one of them has convinced Job that he is a sinner, or has proved that he is. [13] And don't give me that line about 'only God can convince the sinner of his sin.' [14] If Job had been arguing with me, I would not answer with that kind of logic!

[15] "You sit there baffled, with no further replies. [16] Shall I then continue to wait when you are silent? [17] No, I will give my answer too. [18] For I am pent up and full of words, and the spirit within me urges me on. [19] I am like a wine cask without a vent! My words are ready to burst out! [20] I must speak to find relief, so let me give my answers. [21,22] Don't insist that I be cautious lest I insult someone, and don't make me flatter anyone. Let me be frank, lest God should strike me dead.

33 "PLEASE LISTEN, JOB, to what I have to say. [2] I have begun to speak; now let me continue. [3] I will speak the truth with all sincerity. [4] For the Spirit of God has made me, and the breath of the Almighty gives me life. [5] Don't hesitate to answer me if you can.

[6] "Look, I am the one you were wishing for, someone to stand between you and God and to be both his representative and yours. [7] You need not be frightened of me. I am not some person of renown to make you nervous and afraid. I, too, am made of common clay.

[8] "You have said it in my hearing, yes, you've said it again and again— [9] 'I am pure, I am innocent; I have not sinned.' [10] You say God is using a fine-toothed comb to try to find a single fault, and so to count you as his enemy. [11] 'And he puts my feet in the stocks,' you say, 'and watches every move I make.'

[12] "All right, here is my reply: In this very thing, you have sinned by speaking of God that way. For God is greater than man. [13] Why should you fight against him just because he does not give account to you of what he does?

[14] "For God speaks again and again, [15] in dreams, in visions of the night when deep sleep falls on men as they lie on their beds. [16] He opens their ears in times like that, and gives them wisdom and instruction, [17,18] causing them to change their minds, and keeping them from pride, and warning them of the penalties of sin, and keeping them from falling into some trap.

[19] "Or, God sends sickness and pain, even though no bone is broken, [20] so that a man loses all taste and appetite for food and doesn't care for even the daintiest dessert. [21] He becomes thin, mere skin and bones, [22] and draws near to death.

[23,24] "But if a messenger from heaven is there to intercede for him as a friend, to show him what is right, then God pities him and says,[a] 'Set him free. Do not make him die, for I have found a substitute.' [25] Then his body will become as healthy as a child's, firm and youthful again. [26] And when he prays to God, God will hear and answer and

---

a Or, "and if the Angel says."

receive him with joy, and return him to his duties. ²⁷ And he will declare to his friends, 'I sinned, but God let me go. ²⁸ He did not let me die. I will go on living in the realm of light.'

²⁹ "Yes, God often does these things for man— ³⁰ brings back his soul from the pit, so that he may live in the light of the living. ³¹ Mark this well, O Job. Listen to me, and let me say more. ³² But if you have anything to say at this point, go ahead. I want to hear it, for I am anxious to justify you. ³³ But if not, then listen to me. Keep silence and I will teach you wisdom!"

34 ELIHU CONTINUED:

² "Listen to me, you wise men. ³ We can choose the sounds we want to listen to; we can choose the taste we want in food, ⁴ and we should choose to follow what is right. But first of all we must define among ourselves what is good. ⁵ For Job has said, 'I am innocent, but God says I'm not. ⁶ I am called a liar, even though I am innocent. I am horribly punished, even though I have not sinned.'

⁷,⁸ "Who else is as arrogant as Job? He must have spent much time with evil men, ⁹ for he said, 'Why waste time trying to please God?'

¹⁰ "Listen to me, you with understanding. Surely everyone knows that *God doesn't sin!* ¹¹ Rather, he punishes the sinners. ¹² There is no truer statement than this: *God is never wicked or unjust.* ¹³ He alone has authority over the earth and dispenses justice for the world. ¹⁴ If God were to withdraw his Spirit, ¹⁵ all life would disappear and mankind would turn again to dust.

¹⁶ "Listen now and try to understand. ¹⁷ Could God govern if he hated justice? Are you going to condemn the Almighty Judge? ¹⁸ Are you going to condemn this God who says to kings and nobles, 'You are wicked and unjust'? ¹⁹ For he doesn't care how great a man may be, and doesn't pay any more attention to the rich than to the poor. He made them all. ²⁰ In a moment they die, and at midnight great and small shall suddenly pass away, removed by no human hand.

²¹ "For God carefully watches the goings on of all mankind; he sees them all. ²² No darkness is thick enough to hide evil men from his eyes, ²³ so there is no need to wait for some great crime before a man is called before God in judgment. ²⁴ Without making a federal case of it, God simply shatters the greatest of men, and puts others in their place. ²⁵ He watches what they do and in a single night he overturns them, destroying them, ²⁶ or openly strikes them down as wicked men. ²⁷ For they turned aside from following him, ²⁸ causing the cry of the poor to come to the attention of God. Yes, he hears the cries of those being oppressed. ²⁹,³⁰ Yet when he chooses not to speak, who can criticize? Again, he may prevent a vile man from ruling, thus saving a nation from ruin, and he can depose an entire nation just as easily.

³¹ "Why don't people exclaim to their God, 'We have sinned, but we will stop'? ³² Or, 'We know not what evil we have done; only tell us, and we will cease at once.'

³³ "Must God tailor his justice to your demands? Must he change the order of the universe to suit your whims? The answer must be obvious even to you! ³⁴,³⁵ Anyone even half bright will agree with me that you, Job, are speaking like a fool. ³⁶ You should be given the maximum penalty for the wicked way you have talked about God. ³⁷ For now you have added rebellion, arrogance and blasphemy to your other sins."

35 ELIHU CONTINUED:

²,³ "Do you think it is right for you to claim, 'I haven't sinned, but I'm no better off before God than if I had'?

⁴ "I will answer you, and all your friends too. ⁵ Look up there into the sky, high above you. ⁶ If you sin, does that shake the heavens and knock God from his throne? Even if you sin again and again, what effect will it have upon him? ⁷ Or if you are good, is this some great gift to him? ⁸ Your sins may hurt another man, or your good deeds may profit him. ⁹,¹⁰ The oppressed may shriek beneath their wrongs and groan beneath the power of the rich; yet none of them cry to God, asking, 'Where is God my Maker who gives songs in the night, ¹¹ and makes us a little wiser than the animals and birds?'

¹² "But when anyone does cry out this question to him, he never replies by instant

punishment of the tyrants.[a] [13] But it is false to say he doesn't hear those cries; [14,15] and it is even more false to say that he doesn't see what is going on. He *does* bring about justice at last, if you will only wait. But do you cry out against him because he does not instantly respond in anger? [16] Job, you have spoken like a fool."

36 ELIHU CONTINUED: [2] "Let me go on and I will show you the truth of what I am saying. For I have not finished defending God! [3] I will give you many illustrations of the righteousness of my Maker. [4] I am telling you the honest truth, for I am a man of well-rounded knowledge.

[5] "God is almighty and yet does not despise anyone! And he is perfect in his understanding. [6] He does not reward the wicked with his blessings, but gives them their full share of punishment. [7] He does not ignore the good men but honors them by placing them upon eternal, kingly thrones. [8] If troubles come upon them, and they are enslaved and afflicted, [9] then he takes the trouble to point out to them the reason, what they have done that is wrong, or how they have behaved proudly. [10] He helps them hear his instruction to turn away from their sin.

[11] "If they listen and obey him, then they will be blessed with prosperity throughout their lives. [12] If they won't listen to him, they shall perish in battle and die because of their lack of good sense. [13] But the godless reap his anger. They do not even return to him when he punishes them. [14] They die young after lives of dissipation and depravity. [15] He delivers by distress! This makes them listen to him!

[16] "How he wanted to lure you away from danger into a wide and pleasant valley and to prosper you there. [17] But you are too preoccupied with your imagined grievances against others. [18] Watch out! Don't let your anger at others lead you into scoffing at God! Don't let your suffering embitter you at the only one who can deliver you. [19] Do you really think that if you shout loudly enough against God, he will be ashamed and repent? Will this put an end to your chastisement?

[20] "Do not desire the nighttime, with its opportunities for crime. [21] Turn back from evil, for it was to prevent you from getting into a life of evil that God sent this suffering.

[22] "Look, God is all-powerful. Who is a teacher like him? [23] Who can say that what he does is absurd or evil? [24] Instead, glorify him for his mighty works for which he is so famous. [25] Everyone has seen these things from a distance.

[26] "God is so great that we cannot begin to know him. No one can begin to understand eternity. [27] He draws up the water vapor and then distills it into rain, [28] which the skies pour down. [29] Can anyone really understand the spreading of the clouds, and the thunders within? [30] See how he spreads the lightning around him, and blankets the tops of the mountains. [31] By his fantastic powers in nature he punishes or blesses the people, giving them food in abundance. [32] He fills his hands with lightning bolts. He hurls each at its target. [33] We feel his presence in the thunder. May all sinners be warned.[a]

37 "MY HEART TREMBLES at this. [2] Listen, listen to the thunder of his voice. [3] It rolls across the heavens and his lightning flashes out in every direction. [4] Afterwards comes the roaring of the thunder —the tremendous voice of his majesty. [5] His voice is glorious in the thunder. We cannot comprehend the greatness of his power. [6] For he directs the snow, the showers, and storm to fall upon the earth. [7] Man's work stops at such a time, so that all men everywhere may recognize his power. [8] The wild animals hide in the rocks or in their dens.

[9] "From the south comes the rain; from the north, the cold. [10] God blows upon the rivers, and even the widest torrents freeze. [11] He loads the clouds with moisture and they send forth his lightning. [12] The lightning bolts are directed by his hand, and do whatever he commands throughout the earth. [13] He sends the storms[a] as punishment, or, in his lovingkindness, to encour-

---

a Or, "because of man's base pride."   36a Literally, "(even) the cattle (warn us) of the coming storm."
37a Implied.

age.

[14] "Listen, O Job, stop and consider the wonderful miracles of God. [15] Do you know how God controls all nature, and causes the lightning to flash forth from the clouds? [16,17] Do you understand the balancing of the clouds with wonderful perfection and skill? Do you know why you become warm when the south wind is blowing and everything is still? [18] Can you spread out the gigantic mirror of the skies as he does?

[19,20] "You who think you know so much,[b] teach the rest of us how we should approach God. For we are too dull to know! With your wisdom, would we then dare to approach him? Well, does a man wish to be swallowed alive? [21] For as we cannot look at the sun for its brightness when the winds have cleared away the clouds, [22] neither can we gaze at the terrible majesty of God breaking forth upon us from heaven, clothed in dazzling splendor. [23] We cannot imagine the power of the Almighty, and yet he is so just and merciful that he does not destroy us. [24] No wonder men everywhere fear him! For he is not impressed by the world's wisest men!"

38 THEN THE LORD *answered Job from the whirlwind:*

[2] "Why are you using your ignorance to deny my providence? [3] Now get ready to fight, for I am going to demand some answers from you, and you must reply.

[4] "Where were you when I laid the foundations of the earth? Tell me, if you know so much. [5] Do you know how its dimensions were determined, and who did the surveying? [6,7] What supports its foundations, and who laid its cornerstone, as the morning stars sang together and all the angels shouted for joy?

[8,9] "Who decreed the boundaries of the seas when they gushed from the depths? Who clothed them with clouds and thick darkness, [10] and barred them by limiting their shores, [11] and said, 'Thus far and no farther shall you come, and here shall your proud waves stop!'?

[12] "Have you ever once commanded the morning to appear, and caused the dawn to rise in the east? [13] Have you ever told the daylight to spread to the ends of the earth, to end the night's wickedness? [14] Have you ever robed the dawn in red, [15] and disturbed the haunts of wicked men and stopped the arm raised to strike?

[16] "Have you explored the springs from which the seas come, or walked in the sources of their depths? [17,18] Has the location of the gates of Death been revealed to you? Do you realize the extent of the earth? Tell me about it if you know! [19] Where does the light come from, and how do you get there? Or tell me about the darkness. Where does it come from? [20] Can you find its boundaries, or go to its source? [21] But of course you know all this! For you were born before it was all created, and you are so very experienced!

[22,23] "Have you visited the treasuries of the snow, or seen where hail is made and stored? For I have reserved it for the time when I will need it in war. [24] Where is the path to the distribution point of light? Where is the home of the east wind? [25-27] Who dug the valleys for the torrents of rain? Who laid out the path for the lightning, causing the rain to fall upon the barren deserts, so that the parched and barren ground is satisfied with water, and tender grass springs up?

[28] "Has the rain a father? Where does dew come from? [29] Who is the mother of the ice and frost? [30] For the water changes and turns to ice, as hard as rock.

[31] "Can you hold back the stars? Can you restrain Orion or Pleiades? [32] Can you ensure the proper sequence of the seasons, or guide the constellation of the Bear with her satellites across the heavens? [33] Do you know the laws of the universe and how the heavens influence the earth? [34] Can you shout to the clouds and make it rain? [35] Can you make lightning appear and cause it to strike as you direct it?

[36] "Who gives intuition and instinct?[a] [37,38] Who is wise enough to number all the clouds? Who can tilt the water jars of heaven, when everything is dust and clods? [39,40] Can you stalk prey like a lioness, to satisfy the young lions' appetites as they lie in

b Implied.　38a Or, "Who has put wisdom in the inward parts, and given understanding to the mind?"

their dens, or lie in wait in the jungle? [41] Who provides for the ravens when their young cry out to God as they try to struggle up from their nest in hunger?

39 "DO YOU KNOW how mountain goats give birth? Have you ever seen them giving birth to their young? [2,3] Do you know how many months of pregnancy they have before they bow themselves to give birth to their young, and carry their burden no longer? [4] Their young grow up in the open field, then leave their parents and return to them no more.

[5] "Who makes the wild donkeys wild? [6] I have placed them in the wilderness and given them salt plains to live in. [7] For they hate the noise of the city and want no drivers shouting at them! [8] The mountain ranges are their pastureland; there they search for every blade of grass.

[9] "Will the wild ox be your happy servant? Will he stay beside your feeding crib? [10] Can you use a wild ox to plow with? Will he pull the harrow for you? [11] Because he is so strong, will you trust him? Will you let him decide where to work? [12] Can you send him out to bring in the grain from the threshing-floor?

[13] "The ostrich flaps her wings grandly, but has no true motherly love. [14] She lays her eggs on top of the earth, to warm them in the dust. [15] She forgets that someone may step on them and crush them, or the wild animals destroy them. [16] She ignores her young as though they weren't her own, and is unconcerned though they die, [17] for God has deprived her of wisdom. [18] But whenever she jumps up to run, she passes the swiftest horse with its rider.

[19] "Have you given the horse strength, or clothed his neck with a quivering mane? [20] Have you made him able to leap forward like a locust? His majestic snorting is something to hear! [21-23] He paws the earth and rejoices in his strength, and when he goes to war, he is unafraid and does not run away though the arrows rattle against him, or the flashing spear and javelin. [24] Fiercely he paws the ground and rushes forward into battle when the trumpet blows. [25] At the sound of the bugle he shouts, 'Aha!' He smells the battle when far away. He rejoices at the shouts of battle and the roar of the captain's commands.

[26] "Do you know how a hawk soars and spreads her wings to the south? [27] Is it at your command that the eagle rises high upon the cliffs to make her nest? [28] She lives upon the cliffs, making her home in her mountain fortress. [29] From there she spies her prey, from a very great distance. [30] Her nestlings gulp down blood, for she goes wherever the slain are."

40 THE LORD WENT ON: [2] "Do you still want to argue with the Almighty? Or will you yield? Do you—God's critic—have the answers?"

[3] *Then Job replied to God:*

[4] "I am nothing—how could I ever find the answers? I lay my hand upon my mouth in silence. [5] I have said too much already."

[6] *Then the Lord spoke to Job again from the whirlwind:*

[7] "Stand up like a man and brace yourself for battle. Let me ask you a question, and give me the answer. [8] Are you going to discredit my justice and condemn me, so that you can say you are right? [9] Are you as strong as God, and can you shout as loudly as he? [10] All right then, put on your robes of state, your majesty and splendor. [11] Give vent to your anger. Let it overflow against the proud. [12] Humiliate the haughty with a glance; tread down the wicked where they stand. [13] Knock them into the dust, stone-faced in death. [14] If you can do that, then I'll agree with you that your own strength can save you.

[15] "Take a look at the behemoth! I made him, too, just as I made you! He eats grass like an ox. [16] See his powerful loins and the muscles of his belly. [17] His tail is as straight as a cedar. The sinews of his thighs are tightly knit together. [18] His vertebrae lie straight as a tube of brass. His ribs are like iron bars. [19] How ferocious he is among all of God's creation, so let whoever hopes to master him bring a sharp sword! [20] The mountains offer their best food to him—the other wild animals on which he preys. [21] He lies down under the lotus plants, hidden by the reeds, [22] covered by their shade among the willows there beside the stream. [23] He is not disturbed by raging rivers, not even

when the swelling Jordan rushes down upon him. [24] No one can catch him off guard or put a ring in his nose and lead him away.

41 "CAN YOU CATCH leviathan with a hook and line? Or put a noose around his tongue? [2] Can you tie him with a rope through the nose, or pierce his jaw with a spike? [3] Will he beg you to desist or try to flatter you from your intentions? [4] Will he agree to let you make him your slave for life? [5] Can you make a pet of him like a bird, or give him to your little girls to play with? [6] Do fishing partners sell him to the fish-mongers? [7] Will his hide be hurt by darts, or his head with a harpoon?

[8] "If you lay your hands upon him, you will long remember the battle that ensues, and you will never try it again! [9] No, it's useless to try to capture him. It is frightening even to think about it! [10] No one dares to stir *him* up, let alone try to conquer him. And if no one can stand before *him,* who can stand before *me?* [11] I owe no one anything. Everything under the heaven is mine.

[12] "I should mention, too, the tremendous strength in his limbs, and throughout his enormous frame. [13] Who can penetrate his hide, or who dares come within reach of his jaws? [14] For his teeth are terrible. [15-17] His overlapping scales are his pride, making a tight seal, so no air can get between them, and nothing can penetrate.

[18] "When he sneezes, the sunlight sparkles like lightning across the vapor droplets. His eyes glow like sparks. [19] Fire leaps from his mouth. [20] Smoke flows from his nostrils, like steam from a boiling pot that is fired by dry rushes. [21] Yes, his breath would kindle coals—flames leap from his mouth.

[22] "The tremendous strength in his neck strikes terror wherever he goes. [23] His flesh is hard and firm, not soft and fat. [24] His heart is hard as rock, just like a millstone. [25] When he stands up, the strongest are afraid. Terror grips them. [26] No sword can stop him, nor spear nor dart nor pointed shaft. [27,28] Iron is nothing but straw to him, and brass is rotten wood. Arrows cannot make him flee. Slingstones are as ineffective as straw. [29] Clubs do no good, and he laughs at the javelins hurled at him. [30] His belly is covered with scales as sharp as shards; he drags across the ground like a steamroller! [31,32] He makes the water boil with his commotion. He churns the depths. He leaves a shining wake of froth behind him. One would think the sea was made of frost! [33] There is nothing else so fearless anywhere on earth. [34] Of all the beasts, he is the proudest—monarch of all that he sees."

42 THEN JOB REPLIED TO GOD:
[2] "I know that you can do anything and that no one can stop you. [3] You ask who it is who has so foolishly denied your providence. It is I. I was talking about things I knew nothing about and did not understand, things far too wonderful for me.

[4] "[You said,[a]] 'Listen and I will speak! Let me put the questions to you! See if you can answer them!'

[5] "[But now I say,[a]] 'I had heard about you before, but now I have seen you, [6] and I loathe myself and repent in dust and ashes.' "

[7] *After the Lord had finished speaking with Job, he said to Eliphaz the Temanite:*

"I am angry with you and with your two friends, for you have not been right in what you have said about me, as my servant Job was. [8] Now take seven young bulls and seven rams and go to my servant Job and offer a burnt offering for yourselves; and my servant Job will pray for you, and I will accept his prayer on your behalf, and won't destroy you as I should because of your sin, your failure to speak rightly concerning my servant Job."

[9] So Eliphaz the Temanite, and Bildad the Shuhite, and Zophar the Naamathite did as the Lord commanded them, and the Lord accepted Job's prayer on their behalf. [10] Then, when Job prayed for his friends, the Lord restored his wealth and happiness! In fact, the Lord gave him twice as much as before! [11] Then all of his brothers, sisters, and former friends arrived and feasted with him in his home, consoling him for all his sorrow, and comforting him because of all the trials the Lord had brought upon him. And each of them brought him a gift of

---

a Implied.

money, and a gold ring.

[12] So the Lord blessed Job at the end of his life more than at the beginning. For now he had 14,000 sheep, 6,000 camels, 1,000 teams of oxen, and 1,000 female donkeys.

[13,14] God also gave him seven more sons and three more daughters.[b]

These were the names of his daughters:

Jemima, Kezia, Keren.[c]

[15] And in all the land there were no other girls as lovely as the daughters of Job; and their father put them into his will along with their brothers.

[16] Job lived 140 years after that, living to see his grandchildren and great-grandchildren too. [17] Then at last he died, an old, old man, after living a long, good life.

---

b Making a total of twenty children, twice as many as he had before. (Ten were in heaven.)
c Literally, "Keren-Happuch."

Bob Combs

The Way I Feel

The deepest thoughts, the fullest emotions find their outlet in music ... when you can't come out and say what's going on inside, you find (or create) a song ... then you feel relaxed, unthreatened. As one current troubadour said, "If it's done right, a song is almost like a birth. You take many things into your head over which you have very little control, you gestate, and it comes out when ready."

This book, by far the most popular in the entire Old Testament, is a songbook. David, whose ability on the lyre (the early forerunner of the guitar) got him a job with King Saul, is credited with 73 of these psalms, many of them written during personal tragedies and victories. The others were written by Asaph, the sons of Korah, Solomon, and others, some as late as Ezra's time after the captivity. And people have been singing them ever since....

PSALMS

1 OH, THE JOYS of those who do not follow evil men's advice, who do not hang around with sinners, scoffing at the things of God: ² But they delight in doing everything God wants them to, and day and night are always meditating on his laws and thinking about ways to follow him more closely.

³ They are like trees along a river bank bearing luscious fruit each season without fail. Their leaves shall never wither, and all they do shall prosper.

⁴ But for sinners, what a different story! They blow away like chaff before the wind. ⁵ They are not safe on Judgment Day; they shall not stand among the godly.

⁶ For the Lord watches over all the plans and paths of godly men, but the paths of the godless lead to doom.

2 WHAT FOOLS[a] THE nations are to rage against the Lord! How strange that men should try to outwit God![b] ² For a summit conference of the nations has been called to plot against the Lord and his Messiah, Christ the King.[c] ³ "Come, let us break his chains," they say, "and free ourselves from all this slavery to God."

⁴ But God in heaven merely laughs! He is amused by all their puny plans. ⁵ And then in fierce fury he rebukes them and fills them with fear.

⁶ For the Lord declares,[d] "This is the King of my choice, and I have enthroned him in Jerusalem, my holy city."[e]

⁷ His chosen one replies,[d] "I will reveal the everlasting purposes of God, for the Lord has said to me, 'You are my Son. This is your Coronation Day.[f] Today I am giving you your glory.' " ⁸ "Only ask, and I will give you all the nations of the world. ⁹ Rule them with an iron rod; smash them like clay pots!"

¹⁰ O kings and rulers of the earth, listen while there is time. ¹¹ Serve the Lord with reverent fear; rejoice with trembling. ¹² Fall down before his Son and kiss his feet[d] before his anger is roused and you perish. I am warning you—his wrath will soon begin. But oh, the joys of those who put their trust in him!

A Psalm of David when he fled from his son Absalom

3 O LORD, SO many are against me. So many seek to harm me. I have so many enemies. ² So many say that God will never help me. ³ But Lord, you are my shield, my glory, and my only hope. You alone can lift my head, now bowed in shame.[a]

⁴ I cried out to the Lord, and he heard me from his Temple in Jerusalem.[b] ⁵ Then I lay down and slept in peace and woke up safely, for the Lord was watching over me. ⁶ And now, although ten thousand enemies surround me on every side, I am not afraid.

2a Implied; literally, "Why do the heathen rage?"
c Literally, "his anointed."　　d Implied.
f Literally, "This day have I begotten you."
b Literally, "from his holy mountain."

b Literally, "meditate a vain thing."
e Literally, "Upon Zion, my holy mountain."
3a Implied.

473

[7] I will cry to him, "Arise, O Lord! Save me, O my God!" And he will slap them in the face, insulting[c] them and breaking off their teeth.

[8] For salvation comes from God. What joys he gives to all his people.

4 O GOD, YOU have declared me perfect in your eyes;[a] you have always cared for me in my distress; now hear me as I call again. Have mercy on me. Hear my prayer.

[2] The Lord God asks, "Sons of men, will you forever turn my glory into shame by worshiping these silly idols, when every claim that's made for them is false?"

[3] Mark this well: The Lord has set apart the redeemed for himself. Therefore he will listen to me and answer when I call to him. [4] Stand before the Lord in awe,[b] and do not sin against him. Lie quietly upon your bed in silent meditation. [5] Put your trust in the Lord, and offer him pleasing sacrifices.

[6] Many say that God will never help us. Prove them wrong,[c] O Lord, by letting the light of your face shine down upon us. [7] Yes, the gladness you have given me is far greater than their joys at harvest time as they gaze at their bountiful crops. [8] I will lie down in peace and sleep, for though I am alone, O Lord, you will keep me safe.

5 O LORD, HEAR me praying; listen to my plea, O God my King, for I will never pray to anyone but you. [3] Each morning I will look to you in heaven and lay my requests before you, praying earnestly.

[4] I know you get no pleasure from wickedness and cannot tolerate the slightest sin. [5] Therefore proud sinners will not survive your searching gaze, for how you hate their evil deeds. [6] You will destroy them for their lies; how you abhor all murder and deception.

[7] But as for me, I will come into your Temple protected by your mercy and your love; I will worship you with deepest awe. [8] Lord, lead me as you promised me you would; otherwise my enemies will conquer me. Tell me clearly what to do, which way to turn. [9] For they cannot speak one truthful word. Their hearts are filled to the brim with wickedness. Their suggestions are full of the stench of sin and death. Their tongues are filled with flatteries to gain their wicked ends. [10] O God, hold them responsible. Catch them in their own traps; let them fall beneath the weight of their own transgressions, for they rebel against you.

[11] But make everyone rejoice who puts his trust in you. Keep them shouting for joy because you are defending them. Fill all who love you with your happiness. [12] For you bless the godly man, O Lord; you protect him with your shield of love.

6 NO, LORD! DON'T punish me in the heat of your anger. [2] Pity me, O Lord, for I am weak. Heal me, for my body is sick, [3] and I am upset and disturbed. My mind is filled with apprehension and with gloom. Oh, restore me soon.

[4] Come, O Lord, and make me well. In your kindness save me. [5] For if I die I cannot give you glory by praising you before my friends.[a] [6] I am worn out with pain; every night my pillow is wet with tears. [7] My eyes are growing old and dim with grief because of all my enemies.

[8] Go, leave me now, you men of evil deeds, for the Lord has heard my weeping [9] and my pleading. He will answer all my prayers. [10] All my enemies shall be suddenly dishonored, terror-stricken, and disgraced. God will turn them back in shame.

7 I AM DEPENDING on you, O Lord my God, to save me from my persecutors. [2] Don't let them pounce upon me as a lion would and maul me and drag me away with no one to rescue me. [3] It would be different, Lord, if I were doing evil things— [4] if I were paying back evil for good or unjustly attacking those I dislike. [5] Then it would be right for you to let my enemies destroy me, crush me to the ground, and trample my life in the dust.

[6] But Lord! Arise in anger against the anger of my enemies. Awake! Demand justice for me, Lord! [7,8] Gather all peoples before you; sit high above them, judging

---

c Implied.   4a Literally, "God of my righteousness."   b Or, "Be ye angry."   c Implied.
6a Literally, "In the grave, who shall give you thanks?" Isaiah 57:1,2 may indicate that Old Testament saints believed in a conscious and pleasant hereafter for those who love God.

their sins. But justify me publicly; establish my honor and truth before them all. ⁹ End all wickedness, O Lord, and bless all who truly worship God;ᵃ for you, the righteous God, look deep within the hearts of men and examine all their motives and their thoughts.

¹⁰ God is my shield; he will defend me. He saves those whose hearts and lives are true and right.ᵇ

¹¹ God is a judge who is perfectly fair, and he is angry with the wicked every day. ¹² Unless they repent, he will sharpen his sword and slay them.

He has bent and strung his bow ¹³ and fitted it with deadly arrows made from shafts of fire.

¹⁴ The wicked man conceives an evil plot, labors with its dark details, and brings to birth his treachery and lies; ¹⁵ let him fall into his own trap. ¹⁶ May the violence he plans for others boomerang upon himself; let him die.

¹⁷ Oh, how grateful and thankful I am to the Lord because he is so good. I will sing praise to the name of the Lord who is above all lords.

8 O LORD OUR God, the majesty and glory of your name fills all the earth and overflows the heavens. ² You have taught the little children to praise you perfectly. May their example shame and silence your enemies!

³ When I look up into the night skies and see the work of your fingers—the moon and the stars you have made— ⁴ I cannot understand how you can bother with mere puny man, to pay any attention to him! ⁵ And yet you have made him only a little lower than the angels,ᵃ and placed a crown of glory and honor upon his head.

⁶ You have put him in charge of everything you made; everything is put under his authority: ⁷ all sheep and oxen, and wild animals too, ⁸ the birds and fish, and all the life in the sea. ⁹ O Jehovah, our Lord, the majesty and glory of your name fills the earth.

9 O LORD, I will praise you with all my heart, and tell everyone about the marvelous things you do. ² I will be glad, yes, filled with joy because of you. I will sing your praises, O Lord God above all gods.ᵃ

³ My enemies will fall back and perish in your presence; ⁴ you have vindicated me; you have endorsed my work, declaring from your throne that it is good.ᵇ ⁵ You have rebuked the nations and destroyed the wicked, blotting out their names forever and ever. ⁶ O enemies of mine, you are doomed forever. The Lord will destroy your cities; even the memory of them will disappear.

⁷,⁸ But the Lord lives on forever; he sits upon his throne to judge justly the nations of the world. ⁹ All who are oppressed may come to him. He is a refuge for them in their times of trouble. ¹⁰ All those who know your mercy, Lord, will count on you for help. For you have never yet forsaken those who trust in you.

¹¹ Oh, sing out your praises to the God who lives in Jerusalem.ᶜ Tell the world about his unforgettable deeds. ¹² He who avenges murder has an open ear to those who cry to him for justice. He does not ignore the prayers of men in trouble when they call to him for help.

¹³ And now, O Lord, have mercy on me; see how I suffer at the hands of those who hate me. Lord, snatch me back from the jaws of death. ¹⁴ Save me, so that I can praise you publicly before all the people at Jerusalem'sᵈ gates and rejoice that you have rescued me.

¹⁵ The nations fall into the pitfalls they have dug for others; the trap they set has snapped on them. ¹⁶ The Lord is famous for the way he punishes the wicked in their own snares!ᵉ

¹⁷ The wicked shall be sent away to hell; this is the fate of all the nations forgetting the Lord. ¹⁸ For the needs of the needy shall not be ignored forever; the hopes of the poor shall not always be crushed.

¹⁹ O Lord, arise and judge and punish the nations; don't let them conquer you!

a Literally, "the just."   b Literally, "the upright in heart."   a Or, "only a little lower than God!"
9 a Literally, "O Most High."   b Literally, "You sit on the throne, judging righteously."
c Literally, "in Zion."   d Literally, "in the gates of the daughter of Zion."   e The Hebrew text adds here: "Higgaion. Selah." The meanings of these words are not known.

²⁰ Make them tremble in fear; put the nations in their place until at last they know they are but puny men.

10 LORD, WHY ARE you standing aloof and far away? Why do you hide when I need you the most?

² Come and deal with all these proud and wicked men who viciously persecute the poor. Pour upon these men the evil they planned for others! ³ For these men brag of all their evil lusts; they revile God and congratulate those the Lord abhors, whose only goal in life is money.

⁴ These wicked men, so proud and haughty, seem to think that God is dead.ᵃ They wouldn't think of looking for him! ⁵ Yet there is success in everything they do, and their enemies fall before them. They do not see your punishment awaiting them. ⁶ They boast that neither God nor man can ever keep them down—somehow they'll find a way!

⁷ Their mouths are full of profanity and lies and fraud. They are always boasting of their evil plans. ⁸ They lurk in dark alleys of the city and murder passersby. ⁹ Like lions they crouch silently, waiting to pounce upon the poor. Like hunters they catch their victims in their traps. ¹⁰ The unfortunate are overwhelmed by their superior strength and fall beneath their blows. ¹¹ "God isn't watching," they say to themselves; "he'll never know!"

¹² O Lord, arise! O God, crush them! Don't forget the poor or anyone else in need. ¹³ Why do you let the wicked get away with this contempt for God? For they think that God will never call them to account. ¹⁴ Lord, you see what they are doing. You have noted each evil act. You know what trouble and grief they have caused. Now punish them. O Lord, the poor man trusts himself to you; you are known as the helper of the helpless. ¹⁵ Break the arms of these wicked men. Go after them until the last of them is destroyed.

¹⁶ The Lord is King forever and forever. Those who follow other gods shall be swept from his land.

¹⁷ Lord, you know the hopes of humble people. Surely you will hear their cries and comfort their hearts by helping them. ¹⁸ You will be with the orphans and all who are oppressed, so that mere earthly man will terrify them no longer.

11 HOW DARE YOU tell me, "Fleeᵃ to the mountains for safety," when I am trusting in the Lord?

² For the wicked have strung their bows, drawn their arrows tight against the bowstrings, and aimed from ambush at the people of God. ³ "Law and order have collapsed,"ᵇ we are told. "What can the righteous do but flee?"

⁴ But the Lord is still in his holy temple; he still rules from heaven. He closely watches everything that happens here on earth. ⁵ He puts the righteous and the wicked to the test; he hates those loving violence. ⁶ He will rain down fire and brimstone on the wicked and scorch them with his burning wind.

⁷ For God is good, and he loves goodness; the godly shall see his face.ᶜ

12 LORD! HELP! GODLY men are fast disappearing. Where in all the world can dependable men be found? ² Everyone deceives and flatters and lies. There is no sincerity left.

³,⁴ But the Lord will not deal gently with people who act like that; he will destroy those proud liars who say, "We will lie to our hearts' content. Our lips are our own; who can stop us?" ⁵ The Lord replies, "I will arise and defend the oppressed, the poor, the needy. I will rescue them as they have longed for me to do." ⁶ The Lord's promise is sure. He speaks no careless word; all he says is purest truth, like silver seven times refined. ⁷ O Lord, we know that you will forever preserve your own from the reach of evil men, ⁸ although they prowl on every side and vileness is praised throughout the land.

13 HOW LONG WILL you forget me, Lord? Forever? How long will you

---

a Literally, "that there is no God."   11a Literally, "Flee as a bird."   b Literally, "If the foundations have been torn down."   c Or, "His face shines down in mercy and joy upon the good."

look the other way when I am in need?
² How long must I be hiding daily anguish in my heart? How long shall my enemy have the upper hand? ³ Answer me, O Lord my God; give me light in my darkness lest I die. ⁴ Don't let my enemies say, "We have conquered him!" Don't let them gloat that I am down.

⁵ But I will always trust in you and in your mercy and shall rejoice in your salvation. ⁶ I will sing to the Lord because he has blessed me so richly.

14 THAT MAN IS a fool who says to himself, "There is no God!" Anyone who talks like that is warped and evil and cannot really be a good person at all.

² The Lord looks down from heaven on all mankind to see if there are any who are wise, who want to please God. ³ But no, all have strayed away; all are rotten with sin. Not one is good, not one! ⁴ They eat my people like bread and wouldn't think of praying! Don't they really know any better?

⁵ Terror shall grip them, for God is with those who love him. ⁶ He is the refuge of the poor and humble when evildoers are oppressing them. ⁷ Oh, that the time of their rescue were already here, that God would come from Zion now to save his people. What gladness when the Lord has rescued Israel!

15 LORD, WHO MAY go and find refuge and shelter in your tabernacle up on your holy hill?

² Anyone who leads a blameless life and is truly sincere. ³ Anyone who refuses to slander others, does not listen to gossip, never harms his neighbor, ⁴ speaks out against sin, criticizes those committing it, commends the faithful followers of the Lord, keeps a promise even if it ruins him, ⁵ does not crush his debtors with high interest rates, and refuses to testify against the innocent despite the bribes offered him— such a man shall stand firm forever.

16 SAVE ME, O God, because I have come to you for refuge. ² I said to him, "You are my Lord; I have no other help but

yours." ³ I want the company of the godly men and women in the land; they are the true nobility. ⁴ Those choosing other gods shall all be filled with sorrow; I will not offer the sacrifices they do or even speak the names of their gods.

⁵ The Lord himself is my inheritance, my prize. He is my food and drink, my highest joy! He guards all that is mine. ⁶ He sees that I am given pleasant brooks and meadows as my share!ᵃ What a wonderful inheritance! ⁷ I will bless the Lord who counsels me; he gives me wisdom in the night. He tells me what to do.

⁸ I am always thinking of the Lord; and because he is so near, I never need to stumble or to fall. ⁹ Heart, body, and soul are filled with joy. ¹⁰ For you will not leave me among the dead; you will not allow your beloved one to rot in the grave. ¹¹ You have let me experience the joys of life and the exquisite pleasures of your own eternal presence.

17 I AM PLEADING for your help, O Lord; for I have been honest and have done what is right, and you must listen to my earnest cry! ² Publicly acquit me, Lord, for you are always fair. ³ You have tested me and seen that I am good. You have come even in the night and found nothing amiss and know that I have told the truth. ⁴ I have followed your commands and have not gone along with cruel and evil men. ⁵ My feet have not slipped from your paths.

⁶ Why am I praying like this? Because I know you will answer me, O God! Yes, listen as I pray. ⁷ Show me your strong love in wonderful ways, O Savior of all those seeking your help against their foes. ⁸ Protect me as you would the pupil of your eye; hide me in the shadow of your wings as you hover over me.

⁹ My enemies encircle me with murder in their eyes. ¹⁰ They are pitiless and arrogant. Listen to their boasting. ¹¹ They close ·in upon me and are ready to throw me to the ground. ¹² They are like lions eager to tear me apart, like young lions hiding and waiting their chance.

¹³,¹⁴ Lord, arise and stand against them.

---

a Literally, "The boundary lines are fallen unto me in pleasant places."

Push them back! Come and save me from these men of the world whose only concern is earthly gain—these men whom you have filled with your treasures so that their children and grandchildren are rich and prosperous.

¹⁵ But as for me, my contentment is not in wealth but in seeing you and knowing all is well between us. And when I awake in heaven, I will be fully satisfied, for I will see you face to face.

This song of David was written at a time when the Lord had delivered him from his many enemies, including Saul.

18 LORD, HOW I love you! For you have done such tremendous things for me. ² The Lord is my fort where I can enter and be safe; no one can follow me in and slay me. He is a rugged mountain where I hide; he is my Savior, a rock where none can reach me, and a tower of safety. He is my shield. He is like the strong horn of a mighty fighting bull. ³ All I need to do is cry to him—oh, praise the Lord—and I am saved from all my enemies!

⁴ Death bound me with chains, and the floods of ungodliness mounted a massive attack against me. ⁵ Trapped and helpless, I struggled against the ropes that drew me on to death.

⁶ In my distress I screamed to the Lord for his help. And he heard me from heaven;ᵃ my cry reached his ears. ⁷ Then the earth rocked and reeled, and mountains shook and trembled. How they quaked! For he was angry. ⁸ Fierce flames leaped from his mouth, setting fire to the earth;ᵇ smoke blew from his nostrils. ⁹ He bent the heavens down and came to my defense;ᶜ thick darkness was beneath his feet. ¹⁰ Mounted on the cherubim,ᵈ he sped swiftly to my aid with wings of wind. ¹¹ He enshrouded himself with darkness, veiling his approach with dense clouds dark as murky waters. ¹² Suddenly the brilliance of his presence broke through the clouds with lightningᵉ and a mighty storm of hail.

¹³ The Lord thundered in the heavens; the God above all gods has spoken—oh, the hailstones; oh, the fire! ¹⁴ He flashed his fearful arrows of lightning and routed all my enemies. See how they run! ¹⁵ Then at your command, O Lord, the sea receded from the shore. At the blast of your breath the depths were laid bare.

¹⁶ He reached down from heaven and took me and drew me out of my great trials. He rescued me from deep waters. ¹⁷ He delivered me from my strong enemy, from those who hated me—I who was helpless in their hands.

¹⁸ On the day when I was weakest, they attacked. But the Lord held me steady. ¹⁹ He led me to a place of safety, for he delights in me. ²⁰ The Lord rewarded me for doing right and being pure. ²¹ For I have followed his commands and have not sinned by turning back from following him. ²² I kept close watch on all his laws; I did not refuse a single one. ²³ I did my best to keep them all, holding myself back from doing wrong. ²⁴ And so the Lord has paid me with his blessings, for I have done what is right, and I am pure of heart. This he knows, for he watches my every step.

²⁵ Lord, how merciful you are to those who are merciful. And you do not punish those who run from evil.ᶠ ²⁶ You give blessings to the pure but pain to those who leave your paths. ²⁷ You deliver the humble but condemn the proud and haughty ones. ²⁸ You have turned on my light! The Lord my God has made my darkness turn to light. ²⁹ Now in your strength I can scale any wall, attack any troop.

³⁰ What a God he is! How perfect in every way! All his promises prove true. He is a shield for everyone who hides behind him. ³¹ For who is God except our Lord? Who but he is as a rock?

³² He fills me with strength and protects me wherever I go. ³³ He gives me the sure-footedness of a mountain goat upon the crags. He leads me safely along the top of the cliffs. ³⁴ He prepares me for battle and gives me strength to draw an ironᵍ bow!

³⁵ You have given me your salvation as my shield. Your right hand, O Lord, supports me; your gentleness has made me

---

a Literally, "out of his temple."   b Literally, "coals were kindled by it."   c Implied.
d Literally, "a cherub."   e Literally, "coals of fire."   f Literally, "with the upright you show yourself upright."   g Literally, "a bow of bronze."

great. [36] You have made wide steps beneath my feet so that I need never slip. [37] I chased my enemies; I caught up with them and did not turn back until all were conquered. [38] I pinned them to the ground; all were helpless before me. I placed my feet upon their necks. [39] For you have armed me with strong armor for the battle. My enemies quail before me and fall defeated at my feet. [40] You made them turn and run; I destroyed all who hated me. [41] They shouted for help but no one dared to rescue them; they cried to the Lord, but he refused to answer them. [42] So I crushed them fine as dust and cast them to the wind. I threw them away like sweepings from the floor. [43,44,45] You gave me victory in every battle. The nations came and served me. Even those I didn't know before come now and bow before me. Foreigners who have never seen me submit instantly. They come trembling from their strongholds.

[46] God is alive! Praise him who is the great rock of protection. [47] He is the God who pays back those who harm me and subdues the nations before me.

[48] He rescues me from my enemies; he holds me safely out of their reach and saves me from these powerful opponents. [49] For this, O Lord, I will praise you among the nations. [50] Many times you have miraculously rescued me, the king you appointed. You have been loving and kind to me and will be to my descendants.

19 THE HEAVENS ARE telling the glory of God; they are a marvelous display of his craftsmanship. [2] Day and night they keep on telling about God. [3,4] Without a sound or word, silent in the skies, their message reaches out to all the world. The sun lives in the heavens where God placed it [5] and moves out across the skies as radiant[a] as a bridegroom going to his wedding,[b] or as joyous as an athlete looking forward to a race! [6] The sun crosses the heavens from end to end, and nothing can hide from its heat.

[7,8] God's laws are perfect. They protect us, make us wise, and give us joy and light.

[9] God's laws are pure, eternal, just.[c] [10] They are more desirable than gold. They are sweeter than honey dripping from a honeycomb. [11] For they warn us away from harm and give success to those who obey them.

[12] But how can I ever know what sins are lurking in my heart? Cleanse me from these hidden faults. [13] And keep me from deliberate wrongs; help me to stop doing them. Only then can I be free of guilt and innocent of some great crime.

[14] May my spoken words and unspoken thoughts be pleasing even to you, O Lord my Rock and my Redeemer.

20 IN YOUR DAY of trouble, may the Lord be with you! May the God of Jacob keep you from all harm. [2] May he send you aid from his sanctuary in Zion. [3] May he remember with pleasure the gifts you have given him, your sacrifices and burnt offerings. [4] May he grant you your heart's desire and fulfill all your plans. [5] May there be shouts of joy when we hear the news of your victory, flags flying with praise to God for all that he has done for you. May he answer all your prayers!

[6] "God save the king"—I know he does! He hears me from highest heaven and sends great victories. [7] Some nations boast of armies and of weaponry, but our boast is in the Lord our God. [8] Those nations will collapse and perish; we will arise to stand firm and sure!

[9] Give victory to our king, O Lord; oh, hear our prayer.

21 HOW THE KING rejoices in your strength, O Lord! How he exults in your salvation. [2] For you have given him his heart's desire, everything he asks you for!

[3] You welcomed him to the throne with success and prosperity. You set a kingly crown of purest gold upon his head. [4] He asked for a long, good life, and you have granted his request; the days of his life stretch on and on forever. [5] You have given him fame and honor. You have clothed him with splendor and majesty. [6] You have endowed him with eternal happiness. You

---

a Implied. Literally, "is like a bridegroom."   b Implied. Literally, "going forth from his chamber."
c Or, "The rules governing the worship of the Lord are pure and need never be changed."

have given him the unquenchable joy of your presence. ⁷ And because the king trusts in the Lord, he will never stumble, never fall; for he depends upon the steadfast love of the God who is above all gods.

⁸ Your hand, O Lord, will find your enemies, all who hate you. ⁹,¹⁰ When you appear, they will be destroyed in the fierce fire of your presence. The Lord will destroy them and their children. ¹¹ For these men plot against you, Lord, but they cannot possibly succeed. ¹² They will turn and flee when they see your arrows aimed straight at them.

¹³ Accept our praise, O Lord, for all your glorious power. We will write songs to celebrate your mighty acts!

22 MY GOD, MY God, why have you forsaken me? Why do you refuse to help me or even to listen to my groans? ² Day and night I keep on weeping, crying for your help, but there is no reply— ³,⁴ for *you are holy.*

The praises of our fathers surrounded your throne; they trusted you and you delivered them. ⁵ You heard their cries for help and saved them; they were never disappointed when they sought your aid.

⁶ But I am a worm, not a man, scorned and despised by my own people and by all mankind. ⁷ Everyone who sees me mocks and sneers and shrugs. ⁸ "Is this the one who rolled his burden on the Lord?" they laugh. "Is this the one who claims the Lord delights in him? We'll believe it when we see God rescue him!"

⁹,¹⁰,¹¹ Lord, how you have helped me before!ᵃ You took me safely from my mother's womb and brought me through the years of infancy. I have depended upon you since birth; you have always been my God. Don't leave me now, for trouble is near and no one else can possibly help.

¹² I am surrounded by fearsome enemies, strong as the giant bulls from Bashan. ¹³ They come at me with open jaws, like roaring lions attacking their prey. ¹⁴ My strength has drained away like water, and all my bones are out of joint. My heart

melts like wax; ¹⁵ my strength has dried up like sun-baked clay; my tongue sticks to my mouth, for you have laid me in the dust of death. ¹⁶ The enemy, this gang of evil men, circles me like a pack of dogs; they have pierced my hands and feet. ¹⁷ I can count every bone in my body. See these men of evil gloat and stare; ¹⁸ they divide my clothes among themselves by a toss of the dice.

¹⁹ O Lord, don't stay away. O God my Strength, hurry to my aid. ²⁰ Rescue me from death; spare my precious life from all these evil men.ᵇ ²¹ Save me from these lions' jaws and from the horns of these wild oxen. Yes, God will answer me and rescue me.

²² I will praise you to all my brothers; I will stand up before the congregation and testify of the wonderful things you have done. ²³ "Praise the Lord, each one of you who fears him," I will say. "Each of youᶜ must fear and reverence his name. Let all Israel sing his praises, ²⁴ for he has not despised my cries of deep despair; he has not turned and walked away. When I cried to him, he heard and came."

²⁵ Yes, I will stand and praise youᵈ before all the people. I will publicly fulfill my vows in the presence of all who reverence your name. ²⁶ The poorᵉ shall eat and be satisfied; all who seek the Lord shall find him and shall praise his name. Their hearts shall rejoice with everlasting joy. ²⁷ The whole earth shall see it and return to the Lord; the people of every nation shall worship him.

²⁸ For the Lord is King and rules the nations. ²⁹ Both proud and humble together, all who are mortal—born to die—shall worship him. ³⁰ Our children too shall serve him, for they shall hear from us about the wonders of the Lord; ³¹ generations yet unborn shall hear of all the miracles he did for us.

23 BECAUSE THE LORD is my Shepherd, I have everything I need!

²,³ He lets me rest in the meadow grass and leads me beside the quiet streams. He restores my failing health. He helps me do what honors him the most.

---

a Implied.   b Literally, "Deliver my soul from the sword, my only one from the power of the dog!"
c Literally, "all you sons of Jacob."   d Literally, "praise from you."   e Literally, "the afflicted."

[4] Even when walking through the dark valley of death I will not be afraid, for you are close beside me, guarding, guiding all the way.[a]

[5] You provide delicious food for me in the presence of my enemies. You have welcomed me as your guest;[b] blessings overflow!

[6] Your goodness and unfailing kindness shall be with me all of my life, and afterwards I will live with you forever in your home.

24 THE EARTH BELONGS to God! Everything in all the world is his! [2] He is the one who pushed the oceans back to let dry land appear.[a]

[3] Who may climb the mountain of the Lord and enter where he lives? Who may stand before the Lord? [4] Only those with pure hands and hearts, who do not practice dishonesty and lying. [5] They will receive God's own goodness[b] as their blessing from him, planted in their lives by God himself, their Savior. [6] These are the ones who are allowed to stand before the Lord and worship the God of Jacob.

[7] Open up, O ancient gates, and let the King of Glory in. [8] Who is this King of Glory? The Lord, strong and mighty, invincible in battle. [9] Yes, open wide the gates and let the King of Glory in.

[10] Who is this King of Glory? The Commander of all of heaven's armies!

25 TO YOU, O Lord, I pray. [2] Don't fail me, Lord, for I am trusting you. Don't let my enemies succeed. Don't give them victory over me. [3] None who have faith in God will ever be disgraced for trusting him. But all who harm the innocent shall be defeated.

[4] Show me the path where I should go, O Lord; point out the right road for me to walk. [5] Lead me; teach me; for you are the God who gives me salvation. I have no hope except in you. [6,7] Overlook my youthful sins, O Lord! Look at me instead through eyes of mercy and forgiveness, through eyes of everlasting love and kindness.

[8] The Lord is good and glad to teach the proper path to all who go astray; [9] he will teach the ways that are right and best to those who humbly turn to him. [10] And when we obey him, every path he guides us on is fragrant with his lovingkindness and his truth.

[11] But Lord, my sins! How many they are. Oh, pardon them for the honor of your name.

[12] Where is the man who fears the Lord? God will teach him how to choose the best. [13] He shall live within God's circle of blessing, and his children shall inherit the earth.

[14] Friendship with God is reserved for those who reverence him. With them alone he shares the secrets of his promises.

[15] My eyes are ever looking to the Lord for help, for he alone can rescue me. [16] Come, Lord, and show me your mercy, for I am helpless, overwhelmed, in deep distress; [17] my problems go from bad to worse. Oh, save me from them all! [18] See my sorrows; feel my pain; forgive my sins. [19] See how many enemies I have and how viciously they hate me! [20] Save me from them! Deliver my life from their power! Oh, let it never be said that I trusted you in vain!

[21] Assign me Godliness and Integrity as my bodyguards, for I expect you to protect me [22] and to ransom Israel from all her troubles.

26 DISMISS ALL THE charges against me, Lord, for I have tried to keep your laws and have trusted you without wavering. [2] Cross-examine me, O Lord, and see that this is so; test my motives and affections too. [3] For I have taken your lovingkindness and your truth as my ideals. [4] I do not have fellowship with tricky, two-faced men; they are false and hypocritical. [5] I hate the sinners' hangouts and refuse to enter them. [6] I wash my hands to prove my innocence and come before your altar, [7] singing a song of thanksgiving and telling about your miracles.

[8] Lord, I love your home, this shrine where the brilliant, dazzling splendor of

---

a Literally, "Your rod and your staff comfort me." cup runs over." 24a Literally, "He has founded it upon the seas." b Literally, "You have anointed my head with oil, my standing with God.

your presence lives.

⁹,¹⁰ Don't treat me as a common sinner or murderer who plots against the innocent and demands bribes.

¹¹ No, I am not like that, O Lord; I try to walk a straight and narrow path of doing what is right; therefore in mercy save me.

¹² I publicly praise the Lord for keeping me from slipping and falling.

27 THE LORD IS my light and my salvation; whom shall I fear? ² When evil men come to destroy me, they will stumble and fall! ³ Yes, though a mighty army marches against me, my heart shall know no fear! I am confident that God will save me.

⁴ The one thing I want from God, the thing I seek most of all, is the privilege of meditating in his Temple, living in his presence every day of my life, delighting in his incomparable perfections and glory. ⁵ There I'll be when troubles come. He will hide me. He will set me on a high rock ⁶ out of reach of all my enemies. Then I will bring him sacrifices and sing his praises with much joy. ⁷ Listen to my pleading, Lord! Be merciful and send the help I need.

⁸ My heart has heard you say, "Come and talk with me, O my people." And my heart responds, "Lord, I am coming."

⁹ Oh, do not hide yourself when I am trying to find you. Do not angrily reject your servant. You have been my help in all my trials before; don't leave me now. Don't forsake me, O God of my salvation. ¹⁰ For if my father and mother should abandon me, you would welcome and comfort me.

¹¹ Tell me what to do, O Lord, and make it plain because I am surrounded by waiting enemies. ¹² Don't let them get me, Lord! Don't let me fall into their hands! For they accuse me of things I never did, and all the while are plotting cruelty. ¹³ I am expecting the Lord to rescue me again, so that once again I will see his goodness to me here in the land of the living.

¹⁴ Don't be impatient. Wait for the Lord, and he will come and save you! Be brave, stouthearted and courageous. Yes, wait and

he will help you.

28 I PLEAD WITH you to help me, Lord, for you are my Rock of safety. If you refuse to answer me, I might as well give up and die. ² Lord, I lift my hands to heavenª and implore your help. Oh, listen to my cry.

³ Don't punish me with all the wicked ones who speak so sweetly to their neighbors while planning to murder them. ⁴ Give them the punishment they so richly deserve! Measure it out to them in proportion to their wickedness; pay them back for all their evil deeds. ⁵ They care nothing for God or what he has done or what he has made; therefore God will dismantle them like old buildings, never to be rebuilt again.

⁶ Oh, praise the Lord, for he has listened to my pleadings! ⁷ He is my strength, my shield from every danger. I trusted in him, and he helped me. Joy rises in my heart until I burst out in songs of praise to him. ⁸ The Lord protects his people and gives victory to his anointed king.

⁹ Defend your people, Lord; defend and bless your chosen ones. Lead them like a shepherd and carry them forever in your arms.

29 PRAISE THE LORD, you angels of his; praise his glory and his strength. ² Praise him for his majestic glory, the glory of his name. Come before him clothed in sacred garments.

³ The voice of the Lord echoes from the clouds. The God of glory thunders through the skies. ⁴ So powerful is his voice; so full of majesty. ⁵,⁶ It breaks down the cedars. It splits the giant trees of Lebanon. It shakes Mount Lebanon and Mount Sirion. They leap and skip before him like young calves! ⁷ The voice of the Lord thunders through the lightning. ⁸ It resounds through the deserts and shakes the wilderness of Kadesh. ⁹ The voice of the Lord spins and topples the mighty oaks.ª It strips the forests bare. They whirl and sway beneath the blast. But in his temple all are praising, "Glory, glory to the Lord."

¹⁰ At the Flood, the Lord showed his

---

a Literally, "Your innermost shrine," i.e., the Holy of Holies within the Tabernacle.   29a Or, "makes the hinds to calve."

control of all creation. Now he continues to unveil his power. [11] He will give his people strength. He will bless them with peace.

30 I WILL PRAISE you, Lord, for you have saved me from my enemies. You refuse to let them triumph over me. [2] O Lord my God, I pleaded with you, and you gave me my health again. [3] You brought me back from the brink of the grave, from death itself, and here I am alive!

[4] Oh, sing to him you saints of his; give thanks to his holy name. [5] His anger lasts a moment; his favor lasts for life! Weeping may go on all night, but in the morning there is joy.

[6,7] In my prosperity I said, "This is forever; nothing can stop me now! The Lord has shown me his favor. He has made me steady as a mountain." Then, Lord, you turned your face away from me and cut off your river of blessings.[a] Suddenly my courage was gone; I was terrified and panic-stricken. [8] I cried to you, O Lord; oh, how I pled: [9] "What will you gain, O Lord, from killing me? How can I praise you then to all my friends?[a] How can my dust in the grave speak out and tell the world about your faithfulness? [10] Hear me, Lord; oh, have pity and help me." [11] Then he turned my sorrow into joy! He took away my clothes of mourning and gave me gay and festive garments to rejoice in [12] so that I might sing glad praises to the Lord instead of lying in silence in the grave. O Lord my God, I will keep on thanking you forever!

31 LORD, I TRUST in you alone. Don't let my enemies defeat me. Rescue me because you are the God who always does what is right. [2] Answer quickly when I cry to you; bend low and hear my whispered[a] plea. Be for me a great Rock of safety from my foes. [3] Yes, you are my Rock and my fortress; honor your name by leading me out of this peril. [4] Pull me from the trap my enemies have set for me. For you alone are strong enough.[b] [5,6] Into your hand I commit my spirit.

You have rescued me, O God who keeps his promises. I worship only you; how you hate all those who worship idols, those imitation gods. [7] I am radiant with joy because of your mercy, for you have listened to my troubles and have seen the crisis in my soul. [8] You have not handed me over to my enemy, but have given me open ground in which to maneuver.

[9,10] O Lord, have mercy on me in my anguish. My eyes are red from weeping; my health is broken from sorrow. I am pining away with grief; my years are shortened, drained away because of sadness. My sins have sapped my strength; I stoop with sorrow and with shame.[c] [11] I am scorned by all my enemies and even more by my neighbors and friends. They dread meeting me and look the other way when I go by. [12] I am forgotten like a dead man, like a broken and discarded pot. [13] I heard the lies about me, the slanders of my enemies. Everywhere I looked I was afraid, for they were plotting against my life.

[14,15] But I was trusting you, O Lord. I said, "You alone are my God; my times are in your hands. Rescue me from those who hunt me down relentlessly. [16] Let your favor shine again upon your servant; save me just because you are so kind! [17] Don't disgrace me, Lord, by not replying when I call to you for aid. But let the wicked be shamed by what they trust in; let them lie silently in their graves, [18] their lying lips quieted at last—the lips of these arrogant men who are accusing honest men of evil deeds."

[19] Oh, how great is your goodness to those who publicly declare that you will rescue them. For you have stored up great blessings for those who trust and reverence you.

[20] Hide your loved ones in the shelter of your presence, safe beneath your hand, safe from all conspiring men. [21] Blessed is the Lord, for he has shown me that his never-failing love protects me like the walls of a fort! [22] I spoke too hastily when I said, "The Lord has deserted me," for you listened to my plea and answered me.

[23] Oh, love the Lord, all of you who are his people; for the Lord protects those who

---

a Implied.   31a Implied.   b Literally, "for you are my refuge."   c Literally, "Even my bones are rotting away."

are loyal to him, but harshly punishes all who haughtily reject him. [24] So cheer up! Take courage if you are depending on the Lord.

32 WHAT HAPPINESS FOR those whose guilt has been forgiven! What joys when sins are covered over! What relief for those who have confessed their sins and God has cleared their record.

[3] There was a time when I wouldn't admit what a sinner I was.[a] But my dishonesty made me miserable and filled my days with frustration. [4] All day and all night your hand was heavy on me. My strength evaporated like water on a sunny day [5] until I finally admitted all my sins to you and stopped trying to hide them. I said to myself, "I will confess them to the Lord." And you forgave me! All my guilt is gone.

[6] Now I say that each believer should confess his sins to God when he is aware of them, while there is time to be forgiven. Judgment will not touch him[b] if he does.

[7] You are my hiding place from every storm of life; you even keep me from getting into trouble! You surround me with songs of victory. [8] I will instruct you (says the Lord) and guide you along the best pathway for your life; I will advise you and watch your progress. [9] Don't be like a senseless horse or mule that has to have a bit in its mouth to keep it in line!

[10] Many sorrows come to the wicked, but abiding love surrounds those who trust in the Lord. [11] So rejoice in him, all those who are his,[c] and shout for joy, all those who try to obey him.[d]

33 LET ALL THE joys of the godly well up in praise to the Lord, for it is right to praise him. [2] Play joyous melodies of praise upon the lyre and on the harp. [3] Compose new songs of praise to him, accompanied skillfully on the harp; sing joyfully.

[4] For all God's words are right, and everything he does is worthy of our trust. [5] He loves whatever is just and good; the earth is filled with his tender love. [6] He merely spoke, and the heavens were formed, and all the galaxies of stars. [7] He made the oceans, pouring them into his vast reservoirs.

[8] Let everyone in all the world—men, women and children—fear the Lord and stand in awe of him. [9] For when he but spoke, the world began! It appeared at his command! [10] And with a breath he can scatter the plans of all the nations who oppose him, [11] but his own plan stands forever. His intentions are the same for every generation.

[12] Blessed is the nation whose God is the Lord, whose people he has chosen as his own. [13,14,15] The Lord gazes down upon mankind from heaven where he lives. He has made their hearts and closely watches everything they do.

[16,17] The best-equipped army cannot save a king—for great strength is not enough to save anyone. A war horse is a poor risk for winning victories—it is strong but it cannot save.

[18,19] But the eyes of the Lord are watching over those who fear him, who rely upon his steady love. He will keep them from death even in times of famine! [20] We depend upon the Lord alone to save us. Only he can help us; he protects us like a shield. [21] No wonder we are happy in the Lord! For we are trusting him. We trust his holy name. [22] Yes, Lord, let your constant love surround us, for our hopes are in you alone.

34 I WILL PRAISE the Lord no matter what happens. I will constantly speak of his glories and grace.[a] [2] I will boast of all his kindness to me. Let all who are discouraged take heart. [3] Let us praise the Lord together, and exalt his name.

[4] For I cried to him and he answered me! He freed me from all my fears. [5] Others too were radiant at what he did for them. Theirs was no downcast look of rejection! [6] This poor man cried to the Lord—and the Lord heard him and saved him out of his troubles. [7] For the Angel of the Lord guards and rescues all who reverence him.

[8] Oh, put God to the test and see how kind he is! See for yourself the way his mercies shower down on all who trust in him.

---

a Literally, "when I kept silence."   b Literally, "When the great waters overflow they shall not reach him."
c Literally, "you righteous."   d Literally, "all who are upright in heart."   34a Literally, "His praise shall continually be in my mouth."

⁹ If you belong to the Lord, reverence him; for everyone who does this has everything he needs. ¹⁰ Even strong young lions sometimes go hungry, but those of us who reverence the Lord will never lack any good thing.

¹¹ Sons and daughters, come and listen and let me teach you the importance of trusting and fearing the Lord. ¹² Do you want a long, good life? ¹³ Then watch your tongue! Keep your lips from lying. ¹⁴ Turn from all known sin and spend your time in doing good. Try to live in peace with everyone; work hard at it.

¹⁵ For the eyes of the Lord are intently watching all who live good lives, and he gives attention when they cry to him. ¹⁶ But the Lord has made up his mind to wipe out even the memory of evil men from the earth. ¹⁷ Yes, the Lord hears the good man when he calls to him for help, and saves him out of all his troubles.

¹⁸ The Lord is close to those whose hearts are breaking; he rescues those who are humbly sorry for their sins. ¹⁹ The good man does not escape all troubles—he has them too. But the Lord helps him in each and every one. ²⁰ God even protects him from accidents.

²¹ Calamity will surely overtake the wicked; heavy penalties are meted out to those who hate the good. ²² But as for those who serve the Lord, he will redeem them; everyone who takes refuge in him will be freely pardoned.

35 O LORD, FIGHT those fighting me; declare war on them for their attacks on me. ² Put on your armor, take your shield and protect me by standing in front. ³ Lift your spear in my defense, for my pursuers are getting very close. Let me hear you say that you will save me from them. ⁴ Dishonor those who are trying to kill me. Turn them back and confuse them. ⁵ Blow them away like chaff in the wind—wind sent by the Angel of the Lord. ⁶ Make their path dark and slippery before them, with the Angel of the Lord pursuing them. ⁷ For though I did them no wrong, yet they laid a trap for me and dug a pitfall in my path. ⁸ Let them be overtaken by sudden ruin, caught in their own net, and destroyed.

⁹ But I will rejoice in the Lord. He shall rescue me! ¹⁰ From the bottom of my heart praise rises to him. Where is his equal in all of heaven and earth? Who else protects the weak and helpless from the strong, and the poor and needy from those who would rob them?

¹¹ These evil men swear to a lie. They accuse me of things I have never even heard about. ¹² I do them good, but they return me harm. I am sinking down to death. ¹³ When they were ill, I mourned before the Lord in sackcloth, asking him to make them well; I refused to eat; I prayed for them with utmost earnestness, but God did not listen. ¹⁴ I went about sadly as though it were my mother, friend or brother who was sick and nearing death. ¹⁵ But now that I am in trouble they are glad; they come together in meetings filled with slander against me—I didn't even know some of those who were there. ¹⁶ For they gather with the worthless fellows of the town and spend their time cursing me.

¹⁷ Lord, how long will you stand there, doing nothing? Act now and rescue me, for I have but one life and these young lions are out to get it. ¹⁸ Save me, and I will thank you publicly before the entire congregation, before the largest crowd I can find.

¹⁹ Don't give victory to those who fight me without any reason! Don't let them rejoice[a] at my fall—let them die. ²⁰ They don't talk of peace and doing good, but of plots against innocent men who are minding their own business. ²¹ They shout that they have seen *me* doing wrong! "Aha!" they say. "With our own eyes we saw him do it." ²² Lord, you know all about it. Don't stay silent! Don't desert me now!

²³ Rise up, O Lord my God; vindicate me. ²⁴ Declare me "not guilty," for you are just.[b] Don't let my enemies rejoice over me in my troubles. ²⁵ Don't let them say, "Aha! Our dearest wish against him will soon be fulfilled!" and, "At last we have him!" ²⁶ Shame them; let these who boast against me and who rejoice at my troubles be themselves overcome by misfortune that strips

---

a Literally, "wink with the eye."   b Literally, "Judge me according to your righteousness."

them bare of everything they own. Bare them to dishonor. ²⁷ But give great joy to all who wish me well. Let them shout with delight, "Great is the Lord who enjoys helping his child!"ᶜ ²⁸ And I will tell everyone how great and good you are; I will praise you all day long.

36 SIN LURKS DEEP in the hearts of the wicked, forever urging them on to evil deeds. They have no fear of God to hold them back. ² Instead, in their conceit, they think they can hide their evil deeds and not get caught. ³ Everything they say is crooked and deceitful; they are no longer wise and good. ⁴ They lie awake at night to hatch their evil plots, instead of planning how to keep away from wrong.

⁵ Your steadfast love, O Lord, is as great as all the heavens. Your faithfulness reaches beyond the clouds. ⁶ Your justice is as solid as God's mountains. Your decisions are as full of wisdom as the oceans are with water. You are concernedᵃ for men and animals alike. ⁷ How precious is your constant love, O God! All humanity takes refuge in the shadow of your wings. ⁸ You feed them with blessings from your own table and let them drink from your rivers of delight.

⁹ For you are the Fountain of life; our light is from your Light. ¹⁰ Pour out your unfailing love on those who know you! Never stop giving your salvationᵇ to those who long to do your will.

¹¹ Don't let these proud men trample me. Don't let their wicked hands push me around. ¹² Look! They have fallen. They are thrown down and will not rise again.

37 NEVER ENVY THE wicked! ² Soon they fade away like grass and disappear. ³ Trust in the Lord instead. Be kind and good to others; then you will live safely here in the land and prosper, feeding in safety.

⁴ Be delighted with the Lord. Then he will give you all your heart's desires. ⁵ Commit everything you do to the Lord. Trust him to help you do it and he will. ⁶ Your innocence will be clear to everyone. He will vindicate you with the blazing light of jus-

tice shining down as from the noonday sun.

⁷ Rest in the Lord; wait patiently for him to act. Don't be envious of evil men who prosper.

⁸ Stop your anger! Turn off your wrath. Don't fret and worry—it only leads to harm. ⁹ For the wicked shall be destroyed, but those who trust the Lord shall be given every blessing. ¹⁰ Only a little while and the wicked shall disappear. You will look for them in vain. ¹¹ But all who humble themselves before the Lord shall be given every blessing, and shall have wonderful peace.

¹²,¹³ The Lord is laughing at those who plot against the godly, for he knows their judgment day is coming. ¹⁴ Evil men take aim to slay the poor; they are ready to butcher those who do right. ¹⁵ But their swords will be plunged into their own hearts and all their weapons will be broken.

¹⁶ It is better to have little and be godly than to own an evil man's wealth; ¹⁷ for the strength of evil men shall be broken, but the Lord takes care of those he has forgiven.ᵃ

¹⁸ Day by day the Lord observes the good deeds done by godly men,ᵇ and gives them eternal rewards. ¹⁹ He cares for them when times are hard; even in famine, they will have enough. ²⁰ But evil men shall perish. These enemies of God will wither like grass, and disappear like smoke. ²¹ Evil men borrow and "cannot pay it back"! But the good man returns what he owes with some extra besides. ²² Those blessed by the Lord shall inherit the earth, but those cursed by him shall die.

²³ The steps of good men are directed by the Lord. He delights in each step they take. ²⁴ If they fall it isn't fatal, for the Lord holds them with his hand.

²⁵ I have been young and now I am old. And in all my years I have never seen the Lord forsake a man who loves him; nor have I seen the children of the godly go hungry. ²⁶ Instead, the godly are able to be generous with their gifts and loans to others, and their children are a blessing.

²⁷ So if you want an eternal home, leave your evil, low-down ways and live good lives. ²⁸ For the Lord loves justice and fair-

---

c Literally, "servant."   36a Literally, "You preserve."   b Literally, "your righteousness."
37a Literally, "the righteous."   b Literally, "knows the days of the upright."

ness; he will never abandon his people. They will be kept safe forever; but all who love wickedness shall perish.

²⁹ The godly shall be firmly planted in the land, and live there forever. ³⁰,³¹ The godly man is a good counselor because he is just and fair and knows right from wrong.

³² Evil men spy on the godly, waiting for an excuse to accuse them and then demanding their death. ³³ But the Lord will not let these evil men succeed, nor let the godly be condemned when they are brought before the judge.

³⁴ Don't be impatient for the Lord to act! Keep traveling steadily along his pathway and in due season he will honor you with every blessing,ᶜ and you will see the wicked destroyed. ³⁵,³⁶ I myself have seen it happen: a proud and evil man, towering like a cedar of Lebanon, but when I looked again, he was gone! I searched but could not find him! ³⁷ But the good man—what a different story! For the good man—the blameless, the upright, the man of peace—he has a wonderful future ahead of him. For him there is a happy ending. ³⁸ But evil men shall be destroyed, and their posterity shall be cut off.

³⁹ The Lord saves the godly! He is their salvation and their refuge when trouble comes. ⁴⁰ Because they trust in him, he helps them and delivers them from the plots of evil men.

38 O LORD, DON'T punish me while you are angry! ² Your arrows have struck deep; your blows are crushing me. ³,⁴ Because of your anger my body is sick, my health is broken beneath my sins. They are like a flood, higher than my head; they are a burden too heavy to bear. ⁵,⁶ My wounds are festering and full of pus. Because of my sins I am bent and racked with pain. My days are filled with anguish. ⁷ My loins burn with inflammationᵃ and my whole body is diseased. ⁸ I am exhausted and crushed; I groan in despair.ᵇ

⁹ Lord, you know how I long for my health once more. You hear my every sigh. ¹⁰ My heart beats wildly, my strength fails, and I am going blind. ¹¹ My loved ones and

friends stay away, fearing my disease. Even my own family stands at a distance.

¹² Meanwhile my enemies are trying to kill me. They plot my ruin and spend all their waking hours planning treachery. ¹³,¹⁴ But I am deaf to all their threats; I am silent before them as a man who cannot speak. I have nothing to say. ¹⁵ For I am waiting for you, O Lord my God. Come and protect me. ¹⁶ Put an end to their arrogance, these who gloat when I am cast down!

¹⁷ How constantly I find myself upon the verge of sin;ᶜ this source of sorrow always stares me in the face. ¹⁸ I confess my sins; I am sorry for what I have done. ¹⁹ But my enemies persecute with vigor, and continue to hate me—though I have done nothing against them to deserve it. ²⁰ They repay me evil for good and hate me for standing for the right.

²¹ Don't leave me, Lord; don't go away! ²² Come quickly! Help me, O my Savior.

39 I SAID TO myself, I'm going to quit complaining! I'll keep quiet, especially when the ungodly are around me. ²,³ But as I stood there silently the turmoil within me grew to the bursting point. The more I mused, the hotter the fires inside. Then at last I spoke, and pled with God: ⁴ Lord, help me to realize how brief my time on earth will be. Help me to know that I am here for but a moment more. ⁵,⁶ My life is no longer than my hand! My whole lifetime is but a moment to you. Proud man! Frail as breath! A shadow! And all his busy rushing ends in nothing. He heaps up riches for someone else to spend. ⁷ And so, Lord, my only hope is in you.

⁸ Save me from being overpowered by my sins, for even fools will mock me then.

⁹ Lord, I am speechless before you. I will not open my mouth to speak one word of complaint, for my punishment is from you.ᵃ

¹⁰ Lord, don't hit me anymore—I am exhausted beneath your hand. ¹¹ When you punish a man for his sins, he is destroyed, for he is as fragile as a moth-infested cloth; yes, man is frail as breath.

---

c Literally, "to possess the land." **38**a Implied. b Or, "because of the pains in my heart."
c Literally, "I am ready to fall." **39**a Literally, "for you have done it."

¹² Hear my prayer, O Lord; listen to my cry! Don't sit back, unmindful of my tears. For I am your guest. I am a traveler passing through the earth, as all my fathers were. ¹³ Spare me, Lord! Let me recover and be filled with happiness again before my death.

40 I WAITED PATIENTLY for God to help me; then he listened and heard my cry. ² He lifted me out of the pit of despair, out from the bog and the mire, and set my feet on a hard, firm path and steadied me as I walked along. ³ He has given me a new song to sing, of praises to our God. Now many will hear of the glorious things he did for me, and stand in awe before the Lord, and put their trust in him. ⁴ Many blessings are given to those who trust the Lord, and have no confidence in those who are proud, or who trust in idols.

⁵ O Lord my God, many and many a time you have done great miracles for us, and we are ever in your thoughts. Who else can do such glorious things? No one else can be compared with you. There isn't time to tell of all your wonderful deeds.

⁶ It isn't sacrifices and offerings which you really want from your people. Burnt animals bring no special joy to your heart. But you have accepted the offer of my life-long service.ᵃ ⁷ Then Iᵇ said, "See, I have come, just as all the prophets foretold. ⁸ And I delight to do your will, my God, for your law is written upon my heart!"

⁹ I have told everyone the Good News that you forgive men's sins.ᶜ I have not been timid about it, as you well know, O Lord. ¹⁰ I have not kept this Good Newsᶜ hidden in my heart, but have proclaimed your lovingkindness and truth to all the congregation.

¹¹ O Lord, don't hold back your tender mercies from me! My only hope is in your love and faithfulness. ¹² Otherwise I perish, for problems far too big for me to solve are piled higher than my head. Meanwhile my sins, too many to count, have all caught up with me and I am ashamed to look up. My heart quails within me.

¹³ Please, Lord, rescue me! Quick! Come and help me! ¹⁴,¹⁵ Confuse them! Turn them around and send them sprawling—all these who are trying to destroy me. Disgrace these scoffers with their utter failure!

¹⁶ But may the joy of the Lord be given to everyone who loves him and his salvation. May they constantly exclaim, "How great God is!"

¹⁷ I am poor and needy, yet the Lord is thinking about me right now! O my God, you are my helper. You are my Savior; come quickly, and save me. Please don't delay!

41 GOD BLESSES THOSE who are kind to the poor. He helps them out of their troubles. ² He protects them and keeps them alive; he publicly honors them and destroys the power of their enemies. ³ He nurses them when they are sick, and soothes their pains and worries.ᵃ

⁴ "O Lord," I prayed, "be kind and heal me, for I have confessed my sins." ⁵ But my enemies say, "May he soon die and be forgotten!" ⁶ They act so friendly when they come to visit me while I am sick; but all the time they hate me and are glad that I am lying there upon my bed of pain. And when they leave, they laugh and mock. ⁷ They whisper together about what they will do when I am dead. ⁸ "It's fatal, whatever it is," they say. "He'll never get out of that bed!"

⁹ Even my best friend has turned against me—a man I completely trusted; how often we ate together. ¹⁰ Lord, don't you desert me! Be gracious, Lord, and make me well again so I can pay them back! ¹¹ I know you are pleased with me because you haven't let my enemies triumph over me. ¹² You have preserved me because I was honest; you have admitted me forever to your presence.

¹³ Bless the Lord, the God of Israel, who exists from everlasting ages past—and on into everlasting eternity ahead. Amen and amen!

42 AS THE DEER pants for water, so I long for you, O God. ² I thirst for

---

a Literally, "my ears you have dug." b This verse was quoted by Christ as applying to himself. See John 4:34. c Literally, "your righteousness." 41a Literally, "You make all his bed in his sickness."

God, the living God. Where can I find him to come and stand before him? ³ Day and night I weep for his help, and all the while my enemies taunt me. "Where is this God of yours?" they scoff.

⁴,⁵ Take courage, my soul! Do you remember those times (but how could you ever forget them!) when you led a great procession to the Temple on festival days, singing with joy, praising the Lord? Why then be downcast? Why be discouraged and sad? Hope in God! I shall yet praise him again. Yes, I shall again praise him for his help.ᵃ ⁶ Yet I am standing here depressed and gloomy, but I will meditate upon your kindness in this lovely land where the Jordan River flows and where Mount Hermon and Mount Mizar stand. ⁷ All your waves and billows have gone over me, and floods of sorrow pour upon me like a thundering cataract.ᵇ

⁸ Yet day by day the Lord also pours out his steadfast love upon me, and through the night I sing his songs and pray to God who gives me life.

⁹ "O God my Rock," I cry, "why have you forsaken me? Why must I suffer these attacks from my enemies?" ¹⁰ Their taunts pierce me like a fatal wound; again and again they scoff, "Where is that God of yours?" ¹¹ But O my soul, don't be discouraged. Don't be upset. Expect God to act! For I know that I shall again have plenty of reason to praise him for all that he will do. He is my help! He is my God!

43 O GOD, DEFEND me from the charges of these merciless, deceitful men. ² For you are God, my only place of refuge. Why have you tossed me aside? Why must I mourn at the oppression of my enemies?

³ Oh, send out your light and your truth—let them lead me. Let them lead me to your Temple on your holy mountain, Zion. ⁴ There I will go to the altar of God my exceeding joy, and praise him with my harp. O God—my God! ⁵ O my soul, why be so gloomy and discouraged? Trust in God! I shall again praise him for his wondrous help; he will make me smile again,ᵃ

for he is my God!

44 O GOD, WE have heard of the glorious miracles you did in the days of long ago. Our forefathers have told us how you drove the heathen nations from this land and gave it all to us, spreading Israel from one end of the country to the other. ³ They did not conquer by their own strength and skill, but by your mighty power and because you smiled upon them and favored them.

⁴ You are my King and my God. Decree victories for your people. ⁵ For it is only by your power and through your name that we tread down our enemies; ⁶ I do not trust my weapons. They could never save me. ⁷ Only you can give us the victory over those who hate us.

⁸ My constant boast is God. I can never thank you enough! ⁹ And yet for a time, O Lord, you have tossed us aside in dishonor, and have not helped us in our battles. ¹⁰ You have actually fought against us and defeated us before our foes. Our enemies have invaded our land and pillaged the countryside. ¹¹ You have treated us like sheep in a slaughter pen, and scattered us among the nations. ¹² You sold us for a pittance. You valued us at nothing at all. ¹³ The neighboring nations laugh and mock at us because of all the evil you have sent. ¹⁴ You have made the word "Jew" a byword of contempt and shame among the nations, disliked by all. ¹⁵,¹⁶ I am constantly despised, mocked, taunted and cursed by my vengeful enemies.

¹⁷ And all this has happened, Lord, despite our loyalty to you. We have not violated your covenant. ¹⁸ Our hearts have not deserted you! We have not left your path by a single step. ¹⁹ If we had, we could understand your punishing us in the barren wilderness and sending us into darkness and death. ²⁰ If we had turned away from worshiping our God, and were worshiping idols, ²¹ would God not know it? Yes, he knows the secrets of every heart. ²² But that is not our case. For we are facing death threats constantly because of serving you! We are like sheep awaiting slaughter.

---

a Literally, "for the help of his countenance." b Literally, "deep calls to deep at the noise of your waterfalls." **43**a Literally, "He is the help of my countenance."

²³ Waken! Rouse yourself! Don't sleep, O Lord! Are we cast off forever? ²⁴ Why do you look the other way? Why do you ignore our sorrows and oppression? ²⁵ We lie face downward in the dust. ²⁶ Rise up, O Lord, and come and help us. Save us by your constant love.

45 MY HEART IS overflowing with a beautiful thought! I will write a lovely poem to the King, for I am as full of words as the speediest writer pouring out his story.
² You are the fairest of all;
Your words are filled with grace;
God himself is blessing you forever.
³ Arm yourself, O Mighty One,
So glorious, so majestic!
⁴ And in your majesty
Go on to victory,
Defending truth, humility, and justice.
Go forth to awe-inspiring deeds!
⁵ Your arrows are sharp
In your enemies' hearts;
They fall before you.
⁶ Your throne, O God, endures forever.
Justice is your royal scepter.
⁷ You love what is good
And hate what is wrong.
Therefore God, your God,
Has given you more gladness
Than anyone else.
⁸ Your robes are perfumed with myrrh, aloes and cassia. In your inlaid palaces of ivory, lovely music is being played for your enjoyment. ⁹ Kings' daughters are among your concubines.ᵃ Standing beside you is the queen, wearing jewelry of finest gold from Ophir. ¹⁰,¹¹ "I advise you, O daughter, not to fret about your parents in your homeland far away. Your royal husband delights in your beauty. Reverence him, for he is your lord. ¹² The people of Tyre, the richest people of our day, will shower you with gifts and entreat your favors."
¹³ The bride,ᵇ a princess, waits within her chamber, robed in beautiful clothing woven with gold. ¹⁴ Lovelyᶜ she is, led beside her maids of honor to the king! ¹⁵ What

a joyful, glad procession as they enter in the palace gates! ¹⁶ "Your sons will some day be kings like their father. They shall sit on thrones around the world!
¹⁷ "I will cause your name to be honored in all generations; the nations of the earth will praise you forever."

46 GOD IS OUR refuge and strength, a tested help in times of trouble. ² And so we need not fear even if the world blows up, and the mountains crumble into the sea. ³ Let the oceans roar and foam; let the mountains tremble!
⁴ There is a river of joy flowing through the City of our God—the sacred home of the God above all gods. ⁵ God himself is living in that City; therefore it stands unmoved despite the turmoil everywhere. He will not delay his help. ⁶ The nations rant and rave in anger—but when God speaks, the earth melts in submission and kingdoms totter into ruin.
⁷ The Commander of the armies of heaven is here among us. He, the God of Jacob, has come to rescue us. ⁸ Come, see the glorious things that our God does, how he brings ruin upon the world, ⁹ and causes wars to end throughout the earth, breaking and burning every weapon. ¹⁰ "Stand silent! Know that I am God! I will be honored by every nation in the world!"
¹¹ The Commander of the heavenly armies is here among *us!* He, the God of Jacob, has come to rescue *us!*

47 COME, EVERYONE, AND clap for joy! Shout triumphant praises to the Lord! ² For the Lord, the God above all gods, is awesome beyond words; he is the great King of all the earth. ³ He subdues the nations before us, ⁴ and will personally select his choicest blessings for his Jewish peopleᵃ—the very best for those he loves.
⁵ God has ascended with a mighty shout, with trumpets blaring. ⁶,⁷ Sing out your praises to our God, our King. Yes, sing your highest praises to our King, the King of all the earth. Sing thoughtful praises! ⁸ He reigns above the nations, sitting on his holy

---

a Literally, "honorable women."   b Literally, "The king's daughter."   c Literally, "embroidered work."   47a Literally, "the pride of Jacob."

throne. ⁹ The Gentile rulers of the world have joined with us in praising[b] him—praising[b] the God of Abraham—for the battle shields of all the armies of the world are his trophies. He is highly honored everywhere.

48 HOW GREAT IS the Lord! How much we should praise him. He lives upon Mount Zion in Jerusalem. ² What a glorious sight! See Mount Zion rising north of the city[a] high above the plains for all to see—Mount Zion, joy of all the earth, the residence of the great King.

³ God himself is the defender of Jerusalem.[b] ⁴ The kings of the earth have arrived together to inspect the city. ⁵ They marvel at the sight and hurry home again, ⁶ afraid of what they have seen; they are filled with panic like a woman in travail! ⁷ For God destroys the mightiest warships with a breath of wind. ⁸ We have heard of the city's glory—the city of our God, the Commander of the armies of heaven. And now we see it for ourselves! God has established Jerusalem forever.

⁹ Lord, here in your Temple we meditate upon your kindness and your love. ¹⁰ Your name is known throughout the earth, O God. You are praised everywhere for the salvation[c] you have scattered throughout the world. ¹¹ O Jerusalem,[d] rejoice! O people of Judah, rejoice! For God will see to it that you are finally treated fairly. ¹² Go, inspect the city! Walk around and count her many towers! ¹³ Note her walls and tour her palaces, so that you can tell your children.

¹⁴ For this great God is our God forever and ever. He will be our guide until we die.

49 LISTEN, EVERYONE! HIGH and low, rich and poor, all around the world—listen to my words, ³ for they are wise and filled with insight.

⁴ I will tell in song accompanied by harps the answer to one of life's most perplexing problems: ⁵ *There is no need to fear when times of trouble come,* even though surrounded by enemies! ⁶ They trust in their wealth and boast about how rich they are, ⁷ yet not one of them, though rich as kings, can ransom his own brother from the penalty of sin! For God's forgiveness does not come that way.[a] ⁸,⁹ For a soul is far too precious to be ransomed by mere earthly wealth. There is not enough of it in all the earth to buy eternal life for just one soul, to keep it out of hell.[b]

¹⁰ Rich man! Proud man! Wise man! You must die like all the rest! You have no greater lease on life than foolish, stupid men. You must leave your wealth to others. ¹¹ You name your estates after yourselves as though your lands could be forever yours, and you could live on them eternally. ¹² But man with all his pomp must die like any animal. ¹³ Such is the folly of these men, though after they die they will be quoted as having great wisdom.

¹⁴ Death is the shepherd of all mankind. And "in the morning" those who are evil will be the slaves of those who are good. For the power of their wealth[c] is gone when they die; they cannot take it with them.

¹⁵ But as for me, God will redeem my soul from the power of death, for he will receive me. ¹⁶ So do not be dismayed when evil men grow rich and build their lovely homes. ¹⁷ For when they die they carry nothing with them! Their honors will not follow them. ¹⁸ Though a man calls himself happy all through his life—and the world loudly applauds success— ¹⁹ yet in the end he dies like everyone else, and enters eternal darkness.

²⁰ For man with all his pomp[d] must die like any animal.

50 THE MIGHTY GOD, the Lord, has summoned all mankind from east to west! ² God's glory-light shines from the beautiful Temple[a] on Mount Zion. ³ He comes with the noise of thunder,[b] surrounded by devastating fire; a great storm

---

b Implied. **48** a Literally, "on the sides of the north." her palaces for a high tower." c Literally, "Your right hand is filled with righteousness." d Literally, "Mount Zion." **49** a Implied in text. c Literally, "their beauty shall be for Sheol to consume." whether this phrase was part of the original text. b Literally, "comes, and does not keep silence."   b Literally, "God has made himself known in   b Literally, "so that he should not see the Pit."   d Literally, "but without insight." It is uncertain **50** a Literally, "Out of Zion, the perfection of beauty."

rages round about him. ⁴ He has come to judge his people. To heaven and earth he shouts, ⁵ "Gather together my own people who by their sacrifice upon my altar have promised to obey[c] me." ⁶ God will judge them with complete fairness, for all heaven declares that he is just.

⁷ O my people, listen! For I am your God. Listen! Here are my charges against you: ⁸ I have no complaint about the sacrifices you bring to my altar, for you bring them regularly. ⁹ But it isn't sacrificial bullocks and goats that I really want from you. ¹⁰,¹¹ For all the animals of field and forest are mine! The cattle on a thousand hills! And all the birds upon the mountains! ¹² If I were hungry, I would not mention it to you—for all the world is mine, and everything in it. ¹³ No, I don't need your sacrifices of flesh and blood. ¹⁴,¹⁵ What I want from you is your true thanks; I want your promises fulfilled. *I want you to trust me in your times of trouble, so I can rescue you, and you can give me glory.*

¹⁶ But God says to evil men: Recite my laws no longer, and stop claiming my promises, ¹⁷ for you have refused my discipline, disregarding my laws. ¹⁸ You see a thief and help him, and spend your time with evil and immoral men. ¹⁹ You curse and lie, and vile language streams from your mouths. ²⁰ You slander your own brother. ²¹ I remained silent—you thought I didn't care—but now your time of punishment has come, and I list all the above charges against you. ²² This is the last chance for all of you who have forgotten God, before I tear you apart—and no one can help you then.

²³ But true praise is a worthy sacrifice; this really honors me. Those who walk my paths will receive salvation from the Lord.

Written after Nathan the prophet had come to inform David of God's judgment against him because of his adultery with Bathsheba, and his murder of Uriah, her husband.

51 O LOVING AND kind God, have mercy. Have pity upon me and take away the awful stain of my transgressions. ² Oh, wash me, cleanse me from this guilt. Let me be pure again. ³ For I admit my shameful deed—it haunts me day and night. ⁴ It is against you and you alone I sinned, and did this terrible thing. You saw it all, and your sentence against me is just. ⁵ But I was born a sinner, yes, from the moment my mother conceived me. ⁶ You deserve honesty from the heart; yes, utter sincerity and truthfulness. Oh, give me this wisdom.

⁷ Sprinkle me with the cleansing blood[a] and I shall be clean again. Wash me and I shall be whiter than snow. ⁸ And after you have punished me, give me back my joy again. ⁹ Don't keep looking at my sins—erase them from your sight. ¹⁰ Create in me a new, clean heart, O God, filled with clean thoughts and right desires. ¹¹ Don't toss me aside, banished forever from your presence. Don't take your Holy Spirit from me. ¹² Restore to me again the joy of your salvation, and make me willing to obey you. ¹³ Then I will teach your ways to other sinners, and they—guilty like me—will repent and return to you. ¹⁴,¹⁵ Don't sentence me to death. O my God, you alone can rescue me. Then I will sing of your forgiveness,[b] for my lips will be unsealed—oh, how I will praise you.

¹⁶ You don't want penance;[c] if you did, how gladly I would do it! You aren't interested in offerings burned before you on the altar. ¹⁷ It is a broken spirit you want —remorse and penitence. A broken and a contrite heart, O God, you will not ignore.

¹⁸ And Lord, don't punish Israel for my sins—help your people and protect Jerusalem.[d]

¹⁹ And when my heart is right,[e] then you will rejoice in the good that I do[f] and in the bullocks I bring to sacrifice upon your altar.

Written by David to protest against his enemy Doeg (1 Samuel 22), who later slaughtered eighty-five priests and their families.

52 YOU CALL YOURSELF a *hero,* do you? You *boast* about this evil deed of

---

c Literally, "who made a covenant with me by sacrifice." 12:22, Hebrews 9:18–22.   b Literally, "righteousness."

51a Literally, "purge me with hyssop." See Exodus
c Literally, "a sacrifice."

d Literally, "Do good in your good pleasure unto Zion; build the walls of Jerusalem."   e Implied.
f Literally, "then you will delight in the sacrifice of righteousness."

yours against God's people.[a] [2] You are sharp as a tack in plotting your evil tricks. [3] How you love wickedness—far more than good! And lying more than truth! [4] You love to slander—you love to say anything that will do harm, O man with the lying tongue.

[5] But God will strike you down and pull you from your home, and drag you away from the land of the living. [6] The followers of God will see it happen. They will watch in awe. Then they will laugh and say, [7] "See what happens to those who despise God and trust in their wealth, and become ever more bold in their wickedness."[b]

[8] But I am like a sheltered olive tree protected by the Lord himself. I trust in the mercy of God forever and ever. [9] O Lord, I will praise you forever and ever for your punishment.[c] And I will wait for your mercies—for everyone knows what a merciful God you are.

53 ONLY A FOOL would say to himself, "There is no God." And why does he say it?[a] Because of his wicked heart, his dark and evil deeds. His life is corroded with sin.

[2] God looks down from heaven, searching among all mankind to see if there is a single one who does right and really seeks for God. [3] But all have turned their backs on him; they are filthy with sin—corrupt and rotten through and through. Not one is good, not one! [4] How can this be? Can't they understand anything? For they devour my people like bread and refuse to come to God. [5] But soon unheard-of terror will fall on them. God will scatter the bones of these, your enemies. They are doomed, for God has rejected them.

[6] Oh, that God would come from Zion now and save Israel! Only when the Lord himself restores them can they ever be really happy again.

Written by David at the time the men of Ziph tried to betray him to Saul.

54 COME WITH GREAT power,[a] O God, and save me! Defend me with your might! [2] Oh, listen to my prayer. [3] For violent men have risen against me—ruthless men who care nothing for God are seeking my life.

[4] But God is my helper. He is a friend of mine![b] [5] He will cause the evil deeds of my enemies to boomerang upon them. Do as you promised and put an end to these wicked men, O God. [6] Gladly I bring my sacrifices to you; I will praise your name, O Lord, for it is good.

[7] God has rescued me from all my trouble, and triumphed over my enemies.

55 LISTEN TO MY prayer, O God; don't hide yourself when I cry to you. [2] Hear me, Lord! Listen to me! For I groan and weep beneath my burden of woe.

[3] My enemies shout against me and threaten me with death. They surround me with terror and plot to kill me. Their fury and hatred rise to engulf me. [4] My heart is in anguish within me. Stark fear overpowers me. [5] Trembling and horror overwhelm me. [6] Oh, for wings like a dove, to fly away and rest! [7] I would fly to the far off deserts and stay there. [8] I would flee to some refuge from all this storm.

[9] O Lord, make these enemies begin to quarrel among themselves—destroy them with their own violence and strife.[a] [10] Though they patrol their walls night and day against invaders, their real problem is internal—wickedness and dishonesty are entrenched in the heart of the city. [11] There is murder and robbery there, and cheating in the markets and wherever you look.

[12] It was not an enemy who taunted me—then I could have borne it; I could have hidden and escaped. [13] But it was you, a man like myself, my companion and my friend. [14] What fellowship we had, what wonderful discussions as we walked together to the Temple of the Lord on holy days.

[15] Let death seize them and cut them down in their prime, for there is sin in their homes, and they are polluted to the depths of their souls. [16] But I will call upon the

---

a Literally, "the lovingkindness of God continually." ness." c Literally, "because you have done it." b Literally, "The Lord is of them that uphold my soul."
in the city."

b Literally, "strengthened himself in his wickedness."
53a Implied. 54a Literally, "your name."
55a Literally, "for I have seen violence and strife

I hide beneath your wings

Lord to save me—and he will. ¹⁷ I will pray morning, noon, and night, pleading aloud with God; and he will hear and answer. ¹⁸ Though the tide of battle runs strongly against me, for so many are fighting me, yet he will rescue me. ¹⁹ God himself—God from everlasting ages past—will answer them! For they refuse to fear him or even honor his commands.

²⁰ This friend of mine betrayed me—I who was at peace with him. He broke his promises. ²¹ His words were oily smooth, but in his heart was war. His words were sweet, but underneath were daggers.

²² Give your burdens to the Lord. He will carry them. He will not permit the godly to slip or fall. ²³ He will send my enemies to the pit of destruction. Murderers and liars will not live out half their days. But I am trusting you to save me.

56 LORD, HAVE MERCY on me; all day long the enemy troops press in. So many are proud to fight against me; how they long to conquer me.

³,⁴ But when I am afraid, I will put my confidence in you. Yes, I will trust the promises of God. And since I am trusting him, what can mere man do to me? ⁵ They are always twisting what I say. All their thoughts are how to harm me. ⁶ They meet together to perfect their plans; they hide beside the trail, listening for my steps, waiting to kill me. ⁷ They expect to get away with it. Don't let them, Lord. In anger cast them to the ground.

⁸ You have seen me tossing and turning through the night. You have collected all my tears and preserved them in your bottle! You have recorded every one in your book. ⁹ The very day I call for help, the tide of battle turns. My enemies flee! This one thing I *know: God is for me!* ¹⁰,¹¹ I am trusting God—oh, praise his promises! I am not afraid of anything mere man can do to me! Yes, praise his promises. ¹² I will surely do what I have promised, Lord, and thank you for your help. ¹³ For you have saved me from death and my feet from slipping, so that I can walk before the Lord in the land

of the living.

57 O GOD, HAVE pity, for I am trusting you! I will hide beneath the shadow of your wings until this storm is past. ² I will cry to the God of heaven who does such wonders for me. ³ He will send down help from heaven to save me, because of his love and his faithfulness. He will rescue me from these liars who are so intent upon destroying me. ⁴ I am surrounded by fierce lions—hotheads whose teeth are sharp as spears and arrows. Their tongues are like swords. ⁵ Lord, be exalted above the highest heavens! Show your glory high above the earth. ⁶ My enemies have set a trap for me. Frantic fear grips me. They have dug a pitfall in my path. But look! They themselves have fallen into it!

⁷ O God, my heart is quiet and confident. No wonder I can sing your praises! ⁸ Rouse yourself, my soul! Arise, O harp and lyre! Let us greet the dawn with song! ⁹ I will thank you publicly throughout the land. I will sing your praises among the nations. ¹⁰ Your kindness and love are as vast as the heavens. Your faithfulness is higher than the skies.

¹¹ Yes, be exalted, O God, above the heavens. May your glory shine throughout the earth.

58 JUSTICE? YOU HIGH and mighty politicians don't even know the meaning of the word! Fairness? Which of you has any left? Not one! All your dealings are crooked: you give "justice" in exchange for bribes.ᵃ ³ These men are born sinners, lying from their earliest words! ⁴,⁵ They are poisonous as deadly snakes, cobras that close their ears to the most expert of charmers.

⁶ O God, break off their fangs. Tear out the teeth of these young lions, Lord. ⁷ Let them disappear like water into thirsty ground. Make their weapons useless in their hands.ᵇ ⁸ Let them be as snails that dissolve into slime; and as those who die at birth, who never see the sun. ⁹ God will sweep away both old and young. He will destroy them more quickly than a cooking pot can

---

a Literally, "you deal out the violence of your hands in the land."   b Or, "Let them be trodden down and wither like grass."

feel the blazing fire of thorns beneath it.

¹⁰ The godly shall rejoice in the triumph of right;ᶜ they shall walk the blood-stained fields of slaughtered, wicked men. ¹¹ Then at last everyone will know that good is rewarded, and that there is a God who judges justly here on earth.

Written by David at the time King Saul set guards at his home to capture and kill him. 1 Samuel 19:11

59 O MY GOD, save me from my enemies. Protect me from these who have come to destroy me. ² Preserve me from these criminals, these murderers. ³ They lurk in ambush for my life. Strong men are out there waiting. And not, O Lord, because I've done them wrong. ⁴ Yet they prepare to kill me. Lord, waken! See what is happening! Help me! ⁵ (And O Jehovah, God of heaven's armies, God of Israel, arise and punish the heathen nations surrounding us.) Do not spare these evil, treacherous men. ⁶ At evening they come to spy, slinking around like dogs that prowl the city. ⁷ I hear them shouting insults and cursing God, for "No one will hear us," they think. ⁸ Lord, laugh at them! (And scoff at these surrounding nations too.)

⁹ O God my Strength! I will sing your praises, for you are my place of safety. ¹⁰ My God is changeless in his love for me and he will come and help me. He will let me see my wish come true upon my enemies. ¹¹ Don't kill them—for my people soon forget such lessons—but stagger them with your power and bring them to their knees. Bring them to the dust, O Lord our shield. ¹²,¹³ They are proud, cursing liars. Angrily destroy them. Wipe them out. (And let the nations find out too that God rules in Israel and will reign throughout the world.) ¹⁴,¹⁵ Let these evil men slink back at evening, and prowl the city all night before they are satisfied, howling like dogs and searching for food.

¹⁶ But as for me, I will sing each morning about your power and mercy. For you have been my high tower of refuge, a place of safety in the day of my distress. ¹⁷ O my Strength, to you I sing my praises; for you are my high tower of safety, my God of mercy.ᶜ

Written by David at the time he was at war with Syria, with the outcome still uncertain; this was when Joab, captain of his forces, slaughtered 12,000 men of Edom in the Valley of Salt.

60 O GOD, YOU have rejected us and broken our defenses; you have become angry and deserted us. Lord, restore us again to your favor. ² You have caused this nation to tremble in fear; you have torn it apart. Lord, heal it now, for it is shaken to its depths. ³ You have been very hard on us and made us reel beneath your blows.

⁴,⁵ But you have given us a banner to rally to; all who love truthᵃ will rally to it; then you can deliver your beloved people. Use your strong right arm to rescue us. ⁶,⁷ God has promised to help us. He has vowed it by his holiness! No wonder I exult! "Shechem, Succoth, Gilead, Manasseh—still are mine!" he says. "Judah shall continue to produce kings, and Ephraim great warriors. ⁸ Moab shall become my lowly servant, and Edom my slave. And I will shout in triumph over the Philistines."

⁹,¹⁰ Who will bring me in triumph into Edom's strong cities? God will! He who cast us off! He who abandoned us to our foes! ¹¹ Yes, Lord, help us against our enemies, for man's help is useless.

¹² With God's help we shall do mighty things, for he will trample down our foes.

61 O GOD, LISTEN to me! Hear my prayer! ² For wherever I am, though far away at the ends of the earth, I will cry to you for help. When my heart is faint and overwhelmed, lead me to the mighty, towering Rock of safety. ³ For you are my refuge, a high tower where my enemies can never reach me. ⁴ I shall live forever in your tabernacle; oh, to be safe beneath the shelter of your wings! ⁵ For you have heard my vows, O God, to praiseᵃ you every day, and you have given me the blessings you reserve for those who reverence your name.

---

c Literally, "when he sees the vengeance."   60a Literally, "that it may be displayed because of the truth."
61a Implied in verse 8.

⁶ You will give me[b] added years of life, as rich and full as those of many generations, all packed into one. ⁷ And I shall live before the Lord forever. Oh, send your lovingkindness and truth to guard and watch over me, ⁸ and I will praise your name continually, fulfilling my vow of praising you each day.

62 I STAND SILENTLY before the Lord, waiting for him to rescue me. For salvation comes from him alone. ² Yes, he alone is my Rock, my rescuer, defense and fortress. Why then should I be tense with fear when troubles come?

³,⁴ But what is this? They pick on me at a time when my throne[a] is tottering; they plot my death and use lies and deceit to try to force me from the throne.[a] They are so friendly to my face while cursing in their hearts! ⁵ But I stand silently before the Lord, waiting for him to rescue me. For salvation comes from him alone. ⁶ Yes, he alone is my Rock, my rescuer, defense and fortress—why then should I be tense with fear when troubles come?

⁷ My protection and success[b] come from God alone. He is my refuge, a Rock where no enemy can reach me. ⁸ O my people, trust him all the time. Pour out your longings before him, for he can help! ⁹ The greatest of men, or the lowest—both alike are nothing in his sight. They weigh less than air on scales.

¹⁰,¹¹ Don't become rich by extortion and robbery. And don't let the rich men be proud. ¹² He is loving and kind and rewards each one of us according to the work we do for him.

A Psalm of David when he was hiding in the wilderness of Judea.

63 O GOD, MY God! How I search for you! How I thirst for you in this parched and weary land where there is no water. How I long to find you! ² How I wish I could go into your sanctuary to see your strength and glory, ³ for your love and kindness are better to me than life itself. How I praise you! ⁴ I will bless you as long as I live, lifting up my hands to you in prayer. ⁵ At last I shall be fully satisfied; I will praise you with great joy.

⁶ I lie awake at night thinking of you— ⁷ of how much you have helped me—and how I rejoice through the night beneath the protecting shadow of your wings. ⁸ I follow close behind you, protected by your strong right arm. ⁹ But those plotting to destroy me shall go down to the depths of hell. ¹⁰ They are doomed to die by the sword, to become the food of jackals. ¹¹ But I[a] will rejoice in God. All who trust in him exult, while liars shall be silenced.

64 LORD, LISTEN TO my complaint: Oh, preserve my life from the conspiracy of these wicked men, these gangs of criminals. ³ They cut me down with sharpened tongues; they aim their bitter words like arrows straight at my heart. ⁴ They shoot from ambush at the innocent. Suddenly the deed is done, yet they are not afraid. ⁵ They encourage each other to do evil. They meet in secret to set their traps. "He will never notice them here," they say. ⁶ They keep a sharp lookout for opportunities of crime. They spend long hours with all their endless evil thoughts and plans.[a]

⁷ But God himself will shoot them down. Suddenly his arrow will pierce them. ⁸ They will stagger backward, destroyed by those they spoke against. All who see it happening will scoff at them. ⁹ Then everyone shall stand in awe and confess the greatness of the miracles of God; at last they will realize what amazing things he does. ¹⁰ And the godly shall rejoice in the Lord, and trust and praise him.

65 O GOD IN Zion, we wait before you in silent praise, and thus fulfill our vow. And because you answer prayer, all mankind will come to you with their requests. ³ Though sins fill our hearts, you forgive them all. ⁴ How greatly to be envied are those you have chosen to come and live with you within the holy tabernacle courts! What joys await us among all the good things there. ⁵ With dread deeds and awesome

b Literally, "to the days of the king."   62a Implied.   b Literally, "glory."   63a Literally, "the king."
64a Literally, "And the inward thought and the heart of everyone is deep."

power you will defend us from our enemies,[a] O God who saves us. You are the only hope of all mankind throughout the world and far away upon the sea.

⁶ He formed the mountains by his mighty strength. ⁷ He quiets the raging oceans and all the world's clamor. ⁸ In the farthest corners of the earth the glorious acts of God shall startle everyone. The dawn and sunset shout for joy! ⁹ He waters the earth to make it fertile. The rivers of God will not run dry! He prepares the earth for his people and sends them rich harvests of grain. ¹⁰ He waters the furrows with abundant rain. Showers soften the earth, melting the clods and causing seeds to sprout across the land. ¹¹,¹² Then he crowns it all with green, lush pastures in the wilderness; hillsides blossom with joy. ¹³ The pastures are filled with flocks of sheep, and the valleys are carpeted with grain. All the world shouts with joy, and sings.

66 SING TO THE Lord, all the earth! ² Sing of his glorious name! Tell the world how wonderful he is.

³ How awe-inspiring are your deeds, O God! How great your power! No wonder your enemies surrender! ⁴ All the earth shall worship you and sing of your glories. ⁵ Come, see the glorious things God has done. What marvelous miracles happen to his people! ⁶ He made a dry road through the sea for them. They went across on foot. What excitement and joy there was that day!

⁷ Because of his great power he rules forever. He watches every movement of the nations. O rebel lands, he will deflate your pride.

⁸ Let everyone bless God and sing his praises, ⁹ for he holds our lives in his hands. And he holds our feet to the path. ¹⁰ You have purified us with fire,[a] O Lord, like silver in a crucible. ¹¹ You captured us in your net and laid great burdens on our backs. ¹² You sent troops to ride across our broken bodies.[b] We went through fire and flood. But in the end, you brought us into wealth and great abundance.

¹³ Now I have come to your Temple with burnt offerings to pay my vows. ¹⁴ For when I was in trouble I promised you many offerings. ¹⁵ That is why I am bringing you these fat he-goats, rams and calves. The smoke of their sacrifice shall rise before you.

¹⁶ Come and hear, all of you who reverence the Lord, and I will tell you what he did for me: ¹⁷ For I cried to him for help, with praises ready on my tongue. ¹⁸ He would not have listened if I had not confessed my sins. ¹⁹ But he listened! He heard my prayer! He paid attention to it!

²⁰ Blessed be God who didn't turn away when I was praying, and didn't refuse me his kindness and love.

67 O GOD, IN mercy bless us; let your face beam with joy as you look down at us.

² Send us around the world with the news of your saving power and your eternal plan for all mankind. ³ How everyone throughout the earth will praise the Lord! ⁴ How glad the nations will be, singing for joy because you are their King[a] and will give true justice to their people! ⁵ Praise God, O world! May all the peoples of the earth give thanks to you. ⁶,⁷ For the earth has yielded abundant harvests. God, even our own God, will bless us. And peoples from remotest lands will worship him.

68 ARISE, O GOD, and scatter all your enemies! Chase them away! ² Drive them off like smoke before the wind; melt them like wax in fire! So let the wicked perish at the presence of God.

³ But may the godly man exult. May he rejoice and be merry. ⁴ Sing praises to the Lord! Raise your voice in song to him who rides upon the clouds![a] Jehovah is his name —oh, rejoice in his presence. ⁵ He is a father to the fatherless; he gives justice to the widows, for he is holy.[b] ⁶ He gives families to the lonely, and releases prisoners from jail, singing with joy! But for rebels there is famine and distress.

⁷ O God, when you led your people through the wilderness, ⁸ the earth trembled and the heavens shook. Mount Sinai quailed

---

a Literally, "will answer us in righteousness." 66a Implied. b Literally, "You caused men to ride over our heads." 67a Literally, "govern the nations." 68a Or, "deserts." b Literally, "in his holy habitation."

before you—the God of Israel. ⁹,¹⁰ You sent abundant rain upon your land, O God, to refresh it in its weariness! There your people lived, for you gave them this home when they were destitute.

¹¹,¹²,¹³ The Lord speaks. The enemy flees. The women at homeᶜ cry out the happy news: "The armies that came to destroy us have fled!" Now all the women of Israel are dividing the booty. See them sparkle with jewels of silver and gold, covered all over as wings cover doves! ¹⁴ God scattered their enemies like snowflakes melting in the forests of Zalmon.

¹⁵,¹⁶ O mighty mountains in Bashan! O splendid many-peaked ranges! Well may you look with envy at Mount Zion, the mount where God has chosen to live forever. ¹⁷ Surrounded by unnumbered chariots, the Lord moves on from Mount Sinai and comes to his holy temple high upon Mount Zion. ¹⁸ He ascends the heights, leading many captives in his train. He receives gifts forᵈ men, even those who once were rebels. God will live among us here.

¹⁹ What a glorious Lord! He who daily bears our burdens also gives us our salvation.

²⁰ He frees us! He rescues us from death. ²¹ But he will crush his enemies, for they refuse to leave their guilty, stubborn ways. ²² The Lord says, "Come," to all his people's enemies;ᵉ they are hiding on Mount Hermon's highest slopes and deep within the sea! ²³ His people must destroy them. Cover your feet with their blood; dogs will eat them.

²⁴ The procession of God my King moves onward to the sanctuary— ²⁵ singers in front, musicians behind, girls playing the timbrels in between. ²⁶ Let all the people of Israel praise the Lord, who is Israel's fountain. ²⁷ The little tribe of Benjamin leads the way. The princes and elders of Judah, and the princes of Zebulun and Naphtali are right behind.ᶠ ²⁸ Summon your might; display your strength, O God, for you have done such mighty things for us.

²⁹ The kings of the earth are bringing their gifts to your temple in Jerusalem. ³⁰ Rebuke our enemies, O Lord. Bring them—submissive, tax in hand.ᵍ Scatter all who delight in war. ³¹ Egypt will send gifts of precious metals. Ethiopia will stretch out her hands to God in adoration. ³² Sing to the Lord, O kingdoms of the earth—sing praises to the Lord, ³³ to him who rides upon the ancient heavens, whose mighty voice thunders from the sky.

³⁴ Power belongs to God! His majesty shines down on Israel; his strength is mighty in the heavens. ³⁵ What awe we feel, kneeling here before him in the sanctuary. The God of Israel gives strength and mighty power to his people. Blessed be God!

69 SAVE ME, O my God. The floods have risen. Deeper and deeper I sink in the mire; the waters rise around me. ³ I have wept until I am exhausted; my throat is dry and hoarse; my eyes are swollen with weeping, waiting for my God to act. ⁴ I cannot even count all those who hate me without cause. They are influential men, these who plot to kill me though I am innocent. They demand that I be punished for what I didn't do.

⁵ O God, you know so well how stupid I am, and you know all my sins. ⁶ O Lord God of the armies of heaven, don't let me be a stumbling block to those who trust in you. O God of Israel, don't let me cause them to be confused, ⁷ though I am mocked and cursed and shamed for your sake. ⁸ Even my own brothers pretend they don't know me! ⁹ My zeal for God and his workᵃ burns hot within me. And because I advocate your cause, your enemies insult me even as they insult you. ¹⁰ How they scoff and mock me when I mourn and fast before the Lord! ¹¹ How they talk about me when I wear sackcloth to show my humiliation and sorrow for my sins! ¹² I am the talk of the town and the song of the drunkards. ¹³ But I keep right on praying to you, Lord. For now is the time—you are bending down to hear! You are ready with a plentiful sup-

c Literally, "among the sheepfolds."   d Implied in Ephesians 4:8.   e Literally, "I will bring back from Bashan."   f Implied.   g Literally, "everyone submitting himself with pieces of silver." An alternate rendering of verse 30 could be, "Trample upon those who lust after the tribute of smaller nations, and who delight in aggressive wars."   69 a Literally, "for your house."

ply of love and kindness. Now answer my prayer and rescue me as you promised.[b] ¹⁴ Pull me out of this mire. Don't let me sink in. Rescue me from those who hate me, and from these deep waters I am in.

¹⁵ Don't let the floods overwhelm me, or the ocean swallow me; save me from the pit that threatens me. ¹⁶ O Jehovah, answer my prayers, for your lovingkindness is wonderful; your mercy is so plentiful, so tender and so kind. ¹⁷ Don't hide from me,[c] for I am in deep trouble. Quick! Come and save me. ¹⁸ Come, Lord, and rescue me. Ransom me from all my enemies. ¹⁹ You know how they talk about me, and how they so shamefully dishonor me. You see them all and know what each has said.

²⁰ Their contempt has broken my heart; my spirit is heavy within me. If even one would show some pity, if even one would comfort me! ²¹ For food they gave me poison; for my awful thirst they offered me vinegar. ²² Let their joys[d] turn to ashes and their peace disappear; ²³ let darkness, blindness and great feebleness be theirs. ²⁴ Pour out your fury upon them; consume them with the fierceness of your anger. ²⁵ Let their homes be desolate and abandoned. ²⁶ For they persecute the one you have smitten, and scoff at the pain of the one you have pierced. ²⁷ Pile their sins high and do not overlook them. ²⁸ Let these men be blotted from the list[e] of the living; do not give them the joys of life with the righteous.

²⁹ But rescue me, O God, from my poverty and pain. ³⁰ Then I will praise God with my singing! My thanks will be his praise—³¹ that will please him more than sacrificing a bullock or an ox. ³² The humble shall see their God at work for them. No wonder they will be so glad! All who seek for God shall live in joy. ³³ For Jehovah hears the cries of his needy ones, and does not look the other way.

³⁴ Praise him, all heaven and earth! Praise him, all the seas and everything in them! ³⁵ For God will save Jerusalem;[f] he rebuilds the cities of Judah. His people shall live in them and not be dispossessed. ³⁶ Their children shall inherit the land; all who love his name shall live there safely.

70 RESCUE ME, O God! Lord, hurry to my aid! ²,³ They are after my life, and delight in hurting me. Confuse them! Shame them! Stop them! Don't let them keep on mocking me! ⁴ But fill the followers of God with joy. Let those who love your salvation exclaim, "What a wonderful God he is!" ⁵ But I am in deep trouble. Rush to my aid, for only you can help and save me. O Lord, don't delay.

71 LORD, YOU ARE my refuge! Don't let me down! ² Save me from my enemies, for you are just! Rescue me! Bend down your ear and listen to my plea and save me. ³ Be to me a great protecting Rock, where I am always welcome, safe from all attacks. For you have issued the order to save me. ⁴ Rescue me, O God, from these unjust and cruel men. ⁵ O Lord, you alone are my hope; I've trusted you from childhood. ⁶ Yes, you have been with me from birth and have helped me constantly—no wonder I am always praising you! ⁷ My success—at which so many stand amazed—is because you are my mighty protector. ⁸ All day long I'll praise and honor you, O God, for all that you have done for me.

⁹ And now, in my old age, don't set me aside. Don't forsake me now when my strength is failing. ¹⁰ My enemies are whispering, ¹¹ "God has forsaken him! Now we can get him. There is no one to help him now!" ¹² O God, don't stay away! Come quickly! Help! ¹³ Destroy them! Cover them with failure and disgrace—these enemies of mine. ¹⁴ I will keep on expecting you to help me. I praise you more and more. ¹⁵ I cannot count the times when you have faithfully rescued me from danger. I will tell everyone how good you are, and of your constant, daily care. ¹⁶ I walk in the strength of the Lord God. I tell everyone that you alone are just and good. ¹⁷ O God, you have helped me from my earliest childhood—and I have constantly testified to others of the wonderful things you do. ¹⁸ And now that I am old and gray, don't forsake me. Give me time

---

b Literally, "in the truth of your salvation."   c Literally, "your servant."   d Literally, "their table."
e Or, "Let them be blotted out of the book of life."   f Literally, "Zion."

to tell this new generation (and their children too) about all your mighty miracles. [19] Your power and goodness, Lord, reach to the highest heavens. You have done such wonderful things. Where is there another God like you? [20] You have let me sink down deep in desperate problems. But you will bring me back to life again, up from the depths of the earth. [21] You will give me greater honor than before, and turn again and comfort me.

[22] I will praise you with music, telling of your faithfulness to all your promises, O Holy One of Israel. [23] I will shout and sing your praises for redeeming me. [24] I will talk to others all day long about your justice and your goodness. For all who tried to hurt me have been disgraced and dishonored.

72 O GOD, HELP the king to judge as you would, and help his son to walk in godliness. [2] Help him to give justice to your people, even to the poor. [3] May the mountains and hills flourish in prosperity because of his good reign. [4] Help him to defend the poor and needy and to crush their oppressors. [5] May the poor and needy revere you constantly, as long as sun and moon continue in the skies! Yes, forever!

[6] May the reign of this son[a] of mine be as gentle and fruitful as the springtime rains upon the grass—like showers that water the earth! [7] May all good men flourish in his reign, with abundance of peace to the end of time. [8] Let him reign from sea to sea, and from the Euphrates River to the ends of the earth. [9] The desert nomads shall bow before him; his enemies shall fall face downward in the dust. [10] Kings along the Mediterranean coast—the kings of Tarshish and the islands—and those from Sheba and from Seba—all will bring their gifts. [11] Yes, kings from everywhere! All will bow before him! All will serve him!

[12] He will take care of the helpless and poor when they cry to him; for they have no one else to defend them. [13] He feels pity for the weak and needy, and will rescue them. [14] He will save them from oppression and from violence, for their lives are pre-

cious to him.

[15] And he shall live; and to him will be given the gold of Sheba, and there will be constant praise[b] for him. His people[c] will bless him all day long. [16] Bless us with abundant crops throughout the land, even on the highland plains; may there be fruit like that of Lebanon; may the cities be as full of people as the fields are of grass. [17] His name will be honored forever; it will continue as the sun; and all will be blessed in him; all nations will praise him.

[18] Blessed be Jehovah God, the God of Israel, who only does wonderful things! [19] Blessed be his glorious name forever! Let the whole earth be filled with his glory. Amen, and amen!

[20] (This ends the psalms of David, son of Jesse.)

73 HOW GOOD GOD is to Israel—to those whose hearts are pure. [2] But as for me, I came *so* close to the edge of the cliff! My feet were slipping and I was almost gone. [3] For I was envious of the prosperity of the proud and wicked. [4] Yes, all through life their road is smooth![a] They grow sleek and fat. [5] They aren't always in trouble and plagued with problems like everyone else, [6] so their pride sparkles like a jeweled necklace, and their clothing is woven of cruelty! [7] These fat cats have everything their hearts could ever wish for! [8] They scoff at God and threaten his people. How proudly they speak! [9] They boast against the very heavens, and their words strut through the earth.

[10] And so God's people are dismayed and confused, and drink it all in. [11] "Does God realize what is going on?" they ask. [12] "Look at these men of arrogance; they never have to lift a finger—theirs is a life of ease; and all the time their riches multiply."

[13] Have I been wasting my time? Why take the trouble to be pure? [14] All I get out of it is trouble and woe—every day and all day long! [15] If I had really said that, I would have been a traitor to your people. [16] Yet it is so hard to explain it—this prosperity of those who hate the Lord. [17] Then one day

---

a The reference seems to look beyond Solomon's son to Jesus the Messiah.   b Literally, "men shall pray for him continually."   c Implied. Literally, "they" or "he."   73a Or, "they never have any pains."

I went into God's sanctuary to meditate, and thought about the future of these evil men. [18] What a slippery path they are on—suddenly God will send them sliding over the edge of the cliff and down to their destruction: [19] an instant end to all their happiness, an eternity of terror. [20] Their present life is only a dream! They will awaken to the truth as one awakens from a dream of things that never really were!

[21] When I saw this, what turmoil filled my heart! [22] I saw myself so stupid and so ignorant; I must seem like an animal to you, O God. [23] But even so, you love me! You are holding my right hand! [24] You will keep on guiding me all my life with your wisdom and counsel; and afterwards receive me into the glories of heaven![b] [25] Whom have I in heaven but you? And I desire no one on earth as much as you! [26] My health fails; my spirits droop, yet God remains! He is the strength of my heart; he is mine forever!

[27] But those refusing to worship God will perish, for he destroys those serving other gods.

[28] But as for me, I get as close to him as I can! I have chosen him and I will tell everyone about the wonderful ways he rescues me.

74 O GOD, WHY have you cast us away forever? Why is your anger hot against us—the sheep of your own pasture? [2] Remember that we are your people—the ones you chose in ancient times from slavery and made the choicest of your possessions. You chose Jerusalem[a] as your home on earth!

[3] Walk through the awful ruins of the city, and see what the enemy has done to your sanctuary. [4] There they shouted their battle cry and erected their idols to flaunt their victory. [5,6] Everything lies in shambles like a forest chopped to the ground. They came with their axes and sledgehammers and smashed and chopped the carved paneling, [7] and set the sanctuary on fire, and razed it to the ground—your sanctuary, Lord. [8] "Let's wipe out every trace of God," they said, and went through the entire country burning down the assembly places where we worshiped you.

[9,10] There is nothing left to show that we are your people. The prophets are gone, and who can say when it all will end? How long, O God, will you allow our enemies to dishonor your name? Will you let them get away with this forever? [11] Why do you delay? Why hold back your power? Unleash your fist and give them a final blow.

[12] God is my King from ages past; you have been actively helping me everywhere throughout the land. [13,14] You divided the Red Sea with your strength; you crushed the sea-god's heads! You gave him to the desert tribes to eat! [15] At your command the springs burst forth to give your people water; and then you dried a path for them across the ever-flowing Jordan. [16] Day and night alike belong to you; you made the starlight and the sun. [17] All nature is within your hands; you make the summer and the winter too. [18] Lord, see how these enemies scoff at you. O Jehovah, an arrogant nation has blasphemed your name.

[19] O Lord, save me! Protect your turtle-dove from the hawks.[b] Save your beloved people from these beasts. [20] Remember your promise! For the land is full of darkness and cruel men. [21] O Lord, don't let your downtrodden people be constantly insulted. Give cause for these poor and needy ones to praise your name! [22] Arise, O God, and state your case against our enemies. Remember the insults these rebels have hurled against you all day long. [23] Don't overlook the cursing of these enemies of yours; it grows louder and louder.

75 HOW WE THANK you, Lord! Your mighty miracles give proof that you care.

[2] "Yes," the Lord replies, "and when I am ready, I will punish the wicked! [3] Though the earth shakes and all its people live in turmoil, yet its pillars are firm, for I have set them in place!"

[4] I warned the proud to cease their arrogance! I told the wicked to lower their insolent gaze,[a] [5] and to stop being stubborn and

---

b Or, "you will bring me unto honor."   74a Literally, "Mount Zion."   b Literally, "the wild beasts."
75a Literally, "lift not up the horn."

proud. ⁶,⁷ For promotion and power come from nowhere on earth, but only from God. He promotes one and deposes another. ⁸ In Jehovah's hand there is a cup of pale and sparkling wine. It is his judgment, poured out upon the wicked of the earth. They must drain that cup to the dregs. ⁹ But as for me, I shall forever declare the praises of the God of Jacob. ¹⁰ "I will cut off the strength of evil men," says the Lord,ᵇ "and increase the power of good men in their place."

76 GOD'S REPUTATION IS very great in Judah and in Israel. ² His home is in Jerusalem. He lives upon Mount Zion. ³ There he breaks the weapons of our enemies.

⁴ The everlasting mountains cannot compare with you in glory! ⁵ The mightiest of our enemies are conquered. They lie before us in the sleep of death; not one can lift a hand against us. ⁶ When you rebuked them, God of Jacob, steeds and riders fell. ⁷ No wonder you are greatly feared! Who can stand before an angry God? ⁸ You pronounce sentence on them from heaven; the earth trembles and stands silently before you. ⁹ You stand up to punish the evil-doers and to defend the meek of the earth. ¹⁰ Man's futile wrath will bring you glory. You will use it as an ornament! ¹¹ Fulfill all your vows that you have made to Jehovah your God. Let everyone bring him presents. He should be reverenced and feared, ¹² for he cuts down princes and does awesome things to the kings of the earth.

77 I CRY TO the Lord; I call and call to him. Oh, that he would listen. ² I am in deep trouble and I need his help so badly. All night long I pray, lifting my hands to heaven, pleading. There can be no joy for me until he acts. ³ I think of God and moan, overwhelmed with longing for his help. ⁴ I cannot sleep until you act. I am too distressed even to pray!

⁵ I keep thinking of the good old days of the past, long since ended. ⁶ Then my nights were filled with joyous songs. I search my soul and meditate upon the difference now. ⁷ Has the Lord rejected me forever? Will he never again be favorable? ⁸ Is his loving-kindness gone forever? Has his promise failed? ⁹ Has he forgotten to be kind to one so undeserving? Has he slammed the door in anger on his love? ¹⁰ And I said: This is my fate, that the blessings of God have changed to hate.ᵃ ¹¹ I recall the many miracles he did for me so long ago. ¹² Those wonderful deeds are constantly in my thoughts. I cannot stop thinking about them.

¹³ O God, your ways are holy. Where is there any other as mighty as you? ¹⁴ You are the God of miracles and wonders! You still demonstrate your awesome power.

¹⁵ You have redeemed us who are the sons of Jacob and of Joseph by your might. ¹⁶ When the Red Sea saw you, how it feared! It trembled to its depths! ¹⁷ The clouds poured down their rain, the thunder rolled and crackled in the sky. Your lightning flashed. ¹⁸ There was thunder in the whirlwind; the lightning lighted up the world! The earth trembled and shook.

¹⁹ Your road led by a pathway through the sea—a pathway no one knew was there! ²⁰ You led your people along that road like a flock of sheep, with Moses and Aaron as their shepherds.

78 O MY PEOPLE, listen to my teaching. Open your ears to what I am saying. ²,³ For I will show you lessons from our history, stories handed down to us from former generations. ⁴ I will reveal these truths to you so that you can describe these glorious deeds of Jehovah to your children, and tell them about the mighty miracles he did. ⁵ For he gave his laws to Israel, and commanded our fathers to teach them to their children, ⁶ so that they in turn could teach their children too. Thus his laws pass down from generation to generation. ⁷ In this way each generation has been able to obey his laws and to set its hope anew on God and not forget his glorious miracles. ⁸ Thus they did not need to be as their fathers were—stubborn, rebellious, unfaithful, refusing to give their hearts to God.

---

b Implied.　77a Literally, "that the right hand of the Most High has changed."

⁹ The people of Ephraim, though fully armed, turned their backs and fled when the day of battle came, ¹⁰ because they didn't obey his laws. They refused to follow his ways. ¹¹,¹² And they forgot about the wonderful miracles God had done for them, and for their fathers in Egypt. ¹³ For he divided the sea before them and led them through! The water stood banked up along both sides of them! ¹⁴ In the daytime he led them by a cloud, and at night by a pillar of fire. ¹⁵ He split open the rocks in the wilderness to give them plenty of water, as though gushing from a spring. ¹⁶ Streams poured from the rock, flowing like a river! ¹⁷ Yet they kept on with their rebellion, sinning against the God who is above all gods. ¹⁸ They murmured and complained, demanding other food than God was giving them. ¹⁹,²⁰ They even spoke against God himself. "Why can't he give us decent food as well as water?" they grumbled. ²¹ Jehovah heard them and was angry; the fire of his wrath burned against Israel, ²² because they didn't believe in God or trust in him to care for them, ²³ even though he commanded the skies to open—he opened the windows of heaven— ²⁴ and rained down manna for their food. He gave them bread from heaven! ²⁵ They ate angel's food! He gave them all that they could hold.

²⁶ And he led forth the east wind and guided the south wind by his mighty power. ²⁷ He rained down birds as thick as dust, clouds of them like sands along the shore! ²⁸ He caused the birds to fall to the ground among the tents. ²⁹ The people ate their fill. He gave them what they asked for. ³⁰ But they had hardly finished eating, and the meat was yet in their mouths, ³¹ when the anger of the Lord rose against them and killed the finest of Israel's young men. ³² Yet even so the people kept on sinning and refused to believe in miracles. ³³ So he cut their lives short and gave them years of terror and disaster.

³⁴ Then at last, when he had ruined them, they walked awhile behind him; how earnestly they turned around and followed him! ³⁵ Then they remembered that God was their Rock—that their Savior was the God above all gods. ³⁶ But it was only with their words they followed him, not with their hearts; ³⁷ their hearts were far away. They did not keep their promises. ³⁸ Yet he was merciful and forgave their sins and didn't destroy them all. Many and many a time he held back his anger. ³⁹ For he remembered that they were merely mortal men, gone in a moment like a breath of wind.

⁴⁰ Oh, how often they rebelled against him in those desert years and grieved his heart. ⁴¹ Again and again they turned away and tempted God to kill them, and limited the Holy One of Israel from giving them his blessings. ⁴² They forgot his power and love, and how he had rescued them from their enemies; ⁴³ they forgot the plagues he sent upon the Egyptians in Tanis[a]— ⁴⁴ how he turned their rivers into blood, so that no one could drink, ⁴⁵ and how he sent vast swarms of flies to fill the land, and how the frogs had covered all of Egypt!

⁴⁶ He gave their crops to caterpillars. Their harvest was consumed by locusts. ⁴⁷ He destroyed their grapevines and their sycamores with hail. ⁴⁸ Their cattle died in the fields, mortally wounded by iceballs from heaven. Their sheep were killed by lightning. ⁴⁹ He loosed on them the fierceness of his anger, sending sorrow and trouble. He dispatched against them a band of destroying angels. ⁵⁰ He gave free course to his anger and did not spare the Egyptians' lives, but handed them over to plagues and sickness. ⁵¹ Then he killed the eldest son[b] in each Egyptian family—he who was the beginning of its strength and joy.

⁵² But he led forth his own people like a flock, guiding them safely through the wilderness. ⁵³ He kept them safe, so they were not afraid. But the Sea closed in upon their enemies and overwhelmed them. ⁵⁴ He brought them to the border of his land of blessing, to this land of hills he made for them. ⁵⁵ He drove out the nations occupying the land, and gave each tribe of Israel its apportioned place as its home.

⁵⁶ Yet though he did all this for them, they still rebelled against the God above all gods, and refused to follow his commands.

---

a Literally, "the plains of Zoan."   b Literally, "all the firstborn."

⁵⁷ They turned back from entering the Promised Land and disobeyed as their fathers had. Like a crooked arrow, they missed the target of God's will. ⁵⁸ They made him angry by erecting idols and altars to other gods.

⁵⁹ When God saw their deeds, his wrath was strong and he despised his people. ⁶⁰ Then he abandoned his Tabernacle at Shiloh, where he had lived among mankind, ⁶¹ and allowed his Ark to be captured; he surrendered his glory into enemy hands. ⁶² He caused his people to be butchered because his anger was intense. ⁶³ Their young men were killed by fire and their girls died before they were old enough to sing their wedding songs. ⁶⁴ The priests were slaughtered and their widows died before they could even begin their lament. ⁶⁵ Then the Lord rose up as though awakening from sleep, and like a mighty man aroused by wine, ⁶⁶ he routed his enemies and drove them back and sent them to eternal shame. ⁶⁷ But he rejected Joseph's family, the tribe of Ephraim, ⁶⁸ and chose the tribe of Judah —and Mount Zion which he loved. ⁶⁹ There he built his towering temple, solid and enduring as the heavens and the earth. ⁷⁰ He chose his servant David, taking him from feeding sheep, ⁷¹,⁷² and from following the ewes with lambs; God presented David to his people as their shepherd and he cared for them with a true heart and skillful hands.

79 O GOD, YOUR land has been conquered by the heathen nations. Your Temple is defiled and Jerusalem is a heap of ruins. ² The bodies of your people lie exposed— food for birds and animals. ³ The enemy has butchered the entire population of Jerusalem; blood has flowed like water. No one is left even to bury them. ⁴ The nations all around us scoff. They heap contempt on us.

⁵ O Jehovah, how long will you be angry with us? Forever? Will your jealousy burn till every hope is gone? ⁶ Pour out your wrath upon the godless nations, not on us! And on kingdoms that refuse to pray, that will not call upon your name! ⁷ For they have destroyed your people Israel, invading every home. ⁸ Oh, do not hold us guilty for our former sins! Let your tenderhearted mercies meet our needs, for we are brought low to the dust. ⁹ Help us, God of our salvation! Help us for the honor of your name. Oh, save us and forgive our sins. ¹⁰ Why should the heathen nations be allowed to scoff, "Where is their God?" Publicly avenge this slaughter of your people! ¹¹ Listen to the sighing of the prisoners and those condemned to die. Demonstrate the greatness of your power by saving them. ¹² O Lord, take sevenfold vengeance on these nations scorning you.

¹³ Then we your people, the sheep of your pasture, will thank you forever and forever, praising your greatness from generation to generation.

80 O SHEPHERD OF Israel who leads Israel like a flock; O God enthroned above the cherubim, bend down your ear and listen as I plead. Display your power and radiant glory. ² Let Ephraim, Benjamin and Manasseh see you rouse yourself and use your mighty power to rescue us.

³ Turn us again to yourself, O God. Look down on us in joy and love;ᵃ only then shall we be saved. ⁴ O Jehovah, God of heaven's armies, how long will you be angry and reject our prayers? ⁵ You have fed us with sorrow and tears, ⁶ and have made us the scorn of the neighboring nations. They laugh among themselves.

⁷ Turn us again to yourself, O God of Hosts. Look down on us in joy and love;ᵃ only then shall we be saved. ⁸ You brought us from Egypt as though we were a tender vine and drove away the heathen from your land and planted us. ⁹ You cleared the ground and tilled the soil and we took root and filled the land. ¹⁰ The mountains were covered with our shadow; we were like the mighty cedar trees,ᵇ ¹¹ covering the entire land from the Mediterranean Sea to the Euphrates River. ¹² But now you have broken down our walls, leaving us without protection. ¹³ The boar from the forest roots around us, and the wild animals feed on us.

¹⁴ Come back, we beg of you, O God of the armies of heaven, and bless us. Look

---

a Literally, "Cause your face to shine upon us."   b Literally, "the cedars of God."

down from heaven and see our plight and care for this your vine! [15] Protect what you yourself have planted, this son you have raised for yourself. [16] For we are chopped and burned by our enemies. May they perish at your frown. [17] Strengthen the man you love,[c] the son of your choice,[d] [18] and we will never forsake you again. Revive us to trust in you.

[19] Turn us again to yourself, O God of the armies of heaven. Look down on us, your face aglow with joy and love—only then shall we be saved.

81 THE LORD MAKES us strong! Sing praises! Sing to Israel's God! [2] Sing, accompanied by drums; pluck the sweet lyre and harp. [3] Sound the trumpet! Come to the joyous celebrations at full moon, new moon and all the other holidays. [4] For God has given us these times of joy; they are scheduled in the laws of Israel. [5] He gave them as reminders of his war against Egypt where we were slaves on foreign soil.

I heard an unknown voice that said, [6] "Now I will relieve your shoulder of its burden; I will free your hands from their heavy tasks." [7] He said, "You cried to me in trouble and I saved you; I answered from Mount Sinai[a] where the thunder hides. I tested your faith at Meribah, when you complained there was no water. [8] Listen to me, O my people, while I give you stern warnings. O Israel, if you will only listen! [9] *You must never worship any other god,* nor ever have an idol in your home.[b] [10] For it was I, Jehovah your God, who brought you out of the land of Egypt. Only test me![c] Open your mouth wide and see if I won't fill it. You will receive every blessing you can use! [11] But no, my people won't listen. Israel doesn't want me around. [12] So I am letting them go their blind and stubborn way, living according to their own desires.

[13] But oh, that my people would listen to me! Oh, that Israel would follow me, walking in my paths! [14] How quickly then I would subdue her enemies! How soon my hands would be upon her foes! [15] Those who hate the Lord would cringe before him; their desolation would last forever. [16] But he would feed you with the choicest foods. He would satisfy you with honey for the taking."[d]

82 GOD STANDS UP to open heaven's court. He pronounces judgment on the judges.[a] [2] How long will you judges refuse to listen to the evidence? How long will you shower special favors on the wicked? [3] Give fair judgment to the poor man, the afflicted, the fatherless, the destitute. [4] Rescue the poor and needy from the grasp of evil men. [5] But you are so foolish and so ignorant! Because you are in darkness, all the foundations of society[b] are shaken to the core. [6] I have called you all "gods" and "sons of the Most High." [7] But in death you are mere men. You will fall as any prince—for all must die.

[8] Stand up, O God, and judge the earth. For all of it belongs to you. All nations are in your hands.

83 O GOD, DON'T sit idly by, silent and inactive when we pray. Answer us! Deliver us!

[2] Don't you hear the tumult and commotion of your enemies? Don't you see what they are doing, these proud men who hate the Lord? [3] They are full of craftiness and plot against your people, laying plans to slay your precious ones. [4] Come, they say, and let us wipe out Israel as a nation—we will destroy the very memory of her existence. [5] This was their unanimous decision at their summit conference—they signed a treaty to ally themselves against Almighty God— [6] these Ishmaelites and Edomites and Moabites and Hagrites; [7] people from the lands of Gebal, Ammon, Amalek, Philistia and Tyre; [8] Assyria has joined them too, and is allied with the descendants of Lot.[a]

[9] Do to them as once you did to Midian, or as you did to Sisera and Jabin at the river

---

c Literally, "the man of your right hand."   d Literally, "the son of man you made strong for yourself."
81a Implied. Literally, "in the hiding place of thunder."   b Literally, "There shall no foreign god be in you."
c Implied.   d Literally, "honey out of the rock."   82a Implied in verses 2-4 and 6. Literally, "He judges among the gods."   b Literally, "of the earth."   83a The Moabites and Ammonites were among Lot's descendants.

Kishon, [10] and as you did to your enemies at Endor, whose decaying corpses fertilized the soil. [11] Make their mighty nobles die as Oreb did,[b] and Zeeb;[b] let all their princes die like Zebah[c] and Zalmunna,[c] [12] who said, "Let us seize for our own use these pasturelands of God!"

[13] O my God, blow them away like dust; like chaff before the wind— [14] as a forest fire that roars across a mountain. [15] Chase them with your fiery storms, tempests and tornados. [16] Utterly disgrace them until they recognize your power and name, O Lord. [17] Make them failures in everything they do; let them be ashamed and terrified [18] until they learn that you alone, Jehovah, are the God above all gods in supreme charge of all the earth.

84 HOW LOVELY IS your Temple, O Lord of the armies of heaven.

[2] I long, yes, faint with longing to be able to enter your courtyard and come near to the Living God. [3] Even the sparrows and swallows are welcome to come and nest among your altars and there have their young, O Lord of heaven's armies, my King and my God! [4] How happy are those who can live in your Temple, singing your praises.

[5] Happy are those who are strong in the Lord, who want above all else to follow your steps. [6] When they walk through the Valley of Weeping it will become a place of springs where pools of blessing and refreshment collect after rains! [7] They will grow constantly in strength and each of them is invited to meet with the Lord in Zion.

[8] O Jehovah, God of the heavenly armies, hear my prayer! Listen, God of Israel. [9] O God, our Defender and our Shield, have mercy on the one you have anointed as your king.[a]

[10] A single day spent in your Temple is better than a thousand anywhere else! I would rather be a doorman of the Temple of my God than live in palaces[b] of wickedness. [11] For Jehovah God is our Light and our Protector. He gives us grace and glory. No good thing will he withhold from those who walk along his paths.[c]

[12] O Lord of the armies of heaven, blessed are those who trust in you.

85 LORD, YOU HAVE poured out amazing blessings on this land! You have restored the fortunes[a] of Israel, [2] and forgiven the sins of your people—yes, covered over each one, [3] so that all your wrath, your blazing anger, is now ended.

[4] Now bring us back to loving you,[b] O Lord, so that your anger will never need rise against us again. [5] (Or will you be always angry—on and on to distant generations?) [6] Oh, revive us! Then your people can rejoice in you again. [7] Pour out your love and kindness on us, Lord, and grant us your salvation.

[8] I am listening carefully to all the Lord is saying—for he speaks peace to his people, his saints, if they will only stop their sinning. [9] Surely his salvation is near to those who reverence him; our land will be filled with his glory.

[10] Mercy and truth have met together. Grim justice[c] and peace have kissed! [11] Truth rises from the earth and righteousness smiles down from heaven.

[12] Yes, the Lord pours down his blessings on the land and it yields its bountiful crops. [13] Justice goes before him to make a pathway for his steps.[d]

86 BEND DOWN AND hear my prayer, O Lord, and answer me, for I am deep in trouble.

[2] Protect me from death, for I try to follow all your laws. Save me, for I am serving you and trusting you. [3] Be merciful, O Lord, for I am looking up to you in constant hope. [4] Give me happiness, O Lord, for I worship only you. [5] O Lord, you are so good and kind, so ready to forgive; so full of mercy for all who ask your aid.

[6] Listen closely to my prayer, O God. Hear my urgent cry. [7] I will call to you whenever trouble strikes, and you will help me.

[8] Where among the heathen gods is there a god like you? Where are their miracles?

---

b Judges 7:25.   c Judges 8:21.   84a Literally, "your anointed."   b Literally, "tents."
c Literally, "walk uprightly."   85a Literally, "brought back the captivity."   b Or, "Turn to us."
c Literally, "righteousness."   d Or, "set us in the way of his steps."

⁹ All the nations—and you made each one—will come and bow before you, Lord, and praise your great and holy name. ¹⁰ For you are great, and do great miracles. You alone are God.

¹¹ Tell me where you want me to go and I will go there. May every fiber of my being unite in reverence to your name. ¹² With all my heart I will praise you. I will give glory to your name forever, ¹³ for you love me so much! You are constantly so kind! You have rescued me from deepest hell.

¹⁴ O God, proud and insolent men defy me; violent, godless men are trying to kill me. ¹⁵ But you are merciful and gentle, Lord, slow in getting angry, full of constant lovingkindness and of truth; ¹⁶ so look down in pity and grant strength to your servant and save me. ¹⁷ Send me a sign of your favor. When those who hate me see it they will lose face because you help and comfort me.

87 HIGH ON HIS holy mountain stands Jerusalem,ᵃ the city of God, the city he loves more than any other!

³ O city of God, what wondrous tales are told of you! ⁴ Nowadays when I mention among my friends the names of Egypt and Babylonia, Philistia and Tyre, or even distant Ethiopia, someone boasts that he was born in one or another of those countries. ⁵ But someday the highest honor will be to be a native of Jerusalem! For the God above all gods will personally bless this city. ⁶ When he registers her citizens he will place a checkmark beside the names of those who were born here. ⁷ And in the festivals they'll sing, "All my heart is in Jerusalem."

88 O JEHOVAH, GOD of my salvation, I have wept before you day and night. ² Now hear my prayers; oh, listen to my cry, ³ for my life is full of troubles, and death draws near. ⁴ They say my life is ebbing out—a hopeless case. ⁵ They have left me here to die, like those slain on battlefields, from whom your mercies are removed.

⁶ You have thrust me down to the darkest depths. ⁷ Your wrath lies heavy on me; wave after wave engulfs me. ⁸ You have made my friends to loathe me, and they have gone away. I am in a trap with no way out. ⁹ My eyes grow dim with weeping. Each day I beg your help; O Lord, I reach my pleading hands to you for mercy.

¹⁰ Soon it will be too late! Of what use are your miracles when I am in the grave? How can I praise you then? ¹¹ Can those in the grave declare your lovingkindness? Can they proclaim your faithfulness? ¹² Can the darkness speak of your miracles? Can anyone in the Land of Forgetfulness talk about your help?

¹³ O Lord, I plead for my life and will keep on pleading day by day. ¹⁴ O Jehovah, why have you thrown my life away? Why are you turning your face from me, and looking the other way? ¹⁵ From my youth I have been sickly and ready to die. I stand helpless before your terrors. ¹⁶ Your fierce wrath has overwhelmed me. Your terrors have cut me off. ¹⁷ They flow around me all day long. ¹⁸ Lover, friend, acquaintance —all are gone. There is only darkness everywhere.

89 FOREVER AND EVER I will sing about the tender kindness of the Lord! Young and old shall hear about your blessings. ² Your love and kindness are forever; your truth is as enduring as the heavens.

³,⁴ The Lord God says,ᵃ "I have made a solemn agreement with my chosen servant David. I have taken an oath to establish his descendants as kings forever on his throne, from now until eternity!"

⁵ All heaven shall praise your miracles, O Lord; myriads of angelsᵇ will praise you for your faithfulness. ⁶ For who in all of heaven can be compared with God? What mightiest angelᶜ is anything like him? ⁷ The highest of angelic powersᵇ stand in dread and awe of him. Who is as revered as he by those surrounding him? ⁸ O Jehovah, Commander of the heavenly armies, where is there any other Mighty One like you? Faithfulness is your very character.

⁹ You rule the oceans when their waves arise in fearful storms; you speak, and they lie still. ¹⁰ You have cut haughty Egyptᵈ to

---

a Literally, "Zion."   **89a** Implied.   b Literally, "the assembly of the holy ones."   c Literally, "the sons of the mighty."   d Literally, "Rahab."

pieces. Your enemies are scattered by your awesome power. ¹¹ The heavens are yours, the world, everything—for you created them all. ¹² You created north and south! Mount Tabor and Mount Hermon rejoice to be signed by your name as their maker! ¹³ Strong is your arm! Strong is your hand! Your right hand is lifted high in glorious strength.

¹⁴,¹⁵ Your throne is founded on two strong pillars—the one is Justice and the other Righteousness. Mercy and Truth walk before you as your attendants. Blessed are those who hear the joyful blast of the trumpet, for they shall walk in the light of your presence. ¹⁶ They rejoice all day long in your wonderful reputation and in your perfect righteousness. ¹⁷ You are their strength. What glory! Our power is based on your favor! ¹⁸ Yes, our protection is from the Lord himself and he, the Holy One of Israel, has given us our king.

¹⁹ In a vision you spoke to your prophetᵉ and said, "I have chosen a splendid young man from the common people to be the king— ²⁰ he is my servant David! I have anointed him with my holy oil. ²¹ I will steady him and make him strong. ²² His enemies shall not outwit him, nor shall the wicked overpower him. ²³ I will beat down his adversaries before him, and destroy those who hate him. ²⁴ I will protect and bless him constantly and surround him with my love; he will be great because of me. ²⁵ He will hold sway from the Euphrates River to the Mediterranean Sea. ²⁶ And he will cry to me, 'You are my Father, my God, and my Rock of Salvation.'

²⁷ "I will treat him as my firstborn son, and make him the mightiest king in all the earth. ²⁸ I will love him forever, and be kind to him always; my covenant with him will never end. ²⁹ He will always have an heir; his throne will be as endless as the days of heaven. ³⁰,³¹,³² If his children forsake my laws and don't obey them, then I will punish them, ³³ but I will never completely take away my lovingkindness from them, nor let my promise fail. ³⁴ No, I will not break my covenant; I will not take back one word of what I said. ³⁵,³⁶ For I have sworn to David (and a holy God can never lie), that his dynasty will go on forever, and his throne will continue to the end of time.ᶠ ³⁷ It shall be eternal as the moon, my faithful witness in the sky!"

³⁸ Then why cast me off, rejected? Why be so angry with the one you chose as king? ³⁹ Have you renounced your covenant with him? For you have thrown his crown in the dust. ⁴⁰ You have broken down the walls protecting him and laid in ruins every fort defending him. ⁴¹ Everyone who comes along has robbed him while his neighbors mock. ⁴² You have strengthened his enemies against him and made them rejoice. ⁴³ You have struck down his sword and refused to help him in battle. ⁴⁴ You have ended his splendor and overturned his throne. ⁴⁵ You have made him old before his time and publicly disgraced him.

⁴⁶ O Jehovah, how long will this go on? Will you hide yourself from me forever? How long will your wrath burn like fire? ⁴⁷ Oh, remember how short you have made man's lifespan. Is it an empty, futile life you give the sons of men? ⁴⁸ No man can live forever. All will die. Who can rescue his life from the power of the grave?

⁴⁹ Lord, where is the love you used to have for me? Where is your kindness that you promised to David with a faithful pledge? ⁵⁰ Lord, see how all the people are despising me. ⁵¹ Your enemies joke about me, the one you anointed as their king.

⁵² And yet—blessed be the Lord forever! Amen and amen!

A prayer of Moses, the man of God.

90 LORD, THROUGH ALL the generations you have been our home! ² Before the mountains were created, before the earth was formed, you are God without beginning or end.

³ You speak, and man turns back to dust. ⁴ A thousand years are but as yesterday to you! They are like a single hour!ᵃ ⁵,⁶ We glide along the tides of time as swiftly as a racing river, and vanish as quickly as a dream. We are like grass that is green in the

---

e Literally, "your saint"; apparently a reference to Samuel, who was sent to anoint David as king.
f Literally, "his throne as the sun before me."   90a Literally, "as a watch in the night."

morning but mowed down and withered before the evening shadows fall. ⁷ We die beneath your anger; we are overwhelmed by your wrath. ⁸ You spread out our sins before you—our secret sins—and see them all. ⁹ No wonder the years are long and heavy here beneath your wrath. All our days are filled with sighing.

¹⁰ Seventy years are given us! And some may even live to eighty. But even the best of these years are often emptiness and pain; soon they disappear, and we are gone. ¹¹ Who can realize the terrors of your anger? Which of us can fear you as he should?

¹² Teach us to number our days and recognize how few they are; help us to spend them as we should.

¹³ O Jehovah, come and bless us! How long will you delay? Turn away your anger from us. ¹⁴ Satisfy us in our earliest youth[b] with your lovingkindness, giving us constant joy to the end of our lives. ¹⁵ Give us gladness in proportion to our former misery! Replace the evil years with good. ¹⁶ Let us see your miracles again; let our children see glorious things, the kind you used to do, ¹⁷ and let the Lord our God favor us and give us success.

91 WE LIVE WITHIN the shadow of the Almighty, sheltered by the God who is above all gods.

² This I declare, that he alone is my refuge, my place of safety; he is my God, and I am trusting him. ³ For he rescues you from every trap, and protects you from the fatal plague. ⁴ He will shield you with his wings! They will shelter you. His faithful promises are your armor. ⁵ Now you don't need to be afraid of the dark any more, nor fear the dangers of the day; ⁶ nor dread the plagues of darkness, nor disasters in the morning.[a]

⁷ Though a thousand fall at my side, though ten thousand are dying around me, the evil will not touch me. ⁸ I will see how the wicked are punished but I will not share it. ⁹ For Jehovah is my refuge! I choose the God above all gods to shelter me. ¹⁰ How then can evil overtake me or any plague come near? ¹¹ For he orders his angels to protect you wherever you go. ¹² They will steady you with their hands to keep you from stumbling against the rocks on the trail. ¹³ You can safely meet a lion or step on poisonous snakes, yes, even trample them beneath your feet!

¹⁴ For the Lord says, "Because he loves me, I will rescue him; I will make him great because he trusts in my name. ¹⁵ When he calls on me I will answer; I will be with him in trouble, and rescue him and honor him. ¹⁶ I will satisfy him with a full life[b] and give him my salvation."

A song to sing on the Lord's Day[a]

92 IT IS GOOD to say, "Thank you" to the Lord, to sing praises to the God who is above all gods.

² Every morning tell him, "Thank you for your kindness," and every evening rejoice in all his faithfulness. ³ Sing his praises, accompanied by music from the harp and lute and lyre. ⁴ You have done so much for me, O Lord. No wonder I am glad! I sing for joy.

⁵ O Lord, what miracles you do! And how deep are your thoughts! ⁶ Unthinking people do not understand them! No fool can comprehend this: ⁷ that although the wicked flourish like weeds, there is only eternal destruction ahead of them. ⁸ But the Lord continues forever, exalted in the heavens, ⁹ while his enemies—all evil-doers—shall be scattered.

¹⁰ But you have made me as strong as a wild bull. How refreshed I am by your blessings![b] ¹¹ I have heard the doom of my enemies announced and seen them destroyed. ¹² But the godly shall flourish like palm trees, and grow tall as the cedars of Lebanon. ¹³ For they are transplanted into the Lord's own garden, and are under his personal care. ¹⁴ Even in old age they will still produce fruit and be vital and green. ¹⁵ This honors the Lord, and exhibits his faithful care. He is my shelter. There is nothing but goodness in him!

93 JEHOVAH IS KING! He is robed in majesty and strength. The world is his

---

b Literally, "early."   91a Literally, "at noonday."   b Literally, "with long life."   92a Literally, "for the Sabbath day."   b Literally, "anointed with fresh oil."

throne.[a]

O Lord, you have reigned from prehistoric times, from the everlasting past. [3] The mighty oceans thunder your praise. [4] You are mightier than all the breakers pounding on the seashores of the world! [5] Your royal decrees cannot be changed. Holiness is forever the keynote of your reign.

94 LORD GOD, TO whom vengeance belongs, let your glory shine out. Arise and judge the earth; sentence the proud to the penalties they deserve. [3] Lord, how long shall the wicked be allowed to triumph and exult? [4] Hear their insolence! See their arrogance! How these men of evil boast! [5] See them oppressing your people, O Lord, afflicting those you love. [6,7] They murder widows, immigrants, and orphans, for "The Lord isn't looking," they say, "and besides, he[a] doesn't care."

[8] Fools! [9] Is God deaf and blind—he who makes ears and eyes? [10] He punishes the nations—won't he also punish you? He knows everything—doesn't he also know what you are doing?

[11] The Lord is fully aware of how limited and futile the thoughts of mankind are, [12,13] so he helps us by punishing us. This makes us follow his paths, and gives us respite from our enemies while God traps them and destroys them. [14] The Lord will not forsake his people, for they are his prize. [15] Judgment will again be just and all the upright will rejoice.

[16] Who will protect me from the wicked? Who will be my shield? [17] I would have died unless the Lord had helped me. [18] I screamed, "I'm slipping, Lord!" and he was kind and saved me.

[19] Lord, when doubts fill my mind, when my heart is in turmoil, quiet me and give me renewed hope and cheer. [20] Will you permit a corrupt government to rule under your protection—a government permitting wrong to defeat right? [21,22] Do you approve of those who condemn the innocent to death? No! The Lord my God is my fortress—the mighty Rock where I can hide. [23] God has made the sins of evil men to boomerang upon them! He will destroy them by their own plans. Jehovah our God will cut them off.

95 OH, COME, LET us sing to the Lord! Give a joyous shout in honor of the Rock of our salvation!

[2] Come before him with thankful hearts. Let us sing him psalms of praise. [3] For the Lord is a great God, the great King of[a] all gods. [4] He controls the formation of the depths of the earth and the mightiest mountains; all are his. [5] He made the sea and formed the land; they too are his. [6] Come, kneel before the Lord our Maker, [7] for he is our God. We are his sheep and he is our Shepherd. Oh, that you would hear him calling you today and come to him!

[8] Don't harden your hearts as Israel did in the wilderness[b] at Meribah and Massah. [9] For there your fathers doubted me, though they had seen so many of my miracles before. My patience was severely tried by their complaints. [10] "For forty years I watched them in disgust," the Lord God says. "They were a nation whose thoughts and heart were far away from me. They refused to accept my laws. [11] Therefore in mighty wrath I swore that they would never enter the Promised Land, the place of rest I planned for them."

96 SING A NEW song to the Lord! Sing it everywhere around the world! [2] Sing out his praises! Bless his name. Each day tell someone that he saves.

[3] Publish his glorious acts throughout the earth. Tell everyone about the amazing things he does. [4] For the Lord is great beyond description, and greatly to be praised. Worship only him among the gods! [5] For the gods of other nations are merely idols, but our God made the heavens! [6] Honor and majesty surround him; strength and beauty are in his Temple.

[7] O nations of the world, confess that God alone is glorious and strong. [8] Give him the glory he deserves! Bring your offering and come to worship him.[a] [9] Worship the Lord with the beauty of holy lives.[b] Let

---

a Literally, "The world is established . . . your throne is established."   94a Literally, "the God of Jacob."   95a Literally, "above."   b Exodus 17:7.   96a Literally, "enter his courts."   b Or, "in the priestly robes."

the earth tremble before him. [10] Tell the nations that Jehovah reigns! He rules the world. His power can never be overthrown. He will judge all nations fairly.

[11] Let the heavens be glad, the earth rejoice; let the vastness of the roaring seas demonstrate his glory. [12] Praise him for the growing fields, for they display his greatness. Let the trees of the forest rustle with praise. [13] For the Lord is coming to judge the earth; he will judge the nations fairly and with truth!

97 JEHOVAH IS KING! Let all the earth rejoice! Tell the farthest islands to be glad.

[2] Clouds and darkness surround him. Righteousness and justice are the foundation of his throne. [3] Fire goes forth before him and burns up all his foes. [4] His lightning flashes out across the world. The earth sees and trembles. [5] The mountains melt like wax before the Lord of all the earth. [6] The heavens declare his perfect righteousness; every nation sees his glory.

[7] Let those who worship idols be disgraced—all who brag about their worthless gods—for every god must bow to him! [8,9] Jerusalem and all the cities of Judah have heard of your justice, Lord, and are glad that you reign in majesty over the entire earth and are far greater than these other gods.

[10] The Lord loves those who hate evil; he protects the lives of his people, and rescues them from the wicked. [11] Light is sown for the godly and joy for the good. [12] May all who are godly be happy in the Lord and crown[a] him, our holy God.

98 SING A NEW song to the Lord telling about his mighty deeds! For he has won a mighty victory by his power and holiness. [2,3] He has announced this victory and revealed it to every nation by fulfilling his promise to be kind to Israel. The whole earth has seen God's salvation of his people. [4] That is why the earth breaks out in praise to God, and sings for utter joy!

[5] Sing your praise accompanied by music from the harp. [6] Let the cornets and trumpets shout! Make a joyful symphony before the Lord, the King! [7] Let the sea in all its vastness roar with praise! Let the earth and all those living on it shout, "Glory to the Lord."

[8,9] Let the waves clap their hands in glee, and the hills sing out their songs of joy before the Lord, for he is coming to judge the world with perfect justice.

99 JEHOVAH IS KING! Let the nations tremble! He is enthroned upon the cherubim. Let the whole earth shake.

[2] Jehovah sits in majesty in Zion, supreme above all rulers of the earth. [3] Let them reverence your great and holy name.

[4] This mighty King is determined to give justice. Fairness is the touchstone of everything he does. He gives justice throughout Israel. [5] Exalt the Lord our holy God! Bow low before his feet.

[6] When Moses and Aaron and Samuel, his prophet, cried to him for help, he answered them. [7] He spoke to them from the pillar of cloud and they followed his instructions. [8] O Jehovah our God! You answered them and forgave their sins, yet punished them when they went wrong.

[9] Exalt the Lord our God, and worship at his holy mountain in Jerusalem, for he is holy.

100 SHOUT WITH JOY before the Lord, O earth! [2] Obey him gladly; come before him, singing with joy.

[3] Try to realize what this means—the Lord is God! He made us—we are his people, the sheep of his pasture.

[4] Go through his open gates with great thanksgiving; enter his courts with praise. Give thanks to him and bless his name. [5] For the Lord is always good. He is always loving and kind, and his faithfulness goes on and on to each succeeding generation.

101 I WILL SING about your lovingkindness and your justice, Lord. I will sing your praises!

[2] I will try to walk a blameless path, but how I need your help, especially in my own home, where I long to act as I should.

---

a Literally, "give glory to his holy name."

³ Help me to refuse the low and vulgar things; help me to abhor all crooked deals of every kind, to have no part in them. ⁴ I will reject all selfishness and stay away from every evil. ⁵ I will not tolerate anyone who secretly slanders his neighbors; I will not permit conceit and pride. ⁶ I will make the godly of the land my heroes, and invite them to my home. Only those who are truly good shall be my servants. ⁷ But I will not allow those who deceive and lie to stay in my house. ⁸ My daily task will be to ferret out criminals and free the city of God from their grip.

A prayer when overwhelmed with trouble.

102 LORD, HEAR MY prayer! Listen to my plea!

² Don't turn away from me in this time of my distress. Bend down your ear and give me speedy answers, ³,⁴ for my days disappear like smoke. My health is broken and my heart is sick; it is trampled like grass and is withered. My food is tasteless, and I have lost my appetite. ⁵ I am reduced to skin and bones because of all my groaning and despair. ⁶ I am like a vulture in a far-off wilderness, or like an owl alone in the desert. ⁷ I lie awake, lonely as a solitary sparrow on the roof.

⁸ My enemies taunt me day after day and curse at me. ⁹,¹⁰ I eat ashes instead of bread. My tears run down into my drink because of your anger against me, because of your wrath. For you have rejected me and thrown me out. ¹¹ My life is passing swiftly as the evening shadows. I am withering like grass, ¹² while you, Lord, are a famous King forever. Your fame will endure to every generation.

¹³ I know that you will come and have mercy on Jerusalem—and now is the time to pity her—the time you promised help. ¹⁴ For your people love every stone in her walls and feel sympathy for every grain of dust in her streets. ¹⁵ Now let the nations and their rulers tremble before the Lord, before his glory. ¹⁶ For Jehovah will rebuild Jerusalem! He will appear in his glory!

¹⁷ He will listen to the prayers of the destitute, for he is never too busy to heed their requests. ¹⁸ I am recording this so that future generations will also praise the Lord for all that he has done. And a people that shall be created shall praise the Lord. ¹⁹ Tell them that God looked down from his temple in heaven, ²⁰ and heard the groans of his people in slavery—they were children of death—and released them, ²¹,²² so that multitudes would stream to the Temple in Jerusalem to praise him, and his praises were sung throughout the city; and many rulers throughout the earth came to worship him.

²³ He has cut me down in middle life, shortening my days. ²⁴ But I cried to him, "O God, you live forever and forever! Don't let me die half through my years! ²⁵ In ages past you laid the foundations of the earth, and made the heavens with your hands! ²⁶ They shall perish, but you go on forever. They will grow old, like worn-out clothing, and you will change them like a man putting on a new shirt and throwing away the old one! ²⁷ But you yourself never grow old. You are forever, and your years never end.

²⁸ But our families will continue; generation after generation will be preserved by your protection.

103 I BLESS THE holy name of God with all my heart. ² Yes, I will bless the Lord and not forget the glorious things he does for me.

³ He forgives all my sins. He heals me. ⁴ He ransoms me from hell. He surrounds me with lovingkindness and tender mercies. ⁵ He fills my life with good things! My youth is renewed like the eagle's! ⁶ He gives justice to all who are treated unfairly. ⁷ He revealed his will and nature to Moses and the people of Israel.

⁸ He is merciful and tender toward those who don't deserve it; he is slow to get angry and full of kindness and love. ⁹ He never bears a grudge, nor remains angry forever. ¹⁰ He has not punished us as we deserve for all our sins, ¹¹ for his mercy toward those who fear and honor him is as great as the height of the heavens above the earth. ¹² He has removed our sins as far away from us as the east is from the west. ¹³ He is like a father to us, tender and sympathetic to those who reverence him. ¹⁴ For he knows we are but dust, ¹⁵ and that our days are few and brief, like grass, like flowers, ¹⁶ blown

by the wind and gone forever.

[17,18] But the lovingkindness of the Lord is from everlasting to everlasting, to those who reverence him; his salvation is to children's children of those who are faithful to his covenant and remember to obey him!

[19] The Lord has made the heavens his throne; from there he rules over everything there is. [20] Bless the Lord, you mighty angels of his who carry out his orders, listening for each of his commands. [21] Yes, bless the Lord, you armies of his angels who serve him constantly.

[22] Let everything everywhere bless the Lord. And how I bless him too!

104 I BLESS THE Lord: O Lord my God, how great you are! You are robed with honor and with majesty and light! You stretched out the starry curtain of the heavens, [3] and hollowed out the surface of the earth to form the seas. The clouds are his chariots. He rides upon the wings of the wind. [4] The angels[a] are his messengers—his servants of fire!

[5] You bound the world together so that it would never fall apart. [6] You clothed the earth with floods of waters covering up the mountains. [7,8] You spoke, and at the sound of your shout the water collected into its vast ocean beds, and mountains rose and valleys sank to the levels you decreed. [9] And then you set a boundary for the seas, so that they would never again cover the earth.

[10] He placed springs in the valleys, and streams that gush from the mountains. [11] They give water for all the animals to drink. There the wild donkeys quench their thirst, [12] and the birds nest beside the streams and sing among the branches of the trees. [13] He sends rain upon the mountains and fills the earth with fruit. [14] The tender grass grows up at his command to feed the cattle, and there are fruit trees, vegetables and grain for man to cultivate, [15] and wine to make him glad, and olive oil as lotion for his skin, and bread to give him strength. [16] The Lord planted the cedars of Lebanon. They are tall and flourishing. [17] There the birds make their nests, the storks in the firs. [18] High in the mountains are pastures for the wild goats, and rock-badgers burrow in among the rocks and find protection there.

[19] He assigned the moon to mark the months, and the sun to mark the days. [20] He sends the night and darkness, when all the forest folk come out. [21] Then the young lions roar for their food, but they are dependent on the Lord. [22] At dawn they slink back into their dens to rest, [23] and men go off to work until the evening shadows fall again. [24] O Lord, what a variety you have made! And in wisdom you have made them all! The earth is full of your riches.

[25] There before me lies the mighty ocean, teeming with life of every kind, both great and small. [26] And look! See the ships! And over there, the whale you made to play in the sea. [27] Every one of these depends on you to give them daily food. [28] You supply it, and they gather it. You open wide your hand to feed them and they are satisfied with all your bountiful provision.

[29] But if you turn away from them, then all is lost. And when you gather up their breath, they die and turn again to dust. [30] Then you send your Spirit, and new life is born[b] to replenish all the living of the earth. [31] Praise God forever! How he must rejoice in all his work! [32] The earth trembles at his glance; the mountains burst into flame at his touch.

[33] I will sing to the Lord as long as I live. I will praise God to my last breath! [34] May he be pleased by all these thoughts about him, for he is the source of all my joy. [35] Let all sinners perish—all who refuse to praise him. But I will praise him. Hallelujah!

105 THANK THE LORD for all the glorious things he does; proclaim them to the nations. [2] Sing his praises and tell everyone about his miracles. [3] Glory in the Lord; O worshipers of God, rejoice.

[4] Search for him and for his strength, and keep on searching!

[5,6] Think of the mighty deeds he did for us, his chosen ones—descendants of God's servant Abraham, and of Jacob. Remember how he destroyed our enemies. [7] He is the Lord our God. His goodness[a] is seen everywhere throughout the land. [8,9] Though a

---

a Literally, "spirits."   b Literally, "created."   105 a Literally, "His judgments."

thousand generations pass he never forgets his promise, his covenant with Abraham and Isaac, [10,11] and confirmed with Jacob. This is his never-ending treaty with the people of Israel: *"I will give you the land of Canaan as your inheritance."* [12] He said this when they were but few in number, very few, and were only visitors in Canaan. [13] Later they were dispersed among the nations, and were driven from one kingdom to another; [14] but through it all he would not let one thing be done to them apart from his decision.[b] He destroyed many a king who tried! [15] "Touch not these chosen ones of mine," he warned, "and do not hurt my prophets."

[16] He called for a famine on the land of Canaan, cutting off its food supply. [17] Then he sent Joseph as a slave to Egypt to save his people from starvation. [18] There in prison they hurt his feet with fetters, and placed his neck in an iron collar, [19] until God's time finally came—how God tested his patience! [20] Then the king sent for him and set him free. [21] He was put in charge of all the king's possessions. [22] At his pleasure he could imprison the king's aides and teach the king's advisors.

[23] Then Jacob (Israel) arrived in Egypt and lived there with his sons. [24] In the years that followed, the people of Israel multiplied explosively, until they were a greater nation than their rulers. [25] At that point God turned the Egyptians against the Israelis; they hated and enslaved them.

[26] But God sent Moses as his representative, and Aaron with him, [27] to call down miracles of terror upon the land of Egypt. [28] They[c] followed his instructions and he sent thick darkness through the land, [29] and turned the nation's water into blood, poisoning the fish. [30] Then frogs invaded in enormous numbers; they were found even in the king's private rooms. [31] When Moses spoke, the flies and other insects swarmed in vast clouds from one end of Egypt to the other. [32] Instead of rain he sent down murderous hail, and lightning flashes overwhelmed the nation. [33] Their grape vines and fig trees were ruined; all the trees lay broken on the ground. [34] He spoke, and hordes of locusts came, [35] and ate up everything green, destroying all the crops. [36] Then he killed the oldest child in each Egyptian home, their pride and joy— [37] and brought his people safely out from Egypt, loaded with silver and gold; there were no sick and feeble folk among them then. [38] Egypt was glad when they were gone, for the dread of them was great.

[39] He spread out a cloud above them to shield them from the burning sun, and gave them a pillar of flame at night to give them light. [40] They asked for meat and he sent them quail, and gave them manna—bread from heaven. [41] He opened up a rock, and water gushed out to form a river through the dry and barren land; [42] for he remembered his sacred promises to Abraham his servant.

[43] So he brought his chosen ones singing into the Promised Land.[c] [44] He gave them the lands of the Gentiles, complete with their growing crops; they ate what others planted. [45] This was done to make them faithful and obedient to his laws. Hallelujah!

106 HALLELUJAH! THANK YOU, Lord! How good you are! Your love for us continues on forever. [2] Who can ever list the glorious miracles of God? Who can ever praise him half enough?

[3] Happiness comes to those who are fair to others and are always just and good.

[4] Remember me too, O Lord, while you are blessing and saving your people. [5] Let me share in your chosen ones' prosperity and rejoice in all their joys, and receive the glory you give to them.

[6] Both we and our fathers have sinned so much. [7] They weren't impressed by the wonder of your miracles in Egypt, and soon forgot your many acts of kindness to them. Instead they rebelled against you at the Red Sea. [8] Even so you saved them—to defend the honor of your name and demonstrate your power to all the world. [9] You commanded the Red Sea to divide, forming a dry road across its bottom. Yes, as dry as any desert! [10] Thus you rescued them from their enemies. [11] Then the water returned

---

b Literally, "He suffered no man to do them wrong."   c Implied.

and covered the road and drowned their foes; not one survived.

¹² Then at last his people believed him. Then they finally sang his praise.

¹³ Yet how quickly they forgot again! They wouldn't wait for him to act, ¹⁴ but demanded better food,ᵃ testing God's patience to the breaking point. ¹⁵ So he gave them their demands, but sent them leanness in their souls.ᵇ ¹⁶ They were envious of Moses; yes, and Aaron, too, the man anointedᶜ by God as his priest. ¹⁷ Because of this the earth opened and swallowed Dathan, Abiram and his friends; ¹⁸ and fire fell from heaven to consume these wicked men. ¹⁹,²⁰ For they preferred a statue of an ox that eats grass, to the glorious presence of God himself. ²¹,²² Thus they despised their Savior who had done such mighty miracles in Egypt and at the Sea. ²³ So the Lord declared he would destroy them. But Moses, his chosen one, stepped into the breach between the people and their God and begged him to turn from his wrath, and not destroy them.

²⁴ They refused to enter the Promised Land, for they wouldn't believe his solemn oath to care for them. ²⁵ Instead, they pouted in their tents and mourned and despised his command. ²⁶ Therefore he swore that he would kill them in the wilderness ²⁷ and send their children away to distant lands as exiles. ²⁸ Then our fathers joined the worshipers of Baal at Peor and even offered sacrifices to the dead!ᵈ ²⁹ With all these things they angered him—and so a plague broke out upon them ³⁰ and continued until Phineas executed those whose sins had caused the plague to start. ³¹ (For this good deed Phineas will be remembered forever.)

³² At Meribah, too, Israel angered God, causing Moses serious trouble, ³³ for he became angry and spoke foolishly. ³⁴ Nor did Israel destroy the nations in the land as God had told them to, ³⁵ but mingled in among the heathen and learned their evil ways, ³⁶ sacrificing to their idols, and were led away from God. ³⁷,³⁸ They even sacrificed their little children to the demons—the idols of Canaan—shedding innocent blood and polluting the land with murder. ³⁹ Their evil deeds defiled them, for their love of idols was adultery in the sight of God. ⁴⁰ That is why Jehovah's anger burned against his people, and he abhorred them. ⁴¹,⁴² That is why he let the heathen nations crush them. They were ruled by those who hated them and oppressed by their enemies.

⁴³ Again and again he delivered them from their slavery, but they continued to rebel against him, and were finally destroyed by their sin. ⁴⁴ Yet, even so, he listened to their cries and heeded their distress; ⁴⁵ he remembered his promises to them and relented because of his great love, ⁴⁶ and caused even their enemies who captured them to pity them.

⁴⁷ O Lord God, save us! Regather us from the nations so we can thank your holy name and rejoice and praise you.

⁴⁸ Blessed be the Lord, the God of Israel, from everlasting to everlasting. Let all the people say, "Amen!" Hallelujah!

107 SAY "THANK YOU" to the Lord for being so good, for always being so loving and kind. ² Has the Lord redeemed you? Then speak out! Tell others he has saved you from your enemies.

³ He brought the exiles back from the farthest corners of the earth. ⁴ They were wandering homeless in the desert, ⁵ hungry and thirsty and faint. ⁶ "Lord, help!" they cried, and he did! ⁷ He led them straight to safety and a place to live. ⁸ Oh, that these men would praise the Lord for his lovingkindness, and for all of his wonderful deeds! ⁹ For he satisfies the thirsty soul and fills the hungry soul with good.

¹⁰ Who are these who sit in darkness, in the shadow of death, crushed by misery and slavery? ¹¹ They rebelled against the Lord, scorning him who is the God above all gods. ¹² That is why he broke them with hard labor; they fell and none could help them rise again. ¹³ Then they cried to the Lord in their troubles, and he rescued them! ¹⁴ He led them from the darkness and shadow of death and snapped their chains. ¹⁵ Oh, that

---

a Literally, "lusted exceedingly."   b Or, "but sent a plague to punish them."   c Literally, "the holy one of Jehovah."   d Or, "to lifeless idols."

these men would praise the Lord for his lovingkindness and for all of his wonderful deeds! [16] For he broke down their prison gates of brass and cut apart their iron bars. [17] Others, the fools, were ill because of their sinful ways. [18] Their appetites were gone and death was near. [19] Then they cried to the Lord in their troubles, and he helped them and delivered them. [20] He spoke, and they were healed—snatched from the door of death. [21] Oh, that these men would praise the Lord for his lovingkindness and for all of his wonderful deeds! [22] Let them tell him "Thank you" as their sacrifice, and sing about his glorious deeds.

[23] And then there are the sailors sailing the seven seas, plying the trade routes of the world. [24] They, too, observe the power of God in action. [25] He calls to the storm winds; the waves rise high. [26] Their ships are tossed to the heavens and sink again to the depths; the sailors cringe in terror. [27] They reel and stagger like drunkards and are at their wit's end. [28] Then they cry to the Lord in their trouble, and he saves them. [29] He calms the storm and stills the waves. [30] What a blessing is that stillness, as he brings them safely into harbor! [31] Oh, that these men would praise the Lord for his lovingkindness and for all of his wonderful deeds! [32] Let them praise him publicly before the congregation, and before the leaders of the nation.

[33] He dries up rivers, [34] and turns the good land of the wicked into deserts of salt. [35] Again, he turns deserts into fertile, watered valleys. [36] He brings the hungry to settle there and build their cities, [37] to sow their fields and plant their vineyards, and reap their bumper crops! [38] How he blesses them! They raise big families there, and many cattle.

[39] But others become poor through oppression, trouble and sorrow. [40] For God pours contempt upon the haughty and causes princes to wander among ruins; [41] but he rescues the poor who are godly and gives them many children and much prosperity. [42] Good men everywhere will see it and be glad, while evil men are stricken silent.

[43] Listen, if you are wise, to what I am saying. Think about the lovingkindness of the Lord!

108 O GOD, MY heart is ready to praise you! I will sing and rejoice before you.

[2] Wake up, O harp and lyre! We will meet the dawn with song. [3] I will praise you everywhere around the world, in every nation. [4] For your lovingkindness is great beyond measure, high as the heavens. Your faithfulness reaches the skies. [5] His glory is far more vast than the heavens. It towers above the earth. [6] Hear the cry of your beloved child—come with mighty power and rescue me.

[7] God has given sacred promises; no wonder I exult! He has promised to give us all the land of Shechem, and also Succoth Valley. [8] "Gilead is mine to give to you," he says, "and Manasseh as well; the land of Ephraim is the helmet on my head. Judah is my scepter. [9] But Moab and Edom are despised;[a] and I will shout in triumph over the Philistines."

[10] Who but God can give me strength to conquer these fortified cities? Who else can lead me into Edom?

[11] Lord, have you thrown us away? Have you deserted our army? [12] Oh, help us fight against our enemies, for men are useless allies. [13] But with the help of God we shall do mighty acts of valor. For he treads down our foes.

109 O GOD OF my praise, don't stand silent and aloof [2] while the wicked slander me and tell their lies. [3] They have no reason to hate and fight me, yet they do! [4] I love them, but even while I am praying for them, they are trying to destroy me. [5] They return evil for good, and hatred for love.

[6] Show him how it feels![a] Let lies be told about him, and bring him to court before an unfair judge. [7] When his case is called for judgment, let him be pronounced guilty. Count his prayers as sins. [8] Let his years be few and brief; let others step forward to replace him. [9,10] May his children become

---

a Literally, "Moab is my washbasin; upon Edom I cast my shoe." 109a Implied.

fatherless and his wife a widow; may they be evicted from the ruins of their home. [11] May creditors seize his entire estate and strangers take all he has earned. [12,13] Let no one be kind to him; let no one pity his fatherless children. May they die. May his family name be blotted out in a single generation. [14] Punish the sins of his father and mother. Don't overlook them. [15] Think constantly about the evil things he has done, and cut off his name from the memory of man.

[16] For he refused all kindness to others, and persecuted those in need, and hounded brokenhearted ones to death. [17] He loved to curse others; now you curse him. He never blessed others; now don't you bless him. [18] Cursing is as much a part of him as his clothing, or as the water he drinks, or the rich food he eats.

[19] Now may those curses return and cling to him like his clothing or his belt. [20] This is the Lord's punishment upon my enemies who tell lies about me and threaten me with death.

[21] But as for me, O Lord, deal with me as your child, as one who bears your name! Because you are so kind, O Lord, deliver me.

[22,23] I am slipping down the hill to death; I am shaken off from life as easily as a man brushes a grasshopper from his arm. [24] My knees are weak from fasting and I am skin and bones. [25] I am a symbol of failure to all mankind; when they see me they shake their heads.

[26] Help me, O Lord my God! Save me because you are loving and kind. [27] Do it publicly, so all will see that you yourself have done it. [28] Then let them curse me if they like—I won't mind that if you are blessing me! For then all their efforts to destroy me will fail, and I shall go right on rejoicing!

[29] Make them fail in everything they do. Clothe them with disgrace. [30] But I will give repeated thanks to the Lord, praising him to everyone. [31] For he stands beside the poor and hungry to save them from their enemies.

110 JEHOVAH SAID TO my Lord the Messiah,[a] "Rule as my regent—I will subdue your enemies and make them bow low before you."

[2] Jehovah has established your throne[b] in Jerusalem[c] to rule over your enemies. [3] In that day of your power your people shall come to you willingly, dressed in holy altar robes.[d] And your strength shall be renewed day by day like morning dew. [4] Jehovah has taken oath, and will not rescind his vow, that you are a priest forever like[e] Melchizedek. [5] God stands beside you to protect you. He will strike down many kings in the day of his anger. [6] He will punish the nations, and fill them with their dead. He will crush many heads. [7] But he himself shall be refreshed from springs along the way.

111 HALLELUJAH! I WANT to express publicly before his people my heartfelt thanks to God for his mighty miracles. All who are thankful should ponder them with me. [3] For his miracles demonstrate his honor, majesty, and eternal goodness.

[4] Who can forget the wonders he performs—deeds of mercy and of grace? [5] He gives food to those who trust him; he never forgets his promises. [6] He has shown his great power to his people by giving them the land of Israel, though it was the home of many nations living there. [7] All he does is just and good, and all his laws are right, [8] for they are formed from truth and goodness, and stand firm forever. [9] He has paid a full ransom for his people; now they are always free to come to Jehovah (what a holy, awe-inspiring name that is).

[10] How can men be wise? The only way to begin is by reverence for God. For growth in wisdom comes from obeying his laws. Praise his name forever.

112 PRAISE THE LORD! For all who fear God and trust in him are blessed beyond expression. Yes, happy is the man who delights in doing his commands.

[2] His children shall be honored everywhere, for good men's sons have a special heritage. [3] He himself shall be wealthy, and

---

a Implied. In Matthew 22:41–45, Jesus applies these words to himself.   b Literally, "The Lord will send forth the rod of your strength out of Zion."   c Literally, "from Zion."   d Literally, "in holy array." e Literally, "after the manner of."

his good deeds will never be forgotten.[a]
[4] When darkness overtakes him, light will
come bursting in. He is kind and merciful—
[5] and all goes well for the generous man who
conducts his business fairly.

[6] Such a man will not be overthrown by
evil circumstances. God's constant care of
him will make a deep impression on all who
see it. [7] He does not fear bad news, nor live
in dread of what may happen. For he is
settled in his mind that Jehovah will take
care of him. [8] That is why he is not afraid,
but can calmly face his foes. [9] He gives generously to those in need. His deeds will
never be forgotten.[a] He shall have influence
and honor.

[10] Evil-minded men will be infuriated
when they see all this; they will gnash their
teeth in anger and slink away, their hopes
thwarted.

113 HALLELUJAH! O SERVANTS of Jehovah, praise his name. [2] Blessed is his
name forever and forever. [3] Praise him from
sunrise to sunset! [4] For he is high above the
nations; his glory is far greater than the
heavens.

[5] Who can be compared with God enthroned on high? [6] Far below him are the
heavens and the earth; he stoops to look,
[7] and lifts the poor from the dirt, and the
hungry from the garbage dump, [8] and sets
them among princes! [9] He gives children to
the childless wife, so that she becomes a
happy mother.

Hallelujah! Praise the Lord.

114 LONG AGO WHEN the Israelis escaped from Egypt, from that land of
foreign tongue, [2] then the lands of Judah
and of Israel became God's new home and
kingdom.

[3] The Red Sea saw them coming and
quickly broke apart before them. The Jordan River opened up a path for them to
cross. [4] The mountains skipped like rams,
the little hills like lambs! [5] What's wrong,
Red Sea, that made you cut yourself in two?
What happened, Jordan River, to your waters? Why were they held back? [6] Why,

mountains, did you skip like rams? Why,
little hills, like lambs?

[7] Tremble, O earth, at the presence of the
Lord, the God of Jacob. [8] For he caused
gushing streams to burst from flinty rock.

115 GLORIFY YOUR NAME, not ours, O
Lord! Cause everyone to praise your
lovingkindness and your truth. [2] Why let
the nations say, "Their God is dead!"[a]

[3] For he is in the heavens, and does as
he wishes. [4] Their gods are merely man-
made things of silver and of gold. [5] They
can't talk or see, despite their eyes and
mouths! [6] Nor can they hear, nor smell,
[7] nor use their hands or feet! Nor speak!
[8] And those who make and worship them
are just as foolish as their idols are.

[9] O Israel, trust the Lord! He is your
helper. He is your shield. [10] O priests of
Aaron, trust the Lord! He is your helper;
he is your shield. [11] All of you, his people,
trust in him. He is your helper; he is your
shield.

[12] Jehovah is constantly thinking about
us and he will surely bless us. He will bless
the people of Israel and the priests of
Aaron, [13] and all, both great and small, who
reverence him.

[14] May the Lord richly bless both you
and your children. [15] Yes, Jehovah who
made heaven and earth will personally bless
you! [16] The heavens belong to the Lord, but
he has given the earth to all mankind.

[17] The dead cannot sing praises to Jehovah here on earth,[b] [18] but we can! We praise
him forever! Hallelujah! Praise the Lord!

116 I LOVE THE Lord because he hears
my prayers and answers them. [2] Because he bends down and listens, I will pray
as long as I breathe!

[3] Death stared me in the face—I was
frightened and sad. [4] Then I cried, "Lord,
save me!" [5] How kind he is! How good he
is! So merciful, this God of ours! [6] The Lord
protects the simple and the childlike; I was
facing death and then he saved me. [7] Now
I can relax. For the Lord has done this wonderful miracle for me. [8] He has saved me

---

a Literally, "his righteousness endures forever."   115a Literally, "Where is their God?"
b Implied.

from death, my eyes from tears, my feet from stumbling. ⁹ I shall live! Yes, in his presence—here on earth!

¹⁰,¹¹ In my discouragement I thought, "They are lying when they say I will recover."ᵃ ¹² But now what can I offer Jehovah for all he has done for me? ¹³ I will bring him an offering of wineᵇ and praise his name for saving me. ¹⁴ I will publicly bring him the sacrifice I vowed I would. ¹⁵ His loved ones are very precious to him and he does not lightly let them die.ᶜ

¹⁶ O Lord, you have freed me from my bonds and I will serve you forever. ¹⁷ I will worship you and offer you a sacrifice of thanksgiving. ¹⁸,¹⁹ Here in the courts of the Temple in Jerusalem, before all the people, I will pay everything I vowed to the Lord. Praise the Lord.

117 PRAISE THE LORD, all nations everywhere. Praise him, all the peoples of the earth. ² For he loves us very dearly, and his truth endures. Praise the Lord.

118 OH, THANK THE Lord, for he's so good! His lovingkindness is forever. ² Let the congregation of Israel praise him with these same words: "His lovingkindness is forever." ³ And let the priests of Aaron chant, "His lovingkindness is forever." ⁴ Let the Gentile converts chant, "His lovingkindness is forever."

⁵ In my distress I prayed to the Lord and he answered me and rescued me. ⁶ He is for me! How can I be afraid? What can mere man do to me? ⁷ The Lord is on my side, he will help me. Let those who hate me beware.

⁸ It is better to trust the Lord than to put confidence in men. ⁹ It is better to take refuge in him than in the mightiest king!

¹⁰ Though all the nations of the world attack me, I will march out behind his banner and destroy them. ¹¹ Yes, they surround and attack me; but with his flag flying above me I will cut them off. ¹² They swarm around me like bees; they blaze against me

like a roaring flame. Yet beneath his flag I shall destroy them. ¹³ You did your best to kill me, O my enemy, but the Lord helped me. ¹⁴ He is my strength and song in the heat of battle, and now he has given me the victory. ¹⁵,¹⁶ Songs of joy at the news of our rescue are sung in the homes of the godly. The strong arm of the Lord has done glorious things! ¹⁷ I shall not die, but live to tell of all his deeds. ¹⁸ The Lord has punished me, but not handed me over to death.

¹⁹ Open the gates of the Templeᵃ—I will go in and give him my thanks. ²⁰ Those gates are the way into the presence of the Lord, and the godly enter there. ²¹ O Lord, thank you so much for answering my prayer and saving me.

²² The stone rejected by the builders has now become the capstone of the arch!ᵇ ²³ This is the Lord's doing, and it is marvelous to see! ²⁴ This is the day the Lord has made. We will rejoice and be glad in it. ²⁵ O Lord, please help us. Save us. Give us success. ²⁶ Blessed is the one who is coming, the one sentᶜ by the Lord. We bless you from the Temple.

²⁷,²⁸ Jehovah God is our light. I present to him my sacrifice upon the altar, for you are my God, and I shall give you this thanks and this praise. ²⁹ Oh, give thanks to the Lord, for he is so good! For his lovingkindness is forever.

119 HAPPY ARE ALL who perfectly follow the laws of God. ² Happy are all who search for God, and always do his will, ³ rejecting compromise with evil, and walking only in his paths. ⁴ You have given us your laws to obey— ⁵ oh, how I want to follow them consistently. ⁶ Then I will not be disgraced, for I will have a clean record.

⁷ After you have correctedᵃ me I will thank you by living as I should! ⁸ I *will* obey! Oh, don't forsake me and let me slip back into sin again.ᵇ

⁹ How can a young man stay pure? By reading your Word and following its rules. ¹⁰ I have tried my best to find you—don't

---

a Literally, "I said in my alarm, all men are liars." offering of wine for saving me.   c Literally, "Precious in the sight of the Lord is the death of his saints." See context for validity of the paraphrase.   **118a** Literally, "the gates of righteousness." b Literally, "the head of the corner."   c Literally, "in the name of the Lord."   **119a** Literally, "when I learn (have experienced) your righteous judgments." b Literally, "Oh, forsake me not utterly."

let me wander off from your instructions. [11] I have thought much about your words, and stored them in my heart so that they would hold me back from sin.

[12] Blessed Lord, teach me your rules. [13] I have recited your laws, [14] and rejoiced in them more than in riches. [15] I will meditate upon them and give them my full respect. [16] I will delight in them and not forget them.

[17] Bless me with life[c] so that I can continue to obey you. [18] Open my eyes to see wonderful things in your Word. [19] I am but a pilgrim here on earth: how I need a map —and your commands are my chart and guide. [20] I long for your instructions more than I can tell.

[21] You rebuke those cursed proud ones who refuse your commands— [22] don't let them scorn me for obeying you. [23] For even princes sit and talk against me, but I will continue in your plans. [24] Your laws are both my light and my counselors.

[25] I am completely discouraged—I lie in the dust. Revive me by your Word. [26] I told you my plans and you replied. Now give me your instructions. [27] Make me understand what you want; for then I shall see your miracles.

[28] I weep with grief; my heart is heavy with sorrow; encourage and cheer me with your words. [29,30] Keep me far from every wrong; help me, undeserving as I am, to obey your laws, for I have chosen to do right. [31] I cling to your commands and follow them as closely as I can. Lord, don't let me make a mess of things. [32] If you will only help me to want your will, then I will follow your laws even more closely.

[33,34] Just tell me what to do and I will do it, Lord. As long as I live I'll wholeheartedly obey. [35] Make me walk along the right paths for I know how delightful they really are.

[36] Help me to prefer obedience to making money! [37] Turn me away from wanting any other[d] plan than yours. Revive my heart toward you. [38] Reassure me that your promises are for me, for I trust and revere you.

[39] How I dread being mocked for obeying, for your laws are right and good. [40,41,42] I long to obey them! Therefore in fairness renew my life, for this was your promise—yes, Lord, to save me! Now spare me by your kindness and your love. Then I will have an answer for those who taunt me, for I trust your promises.

[43] May I never forget your words; for they are my only hope. [44,45,46] Therefore I will keep on obeying you forever and forever, free within the limits of your laws. I will speak to kings about their value, and they will listen with interest and respect.

[47] How I love your laws! How I enjoy your commands! [48] "Come, come to me," I call to them, for I love them and will let them fill my life.

[49,50] Never forget your promises to me your servant, for they are my only hope. They give me strength in all my troubles; how they refresh and revive me! [51] Proud men hold me in contempt for obedience to God, but I stand unmoved. [52] From my earliest youth I have tried to obey you; your Word has been my comfort.

[53] I am very angry with those who spurn your commands. [54] For these laws of yours have been my source of joy and singing through all these years of my earthly pilgrimage. [55] I obey them even at night and keep my thoughts, O Lord, on you. [56] What a blessing this has been to me—to constantly obey.

[57] Jehovah is mine! And I promise to obey! [58] With all my heart I want your blessings. Be merciful just as you promised. [59,60] I thought about the wrong direction in which I was headed, and turned around and came running back to you. [61] Evil men have tried to drag me into sin, but I am firmly anchored to your laws.

[62] At midnight I will rise to give my thanks to you for your good laws. [63] Anyone is my brother who fears and trusts the Lord and obeys him. [64] O Lord, the earth is full of your lovingkindness! Teach me your good paths.

[65] Lord, I am overflowing with your blessings, just as you promised. [66] Now teach me good judgment as well as knowledge. For your laws are my guide. [67] I used to wander off until you punished me; now I closely follow all you say. [68] You are good

---

c Literally, "deal bountifully that I may live."　　d Literally, "from beholding vanity."

and do only good; make me follow your lead.

⁶⁹ Proud men have made up lies about me, but the truth is that I obey your laws with all my heart. ⁷⁰ Their minds are dull and stupid, but I have sense enough to follow you.

⁷¹,⁷² The punishment you gave me was the best thing that could have happened to me, for it taught me to pay attention to your laws. They are more valuable to me than millions in silver and gold!

⁷³ You made my body, Lord; now give me sense to heed your laws. ⁷⁴ All those who fear and trust in you will welcome me because I too am trusting in your Word.

⁷⁵,⁷⁶,⁷⁷ I know, O Lord, that your decisions are right and that your punishment was right and did me good. Now let your lovingkindness comfort me, just as you promised. Surround me with your tender mercies, that I may live. For your law is my delight.

⁷⁸ Let the proud be disgraced, for they have cut me down with all their lies. But I will concentrate my thoughts upon your laws.

⁷⁹ Let all others join me, who trust and fear you, and we will discuss your laws. ⁸⁰ Help me to love your every wish; then I will never have to be ashamed of myself.

⁸¹ I faint for your salvation; but I expect your help, for you have promised it. ⁸² My eyes are straining to see your promises come true. When will you comfort me with your help? ⁸³ I am shriveled like a wineskin in the smoke, exhausted with waiting. But still I cling to your laws and obey them. ⁸⁴ How long must I wait before you punish those who persecute me? ⁸⁵,⁸⁶ These proud men who hate your truth and laws have dug deep pits for me to fall in. Their lies have brought me into deep trouble. Help me, for you love only truth. ⁸⁷ They had almost finished me off, yet I refused to yield and disobey your laws. ⁸⁸ In your kindness, spare my life; then I can continue to obey you.

⁸⁹ Forever, O Lord, your Word stands firm in heaven. ⁹⁰,⁹¹ Your faithfulness extends to every generation, like the earth you created; it endures by your decree, for everything serves your plans.

⁹² I would have despaired and perished unless your laws had been my deepest delight. ⁹³ I will never lay aside your laws, for you have used them to restore my joy and health. ⁹⁴ I am yours! Save me! For I have tried to live according to your desires. ⁹⁵ Though the wicked hide along the way to kill me, I will quietly keep my mind upon your promises.

⁹⁶ Nothing is perfect except your words. ⁹⁷ Oh, how I love them. I think about them all day long. ⁹⁸ They make me wiser than my enemies, because they are my constant guide. ⁹⁹ Yes, wiser than my teachers, for I am ever thinking of your rules. ¹⁰⁰ They make me even wiser than the aged.

¹⁰¹ I have refused to walk the paths of evil for I will remain obedient to your Word. ¹⁰²,¹⁰³ No, I haven't turned away from what you taught me; your words are sweeter than honey. ¹⁰⁴ And since only your rules can give me wisdom and understanding, no wonder I hate every false teaching.

¹⁰⁵ Your words are a flashlight to light the path ahead of me, and keep me from stumbling. ¹⁰⁶ I've said it once and I'll say it again and again: I will obey these wonderful laws of yours.

¹⁰⁷ I am close to death at the hands of my enemies; oh, give me back my life again, just as you promised me. ¹⁰⁸ Accept my grateful thanks and teach me your desires. ¹⁰⁹ My life hangs in the balance, but I will not give up obedience to your laws. ¹¹⁰ The wicked have set their traps for me along your path, but I will not turn aside. ¹¹¹ Your laws are my joyous treasure forever. ¹¹² I am determined to obey you until I die.

¹¹³ I hate those who are undecided whether or not to obey you; but my choice is clear—I love your law. ¹¹⁴ You are my refuge and my shield, and your promises are my only source of hope. ¹¹⁵ Begone, you evil-minded men. Don't try to stop me from obeying God's commands. ¹¹⁶ Lord, you promised to let me live! Never let it be said that God failed me. ¹¹⁷ Hold me safe above the heads of all my enemies; then I can continue to obey your laws.

¹¹⁸ But you have rejected all who reject your laws. They are only fooling themselves. ¹¹⁹ The wicked are the scum you skim off and throw away; no wonder I love to obey your laws! ¹²⁰ I tremble in fear of you;

I fear your punishments.

¹²¹ Don't leave me to the mercy of my enemies, for I have done what is right; I've been perfectly fair. ¹²² Commit yourself to bless me! Don't let the proud oppress me! ¹²³ My eyes grow dim with longing for you to fulfill your wonderful promise to rescue me. ¹²⁴ Lord, deal with me in lovingkindness, and teach me, your servant, to obey; ¹²⁵ for I am your servant; therefore give me common sense to apply your rules to everything I do.

¹²⁶ Lord, it is time for you to act. For these evil men have violated your laws, ¹²⁷ while I love your commandments more than the finest gold. ¹²⁸ Every law of God is right, whatever it concerns. I hate every other way.

¹²⁹ Your laws are wonderful; no wonder I obey them. ¹³⁰ As your plan unfolds, even the simple can understand it. ¹³¹ No wonder I wait expectantly for each of your commands.

¹³² Come and have mercy on me as is your way with those who love you. ¹³³ Guide me with your laws so that I will not be overcome by evil. ¹³⁴ Rescue me from the oppression of evil men; then I can obey you. ¹³⁵ Look down in love upon me and teach me all your laws. ¹³⁶ I weep because your laws are disobeyed.

¹³⁷ O Lord, you are just and your punishments are fair. ¹³⁸ Your demands are just and right. ¹³⁹ I am indignant and angry because of the way my enemies have disregarded your laws. ¹⁴⁰ I have thoroughly tested your promises and that is why I love them so much. ¹⁴¹ I am worthless and despised, but I don't despise your laws.

¹⁴² Your justice is eternal for your laws are perfectly fair. ¹⁴³ In my distress and anguish, your commandments comfort me. ¹⁴⁴ Your laws are always fair; help me to understand them and I shall live.

¹⁴⁵ I am praying with great earnestness; answer me, O Lord, and I will obey your laws. ¹⁴⁶ "Save me," I cry, "for I am obeying." ¹⁴⁷ Early in the morning, before the sun is up, I was praying and pointing out how much I trust in you. ¹⁴⁸ I stay awake through the night to think about your promises. ¹⁴⁹ Because you are so loving and kind, listen to me and make me well again.

¹⁵⁰ Here come these lawless men to attack me; ¹⁵¹ but you are near, O Lord; all your commandments are based on truth. ¹⁵² I have known from earliest days that your will never changes. ¹⁵³ Look down upon my sorrows and rescue me, for I am obeying your commands. ¹⁵⁴ Yes, rescue me and give me back my life again just as you have promised. ¹⁵⁵ The wicked are far from salvation for they do not care for your laws. ¹⁵⁶ Lord, how great is your mercy; oh, give me back my life again.

¹⁵⁷ My enemies are so many. They try to make me disobey, but I have not swerved from your will. ¹⁵⁸ I loathed these traitors because they care nothing for your laws. ¹⁵⁹ Lord, see how much I really love your demands. Now give me back my life and health because you are so kind. ¹⁶⁰ There is utter truth in all your laws; your decrees are eternal.

¹⁶¹ Great men have persecuted me, though they have no reason to, but I stand in awe of only your words. ¹⁶² I rejoice in your laws like one who finds a great treasure. ¹⁶³ How I hate all falsehood but how I love your laws. ¹⁶⁴ I will praise you seven times a day because of your wonderful laws.

¹⁶⁵ Those who love your laws have great peace of heart and mind and do not stumble. ¹⁶⁶ I long for your salvation, Lord, and so I have obeyed your laws. ¹⁶⁷ I have looked for your commandments and I love them very much; ¹⁶⁸ yes, I have searched for them. You know this because everything I do is known to you.

¹⁶⁹ O Lord, listen to my prayers; give me the common sense you promised. ¹⁷⁰ Hear my prayers; rescue me as you said you would. ¹⁷¹ I praise you for letting me learn your laws. ¹⁷² I will sing about their wonder, for each of them is just. ¹⁷³ Stand ready to help me because I have chosen to follow your will. ¹⁷⁴ O Lord, I have longed for your salvation, and your law is my delight. ¹⁷⁵ If you will let me live, I will praise you; let your laws assist me.

¹⁷⁶ I have wandered away like a lost sheep; come and find me for I have not turned away from your commandments.

120 IN MY TROUBLES I pled with God to help me and he did!

² Deliver me, O Lord, from liars. ³ O lying tongue, what shall be your fate? ⁴ You shall be pierced with sharp arrows and burned with glowing coals.ᵃ

⁵,⁶ My troubles pile high among these haters of the Lord, these men of Meshech and Kedar. I am tired of being here among these men who hate peace. ⁷ I am for peace, but they are for war, and my voice goes unheeded in their councils.

121 SHALL I LOOK to the mountain gods for help? ² No! My help is from Jehovah who made the mountains! And the heavens too! ³,⁴ He will never let me stumble, slip or fall. For he is always watching, never sleeping.

⁵ Jehovah himself is caring for you! He is your defender.ᵃ ⁶ He protects you day and night. ⁷ He keeps you from all evil, and preserves your life. ⁸ He keeps his eye upon you as you come and go, and always guards you.

122 I WAS GLAD for the suggestion of going to Jerusalem, to the Temple of the Lord. ²,³ Now we are standing here inside the crowded city. ⁴ All Israel—Jehovah's people—have come to worship as the law requires, to thank and praise the Lord. ⁵ Look! There are the judges holding court beside the city gates, deciding all the people's arguments.

⁶ Pray for the peace of Jerusalem. May all who love this city prosper. ⁷ O Jerusalem, may there be peace within your walls and prosperity in your palaces. ⁸ This I ask for the sake of all my brothers and my friends who live here; ⁹ and may there be peace as a protection to the Temple of the Lord.

123 O GOD ENTHRONED in heaven, I lift my eyes to you.

² We look to Jehovah our God for his mercy and kindness just as a servant keeps his eyes upon his master or a slave girl watches her mistress for the slightest signal. ³,⁴ Have mercy on us, Lord, have mercy. For we have had our fill of contempt and of the scoffing of the rich and proud.

124 IF THE LORD had not been on our side (let all Israel admit it), if the Lord had not been on our side, ²,³ we would have been swallowed alive by our enemies, destroyed by their anger. ⁴,⁵ We would have drowned beneath the flood of these men's fury and pride.

⁶ Blessed be Jehovah who has not let them devour us. ⁷ We have escaped with our lives as a bird from a hunter's snare. The snare is broken and we are free!

⁸ Our help is from the Lord who made heaven and earth.

125 THOSE WHO TRUST in the Lord are steady as Mount Zion, unmoved by any circumstance.

² Just as the mountains surround and protect Jerusalem, so the Lord surrounds and protects his people. ³ For the wicked shall not rule the godly, lest the godly be forced to do wrong. ⁴ O Lord, do good to those who are good, whose hearts are right with the Lord; ⁵ but lead evil men to execution. And let Israel have quietness and peace.

126 WHEN JEHOVAH BROUGHT back his exiles to Jerusalem, it was like a dream! ² How we laughed and sang for joy. And the other nations said, "What amazing things the Lord has done for them."

³ Yes, glorious things! What wonder! What joy! ⁴ May we be refreshedᵃ as by streams in the desert.

⁵ Those who sow tears shall reap joy. ⁶ Yes, they go out weeping, carrying seed for sowing, and return singing, carrying their sheaves.

127 UNLESS THE LORD builds a house, the builders' work is useless. Unless the Lord protects a city, sentries do no good. ² It is senseless for you to work so hard from early morning until late at night, fearing you will starve to death; for God wants his loved ones to get their proper rest.

³ Children are a gift from God; they are his reward. ⁴ Children born to a young man are like sharp arrows to defend him.

---

a Literally, "with coals of the broom tree."   121a Literally, "your shade at your right hand."
126a Literally, "Restore our fortunes, Lord."

[5] Happy is the man who has his quiver full of them. That man shall have the help he needs when arguing with his enemies.[a]

128 BLESSINGS ON ALL who reverence and trust the Lord—on all who obey him!
[2] Their reward shall be prosperity and happiness. [3] Your wife shall be contented in your home. And look at all those children! There they sit around the dinner table as vigorous and healthy as young olive trees. [4] That is God's reward to those who reverence and trust him.
[5] May the Lord continually bless you with heaven's blessings[a] as well as with human joys.[b] [6] May you live to enjoy your grandchildren! And may God bless Israel!

129 PERSECUTED FROM MY earliest youth (Israel is speaking), [2] and faced with never-ending discrimination—but not destroyed! My enemies have never been able to finish me off!
[3,4] Though my back is cut to ribbons with their whips, the Lord is good. For he has snapped the chains that evil men had bound me with.
[5] May all who hate the Jews be brought to ignominious defeat. [6,7] May they be as grass in shallow soil, turning sere and yellow when half grown, ignored by the reaper, despised by the binder. [8] And may those passing by refuse to bless them by saying, "Jehovah's blessings be upon you; we bless you in Jehovah's name."

130 O LORD, FROM the depths of despair I cry for your help: [2] "Hear me! Answer! Help me!"
[3,4] Lord, if you keep in mind our sins then who can ever get an answer to his prayers? But you forgive! What an awesome thing this is! [5] That is why I wait expectantly, trusting God to help, for he has promised. [6] I long for him more than sentinels long for the dawn.
[7] O Israel, hope in the Lord; for he is loving and kind, and comes to us with arm-

loads of salvation. [8] He himself shall ransom Israel from her slavery to sin.

131 LORD, I AM not proud and haughty. I don't think myself better than others. I don't pretend to "know it all." [2] I am quiet now before the Lord, just as a child who is weaned from the breast. Yes, my begging has been stilled.
[3] O Israel, you too should quietly trust in the Lord—now, and always.

132 LORD, DO YOU remember that time when my[a] heart was so filled with turmoil? [2-5] I couldn't rest, I couldn't sleep, thinking how I ought to build a permanent home for the Ark[b] of the Lord, a Temple for the mighty one of Israel. Then I vowed that I would do it; I made a solemn promise to the Lord.
[6] First the Ark was in[c] Ephrathah, then in the distant countryside of Jaar. [7] But now it will be settled in the Temple, in God's permanent home here on earth. That is where we will go to worship him.[d] [8] Arise, O Lord, and enter your Temple with the Ark, the symbol of your power.
[9] We will clothe the priests in white, the symbol of all purity. May our nation shout for joy.
[10] Do not reject your servant David—the king you chose for your people. [11] For you promised me that my son would sit on my throne and succeed me. And surely you will never go back on a promise! [12] You also promised that if my descendants will obey the terms of your contract with me, then the dynasty of David shall never end.
[13] O Lord, you have chosen Jerusalem[e] as your home: [14] "This is my permanent home where I shall live," you said, "for I have always wanted it this way. [15] I will make this city prosperous and satisfy her poor with food. [16] I will clothe her priests with salvation; her saints shall shout for joy. [17] David's power shall grow, for I have decreed for him a mighty Son.[f] [18] I'll clothe his enemies with shame, but he shall be a glorious King."

---

a Literally, "when they speak with their enemies in the gate."   128a Literally, "from Zion."
b Literally, "of Jerusalem."   132a Literally, "David's soul."   b Implied.   c Literally, "Lo, we heard of it in Ephrathah."   d Literally, "We will go into his tabernacles; we will worship at his footstool."
e Literally, "Zion."   f Literally, "a progeny."

133 HOW WONDERFUL IT is, how pleasant, when brothers live in harmony! [2] For harmony is as precious as the fragrant anointing oil that was poured over Aaron's head, and ran down onto his beard, and onto the border of his robe. [3] Harmony is as refreshing as the dew on Mount Hermon, on the mountains of Israel. And God has pronounced this eternal blessing on Jerusalem,[a] even life forevermore.

134 OH, BLESS THE Lord, you who serve him as watchmen in the Temple every night. [2] Lift your hands in holiness and bless the Lord.
[3] The Lord bless you from Zion—the Lord who made heaven and earth.

135 HALLELUJAH! YES, LET his people praise him as they stand in his Temple courts. [3] Praise the Lord because he is so good; sing to his wonderful name. [4] For the Lord has chosen Israel as his personal possession.
[5] I know the greatness of the Lord—that he is greater far than any other god. [6] He does whatever pleases him throughout all of heaven and earth, and in the deepest seas. [7] He makes mists rise throughout the earth and sends the lightning to bring down the rain; and sends the winds from his treasuries. [8] He destroyed the eldest child in each Egyptian home, along with the firstborn of the flocks. [9] He did great miracles in Egypt before Pharaoh and all his people. [10] He smote great nations, slaying mighty kings— [11] Sihon, king of Amorites; and Og, the king of Bashan; and the kings of Canaan— [12] and gave their land as an eternal gift to his people Israel.
[13] O Jehovah, your name endures forever; your fame is known to every generation. [14] For Jehovah will vindicate his people, and have compassion on his servants.
[15] The heathen worship idols of gold and silver, made by men— [16] idols with speechless mouths and sightless eyes [17] and ears that cannot hear; they cannot even breathe. [18] Those who make them become like them! And so do all who trust in them!

[19] O Israel, bless Jehovah! High priests of Aaron, bless his name. [20] O Levite priests, bless the Lord Jehovah! Oh, bless his name, all of you who trust and reverence him. [21] All people of Jerusalem,[a] praise the Lord, for he lives here in Jerusalem. Hallelujah!

136 OH, GIVE THANKS to the Lord, for he is good; his lovingkindness continues forever.
[2] Give thanks to the God of gods, for his lovingkindness continues forever. [3] Give thanks to the Lord of lords, for his lovingkindness continues forever. [4] Praise him who alone does mighty miracles, for his lovingkindness continues forever. [5] Praise him who made the heavens, for his lovingkindness continues forever. [6] Praise him who planted the water within the earth,[a] for his lovingkindness continues forever. [7] Praise him who made the heavenly lights, for his lovingkindness continues forever: [8] the sun to rule the day, for his lovingkindness continues forever; [9] and the moon and stars at night, for his lovingkindness continues forever. [10] Praise the God who smote the firstborn of Egypt, for his lovingkindness to Israel[b] continues forever. [11,12] He brought them out with mighty power and upraised fist to strike their enemies, for his lovingkindness to Israel[b] continues forever. [13] Praise the Lord who opened the Red Sea to make a path before them, for his lovingkindness continues forever, [14] and led them safely through, for his lovingkindness continues forever— [15] but drowned Pharaoh's army in the sea, for his lovingkindness to Israel[b] continues forever.
[16] Praise him who led his people through the wilderness, for his lovingkindness continues forever. [17] Praise him who saved his people from the power of mighty kings, for his lovingkindness continues forever, [18] and killed famous kings who were their enemies, for his lovingkindness to Israel[b] continues forever: [19] Sihon, king of Amorites—for God's lovingkindness to Israel[b] continues forever— [20] and Og, king of Bashan—for his lovingkindness to Israel[b] continues forever. [21] God gave the land of these kings

---

a Literally, "Zion." 135a Literally, "the Lord be blessed from Zion." 136a Or, "who separated the earth from the oceans." b Implied.

to Israel as a gift forever, for his lovingkindness to Israel[c] continues forever; [22] yes, a permanent gift to his servant Israel, for his lovingkindness continues forever.

[23] He remembered our utter weakness, for his lovingkindness continues forever. [24] And saved us from our foes, for his lovingkindness continues forever.

[25] He gives food to every living thing, for his lovingkindness continues forever. [26] Oh, give thanks to the God of heaven, for his lovingkindness continues forever.

137 WEEPING, WE SAT beside the rivers of Babylon thinking of Jerusalem. [2] We have put away our lyres, hanging them upon the branches of the willow trees, [3,4] for how can we sing? Yet our captors, our tormentors, demand that we sing for them the happy songs of Zion! [5,6] If I forget you, O Jerusalem, let my right hand forget its skill upon the harp. If I fail to love her more than my highest joy, let me never sing again.

[7] O Jehovah, do not forget what these Edomites did on that day when the armies of Babylon captured Jerusalem. "Raze her to the ground!" they yelled. [8] O Babylon, evil beast, you shall be destroyed. Blessed is the man who destroys you as you have destroyed us. [9] Blessed is the man who takes your babies and smashes them against the rocks![a]

138 LORD, WITH ALL my heart I thank you. I will sing your praises before the armies of angels[a] in heaven. [2] I face your Temple as I worship, giving thanks to you for all your lovingkindness and your faithfulness, for your promises are backed by all the honor of your name.[b] [3] When I pray, you answer me, and encourage me by giving me the strength I need.

[4] Every king in all the earth shall give you thanks, O Lord, for all of them shall hear your voice. [5] Yes, they shall sing about Jehovah's glorious ways, for his glory is very great. [6] Yet though he is so great, he respects the humble, but proud men must keep their distance. [7] Though I am surrounded by troubles, you will bring me safely through them. You will clench your fist against my angry enemies! Your power will save me. [8] The Lord will work out his plans for my life—for your lovingkindness, Lord, continues forever. Don't abandon me—for you made me.

139 O LORD, YOU have examined my heart and know everything about me. [2] You know when I sit or stand. When far away you know my every thought. [3] You chart the path ahead of me, and tell me where to stop and rest. Every moment, you know where I am. [4] You know what I am going to say before I even say it. [5] You both precede and follow me, and place your hand of blessing on my head.

[6] This is too glorious, too wonderful to believe! [7] I can *never* be lost to your Spirit! I can *never* get away from my God! [8] If I go up to heaven, you are there; if I go down to the place of the dead, you are there. [9] If I ride the morning winds to the farthest oceans, [10] even there your hand will guide me, your strength will support me. [11] If I try to hide in the darkness, the night becomes light around me. [12] For even darkness cannot hide from God; to you the night shines as bright as day. Darkness and light are both alike to you.

[13] You made all the delicate, inner parts of my body, and knit them together in my mother's womb. [14] Thank you for making me so wonderfully complex! It is amazing to think about. Your workmanship is marvelous—and how well I know it. [15] You were there while I was being formed in utter seclusion! [16] You saw me before I was born and scheduled each day of my life before I began to breathe. Every day was recorded in your Book!

[17,18] How precious it is, Lord, to realize that you are thinking about me constantly! I can't even count how many times a day your thoughts turn towards me.[a] And when I waken in the morning, you are still thinking of me!

[19] Surely you will slay the wicked, Lord! Away, bloodthirsty men! Begone! [20] They blaspheme your name and stand in arro-

---

c Implied.   **137**a Perhaps this could be paraphrased, "Blessed is he who invades and sacks your city."
138a Literally, "before the gods," or "before the idols."   b Literally, "You have exalted your Word above all your name."   **139**a Literally, "how precious are your thoughts to me."

gance against you—how silly can they be? [21] O Lord, shouldn't I hate those who hate you? Shouldn't I be grieved with them? [22] Yes, I hate them, for your enemies are my enemies too.

[23] Search me, O God, and know my heart; test my thoughts. [24] Point out anything you find in me that makes you sad, and lead me along the path of everlasting life.

140 O LORD, DELIVER me from evil men. Preserve me from the violent, [2] who plot and stir up trouble all day long. [3] Their words sting like poisonous snakes. [4] Keep me out of their power. Preserve me from their violence, for they are plotting against me. [5] These proud men have set a trap to catch me, a noose to yank me up and leave me dangling in the air; they wait in ambush with a net to throw over and hold me helpless in its meshes.

[6,7,8] O Jehovah, my Lord and Savior, my God and my shield—hear me as I pray! Don't let these wicked men succeed; don't let them prosper and be proud. [9] Let their plots boomerang! Let them be destroyed by the very evil they have planned for me. [10] Let burning coals fall down upon their heads, or throw them into the fire, or into deep pits from which they can't escape.

[11] Don't let liars prosper here in our land; quickly punish them. [12] But the Lord will surely help those they persecute; he will maintain the rights of the poor. [13] Surely the godly are thanking you, for they shall live in your presence.

141 QUICK, LORD, ANSWER me—for I have prayed. Listen when I cry to you for help! [2] Regard my prayer as my evening sacrifice and as incense wafting up to you.

[3] Help me, Lord, to keep my mouth shut and my lips sealed. [4] Take away my lust for evil things; don't let me want to be with sinners, doing what they do, sharing their dainties. [5] Let the godly smite me! It will be a kindness! If they reprove me, it is medicine! Don't let me refuse it. But I am in constant prayer against the wicked and their deeds. [6,7] When their leaders are condemned, and their bones are strewn across the ground,[a] then these men will finally listen to me and know that I am trying to help them.

[8] I look to you for help, O Lord God. You are my refuge. Don't let them slay me. [9] Keep me out of their traps. [10] Let them fall into their own snares, while I escape.

142 HOW I PLEAD with God, how I implore his mercy, pouring out my troubles before him. [3] For I am overwhelmed and desperate, and you alone know which way I ought to turn to miss the traps my enemies have set for me. [4] (There's one—just over there to the right!) No one gives me a passing thought. No one will help me; no one cares a bit what happens to me. [5] Then I prayed to Jehovah. "Lord," I pled, "you are my only place of refuge. Only you can keep me safe.

[6] "Hear my cry, for I am very low. Rescue me from my persecutors, for they are too strong for me. [7] Bring me out of prison, so that I can thank you. The godly will rejoice with me for all your help."

143 HEAR MY PRAYER, O Lord; answer my plea, because you are faithful to your promises.[a] [2] Don't bring me to trial! For as compared with you, no one is perfect.

[3] My enemies chased and caught me. They have knocked me to the ground. They force me to live in the darkness like those in the grave. [4] I am losing all hope; I am paralyzed with fear.

[5] I remember the glorious miracles you did in days of long ago. [6] I reach out for you. I thirst for you as parched land thirsts for rain. [7] Come quickly, Lord, and answer me, for my depression deepens; don't turn away from me or I shall die. [8] Let me see your kindness to me in the morning, for I am trusting you. Show me where to walk, for my prayer is sincere. [9] Save me from my enemies, O Lord, I run to you to hide me. [10] Help me to do your will, for you are my

---

a Literally, "As when one plows and cleaves the earth, our bones are scattered at the mouth of Sheol."
143 a Literally, "answer me in faithfulness and righteousness."

God. Lead me in good paths, for your Spirit is good.

[11] Lord, saving me will bring glory to your name. Bring me out of all this trouble because you are true to your promises. [12] And because you are loving and kind to me, cut off all my enemies and destroy those who are trying to harm me; for I am your servant.

144 BLESS THE LORD who is my immovable Rock. He gives me strength and skill in battle. [2] He is always kind and loving to me; he is my fortress, my tower of strength and safety, my deliverer. He stands before me as a shield. He subdues my people under me.

[3] O Lord, what is man that you even notice him? Why bother at all with the human race?[a] [4] For man is but a breath; his days are like a passing shadow.

[5] Bend down the heavens, Lord, and come. The mountains smoke beneath your touch. [6] Let loose your lightning bolts, your arrows, Lord, upon your enemies, and scatter them.

[7] Reach down from heaven and rescue me; deliver me from deep waters, from the power of my enemies. [8] Their mouths are filled with lies; they swear to the truth of what is false.

[9] I will sing you a new song, O God, with a ten-stringed harp. [10] For you grant victory to kings! You are the one who will rescue your servant David from the fatal sword. [11] Save me! Deliver me from these enemies, these liars, these treacherous men.

[12-15] Here is my description of[b] a truly happy land where Jehovah is God:

Sons vigorous and tall as growing plants.

Daughters of graceful beauty like the pillars of a palace wall.

Barns full to the brim with crops of every kind.

Sheep by the thousands out in our fields.

Oxen loaded down with produce.

No enemy attacking the walls, but peace everywhere.

No crime in our streets.

Yes, happy are those whose God is Jehovah.

145 I WILL PRAISE you, my God and King, and bless your name each day and forever. [3] Great is Jehovah! Greatly praise him! His greatness is beyond discovery! [4] Let each generation tell its children what glorious things he does. [5] I will meditate about your glory, splendor, majesty and miracles. [6] Your awe-inspiring deeds shall be on every tongue; I will proclaim your greatness. [7] Everyone will tell about how good you are, and sing about your righteousness.

[8] Jehovah is kind and merciful, slow to get angry, full of love. [9] He is good to everyone, and his compassion is intertwined with everything he does. [10] All living things shall thank you, Lord, and your people will bless you. [11] They will talk together about the glory of your kingdom and mention examples of your power. [12] They will tell about your miracles and about the majesty and glory of your reign. [13] For your kingdom never ends. You rule generation after generation.

[14] The Lord lifts the fallen and those bent beneath their loads. [15] The eyes of all mankind look up to you for help; you give them their food as they need it. [16] You constantly satisfy the hunger and thirst of every living thing.

[17] The Lord is fair in everything he does, and full of kindness. [18] He is close to all who call on him sincerely. [19] He fulfills the desires of those who reverence and trust him; he hears their cries for help and rescues them. [20] He protects all those who love him, but destroys the wicked.

[21] I will praise the Lord and call on all men everywhere to bless his holy name forever and forever.

146 PRAISE THE LORD! Yes, really praise him! [2] I will praise him as long as I live, yes, even with my dying breath.

[3] Don't look to men for help; their greatest leaders fail; [4] for every man must die. His breathing stops, life ends, and in a moment all he planned for himself is ended. [5] But

---

a Literally, "or the son of man that you take account of him?"   b Implied.

happy is the man who has the God of Jacob as his helper, whose hope is in the Lord his God— [6] the God who made both earth and heaven, the seas and everything in them. He is the God who keeps every promise, [7] and gives justice to the poor and oppressed, and food to the hungry. He frees the prisoners, [8] and opens the eyes of the blind; he lifts the burdens from those bent down beneath their loads. For the Lord loves good men. [9] He protects the immigrants, and cares for the orphans and widows. But he turns topsy-turvy the plans of the wicked.

[10] The Lord will reign forever. O Jerusalem,[a] your God is King in every generation! Hallelujah! Praise the Lord!

147 HALLELUJAH! YES, PRAISE the Lord! How good it is to sing his praises! How delightful, and how right!

[2] He is rebuilding Jerusalem and bringing back the exiles. [3] He heals the broken-hearted, binding up their wounds. [4] He counts the stars and calls them all by name. [5] How great he is! His power is absolute! His understanding is unlimited. [6] The Lord supports the humble, but brings the wicked into the dust. [7] Sing out your thanks to him; sing praises to our God, accompanied by harps. [8] He covers the heavens with clouds, sends down the showers and makes the green grass grow in mountain pastures. [9] He feeds the wild animals and the young ravens cry to him for food. [10] The speed of a horse is nothing to him. How puny in his sight is the strength of a man. [11] But his joy is in those who reverence him, those who expect him to be loving and kind.

[12] Praise him, O Jerusalem! Praise your God, O Zion! [13] For he has fortified your gates against all enemies, and blessed your children. [14] He sends peace across your nation, and fills your barns with plenty of the finest wheat. [15] He sends his orders to the world. How swiftly his word flies. [16] He sends the snow in all its lovely whiteness, and scatters the frost upon the ground, [17] and hurls the hail upon the earth. Who can stand before his freezing cold? [18] But then he calls for warmer weather, and the spring winds blow and all the river ice is broken. [19] He has made known his laws and ceremonies of worship to Israel— [20] something he has not done with any other nation; they have not known his commands.

Hallelujah! Yes, praise the Lord!

148 PRAISE THE LORD, O heavens! Praise him from the skies! [2] Praise him, all his angels, all the armies of heaven. [3] Praise him, sun and moon, and all you twinkling stars. [4] Praise him, skies above. Praise him, vapors high above the clouds.

[5] Let everything he has made give praise to him. For he issued his command, and they came into being; [6] he established them forever and forever. His orders will never be revoked.

[7] And praise him down here on earth, you creatures of the ocean depths. [8] Let fire and hail, snow, rain, wind and weather, all obey. [9] Let the mountains and hills, the fruit trees and cedars, [10] the wild animals and cattle, the snakes and birds, [11] the kings and all the people, with their rulers and their judges, [12] young men and maidens, old men and children— [13] all praise the Lord together. For he alone is worthy. His glory is far greater than all of earth and heaven. [14] He has made his people strong, honoring his godly ones—the people of Israel, the people closest to him.

Hallelujah! Yes, praise the Lord!

149 HALLELUJAH! YES, PRAISE the Lord! Sing him a new song. Sing his praises, all his people.

[2] O Israel, rejoice in your Maker. O people of Jerusalem, exult in your King. [3] Praise his name with dancing, accompanied by drums and lyre.

[4,5] For Jehovah enjoys his people; he will save the humble. Let his people rejoice in this honor. Let them sing for joy as they lie upon their beds.

[6,7] Adore him, O his people! And take a double-edged sword to execute his punishment upon the nations. [8] Bind their kings and leaders with iron chains, [9] and execute their sentences.

He is the glory of his people. Hallelujah! Praise him!

a Literally, "Zion."

150 HALLELUJAH! YES, PRAISE the Lord!

Praise him in his Temple, and in the heavens he made with mighty power.[a] [2] Praise him for his mighty works. Praise his unequaled greatness. [3] Praise him with the trumpet and with lute and harp. [4] Praise him with the tambourines and processional. Praise him with stringed instruments and horns. [5] Praise him with the cymbals, yes, loud clanging cymbals.

[6] Let everything alive give praises to the Lord! *You* praise him!

Hallelujah!

a Literally, "in the firmament of his power."

Emil Edgren & Al Magacu, San Jose Mercury-News

On a brisk November day, 18-year-old Art DePeralta walked into a San Jose bank with his partner. Minutes later the two reappeared, with two woman hostages and pillowcases stuffed with $119,000 in cash. With the police on their trail, the young robbers screeched off on a hair-raising, bullet-splattering chase. Dizzily weaving through the city at break-neck speed, the police finally forced the car off the road. Art's partner was shot (later recovering) but Art surrendered.

Why would a high school student pull such a caper? "I knew it was wrong, but I wanted to do what I wanted to do," he says.

Art is different now. While in a county jail he became a Christian and has since spoken of his faith publicly. He shares advice with students who might be headed for a life of crime, or who secretly yearn for a big splash like a bank robbery. They listen to Art, because he's been behind both ends of the gun.

Gordon McLean

Learning the Hard Way

Art learned his lessons the hard way. The wisdom Solomon dispenses in the book of Proverbs packs a strong punch. But Solomon's not spouting off on something he hasn't experienced the hard way, too.

Take women, for instance. Proverbs contains much advice about women, such as, "It is better to live in the corner of an attic than with a crabby woman in a lovely home" (21:9). He should know: he had over a thousand wives!

PROVERBS

1 THESE ARE THE proverbs of King Solomon of Israel, David's son:

[2] He wrote them to teach his people how to live—how to act in every circumstance, [3] for he wanted them to be understanding, just and fair in everything they did. [4] "I want to make the simple-minded wise!" he said. "I want to warn young men about some problems they will face. [5,6] I want those already wise to become the wiser and become leaders by exploring the depths of meaning in these nuggets of truth."

[7,8,9] How does a man become wise? The first step is to trust and reverence the Lord! Only fools refuse to be taught. Listen to your father and mother. What you learn from them will stand you in good stead; it will gain you many honors.[a]

[10] If young toughs tell you, "Come and join us"—turn your back on them! [11] "We'll hide and rob and kill," they say. [12] "Good or bad, we'll treat them all alike. [13] And the loot we'll get! All kinds of stuff! [14] Come on, throw in your lot with us; we'll split with you in equal shares."

[15] Don't do it, son! Stay far from men like that, [16] for crime is their way of life, and murder is their specialty. [17] When a bird sees a trap being set, it stays away, [18] but not these men; they trap themselves! They lay a booby trap for their own lives. [19] Such is the fate of all who live by violence and murder.[b] They will die a violent death.

[20] Wisdom shouts in the streets for a hearing. [21] She calls out to the crowds along Main Street, and to the judges in their courts, and to everyone in all the land:

[22] "You simpletons!" she cries. "How long will you go on being fools? How long will you scoff at wisdom and fight the facts? [23] Come here and listen to me! I'll pour out the spirit of wisdom upon you, and make you wise. [24] I have called you so often but still you won't come. I have pleaded, but all in vain. [25] For you have spurned my counsel and reproof. [26] Some day you'll be in trouble, and I'll laugh! Mock me, will you?—I'll mock you! [27] When a storm of terror surrounds you, and when you are engulfed by anguish and distress, [28] then I will not answer your cry for help. It will be too late though you search for me ever so anxiously.

[29] "For you closed your eyes to the facts and did not choose to reverence and trust the Lord, [30] and you turned your back on me, spurning my advice. [31] That is why you must eat the bitter fruit of having your own way, and experience the full terrors of the pathway you have chosen. [32] For you turned away from me—to death; your own complacency will kill you. Fools! [33] But all who listen to me shall live in peace and safety, unafraid."

2 EVERY YOUNG MAN who listens to me and obeys my instructions will be given wisdom and good sense. [3,4,5] Yes, if you want better insight and discernment, and are searching for them as you would for lost money or hidden treasure, then wisdom will be given you, and knowledge of God himself; you will soon learn the importance of reverence for the Lord and of trusting him.

[6] For the Lord grants wisdom! His every

---

a Literally, "a fair garland and adornment."

b Literally, "all who are greedy of gain."

word is a treasure of knowledge and understanding. [7,8] He grants good sense to the godly—his saints. He is their shield, protecting them and guarding their pathway. [9] He shows how to distinguish right from wrong, how to find the right decision every time. [10] For wisdom and truth will enter the very center of your being, filling your life with joy. [11,12,13] You will be given the sense to stay away from evil men who want you to be their partners in crime—men who turn from God's ways to walk down dark and evil paths, [14] and exult in doing wrong, for they thoroughly enjoy their sins. [15] Everything they do is crooked and wrong.

[16,17] Only wisdom from the Lord can save a man from the flattery of prostitutes; these girls have abandoned their husbands and flouted the laws of God. [18] Their houses lie along the road to death and hell. [19] The men who enter them are doomed. None of these men will ever be the same again.[a]

[20] Follow the steps of the godly instead, and stay on the right path, [21] for only good men enjoy life to the full;[b] [22] evil men lose the good things they might have had,[c] and they themselves shall be destroyed.

3 MY SON, NEVER forget the things I've taught you. If you want a long and satisfying life, closely follow my instructions. [3] Never forget to be truthful and kind. Hold these virtues tightly. Write them deep within your heart. [4,5] If you want favor with both God and man, and a reputation for good judgment and common sense, then trust the Lord completely; don't ever trust yourself. [6] In everything you do, put God first, and he will direct you and crown your efforts with success.

[7,8] Don't be conceited, sure of your own wisdom. Instead, trust and reverence the Lord, and turn your back on evil; when you do that, then you will be given renewed health and vitality.

[9,10] Honor the Lord by giving him the first part of all your income, and he will fill your barns with wheat and barley and overflow your wine vats with the finest wines.

[11,12] Young man, do not resent it when God chastens and corrects you, for his punishment is proof of his love. Just as a father punishes a son he delights in to make him better, so the Lord corrects you.

[13,14,15] The man who knows right from wrong[a] and has good judgment and common sense is happier than the man who is immensely rich! For such wisdom is far more valuable than precious jewels. Nothing else compares with it. [16,17] Wisdom gives:

A long, good life
Riches
Honor
Pleasure
Peace

[18] Wisdom is a tree of life to those who eat her fruit; happy is the man who keeps on eating it.

[19] The Lord's wisdom founded the earth; his understanding established all the universe and space. [20] The deep fountains of the earth were broken open by his knowledge, and the skies poured down rain.

[21] Have two goals: wisdom—that is, knowing and doing right—and common sense. Don't let them slip away, [22] for they fill you with living energy, and are a feather in your cap.[b] [23] They keep you safe from defeat and disaster and from stumbling off the trail. [24,25,26] With them on guard you can sleep without fear; you need not be afraid of disaster or the plots of wicked men, for the Lord is with you; he protects you.

[27,28] Don't withhold repayment of your debts. Don't say "some other time," if you can pay now. [29] Don't plot against your neighbor; he is trusting you. [30] Don't get into needless fights. [31] Don't envy violent men. Don't copy their ways. [32] For such men are an abomination to the Lord, but he gives his friendship to the godly.

[33] The curse of God is on the wicked, but his blessing is on the upright. [34] The Lord mocks at mockers, but helps the humble. [35] The wise are promoted to honor, but fools are promoted to shame!

4 YOUNG MEN, LISTEN to me as you would to your father. Listen, and grow wise, for I speak the truth—don't turn

---

a Literally, "never return to the ways of life."
c Literally, "shall be cut off from the land."
b Literally, "be an ornament to your neck."

b Literally, "shall dwell in the land."
3a Literally, "the man that finds wisdom."

away. [3] For I, too, was once a son, tenderly loved by my mother as an only child, and the companion of my father. [4] He told me never to forget his words. "If you follow them," he said, "you will have a long and happy life. [5] *Learn to be wise,* "he said, *"and develop good judgment and common sense! I cannot overemphasize this point.* "[a] [6] Cling to wisdom—she will protect you. Love her—she will guard you.

[7] Determination to be wise is the first step toward becoming wise! And with your wisdom, develop common sense and good judgment. [8,9] If you exalt wisdom, she will exalt you. Hold her fast and she will lead you to great honor; she will place a beautiful crown upon your head. [10] My son, listen to me and do as I say, and you will have a long, good life.

[11] I would have you learn this great fact: that a life of doing right is the wisest life there is. [12] If you live that kind of life, you'll not limp or stumble as you run. [13] Carry out my instructions; don't forget them, for they will lead you to real living.

[14] Don't do as the wicked do. [15] Avoid their haunts—turn away, go somewhere else, [16] for evil men don't sleep until they've done their evil deed for the day. They can't rest unless they cause someone to stumble and fall. [17] They eat and drink wickedness and violence!

[18] But the good man walks along in the ever-brightening light of God's favor; the dawn gives way to morning splendor, [19] while the evil man gropes and stumbles in the dark.

[20] Listen, son of mine, to what I say. Listen carefully. [21] Keep these thoughts ever in mind; let them penetrate deep within your heart, [22] for they will mean real life for you, and radiant health.

[23] *Above all else, guard your affections.* For they influence everything else in your life. [24] Spurn the careless kiss of a prostitute.[b] Stay far from her. [25] Look straight ahead; don't even turn your head to look. [26] Watch your step. Stick to the path and be safe. [27] Don't sidetrack; pull back your foot

from danger.

5 LISTEN TO ME, my son! I know what I am saying; *listen!* [2] Watch yourself, lest you be indiscreet and betray some vital information. [3] For the lips of a prostitute are as sweet as honey, and smooth flattery is her stock in trade. [4] But afterwards only a bitter conscience[a] is left to you, sharp as a double-edged sword. [5] She leads you down to death and hell. [6] For she does not know the path to life. She staggers down a crooked trail, and doesn't even realize where it leads.

[7] Young men, listen to me, and never forget what I'm about to say: [8] *Run from her! Don't go near her house,* [9] lest you fall to her temptation and lose your honor, and give the remainder of your life to the cruel and merciless;[b] [10] lest strangers obtain your wealth, and you become a slave of foreigners. [11] Lest afterwards you groan in anguish and in shame, when syphilis[c] consumes your body, [12] and you say, "Oh, if only I had listened! If only I had not demanded my own way! [13] Oh, why wouldn't I take advice? Why was I so stupid? [14] For now I must face public disgrace."

[15] Drink from your own well, my son—be faithful and true to your wife. [16] Why should you beget children with women of the street? [17] Why share your children with those outside your home? [18] Let your manhood be a blessing; rejoice in the wife of your youth. [19] Let her charms[d] and tender embrace[e] satisfy you. Let her love alone fill you with delight. [20] Why delight yourself with prostitutes, embracing what isn't yours? [21] *For God is closely watching you,* and he weighs carefully everything you do.

[22] The wicked man is doomed by his own sins; they are ropes that catch and hold him. [23] He shall die because he will not listen to the truth; he has let himself be led away into incredible folly.

6 SON, IF YOU endorse a note for someone you hardly know, guaranteeing his debt, you are in serious trouble. [2] You may have

---

a Literally, "Forget not nor turn from the words of my mouth."   b Implied; literally, "Put away from you a wayward mouth."   5a Literally, "But in the end she is bitter as wormwood."   b Perhaps the reference is to blackmail, or to fear of vengeance from the wronged husband.   c Literally, "disease." d Literally, "as a loving hind and a pleasant doe."   e Literally, "breasts."

trapped yourself by your agreement. [3] Quick! Get out of it if you possibly can! Swallow your pride; don't let embarrassment stand in the way. Go and beg to have your name erased. [4] Don't put it off. Do it now. Don't rest until you do. [5] If you can get out of this trap you have saved yourself like a deer that escapes from a hunter, or a bird from the net.

[6] Take a lesson from the ants, you lazy fellow. Learn from their ways and be wise! [7] For though they have no king to make them work, [8] yet they labor hard all summer, gathering food for the winter. [9] But you—all you do is sleep. When will you wake up? [10] "Let me sleep a little longer!" Sure, just a little more! [11] And as you sleep, poverty creeps upon you like a robber and destroys you; want attacks you in full armor.

[12,13] Let me describe for you a worthless and a wicked man; first, he is a constant liar; he signals his true intentions to his friends with eyes and feet and fingers. [14] Next, his heart is full of rebellion. And he spends his time thinking of all the evil he can do, and stirring up discontent. [15] But he will be destroyed suddenly, broken beyond hope of healing.

[16-19] For there are six things the Lord hates—no, seven:

Haughtiness
Lying
Murdering
Plotting evil
Eagerness to do wrong
A false witness
Sowing discord among brothers

[20] Young man, obey your father and your mother. [21] Tie their instructions around your finger so you won't forget. Take to heart all of their advice. [22] Every day and all night long their counsel will lead you and save you from harm; when you wake up in the morning, let their instructions guide you into the new day. [23] For their advice is a beam of light directed into the dark corners of your mind to warn you of danger and to give you a good life. [24] Their counsel will keep you far away from prostitutes with all their flatteries.

[25] Don't lust for their beauty. Don't let their coyness seduce you. [26] For a prostitute will bring a man to poverty, and an adulteress may cost him his very life. [27] Can a man hold fire against his chest and not be burned? [28] Can he walk on hot coals and not blister his feet? [29] So it is with the man who commits adultery with another's wife. He shall not go unpunished for this sin. [30] Excuses might even be found for a thief, if he steals when he is starving! [31] But even so, he is fined seven times as much as he stole, though it may mean selling everything in his house to pay it back.

[32] But the man who commits adultery is an utter fool, for he destroys his own soul. [33] Wounds and constant disgrace are his lot, [34] for the woman's husband will be furious in his jealousy, and he will have no mercy on you in his day of vengeance. [35] You won't be able to buy him off no matter what you offer.

7 FOLLOW MY ADVICE, my son; always keep it in mind and stick to it. [2] Obey me and live! Guard my words as your most precious possession. [3] Write them down,[a] and also keep them deep within your heart. [4] Love wisdom like a sweetheart; make her a beloved member of your family. [5] Let her hold you back from visiting a prostitute, from listening to her flattery.

[6] I was looking out the window of my house one day, [7] and saw a simple-minded lad, a young man lacking common sense, [8,9] walking at twilight down the street to the house of this wayward girl, a prostitute. [10] She approached him, saucy and pert, and dressed seductively. [11,12] She was the brash, coarse type, seen often in the streets and markets, soliciting at every corner for men to be her lovers.

[13] She put her arms around him and kissed him, and with a saucy look she said, [14] "I've decided to forget our quarrel![b] [15] I was just coming to look for you and here you are! [16,17] My bed is spread with lovely, colored sheets of finest linen imported from Egypt, perfumed with myrrh, aloes and cin-

---

a Literally, "Bind them upon your fingers."   b Literally, "Sacrifices of peace offerings were due from me; this day have I paid my vows." If she meant this literally, she was telling him that she had plenty of food on hand, left from her sacrifice at the Temple.

namon. [18] Come on, let's take our fill of love until morning, [19] for my husband is away on a long trip. [20] He has taken a wallet full of money with him, and won't return for several days."

[21] So she seduced him with her pretty speech, her coaxing and her wheedling, until he yielded to her. He couldn't resist her flattery. [22] He followed her as an ox going to the butcher, or as a stag that is trapped, [23] waiting to be killed with an arrow through its heart. He was as a bird flying into a snare, not knowing the fate awaiting it there.

[24] Listen to me, young men, and not only listen but obey; [25] don't let your desires get out of hand; don't let yourself think about her. Don't go near her; stay away from where she walks, lest she tempt you and seduce you. [26] For she has been the ruin of multitudes—a vast host of men have been her victims. [27] If you want to find the road to hell, look for her house.

8 CAN'T YOU HEAR the voice of wisdom? She is standing at the city gates and at every fork in the road, and at the door of every house. Listen to what she says: [4,5] "Listen, men!" she calls. "How foolish and naive you are! Let me give you understanding. O foolish ones, let me show you common sense! [6,7] Listen to me! For I have important information for you. Everything I say is right and true, for I hate lies and every kind of deception. [8] My advice is wholesome and good. There is nothing of evil in it. [9] My words are plain and clear to anyone with half a mind—if it is only open! [10] My instruction is far more valuable than silver or gold."

[11] For the value of wisdom is far above rubies; nothing can be compared with it. [12] Wisdom and good judgment live together, for wisdom knows where to discover knowledge and understanding. [13] If anyone respects and fears God, he will hate evil. For wisdom hates pride, arrogance, corruption and deceit of every kind.

[14,15] "I, Wisdom, give good advice and common sense. Because of my strength, kings reign in power. I show the judges who

is right and who is wrong. [16] Rulers rule well with my help. [17] I love all who love me. Those who search for me shall surely find me. [18] Unending riches, honor, justice and righteousness are mine to distribute. [19] My gifts are better than the purest gold or sterling silver! [20] My paths are those of justice and right. [21] Those who love and follow me are indeed wealthy. I fill their treasuries. [22] The Lord formed me in the beginning, before he created anything else. [23] From ages past, I am. I existed before the earth began. [24] I lived before the oceans were created, before the springs bubbled forth their waters onto the earth; [25] before the mountains and the hills were made. [26] Yes, I was born before God made the earth and fields, and high plateaus.

[27,28,29] "I was there when he established the heavens and formed the great springs in the depths of the oceans. I was there when he set the limits of the seas and gave them his instructions not to spread beyond their boundaries. I was there when he made the blueprint for the earth and oceans. [30] I was always at his side like a little child.[a] I was his constant delight, laughing and playing in his presence. [31] And how happy I was with what he created—his wide world and all his family of mankind! [32] And so, young men, listen to me, for how happy are all who follow my instructions.

[33] "Listen to my counsel—oh, don't refuse it—and be wise. [34] Happy is the man who is so anxious to be with me that he watches for me daily at my gates, or waits for me outside my home! [35] For whoever finds me finds life and wins approval from the Lord. [36] But the one who misses me has injured himself irreparably. Those who refuse me show that they love death."

9 WISDOM HAS BUILT a palace supported on seven pillars, [2] and has prepared a great banquet, and mixed the wines, [3] and sent out her maidens inviting all to come. She calls from the busiest intersections in the city, [4] "Come, you simple ones without good judgment; [5] come to wisdom's banquet and drink the wines that I have mixed. [6] Leave behind your foolishness and begin

a Or, "like a master workman."

to live; learn how to be wise."

[7,8] If you rebuke a mocker, you will only get a smart retort; yes, he will snarl at you. So don't bother with him; he will only hate you for trying to help him. But a wise man, when rebuked, will love you all the more. [9] Teach a wise man, and he will be the wiser; teach a good man, and he will learn more. [10] *For the reverence and fear of God are basic to all wisdom. Knowing God results in every other kind of understanding.* [11] "I, Wisdom, will make the hours of your day more profitable and the years of your life more fruitful." [12] Wisdom is its own reward, and if you scorn her, you hurt only yourself.

[13] A prostitute is loud and brash, and never has enough of lust and shame. [14] She sits at the door of her house or stands at the street corners of the city, [15] whispering to men going by, and to those minding their own business. [16] "Come home with me," she urges simpletons. [17] "Stolen melons[a] are the sweetest; stolen apples[b] taste the best!" [18] But they don't realize that her former guests are now citizens of hell.

These are the proverbs of Solomon:

10 HAPPY IS THE man with a level-headed son; sad the mother of a rebel.

[2] Ill-gotten gain brings no lasting happiness; right living does.

[3] The Lord will not let a good man starve to death, nor will he let the wicked man's riches continue forever.

[4] Lazy men are soon poor; hard workers get rich.

[5] A wise youth makes hay while the sun shines, but what a shame to see a lad who sleeps away his hour of opportunity.

[6] The good man is covered with blessings from head to foot, but an evil man inwardly curses his luck.[a]

[7] We all have happy memories of good men gone to their reward, but the names of wicked men stink after them.

[8] The wise man is glad to be instructed, but a self-sufficient fool falls flat on his face.

[9] A good man has firm footing, but a crook will slip and fall.

[10] Winking at sin leads to sorrow; bold reproof leads to peace.

[11] There is living truth in what a good man says, but the mouth of the evil man is filled with curses.

[12] Hatred stirs old quarrels, but love overlooks insults.

[13] Men with common sense are admired[b] as counselors; those without it are beaten as servants.

[14] A wise man holds his tongue. Only a fool blurts out everything he knows; that only leads to sorrow and trouble.

[15] The rich man's wealth is his only[b] strength. The poor man's poverty is his only[b] curse.

[16] The good man's earnings advance the cause of righteousness. The evil man squanders his on sin.

[17] Anyone willing to be corrected is on the pathway to life. Anyone refusing has lost his chance.

[18] To hate is to be a liar; to slander is to be a fool.

[19] Don't talk so much. You keep putting your foot in your mouth. Be sensible and turn off the flow!

[20] When a good man speaks, he is worth listening to, but the words of fools are a dime a dozen.

[21] A godly man gives good advice, but a rebel is destroyed by lack of common sense.

[22] The Lord's blessing is our greatest wealth. All our work adds nothing to it![c]

[23] A fool's fun is being bad; a wise man's fun is being wise!

[24] The wicked man's fears will all come true, and so will the good man's hopes.

[25] Disaster strikes like a cyclone and the wicked are whirled away. But the good man has a strong anchor.

[26] A lazy fellow is a pain to his employers—like smoke in their eyes or vinegar that sets the teeth on edge.

[27] Reverence for God adds hours to each day;[d] so how can the wicked expect a long, good life?

[28] The hope of good men is eternal happiness; the hopes of evil men are all in vain.

[29] God protects the upright but destroys the wicked.

---

a Literally, "water."   b Literally, "food."   10a Literally, "but the mouth of the wicked conceals violence."   b Implied.   c Or, "and he adds no sorrow therewith."   d Literally, "prolongs days."

³⁰ The good shall never lose God's blessings, but the wicked shall lose everything.

³¹ The good man gives wise advice, but the liar's counsel is shunned.

³² The upright speak what is helpful; the wicked speak rebellion.

11 THE LORD HATES cheating and delights in honesty.

² Proud men end in shame, but the meek become wise.

³ A good man is guided by his honesty; the evil man is destroyed by his dishonesty.

⁴ Your riches won't help you on Judgment Day; only righteousness counts then.

⁵ The upright are directed by their honesty; the wicked shall fall beneath their load of sins.

⁶ The good man's goodness delivers him; the evil man's treachery is his undoing.

⁷ When an evil man dies, his hopes all perish, for they are based upon this earthly life.

⁸ God rescues good men from danger while letting the wicked fall into it.

⁹ Evil words destroy. Godly skill rebuilds.ᵃ

¹⁰ The whole city celebrates a good man's success—and also the godless man's death.

¹¹ The good influence of godly citizens causes a city to prosper, but the moral decay of the wicked drives it downhill.

¹² To quarrel with a neighbor is foolish; a man with good sense holds his tongue.

¹³ A gossip goes around spreading rumors, while a trustworthy man tries to quiet them.

¹⁴ Without wise leadership, a nation is in trouble; but with good counselors there is safety.

¹⁵ Be sure you know a person well before you vouch for his credit! Better refuse than suffer later.

¹⁶ Honor goes to kind and gracious women, mereᵇ money to cruel men.

¹⁷ Your own soul is nourished when you are kind; it is destroyed when you are cruel.

¹⁸ The evil man gets rich for the moment, but the good man's reward lasts forever.

¹⁹ The good man finds life; the evil man, death.

²⁰ The Lord hates the stubborn but delights in those who are good.

²¹ You can be very sure that the evil man will not go unpunished forever. And you can also be very sure that God will rescue the children of the godly.

²² A beautiful woman lacking discretion and modesty is like a fine gold ring in a pig's snout.

²³ The good man can look forward to happiness, while the wicked can expect only wrath.

²⁴,²⁵ It is possible to give away and become richer! It is also possible to hold on too tightly and lose everything. Yes, the liberal man shall be rich! By watering others, he waters himself.

²⁶ People curse the man who holds his grain for higher prices, but they bless the man who sells it to them in their time of need.

²⁷ If you search for good you will find God's favor; if you search for evil you will find his curse.

²⁸ Trust in your money and down you go! Trust in God and flourish as a tree!

²⁹ The fool who provokes his family to anger and resentment will finally have nothing worthwhile left. He shall be the servant of a wiser man.

³⁰ Godly men are growing a tree that bears life-giving fruit, and all who win souls are wise.ᶜ

³¹ Even the godly shall be rewarded here on earth; how much more the wicked!

12 TO LEARN, YOU must want to be taught. To refuse reproof is stupid.

² The Lord blesses good men and condemns the wicked.

³ Wickedness never brings real success; only the godly have that.

⁴ A worthy wife is her husband's joy and crown; the other kind corrodes his strength and tears down everything he does.

⁵ A good man's mind is filled with honest thoughts; an evil man's mind is crammed with lies.

---

a Or, "When a godless man slanders his neighbor, the charges won't stick because everyone knows his reputation."   b Implied.   c Or, "He that is wise wins souls."

⁶ The wicked accuse; the godly defend.

⁷ The wicked shall perish; the godly shall stand.

⁸ Everyone admires a man with good sense, but a man with a warped mind is despised.

⁹ It is better to get your hands dirty —and eat,ᵃ than to be too proud to work —and starve.

¹⁰ A good man is concerned for the welfare of his animals, but even the kindness of godless men is cruel.

¹¹ Hard work means prosperity;ᵇ only a fool idles away his time.

¹² Crooks are jealous of each other's loot, while good men long to help each other.

¹³ Lies will get any man into trouble, but honesty is its own defense.

¹⁴ Telling the truth gives a man great satisfaction, and hard work returns many blessings to him.

¹⁵ A fool thinks he needs no advice, but a wise man listens to others.

¹⁶ A fool is quick-tempered; a wise man stays cool when insulted.

¹⁷ A good man is known by his truthfulness; a false man by deceit and lies.

¹⁸ Some people like to make cutting remarks, but the words of the wise soothe and heal.

¹⁹ Truth stands the test of time; lies are soon exposed.

²⁰ Deceit fills hearts that are plotting for evil; joy fills hearts that are planning for good!

²¹ No realᵃ harm befalls the good, but there is constant trouble for the wicked.

²² God delights in those who keep their promises, and abhors those who don't.

²³ A wise man doesn't display his knowledge, but a fool displays his foolishness.

²⁴ Work hard and become a leader; be lazy and never succeed.

²⁵ Anxious hearts are very heavy but a word of encouragement does wonders!

²⁶ The good man asks advice from friends; the wicked plunge ahead—and fall.

²⁷ A lazy man won't even dress the game he gets while hunting, but the diligent man makes good use of everything he finds.

²⁸ The path of the godly leads to life. So why fear death?

13 A WISE YOUTH accepts his father's rebuke; a young mocker doesn't.

² The good man wins his case by careful argument; the evil-minded only wants to fight.

³ Self-control means controlling the tongue! A quick retort can ruin everything.

⁴ Lazy people want much but get little, while the diligent are prospering.

⁵ A good man hates lies; wicked men lieᵃ constantly and come to shame.

⁶ A man's goodness helps him all through life, while evil men are being destroyed by their wickedness.

⁷ Some rich people are poor, and some poor people have great wealth!

⁸ Being kidnapped and held for ransom never worries the poor man!

⁹ The good man's life is full of light. The sinner's road is dark and gloomy.

¹⁰ Pride leads to arguments; be humble, take advice and become wise.

¹¹ Wealth from gambling quickly disappears; wealth from hard work grows.

¹² Hope deferred makes the heart sick; but when dreams come true at last, there is life and joy.ᵇ

¹³ Despise God's Word and find yourself in trouble. Obey it and succeed.

¹⁴ The advice of a wise man refreshes like water from a mountain spring. Those accepting it become aware of the pitfalls on ahead.

¹⁵ A man with good sense is appreciated. A treacherous man must walk a rocky road.

¹⁶ A wise man thinks ahead; a fool doesn't, and even brags about it!

¹⁷ An unreliable messenger can cause a lot of trouble. Reliable communication permits progress.

¹⁸ If you refuse criticism you will end in poverty and disgrace; if you accept criticism you are on the road to fame.

¹⁹ It is pleasant to see plans develop. That is why fools refuse to give them up even when they are wrong.

²⁰ Be with wise men and become wise. Be

---

a Implied.   b Literally, "He who tills his ground shall have his fill of bread."   13a Implied.

b Literally, "it is a tree of life."

with evil men and become evil.

²¹ Curses chase sinners, while blessings chase the righteous!

²² When a good man dies, he leaves an inheritance to his grandchildren; but when a sinner dies, his wealth is stored up for the godly.

²³ A poor man's farm may have good soil, but injustice robs him of its riches.

²⁴ If you refuse to discipline your son, it proves you don't love him; for if you love him you will be prompt to punish him.

²⁵ The good man eats to live, while the evil man lives to eat.ᶜ

14 A WISE WOMAN builds her house, while a foolish woman tears hers down by her own efforts.

² To do right honors God; to sin is to despise him.

³ A rebel's foolish talk should prick his own pride! But the wise man's speech is respected.

⁴ An empty stable stays clean—but there is no income from an empty stable.

⁵ A truthful witness never lies; a false witness always lies.

⁶ A mocker never finds the wisdom he claims he is looking for, yet it comes easily to the man with common sense.

⁷ If you are looking for advice, stay away from fools.

⁸ The wise man looks ahead. The fool attempts to fool himself and won't face facts.

⁹ The common bond of rebels is their guilt.ᵃ The common bond of godly people is good will.

¹⁰ Only the person involved can know his own bitterness or joy—no one else can really share it.

¹¹ The work of the wicked will perish; the work of the godly will flourish.

¹² Before every man there lies a wide and pleasant road that seems right but ends in death.

¹³ Laughter cannot mask a heavy heart. When the laughter ends, the grief remains.

¹⁴ The backslider gets bored with himself; the godly man's life is exciting.

¹⁵ Only a simpleton believes what he is told! A prudent man checks to see where he is going.

¹⁶ A wise man is cautious and avoids danger; a fool plunges ahead with great confidence.

¹⁷ A short-tempered man is a fool. He hates the man who is patient.

¹⁸ The simpleton is crowned with folly; the wise man is crowned with knowledge.

¹⁹ Evil men shall bow before the godly.

²⁰ Even his own neighbors despise the poor man, while the rich have many "friends."

²¹ To despise the poor is to sin. Blessed are those who pity them.

²² Those who plot evil shall wander away and be lost, but those who plan good shall be granted mercy and quietness.

²³ Work brings profit; talk brings poverty!

²⁴ Wise men are praised for their wisdom; fools are despised for their folly.

²⁵ A witness who tells the truth saves good men from being sentenced to death, but a false witness is a traitor.

²⁶ Reverence for God gives a man deep strength; his children have a place of refuge and security.

²⁷ Reverence for the Lord is a fountain of life; its waters keep a man from death.

²⁸ A growing population is a king's glory; a dwindling nation is his doom.

²⁹ A wise man controls his temper. He knows that anger causes mistakes.

³⁰ A relaxed attitude lengthens a man's life; jealousy rots it away.

³¹ Anyone who oppresses the poor is insulting God who made them. To help the poor is to honor God.

³² The godly have a refuge when they die, but the wicked are crushed by their sins.

³³ Wisdom is enshrined in the hearts of men of common sense, but it must shout loudly before fools will hear it.

³⁴ Godliness exalts a nation, but sin is a reproach to any people.

³⁵ A king rejoices in servants who know what they are doing; he is angry with those who cause trouble.

---

c Literally, "but the wicked never get enough."   14a Or, "Fools make a mock at sin." The Hebrew is obscure.

15 A SOFT ANSWER turns away wrath, but harsh words cause quarrels.

[2] A wise teacher makes learning a joy; a rebellious teacher spouts foolishness.

[3] The Lord is watching everywhere and keeps his eye on both the evil and the good.

[4] Gentle words cause life and health; griping brings discouragement.

[5] Only a fool despises his father's advice; a wise son considers each suggestion.

[6] There is treasure in being good, but trouble dogs the wicked.

[7] Only the good can give good advice. Rebels can't.

[8] The Lord hates the gifts of the wicked, but delights in the prayers of his people.

[9,10] The Lord despises the deeds of the wicked, but loves those who try to be good. If they stop trying, the Lord will punish them; if they rebel against that punishment, they will die.

[11] The depths of hell are open to God's knowledge. How much more the hearts of all mankind!

[12] A mocker stays away from wise men because he hates to be scolded.

[13] A happy face means a glad heart; a sad face means a breaking heart.

[14] A wise man is hungry for truth, while the mocker feeds on trash.

[15] When a man is gloomy, everything seems to go wrong; when he is cheerful, everything seems right!

[16] Better a little with reverence for God, than great treasure and trouble with it.

[17] It is better to eat soup with someone you love than steak with someone you hate.

[18] A quick-tempered man starts fights; a cool-tempered man tries to stop them.

[19] A lazy fellow has trouble all through life; the good man's path is easy!

[20] A sensible son gladdens his father. A rebellious son saddens his mother.[a]

[21] If a man enjoys folly, something is wrong! The sensible stay on the pathways of right.

[22] Plans go wrong with too few counselors; many counselors bring success.

[23] Everyone enjoys giving good advice, and how wonderful it is to be able to say the right thing at the right time!

[24] The road of the godly leads upward, leaving hell behind.

[25] The Lord destroys the possessions of the proud but cares for widows.

[26] The Lord hates the thoughts of the wicked but delights[b] in kind words.

[27] Dishonest money brings grief to all the family, but hating bribes brings happiness.[c]

[28] A good man thinks before he speaks; the evil man pours out his evil words without a thought.

[29] The Lord is far from the wicked, but he hears the prayers of the righteous.

[30] Pleasant sights and good reports give happiness and health.

[31,32] If you profit from constructive criticism you will be elected to the wise men's hall of fame. But to reject criticism is to harm yourself and your own best interests.

[33] Humility and reverence for the Lord will make you both wise and honored.

16 WE CAN MAKE our plans, but the final outcome is in God's hands.

[2] We can always "prove" that we are right, but is the Lord convinced?

[3] Commit your work to the Lord, then it will succeed.

[4] The Lord has made everything for his own purposes—even the wicked, for punishment.

[5] Pride disgusts the Lord. Take my word for it—*proud men shall be punished.*

[6] Iniquity is atoned for by mercy and truth; evil is avoided by reverence for God.

[7] When a man is trying to please God, God makes even his worst enemies to be at peace with him.

[8] A little, gained honestly, is better than great wealth gotten by dishonest means.

[9] We should make plans—counting on God to direct us.

[10] God will help the king to judge the people fairly; there need be no mistakes.

[11] The Lord demands fairness in every business deal.[a] He established this principle.

[12] It is a horrible thing for a king to do evil. His right to rule depends upon his fair-

---

a Literally, "despises his mother."   b Literally, "but kind words are pure."   c Literally, "you will live."   16 a Literally, "a just balance and scales are the Lord's; all the weights in the bag are his work."

ness.[b]

[13] The king rejoices when his people are truthful and fair.

[14] The anger of the king is a messenger of death and a wise man will appease it.

[15] Many favors are showered on those who please the king.

[16] How much better is wisdom than gold, and understanding than silver!

[17] The path of the godly leads away from evil; he who follows that path is safe.

[18] Pride goes before destruction and haughtiness before a fall.

[19] Better poor and humble than proud and rich.

[20] God blesses those who obey him; happy the man who puts his trust in the Lord.

[21] The wise man is known by his common sense, and a pleasant teacher is the best.

[22] Wisdom is a fountain of life to those possessing it, but a fool's burden is his folly.

[23] From a wise mind comes careful and persuasive speech.

[24] Kind words are like honey—enjoyable and healthful.

[25] Before every man there lies a wide and pleasant road he thinks is right, but it ends in death.

[26] Hunger is good—if it makes you work to satisfy it!

[27] Idle hands are the devil's workshop; idle lips are his mouthpiece.[c]

[28] An evil man sows strife; gossip separates the best of friends.

[29] Wickedness loves company—and leads others into sin.[d]

[30] The wicked man stares into space with pursed lips, deep in thought, planning his evil deeds.

[31] White hair is a crown of glory and is seen most among the godly.

[32] It is better to be slow-tempered than famous; it is better to have self-control than to control an army.

[33] We toss the coin,[e] but it is the Lord who controls its decision.

17 A DRY CRUST eaten in peace is better than steak every day along with argument and strife.

[2] A wise slave will rule his master's wicked sons and share their estate.

[3] Silver and gold are purified by fire, but God purifies hearts.

[4] The wicked enjoy fellowship with others who are wicked; liars enjoy liars.

[5] Mocking the poor is mocking the God who made them. He will punish those who rejoice at others' misfortunes.

[6] An old man's grandchildren are his crowning glory. A child's glory is his father.

[7] Truth from a rebel or lies from a king are both unexpected.

[8] A bribe works like magic. Whoever uses it will prosper![a]

[9] Love forgets mistakes; nagging about them parts the best of friends.

[10] A rebuke to a man of common sense is more effective than a hundred lashes on the back of a rebel.

[11] The wicked live for rebellion; they shall be severely punished.[b]

[12] It is safer to meet a bear robbed of her cubs than a fool caught in his folly.

[13] If you repay evil for good, a curse is upon your home.

[14] It is hard to stop a quarrel once it starts,[c] so don't let it begin.

[15] The Lord despises those who say that bad is good, and good is bad.

[16] It is senseless to pay tuition to educate a rebel who has no heart for truth.[d]

[17] A true friend is always loyal, and a brother is born to help in time of need.

[18] It is poor judgment to countersign another's note, to become responsible for his debts.

[19] Sinners love to fight; boasting is looking for trouble.

[20] An evil man is suspicious of everyone[e] and tumbles into constant trouble.

[21] It's no fun to be a rebel's father.

[22] A cheerful heart does good like medicine, but a broken spirit makes one sick.

[23] It is wrong to accept a bribe to twist

---

b Literally, "for the throne is established by righteousness."   c Literally, "A worthless man devises mischief; and in his lips there is a scorching fire."   d Or, "An evil man deceives his neighbor and leads him into loss."   e Literally, "cast dice into the lap."   17a This is a fact, but not to be encouraged!
b Literally, "a stern (ruthless) messenger will be sent against him."   c Literally, "as when one lets out water."   d Literally, "no heart."   e Or, "does not prosper."

justice.

²⁴ Wisdom is the main pursuit of sensible men, but a fool's goals are at the ends of the earth!

²⁵ A rebellious son is a grief to his father and a bitter blow to his mother.

²⁶ How short-sighted to fine the godly for being good! And to punish nobles for being honest!

²⁷,²⁸ The man of few words and settled mind is wise; therefore, even a fool is thought to be wise when he is silent. It pays him to keep his mouth shut.

18 THE SELFISH MAN quarrels against every sound principle of conduct by demanding his own way.

² A rebel doesn't care about the facts. All he wants to do is yell.ᵃ

³ Sin brings disgrace.

⁴ A wise man's words express deep streams of thought.

⁵ It is wrong for a judge to favor the wicked and condemn the innocent.

⁶,⁷ A fool gets into constant fights. His mouth is his undoing! His words endanger him.

⁸ What dainty morsels rumors are. They are eaten with great relish!

⁹ A lazy man is brother to the saboteur.

¹⁰ The Lordᵇ is a strong fortress. The godly run to him and are safe.

¹¹ The rich man thinks of his wealth as an impregnable defense, a high wall of safety. What a dreamer!

¹² Pride ends in destruction; humility ends in honor.

¹³ What a shame—yes, how stupid!—to decide before knowing the facts!

¹⁴ A man's courageᶜ can sustain his broken body, but when courage dies, what hope is left?

¹⁵ The intelligent man is always open to new ideas. In fact, he looks for them.

¹⁶ A bribe does wonders; it will bring you before men of importance!

¹⁷ Any story sounds true until someone tells the other side and sets the record straight.

¹⁸ A coin tossᵈ ends arguments and set-tles disputes between powerful opponents.

¹⁹ It is harder to win back the friendship of an offended brother than to capture a fortified city.ᵉ His anger shuts you out like iron bars.

²⁰ Ability to give wise advice satisfies like a good meal!

²¹ Those who love to talk will suffer the consequences. Men have died for saying the wrong thing!

²² The man who finds a wife finds a good thing; she is a blessing to him from the Lord.

²³ The poor man pleads and the rich man answers with insults.

²⁴ There are "friends" who pretend to be friends, but there is a friend who sticks closer than a brother.

19 BETTER BE POOR and honest than richᵃ and dishonest.

² It is dangerous and sinful to rush into the unknown.

³ A man may ruin his chances by his own foolishness and then blame it on the Lord!

⁴ A wealthy man has many "friends"; the poor man has none left.

⁵ Punish false witnesses. Track down liars.

⁶ Many beg favors from a man who is generous; everyone is his friend!

⁷ A poor man's own brothers turn away from him in embarrassment;ᵇ how much more his friends! He calls after them, but they are gone.

⁸ He who loves wisdom loves his own best interest and will be a success.

⁹ A false witness shall be punished and a liar shall be caught.

¹⁰ It doesn't seem right for a fool to succeed or for a slave to rule over princes!

¹¹ A wise man restrains his anger and overlooks insults. This is to his credit.

¹² The king's anger is as dangerous as a lion's. But his approval is as refreshing as the dew on grass.

¹³ A rebellious son is a calamity to his father, and a nagging wife annoys like constant dripping.

¹⁴ A father can give his sons homes and

---

a Literally, "express his opinion."   b Literally, "The name of the Lord."   c Literally, "spirit."
d Literally, "the lot."   e The Hebrew of this verse is not clear.   19a Literally, "a fool."
b Literally, "despise him."

riches, but only the Lord can give them understanding wives.

¹⁵ A lazy man sleeps soundly—and goes hungry!

¹⁶ Keep the commandments and keep your life; despising them means death.

¹⁷ When you help the poor you are lending to the Lord—and he pays wonderful interest on your loan!

¹⁸ Discipline your son in his early years while there is hope. If you don't you will ruin his life.

¹⁹ A short-tempered man must bear his own penalty; you can't do much to help him. If you try once you must try a dozen times!

²⁰ Get all the advice you can and be wise the rest of your life.

²¹ Man proposes, but God disposes.

²² Kindness makes a man attractive. And it is better to be poor than dishonest.

²³ Reverence for God gives life, happiness, and protection from harm.

²⁴ Some men are so lazy they won't even feed themselves!

²⁵ Punish a mocker and others will learn from his example. Reprove a wise man and he will be the wiser.

²⁶ A son who mistreats his father or mother is a public disgrace.

²⁷ Stop listening to teaching that contradicts what you know is right.

²⁸ A worthless witness cares nothing for truth—he enjoys his sinning too much.

²⁹ Mockers and rebels shall be severely punished.

20 WINE GIVES FALSE courage; hard liquor leads to brawls; what fools men are to let it master them, making them reel drunkenly down the street!

² The king's fury is like that of a roaring lion; to rouse his anger is to risk your life.

³ It is an honor for a man to stay out of a fight. Only fools insist on quarreling.

⁴ If you won't plow in the cold, you won't eat at the harvest.

⁵ Though good advice lies deep within a counselor's heart, the wise man will draw it out.

⁶ Most people will tell you what loyal friends they are, but are they telling the truth?

⁷ It is a wonderful heritage to have an honest father.

⁸ A king sitting as judge weighs all the evidence carefully, distinguishing the true from false.

⁹ Who can ever say, "I have cleansed my heart; I am sinless"?

¹⁰ The Lord despises every kind of cheating.^a

¹¹ The character of even a child can be known by the way he acts—whether what he does is pure and right.

¹² If you have good eyesight and good hearing, thank^b God who gave them to you.

¹³ If you love sleep, you will end in poverty. Stay awake, work hard, and there will be plenty to eat!

¹⁴ "Utterly worthless!" says the buyer as he haggles over the price. But afterwards he brags about his bargain!

¹⁵ Good sense is far more valuable than gold or precious jewels.

¹⁶ It is risky to make loans to strangers!

¹⁷ Some men enjoy cheating, but the cake they buy with such ill-gotten gain will turn to gravel in their mouths.

¹⁸ Don't go ahead with your plans without the advice of others; don't go to war until they agree.

¹⁹ Don't tell^c your secrets to a gossip unless you want them broadcast to the world.

²⁰ God puts out the light of the man who curses his father or mother.

²¹ A fortune can be made from cheating,^d but there is a curse that goes with it.

²² Don't repay evil for evil. Wait for the Lord to handle the matter.

²³ The Lord loathes all cheating and dishonesty.^e

²⁴ Since the Lord is directing our steps, why try to understand everything that happens along the way?

²⁵ It is foolish and rash to make a promise to the Lord before counting the cost.

²⁶ A wise king stamps out crime by severe punishment.

²⁷ A man's conscience^f is the Lord's

---

a Literally, "diverse weights and diverse measures." b Implied. c Literally, "company not with him." d Literally, "quickly gathered." e Literally, "diverse weights . . . false scales." f Literally, "spirit."

searchlight exposing his hidden motives.

²⁸ If a king is kind, honest and fair, his kingdom stands secure.

²⁹ The glory of young men is their strength; of old men, their experience.ᵍ

³⁰ Punishment that hurts chases evil from the heart.

21 JUST AS WATER is turned into irrigation ditches, so the Lord directs the king's thoughts. He turns them wherever he wants to.

² We can justify our every deed but God looks at our motives.

³ God is more pleased when we are just and fair than when we give him gifts.

⁴ Pride, lust, and evil actionsᵃ are all sin.

⁵ Steady plodding brings prosperity; hasty speculation brings poverty.

⁶ Dishonest gain will never last, so why take the risk?

⁷ Because the wicked are unfair, their violence boomerangs and destroys them.

⁸ A man is known by his actions.ᵇ An evil man lives an evil life; a good man lives a godly life.

⁹ It is better to live in the corner of an attic than with a crabby woman in a lovely home.

¹⁰ An evil man loves to harm others; being a good neighbor is out of his line.

¹¹ The wise man learns by listening; the simpleton can learn only by seeing scorners punished.

¹² The godly learn by watching ruin overtake the wicked.

¹³ He who shuts his ears to the cries of the poor will be ignored in his own time of need.

¹⁴ An angry man is silenced by giving him a gift!

¹⁵ A good man loves justice, but it is a calamity to evil-doers.

¹⁶ The man who strays away from common sense will end up dead!

¹⁷ A man who loves pleasure becomes poor; wine and luxury are not the way to riches!

¹⁸ The wicked will finally lose; the right-

eous will finally win.ᶜ

¹⁹ Better to live in the desert than with a quarrelsome, complaining woman.

²⁰ The wise man saves for the future,ᵈ but the foolish man spends whatever he gets.

²¹ The man who tries to be good, loving and kind finds life, righteousness and honor.

²² The wise man conquers the strong man and levels his defenses.

²³ Keep your mouth closed and you'll stay out of trouble.

²⁴ Mockers are proud, haughty and arrogant.

²⁵,²⁶ The lazy man longs for many things but his hands refuse to work. He is greedy to get, while the godly love to give!

²⁷ God loathes the gifts of evil men, especially if they are trying to bribe him!

²⁸ A false witness must be punished; an honest witness is safe.

²⁹ An evil man is stubborn, but a godly man will reconsider.ᵉ

³⁰ No one, regardless of how shrewd or well-advised he is, can stand against the Lord.

³¹ Go ahead and prepare for the conflict,ᶠ but victory comes from God.

22 IF YOU MUST choose, take a good name rather than great riches; for to be held in loving esteem is better than silver and gold.

² The rich and the poor are alike before the Lord who made them all.

³ A prudent man foresees the difficulties ahead and prepares for them; the simpleton goes blindly on and suffers the consequences.

⁴ True humility and respect for the Lord lead a man to riches, honor and long life.

⁵ The rebel walks a thorny, treacherous road; the man who values his soul will stay away.

⁶ Teach a child to choose the right path, and when he is older he will remain upon it.

⁷ Just as the rich rule the poor, so the borrower is servant to the lender.

⁸ The unjust tyrant will reap disaster and

---

g Literally, "the hoary head."   21a Literally, "the tillage of the wicked."   b Implied.
c Literally, "the wicked is a ransom for the righteous."   d Literally, "There is precious treasure and oil in the dwelling of the wise."   e Or, "The wicked man is brazen; the godly man is thoughtful."
f Literally, "The horse is prepared against the day of battle."

his reign of terror shall end.

⁹ Happy is the generous man, the one who feeds the poor.

¹⁰ Throw out the mocker, and you will be rid of tension, fighting and quarrels.

¹¹ He who values grace and truth is the king's friend.

¹² The Lord preserves the upright but ruins the plans^a of the wicked.

¹³ The lazy man is full of excuses. "I can't go to work!" he says. "If I go outside I might meet a lion in the street and be killed!"

¹⁴ A prostitute is a dangerous trap; those cursed of God are caught in it.

¹⁵ A youngster's heart is filled with rebellion, but punishment will drive it out of him.

¹⁶ He who gains by oppressing the poor or by bribing the rich shall end in poverty.

¹⁷,¹⁸,¹⁹ Listen to this wise advice; follow it closely, for it will do you good, and you can pass it on to others: *Trust in the Lord.*

²⁰,²¹ In the past, haven't I been right? Then believe what I am telling you now, and share it with others.

²²,²³ Don't rob the poor and sick! For the Lord is their defender. If you injure them he will punish you.

²⁴,²⁵ Keep away from angry, short-tempered men, lest you learn to be like them and endanger your soul.

²⁶,²⁷ Unless you have the extra cash on hand, don't countersign a note. Why risk everything you own? They'll even take your bed!

²⁸ Do not move the ancient boundary marks. That is stealing.^b

²⁹ Do you know a hard-working man? He shall be successful and stand before kings!

23 WHEN DINING WITH a rich man,^a be on your guard and don't stuff yourself, though it all tastes so good; for he is trying to bribe you, and no good is going to come of his invitation.

⁴,⁵ Don't weary yourself trying to get rich. Why waste your time? For riches can disappear as though they had the wings of a bird!

⁶,⁷,⁸ Don't associate with evil men; don't long for their favors and gifts. Their kindness is a trick; they want to use you as their pawn. The delicious food they serve will turn sour in your stomach and you will vomit it, and have to take back your words of appreciation for their "kindness."

⁹ Don't waste your breath on a rebel. He will despise the wisest advice.

¹⁰,¹¹ Don't steal the land of defenseless orphans by moving their ancient boundary marks, for their Redeemer is strong; he himself will accuse you.

¹² Don't refuse to accept criticism; get all the help^b you can.

¹³,¹⁴ Don't fail to correct your children; discipline won't hurt them! They won't die if you use a stick on them! Punishment will keep them out of hell.

¹⁵,¹⁶ My son, how I will rejoice if you become a man of common sense. Yes, my heart will thrill to your thoughtful, wise words.

¹⁷,¹⁸ Don't envy evil men but continue to reverence the Lord all the time, for surely you have a wonderful future ahead of you. There is hope for you yet!

¹⁹,²⁰,²¹ O my son, be wise and stay in God's paths; don't carouse with drunkards and gluttons, for they are on their way to poverty. And remember that too much sleep clothes a man with rags. ²² Listen to your father's advice and don't despise an old mother's experience. ²³ Get the facts at any price, and hold on tightly to all the good sense you can get. ²⁴,²⁵ The father of a godly man has cause for joy—what pleasure a wise son is! So give your parents joy!

²⁶,²⁷,²⁸ O my son, trust my advice—stay away from prostitutes. For a prostitute is a deep and narrow grave. Like a robber, she waits for her victims as one after another become unfaithful to their wives.

²⁹,³⁰ Whose heart is filled with anguish and sorrow? Who is always fighting and quarreling? Who is the man with bloodshot eyes and many wounds? It is the one who spends long hours in the taverns, trying out new mixtures. ³¹ Don't let the sparkle and the smooth taste of strong wine deceive you. ³² For in the end it bites like a poisonous

---

a Literally, "the words."   b Implied.   23a Literally, "a ruler."   b Literally, "knowledge."

serpent; it stings like an adder. ³³ You will see hallucinations and have delirium tremens, and you will say foolish, silly things that would embarrass you no end when sober. ³⁴ You will stagger like a sailor tossed at sea, clinging to a swaying mast. ³⁵ And afterwards you will say, "I didn't even know it when they beat me up . . . . Let's go and have another drink!"

24 DON'T ENVY GODLESS men; don't even enjoy their company. ² For they spend their days plotting violence and cheating.

³,⁴ Any enterprise is built by wise planning, becomes strong through common sense, and profits wonderfully by keeping abreast of the facts.

⁵ A wise man is mightier than a strong man. Wisdom is mightier than strength.

⁶ Don't go to war without wise guidance; there is safety in many counselors.

⁷ Wisdom is too much for a rebel. He'll not be chosen as a counselor!

⁸ To plan evil is as wrong as doing it.

⁹ The rebel's schemes are sinful, and the mocker is the scourge of all mankind.

¹⁰ You are a poor specimen if you can't stand the pressure of adversity.

¹¹,¹² Rescue those who are unjustly sentenced to death; don't stand back and let them die. Don't try to disclaim responsibility by saying you didn't know about it. For God, who knows all hearts, knows yours, and he knows you knew! And he will reward everyone according to his deeds.

¹³,¹⁴ My son, honey whets the appetite, and so does wisdom! When you enjoy becoming wise, there is hope for you! A bright future lies ahead!

¹⁵,¹⁶ O evil man, leave the upright man alone, and quit trying to cheat him out of his rights. Don't you know that this good man, though you trip him up seven times, will each time rise again? But one calamity is enough to lay you low.

¹⁷ Do not rejoice when your enemy meets trouble. Let there be no gladness when he falls— ¹⁸ for the Lord may be displeased with you and stop punishing him!

¹⁹,²⁰ Don't envy the wicked. Don't covet his riches. For the evil man has no future; his light will be snuffed out.

²¹,²² My son, watch your step before the Lord and the king, and don't associate with radicals. For you will go down with them to sudden disaster, and who knows where it all will end?

Here are some additional proverbs:

²³ It is wrong to sentence the poor, and let the rich go free. ²⁴ He who says to the wicked, "You are innocent," shall be cursed by many people of many nations; ²⁵ but blessings shall be showered on those who rebuke sin fearlessly.

²⁶ It is an honor to receive a frank reply.

²⁷ Develop your business first before building your house.

²⁸,²⁹ Don't testify spitefully against an innocent neighbor. Why lie about him? Don't say, "Now I can pay him back for all his meanness to me!"

³⁰,³¹ I walked by the field of a certain lazy fellow and saw that it was overgrown with thorns, and covered with weeds; and its walls were broken down. ³²,³³ Then, as I looked, I learned this lesson:

"A little extra sleep,
    A little more slumber,
    A little folding of the hands to rest"
³⁴ means that poverty will break in upon you suddenly like a robber, and violently like a bandit.

25 THESE PROVERBS OF Solomonᵃ were discovered and copied by the aides of King Hezekiahᵇ of Judah:

²,³ It is God's privilege to conceal things, and the king's privilege to discover and invent. You cannot understand the height of heaven, the size of the earth, or all that goes on in the king's mind!

⁴,⁵ When you remove dross from silver, you have sterling ready for the silversmith. When you remove corrupt men from the king's court, his reign will be just and fair.

⁶,⁷ Don't demand an audience with the king as though you were some powerful prince. It is better to wait for an invitation rather than to be sent back to the end of the line, publicly disgraced!

⁸,⁹,¹⁰ Don't be hot-headed and rush to

---

a 1 Kings 4:32.   b Hezekiah lived 200 years after Solomon.

court! You may start something you can't finish and go down before your neighbor in shameful defeat. So discuss the matter with him privately. Don't tell anyone else, lest he accuse you of slander and you can't withdraw what you said.

¹¹ Timely advice is as lovely as golden apples in a silver basket.

¹² It is a badge of honor to accept valid criticism.

¹³ A faithful employee is as refreshing as a cool day[c] in the hot summertime.

¹⁴ One who doesn't give the gift he promised is like a cloud blowing over a desert without dropping any rain.

¹⁵ Be patient and you will finally win, for a soft tongue can break hard bones.

¹⁶ Do you like honey? Don't eat too much of it, or it will make you sick!

¹⁷ Don't visit your neighbor too often, or you will outwear your welcome!

¹⁸ Telling lies about someone is as harmful as hitting him with an axe, or wounding him with a sword, or shooting him with a sharp arrow.

¹⁹ Putting confidence in an unreliable man is like chewing with a sore tooth, or trying to run on a broken foot.

²⁰ Being happy-go-lucky around a person whose heart is heavy is as bad as stealing his jacket in cold weather, or rubbing salt in his wounds.[d]

²¹,²² If your enemy is hungry, give him food! If he is thirsty, give him something to drink! This will make him feel ashamed of himself, and God will reward you.

²³ As surely as a wind from the north brings cold,[e] just as surely a retort causes anger!

²⁴ It is better to live in a corner of an attic than in a beautiful home with a cranky, quarrelsome woman.

²⁵ Good news from far away is like cold water to the thirsty.

²⁶ If a godly man compromises with the wicked, it is like polluting a fountain or muddying a spring.

²⁷ Just as it is harmful to eat too much honey, so also it is bad for men to think about all the honors they deserve!

²⁸ A man without self-control is as defenseless as a city with broken-down walls.

26 HONOR DOESN'T GO with fools any more than snow with summertime or rain with harvest time!

² An undeserved curse has no effect. Its intended victim will be no more harmed by it than by a sparrow or swallow flitting through the sky.

³ Guide a horse with a whip, a donkey with a bridle, and a rebel with a rod to his back!

⁴,⁵ When arguing with a rebel, don't use foolish arguments as he does, or you will become as foolish as he is! Prick[a] his conceit with silly replies!

⁶ To trust a rebel to convey a message is as foolish as cutting off your feet and drinking poison!

⁷ In the mouth of a fool a proverb becomes as useless as a paralyzed leg.

⁸ Honoring a rebel will backfire like a stone tied to a slingshot!

⁹ A rebel will misapply an illustration so that its point will no more be felt than a thorn in the hand of a drunkard.

¹⁰ The master may get better work from an untrained apprentice than from a skilled rebel!

¹¹ As a dog returns to his vomit, so a fool repeats his folly.

¹² There is one thing worse than a fool, and that is a man who is conceited.

¹³ The lazy man won't go out and work. "There might be a lion outside!" he says. ¹⁴ He sticks to his bed like a door to its hinges! ¹⁵ He is too tired even to lift his food from his dish to his mouth! ¹⁶ Yet in his own opinion he is smarter than seven wise men.

¹⁷ Yanking a dog's ears is no more foolish than interfering in an argument that isn't any of your business.

¹⁸,¹⁹ A man who is caught lying to his neighbor and says, "I was just fooling," is like a madman throwing around firebrands, arrows and death!

²⁰ Fire goes out for lack of fuel, and tensions disappear when gossip stops.

²¹ A quarrelsome man starts fights as

---

c Literally, "snow."   d Literally, "like vinegar upon soda."   e Literally, "rain."
26a Implied. Literally, "Reply to a fool as his folly requires."

easily as a match[b] sets fire to paper.

²² Gossip is a dainty morsel eaten with great relish.

²³ Pretty words may hide a wicked heart, just as a pretty glaze covers a common clay pot.

²⁴,²⁵,²⁶ A man with hate in his heart may sound pleasant enough, but don't believe him; for he is cursing you in his heart. Though he pretends to be so kind, his hatred will finally come to light for all to see.

²⁷ The man who sets a trap for others will get caught in it himself. Roll a boulder down on someone, and it will roll back and crush you.

²⁸ Flattery is a form of hatred and wounds cruelly.

27 DON'T BRAG ABOUT your plans for tomorrow—wait and see what happens.

² Don't praise yourself; let others do it!

³ A rebel's frustrations are heavier than sand and rocks.

⁴ Jealousy is more dangerous and cruel than anger.

⁵ Open rebuke is better than hidden love!

⁶ Wounds from a friend are better than kisses from an enemy!

⁷ Even honey seems tasteless to a man who is full; but if he is hungry, he'll eat anything!

⁸ A man who strays from home is like a bird that wanders from its nest.

⁹ Friendly suggestions are as pleasant as perfume.

¹⁰ Never abandon a friend—either yours or your father's. Then you won't need to go to a distant relative for help in your time of need.

¹¹ My son, how happy I will be if you turn out to be sensible! It will be a public honor to me.

¹² A sensible man watches for problems ahead and prepares to meet them. The simpleton never looks, and suffers the consequences.

¹³ The world's poorest credit risk is the man who agrees to pay a stranger's debts.

¹⁴ If you shout a pleasant greeting to a friend too early in the morning, he will count it as a curse!

¹⁵ A constant dripping on a rainy day and a cranky woman are much alike! ¹⁶ You can no more stop her complaints than you can stop the wind or hold onto anything with oil-slick hands.

¹⁷ A friendly discussion is as stimulating as the sparks that fly when iron strikes iron.

¹⁸ A workman may eat from the orchard he tends; anyone should be rewarded who protects another's interests.

¹⁹ A mirror reflects a man's face, but what he is really like is shown by the kind of friends he chooses.

²⁰ Ambition[a] and death are alike in this: neither is ever satisfied.

²¹ The purity of silver and gold can be tested in a crucible, but a man is tested by his reaction to men's praise.

²² You can't separate a rebel from his foolishness though you crush him to powder.

²³,²⁴ Riches can disappear fast. And the king's crown doesn't stay in his family forever—so watch your business[b] interests closely. Know the state of your flocks and your herds; ²⁵,²⁶,²⁷ then there will be lamb's wool enough for clothing, and goat's milk enough for food for all your household after the hay is harvested, and the new crop appears, and the mountain grasses are gathered in.

28 THE WICKED FLEE when no one is chasing them! But the godly are bold as lions!

² When there is moral rot within a nation, its government topples easily; but with honest, sensible leaders there is stability.

³ When a poor man oppresses those even poorer, he is like an unexpected flood sweeping away their last hope.

⁴ To complain about the law is to praise wickedness. To obey the law is to fight evil.

⁵ Evil men don't understand the importance of justice, but those who follow the Lord are much concerned about it.

⁶ Better to be poor and honest than rich and a cheater.

---

b Literally, "like hot embers to coals and wood to fire." is to lust.   b Implied.

27a Literally, "a man's eyes." Possibly the reference

⁷ Young men who are wise obey the law; a son who is a member of a lawless gang is a shame to his father.

⁸ Income from exploiting the poor will end up in the hands of someone who pities them.

⁹ God doesn't listen to the prayers of men who flout the law.

¹⁰ A curse on those who lead astray the godly. But men who encourage the upright to do good shall be given a worthwhile reward.

¹¹ Rich men are conceited, but their real poverty is evident to the poor.

¹² When the godly are successful, everyone is glad. When the wicked succeed, everyone is sad.

¹³ A man who refuses to admit his mistakes can never be successful. But if he confesses and forsakes them, he gets another chance.

¹⁴ Blessed is the man who reveres God, but the man who doesn't care is headed for serious trouble.

¹⁵ A wicked ruler is as dangerous to the poor as a lion or bear attacking them.

¹⁶ Only a stupid prince will oppress his people, but a king will have a long reign if he hates dishonesty and bribes.

¹⁷ A murderer's conscience will drive him into hell. Don't stop him!

¹⁸ Good men will be rescued from harm, but cheaters will be destroyed.

¹⁹ Hard work brings prosperity; playing around brings poverty.

²⁰ The man who wants to do right will get a rich reward. But the man who wants to get rich quick will quickly fail.

²¹ Giving preferred treatment to rich people is a clear case of selling one's soul for a piece of bread.

²² Trying to get rich quick is evil and leads to poverty.

²³ In the end, people appreciate frankness more than flattery.

²⁴ A man who robs his parents and says, "What's wrong with that?" is no better than a murderer.

²⁵ Greed causes fighting; trusting God leads to prosperity.

²⁶ A man is a fool to trust himself! But those who use God's wisdom are safe.

²⁷ If you give to the poor, your needs will be supplied! But a curse upon those who close their eyes to poverty.

²⁸ When the wicked prosper, good men go away; when the wicked meet disaster, good men return.

29 THE MAN WHO is often reproved but refuses to accept criticism will suddenly be broken and never have another chance.

² With good men in authority, the people rejoice; but with the wicked in power, they groan.

³ A wise son makes his father happy, but a lad who hangs around with prostitutes disgraces him.

⁴ A just king gives stability to his nation, but one who demands bribes destroys it.

⁵,⁶ Flattery is a trap; evil men are caught in it, but good men stay away and sing for joy.

⁷ The good man knows the poor man's rights; the godless don't care.

⁸ Fools start fights everywhere while wise men try to keep peace.

⁹ There's no use arguing with a fool. He only rages and scoffs, and tempers flare.

¹⁰ The godly pray for those who long to kill them.

¹¹ A rebel shouts in anger; a wise man holds his temper in and cools it.

¹² A wicked ruler will have wicked aides on his staff.

¹³ Rich and poor are alike in this: each depends on God for light.

¹⁴ A king who is fair to the poor shall have a long reign.

¹⁵ Scolding and spanking a child helps him to learn. Left to himself, he brings shame to his mother.

¹⁶ When rulers are wicked, their people are too; but good men will live to see the tyrant's downfall.

¹⁷ Discipline your son and he will give you happiness and peace of mind.

¹⁸ Where there is ignorance of God, the people run wild; but what a wonderful thing it is for a nation to know and keep his laws!

¹⁹ Sometimes[a] mere words are not

---

a Literally, "for a servant."

enough—discipline is needed. For the words may not be heeded.

²⁰ There is more hope for a fool than for a man of quick temper.

²¹ Pamper a servant from childhood, and he will expect you to treat him as a son!

²² A hot-tempered man starts fights and gets into all kinds of trouble.

²³ Pride ends in a fall, while humility brings honor.

²⁴ A man who assists a thief must really hate himself! For he knows the consequence but does it anyway.

²⁵ Fear of man is a dangerous trap, but to trust in God means safety.

²⁶ Do you want justice? Don't fawn on the judge, but ask the Lord for it!

²⁷ The good hate the badness of the wicked. The wicked hate the goodness of the good.

30 *These are the messages of Agur, son of Jakeh, from Massa, addressed to Ithiel and Ucal:*

² I am tired out, O God, and ready to die. I am too stupid even to call myself a human being! ³ I cannot understand man,ᵃ let alone God. ⁴ Who else but God goes back and forth to heaven? Who else holds the wind in his fists, and wraps up the oceans in his cloak? Who but God has created the world? If there is any other, what is his name—and his son's name—if you know it?

⁵ Every word of God proves true. He defends all who come to him for protection. ⁶ Do not add to his words, lest he rebuke you, and you be found a liar.

⁷ O God, I beg two favors from you before I die: ⁸ First, help me never to tell a lie. Second, give me neither poverty nor riches! Give me just enough to satisfy my needs! ⁹ For if I grow rich, I may become content without God. And if I am too poor, I may steal, and thus insult God's holy name.

¹⁰ Never falsely accuse a man to his employer, lest he curse you for your sin.

¹¹,¹² There are those who curse their father and mother, and feel themselves faultless despite their many sins. ¹³,¹⁴ They are proud beyond description, arrogant, disdainful. They devour the poor with teeth as sharp as knives!

¹⁵,¹⁶ There are two things never satisfied, like a leech forever craving more: no, three things! no, four!

Hell
The barren womb
A barren desert
Fire

¹⁷ A man who mocks his father and despises his mother shall have his eye plucked out by ravens and eaten by vultures.

¹⁸,¹⁹ There are three things too wonderful for me to understand—no, four!

How an eagle glides through the sky.
How a serpent crawls upon a rock.
How a ship finds its way across the heaving ocean.
The growth of love between a man and a girl.ᵇ

²⁰ There is another thing too: how a prostitute can sin and then say, "What's wrong with that?"

²¹,²²,²³ There are three things that make the earth tremble—no, four it cannot stand:

A slave who becomes a king.
A rebel who prospers.
A bitter woman when she finally marries.
A servant girl who marries her mistress' husband.ᶜ

²⁴⁻²⁸ There are four things that are small but unusually wise:

Ants: they aren't strong, but store up food for the winter.
Cliff badgers: delicate little animals who protect themselves by living among the rocks.
The locusts: though they have no leader, they stay together in swarms.
The lizards: they are easy to catch and kill, yet are found even in king's palaces!

²⁹,³⁰,³¹ There are three stately monarchs in the earth—no, four:

The lion, king of the animals. He won't turn aside for anyone.
The peacock.

---

a Literally, "I have not learned wisdom."   b Literally "the way of a man with a maid." Some linguists believe the meaning is, "why a girl will let herself be seduced."   c Literally, "who succeeds her mistress."

The he-goat.
A king as he leads his army.
[32] If you have been a fool by being proud or plotting evil, don't brag about it—cover your mouth with your hand in shame.
[33] As the churning of cream yields butter, and a blow to the nose causes bleeding, so anger causes quarrels.

31 *These are the wise sayings of King Lemuel of Massa,[a] taught to him at his mother's knee:*

[2] O my son, whom I have dedicated to the Lord, [3] do not spend your time with women—the royal pathway to destruction.

[4] And it is not for kings, O Lemuel, to drink wine and whiskey. [5] For if they drink they may forget their duties and be unable to give justice to those who are oppressed. [6,7] Hard liquor is for sick men at the brink of death, and wine for those in deep depression. Let them drink to forget their poverty and misery.

[8] You should defend those who cannot help themselves. [9] Yes, speak up for the poor and needy and see that they get justice.

[10] If you can find a truly good wife, she is worth more than precious gems! [11] Her husband can trust her, and she will richly satisfy his needs. [12] She will not hinder him, but help him all her life. [13] She finds wool and flax and busily spins it. [14] She buys imported foods, brought by ship from distant ports. [15] She gets up before dawn to prepare breakfast for her household, and plans the day's work for her servant girls. [16] She goes out to inspect a field, and buys it; with her own hands she plants a vineyard. [17] She is energetic, a hard worker, [18] and watches for bargains. She works far into the night!

[19,20] She sews for the poor, and generously gives to the needy. [21] She has no fear of winter for her household, for she has made warm clothes for all of them. [22] She also upholsters with finest tapestry; her own clothing is beautifully made—a purple gown of pure linen. [23] Her husband is well known, for he sits in the council chamber with the other civic leaders. [24] She makes belted linen garments to sell to the merchants.

[25] She is a woman of strength and dignity, and has no fear of old age. [26] When she speaks, her words are wise, and kindness is the rule for everything she says. [27] She watches carefully all that goes on throughout her household, and is never lazy. [28] Her children stand and bless her; so does her husband. He praises her with these words: [29] "There are many fine women in the world, but you are the best of them all!"

[30] Charm can be deceptive and beauty doesn't last, but a woman who fears and reverences God shall be greatly praised. [31] Praise her for the many fine things she does. These good deeds of hers shall bring her honor and recognition from even the leaders of the nations.[b]

---

a Or, "of King Lemuel the oracle."   b Literally, "Give her of the fruit of her hands; and let her works praise her in the gates."

The Money Scramble

If the market closed tomorrow, would you be caught with your stocks up or down? Does it matter? For more and more people, the gold doesn't lie buried at the rainbow's end, but at the end of a ticker tape readout. On a speculator's whim or as a desperate grab for riches, everything goes—and the changing numbers on the Big Board tell the rest of the story.

Solomon could have been one of the original subscribers to *The Wall Street*

Richard Taylor

Journal, keeping close tabs on his growing and sometimes dwindling investments. But through a series of pleasure-seeking blowouts, he finally admits: "He who loves money shall never have enough. The more you have, the more you spend, right up to the limits of your income, so what is the advantage of wealth—except perhaps to watch it as it runs through your fingers?" (5:10, 11). Solomon knew that the person in the money scramble doesn't make it to the winner's circle.

In this book, he tells about trying to get kicks out of nonessential frills and thrills—some with culture and some without. Solomon was fast becoming the legendary "man who has everything." But his total of fulfilling assets still added up to zero.

When the solution is finally slipped in, you almost miss it. There is no million dollar giveaway, but there is a bedrock *meaning* to life for him—and millions of modern pleasure-seekers.

ECCLESIASTES

1 THE AUTHOR: SOLOMON[a] of Jerusalem, King David's son, "The Preacher."

[2] In my opinion, nothing is worthwhile; everything is futile. [3-7] For what does a man get for all his hard work?

Generations come and go but it makes no difference.[b] The sun rises and sets and hurries around to rise again. The wind blows south and north, here and there, twisting back and forth, getting nowhere.[c]

The rivers run into the sea but the sea is never full, and the water returns again to the rivers, and flows again to the sea . . . [8-11] everything is unutterably weary and tiresome. No matter how much we see, we are never satisfied; no matter how much we hear, we are not content.

History merely repeats itself. Nothing is truly new; it has all been done or said before. What can you point to that is new?

---

a Implied. Literally, "the words of the Preacher, the son (or descendant) of David, King of Jerusalem."   b Literally, "but the earth remains forever."   c Implied.

How do you know it didn't exist long ages ago? We don't remember what happened in those former times, and in the future generations no one will remember what we have done back here.

¹²⁻¹⁵ I, the Preacher, was king of Israel, living in Jerusalem. And I applied myself to search for understanding about everything in the universe. I discovered that the lot of man, which God has dealt to him, is not a happy one. It is all foolishness, chasing the wind. What is wrong cannot be righted; it is water over the dam; and there is no use thinking of what might have been.

¹⁶⁻¹⁸ I said to myself, "Look, I am better educated than any of the kings before me in Jerusalem. I have greater wisdom and knowledge." So I worked hard to be wise instead of foolish[d]—but now I realize that even this was like chasing the wind. For the more my wisdom, the more my grief; to increase knowledge only increases distress.

2 I SAID TO myself, "Come now, be merry; enjoy yourself to the full." But I found that this, too, was futile. For it is silly to be laughing all the time; what good does it do? ³ So, after a lot of thinking, I decided to try the road of drink, while still holding steadily to my course of seeking wisdom.

Next I changed my course again and followed the path of folly, so that I could experience the only happiness most men have throughout their lives.

⁴,⁵,⁶ Then I tried to find fulfillment by inaugurating a great public works program: homes, vineyards, gardens, parks and orchards for myself, and reservoirs to hold the water to irrigate my plantations.

⁷,⁸ Next I bought slaves, both men and women, and others were born within my household. I also bred great herds and flocks, more than any of the kings before me. I collected silver and gold as taxes from many kings and provinces.

In the cultural arts, I organized men's and women's choirs and orchestras.

And then there were my many beautiful concubines.

⁹ So I became greater than any of the kings in Jerusalem before me, and with it all I remained clear-eyed, so that I could evaluate all these things. ¹⁰ Anything I wanted, I took, and did not restrain myself from any joy. I even found great pleasure in hard work. This pleasure was, indeed, my only reward for all my labors.

¹¹ But as I looked at everything I had tried, it was all so useless, a chasing of the wind, and there was nothing really worthwhile anywhere. ¹² Now I began a study of the comparative virtues of wisdom and folly, and anyone else would come to the same conclusion[a] I did— ¹³,¹⁴ that wisdom is of more value than foolishness, just as light is better than darkness; for the wise man sees, while the fool is blind. And yet I noticed that there was one thing that happened to wise and foolish alike— ¹⁵ just as the fool will die, so will I. So of what value is all my wisdom? Then I realized that even wisdom is futile. ¹⁶ For the wise and fool both die, and in the days to come both will be long forgotten. ¹⁷ So now I hate life because it is all so irrational; all is foolishness, chasing the wind.

¹⁸ And I am disgusted about this, that I must leave the fruits of all my hard work to others. ¹⁹ And who can tell whether my son will be a wise man or a fool? And yet all I have will be given to him—how discouraging!

²⁰⁻²³ So I turned in despair from hard work as the answer to my search for satisfaction. For though I spend my life searching for wisdom, knowledge, and skill, I must leave all of it to someone who hasn't done a day's work in his life; he inherits all my efforts, free of charge. This is not only foolish, but unfair. So what does a man get for all his hard work? Days full of sorrow and grief, and restless, bitter nights. It is all utterly ridiculous.

²⁴⁻²⁶ So I decided that there was nothing better for a man to do than to enjoy his food and drink, and his job. Then I realized that even this pleasure is from the hand of God. For who can eat or enjoy apart from him? For God gives those who please him wisdom, knowledge, and joy; but if a sinner

---

d Or, "I sought to learn about composure and madness." after the king?"

2a Literally, "for what can the man do who comes

becomes wealthy, God takes the wealth away from him and gives it to those who please him. So here, too, we see an example of foolishly chasing the wind.

3 THERE IS A right time for everything: [2] A time to be born, a time to die;
A time to plant;
A time to harvest;
[3] A time to kill;
A time to heal;
A time to destroy;
A time to rebuild;
[4] A time to cry;
A time to laugh;
A time to grieve;
A time to dance;
[5] A time for scattering stones;
A time for gathering stones;
A time to hug;
A time not to hug;
[6] A time to find;
A time to lose;
A time for keeping;
A time for throwing away;
[7] A time to tear;
A time to repair;
A time to be quiet;
A time to speak up;
[8] A time for loving;
A time for hating;
A time for war;
A time for peace.

[9] What does one really get from hard work? [10] I have thought about this in connection with all the various kinds of work God has given to mankind. [11] Everything is appropriate in its own time. But though God has planted eternity in the hearts of men, even so, man cannot see the whole scope of God's work from beginning to end. [12] So I conclude that, first, there is nothing better for a man than to be happy and to enjoy himself as long as he can; [13] and second, that he should eat and drink and enjoy the fruits of his labors, for these are gifts from God.

[14] And I know this, that whatever God does is final—nothing can be added or taken from it; God's purpose in this is that man should fear the all-powerful God.[a]

[15] Whatever is, has been long ago; and whatever is going to be has been before; God brings to pass again what was in the distant past and disappeared.[b]

[16] Moreover, I notice that throughout the earth justice is giving way to crime and even the police courts are corrupt. [17] I said to myself, "In due season God will judge everything man does, both good and bad."

[18] And then I realized that God is letting the world go on its sinful way so that he can test mankind, and so that men themselves will see that they are no better than beasts. [19] For men and animals both breathe the same air, and both die. So mankind has no real advantage over the beasts; what an absurdity! [20] All go to one place—the dust from which they came and to which they must return. [21] For who can prove that the spirit of man goes upward and the spirit of animals goes downward into dust? [22] So I saw that there is nothing better for men than that they should be happy in their work, for that is what they are here for, and no one can bring them back to life to enjoy what will be in the future, so let them enjoy it now.

4 NEXT I OBSERVED all the oppression and sadness throughout the earth—the tears of the oppressed, and no one helping them, while on the side of their oppressors were powerful allies. [2] So I felt that the dead were better off than the living. [3] And most fortunate of all are those who have never been born, and have never seen all the evil and crime throughout the earth.

[4] Then I observed that the basic motive for success is the driving force of envy and jealousy! But this, too, is foolishness, chasing the wind. [5,6] The fool won't work and almost starves, but feels that it is better to be lazy and barely get by, than to work hard when, in the long run, it is all so futile.

[7] I also observed another piece of foolishness around the earth. [8] This is the case of a man who is quite alone, without a son or brother, yet he works hard to keep gaining more riches, and to whom will he leave it all? And why is he giving up so much now? It is all so pointless and depressing.

---

a Implied.   b Literally, "God seeks what has been driven away."

⁹ Two can accomplish more than twice as much as one, for the results can be much better. ¹⁰ If one falls, the other pulls him up; but if a man falls when he is alone, he's in trouble. ¹¹ Also, on a cold night, two under the same blanket gain warmth from each other, but how can one be warm alone? ¹² And one standing alone can be attacked and defeated, but two can stand back-to-back and conquer; three is even better, for a triple-braided cord is not easily broken.

¹³ It is better to be a poor but wise youth than to be an old and foolish king who refuses all advice. ¹⁴ Such a lad could come from prison and succeed. He might even become king, though born in poverty. ¹⁵ Everyone is eager to help a youth like that, even to help him usurp the throne. ¹⁶ He can become the leader of millions of people, and be very popular. But, then, the younger generation grows up around him and rejects him! So again, it is all foolishness, chasing the wind.

5 AS YOU ENTER the Temple, keep your ears open and your mouth shut! Don't be a fool who doesn't even realize it is sinful to make rash promises to God, for he is in heaven and you are only here on earth, so let your words be few. Just as being too busy gives you nightmares, so being a fool makes you a blabbermouth. ⁴ So when you talk to God and vow to him that you will do something, don't delay in doing it, for God has no pleasure in fools. Keep your promise to him. ⁵ It is far better not to say you'll do something than to say you will and then not do it. ⁶,⁷ In that case, your mouth is making you sin. Don't try to defend yourself by telling the messenger from God that it was all a mistake [to make the vowᵃ]. That would make God very angry; and he mightᵃ destroy your prosperity. Dreaming instead of doing is foolishness, and there is ruin in a flood of empty words; fear God instead.

⁸ If you see some poor man being oppressed by the rich, with miscarriage of justice anywhere throughout the land, don't be surprised! For every official is under orders from higher up, and the higher officials look up to their superiors. And so the matter is lost in red tape and bureaucracy.ᵇ ⁹ And over them all is the king. Oh, for a king who is devoted to his country! Only he can bring order from this chaos.

¹⁰ He who loves money shall never have enough. The foolishness of thinking that wealth brings happiness! ¹¹ The more you have, the more you spend, right up to the limits of your income, so what is the advantage of wealth—except perhaps to watch it as it runs through your fingers! ¹² The man who works hard sleeps well whether he eats little or much, but the rich must worry and suffer insomnia.

¹³,¹⁴ There is another serious problem I have seen everywhere—savings are put into risky investments that turn sour, and soon there is nothing left to pass on to one's son. ¹⁵ The man who speculates is soon back to where he began—with nothing. ¹⁶ This, as I said, is a very serious problem, for all his hard work has been for nothing; he has been working for the wind. It is all swept away. ¹⁷ All the rest of his life he is under a cloud—gloomy, discouraged, frustrated, and angry.

¹⁸ Well, one thing, at least, is good: it is for a man to eat well, drink a good glass of wine, accept his position in life, and enjoy his work whatever his job may be, for however long the Lord may let him live. ¹⁹,²⁰ And, of course, it is very good if a man has received wealth from the Lord, and the good health to enjoy it. To enjoy your work and to accept your lot in life—that is indeed a gift from God. The person who does that will not need to look back with sorrow on his past, for God gives him joy.

6 YES, BUT THERE is a very serious evil which I have seen everywhere— ² God has given to some men very great wealth and honor, so that they can have everything they want, but he doesn't give them the health to enjoy it, and they die and others get it all! This is absurd, a hollow mockery, and a serious fault.

³ Even if a man has a hundred sons and as many daughters and lives to be very old,

a Implied.   b Literally, "and there are yet higher ones over them."

557

but leaves so little money at his death that his children can't even give him a decent burial—I say that he would be better off born dead. [4] For though his birth would then be futile and end in darkness, without even a name, [5] never seeing the sun or even knowing its existence, yet that is better than to be an old, unhappy man. [6] Though a man lives a thousand years twice over, but doesn't find contentment—well, what's the use?

[7,8] Wise men and fools alike spend their lives scratching for food, and never seem to get enough. Both have the same problem, yet the poor man who is wise lives a far better life. [9] A bird in the hand is worth two in the bush; mere dreaming of nice things is foolish; it's chasing the wind.

[10] All things are decided by fate; it was known long ago what each man would be. So there's no use arguing with God about your destiny.

[11] The more words you speak, the less they mean, so why bother to speak at all?

[12] In these few days of our empty lifetimes, who can say how one's days can best be spent? Who can know what will prove best for the future after he is gone? For who knows the future?

7 A GOOD REPUTATION is more valuable than the most expensive perfume.

The day one dies is better than the day he is born! [2] It is better to spend your time at funerals than at festivals. For you are going to die and it is a good thing to think about it while there is still time. [3] Sorrow is better than laughter, for sadness has a refining influence on us. [4] Yes, a wise man thinks much of death, while the fool thinks only of having a good time now.

[5] It is better to be criticized by a wise man than to be praised by a fool! [6] For a fool's compliment is as quickly gone as paper in fire, and it is silly to be impressed by it.

[7] The wise man is turned into a fool by a bribe; it destroys his understanding.

[8] Finishing is better than starting! Patience is better than pride! [9] Don't be quick-tempered—that is being a fool.

[10] Don't long for "the good old days," for you don't know whether they were any better than these!

[11] To be wise is as good as being rich; in fact, it is better. [12] You can get anything by either wisdom or money, but being wise has many advantages.

[13] See the way God does things and fall into line. Don't fight the facts of nature. [14] Enjoy prosperity whenever you can, and when hard times strike, realize that God gives one as well as the other—so that everyone will realize that nothing is certain in this life.

[15-17] In this silly life I have seen everything, including the fact that some of the good die young and some of the wicked live on and on. So don't be too good or too wise! Why destroy yourself? On the other hand, don't be too wicked either—don't be a fool! Why should you die before your time?

[18] Tackle every task that comes along, and if you fear God you can expect his blessing.

[19] A wise man is stronger than the mayors of ten big cities! [20] And there is not a single man in all the earth who is always good and never sins.

[21,22] Don't eavesdrop! You may hear your servant cursing you! For you know how often you yourself curse others!

[23] I have tried my best to be wise. I declared, "I *will* be wise," but it didn't work. [24] Wisdom is far away, and very difficult to find. [25] I searched everywhere, determined to find wisdom and the reason for things, and to prove to myself the wickedness of folly, and that foolishness is madness.

[26] A prostitute is more bitter than death.[a] May it please God that you escape from her, but sinners don't evade her snares.

[27,28] This is my conclusion, says the Preacher. Step by step I came to this result after researching in every direction: One tenth of one per cent of the men I interviewed could be said to be wise, but not one woman!

[29] And I found that though God has made men upright, each has turned away to follow his own downward road.

a Literally, "the woman whose heart is snares and nets."

8 HOW WONDERFUL TO be wise, to understand things, to be able to analyze them and interpret them. Wisdom lights up a man's face, softening its hardness.

2,3 Obey the king as you have vowed to do. Don't always be trying to get out of doing your duty, even when it's unpleasant. For the king punishes those who disobey. 4 The king's command is backed by great power, and no one can withstand it or question it. 5 Those who obey him will not be punished. The wise man will find a time and a way to do what he says. 6,7 Yes, there is a time and a way for everything, though man's trouble lies heavy upon him; for how can he avoid what he doesn't know is going to happen?

8 No one can hold back his spirit from departing; no one has the power to prevent his day of death, for there is no discharge from that obligation and that dark battle. Certainly a man's wickedness is not going to help him then.

9,10 I have thought deeply about all that goes on here in the world, where people have the power of injuring each other. I have seen wicked men buried and as their friends returned from the cemetery, having forgotten all the dead man's evil deeds, these men were praised in the very city where they had committed their many crimes! How odd! 11 Because God does not punish sinners instantly, people feel it is safe to do wrong. 12 But though a man sins a hundred times and still lives, I know very well that those who fear God will be better off, 13 unlike the wicked, who will not live long, good lives—their days shall pass away as quickly as shadows because they don't fear God.

14 There is a strange thing happening here upon the earth: Providence seems to treat some good men as though they were wicked, and some wicked men as though they were good. This is all very vexing and troublesome!

15 Then I decided to spend my time having fun, because I felt that there was nothing better in all the earth than that a man should eat, drink, and be merry, with the hope that this happiness would stick with him in all the hard work which God gives to mankind everywhere.

16,17 In my search for wisdom I observed all that was going on everywhere across the earth—ceaseless activity, day and night. (Of course, only God can see everything, and even the wisest man who says he knows everything, doesn't!)

9 THIS, TOO, I carefully explored—that godly and wise men are in God's will; no one knows whether he will favor them or not. All is chance! 2,3 The same providence confronts everyone, whether good or bad, religious or irreligious, profane or godly. It seems so unfair, that one fate comes to all. That is why men are not more careful to be good, but instead choose their own mad course, for they have no hope— there is nothing but death ahead anyway.

4 There is hope only for the living. "It is better to be a live dog than a dead lion!" 5 For the living at least know that they will die! But the dead know nothing[a]; they don't even have their memories.[a] 6 Whatever they did in their lifetimes—loving, hating, envying—is long gone, and they have no part in anything here on earth any more. 7 So go ahead, eat, drink, and be merry, for it makes no difference to God! 8 Wear fine clothes— with a dash of cologne! 9 Live happily with the woman you love through the fleeting days of life, for the wife God gives you is your best reward down here for all your earthly toil. 10 Whatever you do, do well, for in death, where you are going, there is no working or planning, or knowing, or understanding.[a]

11 Again I looked throughout the earth and saw that the swiftest person does not always win the race, nor the strongest man the battle, and that wise men are often poor, and skillful men are not necessarily famous; but it is all by chance, by happening to be at the right place at the right time. 12 A man never knows when he is going to run into bad luck. He is like a fish caught in a net, or a bird caught in a snare.

13 Here is another thing that has made

---

a These statements are Solomon's discouraged opinion, and do not reflect a knowledge of God's truth on these points!

a deep impression on me as I have watched human affairs: [14] There was a small city with only a few people living in it, and a great king came with his army and besieged it. [15] There was in the city a wise man, very poor, and he knew what to do to save the city, and so it was rescued. But afterwards no one thought any more about him. [16] Then I realized that though wisdom is better than strength, nevertheless, if the wise man is poor, he will be despised, and what he says will not be appreciated. [17] But even so, the quiet words of a wise man are better than the shout of a king of fools. [18] Wisdom is better than weapons of war, but one rotten apple can spoil a barrelful.

10 DEAD FLIES WILL cause even a bottle of perfume to stink! Yes, a small mistake can outweigh much wisdom and honor. [2] A wise man's heart leads him to do right, and a fool's heart leads him to do evil. [3] You can identify a fool just by the way he walks down the street!

[4] If the boss is angry with you, don't quit! A quiet spirit will quiet his bad temper.

[5] There is another evil I have seen as I have watched the world go by, a sad situation concerning kings and rulers: [6] For I have seen foolish men given great authority, and rich men not given their rightful place of dignity! [7] I have even seen servants riding, while princes walk like servants!

[8,9] Dig a well—and fall into it! Demolish an old wall—and be bitten by a snake! When working in a quarry, stones will fall and crush you! There is risk in each stroke of your axe!

[10] A dull axe requires great strength; be wise and sharpen the blade.

[11] When the horse is stolen, it is too late to lock the barn.[a]

[12,13] It is pleasant to listen to wise words, but a fool's speech brings him to ruin. Since he begins with a foolish premise, his conclusion is sheer madness. [14] A fool knows all about the future and tells everyone in detail! But who can really know what is going to happen? [15] A fool is so upset by a little work that he has no strength for the simplest matter.[b]

[16,17] Woe to the land whose king is a child and whose leaders are already drunk in the morning. Happy the land whose king is a nobleman, and whose leaders work hard before they feast and drink, and then only to strengthen themselves for the tasks ahead! [18] Laziness lets the roof leak, and soon the rafters begin to rot. [19] A party gives laughter, and wine gives happiness, and money gives everything! [20] Never curse the king, not even in your thoughts; nor the rich man, either; for a little bird will tell them what you've said.

11 GIVE GENEROUSLY, FOR your gifts will return to you later. [2] Divide your gifts among many,[a] for in the days ahead you yourself may need much help.

[3] When the clouds are heavy, the rains come down; when a tree falls, whether south or north, the die is cast, for there it lies. [4] If you wait for perfect conditions, you will never get anything done.[b] [5] God's ways are as mysterious as the pathway of the wind, and as the manner in which a human spirit is infused into the little body of a baby while it is yet in its mother's womb. [6] Keep on sowing your seed, for you never know which will grow—perhaps it all will.

[7] It is a wonderful thing to be alive! [8] If a person lives to be very old, let him rejoice in every day of life, but let him also remember that eternity is far longer, and that everything down here is futile in comparison.

[9] Young man, it's wonderful to be young! Enjoy every minute of it! Do all you want to; take in everything, but realize that you must account to God for everything you do. [10] So banish grief and pain, but remember that youth, with a whole life before it, can make serious mistakes.

12 DON'T LET THE excitement of being young cause you to forget about your Creator. Honor him in your youth before the evil years come—when you'll no longer enjoy living. [2] It will be too late then to try to remember him, when the sun and light and moon and stars are dim to your old

a Literally, "If the serpent bites before it is charmed, there is no advantage in a charmer."
b Literally, "for a trip to the city."   11a Literally, "Give a portion to seven, yes, even to eight."
b Literally, "He that observeth the wind shall not sow and he that regardeth the clouds shall not reap."

eyes, and there is no silver lining left among your clouds. ³ For there will come a time when your limbs will tremble with age, and your strong legs will become weak, and your teeth will be too few to do their work, and there will be blindness, too. ⁴ Then let your lips be tightly closed while eating, when your teeth are gone! And you will waken at dawn with the first note of the birds; but you yourself will be deaf and tuneless, with quavering voice. ⁵ You will be afraid of heights and of falling—a white-haired, withered old man, dragging himself along: without sexual desire, standing at death's door, and nearing his everlasting home as the mourners go along the streets.

⁶ Yes, remember your Creator now while you are young, before the silver cord of life snaps, and the golden bowl is broken, and the pitcher is broken at the fountain, and the wheel is broken at the cistern; ⁷ and the dust returns to the earth as it was, and the spirit returns to God who gave it. ⁸ All is futile, says the Preacher; utterly futile.

⁹ But then, because the Preacher was wise, he went on teaching the people all he knew; and he collected proverbs and classified them. ¹⁰ For the Preacher was not only a wise man, but a good teacher; he not only taught what he knew to the people, but taught them in an interesting manner. ¹¹ The wise man's words are like goads that spur to action. They nail down important truths. Students are wise who master what their teachers tell them.

¹² But, my son, be warned: there is no end of opinions ready to be expressed. Studying them can go on forever, and become very exhausting!

¹³ Here is my final conclusion: fear God and obey his commandments, for this is the entire duty of man. ¹⁴ For God will judge us for everything we do, including every hidden thing, good or bad.

Sweet Some-things

Richard T. Lee

If you ever had any doubts that God favored romantic love, leave them here. Solomon's song is a joyful, passionate celebration of married bliss ... a bit too explicit for some western readers, perhaps ... but a beautiful dialogue between two jubilant Asian lovers.

Jews and Christians of all centuries have not only appreciated the human warmth of this book, but have let their imaginations run wild on all sorts of allegorical applications: God and Israel, Christ and his Church, and other variations. Whichever track you prefer, one thing is clear: Love is one of God's most beautiful ideas.

THE SONG OF SOLOMON

1 THIS SONG OF *songs, more wonderful than any other, was composed by King Solomon:*

The Girl: [a] [2] "Kiss me again and again, for your love is sweeter than wine. [3] How fragrant your cologne, and how great your name! No wonder all the young girls love you! [4] Take me with you; come, let's run!"

The Girl: "The king has brought me into his palace. How happy we will be! Your love is better than wine. No wonder all the young girls love you!"

The Girl: [5] "I am dark but beautiful, O girls of Jerusalem, tanned as the dark tents of Kedar."

King Solomon: "But lovely as the silken tents of Solomon!"

The Girl: [6] "Don't look down on me, you city girls,[b] just because my complexion is so dark—the sun has tanned me. My brothers were angry with me and sent me out into the sun[c] to tend the vineyards, but see what it has done to me!"[d]

The Girl: [7] "Tell me, O one I love, where are you leading your flock today? Where will you be at noon? For I will come and join you there instead of wandering like a vagabond among the flocks of your companions."

King Solomon: [8] "If you don't know, O most beautiful woman in all the world, follow the trail of my flock to the shepherds' tents, and there feed your sheep and their lambs. [9] What a lovely filly[e] you are, my love! [10] How lovely your cheeks are, with your hair[f] falling down upon them! How stately your neck with that long string of jewels. [11] We shall make you golden earrings and silver beads."

The Girl: [12] "The king lies on his bed, enchanted by the fragrance of my per-

---

a The headings identifying the speakers are conjectures and are not in the original text.
b Implied in verse 5.   c Implied.   d Literally, "but my own vineyards are neglected."
e Literally, "I compare you to my mare harnessed to Pharaoh's chariot."   f Literally, "ornaments."

fume. [13] My beloved one is a sachet of myrrh lying between my breasts."

King Solomon: [14] "My beloved is a bouquet of flowers in the gardens of Engedi. [15] How beautiful you are, my love, how beautiful! Your eyes are soft as doves'. [16] What a lovely, pleasant thing you are, lying here upon the grass, [17] shaded by the cedar trees and firs."

2 THE GIRL: "I am the rose of Sharon, the lily of the valley."

King Solomon: [2] "Yes, a lily among thorns, so is my beloved as compared with any other girls."

The Girl: [3] "My lover is an apple tree, the finest in the orchard as compared with any of the other youths. I am seated in his much-desired shade and his fruit is lovely to eat. [4] He brings me to the banquet hall and everyone can see how much he loves me. [5] Oh, feed me with your love—your 'raisins' and your 'apples'—for I am utterly lovesick. [6] His left hand is under my head and with his right hand he embraces me. [7] O girls of Jerusalem, I adjure you by the gazelles and deer in the park, that you do not awaken my lover. Let him sleep!"[a]

The Girl: [8] "Ah, I hear him—my beloved! Here he comes, leaping upon the mountains and bounding over the hills. [9] My beloved is like a gazelle or young deer. Look, there he is behind the wall, now looking in at the windows.

[10] "My beloved said to me, 'Rise up, my love, my fair one, and come away. [11] For the winter is past, the rain is over and gone. [12] The flowers are springing up and the time of the singing of birds has come. Yes, spring is here.[b] [13] The leaves are coming out[c] and the grape vines are in blossom. How delicious they smell! Arise, my love, my fair one, and come away.'

[14] "My dove is hiding behind some rocks, behind an outcrop of the cliff.

Call to me and let me hear your lovely voice and see your handsome face.

[15] "The little foxes are ruining the vineyards. Catch them, for the grapes are all in blossom.

[16] "My beloved is mine and I am his. He is feeding among the lilies! [17] Before the dawn comes and the shadows flee away, come to me, my beloved, and be like a gazelle or a young stag on the mountains of spices."

3 THE GIRL: "One night my lover was missing from my bed. I got up to look for him but couldn't find him. [2] I went out into the streets of the city and the roads to seek him, but I searched in vain. [3] The police stopped me and I said to them, 'Have you seen him anywhere, this one I love so much?' [4] It was only a little while afterwards that I found him and held him and would not let him go until I had brought him into my childhood home, into my mother's old bedroom. [5] I adjure you, O women of Jerusalem, by the gazelles and deer of the park, not to awake my lover. Let him sleep."

The Young Women of Jerusalem: [6] "Who is this sweeping in from the deserts like a cloud of smoke along the ground, smelling of myrrh and frankincense and every other spice that can be bought? [7] Look, it is the chariot[a] of Solomon with sixty of the mightiest men of his army surrounding it. [8] They are all skilled swordsmen and experienced bodyguards. Each one has his sword upon his thigh to defend his king against any onslaught in the night. [9] For King Solomon made himself a chariot from the wood of Lebanon. [10] Its posts are silver, its canopy gold, the seat is purple; and the back is inlaid with these words: 'With love from the girls of Jerusalem!'"

---

a Literally, "that you stir not up nor awaken love until it please."   b Literally, "The voice of the turtledove is heard in our land."   c Literally, "The fig tree puts forth its figs."   3a Literally, "litter."

The Girl: [11] "Go out and see King Solomon, O young women of Zion; see the crown with which his mother crowned him on his wedding day, his day of gladness."

4 KING SOLOMON: "How beautiful you are, my love, how beautiful! Your eyes are those of doves. Your hair falls across your face like flocks of goats that frisk across the slopes of Gilead. [2] Your teeth are white as sheep's wool, newly shorn and washed; perfectly matched, without one missing. [3] Your lips are like a thread of scarlet—and how beautiful your mouth. Your cheeks are matched loveliness[a] behind your locks.[b] [4] Your neck is stately[c] as the tower of David, jeweled with a thousand heroes' shields. [5] Your breasts are like twin fawns of a gazelle, feeding among the lilies. [6] Until the morning dawns and the shadows flee away, I will go to the mountain of myrrh and to the hill of frankincense. [7] You are so beautiful, my love, in every part of you.

[8] "Come with me from Lebanon, my bride. We will look down from the summit of the mountain, from the top of Mount Hermon,[d] where the lions have their dens, and panthers prowl. [9] You have ravished my heart, my lovely one, my bride; I am overcome by one glance of your eyes, by a single bead of your necklace. [10] How sweet is your love, my darling, my bride. How much better it is than mere wine. The perfume of your love is more fragrant than all the richest spices. [11] Your lips, my dear, are made of honey. Yes, honey and cream are under your tongue, and the scent of your garments is like the scent of the mountains and cedars of Lebanon.

[12] "My darling bride is like a private garden, a spring that no one else can have, a fountain of my own.

[13,14] You are like a lovely orchard bearing precious fruit,[e] with the rarest of perfumes; nard and saffron, calamus and cinnamon, and perfume from every other incense tree, as well as myrrh and aloes, and every other lovely spice. [15] You are a garden fountain, a well of living water, refreshing as the streams from the Lebanon mountains."

The Girl: [16] "Come, north wind, awaken; come, south wind, blow upon my garden and waft its lovely perfume to my beloved. Let him come into his garden and eat its choicest fruits."

5 KING SOLOMON: "I am here in my garden, my darling, my bride! I gather my myrrh with my spices and eat my honeycomb with my honey. I drink my wine with my milk."

The Young Women of Jerusalem: "Oh, lover and beloved, eat and drink! Yes, drink deeply!"

The Girl: [2] "One night as I was sleeping, my heart awakened in a dream. I heard the voice of my beloved; he was knocking at my bedroom door. 'Open to me, my darling, my lover, my lovely dove,' he said, 'for I have been out in the night and am covered with dew.'

[3] "But I said, 'I have disrobed. Shall I get dressed again? I have washed my feet, and should I get them soiled?'

[4] "My beloved tried to unlatch the door and my heart was moved for him. [5] I jumped up to open it and my hands dripped with perfume, my fingers with lovely myrrh as I pulled back the bolt. [6] I opened to my beloved, but he was gone. My heart stopped. I searched for him but couldn't find him anywhere. I called to him, but there was no reply. [7] The guards found me and struck and wounded me. The watchman on the wall tore off my veil. [8] I adjure you, O women of Jerusalem, if you find

a Literally, "like halves of a pomegranate." b Literally, "behind your veil." c Implied.
d Literally, "Depart from the peak of Amana, from the peak of Senir and Hermon." e Literally, "Your shoots are an orchard of pomegranates . . ."

my beloved one, tell him that I am sick with love."

The Young Women of Jerusalem: [9] "O woman of rare beauty, what is it about your loved one that is better than any other, that you command us this?"

The Girl: [10] "My beloved one is tanned and handsome, better than ten thousand others! [11] His head is purest gold, and he has wavy, raven hair. [12] His eyes are like doves beside the water brooks, deep and quiet. [13] His cheeks are like sweetly scented beds of spices. His lips are perfumed lilies, his breath like myrrh. [14] His arms are round bars of gold set with topaz; his body is bright ivory encrusted with jewels. [15] His legs are as pillars of marble set in sockets of finest gold, like cedars of Lebanon; none can rival him. [16] His mouth is altogether sweet, lovable in every way. Such, O women of Jerusalem, is my beloved, my friend."

6 THE YOUNG WOMEN *of Jerusalem:* "O rarest of beautiful women, where has your loved one gone? We will help you find him."

The Girl: [2] "He has gone down to his garden, to his spice beds, to pasture his flock and to gather the lilies. [3] I am my beloved's and my beloved is mine. He pastures his flock among the lilies!"

King Solomon: [4] "O my beloved, you are as beautiful as the lovely land of Tirzah, yes, beautiful as Jerusalem, and how you capture my heart.[a] [5] Look the other way, for your eyes have overcome me! Your hair, as it falls across your face, is like a flock of goats frisking down the slopes of Gilead. [6] Your teeth are white as freshly washed ewes, perfectly matched and not one missing. [7] Your cheeks are matched loveliness[b] behind your hair. [8] I have

sixty other wives, all queens, and eighty concubines, and unnumbered virgins available to me; [9] but you, my dove, my perfect one, are the only one among them all, without an equal! The women of Jerusalem were delighted when they saw you and even the queens and concubines praise you. [10] 'Who is this,' they ask, 'arising as the dawn, fair as the moon, pure as the sun, so utterly captivating?' "[c]

The Girl: [11] "I went down into the orchard of nuts and out to the valley to see the springtime there, to see whether the grape vines were budding or the pomegranates were blossoming yet. [12] Before I realized it I was stricken with terrible homesickness and wanted to be back among my own people."[d]

The Young Women of Jerusalem: [13] "Return, return to us, O maid of Shulam. Come back, come back, that we may see you once again."

The Girl: "Why should you seek a mere Shulammite?"

King Solomon: "Because you dance so beautifully."[e]

7 KING SOLOMON: "How beautiful your tripping feet, O queenly maiden. Your rounded thighs are like jewels, the work of the most skilled of craftsmen. [2] Your navel is lovely as a goblet filled with wine. Your waist[a] is like a heap of wheat set about with lilies. [3] Your two breasts are like two fawns, yes, lovely twins.[b] [4] Your neck is stately as an ivory tower, your eyes as limpid pools in Heshbon by the gate of Bath-rabbim. Your nose is shapely[c] like the tower of Lebanon overlooking Damascus.

[5] "As Mount Carmel crowns the mountains, so your hair is your crown. The king is held captive in your queenly tresses.

---

a Literally, "You are . . . terrible as an army with banners." nate."   c Literally, "terrible as an army with banners." people." Another possible reading is, "terrible desire to sit beside my beloved in his chariot." e Literally, "as upon a dance before two armies."   7a Literally, "belly." zelle."   c Implied.

b Literally, "like the halves of a pomegra- d Literally, "the chariots of my princely

b Literally, "twins of a ga-

⁶ "Oh, how delightful you are; how pleasant, O love, for utter delight! ⁷ You are tall and slim like a palm tree, and your breasts are like its clusters of dates. ⁸ I said, I will climb up into the palm tree and take hold of its branches. Now may your breasts be like grape clusters, and the scent of your breath like apples, ⁹ and your kisses as exciting as the best of wine, smooth and sweet, causing the lips of those who are asleep to speak."

The Girl: ¹⁰ "I am my beloved's and I am the one he desires. ¹¹ Come, my beloved, let us go out into the fields and stay in the villages. ¹² Let us get up early and go out to the vineyards and see whether the vines have budded and whether the blossoms have opened and whether the pomegranates are in flower. And there I will give you my love. ¹³ There the mandrakes give forth their fragrance and the rarest fruits are at our doors, the new as well as old, for I have stored them up for my beloved."

8 THE GIRL: "Oh, if only you were my brother; then I could kiss you no matter who was watching, and no one would laugh at me. ² I would bring you to my childhood home,ᵃ and there you would teach me. I would give you spiced wine to drink, sweet pomegranate wine. ³ His left hand would be under my head and his right hand would embrace me. ⁴ I adjure you, O women of Jerusalem, not to awaken him until he please."

The Young Women of Jerusalem: ⁵ "Who is this coming up from the desert, leaning on her beloved?"

King Solomon: "Under the apple tree where your mother gave birth to you in her travail, there I awakened your love."

The Girl: ⁶ "Seal me in your heart with permanent betrothal, for love is strong as death and jealousy is as cruel as Sheol. It flashes fire, the very flame of Jehovah. ⁷ Many waters cannot quench the flame of love, neither can the floods drown it. If a man tried to buy it with everything he owned, he couldn't do it."

The Girl: ⁸ "We have a little sister too young for breasts. What shall we do if someone asks to marry her?"

King Solomon: ⁹ "If she has no breastsᵇ we will build upon her a battlement of silver,ᶜ and if she is a door we will enclose her with cedar boards."ᶜ

The Girl: ¹⁰ "I am slim, tall,ᵈ and full-breastedᵉ and I have found favor in my lover's eyes. ¹¹ Solomon had a vineyard at Baal-hamon which he rented out to some farmers there, the rent being one thousand pieces of silver from each. ¹² But as for my own vineyard, you, O Solomon, shall have my thousand pieces of silver and I will give two hundred pieces to those who care for it. ¹³ O my beloved, living in the gardens, how wonderful that your companions may listen to your voice; let me hear it too. ¹⁴ Come quickly, my beloved, and be like a gazelle or young deer upon the mountains of spices."

---

a Literally, "my mother's house." b Literally, "if she be a wall." c The meaning is obscure.
d Literally, "I am as a wall." e Literally, "My breasts are its towers."

Signs of the Times

NO DUMPING

Pete Ceren

Some people just don't read. Well, yes, they do, but it's so easy to rationalize about sign messages (maybe it doesn't really mean it, or maybe I won't get caught, or the sign is dumb and I don't see any good logic to it).

Isaiah, like the other fifteen prophets whose writings fill out the Old Testament, was a man who posted verbal signs for God. He got a better response than some of the others; kings like Hezekiah took him seriously. But most of the time, people passed off God's messages lightly —they just weren't interested, or didn't like what they heard, or found some other way to ignore the divine word.

Times really haven't changed, have they?

ISAIAH

1 *These are the messages that came to Isaiah, son of Amoz, in the visions he saw during the reigns of King Uzziah, King Jotham, King Ahaz and King Hezekiah—all kings of Judah. In these messages God showed him what was going to happen to Judah and Jerusalem in the days ahead.* [2] Listen, O heaven and earth, to what the Lord is saying:

The children I raised and cared for so long and tenderly have turned against me. [3] Even the animals—the donkey and the ox—know their owner and appreciate his care for them, but not my people Israel. No matter what I do for them, they still don't care. [4] Oh, what a sinful nation they are! They walk bent-backed beneath their load of guilt. Their fathers before them were evil too. Born to be bad, they have turned their backs upon the Lord, and have despised the Holy One of Israel. They have cut themselves off from my help.

[5,6] Oh, my people, haven't you had enough of punishment? Why will you force me to whip you again and again? Must you forever rebel? From head to foot you are sick and weak and faint, covered with bruises and welts and infected wounds, unanointed and unbound. [7] Your country lies in ruins; your cities are burned; while you watch, foreigners are destroying and plundering everything they see. [8] You stand there helpless and abandoned like a watchman's shanty in the field when the harvest time is over—or when the crop is stripped and robbed.

[9] *If the Lord of Hosts had not stepped in to save a few of us, we would have been wiped out as Sodom and Gomorrah were.* [10] An apt comparison![a] Listen, you leaders of Israel, you men of Sodom and Gomorrah, as I call you now. Listen to the Lord. Hear what he is telling you! [11] I am sick of your sacrifices. Don't bring me any more of them. I don't want your fat rams; I don't want to see the blood from your offerings. [12,13] Who wants your sacrifices when you have no sorrow for your sins? The incense you bring me is a stench in my nostrils. Your holy celebrations of the new moon and the Sabbath, and your special days for fasting—even your most pious meetings—all are frauds! I want nothing more to do with them. [14] I hate them all; I can't stand the sight of them. [15] From now on, when you pray with your hands stretched out to heaven, I won't look or listen. Even though you make many prayers, I will not hear, for your hands are those of murderers; they are covered with the blood of your innocent victims.

[16] Oh, wash yourselves! Be clean! Let me no longer see you doing all these wicked things; quit your evil ways. [17] Learn to do good, to be fair and to help the poor, the fatherless, and widows.

[18] Come, let's talk this over! says the Lord; no matter how deep the stain of your sins, I can take it out and make you as clean as freshly fallen snow. Even if you are stained as red as crimson, I can make you white as wool! [19] If you will only let me help you, if you will only obey, then I will make you rich! [20] But if you keep on turning your backs and refusing to listen to me, you will be killed by your enemies; I, the Lord, have spoken.

[21] Jerusalem, once my faithful wife! And now a prostitute! Running after other gods! Once "The City of Fair Play," but now a gang of murderers. [22] Once like sterling silver; now mixed with worthless alloy! Once so pure, but now diluted like watered-down wine! [23] Your leaders are rebels, companions of thieves; all of them take bribes and won't defend the widows and orphans. [24] Therefore the Lord of Hosts, the Mighty One of Israel, says: I will pour out my anger on you, my enemies! [25] I myself will melt you in a smelting pot, and skim off your slag.

[26] And afterwards I will give you good judges and wise counselors like those you used to have. Then your city shall again be called "The City of Justice," and "The Faithful Town." [27] Those who return to the Lord, who are just and good, shall be re-

---

a Implied.

deemed.

²⁸ (But all sinners shall utterly perish, for they refuse to come to me.) ²⁹ Shame will cover you, and you will blush to think of all those times you sacrificed to idols in your groves of "sacred" oaks. ³⁰ You will perish like a withered tree or a garden without water. ³¹ The strongest among you will disappear like burning straw; your evil deeds are the spark that sets the straw on fire, and no one will be able to put it out.

2 THIS IS ANOTHER message to Isaiah from the Lord concerning Judah and Jerusalem:

² In the last days Jerusalem and the Temple of the Lord will become the world's greatest attraction,ᵃ and people from many lands will flow there to worship the Lord.

³ "Come," everyone will say, "let us go up the mountain of the Lord, to the Temple of the God of Israel; there he will teach us his laws, and we will obey them." For in those days the world will be ruled from Jerusalem. ⁴ The Lord will settle international disputes; all the nations will convert their weapons of war into implements of peace.ᵇ Then at the last all wars will stop and all military training will end. ⁵ O Israel, come, let us walk in the light of the Lord, and be obedient to his laws!ᶜ

⁶ The Lord has rejected you because you welcome foreigners from the East who practice magic and communicate with evil spirits, as the Philistines do.

⁷ Israel has vast treasures of silver and gold, and great numbers of horses and chariots ⁸ and idols—the land is full of them! They are man-made, and yet you *worship* them! ⁹ Small and great, all bow before them; God will not forgive you for this sin.

¹⁰ Crawl into the caves in the rocks and hide in terror from his glorious majesty, ¹¹ for the day is coming when your proud looks will be brought low; the Lord alone will be exalted. ¹² On that day the Lord of Hosts will move against the proud and haughty and bring them to the dust. ¹³ All the tall cedars of Lebanon and all the mighty oaks of Bashan shall bend low, ¹⁴ and all the high mountains and hills, ¹⁵ and every high tower and wall, ¹⁶ and all the proud ocean ships and trim harbor craft—*all* shall be crushed before the Lord that day. ¹⁷ All the glory of mankind will bow low; the pride of men will lie in the dust, and the Lord alone will be exalted. ¹⁸ And all idols will be utterly abolished and destroyed.

¹⁹ When the Lord stands up from his throne to shake up the earth, his enemies will crawl with fear into the holes in the rocks and into the caves because of the glory of his majesty. ²⁰ Then at last they will abandon their gold and silver idols to the moles and bats, ²¹ and crawl into the caverns to hide among the jagged rocks at the tops of the cliffs to try to get away from the terror of the Lord and the glory of his majesty when he rises to terrify the earth. ²² Puny man! Frail as his breath! Don't ever put your trust in him!

3 THE LORD OF Hosts will cut off Jerusalem's and Judah's food and water supplies ² and kill her leaders; he will destroy her armies, judges, prophets, elders, ³ army officers, businessmen, lawyers, magicians and politicians. ⁴ Israel's kings will be like babies, ruling childishly. ⁵ And the worst sort of anarchy will prevail—everyone stepping on someone else, neighbors fighting neighbors, youths revolting against authority, criminals sneering at honorable men.

⁶ In those days a man will say to his brother, "You have some extra clothing, so you be our king and take care of this mess."

⁷ "No!" he will reply. "I cannot be of any help! I have no extra food or clothes. Don't get me involved!"

⁸ Israel's civil government will be in utter ruin because the Jews have spoken out against their Lord and will not worship him; they offend his glory. ⁹ The very look on their faces gives them away and shows their guilt. And they boast that their sin is equal to the sin of Sodom; they are not even ashamed. What a catastrophe! They have doomed themselves.

---

a Literally, "shall be established as the highest of the mountains." b Literally, "beat their swords into plowshares and their spears into pruning hooks." c Implied.

[10] But all is well for the godly man. Tell him, "What a reward you are going to get!" [11] But say to the wicked, "Your doom is sure. You too shall get your just deserts. Your well-earned punishment is on the way."

[12] O my people! Can't you see what fools your rulers are? Weak as women! Foolish as little children playing king. True leaders? No, misleaders! Leading you down the garden path to destruction.

[13] The Lord stands up! He is the great Prosecuting Attorney presenting his case against his people! [14] First to feel his wrath will be the elders and the princes, for they have defrauded the poor. They have filled their barns with grain extorted from the helpless peasants.

[15] "How dare you grind my people in the dust like that?" the Lord of Hosts will demand of them.

[16] Next, he will judge the haughty Jewish women, who mince along, noses in the air, tinkling bracelets on their ankles, with wanton eyes that rove among the crowds to catch the glances of the men. [17] The Lord will send a plague of scabs to ornament their heads! He will expose their nakedness for all to see. [18] No longer shall they tinkle with self-assurance as they walk. For the Lord will strip away their artful beauty and their ornaments, [19] their necklaces and bracelets and veils of shimmering gauze. [20] Gone shall be their scarves and ankle chains, headbands, earrings, and perfumes; [21] their rings and jewels, [22] and party clothes and negligees and capes and ornate combs and purses; [23] their mirrors, lovely lingerie, beautiful dresses and veils. [24] Instead of smelling of sweet perfume, they'll stink; for sashes they'll use ropes; their well-set hair will all fall out; they'll wear sacks instead of robes.

All their beauty will be gone; all that will be left to them is shame and disgrace. [25,26] Their husbands shall die in battle; the women, ravaged, shall sit crying on the ground.

4 AT THAT TIME so few men will be left alive that seven women will fight over each of them and say, "Let us all marry you! We will furnish our own food and clothing; only let us be called by your name so that we won't be mocked as old maids."

[2,3,4] Those whose names are written down to escape the destruction of Jerusalem will be washed and rinsed of all their moral filth by the horrors and the fire. They will be God's holy people. And the land will produce for them its lushest bounty and its richest fruit.[a] [5] Then the Lord will provide shade on all Jerusalem—over every home and all its public grounds—a canopy of smoke and cloud throughout the day, and clouds of fire at night, covering the Glorious Land, [6] protecting it from daytime heat and from rains and storms.

5 NOW I WILL sing a song about his vineyard to the one I love. *My Beloved has a vineyard on a very fertile hill.* [2] *He plowed it and took out all the rocks and planted his vineyard with the choicest vines. He built a watchtower and cut a winepress in the rocks. Then he waited for the harvest, but the grapes that grew were wild and sour and not at all the sweet ones he expected.*

[3] Now, men of Jerusalem and Judah, you have heard the case! You be the judges! [4] What more could I have done? Why did my vineyard give me wild grapes instead of sweet? [5] I will tear down the fences and let my vineyard go to pasture to be trampled by cattle and sheep. [6] I won't prune it or hoe it, but let it be overgrown with briars and thorns. I will command the clouds not to rain on it any more.

[7] I have given you the story of God's people. They are the vineyard that I spoke about. Israel and Judah are his pleasant acreage! He expected them to yield a crop of justice, but found bloodshed instead. He expected righteousness, but the cries of deep oppression met his ears.[a] [8] You buy up property so others have no place to live. Your homes are built on great estates so you

---

a The term used here, "branch of the Lord," sometimes refers to the coming Messiah (Jeremiah 23:5, Zechariah 3:8). Here it is used differently to describe God's people, as explained by the parallel phrase, "fruit of the land." However, some may prefer to see here a reference to the presence of the Messiah in Jerusalem at that time.
5a Here is an example of serious punning often used by the prophets: the Hebrew words for "justice" and "bloodshed" sound very much alike, as do those for "righteousness" and "cry."

can be alone in the midst of the earth! ⁹ But the Lord of Hosts has sworn your awful fate—with my own ears I heard him say, "Many a beautiful home will lie deserted, their owners killed or gone." ¹⁰ An acre of vineyard will not produce a gallon of juice! Ten bushels of seed will yield but a one-bushel crop!

¹¹ Woe to you who get up early in the morning to go on long drinking bouts that last till late at night—woe to you drunken bums. ¹² You furnish lovely music at your grand parties; the orchestras are superb! But for the Lord you have no thought or care. ¹³ Therefore I will send you into exile far away because you neither know nor care that I have done so much for you. Your great and honored men will starve, and the common people will die of thirst.

¹⁴ Hell is licking its chops in anticipation of this delicious morsel, Jerusalem. Her great and small shall be swallowed up, and all her drunken throngs. ¹⁵ In that day the haughty shall be brought down to the dust; the proud shall be humbled; ¹⁶ but the Lord of Hosts is exalted above all, for he alone is holy, just and good. ¹⁷ In those days flocks will feed among the ruins. Lambs and calves and kids will pasture there!

¹⁸ Woe to those who drag their sins behind them like a bullock[b] on a rope. ¹⁹ They even mock the Holy One of Israel and dare the Lord to punish them.[c] "Hurry up and punish us, O Lord," they say. "We want to see what you can do!" ²⁰ They say that what is right is wrong, and what is wrong is right; that black is white and white is black; bitter is sweet and sweet is bitter.

²¹ Woe to those who are wise and shrewd in their own eyes! ²² Woe to those who are "heroes" when it comes to drinking, and boast about the liquor they can hold. ²³ They take bribes to pervert justice, letting the wicked go free and putting innocent men in jail. ²⁴ Therefore God will deal with them and burn them. They will disappear like straw on fire. Their roots will rot and their flowers wither, for they have thrown away the laws of God and despised the Word of the Holy One of Israel. ²⁵ That is why the anger of the Lord is hot against his

people; that is why he has reached out his hand to smash them. The hills will tremble, and the rotting bodies of his people will be thrown as refuse in the streets. But even so, his anger is not ended; his hand is heavy on them still.

²⁶ He will send a signal to the nations far away, whistling to those at the ends of the earth, and they will come racing toward Jerusalem. ²⁷ They never weary, never stumble, never stop; their belts are tight, their bootstraps strong; they run without stopping for rest or for sleep. ²⁸ Their arrows are sharp; their bows are bent; sparks fly from their horses' hoofs, and the wheels of their chariots spin like the wind. ²⁹ They roar like lions and pounce upon the prey. They seize my people and carry them off into captivity with none to rescue them. ³⁰ They growl over their victims like the roaring of the sea. Over all Israel lies a pall of darkness and sorrow and the heavens are black.

6 THE YEAR KING Uzziah died I saw the Lord! He was sitting on a lofty throne, and the Temple was filled with his glory. ² Hovering about him were mighty, six-winged seraphs. With two of their wings they covered their faces; with two others they covered their feet, and with two they flew. ³ In a great antiphonal chorus they sang, "Holy, holy, holy is the Lord of Hosts; the whole earth is filled with his glory." ⁴ Such singing it was! It shook the Temple to its foundations, and suddenly the entire sanctuary was filled with smoke.

⁵ Then I said, "My doom is sealed, for I am a foul-mouthed sinner, a member of a sinful, foul-mouthed race; and I have looked upon the King, the Lord of heaven's armies."

⁶ Then one of the seraphs flew over to the altar and with a pair of tongs picked out a burning coal. ⁷ He touched my lips with it and said, "Now you are pronounced 'Not guilty' because this coal has touched your lips. Your sins are all forgiven."

⁸ Then I heard the Lord asking, "Whom shall I send as a messenger to my people? Who will go?"

And I said, "Lord, I'll go! Send *me.*"

---

b Or, "with cords of falsehood."   c Implied

⁹ And he said, "Yes, go. But tell my people this: 'Though you hear my words repeatedly, you won't understand them. Though you watch and watch as I perform my miracles, still you won't know what they mean.' ¹⁰ Dull their understanding, close their ears and shut their eyes. I don't want them to see or to hear or to understand, or to turn to me to heal them."ᵃ

¹¹ Then I said, "Lord, how long will it be before they are ready to listen?"

And he replied, "Not until their cities are destroyed—without a person left—and the whole country is an utter wasteland, ¹² and they are all taken away as slaves to other countries far away, and all the land of Israel lies deserted! ¹³ Yet a tenth—a remnant—will survive; and though Israel is invaded again and again and destroyed, yet Israel will be like a tree cut down, whose stump still lives to grow again."

7 DURING THE REIGN of Ahaz (the son of Jotham and grandson of Uzziah), Jerusalem was attacked by King Rezin of Syria and King Pekah of Israel (the son of Remaliah).ᵃ But it was not taken; the city stood. ² However, when the news came to the royal court, "Syria is allied with Israel against us!" the hearts of the king and his people trembled with fear as the trees of a forest shake in a storm.

³ Then the Lord said to Isaiah, "Go out to meet King Ahaz, you and Shear-jashub, your son. You will find him at the end of the aqueduct which leads from Gihon Spring to the upper reservoir, near the road that leads down to the bleaching field. ⁴ Tell him to quit worrying," the Lord said. "Tell him he needn't be frightened by the fierce anger of those two has-beens, Rezin and Pekah. ⁵ Yes, the kings of Syria and Israel are coming against you.

"They say, ⁶ 'We will invade Judah and throw her people into panic. Then we'll fight our way into Jerusalem and install the son of Tabeel as their king.'

⁷ "But the Lord God says, This plan will not succeed, ⁸ for Damascus will remain the capital of Syria alone, and King Rezin's kingdom will not increase its boundaries. And within sixty-five years Ephraim, too, will be crushed and broken.ᵇ ⁹ Samaria is the capital of Ephraim alone and King Pekah's power will not increase. You don't believe me? If you want me to protect you, you must learn to believe what I say."

¹⁰ Not long after this, the Lord sent this further message to King Ahaz:

¹¹ "Ask me for a sign, Ahaz, to prove that I will indeed crush your enemies as I have said. Ask anything you like, in heaven or on earth."ᶜ

¹² But the king refused. "No," he said, "I'll not bother the Lord with anything like that." ¹³ Then Isaiah said, O House of David, you aren't satisfied to exhaust *my* patience; you exhaust the Lord's as well! ¹⁴ All right then, the Lord himself will choose the sign—a child shall be born to a virgin!ᵈ And she shall call him Immanuel (meaning, "God is with us"). ¹⁵,¹⁶ By the time this child is weanedᵉ and knows right from wrong, the two kings you fear so much—the kings of Israel and Syriaᶠ—will both be dead.ᵍ

¹⁷ But later on,ʰ the Lord will bring a terrible curse on you and on your nation and your family. There will be terror, such as has not been known since the division of Solomon's empire into Israel and Judah—the mighty king of Assyria will come with his great army! ¹⁸ At that time the Lord will whistle for the army of Upper Egypt,ⁱ and of Assyria too, to swarm down upon you

---

a Apparently God's patience with their chronic rebellion was finally exhausted.   a "The usurper, the son of Remaliah" is implied.   b Samaria, the capital of "Ephraim," fell to the Assyrian armies in 722 B.C., thirteen years after this oracle—ending the Northern kingdom.   c Literally, "let it be deep as Sheol or high as heaven."   d The controversial Hebrew word used here sometimes means "virgin" and sometimes "young woman." Its immediate use here refers to Isaiah's young wife and her newborn son (Isaiah 8:1–4). This, of course, was not a virgin birth. God's sign was that before this child was old enough to talk (verse 4) the two invading kings would be destroyed. However, the Gospel of Matthew (1:23) tells us that there was a further fulfillment of this prophecy, in that a virgin (Mary) conceived and bore a son, Immanuel, the Christ. We have therefore properly used this higher meaning, "virgin," in verse 14, as otherwise the Matthew account loses its significance.   e Literally, "For before this child shall know (is old enough) to refuse the evil and to choose the good . . . and (is old enough to) eat curds and honey."   f Implied.   g Or, "the lands will be deserted (of their kings)."   h Implied.   i Literally, "sources of the streams of Egypt" refers to Upper Egypt where the powerful 25th Ethiopian Dynasty would soon arise.

like flies and destroy you, like bees to sting and to kill. ¹⁹ They will come in vast hordes, spreading across the whole land, even into the desolate valleys and caves and thorny parts, as well as to all your fertile acres. ²⁰ In that day the Lord will take this "razor"— these Assyrians you have hired to save you[j]—and use it on you to shave off everything you have: your land, your crops, your people.[k]

²¹,²² When they finally stop plundering, the whole nation will be a pastureland; whole flocks and herds will be destroyed, and a farmer will be fortunate to have a cow and two sheep left. But the abundant pastureland will yield plenty of milk, and everyone left will live on curds and wild honey. ²³ At that time the lush vineyards will become patches of briars. ²⁴ All the land will be one vast thornfield, a hunting ground overrun by wildlife. ²⁵ No one will go to the fertile hillsides where once the gardens grew, for thorns will cover them; cattle, sheep and goats will graze there.

8 AGAIN THE LORD sent me a message: "Make a large signboard and write on it the birth announcement of the son I am going to give you. Use capital letters! His name will be Maher-shalal-hash-baz, which means 'Your enemies will soon be destroyed.' "[a] ² I asked Uriah the priest and Zechariah the son of Jeberechiah, both known as honest men, to watch me as I wrote so they could testify that I had written it (before the child was even on the way).[b] ³ Then I had sexual intercourse with my wife and she conceived, and bore me a son, and the Lord said, "Call him Maher-shalal-hash-baz. ⁴ This name prophesies that within a couple of years, before this child is even old enough to say 'Daddy' or 'Mommy,' the king of Assyria will invade both Damascus and Samaria and carry away their riches."

⁵ Then the Lord spoke to me again and said:

⁶ "Since the people of Jerusalem are planning to refuse my gentle care[c] and are enthusiastic about asking King Rezin and King Pekah to come and aid them, ⁷,⁸ therefore I will overwhelm my people with Euphrates' mighty flood; the king of Assyria and all his mighty armies will rage against them. This flood will overflow all its channels and sweep into your land of Judah, O Immanuel, submerging it from end to end."

⁹,¹⁰ Do your worst, O Syria and Israel,[d] our enemies,[b] but you will not succeed —you will be shattered. Listen to me, all you enemies of ours: Prepare for war against us—and perish! Yes! Perish! Call your councils of war, develop your strategies, prepare your plans of attacking us, and perish! For God is with us.[e]

¹¹ The Lord has said in strongest terms: Do not under any circumstances, go along with the plans of Judah to surrender to Syria and Israel. ¹² Don't let people call you a traitor for staying true to God. Don't you panic as so many of your neighbors are doing when they think of Syria and Israel attacking you. ¹³ Don't fear anything except the Lord of the armies of heaven! If you fear him, you need fear nothing else. ¹⁴,¹⁵ He will be your safety; but Israel and Judah have refused his care and thereby stumbled against the Rock of their salvation and lie fallen and crushed beneath it: God's presence among them has endangered them! ¹⁶ Write down all these things I am going to do, says the Lord, and seal it up for the future. Entrust it to some godly man to pass on down to godly men of future generations.

¹⁷ I will wait for the Lord to help us, though he is hiding now. My only hope is in him. ¹⁸ I and the children God has given me have symbolic names that reveal the plans of the Lord of heaven's armies for his people: Isaiah means "Jehovah will save (his people)," Shear-jashub means "A remnant shall return," and Maher-shalal-hash-baz means "Your enemies will soon be destroyed." ¹⁹ So why are you trying to find out the future by consulting witches and mediums? Don't listen to their whisperings and mutterings. Can the living find out the future from the dead? Why not ask your God?

j 2 Kings 16:7–8.   k Implied. Literally, "head-hair, beard, body-hair."   a Literally, "Plundering and despoiling (will) come quickly."   b Implied.   c Literally, "have refused the waters of Shiloah that go softly."   d Literally, "O peoples."   e Or, "Immanuel."

²⁰ "Check these witches' words against the Word of God!" he says. "If their messages are different than mine, it is because I have not sent them; for they have no light or truth in them. ²¹ My people will be led away captive, stumbling, weary and hungry. And because they are hungry they will rave and shake their fists at heaven and curse their King and their God. ²² Wherever they look there will be trouble and anguish and dark despair. And they will be thrust out into the darkness."

9 NEVERTHELESS, THAT TIME of darkness and despair shall not go on forever. Though soon the land of Zebulun and Naphtali will be under God's contempt and judgment, yet in the future these very lands, Galilee and Northern Transjordan, where lies the road to the sea, will be filled with glory. ² The people who walk in darkness shall see a great Light—a Light that will shine on all those who live in the land of the shadow of death. ³ For Israel will again be great, filled with joy like that of reapers when the harvest time has come, and like that of men dividing up the plunder they have won. ⁴ For God will break the chains that bind his people and the whip that scourges them, just as he did when he destroyed the vast host of the Midianites by Gideon's little band. ⁵ In that glorious day of peace there will no longer be the issuing of battle gear; no more the blood-stained uniforms of war; all such will be burned.

⁶ For unto us a Child is born; unto us a Son is given; and the government shall be upon his shoulder. These will be his royal titles: "Wonderful," "Counselor," "The Mighty God," "The Everlasting Father," "The Prince of Peace." ⁷ His ever-expanding, peaceful government will never end. He will rule with perfect fairness and justice from the throne of his father David. He will bring true justice and peace to all the nations of the world. This is going to happen because the Lord of heaven's armies has dedicated himself to do it!

⁸,⁹,¹⁰ The Lord has spoken out against that braggart Israel who says that though our land lies in ruins now, we will rebuild it better than before. The sycamore trees are cut down, but we will replace them with cedars! ¹¹,¹² The Lord's reply to your bragging is to bring yourᵃ enemies against you— the Syrians on the east and the Philistines on the west. With bared fangs they will devour Israel. And even then the Lord's anger against you will not be satisfied—his fist will still be poised to smash you. ¹³ For after all this punishment you will not repent and turn to him, the Lord of heaven's armies. ¹⁴,¹⁵ Therefore the Lord, in one day, will destroy the leaders of Israel and the lying prophets. ¹⁶ For the leaders of his people have led them down the paths of ruin.

¹⁷ That is why the Lord has no joy in their young men, and no mercy upon even the widows and orphans, for they are all filthy-mouthed, wicked liars. That is why his anger is not yet satisfied, but his fist is still poised to smash them all. ¹⁸ He will burn up all this wickedness, these thorns and briars; and the flames will consume the forests, too, and send a vast cloud of smoke billowing up from their burning. ¹⁹,²⁰ The land is blackened by that fire, by the wrath of the Lord of heaven's armies. The people are fuel for the fire. Each fights against his brother to steal his food, but will never have enough. Finally they will even eat their own children! ²¹ Manasseh against Ephraim and Ephraim against Manasseh—and both against Judah. Yet even after all of this, God's anger is not yet satisfied. His hand is still heavy upon them, to crush them.

10 WOE TO UNJUST judges and to those who issue unfair laws, says the Lord, ² so that there is no justice for the poor, the widows and orphans. Yes, it is true that they even rob the widows and fatherless children.

³ Oh, what will you do when I visit you in that day when I send desolation upon you from a distant land? To whom will you turn then for your help? Where will your treasures be safe? ⁴ I will not help you; you will stumble along as prisoners or lie among the slain. And even then my anger will not be satisfied, but my fist will still be poised to strike you. ⁵,⁶ Assyria is the whip of my an-

---

a Or, "Rezin's enemies," in some ancient versions.

ger; his military strength is my weapon upon this godless nation, doomed and damned; he will enslave them and plunder them and trample them like dirt beneath his feet. [7] But the king of Assyria will not know that it is I who sent him. He will merely think he is attacking my people as part of his plan to conquer the world. [8] He will declare that every one of his princes will soon be a king, ruling a conquered land.

[9] "We will destroy Calno just as we did Carchemish," he will say, "and Hamath will go down before us as Arpad did; and we will destroy Samaria just as we did Damascus. [10] Yes, we have finished off many a kingdom whose idols were far greater than those in Jerusalem and Samaria, [11] so when we have defeated Samaria and her idols we will destroy Jerusalem with hers."

[12] After the Lord has used the king of Assyria to accomplish his purpose, then he will turn upon the Assyrians and punish them too—for they are proud and haughty men.

[13] They boast, "We in our own power and wisdom have won these wars. We are great and wise. By our own strength we broke down the walls and destroyed the people and carried off their treasures. [14] In our greatness we have robbed their nests of riches and gathered up kingdoms as a farmer gathers eggs, and no one can move a finger or open his mouth to peep against us!"

[15] But the Lord says, "Shall the axe boast greater power than the man who uses it? Is the saw greater than the man who saws? Can a rod strike unless a hand is moving it? Can a cane walk by itself?"

[16] Because of all your evil boasting, O king of Assyria, the Lord of Hosts will send a plague among your proud troops, and strike them down. [17] God, the Light and Holy One of Israel, will be the fire and flame that will destroy them. In a single night he will burn those thorns and briars, the Assyrians who destroyed the land of Israel.[a] [18] Assyria's vast army is like a glorious forest, yet it will be destroyed. The Lord will destroy them, soul and body, as when a sick man wastes away. [19] Only a few from all that mighty army will be left; so few a child could count them!

[20] Then at last, those left in Israel and in Judah will trust the Lord, the Holy One of Israel, instead of fearing the Assyrians. [21] A remnant of them will return to the mighty God. [22] But though Israel be now as many as the sands along the shore, yet only a few of them will be left to return at that time; God has rightly decided to destroy his people. [23] Yes, it has already been decided by the Lord God of Hosts to consume them.

[24] Therefore the Lord God of Hosts says, "O my people in Jerusalem, don't be afraid of the Assyrians when they oppress you just as the Egyptians did long ago. [25] It will not last very long; in a little while my anger against you will end, and then it will rise against them to destroy them."

[26] The Lord of Hosts will send his angel to slay them in a mighty slaughter like the time when Gideon triumphed over Midian at the rock of Oreb or the time God drowned the Egyptian armies in the sea. [27] On that day God will end the bondage of his people. He will break the slave-yoke off their necks, and destroy it as decreed.[b]

[28,29] Look, the mighty armies of Assyria are coming! Now they are at Aiath, now at Migron; they are storing some of their equipment at Michmash and crossing over the pass; they are staying overnight at Geba. Fear strikes the city of Ramah; all the people of Gibeah—the city of Saul—are running for their lives. [30] Well may you scream in terror, O people of Gallim. Shout out a warning to Laish, for the mighty army comes. O poor Anathoth, what a fate is yours! [31] There go the people of Madmenah, all fleeing, and the citizens of Gebim are preparing to run. [32] But the enemy stops at Nob for the remainder of that day. He shakes his fist at Jerusalem on Mount Zion.

[33] Then, look, look! The Lord, the Lord of the armies of heaven, is chopping down the mighty tree! He is destroying all of that vast army, great and small alike, both officers and men. [34] He, the Mighty One, will

---

a See 2 Kings 19:35 and Isaiah 37:36. b Literally, "because of ointment." Some see here a reference to the Messiah, the Anointed One.

cut down the enemy as a woodsman's axe cuts down the forest trees in Lebanon.

11 THE ROYAL LINE of David[a] will be cut off, chopped down like a tree; but from the stump will grow a Shoot[b]—yes, a new Branch[b] from the old root. [2] And the Spirit of the Lord shall rest upon him, the Spirit of wisdom, understanding, counsel and might; the Spirit of knowledge and of the fear of the Lord. [3] His delight will be obedience to the Lord. He will not judge by appearance, false evidence, or hearsay, [4] but will defend the poor and the exploited. He will rule against the wicked who oppress them. [5] For he will be clothed with fairness and with truth.

[6] In that day the wolf and the lamb will lie down together, and the leopard and goats will be at peace. Calves and fat cattle will be safe among lions, and a little child shall lead them all. [7] The cows will graze among bears; cubs and calves will lie down together, and lions will eat grass like the cows. [8] Babies will crawl safely among poisonous snakes, and a little child who puts his hand in a nest of deadly adders will pull it out unharmed. [9] Nothing will hurt or destroy in all my holy mountain, for as the waters fill the sea, so shall the earth be full of the knowledge of the Lord.

[10] In that day he who created the royal dynasty of David [c] will be a banner of salvation to all the world. The nations will rally to him, for the land where he lives will be a glorious place. [11] At that time the Lord will bring back a remnant of his people for the second time, returning them to the land of Israel from Assyria, Upper and Lower Egypt, Ethiopia, Elam, Babylonia, Hamath and all the distant coastal lands. [12] He will raise a flag among the nations for them to rally to; he will gather the scattered Israelites from the ends of the earth. [13] Then, at last, the jealousy between Israel and Judah will end; they will not fight each other any more. [14] Together they will fly against the nations possessing their land on the east and on the west, uniting forces to destroy them, and they will occupy the nations of Edom and Moab and Ammon.

[15] The Lord will dry a path through the Red Sea,[d] and wave his hand over the Euphrates,[e] sending a mighty wind to divide it into seven streams that can easily be crossed. [16] He will make a highway from Assyria for the remnant there, just as he did for all of Israel long ago when they returned from Egypt.

12 ON THAT DAY you will say, "Praise the Lord! He was angry with me, but now he comforts me. [2] See, God has come to save me! I will trust and not be afraid, for the Lord is my strength and song; he is my salvation. [3] Oh, the joy of drinking deeply from the Fountain of Salvation!"

[4] In that wonderful day you will say, "Thank the Lord! Praise his name! Tell the world about his wondrous love.[a] How mighty he is!" [5] Sing to the Lord, for he has done wonderful things. Make known his praise around the world. [6] Let all the people of Jerusalem shout his praise with joy. For great and mighty is the Holy One of Israel, who lives among you.

13 THIS IS THE vision God showed Isaiah (son of Amoz) concerning Babylon's doom.

[2] See the flags waving as their enemy attacks. Shout to them, O Israel, and wave them on as they march against Babylon to destroy the palaces of the rich and mighty. [3] I, the Lord, have set apart these armies for this task; I have called those rejoicing in their strength to do this work, to satisfy my anger. [4] Hear the tumult on the mountains! Listen as the armies march! It is the tumult and the shout of many nations. The Lord of Hosts has brought them here, [5] from countries far away. They are his weapons against you, O Babylon. They carry his anger with them and will destroy your whole land.

[6] Scream in terror, for the Lord's time has come, the time for the Almighty to crush you. [7] Your arms lie paralyzed with fear; the strongest hearts melt, [8] and are afraid. Fear grips you with terrible pangs,

---

a Literally, "Jesse."   b Christ, the Messiah.   c Literally, "the Root of Jesse." Possibly the meaning is, "the Heir of David's royal line."   d Literally, "the Sea of Egypt."   e Literally, "the River."
12a Literally, "Proclaim his doings among the nations."

like those of a woman in labor. You look at one another, helpless, as the flames of the burning city reflect upon your pallid faces. ⁹ For see, the day of the Lord is coming, the terrible day of his wrath and fierce anger. The land shall be destroyed, and all the sinners with it. ¹⁰ The heavens will be black above them. No light will shine from stars or sun or moon.

¹¹ And I will punish the world for its evil, the wicked for their sin; I will crush the arrogance of the proud man and the haughtiness of the rich. ¹² Few will live when I have finished up my work.

Men will be as scarce as gold—of greater value than the gold of Ophir. ¹³ For I will shake the heavens in my wrath and fierce anger, and the earth will move from its place in the skies.

¹⁴ The armies of Babylon will run until exhausted, fleeing back to their own land like deer chased by dogs, wandering like sheep deserted by their shepherd. ¹⁵ Those who don't run will be butchered. ¹⁶ Their little children will be dashed to death against the pavement right before their eyes; their homes will be sacked, and their wives raped by the attacking hordes. ¹⁷ For I will stir up the Medes against Babylon, and no amount of silver or gold will buy them off. ¹⁸ The attacking armies will have no mercy on the young people of Babylon or the babies or the children.

¹⁹ And so Babylon, the most glorious of kingdoms, the flower of Chaldean culture, will be as utterly destroyed as Sodom and Gomorrah were when God sent fire from heaven; ²⁰ Babylon will never rise again. Generation after generation will come and go, but the land will never again be lived in.ª The nomads will not even camp there. The shepherds won't let their sheep stay overnight. ²¹ The wild animals of the desert will make it their home. The houses will be haunted by howling creatures. Ostriches will live there, and the demons will come there to dance. ²² Hyenas and jackals will den within the palaces. Babylon's days are numbered; her time of doom will soon be here.

14 BUT THE LORD will have mercy on the Israelis; they are still his special ones. He will bring them back to settle once again in the land of Israel. And many nationalities will come and join them there and be their loyal allies. ² The nations of the world will help them to return, and those coming to live in their land will serve them. Those enslaving Israel will be enslaved—Israel shall rule her enemies!

³ In that wonderful day when the Lord gives his people rest from sorrow and fear, from slavery and chains, ⁴ you will jeer at the king of Babylon and say, "You bully, you! At last you have what was coming to you! ⁵ For the Lord has crushed your wicked power, and broken your evil rule." ⁶ You persecuted my people with unceasing blows of rage and held the nations in your angry grip. You were unrestrained in tyranny. ⁷ But at last the whole earth is at rest and is quiet! All the world begins to sing! ⁸ Even the trees of the woods—the fir trees and cedars of Lebanon—sing out this joyous song: "Your power is broken; no one will bother us now; at last we have peace."

⁹ The denizens of hell crowd to meet you as you enter their domain. World leaders and earth's mightiest kings, long dead, are there to see you. ¹⁰ With one voice they all cry out, "Now you are as weak as we are!" ¹¹ Your might and power are gone; they are buried with you. All the pleasant music in your palace has ceased; now maggots are your sheet, worms your blanket!

¹² How you are fallen from heaven, O Lucifer, son of the morning! How you are cut down to the ground—mighty though you were against the nations of the world. ¹³ For you said to yourself, "I will ascend to heaven and rule the angels.ª I will take the highest throne. I will preside on the Mount of Assembly far away in the north.ᵇ ¹⁴ I will climb to the highest heavens and be like the Most High." ¹⁵ But instead, you will be brought down to the pit of hell, down to its lowest depths. ¹⁶ Everyone there will stare at you and ask, "Can this be the one who shook the earth and the kingdoms of the world? ¹⁷ Can this be the one who de-

---

a Babylon, in Iraq, still lies in utter ruin today. **14a** Literally, "the stars of God." b Literally, "I will sit upon the mount of the congregation in the sides of the north" (Psalm 48:2); or, "on the slopes of Mount Saphon."

stroyed the world and made it into a shambles and demolished its greatest cities and had no mercy on his prisoners?"

[18] The kings of the nations lie in stately glory in their graves, [19] but your body is thrown out like a broken branch; it lies in an open grave, covered with the dead bodies of those slain in battle. It lies as a carcass in the road, trampled and mangled by horses' hoofs. [20] No monument will be given you, for you have destroyed your nation and slain your people. Your son will not succeed you as the king. [21] Slay the children of this sinner. Do not let them rise and conquer the land nor rebuild the cities of the world.

[22] I, myself, have risen against him, says the Lord of heaven's armies, and will cut off his children and his children's children from ever sitting on his throne. [23] I will make Babylon into a desolate land of porcupines, full of swamps and marshes. I will sweep the land with the broom of destruction, says the Lord of the armies of heaven. [24] He has taken an oath to do it! For this is his purpose and plan. [25] I have decided to break the Assyrian army when they are in Israel and to crush them on my mountains; my people shall no longer be their slaves. [26] This is my plan for the whole earth—I will do it by my mighty power that reaches everywhere around the world. [27] The Lord, the God of battle, has spoken—who can change his plans? When his hand moves, who can stop him?

[28] This is the message that came to me the year King Ahaz died:

[29] Don't rejoice, Philistines, that the king who smote you is dead.[c] That rod is broken, yes; but his son will be a greater scourge to you than his father ever was! From the snake will be born an adder, a fiery serpent to destroy you! [30] I will shepherd the poor of my people; they shall graze in my pasture! The needy shall lie down in peace. But as for you—I will wipe you out with famine and the sword. [31] Weep, Philistine cities —you are doomed. All your nation is doomed. For a perfectly trained army[d] is coming down from the north against you. [32] What then shall we tell the reporters? Tell them that the Lord has founded Jerusalem and is determined that the poor of his people will find a refuge within her walls.

15 HERE IS GOD'S message to Moab:
In one night your cities of Ar and Kir will be destroyed. [2] Your people in Dibon go mourning to their temples to weep for the fate of Nebo and Medeba; they shave their heads in sorrow and cut off their beards. [3] They wear sackcloth through the streets, and from every home comes the sound of weeping. [4] The cries from the cities of Heshbon and Elealeh are heard far away, even in Jahaz. The bravest warriors of Moab cry in utter terror.

[5] My heart weeps for Moab! His people flee to Zoar and Eglath. Weeping, they climb the upward road to Luhith, and their crying will be heard all along the road to Horonaim. [6] Even Nimrim River is desolate! The grassy banks are dried up and the tender plants are gone. [7] The desperate refugees take only the possessions they can carry, and flee across the Brook of Willows. [8] The whole land of Moab is a land of weeping, from one end to the other. [9] The stream near Dibon will run red with blood, but I am not through with Dibon yet! Lions will hunt down the survivors, both those who escape and those who remain.

16 MOAB'S REFUGEES AT Sela send lambs as a token of alliance with the king of Judah. [2] The women of Moab are left at the fords of the Arnon River like homeless birds. [3] (The ambassadors, who accompany the gift to Jerusalem[a]) plead for advice and help. "Give us sanctuary. Protect us. Do not turn us over to our foes. [4,5] Let our outcasts stay among you; hide them from our enemies! God will reward you for your kindness to us. If you let Moab's fugitives settle among you, then, when the terror is past, God will establish David's throne forever, and on that throne he will place a just and righteous King."

[6] Is this proud Moab, concerning which we heard so much? His arrogance and insolence are all gone now! [7] Therefore all Moab weeps. Yes, Moab, you will mourn for stricken Kir-hareseth, [8] and for the aban-

---

c Shalmaneser V of Assyria.   d Sargon of Assyria.   16a Implied.

doned farms of Heshbon and the vineyards at Sibmah. The enemy war-lords have cut down the best of the grape vines; their armies spread out as far as Jazer in the deserts, and even down to the sea. ⁹ So I wail and lament for Jazer and the vineyards of Sibmah. My tears shall flow for Heshbon and Elealeh, for destruction has come upon their summer fruits and harvests. ¹⁰ Gone now is the gladness, gone the joy of harvest. The happy singing in the vineyards will be heard no more; the treading out of the grapes in the wine presses has ceased forever. I have ended all their harvest joys.

¹¹ I will weep, weep, weep, for Moab; and my sorrow for Kir-haresh will be very great. ¹² The people of Moab will pray in anguish to their idols at the tops of the hills, but it will do no good; they will cry to their gods in their idol temples, but none will come to save them. ¹³,¹⁴ All this concerning Moab has been said before; but now the Lord says that within three years, without fail, the glory of Moab shall be ended, and few of all its people will be left alive.

17 THIS IS GOD'S message to Damascus, capital of Syria:

Look, Damascus is gone! It is no longer a city—it has become a heap of ruins! ² The cities of Aroer are deserted. Sheep pasture there, lying quiet and unafraid, with no one to chase them away. ³ The strength of Israel and the power of Damascus will end, and the remnant of Syria shall be destroyed. For as Israel's glory departed, so theirs, too, will disappear, declares the Lord of Hosts. ⁴ Yes, the glory of Israel will be very dim when poverty stalks the land. ⁵ Israel will be as abandoned as the harvested grain fields in the Valley of Rephaim. ⁶ Oh, a very few of her people will be left, just as a few stray olives are left on the trees when the harvest is ended, two or three in the highest branches, four or five out on the tips of the limbs. That is how it will be in Damascus and Israel—stripped bare of people except for a few of the poor who remain.

⁷ Then at last they will think of God their Creator and have respect for the Holy One of Israel. ⁸ They will no longer ask their idols for help in that day, neither will they worship what their hands have made! They will no longer have respect for the images of Ashtaroth and the sun-idols.

⁹ Their largest cities will be as deserted as the distant wooded hills and mountain tops and become like the abandoned cities of the Amorites, deserted when the Israelites approached (so long agoᵃ). ¹⁰ Why? Because you have turned from the God who can save you—the Rock who can hide you; therefore, even though you plant a wonderful, rare crop of greatest value, ¹¹ and though it grows so well that it will blossom on the very morning that you plant it, yet you will never harvest it—your only harvest will be a pile of grief and incurable pain.

¹² Look, see the armies thundering toward God's land. ¹³ But though they roar like breakers rolling upon a beach, God will silence them. They will flee, scattered like chaff by the wind, like whirling dust before a storm. ¹⁴ In the evening Israel waits in terror, but by dawn her enemies are dead. This is the just reward of those who plunder and destroy the people of God.

18 AH, LAND BEYOND the upper reaches of the Nile,ᵃ where winged sailboats glide along the river! ² Land that sends ambassadors in fast boats down the Nile! Let swift messengers return to you, O strong and supple nation feared far and wide, a conquering, destroying nation whose land the upper Nileᵇ divides. And this is the message sent to you:

³ When I raise my battle flag upon the mountain, let all the world take notice! When I blow the trumpet, listen! ⁴ For the Lord has told me this: Let your mighty army now advance against the land of Israel.ᶜ God will watch quietly from his Temple in Jerusalem—serene as on a pleasant summer day or a lovely autumn morning during harvest time. ⁵ But before you have begun the attack, and while your plans are ripening like grapes, he will cut you off as though with pruning shears. He will snip the spreading tendrils. ⁶ Your mighty army

---

a Implied.   18a Literally, "land beyond the rivers of Ethiopia." Ethiopia was the seat of the powerful 25th Egyptian Dynasty (730–660 B.C.).   b Literally, "whose land the rivers divide."   c Implied.

will be left dead on the field for the mountain birds and wild animals to eat; the vultures will tear bodies all summer, and the wild animals will gnaw bones all winter. ⁷ But the time will come when that strong and mighty nation, a terror to all both far and near, that conquering, destroying nation whose land the rivers divide, will bring gifts to the Lord of Hosts in Jerusalem, where he has placed his name.

19 THIS IS GOD'S message concerning Egypt:

Look, the Lord is coming against Egypt, riding on a swift cloud; the idols of Egypt tremble; the hearts of the Egyptians melt with fear. ² I will set them to fighting against each other—brother against brother, neighbor against neighbor, city against city, province against province. ³ Her wise counselors are all at their wits' ends to know what to do; they plead with their idols for wisdom, and call upon mediums, wizards and witches to show them what to do.

⁴ I will hand over Egypt to a hard, cruel master, to a vicious king, says the Lord of Hosts. ⁵ And the waters of the Nile will fail to rise and flood the fields; the ditches will be parched and dry, ⁶ their channels fouled with rotting reeds. ⁷ All green things along the river bank will wither and blow away. All crops will perish; everything will die. ⁸ The fishermen will weep for lack of work; those who fish with hooks and those who use the nets will all be unemployed. ⁹ The weavers will have no flax or cotton, for the crops will fail. ¹⁰ Great men and small—all will be crushed and broken.

¹¹ What fools the counselors of Zoan are! Their best counsel to the king of Egypt is utterly stupid and wrong. Will they still boast of their wisdom? Will they dare tell Pharaoh about the long line of wise men they have come from? ¹² What has happened to your "wise counselors," O Pharaoh? Where has their wisdom gone? If they are wise, let them tell you what the Lord is going to do to Egypt. ¹³ The "wise men" from Zoan are also fools, and those from Memphis are utterly deluded. They are the best you can find, but they have ruined Egypt with their foolish counsel. ¹⁴ The Lord has sent a spirit of foolishness on them, so that all their suggestions are wrong; they make Egypt stagger like a sick drunkard. ¹⁵ Egypt cannot be saved by anything or anybody—no one can show her the way.

¹⁶ In that day the Egyptians will be as weak as women, cowering in fear beneath the upraised fist of God. ¹⁷ Just to speak the name of Israel will strike deep terror in their hearts, for the Lord of Hosts has laid his plans against them.

¹⁸ At that time five of the cities of Egypt will follow the Lord of Hosts and will begin to speak the Hebrew language.ᵃ One of these will be Heliopolis, "The City of the Sun." ¹⁹ And there will be an altar to the Lord in the heart of Egypt in those days, and a monument to the Lord at its border. ²⁰ This will be for a sign of loyalty to the Lord of Hosts; then when they cry to the Lord for help against those who oppress them, he will send them a Savior—and he shall deliver them.

²¹ In that day the Lord will make himself known to the Egyptians. Yes, they will know the Lord and give their sacrifices and offerings to him; they will make promises to God and keep them. ²² The Lord will smite Egypt and then restore her! For the Egyptians will turn to the Lord and he will listen to their plea and heal them.

²³ In that day Egypt and Iraqᵇ will be connected by a highway, and the Egyptians and the Iraqi will move freely back and forth between their lands, and they shall worship the same God. ²⁴ And Israel will be their ally; the three will be together, and Israel will be a blessing to them. ²⁵ For the Lord will bless Egypt and Iraq because of their friendshipᶜ with Israel. He will say, "Blessed be Egypt, my people; blessed be Iraq, the land I have made; blessed be Israel, my inheritance!"

20 IN THE YEAR when Sargon, king of Assyria, sent the commander-in-chief of his army against the Philistine city of Ashdod and captured it, ² the Lord told Isaiah, the son of Amoz, to take off his

---

a Literally, "the language of Canaan."   b Literally, "Assyria."   c Implied.

clothing, including his shoes, and to walk around naked and barefoot. And Isaiah did as he was told.

³ Then the Lord said, My servant Isaiah, who has been walking naked and barefoot for the last three years, is a symbol of the terrible troubles I will bring upon Egypt and Ethiopia. ⁴ For the king of Assyria will take away the Egyptians and Ethiopians as prisoners, making them walk naked and barefoot, both young and old, their buttocks uncovered, to the shame of Egypt. ⁵,⁶ Then how dismayed the Philistines[a] will be, who counted on "Ethiopia's power" and their "glorious ally," Egypt! And they will say, "If this can happen to Egypt, what chance have we?"

21 THIS IS GOD'S message concerning Babylon:[a]

Disaster is roaring down upon you from the terrible desert, like a whirlwind sweeping from the Negeb. ² I see an awesome vision: oh, the horror of it all! God is telling me what he is going to do. I see you plundered and destroyed. Elamites and Medes will take part in the siege. Babylon will fall, and the groaning of all the nations she enslaved will end. ³ My stomach constricts and burns with pain; sharp pangs of horror are upon me, like the pangs of a woman giving birth to a child. I faint when I hear what God is planning; I am terrified, blinded with dismay. ⁴ My mind reels; my heart races; I am gripped by awful fear. All rest at night—so pleasant once—is gone; I lie awake, trembling.

⁵ Look! They are preparing a great banquet! They load the tables with food; they pull up their chairs[b] to eat . . . . Quick, quick, grab your shields and prepare for battle! You are being attacked![c]

⁶,⁷ Meanwhile (in my vision)[d] the Lord had told me, "Put a watchman on the city wall to shout out what he sees. When he sees riders in pairs on donkeys and camels,[e] tell

him, 'This is it!' "

⁸,⁹ So I put the watchman on the wall, and at last he shouted, "Sir, day after day and night after night I have been here at my post. Now at last—look! Here come riders in pairs!"

Then I heard a Voice shout out, "Babylon is fallen, is fallen; and all the idols of Babylon lie broken on the ground."

¹⁰ O my people, threshed and winnowed, I have told you all that the Lord of Hosts, the God of Israel, has said.

¹¹ This is God's message to Edom:[f]

Someone from among you keeps calling, calling to me: "Watchman, what of the night? Watchman, what of the night? How much time is left?" ¹² The watchman replies, "Your judgment day is dawning now. Turn again to God, so that I can give you better news. Seek for him, then come and ask again!"

¹³ This is God's message concerning Arabia:

O caravans from Dedam, you will hide in the deserts of Arabia. ¹⁴ O people of Tema, bring food and water to these weary fugitives! ¹⁵ They have fled from drawn swords and sharp arrows and the terrors of war! ¹⁶ "But a long year from now,"[g] says the Lord, "the great power of their enemy,[h] the mighty tribe of Kedar, will end. ¹⁷ Only a few of its stalwart archers will survive." The Lord, the God of Israel, has spoken.

22 THIS IS GOD'S message concerning Jerusalem:[a]

What is happening? Where is everyone going? Why are they running to the rooftops? What are they looking at? ² The whole city is in terrible uproar. What's the trouble in this busy, happy city?[b] Bodies! Lying everywhere, slain by plague[b] and not by sword. ³ All your leaders flee; they surrender without resistance. The people slip away but they are captured, too. ⁴ Let me alone

---

a Literally, "inhabitants of the coastland." 21a Implied in verse 9. b Literally, "spread out the rugs."
c More details of the feast are seen in Daniel, chapter 5, as this prophecy was fulfilled when Cyrus captured the city. d Implied. e Literally, "When he sees a troop, horsemen in pairs, riders on asses, riders on camels." Possibly the meaning is that the asses and camels were paired for the attack. The city fell to the Medes and Persians, perhaps represented by these paired riders. f Literally, "Dumah."
g The Dead Sea manuscript reads, "within *three* years, according to the year of a hireling," like 16:14.
h Implied. 22a Literally, "The Valley of Vision." b Implied.

to weep. Don't try to comfort me—let me cry for my people as I watch them being destroyed. [5] Oh, what a day of crushing trouble! What a day of confusion and terror from the Lord God of heaven's armies! The walls of Jerusalem are breached and the cry of death echoes from the mountainsides. [6,7] Elamites are the archers; Syrians drive the chariots; the men of Kir hold up the shields. They fill your choicest valleys and crowd against your gates.

[8] God has removed his protecting care. You run to the armory for your weapons! [9,10,11] You inspect the walls of Jerusalem to see what needs repair! You check over the houses and tear some down for stone for fixing walls. Between the city walls, you build a reservoir for water from the lower pool! But all your feverish plans will not avail, for you never ask for help from God, who lets this come upon you. He is the one who planned it long ago. [12] The Lord God of Hosts called you to repent, to weep and mourn and shave your heads in sorrow for your sins, and to wear clothes made of sackcloth to show your remorse. [13] But instead, you sing and dance and play, and feast and drink. "Let us eat, drink, and be merry," you say: "What's the difference, for tomorrow we die." [14] The Lord of Hosts has revealed to me that this sin will never be forgiven you until the day you die.

[15,16] Furthermore, the same Lord God of the armies of heaven has told me this: Go and say to Shebna, the palace administrator: "And who do you think you are, building this beautiful sepulchre in the rock for yourself? [17] For the Lord who allowed you to be clothed so gorgeously will hurl you away, sending you into captivity, O strong man! [18] He will wad you up in his hands like a ball and toss you away into a distant, barren land; there you will die, O glorious one—you who disgrace your nation!

[19] "Yes, I will drive you out of office," says the Lord, "and pull you down from your high position. [20] And then I will call my servant Eliakim, the son of Hilkiah, to replace you. [21] He shall have your uniform and title and authority, and he will be a father to the people of Jerusalem and all Judah. [22] I will give him responsibility over all my people; whatever he says will be done; none will be able to stop him. [23,24] I will make of him a strong and steady peg to support my people; they will load him with responsibility, and he will be an honor to his family name." [25] But the Lord will pull out that other peg that seems to be so firmly fastened to the wall! It will come out and fall to the ground, and everything it supports will fall with it, for the Lord has spoken.

23 THIS IS GOD'S message to Tyre:

Weep, O ships of Tyre, returning home from distant lands![a] Weep for your harbor, for it is gone! The rumors that you heard in Cyprus are all true. [2,3] Deathly silence is everywhere. Stillness reigns where once your hustling port was full of ships from Sidon, bringing merchandise from far across the ocean, from Egypt and along the Nile. You were the merchandise mart of the world. [4] Be ashamed, O Sidon,[a] stronghold of the sea. For you are childless now! [5] When Egypt hears the news, there will be great sorrow. [6] Flee to Tarshish, men of Tyre, weeping as you go. [7] This silent ruin is all that's left of your once joyous land. What a history was yours! Think of all the colonists you sent to distant lands!

[8] Who has brought this disaster on Tyre, empire builder and top trader of the world? [9] The Commander of the armies of heaven has done it to destroy your pride and show his contempt for all the greatness of mankind. [10] Sail on, O ships of Tarshish, for your harbor is gone. [11] The Lord holds out his hand over the seas; he shakes the kingdoms of the earth; he has spoken out against this great merchant city, to destroy its strength.

[12] He says, "Never again, O dishonored virgin, daughter of Sidon, will you rejoice, will you be strong. Even if you flee to Cyprus, you will find no rest."

[13] It will be the Babylonians, not the Assyrians, who consign Tyre to the wild beasts. They will lay siege to it, raze its palaces and make it a heap of ruins. [14] Wail, you ships that ply the oceans, for your home

---

a Tyre was originally a colony of the mother-city, Sidon.

port is destroyed!

¹⁵,¹⁶ For seventy years Tyre will be forgotten. Then, in the days of another king, the city will come back to life again; she will sing sweet songs as a harlot sings who, long absent from her lovers, walks the streets to look for them again and is remembered. ¹⁷ Yes, after seventy years, the Lord will revive Tyre, but she will be no different than she was before; she will return again to all her evil ways around the world. ¹⁸ Yet [the distant time will come when^b] her businesses will give their profits to the Lord! They will not be hoarded but used for good food and fine clothes for the priests of the Lord!

24 LOOK! THE LORD is overturning the land of Judah and making it a vast wasteland of destruction. See how he is emptying out all its people and scattering them over the face of the earth. ² Priests and people, servants and masters, slave girls and mistresses, buyers and sellers, lenders and borrowers, bankers and debtors—none will be spared. ³ The land will be completely emptied and looted. The Lord has spoken. ⁴,⁵ The land suffers for the sins of its people. The earth languishes, the crops wither, the skies refuse their rain. The land is defiled by crime; the people have twisted the laws of God and broken his everlasting commands. ⁶ Therefore the curse of God is upon them; they are left desolate, destroyed by the drought. Few will be left alive.

⁷ All the joys of life will go: the grape harvest will fail, the wine will be gone, the merrymakers will sigh and mourn. ⁸ The melodious chords of the harp and timbrel are heard no more; the happy days are ended. ⁹ No more are the joys of wine and song; strong drink turns bitter in the mouth. ¹⁰ The city lies in chaos; every home and shop is locked up tight to keep out looters. ¹¹ Mobs form in the streets, crying for wine; joy has reached its lowest ebb; gladness has been banished from the land. ¹² The city is left in ruins; its gates are battered down. ¹³ Throughout the land^a the story is the same—only a remnant is left.

¹⁴ But all who are left will shout and sing for joy; those in the west will praise the majesty of God, ¹⁵,¹⁶ and those in the east will respond with praise. Hear them singing to the Lord from the ends of the earth, singing glory to the Righteous One!

But my heart is heavy with grief, for evil still prevails and treachery is everywhere. ¹⁷ Terror and the captivity of hell are still your lot, O men of the world. ¹⁸ When you flee in terror you will fall into a pit, and if you escape from the pit you will step into a trap, for destruction falls from the heavens upon you; the world is shaken beneath you. ¹⁹ The earth has broken down in utter collapse; everything is lost, abandoned and confused. ²⁰ The world staggers like a drunkard; it shakes like a tent in a storm. It falls and will not rise again, for the sins of the earth are very great.

²¹ On that day the Lord will punish the fallen angels in the heavens, and the proud rulers of the nations on earth. ²² They will be rounded up like prisoners and imprisoned in a dungeon until they are tried and condemned. ²³ Then the Lord of heaven's armies will mount his throne in Zion and rule gloriously in Jerusalem, in the sight of all the elders of his people. Such glory there will be that all the brightness of the sun and moon will seem to fade away.

25 O LORD, I will honor and praise your name, for you are my God; you do such wonderful things! You planned them long ago, and now you have accomplished them, just as you said! ² You turn mighty cities into heaps of ruins. The strongest forts are turned to rubble. Beautiful palaces in distant lands disappear and never will be rebuilt. ³ Therefore strong nations will shake with fear before you; ruthless nations will obey and glorify your name.

⁴ But to the poor, O Lord, you are a refuge from the storm, a shadow from the heat, a shelter from merciless men who are like a driving rain that melts down an earthen wall. ⁵ As a hot, dry land is cooled by clouds, you will cool the pride of ruthless nations. ⁶ Here on Mount Zion in Jerusalem, the Lord of Hosts will spread a wondrous feast for everyone around the

---

b Implied.   24a Or possibly, "throughout the nations of the world."

world—a delicious feast of good food, with clear, well-aged wine and choice beef. ⁷ At that time he will remove the cloud of gloom, the pall of death that hangs over the earth; ⁸ he will swallow up death forever. The Lord God will wipe away all tears and take away forever all insults and mockery against his land and people. The Lord has spoken—he will surely do it!

⁹ In that day the people will proclaim, "This is our God, in whom we trust, for whom we waited. Now at last he is here." What a day of rejoicing! ¹⁰ For the Lord's good hand will rest upon Jerusalem, and Moab will be crushed as straw beneath his feet and left to rot. ¹¹ God will push them down just as a swimmer pushes down the water with his hands. He will end their pride and all their evil works. ¹² The high walls of Moab will be demolished and brought to dust.

26 LISTEN TO THEM singing! In that day the whole land of Judah will sing this song:

"Our city is strong! We are surrounded by the walls of his salvation!" ² Open the gates to everyone, for all may enter in who love the Lord. ³ He will keep in perfect peace all those who trust in him, whose thoughts turn often to the Lord! ⁴ Trust in the Lord God always, for in the Lord Jehovah is your everlasting strength. ⁵ He humbles the proud and brings the haughty city to the dust; its walls come crashing down. ⁶ He presents it to the poor and needy for their use.

⁷ But for good men the path is not uphill and rough! God does not give them a rough and treacherous path, but smooths the road before them. ⁸ O Lord, we love to do your will! Our hearts' desire is to glorify your name. ⁹ All night long I search for you; earnestly I seek for God; for only when you come in judgment on the earth to punish it will people turn away from wickedness and do what is right.

¹⁰ Your kindness to the wicked doesn't make them good; they keep on doing wrong and take no notice of your majesty. ¹¹ They do not listen when you threaten; they will

not look to see your upraised fist. Show them how much you love your people. Perhaps then they will be ashamed! Yes, let them be burned up by the fire reserved for your enemies.

¹² Lord, grant us peace; for all we have and are has come from you. ¹³ O Lord our God, once we worshiped other gods; but now we worship you alone. ¹⁴ Those we served before are dead and gone; never again will they return. You came against them and destroyed them, and they are long forgotten. ¹⁵ O praise the Lord! He has made our nation very great. He has widened the boundaries of our land!

¹⁶ Lord, in their distress they sought for you. When your punishment was on them, they poured forth a whispered prayer. ¹⁷ How we missed your presence, Lord! We suffered as a woman giving birth, who cries and writhes in pain. ¹⁸ We too have writhed in agony, but all to no avail. No deliverance has come from all our efforts. ¹⁹ Yet we have this assurance: Those who belong to God shall live again. Their bodies shall rise again! Those who dwell in the dust shall awake and sing for joy! For God's light of life will fall like dew upon them!

²⁰ Go home, my people, and lock the doors! Hide for a little while until the Lord's wrath against your enemies has passed. ²¹ Look! The Lord is coming from the heavens to punish the people of the earth for their sins. The earth will no longer hide the murderers. The guilty will be found.

27 IN THAT DAY the Lord will take his terrible, swift sword and punish leviathan, the swiftly moving serpent, the coiling, writhing serpent, the dragon of the sea.

² In that day [of Israel's freedomᵃ] let this anthem be their song:

³ Israelᵃ is my vineyard; I, the Lord, will tend the fruitful vines; every day I'll water them, and day and night I'll watch to keep all enemies away. ⁴,⁵ My anger against Israelᵃ is gone. If I find thorns and briars bothering her, I will burn them up, unless these enemies of mine surrender and beg for peace and my protection. ⁶ The time will come when Israel will take root and bud and blos-

---

a Implied.

som and fill the whole earth with her fruit! ⁷,⁸ Has God punished Israel as much as he has punished her enemies? No, for he has devastated her enemies,ᵃ while he has punished Israel but a little, exiling her far from her own land as though blown away in a storm from the east. ⁹ And why did God do it? It was to purge awayᵇ her sins, to rid her of all her idol altars and her idols. They will never be worshiped again. ¹⁰ Her walled cities will be silent and empty, houses abandoned, streets grown up with grass, cows grazing through the city munching on twigs and branches.

¹¹ My people are like the dead branches of a tree, broken off and used to burn beneath the pots. They are a foolish nation, a witless, stupid people, for they turn away from God. Therefore, he who made them will not have pity on them or show them his mercy. ¹² Yet the time will come when the Lord will gather them together one by one like handpicked grain, selecting them here and there from his great threshing floor that reaches all the way from the Euphrates River to the Egyptian boundary. ¹³ In that day the great trumpet will be blown, and many about to perish among their enemies, Assyria and Egypt, will be rescued and brought back to Jerusalem to worship the Lord in his holy mountain.

28 WOE TO THE city of Samaria, surrounded by her rich valley—Samaria, the pride and delight of the drunkards of Israel! Woe to her fading beauty, the crowning glory of a nation of men lying drunk in the streets! ² For the Lord will send a mighty army (the Assyrians) against you; like a mighty hailstorm he will burst upon you and dash you to the ground. ³ The proud city of Samaria—yes, the joy and delight of the drunkards of Israel—will be hurled to the ground and trampled beneath the enemies' feet. ⁴ Once glorious, her fading beauty surrounded by a fertile valley will suddenly be gone, greedily snatched away as an early fig is hungrily snatched and gobbled up! ⁵ Then at last the Lord of Hosts himself will be their crowning glory, the diadem of beauty to his people who are left. ⁶ He will give a longing for justice to your judges and great courage to your soldiers who are battling to the last before your gates. ⁷ But Jerusalem is now led by drunks! Her priests and prophets reel and stagger, making stupid errors and mistakes. ⁸ Their tables are covered with vomit; filth is everywhere.

⁹ "Who does Isaiah think he is," the people say, "to speak to us like this! Are we little children, barely old enough to talk? ¹⁰ He tells us everything over and over again, a line at a time and in such simple words!"

¹¹ But they won't listen; the only language they can understand is punishment! So God will punish them by sending against them foreigners who speak strange gibberish! Only then will they listen to him! ¹² They could have rest in their own land if they would obey him, if they were kind and good. He told them that, but they wouldn't listen to him. ¹³ So the Lord will spell it out for them again, repeating it over and over in simple words whenever he can; yet over this simple, straightforward message they will stumble and fall and be broken, trapped and captured.

¹⁴ Therefore hear the word of the Lord, you scoffing rulers in Jerusalem:

¹⁵ You have struck a bargain with Death, you say, and sold yourselves to the devilᵃ in exchange for his protection against the Assyrians. "They can never touch us," you say, "for we are under the care of one who will deceive and fool them."

¹⁶ But the Lord God says, See, I am placing a Foundation Stone in Zion—a firm, tested, precious Cornerstone that is safe to build on. He who believes need never run away again. ¹⁷ I will take the line and plummet of justice to check the foundation wall you built; it looks so fine, but it is so weak a storm of hail will knock it down! The enemy will come like a flood and sweep it away, and you will be drowned. ¹⁸ I will cancel your agreement of compromise with Death and the devil, so when the terrible enemy floods in, you will be trampled into the ground. ¹⁹ Again and again that flood will come and carry you off, until at last the

a Implied.   b Literally, "atone for."   28 a Literally, "Sheol," "the underworld."

unmixed horror of the truth of my warnings will finally dawn on you.

²⁰ The bed you have made is far too short to lie on; the blankets are too narrow to cover you. ²¹ The Lord will come suddenly and in anger, as at Mount Perazim and Gibeon, to do a strange, unusual thing—to destroy his own people! ²² So scoff no more, lest your punishment be made even greater, for the Lord God of Hosts has plainly told me that he is determined to crush you.

²³,²⁴ Listen to me, listen as I plead: Does a farmer always plow and never sow? Is he forever harrowing the soil and never planting it? ²⁵ Does he not finally plant his many kinds of grain, each in its own section of his land? ²⁶ He knows just what to do, for God has made him see and understand. ²⁷ He doesn't thresh all grains the same. A sledge is never used on dill, but it is beaten with a stick. A threshing wheel is never rolled on cummin, but it is beaten softly with a flail. ²⁸ Bread grain is easily crushed, so he doesn't keep on pounding it. ²⁹ The Lord of Hosts is a wonderful teacher and gives the farmer wisdom.

29 WOE TO JERUSALEM,ᵃ the city of David. Year after year you make your many offerings, ² but I will send heavy judgment upon you and there will be weeping and sorrow. For Jerusalem shall become as her name "Ariel" means—an altar covered with blood. ³ I will be your enemy. I will surround Jerusalem and lay siege against it, and build forts around it to destroy it. ⁴ Your voice will whisper like a ghost from the earth where you lie buried.

⁵ But suddenly your ruthless enemies will be driven away like chaff before the wind. ⁶ In an instant, I, the Lord of Hosts, will come upon them with thunder, earthquake, whirlwind and fire. ⁷ And all the nations fighting Jerusalem will vanish like a dream! ⁸ As a hungry man dreams of eating, but is still hungry, and as a thirsty man dreams of drinking, but is still faint from thirst when he wakes up, so your enemies will dream of victorious conquest, but all to no avail.

⁹ You are amazed, incredulous? You don't believe it? Then go ahead and be blind if you must! You are stupid—and not from drinking, either! Stagger, and not from wine! ¹⁰ For the Lord has poured out upon you a spirit of deep sleep. He has closed the eyes of your prophets and seers, ¹¹ so all of these future events are a sealed book to them. When you give it to one who can read, he says, "I can't, for it's sealed." ¹² When you give it to another, he says, "Sorry, I can't read."

¹³ And so the Lord says, "Since these people say they are mine but they do not obey me, and since their worship amounts to mere words learned by rote, ¹⁴ therefore I will take awesome vengeance on these hypocrites, and make their wisest counselors as fools."

¹⁵ Woe to those who try to hide their plans from God, who try to keep him in the dark concerning what they do! "God can't see us," they say to themselves. "He doesn't know what is going on!" ¹⁶ How stupid can they be! Isn't he, the Potter, greater than you, the jars he makes? Will you say to him, "He didn't make us"? Does a machine call its inventor dumb?

¹⁷ Soon—and it will not be very long—the wilderness of Lebanon will be a fruitful field again, a lush and fertile forest. ¹⁸ In that day the deaf will hear the words of a book, and out of their gloom and darkness the blind will see my plans. ¹⁹ The meek will be filled with fresh joy from the Lord, and the poor shall exult in the Holy One of Israel. ²⁰ Bullies will vanish and scoffers will cease, and all those plotting evil will be killed— ²¹ the violent man who fights at the drop of a hat, the man who waits in hiding to beat up the judge who sentenced him, and the men who use any excuse to be unfair.

²² That is why the Lord who redeemed Abraham says: My people will no longer pale with fear, or be ashamed. ²³ For when they see the surging birth rate and the expanding economy,ᵇ then they will fear and rejoice in my name, and praise the Holy One of Israel, and stand in awe of him. ²⁴ Those in error will believe the truth, and complainers will be willing to be taught!

---

a Literally, "to Ariel."   b Literally, "when he sees his children, the work of my hands, in his midst."

30 WOE TO MY rebellious children, says the Lord; you ask advice from everyone but me, and decide to do what I don't want you to do. You yoke yourselves with unbelievers, thus piling up your sins. ² For without consulting me you have gone down to Egypt to find aid and have put your trust in Pharaoh for his protection.ª ³ But in trusting Pharaoh, you will be disappointed, humiliated and disgraced, for he can't deliver on his promises to save you. ⁴ For though his power extends to Zoan and Hanes, ⁵ yet it will all turn out to your shame—he won't help one little bit!

⁶ See them moving slowly across the terrible desert to Egypt—donkeys and camels laden down with treasure to pay for Egypt's aid. On through the badlands they go, where lions and swift venomous snakes live —and Egypt will give you nothing in return! ⁷ For Egypt's promises are worthless! "The Reluctant Dragon,"ᵇ I call her!

⁸ Now go and write down this word of mine concerning Egypt, so that it will stand until the end of time, forever and forever, as an indictment of Israel's unbelief. ⁹ For if you don't write it, they will claim I never warned them. "Oh, no," they'll say, "you never told us that!"

For they are stubborn rebels. ¹⁰,¹¹.They tell my prophets, "Shut up—we don't want any more of your reports!" Or they say, "Don't tell us the truth; tell us nice things; tell us lies. Forget all this gloom; we've heard more than enough about your 'Holy One of Israel' and all he says."

¹² This is the reply of the Holy One of Israel:

Because you despise what I tell you and trust instead in frauds and lies and won't repent, ¹³ therefore calamity will come upon you suddenly, as upon a bulging wall that bursts and falls; in one moment it comes crashing down. ¹⁴ God will smash you like a broken dish; he will not act sparingly. Not a piece will be left large enough to use for carrying coals from the hearth, or a little water from the well. ¹⁵ For the Lord God, the Holy One of Israel, says: Only in returning to me and waiting for me will you be saved; in quietness and confidence is your strength; but you'll have none of this.

¹⁶ "No," you say. "We will get our help from Egypt; they will give us swift horses for riding to battle." But the only swiftness you are going to see is the swiftness of your enemies chasing you! ¹⁷ One of them will chase a thousand of you! Five of them will scatter you until not two of you are left together. You will be like lonely trees on the distant mountain tops. ¹⁸ Yet the Lord still waits for you to come to him, so he can show you his love; he will conquer you to bless you, just as he said. For the Lord is faithful to his promises. Blessed are all those who wait for him to help them.

¹⁹ O my people in Jerusalem, you shall weep no more, for he will surely be gracious to you at the sound of your cry. He will answer you. ²⁰ Though he give you the bread of adversity and water of affliction, yet he will be with you to teach you—with your own eyes you will see your Teacher. ²¹ And if you leave God's paths and go astray, you will hear a Voice behind you say, "No, this is the way; walk here." ²² And you will destroy all your silver idols and golden images and cast them out like filthy things you hate to touch. "Ugh!" you'll say to them. "Be gone!"

²³ Then God will bless you with rain at planting time and with wonderful harvests and with ample pastures for your cows. ²⁴ The oxen and young donkeys that till the ground will eat grain, its chaff blown away by the wind. ²⁵ In that day when God steps in to destroy your enemies, he will give you streams of water flowing down each mountain and every hill. ²⁶ The moon will be as bright as the sun, and the sunlight brighter than seven days! So it will be when the Lord begins to heal his people and to cure the wounds he gave them.

²⁷ See, the Lord comes from afar, aflame with wrath, surrounded by thick rising smoke. His lips are filled with fury; his words consume like fire. ²⁸ His wrath pours out like floods upon them all, to sweep them all away. He will sift out the proud nations and bridle them and lead them off to their

---

a Hezekiah was seeking a defensive alliance with Ethiopia's Egyptian dynasty against Sennacherib of Assyria.
b Literally, "Rahab who sits still."

doom.

²⁹ But the people of God will sing a song of solemn joy, like songs in the night when holy feasts are held; his people will have gladness of heart, as when a flutist leads a pilgrim band to Jerusalem to the Mountain of the Lord, the Rock of Israel. ³⁰ And the Lord shall cause his majestic voice to be heard and shall crush down his mighty arm upon his enemies with angry indignation and with devouring flames and tornados and terrible storms and huge hailstones. ³¹ The voice of the Lord shall punish the Assyrians, who had been his rod of punishment. ³² And when the Lord smites them, his people will rejoice with music and song. ³³ The funeral pyre has long been ready, prepared for Molech, the Assyrian god; it is piled high with wood. The breath of the Lord, like fire from a volcano, will set it all on fire.

31 WOE TO THOSE who run to Egypt for help, trusting their mighty cavalry and chariots instead of looking to the Holy One of Israel and consulting him. ² In his wisdom, he will send great evil on his people and will not change his mind. He will rise against them for the evil they have done, and crush their allies too. ³ For these Egyptians are mere men, not God! Their horses are puny flesh, not mighty spirits! When the Lord clenches his fist against them, they will stumble and fall among those they are trying to help. All will fail together.

⁴,⁵ But the Lord has told me this: When a lion, even a young one, kills a sheep, he pays no attention to the shepherd's shouts and noise. He goes right on and eats. In such manner the Lord will come and fight upon Mount Zion. He will not be frightened away! He, the Lord of Hosts, will hover over Jerusalem as birds hover round their nests, and he will defend the city and deliver it.

⁶ Therefore, O my people, though you are such wicked rebels, come, return to God. ⁷ I know the glorious day will come when every one of you will throw away his golden idols and silver images—which in your sinfulness you have made. ⁸ And the Assyrians will be destroyed, but not by swords of men. The "sword of God" will

smite them. They will panic and flee, and the strong young Assyrians will be taken away as slaves. ⁹ Even their generals will quake with terror and flee when they see the battle flags of Israel, says the Lord. For the flame of God burns brightly in Jerusalem.

32 LOOK, A RIGHTEOUS King is coming, with honest princes! ² He will shelter Israel from the storm and wind. He will refresh her as a river in the desert and as the cooling shadow of a mighty rock within a hot and weary land. ³ Then at last the eyes of Israel will open wide to God; his people will listen to his voice. ⁴ Even the hotheads among them will be full of sense and understanding, and those who stammer in uncertainty will speak out plainly.

⁵ In those days the ungodly, the atheists, will not be heroes! Wealthy cheaters will not be spoken of as generous, outstanding men! ⁶ Everyone will recognize an evil man when he sees him, and hypocrites will fool no one at all. Their lies about God and their cheating of the hungry will be plain for all to see. ⁷ The smooth tricks of evil men will be exposed, as will all the lies they use to oppress the poor in the courts. ⁸ But good men will be generous to others and will be blessed of God for all they do.

⁹ Listen, you women who loll around in lazy ease; listen to me and I will tell you your reward: ¹⁰ In a short time—in just a little more than a year—suddenly you'll care, O careless ones. For the crops of fruit will fail; the harvest will not take place. ¹¹ Tremble, O women of ease; throw off your unconcern. Strip off your pretty clothes— wear sackcloth for your grief. ¹² Beat your breasts in sorrow for those bountiful farms of yours that will soon be gone, and for those fruitful vines of other years. ¹³ For your lands will thrive with thorns and briars; your joyous homes and happy cities will be gone. ¹⁴ Palaces and mansions will all be deserted, the crowded cities empty. Wild herds of donkeys and goats will graze upon the mountains where the watchtowers are, ¹⁵ until at last the Spirit is poured down on us from heaven. Then once again enormous crops will come. ¹⁶ Then justice will rule through all the land, ¹⁷ and out of justice, peace. Quietness and confidence will

reign forever more.

[18] My people will live in safety, quietly at home, [19] but the Assyrians[a] will be destroyed and their cities laid low. [20] And God will greatly bless his people. Wherever they plant, bountiful crops will spring up, and their flocks and herds will graze in green pastures.

33 WOE TO YOU, Assyrians,[a] who have destroyed everything around you but have never felt destruction for yourselves. You expect others to respect their promises to you, while you betray them! Now you, too, will be betrayed and destroyed.

[2] But to us, O Lord, be merciful, for we have waited for you. Be our strength each day and our salvation in the time of trouble. [3] The enemy runs at the sound of your voice. When you stand up, the nations flee. [4] Just as locusts strip the fields and vines, so Jerusalem will strip the fallen army of Assyria![b]

[5] The Lord is very great, and lives in heaven. He will make Jerusalem the home of justice and goodness and righteousness. [6] An abundance of salvation is stored up for Judah in a safe place, along with wisdom and knowledge and reverence for God.

[7] But now your ambassadors weep in bitter disappointment, for Assyria has refused their cry for peace. [8] Your roads lie in ruins; travelers detour on back roads. The Assyrians have broken their peace pact[c] and care nothing for the promises they made in the presence of witnesses—they have no respect for anyone. [9] All the land of Israel is in trouble; Lebanon has been destroyed; Sharon has become a wilderness; Bashan and Carmel are plundered.

[10] But the Lord says, I will stand up and show my power and might. [11] You Assyrians will gain nothing by all your efforts. Your own breath will turn to fire and kill you. [12] Your armies will be burned to lime, like thorns cut down and tossed in the fire.

[13] Listen to what I have done, O nations far away! And you that are near, acknowledge my might! [14] The sinners among my people shake with fear. "Which one of us," they cry, "can live here in the presence of this all-consuming, Everlasting Fire?" [15] I will tell you who can live here: All who are honest and fair, who reject making profit by fraud, who hold back their hands from taking bribes, who refuse to listen to those who plot murder, who shut their eyes to all enticement to do wrong. [16] Such as these shall dwell on high. The rocks of the mountains will be their fortress of safety; food will be supplied to them and they will have all the water they need.

[17] Your eyes will see the King in his beauty, and the highlands of heaven far away. [18] Your mind will think back to this time of terror when the Assyrian officers outside your walls are counting your towers and estimating how much they will get from your fallen city. [19] But soon they will all be gone. These fierce, violent people, with a strange, jabbering language you can't understand, will disappear.

[20] Instead you will see Jerusalem at peace, a place where God is worshiped, a city quiet and unmoved. [21] The glorious Lord will be to us as a wide river of protection, and no enemy can cross. [22] For the Lord is our Judge, our Lawgiver and our King; he will care for us and save us. [23] The enemies' sails hang loose on broken masts with useless tackle. Their treasure will be divided by the people of God; even the lame will win their share. [24] The people of Israel will no longer say, "We are sick and helpless," for the Lord will forgive them their sins and bless them.

34 COME HERE AND listen, O nations of the earth; let the world and everything in it hear my words. [2] For the Lord is enraged against the nations; his fury is against their armies. He will utterly destroy them and deliver them to slaughter. [3] Their dead will be left unburied, and the stench of rotting bodies will fill the land, and the mountains will flow with their blood. [4] At that time the heavens above will melt away and disappear just like a rolled-up scroll, and the stars will fall as leaves, as ripe fruit from the trees.

[5] And when my sword has finished its work in the heavens, then watch, for it will

a Implied.   33a Implied.   b 2 Kings 19:35.   c 2 Kings 18:14–17.

fall upon Edom, the people I have doomed.
⁶ The sword of the Lord is sated with blood;
it is gorged with flesh as though used for
slaying lambs and goats for sacrifice. For
the Lord will slay a great sacrifice in Edom
and make a mighty slaughter there. ⁷ The
strongest will perish, young boys and veterans
too. The land will be soaked with blood,
and the soil made rich with fat. ⁸ For it is
the day of vengeance, the year of recompense
for what Edom has done to Israel.
⁹ The streams of Edom will be filled with
burning pitch, and the ground will be covered
with fire.

¹⁰ This judgment on Edom will never
end. Its smoke will rise up forever. The land
will lie deserted from generation to generation;
no one will live there anymore.
¹¹ There the hawks and porcupines will live,
and owls and ravens. For God will observe
that land and find it worthy of destruction.
He will test its nobles and find them worthy
of death. ¹² It will be called "The Land of
Nothing," and its princes soon will all be
gone. ¹³ Thorns will overrun the palaces,
and nettles will grow in its forts, and it will
become the haunt of jackals and a home for
ostriches. ¹⁴ The wild animals of the desert
will mingle there with wolves and hyenas.
Their howls will fill the night. There the
night-monsters will scream at each other,
and the demons will come there to rest.
¹⁵ There the owl will make her nest and lay
her eggs and hatch her young and nestle
them beneath her wings, and the kites will
come, each one with its mate.

¹⁶ Search the Book of the Lord and see
all that he will do; not one detail will he
miss; not one kite will be there without a
mate, for the Lord has said it, and his Spirit
will make it all come true. ¹⁷ He has
surveyed and subdivided the land and
deeded it to those doleful creatures; they
shall possess it forever, from generation to
generation.

35 EVEN THE WILDERNESS and desert
will rejoice in those days; the desert
will blossom with flowers. ² Yes, there will
be an abundance of flowers and singing and
joy! The deserts will become as green as the
Lebanon mountains, as lovely as Mount
Carmel's pastures and Sharon's meadows;

for the Lord will display his glory there, the
excellency of our God.

³ With this news bring cheer to all discouraged
ones. ⁴ Encourage those who are
afraid. Tell them, "Be strong, fear not, for
your God is coming to destroy your enemies.
He is coming to save you." ⁵ And
when he comes, he will open the eyes of the
blind, and unstop the ears of the deaf. ⁶ The
lame man will leap up like a deer, and those
who could not speak will shout and sing!
Springs will burst forth in the wilderness,
and streams in the desert. ⁷ The parched
ground will become a pool, with springs of
water in the thirsty land. Where desert jackals
lived, there will be reeds and rushes!

⁸ And a main road will go through that
once-deserted land; it will be named "The
Holy Highway." No evil-hearted men may
walk upon it. God will walk there with you;
even the most stupid cannot miss the way.
⁹ No lion will lurk along its course, nor will
there be any other dangers; only the redeemed
will travel there. ¹⁰ These, the ransomed
of the Lord, will go home along that
road to Zion, singing the songs of everlasting
joy. For them all sorrow and all sighing
will be gone forever; only joy and gladness
will be there.

36 SO IN THE fourteenth year of King
Hezekiah's reign, Sennacherib, king
of Assyria, came to fight against the walled
cities of Judah and conquered them. ² Then
he sent his personal representative with a
great army from Lachish to confer with
King Hezekiah in Jerusalem. He camped
near the outlet of the upper pool, along the
road going past the field where cloth is
bleached.

³ Then Eliakim, Hilkiah's son, who was
the prime minister of Israel, and Shebna,
the king's scribe, and Joah (Asaph's son),
the royal secretary, formed a truce team and
went out of the city to meet with him. ⁴ The
Assyrian ambassador told them to go and
say to Hezekiah, "The mighty king of Assyria
says you are a fool to think that the
king of Egypt will help you. ⁵ What are the
Pharaoh's promises worth? Mere words
won't substitute for strength, yet you rely
on him for help, and have rebelled against
me! ⁶ Egypt is a dangerous ally. She is a

sharpened stick that will pierce your hand if you lean on it. That is the experience of everyone who has ever looked to her for help. [7] But perhaps you say, 'We are trusting in the Lord our God!' Oh? Isn't he the one your king insulted, tearing down his temples and altars in the hills and making everyone in Judah worship only at the altars here in Jerusalem? [8,9] My master, the king of Assyria, wants to make a little bet with you!—that you don't have 2,000 men left in your entire army! If you do, he will give you 2,000 horses for them to ride on! With that tiny army, how can you think of proceeding against even the smallest and worst contingent of my master's troops? For you'll get no help from Egypt. [10] What's more, do you think I have come here without the Lord's telling me to take this land? The Lord said to me, 'Go and destroy it!' "

[11] Then Eliakim and Shebna and Joah said to him, "Please talk to us in Aramaic[a] for we understand it quite well. Don't speak in Hebrew, for the people on the wall will hear."

[12] But he replied, "My master wants everyone in Jerusalem to hear this, not just you. He wants them to know that if you don't surrender, this city will be put under siege until everyone is so hungry and thirsty that he will eat his own dung and drink his own urine."

[13] Then he shouted in Hebrew to the Jews listening on the wall, "Hear the words of the great king, the king of Assyria:

[14] "Don't let Hezekiah fool you—nothing he can do will save you. [15] Don't let him talk you into trusting in the Lord by telling you the Lord won't let you be conquered by the king of Assyria. [16] Don't listen to Hezekiah, for here is the king of Assyria's offer to you: Give me a present as a token of surrender; open the gates and come out, and I will let you each have your own farm and garden and water, [17] until I can arrange to take you to a country very similar to this one—a country where there are bountiful harvests of grain and grapes, a land of plenty. [18] Don't let Hezekiah deprive you of all this by saying the Lord will deliver you from my armies. Have any other nation's gods ever gained victory over the armies of the king of Assyria? [19] Don't you remember what I did to Hamath and Arpad? Did their gods save them? And what about Sepharvaim and Samaria? Where are their gods now? [20] Of all the gods of these lands, which one has ever delivered their people from my power? Name just one! And do you think this God of yours can deliver Jerusalem from me? Don't be ridiculous!"

[21] But the people were silent and answered not a word, for Hezekiah had told them to say nothing in reply. [22] Then Eliakim (son of Hilkiah), the prime minister, and Shebna, the royal scribe, and Joah (son of Asaph), the royal secretary, went back to Hezekiah with clothes ripped to shreds as a sign of their despair and told him all that had happened.

37 WHEN KING HEZEKIAH heard the results of the meeting, he tore his robes and wound himself in coarse cloth used for making sacks, as a sign of humility and mourning, and went over to the Temple to pray. [2] Meanwhile he sent Eliakim his prime minister, and Shebna his royal scribe, and the older priests—all dressed in sackcloth—to Isaiah the prophet, son of Amoz. [3] They brought him this message from Hezekiah:

"This is a day of trouble and frustration and blasphemy; it is a serious time, as when a woman is in heavy labor trying to give birth, and the child does not come. [4] But perhaps the Lord your God heard the blasphemy of the king of Assyria's representative as he scoffed at the Living God. Surely God won't let him get away with this. Surely God will rebuke him for those words. Oh, Isaiah, pray for us who are left!"

[5] So they took the king's message to Isaiah.

[6] Then Isaiah replied, "Tell King Hezekiah that the Lord says, Don't be disturbed by this speech from the servant of the king of Assyria, and his blasphemy. [7] For a report from Assyria will reach the king that he is needed at home at once, and he will return to his own land, where I will have him killed."

---

a Aramaic was the language used in international diplomacy at this time.

[8,9] Now the Assyrian envoy left Jerusalem and went to consult his king, who had left Lachish and was besieging Libnah. But at this point the Assyrian king received word that Tirhakah, crown prince of Ethiopia, was leading an army against him [from the south[a]]. Upon hearing this, he sent messengers back to Jerusalem to Hezekiah with this message:

[10] "Don't let this God you trust in fool you by promising that Jerusalem will not be captured by the king of Assyria! [11] Just remember what has happened wherever the kings of Assyria have gone, for they have crushed everyone who has opposed them. Do you think you will be any different? [12] Did their gods save the cities of Gozan, Haran, or Rezeph, or the people of Eden in Telassar? No, the Assyrian kings completely destroyed them! [13] And don't forget what happened to the king of Hamath, to the king of Arpad, and to the kings of the cities of Sepharvaim, Hena, and Ivvah."

[14] As soon as King Hezekiah had read this letter, he went over to the Temple and spread it out before the Lord, [15] and prayed, saying, [16,17] "O Lord of Hosts, God of Israel enthroned above the cherubim, *you alone* are God of all the kingdoms of the earth. You alone made heaven and earth. Listen as I plead; see me as I pray. Look at this letter from King Sennacherib, for he has mocked the Living God. [18] It is true, O Lord, that the kings of Assyria have destroyed all those nations, just as the letter says, [19] and thrown their gods into the fire; for they weren't gods at all, but merely idols, carved by men from wood and stone. Of course the Assyrians could destroy them. [20] O Lord our God, save us so that all the kingdoms of the earth will know that you are God, and you alone."

[21] Then Isaiah, the son of Amoz, sent this message to King Hezekiah: "The Lord God of Israel says, This is my answer to your prayer against Sennacherib, Assyria's king.

[22] "The Lord says to him: My people—the helpless virgin daughter of Zion—laughs at you and scoffs and shakes her head at you in scorn. [23] Who is it you scoffed against and mocked? Whom did you revile? At whom did you direct your violence and pride? It was against the Holy One of Israel! [24] You have sent your messengers to mock the Lord. You boast, 'I came with my mighty army against the nations of the west. I cut down the tallest cedars and choicest cypress trees. I conquered their highest mountains and destroyed their thickest forests.'

[25] "You boast of wells you've dug in many a conquered land, and Egypt with all its armies is no obstacle to you! [26] But do you not yet know that it was I who decided all this long ago? That it was I who gave you all this power from ancient times? I have caused all this to happen as I planned—that you should crush walled cities into ruined heaps. [27] That's why their people had so little power, and were such easy prey for you. They were as helpless as the grass, as tender plants you trample down beneath your feet, as grass upon the housetops, burnt yellow by the sun. [28] But I know you well—your comings and goings and all you do—and the way you have raged against me. [29] Because of your anger against the Lord —and I heard it all!—I have put a hook in your nose and a bit in your mouth and led you back to your own land by the same road you came."

[30] Then God said to Hezekiah, "Here is the proof that I am the one who is delivering this city from the king of Assyria: This year[a] he will abandon his siege. Although it is too late now to plant your crops, and you will have only volunteer grain this fall, still it will give you enough seed for a small harvest next year, and two years from now[b] you will be living in luxury again. [31] And you who are left in Judah will take root again in your own soil and flourish and multiply. [32] For a remnant shall go out from Jerusalem to repopulate the land; the power of the Lord of Hosts will cause all this to come to pass.

[33] "As for the king of Assyria, his armies shall not enter Jerusalem, nor shoot their arrows there, nor march outside its gates, nor build up an earthen bank against its walls. [34] He will return to his own country

---

a Implied. b The third harvest from then would yield a bumper crop.

by the road he came on, and will not enter this city, says the Lord. [35] For my own honor I will defend it, and in memory of my servant David."

[36] That night the Angel of the Lord went out to the camp of the Assyrians and killed 185,000 soldiers; when the living wakened the next morning, all these lay dead before them. [37] Then Sennacherib, king of Assyria, returned to his own country, to Nineveh. [38] And one day while he was worshiping in the temple of Nisroch his god, his sons Adrammelech and Sharezer killed him with their swords; then they escaped into the land of Ararat, and Esar-haddon his son became king.

38 IT WAS JUST before all this that Hezekiah became deathly sick and Isaiah the prophet (Amoz' son) went to visit him and gave him this message from the Lord: "Set your affairs in order, for you are going to die; you will not recover from this illness."

[2] When Hezekiah heard this, he turned his face to the wall and prayed:

[3] "O Lord, don't you remember how true I've been to you and how I've always tried to obey you in everything you said?" Then he broke down with great sobs.

[4] So the Lord sent another message to Isaiah:

[5] "Go and tell Hezekiah that the Lord God of your forefather David hears you praying and sees your tears and will let you live fifteen more years. [6] He will deliver you and this city from the king of Assyria. I will defend you, says the Lord, [7] and here is my guarantee: [8] I will send the sun backwards ten degrees as measured on Ahaz' sun dial!"

So the sun retraced ten degrees that it had gone down!

[9] When King Hezekiah was well again, he wrote this poem about his experience:

[10] "My life is but half done and I must leave it all. I am robbed of my normal years, and now I must enter the gates of Sheol. [11] Never again will I see the Lord in the land of the living. Never again will I see my friends in this world. [12] My life is blown away like a shepherd's tent; it is cut short as when a weaver stops his working at the loom. In one short day my life hangs by a thread.

[13] "All night I moaned; it was like being torn apart by lions. [14] Delirious, I chattered like a swallow and mourned like a dove; my eyes grew weary of looking up for help. 'O God,' I cried, 'I am in trouble—help me.' [15] But what can I say? For he himself has sent this sickness. All my sleep has fled because of my soul's bitterness. [16] O Lord, your discipline is good and leads to life and health. Oh, heal me and make me live!

[17] "Yes, now I see it all—it was good for me to undergo this bitterness, for you have lovingly delivered me from death; you have forgiven all my sins. [18] For dead men cannot praise you.[a] They cannot be filled with hope and joy. [19] The living, only the living, can praise you as I do today. One generation makes known your faithfulness to the next. [20] Think of it! The Lord healed me! Every day of my life from now on I will sing my songs of praise in the Temple, accompanied by the orchestra."

[21] (For Isaiah had told Hezekiah's servants, "Make an ointment of figs and spread it over the boil, and he will get well again." [22] And then Hezekiah had asked, "What sign will the Lord give me to prove that he will heal me?")

39 SOON AFTERWARDS, THE king of Babylon (Merodach-baladan, the son of Baladan) sent Hezekiah a present and his best wishes,[a] for he had heard that Hezekiah had been very sick and now was well again. [2] Hezekiah appreciated this and took the envoys from Babylon on a tour of the palace, showing them his treasure house full of silver, gold, spices and perfumes. He took them into his jewel rooms, too, and opened to them all his treasures—everything.

[3] Then Isaiah the prophet came to the king and said, "What did they say? Where are they from?"

"From far away in Babylon," Hezekiah

a The meaning is unclear. Perhaps Hezekiah was unaware of the blessedness of the future life for those who trust in God (Isaiah 57:1,2). Or perhaps his meaning is, "Dead bodies cannot praise you."

39a Merodach-baladan was at this time planning a revolt in the east against Sennacherib, so he was especially interested in Hezekiah's activities in the west.

replied.

⁴ "How much have they seen?" asked Isaiah.

And Hezekiah replied, "I showed them everything I own, all my priceless treasures."

⁵ Then Isaiah said to him, "Listen to this message from the Lord of Hosts:

⁶ "The time is coming when everything you have—all the treasures stored up by your fathers—will be carried off to Babylon. Nothing will be left. ⁷ And some of your own sons will become slaves, yes, eunuchs, in the palace of the king of Babylon."

⁸ "All right," Hezekiah replied. "Whatever the Lord says is good. At least there will be peace during my lifetime!"

40 COMFORT, OH, COMFORT my people, says your God. ² Speak tenderly to Jerusalem and tell her that her sad days are gone. Her sins are pardoned, and the Lord will give her twice as many blessings as he gave her punishment before.

³ Listen! I hear the voice of someone shouting, "Make a road for the Lord through the wilderness; make him a straight, smooth road through the desert. ⁴ Fill the valleys; level the hills; straighten out the crooked paths and smooth off the rough spots in the road. ⁵ The glory of the Lord will be seen by all mankind together." The Lord has spoken—it shall be.

⁶ The voice says, "Shout!"

"What shall I shout?" I asked.

"Shout that man is like the grass that dies away, and all his beauty fades like dying flowers. ⁷ The grass withers, the flower fades beneath the breath of God. And so it is with fragile man. ⁸ The grass withers, the flowers fade, but the Word of our God shall stand forever."

⁹ O Crier of Good News, shout to Jerusalem from the mountain tops! Shout louder—don't be afraid—tell the cities of Judah, "Your God is coming!" ¹⁰ Yes, the Lord God is coming with mighty power; he will rule with awesome strength. See, his reward is with him, to each as he has done. ¹¹ He will feed his flock like a shepherd; he will carry the lambs in his arms and gently lead the ewes with young.

¹² Who else has held the oceans in his hands and measured off the heavens with his ruler? Who else knows the weight of all the earth and weighs the mountains and the hills? ¹³ Who can advise the Spirit of the Lord or be his teacher or give him counsel? ¹⁴ Has he ever needed anyone's advice? Did he need instruction as to what is right and best? ¹⁵ No, for all the peoples of the world are nothing in comparison with him—they are but a drop in the bucket, dust on the scales. He picks up the islands as though they had no weight at all. ¹⁶ All of Lebanon's forests do not contain sufficient fuel to consume a sacrifice large enough to honor him, nor are all its animals enough to offer to our God. ¹⁷ All the nations are as nothing to him; in his eyes they are less than nothing—mere emptiness and froth.

¹⁸ How can we describe God? With what can we compare him? ¹⁹ With an idol? An idol, made from a mold, overlaid with gold, and with silver chains around its neck? ²⁰ The man too poor to buy expensive gods like that will find a tree free from rot and hire a man to carve a face on it, and that's his god—a god that cannot even move!

²¹ Are you so ignorant? Are you so deaf to the words of God—the words he gave before the worlds began? Have you never heard nor understood? ²² It is God who sits above the circle of the earth. (The people below must seem to him like grasshoppers!) He is the one who stretches out the heavens like a curtain and makes his tent from them. ²³ He dooms the great men of the world and brings them all to naught. ²⁴ They hardly get started, barely take root, when he blows on them and their work withers and the wind carries them off like straw.

²⁵ "With whom will you compare me? Who is my equal?" asks the Holy One.

²⁶ Look up into the heavens! Who created all these stars? As a shepherd[a] leads his sheep, calling each by its pet name, and counts them to see that none are lost or strayed, so God does with stars and planets!

²⁷ O Jacob, O Israel, how can you say that the Lord doesn't see your troubles and isn't being fair? ²⁸ Don't you yet under-

---

a Implied.

stand? Don't you know by now that the everlasting God, the Creator of the farthest parts of the earth, never grows faint or weary? No one can fathom the depths of his understanding. [29] He gives power to the tired and worn out, and strength to the weak. [30] Even the youths shall be exhausted, and the young men will all give up. [31] But they that wait upon the Lord shall renew their strength. They shall mount up with wings like eagles; they shall run and not be weary; they shall walk and not faint.

41 LISTEN IN SILENCE before me, O lands beyond the sea. Bring your strongest arguments. Come now and speak. The court is ready for your case.

[2] Who has stirred up this one from the east,[a] whom victory meets at every step? Who, indeed, but the Lord? God has given him victory over many nations and permitted him to trample kings underfoot and to put entire armies to the sword. [3] He chases them away and goes on safely, though the paths he treads are new. [4] Who has done such mighty deeds, directing the affairs of generations of mankind as they march by? It is I, the Lord, the First and Last; I alone am he.

[5] The lands beyond the sea watch in fear and wait for word of Cyrus' new campaigns. Remote lands tremble and mobilize for war. [6] Each man encourages his neighbor and says, "Don't worry. He won't win." [7] But they rush to make a new idol; the carver hurries the goldsmith, and the molder helps at the anvil. "Good," they say. "It's coming along fine. Now we can solder on the arms." Carefully they join the parts together, and then fasten the thing in place so it won't fall over!

[8] But as for you, O Israel, you are mine, my chosen ones; for you are Abraham's family, and he was my friend. [9] I have called you back from the ends of the earth and said that you must serve but me alone, for I have chosen you and will not throw you away. [10] Fear not, for I am with you. Do not be dismayed. I am your God. I will strengthen you; I will help you; I will uphold you with my victorious right hand.[b]

[11] See, all your angry enemies lie confused and shattered. Anyone opposing you will die. [12] You will look for them in vain—they will all be gone. [13] I am holding you by your right hand—I, the Lord your God—and I say to you, Don't be afraid; I am here to help you. [14] Despised though you are, fear not, O Israel; for I will help you. I am the Lord, your Redeemer; I am the Holy One of Israel. [15] You shall be a new and sharp-toothed threshing instrument to tear all enemies apart, making chaff of mountains. [16] You shall toss them in the air; the wind shall blow them all away; whirlwinds shall scatter them. And the joy of the Lord shall fill you full; you shall glory in the God of Israel.

[17] When the poor and needy seek water and there is none and their tongues are parched from thirst, then I will answer when they cry to me. I, Israel's God, will not ever forsake them. [18] I will open up rivers for them on high plateaus! I will give them fountains of water in the valleys! In the deserts will be pools of water, and rivers fed by springs shall flow across the dry, parched ground. [19] I will plant trees—cedars, myrtle, olive trees, the cypress, fir and pine—on barren land. [20] Everyone will see this miracle and understand that it is God who did it, Israel's Holy One.

[21] Can your idols make such claims as these? Let them come and show what they can do! says God, the King of Israel. [22] Let them try to tell us what occurred in years gone by, or what the future holds. [23] Yes, that's it! If you are gods, tell what will happen in the days ahead! Or do some mighty miracle that makes us stare, amazed. [24] But no! You are less than nothing, and can do nothing at all. Anyone who chooses you needs to have his head examined!

[25] But I have stirred up (Cyrus) from the north and east; he will come against the nations and call on my name, and I will give him victory over kings and princes. He will tread them as a potter tramples clay.

[26] Who but I have told you this would happen? Who else predicted this, making you admit that he was right? No one else! None other said one word! [27] I was the first

---

a Doubtless Cyrus the Great of Persia. See Isaiah 44:28.　　　b Or, "with the right hand of my righteousness."

to tell Jerusalem, "Look! Look! Help is on the way!" [28] Not one of your idols told you this. Not one gave any answer when I asked. [29] See, they are all foolish, worthless things; your idols are all as empty as the wind.

42 SEE MY SERVANT,[a] whom I uphold; my Chosen One, in whom I delight. I have put my Spirit upon him; he will reveal justice to the nations of the world. [2] He will be gentle—he will not shout nor quarrel in the streets. [3] He will not break the bruised reed, nor quench the dimly burning flame. He will encourage the fainthearted, those tempted to despair. He will see full justice given to all who have been wronged. [4] He won't be satisfied[b] until truth and righteousness prevail throughout the earth, nor until even distant lands beyond the seas have put their trust in him.

[5] The Lord God who created the heavens and stretched them out and created the earth and everything in it, and gives life and breath and spirit to everyone in all the world, he is the one who says [to his Servant, the Messiah[c]],

[6] "I the Lord have called you to demonstrate my righteousness. I will guard and support you, for I have given you to my people as the personal confirmation of my covenant with them.[d] You shall also be a light to guide the nations unto me. [7] You will open the eyes of the blind, and release those who sit in prison darkness and despair. [8] I am the Lord! That is my name, and I will not give my glory to anyone else; I will not share my praise with carved idols. [9] Everything I prophesied came true, and now I will prophesy again. I will tell you the future before it happens."

[10] Sing a new song to the Lord; sing his praises, all you who live in earth's remotest corners! Sing, O sea! Sing, all you who live in distant lands beyond the sea! [11] Join in the chorus, you desert cities—Kedar and Sela! And you, too, dwellers in the mountain tops. [12] Let the western coastlands glorify the Lord and sing his mighty power.

[13] The Lord will be a mighty warrior, full of fury toward his foes. He will give a great shout and prevail. [14] Long has he been silent; he has restrained himself. But now he will give full vent to his wrath; he will groan and cry like a woman delivering her child. [15] He will level the mountains and hills and blight their greenery. He will dry up the rivers and pools. [16] He will bring blind Israel along a path they have not seen before. He will make the darkness bright before them and smooth and straighten out the road ahead. He will not forsake them. [17] But those who trust in idols and call them gods will be greatly disappointed; they will be turned away.

[18] Oh, how blind and deaf you are towards God! Why won't you listen? Why won't you see? [19] Who in all the world is as blind as my own people,[e] who are designed to be my messengers of truth? Who is so blind as my "dedicated one," the "servant of the Lord"? [20] You see and understand what is right but won't heed nor do it; you hear but you won't listen.

[21] The Lord has magnified his law and made it truly glorious. Through it he had planned to show the world that he is righteous. [22] But what a sight his people are— these who were to demonstrate to all the world the glory of his law;[f] for they are robbed, enslaved, imprisoned, trapped, fair game for all, with no one to protect them. [23] Won't even one of you apply these lessons from the past and see the ruin that awaits you up ahead? [24] Who let Israel be robbed and hurt? Did not the Lord? It is the Lord they sinned against, for they would not go where he sent them nor listen to his laws. [25] That is why God poured out such fury and wrath on his people and destroyed them in battle. Yet, though set on fire and burned, they will not understand the reason why— that it is God, wanting them to repent.[c]

43 BUT NOW THE Lord who created you, O Israel, says, Don't be afraid, for I have ransomed you; I have called you by name; you are mine. [2] When you go through deep waters and great trouble, I will be with you. When you go through rivers of difficulty, you will not drown! When you walk

---

a Not Cyrus, as in chapter 41, but Christ.   b Literally, "He will not burn dimly or be bruised until . . ."
c Implied.   d Or, "You will be my covenant with all the people . . ."   e Literally, "as my servant."
f Implied in previous verse.

through the fire of oppression, you will not be burned up—the flames will not consume you. [3] For I am the Lord your God, your Savior, the Holy One of Israel. I gave Egypt and Ethiopia and Seba [to Cyrus[a]] in exchange for your freedom, as your ransom. [4] Others died that you might live; I traded their lives for yours because you are precious to me and honored, and I love you.

[5] Don't be afraid, for I am with you. I will gather you from east and west, [6] from north and south. I will bring my sons and daughters back to Israel from the farthest corners of the earth. [7] All who claim me as their God will come, for I have made them for my glory; I created them. [8] Bring them back to me—blind as they are and deaf when I call (although they see and hear!).

[9] Gather the nations together! Which of all their idols ever has foretold such things? Which can predict a single day ahead? Where are the witnesses of anything they said? If there are no witnesses, then they must confess that only God can prophesy.

[10] But I have witnesses, O Israel, says the Lord! You are my witnesses and my servants, chosen to know and to believe me and to understand that I alone am God. There is no other God; there never was and never will be. [11] I am the Lord, and there is no other Savior. [12] Whenever you have thrown away your idols, I have shown you my power. With one word I have saved you. You have seen me do it; you are my witnesses that it is true. [13] From eternity to eternity I am God. No one can oppose what I do.

[14] The Lord, your Redeemer, the Holy One of Israel, says:

For your sakes I will send an invading army against Babylon, that will walk in almost unscathed. The boasts of the Babylonians will turn to cries of fear. [15] I am the Lord, your Holy One, Israel's Creator and King. [16] I am the Lord, who opens a way through the waters, making a path right through the sea. [17] I called forth the mighty army of Egypt with all its chariots and horses, to lie beneath the waves, dead, their lives snuffed out like candlewicks. [18] But forget all that—it is nothing compared to what I'm going to do! [19] For I'm going to do a brand new thing. See, I have already begun! Don't you see it? I will make a road through the wilderness of the world for my people to go home, and create rivers for them in the desert! [20] The wild animals in the fields will thank me, the jackals and ostriches too, for giving them water in the wilderness, yes, springs in the desert, so that my people, my chosen ones, can be refreshed. [21] I have made Israel for myself, and these my people will some day honor me before the world.

[22] But O my people, you won't ask my help; you have grown tired of me! [23] You have not brought me the lambs for burnt offerings; you have not honored me with sacrifices. Yet my requests for offerings and incense have been very few! I have not treated you as slaves. [24] You have brought me no sweet-smelling incense nor pleased me with the sacrificial fat. No, you have presented me only with sins, and wearied me with all your faults.

[25] I, yes, I alone am he who blots away your sins for my own sake and will never think of them again. [26] Oh, remind me of this promise of forgiveness, for we must talk about your sins. Plead your case for my forgiving you. [27] From the very first your ancestors sinned against me—all your forebears transgressed my law. [28] That is why I have deposed your priests and destroyed Israel, leaving her to shame.

44 LISTEN TO ME, O my servant Israel, O my chosen ones:

[2] The Lord who made you, who will help you, says, O servant of mine, don't be afraid. O Jerusalem, my chosen ones, don't be afraid. [3] For I will give you abundant water for your thirst and for your parched fields. And I will pour out my Spirit and my blessings on your children. [4] They shall thrive like watered grass, like willows on a river bank. [5] "I am the Lord's," they'll proudly[a] say, or, "I am a Jew," and tattoo upon their hands the name of God or the honored name of Israel.

[6] The Lord, the King of Israel, says —yes, it is Israel's Redeemer, the Lord of

---

a Implied.   **44**a Implied

Hosts, who says it—I am the First and Last; there is no other God. [7] Who else can tell you what is going to happen in the days ahead? Let them tell you if they can, and prove their power. Let them do as I have done since ancient times. [8] Don't, don't be afraid. Haven't I proclaimed from ages past [that I would save you[b]]? You are my witnesses —is there any other God? No! None that I know about! There is no other Rock!

[9] What fools they are who manufacture idols for their gods. Their hopes remain unanswered. They themselves are witnesses that this is so, for their idols neither see nor know. No wonder those who worship them are so ashamed. [10] Who but a fool would make his own god—an idol that can help him not one whit! [11] All that worship these will stand before the Lord in shame, along with all these carpenters—mere men—who claim that they have made a god. Together they will stand in terror. [12] The metalsmith stands at his forge to make an axe, pounding on it with all his might. He grows hungry and thirsty, weak and faint. [13] Then the woodcarver takes the axe and uses it to make an idol. He measures and marks out a block of wood and carves the figure of a man. Now he has a wonderful idol that can't so much as move from where it is placed. [14] He cuts down cedars, he selects the cypress and the oak, he plants the ash in the forest to be nourished by the rain. [15] And after his care, he uses part of the wood to make a fire to warm himself and bake his bread, and then—he really does —he takes the rest of it and makes himself a god—a god for men to worship! An idol to fall down before and praise! [16] Part of the tree he burns to roast his meat and to keep him warm and fed and well content, [17] and with what's left he makes his god: a carved idol! He falls down before it and worships it and prays to it. "Deliver me," he says. "You are my god!"

[18] Such stupidity and ignorance! God has shut their eyes so that they cannot see, and closed their minds from understanding. [19] The man never stops to think or figure out, "Why, it's just a block of wood! I've burned it for heat and used it to bake my bread and roast my meat. How can the rest of it be a god? Should I fall down before a chunk of wood?" [20] The poor, deluded fool feeds on ashes; he is trusting what can never give him any help at all. Yet he cannot bring himself to ask, "Is this thing, this idol that I'm holding in my hand, a lie?"

[21] Pay attention, Israel, for you are my servant; I made you, and I will not forget to help you. [22] I've blotted out your sins; they are gone like morning mist at noon! Oh, return to me, for I have paid the price to set you free.

[23] Sing, O heavens, for the Lord has done this wondrous thing. Shout, O earth; break forth into song, O mountains and forests, yes, and every tree; for the Lord redeemed Jacob and is glorified in Israel! [24] The Lord, your Redeemer who made you, says, All things were made by me; I alone stretched out the heavens. By myself I made the earth and everything in it.

[25] I am the one who shows what liars all false prophets are, by causing something else to happen than the things they say. I make wise men give opposite advice to what they should, and make them into fools. [26] But what my prophets say, I do; when they say Jerusalem will be delivered and the cities of Judah lived in once again—it shall be done! [27] When I speak to the rivers and say, "Be dry!" they shall be dry. [28] When I say of Cyrus,[c] "He is my shepherd," he will certainly do as I say; and Jerusalem will be rebuilt and the Temple restored, for I have spoken it.

45 THIS IS JEHOVAH'S message to Cyrus, God's anointed, whom he has chosen to conquer many lands. God shall empower his right hand and he shall crush the strength of mighty kings. God shall open the gates of Babylon to him; the gates shall not be shut against him any more. [2] I will go before you, Cyrus, and level the mountains and smash down the city gates of brass and iron bars. [3] And I will give you treasures hidden in the darkness, secret riches; and you will know that I am doing this—I, the Lord, the God of Israel, the one who calls you by your name.

---

b Implied. c This was written many years before Cyrus began his meteoric rise to power.

⁴ And why have I named you for this work? For the sake of Jacob, my servant —Israel, my chosen. I called you by name when you didn't know me. ⁵ I am Jehovah; there is no other God. I will strengthen you and send you out to victory even though you don't know me, ⁶ and all the world from east to west will know there is no other God. I am Jehovah and there is no one else. I alone am God. ⁷ I form the light and make the dark. I send good times and bad. I, Jehovah, am he who does these things. ⁸ Open up, O heavens. Let the skies pour out their righteousness. Let salvation and righteousness sprout up together from the earth. I, Jehovah, created them.

⁹ Woe to the man who fights with his Creator. Does the pot argue with its maker? Does the clay dispute with him who forms it, saying, "Stop, you're doing it wrong!" or the pot exclaim, "How clumsy can you be!"? ¹⁰ Woe to the baby just being born who squalls to his father and mother, "Why have you produced me? Can't you do anything right at all?"

¹¹ Jehovah, the Holy One of Israel, Israel's Creator, says: What right have you to question what I do? Who are you to command me concerning the work of my hands? ¹² I have made the earth and created man upon it. With my hands I have stretched out the heavens and commanded all the vast myriads of stars. ¹³ I have raised up Cyrusᵃ to fulfill my righteous purpose, and I will direct all his paths. He shall restore my city and free my captive people—and not for a reward!

¹⁴ Jehovah says: The Egyptians, Ethiopians and Sabeans shall be subject to you. They shall come to you with all their merchandise and it shall all be yours. They shall follow you as prisoners in chains, and fall down on their knees before you and say, "The only God there is, is your God!"

¹⁵ Truly, O God of Israel, Savior, you work in strange, mysterious ways. ¹⁶ All who worship idols shall be disappointed and ashamed. ¹⁷ But Israel shall be saved by Jehovah with eternal salvation; they shall never be disappointed in their God through all eternity. ¹⁸ For Jehovah created the heavens and earth and put everything in place, and he made the world to be lived in, not to be an empty chaos. I am Jehovah, he says, and there is no other! ¹⁹ I publicly proclaim bold promises; I do not whisper obscurities in some dark corner so that no one can know what I mean. And I didn't tell Israel to ask me for what I didn't plan to give! No, for I, Jehovah, speak only truth and righteousness.

²⁰ Gather together and come, you nations that escape from Cyrus' hand. What fools they are who carry around the wooden idols and pray to gods that cannot save! ²¹ Consult together, argue your case and state your proofs that idol-worship pays! Who but God has said that these things concerning Cyrus would come true? What idol ever told you they would happen? For there is no other God but me—a just God and a Savior—no, not one! ²² Let all the world look to me for salvation! For I am God; there is no other. ²³ I have sworn by myself and I will never go back on my word, for it is true—that every knee in all the world shall bow to me, and every tongue shall swear allegiance to my name.

²⁴ "In Jehovah is all my righteousness and strength," the people shall declare. And all who were angry with him shall come to him and be ashamed. ²⁵ In Jehovah all the generations of Israel shall be justified, triumphant.

46 THE IDOLS OF Babylon, Bel and Nebo,ᵃ are being hauled away on ox carts! But look! The beasts are stumbling! The cart is turning over! The gods are falling out onto the ground! Is that the best that they can do? If they cannot even save themselves from such a fall, how can they save their worshipers from Cyrus?

³ "Listen to me, all Israel who are left; I have created you and cared for you since you were born. ⁴ I will be your God through all your lifetime, yes, even when your hair is white with age. I made you and I will care for you. I will carry you along and be your Savior.

---

a Literally, "I have raised up him . . ." The reference probably is also to Christ in the more distant future, as well as to Cyrus.   **46**a Names of Marduk and Nabu, the two principal gods in the Babylonian pantheon.

[5] "With what in all of heaven and earth do I compare? Whom can you find who equals me? [6] Will you compare me with an idol made lavishly with silver and with gold? They hire a goldsmith to take your wealth and make a god from it! Then they fall down and worship it! [7] They carry it around on their shoulders, and when they set it down it stays there, for it cannot move! And when someone prays to it there is no answer, for it cannot get him out of his trouble.

[8] "Don't forget this, O guilty ones. [9] And don't forget the many times I clearly told you what was going to happen in the future. For I am God—I only—and there is no other like me [10] who can tell you what is going to happen. All I say will come to pass, for I do whatever I wish. [11] I will call that swift bird of prey from the east—that man Cyrus from far away. And he will come and do my bidding. I have said I would do it and I will. [12] Listen to me, you stubborn, evil men! [13] For I am offering you my deliverance; not in the distant future, but right now! I am ready to save you, and I will restore Jerusalem, and Israel, who is my glory.

47 O BABYLON, THE unconquered, come sit in the dust; for your days of glory, pomp and honor are ended. O daughter of Chaldea, never again will you be the lovely princess, tender and delicate. [2] Take heavy millstones and grind the corn; remove your veil;[a] strip off your robe; expose yourself to public view. [3] You shall be in nakedness and shame. I will take vengeance upon you and will not repent."

[4] So speaks our Redeemer, who will save Israel from Babylon's mighty power; the Lord of Hosts is his name, the Holy One of Israel.

[5] Sit in darkness and silence, O Babylon; never again will you be called "The Queen of Kingdoms." [6] For I was angry with my people Israel and began to punish them a little by letting them fall into your hands, O Babylon. But you showed them no mercy. You have made even the old folks carry heavy burdens. [7] You thought your reign would never end, Queen Kingdom of the world. You didn't care a whit about my people or think about the fate of those who do them harm.

[8] O pleasure-mad kingdom, living at ease, bragging as the greatest in the world—listen to the sentence of my court upon your sins. You say, "I alone am God! I'll never be a widow; I'll never lose my children." [9] Well, those two things shall come upon you in one moment, in full measure in one day: widowhood and the loss of your children, despite all your witchcraft and magic.

[10] You felt secure in all your wickedness. "No one sees me," you said. Your "wisdom" and "knowledge" have caused you to turn away from me and claim that you yourself are Jehovah. [11] That is why disaster shall overtake you suddenly—so suddenly that you won't know where it comes from. And there will be no atonement then to cleanse away your sins.

[12] Call out the demon hordes you've worshiped all these years. Call on them to help you strike deep terror into many hearts again. [13] You have advisors by the ton —your astrologers and stargazers, who try to tell you what the future holds. [14] But they are as useless as dried grass burning in the fire. They cannot even deliver themselves! You'll get no help from them at·all. Theirs is no fire to sit beside to make you warm! [15] And all your friends of childhood days shall slip away and disappear, unable to help.

48 HEAR ME, MY people: you swear allegiance to the Lord without meaning a word of it, when you boast of living in the Holy City and brag about depending on the God of Israel. [3] Time and again I told you what was going to happen in the future. My words were scarcely spoken when suddenly I did just what I said. [4] I knew how hard and obstinate you are. Your necks are as unbending as iron; you are as hardheaded as brass. [5] That is why I told you ahead of time what I was going to do, so that you could never say, "My idol did it; my carved image commanded it to happen!" [6] You have heard my predictions and seen them

---

a In ancient Babylonia (and in many eastern lands today) only harlots were permitted to go without veils.

fulfilled, but you refuse to agree it is so. Now I will tell you new things I haven't mentioned before, secrets you haven't heard.

⁷ Then you can't say, "We knew that all the time!"

⁸ Yes, I'll tell you things entirely new, for I know so well what traitors you are, rebels from earliest childhood, rotten through and through. ⁹ Yet for my own sake and for the honor of my name I will hold back my anger and not wipe you out. ¹⁰ I refined you in the furnace of affliction, but found no silver there. You are worthless, with nothing good in you at all. ¹¹ Yet for my own sake—yes, *for my own sake*—I will save you from my anger and not destroy you lest the heathen say their gods have conquered me. I will not let them have my glory.

¹² Listen to me, my people, my chosen ones! I alone am God. I am the First; I am the Last. ¹³ It was my hand that laid the foundations of the earth; the palm of my right hand spread out the heavens above; I spoke and they came into being.

¹⁴ Come, all of you, and listen. Among all your idols, which one has ever told you this: "The Lord loves Cyrus. He will use him to put an end to the empire of Babylonia. He will utterly rout the armies of the Chaldeans"? ¹⁵ But I am saying it. I have called Cyrus; I have sent him on this errand and I will prosper him.

¹⁶ Come closer and listen. I have always told you plainly what would happen, so that you could clearly understand. And now the Lord God and his Spirit have sent me (with this message): ¹⁷ The Lord, your Redeemer, the Holy One of Israel, says, I am the Lord your God, who punishes you for your own good and leads you along the paths that you should follow.

¹⁸ Oh, that you had listened to my laws! Then you would have had peace flowing like a gentle river, and great waves of righteousness. ¹⁹ Then you would have become as numerous as the sands along the seashores of the world, too many to count, and there would have been no need for your destruction.

²⁰ Yet even now, be free from your cap-tivity! Leave Babylon, singing as you go; shout to the ends of the earth that the Lord has redeemed his servants, the Jews. ²¹ They were not thirsty when he led them through the deserts; he divided the rock, and water gushed out for them to drink. ²² But there is no peace, says the Lord, for the wicked.

49 LISTEN TO ME, all of you in far-off lands: The Lord called me before my birth. From within the womb he called me by my name. ² God will make my words of judgment sharp as swords. He has hidden me in the shadow of his hand; I am like a sharp arrow in his quiver.

³ He said to me: "You are my Servant, a Prince of Power[a] with God, and you shall bring me glory."

⁴ I replied, "But my work for them seems all in vain; I have spent my strength for them without response. Yet I leave it all with God for my reward."

⁵ "And now," said the Lord—the Lord who formed me from my mother's womb to serve him who commissioned me to restore to him his people Israel, who has given me the strength to perform this task and honored me for doing it!— ⁶ "you shall do more than restore Israel to me. I will make you a Light to the nations of the world to bring my salvation to them too."

⁷ The Lord, the Redeemer and Holy One of Israel, says to the one who is despised, rejected by mankind, and kept beneath the heel of earthly rulers: "Kings shall stand at attention when you pass by; princes shall bow low because the Lord has chosen you; he, the faithful Lord, the Holy One of Israel, chooses you."

⁸,⁹ The Lord says, "Your request has come at a favorable time. I will keep you from premature[b] harm and give you as a token and pledge to Israel, proof that I will reestablish the land of Israel and reassign it to its own people again. Through you I am saying to the prisoners of darkness, 'Come out! I am giving you your freedom!' They will be my sheep, grazing in green pastures and on the grassy hills. ¹⁰ They shall neither hunger nor thirst; the searing sun and scorching desert winds will not

a Or, "Israel."　　b Implied.

reach them any more. For the Lord in his mercy will lead them beside the cool waters. [11] And I will make my mountains into level paths for them; the highways shall be raised above the valleys. [12] See, my people shall return from far away, from north and west and south."

[13] Sing for joy, O heavens; shout, O earth. Break forth with song, O mountains, for the Lord has comforted his people, and will have compassion upon them in their sorrow.

[14] Yet they say, "My Lord deserted us; he has forgotten us."

[15] "Never! Can a mother forget her little child and not have love for her own son? Yet even if that should be, I will not forget you. [16] See, I have tattooed your name upon my palm and ever before me is a picture of Jerusalem's walls in ruins. [17] Soon your rebuilders shall come and chase away all those destroying you. [18] Look and see, for the Lord has vowed that all your enemies shall come and be your slaves. They will be as jewels to display, as bridal ornaments.

[19] "Even the most desolate parts of your abandoned land shall soon be crowded with your people, and your enemies who enslaved you shall be far away. [20] The generations born in exile shall return and say, 'We need more room! It's crowded here!' [21] Then you will think to yourself, 'Who has given me all these? For most of my children were killed and the rest were carried away into exile, leaving me here alone. Who bore these? Who raised them for me?' "

[22] The Lord God says, "See, I will give a signal to the Gentiles and they shall carry your little sons back to you in their arms, and your daughters on their shoulders. [23] Kings and queens shall serve you; they shall care for all your needs. They shall bow to the earth before you, and lick the dust from off your feet; then you shall know I am the Lord. Those who wait for me shall never be ashamed."

[24] Who can snatch the prey from the hands of a mighty man? Who can demand that a tyrant let his captives go? [25] But the Lord says, "Even the captives of the most mighty and most terrible shall all be freed; for I will fight those who fight you, and I will save your children. [26] I will feed your enemies with their own flesh and they shall be drunk with rivers of their own blood. All the world shall know that I, the Lord, am your Savior and Redeemer, the Mighty One of Israel."

50 THE LORD ASKS, Did I sell you to my creditors? Is that why you aren't here? Is your mother gone because I divorced her and sent her away? No, you sold yourselves for your sins. And your mother was taken in payment for your debts. [2] Was I too weak to save you? Is that why the house is silent and empty when I come home? Have I no longer power to deliver? No, that is not the reason! For I can rebuke the sea and make it dry! I can turn the rivers into deserts, covered with dying fish. [3] I am the one who sends the darkness out across the skies.

[4] The Lord God has given me his words of wisdom so that I may know what I should say to all these weary ones. Morning by morning he wakens me and opens my understanding to his will. [5] The Lord God has spoken to me and I have listened; I do not rebel nor turn away. [6] I give my back to the whip, and my cheeks to those who pull out the beard. I do not hide from shame—they spit in my face.

[7] Because the Lord God helps me, I will not be dismayed; therefore, I have set my face like flint to do his will, and I know that I will triumph. [8] He who gives me justice is near. Who will dare to fight against me now? Where are my enemies? Let them appear! [9] See, the Lord God is for me! Who shall declare me guilty? All my enemies shall be destroyed like old clothes eaten up by moths!

[10] Who among you fears the Lord and obeys his Servant? If such men walk in darkness, without one ray of light, let them trust the Lord, let them rely upon their God. [11] But see here, you who live in your own light, and warm yourselves from your own fires and not from God's; you will live among sorrows.

51 LISTEN TO ME, all who hope for deliverance, who seek the Lord! Consider the quarry from which you were mined, the rock from which you were cut! Yes, think about your ancestors Abraham and Sarah,

from whom you came. You worry at being so small and few, but Abraham was only *one* when I called him. But when I blessed him, he became a great nation. [3] And the Lord will bless Israel again, and make her deserts blossom; her barren wilderness will become as beautiful as the Garden of Eden. Joy and gladness will be found there, thanksgiving and lovely songs.

[4] Listen to me, my people; listen, O Israel, for I will see that right prevails. [5] My mercy and justice are coming soon; your salvation is on the way. I will rule the nations; they shall wait for me and long for me to come. [6] Look high in the skies and watch the earth beneath, for the skies shall disappear like smoke, the earth shall wear out like a garment, and the people of the earth shall die like flies. But my salvation lasts forever; my righteous rule will never die nor end.

[7] Listen to me, you who know the right from wrong and cherish my laws in your hearts: don't be afraid of people's scorn or their slanderous talk. [8] For the moth shall destroy them like garments; the worm shall eat them like wool; but my justice and mercy shall last forever, and my salvation from generation to generation.

[9] Awake, O Lord! Rise up and robe yourself with strength. Rouse yourself as in the days of old when you slew Egypt, the dragon of the Nile.[a] [10] Are you not the same today, the mighty God who dried up the sea, making a path right through it for your ransomed ones? [11] The time will come when God's redeemed will all come home again. They shall come with singing to Jerusalem, filled with joy and everlasting gladness; sorrow and mourning will all disappear.

[12] I, even I, am he who comforts you and gives you all this joy. So what right have you to fear mere mortal men, who wither like the grass and disappear? [13] And yet you have no fear of God, your Maker—you have forgotten him, the one who spread the stars throughout the skies and made the earth. Will you be in constant dread of men's oppression, and fear their anger all day long? [14] Soon, soon you slaves shall be released; dungeon, starvation and death are

not your fate. [15] For I am the Lord your God, the Lord of Hosts, who dried a path for you right through the sea, between the roaring waves. [16] And I have put my words in your mouth and hidden you safe within my hand. I planted the stars in place and molded all the earth. I am the one who says to Israel, "You are mine."

[17] Wake up, wake up, Jerusalem! You have drunk enough from the cup of the fury of the Lord. You have drunk to the dregs the cup of terror and squeezed out the last drops. [18] Not one of her sons is left alive to help or tell her what to do. [19] These two things have been your lot: desolation and destruction. Yes, famine and the sword. And who is left to sympathize? Who is left to comfort you? [20] For your sons have fainted and lie in the streets, helpless as wild goats caught in a net. The Lord has poured out his fury and rebuke upon them. [21] But listen now to this, afflicted ones—full of troubles and in a stupor (but not from being drunk)— [22] this is what the Lord says, the Lord your God who cares for his people: "See, I take from your hands the terrible cup; you shall drink no more of my fury; it is gone at last. [23] But I will put that terrible cup into the hands of those who tormented you and trampled your souls to the dust and walked upon your backs."

52 WAKE UP, WAKE up, Jerusalem, and clothe yourselves with strength [from God[a]]. Put on your beautiful clothes, O Zion, Holy City; for sinners—those who turn from God—will no longer enter your gates. [2] Rise from the dust, Jerusalem; take off the slave bands from your neck, O captive daughter of Zion. [3] For the Lord says, When I sold you into exile I asked no fee from your oppressors; now I can take you back again and owe them not a cent! [4] My people were tyrannized without cause by Egypt and Assyria, and I delivered them.

[5] And now, what is this? asks the Lord. Why are my people enslaved again, and oppressed without excuse? Those who rule them shout in exultation, and my name is constantly blasphemed, day by day. [6] Therefore I will reveal my name to my

---

a Literally, "Rahab, the dragon." 52a Implied.

people and they shall know the power in that name. Then at last they will recognize that it is I, yes, I, who speaks to them.

⁷ How beautiful upon the mountains are the feet of those who bring the happy news of peace and salvation, the news that the God of Israel reigns. ⁸ The watchmen shout and sing with joy, for right before their eyes they see the Lord God bring his people home again. ⁹ Let the ruins of Jerusalem break into joyous song, for the Lord has comforted his people; he has redeemed Jerusalem. ¹⁰ The Lord has bared his holy arm before the eyes of all the nations; the ends of the earth shall see the salvation of our God.

¹¹ Go now, leave your bonds and slavery. Put Babylon and all it represents far behind you—it is unclean to you. You are the holy people of the Lord; purify yourselves, all you who carry home the vessels of the Lord. ¹² You shall not leave in haste, running for your lives; for the Lord will go ahead of you, and he, the God of Israel, will protect you from behind.

¹³ See, my Servant^b shall prosper; he shall be highly exalted. ¹⁴,¹⁵ Yet many shall be amazed when they see him—yes, even far-off foreign nations and their kings; they shall stand dumbfounded, speechless in his presence. For they shall see and understand what they had not been told before. They shall see my Servant beaten and bloodied, so disfigured one would scarcely know it was a person standing there. So shall he cleanse^c many nations.

53 BUT, OH, HOW few believe it! Who will listen? To whom will God reveal his saving power? ² In God's eyes^a he was like a tender green shoot, sprouting from a root in dry and sterile ground. But in our eyes there was no attractiveness at all, nothing to make us want him. ³ We despised him and rejected him—a man of sorrows, acquainted with bitterest grief. We turned our backs on him and looked the other way when he went by. He was despised and we

didn't care.

⁴ Yet it was *our* grief he bore, *our* sorrows that weighed him down. And we thought his troubles were a punishment from God, for his *own* sins! ⁵ But he was wounded and bruised for *our* sins. He was chastised that we might have peace; he was lashed—and we were healed! ⁶ *We* are the ones who strayed away like sheep! *We*, who left God's paths to follow our own. Yet God laid on *him* the guilt and sins of every one of us!

⁷ He was oppressed and he was afflicted, yet he never said a word. He was brought as a lamb to the slaughter; and as a sheep before her shearers is dumb, so he stood silent before the ones condemning him. ⁸ From prison and trial they led him away to his death. But who among the people of that day realized it was their sins that he was dying for—that he was suffering their punishment? ⁹ He was buried like a criminal in a rich man's grave; but he had done no wrong, and had never spoken an evil word.

¹⁰ Yet it was the Lord's good plan to bruise him and fill him with grief. But when his soul has been made an offering for sin, then he shall have a multitude of children, many heirs. He shall live again^b and God's program shall prosper in his hands. ¹¹ And when he sees all that is accomplished by the anguish of his soul, he shall be satisfied; and because of what he has experienced, my righteous Servant shall make many to be counted righteous before God, for he shall bear all their sins. ¹² Therefore I will give him the honors of one who is mighty and great, because he has poured out his soul unto death. He was counted as a sinner, and he bore the sins of many, and he pled with God for sinners.

54 SING, O CHILDLESS woman! Break out into loud and joyful song, Jerusalem,^a for she who was abandoned has more blessings^b now than she whose husband stayed! ² Enlarge your house; build on additions; spread out your home! ³ For you will

---

b The Servant of the Lord, as the term is used here, is the Messiah, our Lord Jesus. This was the interpretation of this passage by Christ himself, and the writers of the New Testament and orthodox Christianity ever since.
c Or, "So shall he startle many nations." The meaning of the Hebrew word is uncertain.
53a Literally, "before him."   b Literally, "He shall prolong his days."   54a Implied.
b Literally, "children."

soon be bursting at the seams! And your descendants will possess the cities left behind during the exile, and rule the nations that took their lands.

⁴ Fear not; you will no longer live in shame. The shame of your youth and the sorrows of widowhood will be remembered no more, ⁵ for your Creator will be your "husband." The Lord of Hosts is his name; he is your Redeemer, the Holy One of Israel, the God of all the earth. ⁶ For the Lord has called you back from your grief—a young wife abandoned by her husband. ⁷ For a brief moment I abandoned you. But with great compassion I will gather you. ⁸ In a moment of anger I turned my face a little while; but with everlasting love I will have pity on you, says the Lord, your Redeemer. ⁹ Just as in the time of Noah I swore that I would never again permit the waters of a flood to cover the earth and destroy its life, so now I swear that I will never again pour out my anger on you as I have during this exile. ¹⁰ For the mountains may depart and the hills disappear, but my kindness shall not leave you. My promise of peace for you will never be broken, says the Lord who has mercy upon you.

¹¹ O my afflicted people, tempest-tossed and troubled, I will rebuild you on a foundation of sapphires and make the walls of your houses from precious jewels. ¹² I will make your towers of sparkling agate, and your gates and walls of shining gems. ¹³ And all your citizens shall be taught by me, and their prosperity shall be great. ¹⁴ You will live under a government that is just and fair. Your enemies will stay far away; you will live in peace. Terror shall not come near. ¹⁵ If any nation comes to fight you, it will not be sent by me to punish you. Therefore it will be routed, for I am on your side.[c] ¹⁶ I have created the smith who blows the coals beneath the forge and makes the weapons of destruction. And I have created the armies that destroy. ¹⁷ But in that coming day, no weapon turned against you shall succeed, and you will have justice against every courtroom lie. This is the heritage of the servants of the Lord. This is the blessing I have given you, says the Lord.

55 SAY THERE! IS anyone thirsty? Come and drink—even if you have no money! Come, take your choice of wine and milk—it's all free! ² Why spend your money on foodstuffs that don't give you strength? Why pay for groceries that don't do you any good? Listen and I'll tell you where to get good food that fattens up the soul!

³ Come to me with your ears wide open. Listen, for the life of your soul is at stake. I am ready to make an everlasting covenant with you, to give you all the unfailing mercies and love that I had for King David.[a] ⁴ He proved my power by conquering foreign nations.[b] ⁵ You also will command the nations and they will come running to obey, not because of your own power or virtue but because I, the Lord your God, have glorified you.

⁶ Seek the Lord while you can find him. Call upon him now while he is near. ⁷ Let men cast off their wicked deeds; let them banish from their minds the very thought of doing wrong! Let them turn to the Lord that he may have mercy upon them, and to our God, for he will abundantly pardon! ⁸ This plan of mine is not what you would work out, neither are my thoughts the same as yours! ⁹ For just as the heavens are higher than the earth, so are my ways higher than yours, and my thoughts than yours.

¹⁰ As the rain and snow come down from heaven and stay upon the ground to water the earth, and cause the grain to grow and to produce seed for the farmer and bread for the hungry, ¹¹ so also is my Word. I send it out and it always produces fruit. It shall accomplish all I want it to, and prosper everywhere I send it. ¹² You will live in joy and peace. The mountains and hills, the trees of the field—all the world around you—will rejoice. ¹³ Where once were thorns, fir trees will grow; where briars grew, the myrtle trees will sprout up. This miracle will make the Lord's name very great and be an everlasting sign [of God's power and love[b]].

---

c Literally, "because of you." 55a See 2 Samuel 7 for the terms of God's covenant with David, here remembered.   b Implied.

56 BE JUST AND fair to all, the Lord God says. Do what's right and good, for I am coming soon to rescue you. [2] Blessed is the man who refuses to work during my Sabbath days of rest, but honors them; and blessed is the man who checks himself from doing wrong.

[3] And my blessings are for Gentiles, too, when they accept the Lord; don't let them think that I will make them second-class citizens. And this is for the eunuchs too. They can be as much mine as anyone. [4] For I say this to the eunuchs who keep his Sabbaths holy and choose the things that please him, and come to grips with his laws: [5] I will give them—in my house, within my walls —a name far greater than the honor they would receive from having sons and daughters. For the name that I will give them is an everlasting one; it will never disappear.

[6] As for the Gentiles, the outsiders who join the people of the Lord and serve him and love his name, and are his servants and don't desecrate the Sabbath, and have accepted his covenant and promises, [7] I will bring them also to my holy mountain of Jerusalem, and make them full of joy within my House of Prayer.

I will accept their sacrifices and offerings, for my Temple shall be called "A House of Prayer for All People"! [8] For the Lord God who brings back the outcasts of Israel says, I will bring others too besides my people Israel.

[9] Come, wild animals of the field; come, tear apart the sheep; come, wild animals of the forest, devour my people.[a] [10] For the leaders of my people—the Lord's watchmen, his shepherds—are all blind to every danger. They are featherbrained and give no warning when danger comes. They love to lie there, love to sleep, to dream. [11] And they are as greedy as dogs, never satisfied; they are stupid shepherds who only look after their own interest, each trying to get as much as he can for himself from every possible source.

[12] "Come," they say. "We'll get some wine and have a party; let's all get drunk. This is really living; let it go on and on, and tomorrow will be better yet!"

57 THE GOOD MEN perish; the godly die before their time and no one seems to care or wonder why. No one seems to realize that God is taking them away from evil days ahead. [2] For the godly who die shall rest in peace.

[3] But you—come here, you witches' sons, you offspring of adulterers and harlots! [4] Who is it you mock, making faces and sticking out your tongues? You children of sinners and liars! [5] You worship your idols with great zeal beneath the shade of every tree, and slay your children as human sacrifices down in the valleys, under overhanging rocks. [6] Your gods are the smooth stones in the valleys. You worship them and they, not I, are your inheritance. Does all this make me happy? [7,8] You have committed adultery on the tops of the mountains, for you worship idols there, deserting me. Behind closed doors you set your idols up and worship someone other than me. This is adultery, for you are giving these idols your love, instead of loving me. [9] You have taken pleasant incense and perfume to Molech as your gift. You have traveled far, even to hell itself, to find new gods to love. [10] You grew weary in your search, but you never gave up. You strengthened yourself and went on. [11] Why were you more afraid of them than of me? How is it that you gave not even a second thought to me? Is it because I've been too gentle, that you have no fear of me?

[12] And then there is your "righteousness" and your "good works"—none of which will save you. [13] Let's see if the whole collection of your idols can help you when you cry to them to save you! They are so weak that the wind can carry them off! A breath can puff them away. But he who trusts in me shall possess the land and inherit my Holy Mountain. [14] I will say, Rebuild the road! Clear away the rocks and stones. Prepare a glorious highway for my people's return from captivity.

[15] The high and lofty one who inhabits eternity, the Holy One, says this: I live in that high and holy place where those with contrite, humble spirits dwell; and I refresh the humble and give new courage to those with repentant hearts. [16] For I will not fight

a Implied.

against you forever, nor always show my wrath; if I did, all mankind would perish—the very souls that I have made. [17] I was angry and smote these greedy men. But they went right on sinning, doing everything their evil hearts desired. [18] I have seen what they do, but I will heal them anyway! I will lead them and comfort them, helping them to mourn and to confess their sins. [19] Peace, peace to them, both near and far, for I will heal them all. [20] But those who still reject me[a] are like the restless sea, which is never still, but always churns up mire and dirt. [21] There is no peace, says my God, for them!

58 SHOUT WITH THE voice of a trumpet blast; tell my people of their sins! [2] Yet they act so pious! They come to the Temple every day and are so delighted to hear the reading of my laws—just as though they would obey them—just as though they don't despise the commandments of their God! How anxious they are to worship correctly; oh, how they love the Temple services!

[3] "We have fasted before you," they say. "Why aren't you impressed? Why don't you see our sacrifices? Why don't you hear our prayers? We have done much penance, and you don't even notice it!" I'll tell you why! Because you are living in evil pleasure even while you are fasting, and you keep right on oppressing your workers. [4] Look, what good is fasting when you keep on fighting and quarreling? This kind of fasting will never get you anywhere with me. [5] Is this what I want—this doing of penance and bowing like reeds in the wind and putting on sackcloth and covering yourselves with ashes? Is this what you call fasting?

[6] No, the kind of fast I want is that you stop oppressing those who work for you and treat them fairly and give them what they earn. [7] I want you to share your food with the hungry and bring right into your own homes those who are helpless, poor and destitute. Clothe those who are cold and don't hide from relatives who need your help. [8] If you do these things, God will shed his own glorious light upon you. He will heal you; your godliness will lead you forward, and

goodness will be a shield before you, and the glory of the Lord will protect you from behind. [9] Then, when you call, the Lord will answer. "Yes, I am here," he will quickly reply. All you need to do is to stop oppressing the weak, and to stop making false accusations and spreading vicious rumors!

[10] Feed the hungry! Help those in trouble! Then your light will shine out from the darkness, and the darkness around you shall be as bright as day. [11] And the Lord will guide you continually, and satisfy you with all good things, and keep you healthy too; and you will be like a well-watered garden, like an ever-flowing spring. [12] Your sons will rebuild the long-deserted ruins of your cities, and you will be known as "The People Who Rebuild Their Walls and Cities."

[13] If you keep the Sabbath holy, not having your own fun and business on that day, but enjoying the Sabbath and speaking of it with delight as the Lord's holy day, and honoring the Lord in what you do, not following your own desires and pleasure, nor talking idly— [14] then the Lord will be your delight, and I will see to it that you ride high, and get your full share of the blessings I promised to Jacob, your father. The Lord has spoken.

59 LISTEN NOW! THE Lord isn't too weak to save you. And he isn't getting deaf! He can hear you when you call! [2] But the trouble is that your sins have cut you off from God. Because of sin he has turned his face away from you and will not listen anymore. [3] For your hands are those of murderers and your fingers are filthy with sin. You lie and grumble and oppose the good. [4] No one cares about being fair and true. Your lawsuits are based on lies; you spend your time plotting evil deeds and doing them. [5] You spend your time and energy in spinning evil plans which end up in deadly actions. [6] You cheat and shortchange everyone. Everything you do is filled with sin; violence is your trademark. [7] Your feet run to do evil and rush to murder; your thoughts are only of sinning, and wherever you go you leave behind a trail of misery

a Literally, "the wicked."

and death. ⁸ You don't know what true peace is, nor what it means to be just and good; you continually do wrong and those who follow you won't experience any peace, either.

⁹ It is because of all this evil that you aren't finding God's blessings; that's why he doesn't punish those who injure you. No wonder you are in darkness when you expected light. No wonder you are walking in the gloom. ¹⁰ No wonder you grope like blind men and stumble along in broad daylight, yes, even at brightest noontime, as though it were the darkest night! No wonder you are like corpses when compared with vigorous young men! ¹¹ You roar like hungry bears; you moan with mournful cries like doves. You look for God to keep you, but he doesn't. He has turned away. ¹² For your sins keep piling up before the righteous God, and testify against you.

Yes, we know what sinners we are. ¹³ We know our disobedience; we have denied the Lord our God. We know what rebels we are and how unfair we are, for we carefully plan our lies. ¹⁴ Our courts oppose the righteous man; fairness is unknown. Truth falls dead in the streets, and justice is outlawed.

¹⁵ Yes, truth is gone, and anyone who tries a better life is soon attacked. The Lord saw all the evil and was displeased to find no steps taken against sin. ¹⁶ He saw no one was helping you, and wondered that no one intervened. Therefore he himself stepped in to save you through his mighty power and justice. ¹⁷ He put on righteousness as armor, and the helmet of salvation on his head. He clothed himself with robes of vengeance and of godly fury. ¹⁸ He will repay his enemies for their evil deeds—fury for his foes in distant lands. ¹⁹ Then at last they will reverence and glorify the name of God from west to east. For he will come like a flood-tide driven by Jehovah's breath. ²⁰ He will come as a Redeemer to those in Zion who have turned away from sin.

²¹ "As for me, this is my promise to them," says the Lord: "My Holy Spirit shall not leave them, and they shall want the good and hate the wrong—they and their children and their children's children

forever."

60 ARISE, MY PEOPLE! Let your light shine for all the nations to see! For the glory of the Lord is streaming from you. ² Darkness as black as night shall cover all the peoples of the earth, but the glory of the Lord will shine from you. ³ All nations will come to your light; mighty kings will come to see the glory of the Lord upon you.

⁴ Lift up your eyes and see! For your sons and daughters are coming home to you from distant lands. ⁵ Your eyes will shine with joy, your hearts will thrill, for merchants from around the world will flow to you, bringing you the wealth of many lands. ⁶ Vast droves of camels will converge upon you, dromedaries from Midian and Sheba and Ephah, too, bringing gold and incense to add to the praise of God. ⁷ The flocks of Kedar shall be given you, and the rams of Nabaioth for my altars, and I will glorify my glorious Temple in that day.

⁸ And who are these who fly like a cloud to Israel, like doves to their nests? ⁹ I have reserved the ships of many lands, the very best,ᵃ to bring the sons of Israel home again from far away, bringing their wealth with them. For the Holy One of Israel, known around the world, has glorified you in the eyes of all.

¹⁰ Foreigners will come and build your cities. Presidents and kings will send you aid. For though I destroyed you in my anger, I will have mercy on you through my grace. ¹¹ Your gates will stay wide open around the clock to receive the wealth of many lands. The kings of the world will cater to you. ¹² For the nations refusing to be your alliesᵇ will perish; they shall be destroyed. ¹³ The glory of Lebanon will be yours—the forests of firs and pines, and box trees—to beautify my sanctuary. My Temple will be glorious.

¹⁴ The sons of anti-Semites will come and bow before you! They will kiss your feet! They will call Jerusalem "The City of the Lord" and "The Glorious Mountain of the Holy One of Israel." ¹⁵ Though once despised and hated and rebuffed by all, you will be beautiful forever, a joy for all the

---

a Literally, "the ships of Tarshish."   b Literally, "that will not serve you."

generations of the world, for I will make you so. ¹⁶ Powerful kings and mighty nations shall provide you with the choicest of their goods to satisfy your every need, and you will know at last and really understand that I, the Lord, am your Savior and Redeemer, the Mighty One of Israel. ¹⁷ I will exchange your brass for gold, your iron for silver, your wood for brass, your stones for iron. Peace and righteousness shall be your taskmasters! ¹⁸ Violence will disappear out of your land—all war will end. Your walls will be "Salvation" and your gates "Praise."

¹⁹ No longer will you need the sun or moon to give you light, for the Lord your God will be your everlasting light, and he will be your glory. ²⁰ Your sun shall never set; the moon shall not go down—for the Lord will be your everlasting light; your days of mourning all will end. ²¹ All your people will be good. They will possess their land forever, for I will plant them there with my own hands; this will bring me glory. ²² The smallest family shall multiply into a clan; the tiny group shall be a mighty nation. I, the Lord, will bring it all to pass when it is time.

61 THE SPIRIT OF the Lord God is upon me, because the Lord has anointed me to bring good news to the suffering and afflicted. He has sent me to comfort the broken-hearted, to announce liberty to captives and to open the eyes of the blind. ² He has sent me to tell those who mourn that the time of God's favor to them has come, and the day of his wrath to their enemies. ³ To all who mourn in Israel he will give:

Beauty for ashes;
Joy instead of mourning;
Praise instead of heaviness.

For God has planted them like strong and graceful oaks for his own glory.

⁴ And they shall rebuild the ancient ruins, repairing cities long ago destroyed, reviving them though they have lain there many generations. ⁵ Foreigners shall be your servants; they shall feed your flocks and plow your fields and tend your vineyards. ⁶ You shall be called priests of the Lord, ministers of our God. You shall be fed with the treasures of the nations and shall glory in their riches. ⁷ Instead of shame and dishonor, you shall have a double portion of prosperity and everlasting joy.

⁸ For I, the Lord, love justice; I hate robbery and wrong. I will faithfully reward my people for their suffering and make an everlasting covenant with them. ⁹ Their descendants shall be known and honored among the nations; all shall realize that they are a people God has blessed.

¹⁰ Let me tell you how happy God has made me! For he has clothed me with garments of salvation and draped about me the robe of righteousness. I am like a bridegroom in his wedding suit or a bride with her jewels. ¹¹ The Lord will show the nations of the world his justice; all will praise him. His righteousness shall be like a budding tree, or like a garden in early spring, full of young plants springing up everywhere.

62 BECAUSE I LOVE Zion, because my heart yearns for Jerusalem, I will not cease to pray for her or to cry out to God on her behalf until she shines forth in his righteousness and is glorious in his salvation. ² The nations shall see your righteousness. Kings shall be blinded by your glory; and God will confer on you a new name. ³ He will hold you aloft in his hands for all to see—a splendid crown for the King of kings. ⁴ Never again shall you be called "The God-forsaken Land" or the "Land that God Forgot." Your new name will be "The Land of God's Delight" and "The Bride," for the Lord delights in you and will claim you as his own. ⁵ Your children will care for you, O Jerusalem, with joy like that of a young man who marries a virgin; and God will rejoice over you as a bridegroom with his bride.

⁶,⁷ O Jerusalem, I have set intercessors[a] on your walls who shall cry to God all day and all night for the fulfillment of his promises. Take no rest, all you who pray, and give God no rest until he establishes Jerusalem and makes her respected and admired throughout the earth. ⁸ The Lord has sworn

---

a Literally, "watchmen."

to Jerusalem with all his integrity: "I will never again give you to your enemies; never again shall foreign soldiers come and take away your grain and wine. ⁹ You raised it; you shall keep it, praising God. Within the Temple courts you yourselves shall drink the wine you pressed. ¹⁰ Go out! Go out! Prepare the roadway for my people to return! Build the roads, pull out the boulders, raise the flag of Israel."

¹¹ See, the Lord has sent his messengers to every land and said, "Tell my people, I, the Lord your God, am coming to save you and will bring you many gifts." ¹² And they shall be called "The Holy People" and "The Lord's Redeemed," and Jerusalem shall be called "The Land of Desire" and "The City God Has Blessed."

63 WHO IS THIS who comes from Edom, from the city of Bozrah, with his magnificent garments of crimson? Who is this in kingly robes, marching in the greatness of his strength?

"It is I, the Lord, announcing your salvation; I, the Lord, the one who is mighty to save!"

² "Why are your clothes so red, as from treading out the grapes?"

³ "I have trodden the winepress alone. No one was there to help me. In my wrath I have trodden my enemies like grapes. In my fury I trampled my foes. It is their blood you see upon my clothes. ⁴ For the time has come for me to avenge my people, to redeem them from the hands of their oppressors. ⁵ I looked but no one came to help them; I was amazed and appalled. So I executed vengeance alone; unaided, I meted out judgment. ⁶ I crushed the heathen nations in my anger and made them stagger and fall to the ground."

⁷ I will tell of the lovingkindnesses of God. I will praise him for all he has done; I will rejoice in his great goodness to Israel, which he has granted in accordance with his mercy and love. ⁸ He said, "They are my very own; surely they will not be false again." And he became their Savior. ⁹ In all their affliction he was afflicted, and he personally[a] saved them. In his love and pity he redeemed them and lifted them up and carried them through all the years.

¹⁰ But they rebelled against him and grieved his Holy Spirit. That is why he became their enemy and personally fought against them. ¹¹ Then they remembered those days of old when Moses, God's servant, led his people out of Egypt and they cried out, "Where is the one who brought Israel through the sea, with Moses as their shepherd? Where is the God who sent his Holy Spirit to be among his people? ¹² Where is he whose mighty power divided the sea before them when Moses lifted up his hand, and established his reputation forever? ¹³ Who led them through the bottom of the sea? Like fine stallions racing through the desert, they never stumbled. ¹⁴ Like cattle grazing in the valleys, so the Spirit of the Lord gave them rest. Thus he gave himself a magnificent reputation.

¹⁵ O Lord, look down from heaven and see us from your holy, glorious home; where is the love for us you used to show—your power, your mercy and your compassion? Where are they now? ¹⁶ Surely you are still our Father! Even if Abraham and Jacob would disown us, still you would be our Father, our Redeemer from ages past. ¹⁷ O Lord, why have you hardened our hearts and made us sin and turn against you? Return and help us, for we who belong to you need you so.[b] ¹⁸ How briefly we possessed Jerusalem! And now our enemies have destroyed her. ¹⁹ O God, why do you treat us as though we weren't your people, as though we were a heathen nation that never called you "Lord"?

64 OH, THAT YOU would burst forth from the skies and come down! How the mountains would quake in your presence! ² The consuming fire of your glory would burn down the forests and boil the oceans dry. The nations would tremble before you; then your enemies would learn the reason for your fame! ³ So it was before when you came down, for you did awesome things beyond our highest expectations, and how the mountains quaked! ⁴ For since the world began no one has seen or heard of such a

---

a Or, "The Angel of his Presence saved them out of their affliction."   b Literally, "for your servants' sake."

God as ours, who works for those who wait for him! [5] You welcome those who cheerfully do good, who follow godly ways.

But we are not godly; we are constant sinners and have been all our lives. Therefore your wrath is heavy on us. How can such as we be saved? [6] We are all infected and impure with sin. When we put on our prized robes of righteousness we find they are but filthy rags.[a] Like autumn leaves we fade, wither and fall. And our sins, like the wind, sweep us away. [7] Yet no one calls upon your name or pleads with you for mercy. Therefore you have turned away from us and turned us over to our sins.

[8] And yet, O Lord, you are our Father. We are the clay and you are the Potter. We are all formed by your hand. [9] Oh, be not so angry with us, Lord, nor forever remember our sins. Oh, look and see that we are all your people.

[10] Your holy cities are destroyed; Jerusalem is a desolate wilderness. [11] Our holy, beautiful Temple where our fathers praised you is burned down, and all the things of beauty are destroyed. [12] After all of this, must you still refuse to help us, Lord? Will you stand silent and still punish us?

65 THE LORD SAYS, People[a] who never before inquired about me are now seeking me out. Nations[a] who never before searched for me are finding me.

[2] But my own people—though I have been spreading out my arms to welcome them all day long—have rebelled; they follow their own evil paths and thoughts. [3] All day long they insult me to my face by worshiping idols in many gardens and burning incense on the rooftops of their homes. [4] At night they go out among the graves and caves to worship evil spirits, and they eat pork and other forbidden foods. [5] Yet they say to one another, "Don't come too close, you'll defile me! For I am holier than you!" They stifle me. Day in and day out they infuriate me.

[6] See, here is my decree all written out before me: *I will not stand silent; I will repay. Yes, I will repay them—* [7] not only for

their own sins but for those of their fathers too, says the Lord, for they also burned incense on the mountains and insulted me upon the hills. I will pay them back in full.

[8] But I will not destroy them all, says the Lord; for just as good grapes are found among a cluster of bad ones (and someone will say, "Don't throw them all away—there are some good grapes there!") so I will not destroy all Israel, for I have true servants there. [9] I will preserve a remnant of my people to possess the land of Israel; those I select will inherit it and serve me there. [10] As for my people who have sought me, the plains of Sharon shall again be filled with flocks, and the valley of Achor shall be a place to pasture herds.

[11] But because the rest of you have forsaken the Lord and his Temple and worship gods of "Fate" and "Destiny," [12] therefore I will "destine" you to the sword, and your "fate" shall be a dark one; for when I called, you didn't answer; when I spoke, you wouldn't listen. You deliberately sinned before my very eyes, choosing to do what you know I despise. [13] Therefore the Lord God says, You shall starve, but my servants shall eat; you shall be thirsty while they drink; you shall be sad and ashamed, but they shall rejoice. [14] You shall cry in sorrow and vexation and despair, while they sing for joy. [15] Your name shall be a curse word among my people, for the Lord God will slay you and call his true servants by another name.[b]

[16] And yet, the days will come[c] when all who invoke a blessing or take an oath shall swear by the God of Truth; for I will put aside my anger and forget the evil that you did. [17] For see, I am creating new heavens and a new earth—so wonderful that no one will even think about the old ones anymore. [18] Be glad; rejoice forever in my creation. Look! I will recreate Jerusalem as a place of happiness, and her people shall be a joy! [19] And I will rejoice in Jerusalem, and in my people; and the voice of weeping and crying shall not be heard there any more.

[20] No longer will babies die when only a few days old; no longer will men be consid-

a Literally, "filthy as a menstruating woman's rags." as the next applies to Israelites rather than to the nations. See Acts 11:26.   c Implied.

65a Literally, "those." Some believe this verse as well But see Romans 10:20–21.   b i.e., "Christians"?

613

ered old at 100! Only sinners will die that young! [21,22] In those days, when a man builds a house, he will keep on living in it—it will not be destroyed by invading armies as in the past. My people will plant vineyards and eat the fruit themselves—their enemies will not confiscate it. For my people will live as long as trees and will long enjoy their hard-won gains. [23] Their harvests will not be eaten by their enemies; their children will not be born to be cannon fodder. For they are the children of those the Lord has blessed; and their children, too, shall be blessed. [24] I will answer them before they even call to me. While they are still talking to me about their needs, I will go ahead and answer their prayers! [25] The wolf and lamb shall feed together, the lion shall eat straw as the ox does, and poisonous snakes shall strike[d] no more! In those days nothing and no one shall be hurt or destroyed in all my Holy Mountain, says the Lord.

66 HEAVEN IS MY throne and the earth is my footstool: What Temple can you build for me as good as that? [2] My hand has made both earth and skies, and they are mine. Yet I will look with pity on the man who has a humble and a contrite heart, who trembles at my word.

[3] But those who choose their own ways, delighting in their sins, are cursed. God will not accept their offerings. When such men sacrifice an ox on the altar of God, it is no more acceptable to him than human sacrifice. If they sacrifice a lamb, or bring an offering of grain, it is as loathsome to God as putting a dog or the blood of a swine on his altar! When they burn incense to him, he counts it the same as though they blessed an idol. [4] I will send great troubles upon them—all the things they feared, for when I called them, they refused to answer, and when I spoke to them, they would not hear. Instead, they did wrong before my eyes, and chose what they knew I despised.

[5] Hear the words of God, all you who fear him, and tremble at his words: Your brethren hate you and cast you out for being loyal to my name. "Glory to God," they scoff. "Be happy in the Lord!" But they shall be put to shame.

[6] What is all the commotion in the city? What is that terrible noise from the Temple? It is the voice of the Lord taking vengeance upon his enemies.

[7,8] Who has heard or seen anything as strange as this? For in one day, suddenly, a nation, Israel, shall be born, even before the birth pains come. In a moment, just as Israel's anguish starts, the baby is born; the nation begins. [9] Shall I bring to the point of birth and then not deliver? asks the Lord your God. No! Never!

[10] Rejoice with Jerusalem; be glad with her, all you who love her, you who mourned for her. [11] Delight in Jerusalem; drink deep of her glory even as an infant at a mother's generous breasts. [12] Prosperity shall overflow Jerusalem like a river, says the Lord, for I will send it; the riches of the Gentiles will flow to her. Her children shall be nursed at her breasts, carried on her hips and dandled on her knees. [13] I will comfort you there as a little one is comforted by its mother. [14] When you see Jerusalem, your heart will rejoice; vigorous health will be yours. All the world will see the good hand of God upon his people, and his wrath upon his enemies.

[15] For see, the Lord will come with fire and with swift chariots of doom to pour out the fury of his anger and his hot rebuke with flames of fire. [16] For the Lord will punish the world by fire and by his sword, and the slain of the Lord shall be many! [17] Those who worship idols that are hidden behind a tree in the garden, feasting there on pork and mouse and all forbidden meat—they will come to an evil end, says Jehovah. [18] I see full well what they are doing; I know what they are thinking, so I will gather together all nations and people against Jerusalem, where they shall see my glory. [19] I will perform a mighty miracle against them, and I will send those[a] who escape, as missionaries to the nations—to Tarshish, Put, Lud, Meshech, Rosh, Tubal, Javan, and to the lands

---

d Literally, "dust (i.e., not men!) shall be the serpent's food."   66a It is not clear from the Hebrew whether "those who escape" means survivors of the armies of the nations, or survivors of the Jews in Israel. The context seems to favor the former. Put and Lud were in North Africa; Meshech, Rosh and Tubal were in Asia Minor and Armenia.

beyond the sea that have not heard my fame nor seen my glory. There they shall declare my glory to the Gentiles. [20] And they shall bring back all your brethren from every nation as a gift to the Lord, transporting them gently[b] on horses and in chariots, and in litters, and on mules and camels, to my holy mountain, to Jerusalem, says the Lord. It will be like offerings flowing into the Temple of the Lord at harvest time, carried in vessels consecrated to the Lord. [21] And I will appoint some of those returning to be my priests and Levites, says the Lord.

[22] As surely as my new heavens and earth shall remain, so surely shall you always be my people, with a name that shall never disappear. [23] All mankind shall come to worship me from week to week and month to month. [24] And they shall go out and look at the dead bodies of those who have rebelled against me, for their worm shall never die; their fire shall not be quenched, and they shall be a disgusting sight to all mankind.

---

b Implied.

Who? ME?

Rohn Engh

Young men, their futures looming with huge question marks...hoping for success in the tough, competitive world, wondering how closely failure snaps at their heels . . . some better prepared than others, but nearly all a bit hesitant, uncertain . . .

Jeremiah was more fearful than most, a priest's son from the country crossroads of Anathoth, when God laid on him the staggering job of being "my spokesman to the world" (1:5). He protested that he was too young, but God pushed ahead, launching him with two startling visions which illustrated the coming judgment. Before his ministry ended more than 40 years later, Jeremiah had been jeered as a traitor, jailed several times, had his writings burned by King Jehoiakim, and eventually had been deported to Egypt. He was a sensitive, dramatic person, his depth of grief coming through strongest in a second short book called Lamentations, which follows this collection of prophecies.

Was he successful?

That all depends on whose definition of success we use.

JEREMIAH

1 THESE ARE GOD'S messages to Jeremiah the priest (the son of Hilkiah) who lived in the town of Anathoth in the land of Benjamin. The first of these messages came to him in the thirteenth year of the reign of Amon's son Josiah, king of Judah. ³ Others came during the reign of Josiah's son Jehoiakim, king of Judah, and at various other times until July of the eleventh year of the reign of Josiah's son Zedekiah, king of Judah, when Jerusalem was captured and the people were taken away as slaves.

⁴ The Lord said to me, ⁵ "I knew you before you were formed within your mother's womb; before you were born I sanctified you and appointed you as my spokesman to the world."

⁶ "O Lord God," I said, "I can't do that! I'm far too young! I'm only a youth!"

⁷ "Don't say that," he replied, "for you will go wherever I send you and speak whatever I tell you to. ⁸ And don't be afraid of the people, for I, the Lord, will be with you and see you through."

⁹ Then he touched my mouth and said, "See, I have put my words in your mouth! ¹⁰ Today your work begins, to warn the nations and the kingdoms of the world. In accord with my words spoken through your mouth I will tear down some and destroy them, and plant others and nurture them and make them strong and great."

¹¹ Then the Lord said to me, "Look, Jeremiah! What do you see?"

And I replied, "I see a whip made from the branch of an almond tree."

¹² And the Lord replied, "That's right, and it means that I will surely carry out my threats of punishment."ᵃ

¹³ Then the Lord asked me, "What do you see now?"

And I replied, "I see a pot of boiling water, tipping southward, spilling over Judah."ᵇ

¹⁴ "Yes," he said, "for terror from the north will boil out upon all the people of this land. ¹⁵ I am calling the armies of the kingdoms of the north to come to Jerusalem and set their thrones at the gates of the city and all along its walls, and in all the other cities of Judah. ¹⁶ This is the way I will punish my people for deserting me and for worshiping other gods—yes, idols they themselves have made! ¹⁷ Get up and dress and go out and tell them whatever I tell you to say. Don't be afraid of them, or else I will make a fool of you in front of them. ¹⁸ For see, today I have made you impervious to their attacks. They cannot harm you. You are strong like a fortified city that cannot be captured, like an iron pillar and heavy gates of brass. All the kings of Judah and its officers and priests and people will not be able to prevail against you. ¹⁹ They will

---

a There is word play here between *shaqedh* (almond) in verse 11 and *shoqedh* (watching) in verse 12: "For I am watching over my word to perform it."   b Implied.

try, but they will fail. For I am with you," says the Lord. "I will deliver you."

2 AGAIN THE LORD spoke to me and said:
² Go and shout this in Jerusalem's streets: The Lord says, I remember how eager you were to please me as a young bride long ago and how you loved me and followed me even through the barren deserts. ³ In those days Israel was a holy people, the first of my children.[a] All who harmed them were counted deeply guilty, and great evil fell on anyone who touched them.

⁴,⁵ O Israel, says the Lord, why did your fathers desert me? What sin did they find in me that turned them away and changed them into fools who worship idols? ⁶ They ignore the fact that it was I, the Lord, who brought them safely out of Egypt and led them through the barren wilderness, a land of deserts and rocks, of drought and death, where no one lives or even travels. ⁷ And I brought them into a fruitful land, to eat of its bounty and goodness, but they made it into a land of sin and corruption and turned my inheritance into an evil thing. ⁸ Even their priests cared nothing for the Lord, and their judges ignored me; their rulers turned against me, and their prophets worshiped Baal and wasted their time on nonsense.

⁹ But I will not give you up—I will plead for you to return to me, and will keep on pleading; yes, even with your children's children in the years to come!

¹⁰,¹¹ Look around you and see if you can find another nation anywhere that has traded in its old gods for new ones—even though their gods are nothing. Send to the west to the island of Cyprus; send to the east to the deserts of Kedar. See if anyone there has ever heard so strange a thing as this. And yet my people have given up their glorious God for silly idols! ¹² The heavens are shocked at such a thing and shrink back in horror and dismay. ¹³ For my people have done two evil things: They have forsaken me, the Fountain of Life-giving Water; and they have built for themselves broken cisterns that can't hold water!

¹⁴ Why has Israel become a nation of slaves? Why is she captured and led far away?

¹⁵ I see great armies marching on Jerusalem with mighty shouts[b] to destroy her and leave her cities in ruins, burned and desolate. ¹⁶ I see the armies of Egypt rising against her, marching from their cities of Memphis and Tahpanhes to utterly destroy Israel's glory and power. ¹⁷ And you have brought this on yourselves by rebelling against the Lord your God when he wanted to lead you and show you the way!

¹⁸ What have you gained by your alliances with Egypt and with Assyria? ¹⁹ Your own wickedness will punish you. You will see what an evil, bitter thing it is to rebel against the Lord your God, fearlessly forsaking him, says the Lord, the God of Hosts. ²⁰ Long ago you shook off my yoke and broke away from my ties. Defiant, you would not obey me. On every hill and under every tree you've bowed low before idols.

²¹ How could this happen? How could this be? For when I planted you, I chose my seed so carefully—the very best. Why have you become this degenerate race of evil men? ²² No amount of soap or lye can make you clean. You are stained with guilt that cannot ever be washed away. I see it always before me, the Lord God says. ²³ You say it isn't so, that you haven't worshiped idols? How can you say a thing like that? Go and look in any valley in the land! Face the awful sins that you have done, O restless female camel, seeking for a male! ²⁴ You are a wild donkey, sniffing the wind at mating time. (Who can restrain your lust?) Any jack wanting you need not search, for you come running to him! ²⁵ Why don't you turn from all this weary running after other gods? But you say, "Don't waste your breath. I've fallen in love with these strangers and I can't stop loving them now!"

²⁶,²⁷ Like a thief, the only shame that Israel knows is getting caught. Kings, princes, priests and prophets—all are alike in this. They call a carved-up wooden post their father, and for their mother they have an idol chiseled out from stone. Yet in time of trouble they cry to me to save them! ²⁸ Why don't you call on these gods you have made?

---

a Literally, "the firstfruits of his harvest."   b Literally, "The lions have roared against him."

When danger comes, let *them* go out and save you if they can! For you have as many gods as there are cities in Judah. ²⁹ Don't come to me—you are all rebels, says the Lord. ³⁰ I have punished your children but it did them no good; they still will not obey. And you yourselves have killed my prophets as a lion kills its prey.

³¹ O my people, listen to the words of God: Have I been unjust to Israel? Have I been to them a land of darkness and of evil? Why then do my people say, "At last we are free from God; we won't have anything to do with him again!" ³² How can you disown your God like that?ᶜ Can a girl forget her jewels? What bride will seek to hide her wedding dress? Yet for years on end my people have forgotten me—the most precious of their treasures.ᶜ

³³ How you plot and scheme to win your lovers. The most experienced harlot could learn a lot from you! ³⁴ Your clothing is stained with the blood of the innocent and the poor. Brazenly you murder without a cause. ³⁵ And yet you say, "I haven't done a thing to anger God. I'm sure he isn't angry!"ᶜ I will punish you severely because you say, "I haven't sinned!"

³⁶ First here, then there, you flit about, going from one ally to another for their help; but it's all no good—your new friends in Egypt will forsake you as Assyria did before. ³⁷ You will be left in despair, and cover your face with your hands, for the Lord has rejected the ones that you trust. You will not succeed despite their aid.

3 THERE IS A lawᵃ that if a man divorces a woman who then remarries, he is not to take her back again, for she has become corrupted. But though you have left me and married many lovers, yet I have invited you to come to me again, the Lord says. ² Is there a single spot in all the land where you haven't been defiled by your adulteries —your worshiping these other gods?ᵇ You sit like a prostitute beside the road waiting for a client! You sit alone like a Bedouin in the desert. You have polluted the land with your vile prostitution. ³ That is why even the springtime rains have failed. For you are

a prostitute, and completely unashamed. ⁴,⁵ And yet you say to me, "O Father, you have always been my Friend; surely you won't be angry about such a little thing! Surely you will just forget it?" So you talk, and keep right on doing all the evil that you can.

⁶ This message from the Lord came to me during the reign of King Josiah:

Have you seen what Israel does? Like a wanton wife who gives herself to other men at every chance, so Israel has worshiped other gods on every hill, beneath every shady tree. ⁷ I thought that someday she would return to me and once again be mine; but she didn't come back. And her faithless sister Judah saw the continued rebellion of Israel. ⁸ Yet she paid no attention, even though she saw that I divorced faithless Israel. But now Judah too has left me and given herself to prostitution, for she has gone to other gods to worship them. ⁹ She treated it all so lightly—to her it was nothing at all that she should worship idols made of wood and stone. And so the land was greatly polluted and defiled. ¹⁰ Then, afterwards, this faithless one "returned" to me, but her "sorrow" was only faked, the Lord God says. ¹¹ In fact, faithless Israel is less guilty than treacherous Judah!

¹² Therefore go and say to Israel, O Israel, my sinful people, come home to me again, for I am merciful; I will not be forever angry with you. ¹³ Only acknowledge your guilt; admit that you rebelled against the Lord your God and committed adultery against him by worshiping idols under every tree; confess that you refused to follow me. ¹⁴ O sinful children, come home, for I am your Master and I will bring you again to the land of Israel—one from here and two from there, wherever you are scattered. ¹⁵ And I will give you leaders after my own heart, who will guide you with wisdom and understanding.

¹⁶ Then, when your land is once more filled with people, says the Lord, you will no longer wish for "the good old days of long ago" when you possessed the Ark of God's covenant. Those days will not be missed or even thought about, and the Ark

---

ᶜ Implied.   3a Deuteronomy 24:1–4.   b Implied.

will not be reconstructed, [17] for the Lord himself will be among you, and the whole city of Jerusalem will be known as the throne of the Lord, and all nations will come to him there and no longer stubbornly follow their evil desires. [18] At that time the people of Judah and of Israel will return together from their exile in the north, to the land I gave their fathers as an inheritance forever. [19] And I thought how wonderful it would be for you to be here among my children. I planned to give you part of this beautiful land, the finest in the world. I looked forward to your calling me "Father," and thought that you would never turn away from me again. [20] But you have betrayed me; you have gone off and given yourself to a host of foreign gods; you have been like a faithless wife who leaves her husband.

[21] I hear voices high upon the windswept mountains, crying, crying. It is the sons of Israel who have turned their backs on God and wandered far away. [22] O my rebellious children, come back to me again and I will heal you from your sins.

And they reply, Yes, we will come, for you are the Lord our God. [23] We are weary of worshiping idols on the hills and of having orgies on the mountains. It is all a farce. Only in the Lord our God can Israel ever find her help and her salvation. [24] From our childhood we have seen everything our fathers had—flocks and herds and sons and daughters—squandered on priests and idols. [25] We lie in shame and in dishonor, for we and our fathers have sinned from childhood against the Lord our God; we have not obeyed him.

4 O ISRAEL, IF you will truly return to me and absolutely discard your idols, [2] and if you will swear by me alone, the living God, and begin to live good, honest, clean lives, then you will be a testimony to the nations of the world and they will come to me and glorify my name.

[3] The Lord is saying to the men of Judah and Jerusalem, Plow up the hardness of your hearts; otherwise the good seed will be wasted among the thorns. [4] Cleanse[a] your minds and hearts, not just your bodies, or else my anger will burn you to a crisp because of all your sins. And no one will be able to put the fire out.

[5] Shout to Jerusalem and to all Judea, telling them to sound the alarm throughout the land. "Run for your lives! Flee to the fortified cities!" [6] Send a signal from Jerusalem: "Flee now, don't delay!" For I the Lord am bringing vast destruction on you from the north.[b] [7] A lion—a destroyer of nations—stalks from his lair; and he is headed for your land. Your cities will lie in ruin without inhabitant. [8] Put on clothes of mourning and weep with broken hearts, for the fierce anger of the Lord has not stopped yet. [9] In that day, says the Lord, the king and the princes will tremble in fear; and the priests and the prophets will be stricken with horror.

[10] (Then I said, "But Lord, the people have been deceived by what you said, for you promised great blessings on Jerusalem. Yet the sword is even now poised to strike them dead!")

[11,12] At that time he will send a burning wind from the desert upon them—not in little gusts but in a roaring blast—and he will pronounce their doom. [13] The enemy shall roll down upon us like a storm wind; his chariots are like a whirlwind; his steeds are swifter than eagles. Woe, woe upon us, for we are doomed.

[14] O Jerusalem, cleanse your hearts while there is time. You can yet be saved by casting out your evil thoughts. [15] From Dan and from Mount Ephraim your doom has been announced. [16] Warn the other nations that the enemy is coming from a distant land and they shout against Jerusalem and the cities of Judah. [17] They surround Jerusalem like shepherds moving in on some wild animal! For my people have rebelled against me, says the Lord. [18] Your ways have brought this down upon you; it is a bitter dose of your own medicine, striking deep within your hearts.

[19] My heart, my heart—I writhe in pain; my heart pounds within me. I cannot be still

---

a Literally, "Circumcise yourselves . . . remove the foreskin of your hearts."   b i.e., from Babylon. Nabopolasser and Nebuchadnezzar II soon attacked.

because I have heard, O my soul, the blast of the enemies' trumpets and the enemies' battle cries. ²⁰ Wave upon wave of destruction rolls over the land, until it lies in utter ruin; suddenly, in a moment, every house is crushed. ²¹ How long must this go on? How long must I see war and death surrounding me?

²² "Until my people leave their foolishness, for they refuse to listen to me; they are dull, retarded children who have no understanding. They are smart enough at doing wrong, but for doing right they have no talent, none at all."

²³ I looked down upon their land and as far as I could see in all directions everything was ruins. And all the heavens were dark. ²⁴ I looked at the mountains and saw that they trembled and shook. ²⁵ I looked, and mankind was gone and the birds of the heavens had fled.

²⁶ The fertile valleys were wilderness and all the cities were broken down before the presence of the Lord, and crushed by his fierce anger. ²⁷ The Lord's decree of desolation covers all the land.

"Yet," he says, "there will be a little remnant of my people left. ²⁸ The earth shall mourn, the heavens shall be draped with black, because of my decree against my people, but I have made up my mind and I will not change it."

²⁹ All the cities flee in terror at the noise of marching armies coming near. The people hide in the bushes and flee to the mountains. All the cities are abandoned—all have fled in terror. ³⁰ Why do you put on your most beautiful clothing and jewelry and brighten your eyes with mascara? It will do you no good! Your allies despise you and will kill you.

³¹ I have heard great crying like that of a woman giving birth to her first child; it is the cry of my people gasping for breath, pleading for help, prostrate before their murderers.

5 RUN UP AND down through every street in all Jerusalem; search high and low and see if you can find one fair and honest man! Search every square, and if you find just one, I'll not destroy the city! ² Even

under oath, they lie. ³ O Lord, you will take naught but truth. You have tried to get them to be honest, for you have punished them, but they won't change! You have destroyed them but they refuse to turn from their sins. They are determined, with faces hard as rock, not to repent.

⁴ Then I said, "But what can we expect from the poor and ignorant? They don't know the ways of God. How can they obey him?"

⁵ I will go now to their leaders, the men of importance, and speak to them, for they know the ways of the Lord and the judgment that follows sin. But they too had utterly rejected their God.

⁶ So I will send upon them the wild fury of the "lion from the forest"; the "desert wolves" shall pounce upon them, and a "leopard" shall lurk around their cities so that all who go out shall be torn apart. For their sins are very many; their rebellion against me is great.

⁷ How can I pardon you? For even your children have turned away, and worship gods that are not gods at all. I fed my people until they were fully satisfied, and their thanks was to commit adultery wholesale and to gang up at the city's brothels. ⁸ They are well-fed, lusty stallions, each neighing for his neighbor's mate. ⁹ Shall I not punish them for this? Shall I not send my vengeance on such a nation as this? ¹⁰ Go down the rows of the vineyards and destroy them! But leave a scattered few to live. Strip the branches from each vine, for they are not the Lord's.

¹¹ For the people of Israel and Judah are full of treachery against me, says the Lord. ¹² They have lied and said, "He won't bother us! No evil will come upon us! There will be neither famine nor war! ¹³ God's prophets," they say, "are windbags full of words with no divine authority. Their claims of doom will fall upon themselves, not us!"

¹⁴ Therefore this is what the Lord God of Hosts says to his prophets: Because of talk like this I'll take your words and prophecies and turn them into raging fire and burn up these people like kindling wood. ¹⁵ See, I will bring a distant nation

against you, O Israel, says the Lord—a mighty nation, an ancient[a] nation whose language you don't understand. [16] Their weapons are deadly; the men are all mighty. [17] And they shall eat your harvest and your children's bread, and your flocks of sheep and herds of cattle, yes, and your grapes and figs; and they shall sack your walled cities that you think are safe.

[18] But I will not completely blot you out. So says the Lord.

[19] And when your people ask, "Why is it that the Lord is doing this to us?" then you shall say, "You rejected him and gave yourselves to other gods while in your land; now you must be slaves to foreigners in their lands."

[20] Make this announcement to Judah and to Israel:

[21] Listen, O foolish, senseless people—you with the eyes that do not see and the ears that do not listen— [22] have you no respect at all for me? the Lord God asks. How can it be that you don't even tremble in my presence? I set the shorelines of the world by perpetual decrees, so that the oceans, though they toss and roar, can never pass those bounds. Isn't such a God to be feared and worshiped?

[23,24] But my people have rebellious hearts; they have turned against me and gone off into idolatry. Though I am the one who gives them rain each year in spring and fall and sends the harvest times, yet they have no respect or fear for me. [25] And so I have taken away these wondrous blessings from them. This sin has robbed them of all of these good things.

[26] Among my people are wicked men who lurk for victims like a hunter hiding in a blind. They set their traps for men. [27] Like a coop full of chickens their homes are full of evil plots. And the result? Now they are great and rich, [28] and well fed and well groomed, and there is no limit to their wicked deeds. They refuse justice to orphans and the rights of the poor. [29] Should I sit back and act as though nothing is going on? the Lord God asks. Shouldn't I punish a nation such as this?

[30] A horrible thing has happened in this land— [31] the priests are ruled by false prophets, and my people like it so! But your doom is certain.

6 RUN, PEOPLE OF Benjamin, run for your lives! Flee from Jerusalem! Sound the alarm in Tekoa; send up a smoke signal at Beth-haccherem; warn everyone that a powerful army is on the way from the north, coming to destroy this nation! [2] Helpless as a girl, you are beautiful and delicate—and doomed. [3] Evil shepherds shall surround you. They shall set up camp around the city, and divide your pastures for their flocks. [4] See them prepare for battle. At noon it has begun. All afternoon it rages, until the evening shadows fall. [5] "Come," they say. "Let us attack by night and destroy her palaces!"

[6] For the Lord of Hosts has said to them, Cut down her trees for battering rams; smash down the walls of Jerusalem. This is the city to be punished, for she is vile through and through. [7] She spouts evil like a fountain! Her streets echo with the sounds of violence; her sickness and wounds are ever before me.

[8] This is your last warning, O Jerusalem. If you don't listen, I will empty the land. [9] Disaster on disaster shall befall you. Even the few who remain in Israel shall be gleaned again, the Lord of Hosts has said; for as a grape-gatherer checks each vine to pick what he has missed, so the remnant of my people shall be destroyed again. [10] But who will listen when I warn them? Their ears are closed and they refuse to hear. The word of God has angered them; they don't want it at all.

[11] For all this I am full of the wrath of God against them. I am weary of holding it in. I will pour it out over Jerusalem, even upon the children playing in the streets, upon the gatherings of young men, and on husbands and wives and grandparents. [12] Their enemies shall live in their homes and take their fields and wives. For I will punish the people of this land, the Lord has said. [13] They are swindlers and liars, from the least of them right to the top! Yes, even

---

a The kingdom of Babylonia, being revived in Jeremiah's time (around 626 B.C.) had a long and illustrious history. The old Babylonian Empire lasted from about 1900 B.C. to 1550 B.C. (the days of the Hebrew patriarchs), and earlier kingdoms had ruled on Babylonian soil as early as 3000 B.C.

my prophets and priests! [14] You can't heal a wound by saying it's not there! Yet the priests and prophets give assurances of peace when all is war. [15] Were my people ashamed when they worshiped idols? No, not at all—they didn't even blush. Therefore they shall lie among the slain. They shall die beneath my anger.

[16] Yet the Lord pleads with you still: Ask where the good road is, the godly paths you used to walk in, in the days of long ago. Travel there, and you will find rest for your souls. But you reply, "No, that is not the road we want!" [17] I set watchmen over you who warned you: "Listen for the sound of the trumpet! It will let you know when trouble comes." But you said, "No! We won't pay any attention!"

[18,19] This, then, is my decree against my people: (Listen to it, distant lands; listen to it, O my people in Jerusalem; listen to it, all the earth!) I will bring evil upon this people; it will be the fruit of their own sin, because they will not listen to me. They reject my law. [20] There is no use now in burning sweet incense from Sheba before me! Keep your expensive perfumes! I cannot accept your offerings; they have no sweet fragrance for me. [21] I will make an obstacle course of the pathway of my people; fathers and sons shall be frustrated; neighbors and friends shall collapse together. [22] The Lord God says, See the armies marching from the north—a great nation is rising against you. [23] They are a cruel, merciless people, fully armed, mounted for war. The noise of their army is like a roaring sea.

[24] We have heard the fame of their armies and we are weak with fright. Fright and pain have gripped us like that of women in travail. [25] Don't go out to the fields! Don't travel the roads! For the enemy is everywhere, ready to kill; we are terrorized at every turn.

[26] O Jerusalem, pride of my people, put on mourning clothes and sit in ashes and weep bitterly as for an only son. For suddenly the destroying armies will be upon you. [27] Jeremiah, I have made you an assayer of metals, that you may test this my people and determine their value. Listen to what they are saying and watch what they are doing. [28] Are they not the worst of rebels, full of evil talk against the Lord? They are insolent as brass, hard and cruel as iron. [29] The bellows blow fiercely; the refining fire grows hotter, but it can never cleanse them, for there is no pureness in them to bring out. Why continue the process longer? All is dross. No matter how hot the fire, they continue in their wicked ways. [30] I must label them "Impure, Rejected Silver," and I have discarded them.

7 THEN THE LORD said to Jeremiah: [2] Go over to the entrance of the Temple of the Lord and give this message to the people: O Judah, listen to this message from God. Listen to it, all of you who worship here. [3] The Lord of Hosts, the God of Israel says: Even yet, if you quit your evil ways I will let you stay in your own land. [4] But don't be fooled by those who lie to you and say that since the Temple of the Lord is here, God will never let Jerusalem be destroyed. [5] You may remain under these conditions only: If you stop your wicked thoughts and deeds, and are fair to others, [6] and stop exploiting orphans, widows and foreigners. And stop your murdering. And stop worshiping idols as you do now to your hurt. [7] Then, and only then, will I let you stay in this land that I gave to your fathers to keep forever.

[8] You think that because the Temple is here, you will never suffer? Don't fool yourselves! [9] Do you really think that you can steal, murder, commit adultery, lie, and worship Baal and all of those new gods of yours, [10] and then come here and stand before me in my Temple and chant, "We are saved!"—only to go right back to all these evil things again? [11] Is my Temple but a den of robbers in your eyes? For I see all the evil going on in there.

[12] Go to Shiloh, the city I first honored with my name, and see what I did to her because of all the wickedness of my people Israel. [13,14] And now, says the Lord, I will do the same thing here because of all this evil you have done. Again and again I spoke to you about it, rising up early and calling, but you refused to hear or answer. Yes, I will destroy this Temple, as I did in Shiloh—this Temple called by my name, which

you trust for help, and this place I gave to you and to your fathers. ¹⁵ And I will send you into exile, just as I did your brothers, the people of Ephraim.

¹⁶ Pray no more for these people, Jeremiah. Neither weep for them nor pray nor beg that I should help them, for I will not listen. ¹⁷ Don't you see what they are doing throughout the cities of Judah and in the streets of Jerusalem? ¹⁸ No wonder my anger is great! Watch how the children gather wood and the fathers build fires, and the women knead dough and make cakes to offer to "The Queen of Heaven"ᵃ and to their other idol-gods! ¹⁹ Am I the one that they are hurting? asks the Lord. Most of all they hurt themselves, to their own shame. ²⁰ So the Lord God says, I will pour out my anger, yes, my fury on this place—people, animals, trees and plants will be consumed by the unquenchable fire of my anger.

²¹ The Lord of Hosts, the God of Israel says, Away with your offerings and sacrifices! ²² It wasn't offerings and sacrifices I wanted from your fathers when I led them out of Egypt. That was not the point of my command. ²³ But what I told them was: *Obey* me and I will be your God and you shall be my people; only do as I say and all shall be well!

²⁴ But they wouldn't listen; they kept on doing whatever they wanted to, following their own stubborn, evil thoughts. They went backward instead of forward. ²⁵ Ever since the day your fathers left Egypt until now, I have kept on sending them my prophets, day after day. ²⁶ But they wouldn't listen to them or even try to hear. They are hard and stubborn and rebellious—worse even than their fathers were.

²⁷ Tell them everything that I will do to them, but don't expect them to listen. Cry out your warnings, but don't expect them to respond. ²⁸ Say to them: This is the nation that refuses to obey the Lord its God, and refuses to be taught. She continues to live a lie.

²⁹ O Jerusalem, shave your head in shame and weep alone upon the mountains; for the Lord has rejected and forsaken this people of his wrath. ³⁰ For the people of Judah have sinned before my very eyes, says the Lord. They have set up their idols right in my own Temple, polluting it. ³¹ They have built the altar called Topheth in the Valley of Ben-Hinnom, and there they burn to death their little sons and daughters as sacrifices to their gods—a deed so horrible I've never even thought of it, let alone commanded it to be done. ³² The time is coming, says the Lord, when that valley's name will be changed from "Topheth," or the "Valley of Ben-Hinnom," to the "Valley of Slaughter"; for there will be so many slain to bury that there won't be room enough for all the graves and they will dump the bodies in that valley. ³³ The bodies of my people shall be food for the birds and animals, and no one shall be left to scare them away. ³⁴ I will end the happy singing and laughter in the streets of Jerusalem and in the cities of Judah, and the joyous voices of the bridegrooms and brides. For the land shall lie in desolation.

8 THEN, SAYS THE Lord, the enemy shall break open the graves of the kings of Judah and of the princes and priests and prophets and people, ² and dig out their bones and spread them out on the ground before the sun and moon and stars—the gods of my people!—whom they have loved and worshiped. Their bones shall not be gathered up again nor buried but shall be scattered like dung upon the ground. ³ And those of this evil nation who are still left alive shall long to die, rather than live where I will scatter them, says the Lord of Hosts.

⁴,⁵ Once again give them this message from the Lord: When a person falls, he jumps up again; when he is on the wrong road and discovers his mistake, he goes back to the fork where he made the wrong turn. But these people keep on along their evil path, even though I warn them. ⁶ I listen to their conversation and what do I hear? Is anyone sorry for sin? Does anyone say, "What a terrible thing I have done?" No, all are rushing pell-mell down the path

---

a A name by which Ishtar, the Mesopotamian goddess of love and war, was called. After the fall of Jerusalem the refugees who fled to Egypt continued to worship her (chapter 44). A papyrus dating from the 5th century B.C., found at Hermopolis in Egypt, mentions the "Queen of Heaven" among the gods honored by the Jewish community.

of sin as swiftly as a horse rushing to the battle! ⁷ The stork knows the time of her migration, as does the turtledove, and the crane, and the swallow. They all return at God's appointed time each year; but not my people! They don't accept the laws of God.

⁸ How can you say, "We understand his laws," when your teachers have twisted them up to mean a thing I never said? ⁹ These wise teachers of yours will be shamed by exile for this sin, for they have rejected the word of the Lord. Are they then so wise? ¹⁰ I will give their wives and their farms to others; for all of them, great and small, prophet and priest, have one purpose in mind—to get what isn't theirs. ¹¹ They give useless medicine for my people's grievous wounds, for they assure them all is well when that isn't so at all! ¹² Are they ashamed because they worship idols? No, not in the least; they don't even know how to blush! That is why I will see to it that they lie among the fallen. I will visit them with death. ¹³ Their figs and grapes will disappear, their fruit trees will die, and all the good things I prepared for them will soon be gone.

¹⁴ Then the people will say, "Why should we wait here to die? Come, let us go to the walled cities and perish there. For the Lord our God has decreed our doom and given us a cup of poison to drink because of all our sins. ¹⁵ We expected peace, but no peace came; we looked for health but there was only terror."

¹⁶ The noise of war resounds from the northern border.[a] The whole land trembles at the approach of the terrible army, for the enemy is coming, and is devouring the land and everything in it—the cities and people alike. ¹⁷ For I will send these enemy troops among you like poisonous snakes which you cannot charm. No matter what you do, they shall bite you and you will die.

¹⁸ My grief is beyond healing; my heart is broken. ¹⁹ Listen to the weeping of my people all across the land.

"Where is the Lord?" they ask. "Has God deserted us?"

"Oh, why have they angered me with their carved idols and strange evil rites?"

the Lord replies.

²⁰ "The harvest is finished; the summer is over and we are not saved."

²¹ I weep for the hurt of my people; I stand amazed, silent, dumb with grief. ²² Is there no medicine in Gilead? Is there no physician there? Why doesn't God do something? Why doesn't he help?

9 OH, THAT MY eyes were a fountain of tears; I would weep forever; I would sob day and night for the slain of my people! ² Oh, that I could go away and forget them and live in some wayside shack in the desert, for they are all adulterous, treacherous men.

³ "They bend their tongues like bows to shoot their arrows of untruth. They care nothing for right and go from bad to worse; they care nothing for me," says the Lord.

⁴ Beware of your neighbor! Beware of your brother! All take advantage of one another and spread their slanderous lies. ⁵ With practiced tongues they fool and defraud each other; they wear themselves out with all their sinning.

⁶ "They pile evil upon evil, lie upon lie, and utterly refuse to come to me," says the Lord.

⁷ Therefore the Lord of Hosts says this: "See, I will melt them in a crucible of affliction. I will refine them and test them like metal. What else can I do with them? ⁸ For their tongues aim lies like poisoned spears. They speak cleverly to their neighbors while planning to kill them. ⁹ Should not I punish them for such things as this?" asks the Lord. "Shall not my soul be avenged on such a nation as this?"

¹⁰ Sobbing and weeping, I point to their mountains and pastures, for now they are desolate, without a living soul. Gone is the lowing of cattle, gone the birds and wild animals. All have fled.

¹¹ "And I will turn Jerusalem into heaps of ruined houses where only jackals have their dens. The cities of Judah shall be ghost towns, with no one living in them."

¹² Who is wise enough to understand all this? Where is the Lord's messenger to explain it? Why is the land a wilderness so that

---

a Literally, "The snorting of their war horses can be heard all the way from Dan in the north."

no one dares even to travel through? [13] "Because," the Lord replies, "my people have forsaken my commandments and not obeyed my laws. [14] Instead they have done whatever they pleased and worshiped the idols of Baal, as their fathers told them to. [15] Therefore this is what the Lord of Hosts, the God of Israel, says: Lo, I will feed them with bitterness and give them poison to drink. [16] I will scatter them around the world, to be strangers in distant lands; and even there the sword of destruction shall chase them until I have utterly destroyed them.

[17,18] "The Lord of Hosts says: Send for the mourners! Quick! Begin your crying! Let the tears flow from your eyes. [19] Hear Jerusalem weeping in despair. 'We are ruined! Disaster has befallen us! We must leave our land and homes!' " [20] Listen to the words of God, O women who wail. Teach your daughters to wail and your neighbors too. [21] For death has crept in through your windows into your homes. He has killed off the flower of your youth. Children no longer play in the streets; the young men gather no more in the squares.

[22] Tell them this, says the Lord: Bodies shall be scattered across the fields like manure, like sheaves after the mower, and no one will bury them.

[23] The Lord says: Let not the wise man bask in his wisdom, nor the mighty man in his might, nor the rich man in his riches. [24] Let them boast in this alone: That they truly know me, and understand that I am the Lord of justice and of righteousness whose love is steadfast; and that I love to be this way.

[25,26] A time is coming, says the Lord, when I will punish all those who are circumcised in body but not in spirit—the Egyptians, Edomites, Ammonites, Moabites, Arabs, and yes, even you people of Judah. For all these pagan nations also circumcise themselves. Unless you circumcise your hearts by loving me, your circumcision is only a heathen rite like theirs, and nothing more.

10 HEAR THE WORD of the Lord, O Israel:
[2,3] Don't act like the people who make horoscopes and try to read their fate and future in the stars! Don't be frightened by predictions such as theirs, for it is all a pack of lies. Their ways are futile and foolish. They cut down a tree and carve an idol, [4] and decorate it with gold and silver and fasten it securely in place with hammer and nails, so that it won't fall over, [5] and there stands their god like a helpless scarecrow in a garden! It cannot speak, and it must be carried, for it cannot walk. Don't be afraid of such a god for it can neither harm nor help, nor do you any good.

[6] O Lord, there is no other god like you. For you are great and your name is full of power. [7] Who would not fear you, O King of nations? (And that title belongs to you alone!) Among all the wise men of the earth and in all the kingdoms of the world there isn't anyone like you.

[8] The wisest of men who worship idols are altogether stupid and foolish. [9] They bring beaten sheets of silver from Tarshish and gold from Uphaz, and give them to skillful goldsmiths who make their idols; then they clothe these gods in kingly purple robes that expert tailors make.

[10] But the Lord is the only true God, the living God, the everlasting King. The whole earth shall tremble at his anger; the world shall hide before his displeasure.

[11] Say this to those who worship other gods: Your so-called gods, who have not made the heavens and earth, shall vanish from the earth, [12] but our God formed the earth by his power and wisdom, and by his intelligence he hung the stars in space and stretched out the heavens. [13] It is his voice that echoes in the thunder of the storm clouds. He causes mist to rise upon the earth; he sends the lightning and brings the rain, and from his treasuries he brings the wind.

[14] But foolish men without knowledge of God bow before their idols. It is a shameful business that these men are in, for what they make are frauds, gods without life or power in them. [15] All are worthless, silly; they will be crushed when their makers perish. [16] But the God of Jacob is not like these foolish idols. He is the Creator of all, and Israel is his chosen nation. The Lord of Hosts is his name.

¹⁷ Pack your bags, he says. Get ready now to leave; the siege will soon begin. ¹⁸ For suddenly I'll fling you from this land and pour great troubles down; at last you shall feel my wrath.

¹⁹ *Desperate is my wound. My grief is great. My sickness is incurable, but I must bear it.* ²⁰ *My home is gone; my children have been taken away and I will never see them again. There is no one left to help me rebuild my home.* ²¹ The shepherds of my people have lost their senses; they no longer follow God nor ask his will. Therefore they perish and their flocks are scattered. ²² Listen! Hear the terrible sound of great armies coming from the north. The cities of Judah shall become dens of jackals.

²³ O Lord, I know it is not within the power of man to map his life and plan his course— ²⁴ so you correct me, Lord; but please be gentle. Don't do it in your anger, for I would die. ²⁵ Pour out your fury on the nations who don't obey the Lord, for they have destroyed Israel and made a wasteland of this entire country.

11 THEN THE LORD spoke to Jeremiah once again and said:

Remind the men of Judah and all the people of Jerusalem that I made a contract with their fathers—and cursed is the man who does not heed it! ⁴ For I told them at the time I brought them out of slavery in Egypt that if they would obey me and do whatever I commanded them, then they and all their children would be mine and I would be their God. ⁵ And now, Israel, obey me, says the Lord, so that I can do for you the wonderful things I swore I would if you obeyed. I want to give you a land that "flows with milk and honey," as it is today. Then I replied, "So be it, Lord!"

⁶ Then the Lord said: Broadcast this message in Jerusalem's streets—go from city to city throughout the land and say, Remember this agreement that your fathers made with God, and do all the things they promised him they would. ⁷ For I solemnly said to your fathers when I brought them out of Egypt—and have kept on saying it over and over again until this day: Obey my every command! ⁸ But your fathers didn't do it. They wouldn't even listen. Each fol-lowed his own stubborn will and his proud heart. Because they refused to obey, I did to them all the evils stated in the contract.

⁹ Again the Lord spoke to me and said: I have discovered a conspiracy against me among the men of Judah and Jerusalem. ¹⁰ They have returned to the sins of their fathers, refusing to listen to me and wor-shiping idols. The agreement I made with their fathers is broken and canceled. ¹¹ Therefore, the Lord says, I am going to bring calamity down upon them and they shall not escape. Though they cry for mercy, I will not listen to their pleas. ¹² Then they will pray to their idols and burn incense before them, but that cannot save them from their time of anguish and despair. ¹³ O my people, you have as many gods as there are cities, and your altars of shame (your altars to burn incense to Baal) are along every street in Jerusalem.

¹⁴ Therefore, Jeremiah, pray no longer for this people, neither weep nor plead for them; for I will not listen to them when they are finally desperate enough to beg me for help. ¹⁵ What right do my beloved people have to come any more to my Temple? For you have been unfaithful and worshiped other gods. Can promises and sacrifices now avert your doom and give you life and joy again? ¹⁶ The Lord used to call you his green olive tree, beautiful to see and full of good fruit; but now he has sent the fury of your enemies to burn you up and leave you bro-ken and charred. ¹⁷ It is because of the wickedness of Israel and Judah in offering incense to Baal that the Lord of Hosts who planted the tree has ordered it destroyed.

¹⁸ Then the Lord told me all about their plans and showed me their evil plots. ¹⁹ I had been as unsuspecting as a lamb or ox on the way to slaughter. I didn't know that they were planning to kill me! "Let's de-stroy this man and all his messages," they said. "Let's kill him so that his name will be forever forgotten."

²⁰ O Lord of Hosts, you are just. See the hearts and motives of these men. Repay them for all that they have planned! I look to you for justice.

²¹,²² And the Lord replied, The men of the city of Anathoth shall be punished for planning to kill you. They will tell you not

to prophesy in God's name on pain of death. And so their young men shall die in battle; their boys and girls shall starve. ²³ Not one of these plotters of Anathoth shall survive, for I will bring a great disaster upon them. Their time has come.

12 O LORD, YOU always give me justice when I bring a case before you to decide. Now let me bring you this complaint: Why are the wicked so prosperous? Why are evil men so happy? ² You plant them. They take root and their business grows. Their profits multiply, and they are rich. They say, "Thank God!" But in their hearts they give no credit to you. ³ But as for me— Lord, you know my heart—you know how much it longs for you. (And I am poor,ᵃ O Lord!) Lord, drag them off like helpless sheep to the slaughter. Judge them, O God!

⁴ How long must this land of yours put up with all their goings on? Even the grass of the field groans and weeps over their wicked deeds! The wild animals and birds have moved away, leaving the land deserted. Yet the people say, "God won't bring judgment on us. We're perfectly safe!"

⁵ The Lord replied to me: If racing with mere men—these men of Anathothᵃ—has wearied you, how will you race against horses, against the king, his court and all his evil priests?ᵃ If you stumble and fall on open ground, what will you do in Jordan's jungles? ⁶ Even your own brothers, your own family, have turned against you. They have plotted to call for a mob to lynch you. Don't trust them, no matter how pleasantly they speak. Don't believe them.

⁷ Then the Lord said: I have abandoned my people, my inheritance; I have surrendered my dearest ones to their enemies. ⁸ My people have roared at me like a lion of the forest, so I have treated them as though I hated them. ⁹ My people have fallen. I will bring upon them swarms of vultures and wild animals to pick the flesh from their corpses.

¹⁰ Many foreign rulers have ravaged my vineyard, trampling down the vines, and turning all its beauty into barren wilderness.

¹¹ They have made it desolate; I hear its mournful cry. The whole land is desolate and no one cares. ¹² Destroying armies plunder the land; the sword of the Lord devours from one end of the nation to the other; nothing shall escape. ¹³ My people have sown wheat but reaped thorns; they have worked hard but it does them no good. They shall harvest a crop of shame, for the fierce anger of the Lord is upon them.

¹⁴ And now the Lord says this to the evil nations, the nations surrounding the land God gave his people Israel: See, I will force you from your land just as Judah will be forced from hers; ¹⁵ but afterwards I will return and have compassion on all of you, and will bring you home to your own land again, each man to his inheritance. ¹⁶ And if these heathen nations quickly learn my people's ways and claim me as their God instead of Baal (whom they taught my people to worship), then they shall be strong among my people. ¹⁷ But any nation refusing to obey me will be expelled again and finished, says the Lord.

13 THE LORD SAID to me, Go and buy a linen loincloth and wear it, but don't wash it—don't put it in water at all. ² So I bought the loincloth and put it on. ³ Then the Lord's message came to me again. This time he said, ⁴ Take the loincloth out to the Euphrates River and hide it in a hole in the rocks.

⁵ So I did; I hid it as the Lord had told me to. ⁶ Then, a long time afterwards, the Lord said: Go out to the river again and get the loincloth. ⁷ And I did; I dug it out of the hole where I had hidden it. But now it was mildewed and falling apart. It was utterly useless!

⁸,⁹ Then the Lord said: This illustrates the way that I will rot the pride of Judah and Jerusalem. ¹⁰ This evil nation refuses to listen to me, and follows its own evil desires and worships idols; therefore it shall become as this loincloth—good for nothing. ¹¹ Even as a loincloth clings to a man's loins, so I made Judah and Israel to cling to me, says the Lord. They were my people, an honor to my name. But then they turned

---

a Implied.

away.

¹² Tell them this: The Lord God of Israel says, All your jugs will be full of wine. And they will reply, Of course, you don't need to tell us how prosperous we will be!ᵃ ¹³ Then tell them: You're getting the wrong impression.ᵇ I will fill everyone living in this land with helpless bewilderment—from the king sitting on David's throne, and the priests and the prophets right on down to all the people. ¹⁴ And I will smash fathers and sons against each other, says the Lord. I will not let pity nor mercy spare them from utter destruction.

¹⁵ Oh, that you were not so proud and stubborn! Then you would listen to the Lord, for he has spoken. ¹⁶ Give glory to the Lord your God before it is too late, before he causes deep, impenetrable darkness to fall upon you so that you stumble and fall upon the dark mountains; then, when you look for light, you will find only terrible darkness. ¹⁷ Do you still refuse to listen? Then in loneliness my breaking heart shall mourn because of your pride. My eyes will overflow with tears because the Lord's flock shall be carried away as slaves.

¹⁸ Say to the king and queen-mother,ᶜ Come down from your thrones and sit in the dust, for your glorious crowns are removed from your heads. They are no longer yours. ¹⁹ The cities of the Negeb to the south of Jerusalem have closed their gates against the enemy. They must defend themselves, for Jerusalem cannot help;ᵈ and all Judah shall be taken away as slaves. ²⁰ See the armies marching from the north! Where is your flock, Jerusalem,ᵉ your beautiful flock I gave you to take care of? ²¹ How will you feel when I set your allies over you as your rulers? You will writhe in pain like a woman having a child. ²² And if you ask yourself, Why is all this happening to me? It is because of the grossness of your sins; that is why you have been raped and destroyed by the invading army.

²³ Can the Ethiopian change the color of his skin? or a leopard take away his spots? Nor can you who are so used to doing evil now start being good. ²⁴,²⁵ Because you have

put me out of your mind and put your trust in false gods, I will scatter you as chaff is scattered by the fierce winds off the desert. This then is your allotment, that which is due you, which I have measured out especially for you. ²⁶ I myself will expose you to utter shame. ²⁷ I am keenly aware of your apostasy, your faithlessness to me, and your abominable idol worship in the fields and on the hills. Woe upon you, O Jerusalem! How long before you will be pure?

14 THIS MESSAGE CAME to Jeremiah from the Lord, explaining why he was holding back the rain:

² Judah mourns; business has ground to a halt; all the people prostrate themselves to the earth and a great cry rises from Jerusalem. ³ The nobles send servants for water from the wells, but the wells are dry. The servants return, baffled and desperate, and cover their heads in grief. ⁴ The ground is parched and cracked for lack of rain; the farmers are afraid. ⁵ The deer deserts her fawn because there is no grass. ⁶ The wild donkeys stand upon the bare hills panting like thirsty jackals. They strain their eyes looking for grass to eat, but there is none to be found.

⁷ O Lord, we have sinned against you grievously, yet help us for the sake of your own reputation! ⁸ O Hope of Israel, our Savior in times of trouble, why are you as a stranger to us, as one passing through the land who is merely stopping for the night? ⁹ Are you also baffled? Are you helpless to save us? O Lord, you are right here among us, and we carry your name; we are known as your people. O Lord, don't desert us now!

¹⁰ But the Lord replies: You have loved to wander far from me and have not tried to follow in my paths. Now I will no longer accept you as my people; now I will remember all the evil you have done, and punish your sins.

¹¹ The Lord told me again: Don't ask me any more to bless this people. Don't pray for them any more. ¹² When they fast, I will not pay any attention; when they present their offerings and sacrifices to me, I will not

---

a Literally, "that every bottle shall be filled with wine."   b Implied.   c King Jehoiachin and his mother Nehashta.   d Literally, "the cities are closed and none can open them." Perhaps the meaning is that they are permanently abandoned.   e Implied.

accept them. What I will give them in return is war and famine and disease.

¹³ Then I said, O Lord God, their prophets are telling them that all is well—that no war or famine will come. They tell the people you will surely send them peace, that you will bless them.

¹⁴ Then the Lord said: The prophets are telling lies in my name. I didn't send them or tell them to speak or give them any message. They prophesy of visions and revelations they have never seen nor heard; they speak foolishness concocted out of their own lying hearts. ¹⁵ Therefore, the Lord says, I will punish these lying prophets who have spoken in my name though I did not send them, who say no war shall come nor famine. By war and famine they themselves shall die! ¹⁶ And the people to whom they prophesy—their bodies shall be thrown out into the streets of Jerusalem, victims of famine and war; there shall be no one to bury them. Husbands, wives, sons and daughters —all will be gone. For I will pour out terrible punishment upon them for their sins.

¹⁷ Therefore, tell them this: Night and day my eyes shall overflow with tears; I cannot stop my crying, for my people have been run through with a sword and lie mortally wounded on the ground. ¹⁸ If I go out in the fields, there lie the bodies of those the sword has killed; and if I walk in the streets, there lie those dead from starvation and disease. And yet the prophets and priests alike have made it their business to travel through the whole country, reassuring everyone that all was well, speaking of things they knew nothing about.

¹⁹ "O Lord," the people will cry, "have you completely rejected Judah? Do you abhor Jerusalem? Even after punishment, will there be no peace? We thought, Now at last he will heal us and bind our wounds. But no peace has come and there is only trouble and terror everywhere. ²⁰ O Lord, we confess our wickedness, and that of our fathers too. ²¹ Do not hate us, Lord, for the sake of your own name. Do not disgrace yourself and the throne of your glory by forsaking your promise to bless us! ²² What heathen god can give us rain? Who but you alone, O Lord our God, can do such things as this? Therefore we will wait for you to help us."

15 THEN THE LORD said to me, Even if Moses and Samuel stood before me pleading for these people, even then I wouldn't help them—away with them! Get them out of my sight! ² And if they say to you, But where can we go? tell them the Lord says: Those who are destined for death, to death; those who must die by the sword, to the sword; those doomed to starvation, to famine; and those for captivity, to captivity. ³ I will appoint over them four kinds of destroyers, says the Lord—the sword to kill, the dogs to tear, and the vultures and wild animals to finish up what's left. ⁴ Because of the wicked things that Manasseh, son of Hezekiah, king of Judah, did in Jerusalem, I will punish you so severely that your fate will horrify the peoples of the world.

⁵ Who will feel sorry for you, Jerusalem? Who will weep for you? Who will even bother to ask how you are? ⁶ You have forsaken me and turned your backs upon me. Therefore I will clench my fists against you to destroy you. I am tired of always giving you another chance. ⁷ I will sift you at the gates of your cities and take from you all that you hold dear, and I will destroy my own people because they refuse to turn back to me from all their evil ways. ⁸ There shall be countless widows; at noon time I will bring death to the young men and sorrow to their mothers. I will cause anguish and terror to fall upon them suddenly. ⁹ The mother of seven sickens and faints, for all her sons are dead. Her sun is gone down while it is yet day. She sits childless now, disgraced, for all her children have been killed.

¹⁰ Then Jeremiah said, "What sadness is mine, my mother; oh, that I had died at birth. For I am hated everywhere I go. I am neither a creditor soon to foreclose nor a debtor refusing to pay—yet they all curse me. ¹¹ Well, let them curse! Lord, you know how I have pled with you on their behalf— how I have begged you to spare these enemies of mine."

¹²,¹³ Can a man break bars of northern iron or bronze? This people's stubborn will can't be broken either. So, because of all your sins against me, I will deliver your wealth and treasures as spoil to the enemy.

¹⁴ I will have your enemies take you as slaves to a land where you have never been before, for my anger burns like fire, and it shall consume you.

¹⁵ Then Jeremiah replied, "Lord, you know it is for your sake that I am suffering. They are persecuting me because I have proclaimed your word to them. Don't let them kill me! Rescue me from their clutches, and give them what they deserve! ¹⁶ Your words are what sustain me; they are food to my hungry soul. They bring joy to my sorrowing heart and delight me. How proud I am to bear your name, O Lord. ¹⁷,¹⁸ I have not joined the people in their merry feasts. I sit alone beneath the hand of God. I burst with indignation at their sins. Yet you have failed me in my time of need! You have let them keep right on with all their persecutions. Will they never stop hurting me? Your help is as uncertain as a seasonal mountain brook—sometimes a flood, sometimes as dry as a bone."

¹⁹ The Lord replied: "Stop this foolishness and talk some sense! Only if you return to trusting me will I let you continue as my spokesman. You are to influence *them,* not let them influence *you!* ²⁰ They will fight against you like a besieging army against a high city wall. But they will not conquer you for I am with you to protect and deliver you, says the Lord. ²¹ Yes, I will certainly deliver you from these wicked men and rescue you from their ruthless hands."

16 ON YET ANOTHER occasion God spoke to me, and said:

² You must not marry and have children here. ³ For the children born in this city, and their mothers and fathers, ⁴ shall die from terrible diseases. No one shall mourn for them or bury them, but their bodies shall lie on the ground to rot and fertilize the soil. They shall die from war and famine, and their bodies shall be picked apart by vultures and wild animals. ⁵ Do not mourn or weep for them, for I have removed my protection and my peace from them—taken away my lovingkindness and my mercies. ⁶ Both great and small shall die in this land, unburied and unmourned, and

their friends shall not cut themselves nor shave their heads as signs of sorrow (as is their heathen custom). ⁷ No one shall comfort the mourners with a meal, or send them a cup of wine expressing grief for their parents' death.

⁸ As a sign to them of these sad days ahead,[a] don't you join them any more in their feasts and parties—don't even eat a meal with them. ⁹ For the Lord of Hosts, the God of Israel, says: In your own lifetime, before your very eyes, I will end all laughter in this land—the happy songs, the marriage feasts, the songs of bridegrooms and of brides.

¹⁰ And when you tell the people all these things and they ask, "Why has the Lord decreed such terrible things against us? What have we done to merit such treatment? What is our sin against the Lord our God?" ¹¹ tell them the Lord's reply is this: Because your fathers forsook me. They worshiped other gods and served them; they did not keep my laws, ¹² *and you have been worse than your fathers were!* You follow evil to your hearts' content and refuse to listen to me. ¹³ Therefore I will throw you out of this land and chase you into a foreign land where neither you nor your fathers have been before, and there you can go ahead and worship your idols all you like —and I will grant you no favors!

¹⁴,¹⁵ But there will come a glorious day, says the Lord, when the whole topic of conversation will be that God is bringing his people home from the countries of the north, where he had sent them as slaves for punishment. You will look back no longer to the time I brought you out from slavery in Egypt. That mighty miracle will scarcely be mentioned any more. Yes, I will bring you back again, says the Lord, to this same land I gave your fathers.

¹⁶ Now I am sending for many fishermen to fish you from the deeps where you are hiding from my wrath. I am sending for hunters to chase you down like deer in the forests or mountain goats on inaccessible crags. Wherever you run to escape my judgment, I will find you and punish you. ¹⁷ For I am closely watching you and I see every

---

a Implied.

sin. You cannot hope to hide from me. [18] And I will punish you doubly for all your sins because you have defiled my land with your detestable idols, and filled it up with all your evil deeds.

[19] O Lord, my Strength and Fortress, my Refuge in the day of trouble, nations from around the world will come to you saying, "Our fathers have been foolish, for they have worshiped worthless idols! [20] Can men make God? The gods they made are not real gods at all." [21] And when they come in that spirit, I will show them[b] my power and might and make them understand at last that I alone am God.

17 MY PEOPLE SIN as though commanded to, as though their evil were laws chiseled with an iron pen or diamond point upon their stony hearts or on the corners of their altars. [2,3] Their youths do not forget to sin, worshiping idols beneath each tree, high in the mountains or in the open country down below. And so I will give all your treasures to your enemies as the price that you must pay for all your sins. [4] And the wonderful heritage I reserved for you will slip out of your hand, and I will send you away as slaves to your enemies in distant lands. For you have kindled a fire of my anger that shall burn forever.

[5] The Lord says: Cursed is the man who puts his trust in mortal man and turns his heart away from God. [6] He is like a stunted shrub in the desert, with no hope for the future; he lives on the salt-encrusted plains in the barren wilderness; good times pass him by forever.

[7] But blessed is the man who trusts in the Lord and has made the Lord his hope and confidence. [8] He is like a tree planted along a riverbank, with its roots reaching deep into the water—a tree not bothered by the heat nor worried by long months of drought. Its leaves stay green and it goes right on producing all its luscious fruit.

[9] The heart is the most deceitful thing there is, and desperately wicked. No one can really know how bad it is! [10] Only the Lord knows! He searches all hearts and examines deepest motives so he can give to each person his right reward, according to his deeds—how he has lived.

[11] Like a bird that fills her nest with young she has not hatched and which will soon desert her and fly away, so is the man who gets his wealth by unjust means. Sooner or later he will lose his riches and at the end of his life become a poor old fool.

[12] But our refuge is your throne, eternal, high and glorious. [13] O Lord, the Hope of Israel, all who turn away from you shall be disgraced and shamed; they are registered for earth and not for glory, for they have forsaken the Lord, the Fountain of living waters. [14] Lord, you alone can heal me, you alone can save, and my praises are for you alone.

[15] Men scoff at me and say, "What is this word of the Lord you keep talking about? If these threats of yours are really from God, why don't they come true?"

[16] Lord, I don't want the people crushed by terrible calamity. The plan is yours, not mine. It is *your* message I've given them, not my own. *I* don't want them doomed! [17] Lord, don't desert me now! You alone are my hope. [18] Bring confusion and trouble on all who persecute me, but give me peace. Yes, bring double destruction upon them!

[19] Then the Lord said to me, Go and stand in the gates of Jerusalem, first at the gate where the king goes out, and then at each of the other gates, [20] and say to all the people: Hear the word of the Lord, kings of Judah and all the people of this nation, and all you citizens of Jerusalem. [21,22] The Lord says: Take warning and live; do no unnecessary[a] work on the Sabbath day but make it a holy day. I gave this commandment to your fathers, [23] but they didn't listen or obey. They stubbornly refused to pay attention and be taught.

[24] But if you obey me, says the Lord, and refuse to work on the Sabbath day and keep it separate, special and holy, [25] then this nation shall continue forever. There shall always be descendants of David sitting on the throne here in Jerusalem; there shall always be kings and princes riding in pomp and splendor among the people, and this city shall remain forever. [26] And from all around

---

b Literally, "Therefore, behold, I will cause them to know. . . ."   17a Implied.

Jerusalem and from the cities of Judah and Benjamin, and from the Negeb and from the lowlands west of Judah, the people shall come with their burnt offerings and grain offerings and incense, bringing their sacrifices to praise the Lord in his Temple.

²⁷ But if you will not listen to me, if you refuse to keep the Sabbath holy, if on the Sabbath you bring in loads of merchandise through these gates of Jerusalem, just as on other days, then I will set fire to these gates. The fire shall spread to the palaces and utterly destroy them, and no one shall be able to put out the raging flames.

18 HERE IS ANOTHER message to Jeremiah from the Lord:

² Go down to the shop where clay pots and jars are made and I will talk to you there. ³ I did as he told me, and found the potter working at his wheel. ⁴ But the jar that he was forming didn't turn out as he wished, so he kneaded it into a lump and started again.

⁵ Then the Lord said:

⁶ O Israel, can't I do to you as this potter has done to his clay? As the clay is in the potter's hand, so are you in my hand. ⁷ Whenever I announce that a certain nation or kingdom is to be taken up and destroyed, ⁸ then if that nation renounces its evil ways, I will not destroy it as I had planned. ⁹ And if I announce that I will make a certain nation strong and great, ¹⁰ but then that nation changes its mind and turns to evil and refuses to obey me, then I too will change my mind and not bless that nation as I had said I would.

¹¹ Therefore go and warn all Judah and Jerusalem, saying: Hear the word of the Lord. I am planning evil against you now instead of good; turn back from your evil paths and do what is right.

¹² But they replied, "Don't waste your breath. We have no intention whatever of doing what God says. We will continue to live as we want to, free from any restraint, full of stubbornness and wickedness!"

¹³ Then the Lord said: Even among the heathen, no one has ever heard of such a thing! My people have done something too horrible to understand. ¹⁴ The snow never melts high up in the Lebanon mountains.

The cold, flowing streams from the crags of Mount Hermon never run dry. ¹⁵ These can be counted on. But not my people! For they have deserted me and turned to foolish idols. They have turned away from the ancient highways of good, and walk the muddy paths of sin. ¹⁶ Therefore their land shall become desolate, so that all who pass by will gasp and shake their heads in amazement at its utter desolation. ¹⁷ I will scatter my people before their enemies as the east wind scatters dust; and in all their trouble I will turn my back on them and refuse to notice their distress.

¹⁸ Then the people said, "Come, let's get rid of Jeremiah. We have our own priests and wise men and prophets—we don't need his advice. Let's silence him that he may speak no more against us, nor bother us again."

¹⁹ *O Lord, help me! See what they are planning to do to me!* ²⁰ Should they repay evil for good? They have set a trap to kill me, yet I spoke well of them to you and tried to defend them from your anger. ²¹ Now, Lord, let their children starve to death and let the sword pour out their blood! Let their wives be widows and be bereft of all their children! Let their men die in epidemics and their youths die in battle! ²² Let screaming be heard from their homes as troops of soldiers come suddenly upon them, for they have dug a pit for me to fall in, and they have hidden traps along my path. ²³ Lord, you know all their murderous plots against me. Don't forgive them, don't blot out their sin, but let them perish before you; deal with them in your anger.

19 THE LORD SAID, Buy a clay jar and take it out into the valley of Ben-Hinnom by the east gate of the city. Take some of the elders of the people and some of the older priests with you, and speak to them whatever words I give you.

³ Then the Lord spoke to them and said: Listen to the word of the Lord, kings of Judah and citizens of Jerusalem! The Lord of Hosts, the God of Israel, says, I will bring terrible evil upon this place, so terrible that the ears of those who hear it will prickle. ⁴ For Israel has forsaken me and turned this valley into a place of shame and wickedness.

The people burn incense to idols—idols that neither this generation nor their forefathers nor the kings of Judah have worshiped before—and they have filled this place with the blood of innocent children. ⁵ They have built high altars to Baal and there they burn their sons in sacrifice—a thing I never commanded them nor even thought of!

⁶ The day is coming, says the Lord, when this valley shall no longer be called "Topheth" or "Ben-Hinnom Valley," but "The Valley of Slaughter." ⁷ For I will upset the battle plans of Judah and Jerusalem and I will let invading armies kill you here and leave your dead bodies for vultures and wild animals to feed upon. ⁸ And I will wipe Jerusalem off the earth, so that everyone going by will gasp with astonishment at all that I have done to her. ⁹ I will see to it that your enemies lay siege to the city until all food is gone, and those trapped inside begin to eat their own children and friends.

¹⁰ And now, Jeremiah, as these men watch, smash the jar you brought with you, ¹¹ and say to them, This is the message to you from the Lord of Hosts: As this jar lies shattered, so I will shatter the people of Jerusalem; and as this jar cannot be mended, neither can they. The slaughter shall be so great that there won't be room enough for decent burial anywhere, and their bodies shall be heaped in this valley. ¹² And as it will be in this valley, so it will be in Jerusalem. For I will fill Jerusalem with dead bodies too. ¹³ And I will defile all the homes in Jerusalem, including the palace of the kings of Judah—wherever incense has been burned upon the roofs to your star-gods, and libations poured out to them.

¹⁴ As Jeremiah returned from Topheth where he had delivered this message, he stopped in front of the Temple of the Lord and said to all the people, ¹⁵ The Lord of Hosts, the God of Israel, says: I will bring upon this city and her surrounding towns all the evil I have promised, because you have stubbornly refused to listen to the Lord.

20 NOW WHEN PASHHUR (son of Immer), the priest in charge of the Temple of the Lord, heard what Jeremiah was saying, ² he arrested Jeremiah and had him whipped and put in the stocks at Benjamin Gate near the Temple. ³ He left him there all night.

The next day when Pashhur finally released him, Jeremiah said, "Pashhur, the Lord has changed your name. He says from now on to call you 'The Man Who Lives in Terror.' ⁴ For the Lord will send terror on you and all your friends, and you will see them die by the swords of their enemies. I will hand over Judah to the king of Babylon, says the Lord, and he shall take away these people as slaves to Babylon and kill them. ⁵ And I will let your enemies loot Jerusalem. All the famed treasures of the city, with the precious jewels and gold and silver of your kings, shall be carried off to Babylon. ⁶ And as for you, Pashhur, you and all your family and household shall become slaves in Babylon and die there —you and those to whom you lied when you prophesied that everything would be all right."

⁷ Then I said, O Lord, you deceived me when you promised me your help. I have to give them your messages because you are stronger than I am, but now I am the laughingstock of the city, mocked by all. ⁸ You have never once let me speak a word of kindness to them; always it is disaster and horror and destruction. No wonder they scoff and mock and make my name a household joke. ⁹ And I can't quit! For if I say I'll never again mention the Lord —never more speak in his name—then his word in my heart is like fire that burns in my bones, and I can't hold it in any longer. ¹⁰ Yet on every side I hear their whispered threats, and am afraid. "We will report you," they say. Even those who were my friends are watching me, waiting for a fatal slip. "He will trap himself," they say, "and then we will get our revenge on him."

¹¹ But the Lord stands beside me like a great warrior, and before him, the Mighty, Terrible One, they shall stumble. They cannot defeat me; they shall be shamed and thoroughly humiliated, and they shall have a stigma upon them forever. ¹² O Lord of Hosts, who knows those who are righteous and examines the deepest thoughts of hearts and minds, let me see your vengeance on them. For I have committed my cause to

you. [13] Therefore I will sing out in thanks to the Lord! Praise him! For he has delivered me, poor and needy, from my oppressors.

[14] Yet, cursed be the day that I was born! [15] Cursed be the man who brought my father the news that a son was born. [16] Let that messenger be destroyed like the cities of old which God overthrew without mercy. Terrify him all day long with battle shouts, [17] because he did not kill me at my birth! Oh, that I had died within my mother's womb, that it had been my grave! [18] Why was I ever born? For my life has been but trouble and sorrow and shame.

21 THEN KING ZEDEKIAH sent Pashhur (son of Malchiah) and Zephaniah the priest (son of Ma-aseiah) to Jeremiah, and begged, "Ask the Lord to help us, for Nebuchadnezzar, king of Babylon, has declared war on us! Perhaps the Lord will be gracious to us and do a mighty miracle as in olden times[a] and force Nebuchadnezzar to withdraw his forces."

[3,4] Jeremiah replied, "Go back to King Zedekiah and tell him the Lord God of Israel says, I will make all your weapons useless against the king of Babylon and the Chaldeans besieging you. In fact, I will bring your enemies right into the heart of this city, [5] and I myself will fight against you, for I am very angry. [6] And I will send a terrible plague on this city, and both men and animals shall die. [7] And finally I will deliver King Zedekiah himself and all the remnant left in the city into the hands of King Nebuchadnezzar of Babylon, to slaughter them without pity or mercy.

[8] "Tell these people, the Lord says: Take your choice of life or death! [9] Stay here in Jerusalem and die—slaughtered by your enemies, killed by starvation and disease —or go out and surrender to the Chaldean army and live. [10] For I have set my face against this city; I will be its enemy and not its friend, says the Lord. It shall be captured by the king of Babylon and he shall reduce it to ashes.

[11] "And to the king of Judah, the Lord says: [12] I am ready to judge you because of all the evil you are doing. Quick! Give justice to these you judge! Begin doing what is right before my burning fury flashes out upon you like a fire no man can quench. [13] I will fight against this city of Jerusalem, which boasts, 'We are safe; no one can touch us here!' [14] And I myself will destroy you for your sinfulness, says the Lord. I will light a fire in the forests that will burn up everything in its path."

22 THEN THE LORD said to me: Go over and speak directly to the king of Judah and say, [2] Listen to this message from God, O king of Judah, sitting on David's throne; and let your servants and your people listen too.

[3] The Lord says: Be fair-minded. Do what is right! Help those in need of justice! Quit your evil deeds! Protect the rights of aliens and immigrants, orphans and widows; stop murdering the innocent! [4] If you put an end to all these terrible deeds you are doing, then I will deliver this nation and once more give kings to sit on David's throne, and there shall be prosperity for all.

[5] But if you refuse to pay attention to this warning, I swear by my own name, says the Lord, that this palace shall become a shambles. [6] For this is the Lord's message concerning the palace: You are as beloved to me as fruitful Gilead and the green forests of Lebanon; but I will destroy you and leave you deserted and uninhabited. [7] I will call for a wrecking crew to bring out its tools to dismantle you. They will tear out all of your fine cedar beams and throw them on the fire. [8] Men from many nations will pass by the ruins of this city and say to one another, "Why did the Lord do it? Why did he destroy such a great city?" [9] And the answer will be, "Because the people living here forgot the Lord their God and violated his agreement with them, for they worshiped idols."

[10] Don't weep for the dead! Instead weep for the captives led away! For they will never return to see their native land again. [11] For the Lord says this about Jehoahaz

a King Zedekiah doubtless had in mind God's deliverance of Jerusalem from Sennacherib, king of Assyria, in the days of Hezekiah (Isaiah 36–37). But Zedekiah's hopes were dashed. He was Judah's last ruler before the exile of 597 B.C.

who succeeded[a] his father King Josiah, and was taken away as a captive: [12] He shall die in a distant land[b] and never again see his own country.

[13] And woe to you, King Jehoiakim,[c] for you are building your great palace with forced labor. By not paying wages you are building injustice into its walls and oppression into its doorframes and ceilings. [14] You say, "I will build a magnificent palace with huge rooms and many windows, paneled throughout with fragrant cedar and painted a lovely red." [15] But a beautiful palace does not make a great king! Why did your father Josiah reign so long? Because he was just and fair in all his dealings. That is why God blessed him. [16] He saw to it that justice and help were given the poor and the needy and all went well for him. This is how a man lives close to God. [17] But you! You are full of selfish greed and all dishonesty! You murder the innocent, oppress the poor and reign with ruthlessness.

[18] Therefore this is God's decree of punishment against King Jehoiakim, who succeeded his father Josiah on the throne: His family will not weep for him when he dies. His subjects will not even care that he is dead. [19] He shall be buried like a dead donkey—dragged out of Jerusalem and thrown on the garbage dump beyond the gate! [20] Weep, for your allies are gone. Search for them in Lebanon; shout for them at Bashan; seek them at the fording points of Jordan. See, they are all destroyed. Not one is left to help you! [21] When you were prosperous I warned you, but you replied, "Don't bother me." Since childhood you have been that way—you just won't listen! [22] And now all your allies have disappeared with a puff of wind; all your friends are taken off as slaves. Surely at last you will see your wickedness and be ashamed. [23] It's very nice to live graciously in a beautiful palace among the cedars of Lebanon, but soon you will cry and groan in anguish—anguish as of a woman in labor.

[24,25] And as for you, Coniah,[d] son of Jehoiakim king of Judah—even if you were the signet ring on my right hand, I would pull you off and give you to those who seek to kill you, of whom you are so desperately afraid—to Nebuchadnezzar, king of Babylon, and his mighty army. [26] I will throw you and your mother out of this country, and you shall die in a foreign land. [27] You will never again return to the land of your desire. [28] This man Coniah is like a discarded, broken dish. He and his children will be exiled to distant lands.

[29] O earth, earth, earth! Hear the word of the Lord! [30] The Lord says:

Record this man Coniah as childless, for none of his children shall ever sit upon the throne of David or rule in Judah.[e] His life will amount to nothing.

23 THE LORD DECLARES:

I will send disaster upon the leaders of my people—the shepherds of my sheep—for they have destroyed and scattered the very ones they were to care for. [2] Instead of leading my flock to safety, you have deserted them and driven them to destruction. And now I will pour out judgment upon you for the evil you have done to them. [3] And I will gather together the remnant of my flock from wherever I have sent them, and bring them back into their own fold, and they shall be fruitful and increase. [4] And I will appoint responsible shepherds to care for them, and they shall not need to be afraid again; all of them shall be accounted for continually.

[5,6] For the time is coming, says the Lord, when I will place a righteous Branch upon King David's throne. He shall be a King who shall rule with wisdom and justice and cause righteousness to prevail everywhere throughout the earth.[a] And this is his name: *The Lord Our Righteousness.* At that time Judah will be saved and Israel will live in peace.

[7] In that day people will no longer say

---

a Jehoahaz, or Shallum, reigned for three brief months in the year 609 B.C.   b Egypt.
c Implied. See verse 18. He was chosen by the Egyptians to replace Jehoahaz, whom they took back to Egypt with them. He ruled from 609–598 B.C.   d Coniah is an abbreviation—perhaps a disparaging nickname—for Jeconiah and Jehoiachin, his other names. His name means, "The Lord will establish my throne!"
e This man Coniah's grandson, Zerubbabel, was briefly governor, but not king.   23a Or, "throughout the land."

when taking an oath, "As the Lord lives who rescued the people of Israel from the land of Egypt," [8] but they will say, "As the Lord lives who brought the Jews back to their own land of Israel from the countries to which he had exiled them."

[9] My heart is broken for the false prophets, full of deceit. I awake with fear and stagger as a drunkard does from wine, because of the awful fate awaiting them,[b] for God has decreed holy words of judgment against them. [10] For the land is full of adultery and the curse of God is on it. The land itself is mourning—the pastures are dried up—for the prophets do evil and their power is used wrongly. [11] And the priests are like the prophets, all ungodly, wicked men. I have seen their despicable acts right here in my own Temple, says the Lord. [12] Therefore their paths will be dark and slippery; they will be chased down dark and treacherous trails, and fall. For I will bring evil upon them and see to it, when their time has come, that they pay their penalty in full for all their sins.

[13] I knew the prophets of Samaria were unbelievably evil, for they prophesied by Baal and led my people Israel into sin; [14] but the prophets of Jerusalem are even worse! The things they do are horrible; they commit adultery and love dishonesty. They encourage and compliment those who are doing evil, instead of turning them back from their sins. These prophets are as thoroughly depraved as the men of Sodom and Gomorrah were.

[15] Therefore the Lord of Hosts says: I will feed them with bitterness and give them poison to drink. For it is because of them that wickedness fills this land. [16] This is my warning to my people, says the Lord of Hosts. Don't listen to these false prophets when they prophesy to you, filling you with futile hopes. They are making up everything they say. They do not speak for me! [17] They keep saying to these rebels who despise me, "Don't worry! All is well"; and to those who live the way they want to, "The Lord has said you shall have peace!"

[18] But can you name even one of these prophets who lives close enough to God to hear what he is saying? Has even one of them cared enough to listen? [19] See, the Lord is sending a furious whirlwind to sweep away these wicked men. [20] The terrible anger of the Lord will not abate until it has carried out the full penalty he decrees against them. Later, when Jerusalem has fallen,[c] you will see what I mean.

[21] I have not sent these prophets, yet they claim to speak for me; I gave them no message, yet they say their words are mine. [22] If they were mine, they would try to turn my people from their evil ways. [23] Am I a God who is only in one place and cannot see what they are doing? [24] Can anyone hide from me? Am I not everywhere in all of heaven and earth?

[25] "Listen to the dream I had from God last night," they say. And then they proceed to lie in my name. [26] How long will this continue? If they are "prophets," they are prophets of deceit, inventing everything they say. [27] By telling these false dreams they are trying to get my people to forget me in the same way as their fathers did, who turned away to the idols of Baal. [28] Let these false prophets tell their dreams and let my true messengers faithfully proclaim my every word. There is a difference between chaff and wheat! [29] Does not my word burn like fire? asks the Lord. Is it not like a mighty hammer that smashed the rock to pieces? [30,31] So I stand against these "prophets" who get their messages from each other—these smooth-tongued prophets who say, "This message is from God!" [32] Their made-up dreams are flippant lies that lead my people into sin. I did not send them and they have no message at all for my people, says the Lord.

[33] When one of the people or one of their "prophets" or priests asks you, "Well, Jeremiah, what is the sad news from the Lord today?" you shall reply, "What sad news? You are the sad news, for the Lord has cast you away!" [34] And as for the false prophets and priests and people who joke about "today's sad news from God," I will punish them and their families for saying this. [35] You can ask each other, "What is God's message? What is he saying?" [36] But stop

---

b Implied.   c Literally, "in the latter days."

using this term, "God's sad news." For what is sad is you and your lying. You are twisting my words and inventing "messages from God" that I didn't speak. ³⁷ You may respectfully ask Jeremiah, "What is the Lord's message? What has he said to you?" ³⁸,³⁹ But if you ask him about "today's sad news from God," when I have warned you not to mock like that, then I, the Lord God, will unburden myself of the burden^d you are to me. I will cast you out of my presence, you and this city I gave to you and your fathers. ⁴⁰ And I will bring reproach upon you and your name shall be infamous through the ages.

24 AFTER NEBUCHADNEZZAR, KING of Babylon, had captured and enslaved Jeconiah (son of Jehoiakim), king of Judah, and exiled him to Babylon along with the princes of Judah and the skilled tradesmen—the carpenters and blacksmiths—the Lord gave me this vision. ² I saw two baskets of figs placed in front of the Temple in Jerusalem. In one basket there were fresh, just-ripened figs, but in the other the figs were spoiled and moldy—too rotten to eat. ³ Then the Lord said to me, "What do you see, Jeremiah?"

I replied, "Figs, some very good and some very bad."

⁴,⁵ Then the Lord said: "The good figs represent the exiles sent to Babylon. I have done it for their good. ⁶ I will see that they are well treated and I will bring them back here again. I will help them and not hurt them; I will plant them and not pull them up. ⁷ I will give them hearts that respond to me. They shall be my people and I will be their God, for they shall return to me with great joy.

⁸ "But the rotten figs represent Zedekiah, king of Judah, his officials and all the others of Jerusalem left here in this land; those too who live in Egypt. I will treat them like spoiled figs, too bad to use. ⁹ I will make them repulsive to every nation of the earth, and they shall be mocked and taunted and cursed wherever I compel them to go. ¹⁰ And I will send massacre and famine and disease among them until they are destroyed from the land of Israel, which I gave to them and to their fathers."

25 THIS MESSAGE FOR all the people of Judah came from the Lord to Jeremiah during the fourth year of the reign of King Jehoiakim of Judah (son of Josiah). This was the year Nebuchadnezzar, king of Babylon, began his reign.

²,³ For the past twenty-three years, Jeremiah said, from the thirteenth year of the reign of Josiah (son of Amon) king of Judah, until now, God has been sending me his messages. I have faithfully passed them on to you, but you haven't listened. ⁴ Again and again down through the years, God has sent you his prophets, but you have refused to hear. ⁵ Each time the message was this: Turn from the evil road you are traveling and from the evil things you are doing. Only then can you continue to live here in this land which the Lord gave to you and to your ancestors forever. ⁶ *Don't anger me by worshiping idols; but if you are true to me, then I'll not harm you.* ⁷ But you won't listen; you have gone ahead and made me furious with your idols. So you have brought upon yourselves all the evil that has come your way.

⁸,⁹ And now the Lord God of Hosts says, Because you have not listened to me, I will gather together all the armies of the north under Nebuchadnezzar, king of Babylon (I have appointed him as my deputy), and I will bring them all against this land and its people and against the other nations near you, and I will utterly destroy you and make you a byword of contempt forever. ¹⁰ I will take away your joy, your gladness and your wedding feasts; your businesses shall fail and all your homes shall lie in silent darkness. ¹¹ This entire land shall become a desolate wasteland; all the world will be shocked at the disaster that befalls you. Israel and her neighboring lands shall serve the king of Babylon for seventy years. ¹² Then, after these years^a of slavery are ended, I will punish the king of Babylon^b and his people for their sins; I will make the

d Literally, either, "the *burden* of the Lord," or, "the *message* of the Lord." This is a Hebrew pun.
25a Literally, "the seventy years."   b This event is further described in Daniel 5. The troops of Cyrus the Great entered Babylon in 539 B.C. and killed Belshazzar, the last Babylonian ruler.

land of Chaldea an everlasting waste. ¹³ I
will bring upon them all the terrors I have
promised in this book—all the penalties announced by Jeremiah against the nations.
¹⁴ For many nations and great kings shall
enslave the Chaldeans, just as they enslaved
my people; I will punish them in proportion
to their treatment of my people.

¹⁵ For the Lord God said to me: "Take
from my hand this wine cup filled to the
brim with my fury, and make all the nations
to whom I send you drink from it. ¹⁶ They
shall drink from it and reel, crazed by the
death blows I rain upon them."

¹⁷ So I took the cup of fury from the Lord
and made all the nations drink from it—every nation God had sent me to; ¹⁸ I went to
Jerusalem and to the cities of Judah, and
their kings and princes drank of the cup so
that from that day until this they have been
desolate, hated and cursed, just as they are
today. ¹⁹,²⁰ I went to Egypt, and Pharaoh
and his servants, the princes and the people—they too drank from that terrible cup,
along with all the foreign population living
in his land. So did all the kings of the land
of Uz and the kings of the Philistine cities:
Ashkelon, Gaza, Ekron, and what remains
of Ashdod, ²¹ and I visited the nations of
Edom, Moab and Ammon; ²² and all the
kings of Tyre and Sidon, and the kings of
the regions across the sea; ²³ Dedan and
Tema and Buz, and the other heathen there;
²⁴ and all the kings of Arabia and of the
nomadic tribes of the desert; ²⁵ and all the
kings of Zimri, Elam and Media; ²⁶ and all
the kings of the northern countries, far and
near, one after the other; and all the kingdoms of the world. And finally, the king of
Babylon himself drank from this cup of
God's wrath.

²⁷ Tell them, "The Lord of Hosts, the
God of Israel, says, Drink from this cup of
my wrath until you are drunk and vomit
and fall and rise no more, for I am sending
terrible wars upon you." ²⁸ And if they
refuse to accept the cup, tell them, "The
Lord of Hosts says you *must* drink it! You
cannot escape! ²⁹ I have begun to punish my
own people, so should you go free? No, you
shall not evade punishment. I will call for
war against all the peoples of the earth."

³⁰ Therefore prophesy against them. Tell

them the Lord will shout against his own
from his holy temple in heaven, and against
all those living on the earth. He will shout
as the harvesters do who tread the juice
from the grapes. ³¹ That cry of judgment
will reach the farthest ends of the earth, for
the Lord has a case against all the nations
—all mankind. He will slaughter all the
wicked. ³² See, declares the Lord of Hosts,
the punishment shall go from nation to nation—a great whirlwind of wrath shall rise
against the farthest corners of the earth.
³³ On that day those the Lord has slain shall
fill the earth from one end to the other. No
one shall mourn for them nor gather up the
bodies to bury them; they shall fertilize the
earth.

³⁴ Weep and moan, O evil shepherds; let
the leaders of mankind beat their heads
upon the stones, for their time has come to
be slaughtered and scattered; they shall fall
like fragile women. ³⁵ And you will find no
place to hide, no way to escape.

³⁶ Listen to the frantic cries of the
shepherds and to the leaders shouting in
despair, for the Lord has spoiled their pastures. ³⁷ People now living undisturbed will
be cut down by the fierceness of the anger
of the Lord. ³⁸ He has left his lair like a lion
seeking prey; their land has been laid waste
by warring armies—because of the fierce
anger of the Lord.

26 THIS MESSAGE CAME to Jeremiah
from the Lord during the first year of
the reign of Jehoiakim (son of Josiah), king
of Judah:

² Stand out in front of the Temple of the
Lord and make an announcement to all the
people who have come there to worship
from many parts of Judah. Give them the
entire message; don't leave out one word of
all I have for them to hear. ³ For perhaps
they will listen and turn from their evil
ways, and then I can withhold all the punishment I am ready to pour out upon them
because of their evil deeds. ⁴ Tell them the
Lord says: If you will not listen to me and
obey the laws I have given you, ⁵ and if you
will not listen to my servants, the prophets—for I sent them again and again to
warn you, but you would not listen to
them— ⁶ then I will destroy this Temple as

I destroyed the Tabernacle at Shiloh, and I will make Jerusalem a curse word in every nation of the earth.

[7,8] When Jeremiah had finished his message, saying everything the Lord had told him to, the priests and false prophets and all the people in the Temple mobbed him, shouting, "Kill him! Kill him! [9] What right do you have to say the Lord will destroy this Temple like the one at Shiloh?" they yelled. "What do you mean—Jerusalem destroyed and not one survivor?"

[10] When the high officials of Judah heard what was going on, they rushed over from the palace and sat down at the door of the Temple to hold court. [11] Then the priests and the false prophets presented their accusations to the officials and the people. "This man should die!" they said. "You have heard with your own ears what a traitor he is, for he has prophesied against this city."

[12] Then Jeremiah spoke in his defense. "The Lord sent me," he said, "to prophesy against this Temple and this city. He gave me every word of all that I have spoken. [13] But if you stop your sinning and begin obeying the Lord your God, he will cancel all the punishment he has announced against you. [14] As for me, I am helpless and in your power—do with me as you think best. [15] But there is one thing sure, if you kill me, you will be killing an innocent man and the responsibility will lie upon you and upon this city and upon every person living in it; for it is absolutely true that the Lord sent me to speak every word that you have heard from me."

[16] Then the officials and people said to the priests and false prophets, "This man does not deserve the death sentence, for he has spoken to us in the name of the Lord our God."

[17] Then some of the wise old men stood and spoke to all the people standing around and said:

[18] "The decision is right; for back in the days when Micah the Morasthite prophesied in the days of King Hezekiah of Judah, he told the people that God said: 'This hill shall be plowed like an open field and this city of Jerusalem razed into heaps of stone, and a forest shall grow at the top where the great Temple now stands!' [19] But did King Hezekiah and the people kill him for saying this? No, they turned from their wickedness and worshiped the Lord and begged the Lord to have mercy upon them; and the Lord held back the terrible punishment he had pronounced against them. If we kill Jeremiah for giving us the messages of God, who knows what God will do to us!"

[20] Another true prophet of the Lord, Uriah (son of Shemaiah) from Kiriath-jearim, was also denouncing the city and the nation at the same time as Jeremiah was. [21] But when King Jehoiakim and the army officers and officials heard what he was saying, the king sent to kill him. Uriah heard about it and fled to Egypt. [22] Then King Jehoiakim sent Elnathan (son of Achbor) to Egypt along with several other men to capture Uriah. [23] They took him prisoner and brought him back to King Jehoiakim, who butchered him with a sword and had him buried in an unmarked grave.

[24] But Ahikam (son of Shaphan), the royal secretary,[a] stood with Jeremiah and persuaded the court not to turn him over to the mob to kill him.

27 THIS MESSAGE CAME to Jeremiah from the Lord at the beginning of the reign of Jehoiakim[a] (son of Josiah), king of Judah:

[2] Make a yoke and fasten it on your neck with leather thongs as you would strap a yoke on a plow-ox. [3] Then send messages to the kings of Edom, Moab, Ammon, Tyre and Sidon, through their ambassadors in Jerusalem, [4] saying, Tell your masters that the Lord of Hosts, the God of Israel, sends you this message:

[5] "By my great power I have made the earth and all mankind and every animal; and I give these things of mine to anyone I want to. [6] So now I have given all your countries to King Nebuchadnezzar of Babylon, who is my deputy. And I have handed over to him all your cattle for his use. [7] All the nations shall serve him and his son and his grandson until his time is up,

---

a Implied. See 2 Kings 22:12.   27a Some versions read "Zedekiah."

and then many nations and great kings shall conquer Babylon and make him their slave. [8] Submit to him and serve him—put your neck under Babylon's yoke! I will punish any nation refusing to be his slave; I will send war, famine and disease upon that nation until he has conquered it.

[9] "Do not listen to your false prophets, fortune-tellers, dreamers, mediums and magicians who say the king of Babylon will not enslave you. [10] For they are all liars, and if you follow their advice and refuse to submit to the king of Babylon, I will drive you out of your land and send you far away to perish. [11] But the people of any nation submitting to the king of Babylon will be permitted to stay in their own country and farm the land as usual."

[12] Jeremiah repeated all these prophecies to Zedekiah, king of Judah. "If you want to live, submit to the king of Babylon," he said. [13] "Why do you insist on dying—you and your people? Why should you choose war and famine and disease, which the Lord has promised to every nation that will not submit to Babylon's king? [14] Don't listen to the false prophets who keep telling you the king of Babylon will not conquer you, for they are liars. [15] I have not sent them, says the Lord, and they are telling you lies in my name. If you insist on heeding them, I must drive you from this land to die—you and all these 'prophets' too."

[16] I spoke again and again to the priests and all the people and told them: "The Lord says, Don't listen to your prophets who are telling you that soon the golden dishes taken from the Temple will be returned from Babylon. It is all a lie. [17] Don't listen to them. Surrender to the king of Babylon and live, for otherwise this whole city will be destroyed. [18] If they are really God's prophets, then let them pray to the Lord of Hosts that the golden dishes still here in the Temple, left from before, and that those in the palace of the king of Judah and in the palaces in Jerusalem will not be carried away with you to Babylon!

[19,20,21] "For the Lord of Hosts says, The pillars of bronze standing before the Temple, and the great bronze basin in the Tem-

ple court, and the metal stands and all the other ceremonial articles left here by Nebuchadnezzar, king of Babylon, when he exiled all the important people of Judah and Jerusalem to Babylon, along with Jeconiah (son of Jehoiakim), king of Judah, [22] will all yet be carried away to Babylon and will stay there until I send for them. Then I will bring them all back to Jerusalem again."

28 ON A DECEMBER day in that same year—the fourth year of the reign of Zedekiah, king of Judah—Hananiah (son of Azzur), a false prophet from Gibeon, addressed me publicly in the Temple while all the priests and people listened. He said:

[2] "The Lord of Hosts, the God of Israel, declares: I have removed the yoke of the king of Babylon from your necks. [3] Within two years I will bring back all the Temple treasures that Nebuchadnezzar carried off to Babylon, [4] and I will bring back King Jeconiah,[a] son of Jehoiakim, king of Judah, and all the other captives exiled to Babylon, says the Lord. I will surely remove the yoke put on your necks by the king of Babylon."

[5] Then Jeremiah said to Hananiah, in front of all the priests and people, [6] "Amen! May your prophecies come true! I hope the Lord will do everything you say and bring back from Babylon the treasures of this Temple, with all our loved ones. [7] But listen now to the solemn words I speak to you in the presence of all these people. [8] The ancient prophets who preceded you and me spoke against many nations, always warning of *war, famine* and *plague.* [9] So a prophet who foretells *peace* has the burden of proof on him to prove that God has really sent him. Only when his message comes true can it be known that he really is from God."

[10] Then Hananiah, the false prophet, took the yoke off Jeremiah's neck and broke it. [11] And Hananiah said again to the crowd that had gathered, "The Lord has promised that within two years he will release all the nations now in slavery to King Nebuchadnezzar of Babylon." At that point Jeremiah walked out.

[12] Soon afterwards, the Lord gave this

---

a Or, "Jehoiachin," as he is also called.

message to Jeremiah:

13 Go and tell Hananiah that the Lord says, You have broken a wooden yoke but these people have yokes of iron on their necks. 14 The Lord of Hosts, the God of Israel, says: I have put a yoke of iron on the necks of all these nations, forcing them into slavery to Nebuchadnezzar, king of Babylon. And nothing will change this decree, for I have even given him all your flocks and herds.

15 Then Jeremiah said to Hananiah, the false prophet, "Listen, Hananiah, the Lord has not sent you, and the people are believing your lies. 16 Therefore the Lord says you must die. This very year your life will end because you have rebelled against the Lord."

17 And sure enough, two months later Hananiah died.

29 AFTER JECONIAH THE king, and the queen-mother, and the court officials, and the tribal officers and craftsmen had been deported to Babylon by Nebuchadnezzar, Jeremiah wrote them a letter from Jerusalem, addressing it to the Jewish elders and priests and prophets, and to all the people. 3 He sent the letter with Elasah (son of Shaphan) and Gemariah (son of Hilkiah) when they went to Babylon as King Zedekiah's ambassadors to Nebuchadnezzar. And this is what the letter said:

4 The Lord of Hosts, the God of Israel, sends this message to all the captives he has exiled to Babylon from Jerusalem:

5 Build homes and plan to stay; plant vineyards, for you will be there many years. 6 Marry and have children, and then find mates for them and have many grandchildren. Multiply! Don't dwindle away! 7 And work for the peace and prosperity of Babylon. Pray for her, for if Babylon has peace, so will you.

8 The Lord of Hosts, the God of Israel, says: Don't let the false prophets and mediums who are there among you fool you. Don't listen to the dreams that they invent, 9 for they prophesy lies in my name. I have not sent them, says the Lord. 10 The truth

is this: You will be in Babylon for a lifetime.[a] But then I will come and do for you all the good things I have promised, and bring you home again. 11 For I know the plans I have for you, says the Lord. They are plans for good and not for evil, to give you a future and a hope. 12 In those days when you pray, I will listen. 13 You will find me when you seek me, if you look for me in earnest.

14 Yes, says the Lord, I will be found by you, and I will end your slavery and restore your fortunes, and gather you out of the nations where I sent you and bring you back home again to your own land.

15 But now, because you accept the false prophets among you and say the Lord has sent them, 16,17 I will send war, famine and plague upon the people left here in Jerusalem—on your relatives who were not exiled to Babylon, and on the king who sits on David's throne—and make them like rotting figs, too bad to eat. 18 And I will scatter them around the world. And in every nation where I place them they will be cursed and hissed and mocked, 19 for they refuse to listen to me though I spoke to them again and again through my prophets.

20 Therefore listen to the word of God, all you Jewish captives over there in Babylon. 21 The Lord of Hosts, the God of Israel, says this about your false prophets, Ahab (son of Kolaiah) and Zedekiah (son of Maaseiah), who are declaring lies to you in my name: Look, I am turning them over to Nebuchadnezzar to execute publicly. 22 Their fate shall become proverbial of all evil, so that whenever anyone wants to curse someone he will say, "The Lord make you like Zedekiah and Ahab whom the king of Babylon burned alive!" 23 For these men have done a terrible thing among my people. They have committed adultery with their neighbors' wives and have lied in my name. I know, for I have seen everything they do, says the Lord. 24 And say this to Shemaiah the dreamer:[b]

25 The Lord of Hosts, the God of Israel, says: You have written a letter to Zephaniah (son of Ma-aseiah) the priest, and sent

a Literally, "for seventy years."   b Literally, "the Nehelamite." Nehelam was Shemaiah's home town, the name of which means "Dreamer." This seems to be another of the frequent puns in the prophetic books.

copies to all the other priests and to everyone in Jerusalem. [26] And in this letter you have said to Zephaniah, "The Lord has appointed you to replace Jehoiada as priest in Jerusalem. And it is your responsibility to arrest any madman who claims to be a prophet, and to put him in the stocks and collar. [27] Why haven't you done something about this false prophet Jeremiah of Anathoth? [28] For he has written to us here in Babylon saying that our captivity will be long, and that we should build permanent homes and plan to stay many years, that we should plant fruit trees, for we will be here to eat the fruit from them for a long time to come."

[29] Zephaniah took the letter over to Jeremiah and read it to him! [30] Then the Lord gave this message to Jeremiah:

[31] Send an open letter to all the exiles in Babylon and tell them this: The Lord says that because Shemaiah the Nehelamite has "prophesied" to you when I didn't send him, and has fooled you into believing his lies, [32] I will punish him and his family. None of his descendants shall see the good I have waiting for my people, for he has taught you to rebel against the Lord.

30 THIS IS ANOTHER of the Lord's messages to Jeremiah:

[2] The Lord God of Israel says, Write down for the record all that I have said to you. [3] For the time is coming when I will restore the fortunes of my people, Israel and Judah, and I will bring them home to this land that I gave to their fathers; they shall possess it and live here again.

[4] And write this also concerning Israel and Judah:

[5] "Where shall we find peace?" they cry. "There is only fear and trembling. [6] Do men give birth? Then why do they stand there, ashen-faced, hands pressed against their sides like women in labor?"

[7] Alas, in all history when has there ever been a time of terror such as in that coming day? It is a time of trouble for my people— for Jacob—such as they have never known before. Yet God will rescue them! [8] For on that day, says the Lord of Hosts, I will break the yoke from their necks and snap their chains, and foreigners shall no longer be their masters! [9] For they shall serve the Lord their God, and David their King,[a] whom I will raise up for them, says the Lord.

[10] So don't be afraid, O Jacob my servant; don't be dismayed, O Israel; for I will bring you home again from distant lands, and your children from their exile. They shall have rest and quiet in their own land, and no one shall make them afraid. [11] For I am with you and I will save you, says the Lord. Even if I utterly destroy the nations where I scatter you, I will not exterminate you; I will punish you, yes—you will not go unpunished.

[12] For your sin is an incurable bruise, a terrible wound. [13] There is no one to help you or to bind up your wound and no medicine does any good. [14] All your lovers have left you and don't care anything about you any more; for I have wounded you cruelly, as though I were your enemy; mercilessly, as though I were an implacable foe; for your sins are so many, your guilt is so great.

[15] Why do you protest your punishment? Your sin is so scandalous that your sorrow should never end! It is because your guilt is great that I have had to punish you so much.

[16] But in that coming day, all who are destroying you shall be destroyed, and all your enemies shall be slaves. Those who rob you shall be robbed; and those attacking you shall be attacked. [17] I will give you back your health again and heal your wounds. Now you are called "The Outcast" and "Jerusalem, the Place Nobody Wants."

[18] But, says the Lord, when I bring you home again from your captivity and restore your fortunes, Jerusalem will be rebuilt upon her ruins; the palace will be reconstructed as it was before. [19] The cities will be filled with joy and great thanksgiving, and I will multiply my people and make of them a great and honored nation. [20] Their children shall prosper as in David's reign; their nations shall be established before me,

---

a The Messiah, David's greater Son, whom God has raised up for them.

and I will punish anyone who hurts them. [21] They will have their own ruler again.[b] He will not be a foreigner. And I will invite him to be a priest at my altars, and he shall approach me, for who would dare to come unless invited. [22] And you shall be my people and I will be your God.

[23] Suddenly the devastating whirlwind of the Lord roars with fury; it shall burst upon the heads of the wicked. [24] The Lord will not call off the fierceness of his wrath until it has finished all the terrible destruction he has planned. Later on[c] you will understand what I am telling you.

31 AT THAT TIME, says the Lord, all the families of Israel shall recognize me as the Lord; they shall act like my people. [2] I will care for them as I did those who escaped from Egypt, to whom I showed my mercies in the wilderness, when Israel sought for rest. [3] For long ago the Lord had said to Israel: I have loved you, O my people, with an everlasting love; with lovingkindness I have drawn you to me. [4] I will rebuild your nation, O virgin of Israel. You will again be happy and dance merrily with the timbrels. [5] Again you will plant your vineyards upon the mountains of Samaria and eat from your own gardens there.

[6] The day shall come when watchmen on the hills of Ephraim will call out and say, "Arise, and let us go up to Zion to the Lord our God." [7] For the Lord says, Sing with joy for all that I will do for Israel, the greatest of the nations! Shout out with praise and joy: "The Lord has saved his people, the remnant of Israel." [8] For I will bring them from the north and from earth's farthest ends, not forgetting their blind and lame, young mothers with their little ones, those ready to give birth. It will be a great company who comes. [9] Tears of joy shall stream down their faces, and I will lead them home with great care. They shall walk beside the quiet streams and not stumble. For I am a Father to Israel, and Ephraim is my oldest child.

[10] Listen to this message from the Lord, you nations of the world, and publish it abroad: The Lord who scattered his people will gather them back together again and watch over them as a shepherd does his flock. [11] He will save Israel from those who are too strong for them! [12] They shall come home and sing songs of joy upon the hills of Zion, and shall be radiant over the goodness of the Lord—the good crops, the wheat and the wine and the oil, and the healthy flocks and herds. Their life shall be like a watered garden, and all their sorrows shall be gone. [13] The young girls will dance for joy, and men folk—old and young—will take their part in all the fun; for I will turn their mourning into joy and I will comfort them and make them rejoice, for their captivity with all its sorrows will be behind them. [14] I will feast the priests with the abundance of offerings brought to them at the Temple; I will satisfy my people with my bounty, says the Lord.

[15] The Lord spoke to me again, saying: In Ramah there is bitter weeping, Rachel[a] is weeping for her children and she cannot be comforted, for they are gone. [16] But the Lord says: Don't cry any longer, for I have heard your prayers[b] and you will see them again; they will come back to you from the distant land of the enemy. [17] There is hope for your future, says the Lord, and your children will come again to their own land.

[18] I have heard Ephraim's groans: "You have punished me greatly; but I needed it all, as a calf must be trained for the yoke. Turn me again to you and restore me, for you alone are the Lord, my God. [19] I turned away from God but I was sorry afterwards. I kicked myself for my stupidity. I was thoroughly ashamed of all I did in younger days."

[20] And the Lord replies: Ephraim is still my son, my darling child. I had to punish him, but I still love him. I long for him and surely will have mercy on him.

[21] As you travel into exile, set up road signs pointing back to Israel. Mark your pathway well. For you shall return again,

---

b This verse probably refers to the restoration after the Babylonian captivity (the rulers of the Maccabean period were priests as well as kings) as well as to the final restoration under Christ.   c Literally, "in the latter days."   31a Symbolic mother of the northern tribes, who were taken away by the Assyrians as slaves. b Literally, "for your work shall be rewarded."

O virgin Israel, to your cities here. ²² How long will you vacillate, O wayward daughter? For the Lord will cause something new and different to happen—Israel shall seek him!ᶜ

²³ The Lord of Hosts, the God of Israel, says: When I bring them back again they shall say in Judah and her cities, "The Lord bless you, O center of righteousness, O holy hill!" ²⁴ And city dwellers and farmers and shepherds alike shall live together in peace and happiness. ²⁵ For I have given rest to the weary and joy to all the sorrowing.

²⁶ (Then Jeremiah wakened. "Such sleep is very sweet!" he said.)

²⁷ The Lord says: The time will come when I will greatly increase the population and multiply the number of cattle here in Israel. ²⁸ In the past I painstakingly destroyed the nation but now I will carefully build it up. ²⁹ The people shall no longer quote this proverb—"Children pay for their fathers' sins."ᵈ ³⁰ For everyone shall die for his own sins—the person eating sour grapes is the one whose teeth are set on edge.

³¹ The day will come, says the Lord, when I will make a new contract with the people of Israel and Judah. ³² It won't be like the one I made with their fathers when I took them by the hand to bring them out of the land of Egypt—a contract they broke, forcing me to reject them,ᵉ says the Lord. ³³ But this is the new contract I will make with them: I will inscribe my laws upon their hearts,ᶠ so that they shall want to honor me;ᵍ then they shall truly be my people and I will be their God. ³⁴ At that time it will no longer be necessary to admonish one another to know the Lord. For everyone, both great and small, shall really know me then, says the Lord, and I will forgive and forget their sins.

³⁵ The Lord who gives us sunlight in the daytime and the moon and stars to light the night, and who stirs the sea to make the roaring waves—his name is Lord of Hosts—says this:

³⁶ I am as likely to reject my people Israel as I am to do away with these laws of nature! ³⁷ Not until the heavens can be measured and the foundations of the earth explored, will I consider casting them away forever for their sins!

³⁸,³⁹ For the time is coming, says the Lord, when all Jerusalem shall be rebuilt for the Lord, from the Tower of Hananel at the northeast corner,ʰ to the Corner Gate at the northwest;ʰ and from the Hill of Gareb at the southwest,ʰ across to Goah on the southeast.ʰ ⁴⁰ And the entire city including the graveyard and ash dump in the valley shall be holy to the Lord, and so shall all the fields out to the brook of Kidron, and from there to the Horse Gate on the east side of the city; it shall never again be captured or destroyed.

32 THE FOLLOWING MESSAGE came to Jeremiah from the Lord in the tenth year of the reign of Zedekiah, king of Judah (which was the eighteenth year of Nebuchadnezzar's reign). ² At this time Jeremiah was imprisoned in the dungeon beneathᵃ the palace, while the Babylonian army was besieging Jerusalem. ³ King Zedekiah had put him there for continuing to prophesy that the city would be conquered by the king of Babylon, ⁴ and that King Zedekiah would be caught and taken as a prisoner before the king of Babylon for trial and sentencing.

⁵ "He shall take you to Babylon and imprison you there for many years until you die. Why fight the facts? You can't win! Surrender now!" Jeremiah had told him again and again.

⁶,⁷ Then this message from the Lord came to Jeremiah: Your cousin Hanamel (son of Shallum) will soon arrive to ask you to buy the farm he owns in Anathoth, for by law you have a chance to buy before it is offered to anyone else. ⁸ So Hanamel came, as the Lord had said he would, and

---

c Literally, "a woman shall court a suitor," or, "a woman shall encompass a man."   d Literally, "The fathers eat the sour grapes and the children's teeth are set on edge."   e Some versions read, "a covenant they broke, even though I cared for them as a husband does his wife." See Hebrews 8:9b. f i.e., rather than upon tablets of stone, as were the Ten Commandments.   g In Jeremiah 17:1 their sin was inscribed on their hearts, so that they wanted above all to disobey. This change seems to describe an experience very much like, if not the same as, the new birth.   h Implied.   32a Literally, "in the court of the prison in the palace."

visited me in the prison. "Buy my field in Anathoth, in the land of Benjamin," he said, "for the law gives you the first right to purchase it." Then I knew for sure that the message I had heard was really from the Lord.

⁹ So I bought the field, paying Hanamel seventeen shekels of silver. ¹⁰ I signed and sealed the deed of purchase before witnesses, and weighed out the silver and paid him. ¹¹ Then I took the sealed deed containing the terms and conditions, and also the unsealed copy, ¹² and publicly, in the presence of my cousin Hanamel and the witnesses who had signed the deed, and as the prison guards watched, I handed the papers to Baruch (son of Neriah, who was the son of Mahseiah). ¹³ And I said to him as they all listened:

¹⁴ "The Lord of Hosts, God of Israel, says: Take both this sealed deed and the copy and put them into a pottery jar to preserve them for a long time. ¹⁵ For the Lord of Hosts, God of Israel, says, In the future these papers will be valuable.ᵇ Someday people will again own property here in this country and will be buying and selling houses and vineyards and fields."

¹⁶ Then after I had given the papers to Baruch I prayed:

¹⁷ "O Lord God! You have made the heavens and earth by your great power; nothing is too hard for you! ¹⁸ You are loving and kind to thousands, yet children suffer for their fathers' sins; you are the great and mighty God, the Lord of Hosts. ¹⁹ You have all wisdom and do great and mighty miracles; for your eyes are open to all the ways of men, and you reward everyone according to his life and deeds. ²⁰ You have done incredible things in the land of Egypt—things still remembered to this day. And you have continued to do great miracles in Israel and all around the world. You have made your name very great, as it is today.

²¹ "You brought Israel out of Egypt with mighty miracles and great power and terror. ²² You gave Israel this land that you promised their fathers long ago—a wonderful land that 'flows with milk and honey.'

²³ Our fathers came and conquered it and lived in it, but they refused to obey you or to follow your laws; they have hardly done one thing you told them to. That is why you have sent all this terrible evil upon them. ²⁴ See how the siege mounds have been built against the city walls, and the Babylonians shall conquer the city by sword, famine and disease. Everything has happened just as you said—as you determined it should! ²⁵ And yet you say to buy the field—paying good money for it before these witnesses —even though the city will belong to our enemies."

²⁶ Then this message came to Jeremiah:

²⁷ I am the Lord, the God of all mankind; is there anything too hard for me? ²⁸ Yes, I will give this city to the Babylonians and to Nebuchadnezzar, king of Babylon; he shall conquer it. ²⁹ And the Babylonians outside the walls shall come in and set fire to the city and burn down all these houses where the roofs have been used to offer incense to Baal, and to pour out libations to other gods, causing my fury to rise! ³⁰ For Israel and Judah have done nothing but wrong since their earliest days; they have infuriated me with all their evil deeds. ³¹ From the time this city was built until now it has done nothing but anger me; so I am determined to be rid of it.

³² The sins of Israel and Judah—the sins of the people, of their kings, officers, priests and prophets—stir me up. ³³ They have turned their backs upon me and refused to return; day after day, year after year, I taught them right from wrong, but they would not listen or obey. ³⁴ They have even defiled my own Temple by worshiping their abominable idols there. ³⁵ And they have built high altars to Baal in the Valley of Hinnom. There they have burnt their children as sacrifices to Molech—something I never commanded, and cannot imagine suggesting. What an incredible evil, causing Judah to sin so greatly!

³⁶ Now therefore the Lord God of Israel says concerning this city that it will fall to the king of Babylon through warfare, famine and disease, ³⁷ but I will bring my people back again from all the countries where in

ᵇ Implied.

646

my fury I will scatter them. I will bring them back to this very city, and make them live in peace and safety. [38] And they shall be my people and I will be their God. [39] And I will give them one heart and mind to worship me forever, for their own good and for the good of all their descendants.

[40] And I will make an everlasting covenant with them, promising never again to desert them, but only to do them good. I will put a desire into their hearts to worship me, and they shall never leave me. [41] I will rejoice to do them good and will replant them in this land, with great joy. [42] Just as I have sent all these terrors and evils upon them, so will I do all the good I have promised them.

[43] Fields will again be bought and sold in this land, now ravaged by the Babylonians, where men and animals alike have disappeared. [44] Yes, fields shall once again be bought and sold—deeds signed and sealed and witnessed—in the country of Benjamin and here in Jerusalem, in the cities of Judah and in the hill country, in the Philistine plain and in the Negeb too, for some day I will restore prosperity to them.

33 WHILE JEREMIAH WAS still in jail, the Lord sent him this second message: [2] The Lord, the Maker of heaven and earth—Jehovah is his name—says this: [3] Ask me and I will tell you some remarkable secrets about what is going to happen here. [4] For though you have torn down the houses of this city, and the king's palace too, for materials to strengthen the walls against the siege guns of the enemy, [5] yet the Babylonians will enter, and the men of this city are already as good as dead, for I have determined to destroy them in my furious anger. I have abandoned them because of all their wickedness, and I will not pity them when they cry for help.

[6] Nevertheless the time will come when I will heal Jerusalem's damage and give her prosperity and peace. [7] I will rebuild the cities of both Judah and Israel and restore their fortunes. [8] And I will cleanse away all their sins against me, and pardon them.

[9] Then this city will be an honor to me, and it will give me joy and be a source of praise and glory to me before all the nations of the earth! The people of the world will see the good I do for my people and will tremble with awe!

[10,11] The Lord declares that the happy voices of bridegrooms and of brides, and the joyous song of those bringing thanksgiving offerings to the Lord will be heard again in this doomed land. The people will sing: "Praise the Lord! For he is good and his mercy endures forever!" For I will make this land happier and more prosperous than it has ever been before. [12] This land—though every man and animal and city is doomed—will once more see shepherds leading sheep and lambs. [13] Once again their flocks will prosper in the mountain villages and in the cities east of the Philistine plain, in all the cities of the Negeb, in the land of Benjamin, in the vicinity of Jerusalem and in all the cities of Judah. [14] Yes, the day will come, says the Lord, when I will do for Israel and Judah all the good I promised them.

[15] At that time I will bring to the throne the true Son[a] of David, and he shall rule justly. [16] In that day the people of Judah and Jerusalem shall live in safety and their motto will be, "The Lord is our righteousness!" [17] For the Lord declares that from then on, David shall forever have an heir sitting on the throne of Israel. [18] And there shall always be Levites to offer burnt offerings and meal offerings and sacrifices to the Lord.

[19] Then this message came to Jeremiah from the Lord: [20,21] If you can break my covenant with the day and with the night so that day and night don't come on their usual schedule, only then will my covenant with David, my servant, be broken so that he shall not have a son to reign upon his throne; and my covenant with the Levite priests, my ministers, is non-cancelable. [22] And as the stars cannot be counted nor the sand upon the seashores measured, so the descendants of David my servant and the line of the Levites who min-

---

a Or, "the true vine from the roots of David." Christ was the true vine, the only true expression of David, the man after God's own heart.

ister to me will be multiplied.

²³ The Lord spoke to Jeremiah again and said:

²⁴ Have you heard what people are saying?—that the Lord chose Judah and Israel and then abandoned them! They are sneering and saying that Israel isn't worthy to be counted as a nation. ²⁵,²⁶ But this is the Lord's reply: I would no more reject my people than I would change my laws of night and day, of earth and sky. I will never abandon the Jews, or David my servant, or change the plan that his Child will someday rule these descendants of Abraham, Isaac and Jacob. Instead I will restore their prosperity and have mercy on them.

34 THIS IS THE message that came to Jeremiah from the Lord when Nebuchadnezzar, king of Babylon, and all his armies from all the kingdoms he ruled, came and fought against Jerusalem and the cities of Judah:

² Go tell Zedekiah, king of Judah, that the Lord says this: I will give this city to the king of Babylon and he shall burn it. ³ You shall not escape; you shall be captured and taken before the king of Babylon and he shall pronounce sentence against you and you shall be exiled to Babylon. ⁴ But listen to this, O Zedekiah, king of Judah: God says you won't be killed in war and carnage, ⁵ but that you will die quietly among your people, and they will burn incense in your memory, just as they did for your fathers. They will weep for you and say, "Alas, our king is dead!" This I have decreed, says the Lord.

⁶ So Jeremiah delivered the message to King Zedekiah. ⁷ At this time the Babylonian army was besieging Jerusalem, Lachish and Azekah—the only walled cities of Judah still standing.

⁸ This is the message that came to Jeremiah from the Lord after King Zedekiah of Judah had freed all the slaves in Jerusalem— ⁹ (for King Zedekiah had ordered everyone to free his Hebrew slaves, both men and women. He had said that no Jew should be the master of another Jew for all were

brothers. ¹⁰ The princes and all the people had obeyed the king's command and freed their slaves, but the action was only temporary. ¹¹ They changed their minds and made their servants slaves again.ᵃ ¹² That is why the Lord gave the following message to Jerusalem.)

¹³ The Lord, the God of Israel, says:

I made a covenant with your fathers long ago when I brought them from their slavery in Egypt. ¹⁴ I told them that every Hebrew slave must be freed after serving six years. But this was not done. ¹⁵ Recently you began doing what was right, as I commanded you, and freed your slaves. You had solemnly promised me in my Temple that you would do it. ¹⁶ But now you refuse and have defiled my name by shrugging off your oath and have made them slaves again.

¹⁷ Therefore, says the Lord, because you will not listen to me and release them, I will release you to the power of death by war and famine and disease. And I will scatter you over all the world as exiles. ¹⁸,¹⁹ Because you have refused the terms of our contract I will cut you apart just as you cut apart the calf when you walked between its halves to solemnize your vows. Yes, I will butcher you, whether you are princes, court officials, priests or people—for you have broken your oath. ²⁰ I will give you to your enemies and they shall kill you. I will feed your dead bodies to the vultures and wild animals. ²¹ And I will surrender Zedekiah, king of Judah, and his officials to the army of the king of Babylon, though he has departed from the city for a little while. ²² I will summon the Babylonian armies back again and they will fight against it and capture this city and burn it. And I will see to it that the cities of Judah are completely destroyed and left desolate without a living soul.

35 THIS IS THE message the Lord gave Jeremiah when Jehoiakim (son of Josiah) was the king of Judah:ᵃ

² Go to the settlement where the families of the Rechabites live and invite them to the Temple. Take them into one of the inner rooms and offer them a drink of wine.

---

a When the siege was temporarily lifted (Jeremiah 37:6–11) they became bold and returned to their sins.
35a This is apparently an early message to Jeremiah, and is not here in its chronological order with the other messages.

³ So I went over to see Ja-azaniah (son of Jeremiah, who was the son of Habazziniah), and brought him and all his brothers and sons—representing all the Rechab families— ⁴ to the Temple, into the room assigned for the use of the sons of Hanan the prophet (the son of Igdaliah). This room was located next to the one used by the palace official, directly above the room of Ma-aseiah (son of Shallum), who was the temple doorman. ⁵ I set cups and jugs of wine before them and invited them to have a drink, ⁶ but they refused.

"No," they said. "We don't drink, for Jonadab our father (son of Rechab) commanded that none of us should ever drink, neither we nor our children forever. ⁷ He also told us not to build houses or plant crops or vineyards and not to own farms, but always to live in tents; and that if we obeyed we would live long, good lives in our own land. ⁸ And we have obeyed him in all these things. We have never had a drink of wine since then, nor our wives or our sons or daughters either. ⁹ We haven't built houses or owned farms or planted crops. ¹⁰ We have lived in tents and have fully obeyed everything that Jonadab our father commanded us. ¹¹ But when Nebuchadnezzar, king of Babylon, arrived in this country, we were afraid and decided to move to Jerusalem. That's why we are here."

¹² Then the Lord gave this message to Jeremiah:

¹³ The Lord of Hosts, the God of Israel, says: Go and say to Judah and Jerusalem, Won't you learn a lesson from the families of Rechab? ¹⁴ They don't drink, because their father told them not to. But I have spoken to you again and again and you won't listen or obey. ¹⁵ I have sent you prophet after prophet to tell you to turn back from your wicked ways and to stop worshiping other gods and that if you obeyed, then I would let you live in peace here in the land I gave to you and your fathers. But you wouldn't listen or obey. ¹⁶ The families of Rechab have obeyed their father completely, but you have refused to listen to me. ¹⁷ Therefore the Lord God of Hosts, the God of Israel, says: Because you refuse to listen or answer when I call, I will send upon Judah and Jerusalem all the evil I have ever threatened.

¹⁸,¹⁹ Then Jeremiah turned to the Rechabites and said: "The Lord of Hosts, the God of Israel, says that because you have obeyed your father in every respect, he shall always have descendants who will worship me."

36 IN THE FOURTH yearª of the reign of King Jehoiakim of Judah (son of Josiah) the Lord gave this message to Jeremiah:

² "Get a scroll and write down all my messages against Israel, Judah and the other nations. Begin with the first message back in the days of Josiah, and write down every one of them. ³ Perhaps when the people of Judah see in writing all the terrible things I will do to them, they will repent. And then I can forgive them."

⁴ So Jeremiah sent for Baruch (son of Neriah), and as Jeremiah dictated, Baruch wrote down all the prophecies.

⁵ When all was finished, Jeremiah said to Baruch, "Since I am a prisoner here, ⁶ you read the scroll in the Temple on the next Day of Fasting, for on that day people will be there from all over Judah. ⁷ Perhaps even yet they will turn from their evil ways and ask the Lord to forgive them before it is too late, even though these curses of God have been pronounced upon them."

⁸ Baruch did as Jeremiah told him to, and read all these messages to the people at the Temple. ⁹ This occurred on the Day of Fasting held in December of the fifth year of the reign of King Jehoiakim (son of Josiah). People came from all over Judah to attend the services at the Temple that day. ¹⁰ Baruch went to the office of Gemariah the Scribe (son of Shaphan) to read the scroll. (This room was just off the upper assembly hall of the Temple, near the door of the New Gate.) ¹¹ When Micaiah (son of Gemariah, son of Shaphan) heard the messages from God,

---

a Probably in the summer of 605 B.C., shortly after Nebuchadnezzar's victory over the Egyptian army at Carchemish.

¹² he went down to the palace to the conference room where the administrative officials were meeting. Elishama (the scribe) was there, as well as Delaiah (son of Shamaiah), Elnathan (son of Achbor), Gemariah (son of Shaphan), Zedekiah (son of Hananiah), and all the others with similar responsibilities. ¹³ When Micaiah told them about the messages Baruch was reading to the people, ¹⁴,¹⁵ the officials sent Jehudi (son of Nethaniah, son of Shelemiah, son of Cushi) to ask Baruch to come and read the messages to them too, and Baruch did.

¹⁶ By the time he finished they were badly frightened. "We must tell the king," they said. ¹⁷ "But first, tell us how you got these messages. Did Jeremiah himself dictate them to you?" ¹⁸ So Baruch explained that Jeremiah had dictated them to him word by word, and he had written them down in ink upon the scroll. ¹⁹ "You and Jeremiah both hide," the officials said to Baruch. "Don't tell a soul where you are!" ²⁰ Then the officials hid the scroll in the room of Elishama the scribe and went to tell the king.

²¹ The king sent Jehudi to get the scroll. Jehudi brought it from Elishama the scribe and read it to the king as all his officials stood by. ²² The king was in a winterized part of the palace at the time, sitting in front of a fireplace,[b] for it was December, and cold. ²³ And whenever Jehudi finished reading three or four columns, the king would take his knife, and slit off the section and throw it into the fire, until the whole scroll was destroyed. ²⁴,²⁵ And no one protested except Elnathan, Delaiah and Gemariah. They pled with the king not to burn the scroll, but he wouldn't listen to them. Not another of the king's officials showed any signs of fear or anger at what he had done.

²⁶ Then the king commanded Jerahmeel (a member of the royal family[c]) and Seraiah (son of Azri-el) and Shelemiah (son of Abdeel) to arrest Baruch and Jeremiah. But the Lord hid them!

²⁷ After the king had burned the scroll, the Lord said to Jeremiah:

²⁸ Get another scroll and write everything again just as you did before, ²⁹ and say this to the king: "The Lord says, You burned the scroll because it said the king of Babylon would destroy this country and everything in it. ³⁰ And now the Lord adds this concerning you, Jehoiakim, king of Judah: He shall have no one to sit[d] upon the throne of David. His dead body shall be thrown out to the hot sun and frosty nights, ³¹ and I will punish him and his family and his officials because of their sins. I will pour out upon them all the evil I promised—upon them and upon all the people of Judah and Jerusalem, for they wouldn't listen to my warnings."

³² Then Jeremiah took another scroll and dictated again to Baruch all he had written before, only this time the Lord added a lot more!

37 NEBUCHADNEZZAR, KING OF Babylon, did not appoint Coniah (King Jehoiakim's son) to be the new king of Judah.[a] Instead he chose Zedekiah (son of Josiah). ² But neither King Zedekiah nor his officials nor the people who were left in the land listened to what the Lord said through Jeremiah. ³ Nevertheless, King Zedekiah sent Jehucal (son of Shelemiah) and Zephaniah the priest (son of Ma-aseiah) to ask Jeremiah to pray for them. ⁴ (Jeremiah had not been imprisoned yet, so he could go and come as he pleased.)

⁵ When the army of Pharaoh Hophra of Egypt appeared at the southern border of Judah to relieve the besieged city of Jerusalem, the Babylonian army withdrew from Jerusalem to fight the Egyptians.

⁶ Then the Lord sent this message to Jeremiah:

⁷ "The Lord, the God of Israel, says: Tell the king of Judah, who sent you to ask me what is going to happen, that Pharaoh's army, though it came here to help you, is about to return in flight to Egypt! The Babylonians shall defeat them and send

---

b More literally, "a large brazier in which a fire was burning."   c "a son of the king."
d A three-month inter-regnum by his son Jehoiachin (also called Coniah and Jeconiah) evidently did not qualify as "sitting on the throne" under the meaning of permanence in the Hebrew expression used here.
37a The people of Jerusalem who had assassinated King Jehoiakim appointed his son Coniah as ruler before Nebuchadnezzar captured the city. The Babylonians took Coniah to Babylon as a political hostage.

them scurrying home. [8] These Babylonians shall capture this city and burn it to the ground. [9] Don't fool yourselves that the Babylonians are gone for good. They aren't! [10] Even if you destroyed the entire Babylonian army until there was only a handful of survivors and they lay wounded in their tents, yet they would stagger out and defeat you and put this city to the torch!"

[11] When the Babylonian army set out from Jerusalem to engage Pharaoh's army in battle, [12] Jeremiah started to leave the city to go to the land of Benjamin, to see the property he had bought.[b] [13] But as he was walking through the Benjamin Gate, a sentry arrested him as a traitor, claiming he was defecting to the Babylonians. The guard making the arrest was Irijah (son of Shelemiah, grandson of Hananiah).

[14] "That's not true," Jeremiah said. "I have no intention whatever of doing any such thing!"

But Irijah wouldn't listen; he took Jeremiah before the city officials. [15,16] They were incensed with Jeremiah and had him flogged and put into the dungeon under the house of Jonathan the scribe, which had been converted into a prison. Jeremiah was kept there for several days, [17] but eventually King Zedekiah sent for him to come to the palace secretly. The king asked him if there was any recent message from the Lord. "Yes," said Jeremiah, "there is! You shall be defeated by the king of Babylon!"

[18] Then Jeremiah broached the subject of his imprisonment. "What have I ever done to deserve this?" he asked the king. "What crime have I committed? Tell me what I have done against you or your officials or the people? [19] Where are those prophets now who told you that the king of Babylon would not come? [20] Listen, O my lord the king: I beg you, don't send me back to that dungeon, for I'll die there."

[21] Then King Zedekiah commanded that Jeremiah not be returned to the dungeon, but be placed in the palace prison instead, and that he be given a small loaf of fresh bread every day as long as there was any left in the city. So Jeremiah was kept in the palace prison.[c]

38 BUT WHEN SHEPHATIAH (son of Mattan) and Gedaliah (son of Pashhur) and Jucal (son of Shelemiah) and Pashhur (son of Malchiah) heard what Jeremiah had been telling the people— [2] that everyone remaining in Jerusalem would die by sword, starvation or disease, but anyone surrendering to the Babylonians would live, [3] and that the city of Jerusalem would surely be captured by the king of Babylon— [4] they went to the king and said: "Sir, this fellow must die. That kind of talk will undermine the morale of the few soldiers we have left, and of all the people too. This man is a traitor."

[5] So King Zedekiah agreed. "All right," he said. "Do as you like—I can't stop you."

[6] They took Jeremiah from his cell and lowered him by ropes into an empty cistern in the prison yard. (It belonged to Malchiah, a member of the royal family.) There was no water in it, but there was a thick layer of mire at the bottom, and Jeremiah sank down into it.

[7] When Ebed-melech the Ethiopian, an important palace official, heard that Jeremiah was in the cistern, [8] he rushed out to the Gate of Benjamin where the king was holding court.

[9] "My lord the king," he said, "these men have done a very evil thing in putting Jeremiah into the cistern. He will die of hunger, for almost all the bread in the city is gone."

[10] Then the king commanded Ebed-melech to take thirty men with him and pull Jeremiah out before he died. [11] So Ebed-melech took thirty men and went to a palace depot for discarded supplies where used clothing was kept. There he found some old rags and discarded garments which he took to the cistern and lowered to Jeremiah on a rope. [12] Ebed-melech called down to Jeremiah, "Use these rags under your armpits to protect you from the ropes." Then, when Jeremiah was ready, [13] they pulled him out and returned him to the palace prison, where he remained.

[14] One day King Zedekiah sent for Jeremiah to meet him at the side entrance of the

---

b See chapter 32:6–15.　　c Literally, "the court of the guard."

Temple.

"I want to ask you something," the king said, "and don't try to hide the truth."

[15] Jeremiah said, "If I tell you the truth, you will kill me. And you won't listen to me anyway."

[16] So King Zedekiah swore before Almighty God his Creator that he would not kill Jeremiah or give him to the men who were after his life.

[17] Then Jeremiah said to Zedekiah, "The Lord, the God of Hosts, the God of Israel, says: If you will surrender to Babylon, you and your family shall live and the city will not be burned. [18] If you refuse to surrender, this city shall be set afire by the Babylonian army and you will not escape."

[19] "But I am afraid to surrender," the king said, "for the Babylonians will hand me over to the Jews who have defected to them, and who knows what they will do to me?"

[20] Jeremiah replied, "You won't get into their hands if only you will obey the Lord; your life will be spared and all will go well for you. [21,22] But if you refuse to surrender, the Lord has said that all the women left in your palace will be brought out and given to the officers of the Babylonian army; and these women will taunt you with bitterness. 'Fine friends you have,' they'll say, 'those Egyptians. They have betrayed you and left you to your fate!' [23] All your wives and children will be led out to the Babylonians, and you will not escape. You will be seized by the king of Babylon, and this city will be burned."

[24] Then Zedekiah said to Jeremiah, "On pain of death, don't tell anyone you told me this! [25] And if my officials hear that I talked with you and they threaten you with death unless you tell them what we discussed, [26] just say that you begged me not to send you back to the dungeon in Jonathan's house, for you would die there."

[27] And sure enough, it wasn't long before all the city officials came to Jeremiah and asked him why the king had called for him. So he said what the king had told him to, and they left without finding out the truth, for the conversation had not been overheard by anyone. [28] And Jeremiah remained confined to the prison yard until the day that Jerusalem was retaken by the Babylonians.

39 IT WAS IN January of the ninth year of the reign of King Zedekiah of Judah, that King Nebuchadnezzar and all his army came against Jerusalem again and besieged it. [2] Two years later, in the month of July, they breached the wall, and the city fell, [3] and all the officers of the Babylonian army came in and sat in triumph at the middle gate. Nergal-sharezer was there, and Samgar-nebo and Sarsechim and Nergalsharezer the king's chief assistant, and many others.

[4] When King Zedekiah and his soldiers realized that the city was lost, they fled during the night, going out through the gate between the two walls back of the palace garden and across the fields toward the Jordan valley. [5] But the Babylonians chased the king and caught him on the plains of Jericho and brought him to Nebuchadnezzar, king of Babylon who was at Riblah, in the land of Hamath, where he pronounced judgment upon him. [6] The king of Babylon made Zedekiah watch as they killed his children and all the nobles of Judah. [7] Then he gouged out Zedekiah's eyes and bound him in chains to send him away to Babylon as a slave.

[8] Meanwhile the army burned Jerusalem, including the palace, and tore down the walls of the city. [9] Then Nebuzaradan, the captain of the guard, and his men sent the remnant of the population and all those who had defected to him to Babylon. [10] But throughout the land of Judah he left a few people, the very poor, and gave them fields and vineyards.

[11,12] Meanwhile King Nebuchadnezzar had told Nebuzaradan to find Jeremiah. "See that he isn't hurt," he said. "Look after him well and give him anything he wants." [13] So Nebuzaradan, the captain of the guard, and Nebushazban, the chief of the eunuchs, and Nergal-sharezer, the king's advisor, and all the officials took steps to do as the king had commanded. [14] They sent soldiers to bring Jeremiah out of the prison, and put him into the care of Gedaliah (son of Ahikam, son of Shaphan), to take him back to his home. And Jeremiah lived there among his people who were left in the land.

¹⁵ The Lord gave the following message to Jeremiah before the Babylonians arrived, while he was still in prison:

¹⁶ "Send this word to Ebed-melech the Ethiopian: The Lord of Hosts, the God of Israel, says: I will do to this city everything I threatened; I will destroy it before your eyes, ¹⁷ but I will deliver you. You shall not be killed by those you fear so much. ¹⁸ As a reward for trusting me, I will preserve your life and keep you safe."

40 NEBUZARADAN, CAPTAIN OF the guard, took Jeremiah to Ramah along with all the exiled people of Jerusalem and Judah who were being sent to Babylon, but then released him.

²,³ The captain called for Jeremiah and said, "The Lord your God has brought this disaster on this land, just as he said he would. For these people have sinned against the Lord. That is why it happened. ⁴ Now I am going to take off your chains and let you go. If you want to come with me to Babylon, fine; I will see that you are well cared for. But if you don't want to come, don't. The world is before you—go where you like. ⁵ If you decide to stay, then return to Gedaliah, who has been appointed as governor of Judah by the king of Babylon, and stay with the remnant he rules. But it's up to you; go where you like."

Then Nebuzaradan gave Jeremiah some food and money and let him go. ⁶ So Jeremiah returned to Gedaliah and lived in Judah with the people left in the land.

⁷ Now when the leaders of the Jewish guerrilla bands in the countryside heard that the king of Babylon had appointed Gedaliah as governor over the poor of the land who were left behind, and had not exiled everyone to Babylon, ⁸ they came to see Gedaliah at Mizpah, where his headquarters were. These are the names of the leaders who came: Ishmael (son of Nethaniah), Johanan and Jonathan (sons of Kareah), Seraiah (son of Tanhumeth), the sons of Ephai (the Netophathite), Jezaniah (son of a Maacathite), and their men. ⁹ And Gedaliah assured them that it would be safe to surrender to the Babylonians.

"Stay here and serve the king of Babylon," he said, "and all will go well for you.

¹⁰ As for me, I will stay at Mizpah and intercede for you with the Babylonians who will come here to oversee my administration. Settle in any city you wish and live off the land. Harvest the grapes and summer fruits and olives and store them away."

¹¹ When the Jews in Moab and among the Ammonites and in Edom and the other nearby countries heard that a few people were still left in Judah, and that the king of Babylon had not taken them all away, and that Gedaliah was the governor, ¹² they all began to return to Judah from the many places to which they had fled. They stopped at Mizpah to discuss their plans with Gedaliah and then went out to the deserted farms and gathered a great harvest of wine grapes and other crops.

¹³,¹⁴ But soon afterwards Johanan (son of Kareah) and the other guerrilla leaders came to Mizpah to warn Gedaliah that Baalis, king of the Ammonites, had sent Ishmael (son of Nethaniah) to assassinate him. But Gedaliah wouldn't believe them. ¹⁵ Then Johanan had a private conference with Gedaliah. Johanan volunteered to kill Ishmael secretly.

"Why should we let him come and murder you?" Johanan asked. "What will happen then to the Jews who have returned? Why should this remnant be scattered and lost?"

¹⁶ But Gedaliah said, "I forbid you to do any such thing, for you are lying about Ishmael."

41 BUT IN OCTOBER, Ishmael (son of Nethaniah, son of Elishama), who was a member of the royal family and one of the king's top officials, arrived in Mizpah, accompanied by ten men. Gedaliah invited them to dinner. ² While they were eating, Ishmael and the ten men in league with him suddenly jumped up, pulled out their swords and killed Gedaliah. ³ Then they went out and slaughtered all the Jewish officials and Babylonian soldiers who were in Mizpah with Gedaliah.

⁴ The next day, before the outside world knew what had happened, ⁵ eighty men approached Mizpah from Shechem, Shiloh and Samaria, to worship at the Temple of the Lord. They had shaved off their beards,

torn their clothes and cut themselves, and were bringing offerings and incense. ⁶ Ishmael went out from the city to meet them, crying as he went. When he faced them he said, "Oh, come and see what has happened to Gedaliah!"

⁷ Then, when they were all inside the city, Ishmael and his men killed all but ten of them and threw their bodies into a cistern. ⁸ The ten had talked Ishmael into letting them go by promising to bring him their treasures of wheat, barley, oil and honey they had hidden away. ⁹ The cistern where Ishmael dumped the bodies of the men he murdered was the large one constructed by King Asa when he fortified Mizpah to protect himself against Baasha, king of Israel.ᵃ

¹⁰ Ishmael made captives of the king's daughters and of the people who had been left under Gedaliah's care in Mizpah by Nebuzaradan, captain of the guard. Soon after he took them with him when he headed toward the country of the Ammonites.

¹¹ But when Johanan (son of Kareah) and the rest of the guerrilla leaders heard what Ishmael had done, ¹² they took all their men and set out to stop him. They caught up with him at the pool near Gibeon. ¹³,¹⁴ The people with Ishmael shouted for joy when they saw Johanan and his men, and ran to meet them.

¹⁵ Meanwhile Ishmael escaped with eight of his men into the land of the Ammonites.

¹⁶,¹⁷ Then Johanan and his men went to the village of Geruth Chimham, near Bethlehem, taking with them all those they had rescued—soldiers, women, children and eunuchs, to prepare to leave for Egypt. ¹⁸ For they were afraid of what the Babylonians would do when the news reached them that Ishmael had killed Gedaliah the governor, for he had been chosen and appointed by the Babylonian emperor.

42 THEN JOHANAN AND the army captains and all the people, great and small, came to Jeremiah ² and said, "Please pray for us to the Lord your God, for as you know so well, we are only a tiny remnant

of what we were before. ³ Beg the Lord your God to show us what to do and where to go."

⁴ "All right," Jeremiah replied. "I will ask him and I will tell you what he says. I will hide nothing from you."

⁵ Then they said to Jeremiah, "May the curse of God be on us if we refuse to obey whatever he says we should do! ⁶ Whether we like it or not, we will obey the Lord our God, to whom we send you with our plea. For if we obey him, everything will turn out well for us."

⁷ Ten days later the Lord gave his reply to Jeremiah. ⁸ So he called for Johanan and the captains of his forces, and for all the people, great and small, ⁹ and said to them: "You sent me to the Lord, the God of Israel, with your request, and this is his reply:

¹⁰ "Stay here in this land. If you do, I will bless you and no one will harm you. For I am sorry for all the punishment I have had to give to you. ¹¹ Don't fear the king of Babylon any more, for I am with you to save you and to deliver you from his hand. ¹² And I will be merciful to you by making him kind so that he will not kill you or make slaves of you but will let you stay here in your land.

¹³,¹⁴ "But if you refuse to obey the Lord and say, 'We will not stay here,'—and insist on going to Egypt where you think you will be free from war and hunger and alarms, ¹⁵ then this is what the Lord replies, O remnant of Judah: The Lord of Hosts, the God of Israel, says: If you insist on going to Egypt, ¹⁶ the war and famine you fear will follow close behind you and you will perish there. ¹⁷ That is the fate awaiting every one of you who insists on going to live in Egypt. Yes, you will die from sword, famine and disease. None of you will escape from the evil I will bring upon you there.

¹⁸ "For the Lord of Hosts, the God of Israel, says: Just as my anger and fury were poured out upon the people of Jerusalem, so it will be poured out on you when you enter Egypt. You will be received with disgust and with hatred—you will be cursed and reviled. And you will never again see your own land. ¹⁹ For the Lord has said: O

---

a See 1 Kings 15:22. Fifty-three cisterns have been uncovered by excavators at the site of ancient Mizpah.

remnant of Judah, do not go to Egypt!" Jeremiah concluded: "Never forget the warning I have given you today. [20] If you go, it will be at the cost of your lives. For you were deceitful when you sent me to pray for you and said, 'Just tell us what God says and we will do it!' [21] And today I have told you exactly what he said, but you will not obey any more now than you did the other times. [22] Therefore know for a certainty that you will die by sword, famine and disease in Egypt, where you insist on going."

43 WHEN JEREMIAH HAD finished giving this message from God to all the people, [2,3] Azariah (son of Hoshaiah) and Johanan (son of Kareah) and all the other proud men, said to Jeremiah, "You lie! The Lord our God hasn't told you to tell us not to go to Egypt! Baruch (son of Neriah) has plotted against us and told you to say this so that we will stay here and be killed by the Babylonians or carried off to Babylon as slaves."

[4] So Johanan and all the guerrilla leaders and all the people refused to obey the Lord and stay in Judah. [5] All of them, including all those who had returned from the nearby countries where they had fled, now started off for Egypt with Johanan and the other captains in command. [6] In the crowd were men, women and children, the king's daughters and all those whom Nebuzaradan, the captain of the guard, had left with Gedaliah. They even forced Jeremiah and Baruch to go with them too. [7] And so they arrived in Egypt at the city of Tahpanhes, for they would not obey the Lord.

[8] Then at Tahpanhes, the Lord spoke to Jeremiah again and said:

[9] "Call together the men of Judah and, as they watch you, bury large rocks between the pavement stones at the entrance of Pharaoh's palace here in Tahpanhes, [10] and tell the men of Judah this: The Lord of Hosts, the God of Israel, says: I will surely bring Nebuchadnezzar, king of Babylon, here to Egypt, for he is my servant. I will set his throne upon these stones that I have hidden. He shall spread his royal canopy over them. [11] And when he comes he shall destroy the land of Egypt, killing all those I want killed, and capturing those I want

captured, and many shall die of plague. [12] He will set fire to the temples of the gods of Egypt and burn the idols and carry off the people as his captives. And he shall plunder the land of Egypt as a shepherd picks fleas from his cloak! And he himself shall leave unharmed. [13] And he shall break down the obelisks standing in the city of Heliopolis, and burn down the temples of the gods of Egypt."

44 THIS IS THE message God gave to Jeremiah concerning all the Jews who were living in the north of Egypt in the cities of Migdol, Tahpanhes and Memphis, and throughout southern Egypt as well:

[2,3] The Lord of Hosts, the God of Israel, says: You saw what I did to Jerusalem and to all the cities of Judah. Because of all their wickedness they lie in heaps and ashes, without a living soul. For my anger rose high against them for worshiping other gods—"gods" that neither they nor you nor any of your fathers have ever known. [4] I sent my servants, the prophets, to protest over and over again and to plead with them not to do this horrible thing I hate, [5] but they wouldn't listen and wouldn't turn back from their wicked ways; they have kept right on with their sacrifices to these "gods." [6] And so my fury and anger boiled forth and fell as fire upon the cities of Judah and into the streets of Jerusalem, and there is desolation until this day.

[7] And now the Lord, the God of Hosts, the God of Israel, asks you: Why are you destroying yourselves? For not one of you shall live—not a man, woman or child among you who has come here from Judah, not even the babies in arms. [8] For you are rousing my anger with the idols you have made and worshiped here in Egypt, burning incense to them, and causing me to destroy you completely and to make you a curse and a stench in the nostrils of all the nations of the earth. [9] Have you forgotten the sins of your fathers, and the sins of the kings and queens of Judah, and your own sins, and the sins of your wives in Judah and Jerusalem? [10] And even until this very hour there has been no apology; no one has wanted to return to me, or follow the laws I gave you and your fathers before you.

¹¹ Therefore the Lord of Hosts, the God of Israel, says: There is fury in my face and I will destroy every one of you! ¹² I will take this remnant of Judah that insisted on coming here to Egypt and I will consume them. They shall fall here in Egypt, killed by famine and sword; all shall die, from the least to the greatest. They shall be despised and loathed, cursed and hated. ¹³ I will punish them in Egypt just as I punished them in Jerusalem, by sword, famine and disease. ¹⁴ Not one of them shall escape from my wrath except those who repent of their coming and escape from the others by returning again to their own land.

¹⁵ Then all the women present and all the men who knew that their wives had burned incense to idols (it was a great crowd of all the Jews in southern Egypt) answered Jeremiah:

¹⁶ "We will not listen to your false 'Messages from God'! ¹⁷ We will do whatever we want to. We will burn incense to the 'Queen of Heaven'ᵃ and sacrifice to her just as much as we like—just as we and our fathers before us, and our kings and princes have always done in the cities of Judah and in the streets of Jerusalem; for in those days we had plenty to eat and we were well off and happy! ¹⁸ But ever since we quit burning incense to the 'Queen of Heaven' and stopped worshiping her we have been in great trouble and have been destroyed by sword and famine."

¹⁹ "And," the women added, "do you suppose that we were worshiping the 'Queen of Heaven' and pouring out our libations to her and making cakes for her with her image on them, without our husbands knowing it and helping us? Of course not!"

²⁰ Then Jeremiah said to all of them, men and women alike, who had given him that answer:

²¹ "Do you think the Lord didn't know that you and your fathers and your kings and princes and all the people were burning incense to idols in the cities of Judah and in the streets of Jerusalem? ²² It was because he could no longer bear all the evil things you were doing that he made your land desolate, an incredible ruin, cursed, without an inhabitant, as it is today. ²³ The very reason all these terrible things have befallen you is because you have burned incense and sinned against the Lord and refused to obey him."

²⁴ Then Jeremiah said to them all, including the women: "Listen to the word of the Lord, all you citizens of Judah who are here in Egypt! ²⁵ The Lord of Hosts, the God of Israel, says: Both you and your wives have said that you will never give up your devotion and sacrifices to the 'Queen of Heaven,' and you have proved it by your actions. Then go ahead and carry out your promises and vows to her! ²⁶ But listen to the word of the Lord, all you Jews who are living in the land of Egypt: I have sworn by my great name, says the Lord, that it will do you no good to seek my help and blessing any more, saying, 'O Lord our God, help us!' ²⁷ For I will watch over you, but *not* for good! I will see to it that evil befalls you, and you shall be destroyed by war and famine until all of you are dead.

²⁸ "Only those who return to Judah (it will be but a tiny remnant) shall escape my wrath, but all who refuse to go back—who insist on living in Egypt—shall find out who tells the truth, I or they! ²⁹ And this is the proof I give you that all I have threatened will happen to you, and that I will punish you here: ³⁰ I will turn Pharaoh Hophra,ᵇ king of Egypt, over to thoseᶜ who seek his life, just as I turned Zedekiah, king of Judah, over to Nebuchadnezzar, king of Babylon."

45 THIS IS THE messageᵃ Jeremiah gave to Baruch in the fourth year of the reign of King Jehoiakim (son of Josiah), after Baruch had written down all God's messages as Jeremiah was dictating them to him:

² O Baruch, the Lord God of Israel says this to you:

³ You have said, Woe is me! Don't I have troubles enough already? And now the Lord has added more! I am weary of my own sighing and I find no rest. ⁴ But tell

---

a "Queen of Heaven"; see note on chapter 7, verse 18. 568 B.C.   c Pharaoh Hophra was killed by Amasis, one of his generals who had revolted and who was then crowned in his place.   **45**a This message, in point of time, follows chapter 36.   b Hophra, or Apries, ruled Egypt from 588 to

Baruch this, The Lord says: I will destroy this nation that I built; I will wipe out what I established. ⁵ Are you seeking great things for yourself? Don't do it! For though I will bring great evil upon all these people, I will protect you wherever you go, as your reward.

46
HERE ARE THE messages given to Jeremiah concerning foreign nations.

The Egyptians

² This message was given against Egypt at the occasion of the battle of Carchemish when Pharaoh Necho, king of Egypt, and his army were defeated beside the Euphrates River by Nebuchadnezzar, king of Babylon, in the fourth year of the reign of Jehoiakim (son of Josiah), king of Judah:

³ Buckle on your armor, you Egyptians and advance to battle! ⁴ Harness the horses and prepare to mount them—don your helmets, sharpen your spears, put on your armor. ⁵ But look! The Egyptian army flees in terror; the mightiest of its soldiers run without a backward glance. Yes, terror shall surround them on every side, says the Lord. ⁶ The swift will not escape, nor the mightiest of warriors. In the north, by the river Euphrates, they have stumbled and fallen.

⁷ What is this mighty army, rising like the Nile at flood time, overflowing all the land? ⁸ It is the Egyptian army, boasting that it will cover the earth like a flood, destroying every foe. ⁹ Then come, O horses and chariots and mighty soldiers of Egypt! Come, all of you from Cush and Put and Lud who handle the shield and bend the bow! ¹⁰ For this is the day of the Lord God of Hosts, a day of vengeance upon his enemies. The sword shall devour until it is sated, yes, drunk with your blood, for the Lord God of Hosts will receive a sacrifice today in the north country beside the river Euphrates! ¹¹ Go up to Gilead for medicine, O virgin daughter of Egypt! Yet there is no cure for your wounds. Though you have used many medicines, there is no healing for you. ¹² The nations have heard of your shame. The earth is filled with your cry of despair and defeat; your mightiest soldiers will stumble against each other and fall together.

¹³ Then God gave Jeremiah this message concerning the coming of Nebuchadnezzar, king of Babylon, to attack Egypt:

¹⁴ Shout it out in Egypt; publish it in the cities of Migdol, Memphis and Tahpanhes! Mobilize for battle, for the sword of destruction shall devour all around you. ¹⁵ Why has Apis, your bull god, fled in terror? Because the Lord knocked him down before your enemies. ¹⁶ Vast multitudes fall in heaps. (Then the remnant of the Jews will say, "Come, let us return again to Judah where we were born and get away from all this slaughter here!")

¹⁷ Rename Pharaoh Hophra and call him "The Man with No Power But with Plenty of Noise!"

¹⁸ As I live, says the King, the Lord of Hosts, one is coming against Egypt who is as tall as Mount Tabor or Mount Carmel by the sea! ¹⁹ Pack up; get ready to leave for exile, you citizens of Egypt, for the city of Memphis shall be utterly destroyed, and left without a soul alive. ²⁰,²¹ Egypt is sleek as a heifer, but a gadfly sends her running—a gadfly from the north! Even her famed mercenaries have become like frightened calves. They turn and run, for it is the day of great calamity for Egypt, a time of great punishment. ²²,²³ Silent as a serpent gliding away, Egypt flees; the invading army marches in. The numberless soldiers cut down your people like woodsmen who clear a forest of its trees. ²⁴ Egypt is as helpless as a girl before these men from the north.

²⁵ The Lord of Hosts, the God of Israel, says: I will punish Amon, god of Thebes, and all the other gods of Egypt. I will punish Pharaoh too, and all who trust in him. ²⁶ I will deliver them into the hands of those who want them killed—into the hands of Nebuchadnezzar, king of Babylon, and his army. But afterwards the land shall recover from the ravages of war.

²⁷ But don't you be afraid, O my people who return to your own land, don't be dismayed; for I will save you from far away and bring your children from a distant land. Yes, Israel shall return and be at rest and nothing shall make her afraid. ²⁸ Fear not, O Jacob, my servant, says the Lord, for I am with you. I will destroy all the nations to which I have exiled you, but I will not destroy you. I will punish you, but only

enough to correct you.

The Philistines

47 THIS IS GOD'S message to Jeremiah concerning the Philistines of Gaza, before the city was captured[a] by the Egyptian army.

2 The Lord says: A flood is coming from the north to overflow the land of the Philistines; it will destroy their cities and everything in them. Strong men will scream in terror and all the land will weep. 3 Hear the clattering hoofs and rumbling wheels as the chariots go rushing by; fathers flee without a backward glance at their helpless children, 4 for the time has come when all the Philistines and their allies from Tyre and Sidon will be destroyed. For the Lord is destroying the Philistines, those colonists from Caphtor. 5 The cities of Gaza and Ashkelon will be razed to the ground and lie in ruins. O descendants of the Anakim, how you will lament and mourn!

6 O sword of the Lord, when will you be at rest again? Go back into your scabbard; rest and be still! 7 But how can it be still when the Lord has sent it on an errand? For the city of Ashkelon and those living along the sea must be destroyed.

The Moabites

48 THIS IS THE message of the Lord of Hosts, the God of Israel, against Moab:

Woe to the city of Nebo, for it shall lie in ruins. The city of Kiriathaim and its forts are overwhelmed and captured. 2,3,4 No one will ever brag of Moab any more, for there is a plot against her life. In Heshbon, plans have been completed to destroy her. "Come," they say, "we will cut her off from being a nation." In Madmen all is silent. And then the roar of battle will surge against Horonaim, for all Moab is being destroyed. Her crying will be heard as far away as Zoar. 5 Her refugees will climb the hills of Luhith, weeping bitterly, while cries of terror rise from the city below. 6 Flee for your lives; hide in the wilderness! 7 For you trusted in your wealth and skill; therefore you shall perish. Your god Chemosh, with

his priests and princes, shall be taken away to distant lands!

8 All the villages and cities, whether they be on the plateaus or in the valleys, shall be destroyed, for the Lord has said it. 9 Oh, for wings for Moab that she could fly away, for her cities shall be left without a living soul. 10 Cursed be those withholding their swords from your blood, refusing to do the work that God has given them!

11 From her earliest history Moab has lived there undisturbed from all invasions. She is like wine that has not been poured from flask to flask, and is fragrant and smooth. But now she shall have the pouring out of exile! 12 The time is coming soon, the Lord has said, when he will send troublers to spill her out from jar to jar and then shatter the jars! 13 Then at last Moab shall be ashamed of her idol Chemosh, as Israel was of her calf-idol at Bethel.

14 Do you remember that boast of yours: "We are heroes, mighty men of war"? 15 But now Moab is to be destroyed; her destroyer is on the way; her choicest youth are doomed to slaughter, says the King, the Lord of Hosts. 16 Calamity is coming fast to Moab.

17 O friends of Moab, weep for her and cry! See how the strong, the beautiful is shattered! 18 Come down from your glory and sit in the dust, O people of Dibon, for those destroying Moab shall shatter Dibon too, and tear down all her towers. 19 Those in Aroer stand anxiously beside the road to watch, and shout to those who flee from Moab, "What has happened there?"

20 And they reply, "Moab lies in ruins; weep and wail. Tell it by the banks of the Arnon, that Moab is destroyed."

21 All the cities of the tableland lie in ruins too, for God's judgment has been poured out upon them all—on Holon and Jahzah and Mepha-ath, 22 and Dibon and Nebo and Beth-diblathaim, 23 and Kiriathaim and Beth-gamul and Beth-meon, 24 and Keri-oth and Bozrah—and all the cities of the land of Moab, far and near.

25 The strength of Moab is ended—her horns are cut off; her arms are broken. 26 Let her stagger and fall like a drunkard, for she

---

a In 609 B.C., the year King Josiah died.

has rebelled against the Lord. Moab shall wallow in her vomit, scorned by all. [27] For you scorned Israel and robbed her, and were happy at her fall.

[28] O people of Moab, flee from your cities and live in the caves like doves that nest in the clefts of the rocks. [29] We have all heard of the pride of Moab, for it is very great. We know your loftiness, your arrogance and your haughty heart. [30] I know her insolence, the Lord has said, but her boasts are false—her helplessness is great. [31] Yes, I wail for Moab, my heart is broken for the men of Kir-heres.

[32] O men of Sibmah, rich in vineyards, I weep for you even more than for Jazer. For the destroyer has cut off your spreading tendrils and harvested your grapes and summer fruits. He has plucked you bare! [33] Joy and gladness are gone from fruitful Moab. The presses yield no wine; no one treads the grapes with shouts of joy. There is shouting, yes, but not the shouting of joy. [34] Instead the awful cries of terror and pain rise from all over the land—from Heshbon clear across to Elealeh and to Jahaz; from Zoar to Horonaim and to Eglath-she-lishiyah. The pastures of Nimrim are deserted now.

[35] For the Lord says: I have put a stop to Moab's worshiping false gods and burning incense to idols. [36] Sad sings my heart for Moab and Kir-heres, for all their wealth has disappeared. [37] They shave their heads and beards in anguish, and slash their hands and put on clothes of sackcloth. [38] Crying and sorrow will be in every Moabite home and on the streets; for I have smashed and shattered Moab like an old, unwanted bottle. [39] How it is broken! Hear the wails! See the shame of Moab! For she is a sign of horror and of scoffing to her neighbors now.

[40] A vulture circles ominously above the land of Moab, says the Lord. [41] Her cities are fallen; her strongholds are seized. The hearts of her mightiest warriors fail with fear like women in the pains of giving birth. [42] Moab shall no longer be a nation, for she has boasted against the Lord. [43] Fear and traps and treachery shall be your lot, O Moab, says the Lord. [44] He who flees shall

fall in a trap and he who escapes from the trap shall run into a snare. I will see to it that you do not get away, for the time of your judgment has come. [45] They flee to Heshbon, unable to go farther. But a fire comes from Heshbon—Sihon's ancestral home—and devours the land from end to end with all its rebellious people.

[46] Woe to you, O Moab; the people of the god Chemosh are destroyed, and your sons and daughters are taken away as slaves. [47] But in the latter days, says the Lord, I will reestablish Moab.

(Here the prophecy concerning Moab ends.)

The Ammonites

49 WHAT IS THIS you are doing? Why are you living in the cities of the Jews? Aren't the Jews enough to fill them up? Didn't they inherit them from me? Why then have you, who worship Milcom, taken over Gad and all its cities? [2] I will punish you for this, the Lord declares, by destroying your city of Rabbah. It shall become a desolate heap, and the neighboring towns shall be burned. Then Israel shall come and take back her land from you again. She shall dispossess those who dispossessed her, says the Lord.

[3] Cry out, O Heshbon, for Ai is destroyed! Weep, daughter of Rabbah! Put on garments of mourning; weep and wail, hiding in the hedges, for your god Milcom shall be exiled along with his princes and priests. [4] You are proud of your fertile valleys, but they will soon be ruined. O wicked daughter, you trusted in your wealth and thought no one could ever harm you. [5] But see, I will bring terror upon you, says the Lord God of Hosts. For all your neighbors shall drive you from your land and none shall help your exiles as they flee. [6] But afterward I will restore the fortunes of the Ammonites, says the Lord.

The Edomites

[7] The Lord of Hosts says: Where are all your wise men of days gone by? Is there not one left in all of Teman? [8] Flee to the remotest parts of the desert, O people of Dedan[a]; for when I punish Edom, I will

---

a Dedan was in Northern Arabia and was a flourishing caravan city at the time of Jeremiah and Ezekiel.

punish you! [9,10] Those who gather grapes leave a few for the poor, and even thieves don't take everything, but I will strip bare the land of Esau, and there will be no place to hide. Her children, her brothers, her neighbors—all will be destroyed—and she herself will perish too. [11] (But I will preserve your fatherless children who remain, and let your widows depend upon me.)

[12] The Lord says to Edom: If the innocent must suffer, how much more must you! You shall not go unpunished! You must drink this cup of judgment! [13] For I have sworn by my own name, says the Lord, that Bozrah shall become heaps of ruins, cursed and mocked; and her cities shall be eternal wastes.

[14] I have heard this message from the Lord:

He has sent a messenger to call the nations to form a coalition against Edom and destroy her. [15] I will make her weak among the nations and despised by all, says the Lord. [16] You have been fooled by your fame and your pride, living there in the mountains of Petra, in the clefts of the rocks. But though you live among the peaks with the eagles, I will bring you down, says the Lord.

[17] The fate of Edom will be horrible; all who go by will be appalled, and gasp at the sight. [18] Your cities will become as silent as Sodom and Gomorrah and their neighboring towns, says the Lord. No one will live there anymore. [19] I will send against them one who will come like a lion from the wilds of Jordan stalking the sheep in the fold. Suddenly Edom shall be destroyed, and I will appoint over the Edomites the person of my choice. For who is like me and who can call me to account? [20] What shepherd can defy me? Take note: The Lord will certainly do this to Edom and also the people of Teman—even little children will be dragged away as slaves! It will be a shocking thing to see. [21] The earth shakes with the noise of Edom's fall; the cry of the people is heard as far away as the Red Sea. [22] The one who will come will fly as swift as a vulture and will spread his wings against Bozrah. Then the courage of the mightiest warriors will disappear like that of women in labor.

Damascus

[23] The cities of Hamath and Arpad are stricken with fear, for they have heard the news of their doom. Their hearts are troubled like a wild sea in a raging storm. [24] Damascus has become feeble and all her people turn to flee. Fear, anguish and sorrow have gripped her as they do women in labor. [25] O famous city, city of joy, how you are forsaken now! [26] Your young men lie dead in the streets; your entire army shall be destroyed in one day, says the Lord of Hosts. [27] And I will start a fire at the edge of Damascus that shall burn up the palaces of Benhadad.

Kedar and Hazor

[28] This prophecy is about Kedar[b] and the kingdoms of Hazor, which are going to be destroyed by Nebuchadnezzar, king of Babylon, for the Lord will send him to destroy them. [29] Their flocks and their tents will be captured, says the Lord, with all their household goods. Their camels will be taken away, and all around will be the shouts of panic, "We are surrounded and doomed!" [30] Flee for your lives, says the Lord. Go deep into the deserts, O people of Hazor[c], for Nebuchadnezzar, king of Babylon, has plotted against you and is preparing to destroy you.

[31] "Go," said the Lord to King Nebuchadnezzar. "Attack those wealthy Bedouin tribes living alone in the desert without a care in the world, boasting that they are self-sufficient—that they need neither walls nor gates. [32] Their camels and cattle shall all be yours, and I will scatter these heathen[d] to the winds. From all directions I will bring calamity upon them."

[33] Hazor shall be a home for wild animals of the desert. No one shall ever live there again. It shall be desolate forever.

Elam

[34] God's message against Elam came to Jeremiah in the beginning of the reign of Zedekiah, king of Judah:

[35] The Lord of Hosts says: I will destroy the army of Elam, [36] and I will scatter the

---

b An Arab tribe living in the desert east of Palestine. great city north of the Sea of Galilee; but rather, a group of Arab tribes. corners of their hair."

c Not the Hazor mentioned in Joshua and Judges—a d Literally, "those who cut the

people of Elam to the four winds; they shall be exiled to countries throughout the world. [37] My fierce anger will bring great evil upon Elam, says the Lord, and I will cause her enemies to wipe her out. [38] And I will set my throne in Elam, says the Lord. I will destroy her king and princes. [39] But in the latter days I will bring the people back, says the Lord.

Babylon

50 THIS IS THE message from the Lord against Babylon and the Chaldeans, spoken by Jeremiah the prophet:

[2] Tell all the world that Babylon will be destroyed; her god Marduk will be utterly disgraced! [3] For a nation shall come down upon her from the north with such destruction that no one shall live in her again; all shall be gone—both men and animals shall flee.

[4] Then the people of Israel and Judah shall join together, weeping and seeking the Lord their God. [5] They shall ask the way to Zion and start back home again. "Come," they will say, "let us be united to the Lord with an eternal pledge that will never be broken again."

[6] My people have been lost sheep. Their shepherds led them astray and then turned them loose in the mountains. They lost their way and didn't remember how to get back to the fold. [7] All who found them devoured them and said, "We are permitted to attack them freely, for they have sinned against the Lord, the God of justice, the hope of their fathers."

[8] But now, flee from Babylon, the land of the Chaldeans; lead my people home again, [9] for see, I am raising up an army of great nations from the north and I will bring them against Babylon to attack her, and she shall be destroyed. The enemies' arrows go straight to the mark; they do not miss! [10] And Babylon shall be sacked until everyone is sated with loot, says the Lord.

[11] Though you were glad, O Chaldeans, plunderers of my people, and are fat as cows that feed in lush pastures, and neigh like stallions, [12] yet your mother shall be overwhelmed with shame, for you shall become the least of the nations—a wilderness, a dry and desert land. [13] Because of the anger of the Lord, Babylon shall become deserted wasteland, and all who pass by shall be appalled and shall mock at her for all her wounds.

[14] Yes, prepare to fight with Babylon, all you nations round about; let the archers shoot at her; spare no arrows, for she has sinned against the Lord. [15] Shout against her from every side. Look! She surrenders! Her walls have fallen. The Lord has taken vengeance. Do to her as she has done! [16] Let the farm hands all depart. Let them rush back to their own lands as the enemies advance.

[17] The Israelites are like sheep the lions chase. First the king of Assyria ate them up; then Nebuchadnezzar, the king of Babylon, crunched their bones. [18] Therefore the Lord of Hosts, the God of Israel, says: Now I will punish the king of Babylon and his land as I punished the king of Assyria. [19] And I will bring Israel home again to her own land, to feed in the fields of Carmel and Bashan and to be happy once more on Mount Ephraim and Mount Gilead. [20] In those days, says the Lord, no sin shall be found in Israel or in Judah, for I will pardon the remnant I preserve.

[21] Go up, O my warriors, against the land of Merathaim[a] and against the people of Pekod.[b] Yes, march against Babylon, the land of rebels, a land that I will judge! Annihilate them, as I have commanded you. [22] Let there be the shout of battle in the land, a shout of great destruction. [23] Babylon, the mightiest hammer in all the earth, lies broken and shattered. Babylon is desolate among the nations! [24] O Babylon, I have set a trap for you and you are caught, for you have fought against the Lord.

[25] The Lord has opened his armory and brought out weapons to explode his wrath upon his enemies. The terror that befalls Babylon will be the work of the Lord, the God of Hosts. [26] Yes, come against her from distant lands; break open her granaries; knock down her walls and houses into heaps of ruins and utterly destroy her; let nothing be left. [27] Not even her cattle—woe

---

a In southern Babylonia.   b In eastern Babylonia.

to them, too! Kill them all! For the time has come for Babylon to be devastated.

²⁸ But my people will flee; they will escape back to their own country to tell how the Lord their God has broken forth in fury upon those who destroyed his Temple.

²⁹ Send out a call for archers to come to Babylon; surround the city so that none can escape. Do to her as she has done to others, for she has haughtily defied the Lord, the Holy One of Israel. ³⁰ Her young men will fall in the streets and die; her warriors will all be killed. ³¹ For see, I am against you, O people so proud; and now your day of reckoning has come. ³² Land of pride, you will stumble and fall and no one will raise you up, for the Lord will light a fire in the cities of Babylon that will burn everything around them.

³³ The Lord of Hosts says: The people of Israel and Judah have been wronged. Their captors hold them and refuse to let them go. ³⁴ But their Redeemer is strong. His name is the Lord of Hosts. He will plead for them and see that they are freed to live again in quietness in Israel.

As for the people of Babylon—there is no rest for them! ³⁵ The sword of destruction shall smite the Chaldeans, says the Lord. It shall smite the people of Babylon—her princes and wise men too. ³⁶ All her wise counselors shall become fools! Panic shall seize her mightiest warriors! ³⁷ War shall devour her horses and chariots, and her allies from other lands shall become as weak as women. Her treasures shall all be robbed; ³⁸ even her water supply will fail. And why? Because the whole land is full of images, and the people are madly in love with their idols.

³⁹ Therefore this city of Babylon shall become inhabited by ostriches and jackals; it shall be a home for the wild animals of the desert. Never again shall it be lived in by human beings; it shall lie desolate forever. ⁴⁰ The Lord declares that he will destroy Babylon just as he destroyed Sodom and Gomorrah and their neighboring towns. No one has lived in them since, and no one will live again in Babylon.

⁴¹ See them coming! A great army from the north! It is accompanied by many kings called by God from many lands. ⁴² They are fully armed for slaughter; they are cruel and show no mercy; their battle cry roars like the surf against the shoreline. O Babylon, they ride against you fully ready for the battle.

⁴³ When the king of Babylon received the dispatch, his hands fell helpless at his sides; pangs of terror gripped him like the pangs of a woman in labor.

⁴⁴ *I will send against them an invader who will come upon them suddenly, like a lion from the jungles of Jordan that leaps upon the grazing sheep. I will put her defenders to flight and appoint over them whomsoever I please. For who is like me? What ruler can oppose my will? Who can call me to account?* ⁴⁵ *Listen to the plan of the Lord against Babylon, the land of the Chaldeans. For even little children shall be dragged away as slaves; oh, the horror; oh, the terror.* ⁴⁶ The whole earth shall shake at Babylon's fall, and her cry of despair shall be heard around the world.

51 THE LORD SAYS: I will stir up a destroyer against Babylon, against that whole land of the Chaldeans, and destroy it. ² Winnowers shall come and winnow her and blow her away; they shall come from every side to rise against her in her day of trouble. ³ The arrows of the enemy shall strike down the bowmen of Babylon and pierce her warriors in their coats of mail. No one shall be spared; both young and old alike shall be destroyed. ⁴ They shall fall down slain in the land of the Chaldeans, slashed to death in her streets. ⁵ For the Lord of Hosts has not forsaken Israel and Judah. He is still their God, but the land of the Chaldeans[a] is filled with sin against the Holy One of Israel.

⁶ Flee from Babylon! Save yourselves! Don't get trapped! If you stay, you will be destroyed when God takes his vengeance on all of Babylon's sins. ⁷ Babylon has been as a golden cup in the Lord's hands, a cup from which he made the whole earth drink and go mad. ⁸ But now, suddenly Babylon too has fallen. Weep for her; give her medi-

---

a Implied.

662

cine; perhaps she can yet be healed. ⁹ We would help her if we could, but nothing can save her now. Let her go. Abandon her and return to your own land, for God is judging her from heaven. ¹⁰ The Lord has vindicated us. Come, let us declare in Jerusalem all the Lord our God has done.

¹¹ Sharpen the arrows! Lift up the shields! For the Lord has stirred up the spirit of the kings of the Medes to march on Babylon and destroy her. This is his vengeance on those who wronged his people and desecrated his Temple. ¹² Prepare your defenses, Babylon! Set many watchmen on your walls; send out an ambush, for the Lord will do all he has said he would concerning Babylon. ¹³ O wealthy port, great center of commerce, your end has come; the thread of your life is cut. ¹⁴ The Lord of Hosts has taken this vow, and sworn to it in his own name: Your cities shall be filled with enemies, like fields filled with locusts in a plague, and they shall lift to the skies their mighty shouts of victory.

¹⁵ God made the earth by his power and wisdom. He stretched out the heavens by his understanding. ¹⁶ When he speaks there is thunder in the heavens and he causes the vapors to rise around the world; he brings the lightning with the rain and the winds from his treasuries. ¹⁷ Compared to him, all men are stupid beasts. They have no wisdom—none at all! The silversmith is dulled by the images he makes, for in making them he lies; for he calls them gods, when there is not a breath of life in them at all! ¹⁸ Idols are nothing! They are lies! And the time is coming when God will come and see, and shall destroy them all. ¹⁹ But the God of Israel is no idol! For he made everything there is, and Israel is his nation; the Lord of Hosts is his name.

²⁰ Cyrusᵇ is God's battleaxe and sword. I will use you, says the Lord, to break nations in pieces and to destroy many kingdoms. ²¹ With you I will crush armies, destroying the horse and his rider, the chariot and the charioteer— ²² yes, and the civilians too, both old and young, young men and maidens, ²³ shepherds and flocks,

farmers and oxen, captains and rulers; ²⁴ before your eyes I will repay Babylon and all the Chaldeans for all the evil they have done to my people, says the Lord.

²⁵ For see, I am against you, O mighty mountain, Babylon, destroyer of the earth! I will lift my hand against you and roll you down from your heights and leave you, a burnt-out mountain. ²⁶ You shall be desolate foreverᶜ; even your stones shall never be used for building again. You shall be completely wiped out.

²⁷ Signal many nations to mobilize for war on Babylon. Sound the battle cry; bring out the armies of Ararat, Minni, and Ashkenaz. Appoint a leader; bring a multitude of horses! ²⁸ Bring against her the armies of the kings of the Medes and their generals, and the armies of all the countries they rule.

²⁹ Babylon trembles and writhes in pain, for all that the Lord has planned against her stands unchanged. Babylon will be left desolate without a living soul. ³⁰ Her mightiest soldiers no longer fight; they stay in their barracks. Their courage is gone; they have become as women. The invaders have burned the houses and broken down the city gates. ³¹ Messengers from every side come running to the king to tell him all is lost! ³² All the escape routes are blocked; the fortifications are burning and the army is in panic.

³³ For the Lord of Hosts, the God of Israel, says: Babylon is like the wheat upon a threshing floor; in just a little while the flailing will begin.

³⁴,³⁵ The Jews in Babylon say, "Nebuchadnezzar, king of Babylon, has eaten and crushed us and emptied out our strength; he has swallowed us like a great monster and filled his belly with our riches and cast us out of our own country. May Babylon be repaid for all she did to us! May she be paid in full for all our blood she spilled!"

³⁶ And the Lord replies: I will be your lawyer; I will plead your case; I will avenge you. I will dry up her river, her water supply, ³⁷ and Babylon shall become a heap of ruins, haunted by jackals, a land horrible to see, incredible, without a living soul. ³⁸ In

---

b Literally, "You are . . ." Cyrus was used of God to conquer Babylon. See also, Isaiah 44:28; 45:1.
c This complete destruction of the city of Babylon was accomplished by later Persian kings. Jeremiah here sees the long-range picture of the city's history, and does not confine himself to Cyrus.

their drunken feasts, the men of Babylon roar like lions. [39] And while they lie inflamed with all their wine, I will prepare a different kind of feast for them, and make them drink until they fall unconscious to the floor, to sleep forever, never to waken again, says the Lord. [40] I will bring them like lambs to the slaughter, like rams and goats.

[41] How Babylon is fallen—great Babylon, lauded by all the earth! The world can scarcely believe its eyes at Babylon's fall! [42] The sea has risen upon Babylon; she is covered by its waves. [43] Her cities lie in ruins—she is a dry wilderness where no one lives nor even travelers pass by. [44] And I will punish Bel, the god of Babylon, and pull from his mouth what he has taken. The nations shall no longer come and worship him; the wall of Babylon has fallen.

[45] O my people, flee from Babylon; save yourselves from the fierce anger of the Lord. [46] But don't panic when you hear the first rumor of approaching forces. For rumors will keep coming year by year. Then there will be a time of civil war as the governors of Babylon fight against each other. [47] For the time is surely coming when I will punish this great city and all her idols; her dead shall lie in the streets. [48] Heaven and earth shall rejoice, for out of the north shall come destroying armies against Babylon, says the Lord. [49] Just as Babylon killed the people of Israel, so must she be killed. [50] Go, you who escaped the sword! Don't stand and watch—flee while you can! Remember the Lord and return to Jerusalem far away!

[51] *"We are ashamed because the Temple of the Lord has been defiled by foreigners from Babylon."*

[52] Yes, says the Lord. But the time is coming for the destruction of the idols of Babylon. All through the land will be heard the groans of the wounded. [53] Though Babylon be as powerful as heaven, though she increase her strength immeasurably, she shall die, says the Lord.

[54] Listen! Hear the cry of great destruction out of Babylon, the land the Chaldeans rule! [55] For the Lord is destroying Babylon; her mighty voice is stilled as the waves roar in upon her. [56] Destroying armies come and slay her mighty men; all her weapons break in her hands, for the Lord God gives just punishment and is giving Babylon all her due. [57] I will make drunk her princes, wise men, rulers, captains, warriors. They shall sleep and not wake up again! So says the King, the Lord of Hosts. [58] For the wide walls of Babylon shall be leveled to the ground and her high gates shall be burned; the builders from many lands have worked in vain—their work shall be destroyed by fire!

[59] During the fourth year of Zedekiah's reign, this message came to Jeremiah to give to Seraiah (son of Neriah, son of Mahseiah), concerning Seraiah's capture[d] and exile to Babylon along with Zedekiah, king of Judah. (Seraiah was quartermaster of Zedekiah's army.) [60] Jeremiah wrote on a scroll all the terrible things God had scheduled against Babylon—all the words written above— [61,62] and gave the scroll to Seraiah and said to him, "When you get to Babylon, read what I have written and say, 'Lord, you have said that you will destroy Babylon so that not a living creature will remain, and it will be abandoned forever.' [63] Then, when you have finished reading the scroll, tie a rock to it and throw it into the Euphrates River, [64] and say, 'So shall Babylon sink, never more to rise, because of the evil I am bringing upon her.' "

(This ends Jeremiah's messages.)

(Events told about in chapter 39.)

52 ZEDEKIAH WAS TWENTY-ONE years old when he became king, and he reigned eleven years in Jerusalem. His mother's name was Hamutal (daughter of Jeremiah of Libnah). [2] But he was a wicked king, just as Jehoiakim had been. [3] Things became so bad at last that the Lord, in his anger, saw to it that Zedekiah rebelled against the king of Babylon until he and the people of Israel were ejected from the Lord's presence in Jerusalem and Judah, and were taken away as captives to Babylon.

[4] In the ninth year of Zedekiah's reign, on the tenth day of the tenth month, Nebuchadnezzar, king of Babylon, came with all

---

d This event occurred six years after this prophecy.

his army against Jerusalem and built forts around it, [5] and laid siege to the city for two years. [6] Then finally, on the ninth day of the fourth month, when the famine in the city was very serious, with the last of the food entirely gone, [7] the people in the city tore a hole in the city wall and all the soldiers fled from the city during the night, going out by the gate between the two walls near the king's gardens (for the city was surrounded by the Chaldeans), and made a dash for it across the fields, toward Arabah.

[8] But the Chaldean soldiers chased them and caught King Zedekiah in some fields near Jericho—for all his army was scattered from him. [9] They brought him to the king of Babylon who was staying in the city of Riblah in the kingdom of Hamath, and there judgment was passed upon him. [10] He made Zedekiah watch while his sons and all the princes of Judah were killed before his eyes, [11] and then his eyes were gouged out and he was taken in chains to Babylon and put in prison for the rest of his life.

[12] On the tenth day of the fifth month during the nineteenth year[a] of the reign of Nebuchadnezzar, king of Babylon, Nebuzaradan, captain of the guard, arrived in Jerusalem, [13] and burned the Temple and the palace and all the larger homes, [14] and set the Chaldean army to work tearing down the walls of the city. [15] Then he took to Babylon, as captives, some of the poorest of the people—along with those who survived the city's destruction, and those who had deserted Zedekiah and had come over to the Babylonian army, and the tradesmen who were left. [16] But he left some of the poorest people to care for the crops as vinedressers and plowmen.

[17] The Babylonians dismantled the two large bronze pillars that stood at the entrance of the Temple, and the bronze laver and bronze bulls on which it stood, and carted them off to Babylon. [18] And he took along all the bronze pots and kettles, and ash shovels used at the altar, and the snuffers, spoons, bowls, and all the other items used in the Temple. [19] He also took the firepans and the solid gold and silver candlesticks and cups and bowls.

[20] The weight of the two enormous pillars and the laver and twelve bulls was tremendous. They had no way of estimating it. (They had been made in the days of King Solomon.) [21] For the pillars were each twenty-seven feet high and eighteen feet in circumference, hollow, with three-inch walls. [22] The top 7½ feet of each column had bronze carvings, a network of bronze pomegranates. [23] There were ninety-six pomegranates on the sides, and on the network round about there were a hundred more.

[24,25] The captain of the guard took along with him, as his prisoners, Seraiah the chief priest, and Zephaniah his assistant, the three chief Temple guards, one of the commanding officers of the army, seven of the king's special counselors discovered in the city, and the secretary of the general-in-chief of the Jewish army (who was in charge of recruitment) and sixty other men of importance found hiding. [26] He took them to the king of Babylon at Riblah, [27] where the king killed them all.

So it was that Judah's exile was accomplished. [28] The number of captives taken to Babylon in the seventh year of Nebuchadnezzar's reign was 3,023. [29] Then, eleven years later, he took 832 more; [30] five years after that he sent Nebuzaradan, his captain of the guard, and took 745—a total of 4,600 captives in all.

[31] On February 25, of the 37th year of the imprisonment in Babylon of Jehoiachin, king of Judah, Evil-merodach, who became king of Babylon that year, was kind to King Jehoiachin and brought him out of prison, [32] and spoke pleasantly to him and gave him preference over all the other kings in Babylon, [33] and gave him new clothes and fed him from the king's kitchen as long as he lived. [34] And he was given a regular allowance to cover his daily needs until the day of his death.

---

a Late in July, 587 B.C.

LAMENTATIONS

1 JERUSALEM'S STREETS, ONCE thronged with people, are silent now. Like a widow broken with grief, she sits alone in her mourning. She, once queen of nations, is now a slave.

² She sobs through the night; tears run down her cheeks. Among all her lovers,ª there is none to help her. All her friends are now her enemies.

³ Why is Judah led away, a slave? Because of all the wrong she did to others, making them her slaves. Now she sits in exile far away. There is no rest, for those she persecuted have turned and conquered her.

⁴ The roads to Zion mourn, no longer filled with joyous throngs who come to celebrate the Temple feasts; the city gates are silent, her priests groan, her virgins have been dragged away. Bitterly she weeps.

⁵ Her enemies prosper, for the Lord has punished Jerusalem for all her many sins; her young children are captured and taken far away as slaves.

⁶ All her beauty and her majesty are gone; her princes are like starving deer that search for pasture—helpless game too weak to keep on running from their foes.

⁷ And now in the midst of all Jerusalem's sadness she remembers happy bygone days. She thinks of all the precious joys she had before her mocking enemy struck her down—and there was no one to give her aid.

⁸ For Jerusalem sinned so horribly; therefore she is tossed away like dirty rags. All who honored her despise her now, for they have seen her stripped naked and humiliated. She groans and hides her face.

⁹ She indulged herself in immorality, and refused to face the fact that punishment was sure to come. Now she lies in the gutter with no one left to lift her out. "O Lord," she cries, "see my plight. The enemy has triumphed."

¹⁰ Her enemies have plundered her completely, taking everything precious she owns. She has seen foreign nations violate her sacred Temple—foreigners you had forbidden even to enter.

¹¹ Her people groan and cry for bread; they have sold all they have for food to give a little strength. "Look, O Lord," she prays, "and see how I'm despised."

¹² Is it nothing to you, all you who pass by? Look and see if there is any sorrow like my sorrow, because of all the Lord has done to me in the day of his fierce wrath.

¹³ He has sent fire from heaven that burns within my bones; he has placed a pitfall in my path and turned me back. He has left me sick and desolate the whole day through.

¹⁴ He wove my sins into ropes to hitch me to a yoke of slavery. He sapped my strength and gave me to my enemies; I am helpless in their hands.

¹⁵ The Lord has trampled all my mighty men. A great army has come at his command to crush the noblest youth. The Lord has trampled his beloved city as grapes in a winepress.

¹⁶ For all these things I weep; tears flow down my cheeks. My Comforter is far away—he who alone could help me. My children have no future; we are a conquered land.

¹⁷ Jerusalem pleads for help but no one comforts her. For the Lord has spoken: "Let her neighbors be her foes! Let her be thrown out like filthy rags!"

¹⁸ And the Lord is right, for we rebelled. And yet, O people everywhere, behold and see my anguish and despair, for my sons and daughters are taken far away as slaves to distant lands.

¹⁹ I begged my alliesᵇ for their help. False hope—they could not help at all. Nor could my priests and elders—they were starving in the streets while searching through the garbage dumps for bread.

²⁰ *See, O Lord, my anguish;* my heart is broken and my soul despairs, for I have terribly rebelled. In the streets the sword awaits me; at home, disease and death.

²¹ *Hear my groans!* And there is no one

---

a The reference is to Egypt and Israel's other former allies. to Egypt.

b Literally, "lovers." The reference is probably

anywhere to help. All my enemies have heard my troubles and they are glad to see what you have done. And yet, O Lord, the time will surely come—for you have promised it—when you will do to them as you have done to me.

²² Look also on their sins, O Lord, and punish them as you have punished me, for my sighs are many and my heart is faint.

2 A CLOUD OF anger from the Lord has overcast Jerusalem; the fairest city of Israel lies in the dust of the earth, cast from the heights of heaven at his command. In his day of awesome fury he has shown no mercy even to his Temple.[a]

² The Lord without mercy has destroyed every home in Israel. In his wrath he has broken every fortress, every wall. He has brought the kingdom to dust, with all its rulers.

³ All the strength of Israel vanishes beneath his wrath. He has withdrawn his protection as the enemy attacks. God burns across the land of Israel like a raging fire.

⁴ He bends his bow against his people as though he were an enemy. His strength is used against them to kill their finest youth. His fury is poured out like fire upon them.

⁵ Yes, the Lord has vanquished Israel like an enemy. He has destroyed her forts and palaces. Sorrows and tears are his portion for Jerusalem.

⁶ He has violently broken down his Temple as though it were a booth of leaves and branches in a garden! No longer can the people celebrate their holy feasts and Sabbaths. Kings and priests together fall before his wrath.

⁷ The Lord has rejected his own altar, for he despises the false "worship" of his people; he has given their palaces to their enemies, who carouse in the Temple as Israel used to do on days of holy feasts!

⁸ The Lord determined to destroy Jerusalem. He laid out an unalterable line of destruction. Therefore the ramparts and walls fell down before him.

⁹ Jerusalem's gates are useless. All their locks and bars are broken, for he has crushed them. Her kings and princes are enslaved in far-off lands, without a temple, without a divine law to govern them, or prophetic vision to guide them.

¹⁰ The elders of Jerusalem sit upon the ground in silence, clothed in sackcloth; they throw dust upon their heads in sorrow and despair. The virgins of Jerusalem hang their heads in shame.

¹¹ I have cried until the tears no longer come; my heart is broken, my spirit poured out, as I see what has happened to my people; little children and tiny babies are fainting and dying in the streets.

¹² "Mamma, Mamma, we want food," they cry, and then collapse upon their mothers' shrunken breasts. Their lives ebb away like those wounded in battle.

¹³ In all the world has there ever been such sorrow? O Jerusalem, what can I compare your anguish to? How can I comfort you? For your wound is deep as the sea. Who can heal you?

¹⁴ Your "prophets" have said so many foolish things, false to the core. They have not tried to hold you back from slavery by pointing out your sins. They lied and said that all was well.

¹⁵ All who pass by scoff and shake their heads and say, "Is this the city called 'Most Beautiful in All the World,' and 'Joy of All the Earth'?"

¹⁶ All your enemies deride you. They hiss and grind their teeth and say, "We have destroyed her at last! Long have we waited for this hour and it is finally here! With our own eyes we've seen her fall."

¹⁷ But it is the Lord who did it, just as he had warned. He has fulfilled the promises of doom he made so long ago. He has destroyed Jerusalem without mercy and caused her enemies to rejoice over her and boast of their power.

¹⁸ Then the people wept before the Lord. O walls of Jerusalem, let tears fall down upon you like a river; give yourselves no rest from weeping day or night.

¹⁹ Rise in the night and cry to your God. Pour out your hearts like water to the Lord; lift up your hands to him; plead for your children as they faint with hunger in the streets.

---

a Literally, "footstool."

²⁰ *O Lord, think! These are your own people to whom you are doing this.* Shall mothers eat their little children, those they bounced upon their knees? Shall priests and prophets die within the Temple of the Lord? ²¹ See them lying in the streets—old and young, boys and girls, killed by the enemies' swords. You have killed them, Lord, in your anger; you have killed them without mercy.

²² You have deliberately called for this destruction; in the day of your anger none escaped or remained. All my little children lie dead upon the streets before the enemy.

3 I AM THE man who has seen the afflictions that come from the rod of God's wrath. ² He has brought me into deepest darkness, shutting out all light. ³ He has turned against me. Day and night his hand is heavy on me. ⁴ He has made me old and has broken my bones.

⁵ He has built forts against me and surrounded me with anguish and distress. ⁶ He buried me in dark places, like those long dead. ⁷ He has walled me in; I cannot escape; he has fastened me with heavy chains. ⁸ And though I cry and shout, he will not hear my prayers! ⁹ He has shut me into a place of high, smooth walls[a]; he has filled my path with detours.

¹⁰ He lurks like a bear, like a lion, waiting to attack me. ¹¹ He has dragged me into the underbrush and torn me with his claws, and left me bleeding and desolate.

¹² He has bent his bow and aimed it squarely at me, ¹³ and sent his arrows deep within my heart.

¹⁴ My own people laugh at me; all day long they sing their ribald songs.

¹⁵ He has filled me with bitterness, and given me a cup of deepest sorrows to drink. ¹⁶ He has made me eat gravel and broken my teeth; he has rolled me in ashes and dirt. ¹⁷ O Lord, all peace and all prosperity have long since gone, for you have taken them away. I have forgotten what enjoyment is. ¹⁸ All hope is gone; my strength has turned to water, for the Lord has left me. ¹⁹ Oh, remember the bitterness and suffering you have dealt to me! ²⁰ For I can never forget these awful years; always my soul will live in utter shame.

²¹ *Yet there is one ray of hope:* ²² *his compassion never ends.* It is only the Lord's mercies that have kept us from complete destruction. ²³ Great is his faithfulness; his lovingkindness begins afresh each day. ²⁴ My soul claims the Lord as my inheritance; therefore I will hope in him. ²⁵ The Lord is wonderfully good to those who wait for him, to those who seek for him. ²⁶ It is good both to hope and wait quietly for the salvation of the Lord.

²⁷ It is good for a young man to be under discipline, ²⁸ for it causes him to sit apart in silence beneath the Lord's demands, ²⁹ to lie face downward in the dust; then at last there is hope for him. ³⁰ Let him turn the other cheek to those who strike him, and accept their awful insults, ³¹ for the Lord will not abandon him forever. ³² Although God gives him grief, yet he will show compassion too, according to the greatness of his lovingkindness. ³³ For he does not enjoy afflicting men and causing sorrow.

³⁴,³⁵,³⁶ But you have trampled and crushed beneath your feet the lowly of the world, and deprived men of their God-given rights, and refused them justice. No wonder the Lord has had to deal with you! ³⁷ For who can act against you without the Lord's permission? ³⁸ It is the Lord who helps one and harms another.

³⁹ Why then should we, mere humans as we are, murmur and complain when punished for our sins? ⁴⁰ Let us examine ourselves instead, and repent and turn again to the Lord. ⁴¹ Let us lift our hearts and hands to him in heaven, ⁴² for we have sinned; we have rebelled against the Lord, and he has not forgotten it.

⁴³ You have engulfed us by your anger, Lord, and slain us without mercy. ⁴⁴ You have veiled yourself as with a cloud so that our prayers do not reach through. ⁴⁵ You have made us as refuse and garbage among the nations. ⁴⁶ All our enemies have spoken out against us. ⁴⁷ We are filled with fear, for we are trapped and desolate, destroyed.

⁴⁸,⁴⁹ My eyes flow day and night with never-ending streams of tears because of the

---

a Literally, "He has walled up my ways with hewn stone."

destruction of my people. ⁵⁰ Oh, that the Lord might look down from heaven and respond to my cry! ⁵¹ My heart is breaking over what is happening to the young girls of Jerusalem.

⁵² My enemies, whom I have never harmed, chased me as though I were a bird. ⁵³ They threw me in a well and capped it with a rock. ⁵⁴ The water flowed above my head. I thought, This is the end! ⁵⁵ But I called upon your name, O Lord, from deep within the well, ⁵⁶ and you heard me! You listened to my pleading; you heard my weeping! ⁵⁷ Yes, you came at my despairing cry and told me not to fear.

⁵⁸ O Lord, you are my lawyer! Plead my case! For you have redeemed my life. ⁵⁹ You have seen the wrong they did to me; be my Judge, to prove me right. ⁶⁰ You have seen the plots my foes have laid against me. ⁶¹ You have heard the vile names they have called me, ⁶² and all they say about me and their whispered plans. ⁶³ See how they laugh and sing with glee, preparing my doom.

⁶⁴ O Lord, repay them well for all the evil they have done. ⁶⁵ Harden their hearts and curse them, Lord. ⁶⁶ Go after them in fierce pursuit and wipe them off the earth, beneath the heavens of the Lord.

4 HOW THE FINEST gold has lost its luster! For the inlaidᵃ Temple walls are scattered in the streets! ² The cream of our youth—the finest of the gold—are treated as earthenware pots. ³,⁴ Even the jackals feed their young, but not my people, Israel. They are like cruel desert ostriches, heedless of their babies' cries. The children's tongues stick to the roofs of their mouths for thirst, for there is not a drop of water left. Babies cry for bread but no one can give them any. ⁵ Those who used to eat fastidiously are begging in the streets for anything at all. Those brought up in palaces now scratch in garbage pits for food. ⁶ For the sin of my people is greater than that of Sodom, where utter disaster struck in a moment without the hand of man.

⁷ Our princes were lean and tanned,ᵇ the finest specimens of men; ⁸ but now their faces are as black as soot. No one can recognize them. Their skin sticks to their bones; it is dry and hard and withered. ⁹ Those killed by the sword are far better off than those who die of slow starvation. ¹⁰ Tenderhearted women have cooked and eaten their own children; thus they survived the siege.

¹¹ But now at last the anger of the Lord is satisfied; his fiercest anger has been poured out. He started a fire in Jerusalem that burned it down to its foundations. ¹² Not a king in all the earth—no one in all the world—would have believed an enemy could enter through Jerusalem's gates! ¹³ Yet God permitted it because of the sins of her prophets and priests, who defiled the city by shedding innocent blood. ¹⁴ Now these same men are blindly staggering through the streets, covered with blood, defiling everything they touch.

¹⁵ "Get away!" the people shout at them. "You are defiled!" They flee to distant lands and wander there among the foreigners; but none will let them stay. ¹⁶ The Lord himself has dealt with them; he no longer helps them, for they persecuted the priests and elders who stayed true to God.

¹⁷ We look for our alliesᶜ to come and save us, but we look in vain. The nation we expected most to help us makes no move at all.

¹⁸ We can't go into the streets without danger to our lives. Our end is near—our days are numbered. We are doomed. ¹⁹ Our enemies are swifter than the eagles; if we flee to the mountains they find us. If we hide in the wilderness, they are waiting for us there. ²⁰ Our king—the life of our life, the Lord's anointed—was captured in their snares. Yes, even our mighty king, about whom we had boasted that under his protection we could hold our own against any nation on earth!

²¹ Do you rejoice, O people of Edom, in the land of Uz? But you too will feel the awful anger of the Lord. ²² Israel's exile for her sins will end at last, but Edom's never.

5 O LORD, REMEMBER all that has befallen us; see what sorrows we must

---

a Implied.   b Literally, "were purer than snow, whiter than milk, more ruddy than rubies, polished like sapphires."   c The reference is probably to Egypt.

bear! ² Our homes, our nation, now are filled with foreigners. ³ We are orphans—our fathers dead, our mothers widowed. ⁴ We must even pay for water to drink; our fuel is sold to us at the highest of prices. ⁵ We bow our necks beneath the victors' feet; unending work is now our lot. ⁶ We beg for bread from Egypt, and Assyria too.

⁷ Our fathers sinned but died before the hand of judgment fell. We have borne the blow that they deserved!

⁸ Our former servants have become our masters; there is no one left to save us. ⁹ We went into the wilderness to hunt for food, risking death from enemies. ¹⁰ Our skin was black from famine. ¹¹ They rape the women of Jerusalem and the girls in Judah's cities. ¹² Our princes are hanged by their thumbs. Even aged men are treated with contempt. ¹³ They take away the young men to grind their grain and the little children stagger beneath their heavy loads.

¹⁴ The old men sit no longer in the city gates; the young no longer dance and sing. ¹⁵ The joy of our hearts has ended; our dance has turned to death.ᵃ ¹⁶ Our glory is gone. The crown is fallen from our head. Woe upon us for our sins. ¹⁷ Our hearts are faint and weary; our eyes grow dim. ¹⁸ Jerusalem and the Temple of the Lord are desolate, deserted by all but wild animals lurking in the ruins.

¹⁹ O Lord, forever you remain the same! Your throne continues from generation to generation. ²⁰ Why do you forget us forever? Why do you forsake us for so long? ²¹ Turn us around and bring us back to you again! That is our only hope! Give us back the joys we used to have! ²² *Or have you utterly rejected us? Are you angry with us still?*

Dry Bones and Flying Saucers?

---

a Literally, "to mourning."

Ezekiel saw dem dry bones ..." a bouncy spiritual for school chorales to perform—but when Ezekiel first saw the valley of skeleton pieces (chapter 37) he probably froze in his tracks. When the bones began to rattle and reassemble themselves into living people, the prophet may well have shut his eyes in fright.

But then, God seemed to blow Ezekiel's mind regularly during the exile with weird symbols and strange phenomena—wheels soaring across the sky (chapters one and ten) which many readers have thought to be flying saucers, scrolls to be eaten (chapters two and three), and an elaborate new society (chapters 40-48) which has puzzled nearly everyone who's read it. The surrealism of Ezekiel is frankly a puzzle in places—but since it originates with God, it's worth figuring out.

EZEKIEL

1 *Ezekiel was a priest (the son of Buzi)
who lived with the Jewish exiles beside
the Chebar Canal in Babylon.*

One day late in June, when I was thirty
years old,[a] the heavens were suddenly
opened to me and I saw visions from God.
⁴ I saw, in this vision, a great storm coming
toward me from the north, driving before
it a huge cloud glowing with fire, with a
mass of fire inside that flashed continually;
and in the fire there was something that
shone like polished brass.

⁵ Then from the center of the cloud, four
strange forms appeared that looked like
men, ⁶ except that each had four faces and
two pairs of wings! ⁷ Their legs were like
those of men, but their feet were cloven like
calves' feet, and shone like burnished brass.
⁸ And beneath each of their wings I could
see human hands.

⁹ The four living beings were joined wing
to wing, and they flew straight forward
without turning. ¹⁰ Each had the face of a
man [in front[b]], with a lion's face on the
right side [of his head[b]], and the face of an
ox on his left side, and the face of an eagle
at the back of his head! ¹¹ Each had two
pairs of wings spreading out from the middle of his back. One pair stretched out to
attach to the wings of the living beings on
each side, and the other pair covered his
body. ¹² Wherever their spirit[c] went they
went, going straight forward without turning.

¹³ Going up and down among them were
other forms that glowed like bright coals of
fire or brilliant torches, and it was from
these the lightning flashed. ¹⁴ The living beings darted to and fro, swift as lightning.

¹⁵ As I stared at all of this, I saw four
wheels on the ground beneath them, one
wheel belonging to each. ¹⁶ The wheels
looked as if they were made of polished amber and each wheel was constructed with a
second wheel crosswise inside.[d] ¹⁷ They
could go in any of the four directions without having to face around. ¹⁸ The four
wheels had rims and spokes, and the rims

1a Literally, "in the thirtieth year."   b Implied.   c Literally, "the spirit."
d Literally, "a wheel within a wheel," perhaps as in a gyroscope.

672

were filled with eyes around their edges.

19,20,21 When the four living beings flew forward, the wheels moved forward with them. When they flew upwards, the wheels went up too. When the living beings stopped, the wheels stopped. For the spirit of the four living beings was in the wheels; so wherever their spirit went, the wheels and the living beings went there too.

22 The sky spreading out above them looked as though it were made of crystal; it was inexpressibly beautiful.

23 Each being's wings stretched straight out to touch the others' wings, and each had two wings covering his body. 24 And as they flew, their wings roared like waves against the shore, or like the voice of God, or like the shouting of a mighty army. When they stopped they let down their wings. 25 And every time they stopped, there came a voice from the crystal sky[c] above them.

26 For high in the sky above them was what looked like a throne made of beautiful blue sapphire stones, and upon it sat someone who appeared to be a Man.

27,28 From his waist up, he seemed to be all glowing bronze, dazzling like fire; and from his waist down he seemed to be entirely flame, and there was a glowing halo like a rainbow all around him. That was the way the glory of the Lord appeared to me. And when I saw it, I fell face downward on the ground, and heard the voice of someone speaking to me:

2 AND HE SAID to me: "Stand up, son of dust,[a] and I will talk to you."

2 And the Spirit entered into me as he spoke, and set me on my feet.

3 "Son of dust," he said, "I am sending you to the nation of Israel, to a nation rebelling against me. They and their fathers have kept on sinning against me until this very hour. 4 For they are a hardhearted, stiffnecked people. But I am sending you to give them my messages—the messages of the Lord God. 5 And whether they listen or not (for remember, they are rebels), they will at least know they have had a prophet among

them.

6 "Son of dust, don't be afraid of them; don't be frightened even though their threats are sharp and barbed and sting like scorpions. Don't be dismayed by their dark scowls. For remember, they are rebels! 7 You must give them my messages whether they listen or not (but they won't,[b] for they are utter rebels). 8 Listen, son of dust, to what I say to you. Don't you be a rebel too! Open your mouth and eat what I give you."

9,10 Then I looked and saw a hand holding out to me a scroll, with writing on both sides. He unrolled it, and I saw that it was full of warnings and sorrows and pronouncements of doom.

3 AND HE SAID to me: "Son of dust, eat what I am giving you—eat this scroll! Then go and give its message to the people of Israel."

2 So I took the scroll.

3 "Eat it all," he said. And when I ate it, it tasted sweet as honey.

4 Then he said: "Son of dust, I am sending you to the people of Israel with my messages. 5 I am not sending you to some far-off foreign land where you can't understand the language— 6 no, not to tribes with strange, difficult tongues. (If I did, they would listen!) 7 I am sending you to the people of Israel, and they won't listen to you any more than they listened to me! For the whole lot of them are hard, impudent and stubborn. 8 But see, I have made you hard and stubborn too—as tough as they are. 9 I have made your forehead as hard as rock. So don't be afraid of them, or fear their sullen, angry looks, even though they are such rebels."

10 Then he added: "Son of dust, let all my words sink deep into your own heart first; listen to them carefully for yourself. 11 Then, afterward, go to your people in exile, and whether or not they will listen, tell them: This is what the Lord God says!"

12 Then the Spirit lifted me up and the glory of the Lord began to move away, accompanied by the sound of a great earth-

---

e Literally, "from above the firmament, over their heads."   2a Or, "son of man" . . . and so also eighty-seven times throughout the book of Ezekiel. The connotation is "mortal man." In Daniel 7:13, the corresponding Aramaic expression is used for the Messiah as representative of the human race of which he is the head. b Implied.

quake.[a] [13] It was the noise of the wings of the living beings as they touched against each other, and the sound of their wheels beside them.

[14,15] The Spirit lifted me up and took me away to Tel Abib, another colony of Jewish exiles beside the Chebar River. I went in bitterness and anger,[b] but the hand of the Lord was strong upon me. And I sat among them, overwhelmed, for seven days.

[16] At the end of the seven days, the Lord said to me:

[17] "Son of dust, I have appointed you as a watchman for Israel; whenever I send my people a warning, pass it on to them at once. [18] If you refuse to warn the wicked when I want you to tell them, you are under the penalty of death, therefore repent and save your life—they will die in their sins, but I will punish you. I will demand your blood for theirs. [19] But if you warn them and they keep on sinning, and refuse to repent, they will die in their sins, but you are blameless —you have done all you could. [20] And if a good man becomes bad, and you refuse to warn him of the consequences, and the Lord destroys him, his previous good deeds won't help him—he shall die in his sin. But I will hold you responsible for his death, and punish you. [21] But if you warn him and he repents, he shall live and you have saved your own life too."

[22] I was helpless in the hand of God, and when he said to me, "Go out into the valley and I will talk to you there"— [23] I arose and went, and oh, I saw the glory of the Lord there, just as in my first vision! And I fell to the ground on my face.

[24] Then the Spirit entered into me and set me on my feet. He talked to me and said: "Go, imprison yourself in your house, [25] and I will paralyze[c] you so you can't leave; [26] and I will make your tongue stick to the roof of your mouth so that you can't reprove them; for they are rebels. [27] But whenever I give you a message, then I will loosen your tongue and let you speak, and you shall say to them: The Lord God says, Let anyone listen who wants to, and let any-one refuse who wants to, for they are rebels.

4 "AND NOW, SON of dust, take a large brick and lay it before you and draw a map of the city of Jerusalem on it. Draw a picture of siege mounds being built against the city, and enemy camps around it, and battering rams surrounding the walls. [3] And put an iron plate between you and the city, like a wall of iron. Demonstrate how an enemy army will capture Jerusalem!

"There is special meaning in each detail of what I have told you to do. For it is a warning to the people of Israel.

[4,5] "Now lie on your left side for 390[a] days, to show that Israel will be punished for 390 years by captivity and doom. Each day you lie there represents a year of punishment ahead for Israel. [6] Afterwards, turn over and lie on your right side for forty days, to signify the years of Judah's punishment. Each day will represent one year.

[7] "Meanwhile continue your demonstration of the siege of Jerusalem; lie there with your arm bared [to signify great strength and power in the attack against her[b]]. This will prophesy her doom. [8] And I will paralyze[c] you so that you can't turn over from one side to the other until you have completed all the days of your siege.

[9] "During the first 390 days eat bread made of flour mixed from wheat, barley, beans, lentils, and spelt. Mix the various kinds of flour together in a jar. [10] You are to ration this out to yourself at the rate of eight ounces at a time, one meal a day. [11] And use one quart of water a day; don't use more than that. [12] Each day take flour from the barrel and prepare it as you would barley cakes. While all the people are watching, bake it over a fire, using dried human dung as fuel, and eat it. [13] For the Lord declares, Israel shall eat defiled bread in the Gentile lands to which I exile them!"

[14] Then I said, "O Lord God, must I be defiled by using dung? For I have never been defiled before in all my life. From the time I was a child until now I have never eaten any animal that died of sickness or

---

a Literally, "I heard behind me the sound of a great earthquake."
spirit"—not necessarily anger, but indicated here by this reaction.
4a Some versions read, "190 days."   b Implied.

b Literally, "I went in the heat of my
c Literally, "lay bands upon you."
c Literally, "I will lay bands upon you."

that I found injured or dead; and I have never eaten any of the kinds of animals our law forbids."[d]

¹⁵ Then the Lord said, "All right, you may use cow dung instead of human dung."

¹⁶ Then he told me, "Son of dust, bread will be tightly rationed in Jerusalem. It will be weighed out with great care and eaten fearfully. And the water will be portioned out in driblets, and the people will drink it with dismay. ¹⁷ I will cause the people to lack both bread and water, and to look at one another in frantic terror, and to waste away beneath their punishment.

5 "SON OF DUST, take a sharp sword and use it as a barber's razor to shave your head and beard; use balances to weigh the hair into three equal parts. ² Place a third of it at the center of your map of Jerusalem. After your siege, burn it there. Scatter another third across your map and slash at it with a knife. Scatter the last third to the wind, for I will chase my people with the sword. ³ Keep just a bit of the hair and tie it up in your robe; ⁴ then take a few hairs out and throw them into the fire, for a fire shall come from this remnant and destroy all Israel."

⁵,⁶,⁷ The Lord God says, "This illustrates what will happen to Jerusalem, for she has turned away from my laws and has been even more wicked than the nations surrounding her." ⁸ Therefore the Lord God says, I, even I, am against you and will punish you publicly while all the nations watch. ⁹ Because of the terrible sins you have committed, I will punish you more terribly than I have ever done before or will ever do again. ¹⁰ Fathers will eat their own sons, and sons will eat their fathers; and those who survive will be scattered into all the world.

¹¹ "For I promise you: Because you have defiled my Temple with idols and evil sacrifices, therefore I will not spare you nor pity you at all. ¹² One-third of you will die from famine and disease; one-third will be slaughtered by the enemy; and one-third I will scatter to the winds, sending the sword of the enemy chasing after you. ¹³ Then at

last my anger will be appeased. And all Israel will know that what I threaten, I do.

¹⁴ "So I will make a public example of you before all the surrounding nations and before everyone traveling past the ruins of your land. ¹⁵ You will become a laughingstock to the world and an awesome example to everyone, for all to see what happens when the Lord turns against an entire nation in furious rebuke. I, the Lord, have spoken it!

¹⁶ "I will shower you with deadly arrows of famine to destroy you. The famine will become more and more serious until every bit of bread is gone. ¹⁷ And not only famine will come, but wild animals will attack you and kill you and your families; disease and war will stalk your land, and the sword of the enemy will slay you; I, the Lord, have spoken it!"

6 AGAIN A MESSAGE came from the Lord:

² "Son of dust, look over toward the mountains of Israel and prophesy against them. ³ Say to them, O mountains of Israel, hear the message of the Lord God against you and against the rivers and valleys. I, even I the Lord, will bring war upon you to destroy your idols. ⁴⁻⁷ All your cities will be smashed and burned, and the idol altars abandoned. Your gods will be shattered; the bones of their worshipers will lie scattered among the altars. Then at last you will know I am the Lord.

⁸ "But I will let a few of my people escape—to be scattered among the nations of the world. ⁹ Then when they are exiled among the nations, they will remember me, for I will take away their adulterous hearts—their love of idols—and I will blind their lecherous eyes that long for other gods. Then at last they will loathe themselves for all this wickedness. ¹⁰ They will realize that I alone am God, and that I wasn't fooling when I told them that all this would happen to them.

¹¹ "The Lord God says: Raise your hands in horror and shake your head[a] with deep remorse and say, Alas for all the evil

---

d See the dietary laws Ezekiel here refers to, in Leviticus 11.

6a Literally, "clap your hands and stamp your feet."

we have done! For you are going to perish from war and famine and disease. ¹² Disease will strike down those in exile; war will destroy those in the land of Israel; and any who remain will die by famine and siege. So at last I will expend my fury on you. ¹³ When your slain lie scattered among your idols and altars on every hill and mountain and under every green tree and great oak where they offered incense to their gods —you will realize that I alone am God. ¹⁴ I will crush you and make your cities desolate from the wilderness in the south to Riblah in the north. Then you will know I am the Lord."

7 THIS FURTHER MESSAGE came to me from God:
² "Tell Israel, Wherever you look—east, west, north or south—your land is finished. ³ No hope remains, for I will loose my anger on you for your worshiping of idols. ⁴ I will turn my eyes away and show no pity; I will repay you in full, and you shall know I am the Lord."
⁵,⁶ The Lord God says: "With one blow after another I will finish you. The end has come; your final doom is waiting. ⁷ O Israel, the day of your damnation dawns; the time has come; the day of trouble nears. It is a day of shouts of anguish, not shouts of joy! ⁸,⁹ Soon I will pour out my fury and let it finish its work of punishing you for all your evil deeds. I will not spare nor pity you, and you will know that I, the Lord, am doing it. ¹⁰,¹¹ The day of judgment has come; the morning dawns, for your wickedness and pride have run their course and reached their climax—none of these rich and wicked men of pride shall live. All your boasting will die away, and no one will be left to bewail your fate.
¹² "Yes, the time has come; the day draws near. There will be nothing to buy or sell, for the wrath of God is on the land. ¹³ And even if a merchant lives, his business will be gone, for God has spoken against all the people of Israel; all will be destroyed. Not one of those whose lives are filled with sin will recover.
¹⁴ "The trumpets shout to Israel's army,

'Mobilize!' but no one listens, for my wrath is on them all. ¹⁵ If you go outside the walls, there stands the enemy to kill you. If you stay inside, famine and disease will devour you. ¹⁶ Any who escape will be lonely as mourning doves hiding on the mountains, each weeping for his sins. ¹⁷ All hands shall be feeble, and all knees as weak as water. ¹⁸ You shall clothe yourselves with sackcloth, and horror and shame shall cover you; you shall shave your heads in sorrow and remorse.
¹⁹ "Throw away your money! Toss it out like worthless rubbish, for it will have no value in that day of wrath. It will neither satisfy nor feed you, for your love of money is the reason for your sin. ²⁰ I gave you gold to use in decorating the Temple, and you used it instead to make idols! Therefore I will take it all away from you. ²¹ I will give it to foreigners and to wicked men as booty. They shall defile my Temple. ²² I will not look when they defile it, nor will I stop them. Like robbers, they will loot the treasures and leave the Temple in ruins.
²³ "Prepare chains for my people, for the land is full of bloody crimes. Jerusalem is filled with violence, so I will enslave her people. ²⁴ I will crush your pride by bringing to Jerusalem the worst of the nations to occupy your homes, break down your fortifications you are so proud of, and defile your Temple. ²⁵ For the time has come for the cutting off of Israel. You will sue for peace, but you won't get it. ²⁶,²⁷ Calamity upon calamity will befall you; woe upon woe, disaster upon disaster! You will long for a prophet to guide you, but the priests and elders and the kings and princes will stand helpless, weeping in despair. The people will tremble with fear, for I will do to them the evil they have done, and give them all their just deserts. They shall learn that I am the Lord."

8 THEN, LATE IN August of the sixth year of King Jehoiachin's captivity,ᵃ as I was talking with the elders of Judah in my home, the power of the Lord God fell upon me. ² I saw what appeared to be a Man; from his waist down, he was made of fire;

---

a Implied.

from his waist up, he was all amber-colored brightness. ³ He put out what seemed to be a hand and took me by the hair. And the Spirit lifted me up into the sky and seemed to transport me to Jerusalem, to the entrance of the north gate, where the large idol was that had made the Lord so angry. ⁴ Suddenly the glory of the God of Israel was there, just as I had seen it before in the valley.

⁵ He said to me, "Son of dust, look toward the north." So I looked and, sure enough, north of the altar gate, in the entrance, stood the idol.

⁶ And he said: "Son of dust, do you see what they are doing? Do you see what great sins the people of Israel are doing here, to push me from my Temple? But come, and I will show you greater sins than these!"

⁷ Then he brought me to the door of the Temple court, where I made out an opening in the wall.

⁸ "Now dig into the wall," he said. I did, and uncovered a door to a hidden room.

⁹ "Go on in," he said, "and see the wickedness going on in there!"

¹⁰ So I went in. The walls were covered with pictures of all kinds of snakes, lizards and hideous creatures, besides all the various idols worshiped by the people of Israel. ¹¹ Seventy elders of Israel were standing there along with Ja-azaniah (son of Shaphan) worshiping the pictures. Each of them held a censer of burning incense, so there was a thick cloud of smoke above their heads.

¹² Then the Lord said to me: "Son of dust, have you seen what the elders of Israel are doing in their minds? For they say, 'The Lord doesn't see us; he has gone away!'"

¹³ Then he added, "Come, and I will show you greater sins than these!"

¹⁴ He brought me to the north gate of the Temple, and there sat women weeping for Tammuz,ᵇ their god.

¹⁵ "Have you seen this?" he asked. "But I will show you greater evils than these!"

¹⁶ Then he brought me into the inner court of the Temple and there at the door, between the porch and the bronze altar,

were about twenty-five men standing with their backs to the Temple of the Lord, facing east, worshiping the sun!

¹⁷ "Have you seen this?" he asked. "Is it nothing to the people of Judah that they commit these terrible sins, leading the whole nation into idolatry, thumbing their noses at me and arousing my fury against them? ¹⁸ Therefore I will deal with them in fury. I will neither pity nor spare. And though they scream for mercy, I will not listen."

9 THEN HE THUNDERED, "Call those to whom I have given the city! Tell them to bring their weapons with them!"

² Six men appeared at his call, coming from the upper north gate, each one with his sword. One of them wore linen clothing and carried a writer's case strapped to his side. They all went into the Temple and stood beside the bronze altar. ³ And the glory of the God of Israel rose from the cherubim where it had rested and stood above the entranceᵃ to the Temple.

And the Lord called to the man with the writer's case, ⁴ and said to him, "Walk through the streets of Jerusalem and put a mark on the foreheads of the men who weep and sigh because of all the sins they see around them."

⁵ Then I heard the Lord tell the other men: "Follow him through the city and kill everyone whose forehead isn't marked. Spare not nor pity them— ⁶ kill them all —old and young, girls, women and little children; but don't touch anyone with the mark. And begin right here at the Temple." And so they began by killing the seventy elders.

⁷ And he said, "Defile the Temple! Fill its courts with the bodies of those you kill! Go!" And they went out through the city and did as they were told.

⁸ While they were fulfilling their orders, I was alone. I fell to the ground on my face and cried out: "O Lord God! Will your fury against Jerusalem wipe out everyone left in Israel?"

⁹ But he said to me, "The sins of the

---

b The women wept for Tammuz, the god of fertility, because, according to Mesopotamian myths, he had been killed, and fertility had vanished with him.   9a Literally, "above the threshold of . . ."

people of Israel and Judah are very great and all the land is full of murder and injustice, for they say, 'The Lord doesn't see it! He has gone away!' ¹⁰ And so I will not spare them nor have any pity on them, and I will fully repay them for all that they have done."

¹¹ Just then the man in linen clothing, carrying the writer's case, reported back and said, "I have finished the work you gave me to do."

10 SUDDENLY A THRONE of beautiful blue sapphire[a] appeared in the sky above the heads of the cherubim.

² Then the Lord spoke to the man in linen clothing and said: "Go in between the whirling wheels beneath the cherubim and take a handful of glowing coals and scatter them over the city."

He did so while I watched. ³ The cherubim were standing at the south end of the Temple when the man went in. And the cloud of glory filled the inner court. ⁴ Then the glory of the Lord rose from above the cherubim and went over to the door of the Temple. The Temple was filled with the cloud of glory, and the court of the Temple was filled with the brightness of the glory of the Lord. ⁵ And the sound of the wings of the cherubim was as the voice of Almighty God when he speaks and could be heard clear out in the outer court.

⁶ When the Lord told the man in linen clothing to go between the cherubim and take some burning coals from between the wheels, the man went in and stood beside one of the wheels, ^{7,8} and one of the cherubim reached out his hand (for each cherub had, beneath his wings, what looked like human hands) and took some live coals from the flames between the cherubim and put them into the hands of the man in linen clothes, who took them and went out.

⁹⁻¹³ Each of the four cherubim had a wheel beside him—"The Whirl-Wheels," as I heard them called, for each one had a second wheel crosswise within, sparkled like chrysolite, giving off a greenish-yellow glow. Because of the construction of these wheels,[b] the cherubim could go straight forward in each of four directions; they did not turn when they changed direction but could go in any of the four ways their faces looked. Each of the four wheels was covered with eyes, including the rims and spokes. ¹⁴ Each of the four cherubim had four faces—the first was that of an ox;[c] the second, a man's; the third, a lion's; and the fourth, an eagle's.

^{15,16} These were the same beings I had seen beside the Chebar Canal, and when they rose into the air the wheels rose with them, and stayed beside them as they flew. ¹⁷ When the cherubim stood still, so did the wheels, for the spirit[d] of the cherubim was in the wheels. ¹⁸ Then the glory of the Lord moved from the door of the Temple and stood above the cherubim. ¹⁹ And as I watched, the cherubim flew with their wheels beside them to the east gate of the Temple. And the glory of the God of Israel was above them.

²⁰ These were the living beings I had seen beneath the God of Israel beside the Chebar Canal. I knew they were the same, ²¹ for each had four faces and four wings, with what looked like human hands under their wings. ²² Their faces too were identical to the faces of those I had seen at the Canal, and they traveled straight ahead, just as the others did.

11 THEN THE SPIRIT lifted me and brought me over to the east gate of the Temple, where I saw twenty-five of the most prominent men of the city, including two officers, Ja-azaniah (son of Azzur) and Pelatiah (son of Benaiah).

Then the Spirit said to me, "Son of dust, these are the men who are responsible for all of the wicked counsel being given out in this city. ³ For they say to the people, 'It is time to rebuild Jerusalem, for our city is an iron shield and will protect us from all harm.[a] ⁴ Therefore, son of dust, prophesy against them loudly and clearly."

⁵ Then the Spirit of the Lord came upon me and told me to say: "The Lord says to

a Literally, "lapis lazuli."   b Implied.   c Literally, "cherub's face." See Ezekiel 1:10.
d That is, the wheel was a living part of the bodies of the cherubim. Hence it could not be separated from the cherubim.   11a Literally, "this city the caldron and we the flesh."

the people of Israel: Is that what you are saying? Yes, I know it is, for I know everything you think—every thought that comes into your minds. ⁶ You have murdered endlessly and filled your streets with the dead. ⁷ "Therefore the Lord God says: You think this city is an iron shield? No, it isn't! It will not protect you. Your slain will lie within it, but you will be dragged out and slaughtered.ᵇ ⁸ I will expose you to the war you have so greatly feared, says the Lord God, ⁹ and I will take you from Jerusalem and hand you over to foreigners who will carry out my judgments against you. ¹⁰ You will be slaughtered all the way to the borders of Israel, and you will know I am the Lord. ¹¹ No, this city will not be an iron shield for you, and you safe within. I will chase you even to the borders of Israel, ¹² and you will know I am the Lord—you who have not obeyed me, but rather have copied the nations all around you."

¹³ While I was still speaking and telling them this, Pelatiah (son of Benaiah) suddenly died. Then I fell to the ground on my face and cried out: "O Lord God, are you going to kill everyone in all Israel?"

¹⁴ Again a message came from the Lord: ¹⁵ "Son of dust, the remnant left in Jerusalem are saying about your brother exiles: 'It is because they were so wicked that the Lord has deported them. Now the Lord has given us their land!'

¹⁶ "But tell the exiles that the Lord God says: Although I have scattered you in the countries of the world, yet I will be a sanctuary to you for the time that you are there, ¹⁷ and I will gather you back from the nations where you are scattered and give you the land of Israel again. ¹⁸ And when you return you will remove every trace of all this idol worship. ¹⁹ I will give you one heart and a new spirit; I will take from you your hearts of stone and give you tender hearts of love for God, ²⁰ so that you can obey my laws and be my people, and I will be your God. ²¹ But as for those now in Jerusalem,ᶜ who long for idols, I will repay them fully for their sins," the Lord God says.

²² Then the cherubim lifted their wings and rose into the air with their wheels beside them, and the glory of the God of Israel stood above them. ²³ Then the glory of the Lord rose from over the city and stood above the mountain on the east side.

²⁴ Afterwards the Spirit of God carried me back again to Babylon, to the Jews in exile there. And so ended the vision of my visit to Jerusalem. ²⁵ And I told the exiles everything the Lord had shown me.

12 AGAIN A MESSAGE came to me from the Lord:

² "Son of dust," he said, "you live among rebels who could know the truth if they wanted to, but they don't want to; they could hear me if they would listen, but they won't, ³ for they are rebels. So now put on a demonstration, to show them what being exiled will be like. Pack whatever you can carry on your back and leave your home —go somewhere else. Go in the daylight so they can see, for perhaps even yet they will consider what this means, even though they are such rebels. ⁴ Bring your baggage outside your house during the daylight so they can watch. Then leave the house at night, just as captives do when they begin their long march to distant lands. ⁵ Dig a tunnel through the city wall while they are observing and carry your possessions out through the hole. ⁶ As they watch, lift your pack to your shoulders and walk away into the night; muffle your face and don't gaze around. All this is a sign to the people of Israel of the evil that will come upon Jerusalem."

⁷ So I did as I was told. I brought my pack outside in the daylight—all I could take into exile—and in the evening I dug through the wall with my hands. I went out into the darkness with my pack on my shoulder while the people looked on. ⁸ The next morning this message came to me from the Lord:

⁹ "Son of dust, these rebels, the people of Israel, have asked what all this means. ¹⁰ Tell them the Lord God says it is a message to King Zedekiahᵃ in Jerusalem and to all the people of Israel. ¹¹ Explain that what

---

b Literally, "Your slain . . . are the flesh and this is the caldron; but you will be brought out from it."
c Implied.   **12** a Literally, "to the prince in Jerusalem."

you did was a demonstration of what is going to happen to them, for they shall be driven out of their homes and sent away into exile.

¹² "Even King Zedekiah shall go out at night through a hole in the wall, taking only what he can carry with him, with muffled face, for he won't be able to see.ᵇ ¹³ I will capture him in my net and bring him to Babylon, the land of the Chaldeans; but he shall not see it,ᵇ and he shall die there. ¹⁴ I will scatter his servants and guards to the four winds and send the sword after them. ¹⁵ And when I scatter them among the nations, then they shall know I am the Lord. ¹⁶ But I will spare a few of them from death by war and famine and disease. I will save them to confess to the nations how wicked they have been, and they shall know I am the Lord."

¹⁷ Then this message came to me from the Lord:

¹⁸ "Son of dust, tremble as you eat your meals; ration out your water as though it were your last, ¹⁹ and say to the people, the Lord God says that the people of Israel and Jerusalem shall ration their food with utmost care and sip their tiny portions of water in utter despair because of all their sins. ²⁰ Your cities shall be destroyed and your farmlands deserted, and you shall know I am the Lord."

²¹ Again a message came to me from the Lord:

²² "Son of dust, what is that proverb they quote in Israel—'The days as they pass make liars out of every prophet.' ²³ The Lord God says, I will put an end to this proverb and they will soon stop saying it. Give them this one instead: 'The time has come for all these prophecies to be fulfilled.'

²⁴ "Then you will see what becomes of all the false predictions of safety and security for Jerusalem. ²⁵ For I am the Lord! What I threaten always happens. There will be no more delays, O rebels of Israel! I will do it in your own lifetime!" says the Lord God.

²⁶ Then this message came:

²⁷ "Son of dust, the people of Israel say, 'His visions won't come true for a long, long time.' ²⁸ Therefore say to them: 'The Lord God says, All delay has ended! I will do it now!' "

13 THEN THIS MESSAGE came to me: ²,³ "Son of dust, prophesy against the false prophets of Israel who are inventing their own visions and claiming to have messages from me when I have never told them anything at all. Woe upon them!

⁴ "O Israel, these 'prophets' of yours are as useless as foxes for rebuilding your walls! ⁵ O evil prophets, what have you ever done to strengthen the walls of Israel against her enemies—by strengthening Israel in the Lord? ⁶ Instead you have lied when you said, 'My message is from God!' God did not send you. And yet you expect him to fulfill your prophecies. ⁷ Can you deny that you have claimed to see 'visions' you never saw, and that you have said, 'This message is from God,' when I never spoke to you at all?

⁸ "Therefore the Lord God says: I will destroy you for these 'visions' and lies. ⁹ My hand shall be against you, and you shall be cut off from among the leaders of Israel; I will blot out your names and you will never see your own country again. And you shall know I am the Lord. ¹⁰ For these evil men deceive my people by saying, 'God will send peace,' when that is not my plan at all! My people build a flimsy wall and these prophets praise them for it—and cover it with whitewash!

¹¹ "Tell these evil builders that their wall will fall. A heavy rainstorm will undermine it; great hailstones and mighty winds will knock it down. ¹² And when the wall falls, the people will cry out, 'Why didn't you tell us that it wasn't good enough? Why did you whitewash it and cover up its faults?' ¹³ Yes, it will surely fall. The Lord God says: I will sweep it away with a storm of indignation and with a great flood of anger and with hailstones of wrath. ¹⁴ I will break down your whitewashed wall, and it will fall on you and crush you, and you shall know I am the Lord. ¹⁵ Then at last my wrath

---

b Literally, "that he may not see the land with his eyes." Apparently a reference to the fact that his eyes were put out before he was taken to Babylon, Jeremiah 52:11.

against the wall will be completed; and concerning those who praised it, I will say: The wall and its builders both are gone. [16] For they were lying prophets, claiming Jerusalem will have peace when there is no peace, says the Lord God.

[17] "Son of dust, speak out against the women prophets too who pretend the Lord has given them his messages. [18] Tell them the Lord God says: Woe to these women who are damning the souls of my people, of both young and old alike, by tying magic charms on their wrists and furnishing them with magic veils and selling them indulgences. They refuse to even offer help unless they get a profit from it.[a] [19] For the sake of a few paltry handfuls of barley or a piece of bread will you turn away my people from me? You have led those to death who should not die! And you have promised life to those who should not live, by lying to my people—and how they love it!

[20] "And so the Lord says: I will crush you because you hunt my people's souls with all your magic charms. I will tear off the charms and set my people free like birds from cages. [21] I will tear off the magic veils and save my people from you; they will no longer be your victims, and you shall know I am the Lord. [22] Your lies have discouraged the righteous, when I didn't want it so. And you have encouraged the wicked by promising life, though they continue in their sins. [23] But you will lie no more; no longer will you talk of seeing 'visions' that you never saw, nor practice your magic, for I will deliver my people out of your hands by destroying you, and you shall know I am the Lord."

14 THEN SOME OF the elders of Israel visited me, to ask me for a message from the Lord, [2] and this is the message that came to me to give to them:

[3] "Son of dust, these men worship idols in their hearts—should I let them ask me anything? [4] Tell them, the Lord God says: I the Lord will personally deal with anyone in Israel who worships idols and then comes to ask my help. [5] For I will punish the minds and hearts of those who turn from me to idols.

[6,7] "Therefore warn them that the Lord God says: Repent and destroy your idols, and stop worshiping them in your hearts. I the Lord will personally punish everyone, whether people of Israel or the foreigners living among you, who rejects me for idols, and then comes to a prophet to ask for my help and advice. [8] I will turn upon him and make a terrible example of him, destroying him; and you shall know I am the Lord. [9] And if one of the false prophets gives him a message anyway, it is a lie. His prophecy will not come true, and I will stand against that 'prophet' and destroy him from among my people Israel. [10] False prophets and hypocrites—evil people who say they want my words—all will be punished for their sins, [11] so that the people of Israel will learn not to desert me and not to be polluted any longer with sin, but to be my people and I their God. So says the Lord."

[12] Then this message of the Lord came to me:

[13] "Son of dust, when the people of this land sin against me, then I will crush them with my fist and break off their food supply and send famine to destroy both man and beast. [14] If Noah, Daniel and Job were here today, they alone would be saved by their righteousness, and I would destroy the remainder of Israel, says the Lord God.

[15] "When I send an invasion of dangerous wild animals into the land to devastate the land, [16] even if these three men were here, the Lord God swears that it would do no good—it would not save the people from their doom. Those three only would be saved, but the land would be devastated. [17] "Or when I bring war against that land and tell the armies of the enemy to come and destroy everything, [18] even if these three men were in the land, the Lord God declares that they alone would be saved.

[19] "And when I pour out my fury by sending an epidemic of disease into the land, and the plague kills man and beast alike, [20] though Noah, Daniel and Job were living there, the Lord God says that only they would be saved, because of their righteousness.

---

a Literally, "Will you hunt the souls of my people and save your own souls alive?"

²¹ "And the Lord says: Four great punishments await Jerusalem to destroy all life: war, famine, ferocious beasts, plague. ²² If there are survivors and they come here to join you as exiles in Babylon, you will see with your own eyes how wicked they are, and you will know it was right for me to destroy Jerusalem. ²³ You will agree, when you meet them, that it is not without cause that all these things are being done to Israel."

15 THEN THIS MESSAGE came to me from the Lord:

² "Son of dust, what good are vines from the forest? Are they as useful as trees? Are they even as valuable as a single branch? ³ No, for vines can't be used even for making pegs to hang up pots and pans! ⁴ All they are good for is fuel—and even so, they burn but poorly! ^{5,6} So they are useless both before and after being put in the fire!

"This is what I mean, the Lord God says: The people of Jerusalem are like the vines of the forest—useless before being burned and certainly useless afterwards! ⁷ And I will set myself against them to see to it that if they escape from one fire, they will fall into another; and then you shall know I am the Lord. ⁸ And I will make the land desolate because they worship idols," says the Lord God.

16 THEN AGAIN A message came to me from the Lord.

² "Son of dust," he said, "speak to Jerusalem about her loathsome sins. ³ Tell her, the Lord God says: You are no better than the people of Canaan—your father must have been an Amorite and your mother a Hittite!^a ⁴ When you were born, no one cared for you. When I first saw you, your umbilical cord was uncut, and you had been neither washed nor rubbed with salt nor clothed. ⁵ No one had the slightest interest in you; no one pitied you or cared for you. On that day when you were born, you were dumped out into a field and left to die, unwanted.

^{6,7} "But I came by and saw you there, covered with your own blood, and I said, 'Live! Thrive like a plant in the field!' And you did! You grew up and became tall, slender and supple, a jewel among jewels. And when you reached the age of maidenhood your breasts were full-formed and your pubic hair had grown; yet you were naked.

⁸ "Later, when I passed by and saw you again, you were old enough for marriage; and I wrapped my cloak around you to legally declare my marriage vow. I signed a covenant with you, and you became mine. ^{9,10} Then, when the marriage had taken place, I gave you beautiful clothes of linens and silk, embroidered, and sandals made of dolphin hide. ¹¹ I gave you lovely ornaments, bracelets and beautiful necklaces, ¹² a ring for your nose and two more for your ears, and a lovely tiara for your head. ¹³ And so you were made beautiful with gold and silver, and your clothes were silk and linen and beautifully embroidered. You ate the finest foods and became more beautiful than ever. You looked like a queen, and so you were! ¹⁴ Your reputation was great among the nations for your beauty; it was perfect because of all the gifts I gave you, says the Lord God.

¹⁵ "But you thought you could get along without me—you trusted in your beauty instead; and you gave yourself as a prostitute to every man who came along. Your beauty was his for the asking. ¹⁶ You used the lovely things I gave you for making idol shrines and to decorate your bed of prostitution. Unbelievable! There has never been anything like it before! ¹⁷ You took the very jewels and gold and silver ornaments I gave to you and made statues of men and worshiped them, which is adultery against me. ¹⁸ You used the beautifully embroidered clothes I gave you—to cover your idols! And used my oil and incense to worship *them!* ¹⁹ You set before them—imagine it— the fine flour and oil and honey I gave you; you used it as a lovely sacrifice to *them!* ²⁰ And you took my sons and daughters you had borne to me, and sacrificed them to your gods; and they are gone. Wasn't it enough that you should be a prostitute? ²¹ Must you also slay my children in the fires of strange altars?

---

a The Amorites and Hittites were nations who turned their backs to all knowledge of God.

²² "And in all these years of adultery and sin you have not thought of those days long ago when you were naked and covered with blood.

²³ "And then, in addition to all your other wickedness—woe, woe upon you, says the Lord God— ²⁴ you built a spacious brothel for your lovers, and idol altars on every street, ²⁵ and there you offered your beauty to every man who came by, in an endless stream of prostitution. ²⁶ And you added lustful Egypt to your prostitutions by your alliance with her. My anger is great.

²⁷ "Therefore I have crushed you with my fist; I have reduced your boundaries and delivered you into the hands of those who hate you—the Philistines—and even they are ashamed of you.

²⁸ "You have committed adultery with the Assyrians too [by making them your allies and worshiping their gods[b]]; it seems that you can never find enough new gods. After your adultery there, you still weren't satisfied, ²⁹ so you worshiped the gods of that great merchant land of Babylon—and you still weren't satisfied. ³⁰ What a filthy heart you have, says the Lord God, to do such things as these; you are a brazen prostitute, ³¹ building your idol altars, your brothels, on every street. You have been worse than a prostitute, so eager for sin that you have not even charged for your love! ³² Yes, you are an adulterous wife who lives with other men instead of her own husband. ³³,³⁴ Prostitutes charge for their services—men pay with many gifts. But not you, you give *them* gifts, bribing them to come to you! So you are different from other prostitutes. But you had to pay them, for no one wanted you.

³⁵ "O prostitute, hear the word of the Lord:

³⁶ "The Lord God says: Because I see your filthy sins, your adultery with your lovers—your worshiping of idols—and the slaying of your children as sacrifices to your gods, ³⁷ this is what I am going to do: I will gather together all your allies—these lovers of yours you have sinned with, both those you loved and those you hated—and I will make you naked before them, that they may

see you. ³⁸ I will punish you as a murderess is punished and as a woman breaking wedlock living with other men. ³⁹ I will give you to your lovers—these many nations—to destroy, and they will knock down your brothels and idol altars, and strip you and take your beautiful jewels and leave you naked and ashamed. ⁴⁰,⁴¹ They will burn your homes, punishing you before the eyes of many women. And I will see to it that you stop your adulteries with other gods and end your payments to your allies for their love.

⁴² "Then at last my fury against you will die away; my jealousy against you will end, and I will be quiet and not be angry with you anymore. ⁴³ But first, because you have not remembered your youth, but have angered me by all these evil things you do, I will fully repay you for all of your sins, says the Lord. For you are thankless in addition to all your other faults.

⁴⁴ " 'Like mother, like daughter'—that is what everyone will say of you. ⁴⁵ For your mother loathed her husband and her children, and you do too. And you are exactly like your sisters, for they despised their husbands and their children. Truly, your mother must have been a Hittite and your father an Amorite.

⁴⁶ "Your older sister is Samaria, living with her daughters north of you; your younger sister is Sodom and her daughters, in the south. ⁴⁷ You have not merely sinned as they do—no, that was nothing to you; in a very short time you far surpassed them. ⁴⁸ "As I live, the Lord God says, Sodom and her daughters have never been as wicked as you and your daughters. ⁴⁹ Your sister Sodom's sins were pride and laziness and too much food, while the poor and needy suffered outside her door. ⁵⁰ She insolently worshiped many idols as I watched. Therefore. I crushed her.

⁵¹ "Even Samaria has not committed half your sins. You have worshiped idols far more than your sisters have; they seem almost righteous in comparison with you! ⁵² Don't be surprised then by the lighter punishment they get. For your sins are so awful that in comparison with you, your

---

b Implied.

sisters seem innocent![53] (But someday I will restore the fortunes of Sodom and Samaria again, and those of Judah too.)[54] Your terrible punishment will be a consolation to them, for it will be greater than theirs. [55] "Yes, your sisters, Sodom and Samaria, and all their people will be restored again, and Judah too will prosper in that day. [56] In your proud days you held Sodom in unspeakable contempt. [57] But now your greater wickedness has been exposed to all the world, and you are the one who is scorned—by Edom and all her neighbors and by all the Philistines. [58] This is part of your punishment for all your sins, says the Lord.

[59,60] "For the Lord God says: I will repay you for your broken promises. You lightly broke your solemn vows to me, yet I will keep the pledge I made to you when you were young. I will establish an everlasting covenant with you forever, [61] and you will remember with shame all the evil you have done; and you will be overcome by my favor when I take your sisters, Samaria and Sodom, and make them your daughters, for you to rule over. You will know you don't deserve this gracious act, for you did not keep my covenant. [62] I will reaffirm my covenant with you, and you will know I am the Lord. [63] Despite all you have done, I will be kind to you again; you will cover your mouth in silence and in shame when I forgive you all that you have done, says the Lord God."

17 THEN THIS MESSAGE came to me from the Lord:

[2] "Son of dust, give this riddle to the people of Israel:

[3,4] "A great eagle with broad wings full of many-colored feathers came to Lebanon and plucked off the shoot at the top of the tallest cedar tree and carried it into a city filled with merchants. [5] There he planted it[a] in fertile ground beside a broad river, where it would grow as quickly as a willow tree. [6] It took root and grew and became a low but spreading vine that turned toward the eagle and produced strong branches and luxuriant leaves. [7] But when another great,

broad-winged, full-feathered eagle came along, this tree sent its roots and branches out toward him instead, [8] even though it was already in good soil with plenty of water to become a splendid vine, producing leaves and fruit.

[9] "The Lord God asks: Shall I let this tree grow and prosper? No! I will pull it out, roots and all! I will cut off its branches and let its leaves wither and die. It will pull out easily enough—it won't take a big crew or a lot of equipment to do that. [10] Though the vine began so well, will it thrive? No, it will wither away completely when the east wind touches it, dying in the same choice soil where it had grown so well."

[11] Then this message came to me from the Lord:

[12,13] "Ask these rebels of Israel: Don't you understand what this riddle of the eagles means? I will tell you. Nebuchadnezzar, king of Babylon [the first of the two eagles[b]], came to Jerusalem and took away her king and princes [her topmost buds and shoots[b]] and brought them to Babylon. Nebuchadnezzar made a covenant with a member of the royal family [Zedekiah[b]], and made him take an oath of loyalty. He took a seedling and planted it in fertile ground beside a broad river, and he exiled the top men of Israel's government, [14] so that Israel would not be strong again and revolt. But by keeping her promises, Israel could be respected and maintain her identity.

[15] "Nevertheless, Zedekiah rebelled against Babylon, sending ambassadors to Egypt to seek for a great army and many horses to fight against Nebuchadnezzar. But will Israel prosper after breaking all her promises like that? Will she succeed? [16] No! For as I live, says the Lord, the king of Israel shall die. (Nebuchadnezzar will pull out the tree, roots and all!) Zedekiah[b] shall die in Babylon, where the king lives who gave him his power, and whose covenant he despised and broke. [17] Pharaoh and all his mighty army shall fail to help Israel when the king of Babylon lays siege to Jerusalem again and slaughters many lives. [18] For the king of Israel broke his promise after swear-

---

a Literally, "planted the seed of the land."   b Implied.

684

ing to obey; therefore he shall not escape.
¹⁹ "The Lord God says: As I live, surely I will punish him for despising the solemn oath he made in my name. ²⁰ I will throw my net over him and he shall be captured in my snare, and I will bring him to Babylon and deal with him there for this treason against me. ²¹ And all the best soldiers of Israel will be killed by the sword, and those remaining in the city will be scattered to the four winds. Then you will know that I, the Lord, have spoken these words.

²²,²³ "The Lord God says: I, myself, will take the finest and most tender twig from the top of the highest cedar, and I, myself, will plant it on the top of Israel's highest mountain. It shall become a noble cedar, bringing forth branches and bearing fruit. Animals of every sort will gather under it; its branches will shelter every kind of bird. ²⁴ And everyone shall know that it is I, the Lord, who cuts down the high trees and exalts the low, that I make the green tree wither and the dry tree grow. I, the Lord, have said that I would do it, and I will."

18 THEN THE LORD'S message came to me again.
² "Why do people use this proverb about the land of Israel: The children are punished for their fathers' sins?ᵃ ³ As I live, says the Lord God, you will not use this proverb any more in Israel, ⁴ for all souls are mine to judge—fathers and sons alike—and my rule is this: It is for a man's own sins that he will die.

⁵ "But if a man is just and does what is lawful and right, ⁶ and has not gone out to the mountains to feast before the idols of Israel and worship them, and does not commit adultery, nor lie with any woman during the time of her menstruation, ⁷ and is a merciful creditor, not holding on to the items given to him in pledge by poor debtors, and is no robber, but gives food to the hungry and clothes to those in need, ⁸ and grants loans without interest,ᵇ and stays away from sin, and is honest and fair when judging others, ⁹ and obeys my laws—that man is just, says the Lord, and he shall

surely live.
¹⁰ "But if that man has a son who is a robber or murderer and who fulfills none of his responsibilities, ¹¹ who refuses to obey the laws of God, but worships idols on the mountains and commits adultery, ¹² and oppresses the poor and needy, and robs his debtors by refusing to let them redeem what they have given him in pledge, and loves idols and worships them, ¹³ and loans out his money at interestᶜ—shall that man live? No! He shall surely die, and it is his own fault.

¹⁴ "But if this sinful man has, in turn, a son who sees all his father's wickedness, so that he fears God and decides against that kind of life, ¹⁵ and doesn't go up on the mountains to feast before the idols and worship them, and does not commit adultery, ¹⁶ and is fair to those who borrow from him and doesn't rob them, but feeds the hungry and clothes the needy, ¹⁷ and helps the poor and does not loan money at interest,ᶜ and obeys my laws—he shall not die because of his father's sins; he shall surely live. ¹⁸ But his father shall die for his own sins because he is cruel and robs and does wrong.

¹⁹ " 'What?' you ask. 'Doesn't the son pay for his father's sins?' No! For if the son does what is right and keeps my laws, he shall surely live. ²⁰ The one who sins is the one who dies. The son shall not be punished for his father's sins, nor the father for his son's. The righteous person will be rewarded for his own goodness and the wicked person for his wickedness. ²¹ But if a wicked person turns away from all his sins and begins to obey my laws and do what is just and right, he shall surely live and not die. ²² All his past sins will be forgotten, and he shall live because of his goodness.

²³ "Do you think I like to see the wicked die? asks the Lord. Of course not! I only want him to turn from his wicked ways and live. ²⁴ However, if a righteous person turns to sinning and acts like any other sinner, should he be allowed to live? No, of course not. All his previous goodness will be forgotten and he shall die for his sins.

²⁵ "Yet you say: 'The Lord isn't being

---

a Literally, "The fathers have eaten sour grapes and the children's teeth are set on edge."
b Or, "without any usury."   c Or, "at usurious interest."

fair!' Listen to me, O people of Israel. Am I the one who is unfair, or is it you? [26] When a good man turns away from being good and begins sinning and dies in his sins, he dies for the evil he has done. [27] And if a wicked person turns away from his wickedness and obeys the law, and does right, he shall save his soul, [28] for he has thought it over and decided to turn from his sins and live a good life. He shall surely live—he shall not die. [29] "And yet the people of Israel keep saying: 'The Lord is unfair!' O people of Israel, it is you who are unfair, not I. [30] I will judge each of you, O Israel, and punish or reward each according to your own actions. Oh, turn from your sins while there is yet time. [31] Put them behind you and receive a new heart and a new spirit. For why will you die, O Israel? [32] I do not enjoy seeing you die, the Lord God says. Turn, turn and live!

19 "SING THIS DEATH dirge for the leaders of Israel: [2] What a woman your mother was—like a lioness! Her children were like lion's cubs! [3] One of her cubs [King Jehoahaz[a]] grew into a strong young lion, and learned to catch prey and became a man-eater. [4] Then the nations called out their hunters and trapped him in a pit and brought him in chains to Egypt. [5] "When Israel, the mother lion, saw that all her hopes for him were gone, she took another of her cubs [King Jehoiachin[a]] and taught him to be 'king of the beasts.' [6] He became a leader among the lions and learned to catch prey, and he too became a man-eater. [7] He demolished the palaces of the surrounding nations and ruined their cities; their farms were desolated, their crops destroyed; everyone in the land shook with terror when they heard him roar. [8] Then the armies of the nations surrounded him, coming from every side, and trapped him in a pit and captured him. [9] They prodded him into a cage and brought him before the king of Babylon. He was held in captivity so that his voice could never again be heard upon the mountains of Israel.

[10] "Your mother was like a vine beside an irrigation ditch, with lush, green foliage because of all the water. [11] Its strongest branch became a ruler's scepter and it was very great, towering above the others and noticed from far away. [12] But the vine was uprooted in fury and thrown down to the ground. Its branches were broken and withered by a strong wind from the east; the fruit was destroyed by fire. [13] Now the vine is planted in the wilderness where the ground is hard and dry. [14] It is decaying from within;[b] no strong branch remains. The fulfillment of this sad prophecy has already begun, and there is more ahead."

20 LATE IN JULY, six[a] years after King Jeconiah was captured, some of the elders of Israel came to ask instructions from the Lord, and sat before me awaiting his reply.

[2] Then the Lord gave me this message: [3] "Son of dust, say to the elders of Israel: The Lord God says: How dare you come to ask my help? I swear that I will tell you nothing. [4] Judge them, son of dust; condemn them; tell them of all the sins of this nation from the times of their fathers until now. [5,6] Tell them the Lord God says: When I chose Israel and revealed myself to her in Egypt, I swore to her and her descendants that I would bring them out of Egypt to a land I had discovered and explored for them—a good land, flowing as it were with milk and honey, the best of all lands anywhere.

[7] "Then I said to them: Get rid of every idol; do not defile yourselves with the Egyptian gods, for I am the Lord your God. [8] But they rebelled against me and would not listen. They didn't get rid of their idols, nor forsake the gods of Egypt. Then I thought, I will pour out my fury upon them and fulfill my anger against them while they are still in Egypt.

[9,10] "But I didn't do it, for I acted to protect the honor of my name, lest the Egyptians laugh at Israel's God who couldn't keep them back from harm. So I brought my people out of Egypt right before the

---

a Implied.   b Literally, "A fire is gone out of the rods of its branches and devoured its fruit."
20a Literally, "in the seventh year of Jeconiah's captivity."

Egyptians' eyes, and led them into the wilderness. ¹¹ There I gave them my laws so they could live by keeping them. If anyone keeps them, he shall live. ¹² And I gave them the Sabbath—a day of rest every seventh day—as a symbol between them and me, to remind them that it is I, the Lord, who sanctifies them, that they are truly my people.

¹³ "But Israel rebelled against me. There in the wilderness they refused my laws. They would not obey my rules even though obeying them means life. And they misused my Sabbaths. Then I thought, I will pour out my fury upon them and utterly consume them in the desert.

¹⁴ "But again I refrained in order to protect the honor of my name, lest the nations who saw me bring them out of Egypt would say that it was because I couldn't care for them that I destroyed them. ¹⁵ But I swore to them in the wilderness that I would not bring them into the land I had given them, a land full of milk and honey, the choicest spot on earth, ¹⁶ because they laughed at my laws, ignored my wishes, and violated my Sabbaths—their hearts were with their idols! ¹⁷ Nevertheless, I spared them. I didn't finish them off in the wilderness.

¹⁸ "Then I spoke to their children and said: Don't follow your fathers' footsteps. Don't defile yourselves with their idols, ¹⁹ for I am the Lord your God. Follow my laws; keep my ordinances; ²⁰ hallow my Sabbaths; for they are a symbol of the contract between us to help you remember that I am the Lord your God.

²¹ "But their children too rebelled against me. They refused my laws—the laws that, if a person keeps them, he shall live. And they defiled my Sabbaths. So then I said: Now at last I will pour out my fury upon you in the wilderness.

²² "Nevertheless, again I withdrew my judgment against them to protect my name among the nations who had seen my power in bringing them out of Egypt. ²³,²⁴ But I took a solemn oath against them while they

were in the wilderness that I would scatter them, dispersing them to the ends of the earth because they did not obey my laws but scorned them and violated my Sabbaths and longed for their fathers' idols. ²⁵ I let them adopt[b] customs and laws which were worthless. Through the keeping of them they could not attain life.[c] ²⁶ In the hope that they would draw back in horror, and know that I alone am God, I let them pollute themselves with the very gifts I gave them. They burnt their firstborn children as offerings to their gods!

²⁷,²⁸ "Son of dust, tell them that the Lord God says: Your fathers continued to blaspheme and betray me when I brought them into the land I promised them, for they offered sacrifices and incense on every high hill and under every tree! They roused my fury as they offered up their sacrifices to those 'gods.' They brought their perfumes and incense and poured out their drink offerings to them! ²⁹ I said to them: 'What is this place of sacrifice[d] where you go?' And so it is still called 'The Place of Sacrifice'— that is how it got its name.

³⁰ "The Lord God wants to know whether you are going to pollute yourselves just as your fathers did, and keep on worshiping idols? ³¹ For when you offer gifts to them and give your little sons to be burned to ashes as you do even today, shall I listen to you or help you, Israel? As I live, the Lord God says, I will not give you any message, though you have come to me to ask.

³² "What you have in mind will not be done—to be like the nations all around you, serving gods of wood and stone. ³³ I will rule you with an iron fist and in great anger and with power. ³⁴ With might and fury I will bring you out from the lands where you are scattered, ³⁵,³⁶ and will bring you into my desert judgment hall.[e] I will judge you there, and get rid of the rebels, just as I did in the wilderness after I brought you out of Egypt. ³⁷ I will count you carefully and let only a small quota return. ³⁸ And the others—the rebels and all those who sin

---

b Literally, "gave them." c Literally, "ordinances by which they could not have life." Doubtless, the reference is to the pagan customs of verses 18 and 26. In contrast, see verse 11. d Literally, "bamah"—a hilltop area where sacrifices were made to the gods. e Literally, "the wilderness of the people," meaning the Syro-Arabian deserts, peopled by nomadic tribes. This desert would be traversed in returning to Israel from Babylon.

against me—I will purge from among you. They shall not enter Israel, but I will bring them out of the countries where they are in exile. And when that happens, you will know I am the Lord.

[39] "O Israel, the Lord God says: If you insist on worshiping your idols, go right ahead, but then don't bring your gifts to me as well! Such desecration of my holy name must stop! [40] For at Jerusalem in my holy mountain, says the Lord, all Israel shall worship me. There I will accept you, and require you to bring me your offerings and the finest of your gifts. [41] You will be to me as an offering of perfumed incense when I bring you back from exile, and the nations will see the great change in your hearts. [42] Then, when I have brought you home to the land I promised your fathers, you will know I am the Lord. [43] Then you will look back at all your sins and loathe yourselves because of the evil you have done. [44] And when I have honored my name by blessing you despite your wickedness, then, O Israel, you will know I am the Lord."

[45] Then this message came to me from the Lord:

[46] "Son of dust, look toward Jerusalem and speak out against it and the forest lands of the Negeb. [47] Prophesy to it and say: Hear the word of the Lord. I will set you on fire, O forest, and every tree will die, green and dry alike. The terrible flames will not be quenched and they will scorch the world. [48] And all the world will see that I, the Lord, have set the fire. It shall not be put out."

[49] Then I said, "O Lord God, they say of me, 'He only talks in riddles!' "

21 THEN THIS MESSAGE came to me from the Lord:

[2] "Son of dust, face toward Jerusalem and prophesy against Israel and against my Temple![a] [3] For the Lord says: I am against you, Israel. I will unsheath my sword and destroy your people, good and bad alike— [4] I will not spare even the righteous. I will make a clean sweep throughout the land from the Negeb to your northern borders. [5] All the world shall know that it is I, the Lord. His sword is in his hand, and it will

not return to its sheath again until its work is finished.

[6] "Sigh and groan before the people, son of dust, in your bitter anguish; sigh with grief and broken heart. [7] When they ask you why, tell them: Because of the fearsome news that God has given me. When it comes true, the boldest heart will melt with fear; all strength will disappear. Every spirit will faint; strong knees will tremble and become as weak as water. And the Lord God says: Your doom is on the way; my judgments will be fulfilled!"

[8] Then again this message came to me from God:

[9,10,11] "Son of dust, tell them this: A sword is being sharpened and polished for terrible slaughter. Now will you laugh? For those far stronger than you have perished beneath its power. It is ready now to hand to the executioner. [12] Son of dust, with sobbing, beat upon your thigh, for that sword shall slay my people and all their leaders. All alike shall die. [13] It will put them all to the test—and what chance do they have? the Lord God asks.

[14] "Prophesy to them in this way: Clap your hands vigorously, then take a sword and brandish it twice, thrice, to symbolize the great massacre they face! [15] Let their hearts melt with terror, for a sword glitters at every gate; it flashes like lightning; it is razor-edged for slaughter. [16] O sword, slash to the right and slash to the left, wherever you will, wherever you want. [17] And you have prophesied with clapping hands that I, the Lord, will smite Jerusalem and satisfy my fury."

[18] Then this message came to me. The Lord said:

[19,20] "Son of dust, make a map and on it trace two routes for the king of Babylon to follow—one to Jerusalem and the other to Rabbah in Trans-Jordan.[b] And put a signpost at the fork in the road from Babylon. [21] For the king of Babylon stands at a fork, uncertain whether to attack Jerusalem or Rabbah. He will call his magicians to use divination; they will cast lots by shaking arrows from the quiver; they will sacrifice to idols and inspect the liver[c] of their sacri-

---

a Literally, "against the sanctuaries."   b Literally, "Rabbah of the Ammonites."   c A very common type of divination by which ancients thought they could obtain information from the gods.

fice. ²² They will decide to turn toward Jerusalem! With battering rams they will go against the gates, shouting for the kill; they will build siege towers and make a hill against the walls to reach the top. ²³ Jerusalem won't understand this treachery; how could the diviners make this terrible mistake? For Babylon is Judah's ally and has sworn to defend Jerusalem! But (the king of Babylon) will think only of the times the people rebelled. He will attack and defeat them.

²⁴ "The Lord God says: Again and again your guilt cries out against you, for your sins are open and unashamed. Wherever you go, whatever you do, all is filled with sin. And now the time of punishment has come. ²⁵ O King Zedekiah,ᵈ evil prince of Israel, your final day of reckoning is here. ²⁶ Take off your jeweled crown, the Lord God says. The old order changes. Now the poor are exalted, and the rich brought very low. ²⁷ I will overturn, overturn, overturn the kingdom, so that even the new order that emerges will not succeed until the Man appears who has a right to it. And I will give it all to him.

²⁸ "Son of dust, prophesy to the Ammonites too, for they mocked my people in their woe. Tell them this:

"Against you also my glittering sword is drawn from its sheath; it is sharpened and polished and flashes like lightning. ²⁹ Your magicians and false prophets have told you lies of safety and success—that your gods will save you from the king of Babylon. Thus they have caused your death along with all the other wicked, for when the day of final reckoning has come you will be wounded unto death. ³⁰ Shall I return my sword to its sheath before I deal with you? No, I will destroy you in your own country where you were born. ³¹ I will pour out my fury upon you and blow upon the fire of my wrath until it becomes a roaring conflagration, and I will deliver you into the hands of cruel men skilled in destruction. ³² You are the fuel for the fire; your blood will be spilled in your own country and you will be utterly wiped out, your memory lost in his-

tory. For I, the Lord, have spoken it."

22 NOW ANOTHER MESSAGE came from the Lord. He said:

² "Son of dust, indict Jerusalem as the City of Murder. Publicly denounce her terrible deeds. ³ City of Murder, doomed and damned—City of Idols, filthy and foul— ⁴ you are guilty both of murder and idolatry. Now comes your day of doom. You have reached the limit of your years. I will make you a laughingstock and a reproach to all the nations of the world. ⁵ Near and far they will mock you, a city of infamous rebels.

⁶ "Every leader in Israel who lives within your walls is bent on murder. ⁷ Fathers and mothers are contemptuously ignored; immigrants and visitors are forced to pay you for your 'protection'; orphans and widows are wronged and oppressed. ⁸ The things of God are all despised; my Sabbaths are ignored. ⁹ Prisoners are falsely accused and sent to their death. Every mountain top is filled with idols; lewdness is everywhere. ¹⁰ There are men who commit adulteryᵃ with their fathers' wives and lie with menstruous women. ¹¹ Adultery with a neighbor's wife, a daughter-in-law, a half sister—this is common. ¹² Hired murderers, loan racketeers and extortioners are everywhere. You never even think of me and my commands, the Lord God says.

¹³ "But now I snap my fingers and call a halt to your dishonest gain and bloodshed. ¹⁴ How strong and courageous will you be then, in my day of reckoning? For I, the Lord, have spoken, and I will do all that I have said. ¹⁵ I will scatter you throughout the world and burn out the wickedness within you. ¹⁶ You will be dishonored among the nations, and you shall know I am the Lord."

¹⁷ Then the Lord said this:

¹⁸,¹⁹,²⁰ "Son of dust, the people of Israel are the worthless slag left when silver is smelted. They are the dross, compounded from the brass, the tin, the iron and the lead. Therefore the Lord God says: Because you are worthless dross, I will bring you to my crucible in Jerusalem, to smelt you with the

---

ᵈ Implied.   22a Or, "You degrade yourselves through homosexual practices and through lying with women in their time of menstruation."

heat of my wrath. [21] I will blow the fire of my wrath upon you, [22] and you will melt like silver in fierce heat, and you will know that I, the Lord, have poured my wrath upon you."

[23] Again the message of the Lord came to me, saying:

[24] "Son of dust, say to the people of Israel: In the day of my indignation you shall be like an uncleared wilderness, or a desert without rain. [25] Your 'prophets' have plotted against you like lions stalking prey. They devour many lives; they seize treasures and extort wealth; they multiply the widows in the land. [26] Your priests have violated my laws and defiled my Temple and my holiness. To them the things of God are no more important than any daily task. They have not taught my people the difference between right and wrong, and they disregard my Sabbaths, so my holy name is greatly defiled among them. [27] Your leaders are like wolves, who tear apart their victims, and they destroy lives for profit. [28] Your 'prophets' describe false visions and speak false messages they claim are from God, when he hasn't spoken one word to them at all. Thus they repair the walls with whitewash! [29] Even the common people oppress and rob the poor and needy and cruelly extort from aliens.

[30] "I looked in vain for anyone who would build again the wall of righteousness that guards the land, who could stand in the gap and defend you from my just attacks, but I found not one. [31] And so the Lord God says: I will pour out my anger upon you; I will consume you with the fire of my wrath. I have heaped upon you the full penalty for all your sins."

23 THE LORD'S MESSAGE came to me again, saying:

[2,3] "Son of dust, there were two sisters who as young girls became prostitutes in Egypt. [4,5] The older girl was named Oholah; her sister was Oholibah. (I am speaking of Samaria and Jerusalem!) I married them, and they bore me sons and daughters. But then Oholah turned to other gods instead of me, and gave her love to the Assyrians, her neighbors, [6] for they were all attractive young men, captains and commanders, in handsome blue, dashing about on their horses. [7] And so she sinned with them—the choicest men of Assyria—worshiping their idols, defiling herself. [8] For when she left Egypt, she did not leave her spirit of prostitution behind, but was still as lewd as in her youth, when the Egyptians poured out their lusts upon her and robbed her of her virginity.

[9] "And so I delivered her into the evil clutches of the Assyrians whose gods she loved so much. [10] They stripped her and killed her and took away her children as their slaves. Her name was known to every woman in the land as a sinner who had received what she deserved.

[11] "But when Oholibah (Jerusalem) saw what had happened to her sister she went right ahead in the same way, and sinned even more than her sister. [12] She fawned over her Assyrian neighbors,[a] those handsome young men on fine steeds, those army officers in handsome uniforms—all of them desirable. [13] I saw the way she was going, following right along behind her older sister.

[14,15] "She was in fact more debased than Samaria, for she fell in love with pictures she saw painted on a wall! They were pictures of Babylonian military officers, outfitted in striking red uniforms, with handsome belts, and flowing turbans on their heads. [16] When she saw these paintings she longed to give herself to the men pictured, so she sent messengers[b] to Chaldea to invite them to come to her. [17] And they came and committed adultery with her, defiling her in the bed of love, but afterward she hated them and broke off all relations with them.[c]

[18] "And I despised her just as I despised her sister, because she flaunted herself before them and gave herself to their lust. [19,20] But that didn't bother her. She turned to even greater prostitution, sinning with the lustful men she remembered from

---

a i.e., when Ahaz paid "protection money" to Tiglath-pileser II (2 Kings 16:7, 8).·   b This occurred when Hezekiah entertained the embassy from Babylon (Isaiah 38–39), also during the reign of Manasseh.
c The anti-Babylonian party in Judah looked to Egypt for help during the reigns of the last twc Judean kings, Jehoiakim and Zedekiah.

her youth when she was a prostitute in Egypt.[d] [21] And thus you celebrated those former days when as a young girl you gave your virginity to those from Egypt.

[22] "And now the Lord God says that he will raise against you, O Oholibah (Jerusalem), those very nations from which you turned away, disgusted. [23] For the Babylonians will come, and all the Chaldeans from Pekod and Shoa and Koa; and all the Assyrians with them—handsome young men of high rank, riding their steeds. [24] They will come against you from the north with chariots and wagons and a great army fully prepared for attack. They will surround you on every side with armored men and I will let them at you, to do with you as they wish. [25] And I will send my jealousy against you and deal furiously with you, and cut off your nose and ears; your survivors will be killed; your children will be taken away as slaves, and everything left will be burned. [26] They will strip you of your beautiful clothes and jewels.

[27] "And so I will put a stop to your lewdness and prostitution brought from the land of Egypt; you will no more long for Egypt and her gods. [28] For the Lord God says: I will surely deliver you over to your enemies, to those you loathe. [29] They will deal with you in hatred, and rob you of all that you own, leaving you naked and bare. And the shame of your prostitution shall be exposed to all the world.

[30] "You brought all this upon yourself by worshiping the gods of other nations, defiling yourself with all their idols. [31] You have followed in your sister's footsteps, so I will punish you with the same terrors that destroyed her. [32] Yes, the terrors that fell upon her will fall upon you—and the cup from which she drank was full and large. And all the world will mock you for your woe. [33] You will reel like a drunkard beneath the awful blows of sorrow and distress, just as your sister Samaria did. [34] In deep anguish you will drain that cup of terror to the very bottom and will lick the inside to get every drop. For I have spoken, says the Lord. [35] Because you have forgotten me and turned your backs upon me, therefore you

must bear the consequence of all your sin.

[36] "Son of dust, you must accuse Jerusalem and Samaria of all their awful deeds. [37] For they have committed both adultery and murder; they have worshiped idols and murdered my children whom they bore to me, burning them as sacrifices on their altars. [38] On the same day they defiled my Temple and ignored my Sabbaths, [39] for when they had murdered their children in front of their idols, then even that same day they actually came into my Temple to worship! That is how much regard they have for me!

[40] "You even sent away to distant lands for priests to come with other gods for you to serve, and they have come and been welcomed! You bathed yourself, painted your eyelids, and put on your finest jewels for them. [41] You sat together on a beautifully embroidered bed and put my incense and my oil upon a table spread before you. [42] From your apartment came the sound of many men carousing—lewd men and drunkards from the wilderness, who put bracelets on your wrists and beautiful crowns upon your head. [43] Will they commit adultery with these who have become old harlot hags? [44] Yet that is what they did. They went in to them—to Samaria and Jerusalem, these shameless harlots—with all the zest of lustful men who visit prostitutes. [45] But just persons everywhere will judge them for what they really are—adulteresses and murderers. They will mete out to them the sentences the law demands.

[46] "The Lord God says: Bring an army against them and hand them out to be crushed and despised. [47] For their enemies will stone them and kill them with swords; they will butcher their sons and daughters and burn their homes. [48] Thus will I make lewdness and idolatry to cease from the land. My judgment will be a lesson against idolatry for all to see. [49] For you will be fully repaid for all your harlotry, your worshiping of idols. You will suffer the full penalty, and you will know that I alone am God."

24 ONE DAY LATE in December of the ninth year (of King Jehoiachin's cap-

---

d i.e., during the reign of Josiah.

tivity), another message came to me from the Lord.

² "Son of dust," he said, "write down this date, for today the king of Babylon has attacked Jerusalem. ³ And now give this parable to these rebels, Israel; tell them the Lord God says: Put a pot of water on the fire to boil. ⁴ Fill it with choicest mutton, the rump and shoulder and all the most tender cuts. ⁵ Use only the best sheep from the flock, and heap fuel on the fire beneath the pot. Boil the meat well, until the flesh falls off the bones.

⁶ "For the Lord God says: Woe to Jerusalem, City of Murderers; you are a pot that is pitted with rust and with wickedness. So take out the meat chunk by chunk in whatever order it comes—for none is better than any other.ᵃ ⁷ For her wickedness is evident to all—she boldly murders, leaving blood upon the rocks in open view for all to see; she does not even try to cover it. ⁸ And I have left it there, uncovered, to shout to me against her and arouse my wrath and vengeance.

⁹ "Woe to Jerusalem, City of Murderers. I will pile on the fuel beneath her. ¹⁰ Heap on the wood; let the fire roar and the pot boil. Cook the meat well and then empty the pot and burn the bones. ¹¹ Now set it empty on the coals to scorch away the rust and corruption. ¹² But all for naught—it all remains despite the hottest fire. ¹³ It is the rust and corruption of your filthy lewdness, of worshiping your idols. And now, because I wanted to cleanse you and you refused, remain filthy until my fury has accomplished all its terrors upon you! ¹⁴ I, the Lord, have spoken it; it shall come to pass and I will do it."

¹⁵ Again a message came to me from the Lord, saying:

¹⁶ "Son of dust, I am going to take away your lovely wife. Suddenly, she will die. Yet you must show no sorrow. Do not weep; let there be no tears. ¹⁷ You may sigh, but only quietly. Let there be no wailing at her grave; don't bare your head nor feet, and don't accept the food brought to you by consoling friends."

¹⁸ I proclaimed this to the people in the morning, and in the evening my wife died. The next morning I did all the Lord had told me to.

¹⁹ Then the people said: "What does all this mean? What are you trying to tell us?"

²⁰,²¹ And I answered, "The Lord told me to say to the people of Israel: I will destroy my lovely, beautiful Temple, the strength of your nation. And your sons and daughters in Judea will be slaughtered by the sword. ²² And you will do as I have done; you may not mourn in public or console yourself by eating the food brought to you by sympathetic friends. ²³ Your head and feet shall not be bared; you shall not mourn or weep. But you will sorrow to one another for your sins, and mourn privately for all the evil you have done. ²⁴ Ezekiel is an example to you, the Lord God says. You will do as he has done. And when that time comes, then you will know I am the Lord."

²⁵ "Son of dust, on the day I finish taking from them in Jerusalem the joy of their hearts and their glory and joys—their wives and their sons and their daughters— ²⁶ on that day a refugee from Jerusalem will start on a journey to come to you in Babylon to tell you what has happened. ²⁷ And on the day of his arrival, your voice will suddenly return to you so that you can talk with him; and you will be a symbol for these people and they shall know I am the Lord."

25 THEN THE LORD'S message came to me again. He said:

² "Son of dust, look toward the land of Ammon and prophesy against its people. ³ Tell them: Listen to what the Lord God says. Because you scoffed when my Temple was destroyed, and mocked Israel in her anguish, and laughed at Judah when she was marched away captive, ⁴ therefore I will let the Bedouins from the desert to the east of you overrun your land. They will set up their encampments among you. They will harvest all your fruit and steal your dairy cattle. ⁵ And I will turn the city of Rabbah into a pasture for camels and all the country of the Ammonites into a waste land where flocks of sheep can graze. Then you will know I am the Lord.

---

a Literally, "no lot has fallen upon it."

6 "For the Lord God says: Because you clapped and stamped and cheered with glee at the destruction of my people, 7 therefore I will lay my hand heavily upon you, delivering you to many nations for devastation. I will cut you off from being a nation any more. I will destroy you; then you shall know I am the Lord.

8 "And the Lord God says: Because the Moabites have said that Judah is no better off than any other nation, 9,10 therefore I will open up the eastern flank of Moab, wiping out her frontier cities, the glory of the nation—Beth-jeshimoth, Baal-meon and Kiriathaim. And Bedouin tribes from the desert to the east will pour in upon her, just as they will upon Ammon. And Moab will no longer be counted among the nations. 11 Thus I will bring down my judgment upon the Moabites, and they shall know I am the Lord.

12 "And the Lord God says: Because the people of Edom have sinned so greatly by avenging themselves upon the people of Judah, 13 I will smash Edom with my fist and wipe out her people, her cattle and her flocks. The sword will destroy everything from Teman to Dedan. 14 By the hand of my people, Israel, this shall be done. They will carry out my furious vengeance.

15 "And the Lord God says: Because the Philistines have acted against Judah out of revenge and long-standing hatred, 16 I will shake my fist over the land of the Philistines, and I will wipe out the Cherithites and utterly destroy those along the sea coast. 17 I will execute terrible vengeance upon them to rebuke them for what they have done. And when all this happens, then they shall know I am the Lord."

26 ANOTHER MESSAGE CAME to me from the Lord on the first day of the month, in the eleventh year (after King Jehoiachin was taken away to captivity).

2 "Son of dust, Tyre has rejoiced over the fall of Jerusalem, saying, 'Ha! She who controlled the lucrative north-south trade routes along the coast and along the course of the Jordan River[a] has been broken, and

I have fallen heir! Because she has been laid waste, I shall become wealthy!'

3 "Therefore the Lord God says: I stand against you, Tyre, and I will bring nations against you like ocean waves. 4 They will destroy the walls of Tyre and tear down her towers. I will scrape away her soil and make her a bare rock! 5 Her island shall become uninhabited, a place for fishermen to spread their nets, for I have spoken it, says the Lord God. Tyre shall become the prey of many nations, 6 and her mainland city shall perish by the sword. Then they shall know I am the Lord.

7 "For the Lord God says: I will bring Nebuchadnezzar, king of Babylon—the king of kings from the north—against Tyre with a great army and cavalry and chariots. 8 First he will destroy your suburbs; then he will attack your mainland city by building a siege wall and raising a roof of shields against it. 9 He will set up battering rams against your walls and with sledge hammers demolish your forts. 10 The hoofs of his cavalry will choke the city with dust, and your walls will shake as the horses gallop through your broken gates, pulling chariots behind them. 11 Horsemen will occupy every street in the city; they will butcher your people, and your famous, huge pillars will topple.

12 "They will plunder all your riches and merchandise and break down your walls. They will destroy your lovely homes and dump your stones and timber and even your dust into the sea. 13 I will stop the music of your songs. No more will there be the sound of harps among you. 14 I will make your island a bare rock,[b] a place for fishermen to spread their nets. You will never be rebuilt, for I, the Lord, have spoken it. So says the Lord. 15 The whole country will shake with your fall; the wounded will scream as the slaughter goes on.

16 "Then all the seaport rulers shall come down from their thrones and lay aside their robes and beautiful garments and sit on the ground shaking with fear at what they have seen. 17 And they shall wail for you, singing this dirge: 'O mighty island city, with your

---

a Literally, "the gate of the peoples."   b Certain aspects of verses 12 and 14 exceed the actual damage done to Tyre by Nebuchadnezzar, and foreshadow what happened to the island settlement later as a result of the conquest by Alexander the Great.

naval power that terrorized the mainland, how you have vanished from the seas! [18] How the islands tremble at your fall! They watch dismayed.'

[19] "For the Lord God says: I will destroy Tyre to the ground. You will sink beneath the terrible waves of enemy attack. Great seas shall swallow you. [20] I will send you to the pit of hell to lie there with those of long ago. Your city will lie in ruins, dead, like the bodies of those in the underworld who entered long ago the nether world of the dead. Never again will you be inhabited or be given beauty here in the land of those who live. [21] I will bring you to a dreadful end; no search will be enough to find you, says the Lord."

27 THEN THIS MESSAGE came to me from the Lord. He said:

[2] "Son of dust, sing this sad dirge for Tyre:

[3] "O mighty seaport city, merchant center of the world, the Lord God speaks. You say, 'I am the most beautiful city in all the world.' [4] You have extended your boundaries out into the sea; your architects have made you glorious. [5] You are like a ship built of finest fir from Senir. They took a cedar from Lebanon to make a mast for you. [6] They made your oars from oaks of Bashan. The walls of your cabin are of cypress from the southern coast of Cyprus. [7] Your sails are made of Egypt's finest linens; you stand beneath awnings bright with purple and scarlet dyes from eastern Cyprus.

[8] "Your sailors come from Sidon and Arvad; your helmsmen are skilled men from Zemer. [9] Wise old craftsmen from Gebal do the calking. Ships come from every land with all their goods to barter for your trade.

[10] "Your army includes men from far-off Paras, Lud and Put.[a] They serve you—it is a feather in your cap to have their shields hang upon your walls; it is the ultimate of honor. [11] Men from Arvad and from Helech[b] are the sentinels upon your walls; your

towers are manned by men from Gamad. Their shields hang row on row upon the walls, perfecting your glory.

[12] "From Tarshish come all kinds of riches to your markets—silver, iron, tin and lead. [13] Merchants from Javan, Tubal and Meshech[c] bring slaves and bronze dishes, [14] while from Togarmah[c] come chariot horses, steeds and mules.

[15] "Merchants come to you from Rhodes, and many coastlands are your captive markets, giving payment in ebony and ivory. [16] Edom sends her traders to buy your many wares. They bring emeralds, purple dyes, embroidery, fine linen, and jewelry of coral and agate. [17] Judah and the cities in what was once the kingdom of Israel send merchants with wheat from Minnith and Pannag,[d] and with honey, oil and balm. [18] Damascus comes. She brings wines from Helbon, and white Syrian wool to trade for all the rich variety of goods you make. [19] Vedan and Javan bring Arabian yarn,[e] wrought iron, cassia and calamus, [20] while Dedan brings expensive saddlecloths for riding.

[21] "The Arabians, and Kedar's wealthy merchant princes bring you lambs and rams and goats. [22] The merchants of Sheba and Raamah come with all kinds of spices, jewels and gold. [23] Haran and Canneh, Eden, Asshur and Chilmad all send their wares. [24] They bring choice fabrics to trade—blue cloth, embroidery and many-colored carpets bound with cords and made secure. [25] The ships of Tarshish are your ocean caravans; your island warehouse is filled to the brim!

[26] "But now your statesmen bring your ship of state into a hurricane! Your mighty vessel flounders in the heavy eastern gale,[f] and you are wrecked in the heart of the seas! [27] Everything is lost. Your riches and wares, your sailors and pilots, your shipwrights and merchants and soldiers and all the people sink into the sea on the day of your vast ruin.

[28] "The surrounding cities quake at the sound as your pilots scream with fright.

---

a These were three cities of ancient North Africa. records as Hilakku.   c Regions of Asia Minor, now in Turkey.   d Or, "with wheat, minnith and pannag." If these were commodities, their identification is uncertain.   e Or, probably better, "They exchanged wine from Uzal for your wares." The text here is uncertain.   b A region in ancient Cilicia known from Assyrian   f i.e., Nebuchadnezzar of Babylonia.

²⁹ All your sailors out at sea come to land and watch upon the mainland shore, ³⁰ weeping bitterly and casting dust upon their heads and wallowing in ashes. ³¹ They shave their heads in grief and put on sackcloth and weep for you with bitterness of heart and deep mourning.

³² "And this is the song of their sorrow: 'Where in all the world was there ever such a wondrous city as Tyre, destroyed in the midst of the sea? ³³ Your merchandise satisfied the desires of many nations. Kings at the ends of the earth rejoiced in the riches you sent them. ³⁴ Now you lie broken beneath the sea; all your merchandise and all your crew have perished with you. ³⁵ All who live along the coastlands watch, incredulous. Their kings are horribly afraid and look on with twisted faces. ³⁶ The merchants of the nations shake their heads, for your fate is dreadful; you have forever perished.' "

28 HERE IS ANOTHER message given to me from the Lord:

²,³ "Son of dust, say to the prince of Tyre: The Lord God says: You are so proud you think you are God, sitting on the throne of a god on your island home in the midst of the seas. But you are only a man, and not a god, though you boast yourself to be like God. You are wiser than Daniel, for no secret is hidden from you. ⁴ You have used your wisdom and understanding to get great wealth—gold and silver and many treasures. ⁵ Yes, your wisdom has made you very rich and very proud.

⁶ "Therefore the Lord God says: Because you claim that you are as wise as God, ⁷ an enemy army, the terror of the nations, shall suddenly draw their swords against your marvelous wisdom and defile your splendor! ⁸ They will bring you to the pit of hell and you shall die as those pierced with many wounds, there on your island in the heart of the seas. ⁹ Then will you boast as a god? At least to these invaders you will be no god, but merely man! ¹⁰ You will die like an outcast at the hands of foreigners. For I have spoken it, the Lord God says."

¹¹ Then this further message came to me from the Lord:

¹² "Son of dust, weep for the king of Tyre.ᵃ Tell him, the Lord God says: You were the perfection of wisdom and beauty. ¹³ You were in Eden, the garden of God; your clothing was bejeweled with every precious stone—ruby, topaz, diamond, chrysolite, onyx, jasper, sapphire, carbuncle, and emerald—all in beautiful settings of finest gold. They were given to you on the day you were created. ¹⁴ I appointed you to be the anointed guardian cherub. You had access to the holy mountain of God. You walked among the stones of fire.ᵇ

¹⁵ "You were perfect in all you did from the day you were created until that time when wrong was found in you. ¹⁶ Your great wealth filled you with internal turmoil and you sinned. Therefore, I cast you out of the mountain of God like a common sinner. I destroyed you, O overshadowing cherub, from the midst of the stones of fire.ᶜ ¹⁷ Your heart was filled with pride because of all your beauty; you corrupted your wisdom for the sake of your splendor. Therefore I have cast you down to the ground and exposed you helpless before the curious gaze of kings. ¹⁸ You defiled your holiness with lust for gain;ᵈ therefore I brought forth fire from your own actionsᵉ and let it burn you to ashes upon the earth in the sight of all those watching you. ¹⁹ All who know you are appalled at your fate; you are an example of horror; you are destroyed forever."

²⁰ Then another message came to me from the Lord:

²¹ "Son of dust, look toward the city of Sidon and prophesy against it. Say to it:

²² "The Lord God says: I am your enemy, O Sidon, and I will reveal my power over you. When I destroy you and show forth my holiness upon you then all who see shall know I am the Lord. ²³ I will send an epidemic of disease and an army to destroy; the wounded shall be slain in your streets

---

a In this passage (verses 11-19) some descriptive phrases apply to a human king of Tyre, and some seem to apply to Satan. Great care must therefore be taken to apply these verses with discernment.
b Probably a symbol of the angels.   c Or, "and the guardian cherub drove you out from the midst of the stones of fire."   d Literally, "in the unrighteousness of your trade."   e Literally, "I brought fire from the midst of you."

by troops on every side. Then you will know I am the Lord. ²⁴ No longer shall you and Israel's other neighbor nations prick and tear at Israel like thorns and briars, though they formerly despised her and treated her with great contempt.

²⁵ "The people of Israel will once more live in their own land, the land I gave their father Jacob. For I will gather them back again from distant lands where I have scattered them and I will show the nations of the world my holiness among my people. ²⁶ They will live safely in Israel, and build their homes and plant their vineyards. When I punish all the bordering nations that treated them with such contempt, then they shall know I am the Lord their God."

29 LATE IN DECEMBER of the tenth year (of the imprisonment of King Jehoiachin), this message came to me from the Lord:

² "Son of dust, face toward Egypt and prophesy against Pharaoh her king and all her people. ³ Tell them that the Lord God says: I am your enemy, Pharaoh, king of Egypt—mighty dragon lying in the middle of your rivers. For you have said, 'The Nile is mine; I have made it for myself!' ⁴ I will put hooks into your jaws and drag you out onto the land with fish sticking to your scales. ⁵ And I will leave you and all the fish stranded in the desert to die, and you won't be buried, for I have given you as food to the wild animals and birds.

⁶ "Because of the way your might collapsed when Israel called on you for aid [instead of trusting meᵃ], all of you shall know I am the Lord. ⁷ Israel leaned on you but, like a cracked staff, you snapped beneath her hand and wrenched her shoulder out of joint and made her stagger with the pain. ⁸ Therefore the Lord God says: I will bring an army against you, O Egypt, and destroy both men and herds. ⁹ The land of Egypt shall become a desolate wasteland, and the Egyptians will know that I, the Lord, have done it.

¹⁰ "Because you said: 'The Nile is mine! I made it!' therefore I am against you and

your river and I will utterly destroy the land of Egypt, from Migdol to Syene, as far south as the border of Ethiopia. ¹¹ For forty years not a soul will pass that way, neither men nor animals. It will be completely uninhabited. ¹² I will make Egypt desolate, surrounded by desolate nations, and her cities will lie as wastelands for forty years. I will exile the Egyptians to other lands.

¹³ "But the Lord God says that at the end of the forty years he will bring the Egyptians home again from the nations to which they will be banished. ¹⁴ And I will restore the fortunes of Egypt and bring her people back to the land of Pathros in southern Egypt where they were born, but she will be an unimportant, minor kingdom. ¹⁵ She will be the lowliest of all the nations; never again will she raise herself above the other nations; never again will Egypt be great enough for that.

¹⁶ "Israel will no longer expect any help from Egypt. Whenever she thinks of asking for it, then she will remember her sin in seeking it before. Then Israel will know that I alone am God."

¹⁷ In the twenty-seventh year of King Jehoiachin's captivity,ᵃ around the middle of March, this message came to me from the Lord:

¹⁸ "Son of dust, the army of King Nebuchadnezzar of Babylon fought hard against Tyre. The soldiers' heads were bald (from carrying heavy basketfuls of earth); their shoulders were raw and blistered (from burdens of stones for the siege). And Nebuchadnezzar received no compensation and could not pay the army for all this work.ᵇ ¹⁹ Therefore, the Lord God says, I will give the land of Egypt to Nebuchadnezzar, king of Babylon, and he will carry off her wealth, plundering everything she has, for his army. ²⁰ Yes, I have given him the land of Egypt for his salary, because he was working for me during those thirteen years at Tyre,ᵇ says the Lord. ²¹ And the day will come when I will cause the ancient glory of Israel to revive, and then at last her words will be respected, and Egypt shall know I am the Lord."

a Implied.   b Tyre capitulated to Nebuchadnezzar at the end of a 13-year siege (587-574 B.C.). There was little left to pay the "salary" of Nebuchadnezzar, so the Lord was giving Egypt to him to make up for what he was "shortchanged" at Tyre.

30 ANOTHER MESSAGE FROM the Lord! [2,3] "Son of dust, prophesy and say: The Lord God says, Weep, for the terrible day is almost here; the day of the Lord; a day of clouds and gloom; a day of despair for the nations! [4] A sword shall fall on Egypt; the slain shall cover the ground. Her wealth is taken away, her foundations destroyed. The land of Cush has been ravished. [5] For Cush and Put and Lud, Arabia and Libya and all the countries leagued with them shall perish in that war.

[6] "For the Lord says: All Egypt's allies shall fall, and the pride of her power shall end. From Migdol to Syene they shall perish by the sword. [7] She shall be desolate, surrounded by desolate nations, and her cities shall be in ruins, surrounded by other ruined cities. [8] And they will know I am the Lord when I have set Egypt on fire and destroyed her allies. [9] At that time I will send swift messengers to bring panic to the Ethiopians; great terror shall befall them at that time of Egypt's doom. This will all come true.

[10] "For the Lord God says: Nebuchadnezzar, king of Babylon, will destroy the multitudes of Egypt. [11] He and his armies— the terror of the nations—are sent to demolish the land. They shall war against Egypt and cover the ground with the slain. [12] I will dry up the Nile and sell the whole land to wicked men. I will destroy Egypt and everything in it, using foreigners to do it. I, the Lord, have spoken it. [13] And I will smash the idols of Egypt and the images at Memphis, and there will be no king in Egypt; anarchy shall reign!

[14] "The cities of Pathros [along the upper Nile[a]], and Zoan and Thebes shall lie in ruins by my hand. [15] And I will pour out my fury upon Pelusium, the strongest fortress of Egypt, and I will stamp out the people of Thebes. [16] Yes, I will set fire to Egypt, Pelusium will be racked with pain, Thebes will be torn apart, Memphis will be in daily terror. [17] The young men of Heliopolis and Bubastis shall die by the sword and the women will be taken away as slaves.

[18] When I come to break the power of Egypt it will be a dark day for Tehaphnehes too; a dark cloud will cover her, and her daughters will be taken away as captives. [19] And so I will greatly punish Egypt and they shall know I am the Lord."

[20] A year later,[b] around the middle of March of the eleventh year of King Jehoiachin's captivity, this message came to me:

[21] "Son of dust, I have broken the arm[c] of Pharaoh, king of Egypt, and it has not been set nor put into a cast to make it strong enough to hold a sword again. [22] For, the Lord God says, I am against Pharaoh, king of Egypt, and I will break both his arms— the strong one and the one that was broken before, and I will make his sword clatter to the ground. [23] And I will banish the Egyptians to many lands. [24] And I will strengthen the arms of the king of Babylon and place my sword in his hand. But I will break the arms of Pharaoh, king of Egypt, and he shall groan before the king of Babylon as one who has been wounded unto death. [25] I will strengthen the hands of the king of Babylon, while the arms of Pharaoh fall useless to his sides. Yes, when I place my sword into the hand of the king of Babylon, and he swings it over the land of Egypt, Egypt shall know I am the Lord. [26] I will scatter the Egyptians among the nations; then they shall know I am the Lord."

31 IN MID-MAY OF the eleventh year of King Jehoiachin's captivity,[a] this message came to me from the Lord: [2,3] "Son of dust, tell Pharaoh, king of Egypt, and all his people: You are as Assyria was—a great and mighty nation—like a cedar of Lebanon, full of thick branches and forest shade, with its head high up among the clouds. [4] Its roots went deep into the moist earth. It grew luxuriantly and gave streamlets of water to all the trees around. [5] It towered above all the other trees. It prospered and grew long thick branches because of all the water at its roots. [6] The birds nested in its branches, and in its shade the flocks and herds gave birth

---

a Implied.   b 587 B.C., the year Jerusalem fell to Nebuchadnezzar and was destroyed.
c When Pharaoh Hophra sent an army to relieve Jerusalem in 588, Nebuchadnezzar withdrew from the siege just long enough to defeat the Egyptian force. This is what Ezekiel means by the first "broken arm."
31a Implied. It was the year 587 B.C., the year Jerusalem fell.

to young. All the great nations of the world lived beneath its shadow. ⁷ It was strong and beautiful, for its roots went deep to water. ⁸ This tree was taller than any other in the garden of God; no cypress had branches equal to it; none had boughs to compare; none equaled it in beauty. ⁹ Because of the magnificence that I gave it, it was the envy of all the other trees of Eden.

¹⁰ "But Egypt[b] has become proud and arrogant, the Lord God says. Therefore because she has set herself so high above the others, reaching to the clouds, ¹¹ I will deliver her into the hands of a mighty nation, to destroy her as her wickedness deserves. I, myself, will cut her down. ¹² A foreign army (from Babylon)—the terror of the nations—will invade her land and cut her down and leave her fallen on the ground. Her branches will be scattered across the mountains and valleys and rivers of the land. All those who live beneath her shade will go away and leave her lying there. ¹³ The birds will pluck off her twigs and the wild animals will lie among her branches; ¹⁴ let no other nation exult with pride for its own prosperity, though it be higher than the clouds, for all are doomed and they will land in hell, along with all the proud men of the world.

¹⁵ "The Lord God says: When she fell I made the oceans mourn for her and restrained their tides.[c] I clothed Lebanon in black and caused the trees of Lebanon to weep. ¹⁶ I made the nations shake with fear at the sound of her fall, for I threw her down to hell with all the others like her. And all the other proud trees of Eden, the choicest and the best of Lebanon, the ones whose roots went deep into the water, are comforted to find her there with them in hell. ¹⁷ Her allies too are all destroyed and perish with her. They went down with her to the nether world—those nations that had lived beneath her shade.

¹⁸ "O Egypt, you are great and glorious among the trees of Eden—the nations of the world. And you will be brought down to the pit of hell with all these other nations. You will be among the nations you despise,

killed by the sword. This is the fate of Pharaoh and all his teeming masses, says the Lord."

32 IN MID-FEBRUARY OF the twelfth year of King Jehoiachin's captivity, this message came to me from the Lord:

² "Son of dust, mourn for Pharaoh, king of Egypt, and say to him: You think of yourself as a strong young lion among the nations, but you are merely a crocodile[a] along the banks of the Nile, making bubbles and muddying the stream.

³ "The Lord God says: I will send a great army to catch you with my net. I will haul you out, ⁴ and leave you stranded on the land to die. And all the birds of the heavens will light upon you and the wild animals of the whole earth will devour you until they are glutted and full. ⁵ And I will cover the hills with your flesh and fill the valleys with your bones. ⁶ And I will drench the earth with your gushing blood, filling the ravines to the tops of the mountains. ⁷ I will blot you out, and I will veil the heavens and darken the stars. I will cover the sun with a cloud, and the moon shall not give you her light. ⁸ Yes, darkness will be everywhere across your land—even the bright stars will be dark above you.

⁹ "And when I destroy you,[b] grief will be in many hearts among the distant nations you have never seen. ¹⁰ Yes, terror shall strike in many lands, and their kings shall be terribly afraid because of all I do to you. They shall shudder with terror when I brandish my sword before them. They shall greatly tremble for their lives on the day of your fall.

¹¹ "For the Lord God says: The sword of the king of Babylon shall come upon you. ¹² I will destroy you with Babylon's mighty army—the terror of the nations. It will smash the pride of Egypt and all her people; all will perish. ¹³ I will destroy all your flocks and herds that graze beside the streams, and neither man nor animal will disturb those waters any more. ¹⁴ Therefore the waters of Egypt will be as clear and flow as smoothly as olive oil, the Lord God says.

---

b Implied.   c Literally, "the great waters were held back."   32a Or, "sea serpent."
b Or, "when I carry you captive among the nations."

¹⁵ And when I destroy Egypt and wipe out everything she has, then she shall know that I, the Lord, have done it. ¹⁶ Yes, cry for the sorrows of Egypt. Let all the nations weep for her and for her people, says the Lord."

¹⁷ Two weeks later,ᶜ another message came to me from the Lord. He said:

¹⁸ "Son of dust, weep for the people of Egypt and for the other mighty nations. Send them down to the nether world among the denizens of death. ¹⁹ What nation is as beautiful as you, O Egypt? Yet your doom is the pit; you will be laid beside the people you despise. ²⁰ The Egyptians will die with the multitudes slain by the sword, for the sword is drawn against the land of Egypt. She will be drawn down to judgment. ²¹ The mighty warriors in the nether world will welcome her as she arrives with all her friends, to lie there beside the nations she despised, all victims of the sword.

²² "The princes of Assyria lie there surrounded by the graves of all her people, those the sword has slain. ²³ Their graves are in the depths of hell, surrounded by their allies. All these mighty men who once struck terror into the hearts of everyone are now dead at the hands of their foes.

²⁴ "Great kings of Elam lie there with their people. They scourged the nations while they lived, and now they lie undone in hell; their fate is the same as that of ordinary men. ²⁵ They have a resting place among the slain, surrounded by the graves of all their people. Yes, they terrorized the nations while they lived, but now they lie in shame in the pit, slain by the sword.

²⁶ "The princes of Meshech and Tubal are there, surrounded by the graves of all their armies—all of them idolaters—who once struck terror to the hearts of all; now they lie dead. ²⁷ They are buried in a common grave, and not as the fallen lords who are buried in great honor with their weapons beside them, with their shields covering them andᵈ their swords beneath their heads. They were a terror to all while they lived. ²⁸ Now you will lie crushed and broken among the idolaters, among those who are slain by the sword.

²⁹ "Edom is there with her kings and her princes; mighty as they were, they too lie among the others whom the sword has slain, with the idolaters who have gone down to the pit. ³⁰ All the princes of the north are there, and the Sidonians, all slain. Once a terror, now they lie in shame; they lie in ignominy with all the other slain who go down to the pit.

³¹ "When Pharaoh arrives, he will be comforted to find that he is not alone in having all his army slain, says the Lord God. ³² For I have caused my terror to fall upon all the living. And Pharaoh and his army shall lie among the idolaters who are slain by the sword."

33 ONCE AGAIN A message came to me from the Lord. He said:

² "Son of dust, tell your people: When I bring an army against a country, and the people of that land choose a watchman, ³ and when he sees the army coming, and blows the alarm to warn them, ⁴ then anyone who hears the alarm and refuses to heed it—well, if he dies the fault is his own. ⁵ For he heard the warning and wouldn't listen; the fault is his. If he had heeded the warning, he would have saved his life. ⁶ But if the watchman sees the enemy coming and doesn't sound the alarm and warn the people, he is responsible for their deaths. They will die in their sins, but I will charge the watchman with their deaths.

⁷ "So with you, son of dust. I have appointed you as a watchman for the people of Israel; therefore listen to what I say and warn them for me. ⁸ When I say to the wicked, 'O wicked man, you will die!' and you don't tell him what I say, so that he does not repent—that wicked person will die in his sins, but I will hold you responsible for his death. ⁹ But if you warn him to repent and he doesn't, he will die in his sin, and you will not be responsible.

¹⁰ "O people of Israel, you are saying: 'Our sins are heavy upon us; we pine away with guilt. How can we live?' ¹¹ Tell them: As I live, says the Lord God, I have no pleasure in the death of the wicked; *I desire*

---

c Literally, "In the twelfth year, on the fifteenth day of the month."   d Literally, "their iniquity (iniquities) upon their bones."

that the wicked turn from his evil ways and live. Turn, turn from your wickedness, for why will you die, O Israel? ¹² For the good works of a righteous man will not save him if he turns to sin; and the sins of an evil man will not destroy him if he repents and turns from his sins.

¹³ "I have said the good man will live. But if he sins, expecting his past goodness to save him, then none of his good deeds will be remembered. I will destroy him for his sins. ¹⁴ And when I tell the wicked he will die and then he turns from his sins and does what is fair and right— ¹⁵ if he gives back the borrower's pledge and returns what he has stolen and walks along the paths of right, not doing evil—he shall surely live. He shall not die. ¹⁶ None of his past sins shall be brought up against him, for he has turned to the good and shall surely live.

¹⁷ "And yet your people are saying the Lord isn't fair. The trouble is *they* aren't fair. ¹⁸ For again I say, when the good man turns to evil, he shall die. ¹⁹ But if the wicked turns from his wickedness and does what's fair and just, he shall live. ²⁰ Yet you are saying the Lord isn't fair. But I will judge each of you in accordance with his deeds."

²¹ In the eleventh^a year of our exile, late in December, one of those who escaped from Jerusalem arrived to tell me, "The city has fallen!" ²² Now the hand of the Lord had been upon me the previous evening, and he had healed me so that I could speak again by the time the man arrived.

²³ Then this message came to me:

²⁴ "Son of dust, the scattered remnants of Judah living among the ruined cities keep saying, 'Abraham was only one man and yet he got possession of the whole country! We are many, so we should certainly be able to get it back!' ²⁵ But the Lord God says: You are powerless, for you do evil! You eat meat with the blood; you worship idols, and murder. Do you suppose I'll let you have the land? ²⁶ Murderers! Idolators! Adulterers! Should you possess the land?

²⁷ "Tell them: The Lord God says: As I live, surely those living in the ruins shall die by the sword. Those living in the open fields shall be eaten by wild animals, and those in the forts and caves shall die of disease. ²⁸ I will desolate the land and her pride, and her power shall come to an end. And the mountain villages of Israel shall be so ruined that no one will even travel through them. ²⁹ When I have ruined the land because of their sins, then they shall know I am the Lord.

³⁰ "Son of dust, your people are whispering behind your back. They talk about you in their houses and whisper about you at the doors, saying, 'Come on, let's have some fun! Let's go hear him tell us what the Lord is saying!'^b ³¹ So they come as though they are sincere and sit before you listening. But they have no intention of doing what I tell them to; they talk very sweetly about loving the Lord, but with their hearts they are loving their money. ³² You are very entertaining to them, like someone who sings lovely songs with a beautiful voice or plays well on an instrument. They hear what you say but don't pay any attention to it! ³³ But when all these terrible things happen to them—as they will—then they will know a prophet has been among them."

34 THEN THIS MESSAGE came to me from the Lord:

² "Son of dust, prophesy against the shepherds, the leaders of Israel, and say to them: The Lord God says to you: Woe to the shepherds who feed themselves instead of their flocks. Shouldn't shepherds feed the sheep? ³ You eat the best food and wear the finest clothes, but you let your flocks starve. ⁴ You haven't taken care of the weak nor tended the sick nor bound up the broken bones nor gone looking for those who have wandered away and are lost. Instead you have ruled them with force and cruelty. ⁵ So they were scattered, without a shepherd. They have become a prey to every animal that comes along. ⁶ My sheep wandered through the mountains and hills and over the face of the earth, and there was no one to search for them or care about them.

---

a Some manuscripts read, "In the twelfth year." comes from the Lord!"

b Literally, "Come and let us hear what the word is that

⁷ "Therefore, O shepherds, hear the word of the Lord:

⁸ "As I live, says the Lord God, you abandoned my flock, leaving them to be attacked and destroyed, and you were no real shepherds at all, for you didn't search for them. You fed yourselves and let them starve; ⁹,¹⁰ therefore I am against the shepherds, and I will hold them responsible for what has happened to my flock. I will take away their right to feed the flock—and take away their right to eat. I will save my flock from being taken for their food.

¹¹ "For the Lord God says: I will search and find my sheep. ¹² I will be like a shepherd looking for his flock. I will find my sheep and rescue them from all the places they were scattered in that dark and cloudy day. ¹³ And I will bring them back from among the people and nations where they were, back home to their own land of Israel, and I will feed them upon the mountains of Israel and by the rivers where the land is fertile and good. ¹⁴ Yes, I will give them good pasture on the high hills of Israel. There they will lie down in peace and feed in luscious mountain pastures. ¹⁵,¹⁶ I myself will be the Shepherd of my sheep, and cause them to lie down in peace, the Lord God says. I will seek my lost ones, those who strayed away, and bring them safely home again. I will put splints and bandages upon their broken limbs and heal the sick. And I will destroy the powerful, fat shepherds; I will feed them, yes—feed them punishment!

¹⁷ "And as for you, O my flock—my people—the Lord God says, I will distinguish lambs from kids and rams from billy goats!

¹⁸ "Is it a small thing to you, O evil shepherds, that you not only keep the best of the pastures for yourselves, but trample down the rest? That you take the best water for yourselves, and muddy the rest with your feet? ¹⁹ All that's left for my flock is what you've trampled down; all they have to drink is water that you've fouled.

²⁰ "Therefore the Lord God says: I will surely judge between these fat shepherds and their scrawny sheep. ²¹ For these shepherds push and butt and crowd my sick and hungry flock until they're scattered far away. ²² So I myself will save my flock; no more will they be picked on and destroyed. And I will notice which is plump and which is thin, and why! ²³ And I will set one Shepherd over all my people, even my Servant, David. He shall feed them and be a Shepherd to them.

²⁴ "And I, the Lord, will be their God, and my Servant David shall be a Prince among my people. I, the Lord, have spoken it. ²⁵ I will make a peace pact with them, and drive away the dangerous animals from the land so that my people can safely camp in the wildest places and sleep safely in the woods. ²⁶ I will make my people and their homes around my hill a blessing. And there shall be showers, showers of blessing, for I will not shut off the rains but send them in their seasons. ²⁷ Their fruit trees and fields will yield bumper crops, and everyone will live in safety. When I have broken off their chains of slavery and delivered them from those who profiteered at their expense, they shall know I am the Lord. ²⁸ No more will other nations conquer them nor wild animals attack. They shall live in safety and no one shall make them afraid.

²⁹ "And I will raise up a notable Vine [the Messiahª], in Israel so that my people will never again go hungry nor be shamed by heathen conquest. ³⁰ In this way they will know that I, the Lord their God, am with them, and that they, the people of Israel, are my people, says the Lord God. ³¹ You are my flock, the sheep of my pasture. You are my men and I am your God, so says the Lord."

35 AGAIN A MESSAGE came from the Lord. He said:

² "Son of dust, face toward Mount Seir and prophesy against the people saying:

³ "The Lord God says: I am against you and I will smash you with my fist and utterly destroy you. ⁴,⁵ Because you hate my people Israel, I will demolish your cities and make you desolate, and then you shall know I am the Lord. You butchered my people

---

a Literally, "a plant of renown"; so perhaps the meaning is, "I will give them bumper crops." Either translation is permissible, but the word for "plant" is in the singular.

when they were helpless, when I had punished them for all their sins. ⁶ As I live, the Lord God says, since you enjoy blood so much, I will give you a blood bath—your turn has come! ⁷ I will utterly wipe out the people of Mount Seir, killing off all those who try to escape and all those who return. ⁸ I will fill your mountains with the dead —your hills, your valleys and your rivers will be filled with those the sword has killed. ⁹ Never again will you revive. You will be abandoned forever; your cities will never be rebuilt. Then you shall know I am the Lord.

¹⁰ "For you said, 'Both Israel and Judah shall be mine. We will take possession of them. What do we care that God is there!' ¹¹ Therefore as I live, the Lord God says, I will pay back your angry deeds with mine—I will punish you for all your acts of envy and of hate. And I will honor my name in Israel by what I do to you. ¹² And you shall know that I have heard each evil word you spoke against the Lord, saying, 'His people are helpless; they are food for us to eat!' ¹³ Saying that, you boasted great words against the Lord. And I have heard them all!

¹⁴ "The whole world will rejoice when I make you desolate. ¹⁵ You rejoiced at Israel's fearful fate. Now I will rejoice at yours! You will be wiped out, O people of Mount Seir and all who live in Edom! And then you will know I am the Lord!

36 "SON OF DUST, prophesy to Israel's mountains. Tell them: Listen to this message from the Lord.

² "Your enemies have sneered at you and claimed your ancient heights as theirs, ³ and destroyed you on every side and sent you away as slaves to many lands. You are mocked and slandered. ⁴ Therefore, O mountains of Israel, hear the word of the Lord God. He says to the hills and mountains, dales and valleys, and to the ruined farms and the long-deserted cities, destroyed and mocked by heathen nations all around: ⁵ My anger is afire against these nations, especially Edom, for grabbing my land with relish, in utter contempt for me, to take it for themselves.

⁶ "Therefore prophesy and say to the hills and mountains, dales and valleys of Israel: The Lord God says, I am full of fury because you suffered shame before the surrounding nations. ⁷ Therefore I have sworn with hand held high, that those nations are going to have their turn of being covered with shame, ⁸ but for Israel, good times will return. There will be heavy crops of fruit to prepare for my people's return—and they will be coming home again soon! ⁹ See, I am for you, and I will come and help you as you prepare the ground and sow your crops. ¹⁰ I will greatly increase your population throughout all Israel, and the ruined cities will be rebuilt and filled with people. ¹¹ Not only the people, but your flocks and herds will also greatly multiply. O mountains of Israel, again you will be filled with homes. I will do even more for you than I did before. Then you shall know I am the Lord. ¹² My people will walk upon you once again, and you will belong to them again; and you will no longer be a place for burning their children on idol altars.

¹³ "The Lord God says: Now the other nations taunt you, saying, 'Israel is a land that devours her people!' ¹⁴ But they will not say this any more. Your birth rate will rise and your infant mortality rate will drop off sharply, says the Lord. ¹⁵ No longer will those heathen nations sneer, for you will no longer be a nation of sinners, the Lord God says."

¹⁶ Then this further word came to me from the Lord:

¹⁷ "Son of dust, when the people of Israel were living in their own country, they defiled it by their evil deeds; to me their worship was as foul as filthy rags.ᵃ ¹⁸ They polluted the land with murder and with the worshiping of idols, so I poured out my fury upon them. ¹⁹ And I exiled them to many lands; that is how I punished them for the evil way they lived. ²⁰ But when they were scattered out among the nations, then they were a blight upon my holy name because the nations said, 'These are the people of God and he couldn't protect them from harm!' ²¹ I am concerned about my reputation that was ruined by my people through-

---

a Literally, "as a menstruous cloth."

out the world.

²² "Therefore say to the people of Israel: The Lord God says, I am bringing you back again, but not because you deserve it; I am doing it to protect my holy name which you tarnished among the nations. ²³ I will honor my great name that you defiled, and the people of the world shall know I am the Lord. I will be honored before their eyes by delivering you from exile among them.ᵇ ²⁴ For I will bring you back home again to the land of Israel.

²⁵ "Then it will be as though I had sprinkled clean water on you, for you will be clean—your filthiness will be washed away, your idol worship gone. ²⁶ And I will give you a new heart—I will give you new and right desires—and put a new spirit within you. I will take out your stony hearts of sin and give you new hearts of love.ᶜ ²⁷ And I will put my Spirit within you so that you will obey my laws and do whatever I command.

²⁸ "And you shall live in Israel, the land which I gave your fathers long ago. And you shall be my people and I will be your God. ²⁹ I will cleanse away your sins. I will abolish crop failures and famine. ³⁰ I will give you huge harvests from your fruit trees and fields, and never again will the surrounding nations be able to scoff at your land for its famines. ³¹ Then you will remember your past sins and loathe yourselves for all the evils you did. ³² But always remember this: It is not for your own sakes that I will do this, but for mine. O my people Israel, be utterly ashamed of all that you have done!

³³ "The Lord God says: When I cleanse you from your sins, I will bring you home again to Israel, and rebuild the ruins. ³⁴ Acreage will be cultivated again that through the years of exile lay empty as a barren wilderness; all who passed by were shocked to see the extent of ruin in your land. ³⁵ But when I bring you back they will say, 'This God-forsaken land has become like Eden's garden! The ruined cities are rebuilt and walled and filled with people!' ³⁶ Then the nations all around—all those still left—will know that I, the Lord, rebuilt

the ruins and planted lush crops in the wilderness. For I, the Lord, have promised it, and I will do it.

³⁷,³⁸ "The Lord God says: I am ready to hear Israel's prayers for these blessings, and to grant them their requests. Let them but ask and I will multiply them like the flocks that fill Jerusalem's streets at time of sacrifice. The ruined cities will be crowded once more, and everyone will know I am the Lord."

37 THE POWER OF the Lord was upon me and I was carried away by the Spirit of the Lord to a valley full of old, dry bones that were scattered everywhere across the ground. He led me around among them, ³ and then he said to me:

"Son of dust, can these bones become people again?"

I replied, "Lord, you alone know the answer to that."

⁴ Then he told me to speak to the bones and say: "O dry bones, listen to the words of God, ⁵ for the Lord God says, See! I am going to make you live and breathe again! ⁶ I will replace the flesh and muscles on you and cover you with skin. I will put breath into you, and you shall live and know I am the Lord."

⁷ So I spoke these words from God, just as he told me to; and suddenly there was a rattling noise from all across the valley, and the bones of each body came together and attached to each other as they used to be. ⁸ Then, as I watched, the muscles and flesh formed over the bones, and skin covered them, but the bodies had no breath. ⁹ Then he told me to call to the wind and say: "The Lord God says: Come from the four winds, O Spirit, and breathe upon these slain bodies, that they may live again." ¹⁰ So I spoke to the winds as he commanded me and the bodies began breathing; they lived, and stood up—a very great army.

¹¹ Then he told me what the vision meant: "These bones," he said, "represent all the people of Israel. They say: 'We have become a heap of dried-out bones—all hope is gone.' ¹² But tell them, the Lord God says: My people, I will open your graves of exile

---

b Implied.   c Literally, "hearts of flesh," in contrast to "hearts of stone."

and cause you to rise again and return to the land of Israel. [13] And, then at last, O my people, you will know I am the Lord. [14] I will put my Spirit into you, and you shall live and return home again to your own land. Then you will know that I, the Lord, have done just what I promised you."

[15] Again a message from the Lord came to me, saying:

[16] "Take a stick and carve on it these words: 'This stick represents Judah and her allied tribes.' Then take another stick and carve these words on it: 'This stick represents all the other tribes of Israel.' [17] Now hold them together in your hand as one stick. [18,19,20] Tell these people (holding the sticks so they can see what you are doing), the Lord God says: I will take the tribes of Israel and join them to Judah and make them one stick in my hand.

[21] "For the Lord God says: I am gathering the people of Israel from among the nations, and bringing them home from around the world to their own land, [22] to unify them into one nation. One king shall be king of them all; no longer shall they be divided into two nations. [23] They shall stop polluting themselves with idols and their other sins, for I will save them from all this foulness. Then they shall truly be my people and I their God.

[24] "And David, my Servant—the Messiah—shall be their King, their only Shepherd; and they shall obey my laws and all my wishes. [25] They shall live in the land of Israel where their fathers lived, the land I gave my servant Jacob. They and their children after them shall live there, and their grandchildren, for all generations. And my Servant David, their Messiah, shall be their Prince forever. [26] And I will make a covenant of peace with them, an everlasting pact. I will bless them and multiply them and put my Temple among them forever. [27] And I will make my home among them. Yes, I will be their God and they shall be my people. [28] And when my Temple remains among them, then the nations shall know that I, the Lord, have set Israel apart for special blessings."

38 HERE IS ANOTHER message to me from the Lord:

[2,3] "Son of dust, face northward[a] toward the land of Magog, and prophesy against Gog[b] king of Meshech and Tubal. Tell him that the Lord God says: I am against you, Gog. [4] I will put hooks into your jaws and pull you to your doom. I will mobilize your troops and armored cavalry, and make you a mighty host, all fully armed. [5] Peras, Cush and Put shall join you too with all their weaponry, [6] and so shall Gomer and all his hordes and the armies of Togarmah from the distant north, as well as many others. [7] Be prepared! Stay mobilized. You are their leader, Gog!

[8] "A long time from now you will be called to action. In distant years you will swoop down onto the land of Israel, that will be lying in peace after the return of its people from many lands. [9] You and all your allies—a vast and awesome army—will roll down upon them like a storm and cover the land like a cloud. [10] For at that time an evil thought will have come to your mind. [11] You will have said, 'Israel is an unprotected land of unwalled villages! I will march against her and destroy these people living in such confidence! [12] I will go to those once-desolate cities that are now filled with people again—those who have returned from all the nations—and I will capture vast booty and many slaves. For the people are rich with cattle now, and the whole earth revolves around them!'

[13] "But Sheba and Dedan[c] and the merchant princes of Tarshish with whom she trades[d] will ask, 'Who are you to rob them of silver and gold and drive away their cattle and seize their goods and make them poor?'

---

a Implied.   b The names of Gog's confederates (Meshech, Tubal, Gomer, Beth-togarmah) can be identified as Mushki, Tabal, Gimaraya, Tegerama, peoples who lived in the mountainous area southeast of the Black Sea and southwest of the Caspian, currently in central Turkey. It therefore seems that Gog was, or is to be, the leader of one of these nations. But from the context Gog seems to be a symbol rather than an historical figure like Nebuchadnezzar. In any event, he represents the aggregate military might of the forces opposed to God, especially in a mighty battle of the end times. See also Revelation 20:7-9.   c Great trading centers in Arabia.   d Implied.

[14] "The Lord God says to Gog: When my people are living in peace in their land, then you will rouse yourself. [15,16] You will come from all over the north with your vast host of cavalry and cover the land like a cloud. This will happen in the distant future —in the latter years of history.[e] I will bring you against my land, and my holiness will be vindicated in your terrible destruction before their eyes, so that all the nations will know that I am God.

[17] "The Lord God says: You are the one I spoke of long ago through the prophets of Israel, saying that after many years had passed, I would bring you against my people. [18] But when you come to destroy the land of Israel, my fury will rise! [19] For in my jealousy and blazing wrath, I promise a mighty shaking in the land of Israel on that day. [20] All living things shall quake in terror at my presence; mountains shall be thrown down; cliffs shall tumble; walls shall crumble to the earth. [21] I will summon every kind of terror against you, says the Lord God, and you will fight against yourselves in mortal combat! [22] I will fight you with sword, disease, torrential floods, great hailstones, fire and brimstone! [23] Thus will I show my greatness and bring honor upon my name, and all the nations of the world will hear what I have done, and know that I am God!

39 "SON OF DUST, prophesy this also against Gog. Tell him:

I stand against you, Gog, leader of Meshech and Tubal. [2] I will turn you and drive you toward the mountains of Israel, bringing you from the distant north. And I will destroy 85 percent[a] of your army in the mountains. [3] I will knock your weapons from your hands and leave you helpless. [4] You and all your vast armies will die upon the mountains. I will give you to the vultures and wild animals to devour you. [5] You will never reach the cities—you will fall upon the open fields; for I have spoken, the Lord God says. [6] And I will rain down fire on Magog and on all your allies who live safely on the coasts, and they shall know I am the Lord.

[7] "Thus I will make known my holy name among my people Israel; I will not let it be mocked at anymore. And the nations too shall know I am the Lord, the Holy One of Israel. [8] That day of judgment will come; everything will happen just as I have declared it.

[9] "The people of the cities of Israel will go out and pick up your shields and bucklers, bows and arrows, javelins and spears, to use for fuel—enough to last them seven years. [10] For seven years they will need nothing else for their fires. They won't cut wood from the fields or forests, for these weapons will give them all they need. They will use the possessions of those who abused them.

[11] "And I will make a vast graveyard for Gog and his armies in the Valley of the Travelers, east of the Dead Sea. It will block the path of the travelers. There Gog and all his armies will be buried. And they will change the name of the place to "The Valley of Gog's Army." [12] It will take seven months for the people of Israel to bury the bodies. [13] Everyone in Israel will help, for it will be a glorious victory for Israel on that day when I demonstrate my glory, says the Lord. [14] At the end of the seven months, they will appoint men to search the land systematically for any skeletons left and bury them, so that the land will be cleansed. [15,16] Whenever anyone sees some bones, he will put up a marker beside them so that the buriers will see them and take them to the Valley of Gog's Army to bury them. A city named 'Multitude' is there! And so the land will finally be cleansed.

[17] "And now, son of dust, call all the birds and animals and say to them: Gather together for a mighty sacrificial feast. Come from far and near to the mountains of Israel. Come, eat the flesh and drink the blood! [18] Eat the flesh of mighty men and drink the blood of princes—they are the rams, the lambs, the goats and the fat young bulls of Bashan for my feast! [19] Gorge yourselves with flesh until you are glutted, drink blood until you are drunk; this is the sacrificial feast I have prepared for you. [20] Feast

---

e Implied. Literally, "in the latter days," an expression which does not, in Hebrew usage, necessarily mean "the end times." 39a Literally, "leave one-sixth of you."

at my banquet table—feast on horses, riders and valiant warriors, says the Lord God. [21] Thus I will demonstrate my glory among the nations; all shall see the punishment of Gog and know that I have done it.

[22] "And from that time onward, the people of Israel will know I am the Lord their God. [23] And the nations will know why Israel was sent away to exile—it was punishment for sin, for they acted in treachery against their God. Therefore I turned my face away from them and let their enemies destroy them. [24] I turned my face away and punished them in proportion to the vileness of their sins.

[25] "But now, the Lord God says, I will end the captivity of my people and have mercy upon them and restore their fortunes, for I am concerned about my reputation! [26] Their time of treachery and shame will all be in the past; they will be home again, in peace and safety in their own land, with no one bothering them or making them afraid. [27] I will bring them home from the lands of their enemies—and my glory shall be evident to all the nations when I do it. Through them I will vindicate my holiness before the nations. [28] Then my people will know I am the Lord their God—responsible for sending them away to exile, and responsible for bringing them home. I will leave none of them remaining among the nations. [29] And I will never hide my face from them again, for I will pour out my Spirit upon them, says the Lord God."

40 EARLY IN APRIL of the twenty-fifth year of our exile—the fourteenth year after Jerusalem was captured—the hand of the Lord was upon me, [2] and in a vision he took me to the land of Israel and set me down on a high mountain where I saw what appeared to be a city opposite me. [3] Going nearer, I saw a man whose face shone like bronze, standing beside the Temple gate,[a] holding in his hand a measuring tape and a measuring stick.

[4] He said to me: "Son of dust, watch and listen and take to heart everything I show you, for you have been brought here so I can show you many things; and then you are to return to the people of Israel to tell them all you have seen." [5] [b]The man began to measure the wall around the outside of the Temple area with his measuring stick, which was 10½ feet long. He told me, "This wall is 10½ feet high and 10½ feet wide." [6] Then he took me over to the passageway that goes through the eastern wall.[c] We climbed the seven steps into the entrance and he measured the entry hall of the passage; it was 10½ feet wide.

[7-12] Walking on through the passageway I saw that there were three guardrooms on each side; each of these rooms was 10½ feet square, with a distance of 8¾ feet along the wall between them. In front of these rooms was a low barrier eighteen inches high and eighteen inches wide.[d] Beyond the guardrooms was a 10½-foot doorway opening into a 14-foot hall with 3½-foot columns. Beyond this hall, at the inner end of the passageway was a vestibule 22¾ feet wide and 17½ feet long.

[13] Then he measured the entire outside width of the passageway, measuring across the roof from the outside doors of the guardrooms; this distance was 43¾ feet. [14] Then he estimated the pillars on each side of the porch to be about 100 feet high. [15] The full length of the entrance passage was 87½ feet from one end to the other. [16] There were windows that narrowed inward through the walls along both sides of the passageway and along the guardroom walls. The windows were also in the exit and in the entrance halls. The pillars were decorated with palm tree decorations.

[17] And so we passed through the passageway to the court inside. A stone pavement ran around the inside of the walls, and thirty rooms were built against the walls, opening onto this pavement. [18] This was called "the lower pavement." It extended out from the walls into the court the same distance as the passageway did.

[19] Then he measured across to the wall on the other side of this court (which was called "the outer court" of the Temple[e]) and found that the distance was 175 feet.

a Implied.   b See Diagrams 1, 2, 3, pages 787, 788, and 789.   c See Diagram 4, page 789.
d Or, an eighteen-inch pillar in front of (or between) the guardrooms, projecting out into the hallway.
e Implied.

20 As I followed, he left the eastern passageway and went over to the passage through
the northern wall and measured it. 21 Here
too there were three guardrooms on each
side, and all the measurements were the
same as for the east passageway—87½ feet
long and 43¾ feet from side to side across
the top of the guardrooms. 22 There were
windows, an entry hall and the palm tree
decorations just the same as on the east
side. And there were seven steps leading up
to the doorway to the entry hall inside.

23 Here at the north entry, just as at the
east, if one walked through the passageway
into the court, and straight across it, he
came to an inner wall and a passageway
through it to an inner court. The distance
between the two passageways was 175 feet.
24 Then he took me around to the south gate
and measured the various sections of its passageway and found they were just the same
as in the others. 25 It had windows along the
walls as the others did, and an entry hall.
And like the others, it was 87½ feet long
and 43¾ feet wide. 26 It too had a stairway
of seven steps leading up to it, and there
were palm tree decorations along the walls.
27 And here again, if one walked through the
passageway into the court and straight
across it, he came to the inner wall and a
passageway through it to the inner court.
And the distance between the passageways
was 175 feet.

28 Then he took me over to the inner wall
and its south passageway.[f] He measured
this passageway and found that it had the
same measurements as the passageways of
the outer wall.[g] 29,30[h] Its guardrooms, pillars
and entrance and exit hall were identical to
all the others, and so were the windows
along its walls and entry. And, like the others, it was 87½ feet long by 43¾ feet wide.
31 The only difference was that it had eight
steps leading up to it instead of seven. It had
palm tree decorations on the pillars, just as
the others.

32 Then he took me along the court to the
eastern entrance of the inner wall, and
measured it. It too had the same measurements as the others. 33 Its guardrooms, pillars and entrance hall were the same size as
those of the other passageways, and there
were windows along the walls and in the
entry hall; and it was 87½ feet long by 43¾
feet wide. 34 Its entry hall faced the outer
court and there were palm tree decorations
on its columns, but there were eight steps
instead of seven going up to the entrance.

35 Then he took me around to the north
gate of the inner wall, and the measurements there were just like the others: 36 The
guardrooms, pillars and entry hall of this
passageway were the same as the others,
with a length of 87½ feet and a width of
43¾ feet. 37 Its entry hall faced toward the
outer court, and it had palm tree decorations on the walls of each side of the passageway, and there were eight steps leading
up to the entrance.

38 But a door led from its entry hall into
a side room where the flesh of the sacrifices
was washed before being taken to the altar;
39 on each side of the entry hall of the passageway there were two tables where the
animals for sacrifice were slaughtered for
the burnt offerings, sin offerings and guilt
offerings to be presented in the Temple.
40 Outside the entry hall, on each side of the
stairs going up to the north entrance, there
were two more tables. 41 So, in all, there
were eight tables, four inside and four outside, where the sacrifices were cut up and
prepared. 42 There were also four stone tables where the butchering knives and other
implements were laid. These tables were
about 2⅝ feet square and 1¾ feet high.
43 There were hooks, three or four inches
long, fastened along the walls of the entry
hall, and on the tables the flesh of the offering was to be laid.

44 In the inner court, there were two one-
room buildings, one beside the northern entrance, facing south, and one beside the
southern entrance, facing north.

45 And he said to me: "The building beside the inner northern gate is for the priests
who supervise the maintenance. 46 The
building beside the inner southern entrance
is for the priests in charge of the altar—the
descendants of Zadok—for they alone of all

f See Diagram 5, page 790. g Some manuscripts add: "And the arches around it were 37½ feet by 8¾ feet broad." h Verse 30, omitted in the Septuagint and several other of the ancient manuscripts, reads, "There were vestibules round about, and they were 37½ feet long and 8¾ feet broad."

the Levites may come near to the Lord to minister to him."

[47] Then he measured the inner court [in front of the Temple[i]] and found it to be 175 feet square, and there was an altar in the court, standing in front of the Temple. [48,49] Then he brought me to the entrance hall of the Temple. Ten steps led up to it from the inner court. Its walls extended up on either side to form two pillars, each of them 8¾ feet thick. The entrance was 24½ feet wide with 5¼-foot walls. Thus the entry hall was 35 feet wide and 19¼ feet long.

41 AFTERWARD HE BROUGHT me into the nave, the large main room of the Temple, and measured the pillars that formed its doorway. They were 10½ feet square. [2] The entrance hall was 17½ feet wide and 8¾ feet deep. The nave itself was seventy feet long by thirty-five feet.

[3] Then he went into the inner room at the end of the nave and measured the columns at the entrance and found them to be 3½ feet thick; its doorway was 10½ feet wide, with a hallway 12¼ feet deep behind it. [4] The inner room was thirty-five feet square. "This," he told me, "is the Most Holy Place."

[5] Then he measured the wall of the Temple and found that it was 10½ feet thick, with a row of rooms along the outside. Each room was seven feet wide. [6] These rooms were in three tiers, one above the other, with thirty rooms in each tier. The whole structure was supported by girders and not attached to the Temple wall for support. [7] Each tier was wider than the one below it, corresponding to the narrowing of the Temple wall as it rose higher. A stairway at the side of the Temple led up from floor to floor.

[8] I noticed that the Temple was built on a terrace and that the bottom row of rooms extended out 10½ feet onto the terrace. [9] The outer wall of these rooms was 8¾ feet thick, leaving a free space of 8¾ feet out to the edge of the terrace, the same on both sides.

[10] Thirty-five feet away from the terrace, on both sides of the Temple, was another row of rooms down in the inner court.

[11] Two doors opened from the tiers of rooms to the terrace yard, which was 8¾ feet wide; one door faced north and the other south.

[12] A large building stood on the west, facing the Temple yard, measuring 122½ feet wide by 157½ feet long. Its walls were 8¾ feet thick. [13] Then he measured the Temple and its immediately surrounding yards. The area was 175 feet square. [14] The inner court at the east of the Temple was also 175 feet wide, [15,16] and so was the building west of the Temple, including its two walls.

The nave of the Temple and the Holy of Holies and the entry hall were paneled, and all three had recessed windows. The inner walls of the Temple were paneled with wood above and below the windows. [17,18] The space above the door leading into the Holy of Holies was also paneled. The walls were decorated with carvings of cherubim, each with two faces, and of palm trees alternating with the cherubim. [19,20] One face—that of a man—looked toward the palm tree on one side, and the other face—that of a young lion—looked toward the palm tree on the other side. And so it was, all around the inner wall of the Temple.

[21] There were square doorposts at the doors of the nave, and in front of the Holy of Holies was what appeared to be an altar, but it was made of wood. [22] This altar was 3½ feet square, and 5¼ feet high; its corners, base and sides were all of wood. "This," he told me, "is the Table of the Lord."[a]

[23] Both the nave and the Holy of Holies had double doors, [24] each with two swinging sections. [25] The doors leading into the nave were decorated with cherubim and palm trees, just as on the walls. And there was a wooden canopy over the entry hall. [26] There were recessed windows and carved palm trees on both sides of the entry hall, the hallways beside the Temple, and on the canopy over the entrance.

42 THEN HE LED me out of the Temple, back into the inner court to the rooms

---

i Implied.   41a Literally, "the table which is before the Lord."

north of the Temple yard, and to another building. ² This group of structures was 175 feet long by 87½ feet wide. ³ The rows of rooms behind this building were the inner wall of the court. The rooms were in three tiers, overlooking the outer court on one side, and having a 35-foot strip of inner court on the other. ⁴ A 17½-foot walk ran between the building and the tiers of rooms, extending the entire length, with the doors of the building facing north. ⁵ The upper two tiers of rooms were not as wide as the lower one, because the upper tiers had wider walkways beside them. ⁶ And since the building was not built with girders as those in the outer court were, the upper stories were set back from the ground floor.

⁷,⁸ The north tiers, next to the outer court, were 87½ feet long—only half as long as the inner wing that faced the Temple court, which was 175 feet long. But a wall extended from the end of the shorter wing, parallel to the longer wing. ⁹,¹⁰ And there was an entrance from the outer court to these rooms from the east. On the opposite side of the Temple a similar building composed of two units of tiers was on the south side of the inner court, between the Temple and the outer court, arranged the same as the other. ¹¹ There was a walk between the two wings of the building, the same as in the other building across the court—the same length and width and the same exits and doors—they were identical units. ¹² And there was a door from the outer court[a] at the east.

¹³ Then he told me: "These north and south tiers of rooms facing the Temple yard are holy; there the priests who offer up the sacrifices to the Lord shall eat of the most holy offerings and store them—the cereal offerings, sin offerings, and guilt offerings, for these rooms are holy. ¹⁴ When the priests leave the Holy Place—the nave of the Temple—they must change their clothes before going out to the outer court. The special robes in which they have been ministering must first be removed, for these robes are holy. They must put on other clothes before entering the parts of the building open to the public."

¹⁵ When he had finished making these measurements, he led me out through the east passageway to measure the entire Temple area. ¹⁶⁻²⁰ He found that it was in the form of a square, 875 feet long on each side, with a wall all around it to separate the restricted area from the public places.[b]

43 AFTERWARD HE BROUGHT me out again to the passageway through the outer wall leading to the east. ² And suddenly the glory of the God of Israel appeared from the east. The sound of his coming was like the roar of rushing waters and the whole landscape lighted up with his glory. ³ It was just as I had seen it in the other visions, first by the Chebar Canal, and then later at Jerusalem[a] when he came to destroy the city. And I fell down before him with my face in the dust. ⁴ And the glory of the Lord came into the Temple through the eastern passageway.

⁵ Then the Spirit took me up and brought me into the inner court; and the glory of the Lord filled the Temple. ⁶ And I heard the Lord speaking to me from within the Temple (the man who had been measuring was still standing beside me).

⁷ And the Lord said to me:

"Son of dust, this is the place of my throne, and my footstool, where I shall remain, living among the people of Israel forever. They and their kings will not defile my holy name any longer through the adulterous worship of other gods or by worshiping the totem poles erected by their kings. ⁸ They built their idol temples beside mine, with only a wall between, and worshiped their idols. Because they sullied my holy name by such wickedness, I consumed them in my anger. ⁹ Now let them put away their idols and the totem poles[b] erected by their kings, and I will live among them forever.

¹⁰ "Son of dust, describe the Temple I have shown you to the people of Israel. Tell them its appearance and its plan so they will be ashamed of all their sins. ¹¹ And if they are truly ashamed of what they have done, then explain to them the details of its construction—its doors and entrances—and everything about it. Write out all the direc-

---

a Implied.　　b Literally, "between the holy and the common."　　43 a Implied.　　b Literally, "stellae."

tions and the rules for them to keep. ¹² And this is the basic law of the Temple: *Holiness!* The entire top of the hill where the Temple is built is *holy.* Yes, this is the primary law concerning it.

¹³ "And these are the measurements of the altar:ᶜ The base is twenty-one inches high, with a nine-inch rim around its edge, and it extends twenty-one inches beyond the altar on all sides. ¹⁴ The first stage of the altar is a stone platform 3½ feet high. This platform is twenty-one inches narrower than the base block on all sides. Rising from this is a narrower platform, twenty-one inches narrower on all sides, and seven feet high. ¹⁵ From it a still narrower platform rises seven feet, and this is the top of the altar, with four horns projecting twenty-one inches up from the corners. ¹⁶ This top platform of the altar is twenty-one feet square. ¹⁷ The platform beneath it is 24½ feet square with a 10½-inch curb around the edges. The entire platform extends out from the top twenty-one inches on all sides. On the east side are steps to climb the altar."

¹⁸ And he said to me:

"Son of dust, the Lord God says: These are the measurements of the altar to be made in the future, when it is erected for the burning of offerings and the sprinkling of blood upon it. ¹⁹ At that time the Zadok family of the Levite tribe, who are my ministers, are to be given a bullock for a sin offering. ²⁰ You shall take some of its blood and smear it on the four horns of the altar and on the four corners of the top platform and in the curb around it. This will cleanse and make atonement for the altar. ²¹ Then take the bullock for the sin offering and burn it at the appointed place outside the Temple area.

²² "The second day, sacrifice a young male goat without any defects—without sickness, deformities, cuts or scars—for a sin offering. Thus the altar shall be cleansed, as it was by the bullock. ²³ When you have finished this cleansing ceremony, offer another perfect bullock and a perfect ram from the flock. ²⁴ Present them before the Lord, and the priests shall sprinkle salt

upon them as a burnt offering.

²⁵ "Every day for seven days a male goat, a bullock and a ram from the flock shall be sacrificed as a sin offering. None are to have any defects or unhealthiness of any kind. ²⁶ Do this each day for seven days to cleanse and make atonement for the altar, thus consecrating it. ²⁷ On the eighth day, and on each day afterward, the priests will sacrifice on the altar the burnt offerings and thank offerings of the people, and I will accept you, says the Lord God."

44 THEN THE LORD brought me back to the outer wall's eastern passageway, but it was closed. ² And he said to me:

"This gate shall remain closed; it shall never be opened. No man shall pass through it; for the Lord, the God of Israel, entered here and so it shall remain shut. ³ Only the prince—because he is the prince—may sit inside the passageway to feast there before the Lord. But he shall go and come only through the entry hall of the passage."

⁴ Then he brought me through the north passageway to the front of the Temple. I looked and saw that the glory of the Lord filled the Temple of the Lord, and I fell to the ground with my face in the dust.

⁵ And the Lord said to me:

"Son of dust, notice carefully; use your eyes and ears. Listen to all I tell you about the laws and rules of the Temple of the Lord. Note carefully who may be admitted to the Temple, and who is to be excluded from it. ⁶ And say to these rebels, the people of Israel, The Lord God says: O Israel, you have sinned greatly, ⁷ by letting the uncircumcised into my sanctuary—those who have no heart for God—when you offer me my food, the fat and the blood. Thus you have broken my covenant in addition to all your other sins. ⁸ You have not kept the laws I gave you concerning these holy affairs, for you have hired foreigners to take charge of my sanctuary.

⁹ "The Lord God says: No foreigner of all the many among you shall enter my sanctuary if he has not been circumcised and does not love the Lord. ¹⁰ And the men of the tribe of Levi who abandoned me

---

c See Diagram 6, page 790.

710

when Israel strayed away from God to idols must be punished for their unfaithfulness. [11] They may be Temple guards and gatemen; they may slay the animals brought for burnt offerings and be present to help the people. [12] But because they encouraged the people to worship other gods, causing Israel to fall into deep sin, I have raised my hand and taken oath, says the Lord God, that they must be punished. [13] They shall not come near me to minister as priests; they may not touch any of my holy things, for they must bear their shame for all the sins they have committed. [14] They are the Temple caretakers, to do maintenance work and to assist the people in a general way.

[15] "However, the sons of Zadok, of the tribe of Levi, continued as my priests in the Temple when Israel abandoned me for idols. These men shall be my ministers; they shall stand before me to offer the fat and blood of the sacrifices, says the Lord God. [16] They shall enter my sanctuary and come to my Table to minister to me; they shall fulfill my requirements.

[17] "They must wear only linen clothing when they enter the passageway to the inner court, for they must wear no wool while on duty in the inner court or in the Temple. [18] They must wear linen turbans and linen trousers; they must not wear anything that would cause them to perspire. [19] When they return to the outer court, they must take off the clothes they wear while ministering to me, leaving them in the sacred chambers, and put on other clothes lest they consecrate the people by touching them with this clothing.

[20] "They must not let their hair grow too long, nor shave it off. Regular, moderate haircuts are all they are allowed. [21] No priest may drink wine before coming to the inner court. [22] He may marry only a Jewish maiden, or the widow of a priest; he may not marry a divorced woman.

[23] "He shall teach my people the difference between what is holy and what is secular, what is right and what is wrong.[a]

[24] "They will serve as judges to resolve any disagreements among my people. Their decisions must be based upon my laws. And

the priests themselves shall obey my rules and regulations at all the sacred festivals, and they shall see to it that the Sabbath is kept a sacred day.

[25] "A priest must not defile himself by being in the presence of a dead person, unless it is his father, mother, child, brother or unmarried sister. In such cases it is all right. [26] But afterward he must wait seven days before he is cleansed and able to perform his Temple duties again. [27] The first day he returns to work and enters the inner court and the sanctuary, he must offer a sin offering for himself, the Lord God says.

[28] "As to property, they shall not own any, for I am their heritage! That is enough![b]

[29] "Their food shall be the gifts and sacrifices brought to the Temple by the people—the cereal offerings, the sin offerings and the guilt offerings. Whatever anyone gives to the Lord shall be the priests'. [30] The first of the first-ripe fruits and all the gifts for the Lord shall go to the priests. The first samples of each harvest of grain shall be donated to the priests too, so that the Lord will bless your homes. [31] Priests may never eat meat from any bird or animal that dies a natural death or that dies after being attacked by other animals.

45 "WHEN YOU DIVIDE the land among the tribes of Israel, you shall first give a section of it to the Lord as his holy portion. This piece shall be 8¹/₃ miles long and 6²/₃ miles wide. It shall all be holy ground. [2] "A section of this land, 875 feet square, shall be designated for the Temple. An additional 87½-foot strip all around is to be left empty. [3] The Temple shall be built within the area which is 8¹/₃ miles long and 3¹/₃ miles wide. [4] All this section shall be holy land; it will be used by the priests, who minister in the sanctuary, for their homes and for my Temple.

[5] "The strip next to it, 8¹/₃ miles long and 3¹/₃ miles wide, shall be the residence area for the Levites who work at the Temple. [6] Adjacent to the holy lands will be a section 8¹/₃ miles by 1²/₃ miles for a city open to everyone in Israel.

---

a Literally, "between what is ritually clean and ritually unclean."   b Implied.

[7] "Two special sections of land shall be set apart for the prince—one on each side of the holy lands and city; it is contiguous with them in length, and its eastern and western boundaries are the same as those of the tribal sections. [8] This shall be his allotment. My princes shall no longer oppress and rob my people, but shall assign all the remainder of the land to the people, giving a portion to each tribe. [9] For the Lord God says to the rulers: Quit robbing and cheating my people out of their land, and expelling them from their homes. Always be fair and honest.

[10] "You must use honest scales, honest bushels, honest gallons. [11] A homer[a] shall be your standard unit of measurement for both liquid and dry measure. Smaller units shall be the ephah (one-tenth of a homer) for dry measure, and the bath (one-tenth of a homer) for liquid. [12] The unit of weight shall be the silver shekel (about half an ounce); it must always be exchanged for twenty gerahs, no less; five shekels shall be valued at five shekels, no less; and ten shekels at ten shekels! Fifty shekels shall always equal one maneh.

[13] "This is the tax you must give to the prince: a bushel of wheat or barley for every sixty you reap; [14] and one per cent of your olive oil; [15] from each 200 sheep in all your flocks in Israel, give him one sheep. These are the meal offerings, burnt offerings and thank offerings to make atonement for those who bring them, says the Lord God. [16] All the people of Israel shall bring their offerings to the prince.

[17] "The prince shall be required to furnish the people with sacrifices for public worship—sin offerings, burnt offerings, meal offerings, drink offerings and thank offerings—to make reconciliation for the people of Israel. This shall be done at the time of the religious feasts, the new moon ceremonies, the Sabbaths and all other similar occasions.

[18] "The Lord God says: On each New Year's Day[b] sacrifice a young bull with no blemishes, to purify the Temple. [19] The priest shall take some of the blood of this sin offering and put it on the door posts of the Temple and upon the four corners of the base of the altar and upon the walls at the entry of the inner court. [20] Do this also on the seventh day of that month for anyone who has sinned through error or ignorance, and so the Temple will be cleansed.

[21] "On the fourteenth day of the same month, you shall celebrate the Passover. It will be a seven-day feast. Only bread without yeast shall be eaten during those days. [22] On the day of Passover the prince shall provide a young bull for a sin offering for himself and all the people of Israel. [23] On each of the seven days of the feast he shall prepare a burnt offering to the Lord. This daily offering will consist of seven young bulls and seven rams without blemish. A young goat will also be given each day for a sin offering. [24] And the prince shall provide fourteen bushels of grain for the meal offering—one bushel for each bullock and ram; and twenty-one gallons of olive oil—1½ gallons to go with each bushel.

[25] "Early in October, during each of the seven days of the annual feast, he shall provide these same sacrifices for the sin offering, burnt offering, meal offering and oil offering.

46 "THE LORD GOD says, the inner wall's eastern entrance shall be closed during the six work days but open on the Sabbath and on the days of the new moon celebrations. [2] The prince shall enter the outside entry hall of the passageway and proceed to the inner wall at the other end while the priest offers his burnt offering and peace offering. He shall worship inside the passageway and then return back to the entrance, which shall not be closed until evening. [3] The people shall worship the Lord in front of this passageway on the Sabbaths and on the days of the new moon celebrations.

[4] "The burnt offering which the prince sacrifices to the Lord on the Sabbath days shall be six lambs and a ram, all unblemished. [5] He shall present a meal offering of one bushel of flour to go with the ram, and whatever amount he is willing for, to go with each lamb. And he shall bring 1½ gal-

---

a The homer was about 220 litres, or 6½ bushels.   b April was the first month of the Hebrew year.

lons of olive oil for each bushel of flour. ⁶ At the new moon celebration, he shall bring one young bull, in perfect condition; six lambs and one ram, all without any blemish. ⁷ With the young bull, he must bring a bushel[a] of flour for a meal offering. With the ram, he is to bring one bushel[a] of flour. With the lamb, he is to bring whatever he is willing[b] to give. With each bushel he is to bring 1½ gallons of olive oil.

⁸ "The prince shall go in at the entry hall of the passageway and out the same way; ⁹ but when the people come in through the north passageway to sacrifice during the religious feasts, they must go out through the south passageway. Those coming in from the south must go out by the north. They must never go out the same way they come in, but must always use the opposite passageway. ¹⁰ The prince shall enter and leave with the common people on these occasions.

¹¹ "To summarize: At the special feasts and sacred festivals the meal offering shall be one bushel with the young bull; one bushel with the ram; as much as the prince is willing to give with each lamb; and 1½ gallons of oil with each bushel. ¹² Whenever the prince offers an extra burnt offering or peace offering to be sacrificed to the Lord, the inner eastern gate shall be opened up for him to enter and he shall offer his sacrifices just as on the Sabbaths. Then he shall turn around and go out, and the passage shall be shut behind him.

¹³ "Each morning a yearling lamb must be sacrificed as a burnt offering to the Lord. ¹⁴,¹⁵ And there must be a meal offering each morning—⅙ bushel of flour with half a gallon of oil with which to mix it. This is a permanent ordinance—the lamb, the grain offering and the olive oil shall be provided every morning for the daily sacrifice.

¹⁶ "The Lord God says: If the prince gives a gift of land to one of his sons, it will belong to him forever. ¹⁷ But if he gives a gift of land to one of his servants, the servant may keep it only until the Year of Release (every seventh year) when he is set free; then the land returns to the prince.

Only gifts to his sons are permanent. ¹⁸ And the prince may never take anyone's property by force. If he gives property to his sons, it must be from his own land, for I don't want my people losing their property and having to move away."

¹⁹,²⁰ After that, using the door through the wall at the side of the main passageway, he led me through the entrance to the block of sacred chambers that faced north. There, at the extreme west end of these rooms, I saw a place where, my guide told me, the priests boil the meat of the trespass offering and sin offering and bake the flour of the flour offerings into bread. They do it here to avoid the necessity of carrying the sacrifices through the outer court, in case they sanctify the people.

²¹,²² Then he brought me out to the outer court again and led me to each of the four corners of the court. I saw that in each corner there was a room 70 feet long by 52½ feet wide, enclosed by walls. ²³ Around the inside of these walls there ran a line of brick boiling vats, with ovens underneath. ²⁴ He said these rooms were where the Temple assistants—the Levites—boil the sacrifices the people offer.

47 THEN HE BROUGHT me back to the door of the Temple. I saw a stream flowing eastward from beneath the Temple and passing to the right of the altar, that is, on its south side. ² Then he brought me outside the wall through the north passageway[a] and around to the eastern entrance, where I saw the stream flowing along on the south side [of the eastern passageway[b]]. ³ Measuring as he went, he took me 1,500 feet east along the stream and told me to go across. At that point the water was up to my ankles. ⁴ He measured off another 1,500 feet and told me to cross again. This time the water was up to my knees. ⁵ Fifteen hundred feet after that it was up to my waist. Another 1,500 feet and it had become a river so deep I wouldn't be able to get across unless I were to swim. It was too deep to cross on foot.

⁶ He told me to keep in mind what I had

---

a Literally, one ephah.   b Literally, "his hand shall attain unto."   47 a The eastern passageway was closed.   b Implied.

seen, then led me back along the bank. [7] And now, to my surprise,[c] many trees were growing on both sides of the river!

[8] He told me: "This river flows east through the desert and the Jordan Valley to the Dead Sea, where it will heal the salty waters and make them fresh and pure. [9] Everything touching the water of this river shall live. Fish will abound in the Dead Sea, for its waters will be healed. Wherever this water flows, everything will live. [10] Fishermen will stand along the shores of the Dead Sea, fishing all the way from En-gedi to En-eglaim. The shores will be filled with nets drying in the sun. Fish of every kind will fill the Dead Sea just as they do the Mediterranean! [11] But the marshes and swamps will not be healed; they will still be salty. [12] All kinds of fruit trees will grow along the river banks. The leaves will never turn brown and fall, and there will always be fruit. There will be a new crop every month —without fail! For they are watered by the river flowing from the Temple. The fruit will be for food and the leaves for medicine.

[13] "The Lord God says:[d] Here are the instructions for dividing the land to the twelve tribes of Israel: The tribe of Joseph (Ephraim and Manesseh[c]) shall be given two sections. [14] Otherwise, each tribe will have an equal share. I promised with hand raised in oath of truth to give the land to your fathers, and you shall inherit it now.

[15] "The northern boundary will run from the Mediterranean toward Hethlon, then on through Labweh[e] to Zedad; [16] then to Berothah and Sibraim, which are on the border between Damascus and Hamath, and finally to Hazer-hatticon, on the border of Hauran. [17] So the northern border will be from the Mediterranean to Hazar-enon, on the border with Hamath to the north and Damascus to the south.

[18] "The eastern border will run south from Hazar-enon to Mount Hauran, where it will bend westward to the Jordan at the southern tip of the Sea of Galilee, and down along the Jordan River separating Israel from Gilead, past the Dead Sea to Tamar. [19] "The southern border will go west from Tamar to the springs at Meribath-kadesh and then follow the course of the Brook of Egypt (Wadi el-Arish) to the Mediterranean.

[20] "On the west side, the Mediterranean itself will be your boundary, from the southern boundary to the point where the northern boundary begins.

[21] "Divide the land within these boundaries among the tribes of Israel. [22] Distribute the land as an inheritance for yourselves and for the foreigners who live among you with their families. All children born in the land—whether or not their parents are foreigners—are to be considered citizens and have the same rights your own children have. [23] All these immigrants are to be given land according to the tribe where they now live.

48 "HERE IS THE list of the tribes and the territory each is to get. For Dan: From the northwest boundary at the Mediterranean, across to Hethlon, then to Labweh, and then on to Hazar-enon on the border between Damascus to the south and Hamath to the north. Those are the eastern and western limits of the land. [2] Asher's territory lies south of Dan's and has the same east and west boundaries. [3] Naphtali's land lies south of Asher's, with the same boundary lines on the east and the west. [4] Then comes Manasseh, south of Naphtali, with the same eastern and western boundary lines. [5,6,7] Next, to the south, is Ephraim, and then Reuben and then Judah, all with the same boundaries on the east and the west.

[8] "South of Judah is the land set aside for the Temple. It has the same eastern and western boundaries as the tribal units, with the Temple in the center.[a] [9] This Temple area will be 8 1/3 miles long and 6 2/3 miles wide.

[10] "A strip of land measuring 8 1/3 miles long by 3 1/3 miles wide, north to south, surrounds the Temple. [11] It is for the priests, that is, the sons of Zadok who obeyed me and didn't go into sin when the people of Israel and the rest of their tribe of Levi did.

---

c Implied.   d See Diagram 7, page 791.   e The present village on this site is so named. It was originally called Lebo-Hamath.   48a See Diagram 7, page 791.

¹² It is their special portion when the land is distributed, the most sacred land of all. Next to it lies the area where the other Levites will live. ¹³ It will be of the same size and shape as the first. Together they measure 8¹/₃ miles by 6²/₃ miles. ¹⁴ None of this special land shall ever be sold or traded or used by others, for it belongs to the Lord; it is holy.

¹⁵ "The strip of land 8¹/₃ miles long by 1²/₃ miles wide, south of the Temple section, is for public use—homes, pasture and parks, with a city in the center. ¹⁶ The city itself is to be 1½ miles square. ¹⁷ Open land for pastures shall surround the city for approximately^b a tenth of a mile. ¹⁸ Outside the city, stretching east and west for three miles alongside the holy grounds, is garden area belonging to the city, for public use. ¹⁹ It is open to anyone working in the city, no matter where he comes from in Israel.

²⁰ "The entire area—including sacred lands and city lands—is 8¹/₃ miles square.

²¹,²² "The land on both sides of this area, extending clear out to the eastern and western boundaries of Israel, shall belong to the prince. This land, lying between the sections alloted to Judah and Benjamin, is 8¹/₃ miles square on each side of the sacred and city lands.

²³ "The sections given to the remaining tribes are as follows: Benjamin's section extends across the entire country of Israel, from its eastern border clear across to the western border. ²⁴ South of Benjamin's area lies that of Simeon, also extending out to these same eastern and western borders. ²⁵ Next is Issachar, with the same boundaries. ²⁶ Then comes Zebulun, also extending all the way across. ²⁷,²⁸ Then Gad, with the same borders on east and west, while its south border runs from Tamar to the Spring at Meribath-kadesh, and then follows the Brook of Egypt (Wadi el-Arish) to the Mediterranean. ²⁹ These are the allotments to be made to each tribe, says the Lord God.

³⁰,³¹ "Each city gate will be named in honor of one of the tribes of Israel. On the north side, with its 1½-mile wall, there will be three gates, one named for Reuben, one for Judah and one for Levi. ³² On the east side, with its 1½-mile wall, the gates will be named for Joseph, Benjamin and Dan. ³³ The south wall, also the same length, will have the gates of Simeon, Issachar and Zebulun; ³⁴ on the 1½ miles of the west side, they will be named for Gad, Asher and Naphtali.

³⁵ "The entire circumference of the city is six miles. And the name of the city will be 'The City of God.' "^c

---

b Literally, "437½ feet" in every direction.   c Literally, "Jehovah-Shammah," "The Lord is there."

The POWs

Polish Jews, hands upraised, being hustled through the streets of Warsaw in 1943, headed for death . . . Nazi soldiers ambling alongside, fingering their weapons . . . shades of the conquest of Jerusalem in 605 B.C., when the Babylonian war machine crashed into the Jewish city and began rounding up captives.

Nebuchadnezzar was not quite a Hitler, however. He moved the Jews not to concentration camps but to resettlements near his capital. A young man named Daniel and three of his friends were among the most fortunate POWs; they were chosen for a special three-year training program for civil service jobs. That brought some interesting pressures to conform—and the way Daniel not only kept his balance but eventually became one of three presidents under the monarch is a fascinating example of how God never fails his people in spite of their environment.

DANIEL

1 THREE YEARS AFTER King Jehoiakim began to rule in Judah, Babylon's King Nebuchadnezzar attacked Jerusalem with his armies, and the Lord gave him victory over Jehoiakim. When he returned to Babylon, he took along some of the sacred cups from the Temple of God, and placed them in the treasury of his god in the land of Shinar.

3,4 Then he ordered Ashpenaz, who was in charge of his palace personnel,[a] to select some of the Jewish youths brought back as captives—young men of the royal family and nobility of Judah—and to teach them the Chaldean language and literature.[b] "Pick strong, healthy, good-looking lads," he said; "those who have read widely in many fields, are well informed, alert and sensible, and have enough poise to look good around the palace."

5 The king assigned them the best of food and wine from his own kitchen during their three-year training period, planning to make them his counselors when they graduated.

6 Daniel, Hananiah, Misha-el, and Aza-

---

a Literally, "his chief eunuch." See 2 Kings 20:17, 18.   b The language was Aramaic; the literature would have included mathematics, astronomy and history—plus a strong dose of alchemy and magic!

717

riah were four of the young men chosen, all from the tribe of Judah. ⁷ However, their superintendent gave them Babylonian names, as follows:

Daniel was called Belteshazzar;
Hananiah was called Shadrach;
Misha-el was called Meshach;
Azariah was called Abednego.

⁸ But Daniel made up his mind not to eat the food and wine given to them by the king.ᶜ He asked the superintendent for permission to eat other things instead.ᵈ ⁹ Now as it happened, God had given the superintendent a special appreciation for Daniel, and sympathy for his predicament. ¹⁰ But he was alarmed by Daniel's suggestion.

"I'm afraid you will become pale and thin compared with the other youths your age," he said, "and then the king will behead me for neglecting my responsibilities."

¹¹ Daniel talked it over with the steward who was appointed by the superintendent to look after Daniel, Hananiah, Misha-el, and Azariah, ¹² and suggested a ten-day diet of only vegetables and water; ¹³ then, at the end of this trial period the steward could see how they looked in comparison with the other fellows who ate the king's rich food, and decide whether or not to let them continue their diet.

¹⁴ The steward finally agreed to the test. ¹⁵ Well, at the end of the ten days, Daniel and his three friends looked healthier and better nourished than the youths who had been eating the food supplied by the king! ¹⁶ So after that the steward fed them only vegetables and water, without the rich foods and wines!

¹⁷ God gave these four youths great ability to learn and they soon mastered all the literature and science of the time, and God gave to Daniel special ability in understanding the meanings of dreams and visions.

¹⁸,¹⁹ When the three-year training period was completed, the superintendent brought all the young men to the king for oral exams, as he had been ordered to do. King Nebuchadnezzar had long talks with each of them, and none of them impressed him as much as Daniel, Hananiah, Misha-el,

and Azariah. So they were put on his regular staff of advisors. ²⁰ And in all matters requiring information and balanced judgment, the king found these young men's advice ten times better than that of all the skilled magicians and wise astrologers in his realm.

²¹ Daniel held this appointment as the king's counselor until the first year of the reign of King Cyrus.

2 ONE NIGHT IN the second year of his reign, Nebuchadnezzar had a terrifying nightmare, and awoke trembling with fear. And to make matters worse, he couldn't remember his dream! He immediately called in all his magicians, incantationists, sorcerers, and astrologers, and demanded that they tell him what his dream had been.

"I've had a terrible nightmare," he said as they stood before him, "and I can't remember what it was. Tell me, for I fear some tragedy awaits me."

⁴ Then the astrologers (speaking in Aramaic) said to the king, "Sir, tell us the dream and then we can tell you what it means."

⁵ But the king replied, "I tell you, the dream is gone—I can't remember it. And if you won't tell me what it was and what it means, I'll have you torn limb from limb and your houses made into heaps of rubble! ⁶ But I will give you many wonderful gifts and honors if you tell me what the dream was and what it means. So, begin!"

⁷ They said again, "How can we tell you what the dream means unless you tell us what it was?"

⁸,⁹ The king retorted, "I can see your trick! You're trying to stall for time until the calamity befalls me that the dream foretells. But if you don't tell me the dream, you certainly can't expect me to believe your interpretation!"

¹⁰ The Chaldeans replied to the king, "There isn't a man alive who can tell others what they have dreamed! And there isn't a king in all the world who would ask such a thing! ¹¹ This is an impossible thing the king requires. No one except the gods can

---

c Literally, "determined . . . that he would not defile himself." The defilement was probably in eating pork or other foods outlawed in Leviticus.   d Literally, "He asked . . . to allow him not to defile himself."

tell you your dream, and they are not here to help."

¹² Upon hearing this, the king was furious, and sent out orders to execute all the wise men of Babylon. ¹³ And Daniel and his companions were rounded up with the others to be killed.

¹⁴ But when Ari-och, the chief executioner, came to kill them, Daniel handled the situation with great wisdom by asking, ¹⁵ "Why is the king so angry? What is the matter?"

Then Ari-och told him all that had happened.

¹⁶ So Daniel went in to see the king. "Give me a little time," he said, "and I will tell you the dream and what it means."

¹⁷ Then he went home and told Hananiah, Misha-el, and Azariah, his companions. ¹⁸ They asked the God of heaven to show them his mercy by telling them the secret, so they would not die with the others. ¹⁹ And that night in a vision God told Daniel what the king had dreamed.

Then Daniel praised the God of heaven, ²⁰ saying, "Blessed be the name of God forever and ever, for he alone has all wisdom and all power. ²¹ World events are under his control. He removes kings and sets others on their thrones. He gives wise men their wisdom, and scholars their intelligence. ²² He reveals profound mysteries beyond man's understanding. He knows all hidden things, for he is light, and darkness is no obstacle to him. ²³ I thank and praise you, O God of my fathers, for you have given me wisdom and glowing health, and now, even this vision of the king's dream, and the understanding of what it means."

²⁴ Then Daniel went in to see Ari-och, who had been ordered to execute the wise men of Babylon, and said, "Don't kill them. Take me to the king and I will tell him what he wants to know."

²⁵ Then Ari-och hurried Daniel in to the king and said, "I've found one of the Jewish captives who will tell you your dream!"

²⁶ The king said to Daniel, "Is this true? Can you tell me what my dream was and what it means?"

²⁷ Daniel replied, "No wise man, astrologer, magician, or wizard can tell the king such things, ²⁸ but there is a God in heaven who reveals secrets, and he has told you in your dream what will happen in the future. This was your dream:

²⁹ "You dreamed of coming events. He who reveals secrets was speaking to you. ³⁰ (But remember, it's not because I am wiser than any living person that I know this secret of your dream, for God showed it to me for your benefit.)

³¹ "O king, you saw a huge and powerful statue of a man, shining brilliantly, frightening and terrible. ³² The head of the statue was made of purest gold, its chest and arms were of silver, its belly and thighs of brass, ³³ its legs of iron, its feet part iron and part clay. ³⁴ But as you watched, a Rock was cut from the mountainsideᵃ by supernatural means. It came hurtling toward the statue and crushed the feet of iron and clay, smashing them to bits. ³⁵ Then the whole statue collapsed into a heap of iron, clay, brass, silver, and gold; its pieces were crushed as small as chaff, and the wind blew them all away. But the Rock that knocked the statue down became a great mountain that covered the whole earth.

³⁶ "That was the dream; now for its meaning:

³⁷ "Your Majesty, you are a king over many kings, for the God of heaven has given you your kingdom, power, strength and glory. ³⁸ You rule the farthest provinces, and even animals and birds are under your control, as God decreed. You are that head of gold.

³⁹ "But after your kingdom has come to an end, another world powerᵇ will arise to take your place. This empire will be inferior to yours. And after that kingdom has fallen, yet a third great powerᶜ—represented by the bronze belly of the statue—will rise to rule the world. ⁴⁰ Following it, the fourth kingdomᵈ will be strong as iron—smashing, bruising, and conquering. ⁴¹,⁴² The feet and toes you saw—part iron and part clay—show that later on, this kingdom will be divided. Some parts of it will be as strong

---

a Implied.   b The Medo-Persian Empire, whose first great ruler was Cyrus.   c The Greek Empire,
founded by Alexander the Great.   d Apparently the Roman Empire.

as iron, and some as weak as clay. [43] This mixture of iron with clay also shows that these kingdoms will try to strengthen themselves by forming alliances with each other through intermarriage of their rulers; but this will not succeed, for iron and clay don't mix.

[44] "During the reigns of those kings, the God of heaven will set up a kingdom that will never be destroyed; no one will ever conquer it. It will shatter all these kingdoms into nothingness, but it shall stand forever, indestructible. [45] That is the meaning of the Rock cut from the mountain without human hands—the Rock that crushed to powder all the iron and brass, the clay, the silver, and the gold.

"Thus the great God has shown what will happen in the future, and this interpretation of your dream is as sure and certain as my description of it."

[46] Then Nebuchadnezzar fell to the ground before Daniel and worshiped him, and commanded his people to offer sacrifices and burn sweet incense before him.

[47] "Truly, O Daniel," the king said, "your God is the God of gods, Ruler of kings, the Revealer of mysteries, because he has told you this secret."

[48] Then the king made Daniel very great; he gave him many costly gifts, and appointed him to be ruler over the whole province of Babylon, as well as chief over all his wise men.

[49] Then, at Daniel's request, the king appointed Shadrach, Meshach, and Abednego as Daniel's assistants, to be in charge of all the affairs of the province of Babylon; Daniel served as chief magistrate in the king's court.

3 KING NEBUCHADNEZZAR MADE a golden statue ninety feet high and nine feet wide and set it up on the Plain of Dura, in the province of Babylon; [2] then he sent messages to all the princes, governors, captains, judges, treasurers, counselors, sheriffs, and rulers of all the provinces of his empire, to come to the dedication of his statue. [3] When they had all arrived and were standing before the monument, [4] a herald shouted out, "O people of all nations and languages, this is the king's command:

[5] "When the band[a] strikes up, you are to fall flat on the ground to worship King Nebuchadnezzar's golden statue; [6] anyone who refuses to obey will immediately be thrown into a flaming furnace."

[7] So when the band[a] began to play, everyone—whatever his nation, language, or religion[b]—fell to the ground and worshiped the statue.

[8] But some officials went to the king and accused some of the Jews of refusing to worship!

[9] "Your Majesty," they said to him, [10] "you made a law that everyone must fall down and worship the golden statue when the band[a] begins to play, [11] and that anyone who refuses will be thrown into a flaming furnace. [12] But there are some Jews out there—Shadrach, Meshach, and Abednego, whom you have put in charge of Babylonian affairs—who have defied you, refusing to serve your gods or to worship the golden statue you set up."

[13] Then Nebuchadnezzar, in a terrible rage, ordered Shadrach, Meshach, and Abednego to be brought in before him.

[14] "Is it true, O Shadrach, Meshach, and Abednego," he asked, "that you are refusing to serve my gods or to worship the golden statue I set up? [15] I'll give you one more chance. When the music plays, if you fall down and worship the statue, all will be well. But if you refuse, you will be thrown into a flaming furnace within the hour. And what god can deliver you out of my hands then?"

[16] Shadrach, Meshach, and Abednego replied, "O Nebuchadnezzar, we are not worried about what will happen to us. [17] If we are thrown into the flaming furnace, our God is able to deliver us; and he will deliver us out of your hand, Your Majesty. [18] But if he doesn't, please understand, sir, that even then we will never under any circumstance serve your gods or worship the golden statue you have erected."

[19] Then Nebuchadnezzar was filled with

---

a Literally, "the cornet, flute, harp, sackbut, psaltry, dulcimer, and every other sort of instrument."
b Implied.

fury and his face became dark with anger at Shadrach, Meshach, and Abednego. He commanded that the furnace be heated up seven times hotter than usual, ²⁰ and called for some of the strongest men of his army to bind Shadrach, Meshach, and Abednego, and throw them into the fire.

²¹ So they bound them tight with ropes and threw them into the furnace, fully clothed. ²² And because the king, in his anger, had demanded such a hot fire in the furnace, the flames leaped out and killed the soldiers as they threw them in! ²³ So Shadrach, Meshach, and Abednego fell down bound into the roaring flames.

²⁴ But suddenly, as he was watching, Nebuchadnezzar jumped up in amazement and exclaimed to his advisors, "Didn't we throw three men into the furnace?"

"Yes," they said, "we did indeed, Your Majesty."

²⁵ "Well, look!" Nebuchadnezzar shouted. "I see *four* men, unbound, walking around in the fire, and they aren't even hurt by the flames! And the fourth looks like a god!"[c]

²⁶ Then Nebuchadnezzar came as close as he could to the open door of the flaming furnace and yelled: "Shadrach, Meshach, and Abednego, servants of the Most High God! Come out! Come here!" So they stepped out of the fire.

²⁷ Then the princes, governors, captains, and counselors crowded around them and saw that the fire hadn't touched them—not a hair of their heads was singed; their coats were unscorched, and they didn't even smell of smoke!

²⁸ Then Nebuchadnezzar said, "Blessed be the God of Shadrach, Meshach, and Abednego, for he sent his angel to deliver his trusting servants when they defied the king's commandment, and were willing to die rather than serve or worship any god except their own. ²⁹ Therefore, I make this decree, that any person of any nation, language, or religion[d] who speaks a word against the God of Shadrach, Meshach, and Abednego shall be torn limb from limb and his house knocked into a heap of rubble. For no other God can do what this one does."

³⁰ Then the king gave promotions to Shadrach, Meshach, and Abednego, so that they prospered greatly there in the province of Babylon.

4 THIS IS THE proclamation of Nebuchadnezzar the king, which he sent to people of every language in every nation of the world:

Greetings:

² I want you all to know about the strange thing that the Most High God did to me. ³ It was incredible—a mighty miracle! And now I know for sure that his kingdom is everlasting; he reigns forever and ever.

⁴ I, Nebuchadnezzar, was living in peace and prosperity, ⁵ when one night I had a dream that greatly frightened me. ⁶ I called in all the wise men of Babylon to tell me the meaning of my dream, ⁷ but when they came—the magicians, astrologers, fortunetellers, and wizards—and I told them the dream, they couldn't interpret it. ⁸ At last Daniel came in—the man I named Belteshazzar after my god—the man in whom is the spirit of the holy gods, and I told him the dream.

⁹ "O Belteshazzar, master magician," I said, "I know that the spirit of the holy gods is in you and no mystery is too great for you to solve. Tell me what my dream means:

¹⁰,¹¹ "I saw a very tall tree out in a field, growing higher and higher into the sky until it could be seen by everyone in all the world. ¹² Its leaves were fresh and green, and its branches were weighted down with fruit, enough for everyone to eat. Wild animals rested beneath its shade and birds sheltered in its branches, and all the world was fed from it. ¹³ Then as I lay there dreaming, I saw one of God's angels[a] coming down from heaven.

¹⁴ "He shouted, 'Cut down the tree; lop off its branches; shake off its leaves, and scatter its fruit. Get the animals out from under it and the birds from its branches, ¹⁵ but leave its stump and roots in the ground, banded with a chain of iron and brass, surrounded by the tender grass. Let

---

c Literally, "looks like a son of the gods."   d Implied.   4a Literally, "a watcher, a holy one."

the dews of heaven drench him and let him eat grass with the wild animals! [16] For seven years let him have the mind of an animal instead of a man. [17] For this has been decreed by the Watchers, demanded by the Holy Ones. The purpose of this decree is that all the world may understand that the Most High dominates the kingdoms of the world, and gives them to anyone he wants to, even the lowliest of men!'

[18] "O Belteshazzar, that was my dream; now tell me what it means. For no one else can help me; all the wisest men of my kingdom have failed me. But you can tell me, for the spirit of the holy gods is in you."

[19] Then Daniel[b] sat there stunned and silent for an hour, aghast at the meaning of the dream. Finally the king said to him: "Belteshazzar, don't be afraid to tell me what it means."

Daniel replied: "Oh, that the events foreshadowed in this dream would happen to your enemies, my lord, and not to you! [20] For the tree you saw growing so tall, reaching high into the heavens for all the world to see, [21] with its fresh green leaves, loaded with fruit for all to eat, the wild animals living in its shade, with its branches full of birds— [22] that tree, Your Majesty, is you. For you have grown strong and great; your greatness reaches up to heaven, and your rule to the ends of the earth.

[23] "Then you saw God's angel[c] coming down from heaven and saying, 'Cut down the tree and destroy it, but leave the stump and the roots in the earth surrounded by tender grass, banded with a chain of iron and brass. Let him be wet with the dew of heaven. For seven years let him eat grass with the animals of the field.'

[24] "Your Majesty, the Most High God has decreed—and it will surely happen— [25] that your people will chase you from your palace, and you will live in the fields like an animal, eating grass like a cow, your back wet with dew from heaven. For seven years this will be your life, until you learn that the Most High God dominates the kingdoms of men, and gives power to anyone he chooses. [26] But the stump and the roots were left in

the ground! This means that you will get your kingdom back again, when you have learned that heaven rules.

[27] "O King Nebuchadnezzar, listen to me—stop sinning; do what you know is right; be merciful to the poor. Perhaps even yet God will spare you."

[28] But all these things happened to Nebuchadnezzar. [29] Twelve months after this dream, he was strolling on the roof of the royal palace in Babylon, [30] and saying, "I, by my own mighty power, have built this beautiful city as my royal residence, and as the capital of my empire."

[31] While he was still speaking these words, a voice called down from heaven, "O King Nebuchadnezzar, this message is for you: You are no longer ruler of this kingdom. [32] You will be forced out of the palace to live with the animals in the fields, and to eat grass like the cows for seven years until you finally realize that God parcels out the kingdoms of men and gives them to anyone he chooses."

[33] That very same hour this prophecy was fulfilled. Nebuchadnezzar was chased from his palace and ate grass like the cows, and his body was wet with dew; his hair grew as long as eagles' feathers, and his nails were like birds' claws.

[34] "At the end of seven years[d] I, Nebuchadnezzar, looked up to heaven, and my sanity returned, and I praised and worshiped the Most High God and honored him who lives forever, whose rule is everlasting, his kingdom evermore. [35] All the people of the earth are nothing when compared to him; he does whatever he thinks best among the hosts of heaven, as well as here among the inhabitants of earth. No one can stop him or challenge him, saying, 'What do you mean by doing these things?' [36] When my mind returned to me, so did my honor and glory and kingdom. My counselors and officers came back to me and I was reestablished as head of my kingdom, with even greater honor than before.

[37] "Now, I, Nebuchadnezzar, praise and glorify and honor the King of Heaven, the Judge of all, whose every act is right and

---

b Literally, "Daniel, whose name was Belteshazzar."
d Literally, "at the end of the days."

c Literally, "a holy watcher."

good; for he is able to take those who walk proudly and push them into the dust!"

5 BELSHAZZAR THE KING invited a thousand of his officers to a great feast where the wine flowed freely. [2,3,4] While Belshazzar was drinking he was reminded of the gold and silver cups taken long before from the Temple in Jerusalem during Nebuchadnezzar's reign, and brought to Babylon. Belshazzar ordered that these sacred cups be brought in to the feast, and when they arrived he and his princes, wives, and concubines drank toasts from them to their idols made of gold and silver, brass and iron, wood and stone.

[5] Suddenly, as they were drinking from these cups, they saw the fingers of a man's hand writing on the plaster of the wall opposite the lampstand. The king himself saw the fingers as they wrote. [6] His face blanched with fear, and such terror gripped him that his knees knocked together and his legs gave way beneath him.

[7] "Bring the magicians and astrologers!" he screamed. "Bring the Chaldeans! Whoever reads that writing on the wall, and tells me what it means, will be dressed in purple robes of royal honor with a gold chain around his neck, and become the third ruler[a] in the kingdom!"

[8] But when they came, none of them could understand[b] the writing or tell him what it meant.

[9] The king grew more and more hysterical; his face reflected the terror he felt, and his officers too were shaken. [10] But when the queen-mother heard what was happening, she rushed to the banquet hall and said to Belshazzar, "Calm yourself, Your Majesty, don't be so pale and frightened over this. [11] For there is a man in your kingdom who has within him the spirit of the holy gods. In the days of your father this man was found to be as full of wisdom and understanding as though he were himself a god. And in the reign of King Nebuchadnezzar,[c] he was made chief of all the magicians, astrologers, Chaldeans and soothsayers of Babylon. [12] Call for this man, Daniel—or Belteshazzar, as the king called him—for his mind is filled with divine knowledge and understanding. He can interpret dreams, explain riddles, and solve knotty problems. He will tell you what the writing means."

[13] So Daniel was rushed in to see the king. The king asked him, "Are you the Daniel that King Nebuchadnezzar brought from Israel as a Jewish captive? [14] I have heard that you have the spirit of the gods within you and that you are filled with enlightenment and wisdom. [15] My wise men and astrologers have tried to read that writing on the wall, and tell me what it means, but they can't. [16] I am told that you can solve all kinds of mysteries. If you can tell me the meaning of those words, I will clothe you in purple robes, with a golden chain around your neck, and make you the third ruler in the kingdom."

[17] Daniel answered, "Keep your gifts, or give them to someone else, but I will tell you what they mean. [18] Your Majesty, the Most High God gave Nebuchadnezzar, who long ago preceded you, a kingdom and majesty and glory and honor. [19] He gave him such majesty that all the nations of the world trembled before him in fear. He killed any who offended him, and spared any he liked. At his whim they rose or fell. [20] But when his heart and mind were hardened in pride, God removed him from his royal throne and took away his glory, [21] and he was chased out of his palace into the fields. His thoughts and feelings became those of an animal, and he lived among the wild donkeys; he ate grass like the cows and his body was wet with the dew of heaven, until at last he knew that the Most High overrules the kingdoms of men, and that he appoints anyone he desires to reign over them.

[22] "And you, his successor, O Belshazzar —you knew all this, yet you have not been humble. [23] For you have defied the Lord of Heaven, and brought here these cups from his Temple; and you and your officers and wives and concubines have been drinking wine from them while praising gods of sil-

---

a Belshazzar was the second under Nabonidus his father, who was out of town at the time.
b Since the writing was in familiar Aramaic, they could read the words but could not determine their prophetic significance.   c Literally, "King Nebuchadnezzar your father"—the Aramaic word for "father" can also mean "predecessor," in this instance, fifth removed.

ver, gold, brass, iron, wood, and stone—gods that neither see nor hear, nor know anything at all. But you have not praised the God who gives you the breath of life and controls your destiny! [24,25] And so God sent those fingers to write this message: *'Mene,' 'Mene,' 'Tekel,' 'Parsin.'*

[26] "This is what it means:

"Mene means 'numbered'—God has numbered the days of your reign, and they are ended.

[27] *"Tekel* means 'weighed'—you have been weighed in God's balances and have failed the test.

[28] *"Parsin* means 'divided'—your kingdom will be divided and given to the Medes and Persians."

[29] Then at Belshazzar's command, Daniel was robed in purple, and a golden chain was hung around his neck, and he was proclaimed third ruler in the kingdom.

[30] That very night Belshazzar, the Chaldean king, was killed, [31] and Darius the Mede[d] entered the city and began reigning at the age of sixty-two.

6 DARIUS DIVIDED THE kingdom into 120 provinces, each under a governor. [2] The governors were accountable to three presidents (Daniel was one of them) so that the king could administer the kingdom efficiently.

[3] Daniel soon proved himself more capable than all the other presidents and governors, for he had great ability, and the king began to think of placing him over the entire empire as his administrative officer.

[4] This made the other presidents and governors very jealous, and they began searching for some fault in the way Daniel was handling his affairs so that they could complain to the king about him. But they couldn't find anything to criticize! He was faithful and honest, and made no mistakes.

[5] So they concluded, "Our only chance is his religion!"

[6] They decided to go to the king and say, "King Darius, live forever! [7] We presidents, governors, counselors and deputies have unanimously decided that you should make a law, irrevocable under any circumstance, that for the next thirty days anyone who asks a favor of God or man—except from you, Your Majesty—shall be thrown to the lions. [8] Your Majesty, we request your signature on this law; sign it so that it cannot be canceled or changed; it will be a 'law of the Medes and Persians' that cannot be revoked."

[9] So King Darius signed the law.

[10] But though Daniel knew about it, he went home and knelt down as usual in his upstairs bedroom, with its windows open toward Jerusalem, and prayed three times a day, just as he always had, giving thanks to his God.

[11] Then the men thronged to Daniel's house and found him praying there, asking favors of his God. [12] They rushed back to the king and reminded him about his law. "Haven't you signed a decree," they said, "that permits no petitions to any God or man—except you—for thirty days? And anyone disobeying will be thrown to the lions?"

"Yes," the king replied, "it is 'a law of the Medes and Persians,' that cannot be altered or revoked."

[13] Then they told the king, "That fellow Daniel, one of the Jewish captives, is paying no attention to you or your law. He is asking favors of his God three times a day."

[14] Hearing this, the king was very angry with himself for signing the law, and determined to save Daniel. He spent the rest of the day trying to think of some way to get Daniel out of this predicament.

[15] In the evening the men came again to the king and said, "Your Majesty, there is nothing you can do. You signed the law and it cannot be changed."

[16] So at last the king gave the order for Daniel's arrest, and he was taken to the den of lions. The king said to him, "May your God, whom you worship continually, deliver you." And then they threw him in. [17] A stone was brought and placed over the mouth of the den; and the king sealed it with his own signet ring, and that of his government, so that no one could rescue

---

d This Darius is not to be confused with Darius the Persian, mentioned in Ezra, Haggai, and Zechariah, nor with the one in Nehemiah 12:22.

Daniel from the lions.

¹⁸ Then the king returned to his palace and went to bed without dinner. He refused his usual entertainment and didn't sleep all night. ¹⁹ Very early the next morning he hurried out to the lions' den, ²⁰ and called out in anguish, "O Daniel, servant of the Living God, was your God, whom you worship continually, able to deliver you from the lions?"

²¹ Then he heard a voice! "Your Majesty, live forever!" It was Daniel! ²² "My God has sent his angel," he said, "to shut the lions' mouths so that they can't touch me; for I am innocent before God, nor, sir, have I wronged you."

²³ The king was beside himself with joy and ordered that Daniel be lifted from the den. And not a scratch was found on him, because he believed in his God.

²⁴ Then the king issued a command to bring the men who had accused Daniel, and throw them into the den along with their children and wives, and the lions leaped upon them and tore them apart before they even hit the bottom of the den.

²⁵,²⁶ Afterward King Darius wrote this message addressed to everyone in his empire:

"Greetings! I decree that everyone shall tremble and fear before the God of Daniel in every part of my kingdom. For his God is the living, unchanging God whose kingdom shall never be destroyed and whose power shall never end. ²⁷ He delivers his people, preserving them from harm; he does great miracles in heaven and earth; it is he who delivered Daniel from the power of the lions."

²⁸ So Daniel prospered in the reign of Darius, and in the reign of Cyrus the Persian.

7 ONE NIGHT DURING the first year of Belshazzar's reign over the Babylonian empire, Daniel had a dream and he wrote it down. This is his description of what he saw:

² In my dream I saw a great storm on a mighty ocean, with strong winds blowing from every direction. ³ Then four huge animals came up out of the water, each different from the other. ⁴ The first was like a lion, but it had eagle's wings! And as I watched, its wings were pulled off so that it could no longer fly, and it was left standing on the ground, on two feet, like a man; and a man's mind was given to it. ⁵ The second animal looked like a bear with its paw raised, ready to strike. It held three ribs between its teeth, and I heard a voice saying to it, "Get up! Devour many people!" ⁶ The third of these strange animals looked like a leopard, but on its back it had wings like those of birds, and it had four heads! And great power was given to it over all mankind.

⁷ Then, as I watched in my dream, a fourth animal rose up out of the ocean, too dreadful to describe and incredibly strong. It devoured some of its victims by tearing them apart with its huge iron teeth, and others it crushed beneath its feet. It was far more brutal and vicious than any of the other animals, and it had ten horns.

⁸ As I was looking at the horns, suddenly another small horn appeared among them, and three of the first ones were yanked out, roots and all, to give it room; this little horn had a man's eyes and a bragging mouth.

⁹ I watched as thrones were put in place and the Ancient of Days—the Almighty God—sat down to judge. His clothing was as white as snow, his hair like whitest wool. He sat upon a fiery throne brought in on flaming wheels, and ¹⁰ a river of fire flowed from before him. Millions of angels ministered to him and hundreds of millions of people stood before him, waiting to be judged. Then the court began its session and The Books were opened.

¹¹ As I watched, the brutal fourth animal was killed and its body handed over to be burned because of its arrogance against Almighty God, and the boasting of its little horn. ¹² As for the other three animals, their kingdoms were taken from them, but they were allowed to live a short time longer.ᵃ

¹³ Next I saw the arrival of a Man—or so he seemed to be—brought there on clouds from heaven; he approached the Ancient of Days and was presented to him. ¹⁴ He was given the ruling power and glory

---

a Literally, "for a season and a time."

over all the nations of the world, so that all people of every language must obey him. His power is eternal—it will never end; his government shall never fall.

[15] I was confused and disturbed by all I had seen (Daniel wrote in his report), [16] so I approached one of those standing beside the throne and asked him the meaning of all these things, and he explained them to me.

[17] "These four huge animals," he said, "represent four kings who will someday rule the earth. [18] But in the end the people of the Most High God shall rule the governments of the world forever and forever."

[19] Then I asked about the fourth animal, the one so brutal and shocking, with its iron teeth and brass claws that tore men apart and that stamped others to death with its feet. [20] I asked, too, about the ten horns and the little horn that came up afterward and destroyed three of the others—the horn with the eyes, and the loud, bragging mouth, the one which was stronger than the others. [21] For I had seen this horn warring against God's people and winning, [22] until the Ancient of Days came and opened his court and vindicated his people, giving them worldwide powers of government.

[23] "This fourth animal," he told me, "is the fourth world power[b] that will rule the earth. It will be more brutal than any of the others; it will devour the whole world, destroying everything before it. [24] His ten horns are ten kings that will rise out of his empire; then another king[c] will arise, more brutal than the other ten, and will destroy three of them. [25] He will defy the Most High God, and wear down the saints with persecution, and try to change all laws, morals, and customs.[d] God's people will be helpless in his hands for three and a half years.

[26] "But then the Ancient of Days will come[e] and open his court of justice and take all power from this vicious king, to consume and destroy it until the end. [27] Then every

nation under heaven, and all their power, shall be given to the people of God;[f] they shall rule all things forever, and all rulers shall serve and obey them."

[28] That was the end of the dream. When I awoke, I was greatly disturbed, and my face was pale with fright, but I told no one what I had seen.

8 IN THE THIRD year of the reign of King Belshazzar, I had another dream similar to the first.

[2] This time I was at Susa, the capital[a] in the province of Elam, standing beside the Ulai River. [3] As I was looking around, I saw a ram with two long horns standing on the river bank; and as I watched, one of these horns began to grow, so that it was longer than the other. [4] The ram butted everything out of its way and no one could stand against it or help its victims. It did as it pleased and became very great.

[5] While I was wondering what this could mean, suddenly a buck goat appeared from the west, so swiftly that it didn't even touch the ground. This goat, which had one very large horn between its eyes, [6] rushed furiously at the two-horned ram. [7] And the closer he came, the angrier he was. He charged into the ram and broke off both his horns. Now the ram was helpless and the buck goat knocked him down and trampled him, for there was no one to rescue him.

[8] The victor became both proud and powerful, but suddenly, at the height of his power, his horn was broken, and in its place grew four good-sized horns[b] pointing in four directions. [9] One of these, growing slowly at first, soon became very strong and attacked the south and east, and warred against the land of Israel.[c] [10] He fought against the people of God[d] and defeated some of their leaders.[d] [11] He even challenged the Commander[e] of the army of heaven by canceling the daily sacrifices offered to him, and by defiling his Temple.

b Usually believed to be a revived Roman Empire. See 2:40.   c Probably the future Antichrist of 2 Thessalonians 2:3, 4.   d Literally, "change the times and the law." Perhaps the meaning is, "change right to wrong and wrong to right."   e Implied in verse 22.   f Literally, "the people of the saints of the Most High."   8a Susa was one of several capitals of the empire at this time.   b The four principal successors of Alexander the Great were Ptolemy I of Egypt, Seleucus of Babylonia, Antigonus of Syria and Asia Minor, and Antipater of Macedonia and Greece.   c Literally, "the glorious land." Israel was attacked by Antiochus IV Epiphanes, with a further fulfillment of this prophecy indicated for the future; see verses 17, 19, 23. d Literally, "host of heaven" and "the starry host." See 8:24.   e Compare Joshua 5:13–15.

¹² But the army of heaven was restrained from destroying him for this transgression. As a result, truth and righteousness perished, and evil triumphed and prospered.ᶠ ¹³ Then I heard two of the holy angels talking to each other. One of them said, "How long will it be until the daily sacrifice is restored again? How long until the destruction of the Temple is avenged and God's people triumph?" ¹⁴ The other replied, "Twenty-three hundred daysᵍ must first go by."

¹⁵ As I was trying to understand the meaning of this vision, suddenly a man was standing in front of me—or at least he looked like a man— ¹⁶ and I heard a man's voice calling from across the river, "Gabriel, tell Daniel the meaning of his dream." ¹⁷ So Gabriel started toward me. But as he approached, I was too frightened to stand, and fell down with my face to the ground. "Son of man," he said, "you must understand that the events you have seen in your vision will not take place until the end times come." ¹⁸ Then I fainted, lying face downward on the ground. But he roused me with a touch, and helped me to my feet. ¹⁹ "I am here," he said, "to tell you what is going to happen in the last days of the coming time of terror—for what you have seen pertains to that final event in history.

²⁰ "The two horns of the ram you saw are the kings of Media and Persia; ²¹ the shaggy-haired goat is the nation of Greece, and its long horn represents the first great king of that country. ²² When you saw the horn break off, and four smaller horns replace it, this meant that the Grecian Empire will break into four sections with four kings, none of them as great as the first.

²³ "Toward the end of their kingdoms, when they have become morally rotten, an angry king shall rise to power with great shrewdness and intelligence.ʰ ²⁴ His power shall be mighty, but it will be satanicⁱ

strength and not his own. Prospering wherever he turns, he will destroy all who oppose him, though their armies be mighty, and he will devastate God's people.

²⁵ "He will be a master of deception, defeating many by catching them off guard as they bask in false security. Without warning he will destroy them. So great will he fancy himself to be that he will even take on the Prince of Princes in battle; but in so doing he will seal his own doom, for he shall be broken by the hand of God, though no human means could overpower him.

²⁶ "And then in your vision you heard about the twenty-three hundred days to pass before the rights of worship are restored. This number is literal, and means just that.ʲ But none of these things will happen for a long time, so don't tell anyone about them yet."

²⁷ Then I grew faint and was sick for several days. Afterward I was up and around again and performed my duties for the king, but I was greatly distressed by the dream and did not understand it.

9 IT WAS NOW the first year of the reign of King Darius, the son of Ahasuerus. (Darius was a Mede but became king of the Chaldeans.) ² In that first year of his reign, I, Daniel, learned from the book of Jeremiah the prophet, that Jerusalem must lie desolate for seventy years.ᵃ ³ So I earnestly pleaded with the Lord God [to end our captivity and send us back to our own landᵇ].

As I prayed, I fasted, and wore rough sackcloth, and sprinkled myself with ashes, ⁴ and confessed my sins and those of my people.

"O Lord," I prayed, "you are a great and awesome God; you always fulfill your promises of mercy to those who love you and who keep your laws. ⁵ But we have sinned so much; we have rebelled against you and scorned your commands. ⁶ We have refused to listen to your servants the

---

f Or, "and great indignities were perpetrated against the Temple ceremonies, so truth and righteousness perished." The Hebrew text is obscure.   g Literally, "Twenty-three hundred mornings and evenings."
h Literally, "one who understands riddles"; an alternate rendering might read, "skilled in intrigues." Probably a reference to Antiochus Epiphanes and future further fulfillment by the Antichrist at the end of human history.
i Implied. Literally, "but not with his power."   j Literally, "The vision of the evenings and the mornings which has been told is true." Verse 14 is the basis for the meaning expressed in the paraphrase.
9a Jeremiah 25:11-12; 29:10. This interval had now almost expired.   b Implied.

prophets, whom you sent again and again down through the years, with your messages to our kings and princes and to all the people.

⁷ "O Lord, you are righteous; but as for us, we are always shamefaced with sin, just as you see us now; yes, all of us—the men of Judah, the people of Jerusalem, and all Israel, scattered near and far wherever you have driven us because of our disloyalty to you. ⁸ O Lord, we and our kings and princes and fathers are weighted down with shame because of all our sins.

⁹ "But the Lord our God is merciful, and pardons even those who have rebelled against him.

¹⁰ "O Lord our God, we have disobeyed you; we have flouted all the laws you gave us through your servants, the prophets. ¹¹ All Israel has disobeyed; we have turned away from you and haven't listened to your voice. And so the awesome curse of God has crushed us—the curse written in the law of Moses your servant. ¹² And you have done exactly as you warned us you would do, for never in all history has there been a disaster like what happened at Jerusalem to us and our rulers. ¹³ Every curse against us written in the law of Moses has come true; all the evils he predicted—all have come. But even so we still refuse to satisfy the Lord our God by turning from our sins and doing right.

¹⁴ "And so the Lord deliberately crushed us with the calamity he prepared; he is fair in everything he does, but we would not obey. ¹⁵ O Lord our God, you brought lasting honor to your name by removing your people from Egypt in a great display of power. Lord, do it again! Though we have sinned so much and are full of wickedness, ¹⁶ yet because of all your faithful mercies, Lord, please turn away your furious anger from Jerusalem, your own city, your holy mountain. For the heathen mock at you because your city lies in ruins for our sins. ¹⁷ "O our God, hear your servant's prayer! Listen as I plead! Let your face shine again with peace and joy upon your desolate sanctuary—for your own glory, Lord. ¹⁸ "O my God, bend down your ear and listen to my plea. Open your eyes and see our wretchedness, how your city lies in ruins—for everyone knows that it is yours. We don't ask because we merit help, but because you are so merciful despite our grievous sins. ¹⁹ "O Lord, hear; O Lord, forgive. O Lord, listen to me and act! Don't delay—for your own sake, O my God, because your people and your city bear your name."

²⁰ Even while I was praying and confessing my sin and the sins of my people, and desperately pleading with the Lord my God for Jerusalem, his holy mountain, ²¹ Gabriel, whom I had seen in the earlier vision, flew swiftly to me at the time of the evening sacrifice, ²² and said to me, "Daniel, I am here to help you understand God's plans. ²³ The moment you began praying, a command was given. I am here to tell you what it was, for God loves you very much. Listen, and try to understand the meaning of the vision that you saw!

²⁴ "The Lord has commanded 490 yearsᶜ of further punishment upon Jerusalem and your people. Then at last they will learn to stay away from sin, and their guilt will be cleansed; then the kingdom of everlasting righteousness will begin, and the Most Holy Place (in the Temple) will be rededicated, as the prophets have declared. ²⁵ Now listen! It will be forty-nine years plus 434 yearsᵈ from the time the command is given to rebuild Jerusalem, until the Anointed One comes! Jerusalem's streets and walls will be rebuilt despite the perilous times.

²⁶ "After this period of 434 years, the Anointed One will be killed, his kingdom still unrealized . . . and a king will arise whose armies will destroy the city and the Temple. They will be overwhelmed as with a flood, and war and its miseries are decreed from that time to the very end. ²⁷ This king will make a seven-year treaty with the people, but after half that time, he will break

---

c Literally, "seventy weeks" or "seventy sevens" (of years). These were not in uninterrupted sequence. See verses 25–27.   d This totals 483 years, instead of the 490 years mentioned in verse 24, leaving seven years unaccounted for at the time of Messiah's death. For their future fulfillment see verse 27 and the Revelation. Or, consider the destruction of Jerusalem in A.D. 70 by Titus and the subsequent slaughter of 1,000,000 Jews during the following three and a half years as at least a partial fulfillment of this prophecy.

his pledge and stop the Jews from all their sacrifices and their offerings; then, as a climax to all his terrible deeds, the Enemy shall utterly defile the sanctuary of God. But in God's time and plan, his judgment will be poured out upon this Evil One."

10 IN THE THIRD year of the reign of Cyrus, king of Persia, Daniel (also called Belteshazzar) had another vision. It concerned events certain to happen in the future: times of great tribulation—wars and sorrows, and this time he understood what the vision meant.

² When this vision came to me (Daniel said later) I had been in mourning for three full weeks. ³ All that time I tasted neither wine nor meat, and of course I went without desserts. I neither washed nor shaved nor combed my hair.

⁴ Then one day early in April, as I was standing beside the great Tigris River, ⁵,⁶ I looked up and suddenly there before me stood a person robed in linen garments, with a belt of purest gold around his waist, and glowing, lustrous skin! From his face came blinding flashes like lightning, and his eyes were pools of fire; his arms and feet shone like polished brass, and his voice was like the roaring of a vast multitude of people.

⁷ I, Daniel, alone saw this great vision; the men with me saw nothing, but they were suddenly filled with unreasoning terror and ran to hide, ⁸ and I was left alone. When I saw this frightening vision my strength left me, and I grew pale and weak with fright.

⁹ Then he spoke to me, and I fell to the ground face downward in a deep faint. ¹⁰ But a hand touched me and lifted me, still trembling, to my hands and knees. ¹¹ And I heard his voice—"O Daniel, greatly beloved of God," he said, "stand up and listen carefully to what I have to say to you, for God has sent me to you." So I stood up, still trembling with fear.

¹² Then he said, "Don't be frightened, Daniel, for your request has been heard in heaven and was answered the very first day you began to fast before the Lord and pray for understanding; that very day I was sent here to meet you. ¹³ But for twenty-one days the mighty Evil Spirit who overrules the kingdom of Persia[a] blocked my way. Then Michael, one of the top officers of the heavenly army, came to help me, so that I was able to break through these spirit rulers of Persia. ¹⁴ Now I am here to tell you what will happen to your people, the Jews, at the end times—for the fulfillment of this prophecy is many years away."

¹⁵ All this time I was looking down, unable to speak a word. ¹⁶ Then someone—he looked like a man—touched my lips and I could talk again, and I said to the messenger from heaven, "Sir, I am terrified by your appearance and have no strength. ¹⁷ How can such a person as I even talk to you? For my strength is gone and I can hardly breathe."

¹⁸ Then the one who seemed to be a man touched me again, and I felt my strength returning. ¹⁹ "God loves you very much," he said; "don't be afraid! Calm yourself; be strong—yes, strong!"

Suddenly, as he spoke these words, I felt stronger and said to him, "Now you can go ahead and speak, sir, for you have strengthened me."

²⁰,²¹ He replied, "Do you know why I have come? I am here to tell you what is written in the 'Book of the Future.' Then, when I leave, I will go again to fight my way back, past the prince of Persia; and after him, the prince of Greece. Only Michael, the angel who guards your people Israel,[b] will be there to help me.

11 "I WAS THE one sent to strengthen and help Darius the Mede in the first year of his reign. ² But now I will show you what the future holds. Three more Persian kings will reign, to be succeeded by a fourth,[a] far richer than the others. Using his wealth for political advantage, he will plan total war against Greece.

³ "Then a mighty king will rise in Greece, a king who will rule a vast kingdom and accomplish everything he sets out to do.[b] ⁴ But at the zenith of his power, his

---

a Literally, "the prince of Persia."   b Literally, "your prince."   11a Perhaps Xerxes (486–465) who launched an all-out effort against Greece.   b Doubtless Alexander the Great.

kingdom will break apart and be divided into four weaker nations, not even ruled by his sons. For his empire will be torn apart and given to others. ⁵ One of them, the king of Egypt,ᶜ will increase in power, but this king's own officials will rebel against him and take away his kingdom and make it still more powerful.

⁶ "Several years later an alliance will be formed between the king of Syriaᵈ and the king of Egypt. The daughter of the king of Egypt will be given in marriage to the king of Syria as a gesture of peace,ᵉ but she will lose her influence over him and not only will her hopes be blighted, but those of her father, the king of Egypt, and of her ambassador and child. ⁷ But when her brotherᶠ takes over as king of Egypt, he will raise an army against the king of Syria, and march against him and defeat him. ⁸ When he returns again to Egypt he will carry back their idols with him, along with priceless gold and silver dishes and for many years afterward he will leave the Syrian king alone.

⁹ "Meanwhile the king of Syriaᵍ will invade Egypt briefly, but will soon return again to his own land. ¹⁰,¹¹ However, the sons of this Syrian king will assemble a mighty army that will overflow across Israel into Egypt, to a fortress there. Then the king of Egypt,ʰ in great anger, will rally against the vast forces of Syria and defeat them. ¹² Filled with pride after this great victory, he will have many thousands of his enemies killed, but his success will be short-lived.

¹³ "A few years later the Syrian kingⁱ will return with a fully-equipped army far greater than the one he lost, ¹⁴ and other nations will join him in a crusade against Egypt. Insurgents among your own people, the Jews, will join them, thus fulfilling prophecy,ʲ but they will not succeed.

¹⁵ Then the Syrian king and his allies will come and lay siege to a fortified city of Egypt and capture it, and the proud armies of Egypt will go down to defeat.

¹⁶ "The Syrian king will march onward unopposed; none will be able to stop him. And he will also enter 'The Glorious Land' of Israel, and pillage it. ¹⁷ This will be his plot for conquering all Egypt: he too will form an alliance with the Egyptian king, giving him a daughter in marriage, so that she can work for him from within. But the plan will fail.

¹⁸ "After this he will turn his attention to the coastal cities and conquer many. But a general will stop him and cause him to retreat in shame. ¹⁹ He will turn homeward again, but will have trouble on the way, and disappear.

²⁰ "His successorᵏ will be remembered as the king who sent a tax collector into Israel, but after a very brief reign, he will die mysteriously, neither in battle nor in riot.

²¹ "Next to come to power will be an evil man not directly in line for royal succession.ˡ But during a crisis he will take over the kingdom by flattery and intrigue. ²² Then all opposition will be swept away before him, including a leader of the priests.ᵐ ²³ His promises will be worthless. From the first his method will be deceit; with a mere handful of followers, he will become strong. ²⁴ He will enter the richest areas of the land without warning and do something never done before: he will take the property and wealth of the rich and scatter it out among the people. With great success he will besiege and capture powerful strongholds throughout his dominions, but this will last for only a short while. ²⁵ Then he will stir up his courage and raise a great army against Egypt; and Egypt, too, will raise a mighty army, but to no avail, for

c Literally, "the southern king"—Ptolemy II.   d Literally, "the king of the north," and so also throughout this passage. These prophecies seem to have been fulfilled many years later in the Seleucid wars between Egypt and Syria.   e In 252 B.C. Ptolemy II of Egypt gave his daughter Berenice in marriage to Antiochus II of Syria to conclude a treaty of peace between their two lands.   f Literally, "from a branch." Berenice, murdered in Antioch by Antiochus II's former wife Laodice, was the sister of Ptolemy III, who now ascended the Egyptian throne and declared war against the Seleucids to avenge his sister's murder. g Seleucus II.   h Ptolemy IV.   i Possibly Antiochus III the Great, who was later defeated by the Romans at Magnesia. Compare verse 18.   j Literally, "in order to fulfill the vision." k Seleucus IV, successor of Antiochus III, sent Heliodorus to rob and desecrate the Temple in Jerusalem. l This may refer to Antiochus IV Epiphanes who, when his brother Seleucus was assassinated, ingratiated himself with the Romans and took over.   m Probably Jason, treacherously removed by the Hellenist Menelaus.

plots against him will succeed.

²⁶ "Those of his own household will bring his downfall; his army will desert, and many be killed.

²⁷ "Both these kings[n] will be plotting against each other at the conference table, attempting to deceive each other. But it will make no difference, for neither can succeed until God's appointed time has come.

²⁸ "The Syrian king will then return home with great riches, first marching through Israel and destroying it. ²⁹ Then, at the predestined time, he will once again turn his armies southward, as he had threatened, but now it will be a very different story from those first two occasions. ³⁰,³¹ For Roman warships[o] will scare him off, and he will withdraw and return home. Angered by having to retreat, the Syrian king will again pillage Jerusalem and pollute the sanctuary,[p] putting a stop to the daily sacrifices, and worshiping idols inside the Temple.[q] He will leave godless Jews in power when he leaves—men who have abandoned their fathers' faith. ³² He will flatter those who hate the things of God,[r] and win them over to his side. But the people who know their God[s] shall be strong and do great things.

³³ "Those with spiritual understanding will have a wide ministry of teaching in those days. But they will be in constant danger, many of them dying by fire and sword, or being jailed and robbed. ³⁴ Eventually these pressures will subside, and some ungodly men will come, pretending to offer a helping hand, only to take advantage of them.

³⁵ "And some who are most gifted in the things of God will stumble in those days and fall, but this will only refine and cleanse them and make them pure until the final end of all their trials, at God's appointed time.

³⁶ "The king will do exactly as he pleases, claiming to be greater than every god there is, even blaspheming the God of gods, and

prospering—until his time is up. For God's plans are unshakable. ³⁷ He will have no regard for the gods of his fathers, nor for the god beloved of women,[t] nor any other god, for he will boast that he is greater than them all. ³⁸ Instead of these he will worship the Fortress god[u]—a god his fathers never knew—and lavish on him costly gifts! ³⁹ Claiming his help he will have great success against the strongest fortresses. He will honor those who submit to him, appointing them to positions of authority and dividing the land to them as their reward.

⁴⁰ "Then at the time of the end,[v] the king of the south will attack him again, and the northern king will react with the strength and fury of a whirlwind; his vast army and navy will rush out to bury him with their might. ⁴¹ He will invade various lands on the way, including Israel, the Pleasant Land, and overthrow the governments of many nations. Moab, Edom, and most of Ammon will escape, ⁴² but Egypt and many other lands will be occupied. ⁴³ He will capture all the treasures of Egypt, and the Libyans and Ethiopians shall be his servants.

⁴⁴ "But then news from the east and north will alarm him and he will return in great anger to destroy as he goes. ⁴⁵ He will halt between Jerusalem and the sea, and there pitch his royal tents, but while he is there his time will suddenly run out and there will be no one to help him.

12 "AT THAT TIME Michael, the mighty angelic prince who stands guard over your nation, will stand up [and fight for you in heaven against satanic forces[a]], and there will be a time of anguish for the Jews greater than any previous suffering in Jewish history. And yet every one of your people whose names are written in the Book will endure it.

² "And many of those whose bodies lie dead and buried will rise up, some to everlasting life and some to shame and everlast-

---

n Probably Antiochus IV and Ptolemy IV. o Or, from Cyprus. p By offering swine on the altar. This event was fulfilled in 168–167 B.C. q Literally, "they shall set up the abomination that astonished." r Menelaus, the High Priest, who conspired with Antiochus against the Jews who were loyal to God's laws. s Perhaps the valiant Maccabees and their sympathizers. But a further fulfillment may lie in the future. t See Ezekiel 18:14. Tammuz-Adonis, a Babylonian god. u Literally, "the god of Fortresses." v The prophecy takes a turn here. Antiochus IV fades from view and the Antichrist of the last days becomes the center of attention from this point on. 12a Implied.

ing contempt.

³ "And those who are wise—the people of God—shall shine as brightly as the sun's brilliance, and those who turn many to righteousness will glitter like stars forever.

⁴ "But Daniel, keep this prophecy a secret; seal it up so that it will not be understood until the end times, when travel and education shall be vastly increased!"

⁵ Then I, Daniel, looked and saw two men[b] on each bank of a river. ⁶ And one of them asked the man in linen robes who was standing now above the river, "How long will it be until all these terrors end?"

⁷ He replied, with both hands lifted to heaven, taking oath by him who lives forever and ever, that they will not end until three and a half years[c] after the power of God's people has been crushed.

⁸ I heard what he said but I didn't understand what he meant, so I said, "Sir, how will this all come out?"

⁹ But he said, "Go now, Daniel, for what I have said is not to be understood until the time of the end. ¹⁰ Many shall be purified by great trials and persecutions. But the wicked shall continue in their wickedness, and none of them will understand. Only those who are willing to learn will know what it means.

¹¹ "From the time the daily sacrifice is taken away and the Horrible Thing is set up to be worshiped, there will be 1,290 days.[d] ¹² And blessed are those who wait and remain until the 1335th day!

¹³ "But go on now to the end of your life and your rest; for you will rise again and have your full share of those last days."[e]

The End of the Line

---

b Hebrew: "two others," probably angels.
c Literally, "a time, times, and half a time . . . when the shattering of the power of the holy people comes to an end." d Three and a half years (verse 7) plus one month.
e Literally, "at the end of the days."

Jim Green

ove is a magnificent, exhilarating trip, and when it dies, it is worse than almost any other kind of death. You don't want to believe it ... but the ride is over, and you're just not going any further on this track.

That's what happened to the love affair between Israel and her God during the days of Hosea. "The Lord has filed a lawsuit against you," Hosea announced shortly before Samaria was conquered, "listing the following charges: There is no faithfulness, no kindness, no knowledge of God in your land. You swear and lie and kill and steal and commit adultery. There is violence everywhere, with one murder after another ... Your doom is sealed, for you refuse to understand" (4:1, 2, 14).

It's hard to imagine that God really *loves* human beings...maybe that's why their rejection of him is so terrible.

HOSEA

1 THESE ARE THE messages from the Lord to Hosea, son of Beeri, during the reigns of these four kings of Judah: Uzziah, Jotham, Ahaz, and Hezekiah; and one of the kings of Israel, Jeroboam, son of Joash. ² Here is the first message:

The Lord said to Hosea, "Go and marry a girl who is a prostitute, so that some of her children will be born to you from other men. This will illustrate the way my people have been untrue to me, committing open adultery against me by worshiping other gods."

³ So Hosea married Gomer, daughter of Diblaim, and she conceived and bore him a son.

⁴,⁵ And the Lord said, "Name the child Jezreel, for in the Valley of Jezreel I am about to punish King Jehu's dynasty to avenge the murdersª he committed; in fact, I will put an end to Israel as an independent kingdom, breaking the power of the nation in the Valley of Jezreel."ᵇ

⁶ Soon Gomer had another child—this one a daughter. And God said to Hosea, "Name her Lo-ruhamah (meaning 'No more mercy') for I will have no more mercy upon Israel, to forgive her again. ⁷ But I *will* have mercy on the tribe of Judah. I will personally free her from her enemies without any help from her armies or her weapons."ᶜ

⁸ After Gomer had weaned Lo-ruhamah, she again conceived and this time gave birth to a son. ⁹ And God said, "Call him Lo-ammi (meaning 'Not mine'), for Israel is not mine and I am not her God.

¹⁰ "Yet the time will come when Israel shall prosper and become a great nation; in that day her people will be too numerous to count—like sand along a seashore! Then, instead of saying to them, 'You are not my people,' I will tell them, 'You are my sons,

---

a He went far beyond God's command to execute the family of Ahab. See 1 Kings 21:21 and 2 Kings 10:11.   b A prediction of the Assyrian conquest of Israel twenty-five years later.
c Soon after defeating Israel, the Assyrian Emperor Sennacherib invaded Judah and besieged Jerusalem. He was driven off by special intervention of God's angel (Isaiah 36–37).

children of the Living God.' ¹¹ Then the people of Judah and Israel will unite and have one leader; they will return from exile together; what a day that will be—the day when God will sow his people in the fertile soil of their own land again."ᵈ

2 O JEZREEL,ᵃ RENAME your brother and sister. Call your brother Ammi (which means "Now you are mine"); name your sister Ruhamah ("Pitied"), for now God will have mercy upon her! ² Plead with your mother, for she has become another man's wife—I am no longer her husband. Beg her to stop her harlotry, to quit giving herself to others. ³ If she doesn't, I will strip her as naked as the day she was born, and cause her to waste away and die of thirst as in a land riddled with famine and drought. ⁴ And I will not give special favors to her children as I would to my own, for they are not my children; they belong to other men.

⁵ For their mother has committed adultery. She did a shameful thing when she said, "I'll run after other men and sell myself to them for food and drinks and clothes." ⁶ But I will fence her in with briars and thornbushes; I'll block the road before her to make her lose her way, so that ⁷ when she runs after her lovers she will not catch up with them. She will search for them but not find them. Then she will think, "I might as well return to my husband, for I was better off with him than I am now."

⁸ She doesn't realize that all she has, has come from me. It was I who gave her all the gold and silver that she used in worshiping Baal, her god! ⁹ But now I will take back the wine and ripened corn I constantly supplied, and the clothes I gave her to cover her nakedness—I will no longer give her rich harvests of grain in its season, or wine at the time of the grape harvest. ¹⁰ Now I will expose her nakedness in public for all her lovers to see, and no one will be able to rescue her from my hand.

¹¹ I will put an end to all her joys, her parties, holidays, and feasts. ¹² I will destroy her vineyards and her orchards—gifts she claims her lovers gave her—and let them grow into a jungle; wild animals will eat their fruit.

¹³ For all the incense that she burned to Baal her idol and for the times when she put on her earrings and jewels and went out looking for her lovers, and deserted me: for all these things I will punish her, says the Lord.

¹⁴ But I will court her again, and bring her into the wilderness, and speak to her tenderly there. ¹⁵ There I will give back her vineyards to her, and transform her Valley of Troubles into a Door of Hope. She will respond to me there, singing with joy as in days long ago in her youth, after I had freed her from captivity in Egypt.

¹⁶ In that coming day, says the Lord, she will call me "My Husband" instead of "My Master."ᵇ ¹⁷ O Israel, I will cause you to forget your idols, and their names will not be spoken anymore.

¹⁸ At that time I will make a treaty between you and the wild animals, birds, and snakes, not to fear each other any more; and I will destroy all weapons, and all wars will end.

Then you will lie down in peace and safety, unafraid; ¹⁹ and I will bind you to me forever with chains of righteousness and justice and love and mercy. ²⁰ I will betroth you to me in faithfulness and love, and you will really know me then as you never have before.

²¹,²² In that day, says the Lord, I will answer the pleading of the sky for clouds, to pour down water on the earth in answer to its cry for rain. Then the earth can answer the parched cry of the grain, the grapes, and the olive trees for moisture and for dew —and the whole grand chorus shall sing together that "God sows!"ᶜ He has given all!

²³ At that time I will sow a crop of Israelites and raise them for myself! I will pity those who are "not pitied,"ᵈ and I will say to those who are "not my people," "Now you are my people"; and they will reply,

---

d Literally, "the day of Jezreel ('God sows')"; see 2:23. and verse. b Literally, "my Baal," meaning "my Lord," but this was a tainted word because applied to idols, so it will no longer be used in reference to the true God. c Literally, "Jezreel." d See chapter 1, verses 6, 9, and 10.　　2a "Jezreel" is implied in the preceding chapter

"You are our God!"

3 THEN THE LORD said to me, "Go, and get your wife again and bring her back to you and love her, even though she loves adultery. For the Lord still loves Israel though she has turned to other gods and offered them choice gifts."

² So I bought her [back from her slavery[a]] for a couple of dollars and eight bushels of barley, ³ and I said to her, "You must live alone for many days; do not go out with other men nor be a prostitute, and I will wait for you."

⁴ This illustrates the fact that Israel will be a long time without a king or prince, and without an altar, temple, priests, or even idols!

⁵ Afterward they will return to the Lord their God, and to the Messiah, their King,[b] and they shall come trembling, submissive to the Lord and to his blessings, in the end times.

4 HEAR THE WORD of the Lord, O people of Israel. The Lord has filed a lawsuit against you listing the following charges: There is no faithfulness, no kindness, no knowledge of God in your land. ² You swear and lie and kill and steal and commit adultery. There is violence everywhere, with one murder after another.

³ That is why your land is not producing; it is filled with sadness, and all living things grow sick and die; the animals, the birds, and even the fish begin to disappear.

⁴ Don't point your finger at someone else, and try to pass the blame to him! Look, priest, I am pointing my finger at *you*. ⁵ As a sentence for your crimes, you priests will stumble in broad daylight as well as in the night, and so will your false "prophets" too; and I will destroy your mother, Israel. ⁶ My people are destroyed because they don't know me, and it is all your fault, you priests, for you yourselves refuse to know me; therefore I refuse to recognize you as my priests. Since you have forgotten my laws, I will

"forget" to bless your children. ⁷ The more my people multiplied, the more they sinned against me. They exchanged the glory of God for the disgrace of idols.

⁸ The priests rejoice in the sins of the people; they lap it up and lick their lips for more! ⁹ And thus it is: "Like priests, like people"—because the priests are wicked, the people are too. Therefore, I will punish both priests and people for all their wicked deeds. ¹⁰ They will eat and still be hungry. Though they do a big business as prostitutes, they shall have no children, for they have deserted me and turned to other gods.

¹¹ Wine, women, and song have robbed my people of their brains. ¹² For they are asking a piece of wood to tell them what to do. "Divine Truth" comes to them through tea leaves![a] Longing after idols has made them foolish. For they have played the harlot, serving other gods, deserting me. ¹³ They sacrifice to idols on the tops of mountains; they go up into the hills to burn incense in the pleasant shade of oaks and poplars and terebinth trees.

There your daughters turn to prostitution and your brides commit adultery. ¹⁴ But why should I punish them? For you men are doing the same thing, sinning with harlots and temple prostitutes. Fools! Your doom is sealed, for you refuse to understand.

¹⁵ But though Israel is a prostitute, may Judah stay far from such a life. O Judah, do not join with those who insincerely worship me at Gilgal and at Bethel. Their worship is mere pretense. ¹⁶ Don't be like Israel, stubborn as a heifer, resisting the Lord's attempts to lead her in green pastures. ¹⁷ Stay away from her, for she is wedded to idolatry.

¹⁸ The men of Israel finish up their drinking bouts, and off they go to find some whores. Their love for shame is greater than for honor.[b] ¹⁹ Therefore, a mighty wind[c] shall sweep them away; they shall die in shame, because they sacrifice to idols.

a Implied.   b Literally, "to David, their king." Christ was "the greater David."   4a Literally, "their staff." There is no modern parallel to this ancient practice used by sorcerers, whose predictions were based on how their staffs landed on the ground when thrown or allowed to fall.   b The Hebrew text is uncertain. This translation follows the Greek version.   c The Assyrian invasion came about twenty years later and the nation disappeared.

5 LISTEN TO THIS, you priests and all of Israel's leaders; listen, all you men of the royal family: You are doomed! For you have deluded the people with idols at Mizpah and Tabor, ² and dug a deep pit to trap them at Acacia. But never forget—I will settle up with all of you for what you've done.

³ I have seen your evil deeds: Israel, you have left me as a prostitute leaves her husband; you are utterly defiled. ⁴ Your deeds won't let you come to God again, for the spirit of adultery is deep within you, and you cannot know the Lord.

⁵ The very arrogance of Israel testifies against her in my court. She will stumble under her load of guilt, and Judah, too, shall fall. ⁶ Then at last, they will come with their flocks and herds to sacrifice to God, but it will be too late—they will not find him. He has withdrawn from them and they are left alone.

⁷ For they have betrayed the honor of the Lord, bearing children that aren't his. Suddenly they and all their wealth will disappear. ⁸ Sound the alarm! Warn with trumpet blasts in Gibeah and Ramah, and on over to Beth-aven; tremble, land of Benjamin! ⁹ Hear this announcement, Israel: When your day of punishment comes, you will become a heap of rubble.

¹⁰ The leaders of Judah have become the lowest sort of thieves.ᵃ Therefore, I will pour my anger down upon them like a waterfall, ¹¹ and Ephraim will be crushed and broken by my sentence because she is determined to follow idols. ¹² I will destroy her as a moth does wool; I will sap away the strength of Judah like dry rot.

¹³ When Ephraim and Judah see how sick they are, Ephraim will turn to Assyria, to the great king there, but he can neither help nor cure.

¹⁴ I will tear Ephraim and Judah as a lion rips apart its prey; I will carry them off and chase all rescuers away. ¹⁵ I will abandon them and return to my home until they admit their guilt and look to me for help again, for as soon as trouble comes, they will search for me and say:

6 "COME, LET US return to the Lord; it is he who has torn us—he will heal us. He has wounded—he will bind us up. ² In just a couple of days,ᵃ or three at the most, he will set us on our feet again, to live in his kindness! ³ Oh, that we might know the Lord! Let us press on to know him, and he will respond to us as surely as the coming of dawn or the rain of early spring."

⁴ O Ephraim and Judah, what shall I do with you? For your love vanishes like morning clouds, and disappears like dew. ⁵ I sent my prophets to warn you of your doom; I have slain you with the words of my mouth, threatening you with death. Suddenly, without warning, my judgment will strike you as surely as day follows night.

⁶ I don't want your sacrifices—I want your love; I don't want your offerings—I want you to know me.

⁷ But like Adam, you broke my covenant; you refused my love. ⁸ Gilead is a city of sinners, tracked with footprints of blood. ⁹ Her citizens are gangs of robbers, lying in ambush for their victims; packs of priests murder along the road to Shechem and practice every kind of sin. ¹⁰ Yes, I have seen a horrible thing in Israel—Ephraim chasing other gods, Israel utterly defiled.

¹¹ O Judah, for you also there is a plentiful harvest of punishment waiting—and I wanted so much to bless you!

7 I WANTED TO forgive Israel, but her sins were far too great—no one can even live in Samaria without being a liar, thief, and bandit!

² Her people never seem to recognize that I am watching them. Their sinful deeds give them away on every side; I see them all. ³ The king is glad about their wickedness; the princes laugh about their lies. ⁴ They are all adulterers; as a baker's oven is constantly aflame—except while he kneads the dough and waits for it to rise—so are these people constantly aflame with lust.

⁵ On the king's birthday, the princes get him drunk; he makes a fool of himself and drinks with those who mock him. ⁶ Their

---

a Literally, "as those who move a boundary marker." See Deuteronomy 19:14; 27:17.   6a Literally, "In two days."

hearts blaze like a furnace with intrigue. Their plot smolders through the night, and in the morning it flames forth like raging fire.

[7] They kill their kings one after another,[a] and none cries out to me for help. [8] My people mingle with the heathen, picking up their evil ways; thus they become as good-for-nothing as a half-baked cake! [9] Worshiping foreign gods has sapped their strength, but they don't know it. Ephraim's hair is turning gray, and he doesn't even realize how weak and old he is. [10] His pride in other gods has openly condemned him; yet he doesn't return to his God, nor even try to find him.

[11] Ephraim is a silly, witless dove, calling to Egypt, flying to Assyria. [12] But as she flies, I throw my net over her and bring her down like a bird from the sky; I will punish her for all her evil ways.

[13] Woe to my people for deserting me; let them perish, for they have sinned against me. I wanted to redeem them but their hard hearts would not accept the truth. [14] They lie there sleepless with anxiety, but won't ask my help. Instead, they worship heathen gods, asking them for crops and for prosperity.

[15] I have helped them, and made them strong, yet now they turn against me. [16] They look everywhere except to heaven, to the Most High God. They are like a crooked bow that always misses targets; their leaders will perish by the sword of the enemy for their insolence to me. And all Egypt will laugh at them.

8 SOUND THE ALARM! They are coming! Like a vulture, the enemy descends upon the people of God because they have broken my treaty and revolted against my laws. [2] Now Israel pleads with me and says, "Help us, for you are our God!" [3] But it is too late! Israel has thrown away her chance with contempt, and now her enemies will chase her. [4] She has appointed kings and princes, but not with my consent. They have cut themselves off from my help by worshiping the idols that they made from their silver and gold.

[5] O Samaria, I reject this calf—this idol you have made. My fury burns against you. How long will it be before one honest man is found among you? [6] When will you admit this calf you worship was made by human hands! It is not God! Therefore, it must be smashed to bits.

[7] They have sown the wind and they will reap the whirlwind. Their cornstalks stand there barren, withered, sickly, with no grain; if it has any, foreigners will eat it. [8] Israel is destroyed; she lies among the nations as a broken pot. [9] She is a lonely, wandering wild ass. The only friends she has are those she hires; Assyria is one of them.

[10] But though she hires "friends" from many lands, I will send her off to exile. Then for a while at least she will be free of the burden of her wonderful king! [11] Ephraim has built many altars, but they are not to worship me! They are altars of sin! [12] Even if I gave her ten thousand laws, she'd say they weren't for her—that they applied to someone far away. [13] Her people love the ritual of their sacrifice, but to me it is meaningless! I will call for an accounting of their sins and punish them; they shall return to Egypt.

[14] Israel has built great palaces; Judah has constructed great defenses for her cities, but they have forgotten their Maker. Therefore, I will send down fire upon those palaces and burn those fortresses.

9 O ISRAEL, REJOICE no more as others do, for you have deserted your God and sacrificed to other gods on every threshing floor.

[2] Therefore your harvests will be small; your grapes will blight upon the vine. [3] You may no longer stay here in this land of God; you will be carried off to Egypt and Assyria, and live there on scraps of food. [4] There, far from home, you are not allowed to pour out wine for sacrifice to God. For no sacrifice that is offered there can please him; it is polluted, just as food of mourners is; all who eat such sacrifices are defiled. They may eat this food to feed

a Three Israelite kings were assassinated during Hosea's lifetime—Zechariah, Shallum, and Pekahiah.

themselves, but may not offer it to God.
⁵ What then will you do on holy days, on
days of feasting to the Lord, ⁶ when you are
carried off to Assyria as slaves? Who will
inherit your possessions left behind? Egypt
will! She will gather your dead; Memphis
will bury them. And thorns and thistles will
grow up among the ruins.
⁷ The time of Israel's punishment has
come; the day of recompense is almost here
and soon Israel will know it all too well.
"The prophets are crazy"; "The inspired
men are mad." Yes, so they mock, for the
nation is weighted with sin, and shows only
hatred for those who love God.
⁸ I appointed the prophets to guard my
people, but the people have blocked them
at every turn and publicly declared their
hatred, even in the Temple of the Lord.
⁹ The things my people do are as depraved
as what they did in Gibeahᵃ long ago. The
Lord does not forget. He will surely punish
them.
¹⁰ O Israel, how well I remember those
first delightful days when I led you through
the wilderness! How refreshing was your
love! How satisfying, like the early figs of
summer in their first season! But then you
deserted me for Baal-peor,ᵇ to give yourselves to other gods, and soon you were as
foul as they. ¹¹ The glory of Israel flies away
like a bird, for your children will die at
birth, or perish in the womb, or never even
be conceived. ¹² And if your children grow,
I will take them from you; all are doomed.
Yes, it will be a sad day when I turn away
and leave you alone.
¹³ In my vision I have seen the sons of
Israel doomed. The fathers are forced to
lead their sons to slaughter. ¹⁴ O Lord, what
shall I ask for your people? I will ask for
wombs that don't give birth, for breasts that
cannot nourish.
¹⁵ All their wickedness began at Gilgal;ᶜ
there I began to hate them. I will drive them
from my land because of their idolatry. I
will love them no more, for all their leaders
are rebels. ¹⁶ Ephraim is doomed. The roots
of Israel are dried up; she shall bear no more
fruit. And if she gives birth, I will slay even

her beloved child.
¹⁷ My God will destroy the people of Israel because they will not listen or obey.
They will be wandering Jews, homeless
among the nations.

10 HOW PROSPEROUS ISRAEL is—a luxuriant vine all filled with fruit! But the
more wealth I give her, the more she pours
it on the altars of her heathen gods; the
richer the harvests I give her, the more
beautiful the statues and idols she erects.
² The hearts of her people are false toward
God. They are guilty and must be punished.
God will break down their heathen altars
and smash their idols. ³ Then they will say,
"We deserted the Lord and he took away
our king. But what's the difference? We
don't need one anyway!"
⁴ They make promises they don't intend
to keep. Therefore punishment will spring
up among them like poisonous weeds in the
furrows of the field. ⁵ The people of Samaria
tremble lest their calf-god idols at Beth-
aven should be hurt; the priests and people,
too, mourn over the departed honor of their
shattered gods. ⁶ This idol—this calf-god
thing—will be carted with them when they
go as slaves to Assyria, a present to the great
king there. Ephraim will be laughed at for
trusting in this idol; Israel will be put to
shame. ⁷ As for Samaria, her king shall
disappear like a chip of wood upon an ocean
wave. ⁸ And the idol altars of Aven at
Bethel where Israel sinned will crumble.
Thorns and thistles will grow up to surround them. And the people will cry to the
mountains and hills to fall upon them and
crush them.
⁹ O Israel, ever since that awful night in
Gibeah,ᵃ there has been only sin, sin, sin!
You have made no progress whatever. Was
it not right that the men of Gibeah were
wiped out? ¹⁰ I will come against you for
your disobedience; I will gather the armies
of the nations against you to punish you for
your heaped-up sins.
¹¹ Ephraim is accustomed to treading out
the grain—an easy job she loves. I have
never put her under a heavy yoke before; I

a See Judges 19:14ff.   b Baal-peor, the god of Peor, a city of Moab. See Numbers, chapter 23.
c Gilgal, the town where Baal-worship flourished (Hosea 4:15; 12:11), and where the monarchy, hated of God,
was instituted (1 Samuel 11:15).   10 a Judges, chapters 19 and 20.

have spared her tender neck. But now I will harness her to the plow and harrow. Her days of ease are gone.

¹² Plant the good seeds of righteousness and you will reap a crop of my love; plow the hard ground of your hearts, for now is the time to seek the Lord, that he may come and shower salvation upon you.

¹³ But you have cultivated wickedness and raised a thriving crop of sins. You have earned the full reward of trusting in a lie— believing that military might and great armies can make a nation safe!

¹⁴ Therefore the terrors of war shall rise among your people, and all your forts will fall, just as at Beth-arbel, which Shalman[b] destroyed; even mothers and children were dashed to death there. ¹⁵ That will be your fate, too, you people of Israel, because of your great wickedness. In one morning the king of Israel shall be destroyed.

11 WHEN ISRAEL WAS a child I loved him as a son and brought him out of Egypt. ² But the more I called to him, the more he rebelled, sacrificing to Baal and burning incense to idols. ³ I trained him from infancy, I taught him to walk, I held him in my arms. But he doesn't know or even care that it was I who raised him.

⁴ As a man would lead his favorite ox,[a] so I led Israel with my ropes of love. I loosened his muzzle so he could eat. I myself have stooped and fed him. ⁵ But my people shall return to Egypt and Assyria because they won't return to me.

⁶ War will swirl through their cities; their enemies will crash through their gates and trap them in their own fortresses. ⁷ For my people are determined to desert me. And so I have sentenced them to slavery, and no one shall set them free.

⁸ Oh, how can I give you up, my Ephraim? How can I let you go? How can I forsake you like Admah and Zeboiim?[b] My heart cries out within me; how I long to help you! ⁹ No, I will not punish you as much as my fierce anger tells me to. This is the last time I will destroy Ephraim. For I am God and not man; I am the Holy One

living among you, and I did not come to destroy.

¹⁰ For the people shall walk after the Lord. I shall roar as a lion [at their enemies[a]] and my people shall return trembling from the west. ¹¹ Like a flock of birds, they will come from Egypt—like doves flying from Assyria. And I will bring them home again; it is a promise from the Lord.

¹² Israel surrounds me with lies and deceit, but Judah still trusts in God and is faithful to the Holy One.

12 ISRAEL IS CHASING the wind, yes, shepherding a whirlwind—a dangerous game![a] For she has given gifts to Egypt and Assyria to get their help, and in return she gets their worthless promises. ² But the Lord is bringing a lawsuit against Judah,[b] too. Judah also will be justly punished for his ways. ³ When he was born, he struggled with his brother; when he became a man, he even fought with God. ⁴ Yes, he wrestled with the Angel and prevailed. He wept and pleaded for a blessing from him. He met God there at Bethel face to face. God spoke to him— ⁵ the Lord, the God of Hosts; Jehovah is his name.

⁶ Oh, come back to God. Live by the principles of love and justice, and always be expecting much from him, your God.

⁷ But no, my people are like crafty merchants selling from dishonest scales—they love to cheat. ⁸ Ephraim boasts, "I am so rich! I have gotten it all by myself!" But riches can't make up for sin.

⁹ I am the same Lord, the same God, who delivered you from slavery in Egypt, and I am the one who will consign you to living in tents again, as you do each year at the Tabernacle Feast. ¹⁰ I sent my prophets to warn you with many a vision and many a parable and dream. ¹¹ But the sins of Gilgal flourish just the same. Row on row of altars—like furrows in a field—are used for sacrifices to your idols. And Gilead, too, is full of fools[c] who worship idols. ¹² Jacob fled to Syria and earned a wife by tending sheep. ¹³ Then the Lord led his people out of Egypt by a prophet, who guided and protected

---

b Shalman: probably Salaman, king of Moab, who invaded Gilead around 740 B.C.   11a Implied.
b Cities of the plain that perished with Sodom and Gomorrah (Deuteronomy 29:23).   12a Implied.
b Literally, "Jacob."   c Or, "vanity."

them. [14] But Ephraim has bitterly provoked the Lord. The Lord will sentence him to death as payment for his sins.

13 IT USED TO be when Israel spoke, the nations shook with fear, for he was a mighty prince; but he worshiped Baal and sealed his doom.

[2] And now the people disobey more and more. They melt their silver to mold into idols, formed with skill by the hands of men. "Sacrifice to these!" they say—men kissing calves! [3] They shall disappear like morning mist, like dew that quickly dries away, like chaff blown by the wind, like a cloud of smoke.

[4] I alone am God, your Lord, and have been ever since I brought you out from Egypt. You have no God but me, for there is no other Savior. [5] I took care of you in the wilderness, in that dry and thirsty land. [6] But when you had eaten and were satisfied, then you became proud and forgot me. [7] So I will come upon you like a lion, or a leopard lurking along the road. [8] I will rip you to pieces like a bear whose cubs have been taken away, and like a lion I will devour you.

[9] O Israel, if I destroy you, who can save you? [10] Where is your king? Why don't you call on him for help? Where are all the leaders of the land? You asked for them, now let them save you! [11] I gave you kings in my anger, and I took them away[a] in my wrath. [12] Ephraim's sins are harvested and stored away for punishment.

[13] New birth is offered him, but he is like a child resisting in the womb—how stubborn! how foolish! [14] Shall I ransom him from hell? Shall I redeem him from Death? O Death, bring forth your terrors for his tasting! O Grave, demonstrate your plagues! For I will not relent!

[15] He was called the most fruitful of all his brothers, but the east wind—a wind of the Lord from the desert—will blow hard upon him and dry up his land. All his flowing springs and green oases will dry away, and he will die of thirst. [16] Samaria must bear her guilt, for she rebelled against her God. Her people will be killed by the invading army, her babies dashed to death against the ground, her pregnant women ripped open with a sword.

14 O ISRAEL, RETURN to the Lord, your God, for you have been crushed by your sins. [2] Bring your petition. Come to the Lord and say, "O Lord, take away our sins; be gracious to us and receive us, and we will offer you the sacrifice of praise. [3] Assyria cannot save us, nor can our strength in battle; never again will we call the idols we have made 'our gods'; for in you alone, O Lord, the fatherless find mercy."

[4] Then I will cure you of idolatry and faithlessness, and my love will know no bounds, for my anger will be forever gone! [5] I will refresh Israel like the dew from heaven; she will blossom as the lily and root deeply in the soil like cedars in Lebanon. [6] Her branches will spread out, as beautiful as olive trees, fragrant as the forests of Lebanon. [7] Her people will return from exile far away and rest beneath my shadow. They will be a watered garden and blossom like grapes and be as fragrant as the wines of Lebanon.

[8] O Ephraim! Stay away from idols! I am living and strong! I look after you and care for you. I am like an evergreen tree, yielding my fruit to you throughout the year. My mercies never fail.

[9] Whoever is wise, let him understand these things. Whoever is intelligent, let him listen. For the paths of the Lord are true and right, and good men walk along them. But sinners trying it will fail.

---

a Probably an allusion to the kings of Israel assassinated during her last tempestuous years: Zechariah, Shallum, Pekahiah.

Invasion!

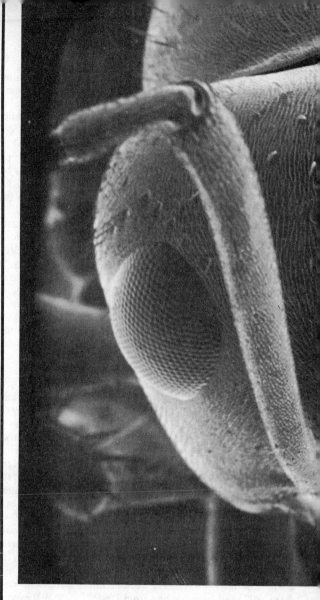

The lowly ant, when seen through the scanning electron microscope at Argonne National Laboratory outside Chicago, looks like a ferocious monster out of a horror movie . . . something like the locusts Joel described in living color in his first chapter. Scholars aren't sure of the date of this invasion and famine, or whether Joel's spellbinding tale of horror also

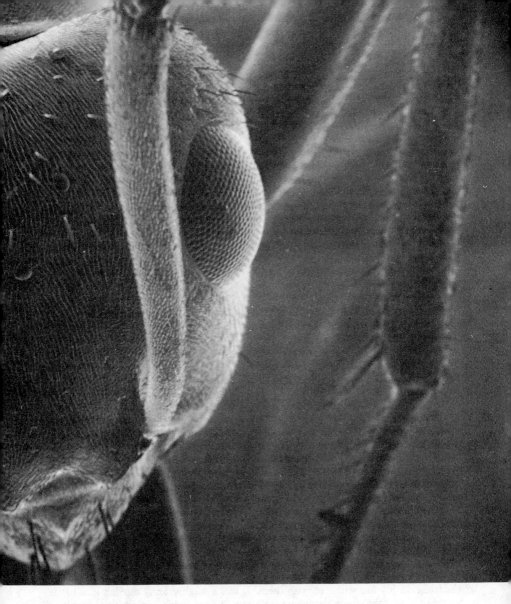

predicted an attack on Judah from human armies.

Just when God's fury seems overwhelming, he turns in love (2:12) and announces the coming of the Holy Spirit (2:28-32). More than a whirlwind of dramatic literature, the prophecy of Joel is evidence of the awesome God at work in this planet.

JOEL

1 THIS MESSAGE CAME from the Lord to Joel, son of Pethuel:

² Listen, you aged men of Israel! Everyone, listen! In all your lifetime, yes, in all your history, have you ever heard of such a thing as I am going to tell you? ³ In years to come, tell your children about it; pass the awful story down from generation to generation. ⁴ After the cutter-locusts finish eating your crops, the swarmer-locusts will take what's left! After them will come the hopper-locusts! And then the stripper-locusts, too!

⁵ Wake up and weep, you drunkards, for all the grapes are ruined and all your wine is gone! ⁶ A vast army of locustsᵃ covers the land. It is a terrible army too numerous to count, with teeth as sharp as those of lions! ⁷ They have ruined my vines and stripped the bark from the fig trees, leaving trunks and branches white and bare.

⁸ Weep with sorrow, as a virgin weeps whose fiancé is dead. ⁹ Gone are the offerings of grain and wine to bring to the Temple of the Lord; the priests are starving. Hear the crying of these ministers of God. ¹⁰ The fields are bare of crops. Sorrow and sadness are everywhere. The grain, the grapes, the olive oil are gone.

¹¹ Well may you farmers stand so shocked and stricken; well may you vinedressers weep. Weep for the wheat and the barley too, for they are gone. ¹² The grapevines are dead; the fig trees are dying; the pomegranates wither; the apples shrivel on the trees; all joy has withered with them.

¹³ O priests, robe yourselves in sackcloth. O ministers of my God, lie all night before the altar, weeping. For there are no more offerings of grain and wine for you. ¹⁴ Announce a fast; call a solemn meeting. Gather the elders and all the people into the Temple of the Lord your God, and weep before him there.

¹⁵ Alas, this terrible day of punishmentᵇ is on the way. Destruction from the Almighty is almost here! ¹⁶ Our food will disappear before our eyes; all joy and gladness will be ended in the Temple of our God. ¹⁷ The seed rots in the ground; the barns and granaries are empty; the grain has dried up in the fields. ¹⁸ The cattle groan with hunger; the herds stand perplexed for there is no pasture for them; the sheep bleat in misery.

¹⁹ Lord, help us! For the heat has withered the pastures and burned up all the trees. ²⁰ Even the wild animals cry to you for help, for there is no water for them. The creeks are dry and the pastures are scorched.

2 SOUND THE ALARM in Jerusalem! Let the blast of the warning trumpet be heard upon my holy mountain! Let everyone tremble in fear, for the day of the Lord's judgment approaches.

² It is a day of darkness and gloom, of black clouds and thick darkness. What a mighty army! It covers the mountains like night! How great, how powerful these "people" are! The likes of them have not been seen before, and never will again throughout the generations of the world! ³ Fire goes before them and follows them on every side! Ahead of them the land lies fair as Eden's Garden in all its beauty, but they destroy it to the ground; not one thing escapes. ⁴ They look like tiny horses, and they run as fast. ⁵ Look at them leaping along the tops of the mountain! Listen to the noise they make, like the rumbling of chariots, or the roar of fire sweeping across a field, and like a mighty army moving into battle.

⁶ Fear grips the waiting people; their faces grow pale with fright. ⁷ These "soldiers" charge like infantry; they scale the walls like picked and trained commandos. Straight forward they march, never breaking ranks. ⁸ They never crowd each other. Each is right in place. No weapon can stop them. ⁹ They swarm upon the city; they run upon the walls; they climb up into the houses, coming like thieves through the windows. ¹⁰ The earth quakes before them and the heavens tremble. The sun and moon

---

ᵃ Literally, "a nation."   ᵇ Or, "the Day of the Lord."

are obscured and the stars are hid.
¹¹ The Lord leads them with a shout.
This is his mighty army and they follow his
orders. The day of the judgment of the Lord
is an awesome, terrible thing. Who can endure it?
¹² That is why the Lord says, "Turn to
me now, while there is time. Give me all
your hearts. Come with fasting, weeping,
mourning. ¹³ Let your remorse tear at your
hearts and not your garments." Return to
the Lord your God, for he is gracious and
merciful. He is not easily angered; he is full
of kindness, and anxious not to punish you.
¹⁴ Who knows? Perhaps even yet he will
decide to let you alone and give you a blessing instead of his terrible curse. Perhaps he
will give you so much that you can offer
your grain and wine to the Lord as before!
¹⁵ Sound the trumpet in Zion! Call a fast
and gather all the people together for a solemn meeting. ¹⁶ Bring everyone—the elders,
the children, and even the babies. Call the
bridegroom from his quarters and the bride
from her privacy.
¹⁷ The priests, the ministers of God, will
stand between the people and the altar,
weeping; and they will pray, "Spare your
people, O our God; don't let the heathen
rule them, for they belong to you. Don't let
them be disgraced by the taunts of the heathen who say, 'Where is this God of theirs?
How weak and helpless he must be!' "
¹⁸ Then the Lord will pity his people and
be indignant for the honor of his land! ¹⁹ He
will reply, "See, I am sending you much
corn and wine and oil, to fully satisfy your
need. No longer will I make you a laughingstock among the nations. ²⁰ I will remove
these armies from the north and send them
far away; I will turn them back into the
parched wastelands where they will die; half
shall be driven into the Dead Sea and the
rest into the Mediterranean, and then their
rotting stench will rise upon the land. The
Lord has done a mighty miracle for you."
²¹ Fear not, my people; be glad now and
rejoice, for he has done amazing things for
you.
²² "Let the flocks and herds forget their
hunger; the pastures will turn green again.

The trees will bear their fruit; the fig trees
and grape vines will flourish once more.
²³ "Rejoice, O people of Jerusalem, rejoice in the Lord your God! For the rains
he sends are tokens of forgiveness. Once
more the autumn rains will come, as well
as those of spring. ²⁴ The threshing floors
will pile high again with wheat, and the
presses overflow with olive oil and wine.
²⁵ And I will give you back the crops the
locusts ate!—my great destroying army that
I sent against you. ²⁶ Once again you will
have all the food you want.

"Praise the Lord, who does these miracles for you. Never again will my people
experience disaster such as this. ²⁷ And you
will know that I am here among my people
Israel, and that I alone am the Lord, your
God. And my people shall never again be
dealt a blow like this.

²⁸ "After I have poured out my rains
again, I will pour out my Spirit upon all of
you! Your sons and daughters will
prophesy; your old men will dream dreams,
and your young men see visions. ²⁹ And I
will pour out my Spirit even on your slaves,
men and women alike, ³⁰ and put strange
symbols in the earth and sky—blood and
fire and pillars of smoke.

³¹ "The sun will be turned into darkness
and the moon to blood before the great and
terrible Day of the Lord shall come.

³² "Everyone who calls upon the name of
the Lord will be saved; even in Jerusalem
some will escape, just as the Lord has promised, for he has chosen some to survive.

3 "AT THAT TIME, when I restore the
prosperity of Judah and Jerusalem,"
says the Lord, ² "I will gather the armies of
the world into the "Valley Where Jehovah
Judges"ᵃ and punish them there for harming my people, for scattering my inheritance
among the nations and dividing up my land.
³ "They divided up my people as their
slaves; they traded a young lad for a prostitute, and a little girl for wine enough to get
drunk. ⁴ Tyre and Sidon, don't you try to
interfere! Are you trying to take revenge on
me, you cities of Philistia? Beware, for I will
strike back swiftly, and return the harm to

a Or, "Valley of Jehoshaphat."

745

your own heads.
⁵ "You have taken my silver and gold and all my precious treasures and carried them off to your heathen temples. ⁶ You have sold the people of Judah and Jerusalem to the Greeks, who took them far from their own land. ⁷ But I will bring them back again from all these places you have sold them to, and I will pay you back for all that you have done. ⁸ I will sell your sons and daughters to the people of Judah and they will sell them to the Sabeans far away. This is a promise from the Lord."

⁹ Announce this far and wide: Get ready for war! Conscript your best soldiers; collect all your armies. ¹⁰ Melt your plowshares into swords and beat your pruning hooks into spears. Let the weak be strong. ¹¹ Gather together and come, all nations everywhere.

And now, O Lord, bring down your warriors! ¹² Collect the nations; bring them to the Valley of Jehoshaphat, for there I will sit to pronounce judgment on them all. ¹³ Now let the sickle do its work; the harvest is ripe and waiting. Tread the winepress, for it is full to overflowing with the wickedness of these men.

¹⁴ Multitudes, multitudes waiting in the valley for the verdict of their doom! For the Day of the Lord is near, in the Valley of Judgment.

¹⁵ The sun and moon will be darkened and the stars withdraw their light. ¹⁶ The Lord shouts from his Temple in Jerusalem and the earth and sky begin to shake. But to his people Israel, the Lord will be very gentle. He is their Refuge and Strength. ¹⁷ "Then you shall know at last that I am the Lord your God in Zion, my holy mountain. Jerusalem shall be mine forever; the time will come when no foreign armies will pass through her any more.

¹⁸ "Sweet wine will drip from the mountains, and the hills shall flow with milk. Water will fill the dry stream beds of Judah, and a fountain will burst forth from the Temple of the Lord to water Acacia Valley. ¹⁹ Egypt will be destroyed, and Edom too, because of their violence against the Jews, for they killed innocent people in those nations.

²⁰ "But Israel will prosper forever, and Jerusalem will thrive as generations pass; ²¹ For I will avenge the blood of my people; I will not clear their oppressors of guilt. For my home is in Jerusalem[b] with my people."

---

b Literally, "Zion."

Some Dream of Food

Consuelo Kanaga

Listen: "Here I am, dirty, smelly, with no proper underwear beneath this rotting dress. The stench of my teeth makes me sick. They're decaying, but they'll never be fixed. That takes money.

"Poverty is dirt. You may say, in your spick and span surroundings, 'Anybody can be clean.' Let me explain housekeeping without money. For breakfast, I give my children grits with no margarine, or cornbread made without eggs or oleo. What dishes there are, I wash in cold water. No soap. Even the cheapest soap is used for the baby's makeshift diapers.

"Look at these cracked, red hands. Every day I have to decide whether I can bear to put these burning, sore hands into that cold water and strong soap. Why don't I use hot water? Hot water is a luxury. We don't have luxuries.

"Poverty is staying up all night when it is

cold watching our feeble fire; a stray spark would ignite our newspaper walls letting us die in the flames. In the summer, poverty is letting gnats and flies drink my baby's tears."

Strong words. They're from a tired and bitter mother in Appalachia who cannot find a decent job and whose husband has left her.

We see people like her on TV. And we hear of mass starvation in Africa and Asia. The book *Population Bomb* tells us that before long half of the world may watch the other half starve to death on TV.

The situation was similar in Amos' time. Amos was a poor country farmer whom God brought to the big city to rail against injustice. Amos simply couldn't abide people who "trample the poor into the dust and kick aside the meek" (2:7). "Seek the Lord and live, or else he will sweep like fire through Israel," he warned (5:6).

How do you react to a word from God like that? Amos was hustled out of town as a branded traitor. How do we respond today to his message, and to that of Obadiah, whose short book follows Amos?

AMOS

1 AMOS WAS A herdsman living in the village of Tekoa. All day long he sat on the hillsides watching the sheep, keeping them from straying.

² One day, in a vision, God told him some of the things that were going to happen to his nation, Israel. This vision came to him at the time Uzziah was king of Judah, and while Jeroboam (son of Joash) was king of Israel—two years before the earthquake.

This is his report of what he saw and heard: The Lord roared—like a ferocious lion from his lair—from his Temple on Mount Zion. And suddenly the lush pastures of Mount Carmel withered and dried, and all the shepherds mourned.

³ The Lord says, "The people of Damascus have sinned again and again, and I will not forget it. I will not leave her unpunished any more. For they have threshed my people in Gilead as grain is threshed with iron rods. ⁴ So I will set fire to King Hazael's palace, destroying the strong fortress of Ben-hadad. ⁵ I will snap the bars that locked the gates of Damascus, and kill her people as far away as the plain of Aven, and the people of Syria shall return to Kir[a] as slaves." The Lord has spoken.

⁶ The Lord says, "Gaza has sinned again

a Decreeing that the Syrians should go back to Kir as slaves was like saying to the Israelites that they must go back to Egypt as slaves, for the Syrians had made their exodus from Kir and now were free. (See 9:7).

and again, and I will not forget it. I will not leave her unpunished any more. For she sent my people into exile, selling them as slaves in Edom. ⁷ So I will set fire to the walls of Gaza, and all her forts shall be destroyed. ⁸ I will kill the people of Ashdod, and destroy Ekron and the king of Ashkelon; all Philistines left will perish." The Lord has spoken.

⁹ The Lord says, "The people of Tyre have sinned again and again and I will not forget it. I will not leave them unpunished any more. For they broke their treaty with their brother, Israel; they attacked and conquered him, and led him into slavery to Edom. ¹⁰ So I will set fire to the walls of Tyre, and it will burn down all his forts and palaces."

¹¹ The Lord says, "Edom has sinned again and again, and I will not forget it. I will not leave him unpunished any more. For he chased his brother, Israel, with the sword; he was pitiless in unrelenting anger. ¹² So I will set fire to Teman, and it will burn down all the forts of Bozrah."ᵇ

¹³ The Lord says, "The people of Ammon have sinned again and again, and I will not forget it. I will not leave them unpunished any more. For in their wars in Gilead to enlarge their borders, they committed cruel crimes, ripping open pregnant women with their swords.

¹⁴ "So I will set fire to the walls of Rabbah, and it will burn down their forts and palaces; there will be wild shouts of battle like a whirlwind in a mighty storm. ¹⁵ And their king and his princes will go into exile together." The Lord has spoken.

2 THE LORD SAYS, "The people of Moab have sinned again and again, and I will not forget it. I will not leave them unpunished any more. For they desecrated the tombs of the kings of Edom, with no respect for the dead. ² Now in return I will send fire upon Moab, and it will destroy all the palaces in Kerioth. Moab shall go down in tumult as the warriors shout and trumpets blare. ³ And I will destroy their king and · slay all the leaders under him." The Lord

has spoken.

⁴ The Lord says, "The people of Judah have sinned again and again, and I will not forget it. I will not leave them unpunished any more. For they have rejected the laws of God, refusing to obey him. They have hardened their hearts and sinned as their fathers did. ⁵ So I will destroy Judah with fire, and burn down all Jerusalem's palaces and forts."

⁶ The Lord says, "The people of Israel have sinned again and again, and I will not forget it. I will not leave them unpunished any more. For they have perverted justice by accepting bribes, and sold into slavery the poor who can't repay their debts; they trade them for a pair of shoes. ⁷ They trample the poor in the dust and kick aside the meek.

"And a man and his father defile the same temple-girl, corrupting my holy name. ⁸ At their religious feasts they lounge in clothing stolen from their debtors,ᵃ and in my own Temple they offer sacrifices of wine they purchased with stolen money.

⁹ "Yet think of all I did for them! I cleared the land of the Amorites before them—the Amorites, as tall as cedar trees, and strong as oaks! But I lopped off their fruit and cut their roots. ¹⁰ And I brought you out from Egypt and led you through the desert forty years, to possess the land of the Amorites. ¹¹ And I chose your sons to be Naziritesᵇ and prophets—can you deny this, Israel?" asks the Lord. ¹² "But you caused the Nazirites to sin by urging them to drink your wine, and you silenced my prophets, telling them, 'Shut up!'

¹³ "Therefore I will make you groan as a wagon groans that is loaded with sheaves. ¹⁴ Your swiftest warriors will stumble in flight. The strong will all be weak, and the great ones can no longer save themselves. ¹⁵ The archer's aim will fail, the swiftest runners won't be fast enough to flee, and even the best of horsemen can't outrun the danger then. ¹⁶ The most courageous of your mighty men will drop their weapons and run for their lives that day." The Lord God has spoken.

b Teman was in the north of Edom, and Bozrah in the south. The entire country would be devastated.
2a Under Mosaic law, it was illegal to keep pledged clothing of debtors overnight. See Exodus 22:26.
b See Numbers, chapter 6.

3 LISTEN! THIS IS your doom! It is spoken by the Lord against both Israel and Judah—against the entire family I brought from Egypt: ² "Of all the peoples of the earth, I have chosen you alone. That is why I must punish you the more for all your sins. ³ For how can we walk together with your sins between us? ⁴ "Would I be roaring as a lion unless I had a reason? The fact is, I am getting ready to destroy you. Even a young lion, when it growls, shows it is ready for its food. ⁵ A trap doesn't snap shut unless it is stepped on; your punishment is well deserved. ⁶ The alarm has sounded—listen and fear! For I, the Lord, am sending disaster into your land.

⁷ "But always, first of all, I warn you through my prophets. This I now have done."

⁸ The Lion has roared—tremble in fear. The Lord God has sounded your doom—I dare not refuse to proclaim it.

⁹ Call together the Assyrian and Egyptian leaders, saying, "Take your seats now on the mountains of Samaria to witness the scandalous spectacle of all Israel's crimes. ¹⁰ My people have forgotten what it means to do right," says the Lord. "Their beautiful homes are full of the loot from their thefts and banditry. ¹¹ Therefore," the Lord God says, "an enemy is coming! He is surrounding them and will shatter their forts and plunder those beautiful homes."

¹² The Lord says, "A shepherd tried to rescue his sheep from a lion, but it was too late; he snatched from the lion's mouth two legs and a piece of ear. So it will be when the Israelites in Samaria are finally rescued —all they will have left is half a chair and a tattered pillow.

¹³ "Listen to this announcement, and publish it throughout all Israel," says the Lord, the God of Hosts: ¹⁴ "On the same day that I punish Israel for her sins, I will also destroy the idol altars at Bethel. The horns of the altar will be cut off and fall to the ground.

¹⁵ "And I will destroy the beautiful homes of the wealthy—their winter mansions and their summer houses, too—and demolish their ivory palaces."

4 LISTEN TO ME, you "fat cows" of Bashan living in Samaria—you women who encourage your husbands to rob the poor and crush the needy—you who never have enough to drink! ² The Lord God has sworn by his holiness that the time will come when he will put hooks in your noses and lead you away like the cattle you are; they will drag the last of you away with fishhooks! ³ You will be hauled from your beautiful homes and tossed out through the nearest breach in the wall. The Lord has said it.

⁴ Go ahead and sacrifice to idols at Bethel and Gilgal. Keep disobeying—your sins are mounting up. Sacrifice each morning and bring your tithes twice a week! ⁵ Go through all your proper forms and give extra offerings. How you pride yourselves and crow about it everywhere!

⁶ "I sent you hunger," says the Lord, "but it did no good; you still would not return to me. ⁷ I ruined your crops by holding back the rain three months before the harvest. I sent rain on one city, but not another. While rain fell on one field, another was dry and withered. ⁸ People from two or three cities would make their weary journey for a drink of water to a city that had rain, but there wasn't ever enough. Yet you wouldn't return to me," says the Lord.

⁹ "I sent blight and mildew on your farms and your vineyards; the locusts ate your figs and olive trees. And still you wouldn't return to me," says the Lord. ¹⁰ "I sent you plagues like those of Egypt long ago. I killed your lads in war and drove away your horses. The stench of death was terrible to smell. And yet you refused to come. ¹¹ I destroyed some of your cities, as I did Sodom and Gomorrah; those left are like half-burned firebrands snatched away from fire. And still you won't return to me," says the Lord.

¹² "Therefore I will bring upon you all these further evils I have spoken of. Prepare to meet your God in judgment, Israel. ¹³ For you are dealing with the one who formed the mountains and made the winds, and knows your every thought; he turns the morning to darkness and crushes down the mountains underneath his feet: Jehovah, the Lord, the God of Hosts, is his name."

5 SADLY I SING this song of grief for you, O Israel:

2 "Beautiful Israel lies broken and crushed upon the ground and cannot rise. No one will help her. She is left alone to die." 3 For the Lord God says, "The city that sends a thousand men to battle, a hundred will return. The city that sends a hundred, only ten will come back alive."

4 The Lord says to the people of Israel, "Seek me—and live. 5 Don't seek the idols of Bethel, Gilgal, or Beer-sheba; for the people of Gilgal will be carried off to exile, and those of Bethel shall surely come to grief."

6 Seek the Lord and live, or else he will sweep like fire through Israel and consume her, and none of the idols in Bethel can put it out.

7 O evil men, you make "justice" a bitter pill for the poor and oppressed. "Righteousness" and "fair play" are meaningless fictions to you!

8 Seek him who created the Seven Stars and the constellation Orion, who turns darkness into morning, and day into night, who calls forth the water from the ocean and pours it out as rain upon the land. The Lord, Jehovah, is his name. 9 With blinding speed and violence he brings destruction on the strong, breaking all defenses.

10 How you hate honest judges! How you despise people who tell the truth! 11 You trample the poor and steal their smallest crumb by all your taxes, fines, and usury; therefore you will never live in the beautiful stone houses you are building, nor drink the wine from the lush vineyards you are planting.

12 For many and great are your sins. I know them all so well. You are the enemies of everything good; you take bribes; you refuse justice to the poor. 13 Therefore those who are wise will not try to interfere with the Lord in the dread day of your punishment.

14 Be good, flee evil—and live! Then the Lord God of Hosts will truly be your Helper, as you have claimed he is. 15 Hate evil and love the good; remodel your courts into true halls of justice. Perhaps even yet the Lord God of Hosts will have mercy on his people who remain.

16 Therefore the Lord God of Hosts says this: "There will be crying in all the streets and every road. Call for the farmers to weep with you, too; call for professional mourners to wail and lament. 17 There will be sorrow and crying in every vineyard, for I will pass through and destroy. 18 You say, 'If only the Day of the Lord were here, for then God would deliver us from all our foes.' But you have no idea what you ask. For that day will *not* be light and prosperity, but darkness and doom! How terrible the darkness will be for you; not a ray of joy or hope will shine. 19 In that day you will be as a man who is chased by a lion—and met by a bear, or a man in a dark room who leans against a wall—and puts his hand on a snake. 20 Yes, that will be a dark and hopeless day for you.

21 "I hate your show and pretense—your hypocrisy of 'honoring' me with your religious feasts and solemn assemblies. 22 I will not accept your burnt offerings and thank offerings. I will not look at your offerings of peace. 23 Away with your hymns of praise—they are mere noise to my ears. I will not listen to your music, no matter how lovely it is.

24 "I want to see a mighty flood of justice—a torrent of doing good.

25,26,27 "You sacrificed to me for forty years while you were in the desert, Israel—but always your real interest has been in your heathen gods—in Sakkuth your king, and in Kaiwan, your god of the stars, and in all the images of them you made. So I will send them into captivity with you far to the east of Damascus," says the Lord, the God of Hosts.

6 WOE TO THOSE lounging in luxury at Jerusalem and Samaria, so famous and popular among the people of Israel. 2 Go over to Calneh and see what happened there; then go to great Hamath and down to Gath in the Philistines' land. Once they were better and greater than you, but look at them now. 3 You push away all thought of punishment awaiting you, but by your deeds you bring the Day of Judgment near.

4 You lie on ivory beds surrounded with luxury, eating the meat of the tenderest lambs and the choicest calves. 5 You sing idle songs to the sound of the harp, and

fancy yourselves to be as great musicians as King David was.

⁶ You drink wine by the bucketful and perfume yourselves with sweet ointments, caring nothing at all that your brothers need your help. ⁷ Therefore you will be the first to be taken as slaves; suddenly your revelry will end.

⁸ Jehovah, the Lord God of Hosts, has sworn by his own name, "I despise the pride and false glory of Israel, and hate their beautiful homes. I will turn over this city and everything in it to her enemies."

⁹ If there are as few as ten of them left, and even one house, they too will perish. ¹⁰ A man's uncle will be the only one left to bury him, and when he goes in to carry his body from the house, he will ask the only one still alive inside, "Are any others left?" And the answer will be, "No," and he will add, "Shhh . . . don't mention the name of the Lord—he might hear you."

¹¹ For the Lord commanded this: That homes both great and small should be smashed to pieces. ¹² Can horses run on rocks? Can oxen plow the sea? Stupid even to ask, but no more stupid than what you do when you make a mockery of justice, and corrupt and sour all that should be good and right. ¹³ And just as stupid is your rejoicing in how great you are, when you are less than nothing! And priding yourselves on your own tiny power!

¹⁴ "O Israel, I will bring against you a nation that will bitterly oppress you from your northern boundary to your southern tip, all the way from Hamath to the brook of Arabah," says the Lord, the God of Hosts.

7 THIS IS WHAT the Lord God showed me in a vision: He was preparing a vast swarm of locusts to destroy all the main crop that sprang up after the first mowing, which went as taxes to the king. ² They ate everything in sight. Then I said, "O Lord God, please forgive your people! Don't send them this plague! If you turn against Israel, what hope is there? For Israel is so small!" ³ So the Lord relented, and did not fulfill the vision. "I won't do it," he told me.

⁴ Then the Lord God showed me a great fire he had prepared to punish them; it had burned up the waters and was devouring the entire land.

⁵ Then I said, "O Lord God, please don't do it. If you turn against them, what hope is there? For Israel is so small!"

⁶ Then the Lord turned from this plan too, and said, "I won't do that either."

⁷ Then he showed me this: The Lord was standing beside a wall built with a plumbline, checking it with a plumbline to see if it was straight. ⁸ And the Lord said to me, "Amos, what do you see?"

I answered, "A plumbline."

And he replied, "I will test my people with a plumbline. I will no longer turn away from punishing. ⁹ The idol altars and temples of Israel will be destroyed, and I will destroy the dynasty of King Jeroboam by the sword."

¹⁰ But when Amaziah, the priest of Bethel, heard what Amos was saying, he rushed a message to Jeroboam, the king: "Amos is a traitor to our nation and is plotting your death. This is intolerable. It will lead to rebellion all across the land. ¹¹ He says you will be killed, and Israel will be sent far away into exile and slavery."

¹² Then Amaziah sent orders to Amos, "Get out of here, you prophet, you! Flee to the land of Judah and do your prophesying there! ¹³ Don't bother us here with your visions, not here in the capital, where the king's chapel is!"

¹⁴ But Amos replied, "I am not really one of the prophets. I do not come from a family of prophets. I am just a herdsman and fruit picker. ¹⁵ But the Lord took me from caring for the flocks and told me, 'Go and prophesy to my people Israel.'

¹⁶ "Now therefore listen to this message to you from the Lord. You say, 'Don't prophesy against Israel.' ¹⁷ The Lord's reply is this: 'Because of your interference, your wife will become a prostitute in this city, and your sons and daughters will be killed and your land divided up. You yourself will die in a heathen land, and the people of Israel will certainly become slaves in exile, far from their land.'"

8 THEN THE LORD God showed me, in a vision, a basket full of ripe fruit. ² "What do you see, Amos?" he asked.

I replied, "A basket full of ripe fruit." Then the Lord said, "This fruit represents my people Israel—ripe for punishment. I will not defer their punishment again. [3] The riotous sound of singing in the Temple will turn to weeping then. Dead bodies will be scattered everywhere. They will be carried out of the city in silence." The Lord has spoken.

[4] Listen, you merchants who rob the poor, trampling on the needy; [5] you who long for the Sabbath to end and the religious holidays to be over, so you can get out and start cheating again—using your weighted scales and under-sized measures; [6] you who make slaves of the poor, buying them for their debt of a piece of silver or a pair of shoes, or selling them your moldy wheat— [7] the Lord, the Pride of Israel, has sworn: "I won't forget your deeds! [8] The land will tremble as it awaits its doom, and everyone will mourn. It will rise up like the river Nile at floodtime, toss about, and sink again. [9] At that time I will make the sun go down at noon and darken the earth in the daytime.

[10] "And I will turn your parties into times of mourning, and your songs of joy will be turned to cries of despair. You will wear funeral clothes and shave your heads as signs of sorrow, as if your only son had died; bitter, bitter will be that day. [11] The time is surely coming," says the Lord God, "when I will send a famine on the land—not a famine of bread or water, but of hearing the words of the Lord. [12] Men will wander everywhere from sea to sea, seeking the Word of the Lord, searching, running here and going there, but will not find it.

[13] "Beautiful girls and fine young men alike will grow faint and weary, thirsting for the Word of God. [14] And those who worship the idols of Samaria, Dan, and Beersheba shall fall and never rise again."

9 I SAW THE Lord standing beside the altar, saying, "Smash the tops of the pillars and shake the Temple until the pillars crumble and the roof crashes down upon the people below. Though they run, they will not escape; they all will be killed.

[2] "Though they dig down to Sheol, I will reach down and pull them up; though they climb into the heavens, I will bring them down. [3] Though they hide among the rocks at the top of Carmel, I will search them out and capture them. Though they hide at the bottom of the ocean, I will send the sea-serpent after them to bite and destroy them. [4] Though they volunteer for exile, I will command the sword to kill them there. I will see to it that they receive evil and not good."

[5] The Lord God of Hosts touches the land and it melts, and all its people mourn. It rises like the river Nile in Egypt, and then sinks again. [6] The upper stories of his home are in the heavens, the first floor on the earth. He calls for the vapor to rise from the ocean and pours it down as rain upon the ground. Jehovah, the Lord, is his name.

[7] "O people of Israel, are you any more to me than the Ethiopians are? Have not I, who brought you out of Egypt, done as much for other people, too? I brought the Philistines from Caphtor and the Syrians out of Kir.

[8] "The eyes of the Lord God are watching Israel, that sinful nation, and I will root her up and scatter her across the world. *Yet I have promised that this rooting out will not be permanent.* [9] For I have commanded that Israel be sifted by the other nations as grain is sifted in a sieve, yet not one true kernel will be lost. [10] But all these sinners who say, 'God will not touch us,' will die by the sword.

[11] "Then, at that time, I will rebuild the City of David, which is now lying in ruins, and return it to its former glory, [12] and Israel will possess what is left of Edom, and of all the nations that belong to me." For so the Lord, who plans it all, has said.

[13] "The time will come when there will be such abundance of crops, that the harvest time will scarcely end before the farmer starts again to sow another crop, and the terraces of grapes upon the hills of Israel will drip sweet wine! [14] I will restore the fortunes of my people Israel, and they shall rebuild their ruined cities, and live in them again, and they shall plant vineyards and gardens and eat their crops and drink their wine. [15] I will firmly plant them there upon the land that I have given them; they shall not be pulled up again," says the Lord your God.

OBADIAH

1 *In a vision the Lord God showed Obadiah the future of the land of Edom.*[a]

"A report has come from the Lord," he said, "that God has sent an ambassador to the nations with this message: 'Attention! You are to send your armies against Edom and destroy her!' "

² I will cut you down to size among the nations, Edom, making you small and despised.

³ You are proud because you live in those high, inaccessible cliffs. "Who can ever reach us way up here!" you boast. Don't fool yourselves! ⁴ Though you soar as high as eagles, and build your nest among the stars, I will bring you plummeting down, says the Lord.

⁵ Far better it would be for you if thieves had come at night to plunder you—for they would not take everything! Or if your vineyards were robbed of all their fruit—for at least the gleanings would be left! ⁶ Every nook and cranny will be searched and robbed, and every treasure found and taken.

⁷ All your allies will turn against you and help to push you out of your land. They will promise peace while plotting your destruction. Your trusted friends will set traps for you and all your counterstrategy will fail. ⁸ In that day not one wise man[b] will be left in all of Edom! says the Lord. For I will fill the wise men of Edom with stupidity. ⁹ The mightiest soldiers of Teman will be confused, and helpless to prevent the slaughter.

¹⁰ And why? Because of what you did to your brother Israel. Now your sins will be exposed for all to see; ashamed and defenseless, you will be cut off forever. ¹¹ For you deserted Israel in his time of need. You stood aloof, refusing to lift a finger to help him when invaders carried off his wealth and divided Jerusalem among them by lot; you were as one of his enemies.

¹² You should not have done it. You should not have gloated when they took him far away to foreign lands; you should not have rejoiced in the day of his misfortune; you should not have mocked in his time of need. ¹³ You yourselves went into the land of Israel in the day of his calamity and looted him. You made yourselves rich at his expense. ¹⁴ You stood at the crossroads and killed those trying to escape; you captured the survivors and returned them to their enemies in that terrible time of his distress.

¹⁵ The Lord's vengeance will soon fall upon all Gentile nations. As you have done to Israel, so will it be done to you. Your acts will boomerang upon your heads. ¹⁶ You drank my cup of punishment upon my holy mountain, and the nations round about will drink it, too; yes, drink and stagger back and disappear from history, no longer nations any more.

¹⁷ But Jerusalem will become a refuge, a way of escape. Israel will reoccupy the land. ¹⁸ Israel will be a fire that sets the dry fields of Edom aflame. There will be no survivors, for the Lord has spoken.

¹⁹ Then my people who live in the Negeb shall occupy the hill country of Edom; those living in Judean lowlands shall possess the Philistine plains, and repossess the fields of Ephraim and Samaria. And the people of Benjamin shall possess Gilead.

²⁰ The Israeli exiles shall return and occupy the Phoenician coastal strip as far north as Zarephath. Those exiled in Asia Minor shall return to their homeland and conquer the Negeb's outlying villages. ²¹ For deliverers will come to Jerusalem and rule all Edom. And the Lord shall be King!

---

a A nation southeast of Israel, including Petra, the city hewn from rocks; her southern boundary was on the Gulf of Aqaba. b Edom was noted for her wise men; Eliphaz, the wisest of Job's three friends, was from Teman, five miles east of Petra, in Edom.

Bob Combs

Runaway

Police estimate that a million American kids are currently missing from home. More than a few of them have come to New York City's Greenwich Village (above) and other similar "crash" areas, melting in with the winos to form a curious montage for the camera-laden tourists. "This city's a great place if you want to hide," says one young New Yorker. "You can just drop completely out of sight from your past."

Jonah tried that—but God was not about to let him off the hook. After all, he wanted the reluctant prophet to go help the people in Nineveh (sort of like dispatching a loyal South Korean to Peking). God eventually won the argument —but in the last episode Jonah was still having trouble handling his responsibility. The important message of this book is not the well-known story of the man-swallowing fish, but God's infinite concern for a city full of lost souls, and his ability to use even an immature and reluctant servant.

JONAH

1 *The Lord sent this message to Jonah, the son of Amittai:*

2 "Go to the great city of Nineveh, and give them this announcement from the Lord: 'I am going to destroy you, for your wickedness rises before me; it smells to highest heaven.' "

3 But Jonah was afraid to go and ran away from the Lord. He went down to the seacoast, to the port of Joppa, where he found a ship leaving for Tarshish. He bought a ticket, went on board, and climbed down into the dark hold of the ship to hide there from the Lord.

4 But as the ship was sailing along, suddenly the Lord flung a terrific wind over the sea, causing a great storm that threatened to send them to the bottom. 5 Fearing for their lives, the desperate sailors shouted to their gods for help and threw the cargo overboard to lighten the ship. And all this time Jonah was sound asleep down in the hold.

6 So the captain went down after him. "What do you mean," he roared, "sleeping at a time like this? Get up and cry to your god, and see if he will have mercy on us and save us!"

7 Then the crew decided to draw straws to see which of them had offended the gods and caused this terrible storm; and Jonah drew the short one.

8 "What have you done," they asked, "to bring this awful storm upon us? Who are you? What is your work? What country are you from? What is your nationality?"

9,10 And he said, "I am a Jew;[a] I worship Jehovah, the God of heaven, who made the earth and sea." Then he told them he was running away from the Lord.

The men were terribly frightened when they heard this. "Oh, why did you do it?" they shouted. 11 "What should we do to you to stop the storm?" For it was getting worse and worse.

12 "Throw me out into the sea," he said, "and it will become calm again. For I know this terrible storm has come because of me."

13 They tried harder to row the boat ashore, but couldn't make it. The storm was too fierce to fight against. 14 Then they shouted out a prayer to Jehovah, Jonah's God. "O Jehovah," they pleaded, "don't make us die for this man's sin, and don't hold us responsible for his death, for it is not our fault—you have sent this storm upon him for your own good reasons."

15 Then they picked up Jonah and threw him overboard into the raging sea—and the storm stopped!

16 The men stood there in awe before Jehovah, and sacrificed to him and vowed to serve him.

17 Now the Lord had arranged for a great fish to swallow Jonah. And Jonah was inside the fish three days and three nights.

2 THEN JONAH PRAYED to the Lord his God from inside the fish:

2 "In my great trouble I cried to the Lord and he answered me; from the depths of death I called, and Lord, you heard me! 3 You threw me into the ocean depths; I sank down into the floods of waters and was covered by your wild and stormy waves. 4 Then I said, 'O Lord, you have rejected me and cast me away. How shall I ever again see your holy Temple?'

5 "I sank beneath the waves, and death was very near. The waters closed above me; the seaweed wrapped itself around my head. 6 I went down to the bottoms of the mountains that rise from off the ocean floor. I was locked out of life and imprisoned in the land of death. But, O Lord my God, you have snatched me from the yawning jaws of death!

7 "When I had lost all hope, I turned my thoughts once more to the Lord. And my earnest prayer went to you in your holy Temple. 8 (Those who worship false gods have turned their backs on all the mercies waiting for them from the Lord!)

9 "I will never worship anyone but you! For how can I thank you enough for all you have done? I will surely fulfill my promises.

---

a Literally, "a Hebrew."

For my deliverance comes from the Lord alone."
[10] And the Lord ordered the fish to spit up Jonah on the beach, and it did.

3 THEN THE LORD spoke to Jonah again: "Go to that great city, Nineveh," he said, "and warn them of their doom, as I told you to before!"
[3] So Jonah obeyed, and went to Nineveh. Now Nineveh was a very large city, with extensive suburbs—so large that it would take three days to walk around it.[a]
[4,5] But the very first day when Jonah entered the city and began to preach, the people repented. Jonah shouted to the crowds that gathered around him, "Forty days from now Nineveh will be destroyed!" And they believed him and declared a fast; from the king on down, everyone put on sackcloth—the rough, coarse garments worn at times of mourning.[b]
[6] For when the king of Nineveh heard what Jonah was saying, he stepped down from his throne and laid aside his royal robes and put on sackcloth and sat in ashes. [7] And the king and his nobles sent this message throughout the city: "Let no one, not even the animals, eat anything at all, nor even drink any water. [8] Everyone must wear sackcloth and cry mightily to God, and let everyone turn from his evil ways, from his violence and robbing. [9] Who can tell? Perhaps even yet God will decide to let us live, and will hold back his fierce anger from destroying us."
[10] And when God saw that they had put a stop to their evil ways, he abandoned his plan to destroy them, and didn't carry it through.

4 THIS CHANGE OF plans made Jonah very angry. [2] He complained to the Lord about it: "This is exactly what I thought you'd do, Lord, when I was there in my own country and you first told me to come here. That's why I ran away to Tarshish. For I knew you were a gracious God, merciful, slow to get angry, and full of kindness; I knew how easily you could cancel your plans for destroying these people. [3] "Please kill me, Lord; I'd rather be dead than alive [when nothing that I told them happens[a]]."
[4] Then the Lord said, "Is it right to be angry about *this?*"
[5] So Jonah went out and sat sulking[a] on the east side of the city, and he made a leafy shelter to shade him as he waited there to see if anything would happen to the city. [6] And when the leaves of the shelter withered in the heat, the Lord arranged for a vine to grow up quickly and spread its broad leaves over Jonah's head to shade him. This made him comfortable and very grateful.
[7] But God also prepared a worm! The next morning the worm ate through the stem of the plant, so that it withered away and died.
[8] Then, when the sun was hot, God ordered a scorching east wind to blow on Jonah, and the sun beat down upon his head until he grew faint and wished to die. For he said, "Death is better than this!"
[9] And God said to Jonah, "Is it right for you to be angry because the plant died?"
"Yes," Jonah said, "it is; it is right for me to be angry enough to die!"
[10] Then the Lord said, "You feel sorry for yourself when your shelter is destroyed, though you did no work to put it there, and it is, at best, short-lived. [11] And why shouldn't I feel sorry for a great city like Nineveh with its 120,000 people in utter spiritual darkness,[b] and all its cattle?"

---

a The Hebrew text makes no distinction between the city proper—the walls of which were only about eight miles in circumference, accommodating a population of about 175,000 persons—and the administrative district of Nineveh which was about thirty to sixty miles across.   b Implied.   4 a Implied.
b Or, "with its 120,000 children who don't know their right hands from their left."

Beautiful?

Bob Combs Photos

What kind of a country are we—sabotaging the physical and moral health of our young by motivating them to buy cigarettes and alcohol, and subjecting them to a bombardment of pornography in books and films? There's more than one kind of garbage in the streets these days. It's easy to blame somebody else, to find alibis, to resign ourselves to living with fraud and greed and apathy ... but God may not put up with that forever. Micah lashed out against Israelis "who lie awake at night, plotting wickedness" (2:1), "who hate justice and love unfairness" (3:9), and promised them the sure judgment of an angry God. Nahum held out the same destruction for Nineveh which, 150 years after Jonah had preached there, was again a "City of Blood, full of lies, crammed with plunder" (3:1).

And it happened: Samaria, 722 B.C., wiped out by the Assyrians from Nineveh; then Nineveh itself, 612 B.C., burned and flooded by the Babylonians; finally Jerusalem overrun, 587 B.C., again by the Babylonians.

The similarities to modern times are too close for comfort.

MICAH

1 *These are messages from the Lord to Micah, who lived in the town of Moresheth during the reigns of King Jotham, King Ahaz, and King Hezekiah, all kings of Judah. The messages were addressed to both Samaria and Judah, and came to Micah in the form of visions.*

² Attention! Let all the peoples of the world listen. For the Lord in his holy Temple has made accusations against you!

³ Look! He is coming! He leaves his throne in heaven and comes to earth, walking on the mountaintops. ⁴ They melt beneath his feet, and flow into the valleys like wax in fire, like water pouring down a hill.

⁵ And why is this happening? Because of the sins of Israel and Judah. What sins? The idolatry and oppression centering in the capital cities, Samaria and Jerusalem!

⁶ Therefore the entire city of Samaria will crumble into a heap of rubble, and become an open field, her streets plowed up for planting grapes! The Lord will tear down her wall and her forts, exposing their foundations, and pour their stones into the valleys below. ⁷ All her carved images will be smashed to pieces; her ornate idol temples, built with the gifts of worshipers, will all be burned.[a]

⁸ I will wail and lament, howling as a jackal, mournful as an ostrich crying across the desert sands at night. I will walk naked and barefoot in sorrow and shame; ⁹ for my people's wound is far too deep to heal. The Lord stands ready at Jerusalem's gates to punish her. ¹⁰ Woe to the city of Gath. Weep, men of Bakah. In Beth-le-aphrah roll in the dust in your anguish and shame. ¹¹ There go the people of Shaphir,[b] led away as slaves—stripped, naked and ashamed. The people of Zaanan[b] dare not show themselves outside their walls. The foundations of Beth-ezel[b] are swept away—the very ground on which it stood. ¹² The people of

Maroth vainly hope for better days, but only bitterness awaits them as the Lord stands poised against Jerusalem.

¹³ Quick! Use your swiftest chariots and flee, O people of Lachish, for you were the first of the cities of Judah to follow Israel in her sin of idol worship. Then all the cities of the south began to follow your example.

¹⁴ Write off Moresheth[c] of Gath; there is no hope of saving her. The town of Achzib has deceived the kings of Israel, for she promised help she cannot give. ¹⁵ You people of Mareshah will be a prize to your enemies. They will penetrate to Adullum, the "Pride of Israel."

¹⁶ Weep, weep for your little ones. For they are snatched away and you will never see them again. They have gone as slaves to distant lands. Shave your heads in sorrow.

2 WOE TO YOU who lie awake at night, plotting wickedness; you rise at dawn to carry out your schemes; because you can, you do. ² You want a certain piece of land, or someone else's house (though it is all he has); you take it by fraud and threats and violence.

³ But the Lord God says, I will reward your evil with evil; nothing can stop me; never again will you be proud and haughty after I am through with you. ⁴ Then your enemies will taunt you and mock your dirge of despair: "We are finished, ruined. God has confiscated our land and sent us far away, and given what is ours to others." ⁵ Others will set your boundaries then. "The People of the Lord" will live where they are sent.

⁶ "Don't say such things," the people say. "Don't harp on things like that. It's disgraceful, that sort of talk. Such evils surely will not come our way."

⁷ Is that the right reply for you to make, O House of Jacob? Do you think the Spirit of the Lord likes to talk to you so roughly?

---

a Literally, "they shall return to the hire of an harlot." verses 10–14. Micah bitterly declaims each town, demonstrating by the use of puns their failures. *Shaphir* sounds like the Hebrew word for "beauty," here contrasted with their shame; *Zaanan* sounds like a verb meaning "to go forth," here contrasted with the fear of its inhabitants to venture outside; *Beth-ezel* sounds like a word for "foundation," which had been taken away from them.

b In the Hebrew, there is frequent word play in c Micah's home town. See verse 1 of chapter 1.

759

No! His threats are for your good, to get you on the path again. [8] Yet to this very hour my people rise against me. For you steal the shirts right off the backs of those who trusted you, who walk in peace. [9] You have driven out the widows from their homes, and stripped their children of every God-given right. [10] Up! Begone! This is no more your land and home, for you have filled it with sin and it will vomit you out. [11] "I'll preach to you the joys of wine and drink"—that is the kind of drunken, lying prophet that you like! [12] The time will come, O Israel, when I will gather you—all that are left—and bring you together again like sheep in a fold, like a flock in a pasture—a noisy, happy crowd. [13] The Messiah[a] will lead you out of exile and bring you through the gates of your cities of captivity, back to your own land. Your King will go before you—the Lord leads on.

3 LISTEN, YOU LEADERS of Israel—you are supposed to know right from wrong, [2] yet you are the very ones who hate good and love evil; you skin my people and strip them to the bone. [3] You devour them, flog them, break their bones, and chop them up like meat for the cooking pot— [4] and then you plead with the Lord for his help in times of trouble! Do you really expect him to listen? He will look the other way! [5] You false prophets! You who lead his people astray! You who cry "Peace" to those who give you food, and threaten those who will not pay!

This is God's message to you: [6] The night will close about you and cut off all your visions; darkness will cover you, with never a word from God. The sun will go down upon you, and your day will end. [7] Then at last you will cover your faces in shame, and admit that your messages were not from God. [8] But as for me, I am filled with power, with the Spirit of the Lord, fearlessly announcing God's punishment on Israel for her sins.

[9] Listen to me, you leaders of Israel who hate justice and love unfairness, [10] and fill Jerusalem with murder and sin of every kind— [11] you leaders who take bribes; you priests and prophets who won't preach and prophesy until you're paid. (And yet you fawn upon the Lord and say, "All is well— the Lord is here among us. No harm can come to us.") [12] It is because of you that Jerusalem will be plowed like a field, and become a heap of rubble; the mountaintop where the Temple stands will be overgrown with brush.

4 BUT IN THE last days Mount Zion will be the most renowned of all the mountains of the world, praised by all nations; people from all over the world will make pilgrimages there. [2] "Come," they will say to one another, "let us visit the mountain of the Lord, and see the Temple of the God of Israel; he will tell us what to do, and we will do it." For in those days the whole world will be ruled by the Lord from Jerusalem! He will issue his laws and announce his decrees from there. [3] He will arbitrate among the nations, and dictate to strong nations far away. They will beat their swords into plowshares and their spears into pruning-hooks; nations shall no longer fight each other, for all war will end. There will be universal peace, and all the military academies and training camps will be closed down. [4] Everyone will live quietly in his own home in peace and prosperity, for there will be nothing to fear. The Lord himself has promised this. [5] (Therefore we will follow the Lord our God forever and ever, even though all the nations around us worship idols!) [6] In that coming day, the Lord says that he will bring back his punished people— sick and lame and dispossessed— [7] and make them strong again in their own land, a mighty nation, and the Lord himself shall be their King from Mount Zion forever. [8] O Jerusalem—the Watchtower of God's people—your royal might and power will come back to you again, just as before.

---

a "He who opens the breach."

⁹ But for now, now you scream in terror. Where is your king to lead you? He is dead! Where are your wise men? All are gone! Pain has gripped you like a woman in labor. ¹⁰ Writhe and groan in your terrible pain, O people of Zion, for you must leave this city and live in the fields; you will be sent far away into exile in Babylon. But there I will rescue you and free you from the grip of your enemies.

¹¹ True, many nations have gathered together against you, calling for your blood, eager to destroy you. ¹² But they do not know my thoughts nor understand my plan, for the time will come when the Lord will gather together the enemies of his people like sheaves upon the threshing floor, ¹³ helpless before Israel.

Rise, thresh, O daughter of Zion; I will give you horns of iron and hoofs of brass and you will trample to pieces many people, and you will give their wealth as offerings to the Lord, the Lord of all the earth.

5 MOBILIZE! THE ENEMY lays siege to Jerusalem! With a rod they shall strike the Judge of Israel on the face.

² O Bethlehem Ephrathah, you are but a small Judean village, yet you will be the birthplace of my King who is alive from everlasting ages past! ³ God will abandon his people to their enemies until the time of Israel's spiritual rebirth;[a] then at last the exile remnants of Israel will rejoin their brethren in their own land.

⁴ And he shall stand and feed his flock in the strength of the Lord, in the majesty of the name of the Lord his God, and his people shall remain there undisturbed, for he will be greatly honored all around the world. ⁵ He will be our Peace. And when the Assyrian invades our land and marches across our hills, he will appoint seven shepherds to watch over us, eight princes to lead us. ⁶ They will rule Assyria with drawn swords and enter the gates of the land of Nimrod. He will deliver us from the Assyrians when they invade our land.

⁷ Then the nation of Israel will refresh the world like a gentle dew or the welcome showers of rain, ⁸ and Israel will be as strong as a lion. The nations will be like helpless sheep before her! ⁹ She will stand up to her foes; all her enemies will be wiped out.

¹⁰ At that same time, says the Lord, I will destroy all the weapons you depend on, ¹¹ and tear down your walls and demolish the defenses of your cities. ¹² I will put an end to all witchcraft—there will be no more fortune-tellers to consult— ¹³ and destroy all your idols. Never again will you worship what you have made, ¹⁴ and I will abolish the heathen shrines from among you, and destroy the cities where your idol temples stand.

¹⁵ And I will pour out my vengeance upon the nations who refuse to obey me.

6 LISTEN TO WHAT the Lord is saying to his people:

Stand up and state your case against me. Let the mountains and hills be called to witness your complaint.

² And now, O mountains, listen to the Lord's complaint! For he has a case against his people Israel! He will prosecute them to the full. ³ O my people, what have I done that makes you turn away from me? Tell me why your patience is exhausted! Answer me! ⁴ For I brought you out of Egypt, and cut your chains of slavery. I gave you Moses, Aaron, and Miriam to help you.

⁵ Don't you remember, O my people, how Balak, king of Moab, tried to destroy you through the curse of Balaam, son of Beor, but I made him bless you instead? That is the kindness I showed you again and again. Have you no memory at all of what happened at Acacia and Gilgal, and how I blessed you there?

⁶ "How can we make up to you for what we've done?" you ask. "Shall we bow before the Lord with offerings of yearling calves?"

Oh, no! ⁷ For if you offered him thousands of rams and ten thousands of rivers of olive oil—would that please him? Would he be satisfied? If you sacrificed your oldest child, would that make him glad? Then would he forgive your sins? Of course not!

⁸ No, he has told you what he wants, and this is all it is: *to be fair and just and merci-*

---

a Literally, "until she who is in travail has brought forth."

ful, and to walk humbly with your God. ⁹ The Lord's voice calls out to all Jerusalem—listen to the Lord if you are wise! The armies of destruction are coming; the Lord is sending them.

¹⁰ For your sins are very great—is there to be no end of getting rich by cheating? The homes of the wicked are full of ungodly treasures and lying scales. ¹¹ Shall I say "Good!" to all your merchants with their bags of false, deceitful weights? How could God be just while saying that? ¹² Your rich men are wealthy through extortion and violence; your citizens are so used to lying that their tongues can't tell the truth!

¹³ Therefore I will wound you! I will make your hearts miserable for all your sins. ¹⁴ You will eat but never have enough; hunger pangs and emptiness will still remain. And though you try and try to save your money, it will come to nothing at the end, and what little you succeed in storing up I'll give to those who conquer you!ᵃ ¹⁵ You will plant crops but not harvest them; you will press out the oil from the olives, and not get enough to anoint yourself! You will trample the grapes, but get no juice to make your wine.

¹⁶ The only commands you keep are those of Omri; the only example you follow is that of Ahab! Therefore I will make an awesome example of you—I will destroy you. I will make you the laughingstock of the world; all who see you will snicker and sneer!

7 WOE IS ME! It is as hard to find an honest man as grapes and figs when harvest days are over. Not a cluster to eat, not a single early fig, however much I long for it! The good men have disappeared from the earth; not one fair-minded man is left. They are all murderers, turning against even their own brothers.

³ They go at their evil deeds with both hands, and how skilled they are in using them! The governor and judge alike demand bribes. The rich man pays them off and tells them whom to ruin. Justice is twisted between them. ⁴ Even the best of them are prickly as briars; the straightest is

more crooked than a hedge of thorns. But your judgment day is coming swiftly now; your time of punishment is almost here; confusion, destruction, and terror will be yours.

⁵ Don't trust anyone, not your best friend—not even your wife! ⁶ For the son despises his father; the daughter defies her mother; the bride curses her mother-in-law. Yes, a man's enemies will be found in his own home.

⁷ As for me, I look to the Lord for his help; I wait for God to save me; he will hear me. ⁸ Do not rejoice against me, O my enemy, for though I fall, I will rise again! When I sit in darkness, the Lord himself will be my Light. ⁹ I will be patient while the Lord punishes me, for I have sinned against him; then he will defend me from my enemies, and punish them for all the evil they have done to me. God will bring me out of my darkness into the light, and I will see his goodness. ¹⁰ Then my enemy will see that God is for me, and be ashamed for taunting me, "Where is that God of yours?" Now with my own eyes I see them trampled down like mud in the street.

¹¹ Your cities, people of God, will be rebuilt, much larger and more prosperous than before. ¹² Citizens of many lands will come and honor you—from Assyria to Egypt, and from Egypt to the Euphrates, from sea to sea and from distant hills and mountains.

¹³ But first comes terrible destruction to Israelᵃ for the great wickedness of her people. ¹⁴ O Lord, come and rule your people; lead your flock; make them live in peace and prosperity; let them enjoy the fertile pastures of Bashan and Gilead as they did long ago.

¹⁵ "Yes," replies the Lord, "I will do mighty miracles for you, like those when I brought you out of slavery in Egypt. ¹⁶ All the world will stand amazed at what I will do for you, and be embarrassed at their puny might. They will stand in silent awe, deaf to all around them." ¹⁷ They will see what snakes they are, lowly as worms crawling from their holes. They will come trembling out from their fortresses to meet

a See Haggai 1:6.   7 a Literally, "But the land will be desolate because of its inhabitants."

the Lord our God. They will fear him; they will stand in awe. [18] Where is another God like you, who pardons the sins of the survivors among his people? You cannot stay angry with your people, for you love to be merciful. [19] Once again you will have compassion on us. You will tread our sins beneath your feet; you will throw them into the depths of the ocean! [20] You will bless us as you promised Jacob long ago. You will set your love upon us, as you promised our father Abraham!

NAHUM

1 THIS IS THE vision God gave to Nahum, who lived in Elkosh, concerning the impending doom of Nineveh:[a]

[2] God is jealous over those he loves; that is why he takes vengeance on those who hurt them. He furiously destroys their enemies. [3] He is slow in getting angry, but when aroused, his power is incredible, and he does not easily forgive. He shows his power in the terrors of the cyclone and the raging storms; clouds are billowing dust beneath his feet! [4] At his command the oceans and rivers become dry sand; the lush pastures of Bashan and Carmel fade away; the green forests of Lebanon wilt. [5] In his presence mountains quake and hills melt; the earth crumbles and its people are destroyed.

[6] Who can stand before an angry God? His fury is like fire; the mountains tumble down before his anger.

[7] The Lord is good. When trouble comes, he is the place to go! And he knows everyone who trusts in him! [8] But he sweeps away his enemies with an overwhelming flood; he pursues them all night long.

[9] What are you thinking of, Nineveh, to defy the Lord? He will stop you with one blow; he won't need to strike again. [10] He tosses his enemies into the fire like a tangled mass of thorns. They burst into flames like straw. [11] Who is this king[b] of yours who dares to plot against the Lord? [12] But the Lord is not afraid of him! "Though he build his army millions strong," the Lord declares, "it will vanish.

"O my people, I have punished you enough! [13] Now I will break your chains and release you from the yoke of slavery to this Assyrian king."[b] [14] And to the king he says, "I have ordered an end to your dynasty; your sons will never sit upon your throne. And I will destroy your gods and temples, and I will bury you! For how you stink with sin!"

[15] See, the messengers come running down the mountains with glad news: "The invaders have been wiped out and we are safe!" O Judah, proclaim a day of thanksgiving, and worship only the Lord, as you have vowed. For this enemy from Nineveh will never come again. He is cut off forever; he will never be seen again.

2 NINEVEH, YOU ARE finished![a] You are already surrounded by enemy armies! Sound the alarm! Man the ramparts! Muster your defenses, full force, and keep a sharp watch for the enemy attack to begin! [2] For the land of the people of God lies empty and broken after your attacks but the Lord will restore their honor and power again!

[3] Shields flash red in the sunlight! The attack begins! See their scarlet uniforms! See their glittering chariots moving forward side by side, pulled by prancing steeds! [4] Your own chariots race recklessly along the streets and through the squares, darting like lightning, gleaming like torches. [5] The king shouts for his officers; they stumble in their haste, rushing to the walls to set up their defenses. [6] But too late! The river gates are open! The enemy has entered! The palace is in panic!

[7] The queen of Nineveh is brought out naked to the streets, and led away, a slave, with all her maidens weeping after her; lis-

---

a Nineveh was the Assyrian capital.　　b Implied in verse 1 and 3:18.　　2a This chapter predicts the events of the year 612 B.C. when the combined armies of the Babylonians and Medes sacked impregnable Nineveh.

ten to them mourn like doves, and beat their breasts! ⁸ Nineveh is like a leaking water tank! Her soldiers slip away, deserting her; she cannot hold them back. "Stop, stop," she shouts, but they keep on running. ⁹ Loot the silver! Loot the gold! There seems to be no end of treasures. Her vast, uncounted wealth is stripped away. ¹⁰ Soon the city is an empty shambles; hearts melt in horror; knees quake; her people stand aghast, pale-faced and trembling. ¹¹ Where now is that great Nineveh, lion of the nations, full of fight and boldness, where even the old and feeble, as well as the young and tender, lived unafraid? ¹² O Nineveh, once mighty lion! You crushed your enemies to feed your children and your wives, and filled your city and your homes with captured goods and slaves. ¹³ But now the Lord of Hosts has turned against you. He destroys your weapons. Your chariots stand there, silent and unused. Your finest youth lie dead. Never again will you bring back slaves from conquered nations; never again will you rule the earth.

3 WOE TO NINEVEH, City of Blood, full of lies, crammed with plunder. ² Listen! Hear the crack of the whips as the chariots rush forward against her, wheels rumbling, horses' hoofs pounding, and chariots clattering as they bump wildly through the streets! ³ See the flashing swords and glittering spears in the upraised arms of the cavalry! The dead are lying in the streets— bodies, heaps of bodies, everywhere. Men stumble over them, scramble to their feet, and fall again. ⁴ All this because Nineveh sold herself to the enemies of God. The beautiful and faithless city, mistress of deadly charms, enticed the nations with her beauty, then taught them all to worship her false gods,ᵃ bewitching people everywhere. ⁵ "No wonder I stand against you," says the Lord of Hosts; "and now all the earth will see your nakedness and shame. ⁶ I will cover you with filth and show the world

how really vile you are." ⁷ All who see you will shrink back in horror: "Nineveh lies in utter ruin." Yet no one anywhere regrets your fate! ⁸ Are you any better than Thebes,ᵇ straddling the Nile, protected on all sides by the river? ⁹ Ethiopia and the whole land of Egypt were her mighty allies, and she could call on them for infinite assistance, as well as Put and Libya. ¹⁰ Yet Thebes fell and her people were led off as slaves; her babies were dashed to death against the stones of the streets. Soldiers drew straws to see who would get her officers as servants. All her leaders were bound in chains. ¹¹ Nineveh, too, will stagger like a drunkard and hide herself in fear. ¹² All your forts will fall. They will be devoured like firstripe figs that fall into the mouths of those who shake the trees. ¹³ Your troops will be weak and helpless as women. The gates of your land will be opened wide to the enemy and set on fire and burned. ¹⁴ Get ready for the siege! Store up water! Strengthen the forts! Prepare many bricks for repairing your walls! Go into the pits to trample the clay, and pack it in the molds! ¹⁵ But in the middle of your preparations, the fire will devour you; the sword will cut you down; the enemy will consume you like young locusts that eat up everything before them. There is no escape, though you multiply like grasshoppers. ¹⁶ Merchants, numerous as stars, filled your city with vast wealth, but your enemies swarm like locusts and carry it away. ¹⁷ Your princes and officials crowd together like grasshoppers in the hedges in the cold, but all of them will flee away and disappear, like locusts when the sun comes up and warms the earth. ¹⁸ O Assyrian king, your princes lie dead in the dust; your people are scattered across the mountains; there is no shepherd now to gather them. ¹⁹ There is no healing for your wound—it is far too deep to cure. All who hear your fate will clap their hands for joy, for where can one be found who has not suffered from your cruelty?

---

a Literally, "who betrays nations with her harlotries." years before this prophecy.

b Thebes was conquered by the Assyrians fifty-one

Bob Combs

What's the Strategy?

If you don't know much about chess, chances are you won't learn much by watching. The players sit there wordlessly, intricate plots and counterplots locked inside their heads. Only an occasional "Check" breaks the silence; then, finally, one of them moves a piece, says "Checkmate"—and the war is over.

How do you find out the strategies? Like Habakkuk watching the course of world events in the last days of Judah's kingdom, you have to ask. Habakkuk knew his decadent country was doomed, but couldn't see why God would use the Chaldeans as his hatchet men, since they were even worse. This book is the record of how God explained his moves.

Zephaniah, who prophesied at about the same time, outlined God's plans even further. After a scorching description of Jerusalem's fall, he comes through in chapter three with the rationale: Jehovah is purifying his people for a future era of happiness and peace.

God is under no obligation to explain his strategy to slow, impertinent humans, of course . . . but it's a great help when he does.

HABAKKUK

1 THIS IS THE message that came to the prophet Habakkuk in a vision from God:

² O Lord, how long must I call for help before you will listen? I shout to you in vain; there is no answer. "Help! Murder!" I cry, but no one comes to save. ³ Must I forever see this sin and sadness all around me?

Wherever I look there is oppression and bribery and men who love to argue and to fight. ⁴ The law is not enforced and there is no justice given in the courts, for the wicked far outnumber the righteous, and bribes and trickery prevail.

⁵ The Lord replied: "Look, and be amazed! You will be astounded at what I am about to do! For I am going to do something in your own lifetime that you will have to see to believe. ⁶ I am raising a new force on the world scene, the Chaldeans,ᵃ a cruel and violent nation who will march across the world and conquer it. ⁷ They are notorious for their cruelty. They do as they like, and no one can interfere. ⁸ Their horses are swifter than leopards. They are a fierce people, more fierce than wolves at dusk. Their cavalry move proudly forward from a distant land; like eagles they come swooping down to pounce upon their prey. ⁹ All opposition melts away before the terror of their presence. They collect captives like sand.

¹⁰ "They scoff at kings and princes, and scorn their forts. They simply heap up dirt against their walls and capture them! ¹¹ᵇ They sweep past like wind and are gone, but their guilt is deep, for they claim their power is from their gods."

¹² O Lord my God, my Holy One, you who are eternal—is your plan in all of this to wipe us out? Surely not! O God our Rock, you have decreed the rise of these Chaldeans to chasten and correct us for our awful sins. ¹³ We are wicked, but they far more! Will you, who cannot allow sin in any form, stand idly by while they swallow us up?

Should you be silent while the wicked destroy those who are better than they? ¹⁴ Are we but fish, to be caught and killed? Are we but creeping things that have no leader to defend them from their foes? ¹⁵ Must we be strung up on their hooks and dragged out in their nets, while they rejoice? ¹⁶ Then they will worship their nets and burn incense before them! "These are the gods who make us rich," they'll say.

¹⁷ Will you let them get away with this forever? Will they succeed forever in their heartless wars?

2 I WILL CLIMB my watchtower now, and wait to see what answer God will give to my complaint.

² And the Lord said to me, "Write my answer on a billboard,ᵃ large and clear, so that anyone can read it at a glance and rush to tell the others. ³ But these things I plan won't happen right away. Slowly, steadily, surely, the time approaches when the vision will be fulfilled. If it seems slow, do not despair, for these things will surely come to pass. Just be patient! They will not be overdue a single day!

⁴ "Note this: Wicked men trust themselves alone [as these Chaldeans doᵇ], and fail; but the righteous man trusts in me, and lives!ᶜ ⁵ What's more, these arrogant Chaldeans are betrayed by all their wine, for it is treacherous. In their greed they have collected many nations, but like death and hell, they are never satisfied. ⁶ The time is coming when all their captives will taunt them, saying: 'You robbers! At last justice has caught up with you! Now you will get your just deserts for your oppression and extortion!'

⁷ "Suddenly your debtors will rise up in anger and turn on you and take all you have, while you stand trembling and helpless. ⁸ You have ruined many nations; now they will ruin you. You murderers! You have filled the countryside with lawlessness and all the cities too.

---

a Chaldeans: a tribe of Semites living between Babylon and the Persian Gulf, who began to assert themselves against the Assyrians around 630 B.C., and twenty-five years later had mastered most of the Near East.
b The Hebrew text of this verse is very uncertain.   2a Literally, "on the tablets."   b Implied.
c Or, "shall live by his faithfulness."

⁹ "Woe to you for getting rich by evil means, attempting to live beyond the reach of danger. ¹⁰ By the murders you commit, you have shamed your name and forfeited your lives. ¹¹ The very stones in the walls of your homes cry out against you, and the beams in the ceilings echo what they say.

¹² "Woe to you who build cities with money gained from murdering and robbery! ¹³ Has not the Lord decreed that godless nations' gains will turn to ashes in their hands? They work so hard, but all in vain! ¹⁴ ("The time will come when all the earth is filled, as the waters fill the sea, with an awareness of the glory of the Lord.)

¹⁵ "Woe to you for making your neighboring lands reel and stagger like drunkards beneath your blows, and then gloating over their nakedness and shame. ¹⁶ Soon your own glory will be replaced by shame. Drink down God's judgment on yourselves. Stagger and fall! ¹⁷ You cut down the forests of Lebanon—now you will be cut down! You terrified the wild animals you caught in your traps—now terror will strike you because of all your murdering and violence in cities everywhere.

¹⁸ "What profit was there in worshiping all your man-made idols? What a foolish lie that they could help! What fools you were to trust what you yourselves had made. ¹⁹ Woe to those who command their lifeless wooden idols to arise and save them, who call out to the speechless stone to tell them what to do. Can images speak for God? They are overlaid with gold and silver, but there is no breath at all inside!

²⁰ "But the Lord is in his holy Temple; let all the earth be silent before him."

3 THIS IS THE prayer of triumph[a] that Habakkuk sang before the Lord:

² O Lord, now I have heard your report, and I worship you in awe for the fearful things you are going to do. In this time of our deep need, begin again to help us, as you did in years gone by. Show us your power to save us. In your wrath, remember mercy.

³ I see God moving across the deserts from Mount Sinai.[b] His brilliant splendor fills the earth and sky; his glory fills the heavens, and the earth is full of his praise! What a wonderful God he is! ⁴ From his hands flash rays of brilliant light. He rejoices[c] in his awesome power. ⁵ Pestilence marches before him; plague follows close behind. ⁶ He stops; he stands still for a moment, gazing at the earth. Then he shakes the nations, scattering the everlasting mountains and leveling the hills. His power is just the same as always! ⁷ I see the people of Cushan and of Midian in mortal fear.

⁸,⁹ [d]Was it in anger, Lord, you smote the rivers and parted the sea? Were you displeased with them? No, you were sending your chariots of salvation! All saw your power! Then springs burst forth upon the earth at your command! ¹⁰ The mountains watched and trembled. Onward swept the raging water. The mighty deep cried out, announcing its surrender to the Lord.[e] ¹¹ The lofty sun and moon began to fade, obscured by brilliance from your arrows and the flashing of your glittering spear.

¹² You marched across the land in awesome anger, and trampled down the nations in your wrath. ¹³ You went out to save your chosen people. You crushed the head of the wicked and laid bare his bones from head to toe. ¹⁴ You destroyed with their own weapons those who came out like a whirlwind, thinking Israel would be an easy prey.

¹⁵ Your horsemen marched across the sea; the mighty waters piled high. ¹⁶ I tremble when I hear all this; my lips quiver with fear. My legs give way beneath me and I shake in terror. I will quietly wait for the day of trouble to come upon the people who invade us.

¹⁷ Even though the fig trees are all destroyed, and there is neither blossom left nor fruit, and though the olive crops all fail, and the fields lie barren; even if the flocks die in the fields and the cattle barns are empty, ¹⁸ yet I will rejoice in the Lord; I will be happy in the God of my salvation. ¹⁹ The

---

a Literally, "according to Shigionoth"—thought by some to mean a mournful dirge.　　b Literally, "from Teman . . . from Mount Paran."　　c Or, "He veils his power."　　d Literally, "Was the Lord displeased against the rivers? Were you angry with them? Was your wrath against their sin that you rode upon your horses? Your chariots were salvation. Your bow was pulled from its sheath and you put arrows to the string. You ribboned the earth with rivers."　　e Literally, "and lifts high its hands."

Lord God is my Strength, and he will give me the speed of a deer and bring me safely over the mountains.

(A note to the choir director: When singing this ode, the choir is to be accompanied by stringed instruments.)

ZEPHANIAH

1 SUBJECT: A MESSAGE from the Lord. *To:* Zephaniah (son of Cushi, grandson of Gedaliah, great-grandson of Amariah, and great-great-grandson of Hezekiah). *When:* During the reign of Josiah (son of Amon) king of Judah.[a]

² "I will sweep away everything in all your land," says the Lord. "I will destroy it to the ground. ³ I will sweep away both men and animals alike. Mankind and all the idols that he worships—all will vanish. Even the birds of the air and the fish in the sea will perish. ⁴ I will crush Judah and Jerusalem with my fist, and destroy every remnant of those who worship Baal; I will put an end to their idolatrous priests, so that even the memory of them will disappear. ⁵ They go up on their roofs and bow to the sun, moon and stars. They 'follow the Lord,' but worship Molech, too! I will destroy them. ⁶ And I will destroy those who formerly worshiped the Lord, but now no longer do, and those who never loved him and never wanted to."

⁷ Stand in silence in the presence of the Lord. For the awesome Day of his Judgment has come; he has prepared a great slaughter of his people and has chosen their executioners.[b] ⁸ "On that Day of Judgment I will punish the leaders and princes of Judah, and all others wearing heathen clothing.[c] ⁹ Yes, I will punish those who follow heathen customs and who rob and kill to fill their masters' homes with evil gain of violence and fraud. ¹⁰ A cry of alarm will begin at the farthest gate of Jerusalem, coming closer and closer until the noise of the advancing army reaches the very top of the hill where the city is built.

¹¹ "Wail in sorrow, you people of Jerusalem. All your greedy businessmen, all your loan sharks—all will die.

¹² "I will search with lanterns in Jerusalem's darkest corners to find and punish those who sit contented in their sins, indifferent to God, thinking he will let them alone. ¹³ They are the very ones whose property will be plundered by the enemy, whose homes will be ransacked; they will never have a chance to live in the new homes they have built. They will never drink wine from the vineyards they have planted."

¹⁴ "That terrible day is near. Swiftly it comes—a day when strong men will weep bitterly. ¹⁵ It is a day of the wrath of God poured out; it is a day of terrible distress and anguish, a day of ruin and desolation, of darkness, gloom, clouds, blackness, ¹⁶ Trumpet calls and battle cries; down go the walled cities and strongest battlements!

¹⁷ "I will make you as helpless as a blind man searching for a path, because you have sinned against the Lord; therefore your blood will be poured out into the dust and your bodies will lie there rotting on the ground."

¹⁸ Your silver and gold will be of no use to you in that day of the Lord's wrath. You cannot ransom yourselves with it.[d] For the whole land will be devoured by the fire of his jealousy. He will make a speedy riddance of all the people of Judah.

2 GATHER TOGETHER AND pray, you shameless nation, ² while there still is time—before judgment begins, and your opportunity is blown away like chaff; before the fierce anger of the Lord falls and the terrible day of his wrath begins. ³ Beg him to save you, all who are humble—all who

---

a Note: The Great Revival under King Josiah followed about ten years after this prophecy, and then, a dozen years later, the deportation and exile. The prophet Jeremiah was active during this same period.
b Literally, "He has prepared a sacrifice and sanctified his guests."   c i.e., showing their desire for foreign gods and foreign ways, and their contempt for the Lord.   d Implied.

have tried to obey.

Walk humbly and do what is right; perhaps even yet the Lord will protect you from his wrath in that day of doom.

⁴ Gaza, Ashkelon, Ashdod, Ekron— these Philistine cities, too, will be rooted out and left in desolation. ⁵ And woe to you Philistines[a] living on the coast and in the land of Canaan, for the judgment is against you, too. The Lord will destroy you until not one of you is left. ⁶ The coastland will become a pasture, a place of shepherd camps and folds for sheep.

⁷ There the little remnant of the tribe of Judah will be pastured. They will lie down to rest in the abandoned houses in Ashkelon. For the Lord God will visit his people in kindness and restore their prosperity again.

⁸ "I have heard the taunts of the people of Moab and Ammon, mocking my people and invading their land. ⁹ Therefore as I live," says the Lord of Hosts, God of Israel, "Moab and Ammon will be destroyed like Sodom and Gomorrah, and become a place of stinging nettles and salt pits and eternal desolation; those of my people who are left will plunder and possess them." ¹⁰ They will receive the wages of their pride, for they have scoffed at the people of the Lord of Hosts. ¹¹ The Lord will do terrible things to them. He will starve out all those gods of foreign powers, and everyone shall worship him, each in his own land throughout the world.

¹² You Ethiopians, too, will be slain by his sword, ¹³ and so will the lands of the north; he will destroy Assyria and make its great capital Nineveh a desolate wasteland like a wilderness. ¹⁴ That once proud city will become a pastureland for sheep. All sorts of wild animals will have their homes in her. Hedgehogs will burrow there; the vultures and the owls will live among the ruins of her palaces, hooting from the gaping windows; the ravens will croak from her doors. All her cedar paneling will lie open

to the wind and weather.

¹⁵ This is the fate of that vast, prosperous city that lived in such security, that said to herself, "In all the world there is no city as great as I." But now—see how she has become a place of utter ruins, a place for animals to live! Everyone passing that way will mock, or shake his head in disbelief.[b]

3 WOE TO FILTHY, sinful Jerusalem, city of violence and crime. ² In her pride she won't listen even to the voice of God. No one can tell her anything; she refuses all correction. She does not trust the Lord, nor seek for God.

³ Her leaders are like roaring lions hunting for their victims—out for everything that they can get. Her judges are like ravenous wolves at evening time, who by dawn have left no trace of their prey.

⁴ Her "prophets" are liars seeking their own gain; her priests defile the Temple by their disobedience to God's laws.

⁵ But the Lord is there within the city, and he does no wrong. Day by day his justice is more evident, but no one heeds—the wicked know no shame.

⁶ "I have cut off many nations, laying them waste to their farthest borders; I have left their streets in silent ruin and their cities deserted without a single survivor to remember what happened. ⁷ I thought, 'Surely they will listen to me now—surely they will heed my warnings, so that I'll not need to strike again.' But no; however much I punish them, they continue all their evil ways from dawn to dusk and dusk to dawn." ⁸ But the Lord says, "Be patient; the time is coming soon when I will stand up and accuse these evil nations. For it is my decision to gather together the kingdoms of the earth, and pour out my fiercest anger and wrath upon them. All the earth shall be devoured with the fire of my jealousy.

⁹ "At that time I will change the speech of my returning people to pure Hebrew[a] so that all can worship the Lord together.

a Literally, "Cherethites (or Cretans)." With the Philistines, they were part of a great wave of immigrants to the southern coast of Palestine around 1200 B.C.   b "Nothing then seemed more improbable than that the capital of so vast an empire, a city of sixty miles around with walls 100 feet high and so thick that three chariots could go abreast on them, and with 1500 towers, should be so totally destroyed that its site is with difficulty discovered."—Jamieson, Fausset and Brown Commentary   3a Literally, ". . . I will change the speech of the peoples to a pure speech. . . ." See Isaiah 19:18.

[10] Those who live far beyond the rivers of Ethiopia will come with their offerings, asking me to be their God again. [11] And then you will no longer need to be ashamed of yourselves, for you will no longer be rebels against me. I will remove all your proud and arrogant men from among you; there will be no pride or haughtiness on my holy mountain. [12] Those who are left will be the poor and the humble, and they will trust in the name of the Lord. [13] They will not be sinners, full of lies and deceit. They will live quietly, in peace, and lie down in safety, and no one will make them afraid."

[14] Sing, O daughter of Zion; shout, O Israel; be glad and rejoice with all your heart, O daughter of Jerusalem. [15] For the Lord will remove his hand of judgment, and disperse the armies of your enemy. And the Lord himself, the King of Israel, will live among you! At last your troubles will be over—you need fear no more.

[16] On that day the announcement to Jerusalem will be, "Cheer up, don't be afraid. [17,18] For the Lord your God has arrived to live among you. He is a mighty Savior. He will give you victory. He will rejoice over you in great gladness; he will love you and not accuse you." Is that a joyous choir I hear? No, it is the Lord himself exulting over you in happy song: "I have gathered your wounded and taken away your reproach. [19] And I will deal severely with all who have oppressed you. I will save the weak and helpless ones, and bring together those who were chased away. I will give glory to my former exiles, mocked and shamed.

[20] "At that time, I will gather you together and bring you home again, and give you a good name, a name of distinction among all the peoples of the earth, and they will praise you when I restore your fortunes before your very eyes," says the Lord.

Horst Ehricht Photos

Don't Give Up Now!

OLD VOLVOS NEVER DIE

A vintage Volvo proves its toughness in an ice race on a hard-frozen Canadian lake. Far from the smooth asphalt and balmy temperatures of Daytona and Sebring, race drivers brave the freezing cold to get their engines started and keep them running around the snowy "track." The speed isn't much—no more than 12 mph can send you spinning gracefully out of some curves!—but ice racing has a hard core of enthusiasts who dig the fancy steering and the battle against freezing gas lines and other hazards they never thought of down south.

It was an unusual set of obstacles for the returning Jewish exiles, too, as they tried to rebuild God's Old Testament house. Contrasted with the high-powered way Solomon had his temple built 450 years earlier, Ezra's workers looked like they were in slow motion. But they didn't have all of the royal forests and federal work crews that Solomon had used; they were doing this on a much smaller scale, and all by themselves.

Eventually, they came to a standstill—and that's when God sent two prophets, Haggai and Zechariah, to get things moving.

The new temple was completed, and the struggling colony had God at the center of things once again. As Zechariah put it, "Not by might, nor by power, but by my Spirit, says the Lord of Hosts— you will succeed because of my Spirit, though you are few and weak" (4:6).

HAGGAI

1 SUBJECT: A MESSAGE from the Lord.
To: Haggai the prophet, who delivered it to Zerubbabel (son of She-alti-el), governor of Judah; and to Joshua (son of Josedech), the High Priest—for it was addressed to them.[a]

When: In late August of the second year of the reign of King Darius I.

[2] "Why is everyone saying it is not the right time for rebuilding my Temple?" asks the Lord.

[3,4] His reply to them is this: "Is it then the right time for you to live in luxurious homes, when the Temple lies in ruins? [5] Look at the result: [6] You plant much but harvest little. You have scarcely enough to eat or drink, and not enough clothes to keep you warm. Your income disappears, as though you were putting it into pockets filled with holes!

[7] "Think it over," says the Lord of Hosts. "Consider how you have acted, and what has happened as a result! [8] Then go up

into the mountains and bring down timber, and rebuild my Temple, and I will be pleased with it and appear there in my glory," says the Lord.

[9] "You hope for much but get so little. And when you bring it home, I blow it away—it doesn't last at all. Why? Because my Temple lies in ruins and you don't care. Your only concern is your own fine homes. [10] That is why I am holding back the rains from heaven and giving you such scant crops. [11] In fact, I have called for a drought upon the land, yes, and in the highlands, too; a drought to wither the grain and grapes and olives and all your other crops, a drought to starve both you and all your cattle, and ruin everything you have worked so hard to get."

[12] Then Zerubbabel (son of She-alti-el), the governor of Judah, and Joshua (son of Josedech), the High Priest, and the few people remaining in the land obeyed Haggai's message from the Lord their God; they be-

a Note: They were among the exiles who had returned from Babylon to rebuild Jerusalem.

gan to worship him in earnest.

[13] Then the Lord told them (again sending the message through Haggai, his messenger), "I am with you; I will bless you." [14,15] And the Lord gave them a desire to rebuild his Temple; so they all gathered in early September of the second year of King Darius' reign, and volunteered their help.

2 IN EARLY OCTOBER of the same year, the Lord sent them this message through Haggai:

[2] Ask this question of the governor and High Priest and everyone left in the land:

[3] "Who among you can remember the Temple as it was before? How glorious it was! In comparison, it is nothing now, is it? [4] But take courage, O Zerubbabel and Joshua and all the people; take courage and work, for 'I am with you,' says the Lord of Hosts. [5] 'For I promised when you left Egypt that my Spirit would remain among you; so don't be afraid.'

[6] "For the Lord of Hosts says, 'In just a little while I will begin to shake the heavens and earth—and the oceans, too, and the dry land— [7] I will shake all nations, and the Desire of All Nations[a] shall come to this Temple, and I will fill this place with my glory,' says the Lord of Hosts. [8,9] 'The future splendor of this Temple will be greater than the splendor of the first one! For I have plenty of silver and gold to do it! And here I will give peace,'[b] says the Lord."

[10] In early December, in the second year of the reign of King Darius, this message came from the Lord through Haggai the prophet:

[11] Ask the priests this question about the law: [12] "If one of you is carrying a holy sacrifice in his robes, and happens to brush against some bread or wine or meat, will it too become holy?"

"No," the priests replied. "Holiness does not pass to other things that way."

[13] Then Haggai asked, "But if someone touches a dead person, and so becomes ceremonially impure, and then brushes against something, does it become contaminated?"

And the priests answered, "Yes."

[14] Haggai then made his meaning clear. "You people," he said (speaking for the Lord), "were contaminating your sacrifices by living with selfish attitudes and evil hearts—and not only your sacrifices, but everything else that you did as a 'service' to me. [15] And so everything you did went wrong. But all is different now, because you have begun to build the Temple. [16,17] Before, when you expected a twenty-bushel crop, there were only ten. When you came to draw fifty gallons from the olive press, there were only twenty. I rewarded all your labor with rust and mildew and hail. Yet, even so, you refused to return to me," says the Lord.

[18,19] "But now note this: From today, this 24th day of the month,[c] as the foundation of the Lord's Temple is finished, and from this day onward, I will bless you. Notice, I am giving you this promise now before you have even begun to rebuild the Temple structure, and before you have harvested your grain, and before the grapes and figs and pomegranates and olives have produced their next crops: *From this day I will bless you.*"

[20] Another message came to Haggai from the Lord that same day:

[21] Tell Zerubbabel, the governor of Judah, "I am about to shake the heavens and the earth, [22] and to overthrow thrones and destroy the strength of the kingdoms of the nations. I will overthrow their armed might, and brothers and companions will kill each other. [23] But when that happens, I will take you, O Zerubbabel my servant, and honor you like a signet ring upon my finger; for I have specially chosen you," says the Lord of Hosts.

---

a i.e., Christ, the Messiah. Literally, "The Treasures" or "that which is choice." But many commentators prefer this rendering: "The treasures of the nations will pour into this Temple, and I will fill it with splendor."
b Peace with God through Christ who, 500 years later, came often to this Temple.   c "The 24th day of Kislev." This corresponds to early in our December.

ZECHARIAH

1 SUBJECT: MESSAGES FROM *the Lord.*

These messages from the Lord were given to Zechariah (son of Berechiah, and grandson of Iddo the prophet) in early November of the second year of the reign of King Darius. [2] The Lord of Hosts was very angry with your fathers. [3] But he will turn again and favor you if only you return to him. [4] Don't be like your fathers were! The earlier prophets pled in vain with them to turn from all their evil ways.

"Come, return to me," the Lord God said. But no, they wouldn't listen; they paid no attention at all.

[5,6] Your fathers and their prophets are now long dead, but remember the lesson they learned, that *God's Word endures!* It caught up with them and punished them. Then at last they repented.

"We have gotten what we deserved from God," they said. "He has done just what he warned us he would."

[7] The following February, still in the second year of the reign of King Darius, another message from the Lord came to Zechariah (son of Berechiah and grandson of Iddo the prophet), in a vision in the night: [8] I saw a Man sitting on a red horse that was standing among the myrtle trees beside a river. Behind him were other horses, red and bay and white, each with its rider.[a]

[9] An angel stood beside me, and I asked him, "Sir, what are all those horses for?"

"I'll tell you," he replied.

[10] Then the rider on the red horse—he was the Angel of the Lord—answered me, "The Lord has sent them to patrol the earth for him."

[11] Then the other riders reported to the Angel of the Lord, "We have patrolled the whole earth, and everywhere there is prosperity and peace."

[12] Upon hearing this, the Angel of the Lord prayed this prayer: "O Lord of Hosts, for seventy years your anger has raged against Jerusalem and the cities of Judah. How long will it be until you again show mercy to them?"

[13] And the Lord answered the angel who stood beside me, speaking words of comfort and assurance.

[14] Then the angel said, "Shout out this message from the Lord of Hosts: Don't you think I care about what has happened to Judah and Jerusalem? I am as jealous as a husband for his captive wife. [15] I am very angry with the heathen nations sitting around at ease, for I was only a little displeased with my people, but the nations afflicted them far beyond my intentions. [16] Therefore the Lord declares: I have returned to Jerusalem filled with mercy; my Temple will be rebuilt, says the Lord of Hosts, and so will all Jerusalem. [17] Say it again: The Lord of Hosts declares that the cities of Israel will again overflow with prosperity, and the Lord will again comfort Jerusalem and bless her and live in her."

[18] Then I looked and saw four animal horns!

[19] "What are these?" I asked the angel.

He replied, "They represent the four world powers that have scattered Judah, Israel, and Jerusalem."

[20] Then the Lord showed me four blacksmiths.

[21] "What have these men come to do?" I asked.

The angel replied, "They have come to take hold of the four horns that scattered Judah so terribly, and to pound them on the anvil and throw them away."

2 WHEN I LOOKED around me again, I saw a man carrying a yardstick in his hand.

[2] "Where are you going?" I asked.

"To measure Jerusalem," he said. "I want to see whether it is big enough for all the people!"

[3] Then the angel who was talking to me went over to meet another angel coming toward him.

[4] "Go tell this young man," said the other angel, "that Jerusalem will some day

---

a Implied.

be so full of people that she won't have room enough for all! Many will live outside the city walls, with all their many cattle —and yet they will be safe. ⁵ For the Lord himself will be a wall of fire protecting them and all Jerusalem; he will be the glory of the city.

⁶,⁷ " 'Come, flee from the land of the north, from Babylon,' says the Lord to all his exiles there; 'I scattered you to the winds but I will bring you back again. Escape, escape to Zion now!' says the Lord.

⁸ "The Lord of Glory has sent meᵃ against the nations that oppressed you, for he who harms you sticks his finger in Jehovah's eye!

⁹ " 'I will smash them with my fist and their slaves will be their rulers! *Then you will know it was the Lord of Hosts who sent me.* ¹⁰ Sing, Jerusalem, and rejoice! For I have come to live among you,' says the Lord. ¹¹,¹² 'At that time many nations will be converted to the Lord, and they too shall be my people; I will live among them all. *Then you will know it was the Lord of Hosts who sent me to you.* And Judah shall be the Lord's inheritance in the Holy Land, for God shall once more choose to bless Jerusalem.'

¹³ "Be silent, all mankind, before the Lord, for he has come to earth from heaven, from his holy home."

3 THEN THE ANGEL showed me (in my vision) Joshua the High Priest standing before the Angel of the Lord; and Satan was there too, at the Angel's right hand, accusing Joshua of many things.

² And the Lord said to Satan, "I reject your accusations,ᵃ Satan; yes, I, the Lord, for I have decided to be merciful to Jerusalem—I rebuke you. I have decreed mercy to Joshua and his nation; they are like a burning stick pulled out of the fire."

³ Joshua's clothing was filthy as he stood before the Angel of the Lord.

⁴ Then the Angel said to the others standing there, "Remove his filthy cloth-

ing." And turning to Joshua he said, "See, I have taken away your sins, and now I am giving you these fine new clothes."

⁵,⁶ Then I said, "Please, could he also have a clean turban on his head?" So they gave him one.

Then the Angel of the Lord spoke very solemnly to Joshua and said, ⁷ "The Lord of Hosts declares: 'If you will follow the paths I set for you and do all I tell you to, then I will put you in charge of my Temple, to keep it holy; and I will let you walk in and out of my presence with these angels. ⁸ Listen to me, O Joshua the High Priest, and all you other priests, you are illustrations of the good things to come. Don't you see?—Joshua represents my servant the Branchᵇ whom I will send. ⁹ He will be the Foundation Stone of the Temple that Joshua is standing beside, and I will engrave this inscription on it seven times:ᶜ *I will remove the sins of this land in a single day.* ¹⁰ And after that,' the Lord of Hosts declares, 'you will all live in peace and prosperity and each of you will own a home of your own where you can invite your neighbors.' "

4 THEN THE ANGEL who had been talking with me woke me, as though I had been asleep.

² "What do you see now?" he asked.

I answered, "I see a golden lampstand holding seven lamps, and at the top there is a reservoir for the olive oil that feeds the lamps, flowing into them through seven tubes. ³ And I see two olive trees carved upon the lampstand, one on each side of the reservoir. ⁴ What is it, sir?" I asked. "What does this mean?"

⁵ "Don't you really know?" the angel asked.

"No, sir," I said, "I don't."

⁶ Then he said, "This is God's message to Zerubbabel:ᵃ 'Not by might, nor by power, but by my Spirit, says the Lord of Hosts—you will succeed because of my Spirit, though you are few and weak.'

---

a This passage evidently refers to the Messiah, here seen as one of the Godhead.   3a Literally, "The Lord rebuke you, O Satan; even the Lord, who has chosen Jerusalem, rebuke you. Is not this a brand plucked out of the fire?"   b i.e., the Messiah, Christ.   c Literally, "See the stone with seven facets I have set before Joshua, and I will engrave its inscription."   4a Governor of Judah, who was given the responsibility for rebuilding the Temple. See Haggai 1:1; 2:23, etc.

⁷ Therefore no mountain, however high, can stand before Zerubbabel! For it will flatten out before him! And Zerubbabel will finish building this Temple[b] with mighty shouts of thanksgiving for God's mercy, declaring that all was done by grace alone."[c]

⁸ Another message that I received from the Lord said:

⁹ "Zerubbabel laid the foundation of this Temple, and he will complete it. (Then you will know these messages are from God, the Lord of Hosts.) ¹⁰ Do not despise this small beginning, for the eyes of the Lord rejoice to see the work begin, to see the plumbline in the hand of Zerubbabel. For these seven lamps represent the eyes of the Lord that see everywhere around the world."

¹¹ Then I asked him about the two olive trees on each side of the lampstand, ¹² and about the two olive branches that emptied oil into golden bowls through two golden tubes.

¹³ "Don't you know?" he asked.

"No, sir," I said.

¹⁴ Then he told me, "They represent the two anointed ones who assist the Lord of all the earth."

5 I LOOKED UP again and saw a scroll flying through the air.

² "What do you see?" he asked.

"A flying scroll!" I replied. "It appears to be about thirty feet long and fifteen feet wide!"

³ "This scroll," he told me, "represents the words of God's curse going out over the entire land. It says that all who steal and lie have been judged and sentenced to death."

⁴ "I am sending this curse into the home of every thief and everyone who swears falsely by my name," says the Lord of Hosts. "And my curse shall remain upon his home and completely destroy it."

⁵ Then the angel left me for awhile, but he returned and said, "Look up! Something is traveling through the sky!"

⁶ "What is it?" I asked.

He replied, "It is a bushel basket filled with the sin prevailing everywhere throughout the land."

⁷ Suddenly the heavy lead cover on the basket was lifted off, and I could see a woman sitting inside the basket!

⁸ He said, "She represents wickedness," and he pushed her back into the basket and clamped down the heavy lid again.

⁹ Then I saw two women flying toward us, with wings like those of a stork. And they took the bushel basket and flew off with it, high in the sky.

¹⁰ "Where are they taking her?" I asked the angel.

¹¹ He replied, "To Babylon[a] where she belongs and where she will stay!"

6 THEN I LOOKED up again and saw four chariots coming from between what looked like two mountains made of brass. ² The first chariot was pulled by red horses, the second by black ones, ³ the third by white horses and the fourth by dappled-greys.

⁴ "And what are these, sir?" I asked the angel.

⁵ He replied, "These are the four heavenly spirits who stand before the Lord of all the earth; they are going out to do his work. ⁶ The chariot pulled by the black horses will go north, and the one pulled by white horses will follow it there,[a] while the dappled-greys will go south. ⁷ The red[b] horses were impatient to be off, to patrol back and forth across the earth, so the Lord said, "Go. Begin your patrol." So they left at once. ⁸ Then the Lord summoned me and said, "Those who went north have executed my judgment and quieted my anger there."

⁹ In another message the Lord said:

¹⁰,¹¹ "Heldai, Tobijah, and Jedaiah will bring gifts of silver and gold from the Jews exiled in Babylon. The same day they arrive, meet them at the home of Josiah (son of Zephaniah), where they will stay. Accept their gifts and make from them a crown from the silver and gold. Then put the crown on the head of Joshua (son of Josedech) the High Priest. ¹² Tell him that the Lord of Hosts says, 'You represent the Man who will come, whose name is "The

---

b Literally, "He will bring forth the capstone."   c Or, "with mighty shouts, 'How beautiful it is!' " or, "The Lord bless it!"   5a Babylon had, by the time of Zechariah, become a symbol, the center of world idolatry and wickedness.   6a Or, "will go west."   b "Red" implied.

Branch"—he will grow up from himself[c] —and will build the Temple of the Lord. [13] To him belongs the royal title. He will rule both as King and as Priest, with perfect harmony between the two!'

[14] "Then put the crown in the Temple of the Lord, to honor those who gave it—Heldai, Tobijah, Jedaiah, and also Josiah. [15] These three who have come from so far away represent many others who will some day come from distant lands to rebuild the Temple of the Lord. And when this happens you will know my messages have been from God, the Lord of Hosts. But none of this will happen unless you carefully obey the commandments of the Lord your God."

7 ANOTHER MESSAGE CAME to me from the Lord in late November of the fourth year of the reign of King Darius.

[2] The Jews of the city of Bethel had sent a group of men headed by Sharezer, the chief administrative officer of the king, and Regem-melech, to the Lord's Temple at Jerusalem, to seek his blessing, [3] and to speak with the priests and prophets about whether they must continue their traditional custom of fasting and mourning during the month of August each year, as they had been doing so long.

[4] This was the Lord's reply:

[5] "When you return to Bethel, say to all your people and your priests, 'During those seventy years of exile when you fasted and mourned in August and October, were you really in earnest about leaving your sins behind, and coming back to me? No, not at all! [6] And even now in your holy feasts to God, you don't think of me, but only of the food and fellowship and fun. [7] Long years ago, when Jerusalem was prosperous and her southern suburbs out along the plain were filled with people, the prophets warned them that this attitude would surely lead to ruin, as it has.' "

[8,9] Then this message from the Lord came to Zechariah. "Tell them to be honest and fair—and not to take bribes—and to be merciful and kind to everyone. [10] Tell them to stop oppressing widows and orphans, foreigners and poor people, and to stop plot-

ting evil against each other. [11] Your fathers would not listen to this message. They turned stubbornly away and put their fingers in their ears to keep from hearing me. [12] They hardened their hearts like flint, afraid to hear the words that God, the Lord of Hosts, commanded them—the laws he had revealed to them by his Spirit through the early prophets. That is why such great wrath came down on them from God. [13] I called but they refused to listen, so when they cried to me, I turned away. [14] I scattered them as with a whirlwind among the far-off nations. Their land became desolate; no one even traveled through it; the Pleasant Land lay bare and blighted."

8 AGAIN THE LORD'S message came to me:

[2] "The Lord of Hosts says, I am greatly concerned—yes, furiously angry—because of all that Jerusalem's enemies have done to her. [3] Now I am going to return to my land and I, myself, will live within Jerusalem, and Jerusalem shall be called 'The Faithful City,' and 'The Holy Mountain,' and 'The Mountain of the Lord of Hosts.' "

[4] The Lord of Hosts declares that Jerusalem will have peace and prosperity so long that there will once again be aged men and women hobbling through her streets on canes, [5] and the streets will be filled with boys and girls at play.

[6] The Lord says, "This seems unbelievable to you—a remnant, small, discouraged as you are—but it is no great thing for me. [7] You can be sure that I will rescue my people from east and west, wherever they are scattered. [8] I will bring them home again to live safely in Jerusalem, and they will be my people, and I will be their God, just and true and yet forgiving them their sins!"[a]

[9] The Lord of Hosts says, "Get on with the job and finish it! You have been listening long enough! For since you began laying the foundation of the Temple, the prophets have been telling you about the blessings that await you when it's finished. [10] Before the work began there were no jobs, no wages, no security; if you left the city, there was no assurance you would ever return, for

c Literally, "He will grow up in his place."   8 a Literally, "I will be their God in truth and in righteousness."

crime was rampant.

[11] "But it is all so different now!" says the Lord of Hosts. [12] "For I am sowing peace and prosperity among you. Your crops will prosper; the grapevines will be weighted down with fruit; the ground will be fertile, with plenty of rain; all these blessings will be given to the people left in the land. [13] 'May you be as poor as Judah,' the heathen used to say to those they cursed! But no longer! For now 'Judah' is a word of blessing, not a curse. 'May you be as prosperous and happy as Judah is,' they'll say. So don't be afraid or discouraged! Get on with rebuilding the Temple! [14,15] If you do, I will certainly bless you. And don't think that I might change my mind. I did what I said I would when your fathers angered me and I promised to punish them, and I won't change this decision of mine to bless you. [16] Here is your part: Tell the truth. Be fair. Live at peace with everyone. [17] Don't plot harm to others; don't swear that something is true when it isn't! How I hate all that sort of thing!" says the Lord.

[18] Here is another message that came to me from the Lord of Hosts:

[19] "The traditional fasts and times of mourning you have kept in July, August, October, and January[b] are ended. They will be changed to joyous festivals if you love truth and peace! [20,21] People from around the world will come on pilgrimages and pour into Jerusalem from many foreign cities to attend these celebrations. People will write their friends in other cities and say, 'Let's go to Jerusalem to ask the Lord to bless us, and be merciful to us. I'm going! Please come with me. Let's go *now!'* [22] Yes, many people, even strong nations, will come to the Lord of Hosts in Jerusalem to ask for his blessing and help. [23] In those days ten men from ten different nations will clutch at the coat sleeves of one Jew and say, 'Please be my friend, for I know that God is with you.'"

9 THIS IS THE message concerning God's curse on the lands of Hadrach and Damascus, for the Lord is closely watching all mankind,[a] as well as Israel.

[2] "Doomed is Hamath, near Damascus, and Tyre, and Zidon, too, shrewd though they be. [3] Though Tyre has armed herself to the hilt, and become so rich that silver is like dirt to her, and fine gold like dust in the streets, [4] yet the Lord will dispossess her, and hurl her fortifications into the sea; and she shall be set on fire and burned to the ground.

[5] "Ashkelon will see it happen and be filled with fear; Gaza will huddle in desperation and Ekron will shake with terror, for their hopes that Tyre would stop the enemies' advance will all be dashed. Gaza will be conquered, her king killed, and Ashkelon will be completely destroyed.

[6] "Foreigners will take over the city of Ashdod, the rich city of the Philistines. [7] I will yank her idolatry out of her mouth, and pull from her teeth her sacrifices that she eats with blood. Everyone left will worship God and be adopted into Israel as a new clan: the Philistines of Ekron will intermarry with the Jews, just as the Jebusites did so long ago. [8] And I will surround my Temple like a guard to keep invading armies from entering Israel. I am closely watching their movements and I will keep them away; no foreign oppressors will again overrun my people's land.

[9] "Rejoice greatly, O my people! Shout with joy! For look—your King is coming! He is the Righteous One, the Victor! Yet he is lowly, riding on a donkey's colt! [10] I will disarm all peoples of the earth, including my people in Israel, and he shall bring peace among the nations. His realm shall stretch from sea to sea, from the river to the ends of the earth.[b] [11] I have delivered you from death in a waterless pit because of the covenant I made with you, sealed with blood. [12] Come to the place of safety, all you prisoners, for there is yet hope! I promise right now, I will repay you two mercies for each of your woes! [13] Judah, you are my bow! Ephraim, you are my arrow! Both of you will be my sword, like the sword of a mighty soldier brandished against the sons of Greece."

---

b Literally, "fourth, fifth, seventh, and tenth months." as much as do the tribes of Israel."   b Or, "to the ends of the land" of Palestine. Either interpretation is possible from the Hebrew text, but many other passages indicate Christ's universal rule.

9a Or, "for the cities of Syria belong to the Lord,

¹⁴ The Lord shall lead his people as they fight! His arrows shall fly like lightning; the Lord God shall sound the trumpet call and go out against his enemies like a whirlwind off the desert from the south. ¹⁵ He will defend his people and they will subdue their enemies, treading them beneath their feet. They will taste victory and shout with triumph. They will slaughter their foes, leaving horrible carnage everywhere. ¹⁶,¹⁷ The Lord their God will save his people in that day, as a Shepherd caring for his sheep. They shall shine in his land as glittering jewels in a crown. How wonderful and beautiful all shall be! The abundance of grain and wine will make the young men and girls flourish; they will be radiant with health and happiness.

10 ASK THE LORD for rain in the springtime, and he will answer with lightning and showers. Every field will become a lush pasture. ² How foolish to ask the idols for anything like that! Fortune-tellers' predictions are all a bunch of silly lies; what comfort is there in promises that don't come true? Judah and Israel have been led astray and wander like lost sheep; everyone attacks them, for they have no shepherd to protect them.

³ "My anger burns against your 'shepherds'—your leaders—and I will punish them—these goats. For the Lord of Hosts has arrived to help his flock of Judah. I will make them strong and glorious like a proud steed in battle. ⁴ From them will come the Cornerstone, the Peg on which all hope hangs, the Bow that wins the battle, the Ruler over all the earth.ᵃ ⁵ They will be mighty warriors for God, grinding their enemies' faces into the dust beneath their feet. The Lord is with them as they fight; their enemy is doomed.

⁶ "I will strengthen Judah, yes, and Israel too; I will re-establish them because I love them. It will be as though I had never cast them all away, for I, the Lord their God, will hear their cries. ⁷ They shall be like mighty warriors. They shall be happy as with wine. Their children, too, shall see

the mercies of the Lord and be glad. Their hearts shall rejoice in the Lord. ⁸ When I whistle to them, they'll come running, for I have bought them back again. From the few that are left, their population will grow again to former size. ⁹ Though I have scattered them like seeds among the nations, still they will remember me and return again to God; with all their children, they will come home again to Israel. ¹⁰ I will bring them back from Egypt and Assyria, and resettle them in Israel—in Gilead and Lebanon; there will scarcely be room for all of them! ¹¹ They shall pass safely through the sea of distress,ᵇ for the waves will be held back. The Nile will become dry—the rule of Assyria and Egypt over my people will end."

¹² The Lord says, "I will make my people strong with power from me! They will go wherever they wish, and wherever they go, they will be under my personal care."

11 OPEN YOUR DOORS, O Lebanon, to judgment.ᵃ You will be destroyed as though by fire raging through your forests. ² Weep, O cypress trees, for all the ruined cedars; the tallest and most beautiful of them are fallen. Cry in fear, you oaks of Bashan, as you watch the thickest forests felled. ³ Listen to the wailing of Israel's leaders—all these evil shepherds—for their wealth is gone. Hear the young lions roaring—the princes are weeping, for their glorious Jordan valley lies in ruins.

⁴ Then said the Lord my God to me, "Go and take a job as shepherd of a flock being fattened for the butcher. ⁵ This will illustrate the way my people have been bought and slain by wicked leaders, who go unpunished. 'Thank God, now I am rich!' say those who have betrayed them—their own shepherds have sold them without mercy. ⁶ And I won't spare them either," says the Lord, "for I will let them fall into the clutches of their own wicked leaders, and they will slay them. They shall turn the land into a wilderness and I will not protect it from them."

⁷ So I took two shepherd's staffs, naming

---

a i.e., the Messiah.   b Or, "the Sea of Egypt," referring to the Red Sea which the people of Israel were miraculously brought through when God brought them out of slavery the first time.   11a Implied.

one "Grace" and the other "Union," and I fed the flock as I had been told to do. ⁸ And I got rid of their three evil shepherds in a single month. But I became impatient with these sheep—this nation—and they hated me too.

⁹ So I told them, "I won't be your shepherd any longer. If you die, you die; if you are killed, I don't care. Go ahead and destroy yourselves!"

¹⁰ And I took my staff called "Grace" and snapped it in two, showing that I had broken my contract to lead and protect them. ¹¹ That was the end of the agreement. Then those who bought and sold sheep, who were watching, realized that God was telling them something through what I did.

¹² And I said to their leaders, "If you like, give me my pay, whatever I am worth; but only if you want to."

So they counted out thirty little silver coins[b] as my wages.

¹³ And the Lord told me, 'Toss it into the Temple treasury[c]—this magnificent sum they value you at!"

So I took the thirty coins and threw them in. ¹⁴ Then I broke my other staff, "Union," to show that the bond of unity between Judah and Israel was broken.

¹⁵ Then the Lord told me to go again and get a job as a shepherd; this time I was to act the part of a worthless, wicked shepherd.

¹⁶ And he said to me, "This illustrates how I will give this nation a shepherd who will not care for the dying ones, nor look after the young, nor heal the broken bones, nor feed the healthy ones, nor carry the lame that cannot walk; instead, he will eat the fat ones, even tearing off their feet. ¹⁷ Woe to this worthless shepherd who doesn't care for the flock. God's sword will cut his arm and pierce through his right eye; his arm will become useless and his right eye blinded."

12 THIS IS THE fate of Israel, as pronounced by the Lord, who stretched out the heavens and laid the foundation of the earth, and formed the spirit of man within him:

² "I will make Jerusalem and Judah like a cup of poison to all the nearby nations that send their armies to surround Jerusalem. ³ Jerusalem will be a heavy stone burdening the world. And though all the nations of the earth unite in an attempt to move her, they will all be crushed.

⁴ "In that day," says the Lord, "I will bewilder the armies drawn up against her, and make fools of them, for I will watch over the people of Judah, but blind all her enemies.

⁵ "And the clans of Judah shall say to themselves, 'The people of Jerusalem have found strength in the Lord of Hosts, their God.'

⁶ "In that day I will make the clans of Judah like a little fire that sets the forest aflame—like a burning match among the sheaves; they will burn up all the neighboring nations right and left, while Jerusalem stands unmoved. ⁷ The Lord will give victory to the rest of Judah first, before Jerusalem, so that the people of Jerusalem and the royal line of David won't be filled with pride at their success.

⁸ "The Lord will defend the people of Jerusalem; the weakest among them will be as mighty as King David! And the royal line will be as God, like the Angel of the Lord who goes before them! ⁹ For my plan is to destroy all the nations that come against Jerusalem.

¹⁰ "Then I will pour out the spirit of grace and prayer on all the people of Jerusalem, and they will look on him they pierced, and mourn for him as for an only son, and grieve bitterly for him as for an oldest child who died. ¹¹ The sorrow and mourning in Jerusalem at that time will be even greater than the grievous mourning for the godly King Josiah,[a] who was killed in the valley of Megiddo.

¹²,¹³,¹⁴ "All of Israel will weep in profound sorrow. The whole nation will be bowed down with universal grief—king, prophet, priest, and people. Each family will go into private mourning, husbands and wives apart, to face their sorrow alone.

---

b The price of a slave. See Exodus 21:32 and Matthew 27:3–9.   c The translation here follows the Syriac version. "Cast it to the potter" is the Hebrew.   12a Implied in 2 Chronicles 35:24, 25. Literally, "Like the mourning of Hadad-rimmon in the valley of Megiddo."

13 "AT THAT TIME a Fountain will be opened to the people of Israel and Jerusalem, a Fountain to cleanse them from all their sins and uncleanness."

² And the Lord of Hosts declares, "In that day I will get rid of every vestige of idol worship throughout the land, so that even the names of the idols will be forgotten. All false prophets and fortune-tellers will be wiped out, ³ and if anyone begins false prophecy again, his own father and mother will slay him! 'You must die,' they will tell him, 'for you are prophesying lies in the name of the Lord.'

⁴ "No one will be boasting then of his prophetic gift! No one will wear prophet's clothes to try to fool the people then.

⁵ " 'No,' he will say. 'I am not a prophet; I am a farmer. The soil has been my livelihood from my earliest youth.'

⁶ "And if someone asks, 'Then what are these scars on your chest and your back?'ᵃ he will say, 'I got into a brawl at the home of a friend!'ᵇ

⁷ "Awake, O sword, against my Shepherd, the man who is my associate and equal," says the Lord of Hosts. "Strike down the Shepherd and the sheep will scatter, but I will come back and comfort and care for the lambs. ⁸ Two-thirds of all the nation of Israel will be cut off and die,ᶜ but a third will be left in the land. ⁹ I will bring the third that remain through the fire and make them pure, as gold and silver are refined and purified by fire. They will call upon my name and I will hear them; I will say, 'These are my people,' and they will say, 'The Lord is our God.' "

14 WATCH, FOR THE day of the Lord is coming soon! On that day the Lord will gather together the nations to fight Jerusalem; the city will be taken, the houses rifled, the loot divided, the women raped; half the population will be taken away as slaves, and half will be left in what remains of the city.

³ Then the Lord will go out fully armed for war, to fight against those nations. ⁴ That day his feet will stand upon the Mount of Olives, to the east of Jerusalem, and the Mount of Olives will split apart, making a very wide valley running from east to west, for half the mountain will move toward the north and half toward the south. ⁵ You will escape through that valley, for it will reach across to the city gate.ᵃ Yes, you will escape as your people did long centuries ago from the earthquake in the days of Uzziah, king of Judah, and the Lord my God shall come, and all his saints and angelsᵇ with him.

⁶ The sun and moon and stars will no longer shine,ᶜ ⁷ yet there will be continuous day! Only the Lord knows how! There will be no normal day and night—at evening time it will still be light. ⁸ Life-giving waters will flow out from Jerusalem, half toward the Dead Sea and half toward the Mediterranean, flowing continuously both in winter and in summer.

⁹ And the Lord shall be King over all the earth. In that day there shall be one Lord—his name alone will be worshiped. ¹⁰ All the land from Geba (the northern border of Judah) to Rimmon (the southern border) will become one vast plain, but Jerusalem will be on an elevated site, covering the area all the way from the Gate of Benjamin over to the site of the old gate, then to the Corner Gate, and from the Tower of Hananel to the king's wine presses. ¹¹ And Jerusalem shall be inhabited, safe at last, never again to be cursed and destroyed.

¹² And the Lord will send a plague on all the people who fought Jerusalem. They will become like walking corpses, their flesh rotting away; their eyes will shrivel in their sockets, and their tongues will decay in their mouths.

¹³ They will be seized with terror, panic-stricken from the Lord, and will fight

---

a Evidently self-inflicted cuts, as practiced by false prophets. See 1 Kings 18:28.   b Literally, "(These are) wounds I received in the house of my friends." That this is not a passage referring to Christ, is clear from the context. This is a false prophet who is lying about the reason for his scars.   c This has already happened twice: Two million Jews perished in the Roman wars, six million under Hitler. Is a yet future disaster foretold here?   14a Literally, "for the valley of my mountain shall touch Azel"—apparently a hamlet on the eastern outskirts of Jerusalem.   b Literally, "his holy ones."   c The Hebrew is uncertain.

against each other in hand-to-hand combat. [14] All Judah will be fighting at[d] Jerusalem. The wealth of all the neighboring nations will be confiscated—great quantities of gold and silver and fine clothing. [15] (This same plague will strike the horses, mules, camels, donkeys, and all the other animals in the enemy camp.)

[16] In the end, those who survive the plague will go up to Jerusalem each year to worship the King, the Lord of Hosts, to celebrate a time[e] of thanksgiving. [17] And any nation anywhere in all the world that refuses to come to Jerusalem to worship the King, the Lord of Hosts, will have no rain. [18] But if Egypt refuses to come, God will punish her with some other plague. [19] And so Egypt and the other nations will all be punished if they refuse to come.

[20] In that day the bells on the horses will have written on them, "These Are Holy Property";[f] and the trash cans in the Temple of the Lord will be as sacred as the bowls beside the altar. [21] In fact, every container in Jerusalem and Judah shall be sacred to the Lord of Hosts; all who come to worship may use any of them free of charge to boil their sacrifices in; there will be no more grasping traders in the Temple of the Lord of Hosts!

No
More
Put-
On

---

d Or, "against Jerusalem."   e Literally, "the Feast of Tabernacles" or "Booths."   f Literally, "Holy to the Lord."

A fed-up shopkeeper in Manhattan puts a sign on his door to get things straight from the very start. No more jive-talk from the customers, no more of the I-was-just-looking bit, no more fooling around.

The people of Nehemiah's time (fifth century B.C.) were playing lots of verbal games with God, and he decided to call their bluff. He sent a prophet named Malachi to cut through the phoniness, quote the people's lines back to them, and tear them apart. For example, God says, "I am your Father and Master, yet you don't honor me, O priests, but you despise my name."

"Who? Us?" you say. "When did we ever despise your name?"

"When you offer polluted sacrifices on my altar."

"Polluted sacrifices? When have we ever done a thing like that?"

"Every time you say, 'Don't bother bringing anything very valuable to offer to God!' " (1:6, 7)

Malachi was the last prophetic messenger before Jesus came to force men into a face-to-face confrontation with God. Both of them were fairly blunt with hypocrites and pretenders—which includes most of us at least some of the time.

MALACHI

1 HERE IS THE Lord's message to Israel, given through the prophet Malachi:

2,3 "I have loved you very deeply," says the Lord.

But you retort, "Really? When was this?"

And the Lord replies, "I showed my love for you by loving your father, Jacob. I didn't need to. I even rejected his very own brother, Esau, and destroyed Esau's mountains and inheritance, to give it to the jackals of the desert. 4 And if his descendants should say, 'We will rebuild the ruins,' then the Lord of Hosts will say, 'Try to if you like, but I will destroy it again,' for their country is named 'The Land of Wickedness' and their people are called 'Those Whom God Does Not Forgive.' "

5 O Israel, lift your eyes to see what God is doing all around the world; then you will say, "Truly, the Lord's great power goes far beyond our borders!"

6 "A son honors his father, a servant honors his master. I am your Father and Master, yet you don't honor me, O priests, but you despise my name."

"Who? Us?" you say. "When did we ever despise your name?"

7 "When you offer polluted sacrifices on my altar."

"Polluted sacrifices? When have we ever done a thing like that?"

"Every time you say, 'Don't bother bringing anything very valuable to offer to God!' 8 You tell the people, 'Lame animals are all right to offer on the altar of the Lord —yes, even the sick and the blind ones.' And you claim this isn't evil? Try it on your governor sometime—give him gifts like that —and see how pleased he is!

9 " 'God have mercy on us,' you recite; 'God be gracious to us!' But when you bring that kind of gift, why should he show you any favor at all?

10 "Oh, to find one priest among you who would shut the doors and refuse this kind of sacrifice. I have no pleasure in you," says the Lord of Hosts, "and I will not accept your offerings.

11 "But my name will be honored by the Gentiles from morning till night. All around the world they will offer sweet incense and pure offerings in honor of my name. For my name shall be great among the nations," says the Lord of Hosts. 12 "But you dishonor it, saying that my altar is not important, and encouraging people to bring cheap, sick animals to offer to me on it.

13 "You say, 'Oh, it's too difficult to serve the Lord and do what he asks.' And you

turn up your noses at the rules he has given you to obey. Think of it! Stolen animals, lame and sick—as offerings to God! Should I accept such offerings as these?" asks the Lord. [14] "Cursed is that man who promises a fine ram from his flock, and substitutes a sick one to sacrifice to God. For I am a Great King," says the Lord of Hosts, "and my name is to be mightily revered among the Gentiles."

2 LISTEN, YOU PRIESTS, to this warning from the Lord of Hosts:

"If you don't change your ways and give glory to my name, then I will send terrible punishment upon you, and instead of giving you blessings as I would like to, I will turn on you with curses. Indeed, I have cursed you already because you haven't taken seriously the things that are most important to me.

[3] "Take note that I will rebuke your children and I will spread on your faces the manure of these animals you offer me, and throw you out like dung. [4] Then at last you will know it was I who sent you this warning to return to the laws I gave your father Levi," says the Lord of Hosts. [5] "The purpose of these laws was to give him life and peace, to be a means of showing his respect and awe for me, by keeping them. [6] He passed on to the people all the truth he got from me. He did not lie or cheat; he walked with me, living a good and righteous life, and turned many from their lives of sin.

[7] "Priests' lips should flow with the knowledge of God so the people will learn God's laws. The priests are the messengers of the Lord of Hosts, and men should come to them for guidance. [8] But not to you! For you have left God's paths. Your 'guidance' has caused many to stumble in sin. You have distorted the covenant of Levi, and made it into a grotesque parody," says the Lord of Hosts. [9] "Therefore I have made you contemptible in the eyes of all the people; for you have not obeyed me, but you let your favorites break the law without rebuke."

[10] We are children of the same father, Abraham, all created by the same God. And yet we are faithless to each other, violating the covenant of our fathers! [11] In Judah, in Israel, and in Jerusalem, there is treachery, for the men of Judah have defiled God's holy and beloved Temple by marrying heathen women who worship idols. [12] May the Lord cut off from his covenant every last man, whether priest or layman, who has done this thing!

[13] Yet you cover the altar with your tears because the Lord doesn't pay attention to your offerings anymore, and you receive no blessing from him. [14] "Why has God abandoned us?" you cry. I'll tell you why; it is because the Lord has seen your treachery in divorcing your wives who have been faithful to you through the years, the companions you promised to care for and keep. [15] You were united to your wife by the Lord. In God's wise plan, when you married, the two of you became one person in his sight. And what does he want? Godly children from your union. Therefore guard your passions! Keep faith with the wife of your youth.

[16] For the Lord, the God of Israel, says he hates divorce and cruel men. Therefore control your passions—let there be no divorcing of your wives.

[17] You have wearied the Lord with your words.

"Wearied him?" you ask in fake surprise. "How have we wearied him?"

By saying that evil is good, that it pleases the Lord! Or by saying that God won't punish us—he doesn't care.

3 "LISTEN: I WILL send my messenger before me to prepare the way. And then the one[a] you are looking for will come suddenly to his Temple—the Messenger of God's promises, to bring you great joy. Yes, he is surely coming," says the Lord of Hosts. [2] "But who can live when he appears? Who can endure his coming? For he is like a blazing fire refining precious metal and he can bleach the dirtiest garments! [3] Like a refiner of silver he will sit and closely watch as the dross is burned away. He will purify the Levites, the ministers of God, refining them like gold or silver, so

---

a Literally, "the Lord."

that they will do their work for God with pure hearts. ⁴ Then once more the Lord will enjoy the offerings brought to him by the people of Judah and Jerusalem, as he did before. ⁵ At that time my punishments will be quick and certain; I will move swiftly against wicked men who trick the innocent, against adulterers, and liars, against all those who cheat their hired hands, or oppress widows and orphans, or defraud strangers, and do not fear me," says the Lord of Hosts. ⁶ "For I am the Lord—I do not change. That is why you are not already utterly destroyed [for my mercy endures foreverᵇ].

⁷ "Though you have scorned my laws from earliest time, yet you may still return to me," says the Lord of Hosts. "Come and I will forgive you.

"But you say, 'We have never even gone away!'

⁸ "Will a man rob God? Surely not! And yet you have robbed me.

" 'What do you mean? When did we ever rob you?'

"You have robbed me of the tithes and offerings due to me. ⁹ And so the awesome curse of God is cursing you, for your whole nation has been robbing me. ¹⁰ Bring all the tithes into the storehouse so that there will be food enough in my Temple; if you do, I will open up the windows of heaven for you and pour out a blessing so great you won't have room enough to take it in!

"Try it! Let me prove it to you! ¹¹ Your crops will be large, for I will guard them from insects and plagues. Your grapes won't shrivel away before they ripen," says the Lord of Hosts. ¹² "And all nations will call you blessed, for you will be a land sparkling with happiness. These are the promises of the Lord of Hosts.

¹³ "Your attitude toward me has been proud and arrogant," says the Lord.

"But you say, 'What do you mean?

What have we said that we shouldn't?'

¹⁴,¹⁵ "Listen; you have said, 'It is foolish to worship God and obey him. What good does it do to obey his laws, and to sorrow and mourn for our sins? From now on, as far as we're concerned, "Blessed are the arrogant." For those who do evil shall prosper, and those who dare God to punish them shall get off scot-free.' "

¹⁶ Then those who feared and loved the Lord spoke often of him to each other. And he had a Book of Remembrance drawn up in which he recorded the names of those who feared him and loved to think about him.

¹⁷ "They shall be mine," says the Lord of Hosts, "in that day when I make up my jewels. And I will spare them as a man spares an obedient and dutiful son. ¹⁸ Then you will see the difference between God's treatment of good men and bad, between those who serve him and those who don't.

4 "WATCH NOW," THE Lord of Hosts declares, "the day of judgment is coming, burning like a furnace. The proud and wicked will be burned up like straw; like a tree, they will be consumed—roots and all.

² "But for you who fear my name, the Sun of Righteousness will rise with healing in his wings. And you will go free, leaping with joy like calves let out to pasture. ³ Then you will tread upon the wicked as ashes underfoot," says the Lord of Hosts. ⁴ "Remember to obey the laws I gave all Israel through Moses my servant on Mount Horeb.

⁵ "See, I will send you another prophet likeᵃ Elijah before the coming of the great and dreadful judgment day of God. ⁶ His preaching will bring fathers and children together again, to be of one mind and heart, for they will know that if they do not repent, I will come and utterly destroy their land."

---

b Implied.   4a Literally, "the prophet Elijah." Compare Matthew 17:10–12 and Luke 1:17.

WEST

Diagram 1

VIEW OF EZEKIEL'S TEMPLE

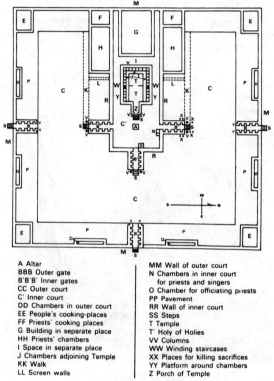

Diagram 2

PLAN OF TEMPLE AREA

A Altar
BBB Outer gate
B'B'B' Inner gates
CC Outer court
C' Inner court
DD Chambers in outer court
EE People's cooking-places
FF Priests' cooking places
G Building in separate place
HH Priests' chambers
I Space in separate place
J Chambers adjoining Temple
KK Walk
LL Screen walls

MM Wall of outer court
N Chambers in inner court
    for priests and singers
O Chamber for officiating priests
PP Pavement
RR Wall of inner court
SS Steps
T Temple
T' Holy of Holies
VV Columns
WW Winding staircases
XX Places for killing sacrifices
YY Platform around chambers
Z Porch of Temple

NORTH

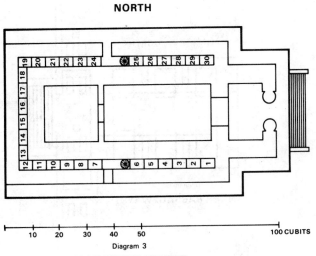

10   20   30   40   50   100 CUBITS

Diagram 3

PLAN OF THE TEMPLE

NORTH

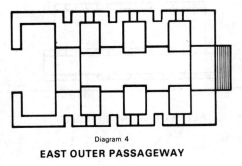

Diagram 4

EAST OUTER PASSAGEWAY

789

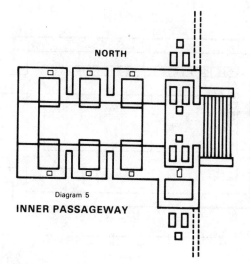

NORTH

Diagram 5

INNER PASSAGEWAY

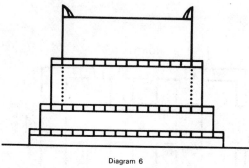

Diagram 6

ALTAR OF BURNT-OFFERING

NORTH

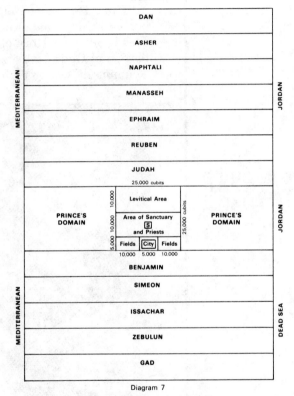

Diagram 7

ALLOTMENT OF THE LAND

REACH OUT

Alienation: of students from parents, of blacks from whites, of Arab from Jew . . . all around us and throughout our world we see the need to reach out in love toward our fellow humans . . . to love people as they are.

In a little Jewish town years ago, God did just this. He reached out in love to every human through his own Son, Jesus Christ. This book is the story of that Man, the extension of God's love and at the same time God himself, who in flesh and blood reached

Roger Bowlin and a partner search for lost climbers (see page 960).

Books, studies,
philosophies—
so many new ideas.
Who's right?
(see page 1061).

out to fishermen, toddlers, and businessmen alike.

It was a rugged world he entered. Men were sold like animals to die for others' amusement. Rumors of insurrection buzzed in cities and towns, and at times when walking along the road one could see the places of mass executions. It was a sordid world— of poverty contrasted with opulence, of men treated as less than human, of women degraded, of racial strife and hatreds.

Into this world he came . . . not as an emperor, but as a low-born person, to taste the poverty, the sorrow, the anguish, to be just one man facing a system in which men exploited men, Jew hated Samaritan, Roman hated Jew, and religion was usually phony.

He entered as a baby and grew up to become a spiritual revolutionary. He, who had created both tiny flowers and distant stars,

entered the corruption of his once perfect creation, and, in his reaching out to people with the *truth*, he revolutionized the religious establishment by transforming individuals.

How? Read through the first four books, the Gospels. Why are there four? Aren't they repetitious? Not when you consider how crucial are these factual, eyewitness accounts of what Jesus said and did! Here is the base on which our knowledge of Jesus Christ rests.

Read through the letters circulated in those early churches and study the depth of how these people were making this new Christ-life part of their very beings, enabling them for world-changing.

Read, too, *The Revelation*, a glimpse of another facet of Jesus Christ, the awesome Creator-God, with the fury of his judgment contrasted with the expanse of his love.

As you read, allow your mind to be stretched by the God behind these words. Let him reach out to your thoughts, your emotions, your will. Then, as he fills you with himself, reach out to others with the fantastic good news!

*A rough
rodeo ride on
cowhide
(see page 1075)
and the strain
for the home run record
(see page 1044).*

It's a Strange World We Live In

A New England high-school junior, bored, took off from home with a few extra clothes, a guitar and $12 and thumbed his way to Pittsburgh, Nashville, then west through Texas, New Mexico, Arizona, California. The $12 gone, he sang for his supper — often just a cup of coffee or two. Months later, forty pounds lighter, finding that "people are much the same wherever you go," he returned home. Reason: boredom.

You've probably felt the same emotions which triggered his trip. He had wanted to get alone to think. What a strange world to face up to . . . so many conflicting ideas . . . so many incomprehensible things. . . . Actually, it was much the same kind of world Jesus entered on the first Christmas. As you read his story in this book written by his follower, Matthew, you see

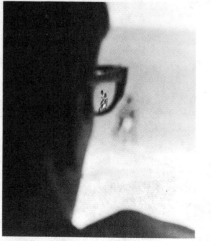

how Jesus introduced a totally new perspective, a jolting set of different ideas and dynamics which many flatly rejected and others allowed to change their lives. There was no middle ground with this Man Jesus— who came as the fulfillment of hundreds of facts the prophets had foretold about him centuries before. He came into a bewildering world of hatreds and confusion with a message and a power available to anybody wanting to listen . . . .

MATTHEW

1 THESE ARE THE ancestors of Jesus Christ, a descendant of King David and of Abraham:

2 Abraham was the father of Isaac; Isaac was the father of Jacob; Jacob was the father of Judah and his brothers.

3 Judah was the father of Perez and Zerah (Tamar was their mother); Perez was the father of Hezron; Hezron was the father of Aram;

4 Aram was the father of Amminadab; Amminadab was the father of Nahshon; Nahshon was the father of Salmon;

5 Salmon was the father of Boaz (Rahab was his mother); Boaz was the father of Obed (Ruth was his mother); Obed was the father of Jesse;

6 Jesse was the father of King David. David was the father of Solomon (his mother was the widow of Uriah);

7 Solomon was the father of Rehoboam; Rehoboam was the father of Abijah; Abijah was the father of Asa;

8 Asa was the father of Jehoshaphat; Jehoshaphat was the father of Joram; Joram was the father of Uzziah;

9 Uzziah was the father of Jotham; Jotham was the father of Ahaz; Ahaz was the father of Hezekiah;

10 Hezekiah was the father of Manasseh; Manasseh was the father of Amos; Amos was the father of Josiah;

11 Josiah was the father of Jechoniah and his brothers (born at the time of the exile to Babylon).

12 After the exile:
Jechoniah was the father of Shealtiel; Shealtiel was the father of Zerubbabel;

13 Zerubbabel was the father of Abiud; Abiud was the father of Eliakim; Eliakim was the father of Azor;

14 Azor was the father of Zadok; Zadok was the father of Achim; Achim was the father of Eliud;

15 Eliud was the father of Eleazar; Eleazar was the father of Matthan; Matthan was the father of Jacob;

16 Jacob was the father of Joseph (who was the husband of Mary, the mother of Jesus Christ the Messiah).

17 These are[a] fourteen of the generations from Abraham to King David; and fourteen from King David's time to the exile; and fourteen from the exile to Christ.

18 These are the facts concerning the birth of Jesus Christ: His mother, Mary, was engaged to be married to Joseph. But while she was still a virgin she became pregnant by the Holy Spirit. 19 Then Joseph, her fiancé,[b] being a man of stern principle,[c] decided to break the engagement but to do it quietly, as he didn't want to publicly disgrace her.

20 As he lay awake[d] considering this, he fell into a dream, and saw an angel standing beside him. "Joseph, son of David," the angel said, "don't hesitate to take Mary as your wife! For the child within her has been conceived by the Holy Spirit. 21 And she will have a Son, and you shall name him Jesus (meaning 'Savior'), for he will save his people from their sins. 22 This will fulfill God's message through his prophets—

23 'Listen! The virgin shall conceive a child! She shall give birth to a Son, and he shall be called "Emmanuel" (meaning "God is with us").' "

24 When Joseph awoke, he did as the angel commanded, and brought Mary home to be his wife, 25 but she remained a virgin until her Son was born; and Joseph named him "Jesus."

a Literally, "So all the generations from Abraham unto David are fourteen." b Literally, "her husband."
c Literally, "a just man." d Implied in remainder of verse.

2 JESUS WAS BORN in the town of Bethlehem, in Judea, during the reign of King Herod.

At about that time some astrologers from eastern lands arrived in Jerusalem, asking, [2] "Where is the newborn King of the Jews? for we have seen his star in far-off eastern lands, and have come to worship him."

[3] King Herod was deeply disturbed by their question, and all Jerusalem was filled with rumors.[a] [4] He called a meeting of the Jewish religious leaders.

"Did the prophets tell us where the Messiah would be born?" he asked.

[5] "Yes, in Bethlehem," they said, "for this is what the prophet Micah[b] wrote:

[6] 'O little town of Bethlehem, you are not just an unimportant Judean village, for a Governor shall rise from you to rule my people Israel.' "

[7] Then Herod sent a private message to the astrologers, asking them to come to see him; at this meeting he found out from them the exact time when they first saw the star. Then he told them, [8] "Go to Bethlehem and search for the child. And when you find him, come back and tell me so that I can go and worship him too!"

[9] After this interview the astrologers started out again. And look! The star appeared to them again, standing over Bethlehem.[c] [10] Their joy knew no bounds!

[11] Entering the house where the baby and Mary his mother were, they threw themselves down before him, worshiping. Then they opened their presents and gave him gold, frankincense and myrrh. [12] But when they returned to their own land, they didn't go through Jerusalem to report to Herod, for God had warned them in a dream to go home another way.

[13] After they were gone, an angel of the Lord appeared to Joseph in a dream. "Get up and flee to Egypt with the baby and his mother," the angel said, "and stay there until I tell you to return, for King Herod is going to try to kill the child." [14] That same[d] night he left for Egypt with Mary and the baby, [15] and stayed there until King Herod's death. This fulfilled the prophet's prediction,

"I have called my Son from Egypt."[e]

[16] Herod was furious when he learned that the astrologers had disobeyed him. Sending soldiers to Bethlehem, he ordered them to kill every baby boy two years old and under, both in the town and on the nearby farms, for the astrologers had told him the star first appeared to them two years before. [17] This brutal action of Herod's fulfilled the prophecy of Jeremiah,[f]

[18] "Screams of anguish come from Ramah,[g]

Weeping unrestrained;

Rachel weeping for her children,

Uncomforted—

For they are dead."

[19] When Herod died, an angel of the Lord appeared in a dream to Joseph in Egypt, and told him, [20] "Get up and take the baby and his mother back to Israel, for those who were trying to kill the child are dead."

[21] So he returned immediately to Israel with Jesus and his mother. [22] But on the way he was frightened to learn that the new king was Herod's son, Archelaus. Then, in another dream, he was warned not to go to Judea, so they went to Galilee instead, [23] and lived in Nazareth. This fulfilled the prediction of the prophets concerning the Messiah,

"He shall be called a Nazarene."

3 WHILE THEY WERE living in Nazareth,[a] John the Baptist began preaching out in the Judean wilderness. His constant theme was, [2] "Turn from your sins . . . turn to God . . . for the Kingdom of Heaven is coming soon."[b] [3] Isaiah the prophet had told about John's ministry centuries before! He had written,

"I hear[c] a shout from the wilderness, 'Prepare a road for the Lord— straighten out the path where he

---

a Literally, "and all Jerusalem with him."   b Implied. Micah 5:2. it came and stood over where the baby was."   d Implied.   c Literally, "went before them until g Or, "the region of Ramah."   3a Literally, "in those days."   hand."   c Implied. Isaiah 40:3.   e Hosea 11:1.   f Jeremiah 31:15.   b Or, "has arrived." Literally, "is at

will walk.' "

4 John's clothing was woven from camel's hair and he wore a leather belt; his food was locusts and wild honey. 5 People from Jerusalem and from all over the Jordan Valley, and, in fact, from every section of Judea went out to the wilderness to hear him preach, 6 and when they confessed their sins, he baptized them in the Jordan River.

7 But when he saw many Pharisees[d] and Sadducees[e] coming to be baptized, he denounced them. "You sons of snakes!" he warned. "Who said that you could escape the coming wrath of God? 8 Before being baptized, prove that you have turned from sin by doing worthy deeds. 9 Don't try to get by as you are, thinking, 'We are safe for we are Jews—descendants of Abraham.' That proves nothing. God can change these stones here into Jews![f]

10 "And even now the axe of God's judgment is poised to chop down every unproductive tree. They will be chopped and burned.

11 "With[g] water I baptize those who repent of their sins; but someone else is coming, far greater than I am, so great that I am not worthy to carry his shoes! He shall baptize you with[h] the Holy Spirit and with fire. 12 He will separate the chaff from the grain, burning the chaff with never-ending fire, and storing away the grain."

13 Then Jesus went from Galilee to the Jordan River to be baptized there by John. 14 John didn't want to do it. "This isn't proper," he said. "I am the one who needs to be baptized by you."

15 But Jesus said, "Please do it, for I must do all that is right."[i] So then John baptized him.

16 After his baptism, as soon as Jesus came up out of the water, the heavens were opened to him and he saw the Spirit of God coming down in the form of a dove. 17 And a voice from heaven said, "This is my beloved Son, and I am wonderfully pleased with him."

4 THEN JESUS WAS led out into the wilderness by the Holy Spirit, to be tempted there by Satan. 2 For forty days and forty nights he ate nothing and became very hungry. 3 Then Satan tempted him to get food by changing stones into loaves of bread.

"It will prove you are the Son of God," he said.

4 But Jesus told him, "No! For the Scriptures tell us that bread won't feed men's souls: obedience to every word of God is what we need."

5 Then Satan took him to Jerusalem to the roof of the Temple. 6 "Jump off," he said, "and prove you are the Son of God; for the Scriptures declare, 'God will send his angels to keep you from harm,' . . . they will prevent you from smashing on the rocks below."

7 Jesus retorted, "It also says not to put the Lord your God to a foolish test!"

8 Next Satan took him to the peak of a very high mountain and showed him the nations of the world and all their glory. 9 "I'll give it all to you," he said, "if you will only kneel and worship me."

10 "Get out of here, Satan," Jesus told him. "The Scriptures say, 'Worship only the Lord God. Obey only him.' "

11 Then Satan went away, and angels came and cared for Jesus.

12,13 When Jesus heard that John had been arrested, he left Judea and returned home[a] to Nazareth in Galilee; but soon he moved to Capernaum, beside the Lake of Galilee, close to Zebulun and Naphtali. 14 This fulfilled Isaiah's prophecy:

15,16 "The land of Zebulun and the
land of Naphtali, beside the Lake,
and the countryside beyond the
Jordan River, and Upper Galilee
where so many foreigners live—
there the people who sat in darkness have seen a great Light; they
sat in the land of death, and the
Light broke through upon
them."[b]

17 From then on, Jesus began to preach,

---

d Jewish religious leaders who strictly followed the letter of the law but often violated its intent.
e Jewish political leaders.　　f Literally, "God is able of these stones to raise up children unto Abraham."
g Or, "in water."　　h Or, "in the Holy Spirit and in fire."　　i Literally, "to fulfill all righteousness."
4a Implied.　　b Isaiah 9:1, 2.

"Turn from sin, and turn to God, for the Kingdom of heaven is near."ᶜ

¹⁸ One day as he was walking along the beach beside the Lake of Galilee, he saw two brothers—Simon, also called Peter, and Andrew—out in a boatᵈ fishing with a net, for they were commercial fishermen. ¹⁹ Jesus called out, "Come along with me and I will show you how to fish for the souls of men!" ²⁰ And they left their nets at once and went with him.

²¹ A little farther up the beach he saw two other brothers, James and John, sitting in a boat with their father Zebedee, mending their nets; and he called to them to come too. ²² At once they stopped their work and, leaving their father behind, went with him.

²³ Jesus traveled all through Galilee teaching in the Jewish synagogues, everywhere preaching the Good News about the Kingdom of Heaven. And he healed every kind of sickness and disease. ²⁴ The report of his miracles spread far beyond the borders of Galilee so that sick folk were soon coming to be healed from as far away as Syria. And whatever their illness and pain, or if they were possessed by demons, or were insane, or paralyzed—he healed them all. ²⁵ Enormous crowds followed him wherever he went—people from Galilee, and the Ten Cities, and Jerusalem, and from all over Judea, and even from across the Jordan River.

5 ONE DAY AS the crowds were gathering, he went up the hillside with his disciples and sat down and taught them there.
³ "Humble men are very fortunate!" he told them, "for the Kingdom of Heaven is given to them. ⁴ Those who mourn are fortunate! for they shall be comforted. ⁵ The meek and lowly are fortunate! for the whole wide world belongs to them.
⁶ "Happy are those who long to be just and good, for they shall be completely satisfied. ⁷ Happy are the kind and merciful, for they shall be shown mercy. ⁸ Happy are those whose hearts are pure, for they shall see God. ⁹ Happy are those who strive for peace—they shall be called the sons of God.

¹⁰ Happy are those who are persecuted because they are good, for the Kingdom of Heaven is theirs.
¹¹ "When you are reviled and persecuted and lied about because you are my followers—wonderful! ¹² Be *happy* about it! Be *very glad!* for a *tremendous reward* awaits you up in heaven. And remember, the ancient prophets were persecuted too.
¹³ "You are the world's seasoning, to make it tolerable. If you lose your flavor, what will happen to the world? And you yourselves will be thrown out and trampled underfoot as worthless. ¹⁴ You are the world's light—a city on a hill, glowing in the night for all to see. ¹⁵,¹⁶ Don't hide your light! Let it shine for all; let your good deeds glow for all to see, so that they will praise your heavenly Father.
¹⁷ "Don't misunderstand why I have come—it isn't to cancel the laws of Moses and the warnings of the prophets. No, I came to fulfill them, and to make them all come true. ¹⁸ With all the earnestness I have I say: Every law in the Book will continue until its purpose is achieved.ᵃ ¹⁹ And so if anyone breaks the least commandment, and teaches others to, he shall be the least in the Kingdom of Heaven. But those who teach God's laws *and obey them* shall be great in the Kingdom of Heaven.
²⁰ "But I warn you—unless your goodnessᵇ is greater than that of the Pharisees and other Jewish leaders, you can't get into the Kingdom of Heaven at all!
²¹ "Under the laws of Moses the rule was, 'If you kill, you must die.' ²² But I have added to that rule,ᶜ and tell you that if you are only *angry*, even in your own home,ᵈ you are in danger of judgment! If you call your friend an idiot, you are in danger of being brought before the court. And if you curse him, you are in danger of the fires of hell.ᵉ
²³ "So if you are standing before the altar in the Temple, offering a sacrifice to God, and suddenly remember that a friend has something against you, ²⁴ leave your sacrifice there beside the altar and go and apologize and be reconciled to him, and then

c Or, "is at hand," or, "has arrived."   d Implied.
b Literally, "righteousness."   c Literally, "But I say."
e Literally, "the hell of fire."
5a Literally, "until all things be accomplished."
          d Literally, "with your brother."

come and offer your sacrifice to God. ²⁵ Come to terms quickly with your enemy before it is too late and he drags you into court and you are thrown into a debtor's cell, ²⁶ for you will stay there until you have paid the last penny.

²⁷ "The laws of Moses said, 'You shall not commit adultery.' ²⁸ But I say: Anyone who even looks at a woman with lust in his eye has already committed adultery with her in his heart. ²⁹ So if your eye—even if it is your best^f eye!—causes you to lust, gouge it out and throw it away. Better for part of you to be destroyed than for all of you to be cast into hell. ³⁰ And if your hand —even your right hand—causes you to sin, cut it off and throw it away. Better that than find yourself in hell.

³¹ "The law of Moses says, 'If anyone wants to be rid of his wife, he can divorce her merely by giving her a letter of dismissal.' ³² But I say that a man who divorces his wife, except for fornication, causes her to commit adultery if she marries again. And he who marries her commits adultery.

³³ "Again, the law of Moses says, 'You shall not break your vows to God, but must fulfill them all.' ³⁴ But I say: Don't make any vows! And even to say, 'By heavens!' is a sacred vow to God, for the heavens are God's throne. ³⁵ And if you say 'By the earth!' it is a sacred vow, for the earth is his footstool. And don't swear 'By Jerusalem!' for Jerusalem is the capital of the great King. ³⁶ Don't even swear 'By my head!' for you can't turn one hair white or black. ³⁷ Say just a simple 'Yes, I will' or 'No, I won't.' Your word is enough. To strengthen your promise with a vow shows that something is wrong.

³⁸ "The law of Moses says, 'If a man gouges out another's eye, he must pay with his own eye. If a tooth gets knocked out, knock out the tooth of the one who did it.'^g ³⁹ But I say: Don't resist violence! If you are slapped on one cheek, turn the other too. ⁴⁰ If you are ordered to court, and your shirt is taken from you, give your coat too. ⁴¹ If the military demand that you carry their gear for a mile, carry it two. ⁴² Give to those who ask, and don't turn away from those who want to borrow.

⁴³ "There is a saying, 'Love your *friends* and hate your enemies.' ⁴⁴ But I say: Love your *enemies!* Pray for those who *persecute* you! ⁴⁵ In that way you will be acting as true sons of your Father in heaven. For he gives his sunlight to both the evil and the good, and sends rain on the just and on the unjust too. ⁴⁶ If you love only those who love you, what good is that? Even scoundrels do that much. ⁴⁷ If you are friendly only to your friends, how are you different from anyone else? Even the heathen do that. ⁴⁸ But you are to be perfect, even as your Father in heaven is perfect.

6 "TAKE CARE! DON'T do your good deeds publicly, to be admired, for then you will lose the reward from your Father in heaven. ² When you give a gift to a beggar, don't shout about it as the hypocrites do—blowing trumpets in the synagogues and streets to call attention to their acts of charity! I tell you in all earnestness, they have received all the reward they will ever get. ³ But when you do a kindness to someone, do it secretly—don't tell your left hand what your right hand is doing. ⁴ And your Father who knows all secrets will reward you.

⁵ "And now about prayer. When you pray, don't be like the hypocrites who pretend piety by praying publicly on street corners and in the synagogues where everyone can see them. Truly, that is all the reward they will ever get. ⁶ But when you pray, go away by yourself, all alone, and shut the door behind you and pray to your Father secretly, and your Father, who knows your secrets, will reward you.

^{7,8} "Don't recite the same prayer over and over as the heathen do, who think prayers are answered only by repeating them again and again. Remember, your Father knows exactly what you need even before you ask him!

⁹ "Pray along these lines: 'Our Father in heaven, we honor your holy name. ¹⁰ We ask that your kingdom will come now. May your will be done here on earth, just as it is in heaven. ¹¹ Give us our food again to-

---

f Literally, "your right eye."   g Literally, "an eye for an eye and a tooth for a tooth."

day, as usual, [12] and forgive us our sins, just as we have forgiven those who have sinned against us. [13] Don't bring us into temptation, but deliver us from the Evil One.[a] Amen.' [14,15] Your heavenly Father will forgive you if you forgive those who sin against you; but if *you* refuse to forgive *them, he* will not forgive *you.*

[16] "And now about fasting. When you fast, declining your food for a spiritual purpose, don't do it publicly, as the hypocrites do, who try to look wan and disheveled so people will feel sorry for them. Truly, that is the only reward they will ever get. [17] But when you fast, put on festive clothing, [18] so that no one will suspect you are hungry, except your Father who knows every secret. And he will reward you.

[19] "Don't store up treasures here on earth where they can erode away or may be stolen. [20] Store them in heaven where they will never lose their value, and are safe from thieves. [21] If your profits are in heaven your heart will be there too.

[22] "If your eye is pure, there will be sunshine in your soul. [23] But if your eye is clouded with evil thoughts and desires, you are in deep spiritual darkness. And oh, how deep that darkness can be!

[24] "You cannot serve two masters: God and money. For you will hate one and love the other, or else the other way around.

[25] "So my counsel is: Don't worry about *things*—food, drink, and clothes. For you already have life and a body—and they are far more important than what to eat and wear. [26] Look at the birds! They don't worry about what to eat—they don't need to sow or reap or store up food—for your heavenly Father feeds them. And you are far more valuable to him than they are. [27] Will all your worries add a single moment to your life?

[28] "And why worry about your clothes? Look at the field lilies! They don't worry about theirs. [29] Yet King Solomon in all his glory was not clothed as beautifully as they. [30] And if God cares so wonderfully for flowers that are here today and gone tomorrow, won't he more surely care for you, O men

of little faith?

[31,32] "So don't worry at all about having enough food and clothing. Why be like the heathen? For they take pride in all these things and are deeply concerned about them. But your heavenly Father already knows perfectly well that you need them, [33] and he will give them to you if you give him first place in your life and live as he wants you to.

[34] "So don't be anxious about tomorrow. God will take care of your tomorrow too. Live one day at a time.[b]

7 "DON'T CRITICIZE, AND then you won't be criticized. [2] For others will treat you as you treat them. [3] And why worry about a speck in the eye of a brother when you have a board in your own? [4] Should you say, 'Friend, let me help you get that speck out of your eye,' when you can't even see because of the board in your own? [5] Hypocrite! First get rid of the board. Then you can see to help your brother.

[6] "Don't give holy things to depraved men. Don't give pearls to swine! They will trample the pearls and turn and attack you.

[7] "Ask, and you will be given what you ask for. Seek, and you will find. Knock, and the door will be opened. [8] For everyone who asks, receives. Anyone who seeks, finds. If only you will knock, the door will open. [9] If a child asks his father for a loaf of bread, will he be given a stone instead? [10] If he asks for fish, will he be given a poisonous snake? Of course not! [11] And if you hardhearted, sinful men know how to give good gifts to your children, won't your Father in heaven even more certainly give good gifts to those who ask him for them?

[12] "Do for others what you want them to do for you. This is the teaching of the laws of Moses in a nutshell.[a]

[13] "Heaven can be entered only through the narrow gate! The highway to hell[b] is broad, and its gate is wide enough for all the multitudes who choose its easy way. [14] But the Gateway to Life is small, and the road is narrow, and only a few ever find it.

[15] "Beware of false teachers who come

---

a Or, "from evil." Some manuscripts add here, "For yours is the kingdom and the power and the glory forever. Amen."   b Literally, "sufficient unto the day is the evil thereof."   7a Literally, "this is the law and the prophets."   b Literally, "the way that leads to destruction."

disguised as harmless sheep, but are wolves and will tear you apart. [16] You can detect them by the way they act, just as you can identify a tree by its fruit. You need never confuse grapevines with thorn bushes or figs with thistles. [17] Different kinds of fruit trees can quickly be identified by examining their fruit. [18] A variety that produces delicious fruit never produces an inedible kind. And a tree producing an inedible kind can't produce what is good. [19] So the trees having the inedible fruit are chopped down and thrown on the fire. [20] Yes, the way to identify a tree or a person[c] is by the kind of fruit produced.

[21] "Not all who sound religious are really godly people. They may refer to me as 'Lord,' but still won't get to heaven. For the decisive question is whether they obey my Father in heaven. [22] At the Judgment[d] many will tell me, 'Lord, Lord, we told others about you and used your name to cast out demons and to do many other great miracles.' [23] But I will reply, 'You have never been mine.[e] Go away, for your deeds are evil.'

[24] "All who listen to my instructions and follow them are wise, like a man who builds his house on solid rock. [25] Though the rain comes in torrents, and the floods rise and the storm winds beat against his house, it won't collapse, for it is built on rock. [26] "But those who hear my instructions and ignore them are foolish, like a man who builds his house on sand. [27] For when the rains and floods come, and storm winds beat against his house, it will fall with a mighty crash." [28] The crowds were amazed at Jesus' sermons, [29] for he taught as one who had great authority, and not as their Jewish leaders.[f]

8 LARGE CROWDS FOLLOWED Jesus as he came down the hillside.

[2] *Look! A leper is approaching. He kneels before him, worshiping. "Sir," the leper pleads, "if you want to, you can heal me."*

[3] *Jesus touches the man. "I want to," he says. "Be healed." And instantly the leprosy disappears.*

[4] *Then Jesus says to him, "Don't stop to talk[a] to anyone; go right over to the priest to be examined; and take with you the offering required by Moses' law for lepers who are healed—a public testimony of your cure."*

[5,6] When Jesus arrived in Capernaum, a Roman army captain came and pled with him to come to his home and heal his servant boy who was in bed paralyzed and racked with pain.

[7] "Yes," Jesus said, "I will come and heal him."

[8,9] Then the officer said, "Sir, I am not worthy to have you in my home; [and it isn't necessary for you to come[b]]. If you will only stand here and say, 'Be healed,' my servant will get well! I know, because I am under the authority of my superior officers and I have authority over my soldiers, and I say to one, 'Go,' and he goes, and to another, 'Come,' and he comes, and to my slave boy, 'Do this or that,' and he does it. And I know you have authority to tell his sickness to go—and it will go!"

[10] Jesus stood there amazed! Turning to the crowd he said, "I haven't seen faith like this in all the land of Israel! [11] And I tell you this, that many Gentiles [like this Roman officer[b]], shall come from all over the world and sit down in the Kingdom of Heaven with Abraham, Isaac, and Jacob. [12] And many an Israelite—those for whom the Kingdom was prepared—shall be cast into outer darkness, into the place of weeping and torment."

[13] Then Jesus said to the Roman officer, "Go on home. What you have believed has happened!" And the boy was healed that same hour!

[14] When Jesus arrived at Peter's house, Peter's mother-in-law was in bed with a high fever. [15] But when Jesus touched her hand, the fever left her; and she got up and prepared a meal[c] for them!

[16] That evening several demon-possessed people were brought to Jesus; and when he spoke a single word, all the demons fled; and all the sick were healed. [17] This fulfilled the prophecy of Isaiah, "He took our sick-

---

c Implied.   d Literally, "in that day."   e Literally, "I never knew you."   f Literally, "not as the scribes." These leaders only quoted others, and did not presume to present any fresh revelation. 8a Literally, "See you tell no man."   b Implied.   c Literally, "ministered unto them."

nesses and bore our diseases."[d]

[18] When Jesus noticed how large the crowd was growing, he instructed his disciples to get ready to cross to the other side of the lake.

[19] Just then[e] one of the Jewish religious teachers[f] said to him, "Teacher, I will follow you no matter where you go!"

[20] But Jesus said, "Foxes have dens and birds have nests, but I, the Messiah,[g] have no home of my own—no place to lay my head."

[21] Another of his disciples said, "Sir, when my father is dead, then I will follow you."[h]

[22] But Jesus told him, "Follow me now![e] Let those who are spiritually[e] dead care for their own dead."

[23] Then he got into a boat and started across the lake with his disciples. [24] Suddenly a terrible storm came up, with waves higher than the boat. But Jesus was asleep.

[25] The disciples went to him and wakened him, shouting, "Lord, save us! We're sinking!"

[26] But Jesus answered, "O you men of little faith! Why are you so frightened?" Then he stood up and rebuked the wind and waves, and the storm subsided and all was calm. [27] The disciples just sat there, awed! "Who is this," they asked themselves, "that even the winds and the sea obey him?"

[28] When they arrived on the other side of the lake, in the country of the Gadarenes, two men with demons in them met him. They lived in a cemetery and were so dangerous that no one could go through that area.

[29] They began screaming at him, "What do you want with us, O Son of God? You have no right to torment us yet."[i]

[30] A herd of pigs was feeding in the distance, [31] so the demons begged, "If you cast us out, send us into that herd of pigs."

[32] "All right," Jesus told them. "Begone."

And they came out of the men and entered the pigs, and the whole herd rushed over a cliff and drowned in the water below.

[33] The herdsmen fled to the nearest city with the story of what had happened, [34] and the entire population came rushing out to see Jesus, and begged him to go away and leave them alone.

9 SO JESUS CLIMBED into a boat and went across the lake to Capernaum, his home town.[a]

[2] Soon some men brought him a paralyzed boy on a mat. When Jesus saw their faith, he said to the sick boy, "Cheer up, son! For I have forgiven your sins!"

[3] "Blasphemy! This man is saying he is God!" exclaimed some of the religious leaders to themselves.

[4] Jesus knew what they were thinking and asked them, "Why are you thinking such evil thoughts? [5,6] I, the Messiah,[b] have the authority on earth to forgive sins. But talk is cheap—anybody could say that. So I'll prove it to you by healing this man." Then, turning to the paralyzed man, he commanded, "Pick up your stretcher and go on home, for you are healed."

[7] And the boy jumped up and left!

[8] A chill of fear swept through the crowd as they saw this happen right before their eyes. How they praised God for giving such authority to a man!

[9] As Jesus was going on down the road, he saw a tax collector, Matthew,[c] sitting at a tax collection booth. "Come and be my disciple," Jesus said to him, and Matthew jumped up and went along with him.

[10] Later, as Jesus and his disciples were eating dinner [at Matthew's house[d]], there were many notorious swindlers there as guests!

[11] The Pharisees were indignant. "Why does your teacher associate with men like that?"

[12] "Because people who are well don't need a doctor! It's the sick people who do!" was Jesus' reply. [13] Then he added, "Now go away and learn the meaning of this verse of Scripture,

'It isn't your sacrifices and your gifts I want—I want you to be merciful.'[e]

---

d Isaiah 53:4.   e Implied.   f Literally, "a scribe."   g Literally, "the Son of Man." h Or, "Let me first go and bury my father."   i Literally, "Have you come here to torment us before the time?"   9a Literally, "his own city."   b Literally, "the Son of Man."   c The Matthew who wrote this book.   d Implied.   e Hosea 6:6.

For I have come to urge sinners, not the self-righteous, back to God."

¹⁴ One day the disciples of John the Baptist came to Jesus and asked him, "Why don't your disciples fast as we do and as the Pharisees do?"

¹⁵ "Should the bridegroom's friends mourn and go without food while he is with them?" Jesus asked. "But the time is coming when I[f] will be taken from them. Time enough then for them to refuse to eat.

¹⁶ "And who would patch an old garment with unshrunk cloth? For the patch would tear away and make the hole worse. ¹⁷ And who would use old wineskins[g] to store new wine? For the old skins would burst with the pressure, and the wine would be spilled and the skins ruined. Only new wineskins are used to store new wine. That way both are preserved."

¹⁸ As he was saying this, the rabbi of the local synagogue came and worshiped him. "My little daughter has just died," he said, "but you can bring her back to life again if you will only come and touch her."

¹⁹ As Jesus and the disciples were going to the rabbi's home, ²⁰ a woman who had been sick for twelve years with internal bleeding came up behind him and touched a tassel of his robe, ²¹ for she thought, "If I only touch him, I will be healed."

²² Jesus turned around and spoke to her. "Daughter," he said, "all is well! Your faith has healed you." And the woman was well from that moment.

²³ When Jesus arrived at the rabbi's home and saw the noisy crowds and heard the funeral music, ²⁴ he said, "Get them out, for the little girl isn't dead; she is only sleeping!" Then how they all scoffed and sneered at him!

²⁵ When the crowd was finally outside, Jesus went in where the little girl was lying and took her by the hand, and she jumped up and was all right again! ²⁶ The report of this wonderful miracle swept the entire countryside.

²⁷ As Jesus was leaving her home, two blind men followed along behind, shouting, "O Son of King David, have mercy on us."

²⁸ They went right into the house where he was staying, and Jesus asked them, "Do you believe I can make you see?"

"Yes, Lord," they told him, "we do."

²⁹ Then he touched their eyes and said, "Because of your faith it will happen."

³⁰ And suddenly they could see! Jesus sternly warned them not to tell anyone about it, ³¹ but instead they spread his fame all over the town.[h]

³² Leaving that place, Jesus met a man who couldn't speak because a demon was inside him. ³³ So Jesus cast out the demon, and instantly the man could talk. How the crowds marveled! "Never in all our lives have we seen anything like this," they exclaimed.

³⁴ But the Pharisees said, "The reason he can cast out demons is that he is demon-possessed himself—possessed by Satan, the demon king!"

³⁵ Jesus traveled around through all the cities and villages of that area, teaching in the Jewish synagogues and announcing the Good News about the Kingdom. And wherever he went he healed people of every sort of illness. ³⁶ And what pity he felt for the crowds that came, because their problems were so great and they didn't know what to do or where to go for help. They were like sheep without a shepherd.

³⁷ "The harvest is so great, and the workers are so few," he told his disciples. ³⁸ "So pray to the one in charge of the harvesting, and ask him to recruit more workers for his harvest fields."

10 JESUS CALLED HIS twelve disciples to him, and gave them authority to cast out evil spirits and to heal every kind of sickness and disease.

²,³,⁴ Here are the names of his twelve disciples:

Simon (also called Peter),
Andrew (Peter's brother),
James (Zebedee's son),
John (James' brother),
Philip,
Bartholomew,
Thomas,

---

f Literally, "the Bridegroom."   g These were leather bags for storing wine.
h Literally, "in all that land."

Matthew (the tax collector), James (Alphaeus' son), Thaddaeus, Simon (a member of "The Zealots," a subversive political party), Judas Iscariot (the one who betrayed him).

⁵ Jesus sent them out with these instructions: "Don't go to the Gentiles or the Samaritans, ⁶ but only to the people of Israel—God's lost sheep. ⁷ Go and announce to them that the Kingdom of Heaven is near. ᵃ ⁸ Heal the sick, raise the dead, cure the lepers, and cast out demons. Give as freely as you have received!

⁹ "Don't take any money with you; ¹⁰ don't even carry a duffle bag with extra clothes and shoes, or even a walking stick; for those you help should feed and care for you. ¹¹ Whenever you enter a city or village, search for a godly man and stay in his home until you leave for the next town. ¹² When you ask permission to stay, be friendly, ¹³ and if it turns out to be a godly home, give it your blessing; if not, keep the blessing. ¹⁴ Any city or home that doesn't welcome you—shake off the dust of that place from your feet as you leave. ¹⁵ Truly, the wicked cities of Sodom and Gomorrah will be better off at Judgment Day than they.

¹⁶ "I am sending you out as sheep among wolves. Be as wary as serpents and harmless as doves. ¹⁷ But beware! For you will be arrested and tried, and whipped in the synagogues. ¹⁸ Yes, and you must stand trial before governors and kings for my sake. This will give you the opportunity to tell them about me, yes, to witness to the world.

¹⁹ "When you are arrested, don't worry about what to say at your trial, for you will be given the right words at the right time. ²⁰ For it won't be you doing the talking—it will be the Spirit of your heavenly Father speaking through you!

²¹ "Brother shall betray brother to death, and fathers shall betray their own children. And children shall rise against their parents and cause their deaths. ²² Everyone shall hate you because you belong to me. But all of you who endure to the end shall be saved.

²³ "When you are persecuted in one city, flee to the next! Iᵇ will return before you have reached them all! ²⁴ A student is not greater than his teacher. A servant is not above his master. ²⁵ The student shares his teacher's fate. The servant shares his master's! And since I, the master of the household, have been called 'Satan,'ᶜ how much more will you! ²⁶ But don't be afraid of those who threaten you. For the time is coming when the truth will be revealed: their secret plots will become public information.

²⁷ "What I tell you now in the gloom, shout abroad when daybreak comes. What I whisper in your ears, proclaim from the housetops!

²⁸ "Don't be afraid of those who can kill only your bodies—but can't touch your souls! Fear only God who can destroy both soul and body in hell. ²⁹ Not one sparrow (What do they cost? Two for a penny?) can fall to the ground without your Father knowing it. ³⁰ And the very hairs of your head are all numbered. ³¹ So don't worry! You are more valuable to him than many sparrows.

³² "If anyone publicly acknowledges me as his friend, I will openly acknowledge him as my friend before my father in heaven. ³³ But if anyone publicly denies me, I will openly deny him before my Father in heaven.

³⁴ "Don't imagine that I came to bring peace to the earth! No, rather, a sword. ³⁵ I have come to set a man against his father, and a daughter against her mother, and a daughter-in-law against her mother-in-law— ³⁶ a man's worst enemies will be right in his own home! ³⁷ If you love your father and mother more than you love me, you are not worthy of being mine; or if you love your son or daughter more than me, you are not worthy of being mine. ³⁸ If you refuse to take up your cross and follow me, you are not worthy of being mine.

³⁹ "If you cling to your life, you will lose it; but if you give it up for me, you will save it.

⁴⁰ "Those who welcome you are welcom-

---

a Or, "at hand," or, "has arrived."   b Literally, "the Son of Man."   c See Matthew 9:34, where they called him this.

ing me. And when they welcome me they are welcoming God who sent me. ⁴¹ If you welcome a prophet because he is a man of God, you will be given the same reward a prophet gets. And if you welcome good and godly men because of their godliness, you will be given a reward like theirs.

⁴² "And if, as my representatives, you give even a cup of cold water to a little child, you will surely be rewarded."

11 WHEN JESUS HAD finished giving these instructions to his twelve disciples, he went off preaching in the cities where they were scheduled to go.ᵃ

² John the Baptist, who was now in prison, heard about all the miracles the Messiah was doing, so he sent his disciples to ask Jesus, ³ "Are you really the one we are waiting for, or shall we keep on looking?"

⁴ Jesus told them, "Go back to John and tell him about the miracles you've seen me do— ⁵ the blind people I've healed, and the lame people now walking without help, and the cured lepers, and the deaf who hear, and the dead raised to life; and tell him about my preaching the Good News to the poor. ⁶ Then give him this message, 'Blessed are those who don't doubt me.' "

⁷ When John's disciples had gone, Jesus began talking about him to the crowds. "When you went out into the barren wilderness to see John, what did you expect him to be like? Grass blowing in the wind? ⁸ Or were you expecting to see a man dressed as a prince in a palace? ⁹ Or a prophet of God? Yes, and he is more than just a prophet. ¹⁰ For John is the man mentioned in the Scriptures—a messenger to precede me, to announce my coming, and prepare people to receive me.ᵇ

¹¹ "Truly, of all men ever born, none shines more brightly than John the Baptist. And yet, even the lesser lights in the Kingdom of Heaven will be greater than he is! ¹² And from the time John the Baptist began

preaching and baptizing until now, ardent multitudes have been crowding toward the Kingdom of Heaven,ᶜ ¹³ for all the laws and prophets looked forward [to the Messiahᵈ]. Then John appeared, ¹⁴ and if you are willing to understand what I mean, he is Elijah, the one the prophets said would come [at the time the Kingdom beginsᵈ]. ¹⁵ If ever you were willing to listen, listen now!

¹⁶ "What shall I say about this nation? These people are like children playing, who say to their little friends, ¹⁷ 'We played wedding and you weren't happy, so we played funeral but you weren't sad.' ¹⁸ For John the Baptist doesn't even drink wine and often goes without food, and you say, 'He's crazy.'ᵉ ¹⁹ And I, the Messiah,ᶠ feast and drink, and you complain that I am 'a glutton and a drinking man, and hang around with the worst sort of sinners!' But brilliant men like you can justify your every inconsistency!"ᵍ

²⁰ Then he began to pour out his denunciations against the cities where he had done most of his miracles, because they hadn't turned to God.

²¹ "Woe to you, Chorazin, and woe to you, Bethsaida! For if the miracles I did in your streets had been done in wicked Tyre and Sidonʰ their people would have repented long ago in shame and humility. ²² Truly, Tyre and Sidon will be better off on the Judgment Day than you! ²³ And Capernaum, though highly honored,ⁱ shall go down to hell! For if the marvelous miracles I did in you had been done in Sodom,ʰ it would still be here today. ²⁴ Truly, Sodom will be better off at the Judgment Day than you."

²⁵ And Jesus prayed this prayer: "O Father, Lord of heaven and earth, thank you for hiding the truth from those who think themselves so wise, and for revealing it to little children. ²⁶ Yes, Father, for it pleased you to do it this way! . . .

²⁷ "Everything has been entrusted to me by my Father. Only the Father knows the

---

a Literally, "to teach and preach in their cities." Luke 10:1 remarks, "The Lord appointed seventy others and sent them two and two before his face, into every city and place where he himself was about to come." b Literally, "prepare your way before you."   c Literally, "the Kingdom of Heaven suffers violence and men of violence take it by force."   d Implied.   e Literally, "he has a demon."   f Literally, "the Son of Man."   g Literally, "wisdom is justified by her children."   h Cities destroyed by God for their wickedness.   i Highly honored by Christ's being there.

Son, and the Father is known only by the Son and by those to whom the Son reveals him. ²⁸ Come to me and I will give you rest —all of you who work so hard beneath a heavy yoke. ²⁹,³⁰ Wear my yoke—for it fits perfectly—and let me teach you; for I am gentle and humble, and you shall find rest for your souls; for I give you only light burdens."

12 ABOUT THAT TIME, Jesus was walking one day through some grainfields with his disciples. It was on the Sabbath, the Jewish day of worship, and his disciples were hungry; so they began breaking off heads of wheat and eating the grain.

² But some Pharisees saw them do it and protested, "Your disciples are breaking the law. They are harvesting on the Sabbath."

³ But Jesus said to them, "Haven't you ever read what King David did when he and his friends were hungry? ⁴ He went into the Temple and they ate the special bread permitted to the priests alone. That was breaking the law too. ⁵ And haven't you ever read in the law of Moses how the priests on duty in the Temple may work on the Sabbath? ⁶ And truly, one is here who is greater than the Temple! ⁷ But if you had known the meaning of this Scripture verse, 'I want you to be merciful more than I want your offerings,' you would not have condemned those who aren't guilty! ⁸ For I, the Messiah,ᵃ am master even of the Sabbath."

⁹ Then he went over to the synagogue, ¹⁰ and noticed there a man with a deformed hand. The Phariseesᵇ asked Jesus, "Is it legal to work by healing on the Sabbath day?" (They were, of course, hoping he would say "Yes," so they could arrestᶜ him!) ¹¹ This was his answer: "If you had just one sheep, and it fell into a well on the Sabbath, would you work to rescue it that day? Of course you would.ᵇ ¹² And how much more valuable is a person than a sheep! Yes, it is right to do good on the Sabbath." ¹³ Then he said to the man, "Stretch out your arm." And as he did, his hand became normal, just like the other one!

¹⁴ Then the Pharisees called a meeting to plot Jesus' arrest and death. ¹⁵ But he knew what they were planning, and left the synagogue, with many following him. He healed all the sick among them, ¹⁶ but he cautioned them against spreading the news about his miracles. ¹⁷ This fulfilled the prophecy of Isaiah concerning him:

¹⁸ "Look at my Servant.
See my Chosen One.
He is my Beloved, in whom my soul
    delights.
I will put my Spirit upon him,
And he will judge the nations.
¹⁹ He does not fight nor shout;
He does not raise his voice!
²⁰ He does not crush the weak,
Or quench the smallest hope;
He will end all conflict with his final
    victory,
²¹ And his name shall be the hope
Of all the world."ᵈ

²² Then a demon-possessed man—he was both blind and unable to talk—was brought to Jesus, and Jesus healed him so that he could both speak and see. ²³ The crowd was amazed. "Maybe Jesus is the Messiah!"ᵉ they exclaimed.

²⁴ But when the Pharisees heard about the miracle they said, "He can cast out demons because he is Satan,ᶠ king of devils."

²⁵ Jesus knew their thoughts and replied, "A divided kingdom ends in ruin. A city or home divided against itself cannot stand. ²⁶ And if Satan is casting out Satan, he is fighting himself, and destroying his own kingdom. ²⁷ And if, as you claim, I am casting out demons by invoking the powers of Satan, then what power do your own people use when they cast them out? Let them answer your accusation! ²⁸ But if I am casting out demons by the Spirit of God, then the Kingdom of God has arrived among you. ²⁹ One cannot rob Satan's kingdom without first binding Satan.ᵍ Only then can his demons be cast out!ʰ ³⁰ Anyone who isn't helping me is harming me.

³¹,³² "Even blasphemy against meᵃ or any other sin, can be forgiven—all except one: speaking against the Holy Spirit shall never be forgiven, either in this world or in the

---

a Literally, "the Son of Man."   b Implied.   c Literally, "accuse."   d Isaiah 42:1–4.
e Literally, "the Son of David."   f Literally, "Beelzebub."   g Literally, "the strong."
h Literally, "then will he spoil his house."

810

world to come. ³³ "A tree is identified by its fruit. A tree from a select variety produces good fruit; poor varieties don't. ³⁴ You brood of snakes! How could evil men like you speak what is good and right? For a man's heart determines his speech. ³⁵ A good man's speech reveals the rich treasures within him. An evil-hearted man is filled with venom, and his speech reveals it. ³⁶ And I tell you this, that you must give account on Judgment Day for every idle word you speak. ³⁷ Your words now reflect your fate then: either you will be justified by them or you will be condemned."

³⁸ One day some of the Jewish leaders, including some Pharisees, came to Jesus asking him to show them a miracle.

^{39,40} But Jesus replied, "Only an evil, faithless nation would ask for further proof; and none will be given except what happened to Jonah the prophet! For as Jonah was in the great fish for three days and three nights, so I, the Messiah,ⁱ shall be in the heart of the earth three days and three nights. ⁴¹ The men of Nineveh shall arise against this nation at the judgment and condemn you. For when Jonah preached to them, they repented and turned to God from all their evil ways. And now a greater than Jonah is here—and you refuse to believe him.^{j 42} The Queen of Sheba shall rise against this nation in the judgment, and condemn it; for she came from a distant land to hear the wisdom of Solomon; and now a greater than Solomon is here—and you refuse to believe him.^j

^{43,44,45} "This evil nation is like a man possessed by a demon. For if the demon leaves, it goes into the deserts^k for a while, seeking rest but finding none. Then it says, 'I will return to the man I came from.' So it returns and finds the man's heart clean but empty! Then the demon finds seven other spirits more evil than itself, and all enter the man and live in him. And so he is worse off than before."

^{46,47} As Jesus was speaking in a crowded house^l his mother and brothers were outside, wanting to talk with him. When some-

one told him they were there, ⁴⁸ he remarked, "Who is my mother? Who are my brothers?" ⁴⁹ He pointed to his disciples. "Look!" he said, "these are my mother and brothers." ⁵⁰ Then he added, "Anyone who obeys my Father in heaven is my brother, sister and mother!"

13 LATER THAT SAME day, Jesus left the house and went down to the shore, ^{2,3} where an immense crowd soon gathered. He got into a boat and taught from it while the people listened on the beach. He used many illustrations such as this one in his sermon:

"A farmer was sowing grain in his fields. ⁴ As he scattered the seed across the ground, some fell beside a path, and the birds came and ate it. ⁵ And some fell on rocky soil where there was little depth of earth; the plants sprang up quickly enough in the shallow soil, ⁶ but the hot sun soon scorched them and they withered and died, for they had so little root. ⁷ Other seeds fell among thorns, and the thorns choked out the tender blades. ⁸ But some fell on good soil, and produced a crop that was thirty, sixty, or even a hundred times as much as he had planted. ⁹ If you have ears, listen!"

¹⁰ His disciples came and asked him, "Why do you always use these hard-to-understand^a illustrations?"

¹¹ Then he explained to them that only they were permitted to understand about the Kingdom of Heaven, and others were not.

^{12,13} "For to him who has will more be given," he told them, "and he will have great plenty; but from him who has not, even the little he has will be taken away. That is why I use these illustrations, so people will hear and see but not understand.^b

¹⁴ "This fulfills the prophecy of Isaiah:
'They hear, but don't understand;
    they look, but don't see!
¹⁵ For their hearts are fat
    and heavy, and their ears
    are dull, and they have
    closed their eyes in sleep,
¹⁶ so they won't see and hear

---

i Literally, "the Son of Man."   j Implied.   k Literally, "passes through waterless places."
l Implied in Mark 3:32.   13a Implied.   b Those who were receptive to spiritual truth understood the illustrations. To others they were only stories without meaning.

and understand and turn to God again, and let me heal them.' But blessed are your eyes, for they see; and your ears, for they hear. [17] Many a prophet and godly man has longed to see what you have seen, and hear what you have heard, but couldn't.

[18] "Now here is the explanation of the story I told about the farmer planting grain: [19] The hard path where some of the seeds fell represents the heart of a person who hears the Good News about the Kingdom and doesn't understand it; then Satan[c] comes and snatches away the seeds from his heart. [20] The shallow, rocky soil represents the heart of a man who hears the message and receives it with real joy, [21] but he doesn't have much depth in his life, and the seeds don't root very deeply, and after a while when trouble comes, or persecution begins because of his beliefs, his enthusiasm fades, and he drops out. [22] The ground covered with thistles represents a man who hears the message, but the cares of this life and his longing for money choke out God's Word, and he does less and less for God. [23] The good ground represents the heart of a man who listens to the message and understands it and goes out and brings thirty, sixty, or even a hundred others into the Kingdom."[d]

[24] Here is another illustration Jesus used: "The Kingdom of Heaven is like a farmer sowing good seed in his field; [25] but one night as he slept, his enemy came and sowed thistles among the wheat. [26] When the crop began to grow, the thistles grew too.

[27] "The farmer's men came and told him, 'Sir, the field where you planted that choice seed is full of thistles!'

[28] " 'An enemy has done it,' he exclaimed.

" 'Shall we pull out the thistles?' they asked.

[29] " 'No,' he replied. 'You'll hurt the wheat if you do. [30] Let both grow together until the harvest, and I will tell the reapers to sort out the thistles and burn them, and put the wheat in the barn.' " [31,32] Here is another of his illustrations: "The Kingdom

of Heaven is like a tiny mustard seed planted in a field. It is the smallest of all seeds, but becomes the largest of plants, and grows into a tree where birds can come and find shelter."

[33] He also used this example: "The Kingdom of Heaven can be compared to a woman making bread. She takes a measure of flour and mixes in the yeast until it permeates every part of the dough."

[34,35] Jesus constantly used these illustrations when speaking to the crowds. In fact, because the prophets said that he would use so many, he never spoke to them without at least one illustration. For it had been prophesied, "I will talk in parables; I will explain mysteries hidden since the beginning of time."[e] [36] Then, leaving the crowds outside, he went into the house. His disciples asked him to explain to them the illustration of the thistles and the wheat.

[37] "All right," he said, "I[f] am the farmer who sows the choice seed. [38] The field is the world, and the seed represents the people of the Kingdom; the thistles are the people belonging to Satan. [39] The enemy who sowed the thistles among the wheat is the devil; the harvest is the end of the world,[g] and the reapers are the angels.

[40] "Just as in this story the thistles are separated and burned, so shall it be at the end of the world:[g] [41] I[f] will send my angels and they will separate out of the Kingdom every temptation and all who are evil, [42] and throw them into the furnace and burn them. There shall be weeping and gnashing of teeth. [43] Then the godly shall shine as the sun in their Father's Kingdom. Let those with ears, listen!

[44] "The Kingdom of Heaven is like a treasure a man discovered in a field. In his excitement, he sold everything he owned to get enough money to buy the field—and get the treasure, too!

[45] "Again, the Kingdom of Heaven is like a pearl merchant on the lookout for choice pearls. [46] He discovered a real bargain—a pearl of great value—and sold everything he owned to purchase it!

[47,48] "Again, the Kingdom of Heaven can

---

c Literally, "the evil." d Literally, "produces a crop many times greater than the amount planted—thirty, sixty, or even a hundred times as much." e Psalm 78:2. f Literally, "the Son of Man." g Or, "age."

be illustrated by a fisherman—he casts a net into the water and gathers in fish of every kind, valuable and worthless. When the net is full, he drags it up onto the beach and sits down and sorts out the edible ones into crates and throws the others away. ⁴⁹ That is the way it will be at the end of the world[h]—the angels will come and separate the wicked people from the godly, ⁵⁰ casting the wicked into the fire; there shall be weeping and gnashing of teeth. ⁵¹ Do you understand?"

"Yes," they said, "we do."

⁵² Then he added, "Those experts in Jewish law who are now my disciples have double treasures—from the Old Testament as well as from the New!"[i]

⁵³,⁵⁴ When Jesus had finished giving these illustrations, he returned to his home town, Nazareth in Galilee,[j] and taught there in the synagogue and astonished everyone with his wisdom and his miracles.

⁵⁵ "How is this possible?" the people exclaimed. "He's just a carpenter's son, and we know Mary his mother and his brothers—James, Joseph, Simon, and Judas. ⁵⁶ And his sisters—they all live here. How can he be so great?" ⁵⁷ And they became angry with him!

Then Jesus told them, "A prophet is honored everywhere except in his own country, and among his own people!" ⁵⁸ And so he did only a few great miracles there, because of their unbelief.

14 WHEN KING[a] HEROD heard about Jesus, ² he said to his men, "This must be John the Baptist, come back to life again. That is why he can do these miracles." ³ For Herod had arrested John and chained him in prison at the demand of[b] his wife Herodias, his brother Philip's ex-wife, ⁴ because John had told him it was wrong for him to marry her. ⁵ He would have killed John but was afraid of a riot, for all the people believed John was a prophet.

⁶ But at a birthday party for Herod, Herodias' daughter performed a dance that greatly pleased him, ⁷ so he vowed to give her anything she wanted. ⁸ Consequently, at her mother's urging, the girl asked for John the Baptist's head on a tray.

⁹ The king was grieved, but because of his oath, and because he didn't want to back down in front of his guests, he issued the necessary orders.

¹⁰ So John was beheaded in the prison, ¹¹ and his head was brought on a tray and given to the girl, who took it to her mother. ¹² Then John's disciples came for his body and buried it, and came to tell Jesus what had happened.

¹³ As soon as Jesus heard the news, he went off by himself in a boat to a remote area to be alone. But the crowds saw where he was headed, and followed by land from many villages.

¹⁴ So when Jesus came out of the wilderness, a vast crowd was waiting for him and he pitied them and healed their sick.

¹⁵ That evening the disciples came to him and said, "It is already past time for supper, and there is nothing to eat here in the desert; send the crowds away so they can go to the villages and buy some food."

¹⁶ But Jesus replied, "That isn't necessary—you feed them!"

¹⁷ "What!" they exclaimed. "We have exactly five small loaves of bread and two fish!"

¹⁸ "Bring them here," he said.

¹⁹ Then he told the people to sit down on the grass; and he took the five loaves and two fish, looked up into the sky and asked God's blessing on the meal, then broke the loaves apart and gave them to the disciples to place before the people. ²⁰ And everyone ate until full! And when the scraps were picked up afterwards, there were twelve basketfuls left over! ²¹ (About 5,000 men were in the crowd that day, besides all the women and children.) ²² Immediately after this, Jesus told his disciples to get into their boat and cross to the other side of the lake while he stayed to get the people started home.

²³,²⁴ Then afterwards he went up into the hills to pray. Night fell, and out on the lake the disciples were in trouble. For the wind had risen and they were fighting heavy seas.

---

h Or, "age."   i Literally, "brings back out of his treasure things both new and old." The paraphrase is of course highly anachronistic!   j Implied.   14a Literally, "the Tetrarch"—he was one of four "kings" over the area, his sovereignty being Galilee and Peraea.   b Literally, "on account of."

²⁵ About four o'clock in the morning Jesus came to them, walking on the water! ²⁶ They screamed in terror, for they thought he was a ghost. ²⁷ But Jesus immediately spoke to them, reassuring them. "Don't be afraid!" he said.

²⁸ Then Peter called to him: "Sir, if it is really you, tell me to come over to you, walking on the water."

²⁹ "All right," the Lord said, "come along!"

So Peter went over the side of the boat and walked on the water toward Jesus. ³⁰ But when he looked around at the high waves, he was terrified and began to sink. "Save me, Lord!" he shouted.

³¹ Instantly Jesus reached out his hand and rescued him. "O man of little faith," Jesus said. "Why did you doubt me?" ³² And when they had climbed back into the boat, the wind stopped.

³³ The others sat there, awestruck. "You really are the Son of God!" they exclaimed.

³⁴ They landed at Gennesaret. ³⁵ The news of their arrival spread quickly throughout the city, and soon people were rushing around, telling everyone to bring in their sick to be healed. ³⁶ The sick begged him to let them touch even the tassel of his robe, and all who did were healed.

15 SOME PHARISEES AND other Jewish leaders now arrived from Jerusalem to interview Jesus.

² "Why do your disciples disobey the ancient Jewish traditions?" they demanded. "For they ignore our ritual of ceremonial handwashing before they eat." ³ He replied, "And why do your traditions violate the direct commandments of God? ⁴ For instance, God's law is 'Honor your father and mother; anyone who reviles his parents must die.' ⁵ˑ⁶ But you say, 'Even if your parents are in need, you may give their support money to the church[a] instead.' And so, by your man-made rule, you nullify the direct command of God to honor and care for your parents. ⁷ You hypocrites! Well did Isaiah prophesy of you, ⁸ 'These people say they honor me, but their hearts are far

away. ⁹ Their worship is worthless, for they teach their man-made laws instead of those from God.' "[b]

¹⁰ Then Jesus called to the crowds and said, "Listen to what I say and try to understand: ¹¹ You aren't made unholy by eating non-kosher food! It is what you *say* and *think*[c] that makes you unclean."

¹² Then the disciples came and told him, "You offended the Pharisees by that remark."

¹³ˑ¹⁴ Jesus replied, "Every plant not planted by my Father shall be rooted up, so ignore them. They are blind guides leading the blind, and both will fall into a ditch."

¹⁵ Then Peter asked Jesus to explain what he meant when he said that people are not defiled by non-kosher food.

¹⁶ "Don't you understand?" Jesus asked him. ¹⁷ "Don't you see that anything you eat passes through the digestive tract and out again? ¹⁸ But evil words come from an evil heart, and defile the man who says them. ¹⁹ For from the heart come evil thoughts, murder, adultery, fornication, theft, lying and slander. ²⁰ These are what defile; but there is no spiritual defilement from eating without first going through the ritual of ceremonial handwashing!"

²¹ Jesus then left that part of the country and walked the fifty miles[d] to Tyre and Sidon.

²² A woman from Canaan who was living there came to him, pleading, "Have mercy on me, O Lord, King David's Son! For my daughter has a demon within her, and it torments her constantly."

²³ But Jesus gave her no reply—not even a word. Then his disciples urged him to send her away. "Tell her to get going," they said, "for she is bothering us with all her begging."

²⁴ Then he said to the woman, "I was sent to help the Jews—the lost sheep of Israel—not the Gentiles."

²⁵ But she came and worshiped him and pled again, "Sir, help me!"

²⁶ "It doesn't seem right to take bread from the children and throw it to the dogs," he said.

---

a Literally, "to God."   b Isaiah 29:13.   c Implied. Literally, "what comes out of a man defiles a man."
d Implied. Literally, "withdrew into the parts of Tyre and Sidon."

²⁷ "Yes, it is!" she replied, "for even the puppies beneath the table are permitted to eat the crumbs that fall."

²⁸ "Woman," Jesus told her, "your faith is large, and your request is granted." And her daughter was healed right then.

²⁹ Jesus now returned to the Sea of Galilee, and climbed a hill and sat there. ³⁰ And a vast crowd brought him their lame, blind, maimed, and those who couldn't speak, and many others, and laid them before Jesus, and he healed them all. ³¹ What a spectacle it was! Those who hadn't been able to say a word before were talking excitedly, and those with missing arms and legs had new ones; the crippled were walking and jumping around, and those who had been blind were gazing about them! The crowds just marveled, and praised the God of Israel.

³² Then Jesus called his disciples to him and said, "I pity these people—they've been here with me for three days now, and have nothing left to eat; I don't want to send them away hungry or they will faint along the road."

³³ The disciples replied, "And where would we get enough here in the desert for all this mob to eat?"

³⁴ Jesus asked them, "How much food do you have?" And they replied, "Seven loaves of bread and a few small fish!"

³⁵ Then Jesus told all of the people to sit down on the ground, ³⁶ and he took the seven loaves and the fish, and gave thanks to God for them, and divided them into pieces, and gave them to the disciples who presented them to the crowd. ³⁷,³⁸ And everyone ate until full—4,000 men besides the women and children! And afterwards, when the scraps were picked up, there were seven basketfuls left over!

³⁹ Then Jesus sent the people home and got into the boat and crossed to Magadan.

16 ONE DAY THE Pharisees and Sadducees[a] came to test Jesus' claim of being the Messiah by asking him to show them some great demonstrations in the skies.

²,³ He replied, "You are good at reading the weather signs of the skies—red sky tonight means fair weather tomorrow; red sky in the morning means foul weather all day—but you can't read the obvious signs of the times! ⁴ This evil, unbelieving nation is asking for some strange sign in the heavens, but no further proof will be given except the miracle that happened to Jonah." Then Jesus walked out on them.

⁵ Arriving across the lake, the disciples discovered they had forgotten to bring any food.

⁶ "Watch out!" Jesus warned them; "beware of the yeast of the Pharisees and Sadducees."

⁷ They thought he was saying this because they had forgotten to bring bread.

⁸ Jesus knew what they were thinking and told them, "O men of little faith! Why are you so worried about having no food? ⁹ Won't you ever understand? Don't you remember at all the 5,000 I fed with five loaves, and the basketfuls left over? ¹⁰ Don't you remember the 4,000 I fed, and all that was left? ¹¹ How could you even think I was talking about food? But again I say, 'Beware of the yeast of the Pharisees and Sadducees.'"

¹² Then at last they understood that by "yeast" he meant the *wrong teaching* of the Pharisees and Sadducees.

¹³ When Jesus came to Caesarea Philippi, he asked his disciples, "Who are the people saying I[b] am?"

¹⁴ "Well," they replied, "some say John the Baptist; some, Elijah; some, Jeremiah or one of the other prophets."

¹⁵ Then he asked them, "Who do *you* think I am?"

¹⁶ Simon Peter answered, "The Christ, the Messiah, the Son of the living God."

¹⁷ "God has blessed you, Simon, son of Jonah," Jesus said, "for my Father in heaven has personally revealed this to you—this is not from any human source. ¹⁸ You are Peter, a stone; and upon this rock I will build my church; and all the powers of hell shall not prevail against it. ¹⁹ And I will give you the keys of the Kingdom of Heaven; whatever doors you lock on earth shall be locked in heaven; and whatever doors you open on earth shall be open in

---

a Jewish politico-religious leaders of two different parties.   b Literally, "the Son of Man."

heaven!"

20 Then he warned the disciples against telling others that he was the Messiah.

21 From then on Jesus began to speak plainly to his disciples about going to Jerusalem, and what would happen to him there—that he would suffer at the hands of the Jewish leaders,c that he would be killed, and that three days later he would be raised to life again.

22 But Peter took him aside to remonstrate with him. "Heaven forbid, sir," he said. "This is not going to happen to you!"

23 Jesus turned on Peter and said, "Get away from me, you Satan! You are a dangerous trap to me. You are thinking merely from a human point of view, and not from God's."

24 Then Jesus said to the disciples, "If anyone wants to be a follower of mine, let him deny himself and take up his cross and follow me. 25 For anyone who keeps his life for himself shall lose it; and anyone who loses his life for me shall find it again. 26 What profit is there if you gain the whole world—and lose eternal life? What can be compared with the value of eternal life? 27 For I, the Son of Mankind, shall come with my angels in the glory of my Father and judge each person according to his deeds. 28 And some of you standing right here now will certainly live to see me coming in my Kingdom."

17 SIX DAYS LATER Jesus took Peter, James, and his brother John to the top of a high and lonely hill, 2 and as they watched, his appearance changed so that his face shone like the sun and his clothing became dazzling white.

3 Suddenly Moses and Elijah appeared and were talking with him. 4 Peter blurted out, "Sir, it's wonderful that we can be here! If you want me to, I'll make three shelters,a one for you and one for Moses and one for Elijah."

5 But even as he said it, a bright cloud came over them, and a voice from the cloud said, *"This* is my beloved Son, and I am wonderfully pleased with him. Obeyb *him.* "

6 At this the disciples fell face downward to the ground, terribly frightened. 7 Jesus came over and touched them. "Get up," he said, "don't be afraid."

8 And when they looked, only Jesus was with them.

9 As they were going down the mountain, Jesus commanded them not to tell anyone what they had seen until after he had risen from the dead.

10 His disciples asked, "Why do the Jewish leaders insist Elijah must return before the Messiah comes?"c

11 Jesus replied, "They are right. Elijah must come and set everything in order. 12 And, in fact, he has already come, but he wasn't recognized, and was badly mistreated by many. And I, the Messiahd, shall also suffer at their hands."

13 Then the disciples realized he was speaking of John the Baptist.

14 When they arrived at the bottom of the hill, a huge crowd was waiting for them. A man came and knelt before Jesus and said, 15 "Sir, have mercy on my son, for he is mentally deranged, and in great trouble, for he often falls into the fire or into the water; 16 so I brought him to your disciples, but they couldn't cure him."

17 Jesus replied, "Oh, you stubborn, faithless people! How long shall I bear with you? Bring him here to me." 18 Then Jesus rebuked the demon in the boy and it left him, and from that moment the boy was well.

19 Afterwards the disciples asked Jesus privately, "Why couldn't we cast that demon out?"

20 "Because of your little faith," Jesus told them. "For if you had faith even as small as a tiny mustard seed you could say to this mountain, 'Move!' and it would go far away. Nothing would be impossible. 21 But this kind of demon won't leave unless you have prayed and gone without food."e

22,23 One day while they were still in Galilee, Jesus told them, "I am going to be betrayed into the power of those who will kill

---

c Literally, "of the elders, and chief priests, and scribes." was in Peter's mind is not explained.   b Literally, "hear him." come first."   d Literally, "the Son of Man." scripts.

17a Literally, "three tabernacles" or "tents." What c Implied. Literally, "that Elijah must e This verse is omitted in many of the ancient manu-

me, and on the third day afterwards I will be brought back to life again." And the disciples' hearts were filled with sorrow and dread.

²⁴ On their arrival in Capernaum, the Temple tax collectors came to Peter and asked him, "Doesn't your master pay taxes?"

²⁵ "Of course he does," Peter replied.

Then he went into the house to talk to Jesus about it, but before he had a chance to speak, Jesus asked him, "What do you think, Peter? Do kings levy assessments against their own people, or against conquered foreigners?"

²⁶,²⁷ "Against the foreigners," Peter replied.

"Well, then," Jesus said, "the citizens are free! However, we don't want to offend them, so go down to the shore and throw in a line, and open the mouth of the first fish you catch. You will find a coin to cover the taxes for both of us; take it and pay them."

18 ABOUT THAT TIME the disciples came to Jesus to ask which of them would be greatest in the Kingdom of Heaven!
² Jesus called a small child over to him and set the little fellow down among them, ³ and said, "Unless you turn to God from your sins and become as little children, you will never get into the Kingdom of Heaven. ⁴ Therefore anyone who humbles himself as this little child, is the greatest in the Kingdom of Heaven. ⁵ And any of you who welcomes a little child like this because you are mine, is welcoming me and caring for me. ⁶ But if any of you causes one of these little ones who trusts in me to lose his faith,ᵃ it would be better for you to have a rock tied to your neck and be thrown into the sea.
⁷ "Woe upon the world for all its evils.ᵇ Temptation to do wrong is inevitable, but woe to the man who does the tempting. ⁸ So if your hand or foot causes you to sin, cut it off and throw it away. Better to enter heaven crippled than to be in hell with both of your hands and feet. ⁹ And if your eye causes you to sin, gouge it out and throw

it away. Better to enter heaven with one eye than to be in hell with two.

¹⁰ "Beware that you don't look down upon a single one of these little children. For I tell you that in heaven their angels have constant accessᶜ to my Father. ¹¹ And I, the Messiah,ᵈ came to save the lost.ᵉ ¹² "If a man has a hundred sheep, and one wanders away and is lost, what will he do? Won't he leave the ninety-nine others and go out into the hills to search for the lost one? ¹³ And if he finds it, he will rejoice over it more than over the ninety-nine others safe at home! ¹⁴ Just so, it is not my Father's will that even one of these little ones should perish.

¹⁵ "If a brother sins against you, go to him privately and confront him with his fault. If he listens and confesses it, you have won back a brother. ¹⁶ But if not, then take one or two others with you and go back to him again, proving everything you say by these witnesses. ¹⁷ If he still refuses to listen, then take your case to the church, and if the church's verdict favors you, but he won't accept it, then the church should excommunicate him.ᶠ ¹⁸ And I tell you this— whatever you bind on earth is bound in heaven, and whatever you free on earth will be freed in heaven.

¹⁹ "I also tell you this—if two of you agree down here on earth concerning anything you ask for, my Father in heaven will do it for you. ²⁰ For where two or three gather together because they are mine, I will be right there among them."

²¹ Then Peter came to him and asked, "Sir, how often should I forgive a brother who sins against me? Seven times?"

²² "No!" Jesus replied, "seventy times seven!

²³ "The Kingdom of Heaven can be compared to a king who decided to bring his accounts up to date. ²⁴ In the process, one of his debtors was brought in who owed him $10,000,000!ᵍ ²⁵ He couldn't pay, so the king ordered him sold for the debt, also his wife and children and everything he had.

²⁶ "But the man fell down before the

---

a Literally, "cause to stumble."   b Literally, "because of occasions of stumbling."   c "Do always behold . . ."   d Literally, "the Son of Man."   e This verse is omitted in many manuscripts, some ancient.   f Literally, "let him be to you as the Gentile and the publican."   g Literally, "10,000 talents." Approximately £3,000,000.

king, his face in the dust, and said, 'Oh, sir, be patient with me and I will pay it all.'

[27] "Then the king was filled with pity for him and released him and forgave his debt.

[28] "But when the man left the king, he went to a man who owed him $2,000[h] and grabbed him by the throat and demanded instant payment.

[29] "The man fell down before him and begged him to give him a little time. 'Be patient and I will pay it,' he pled.

[30] "But his creditor wouldn't wait. He had the man arrested and jailed until the debt would be paid in full.

[31] "Then the man's friends went to the king and told him what had happened. [32] And the king called before him the man he had forgiven and said, 'You evil-hearted wretch! Here I forgave you all that tremendous debt, just because you asked me to— [33] shouldn't you have mercy on others, just as I had mercy on you?'

[34] "Then the angry king sent the man to the torture chamber until he had paid every last penny due. [35] So shall my heavenly Father do to you if you refuse to truly forgive your brothers."

19 AFTER JESUS HAD finished this address, he left Galilee and circled back to Judea from across the Jordan River. [2] Vast crowds followed him, and he healed their sick. [3] Some Pharisees came to interview him, and tried to trap him into saying something that would ruin him.

"Do you permit divorce?" they asked.

[4] "Don't you read the Scriptures?" he replied. "In them it is written that at the beginning God created man and woman, [5,6] and that a man should leave his father and mother, and be forever united to his wife. The two shall become one—no longer two, but one! And no man may divorce what God has joined together."

[7] "Then, why," they asked, "did Moses say a man may divorce his wife by merely writing her a letter of dismissal?"

[8] Jesus replied, "Moses did that in recognition of your hard and evil hearts, but it was not what God had originally intended.

[9] And I tell you this, that anyone who divorces his wife, except for fornication, and marries another, commits adultery."[a]

[10] Jesus' disciples then said to him, "If that is how it is, it is better not to marry!"

[11] "Not everyone can accept this statement," Jesus said. "Only those whom God helps. [12] Some are born without the ability to marry,[b] and some are disabled by men, and some refuse to marry for the sake of the Kingdom of Heaven. Let anyone who can, accept my statement."

[13] Little children were brought for Jesus to lay his hands on them and pray. But the disciples scolded those who brought them. "Don't bother him," they said.

[14] But Jesus said, "Let the little children come to me, and don't prevent them. For of such is the Kingdom of Heaven." [15] And he put his hands on their heads and blessed them before he left.

[16] Someone came to Jesus with this question: "Good master, what must I do to have eternal life?"

[17] "When you call me good you are calling me God," Jesus replied, "for God alone is truly good.[c] But to answer your question, you can get to heaven if you keep the commandments."

[18] "Which ones?" the man asked.

And Jesus replied, "Don't kill, don't commit adultery, don't steal, don't lie, [19] honor your father and mother, and love your neighbor as yourself!"

[20] "I've always obeyed every one of them," the youth replied. "What else must I do?"

[21] Jesus told him, "If you want to be perfect, go and sell everything you have and give the money to the poor, and you will have treasure in heaven; and come, follow me." [22] But when the young man heard this, he went away sadly, for he was very rich.

[23] Then Jesus said to his disciples, "It is almost impossible for a rich man to get into the Kingdom of Heaven. [24] I say it again—it is easier for a camel to go through the eye of a needle than for a rich man to enter the Kingdom of God!"

[25] This remark confounded the disciples.

---

h Approximately £700.   19a "And the man who marries a divorced woman commits adultery." This sentence is added in some ancient manuscripts.   b Literally, "born eunuchs," or, "born emasculated."
c Implied from Luke 18:19.

"Then who in the world can be saved?" they asked.

²⁶ Jesus looked at them intently and said, "Humanly speaking, no one. But with God, everything is possible."

²⁷ Then Peter said to him, "We left everything to follow you. What will we get out of it?"

²⁸ And Jesus replied, "When I, the Messiah,ᵈ shall sit upon my glorious throne in the Kingdom,ᵉ you my disciples shall certainly sit on twelve thrones judging the twelve tribes of Israel. ²⁹ And anyone who gives up his home, brothers, sisters, father, mother, wife,ᶠ children, or property, to follow me, shall receive a hundred times as much in return, and shall have eternal life. ³⁰ But many who are first now will be last then; and some who are last now will be first then."

20 HERE IS ANOTHER illustration of the Kingdom of Heaven. "The owner of an estate went out early one morning to hire workers for his harvest field. ² He agreed to pay them $20 a dayᵃ and sent them out to work.

³ "A couple of hours later he was passing a hiring hall and saw some men standing around waiting for jobs, ⁴ so he sent them also into his fields, telling them he would pay them whatever was right at the end of the day. ⁵ At noon and again around three o'clock in the afternoon he did the same thing.

⁶ "At five o'clock that evening he was in town again and saw some more men standing around and asked them, 'Why haven't you been working today?'

⁷ " 'Because no one hired us,' they replied.

" 'Then go on out and join the others in my fields,' he told them.

⁸ "That evening he told the paymaster to call the men in and pay them, beginning with the last men first. ⁹ When the men hired at five o'clock were paid, each received $20. ¹⁰ So when the men hired earlier came to get theirs, they assumed they would receive much more. But they, too, were paid $20.

¹¹,¹² "They protested, 'Those fellows worked only one hour, and yet you've paid them just as much as those of us who worked all day in the scorching heat.'

¹³ " 'Friend,' he answered one of them, 'I did you no wrong! Didn't you agree to work all day for $20? ¹⁴ Take it and go. It is my desire to pay all the same; ¹⁵ is it against the law to give away my money if I want to? Should you be angry because I am kind?' ¹⁶ And so it is that the last shall be first, and the first, last."

¹⁷ As Jesus was on the way to Jerusalem, he took the twelve disciples aside, ¹⁸ and talked to them about what would happen to him when they arrived.

"Iᵇ will be betrayed to the chief priests and other Jewish leaders, and they will condemn me to die. ¹⁹ And they will hand me over to the Roman government, and I will be mocked and crucified, and the third day I will rise to life again."

²⁰ Then the mother of James and John, the sons of Zebedee, brought them to Jesus and respectfully asked a favor.

²¹ "What is your request?" he asked. She replied, "In your Kingdom, will you let my two sons sit on two thronesᶜ next to yours?"

²² But Jesus told her, "You don't know what you are asking!" Then he turned to James and John and asked them, "Are you able to drink from the terrible cup I am about to drink from?"

"Yes," they replied, "we are able!"

²³ "You shall indeed drink from it," he told them. "But I have no right to say who will sit on the thronesᶜ next to mine. Those places are reserved for the persons my Father selects."

²⁴ The other ten disciples were indignant when they heard what James and John had asked for.

²⁵ But Jesus called them together and said, "Among the heathen, kings are tyrants and each minor official lords it over those beneath him. ²⁶ But among you it is quite different. Anyone wanting to be a leader among you must be your servant. ²⁷ And if you want to be right at the top, you must

---

d Literally, "the Son of Man." scripts, but included in Luke 18:29. to $20 in modern times, or £7.   e Literally, "in the regeneration." 20a Literally, "a denarius," the payment for a day's labor; equivalent b Literally, "the Son of Man."   f Omitted here in many manuc Implied.

serve like a slave. ²⁸ Your attitude^d must be like my own, for I, the Messiah,^e did not come to be served, but to serve, and to give my life as a ransom for many."

²⁹ As Jesus and the disciples left the city of Jericho, a vast crowd surged along behind.

³⁰ Two blind men were sitting beside the road and when they heard that Jesus was coming that way, they began shouting, "Sir, King David's Son, have mercy on us!"

³¹ The crowd told them to be quiet, but they only yelled the louder.

³²,³³ When Jesus came to the place where they were he stopped in the road and called, "What do you want me to do for you?"

"Sir," they said, "we want to see!"

³⁴ Jesus was moved with pity for them and touched their eyes. And instantly they could see, and followed him.

21 AS JESUS AND the disciples approached Jerusalem, and were near the town of Bethphage on the Mount of Olives, Jesus sent two of them into the village ahead.

² "Just as you enter," he said, "you will see a donkey tied there, with its colt beside it. Untie them and bring them here. ³ If anyone asks you what you are doing, just say, 'The Master needs them,' and there will be no trouble."

⁴ This was done to fulfill the ancient prophecy, ⁵ "Tell Jerusalem her King is coming to her, riding humbly on a donkey's colt!"

⁶ The two disciples did as Jesus said, ⁷ and brought the animals to him and threw their garments over the colt^a for him to ride on. ⁸ And some in the crowd threw down their coats along the road ahead of him, and others cut branches from the trees and spread them out before him.

⁹ Then the crowds surged on ahead and pressed along behind, shouting, "God bless King David's Son!" . . . "God's Man is here!^b . . . Bless him, Lord!" . . . "Praise God in highest heaven!"

¹⁰ The entire city of Jerusalem was stirred as he entered. "Who is this?" they asked.

¹¹ And the crowds replied, "It's Jesus, the prophet from Nazareth up in Galilee."

¹² Jesus went into the Temple, drove out the merchants, and knocked over the money-changers' tables and the stalls of those selling doves.

¹³ "The Scriptures say my Temple is a place of prayer," he declared, "but you have turned it into a den of thieves."

¹⁴ And now the blind and crippled came to him and he healed them there in the Temple. ¹⁵ But when the chief priests and other Jewish leaders saw these wonderful miracles, and heard even the little children in the Temple shouting, "God bless the Son of David," they were disturbed and indignant and asked him, "Do you hear what these children are saying?"

¹⁶ "Yes," Jesus replied. "Didn't you ever read the Scriptures? For they say, 'Even little babies shall praise him!' "

¹⁷ Then he returned to Bethany, where he stayed overnight.

¹⁸ In the morning, as he was returning to Jerusalem, he was hungry, ¹⁹ and noticed a fig tree beside the road. He went over to see if there were any figs, but there were only leaves. Then he said to it, "Never bear fruit again!" And soon^c the fig tree withered up.

²⁰ The disciples were utterly amazed and asked, "How did the fig tree wither so quickly?"

²¹ Then Jesus told them, "Truly, if you have faith, and don't doubt, you can do things like this and much more. You can even say to this Mount of Olives, 'Move over into the ocean,' and it will. ²² You can get anything—*anything* you ask for in prayer—if you believe."

²³ When he had returned to the Temple and was teaching, the chief priests and other Jewish leaders came up to him and demanded to know by whose authority he had thrown out the merchants the day before.^d

²⁴ "I'll tell you if you answer one question first," Jesus replied. ²⁵ "Was John the Baptist sent from God, or not?"

They talked it over among themselves. "If we say, 'From God,' " they said, "then

---

d Implied.   e Literally, "the Son of Man."   21 a Implied.   b Literally, "Blessed is he who comes in the name of the Lord."   c Or, "immediately."   d Literally, "By what authority do you do these things?"

he will ask why we didn't believe what John said. ²⁶ And if we deny that God sent him, we'll be mobbed, for the crowd all think he was a prophet." ²⁷ So they finally replied, "We don't know!"

And Jesus said, "Then I won't answer your question either.

²⁸ "But what do you think about this? A man with two sons told the older boy, 'Son, go out and work on the farm today.' ²⁹ 'I won't,' he answered, but later he changed his mind and went. ³⁰ Then the father told the youngest, 'You go!' and he said, 'Yes, sir, I will.' But he didn't. ³¹ Which of the two was obeying his father?"

They replied, "The first, of course."

Then Jesus explained his meaning: "Surely evil men and prostitutes will get into the Kingdom before you do. ³² For John the Baptist told you to repent and turn to God, and you wouldn't, while very evil men and prostitutes did. And even when you saw this happening, you refused to repent, and so you couldn't believe.

³³ "Now listen to this story: A certain landowner planted a vineyard with a hedge around it, and built a platform for the watchman, then leased the vineyard to some farmers on a sharecrop basis, and went away to live in another country.

³⁴ "At the time of the grape harvest he sent his agents to the farmers to collect his share. ³⁵ But the farmers attacked his men, beat one, killed one and stoned another.

³⁶ "Then he sent a larger group of his men to collect for him, but the results were the same. ³⁷ Finally the owner sent his son, thinking they would surely respect him.

³⁸ "But when these farmers saw the son coming they said among themselves, 'Here comes the heir to this estate; come on, let's kill him and get it for ourselves!' ³⁹ So they dragged him out of the vineyard and killed him.

⁴⁰ "When the owner returns, what do you think he will do to those farmers?"

⁴¹ The Jewish leaders replied, "He will put the wicked men to a horrible death, and lease the vineyard to others who will pay him promptly."

⁴² Then Jesus asked them, "Didn't you ever read in the Scriptures: 'The stone rejected by the builders has been made the honored cornerstone;^e how remarkable! what an amazing thing the Lord has done'?

⁴³ "What I mean is that the Kingdom of God shall be taken away from you, and given to a nation that will give God his share of the crop.^f ⁴⁴ All who stumble on this rock of truth^g shall be broken, but those it falls on will be scattered as dust."

⁴⁵ When the chief priests and other Jewish leaders realized that Jesus was talking about them—that they were the farmers in his story— ⁴⁶ they wanted to get rid of him, but were afraid to try because of the crowds, for they accepted Jesus as a prophet.

22 JESUS TOLD SEVERAL other stories to show what the Kingdom of Heaven is like.

"For instance," he said, "it can be illustrated by the story of a king who prepared a great wedding dinner for his son. ³ Many guests were invited, and when the banquet was ready he sent messengers to notify everyone that it was time to come. But all refused! ⁴ So he sent other servants to tell them, 'Everything is ready and the roast is in the oven. Hurry!'

⁵ "But the guests he had invited merely laughed and went on about their business, one to his farm, another to his store; ⁶ others beat up his messengers and treated them shamefully, even killing some of them.

⁷ "Then the angry king sent out his army and destroyed the murderers and burned their city. ⁸ And he said to his servants, 'The wedding feast is ready, and the guests I invited aren't worthy of the honor. ⁹ Now go out to the street corners and invite everyone you see.'

¹⁰ "So the servants did, and brought in all they could find, good and bad alike; and the banquet hall was filled with guests. ¹¹ But when the king came in to meet the guests he noticed a man who wasn't wearing the wedding robe [provided for him^a]. ¹² " 'Friend,' he asked, 'how does it happen that you are here without a wedding

---

e Literally, "the head of the corner."   f Literally, "bringing forth the fruits."   g Literally, "on this stone."   22a Implied.

robe?' And the man had no reply.

[13] "Then the king said to his aides, 'Bind him hand and foot and throw him out into the outer darkness where there is weeping and gnashing of teeth.' [14] For many are called, but few are chosen."

[15] Then the Pharisees met together to try to think of some way to trap Jesus into saying something for which they could arrest him. [16] They decided to send some of their men along with the Herodians[b] to ask him this question: "Sir, we know you are very honest and teach the truth regardless of the consequences, without fear or favor. [17] Now tell us, is it right to pay taxes to the Roman government or not?"

[18] But Jesus saw what they were after. "You hypocrites!" he exclaimed. "Who are you trying to fool with your trick questions? [19] Here, show me a coin." And they handed him a penny.

[20] "Whose picture is stamped on it?" he asked them. "And whose name is this beneath the picture?"

[21] "Caesar's," they replied.

"Well, then," he said, "give it to Caesar if it is his, and give God everything that belongs to God."

[22] His reply surprised and baffled them and they went away.

[23] But that same day some of the Sadducees, who say there is no resurrection after death, came to him and asked, [24] "Sir, Moses said that if a man died without children, his brother should marry the widow and their children would get all the dead man's property. [25] Well, we had among us a family of seven brothers. The first of these men married and then died, without children, so his widow became the second brother's wife. [26] This brother also died without children, and the wife was passed to the next brother, and so on until she had been the wife of each of them. [27] And then she also died. [28] So whose wife will she be in the resurrection? For she was the wife of all seven of them!"

[29] But Jesus said, "Your error is caused by your ignorance of the Scriptures and of God's power! [30] For in the resurrection there is no marriage; everyone is as the angels in heaven. [31] But now, as to whether there is a resurrection of the dead—don't you ever read the Scriptures? Don't you realize that God was speaking directly to you when he said, [32] 'I *am* the God of Abraham, Isaac, and Jacob'? So God is not the God of the dead, but of the *living.*"[c]

[33] The crowds were profoundly impressed by his answers— [34,35] but not the Pharisees! When they heard that he had routed the Sadducees with his reply, they thought up a fresh question of their own to ask him.

One of them, a lawyer, spoke up: [36] "Sir, which is the most important command in the laws of Moses?"

[37] Jesus replied, " 'Love the Lord your God with all your heart, soul, and mind.' [38,39] This is the first and greatest commandment. The second most important is similar: 'Love your neighbor as much as you love yourself.' [40] All the other commandments and all the demands of the prophets stem from these two laws and are fulfilled if you obey them. Keep only these and you will find that you are obeying all the others."

[41] Then, surrounded by the Pharisees, he asked them a question: [42] "What about the Messiah? Whose son is he?" "The son of David," they replied.

[43] "Then why does David, speaking under the inspiration of the Holy Spirit, call him 'Lord'?" Jesus asked. "For David said,

[44] 'God said to my Lord, Sit at my right hand until I put your enemies beneath your feet.'

[45] Since David called him 'Lord,' how can he be merely his son?"

[46] They had no answer. And after that no one dared ask him any more questions.

23 THEN JESUS SAID to the crowds, and to his disciples, [2] "You would think these Jewish leaders and these Pharisees were Moses, the way they keep making up so many laws![a] [3] And of course you should obey their every whim! It may be all right to do what they say, but above anything else, *don't follow their example.* For they

---

b The Herodians were a Jewish political party.   c i.e., if Abraham, Isaac, and Jacob, long dead, were not alive in the presence of God, then God would have said, "I *was* the God of Abraham, etc."
23 a Literally, "sit on Moses' seat."

don't do what they tell you to do. ⁴ They load you with impossible demands that they themselves don't even try to keep. ⁵ "Everything they do is done for show. They act holy[b] by wearing on their arms little prayer boxes with Scripture verses inside,[c] and by lengthening the memorial fringes of their robes. ⁶ And how they love to sit at the head table at banquets, and in the reserved pews in the synagogue! ⁷ How they enjoy the deference paid them on the streets, and to be called 'Rabbi' and 'Master'! ⁸ Don't ever let anyone call you that. For only God is your Rabbi and all of you are on the same level, as brothers. ⁹ And don't address anyone here on earth as 'Father,' for only God in heaven should be addressed like that. ¹⁰ And don't be called 'Master,' for only one is your master, even the Messiah.

¹¹ "The more lowly your service to others, the greater you are. To be the greatest, be a servant. ¹² But those who think themselves great shall be disappointed and humbled; and those who humble themselves shall be exalted.

¹³,¹⁴ "Woe to you, Pharisees, and you other religious leaders. Hypocrites! For you won't let others enter the Kingdom of Heaven, and won't go in yourselves. And you pretend to be holy, with all your long, public prayers in the streets, while you are evicting widows from their homes. Hypocrites! ¹⁵ Yes, woe upon you hypocrites. For you go to all lengths to make one convert, and then turn him into twice the son of hell you are yourselves. ¹⁶ Blind guides! Woe upon you! For your rule is that to swear 'By God's Temple' means nothing—you can break that oath, but to swear 'By the gold in the Temple' is binding! ¹⁷ Blind fools! Which is greater, the gold, or the Temple that sanctifies the gold? ¹⁸ And you say that to take an oath 'By the altar' can be broken, but to swear 'By the gifts on the altar' is binding! ¹⁹ Blind! For which is greater, the gift on the altar, or the altar itself that sanctifies the gift? ²⁰ When you swear 'By the altar' you are swearing by it and everything on it, ²¹ and when you swear 'By the Temple' you are swearing by it, and by God who

lives in it. ²² And when you swear 'By heavens' you are swearing by the Throne of God and by God himself.

²³ "Yes, woe upon you, Pharisees, and you other religious leaders—hypocrites! For you tithe down to the last mint leaf in your garden, but ignore the important things—justice and mercy and faith. Yes, you should tithe, but you shouldn't leave the more important things undone. ²⁴ Blind guides! You strain out a gnat and swallow a camel.

²⁵ "Woe to you, Pharisees, and you religious leaders—hypocrites! You are so careful to polish the outside of the cup, but the inside is foul with extortion and greed. ²⁶ Blind Pharisees! First cleanse the inside of the cup, and then the whole cup will be clean.

²⁷ "Woe to you, Pharisees, and you religious leaders! You are like beautiful mausoleums—full of dead men's bones, and of foulness and corruption. ²⁸ You try to look like saintly men, but underneath those pious robes of yours are hearts besmirched with every sort of hypocrisy and sin.

²⁹,³⁰ "Yes, woe to you, Pharisees, and you religious leaders—hypocrites! For you build monuments to the prophets killed by your fathers and lay flowers on the graves of the godly men they destroyed, and say, 'We certainly would never have acted as our fathers did.'

³¹ "In saying that, you are accusing yourselves of being the sons of wicked men. ³² And you are following in their steps, filling up the full measure of their evil. ³³ Snakes! Sons of vipers! How shall you escape the judgment of hell?

³⁴ "I will send you prophets, and wise men, and inspired writers, and you will kill some by crucifixion, and rip open the backs of others with whips in your synagogues, and hound them from city to city, ³⁵ so that you will become guilty of all the blood of murdered godly men from righteous Abel to Zechariah (son of Barachiah), slain by you in the Temple between the altar and the sanctuary. ³⁶ Yes, all the accumulated judgment of the centuries shall break upon the heads of this very generation.

---

b Implied.   c Literally, "enlarge their phylacteries."

³⁷ "O Jerusalem, Jerusalem, the city that kills the prophets, and stones all those God sends to her! How often I have wanted to gather your children together as a hen gathers her chicks beneath her wings, but you wouldn't let me. ³⁸ And now your house is left to you, desolate. ³⁹ For I tell you this, you will never see me again until you are ready to welcome the one sent to you from God."ᵈ

24 AS JESUS WAS leaving the Temple grounds, his disciples came along and wanted to take him on a tour of the various Temple buildings.

² But he told them, "All these buildings will be knocked down, with not one stone left on top of another!"

³ "When will this happen?" the disciples asked him later, as he sat on the slopes of the Mount of Olives. "What events will signal your return, and the end of the world?"ᵃ

⁴ Jesus told them, "Don't let anyone fool you. ⁵ For many will come claiming to be the Messiah, and will lead many astray. ⁶ When you hear of wars beginning, this does not signal my return; these must come, but the end is not yet. ⁷ The nations and kingdoms of the earth will rise against each other and there will be famines and earthquakes in many places. ⁸ But all this will be only the beginning of the horrors to come.

⁹ "Then you will be tortured and killed and hated all over the world because you are mine, ¹⁰ and many of you shall fall back into sin and betray and hate each other. ¹¹ And many false prophets will appear and lead many astray. ¹² Sin will be rampant everywhere and will cool the love of many. ¹³ But those enduring to the end shall be saved.

¹⁴ "And the Good News about the Kingdom will be preached throughout the whole world, so that all nations will hear it, and then, finally, the end will come.

¹⁵ "So, when you see the horrible thingᵇ

(told about by Danielᶜ the prophet) standing in a holy place (Note to the reader: You know what is meant!),ᵈ ¹⁶ then those in Judea must flee into the Judean hills. ¹⁷ Those on their porchesᵉ must not even go inside to pack before they flee. ¹⁸ Those in the fields should not return to their homes for their clothes.

¹⁹ "And woe to pregnant women and to those with babies in those days. ²⁰ And pray that your flight will not be in winter, or on the Sabbath.ᶠ ²¹ For there will be persecution such as the world has never before seen in all its history, and will never see again. ²² "In fact, unless those days are shortened, all mankind will perish. But they will be shortened for the sake of God's chosenᵍ people.

²³ "Then if anyone tells you, 'The Messiah has arrived at such and such a place, or has appeared here or there,' don't believe it. ²⁴ For false Christs shall arise, and false prophets, and will do wonderful miracles, so that if it were possible, even God's chosenᵍ ones would be deceived. ²⁵ See, I have warned you.

²⁶ "So if someone tells you the Messiah has returned and is out in the desert, don't bother to go and look. Or, that he is hiding at a certain place, don't believe it! ²⁷ For as the lightning flashes across the sky from east to west, so shall my coming be, when I, the Messiah,ʰ return. ²⁸ And wherever the carcass is, there the vultures will gather.

²⁹ "Immediately after the persecution of those days the sun will be darkened, and the moon will not give light, and the stars will seemⁱ to fall from the heavens, and the powers overshadowing the earth will be convulsed.ʲ

³⁰ "And then at last the signal of my comingᵏ will appear in the heavens and there will be deep mourning all around the earth. And the nations of the world will see me arrive in the clouds of heaven, with power and great glory. ³¹ And I shall send forth my angels with the sound of a mighty

---

d Literally, "in the name of the Lord."   24a Literally "age."   b Literally, "the abomination of desolation."   c Daniel 9:27, 11:31, 12:11.   d Literally, "Let the reader take note."   e Literally, "roof tops" which, being flat, were used as porches at that time. See Acts 10:9.   f The city gates were closed on the Sabbath.   g Literally, "the elect."   h Literally, "the Son of Man."   i Literally, "the stars shall fall from heaven."   j Literally, "the powers of the heavens shall be shaken." See Ephesians 6:12. k Literally, "of the coming of the Son of Man."

trumpet blast, and they shall gather my chosen ones from the farthest ends of the earth and heaven.[l]

[32] "Now learn a lesson from the fig tree. When her branch is tender and the leaves begin to sprout, you know that summer is almost here. [33] Just so, when you see all these things beginning to happen, you can know that my[m] return is near, even at the doors. [34] Then at last this age will come to its close.[n]

[35] "Heaven and earth will disappear, but my words remain forever. [36] But no one knows the date and hour when the end will be—not even the angels. No, nor even God's Son.[o] Only the Father knows.

[37,38] "The world will be at ease[p]—banquets and parties and weddings—just as it was in Noah's time before the sudden coming of the flood; [39] people wouldn't believe[q] what was going to happen until the flood actually arrived and took them all away. So shall my coming be.

[40] "Two men will be working together in the fields, and one will be taken, the other left. [41] Two women will be going about their household tasks; one will be taken, the other left.

[42] "So be prepared, for you don't know what day your Lord is coming. [43] Just as a man can prevent trouble from thieves by keeping watch for them, [44] so you can avoid trouble by always being ready for my unannounced return.

[45] "Are you a wise and faithful servant of the Lord? Have I given you the task of managing my household, to feed my children day by day? [46] Blessings on you if I return and find you faithfully doing your work. [47] I will put such faithful ones in charge of everything I own!

[48] "But if you are evil and say to yourself, 'My Lord won't be coming for a while,' [49] and begin oppressing your fellow servants, partying and getting drunk, [50] your Lord will arrive unannounced and unexpected, [51] and severely whip you and send you off to the judgment of the hypocrites; there will be weeping and gnashing of teeth.

25 "THE KINGDOM OF Heaven can be illustrated by the story of ten bridesmaids[a] who took their lamps and went to meet the bridegroom. [2,3,4] But only five of them were wise enough to fill their lamps with oil, while the other five were foolish and forgot.

[5,6] "So, when the bridegroom was delayed, they lay down to rest until midnight, when they were roused by the shout, 'The bridegroom is coming! Come out and welcome him!'

[7,8] "All the girls jumped up and trimmed their lamps. Then the five who hadn't any oil begged the others to share with them, for their lamps were going out.

[9] "But the others replied, 'We haven't enough. Go instead to the shops and buy some for yourselves.'

[10] "But while they were gone, the bridegroom came, and those who were ready went in with him to the marriage feast, and the door was locked.

[11] "Later, when the other five returned, they stood outside, calling, 'Sir, open the door for us!'

[12] "But he called back, 'Go away! It is too late!'[b]

[13] "So stay awake and be prepared, for you do not know the date or moment of my return.[c]

[14] "Again, the Kingdom of Heaven can be illustrated by the story of a man going into another country, who called together his servants and loaned them money to invest for him while he was gone.

[15] "He gave $5,000 to one, $2,000 to another, and $1,000 to the last—dividing it in proportion to their abilities—and then left on his trip. [16] The man who received the $5,000 began immediately to buy and sell with it and soon earned another $5,000. [17] The man with $2,000 went right to work, too, and earned another $2,000. [18] But the man who received the $1,000 dug a hole in the ground and hid the money for safekeeping.

[19] "After a long time their master returned from his trip and called them to him

---

l "From the four winds, from one end of heaven to the other."　　m Literally, "He is nigh."
n Or, "after all these things take place, this generation shall pass away."　　o Literally, "neither the Son."
Many ancient manuscripts omit this phrase.　　p Implied.　　q Literally, "knew not."
25 a Literally, "virgins."　　b Literally, "I know you not!"　　c Implied.

to account for his money. [20] The man to whom he had entrusted the $5,000 brought him $10,000.

[21] "His master praised him for good work. 'You have been faithful in handling this small amount,' he told him, 'so now I will give you many more responsibilities. Begin the joyous tasks I have assigned to you.'

[22] "Next came the man who had received the $2,000, with the report, 'Sir, you gave me $2,000 to use, and I have doubled it.'

[23] " 'Good work,' his master said. 'You are a good and faithful servant. You have been faithful over this small amount, so now I will give you much more.'

[24,25] "Then the man with the $1,000 came and said, 'Sir, I knew you were a hard man, and I was afraid you would rob me of what I earned,[d] so I hid your money in the earth and here it is!'

[26] "But his master replied, 'Wicked man! Lazy slave! Since you knew I would demand your profit, [27] you should at least have put my money into the bank so I could have some interest. [28] Take the money from this man and give it to the man with the $10,000. [29] For the man who uses well what he is given shall be given more, and he shall have abundance. But from the man who is unfaithful, even what little responsibility he has shall be taken from him. [30] And throw the useless servant out into outer darkness: there shall be weeping and gnashing of teeth.'

[31] "But when I, the Messiah,[e] shall come in my glory, and all the angels with me, then I shall sit upon my throne of glory. [32] And all the nations shall be gathered before me. And I will separate the people[f] as a shepherd separates the sheep from the goats, [33] and place the sheep at my right hand, and the goats at my left.

[34] "Then I, the King, shall say to those at my right, 'Come, blessed of my Father, into the Kingdom prepared for you from the founding of the world. [35] For I was hungry and you fed me; I was thirsty and you gave me water; I was a stranger and you invited me into your homes; [36] naked and

you clothed me; sick and in prison, and you visited me.'

[37] "Then these righteous ones will reply, 'Sir, when did we ever see you hungry and feed you? Or thirsty and give you anything to drink? [38] Or a stranger, and help you? Or naked, and clothe you? [39] When did we ever see you sick or in prison, and visit you?'

[40] "And I, the King, will tell them, 'When you did it to these my brothers you were doing it to me!' [41] Then I will turn to those on my left and say, 'Away with you, you cursed ones, into the eternal fire prepared for the devil and his demons. [42] For I was hungry and you wouldn't feed me; thirsty, and you wouldn't give me anything to drink; [43] a stranger, and you refused me hospitality; naked, and you wouldn't clothe me; sick, and in prison, and you didn't visit me.'

[44] "Then they will reply, 'Lord, when did we ever see you hungry or thirsty or a stranger or naked or sick or in prison, and not help you?'

[45] "And I will answer, 'When you refused to help the least of these my brothers, you were refusing help to me.'

[46] "And they shall go away into eternal punishment; but the righteous into everlasting life."

26 WHEN JESUS HAD finished this talk with his disciples, he told them, [2] "As you know, the Passover celebration begins in two days, and I[a] shall be betrayed and crucified."

[3] At that very moment the chief priests and other Jewish officials were meeting at the residence of Caiaphas the High Priest, [4] to discuss ways of capturing Jesus quietly, and killing him. [5] "But not during the Passover celebration," they agreed, "for there would be a riot."

[6] Jesus now proceeded to Bethany, to the home of Simon the leper. [7] While he was eating, a woman came in with a bottle of very expensive perfume, and poured it over his head.

[8,9] The disciples were indignant. "What a waste of good money," they said. "Why,

---

d Literally, "reaping where you didn't sow, and gathering where you didn't scatter, and I was afraid . . ."
e Literally, "the Son of Man."   f Or, "separate the nations."   26a Literally, "the Son of Man."

she could have sold it for a fortune and given it to the poor."

[10] Jesus knew what they were thinking, and said, "Why are you criticizing her? For she has done a good thing to me. [11] You will always have the poor among you, but you won't always have me. [12] She has poured this perfume on me to prepare my body for burial. [13] And she will always be remembered for this deed. The story of what she has done will be told throughout the whole world, wherever the Good News is preached."

[14] Then Judas Iscariot, one of the twelve apostles, went to the chief priests, [15] and asked, "How much will you pay me to get Jesus into your hands?" And they gave him thirty silver coins. [16] From that time on, Judas watched for an opportunity to betray Jesus to them.

[17] On the first day of the Passover ceremonies, when bread made with yeast was purged from every Jewish home, the disciples came to Jesus and asked, "Where shall we plan to eat the Passover?"

[18] He replied, "Go into the city and see Mr. So-and-So, and tell him, 'Our Master says, my time has come, and I will eat the Passover meal with my disciples at your house.' " [19] So the disciples did as he told them, and prepared the supper there.

[20,21] That evening as he sat eating with the Twelve, he said, "One of you will betray me."

[22] Sorrow chilled their hearts, and each one asked, "Am I the one?"

[23] He replied, "It is the one I served first.[b] [24] For I must die[c] just as was prophesied, but woe to the man by whom I am betrayed. Far better for that one if he had never been born."

[25] Judas, too, had asked him, "Rabbi, am I the one?" And Jesus had told him, "Yes."

[26] As they were eating, Jesus took a small loaf of bread and blessed it and broke it apart and gave it to the disciples and said, "Take it and eat it, for this is my body."

[27] And he took a cup of wine and gave thanks for it and gave it to them and said, "Each one drink from it, [28] for this is my

blood, sealing the New Covenant. It is poured out to forgive the sins of multitudes. [29] Mark my words—I will not drink this wine again until the day I drink it new with you in my Father's Kingdom."

[30] And when they had sung a hymn, they went out to the Mount of Olives.

[31] Then Jesus said to them, "Tonight you will all desert me. For it is written in the Scriptures[d] that God will smite the Shepherd, and the sheep of the flock will be scattered. [32] But after I have been brought back to life again I will go to Galilee, and meet you there."

[33] Peter declared, "If everyone else deserts you, I won't."

[34] Jesus told him, "The truth is that this very night, before the cock crows at dawn, you will deny me three times!"

[35] "I would die first!" Peter insisted. And all the other disciples said the same thing.

[36] Then Jesus brought them to a garden grove, Gethsemane, and told them to sit down and wait while he went on ahead to pray. [37] He took Peter with him and Zebedee's two sons James and John, and began to be filled with anguish and despair.

[38] Then he told them, "My soul is crushed with horror and sadness to the point of death . . . stay here . . . stay awake with me."

[39] He went forward a little, and fell face downward on the ground, and prayed, "My Father! If it is possible, let this cup be taken away from me. But I want your will, not mine."

[40] Then he returned to the three disciples and found them asleep. "Peter," he called, "couldn't you even stay awake with me one hour? [41] Keep alert and pray. Otherwise temptation will overpower you. For the spirit indeed is willing, but how weak the body is!"

[42] Again he left them and prayed, "My Father! If this cup cannot go away until I drink it all, your will be done."

[43] He returned to them again and found them sleeping, for their eyes were heavy, [44] so he went back to prayer the third time, saying the same things again.

---

b Literally, "he that dipped his hand with me in the dish."   c Literally, "the Son of Man goes."
d Zechariah 13:7.

⁴⁵ Then he came to the disciples and said, "Sleep on now and take your rest . . . but no! The time has come! I⁰ am betrayed into the hands of evil men! ⁴⁶ Up! Let's be going! Look! Here comes the man who is betraying me!"

⁴⁷ At that very moment while he was still speaking, Judas, one of the Twelve, arrived with a great crowd armed with swords and clubs, sent by the Jewish leaders. ⁴⁸ Judas had told them to arrest the man he greeted, for that would be the one they were after. ⁴⁹ So now Judas came straight to Jesus and said, "Hello, Master!" and embracedᶠ him in friendly fashion.

⁵⁰ Jesus said, "My friend, go ahead and do what you have come for." Then the others grabbed him.

⁵¹ One of the men with Jesus pulled out a sword and slashed off the ear of the High Priest's servant.

⁵² "Put away your sword," Jesus told him. "Those using swords will get killed. ⁵³ Don't you realize that I could ask my Father for thousands of angels to protect us, and he would send them instantly? ⁵⁴ But if I did, how would the Scriptures be fulfilled that describe what is happening now?" ⁵⁵ Then Jesus spoke to the crowd. "Am I some dangerous criminal," he asked, "that you had to arm yourselves with swords and clubs before you could arrest me? I was with you teaching daily in the Temple and you didn't stop me then. ⁵⁶ But this is all happening to fulfill the words of the prophets as recorded in the Scriptures."

At that point, all the disciples deserted him and fled.

⁵⁷ Then the mob led him to the home of Caiaphas the High Priest, where all the Jewish leaders were gathering. ⁵⁸ Meanwhile, Peter was following far to the rear, and came to the courtyard of the High Priest's house and went in and sat with the soldiers, and waited to see what was going to be done to Jesus.

⁵⁹ The chief priests and, in fact, the entire Jewish Supreme Court assembled there and looked for witnesses who would lie about Jesus, in order to build a case against him

that would result in a death sentence. ⁶⁰,⁶¹ But even though they found many who agreed to be false witnesses, these always contradicted each other.

Finally two men were found who declared, "This man said, 'I am able to destroy the Temple of God and rebuild it in three days.' "

⁶² Then the High Priest stood up and said to Jesus, "Well, what about it? Did you say that, or didn't you?" ⁶³ But Jesus remained silent.

Then the High Priest said to him, "I demand in the name of the living God that you tell us whether you claim to be the Messiah, the Son of God."

⁶⁴ "Yes," Jesus said, "I am. And in the future you will see me, the Messiah,ᵉ sitting at the right hand of God and returning on the clouds of heaven."

⁶⁵,⁶⁶ Then the High Priest tore at his own clothing, shouting, "Blasphemy! What need have we for other witnesses? You have all heard him say it! What is your verdict?"

They shouted, "Death!—Death!—Death!"

⁶⁷ Then they spat in his face and struck him and some slapped him, ⁶⁸ saying, "Prophesy to us, you Messiah! Who struck you that time?"

⁶⁹ Meanwhile, as Peter was sitting in the courtyard a girl came over and said to him, "You were with Jesus, for both of you are from Galilee."ᵍ

⁷⁰ But Peter denied it loudly. "I don't even know what you are talking about," he angrily declared.

⁷¹ Later, out by the gate, another girl noticed him and said to those standing around, "This man was with Jesus—from Nazareth."

⁷² Again Peter denied it, this time with an oath. "I don't even know the man," he said.

⁷³ But after a while the men who had been standing there came over to him and said, "We know you are one of his disciples, for we can tell by your Galileanʰ accent."

⁷⁴ Peter began to curse and swear. "I don't even know the man," he said.

---

e Literally, "the Son of Man."   f Literally, "kissed," the greeting still used among men in Eastern lands.
g Literally, "with Jesus the Galilean."   h Implied.

And immediately the cock crowed. [75] Then Peter remembered what Jesus had said, "Before the cock crows, you will deny me three times." And he went away, crying bitterly.

27 WHEN IT WAS morning, the chief priests and Jewish leaders met again to discuss how to induce the Roman government to sentence Jesus to death.[a] [2] Then they sent him in chains to Pilate, the Roman governor.

[3] About that time Judas, who betrayed him, when he saw that Jesus had been condemned to die, changed his mind and deeply regretted what he had done,[b] and brought back the money to the chief priests and other Jewish leaders.

[4] "I have sinned," he declared, "for I have betrayed an innocent man."

"That's your problem," they retorted.

[5] Then he threw the money onto the floor of the Temple and went out and hanged himself. [6] The chief priests picked the money up. "We can't put it in the collection," they said, "since it's against our laws to accept money paid for murder."

[7] They talked it over and finally decided to buy a certain field where the clay was used by potters, and to make it into a cemetery for foreigners who died in Jerusalem. [8] That is why the cemetery is still called "The Field of Blood."

[9] This fulfilled the prophecy of Jeremiah which says,

> "They took the thirty pieces of silver—the price at which he was valued by the people of Israel— [10] and purchased a field from the potters as the Lord directed me."

[11] Now Jesus was standing before Pilate, the Roman governor. "Are you the Jews' Messiah?"[c] the governor asked him.

"Yes," Jesus replied.

[12] But when the chief priests and other Jewish leaders made their many accusations against him, Jesus remained silent.

[13] "Don't you hear what they are saying?" Pilate demanded.

[14] But Jesus said nothing, much to the governor's surprise.

[15] Now the governor's custom was to release one Jewish prisoner each year during the Passover celebration—anyone they wanted. [16] This year there was a particularly notorious criminal in jail named Barabbas, [17] and as the crowds gathered before Pilate's house that morning he asked them, "Which shall I release to you—Barabbas, or Jesus your Messiah?"[d] [18] For he knew very well that the Jewish leaders had arrested Jesus out of envy because of his popularity with the people.

[19] Just then, as he was presiding over the court, Pilate's wife sent him this message: "Leave that good man alone; for I had a terrible nightmare concerning him last night."

[20] Meanwhile the chief priests and Jewish officials persuaded the crowds to ask for Barabbas' release, and for Jesus' death. [21] So when the governor asked again,[e] "Which of these two shall I release to you?" the crowd shouted back their reply: "Barabbas!"

[22] "Then what shall I do with Jesus, your Messiah?" Pilate asked.

And they shouted, "Crucify him!"

[23] "Why?" Pilate demanded. "What has he done wrong?" But they kept shouting, "Crucify! Crucify!"

[24] When Pilate saw that he wasn't getting anywhere, and that a riot was developing, he sent for a bowl of water and washed his hands before the crowd, saying, "I am innocent of the blood of this good man. The responsibility is yours!"

[25] And the mob yelled back, "His blood be on us and on our children!"

[26] Then Pilate released Barabbas to them. And after he had whipped Jesus, he gave him to the Roman soldiers to take away and crucify. [27] But first they took him into the armory and called out the entire contingent. [28] They stripped him and put a scarlet robe on him, [29] and made a crown from long thorns and put it on his head, and placed a stick in his right hand as a scepter and knelt before him in mockery. "Hail, King of the Jews," they yelled. [30] And they spat on him and grabbed the stick and beat

---

a Literally, "took counsel against Jesus to put him to death." They did not have the authority themselves. b Literally, "repented himself."   c Literally, " 'King' of the Jews."   d Literally, "Jesus who is called Christ."   e Implied.

him on the head with it.

³¹ After the mockery, they took off the robe and put his own garment on him again, and took him out to crucify him. ³² As they were on the way to the execution grounds they came across a man from Cyrene, in Africa—Simon was his name—and forced him to carry Jesus' cross. ³³ Then they went out to an area known as Golgotha, that is, "Skull Hill," ³⁴ where the soldiers gave him drugged wine to drink; but when he had tasted it, he refused.

³⁵ After the crucifixion, the soldiers threw dice to divide up his clothes among themselves. ³⁶ Then they sat around and watched him as he hung there. ³⁷ And they put a sign above his head, "This is Jesus, the King of the Jews."

³⁸ Two robbers were also crucified there that morning, one on either side of him. ³⁹ And the people passing by hurled abuse, shaking their heads at him and saying, ⁴⁰ "So! You can destroy the Temple and build it again in three days, can you? Well, then, come on down from the cross if you are the Son of God!"

⁴¹,⁴²,⁴³ And the chief priests and Jewish leaders also mocked him. "He saved others," they scoffed, "but he can't save himself! So you are the King of Israel, are you? Come down from the cross and we'll believe you! He trusted God—let God show his approval by delivering him! Didn't he say, 'I am God's Son'?"

⁴⁴ And the robbers also threw the same in his teeth.

⁴⁵ That afternoon, the whole earth[f] was covered with darkness for three hours, from noon until three o'clock.

⁴⁶ About three o'clock, Jesus shouted, "Eli, Eli, lama sabachthani," which means, "My God, my God, why have you forsaken me?"

⁴⁷ Some of the bystanders misunderstood and thought he was calling for Elijah. ⁴⁸ One of them ran and filled a sponge with sour wine and put it on a stick and held it up to him to drink. ⁴⁹ But the rest said, "Leave him alone. Let's see whether Elijah will come and save him."

⁵⁰ Then Jesus shouted out again, dismissed his spirit, and died. ⁵¹ And look! The curtain secluding the Holiest Place[g] in the Temple was split apart from top to bottom; and the earth shook, and rocks broke, ⁵² and tombs opened, and many godly men and women who had died came back to life again. ⁵³ After Jesus' resurrection, they left the cemetery and went into Jerusalem, and appeared to many people there.

⁵⁴ The soldiers at the crucifixion and their sergeant were terribly frightened by the earthquake and all that happened. They exclaimed, "Surely this was God's Son."[h]

⁵⁵ And many women who had come down from Galilee with Jesus to care for him were watching from a distance. ⁵⁶ Among them were Mary Magdalene and Mary the mother of James and Joseph, and the mother of James and John (the sons of Zebedee).

⁵⁷ When evening came, a rich man from Arimathea named Joseph, one of Jesus' followers, ⁵⁸ went to Pilate and asked for Jesus' body. And Pilate issued an order to release it to him. ⁵⁹ Joseph took the body and wrapped it in a clean linen cloth, ⁶⁰ and placed it in his own new rock-hewn tomb, and rolled a great stone across the entrance as he left. ⁶¹ Both Mary Magdalene and the other Mary were sitting nearby watching.

⁶² The next day—at the close of the first day of the Passover ceremonies[i] —the chief priests and Pharisees went to Pilate, ⁶³ and told him, "Sir, that liar once said, 'After three days I will come back to life again.' ⁶⁴ So we request an order from you sealing the tomb until the third day, to prevent his disciples from coming and stealing his body and then telling everyone he came back to life! If that happens we'll be worse off than we were at first."

⁶⁵ "Use your own Temple police," Pilate told them. "They can guard it safely enough."

⁶⁶ So they sealed[j] the stone and posted guards to protect it from intrusion.

28 EARLY ON SUNDAY morning, as the new day was dawning, Mary Magda-

---

f Or, "land."   g Implied.   h Or, "a godly man."   i Implied; literally, "on the morrow, which is after the Preparation."   j This was done by stringing a cord across the rock, the cord being sealed at each end with clay.

lene and the other Mary went out to the tomb.

² Suddenly there was a great earthquake; for an angel of the Lord came down from heaven and rolled aside the stone and sat on it. ³ His face shone like lightning and his clothing was a brilliant white. ⁴ The guards shook with fear when they saw him, and fell into a dead faint.

⁵ Then the angel spoke to the women. "Don't be frightened!" he said. "I know you are looking for Jesus, who was crucified, ⁶ but he isn't here! For he has come back to life again, just as he said he would. Come in and see where his body was lying . . . . ⁷ And now, go quickly and tell his disciples that he has risen from the dead, and that he is going to Galilee to meet them there. That is my message to them."

⁸ The women ran from the tomb, badly frightened, but also filled with joy, and rushed to find the disciples to give them the angel's message. ⁹ And as they were running, suddenly Jesus was there in front of them!

"Good morning!"ª he said. And they fell to the ground before him, holding his feet and worshiping him.

¹⁰ Then Jesus said to them, "Don't be frightened! Go tell my brothers to leave at once for Galilee, to meet me there."

¹¹ As the women were on the way into the city, some of the Temple police who had been guarding the tomb went to the chief priests and told them what had happened. ¹²,¹³ A meeting of all the Jewish leaders was called, and it was decided to bribe the police to say they had all been asleep when Jesus' disciples came during the night and stole his body.

¹⁴ "If the governor hears about it," the Council promised, "we'll stand up for you and everything will be all right."

¹⁵ So the police accepted the bribe and said what they were told to. Their story spread widely among the Jews, and is still believed by them to this very day.

¹⁶ Then the eleven disciples left for Galilee, going to the mountain where Jesus had said they would find him. ¹⁷ There they met him and worshiped him—but some of them weren't sure it really was Jesus!

¹⁸ He told his disciples, "I have been given all authority in heaven and earth. ¹⁹ Therefore go and make disciples inᵇ all the nations, baptizing them into the name of the Father and of the Son and of the Holy Spirit, ²⁰ and then teach these new disciples to obey all the commands I have given you; and be sure of this—that I am with you always, even to the end of the world."ᶜ

---

a Literally, "All hail!"   b Literally, "of."   c Or, "age."

The Face

Have you ever noticed how important faces are? You spend hours peering at your own in the mirror. You collect wallet-sized photos of other people's. Nobody gives away wallet-sized pictures of his ankle or hand. It's the face that counts.

A face is just a bulbous stretch of skin with all kinds of knobs and holes. There are two shiny, slick balls that never stay still. A loose, spongy slit periodically pulls back to reveal rows of sharp, porcelain knives. Yet, we like faces, we need them. You never feel you know someone until you've seen his face.

For centuries, men had a hard time picturing God. They never saw his face, just brief glimpses of his power. The relationship was always "over the phone." Then something enormous happened that split history in two. God became man, and visited Earth. He

Tim Stafford

took on a face, and was called Jesus. For 33 years he put himself on display, walking our roads, talking our language, wearing our clothes. Anyone could talk to him. Anyone could look him in the eye.

Mark was one of those who knew about Jesus firsthand, and he was the first to record his impressions. He wasted no time with speeches or sermons: his book is the gospel in action. It's such an important source that the other three Gospels quote all but 31 verses of Mark.

Mark never describes Jesus' physical face. He thought Jesus' actions more important. But he packed into 16 chapters an amazing record of what it was like when God finally took on a face and became a man. It was different than you might think. Most men didn't recognize him! They wanted him to be different. Be prepared for some shockers—God's face isn't ordinary.

MARK

1 HERE BEGINS THE wonderful story of Jesus the Messiah, the Son of God.

² In the book written by the prophet Isaiah, God announced that he would send his Son[a] to earth, and that a special messenger would arrive first to prepare the world for his coming.

³ "This messenger will live out in the barren wilderness," Isaiah[b] said, "and will proclaim that everyone must straighten out his life to be ready for the Lord's arrival."[c]

⁴ This messenger was John the Baptist. He lived in the wilderness and taught that all should be baptized as a public announcement of their decision to turn their backs on sin, so that God could forgive them.[d] ⁵ People from Jerusalem and from all over Judea traveled out into the Judean wastelands to see and hear John, and when they confessed their sins he baptized them in the Jordan River. ⁶ His clothes were woven from camel's hair and he wore a leather belt; locusts and wild honey were his food.

---

a Implied.   b Some ancient manuscripts read, "the prophets said."
This quotation, unrecorded in the book of Isaiah, appears in Malachi 3:1.
c Literally, "make ready the way of the Lord; make his paths straight."   d Literally, "preaching
a baptism of repentance for the forgiveness of sins."

⁷ Here is a sample of his preaching:

"Someone is coming soon who is far greater than I am, so much greater that I am not even worthy to be his slave.ᵉ ⁸ I baptize you withᶠ water but he will baptize you withᶠ God's Holy Spirit!"

⁹ Then one day Jesus came from Nazareth in Galilee, and was baptized by John there in the Jordan River. ¹⁰ The moment Jesus came up out of the water, he saw the heavens open and the Holy Spirit in the form of a dove descending on him, ¹¹ and a voice from heaven said, "You are my beloved Son; you are my Delight."

¹²,¹³ Immediately the Holy Spirit urged Jesus into the desert. There, for forty days, alone except for desert animals, he was subjected to Satan's temptations to sin. And afterwardsᵍ the angels came and cared for him.

¹⁴ Later on, after John was arrested by King Herod,ʰ Jesus went to Galilee to preach God's Good News.

¹⁵ "At last the time has come!" he announced. "God's Kingdom is near! Turn from your sins and act on this glorious news!"

¹⁶ One day as Jesus was walking along the shores of the Sea of Galilee, he saw Simon and his brother Andrew fishing with nets, for they were commercial fishermen.

¹⁷ Jesus called out to them, "Come, follow me! And I will make you fishermen for the souls of men!" ¹⁸ At once they left their nets and went along with him.

¹⁹ A little farther up the beach, he saw Zebedee's sons, James and John, in a boat mending their nets. ²⁰ He called them too, and immediately they left their father Zebedee in the boat with the hired men and went with him.

²¹ Jesus and his companions now arrived at the town of Capernaum and on Saturday morning went into the Jewish place of worship—the synagogue—where he preached. ²² The congregation was surprised at his sermon because he spoke as an authority, and didn't try to prove his points by quoting others—quite unlike what they were used to hearing!ⁱ

²³ A man possessed by a demon was present and began shouting, ²⁴ "Why are you bothering us, Jesus of Nazareth—have you come to destroy us demons? I know who you are—the holy Son of God!"

²⁵ Jesus curtly commanded the demon to say no more and to come out of the man. ²⁶ At that the evil spirit screamed and convulsed the man violently and left him. ²⁷ Amazement gripped the audience and they began discussing what had happened.

"What sort of new religion is this?" they asked excitedly. "Why, even evil spirits obey his orders!"

²⁸ The news of what he had done spread quickly through that entire area of Galilee.

²⁹,³⁰ Then, leaving the synagogue, he and his disciples went over to Simon and Andrew's home, where they found Simon's mother-in-law sick in bed with a high fever. They told Jesus about her right away. ³¹ He went to her bedside, and as he took her by the hand and helped her to sit up, the fever suddenly left, and she got up and prepared dinner for them!

³²,³³ By sunset the courtyard was filled with the sick and demon-possessed, brought to him for healing; and a huge crowd of people from all over the city of Capernaum gathered outside the door to watch. ³⁴ So Jesus healed great numbers of sick folk that evening and ordered many demons to come out of their victims. (But he refused to allow the demons to speak, because they knew who he was.)

³⁵ The next morning he was up long before daybreak and went out alone into the wilderness to pray.

³⁶,³⁷ Later, Simon and the others went out to find him, and told him, "Everyone is asking for you."

³⁸ But he replied, "We must go on to other towns as well, and give my message to them too, for that is why I came."

³⁹ So he traveled throughout the province of Galilee, preaching in the synagogues and releasing many from the power of demons. ⁴⁰ Once a leper came and knelt in front of him and begged to be healed. "If you want to, you can make me well again,"

---

e Literally, "Whose shoes I am not worthy to unloose." controversial point. g Implied in parallel passages.

f Or, "in." The Greek word is not clear on this h Implied. i Literally, "not as the scribes."

he pled.

⁴¹ And Jesus, moved with pity, touched him and said, "I want to! Be healed!" ⁴² Immediately the leprosy was gone—the man was healed!

⁴³,⁴⁴ Jesus then told him sternly, "Go and be examined immediately by the Jewish priest. Don't stop to speak to anyone along the way. Take along the offering prescribed by Moses for a leper who is healed, so that everyone will have proof that you are well again."

⁴⁵ But as the man went on his way he began to shout the good news that he was healed; as a result, such throngs soon surrounded Jesus that he couldn't publicly enter a city anywhere, but had to stay out in the barren wastelands. And people from everywhere came to him there.

2 SEVERAL DAYS LATER he returned to Capernaum, and the news of his arrival spread quickly through the city. ² Soon the house where he was staying was so packed with visitors that there wasn't room for a single person more, not even outside the door. And he preached the Word to them. ³ Four men arrived carrying a paralyzed man on a stretcher. ⁴ They couldn't get to Jesus through the crowd, so they dug through the clay roof above his head and lowered the sick man on his stretcher, right down in front of Jesus.ᵃ

⁵ When Jesus saw how strongly they believed that he would help, Jesus said to the sick man, "Son, your sins are forgiven!"

⁶ But some of the Jewish religious leadersᵇ said to themselves as they sat there, ⁷ "What? This is blasphemy! Does he think he is God? For only God can forgive sins."

⁸ Jesus could read their minds and said to them at once, "Why does this bother you? ⁹,¹⁰,¹¹ I, the Messiah,ᶜ have the authority on earth to forgive sins. But talk is cheap—anybody could say that. So I'll prove it to you by healing this man." Then, turning to the paralyzed man, he commanded, "Pick up your stretcher and go on home, for you are healed!"ᵃ

¹² The man jumped up, took the stretcher, and pushed his way through the stunned onlookers! Then how they praised God. "We've never seen anything like this before!" they all exclaimed.

¹³ Then Jesus went out to the seashore again, and preached to the crowds that gathered around him. ¹⁴ As he was walking up the beach he saw Levi, the son of Alphaeus, sitting at his tax collection booth. "Come with me," Jesus told him. "Come be my disciple."

And Levi jumped to his feet and went along.

¹⁵ That night Levi invited his fellow tax collectors and many other notorious sinners to be his dinner guests so that they could meet Jesus and his disciples. (There were many men of this type among the crowds that followed him.) ¹⁶ But when some of the Jewish religious leadersᵈ saw him eating with these men of ill repute, they said to his disciples, "How can he stand it, to eat with such scum?"

¹⁷ When Jesus heard what they were saying, he told them, "Sick people need the doctor, not healthy ones! I haven't come to tell good people to repent, but the bad ones."

¹⁸ John's disciples and the Jewish leaders sometimes fasted, that is, went without food as part of their religion. One day some people came to Jesus and asked why his disciples didn't do this too.

¹⁹ Jesus replied, "Do friends of the bridegroom refuse to eat at the wedding feast? Should they be sad while he is with them? ²⁰ But some day he will be taken away from them, and then they will mourn. ²¹ [Besides, going without food is part of the old way of doing things.ᵃ] It is like patching an old garment with unshrunk cloth! What happens? The patch pulls away and leaves the hole worse than before. ²² You know better than to put new wine into old wineskins. They would burst. The wine would be spilled out and the wineskins ruined. New wine needs fresh wineskins."

²³ Another time, on a Sabbath day as Jesus and his disciples were walking through the fields, the disciples were break-

---

a Implied.　　b Literally, "scribes."　　　c Literally, "Son of Man."　　　d Literally, "the scribes of the Pharisees."

ing off heads of wheat and eating the grain.[e]

[24] Some of the Jewish religious leaders said to Jesus, "They shouldn't be doing that! It's against our laws to work by harvesting grain on the Sabbath."

[25,26] But Jesus replied, "Didn't you ever hear about the time King David and his companions were hungry, and he went into the house of God—Abiathar was High Priest then—and they ate the special bread[f] only priests were allowed to eat? That was against the law too. [27] But the Sabbath was made to benefit man, and not man to benefit the Sabbath. [28] And I, the Messiah,[g] have authority even to decide what men can do on Sabbath days!"

3 WHILE IN CAPERNAUM Jesus went over to the synagogue again, and noticed a man there with a deformed hand.

[2] Since it was the Sabbath, Jesus' enemies watched him closely. Would he heal the man's hand? If he did, they planned to arrest him!

[3] Jesus asked the man to come and stand in front of the congregation. [4] Then turning to his enemies he asked, "Is it all right to do kind deeds on Sabbath days? Or is this a day for doing harm? Is it a day to save lives or to destroy them?" But they wouldn't answer him. [5] Looking around at them angrily, for he was deeply disturbed by their indifference to human need, he said to the man, "Reach out your hand." He did, and instantly his hand was healed!

[6] At once the Pharisees[a] went away and met with the Herodians[b] to discuss plans for killing Jesus. [7,8] Meanwhile, Jesus and his disciples withdrew to the beach, followed by a huge crowd from all over Galilee, Judea, Jerusalem, Idumea, from beyond the Jordan River, and even from as far away as Tyre and Sidon. For the news about his miracles had spread far and wide and vast numbers came to see him for themselves.

[9] He instructed his disciples to bring around a boat and to have it standing ready to rescue him in case he was crowded off the beach. [10] For there had been many healings that day and as a result great numbers of sick people were crowding around him, trying to touch him.

[11] And whenever those possessed by demons caught sight of him they would fall down before him shrieking, "You are the Son of God!" [12] But he strictly warned them not to make him known.

[13] Afterwards he went up into the hills and summoned certain ones he chose, inviting them to come and join him there; and they did. [14,15] Then he selected twelve of them to be his regular companions and to go out to preach and to cast out demons. [16–19] These are the names of the twelve he chose:

> Simon (he renamed him "Peter"),
> James and John (the sons of Zebedee, but Jesus called them "Sons of Thunder"),
> Andrew,
> Philip,
> Bartholomew,
> Matthew,
> Thomas,
> James (the son of Alphaeus),
> Thaddaeus,
> Simon (a member of a political party advocating violent overthrow of the Roman government),
> Judas Iscariot (who later betrayed him).

[20] When he returned to the house where he was staying, the crowds began to gather again, and soon it was so full of visitors that he couldn't even find time to eat. [21] When his friends heard what was happening they came to try to take him home with them.

"He's out of his mind," they said.

[22] But the Jewish teachers of religion who had arrived from Jerusalem said, "His trouble is that he's possessed by Satan, king of demons. That's why demons obey him."

[23] Jesus summoned these men and asked them (using proverbs they all understood), "How can Satan cast out Satan? [24] A kingdom divided against itself will collapse. [25] A home filled with strife and division destroys itself. [26] And if Satan is fighting against himself, how can he accomplish anything? He

---

e Implied.   f Literally, "shewbread."   g Literally, "the Son of Man."   3a The Pharisees were a religious sect of the Jews.   b A pro-Roman political party.

would never survive. [27] [Satan must be bound before his demons are cast out[c]], just as a strong man must be tied up before his house can be ransacked and his property robbed.

[28] "I solemnly declare that any sin of man can be forgiven, even blasphemy against me; [29] but blasphemy against the Holy Spirit can never be forgiven. It is an eternal sin."

[30] He told them this because they were saying he did his miracles by Satan's power [instead of acknowledging it was by the Holy Spirit's power[c]].

[31,32] Now his mother and brothers arrived at the crowded house where he was teaching, and they sent word for him to come out and talk with them. "Your mother and brothers are outside and want to see you," he was told.

[33] He replied, "Who is my mother? Who are my brothers?" [34] Looking at those around him he said, "These are my mother and brothers! [35] Anyone who does God's will is my brother, and my sister, and my mother."

4 ONCE AGAIN AN immense crowd gathered around him on the beach as he was teaching, so he got into a boat and sat down and talked from there. [2] His usual method of teaching was to tell the people stories. One of them went like this:

[3] "Listen! A farmer decided to sow some grain. As he scattered it across his field, [4] some of it fell on a path, and the birds came and picked it off the hard ground and ate it. [5,6] Some fell on thin soil with underlying rock. It grew up quickly enough, but soon wilted beneath the hot sun and died because the roots had no nourishment in the shallow soil. [7] Other seeds fell among thorns that shot up and crowded the young plants so that they produced no grain. [8] But some of the seeds fell into good soil and yielded thirty times as much as he had planted—some of it even sixty or a hundred times as much! [9] If you have ears, listen!"

[10] Afterwards, when he was alone with the Twelve and with his other disciples, they asked him, "What does your story mean?"

[11,12] He replied, "You are permitted to know some truths about the Kingdom of God that are hidden to those outside the Kingdom:

'Though they see and hear, they will not understand or turn to God, or be forgiven for their sins.'

[13] But if you can't understand *this* simple illustration, what will you do about all the others I am going to tell?

[14] "The farmer I talked about is anyone who brings God's message to others, trying to plant good seed within their lives. [15] The hard pathway, where some of the seed fell, represents the hard hearts of some of those who hear God's message; Satan comes at once to try to make them forget it. [16] The rocky soil represents the hearts of those who hear the message with joy, [17] but, like young plants in such soil, their roots don't go very deep, and though at first they get along fine, as soon as persecution begins, they wilt.

[18] "The thorny ground represents the hearts of people who listen to the Good News and receive it, [19] but all too quickly the attractions of this world and the delights of wealth, and the search for success and lure of nice things come in and crowd out God's message from their hearts, so that no crop is produced.

[20] "But the good soil represents the hearts of those who truly accept God's message and produce a plentiful harvest for God—thirty, sixty, or even a hundred times as much as was planted in their hearts."

[21] Then he asked them, "When someone lights a lamp, does he put a box over it to shut out the light? Of course not! The light couldn't be seen or used. A lamp is placed on a stand to shine and be useful.

[22] "All that is now hidden will someday come to light. [23] If you have ears, listen! [24] And be sure to put into practice what you hear. The more you do this, the more you will understand what I tell you. [25] To him who has shall be given; from him who has not shall be taken away even what he has.

[26] "Here is another story illustrating what the Kingdom of God is like:

"A farmer sowed his field, [27] and went

---

c Implied.

away, and as the days went by, the seeds grew and grew without his help. [28] For the soil made the seeds grow. First a leaf-blade pushed through, and later the wheat-heads formed and finally the grain ripened, [29] and then the farmer came at once with his sickle and harvested it."

[30] Jesus asked, "How can I describe the Kingdom of God? What story shall I use to illustrate it? [31,32] It is like a tiny mustard seed! Though this is one of the smallest of seeds, yet it grows to become one of the largest of plants, with long branches where birds can build their nests and be sheltered."

[33] He used many such illustrations to teach the people as much as they were ready to understand.[a] [34] In fact, he taught only by illustrations in his public teaching, but afterwards, when he was alone with his disciples, he would explain his meaning to them.

[35] As evening fell, Jesus said to his disciples, "Let's cross to the other side of the lake." [36] So they took him just as he was and started out, leaving the crowds behind (though other boats followed). [37] But soon a terrible storm arose. High waves began to break into the boat until it was nearly full of water and about to sink. [38] Jesus was asleep at the back of the boat with his head on a cushion. Frantically they wakened him, shouting, "Teacher, don't you even care that we are all about to drown?"

[39] Then he rebuked the wind and said to the sea, "Quiet down!" And the wind fell, and there was a great calm!

[40] And he asked them, "Why were you so fearful? Don't you even yet have confidence in me?"

[41] And they were filled with awe and said among themselves, "Who is this man, that even the winds and seas obey him?"

5 WHEN THEY ARRIVED at the other side of the lake a demon-possessed man ran out from a graveyard, just as Jesus was climbing from the boat.

[3,4] This man lived among the gravestones, and had such strength that whenever he was put into handcuffs and

shackles—as he often was—he snapped the handcuffs from his wrists and smashed the shackles and walked away. No one was strong enough to control him. [5] All day long and through the night he would wander among the tombs and in the wild hills, screaming and cutting himself with sharp pieces of stone.

[6] When Jesus was still far out on the water, the man had seen him and had run to meet him, and fell down before him.

[7,8] Then Jesus spoke to the demon within the man and said, "Come out, you evil spirit."

It gave a terrible scream, shrieking, "What are you going to do to me, Jesus, Son of the Most High God? For God's sake, don't torture me!"

[9] "What is your name?" Jesus asked, and the demon replied, "Legion, for there are many of us here within this man."

[10] Then the demons begged him again and again not to send them to some distant land.

[11] Now as it happened there was a huge herd of hogs rooting around on the hill above the lake. [12] "Send us into those hogs," the demons begged.

[13] And Jesus gave them permission. Then the evil spirits came out of the man and entered the hogs, and the entire herd plunged down the steep hillside into the lake and drowned.

[14] The herdsmen fled to the nearby towns and countryside, spreading the news as they ran. Everyone rushed out to see for themselves. [15] And a large crowd soon gathered where Jesus was; but as they saw the man sitting there, fully clothed and perfectly sane, they were frightened. [16] Those who saw what happened were telling everyone about it, [17] and the crowd began pleading with Jesus to go away and leave them alone! [18] So he got back into the boat. The man who had been possessed by the demons begged Jesus to let him go along. [19] But Jesus said no.

"Go home to your friends," he told him, "and tell them what wonderful things God has done for you; and how merciful he has been."

a Literally, "as they were able to hear."

²⁰ So the man started off to visit the Ten Towns[a] of that region and began to tell everyone about the great things Jesus had done for him; and they were awestruck by his story. ²¹ When Jesus had gone across by boat to the other side of the lake, a vast crowd gathered around him on the shore. ²² The leader of the local synagogue, whose name was Jairus, came and fell down before him, ²³ pleading with him to heal his little daughter.

"She is at the point of death," he said in desperation. "Please come and place your hands on her and make her live."

²⁴ Jesus went with him, and the crowd thronged behind. ²⁵ In the crowd was a woman who had been sick for twelve years with a hemorrhage. ²⁶ She had suffered much from many doctors through the years and had become poor from paying them, and was no better but, in fact, was worse. ²⁷ She had heard all about the wonderful miracles Jesus did, and that is why she came up behind him through the crowd and touched his clothes.

²⁸ For she thought to herself, "If I can just touch his clothing, I will be healed." ²⁹ And sure enough, as soon as she had touched him, the bleeding stopped and she knew she was well!

³⁰ Jesus realized at once that healing power had gone out from him, so he turned around in the crowd and asked, "Who touched my clothes?"

³¹ His disciples said to him, "All this crowd pressing around you, and you ask who touched you?"

³² But he kept on looking around to see who it was who had done it. ³³ Then the frightened woman, trembling at the realization of what had happened to her, came and fell at his feet and told him what she had done. ³⁴ And he said to her, "Daughter, your faith has made you well; go in peace, healed of your disease."

³⁵ While he was still talking to her, messengers arrived from Jairus' home with the news that it was too late—his daughter was dead and there was no point in Jesus' coming now. ³⁶ But Jesus ignored their comments and said to Jairus, "Don't be afraid. Just trust me."

³⁷ Then Jesus halted the crowd and wouldn't let anyone go on with him to Jairus' home except Peter and James and John. ³⁸ When they arrived, Jesus saw that all was in great confusion, with unrestrained weeping and wailing. ³⁹ He went inside and spoke to the people.

"Why all this weeping and commotion?" he asked. "The child isn't dead; she is only asleep!"

⁴⁰ They laughed at him in bitter derision, but he told them all to leave, and taking the little girl's father and mother and his three disciples, he went into the room where she was lying.

⁴¹,⁴² Taking her by the hand he said to her, "Get up, little girl!" (She was twelve years old.) And she jumped up and walked around! Her parents just couldn't get over it. ⁴³ Jesus instructed them very earnestly not to tell what had happened, and told them to give her something to eat.

6 SOON AFTERWARDS HE left that section of the country and returned with his disciples to Nazareth, his home town. ²,³ The next Sabbath he went to the synagogue to teach, and the people were astonished at his wisdom and his miracles because he was just a local man like themselves.

"He's no better than we are," they said. "He's just a carpenter, Mary's boy, and a brother of James and Joseph, Judas and Simon. And his sisters live right here among us." And they were offended!

⁴ Then Jesus told them, "A prophet is honored everywhere except in his home town and among his relatives and by his own family." ⁵ And because of their unbelief he couldn't do any mighty miracles among them except to place his hands on a few sick people and heal them. ⁶ And he could hardly accept the fact that they wouldn't believe in him.

Then he went out among the villages, teaching. ⁷ And he called his twelve disciples together and sent them out two by two, with power to cast out demons. ⁸,⁹ He told

a Or, "to visit Decapolis."

them to take nothing with them except their walking sticks—no food, no knapsack, no money, not even an extra pair of shoes or a change of clothes.

[10] "Stay at one home in each village—don't shift around from house to house while you are there," he said. [11] "And whenever a village won't accept you or listen to you, shake off the dust from your feet as you leave; it is a sign that you have abandoned it to its fate."

[12] So the disciples went out, telling everyone they met to turn from sin. [13] And they cast out many demons, and healed many sick people, anointing them with olive oil.

[14] King Herod soon heard about Jesus, for his miracles were talked about everywhere. The king thought Jesus was John the Baptist come back to life again. So the people were saying, "No wonder he can do such miracles." [15] Others thought Jesus was Elijah the ancient prophet, now returned to life again; still others claimed he was a new prophet like the great ones of the past.

[16] "No," Herod said, "it is John, the man I beheaded. He has come back from the dead."

[17,18] For Herod had sent soldiers to arrest and imprison John because he kept saying it was wrong for the king to marry Herodias, his brother Philip's wife. [19] Herodias wanted John killed in revenge, but without Herod's approval she was powerless. [20] And Herod respected John, knowing that he was a good and holy man, and so he kept him under his protection. Herod was disturbed whenever he talked with John, but even so he liked to listen to him.

[21] Herodias' chance finally came. It was Herod's birthday and he gave a stag party for his palace aides, army officers, and the leading citizens of Galilee. [22,23] Then Herodias' daughter came in and danced before them and greatly pleased them all.

"Ask me for anything you like," the king vowed, "even half of my kingdom, and I will give it to you!"

[24] She went out and consulted her mother, who told her, "Ask for John the Baptist's head!"

[25] So she hurried back to the king and told him, "I want the head of John the Baptist—right now—on a tray!"

[26] Then the king was sorry, but he was embarrassed to break his oath in front of his guests. [27] So he sent one of his bodyguards to the prison to cut off John's head and bring it to him. The soldier killed John in the prison, [28] and brought back his head on a tray, and gave it to the girl and she took it to her mother.

[29] When John's disciples heard what had happened, they came for his body and buried it in a tomb.

[30] The apostles now returned to Jesus from their tour and told him all they had done and what they had said to the people they visited.

[31] Then Jesus suggested, "Let's get away from the crowds for a while and rest." For so many people were coming and going that they scarcely had time to eat. [32] So they left by boat for a quieter spot. [33] But many people saw them leaving and ran on ahead along the shore and met them as they landed. [34] So the usual vast crowd was there as he stepped from the boat; and he had pity on them because they were like sheep without a shepherd, and he taught them many things they needed to know.

[35,36] Late in the afternoon his disciples came to him and said, "Tell the people to go away to the nearby villages and farms and buy themselves some food, for there is nothing to eat here in this desolate spot, and it is getting late."

[37] But Jesus said, "*You* feed them."

"With what?" they asked. "It would take a fortune[a] to buy food for all this crowd!"

[38] "How much food do we have?" he asked. "Go and find out."

They came back to report that there were five loaves of bread and two fish. [39,40] Then Jesus told the crowd to sit down, and soon colorful groups of fifty or a hundred each were sitting on the green grass. [41] He took the five loaves and two fish and looking up to heaven, gave thanks for the food. Breaking the loaves into pieces, he gave some of the bread and fish to each disciple to place before the people. [42] And

---

a Literally, "200 denarii," a year's wage.

the crowd ate until they could hold no more!

[43,44] There were about 5,000 men there for that meal, and afterwards twelve basketfuls of scraps were picked up off the grass!

[45] Immediately after this Jesus instructed his disciples to get back into the boat and strike out across the lake to Bethsaida, where he would join them later. He himself would stay and tell the crowds good-bye and get them started home.

[46] Afterwards he went up into the hills to pray. [47] During the night, as the disciples in their boat were out in the middle of the lake, and he was alone on land, [48] he saw that they were in serious trouble, rowing hard and struggling against the wind and waves.

About three o'clock in the morning he walked out to them on the water. He started past them, [49] but when they saw something walking along beside them they screamed in terror, thinking it was a ghost, [50] for they all saw him.

But he spoke to them at once. "It's all right," he said. "It is I! Don't be afraid." [51] Then he climbed into the boat and the wind stopped!

They just sat there, unable to take it in! [52] For they still didn't realize who he was, even after the miracle the evening before! For they didn't want to believe![b]

[53] When they arrived at Gennesaret on the other side of the lake they moored the boat, [54] and climbed out.

The people standing around there recognized him at once, [55] and ran throughout the whole area to spread the news of his arrival, and began carrying sick folks to him on mats and stretchers. [56] Wherever he went —in villages and cities, and out on the farms—they laid the sick in the market plazas and streets, and begged him to let them at least touch the fringes of his clothes; and as many as touched him were healed.

7 ONE DAY SOME Jewish religious leaders arrived from Jerusalem to investigate him, [2] and noticed that some of his disciples failed to follow the usual Jewish rituals before eating. [3] (For the Jews, especially the Pharisees, will never eat until they have sprinkled their arms to the elbows,[a] as required by their ancient traditions. [4] So when they come home from the market they must always sprinkle themselves in this way before touching any food. This is but one of many examples of laws and regulations they have clung to for centuries, and still follow, such as their ceremony of cleansing for pots, pans and dishes.)

[5] So the religious leaders asked him, "Why don't your disciples follow our age-old customs? For they eat without first performing the washing ceremony."

[6,7] Jesus replied, "You bunch of hypocrites! Isaiah the prophet described you very well when he said, 'These people speak very prettily about the Lord but they have no love for him at all. Their worship is a farce, for they claim that God commands the people to obey their petty rules.' How right Isaiah was! [8] For you ignore God's specific orders and substitute your own traditions. [9] You are simply rejecting God's laws and trampling them under your feet for the sake of tradition. [10] For instance, Moses gave you this law from God: 'Honor your father and mother.' And he said that anyone who speaks against his father or mother must die. [11] But you say it is perfectly all right for a man to disregard his needy parents, telling them, 'Sorry, I can't help you! For I have given to God what I could have given to you.' [12,13] And so you break the law of God in order to protect your man-made tradition. And this is only one example. There are many, many others."

[14] Then Jesus called to the crowd to come and hear. "All of you listen," he said, "and try to understand. [15,16] [b] Your souls aren't harmed by what you eat, but by what you think and say!"[c]

[17] Then he went into a house to get away from the crowds, and his disciples asked him what he meant by the statement he had just made.

[18] "Don't you understand either?" he

---

b Literally, "for their hearts were hardened," perhaps implying jealousy, as in Mark 6:2–6.
7a Literally, "to wash with the fist."　　　b Verse 16 is omitted in many of the ancient manuscripts. "If any man has ears to hear, let him hear."　　　c Literally, "what proceeds out of the man defiles the man."

asked. "Can't you see that what you eat won't harm your soul? ¹⁹ For food doesn't come in contact with your heart, but only passes through the digestive system." (By saying this he showed that every kind of food is kosher.)

²⁰ And then he added, "It is the thought-life that pollutes. ²¹ For from within, out of men's hearts, come evil thoughts of lust, theft, murder, adultery, ²² wanting what belongs to others, wickedness, deceit, lewdness, envy, slander, pride, and all other folly. ²³ All these vile things come from within; they are what pollute you and make you unfit for God."

²⁴ Then he left Galilee and went to the region of Tyre and Sidon,^d and tried to keep it a secret that he was there, but couldn't. For as usual the news of his arrival spread fast.

²⁵ Right away a woman came to him whose little girl was possessed by a demon. She had heard about Jesus and now she came and fell at his feet, ²⁶ and pled with him to release her child from the demon's control. (But she was Syrophoenician—a "despised Gentile!")

²⁷ Jesus told her, "First I should help my own family—the Jews.^e It isn't right to take the children's food and throw it to the dogs."

²⁸ She replied, "That's true, sir, but even the puppies under the table are given some scraps from the children's plates."

²⁹ "Good!" he said, "You have answered well—so well that I have healed your little girl. Go on home, for the demon has left her!"

³⁰ And when she arrived home, her little girl was lying quietly in bed, and the demon was gone.

³¹ From Tyre he went to Sidon, then back to the Sea of Galilee by way of the Ten Towns. ³² A deaf man with a speech impediment was brought to him, and everyone begged Jesus to lay his hands on the man and heal him.

³³ Jesus led him away from the crowd and put his fingers into the man's ears, then spat and touched the man's tongue with the spittle. ³⁴ Then, looking up to heaven, he sighed and commanded, "Open!" ³⁵ Instantly the man could hear perfectly and speak plainly!

³⁶ Jesus told the crowd not to spread the news, but the more he forbade them, the more they made it known, ³⁷ for they were overcome with utter amazement. Again and again they said, "Everything he does is wonderful; he even corrects deafness and stammering!"

8 ONE DAY ABOUT this time as another great crowd gathered, the people ran out of food again. Jesus called his disciples to discuss the situation.

"I pity these people," he said, "for they have been here three days, and have nothing left to eat. ³ And if I send them home without feeding them, they will faint along the road! For some of them have come a long distance."

⁴ "Are we supposed to find food for them here in the desert?" his disciples scoffed.

⁵ "How many loaves of bread do you have?" he asked.

"Seven," they replied. ⁶ So he told the crowd to sit down on the ground. Then he took the seven loaves, thanked God for them, broke them into pieces and passed them to his disciples; and the disciples placed them before the people. ⁷ A few small fish were found, too, so Jesus also blessed these and told the disciples to serve them.

^{8,9} And the whole crowd ate until they were full, and afterwards he sent them home. There were about 4,000 people in the crowd that day and when the scraps were picked up after the meal, there were seven very large basketfuls left over!

¹⁰ Immediately after this he got into a boat with his disciples and came to the region of Dalmanutha. ¹¹ When the local Jewish leaders learned of his arrival they came to argue with him.

"Do a miracle for us," they said. "Make something happen in the sky. Then we will believe in you."^a

¹² He sighed deeply when he heard this and he said, "Certainly not. How many

---

more miracles do you people need?"[b]

[13] So he got back into the boat and left them, and crossed to the other side of the lake. [14] But the disciples had forgotten to stock up on food before they left, and had only one loaf of bread in the boat.

[15] As they were crossing, Jesus said to them very solemnly, "Beware of the yeast of King Herod and of the Pharisees."

[16] "What does he mean?" the disciples asked each other. They finally decided that he must be talking about their forgetting to bring bread.

[17] Jesus realized what they were discussing and said, "No, that isn't it at all! Can't you understand? Are your hearts too hard to take it in? [18] 'Your eyes are to see with—why don't you look? Why don't you open your ears and listen?' Don't you remember anything at all?

[19] "What about the 5,000 men I fed with five loaves of bread? How many basketfuls of scraps did you pick up afterwards?"

"Twelve," they said.

[20] "And when I fed the 4,000 with seven loaves, how much was left?"

"Seven basketfuls," they said.

[21] "And yet you think I'm worried that we have no bread?"[c]

[22] When they arrived at Bethsaida, some people brought a blind man to him and begged him to touch and heal him. [23] Jesus took the blind man by the hand and led him out of the village, and spat upon his eyes, and laid his hands over them.

"Can you see anything now?" Jesus asked him.

[24] The man looked around. "Yes!" he said, "I see men! But I can't see them very clearly; they look like tree trunks walking around!"

[25] Then Jesus placed his hands over the man's eyes again and as the man stared intently, his sight was completely restored, and he saw everything clearly, drinking in the sights around him.

[26] Jesus sent him home to his family. "Don't even go back to the village first," he said.

[27] Jesus and his disciples now left Galilee and went out to the villages of Caesarea Philippi. As they were walking along he asked them, "Who do the people think I am? What are they saying about me?"

[28] "Some of them think you are John the Baptist," the disciples replied, "and others say you are Elijah or some other ancient prophet come back to life again."

[29] Then he asked, "Who do you think I am?" Peter replied, "You are the Messiah."

[30] But Jesus warned them not to tell anyone!

[31] Then he began to tell them about the terrible things he[d] would suffer, and that he would be rejected by the elders and the Chief Priests and the other Jewish leaders —and be killed, and that he would rise again three days afterwards. [32] He talked about it quite frankly with them, so Peter took him aside and chided him.[e] "You shouldn't say things like that," he told Jesus.

[33] Jesus turned and looked at his disciples and then said to Peter very sternly, "Satan, get behind me! You are looking at this only from a human point of view and not from God's."

[34] Then he called his disciples and the crowds to come over and listen. "If any of you wants to be my follower," he told them, "you must put aside your own pleasures and shoulder your cross, and follow me closely. [35] If you insist on saving your life, you will lose it. Only those who throw away their lives for my sake and for the sake of the Good News will ever know what it means to really live.

[36] "And how does a man benefit if he gains the whole world and loses his soul in the process? [37] For is anything worth more than his soul? [38] And anyone who is ashamed of me and my message in these days of unbelief and sin, I, the Messiah,[d] will be ashamed of him when I return in the glory of my Father, with the holy angels."

9 JESUS WENT ON to say to his disciples, "Some of you who are standing here right now will live to see the Kingdom of God arrive in great power!"

[2] Six days later Jesus took Peter, James

---

b Literally, "Why does this generation seek a sign?"   c Literally, "Do you not yet understand?"
d Literally, "the Son of Man."   e Literally, "Peter began to rebuke him."

and John to the top of a mountain. No one else was there.

Suddenly his face began to shine with glory, [3] and his clothing became dazzling white, far more glorious than any earthly process could ever make it! [4] Then Elijah and Moses appeared and began talking with Jesus!

[5] "Teacher, this is wonderful!" Peter exclaimed. "We will make three shelters here, one for each of you . . . ."

[6] He said this just to be talking, for he didn't know what else to say and they were all terribly frightened.

[7] But while he was still speaking these words, a cloud covered them, blotting out the sun, and a voice from the cloud said, *"This* is my beloved Son. Listen to *him."*

[8] Then suddenly they looked around and Moses and Elijah were gone, and only Jesus was with them.

[9] As they descended the mountainside he told them never to mention what they had seen until after he[a] had risen from the dead. [10] So they kept it to themselves, but often talked about it, and wondered what he meant by "rising from the dead."

[11] Now they began asking him about something the Jewish religious leaders often spoke of, that Elijah must return [before the Messiah could come[b]]. [12,13] Jesus agreed that Elijah must come first and prepare the way —and that he had, in fact, already come! And that he had been terribly mistreated, just as the prophets had predicted. Then Jesus asked them what the prophets could have been talking about when they predicted that the Messiah[a] would suffer and be treated with utter contempt.

[14] At the bottom of the mountain they found a great crowd surrounding the other nine disciples, as some Jewish leaders argued with them. [15] The crowd watched Jesus in awe as he came toward them, and then ran to greet him. [16] "What's all the argument about?" he asked.

[17] One of the men in the crowd spoke up and said, "Teacher, I brought my son for you to heal—he can't talk because he is possessed by a demon. [18] And whenever the de-mon is in control of him it dashes him to the ground and makes him foam at the mouth and grind his teeth and become rigid.[c] So I begged your disciples to cast out the demon, but they couldn't do it."

[19] Jesus said [to his disciples[b]], "Oh, what tiny faith you have;[d] how much longer must I be with you until you believe? How much longer must I be patient with you? Bring the boy to me."

[20] So they brought the boy, but when he saw Jesus the demon convulsed the child horribly, and he fell to the ground writhing and foaming at the mouth.

[21] "How long has he been this way?" Jesus asked the father.

And he replied, "Since he was very small, [22] and the demon often makes him fall into the fire or into water to kill him. Oh, have mercy on us and do something if you can."

[23] "If I can?" Jesus asked. *"Anything* is possible if you have faith."

[24] The father instantly replied, "I *do* have faith; oh, help me to have *more!"*

[25] When Jesus saw the crowd was growing he rebuked the demon.

"O demon of deafness and dumbness," he said, "I command you to come out of this child and enter him no more!"

[26] Then the demon screamed terribly and convulsed the boy again and left him; and the boy lay there limp and motionless, to all appearance dead. A murmur ran through the crowd—"He is dead." [27] But Jesus took him by the hand and helped him to his feet and he stood up and was all right! [28] Afterwards, when Jesus was alone in the house with his disciples, they asked him, "Why couldn't we cast that demon out?"

[29] Jesus replied, "Cases like this require prayer."[e]

[30,31] Leaving that region they traveled through Galilee where he tried to avoid all publicity in order to spend more time with his disciples, teaching them. He would say to them, "I, the Messiah,[a] am going to be betrayed and killed and three days later I will return to life again."

[32] But they didn't understand and were

---

a Literally, "the Son of Man."   b Implied.   c Or, "is growing weaker day by day."
d Literally, "O unbelieving generation."   e "And fasting" is added in some manuscripts, but not the most ancient.

afraid to ask him what he meant.

³³ And so they arrived at Capernaum. When they were settled in the house where they were to stay he asked them, "What were you discussing out on the road?"

³⁴ But they were ashamed to answer, for they had been arguing about which of them was the greatest!

³⁵ He sat down and called them around him and said, "Anyone wanting to be the greatest must be the least—the servant of all!"

³⁶ Then he placed a little child among them; and taking the child in his arms he said to them, ³⁷ "Anyone who welcomes a little child like this in my name is welcoming me, and anyone who welcomes me is welcoming my Father who sent me!"

³⁸ One of his disciples, John, told him one day, "Teacher, we saw a man using your name to cast out demons; but we told him not to, for he isn't one of our group."

³⁹ "Don't forbid him!" Jesus said. "For no one doing miracles in my name will quickly turn against me.ᶠ ⁴⁰ Anyone who isn't against us is for us. ⁴¹ If anyone so much as gives you a cup of water because you are Christ's—I say this solemnly—he won't lose his reward. ⁴² But if someone causes one of these little ones who believe in me to lose faith—it would be better for that man if a huge millstone were tied around his neck and he were thrown into the sea.

⁴³,⁴⁴ᵍ "If your hand does wrong, cut it off. Better live forever with one hand than be thrown into the unquenchable fires of hell with two! ⁴⁵,⁴⁶ᵍ If your foot carries you toward evil, cut it off! Better be lame and live forever than have two feet that carry you to hell.

⁴⁷ "And if your eye is sinful, gouge it out. Better enter the Kingdom of God half blind than have two eyes and see the fires of hell, ⁴⁸ where the worm never dies, and the fire never goes out— ⁴⁹ where all are salted with fire.ʰ

⁵⁰ "Good salt is worthless if it loses its saltiness; it can't season anything. So don't lose your flavor! Live in peace with each other."

10 THEN HE LEFT Capernaumᵃ and went southward to the Judean borders and into the area east of the Jordan River. And as always there were the crowds; and as usual he taught them.

² Some Pharisees came and asked him, "Do you permit divorce?" Of course they were trying to trap him.

³ "What did Moses say about divorce?" Jesus asked them.

⁴ "He said it was all right," they replied. "He said that all a man has to do is write his wife a letter of dismissal."

⁵ "And why did he say that?" Jesus asked. "I'll tell you why—it was a concession to your hardhearted wickedness. ⁶,⁷ But it certainly isn't God's way. For from the very first he made man and woman to be joined together permanently in marriage; therefore a man is to leave his father and mother, ⁸ and he and his wife are united so that they are no longer two, but one. ⁹ And no man may separate what God has joined together."

¹⁰ Later, when he was alone with his disciples in the house, they brought up the subject again.

¹¹ He told them, "When a man divorces his wife to marry someone else, he commits adultery against her. ¹² And if a wife divorces her husband and remarries, she, too, commits adultery."

¹³ Once when some mothersᵇ were bringing their children to Jesus to bless them, the disciples shooed them away, telling them not to bother him.

¹⁴ But when Jesus saw what was happening he was very much displeased with his disciples and said to them, "Let the children come to me, for the Kingdom of God belongs to such as they. Don't send them away! ¹⁵ I tell you as seriously as I know how that anyone who refuses to come to God as a little child will never be allowed into his Kingdom."

¹⁶ Then he took the children into his

---

f Literally, "will be able to speak evil of me." omitted in some of the ancient manuscripts.
10 a Literally, "and rising up, he went from there." He never returned until after his death and resurrection.
g Verses 44 and 46 (which are identical with verse 48) are
h Literally, "For everyone shall be salted with fire."
Mentioned here so quietly, this was his final farewell to Galilee.
b Implied.

arms and placed his hands on their heads and he blessed them.

¹⁷ As he was starting out on a trip, a man came running to him and knelt down and asked, "Good Teacher, what must I do to get to heaven?"

¹⁸ "Why do you call me good?" Jesus asked. "Only God is truly good! ¹⁹ But as for your question—you know the commandments: don't kill, don't commit adultery, don't steal, don't lie, don't cheat, respect your father and mother."

²⁰ "Teacher," the man replied, "I've never once^c broken a single one of those laws."

²¹ Jesus felt genuine love for this man as he looked at him. "You lack only one thing," he told him; "go and sell all you have and give the money to the poor—and you shall have treasure in heaven—and come, follow me."

²² Then the man's face fell, and he went sadly away, for he was very rich.

²³ Jesus watched him go, then turned around and said to his disciples, "It's almost impossible for the rich to get into the Kingdom of God!"

²⁴ This amazed them. So Jesus said it again: "Dear children, how hard it is for those who trust in riches^d to enter the Kingdom of God. ²⁵ It is easier for a camel to go through the eye of a needle than for a rich man to enter the Kingdom of God."

²⁶ The disciples were incredulous! "Then who in the world can be saved, if not a rich man?" they asked.

²⁷ Jesus looked at them intently, then said, "Without God, it is utterly impossible. But with God everything is possible."

²⁸ Then Peter began to mention all that he and the other disciples had left behind. "We've given up everything to follow you," he said.

²⁹ And Jesus replied, "Let me assure you that no one has ever given up anything —home, brothers, sisters, mother, father, children, or property—for love of me and to tell others the Good News, ³⁰ who won't be given back, a hundred times over, homes, brothers, sisters, mothers, children, and land—with persecutions!

"All these will be his here on earth, and in the world to come he shall have eternal life. ³¹ But many people who seem to be important now will be the least important then; and many who are considered least here shall be greatest there."

³² Now they were on the way to Jerusalem, and Jesus was walking along ahead; and as the disciples were following they were filled with terror and dread.

Taking them aside, Jesus once more began describing all that was going to happen to him when they arrived at Jerusalem.

³³ "When we get there," he told them, "I, the Messiah,^e will be arrested and taken before the chief priests and the Jewish leaders, who will sentence me to die and hand me over to the Romans to be killed. ³⁴ They will mock me and spit on me and flog me with their whips and kill me; but after three days I will come back to life again."

³⁵ Then James and John, the sons of Zebedee, came over and spoke to him in a low voice.^f "Master," they said, "we want you to do us a favor."

³⁶ "What is it?" he asked.

³⁷ "We want to sit on the thrones next to yours in your kingdom," they said, "one at your right and the other at your left!"

³⁸ But Jesus answered, "You don't know what you are asking! Are you able to drink from the bitter cup of sorrow I must drink from? Or to be baptized with the baptism of suffering I must be baptized with?"

³⁹ "Oh, yes," they said, "we are!"

And Jesus said, "You shall indeed drink from my cup and be baptized with my baptism, ⁴⁰ but I do not have the right to place you on thrones next to mine. Those appointments have already been made."

⁴¹ When the other disciples discovered what James and John had asked, they were very indignant. ⁴² So Jesus called them to him and said, "As you know, the kings and great men of the earth lord it over the people; ⁴³ but among you it is different. Whoever wants to be great among you must be your servant. ⁴⁴ And whoever wants to be greatest of all must be the slave of all. ⁴⁵ For

---

c Literally, "from my youth."   d Some of the ancient manuscripts do not contain the words, "for those who trust in riches."   e Literally, "the Son of Man."   f Literally, "came up to him."

even I, the Messiah,[g] am not here to be served, but to help others, and to give my life as a ransom for many."

[46] And so they reached Jericho. Later, as they left town, a great crowd was following. Now it happened that a blind beggar named Bartimaeus (the son of Timaeus) was sitting beside the road as Jesus was going by.

[47] When Bartimaeus heard that Jesus from Nazareth was near, he began to shout out, "Jesus, Son of David, have mercy on me!"

[48] "Shut up!" some of the people yelled at him.

But he only shouted the louder, again and again, "O Son of David, have mercy on me!"

[49] When Jesus heard him he stopped there in the road and said, "Tell him to come here."

So they called the blind man. "You lucky fellow,"[h] they said, "come on, he's calling you!" [50] Bartimaeus yanked off his old coat and flung it aside, jumped up and came to Jesus.

[51] "What do you want me to do for you?" Jesus asked.

"O Teacher," the blind man said, "I want to see!"

[52] And Jesus said to him, "All right, it's done.[i] Your faith has healed you."

And instantly the blind man could see, and followed Jesus down the road!

11 AS THEY NEARED Bethphage and Bethany on the outskirts of Jerusalem and came to the Mount of Olives, Jesus sent two of his disciples on ahead.

[2] "Go into that village over there," he told them, "and just as you enter you will see a colt tied up that has never been ridden. Untie him and bring him here. [3] And if anyone asks you what you are doing, just say, 'Our Master needs him and will return him soon.' "

[4,5] Off went the two men and found the colt standing in the street, tied outside a house. As they were untying it, some who were standing there demanded, "What are you doing, untying that colt?"

[6] So they said what Jesus had told them

to, and then the men agreed.

[7] So the colt was brought to Jesus and the disciples threw their cloaks across its back for him to ride on. [8] Then many in the crowd spread out their coats along the road before him, while others threw down leafy branches from the fields.

[9] He was in the center of the procession with crowds ahead and behind, and all of them shouting, "Hail to the King!" "Praise God for him who comes in the name of the Lord!" . . . [10] "Praise God for the return of our father David's kingdom . . ." "Hail to the King of the universe!"

[11] And so he entered Jerusalem and went into the Temple. He looked around carefully at everything and then left—for now it was late in the afternoon—and went out to Bethany with the twelve disciples.

[12] The next morning as they left Bethany, he felt hungry. [13] A little way off he noticed a fig tree in full leaf, so he went over to see if he could find any figs on it. But no, there were only leaves, for it was too early in the season for fruit.

[14] Then Jesus said to the tree, "You shall never bear fruit again!" And the disciples heard him say it.

[15] When they arrived back to Jerusalem he went to the Temple and began to drive out the merchants and their customers, and knocked over the tables of the moneychangers and the stalls of those selling doves, [16] and stopped everyone from bringing in loads of merchandise.

[17] He told them, "It is written in the Scriptures, 'My Temple is to be a place of prayer for all nations,' but you have turned it into a den of robbers."

[18] When the chief priests and other Jewish leaders heard what he had done they began planning how best to get rid of him. Their problem was their fear of riots because the people were so enthusiastic about Jesus' teaching.

[19] That evening as usual they left the city. [20] Next morning, as the disciples passed the fig tree he had cursed, they saw that it was withered from the roots! [21] Then Peter remembered what Jesus had said to the tree on the previous day, and exclaimed, "Look,

---

g Literally, "the Son of Man."　　　h Literally, "Be of good cheer."　　　i Literally, "Go your way."

A trap for Jesus

Teacher! The fig tree you cursed has withered!"

^{22,23} In reply Jesus said to the disciples, "If you only have faith in God—this is the absolute truth—you can say to this Mount of Olives, 'Rise up and fall into the Mediterranean,' and your command will be obeyed. All that's required is that you really believe and have no doubt! ²⁴ Listen to me! You can pray for *anything*, and *if you believe, you have it;* it's yours! ²⁵ But when you are praying, first forgive anyone you are holding a grudge against, so that your Father in heaven will forgive you your sins too."

^{26,a27,28} By this time they had arrived in Jerusalem again, and as he was walking through the Temple area, the chief priests and other Jewish leaders^b came up to him demanding, "What's going on here? Who gave you the authority to drive out the merchants?"

²⁹ Jesus replied, "I'll tell you if you answer one question! ³⁰ What about John the Baptist? Was he sent by God, or not? Answer me!"

³¹ They talked it over among themselves. "If we reply that God sent him, then he will say, 'All right, why didn't you accept him?' ³² But if we say God didn't send him, then the people will start a riot." (For the people all believed strongly that John was a prophet.)

³³ So they said, "We can't answer. We don't know."

To which Jesus replied, "Then I won't answer your question either!"

12 HERE ARE SOME of the story-illustrations Jesus gave to the people at that time:

"A man planted a vineyard and built a wall around it and dug a pit for pressing out the grape juice, and built a watchman's tower. Then he leased the farm to tenant farmers and moved to another country. ² At grape-picking time he sent one of his men to collect his share of the crop. ³ But the farmers beat up the man and sent him back empty-handed.

⁴ "The owner then sent another of his men, who received the same treatment, only worse, for his head was seriously injured. ⁵ The next man he sent was killed; and later, others were either beaten or killed, until ⁶ there was only one left—his only son. He finally sent him, thinking they would surely give him their full respect.

⁷ "But when the farmers saw him coming they said, 'He will own the farm when his father dies. Come on, let's kill him—and then the farm will be ours!' ⁸ So they caught him and murdered him and threw his body out of the vineyard.

⁹ "What do you suppose the owner will do when he hears what happened? He will come and kill them all, and lease the vineyard to others. ¹⁰ Don't you remember reading this verse in the Scriptures? 'The Rock the builders threw away became the cornerstone, the most honored stone in the building! ¹¹ This is the Lord's doing and it is an amazing thing to see.' "

¹² The Jewish leaders wanted to arrest him then and there for using this illustration, for they knew he was pointing at them—they were the wicked farmers in his story. But they were afraid to touch him for fear of a mob. So they left him and went away. ¹³ But they sent other religious and political leaders^a to talk with him and try to trap him into saying something he could be arrested for.

¹⁴ "Teacher," these spies said, "we know you tell the truth no matter what! You aren't influenced by the opinions and desires of men, but sincerely teach the ways of God. Now tell us, is it right to pay taxes to Rome, or not?"

¹⁵ Jesus saw their trick and said, "Show me a coin and I'll tell you."

¹⁶ When they handed it to him he asked, "Whose picture and title is this on the coin?" They replied, "The emperor's."

¹⁷ "All right," he said, "if it is his, give it to him. But everything that belongs to God must be given to God!" And they scratched their heads in bafflement at his reply.

¹⁸ Then the Sadducees stepped forward—a group of men who say there is no

---

a Many ancient authorities add verse 26, "but if you do not forgive, neither will your Father who is in heaven forgive your trespasses." All include this in Matthew 6:15.   b Literally, "scribes and elders."
12 a Literally, "Pharisees and Herodians."

resurrection. Here was their question:

[19] "Teacher, Moses gave us a law that when a man dies without children, the man's brother should marry his widow and have children in his brother's name. [20,21,22] Well, there were seven brothers and the oldest married and died, and left no children. So the second brother married the widow, but soon he died too, and left no children. Then the next brother married her, and died without children, and so on until all were dead, and still there were no children; and last of all, the woman died too. [23] "What we want to know is this:[b] In the resurrection, whose wife will she be, for she had been the wife of each of them?"

[24] Jesus replied, "Your trouble is that you don't know the Scriptures, and don't know the power of God. [25] For when these seven brothers and the woman rise from the dead, they won't be married—they will be like the angels.

[26] "But now as to whether there will be a resurrection—have you never read in the book of Exodus about Moses and the burning bush? God said to Moses, 'I *am* the God of Abraham, and I *am* the God of Isaac, and I *am* the God of Jacob.'

[27] "God was telling Moses that these men, though dead for hundreds of years,[b] were still very much alive, for he would not have said, 'I *am* the God' of those who don't exist! You have made a serious error."

[28] One of the teachers of religion who was standing there listening to the discussion realized that Jesus had answered well. So he asked, "Of all the commandments, which is the most important?"

[29] Jesus replied, "The one that says, 'Hear, O Israel! The Lord our God is the one and only God. [30] And you must love him with all your heart and soul and mind and strength.'

[31] "The second is: 'You must love others as much as yourself.' No other commandments are greater than these."

[32] The teacher of religion replied, "Sir, you have spoken a true word in saying that there is only one God and no other. [33] And I know it is far more important to love him with all my heart and understanding and strength, and to love others as myself, than to offer all kinds of sacrifices on the altar of the Temple."

[34] Realizing this man's understanding, Jesus said to him, "You are not far from the Kingdom of God." And after that, no one dared ask him any more questions.

[35] Later, as Jesus was teaching the people in the Temple area, he asked them this question:

"Why do your religious teachers claim that the Messiah must be a descendant of King David? [36] For David himself said —and the Holy Spirit was speaking through him when he said it—'God said to my Lord, sit at my right hand until I make your enemies your footstool.' [37] Since David called him his Lord, how can he be his *son?*"

(This sort of reasoning delighted the crowd and they listened to him with great interest.)

[38] Here are some of the other things he taught them at this time:

"Beware of the teachers of religion! For they love to wear the robes of the rich and scholarly, and to have everyone bow to them as they walk through the markets. [39] They love to sit in the best seats in the synagogues, and at the places of honor at banquets— [40] but they shamelessly cheat widows out of their homes and then, to cover up the kind of men they really are, they pretend to be pious by praying long prayers in public. Because of this, their punishment will be the greater."

[41] Then he went over to the collection boxes in the Temple and sat and watched as the crowds dropped in their money. Some who were rich put in large amounts. [42] Then a poor widow came and dropped in two pennies.

[43,44] He called his disciples to him and remarked, "That poor widow has given more than all those rich men put together! For they gave a little of their extra fat,[c] while she gave up her last penny."

13 AS HE WAS leaving the Temple that day, one of his disciples said, "Teacher, what beautiful buildings these

---

b Implied.   c Literally, "out of their surplus."

are! Look at the decorated stonework on the walls."

[2] Jesus replied, "Yes, look! For not one stone will be left upon another, except as ruins."

[3,4] And as he sat on the slopes of the Mount of Olives across the valley from Jerusalem, Peter, James, John, and Andrew got alone with him and asked him, "Just when is all this going to happen to the Temple? Will there be some warning ahead of time?"

[5] So Jesus launched into an extended reply. "Don't let anyone mislead you," he said, [6] "for many will come declaring themselves to be your Messiah, and will lead many astray. [7] And wars will break out near and far, but this is not the signal of the end-time.

[8] "For nations and kingdoms will proclaim war against each other, and there will be earthquakes in many lands, and famines. These herald only the early stages of the anguish ahead. [9] But when these things begin to happen, watch out! For you will be in great danger. You will be dragged before the courts, and beaten in the synagogues, and accused before governors and kings of being my followers. This is your opportunity to tell them the Good News. [10] And the Good News must first be made known in every nation before the end-time finally comes.[a] [11] But when you are arrested and stand trial, don't worry about what to say in your defense. Just say what God tells you to. Then you will not be speaking, but the Holy Spirit will.

[12] "Brothers will betray each other to death, fathers will betray their own children, and children will betray their parents to be killed. [13] And everyone will hate you because you are mine. But all who endure to the end without renouncing me shall be saved.

[14] "When you see the horrible thing standing in the Temple[b]—reader, pay attention!—flee, if you can, to the Judean hills. [15,16] Hurry! If you are on your rooftop porch, don't even go back into the house. If you are out in the fields, don't even return for

your money or clothes.

[17] "Woe to pregnant women in those days, and to mothers nursing their children. [18] And pray that your flight will not be in winter. [19] For those will be days of such horror as have never been since the beginning of God's creation, nor will ever be again. [20] And unless the Lord shortens that time of calamity, not a soul in all the earth will survive. But for the sake of his chosen ones he will limit those days.

[21] "And then if anyone tells you, 'This is the Messiah,' or, 'That one is,' don't pay any attention. [22] For there will be many false Messiahs and false prophets who will do wonderful miracles that would deceive, if possible, even God's own children.[c] [23] Take care! I have warned you!

[24] "After the tribulation ends, then the sun will grow dim and the moon will not shine, [25] and the stars will fall—the heavens will convulse.

[26] "Then all mankind will see me, the Messiah,[d] coming in the clouds with great power and glory. [27] And I will send out the angels to gather together my chosen ones from all over the world—from the farthest bounds of earth and heaven.

[28] "Now, here is a lesson from a fig tree. When its buds become tender and its leaves begin to sprout, you know that spring has come. [29] And when you see these things happening that I've described, you can be sure that my return is very near, that I am right at the door.

[30] "Yes, these are the events that will signal the end of the age.[e] [31] Heaven and earth shall disappear, but my words stand sure forever.

[32] "However, no one, not even the angels in heaven, nor I myself,[f] knows the day or hour when these things will happen; only the Father knows. [33] And since you don't know when it will happen, stay alert. Be on the watch [for my return[a]].

[34] "My coming[g] can be compared with that of a man who went on a trip to another country. He laid out his employees' work for them to do while he was gone, and told the gatekeeper to watch for his return.

a Implied.   b Literally, "standing where he ought not."   c Literally, "elect of God."
d Literally, "the Son of Man."   e Literally, "of this generation."   f Literally, "the Son."
g Literally, "You do not know when the master of the house will come."

35,36,37 "Keep a sharp lookout! For you do not know when I[h] will come, at evening, at midnight, early dawn or late daybreak. Don't let me find you sleeping. *Watch for my return!* This is my message to you and to everyone else."

14 THE PASSOVER OBSERVANCE began two days later—an annual Jewish holiday when no bread made with yeast was eaten. The chief priests and other Jewish leaders were still looking for an opportunity to arrest Jesus secretly and put him to death. [2] "But we can't do it during the Passover," they said, "or there will be a riot."

[3] Meanwhile Jesus was in Bethany, at the home of Simon the leper; during supper a woman came in with a beautiful flask of expensive perfume. Then, breaking the seal, she poured it over his head.

[4,5] Some of those at the table were indignant among themselves about this "waste," as they called it.

"Why, she could have sold that perfume for a fortune and given the money to the poor!" they snarled.

[6] But Jesus said, "Let her alone; why berate her for doing a good thing? [7] You always have the poor among you, and they badly need your help, and you can aid them whenever you want to; but I won't be here much longer. [8] "She has done what she could, and has anointed my body ahead of time for burial. [9] And I tell you this in solemn truth, that wherever the Good News is preached throughout the world, this woman's deed will be remembered and praised."

[10] Then Judas Iscariot, one of his disciples, went to the chief priests to arrange to betray Jesus to them. [11] When the chief priests heard why he had come, they were excited and happy and promised him a reward. So he began looking for the right time and place to betray Jesus.

[12] On the first day of the Passover, the day the lambs were sacrificed, his disciples asked him where he wanted to go to eat the traditional Passover supper. [13] He sent two of them into Jerusalem to make the arrangements.

"As you are walking along," he told them, "you will see a man coming towards you carrying a pot of water. Follow him. [14] At the house he enters, tell the man in charge, 'Our Master sent us to see the room you have ready for us, where we will eat the Passover supper this evening!' [15] He will take you upstairs to a large room all set up. Prepare our supper there."

[16] So the two disciples went on ahead into the city and found everything as Jesus had said, and prepared the Passover.

[17] In the evening Jesus arrived with the other disciples, [18] and as they were sitting around the table eating, Jesus said, "I solemnly declare that one of you will betray me, one of you who is here eating with me."

[19] A great sadness swept over them, and one by one they asked him, "Am I the one?"

[20] He replied, "It is one of you twelve eating with me now. [21] I[a] must die, as the prophets declared long ago; but, oh, the misery ahead for the man by whom I[a] am betrayed. Oh, that he had never been born!"

[22] As they were eating, Jesus took bread and asked God's blessing on it and broke it in pieces and gave it to them and said, "Eat it—this is my body."

[23] Then he took a cup of wine and gave thanks to God for it and gave it to them; and they all drank from it. [24] And he said to them, "This is my blood, poured out for many, sealing[b] the new agreement between God and man. [25] I solemnly declare that I shall never again taste wine until the day I drink a different kind[c] in the Kingdom of God."

[26] Then they sang a hymn and went out to the Mount of Olives.

[27] "All of you will desert me," Jesus told them, "for God has declared through the prophets, 'I will kill the Shepherd, and the sheep will scatter.' [28] But after I am raised to life again, I will go to Galilee and meet you there."

[29] Peter said to him, "I will never desert you no matter what the others do!"

---

h Implied.   14a Literally, "the Son of Man." ancient manuscripts read, "new covenant."

b Literally, "This is my blood of the covenant." Some
c Literally, "drink it new."

[30] "Peter," Jesus said, "before the cock crows a second time tomorrow morning you will deny me three times."

[31] "No!" Peter exploded. "Not even if I have to die with you! I'll *never* deny you!" And all the others vowed the same.

[32] And now they came to an olive grove called the Garden of Gethsemane, and he instructed his disciples, "Sit here, while I go and pray."

[33] He took Peter, James and John with him and began to be filled with horror and deepest distress. [34] And he said to them, "My soul is crushed by sorrow to the point of death; stay here and watch with me."

[35] He went on a little further and fell to the ground and prayed that if it were possible the awful hour awaiting him might never come.[d]

[36] "Father, Father," he said, "everything is possible for you. Take away this cup from me. Yet I want your will, not mine."

[37] Then he returned to the three disciples and found them asleep.

"Simon!" he said. "Asleep? Couldn't you watch with me even one hour? [38] Watch with me and pray lest the Tempter overpower you. For though the spirit is willing enough, the body is weak."

[39] And he went away again and prayed, repeating his pleadings. [40] Again he returned to them and found them sleeping, for they were very tired. And they didn't know what to say.

[41] The third time when he returned to them he said, "Sleep on; get your rest! But no! The time for sleep has ended! Look! I[e] am betrayed into the hands of wicked men. [42] Come! Get up! We must go! Look! My betrayer is here!"

[43] And immediately, while he was still speaking, Judas (one of his disciples) arrived with a mob equipped with swords and clubs, sent out by the chief priests and other Jewish leaders.

[44] Judas had told them, "You will know which one to arrest when I go over and greet[f] him. Then you can take him easily."

[45] So as soon as they arrived he walked up to Jesus. "Master!" he exclaimed, and embraced him with a great show of friendliness. [46] Then the mob arrested Jesus and held him fast. [47] But someone[g] pulled a sword and slashed at the High Priest's servant, cutting off his ear.

[48] Jesus asked them, "Am I some dangerous robber, that you come like this, armed to the teeth to capture me? [49] Why didn't you arrest me in the Temple? I was there teaching every day. But these things are happening to fulfill the prophecies about me."

[50] Meanwhile, all his disciples had fled. [51,52] There was, however, a young man following along behind, clothed only in a linen nightshirt.[h] When the mob tried to grab him, he escaped, though his clothes were torn off in the process, so that he ran away completely naked.

[53] Jesus was led to the High Priest's home where all of the chief priests and other Jewish leaders soon gathered. [54] Peter followed far behind and then slipped inside the gates of the High Priest's residence and crouched beside a fire among the servants.

[55] Inside, the chief priests and the whole Jewish Supreme Court were trying to find something against Jesus that would be sufficient to condemn him to death. But their efforts were in vain. [56] Many false witnesses volunteered, but they contradicted each other.

[57] Finally some men stood up to lie about him and said, [58] "We heard him say, 'I will destroy this Temple made with human hands and in three days I will build another, made without human hands!'" [59] But even then they didn't get their stories straight!

[60] Then the High Priest stood up before the Court and asked Jesus, "Do you refuse to answer this charge? What do you have to say for yourself?"

[61] To this Jesus made no reply.

Then the High Priest asked him. "Are you the Messiah, the Son of God?"

[62] Jesus said, "I am, and you will see me[e] sitting at the right hand of God, and returning to earth in the clouds of heaven."

[63,64] Then the High Priest tore at his clothes and said, "What more do we need?

---

d Literally, "that the hour might pass away from him."   e Literally, "the Son of Man."
f Literally, "kiss"—the usual oriental greeting, even to this day.   g It was Peter. John 18:10.
h Implied. Literally, "wearing only a linen cloth."

Why wait for witnesses? You have heard his blasphemy. What is your verdict?" And the vote for the death sentence was unanimous.

⁶⁵ Then some of them began to spit at him, and they blindfolded him and began to hammer his face with their fists.

"Who hit you that time, you prophet?" they jeered. And even the bailiffs were using their fists on him as they led him away.

⁶⁶,⁶⁷ Meanwhile Peter was below in the courtyard. One of the maids who worked for the High Priest noticed Peter warming himself at the fire.

She looked at him closely and then announced, *"You* were with Jesus, the Nazarene."

⁶⁸ Peter denied it. "I don't know what you're talking about!" he said, and walked over to the edge of the courtyard.

Just then, a rooster crowed.[i]

⁶⁹ The maid saw him standing there and began telling the others, "There he is! There's that disciple of Jesus!"

⁷⁰ Peter denied it again.

A little later others standing around the fire began saying to Peter, "You are, too, one of them, for you are from Galilee!"

⁷¹ He began to curse and swear. "I don't even know this fellow you are talking about," he said.

⁷² And immediately the rooster crowed the second time. Suddenly Jesus' words flashed through Peter's mind: "Before the cock crows twice, you will deny me three times." And he began to cry.

15 EARLY IN THE morning the chief priests, elders and teachers of religion—the entire Supreme Court—met to discuss their next steps. Their decision was to send Jesus under armed guard to Pilate, the Roman governor.[a]

² Pilate asked him, "Are you the King of the Jews?"

"Yes," Jesus replied, "it is as you say."

³,⁴ Then the chief priests accused him of many crimes, and Pilate asked him, "Why don't you say something? What about all these charges against you?"

⁵ But Jesus said no more, much to Pilate's amazement.

⁶ Now, it was Pilate's custom to release one Jewish prisoner each year at Passover time—any prisoner the people requested. ⁷ One of the prisoners at that time was Barabbas, convicted along with others for murder during an insurrection.

⁸ Now a mob began to crowd in toward Pilate, asking him to release a prisoner as usual.

⁹ "How about giving you the 'King of Jews'?" Pilate asked. "Is he the one you want released?" ¹⁰ (For he realized by now that this was a frameup, backed by the chief priests because they envied Jesus' popularity.)

¹¹ But at this point the chief priests whipped up the mob to demand the release of Barabbas instead of Jesus.

¹² "But if I release Barabbas," Pilate asked them, "what shall I do with this man you call your king?"

¹³ They shouted back, "Crucify him!"

¹⁴ "But why?" Pilate demanded. "What has he done wrong?" They only roared the louder, "Crucify him!"

¹⁵ Then Pilate, afraid of a riot and anxious to please the people, released Barabbas to them. And he ordered Jesus flogged with a leaded whip, and handed him over to be crucified.

¹⁶,¹⁷ Then the Roman soldiers took him into the barracks of the palace, called out the entire palace guard, dressed him in a purple robe, and made a crown of long, sharp thorns and put it on his head. ¹⁸ Then they saluted, yelling, "Yea! King of the Jews!" ¹⁹ And they beat him on the head with a cane, and spit on him and went down on their knees to "worship" him.

²⁰ When they finally tired of their sport, they took off the purple robe and put his own clothes on him again, and led him away to be crucified.

²¹ Simon of Cyrene, who was coming in from the country just then, was pressed into service to carry Jesus' cross. (Simon is the father of Alexander and Rufus.)

²² And they brought Jesus to a place called Golgotha. (Golgotha means skull.) ²³ Wine drugged with bitter herbs was offered to him there, but he refused it. ²⁴ And

---

i This statement is found in only some of the manuscripts.　　15a Implied.

then they crucified him—and threw dice for his clothes.

²⁵ It was about nine o'clock in the morning when the crucifixion took place.

²⁶ A signboard was fastened to the cross above his head, announcing his crime. It read, "The King of the Jews."

²⁷ Two robbers were also crucified that morning, their crosses on either side of his. ²⁸ᵇ And so the Scripture was fulfilled that said, "He was counted among evil men."

²⁹,³⁰ The people jeered at him as they walked by, and wagged their heads in mockery.

"Ha! Look at you now!" they yelled at him. "Sure, you can destroy the Temple and rebuild it in three days! If you're so wonderful, save yourself and come down from the cross."

³¹ The chief priests and religious leaders were also standing around joking about Jesus.

"He's quite clever at 'saving' others," they said, "but he can't save himself!"

³² "Hey there, Messiah!" they yelled at him. "You 'King of Israel'! Come on down from the cross and we'll believe you!"

And even the two robbers dying with him, cursed him.

³³ About noon, darkness fell across the entire land,ᶜ lasting until three o'clock that afternoon.

³⁴ Then Jesus called out with a loud voice, "Eli, Eli, lama sabachthani?"ᵈ ("My God, my God, why have you deserted me?")

³⁵ Some of the people standing there thought he was calling for the prophet Elijah. ³⁶ So one man ran and got a sponge and filled it with sour wine and held it up to him on a stick.

"Let's see if Elijah will come and take him down!" he said.

³⁷ Then Jesus uttered another loud cry, and dismissed his spirit.

³⁸ And the curtainᵉ in the Temple was split apart from top to bottom.

³⁹ When the Roman officer standing beside his cross saw how he dismissed his spirit, he exclaimed, "Truly, this was the Son of God!"

⁴⁰ Some women were there watching from a distance—Mary Magdalene, Mary (the mother of James the Younger and of Joses), Salome, and others. ⁴¹ They and many other Galilean women who were his followers had ministered to him when he was up in Galilee, and had come with him to Jerusalem.

⁴²,⁴³ This all happened the day before the Sabbath. Late that afternoon Joseph from Arimathea, an honored member of the Jewish Supreme Court (who personally was eagerly expecting the arrival of God's Kingdom), gathered his courage and went to Pilate and asked for Jesus' body.

⁴⁴ Pilate couldn't believe that Jesus was already dead so he called for the Roman officer in charge and asked him. ⁴⁵ The officer confirmed the fact, and Pilate told Joseph he could have the body.

⁴⁶ Joseph bought a long sheet of linen cloth and, taking Jesus' body down from the cross, wound it in the cloth and laid it in a rock-hewn tomb, and rolled a stone in front of the entrance.

⁴⁷ (Mary Magdalene and Mary the mother of Joses were watching as Jesus was laid away.)

16 THE NEXT EVENING, when the Sabbath ended, Mary Magdalene and Salome and Mary the mother of James went out and purchased embalming spices.

Early the following morning, just at sunrise, they carried them out to the tomb. ³ On the way they were discussing how they could ever roll aside the huge stone from the entrance.

⁴ But when they arrived they looked up and saw that the stone—a *very* heavy one—was already moved away and the entrance was open! ⁵ So they entered the tomb—and there on the right sat a young man clothed

---

b Verse 28 is omitted in some of the ancient manuscripts. The quotation is from Isaiah 53:12.

c Or, "over the entire world."   d He spoke here in Aramaic. The onlookers, who spoke Greek and Latin, misunderstood his first two words ("Eloi, Eloi") and thought he was calling for the prophet Elijah.

e A heavy veil hung in front of the room in the Temple called "The Holy of Holies," a place reserved by God for himself; the veil separated him from sinful mankind. Now this veil was split from above, showing that Christ's death, for man's sin, had opened up access to the holy God.

in white. The women were startled, [6] but the angel said, "Don't be so surprised. Aren't you looking for Jesus, the Nazarene who was crucified? He isn't here! He has come back to life! Look, that's where his body was lying. [7] Now go and give this message to his disciples including Peter:

" 'Jesus is going ahead of you to Galilee. You will see him there, just as he told you before he died!' "

[8] The women fled from the tomb, trembling and bewildered, too frightened to talk.

[9a] It was early on Sunday morning when Jesus came back to life, and the first person who saw him was Mary Magdalene—the woman from whom he had cast out seven demons. [10,11] She found the disciples wet-eyed with grief and exclaimed that she had seen Jesus, and he was alive! But they didn't believe her!

[12] Later that day[b] he appeared to two who were walking from Jerusalem into the country, but they didn't recognize him at first because he had changed his appearance. [13] When they finally realized who he was, they rushed back to Jerusalem to tell the others, but no one believed them.

[14] Still later he appeared to the eleven disciples as they were eating together. He rebuked them for their unbelief—their stubborn refusal to believe those who had seen him alive from the dead.

[15] And then he told them, "You are to go into all the world and preach the Good News to everyone, everywhere. [16] Those who believe and are baptized will be saved. But those who refuse to believe will be condemned.

[17] "And those who believe shall use my authority to cast out demons, and they shall speak new languages.[c] [18] They will be able even to handle snakes with safety, and if they drink anything poisonous, it won't hurt them; and they will be able to place their hands on the sick and heal them."

[19] When the Lord Jesus had finished talking with them, he was taken up into heaven and sat down at God's right hand.

[20] And the disciples went everywhere preaching, and the Lord was with them and confirmed what they said by the miracles that followed their messages.

---

a Verses 9 through 20 are not found in the most ancient manuscripts, but may be considered an appendix giving additional facts.   b Literally, "after these things."   c Literally, "they will speak in new tongues." Some ancient manuscripts omit "new."

We Won!

Bob Combs

Three girls at a music contest laugh, cry, and gasp as close friends are named winners. In the snap and sizzle, emotions soar, excitement mounts—and then comes the release of the judges' decision. Victory, defeat, joy, pain, birth, death—life is all of these. Jesus knew joy—and tears. He knew birth and life—and death! But after he was murdered, he rose from the dead! And that's what his life was all about. He lived so we could live—*really* live—and that's why he said we can know joy which runs so deep that no disappointment can fully squelch it. All through Luke's account of Christ's life, you'll see him "fleshing out" this kind of living—the integrity and depth and power all of us want, so that when our successes and accomplishments disappear like smoke and all we have left is sand in our mouths, we still have what *he* had. *Life.*

LUKE

1 DEAR FRIEND WHO loves God:[a]
1,2 Several biographies of Christ have already been written using as their source material the reports circulating among us from the early disciples and other eyewitnesses. 3 However, it occurred to me that it would be well to recheck all these accounts from first to last and after thorough investigation to pass this summary on to you,[b] 4 to reassure you of the truth of all you were taught.

5 My story begins with a Jewish priest, Zacharias, who lived when Herod was king of Judea. Zacharias was a member of the Abijah division of the Temple service corps. (His wife Elizabeth was, like himself, a member of the priest tribe of the Jews, a descendant of Aaron.) 6 Zacharias and Elizabeth were godly folk, careful to obey all of God's laws in spirit as well as in letter. 7 But they had no children, for Elizabeth was barren; and now they were both very old.

8,9 One day as Zacharias was going about his work in the Temple—for his division was on duty that week—the honor fell to him by lot[c] to enter the inner sanctuary and burn incense before the Lord. 10 Meanwhile, a great crowd stood outside in the Temple court, praying as they always did during that part of the service when the incense was being burned.

11,12 Zacharias was in the sanctuary when

a From verse 3. Literally, "most excellent Theophilus." The name means "one who loves God."
b Literally, "an account of the things accomplished among us."
c Probably by throwing dice or something similar—"drawing straws" would be a modern equivalent.

suddenly an angel appeared, standing to the right of the altar of incense! Zacharias was startled and terrified.

¹³ But the angel said, "Don't be afraid, Zacharias! For I have come to tell you that God has heard your prayer, and your wife Elizabeth will bear you a son! And you are to name him John. ¹⁴ You will both have great joy and gladness at his birth, and many will rejoice with you. ¹⁵ For he will be one of the Lord's great men. He must never touch wine or hard liquor—and he will be filled with the Holy Spirit, even from before his birth! ¹⁶ And he will persuade many a Jew to turn to the Lord his God. ¹⁷ He will be a man of rugged[d] spirit and power like Elijah, the prophet of old; and he will precede the coming of the Messiah, preparing the people for his arrival. He will soften adult hearts to become like little children's, and will change disobedient minds to the wisdom of faith."[e]

¹⁸ Zacharias said to the angel, "But this is impossible! I'm an old man now, and my wife is also well along in years."

¹⁹ Then the angel said, "I am Gabriel! I stand in the very presence of God. It was he who sent me to you with this good news! ²⁰ And now, because you haven't believed me, you are to be stricken silent, unable to speak until the child is born. For my words will certainly come true at the proper time."

²¹ Meanwhile the crowds outside were waiting for Zacharias to appear and wondered why he was taking so long. ²² When he finally came out, he couldn't speak to them, and they realized from his gestures that he must have seen a vision in the Temple. ²³ He stayed on at the Temple for the remaining days of his Temple duties and then returned home. ²⁴ Soon afterwards Elizabeth his wife became pregnant and went into seclusion for five months.

²⁵ "How kind the Lord is," she exclaimed, "to take away my disgrace of having no children!"

²⁶ The following month God sent the angel Gabriel to Nazareth, a village in Galilee, ²⁷ to a virgin, Mary, engaged to be married to a man named Joseph, a descendant of King David.

²⁸ Gabriel appeared to her and said, "Congratulations, favored lady! The Lord is with you!"[f]

²⁹ Confused and disturbed, Mary tried to think what the angel could mean.

³⁰ "Don't be frightened, Mary," the angel told her, "for God has decided to wonderfully bless you! ³¹ Very soon now, you will become pregnant and have a baby boy, and you are to name him 'Jesus.' ³² He shall be very great and shall be called the Son of God. And the Lord God shall give him the throne of his ancestor David. ³³ And he shall reign over Israel forever; his Kingdom shall never end!"

³⁴ Mary asked the angel, "But how can I have a baby? I am a virgin."

³⁵ The angel replied, "The Holy Spirit shall come upon you, and the power of God shall overshadow you; so the baby born to you will be utterly holy—the Son of God. ³⁶ Furthermore, six months ago your Aunt[g] Elizabeth—'the barren one,' they called her—became pregnant in her old age! ³⁷ For every promise from God shall surely come true."

³⁸ Mary said, "I am the Lord's servant, and I am willing to do whatever he wants. May everything you said come true." And then the angel disappeared.

³⁹,⁴⁰ A few days later Mary hurried to the highlands of Judea to the town where Zacharias lived, to visit Elizabeth.

⁴¹ At the sound of Mary's greeting, Elizabeth's child leaped within her and she was filled with the Holy Spirit.

⁴² She gave a glad cry and exclaimed to Mary, "You are favored by God above all other women, and your child is destined for God's mightiest praise. ⁴³ What an honor this is, that the mother of my Lord should visit me! ⁴⁴ When you came in and greeted me, the instant I heard your voice, my baby moved in me for joy! ⁴⁵ You believed that God would do what he said; that is why he has given you this wonderful blessing."

⁴⁶ Mary responded, "Oh, how I praise the Lord. ⁴⁷ How I rejoice in God my Savior! ⁴⁸ For he took notice of his lowly servant

d Implied.   e Literally, "to turn the hearts of the fathers to the children, and the disobedient to the wisdom of the just."   f Some ancient versions add, "Blessed are you among women," as in verse 42 which appears in all the manuscripts.   g Literally, "relative."

girl, and now generation after generation forever shall call me blest of God. [49] For he, the mighty Holy One, has done great things to me. [50] His mercy goes on from generation to generation, to all who reverence him.

[51] "How powerful is his mighty arm! How he scatters the proud and haughty ones! [52] He has torn princes from their thrones and exalted the lowly. [53] He has satisfied the hungry hearts and sent the rich away with empty hands. [54] And how he has helped his servant Israel! He has not forgotten his promise to be merciful. [55] For he promised our fathers—Abraham and his children—to be merciful to them forever."

[56] Mary stayed with Elizabeth about three months and then went back to her own home.

[57] By now Elizabeth's waiting was over, for the time had come for the baby to be born—and it was a boy. [58] The word spread quickly to her neighbors and relatives of how kind the Lord had been to her, and everyone rejoiced.

[59] When the baby was eight days old, all the relatives and friends came for the circumcision ceremony. They all assumed the baby's name would be Zacharias, after his father.

[60] But Elizabeth said, "No! He must be named John!"

[61] "What?" they exclaimed. "There is no one in all your family by that name." [62] So they asked the baby's father, talking to him by gestures.[h]

[63] He motioned for a piece of paper and to everyone's surprise wrote, "His name is *John!*" [64] Instantly Zacharias could speak again, and he began praising God.

[65] Wonder fell upon the whole neighborhood, and the news of what had happened spread through the Judean hills. [66] And everyone who heard about it thought long thoughts and asked, "I wonder what this child will turn out to be? For the hand of the Lord is surely upon him in some special way."

[67] Then his father Zacharias was filled with the Holy Spirit and gave this prophecy:

[68] "Praise the Lord, the God of Israel, for he has come to visit his people and has redeemed them. [69] He is sending us a Mighty Savior from the royal line of his servant David, [70] just as he promised through his holy prophets long ago— [71] someone to save us from our enemies, from all who hate us.

[72,73] "He has been merciful to our ancestors, yes, to Abraham himself, by remembering his sacred promise to him, [74] and by granting us the privilege of serving God fearlessly, freed from our enemies, [75] and by making us holy and acceptable, ready to stand in his presence forever.

[76] "And you, my little son, shall be called the prophet of the glorious God, for you will prepare the way for the Messiah. [77] You will tell his people how to find salvation through forgiveness of their sins. [78] All this will be because the mercy of our God is very tender, and heaven's dawn is about to break upon us, [79] to give light to those who sit in darkness and death's shadow, and to guide us to the path of peace."

[80] The little boy greatly loved God[i] and when he grew up he lived out in the lonely wilderness until he began his public ministry to Israel.

2 ABOUT THIS TIME Caesar Augustus, the Roman Emperor, decreed that a census should be taken throughout the nation. [2] (This census was taken when Quirinius was governor of Syria.)

[3] Everyone was required to return to his ancestral home for this registration. [4] And because Joseph was a member of the royal line, he had to go to Bethlehem in Judea, King David's ancient home—journeying there from the Galilean village of Nazareth. [5] He took with him Mary, his fiancée, who was obviously pregnant by this time.

[6] And while they were there, the time came for her baby to be born; [7] and she gave birth to her first child, a son. She wrapped him in a blanket[a] and laid him in a manger, because there was no room for them in the village inn.

[8] That night some shepherds were in the fields outside the village, guarding their flocks of sheep. [9] Suddenly an angel ap-

---

h Zacharias was apparently stone deaf as well as speechless, and had not heard what his wife had said.
i Literally, "became strong in spirit."   2a Literally, "swaddling clothes."

peared among them, and the landscape shone bright with the glory of the Lord. They were badly frightened, [10] but the angel reassured them.

"Don't be afraid!" he said. "I bring you the most joyful news ever announced, and it is for everyone! [11] The Savior—yes, the Messiah, the Lord—has been born tonight in Bethlehem![b] [12] How will you recognize him? You will find a baby wrapped in a blanket,[c] lying in a manger!"

[13] Suddenly, the angel was joined by a vast host of others—the armies of heaven—praising God:

[14] "Glory to God in the highest heaven," they sang,[d] "and peace on earth for all those pleasing him."

[15] When this great army of angels had returned again to heaven, the shepherds said to each other, "Come on! Let's go to Bethlehem! Let's see this wonderful thing that has happened, which the Lord has told us about."

[16] They ran to the village and found their way to Mary and Joseph. And there was the baby, lying in the manger. [17] The shepherds told everyone what had happened and what the angel had said to them about this child. [18] All who heard the shepherds' story expressed astonishment, [19] but Mary quietly treasured these things in her heart and often thought about them.

[20] Then the shepherds went back again to their fields and flocks, praising God for the visit of the angels, and because they had seen the child, just as the angel had told them.

[21] Eight days later, at the baby's circumcision ceremony, he was named Jesus, the name given him by the angel before he was even conceived.

[22] When the time came for Mary's purification offering at the Temple, as required by the laws of Moses after the birth of a child, his parents took him to Jerusalem to present him to the Lord; [23] for in these laws God had said, "If a woman's first child is a boy, he shall be dedicated to the Lord."

[24] At that time Jesus' parents also offered their sacrifice for purification—"either a pair of turtledoves or two young pigeons" was the legal requirement. [25] That day a man named Simeon, a Jerusalem resident, was in the Temple. He was a good man, very devout, filled with the Holy Spirit and constantly expecting the Messiah[e] to come soon. [26] For the Holy Spirit had revealed to him that he would not die until he had seen him—God's anointed King. [27] The Holy Spirit had impelled him to go to the Temple that day; and so, when Mary and Joseph arrived to present the baby Jesus to the Lord in obedience to the law, [28] Simeon was there and took the child in his arms, praising God.

[29,30,31] "Lord," he said, "now I can die content! For I have seen him as you promised me I would. I have seen the Savior you have given to the world. [32] He is the Light that will shine upon the nations, and he will be the glory of your people Israel!"

[33] Joseph and Mary just stood there, marveling at what was being said about Jesus.

[34,35] Simeon blessed them but then said to Mary, "A sword shall pierce your soul, for this child shall be rejected by many in Israel, and this to their undoing. But he will be the greatest joy of many others. And the deepest thoughts of many hearts shall be revealed."

[36,37] Anna, a prophetess, was also there in the Temple that day. She was the daughter of Phanuel, of the Jewish tribe of Asher, and was very old, for she had been a widow for eighty-four years following seven years of marriage. She never left the Temple but stayed there night and day, worshiping God by praying and often fasting.

[38] She came along just as Simeon was talking with Mary and Joseph, and she also began thanking God and telling everyone in Jerusalem who had been awaiting the coming of the Savior[f] that the Messiah had finally arrived.

[39] When Jesus' parents had fulfilled all the requirements of the Law of God they returned home to Nazareth in Galilee. [40] There the child became a strong, robust lad, and was known for wisdom beyond his

---

b Literally, "in the City of David."   c Literally, "swaddling clothes."   d Literally, "said."
e Literally, "the Consolation of Israel."   f Literally, "looking for the redemption of Jerusalem."

years; and God poured out his blessings on him.

⁴¹,⁴² When Jesus was twelve years old he accompanied his parents to Jerusalem for the annual Passover Festival, which they attended each year. ⁴³ After the celebration was over they started home to Nazareth, but Jesus stayed behind in Jerusalem. His parents didn't miss him the first day, ⁴⁴ for they assumed he was with friends among the other travelers. But when he didn't show up that evening, they started to look for him among their relatives and friends; ⁴⁵ and when they couldn't find him, they went back to Jerusalem to search for him there.

⁴⁶,⁴⁷ Three days later they finally discovered him. He was in the Temple, sitting among the teachers of Law, discussing deep questions with them and amazing everyone with his understanding and answers.

⁴⁸ His parents didn't know what to think. "Son!" his mother said to him. "Why have you done this to us? Your father and I have been frantic, searching for you everywhere."

⁴⁹ "But why did you need to search?" he asked. "Didn't you realize that I would be here at the Temple, in my Father's House?" ⁵⁰ But they didn't understand what he meant.

⁵¹ Then he returned to Nazareth with them and was obedient to them; and his mother stored away all these things in her heart. ⁵² So Jesus grew both tall and wise, and was loved by God and man.

3 IN THE FIFTEENTH year of the reign of Emperor Tiberius Caesar, a message came from God to John (the son of Zacharias), as he was living out in the deserts. (Pilate was governor over Judea at that time; Herod, over Galilee; his brother Philip, over Iturea and Trachonitis; Lysanias, over Abilene; and Annas and Caiaphas were High Priests.) ³ Then John went from place to place on both sides of the Jordan River, preaching that people should be baptized to show that they had turned to God and away from their sins, in order to be forgiven.ᵃ

⁴ In the words of Isaiah the prophet, John was "a voice shouting from the barren wilderness, 'Prepare a road for the Lord to travel on! Widen the pathway before him! ⁵ Level the mountains! Fill up the valleys! Straighten the curves! Smooth out the ruts! ⁶ And then all mankind shall see the Savior sent from God.' "

⁷ Here is a sample of John's preaching to the crowds that came for baptism: "You brood of snakes! You are trying to escape hell without truly turning to God! That is why you want to be baptized! ⁸ First go and prove by the way you live that you really have repented. And don't think you are safe because you are descendants of Abraham. That isn't enough. God can produce children of Abraham from these desert stones! ⁹ The axe of his judgment is poised over you, ready to sever your roots and cut you down. Yes, every tree that does not produce good fruit will be chopped down and thrown into the fire."

¹⁰ The crowd replied, "What do you want us to do?"

¹¹ "If you have two coats," he replied, "give one to the poor. If you have extra food, give it away to those who are hungry."

¹² Even tax collectors—notorious for their corruption—came to be baptized and asked, "How shall we prove to you that we have abandoned our sins?"

¹³ "By your honesty," he replied. "Make sure you collect no more taxes than the Romanᵇ government requires you to."

¹⁴ "And us," asked some soldiers, "what about us?"

John replied, "Don't extort money by threats and violence; don't accuse anyone of what you know he didn't do; and be content with your pay!"

¹⁵ Everyone was expecting the Messiah to come soon, and eager to know whether or not John was he. This was the question of the hour, and was being discussed everywhere.

¹⁶ John answered the question by saying, "I baptize only with water; but someone is coming soon who has far higher authority than mine; in fact, I am not even worthy of being his slave.ᶜ He will baptize you with

---

a Or, "preaching the baptism of repentance for remission of sins."   b Implied.   c Literally, "of loosing (the sandal strap of) his shoe."

fire—with the Holy Spirit. [17] He will separate chaff from grain, and burn up the chaff with eternal fire and store away the grain." [18] He used many such warnings as he announced the Good News to the people.

[19,20] (But after John had publicly criticized Herod, governor of Galilee, for marrying Herodias, his brother's wife, and for many other wrongs he had done, Herod put John in prison, thus adding this sin to all his many others.) [21] Then one day, after the crowds had been baptized, Jesus himself was baptized; and as he was praying, the heavens opened, [22] and the Holy Spirit in the form of a dove settled upon him, and a voice from heaven said, "You are my much loved Son, yes, my delight."

[23-38] Jesus was about thirty years old when he began his public ministry.

Jesus was known as the son of
Joseph.
Joseph's father was Heli;
Heli's father was Matthat;
Matthat's father was Levi;
Levi's father was Melchi;
Melchi's father was Jannai;
Jannai's father was Joseph;
Joseph's father was Mattathias;
Mattathias' father was Amos;
Amos' father was Nahum;
Nahum's father was Esli;
Esli's father was Naggai;
Naggai's father was Maath;
Maath's father was Mattathias;
Mattathias' father was Semein;
Semein's father was Josech;
Josech's father was Joda;
Joda's father was Joanan;
Joanan's father was Rhesa;
Rhesa's father was Zerubbabel;
Zerubbabel's father was Shealtiel;
Shealtiel's father was Neri;
Neri's father was Melchi;
Melchi's father was Addi;
Addi's father was Cosam;
Cosam's father was Elmadam;
Elmadam's father was Er;
Er's father was Joshua;
Joshua's father was Eliezer;
Eliezer's father was Jorim;
Jorim's father was Matthat;

Matthat's father was Levi;
Levi's father was Simeon;
Simeon's father was Judah;
Judah's father was Joseph;
Joseph's father was Jonam;
Jonam's father was Eliakim;
Eliakim's father was Melea;
Melea's father was Menna;
Menna's father was Mattatha;
Mattatha's father was Nathan;
Nathan's father was David;
David's father was Jesse;
Jesse's father was Obed;
Obed's father was Boaz;
Boaz' father was Salmon;[d]
Salmon's father was Nahshon;
Nahshon's father was Amminadab;
Amminadab's father was Admin;
Admin's father was Arni;
Arni's father was Hezron;
Hezron's father was Perez;
Perez' father was Judah;
Judah's father was Jacob;
Jacob's father was Isaac;
Isaac's father was Abraham;
Abraham's father was Terah;
Terah's father was Nahor;
Nahor's father was Serug;
Serug's father was Reu;
Reu's father was Peleg;
Peleg's father was Eber;
Eber's father was Shelah;
Shelah's father was Cainan;
Cainan's father was Arphaxad;
Arphaxad's father was Shem;
Shem's father was Noah;
Noah's father was Lamech;
Lamech's father was Methuselah;
Methuselah's father was Enoch;
Enoch's father was Jared;
Jared's father was Mahalaleel;
Mahalaleel's father was Cainan;
Cainan's father was Enos;
Enos' father was Seth;
Seth's father was Adam;
Adam's father was God.

4 THEN JESUS, FULL of the Holy Spirit, left the Jordan River, being urged by the Spirit out into the barren wastelands of Judea, where Satan tempted him for forty

d "Sala."

days. He ate nothing all that time, and was very hungry.

[3] Satan said, "If you are God's Son, tell this stone to become a loaf of bread."

[4] But Jesus replied, "It is written in the Scriptures, 'Other things in life are much more important than bread!' "[a]

[5] Then Satan took him up and revealed to him all the kingdoms of the world in a moment of time; [6,7] and the devil told him, "I will give you all these splendid kingdoms and their glory—for they are mine to give to anyone I wish—if you will only get down on your knees and worship me."

[8] Jesus replied, "We must worship God, and him alone. So it is written in the Scriptures."

[9,10,11] Then Satan took him to Jerusalem to a high roof of the Temple and said, "If you are the Son of God, jump off! For the Scriptures say that God will send his angels to guard you and to keep you from crashing to the pavement below!"

[12] Jesus replied, "The Scriptures also say, 'Do not put the Lord your God to a foolish test.' "

[13] When the devil had ended all the temptations, he left Jesus for a while and went away.

[14] Then Jesus returned to Galilee, full of the Holy Spirit's power. Soon he became well known throughout all that region [15] for his sermons in the synagogues; everyone praised him.

[16] When he came to the village of Nazareth, his boyhood home, he went as usual to the synagogue on Saturday, and stood up to read the Scriptures. [17] The book of Isaiah the prophet was handed to him, and he opened it to the place where it says:

[18,19] "The Spirit of the Lord is upon me; he has appointed me to preach Good News to the poor; he has sent me to heal the brokenhearted and to announce that captives shall be released and the blind shall see, that the downtrodden shall be freed from their oppressors, and that God is ready to give blessings to all who come to him."[b]

[20] He closed the book and handed it back to the attendant and sat down, while every-

one in the synagogue gazed at him intently. [21] Then he added, "These Scriptures came true today!"

[22] All who were there spoke well of him and were amazed by the beautiful words that fell from his lips. "How can this be?" they asked. "Isn't this Joseph's son?"

[23] Then he said, "Probably you will quote me that proverb, 'Physician, heal yourself'—meaning, 'Why don't you do miracles here in your home town like those you did in Capernaum?' [24] But I solemnly declare to you that no prophet is accepted in his own home town! [25,26] For example, remember how Elijah the prophet used a miracle to help the widow of Zarephath—a foreigner from the land of Sidon. There were many Jewish widows needing help in those days of famine, for there had been no rain for three and one-half years, and hunger stalked the land; yet Elijah was not sent to them. [27] Or think of the prophet Elisha, who healed Naaman, a Syrian, rather than the many Jewish lepers needing help."

[28] These remarks stung them to fury; [29] and jumping up, they mobbed him and took him to the edge of the hill on which the city was built, to push him over the cliff. [30] But he walked away through the crowd and left them.

[31] Then he returned to Capernaum, a city in Galilee, and preached there in the synagogue every Saturday. [32] Here, too, the people were amazed at the things he said. For he spoke as one who knew the truth, instead of merely quoting the opinions of others as his authority.

[33] Once as he was teaching in the synagogue, a man possessed by a demon began shouting at Jesus, [34] "Go away! We want nothing to do with you, Jesus from Nazareth. You have come to destroy us. I know who you are—the Holy Son of God."

[35] Jesus cut him short. "Be silent!" he told the demon. "Come out!" The demon threw the man to the floor as the crowd watched, and then left him without hurting him further.

[36] Amazed, the people asked, "What is in this man's words that even demons obey

---

a Literally, "Man shall not live by bread alone." Deuteronomy 8:3.   b Literally, "to proclaim the acceptable year of the Lord."

Jesus recruits fishermen

him?" [37] The story of what he had done spread like wildfire throughout the whole region.

[38] After leaving the synagogue that day, he went to Simon's home where he found Simon's mother-in-law very sick with a high fever. "Please heal her," everyone begged. [39] Standing at her bedside he spoke to the fever, rebuking it, and immediately her temperature returned to normal and she got up and prepared a meal[c] for them!

[40] As the sun went down that evening, all the villagers who had any sick people in their homes, no matter what their diseases were, brought them to Jesus; and the touch of his hands healed every one! [41] Some were possessed by demons; and the demons came out at his command, shouting, "You are the Son of God." But because they knew he was the Christ, he stopped them and told them to be silent.

[42] Early the next morning he went out into the desert. The crowds searched everywhere for him and when they finally found him they begged him not to leave them, but to stay at Capernaum. [43] But he replied, "I must preach the Good News of the Kingdom of God in other places too, for that is why I was sent." [44] So he continued to travel around preaching in synagogues throughout Judea.

5 ONE DAY AS he was preaching on the shore of Lake Gennesaret, great crowds pressed in on him to listen to the Word of God. [2] He noticed two empty boats standing at the water's edge while the fishermen washed their nets. [3] Stepping into one of the boats, Jesus asked Simon, its owner, to push out a little into the water, so that he could sit in the boat and speak to the crowds from there.

[4] When he had finished speaking, he said to Simon, "Now go out where it is deeper and let down your nets and you will catch a lot of fish!"

[5] "Sir," Simon replied, "we worked hard all last night and didn't catch a thing. But if you say so, we'll try again."

[6] And this time their nets were so full that they began to tear! [7] A shout for help brought their partners in the other boat and soon both boats were filled with fish and on the verge of sinking.

[8] When Simon Peter realized what had happened, he fell to his knees before Jesus and said, "Oh, sir, please leave us—I'm too much of a sinner for you to have around." [9] For he was awestruck by the size of their catch, as were the others with him, [10] and his partners too—James and John, the sons of Zebedee. Jesus replied, "Don't be afraid! From now on you'll be fishing for the souls of men!"

[11] And as soon as they landed, they left everything and went with him.

[12] One day in a certain village he was visiting, there was a man with an advanced case of leprosy. When he saw Jesus he fell to the ground before him, face downward in the dust, begging to be healed.

"Sir," he said, "if you only will, you can clear me of every trace of my disease."

[13] Jesus reached out and touched the man and said, "Of course I will. Be healed." And the leprosy left him instantly! [14] Then Jesus instructed him to go at once without telling anyone what had happened and be examined by the Jewish priest. "Offer the sacrifice Moses' law requires for lepers who are healed," he said. "This will prove to everyone that you are well." [15] Now the report of his power spread even faster and vast crowds came to hear him preach and to be healed of their diseases. [16] But he often withdrew to the wilderness for prayer.

[17] One day while he was teaching, some Jewish religious leaders[a] and teachers of the Law were sitting nearby. (It seemed that these men showed up from every village in all Galilee and Judea, as well as from Jerusalem.) And the Lord's healing power was upon him.

[18,19] Then—look! Some men came carrying a paralyzed man on a sleeping mat. They tried to push through the crowd to Jesus but couldn't reach him. So they went up on the roof above him, took off some tiles and lowered the sick man down into the crowd, still on his sleeping mat, right in front of Jesus.

[20] Seeing their faith, Jesus said to the

---

c Literally, "ministered unto them." 5a Literally, "Pharisees."

man, "My friend, your sins are forgiven!"

[21] "Who does this fellow think he is?" the Pharisees and teachers of the Law exclaimed among themselves. "This is blasphemy! Who but God can forgive sins?"

[22] Jesus knew what they were thinking, and he replied, "Why is it blasphemy? [23,24] I, the Messiah,[b] have the authority on earth to forgive sins. But talk is cheap—anybody could say that. So I'll prove it to you by healing this man." Then, turning to the paralyzed man, he commanded, "Pick up your stretcher and go on home, for you are healed!"

[25] And immediately, as everyone watched, the man jumped to his feet, picked up his mat and went home praising God! [26] Everyone present was gripped with awe and fear. And they praised God, remarking over and over again, "We have seen strange things today."

[27] Later on as Jesus left the town he saw a tax collector—with the usual reputation for cheating—sitting at a tax collection booth. The man's name was Levi. Jesus said to him, "Come and be one of my disciples!" [28] So Levi left everything, sprang up and went with him.

[29] Soon Levi held a reception in his home with Jesus as the guest of honor. Many of Levi's fellow tax collectors and other guests were there.

[30] But the Pharisees and teachers of the Law complained bitterly to Jesus' disciples about his eating with such notorious sinners.

[31] Jesus answered them, "It is the sick who need a doctor, not those in good health. [32] My purpose is to invite sinners to turn from their sins, not to spend my time with those who think themselves already good enough."

[33] Their next complaint was that Jesus' disciples were feasting instead of fasting. "John the Baptist's disciples are constantly going without food, and praying," they declared, "and so do the disciples of the Pharisees. Why are yours wining and dining?"

[34] Jesus asked, "Do happy men fast? Do wedding guests go hungry while celebrating with the groom? [35] But the time will come

when the bridegroom will be killed;[c] then they won't want to eat."

[36] Then Jesus used this illustration: "No one tears off a piece of a new garment to make a patch for an old one. Not only will the new garment be ruined, but the old garment will look worse with a new patch on it! [37] And no one puts new wine into old wineskins, for the new wine bursts the old skins, ruining the skins and spilling the wine. [38] New wine must be put into new wineskins. [39] But no one after drinking the old wine seems to want the fresh and the new. 'The old ways are best,' they say."

6 ONE SABBATH AS Jesus and his disciples were walking through some grainfields, they were breaking off the heads of wheat, rubbing off the husks in their hands and eating the grains.

[2] But some Pharisees said, "That's illegal! Your disciples are harvesting grain, and it's against the Jewish law to work on the Sabbath."

[3] Jesus replied, "Don't you read the Scriptures? Haven't you ever read what King David did when he and his men were hungry? [4] He went into the Temple and took the shewbread, the special bread that was placed before the Lord, and ate it—illegal as this was—and shared it with others." [5] And Jesus added, "I[a] am master even of the Sabbath."

[6] On another Sabbath he was in the synagogue teaching, and a man was present whose right hand was deformed. [7] The teachers of the Law and the Pharisees watched closely to see whether he would heal the man that day, since it was the Sabbath. For they were eager to find some charge to bring against him.

[8] How well he knew their thoughts! But he said to the man with the deformed hand, "Come and stand here where everyone can see." So he did.

[9] Then Jesus said to the Pharisees and teachers of the Law, "I have a question for you. Is it right to do good on the Sabbath day, or to do harm? To save life, or to destroy it?"

[10] He looked around at them one by one

---

b Literally, "the Son of Man."   c Literally, "taken away from them."   6a Literally, "the Son of Man."

and then said to the man, "Reach out your hand." And as he did, it became completely normal again. [11] At this, the enemies of Jesus were wild with rage, and began to plot his murder.

[12] One day soon afterwards he went out into the mountains to pray, and prayed all night. [13] At daybreak he called together his followers and chose twelve of them to be the inner circle of his disciples. (They were appointed as his "apostles," or "missionaries.") [14,15,16] Here are their names:

Simon (he also called him Peter),
Andrew (Simon's brother),
James,
John,
Philip,
Bartholomew,
Matthew,
Thomas,
James (the son of Alphaeus),
Simon (a member of the Zealots, a subversive political party),
Judas (son of James),
Judas Iscariot (who later betrayed him).

[17,18] When they came down the slopes of the mountain, they stood with Jesus on a large, level area, surrounded by many of his followers who, in turn, were surrounded by the crowds. For people from all over Judea and from Jerusalem and from as far north as the seacoasts of Tyre and Sidon had come to hear him or to be healed. And he cast out many demons. [19] Everyone was trying to touch him, for when they did healing power went out from him and they were cured.

[20] Then he turned to his disciples and said, "What happiness there is for you who are poor, for the Kingdom of God is yours! [21] What happiness there is for you who are now hungry, for you are going to be satisfied! What happiness there is for you who weep, for the time will come when you shall laugh with joy! [22] What happiness it is when others hate you and exclude you and insult you and smear your name because you are mine![b] [23] When that happens, rejoice! Yes, leap for joy! For you will have a great reward awaiting you in heaven. And you will be in good company—the ancient prophets

were treated that way too!

[24] "But, oh, the sorrows that await the rich. For they have their only happiness down here. [25] They are fat and prosperous now, but a time of awful hunger is before them. Their careless laughter now means sorrow then. [26] And what sadness is ahead for those praised by the crowds—for *false* prophets have *always* been praised.

[27] "Listen, all of you. Love your *enemies.* Do *good* to those who *hate* you. [28] Pray for the happiness of those who *curse* you; implore God's blessing on those who *hurt* you.

[29] "If someone slaps you on one cheek, let him slap the other too! If someone demands your coat, give him your shirt besides. [30] Give what you have to anyone who asks you for it; and when things are taken away from you, don't worry about getting them back. [31] Treat others as you want them to treat you.

[32] "Do you think you deserve credit for merely loving those who love you? Even the godless do that! [33] And if you do good only to those who do you good—is that so wonderful? Even sinners do that much! [34] And if you lend money only to those who can repay you, what good is that? Even the most wicked will lend to their own kind for full return!

[35] "Love your *enemies!* Do good to *them!* Lend to *them!* And don't be concerned about the fact that they won't repay. Then your reward from heaven will be very great, and you will truly be acting as sons of God; for he is kind to the *unthankful* and to those who are *very wicked.*

[36] "Try to show as much compassion as your Father does. [37] Never criticize or condemn—or it will all come back on you. Go easy on others; then they will do the same for you.[c] [38] For if you give, you will get! Your gift will return to you in full and overflowing measure, pressed down, shaken together to make room for more, and running over. Whatever measure you use to give—large or small—will be used to measure what is given back to you."

[39] Here are some of the story-illustrations Jesus used in his sermons: "What good is it for one blind man to lead another? He

---

b Literally, "on account of the Son of Man."   c Literally, "release, and you shall be released."

will fall into a ditch and pull the other down with him. ⁴⁰ How can a student know more than his teacher? But if he works hard, he may learn as much.

⁴¹ "And why quibble about the speck in someone else's eye—his little fault^d—when a board is in your own? ⁴² How can you think of saying to him, 'Brother, let me help you get rid of that speck in your eye,' when you can't see past the board in yours? Hypocrite! First get rid of the board, and then perhaps you can see well enough to deal with his speck!

⁴³ "A tree from good stock doesn't produce scrub fruit nor do trees from poor stock produce choice fruit. ⁴⁴ A tree is identified by the kind of fruit it produces. Figs never grow on thorns, or grapes on bramble bushes. ⁴⁵ A good man produces good deeds from a good heart. And an evil man produces evil deeds from his hidden wickedness. Whatever is in the heart overflows into speech.

⁴⁶ "So why do you call me 'Lord' when you won't obey me? ⁴⁷,⁴⁸ But all those who come and listen and obey me are like a man who builds a house on a strong foundation laid upon the underlying rock. When the floodwaters rise and break against the house, it stands firm, for it is strongly built.

⁴⁹ "But those who listen and don't obey are like a man who builds a house without a foundation. When the floods sweep down against that house, it crumbles into a heap of ruins."

7 WHEN JESUS HAD finished his sermon he went back into the city of Capernaum.
² Just at that time the highly prized slave of a Roman^a army captain was sick and near death. ³ When the captain heard about Jesus, he sent some respected Jewish elders to ask him to come and heal his slave. ⁴ So they began pleading earnestly with Jesus to come with them and help the man. They told him what a wonderful person the captain was.
"If anyone deserves your help, it is he," they said, ⁵ "for he loves the Jews and even paid personally to build us a synagogue!"

⁶,⁷,⁸ Jesus went with them; but just before arriving at the house, the captain sent some friends to say, "Sir, don't inconvenience yourself by coming to my home, for I am not worthy of any such honor or even to come and meet you. Just speak a word from where you are, and my servant boy will be healed! I know, because I am under the authority of my superior officers, and I have authority over my men. I only need to say 'Go!' and they go; or 'Come!' and they come; and to my slave, 'Do this or that,' and he does it. So just say, 'Be healed!' and my servant will be well again!"

⁹ Jesus was amazed. Turning to the crowd he said, "Never among all the Jews in Israel have I met a man with faith like this."

¹⁰ And when the captain's friends returned to his house, they found the slave completely healed.

¹¹ Not long afterwards Jesus went with his disciples to the village of Nain, with the usual great crowd at his heels. ¹² A funeral procession was coming out as he approached the village gate. The boy who had died was the only son of his widowed mother, and many mourners from the village were with her.

¹³ When the Lord saw her, his heart overflowed with sympathy. "Don't cry!" he said. ¹⁴ Then he walked over to the coffin and touched it, and the bearers stopped. "Laddie," he said, "come back to life again."

¹⁵ Then the boy sat up and began to talk to those around him! And Jesus gave him back to his mother.

¹⁶ A great fear swept the crowd, and they exclaimed with praises to God, "A mighty prophet has risen among us," and, "We have seen the hand of God at work today."

¹⁷ The report of what he did that day raced from end to end of Judea and even out across the borders.

¹⁸ The disciples of John the Baptist soon heard of all that Jesus was doing. When they told John about it, ¹⁹ he sent two of his disciples to Jesus to ask him, "Are you really the Messiah?^b Or shall we keep on looking for him?"

---

d Implied.   7 a Implied.   b Literally, "the one who is coming."

867

20,21,22 The two disciples found Jesus while he was curing many sick people of their various diseases—healing the lame and the blind and casting out evil spirits. When they asked him John's question, this was his reply: "Go back to John and tell him all you have seen and heard here today: how those who were blind can see. The lame are walking without a limp. The lepers are completely healed. The deaf can hear again. The dead come back to life. And the poor are hearing the Good News. 23 And tell him, 'Blessed is the one who does not lose his faith in me.' "c

24 After they left, Jesus talked to the crowd about John. "Who is this man you went out into the Judean wilderness to see?" he asked. "Did you find him weak as grass, moved by every breath of wind? 25 Did you find him dressed in expensive clothes? No! Men who live in luxury are found in palaces, not out in the wilderness. 26 But did you find a prophet? Yes! And more than a prophet. 27 He is the one to whom the Scriptures refer when they say, 'Look! I am sending my messenger ahead of you, to prepare the way before you.' 28 In all humanity there is no one greater than John. And yet the least citizen of the Kingdom of God is greater than he."

29 And all who heard John preach—even the most wicked of themd—agreed that God's requirements were right, and they were baptized by him. 30 All, that is, except the Pharisees and teachers of Moses' Law. They rejected God's plan for them and refused John's baptism.

31 "What can I say about such men?" Jesus asked. "With what shall I compare them? 32 They are like a group of children who complain to their friends, 'You don't like it if we play "wedding" and you don't like it if we play "funeral" '!e 33 For John the Baptist used to go without food and never took a drop of liquor all his life, and you said, 'He must be crazy!'f 34 But I eat my food and drink my wine, and you say, 'What a glutton Jesus is! And he drinks! And has the lowest sort of friends!'g 35 But

I am sure you can always justify your inconsistencies."h

36 One of the Pharisees asked Jesus to come to his home for lunch and Jesus accepted the invitation. As they sat down to eat, 37 a woman of the streets—a prostitute—heard he was there and brought an exquisite flask filled with expensive perfume. 38 Going in, she knelt behind him at his feet, weeping, with her tears falling down upon his feet; and she wiped them off with her hair and kissed them and poured the perfume on them.

39 When Jesus' host, a Pharisee, saw what was happening and who the woman was, he said to himself, "This proves that Jesus is no prophet, for if God had really sent him, he would know what kind of woman this one is!"

40 Then Jesus spoke up and answered his thoughts. "Simon," he said to the Pharisee, "I have something to say to you."

"All right, Teacher," Simon replied, "go ahead."

41 Then Jesus told him this story: "A man loaned money to two people—$5,000 to one and $500 to the other. 42 But neither of them could pay him back, so he kindly forgave them both, letting them keep the money! Which do you suppose loved him most after that?"

43 "I suppose the one who had owed him the most," Simon answered.

"Correct," Jesus agreed.

44 Then he turned to the woman and said to Simon, "Look! See this woman kneeling here! When I entered your home, you didn't bother to offer me water to wash the dust from my feet, but she has washed them with her tears and wiped them with her hair. 45 You refused me the customary kiss of greeting, but she has kissed my feet again and again from the time I first came in. 46 You neglected the usual courtesy of olive oil to anoint my head, but she has covered my feet with rare perfume. 47 Therefore her sins—and they are many—are forgiven, for she loved me much; but one who is forgiven little, shows little love."

---

c Literally, "Blessed is he who keeps from stumbling over me."   d Literally, "even the tax collectors"; i.e., the publicans.   e Literally, "We played the flute for you and you didn't dance; we sang a dirge and you didn't weep."   f Literally, "He has a demon."   g Literally, "is a friend of tax gatherers and sinners." h Literally, "but wisdom is justified of all her children."

[48] And he said to her, "Your sins are forgiven."

[49] Then the men at the table said to themselves, "Who does this man think he is, going around forgiving sins?"

[50] And Jesus said to the woman, "Your faith has saved you; go in peace."

8 NOT LONG AFTERWARDS he began a tour of the cities and villages of Galilee[a] to announce the coming of the Kingdom of God, and took his twelve disciples with him. [2] Some women went along, from whom he had cast out demons or whom he had healed; among them were Mary Magdalene (Jesus had cast out seven demons from her), [3] Joanna, Chuza's wife (Chuza was King Herod's business manager and was in charge of his palace and domestic affairs), Susanna, and many others who were contributing from their private means to the support of Jesus and his disciples.

[4] One day he gave this illustration to a large crowd that was gathering to hear him—while many others were still on the way, coming from other towns.

[5] "A farmer went out to his field to sow grain. As he scattered the seed on the ground, some of it fell on a footpath and was trampled on; and the birds came and ate it as it lay exposed. [6] Other seed fell on shallow soil with rock beneath. This seed began to grow, but soon withered and died for lack of moisture. [7] Other seed landed in thistle patches, and the young grain stalks were soon choked out. [8] Still other fell on fertile soil; this seed grew and produced a crop one hundred times as large as he had planted." (As he was giving this illustration he said, "If anyone has listening ears, use them now!")

[9] His apostles asked him what the story meant.

[10] He replied, "God has granted you to know the meaning of these parables, for they tell a great deal about the Kingdom of God. But these crowds hear the words and do not understand, just as the ancient prophets predicted.

[11] "This is its meaning: The seed is God's message to men. [12] The hard path where some seed fell represents the hard hearts of those who hear the words of God, but then the devil comes and steals the words away and prevents people from believing and being saved. [13] The stony ground represents those who enjoy listening to sermons, but somehow the message never really gets through to them and doesn't take root and grow. They know the message is true, and sort of believe for awhile; but when the hot winds of persecution blow, they lose interest. [14] The seed among the thorns represents those who listen and believe God's words but whose faith afterwards is choked out by worry and riches and the responsibilities and pleasures of life. And so they are never able to help anyone else to believe the Good News.

[15] "But the good soil represents honest, good-hearted people. They listen to God's words and cling to them and steadily spread them to others who also soon believe."

[16] [Another time he asked,[b]] "Who ever heard of someone lighting a lamp and then covering it up to keep it from shining? No, lamps are mounted in the open where they can be seen. [17] This illustrates the fact that someday everything [in men's hearts[b]] shall be brought to light and made plain to all. [18] So be careful how you listen; for whoever has, to him shall be given more; and whoever does not have, even what he thinks he has shall be taken away from him."

[19] Once when his mother and brothers came to see him, they couldn't get into the house where he was teaching, because of the crowds. [20] When Jesus heard they were standing outside and wanted to see him, [21] he remarked, "My mother and my brothers are all those who hear the message of God and obey it."

[22] One day about that time, as he and his disciples were out in a boat, he suggested that they cross to the other side of the lake. [23] On the way across he lay down for a nap, and while he was sleeping the wind began to rise. A fierce storm developed that threatened to swamp them, and they were in real danger.

[24] They rushed over and woke him up.

---

a Implied.   b Implied. See Matthew 5:16.

"Master, Master, we are sinking!" they screamed.

So he spoke to the storm: "Quiet down," he said, and the wind and waves subsided and all was calm! [25] Then he asked them, "Where is your faith?"

And they were filled with awe and fear of him and said to one another, "Who is this man, that even the winds and waves obey him?"

[26] So they arrived at the other side, in the Gerasene country across the lake from Galilee. [27] As he was climbing out of the boat a man from the city of Gadara came to meet him, a man who had been demon-possessed for a long time. Homeless and naked, he lived in a cemetery among the tombs. [28] As soon as he saw Jesus he shrieked and fell to the ground before him, screaming, "What do you want with me, Jesus, Son of God Most High? Please, I beg you, oh, don't torment me!"

[29] For Jesus was already commanding the demon to leave him. This demon had often taken control of the man so that even when shackled with chains he simply broke them and rushed out into the desert, completely under the demon's power. [30] "What is your name?" Jesus asked the demon. "Legion," they replied—for the man was filled with thousands[c] of them! [31] They kept begging Jesus not to order them into the Bottomless Pit.

[32] A herd of pigs was feeding on the mountainside nearby, and the demons pled with him to let them enter into the pigs. And Jesus said they could. [33] So they left the man and went into the pigs, and immediately the whole herd rushed down the mountainside and fell over a cliff into the lake below, where they drowned. [34] The herdsmen rushed away to the nearby city, spreading the news as they ran.

[35] Soon a crowd came out to see for themselves what had happened and saw the man who had been demon-possessed sitting quietly at Jesus' feet, clothed and sane! And the whole crowd was badly frightened. [36] Then those who had seen it happen told how the demon-possessed man had been healed. [37] And everyone begged Jesus to go away and leave them alone (for a deep wave of fear had swept over them). So he returned to the boat and left, crossing back to the other side of the lake.

[38] The man who had been demon-possessed begged to go too, but Jesus said no. [39] "Go back to your family," he told him, "and tell them what a wonderful thing God has done for you."

So he went all through the city telling everyone about Jesus' mighty miracle.

[40] On the other side of the lake the crowds received him with open arms, for they had been waiting for him.

[41] And now a man named Jairus, a leader of a Jewish synagogue, came and fell down at Jesus' feet and begged him to come home with him, [42] for his only child was dying, a little girl twelve years old. Jesus went with him, pushing through the crowds.

[43,44] As they went a woman who wanted to be healed came up behind and touched him, for she had been slowly bleeding for twelve years, and could find no cure (though she had spent everything she had on doctors[d]). But the instant she touched the edge of his robe, the bleeding stopped.

[45] "Who touched me?" Jesus asked.

Everyone denied it, and Peter said, "Master, so many are crowding against you . . . ."

[46] But Jesus told him, "No, it was someone who deliberately touched me, for I felt healing power go out from me."

[47] When the woman realized that Jesus knew, she began to tremble and fell to her knees before him and told why she had touched him and that now she was well.

[48] "Daughter," he said to her, "your faith has healed you. Go in peace."

[49] While he was still speaking to her, a messenger arrived from the Jairus' home with the news that the little girl was dead. "She's gone," he told her father; "there's no use troubling the Teacher now."

[50] But when Jesus heard what had happened, he said to the father, "Don't be afraid! Just trust me, and she'll be all right."

[51] When they arrived at the house Jesus

---

c Implied; a legion consisted of 6,000 troops. Whether the demons were speaking literally is, of course, unknown.
d This clause is not included in some of the ancient manuscripts.

wouldn't let anyone into the room except Peter, James, John, and the little girl's father and mother. ⁵² The home was filled with mourning people, but he said, "Stop the weeping! She isn't dead; she is only asleep!" ⁵³ This brought scoffing and laughter, for they all knew she was dead.

⁵⁴ Then he took her by the hand and called, "Get up, little girl!" ⁵⁵ And at that moment her life returned and she jumped up! "Give her something to eat!" he said. ⁵⁶ Her parents were overcome with happiness, but Jesus insisted that they not tell anyone the details of what had happened.

9 ONE DAY JESUS called together his twelve apostles and gave them authority over all demons—power to cast them out —and to heal all diseases. ² Then he sent them away to tell everyone about the coming of the Kingdom of God and to heal the sick.

³ "Don't even take along a walking stick," he instructed them, "nor a beggar's bag, nor food, nor money. Not even an extra coat. ⁴ Be a guest in only one home at each village.

⁵ "If the people of a town won't listen to you when you enter it, turn around and leave, demonstrating God's anger against itᵃ by shaking its dust from your feet as you go."

⁶ So they began their circuit of the villages, preaching the Good News and healing the sick.

⁷ When reports of Jesus' miracles reached Herod, the governor,ᵇ he was worried and puzzled, for some were saying, "This is John the Baptist come back to life again"; ⁸ and others, "It is Elijah or some other ancient prophet risen from the dead." These rumors were circulating all over the land.

⁹ "I beheaded John," Herod said, "so who is this man about whom I hear such strange stories?" And he tried to see him.

¹⁰ After the apostles returned to Jesus and reported what they had done, he slipped quietly away with them toward the city of Bethsaida. ¹¹ But the crowds found out where he was going, and followed. And he welcomed them, teaching them again about the Kingdom of God and curing those who were ill.

¹² Late in the afternoon all twelve of the disciples came and urged him to send the people away to the nearby villages and farms, to find food and lodging for the night. "For there is nothing to eat here in this deserted spot," they said.

¹³ But Jesus replied, *"You* feed them!"

"Why, we have only five loaves of bread and two fish among the lot of us," they protested; "or are you expecting us to go and buy enough for this whole mob?" ¹⁴ For there were about 5,000 men there!

"Just tell them to sit down on the ground in groups of about fifty each," Jesus replied. ¹⁵ So they did.

¹⁶ Jesus took the five loaves and two fish and looked up into the sky and gave thanks; then he broke off pieces for his disciples to set before the crowd. ¹⁷ And everyone ate and ate; still, twelve basketfuls of scraps were picked up afterwards!

¹⁸ One day as he was alone, praying, with his disciples nearby, he came over and asked them, "Who are the people saying I am?"

¹⁹ "John the Baptist," they told him, "or perhaps Elijah or one of the other ancient prophets risen from the dead."

²⁰ Then he asked them, "Who do you think I am?"

Peter replied, "The Messiah—the Christ of God!"

²¹ He gave them strict orders not to speak of this to anyone. ²² "For I, the Messiah,ᶜ must suffer much," he said, "and be rejected by the Jewish leaders—the elders, chief priests, and teachers of the Law—and be killed; and three days later I will come back to life again!"

²³ Then he said to all, "Anyone who wants to follow me must put aside his own desires and conveniences and carry his cross with him every day and *keep close to me!* ²⁴ Whoever loses his life for my sake will save it, but whoever insists on keeping his life will lose it; ²⁵ and what profit is there in gaining the whole world when it means for-

---

a Literally, "as a testimony against them."   b Literally, "Herod the Tetrarch."   c Literally, "the Son of Man."

feiting one's self?

²⁶ "When I, the Messiah,ᵈ come in my glory and in the glory of the Father and the holy angels, I will be ashamed then of all who are ashamed of me and of my words now. ²⁷ But this is the simple truth—some of you who are standing here right now will not die until you have seen the Kingdom of God."

²⁸ Eight days later he took Peter, James, and John with him into the hills to pray. ²⁹ And as he was praying, his face began to shine,ᵉ and his clothes became dazzling white and blazed with light. ³⁰ Then two men appeared and began talking with him—Moses and Elijah! ³¹ They were splendid in appearance, glorious to see; and they were speaking of his death at Jerusalem, to be carried out in accordance with God's plan.

³² Peter and the others had been very drowsy and had fallen asleep. Now they woke up and saw Jesus covered with brightness and glory, and the two men standing with him. ³³ As Moses and Elijah were starting to leave, Peter, all confused and not even knowing what he was saying, blurted out, "Master, this is wonderful! We'll put up three shelters—one for you and one for Moses and one for Elijah!"

³⁴ But even as he was saying this, a brightᶠ cloud formed above them; and terror gripped them as it covered them. ³⁵ And a voice from the cloud said, *"This* is my Son, my Chosen One; listen to *him."*

³⁶ Then, as the voice died away, Jesus was there alone with his disciples. They didn't tell anyone what they had seen until long afterwards.

³⁷ The next day as they descended from the hill, a huge crowd met him, ³⁸ and a man in the crowd called out to him, "Teacher, this boy here is my only son, ³⁹ and a demon keeps seizing him, making him scream; and it throws him into convulsions so that he foams at the mouth; it is always hitting him and hardly ever leaves him alone. ⁴⁰ I begged your disciples to cast the demon out, but they couldn't."

⁴¹ "O you stubborn faithless people," Jesus said [to his disciplesᶠ], "how long should I put up with you? Bring him here."

⁴² As the boy was coming the demon knocked him to the ground and threw him into a violent convulsion. But Jesus ordered the demon to come out, and healed the boy and handed him over to his father.

⁴³ Awe gripped the people as they saw this display of the power of God.

Meanwhile, as they were exclaiming over all the wonderful things he was doing, Jesus said to his disciples, ⁴⁴ "Listen to me and remember what I say. I, the Messiah,ᵈ am going to be betrayed." ⁴⁵ But the disciples didn't know what he meant, for their minds had been sealed and they were afraid to ask him.

⁴⁶ Now came an argument among them as to which of them would be greatest [in the coming Kingdomᶠ]! ⁴⁷ But Jesus knew their thoughts, so he stood a little child beside him ⁴⁸ and said to them, "Anyone who takes care of a little child like this is caring for me! And whoever cares for me is caring for God who sent me. Your care for others is the measure of your greatness." ⁴⁹ His disciple John came to him and said, "Master, we saw someone using your name to cast out demons. And we told him not to. After all, he isn't in our group."

⁵⁰ But Jesus said, "You shouldn't have done that! For anyone who is not against you is for you."

⁵¹ As the time drew near for his return to heaven, he moved steadily onward towards Jerusalem with an iron will.

⁵² One day he sent messengers ahead to reserve rooms for them in a Samaritan village. ⁵³ But they were turned away! The people of the village refused to have anything to do with them because they were headed for Jerusalem.ᵍ

⁵⁴ When word came back of what had happened, James and John said to Jesus, "Master, shall we order fire down from heaven to burn them up?" ⁵⁵ But Jesus turned and rebuked them,ʰ ⁵⁶ and they went on to another village.

---

d Literally, "the Son of Man."   e Literally, "the appearance of his face changed."   f Implied.
g A typical case of discrimination (cf. John 4:9). The Jews called the Samaritans "half-breeds," so the Samaritans naturally hated the Jews.   h Later manuscripts add to verses 55 and 56, "And Jesus said, You don't realize what your hearts are like. For the Son of Man has not come to destroy men's lives, but to save them."

[57] As they were walking along someone said to Jesus, "I will always follow you no matter where you go."

[58] But Jesus replied, "Remember, I don't even own a place to lay my head. Foxes have dens to live in, and birds have nests, but I, the Messiah,[i] have no earthly home at all."

[59] Another time, when he invited a man to come with him and to be his disciple, the man agreed—but wanted to wait until his father's death.[j]

[60] Jesus replied, "Let those without eternal life concern themselves with things like that.[k] Your duty is to come and preach the coming of the Kingdom of God to all the world."

[61] Another said, "Yes, Lord, I will come, but first let me ask permission of those at home."[l]

[62] But Jesus told him, "Anyone who lets himself be distracted from the work I plan for him is not fit for the Kingdom of God."

10 THE LORD NOW chose seventy other disciples and sent them on ahead in pairs to all the towns and villages he planned to visit later.

[2] These were his instructions to them: "Plead with the Lord of the harvest to send out more laborers to help you, for the harvest is so plentiful and the workers so few. [3] Go now, and remember that I am sending you out as lambs among wolves. [4] Don't take any money with you, or a beggar's bag, or even an extra pair of shoes. And don't waste time along the way.[a]

[5] "Whenever you enter a home, give it your blessing. [6] If it is worthy of the blessing, the blessing will stand; if not, the blessing will return to you.

[7] "When you enter a village, don't shift around from home to home, but stay in one place, eating and drinking without question whatever is set before you. And don't hesitate to accept hospitality, for the workman is worthy of his wages!

[8,9] "If a town welcomes you, follow these two rules:

(1) Eat whatever is set before you.

(2) Heal the sick; and as you heal them, say, 'The Kingdom of God is very near you now.'

[10] "But if a town refuses you, go out into its streets and say, [11] 'We wipe the dust of your town from our feet as a public announcement of your doom. Never forget how close you were to the Kingdom of God!' [12] Even wicked Sodom will be better off than such a city on the Judgment Day. [13] What horrors await you, you cities of Chorazin and Bethsaida! For if the miracles I did for you had been done in the cities of Tyre and Sidon,[b] their people would have sat in deep repentance long ago, clothed in sackcloth and throwing ashes on their heads to show their remorse. [14] Yes, Tyre and Sidon will receive less punishment on the Judgment Day than you. [15] And you people of Capernaum, what shall I say about you? Will you be exalted to heaven? No, you shall be brought down to hell."

[16] Then he said to the disciples, "Those who welcome you are welcoming me. And those who reject you are rejecting me. And those who reject me are rejecting God who sent me."

[17] When the seventy disciples returned, they joyfully reported to him, "Even the demons obey us when we use your name."

[18] "Yes," he told them, "I saw Satan falling from heaven as a flash of lightning! [19] And I have given you authority over all the power of the Enemy, and to walk among serpents and scorpions and to crush them. Nothing shall injure you! [20] However, the important thing is not that demons obey you, but that your names are registered as citizens of heaven."

[21] Then he was filled with the joy of the Holy Spirit and said, "I praise you, O Father, Lord of heaven and earth, for hiding these things from the intellectuals and worldly wise and for revealing them to those who are as trusting as little children.[c] Yes, thank you, Father, for that is the

---

i Literally, "the Son of Man."   j Literally, "But he said, 'Lord, suffer me first to go and bury my father,' " —perhaps meaning that the man could, when his father died, collect the inheritance and have some security. k Or, "Let those who are spiritually dead care for their own dead."   l Literally, "bid them farewell at home."   10 a Literally, "Salute no one in the way."   b Cities destroyed by God in judgment for their wickedness. For a description of this event, see Ezekiel, chapters 26-28.   c Literally, "babies."

way you wanted it. ²² I am the Agent of my Father in everything; and no one really knows the Son except the Father, and no one really knows the Father except the Son and those to whom the Son chooses to reveal him."

²³ Then, turning to the twelve disciples, he said quietly, "How privileged you are to see what you have seen. ²⁴ Many a prophet and king of old has longed for these days, to see and hear what you have seen and heard!"

²⁵ One day an expert on Moses' laws came to test Jesus' orthodoxy by asking him this question: "Teacher, what does a man need to do to live forever in heaven?"

²⁶ Jesus replied, "What does Moses' law say about it?"

²⁷ "It says," he replied, "that you must love the Lord your God with all your heart, and with all your soul, and with all your strength, and with all your mind. And you must love your neighbor just as much as you love yourself."

²⁸ "Right!" Jesus told him. *"Do* this and *you* shall live!"

²⁹ The man wanted to justify (his lack of love for some kinds of people),^d so he asked, "Which neighbors?"

³⁰ Jesus replied with an illustration: "A Jew going on a trip from Jerusalem to Jericho was attacked by bandits. They stripped him of his clothes and money and beat him up and left him lying half dead beside the road.

³¹ "By chance a Jewish priest came along; and when he saw the man lying there, he crossed to the other side of the road and passed him by. ³² A Jewish Temple-assistant^e walked over and looked at him lying there, but then went on.

³³ "But a despised Samaritan^f came along, and when he saw him, he felt deep pity. ³⁴ Kneeling beside him the Samaritan soothed his wounds with medicine and bandaged them. Then he put the man on his donkey and walked along beside him till they came to an inn, where he nursed him

through the night.^g ³⁵ The next day he handed the innkeeper two twenty-dollar bills^h and told him to take care of the man. 'If his bill runs higher than that,' he said, 'I'll pay the difference the next time I am here.'

³⁶ "Now which of these three would you say was a neighbor to the bandits' victim?"

³⁷ The man replied, "The one who showed him some pity."

Then Jesus said, "Yes, now go and do the same."

³⁸ As Jesus and the disciples continued on their way to Jerusalemⁱ they came to a village where a woman named Martha welcomed them into her home. ³⁹ Her sister Mary sat on the floor, listening to Jesus as he talked.

⁴⁰ But Martha was the jittery type, and was worrying over the big dinner she was preparing.

She came to Jesus and said, "Sir, doesn't it seem unfair to you that my sister just sits here while I do all the work? Tell her to come and help me."

⁴¹ But the Lord said to her, "Martha, dear friend,^j you are so upset over all these details! ⁴² There is really only one thing worth being concerned about. Mary has discovered it—and I won't take it away from her!"

11 ONCE WHEN JESUS had been out praying, one of his disciples came to him as he finished and said, "Lord, teach us a prayer to recite^a just as John taught one to his disciples."

² And this is the prayer he taught them: "Father, may your name be honored for its holiness; send your Kingdom soon. ³ Give us our food day by day. ⁴ And forgive our sins—for we have forgiven those who sinned against us. And don't allow us to be tempted."

^{5,6} Then, teaching them more about prayer,^b he used this illustration: "Suppose you went to a friend's house at midnight, wanting to borrow three loaves of bread.

d Literally, "wanting to justify himself."   e Literally, "Levite."   f Literally, "a Samaritan." All Samaritans were despised by Jews, and the feeling was mutual, due to historic reasons.   g Literally, "took care of him."   h Literally, "two denarii," each the equivalent of a modern day's wage. i Implied.   j Literally, "Martha, Martha."   11a Implied.   b Some ancient manuscripts add at this point additional portions of the Lord's Prayer as recorded in Matthew 6:9-13.

You would shout up to him, 'A friend of mine has just arrived for a visit and I've nothing to give him to eat.' ⁷ He would call down from his bedroom, 'Please don't ask me to get up. The door is locked for the night and we are all in bed. I just can't help you this time.'

⁸ "But I'll tell you this—though he won't do it as a friend, if you keep knocking long enough he will get up and give you everything you want—just because of your persistence. ⁹ And so it is with prayer—keep on asking and you will keep on getting; keep on looking and you will keep on finding; knock and the door will be opened. ¹⁰ Everyone who asks, receives; all who seek, find; and the door is opened to everyone who knocks.

¹¹ "You men who are fathers—if your boy asks for bread, do you give him a stone? If he asks for fish, do you give him a snake? ¹² If he asks for an egg, do you give him a scorpion? [Of course not!ᶜ]

¹³ "And if even sinful persons like yourselves give children what they need, don't you realize that your heavenly Father will do at least as much, and give the Holy Spirit to those who ask for him?"

¹⁴ Once, when Jesus cast out a demon from a man who couldn't speak, his voice returned to him. The crowd was excited and enthusiastic, ¹⁵ but some said, "No wonder he can cast them out. He gets his power from Satan,ᵈ the king of demons!" ¹⁶ Others asked for something to happen in the sky to prove his claim of being the Messiah.ᵉ

¹⁷ He knew the thoughts of each of them, so he said, "Any kingdom filled with civil war is doomed; so is a home filled with argument and strife. ¹⁸ Therefore, if what you say is true, that Satan is fighting against himself by empowering me to cast out his demons, how can his kingdom survive? ¹⁹ And if I am empowered by Satan, what about your own followers? For they cast out demons! Do you think this proves they are possessed by Satan? Ask *them* if you are right! ²⁰ But if I am casting out demons because of power from God, it proves that the Kingdom of God has arrived.

²¹ "For when Satan,ᶠ strong and fully armed, guards his palace, it is safe— ²² until someone stronger and better-armed attacks and overcomes him and strips him of his weapons and carries off his belongings.

²³ "Anyone who is not for me is against me; if he isn't helping me, he is hurting my cause.

²⁴ "When a demon is cast out of a man, it goes to the deserts, searching there for rest; but finding none, it returns to the person it left, ²⁵ and finds that its former home is all swept and clean.ᵍ ²⁶ Then it goes and gets seven other demons more evil than itself, and they all enter the man. And so the poor fellow is seven timesᶜ worse off than he was before."

²⁷ As he was speaking, a woman in the crowd called out, "God bless your mother—the womb from which you came, and the breasts that gave you suck!"

²⁸ He replied, "Yes, but even more blessed are all who hear the Word of God and put it into practice."

²⁹,³⁰ As the crowd pressed in upon him, he preached them this sermon: "These are evil times, with evil people. They keep asking for some strange happening in the skies [to prove I am the Messiahᶜ], but the only proof I will give them is a miracle like that of Jonah, whose experiences proved to the people of Nineveh that God had sent him. My similar experience will prove that God has sent me to these people.

³¹ "And at the Judgment Day the Queen of Shebaʰ shall arise and point her finger at this generation, condemning it, for she went on a long, hard journey to listen to the wisdom of Solomon; but one far greater than Solomon is here [and few pay any attentionᶜ].

³² "The men of Nineveh, too, shall arise and condemn this nation, for they repented at the preaching of Jonah; and someone far greater than Jonah is here [but this nation won't listenᶜ].

³³ "No one lights a lamp and hides it! Instead, he puts it on a lampstand to give light to all who enter the room. ³⁴ Your eyes light up your inward being. A pure eye lets

---

c Implied. d Literally, "from Beelzebub." e Implied; literally, "Others, tempting, sought of him a
sign from heaven." f Literally, "the Strong." g But empty, since the person is neutral about Christ.
h Literally, "Queen of the South." See 1 Kings, chapter 10.

sunshine into your soul. A lustful eye shuts out the light and plunges you into darkness. [35] So watch out that the sunshine isn't blotted out. [36] If you are filled with light within, with no dark corners, then your face will be radiant too, as though a floodlight is beamed upon you."

[37,38] As he was speaking, one of the Pharisees asked him home for a meal. When Jesus arrived, he sat down to eat without first performing the ceremonial washing required by Jewish custom. This greatly surprised his host.

[39] Then Jesus said to him, "You Pharisees wash the outside, but inside you are still dirty—full of greed and wickedness! [40] Fools! Didn't God make the inside as well as the outside? [41] Purity is best demonstrated by generosity.

[42] "But woe to you Pharisees! For though you are careful to tithe even the smallest part of your income, you completely forget about justice and the love of God. You should tithe, yes, but you should not leave these other things undone.

[43] "Woe to you Pharisees! For how you love the seats of honor in the synagogues and the respectful greetings from everyone as you walk through the markets! [44] Yes, awesome judgment is awaiting you. For you are like hidden graves in a field. Men go by you with no knowledge of the corruption they are passing."

[45] "Sir," said an expert in religious law who was standing there, "you have insulted my profession, too, in what you just said."

[46] "Yes," said Jesus, "the same horrors await you! For you crush men beneath impossible religious demands—demands that you yourselves would never think of trying to keep. [47] Woe to you! For you are exactly like your ancestors who killed the prophets long ago. [48] Murderers! You agree with your fathers that what they did was right—you would have done the same yourselves.

[49] "This is what God says about you: 'I will send prophets and apostles to you, and you will kill some of them and chase away the others.'

[50] "And you of this generation will be held responsible for the murder of God's servants from the founding of the world— [51] from the murder of Abel to the murder of Zechariah who perished between the altar and the sanctuary. Yes, it will surely be charged against you.

[52] "Woe to you experts in religion! For you hide the truth from the people. You won't accept it for yourselves, and you prevent others from having a chance to believe it."

[53,54] The Pharisees and legal experts were furious; and from that time on they plied him fiercely with a host of questions, trying to trap him into saying something for which they could have him arrested.

12 MEANWHILE THE CROWDS grew until thousands upon thousands were milling about and crushing each other. He turned now to his disciples and warned them, "More than anything else, beware of these Pharisees and the way they pretend to be good when they aren't. But such hypocrisy cannot be hidden forever. [2] It will become as evident as yeast in dough. [3] Whatever they[a] have said in the dark shall be heard in the light, and what you have whispered in the inner rooms shall be broadcast from the housetops for all to hear!

[4] "Dear friends, don't be afraid of these who want to murder you. They can only kill the body; they have no power over your souls. [5] But I'll tell you whom to fear—fear God who has the power to kill and then cast into hell.

[6] "What is the price of five sparrows? A couple of pennies? Not much more than that. Yet God does not forget a single one of them. [7] And he knows the number of hairs on your head! Never fear, you are far more valuable to him than a whole flock of sparrows.

[8] "And I assure you of this: I, the Messiah,[b] will publicly honor you in the presence of God's angels if you publicly acknowledge me here on earth as your Friend. [9] But I will deny before the angels those who deny me here among men. [10] (Yet those who speak against me[b] may be forgiven—while those who speak against the Holy Spirit shall never be forgiven.)

a Literally, "you."   b Literally, "the Son of Man."

¹¹ "And when you are brought to trial before these Jewish rulers and authorities in the synagogues, don't be concerned about what to say in your defense, ¹² for the Holy Spirit will give you the right words even as you are standing there."

¹³ Then someone called from the crowd, "Sir, please tell my brother to divide my father's estate with me."

¹⁴ But Jesus replied, "Man, who made me a judge over you to decide such things as that? ¹⁵ Beware! Don't always be wishing for what you don't have. For real life and real living are not related to how rich we are."

¹⁶ Then he gave an illustration: "A rich man had a fertile farm that produced fine crops. ¹⁷ In fact, his barns were full to overflowing—he couldn't get everything in. He thought about his problem, ¹⁸ and finally exclaimed, 'I know—I'll tear down my barns and build bigger ones! Then I'll have room enough. ¹⁹ And I'll sit back and say to myself, "Friend, you have enough stored away for years to come. Now take it easy! Wine, women, and song for you!" 'ᶜ

²⁰ "But God said to him, 'Fool! Tonight you die. Then who will get it all?'

²¹ "Yes, every man is a fool who gets rich on earth but not in heaven."

²² Then turning to his disciples he said, "Don't worry about whether you have enough food to eat or clothes to wear. ²³ For life consists of far more than food and clothes. ²⁴ Look at the ravens—they don't plant or harvest or have barns to store away their food, and yet they get along all right—for God feeds them. And you are far more valuable to him than any birds!

²⁵ "And besides, what's the use of worrying? What good does it do? Will it add a single day to your life? Of course not! ²⁶ And if worry can't even do such little things as that, what's the use of worrying over bigger things?

²⁷ "Look at the lilies! They don't toil and spin, and yet Solomon in all his glory was not robed as well as they are. ²⁸ And if God provides clothing for the flowers that are here today and gone tomorrow, don't you suppose that he will provide clothing for you, you doubters? ²⁹ And don't worry about food—what to eat and drink; don't worry at all that God will provide it for you. ³⁰ All mankind scratches for its daily bread, but your heavenly Father knows your needs. ³¹ He will always give you all you need from day to day if you will make the Kingdom of God your primary concern.

³² "So don't be afraid, little flock. For it gives your Father great happiness to give you the Kingdom. ³³ Sell what you have and give to those in need. This will fatten your purses in heaven! And the purses of heaven have no rips or holes in them. Your treasures there will never disappear; no thief can steal them; no moth can destroy them. ³⁴ Wherever your treasure is, there your heart and thoughts will also be.

³⁵ "Be prepared—all dressed and ready— ³⁶ for your Lord's return from the wedding feast. Then you will be ready to open the door and let him in the moment he arrives and knocks. ³⁷ There will be great joy for those who are ready and waiting for his return. He himself will seat them and put on a waiter's uniform and serve them as they sit and eat! ³⁸ He may come at nine o'clock at night—or even at midnight. But whenever he comes there will be joy for his servants who are ready!

³⁹ "Everyone would be ready for him if they knew the exact hour of his return —just as they would be ready for a thief if they knew when he was coming. ⁴⁰ So be ready all the time. For I, the Messiah,ᵈ will come when least expected."

⁴¹ Peter asked, "Lord, are you talking just to us or to everyone?"

⁴²,⁴³,⁴⁴ And the Lord replied, "I'm talking to any faithful, sensible man whose master gives him the responsibility of feeding the other servants. If his master returns and finds that he has done a good job, there will be a reward—his master will put him in charge of all he owns.

⁴⁵ "But if the man begins to think, 'My Lord won't be back for a long time,' and begins to whip the men and women he is supposed to protect, and to spend his time at drinking parties and in drunkenness— ⁴⁶ well, his master will return without notice

---

c Literally, "Eat, drink, and be merry."   d Literally, "the Son of Man."

and remove him from his position of trust and assign him to the place of the unfaithful. ⁴⁷ He will be severely punished, for though he knew his duty he refused to do it.

⁴⁸ "But anyone who is not aware that he is doing wrong will be punished only lightly. Much is required from those to whom much is given, for their responsibility is greater.

⁴⁹ "I have come to bring fire to the earth, and, oh, that my task were completed! ⁵⁰ There is a terrible baptism ahead of me, and how I am pent up until it is accomplished!

⁵¹ "Do you think I have come to give peace to the earth? *No!* Rather, strife and division! ⁵² From now on families will be split apart, three in favor of me, and two against—or perhaps the other way around. ⁵³ A father will decide one way about me; his son, the other; mother and daughter will disagree; and the decision of an honored^e mother-in-law will be spurned by her daughter-in-law."

⁵⁴ Then he turned to the crowd and said, "When you see clouds beginning to form in the west, you say, 'Here comes a shower.' And you are right. ⁵⁵ "When the south wind blows you say, 'Today will be a scorcher.' And it is. ⁵⁶ Hypocrites! You interpret the sky well enough, but you refuse to notice the warnings all around you about the crisis ahead. ⁵⁷ Why do you refuse to see for yourselves what is right?

⁵⁸ "If you meet your accuser on the way to court, try to settle the matter before it reaches the judge, lest he sentence you to jail; ⁵⁹ for if that happens you won't be free again until the last penny is paid in full."

13 ABOUT THIS TIME he was informed that Pilate had butchered some Jews from Galilee as they were sacrificing at the Temple in Jerusalem.

² "Do you think they were worse sinners than other men from Galilee?" he asked. "Is that why they suffered? ³ Not at all! And don't you realize that you also will perish unless you leave your evil ways and turn to God?

⁴ "And what about the eighteen men who died when the Tower of Siloam fell on them? Were they the worst sinners in Jerusalem? ⁵ Not at all! And you, too, will perish unless you repent."

⁶ Then he used this illustration: "A man planted a fig tree in his garden and came again and again to see if he could find any fruit on it, but he was always disappointed. ⁷ Finally he told his gardener to cut it down. 'I've waited three years and there hasn't been a single fig!' he said. 'Why bother with it any longer? It's taking up space we can use for something else.'

⁸ " 'Give it one more chance,' the gardener answered. 'Leave it another year, and I'll give it special attention and plenty of fertilizer. ⁹ If we get figs next year, fine; if not, I'll cut it down.' "

¹⁰ One Sabbath as he was teaching in a synagogue, ¹¹ he saw a seriously handicapped woman who had been bent double for eighteen years and was unable to straighten herself. ¹² Calling her over to him Jesus said, "Woman, you are healed of your sickness!" ¹³ He touched her, and instantly she could stand straight. How she praised and thanked God!

¹⁴ But the local Jewish leader in charge of the synagogue was very angry about it because Jesus had healed her on the Sabbath day. "There are six days of the week to work," he shouted to the crowd. "Those are the days to come for healing, not on the Sabbath!"

¹⁵ But the Lord replied, "You hypocrite! You work on the Sabbath! Don't you untie your cattle from their stalls on the Sabbath and lead them out for water? ¹⁶ And is it wrong for me, just because it is the Sabbath day, to free this Jewish woman from the bondage in which Satan has held her for eighteen years?"

¹⁷ This shamed his enemies. And all the people rejoiced at the wonderful things he did.

¹⁸ Now he began teaching them again about the Kingdom of God: "What is the Kingdom like?" he asked. "How can I illustrate it? ¹⁹ It is like a tiny mustard seed

e Implied by ancient custom.

planted in a garden; soon it grows into a tall bush, and the birds live among its branches. 20,21 It is like yeast kneaded into dough, which works unseen until it has risen high and light."

22 He went from city to city and village to village, teaching as he went, always pressing onward toward Jerusalem.

23 Someone asked him, "Will only a few be saved?"

And he replied, 24,25 "The door to heaven is narrow. Work hard to get in, for the truth is that many will try to enter but when the head of the house has locked the door, it will be too late. Then if you stand outside knocking, and pleading, 'Lord, open the door for us,' he will reply, 'I do not know you.'

26 " 'But we ate with you, and you taught in our streets,' you will say.

27 "And he will reply, 'I tell you, I don't know you. You can't come in here, guilty as you are. Go away.'

28 "And there will be great weeping and gnashing of teeth as you stand outside and see Abraham, Isaac, Jacob, and all the prophets within the Kingdom of God— 29 for people will come from all over the world to take their places there. 30 And note this: some who are despised now will be greatly honored then; and some who are highly thought of now will be least important then."

31 A few minutes later some Pharisees said to him, "Get out of here if you want to live, for King Herod is after you!"

32 Jesus replied, "Go tell that fox that I will keep on casting out demons and doing miracles of healing today and tomorrow; and the third day I will reach my destination. 33 Yes, today, tomorrow, and the next day! For it wouldn't do for a prophet of God to be killed except in Jerusalem!

34 "O Jerusalem, Jerusalem! The city that murders the prophets. The city that stones those sent to help her. How often I have wanted to gather your children together even as a hen protects her brood under her wings, but you wouldn't let me. 35 And now—now your house is left desolate. And you will never again see me until you say, 'Welcome to him who comes in the name of the Lord.' "

14 ONE SABBATH AS he was in the home of a member of the Jewish Council, the Pharisees were watching him like hawks to see if he would heal a man who was present who was suffering from dropsy.

3 Jesus said to the Pharisees and legal experts standing around, "Well, is it within the Law to heal a man on the Sabbath day, or not?"

4 And when they refused to answer, Jesus took the sick man by the hand and healed him and sent him away.

5 Then he turned to them: "Which of you doesn't work on the Sabbath?" he asked. "If your cow falls into a pit, don't you proceed at once to get it out?"

6 Again they had no answer.

7 When he noticed that all who came to the dinner were trying to sit near the head of the table, he gave them this advice: 8 "If you are invited to a wedding feast, don't always head for the best seat. For if someone more respected than you shows up, 9 the host will bring him over to where you are sitting and say, 'Let this man sit here instead.' And you, embarrassed, will have to take whatever seat is left at the foot of the table!

10 "Do this instead—start at the foot; and when your host sees you he will come and say, 'Friend, we have a better place than this for you!' Thus you will be honored in front of all the other guests. 11 For everyone who tries to honor himself shall be humbled; and he who humbles himself shall be honored." 12 Then he turned to his host. "When you put on a dinner," he said, "don't invite friends, brothers, relatives, and rich neighbors! For they will return the invitation. 13 Instead, invite the poor, the crippled, the lame, and the blind. 14 Then at the resurrection of the godly, God will reward you for inviting those who can't repay you."

15 Hearing this, a man sitting at the table with Jesus exclaimed, "What a privilege it would be to get into the Kingdom of God!"

16 Jesus replied with this illustration: "A man prepared a great feast and sent out many invitations. 17 When all was ready, he sent his servant around to notify the guests that it was time for them to arrive. 18 But they all began making excuses. One said he

had just bought a field and wanted to inspect it, and asked to be excused. [19] Another said he had just bought five pair of oxen and wanted to try them out. [20] Another had just been married and for that reason couldn't come.

[21] "The servant returned and reported to his master what they had said. His master was angry and told him to go quickly into the streets and alleys of the city and to invite the beggars, crippled, lame, and blind. [22] But even then, there was still room.

[23] " 'Well, then,' said his master, 'go out into the country lanes and out behind the hedges and urge anyone you find to come, so that the house will be full. [24] For none of those I invited first will get even the smallest taste of what I had prepared for them.' "

[25] Great crowds were following him. He turned around and addressed them as follows: [26] "Anyone who wants to be my follower must love me far more than[a] he does his own father, mother, wife, children, brothers, or sisters—yes, more than his own life—otherwise he cannot be my disciple. [27] And no one can be my disciple who does not carry his own cross and follow me.

[28] "But don't begin until you count the cost.[b] For who would begin construction of a building without first getting estimates and then checking to see if he has enough money to pay the bills? [29] Otherwise he might complete only the foundation before running out of funds. And then how everyone would laugh!

[30] " 'See that fellow there?' they would mock. 'He started that building and ran out of money before it was finished!'

[31] "Or what king would ever dream of going to war without first sitting down with his counselors and discussing whether his army of 10,000 is strong enough to defeat the 20,000 men who are marching against him?

[32] "If the decision is negative, then while the enemy troops are still far away, he will send a truce team to discuss terms of peace. [33] So no one can become my disciple unless he first sits down and counts his blessings —and then renounces them all for me.

[34] "What good is salt that has lost its saltiness?[c] [35] Flavorless salt is fit for nothing—not even for fertilizer. It is worthless and must be thrown out. Listen well, if you would understand my meaning."

15 DISHONEST TAX COLLECTORS and other notorious sinners often came to listen to Jesus' sermons; [2] but this caused complaints from the Jewish religious leaders and the experts on Jewish law because he was associating with such despicable people—even eating with them! [3,4] So Jesus used this illustration: "If you had a hundred sheep and one of them strayed away and was lost in the wilderness, wouldn't you leave the ninety-nine others to go and search for the lost one until you found it? [5] And then you would joyfully carry it home on your shoulders. [6] When you arrived you would call together your friends and neighbors to rejoice with you because your lost sheep was found.

[7] "Well, in the same way heaven will be happier over one lost sinner who returns to God than over ninety-nine others who haven't strayed away!

[8] "Or take another illustration: A woman has ten valuable silver coins and loses one. Won't she light a lamp and look in every corner of the house and sweep every nook and cranny until she finds it? [9] And then won't she call in her friends and neighbors to rejoice with her? [10] In the same way there is joy in the presence of the angels of God when one sinner repents."

To further illustrate the point, he told them this story: [11] "A man had two sons. [12] When the younger told his father, 'I want my share of your estate now, instead of waiting until you die!' his father agreed to divide his wealth between his sons.

[13] "A few days later this younger son packed all his belongings and took a trip to a distant land, and there wasted all his money on parties and prostitutes. [14] About the time his money was gone a great famine swept over the land, and he began to starve. [15] He persuaded a local farmer to hire him to feed his pigs. [16] The boy became so

---

a Literally, "If anyone comes to me and does not hate his father and mother. . . ."　　　b Implied in verse 33.　　　c Perhaps the reference is to impure salt; when wet, the salt dissolves and drains out, leaving a tasteless residue. Matthew 5:13.

hungry that even the pods he was feeding the swine looked good to him. And no one gave him anything.

[17] "When he finally came to his senses, he said to himself, 'At home even the hired men have food enough and to spare, and here I am, dying of hunger! [18] I will go home to my father and say, "Father, I have sinned against both heaven and you, [19] and am no longer worthy of being called your son. Please take me on as a hired man." '

[20] "So he returned home to his father. And while he was still a long distance away, his father saw him coming, and was filled with loving pity and ran and embraced him and kissed him.

[21] "His son said to him, 'Father, I have sinned against heaven and you, and am not worthy of being called your son—'

[22] "But his father said to the slaves, 'Quick! Bring the finest robe in the house and put it on him. And a jeweled ring for his finger; and shoes! [23] And kill the calf we have in the fattening pen. We must celebrate with a feast, [24] for this son of mine was dead and has returned to life. He was lost and is found.' So the party began.

[25] "Meanwhile, the older son was in the fields working; when he returned home, he heard dance music coming from the house, [26] and he asked one of the servants what was going on.

[27] " 'Your brother is back,' he was told, 'and your father has killed the calf we were fattening and has prepared a great feast to celebrate his coming home again unharmed.'

[28] "The older brother was angry and wouldn't go in. His father came out and begged him, [29] but he replied, 'All these years I've worked hard for you and never once refused to do a single thing you told me to; and in all that time you never gave me even one young goat for a feast with my friends. [30] Yet when this son of yours comes back after spending your money on prostitutes, you celebrate by killing the finest calf we have on the place.'

[31] " 'Look, dear son,' his father said to him, 'you and I are very close, and everything I have is yours. [32] But it is right to celebrate. For he is your brother; and he was dead and has come back to life! He was lost and is found!' "

16 JESUS NOW TOLD this story to his disciples: "A rich man hired an accountant to handle his affairs, but soon a rumor went around that the accountant was thoroughly dishonest.

[2] "So his employer called him in and said, 'What's this I hear about your stealing from me? Get your report in order, for you are to be dismissed.'

[3] "The accountant thought to himself, 'Now what? I'm through here, and I haven't the strength to go out and dig ditches, and I'm too proud to beg. [4] I know just the thing! And then I'll have plenty of friends to take care of me when I leave!'

[5,6] "So he invited each one who owed money to his employer to come and discuss the situation. He asked the first one, 'How much do you owe him?' 'My debt is 850 gallons of olive oil,' the man replied. 'Yes, here is the contract you signed,' the accountant told him. 'Tear it up and write another one for half that much!'

[7] " 'And how much do you owe him?' he asked the next man. 'A thousand bushels of wheat,' was the reply. 'Here,' the accountant said, 'take your note and replace it with one for only 800 bushels!'

[8] "The rich man had to admire the rascal for being so shrewd.[a] And it is true that the citizens of this world are more clever [in dishonesty![b]] than the godly[c] are. [9] But shall I tell *you* to act that way, to buy friendship through cheating? Will this ensure your entry into an everlasting home in heaven?[d] [10] *No!*[b] For unless you are honest in small matters, you won't be in large ones. If you cheat even a little, you won't be honest with greater responsibilities. [11] And if you are untrustworthy about worldly wealth, who will trust you with the true riches of

---

a Or, "Do you think the rich man commended the scoundrel for being so shrewd?"   b Implied.
c Literally, "sons of the light."   d Literally, and probably ironically, "Make to yourselves friends by means of the mammon of unrighteousness; that when it shall fail you, they may receive you into the eternal tabernacles!" Some commentators would interpret this to mean: "Use your money for good, so that it will be waiting to befriend you when you get to heaven." But this would imply the end justifies the means, an unbiblical idea.

heaven? [12] And if you are not faithful with other people's money, why should you be entrusted with money of your own?

[13] "For neither you nor anyone else can serve two masters. You will hate one and show loyalty to the other, or else the other way around—you will be enthusiastic about one and despise the other. You cannot serve both God and money."

[14] The Pharisees, who dearly loved their money, naturally scoffed at all this.

[15] Then he said to them, "You wear a noble, pious expression in public, but God knows your evil hearts. Your pretense brings you honor from the people, but it is an abomination in the sight of God. [16] Until John the Baptist began to preach, the laws of Moses and the messages of the prophets were your guides. But John introduced the Good News that the Kingdom of God would come soon. And now eager multitudes are pressing in. [17] But that doesn't mean that the Law has lost its force in even the smallest point. It is as strong and unshakable as heaven and earth.

[18] "So anyone who divorces his wife and marries someone else commits adultery, and anyone who marries a divorced woman commits adultery."

[19] "There was a certain rich man," Jesus said, "who was splendidly clothed and lived each day in mirth and luxury. [20] One day Lazarus, a diseased beggar, was laid at his door. [21] As he lay there longing for scraps from the rich man's table, the dogs would come and lick his open sores. [22] Finally the beggar died and was carried by the angels to be with Abraham in the place of the righteous dead.[e] The rich man also died and was buried, [23] and his soul went into hell.[f] There, in torment, he saw Lazarus in the far distance with Abraham.

[24] " 'Father Abraham,' he shouted, 'have some pity! Send Lazarus over here if only to dip the tip of his finger in water and cool my tongue, for I am in anguish in these flames.'

[25] "But Abraham said to him, 'Son, remember that during your lifetime you had everything you wanted, and Lazarus had nothing. So now he is here being comforted and you are in anguish. [26] And besides, there is a great chasm separating us, and anyone wanting to come to you from here is stopped at its edge; and no one over there can cross to us.'

[27] "Then the rich man said, 'O Father Abraham, then please send him to my father's home— [28] for I have five brothers—to warn them about this place of torment lest they come here when they die.'

[29] "But Abraham said, 'The Scriptures have warned them again and again. Your brothers can read them any time they want to.'

[30] "The rich man replied, 'No, Father Abraham, they won't bother to read them. But if someone is sent to them from the dead, then they will turn from their sins.'

[31] "But Abraham said, 'If they won't listen to Moses and the prophets, they won't listen even though someone rises from the dead.' "[g]

17 "THERE WILL ALWAYS be temptations to sin," Jesus said one day to his disciples, "but woe to the man who does the tempting. [2,3] If he were thrown into the sea with a huge rock tied to his neck, he would be far better off than facing the punishment in store for those who harm these little children's souls. I am warning you!

"Rebuke your brother if he sins, and forgive him if he is sorry. [4] Even if he wrongs you seven times a day and each time turns again and asks forgiveness, forgive him."

[5] One day the apostles said to the Lord, "We need more faith; tell us how to get it."

[6] "If your faith were only the size of a mustard seed," Jesus answered, "it would be large enough to uproot that mulberry tree over there and send it hurtling into the sea! Your command would bring immediate results! [7,8,9] When a servant comes in from plowing or taking care of sheep, he doesn't just sit down and eat, but first prepares his master's meal and serves him his supper before he eats his own. And he is not even thanked, for he is merely doing what he is supposed to do. [10] Just so, if you merely

---

e Literally, "into Abraham's bosom."   f Literally, "into Hades."   g Even Christ's resurrection failed to convince the Pharisees, to whom he gave this illustration.

obey me, you should not consider yourselves worthy of praise. For you have simply done your duty!"

¹¹ As they continued onward toward
Jerusalem, they reached the border between
Galilee and Samaria, ¹² and as they entered
a village there, ten lepers stood at a distance, ¹³ crying out, "Jesus, sir, have mercy
on us!"

¹⁴ He looked at them and said, "Go to
the Jewish priest and show him that you are
healed!" And as they were going, their leprosy disappeared.

¹⁵ One of them came back to Jesus,
shouting, "Glory to God, I'm healed!" ¹⁶ He
fell flat on the ground in front of Jesus,
face downward in the dust, thanking him
for what he had done. This man was a
despised[a] Samaritan.

¹⁷ Jesus asked, "Didn't I heal ten men?
Where are the nine? ¹⁸ Does only this foreigner return to give glory to God?"

¹⁹ And Jesus said to the man, "Stand up
and go; your faith has made you well."

²⁰ One day the Pharisees asked Jesus,
"When will the Kingdom of God begin?"
Jesus replied, "The Kingdom of God isn't
ushered in with visible signs. ²¹ You won't
be able to say, 'It has begun here in this
place or there in that part of the country.'
For the Kingdom of God is within you."[b]

²² Later he talked again about this with
his disciples. "The time is coming when you
will long for me[c] to be with you even for a
single day, but I won't be here," he said.
²³ "Reports will reach you that I have returned and that I am in this place or that;
don't believe it or go out to look for me.
²⁴ For when I return, you will know it
beyond all doubt. It will be as evident as the
lightning that flashes across the skies. ²⁵ But
first I must suffer terribly and be rejected
by this whole nation.

²⁶ "[When I return[d]] the world will be [as
indifferent to the things of God[d]] as the people were in Noah's day. ²⁷ They ate and
drank and married—everything just as
usual right up to the day when Noah went
into the ark and the flood came and de-

stroyed them all.

²⁸ "And the world will be as it was in the
days of Lot: people went about their daily
business—eating and drinking, buying and
selling, farming and building— ²⁹ until the
morning Lot left Sodom. Then fire and
brimstone rained down from heaven and
destroyed them all. ³⁰ Yes, it will be 'business as usual' right up to the hour of my
return.[e]

³¹ "Those away from home that day
must not return to pack; those in the fields
must not return to town— ³² remember
what happened to Lot's wife! ³³ Whoever
clings to his life shall lose it, and whoever
loses his life shall save it. ³⁴ That night two
men will be asleep in the same room, and
one will be taken away, the other left.
³⁵,³⁶ Two women will be working together at
household tasks; one will be taken, the other
left; and so it will be with men working side
by side in the fields."

³⁷ "Lord, where will they be taken?" the
disciples asked.

Jesus replied, "Where the body is, the
vultures gather!"[f]

18 ONE DAY JESUS told his disciples a
story to illustrate their need for constant prayer and to show them that they
must keep praying until the answer comes.

² "There was a city judge," he said, "a
very godless man who had great contempt
for everyone. ³ A widow of that city came
to him frequently to appeal for justice
against a man who had harmed her. ⁴,⁵ The
judge ignored her for a while, but eventually she got on his nerves.

" 'I fear neither God nor man,' he said
to himself, 'but this woman bothers me. I'm
going to see that she gets justice, for she is
wearing me out with her constant coming!' "

⁶ Then the Lord said, "If even an evil
judge can be worn down like that, ⁷ don't
you think that God will surely give justice
to his people who plead with him day and
night? ⁸ Yes! He will answer them quickly!
But the question is: When I, the Messiah,[a]

a Implied. Samaritans were despised by Jews as being only "half-breed" Hebrews.   b Or, "among you."
c Or, "long for the Son of Man."   d Implied.   e Or, "the hour I am revealed."
f This may mean that God's people will be taken out to the execution grounds and their bodies left to the
vultures.   **18** a Literally, "the Son of Man."

return, how many will I find who have faith [and are praying[b]]?"

⁹ Then he told this story to some who boasted of their virtue and scorned everyone else:

¹⁰ "Two men went to the Temple to pray. One was a proud, self-righteous Pharisee, and the other a cheating tax collector. ¹¹ The proud Pharisee 'prayed' this prayer: 'Thank God, I am not a sinner like everyone else, especially like that tax collector over there! For I never cheat, I don't commit adultery, ¹² I go without food twice a week, and I give to God a tenth of everything I earn.'

¹³ "But the corrupt tax collector stood at a distance and dared not even lift his eyes to heaven as he prayed, but beat upon his chest in sorrow, exclaiming, 'God, be merciful to me, a sinner.' ¹⁴ I tell you, this sinner, not the Pharisee, returned home forgiven! For the proud shall be humbled, but the humble shall be honored."

¹⁵ One day some mothers brought their babies to him to touch and bless. But the disciples told them to go away.

¹⁶,¹⁷ Then Jesus called the children over to him and said to the disciples, "Let the little children come to me! Never send them away! For the Kingdom of God belongs to men who have hearts as trusting as these little children's. And anyone who doesn't have their kind of faith will never get within the Kingdom's gates."

¹⁸ Once a Jewish religious leader asked him this question: "Good sir, what shall I do to get to heaven?"

¹⁹ "Do you realize what you are saying when you call me 'good'?" Jesus asked him. "Only God is truly good, and no one else. ²⁰ But as to your question, you know what the ten commandments say—don't commit adultery, don't murder, don't steal, don't lie, honor your parents, and so on."

²¹ The man replied, "I've obeyed every one of these laws since I was a small child."

²² "There is still one thing you lack," Jesus said. "Sell all you have and give the money to the poor—it will become treasure for you in heaven—and come, follow me."

²³ But when the man heard this he went sadly away, for he was very rich.

²⁴ Jesus watched him go and then said to his disciples, "How hard it is for the rich to enter the Kingdom of God! ²⁵ It is easier for a camel to go through the eye of a needle than for a rich man to enter the Kingdom of God."

²⁶ Those who heard him say this exclaimed, "If it is that hard, how can *anyone* be saved?"

²⁷ He replied, "God can do what men can't!"

²⁸ And Peter said, "We have left our homes and followed you."

²⁹ "Yes," Jesus replied, "and everyone who has done as you have, leaving home, wife, brothers, parents, or children for the sake of the Kingdom of God, ³⁰ will be repaid many times over now, as well as receiving eternal life in the world to come."

³¹ Gathering the Twelve around him he told them, "As you know, we are going to Jerusalem. And when we get there, all the predictions of the ancient prophets concerning me will come true. ³² I will be handed over to the Gentiles to be mocked and treated shamefully and spat upon, ³³ and lashed and killed. And the third day I will rise again."

³⁴ But they didn't understand a thing he said. He seemed to be talking in riddles.

³⁵ As they approached Jericho, a blind man was sitting beside the road, begging from travelers. ³⁶ When he heard the noise of a crowd going past, he asked what was happening. ³⁷ He was told that Jesus from Nazareth was going by, ³⁸ so he began shouting, "Jesus, Son of David, have mercy on me!"

³⁹ The crowds ahead of Jesus tried to hush the man, but he only yelled the louder, "Son of David, have mercy on me!"

⁴⁰ When Jesus arrived at the spot, he stopped. "Bring the blind man over here," he said. ⁴¹ Then Jesus asked the man, "What do you want?"

"Lord," he pleaded, "I want to see!"

⁴² And Jesus said, "All right, begin seeing! Your faith has healed you."

⁴³ And instantly the man could see, and followed Jesus, praising God. And all who saw it happen praised God too.

---

b Implied.

19 AS JESUS WAS passing through Jericho, a man named Zacchaeus, one of the most influential Jews in the Roman tax-collecting business (and, of course, a very rich man), ³ tried to get a look at Jesus, but he was too short to see over the crowds. ⁴ So he ran ahead and climbed into a sycamore tree beside the road, to watch from there.

⁵ When Jesus came by he looked up at Zacchaeus and called him by name! "Zacchaeus!" he said. "Quick! Come down! For I am going to be a guest in your home today!"

⁶ Zacchaeus hurriedly climbed down and took Jesus to his house in great excitement and joy.

⁷ But the crowds were displeased. "He has gone to be the guest of a notorious sinner," they grumbled.

⁸ Meanwhile, Zacchaeus stood before the Lord and said, "Sir, from now on I will give half my wealth to the poor, and if I find I have overcharged anyone on his taxes, I will penalize myself by giving him back four times as much!"

⁹,¹⁰ Jesus told him, "This shows[a] that salvation has come to this home today. This man was one of the lost sons of Abraham, and I, the Messiah,[b] have come to search for and to save such souls as his."

¹¹ And because Jesus was nearing Jerusalem, he told a story to correct the impression that the Kingdom of God would begin right away.

¹² "A nobleman living in a certain province was called away to the distant capital of the empire to be crowned king of his province. ¹³ Before he left he called together ten assistants and gave them each $2,000 to invest while he was gone. ¹⁴ But some of his people hated him and sent him their declaration of independence, stating that they had rebelled and would not acknowledge him as their king.

¹⁵ "Upon his return he called in the men to whom he had given the money, to find out what they had done with it, and what their profits were.

¹⁶ "The first man reported a tremendous gain—ten times as much as the original amount!

¹⁷ " 'Fine!' the king exclaimed. 'You are a good man. You have been faithful with the little I entrusted to you, and as your reward, you shall be governor of ten cities.'

¹⁸ "The next man also reported a splendid gain—five times the original amount.

¹⁹ " 'All right!' his master said. 'You can be governor over five cities.'

²⁰ "But the third man brought back only the money he had started with. 'I've kept it safe,' he said, ²¹ 'because I was afraid [you would demand my profits[a]], for you are a hard man to deal with, taking what isn't yours and even confiscating the crops that others plant.' ²² 'You vile and wicked slave,' the king roared. 'Hard, am I? That's exactly how I'll be toward you! If you knew so much about me and how tough I am, ²³ then why didn't you deposit the money in the bank so that I could at least get some interest on it?'

²⁴ "Then turning to the others standing by he ordered, 'Take the money away from him and give it to the man who earned the most.'

²⁵ " 'But, sir,' they said, 'he has enough already!'

²⁶ " 'Yes,' the king replied, 'but it is always true that those who have, get more, and those who have little, soon lose even that. ²⁷ And now about these enemies of mine who revolted—bring them in and execute them before me.' "

²⁸ After telling this story, Jesus went on towards Jerusalem, walking along ahead of his disciples. ²⁹ As they came to the towns of Bethphage and Bethany, on the Mount of Olives, he sent two disciples ahead, ³⁰ with instructions to go to the next village, and as they entered they were to look for a donkey tied beside the road. It would be a colt, not yet broken for riding.

"Untie him," Jesus said, "and bring him here. ³¹ And if anyone asks you what you are doing, just say, 'The Lord needs him.' "

³² They found the colt as Jesus said, ³³ and sure enough, as they were untying it, the owners demanded an explanation.

"What are you doing?" they asked. "Why are you untying our colt?"

³⁴ And the disciples simply replied, "The

a Implied.   b Literally, "the Son of Man."

885

Lord needs him!" ³⁵ So they brought the colt to Jesus and threw some of their clothing across its back for Jesus to sit on.

³⁶,³⁷ Then the crowds spread out their robes along the road ahead of him, and as they reached the place where the road started down from the Mount of Olives, the whole procession began to shout and sing as they walked along, praising God for all the wonderful miracles Jesus had done.

³⁸ "God has given us a King!" they exulted. "Long live the King! Let all heaven rejoice! Glory to God in the highest heavens!"

³⁹ But some of the Pharisees among the crowd said, "Sir, rebuke your followers for saying things like that!"

⁴⁰ He replied, "If they keep quiet, the stones along the road will burst into cheers!"

⁴¹ But as they came closer to Jerusalem and he saw the city ahead, he began to cry. ⁴² "Eternal peace was within your reach and you turned it down," he wept, "and now it is too late. ⁴³ Your enemies will pile up earth against your walls and encircle you and close in on you, ⁴⁴ and crush you to the ground, and your children within you; your enemies will not leave one stone upon another—for you have rejected the opportunity God offered you."

⁴⁵ Then he entered the Temple and began to drive out the merchants from their stalls, ⁴⁶ saying to them, "The Scriptures declare, 'My Temple is a place of prayer; but you have turned it into a den of thieves.' "

⁴⁷ After that he taught daily in the Temple, but the chief priests and other religious leaders and the business communityᶜ were trying to find some way to get rid of him. ⁴⁸ But they could think of nothing, for he was a hero to the people—they hung on every word he said.

20 ON ONE OF those days when he was teaching and preaching the Good News in the Temple, he was confronted by the chief priests and other religious leaders and councilmen. ² They demanded to know by what authority he had driven out the merchants from the Temple.

³ "I'll ask you a question before I answer," he replied. ⁴ "Was John sent by God, or was he merely acting under his own authority?"

⁵ They talked it over among themselves. "If we say his message was from heaven, then we are trapped because he will ask, 'Then why didn't you believe him?' ⁶ But if we say John was not sent from God, the people will mob us, for they are convinced that he was a prophet." ⁷ Finally they replied, "We don't know!"

⁸ And Jesus responded, "Then I won't answer your question either."

⁹ Now he turned to the people again and told them this story: "A man planted a vineyard and rented it out to some farmers, and went away to a distant land to live for several years. ¹⁰ When harvest time came, he sent one of his men to the farm to collect his share of the crops. But the tenants beat him up and sent him back empty-handed. ¹¹ Then he sent another, but the same thing happened; he was beaten up and insulted and sent away without collecting. ¹² A third man was sent and the same thing happened. He, too, was wounded and chased away.

¹³ " 'What shall I do?' the owner asked himself. 'I know! I'll send my cherished son. Surely they will show respect for him.'

¹⁴ "But when the tenants saw his son, they said, 'This is our chance! This fellow will inherit all the land when his father dies. Come on. Let's kill him, and then it will be ours.' ¹⁵ So they dragged him out of the vineyard and killed him.

"What do you think the owner will do? ¹⁶ I'll tell you—he will come and kill them and rent the vineyard to others."

"But they would never do a thing like that," his listeners protested.

¹⁷ Jesus looked at them and said, "Then what does the Scripture mean where it says, 'The Stone rejected by the builders was made the cornerstone'?" ¹⁸ And he added, "Whoever stumbles over that Stone shall be broken; and those on whom it falls will be crushed to dust."

¹⁹ When the chief priests and religious leaders heard about this story he had told, they wanted him arrested immediately, for

---

c Literally, "the leading men among the people."

they realized that he was talking about them. They were the wicked tenants in his illustration. But they were afraid that if they themselves arrested him there would be a riot. So they tried to get him to say something that could be reported to the Roman governor as reason for arrest by him.

²⁰ Watching their opportunity, they sent secret agents pretending to be honest men. ²¹ They said to Jesus, "Sir, we know what an honest teacher you are. You always tell the truth and don't budge an inch in the face of what others think, but teach the ways of God. ²² Now tell us—is it right to pay taxes to the Roman government or not?"

²³ He saw through their trickery and said, ²⁴ "Show me a coin. Whose portrait is this on it? And whose name?"

They replied, "Caesar's—the Roman emperor's."

²⁵ He said, "Then give the emperor all that is his—and give to God all that is his!"

²⁶ Thus their attempt to outwit him before the people failed; and marveling at his answer, they were silent.

²⁷ Then some Sadducees—men who believed that death is the end of existence, that there is no resurrection— ²⁸ came to Jesus with this:

"The laws of Moses state that if a man dies without children, the man's brother shall marry the widow and their children will legally belong to the dead man, to carry on his name. ²⁹ We know of a family of seven brothers. The oldest married and then died without any children. ³⁰ His brother married the widow and he, too, died. Still no children. ³¹ And so it went, one after the other, until each of the seven had married her and died, leaving no children. ³² Finally the woman died also. ³³ Now here is our question: Whose wife will she be in the resurrection? For all of them were married to her!"

³⁴,³⁵ Jesus replied, "Marriage is for people here on earth, but when those who are counted worthy of being raised from the dead get to heaven, they do not marry. ³⁶ And they never die again; in these respects they are like angels, and are sons of God, for they are raised up in new life from the dead.

³⁷,³⁸ "But as to your real question—whether or not there is a resurrection—why, even the writings of Moses himself prove this. For when he describes how God appeared to him in the burning bush, he speaks of God as 'the God of Abraham, the God of Isaac, and the God of Jacob.' To say that the Lord *is* ᵃ some person's God means that person is *alive,* not dead! So from God's point of view, all men are living."

³⁹ "Well said, sir!" remarked some of the experts in the Jewish law who were standing there. ⁴⁰ And that ended their questions, for they dared ask no more!

⁴¹ Then he presented *them* with a question. "Why is it," he asked, "that Christ, the Messiah, is said to be a descendant of King David? ⁴²,⁴³ For David himself wrote in the book of Psalms: 'God said to my Lord, the Messiah, "Sit at my right hand until I place your enemies beneath your feet." ' ⁴⁴ How can the Messiah be both David's son and David's God at the same time?"

⁴⁵ Then, with the crowds listening, he turned to his disciples and said, ⁴⁶ "Beware of these experts in religion, for they love to parade in dignified robes and to be bowed to by the people as they walk along the street. And how they love the seats of honor in the synagogues and at religious festivals! ⁴⁷ But even while they are praying long prayers with great outward piety, they are planning schemes to cheat widows out of their property. Therefore God's heaviest sentence awaits these men."

21 AS HE STOOD in the Temple, he was watching the rich tossing their gifts into the collection box. ² Then a poor widow came by and dropped in two small copper coins.

³ "Really," he remarked, "this poor widow has given more than all the rest of them combined. ⁴ For they have given a little of what they didn't need, but she, poor as she is, has given everything she has."

⁵ Some of his disciples began talking about the beautiful stonework of the Temple and the memorial decorations on the

---

a Otherwise the statement would be, "He *had been* that person's God."

walls.

⁶ But Jesus said, "The time is coming when all these things you are admiring will be knocked down, and not one stone will be left on top of another; all will become one vast heap of rubble."

⁷ "Master!" they exclaimed. "When? And will there be any warning ahead of time?"

⁸ He replied, "Don't let anyone mislead you. For many will come announcing themselves as the Messiah,ᵃ and saying, 'The time has come.' But don't believe them! ⁹ And when you hear of wars and insurrections beginning, don't panic. True, wars must come, but the end won't follow immediately— ¹⁰ for nation shall rise against nation and kingdom against kingdom, ¹¹ and there will be great earthquakes, and famines in many lands, and epidemics, and terrifying things happening in the heavens.

¹² "But before all this occurs, there will be a time of special persecution, and you will be dragged into synagogues and prisons and before kings and governors for my name's sake. ¹³ But as a result, the Messiah will be widely known and honored.ᵇ ¹⁴ Therefore, don't be concerned about how to answer the charges against you, ¹⁵ for I will give you the right words and such logic that none of your opponents will be able to reply! ¹⁶ Even those closest to you—your parents, brothers, relatives, and friends will betray you and have you arrested; and some of you will be killed. ¹⁷ And everyone will hate you because you are mine and are called by my name. ¹⁸ But not a hair of your head will perish! ¹⁹ For if you stand firm, you will win your souls.

²⁰ "But when you see Jerusalem surrounded by armies, then you will know that the time of its destruction has arrived. ²¹ Then let the people of Judea flee to the hills. Let those in Jerusalem try to escape, and those outside the city must not attempt to return. ²² For those will be days of God's judgment,ᶜ and the words of the ancient Scriptures written by the prophets will be abundantly fulfilled. ²³ Woe to expectant mothers in those days, and those with tiny babies. For there will be great distress upon this nationᵈ and wrath upon this people. ²⁴ They will be brutally killed by enemy weapons, or sent away as exiles and captives to all the nations of the world; and Jerusalem shall be conquered and trampled down by the Gentiles until the period of Gentile triumph ends in God's good time.

²⁵ "Then there will be strange events in the skies—warnings, evil omens and portents in the sun, moon and stars; and down here on earth the nations will be in turmoil, perplexed by the roaring seas and strange tides. ²⁶ The courage of many people will falter because of the fearful fate they see coming upon the earth, for the stability of the very heavens will be broken up. ²⁷ Then the peoples of the earth shall see me,ᵉ the Messiah, coming in a cloud with power and great glory. ²⁸ So when all these things begin to happen, stand straight and look up! For your salvation is near."

²⁹ Then he gave them this illustration: "Notice the fig tree, or any other tree. ³⁰ When the leaves come out, you know without being told that summer is near. ³¹ In the same way, when you see the events taking place that I've described you can be just as sure that the Kingdom of God is near.

³² "I solemnly declare to you that when these things happen, the end of this ageᶠ has come. ³³ And though all heaven and earth shall pass away, yet my words remain forever true.

³⁴,³⁵ "Watch out! Don't let my sudden coming catch you unawares; don't let me find you living in careless ease, carousing and drinking, and occupied with the problems of this life, like all the rest of the world. ³⁶ Keep a constant watch. And pray that if possible you may arrive in my presence without having to experience these horrors."ᵍ

³⁷,³⁸ Every day Jesus went to the Temple to teach, and the crowds began gathering early in the morning to hear him. And each evening he returned to spend the night on the Mount of Olives.

---

a Literally, "will come in my name."   b Literally, "It shall turn out unto you for a testimony."
c Literally, "days of vengeance."   d Literally, "upon the land," or, "upon the earth."
e Literally, "the Son of Man."   f Or, "this generation."   g Or, "Pray for strength to pass safely
through these coming horrors."

22 AND NOW THE Passover celebration was drawing near—the Jewish festival when only bread made without yeast was used. [2] The chief priests and other religious leaders were actively plotting Jesus' murder, trying to find a way to kill him without starting a riot—a possibility they greatly feared.

[3] Then Satan entered into Judas Iscariot, who was one of the twelve disciples, [4] and he went over to the chief priests and captains of the Temple guards to discuss the best way to betray Jesus to them. [5] They were, of course, delighted to know that he was ready to help them and promised him a reward. [6] So he began to look for an opportunity for them to arrest Jesus quietly when the crowds weren't around.

[7] Now the day of the Passover celebration arrived, when the Passover lamb was killed and eaten with the unleavened bread. [8] Jesus sent Peter and John ahead to find a place to prepare their Passover meal.

[9] "Where do you want us to go?" they asked.

[10] And he replied, "As soon as you enter Jerusalem,[a] you will see a man walking along carrying a pitcher of water. Follow him into the house he enters, [11] and say to the man who lives there, 'Our Teacher says for you to show us the guest room where he can eat the Passover meal with his disciples.' [12] He will take you upstairs to a large room all ready for us. That is the place. Go ahead and prepare the meal there."

[13] They went off to the city and found everything just as Jesus had said, and prepared the Passover supper.

[14] Then Jesus and the others arrived, and at the proper time all sat down together at the table; [15] and he said, "I have looked forward to this hour with deep longing, anxious to eat this Passover meal with you before my suffering begins. [16] For I tell you now that I won't eat it again until what it represents has occurred in the Kingdom of God."

[17] Then he took a glass of wine, and when he had given thanks for it, he said, "Take this and share it among yourselves. [18] For I will not drink wine again until the Kingdom of God has come."

[19] Then he took a loaf of bread; and when he had thanked God for it, he broke it apart and gave it to them, saying, "This is my body, given for you. Eat it in remembrance of me."

[20] After supper he gave them another glass of wine, saying, "This wine is the token of God's new agreement to save you—an agreement sealed with the blood I shall pour out to purchase back your souls.[b] [21] But here at this table, sitting among us as a friend, is the man who will betray me. [22] I[c] must die. It is part of God's plan. But, oh, the horror awaiting that man who betrays me."

[23] Then the disciples wondered among themselves which of them would ever do such a thing.

[24] And they began to argue among themselves as to who would have the highest rank [in the coming Kingdom[d]].

[25] Jesus told them, "In this world the kings and great men order their slaves around, and the slaves have no choice but to like it![e] [26] But among you, the one who serves you best will be your leader. [27] Out in the world the master sits at the table and is served by his servants. But not here! For I am your servant. [28] Nevertheless, because you have stood true to me in these terrible days,[f] [29] and because my Father has granted me a Kingdom, I, here and now, grant you the right [30] to eat and drink at my table in that Kingdom; and you will sit on thrones judging the twelve tribes of Israel.

[31] "Simon, Simon, Satan has asked to have you, to sift you like wheat, [32] but I have pleaded in prayer for you that your faith should not completely fail.[g] So when you have repented and turned to me again, strengthen and build up the faith of your brothers."

[33] Simon said, "Lord, I am ready to go to jail with you, and even to die with you."

[34] But Jesus said, "Peter, let me tell you something. Between now and tomorrow morning when the rooster crows, you will deny me three times, declaring that you

---

a Literally, "the city."   b Literally, "This cup is the new covenant in my blood, poured out for you."
c Literally, "the Son of Man."   d Implied.   e Literally, "they (the kings and great men) are called 'benefactors.' "   f Literally, "you have continued with me in my temptation."   g Literally, "fail not."

don't even know me."

³⁵ Then Jesus asked them, "When I sent you out to preach the Good News and you were without money, duffle bag, or extra clothing, how did you get along?"

"Fine," they replied.

³⁶ "But now," he said, "take a duffle bag if you have one, and your money. And if you don't have a sword, better sell your clothes and buy one! ³⁷ For the time has come for this prophecy about me to come true: 'He will be condemned as a criminal!' Yes, everything written about me by the prophets will come true."

³⁸ "Master," they replied, "we have two swords among us."

"Enough!" he said.

³⁹ Then, accompanied by the disciples, he left the upstairs room and went as usual to the Mount of Olives. ⁴⁰ There he told them, "Pray God that you will not be overcome[h] by temptation."

⁴¹,⁴² He walked away, perhaps a stone's throw, and knelt down and prayed this prayer: "Father, if you are willing, please take away this cup of horror from me. But I want your will, not mine." ⁴³ Then an angel from heaven appeared and strengthened him, ⁴⁴ for he was in such agony of spirit that he broke into a sweat of blood, with great drops falling to the ground as he prayed more and more earnestly.⁴⁵ At last he stood up again and returned to the disciples—only to find them asleep, exhausted from grief.

⁴⁶ "Asleep!" he said. "Get up! Pray God that you will not fall when you are tempted."

⁴⁷ But even as he said this, a mob approached, led by Judas, one of his twelve disciples. Judas walked over to Jesus and kissed him on the cheek in friendly greeting.[i]

⁴⁸ But Jesus said, "Judas, how can you do this—betray the Messiah with a kiss?"

⁴⁹ When the other disciples saw what was about to happen, they exclaimed, "Master, shall we fight? We brought along the swords!" ⁵⁰ And one of them slashed at the High Priest's servant, and cut off his right ear.

⁵¹ But Jesus said, "Don't resist any more." And he touched the place where the man's ear had been and restored it. ⁵² Then Jesus addressed the chief priests and captains of the Temple guards and the religious leaders who headed the mob. "Am I a robber," he asked, "that you have come armed with swords and clubs to get me? ⁵³ Why didn't you arrest me in the Temple? I was there every day. But this is your moment— the time when Satan's power reigns supreme."

⁵⁴ So they seized him and led him to the High Priest's residence, and Peter followed at a distance. ⁵⁵ The soldiers lit a fire in the courtyard and sat around it for warmth, and Peter joined them there.

⁵⁶ A servant girl noticed him in the firelight and began staring at him. Finally she spoke: "This man was with Jesus!"

⁵⁷ Peter denied it. "Woman," he said, "I don't even know the man!"

⁵⁸ After a while someone else looked at him and said, "You must be one of them!"

"No sir, I am not!" Peter replied.

⁵⁹ About an hour later someone else flatly stated, "I know this fellow is one of Jesus' disciples, for both are from Galilee."

⁶⁰ But Peter said, "Man, I don't know what you are talking about." And as he said the words, a rooster crowed.

⁶¹ At that moment Jesus turned and looked at Peter. Then Peter remembered what he had said—"Before the rooster crows tomorrow morning, you will deny me three times." ⁶² And Peter walked out of the courtyard, crying bitterly.

⁶³,⁶⁴ Now the guards in charge of Jesus began mocking him. They blindfolded him and hit him with their fists and asked, "Who hit you that time, prophet?" ⁶⁵ And they threw all sorts of other insults at him.

⁶⁶ Early the next morning at daybreak the Jewish Supreme Court assembled, including the chief priests and all the top religious authorities of the nation. Jesus was led before this Council, ⁶⁷,⁶⁸ and instructed to state whether or not he claimed to be the Messiah.

---

h Literally, "that you enter not into temptation." the traditional greeting among men in eastern lands.

i Literally, "approached Jesus to kiss him." This is still

But he replied, "If I tell you, you won't believe me or let me present my case. [69] But the time is soon coming when I, the Messiah,[j] shall be enthroned beside Almighty God."

[70] They all shouted, "Then you claim you are the Son of God?"

And he replied, "Yes, I am."

[71] "What need do we have for other witnesses?" they shouted. "For we ourselves have heard him say it."

23 THEN THE ENTIRE Council took Jesus over to Pilate, the governor.[a] [2] They began at once accusing him: "This fellow has been leading our people to ruin by telling them not to pay their taxes to the Roman government and by claiming he is our Messiah—a King."

[3] So Pilate asked him, "Are you their Messiah—their King?"[b]

"Yes," Jesus replied, "it is as you say."

[4] Then Pilate turned to the chief priests and to the mob and said, "So? That isn't a crime!"

[5] Then they became desperate. "But he is causing riots against the government everywhere he goes, all over Judea, from Galilee to Jerusalem!"

[6] "Is he then a Galilean?" Pilate asked.

[7] When they told him yes, Pilate said to take him to King Herod, for Galilee was under Herod's jurisdiction; and Herod happened to be in Jerusalem at the time. [8] Herod was delighted at the opportunity to see Jesus, for he had heard a lot about him and had been hoping to see him perform a miracle.

[9] He asked Jesus question after question, but there was no reply. [10] Meanwhile, the chief priests and the other religious leaders stood there shouting their accusations.

[11] Now Herod and his soldiers began mocking and ridiculing Jesus; and putting a kingly robe on him, they sent him back to Pilate. [12] That day Herod and Pilate —enemies before—became fast friends.

[13] Then Pilate called together the chief priests and other Jewish leaders, along with the people, [14] and announced his verdict:

"You brought this man to me, accusing him of leading a revolt against the Roman government.[c] I have examined him thoroughly on this point and find him innocent. [15] Herod came to the same conclusion and sent him back to us—nothing this man has done calls for the death penalty. [16] I will therefore have him scourged with leaded thongs, and release him."

[17,d][18] But now a mighty roar rose from the crowd as with one voice they shouted, "Kill him, and release Barabbas to us!" [19] (Barabbas was in prison for starting an insurrection in Jerusalem against the government, and for murder.) [20] Pilate argued with them, for he wanted to release Jesus. [21] But they shouted, "Crucify him! Crucify him!"

[22] Once more, for the third time, he demanded, "Why? What crime has he committed? I have found no reason to sentence him to death. I will therefore scourge him and let him go." [23] But they shouted louder and louder for Jesus' death, and their voices prevailed.

[24] So Pilate sentenced Jesus to die as they demanded. [25] And he released Barabbas, the man in prison for insurrection and murder, at their request. But he delivered Jesus over to them to do with as they would.

[26] As the crowd led Jesus away to his death, Simon of Cyrene, who was just coming into Jerusalem from the country, was forced to follow, carrying Jesus' cross. [27] Great crowds trailed along behind, and many grief-stricken women.

[28] But Jesus turned and said to them, "Daughters of Jerusalem, don't weep for me, but for yourselves and for your children. [29] For the days are coming when the women who have no children will be counted fortunate indeed. [30] Mankind will beg the mountains to fall on them and crush them, and the hills to bury them. [31] For if such things as this are done to me, the Living Tree, what will they do to you?"[e]

[32,33] Two others, criminals, were led out to be executed with him at a place called

---

j Literally, "the Son of Man."   23a Implied.   b Literally, "Are you the King of the Jews?"
c Literally, "as one who perverts the people."   d Some ancient authorities add verse 17, "For it was necessary for him to release unto them at the feast one (prisoner)."   e Literally, "For if they do this when the tree is green, what will happen when it is dry?"

"The Skull." There all three were crucified—Jesus on the center cross, and the two criminals on either side. [34] "Father, forgive these people," Jesus said, "for they don't know what they are doing."

And the soldiers gambled for his clothing, throwing dice for each piece. [35] The crowd watched. And the Jewish leaders laughed and scoffed. "He was so good at helping others," they said, "let's see him save himself if he is really God's Chosen One, the Messiah."

[36] The soldiers mocked him, too, by offering him a drink—of sour wine. [37] And they called to him, "If you are the King of the Jews, save yourself!"

[38] A signboard was nailed to the cross above him with these words: "This is the King of the Jews."

[39] One of the criminals hanging beside him scoffed, "So you're the Messiah, are you? Prove it by saving yourself—and us, too, while you're at it!"

[40,41] But the other criminal protested. "Don't you even fear God when you are dying? We deserve to die for our evil deeds, but this man hasn't done one thing wrong." [42] Then he said, "Jesus, remember me when you come into your Kingdom."

[43] And Jesus replied, "Today you will be with me in Paradise. This is a solemn promise."

[44] By now it was noon, and darkness fell across the whole land[f] for three hours, until three o'clock. [45] The light from the sun was gone—and suddenly[g] the thick veil hanging in the Temple split apart.

[46] Then Jesus shouted, "Father, I commit my spirit to you," and with those words he died.[h]

[47] When the captain of the Roman military unit handling the executions saw what had happened, he was stricken with awe before God and said, "Surely this man was innocent."[i]

[48] And when the crowd that came to see the crucifixion saw that Jesus was dead, they went home in deep sorrow. [49] Meanwhile, Jesus' friends, including the women who had followed him down from Galilee, stood in the distance watching.

[50,51,52] Then a man named Joseph, a member of the Jewish Supreme Court, from the city of Arimathea in Judea, went to Pilate and asked for the body of Jesus. He was a godly man who had been expecting the Messiah's coming and had not agreed with the decision and actions of the other Jewish leaders. [53] So he took down Jesus' body and wrapped it in a long linen cloth and laid it in a new, unused tomb hewn into the rock [at the side of a hill[g]]. [54] This was done late on Friday afternoon, the day of preparation for the Sabbath.

[55] As the body was taken away, the women from Galilee followed and saw it carried into the tomb. [56] Then they went home and prepared spices and ointments to embalm him; but by the time they were finished it was the Sabbath, so they rested all that day as required by the Jewish law.

24 BUT VERY EARLY on Sunday morning they took the ointments to the tomb— [2] and found that the huge stone covering the entrance had been rolled aside. [3] So they went in—but the Lord Jesus' body was gone.

[4] They stood there puzzled, trying to think what could have happened to it. Suddenly two men appeared before them, clothed in shining robes so bright their eyes were dazzled. [5] The women were terrified and bowed low before them.

Then the men asked, "Why are you looking in a tomb for someone who is alive? [6,7] He isn't here! He has come back to life again! Don't you remember what he told you back in Galilee—that the Messiah[a] must be betrayed into the power of evil men and be crucified and that he would rise again the third day?"

[8] Then they remembered, [9] and rushed back to Jerusalem[b] to tell his eleven disciples—and everyone else—what had happened. [10] (The women who went to the tomb were Mary Magdalene and Joanna and Mary the mother of James, and several others.) [11] But the story sounded like a fairy tale

f Or, "the whole world." g Implied. h Literally, "yielded up the spirit." i Literally, "righteous." 24 a Literally, "the Son of Man." b Literally, "returned from the tomb."

to the men—they didn't believe it.
[12] However, Peter ran to the tomb to look. Stooping, he peered in and saw the empty linen wrappings; and then he went back home again, wondering what had happened.

[13] That same day, Sunday, two of Jesus' followers were walking to the village of Emmaus, seven miles out of Jerusalem. [14] As they walked along they were talking of Jesus' death, [15] when suddenly Jesus himself came along and joined them and began walking beside them. [16] But they didn't recognize him, for God kept them from it.

[17] "You seem to be in a deep discussion about something," he said. "What are you so concerned about?" They stopped short, sadness written across their faces. [18] And one of them, Cleopas, replied, "You must be the only person in Jerusalem who hasn't heard about the terrible things that happened there last week."[c]

[19] "What things?" Jesus asked.

"The things that happened to Jesus, the Man from Nazareth," they said. "He was a Prophet who did incredible miracles and was a mighty Teacher, highly regarded by both God and man. [20] But the chief priests and our religious leaders arrested him and handed him over to the Roman government to be condemned to death, and they crucified him. [21] We had thought he was the glorious Messiah and that he had come to rescue Israel.

"And now, besides all this—which happened three days ago— [22,23] some women from our group of his followers were at his tomb early this morning and came back with an amazing report that his body was missing, and that they had seen some angels there who told them Jesus is alive! [24] Some of our men ran out to see, and sure enough, Jesus' body was gone, just as the women had said."

[25] Then Jesus said to them, "You are such foolish, foolish people! You find it so hard to believe all that the prophets wrote in the Scriptures! [26] Wasn't it clearly predicted by the prophets that the Messiah would have to suffer all these things before entering his time of glory?"

[27] Then Jesus quoted them passage after passage from the writings of the prophets, beginning with the book of Genesis and going right on through the Scriptures, explaining what the passages meant and what they said about himself. [28] By this time they were nearing Emmaus and the end of their journey. Jesus would have gone on, [29] but they begged him to stay the night with them, as it was getting late. So he went home with them. [30] As they sat down to eat, he asked God's blessing on the food and then took a small loaf of bread and broke it and was passing it over to them, [31] when suddenly—it was as though their eyes were opened—they recognized him! And at that moment he disappeared!

[32] They began telling each other how their hearts had felt strangely warm as he talked with them and explained the Scriptures during the walk down the road. [33,34] Within the hour they were on their way back to Jerusalem, where the eleven disciples and the other followers of Jesus greeted them with these words, "The Lord has really risen! He appeared to Peter!"

[35] Then the two from Emmaus told their story of how Jesus had appeared to them as they were walking along the road and how they had recognized him as he was breaking the bread. [36] And just as they were telling about it, Jesus himself was suddenly standing there among them, and greeted them. [37] But the whole group was terribly frightened, thinking they were seeing a ghost!

[38] "Why are you frightened?" he asked. "Why do you doubt that it is really I? [39] Look at my hands! Look at my feet! You can see that it is I, myself! Touch me and make sure that I am not a ghost! For ghosts don't have bodies, as you see that I do!" [40] As he spoke, he held out his hands for them to see [the marks of the nails[d]], and showed them [the wounds in[d]] his feet.

[41] Still they stood there undecided, filled with joy and doubt.

Then he asked them, "Do you have anything here to eat?" [42] They gave him a piece of broiled fish, [43] and he ate it as they watched!

[44] Then he said, "When I was with you

---

c Literally, "in these days."　　　d Implied.

before, don't you remember my telling you that everything written about me by Moses and the prophets and in the Psalms must all come true?" [45] Then he opened their minds to understand at last these many Scriptures! [46] And he said, "Yes, it was written long ago that the Messiah must suffer and die and rise again from the dead on the third day; [47] and that this message of salvation should be taken from Jerusalem to all the nations: *There is forgiveness of sins for all who turn to me.* [48] You have seen these prophecies come true.

[49] "And now I will send the Holy Spirit[e] upon you, just as my Father promised. Don't begin telling others[f] yet—stay here in the city until the Holy Spirit comes and fills you with power from heaven."

[50] Then Jesus led them out along the road[g] to Bethany, and lifting his hands to heaven, he blessed them, [51] and then began rising into the sky, and went on to heaven. [52] And they worshiped him, and returned to Jerusalem filled with mighty joy, [53] and were continually in the Temple, praising God.

---

e Implied. Literally, "the promise of my Father." paraphrase relates this to verse 47.   f Literally, "but wait here in the city until. . . ." The
Mount of Olives.   g Implied. Bethany was a mile or so away, across the valley on the

Tune In

We live in an exciting world. We who are young in the 20th century balance atop a surfer's wave of accelerating action. This restless, pulsating action affects our lives in many ways . . . scientific advances are changing the way we shop, travel, learn, and relax.

The delegate to the National Youth Conference on the Atom watching an experiment at Argonne National Laboratories is—with us—intensely interested in what's coming next and how it will affect us. Projections about flat TV's, computer-regulated traffic, air travel to anywhere in the world

Vivienne

in forty-five minutes, pocket computers, cities below the surface of the sea—all seem like science fiction, yet reputable scientists are predicting them. But as we read and hear about the widening stream of these innovations, we often get strange concepts about God's role in all these changes. One group of university students was asked, "Do you believe God fully understands the molecule and the atom?" The majority replied that they thought he did not (the story sounds absurd, but it's true!). Somehow, in our modern times, we get the idea that God was able to put together trees and animals and mountains, but that he really can't keep up on such things as jet travel, new cars, satellite TV, contemporary music, and fantastic computer advances. Yet God set up all the principles by which our electronic age functions.

The magnificent truth—for each of us who really cares to find it out—is that the Person who masterminded all creation was once breathing, sleeping, and eating on this planet Earth just as you and I are: and we can get acquainted with him! Carefully read the first five verses of this book. Think them through in relation to all that's going on around you. This flesh-and-blood Jesus caused the most dramatic events that ever happened on this planet. And here, from the original documents—part of the Bible itself—you have the full story. Read this book carefully and see how the contemporary Jesus relates to *you!*

JOHN

1 BEFORE ANYTHING ELSE existed,[a] there was Christ,[b] with God. He has always[a] been alive and is himself God. [3] He created everything there is—nothing exists that he didn't make. [4] Eternal life is in him, and this life gives light to all mankind. [5] His life is the light that shines through the darkness —and the darkness can never extinguish it.

[6,7] God sent John the Baptist as a witness to the fact that Jesus Christ is the true Light. [8] John himself was not the Light; he was only a witness to identify it. [9] Later on, the one who is the true Light arrived to shine on everyone coming into the world.

[10] But although he made the world, the world didn't recognize him when he came. [11,12] Even in his own land and among his own people, the Jews, he was not accepted. Only a few would welcome and receive him. But to all who received him, he gave the right to become children of God. All they needed to do was to trust him to save them.[c] [13] All those who believe this are re-born!—not a physical rebirth[d] resulting from human passion or plan—but from the will of God.

[14] And Christ[b] became a human being and lived here on earth among us and was full of loving forgiveness[e] and truth. And some of us have seen his glory[f]—the glory of the only Son of the heavenly Father![g]

[15] John pointed him out to the people, telling the crowds, "This is the one I was talking about when I said, 'Someone is coming who is greater by far than I am—for he existed long before I did!' " [16] We have all benefited from the rich blessings he brought to us—blessing upon blessing heaped upon us! [17] For Moses gave us only the Law with its rigid demands and merciless justice, while Jesus Christ brought us loving for-giveness as well. [18] No one has ever actually seen God, but, of course, his only Son has, for he is the companion of the Father and has told us all about him.

[19] The Jewish leaders[h] sent priests and assistant priests from Jerusalem to ask John whether he claimed to be the Messiah.

[20] He denied it flatly. "I am not the Christ," he said.

[21] "Well then, who are you?" they asked. "Are you Elijah?"

"No," he replied.

"Are you the Prophet?"[i]

---

a Literally, "In the beginning."   b Literally, "the Word," meaning Christ, the wisdom and power of God and the first cause of all things; God's personal expression of himself to men.
c Literally, "to believe on his name."   d Literally, "not of blood."   e Literally, "grace."
f See Matthew 17:2.   g Or, "his unique Son."   h Literally, "the Jews."
i See Deuteronomy 18:15.

"No."

²² "Then who are you? Tell us, so we can give an answer to those who sent us. What do you have to say for yourself?"

²³ He replied, "I am a voice from the barren wilderness, shouting as Isaiah prophesied, 'Get ready for the coming of the Lord!' "

²⁴,²⁵ Then those who were sent by the Pharisees asked him, "If you aren't the Messiah or Elijah or the Prophet, what right do you have to baptize?"

²⁶ John told them, "I merely baptize withʲ water, but right here in the crowd is someone you have never met, ²⁷ who will soon begin his ministry among you, and I am not even fit to be his slave."

²⁸ This incident took place at Bethany, a village on the other side of the Jordan River where John was baptizing.

²⁹ The next day John saw Jesus coming toward him and said, "Look! There is the Lamb of God who takes away the world's sin! ³⁰ He is the one I was talking about when I said, 'Soon a man far greater than I am is coming, who existed long before me!' ³¹ I didn't know he was the one, but I am here baptizing withʲ water in order to point him out to the nation of Israel."

³² Then John told about seeing the Holy Spirit in the form of a dove descending from heaven and resting upon Jesus.

³³ "I didn't know he was the one," John said again, "but at the time God sent me to baptize he told me, 'When you see the Holy Spirit descending and resting upon someone—he is the one you are looking for. He is the one who baptizes withʲ the Holy Spirit.' ³⁴ I saw it happen to this man, and I therefore testify that he is the Son of God."

³⁵ The following day as John was standing with two of his disciples, ³⁶ Jesus walked by. John looked at him intently and then declared, "See! There is the Lamb of God!"

³⁷ Then John's two disciples turned and followed Jesus.

³⁸ Jesus looked around and saw them following. "What do you want?" he asked them.

"Sir," they replied, "where do you live?"

³⁹ "Come and see," he said. So they went with him to the place where he was staying and were with him from about four o'clock that afternoon until the evening. ⁴⁰ (One of these men was Andrew, Simon Peter's brother.)

⁴¹ Andrew then went to find his brother Peter and told him, "We have found the Messiah!" ⁴² And he brought Peter to meet Jesus.

Jesus looked intently at Peter for a moment and then said, "You are Simon, John's son—but you shall be called Peter, the rock!"

⁴³ The next day Jesus decided to go to Galilee. He found Philip and told him, "Come with me." ⁴⁴ (Philip was from Bethsaida, Andrew and Peter's home town.)

⁴⁵ Philip now went off to look for Nathanael and told him, "We have found the Messiah!—the very person Moses and the prophets told about! His name is Jesus, the son of Joseph from Nazareth!"

⁴⁶ "Nazareth!" exclaimed Nathanael. "Can anything good come from there?"

"Just come and see for yourself," Philip declared.

⁴⁷ As they approached, Jesus said, "Here comes an honest man—a true son of Israel."

⁴⁸ "How do you know what I am like?" Nathanael demanded.

And Jesus replied, "I could see you under the fig tree before Philip found you."

⁴⁹ Nathanael replied, "Sir, you are the Son of God—the King of Israel!"

⁵⁰ Jesus asked him, "Do you believe all this just because I told you I had seen you under the fig tree? You will see greater proofs than this. ⁵¹ You will even see heaven open and the angels of God coming back and forth to me, the Messiah."ᵏ

2 TWO DAYS LATER Jesus' mother was a guest at a wedding in the village of Cana in Galilee, ² and Jesus and his disciples were invited too. ³ The wine supply ran out during the festivities, and Jesus' mother came to him with the problem.

⁴ "I can't help you now," he said.ᵃ "It isn't yet my time for miracles."

⁵ But his mother told the servants, "Do

---

j Or, "in."   k Literally, "the Son of Man."   2a Literally, "Woman, what have I to do with you?"

whatever he tells you to."

⁶ Six stone waterpots were standing there; they were used for Jewish ceremonial purposes and held perhaps twenty to thirty gallons each. ⁷,⁸ Then Jesus told the servants to fill them to the brim with water. When this was done he said, "Dip some out and take it to the master of ceremonies."

⁹ When the master of ceremonies tasted the water that was now wine, not knowing where it had come from (though, of course, the servants did), he called the bridegroom over.

¹⁰ "This is wonderful stuff!" he said. "You're different from most. Usually a host uses the best wine first, and afterwards, when everyone is full and doesn't care, then he brings out the less expensive brands. But you have kept the best for the last!"

¹¹ This miracle at Cana in Galilee was Jesus' first public demonstration of his heaven-sent power. And his disciples believed that he really was the Messiah.ᵇ

¹² After the wedding he left for Capernaum for a few days with his mother, brothers, and disciples.

¹³ Then it was time for the annual Jewish Passover celebration, and Jesus went to Jerusalem.

¹⁴ In the Temple area he saw merchants selling cattle, sheep, and doves for sacrifices, and money changers behind their counters. ¹⁵ Jesus made a whip from some ropes and chased them all out, and drove out the sheep and oxen, scattering the money changers' coins over the floor and turning over their tables! ¹⁶ Then, going over to the men selling doves, he told them, "Get these things out of here. Don't turn my Father's House into a market!"

¹⁷ Then his disciples remembered this prophecy from the Scriptures: "Concern for God's House will be my undoing."

¹⁸ "What right have you to order them out?" the Jewish leadersᶜ demanded. "If you have this authority from God, show us a miracle to prove it."

¹⁹ "All right," Jesus replied, "this is the miracle I will do for you: Destroy this sanctuary and in three days I will raise it up!"

²⁰ "What!" they exclaimed. "It took forty-six years to build this Temple, and you can do it in three days?" ²¹ But by "this sanctuary" he meant his body. ²² After he came back to life again, the disciples remembered his saying this and realized that what he had quoted from the Scriptures really did refer to him, and had all come true!

²³ Because of the miracles he did in Jerusalem at the Passover celebration, many people were convinced that he was indeed the Messiah. ²⁴,²⁵ But Jesus didn't trust them, for he knew mankind to the core. No one needed to tell him how changeable human nature is!

3 AFTER DARK ONE night a Jewish religious leader named Nicodemus, a member of the sect of the Pharisees, came for an interview with Jesus. "Sir," he said, "we all know that God has sent you to teach us. Your miracles are proof enough of this."

³ Jesus replied, "With all the earnestness I possess I tell you this: Unless you are born again, you can never get into the Kingdom of God."

⁴ "Born again!" exclaimed Nicodemus. "What do you mean? How can an old man go back into his mother's womb and be born again?"

⁵ Jesus replied, "What I am telling you so earnestly is this: Unless one is born of waterᵃ and the Spirit, he cannot enter the Kingdom of God. ⁶ Men can only reproduce human life, but the Holy Spirit gives new life from heaven; ⁷ so don't be surprised at my statement that you must be born again! ⁸ Just as you can hear the wind but can't tell where it comes from or where it will go next, so it is with the Spirit. We do not know on whom he will next bestow this life from heaven."

⁹ "What do you mean?" Nicodemus asked.

¹⁰,¹¹ Jesus replied, "You, a respected Jewish teacher, and yet you don't understand these things? I am telling you what I know and have seen—and yet you won't believe me. ¹² But if you don't even believe me when

b Literally, "His disciples believed on him."   c Literally, "the Jews."   3a Or, "Physical birth is not enough. You must also be born spiritually. . . ." This alternate paraphrase interprets "born of water" as meaning the normal process observed during every human birth. Some think this means water baptism.

I tell you about such things as these that happen here among men, how can you possibly believe if I tell you what is going on in heaven? [13] For only I, the Messiah,[b] have come to earth and will return to heaven again. [14] And as Moses in the wilderness lifted up the bronze image of a serpent on a pole, even so I must be lifted up upon a pole, [15] so that anyone who believes in me will have eternal life. [16] For God loved the world so much that he gave his only[c] Son so that anyone who believes in him shall not perish but have eternal life. [17] God did not send his Son into the world to condemn it, but to save it.

[18] "There is no eternal doom awaiting those who trust him to save them. But those who don't trust him have already been tried and condemned for not believing in the only[c] Son of God. [19] Their sentence is based on this fact: that the Light from heaven came into the world, but they loved the darkness more than the Light, for their deeds were evil. [20] They hated the heavenly Light because they wanted to sin in the darkness. They stayed away from that Light for fear their sins would be exposed and they would be punished. [21] But those doing right come gladly to the Light to let everyone see that they are doing what God wants them to."

[22] Afterwards Jesus and his disciples left Jerusalem and stayed for a while in Judea and baptized there.

[23,24] At this time John the Baptist was not yet in prison. He was baptizing at Aenon, near Salim, because there was plenty of water there. [25] One day someone began an argument with John's disciples, telling them that Jesus' baptism was best.[d] [26] So they came to John and said, "Master, the man you met on the other side of the Jordan River—the one you said was the Messiah—he is baptizing too, and everybody is going over there instead of coming here to us."

[27] John replied, "God in heaven appoints each man's work. [28] My work is to prepare the way for that man so that everyone will go to him. You yourselves know how plainly I told you that I am not the Messiah. I am here to prepare the way for him—that is all. [29] The crowds will naturally go to the main attraction[e]—the bride will go where the bridegroom is! A bridegroom's friends rejoice with him. I am the Bridegroom's friend, and I am filled with joy at his success. [30] He must become greater and greater, and I must become less and less.

[31] "He has come from heaven and is greater than anyone else. I am of the earth, and my understanding is limited to the things of earth. [32] He tells what he has seen and heard, but how few believe what he tells them! [33,34] Those who believe him discover that God is a fountain of truth. For this one—sent by God—speaks God's words, for God's Spirit is upon him without measure or limit. [35] The Father loves this man because he is his Son, and God has given him everything there is. [36] And all who trust him—God's Son—to save them have eternal life; those who don't believe and obey him shall never see heaven, but the wrath of God remains upon them."

4 WHEN THE LORD knew that the Pharisees had heard about the greater crowds coming to him than to John to be baptized and to become his disciples—(though Jesus himself didn't baptize them, but his disciples did)— [3] he left Judea and returned to the province of Galilee.

[4] He had to go through Samaria on the way, [5,6] and around noon as he approached the village of Sychar, he came to Jacob's Well, located on the parcel of ground Jacob gave to his son Joseph. Jesus was tired from the long walk in the hot sun and sat wearily beside the well.

[7] Soon a Samaritan woman came to draw water, and Jesus asked her for a drink. [8] He was alone at the time as his disciples had gone into the village to buy some food. [9] The woman was surprised that a Jew would ask a "despised Samaritan" for anything—usually they wouldn't even speak to them! —and she remarked about this to Jesus.

[10] He replied, "If you only knew what a wonderful gift God has for you, and who

---

b Literally, "the Son of Man."   c Or, "the unique Son of God."   d Literally, "about purification."
e Implied.

I am, you would ask me for some *living water!*"

[11] "But you don't have a rope or a bucket," she said, "and this is a very deep well! Where would you get this living water? [12] And besides, are you greater than our ancestor Jacob? How can you offer better water than this which he and his sons and cattle enjoyed?"

[13] Jesus replied that people soon became thirsty again after drinking this water. [14] "But the water I give them," he said, "becomes a perpetual spring within them, watering them forever with eternal life."

[15] "Please, sir," the woman said, "give me some of that water! Then I'll never be thirsty again and won't have to make this long trip out here every day."

[16] "Go and get your husband," Jesus told her.

[17,18] "But I'm not married," the woman replied.

"All too true!" Jesus said. "For you have had five husbands, and you aren't even married to the man you're living with now."

[19] "Sir," the woman said, "you must be a prophet. [20] But say, tell me, why is it that you Jews insist that Jerusalem is the only place of worship, while we Samaritans claim it is here [at Mount Gerazim[a]], where our ancestors worshiped?"

[21-24] Jesus replied, "The time is coming, ma'am, when we will no longer be concerned about whether to worship the Father here or in Jerusalem. For it's not *where* we worship that counts, but *how* we worship —is our worship spiritual and real? Do we have the Holy Spirit's help? For God is Spirit, and we must have his help to worship as we should. The Father wants this kind of worship from us. But you Samaritans know so little about him, worshiping blindly, while we Jews know all about him, for salvation comes to the world through the Jews."

[25] The woman said, "Well, at least I know that the Messiah will come—the one they call Christ—and when he does, he will explain everything to us."

[26] Then Jesus told her, "I am the Messiah!"

[27] Just then his disciples arrived. They were surprised to find him talking to a woman, but none of them asked him why, or what they had been discussing.

[28,29] Then the woman left her waterpot beside the well and went back to the village and told everyone, "Come and meet a man who told me everything I ever did! Can this be the Messiah?" [30] So the people came streaming from the village to see him.

[31] Meanwhile, the disciples were urging Jesus to eat. [32] "No," he said, "I have some food you don't know about."

[33] "Who brought it to him?" the disciples asked each other.

[34] Then Jesus explained: "My nourishment comes from doing the will of God who sent me, and from finishing his work. [35] Do you think the work of harvesting will not begin until the summer ends four months from now? Look around you! Vast fields of human souls are ripening all around us, and are ready now for reaping. [36] The reapers will be paid good wages and will be gathering eternal souls into the granaries of heaven! What joys await the sower and the reaper, both together! [37] For it is true that one sows and someone else reaps. [38] I sent you to reap where you didn't sow; others did the work, and you received the harvest."

[39] Many from the Samaritan village believed he was the Messiah because of the woman's report: "He told me everything I ever did!" [40,41] When they came out to see him at the well, they begged him to stay at their village; and he did, for two days, long enough for many of them to believe in him after hearing him. [42] Then they said to the woman, "Now we believe because we have heard him ourselves, not just because of what you told us. He is indeed the Savior of the world."

[43,44] At the end of the two days' stay he went on into Galilee. Jesus used to say, "A prophet is honored everywhere except in his own country!" [45] But the Galileans welcomed him with open arms, for they had been in Jerusalem at the Passover celebration and had seen some of his miracles.[b]

[46,47] In the course of his journey through

---

a Implied.   b See John 2:23.

Galilee he arrived at the town of Cana, where he had turned the water into wine. While he was there, a man in the city of Capernaum, a government official, whose son was very sick, heard that Jesus had come from Judea and was traveling in Galilee. This man went over to Cana, found Jesus, and begged him to come to Capernaum with him and heal his son, who was now at death's door.

⁴⁸ Jesus asked, "Won't any of you believe in me unless I do more and more miracles?"

⁴⁹ The official pled, "Sir, please come now before my child dies."

⁵⁰ Then Jesus told him, "Go back home. Your son is healed!" And the man believed Jesus and started home. ⁵¹ While he was on his way, some of his servants met him with the news that all was well—his son had recovered. ⁵² He asked them when the lad had begun to feel better, and they replied, "Yesterday afternoon at about one o'clock his fever suddenly disappeared!" ⁵³ Then the father realized it was the same moment that Jesus had told him, "Your son is healed." And the officer and his entire household believed that Jesus was the Messiah.

⁵⁴ This was Jesus' second miracle in Galilee after coming from Judea.

5 AFTERWARDS JESUS RETURNED to Jerusalem for one of the Jewish religious holidays. ² Inside the city, near the Sheep Gate, was Bethesda Pool, with five covered platforms or porches surrounding it. ³ Crowds of sick folks—lame, blind, or with paralyzed limbs—lay on the platforms (waiting for a certain movement of the water, ⁴ for an angel of the Lord came from time to time and disturbed the water, and the first person to step down into it afterwards was healed).ᵃ

⁵ One of the men lying there had been sick for thirty-eight years. ⁶ When Jesus saw him and knew how long he had been ill, he asked him, "Would you like to get well?"

⁷ "I can't," the sick man said, "for I have no one to help me into the pool at the movement of the water. While I am trying to get there, someone else always gets in ahead of me."

⁸ Jesus told him, "Stand up, roll up your sleeping mat and go on home!"

⁹ Instantly, the man was healed! He rolled up the mat and began walking!

But it was on the Sabbath when this miracle was done. ¹⁰ So the Jewish leaders objected. They said to the man who was cured, "You can't work on the Sabbath! It's illegal to carry that sleeping mat!"

¹¹ "The man who healed me told me to," was his reply.

¹² "Who said such a thing as that?" they demanded.

¹³ The man didn't know, and Jesus had disappeared into the crowd. ¹⁴ But afterwards Jesus found him in the Temple and told him, "Now you are well; don't sin as you did before,ᵇ or something even worse may happen to you."

¹⁵ Then the man went to find the Jewish leaders and told them it was Jesus who had healed him.

¹⁶ So they began harassing Jesus as a Sabbath breaker. ¹⁷ But Jesus replied, "My Father constantly does good,ᶜ and I'm following his example."

¹⁸ Then the Jewish leaders were all the more eager to kill him because in addition to disobeying their Sabbath laws, he had spoken of God as his Father, thereby making himself equal with God.

¹⁹ Jesus replied, "The Son can do nothing by himself. He does only what he sees the Father doing, and in the same way. ²⁰ For the Father loves the Son, and tells him everything he is doing; and the Son will do far more awesome miracles than this man's healing. ²¹ He will even raise from the dead anyone he wants to, just as the Father does. ²² And the Father leaves all judgment of sin to his Son, ²³ so that everyone will honor the Son, just as they honor the Father. But if you refuse to honor God's Son, whom he sent to you, then you are certainly not honoring the Father.

²⁴ "I say emphatically that anyone who listens to my message and believes in God who sent me has eternal life, and will never be damned for his sins, but has already

---

a Many of the ancient manuscripts omit the material within the parentheses.   b Implied. Literally, "sin no more."   c Implied. Literally, "My Father works even until now, and I work."

passed out of death into life. [25] And I solemnly declare that the time is coming, in fact, it is here, when the dead shall hear my voice—the voice of the Son of God—and those who listen shall live. [26] The Father has life in himself, and has granted his Son to have life in himself, [27] and to judge the sins of all mankind because he is the Son of Man. [28] Don't be so surprised! Indeed the time is coming when all the dead in their graves shall hear the voice of God's Son, [29] and shall rise again—those who have done good, to eternal life; and those who have continued in evil, to judgment.

[30] "But I pass no judgment without consulting the Father. I judge as I am told. And my judgment is absolutely fair and just, for it is according to the will of God who sent me and is not merely my own.

[31] "When I make claims about myself they aren't believed, [32,33] but someone else, yes, John the Baptist,[d] is making these claims for me too. You have gone out to listen to his preaching, and I can assure you that all he says about me is true! [34] But the truest witness I have is not from a man, though I have reminded you about John's witness so that you will believe in me and be saved. [35] John shone brightly for a while, and you benefited and rejoiced, [36] but I have a greater witness than John. I refer to the miracles I do; these have been assigned me by the Father, and they prove that the Father has sent me. [37] And the Father himself has also testified about me, though not appearing to you personally, or speaking to you directly. [38] But you are not listening to him, for you refuse to believe me—the one sent to you with God's message.

[39] "You search the Scriptures, for you believe they give you eternal life. And the Scriptures point to me! [40] Yet you won't come to me so that I can give you this life eternal!

[41,42] "Your approval or disapproval means nothing to me, for as I know so well, you don't have God's love within you. [43] I know, because I have come to you representing my Father and you refuse to welcome me, though you readily enough receive those who aren't sent from him, but represent only themselves! [44] No wonder you can't believe! For you gladly honor each other, but you don't care about the honor that comes from the only God!

[45] "Yet it is not I who will accuse you of this to the Father—Moses will! Moses, on whose laws you set your hopes of heaven. [46] For you have refused to believe Moses. He wrote about me, but you refuse to believe him, so you refuse to believe in me. [47] And since you don't believe what he wrote, no wonder you don't believe me either."

6 AFTER THIS, JESUS crossed over the Sea of Galilee, also known as the Sea of Tiberias. [2-5] And a huge crowd, many of them pilgrims on their way to Jerusalem for the annual Passover celebration[a], were following him wherever he went, to watch him heal the sick. So when Jesus went up into the hills and sat down with his disciples around him, he soon saw a great multitude of people climbing the hill, looking for him.

Turning to Philip he asked, "Philip, where can we buy bread to feed all these people?" [6] (He was testing Philip, for he already knew what he was going to do.)

[7] Philip replied, "It would take a fortune[b] to begin to do it!"

[8,9] Then Andrew, Simon Peter's brother, spoke up. "There's a youngster here with five barley loaves and a couple of fish! But what good is that with all this mob?"

[10] "Tell everyone to sit down," Jesus ordered. And all of them—the approximate count of the men only was 5,000—sat down on the grassy slopes. [11] Then Jesus took the loaves and gave thanks to God and passed them out to the people. Afterwards he did the same with the fish. And everyone ate until full!

[12] "Now gather the scraps," Jesus told his disciples, "so that nothing is wasted." [13] And twelve baskets were filled with the leftovers!

[14] When the people realized what a great miracle had happened, they exclaimed, "Surely, he is the Prophet we have been expecting!"

---

d Implied. However, most commentators believe the reference is to the witness of his Father. See verse 37. 6a Literally, "Now the Passover, the feast of the Jews, was at hand." b Literally, 200 denarii, a denarius being a full day's wage.

[15] Jesus saw that they were ready to take him by force and make him their king, so he went higher into the mountains alone.

[16] That evening his disciples went down to the shore to wait for him. [17] But as darkness fell and Jesus still hadn't come back, they got into the boat and headed out across the lake toward Capernaum. [18,19] But soon a gale swept down upon them as they rowed, and the sea grew very rough. They were three or four miles out when suddenly they saw Jesus walking toward the boat! They were terrified, [20] but he called out to them and told them not to be afraid. [21] Then they were willing to let him in, and immediately the boat was where they were going![c]

[22,23] The next morning, back across the lake, crowds began gathering on the shore [waiting to see Jesus[d]]. For they knew that he and his disciples had come over together and that the disciples had gone off in their boat, leaving him behind. Several small boats from Tiberias were nearby, [24] so when the people saw that Jesus wasn't there, nor his disciples, they got into the boats and went across to Capernaum to look for him.

[25] When they arrived and found him, they said, "Sir, how did you get here?" [26] Jesus replied, "The truth of the matter is that you want to be with me because I fed you, not because you believe in me. [27] But you shouldn't be so concerned about perishable things like food. No, spend your energy seeking the eternal life that I, the Messiah,[e] can give you. For God the Father has sent me for this very purpose."

[28] They replied, "What should we do to satisfy God?"

[29] Jesus told them, "This is the will of God, that you believe in the one he has sent."

[30,31] They replied, "You must show us more miracles if you want us to believe you are the Messiah. Give us free bread every day, like our fathers had while they journeyed through the wilderness! As the Scriptures say, 'Moses gave them bread from heaven.' "

[32] Jesus said, "Moses didn't give it to them. My Father did.[d] And now he offers you true Bread from heaven. [33] The true Bread is a Person—the one sent by God from heaven, and he gives life to the world."

[34] "Sir," they said, "give us that bread every day of our lives!"

[35] Jesus replied, "I am the Bread of Life. No one coming to me will ever be hungry again. Those believing in me will never thirst. [36] But the trouble is, as I have told you before, you haven't believed even though you have seen me. [37] But some will come to me—those the Father has given me—and I will never, never reject them. [38] For I have come here from heaven to do the will of God who sent me, not to have my own way. [39] And this is the will of God, that I should not lose even one of all those he has given me, but that I should raise them to eternal life at the Last Day. [40] For it is my Father's will that everyone who sees his Son and believes on him should have eternal life—that I should raise him at the Last Day."

[41] Then the Jews began to murmur against him because he claimed to be the Bread from heaven.

[42] "What?" they exclaimed. "Why, he is merely Jesus the son of Joseph, whose father and mother we know. What is this he is saying, that he came down from heaven?"

[43] But Jesus replied, "Don't murmur among yourselves about my saying that. [44] For no one can come to me unless the Father who sent me draws him to me, and at the Last Day I will cause all such to rise again from the dead. [45] As it is written in the Scriptures, 'They shall all be taught of God.' Those the Father speaks to, who learn the truth from him, will be attracted to me. [46] (Not that anyone actually sees the Father, for only I have seen him.)

[47] "How earnestly I tell you this—anyone who believes in me already has eternal life! [48-51] Yes, I am the Bread of Life! When your fathers in the wilderness ate bread from the skies, they all died. But the Bread from heaven gives eternal life to everyone who eats it. I am that Living Bread that came down out of heaven. Anyone eating this Bread shall live forever; this Bread is

---

c Literally, "and straightway the boat was at the land. . . ."   d Implied.   e Literally, "the Son of Man."

904

my flesh given to redeem humanity."

⁵² Then the Jews began arguing with each other about what he meant. "How can this man give us his flesh to eat?" they asked.

⁵³ So Jesus said it again, "With all the earnestness I possess I tell you this: Unless you eat the flesh of the Messiah^f and drink his blood, you cannot have eternal life within you. ⁵⁴ But anyone who does eat my flesh and drink my blood has eternal life, and I will raise him at the Last Day. ⁵⁵ For my flesh is the true food, and my blood is the true drink. ⁵⁶ Everyone who eats my flesh and drinks my blood is in me, and I in him. ⁵⁷ I live by the power of the living Father who sent me, and in the same way those who partake of me shall live because of me! ⁵⁸ I am the true Bread from heaven; and anyone who eats this Bread shall live forever, and not die as your fathers did—though they ate bread from heaven." ⁵⁹ (He preached this sermon in the synagogue in Capernaum.)

⁶⁰ Even his disciples said, "This is very hard to understand. Who can tell what he means?"

⁶¹ Jesus knew within himself that his disciples were complaining and said to them, "Does *this* offend you? ⁶² Then what will you think if you see me, the Messiah,^g return to heaven again? ⁶³ Only the Holy Spirit gives eternal life.^h Those born only once, with physical birth^i, will never receive this gift. But now I have told you how to get this true spiritual life. ⁶⁴ But some of you don't believe me." (For Jesus knew from the beginning who didn't believe and knew the one who would betray him.)

⁶⁵ And he remarked, "That is what I meant when I said that no one can come to me unless the Father attracts him to me."

⁶⁶ At this point many of his disciples turned away and deserted him.

⁶⁷ Then Jesus turned to the Twelve and asked, "Are you going too?"

⁶⁸ Simon Peter replied, "Master, to whom shall we go? You alone have the words that give eternal life, ⁶⁹ and we believe them and know you are the holy Son of

God."

⁷⁰ Then Jesus said, "I chose the twelve of you, and one is a devil." ⁷¹ He was speaking of Judas, son of Simon Iscariot, one of the Twelve, who would betray him.

7 AFTER THIS, JESUS went to Galilee, going from village to village, for he wanted to stay out of Judea where the Jewish leaders were plotting his death. ² But soon it was time for the Tabernacle Ceremonies, one of the annual Jewish holidays, ³ and Jesus' brothers urged him to go to Judea for the celebration.

"Go where more people can see your miracles!" they scoffed. ⁴ "You can't be famous when you hide like this! If you're so great, prove it to the world!" ⁵ For even his brothers didn't believe in him.

⁶ Jesus replied, "It is not the right time for me to go now. But you can go anytime and it will make no difference, ⁷ for the world can't hate you; but it does hate me, because I accuse it of sin and evil. ⁸ You go on, and I'll come later^a when it is the right time." ⁹ So he remained in Galilee.

¹⁰ But after his brothers had left for the celebration, then he went too, though secretly, staying out of the public eye. ¹¹ The Jewish leaders tried to find him at the celebration and kept asking if anyone had seen him. ¹² There was a lot of discussion about him among the crowds. Some said, "He's a wonderful man," while others said, "No, he's duping the public." ¹³ But no one had the courage to speak out for him in public for fear of reprisals from the Jewish leaders.

¹⁴ Then, midway through the festival, Jesus went up to the Temple and preached openly. ¹⁵ The Jewish leaders were surprised when they heard him. "How can he know so much when he's never been to our schools?" they asked.

¹⁶ So Jesus told them, "I'm not teaching you my own thoughts, but those of God who sent me. ¹⁷ If any of you really determines to do God's will, then you will certainly know whether my teaching is from God or is merely my own. ¹⁸ Anyone presenting his own ideas is looking for praise

---

f Implied. Literally, "Son of Man."   g Literally, "the Son of Man."   h Literally, "It is the Spirit who quickens."   i See John 1:13. Literally, "the flesh profits nothing."   7a Literally, "I go not up (yet) unto this feast." The word "yet" is included in the text of many ancient manuscripts.

for himself, but anyone seeking to honor the one who sent him is a good and true person. [19] None of *you* obeys the laws of Moses! So why pick on *me* for breaking them? Why kill *me* for this?"

[20] The crowd replied, "You're out of your mind! Who's trying to kill you?"

[21,22,23] Jesus replied, "I worked on the Sabbath by healing a man, and you were surprised. But you work on the Sabbath, too, whenever you obey Moses' law of circumcision (actually, however, this tradition of circumcision is older than the Mosaic law); for if the correct time for circumcising your children falls on the Sabbath, you go ahead and do it, as you should. So why should I be condemned for making a man completely well on the Sabbath? [24] Think this through and you will see that I am right."

[25] Some of the people who lived there in Jerusalem said among themselves, "Isn't this the man they are trying to kill? [26] But here he is preaching in public, and they say nothing to him. Can it be that our leaders have learned, after all, that he really is the Messiah? [27] But how could he be? For we know where this man was born; when Christ comes, he will just appear and no one will know where he comes from."

[28] So Jesus, in a sermon in the Temple, called out, "Yes, you know me and where I was born and raised, but I am the representative of one you don't know, and he is Truth. [29] I know him because I was with him, and he sent me to you."

[30] Then the Jewish leaders sought to arrest him; but no hand was laid on him, for God's time had not yet come.

[31] Many among the crowds at the Temple believed on him. "After all," they said, "what miracles do you expect the Messiah to do that this man hasn't done?"

[32] When the Pharisees heard that the crowds were in this mood, they and the chief priests sent officers to arrest Jesus. [33] But Jesus told them, "[Not yet![b]] I am to be here a little longer. Then I shall return to the one who sent me. [34] You will search for me but not find me. And you won't be able to come where I am!"

[35] The Jewish leaders were puzzled by this statement. "Where is he planning to go?" they asked. "Maybe he is thinking of leaving the country and going as a missionary among the Jews in other lands, or maybe even to the Gentiles! [36] What does he mean about our looking for him and not being able to find him, and, 'You won't be able to come where I am'?"

[37] On the last day, the climax of the holidays, Jesus shouted to the crowds, "If anyone is thirsty, let him come to me and drink. [38] For the Scriptures declare that rivers of living water shall flow from the inmost being of anyone who believes in me." [39] (He was speaking of the Holy Spirit, who would be given to everyone believing in him; but the Spirit had not yet been given, because Jesus had not yet returned to his glory in heaven.)

[40] When the crowds heard him say this, some of them declared, "This man surely is the prophet who will come just before the Messiah." [41,42] Others said, "He *is* the Messiah." Still others, "But he *can't* be! Will the Messiah come from *Galilee?* For the Scriptures clearly state that the Messiah will be born of the royal line of David, in *Bethlehem,* the village where David was born." [43] So the crowd was divided about him. [44] And some wanted him arrested, but no one touched him.

[45] The Temple police who had been sent to arrest him returned to the chief priests and Pharisees. "Why didn't you bring him in?" they demanded.

[46] "He says such wonderful things!" they mumbled. "We've never heard anything like it."

[47] "So you also have been led astray?" the Pharisees mocked. [48] "Is there a single one of us Jewish rulers or Pharisees who believes he is the Messiah? [49] These stupid crowds do, yes; but what do they know about it? A curse upon them anyway!"[c]

[50] Then Nicodemus spoke up. (Remember him? He was the Jewish leader who came secretly to interview Jesus.) [51] "Is it legal to convict a man before he is even tried?" he asked.

[52] They replied, "Are you a wretched

---

b Implied.   c Literally, "This multitude is accursed."

Galilean too? Search the Scriptures and see for yourself—no prophets will come from Galilee!" [53d] Then the meeting broke up and everybody went home.

8 JESUS RETURNED TO the Mount of Olives, [2] but early the next morning he was back again at the Temple. A crowd soon gathered, and he sat down and talked to them. [3] As he was speaking, the Jewish leaders and Pharisees brought a woman caught in adultery and placed her out in front of the staring crowd.

[4] "Teacher," they said to Jesus, "this woman was caught in the very act of adultery. [5] Moses' law says to kill her. What about it?"

[6] They were trying to trap him into saying something they could use against him, but Jesus stooped down and wrote in the dust with his finger. [7] They kept demanding an answer, so he stood up again and said, "All right, hurl the stones at her until she dies. But only he who never sinned may throw the first!"

[8] Then he stooped down again and wrote some more in the dust. [9] And the Jewish leaders slipped away one by one, beginning with the eldest, until only Jesus was left in front of the crowd with the woman.

[10] Then Jesus stood up again and said to her, "Where are your accusers? Didn't even one of them condemn you?"

[11] "No, sir," she said.

And Jesus said, "Neither do I. Go and sin no more."

[12] Later, in one of his talks, Jesus said to the people, "I am the Light of the world. So if you follow me, you won't be stumbling through the darkness, for living light will flood your path."

[13] The Pharisees replied, "You are boasting—and lying!"

[14] Jesus told them, "These claims are true even though I make them concerning myself. For I know where I came from and where I am going, but you don't know this about me. [15] You pass judgment on me without knowing the facts. I am not judging you now; [16] but if I were, it would be an absolutely correct judgment in every respect, for I have with me the Father who sent me. [17] Your laws say that if two men agree on something that has happened, their witness is accepted as fact. [18] Well, I am one witness, and my Father who sent me is the other."

[19] "Where is your father?" they asked.

Jesus answered, "You don't know who I am, so you don't know who my Father is. If you knew me, then you would know him too."

[20] Jesus made these statements while in the section of the Temple known as the Treasury. But he was not arrested, for his time had not yet run out.

[21] Later he said to them again, "I am going away; and you will search for me, and die in your sins. And you cannot come where I am going."

[22] The Jews asked, "Is he planning suicide? What does he mean, 'You cannot come where I am going'?"

[23] Then he said to them, "You are from below; I am from above. You are of this world; I am not. [24] That is why I said that you will die in your sins; for unless you believe that I am the Messiah, the Son of God, you will die in your sins."

[25] "Tell us who you are," they demanded.

He replied, "I am the one I have always claimed to be. [26] I could condemn you for much and teach you much, but I won't, for I say only what I am told to by the one who sent me; and he is Truth." [27] But they still didn't understand that he was talking to them about God.[a]

[28] So Jesus said, "When you have killed the Messiah,[b] then you will realize that I am he and that I have not been telling you my own ideas, but have spoken what the Father taught me. [29] And he who sent me is with me—he has not deserted me—for I always do those things that are pleasing to him."

[30,31] Then many of the Jewish leaders who heard him say these things began believing him to be the Messiah.

Jesus said to them, "You are truly my disciples if you live as I tell you to, [32] and

---

d Most ancient manuscripts omit John 7:53–8:11. have lifted up the Son of Man."   8a Literally, "the Father."   b Literally, "when you

you will know the truth, and the truth will set you free."

³³ "But we are descendants of Abraham," they said, "and have never been slaves to any man on earth! What do you mean, 'set free'?"

³⁴ Jesus replied, "You are slaves of sin, every one of you. ³⁵ And slaves don't have rights, but the Son has every right there is! ³⁶ So if the Son sets you free, you will indeed be free— ³⁷ (Yes, I realize that you are descendants of Abraham!) And yet some of you are trying to kill me because my message does not find a home within your hearts. ³⁸ I am telling you what I saw when I was with my Father. But you are following the advice of *your* father."

³⁹ "Our father is Abraham," they declared.

"No!" Jesus replied, "for if he were, you would follow his good example. ⁴⁰ But instead you are trying to kill me—and all because I told you the truth I heard from God. Abraham wouldn't do a thing like that! ⁴¹ No, you are obeying your *real* father when you act that way."

They replied, "We were not born out of wedlock—our true Father is God himself."

⁴² Jesus told them, "If that were so, then you would love me, for I have come to you from God. I am not here on my own, but he sent me. ⁴³ Why can't you understand what I am saying? It is because you are prevented from doing so! ⁴⁴ For you are the children of your father the devil and you love to do the evil things he does. He was a murderer from the beginning and a hater of truth—there is not an iota of truth in him. When he lies, it is perfectly normal; for he is the father of liars. ⁴⁵ And so when I tell the truth, you just naturally don't believe it!

⁴⁶ "Which of you can truthfully accuse me of one single sin? [No one!ᶜ] And since I am telling you the truth, why don't you believe me? ⁴⁷ Anyone whose Father is God listens gladly to the words of God. Since you don't, it proves you aren't his children."

⁴⁸ "You Samaritan! Foreigner! Devil!" the Jewish leaders snarled. "Didn't we say all along you were possessed by a demon?"

⁴⁹ "No," Jesus said, "I have no demon in me. For I honor my Father—and you dishonor me. ⁵⁰ And though I have no wish to make myself great, God wants this for me and judges [those who reject meᵈ]. ⁵¹ With all the earnestness I have I tell you this—no one who obeys me shall ever die!"

⁵² The leaders of the Jews said, "Now we know you are possessed by a demon. Even Abraham and the mightiest prophets died, and yet you say that obeying you will keep a man from dying! ⁵³ So you are greater than our father Abraham, who died? And greater than the prophets, who died? Who do you think you are?" ⁵⁴ Then Jesus told them this: "If I am merely boasting about myself, it doesn't count. But it is my Father —and you claim him as your God—who is saying these glorious things about me. ⁵⁵ But you do not even know him. I do. If I said otherwise, I would be as great a liar as you! But it is true—I know him and fully obey him. ⁵⁶ Your father Abraham rejoiced to see my day. He knew I was coming and was glad."

⁵⁷ *The Jewish leaders:* "You aren't even fifty years old—sure, you've seen Abraham!"

⁵⁸ *Jesus:* "The absolute truth is that I was in existence before Abraham was ever born!"

⁵⁹ At that point the Jewish leaders picked up stones to kill him. But Jesus was hidden from them, and walked past them and left the Temple.

9 AS HE WAS walking along, he saw a man blind from birth.

² "Master," his disciples asked him, "why was this man born blind? Was it a result of his own sins or those of his parents?"

³ "Neither," Jesus answered. "But to demonstrate the power of God. ⁴ All of us must quickly carry out the tasks assigned us by the one who sent me, for there is little time left before the night falls and all work comes to an end. ⁵ But while I am still here in the world, I give it my light."

⁶ Then he spat on the ground and made mud from the spittle and smoothed the mud

c Implied.   d Implied. Literally, "There is one who seeks and judges."

over the blind man's eyes, [7] and told him, "Go and wash in the Pool of Siloam" (the word "Siloam" means "Sent"). So the man went where he was sent and washed and came back seeing!

[8] His neighbors and others who knew him as a blind beggar asked each other, "Is this the same fellow—that beggar?"

[9] Some said yes, and some said no. "It can't be the same man," they thought, "but he surely looks like him!"

And the beggar said, "I *am* the same man!"

[10] Then they asked him how in the world he could see. What had happened?

[11] And he told them, "A man they call Jesus made mud and smoothed it over my eyes and told me to go to the Pool of Siloam and wash off the mud. I did, and I can see!"

[12] "Where is he now?" they asked.

"I don't know," he replied.

[13] Then they took the man to the Pharisees. [14] Now as it happened, this all occurred on a Sabbath.[a] [15] Then the Pharisees asked him all about it. So he told them how Jesus had smoothed the mud over his eyes, and when it was washed away, he could see!

[16] Some of them said, "Then this fellow Jesus is not from God, because he is working on the Sabbath."

Others said, "But how could an ordinary sinner do such miracles?" So there was a deep division of opinion among them.

[17] Then the Pharisees turned on the man who had been blind and demanded, "This man who opened your eyes—who do you say he is?"

"I think he must be a prophet sent from God," the man replied.

[18] The Jewish leaders wouldn't believe he had been blind, until they called in his parents [19] and asked them, "Is this your son? Was he born blind? If so, how can he see?"

[20] His parents replied, "We know this is our son and that he was born blind, [21] but we don't know what to make him see, or who did it. He is old enough to speak for himself. Ask him."

[22,23] They said this in fear of the Jewish leaders who had announced that anyone

saying Jesus was the Messiah would be excommunicated.

[24] So for the second time they called in the man who had been blind and told him, "Give the glory to God, not to Jesus, for we know Jesus is an evil person."

[25] "I don't know whether he is good or bad," the man replied, "but I know this: *I was blind, and now I see!*"

[26] "But what did he do?" they asked. "How did he heal you?"

[27] "Look!" the man exclaimed. "I told you once; didn't you listen? Why do you want to hear it again? Do you want to become his disciples too?"

[28] Then they cursed him and said, "You are his disciple, but we are disciples of Moses. [29] We know God has spoken to Moses, but as for this fellow, we don't know anything about him."

[30] "Why, that's very strange!" the man replied. "He can heal blind men, and yet you don't know anything about him! [31] Well, God doesn't listen to evil men, but he has open ears to those who worship him and do his will. [32] Since the world began there has never been anyone who could open the eyes of someone born blind. [33] If this man were not from God, he couldn't do it."

[34] "You illegitimate bastard,[b] you!" they shouted. "Are you trying to teach *us?*" And they threw him out.

[35] When Jesus heard what had happened, he found the man and said, "Do you believe in the Messiah?"[c]

[36] The man answered, "Who is he, sir, for I want to."

[37] "You have seen him," Jesus said, "and he is speaking to you!"

[38] "Yes, Lord," the man said, "I believe!" And he worshiped Jesus.

[39] Then Jesus told him, "I have come into the world to give sight to those who are spiritually blind and to show those who think they see that they are blind."

[40] The Pharisees who were standing there asked, "Are you saying we are blind?"

[41] "If you were blind, you wouldn't be guilty," Jesus replied. "But your guilt re-

---

a i.e., on Saturday, the weekly Jewish holy day when all work was forbidden.　　b Literally, "You were altogether born in sin."　　c Literally, "the Son of Man."

mains because you claim to know what you are doing.

10 "ANYONE REFUSING TO walk through the gate into a sheepfold, who sneaks over the wall, must surely be a thief! [2] For a shepherd comes through the gate. [3] The gatekeeper opens the gate for him, and the sheep hear his voice and come to him; and he calls his own sheep by name and leads them out. [4] He walks ahead of them; and they follow him, for they recognize his voice. [5] They won't follow a stranger but will run from him, for they don't recognize his voice."

[6] Those who heard Jesus use this illustration didn't understand what he meant, [7] so he explained it to them.

"I am the Gate for the sheep," he said. [8] "All others who came before me were thieves and robbers. But the true sheep did not listen to them. [9] Yes, I am the Gate. Those who come in by way of the Gate will be saved and will go in and out and find green pastures. [10] The thief's purpose is to steal, kill and destroy. My purpose is to give life in all its fullness.

[11] "I am the Good Shepherd. The Good Shepherd lays down his life for the sheep. [12] A hired man will run when he sees a wolf coming and will leave the sheep, for they aren't his and he isn't their shepherd. And so the wolf leaps on them and scatters the flock. [13] The hired man runs because he is hired and has no real concern for the sheep.

[14] "I am the Good Shepherd and know my own sheep, and they know me, [15] just as my Father knows me and I know the Father; and I lay down my life for the sheep. [16] I have other sheep, too, in another fold. I must bring them also, and they will heed my voice; and there will be one flock with one Shepherd.

[17] "The Father loves me because I lay down my life that I may have it back again. [18] No one can kill me without my consent—I lay down my life voluntarily. For I have the right and power to lay it down when I want to and also the right and power to take it again. For the Father has given

me this right."

[19] When he said these things, the Jewish leaders were again divided in their opinions about him. [20] Some of them said, "He has a demon or else is crazy. Why listen to a man like that?"

[21] Others said, "This doesn't sound to us like a man possessed by a demon! Can a demon open the eyes of blind men?"

[22,23] It was winter,[a] and Jesus was in Jerusalem at the time of the Dedication Celebration. He was at the Temple, walking through the section known as Solomon's Hall. [24] The Jewish leaders surrounded him and asked, "How long are you going to keep us in suspense? If you are the Messiah, tell us plainly."

[25] "I have already told you,[b] and you don't believe me," Jesus replied. "The proof is in the miracles I do in the name of my Father. [26] But you don't believe me because you are not part of my flock. [27] My sheep recognize my voice, and I know them, and they follow me. [28] I give them eternal life and they shall never perish. No one shall snatch them away from me, [29] for my Father has given them to me, and he is more powerful than anyone else, so no one can kidnap them from me. [30] I and the Father are one."

[31] Then again the Jewish leaders picked up stones to kill him.

[32] Jesus said, "At God's direction I have done many a miracle to help the people. For which one are you killing me?"

[33] They replied, "Not for any good work, but for blasphemy; you, a mere man, have declared yourself to be God."

[34,35,36] "In your own Law it says that men are gods!" he replied. "So if the Scripture, which cannot be untrue, speaks of those as gods to whom the message of God came, do you call it blasphemy when the one sanctified and sent into the world by the Father says, 'I am the Son of God'? [37] Don't believe me unless I do miracles of God. [38] But if I do, believe them even if you don't believe me. Then you will become convinced that the Father is in me, and I in the Father."

[39] Once again they started to arrest him. But he walked away and left them, [40] and

---

a December 25 was the usual date for this celebration of the cleansing of the Temple.   b Chapter 5:19; 8:36, 56, 58, etc.

went beyond the Jordan River to stay near the place where John was first baptizing. ⁴¹ And many followed him.

"John didn't do miracles," they remarked to one another, "but all his predictions concerning this man have come true." ⁴² And many came to the decision that he was the Messiah.ᶜ

11 DO YOU REMEMBER Mary, who poured the costly perfume on Jesus' feet and wiped them with her hair?ᵃ Well, her brother Lazarus, who lived in Bethany with Mary and her sister Martha, was sick. ³ So the two sisters sent a message to Jesus telling him, "Sir, your good friend is very, very sick."

⁴ But when Jesus heard about it he said, "The purpose of his illness is not death, but for the glory of God. I, the Son of God, will receive glory from this situation."

⁵ Although Jesus was very fond of Martha, Mary, and Lazarus, ⁶ he stayed where he was for the next two days and made no move to go to them. ⁷ Finally, after the two days, he said to his disciples, "Let's go to Judea."

⁸ But his disciples objected. "Master," they said, "only a few days ago the Jewish leaders in Judea were trying to kill you. Are you going there again?"

⁹ Jesus replied, "There are twelve hours of daylight every day, and during every hour of it a man can walk safely and not stumble. ¹⁰ Only at night is there danger of a wrong step, because of the dark." ¹¹ Then he said, "Our friend Lazarus has gone to sleep, but now I will go and waken him!"

¹²,¹³ The disciples, thinking Jesus meant Lazarus was having a good night's rest, said, "That means he is getting better!" But Jesus meant Lazarus had died.

¹⁴ Then he told them plainly, "Lazarus is dead. ¹⁵ And for your sake, I am glad I wasn't there, for this will give you another opportunity to believe in me. Come, let's go to him."

¹⁶ Thomas, nicknamed "The Twin," said to his fellow disciples, "Let's go too—and die with him."

¹⁷ When they arrived at Bethany, they were told that Lazarus had already been in his tomb for four days. ¹⁸ Bethany was only a couple of miles down the road from Jerusalem, ¹⁹ and many of the Jewish leaders had come to pay their respects and to console Martha and Mary on their loss. ²⁰ When Martha got word that Jesus was coming, she went to meet him. But Mary stayed at home.

²¹ Martha said to Jesus, "Sir, if you had been here, my brother wouldn't have died. ²² And even now it's not too late, for I know that God will bring my brother back to life again, if you will only ask him to."

²³ Jesus told her, "Your brother will come back to life again."

²⁴ "Yes," Martha said, "when everyone else does, on Resurrection Day."

²⁵ Jesus told her, "I am the one who raises the dead and gives them life again. Anyone who believes in me, even though he dies like anyone else, shall live again. ²⁶ He is given eternal life for believing in me and shall never perish. Do you believe this, Martha?"

²⁷ "Yes, Master," she told him. "I believe you are the Messiah, the Son of God, the one we have so long awaited."

²⁸ Then she left him and returned to Mary and, calling her aside from the mourners, told her, "He is here and wants to see you." ²⁹ So Mary went to him at once.

³⁰ Now Jesus had stayed outside the village, at the place where Martha met him. ³¹ When the Jewish leaders who were at the house trying to console Mary saw her leave so hastily, they assumed she was going to Lazarus' tomb to weep; so they followed her.

³² When Mary arrived where Jesus was, she fell down at his feet, saying, "Sir, if you had been here, my brother would still be alive."

³³ When Jesus saw her weeping and the Jewish leaders wailing with her, he was moved with indignation and deeply troubled. ³⁴ "Where is he buried?" he asked them.

They told him, "Come and see." ³⁵ Tears came to Jesus' eyes.

³⁶ "They were close friends," the Jewish

---

c Literally, "Many believed on him there."   11a See John 12:3.

leaders said. "See how much he loved him."

[37,38] But some said, "This fellow healed a blind man—why couldn't he keep Lazarus from dying?" And again Jesus was moved with deep anger. Then they came to the tomb. It was a cave with a heavy stone rolled across its door.

[39] "Roll the stone aside," Jesus told them.

But Martha, the dead man's sister, said, "By now the smell will be terrible, for he has been dead four days."

[40] "But didn't I tell you that you will see a wonderful miracle from God if you believe?" Jesus asked her.

[41] So they rolled the stone aside. Then Jesus looked up to heaven and said, "Father, thank you for hearing me. [42] (You always hear me, of course, but I said it because of all these people standing here, so that they will believe you sent me.)" [43] Then he shouted, "Lazarus, come out!"

[44] And Lazarus came—bound up in the gravecloth, his face muffled in a head swath. Jesus told them, "Unwrap him and let him go!"

[45] And so at last many of the Jewish leaders who were with Mary and saw it happen, finally believed on him. [46] But some went away to the Pharisees and reported it to them.

[47] Then the chief priests and Pharisees convened a council to discuss the situation. "What are we going to do?" they asked each other. "For this man certainly does miracles. [48] If we let him alone the whole nation will follow him—and then the Roman army will come and kill us and take over the Jewish government."

[49] And one of them, Caiaphas, who was High Priest that year, said, "You stupid idiots— [50] let this one man die for the people—why should the whole nation perish?"

[51] This prophecy that Jesus should die for the entire nation came from Caiaphas in his position as High Priest—he didn't think of it by himself, but was inspired to say it. [52] It was a prediction that Jesus' death would not be for Israel only, but for all the children of God scattered around the world. [53] So from that time on the Jewish leaders began plotting Jesus' death.

[54] Jesus now stopped his public ministry and left Jerusalem; he went to the edge of the desert, to the village of Ephraim, and stayed there with his disciples.

[55] The Passover, a Jewish holy day, was near, and many country people arrived in Jerusalem several days early so that they could go through the cleansing ceremony before the Passover began. [56] They wanted to see Jesus, and as they gossiped in the Temple, they asked each other, "What do you think? Will he come for the Passover?" [57] Meanwhile the chief priests and Pharisees had publicly announced that anyone seeing Jesus must report him immediately so that they could arrest him.

12 SIX DAYS BEFORE the Passover ceremonies began, Jesus arrived in Bethany where Lazarus was—the man he had brought back to life. [2] A banquet was prepared in Jesus' honor. Martha served, and Lazarus sat at the table with him. [3] Then Mary took a jar of costly perfume made from essence of nard, and anointed Jesus' feet with it and wiped them with her hair. And the house was filled with fragrance.

[4] But Judas Iscariot, one of his disciples—the one who would betray him—said, [5] "That perfume was worth a fortune. It should have been sold and the money given to the poor." [6] Not that he cared for the poor, but he was in charge of the disciples' funds and often dipped into them for his own use!

[7] Jesus replied, "Let her alone. She did it in preparation for my burial. [8] You can always help the poor, but I won't be with you very long."

[9] When the ordinary people of Jerusalem heard of his arrival, they flocked to see him and also to see Lazarus—the man who had come back to life again. [10] Then the chief priests decided to kill Lazarus too, [11] for it was because of him that many of the Jewish leaders had deserted and believed in Jesus as their Messiah.

[12] The next day, the news that Jesus was on the way to Jerusalem swept through the city, and a huge crowd of Passover visitors [13] took palm branches and went down the road to meet him, shouting, "The Savior! God bless the King of Israel! Hail to God's

Ambassador!"

¹⁴ Jesus rode along on a young donkey, fulfilling the prophecy that said: ¹⁵ "Don't be afraid of your King, people of Israel, for he will come to you meekly, sitting on a donkey's colt!"

¹⁶ (His disciples didn't realize at the time that this was a fulfillment of prophecy; but after Jesus returned to his glory in heaven, then they noticed how many prophecies of Scripture had come true before their eyes.)

¹⁷ And those in the crowd who had seen Jesus call Lazarus back to life were telling all about it. ¹⁸ That was the main reason why so many went out to meet him— because they had heard about this mighty miracle.

¹⁹ Then the Pharisees said to each other, "We've lost. Look—the whole world has gone after him!"

²⁰ Some Greeks who had come to Jerusalem to attend the Passover ²¹ paid a visit to Philip,ᵃ who was from Bethsaida, and said, "Sir, we want to meet Jesus." ²² Philip told Andrew about it, and they went together to ask Jesus.

²³,²⁴ Jesus replied that the time had come for him to return to his glory in heaven, and that "I must fall and die like a kernel of wheat that falls into the furrows of the earth. Unless I die I will be alone—a single seed. But my death will produce many new wheat kernels—a plentiful harvest of new lives. ²⁵ If you love your life down here —you will lose it. If you despise your life down here—you will exchange it for eternal glory.

²⁶ "If these Greeksᵇ want to be my disciples, tell them to come and follow me, for my servants must be where I am. And if they follow me, the Father will honor them. ²⁷ Now my soul is deeply troubled. Shall I pray, 'Father, save me from what lies ahead'? But that is the very reason why I came! ²⁸ Father, bring glory and honor to your name."

Then a voice spoke from heaven saying, "I have already done this, and I will do it again." ²⁹ When the crowd heard the voice,

some of them thought it was thunder, while others declared an angel had spoken to him.

³⁰ Then Jesus told them, "The voice was for your benefit, not mine. ³¹ The time of judgment for the world has come—and the time when Satan,ᶜ the prince of this world, shall be cast out. ³² And when I am lifted up [on the crossᵈ], I will draw everyone to me." ³³ He said this to indicate how he was going to die.

³⁴ "Die?" asked the crowd. "We understood that the Messiah would live forever and never die. Why are you saying he will die? What Messiah are you talking about?"

³⁵ Jesus replied, "My light will shine out for you just a little while longer. Walk in it while you can, and go where you want to go before the darkness falls, for then it will be too late for you to find your way. ³⁶ Make use of the Light while there is still time; then you will become light bearers."ᵉ After saying these things, Jesus went away and was hidden from them.

³⁷ But despite all the miracles he had done, most of the people would not believe he was the Messiah. ³⁸ This is exactly what Isaiah the prophet had predicted: "Lord, who will believe us? Who will accept God's mighty miracles as proof?"ᶠ ³⁹ But they couldn't believe, for as Isaiah also said: ⁴⁰ "Godᵍ has blinded their eyes and hardened their hearts so that they can neither see nor understand nor turn to me to heal them." ⁴¹ Isaiah was referring to Jesus when he made this prediction, for he had seen a vision of the Messiah's glory.

⁴² However, even many of the Jewish leaders believed him to be the Messiah but wouldn't admit it to anyone because of their fear that the Pharisees would excommunicate them from the synagogue; ⁴³ for they loved the praise of men more than the praise of God.

⁴⁴ Jesus shouted to the crowds, "If you trust me, you are really trusting God. ⁴⁵ For when you see me, you are seeing the one who sent me. ⁴⁶ I have come as a Light to shine in this dark world, so that all who put their trust in me will no longer wander in

---

a Philip's name was Greek, though he was a Jew.   b Literally, "if any man."   c Literally, "prince of this world." See 2 Corinthians 4:4, and Ephesians 2:2 and 6:12.   d Implied.   e Literally, "sons of light."   f Literally, "To whom has the arm of the Lord been revealed?" Isaiah 53:1. g Literally, "He." The Greek here is a very free rendering, or paraphrase, of Isaiah 6:10.

the darkness. ⁴⁷ If anyone hears me and doesn't obey me, I am not his judge—for I have come to save the world and not to judge it. ⁴⁸ But all who reject me and my message will be judged at the Day of Judgment by the truths I have spoken. ⁴⁹ For these are not my own ideas, but I have told you what the Father said to tell you. ⁵⁰ And I know his instructions lead to eternal life; so whatever he tells me to say, I say!"

13 JESUS KNEW ON the evening of Passover Day that it would be his last night on earth before returning to his Father. During supper the devil had already suggested to Judas Iscariot, Simon's son, that this was the night to carry out his plan to betray Jesus. Jesus knew that the Father had given him everything and that he had come from God and would return to God. And how he loved his disciples! ⁴ So he got up from the supper table, took off his robe, wrapped a towel around his loins,ᵃ ⁵ poured water into a basin, and began to wash the disciples' feet and to wipe them with the towel he had around him.

⁶ When he came to Simon Peter, Peter said to him, "Master, you shouldn't be washing our feet like this!"

⁷ Jesus replied, "You don't understand now why I am doing it; some day you will."

⁸ "No," Peter protested, "you shall never wash my feet!"

"But if I don't, you can't be my partner," Jesus replied.

⁹ Simon Peter exclaimed, "Then wash my hands and head as well—not just my feet!"

¹⁰ Jesus replied, "One who has bathed all over needs only to have his feet washed to be entirely clean. Now you are clean—but that isn't true of everyone here." ¹¹ For Jesus knew who would betray him. That is what he meant when he said, "Not all of you are clean."

¹² After washing their feet he put on his robe again and sat down and asked, "Do you understand what I was doing? ¹³ You

call me 'Master' and 'Lord,' and you do well to say it, for it is true. ¹⁴ And since I, the Lord and Teacher, have washed your feet, you ought to wash each other's feet. ¹⁵ I have given you an example to follow: do as I have done to you. ¹⁶ How true it is that a servant is not greater than his master. Nor is the messenger more important than the one who sends him. ¹⁷ You know these things—now do them! That is the path of blessing.

¹⁸ "I am not saying these things to all of you; I know so well each one of you I chose. The Scripture declares, 'One who eats supper with me will betray me,' and this will soon come true. ¹⁹ I tell you this now so that when it happens, you will believe on me.

²⁰ "Truly, anyone welcoming my messenger is welcoming me. And to welcome me is to welcome the Father who sent me."

²¹ Now Jesus was in great anguish of spirit and exclaimed, "Yes, it is true—one of you will betray me." ²² The disciples looked at each other, wondering whom he could mean. ²³ Since Iᵇ was sitting nextᶜ to Jesus at the table, being his closest friend, ²⁴ Simon Peter motioned to me to ask him who it was who would do this terrible deed. ²⁵ So I turnedᵈ and asked him, "Lord, who is it?"

²⁶ He told me, "It is the one I honor by giving the bread dipped in the sauce."ᵉ

And when he had dipped it, he gave it to Judas, son of Simon Iscariot. ²⁷ As soon as Judas had eaten it, Satan entered into him. Then Jesus told him, "Hurry—do it now."

²⁸ None of the others at the table knew what Jesus meant. ²⁹ Some thought that since Judas was their treasurer, Jesus was telling him to go and pay for the food or to give some money to the poor. ³⁰ Judas left at once, going out into the night.

³¹ As soon as Judas left the room, Jesus said, "My time has come; the glory of God will soon surround me—and God shall receive great praise because of all that happens to me. ³² And God shall give me his

---

a As the lowliest of slaves would dress. b Literally, "There was one at the table." All commentators believe him to be John, the writer of this book. c Literally, "reclining on Jesus' bosom." The custom of the period was to recline around the table, leaning on the left elbow. John, next to Jesus, was at his side. d Literally, "leaning back against Jesus' chest," to whisper his inquiry. e Literally, "He it is for whom I shall dip the sop and give it him." The honored guest was thus singled out in the custom of that time.

own glory, and this so very soon. [33] Dear, dear children, how brief are these moments before I must go away and leave you! Then, though you search for me, you cannot come to me—just as I told the Jewish leaders.

[34] "And so I am giving a new commandment to you now—love each other just as much as I love you. [35] Your strong love for each other will prove to the world that you are my disciples."

[36] Simon Peter said, "Master, where are you going?"

And Jesus replied, "You can't go with me now; but you will follow me later."

[37] "But why can't I come now?" he asked, "for I am ready to die for you."

[38] Jesus answered, "Die for me? No— three times before the cock crows tomorrow morning, you will deny that you even know me!

14 "LET NOT YOUR heart be troubled. You are trusting God, now trust in me. [2,3] There are many homes up there where my Father lives, and I am going to prepare them for your coming. When everything is ready, then I will come and get you, so that you can always be with me where I am. If this weren't so, I would tell you plainly. [4] And you know where I am going and how to get there."

[5] "No, we don't," Thomas said. "We haven't any idea where you are going, so how can we know the way?"

[6] Jesus told him, "I am the Way—yes, and the Truth and the Life. No one can get to the Father except by means of me. [7] If you had known who I am, then you would have known who my Father is. From now on you know him—and have seen him!"

[8] Philip said, "Sir, show us the Father and we will be satisfied."

[9] Jesus replied, "Don't you even yet know who I am, Philip, even after all this time I have been with you? Anyone who has seen me has seen the Father! So why are you asking to see him? [10] Don't you believe that I am in the Father and the Father is in me? The words I say are not my own but are from my Father who lives in me. And he does his work through me. [11] Just believe

it—that I am in the Father and the Father is in me. Or else believe it because of the mighty miracles you have seen me do.

[12,13] "In solemn truth I tell you, anyone believing in me shall do the same miracles I have done, and even greater ones, because I am going to be with the Father. You can ask him for *anything,* using my name, and I will do it, for this will bring praise to the Father because of what I, the Son, will do for you. [14] Yes, ask *anything,* using my name, and I will do it!

[15,16] "If you love me, obey me; and I will ask the Father and he will give you another Comforter, and he will never leave you. [17] He is the Holy Spirit, the Spirit who leads into all truth. The world at large cannot receive him, for it isn't looking for him and doesn't recognize him. But you do, for he lives with you now and some day shall be in you. [18] No, I will not abandon you or leave you as orphans in the storm—I will come to you. [19] In just a little while I will be gone from the world, but I will still be present with you. For I will live again—and you will too. [20] When I come back to life again, you will know that I am in my Father, and you in me, and I in you. [21] The one who obeys me is the one who loves me; and because he loves me, my Father will love him; and I will too, and I will reveal myself to him."

[22] Judas (not Judas Iscariot, but his other disciple with that name) said to him, "Sir, why are you going to reveal yourself only to us disciples and not to the world at large?"

[23] Jesus replied, "Because I will only reveal myself to those who love me and obey me. The Father will love them too, and we will come to them and live with them. [24] Anyone who doesn't obey me doesn't love me. And remember, I am not making up this answer to your question! It is the answer given by the Father who sent me. [25] I am telling you these things now while I am still with you. [26] But when the Father sends the Comforter[a] instead of me[b]— and by the Comforter I mean the Holy Spirit—he will teach you much, as well as remind you of everything I myself have told you.

a Or, "Helper." b Literally, "in my name."

[27] "I am leaving you with a gift—peace of mind and heart! And the peace I give isn't fragile like the peace the world gives. So don't be troubled or afraid.[c] [28] Remember what I told you—I am going away, but I will come back to you again. If you really love me, you will be very happy for me, for now I can go to the Father, who is greater than I am. [29] I have told you these things before they happen so that when they do, you will believe [in me[c]].

[30] "I don't have much more time to talk to you, for the evil prince of this world approaches. He has no power over me, [31] but I will freely do what the Father requires of me so that the world will know that I love the Father. Come, let's be going.

15 "I AM THE true Vine, and my Father is the Gardener. [2] He lops off every branch that doesn't produce. And he prunes those branches that bear fruit for even larger crops. [3] He has already tended you by pruning you back for greater strength and usefulness by means of the commands I gave you. [4] Take care to live in me, and let me live in you. For a branch can't produce fruit when severed from the vine. Nor can you be fruitful apart from me.

[5] "Yes, I am the Vine; you are the branches. Whoever lives in me and I in him shall produce a large crop of fruit. For apart from me you can't do a thing. [6] If anyone separates from me, he is thrown away like a useless branch, withers, and is gathered into a pile with all the others and burned. [7] But if you stay in me and obey my commands, you may ask any request you like, and it will be granted! [8] My true disciples produce bountiful harvests. This brings great glory to my Father.

[9] "I have loved you even as the Father has loved me. Live within my love. [10] When you obey me you are living in my love, just as I obey my Father and live in his love. [11] I have told you this so that you will be filled with my joy. Yes, your cup of joy will overflow! [12] I demand that you love each other as much as I love you. [13] And here is how to measure it—the greatest love is shown when a person lays down his life for his friends; [14] and you are my friends if you obey me. [15] I no longer call you slaves, for a master doesn't confide in his slaves; now you are my friends, proved by the fact that I have told you everything the Father told me.

[16] "You didn't choose me! I chose you! I appointed you to go and produce lovely fruit always, so that no matter what you ask for from the Father, using my name, he will give it to you. [17] I demand that you love each other, [18] for you get enough hate from the world! But then, it hated me before it hated you. [19] The world would love you if you belonged to it; but you don't—for I chose you to come out of the world, and so it hates you. [20] Do you remember what I told you? 'A slave isn't greater than his master!' So since they persecuted me, naturally they will persecute you. And if they had listened to me, they would listen to you! [21] The people of the world will persecute you because you belong to me, for they don't know God who sent me.

[22] "They would not be guilty if I had not come and spoken to them. But now they have no excuse for their sin. [23] Anyone hating me is also hating my Father. [24] If I hadn't done such mighty miracles among them they would not be counted guilty. But as it is, they saw these miracles and yet they hated both of us—me and my Father. [25] This has fulfilled what the prophets said concerning the Messiah, 'They hated me without reason.'

[26] "But I will send you the Comforter—the Holy Spirit, the source of all truth. He will come to you from the Father and will tell you all about me. [27] And you also must tell everyone about me, because you have been with me from the beginning.

16 "I HAVE TOLD you these things so that you won't be staggered [by all that lies ahead.[a]] [2] For you will be excommunicated from the synagogues, and indeed the time is coming when those who kill you will think they are doing God a service. [3] This is because they have never known the Father or me. [4] Yes, I'm telling you these things now so that when they happen you

---

c Implied.　　16 a Implied.

will remember I warned you. I didn't tell you earlier because I was going to be with you for a while longer.

5 "But now I am going away to the one who sent me; and none of you seems interested in the purpose of my going; none wonders why.[b] 6 Instead you are only filled with sorrow. 7 But the fact of the matter is that it is best for you that I go away, for if I don't, the Comforter won't come. If I do, he will—for I will send him to you.

8 "And when he has come he will convince the world of its sin, and of the availability of God's goodness, and of deliverance from judgment.[c] 9 The world's sin is unbelief in me; 10 there is righteousness available because I go to the Father and you shall see me no more; 11 there is deliverance from judgment because the prince of this world has already been judged.

12 "Oh, there is so much more I want to tell you, but you can't understand it now. 13 When the Holy Spirit, who is truth, comes, he shall guide you into all truth, for he will not be presenting his own ideas, but will be passing on to you what he has heard. He will tell you about the future. 14 He shall praise me and bring me great honor by showing you my glory. 15 All the Father's glory is mine; this is what I mean when I say that he will show you my glory. 16 In just a little while I will be gone, and you will see me no more; but just a little while after that, and you will see me again!"

17,18 "Whatever is he saying?" some of his disciples asked. "What is this about 'going to the Father'? We don't know what he means."

19 Jesus realized they wanted to ask him so he said, "Are you asking yourselves what I mean? 20 The world will greatly rejoice over what is going to happen to me, and you will weep. But your weeping shall suddenly be turned to wonderful joy [when you see me again[d]]. 21 It will be the same joy as that of a woman in labor when her child is born—her anguish gives place to rapturous joy and the pain is forgotten. 22 You have

sorrow now, but I will see you again and then you will rejoice; and no one can rob you of that joy. 23 At that time you won't need to ask me for anything, for you can go directly to the Father and ask him, and he will give you what you ask for because you use my name. 24 You haven't tried this before, [but begin now[d]]. Ask, using my name, and you will receive, and your cup of joy will overflow.

25 "I have spoken of these matters very guardedly, but the time will come when this will not be necessary and I will tell you plainly all about the Father. 26 Then you will present your petitions over my signature![e] And I won't need to ask the Father to grant you these requests, 27 for the Father himself loves you dearly because you love me and believe that I came from the Father. 28 Yes, I came from the Father into the world and will leave the world and return to the Father."

29 "At last you are speaking plainly," his disciples said, "and not in riddles. 30 Now we understand that you know everything and don't need anyone to tell you anything.[f] From this we believe that you came from God."

31 "Do you finally believe this?" Jesus asked. 32 "But the time is coming—in fact, it is here—when you will be scattered, each one returning to his own home, leaving me alone. Yet I will not be alone, for the Father is with me. 33 I have told you all this so that you will have peace of heart and mind. Here on earth you will have many trials and sorrows; but cheer up, for I have overcome the world."

17 WHEN JESUS HAD finished saying all these things he looked up to heaven and said, "Father, the time has come. Reveal the glory of your Son so that he can give the glory back to you. 2 For you have given him authority over every man and woman in all the earth. He gives eternal life to each one you have given him. 3 And this is the way to have eternal life—by knowing

---

b Literally, "none of you is asking me whither I am going." The question had been asked before (John 13:36, 14:5), but apparently not in this deeper sense.   c Literally, "he will convict the world of sin and righteousness and judgment."   d Implied.   e Literally, "you shall ask *in my name.*" The above paraphrase is the modern equivalent of this idea, otherwise obscure.   f Literally, "and need not that anyone should ask you," i.e., discuss what is true.

you, the only true God, and Jesus Christ, the one you sent to earth! [4] I brought glory to you here on earth by doing everything you told me to. [5] And now, Father, reveal my glory as I stand in your presence, the glory we shared before the world began. [6] "I have told these men all about you. They were in the world, but then you gave them to me. Actually, they were always yours, and you gave them to me; and they have obeyed you. [7] Now they know that everything I have is a gift from you, [8] for I have passed on to them the commands you gave me; and they accepted them and know of a certainty that I came down to earth from you, and they believe you sent me.

[9] "My plea is not for the world but for those you have given me because they belong to you. [10] And all of them, since they are mine, belong to you; and you have given them back to me with everything else of yours, and so *they are my glory!* [11] Now I am leaving the world, and leaving them behind, and coming to you. Holy Father, keep them in your own care—all those you have given me—so that they will be united just as we are, with none missing. [12] During my time here I have kept safe within your family[a] all of these you gave me. I guarded them so that not one perished, except the son of hell, as the Scriptures foretold.

[13] "And now I am coming to you. I have told them many things while I was with them so that they would be filled with my joy. [14] I have given them your commands. And the world hates them because they don't fit in with it, just as I don't. [15] I'm not asking you to take them out of the world, but to keep them safe from Satan's power. [16] They are not part of this world any more than I am. [17] Make them pure and holy through teaching them your words of truth. [18] As you sent me into the world, I am sending them into the world, [19] and I consecrate myself to meet their need for growth in truth and holiness.

[20] "I am not praying for these alone but also for the future believers who will come to me because of the testimony of these. [21] My prayer for all of them is that they will be of one heart and mind, just as you and I are, Father—that just as you are in me and I am in you, so they will be in us, and the world will believe you sent me.

[22] "I have given them the glory you gave me—the glorious unity of being one, as we are— [23] I in them and you in me, all being perfected into one—so that the world will know you sent me and will understand that you love them as much as you love me. [24] Father, I want them with me—these you've given me—so that they can see my glory. You gave me the glory because you loved me before the world began!

[25] "O righteous Father, the world doesn't know you, but I do; and these disciples know you sent me. [26] And I have revealed you to them, and will keep on revealing you so that the mighty love you have for me may be in them, and I in them."

18 AFTER SAYING THESE things Jesus crossed the Kidron ravine with his disciples and entered a grove of olive trees. [2] Judas, the betrayer, knew this place, for Jesus had gone there many times with his disciples.

[3] The chief priests and Pharisees had given Judas a squad of soldiers and police to accompany him. Now with blazing torches, lanterns, and weapons they arrived at the olive grove.

[4,5] Jesus fully realized all that was going to happen to him. Stepping forward to meet them he asked, "Whom are you looking for?"

"Jesus of Nazareth," they replied.

"I am he," Jesus said. [6] And as he said it, they all fell backwards to the ground!

[7] Once more he asked them, "Whom are you searching for?"

And again they replied, "Jesus of Nazareth."

[8] "I told you I am he," Jesus said; "and since I am the one you are after, let these others go." [9] He did this to carry out the prophecy he had just made, "I have not lost a single one of those you gave me . . . ."

[10] Then Simon Peter drew a sword and slashed off the right ear of Malchus, the High Priest's servant.

---

a Literally, "kept in your name those whom you have given me."

¹¹ But Jesus said to Peter, "Put your sword away. Shall I not drink from the cup the Father has given me?"

¹² So the Jewish police, with the soldiers and their lieutenant, arrested Jesus and tied him. ¹³ First they took him to Annas, the father-in-law of Caiaphas, the High Priest that year. ¹⁴ Caiaphas was the one who told the other Jewish leaders, "Better that one should die for all." ¹⁵ Simon Peter followed along behind, as did another of the disciples who was acquainted with the High Priest. So that other disciple was permitted into the courtyard along with Jesus, ¹⁶ while Peter stood outside the gate. Then the other disciple spoke to the girl watching at the gate, and she let Peter in. ¹⁷ The girl asked Peter, "Aren't you one of Jesus' disciples?"

"No," he said, "I am not!"

¹⁸ The police and the household servants were standing around a fire they had made, for it was cold. And Peter stood there with them, warming himself.

¹⁹ Inside, the High Priest began asking Jesus about his followers and what he had been teaching them.

²⁰ Jesus replied, "What I teach is widely known, for I have preached regularly in the synagogue and Temple; I have been heard by all the Jewish leaders and teach nothing in private that I have not said in public. ²¹ Why are you asking me this question? Ask those who heard me. You have some of them here. They know what I said."

²² One of the soldiers standing there struck Jesus with his fist. "Is that the way to answer the High Priest?" he demanded.

²³ "If I lied, prove it," Jesus replied. "Should you hit a man for telling the truth?"

²⁴ Then Annas sent Jesus, bound, to Caiaphas the High Priest.

²⁵ Meanwhile, as Simon Peter was standing by the fire, he was asked again, "Aren't you one of his disciples?"

"Of course not," he replied.

²⁶ But one of the household slaves of the High Priest—a relative of the man whose ear Peter had cut off—asked, "Didn't I see you out there in the olive grove with Jesus?"

²⁷ Again Peter denied it. And immediately a rooster crowed.

²⁸ Jesus' trial before Caiaphas ended in the early hours of the morning. Next he was taken to the palace of the Roman governor. His accusers wouldn't go in themselves for that would "defile"ᵃ them, they said, and they wouldn't be allowed to eat the Passover lamb. ²⁹ So Pilate, the governor, went out to them and asked, "What is your charge against this man? What are you accusing him of doing?"

³⁰ "We wouldn't have arrested him if he weren't a criminal!" they retorted.

³¹ "Then take him away and judge him yourselves by your own laws," Pilate told them.

"But we want him crucified," they demanded, "and your approval is required."ᵇ

³² This fulfilled Jesus' prediction concerning the method of his execution.ᶜ

³³ Then Pilate went back into the palace and called for Jesus to be brought to him. "Are you the King of the Jews?" he asked him.

³⁴ " 'King' as *you* use the word or as the *Jews* use it?" Jesus asked.ᵈ

³⁵ "Am I a Jew?" Pilate retorted. "Your own people and their chief priests brought you here. Why? What have you done?"

³⁶ Then Jesus answered, "I am not an earthly king. If I were, my followers would have fought when I was arrested by the Jewish leaders. But my Kingdom is not of the world."

³⁷ Pilate replied, "But you are a king then?"

"Yes," Jesus said. "I was born for that purpose. And I came to bring truth to the world. All who love the truth are my followers."

---

a By Jewish law, entering the house of a Gentile was a serious offense.　　b Literally, "It is not lawful for us to put any man to death."　　c This prophecy is recorded in Matthew 20:19, which indicates his death by crucifixion, a practice under Roman law.　　d A paraphrase of this verse—that goes beyond the limits of this book's paraphrasing—would be, "Do you mean their King, or their Messiah?" If Pilate was asking as the Roman governor, he would be inquiring whether Jesus was setting up a rebel government. But the Jews were using the word "King" to mean their religious ruler, the Messiah. Literally this verse reads, "Are you saying this of yourself, or did someone else say it about me?"

[38] "What is truth?" Pilate exclaimed. Then he went out again to the people and told them, "He is not guilty of any crime. [39] But you have a custom of asking me to release someone from prison each year at Passover. So if you want me to, I'll release the 'King of the Jews.' "

[40] But they screamed back, "No! Not this man, but Barabbas!" Barabbas was a robber.

19 THEN PILATE LAID open Jesus' back with a leaded whip, [2] and the soldiers made a crown of thorns and placed it on his head and robed him in royal purple. [3] "Hail, 'King of the Jews!' " they mocked, and struck him with their fists.

[4] Pilate went outside again and said to the Jews, "I am going to bring him out to you now, but understand clearly that I find him *not guilty.*"

[5] Then Jesus came out wearing the crown of thorns and the purple robe. And Pilate said, "Behold the man!"

[6] At sight of him the chief priests and Jewish officials began yelling, "Crucify! Crucify!"

"*You* crucify him," Pilate said. "I find him *not guilty.*"

[7] They replied, "By our laws he ought to die because he called himself the Son of God."

[8] When Pilate heard this, he was more frightened than ever. [9] He took Jesus back into the palace again and asked him, "Where are you from?" but Jesus gave no answer.

[10] "You won't talk to me?" Pilate demanded. "Don't you realize that I have the power to release you or to crucify you?"

[11] Then Jesus said, "You would have no power at all over me unless it were given to you from above. So those[a] who brought me to you have the greater sin."

[12] Then Pilate tried to release him, but the Jewish leaders told him, "If you release this man, you are no friend of Caesar's. Anyone who declares himself a king is a rebel against Caesar."

[13] At these words Pilate brought Jesus out to them again and sat down at the judgment bench on the stone-paved platform.[b] [14] It was now about noon of the day before Passover.

And Pilate said to the Jews, "Here is your king!"

[15] "Away with him," they yelled. "Away with him—crucify him!"

"What? Crucify your king?" Pilate asked.

"We have no king but Caesar," the chief priests shouted back.

[16] Then Pilate gave Jesus to them to be crucified.

[17] So they had him at last, and he was taken out of the city, carrying his cross to the place known as "The Skull," in Hebrew, "Golgotha." [18] There they crucified him and two others with him, one on either side, with Jesus between them. [19] And Pilate posted a sign over him reading, "Jesus of Nazareth, the King of the Jews." [20] The place where Jesus was crucified was near the city; and the signboard was written in Hebrew, Latin, and Greek, so that many people read it.

[21] Then the chief priests said to Pilate, "Change it from 'The King of the Jews' to '*He said,* I am King of the Jews.' "

[22] Pilate replied, "What I have written, I have written. It stays exactly as it is."

[23,24] When the soldiers had crucified Jesus, they put his garments into four piles, one for each of them. But they said, "Let's not tear up his robe," for it was seamless. "Let's throw dice to see who gets it." This fulfilled the Scripture that says,

"They divided my clothes among them, and cast lots for my robe."[c]

[25] So that is what they did.

Standing near the cross were Jesus' mother, Mary, his aunt, the wife of Cleopas, and Mary Magdalene. [26] When Jesus saw his mother standing there beside me, his close friend,[d] he said to her, "He is your son."

[27] And to me[e] he said, "She is your mother!" And from then on I took her into my home.

[28] Jesus knew that everything was now

a Literally, "he."　　b Literally, "the judgment seat in a place that is called The Pavement, but in Hebrew, Gabbatha."　　c Psalm 22:18.　　d Literally, "standing by the disciple whom he loved." e Literally, "to the disciple."

finished, and to fulfill the Scriptures said, "I'm thirsty." ²⁹ A jar of sour wine was sitting there, so a sponge was soaked in it and put on a hyssop branch and held up to his lips.

³⁰ When Jesus had tasted^f it, he said, "It is finished," and bowed his head and dismissed his spirit.

³¹ The Jewish leaders didn't want the victims hanging there the next day, which was the Sabbath (and a very special Sabbath at that, for it was the Passover), so they asked Pilate to order the legs of the men broken to hasten death; then their bodies could be taken down. ³² So the soldiers came and broke the legs of the two men crucified with Jesus; ³³ but when they came to him, they saw that he was dead already, so they didn't break his. ³⁴ However, one of the soldiers pierced his side with a spear, and blood and water flowed out. ³⁵ I saw all this myself and have given an accurate report so that you also can believe.^g ³⁶,³⁷ The soldiers did this in fulfillment of the Scripture that says, "Not one of his bones shall be broken," and, "They shall look on him whom they pierced."

³⁸ Afterwards Joseph of Arimathea, who had been a secret disciple of Jesus for fear of the Jewish leaders, boldly asked Pilate for permission to take Jesus' body down; and Pilate told him to go ahead. So he came and took it away. ³⁹ Nicodemus, the man who had come to Jesus at night,^h came too, bringing a hundred pounds of embalming ointment made from myrrh and aloes. ⁴⁰ Together they wrapped Jesus' body in a long linen cloth saturated with the spices, as is the Jewish custom of burial. ⁴¹ The place of crucifixion was near a grove of trees,ⁱ where there was a new tomb, never used before. ⁴² And so, because of the need for haste before the Sabbath, and because the tomb was close at hand, they laid him there.

20 EARLY SUNDAY^a MORNING, while it was still dark, Mary Magdalene came to the tomb and found that the stone was rolled aside from the entrance.

² She ran and found Simon Peter and me^b and said, "They have taken the Lord's body out of the tomb, and I don't know where they have put him!"

³,⁴ We^c ran to the tomb to see; I^d outran Peter and got there first, ⁵ and stooped and looked in and saw the linen cloth lying there, but I didn't go in. ⁶ Then Simon Peter arrived and went on inside. He also noticed the cloth lying there, ⁷ while the swath that had covered Jesus' head was rolled up in a bundle and was lying at the side. ⁸ Then I went in too, and saw, and believed [that he had risen^e]— ⁹ for until then we hadn't realized that the Scriptures said he would come to life again!

¹⁰ We^f went on home, ¹¹ and by that time Mary had returned to the tomb^e and was standing outside crying. And as she wept, she stooped and looked in ¹² and saw two white-robed angels sitting at the head and foot of the place where the body of Jesus had been lying.

¹³ "Why are you crying?" the angels asked her.

"Because they have taken away my Lord," she replied, "and I don't know where they have put him."

¹⁴ She glanced over her shoulder and saw someone standing behind her. It was Jesus, but she didn't recognize him!

¹⁵ "Why are you crying?" he asked her. "Whom are you looking for?"

She thought he was the gardener. "Sir," she said, "if you have taken him away, tell me where you have put him, and I will go and get him."

¹⁶ "Mary!" Jesus said. She turned toward him.

"Master!" she exclaimed.

¹⁷ "Don't touch me," he cautioned, "for I haven't yet ascended to the Father. But go find my brothers and tell them that I ascend to my Father and your Father, my God and your God."

¹⁸ Mary Magdalene found the disciples

f Literally, "had received."   g Literally, "And he who has seen has borne witness, and his witness is true; and he knows what he says is true, that you also may believe."   h See chapter 3.   i Literally "a garden."   20a Literally, "on the first day of the week."   b Literally, "the other disciple whom Jesus loved."   c Literally, "Peter and the other disciple."   d Literally, "the other disciple also, who came first."   e Implied.   f Literally, "the disciples."

and told them, "I have seen the Lord!" Then she gave them his message.

[19] That evening the disciples were meeting behind locked doors, in fear of the Jewish leaders, when suddenly Jesus was standing there among them! After greeting them, [20] he showed them his hands and side. And how wonderful was their joy as they saw their Lord!

[21] He spoke to them again and said, "As the Father has sent me, even so I am sending you." [22] Then he breathed on them and told them, "Receive the Holy Spirit. [23] If you forgive anyone's sins, they are forgiven. If you refuse to forgive them, they are unforgiven."

[24] One of the disciples, Thomas, "The Twin," was not there at the time with the others. [25] When they kept telling him, "We have seen the Lord," he replied, "I won't believe it unless I see the nail wounds in his hands—and put my fingers into them—and place my hand into his side."

[26] Eight days later the disciples were together again, and this time Thomas was with them. The doors were locked; but suddenly, as before, Jesus was standing among them and greeting them.

[27] Then he said to Thomas, "Put your finger into my hands. Put your hand into my side. Don't be faithless any longer. Believe!"

[28] "My Lord and my God!" Thomas said.

[29] Then Jesus told him, "You believe because you have seen me. But blessed are those who haven't seen me and believe anyway."

[30,31] Jesus' disciples saw him do many other miracles besides the ones told about in this book, but these are recorded so that you will believe that he is the Messiah, the Son of God, and that believing in him you will have life.

21 LATER JESUS APPEARED again to the disciples beside the Lake of Galilee. This is how it happened:

[2] A group of us were there—Simon Peter, Thomas, "The Twin," Nathanael from Cana in Galilee, my brother James and I[a] and two other disciples.

[3] Simon Peter said, "I'm going fishing."

"We'll come too," we all said. We did, but caught nothing all night. [4] At dawn we saw a man standing on the beach but couldn't see who he was.

[5] He called, "Any fish, boys?"[b]

"No," we replied.

[6] Then he said, "Throw out your net on the right-hand side of the boat, and you'll get plenty of them!" So we did, and couldn't draw in the net because of the weight of the fish, there were so many!

[7] Then I[c] said to Peter, "It is the Lord!" At that, Simon Peter put on his tunic (for he was stripped to the waist) and jumped into the water [and swam ashore[d]]. [8] The rest of us stayed in the boat and pulled the loaded net to the beach, about 300 feet away. [9] When we got there, we saw that a fire was kindled and fish were frying over it, and there was bread.

[10] "Bring some of the fish you've just caught," Jesus said. [11] So Simon Peter went out and dragged the net ashore. By his count there were 153 large fish; and yet the net hadn't torn.

[12] "Now come and have some breakfast!" Jesus said; and none of us dared ask him if he really was the Lord, for we were quite sure of it. [13] Then Jesus went around serving us the bread and fish.

[14] This was the third time Jesus had appeared to us since his return from the dead.

[15] After breakfast Jesus said to Simon Peter, "Simon, son of John, do you love me more than these others?"[e]

"Yes," Peter replied, "You know I am your friend."

"Then feed my lambs," Jesus told him.

[16] Jesus repeated the question: "Simon, son of John, do you *really* love me?"

"Yes, Lord," Peter said, "you know I am your friend."

"Then take care of my sheep," Jesus said.

[17] Once more he asked him, "Simon, son of John, are you even my friend?"

Peter was grieved at the way Jesus asked

---

a Literally, "the sons of Zebedee." b Literally, "children." c Literally, "that disciple therefore whom Jesus loved." d Implied. e Literally, "more than these." See Mark 14:29.

the question this third time. "Lord, you know my heart;[f] you know I am," he said.

Jesus said, "Then feed my little sheep. [18] When you were young, you were able to do as you liked and go wherever you wanted to; but when you are old, you will stretch out your hands and others will direct you and take you where you don't want to go." [19] Jesus said this to let him know what kind of death he would die to glorify God. Then Jesus told him, "Follow me."

[20] Peter turned around and saw the disciple Jesus loved following, the one who had leaned around at supper that time to ask Jesus, "Master, which of us will betray you?" [21] Peter asked Jesus, "What about him, Lord? What sort of death will he die?"[g]

[22] Jesus replied, "If I want him to live[h] until I return, what is that to you? *You follow me.*"

[23] So the rumor spread among the brotherhood that that disciple wouldn't die! But that isn't what Jesus said at all! He only said, "If I want him to live[h] until I come, what is that to you?"

[24] *I am that disciple!* I saw these events and have recorded them here. And we all know that my account of these things is accurate.

[25] And I suppose that if all the other events in Jesus' life were written, the whole world could hardly contain the books!

---

f Literally, "all things."   g Implied. Literally, "and this man. what?"   h Literally, "tarry."

Speak
Out

Steve Sparks

Picture yourself: ... getting an "A" in the roughest math course of the semester.

... standing alone on a Rocky Mountain peak staring at breathtaking beauty.

... hitting a hole-in-one.

Now, picture yourself not being able to share these experiences with anyone. It would kill half the pleasure! After all, what good's an exciting game or trip without friends along?

In the same way, if Christ lives within you, then talking about him should be as natural as talking about your unexpected "A," or your winning touchdown, or that very special date you just had.

Yet speaking out *isn't* that natural! Not at all. People say they don't want to "discuss religion." And often we overreact, thinking people are even more defensive than they actually are. We quickly lose the desire to communicate Christ beyond our small circle of Christian friends.

Yet how great it is to share Christ with those who don't yet know what he can do—like this speaker telling an outdoor crowd in California, "When this old black body falls off like an overcoat, Jesus will come right alongside and say, 'Baby, cool it, we're going to make this trip together. I'm right here!'"

This dramatic Book of Acts can open the door to witnessing for us ordinary people with extraordinary Life within. These first-century Christians were quite ordinary non-supermen, yet they "turned the world upside down."

God's command to speak out for him is possible to obey. It can become a natural part of your Christian life.

ACTS

1 DEAR FRIEND WHO loves God:

In my first letter[a] I told you about Jesus' life and teachings and how he returned to heaven after giving his chosen apostles further instructions from the Holy Spirit. [3] During the forty days after his crucifixion he appeared to the apostles from time to time, actually alive, and proved to them in many ways that it was really he himself they were seeing. And on these occasions he talked to them about the Kingdom of God.

[4] In one of these meetings he told them not to leave Jerusalem until the Holy Spirit came upon them in fulfillment of the Father's promise, a matter he had previously discussed with them.

[5] "John baptized you with[b] water," he reminded them, "but you shall be baptized with[b] the Holy Spirit in just a few days."

[6] And another time when he appeared to them, they asked him, "Lord, are you going to free Israel [from Rome[c]] now and restore us as an independent nation?"

[7] "The Father sets those dates," he replied, "and they are not for you to know. [8] But when the Holy Spirit has come upon you, you will receive power to testify about me with great effect, to the people in Jerusalem, throughout Judea, in Samaria, and to the ends of the earth, about my death and resurrection."

[9] It was not long afterwards that he rose into the sky and disappeared into a cloud, leaving them staring after him. [10] As they were straining their eyes for another glimpse, suddenly two white-robed men were standing there among them, [11] and said, "Men of Galilee, why are you standing here staring at the sky? Jesus has gone away to heaven, and some day, just as he went, he will return!"

[12] They were at the Mount of Olives when this happened, so now they walked the half mile back to Jerusalem [13] and held a prayer meeting in an upstairs room of the house where they were staying.

[14] Here is the list of those who were present at the meeting:

Peter,
John, James,
Andrew,
Philip, Thomas,
Bartholomew,
Matthew,

---

a i.e., the book of Luke; see footnote chapter 1, verse 1.

b Or, "in."   c Implied.

James (son of Alphaeus),
Simon (also called "The Zealot"),
Judas (son of James),
And the brothers of Jesus.
Several women, including Jesus'
mother, were also there.

¹⁵ This prayer meeting went on for several days. During this time, on a day when about 120 people were present, Peter stood up and addressed them as follows:

¹⁶ "Brothers, it was necessary for the Scriptures to come true concerning Judas, who betrayed Jesus by guiding the mob to him, for this was predicted long ago by the Holy Spirit, speaking through King David. ¹⁷ Judas was one of us, chosen to be an apostle just as we were. ¹⁸ He bought a field with the money he received for his treachery and falling headlong there, he burst open, spilling out his bowels. ¹⁹ The news of his death spread rapidly among all the people of Jerusalem, and they named the place 'The Field of Blood.' ²⁰ King David's prediction of this appears in the Book of Psalms, where he says, 'Let his home become desolate with no one living in it.'ᵈ And again, 'Let his work be given to someone else to do.'ᵉ

²¹,²² "So now we must choose someone else to take Judas' place and to join us as witnesses of Jesus' resurrection. Let us select someone who has been with us constantly from our first association with the Lord—from the time he was baptized by John until the day he was taken from us into heaven."

²³ The assembly nominated two men: Joseph Justus (also called Barsabbas) and Matthias. ²⁴,²⁵ Then they all prayed for the right man to be chosen. "O Lord," they said, "you know every heart; show us which of these men you have chosen as an apostle to replace Judas the traitor, who has gone on to his proper place."

²⁶ Then they drew straws,ᶠ and in this manner Matthias was chosen and became an apostle with the other eleven.

2 SEVEN WEEKS HAD gone by since Jesus' death and resurrection, and the Day of Pentecost had now arrived.ᵃ As the believers met together that day, ² suddenly there was a sound like the roaring of a mighty windstorm in the skies above them and it filled the house where they were meeting. ³ Then, what looked like flames or tongues of fire appeared and settled on their heads. ⁴ And everyone present was filled with the Holy Spirit and began speaking in languages they didn't know,ᵇ for the Holy Spirit gave them this ability.

⁵ Many godly Jews were in Jerusalem that day for the religious celebrations, having arrived from many nations. ⁶ And when they heard the roaring in the sky above the house, crowds came running to see what it was all about, and were stunned to hear their own languages being spoken by the disciples.

⁷ "How can this be?" they exclaimed. "For these men are all from Galilee, ⁸ and yet we hear them speaking all the native languages of the lands where we were born! ⁹ Here we are—Parthians, Medes, Elamites, men from Mesopotamia, Judea, Cappadocia, Pontus, Ausia,ᶜ ¹⁰ Phrygia, Pamphylia, Egypt, the Cyrene language areas of Libya, visitors from Rome—both Jews and Jewish converts— ¹¹ Cretans, and Arabians. And we all hear these men telling in our own languages about the mighty miracles of God!"

¹² They stood there amazed and perplexed. "What can this mean?" they asked each other.

¹³ But others in the crowd were mocking. "They're drunk, that's all!" they said.

¹⁴ Then Peter stepped forward with the eleven apostles, and shouted to the crowd, "Listen, all of you, visitors and residents of Jerusalem alike! ¹⁵ Some of you are saying these men are drunk! It isn't true! It's much too early for that! People don't get drunk by 9 A.M.! ¹⁶ No! What you see this morning was predicted centuries ago by the prophet Joel— ¹⁷ 'In the last days,' God said, 'I will pour out my Holy Spirit upon all mankind, and your sons and daughters shall prophesy, and your young men shall see visions, and your old men dream dreams. ¹⁸ Yes, the Holy Spirit shall come upon all

---

d Psalm 69:25.   e Psalm 109:8.   f Literally, "cast lots," or, "threw dice."   2a This annual celebration came fifty days after the Passover ceremonies, when Christ was crucified. See Leviticus 23:16.
b Literally, "in other tongues."   c Literally, "Asia," a province of what is now Turkey.

my servants, men and women alike, and they shall prophesy. [19] And I will cause strange demonstrations in the heavens and on the earth—blood and fire and clouds of smoke; [20] the sun shall turn black and the moon blood-red before that awesome Day of the Lord arrives. [21] But anyone who asks for mercy from the Lord shall have it and shall be saved.'

[22] "O men of Israel, listen! God publicly endorsed Jesus of Nazareth by doing tremendous miracles through him, as you well know. [23] But God, following his prearranged plan, let you use the Roman[d] government to nail him to the cross and murder him. [24] Then God released him from the horrors of death and brought him back to life again, for death could not keep this man within its grip.

[25] "King David quoted Jesus as saying: 'I know the Lord is always with me. He is helping me. God's mighty power supports me.

[26] 'No wonder my heart is filled with joy and my tongue shouts his praises! For I know all will be well with me in death—

[27] 'You will not leave my soul in hell or let the body of your Holy Son decay.

[28] 'You will give me back my life, and give me wonderful joy in your presence.'

[29] "Dear brothers, think! David wasn't referring to himself when he spoke these words I have quoted,[e] for he died and was buried, and his tomb is still here among us. [30] But he was a prophet, and knew God had promised with an unbreakable oath that one of David's own descendants would [be the Messiah and[e]] sit on David's throne. [31] David was looking far into the future and predicting the Messiah's resurrection, and saying that the Messiah's soul would not be left in hell and his body would not decay. [32] He was speaking of Jesus, and we all are witnesses that Jesus rose from the dead.

[33] "And now he sits on the throne of highest honor in heaven, next to God. And just as promised, the Father gave him the authority to send the Holy Spirit—with the results you are seeing and hearing today.

[34] "[No, David was not speaking of himself in these words of his I have quoted[e]], for he never ascended into the skies. Moreover, he further stated, 'God spoke to my Lord, the Messiah, and said to him, Sit here in honor beside me [35] until I bring your enemies into complete subjection.'

[36] "Therefore I clearly state to everyone in Israel that God has made this Jesus you crucified to be the Lord, the Messiah!"

[37] These words of Peter's moved them deeply, and they said to him and to the other apostles, "Brothers, what should we do?"

[38] And Peter replied, "Each one of you must turn from sin, return to God, and be baptized in the name of Jesus Christ for the forgiveness of your sins; then you also shall receive this gift, the Holy Spirit. [39] For Christ promised him to each one of you who has been called by the Lord our God, and to your children and even to those in distant lands!"

[40] Then Peter preached a long sermon, telling about Jesus and strongly urging all his listeners to save themselves from the evils of their nation. [41] And those who believed Peter were baptized—about 3,000 in all! [42] They joined with the other believers in regular attendance at the apostles' teaching sessions and at the Communion services[f] and prayer meetings. [43] A deep sense of awe was on them all, and the apostles did many miracles.

[44] And all the believers met together constantly and shared everything with each other, [45] selling their possessions and dividing with those in need. [46] They worshiped together regularly at the Temple each day, met in small groups in homes for Communion, and shared their meals with great joy and thankfulness, [47] praising God. The whole city was favorable to them, and each day God added to them all who were being saved.

3 PETER AND JOHN went to the Temple one afternoon to take part in the three

---

d Literally, "men without the Law." See Romans 2:12.   e Implied in verse 31.   f Literally, "the
breaking of bread," i.e., "the Lord's Supper."

o'clock daily prayer meeting. [2] As they approached the Temple, they saw a man lame from birth carried along the street and laid beside the Temple gate—the one called The Beautiful Gate—as was his custom every day. [3] As Peter and John were passing by, he asked them for some money.

[4] They looked at him intently, and then Peter said, "Look here!"

[5] The lame man looked at them eagerly, expecting a gift.

[6] But Peter said, "We don't have any money for you! But I'll give you something else! I command you in the name of Jesus Christ of Nazareth, *walk!*"

[7,8] Then Peter took the lame man by the hand and pulled him to his feet. And as he did, the man's feet and ankle-bones were healed and strengthened so that he came up with a leap, stood there a moment and began walking! Then, walking, leaping, and praising God, he went into the Temple with them.

[9] When the people inside saw him walking and heard him praising God, [10] and realized he was the lame beggar they had seen so often at The Beautiful Gate, they were inexpressibly surprised! [11] They all rushed out to Solomon's Hall, where he was holding tightly to Peter and John! Everyone stood there awed by the wonderful thing that had happened.

[12] Peter saw his opportunity and addressed the crowd. "Men of Israel," he said, "what is so surprising about this? And why look at us as though we by our own power and godliness had made this man walk? [13] For it is the God of Abraham, Isaac, Jacob and of all our ancestors who has brought glory to his servant Jesus by doing this. I refer to the Jesus whom you rejected before Pilate, despite Pilate's determination to release him. [14] You didn't want him freed—this holy, righteous one. Instead you demanded the release of a murderer. [15] And you killed the Author of Life; but God brought him back to life again. And John and I are witnesses of this fact, for after you killed him we saw him alive!

[16] "Jesus' name has healed this man

—and you know how lame he was before. Faith in Jesus' name—faith given us from God—has caused this perfect healing.

[17] "Dear brothers, I realize that what you did to Jesus was done in ignorance; and the same can be said of your leaders. [18] But God was fulfilling the prophecies that the Messiah must suffer all these things. [19] Now change your mind and attitude to God and turn to him so he can cleanse away your sins and send you wonderful times of refreshment from the presence of the Lord [20] and send Jesus your Messiah back to you again. [21,22] For he must remain in heaven until the final recovery of all things from sin, as prophesied from ancient times. Moses, for instance, said long ago, 'The Lord God will raise up a Prophet among you, who will resemble me![a] Listen carefully to everything he tells you. [23] Anyone who will not listen to him shall be utterly destroyed.'[b]

[24] "Samuel and every prophet since have all spoken about what is going on today. [25] You are the children of those prophets; and you are included in God's promise to your ancestors to bless the entire world through the Jewish race—that is the promise God gave to Abraham. [26] And as soon as God had brought his servant to life again, he sent him first of all to you men of Israel, to bless you by turning you back from your sins."

4 WHILE THEY WERE talking to the people, the chief priests, the captain of the Temple police, and some of the Sadducees[a] came over to them, [2] very disturbed that Peter and John were claiming that Jesus had risen from the dead. [3] They arrested them and since it was already evening, jailed them overnight. [4] But many of the people who heard their message believed it, so that the number of believers now reached a new high of about 5,000 men!

[5] The next day it happened that the Council of all the Jewish leaders was in session in Jerusalem— [6] Annas the High Priest was there, and Caiaphas, John, Alexander, and others of the High Priest's relatives. [7] So the two disciples were brought in before

---

a Literally, "like unto me." b Literally, "destroyed from among the people." 4a The Sadducees were members of a Jewish religious sect that denied the resurrection of the dead.

them.

"By what power, or by whose authority have you done this?" the Council demanded.

[8] Then Peter, filled with the Holy Spirit, said to them, "Honorable leaders and elders of our nation, [9] if you mean the good deed done to the cripple, and how he was healed, [10] let me clearly state to you and to all the people of Israel that it was done in the name and power of Jesus from Nazareth, the Messiah, the man you crucified—but God raised back to life again. It is by his authority that this man stands here healed! [11] For Jesus the Messiah is (the one referred to in the Scriptures when they speak of) a 'stone discarded by the builders which became the capstone of the arch.'[b] [12] There is salvation in no one else! Under all heaven there is no other name for men to call upon to save them."

[13] When the Council saw the boldness of Peter and John, and could see that they were obviously uneducated non-professionals, they were amazed and realized what being with Jesus had done for them! [14] And the Council could hardly discredit the healing when the man they had healed was standing right there beside them! [15] So they sent them out of the Council chamber and conferred among themselves.

[16] "What shall we do with these men?" they asked each other. "We can't deny that they have done a tremendous miracle, and everybody in Jerusalem knows about it. [17] But perhaps we can stop them from spreading their propaganda. We'll tell them that if they do it again we'll really throw the book at them." [18] So they called them back in, and told them never again to speak about Jesus.

[19] But Peter and John replied, "You decide whether God wants us to obey you instead of him! [20] We cannot stop telling about the wonderful things we saw Jesus do and heard him say."

[21] The Council then threatened them further, and finally let them go because they didn't know how to punish them without starting a riot. For everyone was praising God for this wonderful miracle— [22] the

healing of a man who had been lame for forty years.

[23] As soon as they were freed, Peter and John found the other disciples and told them what the Council had said.

[24] Then all the believers united in this prayer:

"O Lord, Creator of heaven and earth and of the sea and everything in them— [25,26] you spoke long ago by the Holy Spirit through our ancestor King David, your servant, saying, 'Why do the heathen rage against the Lord, and the foolish nations plan their little plots against Almighty God? The kings of the earth unite to fight against him, and against the anointed Son of God!'

[27] "That is what is happening here in this city today! For Herod the king, and Pontius Pilate the governor, and all the Romans—as well as the people of Israel—are united against Jesus, your anointed Son, your holy servant. [28] They won't stop at anything that you in your wise power will let them do. [29] And now, O Lord, hear their threats, and grant to your servants great boldness in their preaching, [30] and send your healing power, and may miracles and wonders be done by the name of your holy servant Jesus."

[31] After this prayer, the building where they were meeting shook and they were all filled with the Holy Spirit and boldly preached God's message.

[32] All the believers were of one heart and mind, and no one felt that what he owned was his own; everyone was sharing. [33] And the apostles preached powerful sermons about the resurrection of the Lord Jesus, and there was warm fellowship[c] among all the believers, [34,35] and no poverty—for all who owned land or houses sold them and brought the money to the apostles to give to others in need.

[36] For instance, there was Joseph (the one the apostles nicknamed "Barny the Preacher"! He was of the tribe of Levi, from the island of Cyprus). [37] He was one of those who sold a field he owned and brought the money to the apostles for distribution to those in need.

---

b Implied. Literally, "became the head of the corner."   c Literally, "great grace was upon them all."

5 BUT THERE WAS a man named Ananias (with his wife Sapphira) who sold some property, [2] and brought only part of the money, claiming it was the full price. (His wife had agreed to this deception.) [3] But Peter said, "Ananias, Satan has filled your heart. When you claimed this was the full price, you were lying to the Holy Spirit. [4] The property was yours to sell or not, as you wished. And after selling it, it was yours to decide how much to give. How could you do a thing like this? You weren't lying to us, but to God."

[5] As soon as Ananias heard these words, he fell to the floor, dead! Everyone was terrified, [6] and the younger men covered him with a sheet and took him out and buried him.

[7] About three hours later his wife came in, not knowing what had happened. [8] Peter asked her, "Did you people sell your land for such and such a price?"

"Yes," she replied, "we did."

[9] And Peter said, "How could you and your husband even think of doing a thing like this—conspiring together to test the Spirit of God's ability to know what is going on?[a] Just outside that door are the young men who buried your husband, and they will carry you out too."

[10] Instantly she fell to the floor, dead, and the young men came in and, seeing that she was dead, carried her out and buried her beside her husband. [11] Terror gripped the entire church and all others who heard what had happened.

[12] Meanwhile, the apostles were meeting regularly at the Temple in the area known as Solomon's Hall, and they did many remarkable miracles among the people. [13] The other believers didn't dare join them, though, but all had the highest regard for them. [14] And more and more believers were added to the Lord, crowds both of men and women. [15] Sick people were brought out into the streets on beds and mats so that at least Peter's shadow would fall across some of them as he went by! [16] And crowds came in from the Jerusalem suburbs, bringing their sick folk and those possessed by demons; and every one of them was healed.

[17] The High Priest and his relatives and friends among the Sadducees reacted with violent jealousy [18] and arrested the apostles, and put them in the public jail. [19] But an angel of the Lord came at night, opened the gates of the jail and brought them out. Then he told them, [20] "Go over to the Temple and preach about this Life!"

[21] They arrived at the Temple about daybreak, and immediately began preaching! Later that morning[b] the High Priest and his courtiers arrived at the Temple, and, convening the Jewish Council and the entire Senate, they sent for the apostles to be brought for trial. [22] But when the police arrived at the jail, the men weren't there, so they returned to the Council and reported, [23] "The jail doors were locked, and the guards were standing outside, but when we opened the gates, no one was there!"

[24] When the police captain[c] and the chief priests heard this, they were frantic, wondering what would happen next and where all this would end! [25] Then someone arrived with the news that the men they had jailed were out in the Temple, preaching to the people!

[26,27] The police captain went with his officers and arrested them (without violence, for they were afraid the people would kill them if they roughed up the disciples) and brought them in before the Council.

[28] "Didn't we tell you never again to preach about this Jesus?" the High Priest demanded. "And instead you have filled all Jerusalem with your teaching and intend to bring the blame for this man's death on us!"

[29] But Peter and the apostles replied, "We must obey God rather than men. [30] The God of our ancestors brought Jesus back to life again after you had killed him by hanging him on a cross. [31] Then, with mighty power, God exalted him to be a Prince and Savior, so that the people of Israel would have an opportunity for repentance, and for their sins to be forgiven. [32] And we are witnesses of these things, and so is the Holy Spirit, who is given by God to all who obey him."

[33] At this, the Council was furious, and

---

a Literally, "to try the Spirit of the Lord."   b Implied.   c Literally, "the captain of the Temple."

decided to kill them. [34] But one of their members, a Pharisee named Gamaliel (an expert on religious law and very popular with the people), stood up and requested that the apostles be sent outside the Council chamber while he talked.

[35] Then he addressed his colleagues as follows:

"Men of Israel, take care what you are planning to do to these men! [36] Some time ago there was that fellow Theudas, who pretended to be someone great. About 400 others joined him, but he was killed, and his followers were harmlessly dispersed.

[37] "After him, at the time of the taxation, there was Judas of Galilee. He drew away some people as disciples, but he also died, and his followers scattered.

[38] "And so my advice is, leave these men alone. If what they teach and do is merely on their own, it will soon be overthrown. [39] But if it is of God, you will not be able to stop them, lest you find yourselves fighting even against God."

[40] The Council accepted his advice, called in the apostles, had them beaten, and then told them never again to speak in the name of Jesus, and finally let them go. [41] They left the Council chamber rejoicing that God had counted them worthy to suffer dishonor for his name. [42] And every day, in the Temple and in their home Bible classes, they continued to teach and preach that Jesus is the Messiah.

6 BUT WITH THE believers multiplying rapidly, there were rumblings of discontent. Those who spoke only Greek complained that their widows were being discriminated against, that they were not being given as much food, in the daily distribution, as the widows who spoke Hebrew. [2] So the Twelve called a meeting of all the believers.

"We should spend our time preaching, not administering a feeding program," they said [3] "Now look around among yourselves, dear brothers, and select seven men, wise and full of the Holy Spirit, who are well thought of by everyone; and we will put them in charge of this business. [4] Then we

can spend our time in prayer, preaching, and teaching."

[5] This sounded reasonable to the whole assembly, and they elected the following: Stephen (a man unusually full of faith and the Holy Spirit), Philip, Prochorus, Nicanor, Timon, Parmenas, Nicolaus of Antioch (a Gentile convert to the Jewish faith, who had become a Christian).

[6] These seven were presented to the apostles, who prayed for them and laid their hands on them in blessing.

[7] God's message was preached in ever-widening circles, and the number of disciples increased vastly in Jerusalem; and many of the Jewish priests were converted too. [8] Stephen, the man so full of faith and the Holy Spirit's power,[a] did spectacular miracles among the people.

[9] But one day some of the men from the Jewish cult of "The Freedmen" started an argument with him, and they were soon joined by Jews from Cyrene, Alexandria in Egypt, and the Turkish provinces of Cilicia, and Ausia. [10] But none of them were able to stand against Stephen's wisdom and spirit.

[11] So they brought in some men to lie about him, claiming they had heard Stephen curse Moses, and even God.

[12] This accusation roused the crowds to fury against Stephen, and the Jewish leaders[b] arrested him and brought him before the Council. [13] The lying witnesses testified again that Stephen was constantly speaking against the Temple and against the laws of Moses.

[14] They declared, "We have heard him say that this fellow Jesus of Nazareth will destroy the Temple, and throw out all of Moses' laws." [15] At this point everyone in the Council chamber saw Stephen's face become as radiant as an angel's!

7 THEN THE HIGH Priest asked him, "Are these accusations true?"

[2] This was Stephen's lengthy reply: "The

---

a Literally, "full of grace and power." See verse 5.   b Literally, "the elders and the Scribes."

glorious God appeared to our ancestor Abraham in Iraq[a] before he moved to Syria,[b] [3] and told him to leave his native land, to say good-bye to his relatives and to start out for a country that God would direct him to. [4] So he left the land of the Chaldeans and lived in Haran, in Syria, until his father died. Then God brought him here to the land of Israel, [5] but gave him no property of his own, not one little tract of land.

"However, God promised that eventually the whole country would belong to him and his descendants—though as yet he had no children! [6] But God also told him that these descendants of his would leave the land and live in a foreign country and there become slaves for 400 years. [7] 'But I will punish the nation that enslaves them,' God told him, 'and afterwards my people will return to this land of Israel and worship me here.'

[8] "God also gave Abraham the ceremony of circumcision at that time, as evidence of the covenant between God and the people of Abraham. And so Isaac, Abraham's son, was circumcised when he was eight days old. Isaac became the father of Jacob, and Jacob was the father of the twelve patriarchs of the Jewish nation. [9] These men were very jealous of Joseph and sold him to be a slave in Egypt. But God was with him, [10] and delivered him out of all of his anguish, and gave him favor before Pharaoh, king of Egypt. God also gave Joseph unusual wisdom, so that Pharaoh appointed him governor over all Egypt, as well as putting him in charge of all the affairs of the palace.

[11] "But a famine developed in Egypt and Canaan and there was great misery for our ancestors. When their food was gone, [12] Jacob heard that there was still grain in Egypt, so he sent his sons[c] to buy some. [13] The second time they went, Joseph revealed his identity to his brothers, and they were introduced to Pharaoh. [14] Then Joseph sent for his father Jacob and all his brothers' families to come to Egypt, seventy-five persons in all. [15] So Jacob came to Egypt, where he died, and all his sons. [16] All of them were

taken to Shechem and buried in the tomb Abraham bought from the sons of Hamor, Shechem's father.

[17,18] "As the time drew near when God would fulfill his promise to Abraham to free his descendants from slavery, the Jewish people greatly multiplied in Egypt; but then a king was crowned who had no respect for Joseph's memory. [19] This king plotted against our race, forcing parents to abandon their children in the fields.

[20] "About that time Moses was born—a child of divine beauty. His parents hid him at home for three months, [21] and when at last they could no longer keep him hidden, and had to abandon him, Pharaoh's daughter found him and adopted him as her own son, [22] and taught him all the wisdom of the Egyptians, and he became a mighty prince and orator.

[23] "One day as he was nearing his fortieth birthday, it came into his mind to visit his brothers, the people of Israel. [24] During this visit he saw an Egyptian mistreating a man of Israel. So Moses killed the Egyptian. [25] Moses supposed his brothers would realize that God had sent him to help them, but they didn't.

[26] "The next day he visited them again and saw two men of Israel fighting. He tried to be a peacemaker. 'Gentlemen,' he said, 'you are brothers and shouldn't be fighting like this! It is wrong!'

[27] "But the man in the wrong told Moses to mind his own business. 'Who made *you* a ruler and judge over us?' he asked. [28] 'Are you going to kill me as you killed that Egyptian yesterday?'

[29] "At this, Moses fled the country, and lived in the land of Midian, where his two sons were born.

[30] "Forty years later, in the desert near Mount Sinai, an Angel appeared to him in a flame of fire in a bush. [31] Moses saw it and wondered what it was, and as he ran to see, the voice of the Lord called out to him, [32] 'I am the God of your ancestors—of Abraham, Isaac and Jacob.' Moses shook with terror and dared not look.

[33] "And the Lord said to him, 'Take off

---

a Literally, "Mesopotamia."   b Literally, "Haran," a city in the area we now know as Syria.
c Literally, "our fathers."

your shoes, for you are standing on holy ground. [34] I have seen the anguish of my people in Egypt and have heard their cries. I have come down to deliver them. Come, I will send you to Egypt.' [35] And so God sent back the same man his people had previously rejected by demanding, 'Who made *you* a ruler and judge over us?' Moses was sent to be their ruler and savior. [36] And by means of many remarkable miracles he led them out of Egypt and through the Red Sea, and back and forth through the wilderness for forty years.

[37] "Moses himself told the people of Israel, 'God will raise up a Prophet much like me[d] from among your brothers.' [38] How true this proved to be, for in the wilderness, Moses was the go-between—the mediator between the people of Israel and the Angel who gave them the Law of God—the Living Word—on Mount Sinai.

[39] "But our fathers rejected Moses and wanted to return to Egypt. [40] They told Aaron, 'Make idols for us, so that we will have gods to lead us back; for we don't know what has become of this Moses, who brought us out of Egypt.' [41] So they made a calf-idol and sacrificed to it, and rejoiced in this thing they had made.

[42] "Then God turned away from them and gave them up, and let them serve the sun, moon and stars as their gods! In the book of Amos' prophecies the Lord God asks, 'Was it to me you were sacrificing during those forty years in the desert, Israel? [43] No, your real interest was in your heathen gods—Sakkuth, and the star god Kaiway, and in all the images you made. So I will send you into captivity far away beyond Babylon.'

[44] "Our ancestors carried along with them a portable Temple, or Tabernacle, through the wilderness. In it they kept the stone tablets with the Ten Commandments written on them. This building was constructed in exact accordance with the plan shown to Moses by the Angel. [45] Years later, when Joshua led the battles against the Gentile nations, this Tabernacle was taken with them into their new territory, and used

until the time of King David.

[46] "God blessed David greatly, and David asked for the privilege of building a permanent Temple for the God of Jacob. [47] But it was Solomon who actually built it. [48,49] However, God doesn't live in temples made by human hands. 'The heaven is my throne,' says the Lord through his prophets, 'and earth is my footstool. What kind of home could you build?' asks the Lord. 'Would I stay in it? [50] Didn't I make both heaven and earth?'

[51] "You stiff-necked heathen! Must you forever resist the Holy Spirit? But your fathers did, and so do you! [52] Name one prophet your ancestors didn't persecute! They even killed the ones who predicted the coming of the Righteous One—the Messiah whom you betrayed and murdered. [53] Yes, and you deliberately destroyed God's Laws, though you received them from the hands of angels."[e]

[54] The Jewish leaders were stung to fury by Stephen's accusation, and ground their teeth in rage. [55] But Stephen, full of the Holy Spirit, gazed steadily upward into heaven and saw the glory of God and Jesus standing at God's right hand. [56] And he told them, "Look, I see the heavens opened and Jesus the Messiah[f] standing beside God, at his right hand!"

[57] Then they mobbed him, putting their hands over their ears, and drowning out his voice with their shouts, [58] and dragged him out of the city to stone him. The official witnesses—the executioners—took off their coats and laid them at the feet of a young man named Paul.[g]

[59] And as the murderous stones came hurtling at him, Stephen prayed, "Lord Jesus, receive my spirit." [60] And he fell to his knees, shouting, "Lord, don't charge them with this sin!" and with that, he died.

8 PAUL WAS IN complete agreement with the killing of Stephen. And a great wave of persecution of the believers began that day, sweeping over the church in Jerusalem, and everyone except the apostles fled into Judea and Samaria. [2] (But some godly

---

d Literally, "like unto me."   e Literally, "the Law as it was ordained by angels."   f Literally, "the Son of Man."   g Paul is also known as Saul.

Jews[a] came and with great sorrow buried Stephen.) [3] Paul was like a wild man, going everywhere to devastate the believers, even entering private homes and dragging out men and women alike and jailing them. [4] But the believers[b] who had fled Jerusalem went everywhere preaching the Good News about Jesus! [5] Philip, for instance, went to the city of Samaria and told the people there about Christ. [6] Crowds listened intently to what he had to say because of the miracles he did. [7] Many evil spirits were cast out, screaming as they left their victims, and many who were paralyzed or lame were healed, [8] so there was much joy in that city!

[9,10,11] A man named Simon had formerly been a sorcerer there for many years; he was a very influential, proud man because of the amazing things he could do—in fact, the Samaritan people often spoke of him as the Messiah.[c] [12] But now they believed Philip's message that Jesus was the Messiah, and his words concerning the Kingdom of God; and many men and women were baptized. [13] Then Simon himself believed and was baptized and began following Philip wherever he went, and was amazed by the miracles he did.

[14] When the apostles back in Jerusalem heard that the people of Samaria had accepted God's message, they sent down Peter and John. [15] As soon as they arrived, they began praying for these new Christians to receive the Holy Spirit, [16] for as yet he had not come upon any of them. For they had only been baptized in the name of the Lord Jesus. [17] Then Peter and John laid their hands upon these believers, and they received the Holy Spirit.

[18] When Simon saw this—that the Holy Spirit was given when the apostles placed their hands upon people's heads—he offered money to buy this power. [19] "Let me have this power too," he exclaimed, "so that when I lay my hands on people, they will receive the Holy Spirit!"

[20] But Peter replied, "Your money perish with you for thinking God's gift can be bought! [21] You can have no part in this, for your heart is not right before God. [22] Turn from this great wickedness and pray. Perhaps God will yet forgive your evil thoughts— [23] for I can see that there is jealousy[d] and sin in your heart."

[24] "Pray for me," Simon exclaimed, "that these terrible things won't happen to me."

[25] After testifying and preaching in Samaria, Peter and John returned to Jerusalem, stopping at several Samaritan villages along the way to preach the Good News to them too.

[26] But as for Philip, an angel of the Lord said to him, "Go over to the road that runs from Jerusalem through the Gaza Desert, arriving around noon." [27] So he did, and who should be coming down the road but the Treasurer of Ethiopia, a eunuch of great authority under Candace the queen. He had gone to Jerusalem to worship at the Temple, [28] and was now returning in his chariot, reading aloud from the book of the prophet Isaiah.

[29] The Holy Spirit said to Philip, "Go over and walk along beside the chariot."

[30] Philip ran over and heard what he was reading and asked, "Do you understand it?"

[31] "Of course not!" the man replied. "How can I when there is no one to instruct me?" And he begged Philip to come up into the chariot and sit with him.

[32] The passage of Scripture he had been reading from was this:

"He was led as a sheep to the slaughter, and as a lamb is silent before the shearers, so he opened not his mouth; [33] in his humiliation, justice was denied him; and who can express the wickedness of the people of his generation?[e] For his life is taken from the earth."

[34] The eunuch asked Philip, "Was Isaiah talking about himself or someone else?" [35] So Philip began with this same Scripture and then used many others to tell him about Jesus.

[36] As they rode along, they came to a

---

a Literally, "devout men." It is not clear whether these were Christians who braved the persecution, or whether they were godly and sympathetic Jews.   b Literally, "the church."   c Literally, "this man is that Power of God which is called great."   d Literally, "the gall of bitterness."   e Implied. Literally, "Who can declare his generation." Alternatively, "Who will be able to speak of his posterity? For . . ."

small body of water, and the eunuch said, "Look! Water! Why can't I be baptized?" [37f] "You can," Philip answered, "if you believe with all your heart."

And the eunuch replied, "I believe that Jesus Christ is the Son of God."

[38] He stopped the chariot, and they went down into the water and Philip baptized him. [39] And when they came up out of the water, the Spirit of the Lord caught away Philip, and the eunuch never saw him again, but went on his way rejoicing. [40] Meanwhile, Philip found himself at Azotus! He preached the Good News there and in every city along the way, as he traveled to Caesarea.

9 BUT PAUL, THREATENING with every breath and eager to destroy every Christian, went to the High Priest in Jerusalem. [2] He requested a letter addressed to synagogues in Damascus, requiring their cooperation in the persecution of any believers he found there, both men and women, so that he could bring them in chains to Jerusalem.

[3] As he was nearing Damascus on this mission, suddenly a brilliant light from heaven spotted down upon him! [4] He fell to the ground and heard a voice saying to him, "Paul! Paul! Why are you persecuting me?"

[5] "Who is speaking, sir?" Paul asked.

And the voice replied, "I am Jesus, the one you are persecuting! [6] Now get up and go into the city and await my further instructions."

[7] The men with Paul stood speechless with surprise, for they heard the sound of someone's voice but saw no one! [8,9] As Paul picked himself up off the ground, he found that he was blind. He had to be led into Damascus and was there three days, blind, going without food and water all that time.

[10] Now there was in Damascus a believer named Ananias. The Lord spoke to him in a vision, calling, "Ananias!"

"Yes, Lord!" he replied.

[11] And the Lord said, "Go over to Straight Street and find the house of a man named Judas and ask there for Paul of Tarsus. He is praying to me right now, for [12] I

have shown him a vision of a man named Ananias coming in and laying his hands on him so that he can see again!"

[13] "But Lord," exclaimed Ananias, "I have heard about the terrible things this man has done to the believers in Jerusalem! [14] And we hear that he has arrest warrants with him from the chief priests, authorizing him to arrest every believer in Damascus!"

[15] But the Lord said, "Go and do what I say. For Paul is my chosen instrument to take my message to the nations and before kings, as well as to the people of Israel. [16] And I will show him how much he must suffer for me."

[17] So Ananias went over and found Paul and laid his hands on him and said, "Brother Paul, the Lord Jesus, who appeared to you on the road, has sent me so that you may be filled with the Holy Spirit and get your sight back."

[18] Instantly (it was as though scales fell from his eyes) Paul could see, and was immediately baptized. [19] Then he ate and was strengthened. He stayed with the believers in Damascus for a few days [20] and went at once to the synagogue to tell everyone there the Good News about Jesus—that he is indeed the Son of God!

[21] All who heard him were amazed. "Isn't this the same man who persecuted Jesus' followers so bitterly in Jerusalem?" they asked. "And we understand that he came here to arrest them all and take them in chains to the chief priests."

[22] Paul became more and more fervent in his preaching, and the Damascus Jews couldn't withstand his proofs that Jesus was indeed the Christ.

[23] After a while the Jewish leaders determined to kill him. [24] But Paul was told about their plans, that they were watching the gates of the city day and night prepared to murder him. [25] So during the night some of his converts let him down in a basket through an opening in the city wall!

[26] Upon arrival in Jerusalem he tried to meet with the believers, but they were all afraid of him. They thought he was faking! [27] Then Barnabas brought him to the apostles and told them how Paul had seen the

f Many ancient manuscripts omit verse 37 wholly or in part.

Lord on the way to Damascus, what the Lord had said to him, and all about his powerful preaching in the name of Jesus. ²⁸ Then they accepted him, and after that he was constantly with the believers ²⁹ and preached boldly in the name of the Lord. But then some Greek-speaking Jews with whom he had argued plotted to murder him. ³⁰ However, when the other believers heard about his danger, they took him to Caesarea and then sent him to his home[a] in Tarsus.

³¹ Meanwhile, the church had peace throughout Judea, Galilee and Samaria, and grew in strength and numbers. The believers learned how to walk in the fear of the Lord and in the comfort of the Holy Spirit.

³² Peter traveled from place to place to visit them,[a] and in his travels came to the believers in the town of Lydda. ³³ There he met a man named Aeneas, paralyzed and bedridden for eight years. ³⁴ Peter said to him, "Aeneas! Jesus Christ has healed you! Get up and make your bed." And he was healed instantly. ³⁵ Then the whole population of Lydda and Sharon turned to the Lord when they saw Aeneas walking around.

³⁶ In the city of Joppa there was a woman named Dorcas ("Gazelle"), a believer who was always doing kind things for others, especially for the poor. ³⁷ About this time she became ill and died. Her friends prepared her for burial and laid her in an upstairs room. ³⁸ But when they learned that Peter was nearby at Lydda, they sent two men to beg him to return with them to Joppa. ³⁹ This he did; as soon as he arrived, they took him upstairs where Dorcas lay. The room was filled with weeping widows who were showing one another the coats and other garments Dorcas had made for them. ⁴⁰ But Peter asked them all to leave the room; then he knelt and prayed. Turning to the body he said, "Get up, Dorcas,"[b] and she opened her eyes! And when she saw Peter, she sat up! ⁴¹ He gave her his hand and helped her up and called in the believers and widows, presenting her

to them. ⁴² The news raced through the town, and many believed in the Lord. ⁴³ And Peter stayed a long time in Joppa, living with Simon, the tanner.

10 IN CAESAREA THERE lived a Roman army officer, Cornelius, a captain of an Italian regiment. ² He was a godly man, deeply reverent, as was his entire household. He gave generously to charity and was a man of prayer. ³ While wide awake one afternoon he had a vision—it was about three o'clock—and in this vision he saw an angel of God coming toward him.

"Cornelius!" the angel said.

⁴ Cornelius stared at him in terror. "What do you want, sir?" he asked the angel.

And the angel replied, "Your prayers and charities have not gone unnoticed by God! ⁵,⁶ Now send some men to Joppa to find a man named Simon Peter, who is staying with Simon, the tanner, down by the shore, and ask him to come and visit you."

⁷ As soon as the angel was gone, Cornelius called two of his household servants and a godly soldier, one of his personal bodyguard, ⁸ and told them what had happened and sent them off to Joppa.

⁹,¹⁰ The next day, as they were nearing the city, Peter went up on the flat roof of his house to pray. It was noon and he was hungry, but while lunch was being prepared, he fell into a trance. ¹¹ He saw the sky open, and a great canvas[a] sheet, suspended by its four corners, settle to the ground. ¹² In the sheet were all sorts of animals, snakes and birds [forbidden to the Jews for food[b]].

¹³ Then a voice said to him, "Go kill and eat any of them you wish."

¹⁴ "Never, Lord," Peter declared, "I have never in all my life eaten such creatures, for they are forbidden by our Jewish laws."

¹⁵ The voice spoke again, "Don't contradict God! If he says something is kosher, then it is."

¹⁶ The same vision was repeated three

---

a Implied.   b Literally, "Tabitha," her name in Hebrew.   10a Implied.   b Implied; see Leviticus 11
for the forbidden list.

times. Then the sheet was pulled up again to heaven. [17] Peter was very perplexed. What could the vision mean? What was he supposed to do?

Just then the men sent by Cornelius had found the house and were standing outside at the gate, [18] inquiring whether this was the place where Simon Peter lived!

[19] Meanwhile, as Peter was puzzling over the vision, the Holy Spirit said to him, "Three men have come to see you. [20] Go down and meet them and go with them. All is well, I have sent them."

[21] So Peter went down. "I'm the man you're looking for," he said. "Now what is it you want?"

[22] Then they told him about Cornelius the Roman officer, a good and godly man, well thought of by the Jews, and how an angel had instructed him to send for Peter to come and tell him what God wanted him to do.

[23] So Peter invited them in and lodged them overnight. The next day he went with them, accompanied by some other believers from Joppa.

[24] They arrived in Caesarea the following day, and Cornelius was waiting for him, and had called together his relatives and close friends to meet Peter. [25] As Peter entered his home, Cornelius fell to the floor before him in worship.

[26] But Peter said, "Stand up! I'm not a god!"

[27] So he got up and they talked together for a while and then went in where the others were assembled.

[28] Peter told them, "You know it is against the Jewish laws for me to come into a Gentile home like this. But God has shown me in a vision that I should never think of anyone as inferior. [29] So I came as soon as I was sent for. Now tell me what you want."

[30] Cornelius replied, "Four days ago I was praying as usual at this time of the afternoon, when suddenly a man was standing before me clothed in a radiant robe! [31] He told me, 'Cornelius, your prayers are heard and your charities have been noticed by God! [32] Now send some men to Joppa

and summon Simon Peter, who is staying in the home of Simon, a tanner, down by the shore.' [33] So I sent for you at once, and you have done well to come so soon. Now here we are, waiting before the Lord, anxious to hear what he has told you to tell us!"

[34] Then Peter replied, "I see very clearly that the Jews are not God's only favorites! [35] In every nation he has those who worship him and do good deeds and are acceptable to him. [36,37] I'm sure you have heard about the Good News for the people of Israel— that there is peace with God through Jesus, the Messiah, who is Lord of all creation. This message has spread all through Judea, beginning with John the Baptist in Galilee. [38] And you no doubt know that Jesus of Nazareth was anointed by God with the Holy Spirit and with power, and he went around doing good and healing all who were possessed by demons, for God was with him.

[39] "And we apostles are witnesses of all he did throughout Israel and in Jerusalem, where he was murdered on a cross. [40,41] But God brought him back to life again three days later and showed him to certain witnesses God had selected beforehand—not to the general public, but to us who ate and drank with him after he rose from the dead. [42] And he sent us to preach the Good News everywhere and to testify that Jesus is ordained of God to be the Judge of all—living and dead. [43] And all the prophets have written about him, saying that everyone who believes in him will have their sins forgiven through his name."

[44] Even as Peter was saying these things, the Holy Spirit fell upon all those listening! [45] The Jews who came with Peter were amazed that the gift of the Holy Spirit would be given to Gentiles too! [46,47] But there could be no doubt about it,[c] for they heard them speaking in tongues and praising God.

Peter asked, "Can anyone object to my baptizing them, now that they have received the Holy Spirit just as we did?" [48] So he did, baptizing them in the name of Jesus, the Messiah. Afterwards Cornelius begged him to stay with them for several days.

---

c Implied.

11 SOON THE NEWS reached the apostles and other brothers in Judea that Gentiles also were being converted! ² But when Peter arrived back in Jerusalem, the Jewish believers argued with him.

³ "You fellowshiped with Gentiles and even ate with them," they accused.

⁴ Then Peter told them the whole story.

⁵ "One day in Joppa," he said, "while I was praying, I saw a vision—a huge sheet, let down by its four corners from the sky. ⁶ Inside the sheet were all sorts of animals, reptiles and birds [which we are not to eat[a]]. ⁷ And I heard a voice say, 'Kill and eat whatever you wish.'

⁸ " 'Never, Lord,' I replied. 'For I have never yet eaten anything forbidden by our Jewish laws!'

⁹ "But the voice came again, 'Don't say it isn't right when God declares it is!'

¹⁰ "This happened *three times* before the sheet and all it contained disappeared into heaven. ¹¹ Just then three men who had come to take me with them to Caesarea arrived at the house where I was staying! ¹² The Holy Spirit told me to go with them and not to worry about their being Gentiles! These six brothers here accompanied me, and we soon arrived at the home of the man who had sent the messengers. ¹³ He told us how an angel had appeared to him and told him to send messengers to Joppa to find Simon Peter! ¹⁴ 'He will tell you how you and all your household can be saved!' the angel had told him.

¹⁵ "Well, I began telling them the Good News, but just as I was getting started with my sermon, the Holy Spirit fell on them, just as he fell on us at the beginning! ¹⁶ Then I thought of the Lord's words when he said, 'Yes, John baptized with[b] water, but you shall be baptized with[b] the Holy Spirit.'

¹⁷ And since it was *God* who gave these Gentiles the same gift he gave us when we believed on the Lord Jesus Christ, who was I to argue?"

¹⁸ When the others heard this, all their objections were answered and they began praising God! "Yes," they said, "God has given to the Gentiles, too, the privilege of turning to him and receiving eternal life!"

¹⁹ Meanwhile, the believers who fled from Jerusalem during the persecution after Stephen's death traveled as far as Phoenicia, Cyprus, and Antioch, scattering the Good News, but only to Jews. ²⁰ However, some of the believers who went to Antioch from Cyprus and Cyrene also gave their message about the Lord Jesus to some Greeks. ²¹ And the Lord honored this effort so that large numbers of these Gentiles became believers.

²² When the church at Jerusalem heard what had happened, they sent Barnabas to Antioch to help the new converts. ²³ When he arrived and saw the wonderful things God was doing, he was filled with excitement and joy, and encouraged the believers to stay close to the Lord, whatever the cost. ²⁴ Barnabas was a kindly person, full of the Holy Spirit and strong in faith. As a result large numbers of people were added to the Lord.

²⁵ Then Barnabas went on to Tarsus to hunt for Paul. ²⁶ When he found him, he brought him back to Antioch; and both of them stayed there for a full year, teaching the many new converts. (It was there at Antioch that the believers were first called "Christians.")

²⁷ During this time some prophets came down from Jerusalem to Antioch, ²⁸ and one of them, named Agabus, stood up in one of the meetings to predict by the Spirit that a great famine was coming upon the land of Israel.[c] (This was fulfilled during the reign of Claudius.) ²⁹ So the believers decided to send relief to the Christians in Judea, each giving as much as he could. ³⁰ This they did, consigning their gifts to Barnabas and Paul to take to the elders of the church in Jerusalem.

12 ABOUT THAT TIME King Herod moved against some of the believers, ² and killed the apostle[a] James (John's brother). ³ When Herod saw how much this pleased the Jewish leaders, he arrested Peter during the Passover celebration ⁴ and imprisoned him, placing him under the guard of sixteen soldiers. Herod's intention was to deliver Peter to the Jews for execution after

---

a Implied.   b Or, "in."   c Literally, "upon the earth."   12a Implied.

the Passover. ⁵ But earnest prayer was going up to God from the Church for his safety all the time he was in prison.

⁶ The night before he was to be executed, he was asleep, double-chained between two soldiers with others standing guard before the prison gate, ⁷ when suddenly there was a light in the cell and an angel of the Lord stood beside Peter! The angel slapped him on the side to awaken him and said, "Quick! Get up!" And the chains fell off his wrists! ⁸ Then the angel told him, "Get dressed and put on your shoes." And he did. "Now put on your coat and follow me!" the angel ordered.

⁹ So Peter left the cell, following the angel. But all the time he thought it was a dream or vision, and didn't believe it was really happening. ¹⁰ They passed the first and second cell blocks and came to the iron gate to the street, and this opened to them of its own accord! So they passed through and walked along together for a block, and then the angel left him.

¹¹ Peter finally realized what had happened! "It's really true!" he said to himself. "The Lord has sent his angel and saved me from Herod and from what the Jews were hoping to do to me!" ¹² After a little thought he went to the home of Mary, mother of John Mark, where many were gathered for a prayer meeting.

¹³ He knocked at the door in the gate, and a girl named Rhoda came to open it. ¹⁴ When she recognized Peter's voice, she was so overjoyed that she ran back inside to tell everyone that Peter was standing outside in the street. ¹⁵ They didn't believe her. "You're out of your mind," they said. When she insisted they decided, "It must be his angel. [They must have killed him.ᵇ]"

¹⁶ Meanwhile Peter continued knocking. When they finally went out and opened the door, their surprise knew no bounds. ¹⁷ He motioned for them to quiet down and told them what had happened and how the Lord had brought him out of jail. "Tell James and the others what happened," he said —and left for safer quarters.

¹⁸ At dawn, the jail was in great commotion. What had happened to Peter? ¹⁹ When Herod sent for him and found that he wasn't there, he had the sixteen guards arrested, court-martialed and sentenced to death.ᵇ Afterwards he left to live in Caesarea for a while.

²⁰ While he was in Caesarea, a delegation from Tyre and Sidon arrived to see him. He was highly displeased with the people of those two cities, but the delegates made friends with Blastus, the royal secretary, and asked for peace, for their cities were economically dependent upon trade with Herod's country. ²¹ An appointment with Herod was granted, and when the day arrived he put on his royal robes, sat on his throne and made a speech to them. ²² At its conclusion the people gave him a great ovation, shouting, "It is the voice of a god and not of a man!"

²³ Instantly, an angel of the Lord struck Herod with a sickness so that he was filled with maggots and died—because he accepted the people's worship instead of giving the glory to God.

²⁴ God's Good News was spreading rapidly and there were many new believers.

²⁵ Barnabas and Paul now visited Jerusalem and, as soon as they had finished their business, returned to Antioch,ᵇ taking John Mark with them.

13 AMONG THE PROPHETS and teachers of the church at Antioch were Barnabas and Symeon (also called "The Black Man"), Lucius (from Cyrene), Manaen (the foster-brother of King Herod), and Paul. ² One day as these men were worshiping and fasting the Holy Spirit said, "Dedicate Barnabas and Paul for a special job I have for them." ³ So after more fasting and prayer, the men laid their hands on them—and sent them on their way.

⁴ Directed by the Holy Spirit they went to Seleucia and then sailed for Cyprus. ⁵ There, in the town of Salamis, they went to the Jewish synagogue and preached. (John Mark went with them as their assistant.)

⁶,⁷ Afterwards they preached from town to town across the entire island until finally they reached Paphos where they met a Jew-

---

ᵇ Implied.

ish sorcerer, a fake prophet named Bar-Jesus. He had attached himself to the governor, Sergius Paulus, a man of considerable insight and understanding. The governor invited Barnabas and Paul to visit him, for he wanted to hear their message from God. [8] But the sorcerer, Elymas (his name in Greek), interfered and urged the governor to pay no attention to what Paul and Barnabas said, trying to keep him from trusting the Lord.

[9] Then Paul, filled with the Holy Spirit, glared angrily at the sorcerer and said, [10] "You son of the devil, full of every sort of trickery and villainy, enemy of all that is good, will you never end your opposition to the Lord? [11] And now God has laid his hand of punishment upon you, and you will be stricken awhile with blindness."

Instantly mist and darkness fell upon him, and he began wandering around begging for someone to take his hand and lead him. [12] When the governor saw what happened he believed and was astonished at the power of God's message.

[13] Now Paul and those with him left Paphos by ship for Turkey,[a] landing at the port town of Perga. There John deserted[b] them and returned to Jerusalem. [14] But Barnabas and Paul went on to Antioch, a city in the province of Pisidia.

On the Sabbath they went into the synagogue for the services. [15] After the usual readings from the Books of Moses and from the Prophets, those in charge of the service sent them this message: "Brothers, if you have any word of instruction for us come and give it!"

[16] So Paul stood, waved a greeting to them[c] and began. "Men of Israel," he said, "and all others here who reverence God, [let me begin my remarks with a bit of history[d]].

[17] "The God of this nation Israel chose our ancestors and honored them in Egypt by gloriously leading them out of their slavery. [18] And he nursed them through forty years of wandering around in the wilderness. [19,20] Then he destroyed seven nations in Canaan, and gave Israel their land as an inheritance. Judges ruled for about 450 years, and were followed by Samuel the prophet.

[21] "Then the people begged for a king, and God gave them Saul (son of Kish), a man of the tribe of Benjamin, who reigned for forty years. [22] But God removed him and replaced him with David as king, a man about whom God said, 'David (son of Jesse) is a man after my own heart, for he will obey me.' [23] And it is one of King David's descendants, Jesus, who is God's promised Savior of Israel!

[24] "But before he came, John the Baptist preached the need for everyone in Israel to turn from sin to God. [25] As John was finishing his work he asked, 'Do you think I am the Messiah? No! But he is coming soon —and in comparison with him, I am utterly worthless.'

[26] "Brothers—you sons of Abraham, and also all of you Gentiles here who reverence God—this salvation is for all of us! [27] The Jews in Jerusalem and their leaders fulfilled prophecy by killing Jesus; for they didn't recognize him, or realize that he is the one the prophets had written about, though they heard the prophets' words read every Sabbath. [28] They found no just cause to execute him, but asked Pilate to have him killed anyway. [29] When they had fulfilled all the prophecies concerning his death, he was taken from the cross and placed in a tomb.

[30] "But God brought him back to life again! [31] And he was seen many times during the next few days by the men who had accompanied him to Jerusalem from Galilee—these men have constantly testified to this in public witness.

[32,33] "And now Barnabas and I are here to bring you this Good News—that God's promise to our ancestors has come true in our own time, in that God brought Jesus back to life again. This is what the second Psalm is talking about when it says concerning Jesus, 'Today I have honored you as my son.'[e]

[34] "For God had promised to bring him back to life again, no more to die. This is stated in the Scripture that says, 'I will do

---

a Literally, "Pamphylia." b Literally, departed from them." See chapter 15, verse 38.
c Literally, "beckoning with the hand." d Implied. e Literally, "This day have I begotten you."

for you the wonderful thing I promised David.' ³⁵ In another Psalm he explained more fully, saying, 'God will not let his Holy One decay.' ³⁶ This was not a reference to David, for after David had served his generation according to the will of God, he died and was buried, and his body decayed. ³⁷ [No, it was a reference to another^f]—someone God brought back to life, whose body was not touched at all by the ravages of death.^g

³⁸ "Brothers! Listen! In this man Jesus, there is forgiveness for your sins! ³⁹ Everyone who trusts in him is freed from all guilt and declared righteous—something the Jewish law could never do. ⁴⁰ Oh, be careful! Don't let the prophets' words apply to you. For they said, ⁴¹ 'Look and perish, you despisers [of the truth^f], for I am doing something in your day—something that you won't believe when you hear it announced.' "

⁴² As the people left the synagogue that day, they asked Paul to return and speak to them again the next week. ⁴³ And many Jews and godly Gentiles who worshiped at the synagogue followed Paul and Barnabas down the street as the two men urged them to accept the mercies God was offering. ⁴⁴ The following week almost the entire city turned out to hear them preach the Word of God.

⁴⁵ But when the Jewish leaders^h saw the crowds, they were jealous, and cursed^i and argued against whatever Paul said.

⁴⁶ Then Paul and Barnabas spoke out boldly and declared, "It was necessary that this Good News from God should be given first to you Jews. But since you have rejected it, and shown yourselves unworthy of eternal life—well, we will offer it to Gentiles. ⁴⁷ For this is as the Lord commanded when he said, 'I have made you a light to the Gentiles, to lead them from the farthest corners of the earth to my salvation.' "

⁴⁸ When the Gentiles heard this, they were very glad and rejoiced in Paul's message; and as many as wanted^j eternal life, believed. ⁴⁹ So God's message spread all through that region.

⁵⁰ Then the Jewish leaders stirred up both the godly women and the civic leaders of the city and incited a mob against Paul and Barnabas, and ran them out of town. ⁵¹ But they shook off the dust of their feet against the town and went on to the city of Iconium. ⁵² And their converts^k were filled with joy and with the Holy Spirit.

14 AT ICONIUM, PAUL and Barnabas went together to the synagogue and preached with such power that many—both Jews and Gentiles—believed.

² But the Jews who spurned God's message stirred up distrust among the Gentiles against Paul and Barnabas, saying all sorts of evil things about them. ³ Nevertheless, they stayed there a long time, preaching boldly, and the Lord proved their message was from him by giving them power to do great miracles. ⁴ But the people of the city were divided in their opinion about them. Some agreed with the Jewish leaders, and some backed the apostles.

⁵,⁶ When Paul and Barnabas learned of a plot to incite a mob of Gentiles, Jews, and Jewish leaders to attack and stone them, they fled for their lives, going to the cities of Lycaonia, Lystra, Derbe, and the surrounding area, ⁷ and preaching the Good News there.

⁸ While they were at Lystra, they came upon a man with crippled feet who had been that way from birth, so he had never walked. ⁹ He was listening as Paul preached, and Paul noticed him and realized he had faith to be healed. ¹⁰ So Paul called to him, "Stand up!" and the man leaped to his feet and started walking!

¹¹ When the listening crowd saw what Paul had done, they shouted (in their local dialect, of course), "These men are gods in human bodies!" ¹² They decided that Barnabas was the Greek god Jupiter, and that Paul, because he was the chief speaker, was Mercury! ¹³ The local priest of the Temple of Jupiter, located on the outskirts of the city, brought them cartloads of flowers and prepared to sacrifice oxen to them at the city gates before the crowds.

---

f Implied.   g Literally, "saw no corruption."   h Literally, "the Jews."   i Or, "blasphemed."
j Or, "were disposed to," or, "ordained to."   k Literally, "the disciples."

¹⁴ But when Barnabas and Paul saw what was happening they ripped at their clothing in dismay and ran out among the people, shouting, ¹⁵ "Men! What are you doing? We are merely human beings like yourselves! We have come to bring you the Good News that you are invited to turn from the worship of these foolish things and to pray instead to the living God who made heaven and earth and sea and everything in them. ¹⁶ In bygone days he permitted the nations to go their own ways, ¹⁷ but he never left himself without a witness; there were always his reminders—the kind things he did such as sending you rain and good crops and giving you food and gladness."

¹⁸ But even so, Paul and Barnabas could scarcely restrain the people from sacrificing to them!

¹⁹ Yet only a few days later, some Jews arrived from Antioch and Iconium and turned the crowds into a murderous mob that stoned Paul and dragged him out of the city, apparently dead. ²⁰ But as the believers stood around him, he got up and went back into the city!

The next day he left with Barnabas for Derbe. ²¹ After preaching the Good News there and making many disciples, they returned again to Lystra, Iconium and Antioch, ²² where they helped the believers to grow in love for God and each other. They encouraged them to continue in the faith in spite of all the persecution, reminding them that they must enter into the Kingdom of God through many tribulations. ²³ Paul and Barnabas also appointed elders in every church and prayed for them with fasting, turning them over to the care of the Lord in whom they trusted.

²⁴ Then they traveled back through Pisidia to Pamphylia, ²⁵ preached again in Perga, and went on to Attalia.

²⁶ Finally they returned by ship to Antioch, where their journey had begun, and where they had been committed to God for the work now completed.

²⁷ Upon arrival they called together the believers and reported on their trip, telling how God had opened the door of faith to the Gentiles too. ²⁸ And they stayed there with the believers at Antioch for a long while.

15 WHILE PAUL AND Barnabas were at Antioch, some men from Judea arrived and began to teach the believers that unless they adhered to the ancient Jewish custom of circumcision, they could not be saved. ² Paul and Barnabas argued and discussed this with them at length, and finally the believers sent them to Jerusalem, accompanied by some local men, to talk to the apostles and elders there about this question. ³ After the entire congregation had escorted them out of the city the delegates went on to Jerusalem, stopping along the way in the cities of Phoenicia and Samaria to visit the believers, telling them—much to everyone's joy—that the Gentiles, too, were being converted.

⁴ Arriving in Jerusalem, they met with the church leaders—all the apostles and elders were present—and Paul and Barnabas reported on what God had been doing through their ministry. ⁵ But then some of the men who had been Pharisees before their conversion stood to their feet and declared that all Gentile converts must be circumcised and required to follow all the Jewish customs and ceremonies. ⁶ So the apostles and church elders set a further meeting to decide this question.

⁷ At the meeting, after long discussion, Peter stood and addressed them as follows: "Brothers, you all know that God chose me from among you long ago to preach the Good News to the Gentiles, so that they also could believe. ⁸ God, who knows men's hearts, confirmed the fact that he accepts Gentiles by giving them the Holy Spirit, just as he gave him to us. ⁹ He made no distinction between them and us, for he cleansed their lives through faith, just as he did ours. ¹⁰ And now are you going to correct God by burdening the Gentiles with a yoke that neither we nor our fathers were able to bear? ¹¹ Don't you believe that all are saved the same way, by the free gift of the Lord Jesus?"

¹² There was no further discussion, and everyone now listened as Barnabas and Paul told about the miracles God had done through them among the Gentiles.

¹³ When they had finished, James took the floor. "Brothers," he said, "listen to me. ¹⁴ Peter has told you about the time God

first visited the Gentiles to take from them a people to bring honor to his name. [15] And this fact of Gentile conversion agrees with what the prophets predicted. For instance, listen to this passage from the prophet Amos[a]:

> [16] Afterwards' [says the Lord[a]], 'I will return and renew the broken contract with David,[b] [17] so that Gentiles, too, will find the Lord —all those marked with my name.'

[18] That is what the Lord says, who reveals his plans made from the beginning.

[19] "And so my judgment is that we should not insist that the Gentiles who turn to God must obey our Jewish laws, [20] except that we should write to them to refrain from eating meat sacrificed to idols, from all fornication, and also from eating unbled meat of strangled animals. [21] For these things have been preached against in Jewish synagogues in every city on every Sabbath for many generations."

[22] Then the apostles and elders and the whole congregation voted to send delegates to Antioch with Paul and Barnabas, to report on this decision. The men chosen were two of the church leaders—Judas (also called Barsabbas) and Silas.

[23] This is the letter they took along with them:

"*From:* The apostles, elders and brothers at Jerusalem.

"*To:* The Gentile brothers in Antioch, Syria and Cilicia. Greetings!

[24] "We understand that some believers from here have upset you and questioned your salvation,[c] but they had no such instructions from us. [25] So it seemed wise to us, having unanimously agreed on our decision, to send to you these two official representatives, along with our beloved Barnabas and Paul. [26] These men—Judas and Silas, who have risked their lives for the sake of our Lord Jesus Christ—will confirm orally what we have decided concerning your question.

[27,28,29] "For it seemed good to the Holy Spirit and to us to lay no greater burden of Jewish laws on you than to abstain from eating food offered to idols and from unbled meat of strangled animals,[d] and, of course, from fornication. If you do this, it is enough. Farewell."

[30] The four messengers went at once to Antioch, where they called a general meeting of the Christians and gave them the letter. [31] And there was great joy throughout the church that day as they read it.

[32] Then Judas and Silas, both being gifted speakers,[e] preached long sermons to the believers, strengthening their faith. [33] They stayed several days,[f] and then Judas and Silas returned to Jerusalem taking greetings and appreciation to those who had sent them. [34,35] Paul and Barnabas stayed on at Antioch to assist several others who were preaching and teaching there.

[36] Several days later Paul suggested to Barnabas that they return again to Turkey, and visit each city where they had preached before,[g] to see how the new converts were getting along. [37] Barnabas agreed, and wanted to take along John Mark. [38] But Paul didn't like that idea at all, since John had deserted them in Pamphylia. [39] Their disagreement over this was so sharp that they separated. Barnabas took Mark with him and sailed for Cyprus, [40,41] while Paul chose Silas and, with the blessing of the believers, left for Syria and Cilicia, to encourage the churches there.

16 PAUL AND SILAS went first to Derbe and then on to Lystra where they met Timothy, a believer whose mother was a Christian Jewess but his father a Greek. [2] Timothy was well thought of by the brothers in Lystra and Iconium, [3] so Paul asked him to join them on their journey. In deference to the Jews of the area, he circumcised Timothy before they left, for everyone knew that his father was a Greek [and hadn't permitted this before[a]]. [4] Then they went from city to city, making known the decision concerning the Gentiles, as decided by the apostles and elders in Jerusalem. [5] So the

---

a Implied. See Amos 9:11-12.   b Literally, "rebuild the tabernacle of David which is fallen."
c Literally, "subverted your souls."   d Literally, "and from blood."   e Or, "prophets."
f Literally, "spent some time."   g Implied. Literally, "return now and visit every city wherein we proclaimed the word of the Lord."   16a Implied.

church grew daily in faith and numbers.

[6] Next they traveled through Phrygia and Galatia, because the Holy Spirit had told them not to go into the Turkish province of Ausia at that time. [7] Then going along the borders of Mysia they headed north for the province of Bithynia, but again the Spirit of Jesus said no. [8] So instead they went on through Mysia province to the city of Troas.

[9] That night[b] Paul had a vision. In his dream he saw a man over in Macedonia, Greece, pleading with him, "Come over here and help us." [10] Well, that settled it. We[c] would go to Macedonia, for we could only conclude that God was sending us to preach the Good News there.

[11] We went aboard a boat at Troas, and sailed straight across to Samothrace, and the next day on to Neapolis, [12] and finally reached Philippi, a Roman[d] colony just inside the Macedonian border, and stayed there several days.

[13] On the Sabbath, we went a little way outside the city to a river bank where we understood some people met for prayer; and we taught the Scriptures to some women who came. [14] One of them was Lydia, a saleswoman from Thyatira, a merchant of purple cloth. She was already a worshiper of God and, as she listened to us, the Lord opened her heart and she accepted all that Paul was saying. [15] She was baptized along with all her household and asked us to be her guests. "If you agree that I am faithful to the Lord," she said, "come and stay at my home." And she urged us until we did.

[16] One day as we were going down to the place of prayer beside the river, we met a demon-possessed slave girl who was a fortune-teller, and earned much money for her masters. [17] She followed along behind us shouting, "These men are servants of God and they have come to tell you how to have your sins forgiven."

[18] This went on day after day until Paul, in great distress, turned and spoke to the demon within her. "I command you in the name of Jesus Christ to come out of her," he said. And instantly it left her.

[19] Her masters' hopes of wealth were now shattered; they grabbed Paul and Silas and dragged them before the judges at the marketplace.

[20,21] "These Jews are corrupting our city," they shouted. "They are teaching the people to do things that are against the Roman laws."

[22] A mob was quickly formed against Paul and Silas, and the judges ordered them stripped and beaten with wooden whips. [23] Again and again the rods slashed down across their bared backs; and afterwards they were thrown into prison. The jailer was threatened with death if they escaped,[d] [24] so he took no chances, but put them into the inner dungeon and clamped their feet into the stocks.

[25] Around midnight, as Paul and Silas were praying and singing hymns to the Lord—and the other prisoners were listening— [26] suddenly there was a great earthquake; the prison was shaken to its foundations, all the doors flew open—and the chains of every prisoner fell off! [27] The jailer wakened to see the prison doors wide open, and assuming the prisoners had escaped, he drew his sword to kill himself. [28] But Paul yelled to him, "Don't do it! We are all here!"

[29] Trembling with fear, the jailer called for lights and ran to the dungeon and fell down before Paul and Silas. [30] He brought them out and begged them, "Sirs, what must I do to be saved?"

[31] They replied, "Believe on the Lord Jesus and you will be saved, and your entire household."

[32] Then they told him and all his household the Good News from the Lord. [33] That same hour he washed their stripes and he and all his family were baptized. [34] Then he brought them up into his house and set a meal before them. How he and his household rejoiced because all were now believers! [35] The next morning the judges sent police officers over to tell the jailer, "Let those men go!" [36] So the jailer told Paul they were free to leave.

[37] But Paul replied, "Oh, no they don't!

---

b Literally, "in the night."   c Luke, the writer of this book, now joined Paul and accompanied him on his journey.   d Implied.

They have publicly beaten us without trial and jailed us—and we are Roman citizens! So now they want us to leave secretly? Never! Let them come themselves and release us!"

[38] The police officers reported to the judges, who feared for their lives when they heard Paul and Silas were Roman citizens. [39] So they came to the jail and begged them to go, and brought them out and pled with them to leave the city. [40] Paul and Silas then returned to the home of Lydia where they met with the believers and preached to them once more before leaving town.

17 NOW THEY TRAVELED through the cities of Amphipolis and Apollonia and came to Thessalonica, where there was a Jewish synagogue. [2] As was Paul's custom, he went there to preach, and for three Sabbaths in a row he opened the Scriptures to the people, [3] explaining the prophecies about the sufferings of the Messiah and his coming back to life, and proving that Jesus is the Messiah. [4] Some who listened were persuaded and became converts—including a large number of godly Greek men, and also many important women of the city.[a]

[5] But the Jewish leaders were jealous and incited some worthless fellows from the streets to form a mob and start a riot. They attacked the home of Jason, planning to take Paul and Silas to the City Council for punishment.

[6] Not finding them there, they dragged out Jason and some of the other believers, and took them before the Council instead. "Paul and Silas have turned the rest of the world upside down, and now they are here disturbing our city," they shouted, [7] "and Jason has let them into his home. They are all guilty of treason, for they claim another king, Jesus, instead of Caesar."

[8,9] The people of the city, as well as the judges, were concerned at these reports and let them go only after they had posted bail.

[10] That night the Christians hurried Paul and Silas to Beroea, and, as usual,[b] they went to the synagogue to preach. [11] But the people of Beroea were more open minded than those in Thessalonica, and gladly lis-

tened to the message. They searched the Scriptures day by day to check up on Paul and Silas' statements to see if they were really so. [12] As a result, many of them believed, including several prominent Greek women and many men also.

[13] But when the Jews in Thessalonica learned that Paul was preaching in Beroea, they went over and stirred up trouble. [14] The believers acted at once, sending Paul on to the coast, while Silas and Timothy remained behind. [15] Those accompanying Paul went on with him to Athens, and then returned to Beroea with a message for Silas and Timothy to hurry and join him.

[16] While Paul was waiting for them in Athens, he was deeply troubled by all the idols he saw everywhere throughout the city. [17] He went to the synagogue for discussions with the Jews and the devout Gentiles, and spoke daily in the public square to all who happened to be there.

[18] He also had an encounter with some of the Epicurean and Stoic philosophers. Their reaction, when he told them about Jesus and his resurrection, was, "He's a dreamer," or, "He's pushing some foreign religion."

[19] But they invited him to the forum at Mars Hill. "Come and tell us more about this new religion," they said, [20] "for you are saying some rather startling things and we want to hear more." [21] (I should explain that all the Athenians as well as the foreigners in Athens seemed to spend all their time discussing the latest new ideas!)

[22] So Paul, standing before them at the Mars Hill forum, addressed them as follows:

"Men of Athens, I notice that you are very religious, [23] for as I was out walking I saw your many altars, and one of them had this inscription on it—'To the Unknown God.' You have been worshiping him without knowing who he is, and now I wish to tell you about him.

[24] "He made the world and everything in it, and since he is Lord of heaven and earth, he doesn't live in man-made temples; [25] and human hands can't minister to his needs—for he has no needs! He himself gives life

---

a Some manuscripts read, "many of the wives of the leading men."   b Implied.

and breath to everything, and satisfies every need there is. [26] He created all the people of the world from one man, Adam,[c] and scattered the nations across the face of the earth. He decided beforehand which should rise and fall, and when. He determined their boundaries.

[27] "His purpose in all of this is that they should seek after God, and perhaps feel their way toward him and find him—though he is not far from any one of us. [28] For in him we live and move and are! As one of your own poets says it, 'We are the sons of God.' [29] If this is true, we shouldn't think of God as an idol made by men from gold or silver or chipped from stone. [30] God tolerated man's past ignorance about these things, but now he commands everyone to put away idols and worship only him. [31] For he has set a day for justly judging the world by the man he has appointed, and has pointed him out by bringing him back to life again."

[32] When they heard Paul speak of the resurrection of a person who had been dead, some laughed, but others said, "We want to hear more about this later." [33] That ended Paul's discussion with them, [34] but a few joined him and became believers. Among them was Dionysius, a member of the City Council, and a woman named Damaris, and others.

18 THEN PAUL LEFT Athens and went to Corinth. [2,3] There he became acquainted with a Jew named Aquila, born in Pontus, who had recently arrived from Italy with his wife, Priscilla. They had been expelled from Italy as a result of Claudius Caesar's order to deport all Jews from Rome. Paul lived and worked with them, for they were tentmakers just as he was.

[4] Each Sabbath found Paul at the synagogue, trying to convince the Jews and Greeks alike. [5] And after the arrival of Silas and Timothy from Macedonia, Paul spent his full time preaching and testifying to the Jews that Jesus is the Messiah. [6] But when the Jews opposed him and blasphemed,

hurling abuse at Jesus, Paul shook off the dust from his robe and said, "Your blood be upon your own heads—I am innocent—from now on I will preach to the Gentiles."

[7] After that he stayed with Titus Justus, a Gentile[a] who worshiped God and lived next door to the synagogue. [8] However, Crispus, the leader of the synagogue, and all his household believed in the Lord and were baptized—as were many others in Corinth.

[9] One night the Lord spoke to Paul in a vision and told him, "Don't be afraid! Speak out! Don't quit! [10] For I am with you and no one can harm you. Many people here in this city belong to me." [11] So Paul stayed there the next year and a half, teaching the truths of God.

[12] But when Gallio became governor of Achaia, the Jews rose in concerted action against Paul and brought him before the governor for judgment. [13] They accused Paul of "persuading men to worship God in ways that are contrary to Roman law." [14] But just as Paul started to make his defense, Gallio turned to his accusers and said, "Listen, you Jews, if this were a case involving some crime, I would be obliged to listen to you, [15] but since it is merely a bunch of questions of semantics and personalities and your silly Jewish laws, you take care of it. I'm not interested and I'm not touching it." [16] And he drove them out of the courtroom.

[17] Then the mob[a] grabbed Sosthenes, the new leader of the synagogue, and beat him outside the courtroom. But Gallio couldn't have cared less.

[18] Paul stayed in the city several days after that and then said good-bye to the Christians and sailed for the coast of Syria, taking Priscilla and Aquila with him. At Cenchreae, Paul had his head shaved according to Jewish custom, for he had taken a vow.[b] [19] Arriving at the port of Ephesus, he left us aboard ship while he went over to the synagogue for a discussion with the Jews. [20] They asked him to stay for a few days, but he felt that he had no time to lose.[c]

---

c Implied.   18 a Implied.   b Probably a vow to offer a sacrifice in Jerusalem in thanksgiving for answered prayer. The head was shaved thirty days before such gifts and sacrifices were given to God at the Temple. c Possibly in order to arrive in Jerusalem within the prescribed thirty days.

²¹ "I must by all means be at Jerusalem for the holiday,"ᵈ he said. But he promised to return to Ephesus later if God permitted; and so we set sail again.

²² The next stop was at the port of Caesarea from where he visited the church [at Jerusalemᵉ] and then sailed on to Antioch. ²³ After spending some time there, he left for Turkey again, going through Galatia and Phrygia visiting all the believers, encouraging them and helping them grow in the Lord.

²⁴ As it happened, a Jew named Apollos, a wonderful Bible teacher and preacher, had just arrived in Ephesus from Alexandria in Egypt. ²⁵,²⁶ While he was in Egypt, someone had told him about John the Baptist and what John had said about Jesus, but that is all he knew. He had never heard the rest of the story! So he was preaching boldly and enthusiastically in the synagogue, "The Messiah is coming! Get ready to receive him!" Priscilla and Aquila were there and heard him—and it was a powerful sermon. Afterwards they met with him and explained what had happened to Jesus since the time of John, and all that it meant!ᶠ

²⁷ Apollos had been thinking about going to Greece, and the believers encouraged him in this. They wrote to their fellow-believers there, telling them to welcome him. And upon his arrival in Greece, he was greatly used of God to strengthen the church, ²⁸ for he powerfully refuted all the Jewish arguments in public debate, showing by the Scriptures that Jesus is indeed the Messiah.

19 WHILE APOLLOS WAS in Corinth, Paul traveled through Turkey and arrived in Ephesus, where he found several disciples. ² "Did you receive the Holy Spirit when you believed?" he asked them.

"No," they replied, "we don't know what you mean. What is the Holy Spirit?"

³ "Then what beliefs did you acknowledge at your baptism?" he asked.

And they replied, "What John the Baptist taught."

⁴ Then Paul pointed out to them that John's baptism was to demonstrate a desire to turn from sin to God and that those receiving his baptism must then go on to believe in Jesus, the one John said would come later.

⁵ As soon as they heard this, they were baptized inᵃ the name of the Lord Jesus. ⁶ Then, when Paul laid his hands upon their heads, the Holy Spirit came on them, and they spoke in other languages and prophesied. ⁷ The men involved were about twelve in number.

⁸ Then Paul went to the synagogue and preached boldly each Sabbath dayᵇ for three months, telling whatᶜ he believed and why, and persuading many to believe in Jesus. ⁹ But some rejected his message and publicly spoke against Christ, so he left, refusing to preach to them again. Pulling out the believers, he began a separate meeting at the lecture hall of Tyrannus and preached there daily. ¹⁰ This went on for the next two years, so that everyone in the Turkish province of Ausia—both Jews and Greeks—heard the Lord's message. ¹¹ And God gave Paul the power to do unusual miracles, ¹² so that even when his handkerchiefs or parts of his clothing were placed upon sick people, they were healed, and any demons within them came out.

¹³ A team of itinerant Jews who were traveling from town to town casting out demons planned to experiment by using the name of the Lord Jesus. The incantation they decided on was this: "I adjure you by Jesus, whom Paul preaches, to come out!" ¹⁴ Seven sons of Sceva, a Jewish priest, were doing this. ¹⁵ But when they tried it on a man possessed by a demon, the demon replied, "I know Jesus and I know Paul, but who are you?" ¹⁶ And he leaped on two of them and beat them up, so that they fled out of his house naked and badly injured.

¹⁷ The story of what happened spread quickly all through Ephesus, to Jews and Greeks alike; and a solemn fear descended on the city, and the name of the Lord Jesus was greatly honored. ¹⁸,¹⁹ Many of the believers who had been practicing black magic confessed their deeds and brought their in-

---

d Literally, "feast." This entire sentence is omitted in many of the ancient manuscripts.
e Implied.   f Literally, "explained to him the way of God more accurately."   19a Or, "into."
b Implied.   c Literally, "concerning the Kingdom of God."

cantation books and charms and burned them at a public bonfire. (Someone estimated the value of the books at $10,000.[d]) [20] This indicates how deeply the whole area was stirred by God's message.

[21] Afterwards, Paul felt impelled by the Holy Spirit[e] to go across to Greece before returning to Jerusalem. "And after that," he said, "I must go on to Rome!" [22] He sent his two assistants, Timothy and Erastus, on ahead to Greece while he stayed awhile longer in Turkey.

[23] But about that time, a big blowup developed in Ephesus concerning the Christians. [24] It began with Demetrius, a silversmith who employed many craftsmen to manufacture silver shrines of the Greek goddess Diana. [25] He called a meeting of his men, together with others employed in related trades, and addressed them as follows:

"Gentlemen, this business is our income. [26] As you know so well from what you've seen and heard, this man Paul has persuaded many, many people that handmade gods aren't gods at all. As a result, our sales volume is going down! And this trend is evident not only here in Ephesus, but throughout the entire province! [27] Of course, I am not only talking about the business aspects of this situation and our loss of income, but also of the possibility that the temple of the great goddess Diana will lose its influence, and that Diana—this magnificent goddess worshiped not only throughout this part of Turkey but all around the world—will be forgotten!"

[28] At this their anger boiled and they began shouting, "Great is Diana of the Ephesians!"

[29] A crowd began to gather and soon the city was filled with confusion. Everyone rushed to the amphitheater, dragging along Gaius and Aristarchus, Paul's traveling companions, for trial. [30] Paul wanted to go in, but the disciples wouldn't let him. [31] Some of the Roman officers of the province, friends of Paul, also sent a message to him, begging him not to risk his life by entering.

[32] Inside, the people were all shouting, some one thing and some another—everything was in confusion. In fact, most of them didn't even know why they were there.

[33] Alexander was spotted among the crowd by some of the Jews and dragged forward. He motioned for silence and tried to speak. [34] But when the crowd realized he was a Jew, they started shouting again and kept it up for two hours: "Great is Diana of the Ephesians! Great is Diana of the Ephesians!"

[35] At last the mayor was able to quiet them down enough to speak. "Men of Ephesus," he said, "everyone knows that Ephesus is the center[f] of the religion of the great Diana, whose image fell down to us from heaven. [36] Since this is an indisputable fact, you shouldn't be disturbed no matter what is said, and should do nothing rash. [37] Yet you have brought these men here who have stolen nothing from her temple and have not defamed her. [38] If Demetrius and the craftsmen have a case against them, the courts are currently in session and the judges can take the case at once. Let them go through legal channels. [39] And if there are complaints about other matters, they can be settled at the regular City Council meetings; [40] for we are in danger of being called to account by the Roman government for today's riot, since there is no cause for it. And if Rome demands an explanation, I won't know what to say."

[41] Then he dismissed them, and they dispersed.

20 WHEN IT WAS all over, Paul sent for the disciples, preached a farewell message to them, said good-bye and left for Greece, [2] preaching to the believers along the way, in all the cities he passed through. [3] He was in Greece three months and was preparing to sail for Syria when he discovered a plot by the Jews against his life, so he decided to go north to Macedonia first.

[4] Several men were traveling with him, going as far as Turkey;[a] they were Sopater of Beroea, the son of Pyrrhus; Aristarchus

---

d Approximately £3,500.   e Literally, "purposed in the spirit."   f Literally, "is the temple-keeper."
20a Literally, "Asia."

and Secundus, from Thessalonica; Gaius, from Derbe; and Timothy; and Tychicus and Trophimus, who were returning to their homes in Turkey, ⁵ and had gone on ahead and were waiting for us at Troas. ⁶ As soon as the Passover ceremonies ended, we boarded ship at Philippi in northern Greece and five days later arrived in Troas, Turkey, where we stayed a week.

⁷ On Sunday,ᵇ we gathered for a communion service, with Paul preaching. And since he was leaving the next day, he talked until midnight! ⁸ The upstairs room where we met was lighted with many flickering lamps; ⁹ and as Paul spoke on and on, a young man named Eutychus, sitting on the window sill, went fast asleep and fell three stories to his death below. ¹⁰,¹¹,¹² Paul went down and took him into his arms. "Don't worry," he said, "he's all right!" And he was! What a wave of awesome joy swept through the crowd! They all went back upstairs and ate the Lord's Supper together; then Paul preached another long sermon—so it was dawn when he finally left them!

¹³ Paul was going by land to Assos, and we went on ahead by ship. ¹⁴ He joined us there and we sailed together to Mitylene; ¹⁵ the next day we passed Chios; the next, we touched at Samos; and a day later we arrived at Miletus.

¹⁶ Paul had decided against stopping at Ephesus this time, as he was hurrying to get to Jerusalem, if possible, for the celebration of Pentecost. ¹⁷ But when we landed at Miletus, he sent a message to the elders of the church at Ephesus asking them to come down to the boat to meet him.

¹⁸ When they arrived he told them, "You men know that from the day I set foot in Turkey until now ¹⁹ I have done the Lord's work humbly—yes, and with tears—and have faced grave danger from the plots of the Jews against my life. ²⁰ Yet I never shrank from telling you the truth, either publicly or in your homes. ²¹ I have had one message for Jews and Gentiles alike—the necessity of turning from sin to God through faith in our Lord Jesus Christ.

²² "And now I am going to Jerusalem, drawn there irresistibly by the Holy Spirit,ᶜ not knowing what awaits me, ²³ except that the Holy Spirit has told me in city after city that jail and suffering lie ahead. ²⁴ But life is worth nothing unless I use it for doing the work assigned me by the Lord Jesus—the work of telling others the Good News about God's mighty kindness and love.

²⁵ "And now I know that none of you among whom I went about teaching the Kingdom will ever see me again. ²⁶ Let me say plainly that no man's blood can be laid at my door, ²⁷ for I didn't shrink from declaring all God's message to you.

²⁸ "And now beware! Be sure that you feed and shepherd God's flock—his church, purchased with his blood—for the Holy Spirit is holding you responsible as overseers. ²⁹ I know full well that after I leave you, false teachers, like vicious wolves, will appear among you, not sparing the flock. ³⁰ Some of you yourselves will distort the truth in order to draw a following. ³¹ Watch out! Remember the three years I was with you—my constant watchcare over you night and day and my many tears for you.

³² "And now I entrust you to God and his care and to his wonderful words which are able to build your faith and give you all the inheritance of those who are set apart for himself.

³³ "I have never been hungry for money or fine clothing— ³⁴ you know that these hands of mine worked to pay my own way and even to supply the needs of those who were with me. ³⁵ And I was a constant example to you in helping the poor; for I remembered the words of the Lord Jesus, 'It is more blessed to give than to receive.' "

³⁶ When he had finished speaking, he knelt and prayed with them, ³⁷ and they wept aloud as they embraced him in farewell, ³⁸ sorrowing most of all because he said that he would never see them again. Then they accompanied him down to the ship.

21 AFTER PARTING FROM the Ephesian elders, we sailed straight to Cos. The

---

b Or, "on Saturday night." Literally, "the first day of the week," by Jewish reckoning, from sundown to sundown.   c Or, "by an inner compulsion."

next day we reached Rhodes and then went to Patara. [2] There we boarded a ship sailing for the Syrian province of Phoenicia. [3] We sighted the island of Cyprus, passed it on our left and landed at the harbor of Tyre, in Syria, where the ship unloaded. [4] We went ashore, found the local believers and stayed with them a week. These disciples warned Paul—the Holy Spirit prophesying through them—not to go on to Jerusalem. [5] At the end of the week when we returned to the ship, the entire congregation including wives and children walked down to the beach with us where we prayed and said our farewells. [6] Then we went aboard and they returned home.

[7] The next stop after leaving Tyre was Ptolemais where we greeted the believers, but stayed only one day. [8] Then we went on to Caesarea and stayed at the home of Philip the Evangelist, one of the first seven deacons.[a] [9] He had four unmarried[b] daughters who had the gift of prophecy.

[10] During our stay of several days, a man named Agabus, who also had the gift of prophecy, arrived from Judea [11] and visited us. He took Paul's belt, bound his own feet and hands with it and said, "The Holy Spirit declares, 'So shall the owner of this belt be bound by the Jews in Jerusalem and turned over to the Romans.'" [12] Hearing this, all of us—the local believers and his traveling companions—begged Paul not to go on to Jerusalem.

[13] But he said, "Why all this weeping? You are breaking my heart! For I am ready not only to be jailed at Jerusalem, but also to die for the sake of the Lord Jesus." [14] When it was clear that he wouldn't be dissuaded, we gave up and said, "The will of the Lord be done."

[15] So shortly afterwards, we packed our things and left for Jerusalem. [16] Some disciples from Caesarea accompanied us, and on arrival we were guests at the home of Mnason, originally from Cyprus, one of the early believers; [17] and all the believers at Jerusalem welcomed us cordially.

[18] The second day Paul took us with him to meet with James and the elders of the Jerusalem church. [19] After greetings were exchanged, Paul recounted the many things God had accomplished among the Gentiles through his work.

[20] They praised God but then said, "You know, dear brother, how many thousands of Jews have also believed, and they are all very insistent that Jewish believers must continue to follow the Jewish traditions and customs.[c] [21] Our Jewish Christians here at Jerusalem have been told that you are against the laws of Moses, against our Jewish customs, and that you forbid the circumcision of their children. [22] Now what can be done? For they will certainly hear that you have come.

[23] "We suggest this: We have four men here who are preparing to shave their heads and take some vows. [24] Go with them to the Temple and have your head shaved too —and pay for theirs to be shaved.

"Then everyone will know that you approve of this custom for the Hebrew Christians and that you yourself obey the Jewish laws and are in line with our thinking in these matters.

[25] "As for the Gentile Christians, we aren't asking them to follow these Jewish customs at all—except for the ones we wrote to them about: not to eat food offered to idols, not to eat unbled meat from strangled animals, and not to commit fornication."

[26,27] So Paul agreed to their request and the next day went with the men to the Temple for the ceremony, thus publicizing his vow to offer a sacrifice seven[d] days later with the others.

The seven days were almost ended when some Jews from Turkey saw him in the Temple and roused a mob against him. They grabbed him, [28] yelling, "Men of Israel! Help! Help! This is the man who preaches against our people and tells everybody to disobey the Jewish laws. He even talks against the Temple and defiles it by bringing Gentiles in!" [29] (For down in the city earlier that day, they had seen him with Trophimus, a Gentile[e] from Ephesus in Turkey, and assumed that Paul had taken

---

a See Acts 6:5; 8:1-13.   b Literally, "virgins."   c Literally, "they are all zealous for the law"
d Literally, "the days of purification."   e Implied.

him into the Temple.)

[30] The whole population of the city was electrified by these accusations and a great riot followed. Paul was dragged out of the Temple, and immediately the gates were closed behind him. [31] As they were killing him, word reached the commander of the Roman garrison that all Jerusalem was in an uproar. [32] He quickly ordered out his soldiers and officers and ran down among the crowd. When the mob saw the troops coming, they quit beating Paul. [33] The commander arrested him and ordered him bound with double chains. Then he asked the crowd who he was and what he had done. [34] Some shouted one thing and some another. When he couldn't find out anything in all the uproar and confusion, he ordered Paul to be taken to the armory.[f] [35] As they reached the stairs, the mob grew so violent that the soldiers lifted Paul to their shoulders to protect him, [36] and the crowd surged behind shouting, "Away with him, away with him!"

[37,38] As Paul was about to be taken inside, he said to the commander, "May I have a word with you?"

"Do you know Greek?" the commander asked, surprised. "Aren't you that Egyptian who led a rebellion a few years ago[g] and took 4,000 members of the Assassins with him into the desert?"

[39] "No," Paul replied, "I am a Jew from Tarsus in Cilicia which is no small town. I request permission to talk to these people."

[40] The commander agreed, so Paul stood on the stairs and motioned to the people to be quiet; soon a deep silence enveloped the crowd, and he addressed them in Hebrew as follows:

22 "BROTHERS AND FATHERS, listen to me as I offer my defense." [2] (When they heard him speaking in Hebrew, the silence was even greater.) [3] "I am a Jew," he said, "born in Tarsus, a city in Cilicia, but educated here in Jerusalem under Gamaliel, at whose feet I learned to follow our Jewish laws and customs very carefully. I became very anxious to honor God in everything I did, just as you have tried to do

today. [4] And I persecuted the Christians, hounding them to death, binding and delivering both men and women to prison. [5] The High Priest or any member of the Council can testify that this is so. For I asked them for letters to the Jewish leaders in Damascus, with instructions to let me bring any Christians I found to Jerusalem in chains to be punished.

[6] "As I was on the road, nearing Damascus, suddenly about noon a very bright light from heaven shone around me. [7] And I fell to the ground and heard a voice saying to me, 'Saul, Saul, why are you persecuting me?'

[8] "'Who is it speaking to me, sir?' I asked. And he replied, 'I am Jesus of Nazareth, the one you are persecuting.' [9] The men with me saw the light but didn't understand what was said.

[10] "And I said, 'What shall I do, Lord?'

"And the Lord told me, 'Get up and go into Damascus, and there you will be told what awaits you in the years ahead.'

[11] "I was blinded by the intense light, and had to be led into Damascus by my companions. [12] There a man named Ananias, as godly a man as you could find for obeying the law, and well thought of by all the Jews of Damascus, [13] came to me, and standing beside me said, 'Brother Saul, receive your sight!' And that very hour I could see him!

[14] "Then he told me, 'The God of our fathers has chosen you to know his will and to see the Messiah[a] and hear him speak. [15] You are to take his message everywhere, telling what you have seen and heard. [16] And now, why delay? Go and be baptized, and be cleansed from your sins, calling on the name of the Lord.'

[17,18] "One day after my return to Jerusalem, while I was praying in the Temple, I fell into a trance and saw a vision of God saying to me, 'Hurry! Leave Jerusalem, for the people here won't believe you when you give them my message.'

[19] "'But Lord,' I argued, 'they certainly know that I imprisoned and beat those in every synagogue who believed on you. [20] And when your witness Stephen was

---

f Literally, "castle," or "fort."   g Literally, "before these days."   22a Literally, "Righteous One."

killed, I was standing there agreeing—keeping the coats they laid aside as they stoned him.'

²¹ "But God said to me, 'Leave Jerusalem, for I will send you far away to the *Gentiles!*' "

²² The crowd listened until Paul came to that word, then with one voice they shouted, "Away with such a fellow! Kill him! He isn't fit to live!" ²³ They yelled and threw their coats in the air and tossed up handfuls of dust.

²⁴ So the commander brought him inside and ordered him lashed with whips to make him confess his crime. He wanted to find out why the crowd had become so furious!

²⁵ As they tied Paul down to lash him, Paul said to an officer standing there, "Is it legal for you to whip a Roman citizen who hasn't even been tried?"

²⁶ The officer went to the commander and asked, "What are you doing? This man is a Roman citizen!"

²⁷ So the commander went over and asked Paul, "Tell me, are you a Roman citizen?"

"Yes, I certainly am."

²⁸ "I am too," the commander muttered, "and it cost me plenty!"

"But I am a citizen by birth!"

²⁹ The soldiers standing ready to lash him, quickly disappeared when they heard Paul was a Roman citizen, and the commander was frightened because he had ordered him bound and whipped.

³⁰ The next day the commander freed him from his chains and ordered the chief priests into session with the Jewish Council. He had Paul brought in before them to try to find out what the trouble was all about.

23 GAZING INTENTLY AT the Council, Paul began:

"Brothers, I have always lived before God in all good conscience!"

² Instantly Ananias the High Priest commanded those close to Paul to slap him on the mouth.

³ Paul said to him, "God shall slap you, you whitewashed pigpen.ᵃ What kind of

judge are you to break the law yourself by ordering me struck like that?"

⁴ Those standing near Paul said to him, "Is that the way to talk to God's High Priest?"

⁵ "I didn't realize he was the High Priest, brothers," Paul replied, "for the Scriptures say, 'Never speak evil of any of your rulers.' "

⁶ Then Paul thought of something! Part of the Council were Sadducees, and part were Pharisees! So he shouted, "Brothers, I am a Pharisee, as were all my ancestors! And I am being tried here today because I believe in the resurrection of the dead!"

⁷ This divided the Council right down the middle—the Pharisees against the Sadducees— ⁸ for the Sadducees say there is no resurrection or angels or even eternal spirit within us,ᵇ but the Pharisees believe in all of these.

⁹ So a great clamor arose. Some of the Jewish leadersᶜ jumped up to argue that Paul was all right. "We see nothing wrong with him," they shouted. "Perhaps a spirit or angel spoke to him [there on the Damascusᵈ]."

¹⁰ The shouting grew louder and louder, and the men were tugging at Paul from both sides, pulling him this way and that. Finally the commander, fearing they would tear him apart, ordered his soldiers to take him away from them by force and bring him back to the armory.

¹¹ That night the Lord stood beside Paul and said, "Don't worry, Paul; just as you have told the people about me here in Jerusalem, so you must also in Rome."

¹²,¹³ The next morning some forty or more of the Jews got together and bound themselves by a curse neither to eat nor drink until they had killed Paul! ¹⁴ Then they went to the chief priests and elders and told them what they had done. ¹⁵ "Ask the commander to bring Paul back to the Council again," they requested. "Pretend you want to ask a few more questions. We will kill him on the way."

¹⁶ But Paul's nephew got wind of their plan and came to the armory and told Paul.

---

a Literally, "you whitewashed wall."   b Literally, "nor spirit."   c Literally, "scribes."
d Implied.

[17] Paul called one of the officers and said, "Take this boy to the commander. He has something important to tell him."

[18] So the officer did, explaining, "Paul, the prisoner, called me over and asked me to bring this young man to you to tell you something."

[19] The commander took the boy by the hand, and leading him aside asked, "What is it you want to tell me, lad?"

[20] "Tomorrow," he told him, "the Jews are going to ask you to bring Paul before the Council again, pretending they want to get some more information. [21] But don't do it! There are more than forty men hiding along the road ready to jump him and kill him. They have bound themselves under a curse to neither eat nor drink till he is dead. They are out there now, expecting you to agree to their request."

[22] "Don't let a soul know you told me this," the commander warned the boy as he left. [23,24] Then the commander called two of his officers and ordered, "Get 200 soldiers ready to leave for Caesarea at nine o'clock tonight! Take 200 spearmen and 70 mounted cavalry. Give Paul a horse to ride and get him safely to Governor Felix."

[25] Then he wrote this letter to the governor:

[26] *"From:* Claudius Lysias

"To: His Excellency, Governor Felix.

"Greetings!

[27] "This man was seized by the Jews and they were killing him when I sent the soldiers to rescue him, for I learned that he was a Roman citizen. [28] Then I took him to their Council to try to find out what he had done. [29] I soon discovered it was something about their Jewish beliefs, certainly nothing worthy of imprisonment or death. [30] But when I was informed of a plot to kill him, I decided to send him on to you and will tell his accusers to bring their charges before you."

[31] So that night, as ordered, the soldiers took Paul to Antipatris. [32] They returned to the armory the next morning, leaving him with the cavalry to take him on to Caesarea.

[33] When they arrived in Caesarea, they presented Paul and the letter to the gover-nor. [34] He read it and then asked Paul where he was from.

"Cilicia," Paul answered.

[35] "I will hear your case fully when your accusers arrive," the governor told him, and ordered him kept in the prison at King Herod's palace.

24 FIVE DAYS LATER Ananias the High Priest arrived with some of the Jewish leaders[a] and the lawyer[b] Tertullus, to make their accusations against Paul. [2] When Tertullus was called forward, he laid charges against Paul in the following address to the governor:

"Your Excellency, you have given quietness and peace to us Jews and have greatly reduced the discrimination against us. [3] And for this we are very, very grateful to you. [4] But lest I bore you, kindly give me your attention for only a moment as I briefly outline our case against this man. [5] For we have found him to be a troublemaker, a man who is constantly inciting the Jews throughout the entire world to riots and rebellions against the Roman government. He is a ringleader of the sect known as the Nazarenes. [6] Moreover, he was trying to defile the Temple when we arrested him.

"We would have given him what he justly deserves, [7] but Lysias, the commander of the garrison, came and took him violently away from us, [8] demanding that he be tried by Roman law. You can find out the truth of our accusations by examining him yourself."

[9] Then all the other Jews chimed in, declaring that everything Tertullus said was true.

[10] Now it was Paul's turn. The governor motioned for him to rise and speak.

Paul began: "I know, sir, that you have been a judge of Jewish affairs for many years, and this gives me confidence as I make my defense. [11] You can quickly discover that it was no more than twelve days ago that I arrived in Jerusalem to worship at the Temple, [12] and you will discover that I have never incited a riot in any synagogue or on the streets of any city; [13] and these

---

a Literally, "elders."   b Literally, "orator."

men certainly cannot prove the things they accuse me of doing. ¹⁴ "But one thing I do confess, that I believe in the way of salvation, which they refer to as a sect; I follow that system of serving the God of our ancestors; I firmly believe in the Jewish law and everything written in the books of prophecy; ¹⁵ and I believe, just as these men do, that there will be a resurrection of both the righteous and ungodly. ¹⁶ Because of this I try with all my strength to always maintain a clear conscience before God and man.

¹⁷ "After several years away, I returned to Jerusalem with money to aid the Jews, and to offer a sacrifice to God. ¹⁸ My accusers saw me in the Temple as I was presenting my thank offering.ᶜ I had shaved my head as their laws required, and there was no crowd around me, and no rioting! But some Jews from Turkey were there ¹⁹ (who ought to be here if they have anything against me)— ²⁰ but look! Ask these men right here what wrongdoing their Council found in me, ²¹ except that I said one thing I shouldn'tᵈ when I shouted out, 'I am here before the Council to defend myself for believing that the dead will rise again!' "

²² Felix, who knew Christians didn't go around starting riots,ᵉ told the Jews to wait for the arrival of Lysias, the garrison commander, and then he would decide the case. ²³ He ordered Paul to prison but instructed the guards to treat him gently and not to forbid any of his friends from visiting him or bringing him gifts to make his stay more comfortable.

²⁴ A few days later Felix came with Drusilla, his legalᶠ wife, a Jewess. Sending for Paul, they listened as he told them about faith in Christ Jesus. ²⁵ And as he reasoned with them about righteousness and self-control and the judgment to come, Felix was terrified.

"Go away for now," he replied, "and when I have a more convenient time, I'll call for you again."

²⁶ He also hoped that Paul would bribe him, so he sent for him from time to time and talked with him. ²⁷ Two years went by

in this way; then Felix was succeeded by Porcius Festus. And because Felix wanted to gain favor with the Jews, he left Paul in chains.

25 THREE DAYS AFTER Festus arrived in Caesarea to take over his new responsibilities, he left for Jerusalem, ² where the chief priests and other Jewish leaders got hold of him and gave him their story about Paul. ³ They begged him to bring Paul to Jerusalem at once. (Their plan was to waylay and kill him.) ⁴ But Festus replied that since Paul was at Caesarea and he himself was returning there soon, ⁵ those with authority in this affair should return with him for the trial.

⁶ Eight or ten days later he returned to Caesarea and the following day opened Paul's trial.

⁷ On Paul's arrival in court the Jews from Jerusalem gathered around, hurling many serious accusations which they couldn't prove. ⁸ Paul denied the charges: "I am not guilty," he said. "I have not opposed the Jewish laws or desecrated the Temple or rebelled against the Roman government."

⁹ Then Festus, anxious to please the Jews, asked him, "Are you willing to go to Jerusalem and stand trial before me?"

¹⁰,¹¹ But Paul replied, "No! I demand my privilege of a hearing before the Emperor himself. You know very well I am not guilty. If I have done something worthy of death, I don't refuse to die! But if I am innocent, neither you nor anyone else has a right to turn me over to these men to kill me. *I appeal to Caesar.*"

¹² Festus conferred with his advisors and then replied, "Very well! You have appealed to Caesar, and to Caesar you shall go!"

¹³ A few days later King Agrippa arrived with Berniceᵃ for a visit with Festus. ¹⁴ During their stay of several days Festus discussed Paul's case with the king. "There is a prisoner here," he told him, "whose case was left for me by Felix. ¹⁵ When I was in Jerusalem, the chief priests and other Jewish leaders gave me their side of the story

---

c Implied. d Literally, "except it be for this one voice." e Literally, "having more accurate knowledge." f Literally, "his own wife." 25a She was his sister.

and asked me to have him killed. [16] Of course I quickly pointed out to them that Roman law does not convict a man before he is tried. He is given an opportunity to defend himself face to face with his accusers.

[17] "When they came here for the trial, I called the case the very next day and ordered Paul brought in. [18] But the accusations made against him weren't at all what I supposed they would be. [19] It was something about their religion, and about someone called Jesus who died, but Paul insists is alive! [20] I was perplexed as to how to decide a case of this kind and asked him whether he would be willing to stand trial on these charges in Jerusalem. [21] But Paul appealed to Caesar! So I ordered him back to jail until I could arrange to get him to the Emperor."

[22] "I'd like to hear the man myself," Agrippa said.

And Festus replied, "You shall—tomorrow!"

[23] So the next day, after the king and Bernice had arrived at the courtroom with great pomp, accompanied by military officers and prominent men of the city, Festus ordered Paul brought in.

[24] Then Festus addressed the audience: "King Agrippa and all present," he said, "this is the man whose death is demanded both by the local Jews and by those in Jerusalem! [25] But in my opinion he has done nothing worthy of death. However, he appealed his case to Caesar, and I have no alternative but to send him. [26] But what shall I write the Emperor? For there is no real charge against him! So I have brought him before you all, and especially you, King Agrippa, to examine him and then tell me what to write. [27] For it doesn't seem reasonable to send a prisoner to the Emperor without any charges against him!"

26 THEN AGRIPPA SAID to Paul, "Go ahead. Tell us your story."

So Paul, with many gestures,[a] presented his defense:

[2] "I am fortunate, King Agrippa," he began, "to be able to present my answer before you, [3] for I know you are an expert on Jewish laws and customs. Now please listen patiently!

[4] "As the Jews are well aware, I was given a thorough Jewish training from my earliest childhood in Tarsus[b] and later at Jerusalem, and I lived accordingly. [5] If they would admit it, they know that I have always been the strictest of Pharisees when it comes to obedience to Jewish laws and customs. [6] But the real reason behind their accusations is something else—it is because I am looking forward to the fulfillment of God's promise made to our ancestors. [7] The twelve tribes of Israel strive night and day to attain this same hope I have! Yet, O King, for me it is a crime, they say! [8] But is it a crime to believe in the resurrection of the dead? Does it seem incredible to you that God can bring men back to life again?

[9] "I used to believe that I ought to do many horrible things to the followers[c] of Jesus of Nazareth. [10] I imprisoned many of the saints in Jerusalem, as authorized by the High Priests; and when they were condemned to death, I cast my vote against them. [11] I used torture to try to make Christians everywhere curse Christ. I was so violently opposed to them that I even hounded them in distant cities in foreign lands.

[12] "I was on such a mission to Damascus, armed with the authority and commission of the chief priests, [13] when one day about noon, sir, a light from heaven brighter than the sun shone down on me and my companions. [14] We all fell down, and I heard a voice speaking to me in Hebrew, 'Saul, Saul, why are you persecuting me? You are only hurting yourself.'[d]

[15] " 'Who are you, sir?' I asked.

"And the Lord replied, 'I am Jesus, the one you are persecuting. [16] Now stand up! For I have appeared to you to appoint you as my servant and my witness. You are to tell the world about this experience and about the many other occasions when I shall appear to you. [17] And I will protect you from both your own people and the Gentiles. Yes, I am going to send you to the

---

a Literally, "stretched forth his hand."   b Literally, "my own nation."   c Literally, "the name."
d Literally, "It is hard for you to kick against the oxgoad!"

Gentiles [18] to open their eyes to their true condition so that they may repent and live in the light of God instead of in Satan's darkness, so that they may receive forgiveness for their sins and God's inheritance along with all people everywhere whose sins are cleansed away, who are set apart by faith in me.'

[19] "And so, O King Agrippa, I was not disobedient to that vision from heaven! [20] I preached first to those in Damascus, then in Jerusalem and through Judea, and also to the Gentiles that all must forsake their sins and turn to God—and prove their repentance by doing good deeds. [21] The Jews arrested me in the Temple for preaching this, and tried to kill me, [22] but God protected me so that I am still alive today to tell these facts to everyone, both great and small. I teach nothing except what the prophets and Moses said— [23] that the Messiah would suffer, and be the First to rise from the dead, to bring light to Jews and Gentiles alike."

[24] Suddenly Festus shouted, "Paul, you are insane. Your long studying has broken your mind!"

[25] But Paul replied, "I am not insane, Most Excellent Festus. I speak words of sober truth. [26] And King Agrippa knows about these things. I speak frankly for I am sure these events are all familiar to him, for they were not done in a corner! [27] King Agrippa, do you believe the prophets? But I know you do—"

[28] Agrippa interrupted him. "With trivial proofs like these,[e] you expect me to become a Christian?"

[29] And Paul replied, "Would to God that whether my arguments are trivial or strong, both you and everyone here in this audience might become the same as I am, except for these chains."

[30] Then the king, the governor, Bernice, and all the others stood and left. [31] As they talked it over afterwards they agreed, "This man hasn't done anything worthy of death or imprisonment."

[32] And Agrippa said to Festus, "He could be set free if he hadn't appealed to Caesar!"

27 ARRANGEMENTS WERE FINALLY made to start us on our way to Rome by ship; so Paul and several other prisoners were placed in the custody of an officer named Julius, a member of the imperial guard. [2] We left on a boat[a] which was scheduled to make several stops along the Turkish coast.[b] I should add that Aristarchus,[c] a Greek from Thessalonica, was with us.

[3] The next day when we docked at Sidon, Julius was very kind to Paul and let him go ashore to visit with friends and receive their hospitality. [4] Putting to sea from there, we encountered headwinds that made it difficult to keep the ship on course, so we sailed north of Cyprus between the island and the mainland,[d] [5] and passed along the coast of the provinces of Cilicia and Pamphylia, landing at Myra, in the province of Lycia. [6] There our officer found an Egyptian ship from Alexandria, bound for Italy, and put us aboard.

[7,8] We had several days of rough sailing, and finally neared Cnidus;[e] but the winds had become too strong, so we ran across to Crete, passing the port of Salmone. Beating into the wind with great difficulty and moving slowly along the southern coast, we arrived at Fair Havens, near the city of Lasea. [9] There we stayed for several days. The weather was becoming dangerous for long voyages by then, because it was late in the year,[f] and Paul spoke to the ship's officers about it.

[10] "Sirs," he said, "I believe there is trouble ahead if we go on—perhaps shipwreck, loss of cargo, injuries, and death." [11] But the officers in charge of the prisoners listened more to the ship's captain and the owner than to Paul. [12] And since Fair Havens was an exposed[g] harbor—a poor place to spend the winter—most of the crew advised trying to go further up the coast to Phoenix, in order to winter there; Phoenix was a good

---

e Literally, "with little (persuasion)." 27a Literally, "a ship of Adramyttium." b Literally, "the coast of Asia." c See Acts 19:29, 20:4, Philemon 24. d Implied. Literally, "we sailed under the lee of Cyprus." Narratives from that period interpret this as meaning what is indicated in the paraphrase above. e Cnidus was a port on the southeast coast of Turkey. f Literally, "because the Fast was now already gone by." It came at about the time of the autumn equinox. g Implied.

harbor with only a northwest and southwest exposure.

¹³ Just then a light wind began blowing from the south, and it looked like a perfect day for the trip; so they pulled up anchor and sailed along close to shore.

¹⁴,¹⁵ But shortly afterwards, the weather changed abruptly and a heavy wind of typhoon strength (a "northeaster," they called it) caught the ship and blew it out to sea. They tried at first to face back to shore but couldn't, so they gave up and let the ship run before the gale.

¹⁶ We finally sailed behind a small island named Clauda, where with great difficulty we hoisted aboard the lifeboat that was being towed behind us, ¹⁷ and then banded the ship with ropes to strengthen the hull. The sailors were afraid of being driven across to the quicksands of the African coast,ʰ so they lowered the topsails and were thus driven before the wind.

¹⁸ The next day as the seas grew higher, the crew began throwing the cargo overboard. ¹⁹ The following day they threw out the tackle and anything else they could lay their hands on. ²⁰ The terrible storm raged unabated many days,ⁱ until at last all hope was gone.

²¹ No one had eaten for a long time, but finally Paul called the crew together and said, "Men, you should have listened to me in the first place and not left Fair Havens —you would have avoided all this injury and loss! ²² But cheer up! Not one of us will lose our lives, even though the ship will go down.

²³ "For last night an angel of the God to whom I belong and whom I serve stood beside me, ²⁴ and said, 'Don't be afraid, Paul—for you will surely stand trial before Caesar! What's more, God has granted your request and will save the lives of all those sailing with you.' ²⁵ So take courage! For I believe God! It will be just as he said! ²⁶ But we will be shipwrecked on an island."

²⁷ About midnight on the fourteenth night of the storm, as we were being driven to and fro on the Adriatic Sea, the sailors suspected land was near. ²⁸ They sounded,

and found 120 feet of water below them. A little later they sounded again, and found only ninety feet. ²⁹ At this rate they knew they would soon be driven ashore; and fearing rocks along the coast, they threw out four anchors from the stern and prayed for daylight.

³⁰ Some of the sailors planned to abandon the ship, and lowered the emergency boat as though they were going to put out anchors from the prow. ³¹ But Paul said to the soldiers and commanding officer, "You will all die unless everyone stays aboard." ³² So the soldiers cut the ropes and let the boat fall off.

³³ As the darkness gave way to the early morning light, Paul begged everyone to eat. "You haven't touched food for two weeks," he said. ³⁴ "Please eat something now for your own good! For not a hair of your heads shall perish!"

³⁵ Then he took some hardtack and gave thanks to God before them all, and broke off a piece and ate it. ³⁶ Suddenly everyone felt better and began eating, ³⁷ all two hundred seventy-six of us—for that is the number we had aboard. ³⁸ After eating, the crew lightened the ship further by throwing all the wheat overboard.

³⁹ When it was day, they didn't recognize the coastline, but noticed a bay with a beach and wondered whether they could get between the rocks and be driven up onto the beach. ⁴⁰ They finally decided to try. Cutting off the anchors and leaving them in the sea, they lowered the rudders, raised the foresail and headed ashore. ⁴¹ But the ship hit a sandbarʲ and ran aground. The bow of the ship stuck fast, while the stern was exposed to the violence of the waves and began to break apart.

⁴² The soldiers advised their commanding officer to let them kill the prisoners lest any of them swim ashore and escape. ⁴³ But Juliusᵏ wanted to spare Paul, so he told them no. Then he ordered all who could swim to jump overboard and make for land, ⁴⁴ and the rest to try for it on planks and debris from the broken ship. So everyone escaped safely ashore!

---

h Literally, "fearing lest they should be cast upon the Syrtis." upon us."   j Literally, "a place where two seas met."   i Literally, "neither sun nor stars shone k Implied.

28 WE SOON LEARNED that we were on the island of Malta. The people of the island were very kind to us, building a bonfire on the beach to welcome and warm us in the rain and cold. ³ As Paul gathered an armful of sticks to lay on the fire, a poisonous snake, driven out by the heat, fastened itself onto his hand! ⁴ The people of the island saw it hanging there and said to each other, "A murderer, no doubt! Though he escaped the sea, justice will not permit him to live!" ⁵ But Paul shook off the snake into the fire and was unharmed. ⁶ The people waited for him to begin swelling or suddenly fall dead; but when they had waited a long time and no harm came to him, they changed their minds and decided he was a god.

⁷ Near the shore where we landed was an estate belonging to Publius, the governor of the island. He welcomed us courteously and fed us for three days. ⁸ As it happened, Publius' father was ill with fever and dysentery. Paul went in and prayed for him, and laying his hands on him, healed him! ⁹ Then all the other sick people in the island came and were cured. ¹⁰ As a result we were showered with gifts,ᵃ and when the time came to sail, people put on board all sorts of things we would need for the trip.

¹¹ It was three months after the shipwreck before we set sail again, and this time it was in *The Twin Brothers* of Alexandria, a ship that had wintered at the island. ¹² Our first stop was Syracuse, where we stayed three days. ¹³ From there we circled around to Rhegium; a day later a south wind began blowing, so the following day we arrived at Puteoli, ¹⁴ where we found some believers! They begged us to stay with them seven days. Then we went on to Rome. ¹⁵ The brothers in Rome had heard we were coming and came to meet us at the Forumᵇ on the Appian Way. Others joined us at The Three Tavernsᶜ. When Paul saw them, he thanked God and took courage. ¹⁶ When we arrived in Rome, Paul was permitted to live wherever he wanted to,

though guarded by a soldier. ¹⁷ Three days after his arrival, he called together the local Jewish leaders and spoke to them as follows: "Brothers, I was arrested by the Jews in Jerusalem and handed over to the Roman government for prosecution, even though I had harmed no one nor violated the customs of our ancestors. ¹⁸ The Romans gave me a trial and wanted to release me, for they found no cause for the death sentence demanded by the Jewish leaders. ¹⁹ But when the Jews protested the decision, I felt it necessary, with no malice against them, to appeal to Caesar. ²⁰ I asked you to come here today so we could get acquainted and I could tell you that it is because I believe the Messiahᵈ has come that I am bound with this chain."

²¹ They replied, "We have heard nothing against you! We have had no letters from Judea or reports from those arriving from Jerusalem.ᵉ ²² But we want to hear what you believe, for the only thing we know about these Christians is that they are denounced everywhere!"

²³ So a time was set and on that day large numbers came to his house. He told them about the Kingdom of God and taught them about Jesus from the Scriptures—from the five books of Moses and the books of prophecy. He began lecturing in the morning and went on into the evening! ²⁴ Some believed, and some didn't. ²⁵ But after they had argued back and forth among themselves, they left with this final word from Paul ringing in their ears: "The Holy Spirit was right when he said through Isaiah the prophet, ²⁶ " 'Say to the Jews, "You will hear and see but not understand, ²⁷ for your hearts are too fat and your ears don't listen and you have closed your eyes against understanding, for you don't want to see and hear and understand and turn to me to heal you." 'ᶠ ²⁸,²⁹ᵍ So I want you to realize that this salvation from God is available to the Gentiles too, and they will accept it."

³⁰ Paul lived for the next two years in his

a Literally, "honors."   b About forty-three miles from Rome.   c About thirty-five miles from Rome. d Literally, "the hope of Israel." But perhaps he is referring here, as in his other defenses, to his belief in the resurrection of the dead.   e Implied.   f Isaiah 6:9, 10.   g Some of the ancient manuscripts add, "And when he had said these words, the Jews departed, having much dissenting among themselves."

rented house[h] and welcomed all who visited him, [31] telling them with all boldness about the Kingdom of God and about the Lord Jesus Christ; and no one tried to stop him.

h Or, "at his own expense."

Richard T. Lee

Roger Bowlin is in a park in Seattle at midnight. Somewhere in the tangle of bushes is a shivering three-year-old girl. He hears a whimper and a scraping sound. He dives into a blackberry patch through an 18-inch-wide tunnel. He belly-crawls forward, ignoring the stinging briars, and finds the girl, huddled alone in the darkness. He wraps her inside his blanket and begins the difficult trip out.

Another day is gruesome. Roger's party has just found a suicide victim, a young woman on an island. The body is lying in a pasture, behind her home, next to a picture of her husband. A thick trail of blood leads to slit marks on her wrists.

Discoveries like these come regularly to Roger Bowlin. He's a member of Search and Rescue, a highly disciplined band of adventurers who specialize in emergencies. Sometimes they salvage a happy ending, sometimes not. Coming back to school classes on a Monday morning after discovering a suicide victim is bound to have some effect. Roger was puzzled to learn that many kids wouldn't talk about tragedies. "I couldn't understand why any of my friends wouldn't talk about the most important things of life, such as how to prepare for death, and how God fits in. Kids feel very comfortable talking about teachers or clothes or Monday night football. But it's kind of hard to shift gears."

Often what really counts in life gets the least attention. Perhaps that's why Romans is often overlooked. It's the Bible's textbook summary of everything that's important to know. It traces God's love from the very beginning and shows exactly what he wants to accomplish in the world.

Set against the background of Christ's life and the exploits of the early church, Paul gets personal about what must happen within us. Tough tracking for anyone who is serious about letting the Lord take over his life.

What Counts?

ROMANS

1 DEAR FRIENDS IN Rome: [1] This letter is from Paul, Jesus Christ's slave, chosen to be a missionary, and sent out to preach God's Good News. [2] This Good News was promised long ago by God's prophets in the Old Testament. [3] It is the Good News about his Son, Jesus Christ our Lord, who came as a human baby, born into King David's royal family line; [4] and by being raised from the dead he was proved to be the mighty Son of God, with the holy nature of God himself.

[5] And now, through Christ, all the kindness of God has been poured out upon us undeserving sinners; and now he is sending us out around the world to tell all people everywhere the great things God has done for them, so that they, too, will believe and obey him.

[6,7] And you, dear friends in Rome, are among those he dearly loves; you, too, are invited by Jesus Christ to be God's very own—yes, his holy people. May all God's mercies and peace be yours from God our Father and from Jesus Christ our Lord.

[8] Let me say first of all that wherever I go I hear you being talked about! For your faith in God is becoming known around the world. How I thank God through Jesus Christ for this good report, and for each one of you. [9] God knows how often I pray for you. Day and night I bring you and your needs in prayer to the one I serve with all my might, telling others the Good News about his Son.

[10] And one of the things I keep on praying for is the opportunity, God willing,[a] to come at last to see you and, if possible, that I will have a safe trip.[b] [11,12] For I long to visit you so that I can impart to you the faith[c] that will help your church grow strong in the Lord. Then, too, I need your help, for I want not only to share my faith with you but to be encouraged by yours: Each of us will be a blessing to the other.

[13] I want you to know, dear brothers, that I planned to come many times before (but was prevented) so that I could work among you and see good results, just as I have among the other Gentile churches.[d] [14] For I owe a great debt to you and to everyone else, both to civilized people and uncivilized alike; yes, to the educated and uneducated alike. [15] So, to the fullest extent of my ability, I am ready to come also to you in Rome to preach God's Good News.

[16] For I am not ashamed of this Good News about Christ. It is God's powerful method of bringing all who believe it to heaven. This message was preached first to the Jews alone, but now everyone is invited to come to God in this same way. [17] This Good News tells us that God makes us ready for heaven—makes us right in God's sight—when we put our faith and trust in Christ to save us. This is accomplished from start to finish by faith.[e] As the Scripture says it, "The man who finds life will find it through trusting God."[f]

[18] But God shows his anger from heaven against all sinful, evil men who push away the truth from them. [19] For the truth about God is known to them instinctively[g]; God has put this knowledge in their hearts. [20] Since earliest times men have seen the earth and sky and all God made, and have known of his existence and great eternal power. So they will have no excuse [when they stand before God at Judgment Day[h]].

[21] Yes, they knew about him all right, but they wouldn't admit it or worship him or even thank him for all his daily care. And

---

1a Literally, "in the will of God."   b Or, "that I will finally succeed in coming."
c Literally, "some spiritual gift . . . that is, . . . faith."   d Literally, "among the Gentiles."
e Literally: "(this) righteousness of God is *revealed* from faith to faith."   f Habakkuk 2:4.
g Literally, "is manifest in them."   h Implied. Or, "They have no excuse for saying there is no God."

after awhile they began to think up silly ideas of what God was like and what he wanted them to do. The result was that their foolish minds became dark and confused. [22] Claiming themselves to be wise without God, they became utter fools instead. [23] And then, instead of worshiping the glorious, ever-living God, they took wood and stone and made idols for themselves, carving them to look like mere birds and animals and snakes and puny[i] men.

[24] So God let them go ahead into every sort of sex sin, and do whatever they wanted to—yes, vile and sinful things with each other's bodies. [25] Instead of believing what they knew was the truth about God, they deliberately chose to believe lies. So they prayed to the things God made, but wouldn't obey the blessed God who made these things.

[26] That is why God let go of them and let them do all these evil things, so that even their women turned against God's natural plan for them and indulged in sex sin with each other. [27] And the men, instead of having a normal sex relationship with women, burned with lust for each other, men doing shameful things with other men and, as a result, getting paid within their own souls with the penalty they so richly deserved.

[28] So it was that when they gave God up and would not even acknowledge him, God gave them up to doing everything their evil minds could think of. [29] Their lives became full of every kind of wickedness and sin, of greed and hate, envy, murder, fighting, lying, bitterness, and gossip. [30] They were backbiters, haters of God, insolent, proud braggarts, always thinking of new ways of sinning and continually being disobedient to their parents. [31] They tried to misunderstand,[j] broke their promises, and were heartless—without pity. [32] They were fully aware of God's death penalty for these crimes, yet they went right ahead and did them anyway, and encouraged others to do them, too.

2 "WELL," YOU MAY be saying, "what terrible people you have been talking about!" But wait a minute! You are just as bad. When you say they are wicked and should be punished, you are talking about yourselves, for you do these very same things. [2] And we know that God, in justice, will punish anyone who does such things as these. [3] Do you think that God will judge and condemn others for doing them and overlook you when you do them, too? [4] Don't you realize how patient he is being with you? Or don't you care? Can't you see that he has been waiting all this time without punishing you, to give you time to turn from your sin? His kindness is meant to lead you to repentance.

[5] But no, you won't listen; and so you are saving up terrible punishment for yourselves because of your stubbornness in refusing to turn from your sin; for there is going to come a day of wrath when God will be the just Judge of all the world. [6] He will give each one whatever his deeds deserve. [7] He will give eternal life to those who patiently do the will of God,[a] seeking for the unseen[b] glory and honor and eternal life that he offers.[b] [8] But he will terribly punish those who fight against the truth of God and walk in evil ways—God's anger will be poured out upon them. [9] There will be sorrow and suffering for Jews and Gentiles alike who keep on sinning. [10] But there will be glory and honor and peace from God for all who obey him,[c] whether they are Jews or Gentiles. [11] For God treats everyone the same.

[12-15] He will punish sin wherever it is found. He will punish the heathen when they sin, even though they never had God's written laws, for down in their hearts they know right from wrong. God's laws are written within them; their own conscience accuses them, or sometimes excuses them. And God will punish the Jews for sinning because they have his written laws but don't obey them. They know what is right but don't do it. After all, salvation is not given to those who know what to do, unless they do it. [16] The day will surely come when at God's command Jesus Christ will judge the secret lives of everyone, their inmost

---

i Literally, "mortal."   j Or, "were confused fools."   2a Literally, "who patiently do good."
b Implied.   c Literally, "all who do good."

thoughts and motives; this is all part of God's great plan which I proclaim.

¹⁷ You Jews think all is well between yourselves and God because he gave his laws to you;ᵈ you brag that you are his special friends. ¹⁸ Yes, you know what he wants; you know right from wrong and favor the right because you have been taught his laws from earliest youth. ¹⁹ You are so sure of the way to God that you could point it out to a blind man. You think of yourselves as beacon lights, directing men who are lost in darkness to God. ²⁰ You think that you can guide the simple and teach even children the affairs of God, for you really know his laws, which are full of all knowledge and truth.

²¹ Yes, you teach others—then why don't you teach yourselves? You tell others not to steal—do *you* steal? ²² You say it is wrong to commit adultery—do *you* do it? You say, "Don't pray to idols," and then make money your god instead.ᵉ

²³ You are so proud of knowing God's laws, *but you dishonor him by breaking them.* ²⁴ No wonder the Scriptures say that the world speaks evil of God because of you.

²⁵ Being a Jew is worth something if you obey God's laws; but if you don't, then you are no better off than the heathen. ²⁶ And if the heathen obey God's laws, won't God give them all the rights and honors he planned to give the Jews? ²⁷ In fact, those heathen will be much better offᶠ than you Jews who know so much about God and have his promises but don't obey his laws.

²⁸ For you are not real Jews just because you were born of Jewish parents or because you have gone through the Jewish initiation ceremony of circumcision. ²⁹ No, a real Jew is anyone whose heart is right with God. For God is not looking for those who cut their bodies in actual body circumcision, but he is looking for those with changed hearts and minds. Whoever has that kind of change in his life will get his praise from God, even if not from you.

3 THEN WHAT'S THE use of being a Jew? Are there any special benefits for them

from God? Is there any value in the Jewish circumcision ceremony? ² Yes, being a Jew has many advantages.

First of all, God trusted them with his laws [so that they could know and do his willᵃ]. ³ True, some of them were unfaithful, but just because they broke their promises to God, does that mean God will break his promises? ⁴ Of course not! Though everyone else in the world is a liar, God is not. Do you remember what the book of Psalms says about this?ᵇ That God's words will always prove true and right, no matter who questions them.

⁵ "But," some say, "our breaking faith with God is good, our sins serve a good purpose, for people will notice how good God is when they see how bad we are. Is it fair, then, for him to punish us when our sins are helping him?" (That is the way some people talk.) ⁶ God forbid! Then what kind of God would he be, to overlook sin? How could he ever condemn anyone? ⁷ For he could not judge and condemn me as a sinner if my dishonesty brought him glory by pointing up his honesty in contrast to my lies. ⁸ If you follow through with that idea you come to this: the worse we are, the better God likes it! But the damnation of those who say such things is just. Yet some claim that this is what I preach!

⁹ Well, then, are we Jews *better* than others? No, not at all, for we have already shown that all men alike are sinners, whether Jews or Gentiles. ¹⁰ As the Scriptures say,

"No one is good—no one in all the world is innocent."ᶜ

¹¹ No one has ever really followed God's paths, or even truly wanted to.

¹² Every one has turned away; all have gone wrong. No one anywhere has kept on doing what is right; not one.

¹³ Their talk is foul and filthy like the stench from an open grave.ᵈ Their tongues are loaded with lies. Everything they say has in it the sting and poison of deadly snakes.

¹⁴ Their mouths are full of cursing and bitterness.

---

d Or, "you rely upon the law for your salvation."
f Literally, "will condemn" you. 3a Implied.
d Literally, "Their throat is an open grave." Perhaps the meaning is "Their speech injures others."

e Literally, "do you rob temples?"
b Psalm 51:4. c Psalm 14:3.

¹⁵ They are quick to kill, hating anyone who disagrees with them.ᵉ

¹⁶ Wherever they go they leave misery and trouble behind them, ¹⁷ and they have never known what it is to feel secure or enjoy God's blessing.

¹⁸ They care nothing about God nor what he thinks of them.

¹⁹ So the judgment of God lies very heavily upon the Jews, for they are responsible to keep God's laws instead of doing all these evil things; not one of them has any excuse; in fact, all the world stands hushed and guilty before Almighty God.

²⁰ Now do you see it? No one can ever be made right in God's sight by doing what the law commands. For the more we know of God's laws, the clearer it becomes that we aren't obeying them; his laws serve only to make us see that we are sinners.

²¹,²² But now God has shown us a different way to heavenᶠ—not by "being good enough" and trying to keep his laws, but by a new way (though not new, really, for the Scriptures told about it long ago). Now God says he will accept and acquit us—declare us "not guilty"—if we trust Jesus Christ to take away our sins. And we all can be saved in this same way, by coming to Christ, no matter who we are or what we have been like. ²³ Yes, all have sinned; all fall short of God's glorious ideal; ²⁴ yet now God declares us "not guilty" of offending him if we trust in Jesus Christ, who in his kindness freely takes away our sins.

²⁵ For God sent Christ Jesus to take the punishment for our sins and to end all God's anger against us. He used Christ's blood and our faith as the means of saving us from his wrath.ᵍ In this way he was being entirely fair, even though he did not punish those who sinned in former times. For he was looking forward to the time when Christ would come and take away those sins. ²⁶ And now in these days also he can receive sinners in this same way, because Jesus took away their sins.

But isn't this unfair for God to let criminals go free, and say that they are innocent? No, for he does it on the basis of their trust in Jesus who took away their sins.

²⁷ Then what can we boast about doing, to earn our salvation? Nothing at all. Why? Because our acquittal is not based on our good deeds; it is based on what Christ has done and our faith in him. ²⁸ So it is that we are savedʰ by faith in Christ and not by the good things we do.

²⁹ And does God save only the Jews in this way? No, the Gentiles, too, may come to him in this same manner. ³⁰ God treats us all the same; all, whether Jews or Gentiles, are acquitted if they have faith. ³¹ Well then, if we are saved by faith, does this mean that we no longer need obey God's laws? Just the opposite! In fact, only when we trust Jesus can we truly obey him.

4 ABRAHAM WAS, HUMANLY speaking, the founder of our Jewish nation. What were his experiences concerning this question of being saved by faith? Was it because of his good deeds that God accepted him? If so, then he would have something to boast about. But from God's point of view Abraham had no basis at all for pride. ³ For the Scriptures tell us Abraham *believed God,* and that is why God canceled his sins and declared him "not guilty."

⁴,⁵ But didn't he earn his right to heaven by all the good things he did? No, for being saved is a gift; if a person could earn it by being good, then it wouldn't be free—but it is! It is *given* to those who do *not* work for it. For God declares sinners to be good in his sight if they have faith in Christ to save them from God's wrath.ᵃ

⁶ King David spoke of this, describing the happiness of an undeserving sinner who is declared "not guilty"ᵇ by God. ⁷ "Blessed, and to be envied," he said, "are those whose sins are forgiven and put out of sight. ⁸ Yes, what joy there is for anyone whose sins are no longer counted against him by the Lord."ᶜ

⁹ Now then, the question: Is this blessing given only to those who have faith in Christ but also keep the Jewish laws, or is the blessing also given to those who do not keep the Jewish rules, but only trust in Christ? Well,

---

e Implied.   f Implied. Literally, "A righteousness of God has been manifested."   g Literally, "to be a propitiation."   h Literally, "justified."   4a Literally, "faith is reckoned for righteousness."
b Literally, "righteous."   c Psalm 32:1-2.

what about Abraham? We say that he received these blessings through his faith. Was it by faith alone? Or because he also kept the Jewish rules?

[10] For the answer to that question, answer this one: *When* did God give this blessing to Abraham? It was *before he became a Jew*—before he went through the Jewish initiation ceremony of circumcision.

[11] It wasn't until later on, *after* God had promised to bless him *because of his faith,* that he was circumcised. The circumcision ceremony was a sign that Abraham already had faith and that God had already accepted him and declared him just and good in his sight—before the ceremony took place. So Abraham is the spiritual father of those who believe and are saved without obeying Jewish laws. We see, then, that those who do not keep these rules are justified by God through faith. [12] And Abraham is also the spiritual father of those Jews who have been circumcised. They can see from his example that it is not this ceremony that saves them, for Abraham found favor with God by faith alone, *before he was circumcised.*

[13] It is clear, then, that God's promise to give the whole earth to Abraham and his descendants was not because Abraham obeyed God's laws but because he trusted God to keep his promise. [14] So if you still claim that God's blessings go to those who are "good enough," then you are saying that God's promises to those who have faith are meaningless, and faith is foolish. [15] But the fact of the matter is this: when we try to gain God's blessing and salvation by keeping his laws we always end up under his anger, for we always fail to keep them. The only way we can keep from breaking laws is not to have any to break!

[16] So God's blessings are given to us by faith, as a free gift; we are certain to get them whether or not we follow Jewish customs if we have faith like Abraham's, for Abraham is the father of us all when it comes to these matters of faith. [17] That is what the Scriptures mean when they say that God made Abraham the father of many nations. God will accept all people in every nation who trust God as Abraham did. And this promise is from God himself, who makes the dead live again and speaks of future events with as much certainty as though they were already past.

[18] So, when God told Abraham that he would give him a son who would have many descendants and become a great nation, Abraham believed God even though such a promise just couldn't come to pass! [19] And because his faith was strong, he didn't worry about the fact that he was too old to be a father, at the age of one hundred, and that Sarah his wife, at ninety,[d] was also much too old to have a baby.

[20] But Abraham never doubted. He believed God, for his faith and trust grew ever stronger, and he praised God for this blessing even before it happened. [21] He was completely sure that God was well able to do anything he promised. [22] And because of Abraham's faith God forgave his sins and declared him "not guilty."

[23] Now this wonderful statement—that he was accepted and approved through his faith—wasn't just for Abraham's benefit. [24] It was for us, too, assuring us that God will accept us in the same way he accepted Abraham—when we believe the promises of God who brought back Jesus our Lord from the dead. [25] He died for our sins and rose again to make us right with God, filling us with God's goodness.[e]

5 SO NOW, SINCE we have been made right in God's sight by faith in his promises, we can have real peace with him because of what Jesus Christ our Lord has done for us. [2] For because of our faith, he has brought us into this place of highest privilege where we now stand, and we confidently and joyfully look forward to actually becoming all that God has had in mind for us to be.

[3] We can rejoice, too, when we run into problems and trials for we know that they are good for us—they help us learn to be patient. [4] And patience develops strength of character in us and helps us trust God more each time we use it until finally our hope and faith are strong and steady. [5] Then, when that happens, we are able to hold our

---

d Genesis 17:17.   e Literally, "raised for our justification."

heads high no matter what happens and know that all is well, for we know how dearly God loves us, and we feel this warm love everywhere within us because God has given us the Holy Spirit to fill our hearts with his love.

⁶ When we were utterly helpless with no way of escape, Christ came at just the right time and died for us sinners who had no use for him. ⁷ Even if we were good, we really wouldn't expect anyone to die for us, though, of course, that might be barely possible. ⁸ But God showed his great love for us by sending Christ to die for us while we were still sinners. ⁹ And since by his blood he did all this for us as sinners, how much more will he do for us now that he has declared us not guilty? Now he will save us from all of God's wrath to come. ¹⁰ And since, when we were his enemies, we were brought back to God by the death of his Son, what blessings he must have for us now that we are his friends, and he is living within us!

¹¹ Now we rejoice in our wonderful new relationship with God—all because of what our Lord Jesus Christ has done in dying for our sins—making us friends of God.

¹² When Adam sinned, sin entered the entire human race. His sin spread death throughout all the world, so everything began to grow old and die,ᵃ for all sinned. ¹³ [We know that it was Adam's sin that caused thisᵇ] because although, of course, people were sinning from the time of Adam until Moses, God did not in those days judge them guilty of death for breaking his laws—because he had not yet given his laws to them, nor told them what he wanted them to do. ¹⁴ So when their bodies died it was not for their own sinsᵇ since they themselves had never disobeyed God's special law against eating the forbidden fruit, as Adam had.

What a contrast between Adam and Christ who was yet to come! ¹⁵ And what a difference between man's sin and God's forgiveness!

For this one man, Adam, brought death to many through his *sin.* But this one man,

Jesus Christ, brought forgiveness to many through God's *mercy.* ¹⁶ Adam's *one* sin brought the penalty of death to many, while Christ freely takes away *many* sins and gives glorious life instead. ¹⁷ The sin of this one man, Adam, caused *death to be king over all,* but all who will take God's gift of forgiveness and acquittal are *kings of lifeᶜ* because of this one man, Jesus Christ. ¹⁸ Yes, Adam's *sin* brought *punishment* to all, but Christ's *righteousness* makes men *right with God,* so that they can live. ¹⁹ Adam caused many to be sinners because he *disobeyed* God, and Christ caused many to be made acceptable to God because he *obeyed.*

²⁰ The Ten Commandments were given so that all could see the extent of their failure to obey God's laws. But the more we see our sinfulness, the more we see God's abounding grace forgiving us. ²¹ Before, sin ruled over all men and brought them to death, but now God's kindness rules instead, giving us right standing with God and resulting in eternal life through Jesus Christ our Lord.

6 WELL THEN, SHALL we keep on sinning so that God can keep on showing us more and more kindness and forgiveness? ²,³ Of course not! Should we keep on sinning when we don't have to? For sin's power over us was broken when we became Christians and were baptized to become a part of Jesus Christ; through his death the power of your sinful nature was shattered. ⁴ Your old sin-loving nature was buried with him by baptism when he died, and when God the Father, with glorious power, brought him back to life again, you were given his wonderful new life to enjoy.

⁵ For you have become a part of him, and so you died with him, so to speak, when he diedᵃ; and now you share his new life, and shall rise as he did. ⁶ Your old evil desires were nailed to the cross with him; that part of you that loves to sin was crushed and fatally wounded, so that your sin-loving body is no longer under sin's control, no longer needs to be a slave to sin; ⁷ for when

---

a Literally, "Sin entered into the world, and death through sin."   b Implied.   c Literally, "reign in life."   6a Literally, "united with him in the likeness of his death."

you are deadened to sin you are freed from all its allure and its power over you. [8] And since your old sin-loving nature "died" with Christ, we know that you will share his new life. [9] Christ rose from the dead and will never die again. Death no longer has any power over him. [10] He died once for all to end sin's power, but now he lives forever in unbroken fellowship with God. [11] So look upon your old sin nature as dead and unresponsive to sin, and instead be alive to God, alert to him, through Jesus Christ our Lord.

[12] Do not let sin control your puny body any longer; do not give in to its sinful desires. [13] Do not let any part of your bodies become tools of wickedness, to be used for sinning; but give yourselves completely to God—every part of you—for you are back from death and you want to be tools in the hands of God, to be used for his good purposes. [14] Sin need[b] never again be your master, for now you are no longer tied to the law where sin enslaves you, but you are free under God's favor and mercy.

[15] Does this mean that now we can go ahead and sin and not worry about it? (For our salvation does not depend on keeping the law, but on receiving God's grace!) Of course not! [16] Don't you realize that you can choose your own master? You can choose sin (with death) or else obedience (with acquittal). The one to whom you offer yourself—he will take you and be your master and you will be his slave. [17] Thank God that though you once chose to be slaves of sin, now you have obeyed with all your heart the teaching to which God has committed you. [18] And now you are free from your old master, sin; and you have become slaves to your new master, righteousness.

[19] I speak this way, using the illustration of slaves and masters, because it is easy to understand: just as you used to be slaves to all kinds of sin, so now you must let yourselves be slaves to all that is right and holy. [20] In those days when you were slaves of sin you didn't bother much with goodness. [21] And what was the result? Evidently not good, since you are ashamed now even to think about those things you used to do, for all of them end in eternal doom. [22] But now you are free from the power of sin and are slaves of God, and his benefits to you include holiness and everlasting life. [23] For the wages of sin is death, but the free gift of God is eternal life through Jesus Christ our Lord.

7 DON'T YOU UNDERSTAND yet, dear Jewish[a] brothers in Christ, that when a person dies the law no longer holds him in its power?

[2] Let me illustrate: when a woman marries, the law binds her to her husband as long as he is alive. But if he dies, she is no longer bound to him; the laws of marriage no longer apply to her. [3] Then she can marry someone else if she wants to. That would be wrong while he was alive, but it is perfectly all right after he dies.

[4] Your "husband," your master, used to be the Jewish law; but you "died," as it were, with Christ on the cross; and since you are "dead," you are no longer "married to the law," and it has no more control over you. Then you came back to life again when Christ did, and are a new person. And now you are "married," so to speak, to the one who rose from the dead, so that you can produce good fruit, that is, good deeds for God. [5] When your old nature was still active, sinful desires were at work within you, making you want to do whatever God said not to, and producing sinful deeds, the rotting fruit of death. [6] But now you need no longer worry about the Jewish laws and customs[b] because you "died" while in their captivity, and now you can really serve God; not in the old way, mechanically obeying a set of rules, but in the new way, [with all of your hearts and minds[c]].

[7] Well then, am I suggesting that these laws of God are evil? Of course not! No, the law is not sinful but it was the law that showed me my sin. I would never have known the sin in my heart—the evil desires that are hidden there—if the law had not said, "You must not have evil desires in your heart." [8] But sin used this law against

---

b Literally, "Sin will never again be your master."
b Literally, "Now we are delivered from the law."

7a Implied. Literally, "men who know (the) law."
c Implied.

evil desires by reminding me that such desires are wrong and arousing all kinds of forbidden desires within me! Only if there were no laws to break would there be no sinning. ⁹ That is why I felt fine so long as I did not understand what the law really demanded. But when I learned the truth, I realized that I had broken the law and was a sinner, doomed to die. ¹⁰ So as far as I was concerned, the good law which was supposed to show me the way of life resulted instead in my being given the death penalty. ¹¹ Sin fooled me by taking the good laws of God and using them to make me guilty of death. ¹² But still, you see, the law itself was wholly right and good.

¹³ But how can that be? Didn't the law cause my doom? How then can it be good? No, it was sin, devilish stuff that it is, that used what was good to bring about my condemnation. So you can see how cunning and deadly and damnable it is. For it uses God's good laws for its own evil purposes. ¹⁴ The law is good, then, and the trouble is not there but with *me,* because I am sold into slavery with Sin as my owner.

¹⁵ I don't understand myself at all, for I really want to do what is right, but I can't. I do what I don't want to—what I hate. ¹⁶ I know perfectly well that what I am doing is wrong, and my bad conscience proves that I agree with these laws I am breaking. ¹⁷ But I can't help myself, because I'm no longer doing it. It is sin inside me that is stronger than I am that makes me do these evil things.

¹⁸ I know I am rotten through and through so far as my old sinful nature is concerned. No matter which way I turn I can't make myself do right. I want to but I can't. ¹⁹ When I want to do good, I don't; and when I try not to do wrong, I do it anyway. ²⁰ Now if I am doing what I don't want to, it is plain where the trouble is: sin still has me in its evil grasp.

²¹ It seems to be a fact of life that when I want to do what is right, I inevitably do what is wrong. ²² I love to do God's will so far as my new nature is concerned; ²³,²⁴,²⁵ but

there is something else deep within me, in my lower nature, that ıs at war with my mind and wins the fight and makes me a slave to the sin that is still within me. In my mind I want to be God's willing servant but instead I find myself still enslaved to sin.

So you see how it is: my new life tells me to do right, but the old nature that is still inside me loves to sin. Oh, what a terrible predicament I'm in! Who will free me from my slavery to this deadly lower nature? Thank God! It has been done[d] by Jesus Christ our Lord. He has set me free.

8 SO THERE IS now no condemnation awaiting those who belong to Christ Jesus. ² For the power of the life-giving Spirit—and this power is mine through Christ Jesus—has freed me from the vicious circle of sin and death. ³ We aren't saved from sin's grasp by knowing the commandments of God, because we can't and don't keep them, but God put into effect a different plan to save us. He sent his own Son in a human body like ours—except that ours are sinful—and destroyed sin's control over us by giving himself as a sacrifice for our sins. ⁴ So now we can obey God's laws if we follow after the Holy Spirit and no longer obey the old evil nature within us.

⁵ Those who let themselves be controlled by their lower natures live only to please themselves, but those who follow after the Holy Spirit find themselves doing those things that please God. ⁶ Following after the Holy Spirit leads to life and peace, but following after the old nature leads to death, ⁷ because the old sinful nature within us is against God. It never did obey God's laws and it never will. ⁸ That's why those who are still under the control of their old sinful selves, bent on following their old evil desires, can never please God.

⁹ But you are not like that. You are controlled by your new nature if you have the Spirit of God living in you. (And remember that if anyone doesn't have the Spirit of Christ living in him, he is not a Christian at all.) ¹⁰ Yet, even though Christ lives within you, your body will die because of

---

d Or, "It will be done." Literally, "I thank God through Jesus Christ our Lord."

sin; but your spirit will live, for Christ has pardoned it.[a] [11] And if the Spirit of God, who raised up Jesus from the dead, lives in you, he will make your dying bodies live again after you die, by means of this same Holy Spirit living within you.

[12] So, dear brothers, you have no obligations whatever to your old sinful nature to do what it begs you to do. [13] For if you keep on following it you are lost and will perish, but if through the power of the Holy Spirit you crush it and its evil deeds, you shall live. [14] For all who are led by the Spirit of God are sons of God.

[15] And so we should not be like cringing, fearful slaves, but we should behave like God's very own children, adopted into the bosom of his family, and calling to him, "Father, Father." [16] For his Holy Spirit speaks to us deep in our hearts, and tells us that we really are God's children. [17] And since we are his children, we will share his treasures—for all God gives to his Son Jesus is now ours too. But if we are to share his glory, we must also share his suffering.

[18] Yet what we suffer now is nothing compared to the glory he will give us later. [19] For all creation is waiting patiently and hopefully for that future day when God will resurrect his children.[b] [20,21] For on that day thorns and thistles, sin, death, and decay[c] —the things that overcame the world against its will at God's command—will all disappear, and the world around us will share in the glorious freedom from sin which God's children enjoy.

[22] For we know that even the things of nature, like animals and plants, suffer in sickness and death as they await this great event.[d] [23] And even we Christians, although we have the Holy Spirit within us as a foretaste of future glory, also groan to be released from pain and suffering. We, too, wait anxiously for that day when God will give us our full rights as his children, including the new bodies he has promised us—bodies that will never be sick again and will never die.

[24] We are saved by trusting. And trusting means looking forward to getting something we don't yet have—for a man who already has something doesn't need to hope and trust that he will get it. [25] But if we must keep trusting God for something that hasn't happened yet, it teaches us to wait patiently and confidently.

[26] And in the same way—by our faith[e] —the Holy Spirit helps us with our daily problems and in our praying. For we don't even know what we should pray for, nor how to pray as we should; but the Holy Spirit prays for us with such feeling that it cannot be expressed in words. [27] And the Father who knows all hearts knows, of course, what the Spirit is saying as he pleads for us in harmony with God's own will. [28] And we know that all that happens to us is working for our good if we love God and are fitting into his plans.

[29] For from the very beginning God decided that those who came to him—and all along he knew who would—should become like his Son, so that his Son would be the First, with many brothers. [30] And having chosen us, he called us to come to him; and when we came, he declared us "not guilty," filled us with Christ's goodness, gave us right standing with himself, and promised us his glory.

[31] What can we ever say to such wonderful things as these? If God is on our side, who can ever be against us? [32] Since he did not spare even his own Son for us but gave him up for us all, won't he also surely give us everything else?

[33] Who dares accuse us whom God has chosen for his own? Will God? No! He is the one who has forgiven us and given us right standing with himself. [34] Who then will condemn us? Will Christ? *No!* For he is the one who died for us and came back to life again for us and is sitting at the place of highest honor next to God, pleading for us there in heaven.

[35] Who then can ever keep Christ's love from us? When we have trouble or calamity, when we are hunted down or destroyed, is it because he doesn't love us anymore? And

a Or possibly, "but the Holy Spirit who lives in you will give you life, for he has already given you righteousness." Literally, "but the spirit is life because of righteousness."   b Literally, "waiting for the revelation of the sons of God."   c Implied.   d Literally, "The whole creation has been groaning in travail together until now."   e Implied. Literally, "in like manner."

970

if we are hungry, or penniless, or in danger, or threatened with death, has God deserted us?

³⁶ No, for the Scriptures tell us that for his sake we must be ready to face death at every moment of the day—we are like sheep awaiting slaughter; ³⁷ but despite all this, overwhelming victory is ours through Christ who loved us enough to die for us. ³⁸ For I am convinced that nothing can ever separate us from his love. Death can't, and life can't. The angels won't, and all the powers of hell itself cannot keep God's love away. Our fears for today, our worries about tomorrow, ³⁹ or where we are—high above the sky, or in the deepest ocean—nothing will ever be able to separate us from the love of God demonstrated by our Lord Jesus Christ when he died for us.

9 OH, ISRAEL, MY people! Oh, my Jewish brothers! How I long for you to come to Christ. My heart is heavy within me and I grieve bitterly day and night because of you. Christ knows and the Holy Spirit knows that it is no mere pretense when I say that I would be willing to be forever damned if that would save you. ⁴ God has given you so much, but still you will not listen to him. He took you as his own special, chosen people and led you along with a bright cloud of glory and told you how very much he wanted to bless you He gave you his rules for daily life so you would know what he wanted you to do. He let you worship him, and gave you mighty promises. ⁵ Great men of God were your fathers, and Christ himself was one of you, a Jew so far as his human nature is concerned, he who now rules over all things. Praise God forever!

⁶ Well then, has God failed to fulfill his promises to the Jews? No! [For these promises are only to those who are truly Jews.ᵃ] And not everyone born into a Jewish family is truly a Jew! ⁷ Just the fact that they come from Abraham doesn't make them truly Abraham's children. For the Scriptures say that the promises apply only to Abraham's son Isaac and Isaac's descendants, though Abraham had other chil-

dren too. ⁸ This means that not all of Abraham's children are children of God, but only those who believe the promise of salvation which he made to Abraham.

⁹ For God had promised, "Next year I will give you and Sarah a son." ¹⁰⁻¹³ And years later, when this son, Isaac, was grown up and married, and Rebecca his wife was about to bear him twin children, God told her that Esau, the child born first, would be a servant to Jacob, his twin brother. In the words of the Scripture, "I chose to bless Jacob, but not Esau." And God said this before the children were even born, before they had done anything either good or bad. This proves that God was doing what he had decided from the beginning; it was not because of what the children did but because of what God wanted and chose.

¹⁴ Was God being unfair? Of course not. ¹⁵ For God had said to Moses, "If I want to be kind to someone, I will. And I will take pity on anyone I want to." ¹⁶ And so God's blessings are not given just because someone decides to have them or works hard to get them. They are given because God takes pity on those he wants to.

¹⁷ Pharaoh, king of Egypt, was an example of this fact. For God told him he had given him the kingdom of Egypt for the very purpose of displaying the awesome power of God against him: so that all the world would hear about God's glorious name.ᵇ ¹⁸ So you see, God is kind to some just because he wants to be, and he makes some refuse to listen. ¹⁹ Well then, why does God blame them for not listening? Haven't they done what he made them do?

²⁰ No, don't say that. Who are you to criticize God? Should the thing made say to the one who made it, "Why have you made me like this?" ²¹ When a man makes a jar out of clay, doesn't he have a right to use the same lump of clay to make one jar beautiful, to be used for holding flowers, and another to throw garbage into? ²² Does not God have a perfect right to show his fury and power against those who are fit only for destruction, those he has been patient with for all this time? ²³,²⁴ And he has a right to take others such as ourselves, who

---

a Implied.   b Literally, "that my name might be published abroad in all the earth."

have been made for pouring the riches of his glory into, whether we are Jews or Gentiles, and to be kind to us so that everyone can see how very great his glory is.

[25] Remember what the prophecy of Hosea says? There God says that he will find other children for himself (who are not from his Jewish family) and will love them, though no one had ever loved them before. [26] And the heathen, of whom it once was said, "You are not my people," shall be called "sons of the Living God."[c]

[27] Isaiah the prophet cried out concerning the Jews that though there would be millions[d] of them, only a small number would ever be saved. [28] "For the Lord will execute his sentence upon the earth, quickly ending his dealings, justly cutting them short."[e]

[29] And Isaiah says in another place that except for God's mercy all the Jews would be destroyed—all of them—just as everyone in the cities of Sodom and Gomorrah perished.[f]

[30] Well then, what shall we say about these things? Just this, that God has given the Gentiles the opportunity to be acquitted by faith, even though they had not been really seeking God. [31] But the Jews, who tried so hard to get right with God by keeping his laws, never succeeded. [32] Why not? Because they were trying to be saved by keeping the law and being good instead of by depending on faith. They have stumbled over the great stumbling stone. [33] God warned them of this in the Scriptures when he said, "I have put a Rock in the path of the Jews, and many will stumble over him (Jesus). Those who believe in him will never be disappointed."[g]

10 DEAR BROTHERS, THE longing of my heart and my prayer is that the Jewish people might be saved. [2] I know what enthusiasm they have for the honor of God, but it is misdirected zeal. [3] For they don't understand that Christ has died to make them right with God. Instead they are trying to make themselves good enough to gain God's favor by keeping the Jewish laws and customs, but that is not God's way of salvation. [4] They don't understand that Christ gives to those who trust in him everything they are trying to get by keeping his laws. He ends all of that.

[5] For Moses wrote that if a person could be perfectly good and hold out against temptation all his life and never sin once, only then could he be pardoned and saved. [6] But the salvation that comes through faith says, "You don't need to search the heavens to find Christ and bring him down to help you," and, [7] "You don't need to go among the dead to bring Christ back to life again."

[8] For salvation that comes from trusting Christ—which is what we preach—is already within easy reach of each of us; in fact, it is as near as our own hearts and mouths. [9] For if you tell others with your own mouth that Jesus Christ is your Lord, and believe in your own heart that God has raised him from the dead, you will be saved. [10] For it is by believing in his heart that a man becomes right with God; and with his mouth he tells others of his faith, confirming his salvation.[a] [11] For the Scriptures tell us that no one who believes in Christ will ever be disappointed. [12] Jew and Gentile are the same in this respect: they all have the same Lord who generously gives his riches to all those who ask him for them. [13] Anyone who calls upon the name of the Lord will be saved.

[14] But how shall they ask him to save them unless they believe in him? And how can they believe in him if they have never heard about him? And how can they hear about him unless someone tells them? [15] And how will anyone go and tell them unless someone sends him? That is what the Scriptures are talking about when they say, "How beautiful are the feet of those who preach the Gospel of peace with God and bring glad tidings of good things."[b] In other words, how welcome are those who come preaching God's Good News!

[16] But not everyone who hears the Good News has welcomed it, for Isaiah the prophet said, "Lord, who has believed me when I told them?"[c] [17] Yet faith comes from

---

c Hosea 2:23.   d Literally, "as the sand of the sea," i.e., numberless.   e Isaiah 10:22; 28:22.
f Isaiah 1:9.   g Isaiah 28:16..   10a Literally, "Confession is made unto salvation."
b Isaiah 52:7.   c Isaiah 53:1.

listening to this Good News—the Good News about Christ.

[18] But what about the Jews? Have they heard God's Word? Yes, for it has gone wherever they are; the Good News has been told to the ends of the earth. [19] And did they understand [that God would give his salvation to others if they refused to take it[d]]? Yes, for even back in the time of Moses, God had said that he would make his people jealous and try to wake them up by giving his salvation to the foolish heathen nations. [20] And later on Isaiah said boldly that God would be found by people who weren't even looking for him.[e] [21] In the meantime, he keeps on reaching out his hands to the Jews, but they keep arguing[f] and refusing to come.

11 I ASK THEN, has God rejected and deserted his people the Jews? Oh no, not at all. Remember that I myself am a Jew, a descendant of Abraham and a member of Benjamin's family.

[2,3] No, God has not discarded his own people whom he chose from the very beginning. Do you remember what the Scriptures say about this? Elijah the prophet was complaining to God about the Jews, telling God how they had killed the prophets and torn down God's altars; Elijah claimed that he was the only one left in all the land who still loved God, and now they were trying to kill him too.

[4] And do you remember how God replied? God said, "No, you are not the only one left. I have seven thousand others besides you who still love me and have not bowed down to idols!"[a]

[5] It is the same today. Not all the Jews have turned away from God; there are a few being saved as a result of God's kindness in choosing them. [6] And if it is by God's kindness, then it is not by their being good enough. For in that case the free gift would no longer be free—it isn't free when it is earned.

[7] So this is the situation: Most of the Jews have not found the favor of God they are looking for. A few have—the ones God has picked out—but the eyes of the others

have been blinded. [8] This is what our Scriptures refer to when they say that God has put them to sleep, shutting their eyes and ears so that they do not understand what we are talking about when we tell them of Christ. And so it is to this very day.

[9] King David spoke of this same thing when he said, "Let their good food and other blessings trap them into thinking all is well between themselves and God. Let these good things boomerang on them and fall back upon their heads to justly crush them. [10] Let their eyes be dim," he said, "so that they cannot see, and let them walk bent-backed forever with a heavy load."

[11] Does this mean that God has rejected his Jewish people forever? Of course not! His purpose was to make his salvation available to the Gentiles, and then the Jews would be jealous and begin to want God's salvation for themselves. [12] Now if the whole world became rich as a result of God's offer of salvation, when the Jews stumbled over it and turned it down, think how much greater a blessing the world will share in later on when the Jews, too, come to Christ.

[13] As you know, God has appointed me as a special messenger to you Gentiles. I lay great stress on this and remind the Jews about it as often as I can, [14] so that if possible I can make them want what you Gentiles have and in that way save some of them. [15] And how wonderful it will be when they become Christians! When God turned away from them it meant that he turned to the rest of the world to offer his salvation; and now it is even more wonderful when the Jews come to Christ. It will be like dead people coming back to life. [16] And since Abraham and the prophets are God's people, their children will be too. For if the roots of the tree are holy, the branches will be too.

[17] But some of these branches from Abraham's tree, some of the Jews, have been broken off. And you Gentiles who were branches from, we might say, a wild olive tree, were grafted in. So now you, too, receive the blessing God has promised Abraham and his children, sharing in God's

---

d Implied.　　e Isaiah 65:1.　　f Literally, "disobedient, obstinate."　　11a 1 Kings 19:18.

rich nourishment of his own special olive tree.

¹⁸ But you must be careful not to brag about being put in to replace the branches that were broken off. Remember that you are important only because you are now a part of God's tree; you are just a branch, not a root.

¹⁹ "Well," you may be saying, "those branches were broken off to make room for me so I must be pretty good."

²⁰ Watch out! Remember that those branches, the Jews, were broken off because they didn't believe God, and you are there only because you do. Do not be proud; be humble and grateful—and careful. ²¹ For if God did not spare the branches he put there in the first place, he won't spare you either.

²² Notice how God is both kind and severe. He is very hard on those who disobey, but very good to you if you continue to love and trust him. But if you don't, you too will be cut off. ²³ On the other hand, if the Jews leave their unbelief behind them and come back to God, God will graft them back into the tree again. He has the power to do it.

²⁴ For if God was willing to take you who were so far away from him—being part of a wild olive tree—and graft you into his own good tree—a very unusual thing to do—don't you see that he will be far more ready to put the Jews back again, who were there in the first place?

²⁵ I want you to know about this truth from God, dear brothers, so that you will not feel proud and start bragging. Yes, it is true that some of the Jews have set themselves against the Gospel now, but this will last only until all of you Gentiles have come to Christ—those of you who will. ²⁶ And then all Israel will be saved.

Do you remember what the prophets said about this? "There shall come out of Zion a Deliverer, and he shall turn the Jews from all ungodliness. ²⁷ At that time I will take away their sins, just as I promised."

²⁸ Now many of the Jews are enemies of the Gospel. They hate it. But this has been a benefit to you, for it has resulted in God's giving his gifts to you Gentiles. Yet the Jews are still beloved of God because of his promises to Abraham, Isaac, and Jacob. ²⁹ For God's gifts and his call can never be withdrawn; he will never go back on his promises. ³⁰ Once you were rebels against God, but when the Jews refused his gifts God was merciful to you instead. ³¹ And now the Jews are the rebels, but some day they, too, will share in God's mercy upon you. ³² For God has given them all up to sinᵇ so that he could have mercy upon all alike.

³³ Oh, what a wonderful God we have! How great are his wisdom and knowledge and riches! How impossible it is for us to understand his decisions and his methods! ³⁴ For who among us can know the mind of the Lord? Who knows enough to be his counselor and guide? ³⁵ And who could ever offer to the Lord enough to induce him to act? ³⁶ For everything comes from God alone. Everything lives by his power, and everything is for his glory. To him be glory evermore.

12 AND SO, DEAR brothers, I plead with you to give your bodies to God. Let them be a living sacrifice, holy—the kind he can accept. When you think of what he has done for you, is this too much to ask? ² Don't copy the behavior and customs of this world, but be a new and different person with a fresh newness in all you do and think. Then you will learn from your own experience how his ways will really satisfy you.

³ As God's messenger I give each of you God's warning: Be honest in your estimate of yourselves, measuring your value by how much faith God has given you. ⁴,⁵ Just as there are many parts to our bodies, so it is with Christ's body. We are all parts of it, and it takes every one of us to make it complete, for we each have different work to do. So we belong to each other, and each needs all the others.

⁶ God has given each of us the ability to do certain things well. So if God has given you the ability to prophesy, then prophesy whenever you can—as often as your faith is strong enough to receive a message from God. ⁷ If your gift is that of serving others,

---

b Literally, "shut up all unto disobedience."

serve them well. If you are a teacher, do a good job of teaching. [8] If you are a preacher, see to it that your sermons are strong and helpful. If God has given you money, be generous in helping others with it. If God has given you administrative ability and put you in charge of the work of others, take the responsibility seriously. Those who offer comfort to the sorrowing should do so with Christian cheer.

[9] Don't just pretend that you love others: really love them. Hate what is wrong. Stand on the side of the good. [10] Love each other with brotherly affection and take delight in honoring each other. [11] Never be lazy in your work but serve the Lord enthusiastically.

[12] Be glad for all God is planning for you. Be patient in trouble, and prayerful always. [13] When God's children are in need, you be the one to help them out. And get into the habit of inviting guests home for dinner or, if they need lodging, for the night.

[14] If someone mistreats you because you are a Christian, don't curse him; pray that God will bless him. [15] When others are happy, be happy with them. If they are sad, share their sorrow. [16] Work happily together. Don't try to act big. Don't try to get into the good graces of important people, but enjoy the company of ordinary folks. And don't think you know it all!

[17] Never pay back evil for evil. Do things in such a way that everyone can see you are honest clear through. [18] Don't quarrel with anyone. Be at peace with everyone, just as much as possible.

[19] Dear friends, never avenge yourselves. Leave that to God, for he has said that he will repay those who deserve it. [Don't take the law into your own hands.[a]] [20] Instead, feed your enemy if he is hungry. If he is thirsty give him something to drink and you will be "heaping coals of fire on his head." In other words, he will feel ashamed of himself for what he has done to you. [21] Don't let evil get the upper hand but conquer evil by doing good.

13 OBEY THE GOVERNMENT, for God is the one who has put it there. There is no government anywhere that God has not placed in power. [2] So those who refuse to obey the laws of the land are refusing to obey God, and punishment will follow. [3] For the policeman does not frighten people who are doing right; but those doing evil will always fear him. So if you don't want to be afraid, keep the laws and you will get along well. [4] The policeman is sent by God to help you. But if you are doing something wrong, of course you should be afraid, for he will have you punished. He is sent by God for that very purpose. [5] Obey the laws, then, for two reasons: first, to keep from being punished, and second, just because you know you should.

[6] Pay your taxes too, for these same two reasons. For government workers need to be paid so that they can keep on doing God's work, serving you. [7] Pay everyone whatever he ought to have: pay your taxes and import duties gladly, obey those over you, and give honor and respect to all those to whom it is due. [8] Pay all your debts except the debt of love for others—never finish paying that! For if you love them, you will be obeying all of God's laws, fulfilling all his requirements. [9] If you love your neighbor as much as you love yourself you will not want to harm or cheat him, or kill him or steal from him. And you won't sin with his wife or want what is his, or do anything else the Ten Commandments say is wrong. All ten are wrapped up in this one, to love your neighbor as you love yourself. [10] Love does no wrong to anyone. That's why it fully satisfies all of God's requirements. It is the only law you need.

[11] Another reason for right living is this: you know how late it is; time is running out. Wake up, for the coming of the Lord[a] is nearer now than when we first believed. [12,13] The night is far gone, the day of his return[a] will soon be here. So quit the evil deeds of darkness and put on the armor of right living, as we who live in the daylight should! Be decent and true in everything you do so that all can approve your behavior. Don't spend your time in wild parties and getting drunk or in adultery and lust, or fighting, or jealousy. [14] But ask the Lord

---

a Implied.   13a Literally, "our salvation."

Jesus Christ to help you live as you should, and don't make plans to enjoy evil.

14 GIVE A WARM welcome to any brother who wants to join you, even though his faith is weak. Don't criticize him for having different ideas from yours about what is right and wrong.[a] ² For instance, don't argue with him about whether or not to eat meat that has been offered to idols. You may believe there is no harm in this, but the faith of others is weaker; they think it is wrong, and will go without any meat at all and eat vegetables rather than eat that kind of meat. ³ Those who think it is all right to eat such meat must not look down on those who won't. And if you are one of those who won't, don't find fault with those who do. For God has accepted them to be his children. ⁴ They are God's servants, not yours. They are responsible to him, not to you. Let him tell them whether they are right or wrong. And God is able to make them do as they should.

⁵ Some think that Christians should observe the Jewish holidays as special days to worship God, but others say it is wrong and foolish to go to all that trouble, for every day alike belongs to God. On questions of this kind everyone must decide for himself. ⁶ If you have special days for worshiping the Lord, you are trying to honor him; you are doing a good thing. So is the person who eats meat that has been offered to idols; he is thankful to the Lord for it; he is doing right. And the person who won't touch such meat, he, too, is anxious to please the Lord, and is thankful. ⁷ We are not our own bosses to live or die as we ourselves might choose. ⁸ Living or dying we follow the Lord. Either way we are his. ⁹ Christ died and rose again for this very purpose, so that he can be our Lord both while we live and when we die.

¹⁰ You have no right to criticize your brother or look down on him. Remember, each of us will stand personally before the Judgment Seat of God. ¹¹ For it is written, "As I live," says the Lord, "every knee shall bow to me and every tongue confess to God." ¹² Yes, each of us will give an account of himself to God. ¹³ So don't criticize each other any more. Try instead to live in such a way that you will never make your brother stumble by letting him see you doing something he thinks is wrong.

¹⁴ As for myself, I am perfectly sure on the authority of the Lord Jesus that there is nothing really wrong with eating meat that has been offered to idols. But if someone believes it is wrong, then he shouldn't do it because for him it is wrong. ¹⁵ And if your brother is bothered by what you eat, you are not acting in love if you go ahead and eat it. Don't let your eating ruin someone for whom Christ died. ¹⁶ Don't do anything that will cause criticism against yourself even though you know that what you do is right. ¹⁷ For, after all, the important thing for us as Christians is not what we eat or drink but stirring up goodness and peace and joy from the Holy Spirit. ¹⁸ If you let Christ be Lord in these affairs, God will be glad; and so will others. ¹⁹ In this way aim for harmony in the church and try to build each other up.

²⁰ Don't undo the work of God for a chunk of meat. Remember, there is nothing wrong with the meat, but it is wrong to eat it if it makes another stumble. ²¹ The right thing to do is to quit eating meat or drinking wine or doing anything else that offends your brother or makes him sin. ²² You may know that there is nothing wrong with what you do, even from God's point of view, but keep it to yourself; don't flaunt your faith in front of others who might be hurt by it. In this situation, happy is the man who does not sin by doing what he knows is right. ²³ But anyone who believes that something he wants to do is wrong shouldn't do it. He sins if he does, for he thinks it is wrong, and so for him it *is* wrong. Anything that is done apart from what he feels is right is sin.

15 EVEN IF WE believe that it makes no difference to the Lord whether we do these things, still we cannot just go ahead and do them to please ourselves; for we must bear the "burden" of being consider-

---

a Literally, "Receive him that is weak in faith, not for decisions of scruples." Perhaps the meaning is, "Receive those whose consciences hurt them when they do things others have no doubts about." Accepting them might cause discord in the church, but Paul says to welcome them anyway.

ate of the doubts and fears of others—of those who feel these things are wrong. Let's please the other fellow, not ourselves, and do what is for his good and thus build him up in the Lord. ³ Christ didn't please himself. As the Psalmist said, "He came for the very purpose of suffering under the insults of those who were against the Lord." ⁴ These things that were written in the Scriptures so long ago are to teach us patience and to encourage us, so that we will look forward expectantly to the time when God will conquer sin and death.

⁵ May God who gives patience, steadiness, and encouragement help you to live in complete harmony with each other—each with the attitude of Christ toward the other. ⁶ And then all of us can praise the Lord together with one voice, giving glory to God, the Father of our Lord Jesus Christ.

⁷ So, warmly welcome each other into the church, just as Christ has warmly welcomed you; then God will be glorified. ⁸ Remember that Jesus Christ came to show that God is true to his promises and to help the Jews. ⁹ And remember that he came also that the Gentiles might be saved and give glory to God for his mercies to them. That is what the Psalmist meant when he wrote: "I will praise you among the Gentiles, and sing to your name."

¹⁰ And in another place, "Be glad, O you Gentiles, along with his people the Jews."

¹¹ And yet again, "Praise the Lord, O you Gentiles, let everyone praise him."

¹² And the prophet Isaiah said, "There shall be an Heir in the house of Jesse, and he will be King over the Gentiles; they will pin their hopes on him alone."

¹³ So I pray for you Gentiles that God who gives you hope will keep you happy and full of peace as you believe in him. I pray that God will help you overflow with hope in him through the Holy Spirit's power within you.

¹⁴ I know that you are wise and good, my brothers, and that you know these things so well that you are able to teach others all about them. ¹⁵,¹⁶ But even so I have been bold enough to emphasize some of these

points, knowing that all you need is this reminder from me; for I am, by God's grace, a special messenger from Jesus Christ to you Gentiles, bringing you the Gospel and offering you up as a fragrant sacrifice to God; for you have been made pure and pleasing to him by the Holy Spirit. ¹⁷ So it is right for me to be a little proud of all Christ Jesus has done through me. ¹⁸ I dare not judge how effectively he has used others, but I know this: he has used me to win the Gentiles to God. ¹⁹ I have won them by my message and by the good way I have lived before them, and by the miracles done through me as signs from God—all by the Holy Spirit's power. In this way I have preached the full[a] Gospel of Christ all the way from Jerusalem clear over into Illyricum.

²⁰ But all the while my ambition has been to go still farther, preaching where the name of Christ has never yet been heard, rather than where a church has already been started by someone else. ²¹ I have been following the plan spoken of in the Scriptures where Isaiah says that those who have never heard the name of Christ before will see and understand. ²² In fact that is the very reason I have been so long in coming to visit you.

²³ But now at last I am through with my work here, and I am ready to come after all these long years of waiting. ²⁴ For I am planning to take a trip to Spain, and when I do, I will stop off there in Rome; and after we have had a good time together for a little while, you can send me on my way again.

²⁵ But before I come, I must go down to Jerusalem to take a gift to the Jewish Christians there. ²⁶ For you see, the Christians in Macedonia and Achaia have taken up an offering for those in Jerusalem who are going through such hard times. ²⁷ They were very glad to do this, for they feel that they owe a real debt to the Jerusalem Christians. Why? Because the news about Christ came to these Gentiles from the church in Jerusalem. And since they received this wonderful spiritual gift of the Gospel from there, they feel that the least they can do in return is

---

a Or, "I have fully accomplished my Gospel ministry."

to give some material aid.[b] [28] As soon as I have delivered this money and completed this good deed of theirs, I will come to see you on my way to Spain. [29] And I am sure that when I come the Lord will give me a great blessing for you.

[30] Will you be my prayer partners? For the Lord Jesus Christ's sake, and because of your love for me—given to you by the Holy Spirit—pray much with me for my work. [31] Pray that I will be protected in Jerusalem from those who are not Christians. Pray also that the Christians there will be willing to accept the money I am bringing them. [32] Then I will be able to come to you with a happy heart by the will of God, and we can refresh each other.

[33] And now may our God, who gives peace, be with you all. Amen.

16 PHOEBE, A DEAR Christian woman from the town of Cenchreae, will be coming to see you soon. She has worked hard in the church there. Receive her as your sister in the Lord, giving her a warm Christian welcome. Help her in every way you can, for she has helped many in their needs, including me. [3] Tell Priscilla and Aquila "hello." They have been my fellow workers in the affairs of Christ Jesus. [4] In fact, they risked their lives for me; and I am not the only one who is thankful to them: so are all the Gentile churches.

[5] Please give my greetings to all those who meet to worship in their home. Greet my good friend Epaenetus. He was the very first person to become a Christian in Asia. [6] Remember me to Mary, too, who has worked so hard to help us. [7] Then there are Andronicus and Junias, my relatives who were in prison with me. They are respected by the apostles, and became Christians before I did. Please give them my greetings. [8] Say "hello" to Ampliatus, whom I love as one of God's own children, [9] and Urbanus, our fellow worker, and beloved Stachys.

[10] Then there is Apelles, a good man whom the Lord approves; greet him for me. And give my best regards to those working at the house of Aristobulus. [11] Remember me to Herodion my relative. Remember me to the Christian slaves over at Narcissus House. [12] Say "hello" to Tryphaena and Tryphosa, the Lord's workers, and to dear Persis, who has worked so hard for the Lord. [13] Greet Rufus for me, whom the Lord picked out to be his very own; and also his dear mother who has been such a mother to me. [14] And please give my greetings to Asyncritus, Phlegon, Hermes, Patrobas, Hermas, and the other brothers who are with them. [15] Give my love to Philologus, Julia, Nereus and his sister, and to Olympas, and all the Christians who are with them. [16] Shake hands warmly with each other. All the churches here send you their greetings.

[17] And now there is one more thing to say before I end this letter. Stay away from those who cause divisions and are upsetting people's faith, teaching things about Christ that are contrary to what you have been taught. [18] Such teachers are not working for our Lord Jesus, but only want gain for themselves. They are good speakers, and simple-minded people are often fooled by them. [19] But everyone knows that you stand loyal and true. This makes me very happy. I want you always to remain very clear about what is right, and to stay innocent of any wrong. [20] The God of peace will soon crush Satan under your feet. The blessings from our Lord Jesus Christ be upon you.

[21] Timothy my fellow-worker, and Lucius and Jason and Sosipater, my relatives, send you their good wishes. [22] I, Tertius, the one who is writing this letter for Paul, send my greetings too, as a Christian brother. [23] Gaius says to say "hello" to you for him. I am his guest, and the church meets here in his home. Erastus, the city treasurer, sends you his greetings and so does Quartus, a Christian brother. [24] Goodbye. May the grace of our Lord Jesus Christ be with you all.

[25,26,27] I commit you to God, who is able to make you strong and steady in the Lord, just as the Gospel says, and just as I have told you. This is God's plan of salvation for you Gentiles, kept secret from the begin-

---

b Literally, "For if the Gentiles have come to share in their spiritual blessings, they ought also to be of service to them in material blessings."

ning of time. But now as the prophets foretold and as God commands, this message is being preached everywhere, so that people all around the world will have faith in Christ and obey him. To God, who alone is wise, be the glory forever through Jesus Christ our Lord. Amen.

Sincerely,
Paul

Don't Look Too Closely

The glittering Manhattan skyline looks good from a distance—but somewhere between those skyscrapers in a section called the Bowery, New York's alcoholics spend the night on the concrete. For all its splendor, New York has become, according to some, ungovernable. It's just too big, with too many people jammed into too small an area

Bob Combs

with people too uptight trying to live together. Corinth, in ancient Greece, was likewise plagued—it was like New York and Las Vegas combined to the sailors, businessmen, and prostitutes who worked its streets. The practical problems of being a Christian in the urban swirl—that's what Paul wrote about in these two letters after having lived in Corinth a year and a half himself.

1 CORINTHIANS

1 FROM: PAUL, CHOSEN by God to be Jesus Christ's missionary, and from brother Sosthenes.

² *To:* The Christians in Corinth, invited by God to be his people and made acceptable[a] to him by Christ Jesus. *And to:* All Christians everywhere—whoever calls upon the name of Jesus Christ, our Lord and theirs.

³ May God our Father and the Lord Jesus Christ give you all of his blessings, and great peace of heart and mind.

⁴ I can never stop thanking God for all the wonderful gifts he has given you, now that you are Christ's: ⁵ he has enriched your whole life. He has helped you speak out for him and has given you a full understanding of the truth; ⁶ what I told you Christ could do for you has happened! ⁷ Now you have every grace and blessing; every spiritual gift and power for doing his will are yours during this time of waiting for the return of our Lord Jesus Christ. ⁸ And he guarantees right up to the end that you will be counted free from all sin and guilt on that day when he returns. ⁹ God will surely do this for you, for he always does just what he says, and he is the one who invited you into this wonderful friendship with his Son, even Christ our Lord.

¹⁰ But, dear brothers, I beg you in the name of the Lord Jesus Christ to stop arguing among yourselves. Let there be real harmony so that there won't be splits in the church. I plead with you to be of one mind, united in thought and purpose. ¹¹ For some of those who live at Chloe's house have told me of your arguments and quarrels, dear brothers. ¹² Some of you are saying, "I am a follower of Paul"; and others say that they

are for Apollos or for Peter; and some that they alone are the true followers of Christ. ¹³ And so, in effect, you have broken Christ into many pieces.

But did I, Paul, die for your sins? Were any of you baptized in my name? ¹⁴ I am so thankful now that I didn't baptize any of you except Crispus and Gaius. ¹⁵ For now no one can think that I have been trying to start something new, beginning a "Church of Paul." ¹⁶ Oh, yes, and I baptized the family of Stephanas. I don't remember ever baptizing anyone else. ¹⁷ For Christ didn't send me to baptize, but to preach the Gospel; and even my preaching sounds poor, for I do not fill my sermons with profound words and high sounding ideas, for fear of diluting the mighty power there is in the simple message of the cross of Christ.

¹⁸ I know very well how foolish it sounds to those who are[b] lost, when they hear that Jesus died to save them. But we who are[b] saved recognize this message as the very power of God. ¹⁹ For God says, "I will destroy all human plans of salvation no matter how wise they seem to be, and ignore the best ideas of men, even the most brilliant of them."

²⁰ So what about these wise men, these scholars, these brilliant debaters of this world's great affairs? God has made them all look foolish, and shown their wisdom to be useless nonsense. ²¹ For God in his wisdom saw to it that the world would never find God through human brilliance, and then he stepped in and saved all those who believed his message, which the world calls foolish and silly. ²² It seems foolish to the Jews because they want a sign from heaven as proof that what is preached is true; and

---

a Or, "chosen by Christ Jesus." Literally, "sanctified in Christ Jesus."   b Or, "are being . . ."

it is foolish to the Gentiles because they believe only what agrees with their philosophy and seems wise to them. ²³ So when we preach about Christ dying to save them, the Jews are offended and the Gentiles say it's all nonsense. ²⁴ But God has opened the eyes of those called to salvation, both Jews and Gentiles, to see that Christ is the mighty power of God to save them; Christ himself is the center of God's wise plan for their salvation. ²⁵ This so-called "foolish" plan of God is far wiser than the wisest plan of the wisest man, and God in his weakness—Christ dying on the cross—is far stronger than any man.

²⁶ Notice among yourselves, dear brothers, that few of you who follow Christ have big names or power or wealth. ²⁷ Instead, God has deliberately chosen to use ideas the world considers foolish and of little worth in order to shame those people considered by the world as wise and great. ²⁸ He has chosen a plan despised by the world, counted as nothing at all, and used it to bring down to nothing those the world considers great, ²⁹ so that no one anywhere can ever brag in the presence of God.

³⁰ For it is from God alone that you have your life through Christ Jesus. He showed us God's plan of salvation; he was the one who made us acceptable to God; he made us pure and holy[c] and gave himself to purchase our salvation.[d] ³¹ As it says in the Scriptures, "If anyone is going to boast, let him boast only of what the Lord has done."

2 DEAR BROTHERS, EVEN when I first came to you I didn't use lofty words and brilliant ideas to tell you God's message. ² For I decided that I would speak only of Jesus Christ and his death on the cross. ³ I came to you in weakness—timid and trembling. ⁴ And my preaching was very plain, not with a lot of oratory and human wisdom, but the Holy Spirit's power was in my words, proving to those who heard them that the message was from God. ⁵ I did this because I wanted your faith to stand firmly upon God, not on man's great ideas.

⁶ Yet when I am among mature Christians I do speak with words of great wisdom, but not the kind that comes from here on earth, and not the kind that appeals to the great men of this world, who are doomed to fall. ⁷ Our words are wise because they are from God, telling of God's wise plan to bring us into the glories of heaven. This plan was hidden in former times, though it was made for our benefit before the world began. ⁸ But the great men of the world have not understood it; if they had, they never would have crucified the Lord of Glory.

⁹ That is what is meant by the Scriptures which say that no mere man has ever seen, heard or even imagined what wonderful things God has ready for those who love the Lord. ¹⁰ But we know about these things because God has sent his Spirit to tell us, and his Spirit searches out and shows us all of God's deepest secrets. ¹¹ No one can really know what anyone else is thinking, or what he is really like, except that person himself. And no one can know God's thoughts except God's own Spirit. ¹² And God has actually given us his Spirit (not the world's spirit) to tell us about the wonderful free gifts of grace and blessing that God has given us. ¹³ In telling you about these gifts we have even used the very words given to us by the Holy Spirit, not words that we as men might choose. So we use the Holy Spirit's words to explain the Holy Spirit's facts.[a] ¹⁴ But the man who isn't a Christian can't understand and can't accept these thoughts from God, which the Holy Spirit teaches us. They sound foolish to him, because only those who have the Holy Spirit within them can understand what the Holy Spirit means. Others just can't take it in. ¹⁵ But the spiritual man has insight into everything, and that bothers and baffles the man of the world, who can't understand him at all. ¹⁶ How could he? For certainly he has never been one to know the Lord's thoughts, or to discuss them with him, or to move the hands of God by prayer.[b] But, strange as it seems, we Christians actually do have within us a portion of the very thoughts and mind of Christ.

---

c Or, "he brought us near to God." spiritual truth in spiritual language."

d Or, "to free us from slavery to sin."
b Or, "who can advise him?"

2a Or, "interpreting

3 DEAR BROTHERS, I have been talking to you as though you were still just babies in the Christian life, who are not following the Lord, but your own desires; I cannot talk to you as I would to healthy Christians, who are filled with the Spirit. ² I have had to feed you with milk and not with solid food, because you couldn't digest anything stronger. And even now you still have to be fed on milk. ³ For you are still only baby Christians, controlled by your own desires, not God's. When you are jealous of one another and divide up into quarreling groups, doesn't that prove you are still babies, wanting your own way? In fact, you are acting like people who don't belong to the Lord at all. ⁴ There you are, quarreling about whether I am greater than Apollos, and dividing the church. Doesn't this show how little you have grown in the Lord?ᵃ

⁵ Who am I, and who is Apollos, that we should be the cause of a quarrel? Why, we're just God's servants, each of us with certain special abilities, and with our help you believed. ⁶ My work was to plant the seed in your hearts, and Apollos' work was to water it, but it was God, not we, who made the garden grow in your hearts. ⁷ The person who does the planting or watering isn't very important, but God is important because he is the one who makes things grow. ⁸ Apollos and I are working as a team, with the same aim, though each of us will be rewarded for his own hard work. ⁹ We are only God's co-workers. You are *God's* garden, not ours; you are *God's* building, not ours.

¹⁰ God, in his kindness, has taught me how to be an expert builder. I have laid the foundation and Apollos has built on it. But he who builds on the foundation must be very careful. ¹¹ And no one can ever lay any other real foundation than that one we already have—Jesus Christ. ¹² But there are various kinds of materials that can be used to build on that foundation. Some use gold and silver and jewels; and some build with sticks, and hay, or even straw! ¹³ There is going to come a time of testing at Christ's Judgment Day to see what kind of material each builder has used. Everyone's work will

be put through the fire so that all can see whether or not it keeps its value, and what was really accomplished. ¹⁴ Then every workman who has built on the foundation with the right materials, and whose work still stands, will get his pay. ¹⁵ But if the house he has built burns up, he will have a great loss. He himself will be saved, but like a man escaping through a wall of flames.

¹⁶ Don't you realize that all of you together are the house of God, and that the Spirit of God lives among you in his house? ¹⁷ If anyone defiles and spoils God's home, God will destroy him. For God's home is holy and clean, and you are that home.

¹⁸ Stop fooling yourselves. If you count yourself above average in intelligence, as judged by this world's standards, you had better put this all aside and be a fool rather than let it hold you back from the true wisdom from above. ¹⁹ For the wisdom of this world is foolishness to God. As it says in the book of Job, God uses man's own brilliance to trap him; he stumbles over his own "wisdom" and falls. ²⁰ And again, in the book of Psalms, we are told that the Lord knows full well how the human mind reasons, and how foolish and futile it is.

²¹ So don't be proud of following the wise men of this world.ᵇ For God has already given you everything you need. ²² He has given you Paul and Apollos and Peter as your helpers. He has given you the whole world to use, and life and even death are your servants. He has given you all of the present and all of the future. All are yours, ²³ and you belong to Christ, and Christ is God's.

4 SO APOLLOS AND I should be looked upon as Christ's servants who distribute God's blessings by explaining God's secrets. ² Now the most important thing about a servant is that he does just what his master tells him to. ³ What about me? Have I been a good servant? Well, I don't worry over what you think about this, or what anyone else thinks. I don't even trust my own judgment on this point. ⁴ My conscience is clear, but even that isn't final proof. It is the Lord

---

a Literally, "Are you not (mere) men?"   b Literally, "Let no one glory in men."

himself who must examine me and decide. ⁵ So be careful not to jump to conclusions before the Lord returns as to whether someone is a good servant or not. When the Lord comes, he will turn on the light so that everyone can see exactly what each one of us is really like, deep down in our hearts. Then everyone will know why we have been doing the Lord's work. At that time God will give to each one whatever praise is coming to him.

⁶ I have used Apollos and myself as examples to illustrate what I have been saying: that you must not have favorites. You must not be proud of one of God's teachers more than another. ⁷ What are you so puffed up about? What do you have that God hasn't given you? And if all you have is from God, why act as though you are so great, and as though you have accomplished something on your own?

⁸ You seem to think you already have all the spiritual food you need. You are full and spiritually contented, rich kings on your thrones, leaving us far behind! I wish you really were already on your thrones, for when that time comes you can be sure that we will be there, too, reigning with you. ⁹ Sometimes I think God has put us apostles at the very end of the line, like prisoners soon to be killed, put on display at the end of a victor's parade, to be stared at by men and angels alike.

¹⁰ Religion has made us foolish, you say, but of course you are all such wise and sensible Christians! We are weak, but not you! You are well thought of, while we are laughed at. ¹¹ To this very hour we have gone hungry and thirsty, without even enough clothes to keep us warm. We have been kicked around without homes of our own. ¹² We have worked wearily with our hands to earn our living. We have blessed those who cursed us. We have been patient with those who injured us. ¹³ We have replied quietly when evil things have been said about us. Yet right up to the present moment we are like dirt under foot, like garbage.

¹⁴ I am not writing about these things to make you ashamed, but to warn and coun-sel you as beloved children. ¹⁵ For although you may have ten thousand others to teach you about Christ, remember that you have only me as your father. For I was the one who brought you to Christ when I preached the Gospel to you. ¹⁶ So I beg you to follow my example, and do as I do.

¹⁷ That is the very reason why I am sending Timothy—to help you do this. For he is one of those I won to Christ, a beloved and trustworthy child in the Lord. He will remind you of what I teach in all the churches wherever I go.

¹⁸ I know that some of you will have become proud, thinking that I am afraid to come to deal with you. ¹⁹ But I will come, and soon, if the Lord will let me, and then I'll find out whether these proud men are just big talkers or whether they really have God's power. ²⁰ The Kingdom of God is not just talking; it is living by God's power. ²¹ Which do you choose? Shall I come with punishment and scolding, or shall I come with quiet love and gentleness?

5 EVERYONE IS TALKING about the terrible thing that has happened there among you, something so evil that even the heathen don't do it: you have a man in your church who is living in sin with his father's wife.ᵃ ² And are you still so conceited, so "spiritual"? Why aren't you mourning in sorrow and shame, and seeing to it that this man is removed from your membership?

³,⁴ Although I am not there with you, I have been thinking a lot about this, and in the name of the Lord Jesus Christ I have already decided what to do, just as though I were there. You are to call a meeting of the church—and the power of the Lord Jesus will be with you as you meet, and I will be there in spirit— ⁵ and cast out this man from the fellowship of the church and into Satan's hands, to punish him,ᵇ in the hope that his soul will be saved when our Lord Jesus Christ returns.

⁶ What a terrible thing it is that you are boasting about your purity, and yet you let this sort of thing go on. Don't you realize that if even one person is allowed to go on sinning, soon all will be affected? ⁷ Remove

---

a Possibly his stepmother.　　　b Literally, "for the destruction of the flesh."

this evil cancer—this wicked person—from among you, so that you can stay pure. Christ, God's Lamb, has been slain for us. [8] So let us feast upon him and grow strong in the Christian life, leaving entirely behind us the cancerous old life with all its hatreds and wickedness. Let us feast instead upon the pure bread of honor and sincerity and truth.

[9] When I wrote to you before I said not to mix with evil people. [10] But when I said that I wasn't talking about unbelievers who live in sexual sin, or are greedy cheats and thieves and idol worshipers. For you can't live in this world without being with people like that. [11] What I meant was that you are not to keep company with anyone who claims to be a brother Christian but indulges in sexual sins, or is greedy, or is a swindler, or worships idols, or is a drunkard, or abusive. Don't even eat lunch with such a person.

[12] It isn't our job to judge outsiders. But it certainly is our job to judge and deal strongly with those who are members of the church, and who are sinning in these ways. [13] God alone is the Judge of those on the outside. But you yourselves must deal with this man and put him out of your church.

6 HOW IS IT that when you have something against another Christian, you "go to law" and ask a heathen court to decide the matter instead of taking it to other Christians to decide which of you is right? [2] Don't you know that some day we Christians are going to judge and govern the world? So why can't you decide even these little things among yourselves? [3] Don't you realize that we Christians will judge and reward the very angels in heaven? So you should be able to decide your problems down here on earth easily enough. [4] Why then go to outside judges who are not even Christians?[a] [5] I am trying to make you ashamed. Isn't there anyone in all the church who is wise enough to decide these arguments? [6] But, instead, one Christian sues another and accuses his Christian brother in front of unbelievers.

[7] To have such lawsuits at all is a real defeat for you as Christians. Why not just accept mistreatment and leave it at that? It would be far more honoring to the Lord to let yourselves be cheated. [8] But, instead, you yourselves are the ones who do wrong, cheating others, even your own brothers.

[9,10] Don't you know that those doing such things have no share in the Kingdom of God? Don't fool yourselves. Those who live immoral lives, who are idol worshipers, adulterers or homosexuals—will have no share in his kingdom. Neither will thieves or greedy people, drunkards, slanderers, or robbers. [11] There was a time when some of you were just like that but now your sins are washed away, and you are set apart for God, and he has accepted you because of what the Lord Jesus Christ and the Spirit of our God have done for you. [12] I can do anything I want to if Christ has not said no,[b] but some of these things aren't good for me. Even if I am allowed to do them, I'll refuse to if I think they might get such a grip on me that I can't easily stop when I want to. [13] For instance, take the matter of eating. God has given us an appetite for food and stomachs to digest it. But that doesn't mean we should eat more than we need. Don't think of eating as important, because some day God will do away with both stomachs and food.

But sexual sin is never right: our bodies were not made for that, but for the Lord, and the Lord wants to fill our bodies with himself. [14] And God is going to raise our bodies from the dead by his power just as he raised up the Lord Jesus Christ. [15] Don't you realize that your bodies are actually parts and members of Christ? So should I take part of Christ and join him to a prostitute? Never! [16] And don't you know that if a man joins himself to a prostitute she becomes a part of him and he becomes a part of her? For God tells us in the Scripture that in his sight the two become one person. [17] But if you give yourself to the Lord, you and Christ are joined together as one per-

---

a Or, "Even the least capable people in the church should be able to decide these things for you." Both interpretations are possible.   b Literally, "All things are lawful for me." Obviously, Paul is not here permitting sins such as have just been expressly prohibited in verses 8 and 9. He is apparently quoting some in the church of lustful Corinth who were excusing their sins.

son. ¹⁸ That is why I say to run from sex sin. No other sin affects the body as this one does. When you sin this sin it is against your own body. ¹⁹ Haven't you yet learned that your body is the home of the Holy Spirit God gave you, and that he lives within you? Your own body does not belong to you. ²⁰ For God has bought you with a great price. So use every part of your body to give glory back to God, because he owns it.

7 NOW ABOUT THOSE questions you asked in your last letter: my answer is that if you do not marry, it is good. ² But usually it is best to be married, each man having his own wife, and each woman having her own husband, because otherwise you might fall back into sin.

³ The man should give his wife all that is her right as a married woman, and the wife should do the same for her husband: ⁴ for a girl who marries no longer has full right to her own body, for her husband then has his rights to it, too; and in the same way the husband no longer has full right to his own body, for it belongs also to his wife. ⁵ So do not refuse these rights to each other. The only exception to this rule would be the agreement of both husband and wife to refrain from the rights of marriage for a limited time, so that they can give themselves more completely to prayer. Afterwards, they should come together again so that Satan won't be able to tempt them because of their lack of self-control.

⁶ I'm not saying you *must* marry; but you certainly *may* if you wish. ⁷ I wish everyone could get along without marrying, just as I do. But we are not all the same. God gives some the gift of a husband or wife, and others he gives the gift of being able to stay happily unmarried. ⁸ So I say to those who aren't married, and to widows—better to stay unmarried if you can, just as I am. ⁹ But if you can't control yourselves, go ahead and marry. It is better to marry than to burn with lust.

¹⁰ Now, for those who are married I have a command, not just a suggestion. And it is not a command from me, for this is what the Lord himself has said: A wife must not leave her husband. ¹¹ But if she is separated

from him, let her remain single or else go back to him. And the husband must not divorce his wife.

¹² Here I want to add some suggestions of my own. These are not direct commands from the Lord, but they seem right to me: If a Christian has a wife who is not a Christian, but she wants to stay with him anyway, he must not leave her or divorce her. ¹³ And if a Christian woman has a husband who isn't a Christian, and he wants her to stay with him, she must not leave him. ¹⁴ For perhaps the husband who isn't a Christian may become a Christian with the help of his Christian wife. And the wife who isn't a Christian may become a Christian with the help of her Christian husband. Otherwise, if the family separates, the children might never come to know the Lord; whereas a united family may, in God's plan, result in the children's salvation.

¹⁵ But if the husband or wife who isn't a Christian is eager to leave, it is permitted. In such cases the Christian husband or wife should not insist that the other stay, for God wants his children to live in peace and harmony. ¹⁶ For, after all, there is no assurance to you wives that your husbands will be converted if they stay; and the same may be said to you husbands concerning your wives.

¹⁷ But be sure in deciding these matters that you are living as God intended, marrying or not marrying in accordance with God's direction and help, and accepting whatever situation God has put you into. This is my rule for all the churches.

¹⁸ For instance, a man who already has gone through the Jewish ceremony of circumcision before he became a Christian shouldn't worry about it; and if he hasn't been circumcised, he shouldn't do it now. ¹⁹ For it doesn't make any difference at all whether a Christian has gone through this ceremony or not. But it makes a lot of difference whether he is pleasing God and keeping God's commandments. That is the important thing.

²⁰ Usually a person should keep on with the work he was doing when God called him. ²¹ Are you a slave? Don't let that worry you—but of course, if you get a chance to be free, take it. ²² If the Lord calls you, and

you are a slave, remember that Christ has set you free from the awful power of sin; and if he has called you and you are free, remember that you are now a slave of Christ. [23] You have been bought and paid for by Christ, so you belong to him—be free now from all these earthly prides and fears.[a] [24] So, dear brothers, whatever situation a person is in when he becomes a Christian, let him stay there, for now the Lord is there to help him.

[25] Now I will try to answer your other question. What about girls who are not yet married? Should they be permitted to do so? In answer to this question, I have no special command for them from the Lord. But the Lord in his kindness has given me wisdom that can be trusted, and I will be glad to tell you what I think.

[26] Here is the problem: We Christians are facing great dangers to our lives at present. In times like these I think it is best for a person to remain unmarried. [27] Of course, if you already are married, don't separate because of this. But if you aren't, don't rush into it at this time. [28] But if you men decide to go ahead anyway and get married now, it is all right; and if a girl gets married in times like these, it is no sin. However, marriage will bring extra problems that I wish you didn't have to face right now.

[29] The important thing to remember is that our remaining time is very short, [and so are our opportunities for doing the Lord's work[b]]. For that reason those who have wives should stay as free as possible for the Lord;[c] [30] happiness or sadness or wealth should not keep anyone from doing God's work. [31] Those in frequent contact with the exciting things the world offers should make good use of their opportunities without stopping to enjoy them; for the world in its present form will soon be gone. [32] In all you do, I want you to be free from worry. An unmarried man can spend his time doing the Lord's work and thinking how to please him. [33] But a married man can't do that so well; he has to think about his earthly responsibilities and how to please his wife. [34] His interests are divided.

It is the same with a girl who marries. She faces the same problem. A girl who is not married is anxious to please the Lord in all she is and does.[d] But a married woman must consider other things such as housekeeping and the likes and dislikes of her husband.

[35] I am saying this to help you, not to try to keep you from marrying. I want you to do whatever will help you serve the Lord best, with as few other things as possible to distract your attention from him.

[36] But if anyone feels he ought to marry because he has trouble controlling his passions, it is all right, it is not a sin; let him marry. [37] But if a man has the willpower not to marry and decides that he doesn't need to and won't, he has made a wise decision. [38] So the person who marries does well, and the person who doesn't marry does even better.

[39] The wife is part of her husband as long as he lives; if her husband dies, then she may marry again, but only if she marries a Christian. [40] But in my opinion she will be happier if she doesn't marry again; and I think I am giving you counsel from God's Spirit when I say this.

8 NEXT IS YOUR question about eating food that has been sacrificed to idols. On this question everyone feels that only his answer is the right one! But although being a "know-it-all" makes us feel important, what is really needed to build the church is love. [2] If anyone thinks he knows all the answers, he is just showing his ignorance. [3] But the person who truly loves God is the one who is open to God's knowledge.

[4] So now, what about it? Should we eat meat that has been sacrificed to idols? Well, we all know that an idol is not really a god, and that there is only one God, and no other. [5] According to some people, there are a great many gods, both in heaven and on earth. [6] But we know that there is only one God, the Father, who created all things[a] and made us to be his own; and one Lord Jesus Christ, who made everything and gives us life.

---

a Literally, "Become not bondservants of men." wives may be as though they didn't." d Literally, "pure in body and in spirit." b Implied. c Literally, "(that) those who have 8a Literally, "of whom are all things."

⁷ However, some Christians don't realize this. All their lives they have been used to thinking of idols as alive, and have believed that food offered to the idols is really being offered to actual gods. So when they eat such food it bothers them and hurts their tender consciences. ⁸ Just remember that God doesn't care whether we eat it or not. We are no worse off if we don't eat it, and no better off if we do. ⁹ But be careful not to use your freedom to eat it, lest you cause some Christian brother to sin whose conscienceᵇ is weaker than yours.

¹⁰ You see, this is what may happen: Someone who thinks it is wrong to eat this food will see you eating at a temple restaurant, for you know there is no harm in it. Then he will become bold enough to do it too, although all the time he still feels it is wrong. ¹¹ So because you "know it is all right to do it," you will be responsible for causing great spiritual damage to a brother with a tender conscience for whom Christ died. ¹² And it is a sin against Christ to sin against your brother by encouraging him to do something he thinks is wrong. ¹³ So if eating meat offered to idols is going to make my brother sin, I'll not eat any of it as long as I live, because I don't want to do this to him.

9 I AM AN apostle, God's messenger, responsible to no mere man. I am one who has actually seen Jesus our Lord with my own eyes. And your changed lives are the result of my hard work for him. ² If in the opinion of others, I am not an apostle, I certainly am to you, for you have been won to Christ through me. ³ This is my answer to those who question my rights.

⁴ Or don't I have any rights at all? Can't I claim the same privilege the other apostles have of being a guest in your homes? ⁵ Ifᵃ I had a wife, and ifᵃ she were a believer, couldn't I bring her along on these trips just as the other disciples do, and as the Lord's brothers do, and as Peter does? ⁶ And must Barnabas and I alone keep working for our living, while you supply these others? ⁷ What soldier in the army has to pay his own expenses? And have you ever heard of

a farmer who harvests his crop and doesn't have the right to eat some of it? What shepherd takes care of a flock of sheep and goats and isn't allowed to drink some of the milk? ⁸ And I'm not merely quoting the opinions of men as to what is right. I'm telling you what God's law says. ⁹ For in the law God gave to Moses he said that you must not put a muzzle on an ox to keep it from eating when it is treading out the wheat. Do you suppose God was thinking only about oxen when he said this? ¹⁰ Wasn't he also thinking about us? Of course he was. He said this to show us that Christian workers should be paid by those they help. Those who do the plowing and threshing should expect some share of the harvest.

¹¹ We have planted good spiritual seed in your souls. Is it too much to ask, in return, for mere food and clothing? ¹² You give them to others who preach to you, and you should. But shouldn't we have an even greater right to them? Yet we have *never* used this right, but supply our own needs without your help. We have never demanded payment of any kind for fear that, if we did, you might be less interested in our message to you from Christ.

¹³ Don't you realize that God told those working in his temple to take for their own needs some of the food brought there as gifts to him? And those who work at the altar of God get a share of the food that is brought by those offering it to the Lord. ¹⁴ In the same way the Lord has given orders that those who preach the Gospel should be supported by those who accept it. ¹⁵ Yet I have never asked you for one penny. And I am not writing this to hint that I would like to start now. In fact, I would rather die of hunger than lose the satisfaction I get from preaching to you without charge. ¹⁶ For just preaching the Gospel isn't any special credit to me—I couldn't keep from preaching if I wanted to. I would be utterly miserable. Woe unto me if I don't.

¹⁷ If I were volunteering my services of my own free will, then the Lord would give me a special reward; but that is not the situation, for God has picked me out and given me this sacred trust and I have no

---

b Implied. Literally, "faith."   9a Implied. Literally, "Have we no right to lead about a wife that is a believer?"

choice. [18] Under this circumstance, what is my pay? It is the special joy I get from preaching the Good News without expense to anyone, never demanding my rights.

[19] And this has a real advantage: I am not bound to obey anyone just because he pays my salary; yet I have freely and happily become a servant of any and all so that I can win them to Christ. [20] When I am with the Jews I seem as one of them so that they will listen to the Gospel and I can win them to Christ. When I am with Gentiles who follow Jewish customs and ceremonies I don't argue, even though I don't agree, because I want to help them. [21] When with the heathen I agree with them as much as I can, except of course that I must always do what is right as a Christian. And so, by agreeing, I can win their confidence[b] and help them too.

[22] When I am with those whose consciences bother them easily, I don't act as though I know it all and don't say they are foolish; the result is that they are willing to let me help them. Yes, whatever a person is like, I try to find common ground with him so that he will let me tell him about Christ and let Christ save him. [23] I do this to get the Gospel to them and also for the blessing I myself receive when I see them come to Christ.

[24] In a race, everyone runs but only one person gets first prize. So run your race to win. [25] To win the contest you must deny yourselves many things that would keep you from doing your best. An athlete goes to all this trouble just to win a blue ribbon or a silver cup,[c] but we do it for a heavenly reward that never disappears. [26] So I run straight to the goal with purpose in every step. I fight to win. I'm not just shadow-boxing or playing around. [27] Like an athlete I punish my body, treating it roughly, training it to do what it should, not what it wants to. Otherwise I fear that after enlisting others for the race, I myself might be declared unfit and ordered to stand aside.

10 FOR WE MUST never forget, dear brothers, what happened to our people in the wilderness long ago. God guided them by sending a cloud that moved along ahead of them; and he brought them all safely through the waters of the Red Sea. [2] This might be called their "baptism" —baptized both in sea and cloud!—as followers of Moses—their commitment to him as their leader. [3,4] And by a miracle[a] God sent them food to eat and water to drink there in the desert; they drank the water that Christ gave them.[b] He was there with them as a mighty Rock of spiritual refreshment. [5] Yet after all this most of them did not obey God, and he destroyed them in the wilderness.

[6] From this lesson we are warned that we must not desire evil things as they did, [7] nor worship idols as they did. (The Scriptures tell us, "The people sat down to eat and drink and then got up to dance" in worship of the golden calf.)

[8] Another lesson for us is what happened when some of them sinned with other men's wives, and 23,000 fell dead in one day. [9] And don't try the Lord's patience—they did, and died from snake bites. [10] And don't murmur against God and his dealings with you, as some of them did, for that is why God sent his Angel to destroy them.

[11] All these things happened to them as examples—as object lessons to us—to warn us against doing the same things; they were written down so that we could read about them and learn from them in these last days as the world nears its end.

[12] So be careful. If you are thinking, "Oh, I would never behave like that"—let this be a warning to you. For you too may fall into sin. [13] But remember this—the wrong desires that come into your life aren't anything new and different. Many others have faced exactly the same problems before you. And no temptation is irresistible. You can trust God to keep the temptation from becoming so strong that you can't stand up against it, for he has promised this and will do what he says. He will show you how to escape temptation's power so that you can bear up patiently against it. [14] So, dear friends, carefully avoid idol-worship of ev-

---

b Implied.   c Literally, "a wreath that quickly fades," given to the winners of the original Olympic races of Paul's time.   10 a Implied. Literally, "all ate the same supernatural food and drink."
b Literally, "For they drank of a spiritual Rock that followed them, and the Rock was Christ."

ery kind. [15] You are intelligent people. Look now and see for yourselves whether what I am about to say is true. [16] When we ask the Lord's blessing upon our drinking from the cup of wine at the Lord's Table, this means, doesn't it, that all who drink it are sharing together the blessing of Christ's blood? And when we break off pieces of the bread from the loaf to eat there together, this shows that we are sharing together in the benefits of his body. [17] No matter how many of us there are, we all eat from the same loaf, showing that we are all parts of the one body of Christ. [18] And the Jewish people, all who eat the sacrifices, are united by that act.

[19] What am I trying to say? Am I saying that the idols to whom the heathen bring sacrifices are really alive and are real gods, and that these sacrifices are of some value? No, not at all. [20] What I am saying is that those who offer food to these idols are united together in sacrificing to demons, certainly not to God. And I don't want any of you to be partners with demons when you eat the same food, along with the heathen, that has been offered to these idols. [21] You cannot drink from the cup at the Lord's Table and at Satan's table, too. You cannot eat bread both at the Lord's Table and at Satan's table.

[22] What? Are you tempting the Lord to be angry with you? Are you stronger than he is? [23] You are certainly free to eat food offered to idols if you want to; it's not against God's laws to eat such meat, but that doesn't mean that you should go ahead and do it. It may be perfectly legal, but it may not be best and helpful. [24] Don't think only of yourself. Try to think of the other fellow, too, and what is best for him.

[25] Here's what you should do. Take any meat you want that is sold at the market. Don't ask whether or not it was offered to idols, lest the answer hurt your conscience. [26] For the earth and every good thing in it belongs to the Lord and is yours to enjoy.

[27] If someone who isn't a Christian asks you out to dinner, go ahead; accept the invitation if you want to. Eat whatever is on the table and don't ask any questions about it.

Then you won't know whether or not it has been used as a sacrifice to idols, and you won't risk having a bad conscience over eating it. [28] But if someone warns you that this meat has been offered to idols, then don't eat it for the sake of the man who told you, and of his conscience. [29] In this case *his* feeling about it is the important thing, not yours.

But why, you may ask, must I be guided and limited by what someone else thinks? [30] If I can thank God for the food and enjoy it, why let someone spoil everything just because he thinks I am wrong? [31] Well, I'll tell you why. It is because you must do everything for the glory of God, even your eating and drinking. [32] So don't be a stumbling block to anyone, whether they are Jews or Gentiles or Christians. [33] That is the plan I follow, too. I try to please everyone in everything I do, not doing what I like or what is best for me, but what is best for them, so that they may be saved.

11 AND YOU SHOULD follow my example, just as I follow Christ's. [2] I am so glad, dear brothers, that you have been remembering and doing everything I taught you. [3] But there is one matter I want to remind you about: that a wife is responsible to her husband, her husband is responsible to Christ, and Christ is responsible to God. [4] That is why, if a man refuses to remove his hat while praying or preaching, he dishonors Christ. [5] And that is why a woman who publicly prays or prophesies without a covering on her head dishonors her husband [for her covering is a sign of her subjection to him[a]]. [6] Yes, if she refuses to wear a head covering, then she should cut off all her hair. And if it is shameful for a woman to have her head shaved, then she should wear a covering. [7] But a man should not wear anything on his head [when worshiping, for his hat is a sign of subjection to men[b]].

God's glory is man made in his image, and man's glory is the woman. [8] The first man didn't come from woman, but the first woman came out of man.[c] [9] And Adam, the first man, was not made for Eve's benefit, but Eve was made for Adam. [10] So a woman

---

a Implied in verses 7, 10.   b Implied   c Genesis 2:21–22.

should wear a covering on her head as a sign that she is under man's authority,[d] a fact for all the angels to notice and rejoice in.[e]

[11] But remember that in God's plan men and women need each other. [12] For although the first woman came out of man, all men have been born from women ever since, and both men and women come from God their Creator.

[13] What do you yourselves really think about this? Is it right for a woman to pray in public without covering her head? [14,15] Doesn't even instinct itself teach us that women's heads should be covered? For women are proud of their long hair, while a man with long hair tends to be ashamed. [16] But if anyone wants to argue about this, all I can say is that we never teach anything else than this—that a woman should wear a covering when prophesying or praying publicly in the church, and all the churches feel the same way about it.

[17] Next on my list of items to write you about is something else I cannot agree with. For it sounds as if more harm than good is done when you meet together for your communion services. [18] Everyone keeps telling me about the arguing that goes on in these meetings, and the divisions developing among you, and I can just about believe it. [19] But I suppose you feel this is necessary so that you who are always right will become known and recognized!

[20] When you come together to eat, it isn't the Lord's Supper you are eating, [21] but your own. For I am told that everyone hastily gobbles all the food he can without waiting to share with the others, so that one doesn't get enough and goes hungry while another has too much to drink and gets drunk. [22] What? Is this really true? Can't you do your eating and drinking at home, to avoid disgracing the church and shaming those who are poor and can bring no food? What am I supposed to say about these things? Do you want me to praise you? Well, I certainly do not!

[23] For this is what the Lord himself has said about his Table, and I have passed it on to you before: That on the night when Judas betrayed him, the Lord Jesus took bread, [24] and when he had given thanks to God for it, he broke it and gave it to his disciples and said, "Take this and eat it. This is my body, which is given[f] for you. Do this to remember me." [25] In the same way, he took the cup of wine after supper, saying, "This cup is the new agreement between God and you that has been established and set in motion by my blood. Do this in remembrance of me whenever you drink it." [26] For every time you eat this bread and drink this cup you are re-telling the message of the Lord's death, that he has died for you. Do this until he comes again.

[27] So if anyone eats this bread and drinks from this cup of the Lord in an unworthy manner, he is guilty of sin against the body and the blood of the Lord. [28] That is why a man should examine himself carefully before eating the bread and drinking from the cup. [29] For if he eats the bread and drinks from the cup unworthily, not thinking about the body of Christ and what it means, he is eating and drinking God's judgment upon himself; for he is trifling with the death of Christ. [30] That is why many of you are weak and sick, and some have even died.

[31] But if you carefully examine yourselves before eating you will not need to be judged and punished. [32] Yet, when we are judged and punished by the Lord, it is so that we will not be condemned with the rest of the world. [33] So, dear brothers, when you gather for the Lord's Supper—the communion service—wait for each other; [34] if anyone is really hungry he should eat at home so that he won't bring punishment upon himself when you meet together.

I'll talk to you about the other matters after I arrive.

12 AND NOW, BROTHERS, I want to write about the special abilities the Holy Spirit gives to each of you, for I don't want any misunderstanding about them. [2] You will remember that before you became Christians you went around from one idol to another, not one of which could speak a

---

d Literally, "For this cause ought the woman to have power on (her) head."   e Literally, "because of the angels."   f Some ancient manuscripts read, "broken."

single word. ³ But now you are meeting people who claim to speak messages from the Spirit of God. How can you know whether they are really inspired by God or whether they are fakes? Here is the test: no one speaking by the power of the Spirit of God can curse Jesus, and no one can say, "Jesus is Lord," and really mean it, unless the Holy Spirit is helping him.

⁴ Now God gives us many kinds of special abilities, but it is the same Holy Spirit who is the source of them all. ⁵ There are different kinds of service to God, but it is the same Lord we are serving. ⁶ There are many ways in which God works in our lives, but it is the same God who does the work in and through all of us who are his. ⁷ The Holy Spirit displays God's power through each of us as a means of helping the entire church.

⁸ To one person the Spirit gives the ability to give wise advice; someone else may be especially good at studying and teaching, and this is his gift from the same Spirit. ⁹ He gives special faith to another, and to someone else the power to heal the sick. ¹⁰ He gives power for doing miracles to some, and to others power to prophesy and preach. He gives someone else the power to know whether evil spirits are speaking through those who claim to be giving God's messages—or whether it is really the Spirit of God who is speaking. Still another person is able to speak in languages he never learned; and others, who do not know the language either, are given power to understand what he is saying. ¹¹ It is the same and only Holy Spirit who gives all these gifts and powers, deciding which each one of us should have.

¹² Our bodies have many parts, but the many parts make up only one body when they are all put together. So it is with the "body" of Christ. ¹³ Each of us is a part of the one body of Christ. Some of us are Jews, some are Gentiles, some are slaves and some are free. But the Holy Spirit has fitted us all together into one body. We have been baptized into Christ's body by the one Spirit, and have all been given that same Holy Spirit.

¹⁴ Yes, the body has many parts, not just one part. ¹⁵ If the foot says, "I am not a part of the body because I am not a hand," that does not make it any less a part of the body. ¹⁶ And what would you think if you heard an ear say, "I am not part of the body because I am only an ear, and not an eye"? Would that make it any less a part of the body? ¹⁷ Suppose the whole body were an eye—then how would you hear? Or if your whole body were just one big ear, how could you smell anything?

¹⁸ But that isn't the way God has made us. He has made many parts for our bodies and has put each part just where he wants it. ¹⁹ What a strange thing a body would be if it had only one part! ²⁰ So he has made many parts, but still there is only one body.

²¹ The eye can never say to the hand, "I don't need you." The head can't say to the feet, "I don't need you."

²² And some of the parts that seem weakest and least important are really the most necessary. ²³ Yes, we are especially glad to have some parts that seem rather odd! And we carefully protect from the eyes of others those parts that should not be seen, ²⁴ while of course the parts that may be seen do not require this special care. So God has put the body together in such a way that extra honor and care are given to those parts that might otherwise seem less important. ²⁵ This makes for happiness among the parts, so that the parts have the same care for each other that they do for themselves. ²⁶ If one part suffers, all parts suffer with it, and if one part is honored, all the parts are glad.

²⁷ Now here is what I am trying to say: All of you together are the one body of Christ and each one of you is a separate and necessary part of it. ²⁸ Here is a list of some of the parts he has placed in his church, which is his body:

Apostles,
Prophets—those who preach God's Word,
Teachers,
Those who do miracles,
Those who have the gift of healing;
Those who can help others,
Those who can get others to work together,
Those who speak in languages they have never learned.

²⁹ Is everyone an apostle? Of course not. Is everyone a preacher? No. Are all teachers? Does everyone have the power to do miracles? ³⁰ Can everyone heal the sick? Of course not. Does God give all of us the ability to speak in languages we've never learned? Can just anyone understand and translate what those are saying who have that gift of foreign speech? ³¹ No, but try your best to have the more important of these gifts.

First, however, let me tell you about something else that is better than any of them!

13 IF I HAD the gift of being able to speak in other languages without learning them, and could speak in every language there is in all of heaven and earth, but didn't love others, I would only be making noise. ² If I had the gift of prophecy and knew all about what is going to happen in the future, knew everything about *everything,* but didn't love others, what good would it do? Even if I had the gift of faith so that I could speak to a mountain and make it move, I would still be worth nothing at all without love. ³ If I gave everything I have to poor people, and if I were burned alive for preaching the Gospel but didn't love others, it would be of no value whatever.

⁴ Love is very patient and kind, never jealous or envious, never boastful or proud, ⁵ never haughty or selfish or rude. Love does not demand its own way. It is not irritable or touchy. It does not hold grudges and will hardly even notice when others do it wrong. ⁶ It is never glad about injustice, but rejoices whenever truth wins out. ⁷ If you love someone you will be loyal to him no matter what the cost. You will always believe in him, always expect the best of him, and always stand your ground in defending him.

⁸ All the special gifts and powers from God will someday come to an end, but love goes on forever. Someday prophecy, and speaking in unknown languages, and special knowledge—these gifts will disappear. ⁹ Now we know so little, even with our special gifts, and the preaching of those most gifted is still so poor. ¹⁰ But when we have been made perfect and complete, then the need for these inadequate special gifts will

come to an end, and they will disappear. ¹¹ It's like this: when I was a child I spoke and thought and reasoned as a child does. But when I became a man my thoughts grew far beyond those of my childhood, and now I have put away the childish things. ¹² In the same way, we can see and understand only a little about God now, as if we were peering at his reflection in a poor mirror; but someday we are going to see him in his completeness, face to face. Now all that I know is hazy and blurred, but then I will see everything clearly, just as clearly as God sees into my heart right now.

¹³ There are three things that remain— faith, hope, and love—and the greatest of these is love.

14 LET LOVE BE your greatest aim; nevertheless, ask also for the special abilities the Holy Spirit gives, and especially the gift of prophecy, being able to preach the messages of God.

² But if your gift is that of being able to "speak in tongues," that is, to speak in languages you haven't learned, you will be talking to God but not to others, since they won't be able to understand you. You will be speaking by the power of the Spirit but it will all be a secret. ³ But one who prophesies, preaching the messages of God, is helping others grow in the Lord, encouraging and comforting them. ⁴ So a person "speaking in tongues" helps himself grow spiritually, but one who prophesies, preaching messages from God, helps the entire church grow in holiness and happiness.

⁵ I wish you all had the gift of "speaking in tongues" but, even more, I wish you were all able to prophesy, preaching God's messages, for that is a greater and more useful power than to speak in unknown languages —unless, of course, you can tell everyone afterwards what you were saying, so that they can get some good out of it too.

⁶ Dear friends, even if I myself should come to you talking in some language you don't understand, how would that help you? But if I speak plainly what God has revealed to me, and tell you the things I know, and what is going to happen, and the great truths of God's Word—that is what you need; that is what will help you. ⁷ Even

musical instruments—the flute, for instance, or the harp—are examples of the need for speaking in plain, simple English[a] rather than in unknown languages. For no one will recognize the tune the flute is playing unless each note is sounded clearly. [8] And if the army bugler doesn't play the right notes, how will the soldiers know that they are being called to battle? [9] In the same way, if you talk to a person in some language he doesn't understand, how will he know what you mean? You might as well be talking to an empty room.

[10] I suppose that there are hundreds of different languages in the world, and all are excellent for those who understand them, [11] but to me they mean nothing. A person talking to me in one of these languages will be a stranger to me and I will be a stranger to him. [12] Since you are so anxious to have special gifts from the Holy Spirit, ask him for the very best, for those that will be of real help to the whole church.

[13] If someone is given the gift of speaking in unknown tongues, he should pray also for the gift of knowing what he has said, so that he can tell people afterwards, plainly. [14] For if I pray in a language I don't understand, my spirit is praying but I don't know what I am saying. [15] Well, then, what shall I do? I will do both. I will pray in unknown tongues and also in ordinary language that everyone understands. I will sing in unknown tongues and also in ordinary language, so that I can understand the praise I am giving; [16] for if you praise and thank God with the spirit alone, speaking in another language, how can those who don't understand you be praising God along with you? How can they join you in giving thanks when they don't know what you are saying? [17] You will be giving thanks very nicely, no doubt, but the other people present won't be helped.

[18] I thank God that I "speak in tongues" privately[b] more than any of the rest of you. [19] But in public worship I would much rather speak five words that people can understand and be helped by, than ten thousand words while "speaking in tongues" in an unknown language.

[20] Dear brothers, don't be childish in your understanding of these things. Be innocent babies when it comes to planning evil, but be men of intelligence in understanding matters of this kind. [21] We are told in the ancient Scriptures that God would send men from other lands to speak in foreign languages to his people, but even then they would not listen. [22] So you see that being able to "speak in tongues" is not a sign to God's children concerning his power, but is a sign to the unsaved. However, prophecy (preaching the deep truths of God) is what the Christians need, and unbelievers aren't yet ready for it. [23] Even so, if an unsaved person, or someone who doesn't have these gifts, comes to church and hears you all talking in other languages, he is likely to think you are crazy. [24] But if you prophesy, preaching God's Word, [even though such preaching is mostly for believers[c]] and an unsaved person or a new Christian comes in who does not understand about these things, all these sermons will convince him of the fact that he is a sinner, and his conscience will be pricked by everything he hears. [25] As he listens, his secret thoughts will be laid bare and he will fall down on his knees and worship God, declaring that God is really there among you.

[26] Well, my brothers, let's add up what I am saying. When you meet together some will sing, another will teach, or tell some special information God has given him, or speak in an unknown language, or tell what someone else is saying who is speaking in the unknown language, but everything that is done must be useful to all, and build them up in the Lord. [27] No more than two or three should speak in an unknown language, and they must speak one at a time, and someone must be ready to interpret what they are saying. [28] But if no one is present who can interpret, they must not speak out loud. They must talk silently to themselves and to God in the unknown language but not publicly.

[29,30] Two or three may prophesy, one at a time, if they have the gift, while all the others listen. But if, while someone is prophesying, someone else receives a mes-

---

a The local language, whatever it is.　　b Implied. See verses 19 and 28.　　c Implied.

sage or idea from the Lord, the one who is speaking should stop. [31] In this way all who have the gift of prophecy can speak, one after the other, and everyone will learn and be encouraged and helped. [32] Remember that a person who has a message from God has the power to stop himself or wait his turn.[d] [33] God is not one who likes things to be disorderly and upset. He likes harmony, and he finds it in all the other churches.

[34] Women should be silent during the church meetings. They are not to take part in the discussion, for they are subordinate to men[e] as the Scriptures also declare. [35] If they have any questions to ask, let them ask their husbands at home, for it is improper for women to express their opinions in church meetings.

[36] You disagree? And do you think that the knowledge of God's will begins and ends with you Corinthians? Well, you are mistaken! [37] You who claim to have the gift of prophecy or any other special ability from the Holy Spirit should be the first to realize that what I am saying is a commandment from the Lord himself. [38] But if anyone still disagrees—well, we will leave him in his ignorance.[f]

[39] So, my fellow believers, long to be prophets so that you can preach God's message plainly; and never say it is wrong to "speak in tongues"; [40] however, be sure that everything is done properly in a good and orderly way.

15 NOW LET ME remind you, brothers, of what the Gospel really is, for it has not changed—it is the same Good News I preached to you before. You welcomed it then and still do now, for your faith is squarely built upon this wonderful message; [2] and it is this Good News that saves you if you still firmly believe it, unless of course you never really believed it in the first place.

[3] I passed on to you right from the first what had been told to me, that Christ died for our sins just as the Scriptures said he would, [4] and that he was buried, and that three days afterwards he arose from the grave just as the prophets foretold. [5] He was seen by Peter and later by the rest of "the Twelve."[a] [6] After that he was seen by more than five hundred Christian brothers at one time, most of whom are still alive, though some have died by now. [7] Then James saw him and later all the apostles. [8] Last of all I saw him too, long after the others, as though I had been born almost too late for this. [9] For I am the least worthy of all the apostles, and I shouldn't even be called an apostle at all after the way I treated the church of God.

[10] But whatever I am now it is all because God poured out such kindness and grace upon me—and not without results: for I have worked harder than all the other apostles, yet actually I wasn't doing it, but God working in me, to bless me. [11] It makes no difference who worked the hardest, I or they; the important thing is that we preached the Gospel to you, and you believed it.

[12] But tell me this! Since you believe what we preach, that *Christ* rose from the dead, why are some of you saying that dead people will never come back to life again? [13] For if there is no resurrection of the dead, then Christ must still be dead. [14] And if he is still dead, then all our preaching is useless and your trust in God is empty, worthless, hopeless; [15] and we apostles are all liars because we have said that God raised Christ from the grave, and of course that isn't true if the dead do not come back to life again. [16] If they don't, then Christ is still dead, [17] and you are very foolish to keep on trusting God to save you, and you are still under condemnation for your sins; [18] in that case all Christians who have died are lost! [19] And if being a Christian is of value to us only now in this life, we are the most miserable of creatures.

[20] But the fact is that Christ did actually rise from the dead, and has become the first of millions[b] who will come back to life again some day.

[21] Death came into the world because of

---

d Literally, "The spirits of the prophets are subject to the prophets."   e Literally, "They are not authorized to speak." They are permitted to pray and prophesy (1 Cor. 11:5), apparently in public meetings, but not to teach men (1 Tim. 2:12).   f Or, "If he disagrees, ignore his opinion."   15a The name given to Jesus' twelve disciples, and still used after Judas was gone from among them.   b Literally, "the first-fruits of them that are asleep."

what one man (Adam) did, and it is because of what this other man (Christ) has done that now there is the resurrection from the dead. ²² Everyone dies because all of us are related to Adam, being members of his sinful race, and wherever there is sin, death results. But all who are related to Christ will rise again. ²³ Each, however, in his own turn: Christ rose first; then when Christ comes back, all his people will become alive again.

²⁴ After that the end will come when he will turn the kingdom over to God the Father, having put down all enemies of every kind. ²⁵ For Christ will be King until he has defeated all his enemies, ²⁶ including the last enemy—death. This too must be defeated and ended. ²⁷ For the rule and authority over all things has been given to Christ by his Father; except, of course, Christ does not rule over the Father himself, who gave him this power to rule. ²⁸ When Christ has finally won the battle against all his enemies, then he, the Son of God, will put himself also under his Father's orders, so that God who has given him the victory over everything else will be utterly supreme.

²⁹ If the dead will not come back to life again, then what point is there in people being baptized for those who are gone? Why do it unless you believe that the dead will some day rise again?

³⁰ And why should we ourselves be continually risking our lives, facing death hour by hour? ³¹ For it is a fact that I face death daily; that is as true as my pride in your growth in the Lord. ³² And what value was there in fighting wild beasts—those men of Ephesus—if it was only for what I gain in this life down here? If we will never live again after we die, then we might as well go and have ourselves a good time: let us eat, drink, and be merry. What's the difference? For tomorrow we die, and that ends everything!

³³ Don't be fooled by those who say such things. If you listen to them you will start acting like them. ³⁴ Get some sense and quit your sinning. For to your shame I say it, some of you are not even Christians at all

and have never really known God.ᶜ

³⁵ But someone may ask, "How will the dead be brought back to life again? What kind of bodies will they have?" ³⁶ What a foolish question! You will find the answer in your own garden! When you put a seed into the ground it doesn't grow into a plant unless it "dies" first. ³⁷ And when the green shoot comes up out of the seed, it is very different from the seed you first planted. For all you put into the ground is a dry little seed of wheat, or whatever it is you are planting, ³⁸ then God gives it a beautiful new body—just the kind he wants it to have; a different kind of plant grows from each kind of seed. ³⁹ And just as there are different kinds of seeds and plants, so also there are different kinds of flesh. Humans, animals, fish, and birds are all different.

⁴⁰ The angelsᵈ in heaven have bodies far different from ours, and the beauty and the glory of their bodies is different from the beauty and the glory of ours. ⁴¹ The sun has one kind of glory while the moon and stars have another kind. And the stars differ from each other in their beauty and brightness.

⁴² In the same way, our earthly bodies which die and decay are different from the bodies we shall have when we come back to life again, for they will never die. ⁴³ The bodies we have now embarrass us for they become sick and die; but they will be full of glory when we come back to life again. Yes, they are weak, dying bodies now, but when we live again they will be full of strength. ⁴⁴ They are just human bodies at death, but when they come back to life they will be superhuman bodies. For just as there are natural, human bodies, there are also supernatural, spiritual bodies.

⁴⁵ The Scriptures tell us that the first man, Adam, was given a natural, human bodyᵉ but Christᶠ is moreᵍ than that, for he was life-giving Spirit.

⁴⁶ First, then, we have these human bodies and later on God gives us spiritual, heavenly bodies. ⁴⁷ Adam was made from the dust of the earth, but Christ came from heaven above. ⁴⁸ Every human being has a body just like Adam's, made of dust, but all

---

c Or, "there are some who know nothing of God." this may refer to the sun, moon, planets, and stars.
f Literally, "the last Adam."   g Implied.

d Literally, "There are celestial bodies." But perhaps
e Literally, "was made a living soul."

who become Christ's will have the same kind of body as his—a body from heaven. [49] Just as each of us now has a body like Adam's, so we shall some day have a body like Christ's.

[50] I tell you this, my brothers: an earthly body made of flesh and blood cannot get into God's kingdom. These perishable bodies of ours are not the right kind to live forever. [51] But I am telling you this strange and wonderful secret: we shall not all die, but we shall all be given new bodies! [52] It will all happen in a moment, in the twinkling of an eye, when the last trumpet is blown. For there will be a trumpet blast from the sky[h] and all the Christians who have died will suddenly become alive, with new bodies that will never, never die; and then we who are still alive shall suddenly have new bodies too. [53] For our earthly bodies, the ones we have now that can die, must be transformed into heavenly bodies that cannot perish but will live forever.

[54] When this happens, then at last this Scripture will come true—"Death is swallowed up in victory." [55,56] O death, where then your victory? Where then your sting? For sin—the sting that causes death—will all be gone; and the law, which reveals our sins, will no longer be our judge. [57] How we thank God for all of this! It is he who makes us victorious through Jesus Christ our Lord!

[58] So, my dear brothers, since future victory is sure, be strong and steady, always abounding in the Lord's work, for you know that nothing you do for the Lord is ever wasted as it would be if there were no resurrection.

16 NOW HERE ARE the directions about the money you are collecting to send to the Christians in Jerusalem;[a] (and, by the way, these are the same directions I gave to the churches in Galatia). [2] On every Lord's Day each of you should put aside something from what you have earned during the week, and use it for this offering. The amount depends on how much the Lord has helped you earn. Don't wait until I get there and then try to collect it all at once. [3] When

I come I will send your loving gift with a letter to Jerusalem, to be taken there by trustworthy messengers you yourselves will choose. [4] And if it seems wise for me to go along too, then we can travel together.

[5] I am coming to visit you after I have been to Macedonia first, but I will be staying there only for a little while. [6] It could be that I will stay longer with you, perhaps all winter, and then you can send me on to my next destination. [7] This time I don't want to make just a passing visit and then go right on; I want to come and stay awhile, if the Lord will let me. [8] I will be staying here at Ephesus until the holiday of Pentecost, [9] for there is a wide open door for me to preach and teach here. So much is happening, but there are many enemies.

[10] If Timothy comes make him feel at home, for he is doing the Lord's work just as I am. [11] Don't let anyone despise or ignore him [because he is young[b]], but send him back to me happy with his time among you; I am looking forward to seeing him soon, along with the others who are returning. [12] I begged Apollos to visit you along with the others, but he thought that it was not at all God's will for him to go now; he will be seeing you later on when he has the opportunity.

[13] Keep your eyes open for spiritual danger; stand true to the Lord; act like men; be strong; [14] and whatever you do, do it with kindness and love.

[15] Do you remember Stephanas and his family? They were the first to become Christians in Greece and they are spending their lives helping and serving Christians everywhere. [16] Please follow their instructions and do everything you can to help them as well as all others like them who work hard at your side with such real devotion. [17] I am so glad that Stephanas, Fortunatus, and Achaicus have arrived here for a visit. They have been making up for the help you aren't here to give me. [18] They have cheered me greatly and have been a wonderful encouragement to me, as I am sure they were to you, too. I hope you properly appreciate the work of such men as these.

[19] The churches here in Asia send you

---

h Implied.   16a Implied.   b Implied in 1 Timothy 4:12.

their loving greetings. Aquila and Priscilla send you their love and so do all the others who meet in their home for their church service. [20] All the friends here have asked me to say "hello" to you for them. And give each other a loving handshake when you meet. [21] I will write these final words of this letter with my own hand: [22] if anyone does not love the Lord, that person is cursed. Lord Jesus, come! [23] May the love and favor of the Lord Jesus Christ rest upon you. [24] My love to all of you, for we all belong to Christ Jesus.

Sincerely,
Paul

---

2 CORINTHIANS

1 DEAR FRIENDS,

This letter is from me, Paul, appointed by God to be Jesus Christ's messenger; and from our dear brother Timothy. We are writing to all of you Christians there in Corinth and throughout Greece.[a] [2] May God our Father and the Lord Jesus Christ mightily bless each one of you, and give you peace.

[3,4] What a wonderful God we have—he is the Father of our Lord Jesus Christ, the source of every mercy, and the one who so wonderfully comforts and strengthens us in our hardships and trials. And why does he do this? So that when others are troubled, needing our sympathy and encouragement, we can pass on to them this same help and comfort God has given us. [5] You can be sure that the more we undergo sufferings for Christ, the more he will shower us with his comfort and encouragement. [6,7] We are in deep trouble for bringing you God's comfort and salvation. But in our trouble God had comforted us—and this, too, to help you: to show you from our personal experience how God will tenderly comfort you when you undergo these same sufferings. He will give you the strength to endure.

[8] I think you ought to know, dear brothers, about the hard time we went through in Asia. We were really crushed and overwhelmed, and feared we would never live through it. [9] We felt we were doomed to die and saw how powerless we were to help ourselves; but that was good, for then we put everything into the hands of God, who alone could save us, for he can even raise the dead. [10] And he did help us, and saved us from a terrible death; yes, and we expect him to do it again and again. [11] But you must help us too, by praying for us. For much thanks and praise will go to God from you who see his wonderful answers to your prayers for our safety!

[12] We are so glad that we can say with utter honesty that in all our dealings we have been pure and sincere, quietly depending upon the Lord for his help, and not on our own skills. And that is even more true, if possible, about the way we have acted toward you. [13,14] My letters have been straightforward and sincere; nothing is written between the lines! And even though you don't know me very well (I hope someday you will), I want you to try to accept me and be proud of me, as you already are to some extent; just as I shall be of you on that day when our Lord Jesus comes back again. [15,16] It was because I was so sure of your understanding and trust that I planned to stop and see you on my way to Macedonia, as well as afterwards when I returned, so that I could be a double blessing to you and so that you could send me on my way to Judea.

[17] Then why, you may be asking, did I change my plan? Hadn't I really made up my mind yet? Or am I like a man of the world who says "yes" when he really means "no"? [18] Never! As surely as God is true, I am not that sort of person. My "yes" means "yes."

[19] Timothy and Silvanus and I have been telling you about Jesus Christ the Son of

---

a Or, "throughout Achaia."

God. He isn't one to say "yes" when he means "no." He always does exactly what he says. [20] He carries out and fulfills all of God's promises, no matter how many of them there are; and we have told everyone how faithful he is, giving glory to his name. [21] It is this God who has made you and me into faithful Christians and commissioned us apostles to preach the Good News. [22] He has put his brand upon us—his mark of ownership—and given us his Holy Spirit in our hearts as guarantee that we belong to him, and as the first installment of all that he is going to give us.

[23] I call upon this God to witness against me if I am not telling the absolute truth: the reason I haven't come to visit you yet is that I don't want to sadden you with a severe rebuke. [24] When I come, although I can't do much to help your faith, for it is strong already, I want to be able to do something about your joy: I want to make you happy, not sad.

2 "NO," I SAID to myself, "I won't do it. I'll not make them unhappy with another painful visit." [2] For if I make you sad, who is going to make me happy? You are the ones to do it, and how can you if I cause you pain? [3] That is why I wrote as I did in my last letter, so that you will get things straightened out before I come.[a] Then, when I do come, I will not be made sad by the very ones who ought to give me greatest joy. I felt sure that your happiness was so bound up in mine that you would not be happy either, unless I came with joy.

[4] Oh, how I hated to write that letter! It almost broke my heart and I tell you honestly that I cried over it. I didn't want to hurt you, but I had to show you how very much I loved you and cared about what was happening to you.

[5,6] Remember that the man I wrote about, who caused all the trouble, has not caused sorrow to me as much as to all the rest of you—though I certainly have my share in it too. I don't want to be harder on him than I should. He has been punished enough by your united disapproval. [7] Now it is time to forgive him and comfort him.

Otherwise he may become so bitter and discouraged that he won't be able to recover. [8] Please show him now that you still do love him very much.

[9] I wrote to you as I did so that I could find out how far you would go in obeying me. [10] When you forgive anyone, I do too. And whatever I have forgiven (to the extent that this affected me too) has been by Christ's authority, and for your good. [11] A further reason for forgiveness is to keep from being outsmarted by Satan; for we know what he is trying to do.

[12] Well, when I got as far as the city of Troas, the Lord gave me tremendous opportunities to preach the Gospel. [13] But Titus, my dear brother, wasn't there to meet me and I couldn't rest, wondering where he was and what had happened to him. So I said good-bye and went right on to Macedonia to try to find him.

[14] But thanks be to God! For through what Christ has done, he has triumphed over us so that now wherever we go he uses us to tell others about the Lord and to spread the Gospel like a sweet perfume. [15] As far as God is concerned there is a sweet, wholesome fragrance in our lives. It is the fragrance of Christ within us, an aroma to both the saved and the unsaved all around us. [16] To those who are not being saved, we seem a fearful smell of death and doom, while to those who know Christ we are a life-giving perfume. But who is adequate for such a task as this? [17] Only those who, like ourselves, are men of integrity, sent by God, speaking with Christ's power, with God's eye upon us. We are not like those hucksters—and there are many of them—whose idea in getting out the Gospel is to make a good living out of it.

3 ARE WE BEGINNING to be like those false teachers of yours who must tell you all about themselves and bring long letters of recommendation with them? I think you hardly need someone's letter to tell you about us, do you? And we don't need a recommendation from you, either! [2] The only letter I need is you yourselves! By looking at the good change in your hearts, every-

---

a Implied.

one can see that we have done a good work among you. [3] They can see that you are a letter from Christ, written by us. It is not a letter written with pen and ink, but by the Spirit of the living God; not one carved on stone, but in human hearts.

[4] We dare to say these good things about ourselves only because of our great trust in God through Christ, that he will help us to be true to what we say, [5] and not because we think we can do anything of lasting value by ourselves. Our only power and success comes from God. [6] He is the one who has helped us tell others about his new agreement to save them. We do not tell them that they must obey every law of God or die; but we tell them there is life for them from the Holy Spirit. The old way, trying to be saved by keeping the Ten Commandments, ends in death; in the new way, the Holy Spirit gives them life.

[7] Yet that old system of law that led to death began with such glory that people could not bear to look at Moses' face. For as he gave them God's law to obey, his face shone out with the very glory of God—though the brightness was already fading away. [8] Shall we not expect far greater glory in these days when the Holy Spirit is giving life? [9] If the plan that leads to doom was glorious, much more glorious is the plan that makes men right with God. [10] In fact, that first glory as it shone from Moses' face is worth nothing at all in comparison with the overwhelming glory of the new agreement. [11] So if the old system that faded into nothing was full of heavenly glory, the glory of God's new plan for our salvation[a] is certainly far greater, for it is eternal.

[12] Since we know that this new glory will never go away, we can preach with great boldness, [13] and not as Moses did, who put a veil over his face so that the Israelis could not see the glory fade away.

[14] Not only Moses' face was veiled, but his people's minds and understanding were veiled and blinded too. Even now when the Scripture is read it seems as though Jewish hearts and minds are covered by a thick veil, because they cannot see and understand the real meaning of the Scriptures.

For this veil of misunderstanding can be removed only by believing in Christ. [15] Yes, even today when they read Moses' writings their hearts are blind and they think that obeying the Ten Commandments is the way to be saved.

[16] But whenever anyone turns to the Lord from his sins, then the veil is taken away. [17] The Lord is the Spirit who gives them life, and where he is there is freedom [from trying to be saved by keeping the laws of God[a]]. [18] But we Christians have no veil over our faces; we can be mirrors that brightly reflect the glory of the Lord. And as the Spirit of the Lord works within us, we become more and more like him.

4 IT IS GOD himself, in his mercy, who has given us this wonderful work [of telling his Good News to others[a]], and so we never give up. [2] We do not try to trick people into believing—we are not interested in fooling anyone. We never try to get anyone to believe that the Bible teaches what it doesn't. All such shameful methods we forego. We stand in the presence of God as we speak and so we tell the truth, as all who know us will agree.

[3] If the Good News we preach is hidden to anyone, it is hidden from the one who is on the road to eternal death. [4] Satan, who is the god of this evil world, has made him blind, unable to see the glorious light of the Gospel that is shining upon him, or to understand the amazing message we preach about the glory of Christ, who is God.[b] [5] We don't go around preaching about ourselves, but about Christ Jesus as Lord. All we say of ourselves is that we are your slaves because of what Jesus has done for us. [6] For God, who said, "Let there be light in the darkness," has made us understand that it is the brightness of his glory that is seen in the face of Jesus Christ.

[7] But this precious treasure—this light and power that now shine within us[a]—is held in a perishable container, that is, in our weak bodies. Everyone can see that the glorious power within must be from God and is not our own.

[8] We are pressed on every side by trou-

---

a Implied.   4a Implied.   b Literally, "who is the image of God."

bles, but not crushed and broken. We are perplexed because we don't know why things happen as they do, but we don't give up and quit. ⁹ We are hunted down, but God never abandons us. We get knocked down, but we get up again and keep going. ¹⁰ These bodies of ours are constantly facing death just as Jesus did; so it is clear to all that it is only the living Christ within [who keeps us safeᶜ].

¹¹ Yes, we live under constant danger to our lives because we serve the Lord, but this gives us constant opportunities to show forth the power of Jesus Christ within our dying bodies. ¹² Because of our preaching we face death, but it has resulted in eternal life for you.

¹³ We boldly say what we believe [trusting God to care for usᶜ], just as the Psalm writer did when he said, "I believe and therefore I speak." ¹⁴ We know that the same God who brought the Lord Jesus back from death will also bring us back to life again with Jesus, and present us to him along with you. ¹⁵ These sufferings of ours are for your benefit. And the more of you who are won to Christ, the more there are to thank him for his great kindness, and the more the Lord is glorified.

¹⁶ That is why we never give up. Though our bodies are dying, our inner strength in the Lord is growing every day. ¹⁷ These troubles and sufferings of ours are, after all, quite small and won't last very long. Yet this short time of distress will result in God's richest blessing upon us forever and ever! ¹⁸ So we do not look at what we can see right now, the troubles all around us, but we look forward to the joys in heaven which we have not yet seen. The troubles will soon be over, but the joys to come will last forever.

5 FOR WE KNOW that when this tent we live in now is taken down—when we die and leave these bodies—we will have wonderful new bodies in heaven, homes that will be ours forevermore, made for us by God himself, and not by human hands. ² How weary we grow of our present bodies. That is why we look forward eagerly to the day

when we shall have heavenly bodies which we shall put on like new clothes. ³ For we shall not be merely spirits without bodies. ⁴ These earthly bodies make us groan and sigh, but we wouldn't like to think of dying and having no bodies at all. We want to slip into our new bodies so that these dying bodies will, as it were, be swallowed up by everlasting life. ⁵ This is what God has prepared for us and, as a guarantee, he has given us his Holy Spirit.

⁶ Now we look forward with confidence to our heavenly bodies, realizing that every moment we spend in these earthly bodies is time spent away from our eternal home in heaven with Jesus. ⁷ We know these things are true by believing, not by seeing. ⁸ And we are not afraid, but are quite content to die, for then we will be at home with the Lord. ⁹ So our aim is to please him always in everything we do, whether we are here in this body or away from this body and with him in heaven. ¹⁰ For we must all stand before Christ to be judged and have our lives laid bare—before him. Each of us will receive whatever he deserves for the good or bad things he has done in his earthly body.

¹¹ It is because of this solemn fear of the Lord, which is ever present in our minds, that we work so hard to win others. God knows our hearts, that they are pure in this matter, and I hope that, deep within, you really know it too.

¹² Are we trying to pat ourselves on the back again? No, I am giving you some good ammunition! You can use this on those preachers of yours who brag about how well they look and preach, but don't have true and honest hearts. You can boast about us that we, at least, are well intentioned and honest. ¹³,¹⁴ Are we insane [to say such things about ourselvesᵃ]? If so, it is to bring glory to God. And if we are in our right minds, it is for your benefit. Whatever we do, it is certainly not for our own profit, but because Christ's love controls us now. Since we believe that Christ died for all of us, we should also believe that we have died to the old life we used to live. ¹⁵ He died for all so that all who live—having received eternal

---

c Implied.   5a Implied.

life from him—might live no longer for themselves, to please themselves, but to spend their lives pleasing Christ who died and rose again for them. [16] So stop evaluating Christians by what the world thinks about them or by what they seem to be like on the outside. Once I mistakenly thought of Christ that way, merely as a human being like myself. How differently I feel now! [17] When someone becomes a Christian he becomes a brand new person inside. He is not the same any more. A new life has begun!

[18] All these new things are from God who brought us back to himself through what Christ Jesus did. And God has given us the privilege of urging everyone to come into his favor and be reconciled to him. [19] For God was in Christ, restoring the world to himself, no longer counting men's sins against them but blotting them out. This is the wonderful message he has given us to tell others. [20] We are Christ's ambassadors. God is using us to speak to you: we beg you, as though Christ himself were here pleading with you, receive the love he offers you—be reconciled to God. [21] For God took the sinless Christ and poured into him our sins. Then, in exchange, he poured God's goodness into us![b]

6 AS GOD'S PARTNERS we beg you not to toss aside this marvelous message of God's great kindness. [2] For God says, "Your cry came to me at a favorable time, when the doors of welcome were wide open. I helped you on a day when salvation was being offered." Right now God is ready to welcome you. Today he is ready to save you.

[3] We try to live in such a way that no one will ever be offended or kept back from finding the Lord by the way we act, so that no one can find fault with us and blame it on the Lord. [4] In fact, in everything we do we try to show that we are true ministers of God.

We patiently endure suffering and hardship and trouble of every kind. [5] We have been beaten, put in jail, faced angry mobs, worked to exhaustion, stayed awake through sleepless nights of watching, and gone without food. [6] We have proved ourselves to be what we claim by our wholesome lives and by our understanding of the Gospel and by our patience. We have been kind and truly loving and filled with the Holy Spirit. [7] We have been truthful, with God's power helping us in all we do. All of the godly man's arsenal—weapons of defense, and weapons of attack—have been ours.

[8] We stand true to the Lord whether others honor us or despise us, whether they criticize us or commend us. We are honest, but they call us liars.

[9] The world ignores us, but we are known to God; we live close to death, but here we are, still very much alive. We have been injured but kept from death. [10] Our hearts ache, but at the same time we have the joy of the Lord. We are poor, but we give rich spiritual gifts to others. We own nothing, and yet we enjoy everything.

[11] Oh, my dear Corinthian friends! I have told you all my feelings; I love you with all my heart. [12] Any coldness still between us is not because of any lack of love on my part, but because your love is too small and does not reach out to me and draw me in. [13] I am talking to you now as if you truly were my very own children. Open your hearts to us! Return our love!

[14] Don't be teamed with those who do not love the Lord, for what do the people of God have in common with the people of sin? How can light live with darkness? [15] And what harmony can there be between Christ and the devil? How can a Christian be a partner with one who doesn't believe? [16] And what union can there be between God's temple and idols? For you are God's temple, the home of the living God, and God has said of you, "I will live in them and walk among them, and I will be their God and they shall be my people." [17] That is why the Lord has said, "Leave them; separate yourselves from them; don't touch their filthy things, and I will welcome you, [18] and be a Father to you, and you will be my sons and daughters."

---

b Literally, "Him who knew no sin, he made sin on our behalf, that we might become the righteousness of God in him."

Pain can turn you to God

7 HAVING SUCH GREAT promises as these, dear friends, let us turn away from everything wrong, whether of body or spirit, and purify ourselves, living in the wholesome fear of God, giving ourselves to him alone. [2] Please open your hearts to us again, for not one of you has suffered any wrong from us. Not one of you was led astray. We have cheated no one nor taken advantage of anyone. [3] I'm not saying this to scold or blame you, for, as I have said before, you are in my heart forever and I live and die with you. [4] I have the highest confidence in you, and my pride in you is great. You have greatly encouraged me; you have made me so happy in spite of all my suffering.

[5] When we arrived in Macedonia there was no rest for us; outside, trouble was on every hand and all around us; within us, our hearts were full of dread and fear. [6] Then God who cheers those who are discouraged refreshed us by the arrival of Titus. [7] Not only was his presence a joy, but also the news that he brought of the wonderful time he had with you. When he told me how much you were looking forward to my visit, and how sorry you were about what had happened, and about your loyalty and warm love for me, well, I overflowed with joy!

[8] I am no longer sorry that I sent that letter to you, though I was very sorry for a time, realizing how painful it would be to you. But it hurt you only for a little while. [9] Now I am glad I sent it, not because it hurt you, but because the pain turned you to God. It was a good kind of sorrow you felt, the kind of sorrow God wants his people to have, so that I need not come to you with harshness. [10] For God sometimes uses sorrow in our lives to help us turn away from sin and seek eternal life. We should never regret his sending it. But the sorrow of the man who is not a Christian is not the sorrow of true repentance and does not prevent eternal death.

[11] Just see how much good this grief from the Lord did for you! You no longer shrugged your shoulders, but became earnest and sincere, and very anxious to get rid of the sin that I wrote you about. You became frightened about what had happened, and longed for me to come and help. You went right to work on the problem and cleared it up [punishing the man who sinned[a]]. You have done everything you could to make it right.

[12] I wrote as I did so the Lord could show how much you really do care for us. That was my purpose even more than to help the man[a] who sinned, or his father[a] to whom he did the wrong.

[13] In addition to the encouragement you gave us by your love, we were made happier still by Titus' joy when you gave him such a fine welcome and set his mind at ease. [14] I told him how it would be—told him before he left me of my pride in you—and you didn't disappoint me. I have always told you the truth and now my boasting to Titus has also proved true! [15] He loves you more than ever when he remembers the way you listened to him so willingly and received him so anxiously and with such deep concern. [16] How happy this makes me, now that I am sure all is well between us again. Once again I can have perfect confidence in you.

8 NOW I WANT to tell you what God in his grace has done for the churches in Macedonia. [2] Though they have been going through much trouble and hard times, they have mixed their wonderful joy with their deep poverty, and the result has been an overflow of giving to others. [3] They gave not only what they could afford, but far more; and I can testify that they did it because they wanted to, and not because of nagging on my part. [4] They begged us to take the money so they could share in the joy of helping the Christians in Jerusalem. [5] Best of all, they went beyond our highest hopes, for their first action was to dedicate themselves to the Lord and to us, for whatever directions God might give to them through us. [6] They were so enthusiastic about it that we have urged Titus, who encouraged your giving in the first place, to visit you and encourage you to complete your share in this ministry of giving. [7] You people there are leaders in so many ways—you have so much faith, so

a Implied.

many good preachers, so much learning, so much enthusiasm, so much love for us. Now I want you to be leaders also in the spirit of cheerful giving. ⁸ I am not giving you an order; I am not saying you must do it, but others are eager for it. This is one way to prove that your love is real, that it goes beyond mere words.

⁹ You know how full of love and kindness our Lord Jesus was: though he was so very rich, yet to help you he became so very poor, so that by being poor he could make you rich.

¹⁰ I want to suggest that you finish what you started to do a year ago, for you were not only the first to propose this idea, but the first to begin doing something about it. ¹¹ Having started the ball rolling so enthusiastically, you should carry this project through to completion just as gladly, giving whatever you can out of whatever you have. Let your enthusiastic idea at the start be equalled by your realistic action now. ¹² If you are really eager to give, then it isn't important how much you have to give. God wants you to give what you have, not what you haven't.

¹³ Of course, I don't mean that those who receive your gifts should have an easy time of it at your expense, ¹⁴ but you should divide with them. Right now you have plenty and can help them; then at some other time they can share with you when you need it. In this way each will have as much as he needs. ¹⁵ Do you remember what the Scriptures say about this? "He that gathered much had nothing left over, and he that gathered little had enough." So you also should share with those in need.

¹⁶ I am thankful to God that he has given Titus the same real concern for you that I have. ¹⁷ He is glad to follow my suggestion that he visit you again—but I think he would have come anyway, for he is very eager to see you! ¹⁸ I am sending another well-known brother with him, who is highly praised as a preacher of the Good News in all the churches. ¹⁹ In fact, this man was elected by the churches to travel with me to take the gift to Jerusalem. This will glorify the Lord and show our eagerness to help each other. ²⁰ By traveling together we will guard against any suspicion, for we are anxious that no one should find fault with the way we are handling this large gift. ²¹ God knows we are honest, but I want everyone else to know it too. That is why we have made this arrangement.

²² And I am sending you still another brother, whom we know from experience to be an earnest Christian. He is especially interested, as he looks forward to this trip, because I have told him all about your eagerness to help.

²³ If anyone asks who Titus is, say that he is my partner, my helper in helping you, and you can also say that the other two brothers represent the assemblies here and are splendid examples of those who belong to the Lord.

²⁴ Please show your love for me to these men and do for them all that I have publicly boasted you would.

9 I REALIZE THAT I really don't even need to mention this to you, about helping God's people. ² For I know how eager you are to do it, and I have boasted to the friends in Macedonia that you were ready to send an offering a year ago. In fact, it was this enthusiasm of yours that stirred up many of them to begin helping. ³ But I am sending these men just to be sure that you really are ready, as I told them you would be, with your money all collected; I don't want it to turn out that this time I was wrong in my boasting about you. ⁴ I would be very much ashamed—and so would you—if some of these Macedonian people come with me, only to find that you still aren't ready after all I have told them!

⁵ So I have asked these other brothers to arrive ahead of me to see that the gift you promised is on hand and waiting. I want it to be a real gift and not look as if it were being given under pressure. ⁶ But remember this—if you give little, you will get little. A farmer who plants just a few seeds will get only a small crop, but if he plants much, he will reap much. ⁷ Every one must make up his own mind as to how much he should give. Don't force anyone to give more than he really wants to, for cheerful givers are the ones God prizes. ⁸ God is able to make it up to you by giving you everything you need and more, so that there will not only be

enough for your own needs, but plenty left over to give joyfully to others. ⁹ It is as the Scriptures say: "The godly man gives generously to the poor. His good deeds will be an honor to him forever."

¹⁰ For God, who gives seed to the farmer to plant, and later on, good crops to harvest and eat, will give you more and more seed to plant and will make it grow so that you can give away more and more fruit from your harvest. ¹¹ Yes, God will give you much so that you can give away much, and when we take your gifts to those who need them they will break out into thanksgiving and praise to God for your help. ¹² So, two good things happen as a result of your gifts—those in need are helped, and they overflow with thanks to God. ¹³ Those you help will be glad not only because of your generous gifts to themselves and to others, but they will praise God for this proof that your deeds are as good as your doctrine. ¹⁴ And they will pray for you with deep fervor and feeling because of the wonderful grace of God shown through you.

¹⁵ Thank God for his Son—his Gift too wonderful for words.

10 I PLEAD WITH you—yes, I, Paul—and I plead gently, as Christ himself would do. Yet some of you are saying, "Paul's letters are bold enough when he is far away, but when he gets here he will be afraid to raise his voice!"

² I hope I won't need to show you when I come how harsh and rough I can be. I don't want to carry out my present plans against some of you who seem to think my deeds and words are merely those of an ordinary man. ³ It is true that I am an ordinary, weak human being, but I don't use human plans and methods to win my battles. ⁴ I use God's mighty weapons, not those made by men, to knock down the devil's strongholds. ⁵ These weapons can break down every proud argument against God and every wall that can be built to keep men from finding him. With these weapons I can capture rebels and bring them back to God, and change them into men whose hearts' desire is obedience to Christ. ⁶ I will use these weapons against every rebel who remains after I have first used them on you yourselves, and you surrender to Christ.

⁷ The trouble with you is that you look at me and I seem weak and powerless, but you don't look beneath the surface. Yet if anyone can claim the power and authority of Christ, I certainly can. ⁸ I may seem to be boasting more than I should about my authority over you—authority to help you, not to hurt you—but I shall make good every claim. ⁹ I say this so that you will not think I am just blustering when I scold you in my letters.

¹⁰ "Don't bother about his letters," some say. "He sounds big, but it's all noise. When he gets here you will see that there is nothing great about him, and you have never heard a worse preacher!" ¹¹ This time my personal presence is going to be just as rough on you as my letters are!

¹² Oh, don't worry, I wouldn't dare say that I am as wonderful as these other men who tell you how good they are! Their trouble is that they are only comparing themselves with each other, and measuring themselves against their own little ideas. What stupidity!

¹³ But we will not boast of authority we do not have. Our goal is to measure up to God's plan for us, and this plan includes our working there with you. ¹⁴ We are not going too far when we claim authority over you, for we were the first to come to you with the Good News concerning Christ. ¹⁵ It is not as though we were trying to claim credit for the work someone else has done among you. Instead, we hope that your faith will grow and that, still within the limits set for us, our work among you will be greatly enlarged.

¹⁶ After that, we will be able to preach the Good News to other cities that are far beyond you, where no one else is working; then there will be no question about being in someone else's field. ¹⁷ As the Scriptures say, "If anyone is going to boast, let him boast about what the Lord has done and not about himself." ¹⁸ When someone boasts about himself and how well he has done, it doesn't count for much. But when the Lord commends him, that's different!

11 I HOPE YOU will be patient with me as I keep on talking like a fool. Do bear with me and let me say what is on my heart. [2] I am anxious for you with the deep concern of God himself—anxious that your love should be for Christ alone, just as a pure maiden saves her love for one man only, for the one who will be her husband. [3] But I am frightened, fearing that in some way you will be led away from your pure and simple devotion to our Lord, just as Eve was deceived by Satan in the Garden of Eden. [4] You seem so gullible: you believe whatever anyone tells you even if he is preaching about another Jesus than the one we preach, or a different spirit than the Holy Spirit you received, or shows you a different way to be saved. You swallow it all.

[5] Yet I don't feel that these marvelous "messengers from God," as they call themselves, are any better than I am. [6] If I am a poor speaker, at least I know what I am talking about, as I think you realize by now, for we have proved it again and again.

[7] Did I do wrong and cheapen myself and make you look down on me because I preached God's Good News to you without charging you anything? [8,9] Instead I "robbed" other churches by taking what they sent me, and using it up while I was with you, so that I could serve you without cost. And when that was gone[a] and I was getting hungry I still didn't ask you for anything, for the Christians from Macedonia brought me another gift. I have never yet asked you for one cent, and I never will. [10] I promise this with every ounce of truth I possess—that I will tell everyone in Greece about it! [11] Why? Because I don't love you? God knows I do. [12] But I will do it to cut out the ground from under the feet of those who boast that they are doing God's work in just the same way we are.

[13] God never sent those men at all; they are "phonies" who have fooled you into thinking they are Christ's apostles. [14] Yet I am not surprised! Satan can change himself into an angel of light, [15] so it is no wonder his servants can do it too, and seem like godly ministers. In the end they will get every bit of punishment their wicked deeds deserve.

[16] Again I plead, don't think that I have lost my wits to talk like this; but even if you do, listen to me anyway—a witless man, a fool—while I also boast a little as they do. [17] Such bragging isn't something the Lord commanded me to do, for I am acting like a brainless fool. [18] Yet those other men keep telling you how wonderful they are, so here I go: [19,20] (You think you are so wise—yet you listen gladly to those fools; you don't mind at all when they make you their slaves and take everything you have, and take advantage of you, and put on airs, and slap you in the face. [21] I'm ashamed to say that I'm not strong and daring like that! But whatever they can boast about—I'm talking like a fool again—I can boast about it, too.)

[22] They brag that they are Hebrews, do they? Well, so am I. And they say that they are Israelites, God's chosen people? So am I. And they are descendants of Abraham? Well, I am too.

[23] They say they serve Christ? But I have served him far more! (Have I gone mad to boast like this?) I have worked harder, been put in jail oftener, been whipped times without number, and faced death again and again and again. [24] Five different times the Jews gave me their terrible thirty-nine lashes. [25] Three times I was beaten with rods. Once I was stoned. Three times I was shipwrecked. Once I was in the open sea all night and the whole next day. [26] I have traveled many weary miles and have been often in great danger from flooded rivers, and from robbers, and from my own people, the Jews, as well as from the hands of the Gentiles. I have faced grave dangers from mobs in the cities and from death in the deserts and in the stormy seas and from men who claim to be brothers in Christ but are not. [27] I have lived with weariness and pain and sleepless nights. Often I have been hungry and thirsty and have gone without food; often I have shivered with cold, without enough clothing to keep me warm.

[28] Then, besides all this, I have the constant worry of how the churches are getting along: [29] Who makes a mistake and I do not

---

a Implied.

feel his sadness? Who falls without my longing to help him? Who is spiritually hurt without my fury rising against the one who hurt him?

[30] But if I must brag, I would rather brag about the things that show how weak I am. [31] God, the Father of our Lord Jesus Christ, who is to be praised forever and ever, knows I tell the truth. [32] For instance, in Damascus the governor under King Aretas kept guards at the city gates to catch me; [33] but I was let down by rope and basket from a hole in the city wall, and so I got away! [What popularity![b]]

12 THIS BOASTING IS all so foolish, but let me go on. Let me tell about the visions I've had, and revelations from the Lord.

[2,3] Fourteen years ago I[a] was taken up to heaven[b] for a visit. Don't ask me whether my body was there or just my spirit, for I don't know; only God can answer that. But anyway, there I was in paradise, [4] and heard things so astounding that they are beyond a man's power to describe or put in words (and anyway I am not allowed to tell them to others). [5] That experience is something worth bragging about, but I am not going to do it. I am going to boast only about how weak I am and how great God is to use such weakness for his glory. [6] I have plenty to boast about and would be no fool in doing it, but I don't want anyone to think more highly of me than he should from what he can actually see in my life and my message.

[7] I will say this: because these experiences I had were so tremendous, God was afraid I might be puffed up by them; so I was given a physical condition which has been a thorn in my flesh, a messenger from Satan to hurt and bother me, and prick my pride. [8] Three different times I begged God to make me well again. [9] Each time he said, "No. But I am with you; that is all you need. My power shows up best in weak people." Now I am glad to boast about how weak I am; I am glad to be a living demonstration of Christ's power, instead of showing off my own power and abilities. [10] Since I know it is all for Christ's

good, I am quite happy about "the thorn," and about insults and hardships, persecutions and difficulties; for when I am weak, then I am strong—the less I have, the more I depend on him.

[11] You have made me act like a fool—boasting like this—for you people ought to be writing about me and not making me write about myself. There isn't a single thing these other marvelous fellows have that I don't have too, even though I am really worth nothing at all. [12]When I was there I certainly gave you every proof that I was truly an apostle, sent to you by God himself: for I patiently did many wonders and signs and mighty works among you. [13] The only thing I didn't do for you, that I do everywhere else in all other churches, was to become a burden to you—I didn't ask you to give me food to eat and a place to stay. Please forgive me for this wrong!

[14] Now I am coming to you again, the third time; and it is still not going to cost you anything, for I don't want your money. I want *you!* And anyway, you are my children, and little children don't pay for their father's and mother's food—it's the other way around; parents supply food for their children. [15] I am glad to give you myself and all I have for your spiritual good, even though it seems that the more I love you, the less you love me.

[16] Some of you are saying, "It's true that his visits didn't seem to cost us anything, but he is a sneaky fellow, that Paul, and he fooled us. As sure as anything he must have made money from us some way."

[17] But how? Did any of the men I sent to you take advantage of you? [18] When I urged Titus to visit you, and sent our other brother with him, did they make any profit? No, of course not. For we have the same Holy Spirit, and walk in each other's steps, doing things the same way.

[19] I suppose you think I am saying all this to get back into your good graces. That isn't it at all. I tell you, with God listening as I say it, that I have said this to help *you,* dear friends—to build you up spiritually and not to help myself. [20] For I am afraid that when I come to visit you I won't like

---

b Implied.   12a Literally, "A man in Christ."   b Literally, "the third heaven."

what I find, and then you won't like the way I will have to act. I am afraid that I will find you quarreling, and envying each other, and being angry with each other, and acting big, and saying wicked things about each other and whispering behind each other's backs, filled with conceit and disunity. ²¹ Yes, I am afraid that when I come God will humble me before you and I will be sad and mourn because many of you who have sinned became sinners and don't even care about the wicked, impure things you have done: your lust and immorality, and the taking of other men's wives.

13 THIS IS THE third time I am coming to visit you. The Scriptures tell us that if two or three have seen a wrong, it must be punished. [Well, this is my third warning, as I come now for this visit.ᵃ] ² I have already warned those who had been sinning when I was there last; now I warn them again, and all others, just as I did then, that this time I come ready to punish severely and I will not spare them.

³ I will give you all the proof you want that Christ speaks through me. Christ is not weak in his dealings with you, but is a mighty power within you. ⁴ His weak, human body died on the cross, but now he lives by the mighty power of God. We, too, are weak in our bodies, as he was, but now we live and are strong, as he is, and have all of God's power to use in dealing with you.

⁵ Check up on yourselves. Are you really Christians? Do you pass the test? Do you feel Christ's presence and power more and more within you? Or are you just pretending to be Christians when actually you aren't at all? ⁶ I hope you can agree that I have stood that test and truly belong to the Lord.

⁷ I pray that you will live good lives, not because that will be a feather in our capsᵇ, proving that what we teach is right; no, for we want you to do right even if we ourselves are despised. ⁸ Our responsibility is to encourage the right at all times, not to hope for evil.ᶜ ⁹ We are glad to be weak and despised if you are really strong. Our greatest wish and prayer is that you will become mature Christians.

¹⁰ I am writing this to you now in the hope that I won't need to scold and punish when I come; for I want to use the Lord's authority which he has given me, not to punish you but to make you strong.

¹¹ I close my letter with these last words:
Be happy.
Grow in Christ.
Pay attention to what I have said.
Live in harmony and peace.
And may the God of love and peace be with you.

¹² Greet each other warmly in the Lord. ¹³ All the Christians here send you their best regards. ¹⁴ May the grace of our Lord Jesus Christ be with you all. May God's love and the Holy Spirit's friendship be yours.

Paul

---

a Implied.   b Literally, "not that we may appear approved."   c Literally, "For we can do nothing against the truth, but for the truth."

Free at Last

The feeling pulses through you. You kick high in the air and twirl around in the open fields. It's a rare thing—leaving struggles behind and feeling the total freedom and joy of life. More often, we have soiled consciences that fear the future, fear God, fear others.

In Galatians Paul cracks the shell on a wholly new kind of Freedom. To his uptight Jewish audience, the message was earth-shaking. Centuries later, it still sparkles. Read on....

GALATIANS

1 FROM: PAUL THE missionary and all the other Christians here.

To: The churches of Galatia.[a]

I was not called to be a missionary by any group or agency. My call is from Jesus Christ himself, and from God the Father who raised him from the dead. [3] May peace and blessing be yours from God the Father and from the Lord Jesus Christ. [4] He died for our sins just as God our Father planned, and rescued us from this evil world in which we live. [5] All glory to God through all the ages of eternity. Amen.

[6] I am amazed that you are turning away so soon from God who, in his love and mercy, invited you to share the eternal life

---

a Galatia was a province in what is now called Turkey.

he gives through Christ; you are already following a different "way to heaven," which really doesn't go to heaven at all. [7] For there is no other way than the one we showed you; you are being fooled by those who twist and change the truth concerning Christ.

[8] Let God's curses fall on anyone, including myself, who preaches any other way to be saved than the one we told you about; yes, if an angel comes from heaven and preaches any other message, let him be forever cursed. [9] I will say it again: if anyone preaches any other Gospel than the one you welcomed, let God's curse fall upon him.

[10] You can see that I am not trying to please you by sweet talk and flattery; no, I am trying to please God. If I were still trying to please men I could not be Christ's servant.

[11] Dear friends, I solemnly swear that the way to heaven which I preach is not based on some mere human whim or dream. [12] For my message comes from no less a person than Jesus Christ himself, who told me what to say. No one else has taught me.

[13] You know what I was like when I followed the Jewish religion—how I went after the Christians mercilessly, hunting them down and doing my best to get rid of them all. [14] I was one of the most religious Jews of my own age in the whole country, and tried as hard as I possibly could to follow all the old, traditional rules of my religion.

[15] But then something happened! For even before I was born God had chosen me to be his, and called me—what kindness and grace— [16] to reveal his Son within me so that I could go to the Gentiles and show them the Good News about Jesus.

When all this happened to me I didn't go at once and talk it over with anyone else; [17] I didn't go up to Jerusalem to consult with those who were apostles before I was. No, I went away into the deserts of Arabia, and then came back to the city of Damascus. [18] It was not until three years later that I finally went to Jerusalem for a visit with Peter, and stayed there with him for fifteen days. [19] And the only other apostle I met at that time was James, our Lord's brother. [20] (Listen to what I am saying, for I am telling you this in the very presence of God.

This is exactly what happened—I am not lying to you.) [21] Then after this visit I went to Syria and Cilicia. [22] And still the Christians in Judea didn't even know what I looked like. [23] All they knew was what people were saying, that "our former enemy is now preaching the very faith he tried to wreck." [24] And they gave glory to God because of me.

2 THEN FOURTEEN YEARS later I went back to Jerusalem again, this time with Barnabas; and Titus came along too. [2] I went there with definite orders from God to confer with the brothers there about the message I was preaching to the Gentiles. I talked privately to the leaders of the church so that they would all understand just what I had been teaching and, I hoped, agree that it was right. [3] And they did agree; they did not even demand that Titus, my companion, should be circumcised, though he was a Gentile.

[4] Even that question wouldn't have come up except for some so-called "Christians" there—false ones, really—who came to spy on us and see what freedom we enjoyed in Christ Jesus, as to whether we obeyed the Jewish laws or not. They tried to get us all tied up in their rules, like slaves in chains. [5] But we did not listen to them for a single moment, for we did not want to confuse you into thinking that salvation can be earned by being circumcised and by obeying Jewish laws.

[6] And the great leaders of the church who were there had nothing to add to what I was preaching. (By the way, their being great leaders made no difference to me, for all are the same to God.) [7,8,9] In fact, when Peter, James, and John, who were known as the pillars of the church, saw how greatly God had used me in winning the Gentiles, just as Peter had been blessed so greatly in his preaching to the Jews—for the same God gave us each our special gifts—they shook hands with Barnabas and me and encouraged us to keep right on with our preaching to the Gentiles while they continued their work with the Jews. [10] The only thing they did suggest was that we must always remember to help the poor, and I, too, was eager for that.

[11] But when Peter came to Antioch I had to oppose him publicly, speaking strongly against what he was doing for it was very wrong. [12] For when he first arrived he ate with the Gentile Christians [who don't bother with circumcision and the many other Jewish laws[a]]. But afterwards when some Jewish friends of James came, he wouldn't eat with the Gentiles anymore because he was afraid of what these Jewish legalists, who insisted that circumcision was necessary for salvation, would say; [13] and then all the other Jewish Christians and even Barnabas became hypocrites too, following Peter's example, though they certainly knew better. [14] When I saw what was happening and that they weren't being honest about what they really believed, and weren't following the truth of the Gospel, I said to Peter in front of all the others, "Though you are a Jew by birth, you have long since discarded the Jewish laws; so why, all of a sudden, are you trying to make these Gentiles obey them? [15] You and I are Jews by birth, not mere Gentile sinners, [16] and yet we Jewish Christians know very well that we cannot become right with God by obeying our Jewish laws, but only by faith in Jesus Christ to take away our sins. And so we, too, have trusted Jesus Christ, that we might be accepted by God because of faith—and not because we have obeyed the Jewish laws. For no one will ever be saved by obeying them."

[17] But what if we trust Christ to save us and then find that we are wrong, and that we cannot be saved without being circumcised and obeying all the other Jewish laws? Wouldn't we need to say that faith in Christ had ruined us? God forbid that anyone should dare to think such things about our Lord. [18] Rather, we are sinners if we start rebuilding the old systems I have been destroying, of trying to be saved by keeping Jewish laws, [19] for it was through reading the Scripture that I came to realize that I could never find God's favor by trying —and failing—to obey the laws. I came to realize that acceptance with God comes by believing in Christ.[b]

[20] I have been crucified with Christ: and I myself no longer live, but Christ lives in me. And the real life I now have within this body is a result of my trusting in the Son of God, who loved me and gave himself for me. [21] I am not one of those who treats Christ's death as meaningless. For if we could be saved by keeping Jewish laws, then there was no need for Christ to die.

3 OH, FOOLISH GALATIANS! What magician has hypnotized you and cast an evil spell upon you? For you used to see the meaning of Jesus Christ's death as clearly as though I had waved a placard before you with a picture on it of Christ dying on the cross. [2] Let me ask you this one question: Did you receive the Holy Spirit by trying to keep the Jewish laws? Of course not, for the Holy Spirit came upon you only after you heard about Christ and trusted him to save you. [3] Then have you gone completely crazy? For if trying to obey the Jewish laws never gave you spiritual life in the first place, why do you think that trying to obey them now will make you stronger Christians? [4] You have suffered so much for the Gospel. Now are you going to just throw it all overboard? I can hardly believe it!

[5] I ask you again, does God give you the power of the Holy Spirit and work miracles among you as a result of your trying to obey the Jewish laws? No, of course not. It is when you believe in Christ and fully trust him.

[6] Abraham had the same experience— God declared him fit for heaven only because he believed God's promises. [7] You can see from this that the real children of Abraham are all the men of faith who truly trust in God.

[8,9] What's more, the Scriptures looked forward to this time when God would save the Gentiles also, through their faith. God told Abraham about this long ago when he said, "I will bless those in every nation who trust in me as you do." And so it is: all who trust in Christ share the same blessing Abraham received.

[10] Yes, and those who depend on the Jewish laws to save them are under God's curse, for the Scriptures point out very

---

a Implied.   b Literally, "For I through the law died unto the law, that I might live unto God."

clearly, "Cursed is everyone who at any time breaks a single one of these laws that are written in God's Book of the Law." [11] Consequently, it is clear that no one can ever win God's favor by trying to keep the Jewish laws, because God has said that the only way we can be right in his sight is by faith. As the prophet Habakkuk says it, "The man who finds life will find it through trusting God." [12] How different from this way of faith is the way of law which says that a man is saved by obeying every law of God, without one slip. [13] But Christ has bought us out from under the doom of that impossible system by taking the curse for our wrongdoing upon himself. For it is written in the Scripture, "Anyone who is hanged on a tree is cursed" [as Jesus was hung upon a wooden cross[a]].

[14] Now God can bless the Gentiles, too, with this same blessing he promised to Abraham; and all of us as Christians can have the promised Holy Spirit through this faith. [15] Dear brothers, even in everyday life a promise made by one man to another, if it is written down and signed, cannot be changed. He cannot decide afterward to do something else instead.

[16] Now, God gave some promises to Abraham and his Child. And notice that it doesn't say the promises were to his *children,* as it would if all his sons—all the Jews—were being spoken of, but to his *Child*—and that, of course, means Christ. [17] Here's what I am trying to say: God's promise to save through faith—and God wrote this promise down and signed it— could not be canceled or changed four hundred and thirty years later when God gave the Ten Commandments. [18] If *obeying those laws* could save us, then it is obvious that this would be a different way of gaining God's favor than Abraham's way, for he simply accepted God's promise.

[19] Well then, why were the laws given? They were added after the promise was given, to show men how guilty they are of breaking God's laws. But this system of law was to last only until the coming of Christ, the Child to whom God's promise was made. (And there is this further difference.

God gave his laws to angels to give to Moses, who then gave them to the people; [20] but when God gave his promise to Abraham, he did it by himself alone, without angels or Moses as go-betweens.)

[21,22] Well then, are God's laws and God's promises against each other? Of course not! If we could be saved by his laws, then God would not have had to give us a different way to get out of the grip of sin—for the Scriptures insist we are all its prisoners. The only way out is through faith in Jesus Christ; the way of escape is open to all who believe him.

[23] Until Christ came we were guarded by the law, kept in protective custody, so to speak, until we could believe in the coming Savior.

[24] Let me put it another way. The Jewish laws were our teacher and guide until Christ came to give us right standing with God through our faith. [25] But now that Christ has come, we don't need those laws any longer to guard us and lead us to him. [26] For now we are all children of God through faith in Jesus Christ, [27] and we who have been baptized into union with Christ are enveloped by him. [28] We are no longer Jews or Greeks or slaves or free men or even merely men or women, but we are all the same—we are Christians; we are one in Christ Jesus. [29] And now that we are Christ's we are the true descendants of Abraham, and all of God's promises to him belong to us.

4 BUT REMEMBER THIS, that if a father dies and leaves great wealth for his little son, that child is not much better off than a slave until he grows up, even though he actually owns everything his father had. [2] He has to do what his guardians and managers tell him to, until he reaches whatever age his father set.

[3] And that is the way it was with us before Christ came. We were slaves to Jewish laws and rituals for we thought they could save us. [4] But when the right time came, the time God decided on, he sent his Son, born of a woman, born as a Jew, [5] to buy freedom for us who were slaves to the

---

a Implied.

law so that he could adopt us as his very own sons. ⁶ And because we are his sons God has sent the Spirit of his Son into our hearts, so now we can rightly speak of God as our dear Father. ⁷ Now we are no longer slaves, but God's own sons. And since we are his sons, everything he has belongs to us, for that is the way God planned.

⁸ Before you Gentiles knew God you were slaves to so-called gods that did not even exist. ⁹ And now that you have found God (or I should say, now that God has found you) how can it be that you want to go back again and become slaves once more to another poor, weak, useless religion of trying to get to heaven by obeying God's laws? ¹⁰ You are trying to find favor with God by what you do or don't do on certain days or months or seasons or years. ¹¹ I fear for you. I am afraid that all my hard work for you was worth nothing.

¹² Dear brothers, please feel as I do about these things, for I am as free from these chains as you used to be. You did not despise me then when I first preached to you, ¹³ even though I was sick when I first brought you the Good News of Christ. ¹⁴ But even though my sickness was revolting to you, you didn't reject me and turn me away. No, you took me in and cared for me as though I were an angel from God, or even Jesus Christ himself.

¹⁵ Where is that happy spirit that we felt together then? For in those days I know you would gladly have taken out your own eyes and given them to replace mine[a] if that would have helped me.

¹⁶ And now have I become your enemy because I tell you the truth?

¹⁷ Those false teachers who are so anxious to win your favor are not doing it for your good. What they are trying to do is to shut you off from me so that you will pay more attention to them. ¹⁸ It is a fine thing when people are nice to you with good motives and sincere hearts, especially if they aren't doing it just when I am with you! ¹⁹ Oh, my children, how you are hurting me! I am once again suffering for you the pains of a mother waiting for her child to be born —longing for the time when you will finally

be filled with Christ. ²⁰ How I wish I could be there with you right now and not have to reason with you like this, for at this distance I frankly don't know what to do.

²¹ Listen to me, you friends who think you have to obey the Jewish laws to be saved: Why don't you find out what those laws really mean? ²² For it is written that Abraham had two sons, one from his slave-wife and one from his freeborn wife. ²³ There was nothing unusual about the birth of the slave-wife's baby. But the baby of the freeborn wife was born only after God had especially promised he would come.

²⁴,²⁵ Now this true story is an illustration of God's two ways of helping people. One way was by giving them his laws to obey. He did this on Mount Sinai, when he gave the Ten Commandments to Moses. Mount Sinai, by the way, is called "Mount Hagar" by the Arabs—and in my illustration Abraham's slave-wife Hagar represents Jerusalem, the mother-city of the Jews, the center of that system of trying to please God by trying to obey the Commandments; and the Jews, who try to follow that system, are her slave children. ²⁶ But our mother-city is the heavenly Jerusalem, and she is not a slave to Jewish laws.

²⁷ That is what Isaiah meant when he prophesied, "Now you can rejoice, O childless woman; you can shout with joy though you never before had a child. For I am going to give you many children—more children than the slave-wife has."

²⁸ You and I, dear brothers, are the children that God promised, just as Isaac was. ²⁹ And so we who are born of the Holy Spirit are persecuted now by those who want us to keep the Jewish laws, just as Isaac the child of promise was persecuted by Ishmael the slave-wife's son.

³⁰ But the Scriptures say that God told Abraham to send away the slave-wife and her son, for the slave-wife's son could not inherit Abraham's home and lands along with the free woman's son. ³¹ Dear brothers, we are not slave children, obligated to the Jewish laws, but children of the free woman, acceptable to God because of our faith.

---

a It is traditional to suppose that Paul was handicapped by a disease of the eyes.

5 SO CHRIST HAS made us free. Now make sure that you stay free and don't get all tied up again in the chains of slavery to Jewish laws and ceremonies. ² Listen to me, for this is serious: *if you are counting on circumcision and keeping the Jewish laws to make you right with God, then Christ cannot save you.* ³ I'll say it again. Anyone trying to find favor with God by being circumcised must always obey every other Jewish law or perish. ⁴ Christ is useless to you if you are counting on clearing your debt to God by keeping those laws; you are lost from God's grace.

⁵ But we by the help of the Holy Spirit are counting on Christ's death to clear away our sins and make us right with God. ⁶ And we to whom Christ has given eternal life don't need to worry about whether we have been circumcised or not, or whether we are obeying the Jewish ceremonies or not; for all we need is faith working through love.

⁷ You were getting along so well. Who has interfered with you to hold you back from following the truth? ⁸ It certainly isn't God who has done it, for he is the one who has called you to freedom in Christ. ⁹ But it takes only one wrong person among you to infect all the others.

¹⁰ I am trusting the Lord to bring you back to believing as I do about these things. God will deal with that person, whoever he is, who has been troubling and confusing you.

¹¹ Some people even say that I myself am preaching that circumcision and Jewish laws are necessary to the plan of salvation. Well, if I preached that, I would be persecuted no more—for that message doesn't offend anyone. The fact that I am still being persecuted proves that I am still preaching salvation through faith in the cross of Christ alone.

¹² I only wish these teachers who want you to cut yourselves by being circumcised would cut themselves off from you and leave you alone!ᵃ

¹³ For, dear brothers, you have been given freedom: not freedom to do wrong, but freedom to love and serve each other. ¹⁴ For the whole Law can be summed up in this one command: "Love others as you love yourself." ¹⁵ But if instead of showing love among yourselves you are always critical and catty, watch out! Beware of ruining each other.

¹⁶ I advise you to obey only the Holy Spirit's instructions. He will tell you where to go and what to do, and then you won't always be doing the wrong things your evil nature wants you to. ¹⁷ For we naturally love to do evil things that are just the opposite from the things that the Holy Spirit tells us to do; and the good things we want to do when the Spirit has his way with us are just the opposite of our natural desires. These two forces within us are constantly fighting each other to win control over us, and our wishes are never free from their pressures. ¹⁸ When you are guided by the Holy Spirit you need no longer force yourself to obey Jewish laws.

¹⁹ But when you follow your own wrong inclinations your lives will produce these evil results: impure thoughts, eagerness for lustful pleasure, ²⁰ idolatry, spiritism (that is, encouraging the activity of demons), hatred and fighting, jealousy and anger, constant effort to get the best for yourself, complaints and criticisms, the feeling that everyone else is wrong except those in your own little group—and there will be wrong doctrine, ²¹ envy, murder, drunkenness, wild parties, and all that sort of thing. Let me tell you again as I have before, that anyone living that sort of life will not inherit the kingdom of God.

²² But when the Holy Spirit controls our lives he will produce this kind of fruit in us: love, joy, peace, patience, kindness, goodness, faithfulness, ²³ gentleness and self-control; and here there is no conflict with Jewish laws.

²⁴ Those who belong to Christ have nailed their natural evil desires to his cross and crucified them there.

²⁵ If we are living now by the Holy Spirit's power, let us follow the Holy Spirit's leading in every part of our lives. ²⁶ Then we won't need to look for honors and popularity, which lead to jealousy and hard feelings.

---

a Or, "Would that those disturbing you would go and castrate themselves."

6 DEAR BROTHERS, IF a Christian is overcome by some sin, you who are godly should gently and humbly help him back onto the right path, remembering that next time it might be one of you who is in the wrong. ² Share each other's troubles and problems, and so obey our Lord's command. ³ If anyone thinks he is too great to stoop to this, he is fooling himself. He is really a nobody.

⁴ Let everyone be sure that he is doing his very best, for then he will have the personal satisfaction of work well done, and won't need to compare himself with someone else. ⁵ Each of us must bear some faults and burdens of his own. For none of us is perfect!

⁶ Those who are taught the Word of God should help their teachers by paying them.

⁷ Don't be misled; remember that you can't ignore God and get away with it: a man will always reap just the kind of crop he sows! ⁸ If he sows to please his own wrong desires, he will be planting seeds of evil and he will surely reap a harvest of spiritual decay and death; but if he plants the good things of the Spirit, he will reap the everlasting life which the Holy Spirit gives him. ⁹ And let us not get tired of doing what is right, for after a while we will reap a harvest of blessing if we don't get discouraged and give up. ¹⁰ That's why whenever we can we should always be kind to everyone, and especially to our Christian brothers.

¹¹ I will write these closing words in my own handwriting. See how large I have to make the letters! ¹² Those teachers of yours who are trying to convince you to be circumcised are doing it for just one reason: so that they can be popular and avoid the persecution they would get if they admitted that the cross of Christ alone can save. ¹³ And even those teachers who submit to circumcision don't try to keep the other Jewish laws; but they want you to be circumcised in order that they can boast that you are their disciples.

¹⁴ As for me, God forbid that I should boast about anything except the cross of our Lord Jesus Christ. Because of that cross my interest in all the attractive things of the world was killed long ago, and the world's interest in me is also long dead. ¹⁵ It doesn't make any difference now whether we have been circumcised or not; what counts is whether we really have been changed into new and different people.

¹⁶ May God's mercy and peace be upon all of you who live by this principle and upon those everywhere who are really God's own. ¹⁷ From now on please don't argue with me about these things, for I carry on my body the scars of the whippings and wounds from Jesus' enemies that mark me as his slave.

¹⁸ Dear brothers, may the grace of our Lord Jesus Christ be with you all.

Sincerely,
Paul

In the Dumps

The blues. When they hit they wipe out every tingle of joy and excitement. Nothing matters except the depressed, pitying way you feel about yourself. You need a compliment, an uplifter, but you look so miserable no one will even approach you, much less compliment you. Where can you turn?

If you ever feel this way—so low that down is up—take a deep breath and read the next six chapters. Paul cuts loose with an explosion of words about how great you are. Through Jesus, God took away all our sins and cruddiness, Paul says, and showered down upon us his richness. God understands us and knows what is best for us at all times (1:8).

Are things looking up? Read on. God is shaping us so well that we are gifts to him that he delights in! (1:11). Encore upon encore, Paul piles on a stream of applause. He rightly gives the praise for what has happened to God, but *we* are the ones who benefit. Ephesians shows what we look like from God's viewpoint. If we're his children, we look dazzling to him. Even when we're feeling low.

Philip Yancey

EPHESIANS

1 DEAR CHRISTIAN FRIENDS at Ephesus, ever loyal to the Lord: This is Paul writing to you, chosen by God to be Jesus Christ's messenger. [2] May his blessings and peace be yours, sent to you from God our Father and Jesus Christ our Lord. [3] How we praise God, the Father of our Lord Jesus Christ, who has blessed us with every blessing in heaven because we belong to Christ.

[4] Long ago, even before he made the world, God chose us to be his very own, through what Christ would do for us; he decided then to make us holy in his eyes, without a single fault—we who stand before him covered with his love. [5] His unchanging plan has always been to adopt us into his own family by sending Jesus Christ to die for us. And he did this because he wanted to!

[6] Now all praise to God for his wonderful kindness to us and his favor that he has poured out upon us, because we belong to his dearly loved Son. [7] So overflowing is his kindness towards us that he took away all

our sins through the blood of his Son, by whom we are saved; [8] and he has showered down upon us the richness of his grace—for how well he understands us and knows what is best for us at all times.

[9] God has told us his secret reason for sending Christ, a plan he decided on in mercy long ago; [10] and this was his purpose: that when the time is ripe he will gather us all together from wherever we are—in heaven or on earth—to be with him in Christ, forever. [11] Moreover, because of what Christ has done we have become gifts to God that he delights in, for as part of God's sovereign plan we were chosen from the beginning to be his, and all things happen just as he decided long ago. [12] God's purpose in this was that we should praise God and give glory to him for doing these mighty things for us, who were the first to trust in Christ.

[13] And because of what Christ did, all you others too, who heard the Good News about how to be saved, and trusted Christ, were marked as belonging to Christ by the Holy Spirit, who long ago had been promised to all of us Christians. [14] His presence within us is God's guarantee that he really will give us all that he promised; and the Spirit's seal upon us means that God has already purchased us and that he guarantees to bring us to himself. This is just one more reason for us to praise our glorious God.

[15] That is why, ever since I heard of your strong faith in the Lord Jesus and of the love you have for Christians everywhere, [16,17] I have never stopped thanking God for you. I pray for you constantly, asking God, the glorious Father of our Lord Jesus Christ, to give you wisdom to see clearly and really understand who Christ is and all that he has done for you. [18] I pray that your hearts will be flooded with light so that you can see something of the future he has called you to share. I want you to realize that God has been made rich because we who are Christ's have been given to him! [19] I pray that you will begin to understand how incredibly great his power is to help those who believe him. It is that same mighty power [20] that raised Christ from the dead and seated him in the place of honor at God's right hand in heaven, [21] far, far above any other king or ruler or dictator or leader. Yes, his honor is far more glorious than that of anyone else either in this world or in the world to come. [22] And God has put all things under his feet and made him the supreme Head of the church— [23] which is his body, filled with himself, the Author and Giver of everything everywhere.

2 ONCE YOU WERE under God's curse, doomed forever for your sins. [2] You went along with the crowd and were just like all the others, full of sin, obeying Satan, the mighty prince of the power of the air, who is at work right now in the hearts of those who are against the Lord. [3] All of us used to be just as they are, our lives expressing the evil within us, doing every wicked thing that our passions or our evil thoughts might lead us into. We started out bad, being born with evil natures, and were under God's anger just like everyone else.

[4] But God is so rich in mercy; he loved us so much [5] that even though we were spiritually dead and doomed by our sins, he gave us back our lives again[a] when he raised Christ from the dead—only by his undeserved favor have we ever been saved— [6] and lifted us up from the grave into glory along with Christ, where we sit with him in the heavenly realms—all because of what Christ Jesus did. [7] And now God can always point to us as examples of how very, very rich his kindness is, as shown in all he has done for us through Jesus Christ.

[8] Because of his kindness you have been saved through trusting Christ. And even trusting[b] is not of yourselves; it too is a gift from God. [9] Salvation is not a reward for the good we have done, so none of us can take any credit for it. [10] It is God himself who has made us what we are and given us new lives from Christ Jesus; and long ages ago he planned that we should spend these lives in helping others.

[11] Never forget that once you were heathen, and that you were called godless and "unclean" by the Jews. (But their hearts,

---

a Literally, "he made us alive."   b Or, "Salvation is not of yourselves."

too, were still unclean, even though they were going through the ceremonies and rituals of the godly, for they circumcised themselves as a sign of godliness.) [12] Remember that in those days you were living utterly apart from Christ; you were enemies of God's children and he had promised you no help. You were lost, without God, without hope.

[13] But now you belong to Christ Jesus, and though you once were far away from God, now you have been brought very near to him because of what Jesus Christ has done for you with his blood.

[14] For Christ himself is our way of peace. He has made peace between us Jews and you Gentiles by making us all one family,[c] breaking down the wall of contempt[d] that used to separate us. [15] By his death he ended the angry resentment between us, caused by the Jewish laws which favored the Jews and excluded the Gentiles, for he died to annul that whole system of Jewish laws. Then he took the two groups that had been opposed to each other and made them parts of himself; thus he fused us together to become one new person, and at last there was peace. [16] As parts of the same body, our anger against each other has disappeared, for both of us have been reconciled to God. And so the feud ended at last at the cross. [17] And he has brought this Good News of peace to you Gentiles who were very far away from him, and to us Jews who were near. [18] Now all of us, whether Jews or Gentiles, may come to God the Father with the Holy Spirit's help because of what Christ has done for us.

[19] Now you are no longer strangers to God and foreigners to heaven, but you are members of God's very own family, citizens of God's country, and you belong in God's household with every other Christian. [20] What a foundation you stand on now: the apostles and the prophets; and the cornerstone of the building is Jesus Christ himself! [21] We who believe are carefully joined together with Christ as parts of a beautiful, constantly growing temple for God. [22] And you also are joined with him and with each other by the Spirit, and are part of this

dwelling place of God.

3 I PAUL, THE servant of Christ, am here in jail because of you—for preaching that you Gentiles are a part of God's house. [2,3] No doubt you already know that God has given me this special work of showing God's favor to you Gentiles, as I briefly mentioned before in one of my letters. God himself showed me this secret plan of his, that the Gentiles, too, are included in his kindness. [4] I say this to explain to you how I know about these things. [5] In olden times God did not share this plan with his people, but now he has revealed it by the Holy Spirit to his apostles and prophets.

[6] And this is the secret: that the Gentiles will have their full share with the Jews in all the riches inherited by God's sons; both are invited to belong to his church, and all of God's promises of mighty blessings through Christ apply to them both when they accept the Good News about Christ and what he has done for them. [7] God has given me the wonderful privilege of telling everyone about this plan of his; and he has given me his power and special ability to do it well.

[8] Just think! Though I did nothing to deserve it, and though I am the most useless Christian there is, yet I was the one chosen for this special joy of telling the Gentiles the Glad News of the endless treasures available to them in Christ; [9] and to explain to everyone that God is the Savior of the Gentiles too, just as he who made all things had secretly planned from the very beginning.

[10] And his reason? To show to all the rulers in heaven how perfectly wise he is when all of his family—Jews and Gentiles alike—are seen to be joined together in his church, [11] in just the way he had always planned it through Jesus Christ our Lord. [12] Now we can come fearlessly right into God's presence, assured of his glad welcome when we come with Christ and trust in him.

[13] So please don't lose heart at what they are doing to me here. It is for you I am suffering and you should feel honored and encouraged. [14,15] When I think of the wisdom and scope of his plan I fall down on

c Literally, "by making us one."   d Implied.

my knees and pray to the Father of all the great family of God—some of them already in heaven and some down here on earth— [16] that out of his glorious, unlimited resources he will give you the mighty inner strengthening of his Holy Spirit. [17] And I pray that Christ will be more and more at home in your hearts, living within you as you trust in him. May your roots go down deep into the soil of God's marvelous love; [18,19] and may you be able to feel and understand, as all God's children should, how long, how wide, how deep, and how high his love really is; and to experience this love for yourselves, though it is so great that you will never see the end of it or fully know or understand it. And so at last you will be filled up with God himself.

[20] Now glory be to God who by his mighty power at work within us is able to do far more than we would ever dare to ask or even dream of—infinitely beyond our highest prayers, desires, thoughts, or hopes. [21] May he be given glory forever and ever through endless ages because of his master plan of salvation for the church through Jesus Christ.

4 I BEG YOU—I, a prisoner here in jail for serving the Lord—to live and act in a way worthy of those who have been chosen for such wonderful blessings as these. [2] Be humble and gentle. Be patient with each other, making allowance for each other's faults because of your love. [3] Try always to be led along together by the Holy Spirit, and so be at peace with one another.

[4] We are all parts of one body, we have the same Spirit, and we have all been called to the same glorious future. [5] For us there is only one Lord, one faith, one baptism, [6] and we all have the same God and Father who is over us all and in us all, and living through every part of us. [7] However, Christ has given each of us special abilities— whatever he wants us to have out of his rich storehouse of gifts.

[8] The Psalmist tells about this, for he says that when Christ returned triumphantly to heaven after his resurrection and victory over Satan, he gave generous gifts to men. [9] Notice that it says he returned to heaven. This means that he had first come down from the heights of heaven, far down to the lowest parts of the earth. [10] The same one who came down is the one who went back up, that he might fill all things everywhere with himself, from the very lowest to the very highest.[a]

[11] Some of us have been given special ability as apostles; to others he has given the gift of being able to preach well; some have special ability in winning people to Christ, helping them to trust him as their Savior; still others have a gift for caring for God's people as a shepherd does his sheep, leading and teaching them in the ways of God.

[12] Why is it that he gives us these special abilities to do certain things best? It is that God's people will be equipped to do better work for him, building up the church, the body of Christ, to a position of strength and maturity; [13] until finally we all believe alike about our salvation and about our Savior, God's Son, and all become full-grown in the Lord—yes, to the point of being filled full with Christ.

[14] Then we will no longer be like children, forever changing our minds about what we believe because someone has told us something different, or has cleverly lied to us and made the lie sound like the truth. [15,16] Instead, we will lovingly follow the truth at all times—speaking truly, dealing truly, living truly[b]—and so become more and more in every way like Christ who is the Head of his body, the church. Under his direction the whole body is fitted together perfectly, and each part in its own special way helps the other parts, so that the whole body is healthy and growing and full of love.

[17,18] Let me say this, then, speaking for the Lord: Live no longer as the unsaved do, for they are blinded and confused. Their closed hearts are full of darkness; they are far away from the life of God because they have shut their minds against him, and they cannot understand his ways. [19] They don't care anymore about right and wrong and have given themselves over to impure ways. They stop at nothing, being driven by their

a Literally, "that he might fill all things." b Amplified New Testament.

evil minds and reckless lusts.

²⁰ But that isn't the way Christ taught you! ²¹ If you have really heard his voice and learned from him the truths concerning himself, ²² then throw off your old evil nature—the old you that was a partner in your evil ways—rotten through and through, full of lust and sham.

²³ Now your attitudes and thoughts must all be constantly changing for the better. ²⁴ Yes, you must be a new and different person, holy and good. Clothe yourself with this new nature.

²⁵ Stop lying to each other; tell the truth, for we are parts of each other and when we lie to each other we are hurting ourselves. ²⁶ If you are angry, don't sin by nursing your grudge. Don't let the sun go down with you still angry—get over it quickly; ²⁷ for when you are angry you give a mighty foothold to the devil.

²⁸ If anyone is stealing he must stop it and begin using those hands of his for honest work so he can give to others in need. ²⁹ Don't use bad language. Say only what is good and helpful to those you are talking to, and what will give them a blessing.

³⁰ Don't cause the Holy Spirit sorrow by the way you live. Remember, he is the one who marks you to be present[c] on that day when salvation from sin will be complete.

³¹ Stop being mean, bad-tempered and angry. Quarreling, harsh words, and dislike of others should have no place in your lives. ³² Instead, be kind to each other, tenderhearted, forgiving one another, just as God has forgiven you because you belong to Christ.

5 FOLLOW GOD'S EXAMPLE in everything you do just as a much loved child imitates his father. ² Be full of love for others, following the example of Christ who loved you and gave himself to God as a sacrifice to take away your sins. And God was pleased, for Christ's love for you was like sweet perfume to him.

³ Let there be no sex sin, impurity or greed among you. Let no one be able to accuse you of any such things. ⁴ Dirty stories, foul talk and coarse jokes—these are not for you. Instead, remind each other of God's goodness and be thankful.

⁵ You can be sure of this: The kingdom of Christ and of God will never belong to anyone who is impure or greedy, for a greedy person is really an idol worshiper—he loves and worships the good things of this life more than God. ⁶ Don't be fooled by those who try to excuse these sins, for the terrible wrath of God is upon all those who do them. ⁷ Don't even associate with such people. ⁸ For though once your heart was full of darkness, now it is full of light from the Lord, and your behavior should show it! ⁹ Because of this light within you, you should do only what is good and right and true.

¹⁰ Learn as you go along what pleases the Lord.[a] ¹¹ Take no part in the worthless pleasures of evil and darkness, but instead, rebuke and expose them. ¹² It would be shameful even to mention here those pleasures of darkness which the ungodly do. ¹³ But when you expose them, the light shines in upon their sin and shows it up, and when they see how wrong they really are, some of them may even become children of light! ¹⁴ That is why God says in the Scriptures, "Awake, O sleeper, and rise up from the dead; and Christ shall give you light."

¹⁵,¹⁶ So be careful how you act; these are difficult days. Don't be fools; be wise: make the most of every opportunity you have for doing good. ¹⁷ Don't act thoughtlessly, but try to find out and do whatever the Lord wants you to. ¹⁸ Don't drink too much wine, for many evils lie along that path; be filled instead with the Holy Spirit, and controlled by him.

¹⁹ Talk with each other much about the Lord, quoting psalms and hymns and singing sacred songs, making music in your hearts to the Lord. ²⁰ Always give thanks for everything to our God and Father in the name of our Lord Jesus Christ.

²¹ Honor Christ by submitting to each other. ²² You wives must submit to your husbands' leadership in the same way you submit to the Lord. ²³ For a husband is in

---

c Literally, "in whom you were sealed unto the day of redemption."

5a Or, "your lives should be an example."

charge of his wife in the same way Christ is in charge of his body the church. (He gave his very life to take care of it and be its Savior!) ²⁴ So you wives must willingly obey your husbands in everything, just as the church obeys Christ.

²⁵ And you husbands, show the same kind of love to your wives as Christ showed to the church when he died for her, ²⁶ to make her holy and clean, washed by baptism^b and God's Word; ²⁷ so that he could give her to himself as a glorious church without a single spot or wrinkle or any other blemish, being holy and without a single fault. ²⁸ That is how husbands should treat their wives, loving them as parts of themselves. For since a man and his wife are now one, a man is really doing himself a favor and loving himself when he loves his wife! ²⁹,³⁰ No one hates his own body but lovingly cares for it, just as Christ cares for his body the church, of which we are parts.

³¹ (That the husband and wife are one body is proved by the Scripture which says, "A man must leave his father and mother when he marries, so that he can be perfectly joined to his wife, and the two shall be one.") ³² I know this is hard to understand, but it is an illustration of the way we are parts of the body of Christ.

³³ So again I say, a man must love his wife as a part of himself; and the wife must see to it that she deeply respects her husband—obeying, praising and honoring him.

6 CHILDREN, OBEY YOUR parents; this is the right thing to do because God has placed them in authority over you. ² Honor your father and mother. This is the first of God's Ten Commandments that ends with a promise. ³ And this is the promise: that if you honor your father and mother, yours will be a long life, full of blessing.

⁴ And now a word to you parents. Don't keep on scolding and nagging your children, making them angry and resentful. Rather, bring them up with the loving discipline the Lord himself approves, with suggestions and godly advice.

⁵ Slaves, obey your masters; be eager to give them your very best. Serve them as you would Christ. ⁶,⁷ Don't work hard only when your master is watching and then shirk when he isn't looking; work hard and with gladness all the time, as though working for Christ, doing the will of God with all your hearts. ⁸ Remember, the Lord will pay you for each good thing you do, whether you are slave or free.

⁹ And you slave owners must treat your slaves right, just as I have told them to treat you. Don't keep threatening them; remember, you yourselves are slaves to Christ; you have the same Master they do, and he has no favorites.

¹⁰ Last of all I want to remind you that your strength must come from the Lord's mighty power within you. ¹¹ Put on all of God's armor so that you will be able to stand safe against all strategies and tricks of Satan. ¹² For we are not fighting against people made of flesh and blood, but against persons without bodies—the evil rulers of the unseen world, those mighty satanic beings and great evil princes of darkness who rule this world; and against huge numbers of wicked spirits in the spirit world.

¹³ So use every piece of God's armor to resist the enemy whenever he attacks, and when it is all over, you will still be standing up.

¹⁴ But to do this, you will need the strong belt of truth and the breastplate of God's approval. ¹⁵ Wear shoes that are able to speed you on as you preach the Good News of peace with God. ¹⁶ In every battle you will need faith as your shield to stop the fiery arrows aimed at you by Satan. ¹⁷ And you will need the helmet of salvation and the sword of the Spirit—which is the Word of God.

¹⁸ Pray all the time. Ask God for anything in line with the Holy Spirit's wishes. Plead with him, reminding him of your needs, and keep praying earnestly for all Christians everywhere. ¹⁹ Pray for me, too, and ask God to give me the right words as I boldly tell others about the Lord, and as I explain to them that his salvation is for the Gentiles too. ²⁰ I am in chains now for preaching this message from God. But pray that I will keep on speaking out boldly for

b Literally, "having cleansed it by washing of water with the word."

him even here in prison, as I should.

²¹ Tychicus, who is a much loved brother and faithful helper in the Lord's work, will tell you all about how I am getting along. ²² I am sending him to you for just this purpose, to let you know how we are and be encouraged by his report.

²³ May God give peace to you, my Christian brothers, and love, with faith from God the Father and the Lord Jesus Christ. ²⁴ May God's grace and blessing be upon all who sincerely love our Lord Jesus Christ.

Sincerely,
Paul

―――――――――――

Grit and Strain!

I'm gonna win!" That thought is uppermost in the mind of each of these teens competing for top honors in the Sun Valley meet. After months and months of gruelling training, they give it all they've got to win that top prize. Yet even the exhilaration of winning it — even the flush of emotion, the *Wow!* that comes from getting the top trophy — can't be compared with what is talked about in the following letter. "*Nothing* can be compared to it," the writer says. And, as we enjoy the excitement of sports competition or anything else in which we can excel, we know deep down that these thrills of victory God allows us to enjoy are only small fragments of the deeper victories this letter communicates.

PHILIPPIANS

1 FROM: PAUL AND Timothy, slaves of Jesus Christ.

To: The pastors and deacons and all the Christians in the city of Philippi.

[2] May God bless you all. Yes, I pray that God our Father and the Lord Jesus Christ will give each of you his fullest blessings, and his peace in your hearts and your lives. [3] All my prayers for you are full of praise to God! [4] When I pray for you, my heart is full of joy, [5] because of all your wonderful help in making known the Good News about Christ from the time you first heard it until now. [6] And I am sure that God who began the good work within you will keep right on helping you grow in his grace until his task within you is finally finished on that day when Jesus Christ returns.

[7] How natural it is that I should feel as I do about you, for you have a very special place in my heart. We have shared together the blessings of God, both when I was in prison and when I was out, defending the truth and telling others about Christ. [8] Only God knows how deep is my love and longing for you—with the tenderness of Jesus Christ. [9] My prayer for you is that you will overflow more and more with love for others, and at the same time keep on growing in spiritual knowledge and insight, [10] for I want you always to see clearly the difference between right and wrong, and to be inwardly clean, no one being able to criticize you from now until our Lord returns. [11] May you always be doing those good, kind things which show that you are a child of God, for this will bring much praise and glory to the Lord.

[12] And I want you to know this, dear brothers: Everything that has happened to me here has been a great boost in getting out the Good News concerning Christ. [13] For everyone around here, including all the soldiers over at the barracks, knows that I am in chains simply because I am a Christian. [14] And because of my imprisonment many of the Christians here seem to have lost their fear of chains! Somehow my patience has encouraged them and they have become more and more bold in telling others about Christ.

[15] Some, of course, are preaching the Good News because they are jealous of the way God has used me. They want reputations as fearless preachers! But others have purer motives, [16,17] preaching because they love me, for they know that the Lord has brought me here to use me to defend the Truth. And some preach to make me jealous, thinking that their success will add to my sorrows here in jail! [18] But whatever their motive for doing it, the fact remains that the Good News about Christ is being preached and I am glad.

[19] I am going to keep on being glad, for I know that as you pray for me, and as the Holy Spirit helps me, this is all going to turn out for my good. [20] For I live in eager expectation and hope that I will never do anything that will cause me to be ashamed of myself but that I will always be ready to speak out boldly for Christ while I am going through all these trials here, just as I have in the past; and that I will always be an honor to Christ, whether I live or whether I must die. [21] For to me, living means opportunities for Christ, and dying—well, that's better yet! [22] But if living will give me more opportunities to win people to Christ, then I really don't know which is better, to live

or die! [23] Sometimes I want to live and at other times I don't, for I long to go and be with Christ. How much happier for *me* than being here! [24] But the fact is that I can be of more help to *you* by staying!

[25] Yes, I am still needed down here and so I feel certain I will be staying on earth a little longer, to help you grow and become happy in your faith; [26] my staying will make you glad and give you reason to glorify Christ Jesus for keeping me safe, when I return to visit you again.

[27] But whatever happens to me, remember always to live as Christians should, so that, whether I ever see you again or not, I will keep on hearing good reports that you are standing side by side with one strong purpose—to tell the Good News [28] fearlessly, no matter what your enemies may do. They will see this as a sign of their downfall, but for you it will be a clear sign from God that he is with you, and that he has given you eternal life with him. [29] For to you has been given the privilege not only of trusting him but also of suffering for him. [30] We are in this fight together. You have seen me suffer for him in the past; and I am still in the midst of a great and terrible struggle now, as you know so well.

2 IS THERE ANY such thing as Christians cheering each other up? Do you love me enough to want to help me? Does it mean anything to you that we are brothers in the Lord, sharing the same Spirit? Are your hearts tender and sympathetic at all? [2] Then make me truly happy by loving each other and agreeing wholeheartedly with each other, working together with one heart and mind and purpose.

[3] Don't be selfish; don't live to make a good impression on others. Be humble, thinking of others as better than yourself. [4] Don't just think about your own affairs, but be interested in others, too, and in what they are doing.

[5] Your attitude should be the kind that was shown us by Jesus Christ, [6] who, though he was God, did not demand and cling to his rights as God, [7] but laid aside

his mighty power and glory, taking the disguise of a slave and becoming like men.[a] [8] And he humbled himself even further, going so far as actually to die a criminal's death on a cross.[b]

[9] Yet it was because of this that God raised him up to the heights of heaven and gave him a name which is above every other name, [10] that at the name of Jesus every knee shall bow in heaven and on earth and under the earth, [11] and every tongue shall confess that Jesus Christ is Lord, to the glory of God the Father.

[12] Dearest friends, when I was there with you, you were always so careful to follow my instructions. And now that I am away you must be even more careful to do the good things that result from being saved, obeying God with deep reverence, shrinking back from all that might displease him. [13] For God is at work within you, helping you want to obey him, and then helping you do what he wants.

[14] In everything you do, stay away from complaining and arguing, [15] so that no one can speak a word of blame against you. You are to live clean, innocent lives as children of God in a dark world full of people who are crooked and stubborn. Shine out among them like beacon lights, [16] holding out to them the Word of Life.

Then when Christ returns how glad I will be that my work among you was so worthwhile. [17] And if my lifeblood is, so to speak, to be poured out over your faith which I am offering up to God as a sacrifice—that is, if I am to die for you—even then I will be glad, and will share my joy with each of you. [18] For you should be happy about this, too, and rejoice with me for having this privilege of dying for you.

[19] If the Lord is willing, I will send Timothy to see you soon. Then when he comes back he can cheer me up by telling me all about you and how you are getting along. [20] There is no one like Timothy for having a real interest in you; [21] everyone else seems to be worrying about his own plans and not those of Jesus Christ. [22] But you know Timothy. He has been just like a son

a Literally, "was made in the likeness of men." of the cross."
b Literally, "became obedient unto death, even the death of the cross."

to me in helping me preach the Good News. [23] I hope to send him to you just as soon as I find out what is going to happen to me here. [24] And I am trusting the Lord that soon I myself may come to see you.

[25] Meanwhile, I thought I ought to send Epaphroditus back to you. You sent him to help me in my need; well, he and I have been real brothers, working and battling side by side. [26] Now I am sending him home again, for he has been homesick for all of you and upset because you heard that he was ill. [27] And he surely was; in fact, he almost died. But God had mercy on him, and on me too, not allowing me to have this sorrow on top of everything else.

[28] So I am all the more anxious to get him back to you again, for I know how thankful you will be to see him, and that will make me happy and lighten all my cares. [29] Welcome him in the Lord with great joy, and show your appreciation, [30] for he risked his life for the work of Christ and was at the point of death while trying to do for me the things you couldn't do because you were far away.

3 WHATEVER HAPPENS, DEAR friends, be glad in the Lord. I never get tired of telling you this and it is good for you to hear it again and again.

[2] Watch out for those wicked men—dangerous dogs, I call them—who say you must be circumcised to be saved. [3] For it isn't the *cutting of our bodies* that makes us children of God; it is *worshiping him with our spirits.* That is the only true "circumcision." We Christians glory in what Christ Jesus has done for us and realize that we are helpless to save ourselves.

[4] Yet if anyone ever had reason to hope that he could save himself, it would be I. If others could be saved by what they are, certainly I could! [5] For I went through the Jewish initiation ceremony when I was eight days old, having been born into a pureblooded Jewish home that was a branch of the old original Benjamin family. So I was a real Jew if there ever was one! What's more, I was a member of the Pharisees who demand the strictest obedience to every Jewish law and custom. [6] And sincere? Yes, so much so that I greatly persecuted the church; and I tried to obey every Jewish rule and regulation right down to the very last point.

[7] But all these things that I once thought very worthwhile—now I've thrown them all away so that I can put my trust and hope in Christ alone. [8] Yes, everything else is worthless when compared with the priceless gain of knowing Christ Jesus my Lord. I have put aside all else, counting it worth less than nothing, in order that I can have Christ, [9] and become one with him, no longer counting on being saved by being good enough or by obeying God's laws, but by trusting Christ to save me; for God's way of making us right with himself depends on faith—counting on Christ alone. [10] Now I have given up everything else—I have found it to be the only way to really know Christ and to experience the mighty power that brought him back to life again, and to find out what it means to suffer and to die with him. [11] So, whatever it takes, I will be one who lives in the fresh newness of life of those who are alive from the dead.

[12] I don't mean to say I am perfect. I haven't learned all I should even yet, but I keep working toward that day when I will finally be all that Christ saved me for and wants me to be.

[13] No, dear brothers, I am still not all I should be but I am bringing all my energies to bear on this one thing: Forgetting the past and looking forward to what lies ahead, [14] I strain to reach the end of the race and receive the prize for which God is calling us up to heaven because of what Christ Jesus did for us.

[15] I hope all of you who are mature Christians will see eye-to-eye with me on these things, and if you disagree on some point, I believe that God will make it plain to you— [16] if you fully obey the truth you have.

[17] Dear brothers, pattern your lives after mine and notice who else lives up to my example. [18] For I have told you often before, and I say it again now with tears in my eyes, there are many who walk along the Christian road who are really enemies of the cross of Christ. [19] Their future is eternal loss, for their god is their appetite: they are proud of what they should be ashamed of; and all

they think about is this life here on earth. 20 But our homeland is in heaven, where our Savior the Lord Jesus Christ is; and we are looking forward to his return from there. 21 When he comes back he will take these dying bodies of ours and change them into glorious bodies like his own, using the same mighty power that he will use to conquer all else everywhere.

4 DEAR BROTHER CHRISTIANS, I love you and long to see you, for you are my joy and my reward for my work. My beloved friends, stay true to the Lord.

2 And now I want to plead with those two dear women, Euodias and Syntyche. Please, please, with the Lord's help, quarrel no more—be friends again. 3 And I ask you, my true teammate, to help these women, for they worked side by side with me in telling the Good News to others; and they worked with Clement, too, and the rest of my fellow workers whose names are written in the Book of Life.

4 Always be full of joy in the Lord; I say it again, rejoice! 5 Let everyone see that you are unselfish and considerate in all you do. Remember that the Lord is coming soon. 6 Don't worry about anything; instead, pray about everything; tell God your needs and don't forget to thank him for his answers. 7 If you do this you will experience God's peace, which is far more wonderful than the human mind can understand. His peace will keep your thoughts and your hearts quiet and at rest as you trust in Christ Jesus.

8 And now, brothers, as I close this letter let me say this one more thing: Fix your thoughts on what is true and good and right. Think about things that are pure and lovely, and dwell on the fine, good things in others. Think about all you can praise God for and be glad about. 9 Keep putting into practice all you learned from me and saw me doing, and the God of peace will be with you.

10 How grateful I am and how I praise the Lord that you are helping me again. I know you have always been anxious to send what you could, but for a while you didn't have the chance. 11 Not that I was ever in need, for I have learned how to get along happily whether I have much or little. 12 I know how to live on almost nothing or with everything. I have learned the secret of contentment in every situation, whether it be a full stomach or hunger, plenty or want; 13 for I can do everything God asks me to with the help of Christ who gives me the strength and power. 14 But even so, you have done right in helping me in my present difficulty.

15 As you well know, when I first brought the Gospel to you and then went on my way, leaving Macedonia, only you Philippians became my partners in giving and receiving. No other church did this. 16 Even when I was over in Thessalonica you sent help twice. 17 But though I appreciate your gifts, what makes me happiest is the well-earned reward you will have because of your kindness.

18 At the moment I have all I need—more than I need! I am generously supplied with the gifts you sent me when Epaphroditus came. They are a sweet-smelling sacrifice that pleases God well. 19 And it is he who will supply all your needs from his riches in glory, because of what Christ Jesus has done for us. 20 Now unto God our Father be glory forever and ever. Amen.

Sincerely,
Paul

P.S. 21 Say "hello" for me to all the Christians there; the brothers with me send their greetings too. 22 And all the other Christians here want to be remembered to you, especially those who work in Caesar's palace. 23 The blessings of our Lord Jesus Christ be upon your spirits.

Anything Else?

What else do I need when I have Christ? Do I need a certain haircut, or a rigid set of rules? Is there a secret body of knowledge only the enlightened can enter? Most other religions have an appeal of mystery, of being on the "inside"—achieved solely by following their way.

Christianity is different. Paul wrote this book to counter people who talked about some secret path for "members only." *No,* he thunders, *Christ is everything.*

Other religions are a mixture of God and man. Only Christianity holds that all of God became man. Christ wasn't just a cut above us ... he was God. The same God who spun off galaxies and quasars and solar systems. "You have everything when you have Christ," Paul concludes, and he proceeds to describe in detail all that includes.

COLOSSIANS

1 FROM: PAUL, CHOSEN by God to be Jesus Christ's messenger, and from Brother Timothy.

² *To:* The faithful Christian brothers— God's people—in the city of Colosse.

May God our Father shower you with blessings and fill you with his great peace. ³ Whenever we pray for you we always begin by giving thanks to God the Father of our Lord Jesus Christ, ⁴ for we have heard how much you trust the Lord, and how much you love his people. ⁵ And you are looking forward to the joys of heaven, and have been ever since the Gospel first was preached to you. ⁶ The same Good News that came to you is going out all over the world and changing lives everywhere, just as it changed yours that very first day you heard it and understood about God's great kindness to sinners.

⁷ Epaphras, our much-loved fellow worker, was the one who brought you this Good News. He is Jesus Christ's faithful slave, here to help us in your place. ⁸ And he is the one who has told us about the great love for others which the Holy Spirit has given you. ⁹ So ever since we first heard about you we have kept on praying and asking God to help you understand what he wants you to do; asking him to make you wise about spiritual things; ¹⁰ and asking that the way you live will always please the Lord and honor him, so that you will always be doing good, kind things for others, while all the time you are learning to know God better and better.

¹¹ We are praying, too, that you will be filled with his mighty, glorious strength so that you can keep going no matter what happens—always full of the joy of the Lord, ¹² and always thankful to the Father who has made us fit to share all the wonderful things that belong to those who live in the kingdom of light. ¹³ For he has rescued us out of the darkness and gloom of Satan's kingdom and brought us into the kingdom of his dear Son, ¹⁴ who bought our freedom with his blood and forgave us all our sins.

¹⁵ Christ is the exact likeness of the unseen God. He existed before God made anything at all,[a] and, in fact, ¹⁶ Christ himself is the Creator who made everything in heaven and earth, the things we can see and the things we can't; the spirit world with its kings and kingdoms, its rulers and authorities; all were made by Christ for his own use and glory. ¹⁷ He was before all else began and it is his power that holds everything together. ¹⁸ He is the Head of the body made up of his people—that is, his church— which he began; and he is the Leader of all those who arise from the dead,[b] so that he is first in everything; ¹⁹ for God wanted all of himself to be in his Son.

²⁰ It was through what his Son did that God cleared a path for everything to come to him—all things in heaven and on earth— for Christ's death on the cross has made peace with God for all by his blood. ²¹ This includes you who were once so far away from God. You were his enemies and hated him and were separated from him by your evil thoughts and actions, yet now he has brought you back as his friends. ²² He has done this through the death on the cross of his own human body, and now as a result Christ has brought you into the very presence of God, and you are standing there before him with nothing left against you— nothing left that he could even chide you for; ²³ the only condition is that you fully believe the Truth, standing in it steadfast and firm, strong in the Lord, convinced of the Good News that Jesus died for you, and never shifting from trusting him to save you. This is the wonderful news that came to each of you and is now spreading all over the world. And I, Paul, have the joy of telling it to others.

²⁴ But part of my work is to suffer for you; and I am glad, for I am helping to finish up the remainder of Christ's sufferings for his body, the church.

²⁵ God has sent me to help his church

---

a Literally, "he is the firstborn of all creation."
dead."

b Literally, "he is the Beginning, the firstborn from the

and to tell his secret plan to you Gentiles. [26,27] He has kept this secret for centuries and generations past, but now at last it has pleased him to tell it to those who love him and live for him, and the riches and glory of his plan are for you Gentiles too. And this is the secret: *that Christ in your hearts is your only hope of glory.*

[28] So everywhere we go we talk about Christ to all who will listen, warning them and teaching them as well as we know how. We want to be able to present each one to God, perfect because of what Christ has done for each of them. [29] This is my work, and I can do it only because Christ's mighty energy is at work within me.

2 I WISH YOU could know how much I have struggled in prayer for you and for the church at Laodicea, and for my many other friends who have never known me personally. [2] This is what I have asked of God for you: that you will be encouraged and knit together by strong ties of love, and that you will have the rich experience of knowing Christ with real certainty and clear understanding. *For God's secret plan, now at last made known, is Christ himself.* [3] In him lie hidden all the mighty, untapped treasures of wisdom and knowledge.

[4] I am saying this because I am afraid that someone may fool you with smooth talk. [5] For though I am far away from you my heart is with you, happy because you are getting along so well, happy because of your strong faith in Christ. [6] And now just as you trusted Christ to save you, trust him, too, for each day's problems; live in vital union with him. [7] Let your roots grow down into him and draw up nourishment from him. See that you go on growing in the Lord, and become strong and vigorous in the truth you were taught. Let your lives overflow with joy and thanksgiving for all he has done.

[8] Don't let others spoil your faith and joy with their philosophies, their wrong and shallow answers built on men's thoughts and ideas, instead of on what Christ has said. [9] For in Christ there is all of God in a human body; [10] *so you have everything when you have Christ,* and you are filled with God through your union with Christ. He is the highest Ruler, with authority over every other power.

[11] When you came to Christ he set you free from your evil desires, not by a bodily operation of circumcision but by a spiritual operation, the baptism of your souls. [12] For in baptism you see how your old, evil nature died with him and was buried with him; and then you came up out of death with him into a new life because you trusted the Word of the mighty God who raised Christ from the dead.

[13] You were dead in sins, and your sinful desires were not yet cut away. Then he gave you a share in the very life of Christ, for he forgave all your sins, [14] and blotted out the charges proved against you, the list of his commandments which you had not obeyed. He took this list of sins and destroyed it by nailing it to Christ's cross. [15] In this way God took away Satan's power to accuse you of sin, and God openly displayed to the whole world Christ's triumph at the cross where your sins were all taken away.

[16] So don't let anyone criticize you for what you eat or drink, or for not celebrating Jewish holidays and feasts or new moon ceremonies or Sabbaths. [17] For these were only temporary rules that ended when Christ came. They were only shadows of the real thing—of Christ himself. [18] Don't let anyone declare you lost when you refuse to worship angels, as they say you must. They have seen a vision, they say, and know you should. These proud men (though they claim to be so humble) have a very clever imagination. [19] But they are not connected to Christ, the Head to which all of us who are his body are joined; for we are joined together by his strong sinews and we grow only as we get our nourishment and strength from God.

[20] Since you died, as it were, with Christ and this has set you free from following the world's ideas of how to be saved—by doing good and obeying various rules[a]—why do you keep right on following them anyway, still bound by such rules as [21] not eating, tasting, or even touching certain foods?

---

a Literally, "by the rudiments of the world."

²² Such rules are mere human teachings, for food was made to be eaten and used up. ²³ These rules may seem good, for rules of this kind require strong devotion and are humiliating and hard on the body, but they have no effect when it comes to conquering a person's evil thoughts and desires. They only make him proud.

3 SINCE YOU BECAME alive again, so to speak, when Christ arose from the dead, now set your sights on the rich treasures and joys of heaven where he sits beside God in the place of honor and power. ² Let heaven fill your thoughts; don't spend your time worrying about things down here. ³ You should have as little desire for this world as a dead person does. Your real life is in heaven with Christ and God. ⁴ And when Christ who is our real life comes back again, you will shine with him and share in all his glories.

⁵ Away then with sinful, earthly things; deaden the evil desires lurking within you; have nothing to do with sexual sin, impurity, lust and shameful desires; don't worship the good things of life, for that is idolatry. ⁶ God's terrible anger is upon those who do such things. ⁷ You used to do them when your life was still part of this world; ⁸ but now is the time to cast off and throw away all these rotten garments of anger, hatred, cursing, and dirty language.

⁹ Don't tell lies to each other; it was your old life with all its wickedness that did that sort of thing; now it is dead and gone. ¹⁰ You are living a brand new kind of life that is continually learning more and more of what is right, and trying constantly to be more and more like Christ who created this new life within you. ¹¹ In this new life one's nationality or race or education or social position is unimportant; such things mean nothing. Whether a person has Christ is what matters, and he is equally available to all.

¹² Since you have been chosen by God who has given you this new kind of life, and because of his deep love and concern for you, you should practice tenderhearted mercy and kindness to others. Don't worry about making a good impression on them but be ready to suffer quietly and patiently.

¹³ Be gentle and ready to forgive; never hold grudges. Remember, the Lord forgave you, so you must forgive others.

¹⁴ Most of all, let love guide your life, for then the whole church will stay together in perfect harmony. ¹⁵ Let the peace of heart which comes from Christ be always present in your hearts and lives, for this is your responsibility and privilege as members of his body. And always be thankful.

¹⁶ Remember what Christ taught and let his words enrich your lives and make you wise; teach them to each other and sing them out in psalms and hymns and spiritual songs, singing to the Lord with thankful hearts. ¹⁷ And whatever you do or say, let it be as a representative of the Lord Jesus, and come with him into the presence of God the Father to give him your thanks.

¹⁸ You wives, submit yourselves to your husbands, for that is what the Lord has planned for you. ¹⁹ And you husbands must be loving and kind to your wives and not bitter against them, nor harsh.

²⁰ You children must always obey your fathers and mothers, for that pleases the Lord. ²¹ Fathers, don't scold your children so much that they become discouraged and quit trying.

²² You slaves must always obey your earthly masters, not only trying to please them when they are watching you but all the time; obey them willingly because of your love for the Lord and because you want to please him. ²³ Work hard and cheerfully at all you do, just as though you were working for the Lord and not merely for your masters, ²⁴ remembering that it is the Lord Christ who is going to pay you, giving you your full portion of all he owns. He is the one you are really working for. ²⁵ And if you don't do your best for him, he will pay you in a way that you won't like—for he has no special favorites who can get away with shirking.

4 YOU SLAVE OWNERS must be just and fair to all your slaves. Always remember that you, too, have a Master in heaven who is closely watching you.

² Don't be weary in prayer; keep at it; watch for God's answers and remember to be thankful when they come. ³ Don't forget

to pray for us too, that God will give us many chances to preach the Good News of Christ for which I am here in jail. [4] Pray that I will be bold enough to tell it freely and fully, and make it plain, as, of course, I should.

[5] Make the most of your chances to tell others the Good News. Be wise in all your contacts with them. [6] Let your conversation be gracious as well as sensible, for then you will have the right answer for everyone.

[7] Tychicus, our much loved brother, will tell you how I am getting along. He is a hard worker and serves the Lord with me. [8] I have sent him on this special trip just to see how you are, and to comfort and encourage you. [9] I am also sending Onesimus, a faithful and much loved brother, one of your own people. He and Tychicus will give you all the latest news.

[10] Aristarchus, who is with me here as a prisoner, sends you his love, and so does Mark, a relative of Barnabas. And as I said before, give Mark a hearty welcome[a] if he comes your way. [11] Jesus Justus also sends his love. These are the only Jewish Chris-tians working with me here, and what a comfort they have been!

[12] Epaphras, from your city, a servant of Christ Jesus, sends you his love. He is always earnestly praying for you, asking God to make you strong and perfect and to help you know his will in everything you do. [13] I can assure you that he has worked hard for you with his prayers, and also for the Christians in Laodicea and Hierapolis.

[14] Dear doctor Luke sends his love, and so does Demas.

[15] Please give my greeting to the Christian friends at Laodicea, and to Nymphas, and to those who meet in his home. [16] By the way, after you have read this letter will you pass it on to the church at Laodicea? And read the letter I wrote to them. [17] And say to Archippus, "Be sure that you do all the Lord has told you to."

[18] Here is my own greeting in my own handwriting: Remember me here in jail. May God's blessings surround you.

Sincerely,
Paul

---

a Literally, "receive him."

What Are They Saying About Me?

Philip Yancey

When a person looks at another and asks that question, the immediate reaction we get is that it's probably not complimentary! As we talk about others we seem to delight in tearing them down, but we get few kicks out of praising someone.

Paul complimented the people to whom he addressed these next two letters. Others were saying *good* things about them—and this was the kind of spirit shown in the fellowship of those "Christ-ones."

Why shouldn't we *enjoy* saying good things about others? Why aren't we more wrapped up in good feelings of loving others? *How* can we start to live this way instead of enjoying "sweet nastiness"? These two letters go a long way toward answering that.

1 THESSALONIANS

1 FROM: PAUL, SILAS and Timothy.

To: The Church at Thessalonica—to you who belong to God the Father and the Lord Jesus Christ: May blessing and peace of heart be your rich gifts from God our Father, and from Jesus Christ our Lord.

² We always thank God for you and pray for you constantly. ³ We never forget your loving deeds as we talk to our God and Father about you, and your strong faith and steady looking forward to the return of our Lord Jesus Christ.

⁴ We know that God has chosen you, dear brothers, much beloved of God. ⁵ For when we brought you the Good News, it was not just meaningless chatter to you; no, you listened with great interest. What we told you produced a powerful effect upon you, for the Holy Spirit gave you great and full assurance that what we said was true. And you know how our very lives were further proof to you of the truth of our message. ⁶ So you became our followers and the Lord's; for you received our message with joy from the Holy Spirit in spite of the trials and sorrows it brought you.

⁷ Then you yourselves became an example to all the other Christians in Greece. ⁸ And now the Word of the Lord has spread out from you to others everywhere, far beyond your boundaries, for wherever we go we find people telling us about your remarkable faith in God. We don't need to tell *them* about it, ⁹ for *they* keep telling *us* about the wonderful welcome you gave us, and how you turned away from your idols to God so that now the living and true God only is your Master. ¹⁰ And they speak of

how you are looking forward to the return of God's Son from heaven—Jesus, whom God brought back to life—and he is our only Savior from God's terrible anger against sin.

2 YOU YOURSELVES KNOW, dear brothers, how worthwhile that visit was. [2] You know how badly we had been treated at Philippi just before we came to you, and how much we suffered there. Yet God gave us the courage to boldly repeat the same message to you, even though we were surrounded by enemies. [3] So you can see that we were not preaching with any false motives or evil purposes in mind; we were perfectly straightforward and sincere.

[4] For we speak as messengers from God, trusted by him to tell the truth; we change his message not one bit to suit the taste of those who hear it; for we serve God alone, who examines our hearts' deepest thoughts. [5] Never once did we try to win you with flattery, as you very well know, and God knows we were not just pretending to be your friends so that you would give us money! [6] As for praise, we have never asked for it from you or anyone else, although as apostles of Christ we certainly had a right to some honor from you. [7] But we were as gentle among you as a mother feeding and caring for her own children. [8] We loved you dearly—so dearly that we gave you not only God's message, but our own lives too.

[9] Don't you remember, dear brothers, how hard we worked among you? Night and day we toiled and sweated to earn enough to live on so that our expenses would not be a burden to anyone there, as we preached God's Good News among you. [10] You yourselves are our witnesses—as is God—that we have been pure and honest and faultless toward every one of you. [11] We talked to you as a father to his own children—don't you remember?—pleading with you, encouraging you and even demanding [12] that your daily lives should not embarrass God, but bring joy to him who invited you into his kingdom to share his glory.

[13] And we will never stop thanking God for this: that when we preached to you, you didn't think of the words we spoke as being just our own, but you accepted what we said as the very Word of God—which, of course, it was—and it changed your lives when you believed it.

[14] And then, dear brothers, you suffered what the churches in Judea did, persecution from your own countrymen, just as they suffered from their own people the Jews. [15] After they had killed their own prophets, they even executed the Lord Jesus; and now they have brutally persecuted us and driven us out. They are against both God and man, [16] trying to keep us from preaching to the Gentiles for fear some might be saved; and so their sins continue to grow. But the anger of God has caught up with them at last.

[17] Dear brothers, after we left you and had been away from you but a very little while (though our hearts never left you), we tried hard to come back to see you once more. [18] We wanted very much to come and I, Paul, tried again and again, but Satan stopped us. [19] For what is it we live for, that gives us hope and joy and is our proud reward and crown? It is you! Yes, you will bring us much joy as we stand together before our Lord Jesus Christ when he comes back again. [20] For you are our trophy and joy.

3 FINALLY, WHEN I could stand it no longer, I decided to stay alone in Athens [2,3] and send Timothy, our brother and fellow worker, God's minister, to visit you to strengthen your faith and encourage you, and to keep you from becoming fainthearted in all the troubles you were going through. (But of course you know that such troubles are a part of God's plan for us Christians. [4] Even while we were still with you we warned you ahead of time that suffering would soon come—and it did.)

[5] As I was saying, when I could bear the suspense no longer I sent Timothy to find out whether your faith was still strong. I was afraid that perhaps Satan had gotten the best of you and that all our work had been useless. [6] And now Timothy has just returned and brings the welcome news that your faith and love are as strong as ever, and that you remember our visit with joy and want to see us just as much as we want to see you. [7] So we are greatly comforted, dear

brothers, in all of our own crushing troubles and suffering here, now that we know you are standing true to the Lord. [8] We can bear anything as long as we know that you remain strong in him.

[9] How can we thank God enough for you and for the joy and delight you have given us in our praying for you? [10] For night and day we pray on and on for you, asking God to let us see you again, to fill up any little cracks there may yet be in your faith. [11] May God our Father himself and our Lord Jesus send us back to you again. [12] And may the Lord make your love to grow and overflow to each other and to everyone else, just as our love does toward you. [13] This will result in your hearts being made strong, sinless and holy by God our Father, so that you may stand before him guiltless on that day when our Lord Jesus Christ returns with all those who belong to him.[a]

4 LET ME ADD this, dear brothers: You already know how to please God in your daily living, for you know the commands we gave you from the Lord Jesus himself. Now we beg you—yes, we demand of you in the name of the Lord Jesus—that you live more and more closely to that ideal. [3,4] For God wants you to be holy and pure, and to keep clear of all sexual sin so that each of you will marry in holiness and honor— [5] not in lustful passion as the heathen do, in their ignorance of God and his ways.

[6] And this also is God's will: that you never cheat in this matter by taking another man's wife, because the Lord will punish you terribly for this, as we have solemnly told you before. [7] For God has not called us to be dirty-minded and full of lust, but to be holy and clean. [8] If anyone refuses to live by these rules he is not disobeying the rules of men but of God who gives his *Holy* Spirit to you.

[9] But concerning the pure brotherly love that there should be among God's people, I don't need to say very much, I'm sure! For God himself is teaching you to love one another. [10] Indeed, your love is already strong toward all the Christian brothers throughout your whole nation. Even so, dear friends, we beg you to love them more and more. [11] This should be your ambition: to live a quiet life, minding your own business and doing your own work, just as we told you before. [12] As a result, people who are not Christians will trust and respect you, and you will not need to depend on others for enough money to pay your bills.

[13] And now, dear brothers, I want you to know what happens to a Christian when he dies so that when it happens, you will not be full of sorrow, as those are who have no hope. [14] For since we believe that Jesus died and then came back to life again, we can also believe that when Jesus returns, God will bring back with him all the Christians who have died.

[15] I can tell you this directly from the Lord: that we who are still living when the Lord returns will not rise to meet him ahead of those who are in their graves. [16] For the Lord himself will come down from heaven with a mighty shout and with the soul-stirring cry of the archangel and the great trumpet-call of God. And the believers who are dead will be the first to rise to meet the Lord. [17] Then we who are still alive and remain on the earth will be caught up with them in the clouds to meet the Lord in the air and remain with him forever. [18] So comfort and encourage each other with this news.

5 WHEN IS ALL this going to happen? I really don't need to say anything about that, dear brothers, [2] for you know perfectly well that no one knows. That day of the Lord will come unexpectedly like a thief in the night. [3] When people are saying, "All is well, everything is quiet and peaceful"— then, all of a sudden, disaster will fall upon them as suddenly as a woman's birth pains begin when her child is born. And these people will not be able to get away anywhere—there will be no place to hide.

[4] But, dear brothers, you are not in the dark about these things, and you won't be surprised as by a thief when that day of the Lord comes. [5] For you are all children of the light and of the day, and do not belong to

---

a Literally, "with all his saints. Amen."

darkness and night. ⁶ So be on your guard, not asleep like the others. Watch for his return and stay sober. ⁷ Night is the time for sleep and the time when people get drunk. ⁸ But let us who live in the light keep sober, protected by the armor of faith and love, and wearing as our helmet the happy hope of salvation.

⁹ For God has not chosen to pour out his anger upon us, but to save us through our Lord Jesus Christ; ¹⁰ he died for us so that we can live with him forever, whether we are dead or alive at the time of his return. ¹¹ So encourage each other to build each other up, just as you are already doing.

¹² Dear brothers, honor the officers of your church who work hard among you and warn you against all that is wrong. ¹³ Think highly of them and give them your whole-hearted love because they are straining to help you. And remember, no quarreling among yourselves.

¹⁴ Dear brothers, warn those who are lazy; comfort those who are frightened; take tender care of those who are weak; and be patient with everyone. ¹⁵ See that no one pays back evil for evil, but always try to do good to each other and to everyone else. ¹⁶ Always be joyful. ¹⁷ Always keep on praying. ¹⁸ No matter what happens, always be thankful, for this is God's will for you who belong to Christ Jesus.

¹⁹ Do not smother the Holy Spirit. ²⁰ Do not scoff at those who prophesy, ²¹ but test everything that is said to be sure it is true, and if it is, then accept it. ²² Keep away from every kind of evil. ²³ May the God of peace himself make you entirely pure and devoted to God; and may your spirit and soul and body be kept strong and blameless until that day when our Lord Jesus Christ comes back again. ²⁴ God, who called you to become his child, will do all this for you, just as he promised. ²⁵ Dear brothers, pray for us. ²⁶ Shake hands for me with all the brothers there. ²⁷ I command you in the name of the Lord to read this letter to all the Christians. ²⁸ And may rich blessings from our Lord Jesus Christ be with you, every one.

Sincerely,
Paul

2 THESSALONIANS

1 FROM: PAUL, SILAS and Timothy.
To: The church of Thessalonica—kept safe in God our Father and in the Lord Jesus Christ.

² May God the Father and the Lord Jesus Christ give you rich blessings and peace-filled hearts and minds.

³ Dear brothers, giving thanks to God for you is not only the right thing to do, but it is our duty to God, because of the really wonderful way your faith has grown, and because of your growing love for each other. ⁴ We are happy to tell other churches about your patience and complete faith in God, in spite of all the crushing troubles and hardships you are going through. ⁵ This is only one example of the fair, just way God does things, for he is using your sufferings to make you ready for his kingdom, ⁶ while at the same time he is preparing judgment and punishment for those who are hurting you.

⁷ And so I would say to you who are suffering, God will give you rest along with us when the Lord Jesus appears suddenly from heaven in flaming fire with his mighty angels, ⁸ bringing judgment on those who do not wish to know God, and who refuse to accept his plan to save them through our Lord Jesus Christ. ⁹ They will be punished in everlasting hell, forever separated from the Lord, never to see the glory of his power, ¹⁰ when he comes to receive praise and admiration because of all he has done for his people, his saints. And you will be among those praising him, because you have believed what we told you about him.

¹¹ And so we keep on praying for you that our God will make you the kind of children he wants to have—will make you as good as you wish you could be!—rewarding your faith with his power. ¹² Then everyone will be praising the name of the Lord

Jesus Christ because of the results they see in you; and your greatest glory will be that you belong to him. The tender mercy of our God and of the Lord Jesus Christ has made all this possible for you.

2 AND NOW, WHAT about the coming again of our Lord Jesus Christ, and our being gathered together to meet him? Please don't be upset and excited, dear brothers, by the rumor that this day of the Lord has already begun. If you hear of people having visions and special messages from God about this, or letters that are supposed to have come from me, don't believe them. [3] Don't be carried away and deceived regardless of what they say.

For that day will not come until two things happen: first, there will be a time of great rebellion against God, and then the man of rebellion will come—the son of hell. [4] He will defy every god there is, and tear down every other object of adoration and worship. He will go in and sit as God in the temple of God, claiming that he himself is God. [5] Don't you remember that I told you this when I was with you? [6] And you know what is keeping him from being here already; for he can come only when his time is ready.

[7] As for the work this man of rebellion and hell will do when he comes, it is already going on,[a] but he himself will not come until the one who is holding him back steps out of the way. [8] Then this wicked one will appear, whom the Lord Jesus will burn up with the breath of his mouth and destroy by his presence when he returns. [9] This man of sin will come as Satan's tool, full of satanic power, and will trick everyone with strange demonstrations, and will do great miracles. [10] He will completely fool those who are on their way to hell because they have said "no" to the Truth; they have refused to believe it and love it, and let it save them, [11] so God will allow them to believe lies with all their hearts, [12] and all of them will be justly judged for believing falsehood, refusing the Truth, and enjoying their sins. [13] But we must forever give

thanks to God for you, our brothers loved by the Lord, because God chose from the very first to give you salvation,[b] cleansing you by the work of the Holy Spirit and by your trusting in the Truth. [14] Through us he told you the Good News. Through us he called you to share in the glory of our Lord Jesus Christ.

[15] With all these things in mind, dear brothers, stand firm and keep a strong grip on the truth that we taught you in our letters and during the time we were with you.

[16] May our Lord Jesus Christ himself and God our Father, who has loved us and given us everlasting comfort and hope which we don't deserve, [17] comfort your hearts with all comfort, and help you in every good thing you say and do.

3 FINALLY, DEAR BROTHERS, as I come to the end of this letter I ask you to pray for us. Pray first that the Lord's message will spread rapidly and triumph wherever it goes, winning converts everywhere as it did when it came to you. [2] Pray too that we will be saved out of the clutches of evil men, for not everyone loves the Lord. [3] But the Lord is faithful; he will make you strong and guard you from satanic attacks of every kind. [4] And we trust the Lord that you are putting into practice the things we taught you, and that you always will. [5] May the Lord bring you into an ever deeper understanding of the love of God and of the patience that comes from Christ.

[6] Now here is a command, dear brothers, given in the name of our Lord Jesus Christ by his authority: Stay away from any Christian who spends his days in laziness and does not follow the ideal of hard work we set up for you. [7] For you well know that you ought to follow our example: you never saw us loafing; [8] we never accepted food from anyone without buying it; we worked hard day and night for the money we needed to live on, in order that we would not be a burden to any of you. [9] It wasn't that we didn't have the right to ask you to feed us, but we wanted to show you, firsthand, how you should work for your living. [10] Even

---

a Literally, "the mystery of lawlessness is already at work."   b Or, "because God chose you to be among the first to believe."

while we were still there with you we gave you this rule: "He who does not work shall not eat."

[11] Yet we hear that some of you are living in laziness, refusing to work, and wasting your time in gossiping. [12] In the name of the Lord Jesus Christ we appeal to such people—we command them—to quiet down, get to work, and earn their own living. [13] And to the rest of you I say, dear brothers, never be tired of doing right.

[14] If anyone refuses to obey what we say in this letter, notice who he is and stay away from him, that he may be ashamed of himself. [15] Don't think of him as an enemy, but speak to him as you would to a brother who needs to be warned. [16] May the Lord of peace himself give you his peace no matter what happens. The Lord be with you all.

[17] Now here is my greeting which I am writing with my own hand, as I do at the end of all my letters, for proof that it really is from me. This is in my own handwriting. [18] May the blessing of our Lord Jesus Christ be upon you all.

Sincerely,
Paul

Hammerin Henry

Henry made it! The slugger stepped to the plate on opening day, 1974, and sent his 714th home run rocketing over the fence. Number 715 followed a few days later in Atlanta, breaking Babe Ruth's long-standing record.

Henry Aaron disciplined every muscle in his body to work toward that goal. The years of practice, the lightning-fast wrists, the steady eye—they paid off in one of sport's most moving moments.

In the following two letters, Paul challenges the young man Timothy to reach for the very top—giving everything to reach the goal. Timothy and those who want to make the record books have the eyes of Someone more awesome than four billion people watching! You'll find throughout these letters why keeping that Someone in mind is so important.

1 TIMOTHY

1 FROM: PAUL, A missionary of Jesus Christ, sent out by the direct command of God our Savior and by Jesus Christ our Lord—our only hope.

² *To:* Timothy.

Timothy, you are like a son to me in the things of the Lord. May God our Father and Jesus Christ our Lord show you his kindness and mercy and give you great peace of heart and mind.

³,⁴ As I said when I left for Macedonia, please stay there in Ephesus and try to stop the men who are teaching such wrong doctrine. Put an end to their myths and fables, and their idea of being saved by finding favor with an endless chain of angels leading up to God—wild ideas that stir up questions and arguments instead of helping people accept God's plan of faith. ⁵ What I am eager for is that all the Christians there will be filled with love that comes from pure hearts, and that their minds will be clean and their faith strong.

⁶ But these teachers have missed this whole idea and spend their time arguing and talking foolishness. ⁷ They want to become famous as teachers of the laws of Moses when they haven't the slightest idea what those laws really show us. ⁸ Those laws are good when used as God intended. ⁹ But they were not made for us, whom God has saved; they are for sinners who hate God, have rebellious hearts, curse and swear, attack their fathers and mothers, and murder. ¹⁰,¹¹ Yes, these laws are made to identify as sinners all who are immoral and impure: homosexuals, kidnappers, liars, and all others who do things that contradict the glorious Good News of our blessed God, whose messenger I am.

¹² How thankful I am to Christ Jesus our Lord for choosing me as one of his messengers, and giving me the strength to be faithful to him, ¹³ even though I used to scoff at the name of Christ. I hunted down his people, harming them in every way I could. But God had mercy on me because I didn't know what I was doing, for I didn't know Christ at that time. ¹⁴ Oh, how kind our Lord was, for he showed me how to trust him and become full of the love of Christ Jesus.

¹⁵ How true it is, and how I long that everyone should know it, that Christ Jesus came into the world to save sinners—and I was the greatest of them all. ¹⁶ But God had mercy on me so that Christ Jesus could use me as an example to show everyone how patient he is with even the worst sinners, so that others will realize that they, too, can have everlasting life. ¹⁷ Glory and honor to God forever and ever. He is the King of the ages, the unseen one who never dies; he alone is God, and full of wisdom. Amen.

¹⁸ Now, Timothy, my son, here is my command to you: Fight well in the Lord's

battles, just as the Lord told us through his prophets that you would. [19] Cling tightly to your faith in Christ and always keep your conscience clear, doing what you know is right. For some people have disobeyed their consciences and have deliberately done what they knew was wrong. It isn't surprising that soon they lost their faith in Christ after defying God like that. [20] Hymenaeus and Alexander are two examples of this. I had to give them over to Satan to punish them until they could learn not to bring shame to the name of Christ.

2 HERE ARE MY directions: Pray much for others; plead for God's mercy upon them; give thanks for all he is going to do for them.

[2] Pray in this way for kings and all others who are in authority over us, or are in places of high responsibility, so that we can live in peace and quietness, spending our time in godly living and thinking much about the Lord.[a] [3] This is good and pleases God our Savior, [4] for he longs for all to be saved and to understand this truth: [5] *That God is on one side and all the people on the other side, and Christ Jesus, himself man, is between them to bring them together, [6] by giving his life for all mankind.*

This is the message which at the proper time God gave to the world. [7] And I have been chosen—this is the absolute truth—as God's minister and missionary to teach this truth to the Gentiles, and to show them God's plan of salvation through faith. [8] So I want men everywhere to pray with holy hands lifted up to God, free from sin and anger and resentment. [9,10] And the women should be the same way, quiet and sensible in manner and clothing. Christian women should be noticed for being kind and good, not for the way they fix their hair or because of their jewels or fancy clothes. [11] Women should listen and learn quietly and humbly.

[12] I never let women teach men or lord it over them. Let them be silent in your church meetings. [13] Why? Because God made Adam first, and afterwards he made Eve. [14] And it was not Adam who was fooled by Satan, but Eve, and sin was the result. [15] So God sent pain and suffering to women when their children are born, but he will save their souls if they trust in him, living quiet, good, and loving lives.

3 IT IS A true saying that if a man wants to be a pastor[a] he has a good ambition. [2] For a pastor must be a good man whose life cannot be spoken against. He must have only one wife, and he must be hard working and thoughtful, orderly, and full of good deeds. He must enjoy having guests in his home, and must be a good Bible teacher. [3] He must not be a drinker or quarrelsome, but he must be gentle and kind, and not be one who loves money. [4] He must have a well-behaved family, with children who obey quickly and quietly. [5] For if a man can't make his own little family behave, how can he help the whole church?

[6] The pastor must not be a new Christian, because he might be proud of being chosen so soon, and pride comes before a fall. (Satan's downfall is an example.) [7] Also, he must be well spoken of by people outside the church—those who aren't Christians—so that Satan can't trap him with many accusations, and leave him without freedom to lead his flock.

[8] The deacons must be the same sort of good, steady men as the pastors. They must not be heavy drinkers and must not be greedy for money. [9] They must be earnest, wholehearted followers of Christ who is the hidden Source of their faith. [10] Before they are asked to be deacons they should be given other jobs in the church as a test of their character and ability, and if they do well, then they may be chosen as deacons.

[11] Their wives must be thoughtful, not heavy drinkers, not gossipers, but faithful in everything they do. [12] Deacons should have only one wife and they should have happy, obedient families. [13] Those who do well as deacons will be well rewarded both by respect from others and also by developing their own confidence and bold trust in the Lord.

[14] I am writing these things to you now, even though I hope to be with you soon, [15] so that if I don't come for awhile you will

---

a Literally, "in gravity."　　3a More literally, "church leader" or "presiding elder."

know what kind of men you should choose as officers for the church of the living God, which contains and holds high the truth of God. [16] It is quite true that the way to live a godly life is not an easy matter. But the answer lies in Christ, who came to earth as a man, was proved spotless and pure in his Spirit, was served by angels, was preached among the nations, was accepted by men everywhere and was received up again to his glory in heaven.

4 BUT THE HOLY Spirit tells us clearly that in the last times some in the church will turn away from Christ and become eager followers of teachers with devil-inspired ideas. [2] These teachers will tell lies with straight faces and do it so often that their consciences won't even bother them. [3] They will say it is wrong to be married and wrong to eat meat, even though God gave these things to well-taught Christians to enjoy and be thankful for. [4] For everything God made is good, and we may eat it gladly if we are thankful for it, [5] and if we ask God to bless it, for it is made good by the Word of God and prayer.

[6] If you explain this to the others you will be doing your duty as a worthy pastor who is fed by faith and by the true teaching you have followed.

[7] Don't waste time arguing over foolish ideas and silly myths and legends. Spend your time and energy in the exercise of keeping spiritually fit. [8] Bodily exercise is all right, but spiritual exercise is much more important and is a tonic for all you do. So exercise yourself spiritually and practice being a better Christian, because that will help you not only now in this life, but in the next life too. [9,10] This is the truth and everyone should accept it. We work hard and suffer much in order that people will believe it, for our hope is in the living God who died for all, and particularly for those who have accepted his salvation.

[11] Teach these things and make sure everyone learns them well. [12] Don't let anyone think little of you because you are young. Be their ideal; let them follow the way you

teach and live; be a pattern for them in your love, your faith, and your clean thoughts. [13] Until I get there, read and explain the Scriptures to the church; preach God's Word.

[14] Be sure to use the abilities God has given you through his prophets when the elders of the church laid their hands upon your head. [15] Put these abilities to work; throw yourself into your tasks so that everyone may notice your improvement and progress. [16] Keep a close watch on all you do and think. Stay true to what is right and God will bless you and use you to help others.

5 NEVER SPEAK SHARPLY to an older man, but plead with him respectfully just as though he were your own father. Talk to the younger men as you would to much loved brothers. [2] Treat the older women as mothers, and the girls as your sisters, thinking only pure thoughts about them.

[3] The church should take loving care of women whose husbands have died, if they don't have anyone else to help them. [4] But if they have children or grandchildren, these are the ones who should take the responsibility, for kindness should begin at home, supporting needy parents. This is something that pleases God very much.

[5] The church should care for widows who are poor and alone in the world, if they are looking to God for his help and spending much time in prayer; [6] but not if they are spending their time running around gossiping, seeking only pleasure and thus ruining their souls. [7] This should be your church rule so that the Christians will know and do what is right.

[8] But anyone who won't care for his own relatives when they need help, especially those living in his own family, has no right to say he is a Christian. Such a person is worse than the heathen.

[9] A widow who wants to become one of the special church workers[a] should be at least sixty years old and have been married only once. [10] She must be well thought of by everyone because of the good she has done.

---

a Literally, "enrolled as a widow."

Has she brought up her children well? Has she been kind to strangers as well as to other Christians? Has she helped those who are sick and hurt? Is she always ready to show kindness?

[11] The younger widows should not become members of this special group because after awhile they are likely to disregard their vow to Christ and marry again. [12] And so they will stand condemned because they broke their first promise. [13] Besides, they are likely to be lazy and spend their time gossiping around from house to house, getting into other people's business. [14] So I think it is better for these younger widows to marry again and have children, and take care of their own homes; then no one will be able to say anything against them. [15] For I am afraid that some of them have already turned away from the church and been led astray by Satan.

[16] Let me remind you again that a widow's relatives must take care of her, and not leave this to the church to do. Then the church can spend its money for the care of widows who are all alone and have nowhere else to turn.

[17] Pastors who do their work well should be paid well and should be highly appreciated, especially those who work hard at both preaching and teaching. [18] For the Scriptures say, "Never tie up the mouth of an ox when it is treading out the grain—let him eat as he goes along!" And in another place, "Those who work deserve their pay!"

[19] Don't listen to complaints against the pastor unless there are two or three witnesses to accuse him. [20] If he has really sinned, then he should be rebuked in front of the whole church so that no one else will follow his example.

[21] I solemnly command you in the presence of God and the Lord Jesus Christ and of the holy angels to do this whether the pastor is a special friend of yours or not. All must be treated exactly the same. [22] Never be in a hurry about choosing a pastor; you may overlook his sins and it will look as if you approve of them. Be sure that you yourself stay away from all sin. [23] (By the way, this doesn't mean you should completely give up drinking wine. You ought to take a little sometimes as medicine for your stomach because you are sick so often.)

[24] Remember that some men, even pastors, lead sinful lives and everyone knows it. In such situations you can do something about it. But in other cases only the judgment day will reveal the terrible truth. [25] In the same way, everyone knows how much good some pastors do, but sometimes their good deeds aren't known until long afterward.

6 CHRISTIAN SLAVES SHOULD work hard for their owners and respect them; never let it be said that Christ's people are poor workers. Don't let the name of God or his teaching be laughed at because of this. [2] If their owner is a Christian, that is no excuse for slowing down; rather they should work all the harder because a brother in the faith is being helped by their efforts.

Teach these truths, Timothy, and encourage all to obey them. [3] Some may deny these things, but they are the sound, wholesome teachings of the Lord Jesus Christ and are the foundation for a godly life. [4] Anyone who says anything different is both proud and stupid. He is quibbling over the meaning of Christ's words and stirring up arguments ending in jealousy and anger, which only lead to name-calling, accusations, and evil suspicions. [5] These arguers—their minds warped by sin—don't know how to tell the truth; to them the Good News is just a means of making money. Keep away from them.

[6] Do you want to be truly rich? You already are if you are happy and good. [7] After all, we didn't bring any money with us when we came into the world, and we can't carry away a single penny when we die. [8] So we should be well satisfied without money if we have enough food and clothing. [9] But people who long to be rich soon begin to do all kinds of wrong things to get money, things that hurt them and make them evil-minded and finally send them to hell itself. [10] For the love of money is the first step toward all kinds of sin. Some people have even turned away from God because of their love for it, and as a result have pierced themselves with many sorrows.

[11] Oh, Timothy, you are God's man. Run

from all these evil things and work instead at what is right and good, learning to trust him and love others, and to be patient and gentle. [12] Fight on for God. Hold tightly to the eternal life which God has given you, and which you have confessed with such a ringing confession before many witnesses. [13] I command you before God who gives life to all, and before Christ Jesus who gave a fearless testimony before Pontius Pilate, [14] that you fulfill all he has told you to do, so that no one can find fault with you from now until our Lord Jesus Christ returns. [15] For in due season Christ will be revealed from heaven by the blessed and only Almighty God, the King of kings and Lord of lords, [16] who alone can never die, who lives in light so terrible that no human being can approach him. No mere man has ever seen him, nor ever will. Unto him be honor and everlasting power and dominion forever and ever. Amen. [17] Tell those who are rich not to be proud and not to trust in their money, which will soon be gone, but their pride and trust should be in the living God who always richly gives us all we need for our enjoyment. [18] Tell them to use their money to do good. They should be rich in good works and should give happily to those in need, always being ready to share with others whatever God has given them. [19] By doing this they will be storing up real treasure for themselves in heaven—it is the only safe investment for eternity! And they will be living a fruitful Christian life down here as well.

[20] Oh, Timothy, don't fail to do these things that God entrusted to you. Keep out of foolish arguments with those who boast of their "knowledge" and thus prove their lack of it. [21] Some of these people have missed the most important thing in life— they don't know God. May God's mercy be upon you.

Sincerely,

Paul

2 TIMOTHY

1 FROM: PAUL, JESUS Christ's missionary, sent out by God to tell men and women everywhere about the eternal life he has promised them through faith in Jesus Christ.

[2] *To:* Timothy, my dear son. May God the Father and Christ Jesus our Lord shower you with his kindness, mercy and peace.

[3] How I thank God for you, Timothy. I pray for you every day, and many times during the long nights I beg my God to bless you richly. He is my fathers' God, and mine, and my only purpose in life is to please him.

[4] How I long to see you again. How happy I would be, for I remember your tears as we left each other.

[5] I know how much you trust the Lord, just as your mother Eunice and your grandmother Lois do; and I feel sure you are still trusting him as much as ever.

[6] This being so, I want to remind you to stir into flame the strength and boldness[a] that is in you, that entered into you when I laid my hands upon your head and blessed you. [7] For the Holy Spirit, God's gift, does not want you to be afraid of people, but to be wise and strong, and to love them and enjoy being with them. [8] If you will stir up this inner power, you will never be afraid to tell others about our Lord, or to let them know that I am your friend even though I am here in jail for Christ's sake. You will be ready to suffer with me for the Lord, for he will give you strength in suffering.

[9] It is he who saved us and chose us for his holy work, not because we deserved it but because that was his plan long before the world began—to show his love and kindness to us through Christ. [10] And now he has made all of this plain to us by the

---

a Implied. Literally, "stir up the gift of God."

coming of our Savior Jesus Christ, who broke the power of death and showed us the way of everlasting life through trusting him. ¹¹ And God has chosen me to be his missionary, to preach to the Gentiles and teach them.

¹² That is why I am suffering here in jail and I am certainly not ashamed of it, for I know the one in whom I trust, and I am sure that he is able to safely guard all that I have given him until the day of his return.

¹³ Hold tightly to the pattern of truth I taught you, especially concerning the faith and love Christ Jesus offers you.ᵇ ¹⁴ Guard well the splendid, God-given ability you received as a gift from the Holy Spirit who lives within you.

¹⁵ As you know, all the Christians who came here from Asia have deserted me; even Phygellus and Hermogenes are gone. ¹⁶ May the Lord bless Onesiphorus and all his family, because he visited me and encouraged me often. His visits revived me like a breath of fresh air, and he was never ashamed of my being in jail. ¹⁷ In fact, when he came to Rome he searched everywhere trying to find me, and finally did. ¹⁸ May the Lord give him a special blessing at the day of Christ's return. And you know better than I can tell you how much he helped me at Ephesus.

2 OH, TIMOTHY, MY son, be strong with the strength Christ Jesus gives you. ² For you must teach others those things you and many others have heard me speak about. Teach these great truths to trustworthy men who will, in turn, pass them on to others.

³ Take your share of suffering as a good soldier of Jesus Christ, just as I do, ⁴ and as Christ's soldier do not let yourself become tied up in worldly affairs, for then you cannot satisfy the one who has enlisted you in his army. ⁵ Follow the Lord's rules for doing his work, just as an athlete either follows the rules or is disqualified and wins no prize. ⁶ Work hard, like a farmer who gets paid well if he raises a large crop. ⁷ Think over these three illustrations, and may the Lord help you to understand how they apply to you.

⁸ Don't ever forget the wonderful fact that Jesus Christ was a Man, born into King David's family; and that he was God, as shown by the fact that he rose again from the dead. ⁹ It is because I have preached these great truths that I am in trouble here and have been put in jail like a criminal. But the Word of God is not chained, even though I am. ¹⁰ I am more than willing to suffer if that will bring salvation and eternal glory in Christ Jesus to those God has chosen.

¹¹ I am comforted by this truth, that when we suffer and die for Christ it only means that we will begin living with him in heaven. ¹² And if we think that our present service for him is hard, just remember that some day we are going to sit with him and rule with him. But if we give up when we suffer, and turn against Christ, then he must turn against us. ¹³ Even when we are too weak to have any faith left, he remains faithful to us and will help us, for he cannot disown us who are part of himself, and he will always carry out his promises to us.

¹⁴ Remind your people of these great facts, and command them in the name of the Lord not to argue over unimportant things. Such arguments are confusing and useless, and even harmful. ¹⁵ Work hard so God can say to you, "Well done." Be a good workman, one who does not need to be ashamed when God examines your work. Know what his Word says and means. ¹⁶ Steer clear of foolish discussions which lead people into the sin of anger with each other. ¹⁷ Things will be said that will burn and hurt for a long time to come. Hymenaeus and Philetus, in their love of argument, are men like that. ¹⁸ They have left the path of truth, preaching the lie that the resurrection of the dead has already occurred; and they have weakened the faith of some who believe them.

¹⁹ But God's truth stands firm like a great rock, and nothing can shake it. It is a foundation stone with these words written on it: "The Lord knows those who are really his," and "A person who calls himself a Christian should not be doing things that

b Literally, "and love that is in Christ Jesus."

are wrong."

²⁰ In a wealthy home there are dishes made of gold and silver as well as some made from wood and clay. The expensive dishes are used for guests, and the cheap ones are used in the kitchen or to put garbage in. ²¹ If you stay away from sin you will be like one of these dishes made of purest gold—the very best in the house—so that Christ himself can use you for his highest purposes.

²² Run from anything that gives you the evil thoughts that young men often have, but stay close to anything that makes you want to do right. Have faith and love, and enjoy the companionship of those who love the Lord and have pure hearts.

²³ Again I say, don't get involved in foolish arguments which only upset people and make them angry. ²⁴ God's people must not be quarrelsome; they must be gentle, patient teachers of those who are wrong. ²⁵ Be humble when you are trying to teach those who are mixed up concerning the truth. For if you talk meekly and courteously to them they are more likely, with God's help, to turn away from their wrong ideas and believe what is true. ²⁶ Then they will come to their senses and escape from Satan's trap of slavery to sin which he uses to catch them whenever he likes, and then they can begin doing the will of God.

3 YOU MAY AS well know this too, Timothy, that in the last days it is going to be very difficult to be a Christian. ² For people will love only themselves and their money; they will be proud and boastful, sneering at God, disobedient to their parents, ungrateful to them, and thoroughly bad. ³ They will be hardheaded and never give in to others; they will be constant liars and troublemakers and will think nothing of immorality. They will be rough and cruel, and sneer at those who try to be good. ⁴ They will betray their friends; they will be hotheaded, puffed up with pride, and prefer good times to worshiping God. ⁵ They will go to church,ᵃ yes, but they won't really believe anything they hear. Don't be taken in by people like that.

⁶ They are the kind who craftily sneak into other people's homes and make friendships with silly, sin-burdened women and teach them their new doctrines. ⁷ Women of that kind are forever following new teachers, but they never understand the truth. ⁸ And these teachers fight truth just as Jannes and Jambres fought against Moses. They have dirty minds, warped and twisted, and have turned against the Christian faith. ⁹ But they won't get away with all this forever. Some day their deceit will be well known to everyone, as was the sin of Jannes and Jambres.

¹⁰ But you know from watching me that I am not that kind of person. You know what I believe and the way I live and what I want. You know my faith in Christ and how I have suffered. You know my love for you, and my patience. ¹¹ You know how many troubles I have had as a result of my preaching the Good News. You know about all that was done to me while I was visiting in Antioch, Iconium and Lystra, but the Lord delivered me. ¹² Yes, and those who decide to please Christ Jesus by living godly lives will suffer at the hands of those who hate him. ¹³ In fact, evil men and false teachers will become worse and worse, deceiving many, they themselves having been deceived by Satan.

¹⁴ But you must keep on believing the things you have been taught. You know they are true for you know that you can trust those of us who have taught you. ¹⁵ You know how, when you were a small child, you were taught the holy Scriptures; and it is these that make you wise to accept God's salvation by trusting in Christ Jesus. ¹⁶ The whole Bibleᵇ was given to us by inspiration from God and is useful to teach us what is true and to make us realize what is wrong in our lives; it straightens us out and helps us do what is right. ¹⁷ It is God's way of making us well prepared at every point, fully equipped to do good to everyone.

4 AND SO I solemnly urge you before God and before Christ Jesus—who will some day judge the living and the dead when he appears to set up his kingdom— ² to preach

---

a Literally, "having a form of godliness."　　b Literally, "Every Scripture."

the Word of God urgently at all times, whenever you get the chance, in season and out, when it is convenient and when it is not. Correct and rebuke your people when they need it, encourage them to do right, and all the time be feeding them patiently with God's Word.

³ For there is going to come a time when people won't listen to the truth, but will go around looking for teachers who will tell them just what they want to hear. ⁴ They won't listen to what the Bible says but will blithely follow their own misguided ideas.

⁵ Stand steady, and don't be afraid of suffering for the Lord. Bring others to Christ. Leave nothing undone that you ought to do.

⁶ I say this because I won't be around to help you very much longer. My time has almost run out. Very soon now I will be on my way to heaven. ⁷ I have fought long and hard for my Lord, and through it all I have kept true to him. And now the time has come for me to stop fighting and rest. ⁸ In heaven a crown is waiting for me which the Lord, the righteous Judge, will give me on that great day of his return. And not just to me, but to all those whose lives show that they are eagerly looking forward to his coming back again.

⁹ Please come as soon as you can, ¹⁰ for Demas has left me. He loved the good things of this life and went to Thessalonica.

Crescens has gone to Galatia, Titus to Dalmatia. ¹¹ Only Luke is with me. Bring Mark with you when you come, for I need him. ¹² (Tychicus is gone too, as I sent him to Ephesus.) ¹³ When you come, be sure to bring the coat I left at Troas with Brother Carpus, and also the books, but especially the parchments.

¹⁴ Alexander the coppersmith has done me much harm. The Lord will punish him, ¹⁵ but be careful of him, for he fought against everything we said.

¹⁶ The first time I was brought before the judge no one was here to help me. Everyone had run away. I hope that they will not be blamed for it. ¹⁷ But the Lord stood with me and gave me the opportunity to boldly preach a whole sermon for all the world to hear. And he saved me from being thrown to the lions.ᵃ ¹⁸ Yes, and the Lord will always deliver me from all evil and will bring me into his heavenly kingdom. To God be the glory forever and ever. Amen.

¹⁹ Please say "hello" for me to Priscilla and Aquila and those living at the home of Onesiphorus. ²⁰ Erastus stayed at Corinth, and I left Trophimus sick at Miletus.

²¹ Do try to be here before winter. Eubulus sends you greetings, and so do Pudens, Linus, Claudia, and all the others. ²² May the Lord Jesus Christ be with your spirit.

Farewell,
Paul

---

a Literally, "I was delivered out of the mouth of the lion."

Meanwhile, off the Field...

Fred (Number 11 in the small photo) not only filled leadership positions in his school, but shared with many others what Christ meant to him. As a result, his teammates Dave and Doug came to Christ, as did many others. As you read this next letter, note that Paul points out that Titus was left on Crete to do a job. Fred was put by God into his high school to do a job. Each of us is placed in some situation—not only to talk about what it means to be involved with Jesus Christ, but to live with him in charge. Notice how Paul refers to phonies who mouth it but don't live it—yet depicts a way of "enthusiasm for doing kind things for others" and "the purity of mind and heart" that can make our youth a time for meaning and reality instead of frustration.

TITUS

1 FROM: PAUL, THE slave of God and the messenger of Jesus Christ.

I have been sent to bring faith to those God has chosen and to teach them to know God's truth—the kind of truth that changes lives—so that they can have eternal life, which God promised them before the world began—and he cannot lie. ³ And now in his own good time he has revealed this Good News and permits me to tell it to everyone. By command of God our Savior I have been trusted to do this work for him.

⁴ *To:* Titus, who is truly my son in the affairs of the Lord.

May God the Father and Christ Jesus our Savior give you his blessings and his peace.

⁵ I left you there on the island of Crete so that you could do whatever was needed to help strengthen each of its churches, and I asked you to appoint pastors[a] in every city who would follow the instructions I gave you. ⁶ The men you choose must be well thought of for their good lives; they must

a More literally, "elders."

have only one wife and their children must love the Lord and not have a reputation for being wild or disobedient to their parents.

[7] These pastors[a] must be men of blameless lives because they are God's ministers. They must not be proud or impatient; they must not be drunkards or fighters or greedy for money. [8] They must enjoy having guests in their homes and must love all that is good. They must be sensible men, and fair. They must be clean minded and level headed. [9] Their belief in the truth which they have been taught must be strong and steadfast, so that they will be able to teach it to others and show those who disagree with them where they are wrong.

[10] For there are many who refuse to obey; this is especially true among those who say that all Christians must obey the Jewish laws. But this is foolish talk; it blinds people to the truth, [11] and it must be stopped. Already whole families have been turned away from the grace of God. Such teachers are only after your money. [12] One of their own men, a prophet from Crete, has said about them, "These men of Crete are all liars; they are like lazy animals, living only to satisfy their stomachs." [13] And this is true. So speak to the Christians there as sternly as necessary to make them strong in the faith, [14] and to stop them from listening to Jewish folk tales and the demands of men who have turned their backs on the truth.

[15] A person who is pure of heart sees goodness and purity in everything; but a person whose own heart is evil and untrusting finds evil in everything, for his dirty mind and rebellious heart color all he sees and hears. [16] Such persons claim they know God, but from seeing the way they act, one knows they don't. They are rotten and disobedient, worthless so far as doing anything good is concerned.

2 BUT AS FOR you, speak up for the right living that goes along with true Christianity. [2] Teach the older men to be serious and unruffled; they must be sensible, knowing and believing the truth and doing everything with love and patience.

[3] Teach the older women to be quiet and respectful in everything they do. They must not go around speaking evil of others and

must not be heavy drinkers, but they should be teachers of goodness. [4] These older women must train the younger women to live quietly, to love their husbands and their children, [5] and to be sensible and clean minded, spending their time in their own homes, being kind and obedient to their husbands, so that the Christian faith can't be spoken against by those who know them.

[6] In the same way, urge the young men to behave carefully, taking life seriously. [7] And here you yourself must be an example to them of good deeds of every kind. Let everything you do reflect your love of the truth and the fact that you are in dead earnest about it. [8] Your conversation should be so sensible and logical that anyone who wants to argue will be ashamed of himself because there won't be anything to criticize in anything you say!

[9] Urge slaves to obey their masters and to try their best to satisfy them. They must not talk back, [10] nor steal, but must show themselves to be entirely trustworthy. In this way they will make people want to believe in our Savior and God.

[11] For the free gift of eternal salvation is now being offered to everyone; [12] and along with this gift comes the realization that God wants us to turn from godless living and sinful pleasures and to live good, God-fearing lives day after day, [13] looking forward to that wonderful time we've been expecting, when his glory shall be seen—the glory of our great God and Savior Jesus Christ. [14] He died under God's judgment against our sins, so that he could rescue us from constant falling into sin and make us his very own people, with cleansed hearts and real enthusiasm for doing kind things for others. [15] You must teach these things and encourage your people to do them, correcting them when necessary as one who has every right to do so. Don't let anyone think that what you say is not important.

3 REMIND YOUR PEOPLE to obey the government and its officers, and always to be obedient and ready for any honest work. [2] They must not speak evil of anyone, nor quarrel, but be gentle and truly courteous to all.

[3] Once we, too, were foolish and

disobedient; we were misled by others and became slaves to many evil pleasures and wicked desires. Our lives were full of resentment and envy. We hated others and they hated us.

⁴ But when the time came for the kindness and love of God our Savior to appear, ⁵ then he saved us—not because we were good enough to be saved, but because of his kindness and pity—by washing away our sins and giving us the new joy of the indwelling Holy Spirit ⁶ whom he poured out upon us with wonderful fullness—and all because of what Jesus Christ our Savior did ⁷ so that he could declare us good in God's eyes—all because of his great kindness; and now we can share in the wealth of the eternal life he gives us, and we are eagerly looking forward to receiving it. ⁸ These things I have told you are all true. Insist on them so that Christians will be careful to do good deeds all the time, for this is not only right, but it brings results.

⁹ Don't get involved in arguing over unanswerable questions and controversial theological ideas; keep out of arguments and quarrels about obedience to Jewish laws, for this kind of thing isn't worthwhile; it only does harm. ¹⁰ If anyone is causing divisions among you, he should be given a first and second warning. After that have nothing more to do with him, ¹¹ for such a person has a wrong sense of values. He is sinning, and he knows it.

¹² I am planning to send either Artemas or Tychicus to you. As soon as one of them arrives, please try to meet me at Nicopolis as quickly as you can, for I have decided to stay there for the winter. ¹³ Do everything you can to help Zenas the lawyer and Apollos with their trip; see that they are given everything they need. ¹⁴ For our people must learn to help all who need their assistance, that their lives will be fruitful.

¹⁵ Everybody here sends greetings. Please say "hello" to all of the Christian friends there. May God's blessings be with you all.

Sincerely,
Paul

Still Prejudiced

Chicanos, blacks and whites ... they all met together in a special forum in Bakersfield, Calif., to discuss minority groups. Their conclusion: each has developed its own proud identity, but whites, including Christian students, are still prejudiced. As a result, some barriers are tougher to crack than ever. All the rhetoric about equality and acceptance needs to be translated into action.

The panelists have each found Christ's love, and the power it has to melt racial tensions. In this very short, dramatic letter to Philemon, we see some principles the Bible lays out about class systems and what our attitudes should be toward people different from us.

PHILEMON

Ron Engh

1 FROM: PAUL, IN jail for preaching the Good News about Jesus Christ, and from Brother Timothy.

To: Philemon, our much loved fellow worker, and to the church that meets in your home, and to Apphia our sister, and to Archippus who like myself is a soldier of the cross.

[3] May God our Father and the Lord Jesus Christ give you his blessings and his peace.

[4] I always thank God when I am praying for you, dear Philemon, [5] because I keep hearing of your love and trust in the Lord Jesus and in his people. [6] And I pray that as you share your faith with others it will grip their lives too, as they see the wealth of good things in you that come from Christ Jesus. [7] I myself have gained much joy and comfort from your love, my brother, because your kindness has so often refreshed the hearts of God's people.

[8,9] Now I want to ask a favor of you. I could demand it of you in the name of Christ because it is the right thing for you to do, but I love you and prefer just to ask you—I, Paul, an old man now, here in jail for the sake of Jesus Christ. [10] My plea is that you show kindness to my child Onesimus, whom I won to the Lord while here in my chains. [11] Onesimus (whose name means "Useful") hasn't been of much use to you in the past, but now he is going to be of real use to both of us. [12] I am sending him back to you, and with him comes my own heart.

[13] I really wanted to keep him here with me while I am in these chains for preaching the Good News, and you would have been helping me through him, [14] but I didn't want to do it without your consent. I didn't want you to be kind because you had to but because you wanted to. [15] Perhaps you could think of it this way: that he ran away

1059

from you for a little while so that now he can be yours forever, ¹⁶ no longer only a slave, but something much better—a beloved brother, especially to me. Now he will mean much more to you too, because he is not only a servant but also your brother in Christ.

¹⁷ If I am really your friend, give him the same welcome you would give to me if I were the one who was coming. ¹⁸ If he has harmed you in any way or stolen anything from you, charge me for it. ¹⁹ I will pay it back (I, Paul, personally guarantee this by writing it here with my own hand) but I won't mention how much you owe me! The fact is, you even owe me your very soul!

²⁰ Yes, dear brother, give me joy with this loving act and my weary heart will praise the Lord.

²¹ I've written you this letter because I am positive that you will do what I ask and even more!

²² Please keep a guest room ready for me, for I am hoping that God will answer your prayers and let me come to you soon.

²³ Epaphras my fellow prisoner, who is also here for preaching Christ Jesus, sends you his greetings. ²⁴ So do Mark, Aristarchus, Demas and Luke, my fellow workers.

²⁵ The blessings of our Lord Jesus Christ be upon your spirit.

Paul

Bob Combs

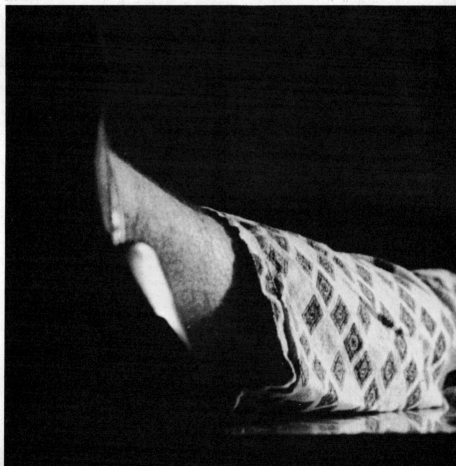

A Guy Could Get a Headache!

Books, tests, studies, philosophies, everybody's believing different things, and a thousand shades of meanings. How does it all fit? How can we piece it all together? Consider this first chapter which indicates where we can get authoritative answers. This book explained to the Jews of that day underlying granite-boulders of truth, which are just as valid today—as are the comments about putting this truth into action.

HEBREWS

1 LONG AGO GOD spoke in many different ways to our fathers through the prophets [in visions, dreams, and even face to face[a]], telling them little by little about his plans.

[2] But now in these days he has spoken to us through his Son to whom he has given everything, and through whom he made the world and everything there is.

[3] God's Son shines out with God's glory, and all that God's Son is and does marks him as God. He regulates the universe by the mighty power of his command. He is the one who died to cleanse us and clear our record of all sin, and then sat down in highest honor beside the great God of heaven.

[4] Thus he became far greater than the angels, as proved by the fact that his name "Son of God," which was passed on to him from his Father, is far greater than the names and titles of the angels. [5,6] For God never said to any angel, "You are my Son, and today I have given you the honor that goes with that name."[b] But God said it about Jesus. Another time he said, "I am his Father and he is my Son." And still another time—when his firstborn Son came to earth—God said, "Let all the angels of God worship him."

[7] God speaks of his angels as messengers swift as the wind and as servants made of flaming fire; [8] but of his Son he says, "Your kingdom, O God, will last forever and ever; its commands are always just and right. [9] You love right and hate wrong; so God, even your God, has poured out more gladness upon you than on anyone else."

[10] God also called him "Lord" when he said, "Lord, in the beginning you made the earth, and the heavens are the work of your hands. [11] They will disappear into nothingness, but you will remain forever. They will become worn out like old clothes, [12] and some day you will fold them up and replace them. But you yourself will never change, and your years will never end."

[13] And did God ever say to an angel, as he does to his Son, "Sit here beside me in honor until I crush all your enemies beneath your feet"?

[14] No, for the angels are only spirit-messengers sent out to help and care for those who are to receive his salvation.

2 SO WE MUST listen very carefully to the truths we have heard, or we may drift away from them. [2] For since the messages from angels have always proved true and

---

a Implied.   b Literally, "this day I have begotten you."

people have always been punished for disobeying them, [3] what makes us think that we can escape if we are indifferent to this great salvation announced by the Lord Jesus himself, and passed on to us by those who heard him speak?

[4] God always has shown us that these messages are true by signs and wonders and various miracles and by giving certain special abilities from the Holy Spirit to those who believe; yes, God has assigned such gifts to each of us.

[5] And the future world we are talking about will not be controlled by angels. [6] No, for in the book of Psalms David says to God, "What is mere man that you are so concerned about him? And who is this Son of Man you honor so highly? [7] For though you made him lower than the angels for a little while, now you have crowned him with glory and honor. [8] And you have put him in complete charge of everything there is. Nothing is left out."

We have not yet seen all of this take place, [9] but we do see Jesus—who for awhile was a little lower than the angels—crowned now by God with glory and honor because he suffered death for us. Yes, because of God's great kindness, Jesus tasted death for everyone in all the world. [10] And it was right and proper that God, who made everything for his own glory, should allow Jesus to suffer, for in doing this he was bringing vast multitudes of God's people to heaven; for his suffering made Jesus a perfect Leader, one fit to bring them into their salvation.

[11] We who have been made holy by Jesus, now have the same Father he has. That is why Jesus is not ashamed to call us his brothers. [12] For he says in the book of Psalms, "I will talk to my brothers about God my Father, and together we will sing his praises." [13] At another time he said, "I will put my trust in God along with my brothers." And at still another time, "See, here am I and the children God gave me."

[14] Since we, God's children, are human beings—made of flesh and blood—he became flesh and blood too by being born in human form; for only as a human being could he die and in dying break the power of the devil who had the power of death. [15] Only in that way could he deliver those who through fear of death have been living all their lives as slaves to constant dread.

[16] We all know he did not come as an angel but as a human being—yes, a Jew. [17] And it was necessary for Jesus to be like us, his brothers, so that he could be our merciful and faithful High Priest before God, a Priest who would be both merciful to us and faithful to God in dealing with the sins of the people. [18] For since he himself has now been through suffering and temptation, he knows what it is like when we suffer and are tempted, and he is wonderfully able to help us.

3 THEREFORE, DEAR BROTHERS whom God has set apart for himself—you who are chosen for heaven—I want you to think now about this Jesus who is God's Messenger and the High Priest of our faith.

[2] For Jesus was faithful to God who appointed him High Priest, just as Moses also faithfully served in God's house. [3] But Jesus has far more glory than Moses, just as a man who builds a fine house gets more praise than his house does. [4] And many people can build houses, but only God made everything.

[5] Well, Moses did a fine job working in God's house, but he was only a servant; and his work was mostly to illustrate and suggest those things that would happen later on. [6] But Christ, God's faithful Son, is in complete charge of God's house. And we Christians are God's house—he lives in us! —if we keep up our courage firm to the end, and our joy and our trust in the Lord.

[7,8] And since Christ is so much superior, the Holy Spirit warns us to listen to him, to be careful to hear his voice today and not let our hearts become set against him, as the people of Israel did. They steeled themselves against his love and complained against him in the desert while he was testing them. [9] But God was patient with them forty years, though they tried his patience sorely; he kept right on doing his mighty miracles for them to see. [10] "But," God says, "I was very angry with them, for their hearts were always looking somewhere else instead of up to me, and they never found the paths I wanted them to follow."

[11] Then God, full of this anger against

them, bound himself with an oath that he would never let them come to his place of rest.

¹² Beware then of your own hearts, dear brothers, lest you find that they, too, are evil and unbelieving and are leading you away from the living God. ¹³ Speak to each other about these things every day while there is still time, so that none of you will become hardened against God, being blinded by the glamor^a of sin. ¹⁴ For if we are faithful to the end, trusting God just as we did when we first became Christians, we will share in all that belongs to Christ.

¹⁵ But *now* is the time. Never forget the warning, *"Today* if you hear God's voice speaking to you, do not harden your hearts against him, as the people of Israel did when they rebelled against him in the desert."

¹⁶ And who were those people I speak of, who heard God's voice speaking to them but then rebelled against him? They were the ones who came out of Egypt with Moses their leader. ¹⁷ And who was it who made God angry for all those forty years? These same people who sinned and as a result died in the wilderness. ¹⁸ And to whom was God speaking when he swore with an oath that they could never go into the land he had promised his people? He was speaking to all those who disobeyed him. ¹⁹ And why couldn't they go in? Because they didn't trust him.

4 ALTHOUGH GOD'S PROMISE still stands—his promise that all may enter his place of rest—we ought to tremble with fear because some of you may be on the verge of failing to get there after all. ² For this wonderful news—the message that God wants to save us—has been given to us just as it was to those who lived in the time of Moses. But it didn't do them any good because they didn't believe it. They didn't mix it with faith. ³ For only we who believe God can enter into his place of rest. He has said, "I have sworn in my anger that those who don't believe me will never get in," even though he has been ready and waiting for them since the world began.

⁴ We know he is ready and waiting be-

cause it is written that God rested on the seventh day of creation, having finished all that he had planned to make.

⁵ Even so they didn't get in, for God finally said, "They shall never enter my rest." ⁶ Yet the promise remains and some get in—but not those who had the first chance, for they disobeyed God and failed to enter.

⁷ But he has set another time for coming in, and that time is now. He announced this through King David long years after man's first failure to enter, saying in the words already quoted, "Today when you hear him calling, do not harden your hearts against him."

⁸ This new place of rest he is talking about does not mean the land of Israel that Joshua led them into. If that were what God meant, he would not have spoken long afterwards about "today" being the time to get in. ⁹ So there is a full complete rest *still waiting* for the people of God. ¹⁰ Christ has already entered there. He is resting from his work, just as God did after the creation. ¹¹ Let us do our best to go into that place of rest, too, being careful not to disobey God as the children of Israel did, thus failing to get in.

¹² For whatever God says to us is full of living power: it is sharper than the sharpest dagger, cutting swift and deep into our innermost thoughts and desires with all their parts, exposing us for what we really are. ¹³ He knows about everyone, everywhere. Everything about us is bare and wide open to the all-seeing eyes of our living God; nothing can be hidden from him to whom we must explain all that we have done.

¹⁴ But Jesus the Son of God is our great High Priest who has gone to heaven itself to help us; therefore let us never stop trusting him. ¹⁵ This High Priest of ours understands our weaknesses, since he had the same temptations we do, though he never once gave way to them and sinned. ¹⁶ So let us come boldly to the very throne of God and stay there to receive his mercy and to find grace to help us in our times of need.

5 THE JEWISH HIGH priest is merely a man like anyone else, but he is chosen

---

a Literally, "deceitfulness."

to speak for all other men in their dealings with God. He presents their gifts to God and offers to him the blood of animals that are sacrificed to cover the sins of the people and his own sins too. And because he is a man he can deal gently with other men, though they are foolish and ignorant, for he, too, is surrounded with the same temptations and understands their problems very well.

⁴ Another thing to remember is that no one can be a high priest just because he wants to be. He has to be called by God for this work in the same way God chose Aaron.

⁵ That is why Christ did not elect himself to the honor of being High Priest; no, he was chosen by God. God said to him, "My Son, today I have honored[a] you." ⁶ And another time God said to him, "You have been chosen to be a priest forever, with the same rank as Melchizedek."

⁷ Yet while Christ was here on earth he pleaded with God, praying with tears and agony of soul to the only one who would save him from [premature[b]] death. And God heard his prayers because of his strong desire to obey God at all times.

⁸ And even though Jesus was God's Son, he had to learn from experience what it was like to obey, when obeying meant suffering. ⁹ It was after he had proved himself perfect in this experience that Jesus became the Giver of eternal salvation to all those who obey him. ¹⁰ For remember that God has chosen him to be a High Priest with the same rank as Melchizedek.

¹¹ There is much more I would like to say along these lines, but you don't seem to listen, so it's hard to make you understand. ¹²,¹³ You have been Christians a long time now, and you ought to be teaching others, but instead you have dropped back to the place where you need someone to teach you all over again the very first principles in God's Word. You are like babies who can drink only milk, not old enough for solid food. And when a person is still living on milk it shows he isn't very far along in the Christian life, and doesn't know much about the difference between right and wrong. He is still a baby-Christian! ¹⁴ You will never be able to eat solid spiritual food and understand the deeper things of God's Word until you become better Christians and learn right from wrong by practicing doing right.

6 LET US STOP going over the same old ground again and again, always teaching those first lessons about Christ. Let us go on instead to other things and become mature in our understanding, as strong Christians ought to be. Surely we don't need to speak further about the foolishness of trying to be saved by being good, or about the necessity of faith in God; ² you don't need further instruction about baptism and spiritual gifts[a] and the resurrection of the dead and eternal judgment.

³ The Lord willing, we will go on now to other things.

⁴ There is no use trying to bring you back to the Lord again if you have once understood the Good News and tasted for yourself the good things of heaven and shared in the Holy Spirit, ⁵ and know how good the Word of God is, and felt the mighty powers of the world to come, ⁶ and then have turned against God. You cannot bring yourself to repent again if you have nailed the Son of God to the cross again by rejecting him, holding him up to mocking and to public shame.

⁷ When a farmer's land has had many showers upon it and good crops come up,

---

a Literally, "begotten you." Probably the reference is to the day of Christ's resurrection.
b Implied. Christ's longing was to live until he could die on the cross for all mankind. There is a strong case to be made that Satan's great desire was that Christ should die prematurely, before the mighty work at the cross could be performed. Christ's body, being human, was frail and weak like ours (except that his was sinless). He had said just a few moments before, "My soul is exceeding sorrowful *unto death.*" And can a human body live long under such pressure of spirit as he underwent in the Garden, that caused sweating of great drops of blood? But God graciously heard and answered his anguished cry in Gethsemane ("Let this cup pass from me") and preserved him from seemingly imminent and premature death: for an angel was sent to strengthen him so that he could live to accomplish God's perfect will at the cross. . . . But some readers may prefer the explanation that Christ's plea was that he be saved *out from* death, at the Resurrection.   6a Literally, "the laying on of hands."

that land has experienced God's blessing upon it. [8] But if it keeps on having crops of thistles and thorns, the land is considered no good and is ready for condemnation and burning off.

[9] Dear friends, even though I am talking like this I really don't believe that what I am saying applies to you. I am confident you are producing the good fruit that comes along with your salvation. [10] For God is not unfair. How can he forget your hard work for him, or forget the way you used to show your love for him—and still do—by helping his children? [11] And we are anxious that you keep right on loving others as long as life lasts, so that you will get your full reward. [12] Then, knowing what lies ahead for you, you won't become bored with being a Christian, nor become spiritually dull and indifferent, but you will be anxious to follow the example of those who receive all that God has promised them because of their strong faith and patience.

[13] For instance, there was God's promise to Abraham: God took an oath in his own name, since there was no one greater to swear by, [14] that he would bless Abraham again and again, and give him a son and make him the father of a great nation of people. [15] Then Abraham waited patiently until finally God gave him a son, Isaac, just as he had promised.

[16] When a man takes an oath, he is calling upon someone greater than himself to force him to do what he has promised, or to punish him if he later refuses to do it; the oath ends all argument about it. [17] God also bound himself with an oath, so that those he promised to help would be perfectly sure and never need to wonder whether he might change his plans.

[18] He has given us both his promise and his oath, two things we can completely count on, for it is impossible for God to tell a lie. Now all those who flee to him to save them can take new courage when they hear such assurances from God; now they can know without doubt that he will give them the salvation he has promised them.

[19] This certain hope of being saved is a strong and trustworthy anchor for our souls, connecting us with God himself behind the sacred curtains of heaven, [20] where Christ has gone ahead to plead for us from his position as[b] our High Priest, with the honor and rank of Melchizedek.

7 THIS MELCHIZEDEK WAS king of the city of Salem, and also a priest of the Most High God. When Abraham was returning home after winning a great battle against many kings, Melchizedek met him and blessed him; [2] then Abraham took a tenth of all he had won in the battle and gave it to Melchizedek.

Melchizedek's name means "Justice," so he is the King of Justice; and he is also the King of Peace because of the name of his city, Salem, which means "Peace." [3] Melchizedek had no father or mother[a] and there is no record of any of his ancestors. He was never born and he never died but his life is like that of the Son of God—a priest forever.

[4] See then how great this Melchizedek is:

(a) Even Abraham, the first and most honored of all God's chosen people, gave Melchizedek a tenth of the spoils he took from the kings he had been fighting. [5] One could understand why Abraham would do this if Melchizedek had been a Jewish priest, for later on God's people were required by law to give gifts to help their priests because the priests were their relatives. [6] But Melchizedek was not a relative, and yet Abraham paid him.

(b) Melchizedek placed a blessing upon mighty Abraham, [7] and as everyone knows, a person who has the power to bless is always greater than the person he blesses.

[8] (c) The Jewish priests, though mortal, received tithes; but we are told that Melchizedek lives on.

[9] (d) One might even say that Levi himself (the ancestor of all Jewish priests, of all who receive tithes), paid tithes to Melchizedek through Abraham. [10] For although Levi wasn't born yet, the seed from which he came was in Abraham when Abraham paid the tithes to Melchizedek.

---

b Literally, "having become our High Priest."   7a No one can be sure whether this means that Melchizedek was Christ appearing to Abraham in human form, or simply that there is no *record* of who Melchizedek's father or mother were, no *record* of his birth or death.

[11] (*e*) If the Jewish priests and their laws had been able to save us, why then did God need to send Christ as a priest with the rank of Melchizedek, instead of sending someone with the rank of Aaron—the same rank all other priests had?

[12,13,14] And when God sends a new kind of priest, his law must be changed to permit it. As we all know, Christ did not belong to the priest-tribe of Levi, but came from the tribe of Judah, which had not been chosen for priesthood; Moses had never given them that work. [15] So we can plainly see that God's method changed, for Christ, the new High Priest who came with the rank of Melchizedek, [16] did not become a priest by meeting the old requirement of belonging to the tribe of Levi, but on the basis of power flowing from a life that cannot end. [17] And the Psalmist points this out when he says of Christ, "You are a priest forever with the rank of Melchizedek."

[18] Yes, the old system of priesthood based on family lines was canceled because it didn't work. It was weak and useless for saving people. [19] It never made anyone really right with God. But now we have a far better hope, for Christ makes us acceptable to God, and now we may draw near to him.

[20] God took an oath that Christ would always be a Priest, [21] although he never said that of other priests. Only to Christ he said, "The Lord has sworn and will never change his mind: You are a Priest forever, with the rank of Melchizedek." [22] Because of God's oath, Christ can guarantee forever the success of this new and better arrangement.

[23] Under the old arrangement there had to be many priests, so that when the older ones died off, the system could still be carried on by others who took their places.

[24] But Jesus lives forever and continues to be a Priest so that no one else is needed. [25] He is able to save completely all who come to God through him. Since he will live forever, he will always be there to remind God that he has paid for their sins with his blood.

[26] He is, therefore, exactly the kind of High Priest we need; for he is holy and blameless, unstained by sin, undefiled by sinners, and to him has been given the place

of honor in heaven. [27] He never needs the daily blood of animal sacrifices, as other priests did, to cover over first their own sins and then the sins of the people; for he finished all sacrifices, once and for all, when he sacrificed himself on the cross. [28] Under the old system, even the high priests were weak and sinful men who could not keep from doing wrong, but later God appointed by his oath his Son who is perfect forever.

8 WHAT WE ARE saying is this: Christ, whose priesthood we have just described, is our High Priest, and is in heaven at the place of greatest honor next to God himself. [2] He ministers in the temple in heaven, the true place of worship built by the Lord and not by human hands.

[3] And since every high priest is appointed to offer gifts and sacrifices, Christ must make an offering too. [4] The sacrifice he offers is far better than those offered by the earthly priests. (But even so, if he were here on earth he wouldn't even be permitted to be a priest, because down here the priests still follow the old Jewish system of sacrifices.) [5] Their work is connected with a mere earthly model of the real tabernacle in heaven; for when Moses was getting ready to build the tabernacle, God warned him to follow exactly the pattern of the heavenly tabernacle as shown to him on Mount Sinai. [6] But Christ, as a Minister in heaven, has been rewarded with a far more important work than those who serve under the old laws, because the new agreement which he passes on to us from God contains far more wonderful promises.

[7] The old agreement didn't even work. If it had, there would have been no need for another to replace it. [8] But God himself found fault with the old one, for he said, "The day will come when I will make a new agreement with the people of Israel and the people of Judah. [9] This new agreement will not be like the old one I gave to their fathers on the day when I took them by the hand to lead them out of the land of Egypt; they did not keep their part in that agreement, so I had to cancel it. [10] But this is the new agreement I will make with the people of Israel, says the Lord: I will write my laws in their minds so that they will know what

I want them to do without my even telling them, and these laws will be in their hearts so that they will want to obey them, and I will be their God and they shall be my people. ¹¹ And no one then will need to speak to his friend or neighbor or brother, saying, 'You, too, should know the Lord,' because everyone, great and small, will know me already. ¹² And I will be merciful to them in their wrongdoings, and I will remember their sins no more."

¹³ God speaks of these new promises, of this new agreement, as taking the place of the old one; for the old one is out of date now and has been put aside forever.

9 NOW IN THAT first agreement between God and his people there were rules for worship and there was a sacred tent down here on earth. Inside this place of worship there were two rooms. The first one contained the golden candlestick and a table with special loaves of holy bread upon it; this part was called the Holy Place. ³ Then there was a curtain and behind the curtain was a room called the Holy of Holies. ⁴ In that room there were a golden incense-altar and the golden chest, called the ark of the covenant, completely covered on all sides with pure gold. Inside the ark were the tablets of stone with the Ten Commandments written on them, and a golden jar with some manna in it, and Aaron's wooden cane that budded. ⁵ Above the golden chest were statues of angels called the cherubim—the guardians of God's glory—with their wings stretched out over the ark's golden cover, called the mercy seat. But enough of such details.

⁶ Well, when all was ready the priests went in and out of the first room whenever they wanted to, doing their work. ⁷ But only the high priest went into the inner room, and then only once a year, all alone, and always with blood which he sprinkled on the mercy seat as an offering to God to cover his own mistakes and sins, and the mistakes and sins of all the people.

⁸ And the Holy Spirit uses all this to point out to us that under the old system the common people could not go into the Holy of Holies as long as the outer room and the entire system it represents were still in use.

⁹ This has an important lesson for us today. For under the old system, gifts and sacrifices were offered, but these failed to cleanse the hearts of the people who brought them. ¹⁰ For the old system dealt only with certain rituals—what foods to eat and drink, rules for washing themselves, and rules about this and that. The people had to keep these rules to tide them over until Christ came with God's new and better way.

¹¹ He came as High Priest of this better system which we now have. He went into that greater, perfect tabernacle in heaven, not made by men nor part of this world, ¹² and once for all took blood into that inner room, the Holy of Holies, and sprinkled it on the mercy seat; but it was not the blood of goats and calves. No, he took his own blood, and with it he, by himself, made sure of our eternal salvation.

¹³ And if under the old system the blood of bulls and goats and the ashes of young cows could cleanse men's bodies from sin, ¹⁴ just think how much more surely the blood of Christ will transform our lives and hearts. His sacrifice frees us from the worry of having to obey the old rules, and makes us want to serve the living God. For by the help of the eternal Holy Spirit, Christ willingly gave himself to God to die for our sins—he being perfect, without a single sin or fault. ¹⁵ Christ came with this new agreement so that all who are invited may come and have forever all the wonders God has promised them. For Christ died to rescue them from the penalty of the sins they had committed while still under that old system.

¹⁶ Now, if someone dies and leaves a will—a list of things to be given away to certain people when he dies—no one gets anything until it is proved that the person who wrote the will is dead. ¹⁷ The will goes into effect only after the death of the person who wrote it. While he is still alive no one can use it to get any of those things he has promised them.

¹⁸ That is why blood was sprinkled [as

proof of Christ's death[a]] before even the first agreement could go into effect. [19] For after Moses had given the people all of God's laws, he took the blood of calves and goats, along with water, and sprinkled the blood over the book of God's laws and over all the people, using branches of hyssop bushes and scarlet wool to sprinkle with. [20] Then he said, "This is the blood that marks the beginning of the agreement between you and God, the agreement God commanded me to make with you." [21] And in the same way he sprinkled blood on the sacred tent and on whatever instruments were used for worship. [22] In fact we can say that under the old agreement almost everything was cleansed by sprinkling it with blood, and without the shedding of blood there is no forgiveness of sins.

[23] That is why the sacred tent down here on earth, and everything in it—all copied from things in heaven—all had to be made pure by Moses in this way, by being sprinkled with the blood of animals. But the real things in heaven, of which these down here are copies, were made pure with far more precious offerings.

[24] For Christ has entered into heaven itself, to appear now before God as our Friend. It was not in the earthly place of worship that he did this, for that was merely a copy of the real temple in heaven. [25] Nor has he offered himself again and again, as the high priest down here on earth offers animal blood in the Holy of Holies each year. [26] If that had been necessary, then he would have had to die again and again, ever since the world began. But no! He came once for all, at the end of the age, to put away the power of sin forever by dying for us.

[27] And just as it is destined that men die only once, and after that comes judgment, [28] so also Christ died only once as an offering for the sins of many people; and he will come again, but not to deal again with our sins.

This time he will come bringing salvation to all those who are eagerly and patiently waiting for him.

10 THE OLD SYSTEM of Jewish laws gave only a dim foretaste of the good things Christ would do for us. The sacrifices under the old system were repeated again and again, year after year, but even so they could never save those who lived under their rules. [2] If they could have, one offering would have been enough; the worshipers would have been cleansed once for all, and their feeling of guilt would be gone.

[3] But just the opposite happened: those yearly sacrifices reminded them of their disobedience and guilt instead of relieving their minds. [4] For it is not possible for the blood of bulls and goats really to take away sins.[a]

[5] That is why Christ said, as he came into the world, "O God, the blood of bulls and goats cannot satisfy you, so you have made ready this body of mine for me to lay as a sacrifice upon your altar. [6] You were not satisfied with the animal sacrifices, slain and burnt before you as offerings for sin. [7] Then I said, 'See, I have come to do your will, to lay down my life, just as the Scriptures said that I would.' "

[8] After Christ said this, about not being satisfied with the various sacrifices and offerings required under the old system, [9] he then added, "Here I am. I have come to give my life."

He cancels the first system in favor of a far better one. [10] Under this new plan we have been forgiven and made clean by Christ's dying for us once and for all. [11] Under the old agreement the priests stood before the altar day after day offering sacrifices that could never take away our sins. [12] But Christ gave himself to God for our sins as one sacrifice for all time, and then sat down in the place of highest honor at God's right hand, [13] waiting for his enemies to be laid under his feet. [14] For by that one offering he made forever perfect in the sight of God all those whom he is making holy.

[15] And the Holy Spirit testifies that this is so, for he has said, [16] "This is the agreement I will make with the people of Israel, though they broke their first agreement: I will write my laws into their minds so that

---

a Implied.   **10** a The blood of bulls and goats merely covered over the sins, taking them out of sight for hundreds of years until Jesus Christ came to die on the cross. There he gave his own blood which forever took those sins away.

they will always know my will, and I will put my laws in their hearts so that they will want to obey them." [17] And then he adds, "I will never again remember their sins and lawless deeds."

[18] Now, when sins have once been forever forgiven and forgotten, there is no need to offer more sacrifices to get rid of them. [19] And so, dear brothers, now we may walk right into the very Holy of Holies where God is, because of the blood of Jesus. [20] This is the fresh, new, life-giving way which Christ has opened up for us by tearing the curtain—his human body—to let us into the holy presence of God.

[21] And since this great High Priest of ours rules over God's household, [22] let us go right in, to God himself, with true hearts fully trusting him to receive us, because we have been sprinkled with Christ's blood to make us clean, and because our bodies have been washed with pure water.

[23] Now we can look forward to the salvation God has promised us. There is no longer any room for doubt, and we can tell others that salvation is ours, for there is no question that he will do what he says.

[24] In response to all he has done for us, let us outdo each other in being helpful and kind to each other and in doing good.

[25] Let us not neglect our church meetings, as some people do, but encourage and warn each other, especially now that the day of his coming back again is drawing near.

[26] If anyone sins deliberately by rejecting the Savior after knowing the truth of forgiveness, this sin is not covered by Christ's death; there is no way to get rid of it. [27] There will be nothing to look forward to but the terrible punishment of God's awful anger which will consume all his enemies. [28] A man who refused to obey the laws given by Moses was killed without mercy if there were two or three witnesses to his sin. [29] Think how much more terrible the punishment will be for those who have trampled underfoot the Son of God and treated his cleansing blood as though it were common and unhallowed, and insulted and outraged the Holy Spirit who brings God's

mercy to his people.

[30] For we know him who said, "Justice belongs to me; I will repay them"; who also said, "The Lord himself will handle these cases." [31] It is a fearful thing to fall into the hands of the living God.

[32] Don't ever forget those wonderful days when you first learned about Christ. Remember how you kept right on with the Lord even though it meant terrible suffering. [33] Sometimes you were laughed at and beaten, and sometimes you watched and sympathized with others suffering the same things. [34] You suffered with those thrown into jail, and you were actually joyful when all you owned was taken from you, knowing that better things were awaiting you in heaven, things that would be yours forever.

[35] Do not let this happy trust in the Lord die away, no matter what happens. Remember your reward! [36] You need to keep on patiently doing God's will if you want him to do for you all that he has promised. [37] His coming will not be delayed much longer. [38] And those whose faith has made them good in God's sight must live by faith, trusting him in everything. Otherwise, if they shrink back, God will have no pleasure in them.

[39] But we have never turned our backs on God and sealed our fate. No, our faith in him assures our souls' salvation.

11 WHAT IS FAITH? It is the confident assurance that something we want is going to happen. It is the certainty that what we hope for is waiting for us, even though we cannot see it up ahead. [2] Men of God in days of old were famous for their faith.

[3] By faith—by believing God—we know that the world and the stars—in fact, all things—were made at God's command; and that they were all made from things that can't be seen.[a]

[4] It was by faith that Abel obeyed God and brought an offering that pleased God more than Cain's offering did. God accepted Abel and proved it by accepting his gift; and though Abel is long dead, we can still learn lessons from him about trusting

a Perhaps the reference is to atoms, electrons, etc.

God.

⁵ Enoch trusted God too, and that is why God took him away to heaven without dying; suddenly he was gone because God took him. Before this happened God had said[b] how pleased he was with Enoch. ⁶ You can never please God without faith, without depending on him. Anyone who wants to come to God must believe that there is a God and that he rewards those who sincerely look for him.

⁷ Noah was another who trusted God. When he heard God's warning about the future, Noah believed him even though there was then no sign of a flood, and wasting no time, he built the ark and saved his family. Noah's belief in God was in direct contrast to the sin and disbelief of the rest of the world—which refused to obey—and because of his faith he became one of those whom God has accepted.

⁸ Abraham trusted God, and when God told him to leave home and go far away to another land which he promised to give him, Abraham obeyed. Away he went, not even knowing where he was going. ⁹ And even when he reached God's promised land, he lived in tents like a mere visitor, as did Isaac and Jacob, to whom God gave the same promise. ¹⁰ Abraham did this because he was confidently waiting for God to bring him to that strong heavenly city whose designer and builder is God.

¹¹ Sarah, too, had faith, and because of this she was able to become a mother in spite of her old age, for she realized that God, who gave her his promise, would certainly do what he said. ¹² And so a whole nation came from Abraham, who was too old to have even one child—a nation with so many millions of people that, like the stars of the sky and the sand on the ocean shores, there is no way to count them.

¹³ These men of faith I have mentioned died without ever receiving all that God had promised them; but they saw it all awaiting them on ahead and were glad, for they agreed that this earth was not their real home but that they were just strangers visiting down here. ¹⁴ And quite obviously when they talked like that, they were looking forward to their real home in heaven.

¹⁵ If they had wanted to, they could have gone back to the good things of this world. ¹⁶ But they didn't want to. They were living for heaven. And now God is not ashamed to be called their God, for he has made a heavenly city for them.

¹⁷ While God was testing him, Abraham still trusted in God and his promises, and so he offered up his son Isaac, and was ready to slay him on the altar of sacrifice; ¹⁸ yes, to slay even Isaac, through whom God had promised to give Abraham a whole nation of descendants! ¹⁹ He believed that if Isaac died God would bring him back to life again; and that is just about what happened, for as far as Abraham was concerned, Isaac was doomed to death, but he came back again alive! ²⁰ It was by faith that Isaac knew God would give future blessings to his two sons, Jacob and Esau.

²¹ By faith Jacob, when he was old and dying, blessed each of Joseph's two sons as he stood and prayed, leaning on the top of his cane.

²² And it was by faith that Joseph, as he neared the end of his life, confidently spoke of God bringing the people of Israel out of Egypt; and he was so sure of it that he made them promise to carry his bones with them when they left!

²³ Moses' parents had faith too. When they saw that God had given them an unusual child, they trusted that God would save him from the death the king commanded, and they hid him for three months, and were not afraid.

²⁴,²⁵ It was by faith that Moses, when he grew up, refused to be treated as the grandson of the king, but chose to share ill-treatment with God's people instead of enjoying the fleeting pleasures of sin. ²⁶ He thought that it was better to suffer for the promised Christ than to own all the treasures of Egypt, for he was looking forward to the great reward that God would give him. ²⁷ And it was because he trusted God that he left the land of Egypt and wasn't afraid of the king's anger. Moses kept right on going; it seemed as though he could see God right there with him. ²⁸ And it was because

---

b Implied.

he believed God would save his people that he commanded them to kill a lamb as God had told them to and sprinkle the blood on the doorposts of their homes, so that God's terrible Angel of Death could not touch the oldest child in those homes, as he did among the Egyptians.

²⁹ The people of Israel trusted God and went right through the Red Sea as though they were on dry ground. But when the Egyptians chasing them tried it, they all were drowned.

³⁰ It was faith that brought the walls of Jericho tumbling down after the people of Israel had walked around them seven days, as God had commanded them. ³¹ By faith —because she believed in God and his power—Rahab the harlot did not die with all the others in her city when they refused to obey God, for she gave a friendly welcome to the spies.

³² Well, how much more do I need to say? It would take too long to recount the stories of the faith of Gideon and Barak and Samson and Jephthah and David and Samuel and all the other prophets. ³³ These people all trusted God and as a result won battles, overthrew kingdoms, ruled their people well, and received what God had promised them; they were kept from harm in a den of lions, ³⁴ and in a fiery furnace. Some, through their faith, escaped death by the sword. Some were made strong again after they had been weak or sick. Others were given great power in battle; they made whole armies turn and run away. ³⁵ And some women, through faith, received their loved ones back again from death. But others trusted God and were beaten to death, preferring to die rather than turn from God and be free—trusting that they would rise to a better life afterwards.

³⁶ Some were laughed at and their backs cut open with whips, and others were chained in dungeons. ³⁷,³⁸ Some died by stoning and some by being sawed in two; others were promised freedom if they would renounce their faith, then were killed with the sword. Some went about in skins of sheep and goats, wandering over deserts and mountains, hiding in dens and caves. They were hungry and sick and ill-treated—too good for this world. ³⁹ And

these men of faith, though they trusted God and won his approval, none of them received all that God had promised them; ⁴⁰ for God wanted them to wait and share the even better rewards that were prepared for us.

12 SINCE WE HAVE such a huge crowd of men of faith watching us from the grandstands, let us strip off anything that slows us down or holds us back, and especially those sins that wrap themselves so tightly around our feet and trip us up; and let us run with patience the particular race that God has set before us.

² Keep your eyes on Jesus, our leader and instructor. He was willing to die a shameful death on the cross because of the joy he knew would be his afterwards; and now he sits in the place of honor by the throne of God. ³ If you want to keep from becoming fainthearted and weary, think about his patience as sinful men did such terrible things to him. ⁴ After all, you have never yet struggled against sin and temptation until you sweat great drops of blood.

⁵ And have you quite forgotten the encouraging words God spoke to you, his child? He said, "My son, don't be angry when the Lord punishes you. Don't be discouraged when he has to show you where you are wrong. ⁶ For when he punishes you, it proves that he loves you. When he whips you it proves you are really his child."

⁷ Let God train you, for he is doing what any loving father does for his children. Whoever heard of a son who was never corrected? ⁸ If God doesn't punish you when you need it, as other fathers punish their sons, then it means that you aren't really God's son at all—that you don't really belong in his family. ⁹ Since we respect our fathers here on earth, though they punish us, should we not all the more cheerfully submit to God's training so that we can begin really to live?

¹⁰ Our earthly fathers trained us for a few brief years, doing the best for us that they knew how, but God's correction is always right and for our best good, that we may share his holiness. ¹¹ Being punished isn't enjoyable while it is happening—it hurts! But afterwards we can see the result, a quiet

growth in grace and character.

¹² So take a new grip with your tired hands, stand firm on your shaky legs, ¹³ and mark out a straight, smooth path for your feet so that those who follow you, though weak and lame, will not fall and hurt themselves, but become strong.

¹⁴ Try to stay out of all quarrels and seek to live a clean and holy life, for one who is not holy will not see the Lord. ¹⁵ Look after each other so that not one of you will fail to find God's best blessings. Watch out that no bitterness takes root among you, for as it springs up it causes deep trouble, hurting many in their spiritual lives. ¹⁶ Watch out that no one becomes involved in sexual sin or becomes careless about God as Esau did: he traded his rights as the oldest son for a single meal. ¹⁷ And afterwards, when he wanted those rights back again, it was too late, even though he wept bitter tears of repentance. So remember, and be careful.

¹⁸ You have not had to stand face to face with terror, flaming fire, gloom, darkness and a terrible storm, as the Israelites did at Mount Sinai when God gave them his laws. ¹⁹ For there was an awesome trumpet blast, and a voice with a message so terrible that the people begged God to stop speaking. ²⁰ They staggered back under God's command that if even an animal touched the mountain it must die. ²¹ Moses himself was so frightened at the sight that he shook with terrible fear.

²² But you have come right up into Mount Zion, to the city of the living God, the heavenly Jerusalem, and to the gathering of countless happy angels; ²³ and to the church, composed of all those registered in heaven; and to God who is Judge of all; and to the spirits of the redeemed in heaven, already made perfect; ²⁴ and to Jesus himself, who has brought us his wonderful new agreement; and to the sprinkled blood which graciously forgives instead of crying out for vengeance as the blood of Abel did.

²⁵ So see to it that you obey him who is speaking to you. For if the people of Israel did not escape when they refused to listen to Moses, the earthly messenger, how terrible our danger if we refuse to listen to God who speaks to us from heaven! ²⁶ When he spoke from Mount Sinai his voice shook the earth, but, "Next time," he says, "I will not only shake the earth, but the heavens too." ²⁷ By this he means that he will sift out everything without solid foundations, so that only unshakable things will be left.

²⁸ Since we have a kingdom nothing can destroy, let us please God by serving him with thankful hearts, and with holy fear and awe. ²⁹ For our God is a consuming fire.

13 CONTINUE TO LOVE each other with true brotherly love. ² Don't forget to be kind to strangers, for some who have done this have entertained angels without realizing it! ³ Don't forget about those in jail. Suffer with them as though you were there yourself. Share the sorrow of those being mistreated, for you know what they are going through.

⁴ Honor your marriage and its vows, and be pure; for God will surely punish all those who are immoral or commit adultery.

⁵ Stay away from the love of money; be satisfied with what you have. For God has said, "I will never, *never* fail you nor forsake you." ⁶ That is why we can say without any doubt or fear, "The Lord is my Helper and I am not afraid of anything that mere man can do to me."

⁷ Remember your leaders who have taught you the Word of God. Think of all the good that has come from their lives, and try to trust the Lord as they do.

⁸ Jesus Christ is the same yesterday, today, and forever. ⁹ So do not be attracted by strange, new ideas. Your spiritual strength comes as a gift from God, not from ceremonial rules about eating certain foods—a method which, by the way, hasn't helped those who have tried it!

¹⁰ We have an altar—the cross where Christ was sacrificed—where those who continue to seek salvation by obeying Jewish laws can never be helped. ¹¹ Under the system of Jewish laws the high priest brought the blood of the slain animals into the sanctuary as a sacrifice for sin, and then the bodies of the animals were burned outside the city. ¹² That is why Jesus suffered and died outside the city, where his blood washed our sins away.

¹³ So let us go out to him beyond the city walls [that is, outside the interests of this

world, being willing to be despised[a]) to suffer with him there, bearing his shame. [14] For this world is not our home; we are looking forward to our everlasting home in heaven.

[15] With Jesus' help we will continually offer our sacrifice of praise to God by telling others of the glory of his name. [16] Don't forget to do good and to share what you have with those in need, for such sacrifices are very pleasing to him. [17] Obey your spiritual leaders and be willing to do what they say. For their work is to watch over your souls, and God will judge them on how well they do this. Give them reason to report joyfully about you to the Lord and not with sorrow, for then you will suffer for it too. [18] Pray for us, for our conscience is clear and we want to keep it that way. [19] I especially need your prayers right now so that I can come back to you sooner.

[20,21] And now may the God of peace, who brought again from the dead our Lord Jesus, equip you with all you need for doing his will. May he who became the great Shepherd of the sheep by an everlasting agreement between God and you, signed with his blood, produce in you through the power of Christ all that is pleasing to him. To him be glory forever and ever. Amen.

[22] Brethren, please listen patiently to what I have said in this letter, for it is a short one. [23] I want you to know that Brother Timothy is now out of jail; if he comes here soon, I will come with him to see you. [24,25] Give my greetings to all your leaders and to the other believers there. The Christians from Italy who are here with me send you their love. God's grace be with you all.

Good-bye.

a Implied.

American Youth Magazine

Youch!

A cowgirl in Phoenix hangs on in rip-snorting competition by riding a hunk of cowhide without falling off. Rough and rugged—but the winning way!

Many people don't mind trying sports that require bruising practice. Rugged times can be appealing, if you have a goal. "It's only when I push my body beyond the hurting point, that I improve," said one cowgirl. The book of James describes a rugged sometimes painful kind of Christian living. James is practical, gutsy and crystal clear in meaning—though we'd like to avoid its impact.

JAMES

1 FROM: JAMES, A servant of God and of the Lord Jesus Christ.

To: Jewish Christians scattered everywhere. Greetings!

² Dear brothers, is your life full of difficulties and temptations? Then be happy, ³ for when the way is rough, your patience has a chance to grow. ⁴ So let it grow, and don't try to squirm out of your problems. For when your patience is finally in full bloom, then you will be ready for anything, strong in character, full and complete.

⁵ If you want to know what God wants you to do, ask him, and he will gladly tell you, for he is always ready to give a bountiful supply of wisdom to all who ask him; he will not resent it. ⁶ But when you ask him, be sure that you really expect him to tell you, for a doubtful mind will be as unsettled as a wave of the sea that is driven and tossed by the wind; ⁷,⁸ and every decision you then make will be uncertain, as you turn first this way, and then that. If you don't ask with faith, don't expect the Lord to give you any solid answer.

⁹ A Christian who doesn't amount to much in this world should be glad, for he is great in the Lord's sight. ¹⁰,¹¹ But a rich man should be glad that his riches mean nothing to the Lord, for he will soon be gone, like a flower that has lost its beauty and fades away, withered—killed by the scorching summer sun. So it is with rich men. They will soon die and leave behind all their busy activities.

¹² Happy is the man who doesn't give in and do wrong when he is tempted, for afterwards he will get as his reward the crown of life that God has promised those who love him. ¹³ And remember, when someone wants to do wrong it is never God who is tempting him, for God never wants to do wrong and never tempts anyone else to do it. ¹⁴ Temptation is the pull of man's own evil thoughts and wishes. ¹⁵ These evil thoughts lead to evil actions and afterwards to the death penalty from God. ¹⁶ So don't be misled, dear brothers.

¹⁷ But whatever is good and perfect comes to us from God, the Creator of all

light, and he shines forever without change or shadow. [18] And it was a happy day for him[a] when he gave us our new lives, through the truth of his Word, and we became, as it were, the first children in his new family.

[19] Dear brothers, don't ever forget that it is best to listen much, speak little, and not become angry; [20] for anger doesn't make us good, as God demands that we must be.

[21] So get rid of all that is wrong in your life, both inside and outside, and humbly be glad for the wonderful message we have received, for it is able to save our souls as it takes hold of our hearts.

[22] And remember, it is a message to obey, not just to listen to. So don't fool yourselves. [23] For if a person just listens and doesn't obey, he is like a man looking at his face in a mirror; [24] as soon as he walks away, he can't see himself anymore or remember what he looks like. [25] But if anyone keeps looking steadily into God's law for free men, he will not only remember it but he will do what it says, and God will greatly bless him in everything he does.

[26] Anyone who says he is a Christian but doesn't control his sharp tongue is just fooling himself, and his religion isn't worth much. [27] The Christian who is pure and without fault, from God the Father's point of view, is the one who takes care of orphans and widows, and who remains true to the Lord—not soiled and dirtied by his contacts with the world.

2 DEAR BROTHERS, HOW can you claim that you belong to the Lord Jesus Christ, the Lord of glory, if you show favoritism to rich people and look down on poor people?

[2] If a man comes into your church dressed in expensive clothes and with valuable gold rings on his fingers, and at the same moment another man comes in who is poor and dressed in threadbare clothes, [3] and you make a lot of fuss over the rich man and give him the best seat in the house and say to the poor man, "You can stand over there if you like, or else sit on the floor"—well, [4] judging a man by his wealth shows that you are guided by wrong motives.

[5] Listen to me, dear brothers: God has chosen poor people to be rich in faith, and the Kingdom of Heaven is theirs, for that is the gift God has promised to all those who love him. [6] And yet, of the two strangers, you have despised the poor man. Don't you realize that it is usually the rich men who pick on you and drag you into court? [7] And all too often they are the ones who laugh at Jesus Christ, whose noble name you bear.

[8] Yes indeed, it is good when you truly obey our Lord's command, "You must love and help your neighbors just as much as you love and take care of yourself." [9] But you are breaking this law of our Lord's when you favor the rich and fawn over them; it is sin.

[10] And the person who keeps every law of God, but makes one little slip, is just as guilty as the person who has broken every law there is. [11] For the God who said you must not marry a woman who already has a husband, also said you must not murder, so even though you have not broken the marriage laws by committing adultery, but have murdered someone, you have entirely broken God's laws and stand utterly guilty before him.

[12] You will be judged on whether or not you are doing what Christ wants you to. So watch what you do and what you think; [13] for there will be no mercy to those who have shown no mercy. But if you have been merciful, then God's mercy toward you will win out over his judgment against you.

[14] Dear brothers, what's the use of saying that you have faith and are Christians if you aren't proving it by helping others? Will *that* kind of faith save anyone? [15] If you have a friend who is in need of food and clothing, [16] and you say to him, "Well, good-bye and God bless you; stay warm and eat hearty," and then don't give him clothes or food, what good does that do?

[17] So you see, it isn't enough just to have faith. You must also do good to prove that you have it. Faith that doesn't show itself by good works is no faith at all—it is dead and useless.

a Literally, "Of his own free will he gave us, etc."

¹⁸ But someone may well argue, "You say the way to God is by faith alone, plus nothing; well, I say that good works are important too, for without good works you can't prove whether you have faith or not; but anyone can see that I have faith by the way I act."

¹⁹ Are there still some among you who hold that "only believing" is enough? Believing in one God? Well, remember that the demons believe this too—so strongly that they tremble in terror! ²⁰ Fool! When will you ever learn that "believing" is useless without *doing* what God wants you to? Faith that does not result in good deeds is not real faith.

²¹ Don't you remember that even our father Abraham was declared good because of what he *did,* when he was willing to obey God, even if it meant offering his son Isaac to die on the altar? ²² You see, he was trusting God so much that he was willing to do whatever God told him to; his faith was made complete by what he did, by his actions, his good deeds. ²³ And so it happened just as the Scriptures say, that Abraham trusted God, and the Lord declared him good in God's sight, and he was even called "the friend of God." ²⁴ So you see, a man is saved by what he does; as well as by what he believes.

²⁵ Rahab, the prostitute, is another example of this. She was saved because of what she did when she hid those messengers and sent them safely away by a different road. ²⁶ Just as the body is dead when there is no spirit in it, so faith is dead if it is not the kind that results in good deeds.

3 DEAR BROTHERS, DON'T be too eager to tell others their faults,ᵃ for we all make many mistakes; and when we teachers of religion, who should know better, do wrong, our punishment will be greater than it would be for others.

If anyone can control his tongue, it proves that he has perfect control over himself in every other way. ³ We can make a large horse turn around and go wherever we want by means of a small bit in his mouth. ⁴ And a tiny rudder makes a huge ship turn wherever the pilot wants it to go, even though the winds are strong.

⁵ So also the tongue is a small thing, but what enormous damage it can do. A great forest can be set on fire by one tiny spark. ⁶ And the tongue is a flame of fire. It is full of wickedness, and poisons every part of the body. And the tongue is set on fire by hell itself, and can turn our whole lives into a blazing flame of destruction and disaster.

⁷ Men have trained, or can train, every kind of animal or bird that lives and every kind of reptile and fish, ⁸ but no human being can tame the tongue. It is always ready to pour out its deadly poison. ⁹ Sometimes it praises our heavenly Father, and sometimes it breaks out into curses against men who are made like God. ¹⁰ And so blessing and cursing come pouring out of the same mouth. Dear brothers, surely this is not right! ¹¹ Does a spring of water bubble out first with fresh water and then with bitter water? ¹² Can you pick olives from a fig tree, or figs from a grape vine? No, and you can't draw fresh water from a salty pool.

¹³ If you are wise, live a life of steady goodness, so that only good deeds will pour forth. And if you don't brag about them, then you will be truly wise! ¹⁴ And by all means don't brag about being wise and good if you are bitter and jealous and selfish; that is the worst sort of lie. ¹⁵ For jealousy and selfishness are not God's kind of wisdom. Such things are earthly, unspiritual, inspired by the devil. ¹⁶ For wherever there is jealousy or selfish ambition, there will be disorder and every other kind of evil.

¹⁷ But the wisdom that comes from heaven is first of all pure and full of quiet gentleness. Then it is peace-loving and courteous. It allows discussion and is willing to yield to others; it is full of mercy and good deeds. It is wholehearted and straightforward and sincere. ¹⁸ And those who are peacemakers will plant seeds of peace and reap a harvest of goodness.

4 WHAT IS CAUSING the quarrels and fights among you? Isn't it because there is a whole army of evil desires within you? ² You want what you don't have, so you kill

---

a Literally, "Not many (of you) should become masters (teachers)."

to get it. You long for what others have, and can't afford it, so you start a fight to take it away from them. And yet the reason you don't have what you want is that you don't ask God for it. ³ And even when you do ask you don't get it because your whole aim is wrong—you want only what will give *you* pleasure.

⁴ You are like an unfaithful wife who loves her husband's enemies. Don't you realize that making friends with God's enemies—the evil pleasures of this world—makes you an enemy of God? I say it again, that if your aim is to enjoy the evil pleasure of the unsaved world, you cannot also be a friend of God. ⁵ Or what do you think the Scripture means when it says that the Holy Spirit, whom God has placed within us, watches over us with tender jealousy? ⁶ But he gives us more and more strength to stand against all such evil longings. As the Scripture says, God gives strength to the humble, but sets himself against the proud and haughty.

⁷ So give yourselves humbly to God. Resist the devil and he will flee from you. ⁸ And when you draw close to God, God will draw close to you. Wash your hands, you sinners, and let your hearts be filled with God alone to make them pure and true to him. ⁹ Let there be tears for the wrong things you have done. Let there be sorrow and sincere grief. Let there be sadness instead of laughter, and gloom instead of joy. ¹⁰ Then when you realize your worthlessness before the Lord, he will lift you up, encourage and help you.

¹¹ Don't criticize and speak evil about each other, dear brothers. If you do, you will be fighting against God's law of loving one another, declaring it is wrong. But your job is not to decide whether this law is right or wrong, but to obey it. ¹² Only he who made the law can rightly judge among us. He alone decides to save us or destroy. So what right do you have to judge or criticize others?

¹³ Look here, you people who say, "Today or tomorrow we are going to such and such a town, stay there a year, and open up a profitable business." ¹⁴ How do you know what is going to happen tomorrow? For the length of your lives is as uncertain as the morning fog—now you see it; soon it is gone. ¹⁵ What you ought to say is, "If the Lord wants us to, we shall live and do this or that." ¹⁶ Otherwise you will be bragging about your own plans, and such self-confidence never pleases God.

¹⁷ Remember, too, that knowing what is right to do and then not doing it is sin.

5 LOOK HERE, YOU rich men, now is the time to cry and groan with anguished grief because of all the terrible troubles ahead of you. ² Your wealth is even now rotting away, and your fine clothes are becoming mere moth-eaten rags. ³ The value of your gold and silver is dropping fast, yet it will stand as evidence against you, and eat your flesh like fire. That is what you have stored up for yourselves, to receive on that coming day of judgment. ⁴ For listen! Hear the cries of the field workers whom you have cheated of their pay. Their cries have reached the ears of the Lord of Hosts.

⁵ You have spent your years here on earth having fun, satisfying your every whim, and now your fat hearts are ready for the slaughter. ⁶ You have condemned and killed good men who had no power to defend themselves against you.

⁷ Now as for you, dear brothers who are waiting for the Lord's return, be patient, like a farmer who waits until the autumn for his precious harvest to ripen. ⁸ Yes, be patient. And take courage, for the coming of the Lord is near.

⁹ Don't grumble about each other, brothers. Are you yourselves above criticism? For see! The great Judge is coming. He is almost here. [Let him do whatever criticizing must be done[a].]

¹⁰ For examples of patience in suffering, look at the Lord's prophets. ¹¹ We know how happy they are now because they stayed true to him then, even though they suffered greatly for it. Job is an example of a man who continued to trust the Lord in sorrow; from his experiences we can see how the Lord's plan finally ended in good, for he is full of tenderness and mercy.

---

a Implied.

¹² But most of all, dear brothers, do not swear either by heaven or earth or anything else; just say a simple yes or no, so that you will not sin and be condemned for it.

¹³ Is anyone among you suffering? He should keep on praying about it. And those who have reason to be thankful should continually be singing praises to the Lord.

¹⁴ Is anyone sick? He should call for the elders of the church and they should pray over him and pour a little oil upon him, calling on the Lord to heal him. ¹⁵ And their prayer, if offered in faith, will heal him, for the Lord will make him well; and if his sickness was caused by some sin, the Lord will forgive him.

¹⁶ Admit your faults to one another and pray for each other so that you may be healed. The earnest prayer of a righteous man has great power and wonderful results. ¹⁷ Elijah was as completely human as we are, and yet when he prayed earnestly that no rain would fall, none fell for the next three and one half years! ¹⁸ Then he prayed again, this time that it *would* rain, and down it poured and the grass turned green and the gardens began to grow again.

¹⁹ Dear brothers, if anyone has slipped away from God and no longer trusts the Lord, and someone helps him understand the Truth again, ²⁰ that person who brings him back to God will have saved a wandering soul from death, bringing about the forgiveness of his many sins.

Sincerely,
James

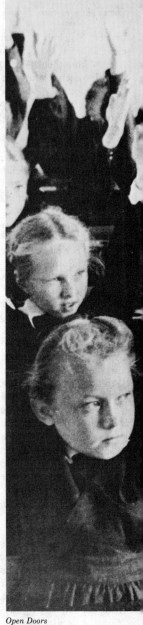

Open Doors

When It Hurts

In America it seldom hurts much to be a Christian. It may involve self-control or some friends' rejection. But you never get horse-whipped for talking about Christ!

Beatings are rare in Russia, too. But persecution against Christians is still blatantly practiced. The faith of Soviet parents may cost them their children. Cases of child stealing are documented with youngsters reappearing in state-operated homes to be educated as atheists. Prison sentences and denial of educational or job opportunities is also a common practice.

Some countries are even more severe. Some Moslem nations have laws against being a Christian. Violation of these laws is punishable by death!

What would you do if your faith met this kind of test—if it really hurt to believe? Peter wrote the next two books to Christians who had been exiled and persecuted for their beliefs. His message is stunning, "Dear friends, don't be bewildered or surprised when you go through the fiery trials ahead, for this is no strange, unusual thing that is going to happen to you. Instead, be really glad ..." (I:4:12). Glad for persecution? Peter goes on to explain why.

1 PETER

1 FROM: PETER, JESUS Christ's missionary.

To: The Jewish Christians driven out of Jerusalem and scattered throughout Pontus, Galatia, Cappadocia, Ausia, and Bithynia.

² Dear friends, God the Father chose you long ago and knew you would become his children. And the Holy Spirit has been at work in your hearts, cleansing you with the blood of Jesus Christ and making you to please him. May God bless you richly and grant you increasing freedom from all anxiety and fear.

³ All honor to God, the God and Father of our Lord Jesus Christ; for it is his boundless mercy that has given us the privilege of being born again, so that we are now members of God's own family. Now we live in the hope of eternal life because Christ rose again from the dead. ⁴ And God has reserved for his children the priceless gift of eternal life; it is kept in heaven for you, pure and undefiled, beyond the reach of change and decay. ⁵ And God, in his mighty power, will make sure that you get there safely to receive it, because you are trusting him. It will be yours in that coming last day for all to see. ⁶ So be truly glad! There is wonderful joy ahead, even though the going is rough for a while down here.

⁷ These trials are only to test your faith, to see whether or not it is strong and pure. It is being tested as fire tests gold and purifies it—and your faith is far more precious to God than mere gold; so if your faith remains strong after being tried in the test tube of fiery trials, it will bring you much praise and glory and honor on the day of his return.

⁸ You love him even though you have never seen him; though not seeing him, you trust him; and even now you are happy with the inexpressible joy that comes from heaven itself. ⁹ And your further reward for trusting him will be the salvation of your souls.

¹⁰ This salvation was something the prophets did not fully understand. Though they wrote about it, they had many questions as to what it all could mean. ¹¹ They wondered what the Spirit of Christ within them was talking about, for he told them to write down the events which, since then, have happened to Christ: his suffering, and his great glory afterwards. And they wondered when and to whom all this would happen.

[12] They were finally told that these things would not occur during their lifetime, but long years later, during yours. And now at last this Good News has been plainly announced to all of us. It was preached to us in the power of the same heaven-sent Holy Spirit who spoke to them; and it is all so strange and wonderful that even the angels in heaven would give a great deal to know more about it. [13] So now you can look forward soberly and intelligently to more of God's kindness to you when Jesus Christ returns.

[14] Obey God because you are his children; don't slip back into your old ways—doing evil because you knew no better. [15] But be holy now in everything you do, just as the Lord is holy, who invited you to be his child. [16] He himself has said, "You must be holy, for I am holy."

[17] And remember that your heavenly Father to whom you pray has no favorites when he judges. He will judge you with perfect justice for everything you do; so act in reverent fear of him from now on until you get to heaven. [18] God paid a ransom to save you from the impossible road to heaven which your fathers tried to take, and the ransom he paid was not mere gold or silver, as you very well know. [19] But he paid for you with the precious lifeblood of Christ, the sinless, spotless Lamb of God. [20] God chose him for this purpose long before the world began, but only recently was he brought into public view, in these last days, as a blessing to you.

[21] Because of this, your trust can be in God who raised Christ from the dead and gave him great glory. Now your faith and hope can rest in him alone. [22] Now you can have real love for everyone because your souls have been cleansed from selfishness and hatred when you trusted Christ to save you; so see to it that you really do love each other warmly, with all your hearts.

[23] For you have a new life. It was not passed on to you from your parents, for the life they gave you will fade away. This new one will last forever, for it comes from Christ, God's ever-living Message to men.

[24] Yes, our natural lives will fade as grass does when it becomes all brown and dry. All our greatness is like a flower that droops and falls; [25] but the Word of the Lord will last forever. And his message is the Good News that was preached to you.

2 SO GET RID of your feelings of hatred. Don't just pretend to be good! Be done with dishonesty and jealousy and talking about others behind their backs. [2,3a] Now that you realize how kind the Lord has been to you, put away all evil, deception, envy, and fraud. Long to grow up into the fullness of your salvation; cry for this as a baby cries for his milk. [4] Come to Christ, who is the living Foundation of Rock upon which God builds; though men have spurned him, he is very precious to God who has chosen him above all others.

[5] And now you have become living building-stones for God's use in building his house. What's more, you are his holy priests; so come to him—[you who are acceptable to him because of Jesus Christ[b]]—and offer to God those things that please him. [6] As the Scriptures express it, "See, I am sending Christ to be the carefully chosen, precious Cornerstone of my church, and I will never disappoint those who trust in him."

[7] Yes, he is very precious to you who believe; and to those who reject him, well —"The same Stone that was rejected by the builders has become the Cornerstone, the most honored and important part of the building." [8] And the Scriptures also say, "He is the Stone that some will stumble over, and the Rock that will make them fall." They will stumble because they will not listen to God's Word, nor obey it, and so this punishment must follow—that they will fall.

[9] But you are not like that, for you have been chosen by God himself—you are priests of the King, you are holy and pure, you are God's very own—all this so that you may show to others how God called you out of the darkness into his wonderful light. [10] Once you were less than nothing;

a An alternative paraphrase of these verses could read: "If you have tasted the Lord's goodness and kindness, cry for more, as a baby cries for milk. Eat God's Word—read it, think about it—and grow strong in the Lord and be saved."   b Implied.

now you are God's own. Once you knew very little of God's kindness; now your very lives have been changed by it. [11] Dear brothers, you are only visitors here. Since your real home is in heaven I beg you to keep away from the evil pleasures of this world; they are not for you, for they fight against your very souls.

[12] Be careful how you behave among your unsaved neighbors; for then, even if they are suspicious of you and talk against you, they will end up praising God for your good works when Christ returns. [13] For the Lord's sake, obey every law of your government: those of the king as head of the state, [14] and those of the king's officers, for he has sent them to punish all who do wrong, and to honor those who do right.

[15] It is God's will that your good lives should silence those who foolishly condemn the Gospel without knowing what it can do for them, having never experienced its power. [16] You are free from the law, but that doesn't mean you are free to do wrong. Live as those who are free to do only God's will at all times.

[17] Show respect for everyone. Love Christians everywhere. Fear God and honor the government.

[18] Servants, you must respect your masters and do whatever they tell you—not only if they are kind and reasonable, but even if they are tough and cruel. [19] Praise the Lord if you are punished for doing right! [20] Of course, you get no credit for being patient if you are beaten for doing wrong; but if you do right and suffer for it, and are patient beneath the blows, God is well pleased.

[21] This suffering is all part of the work God has given you. Christ, who suffered for you, is your example. Follow in his steps: [22] He never sinned, never told a lie, [23] never answered back when insulted; when he suffered he did not threaten to get even; he left his case in the hands of God who always judges fairly. [24] He personally carried the load of our sins in his own body when he died on the cross, so that we can be finished with sin and live a good life from now on. For his wounds have healed ours! [25] Like sheep you wandered away from God, but now you have returned to your Shepherd, the Guardian of your souls who keeps you safe from all attacks.

3 WIVES, FIT IN with your husbands' plans; for then if they refuse to listen when you talk to them about the Lord, they will be won by your respectful, pure behavior. Your godly lives will speak to them better than any words.

[3] Don't be concerned about the outward beauty that depends on jewelry, or beautiful clothes, or hair arrangement. [4] Be beautiful inside, in your hearts, with the lasting charm of a gentle and quiet spirit which is so precious to God. [5] That kind of deep beauty was seen in the saintly women of old, who trusted God and fitted in with their husbands' plans.

[6] Sarah, for instance, obeyed her husband Abraham, honoring him as head of the house. And if you do the same, you will be following in her steps like good daughters and doing what is right; then you will not need to fear [offending your husbands[a]].

[7] You husbands must be careful of your wives, being thoughtful of their needs and honoring them as the weaker sex. Remember that you and your wife are partners in receiving God's blessings, and if you don't treat her as you should, your prayers will not get ready answers.

[8] And now this word to all of you: You should be like one big happy family, full of sympathy toward each other, loving one another with tender hearts and humble minds. [9] Don't repay evil for evil. Don't snap back at those who say unkind things about you. Instead, pray for God's help for them, for we are to be kind to others, and God will bless us for it.

[10] If you want a happy, good life, keep control of your tongue, and guard your lips from telling lies. [11] Turn away from evil and do good. Try to live in peace even if you must run after it to catch and hold it! [12] For the Lord is watching his children, listening to their prayers; but the Lord's face is hard against those who do evil.

a Implied.

1084

[13] Usually no one will hurt you for wanting to do good. [14] But even if they should, you are to be envied, for God will reward you for it. [15] Quietly trust yourself to Christ your Lord and if anybody asks why you believe as you do, be ready to tell him, and do it in a gentle and respectful way.

[16] Do what is right; then if men speak against you, calling you evil names, they will become ashamed of themselves for falsely accusing you when you have only done what is good. [17] Remember, if God wants you to suffer, it is better to suffer for doing good than for doing wrong!

[18] Christ also suffered. He died once for the sins of all us guilty sinners, although he himself was innocent of any sin at any time, that he might bring us safely home to God. But though his body died, his spirit lived on, [19] and it was in the spirit that he visited the spirits in prison, and preached to them— [20] spirits of those who, long before in the days of Noah, had refused to listen to God, though he waited patiently for them while Noah was building the ark. Yet only eight persons were saved from drowning in that terrible flood. [21] (That, by the way, is what baptism pictures for us: In baptism we show that we have been saved from death and doom by the resurrection of Christ;[b] not because our bodies are washed clean by the water, but because in being baptized we are turning to God and asking him to cleanse our *hearts* from sin.) [22] And now Christ is in heaven, sitting in the place of honor next to God the Father, with all the angels and powers of heaven bowing before him and obeying him.

4 SINCE CHRIST SUFFERED and underwent pain, you must have the same attitude he did; you must be ready to suffer, too. For remember, when your body suffers, sin loses its power, [2] and you won't be spending the rest of your life chasing after evil desires, but will be anxious to do the will of God. [3] You have had enough in the past of the evil things the godless enjoy— sex sin, lust, getting drunk, wild parties, drinking bouts, and the worship of idols,

and other terrible sins.[a]

[4] Of course, your former friends will be very surprised when you don't eagerly join them any more in the wicked things they do, and they will laugh at you in contempt and scorn. [5] But just remember that they must face the Judge of all, living and dead; they will be punished for the way they have lived. [6] That is why the Good News was preached even to those who were dead— killed by the flood[b]—so that although their bodies were punished with death, they could still live in their spirits as God lives.

[7] The end of the world is coming soon. Therefore be earnest, thoughtful men of prayer. [8] Most important of all, continue to show deep love for each other, for love makes up for many of your faults.[c] [9] Cheerfully share your home with those who need a meal or a place to stay for the night.

[10] God has given each of you some special abilities; be sure to use them to help each other, passing on to others God's many kinds of blessings. [11] Are you called to preach? Then preach as though God himself were speaking through you. Are you called to help others? Do it with all the strength and energy that God supplies, so that God will be glorified through Jesus Christ—to him be glory and power forever and ever. Amen.

[12] Dear friends, don't be bewildered or surprised when you go through the fiery trials ahead, for this is no strange, unusual thing that is going to happen to you. [13] Instead, be really glad—because these trials will make you partners with Christ in his suffering, and afterwards you will have the wonderful joy of sharing his glory in that coming day when it will be displayed.

[14] Be happy if you are cursed and insulted for being a Christian, for when that happens the Spirit of God will come upon you with great glory.[d] [15] Don't let me hear of your suffering for murdering or stealing or making trouble or being a busybody and prying into other people's affairs. [16] But it is no shame to suffer for being a Christian. Praise God for the privilege of being in Christ's family and being called by his won-

---

b Or, "Baptism, which corresponds to this, now saves you through the Resurrection."   4a Literally, "lawless idolatries."   b Implied. See 1 Peter 3:19, 20.   c Or, "love overlooks each other's many faults."
d Or, "the glory of the Spirit of God is being seen in you."

derful name! [17] For the time has come for judgment, and it must begin first among God's own children. And if even we who are Christians must be judged, what terrible fate awaits those who have never believed in the Lord? [18] If the righteous are barely saved, what chance will the godless have?

[19] So if you are suffering according to God's will, keep on doing what is right and trust yourself to the God who made you, for he will never fail you.

5 AND NOW, A word to you elders of the church. I, too, am an elder; with my own eyes I saw Christ dying on the cross; and I, too, will share his glory and his honor when he returns. Fellow elders, this is my plea to you: [2] Feed the flock of God; care for it willingly, not grudgingly; not for what you will get out of it, but because you are eager to serve the Lord. [3] Don't be tyrants, but lead them by your good example, [4] and when the Head Shepherd comes, your reward will be a never-ending share in his glory and honor.

[5] You younger men, follow the leadership of those who are older. And all of you serve each other with humble spirits, for God gives special blessings to those who are humble, but sets himself against those who are proud. [6] If you will humble yourselves under the mighty hand of God, in his good time he will lift you up.

[7] Let him have all your worries and cares, for he is always thinking about you and watching everything that concerns you.

[8] Be careful—watch out for attacks from Satan, your great enemy. He prowls around like a hungry, roaring lion, looking for some victim to tear apart. [9] Stand firm when he attacks. Trust the Lord; and remember that other Christians all around the world are going through these sufferings too.

[10] After you have suffered a little while, our God, who is full of kindness through Christ, will give you his eternal glory. He personally will come and pick you up, and set you firmly in place, and make you stronger than ever. [11] To him be all power over all things, forever and ever. Amen.

[12] I am sending this note to you through the courtesy of Silvanus who is, in my opinion, a very faithful brother. I hope I have encouraged you by this letter for I have given you a true statement of the way God blesses. What I have told you here should help you to stand firmly in his love.

[13] The church here in Rome[a]—she is your sister in the Lord—sends you her greetings; so does my son Mark. [14] Give each other the handshake of Christian love. Peace be to all of you who are in Christ.

Peter

2 PETER

1 FROM: SIMON PETER, a servant and missionary of Jesus Christ.

To: All of you who have our kind of faith. The faith I speak of is the kind that Jesus Christ our God and Savior gives to us. How precious it is, and how just and good he is to give this same faith to each of us.

[2] Do you want more and more of God's kindness and peace? Then learn to know him better and better. [3] For as you know him better, he will give you, through his great power, everything you need for living a truly good life: he even shares his own glory and his own goodness with us! [4] And by that same mighty power he has given us all the other rich and wonderful blessings he promised; for instance, the promise to save us from the lust and rottenness all around us, and to give us his own character.

[5] But to obtain these gifts, you need more than faith; you must also work hard to be good, and even that is not enough. For then

a Literally, "She who is at Babylon is likewise chosen"; but Babylon was the Christian nickname for Rome, and the "she" is thought by many to be Peter's wife to whom reference is made in Matthew 8:14, 1 Corinthians 9:5, etc. Others believe this should read: "Your sister church here in Babylon salutes you, and so does my son Mark."

you must learn to know God better and discover what he wants you to do. ⁶ Next, learn to put aside your own desires so that you will become patient and godly, gladly letting God have his way with you. ⁷ This will make possible the next step, which is for you to enjoy other people and to like them, and finally you will grow to love them deeply. ⁸ The more you go on in this way, the more you will grow strong spiritually and become fruitful and useful to our Lord Jesus Christ. ⁹ But anyone who fails to go after these additions to faith is blind indeed, or at least very shortsighted, and has forgotten that God delivered him from the old life of sin so that now he can live a strong, good life for the Lord.

¹⁰ So, dear brothers, work hard to prove that you really are among those God has called and chosen, and then you will never stumble or fall away. ¹¹ And God will open wide the gates of heaven for you to enter into the eternal kingdom of our Lord and Savior Jesus Christ.

¹² I plan to keep on reminding you of these things even though you already know them and are really getting along quite well! ¹³,¹⁴ But the Lord Jesus Christ has showed me that my days here on earth are numbered, and I am soon to die. As long as I am still here I intend to keep sending these reminders to you, ¹⁵ hoping to impress them so clearly upon you that you will remember them long after I have gone.

¹⁶ For we have not been telling you fairy tales when we explained to you the power of our Lord Jesus Christ and his coming again. My own eyes have seen his splendor and his glory: ¹⁷,¹⁸ I was there on the holy mountain when he shone out with honor given him by God his Father; I heard that glorious, majestic voice calling down from heaven, saying, "This is my much-loved Son; I am well pleased with him."

¹⁹ So we have seen and proved that what the prophets said came true. You will do well to pay close attention to everything they have written, for, like lights shining into dark corners, their words help us to understand many things that otherwise would be dark and difficult. But when you consider the wonderful truth of the prophets' words, then the light will dawn in your souls and Christ the Morning Star will shine in your hearts. ²⁰,²¹ For no prophecy recorded in Scripture was ever thought up by the prophet himself. It was the Holy Spirit within these godly men who gave them true messages from God.

2 BUT THERE WERE false prophets, too, in those days, just as there will be false teachers among you. They will cleverly tell their lies about God, turning against even their Master who bought them; but theirs will be a swift and terrible end. ² Many will follow their evil teaching that there is nothing wrong with sexual sin. And because of them Christ and his way will be scoffed at.

³ These teachers in their greed will tell you anything to get hold of your money. But God condemned them long ago and their destruction is on the way. ⁴ For God did not spare even the angels who sinned, but threw them into hell, chained in gloomy caves and darkness until the judgment day. ⁵ And he did not spare any of the people who lived in ancient times before the flood except Noah, the one man who spoke up for God, and his family of seven. At that time God completely destroyed the whole world of ungodly men with the vast flood. ⁶ Later, he turned the cities of Sodom and Gomorrah into heaps of ashes and blotted them off the face of the earth, making them an example for all the ungodly in the future to look back upon and fear.

⁷,⁸ But at the same time the Lord rescued Lot out of Sodom because he was a good man, sick of the terrible wickedness he saw everywhere around him day after day. ⁹ So also the Lord can rescue you and me from the temptations that surround us, and continue to punish the ungodly until the day of final judgment comes. ¹⁰ He is especially hard on those who follow their own evil, lustful thoughts, and those who are proud and willful, daring even to scoff at the Glorious Ones[a] without so much as trembling, ¹¹ although the angels in heaven who stand in the very presence of the Lord, and are far greater in power and strength than these

---

a Or, "the glories of the unseen world."

false teachers, never speak out disrespectfully against these evil Mighty Ones.

[12] But false teachers are fools—no better than animals. They do whatever they feel like; born only to be caught and killed, they laugh at the terrifying powers of the underworld[b] which they know so little about; and they will be destroyed along with all the demons and powers of hell.[c]

[13] That is the pay these teachers will have for their sin. For they live in evil pleasures day after day. They are a disgrace and a stain among you, deceiving you by living in foul sin on the side while they join your love feasts as though they were honest men. [14] No woman can escape their sinful stare, and of adultery they never have enough. They make a game of luring unstable women. They train themselves to be greedy; and are doomed and cursed. [15] They have gone off the road and become lost like Balaam, the son of Beor, who fell in love with the money he could make by doing wrong; [16] but Balaam was stopped from his mad course when his donkey spoke to him with a human voice, scolding and rebuking him.

[17] These men are as useless as dried-up springs of water, promising much and delivering nothing; they are as unstable as clouds driven by the storm winds. They are doomed to the eternal pits of darkness. [18] They proudly boast about their sins and conquests, and, using lust as their bait, they lure back into sin those who have just escaped from such wicked living.

[19] "You aren't saved by being good," they say, "so you might as well be bad. Do what you like, be free."

But these very teachers who offer this "freedom" from law are themselves slaves to sin and destruction. For a man is a slave to whatever controls him. [20] And when a person has escaped from the wicked ways of the world by learning about our Lord and Savior Jesus Christ, and then gets tangled up with sin and becomes its slave again, he is worse off than he was before. [21] It would be better if he had never known about Christ at all than to learn of him and then afterwards turn his back on the holy commandments that were given to him. [22] There is an old saying that "A dog comes back to what he has vomited, and a pig is washed only to come back and wallow in the mud again." That is the way it is with those who turn again to their sin.

3 THIS IS MY second letter to you, dear brothers, and in both of them I have tried to remind you—if you will let me—about facts you already know: facts you learned from the holy prophets and from us apostles who brought you the words of our Lord and Savior.

[3] First, I want to remind you that in the last days there will come scoffers who will do every wrong they can think of, and laugh at the truth. [4] This will be their line of argument: "So Jesus promised to come back, did he? Then where is he? He'll never come! Why, as far back as anyone can remember everything has remained exactly as it was since the first day of creation."

[5,6] They deliberately forget this fact: that God did destroy the world with a mighty flood, long after he had made the heavens by the word of his command, and had used the waters to form the earth and surround it. [7] And God has commanded that the earth and the heavens be stored away for a great bonfire at the judgment day, when all ungodly men will perish.

[8] But don't forget this, dear friends, that a day or a thousand years from now is like tomorrow to the Lord. [9] He isn't really being slow about his promised return, even though it sometimes seems that way. But he is waiting, for the good reason that he is not willing that any should perish, and he is giving more time for sinners to repent. [10] The day of the Lord is surely coming, as unexpectedly as a thief, and then the heavens will pass away with a terrible noise and the heavenly bodies will disappear in fire, and the earth and everything on it will be burned up.

[11] And so since everything around us is going to melt away, what holy, godly lives we should be living! [12] You should look forward to that day and hurry it along—the

---

b Literally, "the things they do not understand."
destruction with them."

c Implied. Literally, "will be destroyed in the same

day when God will set the heavens on fire, and the heavenly bodies will melt and disappear in flames. [13] But we are looking forward to God's promise of new heavens and a new earth afterwards, where there will be only goodness.[a]

[14] Dear friends, while you are waiting for these things to happen and for him to come, try hard to live without sinning; and be at peace with everyone so that he will be pleased with you when he returns.

[15,16] And remember why he is waiting. He is giving us time to get his message of salvation out to others. Our wise and beloved brother Paul has talked about these same things in many of his letters. Some of his comments are not easy to understand, and there are people who are deliberately stupid, and always demand some unusual interpretation—they have twisted his letters around to mean something quite different from what he meant, just as they do the other parts of the Scripture—and the result is disaster for them.

[17] I am warning you ahead of time, dear brothers, so that you can watch out and not be carried away by the mistakes of these wicked men, lest you yourselves become mixed up too. [18] But grow in spiritual strength and become better acquainted with our Lord and Savior Jesus Christ. To him be all glory and splendid honor, both now and forevermore. Good-bye.

Peter

---

a Literally, "wherein righteousness dwells."

I'm Comfy Here...

Each of us has his own group he feels at home with. These students, relaxed, casual, know they belong. Yet even in a group like this, arguments come up, friendships splinter, emptiness deepens, frustration at people's lack of understanding boils inside. We depend on our friends to provide something we deeply need. Why does it get spoiled so often? John, now an old, warmhearted man filled with love, shows us in these three letters the path to the kind of camaraderie that gives us what we need to live quality lives with those around us.

1 JOHN

1 CHRIST WAS ALIVE when the world began, yet I myself have seen him with my own eyes and listened to him speak. I have touched him with my own hands. He is God's message of Life. [2] This one who is Life from God has been shown to us and we guarantee that we have seen him; I am speaking of Christ, who is eternal Life. He was with the Father and then was shown to us. [3] Again I say, we are telling you about what we ourselves have actually seen and heard, so that you may share the fellowship and the joys we have with the Father and with Jesus Christ his Son. [4] And if you do as I say in this letter, then you, too, will be full of joy, and so will we.

[5] This is the message God has given us to pass on to you: that God is Light and in him is no darkness at all. [6] So if we say we are his friends, but go on living in spiritual darkness and sin, we are lying. [7] But if we are living in the light of God's presence, just as Christ does, then we have wonderful fellowship and joy with each other, and the blood of Jesus his Son cleanses us from every sin.

[8] If we say that we have no sin, we are only fooling ourselves, and refusing to accept the truth. [9] But if we confess our sins to him,[a] he can be depended on to forgive us and to cleanse us from every wrong. [And it is perfectly proper for God to do this for us because Christ died to wash away our sins.[b]] [10] If we claim we have not sinned, we are lying and calling God a liar, *for he says we have sinned.*

2 MY LITTLE CHILDREN, I am telling you this so that you will stay away from sin. But if you sin, there is someone to plead for you before the Father. His name is Jesus Christ, the one who is all that is good and who pleases God completely. [2] He is the one who took God's wrath against our sins upon himself, and brought us into fellowship with God; and he is the forgiveness[a] for our sins, and not only ours but all the world's.

[3] And how can we be sure that we belong to him? By looking within ourselves: are we really trying to do what he wants us to?

[4] Someone may say, "I am a Christian; I am on my way to heaven; I belong to Christ." But if he doesn't do what Christ tells him to, he is a liar. [5] But those who do

---

a Implied. Literally, "if we confess our sins."
b Literally, "he is . . . just."   2 a Or, "atoning sacrifice."

what Christ tells them to will learn to love God more and more. That is the way to know whether or not you are a Christian. ⁶ Anyone who says he is a Christian should live as Christ did.

⁷ Dear brothers, I am not writing out a new rule for you to obey, for it is an old one you have always had, right from the start. You have heard it all before. ⁸ Yet it is always new, and works for you just as it did for Christ; and as we obey this commandment, *to love one another,* the darkness in our lives disappears and the new light of life in Christ shines in.

⁹ Anyone who says he is walking in the light of Christ but dislikes his fellow man, is still in darkness. ¹⁰ But whoever loves his fellow man is "walking in the light" and can see his way without stumbling around in darkness and sin. ¹¹ For he who dislikes his brother is wandering in spiritual darkness and doesn't know where he is going, for the darkness had made him blind so that he cannot see the way.

¹² I am writing these things to all of you, my little children, because your sins have been forgiven in the name of Jesus our Savior. ¹³ I am saying these things to you older men because you really know Christ, the one who has been alive from the beginning. And you young men, I am talking to you because you have won your battle with Satan. And I am writing to you younger boys and girls because you, too, have learned to know God our Father.

¹⁴ And so I say to you fathers who know the eternal God, and to you young men who are strong, with God's Word in your hearts, and have won your struggle against Satan: ¹⁵ Stop loving this evil world and all that it offers you, for when you love these things you show that you do not really love God; ¹⁶ for all these worldly things, these evil desires—the craze for sex, the ambition to buy everything that appeals to you, and the pride that comes from wealth and importance—these are not from God. They are from this evil world itself. ¹⁷ And this world is fading away, and these evil, forbidden things will go with it, but whoever keeps doing the will of God will live forever.

¹⁸ Dear children, this world's last hour has come. You have heard about the Anti-christ who is coming—the one who is against Christ—and already many such persons have appeared. This makes us all the more certain that the end of the world is near. ¹⁹ These "against-Christ" people used to be members of our churches, but they never really belonged with us or else they would have stayed. When they left us it proved that they were not of us at all.

²⁰ But you are not like that, for the Holy Spirit has come upon you, and you know the truth. ²¹ So I am not writing to you as to those who need to know the truth, but I warn you as those who can discern the difference between true and false.

²² And who is the greatest liar? The one who says that Jesus is not Christ. Such a person is antichrist, for he does not believe in God the Father and in his Son. ²³ For a person who doesn't believe in Christ, God's Son, can't have God the Father either. But he who has Christ, God's Son, has God the Father also.

²⁴ So keep on believing what you have been taught from the beginning. If you do, you will always be in close fellowship with both God the Father and his Son. ²⁵ And he himself has promised us this: *eternal life.*

²⁶ These remarks of mine about the Anti-christ are pointed at those who would dearly love to blindfold you and lead you astray. ²⁷ But you have received the Holy Spirit and he lives within you, in your hearts, so that you don't need anyone to teach you what is right. For he teaches you all things, and he is the Truth, and no liar; and so, just as he has said, you must live in Christ, never to depart from him.

²⁸ And now, my little children, stay in happy fellowship with the Lord so that when he comes you will be sure that all is well, and will not have to be ashamed and shrink back from meeting him. ²⁹ Since we know that God is always good and does only right, we may rightly assume that all those who do right are his children.

3 SEE HOW VERY much our heavenly Father loves us, for he allows us to be called his children—think of it—and we really *are!* But since most people don't know God, naturally they don't understand that we are his children. ² Yes, dear friends,

we are already God's children, right now, and we can't even imagine what it is going to be like later on. But we do know this, that when he comes we will be like him, as a result of seeing him as he really is. ³ And everyone who really believes this will try to stay pure because Christ is pure.

⁴ But those who keep on sinning are against God, for every sin is done against the will of God. ⁵ And you know that he became a man so that he could take away our sins, and that there is no sin in him, no missing of God's will at any time in any way. ⁶ So if we stay close to him, obedient to him, we won't be sinning either; but as for those who keep on sinning, they should realize this: They sin because they have never really known him or become his.

⁷ Oh, dear children, don't let anyone deceive you about this: if you are constantly doing what is good, it is because you *are* good, even as he is. ⁸ But if you keep on sinning, it shows that you belong to Satan, who since he first began to sin has kept steadily at it. But the Son of God came to destroy these works of the devil. ⁹ The person who has been born into God's family does not make a practice of sinning, because now God's life is in him; so he can't keep on sinning, for this new life has been born into him and controls him—he has been *born again.*

¹⁰ So now we can tell who is a child of God and who belongs to Satan. Whoever is living a life of sin and doesn't love his brother shows that he is not in God's family; ¹¹ for the message to us from the beginning has been that we should love one another.

¹² We are not to be like Cain, who belonged to Satan and killed his brother. Why did he kill him? Because Cain had been doing wrong and he knew very well that his brother's life was better than his. ¹³ So don't be surprised, dear friends, if the world hates you.

¹⁴ If we love other Christians it proves that we have been delivered from hell and given eternal life. But a person who doesn't have love for others is headed for eternal

death. ¹⁵ Anyone who hates his Christian brother is really a murderer at heart; and you know that no one wanting to murder has eternal life within. ¹⁶ We know what real love is from Christ's example in dying for us. And so we also ought to lay down our lives for our Christian brothers.

¹⁷ But if someone who is supposed to be a Christian has money enough to live well, and sees a brother in need, and won't help him—how can God's love be within *him?* ¹⁸ Little children, let us stop just *saying* we love people; let us *really* love them, and *show it* by our *actions.* ¹⁹ Then we will know for sure, by our actions, that we are on God's side, and our consciences will be clear, even when we stand before the Lord. ²⁰ But if we have bad consciences and feel that we have done wrong, the Lord will surely feel it even more,ᵃ for he knows everything we do.

²¹ But, dearly loved friends, if our consciences are clear, we can come to the Lord with perfect assurance and trust, ²² and get whatever we ask for because we are obeying him and doing the things that please him. ²³ And this is what God says we must do: Believe on the name of his Son Jesus Christ, and love one another. ²⁴ Those who do what God says—they are living with God and he with them. We know this is true because the Holy Spirit he has given us tells us so.

4 DEARLY LOVED FRIENDS, don't always believe everything you hear just because someone says it is a message from God: test it first to see if it really is. For there are many false teachers around, ² and the way to find out if their message is from the Holy Spirit is to ask: Does it really agree that Jesus Christ, God's Son, actually became man with a human body? If so, then the message is from God. ³ If not, the message is not from God but from one who is against Christ, like the "Antichrist" you have heard about who is going to come, and his attitude of enmity against Christ is already abroad in the world.

⁴ Dear young friends, you belong to God and have already won your fight with those

---

a Or, perhaps, "the Lord will be merciful anyway." Literally, "If our heart condemns us, God is greater than our heart."

who are against Christ, because there is someone in your hearts who is stronger than any evil teacher in this wicked world. ⁵ These men belong to this world, so, quite naturally, they are concerned about worldly affairs and the world pays attention to them. ⁶ But we are children of God; that is why only those who have walked and talked with God will listen to us. Others won't. That is another way to know whether a message is really from God; for if it is, the world won't listen to it.

⁷ Dear friends, let us practice loving each other, for love comes from God and those who are loving and kind show that they are the children of God, and that they are getting to know him better. ⁸ But if a person isn't loving and kind, it shows that he doesn't know God—for God is love.

⁹ God showed how much he loved us by sending his only Son into this wicked world to bring to us eternal life through his death. ¹⁰ In this act we see what real love is: it is not our love for God, but his love for us when he sent his Son to satisfy God's anger against our sins.

¹¹ Dear friends, since God loved us as much as that, we surely ought to love each other too. ¹² For though we have never yet seen God, when we love each other God lives in us and his love within us grows ever stronger. ¹³ And he has put his own Holy Spirit into our hearts as a proof to us that we are living with him and he with us. ¹⁴ And furthermore, we have seen with our own eyes and now tell all the world that God sent his Son to be their Savior. ¹⁵ Anyone who believes and says that Jesus is the Son of God has God living in him, and he is living with God.

¹⁶ We know how much God loves us because we have felt his love and because we believe him when he tells us that he loves us dearly. God is love, and anyone who lives in love is living with God and God is living in him. ¹⁷ And as we live with Christ, our love grows more perfect and complete; so we will not be ashamed and embarrassed at the day of judgment, but can face him with confidence and joy, because he loves us and

we love him too.

¹⁸ We need have no fear of someone who loves us perfectly; his perfect love for us eliminates all dread of what he might do to us. If we are afraid, it is for fear of what he might do to us, and shows that we are not fully convinced that he really loves us. ¹⁹ So you see, our love for him comes as a result of his loving us first.

²⁰ If anyone says "I love God," but keeps on hating his brother, he is a liar; for if he doesn't love his brother who is right there in front of him, how can he love God whom he has never seen? ²¹And God himself has said that one must love not only God, but his brother too.

5 IF YOU BELIEVE that Jesus is the Christ—that he is God's Son and your Savior—then you are a child of God. And all who love the Father love his children too. ² So you can find out how much you love God's children—your brothers and sisters in the Lord—by how much you love and obey God. ³ Loving God means doing what he tells us to do, and really, that isn't hard at all; ⁴ for every child of God can obey him, defeating sin and evil pleasure by trusting Christ to help him.

⁵ But who could possibly fight and win this battle except by believing that Jesus is truly the Son of God? ⁶,⁷,⁸ And we know he is, because God said so with a voice from heaven when Jesus was baptized, and again as he was facing death[a]—yes, not only at his baptism but also as he faced death.[b] And the Holy Spirit, forever truthful, says it too. So we have these three witnesses: the voice of the Holy Spirit in our hearts, the voice from heaven at Christ's baptism, and the voice before he died.[c] And they all say the same thing: that Jesus Christ is the Son of God.[d] ⁹ We believe men who witness in our courts, and so surely we can believe whatever God declares. And God declares that Jesus is his Son. ¹⁰ All who believe this know in their hearts that it is true. If anyone doesn't believe this, he is actually calling God a liar, because he doesn't believe what God has said about his Son.

---

a Literally, "This is he who came by water and blood." See Matthew 3:16, 17; Luke 9:31, 35; John 12:27, 28, 32, 33. Other interpretations of this verse are equally possible.   b Literally, "not by water only, but by water and blood."   c Literally, "the Spirit, and the water, and the blood."   d Implied.

¹¹ And what is it that God has said? That he has given us eternal life, and that this life is in his Son. ¹² So whoever has God's Son has life; whoever does not have his Son, does not have life.

¹³ I have written this to you who believe in the Son of God so that you may know you have eternal life. ¹⁴ And we are sure of this, that he will listen to us whenever we ask him for anything in line with his will. ¹⁵ And if we really know he is listening when we talk to him and make our requests, then we can be sure that he will answer us.

¹⁶ If you see a Christian sinning in a way that does not end in death, you should ask God to forgive him and God will give him life, unless he has sinned that one fatal sin. But there is that one sin which ends in death and if he has done that, there is no use praying for him. ¹⁷ Every wrong is a sin, of course. I'm not talking about these ordinary sins; I am speaking of that one that ends in death.^e

¹⁸ No one who has become part of God's family makes a practice of sinning, for Christ, God's Son, holds him securely and the devil cannot get his hands on him. ¹⁹ We know that we are children of God and that all the rest of the world around us is under Satan's power and control. ²⁰ And we know that Christ, God's Son, has come to help us understand and find the true God. And now we are in God because we are in Jesus Christ his Son, who is the only true God; and he is eternal Life.

²¹ Dear children, keep away from anything that might take God's place in your hearts. Amen.

Sincerely,
John

2 JOHN

1 FROM: JOHN, THE old Elder of the church.

To: That dear woman Cyria, one of God's very own, and to her children whom I love so much, as does everyone else in the church. ² Since the Truth is in our hearts forever, ³ God the Father and Jesus Christ his Son will bless us with great mercy and much peace, and with truth and love.

⁴ How happy I am to find some of your children here, and to see that they are living as they should, following the Truth, obeying God's command.

⁵ And now I want to urgently remind you, dear friends, of the old rule God gave us right from the beginning, that Christians should love one another. ⁶ If we love God, we will do whatever he tells us to. And he has told us from the very first to love each other.

⁷ Watch out for the false leaders—and there are many of them around—who don't believe that Jesus Christ came to earth as a human being with a body like ours. Such people are against the truth and against Christ. ⁸ Beware of being like them, and losing the prize that you and I have been working so hard to get. See to it that you win your full reward from the Lord. ⁹ For if you wander beyond the teaching of Christ, you will leave God behind; while if you are loyal to Christ's teachings, you will have God too. Then you will have both the Father and the Son.

¹⁰ If anyone comes to teach you, and he doesn't believe what Christ taught, don't even invite him into your home. Don't encourage him in any way. ¹¹ If you do you will be a partner with him in his wickedness.

¹² Well, I would like to say much more, but I don't want to say it in this letter, for I hope to come to see you soon and then we can talk over these things together and have a joyous time.

¹³ Greetings from the children of your sister—another choice child of God.

Sincerely,
John

---

e Commentators differ widely in their thoughts about what sin this is, and whether it causes physical death or spiritual death. Blasphemy against the Holy Spirit results in spiritual death (Mark 3:29) but can a Christian ever sin in such a way? Impenitence at the Communion Table sometimes ends in physical death (1 Cor. 11:30). And Hebrews 6:4-8 speaks of the terrible end of those who fall away.

3 JOHN

1 FROM: JOHN, THE Elder.
To: Dear Gaius, whom I truly love.
² Dear friend, I am praying that all is well with you and that your body is as healthy as I know your soul is. ³ Some of the brothers traveling by have made me very happy by telling me that your life stays clean and true, and that you are living by the standards of the Gospel. ⁴ I could have no greater joy than to hear such things about my children.

⁵ Dear friend, you are doing a good work for God in taking care of the traveling teachers and missionaries who are passing through. ⁶ They have told the church here of your friendship and your loving deeds. I am glad when you send them on their way with a generous gift. ⁷ For they are traveling for the Lord, and take neither food, clothing, shelter, nor money from those who are not Christians, even though they have preached to them. ⁸ So we ourselves should take care of them in order that we may become partners with them in the Lord's work.

⁹ I sent a brief letter to the church about this, but proud Diotrephes, who loves to push himself forward as the leader of the Christians there, does not admit my authority over him and refuses to listen to me. ¹⁰ When I come I will tell you some of the things he is doing and what wicked things he is saying about me and what insulting language he is using. He not only refuses to welcome the missionary travelers himself, but tells others not to, and when they do he tries to put them out of the church.

¹¹ Dear friend, don't let this bad example influence you. Follow only what is good. Remember that those who do what is right prove that they are God's children; and those who continue in evil prove that they are far from God. ¹² But everyone, including Truth itself, speaks highly of Demetrius. I myself can say the same for him, and you know I speak the truth.

¹³ I have much to say but I don't want to write it, ¹⁴ for I hope to see you soon and then we will have much to talk about together. ¹⁵ So good-bye for now. Friends here send their love, and please give each of the folks there a special greeting from me.

Sincerely,
John

What Now Brigitt?

Brigitt, a German girl, has just been graduated. What next? She plans to be a school-teacher. Will she find her idealism shattered by the way kids really are at heart? In a way, this is how the writer of Jude felt—he had meant to write of some of the happy things of God and salvation— but instead had to face up to the realism of people "like dirty foam on the beach." Of course, that could be the picture of each of us—if we don't "stay where God's love can reach us" . . . as this letter so aptly indicates.

ANI

JUDE

1 FROM: JUDE, A servant of Jesus Christ, and a brother of James.

To: Christians everywhere—beloved of God and chosen by him. ² May you be given more and more of God's kindness, peace, and love.

³ Dearly loved friends, I had been planning to write you some thoughts about the salvation God has given us, but now I find I must write of something else instead, urging you to stoutly defend the truth which God gave, once for all, to his people to keep without change through the years. ⁴ I say this because some godless teachers have wormed their way in among you, saying that after we become Christians we can do just as we like without fear of God's punishment. The fate of such people was written long ago, for they have turned against our only Master and Lord, Jesus Christ.

⁵ My answer to them is: Remember this fact—which you know already—that the Lord saved a whole nation of people out of the land of Egypt, and then killed every one of them who did not trust and obey him. ⁶ And I remind you of those angels who were once pure and holy, but turned to a life of sin.ᵃ Now God has them chained up in prisons of darkness, waiting for the judgment day. ⁷ And don't forget the cities of

---

a Or, "who abandoned their original rank and left their proper home."

Sodom and Gomorrah and their neighboring towns, all full of lust of every kind including lust of men for other men. Those cities were destroyed by fire and continue to be a warning to us that there is a hell in which sinners are punished.

⁸ Yet these false teachers carelessly go right on living their evil, immoral lives, degrading their bodies and laughing at those in authority over them, even scoffing at the Glorious Ones. ⁹ Yet Michael, one of the mightiest of the angels, when he was arguing with Satan about Moses' body, did not dare to accuse even Satan, or jeer at him, but simply said, "The Lord rebuke you." ¹⁰ But these men mock and curse at anything they do not understand, and, like animals, they do whatever they feel like, thereby ruining their souls.

¹¹ Woe upon them! For they follow the example of Cain who killed his brother; and, like Balaam, they will do anything for money; and like Korah, they have disobeyed God and will die under his curse.

¹² When these men join you at the love feasts of the church, they are evil smears among you, laughing and carrying on, gorging and stuffing themselves without a thought for others. They are like clouds blowing over dry land without giving rain, promising much, but producing nothing. They are like fruit trees without any fruit at picking time. They are not only dead, but doubly dead, for they have been pulled out, roots and all, to be burned.

¹³ All they leave behind them is shame and disgrace like the dirty foam left along the beach by the wild waves. They wander around looking as bright as stars, but ahead of them is the everlasting gloom and darkness that God has prepared for them.

¹⁴ Enoch, who lived seven generations after Adam, knew about these men and said this about them: "See, the Lord is coming with millions of his holy ones. ¹⁵ He will bring the people of the world before him in judgment, to receive just punishment, and to prove the terrible things they have done in rebellion against God, revealing all they have said against him." ¹⁶ These men are constant gripers, never satisfied, doing whatever evil they feel like; they are loud-mouthed "show-offs," and when they show respect for others, it is only to get something from them in return.

¹⁷ Dear friends, remember what the apostles of our Lord Jesus Christ told you, ¹⁸ that in the last times there would come these scoffers whose whole purpose in life is to enjoy themselves in every evil way imaginable. ¹⁹ They stir up arguments; they love the evil things of the world; they do not have the Holy Spirit living in them.

²⁰ But you, dear friends, must build up your lives ever more strongly upon the foundation of our holy faith, learning to pray in the power and strength of the Holy Spirit.

²¹ Stay always within the boundaries where God's love can reach and bless you. Wait patiently for the eternal life that our Lord Jesus Christ in his mercy is going to give you. ²² Try to help those who argue against you. Be merciful to those who doubt. ²³ Save some by snatching them as from the very flames of hell itself. And as for others, help them to find the Lord by being kind to them, but be careful that you yourselves aren't pulled along into their sins. Hate every trace of their sin while being merciful to them as sinners.

²⁴,²⁵ And now—all glory to him who alone is God, who saves us through Jesus Christ our Lord; yes, splendor and majesty, all power and authority are his from the beginning; his they are and his they evermore shall be. And he is able to keep you from slipping and falling away, and to bring you, sinless and perfect, into his glorious presence with mighty shouts of everlasting joy. Amen.

Jude

No Joke

THE END OF THE WORLD! That slogan appears everywhere—scrawled on subway walls, carried by bearded prophets, mocked in *New Yorker* cartoons. It's always good for a few laughs. After all, people have been predicting the end of the world for quite a few thousand years.

Many of the doomsdayers who have been the butts of the biggest laughs found their source right in this book: the Revelation. They took its mysterious symbols and attached dates and specific names to Christ's return, only to find he missed their schedule.

But there's more to Revelation than hints about the future. You meet a side of Jesus hidden through most of the Gospels. He is a person whose "eyes were like flames of fire and voice like waves against the shore." He is power, the one who was here when earth was created and the one who personally holds the destiny of every atom.

No one's sure exactly when the astounding events of this book will take place (not even Jesus knew). But reading through Revelation makes one fact clear—you'd better be aligned on the side of truth ... Jesus Christ. Because when the end of the world finally does happen, it won't be a joke.

THE REVELATION

1 THIS BOOK UNVEILS some of the future activities soon to occur in the life of Jesus Christ.[a] God permitted him to reveal these things to his servant John in a vision; and then an angel was sent from heaven to explain the vision's meaning. [2] John wrote it all down—the words of God and Jesus Christ and everything he heard and saw.

[3] If you read this prophecy aloud to the church, you will receive a special blessing from the Lord. Those who listen to it being read and do what it says will also be blessed. For the time is near when these things will all come true.

[4] *From:* John

To: The seven churches in Turkey.[b]

Dear Friends:

May you have grace and peace from God who is, and was, and is to come! and from the seven-fold Spirit[c] before his throne; [5] and from Jesus Christ who faithfully reveals all truth to us. He was the first to rise from death, to die no more.[d] He is far greater than any king in all the earth. All praise to him who always loves us and who set us free from our sins by pouring out his lifeblood for us. [6] He has gathered us into his kingdom and made us priests of God his Father. Give to him everlasting glory! He rules forever! Amen!

[7] See! He is arriving, surrounded by clouds; and every eye shall see him—yes, and those who pierced him.[e] And the nations will weep in sorrow and in terror when he comes. Yes! Amen! Let it be so!

[8] "I am the A and the Z,[f] the Beginning and the Ending of all things," says God, who is the Lord, the All Powerful One who is, and was, and is coming again![g]

[9] It is I, your brother John, a fellow sufferer for the Lord's sake, who am writing this letter to you. I, too, have shared the patience Jesus gives, and we shall share his kingdom!

I was on the island of Patmos, exiled there for preaching the Word of God, and for telling what I knew about Jesus Christ. [10] It was the Lord's Day and I was worshiping, when suddenly I heard a loud voice behind me, a voice that sounded like a trumpet blast, [11] saying, "I am A and Z, the First and Last!" And then I heard him say, "Write down everything you see, and send your letter to the seven churches in Turkey:[h] to the church in Ephesus, the one in Smyrna, and those in Pergamos, Thyatira, Sardis, Philadelphia, and Laodicea."

[12] When I turned to see who was speaking, there behind me were seven candlesticks of gold. [13] And standing among them was one who looked like Jesus who called himself the Son of Man,[i] wearing a long robe circled with a golden band across his chest. [14] His hair[j] was white as wool or snow, and his eyes penetrated like flames of fire. [15] His feet gleamed like burnished bronze, and his voice thundered like the waves against the shore. [16] He held seven stars in his right hand and a sharp, double-bladed sword in his mouth,[k] and his face shone like the power of the sun in unclouded brilliance.

[17,18] When I saw him, I fell at his feet as dead; but he laid his right hand on me and said, "Don't be afraid! Though I am the First and Last, the Living One who died, who is now alive forevermore, who has the keys of hell and death—don't be afraid! [19] Write down what you have just seen, and what will soon be shown to you. [20] This is

---

a Literally, "the revelation of (*concerning,* or, *from*) Jesus Christ."   b Literally, "in Asia."
c Literally, "the seven spirits." But see Isaiah 11:2, where various aspects of the Holy Spirit are described, and Zechariah 4:2–6, giving probability to the paraphrase; also see Revelation 2:7.   d Literally, "the First-born from the dead." Others (Lazarus, etc.) rose to die again. As used here the expression therefore implies "to die no more."   e John saw this happen with his own eyes—the piercing of Jesus—and never forgot the horror of it.   f Literally, "I am Alpha and Omega"; these are the first and last letters of the Greek alphabet.
g Literally, "who comes" or "who is to come."   h "The seven churches in Asia."   i Literally, "like unto a Son of Man"; John recognizes him from having lived with him for three years, and from seeing him in glory at the Transfiguration.   j Literally, "His head—the hair—was white like wool."
k Literally, "coming out from his mouth."

the meaning of the seven stars you saw in my right hand, and the seven golden candlesticks: The seven stars are the leaders[l] of the seven churches, and the seven candlesticks are the churches themselves.

2 *"Write a letter to the leader[a] of the church at Ephesus and tell him this:*

"I write to inform you of a message from him who walks among the churches[b] and holds their leaders in his right hand.

"He says to you: [2] I know how many good things you are doing. I have watched your hard work and your patience; I know you don't tolerate sin among your members, and you have carefully examined the claims of those who say they are apostles but aren't. You have found out how they lie. [3] You have patiently suffered for me without quitting.

[4] "Yet there is one thing wrong; you don't love me as at first! [5] Think about those times of your first love (how different now!) and turn back to me again and work as you did before; or else I will come and remove your candlestick from its place among the churches.

[6] "But there is this about you that is good: You hate the deeds of the licentious Nicolaitans,[c] just as I do.

[7] "Let this message sink into the ears of anyone who listens to what the Spirit is saying to the churches: To everyone who is victorious, I will give fruit from the Tree of Life in the Paradise of God.

[8] *"To the leader[d] of the church in Smyrna write this letter:*

"This message is from him who is the First and Last, who was dead and then came back to life.

[9] "I know how much you suffer for the Lord, and I know all about your poverty (but you have heavenly riches!). I know the slander of those opposing you, who say that they are Jews—the children of God—but they aren't, for they support the cause of Satan. [10] Stop being afraid of what you are about to suffer—for the devil will soon throw some of you into prison to test you. You will be persecuted for 'ten days.' Remain faithful even when facing death and I will give you the crown of life—an unending, glorious future.[e] [11] Let everyone who can hear, listen to what the Spirit is saying to the churches: He who is victorious shall not be hurt by the Second Death.

[12] *"Write this letter to the leader[d] of the church in Pergamos:*

"This message is from him who wields the sharp and double-bladed sword. [13] I am fully aware that you live in the city where Satan's throne is, at the center of satanic worship; and yet you have remained loyal to me, and refused to deny me, even when Antipas, my faithful witness, was martyred among you by Satan's devotees.

[14] "And yet I have a few things against you. You tolerate some among you who do as Balaam did when he taught Balak how to ruin the people of Israel by involving them in sexual sin and encouraging them to go to idol feasts. [15] Yes, you have some of these very same followers of Balaam[f] among you!

[16] "Change your mind and attitude, or else I will come to you suddenly and fight against them with the sword of my mouth.

[17] "Let everyone who can hear, listen to what the Spirit is saying to the churches: Every one who is victorious shall eat of the hidden manna, the secret nourishment from heaven; and I will give to each a white stone, and on the stone will be engraved a new name that no one else knows except the one receiving it.

[18] *"Write this letter to the leader[d] of the church in Thyatira:*

"This is a message from the Son of God, whose eyes penetrate like flames of fire, whose feet are like glowing brass.

[19] "I am aware of all your good deeds —your kindness to the poor, your gifts and service to them; also I know your love and faith and patience, and I can see your con-

---

l Literally, "angels." Some expositors (Origen, Jerome, etc.) believe from this that an angelic being is appointed by God to oversee each local church.　　2a Literally, "angel," as in 1:20.　　b Literally, "from him who holds the seven stars in his right hand and walks among the golden candlesticks."　　c Nicolaitans, when translated from Greek to Hebrew, becomes Balaamites; followers of the man who induced the Israelites to fall by lust. (See Revelation 2:14 and Numbers 31:15, 16.)　　d Literally, "angel." See note on 1:20. e Implied.　　f Literally, "Nicolaitans," Greek form of "Balaamites."

stant improvement in all these things.

²⁰ "Yet I have this against you: You are permitting that woman Jezebel, who calls herself a prophetess, to teach my servants that sex sin is not a serious matter; she urges them to practice immorality and to eat meat that has been sacrificed to idols. ²¹ I gave her time to change her mind and attitude, but she refused. ²² Pay attention now to what I am saying: I will lay her upon a sickbed of intense affliction, along with all her immoral followers,ᵍ unless they turn again to me, repenting of their sin with her; ²³ and I will strike her children dead. And all the churches shall know that I am he who searches deep within men's hearts, and minds; I will give to each of you whatever you deserve.

²⁴,²⁵ "As for the rest of you in Thyatira who have not followed this false teaching ('deeper truths,' as they call them—depths of Satan, really), I will ask nothing further of you; only hold tightly to what you have until I come.

²⁶ "To every one who overcomes—who to the very end keeps on doing things that please me—I will give power over the nations. ²⁷ You will rule them with a rod of iron just as my Father gave me the authority to rule them; they will be shattered iike a pot of clay that is broken into tiny pieces. ²⁸ And I will give you the Morning Star!

²⁹ "Let all who can hear, listen to what the Spirit says to the churches.

3 *"To the leaderᵃ of the church in Sardis write this letter:*

"This message is sent to you by the one who has the seven-fold Spiritᵇ of God and the seven stars.

"I know your reputation as a live and active church, but you are dead. ² Now wake up! Strengthen what little remains—for even what is left is at the point of death. Your deeds are far from right in the sight of God. ³ Go back to what you heard and believed at first; hold to it firmly and turn

to me again. Unless you do, I will come suddenly upon you, unexpected as a thief, and punish you.

⁴ "Yet even there in Sardis some haven't soiled their garments with the world's filth; they shall walk with me in white, for they are worthy. ⁵ Everyone who conquers will be clothed in white, and I will not erase his name from the Book of Life, but I will announce before my Father and his angels that he is mine.

⁶ "Let all who can hear, listen to what the Spirit is saying to the churches.

⁷ *"Write this letter to the leaderᵃ of the church in Philadelphia.*

"This message is sent to you by the one who is holy and true, and has the key of David to open what no one can shut and to shut what no one can open.

⁸ "I know you well; you aren't strong, but you have tried to obeyᶜ and have not denied my Name. Therefore I have opened a door to you that no one can shut.

⁹ "Note this: I will force those supporting the causes of Satan while claiming to be mineᵈ (but they aren't—they are lying) to fall at your feet and acknowledge that you are the ones I love.

¹⁰ "Because you have patiently obeyed me despite the persecution, therefore I will protect you fromᵉ the time of Great Tribulation and temptation, which will come upon the world to test everyone alive. ¹¹ Look, I am coming soon!ᶠ Hold tightly to the little strength you have—so that no one will take away your crown.

¹² "As for the one who conquers, I will make him a pillar in the temple of my God; he will be secure, and will go out no more; and I will write my God's Name on him, and he will be a citizen in the city of my God—the New Jerusalem, coming down from heaven from my God; and he will have my new Name inscribed upon him.

¹³ "Let all who can hear, listen to what the Spirit is saying to the churches.

¹⁴ *"Write this letter to the leaderᵃ of the church in Laodicea:*

---

g Literally, "together with all those who commit adultery with her."   3a Literally, "angel." See note on 1:20.
b Literally, "the seven spirits of God." See note on 1:4.   c Literally, "you have kept my word."
d Literally, "say they are Jews but are not."   e Or, "I will keep you from failing in the hour of testing . . ."
The inference is not clear in the Greek as to whether this means "kept from" or "kept through" the coming
horror.   f Or, "suddenly," "unexpectedly."

"This message is from the one who stands firm,[g] the faithful and true Witness [of all that is or was or evermore shall be[h]], the primeval source of God's creation:

[15] "I know you well—you are neither hot nor cold; I wish you were one or the other! [16] But since you are merely lukewarm, I will spit you out of my mouth!

[17] "You say, 'I am rich, with everything I want; I don't need a thing!' And you don't realize that spiritually you are wretched and miserable and poor and blind and naked.

[18] "My advice to you is to buy pure gold from me, gold purified by fire—only then will you truly be rich. And to purchase from me white garments, clean and pure, so you won't be naked and ashamed; and to get medicine from me to heal your eyes and give you back your sight. [19] I continually discipline and punish everyone I love; so I must punish you, unless you turn from your indifference and become enthusiastic about the things of God.

[20] "Look! I have been standing at the door and I am constantly knocking. If anyone hears me calling him and opens the door, I will come in and fellowship with him and he with me. [21] I will let every one who conquers sit beside me on my throne, just as I took my place with my Father on his throne when I had conquered. [22] Let those who can hear, listen to what the Spirit is saying to the churches."

4 THEN AS I looked, I saw a door standing open in heaven, and the same voice I had heard before, that sounded like a mighty trumpet blast, spoke to me and said, "Come up here and I will show you what must happen in the future!"

[2] And instantly I was, in spirit, there in heaven and saw—oh, the glory of it!—a throne and someone sitting on it! [3] Great bursts of light flashed forth from him as from a glittering diamond, or from a shining ruby, and a rainbow glowing like an emerald encircled his throne. [4] Twenty-four smaller thrones surrounded his, with twenty-four Elders sitting on them; all were clothed in white, with golden crowns upon

their heads. [5] Lightning and thunder issued from the throne, and there were voices in the thunder. Directly in front of his throne were seven lighted lamps representing the seven-fold Spirit[a] of God. [6] Spread out before it was a shiny crystal sea. Four Living Beings, dotted front and back with eyes, stood at the throne's four sides. [7] The first of these Living Beings was in the form of a lion; the second looked like an ox; the third had the face of a man; and the fourth, the form of an eagle, with wings spread out as though in flight. [8] Each of these Living Beings had six wings, and the central sections of their wings were covered with eyes. Day after day and night after night they kept on saying, "Holy, holy, holy, Lord God Almighty—the one who was, and is, and is to come."

[9] And when the Living Beings gave glory and honor and thanks to the one sitting on the throne, who lives forever and ever, [10] the twenty-four Elders fell down before him and worshiped him, the Eternal Living One, and cast their crowns before the throne, singing, [11] "O Lord, you are worthy to receive. the glory and the honor and the power, for you have created all things. They were created and called into being by your act of will."

5 AND I SAW a scroll in the right hand of the one who was sitting on the throne, a scroll with writing on the inside and on the back, and sealed with seven seals. [2] A mighty angel with a loud voice was shouting out this question: "Who is worthy to break the seals on this scroll, and to unroll it?" [3] But no one in all heaven or earth or from among the dead was permitted to open and read it.

[4] Then I wept with disappointment[a] because no one anywhere was worthy; no one could tell us what it said.

[5] But one of the twenty-four Elders said to me, "Stop crying, for look! The Lion of the tribe of Judah, the Root of David, has conquered, and proved himself worthy to open the scroll and to break its seven seals."

[6] I looked and saw a Lamb standing

---

g Literally, "from the Amen."   h Implied.   4a Literally, "the seven spirits of God." But see Zechariah 4:2–6, where the lamps are equated with the one Spirit.   5a Implied.

there before the twenty-four Elders, in front of the throne and the Living Beings, and on the Lamb were wounds that once had caused his death. He had seven horns and seven eyes, which represent the seven-fold Spirit[b] of God, sent out into every part of the world. [7] He stepped forward and took the scroll from the right hand of the one sitting upon the throne. [8] And as he took the scroll, the twenty-four Elders fell down before the Lamb, each with a harp and golden vials filled with incense—the prayers of God's people!

[9] They were singing[c] him a new song with these words: "You are worthy to take the scroll and break its seals and open it; for you were slain, and your blood has bought people from every nation as gifts for God. [10] And you have gathered them into a kingdom and made them priests of our God; they shall reign upon the earth."

[11] Then in my vision I heard the singing[d] of millions of angels surrounding the throne and the Living Beings and the Elders: [12] "The Lamb is worthy" (loudly they sang[d] it!) "—the Lamb who was slain. He is worthy to receive the power, and the riches, and the wisdom, and the strength, and the honor, and the glory, and the blessing."

[13] And then I heard everyone in heaven and earth, and from the dead beneath the earth and in the sea, exclaiming, "The blessing and the honor and the glory and the power belong to the one sitting on the throne, and to the Lamb forever and ever." [14] And the four Living Beings kept saying, "Amen!" And the twenty-four Elders fell down and worshiped him.

6 AS I WATCHED, the Lamb broke the first seal and began to unroll the scroll. Then one of the four Living Beings, with a voice that sounded like thunder, said, "Come!"

[2] I looked, and there in front of me was a white horse. Its rider carried a bow, and a crown was placed upon his head; he rode out to conquer in many battles and win the war.

[3] Then he unrolled the scroll to the second seal, and broke it open too. And I heard the second Living Being say, "Come!"

[4] This time a red horse rode out. Its rider was given a long sword and the authority to banish peace and bring anarchy to the earth; war and killing broke out everywhere.

[5] When he had broken the third seal, I heard the third Living Being say, "Come!" And I saw a black horse, with its rider holding a pair of balances in his hand. [6] And a voice from among the four Living Beings said, "A loaf of bread for $20, or three pounds of barley flour,[a] but there is no olive oil or wine."[b]

[7] And when the fourth seal was broken, I heard the fourth Living Being say, "Come!" [8] And now I saw a pale horse, and its rider's name was Death. And there followed after him another horse whose rider's name was Hell. They were given control of one-fourth of the earth, to kill with war and famine and disease and wild animals.

[9] And when he broke open the fifth seal, I saw an altar, and underneath it all the souls of those who had been martyred for preaching the Word of God and for being faithful in their witnessing. [10] They called loudly to the Lord and said, "O Sovereign Lord, holy and true, how long will it be before you judge the people of the earth for what they've done to us? When will you avenge our blood against those living on the earth?" [11] White robes were given to each of them, and they were told to rest a little longer until their other brothers, fellow servants of Jesus, had been martyred on the earth and joined them.

[12] I watched as he broke the sixth seal, and there was a vast earthquake; and the sun became dark like black cloth, and the moon was blood-red. [13] Then the stars of heaven appeared to be falling to earth[c] —like green fruit from fig trees buffeted by mighty winds. [14] And the starry heavens disappeared[d] as though rolled up like a

---

b Literally, "the seven spirits of God"; but see Zechariah 4:2–6, 10, where the seven eyes are equated with the seven lamps and the one Spirit.   c Literally, "saying" or "said."   d Literally, "saying" or "said."
6a Literally, "A choenix of wheat for a denarius, and three choenix of barley for a denarius. . . ."
b Literally, "do not damage the oil and wine."   c Literally, "the stars of heaven fell to the earth."
d Literally, "the sky departed."

scroll and taken away; and every mountain and island shook and shifted. [15] The kings of the earth, and world leaders and rich men, and high-ranking military officers, and all men great and small, slave and free, hid themselves in the caves and rocks of the mountains, [16] and cried to the mountains to crush them. "Fall on us," they pleaded, "and hide us from the face of the one sitting on the throne, and from the anger of the Lamb, [17] because the great day of their anger has come, and who can survive it?"

7 THEN I SAW four angels standing at the four corners of the earth, holding back the four winds from blowing, so that not a leaf rustled in the trees, and the ocean became as smooth as glass. [2] And I saw another angel coming from the east, carrying the Great Seal of the Living God. And he shouted out to those four angels who had been given power to injure earth and sea, [3] "Wait! Don't do anything yet—hurt neither earth nor sea nor trees—until we have placed the Seal of God upon the foreheads of his servants."

[4-8] How many were given this mark? I heard the number—it was 144,000; out of all twelve tribes of Israel, as listed here:

Judah	12,000
Reuben	12,000
Gad	12,000
Asher	12,000
Naphtali	12,000
Manasseh	12,000
Simeon	12,000
Levi	12,000
Issachar	12,000
Zebulun	12,000
Joseph	12,000
Benjamin	12,000

[9] After this I saw a vast crowd, too great to count, from all nations and provinces and languages, standing in front of the throne and before the Lamb, clothed in white, with palm branches in their hands. [10] And they were shouting with a mighty shout, "Salvation comes from our God upon the throne, and from the Lamb."

[11] And now all the angels were crowding around the throne and around the Elders and the four Living Beings, and falling face down before the throne and worshiping God. [12] "Amen!" they said. "Blessing, and glory, and wisdom, and thanksgiving, and honor, and power, and might, be to our God forever and forever. Amen!"

[13] Then one of the twenty-four Elders asked me, "Do you know who these are, who are clothed in white, and where they come from?"

[14] "No, sir," I replied. "Please tell me."

"These are the ones coming out of the Great Tribulation," he said; "they washed their robes and whitened them by the blood of the Lamb. [15] That is why they are here before the throne of God, serving him day and night in his temple. The one sitting on the throne will shelter them; [16] they will never be hungry again, nor thirsty, and they will be fully protected from the scorching noontime heat. [17] For the Lamb standing in front of[a] the throne will feed them and be their Shepherd and lead them to the springs of the Water of Life. And God will wipe their tears away."

8 WHEN THE LAMB had broken the seventh seal, there was silence throughout all heaven for what seemed like half an hour. [2] And I saw the seven angels that stand before God, and they were given seven trumpets.

[3] Then another angel with a golden censer came and stood at the altar; and a great quantity of incense was given to him to mix with the prayers of God's people, to offer upon the golden altar before the throne. [4] And the perfume of the incense mixed with prayers ascended up to God from the altar where the angel had poured them out.

[5] Then the angel filled the censer with fire from the altar and threw it down upon the earth; and thunder crashed and rumbled, lightning flashed, and there was a terrible earthquake.

[6] Then the seven angels with the seven trumpets prepared to blow their mighty blasts.

[7] The first angel blew his trumpet, and

a Literally, "in the center of the throne"; i.e., directly in front, not to one side. An alternate rendering might be, "at the heart of the throne."

hail and fire mixed with blood were thrown down upon the earth. One-third of the earth was set on fire so that one-third of the trees were burned, and all the green grass.

[8,9] Then the second angel blew his trumpet, and what appeared to be a huge burning mountain was thrown into the sea, destroying a third of all the ships; and a third of the sea turned red as[a] blood; and a third of the fish were killed.

[10] The third angel blew, and a great flaming star fell from heaven upon a third of the rivers and springs. [11] The star was called "Bitterness"[b] because it poisoned a third of all the water on the earth and many people died.

[12] The fourth angel blew his trumpet and immediately a third of the sun was blighted and darkened, and a third of the moon and the stars, so that the daylight was dimmed by a third, and the nighttime darkness deepened. [13] As I watched, I saw a solitary eagle flying through the heavens crying loudly, "Woe, woe, woe to the people of the earth because of the terrible things that will soon happen when the three remaining angels blow their trumpets."

9 THEN THE FIFTH angel blew his trumpet and I saw one[a] who was fallen to earth from heaven, and to him was given the key to the bottomless pit. [2] When he opened it, smoke poured out as though from some huge furnace, and the sun and air were darkened by the smoke.

[3] Then locusts came from the smoke and descended onto the earth and were given power to sting like scorpions. [4] They were told not to hurt the grass or plants or trees, but to attack those people who did not have the mark of God on their foreheads. [5] They were not to kill them, but to torture them for five months with agony like the pain of scorpion stings. [6] In those days men will try to kill themselves but won't be able to— death will not come. They will long to die— but death will flee away!

[7] The locusts looked like horses armored for battle. They had what looked like golden crowns on their heads, and their faces looked like men's. [8] Their hair was long like women's, and their teeth were those of lions. [9] They wore breastplates that seemed to be of iron, and their wings roared like an army of chariots rushing into battle. [10] They had stinging tails like scorpions, and their power to hurt, given to them for five months, was in their tails. [11] Their king is the Prince of the bottomless pit whose name in Hebrew is Abaddon, and in Greek, Apollyon [and in English, the Destroyer[b]].

[12] One terror now ends, but there are two more coming!

[13] The sixth angel blew his trumpet and I heard a voice speaking from the four horns of the golden altar that stands before the throne of God, [14] saying to the sixth angel, "Release the four mighty demons[c] held bound at the great River Euphrates." [15] They had been kept in readiness for that year and month and day and hour, and now they were turned loose to kill a third of all mankind. [16] They led an army of 200,000,-000[d] warriors[e]—I heard an announcement of how many there were.

[17,18] I saw their horses spread out before me in my vision; their riders wore fiery-red breastplates, though some were sky-blue and others yellow. The horses' heads looked much like lions', and smoke and fire and flaming sulphur billowed from their mouths, killing one-third of all mankind. [19] Their power of death was not only in their mouths, but in their tails as well, for their tails were similar to serpents' heads that struck and bit with fatal wounds.

[20] But the men left alive after these plagues *still refused to worship God!* They would not renounce their demon-worship, nor their idols made of gold and silver, brass, stone, and wood—which neither see nor hear nor walk! [21] Neither did they change their mind and attitude about all their murders and witchcraft, their immo-

---

a Literally, "became blood." b Literally, "Wormwood." 9a Literally, "a star fallen from heaven"; it is unclear whether this person is of satanic origin, as most commentators believe, or whether the reference is to Christ. b Implied. c Literally, "(fallen) angels." d If this is a literal figure, it is no longer incredible, in view of a world population of 6,000,000,000 in the near future. In China alone, in 1961, there were an "estimated 200,000,000 armed and organized militiamen" (Associated Press Release, April 24, 1964). e Literally, "horsemen."

rality and theft.

10 THEN I SAW another mighty angel coming down from heaven, surrounded by a cloud, with a rainbow over his head; his face shone like the sun and his feet flashed with fire. [2] And he held open in his hand a small scroll. He set his right foot on the sea and his left foot on the earth, [3] and gave a great shout—it was like the roar of a lion—and the seven thunders crashed their reply.

[4] I was about to write what the thunders said when a voice from heaven called to me, "Don't do it. Their words are not to be revealed."

[5] Then the mighty angel standing on the sea and land lifted his right hand to heaven, [6] and swore by him who lives forever and ever, who created heaven and everything in it and the earth and all that it contains and the sea and its inhabitants, that there should be no more delay, [7] but that when the seventh angel blew his trumpet, then God's veiled plan—mysterious through the ages ever since it was announced by his servants the prophets—would be fulfilled.

[8] Then the voice from heaven spoke to me again, "Go and get the unrolled scroll from the mighty angel standing there upon the sea and land."

[9] So I approached him and asked him to give me the scroll. "Yes, take it and eat it," he said. "At first it will taste like honey, but when you swallow it, it will make your stomach sour!" [10] So I took it from his hand, and ate it! And just as he had said, it was sweet in my mouth but it gave me a stomach ache when I swallowed it.

[11] Then he told me, "You must prophesy further about many peoples, nations, tribes, and kings."

11 NOW I WAS given a measuring stick and told to go and measure the temple of God, including the inner court where the altar stands, and to count the number of worshipers.[a] [2] "But do not measure the outer court," I was told, "for it has been turned over to the nations. They will tram-ple the Holy City for forty-two months.[b] [3] And I will give power to my two witnesses to prophesy 1,260 days[b] clothed in sackcloth."

[4] These two prophets are the two olive trees,[c] and two candlesticks standing before the God of all the earth. [5] Anyone trying to harm them will be killed by bursts of fire shooting from their mouths. [6] They have power to shut the skies so that no rain will fall during the three and a half years they prophesy, and to turn rivers and oceans to blood, and to send every kind of plague upon the earth as often as they wish.

[7] When they complete the three and a half years of their solemn testimony, the tyrant who comes out of the bottomless pit[d] will declare war against them and conquer and kill them; [8,9] and for three and a half days their bodies will be exposed in the streets of Jerusalem (the city fittingly described as "Sodom" or "Egypt")—the very place where their Lord was crucified. No one will be allowed to bury them, and people from many nations will crowd around to gaze at them. [10] And there will be a worldwide holiday—people everywhere will rejoice and give presents to each other and throw parties to celebrate the death of the two prophets who had tormented them so much!

[11] But after three and a half days, the spirit of life from God will enter them and they will stand up! And great fear will fall on everyone. [12] Then a loud voice will shout from heaven, "Come up!" And they will rise to heaven in a cloud as their enemies watch.

[13] The same hour there will be a terrible earthquake that levels a tenth of the city, leaving 7,000 dead. Then everyone left will, in their terror, give glory to the God of heaven.

[14] The second woe is past, but the third quickly follows:

[15] For just then the seventh angel blew his trumpet, and there were loud voices shouting down from heaven, "The kingdom of this world now belongs to our Lord, and to his Christ; and he shall reign forever and ever."[e]

---

a Literally, "Rise and measure the temple of God, and the altar, and them that worship therein." b 3½ years, as in Daniel 12:7. c Zechariah 4:3, 4, 11. d Revelation 9:11. e Or, "The Lord and his Anointed shall now rule the world from this day to eternity."

¹⁶ And the twenty-four Elders sitting on their thrones before God threw themselves down in worship, saying, ¹⁷ "We give thanks, Lord God Almighty, who is and was, for now you have assumed your great power and have begun to reign. ¹⁸ The nations were angry with you, but now it is your turn to be angry with them. It is time to judge the dead, and reward your servants—prophets and people alike, all who fear your Name, both great and small—and to destroy those who have caused destruction upon the earth."

¹⁹ Then, in heaven, the temple of God was opened and the ark of his covenant could be seen inside. Lightning flashed and thunder crashed and roared, and there was a great hailstorm and the world was shaken by a mighty earthquake.

12 THEN A GREAT pageant appeared in heaven, portraying things to come. I saw a woman clothed with the sun, with the moon beneath her feet, and a crown of twelve stars on her head. ² She was pregnant and screamed in the pain of her labor, awaiting her delivery.

³ Suddenly a red Dragon appeared, with seven heads and ten horns, and seven crowns on his heads. ⁴ His tail drew along behind him a third of the stars, which he plunged to the earth. He stood before the woman as she was about to give birth to her child, ready to eat the baby as soon as it was born. ⁵ She gave birth to a boy who was to rule all nations with a heavy hand, and he was caught up to God and to his throne. ⁶ The woman fled into the wilderness, where God had prepared a place for her, to take care of her for 1,260 days.

⁷ Then there was war in heaven; Michael and the angels under his command fought the Dragon and his hosts of fallen angels. ⁸ And the Dragon lost the battle and was forced from heaven. ⁹ This great Dragon—the ancient serpent called the devil, or Satan, the one deceiving the whole world—was thrown down onto the earth with all his army. ¹⁰ Then I heard a loud voice shouting across the heavens, "It has happened at last!

God's salvation and the power and the rule, and the authority of his Christ are finally here; for the Accuser of our brothers has been thrown down from heaven onto earth—he accused them day and night before our God. ¹¹ They defeated him by the blood of the Lamb, and by their testimony; for they did not love their lives but laid them down for him. ¹² Rejoice, O heavens! You citizens of heaven, rejoice! Be glad! But woe to you people of the world, for the devil has come down to you in great anger, knowing that he has little time."

¹³ And when the Dragon found himself cast down to earth, he persecuted the woman who had given birth to the child. ¹⁴ But she was given two wings like those of a great eagle, to fly into the wilderness to the place prepared for her, where she was cared for and protected from the Serpent, the Dragon, for three and a half years.ᵃ

¹⁵ And from the Serpent's mouth a vast flood of water gushed out and swept toward the woman in an effort to get rid of her; ¹⁶ but the earth helped her by opening its mouth and swallowing the flood! ¹⁷ Then the furious Dragon set out to attack the rest of her children—all who were keeping God's commandments and confessing that they belong to Jesus. He stood waiting on an ocean beach.

13 AND NOW, IN my vision, I saw a strange Creature rising up out of the sea. It had seven heads and ten horns, and ten crowns upon its horns. And written on each head were blasphemous names, each one defying and insulting God. ² This Creature looked like a leopard but had bear's feet and a lion's mouth! And the Dragon gave him his own power and throne and great authority.

³ I saw that one of his heads seemed wounded beyond recovery—but the fatal wound was healed! All the world marveled at this miracle and followed the Creature in awe. ⁴ They worshiped the Dragon for giving him such power, and they worshiped the strange Creature. "Where is there anyone as great as he?" they exclaimed. "Who is able to fight against him?"

a Literally, "a time and times and half a time."

⁵ Then the Dragon encouraged the Creature to speak great blasphemies against the Lord; and gave him authority to control the earth for forty-two months. ⁶ All that time he blasphemed God's Name and his temple and all those living in heaven. ⁷ The Dragon gave him power to fight against God's people[a] and to overcome them, and to rule over all nations and language groups throughout the world. ⁸ And all mankind—whose names were not written down before the founding of the world in the slain[b] Lamb's Book of Life—worshiped the evil Creature.

⁹ Anyone who can hear, listen carefully: ¹⁰ The people of God who are destined for prison will be arrested and taken away; those destined for death will be killed.[c] But do not be dismayed, for here is your opportunity for endurance and confidence.

¹¹ Then I saw another strange animal, this one coming up out of the earth, with two little horns like those of a lamb but a fearsome voice like the Dragon's. ¹² He exercised all the authority of the Creature whose death-wound had been healed, whom he required all the world to worship. ¹³ He did unbelievable miracles such as making fire flame down to earth from the skies while everyone was watching. ¹⁴ By doing these miracles, he was deceiving people everywhere. He could do these marvelous things whenever the first Creature was there to watch him. And he ordered the people of the world to make a great statue of the first Creature, who was fatally wounded and then came back to life. ¹⁵ He was permitted to give breath to this statue and even make it speak! Then the statue ordered that anyone refusing to worship it must die!

¹⁶ He required everyone—great and small, rich and poor, slave and free—to be tattooed with a certain mark on the right hand or on the forehead. ¹⁷ And no one could get a job or even buy in any store without the permit of that mark, which was either the name of the Creature or the code number of his name. ¹⁸ Here is a puzzle that calls for careful thought to solve it. Let those who are able, interpret this code: the numerical values of the letters in his name add to 666![d]

14 THEN I SAW a Lamb standing on Mount Zion in Jerusalem, and with him were 144,000 who had his Name and his Father's Name written on their foreheads. ² And I heard a sound from heaven like the roaring of a great waterfall or the rolling of mighty thunder. It was the singing of a choir accompanied by harps.

³ This tremendous choir—144,000 strong—sang a wonderful new song in front of the throne of God and before the four Living Beings and the twenty-four Elders; and no one could sing this song except those 144,000 who had been redeemed from the earth. ⁴ For they are spiritually undefiled, pure as virgins,[a] following the Lamb wherever he goes. They have been purchased from among the men on the earth as a consecrated offering to God and the Lamb. ⁵ No falsehood can be charged against them; they are blameless.

⁶ And I saw another angel flying through the heavens, carrying the everlasting Good News to preach to those on earth—to every nation, tribe, language and people.

⁷ "Fear God," he shouted, "and extol his greatness. For the time has come when he will sit as Judge. Worship him who made the heaven and the earth, the sea and all its sources."

⁸ Then another angel followed him through the skies, saying, "Babylon is fallen, is fallen—that great city—because she seduced the nations of the world and made them share the wine of her intense impurity and sin."

⁹ Then a third angel followed them shouting, "Anyone worshiping the Creature from the sea[b] and his statue and accepting his mark on the forehead or the hand, ¹⁰ must drink the wine of the anger of God; it is poured out undiluted into God's cup of wrath. And they will be tormented with fire and burning sulphur in the presence of

---

a Literally, "It was permitted to fight against God's people." b Or "those whose names were not written in the Book of Life of the Lamb slain before the founding of the world." That is, regarded as slain in the eternal plan and knowledge of God. c Or, "If anyone imprisons you, he will be imprisoned! If anyone kills you, he will be killed!" d Some manuscripts read "616." 14 a Literally, "They have not defiled themselves with women, for they are virgins." b Implied.

the holy angels and the Lamb. [11] The smoke of their torture rises forever and ever, and they will have no relief day or night, for they have worshiped the Creature and his statue, and have been tattooed with the code of his name. [12] Let this encourage God's people to endure patiently every trial and persecution, for they are his saints who remain firm to the end in obedience to his commands and trust in Jesus."

[13] And I heard a voice in the heavens above me saying, "Write this down: At last the time has come for his martyrs[c] to enter into their full reward. Yes, says the Spirit, they are blest indeed, for now they shall rest from all their toils and trials; for their good deeds follow them to heaven!" [14] Then the scene changed and I saw a white cloud, and someone sitting on it who looked like Jesus, who was called "The Son of Man,"[d] with a crown of solid gold upon his head and a sharp sickle in his hand.

[15] Then an angel came from the temple and called out to him, "Begin to use the sickle, for the time has come for you to reap; the harvest is ripe on the earth." [16] So the one sitting on the cloud swung his sickle over the earth, and the harvest was gathered in. [17] After that another angel came from the temple in heaven, and he also had a sharp sickle.

[18] Just then the angel who has power to destroy the world with fire,[e] shouted to the angel with the sickle, "Use your sickle now to cut off the clusters of grapes from the vines of the earth, for they are fully ripe for judgment." [19] So the angel swung his sickle on the earth and loaded the grapes into the great winepress of God's wrath. [20] And the grapes were trodden in the winepress outside the city, and blood flowed out in a stream 200 miles long and as high as a horse's bridle.

15 AND I SAW in heaven another mighty pageant showing things to come: Seven angels were assigned to carry down to earth the seven last plagues—and then at last God's anger will be finished.

[2] Spread out before me was what seemed to be an ocean of fire and glass, and on it stood all those who had been victorious over the Evil Creature and his statue and his mark and number. All were holding harps of God, [3,4] and they were singing the song of Moses, the servant of God, and the song of the Lamb:

"Great and marvelous
Are your doings,
Lord God Almighty.
Just and true
Are your ways,
O King of Ages.[a]
Who shall not fear,
O Lord,
And glorify your Name?
For you alone are holy.
All nations will come
And worship before you,
For your righteous deeds
Have been disclosed."

[5] Then I looked and saw that the Holy of Holies of the temple in heaven was thrown wide open!

[6] The seven angels who were assigned to pour out the seven plagues then came from the temple, clothed in spotlessly white linen, with golden belts across their chests. [7] And one of the four Living Beings handed each of them a golden flask filled with the terrible wrath of the Living God who lives forever and forever. [8] The temple was filled with smoke from his glory and power; and no one could enter until the seven angels had completed pouring out the seven plagues.

16 AND I HEARD a mighty voice shouting from the temple to the seven angels, "Now go your ways and empty out the seven flasks of the wrath of God upon the earth."

[2] So the first angel left the temple and poured out his flask over the earth, and horrible, malignant sores broke out on everyone who had the mark of the Creature and was worshiping his statue.

[3] The second angel poured out his flask upon the oceans, and they became like the watery blood of a dead man; and everything in all the oceans died.

---

c Literally, "those who die in the faith of Jesus." Verse 12 implies death from persecution for Christ's sake. d Literally, "one like a Son of Man."   e Literally, "who has power over fire."   15a Some manuscripts read, "King of the Nations."

⁴ The third angel poured out his flask upon the rivers and springs and they became blood. ⁵ And I heard this angel of the waters declaring, "You are just in sending this judgment, O Holy One, who is and was, ⁶ for your saints and prophets have been martyred and their blood poured out upon the earth; and now, in turn, you have poured out the blood of those who murdered them; it is their just reward."

⁷ And I heard the angel of the altar[a] say, "Yes, Lord God Almighty, your punishments are just and true."

⁸ Then the fourth angel poured out his flask upon the sun, causing it to scorch all men with its fire. ⁹ Everyone was burned by this blast of heat, and they cursed the name of God who sent the plagues—they did not change their mind and attitude to give him glory.

¹⁰ Then the fifth angel poured out his flask upon the throne of the Creature from the sea,[b] and his kingdom was plunged into darkness. And his subjects gnawed their tongues in anguish, ¹¹ and cursed the God of heaven for their pains and sores, but they refused to repent of all their evil deeds.

¹² The sixth angel poured out his flask upon the great River Euphrates and it dried up so that the kings from the east could march their armies westward without hindrance. ¹³ And I saw three evil spirits disguised as frogs leap from the mouth of the Dragon, the Creature, and his False Prophet.[c] ¹⁴ These miracle-working demons conferred with all the rulers of the world to gather them for battle against the Lord on that great coming Judgment Day of God Almighty.

¹⁵ "Take note: I will come as unexpectedly as a thief! Blessed are all who are awaiting me, who keep their robes in readiness and will not need to walk naked and ashamed."

¹⁶ And they gathered all the armies of the world near a place called, in Hebrew, Armageddon—the Mountain of Megiddo.

¹⁷ Then the seventh angel poured out his flask into the air; and a mighty shout came from the throne of the temple in heaven,

saying, "It is finished!"[d] ¹⁸ Then the thunder crashed and rolled, and lightning flashed; and there was a great earthquake of a magnitude unprecedented in human history. ¹⁹ The great city of "Babylon" split into three sections, and cities around the world fell in heaps of rubble; and so all of "Babylon's" sins were remembered in God's thoughts, and she was punished to the last drop of anger in the cup of the wine of the fierceness of his wrath. ²⁰ And islands vanished, and mountains flattened out, ²¹ and there was an incredible hailstorm from heaven; hailstones weighing a hundred pounds fell from the sky onto the people below, and they cursed God because of the terrible hail.

17 ONE OF THE seven angels who had poured out the plagues came over and talked with me. "Come with me," he said, "and I will show you what is going to happen to the Notorious Prostitute, who sits upon the many waters of the world. ² The kings of the world have had immoral relations with her, and the people of the earth have been made drunk by the wine of her immorality."

³ So the angel took me in spirit into the wilderness. There I saw a woman sitting on a scarlet animal that had seven heads and ten horns,[a] written all over with blasphemies against God. ⁴ The woman wore purple and scarlet clothing and beautiful jewelry made of gold and precious gems and pearls, and held in her hand a golden goblet full of obscenities:

⁵ A mysterious caption was written on her forehead: "Babylon the Great, Mother of Prostitutes and of Idol Worship Everywhere around the World."

⁶ I could see that she was drunk—drunk with the blood of the martyrs of Jesus she had killed. I stared at her in horror.

⁷ "Why are you so surprised?" the angel asked. "I'll tell you who she is and what the animal she is riding represents. ⁸ He was alive but isn't now. And yet, soon he will come up out of the bottomless pit and go to eternal destruction;[b] and the people of

---

a Literally, "I heard the altar cry. . . ."   b Implied.   c Described in 13:11-15 and 19:20.
d Literally, "It has happened." An epoch of human history has come to an end.   17a The Dragon—Satan
—and the Creature from the sea are also described in 12:3, 9 and 13:1.   b Literally, "go to perdition."

earth, whose names have not been written in the Book of Life before the world began, will be dumbfounded at his reappearance after being dead.[c]

⁹ "And now think hard: his seven heads represent a certain city[d] built on seven hills where this woman has her residence. ¹⁰ They also represent seven kings. Five have already fallen, the sixth now reigns, and the seventh is yet to come, but his reign will be brief. ¹¹ The scarlet animal that died is the eighth king, having reigned before as one of the seven; after his second reign, he too, will go to his doom. ¹² His ten horns are ten kings who have not yet risen to power; they will be appointed to their kingdoms for one brief moment, to reign with him. ¹³ They will all sign a treaty giving their power and strength to him. ¹⁴ Together they will wage war against the Lamb, and the Lamb will conquer them; for he is Lord over all lords, and King of kings, and his people are the called and chosen and faithful ones.

¹⁵ "The oceans, lakes and rivers that the woman is sitting on represent masses of people of every race and nation.

¹⁶ "The scarlet animal and his ten horns—which represent ten kings who will reign with him—all hate the woman, and will attack her and leave her naked and ravaged by fire. ¹⁷ For God will put a plan into their minds, a plan that will carry out his purposes: They will mutually agree to give their authority to the scarlet animal, so that the words of God will be fulfilled. ¹⁸ And this woman you saw in your vision represents the great city that rules over the kings of the earth."

18 AFTER ALL THIS I saw another angel come down from heaven with great authority, and the earth grew bright with his splendor.

² He gave a mighty shout, "Babylon the Great is fallen, is fallen; she has become a den of demons, a haunt of devils and every kind of evil spirit.[a] ³ For all the nations have drunk the fatal wine of her intense immorality. The rulers of earth have en-joyed themselves[b] with her, and business-men throughout the world have grown rich from all her luxurious living."

⁴ Then I heard another voice calling from heaven, "Come away from her, my people; do not take part in her sins, or you will be punished with her. ⁵ For her sins are piled as high as heaven and God is ready to judge her for her crimes. ⁶ Do to her as she has done to you, and more—give double penalty for all her evil deeds. She brewed many a cup of woe for others—give twice as much to her. ⁷ She has lived in luxury and pleasure—match it now with torments and with sorrows. She boasts, 'I am queen upon my throne. I am no helpless widow. I will not experience sorrow.' ⁸ Therefore the sorrows of death and mourning and famine shall overtake her in a single day, and she shall be utterly consumed by fire; for mighty is the Lord who judges her."

⁹ And the world leaders, who took part in her immoral acts and enjoyed her favors, will mourn for her as they see the smoke rising from her charred remains. ¹⁰ They will stand far off, trembling with fear and crying out, "Alas, Babylon, that mighty city! In one moment her judgment fell."

¹¹ The merchants of the earth will weep and mourn for her, for there is no one left to buy their goods. ¹² She was their biggest customer for gold and silver, precious stones, pearls, finest linens, purple silks, and scarlet; and every kind of perfumed wood, and ivory goods and most expensive wooden carvings, and brass and iron and marble; ¹³ and spices and perfumes and in-cense, ointment and frankincense, wine, ol-ive oil, and fine flour; wheat, cattle, sheep, horses, chariots, and slaves—and even the souls of men.

¹⁴ "All the fancy things you loved so much are gone," they cry. "The dainty lux-uries and splendor that you prized so much will never be yours again. They are gone forever."

¹⁵ And so the merchants who have become wealthy by selling her these things shall stand at a distance, fearing danger to themselves, weeping and crying, ¹⁶ "Alas,

---

c Literally, "dumbfounded at the ruler who was, and is not, and will be present."   d Implied in verse 18.
18 a Literally, "of every foul and hateful bird."   b Literally, "have committed fornication with her."

that great city, so beautiful—like a woman clothed in finest purple and scarlet linens, decked out with gold and precious stones and pearls! [17] In one moment, all the wealth of the city is gone!"

And all the shipowners and captains of the merchant ships and crews will stand a long way off, [18] crying as they watch the smoke ascend, and saying, "Where in all the world is there another city such as this?" [19] And they will throw dust on their heads in their sorrow and say, "Alas, alas, for that great city! She made us all rich from her great wealth. And now in a single hour all is gone. . . ."

[20] But you, O heaven, rejoice over her fate; and you, O children of God and the prophets and the apostles! For at last God has given judgment against her for you.

[21] Then a mighty angel picked up a boulder shaped like a millstone and threw it into the ocean and shouted, "Babylon, that great city, shall be thrown away as I have thrown away this stone, and she shall disappear forever. [22] Never again will the sound of music be there—no more pianos, saxophones, and trumpets.[c] No industry of any kind will ever again exist there, and there will be no more milling of the grain. [23] Dark, dark will be her nights; not even a lamp in a window will ever be seen again. No more joyous wedding bells and happy voices of the bridegrooms and the brides. Her businessmen were known around the world and she deceived all nations with her sorceries. [24] And she was responsible for the blood of all the martyred prophets and the saints."

19 AFTER THIS I heard the shouting of a vast crowd in heaven, "Hallelujah! Praise the Lord! Salvation is from our God. Honor and authority belong to him alone; [2] for his judgments are just and true. He has punished the Great Prostitute who corrupted the earth with her sin;[a] and he has avenged the murder of his servants."

[3] Again and again their voices rang, "Praise the Lord! The smoke from her burning ascends forever and forever!"

[4] Then the twenty-four Elders and four Living Beings fell down and worshiped God, who was sitting upon the throne, and said, "Amen! Hallelujah! Praise the Lord!"

[5] And out of the throne came a voice that said, "Praise our God, all you his servants, small and great, who fear him."

[6] Then I heard again what sounded like the shouting of a huge crowd, or like the waves of a hundred oceans crashing on the shore, or like the mighty rolling of great thunder, "Praise the Lord. For the Lord our God, the Almighty, reigns. [7] Let us be glad and rejoice and honor him; for the time has come for the wedding banquet of the Lamb, and his bride has prepared herself. [8] She is permitted to wear the cleanest and whitest and finest of linens." (Fine linen represents the good deeds done by the people of God.)

[9] And the angel[b] dictated this sentence to me: "Blessed are those who are invited to the wedding feast of the Lamb." And he added, "God himself has stated this."[c]

[10] Then I fell down at his feet to worship him, but he said, "No! Don't! For I am a servant of God just as you are, and as your brother Christians are, who testify of their faith in Jesus. The purpose of all prophecy and of all I have shown you is to tell about Jesus."[d]

[11] Then I saw heaven opened and a white horse standing there; and the one sitting on the horse was named "Faithful and True" —the one who justly punishes and makes war. [12] His eyes were like flames, and on his head were many crowns. A name was written on his forehead,[e] and only he knew its meaning. [13] He was clothed with garments dipped in blood, and his title was "The Word of God."[f] [14] The armies of heaven, dressed in finest linen, white and clean, followed him on white horses.

[15] In his mouth he held a sharp sword to strike down the nations; he ruled them with an iron grip; and he trod the winepress of the fierceness of the wrath of Almighty

---

c Literally, "harpers . . . pipers . . . and trumpeters." cally through the prophets for the worship of false gods.
c Literally, "These are the true words of God."
prophecy."   e Implied.   f Literally, "The Logos," as in John 1:1—the ultimate method of God's revealing himself to man.

19a Literally, "fornication," the word used symboli-
b Literally, "he"; the exact antecedent is unclear.
d Literally, "The testimony of Jesus is the spirit of

God. [16] On his robe and thigh was written this title: "King of Kings and Lord of Lords."

[17] Then I saw an angel standing in the sunshine, shouting loudly to the birds, "Come! Gather together for the supper of the Great God! [18] Come and eat the flesh of kings, and captains, and great generals; of horses and riders; and of all humanity, both great and small, slave and free."

[19] Then I saw the Evil Creature gathering the governments of the earth and their armies to fight against the one sitting on the horse and his army. [20] And the Evil Creature was captured, and with him the False Prophet,[g] who could do mighty miracles when the Evil Creature was present—miracles that deceived all who had accepted the Evil Creature's mark, and who worshiped his statue. Both of them—the Evil Creature and his False Prophet—were thrown alive into the Lake of Fire that burns with sulphur. [21] And their entire army was killed with the sharp sword in the mouth of the one riding the white horse, and all the birds of heaven were gorged with their flesh.

20 THEN I SAW an angel come down from heaven with the key to the bottomless pit and a heavy chain in his hand. [2] He seized the Dragon—that old Serpent, the devil, Satan—and bound him in chains for 1,000 years, [3] and threw him into the bottomless pit, which he then shut and locked, so that he could not fool the nations any more until the thousand years were finished. Afterwards he would be released again for a little while.

[4] Then I saw thrones, and sitting on them were those who had been given the right to judge. And I saw the souls of those who had been beheaded for their testimony about Jesus, for proclaiming the Word of God, and who had not worshiped the Creature or his statue, nor accepted his mark on their foreheads or their hands. They had come to life again and now they reigned with Christ for a thousand years.

[5] This is the First Resurrection. (The rest of the dead did not come back to life until the thousand years had ended.) [6] Blessed and holy are those who share in the First Resurrection. For them the Second Death holds no terrors, for they will be priests of God and of Christ, and shall reign with him a thousand years.

[7] When the thousand years end, Satan will be let out of his prison. [8] He will go out to deceive the nations of the world and gather them together, with Gog and Magog, for battle—a mighty host, numberless as sand along the shore. [9] They will go up across the broad plain of the earth and surround God's people and the beloved city of Jerusalem[a] on every side. But fire from God in heaven will flash down on the attacking armies and consume them.

[10] Then the devil who had betrayed them will again[b] be thrown into the Lake of Fire burning with sulphur where the Creature and False Prophet are, and they will be tormented day and night forever and ever.

[11] And I saw a great white throne and the one who sat upon it, from whose face the earth and sky fled away, but they found no place to hide.[c] [12] I saw the dead, great and small, standing before God; and The Books were opened, including the Book of Life. And the dead were judged according to the things written in The Books, each according to the deeds he had done. [13] The oceans surrendered the bodies buried in them; and the earth and the underworld gave up the dead in them. Each was judged according to his deeds. [14] And Death and Hell were thrown into the Lake of Fire. This is the Second Death—the Lake of Fire. [15] And if anyone's name was not found recorded in the Book of Life, he was thrown into the Lake of Fire.

21 THEN I SAW a new earth (with no oceans!) and a new sky, for the present earth and sky had disappeared. [2] And I, John, saw the Holy City, the new Jerusalem, coming down from God out of heaven. It was a glorious sight, beautiful as a bride at her wedding.

[3] I heard a loud shout from the throne saying, "Look, the home of God is now among men, and he will live with them and

---

g See chapter 13, verses 11–16.　　20a Implied. was no longer any place for them."　　b Implied; Revelation 20:3.　　c Literally, "There

they will be his people; yes, God himself will be among them.[a] "He will wipe away all tears from their eyes, and there shall be no more death, nor sorrow, nor crying, nor pain. All of that has gone forever."

[5] And the one sitting on the throne said, "See, I am making all things new!" And then he said to me, "Write this down, for what I tell you is trustworthy and true: [6] It is finished! I am the A and the Z—the Beginning and the End. I will give to the thirsty the springs of the Water of Life—as a gift! [7] Everyone who conquers will inherit all these blessings, and I will be his God and he will be my son. [8] But cowards who turn back from following me, and those who are unfaithful to me, and the corrupt, and murderers, and the immoral, and those conversing with demons, and idol worshipers and all liars—their doom is in the Lake that burns with fire and sulphur. This is the Second Death."

[9] Then one of the seven angels, who had emptied the flasks containing the seven last plagues, came and said to me, "Come with me and I will show you the bride, the Lamb's wife."

[10] In a vision he took me to a towering mountain peak and from there I watched that wondrous city, the holy Jerusalem, descending out of the skies from God. [11] It was filled with the glory of God, and flashed and glowed like a precious gem, crystal clear like jasper. [12] Its walls were broad and high, with twelve gates guarded by twelve angels. And the names of the twelve tribes of Israel were written on the gates. [13] There were three gates on each side—north, south, east, and west. [14] The walls had twelve foundation stones, and on them were written the names of the twelve apostles of the Lamb.

[15] The angel held in his hand a golden measuring stick to measure the city and its gates and walls. [16] When he measured it, he found it was a square as wide as it was long; in fact it was in the form of a cube, for its height was exactly the same as its other dimensions—1,500 miles each way. [17] Then he measured the thickness of the walls and

found them to be 216 feet across (the angel called out these measurements to me, using standard units).[b]

[18,19,20] The city itself was pure, transparent gold like glass! The wall was made of jasper, and was built on twelve layers of foundation stones inlaid with gems:

The first layer[c] with jasper;
The second with sapphire;
The third with chalcedony;
The fourth with emerald;
The fifth with sardonyx;
The sixth layer with sardus;
The seventh with chrysolite;
The eighth with beryl;
The ninth with topaz;
The tenth with chrysoprase;
The eleventh with jacinth;
The twelfth with amethyst.

[21] The twelve gates were made of pearls —each gate from a single pearl! And the main street was pure, transparent gold, like glass.

[22] No temple could be seen in the city, for the Lord God Almighty and the Lamb are worshiped in it everywhere.[d] [23] And the city has no need of sun or moon to light it, for the glory of God and of the Lamb illuminate it. [24] Its light will light the nations of the earth, and the rulers of the world will come and bring their glory to it. [25] Its gates never close; they stay open all day long —and there is no night! [26] And the glory and honor of all the nations shall be brought into it. [27] Nothing evil will be permitted in it—no one immoral or dishonest—but only those whose names are written in the Lamb's Book of Life.

22 AND HE POINTED out to me a river of pure Water of Life, clear as crystal, flowing from the throne of God and the Lamb, [2] coursing down the center of the main street. On each side of the river grew Trees[a] of Life, bearing twelve crops of fruit, with a fresh crop each month; the leaves were used for medicine to heal the nations.

[3] There shall be nothing in the city which is evil; for the throne of God and of the

---

a Some manuscripts add, "and be their God."   b Literally, "144 cubits by human measurements." A cubit was the average length of a man's arm—not an angel's! The angel used normal units of measurement that John could understand.   c Implied   d Literally, "are its temple."   22a Literally, "the tree of life"—used here as a collective noun, implying plurality.

Lamb will be there, and his servants will worship him. ⁴ And they shall see his face; and his name shall be written on their foreheads. ⁵ And there will be no night there —no need for lamps or sun—for the Lord God will be their light; and they shall reign forever and ever.

⁶,⁷ Then the angel said to me, "These words are trustworthy and true: 'I am coming soon!'ᵇ God, who tells his prophets what the future holds, has sent his angel to tell you this will happen soon. Blessed are those who believe it and all else written in the scroll."

⁸ I, John, saw and heard all these things, and fell down to worship the angel who showed them to me; ⁹ but again he said, "No, don't do anything like that. I, too, am a servant of Jesus as you are, and as your brothers the prophets are, as well as all those who heed the truth stated in this Book. Worship God alone."

¹⁰ Then he instructed me, "Do not seal up what you have written, for the time of fulfillment is near. ¹¹ And when that time comes, all doing wrong will do it more and more; the vile will become more vile; good men will be better; those who are holy will continue on in greater holiness."

¹² "See, I am coming soon,ᵇ and my reward is with me, to repay everyone according to the deeds he has done. ¹³ I am the A and the Z, the Beginning and the End, the First and Last. ¹⁴ Blessed forever are all who are washing their robes, to have the right to enter in through the gates of the city, and to eat the fruit from the Tree of Life.

¹⁵ "Outside the city are those who have strayed away from God, and the sorcerers and the immoral and murderers and idolaters, and all who love to lie, and do so. ¹⁶ I, Jesus, have sent my angel to you to tell the churches all these things. I am both David's Root and his Descendant. I am the bright Morning Star. ¹⁷ The Spirit and the bride say, 'Come.' Let each one who hears them say the same, 'Come.' Let the thirsty one come—anyone who wants to; let him come and drink the Water of Life without charge. ¹⁸ And I solemnly declare to everyone who reads this book: If anyone adds anything to what is written here, God shall add to him the plagues described in this book. ¹⁹ And if anyone subtracts any part of these prophecies, God shall take away his share in the Tree of Life, and in the Holy City just described.

²⁰ "He who has said all these things declares: Yes, I am coming soon!"ᵇ

Amen! Come, Lord Jesus!

²¹ The grace of our Lord Jesus Christ be with you all. Amen!

ᵇ Or, "suddenly," "unexpectedly."

THE
DEUTEROCANONICAL
BOOKS

Paraphrased by Albert J. Nevins, M.M.
Editor-in-chief and Corporate Vice President
Our Sunday Visitor Inc.

OUR SUNDAY VISITOR
Huntington, Indiana

Nihil Obstat: REV. LAWRENCE A. GOLLNER
           Censor Librorum
Imprimatur: LEO A. PURSLEY
           Bishop of Fort Wayne-South Bend
           January 9, 1976

Printed in the United States of America

What Do You Say to an Angel?

Insurance is a big thing today. We insure our lives, our homes, our cameras, even our airplane rides. We place so high a value on insurance that Americans have invested $250 billion to guard them against loss. When Tobit, the faithful Israelite captive of the Assyrians, decided to send his son into a land unknown to him to collect a family debt, he looked for insurance in the person of a man to guide and guard him. The Book of Tobit tells what happened.

In a delightful blend of Jewish scripture, piety, and folklore, an inspired author uses his talent to illustrate God's providence through four main characters: Tobit; Tobias, his handsome young son; Sarah, who couldn't keep a husband; and Raphael, an angel sent by God to solve their problems. In the story's climax, Tobias leaves Nineveh just before its destruction by God because of its wickedness.

The book has importance in the development of Catholic doctrine on Guardian Angels. However, its real importance is in its moral: God's lasting providence, His concern for those who follow His way, and the triumph of good over evil. As the book develops, its real hero is God Himself, watching over and directing the affairs of His children.

TOBIT

1 THIS IS THE story of Tobit, son of Tobiel, whose father was Hananiel, the son
of Aduel, son of Gabael, who belonged to
the family of Asiel of the tribe of Naphtali.
² During the reign of Shalmaneser, King of
Assyria, Tobit was taken into captivity and
exile from Thisbe in upper Galilee.ᵃ
³ I, Tobit, have tried to live a life of truth
and charity. I performed many charitable
deeds not only for my kinsmen but also for
others held in captivity with me in Nineveh,
Assyria. ⁴ When I was a young man in my
own country of Israel, the whole tribe of
Naphtali left the traditions of David and
Jerusalem. This was the city where all the
tribes of Israel for all time were to offer
sacrifice in the temple, God's dwelling
place. ⁵ Instead, my relatives as well as the
rest of the tribe of Naphtali offered sacrifices on the mountains of Galilee to the
male calf which Jeroboam, King of Israel,
had made in Dan.
⁶ So it was that I alone made the journey
to Jerusalem for the frequent festivals, a
journey commanded for all Israel. I would
bring with me the first fruits of the harvest

and the first born of my flocks, the first wool
from the sheep, and a tenth of my income.
⁷ These I would give to the priests, Aaron's
sons, for the altar. To the Levites who were
on duty, I would give tithes of grain, wine,
olive oil, pomegranates, figs and other
fruits. I would sell another tenth of my income and distribute it in Jerusalem. ⁸ A
third tenth I gave to orphans, widows and
converts as my grandmother, Deborah, had
commanded me because when my father,
Tobiel, died I was left an orphan.
⁹ When I came of age, I married Anna,
a kinswoman, and we had a son whom I
named Tobias. ¹⁰ After I had been taken
captive to Nineveh in Assyria, all of my
kinsmen ate the food of the Gentiles ¹¹ but
I would not.
¹² Because I was faithful to my religion,
¹³ God looked kindly on me and brought
me to the favorable attention of King Shalmaneser who made me his purchasing
agent. ¹⁴ As long as he lived I went frequently to Media to buy supplies. Once I
left $10,000 with my relative, Gabael, son
of Gabris, who lived in Rages in Media.ᵇ

---

a This book alternates between the third and first persons.   b Rages was an important city whose ruins today are close to Teheran, Iran. Media was the northwestern part of modern Iran.

1125

15 When Shalmaneser died and Sennacherib became king, the road to Media was lost to Assyrian control and I could go there no longer.

16 In the time of Shalmaneser, I was able to perform many good deeds for my relatives and my people. 17 I shared my bread with the hungry and clothed the naked. Whenever one of my people died and I saw the body thrown outside the walls of Nineveh, I would bury it. 18 And if Sennacherib put to death any who fled from Judea, I buried them secretly. In his anger Sennacherib put many to death but I used to steal the bodies and bury them in secret. When Sennacherib looked for the bodies he could not find them.

19 A certain Ninevehite told the king what I was doing. When I learned that the king knew all about me and wanted to put me to death, I first went into hiding and then through fear took flight. 20 All my property was taken from me and all that was left to me was my wife, Anna, and my son, Tobias.

21 But in a little more than a month later the king was murdered by two of his sons who escaped into the mountains of Ararat. He was succeeded as king by his son Esarhaddon who named my brother Anael's son, Ahikar, as his chief accountant and administrator. 22 Ahikar put in a good word for me and I was able to return to Nineveh. Under Sennacherib, my nephew, Ahikar, had been head cupbearer, guardian of the king's seal, administrator and treasurer. Esarhaddon not only kept my nephew in office but appointed him second to himself.

2 So when Esarhaddon became king, I returned home to my wife Anna and my son Tobias. It was Pentecost, the Feast of Weeks,[a] and a big dinner was prepared for me. 2 When I saw all the food I said to my son Tobias, "Go, my boy, and seek a poor man among the Israelites captive here and he shall share my dinner. I will wait until you come back." 3 Tobias had hardly left when he returned. "Father!" he exclaimed.

"One of our people has been strangled[b] and his body left in the marketplace!" 4 I hurried from the table without touching my food. I carried the body back to my house and put it in an outbuilding until I could bury it after sunset. 5 I returned to my own quarters, washed myself,[c] and ate my meal in sorrow. 6 I remembered the prophecy of Amos about Bethel:

"And I will turn your parties into times of mourning,
and your songs of joy will be turned to cries of despair."

7 Then I wept. At sunset I went and dug a grave and buried the dead man.

8 My neighbors made fun of me, saying, "Will he never learn? He had to run away the last time for such a thing, and here he is burying the dead again."

9 That same night I took a bath and made my bed along the wall of the courtyard. Because it was a hot night, I left my face uncovered. 10 I did not know there were sparrows above me on the wall until their droppings fell into my eyes, causing white spots. I went to doctors but the more they treated me, the worse my cataracts became, until I was totally blind. My relatives grieved for me and Ahikar took care of me until he went to Elymais.

11 My wife Anna supported us by women's work, mainly weaving. 12 When she delivered the goods to her employers, they would pay her. During the winter, she finished a large piece of cloth and brought it to her employers. When they paid her for the cloth, they gave her a young goat from their herd. 13 When she returned home, the goat began to bleat. I called out to her, "Where did you get that goat? Is it stolen? Give it back to its owners. We cannot eat stolen food." 14 She replied, "It was given to me as a bonus over and above what I earned." But I did not believe her and became angry and told her to take the goat back to where she got it. She answered, "And you're supposed to be a man of charity and righteous deeds! Now your true character is coming out!"

---

a Fifty days after Passover.   b Probably executed and his body left on display as a warning.   c A Jew was made unclean by touching a corpse.

3 I was grief-stricken by my failure. I wept and in my sadness I began to pray,

2 "You are just, O Lord,
and all your deeds are right.
Your ways are merciful and true,
You are the judge of all men.

3 "Remember me, Lord,
and look with kindness upon me.
Do not punish me for my sins, known and unknown,
or for the sins of my ancestors.

4 "They disobeyed your commandments,
and suffered violence, captivity and death.
We became to all a byword of reproach
and you scattered us among the nations.

5 "I admit the justice of your many judgments
and accept the penalty which my own sins
and those of my fathers deserve.
For we have not kept your commandments
nor have we walked in truth before you.

6 "Now deal with me as you please,
and command that my life be taken from me
and that I be returned to the earth as dust.
It is better that I should die than live
because I have heard lies
and I am overwhelmed with grief.
Lord, command that I be freed of this misery
so that I can go to my everlasting abode.
Lord, do not refuse me."

7 On the very same day at Ecbatana, the capital of Media, Sarah, the daughter of Raguel, was abused by her father's maidservants 8 because she had been married to seven husbands, each of whom had been killed by the wicked demon Asmodeus (the Destroyer) before any of the marriages had been consummated. The maids said to her, "Shame! Do you not know that you are a killer of husbands? You have had seven and no children from any of them. 9 Why take it out on us because they are dead. Go and be with them. We never want to see a son or daughter of yours."

10 As a result Sarah was made very sad. She fled upstairs in tears, and was tempted to hang herself. But she regained her senses, saying, "No. People would taunt my father and say, 'Your only daughter killed herself because of her bad luck.' The grief of such a deed would follow my father to his grave. It is better for me to pray to the Lord to let me die because of such insults than to take my own life."

11 She spread out her hands and prayed before a window facing Jerusalem,

"Praise to you, O Lord, God of mercy.
Blessed and honored be your name forever.
May all your work always praise you.

12 "To you, O Lord, I raise my face
and lift my eyes.

13 "Command that I be released
from the bondage of earth,
never more to hear insults.

14 "You know, O Lord, that I am innocent
of any impurity.

15 "I have brought no shame on my name
or that of my father in this land of captivity.
"I am the only child of my father
and there is no other to be his heir.
"There is no kinsman or kinsman's son
for whom I should save myself
in marriage.
"I have already lost seven husbands,
why should I live?
"But if you do not will, Lord,
to take my life,
look on me with favor and pity;
never again let me hear these insults."

16 At that very moment both the prayers of Sarah and Tobit were heard by Almighty God.

17 So Raphael was sent to cure each of them; to remove the cataracts from Tobit's eyes so that he might once again see God's creation, and to give in marriage Sarah, the daughter of Raguel, to Tobias, son of Tobit,

and in doing so to drive the wicked demon Asmodeus from possessing her. For it was God's plan that Tobias and no other should be her husband. It was at this moment that Tobit returned from the courtyard and Sarah, Raguel's daughter, came down from the attic.

4 That same day Tobit remembered the money he had left with Gabael at Rages in Media. He thought, 2 "I have prayed for death, why shouldn't I send for my son Tobias and tell him about this money before I die?" 3 So he summoned his son Tobias and when he came, Tobit said to him, "My son, when I die, give me a fitting burial. Honor your mother and care for her as long as she lives. Do what will please her and do not do anything to bring her sadness. 4 Remember, my son, that she went through many dangers for you before you were even born. When she dies, bury her alongside me.

5 "Remember the Lord every day of your life. Never deliberately do anything evil or break his commandments. As long as you live, walk uprightly and never take the path of wrongdoing. 6 For if you are faithful to the Lord, prosperity will be yours, for the Lord blesses those who live his will.

7 "Give alms from your possessions. If you do not turn your face away from the poor, God will not turn his face from you. 8 Let your giving be according to your possessions. If you have great wealth, give generously; if your possessions be few, give from that little. 9 In this way you will be storing up treasures against a day of adversity. 10 For charity frees one from death and keeps him from going down into the darkness. 11 Charity is pleasing to the Most High.

12 "My son, be on your guard against all immorality. Take a wife from your own ancestry. Do not marry a foreign woman outside our tribe because we have descended from prophets. My son, remember the example of Noah, Isaac and Jacob, our fathers of old who took wives from among their kinsmen. They were blessed in their children and their posterity will inherit the land. 13 Be like them, my son; love your kinsmen. Do not think yourself above the sons and daughters of your people so as to hesitate to take a wife from your own tribe. Pride is the source of ruin and confusion. Wastefulness breeds poverty and waste is the mother of hunger.

14 "Pay your workman the same day, and do not make him wait for the next day. If you so serve God, you will be rewarded. Keep a guard, my son, on your conduct. 15 Do not do to anyone anything you would hate to have done to you. Do not drink to excess for drunkenness can become a habit. 16 Give food to the hungry and clothing to the naked. Whatever you have beyond your needs, give away as alms without being miserly. 17 Offer your bread and pour your wine on the tombs of the just but give nothing to sinners.

18 "Seek advice from every wise man, and do not look down upon any useful suggestions. 19 Bless the Lord at every opportunity and ask him to guide your way so that all your plans and works will prosper. The pagan nations do not have this counsel. It is the Lord himself who gives all good things and who humbles men when he wishes. So, my son, remember my commands and never let them fade from your memory.

20 "Now, son, I want to tell you that I have left a large sum of money in the keeping of Gabri's son Gabael at Rages in Media. 21 Do not worry, my boy, because we have become poor. You will have great wealth if you fear God, avoid all sin, and do what is good in the sight of the Lord."

5 Then Tobias replied, "I will do everything you have told me. 2 But how will I get your money from him, since I do not know him and he does not know me? What proof will I give him to make him believe me and give me the money? I do not even know the way to Media." 3 Tobit told him, "He gave me this receipt and I gave him mine. I divided this in two and gave him half. The other receipt I put in with the money. It is twenty years since I gave him the money! So go, my son, and find a reliable man to accompany you and we will pay him when you get back. Go and reclaim the money from Gabael."

⁴ Tobias went out to find someone who knew the roads to Media and who would accompany him there. He found Raphael, who was an angel, standing outside but Tobias did not know this. ⁵ Tobias asked him, "Who are you, young man?" He replied, "I am an Israelite, one of your countrymen. I am looking for work." Tobias asked him, "Do you know the way to Media?" ⁶ "Yes," he answered, "I have often gone there and know the roads. I used to stay with our tribesman Gabael in Rages. It is a long two days' journey from Ecbatana to Rages,ᵃ for Rages is in the mountains while Ecbatana is on the plains." ⁷ Tobias said to him, "Wait for me, young man, while I go in and tell my father. I need someone to accompany me to Rages, and I will pay you to guide me." ⁸ Raphael replied, "All right, but don't be too long."

⁹ Tobias went in and told his father, "I have found an Israelite who will go with me." Tobit said, "Bring him to me so that I can find out about his family and tribe and decide if he is to be trusted to go with you." Tobias went out and called Raphael, saying, "Young man, my father would like to talk to you."

¹⁰ When Raphael came in, Tobit immediately greeted him. Raphael replied, "And may all be well with you." Tobit responded, "What! Can anything be well with me? I am a blind man who can no longer enjoy God's sunlight but must remain in darkness. Though still alive, I am like one dead who cannot see the day. I hear voices but never see the speakers." "Be brave," Raphael exhorted him. "God will heal you. Be confident." Tobit spoke up, "My son Tobias wishes to go to Media. Can you guide him there? I will of course pay you, brother." "Yes, I can take him there. I know all the roads. I have often been to Media, crossing the plains and the mountains so that I know every route." ¹¹ Tobit inquired, "Tell me, brother, to what tribe and family do you belong?" ¹² "What difference does that make?" replied Raphael. "I thought you were looking for a guide."

Tobit persisted, however, "I really want to know who your family is and your own name."

¹³ Raphael answered, "I am Azarias, son of Ananiasᵇ the elder of your own tribe." ¹⁴ Tobit said, "You are welcome, my brother. Do not be angry with me because I wanted to know your tribe and family. You are a relative of mine, of good and noble stock. I knew Ananias and Jathan, the two sons of Shemaiah the elder. They used to make the pilgrimage to Jerusalem with me and we would worship together, offering the first born of our flocks and tithes of our crops. They did not go astray from the law. Yes, you come from a good line." ¹⁵ He added, "I will pay you a drachmaᶜ a day, plus the same expenses as my son. ¹⁶ I will also add a bonus if you both return safely." Raphael replied, "I will go with him. Don't worry. We will return as healthy as we are now. Besides the route is safe."

¹⁷ Tobit said, "God bless you, brother." Then he called Tobias and said to him, "Son, prepare whatever is necessary for the trip with your kinsman. I pray God will protect both of you on your way and bring you back to me safely. May his angel guard your way." Before setting out on the journey, Tobias kissed his father and mother. Tobit told him, "Have a safe journey." So Tobias and Raphael left and Tobias' dog followed him.ᵈ

¹⁸ Anna began to weep. She said to her husband, "Why have you sent my son away? Is he not the one on whom we depend? Has he not always been at home with us? ¹⁹ What do you want more money for if it costs us our son? ²⁰ Can't we be satisfied with what the Lord has given us?" ²¹ Tobit reassured her: "Don't worry. He leaves in good health and he will return the same way. You will see for yourself when he returns in good health. ²² Don't fret or be anxious about him, my love. A good angel will go with him, his mission will be successful, and he will return safely." At that she stopped.

a The actual distance is 180 miles. The author is merely indicating a long distance and not real time. b Azarias means "Yahweh helps" and Ananias, "Yahweh is merciful." c A drachma, about seventeen cents, was the normal wage for a skilled workman. d The dog is an interesting but incidental note to the story. It appears again at the end.

6 The young man, the angel and the dog traveled until night began to overtake them. 2 They made camp beside the Tigris River.ª 3 When Tobias went down to wash his feet in the river, a large fish jumped from the water and tried to swallow his foot. As he cried out in surprise, 4 the angel shouted, "Catch the fish! Don't let it get away!" The youth caught hold of the fish and pulled it up on the bank. 5 The angel then told him, "Gut the fish and save its heart, liver and gall. Throw away the entrails. The heart, liver and gall make good medicines." 6 Tobias did as the angel told him, then they broiled the fish; what they did not eat, they saved for the journey.

7 They traveled on together until they were near Media. Then the youth asked the angel, "Azarias, my friend, what medicine can be made from the fish's heart, liver and gall?" 8 He replied, "As for the heart and liver, if you burn them and blow the smoke on a man or woman who is bothered with an evil spirit, that spirit will leave and never return. 9 And as for the gall, if you blow its powder into the eyes of a man who has cataracts, he will be cured."

10 When they had entered Media and were getting close to Ecbatana, 11 Raphael spoke to his young companion, "Tobias, my friend!" He replied, "Yes, what is it?" Raphael continued, "Tonight we must stay with your relative, Raguel. He has a daughter named Sarah 12 and no other child. Since you are the only eligible relative, you have the right to marry her and thus gain her inheritance. The girl is also very beautiful and gifted with common sense. 13 Here's what we will do. I will speak to her father to engage her to you and when we return from Rages, we will celebrate the marriage."

14 But Tobias objected to the angel, "Friend Azarias, I have heard that this woman married seven times and that each husband dropped dead on his wedding night in the bridal chamber. I have been told that it was a demon that killed them. 15 I am afraid of this demon. Because he loves the girl, he does not harm her, but he kills anyone who approaches her. I am the only child of my father. My death would lead my mother and father to their own graves. Then there would be no son to bury them."

16 Raphael said to him, "Remember your father's command to take a wife from your own ancestral tribe. Be assured of this, my friend, she will marry you. Do not worry about the demon for this very night she will be given to you in marriage. 17 When you enter the bridal chamber, take the fish's liver and heart and lay them on the embers for incense. 18 The demon will smell the odor and flee, never again to return. Before you retire for the night, both of you must rise up and pray. Beg God's mercy; he will grant it and save you. Sarah was destined for you from all eternity. You will rescue her and she will go with you, and I presume you will have children. So there is nothing to be concerned about." When Tobias heard these things, he felt love stirring within himself and he set his heart on her.

7 When they reached Ecbatana and arrived at Raguel's house, they found him seated by the courtyard gate. They greeted him. He replied, "Greetings to you also, brothers. Welcome and good health to you." Then he brought them into the house 2 and said to his wife Edna, "How greatly this young man looks like my cousin Tobit!" 3 And Raguel asked them, "Where are you from, brothers?" They answered, "We belong to the sons of Naphtali who are exiled in Nineveh." 4 Raguel said to them, "Do you know our brother Tobit?" They replied, "We certainly do!" Then he asked them, "Is he in good health?" 5 They answered, "He is alive and in good health." And Tobias exclaimed, "He is my father!" 6 Raguel embraced and kissed him and wept. Then he blessed him and said, "You are the son of a good and noble man." 7 But when he heard that Tobit had lost his sight, he was saddened and began to weep again. 8 His wife Edna wept for Tobit and even their daughter Sarah began to weep.

---

a Hardly the Tigris unless they went far out of their way. Again the author is not concerned with geography.

⁹ They received the visitors cordially, killing a ram from the flock. And when they had bathed and reclined to eat, Tobias said to Raphael, "Friend Azarias, how about asking Raguel if I can marry my kinswoman Sarah?" ¹⁰ Raguel heard the question and said to the young man, "Eat, drink and be happy. No man is more entitled to my daughter than you. Indeed, I have no right to give her to anyone else since you are my closest kinsman. ¹¹ But I must warn you. I have given her to seven husbands and each of them died when he came to her." But Tobias said, "I will eat nothing until we make a binding agreement."

So Raguel said, "Take her now. She is yours according to the law of Moses. From now on, you are the one to love her. The God of mercy will guide you for the best. May he grant you mercy and peace." ¹² Then he called his daughter Sarah. When she came, he took her by the hand and gave her to Tobias, saying, "Here she is. Take her according to the decrees of Moses to be your wife. Take her to your father safely." ¹³ He then called Edna and told her to bring a scroll on which he wrote the contract and they set their seals to it. ¹⁴ Then they began to eat and drink. ¹⁵ Finally Raguel called Edna and told her, "Sister, prepare the bedroom and take the girl there." ¹⁶ Edna went and made the bed and as she was told, brought her daughter there and the girl began to weep. Edna wiped away the tears and said, ¹⁷ "Be brave, daughter. May the Lord of all grant you joy in place of your sorrow. Be brave, my child." Then she left.

8 And after they had feasted, the young man was taken to the bedroom. ² Tobias remembered Raphael's advice and took part of the liver out of his bag. He put some upon burning incense. ³ Meanwhile, Raphael took the devil and bound him in the desert of upper Egypt.

⁴ Tobias went to the bed and said to Sarah, "Arise! We must pray to God tonight, tomorrow night and the next, because for this time we must think only of God. When the third night is over, our marriage will begin. ⁵ We are children of holy ancestors, and we must not act like heathens who do not know God." ⁶ So they both arose, and prayed earnestly together that protection might be given them. ⁷ Tobias said,

"Lord, God of our fathers,
may the heavens and the earth,
the sea and the springs and the rivers,
and all the creatures you have made
    bless you.
⁸ You created Adam from mud
and gave him Eve for a helper.
⁹ Lord, you know,
I do not take my sister as my wife
for any lustful reason
but solely that our children
may bless your name for ever and
    ever."

¹⁰ Sarah also said, "Have mercy on us, O Lord, have mercy on us, and let us both grow old together." Together they said, "Amen. Amen." Then they lay down to sleep.

¹¹ Raguel called his servants to help him dig a grave. ¹² He thought, "Perhaps he too will die in the same way as the other seven husbands that she married." ¹³ When they had dug the grave, Raguel went back to his wife, and said to her, ¹⁴ "Send one of your maids to find out if Tobias is dead. If he is, we can bury him before it is daylight and anyone knows." ¹⁵ So Edna sent one of her maidservants, who went into the bedroom, and found them safe and sound, sleeping together. ¹⁶ She brought the good news to Raguel and Edna and they blessed the Lord, ¹⁷ saying,

"We bless you, O Lord God of Israel,
because what we expected did not
    happen.
¹⁸ You have shown your mercy to us,
and have kept away the enemy
who has persecuted us.
¹⁹ You have taken pity
upon this only son and only daughter.
Allow them, O Lord, to bless you
    more fully
and to offer up to you a sacrifice of
    praise
for their health,
that all nations may know
that you alone are God in all the
    earth."

²⁰ Immediately Raguel commanded his servants to fill up the grave they had dug while it was yet night.

²¹ He told his wife to make a feast ready, to prepare all kinds of provisions. ²² He also had two fat cows and four sheep killed, and a banquet prepared for all his neighbors and friends. ²³ Raguel begged Tobias to stay with him for two weeks. ²⁴ And of all the goods which Raguel possessed, he gave one half to Tobias, and made a will that gave the other half to Tobias after he and Edna were dead.

9 Then Tobias called the angel, who he thought was a man, and said to him, "Brother Azarias, please listen to me. ² If I should give myself to be your servant, it would not be a worthy reward for your care. ³ However, I beg you, to take camels and servants and to leave for Rages. Go to Gabael's house in the city of the Medes. Give him this receipt and get the money from him. Invite him to return with you to my wedding feast. ⁴ You know that my father is counting the days until we return, and if I stay one day more than necessary, he will be worried unnecessarily. ⁵ You see how Raguel has earnestly begged me to stay and I cannot refuse his request."

⁶ So Raphael took four of Raguel's servants, and two camels, and went to Rages, the city of the Medes. He found Gabael, gave him his receipt, and received from him all the money. ⁷ Raphael told him all that had happened to Tobias, the son of Tobit, and invited him to come with him to the wedding feast.

⁸ When they reached Raguel's house, they found Tobias dining. Tobias hurried to greet Gabael and they kissed each other. Gabael began to weep and he blessed God ⁹ with the words, "The God of Israel bless you, because you are the son of a very good and just man, who fears God and does good deeds. ¹⁰ And may a blessing come upon your wife and upon your parents. ¹¹ And may you see your children, and your children's children, unto the third and fourth generation. May your children be blessed by the God of Israel, who reigns for ever and ever." ¹² And when all had said, "Amen," they began the wedding feast during which they were mindful of the hand of the Lord.

10 Meanwhile, as the days passed and Tobias did not return, Tobit became concerned, saying, "What do you think is keeping my son? What can be detaining him? ² Do you think Gabael has died and there is no one to pay him the money?" ³ Both Tobit and his wife, Anna, were very sad and they began to weep together because their son had not returned on the day appointed. ⁴ Tobias' mother mourned: "Woe, woe is me! Oh, my son, why did we send you into a strange country, you who are the light of our eyes? ⁵ Because you are our hope for the future, we should not have let you go away." ⁶ And Tobit said to her, "Be quiet and stop worrying. Our son is safe. I have confidence in the man we sent with him." ⁷ But Anna could not be comforted. Every day she kept watch for Tobias and even went to stand by the road on which he should return, hoping that she might see him coming in the distance.

⁸ At the same time Raguel urged his son-in-law: "Stay here. I will send a messenger to Tobit your father, telling him you are well." ⁹ But Tobias replied, "My father and mother must be very worried by now. I must go back." ¹⁰ Although Raguel argued with Tobias a long time, he finally gave up when he could not persuade him. So Raguel brought Sarah to him. He also gave Tobias half of his slaves, both men and women, half of his camels, cattle, and money. He bid him farewell and said in blessing, ¹¹ "May the angel of the Lord guard you in your journey, and bring you home safely. May you find your parents well and may my eyes see my grandchildren before I die." ¹² Raguel and Edna kissed their daughter good-bye, ¹³ reminding her to honor her new father- and mother-in-law, to love her husband, to take care of her family, to govern her house, and to behave blamelessly.

11 On the eleventh day the travelers reached Charan, which is halfway to Nineveh. ² Then Raphael said to Tobias, "You know how concerned you left your father. ³ Therefore, let us go ahead to get

things ready while the others follow us."
⁴ Tobias liked the idea. Raphael reminded
Tobias, "Take the gall of the fish with you
because we will need it." So Tobias took the
gall and they went on ahead with the dog
following. ⁵ Anna, as she had been doing
every day, sat on the top of a hill beside the
road so that she could see away off. ⁶ Thus
while she watched for him, she saw two
men far off, and recognized them as her son
and the man who had gone with him. She
hurried to her husband, crying, "Come
look, your son is coming!"

⁷ Raphael told Tobias, "As soon as you
go into your house, first adore the Lord
your God and give thanks to him. Then go
to your father and kiss him. ⁸ Quickly
anoint his eyes with the fish gall you carry.
This will cause the white film to come off
and your father shall see the light of heaven
and rejoice in seeing you." ⁹ Then the dog,
which had traveled all the way with them,
ran ahead, as if he wanted to tell the good
news. He showed his joy by jumping and
wagging his tail. ¹⁰ Despite his blindness,
Tobit stood up and, hurrying to meet his
son, stumbled. A servant caught him and
led him to Tobias. ¹¹ Tobit and Anna kissed
their son, and they began to weep for joy.
¹² After they all had adored God, and given
thanks, they sat down together. ¹³ Then
Tobias took the fish gall and anointed his
father's eyes. ¹⁴ In about half an hour, a
white skin began to come out of Tobit's
eyes, like the skin of an egg. ¹⁵ Tobit took
hold of it and pulled it from his eyes. Immediately he recovered his sight. ¹⁶ All
who were there glorified God. ¹⁷ Tobit said,
"I bless you, O Lord God of Israel, because
you have punished me, and you have saved
me. Behold, I see Tobias my son."

¹⁸ Not long after Sarah and the caravan
arrived, bringing with them the camels, cattle and Sarah's money dowry, plus that
money which Tobias had received from
Gabael. ¹⁹ Tobias told his parents about all
the blessings of God which had come to
him through the man who had been his
guide. ²⁰ Achior and Nabath, Tobit's relatives, came rejoicing for Tobias, congratulating him for all the good things that
God had done for him. ²¹ For seven days
they celebrated Tobias' marriage with great
joy.

12 Then Tobit called Tobias aside and
asked, "What can we give this holy
man who guided you?" ² Tobias replied,
"Father, wages are hardly worthy of his
many benefits. ³ He brought me back safely
to you, he collected the money from
Gabael, he helped me find my wife, he
cured her of an evil spirit, he gave joy to
her parents, he saved me from being devoured by the fish, he has restored your
sight. We have received so many good
things through him that it is difficult to
make any real reward. ⁴ But I beg you, father, to ask him if he would accept one half
of all things that we have brought back with
us." ⁵ So the father and the son summoned
Raphael and took him aside. They asked
him to accept half of all things that they
had brought.

⁶ Raphael replied so no others could
hear, "Rather bless the God of heaven.
Give glory to him before all men because
of the mercy he showed you. ⁷ While it is
good to hide the secret of a king, it is fitting
to reveal and praise the works of God.
⁸ Prayer is good when accompanied by fasting and alms, a far better thing than to lay
up treasures of gold. ⁹ Alms save us from
eternal death and cleanse us of sin. Alms
bring mercy and eternal life. ¹⁰ Those who
do evil and commit sin are enemies to their
own souls. ¹¹ I will tell you the truth, hiding nothing from you. ¹² It was I who
prayed for you to the Lord, while you
prayed with tears and buried the dead.
When you left your dinner to hide a dead
man so that you might bury him by night,
I offered your prayer to the Lord. ¹³ Because you found favor with God, it was
necessary that your faith should be tested.
¹⁴ The Lord sent me to heal you and your
daughter-in-law, Sarah. ¹⁵ I am Raphael,
one of the seven angels,ᵃ who stand before
the Lord."

¹⁶ When father and son had heard these
things, they were overcome with awe. They
fell with their faces to the ground. ¹⁷ But

---

a Only the names of Raphael, Michael and Gabriel appear in the Bible.

the angel said to them, "Peace be with you. Do not be afraid. ¹⁸ When I was with you, I was there by the will of God. Bless and praise him. ¹⁹ If I seemed to eat and drink with you, it was only your imagination. Bless God, and tell all about his wonderful works. ²⁰ It is time now that I must return to the one who sent me." ²¹ After he had said these things, he disappeared from their sight. ²² They lay prostrate with their faces to the ground for three hours, blessing God. Then they arose and told all about the wonderful things that had happened to them.

13 Tobit blessed the Lord in this manner:
"You are great, O Lord, for ever,
and your kingdom is without end.
² For you both punish and pardon;
you send men down to hell and bring them up again.
There is none who can escape your hand.
³ Give glory to the Lord, you children of Israel.
Praise him before the Gentiles
⁴ for if he has scattered you among the unknowing,
it is so that you may declare his wonderful works
and make known to them that there is no other God of might except him.
⁵ Although he punished us for our sins
and he will also save us by his mercy.
⁶ Consider well how he treats us.
Mindful of his majesty give praise to him.
Extol the eternal King by your deeds.
⁷ As for me, I will praise him in the land of my exile,
and make known his majesty
to a nation that sins against him.
⁸ Be converted, therefore, you sinners,
and do justice before God,
believing that he will show his mercy to you.
⁹ For my part, my soul will rejoice in him.
¹⁰ Bless the Lord, you his elect,
and give glory to him.
¹¹ Jerusalem, city of God,

the Lord has punished you for your failures.
¹² Give glory to the Lord for what good you have.
Bless the ever-living God
that your Temple may be rebuilt,
that the exiles may return to you,
and that then you can rejoice for evermore.
¹³ You will shine as a bright light
over all the worshiping nations of the world.
¹⁴ Nations from afar will come to you,
and will bring you gifts,
looking upon your land as holy.
¹⁵ In you they will call upon Yahweh's name.
¹⁶ Those who despise you will be cursed,
and those who blaspheme you will be condemned.
Blessed be those who rebuild you.
¹⁷ Blessed be your children who give you rejoicing
because they will belong to the Lord.
¹⁸ Blessed are all those who love you,
and who rejoice over your peace.
¹⁹ My soul blesses the Lord,
because the Lord our God will deliver Jerusalem his city from all her troubles.
²⁰ I shall be happy if some of my children
live to see the glory of Jerusalem.
²¹ The gates of Jerusalem shall be built of sapphire and emerald,
and all the surrounding walls of precious stones.
²² Its streets shall be paved with white and clean stones.
Songs of joy shall sound in its streets.
²³ Blessed be the Lord, who exalts Jerusalem
and may his reign be for ever and ever.
Amen."

14 So ended the hymn of Tobit.
After Tobit's sight was restored, he lived forty-two years more and saw the children of his grandchildren. ² He died at the age of a hundred and two years and was

buried honorably in Nineveh. ³ He was fifty-six years old when he went blind, and sixty when he saw again. ⁴ His old age was happy, and with full confidence in God, he died in peace.

⁵ As his death approached, he sent for his son Tobias and his seven grandsons and said to them, ⁶ "The destruction of Nineveh is near because the time for the word of the Lord to be fulfilled is at hand. Our brothers, who are scattered in exile from the land of Israel, will return to it. ⁷ All the desert land will be filled with people, and the house of God which has been destroyed will again be rebuilt. All who fear God will return to Jerusalem. ⁸ The Gentiles will leave their idols and will come to Jerusalem, where they will live. ⁹ All the kings of the earth will be converted, adoring the God of Israel. ¹⁰ And now, my children, I give you this task: serve the Lord sincerely, and do what is pleasing to him. ¹¹ Command your children that they do justice and give alms, and that they remember God, blessing him at all times in truth, and with all their power. ¹² And now, my son, obey me, and do not stay here. As soon as you bury your mother alongside me in the tomb, leave without delay, ¹³ for I foresee that sin will bring Nineveh to destruction."

¹⁴ When his mother died, Tobias left Nineveh with his wife and children and children's children to return to Media to his father- and mother-in-law. ¹⁵ He found them in good health in their old age. He took care of them, and when they died, he inherited all of Raguel's belongings. He saw his children's children to the fifth generation. ¹⁶ After he had lived ninety-nine years, all that time serving the Lord, he died and was buried with honor. ¹⁷ His relatives and his descendants continued in a good and holy life, acceptable both to God and men, and to all who lived around Media.

Beauty and the Beast

The Bible is often charged with being a book by men about men. Feminists are not averse to proclaiming it a good example of male chauvinism. There is some truth to the charge because the Bible reflects the cultural settings of its various books, and much of society was male-dominated. But beginning with Eve there were many women who played very important roles in salvation history, some proving that they were more than equal to any man.

One such story is that of the beautiful and valiant Jewish widow, Judith, who singlehandedly saved her nation

and turned back a great invasion by a mighty army from the east. True, she traded on feminine wiles to work her seeming miracle but she showed a courage and resoluteness that her male contemporaries lacked. When they were preparing to surrender, she took violent action.

The purpose of the author of this book is to show the nature of God and His constant care for His people. Man can entreat God for some favor but God replies in His own time and in His own way. While the book makes the point that the Jews were allowed to suffer for past departures from God's law, God permits this suffering in order to bring them back to Him. An unusual thought for a Jewish writer is presented in this book and that is that God not only uses suffering as a punishment but also as a means of purification.

There are some interesting minor characters in this work. Although the book is very nationalistic in its approach, it does devote attention to a natural Jewish enemy, Achior, the Ammonite, who is welcomed into the ranks of the Jews because he is ready to share their suffering and thus gain their salvation. His defense of the Jews, though done obliquely, before the enemy general is something of a classic.

This paraphrase is taken from the Douay version which depended upon the translation by St. Jerome from a lost Aramaic manuscript. Newer translations have had to depend upon Greek originals.

Some have found Judith an embarrassment—a woman who used her wiles to deceive the enemy and who exemplifies the philosophy that the end justifies the means. But this is to miss the point of the book, namely, that those who rely on themselves will fail while those who depend on the aid of God will succeed. The author writes from an Old Testament point of view which does vary from the Christian ethic. The enemy general is not destroyed so much by his murder but by his own lust and cruelty. This book, as other works of the Old Testament, must be regarded with the eyes of its time. The Old Covenant was to be supplanted eventually by the new rule of life given by Jesus, but we must judge Old Testament figures in the light of their own age.

JUDITH

1 NOW ARPHAXAD, King of the Medes, had brought many nations under his rule. He built a fortified city which he called Ecbatana, ² with hewn stone walls. He made these walls seventy cubitsᵃ wide, and thirty cubits high, and its towers he made a hundred cubits high. Each side was extended the space of twenty feet. ³ He made the gates of the city the same height as the towers, ⁴ and he gloried as a mighty one in the strength of his army and in the glory of his chariots.

⁵ Now in the twelfth year of his reign, Nebuchadnezzar, King of the Assyrians,ᵇ who ruled the great city of Nineveh, made war against Arphaxad and overcame him ⁶ on the great plain near Ragae.ᶜ He was joined by the people from along the Euphrates, the Tigris and the Hydaspes and in the plain where Arioch governed the Elymaeans. ⁷ Then the kingdom of Nebuchadnezzar was enlarged, and his heart was elated, and he sent a message to all who lived in Cilicia, Damascus and Lebanon, ⁸ and to the nations of Carmel and Gilead, and to the people of Galilee and in the great plain of Esdraelon, ⁹ and to all who were in Samaria and beyond the river Jordan, even to Jerusalem, and all the land of Jesse, even to the borders of Ethiopia.

¹⁰ To all these, Nebuchadnezzar, King of the Assyrians, sent messengers; ¹¹ but these nations all refused to listen and sent them back emptyhanded, rejecting them without honor. Then King Nebuchadnezzar, being angry with all of them, swore by his throne and kingdom that he would seek revenge on all of those countries.

2 In the eighteenth year of the reign of Nebuchadnezzar, the twenty-second day of the first month, the word was given out in the house of Nebuchadnezzar, King of the Assyrians, that he would seek revenge. ² And he called all the elders, all the governors and his war counselors, revealing to them his secret plan. ³ He said that his intention was to bring all the earth under his empire.

⁴ When his words pleased them all, King Nebuchadnezzar called Holofernes, the general of his armies, ⁵ and said to him,

---

a A cubit equaled 18 inches. These figures seem exaggerated.
c Near modern Teheran.

b He was really King of Babylon.

"Go out against all the kingdoms of the west and especially against those who ignored my invitation. 6 You will not spare any kingdom and you shall bring all the strong cities under my rule."

7 Then Holofernes summoned the leaders and officers of the Assyrian army and as the king commanded him, he recruited men for the expedition: a hundred and twenty thousand fighting men on foot and twelve thousand archers and horsemen. 8 And he made all his warlike preparations, gathering an innumerable multitude of camels to carry abundant provisions for the armies, and uncounted herds of oxen and flocks of sheep. 9 He ordered corn to be stored on his route through Syria. 10 He took gold and silver from the king's palace in great abundance. 11 And he and the army went forth with the chariots, horsemen and archers, covering the face of the earth like locusts. 12 And when he had passed through the borders of the Assyrians, he came to the great mountains of Ange on the left of Cilicia; and going up to all the enemy castles, he took all the fortified places.

13 And he captured the famous city of Melothus by assault, killing all the children of Rassis and Ismahel, a who were on the fringe of the desert and in the south of the land of the Chelleans. 14 And he went along the Euphrates and passed through Mesopotamia, taking all the hilltop cities that were there, from the brook of Abron until one comes to the sea. 15 And he captured the lands from Cilicia to the coasts of Japheth, which are towards Arabia. 16 And he carried away all the children of Midian and stripped them of all their riches; and all who resisted him he killed with the sword. 17 After these things, in the days of the harvest, he went down into the plains of Damascus, set the corn on fire, and caused all the trees and vineyards to be cut down. 18 And the fear of him fell upon all the inhabitants of the land.

3 Then the kings and the princes of all the cities and provinces of Syria, Mesopotamia, Syria Sobal, Libya and Cilicia sent their ambassadors who said to Holofernes, 2 "Let your indignation towards us cease. It is better for us to live and serve Nebuchadnezzar the great king and be subject to you, than to die and perish, or suffer the miseries of slavery. 3 All of our cities and our possessions, all our mountain strongholds, hills and fields, herds of oxen, flocks of sheep, goats, horses and camels, and all our goods and families are in your sight. 4 Let all we have be subject to your law. 5 Both we and our children are your servants. 6 Come to us a peaceable lord and use our service as it shall please you."

7 Then Holofernes went down from the mountains with horsemen in great power, and made himself master of every city and all the inhabitants of the land. 8 And from all the cities he took auxiliaries, valiant men chosen for war. 9 And so great a fear lay upon all those provinces that the inhabitants of all the cities, including princes and nobles, went out to meet him when he came. 10 They received him with garlands, lights, dances, tambourines and flutes. 11 And though they did these things, they could not soften the fierceness of his heart; 12 as he destroyed their sacred groves and demolished their cities. 13 For Nebuchadnezzar the king had commanded him to destroy all the gods of the land, that he alone might be called god by those nations which were brought under his rule by the power of Holofernes.

14 And when he had passed through all of Syria Sobal, Apamea and Mesopotamia, he came to the Idumeans in the land of Geba. 15 He took possession of their cities, staying there for thirty days during which time he organized all the troops of his army.

4 Receiving these reports, the children of Israel, who lived in the land of Judah, were exceedingly afraid of him. 2 Their minds were seized with dread and horror that he would do the same to Jerusalem and to the temple of the Lord as he had done to other cities and their temples. 3 They sent men into all Samaria and round about, as far as Jericho, and seized all the high hilltops; 4 and they fortified their towns

a Bedouins

with walls and stored up food in preparation for war.

5 Joakim the high priest wrote to all who were around Esdrelon, which faces the great plain near Dothan, and to all who controlled the passes through the hills, that they should take control of all the mountain roads which gave access to Jerusalem, and should keep watch where the way was narrow between the mountains. 6 The children of Israel did as the priest of the Lord, Joakim, had ordered them. 7 All the people cried to the Lord with great earnestness, and they and their wives humbled their souls in fastings and prayers.

8 The priests put on sackcloth, and the little children lay prostrate before the temple of the Lord, and they covered the altar of the Lord with sackcloth. 9 They prayed to the Lord the God of Israel with one accord, that their children might not be made captives and their wives carried off, their cities destroyed, their holy things profaned, and that they might not be made a reproach to the Gentiles. 10 Then Joakim the high priest of the Lord went about all Israel and spoke to them, 11 saying, "Know that the Lord will hear your pleas if you continue with perseverance in fastings and prayers in the sight of the Lord. 12 Remember Moses, the servant of the Lord, who overcame Amalec who trusted in his own strength, in his power, in his army, in his shields, in his chariots and in his horsemen; he was defeated not by fighting with the sword but by holy prayers. 13 So shall all the enemies of Israel be turned back, if you persevere in this work which you have begun."

14 So, being moved by his exhortation, they prayed to the Lord and continued faithful in the sight of the Lord. 15 Even they, who offered the holocausts to the Lord, offered the sacrifices to the Lord clothed with sackcloth and with ashes upon their heads. 16 And they begged God with all their hearts that he would remain with his people Israel.

5 When Holofernes, the general of the army of the Assyrians, heard that the children of Israel had prepared themselves to resist and had fortified the mountain passes, 2 he was exceedingly angry. In his indignation, he called all the rulers of Moab and the commanders of Ammon, 3 and said to them, "Tell me who are these people who live on the hill country? What cities do they inhabit? How large and powerful is their army? Who guides and rules them? 4 Why have they, above all others who live in the west, looked down on us and not come out to meet us that they might receive us with peace?"

5 Then Achior, leader of the Ammonites, answered, "If my lord will listen to me, I will tell him the truth concerning this people who dwell in the mountains. No falsehood will come from my mouth. 6 This people have descended from the Chaldeans. 7 Once they lived in Mesopotamia where they would not follow the gods of their fathers, who were in the land of the Chaldeans. 8 Abandoning the worship of their ancestors, which consisted in the worship of many gods, 9 they worshiped one God of heaven. It was this same God who also commanded them to depart from there and to dwell in Canaan. When there was a famine over all the land, they went down into Egypt and there for four hundred years were so multiplied that the number of them could not be counted.

10 "And when the king of Egypt oppressed them and made slaves of them to labor in clay and brick in the building of his cities, they cried to their Lord and he struck the whole land of Egypt with various plagues. 11 When the Egyptians had cast them out from among them, and the plague had ceased from them, and they had a mind to take them again and bring them back to their service, 12 the God of heaven opened the sea to them in their flight so that the waters were made to stand firm as a wall on either side, and they walked through the bottom of the sea and passed without getting their feet wet. 13 And when an innumerable army of the Egyptians pursued after them in that place, they were so overwhelmed by the waters that there was not one left to tell posterity what had happened.

14 "And after they came out of the Red Sea, they built their dwellings in the desert about Mount Sinai, an inhospitable land

that is difficult to work. ¹⁵ There bitter fountains were made sweet for them to drink and for forty years they received food from heaven. ¹⁶ Wheresoever they went in without bow and arrow and without shield and sword, their God fought for them and overcame. ¹⁷ And there was no one who triumphed over this people except when they themselves had departed from the worship of the Lord their God. ¹⁸ Whenever they worshiped any other beside their own God, they were defeated, put to the sword, and humbled. ¹⁹ As often as they repented for having turned from the worship of their God, the God of heaven made them strong again.

²⁰ "So they overthrew the king of the Canaanites, of the Jebusites, of the Perizzites, of the Gergesites, of the Sechemites, of the Ammorites, and all the mighty ones in Heshbon, and they possessed their lands and their cities. ²¹ And as long as they did not sin against their God, it was well with them; for their God hates iniquity. ²² Even some years ago when they revolted against the way which their God had given them to walk, they were destroyed in battles by many nations and very many of them were led away captive into strange lands. ²³ But recently they returned to the Lord their God and have come back from the different places in which they were scattered, they have occupied Jerusalem, where their sanctuary is and have settled in the hill country. ²⁴ Now, therefore, my lord, search if there be any iniquity of theirs in the sight of their God. If so, let us go up against them because their God will surely deliver them to you, and they shall be brought under the yoke of your power. ²⁵ But if there is no offence of this people in the sight of God, we cannot defeat them because their God will defend them and we shall be a reproach to the whole earth."

²⁶ And it came to pass, that when Achior had finished speaking, all the advisors of Holofernes were angry and they had a mind to kill him, saying to each other, ²⁷ "Who is this man who says the children of Israel can resist King Nebuchadnezzar and his armies, men unarmed and without strength and without skill in the art of war? ²⁸ So that Achior, therefore, may know

that he deceives us, let us go up into the hill country, and when the bravest of them shall be captured, we shall put him and his fellows to the sword, ²⁹ so that every nation may know that Nebuchadnezzar is god of the earth and besides him there is no other."

6 Thus when the tumult had died down, Holofernes was in a violent passion and said to Achior, ² "Because you have prophesied to us, saying that the nation of Israel is defended by their God, to show you that there is no god but Nebuchadnezzar, ³ when we shall slay them all as one man, then by the sword of the Assyrians you also will die with them, and all Israel will perish with you. ⁴ You will find that Nebuchadnezzar is lord of the whole earth; and then the sword of my soldiers will pierce your sides, and you will be stabbed and fall among the wounded of Israel, and will breathe no more as you are destroyed with them. ⁵ But, if you think your prophecy true, do not look so downcast and let the paleness that is in your face depart from you, if you think my words cannot be fulfilled. ⁶ And that you may know that you will experience these things together with them, behold from this hour you will be associated to their people, that when they will receive the punishment they deserve from my sword, you may fall under the same vengeance."

⁷ Then Holofernes ordered his servants to seize Achior and take him to Bethulia, and to deliver him into the hands of the children of Israel. ⁸ And the servants of Holofernes taking Achior went out into the plain. When they approached the mountains, the slingers came out against them. ⁹ Avoiding them by taking shelter under the hill, they tied Achior's hands and feet to a tree with ropes and returned to their master.

¹⁰ The children of Israel came down from Bethulia and found him. They untied him and brought him to Bethulia, and setting him in the midst of the people, asked him the reason that the Assyrians had left him bound. ¹¹ In those days the rulers there were Uzziah, the son of Micah of the tribe of Simeon, and Chabris, the son of Gothon-

iel, and Charmis, son of Melchiel. ¹² Achior related in the midst of the elders, and in the presence of all the people, all that he had replied to Holofernes, and how the people of Holofernes would have killed him for this speech; ¹³ how Holofernes himself being angry had commanded him to be delivered for this cause to the Israelites, that when he should conquer the children of Israel, then he might command that Achior himself be put to death by various torments for having said that the God of heaven is their defender.

¹⁴ When Achior had declared all these things, all the people fell upon their faces, adoring the Lord, and all of them together mourning and weeping poured out their prayers with one accord to the Lord, ¹⁵ saying, "O Lord God of heaven and earth, behold their pride, and look on our humiliation, and look upon those consecrated to you, and show that you do not forsake those who trust in you, and that you humble those who presume of themselves and glory in their own strength." ¹⁶ So when their weeping was ended, and the people's prayer, in which they continued all the day, was concluded, they comforted Achior, ¹⁷ saying, "The God of our fathers, whose power you have stated, will make all right with you, that rather than being overcome, you will see their destruction. ¹⁸ And when the Lord our God will give this liberty to his servants, let God be with you also in the midst of us, and as it shall please you, you and your people may be friends with us."

¹⁹ Then Uzziah, after the assembly was broken up, received him into his house, and made him a great supper. ²⁰ All the elders were invited and they refreshed themselves together after their fast was over. ²¹ Afterwards all the people were called together, and they prayed all the night long within the synagogue, asking the help of the God of Israel.

7 The next day Holofernes gave orders to his army to attack Bethulia. ² Now there were in his troops a hundred and seventy thousand infantry and twelve thousand cavalry, together with the baggage handlers and those youths who had been brought from the provinces and cities. ³ All these prepared themselves together to fight the children of Israel, and they made camp in the valley which looked toward Dothan, from the place which is called Balbaim, to Cyamon, which borders Esdraelon. ⁴ When the children of Israel saw the great numbers of them, they prostrated themselves upon the ground, put ashes upon their heads and prayed with one accord that the God of Israel would show his mercy to his people. ⁵ Taking their weapons, they took up their posts along the narrow trails which passed between the mountains, and they guarded these all day and night.

⁶ Now Holofernes, in scouting the area, heard that the spring which supplied the city with water ran through an aqueduct outside the city on the south side, and he commanded that their aqueduct be cut off. ⁷ Nevertheless there were springs not far from the walls, out of which the Israelites secretly drew water, to refresh themselves a little rather than to drink their fill. ⁸ But the children of Esau[a] and Moab came to Holofernes, saying, "The children of Israel do not rely on their spears, nor in their arrows, but the mountains are their defense, and the steep hills and precipices guard them. ⁹ Therefore, that you may overcome them without joining battle, set guards at the springs that they may not draw water out of them, and you will destroy them without sword. They will give up their city, which they imagine is impregnable because it is situated in the mountains." ¹⁰ These words pleased Holofernes and his officers, so he placed about a hundred men at every spring.

¹¹ When they had kept this watch for a full twenty days, the cisterns and the reserve of water failed for the inhabitants of Bethulia, so that there was not within the city enough to satisfy them for a single day, for it was doled out each day by the drink. ¹² Then all the men and women, young men, and children, went in one body to Uzziah, and spoke in one voice ¹³ saying, "God be judge between us and you, for you

a Edomites

have done us evil in not making peace with the Assyrians, and for this God has sold us into their hands. ¹⁴ Therefore there is no one to help us, while we are cast down before their eyes in thirst and utter destruction. ¹⁵ Now assemble all who are in the city, that we may freely surrender to the army of Holofernes. ¹⁶ For it is better, that being captives we should live and bless the Lord, than that we should die and be a reproach to all men for allowing our wives and our infants to die before our eyes. ¹⁷ We call to witness against you this day both heaven and earth and our ancestral God, who punishes us for our sins, demanding that you deliver at once the city to Holofernes. It is better to die quickly by the sword than to die slowly of thirst." ¹⁸ And when they had said these things, there was great weeping and lamentation of all in the assembly, and for many hours with one voice they cried to God, saying, ¹⁹ "We have sinned as did our fathers before us. We have done unjust deeds. We have committed iniquities. ²⁰ Have mercy on us, because you are good, or if you must punish us do it yourself, but do not deliver those who trust in you into the hands of unbelievers. ²¹ Do not let the Gentiles mock: 'Where is their God?' "

²² Finally, being wearied with these cries and tired with these weepings, they held their peace. ²³ Uzziah rising up in tears, said, "Be of good courage, my brothers! Let us hold out for five days more awaiting mercy from the Lord. ²⁴ For perhaps he will put a stop to his indignation and will give glory to his name. ²⁵ But if after five days no help comes, then we will do what you say."

8 Now it happened that Judith, a widow, had heard these things. She was the daughter of Merari, the son of Idox, the son of Joseph, the son of Oziel, the son of Elkiah, the son of Ananias, the son of Gideon, the son of Raphaim, the son of Achitub, the son of Elijah, the son of Eliab, the son of Nathanael, the son of Salamiel, the son of Saracadai, the son of Israel. ² Her husband was Manasses, who died in the time of the barley harvest. ³ He was overseeing the gleaners who bound sheaves in the field and

suffered heat stroke. He died in Bethulia, his own city, and was buried there with his fathers. ⁴ Judith had been a widow for three years and four months. ⁵ She made herself a private room on the roof of her house, in which she lived shut up with her maids. ⁶ She wore sackcloth about her loins and fasted all the days of her widowhood, except the sabbaths, new moons and the feasts of the house of Israel. ⁷ She was exceedingly beautiful, and her husband left her great riches, very many servants and large herds of oxen and flocks of sheep. ⁸ She was greatly renowned among all, because she feared the Lord very much, neither was there any one who spoke an ill word of her.

⁹ When she had heard that Uzziah had promised that he would deliver up the city after the fifth day, she sent for the elders, Chabris and Charmis. ¹⁰ They came to her, and she said to them, "What is this promise which Uzziah has made to surrender the city to the Assyrians if within five days no aid comes to us? ¹¹ Who are you to tempt the Lord? ¹² This is not a promise that may draw down mercy, but rather that may stir up wrath, and enkindle indignation. ¹³ You have set a limit to the mercy of the Lord, and you have told him to act as it pleases you. ¹⁴ But since the Lord acts in his own good time, let us be as patient as he is and with many tears let us beg his pardon. ¹⁵ God is not like man, nor can he be threatened like a human being. ¹⁶ Therefore, let us humble our souls before him and in a humble spirit continue in his service. ¹⁷ Let us ask the Lord with tears to show us mercy if that be his will. If their pride bothers us, we can be consoled by our humility. ¹⁸ We have avoided the sin of our fathers, who forsook their God and worshiped strange gods, ¹⁹ for which crime they were delivered to their enemies, handed over to the sword, plundered and bewildered. We know no other God but him. ²⁰ Let us humbly wait for his consolation, for the Lord our God may require our blood for the affliction of our enemies, yet he will humble all the nations that rise up against us and bring them to disgrace.

²¹ "And now, brethren, as you are the elders among the people of God, and their

very lives depend upon you, comfort their hearts by your speech, that they may be mindful how our fathers were tempted in order that they might be proved, whether they worshiped their God in truth. 22 They must remember how our father Abraham was tempted, and being proved by many tribulations, was made the friend of God. 23 So it was that Isaac, Jacob, Moses and all who have pleased God[a] have passed through many tribulations and remained faithful. 24 But they that did not receive the trials with the fear of the Lord but uttered their impatience and their reproach, murmuring against the Lord, 25 were destroyed by the destroyer, and perished by serpents. 26 As for us, let us not revenge ourselves for these things which we suffer. 27 But judging these very punishments to be less than our sins deserve, let us believe that these scourges of the Lord, with which we are chastised like servants, have happened for our admonishment and not for our destruction."

28 Then Uzziah and the elders said to her, "All that you have said is true and no one can deny your words. 29 So now pray for us, for you are a holy woman who fears God. 30 And Judith said to them, "You recognize what I have said to be of God. 31 Now prove that you are of God by supporting my plan, and pray that God may strengthen my design. 32 You must stand at the city gate tonight and I will go out with my maidservant. You must pray, that as you have said, the Lord may look down upon his people Israel in five days. 33 It is my wish that you do not ask what I am going to do. You yourselves must do nothing but pray to God for me until I bring word of what I have done." And Uzziah, the leader of Judah, said to her, "Go in peace, and the Lord be with you as you take revenge on our enemies." So they left for their posts.

9 And when they were gone, Judith went into her prayer room, and putting on sackcloth, laid ashes on her head, and falling down prostrate before the Lord, she cried to the Lord, saying, 2 "O Lord God of my father Simeon, to whom you gave a sword to execute vengeance against strangers, who had embarrassed and defiled a virgin by stripping her of her clothes. 3 You gave their wives to be made a prey, and their daughters into captivity, and all their booty to be divided among your servants who were zealous for you. Assist me, I beg you, O Lord God, for I am a widow. 4 For you have done great things before and have conceived one thing after another, and what you have designed has been done. 5 For all your ways are prepared, and in your providence you have placed your judgments. 6 Look upon the camp of the Assyrians now, as you were pleased to look upon the camp of the Egyptians when they made armed pursuit of your servants, trusting in their chariots and in their horsemen, and in a multitude of warriors. 7 But you looked over their camp, and darkness wearied them. 8 The bottom of the sea held their feet and the waters overwhelmed them. 9 So may it be with these also, O Lord, who trust in their great numbers, in their chariots, in their lances, in their shields, in their arrows, and glory in their spears, 10 and who do not know that you are our God, who crushes wars when they begin, and the Lord is your name. 11 Lift up your arm as from the beginning and crush their power with your might. Let their strength fall before your wrath, for they intend to violate your sanctuary, defile your tabernacle, and throw down the horn of your altar with their swords. 12 Bring to pass, O Lord, that the pride of Holofernes may be cut down by his own sword. 13 Let him be caught in the net of his own greed for me, and strike him down through the pleasantries of my words. 14 Give me constancy in my mind that I may despise him, and fortitude that I may overthrow him. 15 For this will be a glorious monument for your name, when he shall fall by the hand of a woman. 16 For your power, O Lord, is not in a vast army, nor is your pleasure in the strength of horses; nor from the beginning have the proud been acceptable to you, but the prayer of the humble and the meek has always pleased you. 17 O God of the heavens,

---

a Suffering is more than a penalty for sin.

creator of the waters and Lord of the whole universe, hear me, a pitiable widow making supplication to you and presuming on your mercy. ¹⁸ Remember, O Lord, your covenant, and put your words in my mouth, and strengthen the resolution in my heart, that your house may continue in your holiness ¹⁹ and all nations may acknowledge that you are God, and there is no other besides you."

10 So when she had finished praying to the Lord, she rose from the place where she lay prostrate before the Lord. ² She called her maid and went down into her house where she took off her sackcloth and put away the garments of her widowhood. ³ She washed her body, anointed herself with the finest ointment, plaited her hair, put a tiara upon her head, clothed herself with gay apparel, put sandals on her feet and took her bracelets, anklets, earrings and rings, arraying herself with all her ornaments. ⁴ And the Lord made her even more beautiful because all this dressing up did not proceed from vanity but from virtue, and therefore the Lord increased her beauty, so that she appeared to the eyes of all men as incomparably lovely. ⁵ She gave to her maid a bottle of wine to carry and a flask of oil, parched corn, dry figs, bread and cheese, and they left.

⁶ They went to the city gate and found Uzziah and the elders of the city waiting. ⁷ When they saw her they were astonished and greatly admired her beauty. ⁸ But they asked her no question, letting her pass, saying, "May the God of our fathers grant you favor and may he fulfill your plans by his power so that Jerusalem may glory in you, and your name may be listed among the holy and just." ⁹ And all of them there said with one voice, "Amen! Amen!" ¹⁰ But Judith, praying to the Lord, passed through the gate with her maid.

¹¹ Now it happened that as she went down the hill about the break of day that Assyrian guards met her and halted her, asking, "Where are you coming from? Where are you going?" ¹² And she answered, "I am a daughter of the Hebrews, but I am fleeing from them, because I know they will fall victims to you, for they de-

spised you and would not freely surrender that they might find mercy in your sight. ¹³ For this reason I thought to myself, 'I will go and see General Holofernes so that I may tell him their secrets and show him by what way he may take them without the loss of one man of his army.' " ¹⁴ When the men had heard her words, they beheld her face—she was marvelously beautiful to behold—and ¹⁵ they said to her, "You have saved your life by choosing to come down to see our lord. ¹⁶ Be assured of this, that when you shall stand before him, he will treat you well and you will be most acceptable to his heart." And they brought her to the tent of Holofernes, telling him of her.

¹⁷ And when she was in his presence, Holofernes was caught by her beauty. ¹⁸ His officers said to him, "Who can look down on the Jews when they have such beautiful women. Surely it is worth our lives not to allow such beauty to capture the world." ¹⁹ Judith saw Holofernes sitting under a canopy which was woven of purple and gold, decorated with emeralds and precious stones. ²⁰ She went before him, bowed and prostrated herself. Then at the command of their master, the servants of Holofernes lifted her up.

11 Then Holofernes said to her, "Take courage and don't be afraid. I have never hurt anyone who was willing to serve Nebuchadnezzar, our king. ² If your people had not turned me down, I would never have lifted my spear against them. ³ But now tell me why you left them and why you wish to join us?" ⁴ Judith replied, "Accept the words of your servant and let your handmaid speak to you and God will do wonders through you. ⁵ For as Nebuchadnezzar the king of all the earth lives, and his power endures and is given to you to chastise all who oppose him, so that not only men serve him through you but even the beasts of the field. ⁶ For your wisdom is spoken of among all nations, and it is told through the whole world that you are the one good and powerful man in all his kingdom and your discipline is respected in all the provinces. ⁷ We are aware of what Achior said and we know what you have commanded to be done to him. ⁸ It is also

sure that our God is so offended with sins that he has sent word by his prophets to the people that he will allow them to be overcome for their sins. ⁹ And because the children of Israel know they have offended their God, they stand in fear of you. ¹⁰ Their food supply is gone and thirst is already taking lives. ¹¹ They plan to kill their cattle and to drink their blood. ¹² And the consecrated things of the Lord their God which God forbids them to use—the first fruits of grain, the tithes of wine and oil—they intend to use, although they should not even touch these things with their hands. Because they do these things, it is certain they will be given up to destruction. ¹³ And I your handmaid, knowing this, fled from them, and the Lord has sent me to tell you these very things. ¹⁴ For I worship God even here in your camp and I will pray to God, ¹⁵ and he will tell me when he will punish them for their sins. I will come and tell you, so that I may lead you through Judea to Jerusalem. You shall control all the people of Israel, as sheep that have no shepherd, and there shall not be so much as one dog that will bark against you. ¹⁶ These things are revealed to me by the providence of God. ¹⁷ Because God is angry with Israel, I am sent to tell you all these things."

¹⁸ These words pleased Holofernes and his servants, and they marveled at her wisdom, and said, ¹⁹ "There is not such another woman in all the earth who has her beauty and wisdom." ²⁰ And Holofernes said to her, "God has done well to send you before the people that you might deliver them into our hands. ²¹ If you do as you say and if your God shall do this for me, he shall also be my God, and you shall be great in the house of Nebuchadnezzar, and your name shall be famous through all the earth."

12 Then he ordered that she should be brought to where his silver dishes were kept, and that she remain there and be served food from his own larder. ² Judith said, "I cannot now eat of these things which you have ordered to be given me lest I do wrong, but I will eat of the things which I have brought with me." ³ Holo-

fernes said to her, "If your supply fails where shall we get more such food for you?" ⁴ Judith answered, "As your soul lives, my lord, I shall not use all these things until God carries out that which I intend to do." So his servants brought her into the tent as Holofernes ordered. ⁵ As she was about to enter, she said that she hoped that she had freedom to go out at night and before daybreak to pray to the Lord. ⁶ Holofernes commanded his chamberlains that she should be free to go and come in order to adore her God. ⁷ For three days, she went out at night into the valley of Bethulia, and bathed herself in a spring. ⁸ As she emerged, she prayed to the Lord the God of Israel that he would direct her in the way to deliver his people ⁹ and returning, she remained safely in the tent, until she took her own meal in the evening.

¹⁰ On the fourth day, Holofernes had a banquet for his servants, and said to Bagoas his eunuch, "Go and persuade that Hebrew woman to come freely and dwell with me." ¹¹ It is looked upon as shameful among the Assyrians, if a woman mock a man by refusing his company. ¹² Then Bagoas went to Judith, and said, "Beautiful maiden, will you come to my lord, that you may be honored in his presence, and eat with him and drink wine and be merry." ¹³ Judith replied, "Who am I to refuse my lord? ¹⁴ All that pleases him, I will do. It pleases me to give him pleasure as long as I shall live." ¹⁵ She arose and dressed herself in her finest and went in and stood before him. ¹⁶ The heart of Holofernes was smitten, for he was burning with desire for her. ¹⁷ Holofernes said to her, "Sit down, drink and be merry for you have found favor before me." ¹⁸ Judith answered, "I will drink, my lord, because my life is greater today than any day since I was born." ¹⁹ So she ate and drank before him, but only what her maid had prepared for her. ²⁰ Holofernes was happy with her presence, and drank very much wine, more than he had ever drunk before.

13 When night fell, his servants withdrew to their quarters, and Bagoas closed the tent and went his way ² for they were all sleepy with wine. ³ Judith was alone in the tent ⁴ and Holofernes lay on his bed, fast asleep, being exceedingly drunk. ⁵ Judith had told her maid to keep watch outside the tent. ⁶ Judith stood before the bed praying sadly in her heart, ⁷ saying, "Give me strength, O Lord God of Israel, and in this hour look kindly on the works of my hands, that as you have promised you may rescue your city Jerusalem, and that I may do that which I must, believing that this is your will."

⁸ Then she went to the tent post at the head of the bed and took down the sword that hung there. ⁹ Drawing it from the sheath, she lifted the stupified Holofernes by his hair, saying, "Strengthen me, O Lord God, at this hour." ¹⁰ And she struck twice with all her might at his neck and cut off his head. She rolled his body off the bed, and concealed the head in the bedspread. ¹¹ Then she went out, gave the head of Holofernes to her maid and told her to put it into the food bag.

¹² Then, as it was their custom to go and pray, they went out of the camp, circled the valley and went up to the gate of Bethulia. ¹³ From afar, Judith called out to the watchmen upon the walls, "Open the gates! God is still with us! He has shown his power to Israel."

¹⁴ When the guards heard her voice, they called the elders of the city. ¹⁵ All ran to meet her from the least to the greatest, for they had no hope that they would ever see her again. ¹⁶ Lighting torches they all gathered about her. She climbed up to a higher place and asked for silence. And when it became quiet, ¹⁷ Judith said, "Praise the Lord our God, who has not forsaken those who hope in him. ¹⁸ Through me he has shown his mercy, which he promised to the house of Israel, and by my hand he has killed this night the enemy of his people." ¹⁹ Then she took the head of Holofernes out of the bag, showed it to them, and said, "Behold the head of Holofernes, the general of the army of the Assyrians, and behold his bedspread on which he lay in his drunkenness, where the Lord our God slew him by the hand of a woman. ²⁰ As the same Lord lives, his angel has been my keeper both going there and abiding there and returning from there.

The Lord has not permitted me to be defiled, but has brought me back to you without pollution of sin, rejoicing for his victory, for my escape and for your deliverance. ²¹ Give all of your glory to him, because he is good, since his mercy endures forever."

²² And they all adored the Lord, and cried to her, "The Lord has blessed you by his power, because by you he has brought our enemies to naught." ²³ And Uzziah, the leader of the people of Israel, said to her, "By the Lord the most high God, you are blessed, O daughter, above all women upon earth. ²⁴ Blessed be the Lord who made heaven and earth, who has directed you to cut off the head of the commander of our enemies. ²⁵ Because he has so glorified your name this day, your praise will always be on the lips of men who will remember forever the power of the Lord. You risked your life because of the distress and tribulation of your people, and have prevented our ruin before our God." ²⁶ And all the people said, "Amen! Amen!"

²⁷ Achior was summoned and Judith said to him, "The God of Israel about whom you gave testimony has revenged himself on his enemies. This night he has cut off the head of the commander of the unbelievers by my hand. ²⁸ So that you may believe this, behold the head of Holofernes, who in his contemptuous pride despised the God of Israel and threatened you with death, saying, 'When the people of Israel will be taken, I will command your body to be pierced with the sword.'" ²⁹ Then Achior, seeing the head of Holofernes, was seized with a great fear and fell on his face and his spirit failed him. ³⁰ After he had recovered, he knelt at her feet, and reverenced her, and said, ³¹ "Blessed are you by your God in every tabernacle of Jacob, for in every nation which will hear your name, the God of Israel will be magnified because of you."

14 Judith said to all the people, "Hear me, my brethren, hang this head upon the parapet. ² And as soon as the sun rises, let every man take his arms and rush out, pretending to make an attack, but do not go down to the plain. ³ The guards will run

to awake their prince for the battle. 4 And when their captains run into the tent of Holofernes and find him without his head and wallowing in his blood, fear will fall upon them. 5 And when you see they have taken flight, go after them determinedly, for the Lord will destroy them as they flee.

6 Then Achior seeing the power that the God of Israel had wrought was converted to Judaism. He believed in God, was circumcised and joined the house of Israel with all the generations of his kinsmen even to this present day.

7 As soon as dawn broke, they hung up the head of Holofernes upon the walls, and every man took his weapons and went out with a great clamor and shouting. 8 When the guards saw this, they ran to the tent of Holofernes. 9 They gathered around the tent and made a noise outside the tent to awake him. They wanted to awaken Holofernes by their noise because they did not dare call him. 10 For each was afraid to knock or go into the chamber of the general of the Assyrians. 11 But when his captains and lieutenants arrived, and all the commanders of the royal Assyrian army, they said to the chamberlains, 12 "Go in and awake him, for the mice, coming out of their holes, have presumed to challenge us to fight."

13 So Bagoas went into his tent, stood before the curtain, and made a clapping with his hands, for he thought that he was sleeping with Judith. 14 But when he received no answer, he looked in and saw the empty bed. He entered the bedchamber and saw the body of Holofernes, lying upon the ground, without its head, surrounded by blood. He cried out with a loud voice, wept and rent his garments. 15 And he went to the tent of Judith, and not finding her, he ran out to the soldiers 16 and shouted, "One Hebrew woman has disgraced the house of King Nebuchadnezzar. Look, Holofernes lies upon the ground and his body has no head!" 17 Now when the leaders of the Assyrian army heard this, they rent their garments and an intolerable fear and dread fell upon them, and their minds were confused. 18 And a very great cry went up in the midst of their camp.

15 When the soldiers heard that Holofernes was beheaded, courage and training left them, and being seized with trembling and fear, they thought only to save themselves by flight. 2 No one gave a command but they fled in shame, leaving all things behind, hoping only to escape from the Hebrews, who, they were told, were coming armed upon them. They fled along the paths of the plain and into the hill country. 3 The children of Israel seeing the flight followed after them. They rushed down to the sound of trumpets and with shouts. 4 Because the Assyrians were in disorder, they fled in all directions, but the children of Israel pursued them as one man and put to death all whom they could find.

5 Uzziah sent messengers through all the cities and to the frontiers of Israel. 6 Every region and every city sent their chosen young men armed after the Assyrians, and they pursued them, cutting them down with their swords, until they reached the borders of their country. 7 Those who were in Bethulia went into the camp of the Assyrians and took away the spoils which the Assyrians in their flight had left behind, and they were heavily laden. 8 Those who returned to Bethulia from the slaughter brought with them all things that they had captured, and so there was no numbering the cattle and other animals, plus the other booty. There was so much that from the least to the greatest all were made rich by their booty.

9 Joakim the high priest came to Bethulia from Jerusalem with all his elders to see Judith. 10 When they met her, they all blessed her with one voice, saying, "You are the glory of Jerusalem, you are the joy of Israel, you are the pride of our people. 11 You have done this bravely and your heart is made strong because you have loved chastity, and since your husband is dead you have known no other man. The hand of the Lord has strengthened you, and therefore you shall be blessed forever." 12 And all the people cried, "Amen! Amen!"

13 Thirty days were hardly sufficient time for the people of Israel to gather up the spoils of the Assyrians. 14 All those things that belonged to Holofernes were

given to Judith—his silver plate, gold, precious stones, garments and all his furniture and goods. These were delivered to her by the people. 15 All the people rejoiced, with the women, virgins and young men playing on instruments and harps.

16 Then Judith sang this canticle to the Lord: 2 "Begin a song to my God with tambourines, sing to my Lord with cymbals. Voice unto him a new psalm; exalt him and call upon his name. 3 The Lord puts an end to war, the Lord is his name. 4 He has made his camp in the midst of his people to deliver us from the hand of all our enemies. 5 The Assyrian came down from the mountains of the north with countless warriors. His numbers dammed the streams, his horses covered the valleys. 6 He boasted that he would set my land on fire, and kill my young men with the sword, dash my infants on the ground, and make my virgins captives. 7 But the Almighty Lord has struck him, and delivered him into the hands of a woman, and caused his death. 8 For their mighty one did not fall at the hands of young soldiers, neither did the sons of Titan strike him, nor did tall giants do him battle; but Judith the daughter of Merari was his undoing by the beauty of her face. 9 She shed the garments of widowhood, and put on vestments of joy, to give praise to the children of Israel. 10 She anointed her face with ointment, and fastened her hair with a tiara; she put on a new robe to deceive him. 11 Her sandals ravished his eyes, her beauty captured his soul, with a sword she cut off his head. 12 The Persians trembled at her faithfulness, and the Medes at her daring. 13 Then the camp of the Assyrians wailed, when my lowly ones appeared, parched with thirst. 14 The sons of the maidservants have pierced them through, and they have killed them like children in flight. They perished in battle before the face of the Lord my God. 15 Let us sing a hymn to the Lord, let us sing a new hymn to our God. 16 O Adonai, Lord, you are great and glorious in your power, and no one can overcome you. 17 Let all your creatures serve you, because when you spoke they were made. You sent forth your spirit, and they were created, and there is no one who can resist your voice. 18 The mountains will be shaken from their foundations with the waters. The rocks will melt as water before your glance. 19 But those who fear you will be great with you in all things. 20 Woe to the nation that rises up against my people, for the Lord almighty will take revenge on it; in the day of judgment he will visit it. For he will give fire and worms to the flesh of their people that they may burn and mourn forever."

21 And it came to pass after these things, that all the people, after the victory, went to Jerusalem to adore the Lord. As soon as they were purified, they all made holocausts, offerings and gifts. 22 Judith dedicated to God all the riches of Holofernes which the people had given her, together with the bedspread she had taken from his bedchamber. 23 For three months the people rejoiced before the sanctuary, and Judith was with them.

24 After this all returned home. Judith was held in great esteem in Bethulia, and she was the most renowned woman in all the land of Israel. 25 And her chastity was an enduring virtue, because she knew no man all the days of her life after the death of Manasses her husband. 26 On festival days she came forth to great praise. 27 She lived in her husband's house a hundred and five years, and made her handmaid free, and when she died, she was buried with her husband in Bethulia. 28 All the people mourned for seven days. 29 As long as she lived no man dared trouble Israel, nor for many years after her death. 30 The day of the celebration of this victory is counted by the Hebrews in their calendar of holy days, and has been religiously observed by the Jews from that time until this day.

ADDITIONS TO ESTHER

A1 *(Before Chapter 1)*. In the second year of the reign of King Ahasuerus the Great, in the first day of the month of Nisan, Mordecai, the son of Jair, son of Shimei, son of Kish, of the tribe of Benjamin, had a dream. ² He was a Jew, living in the city of Susa, a great man, among the leaders of the king's court. ³ He was one of the captives whom Nebuchadnezzar, King of Babylon, had taken away from Jerusalem with Jeconiah, King of Judea, and this was his dream:

⁴ "Behold, clamor and confusion, thunders and earthquakes, tumult upon the earth! ⁵ And behold, two great dragons came forward, ready to fight one another. ⁶ At their cry, every nation girded for war, to do battle against the nation of the just. ⁷ It was a day of darkness and gloom, of tribulation and distress, and of great fear upon the earth. ⁸ The nation of the just was troubled, fearing the evils that threatened, and was ready to die. ⁹ The people cried to God, and as they were crying, as though from a small spring there grew a very great river with a flood of waters. ¹⁰ The light of the sun broke out, and the humble were exalted, and they devoured the nobles."
¹¹ When Mordecai had dreamed this he arose from his bed and was thinking what God would do. He kept turning it about in his mind, anxious to know what the dream meant.

A2 At that time he lived at the king's court with Gabatha and Tharra, the king's eunuchs, who were guards of the palace. ² He overheard them plotting, investigated their plans, and learned that they were about to lay violent hands on King Ahasuerus. He told the king of this. ³ Then the king had them both examined, and after they had confessed, commanded them to be put to death. ⁴ The king made a record of what was done, and Mordecai also wrote down the events. ⁵ The king ordered him to serve in the court and gave him a reward. ⁶ But Haman, the son of Hammedatha the Agagite, was in great honor with the king, and he sought to harm Mordecai and his people because of the two eunuchs of the king who were put to death.

B1 *(Following C. 3, v. 13)*. This is a copy of the letter: "Ahasuerus, the great king, who reigns from India to Ethiopia, to the princes and governors of the hundred and twenty-seven provinces which are sub-

1151

ject to his empire, greetings.

2 "Whereas I rule over many nations and have brought all the world under my dominion, I am not willing to abuse the greatness of my power, but choose to govern my subjects with clemency and kindness, that they may live quietly without any fear and might enjoy peace, which is desired by all men.

3 "When I asked my counselors how this might be accomplished, Haman, who excels the rest in wisdom and fidelity, and is second only after the king, 4 told me that there is a people scattered through all the nations which uses laws contrary to those of all nations, despises the commandments of kings, and violates by their opposition our attempt to unify our kingdom. 5 Therefore, having noted this and observing one nation in opposition to all mankind, using perverse laws, going against our commandments and disturbing the peace and concord of the provinces subject to us, 6 we have commanded that all marked out by Haman, who is chief over all the provinces, second after the king and whom we honor as a father, shall be utterly destroyed by their enemies, together with their wives and children, and that none shall have pity on them. This is to happen on the fourteenth day of the twelfth month, Adar, of this present year, 7 so that these wicked men going down to hell in one day may restore to our empire the peace which they have disturbed."

C1 (*Following C. 4, v. 17*). But Mordecai besought the Lord, recalling all his works, and said, 2 "O Lord, Lord, almighty king, all affairs are in your power and there is none who can resist your will if you determine to save Israel. 3 You have made heaven and earth and all things that are under the dome of heaven. 4 You are Lord of all, and there is none who can resist your majesty. 5 You know all things, and you know that it was not out of pride and contempt, or any desire of glory, that I refused to grovel before the proud Haman. 6 For I would willingly and readily for the salvation of Israel have kissed even the soles of his feet. 7 But I did this that I should not place the glory of a man before the glory

of my God, and lest I should adore anyone except my God. 8 And now, O Lord, O King, O God of Abraham, have mercy on your people, because our enemies resolve to destroy us and wipe out your inheritance. 9 Despise not your portion, which you have redeemed for yourself out of Egypt. 10 Hear my supplication and be merciful to your lot and inheritance, and turn our mourning into joy, that we may live and praise your name. O Lord, do not close the mouths of those who sing to you."

11 And all Israel with like mind and supplication cried to the Lord, because they saw certain death hanging over their heads.

C2 Queen Esther, fearing the danger that was at hand, also had recourse to the Lord. 2 Taking off her royal apparel, she put on garments suitable for weeping and mourning. Instead of various precious ointments, she covered her head with ashes and dung and humbled her body by fasting. All the places which she was accustomed to adorn, she covered with her tangled hair.

3 She prayed to the Lord the God of Israel, saying, "O my Lord, who alone are our King, help me, a desolate woman, who has no other helper but you. 4 I am taking my life in my hands. 5 I have heard from my father that you, O Lord, did take Israel from among all nations, and our fathers from all their predecessors, to possess them as an everlasting inheritance, and you have done to them as you have promised. 6 We have sinned in your sight, and therefore you have delivered us into the hands of our enemies 7 because we have worshiped their gods. You are just, O Lord. 8 Now our enemies are not content to oppress us with the most difficult bondage, but attributing their power to the strength of their idols, 9 they plan to change your promises, destroy your inheritance, close the mouths of those who praise you and also extinguish the glory of your temple and altar. 10 This so that they may open the mouths of Gentiles, praise the strength of idols and magnify forever a carnal king. 11 Give not, O Lord, your scepter to those who do not exist. Do not let them laugh at our ruin; but turn their plan against themselves and destroy the man who has begun to rage against us.

¹² Remember, O Lord! Show yourself to us in the time of our tribulation, and give me boldness, O Lord, King of gods, and of all power. ¹³ Put eloquent words in my mouth in the presence of the lion, and turn his heart to hate our enemy so that both he himself may perish and the rest who agree with him. ¹⁴ But deliver us by your hand and help me, who has no other helper but you, O Lord, who has the knowledge of all things. ¹⁵ You know that I hate the glory of the wicked and abhor the bed of the uncircumcised and of any foreigner. ¹⁶ You know my necessity that I abominate the sign of my pride and glory, which is upon my head in the days of my public appearance, and detest it as a menstruous rag and wear it not in the days of my leisure. ¹⁷ I have not eaten at Haman's table, nor has the king's banquet pleased me, nor have I drunk the wine of the libations. ¹⁸ Your handmaid has never rejoiced, since I was brought hither unto this day, but in you, O Lord, God of Abraham. ¹⁹ O God, who are mighty above all, hear the voice of those who have no other hope, and deliver us from the hand of the wicked and deliver me from my fear!"

D1 (*Following C. 5, v. 2*). On the third day she laid away the garments she wore, and put on splendid apparel. ² Glittering in royal robes, she took two maids with her, after she had called upon God the Ruler and Savior of all, ³ and leaned daintily upon one of them with great delicacy as if she were unable to bear her own weight. ⁴ The other maid followed her lady, carrying her flowing train. ⁵ The rosy color of her face and her bright and sparkling eyes hid a mind full of anguish and very great fear.

⁶ She passed through all the doors of the court and stood before the king. He sat upon his royal throne, clothed in his royal robes, shining with gold and precious stones. He was terrifying to behold. ⁷ Looking up, his burning eyes revealed the wrath in his heart. The queen sank down, her color turned pale and she rested her weary head upon her handmaid. ⁸ Then God changed the king's spirit into gentleness. Quickly and with concern, he hurried from his throne and lifted her up in his arms until she came to herself. He comforted her with these words, ⁹ "What is the matter, Esther? I am your brother, fear not. ¹⁰ You shall not die, for this law is not made for you but for all others. ¹¹ Come near and touch the scepter." ¹² And as she held her peace, he took the golden scepter and laid it upon her neck, kissed her and asked, "Why do you not speak to me?" ¹³ She answered, "I saw you, my lord, as an angel of God, and my heart was troubled for fear of your glory. ¹⁴ For you, my lord, are very admirable and your face is full of grace." ¹⁵ While she was speaking, she fell down again, almost in a swoon. ¹⁶ The king was troubled and all his servants comforted her.

D2 (*Following C. 8, v. 12*). The following is a copy of the letter: "The great King Ahasuerus to the governors and princes from India to Ethiopia of the hundred and twenty-seven provinces which obey our command, greetings.

² "Many have turned into pride the goodness of princes and the honor which has been bestowed upon them. ³ They not only seek to oppress the king's subjects, but unable to enjoy the success given them, they have turned against their benefactors. ⁴ Not only do they drive out gratitude from among men but in violating the laws of humanity they think they can also escape the justice of God who sees all things. ⁵ Their madness is so great that they undermine by lies those who seek to carry out diligently the offices entrusted to them. They do it in such a way as to seem worthy of all men's praise. ⁶ With false trickery they deceive the ears of well meaning princes who judge others by their own nature.

⁷ "Now this is proved both from ancient records and by the things which are done daily, which show how the good intentions of kings are made foul by the evil suggestions of certain men. ⁸ Wherefore, we must provide for the peace of all the provinces. ⁹ Neither must you think, if we command different things, that our choice is lightly made, because we make our decision according to the quality and necessity of times as the need of the commonwealth requires. ¹⁰ "That you may more plainly under-

stand what we say, Haman, the son of Hammedatha, a Macedonian both by choice and birth, and having no Persian blood, but by his cruelty betraying our goodness, was received as a guest by us. 11 He found our humanity so great toward him that he was called our father and was bowed down to by all as second to the king. 12 But he was so filled with arrogance that he strove to deprive us of our kingdom and our life. 13 With unimagined craftiness and deceit, he has sought the destruction of Mordecai, by whose fidelity and good services our life was saved, and of Esther, the partner of our kingdom, together with all their nation. 14 He thought that after they were slain, he might work treason against us who would be alone without friends and might transfer the kingdom of the Persians to the Macedonians. 15 But we have found that the Jews, who were slated to be slain by that most wicked man are blameless and on the contrary have just laws, 16 and are the children of the highest, greatest and ever-living God, by whose direction the kingdom was given both to our fathers and to us and is so kept to this day.

17 "Therefore, know that those letters which he sent in our name are void and of no effect. 18 For this crime both he himself who devised it and all his household hang on gibbets before the gates of this city of Susa. God has repaid him as he deserved. 19 But this edict, which we now send, will be published in all cities so that the Jews may freely follow their own laws. 20 On the thirteenth day of the twelfth month, which is called Adar, you must aid them so that they may kill those who had prepared themselves to kill them. 21 For the almighty God has turned this day of sadness and mourning into one of joy for them. 22 Hence you will also count this day among other festival days and celebrate it with all joy, that it may also be known in times to come 23 that all those who faithfully obey the Persians receive a worthy reward for their fidelity, but those who are traitors to their kingdom are destroyed for their wickedness. 24 Let every province and city that will not be partaker of this solemnity perish by sword and fire, and be destroyed in such manner as to be made unliveable both to men and beasts as an example of punishment for contempt and disobedience."

E (*Following C. 10, v. 3*). Mordecai said, "God has done these things. 2 I remember a dream that I had concerning these same things and nothing of it has been unfulfilled: 3 the small spring which grew into a river, and there was light and the sun and bountiful waters—the river is Esther, whom the king married and made queen. 4 The two dragons are Haman and myself. 5 The nations are those who assembled to destroy the name of the Jews. 6 My nation is Israel, who cried to the Lord, and the Lord saved his people. He delivered us from all evils and has wrought great signs and wonders among the nations. 7 He commanded that there should be two lots, one of the people of God and the other of all the nations. 8 These lots came to the appointed day before God and among all nations. 9 And the Lord remembered his people and had mercy on his inheritance. 10 So these days will be observed in the month of Adar, on the fourteenth and fifteenth day of that month, with all the people gathered into one assembly in joy and gladness, from generation to generation forever among the people of Israel."

F In the fourth year of the reign of Ptolemy and Cleopatra, Dositheus, who claimed to be a priest and a Levite, together with Ptolemy his son, brought the above letter of Purim to Egypt, which they asserted was true and had been translated by Lysimachus the son of Ptolemy, a resident of Jerusalem.

What One Family Can Do

The story of the Maccabees sounds almost as if it was written from today's headlines. These two books tell of the Jews hemmed in on all sides by enemies, struggling for national survival. Their chief enemy is Syria but Egypt also causes trouble. The Jews make an alliance with the most powerful nation in the world, the Romans. Despite all their troubles, the faith of one family keeps God alive for the Jewish nation.

The title of these two books is taken from the first great hero they introduce, Judas Maccabeus, thought to be taken from the Hebrew *maqqabah,* meaning "hammer." It is applied throughout these books as a family name. The story is a simple one: how a single family won out over the might of Syria, Jewish traitors, and the turbulence of the times.

The writers stress the deep religiosity of the Maccabees and their unfailing trust in God, their firmness of intention in keeping the land of Judah holy, their military prowess and their skill at taking advantage of the divisions within the Syrian kingdom. There are moments of weakness when their trust is betrayed and some of the Maccabees die. But throughout these pages there is a firmness of faith and trust in God and a determination which at times seems almost to border on the fanatic.

The books are mainly historical and, except for the Maccabee custom of praying for the dead and offering sacrifice for departed souls, add little to theology. But they do tell a story of inspiring and heroic faith.

1 MACCABEES

1 IT HAPPENED THAT after Alexander of Macedonia, son of Philip who reigned first in Greece, had come from the land of Kittim,[a] he overthrew Darius, king of the Persians and Medes. [2] Alexander fought many wars, captured many fortresses, and put the local chiefs to death. [3] He marched to the ends of the earth, and took the spoils of many nations. The earth was quiet before him, and his heart was filled with pride because [4] he had formed a powerful and mighty army that had conquered many nations and kingdoms, all of which paid him tribute. [5] When all these things were done, Alexander took to his bed in sickness, knowing that he was dying. [6] He called his companions, noblemen who had been brought up with him from his youth, and he divided his kingdom among them while he was yet alive. [7] Alexander had reigned twelve years when he died.[b] [8] Each of his comrades took over the kingdom assigned him, [9] and they all put crowns upon themselves after his death. They and their sons ruled for many years, and evils were multiplied over the earth.

[10] From these rulers there came a sinful offshoot, Antiochus the Illustrious, son of King Antiochus, once a hostage at Rome. He became king in the hundred and thirty-seventh year of the kingdom of the Greeks.[c]

[11] In those days there were unfaithful Jews, who tried to persuade many, saying, "Let us have an understanding with the pagans around us, for since we left them, many evils have befallen us." [12] Many thought this to be good advice [13] and decided to do this. They went to the king, who gave them permission to follow pagan practices. [14] They built a gymnasium in Jerusalem, in the pagan manner, [15] hid the fact they were circumcised, and abandoned God's covenant, joining the heathens in doing evil.

[16] Once Antiochus consolidated his power, he decided to make himself King of Egypt, so that he might rule over two countries. [17] He invaded Egypt with a great army; with chariots, elephants and horsemen; and a large number of ships. [18] He waged war against Ptolemy, King of Egypt, but Ptolemy was afraid of his might and fled, leaving behind many wounded and

---

a This term included Cyprus and the Grecian mainland.   b 324 B.C.   c 175 B.C.

1157

dead. [19] Antiochus captured the fortified cities of Egypt, and he plundered the land of Egypt.

[20] After Antiochus had pillaged Egypt in the hundred and forty-third year,[d] he returned and waged war against Israel. [21] He marched into Jerusalem with a great army [22] and arrogantly entered the temple sanctuary where he took away the golden altar, the candlestick of light, all the vessels, the Table of Offering, the pouring vessels, the bowls, the golden censers, the curtain, the crowns and the golden decoration that was on the front of the temple. He stripped the temple of everything of value. [23] He took the silver and gold, and the precious vessels; and he took the hidden treasures which he found. When he had taken everything of value, he departed to his own country.

[24] He slaughtered many men, and bragged about it.
[25] There was great mourning in Israel, and everywhere the people of Israel lived.
[26] The rulers and the elders mourned, and the virgins and the young men trembled, and the beauty of the women became dull.
[27] Every bridegroom and every bride was sorrowful.
[28] The land rocked for the inhabitants and all the house of Jacob was filled with shame.

[29] Two years later the king sent the chief collector of his taxes to the cities of Judah, and he came to Jerusalem with a large force. [30] He deceived the people by speaking of peace and they believed him. [31] But suddenly he attacked the city and killed many Israelites. [32] He plundered the city and put it to the torch. He tore down houses and leveled the walls. [33] He took women and children captives, and confiscated their cattle. [34] The enemy fortified the city of David with large and strong walls and strong towers, making a fortress for themselves. [35] They manned these fortifications with sinful and wicked men, supplying them with armor and food, while they collected and stored the wealth of Jerusalem; [36] and

they became a great threat.
[37] The fortress was an ambush,
an ever present evil in Israel.
[38] They killed the innocent around the sanctuary,
and defiled the holy place.
[39] Because of them, the inhabitants of Jerusalem fled away
and the city became the dwelling place of strangers,
and even a stranger to her own people,
who forsook her.
[40] Her sanctuary was as barren as a desert,
her festival days were turned into mourning,
her sabbaths into days of shame,
her honor was desecrated.
[41] Her dishonor was equal to her former glory,
and her happiness was turned into grief.

[42] King Antiochus issued a proclamation that all his kingdom should be one people, giving up their own religions. [43] The Gentiles agreed to this [44] and many Israelites chose his religion, sacrificing to idols and ignoring the sabbath. [45] The king sent letters by messengers to Jerusalem, and to all the cities of Judah, ordering the people to follow the foreign customs of his kingdom, [46] banning holocausts and sacrifices, and the acts performed in God's temple. [47] He also prohibited keeping the sabbath and celebrating religious holidays. [48] His laws defiled the holy places and profaned God's ministers. [49] He also ordered altars, temples and idols to be built; and pig's flesh and unclean beasts to be sacrificed. [50] Children were not to be circumcised, and they were to practice all kinds of immorality and evil so that they would forget the observance of God's law. [51] Anyone who failed to obey the king's command was to be put to death.

[52] Antiochus sent this command to his whole kingdom. He appointed lieutenants to govern the people and carry out his orders. [53] All the cities of Judah were commanded to offer pagan sacrifices. [54] Many

---

d 169 B.C.

of the people who forsook the law of God came together to commit these evil deeds. ⁵⁵ They drove the faithful Israelites into hiding in those places set aside for refuge.

⁵⁶ On the fifteenth day of Chisleu, in the hundred and forty-fifth year,ᵉ King Antiochus set up the terrible idol of Baal over the very altar of God, and similar altars were built throughout all the cities of Judah. ⁵⁷ They burned incense and sacrificed at the doors of the houses and in the streets. ⁵⁸ They tore up and burned the books containing the law of God. ⁵⁹ By the king's decree, they put to death anyone found with the books of the covenant or observing the law of God. ⁶⁰ Thus month after month throughout Judah they punished the Israelites for their faith. ⁶¹ On the twenty-fifth day of the month they sacrificed to the idol that stood above the altar of holocausts. ⁶² Women who had their children circumcised were killed by order of the king. ⁶³ Their babies were hung around their necks and all who took part in the circumcisions were killed with them.

⁶⁴ Yet there were many Israelites who refused to eat profaned food and who chose death rather than profanation. ⁶⁵ They refused to break the holy law of God, and so died. ⁶⁶ All over Israel God's wrath visited his people.

2 In those days there lived a man named Mattathias, son of John, son of Simeon, a priest of the line of Joarib, who had left Jerusalem to make his home in the mountains of Modein. ² He had five sons, John, known as Gaddi, ³ Simon, called Thassi, ⁴ Judas called Maccabeus, ⁵ Eleazar called Avaran, and Jonathan called Apphus. ⁶ They saw the bad things that were done to the people of Judah and in Jerusalem.

⁷ Mattathias said, "Alas, why was I born to see the destruction of my people, the ruin of the Holy City, and to stand by when it is in the hands of enemies? ⁸ The holy places are controlled by foreigners, and the temple is desecrated. ⁹ The vessels that were its glory have been carried away. Old men are murdered in the streets, and

young men have been killed by the enemy's sword. ¹⁰ Is there a nation that has not claimed its royal privileges? ¹¹ All its ornaments have been plundered. Freedom has given way to slavery. ¹² Look at our sanctuary, how our beauty and our glory are laid waste, profaned by the Gentiles. ¹³ What have we left for which to live?" ¹⁴ Mattathias and his sons tore their garments, covered themselves with sackcloth, and were very sad.

¹⁵ The agents of King Antiochus arrived in Modein to force the exiles to sacrifice and burn incense against the law of God. ¹⁶ Many of the Israelites went along with the pagans, but Mattathias and his sons stood apart. ¹⁷ In response, the agents of Antiochus said to Mattathias, "You are an honored leader and an important man in this city. Your sons and brothers follow you. ¹⁸ Therefore, you must give example in obeying the king's commandment, just as all nations have done, and the men of Judah and those that remain in Jerusalem. Then you and your sons shall be counted among the king's friends, and made rich with gold and silver and many presents."

¹⁹ Mattathias replied in a loud voice, "Although all nations obey King Antiochus, even despite their own ancestral religion, and thus yield to his decrees, ²⁰ I and my sons and my brothers will follow the covenant of our fathers. ²¹ May God have mercy on us. There is no value in forsaking the law and rights of God. ²² We will not obey the orders of King Antiochus, and thus desert our law by making pagan sacrifices or disobeying our commandments."

²³ Now as he finished speaking, a certain Jew came forward to offer sacrifice to the idols in the city of Modein, according to the king's regulations. ²⁴ When Mattathias saw this, he was not only saddened, but his hands trembled and his anger was fired because of his love of the law. He threw himself at the man and killed him on the altar. ²⁵ Moreover, at the same time he killed the agent whom King Antiochus had sent to enforce the pagan sacrifices, and he pulled down the altar. ²⁶ In his zeal for the law he showed the spirit Phinehas showed against

Zimri, the son of Salu.

²⁷ Mattathias went through the city shouting loudly, "Every one who has zeal for the law and wishes to keep it, follow me." ²⁸ Then he and his sons escaped into the mountains, leaving behind all their possessions. ²⁹ Because of the afflictions which had been heaped upon them, many who sought after judgment and justice retreated into the desert ³⁰ and lived there, with their children, wives and cattle.

³¹ The king's agents and the garrison in Jerusalem, in the City of David, received word that these Israelites had broken the king's commands and had gone into secret places in the wilderness, taking many with them. ³² Immediately soldiers were sent after those in the desert, prepared to attack them on the sabbath day. ³³ First they said to them, "Why do you resist? Come forward and obey the edict of King Antiochus, and you shall live." ³⁴ But they replied, "We will not come forward, neither will we profane the sabbath by obeying the king's orders." ³⁵ The king's men moved on the Israelites. ³⁶ They offered no resistance, neither did they throw a stone at them, nor barricade their hideouts. ³⁷ They said, "Let us all die innocent. Heaven and earth are our witnesses, that you put us to death unjustly." ³⁸ The foreigners attacked them on the sabbath and they were killed, together with their wives, children and cattle, to a total of a thousand persons.

³⁹ When Mattathias and his friends heard this news, they were very sad. ⁴⁰ Each man said to his neighbor, "If we all do as our brothers have done, and not fight for our lives and beliefs against the pagans, they will now quickly cause us to disappear from the earth." ⁴¹ So that day they concluded, "Whoever wants to fight with us on the sabbath day will find us ready. We will not die in hiding places as did our brothers."

⁴² Some Hasidaeans,ᵃ strong fighters of Israel, who had great respect for the law, ⁴³ along with others who fled the persecution, joined them, giving added support. ⁴⁴ All these formed an army which in its anger killed sinners and renegades. The subservient Jews fled to the pagans for safety. ⁴⁵ Mattathias and his friends went everywhere and tore down the idolatrous altars, ⁴⁶ and circumcised Israeli children who had not been circumcised. ⁴⁷ They pursued the turncoats and were successful in their fight. ⁴⁸ They wrested the law out of the hands of the pagans and of the kings, and they did not allow the strength of Antiochus to abolish the law and religion of God.

⁴⁹ As the time of Mattathias' death came near, he said to his sons, "Pride and violence are on the increase. It is a time of violence and fury. ⁵⁰ Therefore, O my sons, be zealous for the law, and give your lives to the covenant of your ancestors.

⁵¹ "Remember the deeds of our
    ancestors, which they have done
    generation after generation,
and you shall receive great honor and
    an everlasting fame.
⁵² Was not Abraham found faithful
    in temptation,
and did not this make him a just
    man?
⁵³ Joseph kept the law in the time of
    his trial
and he became lord of Egypt.
⁵⁴ Phinehas, our father, with zealous
    fervor for God
received the covenant of an everlast-
    ing priesthood.
⁵⁵ Joshua, because he fulfilled his
    duty
became a judge of Israel.
⁵⁶ Caleb, for bearing witness before
    the gathered people,
received his inheritance.
⁵⁷ David, by his generosity,
obtained the throne of an everlasting
    kingdom.
⁵⁸ Elias, for his zeal for the law,
was taken up into heaven.
⁵⁹ Ananias, Azarias and Misael
were rescued from the flames by their
    faith.
⁶⁰ Because he was innocent,
Daniel was delivered from the den of

---

a A Jewish group known as the Devout. It supported the law and opposed foreign influence. This group later split into the Pharisees and Essenes of Dead Sea Scrolls fame.

lions.
⁶¹ Remember that through all generations
all who trust in God are strong.
⁶² Do not fear the threats of a sinner
for his reward is dung and worms.
⁶³ Today he is exalted, and tomorrow he can not be found,
because he is returned to the dust of earth,
and his planning has come to nothing.
⁶⁴ Therefore, my sons, be manly and brave in the law:
for by obeying it you shall gain heaven.

⁶⁵ "I know that your brother Simon is a wise man. Listen to him always, for he will take my place. ⁶⁶ Let Judas Maccabeus, who is valiant and strong, be the leader of your army, and direct the war against the pagans. ⁶⁷ All of you who observe the law stay together and avenge the wrong of your people. ⁶⁸ Pay back the pagans as they deserve, but always hold fast to the law."

⁶⁹ Mattathias blessed his sons, and joined his ancestors. ⁷⁰ He died in the hundred and forty-sixth year. He was buried by his sons in the tomb of his fathers in Modein, and all Israel mourned for him with great sadness.

3 His son Judas, called Maccabeus, took his place. ² His brothers, and all who had joined his father, helped him. They gladly fought the battle for Israel.

³ He brought great honor on his people,
and wore the breastplate of a giant,
and carried his warlike armor into battles,
and protected his camps with his sword.
⁴ He was like a lion in his actions
and a lion's cub roaring for his prey.
⁵ He hunted down the wicked and pursued them;
and those who harmed his people he set on fire;
⁶ His enemies fled in fear,
and all the renegades were frightened.

Liberation prospered under his planning.
⁷ He worried many kings,
and made Jacob happy with his actions,
and his memory is blessed for ever.
⁸ He went through the cities of Judah
and destroyed the wicked in them,
turning away wrath from Israel.
⁹ He was famous even to the ends of the earth,
and he helped those who were dying.

¹⁰ Apollonius gathered together the Gentiles and a large army from Samaria to make war against Israel. ¹¹ When Judas heard this, he went out to meet him. He defeated him and killed him. Many others were killed and the rest fled. ¹² He captured their belongings, including the sword of Apollonius, which he fought with all the rest of his life.

¹³ When Seron, commander of the Syrian forces, heard that Judas had formed an army of men faithful to him, ¹⁴ he said, "I will make a reputation for myself, and will become famous in my kingdom by overthrowing Judas and his followers who have scorned the edict of the king." ¹⁵ He organized his troops, a large number of wicked men who were his strong supporters, who sought vengeance on the sons of Israel. ¹⁶ They marched as far as Bethhoron, where Judas went out to meet him with a small army. ¹⁷ When the Israelites saw the advancing army, they said to Judas, "How shall we, being so few, be able to fight against so many who are so strong, when we are ready to faint from fasting today?" ¹⁸ Judas replied, "It is an easy matter for many to be overpowered by a few, for there is no difference in the sight of God whether a few or many are saved. ¹⁹ Success in battle is not in the number of the army, but in the strength that comes from heaven. ²⁰ This arrogant and haughty multitude has come to destroy us, our wives and our children, and to take our belongings. ²¹ We will fight for our lives and our laws, ²² and the Lord himself will vanquish them in our sight. So do not fear them." ²³ As soon as Judas had finished speaking, he rushed his troops at Seron and his army, overpowering the enemy. ²⁴ He pursued them to the plain

of Beth-horon, and there eight hundred men were killed, while the rest fled into the land of the Philistines.

²⁵ All the pagans feared and dreaded Judas and his brothers. ²⁶ The king heard of his reputation, and the pagans told of his battles.

²⁷ When King Antiochus heard these reports, he became angry. He formed an exceedingly strong army out of the forces of all his kingdom. ²⁸ He opened his treasury and paid the army for a year. He told his soldiers to stand prepared. ²⁹ This exhausted the money in his treasury and he realized that the taxes of the country were small because of the dissension and troubles that he had brought on the land when he abolished the ancient laws.

³⁰ He feared that he would not have as much money as previously for his expenses and the gifts which he had bestowed far more freely than the kings who had preceded him. ³¹ He was greatly disturbed and decided to go to Persia to collect taxes from those regions. ³² He left Lysias, a nobleman of royal blood, behind to oversee the affairs of the country, from the river Euphrates to the border of Egypt, ³³ and to take care of his son Antiochus until he returned. ³⁴ He gave Lysias half his soldiers and his elephants, leaving him orders about what was to be done in his absence concerning the inhabitants of Judea and Jerusalem. ³⁵ Lysias was to make war against them to wipe out and destroy the strength of Israel and what remained in Jerusalem; he was to erase all memory of them in those places; ³⁶ and he was to settle foreigners in their country and distribute their land to them. ³⁷ Then the king took the half of the army that remained and left Antioch, the chief city of his country, in the hundred and forty-seventh year. He crossed the Euphrates River and went through the upper provinces.

³⁸ Lysias chose Ptolemy, the son of Dorymenes, and Nicanor and Gorgias, mighty men who were the king's friends, ³⁹ and sent them with forty thousand infantry and seven thousand cavalry into the land of Judah to destroy it, according to the king's orders. ⁴⁰ So the powerful army marched forth and made camp near Emmaus in the plain. ⁴¹ When the merchants of the surrounding lands heard of this might, they took large quantities of silver and gold to the camp to buy the children of Israel for slaves. Forces from Syria and the land of the Philistines joined the army in its camp.

⁴² Judas and his brothers saw that the dangers were increased because the army was camped in their territory. They also knew the king had given orders to destroy their people totally. ⁴³ They said to each other, "Let us raise the morale of our people by fighting for them and our sanctuary." ⁴⁴ They mustered their people to fight and to pray for mercy and compassion. ⁴⁵ Now Jerusalem was left uninhabited like a desert with no one entering or leaving. The sanctuary was defiled and foreigners lived in the citadel. There was no happiness for Jacob and the flute and harp were silent.

⁴⁶ The Israelites assembled at Mizpah near Jerusalem, as it was a traditional place of prayer for them. ⁴⁷ That day, they fasted dressed in sackcloth and put ashes upon their heads while tearing their garments. ⁴⁸ They opened the Book of the Law in which the Gentiles searched for the likeness of their gods; ⁴⁹ they brought out the priestly vestments, and the firstfruits and tithes, and summoned the Nazirites who had completed their vows. ⁵⁰ They cried in a loud voice toward heaven, saying, "What shall we do with these, and where shall we take them? ⁵¹ For your altars are torn down and are profaned; your priests are in mourning and very unhappy. ⁵² The nations are warring against us so that we may be destroyed. You know what their intentions are. ⁵³ How can we stand before them, unless you, O God, help us?" ⁵⁴ Then they sounded the trumpets and cried out with a loud voice.

⁵⁵ Then Judas appointed officers over the people, commanding groups of thousands, hundreds, fifties and tens. ⁵⁶ He told those who were building houses, or soon to be married, or planting vineyards, or were afraid, that they should go home, as the Law permitted. ⁵⁷ They set up a new camp on the south side of Emmaus. ⁵⁸ Judas said, "Prepare yourselves and be brave. Be ready

in the morning to fight those nations which are warring against us in order to destroy us and our holy place. [59] It is better for us to die in battle than to see the ruin of our nation and of our religion. Whatever the outcome, the will of God in heaven shall be done."

4 Gorgias took five thousand infantry and a thousand of the best horsemen and moved out of the camp by night, [2] so that they might find the camp of the Jews and attack them by surprise. The men of the citadel were to guide them. [3] Judas heard of this and he and his valiant men prepared to attack the king's forces in Emmaus [4] while the army was divided. [5] When Gorgias reached the camp of Judas that night, he found no one there, and he began looking for them in the mountains, saying, "These men ran from us."

[6] At daylight Judas was on the plain with only three thousand men, who lacked armor and swords. [7] They saw that the camp of the pagans was strong with men wearing breastplates and horsemen all about, all of whom were trained soldiers. [8] Judas told his soldiers, "Do not be afraid of their numbers or of their attack. [9] Remember how our fathers were saved from the Red Sea when Pharaoh pursued them with a large army. [10] Now let us call on heaven. The Lord will have mercy on us and will remember the faith of our fathers. Today he will destroy this army facing us, [11] so that all nations will know that there is one who redeems and delivers Israel."

[12] The foreigners looked up and saw the Israelites advancing against them. [13] They went out of the camp to join the battle. The trumpet sounded for the army of Judas and [14] it began fighting. The pagans were routed and fled across the plain. [15] The rear guard was killed and Judas followed them as far as Gazara, and even to the plains of Idumea and Azotus and Jamnia. The enemy had three thousand casualties.

[16] Judas returned again with his army [17] and he said to the people, "Forget the booty for we have another battle to face. [18] Gorgias and his army are in the mountain not far from us. Stand first against our enemies and overthrow them. Then you can take booty at your leisure."

[19] While Judas was still speaking, the enemy was spotted on the mountain. [20] Gorgias saw that his men had fled and from the smoke rising from the campsite he realized the Israelites had set it afire. [21] When they had seen this, they were overcome with great fear. Also, seeing Judas and his army in formation on the plain, his troops panicked. [22] They fled to the country of the Philistines.

[23] Then Judas plundered the camp, obtaining much gold and silver, blue and sea-purple silks, and other valuables. [24] On the way home they sang a hymn and blessed God because his goodness and mercy endures for ever. [25] So Israel had a great deliverance that day.

[26] The pagans who had escaped told Lysias all that had happened. [27] When he heard these things he was surprised and dismayed that things had not succeeded in Israel according to his plan and as the king had commanded. [28] So the next year Lysias gathered together sixty thousand picked soldiers and five thousand horsemen so that he might conquer the Israelites. [29] This force marched into Judea, pitched their tents in Beth-horon, where Judas faced them with ten thousand men.

[30] When he saw their military might, he prayed and said, "Blessed are you, O Savior of Israel, who rendered the mighty powerless at the hand of your servant David, and did deliver the Philistine camp into the hands of Jonathan the son of Saul and of his armorbearer. [31] Let this army be surrounded by your people Israel, and let their many soldiers and horsemen become confused. [32] Strike them with fear and undermine their confidence in their own strength. Give them fear for their own destruction. [33] Let those who love you overcome them with their swords so that your followers may praise you with hymns."

[34] The opposing forces engaged in battle and five thousand men of the army of Lysias were killed. [35] When Lysias saw his men in retreat and how bold the Jews were, worrying neither about life or death, he withdrew to Antioch to recruit soldiers so that he might return to Judea with an even larger army.

36 Judas and his brothers said, "Our enemies have been defeated. Now let us go up and repair and purify the Temple." 37 The army was assembled and went up to Mount Zion. 38 They saw the empty sanctuary, the desecrated altar, the gates burned, and weeds growing in the courts as in a forest or on the mountains, and the storerooms adjoining the temple were in ruins. 39 They tore their garments and mourned in grief, putting ashes on their heads. 40 They prostrated themselves on the ground, and sent their pleas heavenward at the sound of the trumpets. 41 Then Judas sent troops to attack the defenders of the citadel, while he purified the holy places. 42 He chose blameless priests, known for their devotion to the law of God. 43 They cleansed the holy places, and took away the stones that had been defiled into an unclean place. 44 Judas wondered what should be done about the altar of holocausts which had been profaned. 45 The suggestion was made to tear it down lest it should be a reproach to them, because the pagans had defiled it. They pulled it down 46 and put up the stones on the Temple hill in a suitable place, until a prophet should come along and tell them what to do concerning them. 47 Then they took uncut stones according to the law and built a new altar like the former, 48 and they restored the holy places and the things that were within the temple. Finally, they sanctified the temple and its courtyards. 49 They made new holy vessels, and brought into the temple the lampstand, the altar of incense and the table. 50 They burned incense on the altar, lighted the lamps that were upon the stand and gave light in the Temple. 51 They set loaves upon the table, and hung up the veils, and finished all the work that they had set out to do.

52 On the twenty-fifth day of the ninth month (Cheslev) in the hundred and forty-eighth year,[a] they arose at dawn. 53 They offered sacrifice according to the law upon the new altar of holocausts which they had made. 54 On the anniversary of the day the pagans had defiled it, the altar was dedicated anew with songs, harps, lutes and cymbals. 55 And all the people prostrated themselves in adoration, and blessed God who had given them good fortune.

56 For eight days they dedicated the altar,[b] and they offered holocausts with joy and sacrifices of salvation and of praise. 57 They adorned the front of the temple with crowns and shields of gold, and they repaired the gates among the people and the shame of the pagans was removed. 59 Judas and his brothers and all the priests of Israel decreed that the anniversary of the dedication of the altar should be observed every year for eight days with joy and gladness, beginning on the twenty-fifth day of the month of Cheslev.

60 They then built high walls and fortified towers around Mount Zion, to stop the pagans from attacking again and destroying it as they did before. 61 He assigned a garrison to guard Mount Zion and he fortified Beth-zur, that the people might have a defense against Idumea.

5 Now when the neighboring nations heard that the altar and sanctuary had been restored, they were very angry. 2 They decided to destroy the descendants of Jacob who lived among them, and began to kill some of the people and to persecute them.

3 Judas fought against the descendants of Esau in Idumea, in the area of Akrabattene, where they besieged the Israelites. They were slaughtered. 4 He was mindful of the evil deeds of the sons of Baean, who were a constant threat to travelers, by ambushing them along the road. 5 He trapped them in their fortified towers, and being determined to destroy them, he set the towers on fire and burned them down and all who were in them.

6 Next, he moved against the Ammonites, where he found a strong and numerous army under Timothy, their captain. 7 He fought many battles with them, and thwarted and overawed them, 8 conquering the city of Gazer and its suburbs. Then he returned to Judea.

9 The pagans in Gilead met together against the Israelites who were among them and plotted to destroy them. The Israelites

a December 164 B.C.   b This is the origin of the Feast of Dedication (Hannakuh).

fled to the fortress of Dathema. ¹⁰ They sent letters to Judas and his brothers, saying, "Timothy is the captain of the army of pagans, surrounding us and planning our destruction. ¹¹ They are preparing to besiege the fortress where we are. ¹² Therefore, come and save us from them for we already have had great losses. ¹³ All our brothers in the cities of Tob are dead. Their wives and children have been taken captives, and their goods confiscated. They have killed almost a thousand men there." ¹⁴ While these letters were being read, other messengers came from Galilee with their clothes torn, who related ¹⁵ that everyone in Ptolemais, Tyre and Sidon had joined the heathen Galileans in order to destroy Israel.

¹⁶ When Judas and the people heard these reports, they held a meeting to decide what action should be taken for their brothers who were in trouble and being attacked by their enemies. ¹⁷ Judas said to his brother Simon, "Choose your men and go and rescue your brothers in Galilee, while my brother Jonathan and I will go into the country of Gilead." ¹⁸ He left Joseph, the son of Zacharias, and Azarias as captains of the people with the remainder of the army to guard Judea. ¹⁹ He gave them orders, saying, "Take charge of our people, but make no war against the pagans until we return." ²⁰ Three thousand men were assigned to accompany Simon into Galilee, while Judas led eight thousand into the land of Gilead.

²¹ Simon went into Galilee and fought many battles with the pagans, driving them away in frustration. He followed them even to the gate of Ptolemais. ²² Almost three thousand pagans were killed and he captured all their belongings. ²³ He led those Jews who were in Galilee and in Arbatta together with their wives and children, and all their belongings, into Judea with great joy.

²⁴ Judas Maccabeus and Jonathan his brother crossed the Jordan River and marched for three days in the desert. ²⁵ The Nabateans met them in peace, and told them all that happened to their brothers in Gilead, ²⁶ and that many Jews were trapped in Bozrah, Bosor, Alma, Chaspho,

Maked and Carnaim; all large and fortified cities. ²⁷ More were also held captives in the other cities of Gilead. The enemy had decided to attack these cities and capture and destroy them all at once.

²⁸ Judas and his army quickly marched back by the desert road to Bosor and took that city. He put every male to the sword, burned the city and carried away all their goods. ²⁹ They left there by night and marched until they came to the fortress of Dathema. ³⁰ At dawn they saw a great number of soldiers carrying ladders and battering rams to attack the fortress and capture the Jews within it. ³¹ Judas saw that the fight had begun, and that the battle cry of the people went up to heaven with trumpets and shouts. ³² He said to his army, "Fight today for your brothers." ³³ Then he advanced on them with three companies while their trumpets sounded and cried aloud in prayer. ³⁴ When the army of Timothy realized that it was Maccabeus, they fled from him. The Israelites killed almost eight thousand men that day. ³⁵ Judas then turned to Alema, assaulted and captured it, and he killed all the males, took the goods from it and burned it. ³⁶ From there he marched and captured Chaspho, Maked, Bosor, and the rest of the cities of Gilead.

³⁷ Following his defeat, Timothy raised another army and camped near Raphon, on the other side of the river. ³⁸ Judas sent out scouts and they returned to report, "All the Gentiles have gathered to form a great army. ³⁹ They have hired the Arabian mercenaries. They are camped on the opposite side of the river, ready to fight against you." Judas went forward to meet them. ⁴⁰ Timothy said to the officers of his army, "If Judas and his army come to the river and ford it, we shall not be able to resist him, and he will certainly defeat us. ⁴¹ But if he hesitates to cross and camps on the other side, we shall cross over and defeat them."

⁴² Now when Judas came near the river, he set the scribes of the people on the bank, ordering them, "Let no man stay behind. Send all into battle." ⁴³ He crossed over at the head of his army and the pagans were confounded. They threw away their weap-

ons and fled to the temple that was in Carnaim. ⁴⁴ He captured that city and burned the temple together with everything inside. Thus Carnaim was subdued and could not resist Judas.

⁴⁵ Judas gathered together all the Israelites that were in the land of Gilead, from the least even to the greatest, their wives, children, and led this large company back into the land of Judah. ⁴⁶ They reached Ephron along the way, a great city and strongly fortified. There was no way of going around it, either to the right or left, so they had to go through it. ⁴⁷ Those who were in the city shut themselves in and barricaded the gates with stones. Judas sent them words of peace, ⁴⁸ saying, "Let us pass through your land to go into our country. No one will harm you. We will only pass through on foot." But they would not open the gates for him. ⁴⁹ Then Judas sent a proclamation to all in his camp, that they should attack from their present positions. ⁵⁰ The army attacked and assaulted the city all day and all night, until the city was captured by him. ⁵¹ They killed every male with their swords, razed and plundered the city. Then they marched through the city over the bodies of the slain.

⁵² They crossed the Jordan to the great plain near Beth-shan. ⁵³ Judas hurried those in the rear and encouraged the people all the way to the land of Judah. ⁵⁴ They went up to Mount Zion with joy and gladness, and offered holocausts, because not one of them was killed, all returning in peace.

⁵⁵ Now while Judas and Jonathan were in the land of Gilead, and Simon his brother was in Galilee before Ptolemais, ⁵⁶ Joseph, the son of Zacharias, and Azarias, commanders of the soldiers, heard of the victories and the battles that were fought. ⁵⁷ They said, "Let us also make a name for ourselves fighting the Gentiles around us." ⁵⁸ Joseph gave orders to those in his army, and they marched against Jamnia. ⁵⁹ Gorgias and his men came out of the city to do battle with them. ⁶⁰ Joseph and Azarias were routed and pursued to the borders of Judea, losing about two thousand Israelites. This great defeat took place ⁶¹ because they did not listen to Judas and

his brothers, thinking that they were self-sufficient. ⁶² But they were not of the family of those by whom salvation was to come to Israel. ⁶³ Judas and his men were greatly honored by all Israel, and their fame spread among the Gentiles. ⁶⁴ People gathered around them with joyful acclamations.

⁶⁵ Judas and his brothers went forth and attacked the sons of Esau, in the land to the south. He captured Hebron and its surrounding towns. He destroyed their fortifications. ⁶⁶ He moved his camp through Samaria into the land of the Philistines. ⁶⁷ That day some priests fell in battle, because desiring to be brave they went out unprepared to fight. ⁶⁸ Judas turned to Azotus into the land of the Philistines. He tore down their altars and burned the statues of their gods. He took the goods of the cities and returned into the land of Judah.

6 King Antiochus was passing through the upper provinces when he heard that the city of Elymais in Persia was famous for its silver and gold. ² There was a temple there that was very rich with golden breastplates and shields which King Alexander, son of Philip the Macedonian and first ruler of Greece, had left there. ³ He came and tried to capture the city in order to pillage it, but he could not because its defenders had learned of his plans. ⁴ They repulsed him in battle, and he fled from there, departing with great sadness, and returned towards Babylon.

⁵ While he was still in Persia, someone told him how his armies that were in the land of Judah had been put to flight, ⁶ that Lysias who had a very powerful army, had been defeated by the Jews, who had grown strong with the armor, war supplies and stores of goods which they had captured from the camps which they had destroyed. ⁷ He was told that they had thrown down the idols which he had set up on the altar in Jerusalem, and that they had surrounded the sanctuary with high walls as previously, as well as the city of Beth-zur.

⁸ When the king heard this news, he grew fearful and was greatly shaken. He became sick with grief and took to his bed, because things had not worked out as he had planned. ⁹ He remained there for many

days as his grief increased until he thought he would die.

¹⁰ He called his friends and said to them, "I cannot sleep, my spirits are low and I have pined away. ¹¹ I said to myself, 'How much trouble have I gotten into and what deep sorrow is now mine. I who was kind and beloved in my power!' ¹² Yet now I remember the evils that I have done in Jerusalem, where I also seized all the spoils of gold and silver there, and ordered the slaughter of the inhabitants of Judah without just cause. ¹³ I know, therefore, that this is why these evils have befallen me. Now I shall perish with great sorrow in a strange land."

¹⁴ He then called Philip, one of his friends, and made him regent of all his kingdom. ¹⁵ He gave him the crown, his robe and his signet ring, so that he should be guardian to Antiochus, his son, to train him to become king. ¹⁶ King Antiochus died there in the year one hundred and forty-nine.[a] ¹⁷ Lysias learned that the king was dead, and set up Antiochus his son to reign, whom he raised. His son was called Eupator.

¹⁸ The army in the citadel hemmed in the Israelites around the sanctuary. They were continually trying to harm the Jews and strengthen the Gentiles. ¹⁹ Judas decided to destroy them, and gathered all the people to wage war. ²⁰ They assembled and attacked the citadel in the year one hundred and fifty,[b] using battering rams and slings. ²¹ Some of the besieged escaped, and some Israeli renegades joined them. ²² They went to the king and said, "How long will you delay the execution of judgment and revenge our brothers? ²³ We agreed to serve your father and do all he ordered, and obey his commands. ²⁴ Because of this, our countrymen are angry with us and have killed as many of us as they could find, and have seized our inheritances. ²⁵ They have not only put forth their hand against us but against all the lands that border us. ²⁶ Today, they have surrounded the citadel of Jerusalem to capture it, and have fortified the strong hold of Beth-zur. ²⁷ Unless you act quickly, they will do worse things than

these, and you will not be able to stop them."

²⁸ The king became angry when he heard this. He called together all his friends, the commanders of his army, and the cavalry. ²⁹ He hired mercenaries from various places, as well as from islands in the sea. ³⁰ The number of his army was a hundred thousand infantry, twenty thousand cavalry men and thirty-two elephants, trained in warfare. ³¹ They went through Idumea and came to Beth-zur and fought many days. They built siege engines but the defenders sallied forth bravely and set them on fire.

³² Judas left the siege of the citadel and moved his camp to Beth-zechariah, opposite the king's camp. ³³ The king rose before daylight and made a forced march toward Beth-zechariah where his armies readied for battle and sounded the trumpets. ³⁴ They showed the elephants the juice of grapes and mulberries to provoke them to fight. ³⁵ They assigned the elephants to the phalanxes and with each elephant, a thousand men armed in coats of mail and brass helmets. Five hundred picked horsemen went with each elephant. ³⁶ These soldiers anticipated the moves of the elephants and went with them, never leaving them. ³⁷ Fastened to each elephant by a harness was a wooden tower, protecting a team of valiant fighting men, while an Indian driver directed the beast. ³⁸ The rest of the cavalry was placed on either flank of the army, with trumpets to arouse the army, and to hasten it forward in massed formation. ³⁹ When the sun reflected from the shields of gold and of brass, the mountains caught the glare and gleamed as if afire. ⁴⁰ Part of the king's army was deployed on the high mountains and the other part on the plain. The soldiers advanced steadily and in good order. ⁴¹ Everyone who heard the noise of this great multitude and the tramp of the army with its clanging armor trembled, for the army was very powerful and numerous.

⁴² Judas and his army marched forward and in the first skirmish six hundred of the king's men were killed. ⁴³ Eleazar, son of Saura, saw one of the elephants equipped

---

a 163 B.C.   b 162 B.C.

with royal harness. It was larger than the other beasts, and he thought that the king was on it. ⁴⁴ He sacrificed himself to win the battle and earn a lasting name. ⁴⁵ He fought his way boldly through the middle of the legion, slashing on the right and on the left, and leaving dead behind him. ⁴⁶ He went under the elephant and plunged his sword into it. It collapsed on him and killed him. ⁴⁷ When the Jews saw the strength and determination of the king's army, they retreated.

⁴⁸ The king's army followed them to Jerusalem, where it made camp in Judea and Mount Zion. ⁴⁹ The king made peace with the people of Beth-zur. They evacuated the city, because they had no food to withstand a siege, since it was a sabbatical year for the land. ⁵⁰ So the king took Beth-zur and left a garrison to hold it. ⁵¹ He began a long siege of the sanctuary. He set up battering rams there, and engines and catapults to hurl fire, stones, javelins and arrows. ⁵² The Jews also made engines of war for defense and they fought for many days. ⁵³ But since it was the sabbatical year, there was no food in the city. Those who had remained behind and those who had fled the pagans had eaten all the stores. ⁵⁴ Only a skeleton force stayed in the sanctuary because of the famine, and the others had gone to their own homes.

⁵⁵ Then Lysias heard that Philip, whom King Antiochus while still alive had appointed to raise his son Antiochus to be king, ⁵⁶ had returned from Persia and Media with the army that had gone with him, and that he sought to seize power. ⁵⁷ Wherefore he quickly went to the king and told him and his commanders, "We daily grow weaker, our provisions are small, and the place that we lay siege to is strong. Besides the affairs of our kingdom are very urgent. ⁵⁸ Therefore, let us make a peace treaty with these men and their nation. ⁵⁹ Let us agree that they may live once more in accordance with their own laws. Because we abolished their laws, we provoked them to be our enemies." ⁶⁰ The proposal pleased the king and his commanders. He sent the Jews a peace offer and they accepted it. ⁶¹ The king and the commanders gave their word and the defenders evacuated the stronghold.

⁶² The king went up Mount Zion and when he saw how strong its defenses were, quickly broke the oath he had taken, and gave orders to tear down the wall around it. ⁶³ He quickly departed and returned to Antioch, where he found Philip in control of the city. He attacked and captured the city.

7 In the hundred and fifty-first year, Demetrius, son of Seleucus, escaped from Rome where he was held hostage and arrived with a few men at a coastal city where he reigned. ² As he was entering the royal palace of his ancestors, the army captured Antiochus and Lysias to bring them to him. ³ When he heard this he said, "I do not want to see them." ⁴ So the army killed them. And Demetrius assumed the throne of his kingdom.

⁵ The wicked and ungodly men of Israel came to him, led by Alcimus who wanted to be made high priest. ⁶ They accused the people of their nation, saying, "Judas and his brothers have destroyed all your friends, and have driven us from our land. ⁷ Therefore, send some man whom you trust to survey the situation and see all the ruin he has brought to us and the king's lands. Let him punish them and all who aid them."

⁸ The king chose Bacchides, one of his friends, who governed beyond the great river in the kingdom and was faithful to the king. He sent him ⁹ and the wicked Alcimus whom he made high priest, to see the havoc that Judas had caused, commanding him to take revenge upon the children of Israel. ¹⁰ They marched forth with a large army into the land of Judah. They sent messengers to Judas and his brothers with deceitful words of peace. ¹¹ But they did not listen to them because they saw that the enemy had come with a large army.

¹² A group of scribes came to Alcimus and Bacchides to inquire about just terms. ¹³ The Hasidaeic Jews were the first to seek peace. ¹⁴ They said, "A priest of the line of Aaron is here. He will not deceive us." ¹⁵ Alcimus spoke words of peace to them and swore to them, saying, "We will do no harm to you or your friends." ¹⁶ They believed him. But he took sixty of them in one

day and killed them, according to the word that is written,

> [17] "The flesh of your saints and their blood
> has been shed around about Jerusalem,
> and there was none to bury them."

[18] Then fear and trembling came over all the people. They said, "There is no truth or justice in them, for they have broken their agreement and the oath which they swore."

[19] Bacchides moved the camp from Jerusalem and pitched it at Beth-zaith. He sent and seized many of those who had deserted to him and some of the people he killed, throwing them into a great pit. [20] Then he entered the country to Alcimus and left some of his troops to help him. So Bacchides went back to the king; [21] Alcimus did what he could to maintain his chief priesthood. [22] Jewish dissenters turned to him, and they took control of the land of Judah and did much harm to Israel. [23] Judas saw all the evils that Alcimus and those that were with him did to the children of Israel. They were worse than the Gentiles. [24] Judas marched along the coasts of Judea and took revenge upon the men who had deserted and prevented city dwellers from going into the country. [25] Alcimus realized that Judas and his followers were gaining control and knew that he could not stand against them, so he went back to the king and accused them of many crimes.

[26] The king sent Nicanor, one of his principal lords, who despised Israel, commanding him to destroy Israel. [27] Nicanor came to Jerusalem with a large army, and he sent Judas and his brothers deceitful words, saying, [28] "Let there be no fighting between us. I will come with a few men to talk of peace." [29] He came to Judas, and they saluted one another peaceably, all the while preparing to seize Judas by force. [30] Judas learned of the treachery, and with caution would not meet him again. [31] Nicanor realized his plan was discovered, so he went out to fight against Judas near Capharsalama. [32] There almost five thousand men of Nicanor's army were killed, and the survivors fled into the city of David. [33] After this Nicanor went to Mount

Zion. Some of the priests and the people came out to salute him peaceably, and to show him the holocausts that were being offered for the king. [34] But he mocked, derided and cursed them. He spoke arrogantly, [35] and angrily swore, "Unless Judas and his army are delivered into my hands, then when I return, I will burn this house." He left in a great rage. [36] The priests went in, and stood facing the altar and the temple. They wept and said,

> [37] "You, O Lord, have chosen this house wherein your name is honored,
> a house of prayer and supplication for your people.
> [38] Take vengeance on this man and his army,
> and let them die by the sword.
> Remember their blasphemies and do not let them live any longer.

[39] Nicanor went out from Jerusalem and encamped near Beth-horon where the Syrian army joined him. [40] Judas pitched his camp in Adasa with three thousand men. He prayed and said, [41] "O Lord, when the messengers of King Sennacherib blasphemed you, an angel went out and killed a hundred and eighty-five thousand of them. [42] In the same way destroy this army before us today, and let the rest know that Nicanor has spoken ill against your sanctuary, and judge him according to his wickedness." [43] The armies joined battle on the thirteenth day of the month Adar. The army of Nicanor was defeated, and he himself was first to fall in battle. [44] When his army saw that Nicanor was dead, they threw away their weapons and fled. [45] The Jews pursued them for a day, from Adasa as far as Gazara, and their trumpets kept sounding the battle call. [46] And men came out of all the towns of Judea and drove the enemy back to their pursuers who put them to the sword until there was not a single man left. [47] The Jews seized all the spoils, and they cut off Nicanor's head and his right hand, which he had so arrogantly extended, and brought them and displayed them in Jerusalem. [48] The people rejoiced very much and they spent that day in happiness. [49] Judas decreed that this day should be celebrated every year, on the thir-

teenth of the month of Adar. ⁵⁰ So the land of Judah had peace for a short time.

8 Judas heard of the fame of the Romans, that they were powerful and strong, and ready to make alliances with anyone who came in friendship, even though they were very powerful. ² They heard of their battles and their heroic deeds against the Gauls, and of how they had conquered them and forced them to pay tribute. ³ They also heard the great things they had done in Spain, of how they had gained control of the silver and gold mines there, and had taken possession of the whole country by their wisdom and patience, ⁴ even though this place was far from them. Kings from everywhere in the world who opposed them had been overthrown with great losses, while others paid them taxes every year. ⁵ They had defeated in battle Philip, and Perseus the king of the Macedonians, and others who had fought against them had been conquered. ⁶ They learned how the Romans defeated Antiochus, the great king of Asia, who fought them with a hundred and twenty elephants, cavalry, chariots and a very large army. They took him alive and ordered that both he and those that would reign after him should pay a large tax, and that he should give hostages and other tribute. ⁸ They took over some of the best provinces—the country of the Indians, Medes, Lydians—and gave to King Eumenes. ⁹ The Greeks decided to go and destroy them. The Romans heard of this ¹⁰ and sent a general against them, who battled with them, and many Greeks were killed. The Romans carried away their wives and their children as captives, and controlled and plundered their land, tore down their walls and made them their servants even to this day. ¹¹ They destroyed and enslaved other kingdoms and islands that at one time had resisted them. ¹² With their friends and those who had alliances with them, they kept peace; otherwise, they conquered kingdoms both far and near and all who heard of them were afraid of them. ¹³ Those they wished to help and make kings, they made kings, and those they did not like, they deposed from their kingdoms; thus they were greatly exalted. ¹⁴ Yet no

Roman wore a crown or was clothed in flattering purple. ¹⁵ They formed a senate of three hundred and twenty men, which met daily in the best interests of the people. ¹⁶ Their government was directed by one man every year who ruled over the whole country and they all obeyed him and there was no envy or jealousy among them.

¹⁷ Judas chose Eupolemus, son of John, the son of Jacob, and Jason, the son of Eleazar, to go to Rome and make a pact of friendship and an alliance with them. ¹⁸ The Jews wanted to be relieved of the oppression of the Greeks, who threatened the kingdom of Israel with servitude. ¹⁹ Eupolemus and Jason went to Rome, which was a very long journey, and they entered the senate house and said, ²⁰ "Judas Maccabeus and his brothers, and the Jewish people have sent us to you to make an alliance and peace with you, that we may be considered as your confederates and friends." ²¹ The proposal was pleasing in their sight.

²² This is the copy of the message to Jerusalem that they sent back, engraved on tablets of bronze, that it might be kept there as a memorial of the peace and alliance. ²³ "May all succeed with the Romans and the Jewish people, at sea and on land forever; and may the sword and enemy be far from them. ²⁴ If war should come to the Romans or any of their friends in all of their dominions, ²⁵ the nation of the Jews will help them befittingly with all their heart. ²⁶ To an enemy who makes war they will not give or supply wheat, arms, money or ships, as Rome has decided. They will keep these obligations without deceit. ²⁹ Thus on these terms the Romans make peace with the Jewish people. ³⁰ And after this if one party or the other decides to add to these articles, or take out anything, they may do it at their choice, and whatsoever they add or take out, will be ratified. ³¹ Moreover, concerning the evils that King Demetrius has done against them, we have written to him, saying, 'Why have you made your yoke heavy upon our friends and allies, the Jews? ³² If, therefore, they come again to us complaining of you, we will obtain them justice, and will make war against you by sea and on land.' "

9 Meanwhile, when Demetrius heard that Nicanor and his army had fallen in battle, he sent Bacchides and Alcimus back into Judea; and they took the right wing of his army with them. ² They marched by the road that leads to Gilgal, and they camped in Mesaloth, in Arbela; they conquered it and killed many people. ³ In the first month of the hundred and fifty-second year[a] they encamped against Jerusalem, ⁴ after which they marched to Berea with twenty thousand infantry and two thousand cavalrymen.

⁵ Judas had pitched his camp in Elasa, together with three thousand picked men. ⁶ When they saw the size of the enemy army, they were seized with great fear and many deserted the camp until no more than eight hundred men remained. ⁷ Judas saw that his army had diminished and the battle was upon him. He was sad and discouraged because he did not have time to gather more forces. ⁸ He said to those who remained, "Let us go and fight our enemies, if we are able." ⁹ His men tried to dissuade him, saying, "We shall not be able, so let us save our lives now and return to our brothers and then fight against them, for now we are but few." ¹⁰ Judas said, "God forbid that we should do this and flee from them. If our time has come, let us die manfully for our brothers and not blemish our honor."

¹¹ The invaders moved out of camp and took positions against the Jews. The cavalry was divided into two groups, and the slingers and the archers went ahead of the army, and those that were in the front were all brave men. ¹² Bacchides was on the right wing, and the army approached on two flanks, sounding its trumpets. ¹³ Judas' soldiers sounded their own trumpets. The earth shook at the noise of the armies. The battle continued from morning until night. ¹⁴ Judas saw that Bacchides and the stronger part of his army was on the right, so leading his bravest men ¹⁵ they attacked the right wing, pursuing them to Mount Azotus. ¹⁶ Those who were on the left flank realized that the right wing was under attack, and they followed Judas and those that were with him; ¹⁷ and the battle was hard fought and many wounded fell on both sides. ¹⁸ Judas was killed and the rest fled.

¹⁹ Jonathan and Simon took Judas their brother and buried him in the tomb of their fathers in the city of Modein. ²⁰ All the people of Israel mourned for him greatly and for many days. ²¹ They said, "How is the mighty man fallen who saved the people of Israel!" ²² All the deeds of Judas concerning his battles, his noble acts and his greatness are not written, there were too many of them.

²³ After the death of Judas the wicked began to reappear throughout Israel, and those guilty of sin came forth. ²⁴ In those days there was a very great famine, and the lawless and as their lands yielded to Bacchides. ²⁵ Bacchides chose ungodly men and made them lords of the country, ²⁶ and they sought and searched for the friends of Judas and brought them to Bacchides, who took vengeance on them and abused them. ²⁷ There was a great sorrow in Israel, such as had not been seen since the day when the last prophet was seen in Israel.

²⁸ All the friends of Judas came and said to Jonathan, ²⁹ "Since your brother Judas died, there is no one like him to battle Bacchides and our enemies, and those of our own people who betray our cause. ³⁰ Therefore, we have chosen you today to be our ruler and commander in his place to fight our battles." ³¹ So Jonathan became leader of the government at that time, and took the place of Judas his brother.

³² Bacchides heard of this and tried to kill him. ³³ Jonathan and Simon his brother and all those that were with them learned of the plot, and they fled into the wilderness of Tekoa, and pitched camp on the shore of Lake Asphar. ³⁴ Bacchides learned of this and he and his army crossed the Jordan on the sabbath day.

³⁵ Jonathan sent his brother, a captain of the people, to ask the Nabateans, his friends, if they would store the Israelites' baggage. ³⁶ However, the sons of Jambri came from Medeba and seized John and all that he had and took him away. ³⁷ After this Jonathan and his brother Simon

---

a 160 B.C.

learned that the sons of Jambri planned a large wedding and were bringing with great splendor the bride from Medeba, who was the daughter of one of the greatest princes of Canaan. ³⁸ They recalled the blood of their brother John and went up and hid themselves in the shelter of the mountain. ³⁹ They raised their eyes and saw much tumult and great possessions; and the bridegroom came out with his relatives and friends to meet them with timbrels and musical instruments and many weapons. ⁴⁰ The Israelites rushed from their ambush. Many were killed and wounded, the rest fled into the mountains. The Jews captured all the goods. ⁴¹ The marriage was turned into mourning, and the sound of their musical instruments into a dirge. ⁴² When they had taken revenge for the death of their brother, they returned to the bank of the Jordan.

⁴³ As soon as Bacchides heard of this, he came on the sabbath day to the bank of the Jordan with a large army. ⁴⁴ Jonathan said to his company, "Let us go and fight our enemies, for it is not like it was yesterday and the day before. ⁴⁵ Now the battle is in front of us. The water of the Jordan is on this side and the banks, marshes and woods on the other. There is no place for us to turn. ⁴⁶ Therefore, pray to heaven that you may be delivered from the hand of your enemies." Then they began to fight. ⁴⁷ Jonathan reached out to strike Bacchides, but he escaped him and retreated. ⁴⁸ Jonathan and those that were with him jumped into the Jordan and swam over to the other side. ⁴⁹ That day a thousand men of Bacchides' army were killed.

⁵⁰ The survivors returned to Jerusalem. They built strong cities in Judea, fortresses with high walls, gates and bars in Jericho, Emmaus, Beth-horon, Bethel, Timnath, Pharathon and Tephon. ⁵¹ Bacchides placed garrisons in them, that they might strike the Israelites. ⁵² He fortified the city of Beth-zur, Gazara and the Citadel, and put troops in them with provisions. ⁵³ He took the sons of the leading men of the country as hostages, and put them in custody in the Citadel of Jerusalem.

⁵⁴ In the year one hundred and fifty-three, in the second month, Alcimus ordered that the walls of the inner court of the sanctuary be torn down. The works of the prophets to be destroyed! ⁵⁵ Alcimus had hardly started this when he had a stroke. Paralyzed and speechless, he could no longer give commands and the work halted. ⁵⁶ Then Alcimus died in great suffering.

⁵⁷ Bacchides saw that Alcimus was dead and he returned to the king, and the land was peaceful for two years. ⁵⁸ Then the lawless began a plot, saying, "Jonathan and those with him live comfortably and without fear. Therefore, let us bring Bacchides back, and he can seize them all in one night." ⁵⁹ So they went and advised him thus. ⁶⁰ He set out with a large army, sending ahead secret letters to his followers in Judea, to seize Jonathan and those that were with him. But this failed because Jonathan learned of this plan through intelligence agents. ⁶¹ He apprehended fifty men of the country, the principal authors of the plot, and killed them. ⁶² Jonathan, Simon and those with them withdrew to Beth-basi, which is in the wilderness, rebuilding and arming the fort.

⁶³ When Bacchides found out, he gathered his army and sent word to his allies in Judea. ⁶⁴ He came and camped above Beth-basi, and fought against it for many days, and made engines of war. ⁶⁵ Jonathan left his brother Simon in the city and went into the country with a number of men. ⁶⁶ He struck down Odomera and his brothers and the children of Phasiron in their tents. Then he began to attack and his forces increased. ⁶⁷ Simon and his troops rushed out of the city and set the war machines on fire. ⁶⁸ They fought against Bacchides, and he was beset by them. They afflicted him greatly, for all his counseling and planning was in vain.

⁶⁹ Bacchides was angry with those lawless Jews who had advised him to come into their country, and he killed many of them. He decided to return with the surviving troops into their own territory. ⁷⁰ When Jonathan heard of this retreat, he sent ambassadors to him to offer peace, provided his captives were set free. ⁷¹ Bacchides accepted the terms and kept his word, swearing that he would do Jonathan no harm as

long as he lived. [72] Bacchides released the prisoners he had taken in Judah, returned to his own country, and never again went past their borders. [73] So war ended in Israel. Jonathan dwelt in Michmash, where he judged the people and he routed the ungodly from Israel.

10 In the hundred and sixtieth year,[a] Alexander, also called the Illustrious,[b] the son of Antiochus, came up and occupied Ptolemais. The people accepted him and he ruled there. [2] When King Demetrius heard of this, he gathered together a very great army and went to fight him.

[3] Demetrius sent a letter to Jonathan with words of peace to appease him, [4] for he reasoned, "Let us first make peace with him before he makes one with Alexander against us. [5] For he will remember all the evils that we have done to him and his brother and his nation." [6] Demetrius gave him authority to recruit and equip an army, hoping thus to make him an ally. He also ordered that the hostages that were in the Citadel be surrendered to Jonathan.

[7] Jonathan came to Jerusalem and read the letter to all the people and those in the Citadel. [8] They were greatly alarmed when they heard that the king had given him authority to recruit an army. [9] The hostages were released to Jonathan, and he returned them to their parents. [10] Jonathan lived in Jerusalem, and began to build and repair the city. [11] He ordered workmen to build the walls with square stones and to continue them around Mount Zion. [12] The foreigners who were in the strongholds which Bacchides had built fled. [13] Every man left his place and returned to his own country. [14] Only in Beth-zur did some remain who had forsaken the law and the commandments of God, for this was a place of refuge for them.

[15] King Alexander heard of the promises that Demetrius had made Jonathan. He was told of the battles fought and the noble deeds done by Jonathan and his brothers, as well as the hardships that they had endured. [16] He said, "Shall we find another man like this? Therefore, we will make him

our friend and our ally." [17] So he wrote a letter and sent it to him saying, [18] "King Alexander to his brother Jonathan, greetings. [19] We have heard of you, that you are a man of great power and fit to be our friend. [20] Therefore, today we make you high priest of your nation, and you shall be called the king's friend (and he sent him a purple robe and a crown of gold), and you will promote our works and keep our friendship." [21] Then Jonathan put on the holy vestments in the seventh month, in the year one hundred and sixty, at the Feast of Tabernacles, and he recruited troops and heavily armed them.

[22] Demetrius heard this and was very grieved, saying, [23] "What have we done, that Alexander has prevented us from gaining the friendship of the Jews in order to strengthen himself? [24] I also will write to them and request their friendship, and offer honors and gifts, that they may be my ally also." [25] He wrote to them in these words, "King Demetrius to the nation of Jews, greetings. [26] Since you have kept your agreement with us and have continued our friendship and have not sided with our enemies, we have heard of this and are glad. [27] So now continue to keep good will towards us and we will reward you with good things for all that you do in our behalf. [28] We will give you many privileges and grant you many gifts.

[29] "I now exempt you and all the Jews from taxes and I release you from the salt tax and crown levies. As regards my share of a third of the grain [30] and half of the fruit harvest, I release you from this day forward, so nothing will be taken from the land of Judah or from the three cities that are added to it from Samaria and Galilee, from this day and forever. [31] Let Jerusalem and its districts, its tithes and taxes, be holy and free. [32] I give up my occupation of the citadel in Jerusalem, and return it to the high priest so that he can defend it with his own men. [33] Every one of the Jews who has been brought captive from the land of Judah into my kingdom, I set free without ransom, and all their taxes, even those on their cattle, are remitted.

---

a 152 B.C.   b In Greek, Epiphanes.

³⁴ "I order that all the feasts and sabbaths and new moons and appointed days, and three days before a feast and three days after, are to be days of immunity and freedom for all the Jews who are in my kingdom. ³⁵ No one will have authority to act against the Jews or molest any of them for any cause.

³⁶ "Let thirty thousand Jews be enrolled in the king's army; rations shall be given them as is due to all the king's armies. Certain ones will be assigned to the great fortresses of the king. ³⁷ Some of them will be entrusted with the affairs of the kingdom. Let their leaders be chosen from their own ranks, and let them keep their own laws, just as the king has commanded in the land of Judah. ³⁸ The three cities that have been added to Judea from the country of Samaria will be annexed to Judea so that they may all be one and obey no other authority than that of the high priest.

³⁹ "Ptolemais and the adjoining lands I give as a free gift for the holy places that are in Jerusalem in order to meet the expenses of the holy places. ⁴⁰ Every year I grant fifteen thousand shekels of silver from the king's treasury. ⁴¹ All the additional funds which were denied in previous years will be given from now on for the upkeep of the Temple. ⁴² Moreover, the five thousand shekels of silver which my agents received every year from the income of the holy places will belong to the priests who minister them. ⁴³ Anyone who flees into the Temple in Jerusalem or wants sanctuaries, because he is indebted to the king for any matter, let him be freed and given back what they own in my kingdom. ⁴⁴ For rebuilding and restoring the holy places let the costs be taken from the king's revenues. ⁴⁵ As for the building of the walls of Jerusalem and its fortifications, the costs will be charged to the king's account. This also applies to rebuilding other walls in Judea."

⁴⁶ When Jonathan and the people heard these words, they did not believe them, because they remembered the great evil that Demetrius had done in Israel, for he had been very repressive. ⁴⁷ Their inclinations, therefore, were towards Alexander, because he had been the foremost promoter of peace in their regard, so they remained his ally.

⁴⁸ King Alexander gathered together a large army and moved his camp near Demetrius. ⁴⁹ The two kings joined battle and the army of Demetrius was routed. Alexander kept up the attack, pressing from all sides. ⁵⁰ The battle was hard fought until sundown and Demetrius was killed that day.

⁵¹ Alexander sent ambassadors to Ptolemy, King of Egypt, with words to this effect: ⁵² "Inasmuch as I have returned to my kingdom and am on the throne of my ancestors and have secured my reign and have overthrown Demetrius, and regained our country, ⁵³ after having met him in battle in which both he and his army were destroyed by us, we now occupy the throne of his kingdom. ⁵⁴ Therefore, let us make a mutual pact of friendship. Give me your daughter as my wife, and I will be your son-in-law, and I will give both you and her gifts worthy of you."

⁵⁵ King Ptolemy answered, "It was a happy day when you returned to the land of your fathers and occupied the throne of their kingdom. ⁵⁶ Now I will do what you wish, but meet me at Ptolemais, so that we may meet one another, and I may give my daughter to you as you requested." ⁵⁷ So Ptolemy left Egypt with Cleopatra, his daughter, and came to Ptolemais in the hundred and sixty-second year.ᵃ ⁵⁸ King Alexander met him and he gave him his daughter Cleopatra. He celebrated her marriage at Ptolemais with great glory, in the manner of kings.

⁵⁹ King Alexander wrote to Jonathan that he should come and meet him. ⁶⁰ He went with ceremony to Ptolemais and there he met the two kings, and he gave them much silver, gold and other presents and found favor in their sight. ⁶¹ Some pernicious men of Israel, who led wicked lives, gathered together against him to accuse him but the king paid no attention to them. ⁶² He commanded that Jonathan's clothes should be taken off, and that he should be dressed in purple, and they did so. And the king made him sit at his side. ⁶³ He said to

---

a 150 B.C.

his officers, "Go out with him to the middle of the city and make a proclamation that no one complain against him for any reason, and that no one annoy him for any reason." ⁶⁴ So when his accusers saw the honor shown him and that he was clothed with purple, they all fled. ⁶⁵ The king praised him, and enrolled him among his chief friends, and made him governor and ally of his dominion. ⁶⁶ Jonathan returned to Jerusalem with peace and joy.

⁶⁷ In the year one hundred and sixty-five, Demetrius, the son of Demetrius, came from Crete into the land of his fathers. ⁶⁸ When King Alexander heard of it, he was very worried and returned to Antioch.

⁶⁹ King Demetrius made Apollonius, who was governor of Coelesyria, his general, and he gathered together a large army and came to Jamnia. He sent a message to Jonathan, the high priest, saying, ⁷⁰ "You are the only one to oppose us. I am laughed at and reproached because you control the hill country. ⁷¹ Now, if you trust in your army, come down and meet us on the plain. There let us test one another, for I am girded for war. ⁷² Ask, and learn who I am, and those who help me, who have told us that you cannot stand up to us since your fathers were twice put to flight in their own land. ⁷³ How will you be able to fight my cavalry and my strong army on the plain, where there is no stone, nor rock, nor place to flee?"

⁷⁴ When Jonathan heard the words of Apollonius, he made a decision. He chose ten thousand men and went out of Jerusalem, and Simon his brother met him to help him. ⁷⁵ They pitched their tents near Joppa, since the gates of the city had been closed because a garrison of Apollonius was in Joppa, so he laid siege to it. ⁷⁶ Those in the city were terrified and they opened the gates to him, so Jonathan took Joppa. ⁷⁷ When Apollonius heard of this, he took three thousand cavalry and a large army ⁷⁸ and went to Azotus as though he was going on. Immediately he went out onto the plain, because he had a large number of horsemen whom he trusted. Jonathan pursued him to Azotus where they fought. ⁷⁹ Apollonius had secretly left a thousand horsemen in the rear. Jonathan realized that there was an ambush behind him, for they surrounded his army and shot arrows at his soldiers from morning till evening. ⁸¹ But his men stood fast, as Jonathan had ordered them, while the enemies' horses became tired.

⁸² Then Simon brought forward his army and attacked the legion for the cavalry was tired. It was overcome by him and fled. ⁸³ Those that were put to flight on the plain fled to Azotus and went into Beth-dagon for safety with their temple's idol. ⁸⁴ But Jonathan set fire to Azotus and the surrounding towns and took booty from them and from the temple of Dagon; all of those that fled into it, he burned. ⁸⁵ Almost eight thousand men were killed by sword or flame. ⁸⁶ Jonathan moved his army away and camped near Askalon where the people came out of the city to greet him with great honor. ⁸⁷ Jonathan returned to Jerusalem with his people, rich with plunder.

⁸⁸ It happened that when King Alexander heard these deeds he honored Jonathan even more. ⁸⁹ He sent him a buckle of gold, as is the custom to give to those of royal blood. He also gave him possession of Ekron and all its borders.

11 The king of Egypt gathered together an army, as numerous as the sands of the seashore, and many ships. He planned to get the kingdom of Alexander by deceit and add it to his own kingdom. ² He marched into Syria with peaceful words. The people opened the gates of their cities and greeted him because King Alexander had ordered them to greet him, because he was his father-in-law.

³ When Ptolemy entered the cities, he stationed garrisons of soldiers in every one. ⁴ When he approached Azotus, the people showed him the ruins of the temple of Dagon which had been destroyed by fire, together with Azotus and its environs which had been leveled; also the bodies lying around, and the graves of those who had been killed in the battle which lined the road. ⁵ They told the king that Jonathan had done these things so that the king would dislike him. But the king said nothing. ⁶ Jonathan came to meet the king at Joppa with great pomp, they greeted one

another, and they lodged there. ⁷ Jonathan went with the king as far as the Eleutherus River; then he returned to Jerusalem.

⁸ King Ptolemy gained control of the coastal cities, as far as Seleucia, and he thought up evil plans against Alexander. ⁹ He sent ambassadors to Demetrius, saying, "Come, let us make a bargain between us, and I will marry you to my daughter whom Alexander has, and you will reign in the kingdom of your father. ¹⁰ For I regret that I gave him my daughter, since he tried to kill me." ¹¹ He slandered him because he coveted his kingdom. ¹² He took away his daughter and gave her to Demetrius, and alienated himself from Alexander, and everyone knew they had become enemies. ¹³ Ptolemy entered Antioch, and now wore two crowns, that of Egypt and that of Asia. ¹⁴ Now King Alexander was in Cilicia at that time, because there was a rebellion there. ¹⁵ When Alexander heard of what had happened, he went forth to do battle. King Ptolemy led his army and met him with great might, putting him to flight. ¹⁶ Alexander fled into Arabia for protection, and King Ptolemy rejoiced.

¹⁷ Zabdiel, the Arab, cut off Alexander's head and sent it to Ptolemy. ¹⁸ However, King Ptolemy died three days later, and his troops in the strongholds were killed by the inhabitants. ¹⁹ Demetrius became king in the hundred and sixty-seventh year.ᵃ

²⁰ In those days Jonathan gathered forces from Judea, to seize the citadel of Jerusalem. They built many engines of war to besiege it. ²¹ Then some wicked men who hated their own nation went to King Demetrius and told him that Jonathan was attacking the Citadel. ²² When Demetrius heard this he was angry, and at once set out for Ptolemais, writing Jonathan to end the siege and meet him there. ²³ When Jonathan heard this, he ordered the siege to continue. Despite the danger, he set out with some of the priests and elders of Israel. ²⁴ He took gold, silver, rich garments and many other presents and went to the king at Ptolemais where he found favor in his sight. ²⁵ Even though certain wicked men of his nation made complaints against him,

²⁶ the king treated him as his predecessors had done, and he exalted Jonathan in the sight of all his friends. ²⁷ He confirmed him in the high priesthood and all the honors he had before, and made him one of his main friends.

²⁸ Jonathan requested that the king make Judea and the three districts of Samaria free from taxes, and he promised him three hundred talents. ²⁹ The king consented. He wrote a letter to Jonathan about all these things in this manner:

³⁰ "King Demetrius to his brother Jonathan, and to the nation of the Jews, greetings. ³¹ We send you here a copy of the letter which we have written to Lasthenes our kinsman, concerning you, that you might know what it contains.

³² "'King Demetrius to Lasthenes his kinsman, greetings. ³³ We are determined to do good to the nation of the Jews who are our friends and keep our agreements with them, for they bear us good will. ³⁴ We have confirmed to them all the borders of Judea, and the three districts of Aphairema, Lydda and Rathamin which were taken from Samaria and added to Judea. To all those who offer sacrifice in Jerusalem, we have freed them from the annual royal taxes, and from payments from their crops and fruit. ³⁵ From this moment on we abolish any other tithes and taxes due us; including the salt tax and crown tax formerly given. ³⁶ We release them from all of these, and nothing hereof shall be revoked from this time forth and forever. ³⁷ Therefore, see that you make a copy of these things, and give it to Jonathan, and post it on the holy mountain in a conspicuous place.'"

³⁸ King Demetrius, seeing that the land was peaceful and no one resisted him, dismissed all his troops, sending every man to his own home, except the foreign army, which he had recruited from the islands of the nations. So all the troops enlisted by his fathers hated him. ³⁹ There was a man called Trypho, who had been Alexander's supporter, who, seeing that all the army murmured against Demetrius, went to Imalkue the Arab, who was raising Antiochus, the son of Alexander. ⁴⁰ He urged the

---

a 145 B.C.

Arab to give Antiochus to him, so that he might make him king in his father's place. He related all that Demetrius had done, and how his soldiers hated him. He remained there for many days.

⁴¹ Jonathan sent word to King Demetrius, asking him to remove the soldiers who were in the Citadel of Jerusalem, and those that were in the strongholds, because they fought against Israel. ⁴² Demetrius replied to Jonathan, saying, "I will not only do this for you and for your people but I will greatly honor you and your country when the opportunity arises. ⁴³ Therefore, you will do well if you send my men to help me because all my army has deserted."

⁴⁴ Jonathan sent three thousand valiant men to him at Antioch. When they arrived before the king, he rejoiced to see them. ⁴⁵ Then the men of the city gathered together, in number a hundred and twenty thousand men, and sought to kill the king. ⁴⁶ He fled into his palace. The insurgents controlled the streets of the city and began to fight. ⁴⁷ The king called the Jews to his aid. They hurried to his assistance and dispersed themselves throughout the city. ⁴⁸ They killed a hundred thousand men that day and set fire to the city, obtaining much spoils that day, and saving the king. ⁴⁹ When the men of the city saw that the Jews controlled the city as they pleased, their courage failed, and they cried to the king, begging him, ⁵⁰ "Grant us peace, and make the Jews halt their attacks on us and our city." ⁵¹ They threw down their arms and made peace and the Jews were honored in the sight of the king and in the sight of all in the country, and became famous throughout the kingdom. They returned to Jerusalem with many riches. ⁵² King Demetrius continued his rule and the land was peaceful. ⁵³ But he broke his word to Jonathan, became estranged, did not repay the favors done him, but gave Jonathan much trouble.

⁵⁴ After this Trypho returned and with him Antiochus, the young boy, who was crowned and made king. ⁵⁵ All the troops that Demetrius had dismissed joined him and they fought against Demetrius, who was forced to flee. ⁵⁶ Trypho captured the elephants and made himself master of Antioch.

⁵⁷ Young Antiochus wrote to Jonathan, saying, "I confirm you in the high priesthood, and I appoint you ruler over the four districts, and confirm you as one of the king's friends." ⁵⁸ He sent him dishes of gold for his table service and he gave him permission to drink from a gold cup and to be clothed in purple and to wear a golden buckle. ⁵⁹ He made his brother Simon governor from the borders of Tyre all the way to the border of Egypt.

⁶⁰ Jonathan marched out and passed through the cities beyond the river, and all the armies of Syria gathered together to help him. When he came to Askalon, the people came out to honor him. ⁶¹ He went from there to Gaza, where he was denied admission, so he attacked it and burned all the environs and plundered them. ⁶² The men of Gaza pleaded with Jonathan and he made peace with them. He took their sons as hostages and sent them to Jerusalem. He went through the country as far as Damascus.

⁶³ Jonathan heard that the officers of Demetrius were treacherously near Kadesh in Galilee with a large army, intending to remove him from his position. ⁶⁴ He went forth to fight them but left his brother Simon in the country. ⁶⁵ Simon encamped near Beth-zur, surrounded it and attacked it for many days. ⁶⁶ The people sought to make peace and he granted it to them. He moved them from their homes, took the city and placed a garrison in it.

⁶⁷ Jonathan and his army encamped by the water of Gennesaret. Before dawn they were already on the plain of Hazor. ⁶⁸ The army of the foreigners met him on the plain, having laid an ambush for him in the mountains where they expected him. He fought against them. ⁶⁹ Those that were in ambush came out of hiding and joined the battle. ⁷⁰ All that were on Jonathan's side fled, and none were left, but the troops of Mattathias, the son of Absalom, and Judas, the son of Chalphi, chief captains of the army. ⁷¹ Jonathan tore his garments and put dirt upon his head and prayed. ⁷² Taking the force left, he returned to battle, and routed the enemy. ⁷³ When those of his own army who had fled saw this, they rejoined him,

and together they pursued the enemies even to their own camp at Kadesh, where they camped opposite. ⁷⁴ That day three thousand of the enemy were killed, and Jonathan returned to Jerusalem.

12 Jonathan saw that the time was right, so he chose certain men and sent them to Rome, to confirm and to renew the friendship with the Romans, ² and he sent letters along the same lines to the Spartans and to other places. ³ So they went to Rome and entered the senate house and said, "Jonathan the high priest and the nation of the Jews have sent us to renew our friendship and alliance as it was before." ⁴ The Romans gave them letters to their governors in every place to provide them safe conduct into the land of Judah.

⁵ This is a copy of the letters which Jonathan wrote to the Spartans: ⁶ "Jonathan the high priest, the elders of the nation, the priests and the rest of the people of the Jews, to the Spartans, their brothers, greetings. ⁷ There were letters sent long ago to Onias the high priest from Arius who reigned then among you, to signify that you are our brothers, as the copy here written does specify. ⁸ Onias received the ambassador with honor and accepted the letter in which was made mention of our alliance and friendship. ⁹ We, though we needed none of these things, having our comfort in the holy books that are in our hands, ¹⁰ chose rather to send to you to renew our brotherhood and friendship, lest we should become strangers to you altogether, for a long time has passed since you wrote to us. ¹¹ We, therefore, at all times without ceasing, both on our festivals and other days when it is convenient, remember you in the sacrifices that we offer, and in our observances, as it is fitting and becoming to remember brothers. ¹² We rejoice at your honor. ¹³ We have had many troubles and wars on every side, and the kings around us have fought against us. ¹⁴ We would not be troublesome to you, nor to the rest of our allies and friends in these wars. ¹⁵ We have had help from heaven, and we have been saved and our enemies are humbled. ¹⁶ We have chosen therefore Numenius, the son of Antiochus, and Antipater, the son of Ja-

son, and have sent them to the Romans to renew our former friendship and alliance. ¹⁷ We have ordered them also to go to you, and to greet you, and to deliver to you our letters concerning the renewing of our brotherhood. ¹⁸ Now you shall do well to give us an answer."

¹⁹ This is the copy of the letter which they sent to Onias: ²⁰ "Arius, king of the Spartans to Onias, the high priest, greetings. ²¹ It is written concerning the Spartans and the Jews that they are brothers and that they are of the family of Abraham. ²² Now that we know this, write us of your prosperity. ²³ We on our part tell you that our cattle and our possessions are yours; and yours, ours. We therefore have ordered that these things should be told to you."

²⁴ Jonathan heard that the generals of Demetrius were coming again to wage war with a larger army than before. ²⁵ He left Jerusalem and met them in the land of Hamath, for he did not want to give them the chance to invade his own country. ²⁶ He sent spies into their camp, who returned and told him that the enemy planned to attack that night. ²⁷ When the sun set, Jonathan commanded his men to be on guard and to keep their arms at hand ready to fight, and he posted sentries around the camp. ²⁸ The enemy learned that Jonathan and his men were ready for battle, and they were afraid and filled with dread. They lit fires in their camp and retreated. ²⁹ Jonathan and his army did not know this until morning because they saw the campfires burning. ³⁰ Jonathan went after them, but did not overtake them, for they had crossed the Eleutherus River. ³¹ Jonathan then went after the Arabians who are called Zabadeans. He defeated them and took their riches. ³² He marched on and came to Damascus, and passed through all that country.

³³ Simon also marched out and went as far as Askalon and the neighboring fortresses, then turned to Joppa and took possession of it ³⁴ (for he heard that they planned to turn over the stronghold to those who sided with Demetrius). He put troops there to guard it.

³⁵ When Jonathan returned, he called together the elders, and drew up plans with

them to build fortresses in Judea, ³⁶ and to raise the walls of Jerusalem, and erect a barrier between the citadel and the city to separate it from the city, that it might have no communication, and that its soldiers could neither buy nor sell. ³⁷ So they assembled to strengthen the city; the wall that bordered the brook towards the east was broken down, and he repaired the part called Chaphenatha. ³⁸ Simon built Adida in Shephelah; he fortified it and erected gates with bars.

³⁹ Then Trypho had tried to make himself King of Asia and take the crown, and fight against King Antiochus. ⁴⁰ Afraid lest Jonathan would fight against him, he sought to attack and kill him. So he came to Beth-shan. ⁴¹ Jonathan went there to meet him in battle with forty thousand picked men.

⁴² When Trypho saw that Jonathan came with a large army, he was afraid to fight against him. ⁴³ So he received him with honor, and praised him to all his friends, and gave him presents. He ordered his troops to obey him as they would himself. ⁴⁴ He said to Jonathan, "Why have you bothered all these people, when we are not at war? ⁴⁵ Send them back home and choose a few men to stay with you, and come with me to Ptolemais. I will give the city to you, as well as the rest of the strongholds and the army and all officials. Then I will go home, for this is why I came."

⁴⁶ Jonathan believed him and did as he said. He sent his army back into the land of Judah, ⁴⁷ keeping three thousand men of whom he sent two thousand into Galilee, while retaining one thousand. ⁴⁸ As soon as Jonathan entered Ptolemais, the men of the city shut the gates and captured him, and all of those that came in with him they killed with swords.

⁴⁹ Trypho dispatched troops and cavalry into Galilee and the great plain to destroy all Jonathan's soldiers. ⁵⁰ When they received word that Jonathan and all who were with him were seized and slain, encouraging one another, they went out ready for battle. ⁵¹ However, when the pursuers realized that they would be fighting for their lives, they turned back. ⁵² So they all reached safety in the land of Judah. They

mourned for Jonathan, especially those that had been with him, and Israel grieved loudly. ⁵³ All the nations surrounding them sought to destroy them, saying, ⁵⁴ "They have no prince, nor anyone to help them. This is the time to make war against them and destroy even the memory of them among men."

13 Simon learned that Trypho was assembling a very large army to invade the land of Judah and to destroy it. ² Realizing that the people were uncertain and fearful, he went to Jerusalem and assembled the people ³ and encouraged them, saying, "You know what great battles I and my brothers and the house of my father have fought for our laws and the sanctuary; and you know the evils we have seen. ⁴ For this reason, all my brothers have lost their lives for Israel's sake, and I alone am left. ⁵ Far be it from me to spare my life in time of trouble, for I am no better than my brothers. ⁶ I will avenge my country and the sanctuary, our children and wives; for all the pagans are assembling to destroy us out of hatred."

⁷ The spirit of the people was rejuvenated as soon as they heard these words. ⁸ They cried out, saying, "You are our leader in the place of Judas and Jonathan your brothers. ⁹ Fight our battles and we will obey you."

¹⁰ Gathering together the army, he hurried to complete the walls of Jerusalem and fortified it on all sides. ¹¹ He sent Jonathan, the son of Absalom, and with him a new army to Joppa, and he cast out those that were in it, and remained there himself.

¹² Trypho moved his large army from Ptolemais to invade the land of Judah, taking Jonathan under guard. ¹³ Simon pitched camp in Adida, near the plain. ¹⁴ When Trypho learned that Simon had taken the place of his brother Jonathan, and that he meant to do battle with him, he sent messengers to Simon, ¹⁵ saying, "We have detained your brother Jonathan for the money that he owed in the king's treasury, when he had management of his affairs. ¹⁶ Send a hundred talents of silver and his two sons as hostages, so that when he is set free he will not rise against us, and we will

release him."

¹⁷ Simon believed that Trypho spoke deceitfully to him, nevertheless he ordered the money and the children to be sent. He did not want to bring upon himself the hatred of the people of Israel, who might say, ¹⁸ "Because he did not send the money and the children, Jonathan died." ¹⁹ So he sent the children and the hundred talents. Trypho lied and did not release Jonathan.

²⁰ After this Trypho entered the country to destroy it. They took the route that leads to Adora, but Simon and his army followed them wherever they went. ²¹ Those that were in the citadel sent messengers to Trypho asking him to hurry and come through the wilderness and bring them food. ²² Trypho readied all his horsemen to leave that night but a very heavy snow fell and he could not get into the country of Gilead. ²³ He marched towards Baskama and killed Jonathan and his sons there. ²⁴ Then Trypho returned to his own country.

²⁵ Simon sent and had the remains of Jonathan his brother brought back and buried him in Modein, the city of his fathers. ²⁶ All Israel wept loudly for him and they mourned for him many days. ²⁷ Simon built a tall building of stone polished in front and back over the sepulcher of his father and of his brother. ²⁸ He erected seven pyramids, opposite one another, for his father, mother and four brothers. ²⁹ He surrounded these with great pillars upon which he hung armor as an eternal memorial, and besides the armor he had ships carved which might be seen by all who sailed on the sea. ³⁰ This is the tomb that remains in Modein even to this day.

³¹ Trypho, when he was on a journey with young King Antiochus, treacherously murdered him. ³² He reigned in his place, assuming the crown of Asia. He brought great evils upon the country.

³³ Simon strengthened the strongholds of Judea, fortifying them with high towers, great walls, gates and bars; and he stored food in them.

³⁴ Simon chose messengers and sent them to King Demetrius, hoping to gain immunity for his nation, for all that Trypho did was to steal. ³⁵ King Demetrius in an-

swering this request wrote a letter in this manner, ³⁶ "King Demetrius to Simon the high priest and friend of kings, and to the elders and to the nation of the Jews, greetings. ³⁷ The golden crown and the palm which you sent have been received. We are ready to make a firm peace with you and to write to the royal officials to release you from all tribute. ³⁸ All that was previously agreed upon remains in force. The fortresses that you have built will be yours. ³⁹ We forgive any oversights or faults committed to this day, and we forgive the crown tax which you owed; and if any other things were taxed in Jerusalem, those taxes are ended. ⁴⁰ If any of you are qualified to join the royal guard, let them be enrolled. Let there be peace between us."

⁴¹ In the one hundred and seventieth year, the yoke of the Gentiles was removed from Israel. ⁴² The people of Israel began to write in their documents and public records, "In the first year of Simon the high priest, the great commander and leader of the Jews."

⁴³ In those days, Simon besieged Gazara, surrounding it. He made siege engines and directed them against the city. He attacked one tower and captured it. ⁴⁴ Those inside the engine jumped out into the city and there was a great uproar in the city. ⁴⁵ The men in the city, together with their wives and children, went up to the wall, tore their clothes and cried out with a loud voice, asking Simon to grant them peace. ⁴⁶ They said, "Deal with us not according to our evil deeds but according to your mercy." ⁴⁷ Simon, being moved, did not destroy them, but he evicted them from the city, and purified the houses where there had been idols. Then he entered the city with hymns, blessing the Lord. ⁴⁸ Having rid it of all uncleanness, he placed men in it who would observe the law. He fortified the city and built a house for himself.

⁴⁹ Those who were in the citadel of Jerusalem were prevented from going out into the country and from buying and selling. They were very hungry and many of them died from famine. ⁵⁰ They begged Simon for peace and he granted it to them. He removed them from there and cleansed the castle from their impurities. ⁵¹ On the

twenty-third day of the second month in the year one hundred and seventy-one, the Jews entered the citadel with thanksgiving, bearing branches of palm trees, and with harps, cymbals, psalms, hymns and canticles, they gave thanks because Israel's great enemy was destroyed. 52 Simon commanded that this occasion should be celebrated every year with gladness. 53 He fortified the temple hill near the citadel and he and his men lived there.

54 Simon saw that his son, John, had reached the bravery of manhood. He made him commander of all the armies and he lived in Gazara.

14 In the year one hundred and seventy-two,ª King Demetrius assembled his army and went into Media to get help to make war against Trypho. 2 When Arsaces, king of Persia and Media, heard that Demetrius had entered his country, he sent one of his commanders to take him alive and bring him to him. 3 The general defeated the army of Demetrius, captured him, and brought him to Arsaces, who kept him prisoner.

4 The land of Judah was at peace all the days of Simon, who sought the good of his country. His power and honor pleased them well all his days. 5 To add to his honor, he took Joppa for a seaport and opened a way to the isles of the sea. 6 He enlarged the boundaries of his nation and kept control of all the land. 7 He assembled a large number of captives and had rule over Gazara, Beth-zur and the citadel from which he removed all impurities. No one opposed him. 8 Every man tilled his land in peace, and the land of Judah yielded its increase and the trees of the plains their fruit. 9 The old men sat in the streets and talked together of the good things of the land, and the young men put on the glory robes of war. 10 He provided food for the cities, and ordered that they should be furnished with ammunition, so that the fame of his name was renowned even to the end of the earth. 11 He made peace in the land, and Israel rejoiced with great joy. 12 Every man sat under his vine, and under his fig tree; and

there was no one to make them fear. 13 There was no one left in the land to fight against them; kings were made powerless in those days. 14 He strengthened all those people of humble state, and he sought out the law, and did away every unjust and wicked man. 15 He honored the sanctuary, and multiplied the vessels of the holy places.

16 It was heard at Rome, and as far as Sparta, that Jonathan was dead, and they were very sorry. 17 When they heard that Simon his brother was made high priest in his place and ruled all the country and the cities there, 18 they wrote to him on tablets of bronze to renew the friendship and alliance which they had made with Judas and with Jonathan his brother. 19 These were read before the assembly in Jerusalem.

This is a copy of the letters that the Spartans sent:20 "The rulers and the cities of the Spartans to Simon the high priest, to the elders, to the priests, and to the rest of the people of the Jews, our brothers, greetings. 21 The ambassadors who were sent to our people have told us of your glory, honor and joy. We rejoiced at their coming. 22 We registered what was said by them in the councils of the people in this way: 'Numenius, the son of Antiochus, and Antipater, the son of Jason, ambassadors of the Jews, came to us to renew the former friendship with us. 23 It pleased our people to receive the men with honor, and to put a copy of their words in the public archives to be a record for the Spartan people. We have sent a copy to Simon the high priest.' "

24 After this Simon sent Numenius to Rome with a great golden shield weighing a thousand minasᵇ to confirm the alliance with them. When the people of Rome had heard 25 these words, they said, "How will we thank Simon and his sons? 26 For he has acted worthily for his brothers, and has repelled the enemies of Israel and kept his people's freedom." They recorded this on bronze tablets and set them upon pillars on Mount Zion.

27 This is a copy of the writing: "On the eighteenth day of the month Elul, in the year one hundred and seventy-two,ᶜ being

---

a 141 B.C.   b A mina was about 20 ounces.   c 140 B.C.

the third year under Simon the high priest in Asaramel, [28] in a great assembly of the priests and of the people and the rulers of the country and the elders, these things were noted: Inasmuch as there have often been wars in our country, [29] Simon the son of Mattathais, a priest of the sons of Joarib, and his brothers, have put themselves in danger, and resisted the enemies of their nation in order to preserve their holy places and the law; and have brought great glory to their nation. [30] Jonathan united his country and was made its high priest and now rests among his people. [31] Their enemies wished to destroy their nation and ravage the holy places. [32] Simon resisted and fought for his nation, spending much of his own money to arm the valiant men of his nation and pay them wages. [33] He fortified the cities of Judea, and Beth-zur that lies on the border of Judea, where once the armor of the enemies was stored, and he placed there a garrison of Jews. [34] He fortified Joppa which is by the sea, and Gazara which borders upon Azotus, where the enemy formerly lived. He settled Jews there and furnished those cities with everything needed for their upkeep.

[35] "The people seeing the acts of Simon and the honor he intended to bring his nation, made him their leader and high priest, because he had done all these things and because of the justice and faith which he kept toward his nation. He sought by all means to advance his people.

[36] "In his days things prospered under his guidance, so that the pagans were driven out of the country, [37] as were also the invaders in the city of David in Jerusalem who occupied the citadel, out of which they sallied forth to defile the sanctuary to defend the country and the city, and he built the high walls of Jerusalem.

[38] "King Demetrius confirmed him in the high priesthood, [39] and made him his friend, and paid him great honor. [40] For he knew that the Romans called the Jews their friends, allies and brothers, and that they had received Simon's ambassadors with honor. [41] The Jews and their priests had consented that he should be their leader and high priest forever, until there should arise a faithful prophet; [42] and that he should be

ruler over them, and that he should take charge of the sanctuary and appoint governors over their works, and over the country, and over the armor and over the fortresses. [43] He should have care of the holy places. He should be obeyed by all, and all the records in the country should be made in his name; and that he should be clothed with purple and wear gold.

[44] "It was unlawful for any of the people or the priests to nullify any of these decisions or question his orders, or to gather an assembly in the country without his permission, or to wear purple or a buckle of gold. [45] Whoever acts contrary to or makes void any of these decisions shall be punished."

[46] It pleased all the people to establish Simon and to do according to these words. [47] Simon accepted the decisions and was happy to carry out the duties of high priest and to command and lead the nation of the Jews and priests, and to govern over all. [48] They commanded that this writing should be put in tablets of bronze and that they should be set up in a conspicuous place within the sanctuary area, [49] and that a copy should be filed in the treasury, that Simon and his sons might have access to it.

15 King Antiochus, the son of Demetrius, sent letters from the isles of the sea to Simon the priest and leader of the Jewish nation and to all the people, [2] and the contents were as follows: "King Antiochus to Simon the high priest, and to the nation of the Jews, greetings. [3] Because certain mischief-makers have seized power in the kingdom of our fathers, and I intend to assert my rightful claims to it and restore it to its former state, I have gathered a large army and have built ships of war. [4] I plan to go through the country that I may take revenge on those who have destroyed our country and who have made desolate many cities in my realm. [5] Therefore, I wish to confirm all tax exemptions that the kings before me granted you, and to continue any other privileges given you. [6] I give you permission to mint your own money in your country. [7] Let Jerusalem be sacred and free. All the armor that has been made and the fortresses which you have built, and those which you control, are to remain yours.

8 Any debts due the king, including future obligations, are canceled from this moment and for all time. 9 When we shall have regained control of our kingdom, we will honor you and your nation, and will make the temple glorious, so that your fame may be known all over."

10 In the year one hundred and seventy-four,[a] Antiochus entered the land of his fathers. Many troops deserted to him, so that few were left with Trypho. 11 King Antiochus pursued him, and he fled along the sea coast and came to Dor. 12 Trypho realized that hard times had come and that his armed strength was weakened. 13 Antiochus camped above Dor with a hundred and twenty thousand soldiers and eight thousand cavalrymen. 14 He surrounded the city, and his ships took up positions off the shore. Antiochus shut off the city by land and by sea, so that no one could go in or come out.

15 Meanwhile, Numenius and his companions arrived from Rome, bearing letters to the kings and countries, which said: 16 "Lucius, consul of the Romans, to King Ptolemy, greetings. 17 The ambassadors of our Jewish friends came to us to renew the former friendship and alliance, being sent from Simon the high priest and the people of the Jews. 18 They brought also a shield of gold weighing a thousand minas. 19 It seems expedient, therefore, for us to write to the kings and countries that they should do them no harm, nor war against them, their cities and country. Neither should anyone give aid to those that fight against them. 20 It has seemed good to us to accept the shield from them. 21 If therefore any trouble makers have fled their country to yours, return them to Simon the high priest, that he may punish them according to their own law."

22 These same things were written to King Demetrius, Attalus, Ariarathes and Arsaces, 23 and to all the nations; and to Sampsames, the Spartans, to Delos, Myndos, Sicyon, Caria, Samos, Pamphylia, Lycia, Halicarnassus, Cos, Side, Aradus, Rhodes, Phaselis, Gortyna, Cnidus, Cyrpus and Cyrene. 24 They sent a copy of the let-

ter to Simon the high priest and to the people of the Jews.

25 King Antiochus besieged Dor anew, assaulting it continually and making war engines. He trapped Trypho so that he could not escape. 26 Simon sent Antiochus two thousand picked men to help him, also silver, gold and much military hardware. 27 Antiochus would not receive them and renounced all agreements that he had made earlier with Simon, and alienated himself from him. 28 He sent Athenobius, one of his friends, to confer with Simon and say, "You control Joppa, Gazara, and the citadel in Jerusalem, which are cities of my kingdom. 29 You have violated their borders and have made great devastation in the land, seizing the power in many places of my kingdom. 30 Therefore, give back the cities that you have taken, and the taxes of the places that you control beyond the borders of Judea. 31 If you do not choose to do so, give me five hundred talents of silver for them for the destruction that you have caused; and to make up the tribute money of the other cities, give me five hundred talents more. Otherwise I will come and fight you." 32 So Athenobius, the king's friend, came to Jerusalem and saw the splendor of Simon and his magnificence of gold and silver, and his many carriages; he was astonished. He related the king's words.

33 Simon answered him, "We have neither taken other men's land, nor other men's goods. What we have is the inheritance of our fathers, which had been unjustly occupied by our enemies. 34 When the chance arose, we reclaimed the inheritance of our fathers. 35 As to your complaints concerning Joppa and Gazara, they did great harm to the people and to our nation, yet for these we will give a hundred talents." Athenobius did not reply 36 but angrily returned to the king, reporting to him what had happened, and of the riches of Simon, and of all that he had seen. The king was enraged.

37 Trypho escaped ship to Orthosia. 38 The king appointed Cendebaeus commander of the coastal areas and gave him an army of infantry and cavalry. 39 He or-

---

a 138 B.C.

dered him to march with his army against Judea. He commanded him to build up Kedron, to fortify its gates, and to wage war against the Jews. Meanwhile, the king himself pursued Trypho.

⁴⁰ Cendebaeus came to Jamnia and began to provoke the people and to raid Judea, taking prisoners and killing them. ⁴¹ He fortified Kedron and stationed troops and cavalry there, so that they might sally out in raids upon Judea, as the king had commanded him.

16 John came up from Gazara and told Simon his father what Cendebaeus had done against their people. ² Simon summoned his two eldest sons, Judas and John, and said to them, "I and my brothers and our father's house have fought against the enemies of Israel from our youth even to this day, and things have gone well in our hands because we have saved Israel many times. ³ Now I am old, but you must take the place of me and my brothers and continue to fight for our nation. May the help of heaven be with you."

⁴ John chose twenty thousand fighting soldiers and horsemen out of the country, and they went to fight Cendebaeus, camping for the night in Modein. ⁵ They arose in the morning and moved out on the plain. A very large army of infantry and horsemen came at them, and there was a running stream between the two armies. ⁶ John and his troops pitched their camp near them and when he saw his troops were afraid to go across the river, he went over first; then the men, seeing him, crossed over after him. ⁷ He divided the army, positioning the horsemen in the center of the infantry, for the enemy cavalry were many. ⁸ They attacked to the sound of the holy trumpets, and Cendebaeus and his army were put to flight. Many of them were wounded, and the survivors fled into the fortress. ⁹ Although Judas, John's brother, was wounded, he pursued the enemy until they arrived at Kedron, which Cendebaeus had fortified. ¹⁰ They also fled to the towers that were in the fields of Azotus, but John burned them with fire. Some two thousand

enemy were killed, and John returned to Judea safely.

¹¹ Ptolemy, the son of Abubus, had been appointed captain over the plain of Jericho, and he had much silver and gold, ¹² for he was son-in-law of the high priest. ¹³ He was happy, and planned to make himself master of the country. So he made treacherous plans against Simon and his sons in order to destroy them.

¹⁴ Simon, as he was going through the cities in the country of Judea, and taking care of their needs, went to Jericho, along with Mattathias and Judas, his sons, in the year one hundred and seventy-seven, in the eleventh month, which is known as Shebat. ¹⁵ The son of Abubus received them treacherously into a small fortress, called Dok, which he had built. He invited them to a great banquet, hiding men in the fortress. ¹⁶ When Simon and his sons had drunk quite a bit, Ptolemy and his men rose up, seized their weapons, entered the banquet place and killed him, his two sons and some of his servants. ¹⁷ He committed a great treachery against Israel, and rendered evil for good.

¹⁸ Ptolemy wrote a report of these things and dispatched it to the king, asking him to send soldiers to help him, promising that he would deliver to him the country and their cities with all their taxes to the king. ¹⁹ He sent others to Gazara to kill John. To the tribunes, he sent letters to come to him and he would give them silver, gold and gifts. ²⁰ He sent others to capture Jerusalem and the temple hill.

²¹ A messenger, running ahead, told John at Gazara that his father and his brothers were dead and that "he has sent men to kill you also." ²² When he heard this, John was exceedingly alarmed. He apprehended the men that came to kill him and he put them to death, for he knew that they sought to do away with him. ²³ The rest of the deeds of John, his wars, his worthy and brave accomplishments, the strengthening of the walls which he built, and his achievements ²⁴ are written in the history of his priesthood, from the time that he succeeded his father as high priest.

2 MACCABEES

1 TO THE JEWISH brethren throughout Egypt, their brother Jews in Jerusalem and in the land of Judea, send health and good peace. ² May God be good to you and remember the covenant he made with Abraham, Isaac and Jacob, his faithful servants, ³ and give you all a desire to worship him, and to do his will with a loving heart and a generous spirit. ⁴ May he open your mind to his law and his commandments, and grant you peace. ⁵ May he hear your prayers, and be reconciled to you, and may he never forsake you in the time of evil. ⁶ We are now praying for you here.

⁷ When Demetrius reigned in the year one hundred and sixty-nine,ᵃ we Jews wrote to you of the trouble and violence that came upon us in those days, after Jason withdrew from the holy land and from the kingdom. ⁸ He burned the city gate and shed innocent blood. Then we prayed to the Lord and were heard, and we offered sacrifices and fine flour and lighted the lamps and set forth the loaves. ⁹ Do keep the Feast of Dedication in the month of Chislev, in the year one hundred and eighty-eight.ᵇ

¹⁰ The people of Jerusalem and Judea, the senate, and Judas, to Aristobolus, the teacher of King Ptolemy, who is of the stock of anointed priests, and to the Jews in Egypt, health and good fortune.

¹¹ Having been delivered by God from perilous times, we give him great thanks, for we have been at war with the king. ¹² He sent many men from Persia to fight against us and the holy city. ¹³ When Antiochus himself was in Persia with a very large army, he was killed in the temple of Nanaea, being deceived by the words of the priests of Nanaea. ¹⁴ Antiochus, with his friends, went to Persia as though he would marry her, hoping to secure large sums of money as dowry. ¹⁵ When the priests of Nanaea set out the treasure, and Antiochus and a few men entered the interior of the temple, they closed the door as soon as he was inside. ¹⁶ Opening a secret door of the temple, they threw stones and killed the leader and those with him, dismembered them, cut off their heads, threw the parts outside. ¹⁷ Blessed be God in all things, who has judged the wicked.

¹⁸ Therefore, since we propose to keep the purification of the temple on the

---

a 143 B.C.   b 124 B.C.

twenty-fifth day of the month of Chislev, we thought it necessary to inform you so that you also may observe the Feast of Dedication and the day when the fire was given to Nehemiah to offer sacrifice, after the temple and altar were built.

19 When our fathers were taken captive into Persia, the holy priests at that time secretly took the fire from the altar and hid it in a valley where there was a dry cistern, and there kept it safe in a place unknown to all other men. 20 When many years had passed, and it pleased God that Nehemiah should be restored by the king of Persia, he sent some of the descendants of those priests who had hidden the fire to get it. They reported that they found no fire but a thick liquid. 21 Nehemiah told them to draw it up and bring it to him. He then commanded that the wood and the sacrifices placed upon them should be sprinkled with this same liquid. 22 When this was done and the sun finally came out, having been hidden by a cloud, a great fire broke out there to the amazement of all. 23 All the priests prayed while the sacrifice was burning, Jonathan leading and the rest answering.

24 The prayer of Nehemiah was this: "O Lord God, Creator of all things, awe-inspiring and strong, just and merciful, you alone are the good King, 25 you alone are gracious, you alone are just and almighty and eternal. It was you who saved Israel from all evil, who did choose the fathers and did sanctify them. 26 Receive the sacrifice for all your people Israel, and preserve your own portion and sanctify it. 27 Gather together our scattered people, free those who are slaves to the Gentiles, and look upon those who are despised and rejected, and let the Gentiles know that you are our God. 28 Punish those who oppress us and who injure us by insolence. 29 Establish your people in your holy place, as Moses promised."

30 Then the priests sang hymns. 31 When the sacrifice was consumed, Nehemiah ordered that the liquid that was left should be poured upon large stones. 32 When this was done, fire broke out on

them but it was put out by the light that shined from the altar. 33 When this matter became known, the king of Persia was told that in the place where the exiled priests had hidden the fire, there appeared a thick liquid with which Nehemiah and those with him had burned the sacrifices. 34 The king investigated the matter and built a temple over the spot as a memorial of what had happened. 35 Because of this evidence, he gave the priests many and various presents, distributing them himself. 36 Nehemiah called this place Nephthar, which means purification. But many call it Naphtha.c

2 One reads in the records that Jeremiah the prophet commanded those who went into captivity to take the fire, as it has been told, and to keep charge of it. 2 He gave them the law that they should not forget the commandments of the Lord and that they should not be confused in their thinking by seeing the gold and silver idols with their ornaments. 3 With similar speeches he told them to keep the law in their hearts. 4 It was also in the same writing how the prophet, being warned by God, commanded that the tabernacle and the ark should accompany him until he came to the mountain where Moses had gone up and received the inheritance of God. 5 When Jeremiah arrived there he found an empty cave into which he carried the tabernacle, the ark and the altar of incense. Then he blocked the entrance. 6 Some of those that followed him came up to mark the place but they could not find it.

7 When Jeremiah heard this, he rebuked them saying, "The place shall be hidden until God gathers together his people and shows them his mercy. 8 Then the Lord will reveal these things, and the majesty of the Lord shall appear, and there shall be a cloud as was shown to Moses, and was again shown when Solomon prayed that the place might be sanctified to the great God. 9 For he treated wisdom in a magnificent manner. Like a wise man, he offered sacrifice for the dedication and finishing of the temple. 10 Just as Moses prayed to the Lord and fire came down from heaven and con-

---

c There is an inflammable substance like naphtha found in Persia.

sumed the sacrifice, so also Solomon prayed and fire came down from heaven and consumed the sacrifice. [11] Moses said, 'Because the sin offering was not eaten, it was consumed.' [12] So Solomon also celebrated the dedication for eight days."

[13] These same things were written in the memoirs and commentaries of Nehemiah and also how he founded a library and gathered together from all the countries the books of the prophets, of David, the epistles of the kings, concerning the votive offerings. [14] Likewise Judas also gathered together all the books which were lost in the war we had, and they now are in our possession. [15] Therefore, if you want these things, send someone to get them for you. [16] We are about to celebrate the purification, which we have written you about. You will be wise if you keep the same days.

[17] We hope that God, who has saved his people and has returned to us our inheritance, kingdom, priesthood and sanctuary, [18] as he promised in the law, will soon have mercy on us and will gather us together from every land under heaven into the holy place. [19] For he has saved us from great dangers and has purified the place.

[20] Now we shall attempt to put into one book all those things concerning Judas Maccabeus and his brothers and the purification of the great temple and the dedication of the altar, [21] and also the wars against Antiochus the Illustrious and his son Eupator, [22] and the appearance which came from heaven to those who behaved themselves manfully on the behalf of the Jews. So that, while being only a few, they made themselves masters of the whole country, and put to flight the barbarian hordes, [23] and regained the most famous temple in all the world, and saved the city, and restored the laws that were abolished. The Lord with all clemency showed mercy to them, [24] and all such things as have been comprised in five books by Jason of Cyrene. [25] For considering the large number of books and the difficulty that exists for those who desire to study the narrations of history, because of the flood of material, [26] we have set about to make it easy for those who are willing to read, and for the studious that they may memorize more easily; so that all

who read might profit. [27] As for ourselves in undertaking this work of abridgment, we have begun a difficult task, yes, one of hard work and loss of sleep. [28] Like those who prepare a banquet and seek to satisfy the pleasure of others, for the sake of many we willingly undertake this labor. [29] We leave to compilers the exact handling of every detail, intending for ourselves to outline a brief digest. [30] Just as the contractor of a new house must take care of the whole building, so he who paints it must concern himself only with its decoration. So must you judge our effort. [31] To collect all that is known, to put the events in order, and searchingly discuss every detail is the duty of the author of a history. [32] But to pursue brevity of speech and to avoid lengthy explanations is allowed one who makes an abridgment. [33] Here then we will begin the narration for this is enough by way of a preface. It is foolish to make a long prologue and have a short story.

3 When the holy city was at peace and the laws as yet were obeyed, because of the holiness of Onias the high priest and the hatred he had of evil, [2] it happened that even the kings and rulers themselves esteemed the place worthy of the highest honor and glorified the temple with very great gifts. [3] Even Seleucus, King of Asia, paid out of his own revenues all the expenses connected with observing the sacrifices.

[4] Simon, of the tribe of Benjamin, who had been appointed manager of the temple, opposed the high priest because of differences over the city markets. [5] When he could not win over Onias, he went to Apollonius of Tarsus, who at that time was governor of Coelesyria and Phoenicia, [6] and reported to him that the treasury in Jerusalem was full of untold sums of money, and that the common store was infinite, and that these did not belong to the sacrificial account, but that it was possible to bring them under the king's control.

[7] Apollonius told the king about this money. The king sent Heliodorus, who was in charge of his affairs, with the commission to bring him these monies. [8] So Heliodorus immediately set out on his journey, under

the guise of visiting the cities of Coelesyria and Phoenicia, when actually he was fulfilling the king's order.

9 When he came to Jerusalem and had been courteously received in the city by the high priest, he told him what information had been given concerning the money. He declared this was the reason for which he came and asked if these things were true. 10 The high priest told him that there were sums deposited to provide for widows and orphans. 11 He also stated that the remainder that the impious Simon had spoken about belonged to Hyrcanus, son of Tobias, a man of great dignity; and that this amounted to four hundred talents of silver and two hundred of gold. 12 He said that he could not alienate these trusts[a] which had been left in the care of the holy place and temple which is honored throughout the whole world. 13 But Heliodorus, by reason of the orders he had received from the king, said that he had no choice but to take the money to the king. 14 So he set a day and entered the treasury to make an accounting.

The people throughout the city were upset. 15 The priests prostrated themselves before the altar in their priestly vestments and called upon him in heaven, who had given the law concerning trusts, that he would preserve them safe for those who had deposited them. 16 It was obvious that the high priest was sick at heart, for his face and his color showed the inward sorrow of his soul. 17 Also his body shook with grief and horror, and those who saw him knew what sorrow he had in his heart. 18 Others hurried from their homes, praying and making public prayer because the holy place was being profaned. 19 The women, with sackcloth tied below their breasts, gathered in the streets. And the virgins also, who were in their homes, came forward, some to Onias, some to the walls, while others peered out of windows. 20 All of them stretched their hands towards heaven in prayer. 21 The groaning of the people and the agony of the high priest should have moved anyone to pity. 22 They fervently called upon Almighty God to keep the things entrusted to them safe and secure for those who had given them.

23 Heliodorus began to do that which he had decided and went with his guard to the treasury. 24 Then, the Spirit of the Almighty God gave so great an evidence of his presence, that all who were under the orders of Heliodorus fell down with weakness and fear because of the power of God. 25 For there appeared to them a horse with a frightening rider, which was covered in very rich ornaments and the rider in armor of gold. The horse reared fiercely and struck Heliodorus with his front hooves. 26 At the same time, there appeared two young men, handsome, strong, bright and glorious, in beautiful dress, who stood on either side of him and scourged him many times without stopping. 27 Heliodorus quickly fell to the ground and he was unconscious when they picked him up. Having put him on a litter, they carried him out. 28 He who came with many servants and all his guard into the treasury was now carried out, and no one was able to help him because of the great power of God which was shown. 29 Indeed, because of God's intervention, he lay speechless and without hope of recovery. 30 The people praised the Lord because he had glorified his sanctuary, and the temple, which a short time before was full of fear and trouble, was filled with joy and gladness after God's might appeared.

31 Because he was dying, some of the friends of Heliodorus begged Onias to call upon the Most High to grant him his life. 32 So the high priest, considering that the king might perhaps suspect that some foul play had been done to Heliodorus by the Jews, offered a sacrifice for his recovery. 33 While the high priest was praying, the same young men dressed in the same clothing, appeared to Heliodorus and said to him, "Give thanks to Onias the priest, because for his sake the Lord has spared your life. 34 And you, having been scourged by God, should declare to all men the great works and power of God." Having said this, they vanished.

35 Heliodorus, after he had offered sacrifice to God and made great vows to him

---

a This is the root of present-day *waqb*, or religious trusts.

who had granted him life, and after giving thanks to Onias, took his troops and returned to the king. [36] He testified to all men the works of the great God, which he had seen with his own eyes. [37] When the king asked Heliodorus who might be suitable to send once more to Jerusalem, he replied, [38] "If you have any enemy or traitor in your country, send him there, and you shall have him returned to you scourged, if he should escape at all, for there is undoubtedly a certain power of God in that place. [39] For he who has his dwelling in heaven is the guardian and protector of that place, and he strikes and destroys those who come with bad intentions." This is what happened to Heliodorus and how the treasury was saved.

4 Simon, already mentioned, who had betrayed his country over the money, maligned Onias, blaming him for what happened to Heliodorus, as if he had caused the trouble. [2] He even dared to brand Onias a traitor to the Jews, despite the fact he was the protector of the city and defender of the nation, as well as a man zealous for God's law. [3] The enmity got to such a point that murders were even committed by some of Simon's friends.

[4] Onias, realizing the danger of this rivalry, and that Apollonius, son of Menestheus, governor of Coelesyria and Phoenicia, was encouraging Simon in his hatred, went to the king, [5] not to be an accuser of any countryman, but with the common good of all the people in mind. [6] He saw that, without the king's intervention, conditions were going to go from bad to worse, because Simon would not give up his folly.

[7] When Seleucus died, Antiochus, who was called the Illustrious,[a] had succeeded to the throne. Jason, the brother of Onias, ambitiously sought the high priesthood, [8] and went to the king, promising him three hundred and sixty talents of silver and, out of other revenues, eighty talents. [9] Besides this, he promised a hundred and fifty more also,[b] if he was granted a license to set up

a gymnasium and youth center, and enroll the men of Jerusalem as citizens of Antioch. [10] When the king approved and he consolidated his rule, Jason immediately began to force the Greek lifestyle on his countrymen. [11] He nullified those royal concessions to the Jews, granted by John, the father of Eupolemus, who had gone to Rome as ambassador to make a treaty of peace and alliance. He destroyed the lawful habits of the citizens and brought in fashions that were perverse. [12] He went so far as to build a gymnasium below the citadel and to make the noblest youths wear the petasos.[c] [13] Jason had sought other ways to introduce foreign and pagan customs because he was a man of abominable and unimagined evil, who lacked every virtue to be a true high priest. [14] Inasmuch as the priests were not now occupied about the duties of the altar, despising the temple and neglecting the sacrifices, they hastened to take part in the unlawful games whenever the call for the discus sounded. [15] Looking down on the values esteemed by their fathers, they held Grecian customs in the highest regard. [16] But those very values which they desired so earnestly and the people they imitated were to prove their enemies and murderers. [17] For contempt for the laws of God does not pass unpunished, a fact which time was to prove.

[18] Now when the quadrennial games were held at Tyre, in the king's presence, [19] the evil Jason sent renegades from Jerusalem to carry three hundred drachmas of silver for the sacrifice to Hercules; but the bearers thought it best not to use it for the sacrifices because it was not needed, but to use it for something else. [20] Although the money was intended by Jason for the sacrifice to Hercules, the messengers contributed it to the construction of a galley.

[21] When Apollonius, the son of Menestheus, went to Egypt as ambassador for the coronation of King Philometor,[d] he learned that Antiochus was no longer held in favor. With his own best interests in mind, he then departed and went to Joppa, and from there

---

a Also Antiochus Epiphanes and Antiochus IV.   b This total of 590 talents equalled approximately a half million dollars.   c A type of Greek hat. It indicates an attempt to supplant Jewish life with Greek customs. d Also, Ptolemy VI.

to Jerusalem, ²² where he was received in a magnificent manner by Jason and the people who welcomed him with torchlights and shouts of praise. From there, he returned with his army to Phoenicia.

²³ Three years later Jason sent Menelaus, brother of the previously mentioned Simon, to carry money to the king and to bring answers from him concerning certain important affairs. ²⁴ He, being thus recommended to the king, exaggerated his own authority and obtained the high priesthood for himself by offering three hundred talents of silver more than Jason paid.

²⁵ Having received the king's authorization, he returned home, bringing nothing worthy of the high priesthood, possessing only the mind of a cruel tyrant and the rage of a savage beast. ²⁶ Then Jason, who had undermined his own brother, being undermined himself, fled as a fugitive into the land of Ammon.

²⁷ Menelaus obtained the leadership but typically he withheld the money he had promised the king, ignoring Sostratus when the governor of the citadel called for it. ²⁸ It was the responsibility of Sostratus to collect taxes. So both men were summoned to the king. ²⁹ Menelaus left his brother Lysimachus, as deputy high priest, and Sostratus left Crates, commander of the Cypriots, to take his place.

³⁰ Meanwhile, a revolt broke out in Tarsus and Mallus because these areas had been given as a present to Antiochis, the king's concubine. ³¹ The king, therefore, went immediately to settle the problem, leaving Andronicus, one of his nobles, as his deputy.

³² Thinking it opportune, Menelaus presented Andronicus with some gold vessels he had stolen from the temple. He also sold others in Tyre and surrounding cities. ³³ When Onias became aware of these acts, he publicly exposed him, but did so from the safety of Daphne near Antioch. ³⁴ Therefore Menelaus, taking Andronicus aside, urged him to kill Onias. Andronicus went to Onias and offered him his right hand as a pledge of friendship (although Onias had some suspicions), and thus persuaded him to leave the sanctuary, whereupon he killed him without any regard to justice. ³⁵ For this reason, not only the Jews but also the other nations were angry and very saddened for the unjust murder of so great a man. ³⁶ When the king returned from Cilicia, the Jews and even the Greeks at Antioch went to him complaining of the unjust murder of Onias. ³⁷ Antiochus therefore was sad because of Onias and, being moved to pity, shed tears, remembering the sobriety and modesty of the dead man. ³⁸ Being also angered, he commanded that Andronicus should be stripped of his purple and led through the city to the very place where he had killed Onias, and there the impious and contemptible man should be put to death, the Lord repaying him with the punishment he deserved.

³⁹ When many sacrileges had been committed in the temple by Lysimachus with the consent of Menelaus, and the report of them spread abroad, the populace turned against Lysimachus, because a large quantity of gold had already been stolen. ⁴⁰ Filled with anger, the people revolted. Lysimachus armed about three thousand men and with Auranus as captain, a man far gone both in age and in madness, began to use violence. ⁴¹ When the Jews saw what Lysimachus was doing, some picked up stones, some strong clubs and some threw ashes at Lysimachus ⁴² and his men. As a result some were wounded, some fell to the ground, but all were put to flight; as for the temple robber himself, he was killed outside the treasury.

⁴³ Charges were filed against Menelaus. ⁴⁴ When the king came to Tyre, three men were sent by the elders to plead their cause. ⁴⁵ Menelaus, already defeated, promised Ptolemy a large bribe if he would persuade the king to favor him. ⁴⁶ So Ptolemy went to the king and took him aside in a colonnade as if for refreshment and caused him to change his mind. ⁴⁷ So Menelaus who was guilty of all the evil was acquitted by the king of the accusations; and those poor men, who, even if they had pleaded their cause before Scythians would have been judged innocent, were condemned to death. ⁴⁸ Thus those who argued the cause for the city, for the people and for the sacred vessels suffered unjust punishment. ⁴⁹ Even the Tyrians were indignant over the deed

and buried them with pomp. [50] So through the covetousness of those in power, Menelaus continued in authority, increasing his evils and betraying the citizens.

5 At this time Antiochus prepared for a second expedition against Egypt. [2] It happened that through the whole city of Jerusalem for forty days, golden clad horsemen were seen charging through the air, armed with lances like bands of soldiers. [3] And cavalry in ranks, attacking and counterattacking, brandishing shields, and a multitude of men in helmets, with drawn swords, throwing spears, and the glitter of golden armor and harnesses of all sorts. [4] Therefore, all men prayed that the apparitions might be a good omen.

[5] Now when a false rumor had gone out that Antiochus was dead, Jason, taking with him no less than a thousand men, suddenly assaulted the city, and though the citizens defended the wall, the city was finally taken and Menelaus took refuge in the citadel. [6] Jason killed his countrymen without mercy, not considering that success against one's own kindred is a great disaster, but imagining that they were enemies and not citizens whom he conquered. [7] He did not gain control of the government but in the end obtained disgrace as the reward for his treachery and was forced to flee again into the country of the Ammonites.

[8] His end was like his life. Pursued by Aretas, King of the Arabians, fleeing from city to city, hated by all men as a miserable betrayer of the law, looked upon as an enemy to his own country and countrymen, he was driven into Egypt. [9] He, who had exiled many of his own countrymen, died in a strange land, for he had gone to Lacedemonia hoping that kinsmen there would give him refuge. [10] So he who had thrown many out to lie unburied, was himself cast out unlamented and without funeral rites, neither having foreign burial nor a place in the tomb of his fathers.

[11] Now when the news of all this reached the king, he suspected that the Jews would break their alliance; whereupon, he left Egypt in a furious state of mind, and

took the city with the force of his army. [12] He commanded the soldiers to kill everyone they met and even to pursue people in the houses and kill them. [13] Thus young and old were slaughtered; women and children, virgins and infants were killed. [14] Within three days, eighty thousand were made victims, forty thousand killed and as many sold into slavery.

[15] But this was not enough. He dared even to enter the temple, the most holy in all the world, with Menelaus, a traitor to the laws and his country, as his guide. [16] Taking in his wicked hands the holy vessels which were given by other kings and cities for the ornament and the glory of the place, he unworthily handled and profaned them. [17] Thus Antiochus, confused in his pride, did not realize that his success was due to the fact that God was angry for a time because of the sins of the inhabitants of the city, and, therefore, God permitted this contempt for the holy place. [18] If the Jews had not been involved in many sins, this man, as soon as he had come, would have been scourged for his presumption and turned back as was Heliodorus when he was sent by King Selecus to rob the treasury. [19] But God did not choose the nation for the sake of the holy place, but the holy place for the sake of the nation. [20] Therefore, the place itself suffered the evils inflicted on the people, just as afterwards it participated in their good fortune. As it was forsaken in the wrath of Almighty God, so will it be exalted again with great glory, when the great Lord shall be reconciled.

[21] After Antiochus had taken one thousand eight hundred talents[a] from the temple, he hurried back to Antioch, believing in his arrogance that he might sail on the land and walk on the sea, so proud was he. [22] He left also governors to afflict the people: at Jerusalem, Philip, a Phrygian by birth, by nature more barbarous than the one who appointed him; [23] and in Gazarim, Andronicus; and Menelaus, who lorded it over his own people even more than the others.

[24] To appease his hatred of the Jews,

---

a Almost a million and a half dollars.

Antiochus sent that spiteful captain, Apollonius, with an army of twenty-two thousand men, commanding him to kill all grown men and sell the women and children. 25 When he came to Jerusalem, under the pretense of peace, he rested until the holy day of the sabbath, then with the Jews observing the holiday, he ordered his men to arms. 26 He killed all who had come to watch them, and dashing through the city with his armed men, he destroyed a very great multitude.

27 Judas Maccabeus with nine others[b] escaped into the wilderness and lived there with his companions as wild beasts in the mountains. They ate nothing but wild plants to avoid defilement.

6 Not long afterwards, the king sent a certain old man of Antioch to compel the Jews to depart from the laws of their fathers and of God, 2 and to defile the temple in Jerusalem and to call it the temple of Jupiter Olympius, and to name the one in Gazarim, Jupiter Hospitalis,[a] as did those who lived there. 3 This invasion of evil was very bad and upsetting to everyone. 4 For the temple was full of debauchery and revellings by the Gentiles, with men lying with lewd women. And women came of their own accord into the holy places, and brought in things that were unclean. 5 The altar also was filled with unclean things, which were strictly forbidden. 6 Neither were the sabbaths kept, nor the solemn days of the ancestors observed, neither did any man openly profess himself to be a Jew. 7 They were forced to attend the pagan sacrifice on the king's birthday; and when the feast of Dionysus was observed, they were made to wear crowns of ivy in honor of Dionysus.[b]

8 At the suggestion of Ptolemy, a decree was sent to neighboring Greek cities that they should act in like manner against the Jews, obliging them to sacrifice, 9 and whoever would not conform to Gentile customs should be put to death. Their misery was obvious. 10 For example, two women were accused of having circumcised their children. They were dragged through the city with their infants in their arms and thrown headlong from the walls. 11 Others who met secretly in nearby caves to keep the sabbath day were betrayed to Philip and were burned together because they refused to make resistance because of the religious observance of the day.

12 Now, I urge those who read this book not to be shocked at these calamities, but to consider the things that happened, not as being for the destruction, but for the correction of our nation. 13 For it is a token of great goodness when sinners are not allowed to proceed in their ways for a long time, but are immediately punished. 14 For in the case of other nations the Lord waits patiently to judge them so that their punishment will be based on the full measure of their sins. 15 But he does not deal so with us, preferring to take his vengeance before our sins reach their height. 16 Therefore he never withdraws his mercy from us. Although he chastises his people with adversity, he never leaves them. 17 But let these few words be sufficient warning to the readers. And now we must go on with the story.

18 Eleazar, one of the chief scribes, a man advanced in years and handsome in appearance, was being forced to open his mouth to eat pork. 19 But he, preferring a most worthy death to a hateful life, went voluntarily to be tortured. 20 He acted as a man should, patiently bearing his wrongs, determined not to do anything unlawful even if it would cost his life. 21 Old friends who stood by, being moved with pity for the man, urged him to bring his own lawful meat to eat and give the appearance that he was eating the sacrificial meat. 22 In this way he might be saved from death, so much did they regard their old friendship with the man. 23 But he decided otherwise after considering his age and his worthy years, the grey hairs which he had reached with honor, his good life even from his childhood. So he answered immediately from a conscience in tune with God that they should send him into another world. 24 "It is unseemly to pretend at my age," he said,

---

b Presumably including his father and brothers.   6a Jupiter, the Friend of Strangers.   b The purpose
was to Hellenize Judea and destroy Judaism.

"or to give young people the idea that Eleazar, at the age of ninety, has yielded to an alien religion [25] lest, through my pretense to gain a few more days of life, I should deceive them, and thus defile and disgrace my old age. [26] For even if I should escape the present punishments of men, whether I live or die, I shall not escape the hand of the Almighty.[c] [27] Therefore, by giving up my life as a man, I show myself worthy of my old age, [28] and I shall leave to the young an example of bravery and how to die an honorable death willingly and with backbone for the revered and holy laws." And having spoken thus, he was immediately taken to be executed.

[29] Those who had just acted kindly suddenly changed because of what he had said, thinking he was utterly mad. [30] When he was about to die from the blows, he moaned and said, "O Lord, who knows all things, you are aware I could have saved my life but instead suffer this agonizing pain; you also know I am happy to suffer these things because I reverence you." [31] Thus did this man die, leaving not only to the young men, but also the entire nation a memorial of virtue and strength.

7 It also happened that seven brothers, together with their mother, were arrested and tortured by the king with whips and scourges in order to make them violate the law by eating pork. [2] One of them, the eldest, said, "What would you ask or learn of us? We are ready to die rather than to sin against God's laws which we received from our fathers." [3] The angry king became enraged and ordered that pans and caldrons be heated. After they were heated, [4] he ordered the tongue of the spokesman be cut out, that he be scalped and have his hands and feet cut off, while the rest of his brothers and his mother watched. [5] When he was completely helpless, the king commanded that while still alive he should be brought to the fire and be fried in the pan. As he was suffering long torments from this, the rest, together with the mother, exhorted one another to die bravely, [6] saying, "The Lord God is watching over us and in truth will take compassion on us, as Moses declared in the hymn which he sang before the people, 'And on his servants he will take compassion.' "

[7] So when the first brother died in this way, they brought forward the second to continue their cruel sport. When they had scalped him, they asked him if he would eat pork before he was tortured limb by limb. [8] He replied, "No!" in Hebrew. Therefore, he underwent the same torments as his brother, [9] and when he was gasping his last, he said, "You blasphemer. You send us from this present life, but the King of the universe will raise us up, to the resurrection of eternal life[a] because we have died for his laws."

[10] After him the third was sent to the same torture, and when he was ordered, he quickly put forth his tongue and courageously stretched out his hands, [11] and said with boldness, "I received these hands from heaven, but for the law of God I willingly give them up, because I hope to receive them again from him." [12] The king and those that were with him marveled at the young man's courage, because he regarded his torments as nothing.

[13] After he was dead, they tortured the fourth in the same way. [14] When he was near death, he spoke, "It is better to die at the hands of men while keeping the hope that God will raise him up again. But for you, there will be no resurrection to life!"

[15] When they brought the fifth son, they molested him as well. But he, looking at the king, [16] said, "Because you have power among men, even though you are only mortal, you do what you will, but do not think that our nation is forsaken by God. [17] Wait patiently for a time and you will see how his great power will torment you and your children."

[18] After him they brought the sixth, and he, being ready to die, declared, "Do not deceive yourself for no reason, for we suffer these things by our own choice because we have sinned against our God. Marvelous things are done to us. [19] But do not think that you will escape unpunished, since you have chosen to fight against God."

---

c A belief in final judgment.   7a An important text because it shows Jewish belief in Resurrection.

20 The mother was particularly admirable and worthy to be remembered by good men. Although she saw her seven sons killed in the space of one day, she bore it with great courage because of her trust in God. With great wisdom, she bravely exhorted each of them in Hebrew. Joining a man's courage to a woman's insight, 22 she said to them, "I do not know how you were formed in my womb; for I neither gave you breath, nor soul, nor life, neither did I create the limbs of any one of you. 23 But the Creator of the world, who planned the beginning of man and conceived the origin of us all, will in his mercy restore both breath and life to you again, since you forget yourselves for the sake of his laws."

24 Antiochus was suspicious at her tone of voice and thought she was mocking him. The youngest brother was still alive, so Antiochus appealed to him by words, and assured him with an oath that he would make him a rich and happy man, if he would desert the laws of his fathers. He said he would make him his friend and give him all kinds of presents. 25 But when the young man was not moved by these offers, the king called the mother, and counselled her to persuade the youth to save his life. 26 After he had argued with her for a long time, she said that she would try to persuade her son. 27 So bending over him, she ignored the cruel tyrant and said in her own language, "My son, have pity upon me, I carried you nine months in my womb, nursed you three years, nourished you, and raised you to this age. 28 I beseech you, my son, look upon heaven and earth and all that is in them, and remember that God made them out of nothing, and mankind as well. 29 So do not fear this torture, but be worthy of your brothers. Accept death so that I may get you back again with your brothers."

30 While she was still speaking, the young man said to his tormentors, "What are you waiting for? I will not obey the commandment of the king but only the commandment of the law which was given to us by Moses. 31 And you Antiochus who have been the author of all evil against the Hebrews, you will not escape the hand of God. 32 We are suffering for our own sins. 33 And if the Lord our God is angry with us for a little while, for our own chastisement and correction, yet he will be reconciled again to his servants. 34 But you, O wicked and most unmerciful of all men, do not be elated in vain, because you are able to torture his servants, 35 for you have not escaped the judgment of the almighty God who sees all things. 36 For my brothers, having undergone a short pain, will now receive eternal life. But you by the judgment of God shall receive just punishment for your pride. 37 But I, like my brothers, offer my body and my life for the laws of our fathers, calling upon God to show quick mercy to our country, and that you by your own torments and pains may confess that he alone is God. 38 Perhaps through the sacrifice of my brothers and myself, the just wrath of God against our nation shall cease." 39 The king then being incensed with anger, raged against him more cruelly than all the rest, being gravely offended that he was ridiculed. 40 So the youth died in his purity, trusting wholly in the Lord.

41 Last of all, after her sons, the mother was put to death. 42 But this is enough, then, of the pollution of sacrifices and of the excessive cruelties.

8 Judas Maccabeus and those that were with him went secretly through the towns, calling together their kinsmen and friends and enlisting those who continued in the Jewish faith. They assembled six thousand men. 2 They called upon the Lord to look down upon his people who were oppressed by all and to have pity on the temple, profaned by the wicked men, 3 and to have mercy also upon the city that was being destroyed and that was about to be leveled, and to hear the voice of the blood that cried to him; 4 and to remember also the unjustified deaths of innocent children, and the blasphemies offered against his name, and to show his indignation for these ills. 5 When Maccabeus had gathered his army, the pagans could not stand against him, because the former wrath of the Lord was turned into mercy. 6 So taking the towns and cities by surprise, he set them on fire. He captured the most strategic places and made no small slaughter of the enemy.

7 He found it advantageous to strike by night, and reports of his valor went abroad everywhere.

8 When Philip saw that the man gained ground little by little and that things for the most part succeeded well for him, he wrote to Ptolemy, the governor of Coelesyria and Phoenicia, to send aid to the king's garrisons. 9 Immediately, he sent Nicanor, the son of Patroclus, one of his special friends, giving him no fewer than twenty thousand armed men of different nations to wipe out the whole Jewish race, assigning to him Gorgias, a good soldier and one of great experience in matters of war. 10 Nicanor proposed to raise for the king the tribute of two thousand talents that was due the Romans by selling into slavery the captured Jews. 11 Therefore he at once sent invitations to dealers in the coastal cities for the purchase of the Jewish slaves, offering ninety slaves for one talent,[a] not imagining the vengeance of the Almighty which was to catch up to him.

12 When Judas discovered that Nicanor was invading, he told the Jews that were with him that the enemy was near. 13 Some of them, being afraid and distrusting the justice of God, ran away. 14 Others sold all their possessions and prayed to the Lord that he would save them from the wicked Nicanor, who had sold them before he even came near them; 15 if not for their own sakes, then for the sake of the covenant that he had made with their fathers, and for the sake of his holy and glorious name that was honored by them. 16 Maccabeus called together the seven thousand that were now with him, exhorted them not to be afraid of the enemy, nor to fear the many pagans who came wrongfully against them, but to fight bravely, 17 reminding them of the outrages done to the holy place and also the harm done to the city, which had been shamefully abused, besides their destroying ancestral customs. 18 "For they trust in their weapons and in their boldness," he said, "but we trust in the Almighty Lord who by a word can utterly destroy both those that fight against us and the whole world." 19 Moreover, he reminded them

also of the help their fathers had received from God; how under Sennacherib a hundred and eighty-five thousand had been destroyed. 20 He recalled the battle that they had fought against the Galatians in Babylonia, with only six thousand soldiers, who when their Macedonian allies were being halted, they alone killed a hundred and twenty thousand, because of the help they had from heaven, and for this they captured much booty. 21 The soldiers were greatly encouraged by these words and resolved even to die for their laws and country.

22 He appointed his brothers—Simon, Joseph and Jonathan—captains over three divisions of his army, giving each one fifteen hundred men. 23 After the holy book had been read to them by Esdras and he had given them "The help of God" as a watchword, he began battle with Nicanor, leading himself the first band, 24 and with the Almighty being their helper, they killed more than nine thousand men; and having wounded and disabled the greater part of Nicanor's army, the enemy were forced to flee. 25 They captured the money of those who came to buy them, and they pursued them on every side. 26 They had to call off the rout because it was approaching the sabbath; therefore, they did not continue their pursuit. 27 When they had gathered together the arms and the spoils of their enemy, they kept the sabbath, blessing the Lord who had saved them that day, and once again began to show his mercy to them. 28 After the sabbath they allotted some of the spoils to the crippled, and the orphans and widows. The rest they took for themselves and their servants. 29 When this was done they all made a common prayer, asking the merciful Lord to be fully reconciled to his servants. 30 In encounters with Timothy and Baccides, they killed more than twenty thousand opponents. They made themselves masters of the high strongholds, and they divided much spoils, giving equal portions to the feeble, the fatherless and the widows, yes, and to the aged also. 31 When they had carefully gathered together the enemy arms, they stored them in convenient places, and the rest of

---

[a] Approximately $725.

their riches they carried to Jerusalem. 32 They also killed Philarches, who was with Timothy, a wicked man, who had in many ways afflicted the Jews. 33 When they celebrated the victory in Jerusalem, they burned Callisthenes, who had set fire to the holy gates, and who had taken refuge in a certain house, thus rewarding him for his impieties.

34 But as for that most wicked man Nicanor, who had brought a thousand merchants to buy the Jews, 35 being conquered through the help of the Lord, laying aside his brilliant uniform, he fled through the midland country and arrived alone at Antioch, bereft by the destruction of his army. 36 Thus he who had promised to raise the tribute for Rome by means of the Jewish captives, now proclaimed that the Jews had God for their protector and therefore they could not be harmed, because they followed the laws appointed by him.

9 At that time, Antiochus had been badly defeated in Persia. 2 He had entered a city called Persepolis and attempted to rob the temple and to bring the city under his domination. However, the inhabitants armed themselves and put the invaders to flight. So Antiochus having been routed, fled in disgrace.

3 When he arrived at Ecbatana, he received the news of what had happened to Nicanor and Timothy. 4 Becoming angry, he decided to make the Jews pay for the humiliation he had already suffered. Therefore he commanded his charioteer to drive without stopping on his journey. But the judgment of heaven was his companion, because in his vanity he had said, "When I get to Jerusalem, I will make it a cemetery for the Jews."

5 The Lord, the God of Israel, who sees all things, struck him with an incurable and an invisible disease. For as soon as he had stopped speaking, a dreadful pain in his stomach came on him and his intestines twisted in pain. 6 A very just retribution, indeed, considering he had tortured the bowels of others with many and new torments. However, this did not end his spite. 7 Since he was filled with pride, he breathed fire in his rage against the Jews, and com-

manded the march to be speeded. It happened as he was hastening on that he was thrown from the chariot, with the result that he was bruised all over his body. 8 Thus he who thought he could command even the waves of the sea in his unnatural insolence, and to weigh high mountains on a scale, was thrown to the ground and carried in a litter, a silent witness to God's manifest power. 9 Maggots swarmed out of the body of this man, and while he still lived in grief and pain, his flesh rotted away, and the stench of his decay made his army sick. 10 No one could stand to bear the litter of this man who thought only a little while earlier that he could touch the stars of heaven.

11 Thus it was, that being humbled in his great pride and being warned by God's curse, he began to come to know himself, for his agony grew by the minute. 12 When he himself could no longer stand his own stench, he said, "It is fitting to be subject to God and no mortal man should make himself like God." 13 Then this wicked man vowed to the Lord, who no longer showed him mercy, 14 that the city to which he was hurrying in order to level it to the ground and to make it a common burying place, he now wished to make free; 15 and the Jews, including their children, whom he said were not worthy to be buried, but only to have their bodies thrown out to be picked over by beasts, he now promised to make equal with the Athenians. 16 The holy temple which he had previously despoiled, he promised to adorn with fine gifts and to donate holy vessels, and he himself would pay the costs of the sacrifices. 17 He even said that he would become a Jew himself, and would go through every place on earth and declare the power of God.

18 But his agony continued (for the just judgment of God had come upon him), so despairing of his life he wrote in the manner of a prayer, a letter to the Jews in these words:

19 "To his very good subjects the Jews, Antiochus, king and ruler, wishes much health, welfare and happiness. 20 If you and your children are well, and if all matters go well with you as you desire, we give very great thanks. 21 As for me, being infirm, but

yet kindly remembering you, returning from the regions of Persia, I became seriously ill and think it necessary to provide for the common good. 22 Not that I despair of my health since I have every expectation to shake off my illness. 23 But recalling that my father, when he led an army into the upper provinces, appointed a successor, 24 with the understanding that if anything contrary to expectation should happen, or any bad news should come, those throughout the realm would not worry about to whom the government was entrusted. 25 Moreover, being aware that the rulers along our borders watch for opportunities and wait to see what happens, I have appointed my son Antiochus king, whom I often recommended to many of you when I went into the upper provinces. I have written to him what I have written here. 26 I urge and beg you, therefore, to recall the public and private favors given you, and to continue to be faithful to me and to my son. 27 For I hope that he will behave with moderation and humanity, and following my intentions, will be gracious to you."

28 So the murderer and blasphemer, so terribly afflicted, much as he had made others suffer, died a miserable death in a strange country among the mountains. 29 Philip, who had grown to manhood with him, carried his body home. Then, fearing the son of Antiochus, he went to Egypt to Ptolemy Philometor.

10 Maccabeus and those that were with him, by the protection of the Lord, recovered the temple and the city again. They tore down the altars which the pagans had set up in the streets and also the temples of the idols. 3 Having purified the temple, they made another altar. Making new fire from flint, they offered sacrifices after a couple of years, burning incense, lighting the lamps and setting out the bread of the Presence. 4 When they had done these things, they fell prostrate to the ground and asked the Lord that they might not fall into any more evils such as before; but if they should at any time sin, that they might be chastised by him more gently, and not be

delivered up to barbarians and blasphemous men. 5 Upon the same day that the temple had been polluted by the strangers, the very same day it was cleansed again, that is, on the twenty-fifth day of the month of Chislev.

6 They celebrated it for eight days with joy, after the manner of the Feast of Tabernacles, remembering how not long before they had kept the Feast of Tabernacles when they were in the mountains in caves like wild beasts. 7 Therefore, they now carried boughs and green branches and palms to honor him who had given them good success in cleansing his holy place. 8 They decreed by public edict and vote that the entire Jewish nation should observe these days every year. 9 Thus was the end of Antiochus, who was called the Illustrious.[a]

10 We will now relate the deeds of Eupator,[b] son of the wicked Antiochus, condensing the account of the calamities that happened in the wars. 11 When he succeeded to the throne, he appointed Lysias, general of the army of Phoenicia and Syria, to govern his kingdom. 12 Ptolemy, who was called Macron, was determined to be fair to the Jews, especially because of the wrong that had been done to them, and to deal with them peacefully. 13 The king's friends accused him to Eupator for his moderation. He was called traitor on every side because he had left his command on Cyprus which Philometor had entrusted to him, and had gone over to Antiochus the Illustrious. Since he had no support, he committed suicide by taking poison.

14 Gorgias, who succeeded to command, using mercenaries,[c] continued fighting the Jews. 15 The Idumeans who controlled fortified strongholds welcomed renegade Jews and pressed the war. 16 Maccabeus and his troops, seeking the Lord's help through prayer, made a strong attack upon the fortresses of the Idumeans, 17 and assaulting them with great power, captured the fortresses, killed all whom they met, altogether no less than twenty thousand. 18 Since some of the enemy had fled into very strong towers with plentiful provisions to sustain a siege,

---

a Epiphanes.   b Antiochus Eupator.   c Philistines.

19 Maccabeus left Simon and Joseph and Zacchaeus, and those who were with them in sufficient number to besiege them; and he departed to more important expeditions. 20 Some of those who were with Simon, being moved by greed, accepted a bribe from some in the towers, and receiving seventy thousand drachmas,d let some of them escape. 21 When Maccabeus heard what had happened, he assembled the leaders of the people and accused those men who had betrayed their brothers for money by letting their enemies escape. 22 He put these traitors to death and quickly captured the two towers. 23 Having success in arms and in all things he undertook, he killed more than twenty thousand in the two fortresses.

24 Timothy, who previously had been defeated by the Jews, mustered a large army of mercenaries and assembled cavalry from Asia. He invaded as though he would take Judea by storm. 25 But Maccabeus and those with him prayed to the Lord as he drew near, sprinkling dust on their heads and wearing sackcloth. 26 They prostrated themselves at the foot of the altar and asked God to be merciful to them, and to be an enemy to their enemies, an adversary to their adversaries, as the law says. 27 So after prayer, they took up their arms, marched from the city until they came into the vicinity of their enemies, where they made camp. 28 As soon as the sun came up, the two forces joined battle; one army having not only its valor but its confidence in the Lord as guarantee for victory and success, while the other made rage its leader in the battle. 29 When they were in the heat of the engagement, there appeared to the enemy at the head of the Jews five men from heaven on horses, brilliant with golden bridles. 30 Two of them protected Maccabeus between them, covered him on every side with their arms and kept him safe. They fired darts and fireballs against the enemy, so that they fell down, being both confounded with blindness and filled with confusion. 31 Twenty thousand five hundred troops and six hundred horsemen were killed. 32 Timothy fled to Gazara, a stronghold, where Chaereas was governor.

33 Maccabeus and his army eagerly laid siege to the fortress for four days. 34 Those who were inside, trusting to the strength of the place, blasphemed exceedingly and uttered abominable words. 35 When the fifth day came, twenty young men who were with Maccabeus, inflamed in their minds because of the blasphemy, bravely approached the wall and pushing forward with fierce courage, breeched it. 36 Moreover, others getting up on it after them, set fire to the towers and the gates in order to burn the blasphemers alive. 37 Having pillaged and sacked the fortress for two days, they killed Timothy, who was found hidden in a secret place. They also killed his brother Chaereas, and Apollophanes. 38 When this was done, they blessed the Lord with hymns and thanksgiving, who had done great things in Israel and given them the victory.

11 A short time after this Lysias, the king's regent and cousin, who was in charge of the government, being greatly displeased with what had happened, 2 gathered together eighty thousand men and all the cavalry and came against the Jews, hoping to take the city and make it a home for the Greeks. 3 He intended to tax the temple, as he did the other temples of the Greeks and to put the high priesthood up for bids every year; 4 he did not consider the power of God, but was proud and trusted in the numbers of his foot soldiers and the thousands of his horsemen and his eighty elephants.

5 He came into Judea and approaching Beth-zur, which was in a narrow place twenty miles from Jerusalem, he began to lay siege to that fortress. 6 When Maccabeus and his army learned that the fortresses were under attack, they and all the people with lamentations and tears asked the Lord to send a good angel to save Israel. 7 Maccabeus himself was the first to take up arms, and he urged the others to risk themselves with him in order to help their brothers. 8 When they were moving forward, there appeared in front of them while still near Jerusalem a horseman in white cloth-

---

d $7,000.

ing and golden armor, brandishing a spear. [9] Together they blessed the merciful Lord, and took great courage, and were determined to break through not only the men but also the fiercest beasts and walls of iron. [10] So they went on bravely, having a helper from heaven in the Lord who showed them mercy. [11] They leaped like lions upon the enemy, killing eleven thousand infantry and sixteen hundred cavalrymen. [12] The rest escaped, many wounded and naked. Even Lysias himself fled shamefully away and escaped.

[13] Lysias was not stupid, so realizing the loss he had suffered and seeing that the Hebrews could not be overcome because they relied upon the help of the almighty God, he sent peace feelers to them, [14] promising that he would agree to just terms and that he would persuade the king to be their friend. [15] Maccabeus, considering the welfare of his people, consented to the request of Lysias. The king in turn consented to all the conditions laid down in behalf of the Jews.

[16] The letter written to the Jews by Lysias went like this: "Lysias to the people of the Jews, greetings. [17] John and Absalom, who were sent by you have delivered your terms and requested that I would grant those things which they asked. [18] Therefore, I have reported all that is pertinent to the king, and he has granted as much as he could. [19] If, therefore, you will remain loyal to him, I will endeavor to help you from now on. [20] As concerning other particulars, I have given verbal orders that these and my emissaries should talk with you. [21] Farewell. Given in the year one hundred and forty-eight,[a] the twenty-fourth day of the month of Dioscorin."

[22] The king's letter contained these words: "King Antiochus to his brother Lysias, greetings. [23] Now that our father is dead, we desire that those in our realm should live quietly, and apply themselves diligently to their own affairs. [24] We understand that the Jews would not accept the Greek customs of my father, but prefer to keep their own ways, and that they request us to allow them to live according to their own laws. [25] Since we desire that this nation also should be at peace, we have ordained and decreed that the temple should be restored to them and that they may live according to the custom of their fathers. [26] You shall do well, therefore, to write to them and grant them peace, so that our pleasure being known, they may rest easy and take care of their own business."

[27] The king's letter to the Jews was like this: "King Antiochus to the senate of the Jews, and to the people of the Jews, greetings. [28] We hope you are well. We ourselves are well. [29] Menelaus came to us saying that you wished to return home and care for your affairs. [30] We therefore grant a safe conduct to all who go home by the thirtieth day of the month of Xanthicus. [31] We also decree that the Jews may use their own foods and follow their own laws as previously, and that none of them shall be molested in any way for things which have been done in ignorance. [32] We have sent also Menelaus to speak to you. [33] Farewell. In the year one hundred and forty-eight, the fifteenth day of the month of Xanthicus."

[34] The Romans also sent them a letter to this effect: "Quintus Memmius, and Titus Manius, ambassadors of the Romans, to the people of the Jews, greetings. [35] Whatever Lysias, the king's cousin, has granted you, we also grant. [36] But regarding such things as he thought should be referred to the king, after you have carefully conferred among yourselves, send someone at once so that we may decree what is befitting you. We are going to Antioch. [37] Therefore, write back immediately that we may know what you are thinking. [38] Farewell. In the year one hundred and forty-eight, the fifteenth day of the month of Xanthicus."

12 When these agreements were made, Lysias returned to the king and the Jews gave themselves to farming. [2] However, some of the governors, namely, Timothy, Apollonius the son of Gennaeus, Hieronymus, Demophon, and Nicanor the governor of Cyprus, would not let them live quietly in peace.

---

a 164 B.C.

³ The men of Joppa also were guilty of this kind of wickedness: they invited the Jews who lived among them to go with their wives and children for a boat ride, which they provided, as though they had no enmity to them, and this was done by public vote. ⁴ They accepted, suspecting nothing because of the peace. When the boats were some distance from the shore, they drowned no less than two hundred of them. ⁵ As soon as Judas heard of this cruelty done to his countrymen, he assembled his men, and after calling upon God the just judge, ⁶ he attacked those murderers of his brethren, and set the port on fire in the night, burned the boats and killed with the sword those who escaped from the fire. ⁷ When he had done these things he departed, threatening to return again and destroy all the people of Joppa.

⁸ When he learned that the men of Jamnia also planned to exterminate the Jews who lived among them, ⁹ he went to Jamnia also at night, set the port and its ships on fire, so that the light of the blaze was seen in Jerusalem, two hundred and forty furlongsᵃ away.

¹⁰ When they had gone nine furlongsᵇ from there, and were marching towards Timotheus, five thousand footmen and five hundred horsemen of the Arabians attacked them. ¹¹ After a hard fight, by the help of God, they won a victory. The surviving Arabs asked Judas for peace, promising to give him pastures and to assist him in other ways. ¹² Judas, thinking that they might be useful indeed in many ways, promised them peace; and after having shaken hands, they departed to their tents.

¹³ He also laid siege to a certain strong city, called Caspin, surrounded by moats and walls, and inhabited by pagans of many nations. ¹⁴ Those who were in it, trusting in the strength of the walls and their supply of food, became careless and taunted Judas with mockery, blasphemies and unmentionable words. ¹⁵ Maccabeus calling upon the great Lord of the world, who without any rams or engines of war crumbled the walls of Jericho in the time of Joshua, fiercely assaulted the walls. ¹⁶ Having taken the city by the will of the Lord, he slaughtered an untold number, so that a lake nearby, two furlongs wide,ᶜ seemed to run over with the blood of those slain.

¹⁷ From there they marched seven hundred and fifty furlongsᵈ to Charax to the Jews who are called Toubiani. ¹⁸ But they did not find Timothy there, for he had left the area without doing anything, except leaving a very strong garrison in a certain fortress. ¹⁹ Dositheus and Sosipater, who were captains under Maccabeus, killed those that were left by Timothy in the fortress, to the number of ten thousand men.

²⁰ Maccabeus organized his six thousand men and made them into divisions. He hastened after Timothy, who had with him twelve thousand infantry and two thousand five hundred cavalry. ²¹ When Timothy learned of the coming of Judas, he sent the women and children and the baggage ahead of him into a fortress called Carnaim, which was impregnable and hard to attack, because of the narrowness of the approach. ²² When the first band of Judas came into sight, his enemies were struck with fear by the presence of God, who sees all things, and they were put to headlong flight so that they were often attacked by their own companions and wounded with their own swords. ²³ Judas went after them vigorously, punishing the sinners, of whom he killed thirty thousand men. ²⁴ Timothy himself was captured by the soldiers of Dositheus and Sosipater, and with many prayers he begged them to let him go alive, because he held the parents and brothers of many of the Jews, who if he died would also perish. ²⁵ When he had given his word that he would restore them according to his promise, they released him without harm, in order to save their brothers. ²⁶ Judas then went to Carnaim where he killed twenty-five thousand persons.

²⁷ After he had destroyed these and put the rest to flight, Judas led his army to Ephron, a fortified city, where many from various nations lived. Strong young men guarding the walls made a vigorous resis-

---

a Thirty miles.   b About a mile.   c About a quarter of a mile.   d Ninety-five miles.

tance; many engines of war and missiles were there. ²⁸ When they had invoked the Almighty, who with his power breaks the strength of enemies, they captured the city and killed twenty-five thousand of those who were inside.

²⁹ From there they journeyed to Scythopolis, which lies six hundred furlongs^e from Jerusalem. ³⁰ The Jews among the Scythopolitans testified that they were used kindly by them, and that even in the times of their adversity the people had treated them with humanity. ³¹ Judas thanked the people, exhorting them to continue to be friendly to his nation. They arrived back at Jerusalem, the feast of weeks being at hand.

³² After Pentecost they marched against Gorgias, the governor of Idumea. ³³ He came out with three thousand infantry and four hundred cavalry. ³⁴ When they began battle, it happened that a few of the Jews were killed. ³⁵ Dositheus, a valiant horseman of Bacenor's band, caught hold of Gorgias. He would have taken him alive when a certain horseman of the Thracians rushed on him and cut off his arm, and so Gorgias escaped to Marisa. ³⁶ Since Esdris and his men had fought a long time and were weary, Judas called upon the Lord to be their helper and leader of the battle. ³⁷ Then in Hebrew he raised the battle cry in hymns, putting the soldiers of Gorgias to flight.

³⁸ Judas assembled his army and went to the city of Adullam. Since it was the seventh day, they purified themselves according to custom and kept the sabbath at that place. ³⁹ The day following, Judas went with his men to remove the bodies of those who had been killed and to bury them with their relatives in the tombs of their fathers. ⁴⁰ They found under the tunics of the dead some of the sacred amulets of the idols of Jamnia, which the law forbids Jews to wear. It was obvious to all that this was why they were killed. ⁴¹ Then they all blessed the just judgment of the Lord, who reveals things that are hidden. ⁴² They began to pray asking the Lord that the sin which had been committed might be forgot-

ten. But the heroic Judas exhorted the people to keep themselves free from sin, since they saw with their own eyes what had happened to those who died because of their sins. ⁴³ Taking up a collection, he sent twelve thousand drachmas of silver to Jerusalem for sacrifice to be offered for the sins of the dead. In so doing he acted well and honorably concerning the resurrection. ⁴⁴ For if he had not expected that those who had fallen would rise again, it would have been superfluous and vain to pray for the dead. ⁴⁵ But he was considering that those who had died in holiness had great grace stored up for them. ⁴⁶ It is therefore a holy and wholesome thought to pray for the dead, that they may be loosed from sins.^f

13 In the year one hundred and forty-nine,^a Judas learned that Antiochus Eupator was marching with a great army on Judea. ² He had with him Lysias, the regent. Together they had an army of a hundred and ten thousand infantry, five thousand cavalry, twenty-two elephants, and three hundred chariots armed with scythes.

³ Menelaus also joined them, and with great hypocrisy urged on Antiochus, not for the welfare of his country but in hope that he would be appointed high priest. ⁴ The King of kings planted suspicion in the mind of Antiochus against the wicked man, and when Lysias suggested that he was the cause of all the evils, Antiochus commanded (as the custom is with them) that Menelaus should be apprehended and put to death in Beroea. ⁵ Now there was a tower fifty cubits^b high in that place, having all around it a heap of ashes, with sides inclined towards the ashes. ⁶ From there any man guilty of sacrilege is thrown down into the ashes to die. ⁷ By such a fate Menelaus, the impious lawbreaker, was put to death, without even burial in the earth. ⁸ It was very just for inasmuch as he had committed many sins against the altar of God, the fire and holy ashes, so was he condemned to die in ashes.

---

e Seventy miles.　　f 43–46. This is theologically one of the most important passages of Maccabees. It gives the clear belief in immortality and the value of prayer for the dead.　　13a 163 B.C.　　b About seventy feet.

⁹ The king, eaten up with anger, revealed himself to the Jews as even worse than his father. ¹⁰ When Judas understood this, he ordered the people to call upon the Lord day and night so he would help them now as he had always done, ¹¹ because they were afraid of being deprived of the law, their country and the holy temple, and not to let his people, only now recovering from past evils, to be again enslaved by blasphemous nations. ¹² When they had all joined in this prayer and had begged mercy of the Lord with weeping, fasting and prostrations, continually for three days, Judas exhorted them to stand ready. ¹³ He and the elders decided that before the king should be able to lead his army into Judea and make himself master of the city, that the Jews should engage the foreigners in battle, counting on the help of the Lord. ¹⁴ So committing all to God, the creator of the world, and having exhorted his people to fight bravely and to stand up even to death for the laws, the temple, the city, their country and its citizens, Judas placed his army around Modein. ¹⁵ He gave his soldiers the watchword, "Victory from God," and with selected and brave young men, he attacked the king's camp at night and killed two thousand men in the camp and the largest of the elephants with its driver. ¹⁶ Having created great fear and confusion in the enemy camp, they left with great success. ¹⁷ This all happened at dawn through the protection and help of the Lord.

¹⁸ The king, having tasted the daring of the Jews, attempted to take the fortresses by strategy. ¹⁹ He marched with his army to Beth-zur, a fortress of the Jews, but he was repulsed, defeated and lost his men. ²⁰ Now Judas sent supplies in to the defenders. ²¹ But Rhodocus, a Jewish soldier, betrayed the secrets to the enemy, so he was hunted down and taken to prison. ²² Again the king made a treaty with those who were in Beth-zur; he gave his right hand, took theirs and went away. He fought with Judas and was defeated. ²³ When the king learned that Philip, who had been left in charge of the government, had rebelled at Antioch, he was worried and sought terms with the

Jews. He yielded to their demands, agreed to all things that seemed reasonable, and being reconciled, offered sacrifice, honored the temple and left gifts. ²⁴ He embraced Maccabeus and appointed Hegemonides as governor from Ptolemais to the Gerar. ²⁵ Then he came to Ptolemais. The people of that city were very displeased with the treaty of the peace; they were so angry that they wanted to break its terms. ²⁶ However, Lysias went up the governor's platform, explained the reason and appeased the people. He then returned to Antioch. This is how the invasion of King Antiochus and his withdrawal took place.

14 Three years later, Judas and his men heard that Demetrius, son of Seleucus, had sailed into the port of Tripolis with a powerful army and navy. ² He made himself master of the country after killing Antiochus and his general Lysias. ³ Now Alcimus, who had been chief priest but had willfully defiled himself during the pagan occupation, seeing that there was no safety for him, nor access to the altar, ⁴ went to King Demetrius in the year one hundred and fifty,ᵃ presenting him with a crown of gold and a palm, and besides these some branches which belonged to the temple. And that day indeed he held his peace. ⁵ But finding an opportunity to further his mad design when he was summoned by Demetrius to a meeting and asked about the plans and intentions of the Jews, ⁶ he answered, "Those of the Jews who are called Hasideans, of whom Judas Maccabeus is leader, begin wars and raise rebellions and will not allow the country to be peaceful. ⁷ Even I am kept from my ancestors' glory (I mean of the high priesthood), and I have now come here— ⁸ first out of fidelity to the king's interests, but also in the second place to provide for the good of my countrymen. All our nation suffers much from the folly of those men. ⁹ Wherefore, O king, seeing you know all these things, be careful, I beg you, both for our country and our nation, according to your humanity which is known to all men. ¹⁰ As long as Judas lives, it is not possible that the state will be at

a 161 B.C.

peace."

11 When he had said all this, the rest of the king's friends, who were also enemies of Judas, aroused Demetrius against him. 12 Immediately the king sent Nicanor, who was the commander of the elephants, appointing him governor of Judea, 13 with orders to capture Judas himself and scatter all of those that were with him; and he was to make Alcimus the high priest of the great temple. 14 The Gentiles, who had fled from Judea before Judas, joined Nicanor in large numbers, thinking the miseries and calamities of the Jews would serve their own good.

15 When the Jews heard of Nicanor's coming, and that the nations were assembled against them, they put dust upon their heads and made prayers to him, who established his own people forever and who protected his share by showing his favor. 16 Then at the order of their leader, the Jews promptly moved out and went to the town of Dessau to meet them.

17 Simon, the brother of Judas, had begun battle with Nicanor, but was halted by the appearance of so many foes. 18 Nevertheless, Nicanor, hearing of the bravery of Judas' soldiers and the greatness of courage with which they fought for their country, was afraid to test the outcome by battle. 19 Wherefore he sent Posidonius, Theodotus and Mattathias ahead to offer and receive a pledge of friendship. 20 After a meeting was held, Judas told the army of the offer and the soldiers consented to the agreement. 21 So a day was chosen when the leaders might come together, and chairs were brought out and set in place. 22 Judas ordered his men to stand by at the ready in case some treachery of the enemy was planned. The conference went off without incident. 23 Nicanor remained in Jerusalem and did no wrong, dismissing the Gentiles who had joined them. 24 Judas remained close to Nicanor, who truly respected him. 25 He urged him to marry and raise a family. So Judas married, settled down and lived the communal life.

26 Alcimus, seeing the affection they had for one another, took his contract and went to Demetrius, complaining that Nicanor served foreign interests, and that he meant to make the traitor Judas his successor.

27 The king became angered and provoked by this man's wicked accusations, so he wrote to Nicanor saying that he was greatly displeased with the agreement of friendship and ordering him nevertheless immediately to send Maccabeus as a prisoner to Antioch. 28 When this message arrived, Nicanor was worried and was concerned that his agreement should be questioned when Judas had done him no wrong. 29 But because he could not oppose the king, he waited for an opportunity to comply with the orders. 30 When Maccabeus saw that Nicanor was not as friendly with him, and that when they met together as was their custom Nicanor was actually rude, he sensed that this changed behavior must come from no reason favorable to him, so he gathered together a few of his men and hid himself from Nicanor.

31 When Nicanor realized that Judas had read him correctly, he went to the great and holy temple and commanded the priests who were offering the customary sacrifices to hand Judas over to him. 32 When they swore to him that they did not know where Judas was, he stretched out his hand to the temple, 33 and swore this oath: "Unless you deliver Judas prisoner to me, I will level this temple to the ground, and will tear down the altar and will dedicate this temple to Dionysus." 34 After speaking these words, he left. The priests, raising their hands to heaven, called upon him who always defended their nation, speaking in this manner: 35 "You, O Lord of all things, who wants nothing, was pleased that the temple of your dwelling should be among us. 36 Therefore now, O Lord, holy of all holies, keep this house forever undefiled which only recently was purified."

37 Razis, one of the elders of Jerusalem, a man who loved the city, of good reputation and who because of his good will was called the father of the Jews, was denounced to Nicanor. 38 For a long time this man held firm in his purpose of keeping himself pure in the Jewish religion and was ready to give up both his body and life so that he might not defect from it. 39 So Nicanor, revealing his hatred for the Jews, sent five hundred soldiers to arrest him.

⁴⁰ He thought that by taking him into custody he would greatly harm the Jews. ⁴¹ Now as the crowd rushed his house to break open the door by setting fire to it, just as he was about to be captured, he killed himself with his sword, ⁴² choosing to die nobly rather than to fall into the hands of the wicked and to suffer abuses unworthy of his noble birth. ⁴³ But through haste he missed giving himself a fatal wound and with the crowd breaking down the doors, he ran boldly to the wall and bravely threw himself down upon the crowd, ⁴⁴ which jumped out of the way so that he landed on his neck. ⁴⁵ Still alive and with his mind being inflamed, he arose and though his blood spurted out and he was seriously injured, he ran through the crowd, ⁴⁶ and standing upon a steep rock, almost drained of blood, he tore out his entrails with both hands and threw them at the crowd, calling upon the Lord of life and spirit to give these back to him again; and so he died.

15 When Nicanor understood that Judas was in the vicinity of Samaria, he decided to fight him with violence on the sabbath day. ² The Jews who were compelled to follow him said, "Do not act so fiercely and barbarously, but respect this day for it is holy, and give reverence to him who beholds all things." ³ That wretch asked if there was a mighty One in heaven who had commanded that the sabbath day be kept. They replied, "It is the living Lord, the sovereign King, who commands the observance of the sabbath." ⁵ Then he said, "I am sovereign upon earth and I command you to take up arms and to do the king's business." Nevertheless he was not able to carry out his plan.

⁶ Nicanor, being filled with exceedingly great pride, thought he would erect a public monument to his victory over Judas. ⁷ But Maccabeus never lost his trust that God would help them. ⁸ He exhorted his people not to fear the attack of the Gentiles but to remember the help they had previously received from heaven, and now to hope for victory from the Almighty. ⁹ Speaking to them of the law and the prophets and finally recalling the battles they had fought before, he made them more optimistic. ¹⁰ Then after he had encouraged them, he showed them the treachery of the Gentiles and their broken oaths. ¹¹ He armed every one of them, not so much with the protection of a shield and spear, but with the inspiration of bold speech, and told them a dream worthy to be believed, whereby they all rejoiced.

¹² Now the vision was this: "Onias, who had been high priest, a good and virtuous man, modest in bearing, gentle in manner, graceful in speech, and who practiced virtue from his childhood, was praying with lifted hands in behalf of all Jews. ¹³ At that moment another man appeared, distinguished by age and glory, and surrounded with great beauty and majesty. ¹⁴ Then Onias spoke, saying 'This is a lover of his brothers and of the people of Israel, this is one who prays much for the people and for the holy city. It is Jeremiah, the prophet of God.' ¹⁵ Whereupon Jeremiah stretched forth his hand and gave Judas a sword of gold, saying, ¹⁶ 'Take this holy sword, a gift from God, with which you shall overthrow the enemies of my people Israel.' "

¹⁷ Thus being urged on by the words of Judas, which were timely and proper to stir up the courage and strengthen the hearts of the young men, they resolved to fight and to attack bravely so that valor might decide the outcome in which the holy city and the temple were in danger. ¹⁸ For their concern was not so much for their wives, children, brothers and kinsfolk, but their greatest and principal fear was for the inviolability of the temple. ¹⁹ Those who were in the city had great concern for those that were to engage in battle.

²⁰ Now when all were anticipating the coming decision and the enemy was at hand, and the army was set in formation, the elephants and horsemen arranged in strategic places, ²¹ Maccabeus, pondering the advancing army with its diversified armor and savage elephants, raised his hands to heaven and called upon the Lord, who works wonders and gives victory to those that are worthy, not according to the power of their arms, but according as he sees fit. ²² In his prayer he said, "You, O Lord, who did send your angel in the days of Hezekiah, king of Judah, killed a hundred and

eighty-five thousand of the army of Sennacherib. ²³ Send now also, O Lord of heaven, your good angel to us, for the fear and dread of the greatness of your arm, ²⁴ that those who come with blasphemy against your holy people may be stricken with fear." And thus he concluded his prayer.

²⁵ Nicanor and those that were with him advanced with trumpets and marching songs. ²⁶ Judas and his men met them, invoking God's help. ²⁷ So fighting with their hands while praying to the Lord with their hearts, they killed no less than thirty-five thousand, and were made happy by God's good grace.

²⁸ When the battle was over and they were returning with joy, they came upon Nicanor, dead in his armor. ²⁹ They shouted in exultation and blessed the Almighty in Hebrew.

³⁰ Judas, who was prepared in body and mind to die for his countrymen, ordered that Nicanor's head and arm be cut off and carried to Jerusalem. ³¹ When he arrived there, having called together his countrymen and the priests to the altar, he sent for those in the citadel also. ³² He showed them the head of Nicanor and his wicked arm, which he had raised in proud boasts against the holy house of the Almighty God. ³³ He commanded also that the tongue of the wicked Nicanor should be cut out and pieces fed to the birds, and that the hand of the wild man be hanged up near the temple. ³⁴ Then all blessed the Lord of heaven, saying, "Blessed is he who has kept his own place undefiled." ³⁵ He impaled Nicanor's head at the top of the citadel that it might be an evident and manifest sign of the help of God.

³⁶ They all ordained by public vote never to let this day pass without solemnity, ³⁷ but to celebrate the thirteenth day of the month which in Syrian is called Adar, the day before Mordecai's day.

³⁸ So this is how things turned out in relation to Nicanor, and from that time on the city has been in the possession of the Hebrews. So I will also make an end of my narration here. ³⁹ I hope I have related the facts as well as they deserve, for that was my purpose. If not, I must be pardoned. ⁴⁰ For just as it is tedious always to drink wine, or always water, but pleasant to vary our drink, so if the story is nicely written, it will fall pleasantly on the ears of the readers. And here will be the end.

Words to the Wise

This book is sometimes called the Wisdom of Solomon, although it was most probably written long after the demise of that famous Jewish king. While some scholars believe that the author was repeating the sayings of Solomon, others believe that the author merely identified himself with one who was his intellectual father.

Both Saints Paul and John draw heavily on this book for their own writings and thus it becomes a bridge between the Old and New Testaments. It is not a book that can be read as a story, as in the case of the Maccabees, for example, but one that is taken in sections and pondered upon.

While the aim of the author is to encourage his reader to seek wisdom which is the key to eternal life, he puts stress on individual responsibility in meeting the dilemma of life and death. The book is somewhat unusual in that it does not look on God solely as the harsh dispenser of justice, as is so common in Jewish tradition, but as One who is wise and just and who loves His creation.

Free will is stressed in Wisdom. Death came into the world because of the Devil, yet the evil one is limited in what he can do. Man chooses whether

he will serve God or the Devil, and thus in the end is master of his own soul. However, God's love for man sometimes brings punishment which is intended to win man back to God. While the author does not mention bodily resurrection, he does see man made in the image of God and therefore eternal.

Wisdom is an important book of the Bible because of the significant and important theology it contains. Although the aim of the author is practical—a love for wisdom which leads to God—the theological implications in what he writes and how he presents his arguments go deeply into the core of Christian belief.

WISDOM

1 LOVE JUSTICE, you rulers of the earth.
Think of the Lord with goodness, and
seek him with simplicity of heart; ² because
he is found by those who do not tempt him,
and he shows himself to those who have
faith in him. ³ Perverse thoughts separate
man from God; and his power when tested
reprimands the unwise. ⁴ Wisdom will not
enter into a wicked soul, nor dwell in a body
given to sin. ⁵ A holy and disciplined spirit
will flee from deceit, and will withdraw
from vain thoughts, and will depart when
sin enters.
⁶ The spirit of wisdom is benevolent,
and will not free the evil speaker from his
words. God is witness to his feelings, and
a true searcher of his heart, and hearer of
his tongue. ⁷ The spirit of the Lord has
filled the whole world, and he who holds all
things together knows what is said. ⁸ Therefore he who speaks unjust things cannot
escape notice; and justice, when it punishes,
will not pass him by. ⁹ Investigation will be
made into the thoughts of the ungodly; and
the sound of his words will arise to God to
convict him of his sins. ¹⁰ A jealous ear
hears all things, and the sound of gossip is
not unheard. ¹¹ Keep yourselves, therefore,
from gossiping, which profits nothing, and

restrain your tongue lest it detract, because
nothing hidden shall go unheard, and a lying tongue destroys the soul.
¹² Seek not death by the error of your
life, nor secure destruction by the works of
your hands. ¹³ God did not make death,
and he takes no pleasure in the destruction
of the living. ¹⁴ He created all things that
they might exist, and the creative forces of
the earth are good. There is no destructive
poison in them, nor in the kingdom of hell
upon earth, ¹⁵ for justice is everlasting.
¹⁶ But the wicked invite death by their
works and words, and considering it a
friend, have fallen away; they made a covenant with death because they are worthy to
belong to its party.

2 They reasoned irrationally, saying to
themselves: "Our life span is short and
sad, and there is no remedy when death
approaches, and neither has any man returned from Sheol. ² We are born by
chance, and after we are gone it is as if we
never existed; the breath in our nostrils is
smoke, and speech a spark kept alive by the
beating of our hearts, ³ which, when extin-
guished, leaves the body in ashes. Our spirit
dissolves into empty air and our life drifts

off as a dissolving cloud, dispersed as a mist dispelled by the sun. ⁴ In time even our name is forgotten and no man remembers our deeds. ⁵ For our days are but the passing of a shadow, and there is no return from our end. It is foreordained, and no man can come back. ⁶ Come, therefore, and let us enjoy the good things that exist and make use of creation as when we were young. ⁷ Let us take our fill of rare wines and rich perfumes, and let not the flower of time pass us by. ⁸ Let us crown ourselves with roses before they fade; let no meadow escape our joyous play. ⁹ Let none seek to avoid luxury; let us leave signs of joy everywhere; for this is our portion, and this our lot.

¹⁰ "Let us oppress the just poor man, and spare not the widow, nor honor the gray hairs of the aged. ¹¹ But let our might be right, for that which is feeble is useless. ¹² Let us, therefore, lie in wait for the just man because he is an embarrassment to us, he is contrary to our doings, and upbraids us for breaking the law, and reveals to others the sins of our way of life. ¹³ He boasts that he has the knowledge of God, and calls himself the son of God. ¹⁴ He has become a censor of our thoughts. ¹⁵ He is troublesome for us to even see; for his life is not like other men's, and his ways are very different. ¹⁶ We are regarded by him as insignificant, and he avoids our ways as dirty. He prefers the latter end of the just, and rejoices that he has God for his father. ¹⁷ Let us see then if his words are true, and let us prove what will happen to him in the end. ¹⁸ If he is the true son of God, God will defend him and will deliver him from the hands of his enemies. ¹⁹ Let us test him by indignities and tortures, that we may know his meekness and try his patience. ²⁰ Let us condemn him to a most shameful death, for, according to him, God will protect him."

²¹ In this manner did they reason, but were deceived, for their own evil blinded them. ²² They did not know the secret plan of God, nor did they hope for the balance of justice, nor esteem the reward for holy souls. ²³ For God created man to be incorruptible, and to the image of his own likeness he made him. ²⁴ But, by the envy of the devil, death came into the world, ²⁵ and those who serve him experience it.

3 But the souls of the just are in the hand of God, and no torment will ever touch them. ² In the sight of the foolish they seemed to die, and their departure was considered a misfortune, ³ and their going away from us to be their destruction. But they are at peace.

⁴ And though in the sight of men they suffered torments, their hope is full of immortality. ⁵ Afflicted in few things, in many they will be well rewarded, for God has tried them and found them worthy of himself. ⁶ As gold in the furnace he has proved them, and as a burnt sacrifice he has received them, and in time honor will be given to them. ⁷ The just will shine and will run like fire through stubble. ⁸ They will govern nations, and rule over people, and the Lord will reign forever. ⁹ Those who trust in him will understand the truth, and those who are faithful will live in him in love, for grace and peace are given to his elect.

¹⁰ But the wicked will be punished as they rightly deserve, because they ignored the just and have rebelled against the Lord. ¹¹ For he who rejects wisdom and instruction is unhappy. Their hope is in vain, and their labors without fruit, and their works unprofitable. ¹² Their wives are foolish and their children spoiled. ¹³ Their offspring is cursed. Happy is the barren woman who is undefiled, who has not entered a sinful relationship; she will be rewarded when God judges her. ¹⁴ Blessed too is the eunuch whose hands have done no wrong, who has thought no wicked things against God; for the precious gift of faith will be given to him, and a most acceptable place in the temple of the Lord. ¹⁵ For the fruit of good labors is famed, and the source of wisdom never fails. ¹⁶ But the children of adulterers will not come to perfection, and the offspring of an unlawful union will be rooted out. ¹⁷ If they live long, they will be regarded as nothing, and finally their old age will be without honor. ¹⁸ And if they die young, they will have no hope nor consolation in the day of judgment. ¹⁹ For the end of a wicked generation is terrible.

4 O how beautiful is the glory of a chaste generation, for the memorial of honor is immortality because it is known both by God and man. ² When it is present, men imitate it; and they desire it when it has gone: forever it marches, crowned in triumph, winning the reward of virtuous conflicts.

³ But the prolific brood of the ungodly will not thrive, and illegitimate cuttings will not take deep root, nor hold fast. ⁴ And if they put forth branches for a time, yet being not deeply rooted, they will be shaken by the wind, and by the force of winds they will be torn out. ⁵ The young branches will be broken off, and their fruit will be useless, sour to eat and unfit for anything. ⁶ For the children who are born of unlawful unions are witnesses of wickedness against their parents at their judgment.

⁷ But the just man, though he dies young, will be at rest. ⁸ Old age is not venerable because of time, nor counted by the number of years, ⁹ but the understanding of a man is grey hairs, and a spotless life is old age. ¹⁰ There was a man who pleased God and was loved by him, and while living among sinners was taken from the earth. ¹¹ He was taken away lest wickedness should alter his understanding, or deceit beguile his soul. ¹² For the fascination of vanity obscures good things, and roving desire perverts the innocent mind. ¹³ Being made perfect in a short space, he fulfilled long years. ¹⁴ His soul pleased God; therefore, he hastened to bring him out of the midst of iniquities. Yet the people saw this and did not understand, nor take such things to heart: ¹⁵ that the grace of God and his mercy are with his saints, and that he guards his elect.

¹⁶ The just who are dead condemn the wicked who are living, and youth quickly made perfect condemns the long life of the unjust. ¹⁷ They will see the end of the wise man, and will not understand what God has designed for him and why the Lord has kept him in safety. ¹⁸ They will see him, and will despise him, but the Lord will laugh them to scorn. ¹⁹ They will fall after this without honor and be a reproach among the dead forever; because he will burst their puffery and speechlessness, and will shake them from the foundations, and they will be utterly abandoned. They will be in sorrow, and their memory will perish. ²⁰ They will come with fear at the thought of their sins, and their iniquities will testify against them to convict them.

5 Then the just man will stand with great constancy against those who have afflicted him and those who make light of his labors. ² Those who see him will be troubled with a terrible fear, and will be amazed at the suddenness of his unexpected salvation. ³ They will speak to each other in repentance and groaning, in anguish of spirit saying, "This is the man we once held in derision and as an example of reproach. ⁴ We fools thought his life was madness and his end without honor. ⁵ Behold how he is numbered among the children of God, and his lot is among the saints. ⁶ It was we who strayed from the way of truth, and the light of justice has not shined on us. The sun of understanding has not risen upon us. ⁷ We filled ourselves with the path of iniquity and destruction, and have walked through difficult trails, but the way of the Lord we have not known. ⁸ What has pride profited us? Or what advantage has the boasting of riches brought us? ⁹ All those things have passed away like a shadow, and like a rumor that slips away. ¹⁰ As a ship that passes through the waves, which when it has gone, no trace can be found, nor the track of its keel in the waters; ¹¹ or as when a bird flies through the air, no track of its passage can be found, but only the sound of wings beating the light air and parting it by the force of its flight; it moved its wings and passed through, and there is no mark found afterwards of its path. ¹² Or as when an arrow is shot at a target, the divided air presently comes together again, so that no one knows its route; ¹³ so we also being born, soon ceased to be and have been able to show no mark of virtue, but are consumed by our wickedness."

¹⁴ Such things as these the sinners repeat in hell, for the hope of the wicked is as dust which is blown away before the wind, and as a thin frost which is dispersed by a storm, like smoke that is dissipated by the wind; ¹⁵ and it is forgotten like the

memory of a guest who stays but one day. 16 But the just will live for evermore; and their reward is with the Lord, and the care of them with the Most High. 17 Therefore, they will receive a kingdom of glory and a crown of beauty at the hand of the Lord; for with his right hand he will cover them, and with his holy arm he will defend them.

18 And his zeal will become his armor and he will arm creation for the revenge of his enemies. 19 He will put on justice as a breastplate and will make true judgment a helmet. 20 He will take holiness for an invincible shield, 21 and he will sharpen his stern wrath as a spear, and the whole world will fight with him against the unwise. 22 Shafts of lightning will go directly from the clouds; as from a bow well-bent, they will be shot out and will fly to the target. 23 And large hailstones will be cast upon them as from a catapult; the water of the sea will rage against them, and the rivers will flood in a torrent. 24 A mighty wind will rise against them, and as a whirlwind it will divide them; their iniquity will lay waste the earth, and wickedness will overthrow the thrones of the mighty.

6 Wisdom is better than strength, and a wise man is better than a strong man. 2 Hear therefore, you kings, and understand; learn, you who are judges to the ends of the earth. 3 Listen, you rulers of the people and those who please yourselves in multitudes of nations, 4 for power is given to you by the Lord, and strength by the Most High. He will examine your works, and search out your thoughts. 5 Because being ministers of his kingdom you have not judged rightly, nor kept the law of justice, nor walked according to the will of God, 6 he will come to you terribly and quickly, because severe judgment will occur for those who rule. 7 To him who is small, mercy is granted; but the mighty will be greatly tested. 8 For God will not exclude any man's person, neither will he stand in awe of any man's greatness; for he made the small and the great and takes equal care of all. 9 But a greater punishment is ready for the mightier. 10 To you, therefore, O kings, these are my words, that you may learn

wisdom and not depart from it. 11 For those who have kept just things justly, will be justified; and those who have learned these things will know what to answer.

12 Set your desire upon my words; love them and you will have instruction. 13 Wisdom is glorious and never fades away and is easily seen by those who love her, and is found by those who seek her. 14 She shows herself first to those who ardently desire her. 15 He who rises early to seek her will not find it hard, for he will find her sitting at his door. 16 To meditate upon her, therefore, is perfect understanding; and he who watches for her will quickly be secure. 17 For she goes about seeking those who are worthy of her, and she shows herself to them cheerfully in their paths and meets them in each thought. 18 For the beginning of wisdom is the most sincere desire for instruction. 19 And the concern of instruction is love; and love is the keeping of her laws; and the keeping of her laws is the firm foundation for immortality, 20 and immortality brings one near to God.

21 Therefore the desire of wisdom brings one to the everlasting kingdom. 22 If, then, your delight is in thrones and scepters, O you kings of the people, love wisdom that you may reign forever. 23 Love the light of wisdom, all who rule over peoples.

24 Now I shall tell what wisdom is and how she came to be, and I shall not hide from you the mysteries of God, but shall seek her out from the beginning of her birth, and bring the knowledge of her to light, and shall not pass over the truth. 25 Neither shall I travel with consuming envy, for envy does not partake of wisdom. 26 Now a host of wise men is the salvation of the whole world; and a wise king is the foundation of his people. 27 Receive, therefore, instruction by my words, and it will be profitable to you.

7 I also am mortal, like all men, and of the race of him who was first made of the earth; in the womb of my mother I was fashioned to be flesh. 2 In the time of ten months, I was alive with blood, fashioned from the seed of man and the pleasures of marriage. 3 And being born, I breathed the common air, and fell upon the common earth, the first sound I uttered was a common cry. ⁴ I was nursed with great care in swaddling clothes. ⁵ And no king had a beginning any different. ⁶ For all men have one entrance into life, and a common exit.

⁶ Therefore I prayed and understanding was given me; I called upon God, and the spirit of wisdom came upon me. ⁸ I preferred her to kingdoms and thrones, and esteemed riches as nothing in comparison to her. ⁹ Neither did I compare her to any precious stone, for all gold is a little sand in comparison to her, and silver in respect to her is counted as clay. ¹⁰ I loved her above health and beauty, and chose to have her instead of light; for her light cannot be put out. ¹¹ Now all good things came to me along with her, and innumerable riches through her hands, ¹² and I rejoiced in all these; for this wisdom went before me, and I did not know that she was the mother of them all. ¹³ I have learned without guile, communicate without envy, and do not hide her riches. ¹⁴ For she is an infinite treasure to men, who, if they use it, become the friends of God, being commended for the gift of discipline.

¹⁵ And God has given to me to speak as I would, and to conceive thoughts worthy of those things that are given me; because he is the guide of wisdom, and the director of the wise. ¹⁶ Both we and our words are in his hands, and all wisdom and the knowledge and skill in crafts. ¹⁷ For he has given me the true knowledge of the things that exist to know the disposition of the whole world and the activity of the elements, ¹⁸ the beginning, the end and the midst of the times, the movement of the heavens and the changes of seasons, ¹⁹ the cycles of the year and the ordering of the stars, ²⁰ the natures of living creatures and dispositions of wild beasts, the power of spirits and reasonings of men, the diversities of plants and the strengths of roots. ²¹ I have learned what is hidden and not foreseen; for wisdom, which is the worker of all things, taught me.

²² For in her is the spirit of understanding: holy, unique, many-faceted, subtle, eloquent, active, undefiled, sure, sweet, loving, good, quick, irresistible, beneficent, ²³ gentle, kind, steadfast, assured, secure, having all power, overseeing all things, and containing all spirits, intelligible, pure, perceptive. ²⁴ Wisdom is busier than all active things, and reaches everywhere by reason of her purity. ²⁵ For she is a breath of the power of God, and a certain pure revelation of the glory of the almighty God; and therefore nothing defiled comes into her. ²⁶ For she is the reflection of eternal light, and the unspotted mirror of God's majesty, and the image of his goodness.

²⁷ And being but one, she can do all things; always remaining herself the same, she renews all things; in every generation she transfers herself into holy souls, and makes them friends of God and prophets. ²⁸ For God loves no one as much as he who dwells with wisdom. ²⁹ For she is more beautiful than the sun, and above all the constellations of the stars; although compared to light, she is found superior. ³⁰ For light is succeeded by night but no evil can overcome wisdom.

8 She reaches mightily from one end of the earth to the other, and ordains all things well. ² I have loved her and have sought her out from my youth, and have desired to take her for my spouse, because I was a lover of her beauty. ³ She crowns her nobility by being conversant with God; yes, and the Lord of all things has loved her. ⁴ For it is she who teaches the knowledge of God and is the helper in his works. ⁵ And if riches are desired in life, what is richer than wisdom which is responsible for all things? ⁶ And if perception is effective, who accomplishes more than wisdom which designs what exists? ⁷ And if a man loves justice, her labors have great virtue; for she teaches temperance, prudence, justice and courage, which are the most valuable things men can have in life. ⁸ And if a man desires much knowledge, she knows things past and foretells what is to come; she knows the subtleties of speeches, and the solutions of arguments; she knows signs and wonders before they are done, and the outcome of times and ages. ⁹ I decided therefore to take her to live with me; knowing that she will communicate to me of her good things, and will be a comfort in my cares and grief. ¹⁰ For her sake I shall have glory among the multitude, and honor with the elders, though I am young. ¹¹ I shall be found to be adept in judgment, and shall be admired in the sight of the mighty, and the faces of princes will wonder at me. ¹² They will wait for me when I am silent, and they will look upon me when I speak, and if I talk much they will lay their hands on their mouths. ¹³ Because of her I shall have immortality, and shall leave behind me an everlasting memory for those who come after me. ¹⁴ I shall rule the people, and nations will be subject to me. ¹⁵ Awesome kings will fear when they hear my name; among the people I shall be found good and valiant in war. ¹⁶ When I go into my house, I shall repose with her; for her conversation has no bitterness, nor her company any monotony, but joy and gladness.

¹⁷ When I pondered these things and weighed them in my mind, that to be allied with wisdom is immortality, ¹⁸ and that there is great delight in her friendship and in the inexhaustible riches of the works of her hands, wisdom and glory in the communication of her words, I went about seeking how I might get her for myself. ¹⁹ I was a bright and blessed child. ²⁰ Since I was quite good, I came into an undefiled body. ²¹ And as I knew I could not otherwise possess wisdom except God gave this to me, this also became a point of wisdom: to know whose gift it was; so I went to the Lord, and besought him, and said with my whole heart:

9 "God of my fathers and Lord of mercy, who has made all things by your word, ² and by your wisdom has appointed man to have dominion over the creatures that you have made, ³ to rule the world in equity and justice, and render judgment with an upright heart, ⁴ give me the wisdom that sits by your throne, and do not reject me from among your children. ⁵ For I am your servant and the son of your handmaid, a weak man, short-lived, with little understanding of judgment and laws. ⁶ If one is perfect among the children of men, yet if your wisdom is not with him, he shall be regarded as nothing.

⁷ You have chosen me to be king of your people and a judge of your sons and daughters. ⁸ You have commanded me to build a temple on your holy mount, and an altar in the city of your dwelling place, a copy of your holy tabernacle which you had prepared from the beginning. ⁹ With you is wisdom, who knows your works, who also was present when you made the world and knew what was pleasant to your sight and what was right according to your commandments. ¹⁰ Send her forth from your holy heaven, and from the throne of your majesty, that she may be with me and may labor with me, that I may know what is acceptable to you. ¹¹ For she knows and understands all things and will guide me soberly in my deeds, and will guard me by her power. ¹² So will my works be acceptable, and I shall govern your people justly, and shall be worthy of the throne of my father.

¹³ For who is there among men who can know the counsel of God? Or who can discern what the will of God is? ¹⁴ For the thoughts of mortal men are fearful, and our counsels uncertain. ¹⁵ For the corruptible body is a weight upon the soul, and the earthly habitation presses down the mind that concerns itself with many things. ¹⁶ We can hardly guess at what is on earth, and with difficulty do we find the things that are before us. But the things that are in heaven, who will search them out? ¹⁷ And who will know your thoughts, except you give wisdom, and send your Holy Spirit from above? ¹⁸ In that manner the ways of those upon the earth may be corrected, and men may learn the things that please you. ¹⁹ For by wisdom they were healed, whosoever have pleased you, O Lord, from the beginning.

10 Wisdom protected the one first formed by God,ᵃ the father of the world, when he was created alone, ² and wisdom freed him from his sin, and gave him power to govern all things. ³ But when the unjust manᵇ went away from her in his anger, he perished by the rage in which he murdered his brother. ⁴ For whose cause,

---

a Adam.   b Cain.

when water destroyed the earth, wisdom healed it again, saving the just man[c] by a mere piece of wood.

⁵ Moreover when the nations conspired together in doing wickedness, she recognized the just man[d] and preserved him without blame before God, and kept him strong to face the compassion for his son. ⁶ She delivered the just man[e] who fled from the wicked who were perishing when the fire came down upon Pentapolis,[f] ⁷ where evidence of their wickedness remains desolate and smokes to this day, where trees bear fruit that do not ripen, and a pillar of salt stands as a monument to an unbelieving soul.[g] ⁸ For ignoring wisdom, not only did they fail to recognize good things, but they also left men a memorial of their folly, so that their shortcomings could never go unnoticed. ⁹ Yet wisdom rescued those who served her. ¹⁰ She guided the just man[h] when he fled from his brother's wrath through the right paths and showed him the kingdom of God, and gave him the knowledge of the holy things, made him honorable and accomplished in his works. ¹¹ In the deceit of those who overreached him, she stood by him and made him honorable. ¹² She kept him safe from his enemies, and she defended him from seducers, and in his difficult fight she gave him victory that he might know that wisdom is mightier than all.

¹³ She did not forsake the just man[i] when he was sold into captivity, but delivered him from sinners; she went down with him into the dungeon. ¹⁴ And she left him not alone in prison until she brought him the scepter of the kingdom, and authority over those who oppressed him; and revealed his accusers as liars and gave him everlasting glory.

¹⁵ She delivered the just people and blameless race from the nations that oppressed them. ¹⁶ She entered into the soul of the servant of God[j] and stood against dread kings with wonders and signs. ¹⁷ And she rendered to the just the wages of their labors and conducted them in a wonderful way; she was to them for a shelter by day and a starry beacon in the night. ¹⁸ She brought them through the Red Sea, and led them through great waters. ¹⁹ But their enemies she drowned in the sea and from the depth of the sea she cast them forth. Therefore the just took the spoils of the wicked. ²⁰ And they sang to your holy name, O Lord, and with one accord they praised your victorious hand. ²¹ For wisdom opened the mouth of the dumb and made the tongues of infants eloquent.

11 She prospered their works in the hands of the holy prophet. ² They went through uninhabited wildernesses and in desert places they pitched their tents. ³ They stood against their enemies and revenged themselves against their adversaries. ⁴ They were thirsty, and called upon you, and water was given to them out of the high rock, and a refreshment of their thirst out of the hard stone.

⁵ For by the very things by which their enemies were punished, when their drink failed them,[a] while the children of Israel found water in abundance and rejoiced, ⁶ they themselves benefitted in their need. ⁷ For instead of a fountain of an ever-running river, you gave blood to the unjust. ⁸ And while they were rebuked as an obvious proof for their murdering infants, you gave them abundant water unexpectedly, ⁹ showing them by their thirst how you exalted your own and did punish their enemies. ¹⁰ For when they were tried and chastised with mercy, they learned how the ungodly were judged in wrath and tormented. ¹¹ For you admonished and tested them as a father; but the others, as a severe king, you examined and condemned. ¹² For whether absent or present, they were alike distressed. ¹³ A double affliction came upon them, and a groaning for the remembrance of things past. ¹⁴ When they heard that by their punishments the righteous were benefitted, they remembered that the Lord ordained what had come to pass. ¹⁵ For he whom they scorned before had been cast out and left to perish, in the end they marveled at him, for their thirst was unlike that

---

c Noah.　　　　d Abraham.　　　　e Lot.　　　　f The Five Cities.　　　　g Lot's wife.　　　　h Jacob.　　　　i Joseph.
j Moses.　　　　11a The Egyptian plague of the Nile.

of the just.

16 But for the foolish thoughts of their iniquity, which falsely led them to worship dumb serpents[b] and worthless beasts, you sent upon them a multitude of irrational creatures to torment them, 17 that they might know that by what things a man sins by the same also he is punished. 18 For your almighty hand, which made a world of matter out of formlessness did not lack the means to send upon them a multitude of bears or fierce lions, 19 or unknown beasts of a new kind, full of rage, either breathing out a fiery breath, or belching forth an acrid smoke, or flashing terrible sparks from their eyes. 20 Not only could their injury harm men, but even the very sight might kill them through fear. 21 Yes, and without these, men might be killed by a single breath, persecuted by their own deeds and scattered by the breath of your power. But you have arranged all things in measure, number and weight.

22 Because great power always belonged to you alone, and who can resist the strength of your arm? 23 For the whole world before you is as the least grain that tips the scales, and as a drop of the morning dew that falls down upon the earth. 24 But you have mercy upon all, because you can do all things, and overlook the sins of men for the sake of repentance. 25 For you love all things that exist, and hate none of the things which you have made, for you would not fashion or make anything if you hated it. 26 And how could anything last if you had not wanted it; or how could it endure, if you had not called it forth? 27 But you spare all things because they are yours, O Lord, who loves souls.

12 O how good and sweet is your spirit, O Lord, in all things! 2 And therefore you chastise little by little those who err, and admonish them, and speak to them concerning the things wherein they offend, so that leaving their wickedness they may believe in you, O Lord. 3 For those ancient inhabitants[a] of your holy land, whom you did abhor, 4 because they did works hateful to you through their sorceries and wicked sacrifices, 5 and those merciless murderers of their own children, and their sacrificial feasting on human flesh and blood,[b] 6 and those parents sacrificing with their own hands helpless lives, you willed to destroy by the hands of our fathers, 7 that the land which of all is most dear to you might receive a worthy colony of the children of God. 8 Yet even these you spared, since they were only men, and sent wasps as forerunners of your army, to destroy them little by little.

9 Not that you were unable to bring the wicked under the just by war, or with one stern word or by cruel beasts to destroy them at once, 10 but judging them little by little you gave them the opportunity to repent, though you knew that they were a wicked generation, and their nature malicious, and that their thought could never be changed. 11 It was a cursed race from the beginning; and it was not because of fear for anyone that you give pardon to their sins. 12 For who will say to you: "What have you done?" Or who will withstand your judgment? Or who will come before you to be an avenger of wicked men? Or who will accuse you of the death of that which you have made? 13 For there is no other God but you, who has care of all, that you should show that you do not give judgment unjustly. 14 Neither can king or tyrant question you about those whom you have destroyed. 15 Because you are just, you order all things justly; deeming it foreign to your power to condemn him who does not deserve to be punished.

16 Your power is the beginning of justice; and because you are Lord of all, you make yourself gracious to all. 17 You show your power when men will not believe you to be absolute in power, and you reject the insolence of those who know you. 18 But you being master of power judge with tranquility; and with great generosity govern us; for your authority is at hand when you will it.

19 You have taught your people by such works that they must be just and humane,

---

b This is an anachronism.   a The Canaanites.
bals except in time of famine.

b There is no evidence that the Canaanites were canni-

and have made your children to be of good hope; because, in judging, you make room for repentance of sins. 20 For if after great deliberation you punished the enemies of your servants and those who deserve to die, giving them time and opportunity to repent of their wickedness, 21 with what strictness have you judged your own children to whose ancestors you have sworn and made covenants of good promises? 22 Therefore, whereas you chastise us, you give us a lesson when you scourge our enemies in moderation, so that when we judge we may think on your goodness; and when we are judged, we may hope for your mercy.

23 Wherefore, you have also greatly tormented those who by their own errors have lived foolishly and unjustly. 24 For they went far astray in the ways of error, regarding as gods the most worthless beasts which all but children would despise. 25 Therefore, as to senseless children, you have sent a judgment upon them to mock them. 26 But those who did not change their ways by admonitions experienced the worthy judgment of God. 27 For realizing that they suffered by those very things they took for gods, they became angry and were punished through them, thus they acknowledged as true God he who in times past they denied that they knew. Therefore the end also of their condemnation came upon them.

13 All men in whom there is no knowledge of God are foolish because they are unable from the good things that are seen to understand him who is. They do not acknowledge the workman although they observe his works, 2 but they have imagined, either the fire, or the wind, or the swift air, or the circle of the stars, or the great water, or the sun and moon to be the gods that rule the world. 3 If because of the beauty of these things men took them to be gods, let them know how much more beautiful is the Lord, their creator, for the author of all beauty made those things. 4 Or if they admired their power and their effects, let them understand from these how much more mighty is he who made them. 5 For from the greatness and beauty of created things, the creator of them may be seen and understood. 6 But yet these are

less to be blamed, for perhaps they erred while seeking God and desiring to find him. 7 For living among his works, they search and are persuaded that the good things are those which they see. 8 But they are not to be pardoned. 9 For if they were able to know so much as to make a judgment of the world, how did they fail to find more quickly the Lord of these things?

10 But with their hope rooted in the dead, unhappy are those who have called "gods" the works of the hands of men; gold and silver, made with skill, resembling animals, or useless stone, the work of an ancient hand. 11 A skilled woodcarver cuts down a tree suitable for the block he needs, and skillfully strips off all the bark, and by his art carefully forms a vessel useful in daily life 12 and uses the fallen chips to heat his food. 13 But a rejected piece, seemingly good for nothing, since it is crooked and full of knots, he carves at his leisure and by the skill of his art fashions it and makes it like the image of a man, 14 or to the likeness of some animal, laying it over with vermilion and painting it red, and covering every blemish that is in it. 15 And he makes a convenient place to put it, and sets it in a wall and fastens it with iron, 16 taking care lest it fall, knowing that it cannot help itself for it is an image and has need of aid. 17 He then makes prayer to it about his possessions, his children, or his marriage. And he is not ashamed to speak to that which has no life. 18 For health, he appeals to that which is weak; for life, he prays to that which is dead; and for help, he calls upon that which is helpless. 19 For a safe journey, he petitions that which cannot walk; and for earning, for working and for success in what he does, he asks of that which is unable to do anything for itself.

14 Again, another planning to sail and about to make a voyage over raging waves calls upon a piece of wood more frail than the wooden ship that carries him. 2 For it was the desire to earn that planned the vessel, and the workman built it by his knowledge. 3 But your providence, O Father, steers it; for you have made a path even in the sea, and a safe way among the waves, 4 showing that you are able to save

from danger, even though a man went to sea without skill. ⁵ But that the works of your wisdom might not be idle, therefore men also trust their lives even to a little wood, and passing over the sea by ship are brought to safe haven. ⁶ And from the beginning also when the proud giants perished, the hope of the world fled in a vessel which was governed by your hand, and left to the world the seed of succeeding generations.

⁷ For blessed is the wood by which justice comes. ⁸ The idol that is made by hands is cursed, as well as he who made it; he, because he made it, and it, because, being futile, is still called a god. ⁹ But to God the wicked doer and his wickedness are alike hateful. ¹⁰ For that which is made, together with him who made it, shall be punished. ¹¹ Therefore, no respect will be given even to the idols of the Gentiles; because the creatures of God are turned to an abomination, and a temptation to the souls of men, and a snare to the feet of the unwise.

¹² The beginning of fornication is the making of idols, and the invention of them is the corruption of life. ¹³ They did not exist from the beginning, nor will they exist forever. ¹⁴ By the vanity of men they came into the world, and therefore they will quickly come to an end.

¹⁵ For a father, being afflicted with bitter grief, made for himself the image of his son who had led a short life, and he who had died as a human began now to be worshiped as a god, and he devised for him rites and sacrifices among his servants. ¹⁶ Then in due time, the wicked custom prevailing, this error was made a law and statues were worshiped by the command of tyrants. ¹⁷ And those whom men could not honor in their presence because they lived far off, they brought in imagination from afar and made a visible image of the king whom they had a mind to recall; that in this manner they might honor the absent one as though present. ¹⁸ The great skill of the sculptor persuaded the ignorant to worship these kings. ¹⁹ For he, being willing to please his employer, labored with all his art to make the likeness as real as possible. ²⁰ And the masses, carried away by the beauty of the work, took now for a god he who a short time before was honored as a man. ²¹ And this was the occasion of deceiving mankind; for men, serving either their inclinations or their king, gave the sacred unshared name[a] to stone and wood.

²² It was not enough for them to err about the knowledge of God, but they live in great conflict due to ignorance and call such evils by the name of peace. ²³ For either they sacrifice their own children, or use secret mysteries, or keep frenzied carousals, ²⁴ so that now they neither keep their lives or their marriages pure, killing one another through envy or injuring another by adultery. ²⁵ All things are mingled together: blood, murder, theft and deceit, corruption and unfaithfulness, quarrels and lying, disturbance of the peace, ²⁶ forgetfulness of God, corruption of souls, unnatural vices, marriage perversions, adultery and sensuality. ²⁷ For the worship of despicable idols is the cause, the beginning and end of all evil. ²⁸ For the worshipers either are intoxicated with festivity, or prophesy lies, or live unjustly, or readily perjure themselves. ²⁹ For while they trust in lifeless idols, they swear falsely and expect no retribution.

³⁰ But for two things they will be justly punished: because they have not thought well of God, giving worship to idols, and because they have been guilty of perjuring while despising justice. ³¹ For it is not the power of the things by which men swear, but the just punishment of sinners, that always avenges the transgression of the unjust.

15 But you, our God, are kind, true, patient, and ruling all things in mercy. ² For even if we sin, we are still yours, aware of your greatness; and if we do not sin, we know you will make us your own. ³ For to know you is perfect justice, and to know your justice and your might is the root of eternal life.

⁴ For the fantasy of mischief makers has not deceived us, nor an unproductive portrait of a painted figure of various colors

---

a God (Yahweh).

5 whose appearance only excites fools so that they yearn for the lifeless presentation. 6 The lovers of evil things deserve no better things to trust in, that includes those who make them and those who love them and those who worship them.

7 The potter also, kneading clay with effort fashions each piece of pottery for our service, and from the same clay he makes both vessels that are for clean uses, and also those that serve to the contrary; but it is the potter who decides what his creations will be used for. 8 He can waste his time by making a useless god, such a man who only a short time before was earth himself and who shortly when his life ends returns to earth again. 9 But his concern is not that he works or that his life is short, but that he competes with the goldsmiths and silversmiths, or the fashioners of bronze, thinking it wonderful to make vain images. 10 His heart is ashes, and his hope like dirt, and his life more base than clay, 11 because he did not know his maker, or the one who gave him his inspiration, or who breathed into him a living soul. 12 Indeed, he thought life but a game, and existence but a quest for profit, and that to make money all is justified, even evil. 13 Yet this man, more than all others, knows that he sins when he makes brittle vessels and fragile gods of earthly clay.

14 How foolish are the enemies of your people who worship these idols, how unhappy, and how inordinately proud. 15 They have believed all their pagan idols to be gods, which neither have eyes to see, noses to breathe, ears to hear, fingers to touch, and as for their feet, they cannot walk. 16 Man made them; and he who owes his very breath to another who fashioned them. No man can make a god like himself. 17 Being mortal himself, he forms a dead thing with his impious hands. He is better than those whom he worships, because he indeed has life, even though temporary, but they never have. 18 Moreover, they worship even the vilest creatures, which are worse than all others because they lack sense. 19 Yes, even beauty escapes these beasts and no man desires them. But they have fled from the praise of God and from his blessing.

16 These men[a] were rightly punished by such creatures and were destroyed by a multitude of beasts.[b]

2 Instead of this punishment, you dealt well with your people, you answered their need for delicious food and sent quail as their meat, 3 so that those men, when they wanted food, by means of those things that were shown and sent among them, might loathe even that which was necessary to satisfy their appetite. While your people, after suffering want for a short time, tasted a new meat. 4 It was necessary that inevitable destruction should come upon those who exercised tyranny; but to yours it was merely shown how their enemies were destroyed.

5 When the rage of wild beasts came upon your people, they, on the other hand, were being destroyed by the bites of writhing serpents. 6 Your wrath endured not forever, but they were troubled for a short time as a warning, having a sign of salvation given them as a remembrance of the ordinances of your law. 7 He who turned towards it was not healed by that which he saw but by you, the Savior of all. 8 And in this you revealed to our enemies that you are the one who delivers all from evil. 9 For they were killed by the bites of locusts and flies.[c] There was no remedy to be found to save them because they deserved to be destroyed by such things. 10 But not even the teeth of venomous serpents overcame your children because your mercy came and healed them. 11 They were tested on how well they remembered your words, and were quickly healed, lest falling into deep forgetfulness, they might not be able to use your help.

12 For it was neither herb nor soothing poultice that healed them, but your word, O Lord, which heals all things. 13 It is you, O Lord, who have power of life and death, taking men to the gates of death and bringing them back again. 14 A man indeed kills through malice, but cannot bring back the departed spirit nor call back the soul that

---

a The Egyptians.   b Refers to the various plagues.   c Two more plagues of Egypt.

has passed beyond. [15] It is impossible to escape your hand.

[16] The wicked who denied knowing you were scourged by the strength of your arm, being persecuted by unusual floods, hail and rain[d] and consumed by fire. [17] And truly marvelous, in the water, which extinguishes all things, the fire had more effect, for the universe defends the just. [18] At one time the fire was banked so that the creatures which were sent against the ungodly might not be burned, that they might see and understand that they were persecuted by the judgment of God. [19] And at another time the fire, against the law of nature, burned in the midst of water to destroy the fruits of a wicked land.

[20] Instead of these things, you fed your people with the food of angels,[e] and gave them bread from heaven prepared without labor, having in it all that is delicious, with sweetness for every taste. [21] Your sustenance showed your sweetness to your children, and ministering to every man's choice, it was turned into what every man liked. [22] But snow and ice endured the power of fire without melting, so that they might know that fire burning in the hail and flashing in the rain destroyed the fruits of their enemies. [23] This same fire forgot its own strength so that the just might be nourished. [24] Creation serving you, the Creator, is made relentless against the unjust in order to give them their just due, yet relaxes for the benefit of those who trust in you.

[25] Therefore, even then it was changed into all things and was obedient to your grace that nourishes all, according to the wants of those who desired it of you, [26] that your children, O Lord, whom you love, might know that it is not the growing of fruits that nourish men, but your word that preserves those who believe in you. [27] What could not be destroyed by fire melted away after being warmed by a little sunbeam, [28] so that it might be known to all that we ought to arise before the sun to bless and adore you. [29] The hope of the unthankful man will melt away as the winter's ice and will run off as waste water.

17 Your judgments, O Lord, are great, and your words cannot be expressed; therefore misguided souls have erred. [2] While the wicked thought they could control the holy nation, they themselves were chained with the bonds of darkness and made prisoners of a long night,[a] exiled from eternal providence. [3] And while they thought to keep their secret sins concealed, hidden under a dark veil of forgetfulness, they were scattered, horribly afraid, and troubled with great astonishment. [4] Neither did the secret room that held them protect them from fear, for noises entering in troubled them and bitter visions frightened them. [5] No power of fire could give them light, nor could the bright flames of the stars enlighten that horrible night. [6] There appeared to them a sudden fire, very dreadful. Being struck with the fear of that face which was not seen, they thought the things which they saw to be worse, [7] and the delusions of their magic art were humbled and their vain wisdom was reproachfully rebuked. [8] Those who promised to drive away the fears and troubles of a sick soul were sick themselves of a fear worthy only to be laughed at. [9] Though no terrible thing provoked them, yet being frightened by the passing by of beasts and hissing of serpents, they died from fear, refusing to look in the air which it was impossible not to do. [10] Whereas wickedness is cowardly, it bears witness to its condemnation; for a troubled conscience[b] always forecasts hurtful things.

[11] Fear is nothing else but a surrender of the aids of reason. [12] And while there is less expectation of help from within, there is also greater ignorance of the cause which brings the torment. [13] During that night, in which nothing could be done, and which came upon them from the lowest and deepest hell, they all slept the same sleep, [14] sometimes molested with the fear of monsters, sometimes fainting away with imaginings when a sudden and unlooked for fear came upon them. [15] If any of them had fallen down, he was kept shut up in prison without bars. [16] If anyone were a farmer or a shepherd or a laborer in the field and were

---

d The seventh plague.   e Manna from heaven. mon word in the Old Testament.

17a The ninth plague.   b Conscience is not a com-

suddenly overwhelmed, he suffered a fate from which there was no escape. 17 They were all bound together with one chain of darkness. Whether it was a whistling wind, or the melodious voice of birds among the spreading branches of trees, or a waterfall tumbling down, 18 or the mighty noise of stones crashing, or the invisible sound of animals playing together, or the roar of wild beasts, or a rebounding echo from the highest mountains, these things made them faint with fear. 19 The whole world was illumined with a bright light, and none were hindered in their labors. 20 Over them alone was spread a deep night, an image of that darkness which was to come upon them. But more grievous than darkness were they to themselves.

18 For your holy ones, there was a very great light, and their enemies heard their voice clearly but did not see their shape. And they glorified you because they did not suffer the same things, 2 and those who before had been wronged gave thanks because they were not hurt now; they asked the gift of being different. 3 Therefore, they received a burning pillar of fire[a] for a guide to the way which they did not know, and you gave them a harmless sun for their celebrated wandering. 4 Their enemies were deemed worthy to be deprived of light and to be imprisoned in darkness, those who kept your chidren shut up, through whom the pure light of law was to be given to the world. 5 And when they decided to kill the babies of the just, one child being cast forth and saved to reprove them[b] you took away a multitude of their children and destroyed them all together in a mighty deluge. 6 For that night[c] was made known beforehand to our fathers, so that they might be reassured knowing in what oaths they had placed their trust. 7 So your people received the salvation of the just and destruction of the unjust. 8 As you punished their adversaries, so you also encouraged and glorified us. 9 In secret the just children of good men were offering sacrifice, and they unani-mously observed a law of justice in which the just received both good and evil alike, already singing the praises of the fathers.

10 But from their enemies there sounded an ominous cry, and a lamentable mourning was heard for their children. 11 The servant suffered the same punishment as the master, and a common man suffered as the king. 12 So all alike had innumerable dead, with one kind of death. Neither were the living sufficient to bury them; for in one moment their beloved children were destroyed. 13 Whereas they would not believe anything before by reason of the magic spell, upon the destruction of the firstborn, they acknowledged your people to be God's children. 14 While all things were in quiet silence and the night was in the midst of its course,[d] 15 your almighty word leapt down from heaven from your royal throne, as a fierce conqueror into the midst of the land of destruction, 16 carrying a sharp sword of your straightforward commandment, and stood and filled all things with death, and reached even to heaven while standing on earth. 17 Then suddenly visions in evil dreams troubled them, and unlooked-for fears came upon them. 18 And one thrown here and another there, half dead, showed the reason why death came. 19 The visions that troubled them foreshowed these things, lest they should perish and not know why they suffered these evils.

20 But even the just did not escape the assault of death, and there was a plague[e] among the multitude in the wilderness, but your wrath did not continue long. 21 A blameless man hurried to pray for the people, bringing forth the shield of his ministry, prayer and the supplication of incense. He withstood the wrath and put an end to the calamity, proving that he was your servant. 22 He overcame the disturbance, not by strength of body nor with force of arms, but with a word he subdued him that punished them, calling upon the oaths and covenant made with our fathers.[f] 23 When the dead had now fallen down in heaps, one upon another, he intervened and stayed the assault, and cut off its way to the living. 24 In

---

18a Ex. 14:24.   b Moses.   c Passover.   d Midnight, c.f. Ex. 11:4.   e Nm. 16: 25–34
f Gn. 15: 9–17

his priestly robe[g] was the whole world shown and in the four rows of the stones the glory of the fathers was engraved, and your majesty was written upon the diadem on his head. [25] To these the destroyer gave place and was afraid of them, for merely the test of wrath was enough.

19 There came upon the wicked wrath without mercy even to the end. God knew in advance what they would do. [2] When the Egyptians had given them permission to depart, and had sent them away with great care, they repented, and pursued them. [3] While they were still mourning and lamenting at the graves of their dead, they took up another foolish device and pursued those as fugitives whom they had urged to leave. [4] A fate which they deserved brought them to this end. They lost the remembrance of those things which had happened, that their punishment might fill up what was wanting in their torments, [5] and that your people might wonderfully pass through, but that they themselves might find a new death.

[6] Every creature according to its nature was fashioned again as from the beginning, obeying your commandments, that your children might be kept without harm. [7] A cloud overshadowed their camp and dry land appeared where water was before, a path through the Red Sea without hindrance, a grassy field out of the great deep, [8] through which the whole nation passed under the protection of your hand, beholding your miracles and wonders. [9] For they pastured like horses and skipped like lambs, praising you, O Lord, who had delivered them. [10] They remembered those things which had been done in the time of their exile, how the ground brought forth flies

instead of cattle, and how the river cast up a multitude of frogs instead of fishes.

[11] At length they saw a new kind of bird, when in their hunger they asked for tasty meats. [12] To satisfy their desire the quail came up to them from the sea. Punishments came upon the sinners, but not without prior signs in peals of thunder, for they suffered justly according to their own wickedness. [13] For they showed a more detestable inhospitality than any people. Others indeed refused to receive strangers unknown to them, but these made slaves of their guests who had served them well. [14] And not only so, but in another respect also they were worse; for the others against their will received the strangers. [15] But these grievously afflicted those whom they had received with joy, and who lived under the same laws. [16] But they were struck with blindness,[a] just as those at the door of the just man,[b] when they were covered with sudden darkness and every one sought the entrance to his own door. [17] For the elements are changed in themselves, as in a musical instrument the note changes the rhythm yet all keep the same sound. This may clearly be perceived by the sight of what happened.

[18] For land animals were turned into water creatures, and the creatures that swim now walked upon the land. [19] Fire even in water kept its normal action, and the water forgot its quenching nature. [20] On the contrary, the flames did not burn the flesh of corruptible animals walking among them, neither did they melt that good food which was as fragile as ice. For in all things you have magnified your people, O Lord, and honored them, and did not despise them, but assisted them at all times, and in every place.

---

g Ex. 28: 4.   19a The punishment of the men of Edom and Sodom.   b Lot.

Ecclesiasticus, or The Wisdom of Jesus the Son of Sirach, is one of the Wisdom books and in the past has simply been referred to as the Book of Sirach. The canonicity of the book was accepted by the Jews of Alexandria and the Christian Church and its text

The Sayings of a Wise Man

has been discovered in the manuscripts of Qumran and Masada. The Essenes supported its canonicity while the Pharisees denied it.

The author's name was Joshua (Hebrew Yesua, Greek Iesous) who was the son of Eleazar, son of Sira; thus in Hebrew fashion he is called Ben Sirach. From the prologue the book was written about 132 B.C.

The book is divided into three sections. In the first wisdom is considered in its relationship to God and how this affects human conduct. The second part is praise for the Fathers of Old and deals with salvation history. The appendix deals with a prayer and hymn of thanksgiving.

The book is rich in wise counsels and much good advice, but the author observes that most older men know these things through experience, while most young are unwilling to accept them, for they must yet learn from their failures.

ECCLESIASTICUS

Translator's Prologue

The knowledge of many great things has been given to us through the law, the prophets and others who followed them; for which things Israel is to be commended for instruction and wisdom, because not only those who read must need to be skillful, but strangers also, both speaking and writing, may by their means become most learned. My grandfather, Jesus, after he had greatly given himself to a diligent reading of the law, the prophets and other books that were delivered to us from our fathers, decided also to write something himself pertaining to instruction and wisdom, that those who are desirous to learn, and are made knowledgeable in these things, may be more and more attentive in mind and be strengthened to live according to the law. I urge you therefore to come with good will and to read with attention, and to pardon us for those things wherein we may seem, while we follow the image of wisdom, to come short in the composition of words; for the Hebrew words have not the same sense in them when translated into another tongue. And not only this work, but even the law itself, the prophecies and the rest of the books differ not a little as expressed in their own language. I came to Egypt in the thirty-eighth year of the reign of Ptolemy Euergetes and stayed for a considerable period. I came across some books there of great learning and wisdom. Therefore, I thought it good and useful for me to devote some effort to translate this book. So with much reading and study over a long time, I finally brought the work to an end, and published it for the service of those who are willing to apply their minds to learn how they ought to conduct themselves, and who intend to lead their lives according to the law of the Lord.

Eulogy of wisdom

1 All wisdom comes from the Lord God and is with him before all time, until eternity. 2 Who has numbered the sands of the sea, the drops of rain and the days of the world? Who has measured the height of heaven, the breadth of the earth and the depth of the abyss? 3 Who has searched out the wisdom of God that goes before all things?

4 Wisdom was created before all things, and prudent understanding from eternity. 5 The word of God on high is the fountain of wisdom, and her ways are everlasting

commandments. 6 To whom has the root of wisdom been revealed, and who has known her wise counsels? 7 To whom has the instruction of wisdom been revealed and made manifest? And who has understood the multiplicity of her ways? 8 There is one most high Creator, Almighty, a powerful King, greatly to be feared, who sits upon his throne and is the God of all authority. 9 He created her in the Holy Spirit, and saw her, numbered her and measured her. 10 And he poured her out upon all flesh as his gift, and has given her to those who love him.

Fear of God

11 The fear of the Lord is honor, glory, gladness and a crown of joy. 12 The fear of the Lord delights the heart and gives joy, gladness and long life. 13 With him who fears the Lord, it will go well in the end and on the day of his death he will be blessed. 14 The love of God is worthy wisdom. 15 And they to whom she reveals herself love her by sight and by the knowledge of her great works. 16 The fear of the Lord is the beginning of wisdom; she is instilled in the faithful in the womb; she walks with chosen women and is known to the just and faithful. 17 The fear of the Lord is the sacredness of knowledge. 18 Piety will keep and justify the heart, it will give joy and gladness. 19 It will go well with him who fears the Lord and in his last days he will be blessed. 20 To fear God is the fullness of wisdom and she satisfies us with her fruits. 21 She will fill all her house with her development, and the storehouses with her treasures. 22 The fear of the Lord is a crown of wisdom, making peace and salvation to flourish. 23 He has seen and taken an account of her, but both are the gifts of God. 24 Wisdom will distribute knowledge and understanding of prudence; she exalts the glory of those who respect her. 25 The root of wisdom is to fear the Lord; and the branches of it are long-lived. 26 In the treasures of wisdom is understanding and sacredness of knowledge, yet to sinners wisdom is an abomination. 27 The fear of the Lord drives out sin. 28 He who is without fear cannot be justified for the anger of his high spirits is his ruin. 29 A patient man will endure for a time, and afterwards joy will be restored to him. 30 A good under-

standing will hide his words for a time, and the lips of many will declare his wisdom. 31 In the treasures of wisdom are important rules, 32 but the worship of God is an abomination to a sinner.

33 Son, if you desire wisdom, keep justice, and God will give her to you. 34 For the fear of the Lord is wisdom and instruction, and that which is agreeable to him 35 is faith and meekness, and he will fill up his treasures. 36 Do not ignore the fear of the Lord and come not to him with a divided mind. 37 Do not be a hypocrite in the sight of men and do not let your lips be a stumbling block to you. 38 Watch over them, lest you fall and bring dishonor upon your soul. 39 God will reveal your secrets and cast you down in the midst of the congregation, 40 because you came to the Lord wickedly, and your heart was full of guile and deceit.

In time of trouble

2 Son, when you come to the service of God, stand in justice and in fear and prepare your soul for temptation. 2 Humble your heart and be steadfast; give heed and receive the words of understanding and make not haste in the time of trouble. 3 Wait on God with patience; join yourself to God and be faithful that you may be honored at the end of your life. 4 Accept whatever comes your way and be patient in your sorrow and when you are humbled. 5 For gold and silver are tried in the fire, but acceptable men in the furnace of humiliation.

6 Believe God and he will strengthen you and direct your way. Trust in him. Be reverent to him and grow old in his ways. 7 You who fear the Lord wait for his mercy; turn not away from him, lest you fall. 8 You who fear the Lord, believe him, and your reward will not be denied. 9 You who fear the Lord hope in him and mercy will come to you for your delight. 10 You who fear the Lord love him and your hearts will be enlightened.

11 My children, behold the generations of men and know that no one has hoped in the Lord and has been put to shame. 12 For who has kept his commandment and been forsaken? Or who has called upon him and

was despised by him? ¹³ For God is compassionate and merciful and will forgive sins in the day of tribulation, and he is a protector to all who seek him in truth.

¹⁴ Woe to those who have a double heart, woe to wicked lips, woe to the hands that do evil, woe to the sinner who is double-faced. ¹⁵ Woe to them who are faint-hearted, who do not believe God; therefore they will not be protected by him. ¹⁶ Woe to those who have lost patience, and who have forsaken the right ways and gone aside into crooked ways. ¹⁷ And what will they do when the Lord renders justice?

¹⁸ Those who fear the Lord will not disbelieve his word, and those who love him will keep his law. ¹⁹ Those who fear the Lord will seek after the things that are well pleasing to him, and those who love him will be filled with his law. ²⁰ Those who fear the Lord will prepare their hearts and in his sight will make their souls holy. ²¹ Those who fear the Lord keep his commandments and will have patience even until his coming. ²² If we do not do penance, we shall fall into the hands of the Lord and not into the hands of men. ²³ For as his greatness is, so also is his mercy.

Duty to parents

3 The sons of wisdom form the church of the just, and their generation gives obedience and love. ² Children, hear the judgment of your father, and act in a way that you may be saved. ³ God has made the father honorable to his children and has confirmed the wisdom of mothers to their children. ⁴ He who loves God will obtain pardon for his sins by prayer, will commit them no more, and will be heard in daily prayer. ⁵ He who honors his mother is as one who lays up a treasure. ⁶ He who honors his father will have joy in his own children, and in the day of his prayer he will be heard. ⁷ He who honors his father will enjoy a long life, and he who obeys his father will be a comfort to his mother. ⁸ He who fears the Lord honors his parents and will serve them as his masters who brought him into the world. ⁹ Honor your father in work and word and all patience, ¹⁰ that a blessing may come upon you from him, and his blessing may remain to your end. ¹¹ The

father's blessing strengthens the homes of the children but a mother's curse roots up the foundation. ¹² Glory not in the dishonor of your father for his shame is no glory to you. ¹³ For the glory of a man comes from honoring his father and a father without honor is the shame of the son.

¹⁴ Son, support the old age of your father and grieve him not in his life; ¹⁵ and, if his understanding fails, have patience with him and despise him not when you are in your maturity, for kindness to a father shall not be forgotten ¹⁶ and your goodness will obtain forgiveness of your sins. ¹⁷ In justice you will be built up, and in the day of affliction you will be remembered. Your sins will melt away as the ice in the fair warm weather. ¹⁸ He who forsakes his father deserves his evil fame and he is cursed of God who angers his mother.

Humility

¹⁹ My son, do your works in meekness, and you will be beloved above the glory of men. ²⁰ The greater you are, the more you should humble yourself in all things, and you will find grace before God. ²¹ Great is the power of God and he is honored by the humble.

²² Seek not the things that are too high for you, and search not into things beyond your ability; but the things that God has commanded you, think on them always, and in many of his works be not curious. ²³ For it is not necessary for you to see with your eyes those things that are hidden. ²⁴ In unnecessary matters do not be over curious and in many of his works you should not be inquisitive. ²⁵ Many things are shown to you above the understanding of men. ²⁶ Hasty judgment has deceived many and has confused their minds by vanity.

Pride

²⁷ A stubborn mind will fear evil at the end and he who loves danger will perish in it. ²⁸ A heart divided in its affections will not have success and the perverse of heart shall be their own victims. ²⁹ A wicked heart will be filled with sorrows and the sinner will add sin to sin. ³⁰ The affliction of the proud will not be healed, for the plant of wickedness will take root in them and it will not be perceived.

³¹ The heart of the wise man is understood by wisdom and a good ear will eagerly listen to wisdom. ³² A wise heart which has understanding will abstain from sins and will have success in the works of justice. ³³ Water quenches a flaming fire and alms resist sin. ³⁴ God provides for him who shows favor, he remembers him afterwards and in the time of his fall he will find a sure support.

Charity to poor

4 Son, do not defraud the poor of alms and do not avert your eyes from the poor. ² Despise not the hungry man and provoke not the poor in his want. ³ Do not afflict the heart of the needy and do not delay in giving to him who is in distress. ⁴ Do not reject the petition of the afflicted and do not turn your face away from the needy. ⁵ Do not turn your eyes away from the poor for fear of anger and let no man because of your hardness curse you behind your back. ⁶ The prayer of him who curses you in the bitterness of his soul will be heard, for he who made him will hear him.

⁷ Make yourself beloved to the congregation of the poor, humble your soul to the elderly and bow your head to a great man. ⁸ Bow down your ear cheerfully to the poor, pay what you owe and answer him peaceably and mildly. ⁹ Deliver him who is wronged from the hand of the wrongdoer and be not fainthearted in your soul. ¹⁰ In judging, be merciful to the fatherless as a father and as a husband to their mother. ¹¹ You will be like an obedient son of the Most High and he will have mercy on you more than does your mother.

Wisdom's hardships and rewards

¹² Wisdom exalts her children and protects those who seek her, and will go before them in the way of justice. ¹³ He who loves her, loves life; and those who watch for her will embrace her sweetness. ¹⁴ They who hold her fast will inherit life; and wherever she enters, God will give a blessing. ¹⁵ Those who serve her will be servants to the holy one and God loves them who love her. ¹⁶ He who obeys her will judge nations and he who obeys her will remain secure. ¹⁷ If he trusts in her, he will inherit her,

and his descendants will possess her. ¹⁸ At first she chooses him and walks with him in temptation. ¹⁹ She will test him with fear and apprehension and she will scourge him with the affliction of her discipline until after testing him by her laws she comes to trust him. ²⁰ Then she will strengthen him and make a straight way for him, and give him joy, ²¹ and will disclose her secrets to him, and will heap upon him treasures of knowledge and understanding of justice. ²² But if he goes astray, she will forsake him and deliver him into the hands of his enemy.

Human respect

²³ Son, heed the time and fly from evil. ²⁴ Let not your soul be ashamed to speak the truth. ²⁵ For there is a shame that brings honor and grace.

²⁶ Do not show partiality to your own hurt. ²⁷ Rejoice not in the fall of your neighbor ²⁸ and do not hesitate to speak when salvation is at stake. Hide not your wisdom in her beauty. ²⁹ For by the tongue wisdom is discerned; and understanding, knowledge, learning by the word of the wise and steadfastness in the works of justice. ³⁰ In no way speak against the truth but be ashamed of the lie of your ignorance. ³¹ Do not be ashamed to confess your sins but do not submit your sins to every man. ³² Resist not the face of the mighty and do not strive against the current of the river. ³³ Strive for justice for your soul, even unto death fight for justice, and God will overthrow your enemies for you. ³⁴ Do not be hasty in your speech and slack or remiss in your works. ³⁵ Do not be like a lion in your home, terrifying those of your household and oppressing those who serve you. ³⁶ Let not your hand be stretched out to receive and closed when you should give.

Wealth

5 Do not set your heart on unjust possessions or say, "I have enough to live on." It will be of no use in the time of punishment and darkness. ² Do not follow your strength and inclinations. ³ Do not say, "How mighty am I? And who will bring me down for my deeds?" For God will surely be avenged. ⁴ Do not say, "I have sinned and what harm has befallen me?" For the

Most High is a patient rewarder. ⁵ Do not be sure your sin is forgiven and add sin upon sin. ⁶ Do not say, "The mercy of the Lord is great, he will have mercy on my many sins." ⁷ Mercy and wrath come quickly from him and his anger rests upon sinners. ⁸ Do not delay to be converted to the Lord or put it off from day to day. ⁹ For his wrath will come suddenly and in the time of vengeance he will destroy you. ¹⁰ Do not take comfort in ill-gotten gains for they will be of no profit on the day of calamity and judgment.

Sincerity

¹¹ Winnow not in every wind or do not go into every path for this is the practice of the two-faced man. ¹² Be steadfast in the way of the Lord and in the truth of your judgment and in knowledge; let the word of peace and justice remain with you.

¹³ Be humble to hear the word that you may understand it and return a true answer with wisdom. ¹⁴ If you have understanding, answer your neighbor; but if not, hold your tongue, lest you say what you do not mean and be confused. ¹⁵ Honor and glory is in the speech of the wise but the tongue of the fool is his ruin.

¹⁶ Do not be called a slanderer and do not be caught in the trap of your own tongue and confounded. ¹⁷ For shame and repentance becomes a thief and the embarrassment of exposure awaits the two-faced, while the scandalmonger earns hatred and enmity and reproach. ¹⁸ Be vindicated in both great and small matters.

6 Be a friend and not an enemy to your neighbor for an evil man will inherit reproach and shame. So too will every sinner who is envious and two-faced. ² Let not your strength be lost through folly or your pride gored by an infuriated bull ³ that eats your leaves and destroys your fruit so that you are left as a withered tree in the wilderness. ⁴ A wicked soul will destroy its owner and thus give joy to his enemies and deliver him to the fate of the wicked.

Friendship

⁵ A gentle word wins friends and appeases enemies, and a gracious speech proves a good man. ⁶ Be at peace with many but let one in a thousand be your counselor. ⁷ If you would find a friend, test him before you accept him and do not trust him easily. ⁸ There is one who is a friend for his own benefit and he will not abide with you in your day of trouble. ⁹ And there is the friend who easily becomes an enemy and returns your confidences with hatred, strife and reproaches. ¹⁰ And there is a friend who dines at your table but will not remain in your day of distress. ¹¹ When things go well he will make himself your equal, ordering your servants around, ¹² but if ever adversity befalls you, he will hide himself from you and be your friend no longer. ¹³ Avoid your enemies and be on guard with your friends. ¹⁴ A faithful friend is a strong defense and he who has found one has found a treasure. ¹⁵ Nothing can be compared to a faithful friend and no weight of gold and silver is able to unbalance the goodness of his fidelity. ¹⁶ A faithful friend is the substance of life and immortality and those who fear the Lord will find one. ¹⁷ He who fears God will likewise make good friends because as a man is so are his friends.

The seeking for wisdom

¹⁸ My son, receive instruction from your youth and even to your old age keep finding wisdom. ¹⁹ Come to her as one who plows and sows and wait for her harvest. ²⁰ In working for her you will labor a little while and will soon eat of her crops. ²¹ How very distasteful is wisdom for the unlearned! The foolish will not remain with her. ²² She will weigh them down as a heavy testing stone and they will soon abandon her. ²³ The wisdom of doctrine is like her name and she is not manifest to many; but with those to whom she is known, she continues faithful before God.

²⁴ Listen, my son, and take wise counsel and do not discard my advice. ²⁵ Put your feet into her fetters and your neck into her harness. ²⁶ Bow down your shoulder and bear her and do not be grieved with her reins. ²⁷ Come to her with all your mind and keep her ways with all your power. ²⁸ Search for her and she will be made known to you; when you have obtained her, do not let her go. ²⁹ In the end you will find rest in her, and she will be turned into your joy. ³⁰ Then her fetters will be a strong de-

fense for you and a firm foundation, and her harness a robe of glory. 31 In her is the beauty of life and her reins are a soothing yoke. 32 You will put her on as a robe of glory and you will set her upon your head as a crown of joy.

33 My son, if you will listen to me, you will learn; and if you will apply your mind, you will be wise. 34 If you will incline your ear, you will receive instruction; and if you love to hear, you will be wise. 35 Stand in the assembly of elders who are wise and join yourself from your heart to their wisdom, that you may hear every discourse of God and the sayings of praise may not escape you. 36 And if you see a man of understanding, go to him early in the morning and let your feet wear out the steps of his doors. 37 Let your thoughts be upon the laws of God and meditate continually on his commandments; he will give you interior knowledge and the desire of wisdom shall be yours.

Various advice

7 Do no evil and no evil will lay hold of you. 2 Depart from the unjust and evil will depart from you. 3 My son, do not sow evil in the furrows of injustice and then you will not reap them sevenfold.

4 Seek not from the Lord a high honor, nor from the king the seat of honor. 5 Do not justify yourself before God for he knows your heart; do not desire to appear wise before the king. 6 Do not seek to be made a judge unless you have strength enough to root out iniquities, lest moved by the person of a powerful man, you place a stumbling block for your integrity.

7 Do not offend the citizens of a city, nor disgrace yourself before the people, 8 nor add sin to sin; even for one you will not go unpunished.

9 Do not be uncertain in your mind. 10 Do not neglect to pray and to give alms. 11 Do not say, "God will respect my many gifts, and when I offer to the Most High God, he will accept it."

12 Do not ridicule any man who is bitter in his soul. God who sees all humbles and exalts.

13 Do not lie about your brother nor about your friend. 14 Be unwilling to make any sort of lie for it is a bad habit.

15 Do not talk on and on before the elders, nor repeat yourself in your prayer.

16 Do not hate tedious work, nor farming, ordained by the Most High.

17 Do not number yourself among the assembly of the disorderly.

18 Remember wrath for it will not long delay retribution.

19 Humble your spirit greatly for the vengeance on the flesh of the ungodly is fire and worms.

20 Do not exchange friendship for money, nor despise your real brother for the sake of gold of Ophir.[a]

21 Do not leave a wise and good wife, whom you married in the fear of the Lord, for the grace of her modesty is above gold.

22 Do not hurt the servant who works faithfully, nor the hired man who gives you his life. 23 Let a wise servant be as dear to you as your own soul; do not defraud him of liberty, nor leave him needy.

24 Have you cattle? Look after them, and if they are profitable, keep them.

Children

25 Have you children? Instruct them, and make them obedient from childhood. 26 Have you daughters? Have concern for their virtue and do not spoil them. 27 Prepare to marry your daughter well and you will do a great work, but give her to a wise man.

28 If you have a wife who pleases you, turn her not out; but if she is hateful do not give her your trust.

Parents

29 With your whole heart, honor your father, and do not forget the birth pangs of your mother. 30 Remember that you owe your very being to them; repay them for all that they have done for you.

Priests

31 With all your soul fear the Lord and reverence his priests. 32 With all your strength love him who made you and do not forsake his ministers. 33 Honor God with all your soul and give honor to the priests and purify yourself by your alms.

a Cf. 1 Kgs. 9:28.

34 As it is commanded you, give him his portion of the firstfruits and the sin offerings and purify yourself for your negligences. 35 Offer to the Lord the gift of your shoulders, the sacrifice of sanctification and the firstfruits of the holy things.

The Poor

36 Stretch out your hand to the poor that your expiation and your blessing may be perfect. 37 A gift has merit in the sight of all the living and restrain not your favor from the dead. 38 Comfort those who weep and share the grief of those who mourn. 39 Do not be slow to visit the sick for by these things you will be loved. 40 In all that you do remember your last end and you will never sin.

Common sense

8 Contend not with a powerful man lest you fall into his hands. 2 Quarrel not with a rich man lest he bring an action against you. 3 For gold and silver has destroyed many and has corrupted even the hearts of kings. 4 Do not argue with a busybody and heap not wood upon his fire.

5 Do not jest with an ignorant man lest he speak ill of your ancestors.

6 Do not despise a man who turns away from sin, nor reproach him for what he did; remember we are all worthy of reproof.

7 Do not despise a man in his old age for we also will become old.

8 Do not rejoice at the death of your enemy. We all die and are not willing that others should rejoice at our death.

Tradition

9 Do not despise the counsels of those who are old and wise but acquaint yourself with their proverbs. 10 From them you can learn wisdom and instruction in understanding and how to serve great men with honor. 11 Do not ignore the talk of old men for they have learned from their fathers. 12 From them you can learn understanding and how to give an answer in time of need.

13 Do not kindle the coals of sinners lest you be burned in the fire of their sins.

14 Do not argue with an insolent person lest he entrap you in your own words.

15 Do not lend to a man who is mightier than yourself, and if you lend, count it as lost. 16 Do not give surety beyond your means; but if you do give bond, presume you will have to pay it.

17 Do not file suit against a judge for his standing will give him the judgment.

18 Do not travel with a carefree man lest his mischief becomes your burden. He will do what he wants to do and you will suffer for his folly.

19 Do not quarrel with a violent man and do not go into a desert with a brutish man; for blood counts as nothing in his sight, and where there is no help to be had, he will strike you down.

20 Do not take the advice of fools for they cannot keep anything secret.

21 Say nothing of import before a stranger for you do not know what he will tell.

22 Do not reveal your thoughts to every man lest he repay you with an evil turn and speak reproachfully of you.

Women

9 Do not be jealous of the wife you love or teach her wicked ways with which she can repay you. 2 Do not give your soul to a woman lest she tread upon your strength and you are put to shame.

3 Look not upon a promiscuous woman lest you fall into her snares.

4 Do not frequent the company of a woman who is a dancer and do not listen to her lest you perish by the force of her charms.

5 Gaze not upon a young girl lest her beauty be a stumbling block to you.

6 Do not give yourself to harlots lest you destroy yourself and your inheritance. 7 Do not look around about you on the streets of the city, nor wander up and down its unfrequented places.

8 Turn your face away from an elegant woman and do not gaze at beauty that belongs to another. 9 For many have perished because of the beauty of a woman, and by it lust is enkindled as a fire. 10 Every woman who is a harlot shall be trodden upon as dung on the road.

11 Many, by admiring the beauty of another man's wife, have fallen into sin, for her conversation burns as fire. 12 Do not sit at table with another man's wife, nor repose upon the bed with her, 13 or spend time

with her over wine, lest you fall victim to her charms and in your ardor fall into ruin.

Relationships with men

¹⁴ Do not forsake an old friend for the new will not compare to him. ¹⁵ A new friend is as new wine; when it grows old, you will drink it with pleasure.

¹⁶ Do not envy the success and riches of a sinner for you do not know what his ruin shall be. ¹⁷ Do not be pleased with the wrong done by the unjust, remember that hell awaits the wicked.

Human greatness

¹⁸ Keep far away from the man who has power to kill and you will not have to worry about the fear of death. ¹⁹ And if you come to him, do not offend, lest he take away your life. ²⁰ Realize that you are in touch with death for you are going in the midst of snares and walking upon the arms of those who are grieved.

²¹ Know your neighbor as well as you can and consult with the wise and prudent. ²² Let just men be your guests and let your glory be in the fear of God. ²³ And let the thought of God be in your mind and all your discourse on the commandments of the Highest.

²⁴ A work will be praised for the skill of the artisan and the leader of the people for the wisdom of his speech, but the word of the elders for its sense.

²⁵ A gossip is feared in his city and he who is rash in his word will be hated.

Government

10 A wise judge will judge his people and the government of a prudent man will be firm. ² As is the judge of the people, so also are his officials; and as is the governor of a city, so are its inhabitants. ³ An unwise king will be the ruin of his people. Cities grow because of the wisdom of their rulers. ⁴ The government of the earth is in the hand of God. He sets the right man over it at the right time. ⁵ The prosperity of man is in the hand of God and upon the person of the scribe he will confer his honor.

Pride

⁶ Forget any injury done to you by your neighbor and do no injury yourself.

⁷ Pride is hateful before God and men and all iniquity of nations is outrageous.

⁸ Control of a kingdom is passed from one people to another because of injustices, wrongs, injuries and various deceits.

⁹ Nothing is more wicked than the covetous man. How can dust and ashes be proud? ¹⁰ There is nothing more wicked than to love money; for such a one sets a price even on his own soul, and while he lives his entrails rot away.

¹¹ All power is short-lived. A long sickness baffles the physician ¹² while a short sickness pleases him. A man is a king today and tomorrow he dies.

¹³ When a man dies, he will inherit serpents, beasts and worms.

¹⁴ The beginning of a man's pride is to depart from God, ¹⁵ because his heart has left him who made him; for pride is the beginning of all sin; he who yields to it will be filled with curses and it will ruin him in the end.

¹⁶ Therefore the Lord has brought down the gatherings of the wicked and has utterly destroyed them. ¹⁷ God has overturned the thrones of proud princes and has set up the meek in their stead. ¹⁸ God has made the roots of proud nations to wither and has planted the humble in their place. ¹⁹ The Lord has overthrown the lands of the Gentiles and has destroyed them even to their very foundations. ²⁰ He has made some of them to wither away and has destroyed them, and has made the memory of them to cease from the earth. ²¹ God has abolished the memory of the proud and has preserved the memory of those who are humble in mind. ²² Pride was not made for men, nor wrath for those born of women.

²³ That seed of men who fear God will be honored but the seed which transgresses the commandments of the Lord will be dishonored.

²⁴ Among brothers their leader is honored, so will those who fear the Lord be rich in his eyes. ²⁵ The fear of God is the glory of the rich and of the noble and of the poor.

²⁶ Despise not a just man who is poor and do not glorify a sinful man who is rich.

²⁷ The great man, the judge and the ruler are honored, yet there is none greater than the man who fears God.

²⁸ Those who are free will serve a servant who is wise, and a man who is prudent

and well instructed will not murmur when he is reproved, and he who is ignorant will not be honored.

Humility

29 Do not show off when doing your work, nor boast in the time of distress. 30 Better is he who labors and has an abundance of everything than he who brags but needs bread. 31 My son, keep your soul in meekness and give it honor according to its worth. 32 Who will justify him who sins against his own soul? And who will honor him who dishonors his own soul?

33 The poor man is glorified by his knowledge and reverence and a rich man is honored for his wealth. 34 But he who is honored in poverty, how much more in wealth? And he who is honored in wealth, let him fear poverty.

Do not judge accidentals

11 The wisdom of the humble man will raise his head and will cause him to sit in the assembly of the great.

2 Do not praise a man for his good looks, nor despise him for his appearance. 3 The bee is small among flying things but her produce has the most sweetness. 4 Do not boast about fine clothes at any time, nor be exalted in the day of your honor; for the works of the Highest only are wonderful and his works are glorious, secret and hidden. 5 Many tyrants have been made to sit on the ground and he whom no man would pick has been given the crown. 6 Many mighty men have been greatly humbled and the honored have been delivered into the hands of others.

Miscellaneous cautions

7 Blame no man before you investigate; and when you have inquired, reprove justly. 8 Listen before you speak and do not interrupt others in the midst of their discourse. 9 Do not strive in a matter which does not concern you, nor sit in judgment with sinners. 10 My son, do not meddle with many affairs; and if you get over-involved, you will suffer for it: hurrying after, you will not overtake; and you will not escape by running away.

11 There is a man who labors, hurries and presses on, yet is so much the more in want. 12 Again, there is a man who does

nothing but wants help. He is very weak in ability and full of poverty. 13 Yet the eye of God has looked upon him for good and has lifted him up from his low estate. He has raised his head, and many have wondered at him and have glorified God.

14 Good and evil things, life and death, poverty and riches, are all from God. 15 Wisdom and discipline and the knowledge of the law are with God. Love and the ways of good things are with him. 16 Error and darkness are created for sinners, and those who dwell in evil grow old in evil. 17 The gift of God abides with the just and what he approves will have success forever.

Trust in God

18 There is one who is made rich by living sparingly and this is the portion of his reward. 19 In that he says: "I have found rest and now I shall enjoy my goods alone." 20 But he does not know how much time is left before death approaches and he must leave them all to others.

21 Be steadfast in your duty and know it well. Grow old in the tasks assigned you. 22 Do not abide in the works of sinners. But trust in God and stay in your place. 23 It is easy in the sight of God to suddenly make the poor man rich. 24 The blessing of God makes haste to reward the just and quickly his blessing bears fruit.

25 Do not say, "What do I need, and what good shall I obtain by this?" 26 Do not say: "I am sufficient for myself, and what misfortune can befall me?" 27 In the day of good things remember evil; and in the day of evil remember the good things. 28 It is easy before God on the day of death to reward every one according to his ways. 29 The affliction of an hour makes one forget great delights and the end of a man is the revealing of his works. 30 Do not praise any man before death for a man is known by his children.

31 Do not bring every man into your home for many are the snares of the deceitful. 32 For as a diseased stomach sends forth a foul breath and as a partridge is decoyed into a cage, and a fish into a snare, so also is the heart of the proud. He is like a spy who waits for the downfall of his neighbor. 33 For he lies in wait and turns good into evil and he will lay blame on the

elect. ³⁴ A great fire comes from one spark and much blood from one deceitful man; a sinful man lies in wait for blood. ³⁵ Beware of a mischievous man who works evil, lest he bring reproach upon you forever. ³⁶ Receive a stranger in and he will overthrow you with disorder and will turn you out of your own home.

Rules for doing good

12 If you do good, know to whom you do it, and there will be much gratitude for your good deeds. ² Do good to the just and you will find great recompense; if not from him, assuredly from the Lord. ³ There is no good for him who is always occupied in evil and does not give alms. The Highest hates sinners and has mercy on the penitent. ⁴ Give to the merciful and uphold not the sinner; God will take vengeance on the ungodly and on sinners and repay them on the day of judgment. ⁵ Give to the good and do not receive a sinner. ⁶ Do good to the humble and do not give to the ungodly; keep your bread and do not give it to him, lest in so doing he overpowers you. ⁷ You will receive twice as much evil for all the good you will have done to him. For the Highest also hates sinners and will repay vengeance to the ungodly.

Friendship

⁸ A friend will not be known in prosperity and an enemy will not be hidden in adversity. ⁹ In the prosperity of a man his enemies are grieved. A friend is proven in his adversity.

¹⁰ Never trust your enemy, for his wickedness tarnishes like a copper pot. ¹¹ Though he humbles himself and goes groveling, yet take good heed and beware of him. ¹² Do not sit him next to you, neither let him sit on your right hand, lest he turn into your place and seek to take your seat; and at the last you realize my words as true and be stung by what I say. ¹³ Who will pity a snake charmer who is struck by a serpent or a man who approaches wild beasts? So it is with him who keeps company with a wicked man and is involved in his sins. ¹⁴ For an hour he will abide with you; but if your fortune declines, he will not endure it. ¹⁵ An enemy speaks sweetly with his lips but in his heart he lies in wait to throw you into a pit. ¹⁶ An enemy weeps with his eyes but if he finds an opportunity he will not be satisfied with blood; ¹⁷ and if evil comes upon you, you will find him ahead of you. ¹⁸ An enemy has tears in his eyes and while he pretends to help you, he will undermine you. ¹⁹ He will shake his head and clap his hands, whisper much and change his expression.

Know your place

13 He who touches pitch will be defiled with it and he who has fellowship with the proud will become proud himself. ² Do not take up a burden too heavy for you, nor associate with one more noble and richer than yourself. ³ What agreement will an earthen pot make with a kettle? For if they knock against one another, the pot will be broken. ⁴ The rich man has done wrong and yet puts on airs, while the poor man is wronged and must hold his peace. ⁵ If you give, he will make use of you; and if you have nothing, he will forsake you. ⁶ If you have any thing, he will live with you, and will consume your goods, and he will not be sorry for you. ⁷ If he has need of you, he will deceive you; he will smile on you and give you hope. He will speak gently to you and ask, "What do you want?" ⁸ And he will shame you by his fine meals until he has drained you dry two or three times, and finally he will laugh at you. Afterwards when he sees you, he will avoid you and shake his head at you. ⁹ Humble yourself to God and wait for his providence. ¹⁰ Beware that you are not deceived into folly and thus humbled. ¹¹ At the same time do not be humble in your wisdom lest you are deceived into folly.

¹² If you are invited by one who is mightier, be reluctant to accept and he will invite you the more. ¹³ Do not push forward, lest you are pushed back; yet keep close to him, lest you are forgotten. ¹⁴ Do not speak to him as an equal or believe his many words, for by much talk he will sift you and by smiling will draw out your secret thoughts. ¹⁵ Cruel is he who stores up your words; he will not hesitate to do you harm and to cast you into prison. ¹⁶ Keep your own counsel and listen diligently to what you hear for you are walking to your own downfall.

17 When you hear those things, see as it were in sleep and you will awake.

18 Love God all your life and call upon him for your salvation.

19 Every beast loves its own kind; so also every man loves the one who is nearest to himself. 20 Every creature will consort with those like to itself and every man will associate himself to his like. 21 Will the wolf at any time have fellowship with the lamb or the sinner with the just? 22 What fellowship has a hyena with a dog or what part has the rich with the poor? 23 The wild ass is the lion's prey in the wilderness, so also the poor are devoured by the rich. 24 Humility is an abomination to the proud man, just as the rich man abhors the poor.

25 When a rich man fails, he is supported by his friends; but when a poor man is down, he is even pushed away by his acquaintances. 26 When a rich man falters, he has many helpers; he speaks proud things and they justify him. 27 The poor man slips, he is even rebuked; he speaks wisely and no one listens. 28 The rich man speaks, and all hold their peace, and what he says they praise to the heavens. 29 The poor man speaks and they ask, "Who is this?" And if he stumbles, they will push him down.

30 Riches are good for the one who has no sin on his conscience, and poverty is very wicked in the estimation of the ungodly. 31 The heart of a man changes his appearance, either for good or for evil. 32 The mask of a good heart is a happy face, but composing proverbs is painful work.

Real happiness

14 Blessed is the man who has not erred in his speech and is not bothered with the remorse for sin. 2 Happy is he who has had no sadness on his mind and who has not given up his hope.

3 Riches are not seemly for a covetous and stingy man and what should an envious man do with gold? 4 He who accumulates wealth by wronging his own soul, gathers for others, and others will squander away his goods in riotous living. 5 If a man is evil to himself, to whom will he be good? He will not enjoy his own wealth. 6 There is none worse than he who envies himself and this is the reward of his wickedness. 7 If he does good, he does it unintentionally and unwillingly; in the end he exposes his wickedness. 8 The eye of the envious is wicked and he averts his face and despises his own soul. 9 The eye of the covetous man is unsatiable in his portion of iniquity; he will not be satisfied till he consumes his own soul, drying it up. 10 An evil eye looks towards evil things; he will not have his fill of bread but shall be needy and pensive at his table.

11 My son, if you have anything, do good to yourself and offer to God worthy offerings. 12 Remember that death advances steadily and that the covenant of Sheol[a] has been shown to you; for the agreements of this world will surely end. 13 Do good to your friend before you die; and according to your ability, reach out your hand and give to the poor. 14 Do not defraud yourself of a good day and do not let your part of a good gift pass by you. 15 Will you not leave your sorrows and labors to others to divide by lot? 16 Give and take, and justify your soul. 17 Before your death, work justice; for in Sheol you cannot find joy. 18 All living things will fade as grass or as the leaf that springs out on a green tree. 19 Some grow and some fall off; so is the generation of flesh and blood, one comes to an end and another is born. 20 Every work that is corruptible will fail in the end and the worker will go with it. 21 And every excellent work will be justified and the worker will be honored in it.

Pursuit of wisdom

22 Blessed is the man who will continue in wisdom, and who will meditate in his justice and in his mind will think of the all-seeing eye of God. 23 He who considers wisdom's ways in his heart and has understanding in her secrets; he who goes after her as a tracker and stays on her trail; 24 he who looks in at her windows and hearkens at her door; 25 he who lodges near her house and who sets up his tent near her, fastening his tent pegs to her wall, will have good things repose in his lodging

---

a The place of the dead.

forever. 26 He will set his children under her shelter and will shelter under her branches; 27 he will be protected under her covering from the heat and will rest in her glory.

15 He who fears God will do good; and he who possesses justice will lay hold of wisdom, 2 and she will meet him as an honorable mother, and will receive him as the wife of his youth. 3 She will feed him with the bread of life and understanding and give him to drink the water of wholesome wisdom. She will be made strong in him and he will not be moved. 4 She will hold him fast and he will not be confused; she will exalt him among his neighbors. 5 And in the midst of the assembly she will open his mouth and will fill him with the spirit of wisdom and understanding and will clothe him with a robe of glory. 6 She will heap upon him a treasure of joy and gladness and will cause him to inherit an everlasting name.

7 Foolish men will not obtain her but wise men will meet her. Foolish men will not see her for she stands off from pride and deceit. 8 Lying men will not be aware of her but men who speak the truth will be found with her and will go forward until they come into the sight of God. 9 Praise is not seemly in the mouth of the sinner 10 for wisdom came forth from God. For praise will be with the wisdom of God and will abound in a faithful mouth and the sovereign Lord will give praise unto it.

Free will

11 Do not say, "It is through God that she is not with me," for he will not do the thing he hates. 12 Do not say, "He has caused me to err," for he has no need of sinful men. 13 The Lord hates every abomination of error and those who fear him will not love it either. 14 God made man from the beginning and left him to his own devices. 15 He added his commandments and precepts. 16 If you will keep the commandments and remain faithful forever, they will preserve you. 17 He has set water and fire before you, stretch forth your hand to which you will. 18 Before man is life and

death, good and evil, and that which he chooses will be given to him; 19 for the wisdom of God is great. He is strong in power, seeing all men without end. 20 The eyes of the Lord are on those who fear him and he knows all the work of man. 21 He has commanded no man to do wickedness and he has given no man license to sin, 22 for he desires not a host of faithless and unprofitable children.

God's justice

16 Do not rejoice in many children if they are ungodly; neither be delighted in them, if the fear of God is not with them. 2 Trust not to their survival and do not respect their number. 3 For it is better for one to fear God than to have a thousand ungodly children. 4 It is better to die without children than to have ungodly children survive you. 5 A country will be made habitable by one who is wise and desolate if it has a tribe[a] of the ungodly. 6 My eyes have seen many such things and greater things than these my ear has heard.

7 In the community of sinners[b] a fire will be kindled and wrath will burn out an unbelieving nation. 8 The ancient giants did not obtain pardon for their sins and they died trusting in their own strength. 9 He spared not the place where Lot sojourned but abhorred them for the pride of their word. 10 He did not have pity on them, destroying the whole nation that extolled themselves in their sins. 11 So he did with the six hundred thousand infantry who were gathered together in the hardness of their heart; and if only one had been stiffnecked, it would be a wonder if he escaped unpunished; 12 for mercy and wrath are with him. He is mighty to forgive, and he pours out indignation. 13 As great as his mercy is, great also is his correction; he judges a man according to his works. 14 The sinner will not escape with his booty and the patience of him who shows mercy will not be delayed. 15 Mercy will make a place for every man according to the merit of his works and each will be treated as he deserves.

16 Do not say, "I shall be hidden from

---

a The Canaanites.   b Sodom and Gomorrah.

God and who will remember me from on high? 17 In such a multitude I shall not be known, for what is my soul in such an immense creation? 18 Behold the heaven and the heavens of heavens, the deep and all the earth, and the things that are in them will be moved at his coming. 19 The mountains also, and the hills, and the foundations of the earth will be shaken with trembling when God looks upon them. 20 In all these things the mind is unthinking, yet every heart is understood by him. 21 Who will understand his ways and the storm which no eye of man can see? 22 Many of his works are hidden. Who will declare the works of his justice? Or who will await them? For the covenant is far from some, yet the examination of all is at the end." 23 Such are the vain thoughts of the man who lacks understanding. The foolish and erring man thinks foolish things.

On creation

24 Listen to me, my son, and learn the discipline of knowledge. Set my words in your heart. 25 I will give instruction by importance and will seek to impart wisdom; listen carefully while with equanimity of spirit I tell you the value that God has put upon his works from the beginning and I show forth his knowledge in truth. 26 The works of God have existed from the beginning and when he formed them he divided them from their origins to their future generations. 27 He beautified their works forever, they neither hunger nor grow weary, nor do they change their appointed actions. 28 Nor do they impose, one upon another, 29 and they obey the law of God. 30 After this God looked upon the earth and filled it with his goods. 31 He covered the surface with every kind of living thing and to it they will all return.

17 God created man of the earth and made him after his own image. 2 He turned him back into it again. He clothed man with strength like his own. 3 He gave him the number of his days and time and gave him power over all the things that are upon the earth. 4 He put the fear of him upon all creatures and he had dominion over beasts and fowls. 5 He created out of him a helpmate like to himself; he gave

them counsel, and a tongue, eyes, ears and a mind for thinking; and he filled them with knowledge and understanding. 6 He created in them the knowledge of the spirit; he filled their hearts with wisdom and showed them both good and evil. 7 He set his light in their hearts to show them the greatness of his works 8 that they might praise the name which he has sanctified and glory in his wondrous acts, that they might declare the glories of his works.

9 Morever, he gave them instructions and the law of life for an inheritance. 10 He made an everlasting covenant with them and he showed them his justice and judgments. 11 Their eyes saw the majesty of his glory and their ears heard his glorious voice and he said to them, "Beware of all iniquity." 12 And he gave to every one of them a commandment concerning his neighbor. 13 Their ways are always before him; they are not hidden from his eyes. 14 Over every nation he set a ruler. 15 But Israel was made the Lord's obvious share.

16 All their works are as the sun in the sight of God and his eyes are continually upon their ways. 17 Their covenants were not hidden by their iniquity and all their sins are seen by God. 18 The alms of a man are as a signet ring with God and he will cherish the grace of a man as the apple of his eye. 19 And afterward he will rise up and will render them their reward, to every one their own, and will return them into the depths of the earth. 20 But to the penitent he has given the way of justice and he has strengthened those whose endurance was failing and has appointed to them the lot of truth.

Repentance

21 Turn to the Lord, forsake your sins, 22 make your prayer before the face of the Lord and offend less. 23 Return to the Lord, turn away from your injustice and greatly hate abomination. 24 Know the justices and judgments of God. Stand firm in the lot set before you and in prayer to the Most High God. 25 Go to the side of the holy age with those who live and give praise to God. 26 Tarry not in the error of the ungodly, give glory before death. Praise from the dead avails nothing. 27 Give thanks while you are living, while you are alive and in

health you will give thanks, and will praise God and will glory in his mercies. ²⁸ How great is the mercy of the Lord and his forgiveness to those who turn to him! ²⁹ All things cannot be in men because the son of man is not immortal, yet they are delighted with the vanity of evil. ³⁰ What is brighter than the sun? Yet it will be eclipsed. Or what is more wicked than that which flesh and blood has invented? And this shall be reproved. ³¹ He beholds the power of the height of heaven and all men are earth and ashes.

Greatness of God

18 He who lives forever created all the universe. God alone will be justified and he remains an invincible King forever. ² Who is able to declare his works? ³ Who will search out his mighty deeds? ⁴ And who will show forth the power of his majesty? Or who will be able to declare his mercy? ⁵ Nothing can be taken away or added, neither is it possible to find out the glorious works of God. ⁶ When a man has done, then will he begin; and when he leaves off, he will be at a loss.

⁷ What is man, and what is his purpose? What is his good or what is his evil? ⁸ The number of the days of men at the most are a hundred years; as a drop of water from the sea or as a grain of sand, so are a few years compared to eternity. ⁹ Therefore God is patient with them and pours forth his mercy upon them. ¹⁰ He has seen the presumption of their heart that it is wicked and has known their end that it is evil. ¹¹ Therefore he has filled up his mercy in their favor and has shown them the way of justice. ¹² The compassion of man is toward his neighbor but the mercy of God is upon all human beings. ¹³ He has mercy, and teaches and corrects, as a shepherd does his flock. ¹⁴ He has compassion on him who receives the discipline of mercy and who is anxious for his judgments.

Advice on bridling the tongue

¹⁵ My son, in your good deeds make no complaint; and when you give anything, do not add grief by an unkind word. ¹⁶ Will not the dew relieve the heat? So also a good word is better than a gift. ¹⁷ Indeed, is not a word better than a present? Yet a gener-ous man gives both. ¹⁸ A fool will upbraid bitterly, and a gift of a boorish man hurts the eye. ¹⁹ Prepare justice before judgment and learn before you speak. ²⁰ Take medicine before sickness and before judgment examine yourself and you will find mercy in the sight of God. ²¹ Humble yourself before you are sick and when you sin show your repentance. ²² Let nothing hinder you from praying always and do not be afraid to be justified even to death, for the reward of God continues forever. ²³ Make your soul ready for prayer and do not be like a man who tempts God. ²⁴ Remember the wrath that will be at the last day and the time of vengeance when he shall turn away his face. ²⁵ Remember poverty in the time of abundance and the necessities of poverty in the day of riches. ²⁶ From the morning until the evening conditions change and all these move swiftly in the eyes of God. ²⁷ A wise man takes care in everything and in the days of sins will be careful not to give offense. ²⁸ Every wise man knows wisdom and will give praise to him who finds her. ²⁹ Those who were of good understanding in words have also done wisely themselves, have understood truth and justice and have poured forth proverbs and judgments.

Self-control

³⁰ Do not go after your evil wishes but turn away your own will. ³¹ If you give to your soul her desires, she will make you a joy to your enemies. ³² Take no pleasure in riotous assemblies, no matter how small; for their cost is great. ³³ Do not make yourself poor by borrowing to contribute to feasts when you have nothing in your pocket for you will be an enemy to your own life.

19 A workman who is a drunkard will not be rich, and he who scorns small things will fall little by little.

² Wine and women corrupt wise men and are a rebuke to the prudent. ³ He who associates himself with prostitutes will be wicked. Rottenness and worms will possess him and he will be an example before all when his soul will be taken away from among men.

Loose talk

⁴ He who trusts others too easily is sim-

ple-minded and will lose out. He who sins only hurts himself. [5] He who takes pleasure in iniquity will be punished, and he who hates chastisement will have less life, and he who hates gossip avoids evil. [6] He who sins will repent, and he who is happy with wickedness will be condemned. [7] Do not repeat a slanderous conversation and you will not be punished. [8] Do not tell it to friend or foe; and unless it would be a sin for you, do not disclose it. [9] For he will listen to you and will watch you, and as if you were defending your own sin, he will hate you; this is what always happens. [10] Have you heard a word against your neighbor? Let it die within you. It will not make you burst. [11] A fool will suffer agony over something told him, as a woman groaning in childbirth. [12] As an arrow that sticks in a man's thigh, so is a word in the heart of a fool. [13] Question a friend, lest he may not have understood, and say, "I did not do it." Or if he did it, that he may do it no more. [14] Question your neighbor for it may be he has not said it, and if he has said it that he may not say it again. [15] Admonish your friends for there is often a fault committed. [16] And do not believe every word. One may make a slip in speech without intending it. [17] For who is there who has not offended with his tongue? Question your neighbor before you threaten him. [18] Give place to the fear of the Most High for the fear of God is all wisdom and in all wisdom the law is kept. [19] But the learning of wickedness is not wisdom and prudence flees the advice of sinners. [20] There is a cleverness that is detestable but the true fool lacks wisdom. [21] Better is a man with less wisdom and an appreciation of the fear of God, than he who abounds in knowledge and sins against the law of the Most High. [22] There is a subtle cleverness which is unjust. [23] And there are those who say too much in telling the truth. There is the man of guile who appears humble while inside he is full of deceit. [24] There is the one who pretends humility, who covers his face and pretends not to see some secret thing. [25] This man may not have the chance to sin, but if he finds the opportunity to do evil, he will do it.

[26] A man is known by his appearance, and a wise man, when you meet him, is recognized by his face. [27] The way a man dresses, his open laughter, and the way he walks will tell you what kind of man he is.

[28] There is a rebuke that is out of place and there is a time for good judgment, and there is the wise man who keeps quiet.

Wisdom teaches silence

20 How much better it is to give a rebuke than to stay angry and [2] to hinder him who admits a mistake! [3] Like the longing of a eunuch for a young girl, so is the man who renders judgments through violence. [4] How good it is when you are reproved to show repentance! So you will escape willful sin.

[5] There is the man who remains silent and is thought wise, while another bold in speech is despised. [6] There is one who keeps quiet because he does not know what to say, and there is another who keeps quiet because it is not the moment to speak. [7] A wise man will keep quiet until the right opportunity, but a babbling fool never knows the right moment. [8] He who uses many words will hurt himself and he who assumes authority unjustly will be hated.

[9] There is the man who finds bad luck good for him and on the other hand a windfall may turn into a loss. [10] There is a gift that is not profitable and there is a gift that repays double. [11] There are losses because of honor and a man of low estate can be lifted up. [12] There is a man who buys much for a small price, yet pays for it seven times over. [13] A man wise in words will make himself beloved but the favors of fools are in vain.

[14] The gift of a fool will do you no good for his eyes seek a sevenfold return. [15] He will give a few things and upbraid much and he opens his mouth as one who knows all. [16] Today he lends and tomorrow he asks for it back; such a man is hateful. [17] A fool will have no friend and there will be no thanks for his good deeds. [18] For those who eat his bread speak uncharitably. How often many will make fun of him! [19] For he does not understand how to give

that which is his to give and that which is not his to give.

20 A slip of the tongue resembles a slip on the pavement for a wicked man will quickly fall. 21 A proverb is empty when it comes from a man without grace for wisdom does not come from fools. 22 A parable coming from a fool's mouth will be rejected because he does not speak it at the right moment.

23 A man may be prevented from sinning by poverty and has pangs of conscience when he rests. 24 There is a man who destroys himself out of shame or destroys himself to earn the respect of a fool. 25 There is a man who for bashfulness makes a promise to a friend and thus gains an enemy for nothing.

Lying

26 A lie is an ugly blot on a man and yet it will be continually in the mouth of the ignorant. 27 A thief is better than a man who is always lying, but even so, both will inherit destruction. 28 Lying is a dishonorable habit.

The wise man

29 A wise man will advance himself with his words and a prudent man will please the mighty.

30 He who tills his land will reap a good harvest and he who works at justice will be exalted. He who pleases great men will escape punishment.

31 Presents and gifts blind the eyes of judges and make them silent so that they do not give correction.

32 What profit is there in wisdom that is hidden and treasure that is unseen? 33 Better is he who hides his folly than the man who hides his wisdom.

Thoughts on sin

21 My son, have you sinned? Do so no more, but also pray that your former sins may be forgiven. 2 Flee from sins as from the bite of a serpent, for if you come near sin, it will bite you. 3 Its teeth are the teeth of a lion, killing the souls of men. 4 All iniquity is like a two-edged sword which has no remedy for its wound. 5 Injuries and wrongs will waste riches

and a mansion will be brought to nothing by an increasing pride. 6 The prayer of a poor man will reach the ears of God and judgment will come for him quickly. 7 He who hates to be reproved walks in the steps of a sinner, and he who fears God is repentant in his own heart. 8 He who is mighty by his bold speech is known afar off but when he makes a slip a wise man detects it. 9 He who builds his house at another's expense is like one who gathers stones for a tomb.

10 The assembly of sinners is like broken fibers heaped together, destined to be thrown in a fire. 11 The way of sinners is paved with stones and in their end is hell,[a] darkness and pains.

12 He who observes justice will get understanding from it. 13 The fear of God is made perfect in wisdom and understanding. 14 He who is not wise in good cannot be taught.

15 There is a wisdom that increases in evil, and there is no understanding where there is bitterness. 16 The knowledge of a wise man will grow like a flood and his counsel like a running fountain. 17 The heart of a fool is like a broken vessel; it will hold no wisdom at all. 18 A man of sense will praise every wise word he hears and will apply it to himself; the indulgent man hears it and it displeases him. He will throw it behind his back.

19 The prattling of a fool is like a burden on a journey but on the lips of the wise grace will be found. 20 The words of the prudent man are sought after in the congregation and they will ponder his words in their hearts. 21 As a house that lies in ruins, so is wisdom to a fool; and the knowledge of the ignorant is but a babbling speech. 22 Education to a fool is like fetters on the feet and like manacles on the right hand. 23 A fool raises his voice when he laughs but a wise man will smile quietly. 24 Learning to the prudent is as an ornament of gold and like a bracelet upon his right arm.

25 The foot of a fool is soon in his neighbor's house but a man of experience approaches with respect. 26 A fool will peer

---

a Sheol, in newer translations.

through the window of a house but he who is well taught will wait outside. ²⁷ It is bad manners for a man to listen at a door and a wise man is grieved by the disgrace.

²⁸ The lips of the unwise relate foolish things but the words of the wise will be weighed in a balance. ²⁹ The mind of the fool is in his mouth but the mouth of wise men is in their minds.

³⁰ When the ungodly curses his adversary, he curses his own soul. ³¹ The talebearer defiles his own soul and is hated by all, and he who abides with him will be hateful. The silent and wise man will be honored.

Lazy children

22 The lazy man is like a filthy stone, and all men whisper his disgrace. ² The idler is like a heap of manure; everyone who touches it will shake it from his hand.

³ A bad mannered son is the disgrace of the father and a foolish daughter will be his loss. ⁴ A wise daughter will bring a dowry to her husband but one who is shameful becomes a disgrace to her father. ⁵ She who is bold shames both her father and husband and is no better than the ungodly, and will be despised by both. ⁶ A tale out of time is like music in mourning but chastisement and discipline are always wise and in tune.

⁷ He who teaches a fool is like one who glues fragments of a pot together. ⁸ He who tells a story to one who does not listen is like one who wakes a man out of a deep sleep. ⁹ While the man is still drowsy he speaks to him, and at the end he will ask, "What did you say?"

¹⁰ Weep for the dead for he lacks light and weep for the fool for he lacks understanding. ¹¹ Weep less for the dead for he is at rest. ¹² For the stupid life of a dumb fool is worse than death. ¹³ The mourning for the dead is seven days but for a fool and an ungodly man we mourn all the days of his life.

¹⁴ Do not talk much with a fool and do not go with him who lacks common sense. ¹⁵ Keep yourself from him that you may avoid trouble and not be defiled by his sin. ¹⁶ Turn away from him and you will find rest and will not be made weary with his folly. ¹⁷ What is heavier than lead? And

what other name has he but "Fool"? ¹⁸ Sand, salt and a piece of iron are easier to carry than a man without sense who is both foolish and wicked.

¹⁹ A wooden beam firmly secured in the frame of a building will not be loosed by an earthquake, so neither will the mind that is rooted in sound counsel. ²⁰ The thinking of one ever wise will not be shaken by fear. ²¹ A fence set on a high place and inexpensive stucco will not stand against the force of the wind, ²² so a timid heart in the imagination of a fool will not resist the onslaughts of fear. ²³ A fool has not enough sense to be afraid and he who keeps the commandments of God has no need to fear.

Friendship

²⁴ Lance an eye and tears will come, lance the heart and feelings pour forth. ²⁵ He who throws a stone at birds scares them off and he who unreasonably scolds his friend breaks his friendship. ²⁶ But even if you have drawn a sword on a friend, do not despair; there is a way back.

Friends

²⁷ If you have reviled a friend, do not fear, for there can be a reconciliation. Only reproach, nagging, arrogance, disclosing of secrets or a treacherous blow are causes for a friend to flee away.

²⁸ Keep faith with a friend in his poverty so that in his prosperity you may also rejoice. ²⁹ In the time of his trouble continue to be faithful to him that you may also be heir with him in his inheritance. ³⁰ As the vapor and smoke arise in the chimney before the flames, so also injurious words, reproaches, and threats precede the shedding of blood. ³¹ I will not be ashamed to shelter a friend, neither will I hide from him; but if any harm should come to me because of him, ³² every one who will hear of it will beware of him.

Watchfulness

³³ Who will set a guard on my mouth and a seal of prudence upon my lips that it may keep me from falling so that my tongue does not destroy me?

23 O Lord, Father, and sovereign Ruler of my life, do not abandon me to their humors or allow me to fall because of them! ² Who will set guards over my thoughts and the discipline of wisdom over my mind that they may not spare me in my errors and that my sins may not be ignored; ³ lest my mistakes increase and my offenses be multiplied and my sins abound and I fall before my adversaries and my enemy rejoices over me? ⁴ O Lord, Father and God of my life, do not leave me to their devices.

Control of the tongue

⁵ Give me not pride of eyes and turn away all evil desires from me. ⁶ Take from me all gluttony, do not let the desires of the flesh take hold of me. Do not surrender me to a shameless and foolish mind. ⁷ Hear, O you children, learn the lesson concerning speech; the one who will deserve it will not perish by his lips, nor be brought to fall into most wicked works. ⁸ A sinner is caught in his own vanity and the proud and the evil fall with the words they utter.

Swearing

⁹ Do not let your mouth become accustomed to swearing for in it there are many pitfalls. ¹⁰ And do not let the name of God be a habit of your lips. Do not meddle with the names of the saints for you will not escape free from fault. ¹¹ As a slave is bruised by daily beatings, so too every one who swears and takes God's name in vain will not be free from sin. ¹² A man who swears much will be filled with iniquity and a scourge will not depart from his house. ¹³ And if he offends, his sin remains upon him; and if he swears without cause, he sins twice. ¹⁴ And if he swears in vain, he will not be justified. His house will be filled with his punishment.

Evil speech

¹⁵ There is also another speech comparable to death, let it not be found in the inheritance of Jacob. ¹⁶ For all these sins will be far from the godly and they will not wallow in sins. ¹⁷ Do not let your mouth be accustomed to lewd vulgarities for therein is the word of sin. ¹⁸ Remember your father and your mother when you sit in the midst of great men, ¹⁹ lest God forget you in their sight. And you, by your daily habit, suffer reproach and wish that you had not been born and curse the day of your birth. ²⁰ The man who is accustomed to vulgar words will never correct the habit all the days of his life.

Sins of the flesh

²¹ Two sorts of men multiply sins and the third brings wrath and destruction. ²² A hot soul is a burning fire; it will never be quenched until it is consumed. ²³ There is a man who lusts for his own flesh and he will not give up until he is devoured by fire. ²⁴ To a man that is a fornicator all food is sweet, he will not be weary of sinning until he dies.

²⁵ Every man who sins against his own marriage bed despises his own soul and says: "Who sees me? ²⁶ Darkness covers me and the walls hide me and no man sees me so who should I fear? The Most High will not remember my sins." ²⁷ And he understands not that God's eye sees all things, for such a man's fear drives from him the fear of God, and he fears the eyes of men. ²⁸ He does not realize that the eyes of the Lord are far brighter than the sun; they look upon all the ways of men and gaze into the hearts of men, even into the most hidden places. ²⁹ For all things were known to the Lord God before they were created, so also after they were finished. ³⁰ This man will be punished in the streets of the city and he will be chased as a colt; and where he does not suspect it, he will be captured. ³¹ And he will be disgraced before all men because he did not understand the fear of the Lord.

The adulteress

³² So it is with every woman who leaves her husband and has an heir by a stranger. ³³ First of all, she has been unfaithful to the law of the Most High; and secondly, she has offended her husband; thirdly, she has committed adultery and has given birth to a child by another man.

³⁴ This woman will be brought before the assembly and punishment will be inherited by her children. ³⁵ Her children will not take root and her branches will bring forth no fruit. ³⁶ She will leave her memory to be cursed and her disgrace will not be blotted out. ³⁷ And those who survive her will know that there is nothing better than the fear of God and that there is nothing sweeter than to have regard for the commandments of the Lord. ³⁸ It is a great glory to follow the Lord, for length of days will be his gift.

Wisdom praises itself

24 Wisdom will praise herself and will be honored in the midst of her people. ² In the assembly of the Most High she will open her mouth and will glorify herself in the sight of his power, ³ and in the midst of her own people she will be exalted, and will be admired in the holy assembly. ⁴ And among the multitude of the elect she will have praise, and among the blessed she will be blessed, saying, ⁵ "I came forth from the mouth of the Most High, the firstborn before all creatures. ⁶ I made a light to rise in the heavens that never fails, and as a cloud I covered all the earth. ⁷ I dwelt in the highest places and my throne is in a pillar of a cloud. ⁸ I alone have made the circuit of heaven and have penetrated into the bottom of the deep and have walked on the waves of the sea.

⁹ "And I have stood in all the earth, and in every people ¹⁰ and in every nation I have had the chief rule. ¹¹ And by my power I have trodden under foot the hearts of all the high and low, and in all these I sought rest and I shall abide in the inheritance of the Lord. ¹² Then the Creator of all things gave me a commandment, and he who made me rested in my tabernacle, ¹³ and he said to me, "Let your dwelling be in Jacob and your inheritance in Israel and take root in my elect." ¹⁴ From the beginning and before the world was made, I was created, and into eternity I shall not cease to be. In the holy tabernacle I have ministered before him. ¹⁵ And so I was established in Zion and in the holy city likewise I rested, and my power was in Jerusalem. ¹⁶ And I took root in an honorable people and in the portion of the Lord, who is his inheritance, and my abode is in the full assembly of saints.

¹⁷ "I was exalted like a cedar in Lebanon and as a cypress tree on Mount Hermon. ¹⁸ I grew tall like a palm tree in Enged, and as a rose plant in Jericho, ¹⁹ as a beautiful olive tree in the plains, and as an elm tree by the water in the streets, so was I exalted. ²⁰ I gave a fragrant aroma like cinnamon and a perfumed balm; I yielded a fragrant odor of the finest myrrh.

²¹ I scented my dwelling with stacte, galbanum, onycha, and aloes, and as fresh frankincense my fragrance is as the purest balm. ²² I have stretched out my branches like the sumac tree and my branches are splendid and graceful. ²³ Like a vine I have brought forth pleasant buds and my flowers became splendid and abundant fruit. ²⁴ I am the mother of fair love and of fear, knowledge and holy hope. ²⁵ In me is all integrity of the way and the truth. In me is all hope of life and of virtue.

²⁶ "Come to me, all you who desire me, and be filled with my fruits. ²⁷ For my spirit is sweeter than honey and my inheritance sweeter than the honeycomb. ²⁸ My memory is for everlasting generations. ²⁹ They who eat and drink of me will hunger and thirst for more. ³⁰ He who listens to me will not be perplexed and those who work with me will not sin. ³¹ Those who explain me will have everlasting life."

³² All these things are the book of life, and the covenant of the Most High, and the knowledge of truth; ³³ the law which Moses commanded in the precepts of justice, an inheritance to the house of Jacob, and the promise to Israel. ³⁴ He appointed David his servant to raise from his progeny a most mighty king who would sit on the throne of glory forever. ³⁵ Who fills men with wisdom like the Phison and like the Tigris in the days of the new fruits. ³⁶ Who makes them full of understanding like the Euphrates and like the Jordan in the time of harvest. ³⁷ Who sends knowledge as the light and rises up like the Gehon in the time of the vintage. ³⁸ Just as the first man did not have perfect knowledge of her and the last one has not searched her out. ³⁹ For her thought is more vast than the sea and her counsel deeper than the great ocean.

⁴⁰ I, wisdom, flowed forth ⁴¹ like a canal out of a river and like an irrigation ditch into a garden. ⁴² I said, "I shall water my orchard and I shall irrigate my gardens." ⁴³ And behold my ditch became a great river and my river became a sea. ⁴⁴ I make teaching shine forth to all as the dawn and I shall make it shine afar. ⁴⁵ I shall penetrate to all the nether regionsᵃ of the earth

---

a Sheol

and shall visit all who sleep and shall enlighten all who hope in the Lord. [46] I shall yet pour out doctrine as prophecy and shall leave it to those who seek wisdom and shall not cease to instruct their offspring even to the holy age. [47] You see that I have not labored for myself only but for all who seek the truth.

Miscellaneous counsels

25 With three things my spirit is pleased which are approved before God and men: [2] the friendship of brothers, the love of neighbors and man and wife who live well together.

[3] Three things my soul hates and I am greatly grieved at their existence: [4] a poor man who is proud, a rich man who is a liar and an adulterous old man who is a fool.

[5] The things which you have not gathered in your youth, how shall you find them in your old age? [6] O how beautiful is judgment in older men and for the aged to know how to counsel! [7] O how attractive is wisdom in the aged and understanding and counsel in men of honor! [8] Much experience is the crown of old men and the fear of God is their glory.

[9] There are nine things I think of that make me happy and a tenth I will tell to men. [10] A man who has the joy of his children, and he who lives and sees the fall of his enemies. [11] Blessed is he who dwells with a wise woman, and who has not slipped with his tongue, and he who has not served those who are unworthy of him. [12] Blessed is he who finds a true friend, and declares justice to one who listens. [13] How great is he who finds wisdom and knowledge! But there is none above him who fears the Lord. [14] The fear of the Lord surpasses all things. [15] Blessed is the man to whom it is given to have the fear of the Lord; he who has it, to whom will he be likened? [16] The fear of God is the beginning of love, and the beginning of faith is closely associated to it.

Good and bad women

[17] How sad is a wound of the heart! How sad is the wickedness of a wife. [18] A man will choose any plague in preference to a plague of the heart, [19] and any wickedness but the wickedness of his wife, [20] any affliction but the affliction from those who hate him, [21] and any revenge but the revenge of enemies. [22] There is no poison worse than the venom of a serpent [23] and there is no anger above the anger of a wife. I would sooner live with a lion and a dragon than to live with an evil wife. [24] The wickedness of a woman changes her appearance and darkens her face like that of a bear, as if she wore haircloth. [25] When her husband goes out to eat with neighbors, he cannot restrain his sighs. [26] All malice is insignificant compared to the malice of a woman; may the fate of sinners fall upon her! [27] As the climbing of a sandy way is difficult for the feet of the aged, so is a rambling and talkative wife to a quiet man.

[28] Do not be taken in by a woman's beauty and desire not a woman for her looks. [29] A woman's anger, impudence and confusion is a great disgrace [30] when a woman of means supports her husband. [31] A wicked wife depletes one's courage, and makes a heavy face and a wounded heart. [32] Feeble hands and weak knees are caused by a woman who does not make her husband happy. [33] From a woman[a] came the beginning of sin and because of her we all die. [34] Give no outlet to water, nor liberty for a wicked wife to gad abroad. [35] If she does not walk at your side, she will confound you in the sight of your enemies. [36] Get rid of her lest she always abuse you.

26 Happy is the husband of a good wife for the number of his years will be double. [2] A virtuous woman makes her husband happy and will fulfill the years of his life in peace. [3] A good wife is a great blessing; she will be given among the blessings of those who fear the Lord. [4] Rich or poor, if his heart is happy, his face will be cheerful at all times.

[5] Of three things my heart has been afraid and at the fourth my face has trembled: [6] the slander of a city, the gathering of a mob [7] and a false calumny, all are more grievous than death.

[8] But there is grief and mourning of the heart when a wife is jealous [9] and everyone

---

a Eve.

knows about it because of the scourge of her tongue. [10] A bad wife chafes like a poorly fitted ox yoke, taking hold of her is like grasping a scorpion.

[11] A drunken woman leads to great anger and her reproach and shame will not be hidden.

[12] A wanton woman is revealed by her bold look and painted eyelids.

[13] Keep a strict watch on a self-willed daughter, lest when she gets the chance she may hurt herself. [14] Take heed of her impudent eyes and do not wonder if she disgraces you. [15] She will open her mouth as a thirsty traveler and drink any water near her and she will sit by every hedge and open her quiver to any arrow.

[16] The charm of a diligent woman will delight her husband and will fatten his bones. [17] Her silence is the gift of God. [18] Of such value is a wise and silent woman that there is nothing worth so much as a well disciplined soul. [19] A holy and modest woman is grace upon grace. [20] And no price can be placed on a chaste soul. [21] Like the sun rising over the world to the high places of God so is the beauty of a good wife the ornament of her house. [22] Like a lamp shining upon the holy candlestick[a] so is the beauty of a mature face. [23] Like golden pillars upon bases of silver so are the shapely legs upon the feet of a steadfast woman. [24] Like everlasting foundations upon solid rock so are the commandments of God in the heart of a holy woman.

Miscellaneous counsels

[25] At two things my heart is grieved and the third brings anger upon me: [26] a warrior in poverty, a man of common sense despised [27] and a man turning from justice to sin. God has prepared such a one for the sword.[b]

[28] Two sorts of callings have appeared to me hard and dangerous: a merchant can hardly keep from doing wrong and a tradesman will not be justified because of the sins of his lips.

Business

27 Many sin for a miserly gain and he who seeks riches avoids his conscience. [2] As a peg holds fast in the joint of two stones, so also is sin wedged between selling and buying. [3] Sin is destroyed with the sinner. [4] Unless you hold yourself diligently in the fear of the Lord, your house will be quickly overthrown.

Speech

[5] When a sieve is shaken the chaff remains. So will a man's defect be revealed in his thoughts. [6] The furnace tries the potter's vessels and the test of a man is in his speech. [7] As the pruning of a tree gives quality to the fruit, so the expression of a thought shows what a man feels. [8] Praise not a man before he speaks for it is then that he is tested.

Virtue

[9] If you pursue justice, you will obtain her; and will wear her as a long robe of honor. You will dwell with her, and she will protect you forever, and in the day of judgment you will find a strong friend. [10] Birds seek their own kind: so truth returns to those who practice it. [11] The lion always lies in wait for prey, so do sins for those who do evil.

[12] A holy man continues in wisdom like the sun but a fool is as changeable as the moon. [13] In the midst of the unwise hold your peace but be continually among men who think. [14] The discourse of sinners is hateful and their laughter is at the pleasures of sin. [15] The talk of those who swear much will make the hair stand on end, and its irreverence will make one stop his ears. [16] The quarrels of the proud lead to bloodshed and their cursing is grievous to hear.

Keeping secrets

[17] He who discloses the secret of a friend loses his credibility and will never find a true friend. [18] Love your neighbor and keep faith with him. [19] But if you discover his secrets, follow him no more. [20] For as a man who destroys his enemy, so also is he who destroys his friendship with his neighbor. [21] And as one who lets a bird go out of his hand, so have you let your neighbor go and you will not get him again. [22] Follow after him no more for he is gone afar off; he has fled as a doe from the snare. [23] Because his soul is wounded, you can no

---

a The seven branched candle of the Temple.　　　b Violent death.

longer bind him up. There is no reconciliation because of a curse and ²⁴ to disclose the secrets of a friend leaves no hope.

The hypocrite

²⁵ He who winks his eye slyly is planning wicked things and no man can dissuade him. ²⁶ In your presence he has a sweet mouth and he admires your words but in the end he will twist his speech and use your own words to condemn you. ²⁷ I have hated many things but not like him, and the Lord will hate him.

²⁸ If one casts a stone straight up, it will fall upon his own head; and a deceitful blow will wound the deceitful. ²⁹ He who digs a pit will fall into it, and he who sets a stone for his neighbor will stumble over it. He who lays a snare for another will be caught in it. ³⁰ Mischievous advice will roll back upon the author and he will not know from where it comes to him. ³¹ Mockery and reproach belong to the proud and vengeance like a lion will lie in wait for him. ³² They will perish in a snare who are delighted with the fall of the just, and sorrow will consume them before they die.

³³ Anger and fury are both abominable and the sinful man will be their victim.

Revenge

28 He who seeks to revenge himself will find vengeance from the Lord and he will surely keep his sins in remembrance. ² Forgive your neighbor if he has hurt you, and then when you pray your sins will be forgiven you. ³ If a man bears anger for another how can he seek remedy from God? ⁴ Does he have no mercy on a man like himself and does he entreat for his own sins? ⁵ If he who is but flesh nourishes anger how can he ask forgiveness of God? Who shall obtain pardon for his sins? ⁶ Remember your last things and let enmity cease. ⁷ Remember, corruption and death hang over you, so keep his commandments. ⁸ Remember the fear of God and do not be angry with your neighbor. ⁹ Remember the covenant of the Most High and overlook the ignorance of your neighbor.

Quarreling

¹⁰ Refrain from strife and you will sin less. ¹¹ An angry man kindles strife and a sinner causes trouble among his friends and brings an argument among those who are at peace. ¹² For as the wood of the forest is, so the fire burns; and as a man's strength is, so shall his anger be, and according to his riches he will increase his anger. ¹³ A hasty quarrel kindles a fire and a quick dispute sheds blood; and a tongue that carries tales brings death. ¹⁴ If you blow the spark, it will burn as a fire; and if you spit upon it, it will be quenched; both come out of the mouth.

¹⁵ The whisperer and the double tongued is cursed for he has troubled many who were at peace. ¹⁶ The slanderer^a has upset many and scattered them from nation to nation. ¹⁷ Slander has destroyed strong and powerful cities and has overthrown the houses of great men. ¹⁸ It has cut armies in pieces and undone strong nations. ¹⁹ Slander has driven valiant women from their homes and deprived them of the fruit of their labors. ²⁰ He who listens to slander will never have rest, nor will he have a friend in whom he may repose. ²¹ The stroke of a whip raises a welt but the stroke of the tongue will break bones. ²² Many have fallen by the edge of the sword but even more have perished by their own tongue.

Loose talk

²³ Blessed is he who is defended from a wicked tongue, who has not suffered its anger, and has not been shackled with its yoke, and has not been bound in its chains. ²⁴ For its yoke is a yoke of iron and its chains are chains of bronze. ²⁵ Its death is a most evil death and Sheol is preferable to it. ²⁶ Its continuance will not be for a long time but it will possess the ways of the unjust, and the just will not be burned with its flame. ²⁷ Those who forsake the Lord will fall into it and it will burn in them, and will not be quenched, and it will be sent upon them as a lion and as a leopard it will tear them apart.

²⁸ Hedge in your ears with thorns; do not hear a wicked tongue and make a door and bolt to your mouth. ²⁹ Melt down your gold and silver and make a scale for your

---

a Lit. "tongue of a third person," meaning the speaker, the listener and the one slandered.

words and a fitting bridle for your mouth. ³⁰ Take heed lest you slip with your tongue and fall in the sight of your enemies who lie in wait for you. Such a fall will result in death.

Borrowing and bonds

29 He who shows mercy lends to his neighbor and he who strengthens him in hand keeps the commandments. ² Lend to your neighbor in the time of his need and pay your neighbor when what you owe is due. ³ Keep your word and deal faithfully with him and you will always find what you need.

⁴ Many look upon a loan as something found and only give trouble to those who help them. ⁵ Until they get what they want, they kiss the hands of the lender and they lower their voice when they make their promises; ⁶ but when they should repay, they will ask more time and will repay in tedious and murmuring words and complain of the time allowed. ⁷ And if he is able to pay, he will hold off or he will scarce pay one half, and will count what he retains as if he had found it. ⁸ But if not, he will defraud him of his money and he will make an enemy without cause, ⁹ and he will repay him with reproaches and curses, and instead of honor and a good turn will repay him with injuries. ¹⁰ Because of such wickedness many have refused to lend, simply because they were afraid to be defrauded without reason.

¹¹ But yet towards the poor you should be more merciful and do not delay to give him alms. ¹² Help the poor man because of the commandment and send him not away empty-handed because of his poverty. ¹³ Lose your money for the sake of your brother or your friend, and do not hide it under a stone to be lost. ¹⁴ Place your treasure in the commandments of the Most High and it will bring you more profit than gold. ¹⁵ Store up alms in the heart of the poor and it will obtain help for you against all evil. ¹⁶ Better than the shield of the mighty and better than the spear; ¹⁷ it will fight for you against your enemy.

¹⁸ A good man goes bond for his neighbor but a man who has lost shame will leave him to himself. ¹⁹ Forget not the kindness of your bond for he has given his life for you. ²⁰ The sinner and the unclean flee from his bond. ²¹ A sinner attributes to himself the goods of his bond and he who is ungrateful will abandon the one who saved him. ²² A man goes bond for his neighbor who, when he has lost all shame, runs out on him. ²³ Going security has ruined many a well-to-do man and has tossed him as a wave on the sea. ²⁴ It has made men of power flee from place to place and they have wandered in strange countries. ²⁵ A sinner who sins against the commandment of the Lord will fall into an evil suretyship; he who undertakes many things will fall into lawsuits. ²⁶ Assist your neighbor according to your ability but take precautions that you do not fall.

Hospitality

²⁷ The essential for life is water and bread, a house and clothing to cover one's nakedness. ²⁸ Better is the life of a poor man under his own roof than sumptuous cheer abroad in another man's house. ²⁹ Be content with little instead of much and you will not hear the reproach of always being away. ³⁰ It is a miserable life to go as a guest from house to house, for where a man is a stranger, he will not behave confidently or open his mouth. ³¹ He will entertain and feed and give drink without thanks and even hear bitter words. ³² "Come, stranger, and set the table, and give these to eat what you have in your hand." ³³ "Make room for my honored friends. I want my house. My brother has come to lodge with me." ³⁴ These things are upsetting to a sensitive man; scolding about rooms and the reproach of the lender.

Bringing up children

30 He who loves his son frequently chastises him so that he may rejoice in the way he turns out. ² He who disciplines his son will be praised in him and will boast about him to all in his household. ³ He who teaches his son makes his enemy jealous and in the presence of his friends he will glory in him. ⁴ When the father is dead, it is as if he were not dead; for he has left one behind who is like himself. ⁵ While he lived, he saw and rejoiced in him; and when he died, he was not sorrowful, neither was he shamed before his enemies. 6 He left behind him a defender of his house against his enemies and one that will repay kindness to his friends. 7 The man who spoils his sons will bind up his wounds and at every cry his heart will be troubled. 8 A horse that is not broken becomes unmanageable and a child left to himself will become headstrong. 9 Give your son his own way and he will cause you fear, pamper him and he will make you sorrowful. 10 Do not laugh with him lest you have sorrow and uncertainty with him. 11 Give him no authority in his youth and wink not at his tricks. 12 Humble him while he is young and spank him while he is a child lest he grow stubborn and have no regard for you and so bring sorrow to your heart. 13 Instruct your son and work with him lest his uncouth behavior be an offense to you.

Health and sickness

14 Better is a poor man who is sound and strong of constitution than a rich man who is weak and afflicted with ills. 15 Health of the soul in the holiness of justice is better than all the gold and silver and a sound body more than immense riches. 16 There is no wealth better than the riches of health of body and there is no pleasure greater than the joy of the heart. 17 Better is death than a miserable life and everlasting rest is preferred to continual sickness. 18 Good things that are poured out on the mouth that is closed are as offerings of meat set about a grave. 19 What good does an offering do to an idol? For it can neither eat nor smell. 20 So is he who is affected by the Lord, bearing the reward of his iniquity. 21 He sees with his eyes and groans as a eunuch embracing a virgin and sighing.

22 Do not yield your soul to sadness and do not afflict yourself by your own advice. 23 Joyfulness of heart is the life of a man and a never failing treasure of holiness; and the joy of a man is length of life. 24 Have pity on your own soul; please God and contain yourself. Gather up your heart in his holiness and drive sadness far away from you. 25 Sadness has killed many and there is no profit in it. 26 Envy and anger shorten a man's days and worry will bring old age before one's time. 27 A cheerful and good heart is always feasting for his banquets are prepared with care.

Wealth

31 Watchfulness over wealth consumes the flesh and the anxiety of it drives away sleep. 2 Worry about what may happen turns away rest and a serious sickness makes the soul sober. 3 The rich man has worked to gather riches together and when he rests he is filled with his goods. 4 The poor man has labored in his hard life and in the end he is still poor. 5 He who loves gold will not be justified, and he who follows after corruption will be filled with it. 6 Many have come to ruin because of gold and the beauty of it has been their ruin. 7 Gold is a stumblingblock to those who are devoted to it; woe to those who eagerly seek it. Every fool will perish by it.

8 Blessed is the rich man who is found without blame and who has not sought after gold nor put his trust in money nor in treasures. 9 Who is he that we shall praise him? For he has done wonderful things in his life. 10 He who has been tested and found perfect will have everlasting glory. He who could have transgressed and did not transgress, he could have done evil things and has not done them, 11 therefore are his goods established in the Lord and all the congregation will declare his charity.

Temperance

12 Are you seated at a great table? Do not be the first to go after the food. 13 Do not say, "There are many things upon it." 14 Remember that a greedy eye is evil. 15 What is created more greedy than the eye? Therefore it weeps over all the face when it sees. 16 Stretch not out your hand first, lest being disgraced by envy you are put to confusion. 17 Do not be hasty at a feast. 18 Judge the feelings of your neighbor by your own. 19 Be frugal in the things that are set before you; because if you are greedy, you will be despised. 20 Be the first to stop eating as good manners demand and do not overdo lest you offend. 21 And if you sit among many, do not reach your hand out first of all, and do not be the first to ask for a drink. 22 How sufficient is a little wine for a man well taught. In sleeping you will not be uneasy with it and you will feel no

cramps. 23 Sleeplessness, nausea, and colic are with an intemperate man, 24 sound and wholesome sleep is with a moderate man; he will sleep until morning and his soul will be delighted with him. 25 And if you over-eat, arise and go outside. It will refresh you and you will not get sick. 26 Hear me, my son, and do not disregard me and in the end you will find my words true. 27 In all your works show restraint and no infirmity will come upon you.

28 The lips of many will bless him who is liberal with his food and their testimony of his truth is faithful. 29 Against the man who is stingy with his food, people will murmur and their testimony of his selfishness is true.

30 Do not match a man drink for drink, for wine has destroyed many. 31 Fire proves steel, so wine drunk to excess will test the hearts of the proud. 32 Wine taken with sobriety is like life to men; if you drink it moderately, you will be sober. 33 What is his life which is shortened with wine? 34 What takes away life? Death. 35 Wine was created from the beginning to make men joyful and not to make them drunk. 36 Wine drunk with moderation is the joy of the soul and the heart. 37 Sober drinking is health to soul and body. 38 Wine drunk with excess raises quarrels, anger and much grief. 39 Wine drunk to excess is bitterness of the soul. 40 Drunkenness is the stumblingblock of the fool, reducing his strength and causing wounds. 41 Rebuke not your neighbor in a banquet of wine and do not despise him in his mirth. 42 Do not speak to him words of reproach or quarrel with him in company.

Manners at a banquet

32 Have they made you the master of ceremonies? Do not be proud, be among them as one of them. 2 Take care of them and then sit down; when you have acquitted yourself of all your charges, take your place 3 that you may be merry for them and receive a wreath as an ornament of favor for your fine leadership.

4 Speak, you who are older, for it is fitting 5 to speak the first word with good judgment and not interrupt the music. 6 If no one is listening, do not talk; do not show off your wisdom at the wrong time. 7 A concert of music at a feast of wine is as a ruby set in gold. 8 As an emerald setting in an ornament of gold so is the melody of music with pleasant and good wine. 9 Listen in silence and for your reverence good grace will come to you.

10 Young man, scarcely speak in your own behalf. 11 If you are asked twice, let your answer be short. 12 In many things be as if you were ignorant and hear in silence and without asking questions. 13 In the company of great men you are not their equal; so when elders are present, do not speak much. 14 Before thunder goes lightning, and before embarrassment goes speech; and for your reverence good grace will come to you. 15 And when the affair is over, do not hang around, but be the first to run home, and there withdraw yourself, and there take your pastime. 16 Do there whatever you wish but do not sin or speak proudly. 17 For all these things bless the Lord who made you and who fills you with all his good things.

Fear of the Lord

18 He who fears the Lord will accept his discipline and those who seek him early will find a blessing. 19 He who seeks the law will be filled with it; he who deals deceitfully will meet his own downfall because of it. 20 Those who fear the Lord will find just judgment and will kindle justice as a light.

21 A sinful man will flee reproof and will find an excuse according to his will. 22 A thoughtful man will not neglect direction while the insolent and proud man is deterred by nothing. 23 Because the latter acts without advice, he will be controlled by his own desires.

24 My son, do nothing without advice and you will not repent what you have done. 25 Do not choose a rocky road and you will not stumble against the stones; trust not yourself to a rugged way, lest you set a stumblingblock for your soul. 26 Beware of your own children and take heed of those of your household. 27 In every work of yours regard your soul in faith for this is the keeping of the commandments. 28 He who believes in God, takes heed of the commandments; and he

who trusts in him will never fare for the worse.

33 No evil will happen to him who fears the Lord but in the time of temptation God will keep him and deliver him from evil. ² A wise man hates not the law and its justice and he will not be dashed in pieces as a ship in a storm. ³ A man of understanding is faithful to the law of God and the law is faithful to him. ⁴ He who would clear up a question will prepare what to say; and having prayed, he will be heard and will recall instruction, and then he will answer. ⁵ The heart of a fool is like a wheel of a cart and his thoughts are like a turning axle. ⁶ A mocker is like a stallion; he neighs under every one who sits on him.

God's governing wisdom

⁷ Why is one day better than another or one light better than another or one year better than another year when all come from the sun? ⁸ By the Lord's will they are different although the sun was created and is keeping his law. ⁹ He gave us the seasons and their feasts. ¹⁰ Some of them God made high and great days and some of them he put in the rank of ordinary days. And all men are from the ground and out of the dust from which Adam was created. ¹¹ With much knowledge the Lord has divided men and diversified their ways. ¹² Some of them he has blessed and exalted;ᵃ some of them he has cursed and brought low and turned them out of their place.ᵇ ¹³ As the potter's clay is in his hand to fashion and design it, ¹⁴ all his ways are according to his own choice, so man is in the hand of him who made him and he will render to him according to his judgment. ¹⁵ Good is opposed to evil and life opposed to death; so also is the sinner opposed to the just man. And so look upon all the works of the Most High: they are in pairs and one against another. ¹⁶ I was last on watch, as one who gathers after the grape gatherers. ¹⁷ In the blessing of God I also have hoped; and as one that gathers grapes, I have filled my winepress. ¹⁸ See that I have not labored for myself only but for all who seek knowledge. ¹⁹ Hear me, you great men and all you people, and listen with your ears, you rulers of the synagogue.

Advice to head of house

²⁰ Do not give to your son or wife, brother or friend power over yourself while you live; and do not give your property to another lest you change and must beg it back. ²¹ As long as you live and have breath in you, let no man change you. ²² It is better that your children should ask from you than that you should depend on the charity of your children. ²³ Excel in all your works. ²⁴ Let no stain sully your honor. In the time when you will end the days of your life and in the time of your death distribute your inheritance.

²⁵ Fodder, a stick and a burden are for an ass; bread, discipline and work are for a servant. ²⁶ He works under discipline and seeks to rest; allow his hands to be idle and he seeks liberty. ²⁷ The yoke and the thong bend a stiff neck and continual labors bow a slave. ²⁸ Torture and fetters are for an ill-disposed slave; send him to work so that he will not be idle ²⁹ for idleness teaches much evil. ³⁰ Set him to work, as is fitting for him, and if he does not obey, put him in bonds; but do not be excessive towards any one and do no serious thing without consideration. ³¹ If you have a faithful servant, let him be as yourself; treat him as a brother because you have bought him with blood. ³² If you hurt him unjustly he will run away. ³³ If he rises up and departs, you would not know whom to ask or where to look for him.

Dreams

34 A man who has no understanding has vain and false hopes and dreams lift up fools. ² The man who gives heed to lying visions is like one who catches at a shadow and follows after the wind. ³ The vision of dreams is the resemblance of one thing to another, as when a man's likeness looks on another likeness. ⁴ What can be made clean by the unclean? And what truth can come from that which is false? ⁵ Deceitful divinations and lying omens and the dreams of evildoers are folly. ⁶ Like a woman in labor, the heart has its fancies; except it be a vision

---

a Israel.   b The Canaanites.

sent forth from the Most High do not set your heart upon them. [7] For dreams have deceived many and they have failed who have put their trust in them. [8] The word of the law will be fulfilled without deception and wisdom will be made plain in the mouth of the faithful.

Travel broadens

[9] What does he know who has not been tried? A man who has much experience will think of many things and he who has learned many things will show forth understanding. [10] He who has no experience knows little and he who has been experienced in many things multiplies prudence. [11] He who has not been tried, what kind of things does he know? He who has been surprised will abound with vigilance. [12] I have seen many things by traveling and many strange customs. [13] Sometimes I have been in danger of death and I have been delivered by the grace of the Lord through my experience.

[14] The spirit of those who fear the Lord is sought after and by his regard will they be blessed. [15] Their hope is in him who saves them and the eyes of God are upon those who love him. [16] He who fears the Lord will not be timid and will not be afraid for the Lord is his hope. [17] The soul of the man who fears the Lord is blessed. [18] To whom does he look and who is his strength? [19] The eyes of the Lord are upon those who fear him; he is their powerful protector and strong support, a shelter from the heat and a cover from the sun at noon, [20] a preservation from stumbling, and a help from falling; he raises up the soul, enlightens the eyes, and gives health, life and blessing.

Worship of the Lord

[21] The sacrifice of the man who offers something wrongfully obtained is blemished and the mockeries of the unjust are not acceptable. [22] The Lord is only for those who wait upon him in the way of truth and justice. [23] The Most High approves not the gifts of the wicked; neither has he respect for the oblations of the unjust, nor will he be pacified for sins by a multitude of sacrifices. [24] He who offers sacrifice of the goods of the poor is like one who sacrifices the son in the presence of his father. [25] The bread of the needy is the life of the poor; he who defrauds them of it is a man of blood. [26] He who takes away the bread gotten by sweat is like the man who kills his neighbor. [27] He who sheds blood and he who defrauds the laborer of his wages are brothers. [28] When one builds up and another pulls down what do they gain but the labor? [29] When one prays and another curses, whose voice will God hear?

[30] He who washes himself after touching the dead, if he touches him again, what does his washing avail? [31] So a man who fasts for his sins and does the same again, what does his humbling himself profit him? Who will hear his prayer?

The law

35 He who keeps the law makes many offerings. [2] It is a wholesome sacrifice to take heed of the commandments and to depart from all iniquity. [3] To depart from injustice is to offer a propitiatory sacrifice for injustices and asking for pardon for sins. [4] He will return thanks who offers fine flour and he who gives charity offers sacrifice. [5] To depart from iniquity is a thing which pleases the Lord and to depart from injustice is to ask pardon for sins. [6] You will not appear empty in the sight of the Lord. [7] All these things are to be done because of the commandment of the Lord. [8] The offerings of the just fill the altar and are an odor of sweetness in the sight of the Most High. [9] The sacrifice of the just is acceptable and the Lord will not forget the memory of it.

[10] Give glory to God with a good heart and do not hold back the firstfruits of your labor. [11] In every gift show a cheerful face and sanctify your tithes with joy. [12] Give to the Most High as he has given to you and generously offer what your hands have produced. [13] The Lord makes recompense and will give you seven times as much.

[14] Do not offer unworthy gifts for such he will not receive. [15] Do not take part in an unjust sacrifice for the Lord is judge and there is no respect of persons with him.

[16] The Lord will not judge personalities in hearing the case of a poor man for he will hear the prayer of the one who is wronged. [17] He will not despise the prayers of the fatherless, nor the widow when she pours out her complaint. [18] Do not the widow's

tears run down her cheek as she cries against him who causes them to fall? ¹⁹ From the cheek they rise to heaven and the Lord who hears will not be delighted with them. ²⁰ He who adores God with joy shall be accepted, and his prayer will reach even to the clouds.

²¹ The prayer of the man who humbles himself will pierce the clouds and until it comes nigh he will not be comforted and he will not depart till the Most High hears him. ²² The Lord will not delay but will judge for the just and will do judgment; the Almighty will not have patience with them that he may crush their back. ²³ He will repay vengeance to the Gentiles until he has taken away the scepters of the unjust, ²⁴ until he has rendered to men according to their deeds and the works of men according to their intentions; ²⁵ until he has judged the cause of his people and delighted the just with his mercy. ²⁶ The mercy of God is as beautiful in the time of affliction, as a cloud of rain in the time of drought.

Prayer for Israel

36 Have mercy upon us,ᵃ O Lord of all, and behold us, and show us the light of your mercies. ² Send your fear upon the nations that have not sought after you, that they may know there is no God but you and that they may show forth your wonders. ³ Lift up your hand over the strange nations that they may see your power. ⁴ For as you have been sanctified in us in their sight so you will be magnified among them in our presence. ⁵ That they may know you, as we also have known you, that there is no God besides you, O Lord.

⁶ Show your signs anew and work new miracles. ⁷ Glorify your hand and your right arm. ⁸ Raise up indignation and pour out wrath. ⁹ Take away the adversary and crush the enemy. ¹⁰ Hasten the time and remember the end that they may declare your wonderful works. ¹¹ Let him who escapes be consumed in fiery wrath and let them perish who oppress your people. ¹² Crush the head of the rulers of the enemy who say, "There is no other but ourselves."

¹³ Gather together all the tribes of Jacob that they may know that there is no God besides you and may declare your great works; ¹⁴ give them their inheritance as you did at the beginning. ¹⁵ Have mercy on Jerusalem, the city which you have sanctified, the city of your rest. ¹⁶ Fill Zion with your unspeakable words and your people with your glory. ¹⁷ Give witness to those whom you did create from the beginning and fulfill the prophecies spoken in your name. ¹⁸ Reward those who patiently wait for you that your prophets may be found faithful; hear the prayers of your servants, ¹⁹ according to your good will to your people. Direct us into the way of justice and let all who dwell upon the earth know that you are the Lord, the God of the ages.

Need for discrimination

²⁰ The stomach will accept any food, yet one is better than another. ²¹ As the palate recognizes the taste of venison so the wise heart knows false speech. ²² A perverse mind will cause grief and a man of experience will resist it.

²³ A woman will accept any man yet one daughter is better than another. ²⁴ The beauty of a woman cheers the countenance of her husband and a man desires nothing more. ²⁵ If she has a tongue that can heal, and likewise forgive and show mercy, her husband is not like other men. ²⁶ He who gets a good wife finds his best possession. She is a helper fit for him and a pillar of rest. ²⁷ Where there is no hedge, the property will be plundered; and where there is no wife, a man mourns his want. ²⁸ Who will trust a man who has no home and who lodges wherever the night finds him. He is like a well equipped robber who skips from city to city.

False friends

37 Every friend will say, "I too am his friend." But there is a friend who is a friend in name only. Is it not a grief unto death ² when a companion and a friend is turned into an enemy? ³ O wicked propensity that turns friendship away, where did you come from to cover the earth with your malice and deceitfulness? ⁴ There is a com-

---

a This passage is reflected in the Eighteen Benedictions of the synagogue liturgy today.

panion who rejoices with his friend in his joys but in the time of trouble he stands aloof. 5 There is a companion who goes with his friend for his stomach's sake and will raise a shield against an assailant. 6 Do not forget your friend in your heart and do not forget him in your riches.

Advice

7 Do not consult with him who lays a snare for you and keep your counsel from those who envy you. 8 Every counselor gives advice but there is one who is a counselor in his own interest. 9 Beware of a counselor and know ahead of time what need he has for he will advise as suits him, 10 lest he cast his lot against you and say to you, 11 "Your way is good," and then stand aside to see what will befall you. 12 Do not consult an irreligious man concerning holiness, nor with an unjust man concerning justice, nor with a woman about her rival, nor with a coward concerning war, nor with a merchant about commerce, nor with a buyer about selling, nor with a stingy man about giving thanks, 13 nor with the ungodly about piety, nor with the dishonest about honesty, nor with a lazy man about work, 14 nor with him who works by the year about finishing sooner, nor with an idle servant about a big job; give no heed to these in any kind of counsel. 15 But be continually with a holy man, whom you know to observe the fear of God, 16 whose soul is according to your own soul; and who, when you will stumble in the dark, will be sorry for you. 17 Establish within yourself a heart of good counsel for there is nothing of more worth to you than it. 18 The soul of a holy man sometimes reveals true things, more than seven watchmen who sit in a high watchtower. 19 But above all these things pray to the Most High that he may direct your way in truth.

20 In all your works let reason go before you and let firm counsel precede every action. 21 A wicked word will change the heart out of which four branches come forth: good, evil, life and death; and the tongue is continually their ruler. There is a man who is shrewd and a teacher to many and yet does nothing for his own soul.

22 A skillful man has taught many and is sweet to his own soul. 23 He who double talks is hateful; he will be destitute of every thing. 24 Grace is not given to him from the Lord for he is deprived of all wisdom.

25 There is a wise man who is wise to his own soul and the fruit of his understanding is commendable. 26 A wise man instructs his own people and the fruits of his understanding are faithful. 27 A wise man will be filled with blessings and those who see will praise him. 28 The life of a man is in the number of his days but the days of Israel are without number. 29 A wise man will inherit honor among his people and his name will live forever.

Moderation

30 My son, test your soul while you live, and learn what is bad for it and give it no such food. 31 For not everything is good for everyone nor does every pleasure please every soul. 32 Do not be greedy for luxury nor give yourself up to your appetite 33 for in many foods there will be sickness and gluttony will turn into colic. 34 By overdoing many have perished, but the temperate man will prolong his life.

Doctors and medical care

38 Honor the physician for the need you have of him, for the Most High has created him. 2 All healing is from God and he will receive gifts from the king. 3 The skill of the physician will lift up his head and in the sight of great men he will be praised. 4 The Most High has created medicines out of the earth and a wise man will not despise them. 5 Was not bitter water made sweet with wood?a 6 The virtue of these things has come to the knowledge of men that he may be honored in his wonders. 7 By these he will cure and will remove their pains and of these the pharmacist makes healing compounds and will make up ointments for health. His works will never end 8 for the peace of God is over the face of the earth.

9 My son, do not neglect yourself in sickness but pray to the Lord and he will heal you. 10 Turn away from sin and order your hands aright and cleanse your heart

---

a Exodus 15:23–26.

from all sin. ¹¹ Offer sweet-smelling sacrifice and a memorial of fine flour and make an offering of oil. ¹² Then give the physician his place for the Lord created him. Let him not depart from you for his works are necessary. ¹³ For there is a time when you must fall into the hands of doctors ¹⁴ and they will beseech the Lord that he bless what they prescribe to relieve and cure for your preservation. ¹⁵ He who sins in the sight of his Maker will fall into the hands of the physician.

Mourning the dead

¹⁶ My son, shed tears for the dead and begin to lament as if you had suffered some great harm and according to the law cover his body and neglect not his burial. ¹⁷ For fear of being spoken ill of, weep bitterly for a day and then comfort yourself in your sadness. ¹⁸ Make mourning for him according to his merit for a day or two for fear of criticism. ¹⁹ From sadness comes death and the sorrow of the heart weakens a person. ²⁰ In calamity sorrow remains and the substance of the poor man is according to his heart. ²¹ Do not give your heart up to sadness but drive it from you and remember the end of life. ²² Do not forget for there is no returning, and you do the dead no good and will hurt yourself. ²³ "Remember my judgment: for yours will be like it; yesterday for me, and today for you." ²⁴ When the dead is at rest, let his remembrance end and be comforted for him in the departure of his spirit.

Worker and sage

²⁵ The wisdom of the scribe depends on his time of leisure and he who is not overly busy may receive wisdom. ²⁶ How can he become wise who directs the plough and who glories in the driving whip and urges on the oxen with it and is occupied in his work and whose whole talk is about the offspring of bulls? ²⁷ He gives his mind to turning up furrows and his worry is to give his cows fodder.

²⁸ So too is every craftsman and master workman who labors night and day, those who cut engraved seals, and each by his continual diligence varies the figure. He gives his attention to making a lifelike image and by his care will finish the work. ²⁹ So does the smith sitting by the anvil contemplating his iron work. The smoke of the fire melts his flesh and he suffers the heat of the furnace. ³⁰ The noise of the hammer is always in his ears and his eye is upon the pattern of the thing he makes. ³¹ He sets his mind to finish his work and his watching to polish it to perfection. ³² So does the potter sitting at his work, turning the wheel with his feet. He takes great care with his work and reckons his success by his output. ³³ He fashions the clay with his arm and kneads it beneath his feet. ³⁴ He gives his attention to finish the glazing and is careful to clean the furnace. ³⁵ All these men trust to their hands and every one is wise in his own art. ³⁶ Without these a city is not built: men cannot dwell in it or walk about it.

³⁷ Yet they are not elected to the council of the people or hold high rank in the assembly. ³⁸ They do not sit upon a judge's seat and the sentence of judgment they do not understand, neither can they teach discipline or judgment, and they are not to be found where proverbs are made. ³⁹ But they strengthen the state of the world and their mind is in the practice of their craft.

The scholar

39 The wise man applies his soul and searches in the law of the Most High. He seeks out the wisdom of all the ancients and is occupied with the prophets. ² He remembers the discourses of renowned men and penetrates the subtleties of parables. ³ He searches out the hidden meanings of proverbs and is conversant in the secrets of parables. ⁴ He serves among great men and appears before the governor. ⁵ He passes into strange countries, for he tests good and evil among men. ⁶ He will give his heart to rise early to seek the Lord who made him and he will pray in the sight of the Most High. ⁷ He will open his mouth in prayer and will make supplication for his sins. ⁸ For if it pleases the great Lord, he will fill him with the spirit of understanding. ⁹ He will pour forth the words of his wisdom as showers, and in his prayer he will confess to the Lord. ¹⁰ He will direct his counsel and his knowledge and meditate on his secrets. ¹¹ He will reveal the knowledge he has learned and will glory in the law of the

covenant of the Lord.

Hymn to the Creator

12 Many will praise his wisdom and it will never be forgotten. 13 His memory will not disappear and his name will be honored from generation to generation. 14 Nations will declare his wisdom and the congregation will proclaim his praise. 15 If he continues, he will leave a name above a thousand; and if he rests, it will be to his advantage.

16 I will yet meditate that I may speak out for I am filled as with a holy delight. 17 Hear me, you divine offspring, and bud forth as the rose planted by a stream of waters. 18 Give a sweet odor as frankincense. 19 Send forth flowers, as the lily; yield a fragrance and bring forth leaves in grace, and praise with canticles, and bless the Lord in his works. 20 Magnify his name, give glory to him with the voice of your lips, with the canticles of your mouths, with harps, and praise him in this manner:

21 "All the works of the Lord are exceedingly good. 22 At his word the waters stood as a mountain, and at the words of his mouth the reservoirs of waters, 23 for at his commandment favor is shown and there is no diminishing of his salvation.

24 "The works of all flesh are before him and there is nothing hidden from his eyes. 25 He sees from eternity to eternity and there is nothing wonderful before him."

26 There is no saying, "What is this? Why is that?" For all things will be sought in their time. 27 His blessing has overflowed like a river. 28 And as a flood has watered the earth so will his wrath inflict the nations that have not sought after him. 29 Even as he turned the waters into dry land, and the earth was made dry, and his ways were made plain for their journey, so to sinners they are stumbling blocks in his wrath. 30 Good things were created for good men from the beginning; so for the wicked, good and evil things. 31 The principal things necessary for the life of men are water, fire, iron, salt, milk, bread of flour, honey, the cluster of the grape, oil and clothing. 32 All these things will be for good to the holy, only to sinners and the ungodly will they be turned into evil.

33 There are winds that are created for vengeance and in their fury they lay on grievous torments. 34 In the time of destruction they will pour out their force and they will appease the wrath of him who made them. 35 Fire, hail, famine and death, all these were created for vengeance. 36 The teeth of beasts, scorpions, serpents, and the sword that punishes the ungodly with destruction. 37 In his commandments they will rejoice and they will be ready upon earth when needed, and when their time has come they will not transgress his word.

38 Therefore from the beginning I have been sure; I have meditated and thought on these things and left them in writing. 39 All the works of the Lord are good and he will supply every need in due time. 40 It is not to be said, "This is worse than that." All things will prove good in their time. 41 Now therefore with the whole heart and voice praise him and bless the name of the Lord.

Life's hardships

40 Tedious work was created for all men and a heavy yoke is upon the children of Adam from the day of their coming out of their mother's womb until the day of their burial into the mother of all. 2 Their thoughts and fears of the heart, their anxieties of things to come, and the day of their death; 3 from the man who sits on a glorious throne, to the man who is humbled in earth and ashes; 4 from the man who wears purple and bears the crown, even to the man who is dressed in rough linen; there is wrath, envy, trouble, unrest, the fear of death, continual anger and strife. 5 And when one rests upon his bed, in his sleep at night his dreams confuse him. 6 He gets little or no rest and afterward in sleep, as if keeping watch, 7 he is troubled by the visions of his mind, as if he had escaped in the day of battle; but at the instant of his rescue, he awakes and wonders that his fear is gone.

8 Such things happen to all flesh, both man and beast, and upon sinners even sevenfold more. 9 Moreover, death and bloodshed, strife and sword, oppressions, famine and affliction and scourges: 10 all these things are created for the wicked, and because of them the flood came. 11 All things that are of the earth will return to the earth again and all waters will return

to the sea. 12 All bribery and injustice will be blotted out but fidelity will stand forever. 13 The riches of the unjust will dry up like a wadi and will pass away like a clap of thunder in the rain. 14 A generous man will rejoice but transgressors will pine away in the end. 15 The children of sinners will not bring forth many branches and will wither as exposed roots on the top of a rock. 16 The reed growing above the water and at the bank of a river will be pulled up before the grass.

Values

17 Grace is like a garden of blessings and mercy remains forever. 18 The life of the laborer who is content with what he has will be sweet and in it you will find a treasure. 19 Children and the building of a city will establish a man's name but a blameless wife will be counted better than both. 20 Wine and music rejoice the heart, but the love of wisdom is better than both. 21 The flute and the harp make a sweet melody but a pleasant tongue is better than both. 22 Your eye seeks grace and beauty but more than these green sown fields. 23 A friend and companion meet together in friendship but better than both is a wife with her husband. 24 Brothers and help are for the time of trouble but mercy will deliver more than them both. 25 Gold and silver make the feet stand sure, wise counsel lifts up the heart, but above these is the fear of the Lord. 26 There is no want in the fear of the Lord and it need not seek for help. 27 The fear of the Lord is like a garden of blessings and covers a man above all glory.

28 My son, in your lifetime do not be a beggar for it is better to die than to beg. 29 When a man must depend on another's table, he exists but does not live; for he feeds his soul with another man's meat. 30 But a man, well instructed and taught, will take care of himself. 31 Begging may be sweet in the mouth of the unwise but in his stomach there will burn a fire.

Death

41 O Death, how bitter is the reminder of you to a man who has peace in his possessions, 2 to a man who is at rest and whose ways are prosperous in all things and who is still able to enjoy food! 3 O death,

your sentence is welcome to the man who is in need and whose strength fails, 4 who is in a decrepit age and who worries about all things, and to the distrustful who loses patience! 5 Do not fear the sentence of death. Remember what things you have done and what will come after you; this sentence is from the Lord upon all flesh, 6 and it will come upon you by the good pleasure of the Most High, whether ten, or a hundred, or a thousand years. 7 There is no inquiring about it in Sheol.

8 The children of sinners become children of abominations and they are found in the vicinity of the houses of the ungodly. 9 The inheritance of the children of sinners will perish and with their posterity will be a perpetual reproach. 10 The children will complain of an ungodly father because they suffer reproach for his sake. 11 Woe to you, ungodly men, who have forsaken the law of the Most High Lord. 12 When you are born, you are born in a curse; and if you die, a curse is your lot. 13 All things that are of the earth will return to the earth; so the ungodly will pass from curse to destruction. 14 The mourning of men is about their bodies but the name of sinners will be blotted out.

15 Protect a good name for it will continue with you, more precious and greater than a thousand treasures. 16 The days of a good life are numbered but a good name will continue forever.

A sense of shame

17 My children, keep instruction in peace: for wisdom that is hidden, and a treasure that is not seen, what profit is there in either of them? 18 Better is the man who hides his folly than the man who hides his wisdom. 19 Therefore have respect for these things about which I am now going to speak. 20 For it is not good to keep all shamefacedness and all things do not please the opinion of all men. 21 Be ashamed of immorality before father or mother, of a lie before a governor or a man in power, 22 of an offense before a prince or a judge, of iniquity before a congregation or the people, 23 of injustice before a companion or friend. And in regard to the place where you dwell, 24 be ashamed of theft, of breaking an oath or the covenant, of stretching

out the elbow at bread, of surliness in giving and taking, ²⁵ of silence before those who salute you, of looking upon a loose woman, and of rejecting the request from your relative, ²⁶ (turn not away your face from your neighbor), and of taking away a portion and not giving it back. ²⁷ Do not gaze upon another man's wife, or ask about his maidservant, and do not approach her bed. ²⁸ Be ashamed of giving reprimands before friends; and after you make a gift, do not backbite.

42 Do not repeat the word which you have heard and do not disclose the thing that is secret. Then you will show proper respect and find favor before all men. Do not be ashamed of any of the following things and do not allow personal respect to cause you to sin thereby: ² of the law of the Most High and of his covenant, of judgment to justify the ungodly, ³ of keeping account with partner and travelers, of the division of the inheritance of friends, ⁴ of exactness of balance and weights, of getting much or little, ⁵ of the corruption of buying from merchants, of much correction of children and of harsh punishment of a wicked slave. ⁶ Safe keeping is good over a wicked wife. ⁷ Where there are many hands, lock up and keep count of all things in number and weight; put all in writing that you give out or take in. ⁸ Do not be ashamed to correct the unwise and foolish, and the aged who quarrel with young men; and you will be well instructed in all things and well approved in the sight of all men.

Care of daughters
⁹ A daughter keeps her father awake in the dark of night, and worry about her takes away his sleep; when she is young, lest she find no husband; and when she is married, lest she be hated; ¹⁰ in her virginity, lest she should be corrupted, and be found with child in her father's house; and having a husband, lest she should misbehave herself or at the least be barren. ¹¹ Keep a strict watch over a brash daughter, lest at any time she makes you become the laughingstock to your enemies, a byword in the city, and a reproach among the people, and she makes you ashamed before all the multitude.

¹² Do not look at everybody's beauty and do not linger among women. ¹³ For from garments comes the moth and from a woman the iniquity of a man. ¹⁴ For the iniquity of a man is better than a woman doing a "good turn," and it is a woman who brings shame and reproach.

Hymn to the Lord
¹⁵ I will now remember the works of the Lord and I will declare the things I have seen. By the words of the Lord his works are made. ¹⁶ The sun looks down on all things with its light and the work of the Lord is full of the glory. ¹⁷ Has not the Lord made the saints to declare all his wonderful works which the Lord Almighty has firmly established for his glory?

¹⁸ He has searched out the deep and the hearts of men and considered their crafty devices. ¹⁹ For the Lord knows all that is known and has seen the signs of the world; he declares the things that are past and the things that are to come and reveals the traces of hidden things. ²⁰ No thought escapes him and no word can hide itself from him.

²¹ He has beautified the glorious works of his wisdom; and he is from eternity to eternity, and to him nothing may be added, ²² nor can he be diminished, and he has no need of any counselor. ²³ O how desirable are all his works and what we can know is but as a spark! ²⁴ All these things live and remain forever and for every use all things obey him. ²⁵ All things are double, one opposite the other, and he has made nothing without its purpose. ²⁶ He has established the good things of every one. And who can have enough of beholding his glory?

The sun
43 The firmament on high is his beauty, the beauty of heaven with its glorious spectacle.

² The sun when it appears reveals him in its rising, an admirable instrument, this work of the Most High. ³ At noon it parches the earth and who can abide its burning heat? ⁴ A man tending a furnace works in heat but the sun burns the mountains three times as much, breathing out fiery vapors, and with its bright beams it blinds the eyes. ⁵ Great is the Lord who

made it and at his command it hastens its course.

The moon

6 He created the moon to serve in its season, to declare the times and to be a sign to the world.[a] 7 From the moon comes the sign of the festival day, a light that wanes when perfectly full. 8 The month is called after the moon, increasing wonderfully in its perfection. 9 Being an instrument of the hosts on high, shining gloriously in the firmament of heaven.

The stars

10 The glory of the stars is the beauty of heaven; the Lord enlightens the world on high. 11 By the words of the holy one they stand as ordered, and never fail in their watches.

The rainbow

12 Look upon the rainbow and bless him who made it; it is very beautiful in its brightness. 13 It encompasses the heaven about with the circle of its glory, the hands of the Most High have displayed it.

Marvels of nature

14 By his commandment he makes the snow to fall in flakes and sends forth swiftly the lightnings of his judgment. 15 Through this is the treasury opened and the clouds fly forth like birds. 16 By his greatness he has fixed the clouds and the hailstones are broken. 17 At his sight the mountains are shaken and at his will the south wind will blow. 18 The noise of his thunder strikes the earth, so does the northern storm and the whirlwind.

19 As birds lighting upon the earth, he scatters snow, and its fall is as the coming down of locusts. 20 The eye admires the beauty of its whiteness and the heart is astonished at its shower. 21 He pours frost as salt upon the earth; and when it freezes, it becomes like the thorns of thistles. 22 The cold north wind blows and the water freezes into crystal. Upon every pool of waters it rests and clothes the waters as a breastplate. 23 And he levels the mountains, burns the wilderness and consumes all that is green like fire. 24 The speedy coming of a mist soon heals all and the dew that comes over-

powers the heat.

25 At his word the wind is still and with his thought he appeases the deep and the Lord has planted islands therein. 26 Let those who sail on the sea tell of its dangers, and when we hear, we will marvel. 27 There are very great and wonderful works, a variety of beasts and of all living things and the huge creatures of the sea. 28 Through him is established their way and purpose and by his will all things are accomplished.

29 We shall say much and yet shall want words. But the sum of our words is, "He is all." 30 Who can extol him as he is? For the Almighty himself is greater than all his works. 31 The Lord is terrible and exceedingly great, and his power is admirable. 32 Glorify the Lord as much as you possibly can, yet he will far exceed your praise, and his magnificence is wonderful. 33 Blessing the Lord, exalt him as much as you can for he is above all praise. 34 When you exalt him put forth all your strength and do not become weary for you can never go far enough. 35 Who has seen him and can describe him? And who will magnify him as he is from the beginning? 36 There are many things hidden from us that are greater than these for we have seen but a few of his works. 37 But the Lord has made all things and to the godly he has given wisdom.

Praise of the ancients

44 Let us now praise men of piety, and our fathers in their generation. 2 The Lord has wrought great glory through his majesty from the beginning. 3 Such as have borne rule in their dominions, men of great power,[a] and endowed with their wisdom, showing forth in their counsel the dignity of prophets, 4 and ruling over the people of their time, and by the strength of wisdom instructing the people in most holy words.[b] 5 Such as by their skill sought out musical tunes and published canticles of the scriptures.[c] 6 Men rich in virtue, studying beauty, and living at peace in their houses.[d] 7 All these have gained glory in their times and were praised in their days. 8 Those who were born of them have left a name

---

a The Hebrew calendar was based on the moon.   a Like Joshua and David.   b Like Elijah and Isaiah.
c The psalmists.   d Solomon.

behind them that their praises might be related.

⁹ There are some for whom there is no memorial; who have perished, as if they had never been, and became as if they had never been born, and their children with them. ¹⁰ These were men of mercy whose godly deeds have not failed. ¹¹ Good things continue with their seed; ¹² their posterity are a holy inheritance and their seed has kept the covenants. ¹³ Their children for their sakes remain forever; their seed and their glory will not be forsaken. ¹⁴ Their bodies are buried in peace and their name lives from generation to generation. ¹⁵ Let the people show forth their wisdom and the assembly declare their praise.

¹⁶ Enoch pleased God and was taken up into paradise as an example of repentance to all generations.

¹⁷ Noah was found perfect and just; in the time of wrath he became a renewer. ¹⁸ Therefore, when the flood came, there was a remnant left on the earth. ¹⁹ The covenants of the world were made with him, that all flesh should not be destroyed with the flood.

²⁰ Abraham was the great father of a multitude of nations and there was not found the like to him in glory, who kept the law of the Most High and was in covenant with him. ²¹ In his flesh he established the covenant and in temptation he was found faithful. ²² Therefore by an oath the Lord gave him glory in his posterity, that he should increase as the dust of the earth, ²³ and that he would exalt his seed as the stars, and they should inherit from sea to sea and from the river to the ends of the earth.

²⁴ He did in like manner with Isaac for the sake of Abraham his father. ²⁵ The blessing of all nations and his covenant the Lord confirmed upon the head of Jacob. ²⁶ He acknowledged him with his blessings, gave him an inheritance and divided his portion among twelve tribes. ²⁷ And from his descendants, the Lord brought from him a man of mercy,ᵉ who found grace in the eyes of all men.

45 Moses was beloved of God and men, whose memory is a benediction. ² He made him like the saints in glory and magnified him in the fear of his enemies, and with his words he made prodigies come to pass.ᵃ ³ The Lord glorified him in the sight of kings, gave him commandments in the sight of his people and revealed to him part of his glory. ⁴ He sanctified him in his faith and meekness and chose him from among all men. ⁵ He made him hear his voice and brought him into a cloud. ⁶ He gave him commandments face to face, the law of life and knowledge that he might teach Jacob his covenant and Israel his judgments.

⁷ He exalted Aaron his brother, like himself of the tribe of Levi. ⁸ He made an everlasting covenant with him and gave him the priesthood of the people and made him blessed in glory. ⁹ He girded him about with a glorious girdle and clothed him with a robe of glory and crowned him with majestic attire. ¹⁰ He put sandals upon his feet, breeches, the sacred priestly vestment, and he surrounded him with many little bells of gold, ¹¹ that as he went there might be a sound and a noise made that might be heard in the temple for a reminder to the sons of his people. ¹² He gave him a holy robe of gold, blue, and purple, a woven work of a wise man; with the oracle of judgment, Urim and Thummin;ᵇ ¹³ with twisted scarlet, the work of an artist, with precious stones cut and set in gold, and graven by the work of a jeweler, as a remembrance of the number of the tribes of Israel. ¹⁴ And a crown of gold upon his turban, whereon was engraved "Holiness," an ornament of honor, a work of power and delightful to the eyes for its beauty. ¹⁵ Before his time there were none so beautiful, even from the beginning. ¹⁶ No stranger was ever clothed with them but only his children alone,ᶜ and his grandchildren forever. ¹⁷ His sacrifices were consumed with fire every day. ¹⁸ Moses ordained him and anointed him with holy oil. ¹⁹ This was made to him an everlasting covenant and to his seed all the days of heaven to execute the office of the priesthood, to give praise and to bless his

---

e Moses, as follows.   45a The plagues of Egypt. was reserved to Aaron's descendants.   b Sacred objects in Ex. 28:30.   c The priesthood

people in the name of the Lord. ²⁰ He chose him out of all men living to offer sacrifice to the Lord, incense, and a good odor, for a memorial to make atonement for his people; ²¹ and he gave him power in his commandments, in the covenants of his judgments, that he should teach Jacob his testimonies and give light to Israel in his law. ²² Outsiders conspired against him and through envy the men who were with Dathan and Abiron and the company of Korah harassed him in the wilderness in their wrath. ²³ The Lord God saw and it did not please him and they were destroyed by his angry indignation. ²⁴ He wrought wonders against them and consumed them with a flame of fire. ²⁵ He added glory to Aaron, gave him an inheritance; he allowed him the firstfruits of the increase of the earth. ²⁶ He prepared bread in the firstfruits in abundance, for they eat the sacrifices of the Lord which he gave to him and to his descendants. ²⁷ But he shall not inherit among the people in the land and he has no portion among the people; for the Lord himself is his portion and inheritance.

²⁸ Phineas, the son of Eleazar, is the third in glory, by imitating him in the fear of the Lord. ²⁹ He stood fast when the people fell away, in the goodness and readiness of his soul he appeased God for Israel. ³⁰ Therefore the Lord made to him a covenant of peace, to be the prince of the sanctuary and of his people, that the dignity of priesthood should be to him and to his descendants forever. ³¹ A covenant was also given to David, the son of Jesse of the tribe of Judah, an inheritance to him and to his descendants, that he might give wisdom unto our hearts to judge his people in justice, that their prosperity might not be abolished. He made their glory everlasting in their nation.

46 Joshua, the son of Nun, who was successor of Moses among the prophets, was great according to his name[a] and mighty in war. He was a very great savior for the elect of God who overthrew the enemies who rose up against them so that he might give Israel its inheritance. ² How glo-

rious was he when he lifted his hands and stretched his sword against cities? ³ Who before him had resisted so strongly? For he fought the enemies of the Lord. ⁴ Was not the sun held back by his anger and one day made as two? ⁵ He called upon the Most High Sovereign when the enemies assaulted him on every side, and the great and holy God answered him by sending hailstones of very great force. ⁶ He made a violent assault against the country of his enemies and in the descent of Bethhoron destroyed his adversaries, so that the nations might know his power and that it is not easy to fight against God. For he followed the Mighty One.

⁷ In the days of Moses he did a deed of mercy, he and Caleb, the son of Jephunneh, who resisted the enemy, and withheld the people from sins, and stilled their wicked rumors. ⁸ The two being appointed were delivered out of the danger from among six hundred thousand infantrymen to bring them into their inheritance, the land that flows with milk and honey. ⁹ The Lord gave strength also to Caleb, and his strength continued even to his old age. So that he went up into the hill country of the land and his descendants obtained it for an inheritance, ¹⁰ that all the children of Israel might understand that it is good to obey the holy God.

¹¹ Then all the judges, every one by name whose heart was not corrupted, who turned not away from the Lord, ¹² that their memory might be blessed, and that their bones revive from their place of rest, ¹³ and may their name continue to flourish forever in their children.

Samuel, the prophet of the Lord, loved by the Lord his God, established a new government and anointed leaders[b] over his people. ¹⁴ By the law of the Lord he judged the congregation and the Lord watched over Jacob. By his fidelity he was proved a prophet. ¹⁵ He was known to be faithful in his words because he saw the God of light ¹⁶ and called upon the name of the Lord Almighty in fighting against the enemies who beset him on every side, and he offered a lamb without blemish as sacri-

---

a i.e. "The Lord saves."   b Saul and David.

fice. [17] The Lord thundered from heaven and made his voice heard with a great noise. [18] He crushed the leaders of Tyre and all the lords of the Philistines, [19] and before the time of the end of his life in the world, he protested before the Lord and his anointed, "I have not taken anything from any man, not money, not even a shoe." And no man did accuse him. [20] Even after he slept, he prophesied to the king and revealed to him the end of his life, and he lifted up his voice from the earth in prophecy to blot out the wickedness of the nation.

47 Then Nathan the prophet arose in the days of David. [2] As the fat is taken away from the flesh,[a] so was David chosen from among the children of Israel. [3] He played with lions as with goats, and with bears as with the lambs of the flock. [4] In his youth did he not kill the giant and take away shame from his people? [5] In lifting up his hand with the stone in the sling he beat down the boasting of Goliath. [6] He called upon the Lord the Almighty to give strength to his right hand to kill the mighty warrior and to exalt the power of his nation. [7] So in ten thousands did they glorify him and praised him in the blessings of the Lord in offering to him a crown of glory. [8] He destroyed the enemies on every side and wiped out the Philistines, his adversaries; even to this day he broke their power. [9] In all his works he gave thanks to the Holy One, the Most High, with words of glory. [10] With all his heart he hymned and loved his Maker who gave him power against his enemies. [11] He assigned singers before the altar to make sweet melody. [12] He added beauty to the festivals and set in order the solemn times throughout the year that they should praise the holy name of the Lord and magnify the holiness of God from the morning. [13] The Lord took away his sins and exalted his power forever; and he gave him a covenant of the kingdom and a throne of glory in Israel.

[14] After him arose up a wise son and for his sake he cast down all the power of the enemies. [15] Solomon reigned in days of peace and the Lord brought all his enemies under him that he might build a house to his name and prepare a sanctuary forever. O how wise were you in your youth! [16] And you were filled as a river with wisdom and your soul covered the earth. [17] And you did multiply riddles and parables; your name went abroad to the islands far off and you were beloved in your peace. [18] The countries wondered at you for your canticles and proverbs, parables and interpretations. [19] In the name of the Lord God, whose surname is God of Israel, [20] you did gather gold as copper and did multiply silver as lead.

[21] And you did bow yourself to women and by your body you were brought under subjection. [22] You put a stain on your honor and defiled your posterity so as to bring wrath upon your children and to have your folly kindled; [23] in that you caused the kingdom to be divided and out of Ephraim a rebellious kingdom came to rule. [24] But God will not forget his mercy and he will not destroy or abolish his own works, neither will he cut off by the roots the offspring of his elect, nor will he utterly take away the seed of him who loves the Lord. [25] Therefore he gave a remnant to Jacob and to David a root of his stock.[b]

[26] Solomon rested with his fathers. [27] He left behind him a son, the folly of the nation: [28] Rehoboam who had little wisdom, who turned away the people through his counsel. [29] Jeroboam, the son of Nabat, caused Israel to sin and showed Ephraim the way of sin, and their sins were multiplied exceedingly. [30] They removed them far away from their land. [31] They followed every kind of iniquity until vengeance came upon them and put an end to all their sins.

48 Elijah the prophet arose like a fire and his word burned like a torch. [2] He brought a famine upon them, and those who provoked him in their envy were reduced to a small number, for they could not endure the commandments of the Lord. [3] By the word of the Lord he shut up the heavens and three times he brought down

---

a In preparing a peace offering.   b The hope of a Davidic Messiah.

fire from heaven. [4] Thus was Elijah magnified in his wondrous works. And who can boast like you? [5] You raised a corpse from death and from Sheol by the word of the Lord God. [6] You brought down kings to destruction and easily broke their power in pieces, and the famed from their bed. [7] Who heard judgment in Sinai, and in Horeb the judgments of vengeance. [8] Who anointed kings to inflict punishment and made prophets to succeed you. [9] You were taken up in a whirlwind of fire, in a chariot of fiery horses. [10] You are ready at the appointed time to appease the wrath of the Lord, to reconcile the heart of the father to the son, and to restore the tribes of Jacob. [11] Blessed are they who saw you and were honored with your friendship. [12] For we live only in our life but after death our name will not be such.

[13] It was Elijah who was covered with the whirlwind, and Elisha was filled with his spirit. In his days he did not fear the prince and no man was more powerful than he. [14] No word could overcome him and after death his body prophesied.[a] [15] In his life he did great wonders and in death he wrought miracles. [16] Despite this the people did not repent, neither did they depart from their sins until they were cast out of their land and were scattered through all the earth. [17] There was left but a small number of people and a ruler in the house of David. [18] Some of them did that which pleased God but others committed many sins.

[19] Hezekiah fortified his city and brought in water into the midst of it and he dug a rock with iron and made a well for water. [20] In his days Sennacherib came up and sent the Rabshakeh. He lifted up his hand against them and he stretched out his hand against Zion and made boasts through his arrogance. [21] Then their hearts and hands trembled and they were in pain like women in labor. [22] They called upon the Lord who is merciful, and spreading their hands, they lifted them up to heaven; and the holy Lord God quickly heard their voice. [23] He was not mindful of their sins, neither did he deliver them up to their enemies, but he purified them by the hand of Isaiah, the holy prophet. [24] He overthrew the army of the Assyrians and the angel of the Lord destroyed them.

[25] Hezekiah did that which pleased the Lord and walked valiantly in the ways of David his father, which Isaiah, the great prophet and faithful man in the sight of God, had commanded him. [26] In his days the sun went backward and he lengthened the king's life. [27] With a great spirit he saw the things that are to come to pass at last and comforted the mourners of Zion. [28] He showed what would come to pass forever and secret things before they came.

49 The memory of Josiah is like the blending of a sweet smell made by the art of a perfumer. [2] His remembrance will be sweet as honey in every mouth and as music at a banquet of wine. [3] He was directed by God to convert the people and he took away the abominations of wickedness. [4] He directed his heart towards the Lord and in the days of sinners he strengthened godliness.

[5] Except for David, Hezekiah and Josiah all committed sin. [6] For the kings of Judah forsook the law of the Most High and despised the fear of God. [7] So their kingdoms were taken from them and their glory given to a strange people [8] who burned the chosen city of the sanctuary and made its streets desolate, according to the prediction of Jeremiah. [9] For they treated him wrongly who was consecrated a prophet from his mother's womb, to overthrow, pluck up, destroy, to build again and plant.

[10] It was Ezekiel who saw the glorious vision, which was shown him upon the chariot of the cherubim. [11] For God remembered his enemies with a storm and did good to those who showed right ways.

[12] May the bones of the twelve prophets spring up from where they rest for they strengthened the people of Jacob and redeemed them by strong faith.

[13] How shall we magnify Zerubbabel? For he was like a signet on the right hand. [14] In like manner was Jeshua, the son of

---

a Referring to a miraculous occurrence after death.

Jozadak? In their days they built the house and set up a temple holy to the Lord, prepared for everlasting glory.

15 Let Nehemiah be remembered for a long time, who raised up for us our walls that were cast down and set up the gates and the bars, who rebuilt our houses.

16 Few like Enoch have been formed on earth, yet he also was taken from the earth. 17 Nor was there any man like Joseph. He was a man born leader of his brothers, the support of his family, the ruler of his brothers, the hope of the people. 18 His bones were cared for, and after death they prophesied.

19 Seth and Shem obtained glory among men and above every soul Adam who was in the beginning.

50 Simon the high priest,[a] the son of Onias, was the leader of his brethren and pride of his people. In his life he repaired the house and fortified the temple. 2 He set the foundations for the high double walls and the high retaining walls of the temple. 3 In his days the wells of water flowed out and they were filled as the sea above measure. 4 He took care of his nation and saved it from destruction. 5 He prevailed to enlarge the city and the entrance of the house and the court, and obtained glory in his conversation with the people.

6 He shone in his days as the morning star in the midst of a cloud and as the moon at its fullest. 7 As the sun when it shines, so did he shine in the temple of God. 8 He was as the rainbow giving light in the bright clouds, and as the flower of roses in the days of the spring, and as the lilies that are on the edge of the water, and as the sprig of frankincense in the time of summer; 9 as the bright fire and frankincense burning in the censer, 10 like a vessel of hammered gold, adorned with every precious stone; 11 as an olive tree budding forth, and a cypress tree rearing itself on high. When he put on the robe of glory and was clothed with the perfection of power, 12 he went up to the holy altar; he honored the sanctuary with holiness. 13 And when he took the portions out of the hands of the priests, he himself stood by the altar. And about him was the garland of his brothers, and as the cedar planted on Mount Libanus, 14 and as branches of palm trees, they stood round about him, all the sons of Aaron in their glory. 15 The oblation of the Lord was in their hands before all the congregation of Israel; and finishing his service on the altar, to honor the offering of the Most High King, 16 he stretched forth his hand to make a libation and offered the blood of the grape. 17 He poured it out at the foot of the altar, a divine odor to the Most High Prince. 18 Then the sons of Aaron shouted, they sounded the trumpets of hammered metal and made a great noise to be heard for a remembrance before God. 19 Then all the people together made haste and fell down to the earth upon their faces, to adore the Lord their God, and to pray to the Almighty God, the Most High. 20 The singers lifted up their voices and in the great house the sound of sweet melody was increased. 21 The people in prayer besought the Lord the Most High, until the worship of the Lord was perfected, and they finished their office. 22 Then coming down, he lifted up his hands over all the congregation of the children of Israel to give glory to God with his lips, and to glory in his name; 23 and he repeated his prayer, willing to show the power of God.

24 Now pray to the God of all who has done great things in all the earth, who has increased our days from our mother's womb, and has done with us according to his mercy. 25 May he grant us joyfulness of heart, and that there be peace in our days of Israel forever, 26 that Israel may believe that the mercy of God is with us, to deliver us in our days.

27 There are two nations which my soul abhors and the third is no nation: 28 those who live on Mount Seir, the Philistines and the foolish people who dwell in Shechem.[b]

29 Jesus, the son of Sirach, of Jerusalem, has written in this book the doctrine of wisdom and instruction and from his heart poured forth wisdom.

30 Blessed is he who concerns himself with these good things, and he who lays

---

a Simeon II, a contemporary of the author.   b The Samaritans.

them up in his heart will be wise always. ³¹ For if he does them, he will be strong to do all things, because the light of God guides his steps.

Appendix

51 A prayer of Jesus, the son of Sirach. I shall give thanks to you, O Lord, O King, and I shall praise you, O God my Savior.

² I shall give glory to your name for you have been a helper and a protector to me. ³ You have preserved my body from destruction, from the snare of an unjust tongue, and from the lips of those who forge lies; and in the sight of those who stood by, you have been my helper. ⁴ And you have delivered me, according to the multitude of the mercy of your name, from those that did roar and were prepared to devour me. ⁵ Out of the hands of those who sought my life and from the walls of afflictions which surrounded me; ⁶ from the oppression of the flame which surrounded me and in the midst of which I was not burned; ⁷ from the depth of the belly of Sheol, and from an unclean tongue, and from lying words, from an unjust king, and from a slanderous tongue. ⁸ My soul will praise the Lord even to death. ⁹ My life was drawing near to Sheol beneath. ¹⁰ They surrounded me on every side and there was no one that would help me. I looked for the aid of men and there was none. ¹¹ Then I remembered your mercy, O Lord, and your works, which are from the beginning of the world; ¹² how you deliver those who wait for you, O Lord, and save them out of the hands of the nations. ¹³ You have exalted my dwelling place upon the earth and I have prayed for death to pass away. ¹⁴ I called upon the Lord, the Father of my lord, that he would not leave me in the day of my trouble, and in the time of the proud, without help. ¹⁵ I shall praise your name continually and shall praise it with thanksgiving. My prayer was heard. ¹⁶ You have saved me from destruction and have delivered me from the evil time. ¹⁷ Therefore, I shall give you thanks and praise and bless the name of the Lord.

¹⁸ When I was yet young, before I wandered about, I sought for wisdom openly in my prayer. ¹⁹ I prayed for her before the temple and unto the very end I shall seek after her. She blossomed as a grape soon ripe. ²⁰ My heart delighted in her, my foot walked in the right path, from my youth up I sought after her. ²¹ I inclined my ear a little and received her. ²² I found much wisdom in myself and profited much from it. ²³ To him who gives me wisdom I shall give glory. ²⁴ For I have determined to follow her. I have had a zeal for good and shall not be confused. ²⁵ My soul has wrestled with her and in doing it I have been confirmed. ²⁶ I stretched forth my hands on high and I mourned my ignorance of her. ²⁷ I directed my soul to her and in knowledge I found her. ²⁸ I possessed my heart with her from the beginning, therefore I shall not be forsaken. ²⁹ My heart was urged to seek her, therefore I shall have a good possession. ³⁰ The Lord has given me a tongue for my reward and with it I shall praise him.

³¹ Draw near to me, you unlearned, and gather yourselves together into my house of instruction. ³² Why are you slow? And what do you say of these things? Your souls are exceedingly thirsty. ³³ I have opened my mouth and have spoken. Buy these things for yourselves without silver, ³⁴ and submit your neck to the yoke and let your soul receive instruction, for it is ready to be found. ³⁵ Behold with your own eyes how I have labored a little and have found much rest for myself. ³⁶ Receive instruction as a great sum of money, and possess abundance of gold by her. ³⁷ Let your soul rejoice in his mercy and you will not be shamed in praising him. ³⁸ Do your work before the assigned time and he will give you your reward in his time.

Getting to the Bottom Line

A good counselor when presented with a problem tries to find the root cause of it. For example, a person's excessive pride can lead to all sorts of faults—lies, uncharitableness, even cheating. This preoccupation with root causes also concerned many biblical writers.

The Babylonian captivity had a great influence on the religious thinking of the Jews. They sought to understand why they, the Chosen People, should endure such a trial. They were looking for the root cause. In the Book of Baruch the answer is given: the infidelity of the Jews to the law of Yahweh. Even so, God will keep His Covenant with His people and they will return to Jerusalem.

This book seems to be the effort of a number of authors, presenting the thought of the prophet Jeremiah. Tradition assigns it to Baruch, who was Jeremiah's secretary. Jeremiah dictated some of his oracles to Baruch, who read them to the Jews. It is said that Baruch died in exile in Egypt. This book is based on many Jewish legalisms to show the falsity of pagan gods. It is included among the Bible's prophetic works.

BARUCH

1 THESE ARE THE words of the book which Baruch, the son of Neriah, the son of Mahseiah, the son of Zedekiah, the son of Hasadiah, the son of Hilkiah, wrote in Babylon ² in the fifth year,ᵃ on the seventh day of the month, at the time when the Chaldeans captured Jerusalem, and destroyed it by fire. ³ Baruch read aloud the words of this book to Jeconiah, son of Jehoiakim, ruler of Judah, and to all those people who came to hear this account. ⁴ Also to the nobles, the court officials, the elders; in short, to everyone, from the least even to the greatest, who lived in Babylon by the river Sud.

⁵ When they had heard it, they wept, fasted and prayed to the Lord. ⁶ They collected all the money each could afford ⁷ and sent it to Jerusalem to Jehoiakim the priest, the son of Hilkiah, the son of Shallum, and to the other priests, and to the Jews who were still with them in Jerusalem. ⁸ It was Baruch who on the tenth of the month of Sivan recovered the silver utensils, which had been looted from the Temple, in order to return them to the land of Judah. They were the silver utensils which

Zedekiah, the son of Josiah, king of Judah, had made ⁹ before Nebuchadnezzar, the king of Babylon, had deported from Jerusalem Jeconiah, the princes, the officials, and all the other people of the land, and brought them captives to Babylon.

¹⁰ They wrote: "We are sending you money to buy sacrifices, incense and meat offerings as atonement for sin to be offered at the altar of the Lord our God. ¹¹ Pray for the health of Nebuchadnezzar, king of Babylon, and for Belshazzar, his son, that their days on earth may last as long as heaven ¹² and that the Lord may give us strength, and enlighten our minds so that we may live under the protection of Nebuchadnezzar, king of Babylon, and that of his son, Belshazzar, and may we serve them many days and win their favor. ¹³ Also pray for us to the Lord our God because we have sinned against him and the anger of the Lord has not yet been turned from us. ¹⁴ Finally, we send you this book to read in the Lord's temple on feasts and meeting days.

¹⁵ You shall say: Justice belongs to the Lord but we people of Judah, ¹⁶ our rulers,

---

a 582 B.C., the anniversary of the fall of Jerusalem.

1267

leaders, prophets, priests, and ancestors bear the look of shame. 17 We have sinned before the Lord our God, and have not believed him nor put our trust in him. 18 We were not obedient to him, nor have we listened to the voice of the Lord our God, nor kept the commandments which he gave us. 19 From the day when the Lord brought our fathers out of the land of Egypt until today, we have been disobedient to the Lord our God. We have turned away from him and have not heard his voice. 20 As a result today many evils have befallen us, as well as the curses which the Lord passed on through Moses his servant who brought our fathers out of the land of Egypt into a land flowing with milk and honey. 21 Despite the warnings of the prophets he sent us, we have not listened to the voice of the Lord our God. 22 Each of us has followed the inclinations of his own wicked heart, to serve strange gods, and to do evil in the sight of the Lord our God.

2 As a result, the Lord our God has carried out the sentence he passed on us, on our judges, on our rulers, on our leaders, and, indeed, on all Israel and Judah. 2 As it is written in the law of Moses, the evils that the Lord inflicted on us and on Jerusalem have never been witnessed before beneath heaven. 3 Who could imagine that a man would eat the flesh of his own son and daughter? 4,5 As a result God allowed us to be captured by the kings who surround us, to be damned and enslaved by the nations among whom the Lord has scattered us; all because we have sinned against the Lord our God by not obeying his voice.

6 Justice is given by the Lord our God, resulting in the downcast faces we bear, as did our forefathers. 7 The Lord has sentenced us to all the evils that have befallen us, 8 and we have not renounced our wicked ways to win back the favor of the Lord our God. 9 The Lord has waited for the right moment and allowed evil to fall on us because the Lord renders justice when his commandments are ignored. 10 The fact is that we have not listened to his voice or obeyed the commandments which he has set before us.

11 And now, O Lord God of Israel, who brought your people out of the land of Egypt with your might, with signs and wonders, with great power and with a strong arm, to make your name holy above all, 12 we have sinned, O Lord our God. We have done wrong, we have acted unjustly against all your commands. 13 Let your anger be turned from us who are a handful among the nations where you scattered us. 14 Hear, O Lord, our prayers and our petitions. Deliver us for your own glory and grant us your favor so that our captors may see it. 15 Let the whole world know that you are the Lord our God, and that Israel and his posterity honors your name. 16 Look down upon us, O Lord, from your holy dwelling place, think of us and hear us. 17 Open your eyes and behold: those who are in the land of the dead, whose souls have been taken from their bodies, cannot give glory and obedience to you, the Lord. 18 But the soul that is sorrowful for the greatness of evil it has done, and goes bowed down and feeble with failing eyes and a spiritual hunger, that soul gives glory and justice to you, the Lord.

19 It is not because of the merits of our ancestors that we pour out our prayers and beg mercy in your sight, O Lord our God; 20 but because you have made known your anger and indignation with us. This you have revealed through your servants the prophets who spoke: 21 "Thus says the Lord: 'Bow your heads and shoulders and serve the king of Babylon, and you will retain title to the land which I have promised your forefathers. 22 But if you will not listen to the voice of the Lord your God and serve the king of Babylon, I will separate you from the cities of Judah and from Jerusalem. 23 I will deprive you of happy and joyful voices, the voice of the bridegroom and of the bride, and all the land shall be desolate of people.' " 24 But we did not listen to your urging to serve the king of Babylon. As a result you have made good your promise which you delivered to us through your prophets with the result that the bones of our rulers and our ancestors have been scattered from their tombs. 25 Indeed, they were cast out to the heat of the sun and to the frost of the night. People have died in severe pain by famine, by the

sword and as refugees. ²⁶ Because of the sin of the house of Israel and the house of Judah, you have made your Temple what it has become today. ²⁷ And yet, O Lord our God, you have dealt with us according to your goodness and great mercy. ²⁸ It has been done as you promised your servant Moses on that day when you commanded him to write your law in the presence of the children of Israel, ²⁹ saying, "If you will not obey my voice, this great multitude will be turned into a very small number among the nations where I will scatter them; ³⁰ and I say this knowing the people will not hear me for they are thickheaded.

"In their exile they will remember these words ³¹ and they will realize that I am the Lord their God. I shall give them an understanding heart and an attentive ear. ³² Then they will praise me in the land of their captivity and will recall my name. ³³ They will turn away from their own wickedness and stubborn ways. ³⁴ Then I will bring them back again to the land which I secured with an oath to Abraham, Isaac, and Jacob, and they will be the masters of it. Their numbers will not grow smaller because I will increase the birth rate. ³⁵ I will renew forever my covenant with them. I shall be their God and they will be my people. I shall never again remove my people, the children of Israel, out of the land that I have given them."

3 And now, O Lord Almighty, God of Israel, a soul in pain, a troubled spirit, cries to you: ² Listen, Merciful Lord, and have pity on us who have sinned in your sight. ³ You are eternal while we are but passing. ⁴ O Lord Almighty, God of Israel, hear the prayer of the dead of Israel and of their children who have sinned in your sight, and who have failed to listen to the voice of the Lord their God, and therefore disaster befell us. ⁵ Remember not the sins of our fathers, but think only of your power and your name. ⁶ You are the Lord our God, and we will praise you, O Lord, ⁷ since you have put your respect in our hearts to help us call upon your name. We praise you in our captivity, for we have turned from the evil of our fathers, who sinned against you. ⁸ Behold us today in

our land of exile, where you have scattered us as a rebuke, accursed offenders, suffering for all the sins of our fathers who had deserted you, O Lord our God.

IN PRAISE OF WISDOM

⁹ Listen, Israel, to the commandments of life;
listen, that you may learn wisdom.
¹⁰ How does it happen, O Israel,
that you are in the land of your enemies?
¹¹ You have grown old in a foreign country,
sharing defilement with the dead.
You are counted among those who go down into hell.
¹² It is because you have abandoned the fountain of wisdom.
¹³ If you had walked in the way of God,
you would have lived in peace for ever.
¹⁴ Learn where wisdom resides,
where strength, where understanding,
and so know where length of days is,
where life, where the light of the eyes, where peace.

¹⁵ Who has discovered wisdom's dwelling place?
Who has gone into her treasury?
¹⁶ Where are the princes of the nations
and those who rule over the beasts of earth?
¹⁷ Those who take their sport with birds?
¹⁸ Those who hoard silver and gold, in which men trust,
and who have no end to their wants?
Those who work meticulously in silver,
creating works beyond our imagination?
¹⁹ They are vanished into the land of the dead,
and others have risen up in their place.
²⁰ A new generation has arisen to inhabit the earth,
but the knowledge of truth is not known to them,

²¹ nor do they know where truth
    treads;
neither have their children received
    it,
for truth is far from their way.
²² Knowledge is not heard of in the
    land of Canaan,
neither has it been seen in Teman.
²³ The children of Agar search after
    worldly wisdom,
the merchants of Midian and of Te-
    man,
the tellers of fables, those who philos-
    ophize,
none have found the way to wisdom
neither have they discovered her
    paths.
²⁴ O Israel, how great is the house of
    God,
and how vast an area is his posses-
    sion!
²⁵ It is great and has no end:
it is high and infinite.
²⁶ In it were born giants,
men renowned from the beginning,
great in stature, expert in war.
²⁷ Yet God did not choose them,
neither did they find the paths of
    knowledge.
²⁸ And because they did not have
    wisdom,
they perished through their own
    folly.

²⁹ Who has gone up into heaven, and
    seized wisdom,
and brought her down from the
    clouds?
³⁰ Who passing over the sea found
    her,
and brought her back to trade for
    gold?
³¹ No one knows her ways, nor
    searches out her paths.

³² But God who knows all knows her
and he has mastered her with his own
    intelligence.
He who gave dimension to the earth
and filled it with cattle and four-
    footed beasts.
³³ He who sends forth light, and it
    speeds away;
who has recalled it and it tremblingly

obeys.
³⁴ The stars shine joyfully in their set
    orbits.
³⁵ When he counts them, they reply:
    "Here we are!"
and they cheerfully shine for their
    creator.
³⁶ This is our God,
and there is no other like him.
³⁷ He who holds all knowledge,
granted a share to his servant Jacob,
and to Israel his beloved.
³⁸ Thus wisdom was seen upon
    earth,
walking with men.

4 This is the book of the command-
    ments of God,
and the law that endures for ever;
those who keep it have life;
those who forsake it, death.
² Come back, O Jacob, and take hold
    of it,
walk in the light of its brightness.
³ Give not your honor to another,
nor your dignity to an unknown na-
    tion.
⁴ We rejoice, O Israel,
because God's pleasures are made
    known to us.

JERUSALEM'S HOPE

⁵ Take courage, O people of God,
memorial of Israel.
⁶ It was not for your destruction that
    you were sold to the Gentiles,
but because you provoked God to an-
    ger,
you were handed over to your ene-
    mies.
⁷ You provoked the eternal God who
    made you
by offering sacrifice to evil spirits.
⁸ You have forgotten God who
    brought you up,
and you have grieved Jerusalem that
    raised you.
⁹ For she saw the wrath of God com-
    ing upon you,
and she said, "Listen, all you that
    live near Zion,
God has brought great sorrow upon
    me,
¹⁰ for I have seen the captivity of my

sons and my daughters,
which the Eternal One has inflicted
on them.
11 Although I nourished them with
joy;
I also sent them away weeping and
mourning.
12 Let no man rejoice over me, widowed and desolate.
I am forsaken for the sins of my children,
because they departed from the law
of God.
13 And they have not heeded his
laws,
nor walked in the light of his commandments,
neither have they trod the paths of
his truth and justice.

14 Let those who live near Zion come
and remember the captivity of my
sons and daughters,
which the Eternal One has brought
upon them.
15 For he has brought against them
a nation from afar,
a wicked nation, speaking a strange
language,
16 who have neither respected old
age nor pitied children,
and have carried away the widow's
only son,
and left me all alone without children.

17 "But as for me, what help can I
give you?
18 For he who brought evil upon you
will deliver you from your enemies.
19 Go your way, my children, go
your way;
for I am left alone.
20 I have taken off the robe of peace
and have put on the sackcloth of supplication,
and I will cry to the Most High all
my days.

21 "Be comforted, my children, cry
to the Lord.
He will deliver you from the trap of
your enemies.

22 I have put my hope in the Eternal
One
to save you;
and joy has come upon me from the
Holy One,
because of the mercy which shall
come to you
from our everlasting Savior.
23 Although I sent you forth with
mourning and weeping,
the Lord will bring you back to me
with joy and gladness for ever.
24 For as the neighbors of Zion have
now seen your captivity
so shall they shortly see your salvation from God,
which will come upon you
with great honor and everlasting
glory.
25 My children, endure patiently the
punishment
that has come upon you.
Although your enemy persecutes
you,
you will quickly see his destruction
and you will grind him into the
ground.
26 My frail children have walked
rough paths,
for they were taken away like a herd,
driven off by their enemies.
27 Be comforted, my children,
and speak out to the Lord,
for you will not be forgotten by him
despite his punishment.
28 Just as it was your choice to stray
from God,
you can likewise seek him again with
tenfold zeal.
29 For he who allowed you to suffer
calamity
will turn your salvation into everlasting joy."

30 Take courage, O Jerusalem,
for he who named you, guides you.
31 The wicked who afflicted you will
perish,
and they who rejoiced at your fall
will be punished.
32 The cities which enslaved your
children
will be chastised, those that took

your sons
will get equal justice.
33 Because they rejoiced at your ruin
and were made happy by your fall,
so will they grieve for their own desolation.
34 The pride of their people will be
humbled,
and their exultation will be turned to
mourning.
35 Lasting fire from the Eternal One
will befall them,
and they will be inhabited by demons
for many years.
36 Look to the east, O Jerusalem,
and see the joy that is coming from
God.
37 Watch your children return,
whom you scattered to the winds.
They will come from the east and the
west,
at the command of the Holy One,
rejoicing in the glory of God.

5   Take off, O Jerusalem, the garment
of your sadness and pain.
Put on the beauty and dignity of that
everlasting glory
which you received from God.
2 Wrap the cloak of God's justice
about you
and put upon your head his crown of
glory.
3 For God will reveal you as his glory
to all nations.
4 The name God gave you will last
for ever:
"The peace of justice and honor of
holiness."
5 Arise, Jerusalem, go to a high
place,
turn your gaze to the east;
see your children gathered together
from the east to west,
by the order of the Holy One,
happy that God has remembered
them.
6 Although they left you
walking, guarded by enemies,
the Lord will return them to you in
honor
and borne on a royal throne.
7 For God has ordered the leveling

of every high mountain,
of the everlasting hills,
and to fill up the valleys to make the
ground level,
so that Israel may walk faithfully in
the glory of God.
8 Moreover the forests and every fragrant tree
will give Israel shade because God
commands it.
9 For God will lead Israel in joy by
the light of his majesty,
with his mercy and justice as its
guides.

JEREMIAH'S LETTER

A copy of the letter that Jeremiah sent
to those who were to be led captives into
Babylon, by the king of Babylon, to tell
them of the instructions God gave him:

6   Because of the sins that you have committed before God, you are to be taken
as captives to Babylon by Nebuchadnezzar,
king of Babylon.2 You will have to spend
many years in Babylon, as much as seven
generations. After that captivity, I will
bring you home in peace. 3 In Babylon, you
will see gods of gold, silver, stone and wood,
carried about upon shoulders, bringing fear
to the pagans. 4 Be careful, therefore, that
you do not imitate these pagan acts, nor
should you be afraid of pagan gods. 5 When
you see the crowds pressing around the images and adoring them, you must say in
your hearts, "You alone must be adored, O
Lord." 6 For my angel is with you, and I
myself will demand an account of your
souls.
7 Plated with gold and silver, their
tongues polished by artisans, they are only
make-believe, unable to speak. 8 As though
for a girl who loves pretty adornments, so
they dress their idols in golden crowns.
9 Sometimes the priests steal the gold and
silver for themselves 10 or give it to the temple prostitutes to buy clothes, or take
money from the prostitutes to adorn their
gods. 11 Yet these gods cannot protect
themselves from tarnish or decay, 12 although they have been dressed in purple
garments; they cannot even clean from
themselves the temple dust which falls on

them. ¹³ One god holds a scepter, like a judge of the country, yet he is powerless to condemn an offender to death. ¹⁴ Another holds a sword or an axe in his hand, yet he cannot protect himself from war or thieves. Therefore do not fear them because they are only powerless idols.

¹⁵ Just as a pot which a man uses becomes worthless when it is broken, so are these gods. ¹⁶ Their eyes are full of dust raised by the feet of those who enter where they are kept. ¹⁷ Just as a prison is securely locked on one who has offended the king, or the grave encloses a dead man, so must the priests secure their doors with bars and locks, lest they be stripped by thieves. ¹⁸ They light candles in great numbers but their gods cannot see any light. They are like beams in a house, ¹⁹ which termites crawling from the ground eat from within, or devour even their garments, yet they feel nothing. ²⁰ Their faces are black from the smoke that rises in the temple. ²¹ Owls, swallows and other birds fly against their bodies, or rest on their heads on which cats also sit. ²² All this tells you they are powerless gods and there is no need to fear them.

²³ The gold with which they are plated may glisten but unless a man has wiped off the tarnish they will not shine. They felt nothing when being cast. ²⁴ Even though they cost much money, there is no life in them. ²⁵ Because they cannot walk, they must be carried on men's shoulders, which proves how false they are. Those who worship them will be damned. ²⁶ If these idols topple over, they cannot straighten themselves; even when they are set in place, they must be supported. Gifts made to them might as well be made to the dead. ²⁷ The things that are offered in sacrifice are defiled when their priests sell them. Sometimes the wives of the priests steal the offerings, not even giving part to the sick or the poor. ²⁸ Even pregnant and unclean women handle the sacrifices. Thus you can see that they are not gods and there is no reason to respect them.

²⁹ How can they even be called gods? Imagine women placing offerings before silver, gold and wood idols, ³⁰ while priests sit in their temples with torn clothing,

heads and beards shaved, yet with their head uncovered! ³¹ These priests roar and shriek before their gods, as if lamenting a dead person. ³² The priests even take away the clothing of the idols to give to their wives and children. ³³ Whether these gods are treated good or bad, they cannot repay in kind. Neither can they appoint a king or overthrow him. ³⁴ Likewise, they cannot shower wealth on a man or correct evil. If a man makes a vow to them and does not keep it, there is nothing they can do. ³⁵ They cannot prevent a man from dying, nor protect the weak from the strong. ³⁶ They cannot restore sight to a blind man, nor save a man from pain. ³⁷ They do not care about widows, nor help orphans. ³⁸ Their wooden and stone gods, even plated in gold and silver, are as useful as a block of stone from a mountain quarry. Thus those who worship them are damned. ³⁹ So how can anyone think or say that they are gods?

⁴⁰ Even the Chaldeans themselves dishonor them. When they find a dumb person, they present him to Bel, asking for the gift of speech ⁴¹ as though he could hear who has no ears. Yet the people fail to understand the contradiction and fail to leave those gods since they have no common sense. ⁴² The temple prostitutes, with cords about them, sit in the streets burning olive pits. ⁴³ And when one of them is picked up by a passer-by and sleeps with him, she mocks her neighbor that she was not thought as good as herself, and thus has not had her cord broken. ⁴⁴ Everything about these gods is fake. So how can anyone say, or even think, they are gods?

⁴⁵ Made by carvers and goldsmiths, they represent only what the priests decide. ⁴⁶ And the very craftsmen who make them are not long for this world, so how can mortal men make gods? ⁴⁷ The only inheritance they leave are lies and disapproval. ⁴⁸ For if war or disaster happens, the priests meet about where they can hide with their gods. ⁴⁹ How can anyone think these idols to be gods when they cannot even save themselves from war or disaster? ⁵⁰ Considering that they are only wood, covered with gold or silver, it should be obvious that they are not gods but only a human creation

without any spirit of God in them. [51] Look at the facts and you will know they are ungodlike and phony.

[52] These gods can appoint no king nor send rain to man. [53] They can make nothing happen or save any land from invaders. They are as useless as crows between heaven and earth. [54] If fire breaks out in the house of these gods of wood, silver and gold, their priests indeed run to safety while the gods burn up like the temple beams. [55] What king and his armies can they halt? So how can anyone think or say that they are gods?

[56] Neither are these gods of wood and stone, overlaid with gold and silver, able to save themselves from thieves or robbers, who prove themselves stronger [57] by stealing the gold and silver, and the garments in which they are clothed, and then go their way while the gods are helpless. [58] Therefore, it is better to be a king who shows his power, or even a useful pot in a house with which the owner is satisfied, or a protective door to the house, than to be such false gods. [59] The sun, moon and stars shine usefully and obey God's laws. [60] Lightning flashes across the sky. The winds blow over all the nations. [61] The clouds obey God's law and pass over the earth. [62] Fire, which God created, burns woods and mountainsides as it was ordained to do. All these are more glorious and powerful than man-made gods. [63] So no one has the right to think or say these idols are gods, since they can neither think or judge or do any good for mankind. [64] Realizing, therefore, that they are not gods, there is no reason to fear them. [65] They can neither curse kings nor bless them. [66] They produce no portents in the heavens for nations to see; they neither shine like the sun, nor give light like the moon. [67] Animals are better off than they are because these can flee to cover and take care of themselves. [68] No one can produce evidence that they are gods, so do not fear them.

[69] These wooden gods, plated in silver or gold, are as productive as a scarecrow in a cucumber patch. [70] They are no better than a thornbush in a garden upon which every bird sits. These gods of wood, overlaid with gold and silver, are like a corpse hidden in the dark. [71] From the purple and scarlet motheaten garments on them, you can tell that they are not gods. In the end they will destroy themselves and be a rebuke to their country. [72] Better, therefore, is a good man with no idols; he will never suffer rebuke.

PRAYER IN THE FIERY FURNACE
(Daniel 3:24-90)

²⁴ And they walked in the middle of the flames, praising God and blessing the Lord. ²⁵ Then Azariah standing in the center of the fire, prayed in a loud voice, saying, ²⁶ "Blessed are you, O Lord, the God of our fathers, and your name is worthy of praise and is glorious forever. ²⁷ You are just in all that you have done to us, and all your works are true; your ways are right, and all your judgments valid. ²⁸ You have executed true justice in all the punishments that you have inflicted upon us, and upon Jerusalem, the holy city of our fathers; for according to truth and judgment, you have brought all these things upon us for our sins.

²⁹ "We have sinned and done wrong, departing from you; and we have trespassed in all things. ³⁰ We have not listened to your commandments, nor have we observed or done as you had commanded us, that it might go well with us.

³¹ "Therefore, all that you have brought upon us, and everything that you have done to us, you have done in true judgment. ³² And you have delivered us into the hands of our enemies who are unjust, most

evil and liars, and to an unjust king, more wicked than all who are upon the earth. ³³ And now we cannot open our mouths; we have become a shame and reproach to your servants and to those who worship you.

³⁴ "Deliver us not up forever, we beseech you for your name's sake, and abolish not your covenant. ³⁵ For the sake of Abraham your beloved, take not away from us your mercy, and for Isaac your servant, and Israel your holy one, ³⁶ to whom you have spoken, promising that you would multiply their offspring as the stars of heaven, and as the sand that is on the seashore. ³⁷ For we, O Lord, are made less than any nation, and are brought low on all the earth this day for our sins. ³⁸ Neither is there at this time prince, or leader, or prophet, or holocaust, or sacrifice, or oblation, or incense, or place of firstfruits before you, ³⁹ that we may find your mercy. Nevertheless, in a contrite heart and humble spirit let us be accepted. ⁴⁰ As in holocausts of rams and bullocks, and as in thousands of fat lambs; so let our sacrifice be made in your sight this day, that it may please

you, for there is no confusion for those who trust in you. 41 And now we follow you with all our heart, we fear you and seek your face.

42 "Put us not to confusion, but deal with us according to your meekness, and according to the multitude of your mercies. 43 Deliver us according to your wonderful works, and give glory to your name, O Lord. 44 Let all those be shamed who show evil to your servants, let them be confounded in all your might, and let their strength be broken. 45 Let them know that you are the Lord, the only God, and glorious over all the world."

46 Now the king's servants who had cast them in continued to heat the furnace with brimstone, chaff, pitch and brush, 47 and the flame mounted high above the furnace forty-nine cubits[a], 48 and it broke forth and burned some of the Chaldeans who were near the furnace. 49 But the angel of the Lord went down into the furnace to be with Azariah and his companions; and he drove the flame of the fire out of the furnace, 50 and made the midst of the furnace like the coolness of a wind bringing dew, and the fire touched them not at all, nor troubled them, nor did them any harm.

51 Then these three in the furnace as with one voice praised, glorified and blessed God, saying,

52 "Blessed are you, O Lord the God of our fathers and worthy to be praised, glorified and exalted above all forever; and blessed is the holy name of your glory, and worthy to be praised, and exalted above all in all ages. 53 Blessed are you in the holy temple of your glory; and greatly to be praised, exceedingly glorious forever. 54 Blessed are you on the throne of your kingdom, and greatly to be praised, and exalted above all forever. 55 Blessed are you, who behold the depths, and sit upon the cherubims: worthy to be praised and exalted above all forever. 56 Blessed are you in the firmament of heaven, and worthy of praise and glorious forever.

57 "All you works of the Lord, bless the Lord; praise and exalt him above all forever. 58 O you angels of the Lord, bless the Lord; praise and exalt him above all forever. 59 O you heavens, bless the Lord; praise and exalt him above all forever. 60 O all you waters that are above the heavens, bless the Lord; praise and exalt him above all forever. 61 O all you powers of the Lord, bless the Lord; praise and exalt him above all forever. 62 O you sun and moon, bless the Lord; praise and exalt him above all forever. 63 O you stars of heaven, bless the Lord; praise and exalt him above all forever. 64 O every shower and dew, bless the Lord; praise and exalt him above all forever. 65 O all you spirits of God, bless the Lord; praise and exalt him above all forever. 66 O you fire and heat, bless the Lord; praise and exalt him above all forever. 67 O you cold and heat, bless the Lord; praise and exalt him above all forever. 68 O you dews and snows, bless the Lord; praise and exalt him above all forever. 69 O you frost and cold, bless the Lord; praise and exalt him above all forever. 70 O you ice and snow, bless the Lord; praise and exalt him above all forever. 71 O you nights and days, bless the Lord; praise and exalt him above all forever. 72 O you light and darkness, bless the Lord; praise and exalt him above all forever. 73 O you lightning and clouds, bless the Lord; praise and exalt him above all forever. 74 O let the earth bless the Lord; let it praise and exalt him above all forever. 75 O you mountains and hills, bless the Lord; praise and exalt him above all forever. 76 O all you things that spring up in the earth, bless the Lord; praise and exalt him above all forever. 77 O you fountains, bless the Lord; praise and exalt him above all forever. 78 O you seas and rivers, bless the Lord; praise and exalt him above all forever.

79 "O you whales, and all that move in the waters, bless the Lord; praise and exalt him above all forever. 80 O all you birds of the air, bless the Lord; praise and exalt him above all forever. 81 O all you beasts and cattle, bless the Lord; praise and exalt him above all forever.

82 "O you sons of men, bless the Lord; praise and exalt him above all forever. 83 O

---

a Approximately 73.5 feet.

let Israel bless the Lord; let it praise and exalt him above all forever. [84] O you priests of the Lord, bless the Lord; praise and exalt him above all forever. [85] O you servants of the Lord, bless the Lord; praise and exalt him above all forever. [86] O you spirits and souls of the just, bless the Lord; praise and exalt him above all forever. [87] O you holy and humble of heart, bless the Lord; praise and exalt him above all forever. [88] O Hananiah, Azariah, and Mishael, bless you the Lord; praise and exalt him above all forever. For he has delivered us from Sheol, and saved us out from the hand of death, and delivered us out of the midst of the burning flame, and saved us out of the midst of the fire. [89] O give thanks to the Lord, because he is good; because his mercy endures forever and ever. [90] O all you holy ones, bless the Lord, the God of gods; praise him and give him thanks, because his mercy endures forever and ever."

SUSANNA AND THE ELDERS
(Daniel 13:1–65)

13 NOW THERE WAS a man who lived in Babylon, and his name was Joakim. ² He took a wife named Susanna, the daughter of Hilkiah, a very beautiful woman who feared God. ³ Her parents being just had instructed their daughter according to the law of Moses. ⁴ Joakim was very rich and had a garden near his house, and the Jews came to him for counsel because he was the most honored of them all.

⁵ And there were two of the elders of the people appointed judges that year, of whom the Lord said: "Iniquity came out of Babylon from the elder-judges who were supposed to govern the people." ⁶ These men frequented the house of Joakim, and all who had any matters of judgment came to them. ⁷ When the people left at noon, Susanna would go out and walk in her husband's garden. ⁸ The old men saw her going out every day and walking, and they were inflamed with lust towards her. ⁹ They darkened their minds and turned away their eyes that they might not look to heaven, nor remember just judgments. ¹⁰ So they were both enfeebled with passion for her, yet they did not make known their feelings to each other; ¹¹ for they were ashamed to declare to one another their lust, desiring to possess her. ¹² They watched carefully every day to see her. And one said to the other: ¹³ "Let us now go home, for it is dinner time." So going out they departed from one another. ¹⁴ Turning back again, they both came to the same place; asking one another the reason, they acknowledged their lust, and then they agreed upon a time when they might find her alone.

¹⁵ And it happened, as they watched on a certain day, she went out at the regular time, accompanied only by two maids, and desired to bathe herself in the garden, for it was hot weather. ¹⁶ There was nobody there, but the two old men who hid themselves and were watching her. ¹⁷ So she said to the maids: "Bring me oil and soap, and shut the gates of the garden, that I may wash myself." ¹⁸ They did as she bade them; and they shut the gates of the garden, and went out by a back gate to get what she had commanded them. They did not know that the elders were hidden within.

¹⁹ Now when the maids had left, the two

elders rose and ran to her, and said: 20 "Behold, the gates of the garden are shut, and nobody sees us, and we are in love with you, so give in to us, and lie with us. 21 But if you will not, we shall bear witness against you, that a young man was with you, and for that reason you sent your maids away." 22 Susanna sighed, and said: "I am trapped no matter where I turn, for if I do this thing, it is death to me; and if I do it not, I shall not escape your hands. 23 But it is better for me to fall into your hands without doing anything wrong than to sin in the sight of the Lord."

24 With that Susanna cried out with a loud voice, and the elders also cried out against her. 25 And one of them ran to the gate of the garden, and opened it. 26 So when the servants of the house heard the cry in the garden, they rushed in by the back gate to see what was the matter. 27 After the old men had spoken, the servants were greatly ashamed; for never had there been any such word said of Susanna.

On the next day, 28 when the people came to her husband Joakim the two elders also came full of a wicked plot against Susanna, to put her to death. 29 They said before the people: "Send for Susanna, daughter of Hilkiah, the wife of Joakim." And they sent for her at once. 30 And she came with her parents, and children, and all her kindred. 31 Now Susanna was exceedingly refined and beautiful to behold. 32 But those wicked men commanded that her face should be uncovered (for she was veiled), that so at least they might be satisfied with her beauty. 33 Therefore her friends and all her acquaintances wept. 34 But the two elders rising up in the midst of the people laid their hands upon her head. 35 And she looked up to heaven weeping, for her heart had confidence in the Lord. 36 The elders said: "As we walked in the garden alone, this woman came in with two maids and shut the doors of the garden, and sent away the maids. 37 Then a young man who was hidden there came to her, and lay with her. 38 But we who were in a corner of the garden, seeing this wickedness, ran up to them, and we saw them lie together. 39 And indeed we could not take him, because he was stronger than we, and

opening the gates he leaped out. 40 Having taken this woman, we asked who the young man was, but she would not tell us. Of this thing we are witnesses." 41 The crowd believed them since they were the elders and the judges of the people, and they condemned her to death.

42 Then Susanna cried out with a loud voice, and said, "O eternal God, who knows hidden things, who knows all things before they come to pass, 43 you know that they have borne false witness against me; and behold I must die, even though I have done none of these things which these men have maliciously made up against me." 44 And the Lord heard her voice.

45 When she was led away to be put to death, the Lord raised up the holy spirit of a young boy whose name was Daniel. 46 He cried out with a loud voice, "I am free of the blood of this woman." 47 Then all the people turning toward him, said: "What is the meaning of this that you have said?" 48 But standing in the midst of them, he said, "Are you so foolish, you children of Israel, that without examination or knowledge of the truth, you have condemned a daughter of Israel? 49 Return to the judgment seat, for they have borne false witness against her."

50 So all the people returned in haste and the old men said to him, "Come, and sit yourself down among us, and show us your reasoning, seeing God has given you the honor of old age." 51 Daniel said to the people, "Separate these two far from one another, and I will examine them." 52 So when they were set apart, one from the other, he called one of them and said to him: "O you who are grown old in evil days, now will your sins be revealed which you have committed before, 53 in judging unjust judgments, oppressing the innocent, and letting the guilty go free, whereas the Lord said, 'The innocent and the just you shall not kill.' 54 Now then, if you saw her, tell me under what tree you saw them conversing together." He said, "Under a mastic tree." 55 And Daniel said, "Well have you lied against your own head, for behold the angel of God having received the sentence of him will cut you in two." 56 And having put him aside, he commanded that the

other should come, and he said to him, "O you seed of Canaan and not of Judah, beauty has deceived you, and lust has perverted your heart. ⁵⁷ Thus have you done to the daughters of Israel, and they for fear were intimate with you; but a daughter of Judah would not abide your wickedness. ⁵⁸ Now therefore tell me, under what tree did you find them conversing together?" And he answered: "Under an evergreen oak." ⁵⁹ And Daniel said to him: "Well have you also lied against your own head; for the angel of the Lord waits with a sword to cut you in two, and to destroy you."

⁶⁰ With that all the assembly cried out with a loud voice, and they blessed God who saved those who trust in him. ⁶¹ And they rose up against the two elders (for Daniel had convicted them of false witness by their own mouth) and they did to them as they had maliciously dealt against their neighbor, ⁶² to fulfill the law of Moses; and they put them to death, and innocent blood was saved that day. ⁶³ But Hilkiah and his wife praised God for their daughter Susanna, as did Joakim her husband, and all her kindred, because there was no dishonesty found in her. ⁶⁴ Daniel became great in the sight of the people from that day forward. ⁶⁵ And King Astyages was gathered to his fathers, and Cyrus the Persian received his kingdom.

DANIEL IN THE LION'S DEN
(Daniel 14:1–42)

14 DANIEL WAS THE king's guest, and was honored above all his friends. ² Now the Babylonians had an idol called Bel; and every day twelve great measures of fine flour, and forty sheep, and sixty vessels of wine were offered to him. ³ The king also worshiped him, and went every day to adore him; but Daniel adored his God. And the king said to him: "Why don't you adore Bel?" ⁴ He answered: "Because I do not worship idols made with hands, but the living God, who created heaven and earth, and rules over all flesh." ⁵ And the king said to him: "Doesn't Bel seem to you to be a living god? Do you not see how much he eats and drinks every day?" ⁶ Then Daniel smiled and said: "O king, be not deceived, for this is but clay within and bronze without, neither has it eaten at any time." ⁷ And the king being angry called for his priests, and said to them: "If you do not tell me who it is that eats up these provisions, you will die. ⁸ But if you can show that Bel eats these things, Daniel will die because he has blasphemed against Bel." And Daniel said to the king: "Be it done according to your word."

⁹ Now the priests of Bel numbered seventy, besides their wives and children. And the king went with Daniel into the temple of Bel. ¹⁰ The priests of Bel said: "Behold we leave; and do you, O king, set forth the food, make ready the wine, lock the door, and seal it with your own signet ring. ¹¹ When you come in the morning, if you do not find that Bel has eaten and drunk everything, we will suffer death, or else it is Daniel who has lied against us." ¹² They were not worried because they had previously made a secret entrance under the altar, and they always came in by it and consumed those things.

¹³ So it came to pass after they had left, the king set the food before Bel; and Daniel commanded his servants, and they brought ashes, and he sifted them all over the temple behind the king as he left; and going forth they shut the door, and having sealed it with the king's ring, they departed. ¹⁴ The priests went in by night, as was their custom, with their wives and their children; and they ate and drank everything.

¹⁵ The king arose early in the morning, and Daniel with him. ¹⁶ And the king said,

1283

"Are the seals whole, Daniel?" He answered, "They are whole, O king." [17] And as soon as he had opened the door, the king looked upon the empty table, and cried out with a loud voice: "Great are you, O Bel, and there is no deceit in you." [18] Daniel laughed; and he restrained the king so that he would not enter, and he said: "Behold the pavement, tell me whose footsteps these are." [19] The king said: "I see the footsteps of men, women and children." And the king was angry. [20] Then he took the priests, their wives and their children; and they showed him the private doors by which they came in, and consumed the things that were on the table. [21] The king therefore put them to death, and delivered Bel into the power of Daniel, who destroyed it and its temple.

[22] And there was a great dragon in that place, and the Babylonians worshiped him. [23] And the king said to Daniel: "Behold, you cannot now say that this is not a living god; adore him therefore." [24] And Daniel said, "I adore the Lord my God; for he is the living God; but that is no living god.

[25] "Give me leave, O king, and I will kill this dragon without sword or club." The king said, "I give you leave." [26] Then Daniel took pitch, fat and hair, and boiled them together; he made cakes and put them into the dragon's mouth, and the dragon burst asunder. And he said, "Behold him whom you worshiped."

[27] When the Babylonians heard this, they became very angry and murmured together against the king, saying: "The king has become a Jew. He has destroyed Bel, he has killed the dragon, and he has put the priests to death." [28] And they came to the king, and said, "Deliver Daniel to us or we will destroy you and your house." [29] The king saw that they intended violence; being pressed by necessity he delivered Daniel to them. [30] They cast him into the den of lions, and he was there six days. [31] And in the den there were seven lions, and they gave them two human carcasses every day and two sheep, but now they were not fed so that they might devour Daniel.

[32] Now there was in Judea a prophet called Habakkuk. He had boiled pottage and had broken bread in a bowl, and was going into the field to carry it to the reapers. [33] The angel of the Lord said to Habakkuk: "Carry the dinner which you have into Babylon to Daniel, who is in the lions' den." [34] And Habakkuk said: "Sir, I never saw Babylon, nor do I know the den." [35] And the angel of the Lord took him by the top of his head, and carried him by the hair of his head, and set him down in Babylon over the den by the force of his spirit. [36] And Habakkuk cried, saying, "O Daniel, you servant of God, take the dinner that God has sent you." [37] And Daniel said: "You have remembered me, O God, and you have not forsaken those who love you." [38] And Daniel rose and ate. And the angel of the Lord presently set Habakkuk again in his own place.

[39] And upon the seventh day the king came to mourn Daniel; and he came to the den and looked in, and behold Daniel was sitting in the midst of the lions. [40] And the king cried out with a loud voice, saying, "Great are you, O Lord, the God of Daniel." And he pulled him out of the lions' den. [41] But those who had been the cause of his destruction, he cast into the den, and they were devoured in a moment before him. [42] Then the king said, "Let all the inhabitants of the whole earth fear the God of Daniel; for his is the Savior, working signs and wonders in the earth; who has delivered Daniel out of the lions' den."